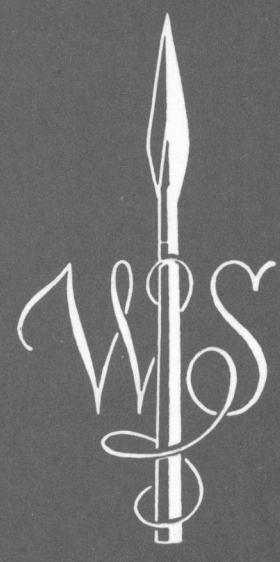

THE COMPLETE WORKS OF
WILLIAM SHAKESPEARE

"*O! how thy worth with manners may I sing,—*"
SONNETS

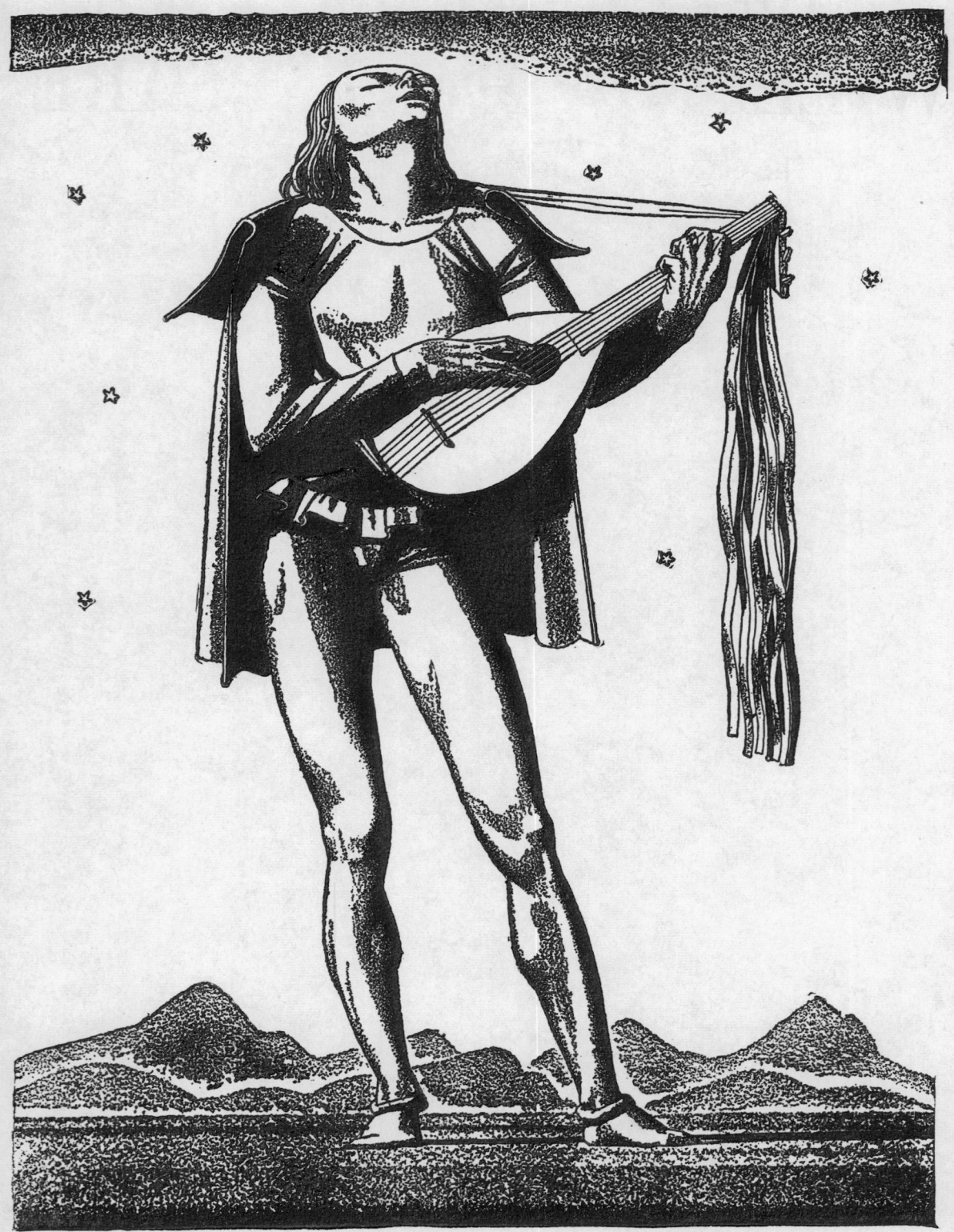

THE COMPLETE WORKS OF
WILLIAM SHAKESPEARE

The CAMBRIDGE EDITION TEXT, as edited by
WILLIAM ALDIS WRIGHT

Including the TEMPLE NOTES

Illustrated by
ROCKWELL KENT

With A Preface by
CHRISTOPHER MORLEY

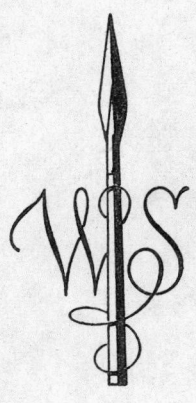

GARDEN CITY BOOKS
Garden City, New York

CONTENTS

CONTENTS

ILLUSTRATIONS

A LETTER TO A READER

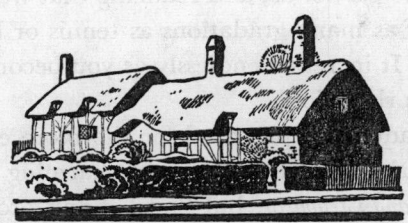

THIS IS NOT an Introduction to Shakespeare, but an Introduction to Yourself-as-a Reader-of-Shakespeare. You excited me when you said you hadn't read "it" since high school. That's what you said, *it;* unconsciously revealing that you had come to think of him as an institution, a monument, a mass of dehumanized classic. In former days, when a publisher wanted to mummify an author he stippled the top of the book with a stone-grain pattern. It was said to be *marbled;* the word was well chosen.

And now you say that, as a man of experience, past forty, you think of trying him again. That's grand. We all did so when young, and under regimented tuition. It was all right, as far as it went; but the Shakespeare we met was only a fraction of the full man. And so, of course, were we.

I wish I could imagine, or share, the experience you will have. Be patient! Your attention, accustomed to the low voltages of modern prose, will blow a fuse here and there: by which I mean you'll be bored, at first, by the heavy load of his verbal richness. You'll have to remind yourself that it's really a different language. (We don't even know how he pronounced it; probably with a strong Warwickshire base, overlaid with some tones of cockney. Stratford, for instance, he called *Stretford*. I strongly suspect that his own name sounded like *Shaxper*. If we heard him talking, we'd very likely think he was an Australian.)

Don't take too ponderously everything I say in this letter. I'm trying to get you interested. The most gorgeous thing you'll discover about Shakespeare is that he's so like yourself. Everyone notices that.

Your taste in reading, I gather, has been for narrative that gets going promptly. Did you suppose Shakespeare was slow? Try the beginning of *Antony and Cleopatra* where the whole situation is set in 13 lines; in fact the two principals come on stage after the 10th line. If the groundlings in the pit were still jostling or clearing their throats they'd miss Cleopatra's first speech, and worldwide question that every man has heard, "How much do you love me?" (And Antony's typically evasive masculine reply.)

Incidentally, if you don't laugh when Cleopatra, feeling moody, suggests a game of billiards, then you're not amused by the things that tickle me. And though you'll weary of some of the inter-

[ix]

mediate scenes, I think you'll find that Cleopatra's death brings the frost on the backbone that only great things cause.

I may be expelled the company of Shakespeare students for writing in this vein; but part of the endless fun of reading him is in exercising and expanding private judgement; cutting our own little paths through the great jungle of his work; discovering (with continuing amazement) how much of him had already become part of us; and realizing that we learn him only bit by bit. Enjoying Shakespeare is a game of as many gradations as tennis or bridge. There is fun to be had even in the crudest amateurism. It increases endlessly as you become a "seeded" player—acquire dexterity and get the pace of his rhetoric.

It's astonishing how few readers are prepared for the more expert strokes of his comedy. I remember once printing a remark that one of the most charming of Shakespeare's improprieties was in a certain scene of *Antony and Cleopatra;* but that I didn't propose to identify the exact line. I received many letters saying that was easy, of course the passage I meant was so-and-so. And in every case they mentioned a crude, coarse, obvious allusion in that scene; not one discerned the really touching and tenderly vulgar line I meant.

So I'm glad you're mature; Shakespeare improves with his readers. You'll find him talking, in perfect simplicity and plainness, of matters that nowadays are too often mentioned with a leer. You, with the bashfulness of a business man, will be a good deal shocked occasionally.

Don't let yourself be grieved by the naïveté of his stage devices: for instance (the first example I think of) the sudden arrival of the English army at just the right moment in Act II of *King John.* The technique of the movies is exactly the same, if you stop to think about it. Nor need you be put off by occasional ghosts, goblins, elves, and apparitions of fantasy. I doubt whether Shakespeare believed in the visible actuality of these any more than you or I; they are purely symbolic; devices to represent imaginations, thoughts, legends, memories. To artists these things do not need to be explained.

For heaven's sake, unless it be Pearsall Smith's chapter *On Not Reading Shakespeare,** don't read anything *about* him, anything biographical or critical.—Well, perhaps Walter Bagehot's *Shakespeare the Man,* written in 1853 and still one of the wisest commentaries not only on W.S. but on authors in general—and written, mark you, by a business man. That you will find in volume I of Bagehot's *Literary Studies,* in the Everyman Series. And whatever you read, including Shakespeare himself, please remember you have the privilege of dissenting from it. For instance, Bagehot's very odd opinion of the Sonnets: that they are ideal reading "for a young man in the spring of the year among green fields and in gentle air." But there are a great many things in the Sonnets that a very young man is unlikely to relish. They require the forty winters that the author mentions; the winters that "feelingly persuade me what I am." I can give an instance of this. It chanced that when I was forty I made a list of the 20 of Shakespeare's Sonnets that then spoke most sharply to my condition. Subsequently, rummaging some old notebooks, I found that I had done exactly the same thing when I was 21, and had forgotten. Only 9 of my favorites at 21 were still in my list chosen at 40.

I'm tempted to say a word more about the Sonnets. Many men, including some of the highest intelligence, have made their study a lifetime hobby. Bagehot's youth, strolling the springtime

*This is the humorous first chapter of Pearsall Smith's brilliant, crotchety, sensitive and superlative little book *On Reading Shakespeare;* unquestionably for the modern reader the most amiable guidebook into the jungle.

fields, was probably perplexed to find those philoprogenitive appeals addressed to one of his own sex. (A man's interest in some other man's begetting children is usually rather detached.) But the wise reader never hesitates to resex the Sonnets to his own purpose. What particular frolicsome conceit Shakespeare had in mind in the first 17 sonnets—perhaps even an ingenious plea to his friend to get married and leave Shakespeare's girl alone—cannot now be guessed, and is immaterial to us. The important thing is not the much scrutinized Dedication, nor the identity of Mr. W. H., but how far do the sonnets themselves prick into the reality of your own heart.

"His sugared sonnets among his private friends" one of Shakespeare's contemporaries called them. And by "sugared" I think an Elizabethan would mean not only sweet but spun into fantastic and dilettante confectionery shapes. The publishers of this present edition once refused Shakespeare's Sonnets for publication, when they were guilefully submitted in modern typescript and under a strange name. Let them not be embarrassed: Shakespeare himself never published them. Thomas Thorpe, a sort of pirating literary agent, got hold of a MS copy and had them printed at the Sign of the White Horse (it should have been Dark Horse) and they were put on sale (for fivepence) at The Parrot. Professional scholars have squawked and scuffled round them like parrots ever since. And it was Don Marquis's imagined Mermaid Tavern parrot (in his book *Archy and Mehitabel*) who uttered one of the shrewdest pieces of Shakespearean criticism. Shakespeare, says the Parrot, was a disappointed man and wept in his beer because his life had largely been spent writing or rewriting stock melodramas for the managers. (Drivel such as *Titus Andronicus*, for instance, which you'd better not try to read.) What Shakespeare really wanted, the Parrot says, was "to write sonnet serials like a gentleman should."

No one should be allowed to write about Shakespeare unless he has himself tried (however humbly) to write poetry and produce plays, and has seen something of the kind of tavern and backstage and lodging-house life that Shakespeare led. Professors, academicians, tamed in years of cautious comfortable living, have been bred to put out of their minds the savage, laughing and despairing world of a mind like Shakespeare's. The scholars have saved the text for us, but the great commentators—the Johnsons, Coleridges, Hazlitts, De Quinceys, to keep safely in the past —have mostly been those who led disorderly and Grub Street lives like his, and understood him by divination. I once tried to discuss Shakespeare before a college community, and a refined old lady was overheard to say afterward that it was "an insult." But bless her heart, I was not trying to talk in the mood a cultured suburban community would understand, but in the mood Shakespeare himself would recognize. It is impossible ever to talk honestly about Shakespeare to well-bred people without appalling them. Canny indeed were the old educators who saw to it, until about the time of McGuffey's Readers, that Shakespeare was excluded from school textbooks. Lindley Murray, the famous grammarian whose influence was potent about a century ago, said—and truly—that Shakespeare caused "fatal wounds to youth's innocence, delicacy, and religion."*

But we were speaking of the Sonnets. Many learned students, uncertain whether the emotions described were platonic or plutonic, fled to the timid theory that Elizabethan sonnet-sequences were a conventionalized artifice; that they dealt with stereotyped themes; in other words that Shakespeare's sonnets don't mean what they say. Perhaps they did begin as formality, but they

*See Henry W. Simon: *The Reading of Shakespeare in American Schools and Colleges.*

soon turned into a bonfire. They are the most definite and passionate onslaught on Time ever undertaken by the perishable human spirit. (I once took the trouble to count, and found the word *Time* occurring 78 times in the series.) Dear old Professor George Herbert Palmer loved to tell how in youth he and another Harvard student agreed to repeat to each other one of the Sonnets every morning at breakfast; in that way he learned 80 of them by heart, and believed it the most valuable experience of his college course. I myself remember at Oxford a parallel episode. On my staircase lived an ambitious young German who was struggling to improve his English. He used to invite some of us to breakfast with him and corrigate his accent. Someone had advised him to memorize the Sonnets and he often asked us to hear him recite them. His fantastic palatals and gutturals were no less comic than the Welsh pronunciation Shakespeare ridiculed in Fluellen.* Indeed his recitations of some of the Sonnets almost spoiled them for me permanently: I can still hear him—

Luff iss not luff
Vich alterss ven it alterration findts

I can imagine Shakespeare's curses when the Sonnets were published. Certainly he would hardly have let them escape into print in the form we have them: some technically imperfect; the later numbers sinking into abominations of carnal vulgarity or an actual madness of mockery; and ending with what seems a realtor's testimonial for the town of Bath.

But if you don't worry about what Shakespeare may have meant, but what the Sonnets mean to *you*, you can agree with Professor Palmer: "no other body of poetry in the language is so precious for internal possession."

II

THERE indeed I think we touch upon a good woodsman's trick for camping in the Forest of Arden. To know exactly what Shakespeare had in mind, to collate his allusions with the history, economics, or metaphysics of his time, is a matter for the expert. But to unprofessional readers, more important is to read with intent to find how it applies to ourselves, to fit his universality to our own particular. Take for instance that extraordinary scene in *Henry V* (Act IV, Scene 1) where King Harry on campaign in France, unknown and disguised in a borrowed cloak, meets Soldiers Three. They are an Englishman, a Scotchman, an Irishman. What an excitement when we suddenly realize what Shakespeare is doing: giving a deliberate cross-section of the B.E.F. of his time. There we find the soldier speaking his blunt mind just as he did in the trenches of the Somme; and arguing the still unanswered question whether the government has a right to call on plain men for such bloody argument. And—as an added verisimilitude—how pleased one is to notice that Bates the cockney and Mike the Irishman are the soldiers who do the talking. Sandy, the Scot, says nothing. It is Mike who gets into quarrel with the incognito king and challenges him to fisticuffs. This magnificent scene could not possibly have meant to readers before 1914 what it

*See the play *Henry V*. You will want to look up Fluellen. Also it was partly from him that descended the modern and continual use of the adjective *lousy*. Very likely you will also discover for yourself the scenes in this play where Shakespeare chaffs the most amusing of human frailties: the difficulties both French and English have with each other's languages.

means to us now when we remember how men of English, Scottish and Irish speech fought again on French fields. So we think of it now (interpreting, as men must, in terms of our own perspective) as the *All Quiet on the Western Front* of its time. One is tempted to say that Shakespeare transfused into the very blood stream of human character, with the result that whatever happens in history serves to consolidate and enrich him.

How much pleasure I had, for instance, during the Prohibition and Racketeering era, in reading *Measure for Measure*—even to the astonishing coincidence of the Duke's lines:—

> We have strict statutes and most biting laws
> Which for this fourteen years we have let sleep. . . .

(The calculation 1919 to 1933, the duration of our Prohibition amendment, = 14 years, was an immediate ecstasy.)

> so our decrees
> Dead to infliction, to themselves are dead,
> And liberty plucks justice by the nose;
> The baby beats the nurse, and quite athwart
> Goes all decorum.

And again, what could be more thrillingly permanent than this:—

> We must not make a scarecrow of the law
> Setting it up to fear [*viz.* frighten] the birds of prey,
> And let it keep one shape, till custom make it
> Their perch and not their terror.

It is not possible for any commentator in England—a relatively law-obeying country—to feel that as tinglingly as does an American. So mark you, Shakespeare gets better and better as time passes; the huge army of the world's desire* is enlisted on his side.

Measure for Measure is as good a play as any to illustrate how invigorating is the drink when you mix the whiskey of Shakespeare with the plain soda of your own mind. First let me say this: don't let yourself be annoyed by the incredible and preposterous plots (which were not, we are assured, Shakespeare's own). Based on twins, disguises, lies or hoaxes, lightning strokes of love or jealousy, they are the crudest beanpoles on which morning glories ever grew. But a queer thought occurs: if the plays were as subtle and shrewd in plot as they are glorious in text, would they not be unbearable? They would not then be art but life itself; which none could endure more than once. And I wonder if the sheer naïveté of the plot did not serve to put the author on his mettle? The rough scantling trellis of his theme is overshaded and beautified by the tenting grapevine of his wit. Did you ever watch the tendrils of the grape making fast with sailorly judgement to the nearest mooring?

Measure for Measure is the story of a municipal clean-up, an attempt to enforce the laws. "Of government the properties to unfold," says the Duke, and the play is partly a satiric on political science. You remember the witty comment that the most Prohibition did was to move the corner saloon to the middle of the block. So how felicitously contemporary is the remark of Pompey, Mrs. Overdone's bartender, in Act I, Scene 2. Mrs. Overdone is the proprietor of a "house of

*Startling line that goes off like a rocket at the beginning of a jejune play, *Love's Labour's Lost*. I say jejune, for so I dimly remember it; but it's a long while since I've read it. It may be a better play by now, since I'm a better reader. Please consider carefully this relativity of Shakespeare to your own experience and capacities.

resort" and is disturbed to hear that her business has fallen under a ban. Have no fear, says the encouraging Pompey, "though you change your place you need not change your trade." But not only in humors of low life is this play perennial: it also rises to universals in serious mood. The next time you see someone fainted on the street and crowded round by well-meaning spectators, look up Act II, Scene 4, line 25; the next time you tread on an insect, III, 1, 79. You know then, this man has had your very own thoughts. It is the subtlest corroboration: he was built (as that oaken word means) of the same tough wood as you. I have said before, we recognize so much of Shakespeare in ourselves, there must have been a good deal of us in him.

There's at least one passage in *Measure for Measure* ("To die, and go we know not where," Act III, Scene 1) which almost everyone, hearing it out of context, will think is from *Hamlet*. This is the most serious criticism one can offer of Shakespeare *as dramatist:* his passages of fine frenzy could too often be put in almost anywhere.

To be honest, observed Anatole France, the critic should say "I am going to talk about myself à propos of Shakespeare." So let me add that *Measure for Measure* is particularly dear to me because I found in it two things I supposed I had invented myself. One was the notion that stewed prunes are funny (see Act II, Scene 1) and the other the phrase *Neither Maid, Wife, Nor Widow* which I tacked on as a subtitle to an old melodrama when we played it in Hoboken. This I truly think was worth thousands to the box-office. But see *M. for M.*, Act V, Scene 1, 177.*

Whether you have read him once or a hundred times, you'll always notice something you hadn't seen before. Somewhere in Keats's Letters—probably, after Shakespeare, the next finest reading our language has—he asks his friend Reynolds to let him know whenever some passage in Shakespeare "comes rather new to you." Only the other day in *Troilus and Cressida* I observed a touch I had never spotted before. It can't be just an accident? Ulysses is making his famous speech (Act IV, Scene 5) about Cressida the wanton:—

> Fie, fie upon her!
> There's language in her eye, her cheek, her lip,
> Nay, her foot speaks; her wanton spirits look out
> At every joint and motive of her body.

And so on; concluding with his description of the Trojan heroine as one of the "daughters of the game." He's interrupted by a trumpet call within, and all the Greek warriors cry out "The Trojans' trumpet!" Surely, surely, this was meant to be also heard by the audience as "The Trojan strumpet!" and a sure-fire laugh.

He keeps pace with the clock. Every new dogma or doctrine can justify itself in him. As I write this, there comes to my table a new book: *Shakespeare, a Marxist Interpretation*, translated from the Russian of A. A. Smirnov. An able little study, I can see at a glance, but devoid of humor. It proves, I gather, that "Shakespeare was the ideologist of the bourgeoisie . . . but the bourgeoisie have never been able to understand him."—Which is, in logic, both eating your cake and having it. Jaggard, Shakespeare's printer, went blind; and most of his thesis-possessed annotators grow curiously cock-eyed.

---

*To forestall argument, my first notion of this title was over 20 years ago, reading a volume of Bertha M. Clay on a park bench. On the back of the paper-bound book was a list of charwomen's classics, including one called *Maid, Wife or Widow* "by Mrs. Alexander." To negative the phrase was obviously funny.—Shakespeare's version was *Neither Maid, Widow, Nor Wife*, less felicitous both in sequence and rhythm.

III

FOR your great purpose of enjoyment you need very little apparatus of knowledge about W.S., but chiefly a readiness to observe your own mind. An adequate glossary of Elizabethan English is helpful, and perhaps also some inkling of the supposed chronology of the plays (the order in which they were written) on which scholars have spent an infinity of argument. But it is your own innocent speculations that I desiderate and solicit. What will you make of *The Tempest*, I'm wondering? Will you see in it, as I do, the most exquisite fable of the human mind cast away on the lonely island of its egotism? Prospero (to me) typifies Thought; Ariel, the magic of Art; Miranda, the soft appeal of loving kindness; Caliban, the various greeds and lusts; and the rest of the shipload is old helterskelter Demos, the public. It matters little to me that the author may have had no conscious intention of any such allegory; that, so baldly suggested, is my own translation. It matters little to me, for instance, that Melville professed amazement when the first readers of *Moby Dick* (two very intelligent people called Mr. and Mrs. Nathaniel Hawthorne) saw in the chase of the White Whale a parable of the soul's heat for certainty. The best of any artist is what he does subconsciously—as true of the writer as of the gymnast's equilibria.

Shakespeare, like all great creators, offers us the chance to collaborate with him. When for instance you see in the line "Your swords are now too massy for your strengths" not merely Ariel magicking the roughnecks, but a comment on our mechanized and militarized civilization, then you have collaborated with Shakespeare; you have brought him home to your present business and bosom; you have put your own exponent above his figure, and raised it to higher power.

Capitalism, or the Profit System as they sometimes call it, is by no means exhausted. You will find it perfectly exemplified in the arts of reading. Two people will read Shakespeare, and how much more profit one will get than another. That is the internal revenue that no tax-collector can plunder.

Or *Hamlet:* how I aspire to hear your sober comments on that play. From the crisp foreboding dialogue of the opening—the thrilling words in the dark: *Who's there?*—down to the "peal of ordnance is shot off", what terrible and ticklish doings! Will you see it (as I do) not only tragedy but also the most humorous satire on parents and the junior generation? Will you note the comic irony of putting the line *Brevity is the soul of wit* in the mouth of gabby old Polonius? Will it occur to you that the dramatic dexterity consists not merely in a play within a play, but in fact two plays within a play: for the whole action is laid inside the confidential reciprocity of Hamlet and the audience. Here some knowledge of the physical structure of the Elizabethan stage (projecting far into the pit, so that Hamlet can be alone with the audience) would be useful. The Elizabethan stage was built just as a man's mind is built, with a forward apron apt for soliloquy.

How many peals of ordnance have been shot off about *Hamlet* by the professors and hierophants. Yet it is not hard to understand if you still have in you anything of the young prince. Youth dies, stabbed by the poisoned sword of living. And all idealists are liegemen to the Dane.

I do not wish to seem to praise ignorance. The full reach and suggestion of that play cannot even be approached without the most absorbing research: not only in the text but in your own living. It is packed with an infinity of small chuckling jests; of which one of my favorites is the groundlings' laugh when, because the family think Hamlet is mad, they wish to send him to England. You, as a solid business man, will enjoy the King and Queen's doubtfulness about Hamlet going back to the university for graduate study. Hamlet, remember, was a Wittenberg student, and Wittenberg (not in Springfield, Ohio, but in Germany) was Martin Luther's college. In other words, they thought Hamlet in danger of becoming (as Wolsey called Anne Boleyn in *Henry VIII*) "a spleeny Lutheran." Some of the commentators have had good frolic in considering that whereas Hamlet was a Protestant, the Ghost was Catholic. How much of the play carries "the tune of the time", and how much is for always, few can profitably conjecture. Of the original printing (the 1603 quarto) only two copies are known to survive. One lacks the last page of text, the other has no title-page. These losses are symbolic. In one's own mind the play either has no beginning or will never end.

Everyone who writes about Shakespeare goes a little mad—a pleasant goofiness, a lunacy only of one point of the compass, as Hamlet said of himself. (As he said so very likely he jerked his thumb in the direction of the King and Queen offstage, to suggest that his antics were put on for their benefit. It would be perfectly characteristic of the spirit in which the play has been studied to conduct an archaeology to determine whether the actors playing King and Queen were actually N.N.W. of Hamlet as he said the lines.) My own kind of mania is to see what gorgeous tricks of alliteration Shakespeare's excitement procured. Read these lines aloud to yourself:—

> The King doth Wake TonighT and TakeS hiS RouSe,
> KeepS WaSSail, and the SWaggering up-SpRing ReelS;
> AnD, as he DRainS hiS DRaughts of Rhenish Down,
> The Kettle-DRum and TRumpet thus BRay out
> The TRiumph of his pledge.

Can you believe that play on consonants was mere chance? See KW changing to WS, then to SR and DR and TR. Or, analyzed more closely still, the sequence is KWS, KSW, SDR, DRT, BRT. All, mark you, harsh percussive thudding sounds, with short vowels for the drum and a long *a* for the brass. That is the sort of fun an author has with himself, taking for granted that few will ever notice it. Sometimes he doesn't notice it himself: it may happen unawares.

You asked me, how much do you need to know of the man himself? A fantastic irony is observable in the few recorded facts. The earliest information we have about the family was when Shakespeare's father was fined for keeping a rubbish heap in the public street. Most of his biographers caught the habit.

We know that he was a country boy, that he apparently left home under a cloud, went up to London, was soon successful enough to rouse the jealousy of playwrights who thought themselves better educated; but that those who actually knew him found him lovable. We know there were lean years: his wife had to borrow money, and he himself was slow in paying taxes. Was it because he went bald early that he lodged at the house of a wigmaker? This wigmaker was a Frenchman, and perhaps from him Shakespeare picked up a smattering of that language. "Daily he gathered the humors of men" John Aubrey noted of him: one of the most significant hearsay comments. He became prosperous, as men may if they are shrewd enough to observe their fellows. He bought a handsome house in Stratford and planted a mulberry tree in the garden. Even in the 18th century there was already so much curiosity about him that the parson who then occupied that house was pestered by visitors. The story is that he tore it down to end the nuisance.

[xvi]

The first doubts as to Shakespeare's authorship, if I read the books correctly, were raised by a United States consul in the rum-drinking port of Santa Cruz. Like the consuls in O. Henry's *Cabbages and Kings* his official duties left much vacation for his mind. His idea was taken up by an eccentric lady whose name oddly enough was Delia Bacon; she inveigled Hawthorne into writing a preface for her book and the fun began. Incidentally, Miss Bacon died *non compos*.

A few days ago I happened to be in the pleasant Falstaff Room of the Biltmore Hotel in Providence, R.I. I asked the waiter if there were a copy of Shakespeare around as I wanted to look up some details in the Boar's Head Tavern scene, illustrated on a mural over the bar. There was no book available, but the cheerful waiter, eager to please, said, "I can tell you where the picture comes from, it's from the third act of Shakespeare."—And later, seeing my interest, and anxious to please, he added (this is exact quotation) "Some people think Bacon wrote it, so they don't know which to read."

IV

THE STORY of Shakespeare and humanity's subsequent dealings with him has no easy consolations for the sharpened mind. It needs not so much a study of documents (though that too is precious) as an intuition of the inward quality of genius; and it is most likely to dismay the house of Grundy. The world tried to dispose of Shakespeare comfortably by turning him over to teachers and troupers, both of whom are people adorably juvenile in their notions. There is a gorgeous hypocrisy in the universal lip-service to Shakespeare: we are safe in praising him because we know that few mature minds really read him. The legend was that his grave was dug 17 feet deep; and the commentators have tried to bury him deeper still.

But the casual reader need not be too humble about Shakespeare. Everyone is a Shakespearean scholar unconsciously. You yourself have probably quoted him today, for his words are the termites of the mind; they infest and honeycomb our thinking. If you said, and I'll wager you did, that the wish was father to the thought, more sinned against than sinning, as sound as a bell, care killed a cat, comparisons are odorous, more in sorrow than in anger, method in his madness,—yes, even if you spoke (I paraphrase) of the heir of a female dog, or said something was lousy, or told someone to laugh that off, or to sell himself to someone else, it was not you speaking but Shakespeare.

"My project was to please," he said—in one of the rare moments when we seem to imagine him speaking in his own person. And he added, though with mannerly qualification, "my ending is despair." He begged us then to set him free from taskwork. He was released long ago; became a marble bust with its right hand resting on a cushion. What hand had ever so earned it?

They say that April 23 was the date of both his birth and death. For the artist (I have said this before) every day should be both birth and death; every day is a complete circle. "His dates", as men say, were 1564–1616. It seems like yesterday; and every day is his birthday in someone's word and thought. Long ago he became far more important to us than the sum total of everything he wrote: he became the symbol of trouble and triumph in the human mind. Be prepared then to go a little mad if you read him sensitively. The surest way to know how great he was is to try to put his own kind of thinking into his own kind of words. Once I imagined him saying:—

> It is the varsal ego in men's bosoms
> That gives them stomach, in their loneliness,
> To chew and savour this our bright pretence
> And take it to themselves.—Haply the author
> Like the matron pelican of adage
> Feeds his unsuspective auditors
> From the red artery of his proper breast.

Christopher Morley

July 1936

THE COMPLETE WORKS OF
WILLIAM SHAKESPEARE

THE FIRST PART OF KING HENRY VI

SYNOPSIS

Aʟʟ England is mourning the death of its great soldier-king, Henry V, conqueror of France, who has died at the height of his glory, leaving his little son, Henry of Windsor, surrounded by jealous relatives, the more contentious being the child's uncle, the Duke of Gloucester, Protector of the Realm during his infancy, and Beaufort, Bishop of Winchester, his arrogant great-uncle. Under cover of the regency, they strive to advance their own interests, and their quarrels extend to clashes in the London streets between the servants of both households, whom the Lord Mayor is forced to disperse.

Neglect of national affairs soon manifests itself in the badly supported English army in France, and the Dauphin seizes the opportunity to regain the possessions lost to Henry V, news soon reaching England of his coronation at Rheims and the imprisonment of Talbot, the valiant commander of the English forces. Talbot is exchanged, however, for a prominent French prisoner, and rejoins his army at Orleans which he defends bravely without supplies and support until his fellow-general, Salisbury, is killed by a French sniper, and the siege is raised by Joan la Pucelle, a shepherd maid who, declaring herself a leader inspired by heavenly visions, wins the confidence and esteem of the Dauphin. The English, scorning Joan's power, scale the walls of Orleans during a celebration of the recent victory, recapture the city at night, and put the French to flight clad only in their shirts.

The French Countess of Auvergne, wishing to make herself famous as the betrayer of the dreaded English general, invites him to visit her, but, suspecting treachery, he stations soldiers outside the door which she locks after him, and, upon his signal, his men break down the barriers.

Disguised as peasants selling corn, La Pucelle and four soldiers with sacks on their backs pass through the gates of Rouen and admit the French forces, compelling the evacuation of the English, but the enraged Talbot quickly reorganizes his men and retakes the city the same day, carrying with him the dying old Duke of Bedford who has refused to leave the fight. While in retreat, Joan meets the noble Duke of Burgundy who has been fighting for the English, and by persisting that Talbot is false to him succeeds in winning him back to France.

Meanwhile, in the Temple Garden in London, with Richard Plantagenet, heir to the house of York, opposing John Beaufort, Earl of Somerset, head of the Lancastrian faction, the bloody civil War of the Roses is initiated, when, to the accompaniment of insults and derision, the followers of York pluck as their badge a white rose and those of Lancaster choose red, thus fulfilling the Bishop

[1]

of Carlisle's prediction at the deposition of Richard II of the future strife of kindred. Edmund Mortimer, dying a prisoner in the Tower, assures Richard Plantagenet that he is Richard II's rightful heir, and denounces as false the taunts of the Lancastrians that his father, the late Duke of Clarence, was a traitor.

In Parliament, where he appears to lay claim to his titles and estates, Plantagenet finds Gloucester and Winchester defying each other in an angry quarrel before the young King who, with the aid of the Earl of Warwick, finally succeeds in his efforts for a makeshift peace between them. Warwick presents Richard's petition to Henry who restores him to the whole inheritance of his house, creates him Duke of York, and the court then leaves for France in order that the young King may be crowned in Paris.

To reward the faithful Talbot for his great services, Henry creates him Earl of Shrewsbury, and to reconcile the York and Lancaster factions, appoints York Regent of France and general of infantry, and Somerset, general of the horse. Owing to their lack of co-operation, Talbot goes down to defeat, fighting desperately against the Dauphin's superior forces at Bordeaux, and dies broken-hearted, clasping in his arms the dead body of his young son who had just joined him after seven years' absence and had refused to desert his soldier-father surrounded by enemies.

In the peace terms offered to the English, a marriage is arranged between the young King Henry and the daughter of the powerful French Earl of Armagnac who offers a large dowry. Winchester, now appointed Cardinal through bribery, is to conclude the peace and bring the bride to England.

But meanwhile, in a battle at Angiers, in which Joan la Pucelle, later to be burned at the stake for witchcraft, is taken prisoner by York, the Earl of Suffolk, a favorite of King Henry, captures Margaret of Anjou, daughter of Reignier, titular King of Naples, falls in love with her, but being already married, resolves to marry her to Henry, and through her influence over the weak young King eventually to gain ruling power for himself. Treacherously acceding to Reignier's terms of marriage, Suffolk uses his artful description of Margaret's charms to induce the King to break his contract to the Earl of Armagnac's daughter. Peace is declared between France and England, with the Dauphin as viceroy of France under Henry, and York, aspiring to both crowns, foresees the loss of England's French possessions.

HISTORICAL DATA

The obscurities caused by the processes of revision and collaboration in the case of these earliest plays attributed to Shakespeare during the time of his apprenticeship present the most difficult problem of authorship of any of the group. Almost all critics agree that the three parts of Henry VI are the work of several hands.

The materials for the first part, which is extremely inaccurate from an historical standpoint, were taken from *Halle's Chronicle* (1548) and Holinshed's *Chronicles* (1577), principally from the former. The dramatist, in the interview between Talbot and his son, actually paraphrased the words used by Halle.

The extent of Shakespeare's contribution to this play is in much dispute but critics usually agree in attributing to him the Temple Garden scene (Act II, Scene iv), the greater part of Act IV, and the wooing of Margaret by Suffolk (Act V, Scene iii). The crude characterization of Joan of Arc is almost never considered to be Shakespeare's.

Due no doubt to the question of authorship, Meres does not include this play in his list of Shakespeare's tragedies in *Palladis Tamia*. Henslowe, however, mentions in his *Diary* the performance of "a new play—*Henry VI*" by Lord Strange's men at the Rose Theatre in 1591, and Nash, in his *Pierce Penniless*, refers to this play as well-known and popular. Gollancz, and most other commentators, think that the play in question was most probably Henry VI, Part I, and that the date of Shakespeare's additions and revamping was about 1590–91.

"*Bring forth that sorceress, condemn'd to burn.*"

HENRY VI, PART I

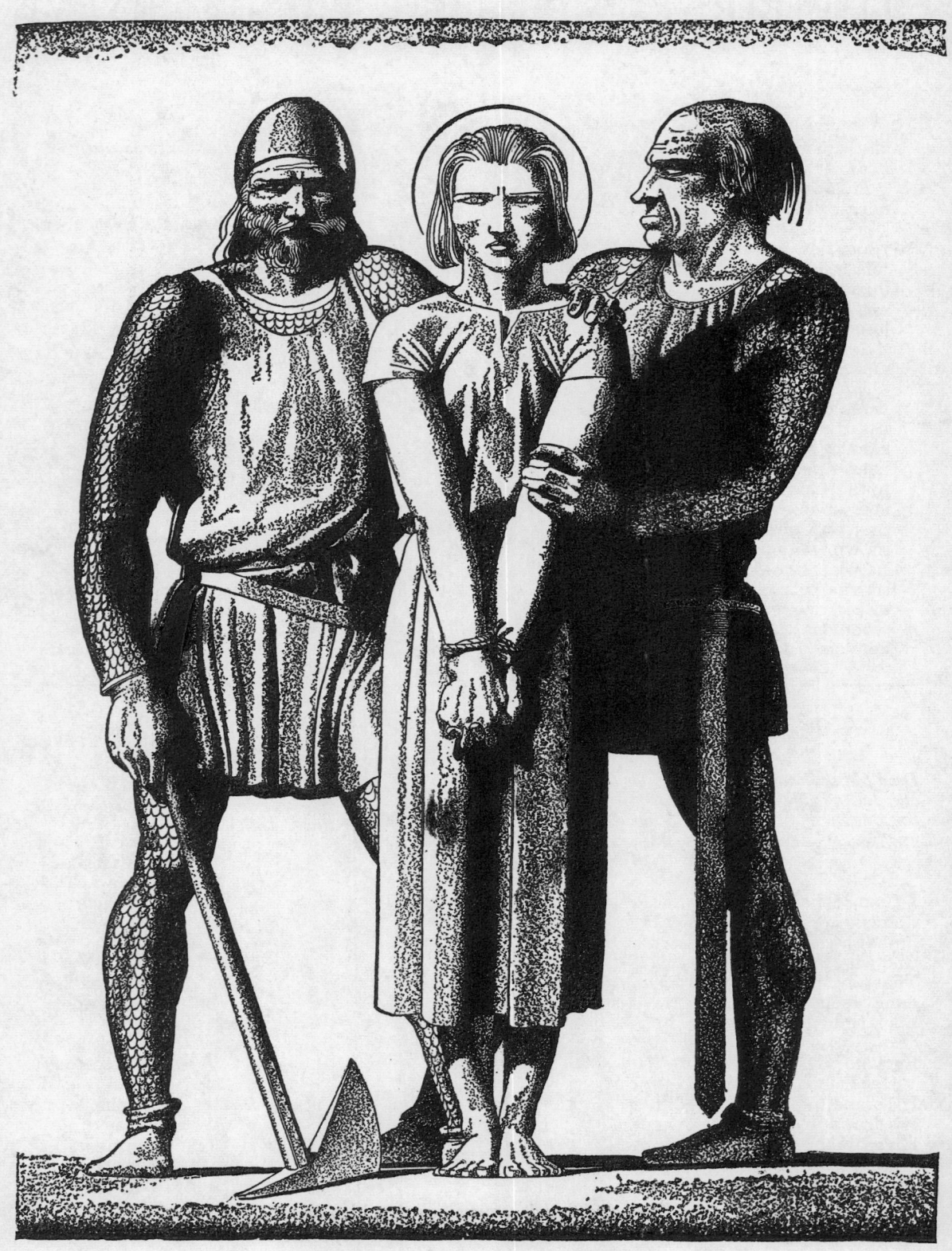

THE FIRST PART OF KING HENRY VI

DRAMATIS PERSONÆ

KING HENRY *the Sixth.*

DUKE OF GLOUCESTER, *uncle to the King, and Protector.*

DUKE OF BEDFORD, *uncle to the King, and Regent of France.*

THOMAS BEAUFORT, *Duke of Exeter, great-uncle to the King.*

HENRY BEAUFORT, *great-uncle to the King, Bishop of Winchester, and afterwards Cardinal.*

JOHN BEAUFORT, *Earl, afterwards Duke, of Somerset.*

RICHARD PLANTAGENET, *son of Richard late Earl of Cambridge, afterwards Duke of York.*

EARL OF WARWICK.

EARL OF SALISBURY.

EARL OF SUFFOLK.

LORD TALBOT, *afterwards Earl of Shrewsbury.*

JOHN TALBOT, *his son.*

EDMUND MORTIMER, *Earl of March.*

SIR JOHN FASTOLFE.

SIR WILLIAM LUCY.

SIR WILLIAM GLANSDALE.

SIR THOMAS GARGRAVE.

MAYOR OF LONDON.

WOODVILE, *Lieutenant of the Tower.*

VERNON, *of the White-Rose or York faction.*

BASSET, *of the Red-Rose or Lancaster faction.*

A LAWYER.

MORTIMER'S KEEPERS.

CHARLES, *Dauphin, and afterwards King, of France*

REIGNIER, *Duke of Anjou, and titular King of Naples.*

DUKE OF BURGUNDY.

DUKE OF ALENÇON.

BASTARD *of Orleans.*

GOVERNOR *of Paris.*

MASTER-GUNNER *of Orleans, and his Son.*

GENERAL *of the French forces in Bourdeaux.*

A FRENCH SERGEANT.

A PORTER.

AN OLD SHEPHERD, *father to Joan la Pucelle.*

MARGARET, *daughter to Reignier, afterwards married to King Henry.*

COUNTESS OF AUVERGNE.

JOAN LA PUCELLE, *commonly called Joan of Arc.*

LORDS, WARDERS *of the Tower,* HERALDS, OFFICERS, SOLDIERS, MESSENGERS, *and* ATTENDANTS.

FIENDS *appearing to La Pucelle.*

SCENE—*Partly in England, and partly in France.*

ACT I

SCENE I. *Westminster Abbey*

Dead March. Enter the Funeral of KING HENRY *the Fifth, attended on by the* DUKE OF BEDFORD, *Regent of France; the* DUKE OF GLOUCESTER, *Protector; the* DUKE OF EXETER, *the* EARL OF WARWICK, *the* BISHOP OF WINCHESTER, HERALDS, &c.

BEDFORD

HUNG be the heavens with black, yield day to night!
Comets, importing change of times and states,
Brandish your crystal tresses in the sky,
And with them scourge the bad revolting stars
That have consented unto Henry's death!
King Henry the Fifth, too famous to live long!
England ne'er lost a king of so much worth.

GLOUCESTER

England ne'er had a king until his time.
Virtue he had, deserving to command:
His brandish'd sword did blind men with his beams:
His arms spread wider than a dragon's wings;
His sparkling eyes, replete with wrathful fire,
More dazzled and drove back his enemies
Than mid-day sun fierce bent against their faces.
What should I say? his deeds exceed all speech:
He ne'er lift up his hand but conquered.

EXETER

We mourn in black: why mourn we not in blood?
Henry is dead and never shall revive:
Upon a wooden coffin we attend,
And death's dishonourable victory
We with our stately presence glorify,
Like captives bound to a triumphant car.
What! shall we curse the planets of mishap
That plotted thus our glory's overthrow?
Or shall we think the subtle-witted French
Conjurers and sorcerers, that afraid of him
By magic verses have contrived his end?

WINCHESTER

He was a king bless'd of the King of kings.
Unto the French the dreadful judgement-day
So dreadful will not be as was his sight.
The battles of the Lord of hosts he fought:
The church's prayers made him so prosperous.

GLOUCESTER

The church! where is it? Had not churchmen pray'd,
His thread of life had not so soon decay'd:
None do you like but an effeminate prince,
Whom, like a school-boy, you may over-awe.

WINCHESTER

Gloucester, whate'er we like, thou art protector,
And lookest to command the prince and realm.

Thy wife is proud; she holdeth thee in awe,
More than God or religious churchmen may.

GLOUCESTER

Name not religion, for thou lovest the flesh,
And ne'er throughout the year to church thou go'st
Except it be to pray against thy foes.

BEDFORD

Cease, cease these jars and rest your minds in peace:
Let's to the altar: heralds, wait on us:
Instead of gold, we'll offer up our arms;
Since arms avail not now that Henry's dead.
Posterity, await for wretched years,
When at their mothers' moist eyes babes shall suck,
Our isle be made a nourish of salt tears,
And none but women left to wail the dead.
Henry the Fifth, thy ghost I invocate:
Prosper this realm, keep it from civil broils,
Combat with adverse planets in the heavens!
A far more glorious star thy soul will make
Than Julius Cæsar or bright—

Enter a MESSENGER

MESSENGER

My honourable lords, health to you all!
Sad tidings bring I to you out of France,
Of loss, of slaughter and discomfiture:
Guienne, Champagne, Rheims, Orleans,
Paris, Guysors, Poictiers, are all quite lost.

BEDFORD

What say'st thou, man, before dead Henry's corse?
Speak softly; or the loss of those great towns
Will make him burst his lead and rise from death.

GLOUCESTER

Is Paris lost? is Rouen yielded up?
If Henry were recall'd to life again,
These news would cause him once more yield the
    ghost.

EXETER

How were they lost? what treachery was used?

MESSENGER

No treachery; but want of men and money.
Amongst the soldiers this is muttered,
That here you maintain several factions,
And whilst a field should be dispatch'd and fought,
You are disputing of your generals:
One would have lingering wars with little cost;
Another would fly swift, but wanteth wings;
A third thinks, without expense at all,
By guileful fair words peace may be obtain'd.
Awake, awake, English nobility!
Let not sloth dim your honours new-begot:
Cropp'd are the flower-de-luces in your arms;
Of England's coat one half is cut away.

EXETER

Were our tears wanting to this funeral,
These tidings would call forth their flowing tides.

BEDFORD

Me they concern; Regent I am of France.
Give me my steeled coat. I'll fight for France.
Away with these disgraceful wailing robes!

Wounds will I lend the French instead of eyes,
To weep their intermissive miseries.

Enter to them another MESSENGER

MESSENGER

Lords, view these letters full of bad mischance.
France is revolted from the English quite,
Except some petty towns of no import:
The Dauphin Charles is crowned king in Rheims;
The Bastard of Orleans with him is join'd;
Reignier, Duke of Anjou, doth take his part;
The Duke of Alençon flieth to his side.

EXETER

The Dauphin crowned king! all fly to him!
O, whither shall we fly from this reproach?

GLOUCESTER

We will not fly, but to our enemies' throats.
Bedford, if thou be slack, I'll fight it out.

BEDFORD

Gloucester, why doubt'st thou of my forwardness?
An army have I muster'd in my thoughts,
Wherewith already France is overrun.

Enter another MESSENGER

MESSENGER

My gracious lords, to add to your laments,
Wherewith you now bedew King Henry's hearse,
I must inform you of a dismal fight
Betwixt the stout Lord Talbot and the French.

WINCHESTER

What! wherein Talbot overcame? is' t so?

MESSENGER

O, no; wherein Lord Talbot was o'erthrown:
The circumstance I'll tell you more at large.
The tenth of August last this dreadful lord,
Retiring from the siege of Orleans,
Having full scarce six thousand in his troop,
By three and twenty thousand of the French
Was round encompassed and set upon.
No leisure had he to enrank his men;
He wanted pikes to set before his archers;
Instead whereof sharp stakes pluck'd out of hedges
They pitched in the ground confusedly,
To keep the horsemen off from breaking in.
More than three hours the fight continued;
Where valiant Talbot above human thought
Enacted wonders with his sword and lance:
Hundreds he sent to hell, and none durst stand him;
Here, there, and every where, enraged he flew:
The French exclaim'd, the devil was in arms;
All the whole army stood agazed on him:
His soldiers spying his undaunted spirit
A Talbot! a Talbot! cried out amain,
And rush'd into the bowels of the battle.
Here had the conquest fully been seal'd up,
If Sir John Fastolfe had not play'd the coward:
He, being in the vaward, placed behind
With purpose to relieve and follow them,
Cowardly fled, not having struck one stroke.
Hence grew the general wreck and massacre;
Enclosed were they with their enemies:
A base Walloon, to win the Dauphin's grace,

[4]

Thrust Talbot with a spear into the back,
Whom all France with their chief assembled strength
Durst not presume to look once in the face.

BEDFORD

Is Talbot slain? then I will slay myself,
For living idly here in pomp and ease,
Whilst such a worthy leader, wanting aid,
Unto his dastard foemen is betray'd.

MESSENGER

O no, he lives; but is took prisoner,
And Lord Scales with him, and Lord Hungerford:
Most of the rest slaughter'd or took likewise.

BEDFORD

His ransom there is none but I shall pay:
I'll hale the Dauphin headlong from his throne:
His crown shall be the ransom of my friend;
Four of their lords I'll change for one of ours.
Farewell, my masters; to my task will I;
Bonfires in France forthwith I am to make,
To keep our great Saint George's feast withal:
Ten thousand soldiers with me I will take,
Whose bloody deeds shall make all Europe quake.

MESSENGER

So you had need; for Orleans is besieged;
The English army is grown weak and faint:
The Earl of Salisbury craveth supply,
And hardly keeps his men from mutiny,
Since they, so few, watch such a multitude.

EXETER

Remember, lords, your oaths to Henry sworn,
Either to quell the Dauphin utterly,
Or bring him in obedience to your yoke.

BEDFORD

I do remember it; and here take my leave,
To go about my preparation.   [Exit

GLOUCESTER

I'll to the Tower with all the haste I can,
To view the artillery and munition;
And then I will proclaim young Henry king.   [Exit

EXETER

To Eltham will I, where the young king is,
Being ordain'd his special governor,
And for his safety there I'll best devise.   [Exit

WINCHESTER

Each hath his place and function to attend:
I am left out; for me nothing remains.
But long I will not be Jack out of office:
The king from Eltham I intend to steal
And sit at chiefest stern of public weal.   [Exeunt

SCENE II. *France. Before Orleans*

Sound a Flourish. Enter CHARLES, ALENÇON, *and*
REIGNIER, *marching with Drum and Soldiers*

CHARLES

Mars his true moving, even as in the heavens
So in the earth, to this day is not known:
Late did he shine upon the English side;
Now we are victors; upon us he smiles.

What towns of any moment but we have?
At pleasure here we lie near Orleans;
Otherwhiles the famish'd English, like pale ghosts,
Faintly besiege us one hour in a month.

ALENÇON

They want their porridge and their fat bull-beeves:
Either they must be dieted like mules,
And have their provender tied to their mouths,
Or piteous they will look, like drowned mice.

REIGNIER

Let's raise the siege: why live we idly here?
Talbot is taken, whom we wont to fear:
Remaineth none but mad-brain'd Salisbury;
And he may well in fretting spend his gall,
Nor men nor money hath he to make war.

CHARLES

Sound, sound alarum! we will rush on them.
Now for the honour of the forlorn French!
Him I forgive my death that killeth me
When he sees me go back one foot or fly.   [*Exeunt*
*Here Alarum; they are beaten back by the English with
great loss. Re-enter* CHARLES, ALENÇON, *and* REIGNIER

CHARLES

Who ever saw the like? what men have I!
Dogs! cowards! dastards! I would ne'er have fled,
But that they left me 'midst my enemies.

REIGNIER

Salisbury is a desperate homicide;
He fighteth as one weary of his life.
The other lords, like lions wanting food,
Do rush upon us as their hungry prey.

ALENÇON

Froissart, a countryman of ours, records,
England all Olivers and Rowlands bred
During the time Edward the Third did reign.
More truly now may this be verified;
For none but Samsons and Goliases
It sendeth forth to skirmish. One to ten!
Lean raw-boned rascals! who would e'er suppose
They had such courage and audacity?

CHARLES

Let's leave this town; for they are hare-brain'd
slaves,
And hunger will enforce them to be more eager:
Of old I know them; rather with their teeth
The walls they'll tear down than forsake the siege.

REIGNIER

I think, by some odd gimmors or device
Their arms are set like clocks, still to strike on;
Else ne'er could they hold out so as they do.
By my consent, we'll even let them alone.

ALENÇON

Be it so.
                    Enter the BASTARD *of Orleans*

BASTARD

Where's the Prince Dauphin? I have news for him.

CHARLES

Bastard of Orleans, thrice welcome to us.

BASTARD

Methinks your looks are sad, your cheer appall'd:
Hath the late overthrow wrought this offence?
Be not dismay'd, for succour is at hand:
A holy maid hither with me I bring,
Which by a vision sent to her from heaven
Ordained is to raise this tedious siege,
And drive the English forth the bounds of France.
The spirit of deep prophecy she hath,
Exceeding the nine sibyls of old Rome:
What's past and what's to come she can descry.
Speak, shall I call her in? Believe my words,
For they are certain and unfallible.

CHARLES

Go, call her in. [Exit BASTARD.] But first, to try her
  skill,
Reignier, stand thou as Dauphin in my place:
Question her proudly; let thy looks be stern:
By this means shall we sound what skill she hath.
  Re-enter the BASTARD *of Orleans, with* JOAN LA
  PUCELLE

REIGNIER

Fair maid, is 't thou wilt do these wondrous feats?

LA PUCELLE

Reignier, is 't thou that thinkest to beguile me?
Where is the Dauphin? Come, come from behind;
I know thee well, though never seen before.
Be not amazed, there's nothing hid from me:
In private will I talk with thee apart.
Stand back, you lords, and give us leave awhile.

REIGNIER

She takes upon her bravely at first dash.

LA PUCELLE

Dauphin, I am by birth a shepherd's daughter,
My wit untrain'd in any kind of art.
Heaven and our Lady gracious hath it pleased
To shine on my contemptible estate:
Lo, whilst I waited on my tender lambs,
And to sun's parching heat display'd my cheeks,
God's mother deigned to appear to me,
And in a vision full of majesty
Will'd me to leave my base vocation,
And free my country from calamity:
Her aid she promised and assured success:
In complete glory she reveal'd herself;
And, whereas I was black and swart before,
With those clear rays which she infused on me
That beauty am I bless'd with which you see.
Ask me what question thou canst possible,
And I will answer unpremeditated:
My courage try by combat, if thou darest,
And thou shalt find that I exceed my sex.
Resolve on this, thou shalt be fortunate,
If thou receive me for thy warlike mate.

CHARLES

Thou hast astonish'd me with thy high terms:
Only this proof I'll of thy valour make,
In single combat thou shalt buckle with me,
And if thou vanquishest, thy words are true;
Otherwise I renounce all confidence.

LA PUCELLE

I am prepared: here is my keen-edged sword,
Deck'd with five flower-de-luces on each side;
The which at Touraine, in Saint Katharine's
  churchyard,
Out of a great deal of old iron I chose forth.

CHARLES

Then come, o' God's name; I fear no woman.

LA PUCELLE

And while I live, I'll ne'er fly from a man.
  [*Here they fight, and* JOAN LA PUCELLE *overcomes*

CHARLES

Stay, stay thy hands! thou art an Amazon,
And fightest with the sword of Deborah.

LA PUCELLE

Christ's mother helps me, else I were too weak.

CHARLES

Whoe'er helps thee, 'tis thou that must help me:
Impatiently I burn with thy desire;
My heart and hands thou hast at once subdued.
Excellent Pucelle, if thy name be so,
Let me thy servant and not sovereign be:
'Tis the French Dauphin sueth to thee thus.

LA PUCELLE

I must not yield to any rites of love,
For my profession's sacred from above:
When I have chased all thy foes from hence,
Then will I think upon a recompense.

CHARLES

Meantime look gracious on thy prostrate thrall.

REIGNIER

My lord, methinks, is very long in talk.

ALENÇON

Doubtless he shrives this woman to her smock;
Else ne'er could he so long protract his speech.

REIGNIER

Shall we disturb him, since he keeps no mean?

ALENÇON

He may mean more than we poor men do know:
These women are shrewd tempters with their
  tongues.

REIGNIER

My lord, where are you? what devise you on?
Shall we give over Orleans, or no?

LA PUCELLE

Why, no, I say, distrustful recreants!
Fight till the last gasp; I will be your guard.

CHARLES

What she says I'll confirm: we'll fight it out.

LA PUCELLE

Assign'd am I to be the English scourge.
This night the siege assuredly I'll raise:
Expect Saint Martin's summer, halcyon days,
Since I have entered into these wars.
Glory is like a circle in the water,
Which never ceaseth to enlarge itself
Till by broad spreading it disperse to nought.
With Henry's death the English circle ends;
Dispersed are the glories it included.

Now am I like that proud insulting ship
Which Cæsar and his fortune bare at once.

CHARLES

Was Mahomet inspired with a dove?
Thou with an eagle art inspired then.
Helen, the mother of great Constantine,
Nor yet Saint Philip's daughters, were like thee.
Bright star of Venus, fall'n down on the earth,
How may I reverently worship thee enough?

ALENÇON

Leave off delays, and let us raise the siege.

REIGNIER

Woman, do what thou canst to save our honours;
Drive them from Orleans and be immortalized.

CHARLES

Presently we'll try: come, let's away about it:
No prophet will I trust, if she prove false.　　[Exeunt

SCENE III. London. Before the Tower

Enter the DUKE OF GLOUCESTER, with his SERVING-MEN
in blue coats

GLOUCESTER

I am come to survey the Tower this day:
Since Henry's death, I fear, there is conveyance.
Where be these warders, that they wait not here?
Open the gates; 'tis Gloucester that calls.

FIRST WARDER

[Within] Who's there that knocks so imperiously?

FIRST SERVANT

It is the noble Duke of Gloucester.

SECOND WARDER

[Within] Whoe'er he be, you may not be let in.

FIRST SERVANT

Villains, answer you so the lord protector?

FIRST WARDER

[Within] The Lord protect him! so we answer him:
We do no otherwise than we are will'd.

GLOUCESTER

Who willed you? or whose will stands but mine?
There's none protector of the realm but I.
Break up the gates, I'll be your warrantize:
Shall I be flouted thus by dunghill grooms?

[GLOUCESTER's men rush at the Tower Gates, and
WOODVILE the Lieutenant speaks within

WOODVILE

What noise is this? what traitors have we here?

GLOUCESTER

Lieutenant, is it you whose voice I hear?
Open the gates; here's Gloucester that would enter.

WOODVILE

Have patience, noble duke; I may not open;
The Cardinal of Winchester forbids:
From him I have express commandment
That thou nor none of thine shall be let in.

GLOUCESTER

Faint-hearted Woodvile, prizest him 'fore me?
Arrogant Winchester, that haughty prelate,
Whom Henry, our late sovereign, ne'er could brook?

Thou art no friend to God or to the king:
Open the gates, or I'll shut thee out shortly.

SERVING-MEN

Open the gates unto the lord protector,
Or we'll burst them open, if that you come not
quickly.

Enter to the Protector at the Tower Gates WINCHESTER
and his men in tawny coats

WINCHESTER

How now, ambitious Humphry! what means this?

GLOUCESTER

Peel'd priest, dost thou command me to be shut out?

WINCHESTER

I do, thou most usurping proditor,
And not protector, of the king or realm.

GLOUCESTER

Stand back, thou manifest conspirator,
Thou that contrivedst to murder our dead lord;
Thou that givest whores indulgences to sin:
I'll canvass thee in thy broad cardinal's hat,
If thou proceed in this thy insolence.

WINCHESTER

Nay, stand thou back; I will not budge a foot:
This be Damascus, be thou cursed Cain,
To slay thy brother Abel, if thou wilt.

GLOUCESTER

I will not slay thee, but I'll drive thee back:
Thy scarlet robes as a child's bearing-cloth
I'll use to carry thee out of this place.

WINCHESTER

Do what thou darest; I beard thee to thy face.

GLOUCESTER

What! am I dared and bearded to my face?
Draw, men, for all this privileged place;
Blue coats to tawny coats. Priest, beware your beard;
I mean to tug it and to cuff you soundly:
Under my feet I stamp thy cardinal's hat:
In spite of pope or dignities of church,
Here by the cheeks I'll drag thee up and down.

WINCHESTER

Gloucester, thou wilt answer this before the pope.

GLOUCESTER

Winchester goose, I cry, a rope! a rope!
Now beat them hence; why do you let them stay?
Thee I'll chase hence, thou wolf in sheep's array.
Out, tawny coats! out, scarlet hypocrite!

Here GLOUCESTER's men beat out the CARDINAL's men,
and enter in the hurly-burly the MAYOR OF LONDON and
his OFFICERS

MAYOR

Fie, lords! that you, being supreme magistrates,
Thus contumeliously should break the peace!

GLOUCESTER

Peace, mayor! thou know'st little of my wrongs:
Here's Beaufort, that regards nor God nor king,
Hath here distrain'd the Tower to his use.

WINCHESTER

Here's Gloucester, a foe to citizens,
One that still motions war and never peace,
O'ercharging your free purses with large fines,

That seeks to overthrow religion,
Because he is protector of the realm,
And would have armour here out of the Tower,
To crown himself king and suppress the prince.

GLOUCESTER

I will not answer thee with words, but blows.
　　　　　　　　　　　　　[Here they skirmish again

MAYOR

Nought rests for me in this tumultuous strife
But to make open proclamation:
Come, officer; as loud as e'er thou canst:
Cry.

OFFICER

All manner of men assembled here in arms this day against
God's peace and the king's, we charge and command you, in
his highness' name, to repair to your several dwelling-places;
and not to wear, handle, or use any sword, weapon, or dagger,
henceforward, upon pain of death.

GLOUCESTER

Cardinal, I'll be no breaker of the law:
But we shall meet, and break our minds at large.

WINCHESTER

Gloucester, we will meet; to thy cost, be sure:
Thy heart-blood I will have for this day's work.

MAYOR

I'll call for clubs, if you will not away.
This cardinal's more haughty than the devil.

GLOUCESTER

Mayor, farewell: thou dost but what thou mayst.

WINCHESTER

Abominable Gloucester, guard thy head;
For I intend to have it ere long.
　　　[Exeunt, severally, GLOUCESTER and WINCHESTER
　　　　　　　　　　　　　with their SERVING-MEN

MAYOR

See the coast clear'd, and then we will depart.
Good God, these nobles should such stomachs bear!
I myself fight not once in forty year.　　[Exeunt

SCENE IV. Orleans

Enter, on the walls, a MASTER GUNNER and his BOY

MASTER GUNNER

Sirrah, thou know'st how Orleans is besieged,
And how the English have the suburbs won.

BOY

Father, I know; and oft have shot at them,
Howe'er unfortunate I miss'd my aim.

MASTER GUNNER

But now thou shalt not. Be thou ruled by me:
Chief master-gunner am I of this town;
Something I must do to procure me grace.
The prince's espials have informed me
How the English, in the suburbs close intrench'd,
Wont through a secret grate of iron bars
In yonder tower to overpeer the city,
And thence discover how with most advantage
They may vex us with shot or with assault.

To intercept this inconvenience,
A piece of ordnance 'gainst it I have placed;
And even these three days have I watch'd,
If I could see them.
Now do thou watch, for I can stay no longer.
If thou spy'st any, run and bring me word;
And thou shalt find me at the governor's.　　[Exit

BOY

Father, I warrant you; take you no care;
I'll never trouble you, if I may spy them.　　[Exit
Enter, on the turrets, the LORDS SALISBURY and TALBOT,
SIR WILLIAM GLANSDALE, SIR THOMAS GARGRAVE, and
　　　　　　　　　　　　others.

SALISBURY

Talbot, my life, my joy, again return'd!
How wert thou handled being prisoner?
Or by what means got'st thou to be released?
Discourse, I prithee, on this turret's top.

TALBOT

The Duke of Bedford had a prisoner
Call'd the brave Lord Ponton de Santrailles;
For him was I exchanged and ransomed.
But with a baser man of arms by far
Once in contempt they would have barter'd me:
Which I disdaining scorn'd, and craved death
Rather than I would be so vile-esteem'd.
In fine, redeem'd I was as I desired.
But, O! the treacherous Fastolfe wounds my heart,
Whom with my bare fists I would execute,
If I now had him brought into my power.

SALISBURY

Yet tell'st thou not how thou wert entertain'd.

TALBOT

With scoffs and scorns and contumelious taunts.
In open market-place produced they me,
To be a public spectacle to all:
Here, said they, is the terror of the French,
The scarecrow that affrights our children so.
Then broke I from the officers that led me,
And with my nails digg'd stones out of the ground,
To hurl at the beholders of my shame:
My grisly countenance made others fly;
None durst come near for fear of sudden death.
In iron walls they deem'd me not secure;
So great fear of my name 'mongst them was spread
That they supposed I could rend bars of steel,
And spurn in pieces posts of adamant:
Wherefore a guard of chosen shot I had,
That walk'd about me every minute while;
And if I did but stir out of my bed,
Ready they were to shoot me to the heart.
　　　　　　　Enter the BOY with a linstock

SALISBURY

I grieve to hear what torments you endured,
But we will be revenged sufficiently.
Now it is supper-time in Orleans:
Here, through this grate, I count each one,
And view the Frenchmen how they fortify:
Let us look in; the sight will much delight thee.
Sir Thomas Gargrave, and Sir William Glansdale,

Let me have your express opinions
Where is best place to make our battery next.
                    GARGRAVE
I think, at the north gate; for there stand lords.
                    GLANSDALE
And I, here, at the bulwark of the bridge.
                    TALBOT
For aught I see, this city must be famish'd,
Or with light skirmishes enfeebled.
            [*Here they shoot.* SALISBURY *and* GARGRAVE *fall*
                    SALISBURY
O Lord, have mercy on us, wretched sinners!
                    GARGRAVE
O Lord, have mercy on me, woful man!
                    TALBOT
What chance is this that suddenly hath cross'd us?
Speak, Salisbury; at least, if thou canst speak:
How farest thou, mirror of all martial men?
One of thy eyes and thy cheek's side struck off!
Accursed tower! accursed fatal hand
That hath contrived this woful tragedy!
In thirteen battles Salisbury o'ercame;
Henry the Fifth he first train'd to the wars;
Whilst any trump did sound, or drum struck up,
His sword did ne'er leave striking in the field.
Yet livest thou, Salisbury? though thy speech doth
        fail,
One eye thou hast, to look to heaven for grace:
The sun with one eye vieweth all the world.
Heaven, be thou gracious to none alive,
If Salisbury wants mercy at thy hands!
Bear hence his body; I will help to bury it.
Sir Thomas Gargrave, hast thou any life?
Speak unto Talbot; nay, look up to him.
Salisbury, cheer thy spirit with this comfort;
Thou shalt not die whiles—
He beckons with his hand and smiles on me,
As who should say 'When I am dead and gone,
Remember to avenge me on the French.'
Plantagenet, I will; and like thee, Nero,
Play on the lute, beholding the towns burn:
Wretched shall France be only in my name.
            [*Here an alarum, and it thunders and lightens*
What stir is this? what tumult's in the heavens?
Whence cometh this alarum, and the noise?
                Enter a MESSENGER
                    MESSENGER
My lord, my lord, the French have gather'd head:
The Dauphin, with one Joan la Pucelle join'd,
A holy prophetess new risen up,
Is come with a great power to raise the siege.
            [*Here* SALISBURY *lifteth himself up and groans*
                    TALBOT
Hear, hear how dying Salisbury doth groan!
It irks his heart he cannot be revenged.
Frenchmen, I'll be a Salisbury to you:
Pucelle or puzzel, dolphin or dogfish,
Your hearts I'll stamp out with my horse's heels,
And make a quagmire of your mingled brains.

Convey me Salisbury into his tent,
And then we'll try what these dastard Frenchmen
dare.   [*Alarum. Exeunt*

                SCENE V. *The same*

Here an alarum again: and TALBOT *pursueth the* DAUPHIN,
and driveth him: then enter JOAN LA PUCELLE, *driving*
Englishmen before her, and exit after them: then re-enter
                    TALBOT
                    TALBOT
Where is my strength, my valour, and my force?
Our English troops retire, I cannot stay them;
A woman clad in armour chaseth them.
                Re-enter LA PUCELLE
Here, here she comes. I'll have a bout with thee;
Devil or devil's dam, I'll conjure thee:
Blood will I draw on thee, thou art a witch,
And straightway give thy soul to him thou servest.
                    LA PUCELLE
Come, come, 'tis only I that must disgrace thee.
                            [*Here they fight*
                    TALBOT
Heavens, can you suffer hell so to prevail?
My breast I'll burst with straining of my courage,
And from my shoulders crack my arms asunder,
But I will chastise this high-minded strumpet.
                            [*They fight again*
                    LA PUCELLE
Talbot, farewell; thy hour is not yet come:
I must go victual Orleans forthwith.
            [*A short alarum: then enter the town with soldiers*
O'ertake me, if thou canst; I scorn thy strength.
Go, go, cheer up thy hungry-starved men;
Help Salisbury to make his testament:
This day is ours, as many more shall be.   [*Exit*
                    TALBOT
My thoughts are whirled like a potter's wheel;
I know not where I am, nor what I do:
A witch, by fear, not force, like Hannibal,
Drives back our troops and conquers as she lists:
So bees with smoke and doves with noisome stench
Are from their hives and houses driven away.
They call'd us for our fierceness English dogs;
Now, like to whelps, we crying run away.
                            [*A short alarum*
Hark, countrymen! either renew the fight,
Or tear the lions out of England's coat;
Renounce your soil, give sheep in lions' stead:
Sheep run not half so treacherous from the wolf,
Or horse or oxen from the leopard,
As you fly from your oft-subdued slaves.
                    [*Alarum. Here another skirmish*
It will not be: retire into your trenches:
You all consented unto Salisbury's death,
For none would strike a stroke in his revenge.
Pucelle is enter'd into Orleans,
In spite of us or aught that we could do.

O, would I were to die with Salisbury!
The shame hereof will make me hide my head.
           [*Exit* TALBOT. *Alarum; retreat; flourish*

SCENE VI. *The same*

Enter, on the walls, LA PUCELLE, CHARLES, REIGNIER,
ALENÇON, *and* SOLDIERS

LA PUCELLE

Advance our waving colours on the walls;
Rescued is Orleans from the English:
Thus Joan la Pucelle hath perform'd her word.

CHARLES

Divinest creature, Astræa's daughter,
How shall I honour thee for this success?
Thy promises are like Adonis' gardens
That one day bloom'd and fruitful were the next.
France, triumph in thy glorious prophetess!
Recover'd is the town of Orleans:
More blessed hap did ne'er befall our state.

REIGNIER

Why ring not out the bells aloud throughout the
    town?
Dauphin, command the citizens make bonfires
And feast and banquet in the open streets,
To celebrate the joy that God hath given us.

ALENÇON

All France will be replete with mirth and joy,
When they shall hear how we have play'd the men.

CHARLES

'Tis Joan, not we, by whom the day is won;
For which I will divide my crown with her,
And all the priests and friars in my realm
Shall in procession sing her endless praise.
A statelier pyramis to her I'll rear
Than Rhodope's or Memphis' ever was:
In memory of her when she is dead,
Her ashes, in an urn more precious
Than the rich-jewel'd coffer of Darius,
Transported shall be at high festivals
Before the kings and queens of France.
No longer on Saint Denis will we cry,
But Joan la Pucelle shall be France's saint.
Come in, and let us banquet royally,
After this golden day of victory.   [*Flourish. Exeunt*

ACT II

SCENE I. *Before Orleans*

Enter a SERGEANT *of a band, with two* SENTINELS

SERGEANT

Sirs, take your places and be vigilant:
If any noise or soldier you perceive
Near to the walls, by some apparent sign
Let us have knowledge at the court of guard.

FIRST SENTINEL

Sergeant, you shall. [*Exit* SERGEANT.] Thus are poor
    servitors,
When others sleep upon their quiet beds,
Constrain'd to watch in darkness, rain and cold.

Enter TALBOT, BEDFORD, BURGUNDY, *and forces, with
scaling-ladders, their drums beating a dead march*

TALBOT

Lord Regent, and redoubted Burgundy,
By whose approach the regions of Artois,
Wallon and Picardy are friends to us,
This happy night the Frenchmen are secure,
Having all day caroused and banqueted:
Embrace we then this opportunity,
As fitting best to quittance their deceit
Contrived by art and baleful sorcery.

BEDFORD

Coward of France! how much he wrongs his fame,
Despairing of his own arm's fortitude,
To join with witches and the help of hell!

BURGUNDY

Traitors have never other company.
But what's that Pucelle whom they term so pure?

TALBOT

A maid, they say.

BEDFORD

          A maid! and be so martial!

BURGUNDY

Pray God she prove not masculine ere long,
If underneath the standard of the French
She carry armour as she hath begun.

TALBOT

Well, let them practise and converse with spirits:
God is our fortress, in whose conquering name
Let us resolve to scale their flinty bulwarks.

BEDFORD

Ascend, brave Talbot; we will follow thee.

TALBOT

Not all together: better far, I guess,
That we do make our entrance several ways;
That, if it chance the one of us do fail,
The other yet may rise against their force.

BEDFORD

Agreed: I'll to yond corner.

BURGUNDY

              And I to this.

TALBOT

And here will Talbot mount, or make his grave.
Now, Salisbury, for thee, and for the right
Of English Henry, shall this night appear
How much in duty I am bound to both.

SENTINEL

Arm! arm! the enemy doth make assault!
        [*Cry:* 'St George,' 'A Talbot'
*The French leap over the walls in their shirts. Enter, several
ways, the* BASTARD *of Orleans,* ALENÇON, *and* REIGNIER,
half ready, and half unready

ALENÇON

How now, my lords! what, all unready so?

BASTARD

Unready! ay, and glad we 'scaped so well.

REIGNIER

'Twas time, I trow, to wake and leave our beds,
Hearing alarums at our chamber-doors.

ALENÇON

Of all exploits since first I follow'd arms,
Ne'er heard I of a warlike enterprise
More venturous or desperate than this.

BASTARD

I think this Talbot be a fiend of hell.

REIGNIER

If not of hell, the heavens, sure, favour him.

ALENÇON

Here cometh Charles: I marvel how he sped.

BASTARD

Tut, holy Joan was his defensive guard.

Enter CHARLES *and* LA PUCELLE

CHARLES

Is this thy cunning, thou deceitful dame?
Didst thou at first, to flatter us withal,
Make us partakers of a little gain,
That now our loss might be ten times so much?

LA PUCELLE

Wherefore is Charles impatient with his friend?
At all times will you have my power alike?
Sleeping or waking must I still prevail,
Or will you blame and lay the fault on me?
Improvident soldiers! had your watch been good,
This sudden mischief never could have fall'n.

CHARLES

Duke of Alençon, this was your default,
That, being captain of the watch to-night,
Did look no better to that weighty charge.

ALENÇON

Had all your quarters been as safely kept
As that whereof I had the government,
We had not been thus shamefully surprised.

BASTARD

Mine was secure.

REIGNIER

And so was mine, my lord.

CHARLES

And, for myself, most part of all this night,
Within her quarter and mine own precinct
I was employ'd in passing to and fro,
About relieving of the sentinels:
Then how or which way should they first break in?

LA PUCELLE

Question, my lords, no further of the case,
How or which way: 'tis sure they found some place
But weakly guarded, where the breach was made.
And now there rests no other shift but this;
To gather our soldiers, scatter'd and dispersed,
And lay new platforms to endamage them.

Alarum. Enter an ENGLISH SOLDIER, *crying* 'A Talbot!
a Talbot!' *They fly, leaving their clothes behind*

SOLDIER

I'll be so bold to take what they have left.
The cry of Talbot serves me for a sword;

For I have loaden me with many spoils,
Using no other weapon but his name.   [*Exit*

SCENE II. *Orleans. Within the town*

Enter TALBOT, BEDFORD, BURGUNDY, *a* CAPTAIN, *and
others*

BEDFORD

The day begins to break, and night is fled,
Whose pitchy mantle over-veil'd the earth.
Here sound retreat, and cease our hot pursuit.

[*Retreat sounded*

TALBOT

Bring forth the body of old Salisbury,
And here advance it in the market-place,
The middle centre of this cursed town.
Now have I paid my vow unto his soul;
For every drop of blood was drawn from him
There hath at least five Frenchmen died to-night.
And that hereafter ages may behold
What ruin happen'd in revenge of him,
Within their chiefest temple I'll erect
A tomb, wherein his corpse shall be interr'd:
Upon the which, that every one may read,
Shall be engraved the sack of Orleans,
The treacherous manner of his mournful death
And what a terror he had been to France.
But, lords, in all our bloody massacre,
I muse we met not with the Dauphin's grace,
His new-come champion, virtuous Joan of Arc,
Nor any of his false confederates.

BEDFORD

'Tis thought, Lord Talbot, when the fight began,
Roused on the sudden from their drowsy beds,
They did amongst the troops of armed men
Leap o'er the walls for refuge in the field.

BURGUNDY

Myself, as far as I could well discern
For smoke and dusky vapours of the night,
Am sure I scared the Dauphin and his trull,
When arm in arm they both came swiftly running,
Like to a pair of loving turtle-doves
That could not live asunder day or night.
After that things are set in order here,
We'll follow them with all the power we have.

Enter a MESSENGER

MESSENGER

All hail, my lords! Which of this princely train
Call ye the warlike Talbot, for his acts
So much applauded through the realm of France?

TALBOT

Here is the Talbot: who would speak with him?

MESSENGER

The virtuous lady, Countess of Auvergne,
With modesty admiring thy renown,
By me entreats, great lord, thou wouldst vouchsafe
To visit her poor castle where she lies,
That she may boast she hath beheld the man
Whose glory fills the world with loud report.

BURGUNDY

Is it even so? Nay, then, I see our wars
Will turn unto a peaceful comic sport,
When ladies crave to be encounter'd with.
You may not, my lord, despise her gentle suit.

TALBOT

Ne'er trust me, then; for when a world of men
Could not prevail with all their oratory,
Yet hath a woman's kindness over-ruled:
And therefore tell her I return great thanks,
And in submission will attend on her.
Will not your honours bear me company?

BEDFORD

No, truly; it is more than manners will:
And I have heard it said, unbidden guests
Are often welcomest when they are gone.

TALBOT

Well then, alone, since there's no remedy,
I mean to prove this lady's courtesy.
Come hither, captain. [Whispers.] You perceive my
    mind?

CAPTAIN

I do, my lord, and mean accordingly.   [Exeunt

SCENE III. *Auvergne. The* COUNTESS's *castle.*

Enter the COUNTESS *and her* PORTER

COUNTESS

Porter, remember what I gave in charge;
And when you have done so, bring the keys to me.

PORTER

Madam, I will.   [Exit

COUNTESS

The plot is laid: if all things fall out right,
I shall as famous be by this exploit
As Scythian Tomyris by Cyrus' death.
Great is the rumour of this dreadful knight,
And his achievements of no less account:
Fain would mine eyes be witness with mine ears,
To give their censure of these rare reports.

Enter MESSENGER *and* TALBOT

MESSENGER

Madam,
According as your ladyship desired,
By message craved, so is Lord Talbot come.

COUNTESS

And he is welcome. What! is this the man?

MESSENGER

Madam, it is.

COUNTESS

          Is this the scourge of France?
Is this the Talbot, so much fear'd abroad
That with his name the mothers still their babes?
I see report is fabulous and false:
I thought I should have seen some Hercules,
A second Hector, for his grim aspect,
And large proportion of his strong-knit limbs.
Alas, this is a child, a silly dwarf!

It cannot be this weak and writhled shrimp
Should strike such terror to his enemies.

TALBOT

Madam, I have been bold to trouble you;
But since your ladyship is not at leisure,
I'll sort some other time to visit you.

COUNTESS

What means he now? Go ask him whither he goes.

MESSENGER

Stay, my Lord Talbot; for my lady craves
To know the cause of your abrupt departure.

TALBOT

Marry, for that she's in a wrong belief,
I go to certify her Talbot's here.

Re-enter PORTER *with keys*

COUNTESS

If thou be he, then art thou prisoner.

TALBOT

Prisoner! to whom?

COUNTESS

          To me, blood-thirsty lord;
And for that cause I train'd thee to my house.
Long time thy shadow hath been thrall to me,
For in my gallery thy picture hangs:
But now the substance shall endure the like,
And I will chain these legs and arms of thine,
That hast by tyranny these many years
Wasted our country, slain our citizens,
And sent our sons and husbands captivate.

TALBOT

Ha, ha, ha!

COUNTESS

Laughest thou, wretch? thy mirth shall turn to
    moan.

TALBOT

I laugh to see your ladyship so fond
To think that you have aught but Talbot's shadow
Whereon to practise your severity.

COUNTESS

Why, art not thou the man?

TALBOT

          I am indeed.

COUNTESS

Then have I substance too.

TALBOT

No, no, I am but shadow of myself:
You are deceived, my substance is not here;
For what you see is but the smallest part
And least proportion of humanity:
I tell you, madam, were the whole frame here,
It is of such a spacious lofty pitch,
Your roof were not sufficient to contain 't.

COUNTESS

This is a riddling merchant for the nonce;
He will be here, and yet he is not here:
How can these contrarieties agree?

TALBOT

That will I show you presently.
        [Winds his horn. Drums strike up: a peal
               of ordnance. Enter SOLDIERS

How say you, madam? are you now persuaded
That Talbot is but shadow of himself?
These are his substance, sinews, arms and strength,
With which he yoketh your rebellious necks,
Razeth your cities and subverts your towns
And in a moment makes them desolate.

COUNTESS

Victorious Talbot! pardon my abuse:
I find thou art no less than fame hath bruited,
And more than may be gather'd by thy shape.
Let my presumption not provoke thy wrath;
For I am sorry that with reverence
I did not entertain thee as thou art.

TALBOT

Be not dismay'd, fair lady; nor misconstrue
The mind of Talbot, as you did mistake
The outward composition of his body.
What you have done hath not offended me;
Nor other satisfaction do I crave,
But only, with your patience, that we may
Taste of your wine and see what cates you have;
For soldiers' stomachs always serve them well.

COUNTESS

With all my heart, and think me honoured
To feast so great a warrior in my house.   [Exeunt

SCENE IV. London. The Temple-garden

Enter the EARLS OF SOMERSET, SUFFOLK, and WARWICK;
RICHARD PLANTAGENET, VERNON, and another LAWYER

PLANTAGENET

Great lords and gentlemen, what means this silence?
Dare no man answer in a case of truth?

SUFFOLK

Within the Temple-hall we were too loud;
The garden here is more convenient.

PLANTAGENET

Then say at once if I maintain'd the truth;
Or else was wrangling Somerset in the error?

SUFFOLK

Faith, I have been a truant in the law,
And never yet could frame my will to it;
And therefore frame the law unto my will.

SOMERSET

Judge you, my lord of Warwick, then, between us.

WARWICK

Between two hawks, which flies the higher pitch;
Between two dogs, which hath the deeper mouth;
Between two blades, which bears the better temper:
Between two horses, which doth bear him best;
Between two girls, which hath the merriest eye;
I have perhaps some shallow spirit of judgement·
But in these nice sharp quillets of the law,
Good faith, I am no wiser than a daw.

PLANTAGENET

Tut, tut, here is a mannerly forbearance:
The truth appears so naked on my side
That any purblind eye may find it out.

SOMERSET

And on my side it is so well apparell'd,
So clear, so shining and so evident
That it will glimmer through a blind man's eye.

PLANTAGENET

Since you are tongue-tied and so loath to speak,
In dumb significants proclaim your thoughts:
Let him that is a true-born gentleman,
And stands upon the honour of his birth,
If he suppose that I have pleaded truth,
From off this brier pluck a white rose with me.

SOMERSET

Let him that is no coward nor no flatterer,
But dare maintain the party of the truth,
Pluck a red rose from off this thorn with me.

WARWICK

I love no colours, and without all colour
Of base insinuating flattery
I pluck this white rose with Plantagenet.

SUFFOLK

I pluck this red rose with young Somerset,
And say withal I think he held the right.

VERNON

Stay, lords and gentlemen, and pluck no more,
Till you conclude that he, upon whose side
The fewest roses are cropp'd from the tree,
Shall yield the other in the right opinion.

SOMERSET

Good Master Vernon, it is well objected:
If I have fewest, I subscribe in silence.

PLANTAGENET

And I.

VERNON

Then for the truth and plainness of the case,
I pluck this pale and maiden blossom here,
Giving my verdict on the white rose side.

SOMERSET

Prick not your finger as you pluck it off,
Lest bleeding you do paint the white rose red,
And fall on my side so, against your will.

VERNON

If I, my lord, for my opinion bleed,
Opinion shall be surgeon to my hurt
And keep me on the side where still I am.

SOMERSET

Well, well, come on: who else?

LAWYER

Unless my study and my books be false,
The argument you held was wrong in you;
                                    [To SOMERSET
In sign whereof I pluck a white rose too.

PLANTAGENET

Now, Somerset, where is your argument?

SOMERSET

Here in my scabbard, meditating that
Shall dye your white rose in a bloody red.

PLANTAGENET

Meantime your cheeks do counterfeit our roses;
For pale they look with fear, as witnessing
The truth on our side.

[13]

SOMERSET

No, Plantagenet,
'Tis not for fear but anger that thy cheeks
Blush for pure shame to counterfeit our roses,
And yet thy tongue will not confess thy error.

PLANTAGENET

Hath not thy rose a canker, Somerset?

SOMERSET

Hath not thy rose a thorn, Plantagenet?

PLANTAGENET

Ay, sharp and piercing, to maintain his truth;
Whiles thy consuming canker eats his falsehood.

SOMERSET

Well, I'll find friends to wear my bleeding roses,
That shall maintain what I have said is true,
Where false Plantagenet dare not be seen.

PLANTAGENET

Now, by this maiden blossom in my hand,
I scorn thee and thy fashion, peevish boy.

SUFFOLK

Turn not thy scorns this way, Plantagenet.

PLANTAGENET

Proud Pole, I will, and scorn both him and thee.

SUFFOLK

I'll turn my part thereof into thy throat.

SOMERSET

Away, away, good William de la Pole!
We grace the yeoman by conversing with him.

WARWICK

Now, by God's will, thou wrong'st him, Somerset;
His grandfather was Lionel Duke of Clarence,
Third son to the third Edward King of England:
Spring crestless yeomen from so deep a root?

PLANTAGENET

He bears him on the place's privilege,
Or durst not, for his craven heart, say thus.

SOMERSET

By him that made me, I'll maintain my words
On any plot of ground in Christendom.
Was not thy father, Richard Earl of Cambridge,
For treason executed in our late king's days?
And, by his treason, stand'st not thou attainted,
Corrupted, and exempt from ancient gentry?
His trespass yet lives guilty in thy blood;
And, till thou be restored, thou art a yeoman.

PLANTAGENET

My father was attached, not attainted,
Condemn'd to die for treason, but no traitor;
And that I'll prove on better men than Somerset,
Were growing time once ripen'd to my will.
For your partaker Pole and you yourself,
I'll note you in my book of memory,
To scourge you for this apprehension:
Look to it well and say you are well warn'd.

SOMERSET

Ah, thou shalt find us ready for thee still;
And know us by these colours for thy foes,
For these my friends in spite of thee shall wear.

PLANTAGENET

And, by my soul, this pale and angry rose,

As cognizance of my blood-drinking hate,
Will I for ever and my faction wear,
Until it wither with me to my grave,
Or flourish to the height of my degree.

SUFFOLK

Go forward and be choked with thy ambition!
And so farewell until I meet thee next.　　　[Exit

SOMERSET

Have with thee, Pole. Farewell, ambitious Richard.
　　　　　　　　　　　　　　　　　　　　[Exit

PLANTAGENET

How I am braved and must perforce endure it!

WARWICK

This blot that they object against your house
Shall be wiped out in the next parliament
Call'd for the truce of Winchester and Gloucester;
And if thou be not then created York,
I will not live to be accounted Warwick.
Meantime, in signal of my love to thee,
Against proud Somerset and William Pole,
Will I upon thy party wear this rose:
And here I prophesy: this brawl to-day,
Grown to this faction in the Temple-garden,
Shall send between the red rose and the white
A thousand souls to death and deadly night.

PLANTAGENET

Good Master Vernon, I am bound to you,
That you on my behalf would pluck a flower.

VERNON

In your behalf still will I wear the same.

LAWYER

And so will I.

PLANTAGENET

Thanks, gentle sir.
Come, let us four to dinner: I dare say
This quarrel will drink blood another day.　[Exeunt

SCENE V. _The Tower of London_

Enter MORTIMER, _brought in a chair, and_ GAOLERS

MORTIMER

Kind keepers of my weak decaying age,
Let dying Mortimer here rest himself.
Even like a man new haled from the rack,
So fare my limbs with long imprisonment;
And these grey locks, the pursuivants of death,
Nestor-like aged in an age of care,
Argue the end of Edmund Mortimer.
These eyes, like lamps whose wasting oil is spent,
Wax dim, as drawing to their exigent;
Weak shoulders, overborne with burthening grief,
And pithless arms, like to a wither'd vine
That droops his sapless branches to the ground:
Yet are these feet, whose strengthless stay is numb,
Unable to support this lump of clay,
Swift-winged with desire to get a grave,
As witting I no other comfort have.
But tell me, keeper, will my nephew come?

FIRST GAOLER

Richard Plantagenet, my lord, will come:
We sent unto the Temple, unto his chamber;
And answer was return'd that he will come.

MORTIMER

Enough: my soul shall then be satisfied.
Poor gentleman! his wrong doth equal mine.
Since Henry Monmouth first began to reign,
Before whose glory I was great in arms,
This loathsome sequestration have I had;
And even since then hath Richard been obscured,
Deprived of honour and inheritance.
But now the arbitrator of despairs,
Just death, kind umpire of men's miseries,
With sweet enlargement doth dismiss me hence:
I would his troubles likewise were expired,
That so he might recover what was lost.

Enter RICHARD PLANTAGENET

FIRST GAOLER

My lord, your loving nephew now is come.

MORTIMER

Richard Plantagenet, my friend, is he come?

PLANTAGENET

Ay, noble uncle, thus ignobly used,
Your nephew, late despised Richard, comes.

MORTIMER

Direct mine arms I may embrace his neck,
And in his bosom spend my latter gasp:
O, tell me when my lips do touch his cheeks,
That I may kindly give one fainting kiss.
And now declare, sweet stem from York's great
    stock,
Why didst thou say of late thou wert despised?

PLANTAGENET

First, lean thine aged back against mine arm;
And, in that ease, I'll tell thee my disease.
This day, in argument upon a case,
Some words there grew 'twixt Somerset and me;
Among which terms he used his lavish tongue
And did upbraid me with my father's death:
Which obloquy set bars before my tongue,
Else with the like I had requited him.
Therefore, good uncle, for my father's sake,
In honour of a true Plantagenet
And for alliance sake, declare the cause
My father, Earl of Cambridge, lost his head.

MORTIMER

That cause, fair nephew, that imprison'd me
And hath detain'd me all my flowering youth
Within a loathsome dungeon, there to pine,
Was cursed instrument of his decease.

PLANTAGENET

Discover more at large what cause that was,
For I am ignorant and cannot guess.

MORTIMER

I will, if that my fading breath permit,
And death approach not ere my tale be done.
Henry the Fourth, grandfather to this king,
Deposed his nephew Richard, Edward's son,
The first-begotten and the lawful heir

Of Edward king, the third of that descent:
During whose reign the Percies of the north,
Finding his usurpation most unjust,
Endeavour'd my advancement to the throne:
The reason moved these warlike lords to this
Was, for that—young King Richard thus removed,
Leaving no heir begotten of his body—
I was the next by birth and parentage;
For by my mother I derived am
From Lionel Duke of Clarence, the third son
To King Edward the Third; whereas he
From John of Gaunt doth bring his pedigree,
Being but fourth of that heroic line.
But mark: as in this haughty great attempt
They laboured to plant the rightful heir,
I lost my liberty and they their lives.
Long after this, when Henry the Fifth,
Succeeding his father Bolingbroke, did reign,
Thy father, Earl of Cambridge, then derived
From famous Edmund Langley, Duke of York,
Marrying my sister that thy mother was,
Again in pity of my hard distress
Levied an army, weening to redeem
And have install'd me in the diadem:
But, as the rest, so fell that noble earl
And was beheaded. Thus the Mortimers,
In whom the title rested, were suppress'd.

PLANTAGENET

Of which, my lord, your honour is the last.

MORTIMER

True; and thou seest that I no issue have,
And that my fainting words do warrant death:
Thou art my heir; the rest I wish thee gather:
But yet be wary in thy studious care.

PLANTAGENET

Thy grave admonishments prevail with me:
But yet, methinks, my father's execution
Was nothing less than bloody tyranny.

MORTIMER

With silence, nephew, be thou politic:
Strong-fixed is the house of Lancaster,
And like a mountain not to be removed.
But now thy uncle is removing hence;
As princes do their courts, when they are cloy'd
With long continuance in a settled place.

PLANTAGENET

O, uncle, would some part of my young years
Might but redeem the passage of your age!

MORTIMER

Thou dost then wrong me, as that slaughterer doth
Which giveth many wounds when one will kill.
Mourn not, except thou sorrow for my good;
Only give order for my funeral:
And so farewell, and fair be all thy hopes,
And prosperous be thy life in peace and war! [*Dies*

PLANTAGENET

And peace, no war, befall thy parting soul!
In prison hast thou spent a pilgrimage,
And like a hermit overpass'd thy days.
Well, I will lock his counsel in my breast;

And what I do imagine let that rest.
Keepers, convey him hence, and I myself
Will see his burial better than his life.

[*Exeunt* GAOLERS, *bearing out the body of* MORTIMER

Here dies the dusky torch of Mortimer,
Choked with ambition of the meaner sort:
And for those wrongs, those bitter injuries,
Which Somerset hath offer'd to my house,
I doubt not but with honour to redress;
And therefore haste I to the parliament,
Either to be restored to my blood,
Or make my ill the advantage of my good.   [*Exit*

ACT III

SCENE I. *London. The Parliament-house*

Flourish. Enter KING, EXETER, GLOUCESTER, WARWICK,
SOMERSET, *and* SUFFOLK; *the* BISHOP OF WINCHESTER,
RICHARD PLANTAGENET, *and others*. GLOUCESTER
offers to put up a bill; WINCHESTER *snatches it, tears it*

WINCHESTER

Comest thou with deep premeditated lines,
With written pamphlets studiously devised,
Humphrey of Gloucester? If thou canst accuse,
Or aught intend'st to lay unto my charge,
Do it without invention, suddenly;
As I with sudden and extemporal speech
Purpose to answer what thou canst object.

GLOUCESTER

Presumptuous priest! this place commands my
      patience,
Or thou shouldst find thou hast dishonour'd me.
Think not, although in writing I preferr'd
The manner of thy vile outrageous crimes,
That therefore I have forged, or am not able
Verbatim to rehearse the method of my pen:
No, prelate; such is thy audacious wickedness,
Thy lewd, pestiferous and dissentious pranks,
As very infants prattle of thy pride.
Thou art a most pernicious usurer,
Froward by nature, enemy to peace;
Lascivious, wanton, more than well beseems
A man of thy profession and degree;
And for thy treachery, what's more manifest?
In that thou laid'st a trap to take my life,
As well at London-bridge as at the Tower.
Beside, I fear me, if thy thoughts were sifted,
The king, thy sovereign, is not quite exempt
From envious malice of thy swelling heart.

WINCHESTER

Gloucester, I do defy thee. Lords, vouchsafe
To give me hearing what I shall reply.
If I were covetous, ambitious or perverse,
As he will have me, how am I so poor?
Or how haps it I seek not to advance
Or raise myself, but keep my wonted calling?
And for dissension, who preferreth peace

More than I do?—except I be provoked.
No, my good lords, it is not that offends;
It is not that that hath incensed the duke:
It is, because no one should sway but he;
No one but he should be about the king;
And that engenders thunder in his breast,
And makes him roar these accusations forth.
But he shall know I am as good—

GLOUCESTER

                            As good!
Thou bastard of my grandfather!

WINCHESTER

Ay, lordly sir; for what are you, I pray,
But one imperious in another's throne?

GLOUCESTER

Am I not protector, saucy priest?

WINCHESTER

And am not I a prelate of the church?

GLOUCESTER

Yes, as an outlaw in a castle keeps
And useth it to patronage his theft.

WINCHESTER

Unreverent Gloster!

GLOUCESTER

                    Thou art reverent
Touching thy spiritual function, not thy life.

WINCHESTER

Rome shall remedy this.

WARWICK

                    Roam thither, then.

SOMERSET

My lord, it were your duty to forbear.

WARWICK

Ay, see the bishop be not overborne.

SOMERSET

Methinks my lord should be religious,
And know the office that belongs to such.

WARWICK

Methinks his lordship should be humbler;
It fitteth not a prelate so to plead.

SOMERSET

Yes, when his holy state is touch'd so near.

WARWICK

State holy or unhallow'd, what of that?
Is not his grace protector to the king?

PLANTAGENET

[*Aside*] Plantagenet, I see, must hold his tongue,
Lest it be said 'Speak, sirrah, when you should;
Must your bold verdict enter talk with lords?'
Else would I have a fling at Winchester.

KING

Uncles of Gloucester and of Winchester,
The special watchmen of our English weal,
I would prevail, if prayers might prevail,
To join your hearts in love and amity.
O, what a scandal is it to our crown,
That two such noble peers as ye should jar!
Believe me, lords, my tender years can tell
Civil dissension is a viperous worm
That gnaws the bowels of the commonwealth.

[*A noise within,* 'Down with the tawny-coats!'
What tumult's this?

WARWICK
          An uproar, I dare warrant,
Begun through malice of the bishop's men.
          [*A noise again,* 'Stones! stones!'
Enter MAYOR

MAYOR
O, my good lords, and virtuous Henry,
Pity the city of London, pity us!
The bishop and the Duke of Gloucester's men,
Forbidden late to carry any weapon,
Have fill'd their pockets full of pebble stones,
And banding themselves in contrary parts
Do pelt so fast at one another's pate
That many have their giddy brains knock'd out:
Our windows are broke down in every street,
And we for fear compell'd to shut our shops.
          Enter SERVING-MEN, *in skirmish, with bloody pates*

KING
We charge you, on allegiance to ourself,
To hold your slaughtering hands and keep the
          peace.
Pray, uncle Gloucester, mitigate this strife.

FIRST SERVANT
Nay, if we be forbidden stones, we'll fall to it with
          our teeth.

SECOND SERVANT
Do what ye dare, we are as resolute. [*Skirmish again*

GLOUCESTER
You of my household, leave this peevish broil
And set this unaccustom'd fight aside.

THIRD SERVANT
My lord, we know your grace to be a man
Just and upright; and, for your royal birth,
Inferior to none but to his majesty:
And ere that we will suffer such a prince,
So kind a father of the commonweal,
To be disgraced by an inkhorn mate,
We and our wives and children all will fight,
And have our bodies slaughter'd by thy foes.

FIRST SERVANT
Ay, and the very parings of our nails
Shall pitch a field when we are dead.   [*Begin again*

GLOUCESTER
                              Stay, stay, I say!
And if you love me, as you say you do,
Let me persuade you to forbear awhile.

KING
O, how this discord doth afflict my soul!
Can you, my Lord of Winchester, behold
My sighs and tears and will not once relent?
Who should be pitiful, if you be not?
Or who should study to prefer a peace,
If holy churchmen take delight in broils?

WARWICK
Yield, my lord protector; yield, Winchester;
Except you mean with obstinate repulse

To slay your sovereign and destroy the realm.
You see what mischief and what murder too
Hath been enacted through your enmity;
Then be at peace, except ye thirst for blood.

WINCHESTER
He shall submit, or I will never yield.

GLOUCESTER
Compassion on the king commands me stoop;
Or I would see his heart out, ere the priest
Should ever get that privilege of me.

WARWICK
Behold, my Lord of Winchester, the duke
Hath banish'd moody discontented fury,
As by his smoothed brows it doth appear:
Why look you still so stern and tragical?

GLOUCESTER
Here, Winchester, I offer thee my hand.

KING
Fie, uncle Beaufort! I have heard you preach
That malice was a great and grievous sin;
And will not you maintain the thing you teach,
But prove a chief offender in the same?

WARWICK
Sweet king! the bishop hath a kindly gird.
For shame, my lord of Winchester, relent!
What, shall a child instruct you what to do?

WINCHESTER
Well, Duke of Gloucester, I will yield to thee;
Love for thy love and hand for hand I give.

GLOUCESTER
[*Aside*] Ay, but, I fear me, with a hollow heart.—
See here, my friends and loving countrymen;
This token serveth for a flag of truce
Betwixt ourselves and all our followers:
So help me God, as I dissemble not!

WINCHESTER
[*Aside*] So help me God, as I intend it not!

KING
O loving uncle, kind Duke of Gloucester,
How joyful am I made by this contract!
Away, my masters! trouble us no more;
But join in friendship, as your lords have done.

FIRST SERVANT
Content: I'll to the surgeon's.

SECOND SERVANT
                              And so will I.

THIRD SERVANT
And I will see what physic the tavern affords.
          [*Exeunt* SERVING-MEN, MAYOR, &c.

WARWICK
Accept this scroll, most gracious sovereign,
Which in the right of Richard Plantagenet
We do exhibit to your majesty.

GLOUCESTER
Well urged, my Lord of Warwick: for, sweet prince,
An if your grace mark every circumstance,
You have great reason to do Richard right;
Especially for those occasions
At Eltham place I told your majesty.

KING

And those occasions, uncle, were of force:
Therefore, my loving lords, our pleasure is
That Richard be restored to his blood.

WARWICK

Let Richard be restored to his blood;
So shall his father's wrongs be recompensed.

WINCHESTER

As will the rest, so willeth Winchester.

KING

If Richard will be true, not that alone
But all the whole inheritance I give
That doth belong unto the house of York,
From whence you spring by lineal descent.

PLANTAGENET

Thy humble servant vows obedience
And humble service till the point of death.

KING

Stoop then and set your knee against my foot;
And, in reguerdon of that duty done,
I gird thee with the valiant sword of York:
Rise, Richard, like a true Plantagenet,
And rise created princely Duke of York.

PLANTAGENET

And so thrive Richard as thy foes may fall!
And as my duty springs, so perish they
That grudge one thought against your majesty!

ALL

Welcome, high prince, the mighty Duke of York!

SOMERSET

[Aside] Perish, base prince, ignoble Duke of York!

GLOUCESTER

Now will it best avail your majesty
To cross the seas and to be crown'd in France:
The presence of a king engenders love
Amongst his subjects and his loyal friends,
As it disanimates his enemies.

KING

When Gloucester says the word, King Henry goes;
For friendly counsel cuts off many foes.

GLOUCESTER

Your ships already are in readiness.

[Sennet. Flourish. Exeunt all but EXETER

EXETER

Ay, we may march in England or in France,
Not seeing what is likely to ensue.
This late dissension grown betwixt the peers
Burns under feigned ashes of forged love,
And will at last break out into a flame:
As fester'd members rot but by degree,
Till bones and flesh and sinews fall away,
So will this base and envious discord breed.
And now I fear that fatal prophecy
Which in the time of Henry named the Fifth
Was in the mouth of every sucking babe;
That Henry born at Monmouth should win all
And Henry born at Windsor lose all:
Which is so plain, that Exeter doth wish
His days may finish ere that hapless time.   [Exit

SCENE II. *France. Before Rouen*

Enter LA PUCELLE *disguised, with four* SOLDIERS *with
sacks upon their backs*

LA PUCELLE

These are the city gates, the gates of Rouen,
Through which our policy must make a breach:
Take heed, be wary how you place your words;
Talk like the vulgar sort of market men
That come to gather money for their corn.
If we have entrance, as I hope we shall,
And that we find the slothful watch but weak,
I'll by a sign give notice to our friends,
That Charles the Dauphin may encounter them.

FIRST SOLDIER

Our sacks shall be a mean to sack the city,
And we be lords and rulers over Rouen;
Therefore we'll knock.   [Knocks

WATCH

[Within] Qui est là?

LA PUCELLE

Paysans, pauvres gens de France;
Poor market folks that come to sell their corn.

WATCH

Enter, go in; the market bell is rung.

LA PUCELLE

Now, Rouen, I'll shake thy bulwarks to the ground.

[Exeunt

Enter CHARLES, *the* BASTARD *of Orleans*, ALENÇON,
REIGNIER, *and* FORCES

CHARLES

Saint Denis bless this happy stratagem!
And once again we'll sleep secure in Rouen.

BASTARD

Here enter'd Pucelle and her practisants;
Now she is there, how will she specify
Where is the best and safest passage in?

REIGNIER

By thrusting out a torch from yonder tower;
Which, once discern'd, shows that her meaning is,
No way to that, for weakness, which she enter'd.

Enter LA PUCELLE *on the top, thrusting out a torch burning*

LA PUCELLE

Behold, this is the happy wedding torch
That joineth Rouen unto her countrymen,
But burning fatal to the Talbotites!   [Exit

BASTARD

See, noble Charles, the beacon of our friend;
The burning torch in yonder turret stands.

CHARLES

Now shine it like a comet of revenge,
A prophet to the fall of all our foes!

REIGNIER

Defer no time, delays have dangerous ends;
Enter, and cry 'The Dauphin!' presently,
And then do execution on the watch.

[Alarum. Exeunt

An alarum. Enter TALBOT *in an excursion*

TALBOT

France, thou shalt rue this treason with thy tears,

If Talbot but survive thy treachery.
Pucelle, that witch, that damned sorceress,
Hath wrought this hellish mischief unawares,
That hardly we escaped the pride of France. [*Exit*
An alarum: excursions. BEDFORD, *brought in sick in a*
chair. Enter TALBOT *and* BURGUNDY *without: within* LA
PUCELLE, CHARLES, BASTARD, ALENÇON, *and* REI-
GNIER, *on the walls*

LA PUCELLE

Good morrow, gallants! want ye corn for bread?
I think the Duke of Burgundy will fast
Before he'll buy again at such a rate:
'Twas full of darnel; do you like the taste?

BURGUNDY

Scoff on, vile fiend and shameless courtezan!
I trust ere long to choke thee with thine own,
And make thee curse the harvest of that corn.

CHARLES

Your grace may starve perhaps before that time.

BEDFORD

O, let no words, but deeds, revenge this treason!

LA PUCELLE

What will you do, good grey-beard? break a lance,
And run a tilt at death within a chair?

TALBOT

Foul fiend of France, and hag of all despite,
Encompass'd with thy lustful paramours!
Becomes it thee to taunt his valiant age,
And twit with cowardice a man half dead?
Damsel, I'll have a bout with you again,
Or else let Talbot perish with this shame.

LA PUCELLE

Are ye so hot, sir? yet, Pucelle, hold thy peace;
If Talbot do but thunder, rain will follow.
          [*The English whisper together in council*
God speed the parliament! who shall be the speaker?

TALBOT

Dare ye come forth and meet us in the field?

LA PUCELLE

Belike your lordship takes us then for fools,
To try if that our own be ours or no.

TALBOT

I speak not to that railing Hecate,
But unto thee, Alençon, and the rest;
Will ye, like soldiers, come and fight it out?

ALENÇON

Signior, no.

TALBOT

Signior, hang! base muleters of France!
Like peasant foot-boys do they keep the walls,
And dare not take up arms like gentlemen.

LA PUCELLE

Away, captains! let's get us from the walls;
For Talbot means no goodness by his looks.
God be wi' you, my lord! we came but to tell you
That we are here.   [*Exeunt from the walls*

TALBOT

And there will we be too, ere it be long,
Or else reproach be Talbot's greatest fame!
Vow, Burgundy, by honour of thy house,

Prick'd on by public wrongs sustain'd in France,
Either to get the town again or die:
And I, as sure as English Henry lives,
And as his father here was conqueror,
As sure as in this late-betrayed town
Great Cœur-de-lion's heart was buried,
So sure I swear to get the town or die.

BURGUNDY

My vows are equal partners with thy vows.

TALBOT

But, ere we go, regard this dying prince,
The valiant Duke of Bedford. Come, my lord,
We will bestow you in some better place,
Fitter for sickness and for crazy age.

BEDFORD

Lord Talbot, do not so dishonour me:
Here will I sit before the walls of Rouen
And will be partner of your weal or woe.

BURGUNDY

Courageous Bedford, let us now persuade you.

BEDFORD

Not to be gone from hence; for once I read
That stout Pendragon in his litter sick
Came to the field and vanquished his foes:
Methinks I should revive the soldiers' hearts,
Because I ever found them as myself.

TALBOT

Undaunted spirit in a dying breast!
Then be it so: heavens keep old Bedford safe!
And now no more ado, brave Burgundy,
But gather we our forces out of hand
And set upon our boasting enemy.
          [*Exeunt all but* BEDFORD *and* ATTENDANTS
An alarum: excursions. Enter SIR JOHN FASTOLFE *and a*
CAPTAIN

CAPTAIN

Whither away, Sir John Fastolfe, in such haste?

FASTOLFE

Whither away! to save myself by flight:
We are like to have the overthrow again.

CAPTAIN

What! will you fly, and leave Lord Talbot?

FASTOLFE

                              Ay,
All the Talbots in the world, to save my life. [*Exit*

CAPTAIN

Cowardly knight! ill fortune follow thee!   [*Exit*
          Retreat: excursions. LA PUCELLE, ALENÇON, *and*
CHARLES *fly*

BEDFORD

Now, quiet soul, depart when heaven please,
For I have seen our enemies' overthrow.
What is the trust or strength of foolish man?
They that of late were daring with their scoffs
Are glad and fain by flight to save themselves.
          [BEDFORD *dies, and is carried in by two in his chair*
          An alarum. Re-enter TALBOT, BURGUNDY, *and the rest*

TALBOT

Lost, and recover'd in a day again!

This is a double honour, Burgundy:
Yet heavens have glory for this victory!

BURGUNDY

Warlike and martial Talbot, Burgundy
Enshrines thee in his heart and there erects
Thy noble deeds as valour's monuments.

TALBOT

Thanks, gentle duke. But where is Pucelle now?
I think her old familiar is asleep:
Now where's the Bastard's braves, and Charles his
    gleeks?
What, all amort? Rouen hangs her head for grief
That such a valiant company are fled.
Now will we take some order in the town,
Placing therein some expert officers,
And then depart to Paris to the king,
For there young Henry with his nobles lie.

BURGUNDY

What wills Lord Talbot pleaseth Burgundy.

TALBOT

But yet, before we go, let's not forget
The noble Duke of Bedford late deceased,
But see his exequies fulfill'd in Rouen:
A braver soldier never couched lance,
A gentler heart did never sway in court;
But kings and mightiest potentates must die,
For that's the end of human misery.   [Exeunt

SCENE III. *The plains near Rouen*

Enter CHARLES, *the* BASTARD *of Orleans*, ALENÇON, LA
PUCELLE, *and* FORCES

LA PUCELLE

Dismay not, princes, at this accident,
Nor grieve that Rouen is so recovered:
Care is no cure, but rather corrosive,
For things that are not to be remedied.
Let frantic Talbot triumph for a while
And like a peacock sweep along his tail;
We'll pull his plumes and take away his train,
If Dauphin and the rest will be but ruled.

CHARLES

We have been guided by thee hitherto,
And of thy cunning had no diffidence:
One sudden foil shall never breed distrust.

BASTARD

Search out thy wit for secret policies,
And we will make thee famous through the world.

ALENÇON

We'll set thy statue in some holy place,
And have thee reverenced like a blessed saint:
Employ thee then, sweet virgin, for our good.

LA PUCELLE

Then thus it must be; this doth Joan devise:
By fair persuasions mix'd with sugar'd words
We will entice the Duke of Burgundy
To leave the Talbot and to follow us.

CHARLES

Ay, marry, sweeting, if we could do that,

France were no place for Henry's warriors;
Nor should that nation boast it so with us,
But be extirped from our provinces.

ALENÇON

For ever should they be expulsed from France,
And not have title of an earldom here.

LA PUCELLE

Your honours shall perceive how I will work
To bring this matter to the wished end.
                          [*Drum sounds afar off*
Hark! by the sound of drum you may perceive
Their powers are marching unto Paris-ward.
*Here sound an English march. Enter, and pass over at a
                 distance,* TALBOT *and his* FORCES
There goes the Talbot, with his colours spread,
And all the troops of English after him.
French march. Enter the DUKE OF BURGUNDY *and* FORCES
Now in the rearward comes the duke and his:
Fortune in favour makes him lag behind.
Summon a parley; we will talk with him.
                          [*Trumpets sound a parley*

CHARLES

A parley with the Duke of Burgundy!

BURGUNDY

Who craves a parley with the Burgundy?

LA PUCELLE

The princely Charles of France, thy countryman.

BURGUNDY

What say'st thou, Charles? for I am marching hence.

CHARLES

Speak, Pucelle, and enchant him with thy words.

LA PUCELLE

Brave Burgundy, undoubted hope of France!
Stay, let thy humble handmaid speak to thee.

BURGUNDY

Speak on; but be not over-tedious.

LA PUCELLE

Look on thy country, look on fertile France,
And see the cities and the towns defaced
By wasting ruin of the cruel foe.
As looks the mother on her lowly babe
When death doth close his tender dying eyes,
See, see the pining malady of France;
Behold the wounds, the most unnatural wounds,
Which thou thyself hast given her woful breast.
O, turn thy edged sword another way;
Strike those that hurt, and hurt not those that help.
One drop of blood drawn from thy country's bosom
Should grieve thee more than streams of foreign
    gore:
Return thee therefore with a flood of tears,
And wash away thy country's stained spots.

BURGUNDY

Either she hath bewitch'd me with her words,
Or nature makes me suddenly relent.

LA PUCELLE

Besides, all French and France exclaims on thee,
Doubting thy birth and lawful progeny.
Who join'st thou with but with a lordly nation
That will not trust thee but for profit's sake?

When Talbot hath set footing once in France
And fashion'd thee that instrument of ill,
Who then but English Henry will be lord,
And thou be thrust out like a fugitive?
Call we to mind, and mark but this for proof,
Was not the Duke of Orleans thy foe?
And was he not in England prisoner?
But when they heard he was thine enemy,
They set him free without his ransom paid,
In spite of Burgundy and all his friends.
See, then, thou fight'st against thy countrymen
And join'st with them will be thy slaughter-men.
Come, come, return; return, thou wandering lord;
Charles and the rest will take thee in their arms.

BURGUNDY

I am vanquished; these haughty words of hers
Have batter'd me like roaring cannon-shot,
And made me almost yield upon my knees.
Forgive me, country, and sweet countrymen,
And, lords, accept this hearty kind embrace:
My forces and my power of men are yours:
So farewell, Talbot; I'll no longer trust thee.

LA PUCELLE

[Aside] Done like a Frenchman: turn, and turn
    again!

CHARLES

Welcome, brave duke! thy friendship makes us
    fresh.

BASTARD

And doth beget new courage in our breasts.

ALENÇON

Pucelle hath bravely play'd her part in this,
And doth deserve a coronet of gold.

CHARLES

Now let us on, my lords, and join our powers,
And seek how we may prejudice the foe.   [Exeunt

SCENE IV. Paris. The palace

Enter the KING, GLOUCESTER, BISHOP OF WINCHESTER,
YORK, SUFFOLK, SOMERSET, WARWICK, EXETER: VER-
NON, BASSET, and others. To them with his SOLDIERS,
TALBOT

TALBOT

My gracious prince, and honourable peers,
Hearing of your arrival in this realm,
I have awhile given truce unto my wars,
To do my duty to my sovereign:
In sign whereof, this arm, that hath reclaim'd
To your obedience fifty fortresses,
Twelve cities and seven walled towns of strength,
Beside five hundred prisoners of esteem,
Lets fall his sword before your highness' feet,
And with submissive loyalty of heart
Ascribes the glory of his conquest got
First to my God and next unto your grace.   [Kneels

KING

Is this the Lord Talbot, uncle Gloucester,
That hath so long been resident in France?

GLOUCESTER

Yes, if it please your majesty, my liege.

KING

Welcome, brave captain and victorious lord!
When I was young, as yet I am not old,
I do remember how my father said
A stouter champion never handled sword.
Long since we were resolved of your truth,
Your faithful service and your toil in war;
Yet never have you tasted our reward,
Or been reguerdon'd with so much as thanks,
Because till now we never saw your face:
Therefore, stand up; and, for these good deserts,
We here create you Earl of Shrewsbury;
And in our coronation take your place.
    [Sennet. Flourish. Exeunt all but VERNON and BASSET

VERNON

Now, sir, to you, that were so hot at sea,
Disgracing of these colours that I wear
In honour of my noble Lord of York:—
Darest thou maintain the former words thou
    spakest?

BASSET

Yes, sir; as well as you dare patronage
The envious barking of your saucy tongue
Against my lord the Duke of Somerset.

VERNON

Sirrah, thy lord I honour as he is.

BASSET

Why, what is he? as good a man as York.

VERNON

Hark ye; not so: in witness, take ye that. [Strikes him

BASSET

Villain, thou know'st the law of arms is such
That whoso draws a sword, 'tis present death,
Or else this blow should broach thy dearest blood.
But I'll unto his majesty, and crave
I may have liberty to venge this wrong;
When thou shalt see I'll meet thee to thy cost.

VERNON

Well, miscreant, I'll be there as soon as you;
And, after, meet you sooner than you would.
    [Exeunt

ACT IV

SCENE I. Paris. A hall of state

Enter the KING, GLOUCESTER, BISHOP OF WINCHESTER,
YORK, SUFFOLK, SOMERSET, WARWICK, TALBOT,
EXETER, the GOVERNOR OF PARIS, and others

GLOUCESTER

Lord bishop, set the crown upon his head.

WINCHESTER

God save King Henry, of that name the sixth!

GLOUCESTER

Now, governor of Paris, take your oath,
That you elect no other king but him;

Esteem none friends but such as are his friends,
And none your foes but such as shall pretend
Malicious practices against his state:
This shall ye do, so help you righteous God!

Enter SIR JOHN FASTOLFE

FASTOLFE

My gracious sovereign, as I rode from Calais,
To haste unto your coronation,
A letter was deliver'd to my hands,
Writ to your grace from the Duke of Burgundy.

TALBOT

Shame to the Duke of Burgundy and thee!
I vow'd, base knight, when I did meet thee next,
To tear the garter from thy craven's leg,

[Plucking it off

Which I have done, because unworthily
Thou wast installed in that high degree.
Pardon me, princely Henry, and the rest:
This dastard, at the battle of Patay,
When but in all I was six thousand strong
And that the French were almost ten to one,
Before we met or that a stroke was given,
Like to a trusty squire did run away:
In which assault we lost twelve hundred men;
Myself and divers gentlemen beside
Were there surprised and taken prisoners.
Then judge, great lords, if I have done amiss;
Or whether that such cowards ought to wear
This ornament of knighthood, yea or no.

GLOUCESTER

To say the truth, this fact was infamous
And ill beseeming any common man,
Much more a knight, a captain and a leader.

TALBOT

When first this order was ordain'd, my lords,
Knights of the garter were of noble birth,
Valiant and virtuous, full of haughty courage,
Such as were grown to credit by the wars;
Not fearing death, nor shrinking for distress,
But always resolute in most extremes.
He then that is not furnish'd in this sort
Doth but usurp the sacred name of knight,
Profaning this most honourable order,
And should, if I were worthy to be judge,
Be quite degraded, like a hedge-born swain
That doth presume to boast of gentle blood.

KING

Stain to thy countrymen, thou hear'st thy doom!
Be packing, therefore, thou that wast a knight:
Henceforth we banish thee, on pain of death.

[Exit FASTOLFE

And now, my lord protector, view the letter
Sent from our uncle Duke of Burgundy.

GLOUCESTER

What means his grace, that he hath changed his
style?
No more but, plain and bluntly,

'To the king!'

Hath he forgot he is his sovereign?

Or doth this churlish superscription
Pretend some alteration in good will?
What's here?

[Reads] 'I have, upon especial cause,
Moved with compassion of my country's wreck,
Together with the pitiful complaints
Of such as your oppression feeds upon,
Forsaken your pernicious faction,
And join'd with Charles, the rightful King of France.'

O monstrous treachery! can this be so,
That in alliance, amity and oaths,
There should be found such false dissembling guile?

KING

What! doth my uncle Burgundy revolt?

GLOUCESTER

He doth, my lord, and is become your foe.

KING

Is that the worst this letter doth contain?

GLOUCESTER

It is the worst, and all, my lord, he writes.

KING

Why, then, Lord Talbot there shall talk with him,
And give him chastisement for this abuse.
How say you, my lord? are you not content?

TALBOT

Content, my liege! yes, but that I am prevented,
I should have begg'd I might have been employ'd.

KING

Then gather strength, and march unto him straight:
Let him perceive how ill we brook his treason,
And what offence it is to flout his friends.

TALBOT

I go, my lord, in heart desiring still
You may behold confusion of your foes.   *[Exit*

Enter VERNON *and* BASSET

VERNON

Grant me the combat, gracious sovereign.

BASSET

And me, my lord, grant me the combat too.

YORK

This is my servant: hear him, noble prince.

SOMERSET

And this is mine: sweet Henry, favour him.

KING

Be patient, lords; and give them leave to speak.
Say, gentlemen, what makes you thus exclaim?
And wherefore crave you combat? or with whom?

VERNON

With him, my lord; for he hath done me wrong.

BASSET

And I with him; for he hath done me wrong.

KING

What is that wrong whereof you both complain?
First let me know, and then I'll answer you.

BASSET

Crossing the sea from England into France,
This fellow here, with envious carping tongue,
Upbraided me about the rose I wear;
Saying, the sanguine colour of the leaves
Did represent my master's blushing cheeks,

When stubbornly he did repugn the truth
About a certain question in the law
Argued betwixt the Duke of York and him;
With other vile and ignominious terms:
In confutation of which rude reproach,
And in defence of my lord's worthiness,
I crave the benefit of law of arms.

VERNON

And that is my petition, noble lord:
For though he seem with forged quaint conceit
To set a gloss upon his bold intent,
Yet know, my lord, I was provoked by him;
And he first took exceptions at this badge,
Pronouncing that the paleness of this flower
Bewray'd the faintness of my master's heart.

YORK

Will not this malice, Somerset, be left?

SOMERSET

Your private grudge, my Lord of York, will out,
Though ne'er so cunningly you smother it.

KING

Good Lord, what madness rules in brainsick men,
When for so slight and frivolous a cause
Such factious emulations shall arise!
Good cousins both, of York and Somerset,
Quiet yourselves, I pray, and be at peace.

YORK

Let this dissension first be tried by fight,
And then your highness shall command a peace.

SOMERSET

The quarrel toucheth none but us alone;
Betwixt ourselves let us decide it then.

YORK

There is my pledge; accept it, Somerset.

VERNON

Nay, let it rest where it began at first.

BASSET

Confirm it so, mine honourable lord.

GLOUCESTER

Confirm it so! Confounded be your strife!
And perish ye, with your audacious prate!
Presumptuous vassals, are you not ashamed
With this immodest clamorous outrage
To trouble and disturb the king and us?
And you, my lords, methinks you do not well
To bear with their perverse objections;
Much less to take occasion from their mouths
To raise a mutiny betwixt yourselves:
Let me persuade you take a better course.

EXETER

It grieves his highness: good my lords, be friends.

KING

Come hither, you that would be combatants:
Henceforth I charge you, as you love our favour,
Quite to forget this quarrel and the cause.
And you, my lords, remember where we are;
In France, amongst a fickle wavering nation:
If they perceive dissension in our looks
And that within ourselves we disagree,
How will their grudging stomachs be provoked

To wilful disobedience, and rebel!
Beside, what infamy will there arise,
When foreign princes shall be certified
That for a toy, a thing of no regard,
King Henry's peers and chief nobility
Destroy'd themselves, and lost the realm of France!
O, think upon the conquest of my father,
My tender years, and let us not forgo
That for a trifle that was bought with blood!
Let me be umpire in this doubtful strife.
I see no reason, if I wear this rose,

[Putting on a red rose

That any one should therefore be suspicious
I more incline to Somerset than York:
Both are my kinsmen, and I love them both:
As well they may upbraid me with my crown,
Because, forsooth, the king of Scots is crown'd.
But your discretions better can persuade
Than I am able to instruct or teach:
And therefore, as we hither came in peace,
So let us still continue peace and love.
Cousin of York, we institute your grace
To be our regent in these parts of France:
And, good my Lord of Somerset, unite
Your troops of horsemen with his bands of foot;
And, like true subjects, sons of your progenitors,
Go cheerfully together and digest
Your angry choler on your enemies.
Ourself, my lord protector and the rest
After some respite will return to Calais;
From thence to England; where I hope ere long
To be presented, by your victories,
With Charles, Alençon and that traitorous rout.

[Flourish. Exeunt all but YORK, WARWICK,
EXETER and VERNON

WARWICK

My Lord of York, I promise you, the king
Prettily, methought, did play the orator.

YORK

And so he did; but yet I like it not,
In that he wears the badge of Somerset.

WARWICK

Tush, that was but his fancy, blame him not;
I dare presume, sweet prince, he thought no harm

YORK

An if I wist he did,—but let it rest;
Other affairs must now be managed.

[Exeunt all but EXETER

EXETER

Well didst thou, Richard, to suppress thy voice;
For, had the passions of thy heart burst out,
I fear we should have seen decipher'd there
More rancorous spite, more furious raging broils,
Than yet can be imagined or supposed.
But howsoe'er, no simple man that sees
This jarring discord of nobility,
This shouldering of each other in the court,
This factious bandying of their favourites,
But that it doth presage some ill event.
'Tis much when sceptres are in children's hands;

But more when envy breeds unkind division;
There comes the ruin, there begins confusion. [*Exit*

Scene II. *Before Bordeaux*

Enter TALBOT, *with trump and drum*

TALBOT

Go to the gates of Bordeaux, trumpeter;
Summon their general unto the wall.
   Trumpet sounds. Enter GENERAL *and others, aloft*
English John Talbot, captains, calls you forth,
Servant in arms to Harry King of England;
And thus he would: Open your city-gates;
Be humble to us; call my sovereign yours,
And do him homage as obedient subjects;
And I'll withdraw me and my bloody power:
But, if you frown upon this proffer'd peace,
You tempt the fury of my three attendants,
Lean famine, quartering steel, and climbing fire;
Who in a moment even with the earth
Shall lay your stately and air-braving towers,
If you forsake the offer of their love.

GENERAL

Thou ominous and fearful owl of death,
Our nation's terror and their bloody scourge!
The period of thy tyranny approacheth.
On us thou canst not enter but by death;
For, I protest, we are well fortified
And strong enough to issue out and fight:
If thou retire, the Dauphin, well appointed,
Stands with the snares of war to tangle thee:
On either hand thee there are squadrons pitch'd,
To wall thee from the liberty of flight;
And no way canst thou turn thee for redress,
But death doth front thee with apparent spoil,
And pale destruction meets thee in the face.
Ten thousand French have ta'en the sacrament
To rive their dangerous artillery
Upon no Christian soul but English Talbot.
Lo, there thou stand'st, a breathing valiant man,
Of an invincible unconquer'd spirit!
This is the latest glory of thy praise
That I, thy enemy, due thee withal;
For ere the glass, that now begins to run,
Finish the process of his sandy hour,
These eyes, that see thee now well coloured,
Shall see thee wither'd, bloody, pale and dead.
   [*Drum afar off*
Hark! hark! the Dauphin's drum, a warning bell,
Sings heavy music to thy timorous soul;
And mine shall ring thy dire departure out.
   [*Exeunt* GENERAL, *&c.*

TALBOT

He fables not; I hear the enemy:
Out, some light horsemen, and peruse their wings.
O, negligent and heedless discipline!
How are we park'd and bounded in a pale,
A little herd of England's timorous deer,
Mazed with a yelping kennel of French curs!

If we be English deer, be then in blood;
Not rascal-like, to fall down with a pinch,
But rather, moody-mad and desperate stags,
Turn on the bloody hounds with heads of steel
And make the cowards stand aloof at bay:
Sell every man his life as dear as mine,
And they shall find dear deer of us, my friends.
God and Saint George, Talbot and England's right,
Prosper our colours in this dangerous fight! [*Exeunt*

Scene III. *Plains in Gascony*

Enter a MESSENGER *that meets* YORK. *Enter* YORK *with trumpet and many* SOLDIERS

YORK

Are not the speedy scouts return'd again,
That dogg'd the mighty army of the Dauphin?

MESSENGER

They are return'd, my lord, and give it out
That he is march'd to Bordeaux with his power,
To fight with Talbot: as he march'd along,
By your espials were discovered
Two mightier troops than that the Dauphin led,
Which join'd with him and made their march for
   Bordeaux.

YORK

A plague upon that villain Somerset,
That thus delays my promised supply
Of horsemen, that were levied for this siege!
Renowned Talbot doth expect my aid,
And I am lowted by a traitor villain,
And cannot help the noble chevalier:
God comfort him in this necessity!
If he miscarry, farewell wars in France.

Enter SIR WILLIAM LUCY

SIR WILLIAM LUCY

Thou princely leader of our English strength,
Never so needful on the earth of France,
Spur to the rescue of the noble Talbot,
Who now is girdled with a waist of iron,
And hemm'd about with grim destruction:
To Bordeaux, warlike duke! to Bordeaux, York!
Else, farewell Talbot, France, and England's hon-
   our.

YORK

O God, that Somerset, who in proud heart
Doth stop my cornets, were in Talbot's place!
So should we save a valiant gentleman
By forfeiting a traitor and a coward.
Mad ire and wrathful fury makes me weep,
That thus we die, while remiss traitors sleep.

SIR WILLIAM LUCY

O, send some succour to the distress'd lord!

YORK

He dies, we lose; I break my warlike word;
We mourn, France smiles; we lose, they daily get;
All 'long of this vile traitor Somerset.

SIR WILLIAM LUCY

Then God take mercy on brave Talbot's soul;

And on his son young John, who two hours since
I met in travel toward his warlike father!
This seven years did not Talbot see his son;
And now they meet where both their lives are done.

YORK

Alas, what joy shall noble Talbot have
To bid his young son welcome to his grave?
Away! vexation almost stops my breath,
That sunder'd friends greet in the hour of death.
Lucy, farewell: no more my fortune can,
But curse the cause I cannot aid the man.
Maine, Blois, Poictiers, and Tours, are won away,
'Long all of Somerset and his delay.

[Exit, with his SOLDIERS

SIR WILLIAM LUCY

Thus, while the vulture of sedition
Feeds in the bosom of such great commanders,
Sleeping neglection doth betray to loss
The conquest of our scarce cold conqueror,
That ever living man of memory,
Henry the Fifth: whiles they each other cross,
Lives, honours, lands and all hurry to loss.   [Exit

SCENE IV. *Other plains in Gascony*

Enter SOMERSET, *with his* ARMY; *a* CAPTAIN *of* TALBOT'S
with him

SOMERSET

It is too late; I cannot send them now:
This expedition was by York and Talbot
Too rashly plotted: all our general force
Might with a sally of the very town
Be buckled with: the over-daring Talbot
Hath sullied all his gloss of former honour
By this unheedful, desperate, wild adventure:
York set him on to fight and die in shame,
That, Talbot dead, great York might bear the name.

CAPTAIN

Here is Sir William Lucy, who with me
Set from our o'er-match'd forces forth for aid.

Enter SIR WILLIAM LUCY

SOMERSET

How now, Sir William! whither were you sent?

SIR WILLIAM LUCY

Whither, my lord? from bought and sold Lord
Talbot;
Who, ring'd about with bold adversity,
Cries out for noble York and Somerset,
To beat assailing death from his weak legions:
And whiles the honourable captain there
Drops bloody sweat from his war-wearied limbs,
And, in advantage lingering, looks for rescue,
You, his false hopes, the trust of England's honour,
Keep off aloof with worthless emulation.
Let not your private discord keep away
The levied succours that should lend him aid,
While he, renowned noble gentleman,
Yields up his life unto a world of odds:
Orleans the Bastard, Charles, Burgundy,

Alençon, Reignier, compass him about,
And Talbot perisheth by your default.

SOMERSET

York set him on; York should have sent him aid.

SIR WILLIAM LUCY

And York as fast upon your grace exclaims;
Swearing that you withhold his levied host,
Collected for this expedition.

SOMERSET

York lies; he might have sent and had the horse:
I owe him little duty, and less love;
And take foul scorn to fawn on him by sending.

SIR WILLIAM LUCY

The fraud of England, not the force of France,
Hath now entrapp'd the noble-minded Talbot:
Never to England shall he bear his life;
But dies, betray'd to fortune by your strife.

SOMERSET

Come, go; I will dispatch the horsemen straight:
Within six hours they will be at his aid.

SIR WILLIAM LUCY

Too late comes rescue: he is ta'en or slain;
For fly he could not, if he would have fled;
And fly would Talbot never, though he might.

SOMERSET

If he be dead, brave Talbot, then adieu!

SIR WILLIAM LUCY

His fame lives in the world, his shame in you.

[Exeunt

SCENE V. *The English camp near Bourdeaux*

Enter TALBOT *and* JOHN *his son*

TALBOT

O young John Talbot! I did send for thee
To tutor thee in stratagems of war,
That Talbot's name might be in thee revived,
When sapless age and weak unable limbs
Should bring thy father to his drooping chair.
But, O malignant and ill-boding stars!
Now thou art come unto a feast of death,
A terrible and unavoided danger:
Therefore, dear boy, mount on my swiftest horse;
And I'll direct thee how thou shalt escape
By sudden flight: come, dally not, be gone.

JOHN

Is my name Talbot? and am I your son?
And shall I fly? O, if you love my mother,
Dishonour not her honourable name,
To make a bastard and a slave of me!
The world will say, he is not Talbot's blood,
That basely fled when noble Talbot stood.

TALBOT

Fly, to revenge my death, if I be slain.

JOHN

He that flies so will ne'er return again.

TALBOT

If we both stay, we both are sure to die.

JOHN

Then let me stay; and, father, do you fly:
Your loss is great, so your regard should be;
My worth unknown, no loss is known in me.
Upon my death the French can little boast;
In yours they will, in you all hopes are lost.
Flight cannot stain the honour you have won;
But mine it will, that no exploit have done:
You fled for vantage, every one will swear;
But, if I bow, they'll say it was for fear.
There is no hope that ever I will stay,
If the first hour I shrink and run away.
Here on my knee I beg mortality,
Rather than life preserved with infamy.

TALBOT

Shall all thy mother's hopes lie in one tomb?

JOHN

Ay, rather than I'll shame my mother's womb.

TALBOT

Upon my blessing, I command thee go.

JOHN

To fight I will, but not to fly the foe.

TALBOT

Part of thy father may be saved in thee.

JOHN

No part of him but will be shame in me.

TALBOT

Thou never hadst renown, nor canst not lose it.

JOHN

Yes, your renowned name: shall flight abuse it?

TALBOT

Thy father's charge shall clear thee from that stain.

JOHN

You cannot witness for me, being slain.
If death be so apparent, then both fly.

TALBOT

And leave my followers here to fight and die?
My age was never tainted with such shame.

JOHN

And shall my youth be guilty of such blame?
No more can I be sever'd from your side,
Than can yourself yourself in twain divide:
Stay, go, do what you will, the like do I;
For live I will not, if my father die.

TALBOT

Then here I take my leave of thee, fair son,
Born to eclipse thy life this afternoon.
Come, side by side together live and die;
And soul with soul from France to heaven fly.

[Exeunt

SCENE VI. *A field of battle*

Alarum: excursions, wherein TALBOT'S SON *is hemmed about, and* TALBOT *rescues him*

TALBOT

Saint George and victory! fight, soldiers, fight:
The regent hath with Talbot broke his word,
And left us to the rage of France his sword.

Where is John Talbot? Pause, and take thy breath;
I gave thee life and rescued thee from death.

JOHN

O, twice my father, twice am I thy son!
The life thou gavest me first was lost and done,
Till with thy warlike sword, despite of fate,
To my determined time thou gavest new date.

TALBOT

When from the Dauphin's crest thy sword struck
    fire,
It warm'd thy father's heart with proud desire
Of bold-faced victory. Then leaden age,
Quicken'd with youthful spleen and warlike rage,
Beat down Alençon, Orleans, Burgundy,
And from the pride of Gallia rescued thee.
The ireful bastard Orleans, that drew blood
From thee, my boy, and had the maidenhood
Of thy first fight, I soon encountered,
And interchanging blows I quickly shed
Some of his bastard blood; and in disgrace
Bespoke him thus; 'Contaminated base
And misbegotten blood I spill of thine,
Mean and right poor, for that pure blood of mine,
Which thou didst force from Talbot, my brave boy:'
Here, purposing the Bastard to destroy,
Came in strong rescue. Speak, thy father's care,
Art thou not weary, John? how dost thou fare?
Wilt thou yet leave the battle, boy, and fly,
Now thou art seal'd the son of chivalry?
Fly, to revenge my death when I am dead:
The help of one stands me in little stead.
O, too much folly is it, well I wot,
To hazard all our lives in one small boat!
If I to-day die not with Frenchmen's rage,
To-morrow I shall die with mickle age:
By me they nothing gain an if I stay;
'Tis but the shortening of my life one day:
In thee thy mother dies, our household's name,
My death's revenge, thy youth, and England's fame:
All these and more we hazard by thy stay;
All these are saved if thou wilt fly away.

JOHN

The sword of Orleans hath not made me smart;
These words of yours draw life-blood from my heart:
On that advantage, bought with such a shame,
To save a paltry life and slay bright fame,
Before young Talbot from old Talbot fly,
The coward horse that bears me fall and die!
And like me to the peasant boys of France,
To be shame's scorn and subject of mischance!
Surely, by all the glory you have won,
An if I fly, I am not Talbot's son:
Then talk no more of flight, it is no boot;
If son to Talbot, die at Talbot's foot.

TALBOT

Then follow thou thy desperate sire of Crete,
Thou Icarus; thy life to me is sweet:
If thou wilt fight, fight by thy father's side;
And, commendable proved, let's die in pride.

[Exeunt

SCENE VII. *Another part of the field*

Alarum: excursions. Enter old TALBOT *led by a* SERVANT

TALBOT

Where is my other life? mine own is gone;
O, where's young Talbot? where is valiant John?
Triumphant death, smear'd with captivity,
Young Talbot's valour makes me smile at thee:
When he perceived me shrink and on my knee,
His bloody sword he brandish'd over me,
And, like a hungry lion, did commence
Rough deeds of rage and stern impatience;
But when my angry guardant stood alone,
Tendering my ruin and assail'd of none,
Dizzy-eyed fury and great rage of heart
Suddenly made him from my side to start
Into the clustering battle of the French;
And in that sea of blood my boy did drench
His over-mounting spirit, and there died,
My Icarus, my blossom, in his pride.

SERVANT

O my dear lord, lo, where your son is borne!

Enter SOLDIERS, *with the body of young* TALBOT

TALBOT

Thou antic death, which laugh'st us here to scorn,
Anon, from thy insulting tyranny,
Coupled in bonds of perpetuity,
Two Talbots, winged through the lither sky,
In thy despite shall 'scape mortality.
O thou, whose wounds become hard-favour'd death,
Speak to thy father ere thou yield thy breath!
Brave death by speaking, whether he will or no;
Imagine him a Frenchman and thy foe.
Poor boy! he smiles, methinks, as who should say,
Had death been French, then death had died to-
  day.
Come, come and lay him in his father's arms:
My spirit can no longer bear these harms.
Soldiers, adieu! I have what I would have,
Now my old arms are young John Talbot's grave.
                                          [*Dies*

Enter CHARLES, ALENÇON, BURGUNDY, BASTARD, LA
  PUCELLE, *and* FORCES

CHARLES

Had York and Somerset brought rescue in,
We should have found a bloody day of this.

BASTARD

How the young whelp of Talbot's, raging-wood,
Did flesh his puny sword in Frenchmen's blood!

LA PUCELLE

Once I encounter'd him, and thus I said:
'Thou maiden youth, be vanquish'd by a maid:'
But, with a proud majestical high scorn,
He answer'd thus: 'Young Talbot was not born
To be the pillage of a giglot wench:'
So, rushing in the bowels of the French,
He left me proudly, as unworthy fight.

BURGUNDY

Doubtless he would have made a noble knight:

See, where he lies inhearsed in the arms
Of the most bloody nurser of his harms!

BASTARD

Hew them to pieces, hack their bones asunder,
Whose life was England's glory, Gallia's wonder.

CHARLES

O, no, forbear! for that which we have fled
During the life, let us not wrong it dead.

Enter SIR WILLIAM LUCY, *attended;* HERALD *of the
  French preceding*

SIR WILLIAM LUCY

Herald, conduct me to the Dauphin's tent,
To know who hath obtain'd the glory of the day.

CHARLES

On what submissive message art thou sent?

SIR WILLIAM LUCY

Submission, Dauphin! 'tis a mere French word;
We English warriors wot not what it means.
I come to know what prisoners thou hast ta'en,
And to survey the bodies of the dead.

CHARLES

For prisoners ask'st thou? hell our prison is.
But tell me whom thou seek'st.

SIR WILLIAM LUCY

But where's the great Alcides of the field,
Valiant Lord Talbot, Earl of Shrewsbury,
Created, for his rare success in arms,
Great Earl of Washford, Waterford and Valence;
Lord Talbot of Goodrig and Urchinfield,
Lord Strange of Blackmere, Lord Verdun of Alton,
Lord Cromwell of Wingfield, Lord Furnival of
  Sheffield,
The thrice-victorious Lord of Falconbridge;
Knight of the noble order of Saint George,
Worthy Saint Michael and the Golden Fleece;
Great marshal to Henry the Sixth
Of all his wars within the realm of France?

LA PUCELLE

Here is a silly stately style indeed!
The Turk, that two and fifty kingdoms hath,
Writes not so tedious a style as this.
Him that thou magnifiest with all these titles
Stinking and fly-blown lies here at our feet.

SIR WILLIAM LUCY

Is Talbot slain, the Frenchmen's only scourge,
Your kingdom's terror and black Nemesis?
O, were mine eye-balls into bullets turn'd,
That I in rage might shoot them at your faces!
O, that I could but call these dead to life!
It were enough to fright the realm of France:
Were but his picture left amongst you here,
It would amaze the proudest of you all.
Give me their bodies, that I may bear them hence
And give them burial as beseems their worth.

LA PUCELLE

I think this upstart is old Talbot's ghost,
He speaks with such a proud commanding spirit.
For God's sake, let him have 'em; to keep them here,
They would but stink, and putrefy the air.

CHARLES

Go, take their bodies hence.

SIR WILLIAM LUCY

I'll bear them hence; but from their ashes shall be
    rear'd
A phœnix that shall make all France afeard.

CHARLES

So we be rid of them, do with 'em what thou wilt.
And now to Paris, in this conquering vein:
All will be ours, now bloody Talbot's slain. [*Exeunt*

ACT V

SCENE I. *London. The palace*

Sennet. Enter KING, GLOUCESTER, *and* EXETER

KING

Have you perused the letters from the pope,
The emperor, and the Earl of Armagnac?

GLOUCESTER

I have, my lord: and their intent is this:
They humbly sue unto your excellence
To have a godly peace concluded of
Between the realms of England and of France.

KING

How doth your grace affect their motion?

GLOUCESTER

Well, my good lord; and as the only means
To stop effusion of our Christian blood
And stablish quietness on every side.

KING

Ay, marry, uncle; for I always thought
It was both impious and unnatural
That such immanity and bloody strife
Should reign among professors of one faith.

GLOUCESTER

Beside, my lord, the sooner to effect
And surer bind this knot of amity,
The Earl of Armagnac, near knit to Charles,
A man of great authority in France,
Proffers his only daughter to your grace
In marriage, with a large and sumptuous dowry.

KING

Marriage, uncle! alas, my years are young!
And fitter is my study and my books
Than wanton dalliance with a paramour.
Yet call the ambassadors; and, as you please,
So let them have their answers every one:
I shall be well content with any choice
Tends to God's glory and my country's weal.

Enter WINCHESTER *in Cardinal's habit, a* LEGATE *and*
two AMBASSADORS

EXETER

What! is my Lord of Winchester install'd,
And call'd unto a cardinal's degree?
Then I perceive that will be verified
Henry the Fifth did sometime prophesy,

'If once he come to be a cardinal,
He'll make his cap co-equal with the crown.'

KING

My lords ambassadors, your several suits
Have been consider'd and debated on.
Your purpose is both good and reasonable;
And therefore are we certainly resolved
To draw conditions of a friendly peace;
Which by my Lord of Winchester we mean
Shall be transported presently to France.

GLOUCESTER

And for the proffer of my lord your master,
I have inform'd his highness so at large,
As liking of the lady's virtuous gifts,
Her beauty and the value of her dower,
He doth intend she shall be England's queen.

KING

In argument and proof of which contract,
Bear her this jewel, pledge of my affection.
And so, my lord protector, see them guarded
And safely brought to Dover; where inshipp'd
Commit them to the fortune of the sea.

[*Exeunt all but* WINCHESTER *and* LEGATE

WINCHESTER

Stay, my lord legate: you shall first receive
The sum of money which I promised
Should be deliver'd to his holiness
For clothing me in these grave ornaments.

LEGATE

I will attend upon your lordship's leisure.

WINCHESTER

[*Aside*] Now Winchester will not submit, I trow,
Or be inferior to the proudest peer.
Humphrey of Gloucester, thou shalt well perceive
That, neither in birth or for authority,
The bishop will be overborne by thee:
I'll either make thee stoop and bend thy knee,
Or sack this country with a mutiny.   [*Exeunt*

SCENE II. *France. Plains in Anjou*

Enter CHARLES, BURGUNDY, ALENÇON, BASTARD,
REIGNIER, LA PUCELLE, *and* FORCES

CHARLES

These news, my lords, may cheer our drooping
    spirits:
'Tis said the stout Parisians do revolt
And turn again unto the warlike French.

ALENÇON

Then March to Paris, royal Charles of France,
And keep not back your powers in dalliance.

LA PUCELLE

Peace be amongst them, if they turn to us;
Else, ruin combat with their palaces!

Enter SCOUT

SCOUT

Success unto our valiant general,
And happiness to his accomplices!

[28]

CHARLES

What tidings send our scouts? I prithee, speak.

SCOUT

The English army, that divided was
Into two parties, is now conjoin'd in one,
And means to give you battle presently.

CHARLES

Somewhat too sudden, sirs, the warning is;
But we will presently provide for them.

BURGUNDY

I trust the ghost of Talbot is not there:
Now he is gone, my lord, you need not fear.

LA PUCELLE

Of all base passions, fear is most accursed.
Command the conquest, Charles, it shall be thine,
Let Henry fret and all the world repine.

CHARLES

Then on, my lords; and France be fortunate!

[Exeunt

SCENE III. Before Angiers

Alarum. Excursions. Enter LA PUCELLE

LA PUCELLE

The regent conquers, and the Frenchmen fly.
Now help, ye charming spells and periapts;
And ye choice spirits that admonish me,
And give me signs of future accidents.　　[*Thunder*
You speedy helpers, that are substitutes
Under the lordly monarch of the north,
Appear and aid me in this enterprise.

Enter FIENDS

This speedy and quick appearance argues proof
Of your accustom'd diligence to me.
Now, ye familiar spirits, that are cull'd
Out of the powerful regions under earth,
Help me this once, that France may get the field.
　　　　　　　　　　　[*They walk, and speak not*
O, hold me not with silence over-long!
Where I was wont to feed you with my blood,
I'll lop a member off and give it you
In earnest of a further benefit,
So you do condescend to help me now.
　　　　　　　　　　　　[*They hang their heads*
No hope to have redress? My body shall
Pay recompense, if you will grant my suit.
　　　　　　　　　　　　[*They shake their heads*
Cannot my body nor blood-sacrifice
Entreat you to your wonted furtherance?
Then take my soul, my body, soul and all,
Before that England give the French the foil.
　　　　　　　　　　　　　　[*They depart*
See, they forsake me! Now the time is come
That France must vail her lofty-plumed crest,
And let her head fall into England's lap.
My ancient incantations are too weak,
And hell too strong for me to buckle with.
Now, France, thy glory droopeth to the dust. [*Exit*

Excursions. Re-enter LA PUCELLE *fighting hand to hand
with* YORK; LA PUCELLE *is taken. The French fly*

YORK

Damsel of France, I think I have you fast:
Unchain your spirits now with spelling charms,
And try if they can gain your liberty.
A goodly prize, fit for the devil's grace!
See, how the ugly witch doth bend her brows,
As if with Circe she would change my shape!

LA PUCELLE

Changed to a worser shape thou canst not be.

YORK

O, Charles the Dauphin is a proper man;
No shape but his can please your dainty eye.

LA PUCELLE

A plaguing mischief light on Charles and thee!
And may ye both be suddenly surprised
By bloody hands, in sleeping on your beds!

YORK

Fell banning hag, enchantress, hold thy tongue!

LA PUCELLE

I prithee, give me leave to curse awhile.

YORK

Curse, miscreant, when thou comest to the stake.
　　　　　　　　　　　　　　　　　[*Exeunt*
Alarum. Enter SUFFOLK, *with* MARGARET *in his hand*

SUFFOLK

Be what thou wilt, thou art my prisoner.
　　　　　　　　　　　　　　　　[*Gazes on her*
O fairest beauty, do not fear nor fly!
For I will touch thee but with reverent hands;
I kiss these fingers for eternal peace,
And lay them gently on thy tender side.
Who art thou? say, that I may honour thee.

MARGARET

Margaret my name, and daughter to a king,
The King of Naples, whosoe'er thou art.

SUFFOLK

An earl I am, and Suffolk am I call'd.
Be not offended, nature's miracle,
Thou art allotted to be ta'en by me:
So doth the swan her downy cygnets save,
Keeping them prisoner underneath her wings.
Yet, if this servile usage once offend,
Go and be free again as Suffolk's friend. [*She is going*
O, stay! I have no power to let her pass;
My hand would free her, but my heart says no.
As plays the sun upon the glassy streams,
Twinkling another counterfeited beam,
So seems this gorgeous beauty to mine eyes.
Fain would I woo her, yet I dare not speak:
I'll call for pen and ink, and write my mind.
Fie, de la Pole! disable not thyself;
Hast not a tongue? is she not here?
Wilt thou be daunted at a woman's sight?
Ay, beauty's princely majesty is such,
Confounds the tongue and makes the senses rough.

MARGARET

Say, Earl of Suffolk,—if thy name be so—

What ransom must I pay before I pass?
For I perceive I am thy prisoner.
SUFFOLK
How canst thou tell she will deny thy suit,
Before thou make a trial of her love?
MARGARET
Why speak'st thou not? what ransom must I pay?
SUFFOLK
She's beautiful and therefore to be woo'd;
She is a woman, therefore to be won.
MARGARET
Wilt thou accept of ransom? yea, or no.
SUFFOLK
Fond man, remember that thou hast a wife;
Then how can Margaret be thy paramour?
MARGARET
I were best to leave him, for he will not hear.
SUFFOLK
There all is marr'd; there lies a cooling card.
MARGARET
He talks at random; sure, the man is mad.
SUFFOLK
And yet a dispensation may be had.
MARGARET
And yet I would that you would answer me.
SUFFOLK
I'll win this Lady Margaret. For whom?
Why, for my king: tush, that's a wooden thing!
MARGARET
He talks of wood: it is some carpenter.
SUFFOLK
Yet so my fancy may be satisfied,
And peace established between these realms.
But there remains a scruple in that too;
For though her father be the King of Naples,
Duke of Anjou and Maine, yet is he poor,
And our nobility will scorn the match.
MARGARET
Hear ye, captain, are you not at leisure?
SUFFOLK
It shall be so, disdain they ne'er so much:
Henry is youthful and will quickly yield.
Madam, I have a secret to reveal.
MARGARET
What though I be enthrall'd? he seems a knight,
And will not any way dishonour me.
SUFFOLK
Lady, vouchsafe to listen what I say.
MARGARET
Perhaps I shall be rescued by the French;
And then I need not crave his courtesy.
SUFFOLK
Sweet madam, give me hearing in a cause—
MARGARET
Tush, women have been captivate ere now.
SUFFOLK
Lady, wherefore talk you so?
MARGARET
I cry you mercy, 'tis but Quid for Quo.

SUFFOLK
Say, gentle princess, would you not suppose
Your bondage happy, to be made a queen?
MARGARET
To be a queen in bondage is more vile
Than is a slave in base servility;
For princes should be free.
SUFFOLK
                              And so shall you,
If happy England's royal king be free.
MARGARET
Why, what concerns his freedom unto me?
SUFFOLK
I'll undertake to make thee Henry's queen,
To put a golden sceptre in thy hand
And set a precious crown upon thy head,
If thou wilt condescend to be my—
MARGARET
                                        What?
SUFFOLK
His love.
MARGARET
I am unworthy to be Henry's wife.
SUFFOLK
No, gentle madam; I unworthy am
To woo so fair a dame to be his wife,
And have no portion in the choice myself.
How say you, madam, are ye so content?
MARGARET
An if my father please, I am content.
SUFFOLK
Then call our captains and our colours forth.
And, madam, at your father's castle walls
We'll crave a parley, to confer with him.
    A parley sounded. Enter REIGNIER *on the walls*
See, Reignier, see, thy daughter prisoner!
REIGNIER
To whom?
SUFFOLK
    To me.
REIGNIER
              Suffolk, what remedy?
I am a soldier, and unapt to weep,
Or to exclaim on fortune's fickleness.
SUFFOLK
Yes, there is remedy enough, my lord:
Consent, and for thy honour give consent,
Thy daughter shall be wedded to my king;
Whom I with pain have woo'd and won thereto;
And this her easy-held imprisonment
Hath gain'd thy daughter princely liberty.
REIGNIER
Speaks Suffolk as he thinks?
SUFFOLK
                                Fair Margaret knows
That Suffolk doth not flatter, face, or feign.
REIGNIER
Upon thy princely warrant, I descend
To give thee answer of thy just demand.
                              [*Exit from the walls*

SUFFOLK

And here I will expect thy coming.
Trumpets sound. Enter REIGNIER, *below*

REIGNIER

Welcome, brave earl, into our territories:
Command in Anjou what your honour pleases.

SUFFOLK

Thanks, Reignier, happy for so sweet a child,
Fit to be made companion with a king:
What answer makes your grace unto my suit?

REIGNIER

Since thou dost deign to woo her little worth
To be the princely bride of such a lord;
Upon condition I may quietly
Enjoy mine own, the country Maine and Anjou,
Free from oppression or the stroke of war,
My daughter shall be Henry's, if he please.

SUFFOLK

That is her ransom; I deliver her;
And those two counties I will undertake
Your grace shall well and quietly enjoy.

REIGNIER

And I again, in Henry's royal name,
As deputy unto that gracious king,
Give thee her hand, for sign of plighted faith.

SUFFOLK

Reignier of France, I give thee kingly thanks,
Because this is in traffic of a king.
[*Aside*] And yet, methinks, I could be well content
To be mine own attorney in this case.
I'll over then to England with this news,
And make this marriage to be solemnized.
So farewell, Reignier: set this diamond safe
In golden palaces, as it becomes.

REIGNIER

I do embrace thee, as I would embrace
The Christian prince, King Henry, were he here.

MARGARET

Farewell, my lord: good wishes, praise and prayers
Shall Suffolk ever have of Margaret.   [*Going*

SUFFOLK

Farewell, sweet madam: but hark you, Margaret;
No princely commendations to my king?

MARGARET

Such commendations as becomes a maid,
A virgin and his servant, say to him.

SUFFOLK

Words sweetly placed and modestly directed.
But, madam, I must trouble you again;
No loving token to his majesty?

MARGARET

Yes, my good lord, a pure unspotted heart,
Never yet taint with love, I send the king.

SUFFOLK

And this withal.   [*Kisses her*

MARGARET

That for thyself: I will not so presume
To send such peevish tokens to a king.

[*Exeunt* REIGNIER *and* MARGARET

SUFFOLK

O, wert thou for myself! But, Suffolk, stay;
Thou mayst not wander in that labyrinth;
There Minotaurs and ugly treasons lurk.
Solicit Henry with her wondrous praise:
Bethink thee on her virtues that surmount,
And natural graces that extinguish art;
Repeat their semblance often on the seas,
That, when thou comest to kneel at Henry's feet,
Thou mayst bereave him of his wits with wonder.
[*Exit*

SCENE IV. *Camp of the* DUKE OF YORK *in Anjou*

Enter YORK, WARWICK, *and others*

YORK

Bring forth that sorceress condemn'd to burn.
Enter LA PUCELLE, *guarded, and a* SHEPHERD

SHEPHERD

Ah, Joan, this kills thy father's heart outright!
Have I sought every country far and near,
And, now it is my chance to find thee out,
Must I behold thy timeless cruel death?
Ah, Joan, sweet daughter Joan, I'll die with thee!

LA PUCELLE

Decrepit miser! base ignoble wretch!
I am descended of a gentler blood:
Thou art no father nor no friend of mine.

SHEPHERD

Out, out! My lords, an please you, 'tis not so;
I did beget her, all the parish knows:
Her mother liveth yet, can testify
She was the first fruit of my bachelorship.

WARWICK

Graceless! wilt thou deny thy parentage?

YORK

This argues what her kind of life hath been,
Wicked and vile; and so her death concludes.

SHEPHERD

Fie, Joan, that thou wilt be so obstacle!
God knows thou art a collop of my flesh;
And for thy sake have I shed many a tear:
Deny me not, I prithee, gentle Joan.

LA PUCELLE

Peasant, avaunt! You have suborn'd this man,
Of purpose to obscure my noble birth.

SHEPHERD

'Tis true, I gave a noble to the priest
The morn that I was wedded to her mother.
Kneel down and take my blessing, good my girl.
Wilt thou not stoop? Now cursed be the time
Of thy nativity! I would the milk
Thy mother gave thee when thou suck'dst her
        breast,
Had been a little ratsbane for thy sake!
Or else, when thou didst keep my lambs a-field,
I wish some ravenous wolf had eaten thee!
Dost thou deny thy father, cursed drab?
O, burn her, burn her! hanging is too good.   [*Exit*

YORK

Take her away; for she hath lived too long,
To fill the world with vicious qualities.

LA PUCELLE

First, let me tell you whom you have condemn'd:
Not me begotten of a shepherd swain,
But issued from the progeny of kings;
Virtuous and holy; chosen from above,
By inspiration of celestial grace,
To work exceeding miracles on earth.
I never had to do with wicked spirits:
But you, that are polluted with your lusts,
Stain'd with the guiltless blood of innocents,
Corrupt and tainted with a thousand vices,
Because you want the grace that others have,
You judge it straight a thing impossible
To compass wonders but by help of devils.
No, misconceived! Joan of Arc hath been
A virgin from her tender infancy,
Chaste and immaculate in very thought;
Whose maiden blood, thus rigorously effused,
Will cry for vengeance at the gates of heaven.

YORK

Ay, ay: away with her to execution!

WARWICK

And hark ye, sirs; because she is a maid,
Spare for no faggots, let there be enow:
Place barrels of pitch upon the fatal stake,
That so her torture may be shortened.

LA PUCELLE

Will nothing turn your unrelenting hearts?
Then, Joan, discover thine infirmity,
That warranteth by law to be thy privilege.
I am with child, ye bloody homicides:
Murder not then the fruit within my womb,
Although ye hale me to a violent death.

YORK

Now heaven forfend! the holy maid with child!

WARWICK

The greatest miracle that e'er ye wrought:
Is all your strict preciseness come to this?

YORK

She and the Dauphin have been juggling:
I did imagine what would be her refuge.

WARWICK

Well, go to; we'll have no bastards live;
Especially since Charles must father it.

LA PUCELLE

You are deceived; my child is none of his:
It was Alençon that enjoy'd my love.

YORK

Alençon! that notorious Machiavel!
It dies, an if it had a thousand lives.

LA PUCELLE

O, give me leave, I have deluded you:
'Twas neither Charles nor yet the duke I named,
But Reignier, king of Naples, that prevail'd.

WARWICK

A married man! that's most intolerable.

YORK

Why, here's a girl! I think she knows not well,
There were so many, whom she may accuse.

WARWICK

It's sign she hath been liberal and free.

YORK

And yet, forsooth, she is a virgin pure.
Strumpet, thy words condemn thy brat and thee:
Use no entreaty, for it is in vain.

LA PUCELLE

Then lead me hence; with whom I leave my curse:
May never glorious sun reflex his beams
Upon the country where you make abode;
But darkness and the gloomy shade of death
Environ you, till mischief and despair
Drive you to break your necks or hang yourselves!
[*Exit, guarded*

YORK

Break thou in pieces and consume to ashes,
Thou foul accursed minister of hell!

Enter CARDINAL BEAUFORT, BISHOP OF WINCHESTER,
attended

CARDINAL

Lord regent, I do greet your excellence
With letters of commission from the king.
For know, my lords, the states of Christendom,
Moved with remorse of these outrageous broils,
Have earnestly implored a general peace
Betwixt our nation and the aspiring French;
And here at hand the Dauphin and his train
Approacheth, to confer about some matter.

YORK

Is all our travail turn'd to this effect?
After the slaughter of so many peers,
So many captains, gentlemen and soldiers,
That in this quarrel have been overthrown,
And sold their bodies for their country's benefit,
Shall we at last conclude effeminate peace?
Have we not lost most part of all the towns,
By treason, falsehood and by treachery,
Our great progenitors had conquered?
O, Warwick, Warwick! I foresee with grief
The utter loss of all the realm of France.

WARWICK

Be patient, York: if we conclude a peace,
It shall be with such strict and severe covenants
As little shall the Frenchmen gain thereby.

Enter CHARLES, ALENÇON, BASTARD, REIGNIER, *and*
OTHERS

CHARLES

Since, lords of England, it is thus agreed
That peaceful truce shall be proclaim'd in France,
We come to be informed by yourselves
What the conditions of that league must be.

YORK

Speak, Winchester; for boiling choler chokes
The hollow passage of my poison'd voice,
By sight of these our baleful enemies.

CARDINAL

Charles, and the rest, it is enacted thus:

That, in regard King Henry gives consent,
Of mere compassion and of lenity,
To ease your country of distressful war,
And suffer you to breathe in fruitful peace,
You shall become true liegemen to his crown:
And, Charles, upon condition thou wilt swear
To pay him tribute, and submit thyself,
Thou shalt be placed as viceroy under him,
And still enjoy thy regal dignity.

ALENÇON

Must he be then as shadow of himself?
Adorn his temples with a coronet,
And yet, in substance and authority,
Retain but privilege of a private man?
This proffer is absurd and reasonless.

CHARLES

'Tis known already that I am possess'd
With more than half the Gallian territories,
And therein reverenced for their lawful king:
Shall I, for lucre of the rest unvanquish'd,
Detract so much from that prerogative,
As to be call'd but viceroy of the whole?
No, lord ambassador, I'll rather keep
That which I have than, coveting for more,
Be cast from possibility of all.

YORK

Insulting Charles! hast thou by secret means
Used intercession to obtain a league,
And, now the matter grows to compromise,
Stand'st thou aloof upon comparison?
Either accept the title thou usurp'st,
Of benefit proceeding from our king
And not of any challenge of desert,
Or we will plague thee with incessant wars.

REIGNIER

My lord, you do not well in obstinacy
To cavil in the course of this contract:
If once it be neglected, ten to one
We shall not find like opportunity.

ALENÇON

To say the truth, it is your policy
To save your subjects from such massacre
And ruthless slaughters, as are daily seen,
By our proceeding in hostility;
And therefore take this compact of a truce,
Although you break it when your pleasure serves.

WARWICK

How say'st thou, Charles? shall our condition stand?

CHARLES

It shall;
Only reserved, you claim no interest
In any of our towns of garrison.

YORK

Then swear allegiance to his majesty,
As thou art knight, never to disobey
Nor be rebellious to the crown of England,
Thou, nor thy nobles, to the crown of England.
So, now dismiss your army when ye please;

Hang up your ensigns, let your drums be still,
For here we entertain a solemn peace.   [Exeunt

SCENE V. London. The royal palace

Enter SUFFOLK in conference with the KING, GLOUCESTER,
and EXETER

KING

Your wondrous rare description, noble earl,
Of beauteous Margaret hath astonish'd me:
Her virtues graced with external gifts
Do breed love's settled passions in my heart:
And like as rigour of tempestuous gusts
Provokes the mightiest hulk against the tide,
So am I driven by breath of her renown,
Either to suffer shipwreck or arrive
Where I may have fruition of her love.

SUFFOLK

Tush, my good lord, this superficial tale
Is but a preface of her worthy praise;
The chief perfections of that lovely dame,
Had I sufficient skill to utter them,
Would make a volume of enticing lines,
Able to ravish any dull conceit:
And, which is more, she is not so divine,
So full-replete with choice of all delights,
But with as humble lowliness of mind
She is content to be at your command;
Command, I mean, of virtuous chaste intents,
To love and honour Henry as her lord.

KING

And otherwise will Henry ne'er presume.
Therefore, my lord protector, give consent
That Margaret may be England's royal queen.

GLOUCESTER

So should I give consent to flatter sin.
You know, my lord, your highness is betroth'd
Unto another lady of esteem:
How shall we then dispense with that contract,
And not deface your honour with reproach?

SUFFOLK

As doth a ruler with unlawful oaths;
Or one that, at a triumph having vow'd
To try his strength, forsaketh yet the lists
By reason of his adversary's odds:
A poor earl's daughter is unequal odds,
And therefore may be broke without offence.

GLOUCESTER

Why, what, I pray, is Margaret more than that?
Her father is no better than an earl,
Although in glorious titles he excel.

SUFFOLK

Yes, my lord, her father is a king,
The King of Naples and Jerusalem;
And of such great authority in France,
As his alliance will confirm our peace,
And keep the Frenchmen in allegiance.

GLOUCESTER

And so the Earl of Armagnac may do,
Because he is near kinsman unto Charles.

EXETER

Beside, his wealth doth warrant a liberal dower,
Where Reignier sooner will receive than give.

SUFFOLK

A dower, my lords! disgrace not so your king,
That he should be so abject, base and poor,
To choose for wealth and not for perfect love.
Henry is able to enrich his queen,
And not to seek a queen to make him rich:
So worthless peasants bargain for their wives,
As market-men for oxen, sheep, or horse.
Marriage as a matter of more worth
Than to be dealt in by attorneyship;
Not whom we will, but whom his grace affects,
Must be companion of his nuptial bed:
And therefore, lords, since he affects her most,
It most of all these reasons bindeth us,
In our opinions she should be preferr'd.
For what is wedlock forced but a hell,
An age of discord and continual strife?
Whereas the contrary bringeth bliss,
And is a pattern of celestial peace.
Whom should we match with Henry, being a king,
But Margaret, that is daughter to a king?
Her peerless feature, joined with her birth,
Approves her fit for none but for a king:
Her valiant courage and undaunted spirit,
More than in women commonly is seen,
Will answer our hope in issue of a king;
For Henry, son unto a conqueror,
Is likely to beget more conquerors,
If with a lady of so high resolve
As is fair Margaret he be link'd in love.

Then yield, my lords; and here conclude with me
That Margaret shall be queen, and none but she.

KING

Whether it be through force of your report,
My noble Lord of Suffolk, or for that
My tender youth was never yet attaint
With any passion of inflaming love,
I cannot tell; but this I am assured,
I feel such sharp dissension in my breast,
Such fierce alarums both of hope and fear,
As I am sick with working of my thoughts.
Take, therefore, shipping; post, my lord, to France;
Agree to any covenants, and procure
That Lady Margaret do vouchsafe to come
To cross the seas to England, and be crown'd
King Henry's faithful and anointed queen:
For your expenses and sufficient charge,
Among the people gather up a tenth.
Be gone, I say; for, till you do return,
I rest perplexed with a thousand cares.
And you, good uncle, banish all offence:
If you do censure me by what you were,
Not what you are, I know it will excuse
This sudden execution of my will.
And so, conduct me where, from company,
I may revolve and ruminate my grief.   [Exit

GLOUCESTER

Ay, grief, I fear me, both at first and last.
       [Exeunt GLOUCESTER and EXETER

SUFFOLK

Thus Suffolk hath prevail'd; and thus he goes,
As did the youthful Paris once to Greece,
With hope to find the like event in love,
But prosper better than the Trojan did.
Margaret shall now be queen, and rule the king;
But I will rule both her, the king and realm.   [Exit

THE SECOND PART OF KING HENRY VI

SYNOPSIS

WHEN Margaret of Anjou arrives at the English court as Henry VI's bride, it at once becomes known that the disgraceful marriage terms arranged by the scheming Duke of Suffolk include the surrender of the duchies of Anjou and Maine, and the omission of the dowry with the bride who is brought to England at Henry's expense. The young King is delighted with his wife, raises Suffolk to a dukedom, and relieves York of his regency in France, but the upright Gloucester, Lord Protector, reads the conditions in utter dismay, Warwick and Salisbury who have fought hard for the relinquished duchies are indignant, while York doggedly awaits an opportunity to seize the throne.

The Lancastrian party rallies around the fair but cruel, imperious Queen who is determined to get control over her weak, religiously minded husband by ousting the faithful Gloucester from his post as Protector, and, extremely jealous of his ambitious wife Eleanor, plots the downfall of both with the assistance of Gloucester's old enemy, Winchester, now Cardinal Beaufort, and the connivance of York himself who sees in the conspiracy the destruction of the entire faction. Eleanor is betrayed into meeting some sorcerers who give her a message from the spirits that the duke yet lives that shall depose King Henry, that the Duke of Suffolk shall die by water, and that the Duke of Somerset should avoid castles. Arrested and tried as a traitor and sorcerer, the Duchess is banished to the Isle of Man, and her sad husband justly abides by the law but in his grief and shame begs the King to retire him.

Shortly after Gloucester receives an unexpected summons to Parliament where the Queen and Suffolk, the Cardinal and York, are doing their utmost to convince Henry of his old counsellor's deceit, and when he appears they accuse him of high treason and send him to prison. Since they have no evidence to support their charges and knowing Gloucester's popularity with the Commons and the affection of the King, the conspirators have him strangled when sleeping, the Cardinal providing the murderers, and Suffolk directing the act and afterwards censuring it in public. The crime is investigated, and the Commons, appointing Salisbury and Warwick as spokesmen, storm the King's palace and accuse the foul Suffolk whom Henry agrees to banish and who is later captured and killed by a seaman off the Kentish coast, thus fulfilling the prophecy made to the Duchess of Gloucester that he should die by water. Suffolk's head is sent to the grieving Queen, and, suddenly taken ill, the Cardinal dies in mental torture without a sign of hope of forgiveness.

York's lineage having proved to Warwick and Salisbury that by right of descent he is the lawful heir to the throne, they promise him their support, and his plans are further advanced by being placed at the head of an army raised to suppress an Irish rebellion. Before leaving England, York encourages Jack Cade of Ashford, a common bullying laborer, to take the name of John Mortimer whom he strongly resembles and foment a rebellion on which the Yorks may later capitalize in seizing the throne. The headstrong Cade, followed by a rabble of citizens, has a few small successes and is soon at London where he seizes London Bridge, lays claim to the city, urges his followers to destroy the Tower, defeats a royal force, beheads Lord Say, the King's messenger, and, with his victims' heads on poles, is proceeding to ride in triumph through the city when Lord Clifford, gaining the attention of the fickle mob, turns it against their leader through an adroit appeal to their patriotism and the King's offer of pardon. Cade flees, and after hiding for several days seeks for food in the garden of Alexander Iden, a Kentish squire, who kills him and is afterwards knighted by the King.

York, back from Ireland, marches on London with a large army, proclaiming that he wishes only the removal of Somerset, head of the Lancaster party, whom he calls a traitor, whereupon the conciliatory Henry sends Somerset temporarily to the Tower. While in audience with the King, to whom he has again professed his allegiance, the dissembling York is suddenly confronted by the Queen with the released Somerset, becomes openly defiant, declares himself the rightful King and is denounced as a traitor. His sons, Edward and Richard, with Warwick and Salisbury, come quickly to his aid. Clifford and his son join the King, and at St. Albans the houses of York and Lancaster meet in pitched battle. York, who is victorious, fights and kills the elder Clifford, whose son upon finding his father's dead body vows an awful vengeance upon his enemies. Somerset is killed by York's deformed, hunchback son Richard near the Castle Inn, whereby the third prophecy to the Duchess of Gloucester is fulfilled; and old Salisbury, fighting like a raging lion, has to be helped back on his horse three times.

The King and Queen having fled to London, Warwick urges York to reach the city before Henry can summon Parliament.

HISTORICAL DATA

Part Two of this historical trilogy first appeared in quarto form in 1594, under the title *The First Part of the Contention of the two Famous Houses of Yorke and Lancaster*. The material was again taken from Holinshed and Halle.

As the Second and Third Parts of Henry VI the plays are found first in the folio of 1623. A great variety of views as to the original authorship have been put forth, and the subject provides the most perplexing problem in Shakespearean scholarship. The principal theories are, briefly:

Knight's, crediting Shakespeare with the authorship of both the original and the revisions;

Malone's, that Greene and Peele were the authors of the original plays, which Shakespeare revised;

Grant White's, that Marlowe, Greene, Shakespeare, and *possibly* Peele, wrote the original plays, and

Miss Jane Lee's, that Marlowe, Greene, and perhaps Peele, were the authors of the original plays and that Shakespeare and Marlowe collaborated in their revision.

The recasting of the plays was probably done by Shakespeare, perhaps with Marlowe's help, during the years 1591-92.

"*From Ireland thus comes York to claim his right.*"
HENRY VI, PART II

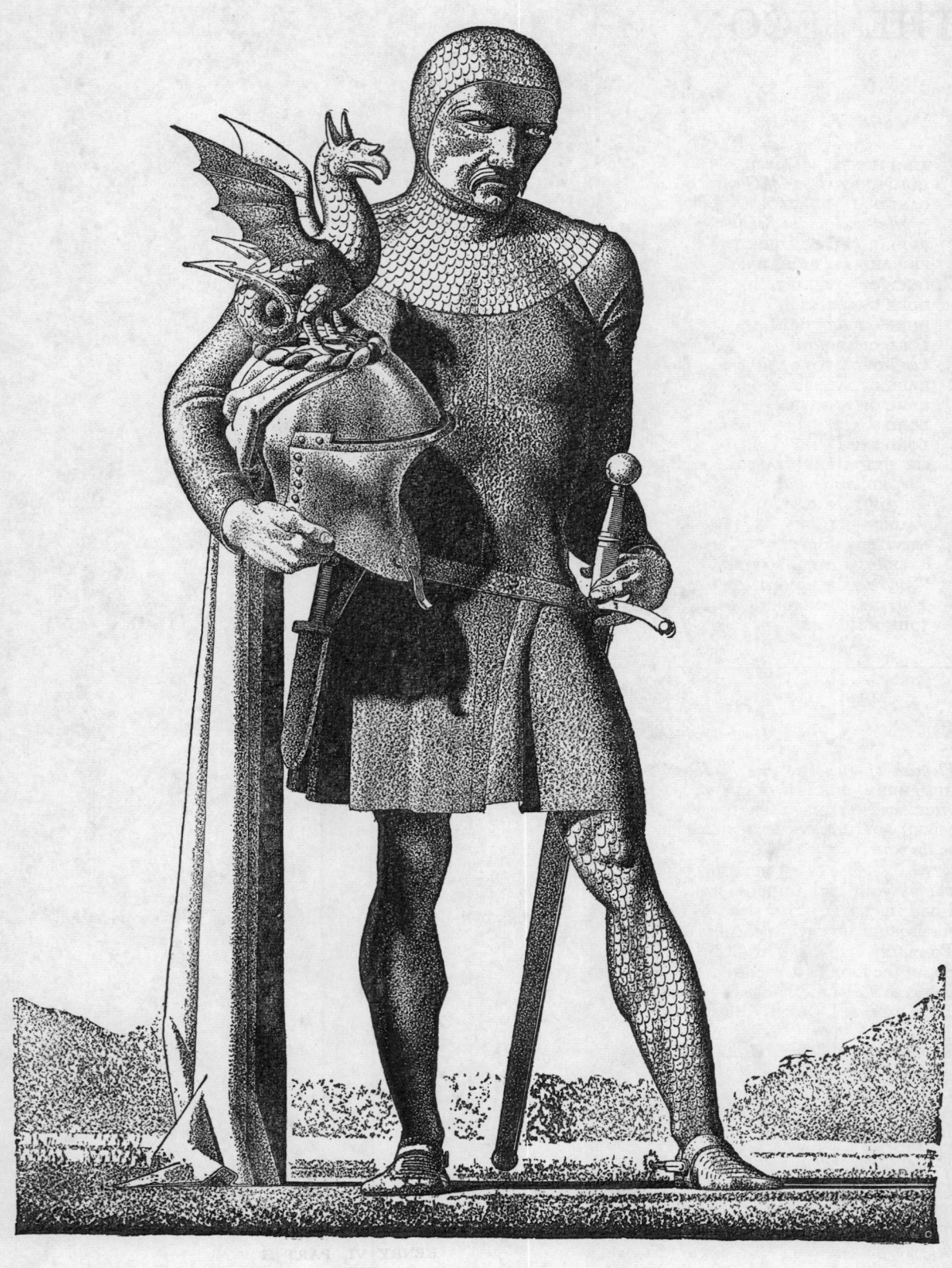

THE SECOND PART OF KING HENRY VI

DRAMATIS PERSONÆ

KING HENRY, *the Sixth.*
HUMPHREY, *Duke of Gloucester, his uncle.*
CARDINAL BEAUFORT, *Bishop of Winchester, great-uncle to the King.*
RICHARD PLANTAGENET, *Duke of York.*
EDWARD *and* RICHARD, *his sons.*
DUKE OF SOMERSET.
DUKE OF SUFFOLK.
DUKE OF BUCKINGHAM.
LORD CLIFFORD.
YOUNG CLIFFORD, *his son.*
EARL OF SALISBURY.
EARL OF WARWICK.
LORD SCALES.
LORD SAY.
SIR HUMPHREY STAFFORD, *and* WILLIAM STAFFORD, *his brother.*
SIR JOHN STANLEY.
VAUX.
MATTHEW GOFFE.
A SEA-CAPTAIN, MASTER, *and* MASTER'S-MATE, *and* WALTER WHITMORE.
TWO GENTLEMEN, *prisoners with Suffolk.*
JOHN HUME *and* JOHN SOUTHWELL, *priests.*

BOLINGBROKE, *a conjurer.*
THOMAS HORNER, *an armourer.*
PETER, *his man.*
CLERK *of Chatham.*
MAYOR *of Saint Alban's.*
SIMPCOX, *an impostor.*
ALEXANDER IDEN, *a Kentish gentleman.*
JACK CADE, *a rebel.*
GEORGE BEVIS, JOHN HOLLAND, DICK *the butcher,* SMITH *the weaver,* MICHAEL, *&c., followers of Cade.*
TWO MURDERERS.

MARGARET, *Queen to King Henry.*
ELEANOR, *Duchess of Gloucester.*
MARGARET JOURDAIN, *a witch.*
WIFE *to Simpcox.*

LORDS, LADIES, *and* ATTENDANTS, PETITIONERS, ALDERMEN, *a* HERALD, *a* BEADLE, SHERIFF, *and* OFFICERS, CITIZENS, 'PRENTICES, FALCONERS, GUARDS, SOLDIERS, MESSENGERS, *&c.*
A SPIRIT.

SCENE—*England.*

ACT I

SCENE I. *London. The palace*

Flourish of trumpets: then hautboys. Enter, THE KING, HUMPHREY, DUKE OF GLOUCESTER, SALISBURY, WARWICK, *and* CARDINAL BEAUFORT, *on the one side;* THE QUEEN, SUFFOLK, YORK, SOMERSET, *and* BUCKINGHAM, *on the other*

SUFFOLK

As by your high imperial majesty
I had in charge at my depart for France,
As procurator to your excellence,
To marry Princess Margaret for your grace,
So, in the famous ancient city Tours,
In presence of the Kings of France and Sicil,
The Dukes of Orleans, Calaber, Bretagne and Alençon,
Seven earls, twelve barons, and twenty reverend bishops,
I have perform'd my task and was espoused:
And humbly now upon my bended knee,
In sight of England and her lordly peers,
Deliver up my title in the queen
To your most gracious hands, that are the substance
Of that great shadow I did represent;
The happiest gift that ever marquess gave,
The fairest queen that ever king received.

KING

Suffolk, arise. Welcome, Queen Margaret:
I can express no kinder sign of love
Than this kind kiss. O Lord, that lends me life,
Lend me a heart replete with thankfulness!
For Thou hast given me in this beauteous face
A world of earthly blessings to my soul,
If sympathy of love unite our thoughts.

QUEEN

Great King of England and my gracious lord,
The mutual conference that my mind hath had,
By day, by night, waking and in my dreams,
In courtly company or at my beads,
With you, mine alder-liefest sovereign,
Makes me the bolder to salute my king
With ruder terms, such as my wit affords
And over-joy of heart doth minister.

KING

Her sight did ravish; but her grace in speech,
Her words y-clad with wisdom's majesty,
Makes me from wondering fall to weeping joys;
Such is the fulness of my heart's content.
Lords, with one cheerful voice welcome my love.

ALL

[*Kneeling*] Long live Queen Margaret, England's happiness!

QUEEN

We thank you all.   [Flourish

SUFFOLK

My lord protector, so it please your grace,
Here are the articles of contracted peace
Between our sovereign and the French king Charles,
For eighteen months concluded by consent.

GLOUCESTER

[Reads] 'Imprimis, It is agreed between the French king Charles
and William de la Pole, Marquess of Suffolk, ambassador
for Henry King of England, that the said Henry shall espouse
the Lady Margaret, daughter unto Reignier King of Naples,
Sicilia and Jerusalem, and crown her Queen of England ere
the thirtieth of May next ensuing. Item, that the duchy of Anjou and the county of Maine shall be released and delivered to
the king her father—'   [Lets the paper fall

KING

Uncle, how now!

GLOUCESTER

Pardon me, gracious lord;
Some sudden qualm hath struck me at the heart,
And dimm'd mine eyes, that I can read no further.

KING

Uncle of Winchester, I pray, read on.

CARDINAL

[Reads] 'Item, It is further agreed between them, that the
duchies of Anjou and Maine shall be released and delivered
over to the king her father, and she sent over of the King of
England's own proper cost and charges, without having any
dowry.'

KING

They please us well. Lord Marquess, kneel down:
We here create thee the first duke of Suffolk,
And gird thee with the sword. Cousin of York,
We here discharge your grace from being regent
I' the parts of France, till term of eighteen months
Be full expired. Thanks, uncle Winchester,
Gloucester, York, Buckingham, Somerset,
Salisbury, and Warwick;
We thank you all for this great favour done,
In entertainment to my princely queen.
Come, let us in, and with all speed provide
To see her coronation be perform'd.
                [Exeunt KING, QUEEN, and SUFFOLK

GLOUCESTER

Brave peers of England, pillars of the state,
To you Duke Humphrey must unload his grief,
Your grief, the common grief of all the land.
What! did my brother Henry spend his youth,
His valour, coin, and people, in the wars?
Did he so often lodge in open field,
In winter's cold and summer's parching heat,
To conquer France, his true inheritance?
And did my brother Bedford toil his wits,
To keep by policy what Henry got?
Have you yourselves, Somerset, Buckingham,
Brave York, Salisbury, and victorious Warwick,
Received deep scars in France and Normandy?
Or hath mine uncle Beaufort and myself,
With all the learned council of the realm,
Studied so long, sat in the council-house

Early and late, debating to and fro
How France and Frenchmen might be kept in awe,
And had his highness in his infancy
Crowned in Paris in despite of foes?
And shall these labours and these honours die?
Shall Henry's conquest, Bedford's vigilance,
Your deeds of war and all our counsel die?
O peers of England, shameful is this league!
Fatal this marriage, cancelling your fame,
Blotting your names from books of memory,
Razing the characters of your renown,
Defacing monuments of conquer'd France,
Undoing all, as all had never been!

CARDINAL

Nephew, what means this passionate discourse,
This peroration with such circumstance?
For France, 'tis ours; and we will keep it still.

GLOUCESTER

Ay, uncle, we will keep it, if we can;
But now it is impossible we should:
Suffolk, the new-made duke that rules the roast,
Hath given the duchy of Anjou and Maine
Unto the poor King Reignier, whose large style
Agrees not with the leanness of his purse.

SALISBURY

Now, by the death of Him that died for all,
These counties were the keys of Normandy.
But wherefore weeps Warwick, my valiant son?

WARWICK

For grief that they are past recovery:
For, were there hope to conquer them again,
My sword should shed hot blood, mine eyes no tears.
Anjou and Maine! myself did win them both;
Those provinces these arms of mine did conquer:
And are the cities, that I got with wounds,
Deliver'd up again with peaceful words?
Mort Dieu!

YORK

For Suffolk's duke, may he be suffocate,
That dims the honour of this warlike isle!
France should have torn and rent my very heart,
Before I would have yielded to this league.
I never read but England's kings have had
Large sums of gold and dowries with their wives;
And our King Henry gives away his own,
To match with her that brings no vantages.

GLOUCESTER

A proper jest, and never heard before,
That Suffolk should demand a whole fifteenth
For costs and charges in transporting her!
She should have stay'd in France and starved in
    France,
Before—

CARDINAL

My lord of Gloucester, now ye grow too hot:
It was the pleasure of my lord the king.

GLOUCESTER

My lord of Winchester, I know your mind;
'Tis not my speeches that you do mislike,
But 'tis my presence that doth trouble ye.

Rancour will out: proud prelate, in thy face
I see thy fury: if I longer stay,
We shall begin our ancient bickerings.
Lordings, farewell; and say, when I am gone,
I prophesied France will be lost ere long.   [*Exit*

CARDINAL

So, there goes our protector in a rage.
'Tis known to you he is mine enemy,
Nay, more, an enemy unto you all,
And no great friend, I fear me, to the king.
Consider, lords, he is the next of blood,
And heir apparent to the English crown:
Had Henry got an empire by his marriage,
And all the wealthy kingdoms of the west,
There's reason he should be displeased at it.
Look to it, lords; let not his smoothing words
Bewitch your hearts; be wise and circumspect.
What though the common people favour him,
Calling him 'Humphrey, the good Duke of Glou-
    cester,'
Clapping their hands, and crying with loud voice,
'Jesu maintain your royal excellence!'
With 'God preserve the good Duke Humphrey!'
I fear me, lords, for all this flattering gloss,
He will be found a dangerous protector.

BUCKINGHAM

Why should he, then, protect our sovereign,
He being of age to govern of himself?
Cousin of Somerset, join you with me,
And all together, with the Duke of Suffolk,
We'll quickly hoise Duke Humphrey from his seat.

CARDINAL

This weighty business will not brook delay;
I'll to the Duke of Suffolk presently.   [*Exit*

SOMERSET

Cousin of Buckingham, though Humphrey's pride
And greatness of his place be grief to us,
Yet let us watch the haughty cardinal:
His insolence is more intolerable
Than all the princes in the land beside:
If Gloucester be displaced, he'll be protector.

BUCKINGHAM

Or thou or I, Somerset, will be protector,
Despite Duke Humphrey or the cardinal.
        [*Exeunt* BUCKINGHAM *and* SOMERSET

SALISBURY

Pride went before, ambition follows him.
While these do labour for their own preferment,
Behoves it us to labour for the realm.
I never saw but Humphrey Duke of Gloucester
Did bear him like a noble gentleman.
Oft have I seen the haughty cardinal,
More like a soldier than a man o' the church,
As stout and proud as he were lord of all,
Swear like a ruffian, and demean himself
Unlike the ruler of a commonweal.
Warwick, my son, the comfort of my age,
Thy deeds, thy plainness, and thy housekeeping,
Hath won the greatest favour of the commons,
Excepting none but good Duke Humphrey:

And, brother York, thy acts in Ireland,
In bringing them to civil discipline,
Thy late exploits done in the heart of France,
When thou wert regent for our sovereign,
Have made thee fear'd and honour'd of the people:
Join we together, for the public good,
In what we can, to bridle and suppress
The pride of Suffolk and the cardinal,
With Somerset's and Buckingham's ambition;
And, as we may, cherish Duke Humphrey's deeds,
While they do tend the profit of the land.

WARWICK

So God help Warwick, as he loves the land,
And common profit of his country!

YORK

[*Aside*] And so says York, for he hath greatest cause.

SALISBURY

Then let's make haste away, and look unto the
    main.

WARWICK

Unto the main! O father, Maine is lost;
That Maine which by main force Warwick did win,
And would have kept so long as breath did last!
Main chance, father, you meant; but I meant
    Maine,
Which I will win from France, or else be slain.
        [*Exeunt* WARWICK *and* SALISBURY

YORK

Anjou and Maine are given to the French;
Paris is lost; the state of Normandy
Stands on a tickle point, now they are gone:
Suffolk concluded on the articles,
The peers agreed, and Henry was well pleased
To change two dukedoms for a duke's fair daughter.
I cannot blame them all: what is 't to them?
'Tis thine they give away, and not their own.
Pirates may make cheap pennyworths of their pil-
    lage,
And purchase friends and give to courtezans,
Still revelling like lords till all be gone;
While as the silly owner of the goods
Weeps over them and wrings his hapless hands,
And shakes his head and trembling stands aloof,
While all is shared and all is borne away,
Ready to starve and dare not touch his own:
So York must sit and fret and bite his tongue,
While his own lands are bargain'd for and sold.
Methinks the realms of England, France and Ire-
    land
Bear that proportion to my flesh and blood
As did the fatal brand Althæa burn'd
Unto the prince's heart of Calydon.
Anjou and Maine both given unto the French!
Cold news for me, for I had hope of France,
Even as I have of fertile England's soil.
A day will come when York shall claim his own;
And therefore I will take the Nevils' parts
And make a show of love to proud Duke Humphrey,
And, when I spy advantage, claim the crown,
For that's the golden mark I seek to hit:

Nor shall proud Lancaster usurp my right,
Nor hold the sceptre in his childish fist,
Nor wear the diadem upon his head,
Whose church-like humours fits not for a crown.
Then, York, be still awhile, till time do serve:
Watch thou and wake when others be asleep,
To pry into the secrets of the state;
Till Henry, surfeiting in joys of love,
With his new bride and England's dear-bought
    queen,
And Humphrey with the peers be fall'n at jars:
Then will I raise aloft the milk-white rose,
With whose sweet smell the air shall be perfumed;
And in my standard bear the arms of York,
To grapple with the house of Lancaster;
And, force perforce, I'll make him yield the crown,
Whose bookish rule hath pull'd fair England down.
                                     [*Exit*

Scene II. *The* Duke of Gloucester's *house*

Enter Duke Humphrey *and his wife* Eleanor

DUCHESS

Why droops my lord, like over-ripen'd corn,
Hanging the head at Ceres' plenteous load?
Why doth the great Duke Humphrey knit his brows,
As frowning at the favours of the world?
Why are thine eyes fix'd to the sullen earth,
Gazing on that which seems to dim thy sight?
What seest thou there? King Henry's diadem,
Enchased with all the honours of the world?
If so, gaze on, and grovel on thy face,
Until thy head be circled with the same.
Put forth thy hand, reach at the glorious gold.
What, is 't too short? I'll lengthen it with mine;
And, having both together heaved it up,
We'll both together lift our heads to heaven,
And never more abase our sight so low
As to vouchsafe one glance unto the ground.

GLOUCESTER

O Nell, sweet Nell, if thou dost love thy lord,
Banish the canker of ambitious thoughts.
And may that thought, when I imagine ill
Against my king and nephew, virtuous Henry,
Be my last breathing in this mortal world!
My troublous dream this night doth make me sad.

DUCHESS

What dream'd my lord? tell me, and I'll requite it
With sweet rehearsal of my morning's dream.

GLOUCESTER

Methought this staff, mine office-badge in court,
Was broke in twain; by whom I have forgot,
But, as I think, it was by the cardinal;
And on the pieces of the broken wand
Were placed the heads of Edmund Duke of Somer-
    set,
And William de la Pole, first duke of Suffolk.
This was my dream: what it doth bode, God knows.

DUCHESS

Tut, this was nothing but an argument,
That he that breaks a stick of Gloucester's grove
Shall lose his head for his presumption.
But list to me, my Humphrey, my sweet duke:
Methought I sat in seat of majesty,
In the cathedral church of Westminster,
And in that chair where kings and queens are
    crown'd;
Where Henry and dame Margaret kneel'd to me,
And on my head did set the diadem.

GLOUCESTER

Nay, Eleanor, then must I chide outright:
Presumptuous dame, ill-nurtured Eleanor,
Art thou not second woman in the realm,
And the protector's wife, beloved of him?
Hast thou not worldly pleasure at command,
Above the reach or compass of thy thought?
And wilt thou still be hammering treachery,
To tumble down thy husband and thyself
From top of honour to disgrace's feet?
Away from me, and let me hear no more!

DUCHESS

What, what, my lord! are you so choleric
With Eleanor, for telling but her dream?
Next time I'll keep my dreams unto myself,
And not be check'd.

GLOUCESTER

Nay, be not angry; I am pleased again.

Enter MESSENGER

MESSENGER

My lord protector, 'tis his highness' pleasure
You do prepare to ride unto Saint Alban's,
Where as the king and queen do mean to hawk.

GLOUCESTER

I go. Come, Nell, thou wilt ride with us?

DUCHESS

Yes, my good lord, I'll follow presently.
            [*Exeunt* GLOUCESTER *and* MESSENGER
Follow I must; I cannot go before,
While Gloucester bears this base and humble mind.
Were I a man, a duke, and next of blood,
I would remove these tedious stumbling-blocks
And smooth my way upon their headless necks;
And, being a woman, I will not be slack
To play my part in Fortune's pageant.
Where are you there? Sir John! nay, fear not, man,
We are alone; here's none but thee and I.

Enter HUME

HUME

Jesus preserve your royal majesty!

DUCHESS

What say'st thou? majesty! I am but grace.

HUME

But, by the grace of God, and Hume's advice,
Your grace's title shall be multiplied.

DUCHESS

What say'st thou, man? hast thou as yet conferr'd
With Margery Jourdain, the cunning witch,

With Roger Bolingbroke, the conjurer?
And will they undertake to do me good?

HUME

This they have promised, to show your highness
A spirit raised from depth of under-ground,
That shall make answer to such questions
As by your grace shall be propounded him.

DUCHESS

It is enough; I'll think upon the questions:
When from Saint Alban's we do make return,
We'll see these things effected to the full.
Here, Hume, take this reward; make merry, man,
With thy confederates in this weighty cause.   [Exit

HUME

Hume must make merry with the duchess' gold;
Marry, and shall. But, how now, Sir John Hume!
Seal up your lips, and give no words but mum:
The business asketh silent secrecy.
Dame Eleanor gives gold to bring the witch:
Gold cannot come amiss, were she a devil.
Yet have I gold flies from another coast;
I dare not say, from the rich cardinal,
And from the great and new-made Duke of Suffolk,
Yet I do find it so; for, to be plain,
They, knowing Dame Eleanor's aspiring humour,
Have hired me to undermine the duchess,
And buz these conjurations in her brain.
They say 'A crafty knave does need no broker;'
Yet am I Suffolk and the cardinal's broker.
Hume, if you take not heed, you shall go near
To call them both a pair of crafty knaves.
Well, so it stands; and thus, I fear, at last
Hume's knavery will be the duchess' wreck,
And her attainture will be Humphrey's fall:
Sort how it will, I shall have gold for all.   [Exit

SCENE III. *The palace*

Enter three or four PETITIONERS, PETER, *the*
ARMOURER'S *man, being one*

FIRST PETITIONER

My masters, let's stand close: my lord protector will
come this way by and by, and then we may deliver
our supplications in the quill.

SECOND PETITIONER

Marry, the Lord protect him, for he's a good man!
Jesu bless him!

Enter SUFFOLK *and* QUEEN

PETER

Here a' comes, methinks, and the queen with him.
I'll be the first, sure.

SECOND PETITIONER

Come back, fool; this is the Duke of Suffolk, and not
my lord protector.

SUFFOLK

How now, fellow! wouldst any thing with me?

FIRST PETITIONER

I pray, my lord, pardon me; I took ye for my lord
protector.

QUEEN

[*Reading*] 'To my Lord Protector!' Are your supplications to his lordship? Let me see them: what is
thine?

FIRST PETITIONER

Mine is, an 't please your grace, against John Goodman, my lord cardinal's man, for keeping my house,
and lands, and wife and all, from me.

SUFFOLK

Thy wife too! that's some wrong, indeed. What's
yours? What's here! [*Reads*] 'Against the Duke of
Suffolk, for enclosing the commons of Melford.'
How now, sir knave!

SECOND PETITIONER

Alas, sir, I am but a poor petitioner of our whole
township.

PETER

[*Giving his petition*] Against my master, Thomas
Horner, for saying that the Duke of York was rightful heir to the crown.

QUEEN

What say'st thou? did the Duke of York say he was
rightful heir to the crown?

PETER

That my master was? no, forsooth: my master said
that he was, and that the king was an usurper.

SUFFOLK

Who is there? [*Enter* SERVANT] Take this fellow in,
and send for his master with a pursuivant presently:
we'll hear more of your matter before the king.

[*Exit* SERVANT *with* PETER

QUEEN

And as for you, that love to be protected
Under the wings of our protector's grace,
Begin your suits anew, and sue to him.

[*Tears the supplications*

Away, base cullions! Suffolk, let them go.

ALL

Come, let's be gone.   [*Exeunt*

QUEEN

My Lord of Suffolk, say, is this the guise,
Is this the fashion in the court of England?
Is this the government of Britain's isle,
And this the royalty of Albion's king?
What, shall King Henry be a pupil still
Under the surly Gloucester's governance?
Am I a queen in title and in style,
And must be made a subject to a duke?
I tell thee, Pole, when in the city Tours
Thou ran'st a tilt in honour of my love,
And stolest away the ladies' hearts of France,
I thought King Henry had resembled thee
In courage, courtship and proportion:
But all his mind is bent to holiness,
To number Ave-Maries on his beads;
His champions are the prophets and apostles,
His weapons holy saws of sacred writ,
His study is his tilt-yard, and his loves
Are brazen images of canonized saints.
I would the college of the cardinals

Would choose him pope and carry him to Rome,
And set the triple crown upon his head:
That were a state fit for his holiness.

SUFFOLK

Madam, be patient: as I was cause
Your highness came to England, so will I
In England work your grace's full content.

QUEEN

Beside the haughty protector, have we Beaufort,
The imperious churchman, Somerset, Buckingham,
And grumbling York; and not the least of these
But can do more in England than the king.

SUFFOLK

And he of these that can do most of all
Cannot do more in England than the Nevils:
Salisbury and Warwick are no simple peers.

QUEEN

Not all these lords do vex me half so much
As that proud dame, the lord protector's wife.
She sweeps it through the court with troops of ladies,
More like an empress than Duke Humphrey's wife:
Strangers in court do take her for the queen:
She bears a duke's revenues on her back,
And in her heart she scorns our poverty:
Shall I not live to be avenged on her?
Contemptuous base-born callet as she is,
She vaunted 'mongst her minions t' other day,
The very train of her worst wearing gown
Was better worth than all my father's lands,
Till Suffolk gave two dukedoms for his daughter.

SUFFOLK

Madam, myself have limed a bush for her,
And placed a quire of such enticing birds,
That she will light to listen to the lays,
And never mount to trouble you again.
So, let her rest: and, madam, list to me;
For I am bold to counsel you in this.
Although we fancy not the cardinal,
Yet must we join with him and with the lords,
Till we have brought Duke Humphrey in disgrace.
As for the Duke of York, this late complaint
Will make but little for his benefit.
So, one by one, we'll weed them all at last,
And you yourself shall steer the happy helm.
Sound a Sennet. Enter the KING, DUKE HUMPHREY OF
GLOUCESTER, CARDINAL BEAUFORT, BUCKINGHAM,
YORK, SOMERSET, SALISBURY, WARWICK, *and the*
DUCHESS OF GLOUCESTER

KING

For my part, noble lords, I care not which;
Or Somerset or York, all's one to me.

YORK

If York have ill demean'd himself in France,
Then let him be denay'd the regentship.

SOMERSET

If Somerset be unworthy of the place,
Let York be regent; I will yield to him.

WARWICK

Whether your grace be worthy, yea or no,
Dispute not that: York is the worthier.

CARDINAL

Ambitious Warwick, let thy betters speak.

WARWICK

The cardinal's not my better in the field.

BUCKINGHAM

All in this presence are thy betters, Warwick.

WARWICK

Warwick may live to be the best of all.

SALISBURY

Peace, son! and show some reason, Buckingham,
Why Somerset should be preferr'd in this.

QUEEN

Because the king, forsooth, will have it so.

GLOUCESTER

Madam, the king is old enough himself
To give his censure: these are no women's matters.

QUEEN

If he be old enough, what needs your grace
To be protector of his excellence?

GLOUCESTER

Madam, I am protector of the realm;
And, at his pleasure, will resign my place.

SUFFOLK

Resign it then and leave thine insolence.
Since thou wert king—as who is king but thou?—
The commonwealth hath daily run to wreck;
The Dauphin hath prevail'd beyond the seas;
And all the peers and nobles of the realm
Have been as bondmen to thy sovereignty.

CARDINAL

The commons hast thou rack'd; the clergy's bags
Are lank and lean with thy extortions.

SOMERSET

Thy sumptuous buildings and thy wife's attire
Have cost a mass of public treasury.

BUCKINGHAM

Thy cruelty in execution
Upon offenders hath exceeded law,
And left thee to the mercy of the law.

QUEEN

Thy sale of offices and towns in France,
If they were known, as the suspect is great,
Would make thee quickly hop without thy head.
     [*Exit* GLOUCESTER. *The* QUEEN *drops her fan*
Give me my fan: what, minion! can ye not?
     [*She gives the* DUCHESS *a box on the ear*
I cry you mercy, madam; was it you?

DUCHESS

Was 't I! yea, I it was, proud Frenchwoman:
Could I come near your beauty with my nails,
I'ld set my ten commandments in your face.

KING

Sweet aunt, be quiet; 'twas against her will.

DUCHESS

Against her will! good king, look to 't in time;
She'll hamper thee, and dandle thee like a baby:
Though in this place most master wear no breeches,
She shall not strike Dame Eleanor unrevenged.
     [*Exit*

BUCKINGHAM

Lord cardinal, I will follow Eleanor,
And listen after Humphrey, how he proceeds:
She's tickled now; her fume needs no spurs,
She'll gallop far enough to her destruction.   [*Exit*

Re-enter GLOUCESTER

GLOUCESTER

Now, lords, my choler being over-blown
With walking once about the quadrangle,
I come to talk of commonwealth affairs.
As for your spiteful false objections,
Prove them, and I lie open to the law:
But God in mercy so deal with my soul,
As I in duty love my king and country!
But, to the matter that we have in hand:
I say, my sovereign, York is meetest man
To be your regent in the realm of France.

SUFFOLK

Before we make election, give me leave
To show some reason, of no little force,
That York is most unmeet of any man.

YORK

I'll tell thee, Suffolk, why I am unmeet:
First, for I cannot flatter thee in pride;
Next, if I be appointed for the place,
My Lord of Somerset will keep me here,
Without discharge, money, or furniture,
Till France be won into the Dauphin's hands:
Last time, I danced attendance on his will
Till Paris was besieged, famish'd, and lost.

WARWICK

That can I witness; and a fouler fact
Did never traitor in the land commit.

SUFFOLK

Peace, headstrong Warwick!

WARWICK

Image of pride, why should I hold my peace?
Enter HORNER, *the Armourer, and his man* PETER, *guarded*

SUFFOLK

Because here is a man accused of treason:
Pray God the Duke of York excuse himself!

YORK

Doth any one accuse York for a traitor?

KING

What mean'st thou, Suffolk? tell me, what are these?

SUFFOLK

Please it your majesty, this is the man
That doth accuse his master of high treason:
His words were these: that Richard Duke of York
Was rightful heir unto the English crown,
And that your majesty was an usurper.

KING

Say, man, were these thy words?

HORNER

An 't shall please your majesty, I never said nor
thought any such matter: God is my witness, I am
falsely accused by the villain.

PETER

By these ten bones, my lords, he did speak them to
me in the garret one night, as we were scouring my
Lord of York's armour.

YORK

Base dunghill villain and mechanical,
I'll have thy head for this thy traitor's speech.
I do beseech your royal majesty,
Let him have all the rigour of the law.

HORNER

Alas, my lord, hang me, if ever I spake the words.
My accuser is my 'prentice; and when I did correct
him for his fault the other day, he did vow upon his
knees he would be even with me: I have good witness of this; therefore I beseech your majesty, do not
cast away an honest man for a villain's accusation.

KING

Uncle, what shall we say to this in law?

GLOUCESTER

This doom, my lord, if I may judge:
Let Somerset be regent o'er the French,
Because in York this breeds suspicion:
And let these have a day appointed them
For single combat in convenient place,
For he hath witness of his servant's malice:
This is the law, and this Duke Humphrey's doom.

SOMERSET

I humbly thank your royal majesty.

HORNER

And I accept the combat willingly.

PETER

Alas, my lord, I cannot fight; for God's sake, pity
my case. The spite of man prevaileth against me. O
Lord, have mercy upon me! I shall never be able to
fight a blow. O Lord, my heart!

GLOUCESTER

Sirrah, or you must fight, or else be hang'd.

KING

Away with them to prison; and the day of combat
shall be the last of the next month. Come, Somerset, we'll see thee sent away.   [*Flourish. Exeunt*

SCENE IV. GLOUCESTER'S *garden*

Enter MARGARET JOURDAIN, HUME, SOUTHWELL, *and*
BOLINGBROKE

HUME

Come, my masters; the duchess, I tell you, expects
performance of your promises.

OLINGBROKE

Master Hume, we are therefore provided: will her
ladyship behold and hear our exorcisms?

HUME

Ay, what else? fear you not her courage.

BOLINGBROKE

I have heard her reported to be a woman of an invincible spirit: but it shall be convenient, Master
Hume, that you be by her aloft, while we be busy
below; and so, I pray you, go, in God's name, and
leave us. [*Exit* HUME] Mother Jourdain, be you

prostrate and grovel on the earth; John Southwell,
read you; and let us to our work.

Enter DUCHESS *aloft,* HUME *following*

DUCHESS

Well said, my masters; and welcome all. To this
gear the sooner the better.

BOLINGBROKE

Patience, good lady; wizards know their times:
Deep night, dark night, the silent of the night,
The time of night when Troy was set on fire;
The time when screech-owls cry, and ban-dogs
howl,
And spirits walk, and ghosts break up their graves,
That time best fits the work we have in hand.
Madam, sit you and fear not: whom we raise,
We will make fast within a hallow'd verge.

[*Here they do the ceremonies belonging, and make the circle;*
BOLINGBROKE *or* SOUTHWELL *reads,* Con-
juro te, &c. *It thunders and lightens
terribly; then the* SPIRIT *riseth*

SPIRIT

Adsum.

MARGARET JOURDAIN

Asmath,
By the eternal God, whose name and power
Thou tremblest at, answer that I shall ask;
For, till thou speak, thou shalt not pass from hence.

SPIRIT

Ask what thou wilt. That I had said and done!

BOLINGBROKE

'First of the king: what shall of him become?'

[*Reading out of a paper*

SPIRIT

The duke yet lives that Henry shall depose;
But him outlive, and die a violent death.

[*As the* SPIRIT *speaks,* SOUTHWELL *writes the answer*

BOLINGBROKE

'What fates await the Duke of Suffolk?'

SPIRIT

By water shall he die, and take his end.

BOLINGBROKE

'What shall befall the Duke of Somerset?'

SPIRIT

Let him shun castles;
Safer shall he be upon the sandy plains
Than where castles mounted stand.
Have done, for more I hardly can endure.

BOLINGBROKE

Descend to darkness and the burning lake!
False fiend, avoid! [*Thunder and lightning. Exit* SPIRIT
Enter the DUKE OF YORK *and the* DUKE OF BUCKINGHAM
with their GUARD *and break in*

YORK

Lay hands upon these traitors and their trash.
Beldam, I think we watch'd you at an inch.
What, madam, are you there? the king and com-
monweal
Are deeply indebted for this piece of pains:
My lord protector will, I doubt it not,
See you well guerdon'd for these good deserts.

DUCHESS

Not half so bad as thine to England's king,
Injurious duke, that threatest where's no cause.

BUCKINGHAM

True, madam, none at all: what call you this?
Away with them! let them be clapp'd up close,
And kept asunder. You, madam, shall with us.
Stafford, take her to thee.

[*Exeunt above* DUCHESS *and* HUME, *guarded*
We'll see your trinkets here all forthcoming.
All, away!

[*Exeunt* GUARD *with* JOURDAIN, SOUTHWELL, &c.

YORK

Lord Buckingham, methinks, you watch'd her well:
A pretty plot, well chosen to build upon!
Now, pray, my lord, let's see the devil's writ.
What have we here?   [*Reads*
'The duke yet lives, that Henry shall depose;
But him outlive, and die a violent death.'
Why, this is just
'Aio te, Æacida, Romanos vincere posse.'
Well, to the rest:
'Tell me, what fate awaits the Duke of Suffolk?
By water shall he die, and take his end.
What shall betide the Duke of Somerset?
Let him shun castles;
Safer shall he be upon the sandy plains
Than where castles mounted stand.'
Come, come my lords;
These oracles are hardly attain'd,
And hardly understood.
The king is now in progress towards Saint Alban's,
With him the husband of this lovely lady:
Thither go these news, as fast as horse can carry
them:
A sorry breakfast for my lord protector.

BUCKINGHAM

Your grace shall give me leave, my Lord of York,
To be the post, in hope of his reward.

YORK

At your pleasure, my good lord. Who's within there,
ho!

Enter a SERVING-MAN

Invite my Lords of Salisbury and Warwick
To sup with me to-morrow night. Away!   [*Exeunt*

ACT II

SCENE I. *Saint Alban's*

Enter the KING, QUEEN, GLOUCESTER, CARDINAL,
and SUFFOLK, *with* FALCONERS *halloing*

QUEEN

Believe me, lords, for flying at the brook,
I saw not better sport these seven years' day:
Yet, by your leave, the wind was very high;
And, ten to one, old Joan had not gone out.

KING

But what a point, my lord, your falcon made,
And what a pitch she flew above the rest!
To see how God in all His creatures works!
Yea, man and birds are fain of climbing high.

SUFFOLK

No marvel, an it like your majesty,
My lord protector's hawks do tower so well;
They know their master loves to be aloft,
And bears his thoughts above his falcon's pitch.

GLOUCESTER

My lord, 'tis but a base ignoble mind
That mounts no higher than a bird can soar.

CARDINAL

I thought as much; he would be above the clouds.

GLOUCESTER

Ay, my lord cardinal? how think you by that?
Were it not good your grace could fly to heaven?

KING

The treasury of everlasting joy.

CARDINAL

Thy heaven is on earth; thine eyes and thoughts
Beat on a crown, the treasure of thy heart;
Pernicious protector, dangerous peer,
That smooth'st it so with king and commonweal!

GLOUCESTER

What, cardinal, is your priesthood grown peremp-
tory?
Tantæne animis cœlestibus iræ?
Churchmen so hot? good uncle, hide such malice;
With such holiness can you do it?

SUFFOLK

No malice, sir; no more than well becomes
So good a quarrel and so bad a peer.

GLOUCESTER

As who, my lord?

SUFFOLK

Why, as you, my lord,
An 't like your lordly lord-protectorship.

GLOUCESTER

Why, Suffolk, England knows thine insolence.

QUEEN

And thy ambition, Gloucester.

KING

I prithee, peace, good queen,
And whet not on these furious peers;
For blessed are the peacemakers on earth.

CARDINAL

Let me be blessed for the peace I make,
Against this proud protector, with my sword!

GLOUCESTER

[*Aside to* CARDINAL] Faith, holy uncle, would 'twere
come to that!

CARDINAL

[*Aside to* GLOUCESTER] Marry, when thou darest.

GLOUCESTER

[*Aside to* CARDINAL] Make up no factious numbers for
the matter;
In thine own person answer thy abuse.

CARDINAL

[*Aside to* GLOUCESTER] Ay, where thou darest not
peep: an if thou darest,
This evening, on the east side of the grove.

KING

How now, my lords!

CARDINAL

Believe me, cousin Gloucester,
Had not your man put up the fowl so suddenly,
We had had more sport. [*Aside to* GLOUCESTER]
Come with thy two-hand sword.

GLOUCESTER

True, uncle.

CARDINAL

[*Aside to* GLOUCESTER] Are ye advised? the east side
of the grove?

GLOUCESTER

[*Aside to* CARDINAL] Cardinal, I am with you.

KING

Why, how now, uncle Gloucester!

GLOUCESTER

Talking of hawking; nothing else, my lord.
[*Aside to* CARDINAL] Now, by God's mother, priest,
I'll shave your crown for this,
Or all my fence shall fail.

CARDINAL

[*Aside to* GLOUCESTER] Medice, teipsum—
Protector, see to 't well, protect yourself.

KING

The winds grow high; so do your stomachs, lords.
How irksome is this music to my heart!
When such strings jar, what hope of harmony?
I pray, my lords, let me compound this strife.
Enter a TOWNSMAN *of Saint Alban's, crying* 'A miracle!'

GLOUCESTER

What means this noise?
Fellow, what miracle dost thou proclaim?

TOWNSMAN

A miracle! a miracle!

SUFFOLK

Come to the king and tell him what miracle.

TOWNSMAN

Forsooth, a blind man at Saint Alban's shrine,
Within this half-hour, hath received his sight;
A man that ne'er saw in his life before.

KING

Now, God be praised, that to believing souls
Gives light in darkness, comfort in despair!
Enter the MAYOR *of Saint Alban's and his brethren,
bearing* SIMPCOX, *between two in a chair,* SIMPCOX'S
WIFE *following*

CARDINAL

Here comes the townsmen on procession,
To present your highness with the man.

KING

Great is his comfort in this earthly vale,
Although by his sight his sin be multiplied.

GLOUCESTER

Stand by, my masters: bring him near the king;
His highness' pleasure is to talk with him.

KING

Good fellow, tell us here the circumstance,
That we for thee may glorify the Lord.
What, hast thou been long blind and now restored?

SIMPCOX

Born blind, an 't please your grace.

WIFE

Ay, indeed, was he.

SUFFOLK

What woman is this?

WIFE

His wife, an 't like your worship.

GLOUCESTER

Hadst thou been his mother, thou couldst have better told.

KING

Where wert thou born?

SIMPCOX

At Berwick in the north, an 't like your grace.

KING

Poor soul, God's goodness hath been great to thee:
Let never day nor night unhallow'd pass,
But still remember what the Lord hath done.

QUEEN

Tell me, good fellow, camest thou here by chance,
Or of devotion, to this holy shrine?

SIMPCOX

God knows, of pure devotion; being call'd
A hundred times and oftener, in my sleep,
By good Saint Alban; who said, 'Simpcox, come,
Come, offer at my shrine, and I will help thee.'

WIFE

Most true, forsooth; and many time and oft
Myself have heard a voice to call him so.

CARDINAL

What, art thou lame?

SIMPCOX

Ay, God Almighty help me!

SUFFOLK

How camest thou so?

SIMPCOX

A fall off of a tree.

WIFE

A plum-tree, master.

GLOUCESTER

How long hast thou been blind?

SIMPCOX

O, born so, master.

GLOUCESTER

What, and wouldst climb a tree?

SIMPCOX

But that in all my life, when I was a youth.

WIFE

Too true; and bought his climbing very dear.

GLOUCESTER

Mass, thou lovedst plums well, that wouldst venture
so.

SIMPCOX

Alas, good master, my wife desired some damsons,
And made me climb, with danger of my life.

GLOUCESTER

A subtle knave! but yet it shall not serve.
Let me see thine eyes: wink now: now open them:
In my opinion yet thou see'st not well.

SIMPCOX

Yes, master, clear as day, I thank God and Saint
Alban.

GLOUCESTER

Say'st thou me so? What colour is this cloak of?

SIMPCOX

Red, master; red as blood.

GLOUCESTER

Why, that's well said. What colour is my gown of?

SIMPCOX

Black, forsooth: coal-black as jet.

KING

Why, then, thou know'st what colour jet is of?

SUFFOLK

And yet, I think, jet did he never see.

GLOUCESTER

But cloaks and gowns, before this day, a many.

WIFE

Never, before this day, in all his life.

GLOUCESTER

Tell me, sirrah, what's my name?

SIMPCOX

Alas, master, I know not.

GLOUCESTER

What's his name?

SIMPCOX

I know not.

GLOUCESTER

Nor his?

SIMPCOX

No, indeed, master.

GLOUCESTER

What's thine own name?

SIMPCOX

Saunder Simpcox, an if it please you, master.

GLOUCESTER

Then, Saunder, sit there, the lyingest knave in
Christendom. If thou hadst been born blind, thou
mightst as well have known all our names as thus
to name the several colours we do wear. Sight may
distinguish of colours, but suddenly to nominate
them all, it is impossible. My lords, Saint Alban
here hath done a miracle; and would ye not think
his cunning to be great, that could restore this cripple to his legs again?

SIMPCOX

O master, that you could!

GLOUCESTER

My masters of Saint Alban's, have you not beadles
in your town, and things called whips?

MAYOR

Yes, my lord, if it please your grace.

GLOUCESTER

Then send for one presently.

MAYOR

Sirrah, go fetch the beadle hither straight.

[*Exit an* ATTENDANT

GLOUCESTER

Now fetch me a stool hither by and by. Now, sirrah,
if you mean to save yourself from whipping, leap
me over this stool and run away.

SIMPCOX

Alas, master, I am not able to stand alone:
You go about to torture me in vain.

Enter a BEADLE *with whips*

GLOUCESTER

Well, sir, we must have you find your legs.
Sirrah beadle, whip him till he leap over that same
  stool.

BEADLE

I will, my lord. Come on, sirrah; off with your
doublet quickly.

SIMPCOX

Alas, master, what shall I do? I am not able to stand.
[*After the* BEADLE *hath hit him once, he leaps over the stool
and runs away; and they follow and cry, 'A miracle!'*

KING

O God, seest Thou this, and bearest so long?

QUEEN

It made me laugh to see the villain run.

GLOUCESTER

Follow the knave; and take this drab away.

WIFE

Alas, sir, we did it for pure need.

GLOUCESTER

Let them be whipped through every market-town,
till they come to Berwick, from whence they came.
[*Exeunt* WIFE, BEADLE, MAYOR, &c.

CARDINAL

Duke Humphrey has done a miracle to-day.

SUFFOLK

True; made the lame to leap and fly away.

GLOUCESTER

But you have done more miracles than I;
You made in a day, my lord, whole towns to fly.

Enter BUCKINGHAM

KING

What tidings with our cousin Buckingham?

BUCKINGHAM

Such as my heart doth tremble to unfold.
A sort of naughty persons, lewdly bent,
Under the countenance and confederacy
Of Lady Eleanor, the protector's wife,
The ringleader and head of all this rout,
Have practised dangerously against your state,
Dealing with witches and with conjurers:
Whom we have apprehended in the fact;
Raising up wicked spirits from under ground,
Demanding of King Henry's life and death,
And other of your highness' privy-council;
As more at large your grace shall understand.

CARDINAL

[*Aside to* GLOUCESTER] And so, my lord protector, by
  this means

Your lady is forthcoming yet at London.
This news, I think, hath turn'd your weapon's edge;
'Tis like, my lord, you will not keep your hour.

GLOUCESTER

Ambitious churchman, leave to afflict my heart:
Sorrow and grief have vanquish'd all my powers;
And, vanquish'd as I am, I yield to thee,
Or to the meanest groom.

KING

O God, what mischiefs work the wicked ones,
Heaping confusion on their own heads thereby!

QUEEN

Gloucester, see here the tainture of thy nest,
And look thyself be faultless, thou wert best.

GLOUCESTER

Madam, for myself, to heaven I do appeal,
How I have loved my king and commonweal:
And, for my wife, I know not how it stands;
Sorry I am to hear what I have heard:
Noble she is, but if she have forgot
Honour and virtue and conversed with such
As, like to pitch, defile nobility,
I banish her my bed and company,
And give her as a prey to law and shame,
That hath dishonour'd Gloucester's honest name.

KING

Well, for this night we will repose us here:
To-morrow toward London back again,
To look into this business thoroughly,
And call these foul offenders to their answers,
And poise the cause in justice' equal scales,
Whose beam stands sure, whose rightful cause pre-
  vails.
[*Flourish. Exeunt*

SCENE II. *London. The* DUKE OF YORK'S *garden*

Enter YORK, SALISBURY, *and* WARWICK

YORK

Now, my good Lords of Salisbury and Warwick,
Our simple supper ended, give me leave
In this close walk to satisfy myself,
In craving your opinion of my title,
Which is infallible, to England's crown.

SALISBURY

My lord, I long to hear it at full.

WARWICK

Sweet York, begin: and if thy claim be good,
The Nevils are thy subjects to command.

YORK

Then thus:
Edward the Third, my lords, had seven sons:
The first, Edward the Black Prince, Prince of Wales;
The second, William of Hatfield, and the third,
Lionel Duke of Clarence; next to whom
Was John of Gaunt, the Duke of Lancaster;
The fifth was Edmund Langley, Duke of York;
The sixth was Thomas of Woodstock, Duke of Glou-
  cester;
William of Windsor was the seventh and last.

[47]

Edward the Black Prince died before his father,
And left behind him Richard, his only son,
Who after Edward the Third's death reign'd as
    king;
Till Henry Bolingbroke, Duke of Lancaster,
The eldest son and heir of John of Gaunt,
Crown'd by the name of Henry the Fourth,
Seized on the realm, deposed the rightful king,
Sent his poor queen to France, from when she came,
And him to Pomfret; where, as all you know,
Harmless Richard was murder'd traitorously.

WARWICK

Father, the duke hath told the truth;
Thus got the house of Lancaster the crown.

YORK

Which now they hold by force and not by right;
For Richard, the first son's heir, being dead,
The issue of the next son should have reign'd.

SALISBURY

But William of Hatfield died without an heir.

YORK

The third son, Duke of Clarence, from whose line
I claim the crown, had issue, Philippe, a daughter,
Who married Edmund Mortimer, Earl of March:
Edmund had issue, Roger Earl of March;
Roger had issue, Edmund, Anne and Eleanor.

SALISBURY

This Edmund, in the reign of Bolingbroke,
As I have read, laid claim unto the crown;
And, but for Owen Glendower, had been king,
Who kept him in captivity till he died.
But to the rest.

YORK

His eldest sister, Anne,
My mother, being heir unto the crown,
Married Richard Earl of Cambridge; who was son
To Edmund Langley, Edward the Third's fifth son.
By her I claim the kingdom: she was heir
To Roger Earl of March, who was the son
Of Edmund Mortimer, who married Philippe,
Sole daughter unto Lionel Duke of Clarence:
So, if the issue of the elder son
Succeed before the younger, I am king.

WARWICK

What plain proceeding is more plain than this?
Henry doth claim the crown from John of Gaunt,
The fourth son; York claims it from the third.
Till Lionel's issue fails, his should not reign:
It fails not yet, but flourishes in thee
And in thy sons, fair slips of such a stock.
Then, father Salisbury, kneel we together;
And in this private plot be we the first
That shall salute our rightful sovereign
With honour of his birthright to the crown.

BOTH

Long live our sovereign Richard, England's king!

YORK

We thank you, lords. But I am not your king
Till I be crown'd, and that my sword be stain'd
With heart-blood of the house of Lancaster;

And that's not suddenly to be perform'd,
But with advice and silent secrecy.
Do you as I do in these dangerous days:
Wink at the Duke of Suffolk's insolence,
At Beaufort's pride, at Somerset's ambition,
At Buckingham and all the crew of them,
Till they have snared the shepherd of the flock,
That virtuous prince, the good Duke Humphrey:
'Tis that they seek, and they in seeking that
Shall find their deaths, if York can prophesy.

SALISBURY

My lord, break we off; we know your mind at full.

WARWICK

My heart assures me that the Earl of Warwick
Shall one day make the Duke of York a king.

YORK

And, Nevil, this I do assure myself:
Richard shall live to make the Earl of Warwick
The greatest man in England but the king. [Exeunt

SCENE III. *A hall of justice*

Sound trumpets. Enter the KING, *the* QUEEN, GLOUCESTER,
    YORK, SUFFOLK, *and* SALISBURY; *the* DUCHESS OF
    GLOUCESTER, MARGARET JOURDAIN, SOUTHWELL,
    HUME, *and* BOLINGBROKE, *under guard*

KING

Stand forth, Dame Eleanor Cobham, Gloucester's
    wife:
In sight of God and us, your guilt is great:
Receive the sentence of the law for sins
Such as by God's book are adjudged to death.
You four, from hence to prison back again;
From thence unto the place of execution:
The witch in Smithfield shall be burn'd to ashes,
And you three shall be strangled on the gallows.
You, madam, for you are more nobly born,
Despoiled of your honour in your life,
Shall, after three days' open penance done,
Live in your country here in banishment,
With Sir John Stanley, in the Isle of Man.

DUCHESS

Welcome is banishment; welcome were my death.

GLOUCESTER

Eleanor, the law, thou see'st, hath judged thee:
I cannot justify whom the law condemns.
    [*Exeunt* DUCHESS *and other prisoners, guarded*
Mine eyes are full of tears, my heart of grief.
Ah, Humphrey, this dishonour in thine age
Will bring thy head with sorrow to the ground!
I beseech your majesty, give me leave to go;
Sorrow would solace and mine age would ease.

KING

Stay, Humphrey Duke of Gloucester: ere thou go,
Give up thy staff: Henry will to himself
Protector be; and God shall be my hope,
My stay, my guide and lantern to my feet:
And go in peace, Humphrey, no less beloved
Than when thou wert protector to thy king.

QUEEN

I see no reason why a king of years
Should be to be protected like a child.
God and King Henry govern England's realm.
Give up your staff, sir, and the king his realm.

GLOUCESTER

My staff? here, noble Henry, is my staff:
As willingly do I the same resign
As e'er thy father Henry made it mine;
And even as willingly at thy feet I leave it
As others would ambitiously receive it.
Farewell, good king: when I am dead and gone,
May honourable peace attend thy throne! 　　[Exit

QUEEN

Why, now is Henry king, and Margaret queen;
And Humphrey Duke of Gloucester scarce himself,
That bears so shrewd a maim; two pulls at once;
His lady banish'd, and a limb lopp'd off.
This staff of honour raught, there let it stand
Where it best fits to be, in Henry's hand.

SUFFOLK

Thus droops this lofty pine and hangs his sprays;
Thus Eleanor's pride dies in her youngest days.

YORK

Lords, let him go. Please it your majesty,
This is the day appointed for the combat;
And ready are the appellant and defendant,
The armourer and his man, to enter the lists,
So please your highness to behold the fight.

QUEEN

Ay, good my lord; for purposely therefore
Left I the court, to see this quarrel tried.

KING

O' God's name, see the lists and all things fit:
Here let them end it; and God defend the right!

YORK

I never saw a fellow worse bested,
Or more afraid to fight, than is the appellant,
The servant of this armourer, my lords.

Enter at one door, HORNER, the Armourer, and his NEIGH-BOURS, drinking to him so much that he is drunk; and he enters with a drum before him and his staff with a sand-bag fastened to it; and at the other door PETER, his man, with a drum and sand-bag, and 'PRENTICES drinking to him

FIRST NEIGHBOUR

Here, neighbour Horner, I drink to you in a cup of sack: and fear not, neighbour, you shall do well enough.

SECOND NEIGHBOUR

And here, neighbour, here's a cup of charneco.

THIRD NEIGHBOUR

And here's a pot of good double beer, neighbour: drink, and fear not your man.

HORNER

Let it come, i' faith, and I'll pledge you all; and a fig for Peter!

FIRST 'PRENTICE

Here, Peter, I drink to thee: and be not afraid.

SECOND 'PRENTICE

Be merry, Peter, and fear not thy master: fight for credit of the 'prentices.

PETER

I thank you all: drink, and pray for me, I pray you; for I think I have taken my last draught in this world. Here, Robin, an if I die, I give thee my apron: and, Will, thou shalt have my hammer: and here, Tom, take all the money that I have. O Lord bless me! I pray God! for I am never able to deal with my master, he hath learnt so much fence already.

SALISBURY

Come, leave your drinking, and fall to blows. Sirrah, what's thy name?

PETER

Peter, forsooth.

SALISBURY

Peter! what more?

PETER

Thump.

SALISBURY

Thump! then see thou thump thy master well.

HORNER

Masters, I am come hither, as it were upon my man's instigation, to prove him a knave and myself an honest man: and touching the Duke of York, I will take my death, I never meant him any ill, nor the king, nor the queen: and therefore, Peter, have at thee with a downright blow!

YORK

Dispatch: this knave's tongue begins to double.
Sound, trumpets, alarum to the combatants!
　　[*Alarum. They fight, and* PETER *strikes him down*

HORNER

Hold, Peter, hold! I confess, I confess treason. [*Dies*

YORK

Take away his weapon. Fellow, thank God, and the good wine in thy master's way.

PETER

O God, have I overcome mine enemy in this presence? O Peter, thou hast prevailed in right!

KING

Go, take hence that traitor from our sight;
For by his death we do perceive his guilt:
And God in justice hath reveal'd to us
The truth and innocence of this poor fellow,
Which he had thought to have murder'd wrongfully.
Come, fellow, follow us for thy reward.
　　[*Sound a flourish. Exeunt*

SCENE IV. *A street*

Enter GLOUCESTER and his SERVING-MEN, in mourning cloaks

GLOUCESTER

Thus sometimes hath the brightest day a cloud;
And after summer evermore succeeds
Barren winter, with his wrathful nipping cold:

So cares and joys abound, as seasons fleet.
Sirs, what's o'clock?

SERVING-MEN
Ten, my lord.

GLOUCESTER
Ten is the hour that was appointed me
To watch the coming of my punish'd duchess:
Uneath may she endure the flinty streets,
To tread them with her tender-feeling feet.
Sweet Nell, ill can thy noble mind abrook
The abject people gazing on thy face,
With envious looks laughing at thy shame,
That erst did follow thy proud chariot-wheels,
When thou didst ride in triumph through the streets.
But, soft! I think she comes; and I'll prepare
My tear-stain'd eyes to see her miseries.

Enter the DUCHESS OF GLOUCESTER *in a white sheet, and
a taper burning in her hand; with* SIR JOHN STANLEY, *the*
SHERIFF, *and* OFFICERS

SERVING-MEN
So please your grace, we'll take her from the sheriff.

GLOUCESTER
No, stir not, for your lives; let her pass by.

DUCHESS
Come you, my lord, to see my open shame?
Now thou dost penance too. Look how they gaze!
See how the giddy multitude do point,
And nod their heads, and throw their eyes on thee!
Ah, Gloucester, hide thee from their hateful looks,
And, in thy closet pent up, rue my shame,
And ban thine enemies, both mine and thine!

GLOUCESTER
Be patient, gentle Nell; forget this grief.

DUCHESS
Ah, Gloucester, teach me to forget myself!
For whilst I think I am thy married wife,
And thou a prince, protector of this land,
Methinks I should not thus be led along,
Mail'd up in shame, with papers on my back,
And follow'd with a rabble that rejoice
To see my tears and hear my deep-fet groans.
The ruthless flint doth cut my tender feet,
And when I start, the envious people laugh,
And bid me be advised how I tread.
Ah, Humphrey, can I bear this shameful yoke?
Trow'st thou that e'er I'll look upon the world,
Or count them happy that enjoy the sun?
No; dark shall be my light and night my day;
To think upon my pomp shall be my hell.
Sometime I'll say, I am Duke Humphrey's wife,
And he a prince and ruler of the land:
Yet so he ruled, and such a prince he was,
As he stood by whilst I, his forlorn duchess,
Was made a wonder and a pointing-stock
To every idle rascal follower.
But be thou mild and blush not at my shame,
Nor stir at nothing till the axe of death
Hang over thee, as, sure, it shortly will;
For Suffolk—he that can do all in all
With her that hateth thee and hates us all—

And York and impious Beaufort, that false priest,
Have all limed bushes to betray thy wings,
And, fly thou how thou canst, they'll tangle thee:
But fear not thou, until thy foot be snared,
Nor never seek prevention of thy foes.

GLOUCESTER
Ah, Nell, forbear! thou aimest all awry;
I must offend before I be attainted;
And had I twenty times so many foes,
And each of them had twenty times their power,
All these could not procure me any scathe,
So long as I am loyal, true and crimeless.
Wouldst have me rescue thee from this reproach?
Why, yet thy scandal were not wiped away,
But I in danger for the breach of law.
Thy greatest help is quiet, gentle Nell:
I pray thee, sort thy heart to patience;
These few days' wonder will be quickly worn.

Enter a HERALD

HERALD
I summon your grace to his majesty's parliament,
Holden at Bury the first of this next month.

GLOUCESTER
And my consent ne'er ask'd herein before!
This is close dealing. Well, I will be there.

[*Exit* HERALD

My Nell, I take my leave: and, master sheriff,
Let not her penance exceed the king's commission.

SHERIFF
An 't please your grace, here my commission stays,
And Sir John Stanley is appointed now
To take her with him to the Isle of Man.

GLOUCESTER
Must you, Sir John, protect my lady here?

STANLEY
So am I given in charge, may 't please your grace.

GLOUCESTER
Entreat her not the worse in that I pray
You use her well: the world may laugh again;
And I may live to do you kindness if
You do it her: and so, Sir John, farewell!

DUCHESS
What, gone, my lord, and bid me not farewell!

GLOUCESTER
Witness my tears, I cannot stay to speak.

[*Exeunt* GLOUCESTER *and* SERVING-MEN

DUCHESS
Art thou gone too? all comfort go with thee!
For none abides with me: my joy is death,—
Death, at whose name I oft have been afear'd,
Because I wish'd this world's eternity.
Stanley, I prithee, go, and take me hence;
I care not whither, for I beg no favour,
Only convey me where thou art commanded.

STANLEY
Why, madam, that is to the Isle of Man;
There to be used according to your state.

DUCHESS
That's bad enough, for I am but reproach:
And shall I then be used reproachfully?

STANLEY
Like to a duchess, and Duke Humphrey's lady;
According to that state you shall be used.
DUCHESS
Sheriff, farewell, and better than I fare,
Although thou hast been conduct of my shame.
SHERIFF
It is my office; and, madam, pardon me.
DUCHESS
Ay, ay, farewell; thy office is discharged.
Come, Stanley, shall we go?
STANLEY
Madam, your penance done, throw off this sheet,
And go we to attire you for our journey.
DUCHESS
My shame will not be shifted with my sheet:
No, it will hang upon my richest robes,
And show itself, attire me how I can.
Go, lead the way; I long to see my prison.   [Exeunt

ACT III
SCENE I. *The Abbey at Bury St. Edmund's*

Sound a Sennet. Enter KING, QUEEN, CARDINAL BEAU-
FORT, SUFFOLK, YORK, BUCKINGHAM, SALISBURY *and*
WARWICK *to the Parliament*
KING
I muse my Lord of Gloucester is not come:
'Tis not his wont to be the hindmost man,
Whate'er occasion keeps him from us now.
QUEEN
Can you not see? or will ye not observe
The strangeness of his alter'd countenance?
With what a majesty he bears himself,
How insolent of late he is become,
How proud, how peremptory, and unlike himself?
We know the time since he was mild and affable,
And if we did but glance a far-off look,
Immediately he was upon his knee,
That all the court admired him for submission:
But meet him now, and, be it in the morn,
When every one will give the time of day,
He knits his brow and shows an angry eye,
And passeth by with stiff unbowed knee,
Disdaining duty that to us belongs.
Small curs are not regarded when they grin;
But great men tremble when the lion roars;
And Humphrey is no little man in England.
First note that he is near you in descent,
And should you fall, he is the next will mount.
Me seemeth then it is no policy,
Respecting what a rancorous mind he bears,
And his advantage following your decease,
That he should come about your royal person,
Or be admitted to your highness' council.
By flattery hath he won the commons' hearts,
And when he please to make commotion,

'Tis to be fear'd they all will follow him.
Now 'tis the spring, and weeds are shallow-rooted;
Suffer them now, and they'll o'ergrow the garden,
And choke the herbs for want of husbandry.
The reverent care I bear unto my lord
Made me collect these dangers in the duke.
If it be fond, call it a woman's fear;
Which fear if better reasons can supplant,
I will subscribe and say I wrong'd the duke.
My Lord of Suffolk, Buckingham, and York,
Reprove my allegation, if you can;
Or else conclude my words effectual.
SUFFOLK
Well hath your highness seen into this duke;
And, had I first been put to speak my mind,
I think I should have told your grace's tale.
The duchess by his subornation,
Upon my life, began her devilish practices:
Or, if he were not privy to those faults,
Yet, by reputing of his high descent,
As next the king he was successive heir,
And such high vaunts of his nobility,
Did instigate the bedlam brain-sick duchess
By wicked means to frame our sovereign's fall.
Smooth runs the water where the brook is deep;
And in his simple show he harbours treason.
The fox barks not when he would steal the lamb.
No, no, my sovereign; Gloucester is a man
Unsounded yet and full of deep deceit.
CARDINAL
Did he not, contrary to form of law,
Devise strange deaths for small offences done?
YORK
And did he not, in his protectorship,
Levy great sums of money through the realm
For soldiers' pay in France, and never sent it?
By means whereof the towns each day revolted.
BUCKINGHAM
Tut, these are petty faults to faults unknown,
Which time will bring to light in smooth Duke
    Humphrey.
KING
My lords, at once: the care you have of us,
To mow down thorns that would annoy our foot,
Is worthy praise: but, shall I speak my conscience,
Our kinsman Gloucester is as innocent
From meaning treason to our royal person,
As is the sucking lamb or harmless dove:
The duke is virtuous, mild and too well given
To dream on evil or to work my downfall.
QUEEN
Ah, what's more dangerous than this fond affiance!
Seems he a dove? his feathers are but borrow'd,
For he's disposed as the hateful raven:
Is he a lamb? his skin is surely lent him,
For he's inclined as is the ravenous wolf.
Who cannot steal a shape that means deceit?
Take heed, my lord; the welfare of us all
Hangs on the cutting short that fraudful man.
Enter SOMERSET

[51]

SOMERSET
All health unto my gracious sovereign!
KING
Welcome, Lord Somerset. What news from France?
SOMERSET
That all your interest in those territories
Is utterly bereft you; all is lost.
KING
Cold news, Lord Somerset: but God's will be done!
YORK
[Aside] Cold news for me; for I had hope of France
As firmly as I hope for fertile England.
Thus are my blossoms blasted in the bud,
And caterpillars eat my leaves away;
But I will remedy this gear ere long,
Or sell my title for a glorious grave.
Enter GLOUCESTER
GLOUCESTER
All happiness unto my lord the king!
Pardon, my liege, that I have stay'd so long.
SUFFOLK
Nay, Gloucester, know that thou art come too soon,
Unless thou wert more loyal than thou art:
I do arrest thee of high treason here.
GLOUCESTER
Well, Suffolk, thou shalt not see me blush,
Nor change my countenance for this arrest:
A heart unspotted is not easily daunted.
The purest spring is not so free from mud
As I am clear from treason to my sovereign:
Who can accuse me? wherein am I guilty?
YORK
'Tis thought, my lord, that you took bribes of
     France,
And, being protector, stay'd the soldiers' pay;
By means whereof his highness hath lost France.
GLOUCESTER
Is it but thought so? what are they that think it?
I never robb'd the soldiers of their pay,
Nor ever had one penny bribe from France.
So help me God, as I have watch'd the night,
Ay, night by night, in studying good for England!
That doit that e'er I wrested from the king,
Or any groat I hoarded to my use,
Be brought against me at my trial-day!
No; many a pound of mine own proper store,
Because I would not tax the needy commons,
Have I dispursed to the garrisons,
And never ask'd for restitution.
CARDINAL
It serves you well, my lord, to say so much.
GLOUCESTER
I say no more than truth, so help me God!
YORK
In your protectorship you did devise
Strange tortures for offenders never heard of,
That England was defamed by tyranny.
GLOUCESTER
Why, 'tis well known that, whiles I was protector,

Pity was all the fault that was in me;
For I should melt at an offender's tears,
And lowly words were ransom for their fault.
Unless it were a bloody murderer,
Or foul felonious thief that fleeced poor passengers,
I never gave them condign punishment:
Murder indeed, that bloody sin, I tortured
Above the felon or what trespass else.
SUFFOLK
My lord, these faults are easy, quickly answer'd:
But mightier crimes are laid unto your charge,
Whereof you cannot easily purge yourself.
I do arrest you in his highness' name;
And here commit you to my lord cardinal
To keep, until your further time of trial.
KING
My Lord of Gloucester, 'tis my special hope
That you will clear yourself from all suspect:
My conscience tells me you are innocent.
GLOUCESTER
Ah, gracious lord, these days are dangerous:
Virtue is choked with foul ambition,
And charity chased hence by rancour's hand;
Foul subornation is predominant,
And equity exiled your highness' land.
I know their complot is to have my life,
And if my death might make this island happy,
And prove the period of their tyranny,
I would expend it with all willingness:
But mine is made the prologue to their play;
For thousands more, that yet suspect no peril,
Will not conclude their plotted tragedy.
Beaufort's red sparkling eyes blab his heart's malice,
And Suffolk's cloudy brow his stormy hate;
Sharp Buckingham unburthens with his tongue
The envious load that lies upon his heart;
And dogged York, that reaches at the moon,
Whose overweening arm I have pluck'd back,
By false accuse doth level at my life:
And you, my sovereign lady, with the rest,
Causeless have laid disgraces on my head,
And with your best endeavour have stirr'd up
My liefest liege to be mine enemy:
Ay, all of you have laid your heads together—
Myself had notice of your conventicles—
And all to make away my guiltless life.
I shall not want false witness to condemn me,
Nor store of treasons to augment my guilt;
The ancient proverb will be well effected:
'A staff is quickly found to beat a dog.'
CARDINAL
My liege, his railing is intolerable:
If those that care to keep your royal person
From treason's secret knife and traitors' rage
Be thus upbraided, chid and rated at,
And the offender granted scope of speech,
'Twill make them cool in zeal unto your grace.
SUFFOLK
Hath he not twit our sovereign lady here
With ignominious words, though clerkly couch'd,

As if she had suborned some to swear
False allegations to o'erthrow his state?

QUEEN

But I can give the loser leave to chide.

GLOUCESTER

Far truer spoke than meant: I lose, indeed;
Beshrew the winners, for they play'd me false!
And well such losers may have leave to speak.

BUCKINGHAM

He'll wrest the sense and hold us here all day:
Lord cardinal, he is your prisoner.

CARDINAL

Sirs, take away the duke, and guard him sure.

GLOUCESTER

Ah! thus King Henry throws away his crutch,
Before his legs be firm to bear his body.
Thus is the shepherd beaten from thy side,
And wolves are gnarling who shall gnaw thee first.
Ah, that my fear were false! ah, that it were!
For, good King Henry, thy decay I fear.

[Exit, guarded

KING

My lords, what to your wisdoms seemeth best,
Do or undo, as if ourself were here.

QUEEN

What, will your highness leave the parliament?

KING

Ay, Margaret; my heart is drown'd with grief,
Whose flood begins to flow within mine eyes,
My body round engirt with misery,
For what's more miserable than discontent?
Ah, uncle Humphrey! in thy face I see
The map of honour, truth and loyalty:
And yet, good Humphrey, is the hour to come
That e'er I proved thee false or fear'd thy faith.
What louring star now envies thy estate,
That these great lords and Margaret our queen
Do seek subversion of thy harmless life?
Thou never didst them wrong nor no man wrong;
And as the butcher takes away the calf,
And binds the wretch, and beats it when it strays,
Bearing it to the bloody slaughter-house,
Even so remorseless have they borne him hence;
And as the dam runs lowing up and down,
Looking the way her harmless young one went,
And can do nought but wail her darling's loss,
Even so myself bewails good Gloucester's case
With sad unhelpful tears, and with dimm'd eyes
Look after him and cannot do him good,
So mighty are his vowed enemies.
His fortunes I will weep, and 'twixt each groan
Say 'Who's a traitor? Gloucester he is none.'

[Exeunt all but QUEEN, CARDINAL BEAUFORT, SUFFOLK,
and YORK. SOMERSET remains apart

QUEEN

Free lords, cold snow melts with the sun's hot beams.
Henry my lord is cold in great affairs,
Too full of foolish pity, and Gloucester's show
Beguiles him, as the mournful crocodile
With sorrow snares relenting passengers,

Or as the snake roll'd in a flowering bank,
With shining checker'd slough, doth sting a child
That for the beauty thinks it excellent.
Believe me, lords, were none more wise than I—
And yet herein I judge mine own wit good—
This Gloucester should be quickly rid the world,
To rid us from the fear we have of him.

CARDINAL

That he should die is worthy policy;
But yet we want a colour for his death:
'Tis meet he be condemn'd by course of law.

SUFFOLK

But, in my mind, that were no policy:
The king will labour still to save his life,
The commons haply rise, to save his life;
And yet we have but trivial argument,
More than mistrust, that shows him worthy death.

YORK

So that, by this, you would not have him die.

SUFFOLK

Ah, York, no man alive so fain as I!

YORK

'Tis York that hath more reason for his death.
But, my lord cardinal, and you, my Lord of Suffolk,
Say as you think, and speak it from your souls:
Were 't not all one, an empty eagle were set
To guard the chicken from a hungry kite,
As place Duke Humphrey for the king's protector?

QUEEN

So the poor chicken should be sure of death.

SUFFOLK

Madam, 'tis true; and were 't not madness, then,
To make the fox surveyor of the fold?
Who being accused a crafty murderer,
His guilt should be but idly posted over,
Because his purpose is not executed.
No; let him die, in that he is a fox,
By nature proved an enemy to the flock,
Before his chaps be stain'd with crimson blood,
As Humphrey, proved by reasons, to my liege.
And do not stand on quillets how to slay him:
Be it by gins, by snares, by subtlety,
Sleeping or waking, 'tis no matter how,
So he be dead; for that is good deceit
Which mates him first that first intends deceit.

QUEEN

Thrice-noble Suffolk, 'tis resolutely spoke.

SUFFOLK

Not resolute, except so much were done;
For things are often spoke and seldom meant:
But that my heart accordeth with my tongue,
Seeing the deed is meritorious,
And to preserve my sovereign from his foe,
Say but the word, and I will be his priest.

CARDINAL

But I would have him dead, my Lord of Suffolk,
Ere you can take due orders for a priest:
Say you consent and censure well the deed,
And I'll provide his executioner,
I tender so the safety of my liege.

SUFFOLK
Here is my hand, the deed is worthy doing.

QUEEN
And so say I.

YORK
And I: and now we three have spoke it,
It skills not greatly who impugns our doom.

Enter a POST

POST
Great lords, from Ireland am I come amain,
To signify that rebels there are up,
And put the Englishmen unto the sword:
Send succours, lords, and stop the rage betime,
Before the wound to grow uncurable;
For, being green, there is great hope of help.

CARDINAL
A breach that craves a quick expedient stop!
What counsel give you in this weighty cause?

YORK
That Somerset be sent as regent thither:
'Tis meet that lucky ruler be employ'd;
Witness the fortune he hath had in France.

SOMERSET
If York, with all his far-fet policy,
Had been the regent there instead of me,
He never would have stay'd in France so long.

YORK
No, not to lose it all, as thou hast done,
I rather would have lost my life betimes
Than bring a burthen of dishonour home,
By staying there so long till all were lost.
Show me one scar character'd on thy skin:
Men's flesh preserved so whole do seldom win.

QUEEN
Nay, then, this spark will prove a raging fire,
If wind and fuel be brought to feed it with:
No more, good York; sweet Somerset, be still:
Thy fortune, York, hadst thou been regent there,
Mighty happily have proved far worse than his.

YORK
What, worse than nought? nay, then, a shame take
all!

SOMERSET
And, in the number, thee that wishest shame!

CARDINAL
My Lord of York, try what your fortune is.
The uncivil kernes of Ireland are in arms,
And temper clay with blood of Englishmen:
To Ireland will you lead a band of men,
Collected choicely, from each county some,
And try your hap against the Irishmen?

YORK
I will, my lord, so please his majesty.

SUFFOLK
Why, our authority is his consent,
And what we do establish he confirms:
Then, noble York, take thou this task in hand.

YORK
I am content: provide me soldiers, lords,
Whiles I take order for mine own affairs.

SUFFOLK
A charge, Lord York, that I will see perform'd.
But now return we to the false Duke Humphrey.

CARDINAL
No more of him; for I will deal with him,
That henceforth he shall trouble us no more.
And so break off; the day is almost spent:
Lord Suffolk, you and I must talk of that event.

YORK
My Lord of Suffolk, within fourteen days
At Bristol I expect my soldiers;
For there I'll ship them all for Ireland.

SUFFOLK
I'll see it truly done, my Lord of York.

[*Exeunt all but* YORK

YORK
Now, York, or never, steel thy fearful thoughts,
And change misdoubt to resolution:
Be that thou hopest to be, or what thou art
Resign to death; it is not worth the enjoying:
Let pale-faced fear keep with the mean-born man,
And find no harbour in a royal heart.
Faster than spring-time showers comes thought on
thought,
And not a thought but thinks on dignity.
My brain more busy than the labouring spider
Weaves tedious snares to trap mine enemies.
Well, nobles, well, 'tis politicly done,
To send me packing with an host of men:
I fear me you but warm the starved snake,
Who, cherish'd in your breasts, will sting your
hearts.
'Twas men I lack'd, and you will give them me:
I take it kindly; yet be well assured
You put sharp weapons in a madman's hands.
Whiles I in Ireland nourish a mighty band,
I will stir up in England some black storm
Shall blow ten thousand souls to heaven or hell;
And this fell tempest shall not cease to rage
Until the golden circuit on my head,
Like to the glorious sun's transparent beams,
Do calm the fury of this mad-bred flaw.
And, for a minister of my intent,
I have seduced a headstrong Kentishman,
John Cade of Ashford,
To make commotion, as full well he can,
Under the title of John Mortimer.
In Ireland have I seen this stubborn Cade
Oppose himself against a troop of kernes
And fought so long, till that his thighs with darts
Were almost like a sharp-quill'd porpentine;
And, in the end being rescued, I have seen
Him caper upright like a wild Morisco,
Shaking the bloody darts as he his bells.
Full often, like a shag-hair'd crafty kerne,
Hath he conversed with the enemy,
And undiscover'd come to me again,
And given me notice of their villanies.
This devil here shall be my substitute;
For that John Mortimer, which now is dead,

In face, in gait, in speech, he doth resemble:
By this I shall perceive the commons' mind,
How they affect the house and claim of York.
Say he be taken, rack'd and tortured,
I know no pain they can inflict upon him
Will make him say I moved him to those arms.
Say that he thrive, as 'tis great like he will,
Why, then from Ireland Come I with my strength,
And reap the harvest which that rascal sow'd;
For Humphrey being dead, as he shall be,
And Henry put apart, the next for me.   [*Exit*

Scene II. *Bury St. Edmund's. A room of state*

Enter certain MURDERERS, *hastily*
FIRST MURDERER
Run to my Lord of Suffolk; let him know
We have dispatch'd the duke, as he commanded.
SECOND MURDERER
O that it were to do! What have we done?
Didst ever hear a man so penitent?
Enter SUFFOLK
FIRST MURDERER
Here comes my lord.
SUFFOLK
Now, sirs, have you dispatch'd this thing?
FIRST MURDERER
Ay, my good lord, he's dead.
SUFFOLK
Why, that's well said. Go, get you to my house;
I will reward you for this venturous deed.
The king and all the peers are here at hand.
Have you laid fair the bed? Is all things well,
According as I gave directions?
FIRST MURDERER
'Tis, my good lord.
SUFFOLK
Away! be gone.   [*Exeunt* MURDERERS
Sound trumpets. Enter the KING, *the* QUEEN, CARDINAL
BEAUFORT, SOMERSET, *with* ATTENDANTS
KING
Go, call our uncle to our presence straight;
Say we intend to try his grace to-day,
If he be guilty, as 'tis published.
SUFFOLK
I'll call him presently, my noble lord.   [*Exit*
KING
Lords, take your places; and, I pray you all,
Proceed no straiter 'gainst our uncle Gloucester
Than from true evidence of good esteem
He be approved in practice culpable.
QUEEN
God forbid any malice should prevail,
That faultless may condemn a nobleman!
Pray God he may acquit him of suspicion!
KING
I thank thee, Nell; these words content me much.
Re-enter SUFFOLK

How now! why look'st thou pale? why tremblest
    thou?
Where is our uncle? what's the matter, Suffolk?
SUFFOLK
Dead in his bed, my lord; Gloucester is dead.
QUEEN
Marry, God forfend!
CARDINAL
God's secret judgement: I did dream to-night
The duke was dumb and could not speak a word.
        [*The* KING *swoons*
QUEEN
How fares my lord? Help, lords! the king is dead.
SOMERSET
Rear up his body; wring him by the nose.
QUEEN
Run, go, help, help! O Henry, ope thine eyes!
SUFFOLK
He doth revive again: madam, be patient.
KING
O heavenly God!
QUEEN
        How fares my gracious lord?
SUFFOLK
Comfort, my sovereign! gracious Henry, comfort!
KING
What, doth my Lord of Suffolk comfort me?
Came he right now to sing a raven's note,
Whose dismal tune bereft my vital powers;
And thinks he that the chirping of a wren,
By crying comfort from a hollow breast,
Can chase away the first-conceived sound?
Hide not thy poison with such sugar'd words;
Lay not thy hands on me; forbear, I say;
Their touch affrights me as a serpent's sting.
Thou baleful messenger, out of my sight!
Upon thy eye-balls murderous tyranny
Sits in grim majesty, to fright the world.
Look not upon me, for thine eyes are wounding:
Yet do not go away: come, basilisk,
And kill the innocent gazer with thy sight;
For in the shade of death I shall find joy;
In life but double death, now Gloucester's dead.
QUEEN
Why do you rate my Lord of Suffolk thus?
Although the duke was enemy to him,
Yet he most Christian-like laments his death:
And for myself, foe as he was to me,
Might liquid tears, or heart-offending groans,
Or blood-consuming sighs recall his life,
I would be blind with weeping, sick with groans,
Look pale as primrose with blood-drinking sighs,
And all to have the noble duke alive.
What know I how the world may deem of me?
For it is known we were but hollow friends:
It may be judged I made the duke away;
So shall my name with slander's tongue be wounded
And princes' courts be fill'd with my reproach.
This get I by his death: ay me, unhappy!
To be a queen, and crown'd with infamy!

KING

Ah, woe is me for Gloucester, wretched man!

QUEEN

Be woe for me, more wretched than he is.
What, dost thou turn away and hide thy face?
I am no loathsome leper; look on me.
What! art thou, like the adder, waxen deaf?
Be poisonous too and kill thy forlorn queen.
Is all thy comfort shut in Gloucester's tomb?
Why, then, dame Eleanor was ne'er thy joy.
Erect his statuë and worship it,
And make my image but an alehouse sign.
Was I for this nigh wreck'd upon the sea,
And twice by awkward wind from England's bank
Drove back again unto my native clime?
What boded this, but well forewarning wind
Did seem to say 'Seek not a scorpion's nest,
Nor set no footing on this unkind shore'?
What did I then, but cursed the gentle gusts,
And he that loosed them forth their brazen caves;
And bid them blow towards England's blessed shore,
Or turn our stern upon a dreadful rock?
Yet Æolus would not be a murderer,
But left that hateful office unto thee:
The pretty-vaulting sea refused to drown me,
Knowing that thou wouldst have me drown'd on
     shore,
With tears as salt as sea, through thy unkindness:
The splitting rocks cower'd in the sinking sands,
And would not dash me with their ragged sides,
Because thy flinty heart, more hard than they,
Might in thy palace perish Eleanor.
As far as I could ken thy chalky cliffs,
When from thy shore the tempest beat us back,
I stood upon the hatches in the storm,
And when the dusky sky began to rob
My earnest-gaping sight of thy land's view,
I took a costly jewel from my neck—
A heart it was, bound in with diamonds—
And threw it towards thy land: the sea received it,
And so I wish'd thy body might my heart:
And even with this I lost fair England's view,
And bid mine eyes be packing with my heart,
And call'd them blind and dusky spectacles,
For losing ken of Albion's wished coast.
How often have I tempted Suffolk's tongue,
The agent of thy foul inconstancy,
To sit and witch me, as Ascanius did,
When he to madding Dido would unfold
His father's acts commenced in burning Troy!
Am I not witch'd like her? or thou not false like him?
Ay me, I can no more! died, Eleanor!
For Henry weeps that thou dost live so long.

Noise within. Enter WARWICK, SALISBURY, *and
many* COMMONS

WARWICK

It is reported, mighty sovereign,
That good Duke Humphrey traitorously is murder'd
By Suffolk and the Cardinal Beaufort's means.
The commons, like an angry hive of bees

That want their leader, scatter up and down,
And care not who they sting in his revenge.
Myself have calm'd their spleenful mutiny,
Until they hear the order of his death.

KING

That he is dead, good Warwick, 'tis too true;
But how he died God knows, not Henry:
Enter his chamber, view his breathless corpse,
And comment then upon his sudden death.

WARWICK

That shall I do, my liege. Stay, Salisbury,
With the rude multitude till I return.   [*Exit*

KING

O Thou that judgest all things, stay my thoughts,
My thoughts, that labour to persuade my soul
Some violent hands were laid on Humphrey's life!
If my suspect be false, forgive me, God;
For judgement only doth belong to Thee.
Fain would I go to chafe his paly lips
With twenty thousand kisses, and to drain
Upon his face an ocean of salt tears,
To tell my love unto his dumb deaf trunk,
And with my fingers feel his hand unfeeling:
But all in vain are these mean obsequies;
And to survey his dead and earthly image,
What were it but to make my sorrow greater?

Re-enter WARWICK *and others, bearing* GLOUCESTER'S
body on a bed

WARWICK

Come hither, gracious sovereign, view this body.

KING

That is to see how deep my grave is made;
For with his soul fled all my worldly solace,
For seeing him I see my life in death.

WARWICK

As surely as my soul intends to live
With that dread King, that took our state upon him
To free us from his father's wrathful curse,
I do believe that violent hands were laid
Upon the life of this thrice-famed duke.

SUFFOLK

A dreadful oath, sworn with a solemn tongue!
What instance gives Lord Warwick for his vow?

WARWICK

See how the blood is settled in his face.
Oft have I seen a timely-parted ghost,
Of ashy semblance, meagre, pale and bloodless
Being all descended to the labouring heart;
Who, in the conflict that it holds with death,
Attracts the same for aidance 'gainst the enemy;
Which with the heart there cools and ne'er returneth
To blush and beautify the cheek again.
But see, his face is black and full of blood,
His eye-balls further out than when he lived,
Staring full ghastly like a strangled man;
His hair uprear'd, his nostrils stretch'd with strug-
     gling;
His hands abroad display'd, as one that grasp'd
And tugg'd for life and was by strength subdued:
Look, on the sheets his hair, you see, is sticking;

His well-proportion'd beard made rough and
    rugged,
Like to the summer's corn by tempest lodged.
It cannot be but he was murder'd here;
The least of all these signs were probable.

SUFFOLK

Why, Warwick, who should do the duke to death?
Myself and Beaufort had him in protection;
And we, I hope, sir, are no murderers.

WARWICK

But both of you were vow'd Duke Humphrey's foes,
And you, forsooth, had the good duke to keep:
'Tis like you would not feast him like a friend;
And 'tis well seen he found an enemy.

QUEEN

Then you, belike, suspect these noblemen
As guilty of Duke Humphrey's timeless death.

WARWICK

Who finds the heifer dead and bleeding fresh,
And sees fast by a butcher with an axe,
But will suspect 'twas he that made the slaughter?
Who finds the partridge in the puttock's nest,
But may imagine how the bird was dead,
Although the kite soar with unbloodied beak?
Even so suspicious is this tragedy.

QUEEN

Are you the butcher, Suffolk? Where's your knife?
Is Beaufort term'd a kite? Where are his talons?

SUFFOLK

I wear no knife to slaughter sleeping men;
But here's a vengeful sword, rusted with ease,
That shall be scoured in his rancorous heart
That slanders me with murder's crimson badge.
Say, if thou darest, proud Lord of Warwickshire,
That I am faulty in Duke Humphrey's death.

[Exeunt CARDINAL, SOMERSET, and others

WARWICK

What dares not Warwick, if false Suffolk dare him?

QUEEN

He dares not calm his contumelious spirit,
Nor cease to be an arrogant controller,
Though Suffolk dare him twenty thousand times.

WARWICK

Madam, be still; with reverence may I say;
For every word you speak in his behalf
Is slander to your royal dignity.

SUFFOLK

Blunt-witted lord, ignoble in demeanour!
If ever lady wrong'd her lord so much,
Thy mother took into her blameful bed
Some stern untutor'd churl, and noble stock
Was graft with crab-tree slip; whose fruit thou art
And never of the Nevils' noble race.

WARWICK

But that the guilt of murder bucklers thee,
And I should rob the deathsman of his fee,
Quitting thee thereby of ten thousand shames,
And that my sovereign's presence makes me mild,
I would, false murderous coward, on thy knee
Make thee beg pardon for thy passed speech,

And say it was thy mother that thou meant'st,
That thou thyself wast born in bastardy;
And after all this fearful homage done,
Give thee thy hire and send thy soul to hell,
Pernicious blood-sucker of sleeping men!

SUFFOLK

Thou shalt be waking while I shed thy blood,
If from this presence thou darest go with me.

WARWICK

Away even now, or I will drag thee hence:
Unworthy though thou art, I'll cope with thee
And do some service to Duke Humphrey's ghost.

[Exeunt SUFFOLK and WARWICK

KING

What stronger breastplate than a heart untainted!
Thrice is he arm'd that hath his quarrel just,
And he but naked, though lock'd up in steel,
Whose conscience with injustice is corrupted.

[A noise within

QUEEN

What noise is this?

Re-enter SUFFOLK and WARWICK, with their weapons
drawn

KING

Why, how now, lords! your wrathful weapons drawn
Here in our presence! dare you be so bold?
Why, what tumultuous clamour have we here?

SUFFOLK

The traitorous Warwick with the men of Bury
Set all upon me, mighty sovereign.

SALISBURY

[To the COMMONS, entering] Sirs, stand apart; the king
    shall know your mind.
Dread lord, the commons send you word by me,
Unless Lord Suffolk straight be done to death,
Or banished fair England's territories,
They will by violence tear him from your palace,
And torture him with grievous lingering death.
They say, by him the good Duke Humphrey died;
They say, in him they fear your highness' death;
And mere instinct of love and loyalty,
Free from a stubborn opposite intent,
As being thought to contradict your liking,
Makes them thus forward in his banishment.
They say, in care of your most royal person,
That if your highness should intend to sleep,
And charge that no man should disturb your rest
In pain of your dislike or pain of death,
Yet, notwithstanding such a strait edict,
Were there a serpent seen, with forked tongue,
That slily glided towards your majesty,
It were but necessary you were waked,
Lest, being suffer'd in that harmful slumber,
The mortal worm might make the sleep eternal;
And therefore do they cry, though you forbid,
That they will guard you, whether you will or no,
From such fell serpents as false Suffolk is,
With whose envenomed and fatal sting,
Your loving uncle, twenty times his worth,
They say, is shamefully bereft of life.

COMMONS

[*Within*] An answer from the king, my Lord of Salisbury!

SUFFOLK

'Tis like the commons, rude unpolish'd hinds,
Could send such message to their sovereign:
But you, my lord, were glad to be employ'd,
To show how quaint an orator you are:
But all the honour Salisbury hath won
Is, that he was the lord ambassador
Sent from a sort of tinkers to the king.

COMMONS

[*Within*] An answer from the king, or we will all break in!

KING

Go, Salisbury, and tell them all from me,
I thank them for their tender loving care;
And had I not been cited so by them,
Yet did I purpose as they do entreat;
For, sure, my thoughts do hourly prophesy
Mischance unto my state by Suffolk's means:
And therefore, by His majesty I swear,
Whose far unworthy deputy I am,
He shall not breathe infection in this air
But three days longer, on the pain of death.
[*Exit* SALISBURY

QUEEN

O Henry, let me plead for gentle Suffolk!

KING

Ungentle queen, to call him gentle Suffolk!
No more, I say: if thou dost plead for him,
Thou wilt but add increase unto my wrath.
Had I but said, I would have kept my word,
But when I swear, it is irrevocable.
If, after three days' space, thou here be'st found
On any ground that I am ruler of,
The world shall not be ransom for thy life.
Come, Warwick, come, good Warwick, go with me;
I have great matters to impart to thee.
[*Exeunt all but* QUEEN *and* SUFFOLK

QUEEN

Mischance and sorrow go along with you!
Heart's discontent and sour affliction
Be playfellows to keep you company!
There's two of you; the devil make a third!
And threefold vengeance tend upon your steps!

SUFFOLK

Cease, gentle queen, these execrations,
And let thy Suffolk take his heavy leave.

QUEEN

Fie, coward woman and soft-hearted wretch!
Hast thou not spirit to curse thine enemy?

SUFFOLK

A plague upon them! wherefore should I curse them?
Would curses kill, as doth the mandrake's groan,
I would invent as bitter-searching terms,
As curst, as harsh and horrible to hear,
Deliver'd strongly through my fixed teeth,

With full as many signs of deadly hate,
As lean-faced Envy in her loathsome cave:
My tongue should stumble in mine earnest words;
Mine eyes should sparkle like the beaten flint;
Mine hair be fix'd on end, as one distract;
Ay, every joint should seem to curse and ban:
And even now my burthen'd heart would break,
Should I not curse them. Poison be their drink!
Gall, worse than gall, the daintiest that they taste!
Their sweetest shade a grove of cypress trees!
Their chiefest prospect murdering basilisks!
Their softest touch as smart as lizards' stings!
Their music frightful as the serpent's hiss,
And boding screech-owls make the concert full!
All the foul terrors in dark-seated hell—

QUEEN

Enough, sweet Suffolk; thou torment'st thyself;
And these dread curses, like the sun 'gainst glass,
Or like an overcharged gun, recoil,
And turn the force of them upon thyself.

SUFFOLK

You bade me ban, and will you bid me leave?
Now, by the ground that I am banish'd from,
Well could I curse away a winter's night,
Though standing naked on a mountain top,
Where biting cold would never let grass grow,
And think it but a minute spent in sport.

QUEEN

O, let me entreat thee cease. Give me thy hand,
That I may dew it with my mournful tears;
Nor let the rain of heaven wet this place,
To wash away my woful monuments.
O, could this kiss be printed in thy hand,
That thou mightst think upon these by the seal,
Through whom a thousand sighs are breathed for thee!
So, get thee gone, that I may know my grief;
'Tis but surmised whiles thou art standing by,
As one that surfeits thinking on a want.
I will repeal thee, or, be well assured,
Adventure to be banished myself:
And banished I am, if but from thee.
Go; speak not to me; even now be gone.
O, go not yet! Even thus two friends condemn'd
Embrace and kiss and take ten thousand leaves,
Loather a hundred times to part than die.
Yet now farewell; and farewell life with thee!

SUFFOLK

Thus is poor Suffolk ten times banished;
Once by the king, and three times thrice by thee.
'Tis not the land I care for, wert thou thence;
A wilderness is populous enough,
So Suffolk had thy heavenly company:
For where thou art, there is the world itself,
With every several pleasure in the world,
And where thou art not, desolation.
I can no more: live thou to joy thy life;
Myself no joy in nought but that thou livest.
Enter VAUX

[58]

QUEEN

Whither goes Vaux so fast? what news, I prithee?

VAUX

To signify unto his majesty
That Cardinal Beaufort is at point of death;
For suddenly a grievous sickness took him,
That makes him gasp and stare and catch the air,
Blaspheming God and cursing men on earth.
Sometime he talks as if Duke Humphrey's ghost
Were by his side; sometime he calls the king,
And whispers to his pillow as to him
The secrets of his overcharged soul:
And I am sent to tell his majesty,
That even now he cries aloud for him.

QUEEN

Go tell this heavy message to the king.
[Exit VAUX

Ay me! what is this world! what news are these!
But wherefore grieve I at an hour's poor loss,
Omitting Suffolk's exile, my soul's treasure?
Why only, Suffolk, mourn I not for thee,
And with the southern clouds contend in tears,
Theirs for the earth's increase, mine for my sorrows?
Now get thee hence: the king, thou know'st, is com-
ing;
If thou be found by me, thou art but dead.

SUFFOLK

If I depart from thee, I cannot live;
And in thy sight to die, what were it else
But like a pleasant slumber in thy lap?
Here could I breathe my soul into the air,
As mild and gentle as the cradle-babe,
Dying with mother's dug between its lips:
Where, from thy sight, I should be raging mad,
And cry out for thee to close up mine eyes,
To have thee with thy lips to stop my mouth;
So shouldst thou either turn my flying soul,
Or I should breathe it so into thy body,
And then it lived in sweet Elysium.
To die by thee were but to die in jest;
From thee to die were torture more than death:
O, let me stay, befall what may befall!

QUEEN

Away! though parting be a fretful corrosive,
It is applied to a deathful wound.
To France, sweet Suffolk: let me hear from thee;
For wheresoe'er thou art in this world's globe,
I'll have an Iris that shall find thee out.

SUFFOLK

I go.

QUEEN

And take my heart with thee.

SUFFOLK

A jewel, lock'd into the wofull'st cask
That ever did contain a thing of worth.
Even as a splitted bark, so sunder we:
This way fall I to death.

QUEEN

This way for me. [Exeunt severally

SCENE III. A bedchamber

Enter the KING, SALISBURY, WARWICK, to the CARDINAL
in bed

KING

How fares my lord? speak, Beaufort, to thy sovereign.

CARDINAL

If thou be'st death, I'll give thee England's treasure,
Enough to purchase such another island,
So thou wilt let me live, and feel no pain.

KING

Ah, what a sign it is of evil life,
Where death's approach is seen so terrible!

WARWICK

Beaufort, it is thy sovereign speaks to thee.

CARDINAL

Bring me unto my trial when you will.
Died he not in his bed? where should he die?
Can I make men live, whether they will or no?
O, torture me no more! I will confess.
Alive again? then show me where he is:
I'll give a thousand pound to look upon him.
He hath no eyes, the dust hath blinded them.
Comb down his hair; look, look! it stands upright,
Like lime-twigs set to catch my winged soul.
Give me some drink; and bid the apothecary
Bring the strong poison that I bought of him.

KING

O thou eternal mover of the heavens,
Look with a gentle eye upon this wretch!
O, beat away the busy meddling fiend
That lays strong siege unto this wretch's soul,
And from his bosom purge this black despair!

WARWICK

See, how the pangs of death do make him grin!

SALISBURY

Disturb him not; let him pass peaceably.

KING

Peace to his soul, if God's good pleasure be!
Lord cardinal, if thou think'st on heaven's bliss,
Hold up thy hand, make signal of thy hope.
He dies, and makes no sign. O God, forgive him!

WARWICK

So bad a death argues a monstrous life.

KING

Forbear to judge, for we are sinners all.
Close up his eyes and draw the curtain close;
And let us all to meditation.   [Exeunt

ACT IV

SCENE I. The coast of Kent

Alarum. Fight at sea. Ordnance goes off. Enter a CAPTAIN,
a MASTER, a MASTER'S-MATE, WALTER WHITMORE, and
others; with them SUFFOLK, and others, PRISONERS

CAPTAIN

The gaudy, blabbing and remorseful day
Is crept into the bosom of the sea;

And now loud-howling wolves arouse the jades
That drag the tragic melancholy night;
Who, with their drowsy, slow and flagging wings,
Clip dead men's graves, and from their misty jaws
Breathe foul contagious darkness in the air.
Therefore bring forth the soldiers of our prize;
For, whilst our pinnace anchors in the Downs,
Here shall they make their ransom on the sand,
Or with their blood stain this discoloured shore.
Master, this prisoner freely give I thee;
And thou that art his mate, make boot of this;
The other, Walter Whitmore, is thy share.

FIRST GENTLEMAN
What is my ransom, master? let me know.

MASTER
A thousand crowns, or else lay down your head.

MATE
And so much shall you give, or off goes yours.

CAPTAIN
What, think you much to pay two thousand crowns,
And bear the name and port of gentlemen?
Cut both the villains' throats; for die you shall:
The lives of those which we have lost in fight
Be counterpoised with such a petty sum!

FIRST GENTLEMAN
I'll give it, sir; and therefore spare my life.

SECOND GENTLEMAN
And so will I, and write home for it straight.

WHITMORE
I lost mine eye in laying the prize aboard,
And therefore to revenge it, shalt thou die;
                              [To SUFFOLK
And so should these, if I might have my will.

CAPTAIN
Be not so rash; take ransom, let him live.

SUFFOLK
Look on my George; I am a gentleman:
Rate me at what thou wilt, thou shalt be paid.

WHITMORE
And so am I; my name is Walter Whitmore.
How now! why start'st thou? what, doth death af-
    fright?

SUFFOLK
Thy name affrights me, in whose sound is death.
A cunning man did calculate my birth,
And told me that by water I should die:
Yet let not this make thee be bloody-minded;
Thy name is Gaultier, being rightly sounded.

WHITMORE
Gaultier or Walter, which it is, I care not:
Never yet did base dishonour blur our name,
But with our sword we wiped away the blot;
Therefore, when merchant-like I sell revenge,
Broke be my sword, my arms torn and defaced,
And I proclaim'd a coward through the world!

SUFFOLK
Stay, Whitmore; for thy prisoner is a prince,
The Duke of Suffolk, William de la Pole.

WHITMORE
The Duke of Suffolk, muffled up in rags!

SUFFOLK
Ay, but these rags are no part of the duke:
Jove sometime went disguised, and why not I?

CAPTAIN
But Jove was never slain, as thou shalt be.

SUFFOLK
Obscure and lowly swain, King Henry's blood,
The honourable blood of Lancaster,
Must not be shed by such a jaded groom.
Hast thou not kiss'd thy hand and held my stirrup?
Bare-headed plodded by my foot-cloth mule,
And thought thee happy when I shook my head?
How often hast thou waited at my cup,
Fed from my trencher, kneel'd down at the board,
When I have feasted with Queen Margaret?
Remember it and let it make thee crest-fall'n.
Ay, and allay this thy abortive pride;
How in our voiding lobby hast thou stood
And duly waited for my coming forth?
This hand of mine hath writ in thy behalf,
And therefore shall it charm thy riotous tongue.

WHITMORE
Speak, captain, shall I stab the forlorn swain?

CAPTAIN
First let my words stab him, as he hath me.

SUFFOLK
Base slave, thy words are blunt, and so art thou.

CAPTAIN
Convey him hence and on our long-boat's side
Strike off his head.

SUFFOLK
            Thou darest not, for thy own.

CAPTAIN
Yes, Pole.

SUFFOLK
        Pole!

CAPTAIN
            Pool! Sir Pool! lord!
Ay, kennel, puddle, sink; whose filth and dirt
Troubles the silver spring where England drinks.
Now will I dam up this thy yawning mouth,
For swallowing the treasure of the realm:
Thy lips that kiss'd the queen shall sweep the
    ground;
And thou that smiledest at good Duke Humphrey's
    death
Against the senseless winds shalt grin in vain,
Who in contempt shall hiss at thee again:
And wedded be thou to the hags of hell,
For daring to affy a mighty lord
Unto the daughter of a worthless king,
Having neither subject, wealth, nor diadem.
By devilish policy art thou grown great,
And, like ambitious Sylla, overgorged
With gobbets of thy mother's bleeding heart.
By thee Anjou and Maine were sold to France,
The false revolting Normans thorough thee
Disdain to call us lord, and Picardy
Hath slain their governors, surprised our forts,
And sent the ragged soldiers wounded home.

The princely Warwick, and the Nevils all,
Whose dreadful swords were never drawn in vain,
As hating thee, are rising up in arms:
And now the house of York, thrust from the crown
By shameful murder of a guiltless king,
And lofty proud encroaching tyranny,
Burns with revenging fire; whose hopeful colours
Advance our half-faced sun, striving to shine,
Under the which is writ 'Invitis nubibus.'
The commons here in Kent are up in arms:
And, to conclude, reproach and beggary
Is crept into the palace of our king,
And all by thee. Away! convey him hence.

SUFFOLK

O that I were a god, to shoot forth thunder
Upon these paltry, servile, abject drudges!
Small things make base men proud: this villain here,
Being captain of a pinnace, threatens more
Than Bargulus the strong Illyrian pirate.
Drones suck not eagles' blood, but rob bee-hives:
It is impossible that I should die
By such a lowly vassal as thyself.
Thy words move rage and not remorse in me:
I go of message from the queen to France;
I charge thee waft me safely cross the Channel.

CAPTAIN

Walter,—

WHITMORE

Come, Suffolk, I must waft thee to thy death.

SUFFOLK

Gelidus timor occupat artus: it is thee I fear.

WHITMORE

Thou shalt have cause to fear before I leave thee.
What, are ye daunted now? now will ye stoop?

FIRST GENTLEMAN

My gracious lord, entreat him, speak him fair.

SUFFOLK

Suffolk's imperial tongue is stern and rough,
Used to command, untaught to plead for favour.
Far be it we should honour such as these
With humble suit: no, rather let my head
Stoop to the block than these knees bow to any
Save to the God of heaven and to my king;
And sooner dance upon a bloody pole
Than stand uncover'd to the vulgar groom.
True nobility is exempt from fear:
More can I bear than you dare execute.

CAPTAIN

Hale him away, and let him talk no more.

SUFFOLK

Come, soldiers, show what cruelty ye can,
That this my death may never be forgot!
Great men oft die by vile bezonians:
A Roman sworder and banditto slave
Murder'd sweet Tully; Brutus' bastard hand
Stabb'd Julius Cæsar; savage islanders
Pompey the Great; and Suffolk dies by pirates.
                [Exeunt WHITMORE and others with SUFFOLK

CAPTAIN

And as for these whose ransom we have set,

It is our pleasure one of them depart:
Therefore come you with us and let him go.
                [Exeunt all but the FIRST GENTLEMAN
           Re-enter WHITMORE with SUFFOLK'S BODY

WHITMORE

There let his head and lifeless body lie,
Until the queen his mistress bury it.   [Exit

FIRST GENTLEMAN

O barbarous and bloody spectacle!
His body will I bear unto the king:
If he revenge it not, yet will his friends;
So will the queen, that living held him dear.
                [Exit with the body

SCENE II. Blackheath

Enter GEORGE BEVIS and JOHN HOLLAND

BEVIS

Come, and get thee a sword, though made of a lath:
they have been up these two days.

HOLLAND

They have the more need to sleep now, then.

BEVIS

I tell thee, Jack Cade the clothier means to dress the
commonwealth, and turn it, and set a new nap
upon it.

HOLLAND

So he had need, for 'tis threadbare. Well, I say it
was never merry world in England since gentlemen
came up.

BEVIS

O miserable age! virtue is not regarded in
handicrafts-men.

HOLLAND

The nobility think scorn to go in leather aprons.

BEVIS

Nay, more, the king's council are no good workmen.

HOLLAND

True; and yet it is said, labour in thy vocation;
which is as much to say as, let the magistrates be
labouring men; and therefore should we be magistrates.

BEVIS

Thou hast hit it; for there's no better sign of a brave
mind than a hard hand.

HOLLAND

I see them! I see them! There's Best's son, the tanner of Wingham,—

BEVIS

He shall have the skins of our enemies, to make
dog's-leather of.

HOLLAND

And Dick the butcher,—

BEVIS

Then is sin struck down like an ox, and iniquity's
throat cut like a calf.

HOLLAND

And Smith the weaver,—

BEVIS

Argo, their thread of life is spun.

HOLLAND

Come, come, let's fall in with them.

Drum. Enter CADE, DICK *the Butcher*, SMITH *the Weaver, and a* SAWYER, *with infinite numbers*

CADE

We John Cade, so termed of our supposed father,—

DICK

[*Aside*] Or rather, of stealing a cade of herrings.

CADE

For our enemies shall fall before us, inspired with the spirit of putting down kings and princes,— Command silence.

DICK

Silence!

CADE

My father was a Mortimer,—

DICK

[*Aside*] He was an honest man, and a good brick-layer.

CADE

My mother a Plantagenet,—

DICK

[*Aside*] I knew her well; she was a midwife.

CADE

My wife descended of the Lacies,—

DICK

[*Aside*] She was, indeed, a pedler's daughter, and sold many laces.

SMITH

[*Aside*] But now of late, not able to travel with her furred pack, she washes bucks here at home.

CADE

Therefore am I of an honourable house.

DICK

[*Aside*] Ay, by my faith, the field is honourable; and there was he born, under a hedge, for his father had never a house but the cage.

CADE

Valiant I am.

SMITH

[*Aside*] A' must needs; for beggary is valiant.

CADE

I am able to endure much.

DICK

[*Aside*] No question of that; for I have seen him whipped three market-days together.

CADE

I fear neither sword nor fire.

SMITH

[*Aside*] He need not fear the sword; for his coat is of proof.

DICK

[*Aside*] But methinks he should stand in fear of fire, being burnt i' the hand for stealing of sheep.

CADE

Be brave, then; for your captain is brave, and vows reformation. There shall be in England seven half-penny loaves sold for a penny: the three-hooped pot

shall have ten hoops; and I will make it felony to drink small beer: all the realm shall be in common; and in Cheapside shall my palfry go to grass: and when I am king, as king I will be,—

ALL

God save your majesty!

CADE

I thank you, good people: there shall be no money; all shall eat and drink on my score; and I will apparel them all in one livery, that they may agree like brothers, and worship me their lord.

DICK

The first thing we do, let's kill all the lawyers.

CADE

Nay, that I mean to do. Is not this a lamentable thing, that of the skin of an innocent lamb should be made parchment? that parchment, being scribbled o'er, should undo a man? Some say the bee stings: but I say, 'tis the bee's wax; for I did but seal once to a thing, and I was never mine own man since. How now! who's there?

Enter some, bringing forward the CLERK OF CHATHAM

SMITH

The clerk of Chatham: he can write and read and cast accompt.

CADE

O monstrous!

SMITH

We took him setting of boys' copies.

CADE

Here's a villain!

SMITH

Has a book in his pocket with red letters in 't.

CADE

Nay, then, he is a conjuror.

DICK

Nay, he can make obligations, and write court-hand.

CADE

I am sorry for 't: the man is a proper man, of mine honour; unless I find him guilty, he shall not die. Come hither, sirrah, I must examine thee: what is thy name?

CLERK

Emmanuel.

DICK

They use to write it on the top of letters: 'twill go hard with you.

CADE

Let me alone. Dost thou use to write thy name? or hast thou a mark to thyself, like an honest plain-dealing man?

CLERK

Sir, I thank God, I have been so well brought up that I can write my name.

ALL

He hath confessed: away with him! he's a villain and a traitor.

CADE

Away with him, I say! hang him with his pen and

ink-horn about his neck. [*Exit one with the* CLERK
Enter MICHAEL

MICHAEL

Where's our general?

CADE

Here I am, thou particular fellow.

MICHAEL

Fly, fly, fly! Sir Humphrey Stafford and his brother
are hard by, with the king's forces.

CADE

Stand, villain, stand, or I'll fell thee down. He shall
be encountered with a man as good as himself: he
is but a knight, is a'?

MICHAEL

No.

CADE

To equal him, I will make myself a knight presently.
[*Kneels*] Rise up, Sir John Mortimer. [*Rises*] Now
have at him!
Enter SIR HUMPHREY STAFFORD *and his* BROTHER, *with
drum and* SOLDIERS

STAFFORD

Rebellious hinds, the filth and scum of Kent,
Mark'd for the gallows, lay your weapons down;
Home to your cottages, forsake this groom:
The king is merciful, if you revolt.

BROTHER

But angry, wrathful, and inclined to blood,
If you go forward; therefore yield, or die.

CADE

As for these silken-coated slaves, I pass not:
It is to you, good people, that I speak,
Over whom, in time to come, I hope to reign;
For I am rightful heir unto the crown.

STAFFORD

Villain, thy father was a plasterer;
And thou thyself a shearman, art thou not?

CADE

And Adam was a gardener.

BROTHER

And what of that?

CADE

Marry, this: Edmund Mortimer, Earl of March,
Married the Duke of Clarence' daughter, did he not?

STAFFORD

Ay, sir.

CADE

By her he had two children at one birth.

BROTHER

That's false.

CADE

Ay, there's the question; but I say, 'tis true:
The elder of them, being put to nurse,
Was by a beggar-woman stolen away;
And, ignorant of his birth and parentage,
Became a bricklayer when he came to age:
His son am I; deny it, if you can.

DICK

Nay, 'tis too true; therefore he shall be king.

SMITH

Sir, he made a chimney in my father's house, and
the bricks are alive at this day to testify it; therefore
deny it not.

STAFFORD

And will you credit this base drudge's words,
That speaks he knows not what?

ALL

Ay, marry, will we; therefore get ye gone.

BROTHER

Jack Cade, the Duke of York hath taught you this.

CADE

[*Aside*] He lies, for I invented it myself.
Go to, sirrah, tell the king from me, that, for his
father's sake, Henry the fifth, in whose time boys
went to span-counter for French crowns, I am content he shall reign; but I'll be protector over him.

DICK

And furthermore, we'll have the Lord Say's head
for selling the dukedom of Maine.

CADE

And good reason; for thereby is England mained,
and fain to go with a staff, but that my puissance
holds it up. Fellow kings, I tell you that that Lord
Say hath gelded the commonwealth, and made it
an eunuch: and more than that, he can speak
French; and therefore he is a traitor.

STAFFORD

O gross and miserable ignorance!

CADE

Nay, answer, if you can: the Frenchmen are our
enemies; go to, then, I ask but this: can he that
speaks with the tongue of an enemy be a good counsellor, or no?

ALL

No, no; and therefore we'll have his head.

BROTHER

Well, seeing gentle words will not prevail,
Assail them with the army of the king.

STAFFORD

Herald, away; and throughout every town
Proclaim them traitors that are up with Cade;
That those which fly before the battle ends
May, even in their wives' and children's sight,
Be hang'd up for example at their doors:
And you that be the king's friends, follow me.
[*Exeunt the two* STAFFORDS, *and* SOLDIERS

CADE

And you that love the commons, follow me.
Now show yourselves men; 'tis for liberty.
We will not leave one lord, one gentleman:
Spare none but such as go in clouted shoon;
For they are thrifty honest men, and such
As would, but that they dare not, take our parts.

DICK

They are all in order and march toward us.

CADE

But then are we in order when we are most out of
order. Come, march forward. [*Exeunt*

SCENE III. *Another part of Blackheath*

Alarums to the fight, wherein both the STAFFORDS *are slain. Enter* CADE *and the rest*

CADE

Where's Dick, the butcher of Ashford?

DICK

Here, sir.

CADE

They fell before thee like sheep and oxen, and thou behavedst thyself as if thou hadst been in thine own slaughter-house: therefore thus will I reward thee, the Lent shall be as long again as it is; and thou shalt have a license to kill for a hundred lacking one.

DICK

I desire no more

CADE

And, to speak truth, thou deservest no less. This monument of the victory will I bear [*putting on* SIR HUMPHREY's *brigandine*]; and the bodies shall be dragged at my horse heels till I do come to London, where we will have the mayor's sword borne before us.

DICK

If we mean to thrive and do good, break open the gaols and let out the prisoners.

CADE

Fear not that, I warrant thee. Come, let's march towards London.   [*Exeunt*

SCENE IV. *London. The palace*

Enter the KING *with a supplication, and the* QUEEN *with* SUFFOLK's *head, the* DUKE OF BUCKINGHAM *and the* LORD SAY

QUEEN

Oft have I heard that grief softens the mind,
And makes it fearful and degenerate;
Think therefore on revenge and cease to weep.
But who can cease to weep and look on this?
Here may his head lie on my throbbing breast:
But where's the body that I should embrace?

BUCKINGHAM

What answer makes your grace to the rebels' supplication?

KING

I'll send some holy bishop to entreat;
For God forbid so many simple souls
Should perish by the sword! And I myself,
Rather than bloody war shall cut them short,
Will parley with Jack Cade their general:
But stay, I'll read it over once again.

QUEEN

Ah, barbarous villains! hath this lovely face
Ruled, like a wandering planet, over me,
And could it not enforce them to relent,
That were unworthy to behold the same?

KING

Lord Say, Jack Cade hath sworn to have thy head.

SAY

Ay, but I hope your highness shall have his.

KING

How now, madam!
Still lamenting and mourning for Suffolk's death?
I fear me, love, if that I had been dead,
Thou wouldest not have mourn'd so much for me.

QUEEN

No, my love, I should not mourn, but die for thee.

Enter a MESSENGER

KING

How now! what news? why comest thou in such haste?

MESSENGER

The rebels are in Southwark; fly, my lord!
Jack Cade proclaims himself Lord Mortimer,
Descended from the Duke of Clarence' house,
And calls your grace usurper openly,
And vows to crown himself in Westminster.
His army is a ragged multitude
Of hinds and peasants, rude and merciless:
Sir Humphrey Stafford and his brother's death
Hath given them heart and courage to proceed:
All scholars, lawyers, courtiers, gentlemen,
They call false caterpillars and intend their death.

KING

O graceless men! they know not what they do.

BUCKINGHAM

My gracious lord, retire to Killingworth,
Until a power be raised to put them down.

QUEEN

Ah, were the Duke of Suffolk now alive,
These Kentish rebels would be soon appeased!

KING

Lord Say, the traitors hate thee;
Therefore away with us to Killingworth.

SAY

So might your grace's person be in danger.
The sight of me is odious in their eyes;
And therefore in this city will I stay,
And live alone as secret as I may.

Enter another MESSENGER

MESSENGER

Jack Cade hath gotten London bridge:
The citizens fly and forsake their houses:
The rascal people, thirsting after prey,
Join with the traitor, and they jointly swear
To spoil the city and your royal court.

BUCKINGHAM

Then linger not, my lord; away, take horse.

KING

Come, Margaret; God, our hope, will succour us.

QUEEN

My hope is gone, now Suffolk is deceased.

KING

Farewell, my lord: trust not the Kentish rebels.

BUCKINGHAM

Trust nobody, for fear you be betray'd.

SAY

The trust I have is in mine innocence,
And therefore am I bold and resolute.   [Exeunt

Scene V. London. The Tower

Enter LORD SCALES *upon the Tower, walking. Then enter
two or three* CITIZENS *below*

SCALES

How now! is Jack Cade slain?

FIRST CITIZEN

No, my lord, nor likely to be slain; for they have
won the bridge, killing all those that withstand
them: the lord mayor craves aid of your honour
from the Tower to defend the city from the rebels.

SCALES

Such aid as I can spare you shall command;
But I am troubled here with them myself;
The rebels have assay'd to win the Tower.
But get you to Smithfield and gather head,
And thither I will send you Matthew Goffe;
Fight for your king, your country, and your lives;
And so, farewell, for I must hence again.   [Exeunt

Scene VI. London. Cannon Street

Enter JACK CADE *and the rest, and strikes his staff on
London-stone*

CADE

Now is Mortimer lord of this city. And here, sitting
upon London-stone, I charge and command that,
of the city's cost, the pissing-conduit run nothing
but claret wine this first year of our reign. And now
henceforward it shall be treason for any that calls
me other than Lord Mortimer.

Enter a SOLDIER, *running*

SOLDIER

Jack Cade! Jack Cade!

CADE

Knock him down there.   [*They kill them*

SMITH

If this fellow be wise, he'll never call ye Jack Cade
more: I think he hath a very fair warning.

DICK

My lord, there's an army gathered together in
Smithfield.

CADE

Come, then, let's go fight with them: but first, go
and set London bridge on fire; and, if you can, burn
down the Tower too. Come, let's away.   [*Exeunt*

Scene VII. London. Smithfield

Alarums. MATTHEW GOFFE *is slain, and all the rest. Then
enter* JACK CADE, *with his company*

CADE

So, sirs: now go some and pull down the Savoy;
others to the inns of court; down with them all.

DICK

I have a suit unto your lordship.

CADE

Be it a lordship, thou shalt have it for that word.

DICK

Only that the laws of England may come out of
your mouth.

HOLLAND

[*Aside*] Mass, 'twill be sore law, then; for he was
thrust in the mouth with a spear, and 'tis not whole
yet.

SMITH

[*Aside*] Nay, John, it will be stinking law; for his
breath stinks with eating toasted cheese.

CADE

I have thought upon it, it shall be so. Away, burn
all the records of the realm: my mouth shall be the
parliament of England.

HOLLAND

[*Aside*] Then we are like to have biting statutes, unless his teeth be pulled out.

CADE

And henceforward all things shall be in common.

Enter a MESSENGER

MESSENGER

My lord, a prize, a prize! here's the Lord Say, which
sold the towns in France; he that made us pay one
and twenty fifteens, and one shilling to the pound,
the last subsidy.

Enter GEORGE BEVIS, *with the* LORD SAY

CADE

Well, he shall be beheaded for it ten times. Ah, thou
say, thou serge, nay, thou buckram lord! now art
thou within point-blank of our jurisdiction regal.
What canst thou answer to my majesty for giving up
of Normandy unto Mounsieur Basimecu, the dauphin of France? Be it known unto thee by these
presence, even the presence of Lord Mortimer, that
I am the besom that must sweep the court clean of
such filth as thou art. Thou hast most traitorously
corrupted the youth of the realm in erecting a grammar school: and whereas, before, our forefathers
had no other books but the score and the tally, thou
hast caused printing to be used, and, contrary to the
king, his crown and dignity, thou hast built a paper-
mill. It will be proved to thy face that thou hast men
about thee that usually talk of a noun and a verb,
and such abominable words as no Christian ear can
endure to hear. Thou hast appointed justices of
peace, to call poor men before them about matters
they were not able to answer. Moreover, thou hast
put them in prison; and because they could not read,
thou hast hanged them; when, indeed, only for that
cause they have been most worthy to live. Thou
dost ride in a foot-cloth, dost thou not?

SAY

What of that?

CADE

Marry, thou oughtest not to let thy horse wear a

cloak, when honester men than thou go in their hose and doublets.

DICK

And work in their shirt too; as myself, for example, that am a butcher.

SAY

You men of Kent,—

DICK

What say you of Kent?

SAY

Nothing but this; 'tis 'bona terra, mala gens.'

CADE

Away with him, away with him! he speaks Latin.

SAY

Hear me but speak, and bear me where you will.
Kent, in the Commentaries Cæsar writ,
Is term'd the civil'st place of all this isle:
Sweet is the country, because full of riches;
The people liberal, valiant, active, wealthy;
Which makes me hope you are not void of pity.
I sold not Maine, I lost not Normandy,
Yet, to recover them, would lose my life.
Justice with favour have I always done;
Prayers and tears have moved me, gifts could never.
When have I aught exacted at your hands,
But to maintain the king, the realm, and you?
Large gifts have I bestow'd on learned clerks,
Because my book preferr'd me to the king,
And seeing ignorance is the curse of God,
Knowledge the wing wherewith we fly to heaven,
Unless you be possess'd with devilish spirits,
You cannot but forbear to murder me:
This tongue hath parley'd unto foreign kings
For your behoof,—

CADE

Tut, when struck'st thou one blow in the field?

SAY

Great men have reaching hands: oft have I struck
Those that I never saw and struck them dead.

GEORGE

O monstrous coward! what, to come behind folks?

SAY

These cheeks are pale for watching for your good.

CADE

Give him a box o' the ear and that will make 'em red again.

SAY

Long sitting to determine poor men's causes
Hath made me full of sickness and diseases.

CADE

Ye shall have a hempen caudle then and the help of hatchet.

DICK

Why dost thou quiver, man?

SAY

The palsy, and not fear, provokes me.

CADE

Nay, he nods at us, as who should say, I'll be even with you: I'll see if his head will stand steadier on a pole, or no. Take him away, and behead him.

SAY

Tell me wherein have I offended most?
Have I affected wealth or honour? speak.
Are my chests fill'd up with extorted gold?
Is my apparel sumptuous to behold?
Whom have I injured, that ye seek my death?
These hands are free from guiltless blood-shedding,
This breast from harbouring foul deceitful thoughts.
O, let me live!

CADE

[Aside] I feel remorse in myself with his words; but I'll bridle it: he shall die, an it be but for pleading so well for his life. Away with him! he has a familiar under his tongue; he speaks not o' God's name. Go, take him away, I say, and strike off his head presently; and then break into his son-in-law's house, Sir James Cromer, and strike off his head, and bring them both upon two poles hither.

ALL

It shall be done.

SAY

Ah, countrymen! if when you make your prayers,
God should be so obdurate as yourselves,
How would it fare with your departed souls?
And therefore yet relent, and save my life.

CADE

Away with him! and do as I command ye.

[Exeunt some with LORD SAY

The proudest peer in the realm shall not wear a head on his shoulders, unless he pay me tribute; there shall not a maid be married, but she shall pay to me her maidenhead ere they have it: men shall hold of me in capite; and we charge and command that their wives be as free as heart can wish or tongue can tell.

DICK

My lord, when shall we go to Cheapside and take up commodities upon our bills?

CADE

Marry, presently.

ALL

O, brave!

Re-enter one with the heads

CADE

But is not this braver? Let them kiss one another, for they loved well when they were alive. Now part them again, lest they consult about the giving up of some more towns in France. Soldiers, defer the spoil of the city until night: for with these borne before us, instead of maces, will we ride through the streets; and at every corner have them kiss. Away! [Exeunt

SCENE VIII. *Southwark*

Alarum and retreat. Enter CADE and all his rabblement

CADE

Up Fish Street! down Saint Magnus' Corner! kill and knock down! throw them into Thames! [Sound a parley.] What noise is this I hear? Dare any be so

bold to sound retreat or parley, when I command
them kill?

Enter BUCKINGHAM *and* CLIFFORD, *attended*

BUCKINGHAM

Ay, here they be that dare and will disturb thee:
Know, Cade, we come ambassadors from the king
Unto the commons whom thou hast misled;
And here pronounce free pardon to them all,
That will forsake thee and go home in peace.

CLIFFORD

What say ye, countrymen? will ye relent,
And yield to mercy whilst 'tis offer'd you;
Or let a rebel lead you to your deaths?
Who loves the king and will embrace his pardon,
Fling up his cap, and say 'God save his majesty!'
Who hateth him and honours not his father,
Henry the fifth, that made all France to quake,
Shake he his weapon at us and pass by.

ALL

God save the king! God save the king!

CADE

What, Buckingham and Clifford, are ye so brave?
And you, base peasants, do ye believe him? will you
needs be hanged with your pardons about your
necks? Hath my sword therefore broke through
London gates, that you should leave me at the White
Hart in Southwark? I thought ye would never have
given out these arms till you had recovered your ancient freedom: but you are all recreants and dastards, and delight to live in slavery to the nobility.
Let them break your backs with burthens, take your
houses over your heads, ravish your wives and
daughters before your faces: for me, I will make
shift for one; and so, God's curse light upon you all!

ALL

We'll follow Cade, we'll follow Cade!

CLIFFORD

Is Cade the son of Henry the Fifth,
That thus you do exclaim you'll go with him?
Will he conduct you through the heart of France,
And make the meanest of you earls and dukes?
Alas, he hath no home, no place to fly to;
Nor knows he how to live but by the spoil,
Unless by robbing of your friends and us.
Were 't not a shame, that whilst you live at jar,
The fearful French, whom you late vanquished,
Should make a start o'er seas and vanquish you?
Methinks already in this civil broil
I see them lording it in London streets,
Crying 'Villiago!' unto all they meet.
Better ten thousand base-born Cades miscarry,
Than you should stoop unto a Frenchman's mercy.
To France, to France, and get what you have lost;
Spare England, for it is your native coast:
Henry hath money, you are strong and manly;
God on our side, doubt not of victory.

ALL

A Clifford! a Clifford! we'll follow the king and
Clifford.

CADE

Was ever feather so lightly blown to and fro as this
multitude? The name of Henry the Fifth hales them
to an hundred mischiefs and makes them leave me
desolate. I see them lay their heads together to surprise me. My sword make way for me, for here is no
staying. In despite of the devils and hell, have
through the very middest of you! and heavens and
honour be witness that no want of resolution in me,
but only my followers' base and ignominious treasons, makes me betake me to my heels. [*Exit*

BUCKINGHAM

What, is he fled? Go some, and follow him;
And he that brings his head unto the king
Shall have a thousand crowns for his reward.

[*Exeunt some of then.*

Follow me, soldiers: we'll devise a mean
To reconcile you all unto the king. [*Exeunt*

SCENE IX. *Kenilworth Castle*

Sound trumpets. Enter KING, QUEEN, *and* SOMERSET,
on the terrace

KING

Was ever king that joy'd an earthly throne,
And could command no more content than I?
No sooner was I crept out of my cradle
But I was made a king, at nine months old.
Was never subject long'd to be a king
As I do long and wish to be a subject.

Enter BUCKINGHAM *and* CLIFFORD

BUCKINGHAM

Health and glad tidings to your majesty!

KING

Why, Buckingham, is the traitor Cade surprised?
Or is he but retired to make him strong?

Enter, below, multitudes, with halters about their necks

CLIFFORD

He is fled, my lord, and all his powers do yield;
And humbly thus, with halters on their necks,
Expect your highness' doom, of life or death.

KING

Then, heaven, set ope thy everlasting gates,
To entertain my vows of thanks and praise!
Soldiers, this day have you redeem'd your lives,
And show'd how well you love your prince and
  country:
Continue still in this so good a mind,
And Henry, though he be infortunate,
Assure yourselves, will never be unkind:
And so, with thanks and pardon to you all,
I do dismiss you to your several countries.

ALL

God save the king! God save the king!

Enter a MESSENGER

MESSENGER

Please it your grace to be advertised
The Duke of York is newly come from Ireland,
And with a puissant and a mighty power
Of gallowglasses and stout kernes

Is marching hitherward in proud array,
And still proclaimeth, as he comes along,
His arms are only to remove from thee
The Duke of Somerset, whom he terms a traitor.

KING

Thus stands my state, 'twixt Cade and York distress'd;
Like to a ship that, having 'scaped a tempest,
Is straightway calm'd and boarded with a pirate:
But now is Cade driven back, his men dispersed;
And now is York in arms to second him.
I pray thee, Buckingham, go and meet him,
And ask him what's the reason of these arms.
Tell him I'll send Duke Edmund to the Tower;
And, Somerset, we will commit thee thither,
Until his army be dismiss'd from him.

SOMERSET

My lord,
I'll yield myself to prison willingly,
Or unto death, to do my country good.

KING

In any case, be not too rough in terms;
For he is fierce and cannot brook hard language.

BUCKINGHAM

I will, my lord; and doubt not so to deal
As all things shall redound unto your good.

KING

Come, wife, let's in, and learn to govern better;
For yet may England curse my wretched reign.
[Flourish. Exeunt

SCENE X. Kent. IDEN's garden

Enter CADE

CADE

Fie on ambition! fie on myself, that have a sword,
and yet am ready to famish! These five days have I
hid me in these woods and durst not peep out, for
all the country is laid for me; but now am I so hungry
that if I might have a lease of my life for a thousand
years I could stay no longer. Wherefore, on a
brick wall have I climbed into this garden, to see if
I can eat grass, or pick a sallet another while, which
is not amiss to cool a man's stomach this hot weather.
And I think this word 'sallet' was born to do me
good: for many a time, but for a sallet, my brain-pan
had been cleft with a brown bill; and many a
time, when I have been dry and bravely marching,
it hath served me instead of a quart pot to drink in;
and now the word 'sallet' must serve me to feed on.

Enter IDEN

IDEN

Lord, who would live turmoiled in the court,
And may enjoy such quiet walks as these?
This small inheritance my father left me
Contenteth me, and worth a monarchy.
I seek not to wax great by others' waning,
Or gather wealth, I care not with what envy:
Sufficeth that I have maintains my state,
And sends the poor well pleased from my gate.

CADE

Here's the lord of the soil come to seize me for a
stray, for entering his fee-simple without leave. Ah,
villain, thou wilt betray me, and get a thousand
crowns of the king by carrying my head to him: but
I'll make thee eat iron like an ostrich, and swallow
my sword like a great pin, ere thou and I part.

IDEN

Why, rude companion, whatsoe'er thou be,
I know thee not; why then should I betray thee?
Is 't not enough to break into my garden,
And, like a thief, to come to rob my grounds,
Climbing my walls in spite of me the owner,
But thou wilt brave me with these saucy terms?

CADE

Brave thee! ay, by the best blood that ever was
broached, and beard thee too. Look on me well: I
have eat no meat these five days; yet, come thou and
thy five men, and if I do not leave you all as dead as
a door-nail, I pray God I may never eat grass more.

IDEN

Nay, it shall ne'er be said, while England stands,
That Alexander Iden, an esquire of Kent,
Took odds to combat a poor famish'd man.
Oppose thy steadfast-gazing eyes to mine,
See if thou canst outface me with thy looks:
Set limb to limb, and thou art far the lesser;
Thy hand is but a finger to my fist,
Thy leg a stick compared with this truncheon;
My foot shall fight with all the strength thou hast;
And if mine arm be heaved in the air,
Thy grave is digg'd already in the earth.
As for words, whose greatness answers words,
Let this my sword report what speech forbears.

CADE

By my valour, the most complete champion that
ever I heard! Steel, if thou turn the edge, or cut not
out the burly-boned clown in chines of beef ere thou
sleep in thy sheath, I beseech God on my knees thou
mayst be turned to hobnails.
[Here they fight. CADE falls
O, I am slain! famine and no other hath slain me:
let ten thousand devils come against me, and give
me but the ten meals I have lost, and I'ld defy
them all. Wither, garden; and be henceforth a
burying-place to all that do dwell in this house, because
the unconquered soul of Cade is fled.

IDEN

Is 't Cade that I have slain, that monstrous traitor?
Sword, I will hallow thee for this thy deed,
And hang thee o'er my tomb when I am dead:
Ne'er shall this blood be wiped from thy point;
But thou shalt wear it as a herald's coat,
To emblaze the honour that thy master got.

CADE

Iden, farewell, and be proud of thy victory. Tell
Kent from me, she hath lost her best man, and exhort
all the world to be cowards; for I, that never
feared any, am vanquished by famine, not by
valour.
[Dies

IDEN

How much thou wrong'st me, heaven be my judge.
Die, damned wretch, the curse of her that bare thee;
And as I thrust thy body in with my sword,
So wish I, I might thrust thy soul to hell.
Hence will I drag thee headlong by the heels
Unto a dunghill which shall be thy grave,
And there cut off thy most ungracious head;
Which I will bear in triumph to the king,
Leaving thy trunk for crows to feed upon.   [*Exit*

ACT V

SCENE I. *Fields between Dartford and Blackheath*

Enter YORK, *and his army of Irish, with drum and colours*

YORK

From Ireland thus comes York to claim his right,
And pluck the crown from feeble Henry's head:
Ring, bells, aloud; burn, bonfires, clear and bright,
To entertain great England's lawful king.
Ah! sancta majestas, who would not buy thee dear?
Let them obey that know not how to rule;
This hand was made to handle nought but gold.
I cannot give due action to my words,
Except a sword or sceptre balance it:
A sceptre shall it have, have I a soul,
On which I'll toss the flower-de-luce of France.

Enter BUCKINGHAM

Whom have we here? Buckingham, to disturb me?
The king hath sent him, sure: I must dissemble.

BUCKINGHAM

York, if thou meanest well, I greet thee well.

YORK

Humphrey of Buckingham, I accept thy greeting.
Art thou a messenger, or come of pleasure?

BUCKINGHAM

A messenger from Henry, our dread liege,
To know the reason of these arms in peace;
Or why thou, being a subject as I am,
Against thy oath and true allegiance sworn,
Should raise so great a power without his leave,
Or dare to bring thy force so near the court.

YORK

[*Aside*] Scarce can I speak, my choler is so great:
O, I could hew up rocks and fight with flint,
I am so angry at these abject terms;
And now, like Ajax Telamonius,
On sheep or oxen could I spend my fury.
I am far better born than is the king,
More like a king, more kingly in my thoughts:
But I must make fair weather yet a while,
Till Henry be more weak and I more strong.—
Buckingham, I prithee, pardon me,
That I have given no answer all this while;
My mind was troubled with deep melancholy.
The cause why I have brought this army hither
Is to remove proud Somerset from the king,
Seditious to his grace and to the state.

BUCKINGHAM

That is too much presumption on thy part:
But if thy arms be to no other end,
The king hath yielded unto thy demand:
The Duke of Somerset is in the Tower.

YORK

Upon thine honour, is he prisoner?

BUCKINGHAM

Upon mine honour, he is prisoner.

YORK

Then, Buckingham, I do dismiss my powers.
Soldiers, I thank you all; disperse yourselves;
Meet me to-morrow in Saint George's field,
You shall have pay and every thing you wish.
And let my sovereign, virtuous Henry,
Command my eldest son, nay, all my sons,
As pledges of my fealty and love;
I'll send them all as willing as I live:
Lands, goods, horse, armour, any thing I have,
Is his to use, so Somerset may die.

BUCKINGHAM

York, I commend this kind submission:
We twain will go into his highness' tent.

Enter KING *and* ATTENDANTS

KING

Buckingham, doth York intend no harm to us,
That thus he marcheth with thee arm in arm?

YORK

In all submission and humility
York doth present himself unto your highness.

KING

Then what intends these forces thou dost bring?

YORK

To heave the traitor Somerset from hence,
And fight against that monstrous rebel Cade,
Who since I heard to be discomfited.

Enter IDEN, *with* CADE's *head*

IDEN

If one so rude and of so mean condition
May pass into the presence of a king,
Lo, I present your grace a traitor's head,
The head of Cade, whom I in combat slew.

KING

The head of Cade! Great God, how just art Thou!
O, let me view his visage, being dead,
That living wrought me such exceeding trouble.
Tell me, my friend, art thou the man that slew him?

IDEN

I was, an 't like your majesty.

KING

How art thou call'd? and what is thy degree?

IDEN

Alexander Iden, that's my name;
A poor esquire of Kent, that loves his king.

BUCKINGHAM

So please it you, my lord, 'twere not amiss
He were created knight for his good service.

KING

Iden, kneel down. [*He kneels.*] Rise up a knight.

We give thee for reward a thousand marks,
And will that thou henceforth attend on us.

IDEN

May Iden live to merit such a bounty,
And never live but true unto his liege!　　　[*Rises*

Enter QUEEN *and* SOMERSET

KING

See, Buckingham, Somerset comes with the queen:
Go, bid her hide him quickly from the duke.

QUEEN

For thousand Yorks he shall not hide his head,
But boldly stand and front him to his face.

YORK

How now! is Somerset at liberty?
Then, York, unloose thy long-imprison'd thoughts,
And let thy tongue be equal with thy heart.
Shall I endure the sight of Somerset?
False king! why hast thou broken faith with me,
Knowing how hardly I can brook abuse?
King did I call thee? no, thou art not king,
Not fit to govern and rule multitudes,
Which darest not, no, nor canst not rule a traitor.
That head of thine doth not become a crown;
Thy hand is made to grasp a palmer's staff,
And not to grace an awful princely sceptre.
That gold must round engirt these brows of mine,
Whose smile and frown, like to Achilles' spear,
Is able with the change to kill and cure.
Here is a hand to hold a sceptre up,
And with the same to act controlling laws.
Give place: by heaven, thou shalt rule no more
O'er him whom heaven created for thy ruler.

SOMERSET

O monstrous traitor! I arrest thee, York,
Of capital treason 'gainst the king and crown:
Obey, audacious traitor; kneel for grace.

YORK

Wouldst have me kneel? first let me ask of these,
If they can brook I bow a knee to man.
Sirrah, call in my sons to be my bail:

[*Exit* ATTENDANT

I know, ere they will have me go to ward,
They'll pawn their swords for my enfranchisement.

QUEEN

Call hither Clifford; bid him come amain,
To say if that the bastard boys of York
Shall be the surety for their traitor father.

[*Exit* BUCKINGHAM

YORK

O blood-bespotted Neapolitan,
Outcast of Naples, England's bloody scourge!
The sons of York, thy betters in their birth,
Shall be their father's bail; and bane to those
That for my surety will refuse the boys!

Enter EDWARD *and* RICHARD

See where they come: I'll warrant they'll make it
　　good.

Enter CLIFFORD *and her son*

QUEEN

And here comes Clifford to deny their bail.

CLIFFORD

Health and all happiness to my lord the king!

[*Kneels*

YORK

I thank thee, Clifford: say, what news with thee?
Nay, do not fright us with an angry look:
We are thy sovereign, Clifford, kneel again;
For thy mistaking so, we pardon thee.

CLIFFORD

This is my king, York, I do not mistake;
But thou mistakest me much to think I do:
To Bedlam with him! is the man grown mad?

KING

Ay, Clifford; a bedlam and ambitious humour
Makes him oppose himself against his king.

CLIFFORD

He is a traitor; let him to the Tower,
And chop away that factious pate of his.

QUEEN

He is arrested, but will not obey;
His sons, he says, shall give their words for him.

YORK

Will you not, sons?

EDWARD

Ay, noble father, if our words will serve.

RICHARD

And if words will not, then our weapons shall.

CLIFFORD

Why, what a brood of traitors have we here!

YORK

Look in a glass, and call thy image so:
I am thy king, and thou a false-heart traitor.
Call hither to the stake my two brave bears,
That with the very shaking of their chains
They may astonish these fell-lurking curs:
Bid Salisbury and Warwick come to me.

Enter the EARLS OF WARWICK *and* SALISBURY

CLIFFORD

Are these thy bears? we'll bait thy bears to death,
And manacle the bear-ward in their chains,
If thou darest bring them to the baiting place.

RICHARD

Oft have I seen a hot o'erweening cur
Run back and bite, because he was withheld;
Who, being suffer'd with the bear's fell paw,
Hath clapp'd his tail between his legs and cried:
And such a piece of service will you do,
If you oppose yourselves to match Lord Warwick.

CLIFFORD

Hence, heap of wrath, foul indigested lump,
As crooked in thy manners as thy shape!

YORK

Nay, we shall heat you thoroughly anon.

CLIFFORD

Take heed, lest by your heat you burn yourselves.

KING

Why, Warwick, hath thy knee forgot to bow?
Old Salisbury, shame to thy silver hair,
Thou mad misleader of thy brain-sick son!
What, wilt thou on thy death-bed play the ruffian,

And seek for sorrow with thy spectacles?
O, where is faith? O, where is loyalty?
If it be banish'd from the frosty head,
Where shall it find a harbour in the earth?
Wilt thou go dig a grave to find out war,
And shame thine honourable age with blood?
Why art thou old, and want'st experience?
Or wherefore dost abuse it, if thou hast it?
For shame! in duty bend thy knee to me,
That bows unto the grave with mickle age.

SALISBURY

My lord, I have consider'd with myself
The title of this most renowned duke;
And in my conscience do repute his grace
The rightful heir to England's royal seat.

KING

Hast thou not sworn allegiance unto me?

SALISBURY

I have.

KING

Canst thou dispense with heaven for such an oath?

SALISBURY

It is great sin to swear unto a sin,
But greater sin to keep a sinful oath.
Who can be bound by any solemn vow
To do a murderous deed, to rob a man,
To force a spotless virgin's chastity,
To reave the orphan of his patrimony,
To wring the widow from her custom'd right,
And have no other reason for this wrong
But that he was bound by a solemn oath?

QUEEN

A subtle traitor needs no sophister.

KING

Call Buckingham, and bid him arm himself.

YORK

Call Buckingham, and all the friends thou hast,
I am resolved for death or dignity.

CLIFFORD

The first I warrant thee, if dreams prove true.

WARWICK

You were best to go to bed and dream again,
To keep thee from the tempest of the field.

CLIFFORD

I am resolved to bear a greater storm
Than any thou canst conjure up to-day;
And that I'll write upon thy burgonet,
Might I but know thee by thy household badge.

WARWICK

Now, by my father's badge, old Nevil's crest,
The rampant bear chain'd to the ragged staff,
This day I'll wear aloft my burgonet,
As on a mountain top the cedar shows
That keeps his leaves in spite of any storm,
Even to affright thee with the view thereof.

CLIFFORD

And from thy burgonet I'll rend thy bear,
And tread it under foot with all contempt,
Despite the bear-ward that protects the bear.

YOUNG CLIFFORD

And so to arms, victorious father,
To quell the rebels and their complices.

RICHARD

Fie! charity, for shame! speak not in spite,
For you shall sup with Jesu Christ to-night.

YOUNG CLIFFORD

Foul stigmatic, that's more than thou canst tell.

RICHARD

If not in heaven, you'll surely sup in hell.

[Exeunt severally

SCENE II. Saint Alban's

Alarums to the battle. Enter WARWICK

WARWICK

Clifford of Cumberland, 'tis Warwick calls:
And if thou dost not hide thee from the bear,
Now, when the angry trumpet sounds alarum,
And dead men's cries do fill the empty air,
Clifford, I say, come forth and fight with me:
Proud northern lord, Clifford of Cumberland,
Warwick is hoarse with calling thee to arms.

Enter YORK

How now, my noble lord! what, all a-foot?

YORK

The deadly-handed Clifford slew my steed,
But match to match I have encounter'd him,
And made a prey for carrion kites and crows
Even of the bonny beast he loved so well.

Enter CLIFFORD

WARWICK

Of one or both of us the time is come.

YORK

Hold, Warwick, seek thee out some other chase,
For I myself must hunt this deer to death.

WARWICK

Then, nobly, York; 'tis for a crown thou fight'st.
As I intend, Clifford, to thrive to-day,
It grieves my soul to leave thee unassail'd.   [Exit

CLIFFORD

What seest thou in me, York? why dost thou pause?

YORK

With thy brave bearing should I be in love,
But that thou art so fast mine enemy.

CLIFFORD

Nor should thy prowess want praise and esteem
But that 'tis shown ignobly and in treason.

YORK

So let it help me now against thy sword,
As I in justice and true right express it.

CLIFFORD

My soul and body on the action both!

YORK

A dreadful lay! Address thee instantly.

[They fight, and CLIFFORD falls

CLIFFORD

La fin couronne les œuvres.   [Dies

YORK

Thus war hath given thee peace, for thou art still.

[71]

Peace with his soul, heaven, if it be thy will!   [*Exit*
Enter YOUNG CLIFFORD
YOUNG CLIFFORD
Shame and confusion! all is on the rout;
Fear frames disorder, and disorder wounds
Where it should guard. O war, thou son of hell,
Whom angry heavens do make their minister,
Throw in the frozen bosoms of our part
Hot coals of vengeance! Let no soldier fly.
He that is truly dedicate to war
Hath no self-love, nor he that loves himself
Hath not essentially but by circumstance
The name of valour. [*Seeing his dead father*] O, let
    the vile world end,
And the premised flames of the last day
Knit earth and heaven together!
Now let the general trumpet blow his blast,
Particularities and petty sounds
To cease! Wast thou ordain'd, dear father,
To lose thy youth in peace, and to achieve
The silver livery of advised age,
And, in thy reverence and thy chair-days, thus
To die in ruffian battle? Even at this sight
My heart is turn'd to stone: and while 'tis mine,
It shall be stony. York not our old men spares;
No more will I their babes: tears virginal
Shall be to me even as the dew to fire,
And beauty that the tyrant oft reclaims
Shall to my flaming wrath be oil and flax.
Henceforth I will not have to do with pity:
Meet I an infant of the house of York,
Into as many gobbets will I cut it
As wild Medea young Absyrtus did:
In cruelty will I seek out my fame.
Come, thou new ruin of old Clifford's house:
As did Æneas old Anchises bear,
So bear I thee upon my manly shoulders;
But then Æneas bare a living load,
Nothing so heavy as these woes of mine.
    [*Exit, bearing off his father*
Enter RICHARD *and* SOMERSET *to fight.* SOMERSET IS
    killed
RICHARD
So, lie thou there;
For underneath an alehouse' paltry sign,
The Castle in Saint Alban's, Somerset
Hath made the wizard famous in his death.
Sword, hold thy temper; heart, be wrathful still:
Priests pray for enemies, but princes kill.   [*Exit*
Fight. Excursions. Enter KING, QUEEN, *and others*
QUEEN
Away, my lord! you are slow; for shame, away!
KING
Can we outrun the heavens? good Margaret, stay.
QUEEN
What are you made of? you'll nor fight nor fly:
Now is it manhood, wisdom and defence,
To give the enemy way, and to secure us
By what we can, which can no more but fly.
    [*Alarum afar off*

If you be ta'en, we then should see the bottom
Of all our fortunes: but if we haply scape,
As well we may, if not through your neglect,
We shall to London get, where you are loved,
And where this breach now in our fortunes made
May readily be stopp'd.
    Re-enter YOUNG CLIFFORD
YOUNG CLIFFORD
But that my heart's on future mischief set,
I would speak blasphemy ere bid you fly:
But fly you must; uncurable discomfit
Reigns in the hearts of all our present parts.
Away, for your relief! and we will live
To see their day and them our fortune give:
Away, my lord, away!   [*Exeunt*

SCENE III. *Fields near St. Alban's*

Alarum. Retreat. Enter YORK, RICHARD, WARWICK,
and SOLDIERS, *with drum and colours*
YORK
Of Salisbury, who can report of him,
That winter lion, who in rage forgets
Aged contusions and all brush of time,
And, like a gallant in the brow of youth,
Repairs him with occasion? This happy day
Is not itself, nor have we won one foot,
If Salisbury be lost.
RICHARD
My noble father,
Three times to-day I holp him to his horse,
Three times bestrid him; thrice I led him off,
Persuaded him from any further act:
But still, where danger was, still there I met him;
And like rich hangings in a homely house,
So was his will in his old feeble body.
But, noble as he is, look where he comes.
Enter SALISBURY
SALISBURY
Now, by my sword, well hast thou fought to-day;
By the mass, so did we all. I thank you, Richard:
God knows how long it is I have to live;
And it hath pleased him that three times to-day
You have defended me from imminent death.
Well, lords, we have not got that which we have:
'Tis not enough our foes are this time fled,
Being opposites of such repairing nature.
YORK
I know our safety is to follow them;
For, as I hear, the king is fled to London,
To call a present court of parliament.
Let us pursue him ere the writs go forth.
What says Lord Warwick? shall we after them?
WARWICK
After them! nay, before them, if we can.
Now, by my faith, lords, 'twas a glorious day:
Saint Alban's battle won by famous York
Shall be eternized in all age to come.
Sound drums and trumpets, and to London all:
And more such days as these to us befall!   [*Exeunt*

THE THIRD PART OF KING HENRY VI

SYNOPSIS

Henry VI and his adherents arrive in London after the battle of St. Albans to find Richard of York seated on the throne in the House of Parliament, surrounded by his sons and followers, and upheld in his demand for the crown by the Earl of Warwick, now known as the king-maker. Each contends that the other must yield, York arguing that Henry has held the crown through the usurpation of his rebellious grandfather, Henry IV, but when upon a signal from Warwick the chamber is filled with armed men, Henry surrenders, disinheriting his own son Prince Edward of Wales and weakly begging to be allowed to wear the crown during his lifetime, with York as Protector of the Realm and Warwick as Chancellor. The King's noblemen denounce his act with bitter speech, leaving him alone to face the railing of the irate Queen Margaret who proceeds to raise an army against the York faction.

At his home in Sandal Castle, York has just yielded to the ambitious plans of his sons, Edward and Richard, to claim the throne without further delay, when word is brought of Margaret advancing with an army greatly outnumbering their forces, and, sneering in over-confidence at the woman-general, his family goes down to defeat in a battle near Wakefield.

Encountering York's youngest son, the Earl of Rutland, as he tries to escape from the castle with his tutor, the raging Clifford, thirsting for revenge, kills the lad as he pleads piteously for his life. York himself is captured in a moment of exhaustion after the fierce fighting, and the Queen mocks him by placing a paper crown on his head before Clifford and she brutally stab him to death, afterwards ordering his head set up over the gates of York.

Warwick, whose forces have suffered defeat in an engagement with the Queen's army at St. Albans, now joins Edward and Richard, sons of the dead York, and together they resolve to fight to the finish. After defying each other in a parley of insults and recriminations, the enemy factions meet near Towton in Yorkshire, where the King, reproached by Clifford and the Queen for his lack of pluck, awaits the fate of battle from a distance and grieves as he witnesses father slaying son, and son, father, in civil war. Margaret is defeated and flees to France with her son Prince Edward; the King takes refuge in Scotland; Clifford dies of wounds and is beheaded; while Edward of York is declared King Edward IV, his brother George is made Duke of Clarence, and the hunchback Richard, Duke of Gloucester. Soon pining for the sight of his own country, the deposed King Henry steals back to England through a forest where he is recognized by two gamekeepers, sent to London and imprisoned in the Tower.

Immediately after Edward's coronation, Warwick hastens to France to cement relations between the two countries by obtaining for the new monarch the hand of Lewis XI's sister-in-law Bona, but in his absence Edward falls in love with the Lady Elizabeth Grey when she appears before him to beg for the rights of her fatherless children, and since she will not consider dishonorable relations he imprudently marries her. At the French court, Warwick meets and is hotly denounced by Queen Margaret who is bent on securing Lewis' help to regain the English crown for Henry, but in spite of her opposition the proposed marriage is arranged. Just as the negotiations are being completed, however, news of Edward's marriage to Lady Grey arrives, and, thoroughly incensed at this breach of honor with the French and the insult to himself, Warwick renounces his allegiance to King Edward and joins forces with Lewis and Margaret to restore Henry to the throne, offering, as a pledge of good faith, the hand of his eldest daughter to the manly young Prince Edward of Wales.

York's treacherous sons, Gloucester and Clarence, having quarreled, Gloucester, to further his own dark schemes, supports Edward, while Clarence joins Warwick and is betrothed to his second daughter. The invading forces are successful, Edward is captured and deposed, Henry is released from the Tower and placed on the throne, but resigns his government to Warwick and Clarence in order to retire to a simple life.

Escaping to Burgundy by Gloucester's aid, Edward soon returns with an army with which he recovers the York estates, marches on London, throws Henry back in prison, and, resuming the crown, sets out to Coventry to meet Warwick. Just as the Earl is mustering all his available forces for the battle, the deceitful Clarence, at the instigation of Gloucester, removes the red rose from his helmet, deserts Warwick with a large body of troops, and the great king-maker is overthrown and slain, fighting valiantly. Margaret, bringing reinforcements from France, is defeated near Tewkesbury and taken prisoner with Prince Edward who is cruelly stabbed by the three York brothers as he stoutly maintains his rights to the throne. Gloucester, intent on paving his own way to the throne, hastens to the Tower in London and kills Henry as he is quietly reading. Edward and Elizabeth with their infant son reclaim the throne; Queen Margaret is ransomed by her father; and the sinister Gloucester bides his time.

HISTORICAL DATA

This continuation of the history of the Houses of Yorke and Lancaster appears to have come directly from *The True Tragedie of Richard Duke of Yorke and the Death of good King Henrie the Sixt* which was published in quarto form in 1595, and is one of the plays attributed variously to Marlowe, Greene, Peele and Shakespeare himself.

In general, authorities incline to the opinion that the quarto editions of both Part Two and Part Three (1594–1595) are garbled acting versions, and that from correct copies Shakespeare prepared the revised versions that, with a few important additions, appeared in the First Folio.

"*A crown to York;—and, lords, bow low to him.—*"
HENRY VI, PART III

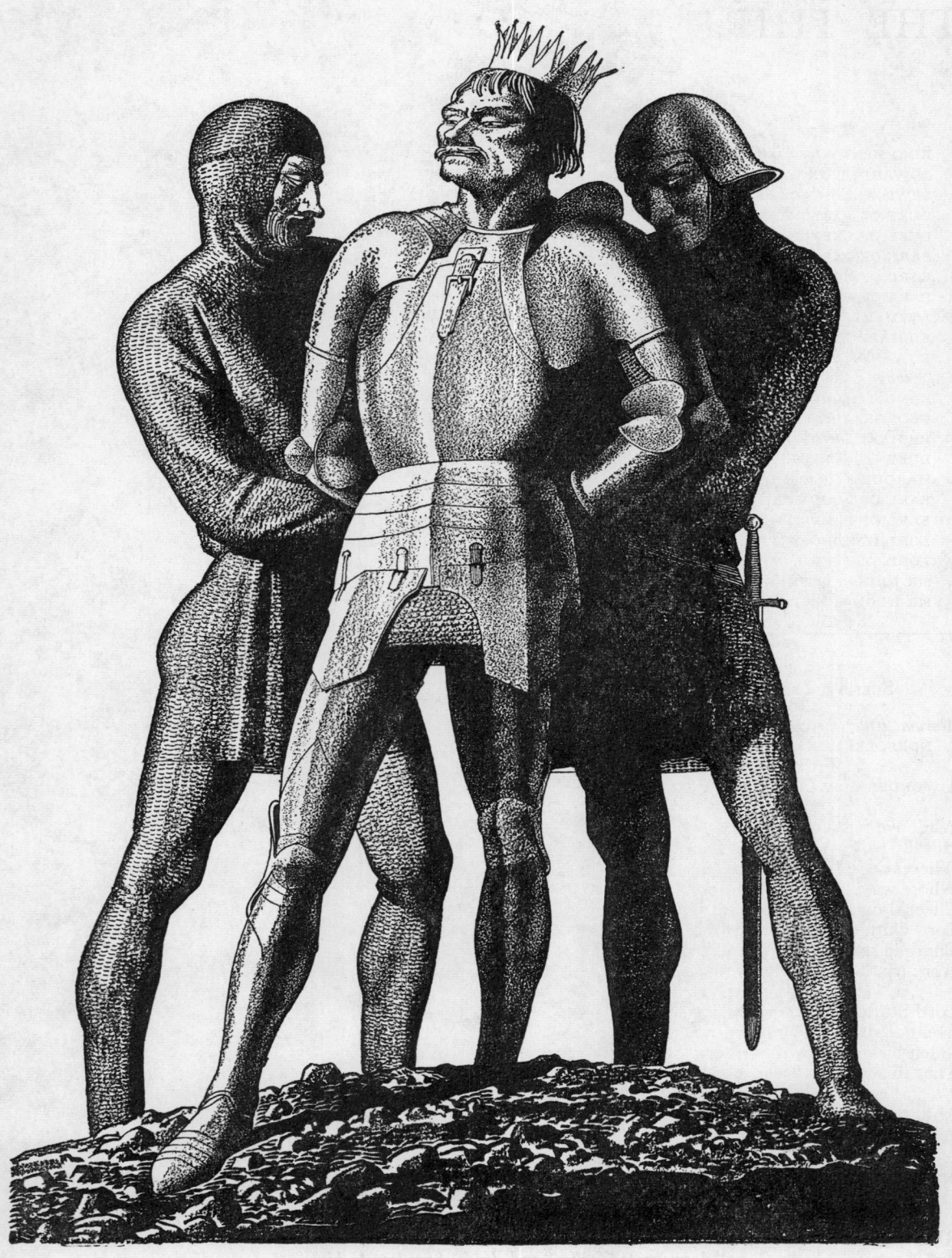

A group in York Minster Tomb, dating from King Henry VI, Part III

THE THIRD PART OF KING HENRY VI

DRAMATIS PERSONÆ

KING HENRY the Sixth.
EDWARD, PRINCE OF WALES, his son.
LEWIS XI. KING OF FRANCE.
DUKE OF SOMERSET.
DUKE OF EXETER.
EARL OF OXFORD.
EARL OF NORTHUMBERLAND.
EARL OF WESTMORELAND.
LORD CLIFFORD.
RICHARD PLANTAGENET, Duke of York.
EDWARD, Earl of March, afterwards
    King Edward IV.,
EDMUND, Earl of Rutland, } his sons.
GEORGE, afterwards Duke of Clarence,
RICHARD, afterwards Duke of Gloucester,
DUKE OF NORFOLK.
MARQUESS OF MONTAGUE.
EARL OF WARWICK.
EARL OF PEMBROKE.
LORD HASTINGS.
LORD STAFFORD.
SIR JOHN MORTIMER, } uncles to the Duke of York.
SIR HUGH MORTIMER,

HENRY, Earl of Richmond, a youth.
LORD RIVERS, brother to Lady Grey.
SIR WILLIAM STANLEY.
SIR JOHN MONTGOMERY.
SIR JOHN SOMERVILE.
TUTOR to Rutland.
MAYOR of York.
LIEUTENANT of the Tower.
A NOBLEMAN.
TWO KEEPERS.
A HUNTSMAN.
A SON that has killed his father.
A FATHER that has killed his son.

QUEEN MARGARET.
LADY GREY, afterwards Queen to Edward IV.
BONA, sister to the French Queen.

SOLDIERS, ATTENDANTS, MESSENGERS, WATCH-
    MEN, &c.

SCENE—England and France.

ACT I
SCENE I. London. The Parliament-house

Alarum. Enter the DUKE OF YORK, EDWARD, RICHARD,
NORFOLK, MONTAGUE, WARWICK, *and* SOLDIERS

WARWICK

I WONDER how the king escaped our hands.

YORK

While we pursued the horsemen of the north,
He slily stole away and left his men:
Whereat the great Lord of Northumberland,
Whose warlike ears could never brook retreat,
Cheer'd up the drooping army; and himself,
Lord Clifford and Lord Stafford, all a-breast,
Charged our main battle's front, and breaking in
Were by the swords of common soldiers slain.

EDWARD

Lord Stafford's father, Duke of Buckingham,
Is either slain or wounded dangerously;
I cleft his beaver with a downright blow:
That this is true, father, behold his blood.

MONTAGUE

And, brother, here's the Earl of Wiltshire's blood,
Whom I encounter'd as the battles join'd.

RICHARD

Speak thou for me and tell them what I did.
    [*Throwing down the* DUKE OF SOMERSET's *head*

YORK

Richard hath best deserved of all my sons.
But is your grace dead, my Lord of Somerset?

NORFOLK

Such hope have all the line of John of Gaunt!

RICHARD

Thus do I hope to shake King Henry's head.

WARWICK

And so do I. Victorious Prince of York,
Before I see thee seated in that throne
Which now the house of Lancaster usurps,
I vow by heaven these eyes shall never close.
This is the palace of the fearful king,
And this the regal seat: possess it, York;
For this is thine, and not King Henry's heirs'.

YORK

Assist me, then, sweet Warwick, and I will;
For hither we have broken in by force.

NORFOLK

We'll all assist you; he that flies shall die.

YORK

Thanks, gentle Norfolk: stay by me, my lords;
And, soldiers, stay and lodge by me this night.
    [*They go up*

WARWICK

And when the king comes, offer him no violence,
Unless he seek to thrust you out perforce.

YORK

The queen this day here holds her parliament,
But little thinks we shall be of her council:
By words or blows here let us win our right.

RICHARD

Arm'd as we are, let's stay within this house.

WARWICK

The bloody parliament shall this be call'd,
Unless Plantagenet, Duke of York, be king,
And bashful Henry deposed, whose cowardice
Hath made us by-words to our enemies.

YORK

Then leave me not, my lords; be resolute:
I mean to take possession of my right.

WARWICK

Neither the king, nor he that loves him best,
The proudest he that holds up Lancaster,
Dares stir a wing, if Warwick shake his bells.
I'll plant Plantagenet, root him up who dares:
Resolve thee, Richard; claim the English crown.

Flourish. Enter KING HENRY, CLIFFORD, NORTHUMBER-
LAND, WESTMORELAND, EXETER, *and the rest*

KING HENRY

My lords, look where the sturdy rebel sits,
Even in the chair of state: belike he means,
Back'd by the power of Warwick, that false peer,
To aspire unto the crown and reign as king.
Earl of Northumberland, he slew thy father,
And thine, Lord Clifford; and you both have vow'd
    revenge
On him, his sons, his favourites and his friends.

NORTHUMBERLAND

If I be not, heavens be revenged on me!

CLIFFORD

The hope thereof makes Clifford mourn in steel.

WESTMORELAND

What, shall we suffer this? let's pluck him down:
My heart for anger burns; I cannot brook it.

KING HENRY

Be patient, gentle Earl of Westmoreland.

CLIFFORD

Patience is for poltroons, such as he:
He durst not sit there, had your father lived.
My gracious lord, here in the parliament
Let us assail the family of York.

NORTHUMBERLAND

Well hast thou spoken, cousin: be it so.

KING HENRY

Ah, know you not the city favours them,
And they have troops of soldiers at their beck?

EXETER

But when the duke is slain, they'll quickly fly.

KING HENRY

Far be the thought of this from Henry's heart,
To make a shambles of the parliament-house!
Cousin of Exeter, frowns, words and threats
Shall be the war that Henry means to use.
Thou factious Duke of York, descend my throne,
And kneel for grace and mercy at my feet;
I am thy sovereign.

YORK
I am thine.

EXETER

For shame, come down: he made thee Duke of
    York.

YORK

'Twas my inheritance, as the earldom was.

EXETER

Thy father was a traitor to the crown.

WARWICK

Exeter, thou art a traitor to the crown,
In following this usurping Henry.

CLIFFORD

Whom should he follow but his natural king?

WARWICK

True, Clifford; and that's Richard Duke of York.

KING HENRY

And shall I stand, and thou sit in my throne?

YORK

It must and shall be so: content thyself.

WARWICK

Be Duke of Lancaster; let him be king.

WESTMORELAND

He is both king and Duke of Lancaster;
And that the Lord of Westmoreland shall maintain.

WARWICK

And Warwick shall disprove it. You forget
That we are those which chased you from the field,
And slew your fathers, and with colours spread
March'd through the city to the palace gates.

NORTHUMBERLAND

Yes, Warwick, I remember it to my grief;
And, by his soul, thou and thy house shall rue it.

WESTMORELAND

Plantagenet, of thee and these thy sons,
Thy kinsmen and thy friends, I'll have more lives
Than drops of blood were in my father's veins.

CLIFFORD

Urge it no more; lest that, instead of words,
I send thee, Warwick, such a messenger
As shall revenge his death before I stir.

WARWICK

Poor Clifford! how I scorn his worthless threats!

YORK

Will you we show our title to the crown?
If not, our swords shall plead it in the field.

KING HENRY

What title hast thou, traitor, to the crown?
Thy father was, as thou art, Duke of York;
Thy grandfather, Roger Mortimer, Earl of March:
I am the son of Henry the Fifth,
Who made the Dauphin and the French to stoop,
And seized upon their towns and provinces.

WARWICK

Talk not of France, sith thou hast lost it all.

KING HENRY

The lord protector lost it, and not I:
When I was crown'd I was but nine months old.

RICHARD

You are old enough now, and yet, methinks, you
    lose.
Father, tear the crown from the usurper's head.

EDWARD

Sweet father, do so; set it on your head.

MONTAGUE

Good brother, as thou lovest and honourest arms,
Let's fight it out and not stand cavilling thus.

RICHARD

Sound drums and trumpets, and the king will fly.

YORK

Sons, peace!

KING HENRY

Peace, thou! and give King Henry leave to speak.

WARWICK

Plantagenet shall speak first: hear him, lords;
And be you silent and attentive too,
For he that interrupts him shall not live.

KING HENRY

Think'st thou that I will leave my kingly throne,
Wherein my grandsire and my father sat?
No: first shall war unpeople this my realm;
Ay, and their colours, often borne in France,
And now in England to our heart's great sorrow,
Shall be my winding-sheet. Why faint you, lords?
My title's good, and better far than his.

WARWICK

Prove it, Henry, and thou shalt be king.

KING HENRY

Henry the Fourth by conquest got the crown.

YORK

'Twas by rebellion against his king.

KING HENRY

[Aside] I know not what to say; my title's weak.
Tell me, may not a king adopt an heir?

YORK

What then?

KING HENRY

An if he may, then am I lawful king;
For Richard, in the view of many lords,
Resign'd the crown to Henry the Fourth,
Whose heir my father was, and I am his.

YORK

He rose against him, being his sovereign,
And made him to resign his crown perforce.

WARWICK

Suppose, my lords, he did it unconstrain'd,
Think you 'twere prejudicial to his crown?

EXETER

No; for he could not so resign his crown
But that the next heir should succeed and reign.

KING HENRY

Art thou against us, Duke of Exeter?

EXETER

His is the right, and therefore pardon me.

YORK

Why whisper you, my lords, and answer not?

EXETER

My conscience tells me he is lawful king.

KING HENRY

[Aside] All will revolt from me, and turn to him.

NORTHUMBERLAND

Plantagenet, for all the claim thou lay'st,
Think not that Henry shall be so deposed.

WARWICK

Deposed he shall be, in despite of all.

NORTHUMBERLAND

Thou art deceived: 'tis not thy southern power,
Of Essex, Norfolk, Suffolk, nor of Kent,
Which makes thee thus presumptuous and proud
Can set the duke up in despite of me.

CLIFFORD

King Henry, be thy title right or wrong,
Lord Clifford vows to fight in thy defence:
May that ground gape and swallow me alive,
Where I shall kneel to him that slew my father!

KING HENRY

O Clifford, how thy words revive my heart!

YORK

Henry of Lancaster, resign thy crown.
What mutter you, or what conspire you, lords?

WARWICK

Do right unto this princely Duke of York,
Or I will fill the house with armed men,
And over the chair of state, where now he sits,
Write up his title with usurping blood.
[He stamps with his foot, and the SOLDIERS show them-
selves

KING HENRY

My Lord of Warwick, hear me but one word:
Let me for this my life-time reign as king.

YORK

Confirm the crown to me and to mine heirs,
And thou shalt reign in quiet while thou livest.

KING HENRY

I am content: Richard Plantagenet,
Enjoy the kingdom after my decease.

CLIFFORD

What wrong is this unto the prince your son!

WARWICK

What good is this to England and himself!

WESTMORELAND

Base, fearful and despairing Henry!

CLIFFORD

How hast thou injured both thyself and us!

WESTMORELAND

I cannot stay to hear these articles.

NORTHUMBERLAND

Nor I.

CLIFFORD

Come, cousin, let us tell the queen these news.

WESTMORELAND

Farewell, faint-hearted and degenerate king,
In whose cold blood no spark of honour bides.

NORTHUMBERLAND

Be thou a prey unto the house of York,
And die in bands for this unmanly deed!

CLIFFORD

In dreadful war mayst thou be overcome,
Or live in peace abandon'd and despised!
[Exeunt
NORTHUMBERLAND, CLIFFORD, and WESTMORELAND

WARWICK

Turn this way, Henry, and regard them not.

EXETER

They seek revenge and therefore will not yield.

KING HENRY

Ah, Exeter!

WARWICK

Why should you sigh, my lord?

KING HENRY

Not for myself, Lord Warwick, but my son,
Whom I unnaturally shall disinherit.
But be it as it may: I here entail
The crown to thee and to thine heirs for ever;
Conditionally, that here thou take an oath
To cease this civil war, and, whilst I live,
To honour me as thy king and sovereign,
And neither by treason nor hostility
To seek to put me down and reign thyself.

YORK

This oath I willingly take and will perform.

WARWICK

Long live King Henry! Plantagenet, embrace him.

KING HENRY

And long live thou and these thy forward sons!

YORK

Now York and Lancaster are reconciled.

EXETER

Accursed be he that seeks to make them foes!

[Sennet. Here they come down

YORK

Farewell, my gracious lord; I'll to my castle.

WARWICK

And I'll keep London with my soldiers.

NORFOLK

And I to Norfolk with my followers.

MONTAGUE

And I unto the sea from whence I came.

[Exeunt YORK and his SONS, WARWICK, NORFOLK,
MONTAGUE, their SOLDIERS, and ATTENDANTS

KING HENRY

And I, with grief and sorrow, to the court.

Enter QUEEN MARGARET and the PRINCE OF WALES

EXETER

Here comes the queen, whose looks bewray her
anger:
I'll steal away.

KING HENRY

Exeter, so will I.

QUEEN MARGARET

Nay, go not from me; I will follow thee.

KING HENRY

Be patient, gentle queen, and I will stay.

QUEEN MARGARET

Who can be patient in such extremes?
Ah, wretched man! would I had died a maid,
And never seen thee, never borne thee son,
Seeing thou hast proved so unnatural a father!
Hath he deserved to lose his birthright thus?
Hadst thou but loved him half so well as I,
Or felt that pain which I did for him once,
Or nourish'd him as I did with my blood,

Thou wouldst have left thy dearest heart-blood
there,
Rather than have made that savage duke thine
heir,
And disinherited thine only son.

PRINCE

Father, you cannot disinherit me:
If you be king, why should not I succeed?

KING HENRY

Pardon me, Margaret; pardon me, sweet son:
The Earl of Warwick and the duke enforced me.

QUEEN MARGARET

Enforced thee! art thou king, and wilt be forced?
I shame to hear thee speak. Ah, timorous wretch!
Thou hast undone thyself, thy son, and me;
And given unto the house of York such head,
As thou shalt reign but by their sufferance.
To entail him and his heirs unto the crown,
What is it, but to make thy sepulchre,
And creep into it far before thy time?
Warwick is chancellor and the lord of Calais;
Stern Falconbridge commands the narrow seas;
The duke is made protector of the realm;
And yet shalt thou be safe? such safety finds
The trembling lamb environed with wolves.
Had I been there, which am a silly woman,
The soldiers should have toss'd me on their pikes,
Before I would have granted to that act.
But thou preferr'st thy life before thine honour:
And seeing thou dost, I here divorce myself
Both from thy table, Henry, and thy bed,
Until that act of parliament be repeal'd,
Whereby my son is disinherited.
The northern lords that have forsworn thy colours
Will follow mine, if once they see them spread;
And spread they shall be, to thy foul disgrace
And utter ruin of the house of York.
Thus do I leave thee. Come, son, let's away;
Our army is ready; come, we'll after them.

KING HENRY

Stay, gentle Margaret, and hear me speak.

QUEEN MARGARET

Thou hast spoke too much already: get thee gone.

KING HENRY

Gentle son Edward, thou wilt stay with me?

QUEEN MARGARET

Ay, to be murder'd by his enemies.

PRINCE

When I return with victory from the field
I'll see your grace: till then I'll follow her.

QUEEN MARGARET

Come, son, away; we may not linger thus.

[Exeunt QUEEN MARGARET and the PRINCE

KING HENRY

Poor queen! how love to me and to her son
Hath made her break out into terms of rage!
Revenged may she be on that hateful duke,
Whose haughty spirit, winged with desire,
Will cost my crown, and like an empty eagle
Tire on the flesh of me and of my son!

The loss of those three lords torments my heart:
I'll write unto them and entreat them fair.
Come, cousin, you shall be the messenger.

EXETER

And I, I hope, shall reconcile them all.   [*Exeunt*

SCENE II. *Sandal Castle*

Enter RICHARD, EDWARD, *and* MONTAGUE

RICHARD

Brother, though I be youngest, give me leave.

EDWARD

No, I can better play the orator.

MONTAGUE

But I have reasons strong and forcible.

Enter the DUKE OF YORK

YORK

Why, how now, sons and brother! at a strife?
What is your quarrel? how began it first?

EDWARD

No quarrel, but a slight contention.

YORK

About what?

RICHARD

About that which concerns your grace and us;
The crown of England, father, which is yours.

YORK

Mine, boy? not till King Henry be dead.

RICHARD

Your right depends not on his life or death.

EDWARD

Now you are heir, therefore enjoy it now:
By giving the house of Lancaster leave to breathe,
It will outrun you, father, in the end.

YORK

I took an oath that he should quietly reign.

EDWARD

But for a kingdom any oath may be broken:
I would break a thousand oaths to reign one year.

RICHARD

No; God forbid your grace should be forsworn.

YORK

I shall be, if I claim by open war.

RICHARD

I'll prove the contrary, if you'll hear me speak.

YORK

Thou canst not, son; it is impossible.

RICHARD

An oath is of no moment, being not took
Before a true and lawful magistrate,
That hath authority over him that swears:
Henry had none, but did usurp the place;
Then, seeing 'twas he that made you to depose,
Your oath, my lord, is vain and frivolous.
Therefore, to arms! And, father, do but think
How sweet a thing it is to wear a crown;
Within whose circuit is Elysium,
And all that poets feign of bliss and joy.
Why do we linger thus? I cannot rest

Until the white rose that I wear be dyed
Even in the lukewarm blood of Henry's heart.

YORK

Richard, enough; I will be king, or die.
Brother, thou shalt to London presently,
And whet on Warwick to this enterprise.
Thou, Richard, shalt to the Duke of Norfolk,
And tell him privily of our intent.
You, Edward, shall unto my Lord Cobham,
With whom the Kentishmen will willingly rise:
In them I trust; for they are soldiers,
Witty, courteous, liberal, full of spirit.
While you are thus employ'd, what resteth more,
But that I seek occasion how to rise,
And yet the king not privy to my drift,
Nor any of the house of Lancaster?

Enter a MESSENGER

But, stay: what news? Why comest thou in such
    post?

MESSENGER

The queen with all the northern earls and lords
Intend here to besiege you in your castle:
She is hard by with twenty thousand men;
And therefore fortify your hold, my lord.

YORK

Ay, with my sword. What! think'st thou that we
    fear them?
Edward and Richard, you shall stay with me;
My brother Montague shall post to London:
Let noble Warwick, Cobham, and the rest,
Whom we have left protectors of the king,
With powerful policy strengthen themselves,
And trust not simple Henry nor his oaths.

MONTAGUE

Brother, I go; I'll win them, fear it not:
And thus most humbly I do take my leave.   [*Exit*

Enter SIR JOHN MORTIMER *and* SIR HUGH MORTIMER

YORK

Sir John and Sir Hugh Mortimer, mine uncles,
You are come to Sandal in a happy hour;
The army of the queen mean to besiege us.

SIR JOHN

She shall not need; we'll meet her in the field.

YORK

What, with five thousand men?

RICHARD

Ay, with five hundred, father, for a need:
A woman's general; what should we fear?

[*A march afar off*

EDWARD

I hear their drums: let's set our men in order,
And issue forth and bid them battle straight.

YORK

Five men to twenty! though the odds be great,
I doubt not, uncle, of our victory.
Many a battle have I won in France,
When as the enemy hath been ten to one:
Why should I not now have the like success?

[*Alarum. Exeunt*

SCENE III. *Field of battle betwixt Sandal Castle and*
Wakefield

Alarums. Enter RUTLAND *and his* TUTOR

RUTLAND

Ah, whither shall I fly to 'scape their hands?
Ah, tutor, look where bloody Clifford comes!

Enter CLIFFORD *and* SOLDIERS

CLIFFORD

Chaplain, away! thy priesthood saves thy life.
As for the brat of this accursed duke,
Whose father slew my father, he shall die.

TUTOR

And I, my lord, will bear him company.

CLIFFORD

Soldiers, away with him!

TUTOR

Ah, Clifford, murder not this innocent child,
Lest thou be hated both of God and man!

[*Exit, dragged off by* SOLDIERS

CLIFFORD

How now! is he dead already? or is it fear
That makes him close his eyes? I'll open them.

RUTLAND

So looks the pent-up lion o'er the wretch
That trembles under his devouring paws;
And so he walks, insulting o'er his prey,
And so he comes, to rend his limbs asunder.
Ah, gentle Clifford, kill me with thy sword,
And not with such a cruel threatening look.
Sweet Clifford, hear me speak before I die.
I am too mean a subject for thy wrath:
Be thou revenged on men, and let me live.

CLIFFORD

In vain thou speak'st, poor boy; my father's blood
Hath stopp'd the passage where thy words should
　enter.

RUTLAND

Then let my father's blood open it again:
He is a man, and, Clifford, cope with him.

CLIFFORD

Had I thy brethren here, their lives and thine
Were not revenge sufficient for me;
No, if I digg'd up thy forefathers' graves,
And hung their rotten coffins up in chains,
It could not slake mine ire, nor ease my heart.
The sight of any of the house of York
Is as a fury to torment my soul;
And till I root out their accursed line
And leave not one alive, I live in hell.
Therefore— 　　　　　　　　　　　[*Lifting his hand*

RUTLAND

O, let me pray before I take my death!
To thee I pray; sweet Clifford, pity me!

CLIFFORD

Such pity as my rapier's point affords.

RUTLAND

I never did thee harm: why wilt thou slay me?

CLIFFORD

Thy father hath.

RUTLAND

　　　　　　　　But 'twas ere I was born.
Thou hast one son; for his sake pity me,
Lest in revenge thereof, sith God is just,
He be as miserably slain as I.
Ah, let me live in prison all my days;
And when I give occasion of offence,
Then let me die, for now thou hast no cause.

CLIFFORD

No cause!
Thy father slew my father; therefore, die. [*Stabs him*

RUTLAND

Di faciant laudis summa sit ista tuæ! 　　　　[*Dies*

CLIFFORD

Plantagenet! I come, Plantagenet!
And this thy son's blood cleaving to my blade
Shall rust upon my weapon, till thy blood,
Congeal'd with this, do make me wipe off both.

[*Exit*

SCENE IV. *Another part of the field*

Alarum. Enter RICHARD, *Duke of York*

YORK

The army of the queen hath got the field:
My uncles both are slain in rescuing me;
And all my followers to the eager foe
Turn back and fly, like ships before the wind,
Or lambs pursued by hunger-starved wolves.
My sons, God knows what hath bechanced them:
But this I know, they have demean'd themselves
Like men born to renown by life or death.
Three times did Richard make a lane to me,
And thrice cried 'Courage, father! fight it out!'
And full as oft came Edward to my side,
With purple falchion, painted to the hilt
In blood of those that had encounter'd him:
And when the hardiest warriors did retire,
Richard cried, 'Charge! and give no foot of ground!'
And cried, 'A crown, or else a glorious tomb!
A sceptre, or an earthly sepulchre!'
With this, we charged again: but, out, alas!
We bodged again; as I have seen a swan
With bootless labour swim against the tide
And spend her strength with over-matching waves.

[*A short alarum within*

Ah, hark! the fatal followers do pursue;
And I am faint, and cannot fly their fury:
And were I strong, I would not shun their fury:
The sands are number'd that make up my life;
Here must I stay, and here my life must end.

Enter QUEEN MARGARET, CLIFFORD,
NORTHUMBERLAND, *the young* PRINCE, *and* SOLDIERS

Come, bloody Clifford, rough Northumberland,
I dare your quenchless fury to more rage:
I am your butt, and I abide your shot.

NORTHUMBERLAND

Yield to our mercy, proud Plantagenet.

[80]

CLIFFORD

Ay, to such mercy as his ruthless arm,
With downright payment, show'd unto my father.
Now Phaëthon hath tumbled from his car,
And made an evening at the noontide prick.

YORK

My ashes, as the phœnix, may bring forth
A bird that will revenge upon you all:
And in that hope I throw mine eyes to heaven,
Scorning whate'er you can afflict me with.
Why come you not? what! multitudes, and fear?

CLIFFORD

So cowards fight when they can fly no further;
So doves do peck the falcon's piercing talons;
So desperate thieves, all hopeless of their lives,
Breathe out invectives 'gainst the officers.

YORK

O Clifford, but bethink thee once again,
And in thy thought o'er-run my former time;
And, if thou canst for blushing, view this face,
And bite thy tongue, that slanders him with cow-
ardice
Whose frown hath made thee faint and fly ere this!

CLIFFORD

I will not bandy with thee word for word,
But buckle with thee blows, twice two for one.

QUEEN MARGARET

Hold, valiant Clifford! for a thousand causes
I would prolong awhile the traitor's life.
Wrath makes him deaf: speak thou, Northumber-
land.

NORTHUMBERLAND

Hold, Clifford! do not honour him so much
To prick thy finger, though to wound his heart:
What valour were it, when a cur doth grin,
For one to thrust his hand between his teeth,
When he might spurn him with his foot away?
It is war's prize to take all vantages;
And ten to one is no impeach of valour.

[They lay hands on YORK, who struggles
CLIFFORD

Ay, ay, so strives the woodcock with the gin.

NORTHUMBERLAND

So doth the cony struggle in the net.

YORK

So triumph thieves upon their conquer'd booty;
So true men yield, with robbers so o'er-match'd.

NORTHUMBERLAND

What would your grace have done unto him now?

QUEEN MARGARET

Brave warriors, Clifford and Northumberland,
Come, make him stand upon this molehill here,
That raught at mountains with outstretched arms,
Yet parted but the shadow with his hand.
What! was it you that would be England's king?
Was 't you that revell'd in our parliament,
And made a preachment of your high descent?
Where are your mess of sons to back you now?
The wanton Edward, and the lusty George?
And where's that valiant crook-back prodigy,

Dicky your boy, that with his grumbling voice
Was wont to cheer his dad in mutinies?
Or, with the rest, where is your darling Rutland?
Look, York: I stain'd this napkin with the blood
That valiant Clifford, with his rapier's point,
Made issue from the bosom of the boy;
And if thine eyes can water for his death,
I give thee this to dry thy cheeks withal.
Alas, poor York! but that I hate thee deadly,
I should lament thy miserable state.
I prithee, grieve, to make me merry, York.
What, hath thy fiery heart so parch'd thine entrails
That not a tear can fall for Rutland's death?
Why art thou patient, man? thou shouldst be mad;
And I, to make thee mad, do mock thee thus.
Stamp, rave, and fret, that I may sing and dance.
Thou wouldst be fee'd, I see, to make me sport:
York cannot speak, unless he wear a crown.
A crown for York! and, lords, bow low to him:
Hold you his hands, whilst I do set it on.

[Putting a paper crown on his head
Ay, marry, sir, now looks he like a king!
Ay, this is he that took King Henry's chair;
And this is he was his adopted heir.
But how is it that great Plantagenet
Is crown'd so soon, and broke his solemn oath?
As I bethink me, you should not be king
Till our King Henry had shook hands with death.
And will you pale your head in Henry's glory,
And rob his temples of the diadem,
Now in his life, against your holy oath?
O, 'tis a fault too too unpardonable!
Off with the crown; and, with the crown, his head;
And, whilst we breathe, take time to do him dead.

CLIFFORD

That is my office, for my father's sake.

QUEEN MARGARET

Nay, stay; let's hear the orisons he makes.

YORK

She-wolf of France, but worse than wolves of
France,
Whose tongue more poisons than the adder's tooth!
How ill-beseeming is it in thy sex
To triumph, like an Amazonian trull,
Upon their woes whom fortune captivates!
But that thy face is, visard-like, unchanging,
Made impudent with use of evil deeds,
I would assay, proud queen, to make thee blush.
To tell thee whence thou camest, of whom derived,
Were shame enough to shame thee, wert thou not
shameless.
Thy father bears the type of King of Naples,
Of both the Sicils and Jerusalem,
Yet not so wealthy as an English yeoman.
Hath that poor monarch taught thee to insult?
It needs not, nor it boots thee not, proud queen,
Unless the adage must be verified,
That beggars mounted run their horse to death.
'Tis beauty that doth oft make women proud;
But, God He knows, thy share thereof is small:

'Tis virtue that doth make them most admired;
The contrary doth make thee wonder'd at:
'Tis government that makes them seem divine;
The want thereof makes thee abominable:
Thou art as opposite to every good
As the Antipodes are unto us,
Or as the south to the septentrion.
O tiger's heart wrapp'd in a woman's hide!
How couldst thou drain the life-blood of the child,
To bid the father wipe his eyes withal,
And yet be seen to bear a woman's face?
Women are soft, mild, pitiful and flexible;
Thou stern, obdurate, flinty, rough, remorseless.
Bid'st thou me rage? why, now thou hast thy wish:
Wouldst have me weep? why, now thou hast thy
     will:
For raging wind blows up incessant showers,
And when the rage allays, the rain begins.
These tears are my sweet Rutland's obsequies:
And every drop cries vengeance for his death,
'Gainst thee, fell Clifford, and thee, false French-
     woman.

NORTHUMBERLAND
Beshrew me, but his passion moves me so
That hardly can I check my eyes from tears.

YORK
That face of his the hungry cannibals
Would not have touch'd, would not have stain'd
     with blood:
But you are more inhuman, more inexorable,
O, ten times more, than tigers of Hyrcania.
See, ruthless queen, a hapless father's tears:
This cloth thou dip'dst in blood of my sweet boy,
And I with tears do wash the blood away.
Keep thou the napkin, and go boast of this:
And if thou tell'st the heavy story right,
Upon my soul, the hearers will shed tears;
Yea, even my foes will shed fast-falling tears,
And say 'Alas, it was a piteous deed!'
There, take the crown, and, with the crown, my
     curse;
And in thy need such comfort come to thee
As now I reap at thy too cruel hand!
Hard-hearted Clifford, take me from the world:
My soul to heaven, my blood upon your heads!

NORTHUMBERLAND
Had he been slaughter-man to all my kin,
I should not for my life but weep with him,
To see how inly sorrow gripes his soul.

QUEEN MARGARET
What, weeping-ripe, my Lord Northumberland?
Think but upon the wrong he did us all,
And that will quickly dry thy melting tears.

CLIFFORD
Here's for my oath, here's for my father's death.
                                        [Stabbing him

QUEEN MARGARET
And here's to right our gentle-hearted king.
                                        [Stabbing him

YORK
Open Thy gate of mercy, gracious God!
My soul flies through these wounds to seek out Thee.
                                        [Dies

QUEEN MARGARET
Off with his head, and set it on York gates;
So York may overlook the town of York.
                                        [Flourish. Exeunt

ACT II

SCENE I. *A plain near Mortimer's Cross in Herefordshire*

A march. Enter EDWARD, RICHARD, *and their power*

EDWARD
I wonder how our princely father 'scaped,
Or whether he be 'scaped away or no
From Clifford's and Northumberland's pursuit:
Had he been ta'en, we should have heard the news;
Had he been slain, we should have heard the news;
Or had he 'scaped, methinks we should have heard
The happy tidings of his good escape.
How fares my brother? why is he so sad?

RICHARD
I cannot joy, until I be resolved
Where our right valiant father is become.
I saw him in the battle range about;
And watch'd him how he singled Clifford forth.
Methought he bore him in the thickest troop
As doth a lion in a herd of neat;
Or as a bear, encompass'd round with dogs,
Who having pinch'd a few and made them cry,
The rest stand all aloof, and bark at him.
So fared our father with his enemies;
So fled his enemies my warlike father:
Methinks, 'tis prize enough to be his son.
See how the morning opes her golden gates,
And takes her farewell of the glorious sun!
How well resembles it the prime of youth,
Trimm'd like a younker prancing to his love!

EDWARD
Dazzle mine eyes, or do I see three suns?

RICHARD
Three glorious suns, each one a perfect sun;
Not separated with the racking clouds,
But sever'd in a pale clear-shining sky.
See, see! they join, embrace, and seem to kiss,
As if they vow'd some league inviolable:
Now are they but one lamp, one light, one sun.
In this the heaven figures some event.

EDWARD
'Tis wondrous strange, the like yet never heard of.
I think it cites us, brother, to the field,
That we, the sons of brave Plantagenet,
Each one already blazing by our meeds,
Should notwithstanding join our lights together,
And over-shine the earth as this the world.

Whate'er it bodes, henceforward will I bear
Upon my target three fair-shining suns.

RICHARD

Nay, bear three daughters: by your leave I speak it,
You love the breeder better than the male.

Enter a MESSENGER

But what art thou, whose heavy looks foretell
Some dreadful story hanging on thy tongue?

MESSENGER

Ah, one that was a woful looker-on
When as the noble Duke of York was slain,
Your princely father and my loving lord!

EDWARD

O, speak no more, for I have heard too much.

RICHARD

Say how he died, for I will hear it all.

MESSENGER

Environed he was with many foes,
And stood against them, as the hope of Troy
Against the Greeks that would have enter'd Troy.
But Hercules himself must yield to odds;
And many strokes, though with a little axe,
Hew down and fell the hardest-timber'd oak.
By many hands your father was subdued;
But only slaughter'd by the ireful arm
Of unrelenting Clifford and the queen,
Who crown'd the gracious duke in high despite,
Laugh'd in his face; and when with grief he wept,
The ruthless queen gave him to dry his cheeks
A napkin steeped in the harmless blood
Of sweet young Rutland, by rough Clifford slain:
And after many scorns, many foul taunts,
They took his head, and on the gates of York
They set the same; and there it doth remain,
The saddest spectacle that e'er I view'd.

EDWARD

Sweet Duke of York, our prop to lean upon,
Now thou art gone, we have no staff, no stay.
O Clifford, boisterous Clifford! thou hast slain
The flower of Europe for his chivalry;
And treacherously hast thou vanquish'd him,
For hand to hand he would have vanquish'd thee.
Now my soul's palace is become a prison:
Ah, would she break from hence, that this my body
Might in the ground be closed up in rest!
For never henceforth shall I joy again,
Never, O never, shall I see more joy!

RICHARD

I cannot weep; for all my body's moisture
Scarce serves to quench my furnace-burning heart:
Nor can my tongue unload my heart's great bur-
    then;
For selfsame wind that I should speak withal
Is kindling coals that fires all my breast,
And burns me up with flames that tears would
    quench.
To weep is to make less the depth of grief:
Tears then for babes; blows and revenge for me!
Richard, I bear thy name; I'll venge thy death,
Or die renowned by attempting it.

EDWARD

His name that valiant duke hath left with thee;
His dukedom and his chair with me is left.

RICHARD

Nay, if thou be that princely eagle's bird,
Show thy descent by gazing 'gainst the sun:
For chair and dukedom, throne and kingdom say;
Either that is thine, or else thou wert not his.

March. Enter WARWICK, MARQUESS OF MONTAGUE, *and
    their army*

WARWICK

How now, fair lords! What fare? what news abroad?

RICHARD

Great Lord of Warwick, if we should recount
Our baleful news, and at each word's deliverance
Stab poniards in our flesh till all were told,
The words would add more anguish than the
    wounds.
O valiant lord, the Duke of York is slain!

EDWARD

O Warwick, Warwick! that Plantagenet,
Which held thee dearly as his soul's redemption,
Is by the stern Lord Clifford done to death.

WARWICK

Ten days ago I drown'd these news in tears;
And now, to add more measure to your woes,
I come to tell you things sith then befall'n.
After the bloody fray at Wakefield fought,
Where your brave father breathed his latest gasp,
Tidings, as swiftly as the posts could run,
Were brought me of your loss and his depart.
I, then in London, keeper of the king,
Muster'd my soldiers, gather'd flocks of friends,
And very well appointed, as I thought,
March'd toward Saint Alban's to intercept the
    queen,
Bearing the king in my behalf along;
For by my scouts I was advertised,
That she was coming with a full intent
To dash our late decree in parliament,
Touching King Henry's oath and your succession.
Short tale to make, we at Saint Alban's met,
Our battles join'd, and both sides fiercely fought:
But whether 'twas the coldness of the king,
Who look'd full gently on his warlike queen,
That robb'd my soldiers of their heated spleen;
Or whether 'twas report of her success;
Or more than common fear of Clifford's rigour,
Who thunders to his captives blood and death,
I cannot judge: but, to conclude with truth,
Their weapons like to lightning came and went;
Our soldiers', like the night-owl's lazy flight,
Or like an idle thresher with a flail,
Fell gently down, as if they struck their friends.
I cheer'd them up with justice of our cause,
With promise of high pay and great rewards:
But all in vain; they had no heart to fight,
And we in them no hope to win the day;
So that we fled; the king unto the queen;
Lord George your brother, Norfolk and myself,

[83]

In haste, post-haste, are come to join with you;
For in the marches here we heard you were,
Making another head to fight again.

EDWARD

Where is the Duke of Norfolk, gentle Warwick?
And when came George from Burgundy to England?

WARWICK

Some six miles off the duke is with the soldiers;
And for your brother, he was lately sent
From your kind aunt, Duchess of Burgundy,
With aid of soldiers to this needful war.

RICHARD

'Twas odds, belike, when valiant Warwick fled:
Oft have I heard his praises in pursuit,
But ne'er till now his scandal of retire.

WARWICK

Nor now my scandal, Richard, dost thou hear;
For thou shalt know this strong right hand of mine
Can pluck the diadem from faint Henry's head,
And wring the awful sceptre from his fist,
Were he as famous and as bold in war,
As he is famed for mildness, peace, and prayer.

RICHARD

I know it well, Lord Warwick; blame me not:
'Tis love I bear thy glories makes me speak.
But in this troublous time what's to be done?
Shall we go throw away our coats of steel,
And wrap our bodies in black mourning gowns,
Numbering our Ave-Maries with our beads?
Or shall we on the helmets of our foes
Tell our devotion with revengeful arms?
If for the last, say ay, and to it, lords.

WARWICK

Why, therefore Warwick came to seek you out;
And therefore comes my brother Montague.
Attend me, lords. The proud insulting queen,
With Clifford and the haught Northumberland,
And of their feather many moe proud birds,
Have wrought the easy-melting king like wax.
He swore consent to your succession,
His oath enrolled in the parliament;
And now to London all the crew are gone,
To frustrate both his oath and what beside
May make against the house of Lancaster.
Their power, I think, is thirty thousand strong:
Now, if the help of Norfolk and myself,
With all the friends that thou, brave Earl of March,
Amongst the loving Welshmen canst procure,
Will but amount to five and twenty thousand,
Why, Via! to London will we march amain,
And once again bestride our foaming steeds,
And once again cry 'Charge upon our foes!'
But never once again turn back and fly.

RICHARD

Ay, now methinks I hear great Warwick speak:
Ne'er may he live to see a sunshine day,
That cries 'Retire,' if Warwick bid him stay.

EDWARD

Lord Warwick, on thy shoulder will I lean;

And when thou fail'st—as God forbid the hour!—
Must Edward fall, which peril heaven forfend!

WARWICK

No longer Earl of March, but Duke of York:
The next degree is England's royal throne;
For King of England shalt thou be proclaim'd
In every borough as we pass along;
And he that throws not up his cap for joy
Shall for the fault make forfeit of his head.
King Edward, valiant Richard, Montague,
Stay we no longer, dreaming of renown,
But sound the trumpets, and about our task.

RICHARD

Then, Clifford, were thy heart as hard as steel,
As thou hast shown it flinty by thy deeds,
I come to pierce it, or to give thee mine.

EDWARD

Then strike up drums: God and Saint George for
us!

Enter a MESSENGER

WARWICK

How now! what news?

MESSENGER

The Duke of Norfolk sends you word by me,
The queen is coming with a puissant host;
And craves your company for speedy counsel.

WARWICK

Why then it sorts, brave warriors, let's away.

[*Exeunt*

SCENE II. *Before York*

Flourish. Enter KING HENRY, QUEEN MARGARET, *the*
PRINCE OF WALES, CLIFFORD, *and* NORTHUMBERLAND,
with drum and trumpets

QUEEN MARGARET

Welcome, my lord, to this brave town of York.
Yonder's the head of that arch-enemy
That sought to be encompass'd with your crown:
Doth not the object cheer your heart, my lord?

KING HENRY

Ay, as the rocks cheer them that fear their wreck:
To see this sight, it irks my very soul.
Withhold revenge, dear God! 'tis not my fault,
Nor wittingly have I infringed my vow.

CLIFFORD

My gracious liege, this too much lenity
And harmful pity must be laid aside.
To whom do lions cast their gentle looks?
Not to the beast that would usurp their den.
Whose hand is that the forest bear doth lick?
Not his that spoils her young before her face.
Who 'scapes the lurking serpent's mortal sting?
Not he that sets his foot upon her back.
The smallest worm will turn being trodden on,
And doves will peck in safeguard of their brood.
Ambitious York did level at thy crown,
Thou smiling while he knit his angry brows:
He, but a duke, would have his son a king,
And raise his issue, like a loving sire;

Thou, being a king, blest with a goodly son,
Didst yield consent to disinherit him,
Which argued thee a most unloving father.
Unreasonable creatures feed their young;
And though man's face be fearful to their eyes,
Yet, in protection of their tender ones,
Who hath not seen them, even with those wings
Which sometime they have used with fearful flight,
Make war with him that climb'd unto their nest,
Offering their own lives in their young's defence?
For shame, my liege, make them your precedent!
Were it not pity that this goodly boy
Should lose his birthright by his father's fault,
And long hereafter say unto his child,
'What my great-grandfather and grandsire got
My careless father fondly gave away'?
Ah, what a shame were this! Look on the boy;
And let his manly face, which promiseth
Successful fortune, steel thy melting heart
To hold thine own, and leave thine own with him.

KING HENRY

Full well hath Clifford play'd the orator,
Inferring arguments of mighty force.
But, Clifford, tell me, didst thou never hear
That things ill-got had ever bad success?
And happy always was it for that son
Whose father for his hoarding went to hell?
I'll leave my son my virtuous deeds behind;
And would my father had left me no more!
For all the rest is held at such a rate
As brings a thousand-fold more care to keep
Than in possession any jot of pleasure.
Ah, cousin York! would thy best friends did know
How it doth grieve me that thy head is here!

QUEEN MARGARET

My lord, cheer up your spirits: our foes are nigh,
And this soft courage makes your followers faint.
You promised knighthood to our forward son:
Unsheathe your sword, and dub him presently.
Edward, kneel down.

KING HENRY

Edward Plantagenet, arise a knight;
And learn this lesson, draw thy sword in right.

PRINCE

My gracious father, by your kingly leave,
I'll draw it as apparent to the crown,
And in that quarrel use it to the death.

CLIFFORD

Why, that is spoken like a toward prince.

Enter a MESSENGER

MESSENGER

Royal commanders, be in readiness:
For with a band of thirty thousand men
Comes Warwick, backing of the Duke of York;
And in the towns, as they do march along,
Proclaims him king, and many fly to him:
Darraign your battle, for they are at hand.

CLIFFORD

I would your highness would depart the field:
The queen hath best success when you are absent.

QUEEN MARGARET

Ay, good my lord, and leave us to our fortune.

KING HENRY

Why, that's my fortune too; therefore I'll stay.

NORTHUMBERLAND

Be it with resolution then to fight.

PRINCE

My royal father, cheer these noble lords,
And hearten those that fight in your defence:
Unsheathe your sword, good father; cry 'Saint
George!'

March. Enter EDWARD, GEORGE, RICHARD, WARWICK,
NORFOLK, MONTAGUE, *and* SOLDIERS

EDWARD

Now, perjured Henry! wilt thou kneel for grace,
And set thy diadem upon my head;
Or bide the mortal fortune of the field?

QUEEN MARGARET

Go, rate thy minions, proud insulting boy!
Becomes it thee to be thus bold in terms
Before thy sovereign and thy lawful king?

EDWARD

I am his king, and he should bow his knee;
I was adopted heir by his consent:
Since when, his oath is broke; for, as I hear,
You, that are king, though he do wear the crown,
Have caused him, by new act of parliament,
To blot out me, and put his own son in.

CLIFFORD

And reason too:
Who should succeed the father but the son?

RICHARD

Are you there, butcher? O, I cannot speak!

CLIFFORD

Ay, crook-back, here I stand to answer thee,
Or any he the proudest of thy sort.

RICHARD

'Twas you that kill'd young Rutland, was it not?

CLIFFORD

Ay, and old York, and yet not satisfied.

RICHARD

For God's sake, lords, give signal to the fight.

WARWICK

What say'st thou, Henry, wilt thou yield the crown?

QUEEN MARGARET

Why, how now, long-tongued Warwick! dare you
speak?
When you and I met at Saint Alban's last,
Your legs did better service than your hands.

WARWICK

Then 'twas my turn to fly, and now 'tis thine.

CLIFFORD

You said so much before, and yet you fled.

WARWICK

'Twas not your valour, Clifford, drove me thence.

NORTHUMBERLAND

No, nor your manhood that durst make you stay.

RICHARD

Northumberland, I hold thee reverently.
Break off the parley; for scarce I can refrain

The execution of my big-swoln heart
Upon that Clifford, that cruel child-killer.

CLIFFORD
I slew thy father, call'st thou him a child?

RICHARD
Ay, like a dastard and a treacherous coward,
As thou didst kill our tender brother Rutland;
But ere sunset I'll make thee curse the deed.

KING HENRY
Have done with words, my lords, and hear me
  speak.

QUEEN MARGARET
Defy them then, or else hold close thy lips.

KING HENRY
I prithee, give no limits to my tongue:
I am a king, and privileged to speak.

CLIFFORD
My liege, the wound that bred this meeting here
Cannot be cured by words; therefore be still.

RICHARD
Then, executioner, unsheathe thy sword:
By Him that made us all, I am resolved
That Clifford's manhood lies upon his tongue.

EDWARD
Say, Henry, shall I have my right, or no?
A thousand men have broke their fasts to-day,
That ne'er shall dine unless thou yield the crown.

WARWICK
If thou deny, their blood upon thy head;
For York in justice puts his armour on.

PRINCE
If that be right which Warwick says is right,
There is no wrong, but every thing is right.

RICHARD
Whoever got thee, there thy mother stands;
For, well I wot, thou hast thy mother's tongue.

QUEEN MARGARET
But thou art neither like thy sire nor dam;
But like a foul mis-shapen stigmatic,
Mark'd by the destinies to be avoided,
As venom toads, or lizards' dreadful stings.

RICHARD
Iron of Naples hid with English gilt,
Whose father bears the title of a king,—
As if a channel should be call'd the sea,—
Shamest thou not, knowing whence thou art ex-
  traught,
To let thy tongue detect thy base-born heart?

EDWARD
A wisp of straw were worth a thousand crowns,
To make this shameless callet know herself.
Helen of Greece was fairer far than thou,
Although thy husband may be Menelaus;
And ne'er was Agamemnon's brother wrong'd
By that false woman, as this king by thee.
His father revell'd in the heart of France,
And tamed the king, and made the dauphin stoop;
And had he match'd according to his state,
He might have kept that glory to this day;
But when he took a beggar to his bed,

And graced thy poor sire with his bridal-day,
Even then that sunshine brew'd a shower for him,
That wash'd his father's fortunes forth of France,
And heap'd sedition on his crown at home.
For what hath broach'd this tumult but thy pride?
Hadst thou been meek, our title still had slept;
And we, in pity of the gentle king,
Had slipp'd our claim until another age.

GEORGE
But when we saw our sunshine made thy spring,
And that thy summer bred us no increase,
We set the axe to thy usurping root;
And though the edge hath something hit ourselves,
Yet, know thou, since we have begun to strike,
We'll never leave till we have hewn thee down,
Or bathed thy growing with our heated bloods.

EDWARD
And, in this resolution, I defy thee;
Not willing any longer conference,
Since thou deniest the gentle king to speak.
Sound trumpets! let our bloody colours wave!
And either victory, or else a grave.

QUEEN MARGARET
Stay, Edward.

EDWARD
No, wrangling woman, we'll no longer stay:
These words will cost ten thousand lives this day.
                                        [Exeunt

SCENE III. *A field of battle between Towton and Saxton,
                    in Yorkshire*

Alarum. Excursions. Enter WARWICK

WARWICK
Forspent with toil, as runners with a race,
I lay me down a little while to breathe;
For strokes received, and many blows repaid,
Have robb'd my strong-knit sinews of their strength,
And spite of spite needs must I rest awhile.

Enter EDWARD, *running*

EDWARD
Smile, gentle heaven! or strike, ungentle death!
For this world frowns, and Edward's sun is clouded

WARWICK
How now, my lord! what hap? what hope of good?

Enter GEORGE

GEORGE
Our hap is loss, our hope but sad despair;
Our ranks are broke, and ruin follows us:
What counsel give you? whither shall we fly?

EDWARD
Bootless is flight, they follow us with wings;
And weak we are and cannot shun pursuit.

Enter RICHARD

RICHARD
Ah, Warwick, why hast thou withdrawn thyself?
Thy brother's blood the thirsty earth hath drunk,
Broach'd with the steely point of Clifford's lance;

[86]

And in the very pangs of death he cried,
Like to a dismal clangor heard from far,
'Warwick, revenge! brother, revenge my death!'
So, underneath the belly of their steeds,
That stain'd their fetlocks in his smoking blood,
The noble gentleman gave up the ghost.

WARWICK

Then let the earth be drunken with our blood:
I'll kill my horse, because I will not fly.
Why stand we like soft-hearted women here,
Wailing our losses, whiles the foe doth rage;
And look upon, as if the tragedy
Were play'd in jest by counterfeiting actors?
Here on my knee I vow to God above,
I'll never pause again, never stand still,
Till either death hath closed these eyes of mine,
Or fortune given me measure of revenge.

EDWARD

O Warwick, I do bend my knee with thine;
And in this vow do chain my soul to thine!
And, ere my knee rise from the earth's cold face,
I throw my hands, mine eyes, my heart to Thee,
Thou setter up and plucker down of kings,
Beseeching Thee, if with Thy will it stands
That to my foes this body must be prey,
Yet that Thy brazen gates of heaven may ope,
And give sweet passage to my sinful soul!
Now, lords, take leave until we meet again,
Where'er it be, in heaven or in earth.

RICHARD

Brother, give me thy hand; and, gentle Warwick,
Let me embrace thee in my weary arms:
I, that did never weep, now melt with woe
That winter should cut off our spring-time so.

WARWICK

Away, away! Once more, sweet lords, farewell.

GEORGE

Yet let us all together to our troops,
And give them leave to fly that will not stay;
And call them pillars that will stand to us;
And, if we thrive, promise them such rewards
As victors wear at the Olympian games:
This may plant courage in their quailing breasts;
For yet is hope of life and victory.
Forslow no longer, make we hence amain. [Exeunt

SCENE IV. *Another part of the field*

Excursions. Enter RICHARD *and* CLIFFORD

RICHARD

Now, Clifford, I have singled thee alone:
Suppose this arm is for the Duke of York,
And this for Rutland; both bound to revenge,
Wert thou environ'd with a brazen wall.

CLIFFORD

Now, Richard, I am with thee here alone:
This is the hand that stabb'd thy father York;
And this the hand that slew thy brother Rutland;
And here's the heart that triumphs in their death,

And cheers these hands that slew thy sire and
    brother
To execute the like upon thyself;
And so, have at thee!

[*They fight.* WARWICK *comes;* CLIFFORD *flies*

RICHARD

Nay, Warwick, single out some other chase;
For I myself will hunt this wolf to death. [*Exeunt*

SCENE V. *Another part of the field*

Alarum. Enter KING HENRY *alone*

KING HENRY

This battle fares like to the morning's war,
When dying clouds contend with growing light,
What time the shepherd, blowing of his nails,
Can neither call it perfect day nor night.
Now sways it this way, like a mighty sea
Forced by the tide to combat with the wind;
Now sways it that way, like the selfsame sea
Forced to retire by fury of the wind:
Sometime the flood prevails, and then the wind;
Now one the better, then another best;
Both tugging to be victors, breast to breast,
Yet neither conqueror nor conquered:
So is the equal poise of this fell war.
Here on this molehill will I sit me down.
To whom God will, there be the victory!
For Margaret my queen, and Clifford too,
Have chid me from the battle; swearing both
They prosper best of all when I am thence.
Would I were dead! if God's good will were so;
For what is in this world but grief and woe?
O God! methinks it were a happy life,
To be no better than a homely swain;
To sit upon a hill, as I do now,
To carve out dials quaintly, point by point,
Thereby to see the minutes how they run,
How many make the hour full complete;
How many hours bring about the day;
How many days will finish up the year;
How many years a mortal man may live.
When this is known, then to divide the times:
So many hours must I tend my flock;
So many hours must I take my rest;
So many hours must I contemplate;
So many hours must I sport myself;
So many days my ewes have been with young;
So many weeks ere the poor fools will ean;
So many years ere I shall shear the fleece:
So minutes, hours, days, months, and years,
Pass'd over to the end they were created,
Would bring white hairs unto a quiet grave.
Ah, what a life were this! how sweet! how lovely!
Gives not the hawthorn-bush a sweeter shade
To shepherds looking on their silly sheep,
Than doth a rich embroider'd canopy
To kings that fear their subjects' treachery?
O, yes, it doth; a thousand-fold it doth.

And to conclude, the shepherd's homely curds,
His cold thin drink out of his leather bottle,
His wonted sleep under a fresh tree's shade,
All which secure and sweetly he enjoys,
Is far beyond a prince's delicates,
His viands sparkling in a golden cup,
His body couched in a curious bed,
When care, mistrust, and treason waits on him.

Alarum. Enter a SON *that has killed his father, dragging in the body*

SON

Ill blows the wind that profits nobody.
This man, whom hand to hand I slew in fight,
May be possessed with some store of crowns;
And I, that haply take them from him now,
May yet ere night yield both my life and them
To some man else, as this dead man doth me.
Who's this? O God! it is my father's face,
Whom in this conflict I unwares have kill'd.
O heavy times, begetting such events!
From London by the king was I press'd forth;
My father, being the Earl of Warwick's man,
Came on the part of York, press'd by his master;
And I, who at his hands received my life,
Have by my hands of life bereaved him.
Pardon me, God, I knew not what I did!
And pardon, father, for I knew not thee!
My tears shall wipe away these bloody marks;
And no more words till they have flow'd their fill.

KING HENRY

O piteous spectacle! O bloody times!
Whiles lions war and battle for their dens,
Poor harmless lambs abide their enmity.
Weep, wretched man, I'll aid thee tear for tear;
And let our hearts and eyes, like civil war,
Be blind with tears, and break o'ercharged with grief.

Enter a FATHER *that has killed his son, bringing in the body*

FATHER

Thou that so stoutly hast resisted me,
Give me thy gold, if thou hast any gold;
For I have bought it with an hundred blows.
But let me see: is this our foeman's face?
Ah, no, no, no, it is mine only son!
Ah, boy, if any life be left in thee,
Throw up thine eye! see, see what showers arise,
Blown with the windy tempest of my heart,
Upon thy wounds, that kill mine eye and heart!
O, pity, God, this miserable age!
What stratagems, how fell, how butcherly,
Erroneous, mutinous and unnatural,
This deadly quarrel daily doth beget!
O boy, thy father gave thee life too soon,
And hath bereft thee of thy life too late!

KING HENRY

Woe above woe! grief more than common grief!
O that my death would stay these ruthful deeds!
O, pity, pity, gentle heaven, pity!
The red rose and the white are on his face,

The fatal colours of our striving houses:
The one his purple blood right well resembles;
The other his pale cheeks, methinks, presenteth:
Wither one rose, and let the other flourish;
If you contend, a thousand lives must wither.

SON

How will my mother for a father's death
Take on with me and ne'er be satisfied!

FATHER

How will my wife for slaughter of my son
Shed seas of tears and ne'er be satisfied!

KING HENRY

How will the country for these woful chances
Misthink the king and not be satisfied!

SON

Was ever son so rued a father's death?

FATHER

Was ever father so bemoan'd his son?

KING HENRY

Was ever king so grieved for subjects' woe?
Much is your sorrow; mine ten times so much.

SON

I'll bear thee hence, where I may weep my fill.

[*Exit with the body*

FATHER

These arms of mine shall be thy winding-sheet;
My heart, sweet boy, shall be thy sepulchre,
For from my heart thine image ne'er shall go;
My sighing breast shall be thy funeral bell;
And so obsequious will thy father be,
Even for the loss of thee, having no more,
As Priam was for all his valiant sons.
I'll bear thee hence; and let them fight that will,
For I have murdered where I should not kill.

[*Exit with the body*

KING HENRY

Sad-hearted men, much overgone with care,
Here sits a king more woful than you are.

Alarums. Excursions. Enter QUEEN MARGARET, *the* PRINCE, *and* EXETER

PRINCE

Fly, father, fly! for all your friends are fled,
And Warwick rages like a chafed bull:
Away! for death doth hold us in pursuit.

QUEEN MARGARET

Mount you, my lord; towards Berwick post amain:
Edward and Richard, like a brace of greyhounds
Having the fearful flying hare in sight,
With fiery eyes sparkling for very wrath,
And bloody steel grasp'd in their ireful hands,
Are at our backs; and therefore hence amain.

EXETER

Away! for vengeance comes along with them:
Nay, stay not to expostulate, make speed;
Or else come after: I'll away before.

KING HENRY

Nay, take me with thee, good sweet Exeter:
Not that I fear to stay, but love to go
Whither the queen intends. Forward; away! [*Exeunt*

SCENE VI. *Another part of the field*

A loud alarum. Enter CLIFFORD, *wounded*
CLIFFORD
Here burns my candle out; ay, here it dies,
Which, whiles it lasted, gave King Henry light.
O Lancaster, I fear thy overthrow
More than my body's parting with my soul!
My love and fear glued many friends to thee;
And, now I fall, thy tough commixture melts.
Impairing Henry, strengthening misproud York,
The common people swarm like summer flies;
And whither fly the gnats but to the sun?
And who shines now but Henry's enemies?
O Phœbus, hadst thou never given consent
That Phaëthon should check thy fiery steeds,
Thy burning car never had scorch'd the earth!
And, Henry, hadst thou sway'd as kings should do,
Or as thy father and his father did,
Giving no ground unto the house of York,
They never then had sprung like summer flies;
I and ten thousand in this luckless realm
Had left no mourning widows for our death;
And thou this day hadst kept thy chair in peace.
For what doth cherish weeds but gentle air?
And what makes robbers bold but too much lenity?
Bootless are plaints, and cureless are my wounds;
No way to fly, nor strength to hold out flight:
The foe is merciless, and will not pity;
For at their hands I have deserved no pity.
The air hath got into my deadly wounds,
And much effuse of blood doth make me faint.
Come, York and Richard, Warwick and the rest;
I stabb'd your fathers' bosoms, split my breast.
[*He faints*
Alarum and retreat. Enter EDWARD, GEORGE, RICHARD,
    MONTAGUE, WARWICK, *and* SOLDIERS
EDWARD
Now breathe we, lords: good fortune bids us pause,
And smooth the frowns of war with peaceful looks.
Some troops pursue the bloody-minded queen,
That led calm Henry, though he were a king,
As doth a sail, fill'd with a fretting gust,
Command an argosy to stem the waves.
But think you, lords, that Clifford fled with them?
WARWICK
No, 'tis impossible he should escape;
For, though before his face I speak the words,
Your brother Richard mark'd him for the grave:
And wheresoe'er he is, he's surely dead.
[CLIFFORD *groans, and dies*
EDWARD
Whose soul is that which takes her heavy leave?
RICHARD
A deadly groan, like life and death's departing.
EDWARD
See who it is: and, now the battle's ended,
If friend or foe, let him be gently used.
RICHARD
Revoke that doom of mercy, for 'tis Clifford;

Who not contented that he lopp'd the branch
In hewing Rutland when his leaves put forth,
But set his murdering knife unto the root
From whence that tender spray did sweetly spring,
I mean our princely father, Duke of York.
WARWICK
From off the gates of York fetch down the head,
Your father's head, which Clifford placed there;
Instead whereof let this supply the room:
Measure for measure must be answered.
EDWARD
Bring forth that fatal screech-owl to our house,
That nothing sung but death to us and ours:
Now death shall stop his dismal threatening sound,
And his ill-boding tongue no more shall speak.
WARWICK
I think his understanding is bereft.
Speak, Clifford, dost thou know who speaks to thee?
Dark cloudy death o'ershades his beams of life,
And he nor sees, nor hears us what we say.
RICHARD
O, would he did! and so perhaps he doth:
'Tis but his policy to counterfeit,
Because he would avoid such bitter taunts
Which in the time of death he gave our father.
GEORGE
If so thou think'st, vex him with eager words.
RICHARD
Clifford, ask mercy and obtain no grace.
EDWARD
Clifford, repent in bootless penitence.
WARWICK
Clifford, devise excuses for thy faults.
GEORGE
While we devise fell tortures for thy faults.
RICHARD
Thou didst love York, and I am son to York.
EDWARD
Thou pitied'st Rutland; I will pity thee.
GEORGE
Where's Captain Margaret, to fence you now?
WARWICK
They mock thee, Clifford: swear as thou wast wont.
RICHARD
What, not an oath? nay, then the world goes hard,
When Clifford cannot spare his friends an oath.
I know by that he's dead; and, by my soul,
If this right hand would buy two hours' life,
That I in all despite might rail at him,
This hand should chop it off, and with the issuing
    blood
Stifle the villain, whose unstanched thirst
York and young Rutland could not satisfy.
WARWICK
Ay, but he's dead: off with the traitor's head,
And rear it in the place your father's stands.
And now to London with triumphant march,
There to be crowned England's royal king:
From whence shall Warwick cut the sea to France,
And ask the Lady Bona for thy queen:

So shalt thou sinew both these lands together;
And, having France thy friend, thou shalt not dread
The scatter'd foe that hopes to rise again;
For though they cannot greatly sting to hurt,
Yet look to have them buzz to offend thine ears.
First will I see the coronation;
And then to Brittany I'll cross the sea,
To effect this marriage, so it please my lord.

EDWARD

Even as thou wilt, sweet Warwick, let it be;
For in thy shoulder do I build my seat,
And never will I undertake the thing
Wherein thy counsel and consent is wanting.
Richard, I will create thee Duke of Gloucester,
And George, of Clarence: Warwick, as ourself,
Shall do and undo as him pleaseth best.

RICHARD

Let me be Duke of Clarence, George of Gloucester;
For Gloucester's dukedom is too ominous.

WARWICK

Tut, that's a foolish observation:
Richard, be Duke of Gloucester. Now to London,
To see these honours in possession.   [*Exeunt*

ACT III

SCENE I. *A forest in the north of England*

Enter two KEEPERS, *with cross-bows in their hands*

FIRST KEEPER

Under this thick-grown brake we'll shroud our-
  selves;
For through this laund anon the deer will come;
And in this covert will we make our stand,
Culling the principal of all the deer.

SECOND KEEPER

I'll stay above the hill, so both may shoot.

FIRST KEEPER

That cannot be; the noise of thy cross-bow
Will scare the herd, and so my shoot is lost.
Here stand we both, and aim we at the best:
And, for the time shall not seem tedious,
I'll tell thee what befel me on a day
In this self-place where now we mean to stand.

SECOND KEEPER

Here comes a man; let's stay till he be past.

Enter KING HENRY, *disguised, with a prayer-book*

KING HENRY

From Scotland am I stol'n, even of pure love,
To greet mine own land with my wishful sight.
No, Harry, Harry, 'tis no land of thine;
Thy place is fill'd, thy sceptre wrung from thee,
Thy balm wash'd off wherewith thou wast a-
  nointed:
No bending knee will call thee Cæsar now,
No humble suitors press to speak for right,
No, not a man comes for redress of thee;
For how can I help them, and not myself?

FIRST KEEPER

Ay, here's a deer whose skin's a keeper's fee:
This is the quondam king; let's seize upon him.

KING HENRY

Let me embrace thee, sour adversity,
For wise men say it is the wisest course.

SECOND KEEPER

Why linger we? let us lay hands upon him.

FIRST KEEPER

Forbear awhile; we'll hear a little more.

KING HENRY

My queen and son are gone to France for aid;
And, as I hear, the great commanding Warwick
Is thither gone, to crave the French king's sister
To wife for Edward: if this news be true,
Poor queen and son, your labour is but lost;
For Warwick is a subtle orator,
And Lewis a prince soon won with moving words.
By this account then Margaret may win him;
For she's a woman to be pitied much:
Her sighs will make a battery in his breast;
Her tears will pierce into a marble heart;
The tiger will be mild whiles she doth mourn;
And Nero will be tainted with remorse,
To hear and see her plaints, her brinish tears.
Ay, but she's come to beg, Warwick, to give;
She, on his left side, craving aid for Henry,
He, on his right, asking a wife for Edward.
She weeps, and says her Henry is deposed;
He smiles, and says his Edward is install'd;
That she, poor wretch, for grief can speak no more;
Whiles Warwick tells his title, smooths the wrong,
Inferreth arguments of mighty strength,
And in conclusion wins the king from her,
With promise of his sister, and what else,
To strengthen and support King Edward's place.
O Margaret, thus 'twill be; and thou, poor soul,
Art then forsaken, as thou went'st forlorn!

SECOND KEEPER

Say, what art thou that talk'st of kings and queens?

KING HENRY

More than I seem, and less than I was born to:
A man at least, for less I should not be;
And men may talk of kings, and why not I?

SECOND KEEPER

Ay, but thou talk'st as if thou wert a king.

KING HENRY

Why, so I am, in mind; and that's enough.

SECOND KEEPER

But, if thou be a king, where is thy crown?

KING HENRY

My crown is in my heart, not on my head;
Not deck'd with diamonds and Indian stones,
Nor to be seen: my crown is call'd content:
A crown it is that seldom kings enjoy.

SECOND KEEPER

Well, if you be a king crown'd with content,
Your crown content and you must be contented
To go along with us; for, as we think,
You are the king King Edward hath deposed;

And we his subjects sworn in all allegiance
Will apprehend you as his enemy.

KING HENRY
But did you never swear, and break an oath?

SECOND KEEPER
No, never such an oath; nor will not now.

KING HENRY
Where did you dwell when I was King of England?

SECOND KEEPER
Here in this country, where we now remain.

KING HENRY
I was anointed king at nine months old;
My father and my grandfather were kings,
And you were sworn true subjects unto me:
And tell me, then, have you not broke your oaths?

FIRST KEEPER
No;
For we were subjects but while you were king.

KING HENRY
Why, am I dead? do I not breathe a man?
Ah, simple men, you know not what you swear!
Look, as I blow this feather from my face,
And as the air blows it to me again,
Obeying with my wind when I do blow,
And yielding to another when it blows,
Commanded always by the greater gust;
Such is the lightness of you common men.
But do not break your oaths; for of that sin
My mild entreaty shall not make you guilty.
Go where you will, the king shall be commanded;
And be you kings, command, and I'll obey.

FIRST KEEPER
We are true subjects to the king, King Edward.

KING HENRY
So would you be again to Henry,
If he were seated as King Edward is.

FIRST KEEPER
We charge you, in God's name, and the king's,
To go with us unto the officers.

KING HENRY
In God's name, lead; your king's name be obey'd:
And what God will, that let your king perform;
And what he will, I humbly yield unto.   [Exeunt

SCENE II. *London. The palace*

Enter KING EDWARD, GLOUCESTER, CLARENCE, *and*
LADY GREY

KING EDWARD
Brother of Gloucester, at Saint Alban's field
This lady's husband, Sir Richard Grey, was slain,
His lands then seized on by the conqueror:
Her suit is now to repossess those lands;
Which we in justice cannot well deny,
Because in quarrel of the house of York
The worthy gentleman did lose his life.

GLOUCESTER
Your highness shall do well to grant her suit;
It were dishonour to deny it her.

KING EDWARD
It were no less; but yet I'll make a pause.

GLOUCESTER
[*Aside to* CLARENCE] Yea, is it so?
I see the lady hath a thing to grant,
Before the king will grant her humble suit.

CLARENCE
[*Aside to* GLOUCESTER] He knows the game: how true
   he keeps the wind!

GLOUCESTER
[*Aside to* CLARENCE] Silence!

KING EDWARD
Widow, we will consider of your suit;
And come some other time to know our mind.

LADY GREY
Right gracious lord, I cannot brook delay:
May it please your highness to resolve me now;
And what your pleasure is, shall satisfy me.

GLOUCESTER
[*Aside to* CLARENCE] Ay, widow? then I'll warrant
   you all your lands,
An if what pleases him shall pleasure you.
Fight closer, or, good faith, you'll catch a blow.

CLARENCE
[*Aside to* GLOUCESTER] I fear her not, unless she
   chance to fall.

GLOUCESTER
[*Aside to* CLARENCE] God forbid that! for he'll take
   vantages.

KING EDWARD
How many children hast thou, widow? tell me.

CLARENCE
[*Aside to* GLOUCESTER] I think he means to beg a
   child of her.

GLOUCESTER
[*Aside to* CLARENCE] Nay, whip me then: he'll rather
   give her two.

LADY GREY
Three, my most gracious lord.

GLOUCESTER
[*Aside to* CLARENCE] You shall have four, if you'll be
   ruled by him.

KING EDWARD
'Twere pity they should lose their father's lands.

LADY GREY
Be pitiful, dread lord, and grant it then.

KING EDWARD
Lords, give us leave: I'll try this widow's wit.

GLOUCESTER
[*Aside to* CLARENCE] Ay, good leave have you; for
   you will have leave,
Till youth take leave and leave you to the crutch.
       [GLOUCESTER *and* CLARENCE *retire*

KING EDWARD
Now tell me, madam, do you love your children?

LADY GREY
Ay, full as dearly as I love myself.

KING EDWARD
And would you not do much to do them good?

LADY GREY

To do them good, I would sustain some harm.

KING EDWARD

Then get your husband's lands, to do them good.

LADY GREY

Therefore I came unto your majesty.

KING EDWARD

I'll tell you how these lands are to be got.

LADY GREY

So shall you bind me to your highness' service.

KING EDWARD

What **service wil**t thou do me, if I give them?

LADY GREY

What you command, that rests in me to do.

KING EDWARD

But you will take exceptions to my boon.

LADY GREY

No, gracious lord, except I cannot do it.

KING EDWARD

Ay, but thou canst do what I mean to ask.

LADY GREY

Why, then I will do what your grace commands.

GLOUCESTER

[*Aside to* CLARENCE] He plies her hard; and much
rain wears the marble.

CLARENCE

[*Aside to* GLOUCESTER] As red as fire! nay, then her
wax must melt.

LADY GREY

Why stops my lord? shall I not hear my task?

KING EDWARD

An easy task; 'tis but to love a king.

LADY GREY

That's soon perform'd, because I am a subject.

KING EDWARD

Why, then, thy husband's lands I freely give thee.

LADY GREY

I take my leave with many thousand thanks.

GLOUCESTER

[*Aside to* CLARENCE] The match is made; she seals it
with a curt'sy.

KING EDWARD

But stay thee, 'tis the fruits of love I mean.

LADY GREY

The fruits of love I mean, my loving liege.

KING EDWARD

Ay, but, I fear me, in another sense.
What love, think'st thou, I sue so much to get?

LADY GREY

My love till death, my humble thanks, my prayers;
That love which virtue begs and virtue grants.

KING EDWARD

No, by my troth, I did not mean such love.

LADY GREY

Why, then you mean not as I thought you did.

KING EDWARD

But now you partly may perceive my mind.

LADY GREY

My mind will never grant what I perceive
Your highness aims at, if I aim aright.

KING EDWARD

To tell thee plain, I aim to lie with thee.

LADY GREY

To tell you plain, I had rather lie in prison.

KING EDWARD

Why, then thou shalt not have thy husband's lands.

LADY GREY

Why, then mine honesty shall be my dower;
For by that loss I will not purchase them.

KING EDWARD

Therein thou wrong'st thy children mightily.

LADY GREY

Herein your highness wrongs both them and me.
But, mighty lord, this merry inclination
Accords not with the sadness of my suit:
Please you dismiss me, either with 'ay' or 'no.'

KING EDWARD

Ay, if thou wilt say 'ay' to my request;
No, if thou dost say 'no' to my demand.

LADY GREY

Then, no, my lord. My suit is at an end.

GLOUCESTER

[*Aside to* CLARENCE] The widow likes him not, she
knits her brows.

CLARENCE

[*Aside to* GLOUCESTER] He is the bluntest wooer in
Christendom.

KING EDWARD

[*Aside*] Her looks do argue her replete with mod-
esty;
Her words do show her wit incomparable;
All her perfections challenge sovereignty:
One way or other, she is for a king;
And she shall be my love, or else my queen.—
Say that King Edward take thee for his queen?

LADY GREY

'Tis better said than done, my gracious lord:
I am a subject fit to jest withal,
But far unfit to be a sovereign.

KING EDWARD

Sweet widow, by my state I swear to thee,
I speak no more than what my soul intends;
And that is, to enjoy thee for my love.

LADY GREY

And that is more than I will yield unto:
I know I am too mean to be your queen,
And yet too good to be your concubine.

KING EDWARD

You cavil, widow: I did mean, my queen.

LADY GREY

'Twill grieve your grace my sons should call you
father.

KING EDWARD

No more than when my daughters call thee mother.
Thou art a widow, and thou hast some children;
And, by God's mother, I, being but a bachelor,
Have other some: why, 'tis a happy thing
To be the father unto many sons.
Answer no more, for thou shalt be my queen.

GLOUCESTER

[*Aside to* CLARENCE] The ghostly father now hath
done his shrift.

CLARENCE

[*Aside to* GLOUCESTER] When he was made a shriver,
'twas for shift.

KING EDWARD

Brothers, you muse what chat we two have had.

GLOUCESTER

The widow likes it not, for she looks very sad.

KING EDWARD

You'ld think it strange if I should marry her.

CLARENCE

To whom, my lord?

KING EDWARD

Why, Clarence, to myself.

GLOUCESTER

That would be ten days' wonder at the least.

CLARENCE

That's a day longer than a wonder lasts.

GLOUCESTER

By so much is the wonder in extremes.

KING EDWARD

Well, jest on, brothers: I can tell you both,
Her suit is granted for her husband's lands.

Enter a NOBLEMAN

NOBLEMAN

My gracious lord, Henry your foe is taken,
And brought your prisoner to your palace gate.

KING EDWARD

See that he be convey'd unto the Tower:
And go we, brothers, to the man that took him,
To question of his apprehension.
Widow, go you along. Lords, use her honourably.

[*Exeunt all but* GLOUCESTER

GLOUCESTER

Ay, Edward will use women honourably.
Would he were wasted, marrow, bones and all,
That from his loins no hopeful branch may spring,
To cross me from the golden time I look for!
And yet, between my soul's desire and me—
The lustful Edward's title buried—
Is Clarence, Henry, and his son young Edward,
And all the unlook'd for issue of their bodies,
To take their rooms, ere I can place myself:
A cold premeditation for my purpose!
Why, then, I do but dream on sovereignty;
Like one that stands upon a promontory,
And spies a far-off shore where he would tread,
Wishing his foot were equal with his eye,
And chides the sea that sunders him from thence,
Saying, he'll lade it dry to have his way:
So do I wish the crown, being so far off;
And so I chide the means that keeps me from it;
And so I say, I'll cut the causes off,
Flattering me with impossibilities.
My eye's too quick, my heart o'erweens too much,
Unless my hand and strength could equal them.
Well, say there is no kingdom then for Richard;

What other pleasure can the world afford?
I'll make my heaven in a lady's lap,
And deck my body in gay ornaments,
And witch sweet ladies with my words and looks.
O miserable thought! and more unlikely
Than to accomplish twenty golden crowns!
Why, love forswore me in my mother's womb
And, for I should not deal in her soft laws,
She did corrupt frail nature with some bribe,
To shrink mine arm up like a wither'd shrub;
To make an envious mountain on my back,
Where sits deformity to mock my body;
To shape my legs of an unequal size;
To disproportion me in every part,
Like to a chaos, or an unlick'd bear-whelp
That carries no impression like the dam.
And am I then a man to be beloved?
O monstrous fault, to harbour such a thought!
Then, since this earth affords no joy to me,
But to command, to check, to o'erbear such
As are of better person than myself,
I'll make my heaven to dream upon the crown,
And, whiles I live, to account this world but hell,
Until my mis-shaped trunk that bears this head
Be round impaled with a glorious crown.
And yet I know not how to get the crown,
For many lives stand between me and home:
And I,—like one lost in a thorny wood,
That rends the thorns and is rent with the thorns,
Seeking a way and straying from the way;
Not knowing how to find the open air,
But toiling desperately to find it out,—
Torment myself to catch the English crown:
And from that torment I will free myself,
Or hew my way out with a bloody axe.
Why, I can smile, and murder whiles I smile,
And cry 'Content' to that which grieves my heart,
And wet my cheeks with artificial tears,
And frame my face to all occasions.
I'll drown more sailors than the mermaid shall;
I'll slay more gazers than the basilisk;
I'll play the orator as well as Nestor,
Deceive more slily than Ulysses could,
And, like a Sinon, take another Troy.
I can add colours to the chameleon,
Change shapes with Proteus for advantages,
And set the murderous Machiavel to school.
Can I do this, and cannot get a crown?
Tut, were it farther off, I'll pluck it down.   [*Exit*

SCENE III. *France. The* KING'S *palace*

Flourish. Enter LEWIS *the French King, his sister* BONA,
his Admiral, called BOURBON: PRINCE EDWARD, QUEEN
MARGARET, *and the* EARL OF OXFORD. LEWIS *sits, and
riseth up again*

KING LEWIS

Fair Queen of England, worthy Margaret,
Sit down with us: it ill befits thy state

And birth, that thou shouldst stand while Lewis
doth sit.

QUEEN MARGARET

No, mighty King of France: now Margaret
Must strike her sail and learn a while to serve
Where kings command. I was, I must confess,
Great Albion's queen in former golden days:
But now mischance hath trod my title down,
And with dishonour laid me on the ground;
Where I must take like seat unto my fortune,
And to my humble seat conform myself.

KING LEWIS

Why, say, fair queen, whence springs this deep
despair?

QUEEN MARGARET

From such a cause as fills mine eyes with tears,
And stops my tongue, while heart is drown'd in
cares.

KING LEWIS

Whate'er it be, be thou still like thyself,
And sit thee by our side: [Seats her by him] yield not
thy neck
To fortune's yoke, but let thy dauntless mind
Still ride in triumph over all mischance.
Be plain, Queen Margaret, and tell thy grief;
It shall be eased, if France can yield relief.

QUEEN MARGARET

Those gracious words revive my drooping thoughts,
And give my tongue-tied sorrows leave to speak.
Now, therefore, be it known to noble Lewis,
That Henry, sole possessor of my love,
Is of a king become a banish'd man,
And forced to live in Scotland a forlorn;
While proud ambitious Edward Duke of York
Usurps the regal title, and the seat
Of England's true-anointed lawful king.
This is the cause that I, poor Margaret,
With this my son, Prince Edward, Henry's heir,
Am come to crave thy just and lawful aid;
And if thou fail us, all our hope is done:
Scotland hath will to help, but cannot help;
Our people and our peers are both misled,
Our treasure seized, our soldiers put to flight,
And, as thou seest, ourselves in heavy plight.

KING LEWIS

Renowned queen, with patience calm the storm,
While we bethink a means to break it off.

QUEEN MARGARET

The more we stay, the stronger grows our foe.

KING LEWIS

The more I stay, the more I'll succour thee.

QUEEN MARGARET

O, but impatience waiteth on true sorrow.
And see where comes the breeder of my sorrow!

Enter WARWICK

KING LEWIS

What's he approacheth boldly to our presence?

QUEEN MARGARET

Our Earl of Warwick, Edward's greatest friend.

KING LEWIS

Welcome, brave Warwick! What brings thee to
France?   [He descends. She ariseth

QUEEN MARGARET

Ay, now begins a second storm to rise;
For this is he that moves both wind and tide.

WARWICK

From worthy Edward, king of Albion,
My lord and sovereign, and thy vowed friend,
I come, in kindness and unfeigned love,
First, to do greetings to thy royal person;
And then to crave a league of amity;
And lastly, to confirm that amity
With nuptial knot, if thou vouchsafe to grant
That virtuous Lady Bona, thy fair sister,
To England's king in lawful marriage.

QUEEN MARGARET

[Aside] If that go forward, Henry's hope is done.

WARWICK

[To BONA] And, gracious madam, in our king's be-
half,
I am commanded, with your leave and favour,
Humbly to kiss your hand, and with my tongue
To tell the passion of my sovereign's heart;
Where fame, late entering at his heedful ears,
Hath placed thy beauty's image and thy virtue.

QUEEN MARGARET

King Lewis and Lady Bona, hear me speak,
Before you answer Warwick. His demand
Springs not from Edward's well-meant honest love,
But from deceit bred by necessity;
For how can tyrants safely govern home,
Unless abroad they purchase great alliance?
To prove him tyrant this reason may suffice,
That Henry liveth still; but were he dead,
Yet here Prince Edward stands, King Henry's son.
Look, therefore, Lewis, that by this league and mar-
riage
Thou draw not on thy danger and dishonour;
For though usurpers sway the rule a while,
Yet heavens are just, and time suppresseth wrongs.

WARWICK

Injurious Margaret!

PRINCE

And why not queen?

WARWICK

Because thy father Henry did usurp;
And thou no more art prince than she is queen.

OXFORD

Then Warwick disannuls great John of Gaunt,
Which did subdue the greatest part of Spain;
And, after John of Gaunt, Henry the Fourth,
Whose wisdom was a mirror to the wisest;
And, after that wise prince, Henry the Fifth,
Who by his prowess conquered all France:
From these our Henry lineally descends.

WARWICK

Oxford, how haps it, in this smooth discourse,
You told not how Henry the Sixth hath lost
All that which Henry the Fifth had gotten?

Methinks these peers of France should smile at that.
But for the rest, you tell a pedigree
Of threescore and two years; a silly time
To make prescription for a kingdom's worth.

OXFORD

Why, Warwick, canst thou speak against thy liege,
Whom thou obeyed'st thirty and six years,
And not bewray thy treason with a blush?

WARWICK

Can Oxford, that did ever fence the right,
Now buckler falsehood with a pedigree?
For shame! leave Henry, and call Edward king.

OXFORD

Call him my king by whose injurious doom
My elder brother, the Lord Aubrey Vere,
Was done to death? and more than so, my father,
Even in the downfall of his mellow'd years,
When nature brought him to the door of death?
No, Warwick, no; while life upholds this arm,
This arm upholds the house of Lancaster.

WARWICK

And I the house of York.

KING LEWIS

Queen Margaret, Prince Edward, and Oxford,
Vouchsafe, at our request, to stand aside,
While I use further conference with Warwick.

[They stand aloof

QUEEN MARGARET

Heavens grant that Warwick's words bewitch him
not!

KING LEWIS

Now, Warwick, tell me, even upon thy conscience,
Is Edward your true king? for I were loath
To link with him that were not lawful chosen.

WARWICK

Thereon I pawn my credit and mine honour.

KING LEWIS

But is he gracious in the people's eye?

WARWICK

The more that Henry was unfortunate.

KING LEWIS

Then further, all dissembling set aside,
Tell me for truth the measure of his love
Unto our sister Bona.

WARWICK

Such it seems
As may beseem a monarch like himself.
Myself have often heard him say and swear
That this his love was an eternal plant,
Whereof the root was fix'd in virtue's ground,
The leaves and fruit maintain'd with beauty's sun,
Exempt from envy, but not from disdain,
Unless the Lady Bona quit his pain.

KING LEWIS

Now, sister, let us hear your firm resolve.

BONA

Your grant, or your denial, shall be mine:
[To WARWICK] Yet I confess that often ere this day,
When I have heard your king's desert recounted,
Mine ear hath tempted judgement to desire.

KING LEWIS

Then, Warwick, thus: our sister shall be Edward's;
And now forthwith shall articles be drawn
Touching the jointure that your king must make,
Which with her dowry shall be counterpoised.
Draw near, Queen Margaret, and be a witness
That Bona shall be wife to the English king.

PRINCE

To Edward, but not to the English king.

QUEEN MARGARET

Deceitful Warwick! it was thy device
By this alliance to make void my suit:
Before thy coming Lewis was Henry's friend.

KING LEWIS

And still is friend to him and Margaret:
But if your title to the crown be weak,
As may appear by Edward's good success,
Then 'tis but reason that I be released
From giving aid which late I promised.
Yet shall you have all kindness at my hand
That your estate requires and mine can yield.

WARWICK

Henry now lives in Scotland at his ease,
Where having nothing, nothing can he lose.
And as for you yourself, our quondam queen,
You have a father able to maintain you;
And better 'twere you troubled him than France.

QUEEN MARGARET

Peace, impudent and shameless Warwick, peace,
Proud setter up and puller down of kings!
I will not hence, till, with my talk and tears,
Both full of truth, I make King Lewis behold
Thy sly conveyance, and thy lord's false love;
For both of you are birds of selfsame feather.

[POST blows a horn within

KING LEWIS

Warwick, this is some post to us or thee.

Enter a POST

POST

[To WARWICK] My lord ambassador, these letters
are for you,
Sent from your brother, Marquess Montague:
[To LEWIS] These from our king unto your majesty:
[To MARGARET] And, madam, these for you; from
whom I know not.   [They all read their letters

OXFORD

I like it well that our fair queen and mistress
Smiles at her news, while Warwick frowns at his.

PRINCE

Nay, mark how Lewis stamps, as he were nettled:
I hope all's for the best.

KING LEWIS

Warwick, what are thy news? and yours, fair queen?

QUEEN MARGARET

Mine, such as fill my heart with unhoped joys.

WARWICK

Mine, full of sorrow and heart's discontent.

KING LEWIS

What! has your king married the Lady Grey?

And now, to soothe your forgery and his,
Sends me a paper to persuade me patience?
Is this the alliance that he seeks with France?
Dare he presume to scorn us in this manner?

QUEEN MARGARET

I told your majesty as much before:
This proveth Edward's love and Warwick's honesty.

WARWICK

King Lewis, I here protest, in sight of heaven,
And by the hope I have of heavenly bliss,
That I am clear from this misdeed of Edward's,
No more my king, for he dishonours me,
But most himself, if he could see his shame.
Did I forget that by the house of York
My father came untimely to his death?
Did I let pass the abuse done to my niece?
Did I impale him with the regal crown?
Did I put Henry from his native right?
And am I guerdon'd at the last with shame?
Shame on himself! for my desert is honour:
And to repair my honour lost for him,
I here renounce him and return to Henry.
My noble queen, let former grudges pass,
And henceforth I am thy true servitor:
I will revenge his wrong to Lady Bona,
And replant Henry in his former state.

QUEEN MARGARET

Warwick, these words have turn'd my hate to love;
And I forgive and quite forget old faults,
And joy that thou becomest King Henry's friend.

WARWICK

So much his friend, ay, his unfeigned friend,
That, if King Lewis vouchsafe to furnish us
With some few bands of chosen soldiers,
I'll undertake to land them on our coast,
And force the tyrant from his seat by war.
'Tis not his new-made bride shall succour him:
And as for Clarence, as my letters tell me,
He's very likely now to fall from him,
For matching more for wanton lust than honour,
Or than for strength and safety of our country.

BONA

Dear brother, how shall Bona be revenged
But by thy help to this distressed queen?

QUEEN MARGARET

Renowned prince, how shall poor Henry live,
Unless thou rescue him from foul despair?

BONA

My quarrel and this English queen's are one.

WARWICK

And mine, fair Lady Bona, joins with yours.

KING LEWIS

And mine with hers, and thine, and Margaret's.
Therefore at last I firmly am resolved
You shall have aid.

QUEEN MARGARET

Let me give humble thanks for all at once.

KING LEWIS

Then, England's messenger, return in post,
And tell false Edward, thy supposed king,
That Lewis of France is sending over masquers,
To revel it with him and his new bride:
Thou seest what's past, go fear thy king withal.

BONA

Tell him, in hope he'll prove a widower shortly,
I'll wear the willow garland for his sake.

QUEEN MARGARET

Tell him, my mourning weeds are laid aside,
And I am ready to put armour on.

WARWICK

Tell him from me that he hath done me wrong,
And therefore I'll uncrown him ere 't be long.
There's thy reward: be gone.　　　[Exit POST

KING LEWIS

　　　　　　　　But, Warwick,
Thou and Oxford, with five thousand men,
Shall cross the seas, and bid false Edward battle;
And, as occasion serves, this noble queen
And prince shall follow with a fresh supply.
Yet, ere thou go, but answer me one doubt,
What pledge have we of thy firm loyalty?

WARWICK

This shall assure my constant loyalty,
That if our queen and this young prince agree,
I'll join mine eldest daughter and my joy
To him forthwith in holy wedlock bands.

QUEEN MARGARET

Yes, I agree, and thank you for your motion.
Son Edward, she is fair and virtuous,
Therefore delay not, give thy hand to Warwick;
And, with thy hand, thy faith irrevocable,
That only Warwick's daughter shall be thine.

PRINCE

Yes, I accept her, for she well deserves it;
And here, to pledge my vow, I give my hand.
　　　　　[He gives his hand to WARWICK

KING LEWIS

Why stay we now? These soldiers shall be levied,
And thou, Lord Bourbon, our high admiral,
Shalt waft them over with our royal fleet.
I long till Edward fall by war's mischance,
For mocking marriage with a dame of France.
　　　　　[Exeunt all but WARWICK

WARWICK

I came from England as ambassador,
But I return his sworn and mortal foe:
Matter of marriage was the charge he gave me,
But dreadful war shall answer his demand.
Had he none else to make a stale but me?
Then none but I shall turn his jest to sorrow.
I was the chief that raised him to the crown,
And I'll be chief to bring him down again:
Not that I pity Henry's misery,
But seek revenge on Edward's mockery.　　　[Exit

ACT IV

Scene I. *London. The palace*

Enter GLOUCESTER, CLARENCE, SOMERSET, *and* MONTAGUE

GLOUCESTER

Now tell me, brother Clarence, what think you
Of this new marriage with the Lady Grey?
Hath not our brother made a worthy choice?

CLARENCE

Alas, you know, 'tis far from hence to France;
How could he stay till Warwick made return?

SOMERSET

My lords, forbear this talk; here comes the king.

GLOUCESTER

And his well-chosen bride.

CLARENCE

I mind to tell him plainly what I think.

Flourish. Enter KING EDWARD, *attended;* LADY GREY, *as Queen;* PEMBROKE, STAFFORD, HASTINGS, *and others*

KING EDWARD

Now, brother of Clarence, how like you our choice,
That you stand pensive, as half malcontent?

CLARENCE

As well as Lewis of France, or the Earl of Warwick,
Which are so weak of courage and in judgement
That they'll take no offence at our abuse.

KING EDWARD

Suppose they take offence without a cause,
They are but Lewis and Warwick: I am Edward,
Your king and Warwick's, and must have my will.

GLOUCESTER

And shall have your will, because our king:
Yet hasty marriage seldom proveth well.

KING EDWARD

Yea, brother Richard, are you offended too?

GLOUCESTER

Not I:
No, God forbid that I should wish them sever'd
Whom God hath join'd together; ay, and 'twere
pity
To sunder them that yoke so well together.

KING EDWARD

Setting your scorns and your mislike aside,
Tell me some reason why the Lady Grey
Should not become my wife and England's queen.
And you too, Somerset and Montague,
Speak freely what you think.

CLARENCE

Then this is mine opinion: that King Lewis
Becomes your enemy, for mocking him
About the marriage of the Lady Bona.

GLOUCESTER

And Warwick, doing what you gave in charge,
Is now dishonoured by this new marriage.

KING EDWARD

What if both Lewis and Warwick be appeased
By such invention as I can devise?

MONTAGUE

Yet, to have join'd with France in such alliance
Would more have strengthen'd this our commonwealth
'Gainst foreign storms than any home-bred marriage.

HASTINGS

Why, knows not Montague that of itself
England is safe, if true within itself?

MONTAGUE

But the safer when 'tis back'd with France.

HASTINGS

'Tis better using France than trusting France:
Let us be back'd with God and with the seas,
Which He hath given for fence impregnable,
And with their helps only defend ourselves;
In them and in ourselves our safety lies.

CLARENCE

For this one speech Lord Hastings well deserves
To have the heir of the Lord Hungerford.

KING EDWARD

Ay, what of that? it was my will and grant;
And for this once my will shall stand for law.

GLOUCESTER

And yet methinks your grace hath not done well,
To give the heir and daughter of Lord Scales
Unto the brother of your loving bride;
She better would have fitted me or Clarence:
But in your bride you bury brotherhood.

CLARENCE

Or else you would not have bestow'd the heir
Of the Lord Bonville on your new wife's son,
And leave your brothers to go speed elsewhere.

KING EDWARD

Alas, poor Clarence! is it for a wife
That thou art malcontent? I will provide thee.

CLARENCE

In choosing for yourself, you show'd your judge-
ment,
Which being shallow, you shall give me leave
To play the broker in mine own behalf;
And to that end I shortly mind to leave you.

KING EDWARD

Leave me, or tarry, Edward will be king,
And not be tied unto his brother's will.

QUEEN ELIZABETH

My lords, before it pleased his majesty
To raise my state to title of a queen,
Do me but right, and you must all confess
That I was not ignoble of descent;
And meaner than myself have had like fortune.
But as this title honours me and mine,
So your dislike, to whom I would be pleasing,
Doth cloud my joys with danger and with sorrow.

KING EDWARD

My love, forbear to fawn upon their frowns:
What danger or what sorrow can befall thee,
So long as Edward is thy constant friend,
And their true sovereign, whom they must obey?
Nay, whom they shall obey, and love thee too,

Unless they seek for hatred at my hands;
Which if they do, yet will I keep thee safe,
And they shall feel the vengeance of my wrath.

GLOUCESTER

I hear, yet say not much, but think the more. [Aside

Enter a POST

KING EDWARD

Now, messenger, what letters or what news
From France?

POST

My sovereign liege, no letters; and few words,
But such as I, without your special pardon,
Dare not relate.

KING EDWARD

Go to, we pardon thee: therefore, in brief,
Tell me their words as near as thou canst guess
them.
What answer makes King Lewis unto our letters?

POST

At my depart, these were his very words:
'Go tell false Edward, thy supposed king,
That Lewis of France is sending over masquers
To revel it with him and his new bride.'

KING EDWARD

Is Lewis so brave? belike he thinks me Henry.
But what said Lady Bona to my marriage?

POST

These were her words, utter'd with mild disdain:
'Tell him, in hope he'll prove a widower shortly,
I'll wear the willow garland for his sake.'

KING EDWARD

I blame not her, she could say little less;
She had the wrong. But what said Henry's queen?
For I have heard that she was there in place.

POST

'Tell him,' quoth she, 'my mourning weeds are
done,
And I am ready to put armour on.'

KING EDWARD

Belike she minds to play the Amazon.
But what said Warwick to these injuries?

POST

He, more incensed against your majesty
Than all the rest, discharged me with these words:
'Tell him from me that he hath done me wrong,
And therefore I'll uncrown him ere 't be long.'

KING EDWARD

Ha! durst the traitor breathe out so proud words?
Well, I will arm me, being thus forewarn'd:
They shall have wars and pay for their presumption.
But say, is Warwick friends with Margaret?

POST

Ay, gracious sovereign; they are so link'd in friendship,
That young Prince Edward marries Warwick's
daughter.

CLARENCE

Belike the elder; Clarence will have the younger.
Now, brother king, farewell, and sit you fast,
For I will hence to Warwick's other daughter;

That, though I want a kingdom, yet in marriage
I may not prove inferior to yourself.
You that love me and Warwick, follow me.

[Exit CLARENCE, and SOMERSET follows

GLOUCESTER

[Aside] Not I:
My thoughts aim at a further matter; I
Stay not for the love of Edward, but the crown.

KING EDWARD

Clarence and Somerset both gone to Warwick!
Yet am I arm'd against the worst can happen;
And haste is needful in this desperate case.
Pembroke and Stafford, you in our behalf
Go levy men, and make prepare for war;
They are already, or quickly will be landed:
Myself in person will straight follow you.

[Exeunt PEMBROKE and STAFFORD

But, ere I go, Hastings and Montague,
Resolve my doubt. You twain, of all the rest,
Are near to Warwick by blood and by alliance:
Tell me if you love Warwick more than me;
If it be so, then both depart to him;
I rather wish you foes than hollow friends:
But if you mind to hold your true obedience,
Give me assurance with some friendly vow,
That I may never have you in suspect.

MONTAGUE

So God help Montague as he proves true!

HASTINGS

And Hastings as he favours Edward's cause!

KING EDWARD

Now, brother Richard, will you stand by us?

GLOUCESTER

Ay, in despite of all that shall withstand you.

KING EDWARD

Why, so! them am I sure of victory.
Now therefore let us hence; and lose no hour,
Till we meet Warwick with his foreign power.

[Exeunt

SCENE II. A plain in Warwickshire

Enter WARWICK and OXFORD, with FRENCH SOLDIERS

WARWICK

Trust me, my lord, all hitherto goes well;
The common people by numbers swarm to us.

Enter CLARENCE and SOMERSET

But see where Somerset and Clarence comes!
Speak suddenly, my lords, are we all friends?

CLARENCE

Fear not that, my lord.

WARWICK

Then, gentle Clarence, welcome unto Warwick;
And welcome, Somerset: I hold it cowardice
To rest mistrustful where a noble heart
Hath pawn'd an open hand in sign of love;
Else might I think that Clarence, Edward's brother,
Were but a feigned friend to our proceedings:
But welcome, sweet Clarence; my daughter shall be
thine.

And now what rests but, in night's coverture,
Thy brother being carelessly encamp'd,
His soldiers lurking in the towns about,
And but attended by a simple guard,
We may surprise and take him at our pleasure?
Our scouts have found the adventure very easy:
That as Ulysses and stout Diomede
With sleight and manhood stole to Rhesus' tents,
And brought from thence the Thracian fatal steeds,
So we, well cover'd with the night's black mantle,
At unawares may beat down Edward's guard,
And seize himself; I say not, slaughter him,
For I intend but only to surprise him.
You that will follow me to this attempt,
Applaud the name of Henry with your leader.
                                        [*They all cry, 'Henry!'*
Why, then, let's on our way in silent sort:
For Warwick and his friends, God and Saint George!
                                        [*Exeunt*

SCENE III. EDWARD'S *camp, near* WARWICK

Enter three WATCHMEN, *to guard the* KING'S *tent*
                    FIRST WATCHMAN
Come on, my masters, each man take his stand:
The king by this is set him down to sleep.
                    SECOND WATCHMAN
What, will he not to bed?
                    FIRST WATCHMAN
Why, no; for he hath made a solemn vow,
Never to lie and take his natural rest,
Till Warwick or himself be quite suppress'd.
                    SECOND WATCHMAN
To-morrow then belike shall be the day,
If Warwick be so near as men report.
                    THIRD WATCHMAN
But say, I pray, what nobleman is that,
That with the king here resteth in his tent?
                    FIRST WATCHMAN
'Tis the Lord Hastings, the king's chiefest friend.
                    THIRD WATCHMAN
O, is it so? But why commands the king
That his chief followers lodge in towns about him,
While he himself keeps in the cold field?
                    SECOND WATCHMAN
'Tis the more honour, because more dangerous.
                    THIRD WATCHMAN
Ay, but give me worship and quietness;
I like it better than a dangerous honour.
If Warwick knew in what estate he stands,
'Tis to be doubted he would waken him.
                    FIRST WATCHMAN
Unless our halberds did shut up his passage.
                    SECOND WATCHMAN
Ay, wherefore else guard we his royal tent,
But to defend his person from night-foes?
Enter WARWICK, CLARENCE, OXFORD, SOMERSET, *and*
          FRENCH SOLDIERS, *silent all*

                    WARWICK
This is his tent; and see where stand his guard.
Courage, my masters! honour now or never!
But follow me, and Edward shall be ours.
                    FIRST WATCHMAN
Who goes there?
                    SECOND WATCHMAN
Stay, or thou diest!
[WARWICK *and the rest cry all, 'Warwick! Warwick!'*
and set upon the GUARD, *who fly, crying, 'Arm! arm!'*
          WARWICK *and the rest following them*
The drum playing and trumpet sounding, re-enter WAR-
WICK, SOMERSET, *and the rest, bringing the* KING *out in*
his gown, sitting in a chair. RICHARD *and* HASTINGS *fly*
                    over the stage
                    SOMERSET
What are they that fly there?
                    WARWICK
Richard and Hastings: let them go; here is
The duke.
                    KING EDWARD
The duke! Why, Warwick, when we parted,
Thou call'dst me king.
                    WARWICK
                    Ay, but the case is alter'd:
When you disgraced me in my embassade,
Then I degraded you from being king,
And come now to create you Duke of York.
Alas! how should you govern any kingdom,
That know not how to use ambassadors,
Nor how to be contented with one wife,
Nor how to use your brothers brotherly,
Nor how to study for the people's welfare,
Nor how to shroud yourself from enemies?
                    KING EDWARD
Yea, brother of Clarence, art thou here too.
Nay, then I see that Edward needs must down.
Yet, Warwick, in despite of all mischance,
Of thee thyself and all thy complices,
Edward will always bear himself as king:
Though fortune's malice overthrow my state,
My mind exceeds the compass of her wheel.
                    WARWICK
Then, for his mind, be Edward England's king:
                              [*Takes off his crown*
But Henry now shall wear the English crown,
And be true king indeed, thou but the shadow.
My Lord of Somerset, at my request,
See that forthwith Duke Edward be convey'd
Unto my brother, Archbishop of York.
When I have fought with Pembroke and his fellows,
I'll follow you, and tell what answer
Lewis and the Lady Bona send to him.
Now, for a while farewell, good Duke of York.
                              [*They lead him out forcibly*
                    KING EDWARD
What fates impose, that men must needs abide;
It boots not to resist both wind and tide.
                              [*Exit, guarded*

OXFORD

What now remains, my lords, for us to do,
But march to London with our soldiers?

WARWICK

Ay, that's the first thing that we have to do;
To free king Henry from imprisonment,
And see him seated in the regal throne.   [Exeunt

SCENE IV. London. The palace

Enter QUEEN ELIZABETH *and* RIVERS

RIVERS

Madam, what makes you in this sudden change?

QUEEN ELIZABETH

Why, brother Rivers, are you yet to learn
What late misfortune is befall'n King Edward?

RIVERS

What! loss of some pitch'd battle against Warwick?

QUEEN ELIZABETH

No, but the loss of his own royal person.

RIVERS

Then is my sovereign slain?

QUEEN ELIZABETH

Ay, almost slain, for he is taken prisoner,
Either betray'd by falsehood of his guard,
Or by his foe surprised at unawares:
And, as I further have to understand,
Is new committed to the Bishop of York,
Fell Warwick's brother and by that our foe.

RIVERS

These news I must confess are full of grief;
Yet, gracious madam, bear it as you may:
Warwick may lose, that now hath won the day.

QUEEN ELIZABETH

Till then fair hope must hinder life's decay.
And I the rather wean me from despair
For love of Edward's offspring in my womb:
This is it that makes me bridle passion,
And bear with mildness my misfortune's cross;
Ay, ay, for this I draw in many a tear
And stop the rising of blood-sucking sighs,
Lest with my sighs or tears I blast or drown
King Edward's fruit, true heir to the English crown.

RIVERS

But, madam, where is Warwick then become?

QUEEN ELIZABETH

I am inform'd that he comes towards London,
To set the crown once more on Henry's head:
Guess thou the rest; King Edward's friends must
    down,
But, to prevent the tyrant's violence,—
For trust not him that hath once broken faith,—
I'll hence forthwith unto the sanctuary,
To save at least the heir of Edward's right:
There shall I rest secure from force and fraud.
Come, therefore, let us fly while we may fly:
If Warwick take us we are sure to die.   [Exeunt

SCENE V. A park near Middleham Castle in Yorkshire

Enter GLOUCESTER, LORD HASTINGS, SIR WILLIAM
STANLEY, *and others*

GLOUCESTER

Now, my Lord Hastings and Sir William Stanley,
Leave off to wonder why I drew you hither,
Into this chiefest thicket of the park.
Thus stands the case: you know our king, my
    brother,
Is prisoner to the bishop here, at whose hands
He hath good usage and great liberty,
And, often but attended with weak guard,
Comes hunting this way to disport himself.
I have advertised him by secret means,
That if about this hour he make this way
Under the colour of his usual game,
He shall here find his friends with horse and men
To set him free from his captivity.

Enter KING EDWARD *and a* HUNTSMAN *with him*

HUNTSMAN

This way, my lord; for this way lies the game.

KING EDWARD

Nay, this way, man: see where the huntsmen stand
Now, brother of Gloucester, Lord Hastings, and the
    rest,
Stand you thus close, to steal the bishop's deer?

GLOUCESTER

Brother, the time and case requireth haste:
Your horse stands ready at the park-corner.

KING EDWARD

But whither shall we then?

HASTINGS

                            To Lynn, my lord,
And ship from thence to Flanders.

GLOUCESTER

Well guess'd, believe me; for that was my meaning.

KING EDWARD

Stanley, I will requite thy forwardness.

GLOUCESTER

But wherefore stay we? 'tis no time to talk.

KING EDWARD

Huntsman, what say'st thou? wilt thou go along?

HUNTSMAN

Better do so than tarry and be hang'd.

GLOUCESTER

Come then, away; let's ha' no more ado.

KING EDWARD

Bishop, farewell: shield thee from Warwick's frown;
And pray that I may repossess the crown.   [Exeunt

SCENE VI. London. The Tower

Flourish. Enter KING HENRY, CLARENCE, WARWICK,
SOMERSET, *young* RICHMOND, OXFORD, MONTAGUE, *and*
LIEUTENANT *of the Tower*

KING HENRY

Master lieutenant, now that God and friends
Have shaken Edward from the regal seat,

And turn'd my captive state to liberty,
My fear to hope, my sorrows unto joys,
At our enlargement what are thy due fees?

LIEUTENANT

Subjects may challenge nothing of their sovereigns;
But if an humble prayer may prevail,
I then crave pardon of your majesty.

KING HENRY

For what, lieutenant? for well using me?
Nay, be thou sure I'll well requite thy kindness,
For that it made my imprisonment a pleasure;
Ay, such a pleasure as incaged birds
Conceive, when after many moody thoughts,
At last, by notes of household harmony,
They quite forget their loss of liberty.
But, Warwick, after God, thou set'st me free,
And chiefly therefore I thank God and thee;
He was the author, thou the instrument.
Therefore, that I may conquer fortune's spite
By living low, where fortune cannot hurt me,
And that the people of this blessed land
May not be punish'd with my thwarting stars,
Warwick, although my head still wear the crown,
I here resign my government to thee,
For thou art fortunate in all thy deeds.

WARWICK

Your grace hath still been famed for virtuous;
And now may seem as wise as virtuous,
By spying and avoiding fortune's malice,
For few men rightly temper with the stars:
Yet in this one thing let me blame your grace,
For choosing me when Clarence is in place.

CLARENCE

No, Warwick, thou art worthy of the sway,
To whom the heavens in thy nativity
Adjudged an olive branch and laurel crown,
As likely to be blest in peace and war;
And therefore I yield thee my free consent.

WARWICK

And I choose Clarence only for protector.

KING HENRY

Warwick and Clarence, give me both your hands:
Now join your hands, and with your hands your
hearts,
That no dissension hinder government:
I make you both protectors of this land,
While I myself will lead a private life,
And in devotion spend my latter days,
To sin's rebuke and my Creator's praise.

WARWICK

What answers Clarence to his sovereign's will?

CLARENCE

That he consents, if Warwick yield consent;
For on thy fortune I repose myself.

WARWICK

Why, then, though loath, yet must I be content:
We'll yoke together, like a double shadow
To Henry's body, and supply his place;
I mean, in bearing weight of government,
While he enjoys the honour and his ease.

And, Clarence, now then it is more than needful
Forthwith that Edward be pronounced a traitor,
And all his lands and goods be confiscate.

CLARENCE

What else? and that succession be determined.

WARWICK

Ay, therein Clarence shall not want his part.

KING HENRY

But, with the first of all your chief affairs,
Let me entreat, for I command no more,
That Margaret your queen and my son Edward
Be sent for, to return from France with speed;
For, till I see them here, by doubtful fear
My joy of liberty is half eclipsed.

CLARENCE

It shall be done, my sovereign, with all speed.

KING HENRY

My Lord of Somerset, what youth is that,
Of whom you seem to have so tender care?

SOMERSET

My liege, it is young Henry, earl of Richmond.

KING HENRY

Come hither, England's hope. [Lays his hand on his
head] If secret powers
Suggest but truth to my divining thoughts,
This pretty lad will prove our country's bliss.
His looks are full of peaceful majesty,
His head by nature framed to wear a crown,
His hand to wield a sceptre, and himself
Likely in time to bless a regal throne.
Make much of him, my lords, for this is he
Must help you more than you are hurt by me.

Enter a POST

WARWICK

What news, my friend?

POST

That Edward is escaped from your brother,
And fled, as he hears since, to Burgundy.

WARWICK

Unsavoury news! but how made he escape?

POST

He was convey'd by Richard duke of Gloucester
And the Lord Hastings, who attended him
In secret ambush on the forest side,
And from the bishop's huntsmen rescued him;
For hunting was his daily exercise.

WARWICK

My brother was too careless of his charge.
But let us hence, my sovereign, to provide
A salve for any sore that may betide.

[Exeunt all but SOMERSET, RICHMOND, and OXFORD

SOMERSET

My lord, I like not of this flight of Edward's;
For doubtless Burgundy will yield him help,
And we shall have more wars before 't be long.
As Henry's late presaging prophecy
Did glad my heart with hope of this young Rich-
mond,
So doth my heart misgive me, in these conflicts
What may befall him, to his harm and ours:

Therefore, Lord Oxford, to prevent the worst,
Forthwith we'll send him hence to Brittany,
Till storms be past of civil enmity.

OXFORD

Ay, for if Edward repossess the crown,
'Tis like that Richmond with the rest shall down.

SOMERSET

It shall be so; he shall to Brittany.
Come, therefore, let's about it speedily. 　　　[Exeunt

SCENE VII. *Before York*

Flourish. Enter KING EDWARD, GLOUCESTER, HASTINGS,
and SOLDIERS

KING EDWARD

Now, brother Richard, Lord Hastings, and the rest,
Yet thus far fortune maketh us amends,
And says that once more I shall interchange
My waned state for Henry's regal crown.
Well have we pass'd and now repass'd the seas,
And brought desired help from Burgundy:
What then remains, we being thus arrived
From Ravenspurgh haven before the gates of York,
But that we enter, as into our dukedom?

GLOUCESTER

The gates made fast! Brother, I like not this;
For many men that stumble at the threshold
Are well foretold that danger lurks within.

KING EDWARD

Tush, man, abodements must not now affright us:
By fair or foul means we must enter in,
For hither will our friends repair to us.

HASTINGS

My liege, I'll knock once more to summon them.

Enter, on the walls, the MAYOR OF YORK *and his Brethren*

MAYOR

My lords, we were forewarned of your coming,
And shut the gates for safety of ourselves;
For now we owe allegiance unto Henry.

KING EDWARD

But, master mayor, if Henry be your king,
Yet Edward at the least is Duke of York.

MAYOR

True, my good lord; I know you for no less.

KING EDWARD

Why, and I challenge nothing but my dukedom,
As being well content with that alone.

GLOUCESTER

[*Aside*] But when the fox hath once got in his nose,
He'll soon find means to make the body follow.

HASTINGS

Why, master mayor, why stand you in a doubt?
Open the gates; we are King Henry's friends.

MAYOR

Ay, say you so? the gates shall then be open'd.
　　　　　　　　　　　　　　　　[*They descend*

GLOUCESTER

A wise stout captain, and soon persuaded!

HASTINGS

The good old man would fain that all were well,
So 'twere not 'long of him; but being enter'd,
I doubt not, I, but we shall soon persuade
Both him and all his brothers unto reason.

Enter the MAYOR *and two* ALDERMEN, *below*

KING EDWARD

So, master mayor: these gates must not be shut
But in the night or in the time of war.
What! fear not, man, but yield me up the keys;
　　　　　　　　　　　　　　　[*Takes his keys*
For Edward will defend the town and thee,
And all those friends that deign to follow me.

March. Enter MONTGOMERY, *with drum and* SOLDIERS

GLOUCESTER

Brother, this is Sir John Montgomery,
Our trusty friend, unless I be deceived.

KING EDWARD

Welcome, Sir John! But why come you in arms?

MONTGOMERY

To help King Edward in his time of storm,
As every loyal subject ought to do.

KING EDWARD

Thanks, good Montgomery; but we now forget
Our title to the crown, and only claim
Our dukedom till God please to send the rest.

MONTGOMERY

Then fare you well, for I will hence again:
I came to serve a king, and not a duke.
Drummer, strike up, and let us march away.
　　　　　　　　　　　　　　[*The drum begins to march*

KING EDWARD

Nay, stay, Sir John, a while, and we'll debate
By what safe means the crown may be recover'd.

MONTGOMERY

What talk you of debating? in few words,
If you'll not here proclaim yourself our king,
I'll leave you to your fortune, and be gone
To keep them back that come to succour you:
Why shall we fight, if you pretend no title?

GLOUCESTER

Why, brother, wherefore stand you on nice points?

KING EDWARD

When we grow stronger, then we'll make our claim:
Till then, 'tis wisdom to conceal our meaning.

HASTINGS

Away with scrupulous wit! now arms must rule.

GLOUCESTER

And fearless minds climb soonest unto crowns.
Brother, we will proclaim you out of hand;
The bruit thereof will bring you many friends.

KING EDWARD

Then be it as you will; for 'tis my right,
And Henry but usurps the diadem.

MONTGOMERY

Ay, now my sovereign speaketh like himself;
And now will I be Edward's champion.

HASTINGS

Sound trumpet; Edward shall be here proclaim'd:
Come, fellow-soldier, make thou proclamation.
                                        [*Flourish*

SOLDIERS

Edward the Fourth, by the grace of God, king of
England and France, and lord of Ireland, &c.

MONTGOMERY

And whosoe'er gainsays King Edward's right,
By this I challenge him to single fight.
                            [*Throws down his gauntlet*

ALL

Long live Edward the Fourth!

KING EDWARD

Thanks, brave Montgomery; and thanks unto you
    all:
If fortune serve me, I'll requite this kindness.
Now, for this night, let's harbour here in York;
And when the morning sun shall raise his car
Above the border of this horizon,
We'll forward towards Warwick and his mates;
For well I wot that Henry is no soldier.
Ah, froward Clarence! how evil it beseems thee,
To flatter Henry and forsake thy brother!
Yet, as we may, we'll meet both thee and Warwick.
Come on, brave soldiers: doubt not of the day,
And, that once gotten, doubt not of large pay.
                                        [*Exeunt*

SCENE VIII. *London. The palace*

Flourish. Enter KING HENRY, WARWICK, MONTAGUE,
CLARENCE, EXETER, *and* OXFORD

WARWICK

What counsel, lords? Edward from Belgia,
With hasty Germans and blunt Hollanders,
Hath pass'd in safety through the narrow seas,
And with his troops doth march amain to London;
And many giddy people flock to him.

KING HENRY

Let's levy men, and beat him back again.

CLARENCE

A little fire is quickly trodden out;
Which, being suffer'd, rivers cannot quench.

WARWICK

In Warwickshire I have true-hearted friends,
Not mutinous in peace, yet bold in war;
Those will I muster up: and thou, son Clarence,
Shalt stir up in Suffolk, Norfolk and in Kent,
The knights and gentlemen to come with thee:
Thou, brother Montague, in Buckingham,
Northampton and in Leicestershire, shalt find
Men well inclined to hear what thou command'st:
And thou, brave Oxford, wondrous well beloved,
In Oxfordshire shalt muster up thy friends.
My sovereign, with the loving citizens,
Like to his island girt in with the ocean,
Or modest Dian circled with her nymphs,
Shall rest in London till we come to him.

Fair lords, take leave and stand not to reply.
Farewell, my sovereign.

KING HENRY

Farewell, my Hector, and my Troy's true hope.

CLARENCE

In sign of truth, I kiss your highness' hand.

KING HENRY

Well-minded Clarence, be thou fortunate!

MONTGOMERY

Comfort, my lord; and so I take my leave.

OXFORD

And thus I seal my truth, and bid adieu.

KING HENRY

Sweet Oxford, and my loving Montague,
And all at once, once more a happy farewell.

WARWICK

Farewell, sweet lords: let's meet at Coventry.
            [*Exeunt all but* KING HENRY *and* EXETER

KING HENRY

Here at the palace will I rest a while.
Cousin of Exeter, what thinks your lordship?
Methinks the power that Edward hath in field
Should not be able to encounter mine.

EXETER

The doubt is that he will seduce the rest.

KING HENRY

That's not my fear; my meed hath got me fame:
I have not stopp'd mine ears to their demands,
Nor posted off their suits with slow delays;
My pity hath been balm to heal their wounds,
My mildness hath allay'd their swelling griefs,
My mercy dried their water-flowing tears;
I have not been desirous of their wealth,
Nor much oppress'd them with great subsidies,
Nor forward of revenge, though they much err'd:
Then why should they love Edward more than me?
No, Exeter, these graces challenge grace:
And when the lion fawns upon the lamb,
The lamb will never cease to follow him.
            [*Shout within*, 'A Lancaster! A Lancaster!'

EXETER

Hark, hark, my lord! what shouts are these?

Enter KING EDWARD, GLOUCESTER, *and* SOLDIERS

KING EDWARD

Seize on the shame-faced Henry, bear him hence;
And once again proclaim us king of England.
You are the fount that makes small brooks to flow:
Now stops thy spring; my sea shall suck them dry,
And swell so much the higher by their ebb.
Hence with him to the Tower; let him not speak.
                    [*Exeunt some with* KING HENRY

And, lords, towards Coventry bend we our course,
Where peremptory Warwick now remains:
The sun shines hot; and, if we use delay,
Cold biting winter mars our hoped-for hay.

GLOUCESTER

Away betimes, before his forces join,
And take the great-grown traitor unawares:
Brave warriors, march amain towards Coventry.
                                        [*Exeunt*

ACT V

Scene I. *Coventry*

Enter WARWICK, *the* MAYOR OF COVENTRY, *two* MESSENGERS, *and others upon the walls*

WARWICK
Where is the post that came from valiant Oxford?
How far hence is thy lord, mine honest fellow?

FIRST MESSENGER
By this at Dunsmore, marching hitherward.

WARWICK
How far off is our brother Montague?
Where is the post that came from Montague?

SECOND MESSENGER
By this at Daintry, with a puissant troop.

Enter SIR JOHN SOMERVILE

WARWICK
Say, Somervile, what says my loving son?
And, by thy guess, how nigh is Clarence now?

SOMERVILE
At Southam I did leave him with his forces,
And do expect him here some two hours hence.
                                        [*Drum heard*

WARWICK
Then Clarence is at hand; I hear his drum.

SOMERVILE
It is not his, my lord; here Southam lies:
The drum your honour hears marcheth from War-
    wick.

WARWICK
Who should that be? belike, unlook'd-for friends.

SOMERVILE
They are at hand, and you shall quickly know.
March. Flourish. Enter KING EDWARD, GLOUCESTER,
and SOLDIERS

KING EDWARD
Go, trumpet, to the walls, and sound a parle.

GLOUCESTER
See how the surly Warwick mans the wall!

WARWICK
O unbid spite! is sportful Edward come?
Where slept our scouts, or how are they seduced,
That we could hear no news of his repair?

KING EDWARD
Now, Warwick, wilt thou ope the city gates,
Speak gentle words and humbly bend thy knee,
Call Edward king and at his hands beg mercy?
And he shall pardon thee these outrages.

WARWICK
Nay, rather, wilt thou draw thy forces hence,
Confess who set thee up and pluck'd thee down,
Call Warwick patron and be penitent?
And thou shalt still remain the Duke of York.

GLOUCESTER
I thought, at least, he would have said the king;
Or did he make the jest against his will?

WARWICK
Is not a dukedom, sir, a goodly gift?

GLOUCESTER
Ay, by my faith, for a poor earl to give:
I'll do thee service for so good a gift.

WARWICK
'Twas I that gave the kingdom to thy brother.

KING EDWARD
Why then 'tis mine, if but by Warwick's gift.

WARWICK
Thou art no Atlas for so great a weight:
And, weakling, Warwick takes his gift again;
And Henry is my king, Warwick his subject.

KING EDWARD
But Warwick's king is Edward's prisoner:
And, gallant Warwick, do but answer this:
What is the body when the head is off?

GLOUCESTER
Alas, that Warwick had no more forecast,
But, whiles he thought to steal the single ten,
The king was slily finger'd from the deck!
You left poor Henry at the bishop's palace,
And, ten to one, you'll meet him in the Tower.

KING EDWARD
'Tis even so; yet you are Warwick still.

GLOUCESTER
Come, Warwick, take the time; kneel down, kneel
    down:
Nay, when? strike now, or else the iron cools.

WARWICK
I had rather chop this hand off at a blow,
And with the other fling it at thy face,
Than bear so low a sail, to strike to thee.

KING EDWARD
Sail how thou canst, have wind and tide thy friend,
This hand, fast wound about thy coal-black hair,
Shall, whiles thy head is warm and new cut off,
Write in the dust this sentence with thy blood,
'Wind-changing Warwick now can change no
    more.'
                Enter OXFORD, *with drum and colours*

WARWICK
O cheerful colours! see where Oxford comes!

OXFORD
Oxford, Oxford, for Lancaster!
                    [*He and his forces enter the city*

GLOUCESTER
The gates are open, let us enter too.

KING EDWARD
So other foes may set upon our backs.
Stand we in good array; for they no doubt
Will issue out again and bid us battle:
If not, the city being but of small defence,
We'll quickly rouse the traitors in the same.

WARWICK
O, welcome, Oxford! for we want thy help.
                Enter MONTAGUE, *with drum and colours*

MONTAGUE
Montague, Montague, for Lancaster!
                    [*He and his forces enter the city*

GLOUCESTER

Thou and thy brother both shall buy this treason
Even with the dearest blood your bodies bear.

KING EDWARD

The harder match'd, the greater victory:
My mind presageth happy gain and conquest.

Enter SOMERSET, *with drum and colours.*

SOMERSET

Somerset, Somerset, for Lancaster!

[*He and his forces enter the city*

GLOUCESTER

Two of thy name, both Dukes of Somerset,
Have sold their lives unto the house of York;
And thou shalt be the third, if this sword hold.

Enter CLARENCE, *with drum and colours*

WARWICK

And lo, where George of Clarence sweeps along,
Of force enough to bid his brother battle;
With whom an upright zeal to right prevails
More than the nature of a brother's love!
Come, Clarence, come; thou wilt, if Warwick call.

CLARENCE

Father of Warwick, know you what this means?

[*Taking his red rose out of his hat*

Look here, I throw my infamy at thee:
I will not ruinate my father's house,
Who gave his blood to lime the stones together,
And set up Lancaster. Why, trow'st thou, Warwick,
That Clarence is so harsh, so blunt, unnatural,
To bend the fatal instruments of war
Against his brother and his lawful king?
Perhaps thou wilt object my holy oath:
To keep that oath were more impiety
Than Jephthah's, when he sacrificed his daughter.
I am so sorry for my trespass made
That, to deserve well at my brother's hands,
I here proclaim myself thy mortal foe,
With resolution, wheresoe'er I meet thee—
As I will meet thee, if thou stir abroad—
To plague thee for thy foul misleading me.
And so, proud-hearted Warwick, I defy thee,
And to my brother turn my blushing cheeks.
Pardon me, Edward, I will make amends:
And, Richard, do not frown upon my faults,
For I will henceforth be no more unconstant.

KING EDWARD

Now welcome more, and ten times more beloved,
Than if thou never hadst deserved our hate.

GLOUCESTER

Welcome, good Clarence; this is brother-like.

WARWICK

O passing traitor, perjured and unjust!

KING EDWARD

What, Warwick, wilt thou leave the town, and fight?
Or shall we beat the stones about thine ears?

WARWICK

Alas, I am not coop'd here for defence!
I will away towards Barnet presently,
And bid thee battle, Edward, if thou darest.

KING EDWARD

Yes, Warwick, Edward dares, and leads the way.
Lords, to the field; Saint George and victory!

[*Exeunt* KING EDWARD *and his company. March.*
WARWICK *and his company follow*

SCENE II. *A field of battle near Barnet*

Alarum and excursions. Enter KING EDWARD, *bringing
forth* WARWICK *wounded*

KING EDWARD

So, lie thou there: die thou, and die our fear;
For Warwick was a bug that fear'd us all.
Now, Montague, sit fast; I seek for thee,
That Warwick's bones may keep thine company.

[*Exit*

WARWICK

Ah, who is nigh? come to me, friend or foe,
And tell me, who is victor, York or Warwick?
Why ask I that? my mangled body shows,
My blood, my want of strength, my sick heart shows,
That I must yield my body to the earth
And, by my fall, the conquest to my foe.
Thus yields the cedar to the axe's edge,
Whose arms gave shelter to the princely eagle,
Under whose shade the ramping lion slept,
Whose top-branch overpeer'd Jove's spreading tree,
And kept low shrubs from winter's powerful wind.
These eyes, that now are dimm'd with death's black
  veil,
Have been as piercing as the mid-day sun,
To search the secret treasons of the world:
The wrinkles in my brows, now fill'd with blood,
Were liken'd oft to kingly sepulchres;
For who lived king, but I could dig his grave?
And who durst smile when Warwick bent his brow?
Lo, now my glory smear'd in dust and blood!
My parks, my walks, my manors that I had,
Even now forsake me, and of all my lands
Is nothing left me but my body's length.
Why, what is pomp, rule, reign, but earth and dust?
And, live we how we can, yet die we must.

Enter OXFORD *and* SOMERSET

SOMERSET

Ah, Warwick, Warwick! wert thou as we are,
We might recover all our loss again:
The queen from France hath brought a puissant
  power:
Even now we heard the news: ah, couldst thou fly!

WARWICK

Why, then I would not fly. Ah, Montague,
If thou be there, sweet brother, take my hand,
And with thy lips keep in my soul a while!
Thou lovest me not; for, brother, if thou didst,
Thy tears would wash this cold congealed blood,
That glues my lips and will not let me speak.
Come quickly, Montague, or I am dead.

SOMERSET

Ah, Warwick! Montague hath breathed his last;

And to the latest gasp cried out for Warwick,
And said 'Commend me to my valiant brother.'
And more he would have said, and more he spoke,
Which sounded like a clamour in a vault,
That mought not be distinguish'd; but at last
I well might hear, delivered with a groan,
'O, farewell, Warwick!'

WARWICK

Sweet rest his soul! Fly, lords, and save yourselves;
For Warwick bids you all farewell, to meet in
    heaven.   [Dies

OXFORD

Away, away, to meet the queen's great power!
        [Here they bear away his body. Exeunt

SCENE III. Another part of the field

Flourish. Enter KING EDWARD in triumph; with
    GLOUCESTER, CLARENCE, and the rest

KING EDWARD

Thus far our fortune keeps an upward course,
And we are graced with wreaths of victory.
But, in the midst of this bright-shining day,
I spy a black, suspicious, threatening cloud,
That will encounter with our glorious sun,
Ere he attain his easeful western bed:
I mean, my lords, those powers that the queen
Hath raised in Gallia have arrived our coast,
And, as we hear, march on to fight with us.

CLARENCE

A little gale will soon disperse that cloud,
And blow it to the source from whence it came:
Thy very beams will dry those vapours up,
For every cloud engenders not a storm.

GLOUCESTER

The queen is valued thirty thousand strong,
And Somerset, with Oxford, fled to her:
If she have time to breathe, be well assured
Her faction will be full as strong as ours.

KING EDWARD

We are advertised by our loving friends
That they do hold their course toward Tewksbury:
We, having now the best at Barnet field,
Will thither straight, for willingness rids way;
And, as we march, our strength will be augmented
In every county as we go along.
Strike up the drum; cry 'Courage!' and away.
                                    [Exeunt

SCENE IV. Plains near Tewksbury

March. Enter QUEEN MARGARET, PRINCE EDWARD,
    SOMERSET, OXFORD, and SOLDIERS

QUEEN MARGARET

Great lords, wise men ne'er sit and wail their loss,
But cheerly seek how to redress their harms.
What though the mast be now blown overboard,
The cable broke, the holding-anchor lost,

And half our sailors swallow'd in the flood?
Yet lives our pilot still. Is 't meet that he
Should leave the helm, and like a fearful lad
With tearful eyes add water to the sea,
And give more strength to that which hath too
    much,
Whiles, in his moan, the ship splits on the rock,
Which industry and courage might have saved?
Ah, what a shame! ah, what a fault were this!
Say Warwick was our anchor; what of that?
And Montague our topmast; what of him?
Our slaughter'd friends the tackles; what of these?
Why, is not Oxford here another anchor?
And Somerset another goodly mast?
The friends of France our shrouds and tacklings?
And, though unskilful, why not Ned and I
For once allow'd the skilful pilot's charge?
We will not from the helm to sit and weep,
But keep our course, though the rough wind say no,
From shelves and rocks that threaten us with wreck.
As good to chide the waves as speak them fair.
And what is Edward but a ruthless sea?
What Clarence but a quicksand of deceit?
And Richard but a ragged fatal rock?
All these the enemies to our poor bark.
Say you can swim; alas, 'tis but a while!
Tread on the sand; why, there you quickly sink:
Bestride the rock; the tide will wash you off,
Or else you famish; that's a threefold death.
This speak I, lords, to let you understand,
If case some one of you would fly from us,
That there's no hoped-for mercy with the brothers,
More than with ruthless waves, with sands and
    rocks.
Why, courage then! what cannot be avoided
'Twere childish weakness to lament or fear.

PRINCE

Methinks a woman of this valiant spirit
Should, if a coward heard her speak these words,
Infuse his breast with magnanimity,
And make him, naked, foil a man at arms.
I speak not this as doubting any here;
For did I but suspect a fearful man,
He should have leave to go away betimes,
Lest in our need he might infect another,
And make him of like spirit to himself.
If any such be here—as God forbid!—
Let him depart before we need his help.

OXFORD

Women and children of so high a courage,
And warriors faint! why, 'twere perpetual shame.
O brave young prince! thy famous grandfather
Doth live again in thee: long mayst thou live
To bear his image and renew his glories!

SOMERSET

And he that will not fight for such a hope,
Go home to bed, and like the owl by day,
If he arise, be mock'd and wonder'd at.

QUEEN MARGARET

Thanks, gentle Somerset; sweet Oxford, thanks.

PRINCE

And take his thanks that yet hath nothing else.

Enter a MESSENGER

MESSENGER

Prepare you, lords, for Edward is at hand,
Ready to fight; therefore be resolute.

OXFORD

I thought no less: it is his policy
To haste thus fast, to find us unprovided.

SOMERSET

But he's deceived; we are in readiness.

QUEEN MARGARET

This cheers my heart, to see your forwardness.

OXFORD

Here pitch our battle; hence we will not budge.

Flourish and March. Enter KING EDWARD, GLOUCESTER,
CLARENCE, *and* SOLDIERS

KING EDWARD

Brave followers, yonder stands the thorny wood,
Which, by the heavens' assistance and your strength,
Must by the roots be hewn up yet ere night.
I need not add more fuel to your fire,
For well I wot ye blaze to burn them out:
Give signal to the fight, and to it, lords!

QUEEN MARGARET

Lords, knights, and gentlemen, what I should say
My tears gainsay; for every word I speak,
Ye see, I drink the water of mine eyes.
Therefore, no more but this: Henry, your sovereign,
Is prisoner to the foe; his state usurp'd,
His realm a slaughter-house, his subjects slain,
His statutes cancell'd, and his treasure spent;
And yonder is the wolf that makes this spoil.
You fight in justice: then, in God's name, lords,
Be valiant, and give signal to the fight.

[*Alarum: Retreat: Excursions. Exeunt*

SCENE V. *Another part of the field*

Flourish. Enter KING EDWARD, GLOUCESTER,
CLARENCE, *and* SOLDIERS; *with* QUEEN MARGARET,
OXFORD, *and* SOMERSET, *prisoners*

KING EDWARD

Now here a period of tumultuous broils.
Away with Oxford to Hames Castle straight:
For Somerset, off with his guilty head.
Go, bear them hence; I will not hear them speak.

OXFORD

For my part, I'll not trouble thee with words.

SOMERSET

Nor I, but stoop with patience to my fortune.

[*Exeunt* OXFORD *and* SOMERSET, *guarded*

QUEEN MARGARET

So part we sadly in this troublous world,
To meet with joy in sweet Jerusalem.

KING EDWARD

Is proclamation made, that who finds Edward
Shall have a high reward, and he his life?

GLOUCESTER

It is: and lo, where youthful Edward comes!

Enter SOLDIERS, *with* PRINCE EDWARD

KING EDWARD

Bring forth the gallant, let us hear him speak.
What! can so young a thorn begin to prick?
Edward, what satisfaction canst thou make
For bearing arms, for stirring up my subjects,
And all the trouble thou hast turn'd me to?

PRINCE

Speak like a subject, proud ambitious York!
Suppose that I am now my father's mouth;
Resign thy chair, and where I stand kneel thou,
Whilst I propose the selfsame words to thee,
Which, traitor, thou wouldst have me answer to.

QUEEN MARGARET

Ah, that thy father had been so resolved!

GLOUCESTER

That you might still have worn the petticoat,
And ne'er have stol'n the breech from Lancaster.

PRINCE

Let Æsop fable in a winter's night;
His currish riddles sort not with this place.

GLOUCESTER

By heaven, brat, I'll plague ye for that word.

QUEEN MARGARET

Ay, thou wast born to be a plague to men.

GLOUCESTER

For God's sake, take away this captive scold.

PRINCE

Nay, take away this scolding crook-back rather.

KING EDWARD

Peace, wilful boy, or I will charm your tongue.

CLARENCE

Untutor'd lad, thou art too malapert.

PRINCE

I know my duty; you are all undutiful:
Lascivious Edward, and thou perjured George,
And thou mis-shapen Dick, I tell ye all
I am your better, traitors as ye are:
And thou usurp'st my father's right and mine.

KING EDWARD

Take that, thou likeness of this railer here. [*Stabs him*

GLOUCESTER

Sprawl'st thou? take that, to end thy agony.

[*Stabs him*

CLARENCE

And there's for twitting me with perjury. [*Stabs him*

QUEEN MARGARET

O, kill me too!

GLOUCESTER

Marry, and shall.   [*Offers to kill her*

KING EDWARD

Hold, Richard, hold; for we have done too much.

GLOUCESTER

Why should she live, to fill the world with words?

KING EDWARD

What, doth she swoon? use means for her recovery.

GLOUCESTER

Clarence, excuse me to the king my brother;
I'll hence to London on a serious matter:
Ere ye come there, be sure to hear some news.

CLARENCE

What? what?

GLOUCESTER

The Tower, the Tower.   [Exit

QUEEN MARGARET

O Ned, sweet Ned! speak to thy mother, boy!
Canst thou not speak? O traitors! murderers!
They that stabb'd Cæsar shed no blood at all,
Did not offend, nor were not worthy blame,
If this foul deed were by to equal it:
He was a man; this, in respect, a child:
And men ne'er spend their fury on a child.
What's worse than murderer, that I may name it?
No, ho, my heart will burst, an if I speak:
And I will speak, that so my heart may burst.
Butchers and villains! bloody cannibals!
How sweet a plant have you untimely cropp'd!
You have no children, butchers! if you had,
The thought of them would have stirr'd up remorse:
But if you ever chance to have a child,
Look in his youth to have him so cut off,
As, deathsmen, you have rid this sweet young
    prince!

KING EDWARD

Away with her; go, bear her hence perforce.

QUEEN MARGARET

Nay, never bear me hence, dispatch me here;
Here sheathe thy sword, I'll pardon thee my death:
What, wilt thou not? then, Clarence, do it thou.

CLARENCE

By heaven, I will not do thee so much ease.

QUEEN MARGARET

Good Clarence, do; sweet Clarence, do thou do it.

CLARENCE

Didst thou not hear me swear I would not do it?

QUEEN MARGARET

Ay, but thou usest to forswear thyself:
'Twas sin before, but now 'tis charity.
What, wilt thou not? Where is that devil's butcher,
Hard-favour'd Richard? Richard, where art thou?
Thou art not here: murder is thy alms-deed;
Petitioners for blood thou ne'er put'st back.

KING EDWARD

Away, I say; I charge ye, bear her hence.

QUEEN MARGARET

So come to you and yours, as to this prince!
       [Exit, led out forcibly

KING EDWARD

Where's Richard gone?

CLARENCE

To London, all in post; and, as I guess,
To make a bloody supper in the Tower.

KING EDWARD

He's sudden, if a thing comes in his head.
Now march we hence: discharge the common sort
With pay and thanks, and let's away to London,
And see our gentle queen how well she fares:
By this, I hope, she hath a son for me.   [Exeunt

SCENE VI. London. The Tower

Enter KING HENRY and GLOUCESTER, with the
LIEUTENANT, on the walls

GLOUCESTER

Good day, my lord. What, at your book so hard?

KING HENRY

Ay, my good lord:—my lord, I should say rather;
'Tis sin to flatter; 'good' was little better:
'Good Gloucester' and 'good devil' were alike,
And both preposterous; therefore, not 'good lord.'

GLOUCESTER

Sirrah, leave us to ourselves: we must confer.
       [Exit LIEUTENANT

KING HENRY

So flies the reckless shepherd from the wolf;
So first the harmless sheep doth yield his fleece,
And next his throat unto the butcher's knife.
What scene of death hath Roscius now to act?

GLOUCESTER

Suspicion always haunts the guilty mind;
The thief doth fear each bush an officer.

KING HENRY

The bird that hath been limed in a bush,
With trembling wings misdoubteth every bush;
And I, the hapless male to one sweet bird,
Have now the fatal object in my eye,
Where my poor young was limed, was caught and
    kill'd.

GLOUCESTER

Why, what a peevish fool was that of Crete,
That taught his son the office of a fowl!
And yet, for all his wings, the fool was drown'd.

KING HENRY

I, Dædalus; my poor boy, Icarus;
Thy father, Minos, that denied our course;
The sun that sear'd the wings of my sweet boy
Thy brother Edward, and thyself the sea
Whose envious gulf did swallow up his life.
Ah, kill me with thy weapon, not with words!
My breast can better brook thy dagger's point,
Than can my ears that tragic history.
But wherefore dost thou come? is 't for my life?

GLOUCESTER

Think'st thou I am an executioner?

KING HENRY

A persecutor, I am sure, thou art:
If murdering innocents be executing,
Why, then thou art an executioner.

GLOUCESTER
Thy son I kill'd for his presumption.
KING HENRY
Hadst thou been kill'd when first thou didst pre-
   sume,
Thou hadst not lived to kill a son of mine.
And thus I prophesy, that many a thousand,
Which now mistrust no parcel of my fear,
And many an old man's sigh and many a widow's,
And many an orphan's water-standing eye—
Men for their sons, wives for their husbands,
And orphans for their parents' timeless death—
Shall rue the hour that ever thou wast born.
The owl shriek'd at thy birth,—an evil sign;
The night-crow cried, aboding luckless time;
Dogs howl'd, and hideous tempest shook down trees;
The raven rook'd her on the chimney's top,
And chattering pies in dismal discords sung.
Thy mother felt more than a mother's pain,
And yet brought forth less than a mother's hope,
To wit, an indigested and deformed lump,
Not like the fruit of such a goodly tree.
Teeth hadst thou in thy head when thou wast born,
To signify thou camest to bite the world:
And, if the rest be true which I have heard,
Thou camest—

GLOUCESTER
I'll hear no more: die, prophet, in thy speech:
                         [Stabs him
For this, amongst the rest, was I ordain'd.
KING HENRY
Ay, and for much more slaughter after this.
O, God forgive my sins, and pardon thee!   [Dies
GLOUCESTER
What, will the aspiring blood of Lancaster
Sink in the ground? I thought it would have
   mounted.
See how my sword weeps for the poor king's death!
O, may such purple tears be always shed
From those that wish the downfall of our house!
If any spark of life be yet remaining,
Down, down to hell; and say I sent thee thither:
                     [Stabs him again
I, that have neither pity, love, nor fear.
Indeed, 'tis true that Henry told me of;
For I have often heard my mother say
I came into the world with my legs forward:
Had I not reason, think ye, to make haste,
And seek their ruin that usurp'd our right?
The midwife wonder'd, and the women cried
'O, Jesus bless us, he is born with teeth!'
And so I was; which plainly signified
That I should snarl and bite and play the dog.
Then, since the heavens have shaped my body so,
Let hell make crook'd my mind to answer it.
I have no brother, I am like no brother;
And this word 'love,' which greybeards call divine,
Be resident in men like one another,
And not in me: I am myself alone.

Clarence, beware; thou keep'st me from the light:
But I will sort a pitchy day for thee;
For I will buz abroad such prophecies
That Edward shall be fearful of his life,
And then, to purge his fear, I'll be thy death.
King Henry and the prince his son are gone:
Clarence, thy turn is next, and then the rest,
Counting myself but bad till I be best.
I'll throw thy body in another room,
And triumph, Henry, in thy day of doom.
                    [Exit, with the body

SCENE VII. London. The palace

Flourish. Enter KING EDWARD, QUEEN ELIZABETH,
CLARENCE, GLOUCESTER, HASTINGS, a NURSE with the
   young PRINCE, and ATTENDANTS

KING EDWARD
Once more we sit in England's royal throne,
Re-purchased with the blood of enemies.
What valiant foemen, like to autumn's corn,
Have we mow'd down in tops of all their pride!
Three Dukes of Somerset, threefold renown'd
For hardy and undoubted champions;
Two Cliffords, as the father and the son;
And two Northumberlands; two braver men
Ne'er spurr'd their coursers at the trumpet's sound;
With them, the two brave bears, Warwick and
   Montague,
That in their chains fetter'd the kingly lion,
And made the forest tremble when they roar'd.
Thus have we swept suspicion from our seat,
And made our footstool of security.
Come hither, Bess, and let me kiss my boy.
Young Ned, for thee, thine uncles and myself
Have in our armours watch'd the winter's night,
Went all afoot in summer's scalding heat,
That thou mightst repossess the crown in peace:
And of our labours thou shalt reap the gain.

GLOUCESTER
[Aside] I'll blast his harvest, if your head were laid;
For yet I am not look'd on in the world.
This shoulder was ordain'd so thick to heave;
And heave it shall some weight, or break my back:
Work thou the way,—and thou shalt execute.

KING EDWARD
Clarence and Gloucester, love my lovely queen;
And kiss your princely nephew, brothers both.

CLARENCE
The duty that I owe unto your majesty
I seal upon the lips of this sweet babe.

QUEEN ELIZABETH
Thanks, noble Clarence; worthy brother, thanks.
GLOUCESTER
And, that I love the tree from whence thou
   sprang'st,

Witness the loving kiss I give the fruit.
[*Aside*] To say the truth, so Judas kiss'd his master,
And cried, 'all hail!' when as he meant all harm.

KING EDWARD

Now am I seated as my soul delights,
Having my country's peace and brothers' loves.

CLARENCE

What will your grace have done with Margaret?
Reignier, her father, to the King of France

Hath pawn'd the Sicils and Jerusalem,
And hither have they sent it for her ransom.

KING EDWARD

Away with her, and waft her hence to France.
And now what rests but that we spend the time
With stately triumphs, mirthful comic shows,
Such as befits the pleasure of the court?
Sound drums and trumpets! farewell sour annoy!
For here, I hope, begins our lasting joy.   [*Exeunt*

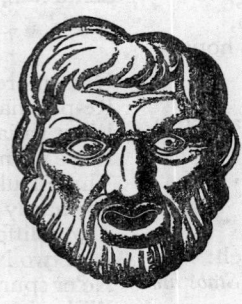

THE TRAGEDY OF KING RICHARD III

SYNOPSIS

THE deformed Richard, Duke of Gloucester, loses no time, once the wars are over, in promoting his evil plots to gain the throne, and immediately revives an old prophecy made to Edward IV that his issue would be disinherited by one of his heirs whose name begins with the letter G, thereby drawing the King's suspicions upon his brother George, Duke of Clarence, who is arrested. Richard blames the King's hatred on the influence of his wife, Queen Elizabeth, promises his brother to free him, then gives orders for his secret murder in the Tower.

While his victim, King Henry VI, is being buried, he interrupts the funeral procession attended by the Lady Anne, widow of the young Prince of Wales whom his brothers and he had stabbed to death, and, with artful persuasion, he swears that his great love for her had forced him to these murders, finally prevailing upon her to stop cursing him and accept an engagement ring. He then visits the court to inquire for the sick Edward, and by professing saintliness and complaining of his wrongs he succeeds in convincing Derby, Hastings and Buckingham that Queen Elizabeth and her supporters had poisoned the King's mind against Clarence whose death, supposedly by the King's order, has greatly shaken them all. Edward dies after trying to make peace among the hostile factions, and the young Prince Edward is brought to London to be crowned.

Richard having imprisoned the Queen's adherents, Lord Rivers, Lord Grey and Sir Thomas Vaughan, whom he later executes, the Archbishop of York offers sanctuary to the fearful Elizabeth and her second son, the little Duke of York, but Gloucester contrives to get the boy away from his mother, and with a great parade of affection and consideration has both children lodged in the Tower under his supervision, as though in preparation for little Edward's coronation. Through his henchman Catesby, he finds out that the powerful Lord Hastings is a staunch adherent to the young Prince, and at a council meeting called to arrange for the coronation Richard suddenly accuses the nobleman of treason and orders him immediately executed, then, accompanied by his ally, Buckingham, in rusty battered armor, he pretends to the Lord Mayor that they are in great danger from a plot of Hastings which necessitated his hurried execution.

Buckingham is instructed to emphasize at the Guildhall the immorality of the late King Edward, to imply the illegitimacy of his children, and also to hint that Edward himself was a bastard. As a result of this propaganda, the citizens of London, headed by the Lord Mayor, wait upon Richard to offer him the crown, and acting upon Buckingham's suggestion he appears on a balcony attended by two bishops and apparently absorbed in his prayer book, giving the people a profound

[111]

impression of his piety. Hypocritically affecting a great reluctance, he at length yields to the entreaties of the Lord Mayor, seconded by Buckingham and upheld by Catesby, and accepts the crown, arrangements being rapidly pushed ahead for the coronation.

At the Tower, where they have come to visit the beloved little Princes, the Queen Mother, the old Duchess of York and Lady Anne are denied admission by the lieutenant in charge. They then hear in abject despair of Richard's usurpation of the throne, and the miserable Lady Anne is summoned to Westminster to be crowned. Richard now suggests to Buckingham that the death of the little Princes is necessary for the security of his crown, but the Duke hesitates, whereupon the new King with sudden coolness ignores his request for the promised earldom of Hereford, and proceeds in secret with his foul plots. Rumors are given out that his wife Anne is mortally ill, and she later dies, as planned, so that Richard may strengthen his position by marrying his niece, Elizabeth of York, daughter of the late Edward IV. He imprisons Clarence's son; arranges a marriage to lower the standing of Clarence's daughter; and by promising preferment to the discontented Sir James Tyrrel he has the little Princes smothered to death as they sleep in each other's arms in the Tower.

Each day, however, brings tidings of English noblemen who have fled to Brittany to join the forces of Henry Tudor, Duke of Richmond, whom as a boy Henry VI had acclaimed as England's hope, and Richmond soon lands at Milford with a great army to gain the crown. Buckingham, knowing well what he may expect from the villainous Richard, is among the noblemen who gather to Richmond's standard as he marches inland, but he is soon captured and executed by the King's order.

The two armies meet on Bosworth Field, and on the night before the battle Richard is terrified by a parade of the ghosts of all his victims who prophesy his defeat. The same ghosts visit Richmond and, assuring him of victory, leave him calm and confident for the battle. Richard fights desperately but is slain in personal combat with Richmond, who mounts the throne, and, by marrying Elizabeth of York, ends the civil strife by uniting the factions of the white and red roses.

HISTORICAL DATA

The material for this play, as in the case of most of the historical dramas attributed to Shakespeare, is drawn in large part from Holinshed's *Chronicles*. In the case of the characterization of Richard III these derive from Sir Thomas More's *History of Edward V and Richard III*. Shakespeare evidently used the second edition of Holinshed (1586–7) as only this edition contains a mistake which was copied in the quarto edition of the play in 1597.

The theme of the tragedy of Richard III had been a popular one and Shakespeare probably benefited by several earlier works, notably *The True Tragedie of Richard the Third* by an unknown author, Dr. Legge's Latin chronicles play, *Richardus Tertius*, written for performance at Cambridge University, and *Richard Crookback*, a play generally attributed to Ben Jonson.

Courtenay, in his *Commentaries*, considers the wooing of Queen Anne, and the two great cursing scenes in which Margaret of Anjou plays the chief part, as well as several other scenes, entirely Shakespeare's own inventions. Certainly there is no foundation for them in Holinshed.

Basing their opinion upon the marks of Shakespeare's early style, and in particular upon the strong evidences of the influence of Marlowe, authorities generally agree that this play was written "not later than 1593." It is included by Meres in *Palladis Tamia* in 1598.

"A horse! a horse!"
RICHARD III

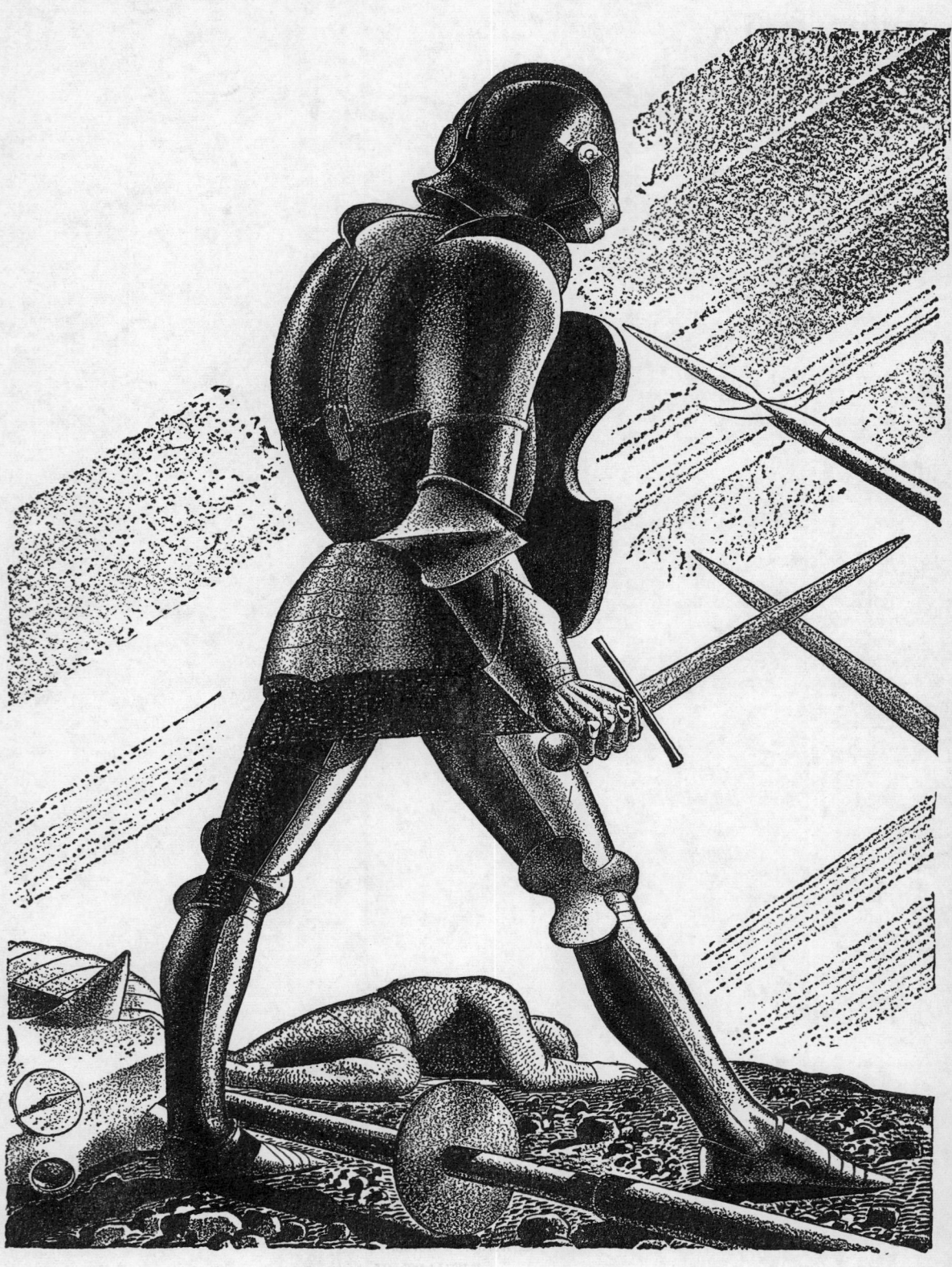

THE TRAGEDY OF KING RICHARD III

DRAMATIS PERSONÆ

KING EDWARD *the Fourth.*
EDWARD, *Prince of Wales, afterwards King Edward V.,*
RICHARD, *Duke of York,* } *sons to the King.*
GEORGE, *Duke of Clarence,*
RICHARD, *Duke of Gloucester, afterwards King Richard III.,* } *brothers to the King.*
A young son of Clarence.
HENRY, *Earl of Richmond, afterwards King Henry VII.*
CARDINAL BOURCHIER, *Archbishop of Canterbury.*
THOMAS ROTHERHAM, *Archbishop of York.*
JOHN MORTON, *Bishop of Ely.*
DUKE OF BUCKINGHAM.
DUKE OF NORFOLK.
EARL OF SURREY, *his son.*
EARL RIVERS, *brother to Elizabeth.*
MARQUIS OF DORSET *and* LORD GREY, *sons to Elizabeth.*
EARL OF OXFORD.
LORD HASTINGS.
LORD STANLEY, *called also* EARL OF DERBY.
LORD LOVEL.
SIR THOMAS VAUGHAN.
SIR RICHARD RATCLIFF.
SIR WILLIAM CATESBY.

SIR JAMES TYRREL.
SIR JAMES BLOUNT.
SIR WALTER HERBERT.
SIR ROBERT BRAKENBURY, *Lieutenant of the Tower.*
SIR WILLIAM BRANDON.
CHRISTOPHER URSWICK, *a priest. Another Priest.*
TRESSEL *and* BERKELEY, *gentlemen attending on the Lady Anne.*
LORD MAYOR *of London.*
SHERIFF *of Wiltshire.*

ELIZABETH, *queen to King Edward IV.*
MARGARET, *widow of King Henry VI.*
DUCHESS OF YORK, *mother to King Edward IV.*
LADY ANNE, *widow of Edward Prince of Wales, son to King Henry VI.; afterwards married to Richard.*
A young daughter of Clarence (MARGARET PLANTAGENET).

GHOSTS *of those murdered by Richard III., LORDS and other ATTENDANTS; a PURSUIVANT, SCRIVENER, CITIZENS, MURDERERS, MESSENGERS, SOLDIERS, &c.*

SCENE—*England.*

ACT I

SCENE I. *London. A street*

Enter RICHARD, DUKE OF GLOUCESTER, *solus*

GLOUCESTER

Now is the winter of our discontent
Made glorious summer by this sun of York;
And all the clouds that lour'd upon our house
In the deep bosom of the ocean buried.
Now are our brows bound with victorious wreaths;
Our bruised arms hung up for monuments;
Our stern alarums changed to merry meetings,
Our dreadful marches to delightful measures.
Grim-visaged war hath smooth'd his wrinkled front;
And now, instead of mounting barbed steeds
To fright the souls of fearful adversaries,
He capers nimbly in a lady's chamber
To the lascivious pleasing of a lute.
But I, that am not shaped for sportive tricks,
Nor made to court an amorous looking-glass;
I, that am rudely stamp'd, and want love's majesty
To strut before a wanton ambling nymph;
I, that am curtail'd of this fair proportion,
Cheated of feature by dissembling nature,
Deform'd, unfinish'd, sent before my time

Into this breathing world, scarce half made up,
And that so lamely and unfashionable
That dogs bark at me as I halt by them;
Why, I, in this weak piping time of peace,
Have no delight to pass away the time,
Unless to spy my shadow in the sun,
And descant on mine own deformity:
And therefore, since I cannot prove a lover,
To entertain these fair well-spoken days,
I am determined to prove a villain,
And hate the idle pleasures of these days.
Plots have I laid, inductions dangerous,
By drunken prophecies, libels and dreams,
To set my brother Clarence and the king
In deadly hate the one against the other:
And if King Edward be as true and just
As I am subtle, false and treacherous,
This day should Clarence closely be mew'd up,
About a prophecy, which says that G
Of Edward's heirs the murderer shall be.
Dive, thoughts, down to my soul: here Clarence
  comes.

Enter CLARENCE, *guarded, and* BRAKENBURY

Brother, good day: what means this armed guard
That waits upon your grace?

[113]

CLARENCE

　　　　　His majesty,
Tendering my person's safety, hath appointed
This conduct to convey me to the Tower.

GLOUCESTER

Upon what cause?

CLARENCE

　　　　　Because my name is George.

GLOUCESTER

Alack, my lord, that fault is none of yours;
He should, for that, commit your godfathers:
O, belike his majesty hath some intent
That you shall be new-christen'd in the Tower.
But what's the matter, Clarence? may I know?

CLARENCE

Yea, Richard, when I know; for I protest
As yet I do not: but, as I can learn,
He hearkens after prophecies and dreams;
And from the cross-row plucks the letter G,
And says a wizard told him that by G
His issue disinherited should be;
And, for my name of George begins with G,
It follows in his thought that I am he.
These, as I learn, and such like toys as these
Have moved his highness to commit me now.

GLOUCESTER

Why, this it is, when men are ruled by women:
'Tis not the king that sends you to the Tower;
My Lady Grey his wife, Clarence, 'tis she
That tempers him to this extremity.
Was it not she and that good man of worship,
Anthony Woodville, her brother there,
That made him send Lord Hastings to the Tower,
From whence this present day he is deliver'd?
We are not safe, Clarence; we are not safe.

CLARENCE

By heaven, I think there's no man is secure,
But the queen's kindred and night-walking heralds,
That trudge betwixt the king and Mistress Shore.
Heard ye not what an humble suppliant
Lord Hastings was to her for his delivery?

GLOUCESTER

Humbly complaining to her deity
Got my lord chamberlain his liberty.
I'll tell you what; I think it is our way,
If we will keep in favour with the king,
To be her men and wear her livery:
The jealous o'erworn widow and herself,
Since that our brother dubb'd them gentlewomen,
Are mighty gossips in this monarchy.

BRAKENBURY

I beseech your graces both to pardon me;
His majesty hath straitly given in charge
That no man shall have private conference,
Of what degree soever, with his brother.

GLOUCESTER

Even so; an 't please your worship, Brakenbury,
You may partake of any thing we say:
We speak no treason, man: we say the king

Is wise and virtuous, and his noble queen
Well struck in years, fair, and not jealous;
We say that Shore's wife hath a pretty foot,
A cherry lip, a bonny eye, a passing pleasing tongue;
And that the queen's kindred are made gentle-folks:
How say you, sir? can you deny all this?

BRAKENBURY

With this, my lord, myself have nought to do.

GLOUCESTER

Naught to do with Mistress Shore! I tell thee, fellow,
He that doth naught with her, excepting one,
Were best he do it secretly alone.

BRAKENBURY

What one, my lord?

GLOUCESTER

Her husband, knave: wouldst thou betray me?

BRAKENBURY

I beseech your grace to pardon me, and withal
Forbear your conference with the noble duke.

CLARENCE

We know thy charge, Brakenbury, and will obey.

GLOUCESTER

We are the queen's abjects, and must obey.
Brother, farewell: I will unto the king;
And whatsoever you will employ me in,
Were it to call King Edward's widow sister,
I will perform it to enfranchise you.
Meantime, this deep disgrace in brotherhood
Touches me deeper than you can imagine.

CLARENCE

I know it pleaseth neither of us well.

GLOUCESTER

Well, your imprisonment shall not be long;
I will deliver you, or else lie for you:
Meantime, have patience.

CLARENCE

　　　　　I must perforce. Farewell.
[Exeunt CLARENCE, BRAKENBURY, and GUARD

GLOUCESTER

Go tread the path that thou shalt ne'er return,
Simple, plain Clarence! I do love thee so,
That I will shortly send thy soul to heaven,
If heaven will take the present at our hands.
But who comes here? the new-deliver'd Hastings?

Enter LORD HASTINGS

HASTINGS

Good time of day unto my gracious lord!

GLOUCESTER

As much unto my good lord chamberlain!
Well are you welcome to the open air.
How hath your lordship brook'd imprisonment?

HASTINGS

With patience, noble lord, as prisoners must:
But I shall live, my lord, to give them thanks
That were the cause of my imprisonment.

GLOUCESTER

No doubt, no doubt; and so shall Clarence too;
For they that were your enemies are his,
And have prevail'd as much on him as you.

HASTINGS
More pity that the eagle should be mew'd,
While kites and buzzards prey at liberty.
GLOUCESTER
What news abroad?
HASTINGS
No news so bad abroad as this at home;
The king is sickly, weak and melancholy,
And his physicians fear him mightily.
GLOUCESTER
Now, by Saint Paul, this news is bad indeed.
O, he hath kept an evil diet long,
And overmuch consumed his royal person:
'Tis very grievous to be thought upon.
What, is he in his bed?
HASTINGS
H^ is.
GLOUCESTER
Go you before, and I will follow you. [Exit HASTINGS
He cannot live, I hope; and must not die,
Till George be pack'd with post-horse up to heaven.
I'll in, to urge his hatred more to Clarence,
With lies well steel'd with weighty arguments;
And, if I fail not in my deep intent,
Clarence hath not another day to live:
Which done, God take King Edward to his mercy,
And leave the world for me to bustle in!
For then I'll marry Warwick's youngest daughter.
What though I kill'd her husband and her father?
The readiest way to make the wench amends
Is to become her husband and her father:
The which will I; not all so much for love,
As for another secret close intent,
By marrying her which I must reach unto.
But yet I run before my horse to market:
Clarence still breathes; Edward still lives and
   reigns:
When they are gone, then must I count my gains.
                            [Exit

SCENE II. *The same. Another street*

Enter the corpse of KING HENRY *the Sixth,* GENTLEMEN
with halberds to guard it; LADY ANNE *being the mourner*
ANNE
Set down, set down your honourable load—
If honour may be shrouded in a hearse—
Whilst I awhile obsequiously lament
The untimely fall of virtuous Lancaster.
Poor key-cold figure of a holy king!
Pale ashes of the house of Lancaster!
Thou bloodless remnant of that royal blood!
Be it lawful that I invocate thy ghost,
To hear the lamentations of poor Anne,
Wife to thy Edward, to thy slaughtered son,
Stabb'd by the selfsame hand that made these
   wounds!
Lo, in these windows that let forth thy life
I pour the helpless balm of my poor eyes.
Cursed be the hand that made these fatal holes!

Cursed be the heart that had the heart to do it!
Cursed the blood that let this blood from hence!
More direful hap betide that hated wretch,
That makes us wretched by the death of thee,
Than I can wish to adders, spiders, toads,
Or any creeping venom'd thing that lives!
If ever he have child, abortive be it,
Prodigious, and untimely brought to light,
Whose ugly and unnatural aspect
May fright the hopeful mother at the view;
And that be heir to his unhappiness!
If ever he have wife, let her be made
As miserable by the death of him,
As I am made by my poor lord and thee!
Come, now towards Chertsey with your holy load,
Taken from Paul's to be interred there;
And still, as you are weary of the weight,
Rest you, whiles I lament King Henry's corse.
          Enter GLOUCESTER
GLOUCESTER
Stay, you that bear the corse, and set it down.
ANNE
What black magician conjures up this fiend,
To stop devoted charitable deeds?
GLOUCESTER
Villains, set down the corse; or, by Saint Paul,
I'll make a corse of him that disobeys.
GENTLEMAN
My lord, stand back, and let the coffin pass.
GLOUCESTER
Unmanner'd dog! stand thou, when I command:
Advance thy halberd higher than my breast,
Or, by Saint Paul, I'll strike thee to my foot,
And spurn upon thee, beggar, for thy boldness.
ANNE
What, do you tremble? are you all afraid?
Alas, I blame you not; for you are mortal,
And mortal eyes cannot endure the devil.
Avaunt, thou dreadful minister of hell!
Thou hadst but power over his mortal body,
His soul thou canst not have; therefore, be gone.
GLOUCESTER
Sweet saint, for charity, be not so curst.
ANNE
Foul devil, for God's sake, hence, and trouble us
   not;
For thou hast made the happy earth thy hell,
Fill'd it with cursing cries and deep exclaims.
If thou delight to view thy heinous deeds,
Behold this pattern of thy butcheries.
O, gentlemen, see, see! dead Henry's wounds
Open their congeal'd mouths and bleed afresh.
Blush, blush, thou lump of foul deformity;
For 'tis thy presence that exhales this blood
From cold and empty veins, where no blood dwells;
Thy deed, inhuman and unnatural,
Provokes this deluge most unnatural.
O God, which this blood madest, revenge his death!
O earth, which this blood drink'st, revenge his
   death!

Either heaven with lightning strike the murderer
    dead,
Or earth, gape open wide and eat him quick,
As thou dost swallow up this good king's blood,
Which his hell-govern'd arm hath butchered!

GLOUCESTER

Lady, you know no rules of charity,
Which renders good for bad, blessings for curses.

ANNE

Villain, thou know'st no law of God nor man:
No beast so fierce but knows some touch of pity.

GLOUCESTER

But I know none, and therefore am no beast.

ANNE

O wonderful, when devils tell the truth!

GLOUCESTER

More wonderful, when angels are so angry.
Vouchsafe, divine perfection of a woman,
Of these supposed evils, to give me leave,
By circumstance, but to acquit myself.

ANNE

Vouchsafe, defused infection of a man,
For these known evils, but to give me leave,
By circumstance, to curse thy cursed self.

GLOUCESTER

Fairer than tongue can name thee, let me have
Some patient leisure to excuse myself.

ANNE

Fouler than heart can think thee, thou canst make
No excuse current, but to hang thyself.

GLOUCESTER

By such despair, I should accuse myself.

ANNE

And, by despairing, shouldst thou stand excused
For doing worthy vengeance on thyself,
Which didst unworthy slaughter upon others.

GLOUCESTER

Say that I slew them not?

ANNE

               Why, then they are not dead:
But dead they are, and, devilish slave, by thee.

GLOUCESTER

I did not kill your husband.

ANNE

               Why, then he is alive.

GLOUCESTER

Nay, he is dead; and slain by Edward's hand.

ANNE

In thy foul throat thou liest: Queen Margaret saw
Thy murderous falchion smoking in his blood;
The which thou once didst bend against her breast,
But that thy brothers beat aside the point.

GLOUCESTER

I was provoked by her slanderous tongue,
Which laid their guilt upon my guiltless shoulders.

ANNE

Thou wast provoked by thy bloody mind,
Which never dreamt on aught but butcheries:
Didst thou not kill this king?

GLOUCESTER

               I grant ye.

ANNE

Dost grant me, hedgehog? then, God grant me too
Thou mayst be damned for that wicked deed!
O, he was gentle, mild, and virtuous!

GLOUCESTER

The fitter for the King of heaven, that hath him.

ANNE

He is in heaven, where thou shalt never come.

GLOUCESTER

Let him thank me, that holp to send him thither;
For he was fitter for that place than earth.

ANNE

And thou unfit for any place but hell.

GLOUCESTER

Yes, one place else, if you will hear me name it.

ANNE

Some dungeon.

GLOUCESTER

               Your bed-chamber.

ANNE

Ill rest betide the chamber where thou liest!

GLOUCESTER

So will it, madam, till I lie with you.

ANNE

I hope so.

GLOUCESTER

               I know so. But, gentle Lady Anne,
To leave this keen encounter of our wits,
And fall somewhat into a slower method,
Is not the causer of the timeless deaths
Of these Plantagenets, Henry and Edward,
As blameful as the executioner?

ANNE

Thou art the cause, and most accursed effect.

GLOUCESTER

Your beauty was the cause of that effect;
Your beauty, which did haunt me in my sleep
To undertake the death of all the world,
So I might live one hour in your sweet bosom.

ANNE

If I thought that, I tell thee, homicide,
These nails should rend that beauty from my
    cheeks.

GLOUCESTER

These eyes could never endure sweet beauty's
    wreck;
You should not blemish it, if I stood by:
As all the world is cheered by the sun,
So I by that; it is my day, my life.

ANNE

Black night o'ershade thy day, and death thy life!

GLOUCESTER

Curse not thyself, fair creature; thou art both.

ANNE

I would I were, to be revenged on thee.

GLOUCESTER

It is a quarrel most unnatural,
To be revenged on him that loveth you.

ANNE

It is a quarrel just and reasonable,
To be revenged on him that slew my husband.

GLOUCESTER

He that bereft thee, lady, of thy husband,
Did it to help thee to a better husband.

ANNE

His better doth not breathe upon the earth.

GLOUCESTER

He lives that loves you better than he could.

ANNE

Name him.

GLOUCESTER

Plantagenet.

ANNE

Why, that was he.

GLOUCESTER

The selfsame name, but one of better nature.

ANNE

Where is he?

GLOUCESTER

Here. [*She spitteth at him.*] Why dost
thou spit at me?

ANNE

Would it were mortal poison, for thy sake!

GLOUCESTER

Never came poison from so sweet a place.

ANNE

Never hung poison on a fouler toad.
Out of my sight! thou dost infect my eyes.

GLOUCESTER

Thine eyes, sweet lady, have infected mine.

ANNE

Would they were basilisks, to strike thee dead!

GLOUCESTER

I would they were, that I might die at once;
For now they kill me with a living death.
Those eyes of thine from mine have drawn salt tears,
Shames their aspect with store of childish drops:
These eyes, which never shed remorseful tear,
No, when my father York and Edward wept,
To hear the piteous moan that Rutland made
When black-faced Clifford shook his sword at him;
Nor when thy warlike father, like a child,
Told the sad story of my father's death,
And twenty times made pause to sob and weep,
That all the standers-by had wet their cheeks,
Like trees bedash'd with rain: in that sad time
My manly eyes did scorn an humble tear;
And what these sorrows could not thence exhale,
Thy beauty hath, and made them blind with
    weeping.
I never sued to friend nor enemy;
My tongue could never learn sweet smoothing
    words;
But, now thy beauty is proposed my fee,
My proud heart sues, and prompts my tongue to
    speak.   [*She looks scornfully at him*
Teach not thy lips such scorn, for they were made
For kissing, lady, not for such contempt.

If thy revengeful heart cannot forgive,
Lo, here I lend thee this sharp-pointed sword;
Which if thou please to hide in this true bosom,
And let the soul forth that adoreth thee,
I lay it naked to the deadly stroke,
And humbly beg the death upon my knee.
    [*He lays his breast open: she offers at it with his sword*
Nay, do not pause; for I did kill King Henry,
But 'twas thy beauty that provoked me.
Nay, now dispatch; 'twas I that stabb'd young
    Edward,
But 'twas thy heavenly face that set me on.
    [*Here she lets fall the sword*
Take up the sword again, or take up me.

ANNE

Arise, dissembler: though I wish thy death,
I will not be the executioner.

GLOUCESTER

Then bid me kill myself, and I will do it.

ANNE

I have already.

GLOUCESTER

Tush, that was in thy rage:
Speak it again, and, even with the word,
That hand, which, for thy love, did kill thy love,
Shall, for thy love, kill a far truer love;
To both their deaths shalt thou be accessary.

ANNE

I would I knew thy heart.

GLOUCESTER

'Tis figured in my tongue.

ANNE

I fear me both are false.

GLOUCESTER

Then never man was true.

ANNE

Well, well, put up your sword.

GLOUCESTER

Say, then, my peace is made.

ANNE

That shall you know hereafter.

GLOUCESTER

But shall I live in hope?

ANNE

All men, I hope, live so.

GLOUCESTER

Vouchsafe to wear this ring.

ANNE

To take is not to give.

GLOUCESTER

Look, how this ring encompasseth thy finger,
Even so thy breast encloseth my poor heart;
Wear both of them, for both of them are thine.
And if thy poor devoted suppliant may
But beg one favour at thy gracious hand,
Thou dost confirm his happiness for ever.

ANNE

What is it?

GLOUCESTER

That it would please thee leave these sad designs

To him that hath more cause to be a mourner,
And presently repair to Crosby Place;
Where, after I have solemnly interr'd
At Chertsey monastery this noble king,
And wet his grave with my repentant tears,
I will with all expedient duty see you:
For divers unknown reasons, I beseech you,
Grant me this boon.

ANNE

With all my heart; and much it joys me too,
To see you are become so penitent.
Tressel and Berkeley, go along with me.

GLOUCESTER

Bid me farewell.

ANNE

          'Tis more than you deserve;
But since you teach me how to flatter you,
Imagine I have said farewell already.

[*Exeunt* LADY ANNE, TRESSEL, *and* BERKELEY

GLOUCESTER

Sirs, take up the corse.

GENTLEMAN

          Towards Chertsey, noble lord?

GLOUCESTER

No, to White-Friars; there attend my coming.

[*Exeunt all but* GLOUCESTER

Was ever woman in this humour woo'd?
Was ever woman in this humour won?
I'll have her; but I will not keep her long.
What! I, that kill'd her husband and his father,
To take her in her heart's extremest hate,
With curses in her mouth, tears in her eyes,
The bleeding witness of her hatred by;
Having God, her conscience, and these bars against
   me,
And I nothing to back my suit at all,
But the plain devil and dissembling looks,
And yet to win her, all the world to nothing!
Ha!
Hath she forgot already that brave prince,
Edward, her lord, whom I, some three months
   since,
Stabb'd in my angry mood at Tewksbury?
A sweeter and a lovelier gentleman,
Framed in the prodigality of nature,
Young, valiant, wise, and, no doubt, right royal,
The spacious world cannot again afford:
And will she yet debase her eyes on me,
That cropp'd the golden prime of this sweet prince,
And made her widow to a woful bed?
On me, whose all not equals Edward's moiety?
On me, that halt and am unshapen thus?
My dukedom to a beggarly denier,
I do mistake my person all this while:
Upon my life, she finds, although I cannot,
Myself to be a marvellous proper man.
I'll be at charges for a looking-glass,
And entertain some score or two of tailors,
To study fashions to adorn my body:
Since I am crept in favour with myself,

I will maintain it with some little cost.
But first I'll turn yon fellow in his grave;
And then return lamenting to my love.
Shine out, fair sun, till I have bought a glass,
That I may see my shadow as I pass. [*Exit*

SCENE III. *The palace*

Enter QUEEN ELIZABETH, LORD RIVERS, *and*
LORD GREY

RIVERS

Have patience, madam: there's no doubt his majesty
Will soon recover his accustom'd health.

GREY

In that you brook it ill, it make. him worse:
Therefore, for God's sake, entertain good comfort,
And cheer his grace with quick and merry words.

QUEEN ELIZABETH

If he were dead, what would betide of me?

RIVERS

No other harm but loss of such a lord.

QUEEN ELIZABETH

The loss of such a lord includes all harm.

GREY

The heavens have bless'd you with a goodly son,
To be your comforter when he is gone.

QUEEN ELIZABETH

Oh, he is young, and his minority
Is put unto the trust of Richard Gloucester,
A man that loves not me, nor none of you.

RIVERS

Is it concluded he shall be protector?

QUEEN ELIZABETH

It is determined, not concluded yet:
But so it must be, if the king miscarry.

Enter BUCKINGHAM *and* DERBY

GREY

Here come the lords of Buckingham and Derby.

BUCKINGHAM

Good time of day unto your royal grace!

DERBY

God make your majesty joyful as you have been!

QUEEN ELIZABETH

The Countess Richmond, good my Lord of Derby,
To your good prayers will scarcely say amen.
Yet, Derby, notwithstanding she's your wife,
And loves not me, be you, good lord, assured
I hate not you for her proud arrogance.

DERBY

I do beseech you, either not believe
The envious slanders of her false accusers;
Or, if she be accused in true report,
Bear with her weakness, which, I think, proceeds
From wayward sickness, and no grounded malice.

RIVERS

Saw you the king to-day, my Lord of Derby?

DERBY

But now the Duke of Buckingham and I
Are come from visiting his majesty.

QUEEN ELIZABETH

What likelihood of his amendment, lords?

BUCKINGHAM

Madam, good hope; his grace speaks cheerfully.

QUEEN ELIZABETH

God grant him health! Did you confer with him?

BUCKINGHAM

Madam, we did: he desires to make atonement
Betwixt the Duke of Gloucester and your brothers,
And betwixt them and my lord chamberlain;
And sent to warn them to his royal presence.

QUEEN ELIZABETH

Would all were well! but that will never be:
I fear our happiness is at the highest.

Enter GLOUCESTER, HASTINGS, *and* DORSET

GLOUCESTER

They do me wrong, and I will not endure it:
Who are they that complain unto the king,
That I, forsooth, am stern and love them not?
By holy Paul, they love his grace but lightly
That fill his ears with such dissentious rumours.
Because I cannot flatter and speak fair,
Smile in men's faces, smooth, deceive and cog,
Duck with French nods and apish courtesy,
I must be held a rancorous enemy.
Cannot a plain man live and think no harm,
But thus his simple truth must be abused
By silken, sly, insinuating Jacks?

RIVERS

To whom in all this presence speaks your grace?

GLOUCESTER

To thee, that hast nor honesty nor grace.
When have I injured thee? when done thee wrong?
Or thee? or thee? or any of your faction?
A plague upon you all! His royal person—
Whom God preserve better than you would wish!—
Cannot be quiet scarce a breathing-while,
But you must trouble him with lewd complaints.

QUEEN ELIZABETH

Brother of Gloucester, you mistake the matter.
The king, of his own royal disposition,
And not provoked by any suitor else;
Aiming, belike, at your interior hatred,
Which in your outward actions shows itself
Against my kindred, brothers, and myself,
Makes him to send; that thereby he may gather
The ground of your ill-will, and to remove it.

GLOUCESTER

I cannot tell: the world is grown so bad,
That wrens make prey where eagles dare not perch:
Since every Jack became a gentleman,
There's many a gentle person made a Jack.

QUEEN ELIZABETH

Come, come, we know your meaning, brother
  Gloucester;
You envy my advancement and my friends':
God grant we never may have need of you!

GLOUCESTER

Meantime, God grants that we have need of you:
Our brother is imprison'd by your means,

Myself disgraced, and the nobility
Held in contempt; whilst many fair promotions
Are daily given to ennoble those
That scarce, some two days since, were worth a
  noble.

QUEEN ELIZABETH

By Him that raised me to this careful height
From that contented hap which I enjoy'd,
I never did incense his majesty
Against the Duke of Clarence, but have been
An earnest advocate to plead for him.
My lord, you do me shameful injury,
Falsely to draw me in these vile suspects.

GLOUCESTER

You may deny that you were not the cause
Of my Lord Hastings' late imprisonment.

RIVERS

She may, my lord, for—

GLOUCESTER

She may, Lord Rivers! why, who knows not so?
She may do more, sir, than denying that:
She may help you to many fair preferments;
And then deny her aiding hand therein,
And lay those honours on your high deserts.
What may she not? She may, yea, marry, may
  she,—

RIVERS

What, marry, may she?

GLOUCESTER

What, marry, may she! marry with a king,
A bachelor, a handsome stripling too:
I wis your grandam had a worser match.

QUEEN ELIZABETH

My Lord of Gloucester, I have too long borne
Your blunt upbraidings and your bitter scoffs:
By heaven, I will acquaint his majesty
With those gross taunts I often have endured.
I had rather be a country servant-maid
Than a great queen, with this condition,
To be thus taunted, scorn'd, and baited at:

Enter QUEEN MARGARET, *behind*

Small joy have I in being England's queen.

QUEEN MARGARET

And lessen'd be that small, God, I beseech thee!
Thy honour, state and seat is due to me.

GLOUCESTER

What! threat you me with telling of the king?
Tell him, and spare not: look, what I have said
I will avouch in presence of the king:
I dare adventure to be sent to the Tower.
'Tis time to speak; my pains are quite forgot.

QUEEN MARGARET

Out, devil! I remember them too well:
Thou slewest my husband Henry in the Tower,
And Edward, my poor son, at Tewksbury.

GLOUCESTER

Ere you were queen, yea, or your husband king,
I was a pack-horse in his great affairs;
A weeder out of his proud adversaries,

A liberal rewarder of his friends:
To royalise his blood I spilt mine own.

QUEEN MARGARET

Yea, and much better blood than his or thine.

GLOUCESTER

In all which time you and your husband Grey
Were factious for the house of Lancaster;
And, Rivers, so were you. Was not your husband
In Margaret's battle at Saint Alban's slain?
Let me put in your minds, if you forget,
What you have been ere now, and what you are;
Withal, what I have been, and what I am.

QUEEN MARGARET

A murderous villain, and so still thou art.

GLOUCESTER

Poor Clarence did forsake his father, Warwick;
Yea, and forswore himself,—which Jesu pardon!—

QUEEN MARGARET

Which God revenge!

GLOUCESTER

To fight on Edward's party for the crown;
And for his meed, poor lord, he is mew'd up.
I would to God my heart were flint, like Edward's;
Or Edward's soft and pitiful, like mine:
I am too childish-foolish for this world.

QUEEN MARGARET

Hie thee to hell for shame, and leave the world,
Thou cacodemon! there thy kingdom is.

RIVERS

My Lord of Gloucester, in those busy days
Which here you urge to prove us enemies,
We follow'd then our lord, our lawful king:
So should we you, if you should be our king.

GLOUCESTER

If I should be! I had rather be a pedlar:
Far be it from my heart, the thought of it!

QUEEN ELIZABETH

As little joy, my lord, as you suppose
You should enjoy, were you this country's king,
As little joy may you suppose in me,
That I enjoy, being the queen thereof.

QUEEN MARGARET

A little joy enjoys the queen thereof;
For I am she, and altogether joyless.
I can no longer hold me patient.   [Advancing
Hear me, you wrangling pirates, that fall out
In sharing that which you have pill'd from me!
Which of you trembles not that looks on me?
If not, that, I being queen, you bow like subjects,
Yet that, by you deposed, you quake like rebels?
O gentle villain, do not turn away!

GLOUCESTER

Foul wrinkled witch, what makest thou in my sight?

QUEEN MARGARET

But repetition of what thou hast marr'd;
That will I make before I let thee go.

GLOUCESTER

Wert thou not banished on pain of death?

QUEEN MARGARET

I was; but I do find more pain in banishment,

Than death can yield me here by my abode.
A husband and a son thou owest to me;
And thou a kingdom; all of you allegiance:
The sorrow that I have, by right is yours,
And all the pleasures you usurp are mine.

GLOUCESTER

The curse my noble father laid on thee,
When thou didst crown his warlike brows with
     paper,
And with thy scorns drew'st rivers from his eyes,
And then, to dry them, gavest the duke a clout,
Steep'd in the faultless blood of pretty Rutland,—
His curses, then from bitterness of soul
Denounced against thee, are all fall'n upon thee;
And God, not we, hath plagued thy bloody deed.

QUEEN ELIZABETH

So just is God, to right the innocent.

HASTINGS

O, 'twas the foulest deed to slay that babe,
And the most merciless that e'er was heard of!

RIVERS

Tyrants themselves wept when it was reported.

DORSET

No man but prophesied revenge for it.

BUCKINGHAM

Northumberland, then present, wept to see it.

QUEEN MARGARET

What! were you snarling all before I came,
Ready to catch each other by the throat,
And turn you all your hatred now on me?
Did York's dread curse prevail so much with heaven,
That Henry's death, my lovely Edward's death,
Their kingdom's loss, my woful banishment,
Could all but answer for that peevish brat?
Can curses pierce the clouds and enter heaven?
Why, then, give way, dull clouds, to my quick
     curses!
If not by war, by surfeit die your king,
As ours by murder, to make him a king!
Edward thy son, which now is Prince of Wales,
For Edward my son, which was Prince of Wales,
Die in his youth by like untimely violence!
Thyself a queen, for me that was a queen,
Outlive thy glory, like my wretched self!
Long mayst thou live to wail thy children's loss;
And see another, as I see thee now,
Deck'd in thy rights, as thou art stall'd in mine!
Long die thy happy days before thy death;
And, after many lengthen'd hours of grief,
Die neither mother, wife, nor England's queen!
Rivers and Dorset, you were standers by,
And so wast thou, Lord Hastings, when my son
Was stabb'd with bloody daggers: God, I pray him,
That none of you may live your natural age,
But by some unlook'd accident cut off!

GLOUCESTER

Have done thy charm, thou hateful withered hag!

QUEEN MARGARET

And leave out thee? stay, dog, for thou shalt hear
     me.

If heaven have any grievous plague in store
Exceeding those that I can wish upon thee,
O, let them keep it till thy sins be ripe,
And then hurl down their indignation
On thee, the troubler of the poor world's peace!
The worm of conscience still begnaw thy soul!
Thy friends suspect for traitors while thou livest,
And take deep traitors for thy dearest friends!
No sleep close up that deadly eye of thine,
Unless it be whilst some tormenting dream
Affrights thee with a hell of ugly devils!
Thou elvish-mark'd, abortive, rooting hog!
Thou that wast seal'd in thy nativity
The slave of nature and the son of hell!
Thou slander of thy mother's heavy womb!
Thou loathed issue of thy father's loins!
Thou rag of honour! thou detested—

GLOUCESTER

Margaret.

QUEEN MARGARET

Richard!

GLOUCESTER

Ha!

QUEEN MARGARET

I call thee not.

GLOUCESTER

I cry thee mercy then, for I had thought
That thou hadst call'd me all these bitter names.

QUEEN MARGARET

Why, so I did; but look'd for no reply.
O, let me make the period to my curse!

GLOUCESTER

'Tis done by me, and ends in 'Margaret.'

QUEEN ELIZABETH

Thus have you breathed your curse against yourself.

QUEEN MARGARET

Poor painted queen, vain flourish of my fortune!
Why strew'st thou sugar on that bottled spider,
Whose deadly web ensnareth thee about?
Fool, fool! thou whet'st a knife to kill thyself.
The time will come that thou shalt wish for me
To help thee curse that poisonous bunch-back'd
toad.

HASTINGS

False-boding woman, end thy frantic curse,
Lest to thy harm thou move our patience.

QUEEN MARGARET

Foul shame upon you! you have all moved mine.

RIVERS

Were you well served, you would be taught your
duty.

QUEEN MARGARET

To serve me well, you all should do me duty,
Teach me to be your queen, and you my subjects:
O, serve me well, and teach yourselves that duty!

DORSET

Dispute not with her; she is lunatic.

QUEEN MARGARET

Peace, master marquess, you are malapert:
Your fire-new stamp of honour is scarce current.

O, that your young nobility could judge
What 'twere to lose it, and be miserable!
They that stand high have many blasts to shake
them;
And if they fall, they dash themselves to pieces.

GLOUCESTER

Good counsel, marry: learn it, learn it, marquess.

DORSET

It toucheth you, my lord, as much as me.

GLOUCESTER

Yea, and much more: but I was born so high,
Our aery buildeth in the cedar's top,
And dallies with the wind and scorns the sun.

QUEEN MARGARET

And turns the sun to shade; alas! alas!
Witness my son, now in the shade of death;
Whose bright out-shining beams thy cloudy wrath
Hath in eternal darkness folded up.
Your aery buildeth in our aery's nest.
O God, that seest it, do not suffer it;
As it was won with blood, lost be it so!

BUCKINGHAM

Have done! for shame, if not for charity.

QUEEN MARGARET

Urge neither charity nor shame to me:
Uncharitably with me have you dealt,
And shamefully by you my hopes are butcher'd.
My charity is outrage, life my shame;
And in that shame still live my sorrow's rage!

BUCKINGHAM

Have done, have done.

QUEEN MARGARET

O princely Buckingham, I'll kiss thy hand,
In sign of league and amity with thee:
Now fair befall thee and thy noble house!
Thy garments are not spotted with our blood,
Nor thou within the compass of my curse.

BUCKINGHAM

Nor no one here; for curses never pass
The lips of those that breathe them in the air.

QUEEN MARGARET

I'll not believe but they ascend the sky,
And there awake God's gentle-sleeping peace.
O Buckingham, take heed of yonder dog!
Look, when he fawns, he bites; and when he bites,
His venom tooth will rankle to the death:
Have not to do with him, beware of him;
Sin, death, and hell have set their marks on him,
And all their ministers attend on him.

GLOUCESTER

What doth she say, my Lord of Buckingham?

BUCKINGHAM

Nothing that I respect, my gracious lord.

QUEEN MARGARET

What, dost thou scorn me for my gentle counsel?
And soothe the devil that I warn thee from?
O, but remember this another day,
When he shall split thy very heart with sorrow,
And say poor Margaret was a prophetess.

Live each of you the subjects to his hate,
And he to yours, and all of you to God's!   [*Exit*

HASTINGS
My hair doth stand on end to hear her curses.

RIVERS
And so doth mine: I muse why she's at liberty.

GLOUCESTER
I cannot blame her: by God's holy mother,
She hath had too much wrong; and I repent
My part thereof that I have done to her.

QUEEN ELIZABETH
I never did her any, to my knowledge.

GLOUCESTER
But you have all the vantage of her wrong.
I was too hot to do somebody good,
That is too cold in thinking of it now.
Marry, as for Clarence, he is well repaid;
He is frank'd up to fatting for his pains:
God pardon them that are the cause of it!

RIVERS
A virtuous and a Christian-like conclusion,
To pray for them that have done scathe to us.

GLOUCESTER
So do I ever: [*Aside*] being well advised:
For had I cursed now, I had cursed myself.

Enter CATESBY

CATESBY
Madam, his majesty doth call for you;
And for your grace; and you, my noble lords.

QUEEN ELIZABETH
Catesby, we come. Lords, will you go with us?

RIVERS
Madam, we will attend your grace.
                    [*Exeunt all but* GLOUCESTER

GLOUCESTER
I do the wrong, and first begin to brawl.
The secret mischiefs that I set abroach
I lay unto the grievous charge of others.
Clarence, whom I, indeed, have laid in darkness,
I do beweep to many simple gulls;
Namely, to Hastings, Derby, Buckingham;
And say it is the queen and her allies
That stir the king against the duke my brother.
Now, they believe it; and withal whet me
To be revenged on Rivers, Vaughan, Grey:
But then I sigh; and, with a piece of Scripture,
Tell them that God bids us do good for evil:
And thus I clothe my naked villany
With old odd ends stolen out of holy writ;
And seem a saint, when most I play the devil.

Enter two MURDERERS

But, soft! here come my executioners.
How now, my hardy stout resolved mates!
Are you now going to dispatch this deed?

FIRST MURDERER
We are, my lord; and come to have the warrant,
That we may be admitted where he is.

GLOUCESTER
Well thought upon; I have it here about me.
                    [*Gives the warrant*

When you have done, repair to Crosby Place.
But, sirs, be sudden in the execution,
Withal obdurate, do not hear him plead;
For Clarence is well-spoken, and perhaps
May move your hearts to pity, if you mark him.

FIRST MURDERER
Tush!
Fear not, my lord, we will not stand to prate;
Talkers are no good doers: be assured
We come to use our hands and not our tongues.

GLOUCESTER
Your eyes drop millstones, when fools' eyes drop
    tears.
I like you, lads: about your business straight.
Go, go, dispatch.

FIRST MURDERER
We will, my noble lord.   [*Exeunt*

SCENE IV. *London. The Tower*

Enter CLARENCE *and* BRAKENBURY

BRAKENBURY
Why looks your grace so heavily to-day?

CLARENCE
O, I have pass'd a miserable night,
So full of ugly sights, of ghastly dreams,
That, as I am a Christian faithful man,
I would not spend another such a night,
Though 'twere to buy a world of happy days,
So full of dismal terror was the time!

BRAKENBURY
What was your dream? I long to hear you tell it.

CLARENCE
Methoughts that I had broken from the Tower,
And was embark'd to cross to Burgundy;
And, in my company, my brother Gloucester;
Who from my cabin tempted me to walk
Upon the hatches: thence we look'd toward Eng-
    land,
And cited up a thousand fearful times,
During the wars of York and Lancaster,
That had befall'n us. As we paced along
Upon the giddy footing of the hatches,
Methought that Gloucester stumbled; and, in fall-
    ing,
Struck me, that thought to stay him, overboard,
Into the tumbling billows of the main.
Lord, Lord! methought, what pain it was to drown!
What dreadful noise of waters in mine ears!
What ugly sights of death within mine eyes!
Methought I saw a thousand fearful wrecks;
Ten thousand men that fishes gnaw'd upon;
Wedges of gold, great anchors, heaps of pearl,
Inestimable stones, unvalued jewels,
All scattered in the bottom of the sea:
Some lay in dead men's skulls; and in those holes
Where eyes did once inhabit, there were crept,
As 'twere in scorn of eyes, reflecting gems,

Which woo'd the slimy bottom of the deep,
And mock'd the dead bones that lay scattered by.
BRAKENBURY
Had you such leisure in the time of death
To gaze upon the secrets of the deep?
CLARENCE
Methought I had; and often did I strive
To yield the ghost: but still the envious flood
Kept in my soul, and would not let it forth
To seek the empty, vast and wandering air;
But smothered it within my panting bulk,
Which almost burst to belch it in the sea.
BRAKENBURY
Awaked you not with this sore agony?
CLARENCE
O no, my dream was lengthened after life;
O, then began the tempest to my soul,
Who pass'd, methought, the melancholy flood,
With that grim ferryman which poets write of,
Unto the kingdom of perpetual night.
The first that there did greet my stranger soul,
Was my great father-in-law, renowned Warwick;
Who cried aloud, 'What scourge for perjury
Can this dark monarchy afford false Clarence?'
And so he vanish'd: then came wandering by
A shadow like an angel, with bright hair
Dabbled in blood; and he squeak'd out aloud,
'Clarence is come; false, fleeting, perjured Clarence,
That stabb'd me in the field by Tewksbury:
Seize on him, Furies, take him to your torments!'
With that, methoughts, a legion of foul fiends
Environ'd me about, and howled in mine ears
Such hideous cries, that with the very noise
I trembling waked, and for a season after
Could not believe but that I was in hell,
Such terrible impression made the dream.
BRAKENBURY
No marvel, my lord, though it affrighted you;
I promise you, I am afraid to hear you tell it.
CLARENCE
O Brakenbury, I have done those things,
Which now bear evidence against my soul,
For Edward's sake; and see how he requites me!
O God! if my deep prayers cannot appease thee,
But thou wilt be avenged on my misdeeds,
Yet execute thy wrath in me alone;
O, spare my guiltless wife and my poor children!
I pray thee, gentle keeper, stay by me;
My soul is heavy, and I fain would sleep.
BRAKENBURY
I will, my lord: God give your grace good rest!
[CLARENCE sleeps
Sorrow breaks seasons and reposing hours,
Makes the night morning and the noon-tide night.
Princes have but their titles for their glories,
An outward honour for an inward toil;
And, for unfelt imagination,
They often feel a world of restless cares:
So that, betwixt their titles and low names,
There's nothing differs but the outward fame.

Enter the two MURDERERS
FIRST MURDERER
Ho! who's here?
BRAKENBURY
In God's name what are you, and how came you
hither?
FIRST MURDERER
I would speak with Clarence, and I came hither on
my legs.
BRAKENBURY
Yea, are you so brief?
SECOND MURDERER
O sir, it is better to be brief than tedious.
Show him our commission; talk no more.
[BRAKENBURY *reads it*
BRAKENBURY
I am in this commanded to deliver
The noble Duke of Clarence to your hands:
I will not reason what is meant hereby,
Because I will be guiltless of the meaning.
Here are the keys, there sits the duke asleep:
I'll to the king; and signify to him
That thus I have resign'd my charge to you.
FIRST MURDERER
Do so, it is a point of wisdom: fare you well.
[Exit BRAKENBURY
SECOND MURDERER
What, shall we stab him as he sleeps?
FIRST MURDERER
No; then he will say 'twas done cowardly, when he
wakes.
SECOND MURDERER
When he wakes! why, fool, he shall never wake till
the judgement-day.
FIRST MURDERER
Why, then he will say we stabbed him sleeping.
SECOND MURDERER
The urging of that word 'judgement' hath bred a
kind of remorse in me.
FIRST MURDERER
What, art thou afraid?
SECOND MURDERER
Not to kill him, having a warrant for it; but to be
damned for killing him, from which no warrant can
defend us.
FIRST MURDERER
I thought thou hadst been resolute.
SECOND MURDERER
So I am, to let him live.
FIRST MURDERER
Back to the Duke of Gloucester, tell him so.
SECOND MURDERER
I pray thee, stay a while: I hope my holy humour
will change; 'twas wont to hold me but while one
would tell twenty.
FIRST MURDERER
How dost thou feel thyself now?
SECOND MURDERER
Faith, some certain dregs of conscience are yet
within me.

FIRST MURDERER

Remember our reward, when the deed is done.

SECOND MURDERER

'Zounds, he dies: I had forgot the reward.

FIRST MURDERER

Where is thy conscience now?

SECOND MURDERER

In the Duke of Gloucester's purse.

FIRST MURDERER

So when he opens his purse to give us our reward, thy conscience flies out.

SECOND MURDERER

Let it go; there's few or none will entertain it.

FIRST MURDERER

How if it come to thee again?

SECOND MURDERER

I'll not meddle with it: it is a dangerous thing: it makes a man a coward: a man cannot steal, but it accuseth him; he cannot swear, but it checks him; he cannot lie with his neighbour's wife, but it detects him: it is a blushing shamefast spirit that mutinies in a man's bosom; it fills one full of obstacles: it made me once restore a purse of gold, that I found; it beggars any man that keeps it: it is turned out of all towns and cities for a dangerous thing; and every man that means to live well endeavours to trust to himself and to live without it.

FIRST MURDERER

'Zounds, it is even now at my elbow, persuading me not to kill the duke.

SECOND MURDERER

Take the devil in thy mind, and believe him not: he would insinuate with thee but to make thee sigh.

FIRST MURDERER

Tut, I am strong-framed, he cannot prevail with me, I warrant thee.

SECOND MURDERER

Spoke like a tall fellow that respects his reputation. Come, shall we to this gear?

FIRST MURDERER

Take him over the costard with the hilts of thy sword, and then we will chop him in the malmsey-butt in the next room.

SECOND MURDERER

O excellent device! make a sop of him.

FIRST MURDERER

Hark! he stirs: shall I strike?

SECOND MURDERER

No, first let's reason with him.

CLARENCE

Where art thou, keeper? give me a cup of wine.

SECOND MURDERER

You shall have wine enough, my lord, anon.

CLARENCE

In God's name, what art thou?

SECOND MURDERER

A man, as you are.

CLARENCE

But not, as I am, royal.

SECOND MURDERER

Nor you, as we are, loyal.

CLARENCE

Thy voice is thunder, but thy looks are humble.

SECOND MURDERER

My voice is now the king's, my looks mine own.

CLARENCE

How darkly and how deadly dost thou speak!
Your eyes do menace me: why look you pale?
Who sent you hither? Wherefore do you come?

BOTH

To, to, to—

CLARENCE

To murder me?

BOTH

Ay, ay.

CLARENCE

You scarcely have the hearts to tell me so,
And therefore cannot have the hearts to do it.
Wherein, my friends, have I offended you?

FIRST MURDERER

Offended us you have not, but the king.

CLARENCE

I shall be reconciled to him again.

SECOND MURDERER

Never, my lord; therefore prepare to die.

CLARENCE

Are you call'd forth from out a world of men
To slay the innocent? What is my offence?
Where are the evidence that do accuse me?
What lawful quest have given their verdict up
Unto the frowning judge? or who pronounced
The bitter sentence of poor Clarence' death?
Before I be convict by course of law,
To threaten me with death is most unlawful.
I charge you, as you hope to have redemption
By Christ's dear blood shed for our grievous sins,
That you depart and lay no hands on me:
The deed you undertake is damnable.

FIRST MURDERER

What we will do, we do upon command.

SECOND MURDERER

And he that hath commanded is the king.

CLARENCE

Erroneous vassal! the great King of kings
Hath in the tables of his law commanded
That thou shalt do no murder: and wilt thou then
Spurn at his edict, and fulfil a man's?
Take heed; for he holds vengeance in his hands,
To hurl upon their heads that break his law.

SECOND MURDERER

And that same vengeance doth he hurl on thee,
For false forswearing, and for murder too:
Thou didst receive the holy sacrament,
To fight in quarrel of the house of Lancaster.

FIRST MURDERER

And, like a traitor to the name of God,

Didst break that vow; and with thy treacherous
    blade
Unrip'dst the bowels of thy sovereign's son.

SECOND MURDERER
Whom thou wert sworn to cherish and defend.

FIRST MURDERER
How canst thou urge God's dreadful law to us,
When thou hast broke it in so dear degree?

CLARENCE
Alas! for whose sake did I that ill deed?
For Edward, for my brother, for his sake:
Why, sirs,
He sends ye not to murder me for this;
For in this sin he is as deep as I.
If God will be revenged for this deed,
O, know you yet, he doth it publicly:
Take not the quarrel from his powerful arm;
He needs no indirect nor lawless course
To cut off those that have offended him.

FIRST MURDERER
Who made thee then a bloody minister,
When gallant-springing brave Plantagenet,
That princely novice, was struck dead by thee?

CLARENCE
My brother's love, the devil, and my rage.

FIRST MURDERER
Thy brother's love, our duty, and thy fault,
Provoke us hither now to slaughter thee.

CLARENCE
Oh, if you love my brother, hate not me;
I am his brother, and I love him well.
If you be hired for meed, go back again,
And I will send you to my brother Gloucester,
Who shall reward you better for my life,
Than Edward will for tidings of my death.

SECOND MURDERER
You are deceived, your brother Gloucester hates
    you.

CLARENCE
O, no, he loves me, and he holds me dear:
Go you to him from me.

BOTH
        Ay, so we will.

CLARENCE
Tell him, when that our princely father York
Bless'd his three sons with his victorious arm,
And charged us from his soul to love each other,
He little thought of this divided friendship:
Bid Gloucester think of this, and he will weep.

FIRST MURDERER
Ay, millstones; as he lesson'd us to weep.

CLARENCE
O, do not slander him, for he is kind.

FIRST MURDERER
Right,
As snow in harvest. Thou deceivest thyself:
'Tis he that sent us hither now to slaughter thee.

CLARENCE
It cannot be; for when I parted with him,
He hugg'd me in his arms, and swore, with sobs,
That he would labour my delivery.

SECOND MURDERER
Why, so he doth, now he delivers thee
From this world's thraldom to the joys of heaven.

FIRST MURDERER
Make peace with God, for you must die, my lord.

CLARENCE
Hast thou that holy feeling in thy soul,
To counsel me to make my peace with God,
And art thou yet to thy own soul so blind,
That thou wilt war with God by murdering me?
Ah, sirs, consider, he that set you on
To do this deed will hate you for the deed.

SECOND MURDERER
What shall we do?

CLARENCE
      Relent, and save your souls.

FIRST MURDERER
Relent! 'tis cowardly and womanish.

CLARENCE
Not to relent is beastly, savage, devilish.
Which of you, if you were a prince's son,
Being pent from liberty, as I am now,
If two such murderers as yourselves came to you,
Would not entreat for life?
My friend, I spy some pity in thy looks;
O, if thine eye be not a flatterer,
Come thou on my side, and entreat for me,
As you would beg, were you in my distress:
A begging prince what beggar pities not?

SECOND MURDERER
Look behind you, my lord.

FIRST MURDERER
Take that, and that: if all this will not do, [Stabs him
I'll drown you in the malmsey-butt within.
                    [Exit, with the body

SECOND MURDERER
A bloody deed, and desperately dispatch'd!
How fain, like Pilate, would I wash my hands
Of this most grievous guilty murder done!

Re-enter FIRST MURDERER

FIRST MURDERER
How now! what mean'st thou, that thou help'st me
    not?
By heavens, the duke shall know how slack thou art!

SECOND MURDERER
I would he knew that I had saved his brother!
Take thou the fee, and tell him what I say;
For I repent me that the duke is slain.   [Exit

FIRST MURDERER
So do not I: go, coward as thou art.
Now must I hide his body in some hole,
Until the duke take order for his burial:
And when I have my meed, I must away;
For this will out, and here I must not stay.   [Exit

ACT II

Scene I. *London. The palace*

Flourish. Enter KING EDWARD *sick*, QUEEN ELIZABETH,
DORSET, RIVERS, HASTINGS, BUCKINGHAM, GREY, *and others*

KING EDWARD

Why, so: now have I done a good day's work:
You peers, continue this united league:
I every day expect an embassage
From my Redeemer to redeem me hence;
And now in peace my soul shall part to heaven,
Since I have set my friends at peace on earth.
Rivers and Hastings, take each other's hand;
Dissemble not your hatred, swear your love.

RIVERS

By heaven, my soul is purged from grudging hate;
And with my hand I seal my true heart's love.

HASTINGS

So thrive I, as I truly swear the like!

KING EDWARD

Take heed you dally not before your king;
Lest he that is the supreme King of kings
Confound your hidden falsehood, and award
Either of you to be the other's end.

HASTINGS

So prosper I, as I swear perfect love!

RIVERS

And I, as I love Hastings with my heart!

KING EDWARD

Madam, yourself are not exempt in this,
Nor your son Dorset; Buckingham, nor you;
You have been factious one against the other.
Wife, love Lord Hastings, let him kiss your hand;
And what you do, do it unfeignedly.

QUEEN ELIZABETH

Here, Hastings; I will never more remember
Our former hatred, so thrive I and mine!

KING EDWARD

Dorset, embrace him; Hastings, love lord marquess.

DORSET

This interchange of love, I here protest,
Upon my part shall be unviolable.

HASTINGS

And so swear I, my lord.   [*They embrace*

KING EDWARD

Now, princely Buckingham, seal thou this league
With thy embracements to my wife's allies,
And make me happy in your unity.

BUCKINGHAM

[*To the* QUEEN] Whenever Buckingham doth turn
  his hate
On you or yours, but with all duteous love
Doth cherish you and yours, God punish me
With hate in those where I expect most love!
When I have most need to employ a friend,
And most assured that he is a friend,
Deep, hollow, treacherous and full of guile,

Be he unto me! this do I beg of God,
When I am cold in zeal to your or yours.
     [*They embrace*

KING EDWARD

A pleasing cordial, princely Buckingham,
Is this thy vow unto my sickly heart.
There wanteth now our brother Gloucester here,
To make the perfect period of this peace.

BUCKINGHAM

And, in good time, here comes the noble duke.

Enter GLOUCESTER

GLOUCESTER

Good morrow to my sovereign king and queen;
And, princely peers, a happy time of day!

KING EDWARD

Happy indeed, as we have spent the day.
Brother, we have done deeds of charity;
Made peace of enmity, fair love of hate,
Between these swelling wrong-incensed peers.

GLOUCESTER

A blessed labour, my most sovereign liege:
Amongst this princely heap, if any here,
By false intelligence, or wrong surmise,
Hold me a foe;
If I unwittingly, or in my rage,
Have aught committed that is hardly borne
By any in this presence, I desire
To reconcile me to his friendly peace:
'Tis death to me to be at enmity;
I hate it, and desire all good men's love.
First, madam, I entreat true peace of you,
Which I will purchase with my duteous service;
Of you, my noble cousin Buckingham,
If ever any grudge were lodged between us;
Of you, Lord Rivers, and, Lord Grey, of you,
That all without desert have frown'd on me;
Dukes, earls, lords, gentlemen; indeed, of all.
I do not know that Englishman alive
With whom my soul is any jot at odds,
More than the infant that is born to-night:
I thank my God for my humility.

QUEEN ELIZABETH

A holy day shall this be kept hereafter:
I would to God all strifes were well compounded.
My sovereign liege, I do beseech your majesty
To take our brother Clarence to your grace.

GLOUCESTER

Why, madam, have I offer'd love for this,
To be so flouted in this royal presence?
Who knows not that the noble duke is dead?
     [*They all start*

You do him injury to scorn his corse.

RIVERS

Who knows not he is dead! who knows he is?

QUEEN ELIZABETH

All-seeing heaven, what a world is this!

BUCKINGHAM

Look I so pale, Lord Dorset, as the rest?

DORSET

Ay, my good lord; and no one in this presence
But his red colour hath forsook his cheeks.

KING EDWARD

Is Clarence dead? the order was reversed.

GLOUCESTER

But he, poor soul, by your first order died,
And that a winged Mercury did bear;
Some tardy cripple bore the countermand,
That came too lag to see him buried.
God grant that some, less noble and less loyal,
Nearer in bloody thoughts, but not in blood,
Deserve not worse than wretched Clarence did,
And yet go current from suspicion!

Enter DERBY

DERBY

A boon, my sovereign, for my service done!

KING EDWARD

I pray thee, peace: my soul is full of sorrow.

DERBY

I will not rise, unless your highness grant.

KING EDWARD

Then speak at once what is it thou demand'st.

DERBY

The forfeit, sovereign, of my servant's life;
Who slew to-day a riotous gentleman
Lately attendant on the Duke of Norfolk.

KING EDWARD

Have I a tongue to doom my brother's death,
And shall that tongue give pardon to a slave?
My brother slew no man; his fault was thought,
And yet his punishment was cruel death.
Who sued to me for him? who, in my rage,
Kneel'd at my feet and bade me be advised?
Who spake of brotherhood? who spake of love?
Who told me how the poor soul did forsake
The mighty Warwick, and did fight for me?
Who told me, in the field by Tewksbury,
When Oxford had me down, he rescued me,
And said 'Dear brother, live, and be a king'?
Who told me, when we both lay in the field
Frozen almost to death, how he did lap me
Even in his own garments, and gave himself,
All thin and naked, to the numb cold night?
All this from my remembrance brutish wrath
Sinfully pluck'd, and not a man of you
Had so much grace to put it in my mind.
But when your carters or your waiting-vassals
Have done a drunken slaughter, and defaced
The precious image of our dear Redeemer,
You straight are on your knees for pardon, pardon;
And I, unjustly too, must grant it you:
But for my brother not a man would speak,
Nor I, ungracious, speak unto myself
For him, poor soul. The proudest of you all
Have been beholding to him in his life;
Yet none of you would once plead for his life.
O God, I fear thy justice will take hold
On me, and you, and mine, and yours for this!

Come, Hastings, help me to my closet. Oh, poor
Clarence!

[Exeunt some with KING *and* QUEEN

GLOUCESTER

This is the fruit of rashness. Mark'd you not
How that the guilty kindred of the queen
Look'd pale when they did hear of Clarence' death?
O, they did urge it still unto the king!
God will revenge it. But come, let us in,
To comfort Edward with our company.

BUCKINGHAM

We wait upon your grace.

[Exeunt

SCENE II. *The palace*

Enter the DUCHESS OF YORK, *with the two children of*
CLARENCE

BOY

Tell me, good grandam, is our father dead?

DUCHESS

No, boy.

BOY

Why do you wring your hands, and beat your breast,
And cry 'O Clarence, my unhappy son'?

GIRL

Why do you look on us, and shake your head,
And call us wretches, orphans, castaways,
If that our noble father be alive?

DUCHESS

My pretty cousins, you mistake me much.
I do lament the sickness of the king,
As loath to lose him; not your father's death;
It were lost sorrow to wail one that's lost.

BOY

Then, grandam, you conclude that he is dead.
The king my uncle is to blame for this:
God will revenge it; whom I will importune
With daily prayers all to that effect.

GIRL

And so will I.

DUCHESS

Peace, children, peace! the king doth love you well:
Incapable and shallow innocents,
You cannot guess who caused your father's death.

BOY

Grandam, we can; for my good uncle Gloucester
Told me, the king, provoked by the queen,
Devised impeachments to imprison him:
And when my uncle told me so, he wept,
And hugg'd me in his arm, and kindly kiss'd my
    cheek;
Bade me rely on him as on my father,
And he would love me dearly as his child.

DUCHESS

Oh, that deceit should steal such gentle shapes,
And with a virtuous vizard hide foul guile!
He is my son; yea, and therein my shame;
Yet from my dugs he drew not this deceit.

BOY

Think you my uncle did dissemble, grandam?

DUCHESS

Ay, boy.

BOY

I cannot think it. Hark! what noise is this?

Enter QUEEN ELIZABETH, *with her hair about her ears;*
RIVERS *and* DORSET *after her*

QUEEN ELIZABETH

Oh, who shall hinder me to wail and weep,
To chide my fortune and torment myself?
I'll join with black despair against my soul,
And to myself become an enemy.

DUCHESS

What means this scene of rude impatience?

QUEEN ELIZABETH

To make an act of tragic violence:
Edward, my lord, your son, our king, is dead.
Why grow the branches now the root is wither'd?
Why wither not the leaves the sap being gone?
If you will live, lament; if die, be brief,
That our swift-winged souls may catch the king's,
Or, like obedient subjects, follow him
To his new kingdom of perpetual rest.

DUCHESS

Ah, so much interest have I in thy sorrow
As I had title in thy noble husband!
I have bewept a worthy husband's death,
And lived by looking on his images:
But now two mirrors of his princely semblance
Are crack'd in pieces by malignant death,
And I for comfort have but one false glass,
Which grieves me when I see my shame in him.
Thou art a widow; yet thou art a mother,
And hast the comfort of thy children left thee:
But death hath snatch'd my husband from mine
    arms,
And pluck'd two crutches from my feeble limbs,
Edward and Clarence. O, what cause have I,
Thine being but a moiety of my grief,
To overgo thy plaints and drown thy cries!

BOY

Good aunt, you wept not for our father's death,
How can we aid you with our kindred tears?

GIRL

Our fatherless distress was left unmoan'd;
Your widow-dolour likewise be unwept!

QUEEN ELIZABETH

Give me no help in lamentation;
I am not barren to bring forth complaints:
All springs reduce their currents to mine eyes,
That I, being govern'd by the watery moon,
May send forth plenteous tears to drown the world!
Oh for my husband, for my dear lord Edward!

CHILDREN

Oh for our father, for our dear lord Clarence!

DUCHESS

Alas for both, both mine, Edward and Clarence!

QUEEN ELIZABETH

What stay had I but Edward? and he's gone.

CHILDREN

What stay had we but Clarence? and he's gone.

DUCHESS

What stays had I but they? and they are gone.

QUEEN ELIZABETH

Was never widow had so dear a loss.

CHILDREN

Were never orphans had so dear a loss.

DUCHESS

Was never mother had so dear a loss.
Alas, I am the mother of these moans!
Their woes are parcell'd, mine are general.
She for an Edward weeps, and so do I;
I for a Clarence weep, so doth not she:
These babes for Clarence weep, and so do I;
I for an Edward weep, so do not they:
Alas, you three, on me threefold distress'd
Pour all your tears! I am your sorrow's nurse,
And I will pamper it with lamentations.

DORSET

Comfort, dear mother: God is much displeased
That you take with unthankfulness his doing:
In common worldly things, 'tis call'd ungrateful,
With dull unwillingness to repay a debt
Which with a bounteous hand was kindly lent;
Much more to be thus opposite with heaven,
For it requires the royal debt it lent you.

RIVERS

Madam, bethink you, like a careful mother,
Of the young prince your son: send straight for him;
Let him be crown'd; in him your comfort lives:
Drown desperate sorrow in dead Edward's grave,
And plant your joys in living Edward's throne.

Enter GLOUCESTER, BUCKINGHAM, DERBY, HASTINGS,
    and RATCLIFF

GLOUCESTER

Madam, have comfort: all of us have cause
To wail the dimming of our shining star;
But none can cure their harms by wailing them.
Madam, my mother, I do cry you mercy;
I did not see your grace: humbly on my knee
I crave your blessing.

DUCHESS

God bless thee, and put meekness in thy mind,
Love, charity, obedience, and true duty!

GLOUCESTER

[*Aside*] Amen; and make me die a good old man!
That is the butt-end of a mother's blessing:
I marvel why her grace did leave it out.

BUCKINGHAM

You cloudy princes and heart-sorrowing peers,
That bear this mutual heavy load of moan,
Now cheer each other in each other's love:
Though we have spent our harvest of this king,
We are to reap the harvest of his son.
The broken rancour of your high-swoln hearts,
But lately splinter'd, knit and join'd together,
Must gently be preserved, cherish'd, and kept:
Me seemeth good, that, with some little train.

Forthwith from Ludlow the young prince be fetch'd
Hither to London, to be crown'd our king.

RIVERS

Why with some little train, my Lord of Buckingham?

BUCKINGHAM

Marry, my lord, lest, by a multitude,
The new-heal'd wound of malice should break out;
Which would be so much the more dangerous,
By how much the estate is green and yet ungovern'd:
Where every horse bears his commanding rein,
And may direct his course as please himself,
As well the fear of harm as harm apparent,
In my opinion, ought to be prevented.

GLOUCESTER

I hope the king made peace with all of us;
And the compact is firm and true in me.

RIVERS

And so in me; and so, I think, in all:
Yet, since it is but green, it should be put
To no apparent likelihood of breach,
Which haply by much company might be urged:
Therefore I say with noble Buckingham,
That it is meet so few should fetch the prince.

HASTINGS

And so say I.

GLOUCESTER

Then be it so; and go we to determine
Who they shall be that straight shall post to Ludlow.
Madam, and you, my mother, will you go
To give your censures in this weighty business?

QUEEN ELIZABETH and DUCHESS

With all our hearts.

    [Exeunt all but BUCKINGHAM and GLOUCESTER

BUCKINGHAM

My lord, whoever journeys to the prince,
For God's sake, let not us two stay behind;
For, by the way, I'll sort occasion,
As index to the story we late talk'd of,
To part the queen's proud kindred from the king.

GLOUCESTER

My other self, my counsel's consistory,
My oracle, my prophet!—My dear cousin,
I, like a child, will go by thy direction.
Towards Ludlow then, for we'll not stay behind.

         [Exeunt

SCENE III. *London. A street*

Enter two CITIZENS, *meeting*

FIRST CITIZEN

Neighbour, well met: whither away so fast?

SECOND CITIZEN

I promise you, I scarcely know myself:
Hear you the news abroad?

FIRST CITIZEN

      Ay, that the king is dead.

SECOND CITIZEN

Bad news, by 'r lady, seldom comes the better:
I fear, I fear, 'twill prove a troublous world.

Enter another CITIZEN

THIRD CITIZEN

Neighbours, God speed!

FIRST CITIZEN

      Give you good morrow, sir.

THIRD CITIZEN

Doth this news hold of good King Edward's death?

SECOND CITIZEN

Ay, sir, it is too true; God help the while!

THIRD CITIZEN

Then, masters, look to see a troublous world.

FIRST CITIZEN

No, no; by God's good grace his son shall reign.

THIRD CITIZEN

Woe to that land that's govern'd by a child!

SECOND CITIZEN

In him there is a hope of government,
That in his nonage council under him,
And in his full and ripen'd years himself,
No doubt, shall then and till then govern well.

FIRST CITIZEN

So stood the state when Henry the Sixth
Was crown'd in Paris but at nine months old.

THIRD CITIZEN

Stood the state so? No, no, good friends, God wot;
For then this land was famously enrich'd
With politic grave counsel; then the king
Had virtuous uncles to protect his grace.

FIRST CITIZEN

Why, so hath this, both by the father and mother.

THIRD CITIZEN

Better it were they all came by the father,
Or by the father there were none at all;
For emulation now, who shall be nearest,
Will touch us all too near, if God prevent not.
O, full of danger is the Duke of Gloucester!
And the queen's sons and brothers haught and
  proud:
And were they to be ruled, and not to rule,
This sickly land might solace as before.

FIRST CITIZEN

Come, come, we fear the worst; all shall be well.

THIRD CITIZEN

When clouds appear, wise men put on their cloaks;
When great leaves fall, the winter is at hand;
When the sun sets, who doth not look for night?
Untimely storms make men expect a dearth.
All may be well; but, if God sort it so,
'Tis more than we deserve, or I expect.

SECOND CITIZEN

Truly, the souls of men are full of dread:
Ye cannot reason almost with a man
That looks not heavily and full of fear.

THIRD CITIZEN

Before the times of change, still is it so:
By a divine instinct men's minds mistrust
Ensuing dangers; as, by proof, we see
The waters swell before a boisterous storm.
But leave it all to God. Whither away?

SECOND CITIZEN

Marry, we were sent for to the justices.

THIRD CITIZEN

And so was I: I'll bear you company.   [*Exeunt*

SCENE IV. *London. The palace*

Enter the ARCHBISHOP OF YORK, *the young* DUKE OF
YORK, QUEEN ELIZABETH, *and the* DUCHESS OF YORK

ARCHBISHOP

Last night, I hear, they lay at Northampton;
At Stony-Stratford will they be to-night:
To-morrow, or next day, they will be here.

DUCHESS

I long with all my heart to see the prince:
I hope he is much grown since last I saw him.

QUEEN ELIZABETH

But I hear, no; they say my son of York
Hath almost overta'en him in his growth.

YORK

Ay, mother; but I would not have it so.

DUCHESS

Why, my young cousin, it is good to grow.

YORK

Grandam, one night, as we did sit at supper,
My uncle Rivers talk'd how I did grow
More than my brother: 'Ay,' quoth my uncle
    Gloucester,
'Small herbs have grace, great weeds do grow
    apace:'
And since, methinks, I would not grow so fast,
Because sweet flowers are slow and weeds make
    haste.

DUCHESS

Good faith, good faith, the saying did not hold
In him that did object the same to thee:
He was the wretched'st thing when he was young,
So long a-growing and so leisurely,
That, if this rule were true, he should be gracious.

ARCHBISHOP

Why, madam, so, no doubt, he is.

DUCHESS

I hope so too; but yet let mothers doubt.

YORK

Now, by my troth, if I had been remember'd,
I could have given my uncle's grace a flout,
To touch his growth nearer than he touch'd mine.

DUCHESS

How, my pretty York? I pray thee, let me hear it.

YORK

Marry, they say my uncle grew so fast
That he could gnaw a crust at two hours old:
'Twas full two years ere I could get a tooth.
Grandam, this would have been a biting jest.

DUCHESS

I pray thee, pretty York, who told thee this?

YORK

Grandam, his nurse.

DUCHESS

His nurse! why, she was dead ere thou wert born.

YORK

If 'twere not she, I cannot tell who told me.

QUEEN ELIZABETH

A parlous boy: go to, you are too shrewd.

ARCHBISHOP

Good madam, be not angry with the child.

QUEEN ELIZABETH

Pitchers have ears.

Enter a MESSENGER

ARCHBISHOP

Here comes a messenger. What news?

MESSENGER

Such news, my lord, as grieves me to unfold.

QUEEN ELIZABETH

How fares the prince?

MESSENGER

                Well, madam, and in health.

DUCHESS

What is thy news then?

MESSENGER

Lord Rivers and Lord Grey are sent to Pomfret,
With them Sir Thomas Vaughan, prisoners.

DUCHESS

Who hath committed them?

MESSENGER

                The mighty dukes,
Gloucester and Buckingham.

QUEEN ELIZABETH

                For what offence?

MESSENGER

The sum of all I can, I have disclosed;
Why or for what these nobles were committed
Is all unknown to me, my gracious lady.

QUEEN ELIZABETH

Ay me, I see the downfall of our house!
The tiger now hath seized the gentle hind;
Insulting tyranny begins to jet
Upon the innocent and aweless throne:
Welcome, destruction, death, and massacre!
I see, as in a map, the end of all.

DUCHESS

Accursed and unquiet wrangling days,
How many of you have mine eyes beheld!
My husband lost his life to get the crown;
And often up and down my sons were toss'd,
For me to joy and weep their gain and loss:
And being seated, and domestic broils
Clean over-blown, themselves, the conquerors,
Make war upon themselves; blood against blood,
Self against self: O, preposterous
And frantic outrage, end thy damned spleen;
Or let me die, to look on death no more!

QUEEN ELIZABETH

Come, come, my boy; we will to sanctuary.
Madam, farewell.

DUCHESS

                I'll go along with you.

QUEEN ELIZABETH

You have no cause.

ARCHBISHOP

My gracious lady, go;
And thither bear your treasure and your goods.
For my part, I'll resign unto your grace
The seal I keep: and so betide to me
As well I tender you and all of yours!
Come, I'll conduct you to the sanctuary.   [*Exeunt*

ACT III

SCENE I. *London. A street*

The trumpets sound. Enter the young PRINCE, *the* DUKES OF
GLOUCESTER *and* BUCKINGHAM, CARDINAL
BOURCHIER, CATESBY, *and others*

BUCKINGHAM

Welcome, sweet prince, to London, to your chamber.

GLOUCESTER

Welcome, dear cousin, my thoughts' sovereign:
The weary way hath made you melancholy.

PRINCE

No, uncle; but our crosses on the way
Have made it tedious, wearisome, and heavy:
I want more uncles here to welcome me.

GLOUCESTER

Sweet prince, the untainted virtue of your years
Hath not yet dived into the world's deceit:
Nor more can you distinguish of a man
Than of his outward show; which, God he knows,
Seldom or never jumpeth with the heart.
Those uncles which you want were dangerous;
Your grace attended to their sugar'd words,
But look'd not on the poison of their hearts:
God keep you from them, and from such false
friends!

PRINCE

God keep me from false friends! but they were none.

GLOUCESTER

My lord, the mayor of London comes to greet you.

Enter the LORD MAYOR, *and his train*

MAYOR

God bless your grace with health and happy days!

PRINCE

I thank you, good my lord; and thank you all.
I thought my mother and my brother York
Would long ere this have met us on the way:
Fie, what a slug is Hastings, that he comes not
To tell us whether they will come or no!

Enter LORD HASTINGS

BUCKINGHAM

And, in good time here comes the sweating lord.

PRINCE

Welcome, my lord: what, will our mother come?

HASTINGS

On what occasion, God he knows, not I,
The queen your mother and your brother York
Have taken sanctuary: the tender prince

Would fain have come with me to meet your grace,
But by his mother was perforce withheld.

BUCKINGHAM

Fie, what an indirect and peevish course
Is this of hers! Lord cardinal, will your grace
Persuade the queen to send the Duke of York
Unto his princely brother presently?
If she deny, Lord Hastings, go with him,
And from her jealous arms pluck him perforce.

CARDINAL

My Lord of Buckingham, if my weak oratory
Can from his mother win the Duke of York,
Anon expect him here; but if she be obdurate
To mild entreaties, God in heaven forbid
We should infringe the holy privilege
Of blessed sanctuary! not for all this land
Would I be guilty of so deep a sin.

BUCKINGHAM

You are too senseless-obstinate, my lord,
Too ceremonious and traditional:
Weigh it but with the grossness of this age,
You break not sanctuary in seizing him.
The benefit thereof is always granted
To those whose dealings have deserved the place,
And those who have the wit to claim the place:
This prince hath neither claim'd it nor deserved it;
And therefore, in mine opinion, cannot have it:
Then, taking him from thence that is not there,
You break no privilege nor charter there.
Oft have I heard of sanctuary men;
But sanctuary children ne'er till now.

CARDINAL

My lord, you shall o'er-rule my mind for once.
Come on, Lord Hastings, will you go with me?

HASTINGS

I go, my lord.

PRINCE

Good lords, make all the speedy haste you may.

[*Exeunt* CARDINAL *and* HASTINGS

Say, uncle Gloucester, if our brother come,
Where shall we sojourn till our coronation?

GLOUCESTER

Where it seems best unto your royal self.
If I may counsel you, some day or two
Your highness shall repose you at the Tower:
Then where you please, and shall be thought most
fit
For your best health and recreation.

PRINCE

I do not like the Tower, of any place.
Did Julius Cæsar build that place, my lord?

BUCKINGHAM

He did, my gracious lord, begin that place;
Which, since, succeeding ages have re-edified.

PRINCE

Is it upon record, or else reported
Successively from age to age, he built it?

BUCKINGHAM

Upon record, my gracious lord.

PRINCE

But say, my lord, it were not register'd,
Methinks the truth should live from age to age,
As 'twere retail'd to all posterity,
Even to the general all-ending day.

GLOUCESTER

[*Aside*] So wise so young, they say, do never live
  long.

PRINCE

What say you, uncle?

GLOUCESTER

I say, without characters, fame lives long.
[*Aside*] Thus, like the formal vice, Iniquity
I moralize two meanings in one word.

PRINCE

That Julius Cæsar was a famous man;
With what his valour did enrich his wit,
His wit set down to make his valour live:
Death makes no conquest of this conqueror;
For now he lives in fame, though not in life.
I'll tell you what, my cousin Buckingham,—

BUCKINGHAM

What, my gracious lord?

PRINCE

An if I live until I be a man,
I'll win our ancient right in France again,
Or die a soldier, as I lived a king.

GLOUCESTER

[*Aside*] Short summers lightly have a forward
  spring.
  Enter young YORK, HASTINGS, *and the* CARDINAL

BUCKINGHAM

Now, in good time, here comes the Duke of York.

PRINCE

Richard of York! how fares our loving brother?

YORK

Well, my dread lord; so must I call you now.

PRINCE

Ay, brother, to our grief, as it is yours:
Too late he died that might have kept that title,
Which by his death hath lost much majesty.

GLOUCESTER

How fares our cousin, noble Lord of York?

YORK

I thank you, gentle uncle. O, my lord,
You said that idle weeds are fast in growth:
The prince my brother hath outgrown me far.

GLOUCESTER

He hath, my lord.

YORK

                And therefore is he idle?

GLOUCESTER

O, my fair cousin, I must not say so.

YORK

Then he is more beholding to you than I.

GLOUCESTER

He may command me as my sovereign;
But you have power in me as in a kinsman.

YORK

I pray you, uncle, give me this dagger.

GLOUCESTER

My dagger, little cousin? with all my heart.

PRINCE

A beggar, brother?

YORK

Of my kind uncle, that I know will give;
And being but a toy, which is no grief to give.

GLOUCESTER

A greater gift than that I'll give my cousin.

YORK

A greater gift! O, that's the sword to it.

GLOUCESTER

Ay, gentle cousin, were it light enough.

YORK

O, then, I see, you will part but with light gifts;
In weightier things you'll say a beggar nay.

GLOUCESTER

It is too heavy for your grace to wear.

YORK

I weigh it lightly, were it heavier.

GLOUCESTER

What, would you have my weapon, little lord?

YORK

I would, that I might thank you as you call me.

GLOUCESTER

How?

YORK

Little.

PRINCE

My Lord of York will still be cross in talk:
Uncle, your grace knows how to bear with him.

YORK

You mean, to bear me, not to bear with me:
Uncle, my brother mocks both you and me;
Because that I am little, like an ape,
He thinks that you should bear me on your
  shoulders.

BUCKINGHAM

With what a sharp-provided wit he reasons!
To mitigate the scorn he gives his uncle,
He prettily and aptly taunts himself:
So cunning and so young is wonderful.

GLOUCESTER

My lord, will 't please you pass along?
Myself and my good cousin Buckingham
Will to your mother, to entreat of her
To meet you at the Tower and welcome you.

YORK

What, will you go unto the Tower, my lord?

PRINCE

My lord protector needs will have it so.

YORK

I shall not sleep in quiet at the Tower.

GLOUCESTER

Why, what should you fear?

YORK

Marry, my uncle Clarence' angry ghost:
My grandam told me he was murder'd there.

PRINCE

I fear no uncles dead.

GLOUCESTER

Nor none that live, I hope.

PRINCE

An if they live, I hope I need not fear.
But come, my lord; and with a heavy heart,
Thinking on them, go I unto the Tower. [*A Sennet.*
Exeunt all but GLOUCESTER, BUCKINGHAM *and* CATESBY

BUCKINGHAM

Think you, my lord, this little prating York
Was not incensed by his subtle mother
To taunt and scorn you thus opprobriously?

GLOUCESTER

No doubt, no doubt: O, 'tis a parlous boy;
Bold, quick, ingenious, forward, capable:
He is all the mother's, from the top to toe.

BUCKINGHAM

Well, let them rest. Come hither, Catesby.
Thou art sworn as deeply to effect what we intend,
As closely to conceal what we impart:
Thou know'st our reasons urged upon the way;
What think'st thou? is it not an easy matter
To make William Lord Hastings of our mind,
For the instalment of this noble duke
In the seat royal of this famous isle?

CATESBY

He for his father's sake so loves the prince,
That he will not be won to aught against him.

BUCKINGHAM

What think'st thou then of Stanley? what will he?

CATESBY

He will do all in all as Hastings doth.

BUCKINGHAM

Well, then, no more but this: go, gentle Catesby,
And, as it were far off, sound thou Lord Hastings,
How he doth stand affected to our purpose;
And summon him to-morrow to the Tower,
To sit about the coronation.
If thou dost find him tractable to us,
Encourage him, and show him all our reasons:
If he be leaden, icy-cold, unwilling,
Be thou so too; and so break off your talk,
And give us notice of his inclination:
For we to-morrow hold divided councils,
Wherein thyself shalt highly be employ'd.

GLOUCESTER

Commend me to Lord William: tell him, Catesby,
His ancient knot of dangerous adversaries
To-morrow are let blood at Pomfret-castle;
And bid my friend, for joy of this good news,
Give Mistress Shore one gentle kiss the more.

BUCKINGHAM

Good Catesby, go, effect this business soundly.

CATESBY

My good lords both, with all the heed I may.

GLOUCESTER

Shall we hear from you, Catesby, ere we sleep?

CATESBY

You shall, my lord.

GLOUCESTER

At Crosby Place, there shall you find us both. [*Exit* CATESBY

BUCKINGHAM

Now, my lord, what shall we do, if we perceive Lord
Hastings will not yield to our complots?

GLOUCESTER

Chop off his head, man; somewhat we will do:
And, look, when I am king, claim thou of me
The earldom of Hereford, and the moveables
Whereof the king my brother stood possess'd.

BUCKINGHAM

I'll claim that promise at your grace's hands.

GLOUCESTER

And look to have it yielded with all willingness.
Come, let us sup betimes, that afterwards
We may digest our complots in some form. [*Exeunt*

SCENE II. *Before* LORD HASTINGS' *house*

Enter a MESSENGER

MESSENGER

What, ho! my lord!

HASTINGS

[*Within*] Who knocks at the door?

MESSENGER

A messenger from the Lord Stanley.

Enter LORD HASTINGS

HASTINGS

What is 't o'clock?

MESSENGER

Upon the stroke of four.

HASTINGS

Cannot thy master sleep these tedious nights?

MESSENGER

So it should seem by that I have to say.
First, he commends him to your noble lordship.

HASTINGS

And then?

MESSENGER

And then he sends you word
He dreamt to-night the boar had razed his helm:
Besides, he says there are two councils held;
And that may be determined at the one
Which may make you and him to rue at the other.
Therefore he sends to know your lordship's
   pleasure,
If presently you will take horse with him,
And with all speed post with him toward the north,
To shun the danger that his soul divines.

HASTINGS

Go, fellow, go, return unto thy lord;
Bid him not fear the separated councils:
His honour and myself are at the one,
And at the other is my servant Catesby;
Where nothing can proceed that toucheth us,
Whereof I shall not have intelligence.
Tell him his fears are shallow, wanting instance:
And for his dreams, I wonder he is so fond

To trust the mockery of unquiet slumbers:
To fly the boar before the boar pursues,
Were to incense the boar to follow us,
And make pursuit where he did mean no chase.
Go, bid thy master rise and come to me;
And we will both together to the Tower,
Where, he shall see, the boar will use us kindly.

MESSENGER

My gracious lord, I'll tell him what you say.   [Exit

Enter CATESBY

CATESBY

Many good morrows to my noble lord!

HASTINGS

Good morrow, Catesby; you are early stirring:
What news, what news, in this our tottering state?

CATESBY

It is a reeling world indeed, my lord;
And I believe 'twill never stand upright
Till Richard wear the garland of the realm.

HASTINGS

How! wear the garland! dost thou mean the crown?

CATESBY

Ay, my good lord.

HASTINGS

I'll have this crown of mine cut from my shoulders,
Ere I will see the crown so foul misplaced.
But canst thou guess that he doth aim at it?

CATESBY

Ay, on my life, and hopes to find you forward
Upon his party for the gain thereof:
And thereupon he sends you this good news,
That this same very day your enemies,
The kindred of the queen, must die at Pomfret.

HASTINGS

Indeed, I am no mourner for that news,
Because they have been still mine enemies:
But, that I'll give my voice on Richard's side,
To bar my master's heirs in true descent,
God knows I will not do it, to the death.

CATESBY

God keep your lordship in that gracious mind!

HASTINGS

But I shall laugh at this a twelve-month hence,
That they who brought me in my master's hate,
I live to look upon their tragedy.
I tell thee, Catesby,—

CATESBY

What, my lord?

HASTINGS

Ere a fortnight make me elder,
I'll send some packing that yet think not on it.

CATESBY

'Tis a vile thing to die, my gracious lord,
When men are unprepared and look not for it.

HASTINGS

O monstrous, monstrous! and so falls it out
With Rivers, Vaughan, Grey: and so 'twill do
With some men else, who think themselves as safe
As thou and I; who, as thou know'st, are dear
To princely Richard and to Buckingham.

CATESBY

The princes both make high account of you;
[Aside] For they account his head upon the bridge.

HASTINGS

I know they do; and I have well deserved it.

Enter LORD STANLEY

Come on, come on; where is your boar-spear, man?
Fear you the boar, and go so unprovided?

STANLEY

My lord, good morrow; good morrow, Catesby:
You may jest on, but, by the holy rood,
I do not like these several councils, I.

HASTINGS

My lord,
I hold my life as dear as you do yours;
And never in my life, I do protest,
Was it more precious to me than 'tis now:
Think you, but that I know our state secure,
I would be so triumphant as I am?

STANLEY

The lords at Pomfret, when they rode from London,
Were jocund and supposed their state was sure,
And they indeed had no cause to mistrust;
But yet, you see, how soon the day o'ercast.
This sudden stab of rancour I misdoubt:
Pray God, I say, I prove a needless coward!
What, shall we toward the Tower? the day is spent.

HASTINGS

Come, come, have with you. Wot you what, my
     lord?
To-day the lords you talk of are beheaded.

STANLEY

They, for their truth, might better wear their heads,
Than some that have accused them wear their hats.
But come, my lord, let us away.

Enter a PURSUIVANT

HASTINGS

Go on before; I'll talk with this good fellow.
       [Exeunt STANLEY and CATESBY
How now, sirrah! how goes the world with thee?

PURSUIVANT

The better that your lordship please to ask.

HASTINGS

I tell thee, man, 'tis better with me now,
Than when I met thee last where now we meet:
Then was I going prisoner to the Tower,
By the suggestion of the queen's allies;
But now, I tell thee—keep it to thyself—
This day those enemies are put to death,
And I in better state than e'er I was.

PURSUIVANT

God hold it, to your honour's good content!

HASTINGS

Gramercy, fellow: there, drink that for me.
       [Throws him his purse

PURSUIVANT

God save your lordship.   [Exit

Enter a PRIEST

PRIEST

Well met, my lord; I am glad to see your honour.

HASTINGS

I thank thee, good Sir John, with all my heart.
I am in your debt for your last exercise;
Come the next Sabbath, and I will content you.

[*He whispers in his ear*

Enter BUCKINGHAM

BUCKINGHAM

What, talking with a priest, lord chamberlain?
Your friends at Pomfret, they do need the priest;
Your honour hath no shriving work in hand.

HASTINGS

Good faith, and when I met this holy man,
Those men you talk of came into my mind.
What, go you toward the Tower?

BUCKINGHAM

I do, my lord; but long I shall not stay:
I shall return before your lordship thence.

HASTINGS

'Tis like enough, for I stay dinner there.

BUCKINGHAM

[*Aside*] And supper too, although thou know'st it
not.
Come, will you go?

HASTINGS

I'll wait upon your lordship.

[*Exeunt*

SCENE III. *Pomfret Castle*

Enter SIR RICHARD RATCLIFF, *with halberds, carrying*
RIVERS, GREY, *and* VAUGHAN *to death*

RATCLIFF

Come, bring forth the prisoners.

RIVERS

Sir Richard Ratcliff, let me tell thee this:
To-day shalt thou behold a subject die
For truth, for duty, and for loyalty.

GREY

God keep the prince from all the pack of you!
A knot you are of damned blood-suckers.

VAUGHAN

You live that shall cry woe for this hereafter.

RATCLIFF

Dispatch; the limit of your lives is out.

RIVERS

O Pomfret, Pomfret! O thou bloody prison,
Fatal and ominous to noble peers!
Within the guilty closure of thy walls
Richard the second here was hack'd to death;
And, for more slander to thy dismal seat,
We give thee up our guiltless blood to drink.

GREY

Now Margaret's curse is fall'n upon our heads,
For standing by when Richard stabb'd her son.

RIVERS

Then cursed she Hastings, then cursed she Bucking-
ham,
Then cursed she Richard. O, remember, God,
To hear her prayers for them, as now for us!
And for my sister and her princely sons,

Be satisfied, dear God, with our true blood,
Which, as thou know'st, unjustly must be spilt.

RATCLIFF

Make haste; the hour of death is expiate.

RIVERS

Come, Grey, come, Vaughan, let us all embrace:
And take our leave, until we meet in heaven.

[*Exeunt*

SCENE IV. *The Tower of London*

Enter BUCKINGHAM, DERBY, HASTINGS, *the* BISHOP OF
ELY, RATCLIFF, LOVEL, *with others, and take
their seats at a table*

HASTINGS

My lords, at once: the cause why we are met
Is, to determine of the coronation.
In God's name, speak: when is the royal day?

BUCKINGHAM

Are all things fitting for that royal time?

DERBY

It is, and wants but nomination.

ELY

To-morrow then I judge a happy day.

BUCKINGHAM

Who knows the lord protector's mind herein?
Who is most inward with the noble duke?

ELY

Your grace, we think, should soonest know his
mind.

BUCKINGHAM

Who, I, my lord! We know each other's faces,
But for our hearts, he knows no more of mine
Than I of yours;
Nor I no more of his, than you of mine.
Lord Hastings, you and he are near in love.

HASTINGS

I thank his grace, I know he loves me well;
But, for his purpose in the coronation,
I have not sounded him, nor he deliver'd
His gracious pleasure any way therein:
But you, my noble lords, may name the time;
And in the duke's behalf I'll give my voice,
Which, I presume, he'll take in gentle part.

Enter GLOUCESTER

ELY

Now in good time, here comes the duke himself.

GLOUCESTER

My noble lords and cousins all, good morrow.
I have been long a sleeper; but, I hope,
My absence doth neglect no great designs,
Which by my presence might have been concluded.

BUCKINGHAM

Had not you come upon your cue, my lord,
William Lord Hastings had pronounced your
part,—
I mean, your voice,—for crowning of the king.

GLOUCESTER

Than my Lord Hastings no man might be bolder;
His lordship knows me well, and loves me well.

HASTINGS

I thank your grace.

GLOUCESTER

My Lord of Ely!

ELY

My lord?

GLOUCESTER

When I was last in Holborn,
I saw good strawberries in your garden there:
I do beseech you send for some of them.

ELY

Marry, and will, my lord, with all my heart.   [*Exit*

GLOUCESTER

Cousin of Buckingham, a word with you.
                                   [*Drawing him aside*
Catesby hath sounded Hastings in our business,
And finds the testy gentleman so hot,
As he will lose his head ere give consent
His master's son, as worshipful he terms it,
Shall lose the royalty of England's throne.

BUCKINGHAM

Withdraw you hence, my lord, I'll follow you.
          [*Exit* GLOUCESTER, BUCKINGHAM *following*

DERBY

We have not yet set down this day of triumph.
To-morrow, in mine opinion, is too sudden;
For I myself am not so well provided
As else I would be, were the day prolong'd.

Re-enter BISHOP OF ELY

ELY

Where is my lord protector? I have sent for these
strawberries.

HASTINGS

His grace looks cheerfully and smooth to-day;
There's some conceit or other likes him well,
When he doth bid good morrow with such a spirit.
I think there's never a man in Christendom
That can less hide his love or hate than he;
For by his face straight shall you know his heart.

DERBY

What of his heart perceive you in his face
By any likelihood he show'd to-day?

HASTINGS

Marry, that with no man here he is offended;
For, were he, as had shown it in his looks.

DERBY

I pray God he be not, I say.

Re-enter GLOUCESTER *and* BUCKINGHAM

GLOUCESTER

I pray you all, tell me what they deserve
That do conspire my death with devilish plots
Of damned witchcraft, and that have prevail'd
Upon my body with their hellish charms?

HASTINGS

The tender love I bear your grace, my lord,
Makes me most forward in this noble presence
To doom the offenders, whatsoever they be:
I say, my lord, they have deserved death.

GLOUCESTER

Then be your eyes the witness of this ill:

See how I am bewitch'd; behold, mine arm
Is like a blasted sapling, withered up:
And this is Edward's wife, that monstrous witch,
Consorted with that harlot strumpet Shore,
That by their witchcraft thus have marked me.

HASTINGS

If they have done this thing, my gracious lord,—

GLOUCESTER

If! thou protector of this damned strumpet,
Tellest thou me of 'if'? Thou art a traitor:
Off with his head! Now, by Saint Paul I swear,
I will not dine until I see the same.
Lovel and Ratcliff, look that it be done:
The rest that love me, rise and follow me.
          [*Exeunt all but* HASTINGS, RATCLIFF *and* LOVEL

HASTINGS

Woe, woe for England! not a whit for me;
For I, too fond, might have prevented this.
Stanley did dream the boar did raze his helm;
But I disdain'd it, and did scorn to fly:
Three times to-day my foot-cloth horse did stumble,
And startled, when he look'd upon the Tower
As loath to bear me to the slaughter-house.
O, now I want the priest that spake to me:
I now repent I told the pursuivant,
As 'twere triumphing at mine enemies,
How they at Pomfret bloodily were butcher'd,
And I myself secure in grace and favour.
O Margaret, Margaret, now thy heavy curse
Is lighted on poor Hastings' wretched head!

RATCLIFF

Dispatch, my lord; the duke would be at dinner:
Make a short shrift; he longs to see your head.

HASTINGS

O momentary grace of mortal men,
Which we more hunt for than the grace of God!
Who builds his hopes in air of your fair looks,
Lives like a drunken sailor on a mast,
Ready, with every nod, to tumble down
Into the fatal bowels of the deep.

LOVEL

Come, come, dispatch; 'tis bootless to exclaim.

HASTINGS

O bloody Richard! miserable England!
I prophesy the fearfull'st time to thee
That ever wretched age hath look'd upon.
Come, lead me to the block; bear him my head;
They smile at me that shortly shall be dead.   [*Exeunt*

SCENE V. *The Tower-walls*

Enter GLOUCESTER *and* BUCKINGHAM, *in rotten armour,
marvellous ill-favoured*

GLOUCESTER

Come, cousin, canst thou quake, and change thy
     colour,
Murder thy breath in middle of a word,
And then begin again, and stop again,
As if thou wert distraught and mad with terror?

BUCKINGHAM

Tut, I can counterfeit the deep tragedian,
Speak and look back, and pry on every side,
Tremble and start at wagging of a straw,
Intending deep suspicion: ghastly looks
Are at my service, like enforced smiles;
And both are ready in their offices,
At any time, to grace my stratagems.
But what, is Catesby gone?

GLOUCESTER

He is; and, see, he brings the mayor along.

Enter the MAYOR *and* CATESBY

BUCKINGHAM

Lord mayor,—

GLOUCESTER

Look to the drawbridge there!

BUCKINGHAM

Hark! a drum.

GLOUCESTER

Catesby, o'erlook the walls.

BUCKINGHAM

Lord mayor, the reason we have sent—

GLOUCESTER

Look back, defend thee, here are enemies.

BUCKINGHAM

God and our innocency defend and guard us!

GLOUCESTER

Be patient, they are friends, Ratcliff and Lovel.

Enter LOVEL *and* RATCLIFF, *with* HASTINGS' *head*

LOVEL

Here is the head of that ignoble traitor,
The dangerous and unsuspected Hastings.

GLOUCESTER

So dear I loved the man, that I must weep.
I took him for the plainest harmless creature
That breathed upon this earth a Christian;
Made him my book, wherein my soul recorded
The history of all her secret thoughts:
So smooth he daub'd his vice with show of virtue
That, his apparent open guilt omitted,
I mean, his conversation with Shore's wife,
He lived from all attainder of suspect.

BUCKINGHAM

Well, well, he was the covert'st shelter'd traitor
That ever lived.
Would you imagine, or almost believe,
Were 't not that, by great preservation,
We live to tell it you, the subtle traitor
This day had plotted, in the council-house
To murder me and my good Lord of Gloucester?

MAYOR

What, had he so?

GLOUCESTER

What, think you we are Turks or infidels?
Or that we would, against the form of law,
Proceed thus rashly to the villain's death,
But that the extreme peril of the case,
The peace of England and our persons' safety,
Enforced us to this execution?

MAYOR

Now, fair befall you! he deserved his death;
And you, my good lords both, have well proceeded,
To warn false traitors from the like attempts.
I never look'd for better at his hands,
After he once fell in with Mistress Shore.

GLOUCESTER

Yet had not we determined he should die,
Until your lordship came to see his death;
Which now the loving haste of these our friends,
Somewhat against our meaning, have prevented:
Because, my lord, we would have had you heard
The traitor speak and timorously confess
The manner and the purpose of his treason;
That you might well have signified the same
Unto the citizens, who haply may
Misconstrue us in him and wail his death.

MAYOR

But, my good lord, your grace's word shall serve,
As well as I had seen and heard him speak:
And doubt you not, right noble princes both,
But I'll acquaint our duteous citizens
With all your just proceedings in this cause.

GLOUCESTER

And to that end we wish'd your lordship here,
To avoid the carping censures of the world.

BUCKINGHAM

But since you come too late of our intents,
Yet witness what you hear we did intend:
And so, my good lord mayor, we bid farewell.

[*Exit* MAYOR

GLOUCESTER

Go, after, after, cousin Buckingham.
The mayor towards Guildhall hies him in all post:
There, at your meet'st advantage of the time,
Infer the bastardy of Edward's children:
Tell them how Edward put to death a citizen,
Only for saying he would make his son
Heir to the crown, meaning indeed his house,
Which, by the sign thereof, was termed so.
Moreover, urge his hateful luxury
And bestial appetite in change of lust;
Which stretched to their servants, daughters, wives,
Even where his lustful eye or savage heart,
Without control, listed to make his prey.
Nay, for a need, thus far come near my person:
Tell them, when that my mother went with child
Of that unsatiate Edward, noble York,
My princely father, then had wars in France;
And, by just computation of the time,
Found that the issue was not his begot;
Which well appeared in his lineaments,
Being nothing like the noble duke my father:
But touch this sparingly, as 'twere far off;
Because you know, my lord, my mother lives.

BUCKINGHAM

Fear not, my lord, I'll play the orator,
As if the golden fee for which I plead
Were for myself: and so, my lord, adieu.

GLOUCESTER

If you thrive well, bring them to Baynard's Castle;
Where you shall find me well accompanied
With reverend fathers and well-learned bishops.

BUCKINGHAM

I go; and towards three or four o'clock
Look for the news that the Guildhall affords.   [Exit

GLOUCESTER

Go, Lovel, with all speed to Doctor Shaw;
[To CATESBY] Go thou to Friar Penker; bid them
    both
Meet me within this hour at Baynard's Castle.
                              [Exeunt all but GLOUCESTER
Now will I in, to take some privy order,
To draw the brats of Clarence out of sight;
And to give notice, that no manner of person
At any time have recourse unto the princes.   [Exit

SCENE VI. *The same. A street*

Enter a SCRIVENER, *with a paper in his hand*

SCRIVENER

This is the indictment of the good Lord Hastings;
Which in a set hand fairly is engross'd,
That it may be this day read o'er in Paul's.
And mark how well the sequel hangs together:
Eleven hours I spent to write it over,
For yesternight by Catesby was it brought me;
The precedent was full as long a-doing:
And yet within these five hours lived Lord Hastings,
Untainted, unexamined, free, at liberty.
Here's a good world the while! Why, who's so gross,
That seeth not this palpable device?
Yet who's so blind, but says he sees it not?
Bad is the world; and all will come to nought,
When such bad dealing must be seen in thought.
                                                    [Exit

SCENE VII. *Baynard's Castle*

Enter GLOUCESTER *and* BUCKINGHAM, *at several doors*

GLOUCESTER

How now, my lord, what say the citizens?

BUCKINGHAM

Now, by the holy mother of our Lord,
The citizens are mum, and speak not a word.

GLOUCESTER

Touch'd you the bastardy of Edward's children?

BUCKINGHAM

I did; with his contract with Lady Lucy,
And his contract by deputy in France;
The insatiate greediness of his desires,
And his enforcement of the city wives;
His tyranny for trifles; his own bastardy,
As being got, your father then in France,
And his resemblance, being not like the duke:
Withal I did infer your lineaments,
Being the right idea of your father,
Both in your form and nobleness of mind;

Laid open all your victories in Scotland,
Your discipline in war, wisdom in peace,
Your bounty, virtue, fair humility;
Indeed left nothing fitting for the purpose
Untouch'd or slightly handled in discourse:
And when mine oratory grew to an end,
I bid them that did love their country's good
Cry 'God save Richard, England's royal king!'

GLOUCESTER

Ah! and did they so?

BUCKINGHAM

No, so God help me, they spake not a word;
But, like dumb statuës or breathing stones,
Gazed each on other, and look'd deadly pale.
Which when I saw, I reprehended them;
And ask'd the mayor what meant this wilful silence:
His answer was, the people were not wont
To be spoke to but by the recorder.
Then he was urged to tell my tale again:
'Thus saith the duke, thus hath the duke inferr'd;'
But nothing spake in warrant from himself.
When he had done, some followers of mine own
At the lower end of the hall hurl'd up their caps,
And some ten voices cried 'God save King Richard!'
And thus I took the vantage of those few,
'Thanks, gentle citizens and friends!' quoth I,
'This general applause and loving shout
Argues your wisdoms and your love to Richard;'
And even here brake off, and came away.

GLOUCESTER

What tongueless blocks were they! would they not
    speak?

BUCKINGHAM

No, by my troth, my lord.

GLOUCESTER

Will not the mayor then and his brethren come?

BUCKINGHAM

The mayor is here at hand: intend some fear;
Be not you spoke with, but by mighty suit:
And look you get a prayer-book in your hand,
And stand betwixt two churchmen, good my lord;
For on that ground I'll build a holy descant:
And be not easily won to our request;
Play the maid's part, still answer nay, and take it.

GLOUCESTER

I go; and if you plead as well for them
As I can say nay to thee for myself,
No doubt we'll bring it to a happy issue.

BUCKINGHAM

Go, go up to the leads; the lord mayor knocks.
                                        [Exit GLOUCESTER

Enter the MAYOR *and* CITIZENS

Welcome, my lord: I dance attendance here;
I think the duke will not be spoke withal.

Enter CATESBY

Here comes his servant: how now, Catesby,
What says he?

CATESBY

          My lord, he doth entreat your grace
To visit him to-morrow or next day:

He is within, with two right reverend fathers,
Divinely bent to meditation;
And in no worldly suit would he be moved,
To draw him from his holy exercise.
BUCKINGHAM
Return, good Catesby, to thy lord again;
Tell him, myself, the mayor and citizens,
In deep designs and matters of great moment,
No less importing than our general good,
Are come to have some conference with his grace.
CATESBY
I'll tell him what you say, my lord.   [Exit
BUCKINGHAM
Ah, ha, my lord, this prince is not an Edward!
He is not lolling on a lewd day-bed,
But on his knees at meditation;
Not dallying with a brace of courtezans,
But meditating with two deep divines;
Not sleeping, to engross his idle body,
But praying, to enrich his watchful soul:
Happy were England, would this gracious prince
Take on himself the sovereignty thereof:
But, sure, I fear, we shall ne'er win him to it.
MAYOR
Marry, God forbid his grace should say us nay!
BUCKINGHAM
I fear he will.
Re-enter CATESBY
How now, Catesby, what says your lord?
CATESBY
                              My lord,
He wonders to what end you have assembled
Such troops of citizens to speak with him,
His grace not being warn'd thereof before:
My lord, he fears you mean no good to him.
BUCKINGHAM
Sorry I am my noble cousin should
Suspect me, that I mean no good to him:
By heaven, I come in perfect love to him;
And so once more return and tell his grace.
                              [Exit CATESBY
When holy and devout religious men
Are at their beads, 'tis hard to draw them thence,
So sweet is zealous contemplation.
Enter GLOUCESTER aloft, between two BISHOPS.
CATESBY returns
MAYOR
See, where he stands between two clergymen!
BUCKINGHAM
Two props of virtue for a Christian prince,
To stay him from the fall of vanity:
And, see, a book of prayer in his hand,
True ornaments to know a holy man.
Famous Plantagenet, most gracious prince,
Lend favourable ears to our request;
And pardon us the interruption
Of thy devotion and right Christian zeal.
GLOUCESTER
My lord, there needs no such apology:
I rather do beseech you pardon me,

Who, earnest in the service of my God,
Neglect the visitation of my friends.
But, leaving this, what is your grace's pleasure?
BUCKINGHAM
Even that, I hope, which pleaseth God above,
And all good men of this ungovern'd isle.
GLOUCESTER
I do suspect I have done some offence
That seems disgracious in the city's eyes,
And that you come to reprehend my ignorance.
BUCKINGHAM
You have, my lord: would it might please your
    grace,
At our entreaties, to amend that fault!
GLOUCESTER
Else wherefore breathe I in a Christian land?
BUCKINGHAM
Then know, it is your fault that you resign
The supreme seat, the throne majestical,
The scepter'd office of your ancestors,
Your state of fortune and your due of birth,
The lineal glory of your royal house,
To the corruption of a blemish'd stock:
Whilst, in the mildness of your sleepy thoughts,
Which here we waken to our country's good,
This noble isle doth want her proper limbs;
Her face defaced with scars of infamy,
Her royal stock graft with ignoble plants,
And almost shoulder'd in the swallowing gulf
Of blind forgetfulness and dark oblivion.
Which to recure, we heartily solicit
Your gracious self to take on you the charge
And kingly government of this your land;
Not as protector, steward, substitute,
Or lowly factor for another's gain;
But as successively, from blood to blood,
Your right of birth, your empery, your own.
For this, consorted with the citizens,
Your very worshipful and loving friends,
And by their vehement instigation,
In this just suit come I to move your grace.
GLOUCESTER
I know not whether to depart in silence,
Or bitterly to speak in your reproof,
Best fitteth my degree or your condition:
If not to answer, you might haply think
Tongue-tied ambition, not replying, yielded
To bear the golden yoke of sovereignty,
Which fondly you would here impose on me;
If to reprove you for this suit of yours
So season'd with your faithful love to me,
Then, on the other side, I check'd my friends.
Therefore, to speak, and to avoid the first,
And then, in speaking, not to incur the last,
Definitively thus I answer you.
Your love deserves my thanks, but my desert
Unmeritable shuns your high request.
First, if all obstacles were cut away
And that my path were even to the crown,
As my ripe revenue and due by birth;

Yet so much is my poverty of spirit,
So mighty and so many my defects,
As I had rather hide me from my greatness,
Being a bark to brook no mighty sea,
Than in my greatness covet to be hid,
And in the vapour of my glory smother'd.
But, God be thanked, there's no need of me,
And much I need to help you, if need were;
The royal tree hath left us royal fruit,
Which, mellow'd by the stealing hours of time,
Will well become the seat of majesty,
And make, no doubt, us happy by his reign.
On him I lay what you would lay on me,
The right and fortune of his happy stars;
Which God defend that I should wring from him!

BUCKINGHAM

My lord, this argues conscience in your grace;
But the respects thereof are nice and trivial,
All circumstances well considered.
You say that Edward is your brother's son:
So say we too, but not by Edward's wife;
For first he was contract to Lady Lucy—
Your mother lives a witness to that vow—
And afterward by substitute betroth'd
To Bona, sister to the King of France.
These both put by, a poor petitioner,
A care-crazed mother of a many children,
A beauty-waning and distressed widow,
Even in the afternoon of her best days,
Made prize and purchase of his lustful eye,
Seduced the pitch and height of all his thoughts
To base declension and loathed bigamy:
By her, in his unlawful bed, he got
This Edward, whom our manners term the prince.
More bitterly could I expostulate,
Save that, for reverence to some alive,
I give a sparing limit to my tongue.
Then, good my lord, take to your royal self
This proffer'd benefit of dignity;
If not to bless us and the land withal,
Yet to draw forth your noble ancestry
From the corruption of abusing times,
Unto a lineal true-derived course.

MAYOR

Do, good my lord, your citizens entreat you.

BUCKINGHAM

Refuse not, mighty lord, this proffer'd love.

CATESBY

O, make them joyful, grant their lawful suit!

GLOUCESTER

Alas, why would you heap these cares on me?
I am unfit for state and majesty:
I do beseech you, take it not amiss;
I cannot nor I will not yield to you.

BUCKINGHAM

If you refuse it,—as, in love and zeal,
Loath to depose the child, your brother's son;
As well we know your tenderness of heart
And gentle, kind, effeminate remorse,
Which we have noted in you to your kin,

And egally indeed to all estates,—
Yet whether you accept our suit or no,
Your brother's son shall never reign our king;
But we will plant some other in the throne,
To the disgrace and downfall of your house:
And in this resolution here we leave you.
Come, citizens: 'zounds! I'll entreat no more.

GLOUCESTER

O, do not swear, my lord of Buckingham.

[Exit BUCKINGHAM with the CITIZENS

CATESBY

Call them again, my lord, and accept their suit:

ANOTHER

Do, good my lord, lest all the land do rue it.

GLOUCESTER

Would you enforce me to a world of care?
Well, call them again. I am not made of stones,
But penetrable to your kind entreats,
Albeit against my conscience and my soul.

Re-enter BUCKINGHAM and the rest

Cousin of Buckingham, and you sage, grave men,
Since you will buckle fortune on my back,
To bear her burthen, whether I will or no,
I must have patience to endure the load:
But if black scandal or foul-faced reproach
Attend the sequel of your imposition,
Your mere enforcement shall acquittance me
From all the impure blots and stains thereof;
For God he knows, and you may partly see,
How far I am from the desire thereof.

MAYOR

God bless your grace! we see it, and will say it.

GLOUCESTER

In saying so, you shall but say the truth.

BUCKINGHAM

Then I salute you with this kingly title:
Long live Richard, England's royal king!

MAYOR and CITIZEN

Amen.

BUCKINGHAM

To-morrow will it please you to be crown'd?

GLOUCESTER

Even when you please, since you will have it so.

BUCKINGHAM

To-morrow then we will attend your grace:
And so most joyfully we take our leave.

GLOUCESTER

Come, let us to our holy task again.
Farewell, good cousin: farewell, gentle friends.

[Exeunt

ACT IV

SCENE I. Before the Tower

Enter, on one side, QUEEN ELIZABETH, DUCHESS OF
YORK, and MARQUESS OF DORSET; on the other, ANNE,
DUCHESS OF GLOUCESTER, leading LADY MARGARET
PLANTAGENET, CLARENCE'S young daughter

DUCHESS

Who meets us here? my niece Plantagenet
Led in the hand of her kind aunt of Gloucester?
Now, for my life, she's wandering to the Tower,
On pure heart's love to greet the tender princes.
Daughter, well met.

ANNE

God give your graces both
A happy and a joyful time of day!

QUEEN ELIZABETH

As much to you, good sister! Whither away?

ANNE

No farther than the Tower, and, as I guess,
Upon the like devotion as yourselves,
To gratulate the gentle princes there.

QUEEN ELIZABETH

Kind sister, thanks: we'll enter all together.

Enter BRAKENBURY

And, in good time, here the lieutenant comes.
Master lieutenant, pray you, by your leave,
How doth the prince, and my young son of York?

BRAKENBURY

Right well, dear madam. By your patience,
I may not suffer you to visit them;
The king hath straitly charged the contrary.

QUEEN ELIZABETH

The king! why, who's that?

BRAKENBURY

I cry you mercy: I mean the lord protector.

QUEEN ELIZABETH

The Lord protect him from that kingly title!
Hath he set bounds betwixt their love and me?
I am their mother; who should keep me from them?

DUCHESS

I am their father's mother; I will see them.

ANNE

Their aunt I am in law, in love their mother:
Then bring me to their sights; I'll bear thy blame,
And take thy office from thee, on my peril.

BRAKENBURY

No, madam, no; I may not leave it so:
I am bound by oath, and therefore pardon me.

[*Exit*

Enter LORD STANLEY

STANLEY

Let me but meet you, ladies, one hour hence,
And I'll salute your grace of York as mother,
And reverend looker on, of two fair queens.
[*To* ANNE] Come, madam, you must straight to
   Westminster,
There to be crowned Richard's royal queen.

QUEEN ELIZABETH

O, cut my lace in sunder, that my pent heart
May have some scope to beat, or else I swoon
With this dead-killing news!

ANNE

Despiteful tidings! O unpleasing news!

DORSET

Be of good cheer: mother, how fares your grace?

QUEEN ELIZABETH

O Dorset, speak not to me, get thee hence!
Death and destruction dog thee at the heels;
Thy mother's name is ominous to children.
If thou wilt outstrip death, go cross the seas,
And live with Richmond, from the reach of hell:
Go, hie thee, hie thee from this slaughter-house,
Lest thou increase the number of the dead;
And make me die the thrall of Margaret's curse,
Nor mother, wife, nor England's counted queen.

STANLEY

Full of wise care is this your counsel, madam.
Take all the swift advantage of the hours;
You shall have letters from me to my son
To meet you on the way, and welcome you.
Be not ta'en tardy by unwise delay.

DUCHESS

O ill-dispersing wind of misery!
O my accursed womb, the bed of death!
A cockatrice hast thou hatch'd to the world,
Whose unavoided eye is murderous.

STANLEY

Come, madam, come; I in all haste was sent.

ANNE

And I in all unwillingness will go.
I would to God that the inclusive verge
Of golden metal that must round my brow
Were red-hot steel, to sear me to the brain!
Anointed let me be with deadly venom,
And die, ere men can say, God save the queen!

QUEEN ELIZABETH

Go, go, poor soul, I envy not thy glory;
To feed my humour, wish thyself no harm.

ANNE

No! why? When he that is my husband now
Came to me, as I follow'd Henry's corse,
When scarce the blood was well wash'd from his
   hands
Which issued from my other angel husband,
And that dead saint which then I weeping follow'd;
O, when, I say, I look'd on Richard's face,
This was my wish: 'Be thou,' quoth I, 'accursed,
For making me, so young, so old a widow!
And, when thou wed'st, let sorrow haunt thy bed;
And be thy wife—if any be so mad—
As miserable by the death of thee
As thou hast made me by my dear lord's death!'
Lo, ere I can repeat this curse again,
Even in so short a space, my woman's heart
Grossly grew captive to his honey words,
And proved the subject of my own soul's curse,
Which ever since hath kept my eyes from rest;
For never yet one hour in his bed
Have I enjoy'd the golden dew of sleep,
But have been waked by his timorous dreams.
Besides, he hates me for my father Warwick;
And will, no doubt, shortly be rid of me.

QUEEN ELIZABETH

Poor heart, adieu! I pity thy complaining.

ANNE

No more than from my soul I mourn for yours.

DORSET

Farewell, thou woful welcomer of glory!

ANNE

Adieu, poor soul, that takest thy leave of it!

DUCHESS

[To DORSET] Go thou to Richmond, and good fortune guide thee!

[To ANNE] Go thou to Richard, and good angels guard thee!

[To QUEEN ELIZABETH] Go thou to sanctuary, and good thoughts possess thee!

I to my grave, where peace and rest lie with me!
Eighty odd years of sorrow have I seen,
And each hour's joy wreck'd with a week of teen.

QUEEN ELIZABETH

Stay, yet look back with me unto the Tower.
Pity, you ancient stones, those tender babes
Whom envy hath immured within your walls!
Rough cradle for such little pretty ones!
Rude ragged nurse, old sullen playfellow
For tender princes, use my babies well!
So foolish sorrow bids your stones farewell. [*Exeunt*

SCENE II. *London. The palace*

Sennet. Enter RICHARD, *in pomp, crowned;* BUCKINGHAM, CATESBY, *a* PAGE, *and others*

KING RICHARD

Stand all apart. Cousin of Buckingham!

BUCKINGHAM

My gracious sovereign?

KING RICHARD

Give me thy hand. [*Here he ascendeth the throne.*]
 Thus high, by thy advice
And thy assistance, is king Richard seated:
But shall we wear these honours for a day?
Or shall they last, and we rejoice in them?

BUCKINGHAM

Still live they, and for ever may they last!

KING RICHARD

O Buckingham, now do I play the touch,
To try if thou be current gold indeed:
Young Edward lives: think now what I would say.

BUCKINGHAM

Say on, my loving lord.

KING RICHARD

Why, Buckingham, I say, I would be king.

BUCKINGHAM

Why, so you are, my thrice renowned liege.

KING RICHARD

Ha! am I king? 'tis so: but Edward lives.

BUCKINGHAM

True, noble prince.

KING RICHARD

   O bitter consequence,
That Edward still should live true noble prince!
Cousin, thou wert not wont to be so dull:
Shall I be plain? I wish the bastards dead;

And I would have it suddenly perform'd.
What sayest thou? speak suddenly; be brief.

BUCKINGHAM

Your grace may do your pleasure.

KING RICHARD

Tut, tut, thou art all ice, thy kindness freezeth:
Say, have I thy consent that they shall die?

BUCKINGHAM

Give me some breath, some little pause, my lord,
Before I positively speak herein:
I will resolve your grace immediately.   [*Exit*

CATESBY

[*Aside to a stander by*] The king is angry: see, he bites the lip.

KING RICHARD

I will converse with iron-witted fools
And unrespective boys: none are for me
That look into me with considerate eyes:
High-reaching Buckingham grows circumspect.
Boy!

PAGE

My lord?

KING RICHARD

Know'st thou not any whom corrupting gold
Would tempt unto a close exploit of death?

PAGE

My lord, I know a discontented gentleman,
Whose humble means match not his haughty mind:
Gold were as good as twenty orators,
And will, no doubt, tempt him to any thing.

KING RICHARD

What is his name?

PAGE

   His name, my lord, is Tyrrel.

KING RICHARD

I partly know the man: go, call him hither.
          [*Exit* PAGE
The deep-revolving witty Buckingham
No more shall be the neighbour to my counsel:
Hath he so long held out with me untired,
And stops he now for breath?

Enter STANLEY

How now! what news with you?

STANLEY

My lord, I hear the Marquis Dorset's fled
To Richmond, in those parts beyond the seas
Where he abides.   [*Stands apart*

KING RICHARD

Catesby!

CATESBY

My lord?

KING RICHARD

Rumour it abroad
That Anne, my wife, is sick and like to die:
I will take order for her keeping close.
Inquire me out some mean-born gentleman,
Whom I will marry straight to Clarence' daughter:
The boy is foolish, and I fear not him.
Look, how thou dream'st! I say again, give out
That Anne my wife is sick, and like to die·

About it; for it stands me much upon,
To stop all hopes whose growth may damage me.
                              [*Exit* CATESBY
I must be married to my brother's daughter,
Or else my kingdom stands on brittle glass.
Murder her brothers, and then marry her!
Uncertain way of gain! But I am in
So far in blood that sin will pluck on sin:
Tear-falling pity dwells not in this eye.
              Re-enter PAGE, *with* TYRREL
Is thy name Tyrrel?

TYRREL
James Tyrrel, and your most obedient subject.

KING RICHARD
Art thou, indeed?

TYRREL
              Prove me, my gracious sovereign.

KING RICHARD
Darest thou resolve to kill a friend of mine?

TYRREL
Ay, my lord;
But I had rather kill two enemies.

KING RICHARD
Why, there thou hast it: two deep enemies,
Foes to my rest and my sweet sleep's disturbers
Are they that I would have thee deal upon:
Tyrrel, I mean those bastards in the Tower.

TYRREL
Let me have open means to come to them,
And soon I'll rid you from the fear of them.

KING RICHARD
Thou sing'st sweet music. Hark, come hither,
    Tyrrel:
Go, by this token: rise, and lend thine ear: [*Whispers*
There is no more but so: say it is done,
And I will love thee, and prefer thee too.

TYRREL
'Tis done, my gracious lord.

KING RICHARD
Shall we hear from thee, Tyrrel, ere we sleep?

TYRREL
Ye shall, my lord.   [*Exit*
              Re-enter BUCKINGHAM

BUCKINGHAM
My lord, I have consider'd in my mind
The late demand that you did sound me in.

KING RICHARD
Well, let that pass. Dorset is fled to Richmond.

BUCKINGHAM
I hear that news, my lord.

KING RICHARD
Stanley, he is your wife's son: well, look to it.

BUCKINGHAM
My lord, I claim your gift, my due by promise,
For which your honour and your faith is pawn'd;
The earldom of Hereford and the moveables
The which you promised I should possess.

KING RICHARD
Stanley, look to your wife: if she convey
Letters to Richmond, you shall answer it.

BUCKINGHAM
What says your highness to my just demand?

KING RICHARD
As I remember, Henry the Sixth
Did prophesy that Richmond should be king,
When Richmond was a little peevish boy.
A king, perhaps, perhaps,—

BUCKINGHAM
My lord!

KING RICHARD
How chance the prophet could not at that time
Have told me, I being by, that I should kill him?

BUCKINGHAM
My lord, your promise for the earldom,—

KING RICHARD
Richmond! When last I was at Exeter,
The mayor in courtesy show'd me the castle,
And call'd it Rougemont: at which name I started,
Because a bard of Ireland told me once,
I should not live long after I saw Richmond.

BUCKINGHAM
My lord!

KING RICHARD
Ay, what's o'clock?

BUCKINGHAM
I am thus bold to put your grace in mind
Of what you promised me.

KING RICHARD
                  Well, but what's o'clock?

BUCKINGHAM
Upon the stroke of ten.

KING RICHARD
                  Well, let it strike.

BUCKINGHAM
Why let it strike?

KING RICHARD
Because that, like a Jack, thou keep'st the stroke
Betwixt thy begging and my meditation.
I am not in the giving vein to-day.

BUCKINGHAM
Why, then resolve me whether you will or no.

KING RICHARD
Tut, tut,
Thou troublest me; I am not in the vein.
                        [*Exeunt all but* BUCKINGHAM

BUCKINGHAM
Is it even so? rewards he my true service
With such deep contempt? made I him king for this?
O, let me think on Hastings, and be gone
To Brecknock, while my fearful head is on! [*Exit*

SCENE III. *The same*

Enter TYRREL

TYRREL
The tyrannous and bloody deed is done,
The most arch act of piteous massacre
That ever yet this land was guilty of.
Dighton and Forrest, whom I did suborn

To do this ruthless piece of butchery,
Although they were flesh'd villains, bloody dogs,
Melting with tenderness and kind compassion
Wept like two children in their deaths' sad stories.
'Lo, thus,' quoth Dighton, 'lay those tender babes:'
'Thus, thus,' quoth Forrest, 'girdling one another
Within their innocent alabaster arms:
Their lips were four red roses on a stalk,
Which in their summer beauty kiss'd each other.
A book of prayers on their pillow lay;
Which once,' quoth Forrest, 'almost changed my
    mind;
But O! the devil'—there the villain stopp'd;
Whilst Dighton thus told on: 'We smothered
The most replenished sweet work of nature
That from the prime creation e'er she framed.'
Thus both are gone with conscience and remorse;
They could not speak; and so I left them both,
To bring this tidings to the bloody king.
And here he comes.

Enter KING RICHARD

        All hail, my sovereign liege!

KING RICHARD

Kind Tyrrel, am I happy in thy news?

TYRREL

If to have done the thing you gave in charge
Beget your happiness, be happy then,
For it is done, my lord.

KING RICHARD

        But didst thou see them dead?

TYRREL

I did, my lord.

KING RICHARD

        And buried, gentle Tyrrel?

TYRREL

The chaplain of the Tower hath buried them;
But how or in what place I do not know.

KING RICHARD

Come to me, Tyrrel, soon at after supper,
And thou shalt tell the process of their death.
Meantime, but think how I may do thee good,
And be inheritor of thy desire.
Farewell till soon.   [*Exit* TYRREL
The son of Clarence have I pent up close;
His daughter meanly have I match'd in marriage;
The sons of Edward sleep in Abraham's bosom,
And Anne my wife hath bid the world good night.
Now, for I know the Breton Richmond aims
At young Elizabeth, my brother's daughter,
And, by that knot, looks proudly o'er the crown,
To her I go, a jolly thriving wooer.

Enter CATESBY

CATESBY

My lord!

KING RICHARD

Good news or bad, that thou comest in so bluntly?

CATESBY

Bad news, my lord: Ely is fled to Richmond;
And Buckingham, back'd with the hardy Welshmen,
Is in the field, and still his power increaseth.

KING RICHARD

Ely with Richmond troubles me more near
Than Buckingham and his rash-levied army.
Come, I have heard that fearful commenting
Is leaden servitor to dull delay;
Delay leads impotent and snail-paced beggary:
Then fiery expedition be my wing,
Jove's Mercury, and herald for a king!
Come, muster men: my counsel is my shield;
We must be brief when traitors brave the field.
                         [*Exeunt*

SCENE IV. *Before the palace*

Enter QUEEN MARGARET

QUEEN MARGARET

So, now prosperity begins to mellow
And drop into the rotten mouth of death.
Here in these confines slily have I lurk'd,
To watch the waning of mine adversaries.
A dire induction am I witness to,
And will to France, hoping the consequence
Will prove as bitter, black, and tragical.
Withdraw thee, wretched Margaret: who comes
    here?

Enter QUEEN ELIZABETH *and the* DUCHESS OF YORK

QUEEN ELIZABETH

Ah, my young princes! ah, my tender babes!
My unblown flowers, new-appearing sweets!
If yet your gentle souls fly in the air,
And be not fix'd in doom perpetual,
Hover about me with your airy wings,
And hear your mother's lamentation!

QUEEN MARGARET

Hover about her; say, that right for right
Hath dimm'd your infant morn to aged night.

DUCHESS

So many miseries have crazed my voice,
That my woe-wearied tongue is mute and dumb.
Edward Plantagenet, why art thou dead?

QUEEN MARGARET

Plantagenet doth quit Plantagenet,
Edward for Edward pays a dying debt.

QUEEN ELIZABETH

Wilt thou, O God, fly from such gentle lambs,
And throw them in the entrails of the wolf?
When didst thou sleep when such a deed was done?

QUEEN MARGARET

When holy Harry died, and my sweet son.

DUCHESS

Blind sight, dead life, poor mortal living ghost,
Woe's scene, world's shame, grave's due by life
    usurp'd,
Brief abstract and record of tedious days,
Rest thy unrest on England's lawful earth,
                     [*Sitting down*
Unlawfully made drunk with innocents' blood!

QUEEN ELIZABETH

O, that thou wouldst as well afford a grave

As thou canst yield a melancholy seat!
Then would I hide my bones, not rest them here.
O, who hath any cause to mourn but I?
                    [*Sitting down by her*
                QUEEN MARGARET
If ancient sorrow be most reverend,
Give mine the benefit of seniory,
And let my woes frown on the upper hand.
If sorrow can admit society, [*Sitting down with them*
Tell o'er your woes again by viewing mine:
I had an Edward, till a Richard kill'd him;
I had a Harry, till a Richard kill'd him:
Thou hadst an Edward, till a Richard kill'd him;
Thou hadst a Richard, till a Richard kill'd him.
                    DUCHESS
I had a Richard too, and thou didst kill him;
I had a Rutland too, thou holp'st to kill him.
                QUEEN MARGARET
Thou hadst a Clarence too, and Richard kill'd him.
From forth the kennel of thy womb hath crept
A hell-hound that doth hunt us all to death:
That dog, that had his teeth before his eyes,
To worry lambs and lap their gentle blood,
That foul defacer of God's handiwork,
That excellent grand tyrant of the earth,
That reigns in galled eyes of weeping souls,
Thy womb let loose, to chase us to our graves.
O upright, just, and true-disposing God,
How do I thank thee, that this carnal cur
Preys on the issue of his mother's body,
And makes her pew-fellow with others' moan!
                    DUCHESS
O Harry's wife, triumph not in my woes!
God witness with me, I have wept for thine.
                QUEEN MARGARET
Bear with me; I am hungry for revenge,
And now I cloy me with beholding it.
Thy Edward he is dead, that stabb'd my Edward;
Thy other Edward dead, to quit my Edward;
Young York he is but boot, because both they
Match not the high perfection of my loss:
Thy Clarence he is dead that kill'd my Edward;
And the beholders of this tragic play,
The adulterate Hastings, Rivers, Vaughan, Grey,
Untimely smother'd in their dusky graves.
Richard yet lives, hell's black intelligencer,
Only reserved their factor, to buy souls
And send them thither: but at hand, at hand,
Ensues his piteous and unpitied end:
Earth gapes, hell burns, fiends roar, saints pray,
To have him suddenly convey'd away.
Cancel his bond of life, dear God, I pray,
That I may live to say, The dog is dead!
                QUEEN ELIZABETH
O, thou didst prophesy the time would come
That I should wish for thee to help me curse
That bottled spider, that foul bunch-back'd toad!
                QUEEN MARGARET
I call'd thee then vain flourish of my fortune;
I call'd thee then poor shadow, painted queen;

The presentation of but what I was;
The flattering index of a direful pageant;
One heaved a-high, to be hurl'd down below;
A mother only mock'd with two sweet babes;
A dream of what thou wert, a breath, a bubble,
A sign of dignity, a garish flag
To be the aim of every dangerous shot;
A queen in jest, only to fill the scene.
Where is thy husband now? where be thy brothers?
Where are thy children? wherein dost thou joy?
Who sues to thee, and cries 'God save the queen'?
Where be the bending peers that flattered thee?
Where be the thronging troops that followed thee?
Decline all this, and see what now thou art:
For happy wife, a most distressed widow;
For joyful mother, one that wails the name;
For queen, a very caitiff crown'd with care;
For one being sued to, one that humbly sues;
For one that scorn'd at me, now scorn'd of me;
For one being fear'd of all, now fearing one;
For one commanding all, obey'd of none.
Thus hath the course of justice wheel'd about,
And left thee but a very prey to time;
Having no more but thought of what thou wert,
To torture thee the more, being what thou art.
Thou didst usurp my place, and dost thou not
Usurp the just proportion of my sorrow?
Now thy proud neck bears half my burthen'd yoke;
From which even here I slip my weary neck,
And leave the burthen of it all on thee.
Farewell, York's wife, and queen of sad mischance:
These English woes will make me smile in France.
                QUEEN ELIZABETH
O thou well skill'd in curses, stay awhile,
And teach me how to curse mine enemies!
                QUEEN MARGARET
Forbear to sleep the nights, and fast the days;
Compare dead happiness with living woe;
Think that thy babes were fairer than they were,
And he that slew them fouler than he is:
Bettering thy loss makes the bad causer worse:
Revolving this will teach thee how to curse.
                QUEEN ELIZABETH
My words are dull; O, quicken them with thine!
                QUEEN MARGARET
Thy woes will make them sharp and pierce like
    mine.   [*Exit*
                    DUCHESS
Why should calamity be full of words?
                QUEEN ELIZABETH
Windy attorneys to their client woes,
Airy succeeders of intestate joys,
Poor breathing orators of miseries!
Let them have scope: though what they do impart
Help not at all, yet do they ease the heart.
                    DUCHESS
If so, then be not tongue-tied: go with me,
And in the breath of bitter words let's smother
My damned son, which thy two sweet sons smother'd.
I hear his drum: be copious in exclaims.

Enter KING RICHARD, *marching, with drums and trumpets*

KING RICHARD
Who intercepts my expedition?

DUCHESS
O, she that might have intercepted thee,
By strangling thee in her accursed womb,
From all the slaughters, wretch, that thou hast done!

QUEEN ELIZABETH
Hidest thou that forehead with a golden crown,
Where should be graven, if that right were right,
The slaughter of the prince that owed that crown,
And the dire death of my two sons and brothers?
Tell me, thou villain slave, where are my children?

DUCHESS
Thou toad, thou toad, where is thy brother
    Clarence?
And little Ned Plantagenet, his son?

QUEEN ELIZABETH
Where is kind Hastings, Rivers, Vaughan, Grey?

KING RICHARD
A flourish, trumpets! strike alarum, drums!
Let not the heavens hear these tell-tale women
Rail on the Lord's anointed: strike, I say!
                              [*Flourish. Alarums*
Either be patient, and entreat me fair,
Or with the clamorous report of war
Thus will I drown your exclamations.

DUCHESS
Art thou my son?

KING RICHARD
Ay, I thank God, my father, and yourself.

DUCHESS
Then patiently hear my impatience.

KING RICHARD
Madam, I have a touch of your condition,
Which cannot brook the accent of reproof.

DUCHESS
O, let me speak!

KING RICHARD
              Do then; but I'll not hear.

DUCHESS
I will be mild and gentle in my speech.

KING RICHARD
And brief, good mother; for I am in haste.

DUCHESS
Art thou so hasty? I have stay'd for thee,
God knows, in anguish, pain and agony.

KING RICHARD
And came I not at last to comfort you?

DUCHESS
No, by the holy rood, thou know'st it well,
Thou camest on earth to make the earth my hell.
A grievous burthen was thy birth to me;
Tetchy and wayward was thy infancy;
Thy school-days frightful, desperate, wild, and
    furious,
Thy prime of manhood daring, bold, and venturous,
Thy age confirm'd, proud, subtle, bloody, treach-
    erous;
More mild, but yet more harmful, kind in hatred:

What comfortable hour canst thou name,
That ever graced me in thy company?

KING RICHARD
Faith, none, but Humphrey Hour, that call'd your
    grace
To breakfast once forth of my company.
If I be so disgracious in your sight,
Let me march on, and not offend your grace.
Strike up the drum.

DUCHESS
              I prithee, hear me speak.

KING RICHARD
You speak too bitterly.

DUCHESS
              Hear me a word;
For I shall never speak to thee again.

KING RICHARD
So.

DUCHESS
Either thou wilt die, by God's just ordinance,
Ere from this war thou turn a conqueror,
Or I with grief and extreme age shall perish
And never look upon thy face again.
Therefore take with thee my most heavy curse;
Which, in the day of battle, tire thee more
Than all the complete armour that thou wear'st!
My prayers on the adverse party fight;
And there the little souls of Edward's children
Whisper the spirits of thine enemies,
And promise them success and victory.
Bloody thou art, bloody will be thy end;
Shame serves thy life and doth thy death attend.
                              [*Exit*

QUEEN ELIZABETH
Though far more cause, yet much less spirit to curse
Abides in me; I say amen to all.

KING RICHARD
Stay, madam; I must speak a word with you.

QUEEN ELIZABETH
I have no moe sons of the royal blood
For thee to murder: for my daughters, Richard,
They shall be praying nuns, not weeping queens:
And therefore level not to hit their lives.

KING RICHARD
You have a daughter call'd Elizabeth,
Virtuous and fair, royal and gracious.

QUEEN ELIZABETH
And must she die for this? O, let her live,
And I'll corrupt her manners, stain her beauty;
Slander myself as false to Edward's bed;
Throw over her the veil of infamy:
So she may live unscarr'd of bleeding slaughter,
I will confess she was not Edward's daughter.

KING RICHARD
Wrong not her birth, she is of royal blood.

QUEEN ELIZABETH
To save her life, I'll say she is not so.

KING RICHARD
Her life is only safest in her birth.

[146]

QUEEN ELIZABETH
And only in that safety died her brothers.

KING RICHARD
Lo, at their births good stars were opposite.

QUEEN ELIZABETH
No, to their lives bad friends were contrary.

KING RICHARD
All unavoided is the doom of destiny.

QUEEN ELIZABETH
True, when avoided grace makes destiny:
My babes were destined to a fairer death,
If grace had bless'd thee with a fairer life.

KING RICHARD
You speak as if that I had slain my cousins.

QUEEN ELIZABETH
Cousins, indeed; and by their uncle cozen'd
Of comfort, kingdom, kindred, freedom, life.
Whose hand soever lanced their tender hearts,
Thy head, all indirectly, gave direction:
No doubt the murderous knife was dull and blunt,
Till it was whetted on thy stone-hard heart,
To revel in the entrails of my lambs.
But that still use of grief makes wild grief tame,
My tongue should to thy ears not name my boys,
Till that my nails were anchor'd in thine eyes;
And I, in such a desperate bay of death,
Like a poor bark, of sails and tackling reft,
Rush all to pieces on thy rocky bosom.

KING RICHARD
Madam, so thrive I in my enterprise,
And dangerous success of bloody wars,
As I intend more good to you and yours,
Than ever you or yours were by me wrong'd!

QUEEN ELIZABETH
What good is cover'd with the face of heaven,
To be discover'd, that can do me good?

KING RICHARD
The advancement of your children, gentle lady.

QUEEN ELIZABETH
Up to some scaffold, there to lose their heads?

KING RICHARD
No, to the dignity and height of honour,
The high imperial type of this earth's glory.

QUEEN ELIZABETH
Flatter my sorrows with report of it;
Tell me what state, what dignity, what honour,
Canst thou demise to any child of mine?

KING RICHARD
Even all I have; yea, and myself and all,
Will I withal endow a child of thine;
So in the Lethe of thy angry soul
Thou drown the sad remembrance of those wrongs,
Which thou supposest I have done to thee.

QUEEN ELIZABETH
Be brief, lest that the process of thy kindness
Last longer telling than thy kindness' date.

KING RICHARD
Then know, that from my soul I love thy daughter.

QUEEN ELIZABETH
My daughter's mother thinks it with her soul.

KING RICHARD
What do you think?

QUEEN ELIZABETH
That thou dost love my daughter from thy soul:
So from thy soul's love didst thou love her brothers;
And from my heart's love I do thank thee for it.

KING RICHARD
Be not so hasty to confound my meaning:
I mean, that with my soul I love thy daughter,
And mean to make her queen of England.

QUEEN ELIZABETH
Say then, who dost thou mean shall be her king?

KING RICHARD
Even he that makes her queen: who should be else?

QUEEN ELIZABETH
What, thou?

KING RICHARD
I, even I: what think you of it, madam?

QUEEN ELIZABETH
How canst thou woo her?

KING RICHARD
                 That would I learn of you,
As one that are best acquainted with her humour.

QUEEN ELIZABETH
And wilt thou learn of me?

KING RICHARD
                 Madam, with all my heart.

QUEEN ELIZABETH
Send to her, by the man that slew her brothers,
A pair of bleeding hearts; thereon engrave
Edward and York; then haply she will weep:
Therefore present to her,—as sometime Margaret
Did to thy father, steep'd in Rutland's blood,—
A handkerchief; which, say to her, did drain
The purple sap from her sweet brother's body,
And bid her dry her weeping eyes therewith.
If this inducement force her not to love,
Send her a story of thy noble acts;
Tell her thou madest away her uncle Clarence,
Her uncle Rivers; yea, and, for her sake,
Madest quick conveyance with her good aunt Anne.

KING RICHARD
Come, come, you mock me; this is not the way
To win your daughter.

QUEEN ELIZABETH
                 There is no other way;
Unless thou couldst put on some other shape,
And not be Richard that hath done all this.

KING RICHARD
Say that I did all this for love of her.

QUEEN ELIZABETH
Nay, then indeed she cannot choose but hate thee
Having bought love with such a bloody spoil.

KING RICHARD
Look, what is done cannot be now amended:
Men shall deal unadvisedly sometimes,
Which after-hours give leisure to repent.
If I did take the kingdom from your sons,
To make amends, I'll give it to your daughter.
If I have kill'd the issue of your womb,

To quicken your increase, I will beget
Mine issue of your blood upon your daughter:
A grandam's name is little less in love
Than is the doting title of a mother;
They are as children but one step below,
Even of your mettle, of your very blood;
Of all one pain, save for a night of groans
Endured of her, for whom you bid like sorrow.
Your children were vexation to your youth,
But mine shall be a comfort to your age.
The loss you have is but a son being king,
And by that loss your daughter is made queen.
I cannot make you what amends I would,
Therefore accept such kindness as I can.
Dorset your son, that with a fearful soul
Leads discontented steps in foreign soil,
This fair alliance quickly shall call home
To high promotions and great dignity:
The king, that calls your beauteous daughter wife,
Familiarly shall call thy Dorset brother;
Again shall you be mother to a king,
And all the ruins of distressful times
Repair'd with double riches of content.
What! we have many goodly days to see:
The liquid drops of tears that you have shed
Shall come again, transform'd to orient pearl,
Advantaging their loan with interest
Of ten times double gain of happiness.
Go then, my mother, to thy daughter go;
Make bold her bashful years with your experience;
Prepare her ears to hear a wooer's tale;
Put in her tender heart the aspiring flame
Of golden sovereignty; acquaint the princess
With the sweet silent hours of marriage joys:
And when this arm of mine hath chastised
The petty rebel, dull-brain'd Buckingham,
Bound with triumphant garlands will I come,
And lead thy daughter to a conqueror's bed;
To whom I will retail my conquest won,
And she shall be sole victress, Cæsar's Cæsar.

QUEEN ELIZABETH
What were I best to say? her father's brother
Would be her lord? or shall I say, her uncle?
Or, he that slew her brothers and her uncles?
Under what title shall I woo for thee,
That God, the law, my honour and her love,
Can make seem pleasing to her tender years?

KING RICHARD
Infer fair England's peace by this alliance.

QUEEN ELIZABETH
Which she shall purchase with still lasting war.

KING RICHARD
Say that the king, which may command, entreats.

QUEEN ELIZABETH
That at her hands which the king's King forbids.

KING RICHARD
Say, she shall be a high and mighty queen.

QUEEN ELIZABETH
To wail the title, as her mother doth.

KING RICHARD
Say, I will love her everlastingly.

QUEEN ELIZABETH
But how long shall that title 'ever' last?

KING RICHARD
Sweetly in force unto her fair life's end.

QUEEN ELIZABETH
But how long fairly shall her sweet life last?

KING RICHARD
So long as heaven and nature lengthens it.

QUEEN ELIZABETH
So long as hell and Richard likes of it.

KING RICHARD
Say, I, her sovereign, am her subject love.

QUEEN ELIZABETH
But she, your subject, loathes such sovereignty.

KING RICHARD
Be eloquent in my behalf to her.

QUEEN ELIZABETH
An honest tale speeds best being plainly told.

KING RICHARD
Then in plain terms tell her my loving tale.

QUEEN ELIZABETH
Plain and not honest is too harsh a style.

KING RICHARD
Your reasons are too shallow and too quick.

QUEEN ELIZABETH
O no, my reasons are too deep and dead;
Too deep and dead, poor infants, in their grave.

KING RICHARD
Harp not on that string, madam; that is past.

QUEEN ELIZABETH
Harp on it still shall I till heart-strings break.

KING RICHARD
Now, by my George, my garter, and my crown,—

QUEEN ELIZABETH
Profaned, dishonour'd, and the third usurp'd.

KING RICHARD
I swear—

QUEEN ELIZABETH
By nothing; for this is no oath:
The George, profaned, hath lost his holy honour;
The garter, blemish'd, pawn'd his knightly virtue;
The crown, usurp'd, disgraced his kingly glory.
If something thou wilt swear to be believed,
Swear then by something that thou hast not
wrong'd.

KING RICHARD
Now, by the world—

QUEEN ELIZABETH
'Tis full of thy foul wrongs.

KING RICHARD
My father's death—

QUEEN ELIZABETH
Thy life hath that dishonour'd.

KING RICHARD
Then, by myself—

QUEEN ELIZABETH
Thyself thyself misusest.

KING RICHARD
Why then, by God—
QUEEN ELIZABETH
                    God's wrong is most of all.
If thou hadst fear'd to break an oath by Him,
The unity the king thy brother made
Had not been broken, nor my brother slain:
If thou hadst fear'd to break an oath by Him,
The imperial metal, circling now thy brow,
Had graced the tender temples of my child,
And both the princes had been breathing here,
Which now, two tender playfellows for dust,
Thy broken faith hath made a prey for worms.
What canst thou swear by now?
KING RICHARD
                    The time to come.
QUEEN ELIZABETH
That thou hast wronged in the time o'erpast;
For I myself have many tears to wash
Hereafter time, for time past wrong'd by thee.
The children live, whose parents thou hast slaugh-
    ter'd,
Ungovern'd youth, to wail it in their age;
The parents live, whose children thou hast butch-
    er'd,
Old withered plants, to wail it with their age.
Swear not by time to come; for that thou hast
Misused ere used, by time misused o'erpast.
KING RICHARD
As I intend to prosper and repent,
So thrive I in my dangerous attempt
Of hostile arms! myself myself confound!
Heaven and fortune bar me happy hours!
Day, yield me not thy light; nor, night, thy rest!
Be opposite all planets of good luck
To my proceedings, if, with pure heart's love,
Immaculate devotion, holy thoughts,
I tender not thy beauteous princely daughter!
In her consists my happiness and thine;
Without her, follows to this land and me,
To thee, herself, and many a Christian soul,
Death, desolation, ruin and decay:
It cannot be avoided but by this;
It will not be avoided but by this.
Therefore, good mother,—I must call you so—
Be the attorney of my love to her:
Plead what I will be, not what I have been;
Not my deserts, but what I will deserve:
Urge the necessity and state of times,
And be not peevish-fond in great designs.
QUEEN ELIZABETH
Shall I be tempted of the devil thus?
KING RICHARD
Ay, if the devil tempt thee to do good.
QUEEN ELIZABETH
Shall I forget myself to be myself?
KING RICHARD
Ay, if yourself's remembrance wrong yourself.
QUEEN ELIZABETH
But thou didst kill my children.

KING RICHARD
But in your daughter's womb I bury them:
Where in that nest of spicery they shall breed
Selves of themselves, to your recomforture.
QUEEN ELIZABETH
Shall I go win my daughter to thy will?
KING RICHARD
And be a happy mother by the deed.
QUEEN ELIZABETH
I go. Write to me very shortly,
And you shall understand from me her mind.
KING RICHARD
Bear her my true love's kiss; and so, farewell.
                              [Exit QUEEN ELIZABETH
Relenting fool, and shallow, changing woman!
        Enter RATCLIFF; CATESBY following
How now! what news?
RATCLIFF
My gracious sovereign, on the western coast
Rideth a puissant navy; to the shore
Throng many doubtful hollow-hearted friends,
Unarm'd, and unresolved to beat them back:
'Tis thought that Richmond is their admiral;
And there they hull, expecting but the aid
Of Buckingham to welcome them ashore.
KING RICHARD
Some light-foot friend post to the Duke of Norfolk:
Ratcliff, thyself, or Catesby; where is he?
CATESBY
Here, my lord.
KING RICHARD
Fly to the duke. [To RATCLIFF] Post thou to Salisbury:
When thou comest thither,— [To CATESBY] Dull un-
    mindful villain,
Why stand'st thou still, and go'st not to the duke?
CATESBY
First, mighty sovereign, let me know your mind,
What from your grace I shall deliver to him.
KING RICHARD
O, true, good Catesby: bid him levy straight
The greatest strength and power he can make,
And meet me presently at Salisbury.
CATESBY
I go.   [Exit
RATCLIFF
What is 't your highness' pleasure I shall do
At Salisbury?
KING RICHARD
Why, what wouldst thou do there before I go?
RATCLIFF
Your highness told me I should post before.
KING RICHARD
My mind is changed, sir, my mind is changed.
              Enter LORD STANLEY
How now, what news with you?
STANLEY
None good, my lord, to please you with the hearing;
Nor none so bad, but it may well be told.
KING RICHARD
Hoyday, a riddle! neither good nor bad

Why dost thou run so many mile about,
When thou mayst tell thy tale a nearer way?
Once more, what news?

STANLEY
            Richmond is on the seas.

KING RICHARD
There let him sink, and be the seas on him!
White-liver'd runagate, what doth he there?

STANLEY
I know not, mighty sovereign, but by guess.

KING RICHARD
Well, sir, as you guess, as you guess?

STANLEY
Stirr'd up by Dorset, Buckingham, and Ely,
He makes for England, there to claim the crown.

KING RICHARD
Is the chair empty? is the sword unsway'd?
Is the king dead? the empire unpossess'd?
What heir of York is there alive but we?
And who is England's king but great York's heir?
Then, tell me, what doth he upon the sea?

STANLEY
Unless for that, my liege, I cannot guess.

KING RICHARD
Unless for that he comes to be your liege,
You cannot guess wherefore the Welshman comes.
Thou wilt revolt and fly to him, I fear.

STANLEY
No, mighty liege; therefore mistrust me not.

KING RICHARD
Where is thy power then to beat him back?
Where are thy tenants and thy followers?
Are they not now upon the western shore,
Safe-conducting the rebels from their ships?

STANLEY
No, my good lord, my friends are in the north.

KING RICHARD
Cold friends to Richard: what do they in the north,
When they should serve their sovereign in the west?

STANLEY
They have not been commanded, mighty sovereign:
Please it your majesty to give me leave,
I'll muster up my friends, and meet your grace
Where and what time your majesty shall please.

KING RICHARD
Ay, ay, thou wouldst be gone to join with Rich-
  mond:
I will not trust you, sir.

STANLEY
           Most mighty sovereign,
You have no cause to hold my friendship doubtful:
I never was nor never will be false.

KING RICHARD
Well,
Go muster men; but, hear you, leave behind
Your son, George Stanley: look your faith be firm,
Or else his head's assurance is but frail.

STANLEY
So deal with him as I prove true to you.   [Exit
        Enter a MESSENGER

MESSENGER
My gracious sovereign, now in Devonshire,
As I by friends am well advertised,
Sir Edward Courtney, and the haughty prelate
Bishop of Exeter, his brother there,
With many moe confederates, are in arms.
        Enter another MESSENGER

SECOND MESSENGER
My liege, in Kent, the Guildfords are in arms;
And every hour more competitors
Flock to their aid, and still their power increaseth.
        Enter another MESSENGER

THIRD MESSENGER
My lord, the army of the Duke of Buckingham—

KING RICHARD
Out on you, owls! nothing but songs of death?
               [He striketh him
Take that, until thou bring me better news.

THIRD MESSENGER
The news I have to tell your majesty
Is, that by sudden floods and fall of waters,
Buckingham's army is dispersed and scatter'd;
And he himself wander'd away alone,
No man knows whither.

KING RICHARD
           I cry thee mercy:
There is my purse to cure that blow of thine.
Hath any well-advised friend proclaim'd
Reward to him that brings the traitor in?

THIRD MESSENGER
Such proclamation hath been made, my liege.
        Enter another MESSENGER

FOURTH MESSENGER
Sir Thomas Lovel and Lord Marquess Dorset,
'Tis said, my liege, in Yorkshire are in arms.
Yet this good comfort bring I to your grace,
The Breton navy is dispersed by tempest:
Richmond, in Dorsetshire, sent out a boat
Unto the shore, to ask those on the banks
If they were his assistants, yea or no;
Who answer'd him, they came from Buckingham
Upon his party: he, mistrusting them,
Hoised sail and made away for Brittany.

KING RICHARD
March on, march on, since we are up in arms;
If not to fight with foreign enemies,
Yet to beat down these rebels here at home.
          Re-enter CATESBY

CATESBY
My liege, the Duke of Buckingham is taken;
That is the best news: that the Earl of Richmond
Is with a mighty power landed at Milford,
Is colder tidings, yet they must be told.

KING RICHARD
Away towards Salisbury! while we reason here,
A royal battle might be won and lost:
Some one take order Buckingham be brought
To Salisbury; the rest march on with me.
              [Flourish. Exeunt

SCENE V. LORD DERBY'S *house*

Enter DERBY *and* SIR CHRISTOPHER URSWICK

DERBY

Sir Christopher, tell Richmond this from me:
That in the sty of this most bloody boar
My son George Stanley is frank'd up in hold:
If I revolt, off goes young George's head;
The fear of that withholds my present aid.
But, tell me, where is princely Richmond now?

CHRISTOPHER

At Pembroke, or at Ha'rford-west, in Wales.

DERBY

What men of name resort to him?

CHRISTOPHER

Sir Walter Herbert, a renowned soldier;
Sir Gilbert Talbot, Sir William Stanley;
Oxford, redoubted Pembroke, Sir James Blunt,
And Rice ap Thomas, with a valiant crew,
And many moe of noble fame and worth:
And towards London they do bend their course,
If by the way they be not fought withal.

DERBY

Return unto thy lord; commend me to him:
Tell him the queen hath heartily consented
He shall espouse Elizabeth her daughter.
These letters will resolve him of my mind.
Farewell.

[*Exeunt*

ACT V

SCENE I. *Salisbury. An open place*

Enter the SHERIFF, *and* BUCKINGHAM, *with halberds, led to execution*

BUCKINGHAM

Will not King Richard let me speak with him?

SHERIFF

No, my good lord; therefore be patient.

BUCKINGHAM

Hastings, and Edward's children, Rivers, Grey,
Holy King Henry, and thy fair son Edward,
Vaughan, and all that have miscarried
By underhand corrupted foul injustice,
If that your moody discontented souls
Do through the clouds behold this present hour,
Even for revenge mock my destruction!
This is All-Souls' day, fellows, is it not?

SHERIFF

It is, my lord.

BUCKINGHAM

Why, then All-Souls' day is my body's doomsday.
This is the day that, in King Edward's time,
I wish'd might fall on me when I was found
False to his children or his wife's allies;
This is the day wherein I wish'd to fall
By the false faith of him I trusted most;
This, this All-Souls' day to my fearful soul
Is the determined respite of my wrongs:

That high All-seer that I dallied with
Hath turn'd my feigned prayer on my head,
And given in earnest what I begg'd in jest.
Thus doth he force the swords of wicked men
To turn their own points on their masters' bosoms:
Now Margaret's curse is fallen upon my head;
'When he,' quoth she, 'shall split thy heart with sorrow,
Remember Margaret was a prophetess.'
Come, sirs, convey me to the block of shame;
Wrong hath but wrong, and blame the due of blame.

[*Exeunt*

SCENE II. *The camp near Tamworth*

Enter RICHMOND, OXFORD, BLUNT, HERBERT, *and others, with drum and colours*

RICHMOND

Fellows in arms, and my most loving friends,
Bruised underneath the yoke of tyranny,
Thus far into the bowels of the land
Have we march'd on without impediment;
And here receive we from our father Stanley
Lines of fair comfort and encouragement.
The wretched, bloody, and usurping board,
That spoil'd your summer fields and fruitful vines,
Swills your warm blood like wash, and makes his trough
In your embowell'd bosoms, this foul swine
Lies now even in the centre of this isle,
Near to the town of Leicester, as we learn:
From Tamworth thither is but one day's march.
In God's name, cheerly on, courageous friends,
To reap the harvest of perpetual peace
By this one bloody trial of sharp war.

OXFORD

Every man's conscience is a thousand swords,
To fight against that bloody homicide.

HERBERT

I doubt not but his friends will fly to us.

BLUNT

He hath no friends but who are friends for fear,
Which in his greatest need will shrink from him.

RICHMOND

All for our vantage. Then, in God's name, march:
True hope is swift, and flies with swallow's wings;
Kings it makes gods, and meaner creatures kings.

[*Exeunt*

SCENE III. *Bosworth Field*

Enter KING RICHARD *in arms with* NORFOLK, *the* EARL OF SURREY, *and others*

KING RICHARD

Here pitch our tents, even here in Bosworth field.
My Lord of Surrey, why look you so sad?

SURREY

My heart is ten times lighter than my looks.

KING RICHARD

My Lord of Norfolk,—

NORFOLK

Here, most gracious liege.

KING RICHARD

Norfolk, we must have knocks; ha! must we not?

NORFOLK

We must both give and take, my gracious lord.

KING RICHARD

Up with my tent there! here will I lie to-night:
But where to-morrow? Well, all's one for that.
Who hath descried the number of the foe?

NORFOLK

Six or seven thousand is their utmost power.

KING RICHARD

Why, our battalion trebles that account:
Besides, the king's name is a tower of strength,
Which they upon the adverse party want.
Up with my tent there! Valiant gentlemen,
Let us survey the vantage of the field;
Call for some men of sound direction:
Let's want no discipline, make no delay;
For, lords, to-morrow is a busy day.   [Exeunt
          Enter, on the other side of the field, RICHMOND, SIR
          WILLIAM BRANDON, OXFORD, and others. Some of
          the SOLDIERS pitch RICHMOND'S tent

RICHMOND

The weary sun hath made a golden set,
And by the bright track of his fiery car
Gives signal of a goodly day to-morrow.
Sir William Brandon, you shall bear my standard.
Give me some ink and paper in my tent:
I'll draw the form and model of our battle,
Limit each leader to his several charge,
And part in just proportion our small strength.
My Lord of Oxford, you, Sir William Brandon,
And you, Sir Walter Herbert, stay with me.
The Earl of Pembroke keeps his regiment:
Good Captain Blunt, bear my good-night to him,
And by the second hour in the morning
Desire the earl to see me in my tent:
Yet one thing more, good Blunt, before thou go'st,
Where is Lord Stanley quarter'd, dost thou know?

BLUNT

Unless I have mista'en his colours much,
Which well I am assured I have not done,
His regiment lies half a mile at least
South from the mighty power of the king.

RICHMOND

If without peril it be possible,
Good Captain Blunt, bear my good-night to him,
And give him from me this most needful scroll.

BLUNT

Upon my life, my lord, I'll undertake it;
And so, God give you quiet rest to-night!

RICHMOND

Good night, good Captain Blunt. Come, gentlemen,
Let us consult upon to-morrow's business:
In to our tent! the air is raw and cold.
          [They withdraw into the tent
Enter, to his tent, KING RICHARD, NORFOLK, RATCLIFF,
          CATESBY, and others

KING RICHARD

What is 't o'clock?

CATESBY

It's supper-time, my lord;
It's nine o'clock.

KING RICHARD

I will not sup to-night.
Give me some ink and paper.
What, is my beaver easier than it was!
And all my armour laid into my tent?

CATESBY

It is, my liege; and all things are in readiness.

KING RICHARD

Good Norfolk, hie thee to thy charge;
Use careful watch, choose trusty sentinels.

NORFOLK

I go, my lord.

KING RICHARD

Stir with the lark to-morrow, gentle Norfolk.

NORFOLK

I warrant you, my lord.   [Exit

KING RICHARD

Catesby!

CATESBY

My lord?

KING RICHARD

Send out a pursuivant at arms
To Stanley's regiment; bid him bring his power
Before sunrising, lest his son George fall
Into the blind cave of eternal night.   [Exit CATESBY
Fill me a bowl of wine. Give me a watch.
Saddle white Surrey for the field to-morrow.
Look that my staves be sound, and not too heavy.
Ratcliff!

RATCLIFF

My lord?

KING RICHARD

Saw'st thou the melancholy Lord Northumberland?

RATCLIFF

Thomas the Earl of Surrey, and himself,
Much about cock-shut time, from troop to troop
Went through the army, cheering up the soldiers.

KING RICHARD

So, I am satisfied. Give me a bowl of wine:
I have not that alacrity of spirit,
Nor cheer of mind, that I was wont to have.
Set it down. Is ink and paper ready?

RATCLIFF

It is, my lord.

KING RICHARD

Bid my guard watch. Leave me. Ratcliff,
About the mid of night come to my tent,
And help to arm me. Leave me, I say.
          [Exeunt RATCLIFF and the other ATTENDANTS
Enter DERBY to RICHMOND in his tent, LORDS and others
          attending

DERBY

Fortune and victory sit on thy helm!

RICHMOND

All comfort that the dark night can afford

Be to thy person, noble father-in-law!
Tell me, how fares our loving mother?
DERBY
I, by attorney, bless thee from thy mother,
Who prays continually for Richmond's good:
So much for that. The silent hours steal on,
And flaky darkness breaks within the east.
In brief, for so the season bids us be,
Prepare thy battle early in the morning,
And put thy fortune to the arbitrement
Of bloody strokes and mortal-staring war.
I, as I may—that which I would I cannot,—
With best advantage will deceive the time,
And aid thee in this doubtful shock of arms:
But on thy side I may not be too forward,
Lest, being seen, thy brother, tender George,
Be executed in his father's sight.
Farewell: the leisure and the fearful time
Cuts off the ceremonious vows of love,
And ample interchange of sweet discourse,
Which so long sunder'd friends should dwell upon,
God give us leisure for these rites of love!
Once more, adieu: be valiant, and speed well!
RICHMOND
Good lords, conduct him to his regiment:
I'll strive, with troubled thoughts, to take a nap,
Lest leaden slumber peise me down to-morrow,
When I should mount with wings of victory:
Once more, good night, kind lords and gentlemen.
                     [Exeunt all but RICHMOND
O Thou, whose captain I account myself,
Look on my forces with a gracious eye;
Put in their hands thy bruising irons of wrath,
That they may crush down with a heavy fall
The usurping helmets of our adversaries!
Make us thy ministers of chastisement,
That we may praise thee in the victory!
To thee I do commend my watchful soul,
Ere I let fall the windows of mine eyes:
Sleeping and waking, O, defend me still!   [Sleeps
Enter the GHOST OF PRINCE EDWARD, son to HENRY the
                   Sixth
                GHOST
[To RICHARD] Let me sit heavy on thy soul to-
   morrow!
Think, how thou stab'dst me in my prime of youth
At Tewksbury: despair, therefore, and die!
[To RICHMOND] Be cheerful, Richmond; for the
   wronged souls
Of butcher'd princes fight in thy behalf:
King Henry's issue, Richmond, comforts thee.
     Enter the GHOST OF HENRY THE SIXTH
                GHOST
['To RICHARD] When I was mortal, my anointed
   body
By thee was punched full of deadly holes:
Think on the Tower and me: despair, and die!
Harry the Sixth bids thee despair and die!
[To RICHMOND] Virtuous and holy, be thou con-
   queror!

Harry, that prophesied thou shouldst be king,
Doth comfort thee in thy sleep: live, and flourish!
        Enter the GHOST OF CLARENCE
                GHOST
[To RICHARD] Let me sit heavy on thy soul to-
   morrow!
I, that was wash'd to death with fulsome wine,
Poor Clarence, by thy guile betray'd to death.
To-morrow in the battle think on me,
And fall thy edgeless sword: despair, and die!
[To RICHMOND] Thou offspring of the house of Lan-
   caster,
The wronged heirs of York do pray for thee:
Good angels guard thy battle! live, and flourish!
   Enter the GHOSTS OF RIVERS, GREY, and VAUGHAN
           GHOST OF RIVERS
[To RICHARD] Let me sit heavy on thy soul to-
   morrow,
Rivers, that died at Pomfret! despair, and die!
            GHOST OF GREY
[To RICHARD] Think upon Grey, and let thy soul
   despair!
          GHOST OF VAUGHAN
[To RICHARD] Think upon Vaughan, and, with
   guilty fear,
Let fall thy lance: despair, and die!
                ALL
[To RICHMOND] Awake, and think our wrongs in
   Richard's bosom
Will conquer him! awake, and win the day!
      Enter the GHOST OF HASTINGS
                GHOST
[To RICHARD] Bloody and guilty, guiltily awake,
And in a bloody battle end thy days!
Think on Lord Hastings: despair, and die!
[To RICHMOND] Quiet untroubled soul, awake,
   awake!
Arm, fight, and conquer, for fair England's sake!
   Enter the GHOSTS OF THE TWO YOUNG PRINCES
                GHOSTS
[To RICHARD] Dream on thy cousins smothered in
   the Tower:
Let us be lead within thy bosom, Richard,
And weigh thee down to ruin, shame, and death!
Thy nephews' souls bid thee despair and die!
[To RICHMOND] Sleep, Richmond, sleep in peace,
   and wake in joy;
Good angels guard thee from the boar's annoy!
Live, and beget a happy race of kings!
Edward's unhappy sons do bid thee flourish.
     Enter the GHOST OF LADY ANNE his wife
                GHOST
[To RICHARD] Richard, thy wife, that wretched
   Anne thy wife,
That never slept a quiet hour with thee,
Now fills thy sleep with perturbations:
To-morrow in the battle think on me,
And fall thy edgeless sword: despair, and die!
[To RICHMOND] Thou quiet soul, sleep thou a quiet
   sleep:

[153]

Dream of success and happy victory!
Thy adversary's wife doth pray for thee.
Enter the GHOST OF BUCKINGHAM

GHOST

[*To* RICHARD] The first was I that help'd thee to the
    crown;
The last was I that felt thy tyranny:
O, in the battle think on Buckingham,
And die in terror of thy guiltiness!
Dream on, dream on, of bloody deeds and death:
Fainting, despair; despairing, yield thy breath!
[*To* RICHMOND] I died for hope ere I could lend thee
    aid:
But cheer thy heart, and be thou not dismay'd:
God and good angels fight on Richmond's side;
And Richard falls in height of all his pride.
[*The* GHOSTS *vanish.* KING RICHARD *starts out of his dream.*

KING RICHARD

Give me another horse: bind up my wounds.
Have mercy, Jesu!—Soft! I did but dream.
O coward conscience, how dost thou afflict me!
The lights burn blue. It is now dead midnight.
Cold fearful drops stand on my trembling flesh.
What do I fear? myself? there's none else by:
Richard loves Richard; that is, I am I.
Is there a murderer here? No. Yes, I am:
Then fly. What, from myself? Great reason why:
Lest I revenge. What, myself upon myself?
Alack, I love myself. Wherefore? for any good
That I myself have done unto myself?
O, no! alas, I rather hate myself
For hateful deeds committed by myself!
I am a villain: yet I lie, I am not.
Fool, of thyself speak well: fool, do not flatter.
My conscience hath a thousand several tongues,
And every tongue brings in a several tale,
And every tale condemns me for a villain.
Perjury, perjury, in the high'st degree;
Murder, stern murder, in the direst degree;
All several sins, all used in each degree,
Throng to the bar, crying all 'Guilty! guilty!'
I shall despair. There is no creature loves me;
And if I die, no soul will pity me:
Nay, wherefore should they, since that I myself
Find in myself no pity to myself?
Methought the souls of all that I had murder'd
Came to my tent, and every one did threat
To-morrow's vengeance on the head of Richard.
Enter RATCLIFF

RATCLIFF

My lord!

KING RICHARD

'Zounds! who is there?

RATCLIFF

Ratcliff, my lord; 'tis I. The early village-cock
Hath twice done salutation to the morn;
Your friends are up, and buckle on their armour.

KING RICHARD

O Ratcliff, I have dream'd a fearful dream!
What thinkest thou, will our friends prove all true?

RATCLIFF

No doubt, my lord.

KING RICHARD

      O Ratcliff, I fear, I fear,—

RATCLIFF

Nay, good my lord, be not afraid of shadows.

KING RICHARD

By the apostle Paul, shadows to-night
Have struck more terror to the soul of Richard,
Than can the substance of ten thousand soldiers
Armed in proof, and led by shallow Richmond.
It is not yet near day. Come, go with me;
Under our tents I'll play the eaves-dropper,
To see if any mean to shrink from me.   [*Exeunt*
Enter the LORDS *to* RICHMOND, *sitting in his tent*

LORDS

Good morrow, Richmond!

RICHMOND

Cry mercy, lords and watchful gentlemen,
That you have ta'en a tardy sluggard here.

LORDS

How have you slept, my lord?

RICHMOND

The sweetest sleep, and fairest-boding dreams
That ever enter'd in a drowsy head,
Have I since your departure had, my lords.
Methought their souls, whose bodies Richard mur-
    der'd,
Came to my tent, and cried on victory:
I promise you, my soul is very jocund
In the remembrance of so fair a dream.
How far into the morning is it, lords?

LORDS

Upon the stroke of four.

RICHMOND

Why, then 'tis time to arm and give direction.
His oration to his SOLDIERS

More than I have said, loving countrymen,
The leisure and enforcement of the time
Forbids to dwell upon: yet remember this,
God and our good cause fight upon our side;
The prayers of holy saints and wronged souls,
Like high-rear'd bulwarks, stand before our faces.
Richard except, those whom we fight against
Had rather have us win than him they follow:
For what is he they follow? truly, gentlemen,
A bloody tyrant and a homicide;
One raised in blood, and one in blood establish'd;
One that made means to come by what he hath,
And slaughter'd those that were the means to help
    him;
A base foul stone, made precious by the foil
Of England's chair, where he is falsely set;
One that hath ever been God's enemy:
Then, if you fight against God's enemy,
God will in justice ward you as his soldiers;
If you do sweat to put a tyrant down,
You sleep in peace, the tyrant being slain;
If you do fight against your country's foes,
Your country's fat shall pay your pains the hire:

If you do fight in safeguard of your wives,
Your wives shall welcome home the conquerors;
If you do free your children from the sword,
Your children's children quit it in your age.
Then, in the name of God and all these rights,
Advance your standards, draw your willing swords.
For me, the ransom of my bold attempt
Shall be this cold corpse on the earth's cold face;
But if I thrive, the gain of my attempt
The least of you shall share his part thereof.
Sound drums and trumpets boldly and cheerfully;
God and Saint George! Richmond and victory!
                                        [*Exeunt*

Re-enter KING RICHARD, RATCLIFF, ATTENDANTS
and FORCES

KING RICHARD
What said Northumberland as touching Richmond?

RATCLIFF
That he was never trained up in arms.

KING RICHARD
He said the truth: and what said Surrey, then?

RATCLIFF
He smiled and said 'The better for our purpose.'

KING RICHARD
He was in the right; and so indeed it is.
                                [*The clock striketh*
Tell the clock there. Give me a calendar.
Who saw the sun to-day?

RATCLIFF
                    Not I, my lord.

KING RICHARD
Then he disdains to shine; for by the book
He should have braved the east an hour ago:
A black day will it be to somebody.
Ratcliff!

RATCLIFF
My lord?

KING RICHARD
        The sun will not be seen to-day;
The sky doth frown and lour upon our army.
I would these dewy tears were from the ground.
Not shine to-day! Why, what is that to me
More than to Richmond? for the selfsame heaven
That frowns on me looks sadly upon him.

Re-enter NORFOLK

NORFOLK
Arm, arm, my lord; the foe vaunts in the field.

KING RICHARD
Come, bustle, bustle. Caparison my horse.
Call up Lord Stanley, bid him bring his power:
I will lead forth my soldiers to the plain,
And thus my battle shall be ordered:
My foreward shall be drawn out all in length,
Consisting equally of horse and foot;
Our archers shall be placed in the midst:
John Duke of Norfolk, Thomas Earl of Surrey,
Shall have the leading of this foot and horse.
They thus directed, we will follow
In the main battle, whose puissance on either side
Shall be well winged with our chiefest horse.

This, and Saint George to boot! What think'st thou,
    Norfolk?

NORFOLK
A good direction, warlike sovereign.
This found I on my tent this morning.
                            [*He sheweth him a paper*

KING RICHARD
[*Reads*] 'Jockey of Norfolk, be not so bold,
For Dickon thy master is bought and sold.'
A thing devised by the enemy.
Go, gentlemen, every man unto his charge:
Let not our babbling dreams affright our souls:
Conscience is but a word that cowards use,
Devised at first to keep the strong in awe:
Our strong arms be our conscience, swords our law.
March on, join bravely, let us to 't pell-mell;
If not to heaven, then hand in hand to hell.

His oration to his ARMY
What shall I say more than I have inferr'd?
Remember whom you are to cope withal;
A sort of vagabonds, rascals, and runaways,
A scum of Bretons, and base lackey peasants,
Whom their o'er-cloyed country vomits forth
To desperate ventures and assured destruction.
You sleeping safe, they bring to you unrest;
You having lands and blest with beauteous wives,
They would restrain the one, distain the other.
And who doth lead them but a paltry fellow,
Long kept in Bretagne at our mother's cost?
A milk-sop, one that never in his life
Felt so much cold as over shoes in snow?
Let's whip these stragglers o'er the seas again,
Lash hence these overweening rags of France,
These famish'd beggars, weary of their lives,
Who, but for dreaming on this fond exploit,
For want of means, poor rats, had hang'd them-
    selves:
If we be conquer'd, let men conquer us,
And not these bastard Bretons, whom our fathers
Have in their own land beaten, bobb'd, and
    thump'd,
And in record left them the heirs of shame.
Shall these enjoy our lands? lie with our wives?
Ravish our daughters? [*Drum afar off*] Hark! I hear
    their drum.
Fight, gentlemen of England! fight, bold yeomen!
Draw, archers, draw your arrows to the head!
Spur your proud horses hard, and ride in blood;
Amaze the welkin with your broken staves!

Enter a MESSENGER
What says Lord Stanley? will he bring his power?

MESSENGER
My lord, he doth deny to come.

KING RICHARD
Off with his son George's head!

NORFOLK
My lord, the enemy is past the marsh:
After the battle let George Stanley die.

KING RICHARD
A thousand hearts are great within my bosom:

Advance our standards, set upon our foes;
Our ancient word of courage, fair Saint George,
Inspire us with the spleen of fiery dragons!
Upon them! Victory sits on our helms.   [*Exeunt*

SCENE IV. *Another part of the field*

Alarum: excursions. Enter NORFOLK *and* FORCES *fighting;
to him* CATESBY

CATESBY

Rescue, my Lord of Norfolk, rescue, rescue!
The king enacts more wonders than a man,
Daring an opposite to every danger:
His horse is slain, and all on foot he fights,
Seeking for Richmond in the throat of death.
Rescue, fair lord, or else the day is lost!

Alarums. Enter KING RICHARD

KING RICHARD

A horse! a horse! my kingdom for a horse!

CATESBY

Withdraw, my lord; I'll help you to a horse.

KING RICHARD

Slave, I have set my life upon a cast,
And I will stand the hazard of the die.
I think there be six Richmonds in the field;
Five have I slain to-day instead of him.
A horse! a horse! my kingdom for a horse!   [*Exeunt*

SCENE V. *Another part of the field*

Alarum. Enter RICHARD *and* RICHMOND; *they fight.*
RICHARD *is slain. Retreat and flourish. Re-enter*
RICHMOND, DERBY *bearing the crown,
with divers other* LORDS

RICHMOND

God and your arms be praised, victorious friends!
The day is ours; the bloody dog is dead.

DERBY

Courageous Richmond, well hast thou acquit thee.
Lo, here, this long usurped royalty
From the dead temples of this bloody wretch
Have I pluck'd off, to grace thy brows withal:
Wear it, enjoy it, and make much of it.

RICHMOND

Great God of heaven, say amen to all!
But, tell me, is young George Stanley living?

DERBY

He is, my lord, and safe in Leicester town;
Whither, if it please you, we may now withdraw us.

RICHMOND

What men of name are slain on either side?

DERBY

John Duke of Norfolk, Walter Lord Ferrers,
Sir Robert Brakenbury, and Sir William Brandon.

RICHMOND

Inter their bodies as becomes their births:
Proclaim a pardon to the soldiers fled,
That in submission will return to us:
And then, as we have ta'en the sacrament,
We will unite the white rose and the red.
Smile heaven upon this fair conjunction,
That long have frown'd upon their enmity!
What traitor hears me, and says not amen?
England hath long been mad, and scarr'd herself;
The brother blindly shed the brother's blood,
The father rashly slaughter'd his own son,
The son, compell'd, been butcher to the sire:
All this divided York and Lancaster,
Divided in their dire division,
O, now let Richmond and Elizabeth,
The true succeeders of each royal house,
By God's fair ordinance conjoin together!
And let their heirs, God, if thy will be so,
Enrich the time to come with smooth-faced peace,
With smiling plenty and fair prosperous days!
Abate the edge of traitors, gracious Lord,
That would reduce these bloody days again,
And make poor England weep in streams of blood!
Let them not live to taste this land's increase,
That would with treason wound this fair land's
     peace!
Now civil wounds are stopp'd, peace lives again:
That she may long live here, God say amen!
         [*Exeunt*

THE COMEDY OF ERRORS

SYNOPSIS

A SYRACUSE merchant named Ægeon was shipwrecked when returning home from a business trip to Epidamnum with his wife, Æmilia, their twin infant sons and twin boy slaves whom Ægeon had bought to be attendants to his children. Himself rescued with one child and one little slave by a ship going to Epidaurus, he had been separated from his wife who, lashed to a spar with the two other children, was carried away by a Corinthian fisherman's boat, and never heard of again.

When a boy of eighteen, his son obtained Ægeon's permission to go accompanied by the slave to search for his lost parent and brother, but, not returning, the father set out to trace him and after five years of futile wandering he arrives in Ephesus on his way home. Here he is arrested and, unable to pay the ransom, is sentenced to death under a recent law enacted to prevent traffic between the enemy cities of Syracuse and Ephesus. The sympathetic Duke Solinus, touched by the unoffending old man's story of bereavement, grants him one day's grace to seek out friends and raise the amount of the ransom.

Ignorant of his father's whereabouts and unaware that his twin brother is living in Ephesus, Antipholus of Syracuse has just arrived in the city with his slave Dromio and, warned about the law, professes to be from Epidamnum. The second Antipholus, on the other hand, who, with his slave, the second Dromio, had been parted from Æmilia after their rescue from the shipwreck and become a prosperous citizen of Ephesus in high favor with the Duke, knows nothing about the visitors' presence in the city, but when his wife Adriana, a shrewish woman of rank, sends the Ephesian Dromio to summon her husband home to dinner, she is perplexed and angry when the slave returns badly beaten in an encounter with Antipholus of Syracuse, who, being unmarried, is exasperated at the man's insistence, especially when he denies any knowledge of the gold which the Syracusian has just sent by his own Dromio to his inn for safe-keeping. He finds his money secure, however, but beats his own slave for his apparent impudence in the invitation to dinner and also for lying about the gold.

Just then Adriana, impatient at waiting for the gold chain her husband had promised her, appears with her sister Luciana, addresses the bewildered man by name, reproves him for his delay, and takes him home to dinner. His slave Dromio, who incurs both his master's and Adriana's wrath by vowing he knows nothing about the previous invitation, is stationed at the gate with strict orders to admit no visitors. The tardy master of the house now arrives home for dinner with two guests, Angelo and Balthazar, and furious with indignation at being ordered away from the locked doors of his own home, he takes his friends to dine with a courtezan, and declaring that he will give Adriana's gold chain to this girl sends Angelo, the goldsmith, to get it.

Meanwhile, at his home his twin brother is making love to the smitten but protesting Luciana, and Dromio is embarrassed by a fat kitchen wench who claims him as husband. Convinced that they are being victimized by witchcraft, the Syracusian sends his Dromio to engage passage on the next ship leaving port, and is suddenly confronted by Angelo who insists upon him taking the gold chain his brother ordered.

Later in the day, Angelo, on the point of being arrested for debt, asks for payment of the chain from Antipholus of Ephesus who denies ever having received it, and is arrested. At this juncture Dromio of Syracuse comes with news of a vessel about to sail, and the Ephesian orders the slave he mistakes for his own to get money from his wife to bail him out. Meeting his own master as he returns, Dromio is surprised to find him at liberty but hands him Adriana's ducats just as the courtezan appears to demand the gold chain about the distracted man's neck in exchange for a diamond she swears she gave him at dinner. He refuses and, rather than lose her ring, the woman goes to tell Adriana that her husband has become insane. Adriana, with Luciana and the courtezan, brings Dr. Pinch, a conjuror, to expel the evil spirit from her husband who beats the doctor but is overpowered and led away, after Adriana pays the fee, to be locked up in his own house. On the way to his ship with Dromio, Antipholus of Syracuse meets Angelo who points out the gold chain the Syracusian is wearing. A quarrel ensues during which Adriana and Luciana reappear, and the harassed man and slave flee for protection to a near-by priory where the Lady Abbess staunchly refuses to surrender them. Adriana appeals to the Duke who is passing by with the bare-headed old Ægeon, the headsman and officers, to the place of execution, and Antipholus of Ephesus, who with his slave has escaped from confinement, presents his case to the Duke for justice.

Charge and countercharge result in still more confusion, in the midst of which the Lady Abbess appears with Antipholus and Dromio of Syracuse who recognize Ægeon, as also does the Abbess who is his own wife Æmilia. The Duke gladly releases the overjoyed old man, as the two pairs of twin brothers embrace. Antipholus of Ephesus is reconciled with his wife, and his brother proceeds happily to court the fair Luciana.

HISTORICAL DATA

The subject of the main plot of *The Comedy of Errors*, Shakespeare's only farce, is similar to that of the *Menaechmi* of Plautus, a comedy of the mistakes in identity of twin-born children. The theme, long popular with Italian and French dramatists, seems to have had its earliest appearance in England in the interlude *Jack Juggler* (1563), a play, however, which was probably unfamiliar to Shakespeare.

Authorities are uncertain as to whether or not he was acquainted with the earliest translation of the *Menaechmi* by William Warner (1595) in manuscript form or whether he derived his plot from some earlier non-extant comedies from the same source, one of which, *The Historie of Error*, is known to have been acted in Hampton Court in 1576.

The scene in which Antipholus of Ephesus is shut out of his own house (Act III, Scene i) was probably derived from the *Amphitruo* of Plautus, as well as the notion of "doubling" the slaves as well as the masters. The entire serious background and the element of pathos is credited wholly to Shakespeare.

A play called *The Comedy of Errors* was performed at Gray's Inn on December 28, 1594, and there seems no reason to doubt that it was Shakespeare's play. It was included in *Palladis Tamia* (1598) and first published in the First Folio of 1623. From an allusion to the civil war in France (Act II, Scene ii), and from its general style the play is usually considered to have been written in 1591 or slightly earlier.

"Who talks within there? ho! open the door."
THE COMEDY OF ERRORS

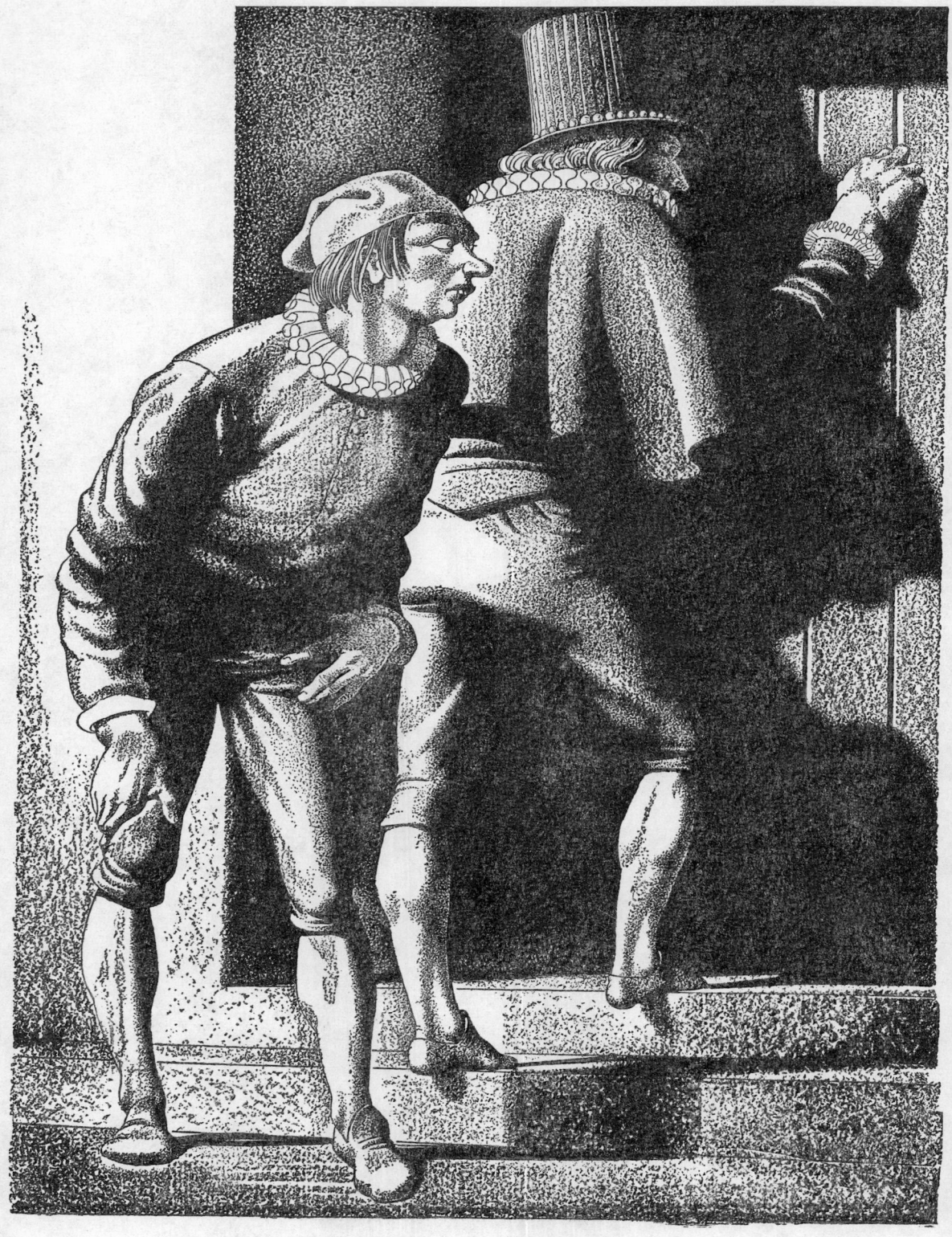

THE COMEDY OF ERRORS

DRAMATIS PERSONÆ

SOLINUS, *duke of Ephesus.*
ÆGEON, *a merchant of Syracuse.*
ANTIPHOLUS OF EPHESUS, } *twin brothers, and sons*
ANTIPHOLUS OF SYRACUSE, } *to Ægeon and Æmilia.*
DROMIO OF EPHESUS, } *twin brothers, and attendants*
DROMIO OF SYRACUSE, } *on the two Antipholuses.*
BALTHAZAR, *a merchant.*
ANGELO, *a goldsmith.*
FIRST MERCHANT, *friend to Antipholus of Syracuse.*
SECOND MERCHANT, *to whom Angelo is a debtor.*

PINCH, *a schoolmaster.*

ÆMILIA, *wife to Ægeon, an abbess at Ephesus.*
ADRIANA, *wife to Antipholus of Ephesus.*
LUCIANA, *her sister.*
LUCE, *servant to Adriana.*
A COURTEZAN.

GAOLER, OFFICERS, *and other* ATTENDANTS

SCENE—*Ephesus.*

ACT I

SCENE I. *A hall in the* DUKE'S *palace*

Enter DUKE, ÆGEON, GAOLER, OFFICERS, *and other*
ATTENDANTS

ÆGEON

Proceed, Solinus, to procure my fall,
And by the doom of death end woes and all.

DUKE

Merchant of Syracusa, plead no more;
I am not partial to infringe our laws:
The enmity and discord which of late
Sprung from the rancorous outrage of your duke
To merchants, our well-dealing countrymen,
Who, wanting guilders to redeem their lives,
Have seal'd his rigorous statutes with their bloods,
Excludes all pity from our threatening looks.
For, since the mortal and intestine jars
'Twixt thy seditious countrymen and us,
It hath in solemn synods been decreed,
Both by the Syracusians and ourselves,
To admit no traffic to our adverse towns:
Nay, more,
If any born at Ephesus be seen
At any Syracusian marts and fairs;
Again: if any Syracusian born
Come to the bay of Ephesus, he dies,
His goods confiscate to the duke's dispose;
Unless a thousand marks be levied,
To quit the penalty and to ransom him.
Thy substance, valued at the highest rate,
Cannot amount unto a hundred marks;
Therefore by law thou art condemn'd to die.

ÆGEON

Yet this my comfort: when your words are done,
My woes end likewise with the evening sun.

DUKE

Well, Syracusian, say, in brief, the cause
Why thou departed'st from thy native home,
And for what cause thou camest to Ephesus.

ÆGEON

A heavier task could not have been imposed

Than I to speak my griefs unspeakable:
Yet, that the world may witness that my end
Was wrought by nature, not by vile offence,
I'll utter what my sorrow gives me leave.
In Syracusa was I born; and wed
Unto a woman, happy but for me,
And by me, had not our hap been bad.
With her I lived in joy; our wealth increased
By prosperous voyages I often made
To Epidamnum; till my factor's death,
And the great care of goods at random left,
Drew me from kind embracements of my spouse:
From whom my absence was not six months old,
Before herself, almost at fainting under
The pleasing punishment that women bear,
Had made provision for her following me,
And soon and safe arrived where I was.
There had she not been long but she became
A joyful mother of two goodly sons;
And, which was strange, the one so like the other
As could not be distinguish'd but by names.
That very hour, and in the self-same inn,
A meaner woman was delivered
Of such a burthen, male twins, both alike:
Those, for their parents were exceeding poor,
I bought, and brought up to attend my sons.
My wife, not meanly proud of two such boys,
Made daily motions for our home return:
Unwilling I agreed; alas! too soon
We came aboard.
A league from Epidamnum had we sail'd,
Before the always-wind-obeying deep
Gave any tragic instance of our harm:
But longer did we not retain much hope;
For what obscured light the heavens did grant
Did but convey unto our fearful minds
A doubtful warrant of immediate death;
Which though myself would gladly have embraced,
Yet the incessant weepings of my wife,
Weeping before for what she saw must come,
And piteous plainings of the pretty babes,
That mourn'd for fashion, ignorant what to fear,

Forced me to seek delays for them and me.
And this it was, for other means was none:
The sailors sought for safety by our boat,
And left the ship, then sinking-ripe, to us:
My wife, more careful for the latter-born,
Had fasten'd him unto a small spare mast,
Such as seafaring men provide for storms;
To him one of the other twins was bound,
Whilst I had been like heedful of the other:
The children thus disposed, my wife and I,
Fixing our eyes on whom our care was fix'd,
Fasten'd ourselves at either end the mast;
And floating straight, obedient to the stream,
Was carried towards Corinth, as we thought.
At length the sun, gazing upon the earth,
Dispersed those vapours that offended us;
And, by the benefit of his wished light,
The seas wax'd calm, and we discovered
Two ships from far making amain to us,
Of Corinth that, of Epidaurus this:
But ere they came,—O, let me say no more!
Gather the sequel by that went before.

DUKE

Nay, forward, old man; do not break off so;
For we may pity, though not pardon thee.

ÆGEON

O, had the gods done so, I had not now
Worthily term'd them merciless to us!
For, ere the ships could meet by twice five leagues,
We were encounter'd by a mighty rock;
Which being violently borne upon,
Our helpful ship was splitted in the midst;
So that, in this unjust divorce of us,
Fortune had left to both of us alike
What to delight in, what to sorrow for.
Her part, poor soul! seeming as burdened
With lesser weight, but not with lesser woe,
Was carried with more speed before the wind;
And in our sight they three were taken up
By fishermen of Corinth, as we thought.
At length, another ship had seized on us;
And, knowing whom it was their hap to save,
Gave healthful welcome to their shipwreck'd guests;
And would have reft the fishers of their prey,
Had not their bark been very slow of sail;
And therefore homeward did they bend their course.
Thus have you heard me sever'd from my bliss;
That by misfortunes was my life prolong'd,
To tell sad stories of my own mishaps.

DUKE

And, for the sake of them thou sorrowest for,
Do me the favour to dilate at full
What hath befall'n of them and thee till now.

ÆGEON

My youngest boy, and yet my eldest care,
At eighteen years became inquisitive
After his brother: and importuned me
That his attendant—so his case was like,
Reft of his brother, but retain'd his name—
Might bear him company in the quest of him:

Whom whilst I labour'd of a love to see,
I hazarded the loss of whom I loved.
Five summers have I spent in farthest Greece,
Roaming clean through the bounds of Asia,
And, coasting homeward, came to Ephesus;
Hopeless to find, yet loath to leave unsought
Or that, or any place that harbours men.
But here must end the story of my life;
And happy were I in my timely death,
Could all my travels warrant me they live.

DUKE

Hapless Ægeon, whom the fates have mark'd
To bear the extremity of dire mishap!
Now, trust me, were it not against our laws,
Against my crown, my oath, my dignity,
Which princes, would they, may not disannul,
My soul should sue as advocate for thee.
But, though thou art adjudged to the death,
And passed sentence may not be recall'd
But to our honour's great disparagement,
Yet will I favour thee in what I can.
Therefore, merchant, I'll limit thee this day
To seek thy help by beneficial help:
Try all the friends thou hast in Ephesus;
Beg thou, or borrow, to make up the sum,
And live; if no, then thou art doom'd to die.
Gaoler, take him to thy custody.

GAOLER

I will, my lord.

ÆGEON

Hopeless and helpless doth Ægeon wend,
But to procrastinate his lifeless end.   [Exeunt

SCENE II. The Mart

Enter ANTIPHOLUS OF SYRACUSE, DROMIO OF SYRACUSE,
and FIRST MERCHANT

FIRST MERCHANT

Therefore give out you are of Epidamnum,
Lest that your goods too soon be confiscate.
This very day a Syracusian merchant
Is apprehended for arrival here;
And, not being able to buy out his life,
According to the statute of the town,
Dies ere the weary sun set in the west.
There is your money that I had to keep.

ANTIPHOLUS S.

Go bear it to the Centaur, where we host,
And stay there, Dromio, till I come to thee.
Within this hour it will be dinner-time:
Till that, I'll view the manners of the town,
Peruse the traders, gaze upon the buildings,
And then return, and sleep within mine inn;
For with long travel I am stiff and weary.
Get thee away.

DROMIO S.

Many a man would take you at your word,
And go indeed, having so good a mean.   [Exit

ANTIPHOLUS S.

A trusty villain, sir; that very oft,
When I am dull with care and melancholy,
Lightens my humour with his merry jests.
What, will you walk with me about the town,
And then go to my inn, and dine with me?

FIRST MERCHANT

I am invited, sir, to certain merchants,
Of whom I hope to make much benefit;
I crave your pardon. Soon at five o'clock,
Please you, I'll meet with you upon the mart,
And afterward consort you till bed-time:
My present business calls me from you now.

ANTIPHOLUS S.

Farewell till then: I will go lose myself,
And wander up and down to view the city.

FIRST MERCHANT

Sir, I commend you to your own content.   [*Exit*

ANTIPHOLUS S.

He that commends me to mine own content
Commends me to the thing I cannot get.
I to the world am like a drop of water,
That in the ocean seeks another drop;
Who, falling there to find his fellow forth,
Unseen, inquisitive, confounds himself:
So I, to find a mother and a brother,
In quest of them, unhappy, lose myself.

Enter DROMIO OF EPHESUS

Here comes the almanac of my true date.
What now? how chance thou art return'd so soon?

DROMIO E.

Return'd so soon! rather approach'd too late:
The capon burns, the pig falls from the spit;
The clock hath strucken twelve upon the bell;
My mistress made it one upon my cheek:
She is so hot, because the meat is cold;
The meat is cold, because you come not home;
You come not home, because you have no stomach;
You have no stomach, having broke your fast;
But we, that know what 'tis to fast and pray,
Are penitent for your default to-day.

ANTIPHOLUS S.

Stop in your wind, sir: tell me this, I pray:
Where have you left the money that I gave you?

DROMIO E.

O,—sixpence, that I had o' Wednesday last
To pay the saddler for my mistress' crupper?
The saddler had it, sir; I kept it not.

ANTIPHOLUS S.

I am not in a sportive humour now:
Tell me, and dally not, where is the money?
We being strangers here, how darest thou trust
So great a charge from thine own custody?

DROMIO E.

I pray you, jest, sir, as you sit at dinner:
I from my mistress come to you in post;
If I return, I shall be post indeed,
For she will score your fault upon my pate.
Methinks your maw, like mine, should be your clock,
And strike you home without a messenger.

ANTIPHOLUS S.

Come, Dromio, come, these jests are out of season;
Reserve them till a merrier hour than this.
Where is the gold I gave in charge to thee?

DROMIO E.

To me, sir? why, you gave no gold to me.

ANTIPHOLUS S.

Come on, sir knave, have done your foolishness,
And tell me how thou hast disposed thy charge.

DROMIO E.

My charge was but to fetch you from the mart
Home to your house, the Phœnix, sir, to dinner:
My mistress and her sister stays for you.

ANTIPHOLUS S.

Now, as I am a Christian, answer me,
In what safe place you have bestow'd my money;
Or I shall break that merry sconce of yours,
That stands on tricks when I am undisposed:
Where is the thousand marks thou had'st of me?

DROMIO E.

I have some marks of yours upon my pate,
Some of my mistress' marks upon my shoulders;
But not a thousand marks between you both.
If I should pay your worship those again,
Perchance you will not bear them patiently.

ANTIPHOLUS S.

Thy mistress' marks? what mistress, slave, hast thou?

DROMIO E.

Your worship's wife, my mistress at the Phœnix;
She that doth fast till you come home to dinner,
And prays that you will hie you home to dinner.

ANTIPHOLUS S.

What, wilt thou flout me thus unto my face,
Being forbid? There, take you that, sir knave.

DROMIO E.

What mean you, sir? for God's sake, hold your hands!
Nay, an you will not, sir, I'll take my heels.   [*Exit*

ANTIPHOLUS S.

Upon my life, by some device or other
The villain is o'er-raught of all my money.
They say this town is full of cozenage;
As, nimble jugglers that deceive the eye,
Dark-working sorcerers that change the mind,
Soul-killing witches that deform the body,
Disguised cheaters, prating mountebanks,
And many such-like liberties of sin:
If it prove so, I will be gone the sooner.
I'll to the Centaur, to go seek this slave:
I greatly fear my money is not safe.   [*Exit*

ACT II

SCENE I. *The house of* ANTIPHOLUS E.

Enter ADRIANA *and* LUCIANA

ADRIANA

Neither my husband nor the slave return'd,
That in such haste I sent to seek his master!
Sure, Luciana, it is two o'clock.

LUCIANA

Perhaps some merchant hath invited him,
And from the mart he's somewhere gone to dinner.
Good sister, let us dine, and never fret:
A man is master of his liberty:
Time is their master; and when they see time,
They'll go or come: if so, be patient, sister.

ADRIANA

Why should their liberty than ours be more?

LUCIANA

Because their business still lies out o' door.

ADRIANA

Look, when I serve him so, he takes it ill.

LUCIANA

O, know he is the bridle of your will.

ADRIANA

There's none but asses will be bridled so.

LUCIANA

Why, headstrong liberty is lash'd with woe.
There's nothing situate under heaven's eye
But hath his bound, in earth, in sea, in sky:
The beasts, the fishes, and the winged fowls,
Are their males' subjects and at their controls:
Men more divine, the masters of all these,
Lords of the wide world and wild watery seas,
Indued with intellectual sense and souls,
Or more pre-eminence than fish and fowls,
Are masters to their females, and their lords:
Then let your will attend on their accords.

ADRIANA

This servitude makes you to keep unwed.

LUCIANA

Not this, but troubles of the marriage-bed.

ADRIANA

But, were you wedded, you would bear some sway.

LUCIANA

Ere I learn love, I'll practise to obey.

ADRIANA

How if your husband start some other where?

LUCIANA

Till he come home again, I would forbear.

ADRIANA

Patience unmoved! no marvel though she pause;
They can be meek that have no other cause.
A wretched soul, bruised with adversity,
We bid be quiet when we hear it cry;
But were we burden'd with like weight of pain,
As much, or more, we should ourselves complain:
So thou, that hast no unkind mate to grieve thee,
With urging helpless patience wouldst relieve me;
But, if thou live to see like right bereft,
This fool-begg'd patience in thee will be left.

LUCIANA

Well, I will marry one day, but to try.
Here comes your man; now is your husband nigh.

Enter DROMIO E.

ADRIANA

Say, is your tardy master now at hand?

DROMIO E.

Nay, he's at two hands with me, and that my two
ears can witness.

ADRIANA

Say, didst thou speak with him? know'st thou his
mind?

DROMIO E.

Ay, ay, he told his mind upon mine ear:
Beshrew his hand, I scarce could understand it.

LUCIANA

Spake he so doubtfully, thou couldst not feel his
meaning?

DROMIO E.

Nay, he struck so plainly, I could too well feel his
blows; and withal so doubtfully, that I could scarce
understand them.

ADRIANA

But say, I prithee, is he coming home?
It seems he hath great care to please his wife.

DROMIO E.

Why, mistress, sure my master is horn-mad.

ADRIANA

Horn-mad, thou villain!

DROMIO E.

                              I mean not cuckold-mad;
But, sure, he is stark mad.
When I desired him to come home to dinner,
He ask'd me for a thousand marks in gold:
''Tis dinner-time,' quoth I; 'My gold!' quoth he:
'Your meat doth burn,' quoth I; 'My gold!' quoth
  he:
'Will you come home?' quoth I; 'My gold!' quoth he,
'Where is the thousand marks I gave thee, villain?'
'The pig,' quoth I, 'is burn'd;' 'My gold!' quoth he:
'My mistress, sir,' quoth I; 'Hang up thy mistress!
I know not thy mistress; out on thy mistress!'

LUCIANA

Quoth who?

DROMIO E.

Quoth my master:
'I know,' quoth he, 'no house, no wife, no mistress.'
So that my errand, due unto my tongue,
I thank him, I bare home upon my shoulders;
For, in conclusion, he did beat me there.

ADRIANA

Go back again, thou slave, and fetch him home.

DROMIO E.

Go back again, and be new beaten home?
For God's sake, send some other messenger.

ADRIANA

Back, slave, or I will break thy pate across.

DROMIO E.

And he will bless that cross with other beating:
Between you I shall have a holy head.

ADRIANA

Hence, prating peasant! fetch thy master home.

DROMIO E.

Am I so round with you as you with me,
That like a football you do spurn me thus?

You spurn me hence, and he will spurn me hither:
If I last in this service, you must case me in leather.
                                                    [Exit

LUCIANA

Fie, how impatience loureth in your face!

ADRIANA

His company must do his minions grace,
Whilst I at home starve for a merry look.
Hath homely age the alluring beauty took
From my poor cheek? then he hath wasted it:
Are my discourses dull? barren my wit?
If voluble and sharp discourse be marr'd,
Unkindness blunts it more than marble hard:
Do their gay vestments his affections bait?
That's not my fault; he's master of my state:
What ruins are in me that can be found,
By him not ruin'd? then is he the ground
Of my defeatures. My decayed fair
A sunny look of his would soon repair:
But, too unruly deer, he breaks the pale,
And feeds from home; poor I am but his stale.

LUCIANA

Self-harming jealousy! fie, beat it hence!

ADRIANA

Unfeeling fools can with such wrongs dispense.
I know his eye doth homage otherwhere;
Or else what lets it but he would be here?
Sister, you know he promised me a chain;
Would that alone, alone he would detain,
So he would keep fair quarter with his bed!
I see the jewel best enamelled
Will lose his beauty; yet the gold bides still,
That others touch, and often touching will
Wear gold: and no man that hath a name,
By falsehood and corruption doth it shame.
Since that my beauty cannot please his eye,
I'll weep what's left away, and weeping die.

LUCIANA

How many fond fools serve mad jealousy!   *[Exeunt*

SCENE II. *A public place*

Enter ANTIPHOLUS S.

ANTIPHOLUS S.

The gold I gave to Dromio is laid up
Safe at the Centaur; and the heedful slave
Is wander'd forth, in care to seek me out
By computation and mine host's report.
I could not speak with Dromio since at first
I sent him from the mart. See, here he comes.

Enter DROMIO S.

How now, sir! is your merry humour alter'd?
As you love strokes, so jest with me again.
You know no Centaur? you received no gold?
Your mistress sent to have me home to dinner?
My house was at the Phœnix? Wast thou mad,
That thus so madly thou didst answer me?

DROMIO S.

What answer, sir? when spake I such a word?

ANTIPHOLUS S.

Even now, even here, not half an hour since.

DROMIO S.

I did not see you since you sent me hence,
Home to the Centaur, with the gold you gave me.

ANTIPHOLUS S.

Villain, thou didst deny the gold's receipt,
And told'st me of a mistress and a dinner;
For which, I hope, thou felt'st I was displeased.

DROMIO S.

I am glad to see you in this merry vein:
What means this jest? I pray you, master, tell me.

ANTIPHOLUS S.

Yea, dost thou jeer and flout me in the teeth?
Think'st thou I jest? Hold, take thou that, and that.
                                      [Beating him

DROMIO S.

Hold, sir, for God's sake! now your jest is earnest:
Upon what bargain do you give it me?

ANTIPHOLUS S.

Because that I familiarly sometimes
Do use you for my fool, and chat with you,
Your sauciness will jest upon my love,
And make a common of my serious hours.
When the sun shines let foolish gnats make sport,
But creep in crannies when he hides his beams.
If you will jest with me, know my aspect,
And fashion your demeanour to my looks,
Or I will beat this method in your sconce.

DROMIO S.

Sconce call you it? so you would leave battering, I
had rather have it a head: an you use these blows
long, I must get a sconce for my head, and insconce
it too; or else I shall seek my wit in my shoulders.
But, I pray, sir, why am I beaten?

ANTIPHOLUS S.

Dost thou not know?

DROMIO S.

Nothing, sir, but that I am beaten.

ANTIPHOLUS S.

Shall I tell you why?

DROMIO S.

Ay, sir, and wherefore; for they say every why hath
a wherefore.

ANTIPHOLUS S.

Why, first,—for flouting me; and then, wherefore,—
For urging it the second time to me.

DROMIO S.

Was there ever any man thus beaten out of season,
When in the why and the wherefore is neither
   rhyme nor reason?
Well, sir, I thank you.

ANTIPHOLUS S.

Thank me, sir! for what?

DROMIO S.

Marry, sir, for this something that you gave me for
nothing.

ANTIPHOLUS S.

I'll make you amends next, to give you nothing for
something. But say, sir, is it dinner-time?

DROMIO S.
No, sir: I think the meat wants that I have.

ANTIPHOLUS S.
In good time, sir; what's that?

DROMIO S.
Basting.

ANTIPHOLUS S.
Well, sir, then 'twill be dry.

DROMIO S.
If it be, sir, I pray you, eat none of it.

ANTIPHOLUS S.
Your reason?

DROMIO S.
Lest it make you choleric, and purchase me another dry basting.

ANTIPHOLUS S.
Well, sir, learn to jest in good time: there's a time for all things.

DROMIO S.
I durst have denied that, before you were so choleric.

ANTIPHOLUS S.
By what rule, sir?

DROMIO S.
Marry, sir, by a rule as plain as the plain bald pate of father Time himself.

ANTIPHOLUS S.
Let's hear it.

DROMIO S.
There's no time for a man to recover his hair that grows bald by nature.

ANTIPHOLUS S.
May he not do it by fine and recovery?

DROMIO S.
Yes, to pay a fine for a periwig, and recover the lost hair of another man.

ANTIPHOLUS S.
Why is Time such a niggard of hair, being, as it is, so plentiful an excrement?

DROMIO S.
Because it is a blessing that he bestows on beasts: and what he hath scanted men in hair, he hath given them in wit.

ANTIPHOLUS S.
Why, but there's many a man hath more hair than wit.

DROMIO S.
Not a man of those but he hath the wit to lose his hair.

ANTIPHOLUS S.
Why, thou didst conclude hairy men plain dealers without wit.

DROMIO S.
The plainer dealer, the sooner lost: yet he loseth it in a kind of jollity.

ANTIPHOLUS S.
For what reason?

DROMIO S.
For two; and sound ones too.

ANTIPHOLUS S.
Nay, not sound, I pray you.

DROMIO S.
Sure ones, then.

ANTIPHOLUS S.
Nay, not sure, in a thing falsing.

DROMIO S.
Certain ones, then.

ANTIPHOLUS S.
Name them.

DROMIO S.
The one, to save the money that he spends in tiring; the other, that at dinner they should not drop in his porridge.

ANTIPHOLUS S.
You would all this time have proved there is no time for all things.

DROMIO S.
Marry, and I did, sir; namely, no time to recover hair lost by nature.

ANTIPHOLUS S.
But your reason was not substantial, why there is no time to recover.

DROMIO S.
Thus I mend it: Time himself is bald, and therefore to the world's end will have bald followers.

ANTIPHOLUS S.
I knew 'twould be a bald conclusion:
But, soft! who wafts us yonder?

Enter ADRIANA *and* LUCIANA

ADRIANA
Ay, ay, Antipholus, look strange and frown:
Some other mistress hath thy sweet aspects;
I am not Adriana nor thy wife.
The time was once when thou unurged wouldst vow
That never words were music to thine ear,
That never object pleasing in thine eye,
That never touch well welcome to thy hand,
That never meat sweet-savour'd in thy taste,
Unless I spake, or look'd, or touch'd, or carved to thee.
How comes it now, my husband, O, how comes it,
That thou art then estranged from thyself?
Thyself I call it, being strange to me,
That, undividable, incorporate,
Am better than thy dear selfs better part.
Ah, do not tear away thyself from me!
For know, my love, as easy mayst thou fall
A drop of water in the breaking gulf,
And take unmingled thence that drop again,
Without addition or diminishing,
As take from me thyself, and not me too.
How dearly would it touch thee to the quick,
Shouldst thou but hear I were licentious,
And that this body, consecrate to thee,
By ruffian lust should be contaminate!
Wouldst thou not spit at me and spurn at me,
And hurl the name of husband in my face,
And tear the stain'd skin off my harlot-brow,
And from my false hand cut the wedding-ring,
And break it with a deep-divorcing vow?
I know thou canst; and therefore see thou do it.

I am possess'd with an adulterate blot;
My blood is mingled with the crime of lust:
For if we two be one, and thou play false,
I do digest the poison of thy flesh,
Being strumpeted by thy contagion.
Keep, then, fair league and truce with thy true bed;
I live distain'd, thou undishonoured.

ANTIPHOLUS S.
Plead you to me, fair dame? I know you not:
In Ephesus I am but two hours old,
As strange unto your town as to your talk;
Who, every word by all my wit being scann'd,
Wants wit in all one word to understand.

LUCIANA
Fie, brother! how the world is changed with you!
When were you wont to use my sister thus?
She sent for you by Dromio home to dinner.

ANTIPHOLUS S.
By Dromio?

DROMIO S.
By me?

ADRIANA
By thee; and this thou didst return from him,
That he did buffet thee, and, in his blows,
Denied my house for his, me for his wife.

ANTIPHOLUS S.
Did you converse, sir, with this gentlewoman?
What is the course and drift of your compact?

DROMIO S.
I, sir? I never saw her till this time.

ANTIPHOLUS S.
Villain, thou liest; for even her very words
Didst thou deliver to me on the mart.

DROMIO S.
I never spake with her in all my life.

ANTIPHOLUS S.
How can she thus then call us by our names?
Unless it be by inspiration.

ADRIANA
How ill agrees it with your gravity
To counterfeit thus grossly with your slave,
Abetting him to thwart me in my mood!
Be it my wrong you are from me exempt,
But wrong not that wrong with a more contempt.
Come, I will fasten on this sleeve of thine:
Thou art an elm, my husband, I a vine,
Whose weakness, married to thy stronger state,
Makes me with thy strength to communicate:
If aught possess thee from me, it is dross,
Usurping ivy, brier, or idle moss;
Who, all for want of pruning, with intrusion
Infect thy sap, and live on thy confusion.

ANTIPHOLUS S.
To me she speaks; she moves me for her theme:
What, was I married to her in my dream?
Or sleep I now, and think I hear all this?
What error drives our eyes and ears amiss?
Until I know this sure uncertainty,
I'll entertain the offer'd fallacy.

LUCIANA
Dromio, go bid the servants spread for dinner.

DROMIO S.
O, for my beads! I cross me for a sinner.
This is the fairy land: O spite of spites!
We talk with goblins, owls, and sprites:
If we obey them not, this will ensue,
They'll suck our breath, or pinch us black and blue.

LUCIANA
Why pratest thou to thyself, and answer'st not?
Dromio, thou drone, thou snail, thou slug, thou sot!

DROMIO S.
I am transformed, master, am not I?

ANTIPHOLUS S.
I think thou art in mind, and so am I.

DROMIO S.
Nay, master, both in mind and in my shape.

ANTIPHOLUS S.
Thou hast thine own form.

DROMIO S.
                    No, I am an ape.

LUCIANA
If thou art changed to aught, 'tis to an ass.

DROMIO S.
'Tis true; she rides me, and I long for grass.
'Tis so, I am an ass; else it could never be
But I should know her as well as she knows me.

ADRIANA
Come, come, no longer will I be a fool,
To put the finger in the eye and weep,
Whilst man and master laughs my woes to scorn.
Come, sir, to dinner. Dromio, keep the gate.
Husband, I'll dine above with you to-day,
And shrive you of a thousand idle pranks.
Sirrah, if any ask you for your master,
Say he dines forth, and let no creature enter.
Come, sister. Dromio, play the porter well.

ANTIPHOLUS S.
Am I in earth, in heaven, or in hell?
Sleeping or waking? mad or well-advised?
Known unto these, and to myself disguised!
I'll say as they say, and persever so,
And in this mist at all adventures go.

DROMIO S.
Master, shall I be porter at the gate?

ADRIANA
Ay; and let none enter, lest I break your pate.

LUCIANA
Come, come, Antipholus, we dine too late. [*Exeunt*

ACT III

SCENE I. *Before the house of* ANTIPHOLUS E.

Enter ANTIPHOLUS E., DROMIO E., ANGELO,
and BALTHAZAR

ANTIPHOLUS E.
Good Signior Angelo, you must excuse us all;

My wife is shrewish when I keep not hours:
Say that I linger'd with you at your shop
To see the making of her carcanet,
And that to-morrow you will bring it home.
But here's a villain that would face me down
He met me on the mart, and that I beat him,
And charged him with a thousand marks in gold,
And that I did deny my wife and house.
Thou drunkard, thou, what didst thou mean by
   this?

DROMIO E.

Say what you will, sir, but I know what I know;
That you beat me at the mart, I have your hand to
   show:
If the skin were parchment, and the blows you gave
   were ink,
Your own handwriting would tell you what I think.

ANTIPHOLUS E.

I think thou art an ass.

DROMIO E.

        Marry, so it doth appear
By the wrongs I suffer, and the blows I bear.
I should kick, being kick'd; and, being at that pass,
You would keep from my heels, and beware of an
   ass.

ANTIPHOLUS E.

You're sad, Signior Balthazar: pray God our cheer
May answer my good will and your good welcome
   here.

BALTHAZAR

I hold your dainties cheap, sir, and your welcome
   dear.

ANTIPHOLUS E.

O, Signior Balthazar, either at flesh or fish,
A table full of welcome makes scarce one dainty
   dish.

BALTHAZAR

Good meat, sir, is common: that every churl affords.

ANTIPHOLUS E.

And welcome more common; for that's nothing but
   words.

BALTHAZAR

Small cheer and great welcome makes a merry
   feast.

ANTIPHOLUS E.

Ay, to a niggardly host and more sparing guest:
But though my cates be mean, take them in good
   part;
Better cheer may you have, but not with better
   heart.
But, soft! my door is lock'd.—Go bid them let us in.

DROMIO E.

Maud, Bridget, Marian, Cicely, Gillian, Ginn!

DROMIO S.

[Within] Mome, malt-horse, capon, coxcomb, idiot,
   patch!
Either get thee from the door, or sit down at the
   hatch.

Dost thou conjure for wenches, that thou call'st for
   such store,
When one is too many? Go get thee from the
   door.

DROMIO E.

What patch is made our porter? My master stays in
   the street.

DROMIO S.

[Within] Let him walk from whence he came, lest
   he catch cold on's feet.

ANTIPHOLUS E.

Who talks within there? ho, open the door!

DROMIO S.

[Within] Right, sir; I'll tell you when, an you'll tell
   me wherefore.

ANTIPHOLUS E.

Wherefore? for my dinner: I have not dined to-day.

DROMIO S.

[Within] Nor to-day here you must not; come again
   when you may.

ANTIPHOLUS E.

What art thou that keepest me out from the house I
   owe?

DROMIO S.

[Within] The porter for this time, sir, and my name
   is Dromio.

DROMIO E.

O villain, thou hast stolen both mine office and my
   name!
The one ne'er got me credit, the other mickle blame.
If thou hadst been Dromio to-day in my place,
Thou wouldst have changed thy face for a name, or
   thy name for an ass.

LUCE

[Within] What a coil is there, Dromio? Who are
   those at the gate!

DROMIO E.

Let my master in, Luce.

LUCE

       [Within] 'Faith, no; he comes too late;
And so tell your master.

DROMIO E.

       O Lord, I must laugh!
Have at you with a proverb;—Shall I set in my
   staff?

LUCE

[Within] Have at you with another; that's,—When?
   can you tell?

DROMIO S.

[Within] If thy name be call'd Luce,—Luce, thou
   hast answer'd him well.

ANTIPHOLUS E.

Do you hear, you minion? you'll let us in, I hope?

LUCE

[Within] I thought to have ask'd you.

DROMIO S.

       [Within] And you said no.

DROMIO E.

So, come, help: well struck! there was blow for blow.

ANTIPHOLUS E.

Thou baggage, let me in.

LUCE

[*Within*] Can you tell for whose sake?

DROMIO E.

Master, knock the door hard.

LUCE

[*Within*] Let him knock till it ache.

ANTIPHOLUS E.

You'll cry for this, minion, if I beat the door down.

LUCE

[*Within*] What needs all that, and a pair of stocks in the town?

ADRIANA

[*Within*] Who is that at the door that keeps all this noise?

DROMIO S.

[*Within*] By my troth, your town is troubled with unruly boys.

ANTIPHOLUS E.

Are you there, wife? you might have come before.

ADRIANA

[*Within*] Your wife, sir knave! go get you from the door.

DROMIO E.

If you went in pain, master, this 'knave' would go sore.

ANGELO

Here is neither cheer, sir, nor welcome: we would fain have either.

BALTHAZAR

In debating which was best, we shall part with neither.

DROMIO E.

They stand at the door, master; bid them welcome hither.

ANTIPHOLUS E.

There is something in the wind, that we cannot get in.

DROMIO E.

You would say so, master, if your garments were thin.

Your cake here is warm within; you stand here in the cold:

It would make a man mad as a buck, to be so bought and sold.

ANTIPHOLUS E.

Go fetch me something: I'll break ope the gate.

DROMIO S.

[*Within*] Break any breaking here, and I'll break your knave's pate.

DROMIO E.

A man may break a word with you, sir; and words are but wind;

Ay, and break it in your face, so he break it not behind.

DROMIO S.

[*Within*] It seems thou want'st breaking: out upon thee, hind!

DROMIO E.

Here's too much 'out upon thee!' I pray thee, let me in.

DROMIO S.

[*Within*] Ay, when fowls have no feathers, and fish have no fin.

ANTIPHOLUS E.

Well, I'll break in: go borrow me a crow.

DROMIO E.

A crow without feather? Master, mean you so?

For a fish without a fin, there's a fowl without a feather:

If a crow help us in, sirrah, we'll pluck a crow together.

ANTIPHOLUS E.

Go get thee gone; fetch me an iron crow.

BALTHAZAR

Have patience, sir: O, let it not be so!

Herein you war against your reputation,

And draw within the compass of suspect

The unviolated honour of your wife.

Once this,—your long experience of her wisdom,

Her sober virtue, years, and modesty,

Plead on her part some cause to you unknown;

And doubt not, sir, but she will well excuse

Why at this time the doors are made against you.

Be ruled by me: depart in patience,

And let us to the Tiger all to dinner;

And about evening come yourself alone

To know the reason of this strange restraint.

If by strong hand you offer to break in

Now in the stirring passage of the day,

A vulgar comment will be made of it,

And that supposed by the common rout

Against your yet ungalled estimation,

That may with foul intrusion enter in,

And dwell upon your grave when you are dead;

For slander lives upon succession,

For ever housed where it gets possession.

ANTIPHOLUS E.

You have prevail'd: I will depart in quiet,

And, in despite of mirth, mean to be merry.

I know a wench of excellent discourse,

Pretty and witty; wild, and yet, too, gentle:

There will we dine. This woman that I mean,

My wife—but, I protest, without desert—

Hath oftentimes upbraided me withal:

To her will we to dinner. [*To* ANGELO] Get you home,

And fetch the chain; by this I know 'tis made:

Bring it, I pray you, to the Porpentine;

For there's the house: that chain will I bestow—

Be it for nothing but to spite my wife—

Upon mine hostess there: good sir, make haste.

Since mine own doors refuse to entertain me,

I'll knock elsewhere, to see if they'll disdain me.

ANGELO

I'll meet you at that place some hour hence.

ANTIPHOLUS E.

Do so. This jest shall cost me some expense. [*Exeunt*

SCENE II. *The same*

Enter LUCIANA, *with* ANTIPHOLUS S.

LUCIANA

And may it be that you have quite forgot
A husband's office? shall, Antipholus,
Even in the spring of love, thy love-springs rot?
    Shall love, in building, grow so ruinous?
If you did wed my sister for her wealth,
    Then for her wealth's sake use her with more
        kindness:
Or if you like elsewhere, do it by stealth;
    Muffle your false love with some show of blind-
        ness:
Let not my sister read it in your eye;
    Be not thy tongue thy own shame's orator;
Look sweet, speak fair, become disloyalty;
    Apparel vice like virtue's harbinger;
Bear a fair presence, though your heart be tainted;
    Teach sin the carriage of a holy saint;
Be secret-false: what need she be acquainted?
    What simple thief brags of his own attaint?
'Tis double wrong, to truant with your bed,
    And let her read it in thy looks at board:
Shame hath a bastard fame, well managed;
    Ill deeds are doubled with an evil word.
Alas, poor women! make us but believe,
    Being compact of credit, that you love us;
Though others have the arm, show us the sleeve;
    We in your motion turn, and you may move us.
Then, gentle brother, get you in again;
    Comfort my sister, cheer her, call her wife
'Tis holy sport, to be a little vain,
    When the sweet breath of flattery conquers strife.

ANTIPHOLUS S.

Sweet mistress,—what your name is else, I know not
    Nor by what wonder you do hit of mine,—
Less in your knowledge and your grace you show
        not
    Than our earth's wonder; more than earth divine.
Teach me, dear creature, how to think and speak;
    Lay open to my earthly-gross conceit,
Smother'd in errors, feeble, shallow, weak,
    The folded meaning of your words' deceit.
Against my soul's pure truth why labour you
    To make it wander in an unknown field?
Are you a god? would you create me new?
    Transform me, then, and to your power I'll yield.
But if that I am I, then well I know
    Your weeping sister is no wife of mine,
Nor to her bed no homage do I owe:
    Far more, far more to you do I decline.
O, train me not, sweet mermaid, with thy note,
    To drown me in thy sister's flood of tears:
Sing, siren, for thyself, and I will dote:
    Spread o'er the silver waves thy golden hairs,
And as a bed I'll take them, and there lie;
    And, in that glorious supposition, think
He gains by death that hath such means to die:
    Let Love, being light, be drowned if she sink!

LUCIANA

What, are you mad, that you do reason so?

ANTIPHOLUS S.

Not mad, but mated; how, I do not know.

LUCIANA

It is a fault that springeth from your eye.

ANTIPHOLUS S.

For gazing on your beams, fair sun, being by.

LUCIANA

Gaze where you should, and that will clear your
    sight.

ANTIPHOLUS S.

As good to wink, sweet love, as look on night.

LUCIANA

Why call you me love? call my sister so.

ANTIPHOLUS S.

Thy sister's sister.

LUCIANA

That's my sister.

ANTIPHOLUS S.

                No;
It is thyself, mine own self's better part,
Mine eye's clear eye, my dear heart's dearer heart,
My food, my fortune, and my sweet hope's aim,
My sole earth's heaven, and my heaven's claim.

LUCIANA

All this my sister is, or else should be.

ANTIPHOLUS S.

Call thyself sister, sweet, for I am thee.
Thee will I love, and with thee lead my life:
Thou hast no husband yet, nor I no wife.
Give me thy hand.

LUCIANA

            O, soft, sir! hold you still:
I'll fetch my sister, to get her good will.   [*Exit*

Enter DROMIO S.

ANTIPHOLUS S.

Why, how now, Dromio! where runn'st thou so fast?

DROMIO S.

Do you know me, sir? am I Dromio? am I your
man? am I myself?

ANTIPHOLUS S.

Thou art Dromio, thou art my man, thou art thyself.

DROMIO S.

I am an ass, I am a woman's man, and besides myself.

ANTIPHOLUS S.

What woman's man? and how besides thyself?

DROMIO S.

Marry, sir, besides myself, I am due to a woman;
one that claims me, one that haunts me, one that
will have me.

ANTIPHOLUS S.

What claim lays she to thee?

DROMIO S.

Marry, sir, such claim as you would lay to your
horse; and she would have me as a beast: not that,
I being a beast, she would have me; but that she,
being a very beastly creature, lays claim to me.

ANTIPHOLUS S.

What is she?

DROMIO S.

A very reverent body; ay, such a one as a man may not speak of, without he say Sir-reverence. I have but lean luck in the match, and yet is she a wondrous fat marriage.

ANTIPHOLUS S.

How dost thou mean a fat marriage?

DROMIO S.

Marry, sir, she's the kitchen-wench, and all grease; and I know not what use to put her to, but to make a lamp of her, and run from her by her own light. I warrant, her rags, and the tallow in them, will burn a Poland winter: if she lives till doomsday, she'll burn a week longer than the whole world.

ANTIPHOLUS S.

What complexion is she of?

DROMIO S.

Swart, like my shoe, but her face nothing like so clean kept: for why she sweats; a man may go over shoes in the grime of it.

ANTIPHOLUS S.

That's a fault that water will mend.

DROMIO S.

No, sir, 'tis in grain; Noah's flood could not do it.

ANTIPHOLUS S.

What's her name?

DROMIO S.

Nell, sir; but her name and three quarters, that's an ell and three quarters, will not measure her from hip to hip.

ANTIPHOLUS S.

Then she bears some breadth?

DROMIO S.

No longer from head to foot than from hip to hip: she is spherical, like a globe; I could find out countries in her.

ANTIPHOLUS S.

In what part of her body stands Ireland?

DROMIO S.

Marry, sir, in her buttocks: I found it out by the bogs.

ANTIPHOLUS S.

Where Scotland?

DROMIO S.

I found it by the barrenness; hard in the palm of the hand.

ANTIPHOLUS S.

Where France?

DROMIO S.

In her forehead; armed and reverted, making war against her heir.

ANTIPHOLUS S.

Where England?

DROMIO S.

I looked for the chalky cliffs, but I could find no whiteness in them; but I guess it stood in her chin, by the salt rheum that ran between France and it.

ANTIPHOLUS S.

Where Spain?

DROMIO S.

'Faith, I saw it not; but I felt it hot in her breath.

ANTIPHOLUS S.

Where America, the Indies?

DROMIO S.

Oh, sir, upon her nose, all o'er embellished with rubies, carbuncles, sapphires, declining their rich aspect to the hot breath of Spain; who sent whole armadoes of caracks to be ballast at her nose.

ANTIPHOLUS S.

Where stood Belgia, the Netherlands?

DROMIO S.

Oh, sir, I did not look so low. To conclude, this drudge, or diviner, laid claim to me; called me Dromio; swore I was assured to her; told me what privy marks I had about me, as, the mark of my shoulder, the mole in my neck, the great wart on my left arm, that I, amazed, ran from her as a witch:

And, I think, if my breast had not been made of faith, and my heart of steel,

She had transform'd me to a curtal dog, and made me turn i' the wheel.

ANTIPHOLUS S.

Go hie thee presently, post to the road:
An if the wind blow any way from shore,
I will not harbour in this town to-night:
If any bark put forth, come to the mart,
Where I will walk till thou return to me.
If every one knows us, and we know none,
'Tis time, I think, to trudge, pack, and be gone.

DROMIO S.

As from a bear a man would run for life,
So fly I from her that would be my wife.   [Exit

ANTIPHOLUS S.

There's none but witches do inhabit here;
And therefore 'tis high time that I were hence.
She that doth call me husband, even my soul
Doth for a wife abhor. But her fair sister,
Possess'd with such a gentle sovereign grace,
Of such enchanting presence and discourse,
Hath almost made me traitor to myself:
But, lest myself be guilty to self-wrong,
I'll stop mine ears against the mermaid's song.

Enter ANGELO *with the chain*

ANGELO

Master Antipholus,—

ANTIPHOLUS S.

Ay, that's my name.

ANGELO

I know it well, sir: lo, here is the chain.
I thought to have ta'en you at the Porpentine:
The chain unfinish'd made me stay thus long.

ANTIPHOLUS S.

What is your will that I shall do with this?

ANGELO

What please yourself, sir: I have made it for you.

ANTIPHOLUS S.

Made it for me sir! I bespoke it not.

ANGELO

Not once, nor twice, but twenty times you have.
Go home with it, and please your wife withal;
And soon at supper-time I'll visit you,
And then receive my money for the chain.

ANTIPHOLUS S.

I pray you, sir, receive the money now,
For fear you ne'er see chain nor money more.

ANGELO

You are a merry man, sir: fare you well.   [*Exit*

ANTIPHOLUS S.

What I should think of this, I cannot tell:
But this I think, there's no man is so vain
That would refuse so fair an offer'd chain.
I see a man here needs not live by shifts,
When in the streets he meets such golden gifts.
I'll to the mart, and there for Dromio stay:
If any ship put out, then straight away.   [*Exit*

ACT IV

SCENE I. *A public place*

Enter SECOND MERCHANT, ANGELO, *and an* OFFICER

SECOND MERCHANT

You know since Pentecost the sum is due,
And since I have not much importuned you;
Nor now I had not, but that I am bound
To Persia, and want guilders for my voyage:
Therefore make present satisfaction,
Or I'll attach you by this officer.

ANGELO

Even just the sum that I do owe to you
Is growing to me by Antipholus;
And in the instant that I met with you
He had of me a chain: at five o'clock
I shall receive the money for the same.
Pleaseth you walk with me down to his house,
I will discharge my bond, and thank you too.

Enter ANTIPHOLUS E. *and* DROMIO E. *from the courtezan's*

OFFICER

That labour may you save: see where he comes.

ANTIPHOLUS E.

While I go to the goldsmith's house, go thou
And buy a rope's end: that will I bestow
Among my wife and her confederates,
For locking me out of my doors by day.
But, soft! I see the goldsmith. Get thee gone;
Buy thou a rope, and bring it home to me.

DROMIO E.

I buy a thousand pound a year: I buy a rope. [*Exit*

ANTIPHOLUS E.

A man is well holp up that trusts to you:
I promised your presence and the chain;
But neither chain nor goldsmith came to me.

Belike you thought our love would last too long,
If it were chain'd together, and therefore came not.

ANGELO

Saving your merry humour, here's the note
How much your chain weighs to the utmost carat,
The fineness of the gold, and chargeful fashion,
Which doth amount to three odd ducats more
Than I stand debted to this gentleman:
I pray you, see him presently discharged,
For he is bound to sea, and stays but for it.

ANTIPHOLUS E.

I am not furnish'd with the present money;
Besides, I have some business in the town.
Good signior, take the stranger to my house,
And with you take the chain, and bid my wife
Disburse the sum on the receipt thereof:
Perchance I will be there as soon as you.

ANGELO

Then you will bring the chain to her yourself?

ANTIPHOLUS E.

No; bear it with you, lest I come not time enough.

ANGELO

Well, sir, I will. Have you the chain about you?

ANTIPHOLUS E.

And if I have not, sir, I hope you have;
Or else you may return without your money.

ANGELO

Nay, come, I pray you, sir, give me the chain:
Both wind and tide stays for this gentleman,
And I, to blame, have held him here too long.

ANTIPHOLUS E.

Good Lord! you use this dalliance to excuse
Your breach of promise to the Porpentine.
I should have chid you for not bringing it,
But, like a shrew, you first begin to brawl.

SECOND MERCHANT

The hour steals on; I pray you, sir, dispatch.

ANGELO

You hear how he importunes me;—the chain!

ANTIPHOLUS E.

Why, give it to my wife, and fetch your money.

ANGELO

Come, come, you know I gave it you even now.
Either send the chain, or send me by some token.

ANTIPHOLUS E.

Fie, now you run this humour out of breath.
Come, where's the chain? I pray you, let me see it.

SECOND MERCHANT

My business cannot brook this dalliance.
Good sir, say whether you'll answer me or no:
If not, I'll leave him to the officer.

ANTIPHOLUS E.

I answer you! what should I answer you?

ANGELO

The money that you owe me for the chain.

ANTIPHOLUS E.

I owe you none till I receive the chain.

ANGELO

You know I gave it you half an hour since.

ANTIPHOLUS E.

You gave me none: you wrong me much to say so.

ANGELO

You wrong me more, sir, in denying it:
Consider how it stands upon my credit.

SECOND MERCHANT

Well, officer, arrest him at my suit.

OFFICER

I do; and charge you in the duke's name to obey
me.

ANGELO

This touches me in reputation.
Either consent to pay this sum for me,
Or I attach you by this officer.

ANTIPHOLUS E.

Consent to pay thee that I never had!
Arrest me, foolish fellow, if thou darest.

ANGELO

Here is thy fee; arrest him, officer.
I would not spare my brother in this case,
If he should scorn me so apparently.

OFFICER

I do arrest you, sir: you hear the suit.

ANTIPHOLUS E.

I do obey thee till I give thee bail.
But, sirrah, you shall buy this sport as dear
As all the metal in your shop will answer.

ANGELO

Sir, sir, I shall have law in Ephesus,
To your notorious shame; I doubt it not.

Enter DROMIO S., *from the bay*

Master, there is a bark of Epidamnum
That stays but till her owner comes aboard,
And then, sir, she bears away. Our fraughtage, sir,
I have convey'd aboard; and I have bought
The oil, the balsamum, and aqua-vitæ.
The ship is in her trim; the merry wind
Blows fair from land: they stay for nought at all
But for their owner, master, and yourself.

ANTIPHOLUS E.

How now! a madman! Why, thou peevish sheep,
What ship of Epidamnum stays for me?

DROMIO S.

A ship you sent me to, to hire waftage.

ANTIPHOLUS E.

Thou drunken slave, I sent thee for a rope,
And told thee to what purpose and what end.

DROMIO S.

You sent me for a rope's end as soon:
You sent me to the bay, sir, for a bark.

ANTIPHOLUS E.

I will debate this matter at more leisure,
And teach your ears to list me with more heed.
To Adriana, villain, hie thee straight:
Give her this key, and tell her, in the desk
That's cover'd o'er with Turkish tapestry
There is a purse of ducats; let her send it:
Tell her I am arrested in the street,
And that shall bail me: hie thee, slave, be gone!

On, officer, to prison till it come.
[*Exeunt* SECOND MERCHANT, ANGELO, OFFICER, *and*
ANTIPHOLUS E.

DROMIO S.

To Adriana! that is where we dined,
Where Dowsabel did claim me for her husband:
She is too big, I hope, for me to compass.
Thither I must, although against my will,
For servants must their masters' minds fulfil. [*Exit*

SCENE II. *The house of* ANTIPHOLUS E.

Enter ADRIANA *and* LUCIANA

ADRIANA

Ah, Luciana, did he tempt thee so?
  Mightst thou perceive austerely in his eye
That he did plead in earnest? yea or no?
  Look'd he or red or pale, or sad or merrily?
What observation madest thou, in this case,
Of his heart's meteors tilting in his face?

LUCIANA

First he denied you had in him no right.

ADRIANA

He meant he did me none; the more my spite.

LUCIANA

Then swore he that he was a stranger here.

ADRIANA

And true he swore, though yet forsworn he were.

LUCIANA

Then pleaded I for you.

ADRIANA

                    And what said he?

LUCIANA

That love I begg'd for you he begg'd of me.

ADRIANA

With what persuasion did he tempt thy love?

LUCIANA

With words that in an honest suit might move,
First he did praise my beauty, then my speech.

ADRIANA

Didst speak him fair?

LUCIANA

                    Have patience, I beseech.

ADRIANA

I cannot, nor I will not, hold me still;
My tongue, though not my heart, shall have his will.
He is deformed, crooked, old, and sere,
Ill-faced, worse bodied, shapeless everywhere;
Vicious, ungentle, foolish, blunt, unkind;
Stigmatical in making, worse in mind.

LUCIANA

Who would be jealous, then, of such a one?
No evil lost is wail'd when it is gone.

ADRIANA

Ah, but I think him better than I say,
  And yet would herein others' eyes were worse.
Far from her nest the lapwing cries away:
  My heart prays for him, though my tongue do
  curse.

Enter DROMIO S.

DROMIO S.

Here! go; the desk, the purse! sweet, now, make
haste.

LUCIANA

How hast thou lost thy breath?

DROMIO S.

                              By running fast.

ADRIANA

Where is thy master, Dromio? is he well?

DROMIO S.

No, he's in Tartar limbo, worse than hell.
A devil in an everlasting garment hath him;
One whose hard heart is button'd up with steel;
A fiend, a fury, pitiless and rough;
A wolf, nay, worse; a fellow all in buff;
A back-friend, a shoulder-clapper, one that coun-
termands
The passages of alleys, creeks, and narrow lands;
A hound that runs counter, and yet draws dry-foot
well;
One that, before the Judgement, carries poor souls
to hell.

ADRIANA

Why, man, what is the matter?

DROMIO S.

I do not know the matter: he is 'rested on the case.

ADRIANA

What, is he arrested? Tell me at whose suit.

DROMIO S.

I know not at whose suit he is arrested well;
But he's in a suit of buff which 'rested him, that can
I tell.
Will you send him, mistress, redemption, the money
in his desk?

ADRIANA

Go fetch it, sister. [*Exit* LUCIANA] This I wonder at,
That he, unknown to me, should be in debt.
Tell me, was he arrested on a band?

DROMIO S.

Not on a band, but on a stronger thing;
A chain, a chain! Do you not hear it ring?

ADRIANA

What, the chain?

DROMIO S.

No, no, the bell: 'tis time that I were gone:
It was two ere I left him, and now the clock strikes
one.

ADRIANA

The hours come back! that did I never hear.

DROMIO S.

Oh, yes; if any hour meet a sergeant, 'a turns back
for very fear.

ADRIANA

As if Time were in debt! how fondly dost thou
reason!

DROMIO S.

Time is a very bankrupt, and owes more than he's
worth to season.
Nay, he's a thief too: have you not heard men say,

That Time comes stealing on by night and day?
If Time be in debt and theft, and a sergeant in the
way,
Hath he not reason to turn back an hour in a day?

Re-enter LUCIANA *with a purse*

ADRIANA

Go, Dromio; there's the money, bear it straight;
And bring thy master home immediately.
Come, sister: I am press'd down with conceit,—
Conceit, my comfort and my injury.   [*Exeunt*

SCENE III. *A public place*

Enter ANTIPHOLUS S.

ANTIPHOLUS S.

There's not a man I meet but doth salute me
As if I were their well-acquainted friend;
And every one doth call me by my name.
Some tender money to me; some invite me;
Some other give me thanks for kindnesses;
Some offer me commodities to buy:
Even now a tailor call'd me in his shop,
And show'd me silks that he had bought for me,
And therewithal took measure of my body.
Sure, these are but imaginary wiles,
And Lapland sorcerers inhabit here.

Enter DROMIO S.

DROMIO S.

Master, here's the gold you sent me for. What, have
you got the picture of old Adam new-apparelled?

ANTIPHOLUS S.

What gold is this? what Adam dost thou mean?

DROMIO S.

Not that Adam that kept the Paradise, but that
Adam that keeps the prison: he that goes in the
calf's skin that was killed for the Prodigal; he that
came behind you, sir, like an evil angel, and bid you
forsake your liberty.

ANTIPHOLUS S.

I understand thee not.

DROMIO S.

No? why, 'tis a plain case: he that went, like a base-
viol, in a case of leather; the man, sir, that, when
gentlemen are tired, gives them a sob, and 'rests
them; he, sir, that takes pity on decayed men, and
gives them suits of durance; he that sets up his rest
to do more exploits with his mace than a morris-
pike.

ANTIPHOLUS S.

What, thou meanest an officer?

DROMIO S.

Ay, sir, the sergeant of the band; he that brings
any man to answer it that breaks his band; one that
thinks a man always going to bed, and says, 'God
give you good rest!'

ANTIPHOLUS S.

Well, sir, there rest in your foolery. Is there any
ship puts forth to-night? may we be gone?

DROMIO S.

Why, sir, I brought you word an hour since, that the bark Expedition put forth to-night; and then were you hindered by the sergeant, to tarry for the hoy Delay. Here are the angels that you sent for to deliver you.

ANTIPHOLUS S.

The fellow is distract, and so am I;
And here we wander in illusions:
Some blessed power deliver us from hence!

Enter a COURTEZAN

COURTEZAN

Well met, well met, Master Antipholus,
I see, sir, you have found the goldsmith now:
Is that the chain you promised me to-day?

ANTIPHOLUS S.

Satan, avoid! I charge thee, tempt me not.

DROMIO S.

Master, is this Mistress Satan?

ANTIPHOLUS S.

It is the devil.

DROMIO S.

Nay, she is worse, she is the devil's dam; and here she comes in the habit of a light wench: and thereof comes that the wenches say, 'God damn me;' that's as much to say, 'God make me a light wench.' It is written, they appear to men like angels of light: light is an effect of fire, and fire will burn; ergo, light wenches will burn. Come not near her.

COURTEZAN

Your man and you are marvellous merry, sir.
Will you go with me? We'll mend our dinner here?

DROMIO S.

Master, if you do, expect spoon-meat; or bespeak a long spoon.

ANTIPHOLUS S.

Why, Dromio?

DROMIO S.

Marry, he must have a long spoon that must eat with the devil.

ANTIPHOLUS S.

Avoid then, fiend! what tell'st thou me of supping?
Thou art, as you are all, a sorceress:
I conjure thee to leave me and be gone.

COURTEZAN

Give me the ring of mine you had at dinner,
Or, for my diamond, the chain you promised,
And I'll be gone, sir, and not trouble you.

DROMIO S.

Some devils ask but the parings of one's nail,
A rush, a hair, a drop of blood, a pin,
A nut, a cherry-stone;
But she, more covetous, would have a chain.
Master, be wise: an if you give it her,
The devil will shake her chain, and fright us with it.

COURTEZAN

I pray you, sir, my ring, or else the chain:
I hope you do not mean to cheat me so.

ANTIPHOLUS S.

Avaunt, thou witch! Come, Dromio, let us go.

DROMIO S.

'Fly pride,' says the peacock: mistress, that you know.　　[*Exeunt* ANTIPHOLUS S. *and* DROMIO S.

COURTEZAN

Now, out of doubt Antipholus is mad,
Else would he never so demean himself.
A ring he hath of mine worth forty ducats,
And for the same he promised me a chain:
Both one and other he denies me now.
The reason that I gather he is mad,
Besides this present instance of his rage,
Is a mad tale he told to-day at dinner,
Of his own doors being shut against his entrance.
Belike his wife, acquainted with his fits,
On purpose shut the doors against his way.
My way is now to hie home to his house,
And tell his wife that, being lunatic,
He rush'd into my house, and took perforce
My ring away. This course I fittest choose;
For forty ducats is too much to lose.　　[*Exit*

SCENE IV. *A street*

Enter ANTIPHOLUS E. *and the* OFFICER

ANTIPHOLUS E.

Fear me not, man; I will not break away:
I'll give thee, ere I leave thee, so much money,
To warrant thee, as I am 'rested for.
My wife is in a wayward mood to-day,
And will not lightly trust the messenger.
That I should be attach'd in Ephesus,
I tell you, 'twill sound harshly in her ears.

Enter DROMIO E. *with a rope's-end*

Here comes my man; I think he brings the money.
How now, sir! have you that I sent you for?

DROMIO E.

Here's that, I warrant you, will pay them all.

ANTIPHOLUS E.

But where's the money?

DROMIO E.

Why, sir, I gave the money for the rope.

ANTIPHOLUS E.

Five hundred ducats, villain, for a rope?

DROMIO E.

I'll serve you, sir, five hundred at the rate.

ANTIPHOLUS E.

To what end did I bid thee hie thee home?

DROMIO E.

To a rope's-end, sir; and to that end am I returned.

ANTIPHOLUS E.

And to that end, sir, I will welcome you.
　　　　　　　　　　　　　　　　[*Beating him*

OFFICER

Good sir, be patient.

DROMIO E.

Nay, 'tis for me to be patient; I am in adversity.

OFFICER

Good now, hold thy tongue.

DROMIO E.

Nay, rather persuade him to hold his hands.

ANTIPHOLUS E.

Thou whoreson, senseless villain!

DROMIO E.

I would I were senseless, sir, that I might not feel your blows.

ANTIPHOLUS E.

Thou art sensible in nothing but blows, and so is an ass.

DROMIO E.

I am an ass, indeed; you may prove it by my long ears. I have served him from the hour of my nativity to this instant, and have nothing at his hands for my service but blows. When I am cold, he heats me with beating; when I am warm, he cools me with beating: I am waked with it when I sleep; raised with it when I sit; driven out of doors with it when I go from home; welcomed home with it when I return: nay, I bear it on my shoulders, as a beggar wont her brat; and, I think, when he hath lamed me, I shall beg with it from door to door.

ANTIPHOLUS E.

Come, go along; my wife is coming yonder.

Enter ADRIANA, LUCIANA, *the* COURTEZAN, *and* PINCH

DROMIO E.

Mistress, 'respice finem,' respect your end; or rather, the prophecy like the parrot, 'beware the rope's-end.'

ANTIPHOLUS E.

Wilt thou still talk?　　　　　　　　　[*Beating him*

COURTEZAN

How say you now? is not your husband mad?

ADRIANA

His incivility confirms no less.

Good Doctor Pinch, you are a conjurer;

Establish him in his true sense again,

And I will please you what you will demand.

LUCIANA

Alas, how fiery and how sharp he looks!

COURTEZAN

Mark how he trembles in his ecstasy!

PINCH

Give me your hand, and let me feel your pulse.

ANTIPHOLUS E.

There is my hand, and let it feel your ear.

[*Striking him*

PINCH

I charge thee, Satan, housed within this man,

To yield possession to my holy prayers,

And to thy state of darkness hie thee straight:

I conjure thee by all the saints in heaven!

ANTIPHOLUS E.

Peace, doting wizard, peace! I am not mad.

ADRIANA

O, that thou wert not, poor distressed soul!

ANTIPHOLUS E.

You minion, you, are these your customers?

Did this companion with the saffron face

Revel and feast it at my house to-day,

Whilst upon me the guilty doors were shut,

And I denied to enter in my house?

ADRIANA

O husband, God doth know you dined at home;

Where would you had remain'd until this time,

Free from these slanders and this open shame!

ANTIPHOLUS E.

Dined at home! Thou villain, what sayest thou?

DROMIO E.

Sir, sooth to say, you did not dine at home.

ANTIPHOLUS E.

Were not my doors lock'd up, and I shut out?

DROMIO E.

Perdie, your doors were lock'd, and you shut out.

ANTIPHOLUS E.

And did not she herself revile me there?

DROMIO E.

Sans fable, she herself reviled you there.

ANTIPHOLUS E.

Did not her kitchen-maid rail, taunt, and scorn me?

DROMIO E.

Certes, she did; the kitchen-vestal scorn'd you.

ANTIPHOLUS E.

And did not I in rage depart from thence?

DROMIO E.

In verity you did; my bones bear witness,

That since have felt the vigour of his rage.

ADRIANA

Is't good to soothe him in these contraries?

PINCH

It is no shame: the fellow finds his vein,

And, yielding to him, humours well his frenzy.

ANTIPHOLUS E.

Thou hast suborn'd the goldsmith to arrest me.

ADRIANA

Alas, I sent you money to redeem you,

By Dromio here, who came in haste for it.

DROMIO E.

Money by me! heart and good-will you might;

But surely, master, not a rag of money.

ANTIPHOLUS E.

Went'st not thou to her for a purse of ducats?

ADRIANA

He came to me, and I deliver'd it.

LUCIANA

And I am witness with her that she did.

DROMIO E.

God and the rope-maker bear me witness

That I was sent for nothing but a rope!

PINCH

Mistress, both man and master is possess'd;

I know it by their pale and deadly looks:

They must be bound, and laid in some dark room.

ANTIPHOLUS E.

Say, wherefore didst thou lock me forth to-day?

And why dost thou deny the bag of gold?

ADRIANA

I did not, gentle husband, lock thee forth.

DROMIO E.

And, gentle master, I received no gold;
But I confess, sir, that we were lock'd out.

ADRIANA

Dissembling villain, thou speak'st false in both.

ANTIPHOLUS E.

Dissembling harlot, thou art false in all,
And art confederate with a damned pack
To make a loathsome abject scorn of me:
But with these nails I'll pluck out these false eyes,
That would behold in me this shameful sport.

Enter three or four, and offer to bind him. He strives

ADRIANA

O, bind him, bind him! let him not come near me.

PINCH

More company! The fiend is strong within him.

LUCIANA

Ay me, poor man, how pale and wan he looks!

ANTIPHOLUS E.

What, will you murder me? Thou gaoler, thou,
I am thy prisoner: wilt thou suffer them
To make a rescue?

OFFICER

Masters, let him go:
He is my prisoner, and you shall not have him.

PINCH

Go bind this man, for he is frantic too.

[*They offer to bind* DROMIO E.

ADRIANA

What wilt thou do, thou peevish officer?
Hast thou delight to see a wretched man
Do outrage and displeasure to himself?

OFFICER

He is my prisoner: if I let him go,
The debt he owes will be required of me.

ADRIANA

I will discharge thee ere I go from thee:
Bear me forthwith unto his creditor,
And, knowing how the debt grows, I will pay it.
Good master doctor, see him safe convey'd
Home to my house. O most unhappy day!

ANTIPHOLUS E.

O most unhappy strumpet!

DROMIO E.

Master, I am here enter'd in bond for you.

ANTIPHOLUS E.

Out on thee, villain! wherefore dost thou mad me?

DROMIO E.

Will you be bound for nothing? be mad, good master: cry, The devil!

LUCIANA

God help, poor souls, how idly do they talk!

ADRIANA

Go bear him hence. Sister, go you with me.

[*Exeunt all but* ADRIANA, LUCIANA, OFFICER *and*
COURTEZAN

Say now; whose suit is he arrested at?

OFFICER

One Angelo, a goldsmith; do you know him?

ADRIANA

I know the man. What is the sum he owes?

OFFICER

Two hundred ducats.

ADRIANA

Say, how grows it due?

OFFICER

Due for a chain your husband had of him.

ADRIANA

He did bespeak a chain for me, but had it not.

COURTEZAN

When as your husband, all in rage, to-day
Came to my house, and took away my ring,—
The ring I saw upon his finger now,—
Straight after did I meet him with a chain.

ADRIANA

It may be so, but I did never see it.
Come, gaoler, bring me where the goldsmith is:
I long to know the truth hereof at large.

Enter ANTIPHOLUS S. *with his rapier drawn, and*
DROMIO S.

LUCIANA

God, for thy mercy! they are loose again.

ADRIANA

And come with naked swords.
Let's call more help to have them bound again.

OFFICER

Away! they'll kill us.

[*Exeunt all but* ANTIPHOLUS S. *and* DROMIO S.

ANTIPHOLUS S.

I see these witches are afraid of swords.

DROMIO S.

She that would be your wife now ran from you.

ANTIPHOLUS S.

Come to the Centaur; fetch our stuff from thence:
I long that we were safe and sound aboard.

DROMIO S.

Faith, stay here this night; they will surely do us no
harm: you saw they speak us fair, give us gold: methinks they are such a gentle nation, that, but for
the mountain of mad flesh that claims marriage of
me, I could find in my heart to stay here still, and
turn witch.

ANTIPHOLUS S.

I will not stay to-night for all the town;
Therefore away, to get our stuff aboard.   [*Exeunt*

ACT V

SCENE I. *A street before a Priory*

Enter SECOND MERCHANT *and* ANGELO

ANGELO

I am sorry, sir, that I have hinder'd you;
But, I protest, he had the chain of me,
Though most dishonestly he doth deny it.

SECOND MERCHANT

How is the man esteem'd here in the city?

ANGELO

Of very reverent reputation, sir,
Of credit infinite, highly beloved,
Second to none that lives here in the city:
His word might bear my wealth at any time.

SECOND MERCHANT

Speak softly: yonder, as I think, he walks.

Enter ANTIPHOLUS S. *and* DROMIO S.

ANGELO

'Tis so; and that self chain about his neck,
Which he forswore most monstrously to have.
Good sir, draw near to me, I'll speak to him;
Signior Antipholus, I wonder much
That you would put me to this shame and trouble;
And, not without some scandal to yourself,
With circumstance and oaths so to deny
This chain which now you wear so openly:
Beside the charge, the shame, imprisonment,
You have done wrong to this my honest friend;
Who, but for staying on our controversy,
Had hoisted sail and put to sea to-day:
This chain you had of me; can you deny it?

ANTIPHOLUS S.

I think I had; I never did deny it.

SECOND MERCHANT

Yes, that you did, sir, and forswore it too.

ANTIPHOLUS S.

Who heard me to deny it or forswear it?

SECOND MERCHANT

These ears of mine, thou know'st, did hear thee.
Fie on thee, wretch! 'tis pity that thou livest
To walk where any honest men resort.

ANTIPHOLUS S.

Thou art a villain to impeach me thus:
I'll prove mine honour and mine honesty
Against thee presently, if thou darest stand.

SECOND MERCHANT

I dare, and do defy thee for a villain. [*They draw*

Enter ADRIANA, LUCIANA, *the* COURTEZAN, *and*
OTHERS

ADRIANA

Hold, hurt him not, for God's sake! he is mad.
Some get within him, take his sword away:
Bind Dromio too, and bear them to my house.

DROMIO S.

Run, master, run; for God's sake, take a house!
This is some priory. In, or we are spoil'd!

[*Exeunt* ANTIPHOLUS S. *and* DROMIO S. *to the Priory*
Enter ÆMILIA

ÆMILIA

Be quiet, people. Wherefore throng you hither?

ADRIANA

To fetch my poor distracted husband hence.
Let us come in, that we may bind him fast,
And bear him home for his recovery.

ANGELO

I knew he was not in his perfect wits.

SECOND MERCHANT

I am sorry now that I did draw on him.

ÆMILIA

How long hath this possession held the man?

ADRIANA

This week he hath been heavy, sour, sad,
And much different from the man he was;
But till this afternoon his passion
Ne'er brake into extremity of rage.

ÆMILIA

Hath he not lost much wealth by wreck of sea?
Buried some dear friend? Hath not else his eye
Stray'd his affection in unlawful love?
A sin prevailing much in youthful men,
Who give their eyes the liberty of gazing.
Which of these sorrows is he subject to?

ADRIANA

To none of these, except it be the last;
Namely, some love that drew him oft from home.

ÆMILIA

You should for that have reprehended him.

ADRIANA

Why, so I did.

ÆMILIA

Ay, but not rough enough.

ADRIANA

As roughly as my modesty would let me.

ÆMILIA

Haply, in private.

ADRIANA

And in assemblies too.

ÆMILIA

Ay, but not enough.

ADRIANA

It was the copy of our conference:
In bed, he slept not for my urging it;
At board, he fed not for my urging it;
Alone, it was the subject of my theme;
In company I often glanced it;
Still did I tell him it was vile and bad.

ÆMILIA

And thereof came it that the man was mad.
The venom clamours of a jealous woman
Poisons more deadly than a mad dog's tooth.
It seems his sleeps were hinder'd by thy railing:
And thereof comes it that his head is light.
Thou say'st his meat was sauced with thy upbraid-
ings:
Unquiet meals make ill digestions;
Thereof the raging fire of fever bred;
And what's a fever but a fit of madness?
Thou say'st his sports were hinder'd by thy brawls
Sweet recreation barr'd, what doth ensue
But moody and dull melancholy,
Kinsman to grim and comfortless despair;
And at her heels a huge infectious troop
Of pale distemperatures and foes to life?
In food, in sport, and life-preserving rest
To be disturb'd, would mad or man or beast:
The consequence is, then, thy jealous fits
Have scared thy husband from the use of wits.

LUCIANA

She never reprehended him but mildly,
When he demean'd himself rough, rude, and wildly.
Why bear you these rebukes, and answer not?

ADRIANA

She did betray me to my own reproof.
Good people, enter, and lay hold on him.

ÆMILIA

No, not a creature enters in my house.

ADRIANA

Then let your servants bring my husband forth.

ÆMILIA

Neither: he took this place for sanctuary,
And it shall privilege him from your hands
Till I have brought him to his wits again,
Or lose my labour in assaying it.

ADRIANA

I will attend my husband, be his nurse,
Diet his sickness, for it is my office,
And will have no attorney but myself;
And therefore let me have him home with me.

ÆMILIA

Be patient; for I will not let him stir
Till I have used the approved means I have,
With wholesome syrups, drugs and holy prayers.
To make of him a formal man again:
It is a branch and parcel of mine oath,
A charitable duty of my order.
Therefore depart, and leave him here with me.

ADRIANA

I will not hence, and leave my husband here:
And ill it doth beseem your holiness
To separate the husband and the wife.

ÆMILIA

Be quiet, and depart: thou shalt not have him. [Exit

LUCIANA

Complain unto the Duke of this indignity.

ADRIANA

Come, go: I will fall prostrate at his feet,
And never rise until my tears and prayers
Have won his Grace to come in person hither,
And take perforce my husband from the abbess.

SECOND MERCHANT

By this, I think, the dial points at five:
Anon, I'm sure, the Duke himself in person
Comes this way to the melancholy vale,
The place of death and sorry execution,
Behind the ditches of the abbey here.

ANGELO

Upon what cause?

SECOND MERCHANT

To see a reverend Syracusian merchant,
Who put unluckily into this bay
Against the laws and statutes of this town,
Beheaded publicly for his offence.

ANGELO

See where they come: we will behold his death.

LUCIANA

Kneel to the Duke before he pass the abbey.

Enter DUKE, *attended;* ÆGEON *bareheaded; with
the* HEADSMAN *and other* OFFICERS

DUKE

Yet once again proclaim it publicly,
If any friend will pay the sum for him,
He shall not die; so much we tender him.

ADRIANA

Justice, most sacred Duke, against the abbess!

DUKE

She is a virtuous and a reverend lady:
It cannot be that she hath done thee wrong.

ADRIANA

May it please your Grace, Antipholus my hus-
    band,—
Whom I made lord of me and all I had,
At your important letters,—this ill day
A most outrageous fit of madness took him;
That desperately he hurried through the street,—
With him his bondman, all as mad as he,—
Doing displeasure to the citizens
By rushing in their houses, bearing thence
Rings, jewels, any thing his rage did like.
Once did I get him bound, and sent him home,
Whilst to take order for the wrongs I went,
That here and there his fury had committed.
Anon, I wot not by what strong escape,
He broke from those that had the guard of him;
And with his mad attendant and himself,
Each one with ireful passion, with drawn swords,
Met us again, and, madly bent on us,
Chased us away; till, raising of more aid,
We came again to bind them. Then they fled
Into this abbey, whither we pursued them;
And here the abbess shuts the gates on us,
And will not suffer us to fetch him out,
Nor send him forth, that we may bear him hence.
Therefore, most gracious Duke, with thy command
Let him be brought forth, and borne hence for help.

DUKE

Long since thy husband served me in my wars;
And I to thee engaged a prince's word,
When thou didst make him master of thy bed,
To do him all the grace and good I could.
Go, some of you, knock at the abbey-gate,
And bid the lady abbess come to me.
I will determine this before I stir.

Enter a SERVANT

SERVANT

O mistress, mistress, shift and save yourself!
My master and his man are both broke loose,
Beaten the maids a-row, and bound the doctor,
Whose beard they have singed off with brands of
    fire;
And ever, as it blazed, they threw on him
Great pails of puddled mire to quench the hair:
My master preaches patience to him, and the while
His man with scissors nicks him like a fool;
And sure, unless you send some present help,
Between them they will kill the conjurer.

ADRIANA

Peace, fool! thy master and his man are here;
And that is false thou dost report to us.

SERVANT

Mistress, upon my life, I tell you true;
I have not breathed almost since I did see it.
He cries for you, and vows, if he can take you,
To scorch your face and to disfigure you. [Cry within
Hark, hark! I hear him, mistress: fly, be gone!

DUKE

Come, stand by me; fear nothing. Guard with halberds!

ADRIANA

Ay me, it is my husband! Witness you,
That he is borne about invisible:
Even now we housed him in the abbey here;
And now he's there, past thought of human reason.

Enter ANTIPHOLUS E. *and* DROMIO E.

ANTIPHOLUS E.

Justice, most gracious Duke, O, grant me justice!
Even for the service that long since I did thee,
When I bestrid thee in the wars, and took
Deep scars to save thy life; even for the blood
That then I lost for thee, now grant me justice.

ÆGEON

Unless the fear of death doth make me dote,
I see my son Antipholus, and Dromio.

ANTIPHOLUS E.

Justice, sweet prince, against that woman there!
She whom thou gavest to me to be my wife,
That hath abused and dishonour'd me
Even in the strength and height of injury:
Beyond imagination is the wrong
That she this day hath shameless thrown on me.

DUKE

Discover how, and thou shalt find me just.

ANTIPHOLUS E.

This day, great Duke, she shut the doors upon me,
While she with harlots feasted in my house.

DUKE

A grievous fault! Say, woman, didst thou so?

ADRIANA

No, my good lord: myself, he and my sister
To-day did dine together. So befal my soul
As this is false he burthens me withal!

LUCIANA

Ne'er may I look on day, nor sleep on night,
But she tells to your Highness simple truth!

ANGELO

O perjured woman! They are both forsworn:
In this the madman justly chargeth them.

ANTIPHOLUS E.

My liege, I am advised what I say;
Neither disturbed with the effect of wine,
Nor heady-rash, provoked with raging ire,
Albeit my wrongs might make one wiser mad.
This woman lock'd me out this day from dinner:
That goldsmith there, were he not pack'd with her,
Could witness it, for he was with me then;

Who parted with me to go fetch a chain,
Promising to bring it to the Porpentine,
Where Balthazar and I did dine together.
Our dinner done, and he not coming thither,
I went to seek him: in the street I met him,
And in his company that gentleman.
There did this perjured goldsmith swear me down
That I this day of him received the chain,
Which, God he knows, I saw not: for the which
He did arrest me with an officer.
I did obey; and sent my peasant home
For certain ducats: he with none return'd.
Then fairly I bespoke the officer
To go in person with me to my house.
By the way we met my wife, her sister, and a rabble
more
Of vile confederates. Along with them
They brought one Pinch, a hungry lean-faced vil-
lain,
A mere anatomy, a mountebank,
A threadbare juggler, and a fortune-teller,
A needy, hollow-eyed, sharp-looking wretch,
A living dead man: this pernicious slave,
Forsooth, took on him as a conjurer;
And, gazing in mine eyes, feeling my pulse,
And with no face, as 'twere, outfacing me,
Cries out, I was possess'd. Then all together
They fell upon me, bound me, bore me thence,
And in a dark and dankish vault at home
There left me and my man, both bound together;
Till, gnawing with my teeth my bonds in sunder,
I gain'd my freedom, and immediately
Ran hither to your Grace; whom I beseech
To give me ample satisfaction
For these deep shames and great indignities.

ANGELO

My lord, in truth, thus far I witness with him,
That he dined not at home, but was lock'd out.

DUKE

But had he such a chain of thee or no?

ANGELO

He had, my lord: and when he ran in here,
These people saw the chain about his neck.

SECOND MERCHANT

Besides, I will be sworn these ears of mine
Heard you confess you had the chain of him,
After you first forswore it on the mart:
And thereupon I drew my sword on you;
And then you fled into this abbey here,
From whence, I think, you are come by miracle.

ANTIPHOLUS E.

I never came within these abbey-walls;
Nor ever didst thou draw thy sword on me:
I never saw the chain, so help me Heaven!
And this is false you burthen me withal.

DUKE

Why, what an intricate impeach is this!
I think you all have drunk of Circe's cup.
If here you housed him, here he would have been;
If he were mad, he would not plead so coldly:

You say he dined at home; the goldsmith here
Denies that saying. Sirrah, what say you?
DROMIO E.
Sir, he dined with her there, at the Porpentine.
COURTEZAN
He did; and from my finger snatch'd that ring.
ANTIPHOLUS E.
'Tis true, my liege; this ring I had of her.
DUKE
Saw'st thou him enter at the abbey here?
COURTEZAN
As sure, my liege, as I do see your Grace.
DUKE
Why, this is strange. Go call the abbess hither.
I think you are all mated, or stark mad.
[Exit one to ÆMILIA
ÆGEON
Most mighty Duke, vouchsafe me speak a word:
Haply I see a friend will save my life,
And pay the sum that may deliver me.
DUKE
Speak freely, Syracusian, what thou wilt.
ÆGEON
Is not your name, sir, call'd Antipholus?
And is not that your bondman, Dromio?
DROMIO E.
Within this hour I was his bondman, sir,
But he, I thank him, gnaw'd in two my cords:
Now am I Dromio, and his man unbound.
ÆGEON
I am sure you both of you remember me.
DROMIO E.
Ourselves we do remember, sir, by you;
For lately we were bound, as you are now.
You are not Pinch's patient, are you, sir?
ÆGEON
Why look you strange on me? you know me well.
ANTIPHOLUS E.
I never saw you in my life till now.
ÆGEON
O, grief hath changed me since you saw me last,
And careful hours with time's deformed hand
Have written strange defeatures in my face:
But tell me yet, dost thou not know my voice?
ANTIPHOLUS E.
Neither.
ÆGEON
Dromio, nor thou?
DROMIO E.
No, trust me, sir, nor I.
ÆGEON
I am sure thou dost.
DROMIO E.
Ay, sir, but I am sure I do not; and whatsoever a
man denies, you are now bound to believe him.
ÆGEON
Not know my voice! O time's extremity,
Hast thou so crack'd and splitted my poor tongue
In seven short years, that here my only son
Knows not my feeble key of untuned cares?

Though now this grained face of mine be hid
In sap-consuming winter's drizzled snow,
And all the conduits of my blood froze up,
Yet hath my night of life some memory,
My wasting lamps some fading glimmer left,
My dull deaf ears a little use to hear:
All these old witnesses—I cannot err—
Tell me thou art my son Antipholus.
ANTIPHOLUS E.
I never saw my father in my life.
ÆGEON
But seven years since, in Syracusa, boy,
Thou know'st we parted: but perhaps, my son,
Thou shamest to acknowledge me in misery.
ANTIPHOLUS E.
The Duke and all that know me in the city
Can witness with me that it is not so:
I ne'er saw Syracusa in my life.
DUKE
I tell thee, Syracusian, twenty years
Have I been patron to Antipholus,
During which time he ne'er saw Syracusa:
I see thy age and dangers make thee dote.
Re-enter ÆMILIA, with ANTIPHOLUS S. and DROMIO S.
ÆMILIA
Most mighty Duke, behold a man much wrong'd.
[All gather to see them
ADRIANA
I see two husbands, or mine eyes deceive me.
DUKE
One of these men is Genius to the other;
And so of these. Which is the natural man,
And which the spirit? who deciphers them?
DROMIO S.
I, sir, am Dromio: command him away.
DROMIO E.
I, sir, am Dromio; pray, let me stay.
ANTIPHOLUS S.
Ægeon art thou not? or else his ghost?
DROMIO S.
O, my old master! who hath bound him here?
ÆMILIA
Whoever bound him, I will loose his bonds,
And gain a husband by his liberty.
Speak, old Ægeon, if thou be'st the man
That hadst a wife once call'd Æmilia,
That bore thee at a burthen two fair sons:
O, if thou be'st the same Ægeon, speak,
And speak unto the same Æmilia!
ÆGEON
If I dream not, thou art Æmilia:
If thou art she, tell me, where is that son
That floated with thee on the fatal raft?
ÆMILIA
By men of Epidamnum he and I
And the twin Dromio, all were taken up;
But by and by rude fishermen of Corinth
By force took Dromio and my son from them,
And me they left with those of Epidamnum.

What then became of them I cannot tell;
I to this fortune that you see me in.

DUKE

Why, here begins this morning story right:
These two Antipholuses, these two so like,
And these two Dromios, one in semblance,—
Besides her urging of her wreck at sea,—
These are the parents to these children,
Which accidentally are met together.
Antipholus, thou camest from Corinth first?

ANTIPHOLUS S.

No, sir, not I; I came from Syracuse.

DUKE

Stay, stand apart; I know not which is which.

ANTIPHOLUS E.

I came from Corinth, my most gracious lord,—

DROMIO E.

And I with him.

ANTIPHOLUS E.

Brought to this town by that most famous warrior,
Duke Menaphon, your most renowned uncle.

ADRIANA

Which of you two did dine with me to-day?

ANTIPHOLUS S.

I, gentle mistress.

ADRIANA

And are not you my husband?

ANTIPHOLUS E.

No; I say nay to that.

ANTIPHOLUS S.

And so do I; yet did she call me so:
And this fair gentlewoman, her sister here,
Did call me brother. [To LUCIANA] What I told you
        then,
I hope I shall have leisure to make good;
If this be not a dream I see and hear.

ANGELO

That is the chain, sir, which you had of me.

ANTIPHOLUS S.

I think it be, sir; I deny it not.

ANTIPHOLUS E.

And you, sir, for this chain arrested me.

ANGELO

I think I did, sir; I deny it not.

ADRIANA

I sent you money, sir, to be your bail,
By Dromio; but I think he brought it not.

DROMIO E.

No, none by me.

ANTIPHOLUS S.

This purse of ducats I received from you,
And Dromio my man did bring them me.
I see we still did meet each other's man;
And I was ta'en for him, and he for me;
And thereupon these ERRORS are arose.

ANTIPHOLUS E.

These ducats pawn I for my father here.

DUKE

It shall not need; thy father hath his life.

COURTEZAN

Sir, I must have that diamond from you.

ANTIPHOLUS E.

There, take it; and much thanks for my good cheer.

ÆMILIA

Renowned Duke, vouchsafe to take the pains
To go with us into the abbey here,
And hear at large discoursed all our fortunes:
And all that are assembled in this place,
That by this sympathized one day's error
Have suffer'd wrong, go keep us company,
And we shall make full satisfaction.
Thirty-three years have I but gone in travail
Of you, my sons; and till this present hour
My heavy burthen ne'er delivered.
The Duke, my husband, and my children both,
And you the calendars of their nativity,
Go to a gossips' feast, and go with me;
After so long grief, such nativity!

DUKE

With all my heart, I'll gossip at this feast.
[Exeunt all but ANTIPHOLUS S., ANTIPHOLUS E., DROMIO S.,
                                    and DROMIO E.

DROMIO S.

Master, shall I fetch your stuff from shipboard?

ANTIPHOLUS E.

Dromio, what stuff of mine hast thou embark'd?

DROMIO S.

Your goods that lay at host, sir, in the Centaur.

ANTIPHOLUS S.

He speaks to me. I am your master, Dromio:
Come, go with us; we'll look to that anon:
Embrace thy brother there; rejoice with him.
    [Exeunt ANTIPHOLUS S. and ANTIPHOLUS E.

DROMIO S.

There is a fat friend at your master's house,
That kitchen'd me for you to-day at dinner:
She now shall be my sister, not my wife.

DROMIO E.

Methinks you are my glass, and not my brother:
I see by you I am a sweet-faced youth.
Will you walk in to see their gossiping?

DROMIO S.

Not I, sir; you are my elder.

DROMIO E.

That's a question: how shall we try it?

DROMIO S.

We'll draw cuts for the senior: till then lead thou
    first.

DROMIO E.

Nay, then, thus:
We came into the world like brother and brother;
And now let's go hand in hand, not one before an-
        other.   [Exeunt

THE TRAGEDY OF TITUS ANDRONICUS

SYNOPSIS

Even in the supreme hour of his triumph as he receives the acclamations of the cheering Roman populace upon his return from the Gothic wars with Tamora, Queen of the Goths, and her three sons as captives, the victorious general, Titus Andronicus, mourns the death of his twenty-one slain sons, and revengefully demands, as a fiery sacrifice to appease their souls, the eldest son of the conquered Queen who pleads tearfully but in vain for his life.

His sons buried, Titus turns to affairs of state and, although offered the Roman crown, he upholds in strict justice the claim of Saturninus, elder son of the late Emperor, who disputes the inheritance with his brother Bassianus. Through the general's influence, the treacherous Saturninus ascends the throne, offering to wed Titus' daughter Lavinia, though the Gothic queen had already caught his fancy. Bassianus wrathfully declares that Lavinia is betrothed to him, and with the support of her brothers abducts and marries her. Enraged at this open breach of faith to the new Emperor, Titus starts in pursuit of his daughter, and finding his way blocked by one of his sons he kills him. Saturninus seizes the opportunity to choose Tamora for his bride and to disgrace the noble Titus, but the wily Queen urges him publicly to restore the general and his sons to his favor and forgive Bassianus, while in secret she ruthlessly plans with the Emperor and her foul Moorish lover Aaron the destruction of the entire Andronicus family in revenge for the death of her son.

During a royal hunt in the forest Aaron hears Tamora's evil sons, Chiron and Demetrius, quarreling over the prospect of possessing Lavinia whom they both desire, and he incites the bestial pair to ravish her in turn and to insure secrecy by tearing out her tongue and cutting off her hands. Straying through the wood while the hunt is in progress, Bassianus and Lavinia discover the love affair of Tamora and Aaron, and, fearing their disclosures, Tamora calls her sons, telling them that her brother-in-law and his wife have insulted her and threatened her with torture. The sons kill Bassianus, throw his body into a deep pit, and drag Lavinia away to defilement and mutilation as she begs them for death. Aaron, enticing two of Titus' sons to the pit into which they fall on top of Bassianus' body, quickly summons Saturninus, points to the young men struggling to escape, produces a falsely incriminating letter arranging for the payment of the murder, and discloses a bag of gold which he had previously placed near the spot.

The Emperor accuses the Andronici of his brother's death, and, regardless of Titus' pleadings, they are sentenced to death, but before the execution the lying Aaron brings word that their lives will be spared if either Lucius, the third son, or Marcus, his uncle, will chop off one of his hands

and send it to the Emperor as a token of good faith. With Aaron's vicious help, the old father fore-
stalls the others and sends his own hand, which is later scornfully returned with the heads of his
two sons.

Titus, Marcus and Lucius vow a terrible requital, and Lucius, whom the Emperor has just
banished, is instructed to raise an invading army among the Goths. Lavinia contrives to fasten
their crime of ravishment and mutilation on Chiron and Demetrius by turning the pages of Ovid's
Metamorphoses with the stumps of her arms until she reaches the tragic tale of Philomela, and,
with a staff held in her mouth and guided by her arms, writing in the sand the names of her
assaulters. Pretending to be mad, Titus sends presents to Chiron and Demetrius and shoots arrows
into the Roman streets and the palace, all of which bear messages to the gods proclaiming his
wrongs.

Meanwhile, Tamora gives birth to a black child, of which Aaron is father, and her sons try
to kill it, but Aaron takes possession of it, kills the nurse and midwife to prevent gossip, and has a
white baby substituted in his child's place as the Emperor's son. Taking the infant away to be
brought up by the Goths, Aaron is captured by a soldier in the army of Lucius and exultingly
relates to the general the full story of his crimes after extracting a promise for his child's protection.
Saturninus, knowing the popularity of Lucius, is greatly disturbed when news reaches him of the
huge forces drawing near the city, and he endeavors to arrange a banquet and parley at Titus'
house where Tamora will separate the general from his army and stir up enmity between them.

To win the support of the supposedly insane Titus, Tamora goes to him disguised as Revenge,
stating that her great desire is to avenge his wrongs at the banquet, and Titus promises to send for
Lucius. She returns in glee to the Emperor to make ready for the feast, leaving her two sons at the
home of Titus. He has them overpowered, cuts their throats, as Lavinia holds a basin to catch their
blood, and, grinding their bodies to a pulp, bakes it in a pie which, in the costume of a cook, he
serves to Tamora. Titus informs Saturninus of the crime of Chiron and Demetrius, and tells
Tamora she has just eaten their bodies in the pie. He kills Lavinia to put an end to her shame, and
stabs Tamora. Saturninus kills Titus, and is himself killed by Lucius. Lucius tells the Roman people
the complete story of his father's tragedy, and is proclaimed Emperor. Aaron is condemned to
death by torture.

HISTORICAL DATA

Popular as was the story of Titus Andronicus
among sixteenth-century writers there seems to be
no direct source of the tragedy, the plot of which is
without foundation in authentic history. It is possible that Shakespeare may have obtained some part
of the plot from an older play, as at least three upon
this subject were entered on the Stationers' Register, and Henslowe's *Diary* mentions one *Tittus and
Vespacia* as having been performed by Lord
Strange's men in 1591, of which only the German
acting version is extant.

The actual authorship of the play in its present
form is in some doubt for, although it was credited

to him during his lifetime, authorities are reasonably in agreement that it gives very little evidence
of his genius save "a few fine touches." It cannot be
denied, however, that it is listed among Shakespeare's tragedies in Meres's *Palladis Tamia* (1598)
and Condell and Heminge, Shakespeare's friends
and fellow actors, include it in their collected edition of his plays published in 1623.

There is good evidence that the play was written
not later than 1593, and a reference in Ben Jonson's
Bartholomew Fair (1614) has led more than one
commentator to fix the date of its composition as
even earlier.

"Confusion fall——"
TITUS ANDRONICUS

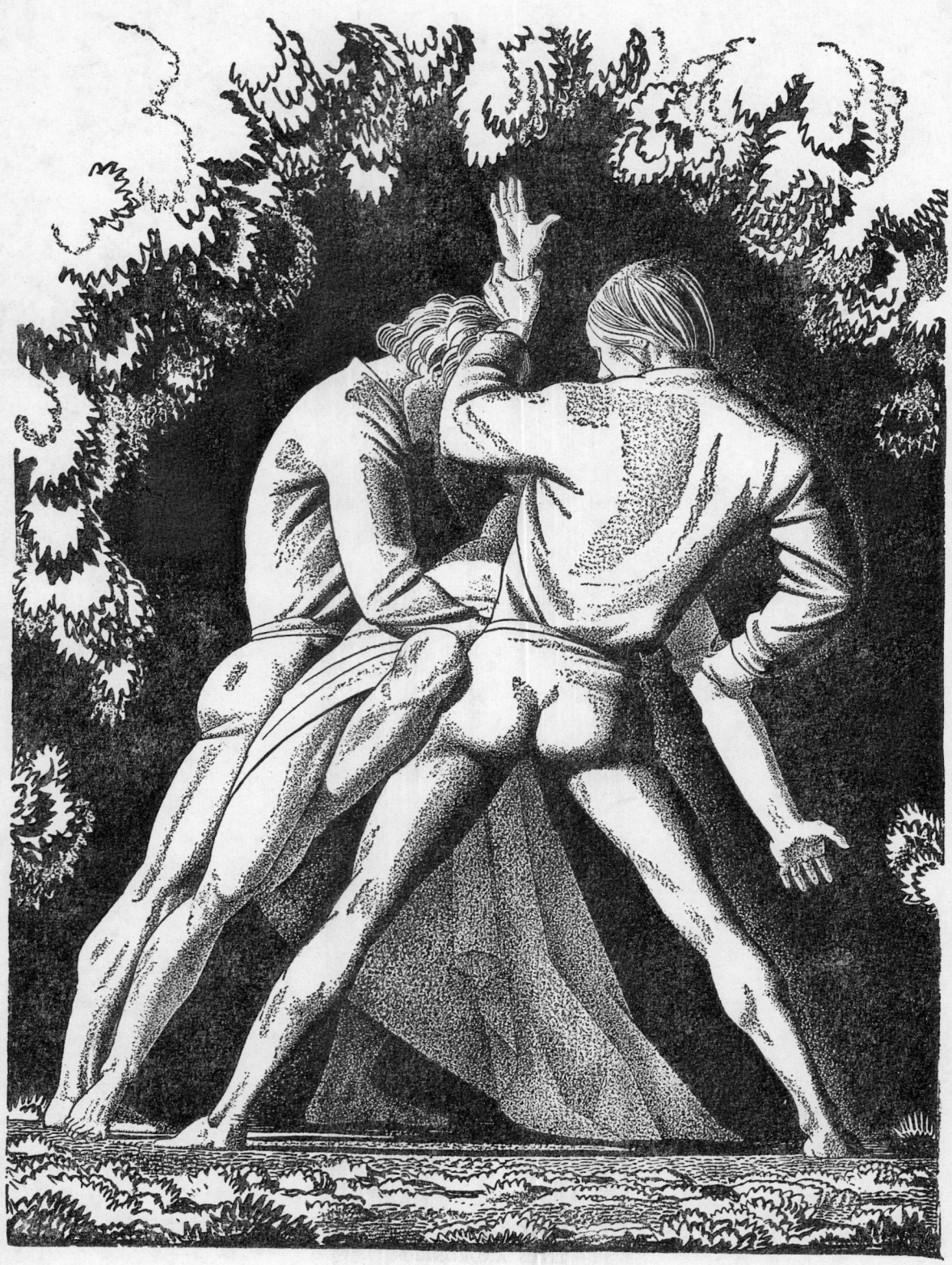

THE TRAGEDY OF TITUS ANDRONICUS

DRAMATIS PERSONÆ

SATURNINUS, *son to the late Emperor of Rome, afterwards emperor.*
BASSIANUS, *brother to Saturninus.*
TITUS ANDRONICUS, *a noble Roman.*
MARCUS ANDRONICUS, *tribune of the people, and brother to Titus.*
LUCIUS,
QUINTUS,
MARTIUS, } *sons to Titus Andronicus.*
MUTIUS,
YOUNG LUCIUS, *a boy, son to Lucius.*
PUBLIUS, *son to Marcus Andronicus.*
ÆMILIUS, *a noble Roman.*

ALARBUS,
DEMETRIUS, } *sons to Tamora.*
CHIRON,
AARON, *a Moor, beloved by Tamora.*
A CAPTAIN, TRIBUNE, MESSENGER, *and* CLOWN; ROMANS *and* GOTHS.

TAMORA, *Queen of the Goths.*
LAVINIA, *daughter to Titus Andronicus.*
A NURSE, *and a black Child.*

KINSMEN *of* Titus, SENATORS, TRIBUNES, OFFICERS, SOLDIERS, *and* ATTENDANTS.

SCENE—*Rome, and the country near it.*

ACT I

SCENE I. *Rome. Before the Capitol. The Tomb of the Andronici appearing.*

Flourish. Enter the TRIBUNES *and* SENATORS *aloft. And then enter below,* SATURNINUS *and his* FOLLOWERS *from one side, and* BASSIANUS *and his* FOLLOWERS *from the other side, with drum and colours*

SATURNINUS
NOBLE patricians, patrons of my right,
Defend the justice of my cause with arms;
And, countrymen, my loving followers,
Plead my successive title with your swords:
I am his first-born son, that was the last
That ware the imperial diadem of Rome;
Then let my father's honours live in me,
Nor wrong mine age with this indignity.

BASSIANUS
Romans, friends, followers, favourers of my right,
If ever Bassianus, Cæsar's son,
Were gracious in the eyes of royal Rome,
Keep then this passage to the Capitol;
And suffer not dishonour to approach
The imperial seat, to virtue consecrate,
To justice, continence and nobility;
But let desert in pure election shine;
And, Romans, fight for freedom in your choice.

Enter MARCUS ANDRONICUS, *aloft, with the crown*

MARCUS
Princes, that strive by factions and by friends
Ambitiously for rule and empery,
Know that the people of Rome, for whom we stand
A special party, have by common voice,
In election for the Roman empery,
Chosen Andronicus, surnamed Pius
For many good and great deserts to Rome:
A nobler man, a braver warrior,
Lives not this day within the city walls:

He by the senate is accited home
From weary wars against the barbarous Goths;
That, with his sons, a terror to our foes,
Hath yoked a nation strong, train'd up in arms.
Ten years are spent since first he undertook
This cause of Rome, and chastised with arms
Our enemies' pride: five times he hath return'd
Bleeding to Rome, bearing his valiant sons
In coffins from the field.
And now at last, laden with honour's spoils,
Returns the good Andronicus to Rome,
Renowned Titus, flourishing in arms.
Let us entreat, by honour of his name,
Whom worthily you would have now succeed,
And in the Capitol and senate's right,
Whom you pretend to honour and adore,
That you withdraw you and abate your strength,
Dismiss your followers and, as suitors should,
Plead your deserts in peace and humbleness.

SATURNINUS
How fair the tribune speaks to calm my thoughts!

BASSIANUS
Marcus Andronicus, so I do affy
In thy uprightness and integrity,
And so I love and honour thee and thine,
Thy noble brother Titus and his sons,
And her to whom my thoughts are humbled all,
Gracious Lavinia, Rome's rich ornament,
That I will here dismiss my loving friends,
And to my fortunes and the people's favour
Commit my cause in balance to be weigh'd.

[Exeunt the FOLLOWERS OF BASSIANUS

SATURNINUS
Friends, that have been thus forward in my right,
I thank you all, and here dismiss you all,
And to the love and favour of my country
Commit myself, my person and the cause.

[Exeunt the FOLLOWERS OF SATURNINUS

[183]

Rome, be as just and gracious unto me,
As I am confident and kind to thee.
Open the gates, and let me in.

BASSIANUS

Tribunes, and me, a poor competitor.
[*Flourish.* SATURNINUS *and* BASSIANUS *go up
into the Capitol*
Enter a CAPTAIN

CAPTAIN

Romans, make way: the good Andronicus,
Patron of virtue, Rome's best champion,
Successful in the battles that he fights,
With honour and with fortune is return'd
From where he circumscribed with his sword,
And brought to yoke, the enemies of Rome.
Drums and trumpets sounded. Enter MARTIUS *and* MUTIUS;
after them, two MEN *bearing a coffin covered with black;
then* LUCIUS *and* QUINTUS. *After them,* TITUS ANDRON-
ICUS; *and then* TAMORA QUEEN OF GOTHS, *with* ALARBUS,
DEMETRIUS, CHIRON, AARON, *and other* GOTHS, *prisoners;*
SOLDIERS *and* PEOPLE *following. The* BEARERS *set down
the coffin, and* TITUS *speaks*

TITUS

Hail, Rome, victorious in thy mourning weeds!
Lo, as the bark that hath discharged her fraught
Returns with precious lading to the bay
From whence at first she weigh'd her anchorage,
Cometh Andronicus, bound with laurel boughs,
To re-salute his country with his tears,
Tears of true joy for his return to Rome.
Thou great defender of this Capitol,
Stand gracious to the rites that we intend!
Romans, of five and twenty valiant sons,
Half of the number that King Priam had,
Behold the poor remains, alive and dead!
These that survive let Rome reward with love;
These that I bring unto their latest home,
With burial amongst their ancestors:
Here Goths have given me leave to sheathe my
    sword.
Titus, unkind, and careless of thine own,
Why suffer'st thou thy sons, unburied yet,
To hover on the dreadful shore of Styx?
Make way to lay them by their brethren.
                              [*They open the tomb*
There greet in silence, as the dead are wont,
And sleep in peace, slain in your country's wars!
O sacred receptacle of my joys,
Sweet cell of virtue and nobility,
How many sons hast thou of mine in store,
That thou wilt never render to me more!

LUCIUS

Give us the proudest prisoner of the Goths,
That we may hew his limbs and on a pile
'Ad manes fratrum' sacrifice his flesh,
Before this earthy prison of their bones,
That so the shadows be not unappeased,
Nor we disturb'd with prodigies on earth.

TITUS

I give him you, the noblest that survives,
The eldest son of this distressed queen.

TAMORA

Stay, Roman brethren! Gracious conqueror,
Victorious Titus, rue the tears I shed,
A mother's tears in passion for her son:
And if thy sons were ever dear to thee,
O, think my son to be as dear to me!
Sufficeth not, that we are brought to Rome,
To beautify thy triumphs and return,
Captive to thee and to thy Roman yoke;
But must my sons be slaughter'd in the streets,
For valiant doings in their country's cause?
O, if to fight for king and commonweal
Were piety in thine, it is in these.
Andronicus, stain not thy tomb with blood.
Wilt thou draw near the nature of the gods?
Draw near them then in being merciful:
Sweet mercy is nobility's true badge:
Thrice-noble Titus, spare my first-born son.

TITUS

Patient yourself, madam, and pardon me.
These are their brethren, whom you Goths beheld
Alive and dead; and for their brethren slain
Religiously they ask a sacrifice:
To this your son is mark'd, and die he must,
To appease their groaning shadows that are gone

LUCIUS

Away with him! and make a fire straight;
And with our swords, upon a pile of wood,
Let's hew his limbs till they be clean consumed.
        [*Exeunt the sons of* ANDRONICUS *with* ALARBUS

TAMORA

O cruel, irreligious piety!

CHIRON

Was ever Scythia half so barbarous?

DEMETRIUS

Oppose not Scythia to ambitious Rome.
Alarbus goes to rest, and we survive
To tremble under Titus' threatening look.
Then, madam, stand resolved; but hope withal,
The self-same gods that arm'd the Queen of Troy
With opportunity of sharp revenge
Upon the Thracian tyrant in his tent,
May favour Tamora, the queen of Goths,
When Goths were Goths and Tamora was queen,
To quit the bloody wrongs upon her foes.
Re-enter the SONS OF ANDRONICUS, *with their swords
bloody*

LUCIUS

See, lord and father, how we have perform'd
Our Roman rites: Alarbus' limbs are lopp'd,
And entrails feed the sacrificing fire,
Whose smoke, like incense, doth perfume the sky.
Remaineth nought but to inter our brethren,
And with loud 'larums welcome them to Rome.

TITUS

Let it be so; and let Andronicus

Make this his latest farewell to their souls.
            [*Trumpets sounded, and the coffin laid in the tomb*
In peace and honour rest you here, my sons;
Rome's readiest champions, repose you here in rest,
Secure from worldly chances and mishaps!
Here lurks no treason, here no envy swells,
Here grow no damned drugs; here are no storms,
No noise, but silence and eternal sleep:
In peace and honour rest you here, my sons!

                    Enter LAVINIA

                        LAVINIA
In peace and honour live Lord Titus long;
My noble lord and father, live in fame!
Lo, at this tomb my tributary tears
I render, for my brethren's obsequies;
And at thy feet I kneel, with tears of joy
Shed on the earth, for thy return to Rome:
O, bless me here with thy victorious hand,
Whose fortunes Rome's best citizens applaud!

                        TITUS
Kind Rome, that hast thus lovingly reserved
The cordial of mine age to glad my heart!
Lavinia, live; outlive thy father's days,
And fame's eternal date, for virtue's praise!
Enter, below, MARCUS ANDRONICUS *and* TRIBUNES; *re-
enter* SATURNINUS *and* BASSIANUS, *attended*

                        MARCUS
Long live Lord Titus, my beloved brother,
Gracious triumpher in the eyes of Rome!

                        TITUS
Thanks, gentle tribune, noble brother Marcus.

                        MARCUS
And welcome, nephews, from successful wars,
You that survive, and you that sleep in fame!
Fair lords, your fortunes are alike in all,
That in your country's service drew your swords:
But safer triumph is this funeral pomp,
That hath aspired to Solon's happiness,
And triumphs over chance in honour's bed.
Titus Andronicus, the people of Rome,
Whose friend in justice thou hast ever been,
Send thee by me, their tribune and their trust,
This palliament of white and spotless hue;
And name thee in election for the empire,
With these our late-deceased emperor's sons:
Be candidatus then, and put it on,
And help to set a head on headless Rome.

                        TITUS
A better head her glorious body fits
Than his that shakes for age and feebleness:
What should I don this robe, and trouble you?
Be chosen with proclamations to-day,
To-morrow yield up rule, resign my life,
And set abroad new business for you all?
Rome, I have been thy soldier forty years,
And led my country's strength successfully,
And buried one and twenty valiant sons,
Knighted in field, slain manfully in arms,
In right and service of their noble country:
Give me a staff of honour for mine age,

But not a sceptre to control the world:
Upright he held it, lords, that held it last.

                        MARCUS
Titus, thou shalt obtain and ask the empery.

                        SATURNINUS
Proud and ambitious tribune, canst thou tell?

                        TITUS
Patience, Prince Saturninus.

                        SATURNINUS
                            Romans, do me right;
Patricians, draw your swords, and sheathe them not
Till Saturninus be Rome's emperor.
Andronicus, would thou wert shipp'd to hell,
Rather than rob me of the people's hearts!

                        LUCIUS
Proud Saturnine, interrupter of the good
That noble-minded Titus means to thee!

                        TITUS
Content thee, prince; I will restore to thee
The people's hearts, and wean them from them-
    selves.

                        BASSIANUS
Andronicus, I do not flatter thee,
But honour thee, and will do till I die:
My faction if thou strengthen with thy friends,
I will most thankful be; and thanks to men
Of noble minds is honourable meed.

                        TITUS
People of Rome, and people's tribunes here,
I ask your voices and your suffrages:
Will you bestow them friendly on Andronicus?

                        TRIBUNES
To gratify the good Andronicus,
And gratulate his safe return to Rome,
The people will accept whom he admits.

                        TITUS
Tribunes, I thank you: and this suit I make,
That you create your emperor's eldest son,
Lord Saturnine; whose virtues will, I hope,
Reflect on Rome as Titan's rays on earth,
And ripen justice in this commonweal:
Then, if you will elect by my advice,
Crown him, and say 'Long live our emperor!'

                        MARCUS
With voices and applause of every sort,
Patricians and plebeians, we create
Lord Saturninus Rome's great emperor,
And say 'Long live our Emperor Saturnine!'
                    [*A long flourish till they come down*

                        SATURNINUS
Titus Andronicus, for thy favours done
To us in our election this day,
I give thee thanks in part of thy deserts,
And will with deeds requite thy gentleness:
And, for an onset, Titus, to advance
Thy name and honourable family,
Lavinia will I make my empress,
Rome's royal mistress, mistress of my heart,
And in the sacred Pantheon her espouse:
Tell me, Andronicus, doth this motion please thee?

                        [185]

TITUS

It doth, my worthy lord; and in this match
I hold me highly honour'd of your grace:
And here, in sight of Rome, to Saturnine,
King and commander of our commonweal,
The wide world's emperor, do I consecrate
My sword, my chariot and my prisoners;
Presents well worthy Rome's imperious lord:
Receive them then, the tribute that I owe,
Mine honour's ensigns humbled at thy feet.

SATURNINUS

Thanks, noble Titus, father of my life!
How proud I am of thee and of thy gifts,
Rome shall record; and when I do forget
The least of these unspeakable deserts,
Romans, forget your fealty to me.

TITUS

[To TAMORA] Now, madam, are you prisoner to an
    emperor;
To him that, for your honour and your state,
Will use you nobly and your followers.

SATURNINUS

A goodly lady, trust me; of the hue
That I would choose, were I to choose anew.
Clear up, fair queen, that cloudy countenance:
Though chance of war hath wrought this change of
    cheer,
Thou comest not to be made a scorn in Rome:
Princely shall be thy usage every way.
Rest on my word, and let not discontent
Daunt all your hopes: madam, he comforts you
Can make you greater than the Queen of Goths.
Lavinia, you are not displeased with this?

LAVINIA

Not I, my lord; sith true nobility
Warrants these words in princely courtesy.

SATURNINUS

Thanks, sweet Lavinia. Romans, let us go:
Ransomless here we set our prisoners free:
Proclaim our honours, lords, with trump and drum.
    [Flourish. SATURNINUS courts TAMORA in
        dumb show

BASSIANUS

[Seizing LAVINIA] Lord Titus, by your leave, this
    maid is mine.

TITUS

How, sir! are you in earnest then, my lord?

BASSIANUS

Ay, noble Titus, and resolved withal
To do myself this reason and this right.

MARCUS

'Suum cuique' is our Roman justice:
This prince in justice seizeth but his own.

LUCIUS

And that he will, and shall, if Lucius live.

TITUS

Traitors, avaunt! Where is the emperor's guard?
Treason, my lord! Lavinia is surprised!

SATURNINUS

Surprised! by whom?

BASSIANUS

By him that justly may
Bear his betroth'd from all the world away.
    [Exeunt BASSIANUS and MARCUS with LAVINIA

MUTIUS

Brothers, help to convey her hence away,
And with my sword I'll keep this door safe.
    [Exeunt LUCIUS, QUINTUS, and MARTIUS

TITUS

Follow, my lord, and I'll soon bring her back.

MUTIUS

My lord, you pass not here.

TITUS

What, villain boy!
Barr'st me my way in Rome?   [Stabbing MUTIUS

MUTIUS

Help, Lucius, help. Dies
[During the fray, SATURNINUS, TAMORA, DEMETRIUS,
    CHIRON and AARON go out, and re-enter above
    Re-enter LUCIUS

LUCIUS

My lord, you are unjust; and, more than so,
In wrongful quarrel you have slain your son.

TITUS

Nor thou, nor he, are any sons of mine;
My sons would never so dishonour me:
Traitor, restore Lavinia to the emperor.

LUCIUS

Dead, if you will; but not to be his wife,
That is another's lawful promised love.   [Exit

SATURNINUS

No, Titus, no; the emperor needs her not,
Nor her, nor thee, nor any of thy stock:
I'll trust by leisure him that mocks me once:
Thee never, nor thy traitorous haughty sons,
Confederates all thus to dishonour me.
Was none in Rome to make a stale
But Saturnine? Full well, Andronicus,
Agree these deeds with that proud brag of thine,
That saidst I begg'd the empire at thy hands.

TITUS

O monstrous! what reproachful words are these?

SATURNINUS

But go thy ways; go give that changing piece
To him that flourish'd for her with his sword:
A valiant son-in-law thou shalt enjoy;
One fit to bandy with thy lawless sons,
To ruffle in the commonwealth of Rome.

TITUS

These words are razors to my wounded heart.

SATURNINUS

And therefore, lovely Tamora, Queen of Goths,
That, like the stately Phœbe 'mongst her nymphs,
Dost overshine the gallant'st dames of Rome,
If thou be pleased with this my sudden choice,
Behold, I choose thee, Tamora, for my bride,
And will create thee empress of Rome.
Speak, Queen of Goths, dost thou applaud my
    choice?
And here I swear by all the Roman gods,

Sith priest and holy water are so near,
And tapers burn so bright, and every thing
In readiness for Hymenæus stand,
I will not re-salute the streets of Rome,
Or climb my palace, till from forth this place
I lead espoused my bride along with me.

TAMORA

And here, in sight of heaven, to Rome I swear,
If Saturnine advance the Queen of Goths,
She will a handmaid be to his desires,
A loving nurse, a mother to his youth.

SATURNINUS

Ascend, fair queen, Pantheon. Lords, accompany
Your noble emperor and his lovely bride,
Sent by the heavens for Prince Saturnine,
Whose wisdom hath her fortune conquered:
There shall we consummate our spousal rites.

[Exeunt all but TITUS

TITUS

I am not bid to wait upon this bride.
Titus, when wert thou wont to walk alone,
Dishonour'd thus and challenged of wrongs?

Re-enter MARCUS, LUCIUS, QUINTUS, and MARTIUS

MARCUS

O Titus, see, O, see what thou hast done!
In a bad quarrel slain a virtuous son.

TITUS

No, foolish tribune, no; no son of mine,
Nor thou, nor these, confederates in the deed
That hath dishonour'd all our family;
Unworthy brother, and unworthy sons!

LUCIUS

But let us give him burial, as becomes;
Give Mutius burial with our brethren.

TITUS

Traitors, away! he rests not in this tomb:
This monument five hundred years hath stood,
Which I have sumptuously re-edified:
Here none but soldiers and Rome's servitors
Repose in fame; none basely slain in brawls:
Bury him where you can, he comes not here.

MARCUS

My lord, this is impiety in you:
My nephew Mutius' deeds do plead for him;
He must be buried with his brethren.

QUINTUS and MARTIUS

And shall, or him we will accompany.

TITUS

And shall! what villain was it spake that word?

QUINTUS

He that would vouch it in any place but here.

TITUS

What, would you bury him in my despite?

MARCUS

No, noble Titus; but entreat of thee
To pardon Mutius and to bury him.

TITUS

Marcus, even thou hast struck upon my crest,

And with these boys mine honour thou hast
　　wounded:
My foes I do repute you every one;
So trouble me no more, but get you gone.

MARTIUS

He is not with himself; let us withdraw.

QUINTUS

Not I, till Mutius' bones be buried.

[MARCUS and the SONS OF TITUS kneel

MARCUS

Brother, for in that name doth nature plead,—

QUINTUS

Father, and in that name doth nature speak,—

TITUS

Speak thou no more, if all the rest will speed.

MARCUS

Renowned Titus, more than half my soul,—

LUCIUS

Dear father, soul and substance of us all,—

MARCUS

Suffer thy brother Marcus to inter
His noble nephew here in virtue's nest,
That died in honour and Lavinia's cause.
Thou art a Roman; be not barbarous:
The Greeks upon advice did bury Ajax
That slew himself; and wise Laertes' son
Did graciously plead for his funerals:
Let not young Mutius then, that was thy joy,
Be barr'd his entrance here.

TITUS

　　　　　Rise, Marcus, rise:
The dismall'st day is this that e'er I saw,
To be dishonour'd by my sons in Rome!
Well, bury him, and bury me the next.

[MUTIUS is put into the tomb

LUCIUS

There lie thy bones, sweet Mutius, with thy friends,
Till we with trophies do adorn thy tomb.

ALL

[Kneeling] No man shed tears for noble Mutius;
He lives in fame that died in virtue's cause.

MARCUS

My lord, to step out of these dreary dumps,
How comes it that the subtle Queen of Goths
Is of a sudden thus advanced in Rome?

TITUS

I know not, Marcus; but I know it is,
Whether by device or no, the heavens can tell:
Is she not then beholding to the man
That brought her for this high good turn so far?
Yes, and will nobly him remunerate

Flourish. Re-enter, from one side, SATURNINUS attended,
TAMORA, DEMETRIUS, CHIRON, and AARON; from the
　　other, BASSIANUS, LAVINIA, with others

SATURNINUS

So, Bassianus, you have play'd your prize:
God give you joy, sir, of your gallant bride!

[187]

BASSIANUS

And you of yours, my lord! I say no more,
Nor wish no less; and so I take my leave.

SATURNINUS

Traitor, if Rome have law, or we have power,
Thou and thy faction shall repent this rape.

BASSIANUS

Rape, call you it, my lord, to seize my own,
My true-betrothed love, and now my wife?
But let the laws of Rome determine all;
Meanwhile I am possess'd of that is mine.

SATURNINUS

'Tis good, sir: you are very short with us;
But, if we live, we'll be as sharp with you.

BASSIANUS

My lord, what I have done, as best I may,
Answer I must, and shall do with my life.
Only thus much I give your grace to know:
By all the duties that I owe to Rome,
This noble gentleman, Lord Titus here,
Is in opinion and in honour wrong'd;
That, in the rescue of Lavinia,
With his own hand did slay his youngest son,
In zeal to you and highly moved to wrath
To be controll'd in that he frankly gave:
Receive him then to favour, Saturnine,
That hath express'd himself in all his deeds
A father and a friend to thee and Rome.

TITUS

Prince Bassianus, leave to plead my deeds:
'Tis thou and those that have dishonour'd me.
Rome and the righteous heavens be my judge,
How I have loved and honour'd Saturnine!

TAMORA

My worthy lord, if ever Tamora
Were gracious in those princely eyes of thine,
Then hear me speak indifferently for all;
And at my suit, sweet, pardon what is past.

SATURNINUS

What, madam! be dishonour'd openly,
And basely put it up without revenge?

TAMORA

Not so, my lord; the gods of Rome forfend
I should be author to dishonour you!
But on mine honour dare I undertake
For good Lord Titus' innocence in all;
Whose fury not dissembled speaks his griefs:
Then, at my suit, look graciously on him;
Lose not so noble a friend on vain suppose,
Nor with sour looks afflict his gentle heart.
[Aside to SATURNINUS] My lord, be ruled by me, be
　　won at last;
Dissemble all your griefs and discontents:
You are but newly planted in your throne;
Lest then the people, and patricians too,
Upon a just survey, take Titus' part,
And so supplant you for ingratitude,
Which Rome reputes to be a heinous sin,

Yield at entreats, and then let me alone:
I'll find a day to massacre them all,
And raze their faction and their family,
The cruel father and his traitorous sons,
To whom I sued for my dear son's life;
And make them know what 'tis to let a queen
Kneel in the streets and beg for grace in vain.—
Come, come, sweet emperor; come, Andronicus;
Take up this good old man, and cheer the heart
That dies in tempest of thy angry frown.

SATURNINUS

Rise, Titus, rise; my empress hath prevail'd.

TITUS

I thank your majesty, and her, my lord:
These words, these looks, infuse new life in me.

TAMORA

Titus, I am incorporate in Rome,
A Roman now adopted happily,
And must advise the emperor for his good.
This day all quarrels die, Andronicus.
And let it be mine honour, good my lord,
That I have reconciled your friends and you.
For you, Prince Bassianus, I have pass'd
My word and promise to the emperor,
That you will be more mild and tractable.
And fear not, lords, and you, Lavinia;
By my advice, all humbled on your knees,
You shall ask pardon of his majesty.

LUCIUS

We do; and vow to heaven, and to his highness,
That what we did was mildly as we might,
Tendering our sister's honour and our own.

MARCUS

That, on mine honour, here I do protest.

SATURNINUS

Away, and talk not; trouble us no more.

TAMORA

Nay, nay, sweet emperor, we must all be friends:
The tribune and his nephews kneel for grace;
I will not be denied: sweet heart, look back.

SATURNINUS

Marcus, for thy sake and thy brother's here,
And at my lovely Tamora's entreats,
I do remit these young men's heinous faults:
Stand up.
Lavinia, though you left me like a churl,
I found a friend; and sure as death I swore
I would not part a bachelor from the priest.
Come, if the emperor's court can feast two brides,
You are my guest, Lavinia, and your friends.
This day shall be a love-day, Tamora.

TITUS

To-morrow, an it please your majesty
To hunt the panther and the hart with me,
With horn and hound we'll give your grace bonjour.

SATURNINUS

Be it so, Titus, and gramercy too.

[Flourish. Exeunt

ACT II

Scene I. *Rome. Before the palace*

Enter AARON

AARON

Now climbeth Tamora Olympus' top,
Safe out of fortune's shot, and sits aloft,
Secure of thunder's crack or lightning flash,
Advanced above pale envy's threatening reach.
As when the golden sun salutes the morn,
And, having gilt the ocean with his beams,
Gallops the zodiac in his glistering coach,
And overlooks the highest-peering hills;
So Tamora:
Upon her wit doth earthly honour wait,
And virtue stoops and trembles at her frown.
Then, Aaron, arm thy heart, and fit thy thoughts,
To mount aloft with thy imperial mistress,
And mount her pitch, whom thou in triumph long
Hast prisoner held, fetter'd in amorous chains,
And faster bound to Aaron's charming eyes
Than is Prometheus tied to Caucasus.
Away with slavish weeds and servile thoughts!
I will be bright, and shine in pearl and gold,
To wait upon this new-made empress.
To wait, said I? to wanton with this queen,
This goddess, this Semiramis, this nymph,
This siren, that will charm Rome's Saturnine,
And see his shipwreck and his commonweal's.
Holloa! what storm is this?

Enter DEMETRIUS *and* CHIRON, *braving*

DEMETRIUS

Chiron, thy years want wit, thy wit wants edge,
And manners, to intrude where I am graced,
And may, for aught thou know'st, affected be.

CHIRON

Demetrius, thou dost over-ween in all,
And so in this, to bear me down with braves.
'Tis not the difference of a year or two
Makes me less gracious, or thee more fortunate:
I am as able and as fit as thou
To serve, and to deserve my mistress' grace;
And that my sword upon thee shall approve,
And plead my passions for Lavinia's love.

AARON

[*Aside*] Clubs, clubs! these lovers will not keep the
   peace.

DEMETRIUS

Why, boy, although our mother, unadvised,
Gave you a dancing-rapier by your side,
Are you so desperate grown, to threat your friends?
Go to; have your lath glued within your sheath
Till you know better how to handle it.

CHIRON

Meanwhile, sir, with the little skill I have,
Full well shalt thou perceive how much I dare.

DEMETRIUS

Ay, boy, grow ye so brave?   [*They draw*

AARON

[*Coming forward*] Why, how now, lords!

So near the emperor's palace dare you draw,
And maintain such a quarrel openly?
Full well I wot the ground of all this grudge:
I would not for a million of gold
The cause were known to them it most concerns;
Nor would your noble mother for much more
Be so dishonour'd in the court of Rome.
For shame, put up.

DEMETRIUS

            Not I, till I have sheathed
My rapier in his bosom, and withal
Thrust those reproachful speeches down his throat,
That he hath breathed in my dishonour here.

CHIRON

For that I am prepared and full resolved.
Foul-spoken coward! that thunder'st with thy
   tongue,
And with thy weapon nothing darest perform.

AARON

Away, I say!
Now, by the gods that warlike Goths adore,
This petty brabble will undo us all.
Why, lords, and think you not how dangerous
It is to jet upon a prince's right?
What, is Lavinia then become so loose,
Or Bassianus so degenerate,
That for her love such quarrels may be broach'd
Without controlment, justice, or revenge?
Young lords, beware! an should the empress know
This discord's ground, the music would not please.

CHIRON

I care not, I, knew she and all the world:
I love Lavinia more than all the world.

DEMETRIUS

Youngling, learn thou to make some meaner choice:
Lavinia is thine elder brother's hope.

AARON

Why, are ye mad? or know ye not, in Rome
How furious and impatient they be,
And cannot brook competitors in love?
I tell you, lords, you do but plot your deaths
By this device.

CHIRON

            Aaron, a thousand deaths
Would I propose to achieve her whom I love.

AARON

To achieve her! how?

DEMETRIUS

            Why makest thou it so strange?
She is a woman, therefore may be woo'd;
She is a woman, therefore may be won;
She is Lavinia, therefore must be loved.
What, man! more water glideth by the mill
Than wots the miller of; and easy it is
Of a cut loaf to steal a shive, we know:
Though Bassianus be the emperor's brother,
Better than he have worn Vulcan's badge.

AARON

[*Aside*] Ay, and as good as Saturninus may.

[189]

DEMETRIUS
Then why should he despair that knows to court it
With words, fair looks, and liberality?
What, hast not thou full often struck a doe,
And borne her cleanly by the keeper's nose?

AARON
Why, then, it seems, some certain snatch or so
Would serve your turns.

CHIRON
          Ay, so the turn were served.

DEMETRIUS
Aaron, thou hast hit it.

AARON
          Would you had hit it too!
Then should not we be tired with this ado.
Why, hark ye, hark ye! and are you such fools
To square for this? would it offend you, then,
That both should speed?

CHIRON
Faith, not me.

DEMETRIUS
          Nor me, so I were one.

AARON
For shame, be friends, and join for that you jar:
'Tis policy and stratagem must do
That you affect; and so must you resolve,
That what you cannot as you would achieve,
You must perforce accomplish as you may.
Take this of me: Lucrece was not more chaste
Than this Lavinia, Bassianus' love.
A speedier course than lingering languishment
Must we pursue, and I have found the path.
My lords, a solemn hunting is in hand;
There will the lovely Roman ladies troop:
The forest walks are wide and spacious;
And many unfrequented plots there are
Fitted by kind for rape and villany:
Single you thither then this dainty doe,
And strike her home by force, if not by words:
This way, or not at all, stand you in hope.
Come, come, our empress, with her sacred wit
To villany and vengeance consecrate,
Will we acquaint with all that we intend;
And she shall file our engines with advice,
That will not suffer you to square yourselves,
But to your wishes' height advance you both.
The emperor's court is like the house of Fame,
The palace full of tongues, of eyes and ears:
The woods are ruthless, dreadful, deaf and dull;
There speak, and strike, brave boys, and take your
   turns;
There serve your lust, shadow'd from heaven's eye,
And revel in Lavinia's treasury.

CHIRON
Thy counsel, lad, smells of no cowardice.

DEMETRIUS
Sit fas aut nefas, till I find the stream
To cool this heat, a charm to calm these fits,
Per Styga, per manes vehor.   [Exeunt

SCENE II. *A forest near Rome. Horns and cry of hounds*
heard.

Enter TITUS ANDRONICUS, *with* HUNTERS, &c., MARCUS,
LUCIUS, QUINTUS, *and* MARTIUS

TITUS
The hunt is up, the morn is bright and grey,
The fields are fragrant, and the woods are green:
Uncouple here, and let us make a bay,
And wake the emperor and his lovely bride,
And rouse the prince, and ring a hunter's peal,
That all the court may echo with the noise.
Sons, let it be your charge, as it is ours,
To attend the emperor's person carefully.
I have been troubled in my sleep this night,
But dawning day new comfort hath inspired.

A cry of hounds, and horns winded in a peal. Enter
SATURNINUS, TAMORA, BASSIANUS, LAVINIA,
DEMETRIUS, CHIRON, *and their* ATTENDANTS

Many good morrows to your majesty;
Madam, to you as many and as good:
I promised your grace a hunter's peal.

SATURNINUS
And you have rung it lustily, my lords;
Somewhat too early for new-married ladies.

BASSIANUS
Lavinia, how say you?

LAVINIA
          I say, no;
I have been broad awake two hours and more.

SATURNINUS
Come on then; horse and chariots let us have,
And to our sport. [*To* TAMORA] Madam, now shall
  ye see
Our Roman hunting.

MARCUS
          I have dogs, my lord,
Will rouse the proudest panther in the chase,
And climb the highest promontory top.

TITUS
And I have horse will follow where the game
Makes way, and run like swallows o'er the plain.

DEMETRIUS
Chiron, we hunt not, we, with horse nor hound,
But hope to pluck a dainty doe to ground.   [Exeunt

SCENE III. *A lonely part of the forest*

Enter AARON, *with a bag of gold*

AARON
He that had wit would think that I had none,
To bury so much gold under a tree,
And never after to inherit it.
Let him that thinks of me so abjectly
Know that this gold must coin a stratagem,
Which, cunningly effected, will beget
A very excellent piece of villany:
And so repose, sweet gold, for their unrest
                [Hides the gold
That have their alms out of the empress' chest.

Enter TAMORA

TAMORA

My lovely Aaron, wherefore look'st thou sad,
When every thing doth make a gleeful boast?
The birds chant melody on every bush;
The snake lies rolled in the cheerful sun;
The green leaves quiver with the cooling wind,
And make a chequer'd shadow on the ground:
Under their sweet shade, Aaron, let us sit,
And, whilst the babbling echo mocks the hounds,
Replying shrilly to the well-tuned horns,
As if a double hunt were heard at once,
Let us sit down and mark their yellowing noise;
And, after conflict such as was supposed
The wandering prince and Dido once enjoy'd,
When with a happy storm they were surprised,
And curtain'd with a counsel-keeping cave,
We may, each wreathed in the other's arms,
Our pastimes done, possess a golden slumber;
Whiles hounds and horns and sweet melodious birds
Be unto us as is a nurse's song
Of lullaby to bring her babe asleep.

AARON

Madam, though Venus govern your desires,
Saturn is dominator over mine:
What signifies my deadly-standing eye,
My silence and my cloudy melancholy,
My fleece of woolly hair that now uncurls
Even as an adder when she doth unroll
To do some fatal execution?
No, madam, these are no venereal signs:
Vengeance is in my heart, death in my hand,
Blood and revenge are hammering in my head.
Hark, Tamora, the empress of my soul,
Which never hopes more heaven than rests in thee,
This is the day of doom for Bassianus:
His Philomel must lose her tongue to-day,
Thy sons make pillage of her chastity,
And wash their hands in Bassianus' blood.
Seest thou this letter? take it up, I pray thee,
And give the king this fatal-plotted scroll.
Now question me no more; we are espied;
Here comes a parcel of our hopeful booty,
Which dreads not yet their lives' destruction.

TAMORA

Ah, my sweet Moor, sweeter to me than life!

AARON

No more, great empress; Bassianus comes:
Be cross with him, and I'll go fetch thy sons
To back thy quarrels, whatsoe'er they be.   [*Exit*

Enter BASSIANUS *and* LAVINIA

BASSIANUS

Who have we here? Rome's royal empress,
Unfurnish'd of her well-beseeming troop?
Or is it Dian, habited like her,
Who hath abandoned her holy groves
To see the general hunting in this forest?

TAMORA

Saucy controller of my private steps.
Had I the power that some say Dian had,

Thy temples should be planted presently
With horns, as was Actæon's, and the hounds
Should drive upon thy new-transformed limbs,
Unmannerly intruder as thou art!

LAVINIA

Under your patience, gentle empress,
'Tis thought you have a goodly gift in horning;
And to be doubted that your Moor and you
Are singled forth to try experiments:
Jove shield your husband from his hounds to-day!
'Tis pity they should take him for a stag.

BASSIANUS

Believe me, queen, your swarth Cimmerian
Doth make your honour of his body's hue,
Spotted, detested, and abominable.
Why are you sequester'd from all your train,
Dismounted from your snow-white goodly steed,
And wander'd hither to an obscure plot,
Accompanied but with a barbarous Moor,
If foul desire had not conducted you?

LAVINIA

And, being intercepted in your sport,
Great reason that my noble lord be rated
For sauciness. I pray you, let us hence,
And let her joy her raven-colour'd love;
This valley fits the purpose passing well.

BASSIANUS

The king my brother shall have note of this.

LAVINIA

Ay, for these slips have made him noted long:
Good king, to be so mightily abused!

TAMORA

Why have I patience to endure all this?

Enter DEMETRIUS *and* CHIRON

DEMETRIUS

How now, dear sovereign, and our gracious mother!
Why doth your highness look so pale and wan?

TAMORA

Have I not reason, think you, to look pale?
These two have ticed me hither to this place:
A barren detested vale, you see it is;
The trees, though summer, yet forlorn and lean,
O'ercome with moss and baleful mistletoe:
Here never shines the sun; here nothing breeds,
Unless the nightly owl or fatal raven:
And when they show'd me this abhorred pit,
They told me, here, at dead time of the night,
A thousand fiends, a thousand hissing snakes,
Ten thousand swelling toads, as many urchins,
Would make such fearful and confused cries,
As any mortal body hearing it
Should straight fall mad, or else die suddenly.
No sooner had they told this hellish tale,
But straight they told me they would bind me **here**
Unto the body of a dismal yew,
And leave me to this miserable death:
And then they call'd me foul adulteress,
Lascivious Goth, and all the bitterest terms
That ever ear did hear to such effect:
And, had you not by wondrous fortune come,

This vengeance on me, had they executed.
Revenge it, as you love your mother's life,
Or be ye not henceforth call'd my children.

DEMETRIUS

This is a witness that I am thy son.
[*Stabs* BASSIANUS

CHIRON

And this for me, struck home to show my strength.
[*Also stabs* BASSIANUS, *who dies*

LAVINIA

Ay, come, Semiramis, nay, barbarous Tamora,
For no name fits thy nature but thy own!

TAMORA

Give me the poniard; you shall know, my boys,
Your mother's hand shall right your mother's
wrong.

DEMETRIUS

Stay, madam; here is more belongs to her;
First thrash the corn, then after burn the straw;
This minion stood upon her chastity,
Upon her nuptial vow, her loyalty,
And with that painted hope braves your mightiness:
And shall she carry this unto her grave?

CHIRON

An if she do, I would I were an eunuch.
Drag hence her husband to some secret hole,
And make his dead trunk pillow to our lust.

TAMORA

But when ye have the honey ye desire,
Let not this wasp outlive us both to sting.

CHIRON

I warrant you, madam, we will make that sure.
Come, mistress, now perforce we will enjoy
That nice-preserved honesty of yours.

LAVINIA

O Tamora! thou bear'st a woman's face—

TAMORA

I will not hear her speak; away with her!

LAVINIA

Sweet lords, entreat her hear me but a word.

DEMETRIUS

Listen, fair madam: let it be your glory
To see her tears, but be your heart to them
As unrelenting flint to drops of rain.

LAVINIA

When did the tiger's young ones teach the dam?
O, do not learn her wrath; she taught it thee;
The milk thou suck'dst from her did turn to marble;
Even at thy teat thou hadst thy tyranny.
Yet every mother breeds not sons alike:
[*To* CHIRON] Do thou entreat her show a woman
pity.

CHIRON

What, wouldst thou have me prove myself a
bastard?

LAVINIA

'Tis true; the raven doth not hatch a lark:
Yet have I heard,—O, could I find it now!—
The lion, moved with pity, did endure
To have his princely paws pared all away:

Some say that ravens foster forlorn children,
The whilst their own birds famish in their nests:
O, be to me, though thy hard heart say no,
Nothing so kind, but something pitiful!

TAMORA

I know not what it means: away with her!

LAVINIA

O, let me teach thee! for my father's sake,
That gave thee life, when well he might have slain
thee,
Be not obdurate, open thy deaf ears.

TAMORA

Hadst thou in person ne'er offended me,
Even for his sake am I pitiless.
Remember, boys, I pour'd forth tears in vain,
To save your brother from the sacrifice;
But fierce Andronicus would not relent:
Therefore, away with her, and use her as you will;
The worse to her, the better loved of me.

LAVINIA

O Tamora, be call'd a gentle queen,
And with thine own hands kill me in this place!
For 'tis not life that I have begg'd so long;
Poor I was slain when Bassianus died.

TAMORA

What begg'st thou then? fond woman, let me go.

LAVINIA

'Tis present death I beg; and one thing more
That womanhood denies my tongue to tell:
O, keep me from their worse than killing lust,
And tumble me into some loathsome pit,
Where never man's eye may behold my body:
Do this, and be a charitable murderer.

TAMORA

So should I rob my sweet sons of their fee:
No, let them satisfy their lust on thee.

DEMETRIUS

Away! for thou hast stay'd us here too long.

LAVINIA

No grace? no womanhood? Ah, beastly creature!
The blot and enemy to our general name!
Confusion fall—

CHIRON

Nay, then I'll stop your mouth. Bring thou her
husband:
This is the hole where Aaron bid us hide him.
[DEMETRIUS *throws the body of* BASSIANUS
into the pit; then exeunt DEMETRIUS *and*
CHIRON, *dragging off* LAVINIA

TAMORA

Farewell, my sons; see that you make her sure.
Ne'er let my heart know merry cheer indeed,
Till all the Andronici be made away.
Now will I hence to seek my lovely Moor,
And let my spleenful sons this trull deflower. [*Exit*
Re-enter AARON, *with* QUINTUS *and* MARTIUS

AARON

Come on, my lords, the better foot before:
Straight will I bring you to the loathsome pit
Where I espied the panther fast asleep.

QUINTUS
My sight is very dull, whate'er it bodes.
MARTIUS
And mine, I promise you; were it not for shame,
Well could I leave our sport to sleep awhile.
[Falls into the pit
QUINTUS
What, art thou fall'n? What subtle hole is this,
Whose mouth is cover'd with rude-growing briers,
Upon whose leaves are drops of new-shed blood
As fresh as morning dew distill'd on flowers?
A very fatal place it seems to me.
Speak, brother, hast thou hurt thee with the fall?
MARTIUS
O brother, with the dismal'st object hurt
That ever eye with sight made heart lament!
AARON
[Aside] Now will I fetch the king to find them here,
That he thereby may have a likely guess
How these were they that made away his brother.
[Exit
MARTIUS
Why dost not comfort me, and help me out
From this unhallow'd and blood-stained hole?
QUINTUS
I am surprised with an uncouth fear;
A chilling sweat o'er-runs my trembling joints;
My heart suspects more than mine eye can see.
MARTIUS
To prove thou hast a true-divining heart,
Aaron and thou look down into this den,
And see a fearful sight of blood and death.
QUINTUS
Aaron is gone; and my compassionate heart
Will not permit mine eyes once to behold
The thing whereat it trembles by surmise:
O, tell me how it is; for ne'er till now
Was I a child to fear I know not what.
MARTIUS
Lord Bassianus lies embrewed here,
All on a heap, like to a slaughter'd lamb,
In this detested, dark, blood-drinking pit.
QUINTUS
If it be dark, how dost thou know 'tis he?
MARTIUS
Upon his bloody finger he doth wear
A precious ring, that lightens all the hole,
Which, like a taper in some monument,
Doth shine upon the dead man's earthy cheeks,
And shows the ragged entrails of the pit:
So pale did shine the moon on Pyramus
When he by night lay bathed in maiden blood.
O brother, help me with thy fainting hand—
If fear hath made thee faint, as me it hath—
Out of this fell devouring receptacle,
As hateful as Cocytus' misty mouth.
QUINTUS
Reach me thy hand, that I may help thee out;
Or, wanting strength to do thee so much good,
I may be pluck'd into the swallowing womb

Of this deep pit, poor Bassianus' grave.
I have no strength to pluck thee to the brink.
MARTIUS
Nor I no strength to climb without thy help.
QUINTUS
Thy hand once more; I will not loose again,
Till thou art here aloft, or I below:
Thou canst not come to me: I come to thee.
[Falls in
Enter SATURNINUS with AARON
SATURNINUS
Along with me: I'll see what hole is here,
And what he is that now is leap'd into it.
Say, who art thou that lately didst descend
Into this gaping hollow of the earth?
MARTIUS
The unhappy son of old Andronicus;
Brought hither in a most unlucky hour,
To find thy brother Bassianus dead.
SATURNINUS
My brother dead! I know thou dost but jest:
He and his lady both are at the lodge
Upon the north side of this pleasant chase;
'Tis not an hour since I left them there.
MARTIUS
We know not where you left them all alive;
But, out, alas! here have we found him dead.
Re-enter TAMORA, with ATTENDANTS; TITUS ANDRONICUS,
and LUCIUS
TAMORA
Where is my lord the king?
SATURNINUS
Here, Tamora; though grieved with killing grief.
TAMORA
Where is thy brother Bassianus?
SATURNINUS
Now to the bottom dost thou search my wound:
Poor Bassianus here lies murdered.
TAMORA
[Giving a letter] Then all too late I bring this fatal
writ,
The complot of this timeless tragedy;
And wonder greatly that man's face can fold
In pleasing smiles such murderous tyranny.
SATURNINUS
[Reads] 'An if we miss to meet him handsomely—
Sweet huntsman, Bassianus 'tis we mean—
Do thou so much as dig the grave for him:
Thou know'st our meaning. Look for thy reward
Among the nettles at the elder-tree,
Which overshades the mouth of that same pit
Where we decreed to bury Bassianus.
Do this and purchase us thy lasting friends.'
O Tamora! was ever heard the like?
This is the pit, and this the elder-tree.
Look, sirs, if you can find the huntsman out
That should have murder'd Bassianus here.
AARON
My gracious lord, here is the bag of gold.

[193]

SATURNINUS

[*To* TITUS] Two of thy whelps, fell curs of bloody kind,
Have here bereft my brother of his life.
Sirs, drag them from the pit unto the prison:
There let them bide until we have devised
Some never-heard-of torturing pain for them.

TAMORA

What, are they in this pit? O wondrous thing!
How easily murder is discovered!

TITUS

High emperor, upon my feeble knee
I beg this boon, with tears not lightly shed,
That this fell fault of my accursed sons,
Accursed, if the fault be proved in them—

SATURNINUS

If it be proved! you see it is apparent.
Who found this letter? Tamora, was it you?

TAMORA

Andronicus himself did take it up.

TITUS

I did, my lord: yet let me be their bail;
For, by my fathers' reverend tomb, I vow
They shall be ready at your highness' will,
To answer their suspicion with their lives.

SATURNINUS

Thou shalt not bail them: see thou follow me.
Some bring the murder'd body, some the murder-
   ers:
Let them not speak a word; the guilt is plain;
For, by my soul, were there worse end than death,
That end upon them should be executed.

TAMORA

Andronicus, I will entreat the king:
Fear not thy sons; they shall do well enough.

TITUS

Come, Lucius, come; stay not to talk with them.
                                 [*Exeunt*

SCENE IV. *Another part of the forest*

Enter DEMETRIUS *and* CHIRON, *with* LAVINIA, *ravished;*
   her hands cut off, and her tongue cut out

DEMETRIUS

So, now go tell, an if thy tongue can speak,
Who 'twas that cut thy tongue and ravish'd thee.

CHIRON

Write down thy mind, bewray thy meaning so,
An if thy stumps will let thee play the scribe.

DEMETRIUS

See, how with signs and tokens she can scrowl.

CHIRON

Go home, call for sweet water, wash thy hands.

DEMETRIUS

She hath no tongue to call, nor hands to wash;
And so let's leave her to her silent walks.

CHIRON

An 'twere my case, I should go hang myself.

DEMETRIUS

If thou hadst hands to help thee knit the cord.
             [*Exeunt* DEMETRIUS *and* CHIRON

Horns winded within. Enter MARCUS, *from hunting*

MARCUS

Who is this? my niece, that flies away so fast!
Cousin, a word; where is your husband?
If I do dream, would all my wealth would wake me!
If I do wake, some planet strike me down,
That I may slumber in eternal sleep!
Speak, gentle niece, what stern ungentle hands
Have lopp'd and hew'd and made thy body bare
Of her two branches, those sweet ornaments,
Whose circling shadows kings have sought to sleep
   in,
And might not gain so great a happiness
As have thy love? Why dost not speak to me?
Alas, a crimson river of warm blood,
Like to a bubbling fountain stirr'd with wind,
Doth rise and fall between thy rosed lips,
Coming and going with thy honey breath.
But, sure, some Tereus hath deflowered thee,
And, lest thou shouldst detect him, cut thy tongue.
Ah, now thou turn'st away thy face for shame!
And, notwithstanding all this loss of blood,
As from a conduit with three issuing spouts,
Yet do thy cheeks look red as Titan's face
Blushing to be encounter'd with a cloud.
Shall I speak for thee? shall I say 'tis so?
O, that I knew thy heart; and knew the beast,
That I might rail at him, to ease my mind!
Sorrow concealed, like an oven stopp'd,
Doth burn the heart to cinders where it is.
Fair Philomel, why she but lost her tongue,
And in a tedious sampler sew'd her mind:
But, lovely niece, that mean is cut from thee;
A craftier Tereus, cousin, hast thou met,
And he hath cut those pretty fingers off,
That could have better sew'd than Philomel.
O, had the monster seen those lily hands
Tremble, like aspen-leaves, upon a lute,
And make the silken strings delight to kiss them,
He would not then have touch'd them for his life!
Or, had he heard the heavenly harmony
Which that sweet tongue hath made,
He would have dropp'd his knife, and fell asleep
As Cerberus at the Thracian poet's feet.
Come, let us go and make thy father blind;
For such a sight will blind a father's eye:
One hour's storm will drown the fragrant meads;
What will whole months of tears thy father's eyes?
Do not draw back, for we will mourn with thee:
O, could our mourning ease thy misery!   [*Exeunt*

ACT III

SCENE I. *Rome. A street*

Enter JUDGES, SENATORS, *and* TRIBUNES, *with* MARTIUS
and QUINTUS, *bound, passing on to the place of execution;*
    TITUS *going before, pleading*

TITUS

Hear me, grave fathers! noble tribunes, stay!

[194]

For pity of mine age, whose youth was spent
In dangerous wars, whilst you securely slept;
For all my blood in Rome's great quarrel shed;
For all the frosty nights that I have watch'd;
And for these bitter tears, which now you see
Filling the aged wrinkles in my cheeks;
Be pitiful to my condemned sons,
Whose souls are not corrupted as 'tis thought.
For two and twenty sons I never wept,
Because they died in honour's lofty bed.

    [Lieth down; the JUDGES, *&c. pass by him, and exeunt*
For these, tribunes, in the dust I write
My heart's deep languor and my soul's sad tears:
Let my tears stanch the earth's dry appetite;
My sons' sweet blood will make it shame and blush.
O earth, I will befriend thee more with rain,
That shall distil from these two ancient urns,
Than youthful April shall with all his showers:
In summer's drought I'll drop upon thee still;
In winter with warm tears I'll melt the snow,
And keep eternal spring-time on thy face,
So thou refuse to drink my dear sons' blood.

    Enter LUCIUS, *with his weapon drawn*
O reverend tribunes! O gentle, aged men!
Unbind my sons, reverse the doom of death;
And let me say, that never wept before,
My tears are now prevailing orators.

LUCIUS
O noble father, you lament in vain:
The tribunes hear you not; no man is by;
And you recount your sorrows to a stone.

TITUS
Ah, Lucius, for thy brothers let me plead.
Grave tribunes, once more I entreat of you,—

LUCIUS
My gracious lord, no tribune hears you speak.

TITUS
Why, 'tis no matter, man: if they did hear,
They would not mark me; or if they did mark,
They would not pity me; yet plead I must,
And bootless unto them. . . .
Therefore I tell my sorrows to the stones;
Who, though they cannot answer my distress,
Yet in some sort they are better than the tribunes,
For that they will not intercept my tale:
When I do weep, they humbly at my feet
Receive my tears, and seem to weep with me;
And, were they but attired in grave weeds,
Rome could afford no tribune like to these.
A stone is soft as wax, tribunes more hard than
    stones;
A stone is silent and offendeth not,
And tribunes with their tongues doom men to
    death.   *[Rises*
But wherefore stand'st thou with thy weapon
    drawn?

LUCIUS
To rescue my two brothers from their death:
For which attempt the judges have pronounced
My everlasting doom of banishment.

TITUS
O happy man! they have befriended thee.
Why, foolish Lucius, dost thou not perceive
That Rome is but a wilderness of tigers?
Tigers must prey, and Rome affords no prey
But me and mine: how happy art thou then,
From these devourers to be banished!
But who comes with our brother Marcus here?

    Enter MARCUS *and* LAVINIA
MARCUS
Titus, prepare thy aged eyes to weep;
Or, if not so, thy noble heart to break:
I bring consuming sorrow to thine age.

TITUS
Will it consume me? let me see it then.

MARCUS
This was thy daughter.

TITUS
               Why, Marcus, so she is.

LUCIUS
Ay me, this object kills me!

TITUS
Faint-hearted boy, arise, and look upon her.
Speak, Lavinia, what accursed hand
Hath made thee handless in thy father's sight?
What fool hath added water to the sea,
Or brought a faggot to bright-burning Troy?
My grief was at the height before thou camest;
And now, like Nilus, it disdaineth bounds.
Give me a sword, I'll chop off my hands too;
For they have fought for Rome, and all in vain;
And they have nursed this woe, in feeding life;
In bootless prayer have they been held up,
And they have served me to effectless use:
Now all the service I require of them
Is, that the one will help to cut the other.
'Tis well, Lavinia, that thou hast no hands;
For hands to do Rome service is but vain.

LUCIUS
Speak, gentle sister, who hath martyr'd thee?

MARCUS
O, that delightful engine of her thoughts,
That blabb'd them with such pleasing eloquence,
Is torn from forth that pretty hollow cage,
Where, like a sweet melodious bird, it sung
Sweet varied notes, enchanting every ear!

LUCIUS
O, say thou for her, who hath done this deed?

MARCUS
O, thus I found her, straying in the park,
Seeking to hide herself, as doth the deer
That hath received some unrecuring wound.

TITUS
It was my dear; and he that wounded her
Hath hurt me more than had he kill'd me dead:
For now I stand as one upon a rock,
Environ'd with a wilderness of sea;
Who marks the waxing tide grow wave by wave,
Expecting ever when some envious surge
Will in his brinish bowels swallow him.

This way to death my wretched sons are gone;
Here stands my other son, a banish'd man;
And here my brother, weeping at my woes:
But that which gives my soul the greatest spurn,
Is dear Lavinia, dearer than my soul.
Had I but seen thy picture in this plight,
It would have madded me: what shall I do,
Now I behold thy lively body so?
Thou hast no hands, to wipe away thy tears;
Nor tongue, to tell me who hath martyr'd thee:
Thy husband he is dead; and for his death
Thy brothers are condemn'd, and dead by this.
Look, Marcus! ah, son Lucius, look on her!
When I did name her brothers, then fresh tears
Stood on her cheeks, as doth the honey-dew
Upon a gather'd lily almost wither'd.

MARCUS
Perchance she weeps because they kill'd her hus-
    band;
Perchance because she knows them innocent.

TITUS
If they did kill thy husband, then be joyful,
Because the law hath ta'en revenge on them.
No, no, they would not do so foul a deed;
Witness the sorrow that their sister makes.
Gentle Lavinia, let me kiss thy lips;
Or make some sign how I may do thee ease:
Shall thy good uncle, and thy brother Lucius,
And thou, and I, sit round about some fountain,
Looking all downwards, to behold our cheeks
How they are stain'd, as meadows yet not dry
With miry slime left on them by a flood?
And in the fountain shall we gaze so long
Till the fresh taste be taken from that clearness,
And made a brine-pit with our bitter tears?
Or shall we cut away our hands, like thine?
Or shall we bite our tongues, and in dumb shows
Pass the remainder of our hateful days?
What shall we do? let us, that have our tongues,
Plot some device of further misery,
To make us wonder'd at in time to come.

LUCIUS
Sweet father, cease your tears; for, at your grief,
See how my wretched sister sobs and weeps.

MARCUS
Patience, dear niece. Good Titus, dry thine eyes.

TITUS
Ah, Marcus, Marcus! brother, well I wot
Thy napkin cannot drink a tear of mine,
For thou, poor man, hast drown'd it with thine own.

LUCIUS
Ah, my Lavinia, I will wipe thy cheeks.

TITUS
Mark, Marcus, mark! I understand her signs:
Had she a tongue to speak, now would she say
That to her brother which I said to thee:
His napkin, with his true tears all bewet,
Can do no service on her sorrowful cheeks.
O, what a sympathy of woe is this,
As far from help as Limbo is from bliss!

Enter AARON

AARON
Titus Andronicus, my lord the emperor
Sends thee this word, that, if thou love thy sons,
Let Marcus, Lucius, or thyself, old Titus,
Or any one of you, chop off your hand,
And send it to the king: he for the same
Will send thee hither both thy sons alive;
And that shall be the ransom for their fault.

TITUS
O gracious emperor! O gentle Aaron!
Did ever raven sing so like a lark,
That gives sweet tidings of the sun's uprise?
With all my heart, I'll send the emperor
My hand:
Good Aaron, wilt thou help to chop it off?

LUCIUS
Stay, father! for that noble hand of thine,
That hath thrown down so many enemies,
Shall not be sent: my hand will serve the turn:
My youth can better spare my blood than you;
And therefore mine shall save my brothers' lives.

MARCUS
Which of your hands hath not defended Rome,
And rear'd aloft the bloody battle-axe,
Writing destruction on the enemy's castle?
O, none of both but are of high desert:
My hand hath been but idle; let it serve
To ransom my two nephews from their death;
Then have I kept it to a worthy end.

AARON
Nay, come, agree whose hand shall go along,
For fear they die before their pardon come.

MARCUS
My hand shall go.

LUCIUS
            By heaven, it shall not go!

TITUS
Sirs, strive no more: such wither'd herbs as these
Are meet for plucking up, and therefore mine.

LUCIUS
Sweet father, if I shall be thought thy son,
Let me redeem my brothers both from death.

MARCUS
And, for our father's sake and mother's care,
Now let me show a brother's love to thee.

TITUS
Agree between you; I will spare my hand.

LUCIUS
Then I'll go fetch an axe.

MARCUS
But I will use the axe.

            [*Exeunt* LUCIUS *and* MARCUS

TITUS
Come hither, Aaron; I'll deceive them both:
Lend me thy hand, and I will give thee mine.

AARON
[*Aside*] If that be call'd deceit, I will be honest,
And never, whilst I live, deceive men so:

But I'll deceive you in another sort,
And that you'll say, ere half an hour pass.
                       [Cuts off TITUS's *hand*
        Re-enter LUCIUS *and* MARCUS
                TITUS
Now stay your strife: what shall be is dispatch'd.
Good Aaron, give his majesty my hand:
Tell him it was a hand that warded him
From thousand dangers; bid him bury it;
More hath it merited; that let it have.
As for my sons, say I account of them
As jewels purchased at an easy price;
And yet dear too, because I bought mine own.
                AARON
I go, Andronicus: and for thy hand
Look by and by to have thy sons with thee.
[Aside] Their heads, I mean. O, how this villany
Doth fat me with the very thoughts of it!
Let fools do good, and fair men call for grace,
Aaron will have his soul black like his face.   *[Exit*
                TITUS
O, here I lift this one hand up to heaven,
And bow this feeble ruin to the earth:
If any power pities wretched tears,
To that I call! *[To* LAVINIA] What, would thou
    kneel with me?
Do. then, dear heart; for heaven shall hear our
    prayers;
Or with our sighs we'll breathe the welkin dim,
And stain the sun with fog, as sometime clouds
When they do hug him in their melting bosoms.
               MARCUS
O brother, speak with possibilities,
And do not break into these deep extremes.
                TITUS
Is not my sorrow deep, having no bottom?
Then be my passions bottomless with them.
               MARCUS
But yet let reason govern thy lament.
                TITUS
If there were reason for these miseries,
Then into limits could I bind my woes:
When heaven doth weep, doth not the earth o'er-
    flow?
If the winds rage, doth not the sea wax mad,
Threatening the welkin with his big-swoln face?
And wilt thou have a reason for this coil?
I am the sea; hark, how her sighs do blow!
She is the weeping welkin, I the earth:
Then must my sea be moved with her sighs;
Then must my earth with her continual tears
Become a deluge, overflow'd and drown'd:
For why my bowels cannot hide her woes,
But like a drunkard must I vomit them.
Then give me leave; for losers will have leave
To ease their stomachs with their bitter tongues.
     Enter a MESSENGER, *with two heads and a hand*
              MESSENGER
Worthy Andronicus, ill art thou repaid
For that good hand thou sent'st the emperor.

Here are the heads of thy two noble sons;
And here's thy hand, in scorn to thee sent back,
Thy griefs their sports, thy resolution mock'd:
That woe is me to think upon thy woes,
More than remembrance of my father's death.
                            [Exit
               MARCUS
Now let hot Ætna cool in Sicily,
And be my heart an ever-burning hell!
These miseries are more than may be borne.
To weep with them that weep doth ease some deal,
But sorrow flouted at is double death.
               LUCIUS
Ah, that this sight should make so deep a wound,
And yet detested life not shrink thereat!
That ever death should let life bear his name,
Where life hath no more interest but to breathe!
            *[*LAVINIA *kisses* TITUS
               MARCUS
Alas, poor heart, that kiss is comfortless
As frozen water to a starved snake.
                TITUS
When will this fearful slumber have an end?
               MARCUS
Now, farewell, flattery: die, Andronicus;
Thou dost not slumber: see, thy two sons' heads,
Thy warlike hand, thy mangled daughter here,
Thy other banish'd son with this dear sight
Struck pale and bloodless, and thy brother, I,
Even like a stony image, cold and numb.
Ah, now no more will I control thy griefs:
Rend off thy silver hair, thy other hand
Gnawing with thy teeth; and be this dismal sight
The closing up of our most wretched eyes:
Now is a time to storm; why art thou still?
                TITUS
Ha, ha, ha!
               MARCUS
Why dost thou laugh? it fits not with this hour.
                TITUS
Why, I have not another tear to shed:
Besides, this sorrow is an enemy,
And would usurp upon my watery eyes,
And make them blind with tributary tears:
Then which way shall I find Revenge's cave?
For these two heads do seem to speak to me,
And threat me I shall never come to bliss
Till all these mischiefs be return'd again
Even in their throats that have committed them.
Come, let me see what task I have to do.
You heavy people, circle me about,
That I may turn me to each one of you,
And swear unto my soul to right your wrongs.
The vow is made. Come, brother, take a head;
And in this hand the other will I bear.
Lavinia, thou shalt be employ'd in these things:
Bear thou my hand, sweet wench, between thy
    teeth.
As for thee, boy, go get thee from my sight;
Thou art an exile, and thou must not stay:

Hie to the Goths, and raise an army there:
And, if you love me, as I think you do,
Let's kiss and part, for we have much to do.

                    [*Exeunt all but* LUCIUS

LUCIUS

Farewell, Andronicus, my noble father,
The wofull'st man that ever lived in Rome:
Farewell, proud Rome; till Lucius come again,
He leaves his pledges dearer than his life:
Farewell, Lavinia, my noble sister;
O, would thou wert as thou tofore hast been!
But now nor Lucius nor Lavinia lives
But in oblivion and hateful griefs.
If Lucius live, he will requite your wrongs;
And make proud Saturnine and his empress
Beg at the gates, like Tarquin and his queen.
Now will I to the Goths and raise a power,
To be revenged on Rome and Saturnine.   [*Exit*

SCENE II. *A room in* TITUS's *house. A banquet set out*

Enter TITUS, MARCUS, LAVINIA, *and young* LUCIUS, *a*
BOY

TITUS

So, so; now sit: and look you eat no more
Than will preserve just so much strength in us
As will revenge these bitter woes of ours.
Marcus, unknit that sorrow-wreathen knot:
Thy niece and I, poor creatures, want our hands,
And cannot passionate our tenfold grief
With folded arms. This poor right hand of mine
Is left to tyrannize upon my breast;
Who, when my heart, all mad with misery,
Beats in this hollow prison of my flesh,
Then thus I thump it down.
[*To* LAVINIA] Thou map of woe, that thus dost talk
   in signs!
When thy poor heart beats with outrageous beating,
Thou canst not strike it thus to make it still.
Wound it with sighing, girl, kill it with groans;
Or get some little knife between thy teeth,
And just against thy heart make thou a hole;
That all the tears that thy poor eyes let fall
May run into that sink, and soaking in
Drown the lamenting fool in sea-salt tears.

MARCUS

Fie, brother, fie! teach her not thus to lay
Such violent hands upon her tender life.

TITUS

How now! has sorrow made thee dote already?
Why, Marcus, no man should be mad but I.
What violent hands can she lay on her life?
Ah, wherefore dost thou urge the name of hands;
To bid Æneas tell the tale twice o'er,
How Troy was burnt and he made miserable?
O, handle not the theme, to talk of hands,
Lest we remember still that we have none.
Fie, fie, how franticly I square my talk,
As if we should forget we had no hands,

If Marcus did not name the word of hands!
Come, let's fall to; and, gentle girl, eat this:
Here is no drink. Hark, Marcus, what she says;
I can interpret all her martyr'd signs;
She says she drinks no other drink but tears,
Brew'd with her sorrow, mesh'd upon her cheeks:
Speechless complainer, I will learn thy thought;
In thy dumb action will I be as perfect
As begging hermits in their holy prayers:
Thou shalt not sigh, nor hold thy stumps to heaven,
Nor wink, nor nod, nor kneel, nor make a sign,
But I of these will wrest an alphabet,
And by still practice learn to know thy meaning.

BOY

Good grandsire, leave these bitter deep laments:
Make my aunt merry with some pleasing tale.

MARCUS

Alas, the tender boy, in passion moved,
Doth weep to see his grandsire's heaviness.

TITUS

Peace, tender sapling; thou art made of tears,
And tears will quickly melt thy life away.
        [MARCUS *strikes the dish with a knife*
What dost thou strike at, Marcus, with thy knife?

MARCUS

At that that I have kill'd, my lord,—a fly.

TITUS

Out on thee, murderer! thou kill'st my heart;
Mine eyes are cloy'd with view of tyranny:
A deed of death done on the innocent
Becomes not Titus' brother: get thee gone;
I see thou art not for my company.

MARCUS

Alas, my lord, I have but kill'd a fly.

TITUS

'But!' How, if that fly had a father and mother?
How would he hang his slender gilded wings,
And buzz lamenting doings in the air!
Poor harmless fly,
That, with his pretty buzzing melody,
Came here to make us merry! and thou hast kill'd
   him.

MARCUS

Pardon me, sir; it was a black ill-favour'd fly,
Like to the empress' Moor; therefore I kill'd him.

TITUS

O, O, O,
Then pardon me for reprehending thee,
For thou hast done a charitable deed.
Give me thy knife, I will insult on him;
Flattering myself, as if it were the Moor
Come hither purposely to poison me.
There's for thyself, and that's for Tamora.
Ah, sirrah!
Yet, I think, we are not brought so low,
But that between us we can kill a fly
That comes in likeness of a coal-black Moor.

MARCUS

Alas, poor man! grief has so wrought on him,
He takes false shadows for true substances.

TITUS

Come, take away. Lavinia, go with me:
I'll to thy closet; and go read with thee
Sad stories chanced in the times of old.
Come, boy, and go with me: thy sight is young,
And thou shalt read when mine begin to dazzle.

[*Exeunt*

ACT IV

SCENE I. *Rome.* TITUS's *garden*

Enter young LUCIUS *and* LAVINIA *running after him, and
the* BOY *flies from her, with his books under his arm. Then
enter* TITUS *and* MARCUS

BOY

Help, grandsire, help! my aunt Lavinia
Follows me every where, I know not why:
Good uncle Marcus, see how swift she comes.
Alas, sweet aunt, I know not what you mean.

MARCUS

Stand by me, Lucius; do not fear thine aunt.

TITUS

She loves thee, boy, too well to do thee harm.

BOY

Ay, when my father was in Rome she did.

MARCUS

What means my niece Lavinia by these signs?

TITUS

Fear her not, Lucius: somewhat doth she mean:
See, Lucius, see how much she makes of thee:
Somewhither would she have thee go with her.
Ah, boy, Cornelia never with more care
Read to her sons than she hath read to thee
Sweet poetry and Tully's Orator.

MARCUS

Canst thou not guess wherefore she plies thee thus?

BOY

My lord, I know not, I, nor can I guess,
Unless some fit or frenzy do possess her:
For I have heard my grandsire say full oft,
Extremity of griefs would make men mad;
And I have read that Hecuba of Troy
Ran mad for sorrow: that made me to fear;
Although, my lord, I know my noble aunt
Loves me as dear as e'er my mother did,
And would not, but in fury, fright my youth:
Which made me down to throw my books and fly,
Causeless perhaps. But pardon me, sweet aunt:
And, madam, if my uncle Marcus go,
I will most willingly attend your ladyship.

MARCUS

Lucius, I will. [LAVINIA *turns over with her stumps the
books which* LUCIUS *has let fall*

TITUS

How now, Lavinia! Marcus, what means this?
Some book there is that she desires to see.
Which is it, girl, of these? Open them, boy.
But thou art deeper read, and better skill'd:
Come, and take choice of all my library,

And so beguile thy sorrow, till the heavens
Reveal the damn'd contriver of this deed.
Why lifts she up her arms in sequence thus?

MARCUS

I think she means that there were more than one
Confederate in the fact; ay, more there was;
Or else to heaven she heaves them for revenge.

TITUS

Lucius, what book is that she tosseth so?

BOY

Grandsire, 'tis Ovid's Metamorphoses:
My mother gave it me.

MARCUS

         For love of her that's gone,
Perhaps she cull'd it from among the rest.

TITUS

Soft! so busily she turns the leaves!
Help her:
What would she find? Lavinia, shall I read?
This is the tragic tale of Philomel,
And treats of Tereus' treason and his rape;
And rape, I fear, was root of thine annoy.

MARCUS

See, brother, see; note how she quotes the leaves.

TITUS

Lavinia, wert thou thus surprised, sweet girl,
Ravish'd and wrong'd, as Philomela was,
Forced in the ruthless, vast, and gloomy woods?
See, see!
Ay, such a place there is, where we did hunt,—
O, had we never, never hunted there!—
Pattern'd by that the poet here describes,
By nature made for murders and for rapes.

MARCUS

O, why should nature build so foul a den,
Unless the gods delight in tragedies?

TITUS

Give signs, sweet girl, for here are none but friends,
What Roman lord it was durst do the deed:
Or slunk not Saturnine, as Tarquin erst,
That left the camp to sin in Lucrece' bed?

MARCUS

Sit down, sweet niece: brother, sit down by me.
Apollo, Pallas, Jove, or Mercury,
Inspire me, that I may this treason find!
My lord, look here: look here, Lavinia:
This sandy plot is plain; guide, if thou canst,
This after me. [*He writes his name with his staff, and
guides it with feet and mouth.*] I have writ my name
Without the help of any hand at all.
Cursed be that heart that forced us to this shift!
Write thou, good niece; and here display at last
What God will have discovered for revenge:
Heaven guide thy pen to print thy sorrows plain,
That we may know the traitors and the truth!
[*She takes the staff in her mouth, and guides it with her
                             stumps, and writes*

TITUS

O, do ye read, my lord, what she hath writ?
'Stuprum. Chiron. Demetrius.'

MARCUS

What, what! the lustful sons of Tamora
Performers of this heinous, bloody deed?

TITUS

Magni Dominator poli,
Tam lentus audis scelera? tam lentus vides?

MARCUS

O, calm thee, gentle lord; although I know
There is enough written upon this earth
To stir a mutiny in the mildest thoughts,
And arm the minds of infants to exclaims.
My lord, kneel down with me; Lavinia, kneel;
And kneel, sweet boy, the Roman Hector's hope;
And swear with me, as, with the woful fere
And father of that chaste dishonour'd dame,
Lord Junius Brutus sware for Lucrece' rape,
That we will prosecute by good advice
Mortal revenge upon these traitorous Goths,
And see their blood, or die with this reproach.

TITUS

'Tis sure enough, an you knew how.
But if you hunt these bear-whelps, then beware:
The dam will wake; and if she wind you once,
She's with the lion deeply still in league,
And lulls him whilst she playeth on her back,
And when he sleeps will she do what she list.
You are a young huntsman, Marcus; let alone;
And, come, I will go get a leaf of brass,
And with a gad of steel will write these words,
And lay it by: the angry northern wind
Will blow these sands, like Sibyl's leaves, abroad,
And where's your lesson then? Boy, what say you?

BOY

I say, my lord, that if I were a man,
Their mother's bed-chamber should not be safe
For these bad bondmen to the yoke of Rome.

MARCUS

Ay, that's my boy! thy father hath full oft
For his ungrateful country done the like.

BOY

And, uncle, so will I, an if I live.

TITUS

Come, go with me into mine armoury;
Lucius, I'll fit thee, and withal, my boy
Shall carry from me to the empress' sons
Presents that I intend to send them both:
Come, come; thou'lt do thy message, wilt thou not?

BOY

Ay, with my dagger in their bosoms, grandsire.

TITUS

No, boy, not so; I'll teach thee another course.
Lavinia, come. Marcus, look to my house:
Lucius and I'll go brave it at the court;
Ay, marry, will we, sir; and we'll be waited on.
[Exeunt TITUS, LAVINIA, and young LUCIUS

MARCUS

O heavens, can you hear a good man groan,
And not relent, or not compassion him?
Marcus, attend him in his ecstasy,
That hath more scars of sorrow in his heart

Than foemen's marks upon his batter'd shield,
But yet so just that he will not revenge.
Revenge, ye heavens, for old Andronicus!   [Exit

SCENE II. *The same. A room in the palace*

Enter AARON, CHIRON, *and* DEMETRIUS *at one door; and
at another door, young* LUCIUS, *and an* ATTENDANT, *with
a bundle of weapons, and verses writ upon them*

CHIRON

Demetrius, here's the son of Lucius;
He hath some message to deliver us.

AARON

Ay, some mad message from his mad grandfather.

BOY

My lords, with all the humbleness I may,
I greet your honours from Andronicus.
[Aside] And pray the Roman gods confound you both!

DEMETRIUS

Gramercy, lovely Lucius: what's the news?

BOY

[Aside] That you are both decipher'd, that's the
news,
For villains mark'd with rape.—May it please you,
My grandsire, well advised, hath sent by me
The goodliest weapons of his armoury
To gratify your honourable youth,
The hope of Rome; for so he bid me say;
And so I do, and with his gifts present
Your lordships, that, whenever you have need,
You may be armed and appointed well:
And so I leave you both, [Aside] like bloody villains.
[Exeunt BOY and ATTENDANT

DEMETRIUS

What's here? A scroll, and written round about!
Let's see:
[Reads] 'Integer vitæ, scelerisque purus,
          Non eget Mauri jaculis, nec arcu.'

CHIRON

O, 'tis a verse in Horace; I know it well:
I read it in the grammar long ago.

AARON

Ay, just; a verse in Horace; right, you have it.
[Aside] Now, what a thing it is to be an ass!
Here's no sound jest: the old man hath found their
guilt,
And sends them weapons wrapp'd about with lines,
That wound, beyond their feeling, to the quick.
But were our witty empress well afoot,
She would applaud Andronicus' conceit:
But let her rest in her unrest awhile.—
And now, young lords, was 't not a happy star
Led us to Rome, strangers, and more than so,
Captives, to be advanced to this height?
It did me good, before the palace gate
To brave the tribune in his brother's hearing.

DEMETRIUS

But me more good, to see so great a lord
Basely insinuate and send us gifts.

AARON
Had he not reason, Lord Demetrius?
Did you not use his daughter very friendly?

DEMETRIUS
I would we had a thousand Roman dames
At such a bay, by turn to serve our lust.

CHIRON
A charitable wish and full of love.

AARON
Here lacks but your mother for to say amen.

CHIRON
And that would she for twenty thousand more.

DEMETRIUS
Come, let us go, and pray to all the gods
For our beloved mother in her pains.

AARON
[Aside] Pray to the devils; the gods have given us
 over.   [Trumpets sound within

DEMETRIUS
Why do the emperor's trumpets flourish thus?

CHIRON
Belike, for joy the emperor hath a son.

DEMETRIUS
Soft! who comes here?

  Enter NURSE, with a blackamoor CHILD

NURSE
    Good morrow, lords:
O, tell me, did you see Aaron the Moor?

AARON
Well, more or less, or ne'er a whit at all,
Here Aaron is; and what with Aaron now?

NURSE
O gentle Aaron, we are all undone!
Now help, or woe betide thee evermore!

AARON
Why, what a caterwauling dost thou keep!
What dost thou wrap and fumble in thine arms?

NURSE
O, that which I would hide from heaven's eye,
Our empress' shame and stately Rome's disgrace!
She is deliver'd, lords, she is deliver'd.

AARON
To whom?

NURSE
   I mean, she is brought a-bed.

AARON
Well, God give her good rest! What hath he sent
 her?

NURSE
A devil.

AARON
  Why, then she is the devil's dam;
A joyful issue.

NURSE
A joyless, dismal, black and sorrowful issue:
Here is the babe, as loathsome as a toad
Amongst the fairest breeders of our clime:
The empress sends it thee, thy stamp, thy seal,
And bids thee christen it with thy dagger's point.

AARON
'Zounds, ye whore! is black so base a hue?
Sweet blowse, you are a beauteous blossom. sure.

DEMETRIUS
Villain, what hast thou done?

AARON
That which thou canst not undo.

CHIRON
Thou hast undone our mother.

AARON
Villain, I have done thy mother.

DEMETRIUS
And therein, hellish dog, thou hast undone her.
Woe to her chance, and damn'd her loathed choice!
Accursed the offspring of so foul a fiend!

CHIRON
It shall not live.

AARON
It shall not die.

NURSE
Aaron, it must; the mother wills it so.

AARON
What, must it, nurse? then let no man but I
Do execution on my flesh and blood.

DEMETRIUS
I'll broach the tadpole on my rapier's point:
Nurse, give it me; my sword shall soon dispatch it.

AARON
Sooner this sword shall plough thy bowels up.
   [Takes the CHILD from the NURSE, and draws
Stay, murderous villains! will you kill your brother?
Now, by the burning tapers of the sky,
That shone so brightly when this boy was got,
He dies upon my scimitar's sharp point
That touches this my first-born son and heir!
I tell you, younglings, not Enceladus,
With all his threatening band of Typhon's brood,
Nor great Alcides, nor the god of war,
Shall seize this prey out of his father's hands.
What, what, ye sanguine, shallow-hearted boys!
Ye white-limed walls! ye alehouse painted signs!
Coal-black is better than another hue,
In that it scorns to bear another hue;
For all the water in the ocean
Can never turn the swan's black legs to white,
Although she lave them hourly in the flood.
Tell the empress from me, I am of age
To keep mine own, excuse it how she can.

DEMETRIUS
Wilt thou betray thy noble mistress thus?

AARON
My mistress is my mistress, this myself,
The vigour and the picture of my youth:
This before all the world do I prefer;
This maugre all the world will I keep safe,
Or some of you shall smoke for it in Rome.

DEMETRIUS
By this our mother is for ever shamed.

CHIRON
Rome will despise her for this foul escape.

NURSE
The emperor in his rage will doom her death.
CHIRON
I blush to think upon this ignomy.
AARON
Why, there's the privilege your beauty bears:
Fie, treacherous hue, that will betray with blushing
The close enacts and counsels of the heart!
Here's a young lad framed of another leer:
Look, how the black slave smiles upon the father,
As who should say 'Old lad, I am thine own.'
He is your brother, lords, sensibly fed
Of that self-blood that first gave life to you;
And from that womb where you imprison'd were
He is enfranchised and come to light:
Nay, he is your brother by the surer side,
Although my seal be stamped in his face.
NURSE
Aaron, what shall I say unto the empress?
DEMETRIUS
Advise thee, Aaron, what is to be done,
And we will all subscribe to thy advice:
Save thou the child, so we may all be safe.
AARON
Then sit we down, and let us all consult.
My son and I will have the wind of you:
Keep there: now talk at pleasure of your safety.
[They sit
DEMETRIUS
How many women saw this child of his?
AARON
Why, so, brave lords! when we join in league,
I am a lamb: but if you brave the Moor,
The chafed boar, the mountain lioness,
The ocean swells not so as Aaron storms.
But say, again, how many saw the child?
NURSE
Cornelia the midwife and myself;
And no one else but the deliver'd empress.
AARON
The empress, the midwife, and yourself:
Two may keep counsel when the third's away:
Go to the empress, tell her this I said.
[He kills the NURSE
Weke, weke!
So cries a pig prepared to the spit.
DEMETRIUS
What mean'st thou, Aaron? wherefore didst thou this?
AARON
O Lord, sir, 'tis a deed of policy:
Shall she live to betray this guilt of ours,
A long-tongued babbling gossip? no, lords, no:
And now be it known to you my full intent.
Not far, one Muliteus, my countryman,
His wife but yesternight was brought to bed;
His child is like to her, fair as you are:
Go pack with him, and give the mother gold,
And tell them both the circumstance of all;
And how by this their child shall be advanced,

And be received for the emperor's heir,
And substituted in the place of mine,
To calm this tempest whirling in the court;
And let the emperor dandle him for his own.
Hark ye, lords; you see I have given her physic,
[Pointing to the NURSE
And you must needs bestow her funeral;
The fields are near, and you are gallant grooms:
This done, see that you take no longer days,
But send the midwife presently to me.
The midwife and the nurse well made away,
Then let the ladies tattle what they please.
CHIRON
Aaron, I see thou wilt not trust the air
With secrets.
DEMETRIUS
For this care of Tamora,
Herself and hers are highly bound to thee.   [Exeunt
DEMETRIUS and CHIRON bearing off the NURSE's body
AARON
Now to the Goths, as swift as swallow flies;
There to dispose this treasure in mine arms,
And secretly to greet the empress' friends.
Come on, you thick-lipp'd slave, I'll bear you hence;
For it is you that puts us to our shifts:
I'll make you feed on berries and on roots,
And feed on curds and whey, and suck the goat,
And cabin in a cave, and bring you up
To be a warrior and command a camp.   [Exit

SCENE III. *The same. A public place*

Enter TITUS, *bearing arrows with letters at the ends of them; with him,* MARCUS, *young* LUCIUS, *and other* GENTLEMEN (PUBLIUS, SEMPRONIUS, *and* CAIUS), *with bows*
TITUS
Come, Marcus, come; kinsmen, this is the way.
Sir boy, let me see your archery;
Look ye draw home enough, and 'tis there straight.
Terras Astræa reliquit:
Be you remember'd, Marcus, she's gone, she's fled.
Sirs, take you to your tools. You, cousins, shall
Go sound the ocean, and cast your nets;
Happily you may catch her in the sea;
Yet there's as little justice as at land:
No; Publius and Sempronius, you must do it;
'Tis you must dig with mattock and with spade,
And pierce the inmost center of the earth:
Then, when you come to Pluto's region,
I pray you, deliver him this petition;
Tell him, it is for justice and for aid,
And that it comes from old Andronicus,
Shaken with sorrows in ungrateful Rome.
Ah, Rome! Well, well; I made thee miserable
What time I threw the people's suffrages
On him that thus doth tyrannize o'er me.
Go get you gone; and pray be careful all,

And leave you not a man-of-war unsearch'd:
This wicked emperor may have shipp'd her hence;
And, kinsmen, then we may go pipe for justice.

MARCUS

O Publius, is not this a heavy case,
To see thy noble uncle thus distract?

PUBLIUS

Therefore, my lord, it highly us concerns
By day and night to attend him carefully,
And feed his humour kindly as we may,
Till time beget some careful remedy.

MARCUS

Kinsmen, his sorrows are past remedy.
Join with the Goths, and with revengeful war
Take wreak on Rome for this ingratitude,
And vengeance on the traitor Saturnine.

TITUS

Publius, how now! how now, my masters!
What, have you met with her?

PUBLIUS

No, my good lord; but Pluto sends you word,
If you will have Revenge from hell, you shall:
Marry, for Justice, she is so employ'd,
He thinks, with Jove in heaven, or somewhere else,
So that perforce you must needs stay a time.

TITUS

He doth me wrong to feed me with delays.
I'll dive into the burning lake below,
And pull her out of Acheron by the heels.
Marcus, we are but shrubs, no cedars we,
No big-boned men framed of the Cyclops' size;
But metal, Marcus, steel to the very back,
Yet wrung with wrongs more than our backs can
   bear:
And sith there's no justice in earth nor hell,
We will solicit heaven, and move the gods
To send down Justice for to wreak our wrongs.
Come, to this gear. You are a good archer, Marcus;
          [*He gives them the arrows*
'Ad Jovem,' that's for you: here, 'Ad Apollinem:'
'Ad Martem,' that's for myself:
Here, boy, to Pallas: here, to Mercury:
To Saturn, Caius, not to Saturnine;
You were as good to shoot against the wind.
To it, boy! Marcus, loose when I bid.
Of my word, I have written to effect;
There's not a god left unsolicited.

MARCUS

Kinsmen, shoot all your shafts into the court:
We will afflict the emperor in his pride.

TITUS

Now, masters, draw. [*They shoot*] O, well said,
   Lucius!
Good boy, in Virgo's lap; give it Pallas.

MARCUS

My lord, I aim a mile beyond the moon;
Your letter is with Jupiter by this.

TITUS

Ha, ha!

Publius, Publius, what hast thou done?
See, see, thou hast shot off one of Taurus' horns.

MARCUS

This was the sport, my lord: when Publius shot,
The Bull, being gall'd, gave Aries such a knock
That down fell both the Ram's horns in the court;
And who should find them but the empress' villain?
She laugh'd, and told the Moor he should not
   choose
But give them to his master for a present.

TITUS

Why, there it goes: God give his lordship joy!
   Enter a CLOWN, *with a basket, and two pigeons in it*
News, news from heaven! Marcus, the post is come.
Sirrah, what tidings? have you any letters?
Shall I have justice? what says Jupiter?

CLOWN

O, the gibbet-maker! he says that he hath taken
them down again, for the man must not be hanged
till the next week.

TITUS

But what says Jupiter, I ask thee?

CLOWN

Alas, sir, I know not Jupiter; I never drank with
him in all my life.

TITUS

Why, villain, art not thou the carrier?

CLOWN

Ay, of my pigeons, sir; nothing else.

TITUS

Why, didst thou not come from heaven?

CLOWN

From heaven! alas, sir, I never came there: God
forbid I should be so bold to press to heaven in my
young days. Why, I am going with my pigeons to
the tribunal plebs, to take up a matter of brawl betwixt my uncle and one of the emperial's men.

MARCUS

Why, sir, that is as fit as can be to serve for your
oration; and let him deliver the pigeons to the
emperor from you.

TITUS

Tell me, can you deliver an oration to the emperor
with a grace?

CLOWN

Nay, truly, sir, I could never say grace in all my life.

TITUS

Sirrah, come hither: make no more ado,
But give your pigeons to the emperor:
By me thou shalt have justice at his hands.
Hold, hold; meanwhile here's money for thy
   charges.
Give me pen and ink.
Sirrah, can you with a grace deliver a supplication?

CLOWN

Ay, sir.

TITUS

Then here is a supplication for you. And when you
come to him, at the first approach you must kneel;
then kiss his foot; then deliver up your pigeons; and

then look for your reward. I'll be at hand, sir; see
you do it bravely.

CLOWN

I warrant you, sir, let me alone.

TITUS

Sirrah, hast thou a knife? come, let me see it.
Here, Marcus, fold it in the oration;
For thou hast made it like an humble suppliant:
And when thou hast given it to the emperor,
Knock at my door, and tell me what he says.

CLOWN

God be with you, sir; I will.   [*Exit*

TITUS

Come, Marcus, let us go. Publius, follow me.
    [*Exeunt*

SCENE IV. *The same. Before the palace*

Enter SATURNINUS, TAMORA, CHIRON, DEMETRIUS,
    LORDS, *and others;* SATURNINUS *with the arrows
    in his hand that* TITUS *shot*

SATURNINUS

Why, lords, what wrongs are these! was ever seen
An emperor in Rome thus overborne,
Troubled, confronted thus, and for the extent
Of egal justice used in such contempt?
My lords, you know, as know the mightful gods,
However these disturbers of our peace
Buzz in the people's ears, there nought hath pass'd
But even with law against the wilful sons
Of old Andronicus. And what an if
His sorrows have so overwhelm'd his wits,
Shall we be thus afflicted in his wreaks,
His fits, his frenzy and his bitterness?
And now he writes to heaven for his redress:
See, here's to Jove, and this to Mercury;
This to Apollo; this to the god of war;
Sweet scrolls to fly about the streets of Rome!
What's this but libelling against the senate,
And blazoning our unjustice every where?
A goodly humour, is it not, my lords?
As who would say, in Rome no justice were.
But if I live, his feigned ecstasies
Shall be no shelter to these outrages:
But he and his shall know that justice lives
In Saturninus' health; whom, if he sleep,
He'll so awake, as he in fury shall
Cut off the proud'st conspirator that lives.

TAMORA

My gracious lord, my lovely Saturnine,
Lord of my life, commander of my thoughts,
Calm thee, and bear the faults of Titus' age,
The effects of sorrow for his valiant sons,
Whose loss hath pierced him deep and scarr'd his
    heart;
And rather comfort his distressed plight
Than prosecute the meanest or the best
For these contempts. [*Aside*] Why, thus it shall be-
    come

High-witted Tamora to gloze with all:
But, Titus, I have touch'd thee to the quick,
Thy life-blood out: if Aaron now be wise,
Then is all safe, the anchor in the port.

Enter CLOWN

How now, good fellow! wouldst thou speak with us?

CLOWN

Yea, forsooth, an your mistership be emperial.

TAMORA

Empress I am, but yonder sits the emperor.

CLOWN

'Tis he. God and Saint Stephen give you godden: I
have brought you a letter and a couple of pigeons
here.   [SATURNINUS *reads the letter*

SATURNINUS

Go, take him away, and hang him presently.

CLOWN

How much money must I have?

TAMORA

Come, sirrah, you must be hanged.

CLOWN

Hanged! by 'r lady, then I have brought up a neck
to a fair end.   [*Exit, guarded*

SATURNINUS

Despiteful and intolerable wrongs!
Shall I endure this monstrous villany?
I know from whence this same device proceeds:
May this be borne? As if his traitorous sons,
That died by law for murder of our brother,
Have by my means been butcher'd wrongfully!
Go, drag the villain hither by the hair;
Nor age nor honour shall shape privilege:
For this proud mock I'll be thy slaughter-man;
Sly frantic wretch, that holp'st to make me great,
In hope thyself should govern Rome and me.

Enter ÆMILIUS

What news with thee, Æmilius?

ÆMILIUS

Arm, my lords; Rome never had more cause.
The Goths have gather'd head, and with a power
Of high-resolved men, bent to the spoil,
They hither march amain, under conduct
Of Lucius, son to old Andronicus;
Who threats, in course of this revenge, to do
As much as ever Coriolanus did.

SATURNINUS

Is warlike Lucius general of the Goths?
These tidings nip me, and I hang the head
As flowers with frost or grass beat down with
    storms:
Ay, now begin our sorrows to approach:
'Tis he the common people love so much;
Myself hath often heard them say,
When I have walked like a private man,
That Lucius' banishment was wrongfully,
And they have wish'd that Lucius were their em-
    peror.

TAMORA

Why should you fear? is not your city strong?

SATURNINUS

Ay, but the citizens favour Lucius,
And will revolt from me to succour him.

TAMORA

King, be thy thoughts imperious, like thy name.
Is the sun dimm'd, that gnats do fly in it?
The eagle suffers little birds to sing,
And is not careful what they mean thereby,
Knowing that with the shadow of his wings
He can at pleasure stint their melody:
Even so mayst thou the giddy men of Rome.
Then cheer thy spirit: for know, thou emperor,
I will enchant the old Andronicus
With words more sweet, and yet more dangerous,
Than baits to fish, or honey-stalks to sheep;
Whenas the one is wounded with the bait,
The other rotted with delicious feed.

SATURNINUS

But he will not entreat his son for us.

TAMORA

If Tamora entreat him, then he will:
For I can smooth, and fill his aged ears
With golden promises; that, were his heart
Almost impregnable, his old ears deaf,
Yet should both ear and heart obey my tongue.
[To ÆMILIUS] Go thou before, be our ambassador:
Say that the emperor requests a parley
Of warlike Lucius, and appoint the meeting
Even at his father's house, the old Andronicus.

SATURNINUS

Æmilius, do this message honourably:
And if he stand on hostage for his safety,
Bid him demand what pledge will please him best.

ÆMILIUS

Your bidding shall I do effectually.   [Exit

TAMORA

Now will I to that old Andronicus,
And temper him with all the art I have,
To pluck proud Lucius from the warlike Goths.
And now, sweet emperor, be blithe again,
And bury all thy fear in my devices.

SATURNINUS

Then go successantly, and plead to him.   [Exeunt

ACT V

Scene I. *Plains near Rome*

Flourish. Enter LUCIUS *and* GOTHS, *with drum and colours*

LUCIUS

Approved warriors, and my faithful friends,
I have received letters from great Rome,
Which signify what hate they bear their emperor,
And how desirous of our sight they are.
Therefore, great lords, be, as your titles witness,
Imperious, and impatient of your wrongs;
And wherein Rome hath done you any scath,
Let him make treble satisfaction.

FIRST GOTH

Brave slip, sprung from the great Andronicus,
Whose name was once our terror, now our comfort;
Whose high exploits and honourable deeds
Ingrateful Rome requites with foul contempt,
Be bold in us: we'll follow where thou lead'st,
Like stinging bees in hottest summer's day,
Led by their master to the flowered fields,
And be avenged on cursed Tamora.

ALL THE GOTHS

And as he saith, so say we all with him.

LUCIUS

I humbly thank him, and I thank you all.
But who comes here, led by a lusty Goth?

Enter a GOTH, *leading* AARON *with his* CHILD *in his arms*

SECOND GOTH

Renowned Lucius, from our troops I stray'd
To gaze upon a ruinous monastery;
And, as I earnestly did fix mine eye
Upon the wasted building, suddenly
I heard a child cry underneath a wall.
I made unto the noise; when soon I heard
The crying babe controll'd with this discourse:
'Peace, tawny slave, half me and half thy dam!
Did not thy hue bewray whose brat thou art,
Had nature lent thee but thy mother's look,
Villain, thou mightst have been an emperor:
But where the bull and cow are both milk-white,
They never do beget a coal-black calf.
Peace, villain, peace!'—even thus he rates the babe—
'For I must bear thee to a trusty Goth;
Who, when he knows thou art the empress' babe,
Will hold thee dearly for thy mother's sake.'
With this, my weapon drawn, I rush'd upon him,
Surprised him suddenly, and brought him hither,
To use as you think needful of the man.

LUCIUS

O worthy Goth, this is the incarnate devil
That robb'd Andronicus of his good hand;
This is the pearl that pleased your empress' eye;
And here's the base fruit of his burning lust.
Say, wall-eyed slave, whither wouldst thou convey
This growing image of thy fiend-like face?
Why dost not speak? what, deaf? not a word?
A halter, soldiers! hang him on this tree,
And by his side his fruit of bastardy.

AARON

Touch not the boy; he is of royal blood.

LUCIUS

Too like the sire for ever being good.
First hang the child, that he may see it sprawl;
A sight to vex the father's soul withal.
Get me a ladder.

[A ladder brought, which AARON *is made to ascend*

AARON

Lucius, save the child,
And bear it from me to the empress.
If thou do this, I'll show thee wondrous things,
That highly may advantage thee to hear:

If thou wilt not, befall what may befall,
I'll speak no more but 'Vengeance rot you all!'

LUCIUS

Say on: an if it please me which thou speak'st,
Thy child shall live, and I will see it nourish'd.

AARON

An if it please thee! why, assure thee, Lucius,
'Twill vex thy soul to hear what I shall speak;
For I must talk of murders, rapes and massacres,
Acts of black night, abominable deeds,
Complots of mischief, treason, villanies
Ruthful to hear, yet piteously perform'd:
And this shall all be buried in my death,
Unless thou swear to me my child shall live.

LUCIUS

Tell on thy mind; I say thy child shall live.

AARON

Swear that he shall, and then I will begin.

LUCIUS

Who should I swear by? thou believest no god:
That granted, how canst thou believe an oath?

AARON

What if I do not? as, indeed, I do not;
Yet, for I know thou art religious,
And hast a thing within thee called conscience,
With twenty popish tricks and ceremonies,
Which I have seen thee careful to observe,
Therefore I urge thy oath; for that I know
An idiot holds his bauble for a god,
And keeps the oath which by that god he swears,
To that I'll urge him: therefore thou shalt vow
By that same god, what god soe'er it be,
That thou adorest and hast in reverence,
To save my boy, to nourish and bring him up;
Or else I will discover nought to thee.

LUCIUS

Even by my god I swear to thee I will.

AARON

First know thou, I begot him on the empress.

LUCIUS

O most insatiate, and luxurious woman!

AARON

Tut, Lucius, this was but a deed of charity
To that which thou shalt hear of me anon.
'Twas her two sons that murder'd Bassianus;
They cut thy sister's tongue, and ravish'd her,
And cut her hands, and trimm'd her as thou saw'st.

LUCIUS

O detestable villain! call'st thou that trimming?

AARON

Why, she was wash'd and cut and trimm'd, and
  'twas
Trim sport for them that had the doing of it.

LUCIUS

O barbarous, beastly villains, like thyself!

AARON

Indeed, I was their tutor to instruct them:
That codding spirit had they from their mother,

As sure a card as ever won the set;
That bloody mind, I think, they learn'd of me,
As true a dog as ever fought at head.
Well, let my deeds be witness of my worth.
I train'd thy brethren to that guileful hole,
Where the dead corpse of Bassianus lay:
I wrote the letter that thy father found,
And hid the gold within the letter mention'd,
Confederate with the queen and her two sons:
And what not done, that thou hast cause to rue,
Wherein I had no stroke of mischief in it?
I play'd the cheater for thy father's hand;
And, when I had it, drew myself apart,
And almost broke my heart with extreme laughter:
I pried me through the crevice of a wall
When for his hand he had his two sons' heads;
Beheld his tears and laugh'd so heartily,
That both mine eyes were rainy like to his:
And when I told the empress of this sport,
She swounded almost at my pleasing tale,
And for my tidings gave me twenty kisses.

FIRST GOTH

What, canst thou say all this, and never blush?

AARON

Ay, like a black dog, as the saying is.

LUCIUS

Art thou not sorry for these heinous deeds?

AARON

Ay, that I had not done a thousand more.
Even now I curse the day—and yet, I think,
Few come within the compass of my curse—
Wherein I did not some notorious ill:
As kill a man, or else devise his death;
Ravish a maid, or plot the way to do it;
Accuse some innocent, and forswear myself;
Set deadly enmity between two friends;
Make poor men's cattle break their necks;
Set fire on barns and hay-stacks in the night,
And bid the owners quench them with their tears.
Oft have I digg'd up dead men from their graves,
And set them upright at their dear friends' doors,
Even when their sorrows almost were forgot;
And on their skins, as on the bark of trees,
Have with my knife carved in Roman letters
'Let not your sorrow die, though I am dead.'
Tut, I have done a thousand dreadful things
As willingly as one would kill a fly;
And nothing grieves me heartily indeed,
But that I cannot do ten thousand more.

LUCIUS

Bring down the devil; for he must not die
So sweet a death as hanging presently.

AARON

If there be devils, would I were a devil,
To live and burn in everlasting fire,
So I might have your company in hell,
But to torment you with my bitter tongue!

LUCIUS

Sirs, stop his mouth, and let him speak no more.

Enter a GOTH

THIRD GOTH

My lord, there is a messenger from Rome
Desires to be admitted to your presence.

LUCIUS

Let him come near.

Enter ÆMILIUS

Welcome, Æmilius: what's the news from Rome?

ÆMILIUS

Lord Lucius, and you princes of the Goths,
The Roman emperor greets you all by me;
And, for he understands you are in arms,
He craves a parley at your father's house,
Willing you to demand your hostages,
And they shall be immediately deliver'd.

FIRST GOTH

What says our general?

LUCIUS

Æmilius, let the emperor give his pledges
Unto my father and my uncle Marcus,
And we will come. March away.   [*Flourish. Exeunt*

SCENE II. *Rome. Before* TITUS's *house*

Enter TAMORA, DEMETRIUS, *and* CHIRON, *disguised*

TAMORA

Thus, in this strange and sad habiliment,
I will encounter with Andronicus,
And say I am Revenge, sent from below
To join with him and right his heinous wrongs.
Knock at his study, where, they say, he keeps,
To ruminate strange plots of dire revenge;
Tell him Revenge is come to join with him,
And work confusion on his enemies.   [*Knock*

Enter TITUS, *above*

TITUS

Who doth molest my contemplation?
Is it your trick to make me ope the door,
That so my sad decrees may fly away,
And all my study be to no effect?
You are deceived: for what I mean to do
See here in bloody lines I have set down;
And what is written shall be executed.

TAMORA

Titus, I am come to talk with thee.

TITUS

No, not a word: how can I grace my talk,
Wanting a hand to give it action?
Thou hast the odds of me; therefore no more.

TAMORA

If thou didst know me, thou wouldst talk with me.

TITUS

I am not mad; I know thee well enough:
Witness this wretched stump, witness these crimson
     lines;
Witness these trenches made by grief and care;
Witness the tiring day and heavy night;
Witness all sorrow, that I know thee well

For our proud empress, mighty Tamora:
Is not thy coming for my other hand?

TAMORA

Know, thou sad man, I am not Tamora;
She is thy enemy, and I thy friend:
I am Revenge; sent from the infernal kingdom,
To ease the gnawing vulture of thy mind,
By working wreakful vengeance on thy foes.
Come down and welcome me to this world's light.
Confer with me of murder and of death:
There's not a hollow cave or lurking-place,
No vast obscurity or misty vale,
Where bloody murder or detested rape
Can couch for fear, but I will find them out,
And in their ears tell them my dreadful name,
Revenge, which makes the foul offender quake.

TITUS

Art thou Revenge? and art thou sent to me,
To be a torment to mine enemies?

TAMORA

I am; therefore come down and welcome me.

TITUS

Do me some service ere I come to thee.
Lo, by thy side where Rape and Murder stands
Now give some surance that thou art Revenge,
Stab them, or tear them on thy chariot-wheels;
And then I'll come and be thy waggoner,
And whirl along with thee about the globes.
Provide thee two proper palfreys, black as jet,
To hale thy vengeful waggon swift away,
And find out murderers in their guilty caves:
And when thy car is loaden with their heads,
I will dismount, and by the waggon-wheel
Trot like a servile footman all day long,
Even from Hyperion's rising in the east
Until his very downfall in the sea:
And day by day I'll do this heavy task,
So thou destroy Rapine and Murder there.

TAMORA

These are my ministers and come with me.

TITUS

Are these thy ministers? what are they call'd?

TAMORA

Rapine and Murder; therefore called so,
'Cause they take vengeance of such kind of men.

TITUS

Good Lord, how like the empress' sons they are,
And you the empress! but we worldly men
Have miserable, mad, mistaking eyes.
O sweet Revenge, now do I come to thee;
And, if one arm's embracement will content thee,
I will embrace thee in it by and by.   [*Exit above*

TAMORA

This closing with him fits his lunacy:
Whate'er I forge to feed his brain-sick fits,
Do you uphold and maintain in your speeches,
For now he firmly takes me for Revenge;
And, being credulous in this mad thought,
I'll make him send for Lucius his son;
And, whilst I at a banquet hold him sure,

I'll find some cunning practice out of hand,
To scatter and disperse the giddy Goths,
Or at the least make them his enemies.
See, here he comes, and I must ply my theme.

Enter TITUS, *below*

TITUS

Long have I been forlorn, and all for thee:
Welcome, dread Fury, to my woful house:
Rapine and Murder, you are welcome too:
How like the empress and her sons you are!
Well are you fitted, had you but a Moor:
Could not all hell afford you such a devil?
For well I wot the empress never wags
But in her company there is a Moor;
And, would you represent our queen aright,
It were convenient you had such a devil:
But welcome, as you are. What shall we do?

TAMORA

What wouldst thou have us do, Andronicus?

DEMETRIUS

Show me a murderer, I'll deal with him.

CHIRON

Show me a villain that hath done a rape,
And I am sent to be revenged on him.

TAMORA

Show me a thousand that have done thee wrong,
And I will be revenged on them all.

TITUS

Look round about the wicked streets of Rome,
And when thou find'st a man that's like thyself,
Good Murder, stab him; he's a murderer.
Go thou with him, and when it is thy hap
To find another that is like to thee,
Good Rapine, stab him; he's a ravisher.
Go thou with them; and in the emperor's court
There is a queen, attended by a Moor;
Well mayst thou know her by thine own proportion,
For up and down she doth resemble thee:
I pray thee, do on them some violent death;
They have been violent to me and mine.

TAMORA

Well hast thou lesson'd us; this shall we do.
But would it please thee, good Andronicus,
To send for Lucius, thy thrice valiant son,
Who leads towards Rome a band of warlike Goths,
And bid him come and banquet at thy house;
When he is here, even at thy solemn feast,
I will bring in the empress and her sons,
The emperor himself, and all thy foes;
And at thy mercy shall they stoop and kneel,
And on them shalt thou ease thy angry heart.
What says Andronicus to this device?

TITUS

Marcus, my brother! 'tis sad Titus calls.

Enter MARCUS

Go, gentle Marcus, to thy nephew Lucius;
Thou shalt inquire him out among the Goths:
Bid him repair to me and bring with him
Some of the chiefest princes of the Goths:
Bid him encamp his soldiers where they are:

Tell him the emperor and the empress too
Feast at my house, and he shall feast with them.
This do thou for my love, and so let him,
As he regards his aged father's life.

MARCUS

This will I do, and soon return again.   [*Exit*

TAMORA

Now will I hence about thy business,
And take my ministers along with me.

TITUS

Nay, nay, let Rape and Murder stay with me;
Or else I'll call my brother back again,
And cleave to no revenge but Lucius.

TAMORA

[*Aside to her sons*] What say you, boys? will you bide
   with him,
Whiles I go tell my lord the emperor
How I have govern'd our determined jest?
Yield to his humour, smooth and speak him fair,
And tarry with him till I turn again.

TITUS

[*Aside*] I know them all, though they suppose me
   mad;
And will o'er-reach them in their own devices:
A pair of cursed hell-hounds and their dam.

DEMETRIUS

Madam, depart at pleasure; leave us here.

TAMORA

Farewell, Andronicus: Revenge now goes
To lay a complot to betray thy foes.

TITUS

I know thou dost; and, sweet Revenge, farewell.
                           [*Exit* TAMORA

CHIRON

Tell us, old man, how shall we be employ'd?

TITUS

Tut, I have work enough for you to do.
Publius, come hither, Caius, and Valentine!

Enter PUBLIUS *and others*

PUBLIUS

What is your will?

TITUS

Know you these two?

PUBLIUS

The empress' sons, I take them, Chiron and
   Demetrius.

TITUS

Fie, Publius, fie! thou art too much deceived;
The one is Murder, Rape is the other's name;
And therefore bind them, gentle Publius:
Caius and Valentine, lay hands on them:
Oft have you heard me wish for such an hour,
And now I find it; therefore bind them sure;
And stop their mouths, if they begin to cry.   [*Exit*
[PUBLIUS, *&c. lay hold on* CHIRON *and* DEMETRIUS

CHIRON

Villains, forbear! we are the empress' sons.

PUBLIUS

And therefore do we what we are commanded.

Stop close their mouths, let them not speak a word.
Is he sure bound? look that you bind them fast.
Re-enter TITUS, *with* LAVINIA; *he bearing a knife, and
she a basin*

TITUS

Come, come, Lavinia; look, thy foes are bound.
Sirs, stop their mouths, let them not speak to me;
But let them hear what fearful words I utter.
O villains, Chiron and Demetrius!
Here stands the spring whom you have stain'd with
  mud,
This goodly summer with your winter mix'd.
You kill'd her husband, and for that vile fault
Two of her brothers were condemn'd to death,
My hand cut off and made a merry jest;
Both her sweet hands, her tongue, and that more
  dear
Than hands or tongue, her spotless chastity,
Inhuman traitors, you constrain'd and forced.
What would you say, if I should let you speak?
Villains, for shame you could not beg for grace.
Hark, wretches! how I mean to martyr you.
This one hand yet is left to cut your throats,
Whilst that Lavinia 'tween her stumps doth hold
The basin that receives your guilty blood.
You know your mother means to feast with me,
And calls herself Revenge, and thinks me mad:
Hark, villains! I will grind your bones to dust,
And with your blood and it I'll make a paste;
And of the paste a coffin I will rear,
And make two pasties of your shameful heads;
And bid that strumpet, your unhallow'd dam,
Like to the earth, swallow her own increase.
This is the feast that I have bid her to,
And this the banquet she shall surfeit on;
For worse than Philomel you used my daughter,
And worse than Progne I will be revenged:
And now prepare your throats. Lavinia, come,
                    [*He cuts their throats*
Receive the blood: and when that they are dead,
Let me go grind their bones to powder small,
And with this hateful liquor temper it;
And in that paste let their vile heads be baked.
Come, come, be every one officious
To make this banquet; which I wish may prove
More stern and bloody than the Centaurs' feast.
So, now bring them in, for I'll play the cook,
And see them ready against their mother comes.
                    [*Exeunt, bearing the dead bodies*

SCENE III. *Court of* TITUS's *house. A banquet set out*

Enter LUCIUS, MARCUS, *and* GOTHS, *with* AARON,
prisoner

LUCIUS

Uncle Marcus, since it is my father's mind
That I repair to Rome, I am content.

FIRST GOTH

And ours with thine, befall what fortune will.

LUCIUS

Good uncle, take you in this barbarous Moor,
This ravenous tiger, this accursed devil;
Let him receive no sustenance, fetter him,
Till he be brought unto the empress' face,
For testimony of her foul proceedings:
And see the ambush of our friends be strong;
I fear the emperor means no good to us.

AARON

Some devil whisper curses in mine ear,
And prompt me, that my tongue may utter forth
The venomous malice of my swelling heart!

LUCIUS

Away, inhuman dog! unhallow'd slave!
Sirs, help our uncle to convey him in,
    [*Exeunt* GOTHS, *with* AARON. *Flourish within*
The trumpets show the emperor is at hand.
    Enter SATURNINUS *and* TAMORA, *with* ÆMILIUS,
        TRIBUNES, SENATORS, *and others*

SATURNINUS

What, hath the firmament moe suns than one?

LUCIUS

What boots it thee to call thyself a sun?

MARCUS

Rome's emperor, and nephew, break the parle;
These quarrels must be quietly debated.
The feast is ready, which the careful Titus
Hath ordain'd to an honourable end,
For peace, for love, for league and good to Rome:
Please you, therefore, draw nigh, and take your
  places.

SATURNINUS

Marcus, we will.
    [*Hautboys sound. The Company sit down at table
Enter* TITUS, *like a Cook, placing the meat on the table,
and* LAVINIA *with a veil over her face, young* LUCIUS, *and
others*

TITUS

Welcome, my gracious lord; welcome, dread queen;
Welcome, ye warlike Goths; welcome, Lucius;
And welcome, all: although the cheer be poor,
'Twill fill your stomachs; please you eat of it.

SATURNINUS

Why art thou thus attired, Andronicus?

TITUS

Because I would be sure to have all well,
To entertain your highness and your empress.

TAMORA

We are beholding to you, good Andronicus.

TITUS

An if your highness knew my heart, you were.
My lord the emperor, resolve me this:
Was it well done of rash Virginius
To slay his daughter with his own right hand,
Because she was enforced, stain'd, and deflower'd?

SATURNINUS

It was, Andronicus.

TITUS

Your reason, mighty lord?

[209]

SATURNINUS

Because the girl should not survive her shame,
And by her presence still renew his sorrows.

TITUS

A reason mighty, strong and effectual,
A pattern, precedent, and lively warrant,
For me, most wretched, to perform the like.
Die, die, Lavinia, and thy shame with thee,
And with thy shame thy father's sorrow die!

                [Kills LAVINIA

SATURNINUS

What hast thou done, unnatural and unkind?

TITUS

Kill'd her, for whom my tears have made me blind.
I am as woful as Virginius was,
And have a thousand times more cause than he
To do this outrage, and it now is done.

SATURNINUS

What, was she ravish'd? tell who did the deed.

TITUS

Will 't please you eat? will 't please your highness
   feed?

TAMORA

Why hast thou slain thine only daughter thus?

TITUS

Not I; 'twas Chiron and Demetrius:
They ravish'd her, and cut away her tongue;
And they, 'twas they, that did her all this wrong.

SATURNINUS

Go fetch them hither to us presently.

TITUS

Why, there they are both, baked in that pie;
Whereof their mother daintily hath fed,
Eating the flesh that she herself hath bred.
'Tis true, 'tis true; witness my knife's sharp point.

                [Kills TAMORA

SATURNINUS

Die, frantic wretch, for this accursed deed!

                [Kills TITUS

LUCIUS

Can the son's eye behold his father bleed?
There's meed for meed, death for a deadly deed!

   [Kills SATURNINUS. A great tumult. LUCIUS,
     MARCUS, and others go up into the balcony

MARCUS

You sad-faced men, people and sons of Rome,
By uproars sever'd, as a flight of fowl
Scatter'd by winds and high tempestuous gusts,
O, let me teach you how to knit again
This scatter'd corn into one mutual sheaf,
These broken limbs again into one body;
Lest Rome herself be bane unto herself,
And she whom mighty kingdoms court'sy to,
Like a forlorn and desperate castaway,
Do shameful execution on herself.
But if my frosty signs and chaps of age,
Grave witnesses of true experience,
Cannot induce you to attend my words,—
[To LUCIUS] Speak, Rome's dear friend: as erst our
   ancestor,

When with his solemn tongue he did discourse
To love-sick Dido's sad attending ear
The story of that baleful burning night,
When subtle Greeks surprised King Priam's Troy;
Tell us what Sinon hath bewitch'd our ears,
Or who hath brought the fatal engine in
That gives our Troy, our Rome, the civil wound.
My heart is not compact of flint nor steel;
Nor can I utter all our bitter grief,
But floods of tears will drown my oratory,
And break my utterance, even in the time
When it should move you to attend me most,
Lending your kind commiseration.
Here is a captain, let him tell the tale;
Your hearts will throb and weep to hear him speak.

LUCIUS

Then, noble auditory, be it known to you,
That cursed Chiron and Demetrius
Were they that murdered our emperor's brother;
And they it were that ravished our sister:
For their fell faults our brothers were beheaded,
Our father's tears despised, and basely cozen'd
Of that true hand that fought Rome's quarrel out,
And sent her enemies unto the grave.
Lastly, myself unkindly banished,
The gates shut on me, and turn'd weeping out,
To beg relief among Rome's enemies;
Who drown'd their enmity in my true tears,
And oped their arms to embrace me as a friend.
I am the turned forth, be it known to you,
That have preserved her welfare in my blood,
And from her bosom took the enemy's point,
Sheathing the steel in my adventurous body.
Alas, you know I am no vaunter, I;
My scars can witness, dumb although they are,
That my report is just and full of truth.
But, soft! methinks I do digress too much,
Citing my worthless praise: O, pardon me;
For when no friends are by, men praise themselves.

MARCUS

Now is my turn to speak. Behold the child:
   [Pointing to the CHILD in the arms of an ATTENDANT
Of this was Tamora delivered;
The issue of an irreligious Moor,
Chief architect and plotter of these woes:
The villain is alive in Titus' house,
And as he is, to witness this is true.
Now judge what cause had Titus to revenge
These wrongs, unspeakable, past patience,
Or more than any living man could bear.
Now you have heard the truth, what say you,
   Romans?
Have we done aught amiss, show us wherein,
And, from the place where you behold us now,
The poor remainder of Andronici
Will, hand in hand, all headlong cast us down,
And on the ragged stones beat forth our brains,
And make a mutual closure of our house.
Speak, Romans, speak, and if you say we shall,
Lo, hand in hand, Lucius and I will fall.

ÆMILIUS

Come, come, thou reverend man of Rome,
And bring our emperor gently in thy hand,
Lucius our emperor; for well I know
The common voice do cry it shall be so.

ALL

Lucius, all hail, Rome's royal emperor!

MARCUS

Go, go into old Titus' sorrowful house,
　　　　　　　　　　　　[*To* ATTENDANTS
And hither hale that misbelieving Moor,
To be adjudged some direful slaughtering death,
As punishment for his most wicked life.
　　　　　　　　　　　[*Exeunt* ATTENDANTS
LUCIUS, MARCUS, *and the others descend*

ALL

Lucius, all hail, Rome's gracious governor!

LUCIUS

Thanks, gentle Romans: may I govern so,
To heal Rome's harms and wipe away her woe!
But, gentle people, give me aim awhile,
For nature puts me to a heavy task;
Stand all aloof; but, uncle, draw you near,
To shed obsequious tears upon this trunk.
O, take this warm kiss on thy pale cold lips,
　　　　　　　　　　　　[*Kissing* TITUS
These sorrowful drops upon thy blood-stain'd face,
The last true duties of thy noble son!

MARCUS

Tear for tear and loving kiss for kiss
Thy brother Marcus tenders on thy lips:
O, were the sum of these that I should pay
Countless and infinite, yet would I pay them!

LUCIUS

Come hither, boy; come, come, and learn of us
To melt in showers: thy grandsire loved thee well:
Many a time he danced thee on his knee,
Sung thee asleep, his loving breast thy pillow;
Many a matter hath he told to thee,
Meet and agreeing with thine infancy;
In that respect then, like a loving child,
Shed yet some small drops from thy tender spring,
Because kind nature doth require it so:

Friends should associate friends in grief and woe:
Bid him farewell; commit him to the grave;
Do him that kindness, and take leave of him.

BOY

O grandsire, grandsire! even with all my heart
Would I were dead, so you did live again!
O Lord, I cannot speak to him for weeping;
My tears will choke me, if I ope my mouth.
　　　　　　　Re-enter ATTENDANTS *with* AARON

A ROMAN

You sad Andronici, have done with woes:
Give sentence on this execrable wretch,
That hath been breeder of these dire events.

LUCIUS

Set him breast-deep in earth, and famish him;
There let him stand and rave and cry for food:
If any one relieves or pities him,
For the offence he dies. This is our doom:
Some stay to see him fasten'd in the earth.

AARON

O, why should wrath be mute, and fury dumb?
I am no baby, I, that with base prayers
I should repent the evils I have done:
Ten thousand worse than ever yet I did
Would I perform, if I might have my will:
If one good deed in all my life I did,
I do repent it from my very soul.

LUCIUS

Some loving friends convey the emperor hence,
And give him burial in his father's grave:
My father and Lavinia shall forthwith
Be closed in our household's monument.
As for that heinous tiger, Tamora,
No funeral rite, nor man in mourning weeds,
No mournful bell shall ring her burial;
But throw her forth to beasts and birds of prey:
Her life was beastly and devoid of pity,
And, being so, shall have like want of pity.
See justice done on Aaron, that damn'd Moor,
By whom our heavy haps had their beginning:
Then, afterwards, to order well the state,
That like events may ne'er it ruinate.　　　[*Exeunt*

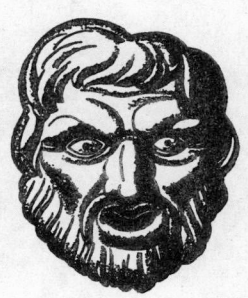

THE TAMING OF THE SHREW

SYNOPSIS

A NOBLEMAN with a fancy for practical jokes finds Christopher Sly, a tinker, dead drunk, and has him carried to the best room of his castle and finely dressed, waited upon by solicitous servants and a beautiful wife, in reality the nobleman's page in disguise. When Sly wakes up he is persuaded to believe that he is a nobleman who has been insane for fifteen years, and in order to make him merry and prevent a return of his mental delusions a company of players perform for his benefit this comedy called The Taming of the Shrew.

Baptista, a rich merchant of Padua, has two beautiful daughters, Katharina, a shrewish, bad-tempered, unruly woman, and Bianca who is sweet and lovable. Bianca's many suitors are greatly dismayed when Baptista decides to refuse all petitions for her hand while the elder daughter remains unmarried.

Lucentio, a young student from Pisa, who is in love with Bianca, changes clothes with his serv-ant Tranio and obtains a position as tutor in languages to Baptista's daughters, while Tranio looks after his interests elsewhere. Hortensio, another lover, is much encouraged when his friend, Petruchio of Verona, comes to town to find a wealthy wife and, in spite of what he hears of Katha-rina's notorious disposition, declares that he will woo and wed any shrew with such a large dowry. When Petruchio, whose father Baptista knows well, presents himself as an aspirant to Katharina's hand, he brings with him Hortensio disguised as a music teacher and Baptista engages him to teach his daughters. While Petruchio is waiting to begin his courting, Hortensio appears to say that Katharina in a fit of temper has just broken his lute over his head. When left alone with Petruchio, she flouts and scorns and strikes at him, but he calmly praises and compliments her, finally over-riding all her harshness and disdain by abruptly declaring that they will be married the following Sunday.

In the meantime the new tutor in languages, Lucentio, is making headway in gaining Bianca's love under the pretext of a Latin lesson, while Hortensio with his lute is being continually discour-aged. Tranio, acting in disguise for Lucentio, persistently presses his master's suit against the third lover, Gremio, until Baptista at length agrees that Bianca will marry the supposed Lucentio who has promised her a larger dowry than Gremio, provided his father vouches for the agreement; otherwise Bianca will marry Gremio on the Sunday following Katharina's wedding. The resource-ful Tranio induces an old pedant to impersonate Lucentio's father, Vincentio of Pisa, and the wooing of Bianca progresses happily.

On his wedding day Petruchio arrives at the church very late, to the great humiliation of his lady, and insists on being married in the disreputable clothes he is wearing. He curses as he makes the responses, cuffs the priest, kisses Katharina with a resounding smack, calls for wine, then peremptorily refuses to stay to the wedding feast and carries his protesting wife away to his country house on an old broken-down horse. On the journey he contrives to have the horses run away, so that Katharina falls on the muddy road, then, because her horse has stumbled, he beats a servant so unmercifully that she wades through the mire to protect the man.

At their home, under the pretense of love for her, he curses the attendants for their lack of service and throws the food on the floor before Katharina can taste it, declaring it badly cooked, while at night she gets no rest whatever because her husband, complaining that the bed is uncomfortable, flings the pillows, bolster, coverlet and sheets in every direction. Suddenly deciding to return to Padua for a visit to Baptista, Petruchio orders fine new clothes for Katharina but when the tailor brings them he rejects them scornfully and tells his wife they will go in their old clothes. Worn from lack of sleep and food, Katharina will now consent to anything to keep her husband quiet and when on their way to town they meet an old traveller whom Petruchio praises as a young girl, his wife agrees with him, likewise, when he rebukes her, she again agrees that their new companion is old and wrinkled. The traveller turns out to be the wealthy, honored Vincentio of Pisa who is amazed and angry to find two impostors at the house of Lucentio, his son, in the shape of Tranio and the pedant, and is about to have them arrested when Lucentio himself appears to ask his father's blessing on his marriage to Bianca with whom he has just eloped.

Hortensio consoles himself by marrying a widow of long acquaintance, and a joyous triple-wedding feast is held at which Petruchio wagers one hundred crowns that of the three brides Katharina is the most obedient. One by one, the two other husbands send messengers for their wives to come to them, but they either refuse or make excuses; then Petruchio sends for Katharina who not only comes promptly but brings the other brides with her and gives them a lecture on wifely obedience.

HISTORICAL DATA

This comedy is an adaptation of an older play *The Taming of a Shrew*, by an unknown author, published in 1594. It is generally agreed that in the working over of this play into its final form another hand than Shakespeare's is evident. Some critics have suggested Marlowe as his collaborator.

The plot follows closely that of the older play, but the style and diction are completely changed. The enlargement of the character of Petruchio, the subplot of Bianca and her lovers, and the genuine spirit of high comedy appear to have been added by Shakespeare.

The Induction, which is taken direct from *A Shrew*, is Oriental in derivation, a similar story having appeared in the *Arabian Nights*. The source of the main plot may be found in an Elizabethan poem *A Merry Geste of a Shrewd and Curst Wife*, written about 1575. Similar stories appear in Italian literature, notably the *Notte Piacevoli* by Straparolo (1550), in which Shakespeare probably found the name of his hero.

The underplot, Bianca and her disguised lovers, is parallel to passages in Gascoigne's *Supposes*, an adaptation of Ariosto's *I Suppositi*, performed at Gray's Inn in 1566.

There is considerable doubt as to the exact date of *The Taming of the Shrew*, opinion ranging from 1594 to 1606, but such evidence as there is would seem to indicate that Shakespeare made his contributions to the comedy within a year or two of 1597.

[214]

"Well, come, my Kate; and we will to your father's,"
THE TAMING OF THE SHREW

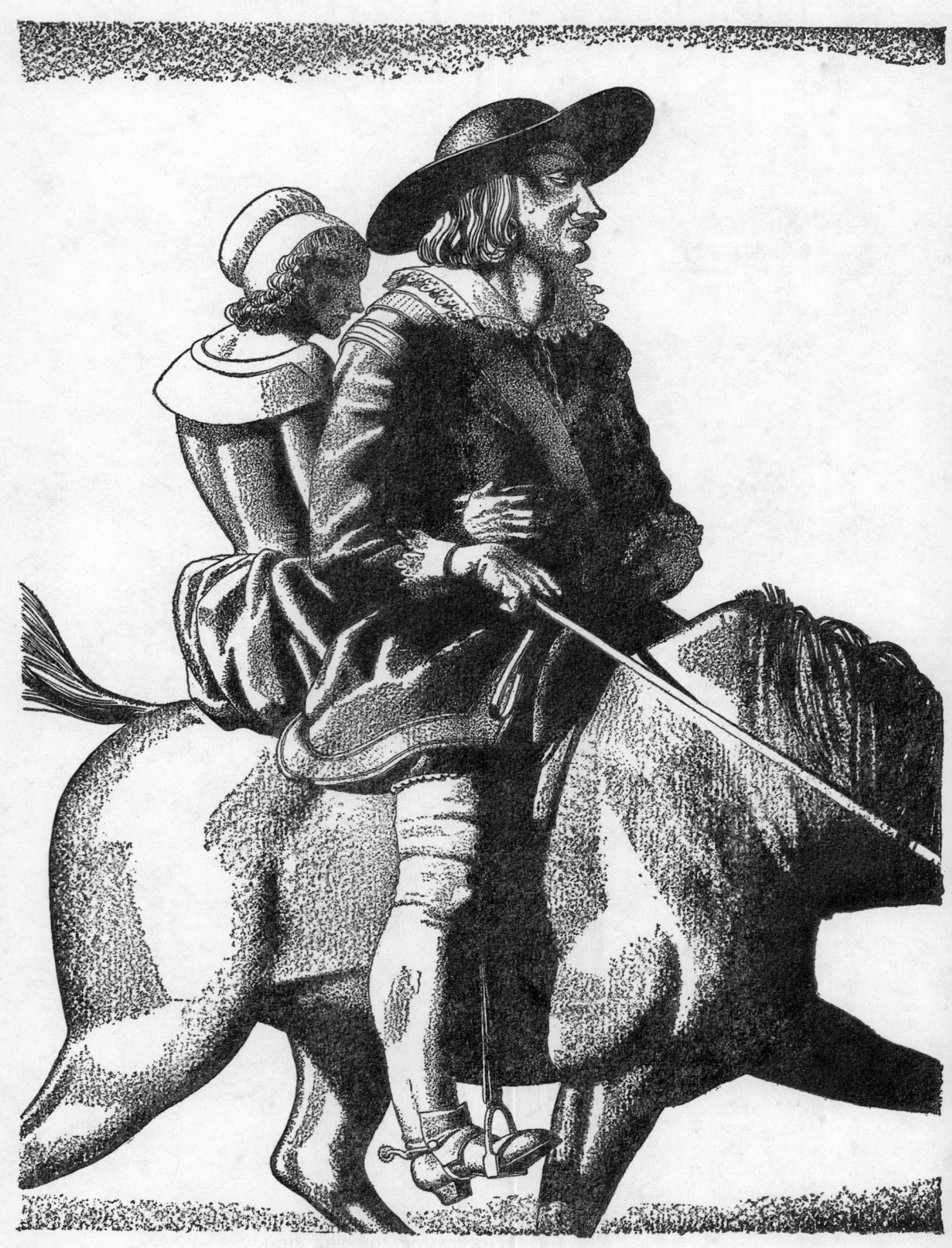

THE TAMING OF THE SHREW

DRAMATIS PERSONÆ

A LORD.
CHRISTOPHER SLY, *a tinker.*
HOSTESS, PAGE, PLAYERS, HUNTSMEN, *and* SERVANTS. } *Persons in the Induction.*

BAPTISTA, *a rich gentleman of Padua.*
VINCENTIO, *an old gentleman of Pisa.*
LUCENTIO, *son to Vincentio, in love with Bianca.*
PETRUCHIO, *a gentleman of Verona, a suitor to Katharina.*
GREMIO, } *suitors to Bianca.*
HORTENSIO, }
TRANIO, } *servants to Lucentio.*
BIONDELLO, }

GRUMIO, } *servants to Petruchio.*
CURTIS, }
A PEDANT.

KATHARINA, *the shrew,* } *daughters to Baptista.*
BIANCA, }
WIDOW.

TAILOR, HABERDASHER, *and* SERVANTS *attending on Baptista and Petruchio.*

SCENE—*Padua, and Petruchio's country house.*

INDUCTION

SCENE I. *Before an alehouse on a heath*

Enter HOSTESS *and* SLY

SLY
I'LL PHEEZE you, in faith.
HOSTESS
A pair of stocks, you rogue!
SLY
Y'are a baggage: the Slys are no rogues; look in the chronicles; we came in with Richard Conqueror. Therefore paucas pallabris; let the world slide: sessa!
HOSTESS
You will not pay for the glasses you have burst?
SLY
No, not a denier. Go by, Jeronimy: go to thy cold bed, and warm thee.
HOSTESS
I know my remedy; I must go fetch the third-borough. [*Exit*
SLY
Third, or fourth, or fifth borough, I'll answer him by law: I'll not budge an inch, boy: let him come, and kindly. [*Falls asleep*
Horns winded. Enter a LORD *from hunting, with his train*
LORD
Huntsman, I charge thee, tender well my hounds:
Brach Merriman, the poor cur is emboss'd;
And couple Clowder with the deep-mouth'd brach.
Saw'st thou not, boy, how Silver made it good
At the hedge-corner, in the coldest fault?
I would not lose the dog for twenty pound.
FIRST HUNTSMAN
Why, Belman is as good as he, my lord;
He cried upon it at the merest loss,
And twice to-day pick'd out the dullest scent:
Trust me, I take him for the better dog.
LORD
Thou art a fool: if Echo were as fleet,

I would esteem him worth a dozen such.
But sup them well and look unto them all:
To-morrow I intend to hunt again.
FIRST HUNTSMAN
I will, my lord.
LORD
What's here? one dead, or drunk? See, doth he breathe?
SECOND HUNTSMAN
He breathes, my lord. Were he not warm'd with ale,
This were a bed but cold to sleep so soundly.
LORD
O monstrous beast! how like a swine he lies!
Grim death, how foul and loathsome is thine image!
Sirs, I will practise on this drunken man.
What think you, if he were convey'd to bed,
Wrapp'd in sweet clothes, rings put upon his fingers,
A most delicious banquet by his bed,
And brave attendants near him when he wakes,
Would not the beggar then forget himself?
FIRST HUNTSMAN
Believe me, lord, I think he cannot choose.
SECOND HUNTSMAN
It would seem strange unto him when he waked.
LORD
Even as a flattering dream or worthless fancy.
Then take him up and manage well the jest:
Carry him gently to my fairest chamber
And hang it round with all my wanton pictures:
Balm his foul head in warm distilled waters
And burn sweet wood to make the lodging sweet:
Procure me music ready when he wakes,
To make a dulcet and a heavenly sound;
And if he chance to speak, be ready straight
And with a low submissive reverence
Say 'What is it your honour will command?'
Let one attend him with a silver basin
Full of rose-water and bestrew'd with flowers;
Another bear the ewer, the third a diaper,

And say 'Will't please your lordship cool your
    hands?'
Some one be ready with a costly suit,
And ask him what apparel he will wear;
Another tell him of his hounds and horse,
And that his lady mourns at his disease:
Persuade him that he hath been lunatic;
And when he says he is, say that he dreams,
For he is nothing but a mighty lord.
This do and do it kindly, gentle sirs:
It will be pastime passing excellent,
If it be husbanded with modesty.

FIRST HUNTSMAN

My lord, I warrant you we will play our part,
As he shall think by our true diligence
He is no less than what we say he is.

LORD

Take him up gently and to bed with him;
And each one to his office when he wakes.
    [Some bear out SLY. *A trumpet sounds*
Sirrah, go see what trumpet 'tis that sounds:
    [Exit SERVINGMAN
Belike, some noble gentleman that means,
Travelling some journey, to repose him here.
    Re-enter SERVINGMAN
How now! who is it?

SERVINGMAN

          An't please your honour, players
That offer service to your lordship.

LORD

Bid them come near.
    Enter PLAYERS
        Now, fellows, you are welcome.

PLAYERS

We thank your honour.

LORD

Do you intend to stay with me to-night?

A PLAYER

So please your lordship to accept our duty.

LORD

With all my heart. This fellow I remember,
Since once he play'd a farmer's eldest son:
'Twas where you woo'd the gentlewoman so well:
I have forgot your name; but, sure, that part
Was aptly fitted and naturally perform'd.

A PLAYER

I think 'twas Soto that your honour means.

LORD

'Tis very true: thou didst it excellent.
Well, you are come to me in happy time;
The rather for I have some sport in hand
Wherein your cunning can assist me much.
There is a lord will hear you play to-night:
But I am doubtful of your modesties;
Lest over-eyeing of his odd behaviour,—
For yet his honour never heard a play,—
You break into some merry passion
And so offend him; for I tell you, sirs,
If you should smile he grows impatient.

A PLAYER

Fear not, my lord: we can contain ourselves,
Were he the veriest antic in the world.

LORD

Go, sirrah, take them to the buttery,
And give them friendly welcome every one:
Let them want nothing that my house affords.
    [Exit one with the PLAYERS
Sirrah, go you to Barthol'mew my page,
And see him dress'd in all suits like a lady:
That done, conduct him to the drunkard's chamber;
And call him 'madam,' do him obeisance.
Tell him from me, as he will win my love,
He bear himself with honourable action,
Such as he hath observed in noble ladies
Unto their lords, by them accomplished:
Such duty to the drunkard let him do
With soft low tongue and lowly courtesy,
And say, 'What is't your honour will command,
Wherein your lady and your humble wife
May show her duty and make known her love?'
And then with kind embracements, tempting kisses,
And with declining head into his bosom,
Bid him shed tears, as being overjoy'd
To see her noble lord restored to health,
Who for this seven years hath esteemed him
No better than a poor and loathsome beggar:
And if the boy have not a woman's gift
To rain a shower of commanded tears,
An onion will do well for such a shift,
Which in a napkin being close convey'd
Shall in despite enforce a watery eye.
See this dispatch'd with all the haste thou canst:
Anon I'll give thee more instructions.
    [Exit a SERVINGMAN
I know the boy will well usurp the grace,
Voice, gait and action of a gentlewoman:
I long to hear him call the drunkard husband,
And how my men will stay themselves from laugh-
    ter
When they do homage to this simple peasant.
I'll in to counsel them; haply my presence
May well abate the over-merry spleen
Which otherwise would grow into extremes. *[Exeunt*

SCENE II. *A bedchamber in the* LORD's *house*

Enter aloft SLY, *with* ATTENDANTS; *some with apparel,
others with basin and ewer and other appurtenances, and*
LORD

SLY

For God's sake, a pot of small ale.

FIRST SERVANT

Will't please your lordship drink a cup of sack?

SECOND SERVANT

Will't please your honour taste of these conserves?

THIRD SERVANT

What raiment will your honour wear to-day?

SLY

I am Christophero Sly; call not me 'honour' nor 'lordship:' I ne'er drank sack in my life; and if you give me any conserves, give me conserves of beef: ne'er ask me what raiment I'll wear; for I have no more doublets than backs, no more stockings than legs, nor no more shoes than feet; nay, sometime more feet than shoes, or such shoes as my toes look through the overleather.

LORD

Heaven cease this idle humour in your honour!
O, that a mighty man of such descent,
Of such possessions and so high esteem,
Should be infused with so foul a spirit!

SLY

What, would you make me mad? Am not I Christopher Sly, old Sly's son of Burton-heath, by birth a pedlar, by education a card-maker, by transmutation a bear-herd, and now by present profession a tinker? Ask Marian Hacket, the fat ale-wife of Wincot, if she know me not: if she say I am not fourteen pence on the score for sheer ale, score me up for the lyingest knave in Christendom. What! I am not bestraught: here's—

THIRD SERVANT

O, this it is that makes your lady mourn!

SECOND SERVANT

O, this is it that makes your servants droop!

LORD

Hence comes it that your kindred shuns your house,
As beaten hence by your strange lunacy.
O noble lord, bethink thee of thy birth,
Call home thy ancient thoughts from banishment,
And banish hence these abject lowly dreams.
Look how thy servants do attend on thee,
Each in his office ready at thy beck.
Wilt thou have music? hark! Apollo plays,   [Music
And twenty caged nightingales do sing:
Or wilt thou sleep? we'll have thee to a couch
Softer and sweeter than the lustful bed
On purpose trimm'd up for Semiramis.
Say thou wilt walk; we will bestrew the ground:
Or wilt thou ride? thy horses shall be trapp'd,
Their harness studded all with gold and pearl.
Dost thou love hawking? thou hast hawks will soar
Above the morning lark: or wilt thou hunt?
Thy hounds shall make the welkin answer them,
And fetch shrill echoes from the hollow earth.

FIRST SERVANT

Say thou wilt course; thy greyhounds are as swift
As breathed stags, ay, fleeter than the roe.

SECOND SERVANT

Dost thou love pictures? we will fetch thee straight
Adonis painted by a running brook,
And Cytherea all in sedges hid,
Which seem to move and wanton with her breath,
Even as the waving sedges play with wind.

LORD

We'll show thee Io as she was a maid

And how she was beguiled and surprised,
As lively painted as the deed was done.

THIRD SERVANT

Or Daphne roaming through a thorny wood,
Scratching her legs that one shall swear she bleeds,
And at that sight shall sad Apollo weep,
So workmanly the blood and tears are drawn.

LORD

Thou art a lord and nothing but a lord:
Thou hast a lady far more beautiful
Than any woman in this waning age.

FIRST SERVANT

And till the tears that she hath shed for thee
Like envious floods o'er-run her lovely face,
She was the fairest creature in the world;
And yet she is inferior to none.

SLY

Am I a lord? and have I such a lady?
Or do I dream? or have I dream'd till now?
I do not sleep: I see, I hear, I speak;
I smell sweet savours and I feel soft things:
Upon my life, I am a lord indeed,
And not a tinker nor Christophero Sly.
Well, bring our lady hither to our sight;
And once again, a pot o' the smallest ale.

SECOND SERVANT

Will't please your mightiness to wash your hands?
O, how we joy to see your wit restored!
O, that once more you knew but what you are!
These fifteen years you have been in a dream;
Or when you waked, so waked as if you slept.

SLY

These fifteen years! by my fay, a goodly nap.
But did I never speak of all that time?

FIRST SERVANT

O, yes, my lord, but very idle words:
For though you lay here in this goodly chamber,
Yet would you say ye were beaten out of door;
And rail upon the hostess of the house;
And say you would present her at the leet,
Because she brought stone jugs and no seal'd quarts:
Sometimes you would call out for Cicely Hacket.

SLY

Ay, the woman's maid of the house.

THIRD SERVANT

Why, sir, you know no house nor no such maid,
Nor no such men as you have reckon'd up,
As Stephen Sly and old John Naps of Greece
And Peter Turph and Henry Pimpernell
And twenty more such names and men as these
Which never were nor no man ever saw.

SLY

Now Lord be thanked for my good amends!

ALL

Amen.

SLY

I thank thee: thou shalt not lose by it.
Enter the PAGE *as a lady, attended*

PAGE

How fares my noble lord?

SLY

Marry, I fare well; for here is cheer enough. Where
is my wife?

PAGE

Here, noble lord: what is thy will with her?

SLY

Are you my wife and will not call me husband?
My men should call me 'lord:' I am your good-man.

PAGE

My husband and my lord, my lord and husband;
I am your wife in all obedience.

SLY

I know it well. What must I call her?

LORD

Madam.

SLY

Al'ce madam, or Joan madam?

LORD

'Madam' and nothing else: so lords call ladies.

SLY

Madam wife, they say that I have dream'd
And slept above some fifteen year or more.

PAGE

Ay, and the time seems thirty unto me,
Being all this time abandon'd from your bed.

SLY

'Tis much. Servants, leave me and her alone.
Madam, undress you and come now to bed.

PAGE

Thrice-noble lord, let me entreat of you
To pardon me yet for a night or two;
Or, if not so, until the sun be set:
For your physicians have expressly charged,
In peril to incur your former malady,
That I should yet absent me from your bed:
I hope this reason stands for my excuse.

SLY

Ay, it stands so that I may hardly tarry so long. But
I would be loath to fall into my dreams again: I will
therefore tarry in despite of the flesh and the blood.

Enter a MESSENGER

MESSENGER

Your honour's players, hearing your amendment,
Are come to play a pleasant comedy;
For so your doctors hold it very meet,
Seeing too much sadness hath congeal'd your blood,
And melancholy is the nurse of frenzy:
Therefore they thought it good you hear a play
And frame your mind to mirth and merriment,
Which bars a thousand harms and lengthens life.

SLY

Marry, I will, let them play it. Is not a comonty a
Christmas gambold or a tumbling-trick?

PAGE

No, my good lord; it is more pleasing stuff.

SLY

What, household stuff?

PAGE

It is a kind of history.

SLY

Well, we'll see't. Come, madam wife, sit by my side
and let the world slip: we shall ne'er be younger.

[Flourish

ACT I

SCENE I. *Padua. A public place*

Enter LUCENTIO *and his man* TRANIO

LUCENTIO

Tranio, since for the great desire I had
To see fair Padua, nursery of arts,
I am arrived for fruitful Lombardy,
The pleasant garden of great Italy;
And by my father's love and leave am arm'd
With his good will and thy good company,
My trusty servant, well approved in all,
Here let us breathe and haply institute
A course of learning and ingenious studies.
Pisa renowned for grave citizens
Gave me my being and my father first,
A merchant of great traffic through the world,
Vincentio, come of the Bentivolii.
Vincentio's son brought up in Florence
It shall become to serve all hopes conceived,
To deck his fortune with his virtuous deeds:
And therefore, Tranio, for the time I study,
Virtue and that part of philosophy
Will I apply that treats of happiness
By virtue specially to be achieved.
Tell me thy mind; for I have Pisa left
And am to Padua come, as he that leaves
A shallow plash to plunge him in the deep,
And with satiety seeks to quench his thirst.

TRANIO

Mi perdonato, gentle master mine,
I am in all affected as yourself;
Glad that you thus continue your resolve
To suck the sweets of sweet philosophy.
Only, good master, while we do admire
This virtue and this moral discipline,
Let's be no stoics nor no stocks, I pray;
Or so devote to Aristotle's checks
As Ovid be an outcast quite abjured:
Balk logic with acquaintance that you have,
And practise rhetoric in your common talk;
Music and poesy use to quicken you;
The mathematics and the metaphysics,
Fall to them as you find your stomach serves you;
No profit grows where is no pleasure ta'en:
In brief, sir, study what you most affect.

LUCENTIO

Gramercies, Tranio, well dost thou advise.
If, Biondello, thou wert come ashore,
We could at once put us in readiness,
And take a lodging fit to entertain
Such friends as time in Padua shall beget.
But stay a while: what company is this?

TRANIO

Master, some show to welcome us to town.

Enter BAPTISTA, KATHARINA, BIANCA, GREMIO, *and*
HORTENSIO. LUCENTIO *and* TRANIO *stand by*

BAPTISTA

Gentlemen, importune me no farther,
For how I firmly am resolved you know;
That is, not to bestow my youngest daughter
Before I have a husband for the elder:
If either of you both love Katharina,
Because I know you well and love you well,
Leave shall you have to court her at your pleasure.

GREMIO

[*Aside*] To cart her rather: she's too rough for me.
There, there, Hortensio, will you any wife?

KATHARINA

I pray you, sir, is it your will
To make a stale of me amongst these mates?

HORTENSIO

Mates, maid! how mean you that? no mates for you,
Unless you were of gentler, milder mould.

KATHARINA

I'faith, sir, you shall never need to fear:
I wis it is not half way to her heart;
But if it were, doubt not her care should be
To comb your noddle with a three-legg'd stool
And paint your face and use you like a fool.

HORTENSIO

From all such devils, good Lord deliver us!

GREMIO

And me too, good Lord!

TRANIO

Husht, master! here's some good pastime toward:
That wench is stark mad or wonderful froward.

LUCENTIO

But in the other's silence do I see
Maid's mild behaviour and sobriety.
Peace, Tranio!

TRANIO

Well said, master; mum! and gaze your fill.

BAPTISTA

Gentlemen, that I may soon make good
What I have said, Bianca, get you in:
And let it not displease thee, good Bianca,
For I will love thee ne'er the less, my girl.

KATHARINA

A pretty peat! it is best
Put finger in the eye, an she knew why.

BIANCA

Sister, content you in my discontent.
Sir, to your pleasure humbly I subscribe:
My books and instruments shall be my company,
On them to look and practise by myself.

LUCENTIO

Hark, Tranio! thou may'st hear Minerva speak.

HORTENSIO

Signior Baptista, will you be so strange?
Sorry am I that our good will effects
Bianca's grief.

GREMIO

Why will you mew her up,
Signior Baptista, for this fiend of hell,
And make her bear the penance of her tongue?

BAPTISTA

Gentlemen, content ye; I am resolved:
Go in, Bianca: [*Exit* BIANCA
And for I know she taketh most delight
In music, instruments and poetry,
Schoolmasters will I keep within my house,
Fit to instruct her youth. If you, Hortensio,
Or Signior Gremio, you, know any such,
Prefer them hither; for to cunning men
I will be very kind, and liberal
To mine own children in good bringing-up
And so farewell. Katharina, you may stay;
For I have more to commune with Bianca.   [*Exit*

KATHARINA

Why, and I trust I may go too, may I not?
What, shall I be appointed hours; as though, belike,
I knew not what to take, and what to leave, ha?
    [*Exit*

GREMIO

You may go to the devil's dam: your gifts are so good, here's none will hold you. Their love is not so great, Hortensio, but we may blow our nails together, and fast it fairly out: our cake's dough on both sides. Farewell: yet, for the love I bear my sweet Bianca, if I can by any means light on a fit man to teach her that wherein she delights, I will wish him to her father.

HORTENSIO

So will I, Signior Gremio: but a word, I pray. Though the nature of our quarrel yet never brooked parle, know now, upon advice, it toucheth us both, that we may yet again have access to our fair mistress, and be happy rivals in Bianca's love, to labour and effect one thing specially.

GREMIO

What's that, I pray?

HORTENSIO

Marry, sir, to get a husband for her sister.

GREMIO

A husband! a devil.

HORTENSIO

I say, a husband.

GREMIO

I say, a devil. Thinkest thou, Hortensio, though her father be very rich, any man is so very a fool to be married to hell?

HORTENSIO

Tush, Gremio, though it pass your patience and mine to endure her loud alarums, why, man, there be good fellows in the world, an a man could light on them, would take her with all faults, and money enough.

GREMIO

I cannot tell; but I had as lief take her dowry with this condition, to be whipped at the high-cross every morning.

HORTENSIO

Faith, as you say, there's small choice in rotten
apples. But come; since this bar in law makes us
friends, it shall be so far forth friendly maintained
till by helping Baptista's eldest daughter to a husband we set his youngest free for a husband, and
then have to't afresh. Sweet Bianca! Happy man
be his dole! He that runs fastest gets the ring. How
say you, Signior Gremio?

GREMIO

I am agreed; and would I had given him the best
horse in Padua to begin his wooing that would thoroughly woo her, wed her and bed her and rid the
house of her! Come on.

[Exeunt GREMIO and HORTENSIO

TRANIO

I pray, sir, tell me, is it possible
That love should of a sudden take such hold?

LUCENTIO

O Tranio, till I found it to be true,
I never thought it possible or likely;
But see, while idly I stood looking on,
I found the effect of love in idleness:
And now in plainness do confess to thee,
That art to me as secret and as dear
As Anna to the Queen of Carthage was,
Tranio, I burn, I pine, I perish, Tranio,
If I achieve not this young modest girl.
Counsel me, Tranio, for I know thou canst;
Assist me, Tranio, for I know thou wilt.

TRANIO

Master, it is no time to chide you now;
Affection is not rated from the heart:
If love have touch'd you, nought remains but so,
'Redime te captum quam queas minimo.'

LUCENTIO

Gramercies, lad, go forward; this contents:
The rest will comfort, for thy counsel's sound.

TRANIO

Master, you look'd so longly on the maid,
Perhaps you mark'd not what's the pith of all.

LUCENTIO

O yes, I saw sweet beauty in her face,
Such as the daughter of Agenor had,
That made great Jove to humble him to her hand,
When with his knees he kiss'd the Cretan strond.

TRANIO

Saw you no more? mark'd you not how her sister
Began to scold and raise up such a storm
That mortal ears might hardly endure the din?

LUCENTIO

Tranio, I saw her coral lips to move
And with her breath she did perfume the air:
Sacred and sweet was all I saw in her.

TRANIO

Nay, then, 'tis time to stir him from his trance.
I pray, awake, sir: if you love the maid,
Bend thoughts and wits to achieve her. Thus it
    stands:
Her elder sister is so curst and shrewd

That till the father rid his hands of her,
Master, your love must live a maid at home;
And therefore has he closely mew'd her up,
Because she will not be annoy'd with suitors.

LUCENTIO

Ah, Tranio, what a cruel father's he!
But art thou not advised, he took some care
To get her cunning schoolmasters to instruct her?

TRANIO

Ay, marry, am I, sir; and now 'tis plotted.

LUCENTIO

I have it, Tranio.

TRANIO

                    Master, for my hand,
Both our inventions meet and jump in one.

LUCENTIO

Tell me thine first.

TRANIO

                    You will be schoolmaster
And undertake the teaching of the maid:
That's your device.

LUCENTIO

                    It is: may it be done?

TRANIO

Not possible; for who shall bear your part,
And be in Padua here Vincentio's son;
Keep house and ply his book, welcome his friends,
Visit his countrymen and banquet them?

LUCENTIO

Basta; content thee, for I have it full.
We have not yet been seen in any house,
Nor can we be distinguish'd by our faces
For man or master; then it follows thus;
Thou shalt be master, Tranio, in my stead,
Keep house and port and servants, as I should:
I will some other be; some Florentine,
Some Neapolitan, or meaner man of Pisa.
'Tis hatch'd and shall be so: Tranio, at once
Uncase thee; take my colour'd hat and cloak:
When Biondello comes, he waits on thee;
But I will charm him first to keep his tongue.

TRANIO

So had you need.
In brief, sir, sith it your pleasure is,
And I am tied to be obedient,
For so your father charged me at our parting;
'Be serviceable to my son,' quoth he,
Although I think 'twas in another sense;
I am content to be Lucentio,
Because so well I love Lucentio.

LUCENTIO

Tranio, be so, because Lucentio loves:
And let me be a slave, to achieve that maid
Whose sudden sight hath thrall'd my wounded eye
Here comes the rogue.

Enter BIONDELLO

                    Sirrah, where have you been

BIONDELLO

Where have I been! Nay, how now! where are you

Master, has my fellow Tranio stolen your clothes?
Or you stolen his? or both? pray, what's the news?

LUCENTIO

Sirrah, come hither: 'tis no time to jest.
And therefore frame your manners to the time.
Your fellow Tranio here, to save my life,
Puts my apparel and my countenance on,
And I for my escape have put on his;
For in a quarrel since I came ashore
I kill'd a man and fear I was descried:
Wait you on him, I charge you, as becomes,
While I make way from hence to save my life:
You understand me?

BIONDELLO

I, sir! ne'er a whit.

LUCENTIO

And not a jot of Tranio in your mouth:
Tranio is changed into Lucentio.

BIONDELLO

The better for him: would I were so too!

TRANIO

So could I, faith, boy, to have the next wish after,
That Lucentio indeed had Baptista's youngest
   daughter.
But, sirrah, not for my sake, but your master's, I ad-
   vise
You use your manners discreetly in all kind of com-
   panies:
When I am alone, why, then I am Tranio;
But in all places else your master Lucentio.

LUCENTIO

Tranio, let's go: one thing more rests, that thyself
execute, to make one among these wooers: if thou
ask me why, sufficeth, my reasons are both good
and weighty.   [Exeunt

The presenters above speak

FIRST SERVANT

My lord, you nod; you do not mind the play.

SLY

Yes, by Saint Anne, do I. A good matter, surely:
comes there any more of it?

PAGE

My lord, 'tis but begun.

SLY

'Tis a very excellent piece of work, madam lady:
would 'twere done!   [*They sit and mark*

SCENE II. *Padua. Before* HORTENSIO's *house*

Enter PETRUCHIO *and his man* GRUMIO

PETRUCHIO

Verona, for a while I take my leave,
To see my friends in Padua, but of all
My best beloved and approved friend,
Hortensio; and I trow this is his house.
Here, sirrah Grumio; knock, I say.

GRUMIO

Knock, sir! whom should I knock? is there any man
has rebused your worship?

PETRUCHIO

Villain, I say, knock me here soundly.

GRUMIO

Knock you here, sir! why, sir, what am I, sir, that I
should knock you here, sir?

PETRUCHIO

Villain, I say, knock me at this gate
And rap me well, or I'll knock your knave's pate.

GRUMIO

My master is grown quarrelsome. I should knock
   you first,
And then I know after who comes by the worst.

PETRUCHIO

Will it not be?
Faith, sirrah, an you'll not knock, and I'll ring it;
I'll try how you can *sol, fa,* and sing it.
                              [*He wrings him by the ears*

GRUMIO

Help, masters, help! my master is mad.

PETRUCHIO

Now, knock when I bid you, sirrah villain!
                              Enter HORTENSIO

HORTENSIO

How now! what's the matter? My old friend
Grumio! and my good friend Petruchio! How do
you all at Verona?

PETRUCHIO

Signior Hortensio, come you to part the fray?
'Con tutto il core ben trovato,' may I say.

HORTENSIO

'Alla nostra casa ben venuto, molto honorato signor
mio Petrucio.'
Rise, Grumio, rise: we will compound this quarrel.

GRUMIO

Nay, 'tis no matter, sir, what he 'leges in Latin. If
this be not a lawful cause for me to leave his service,
look you, sir, he bid me knock him and rap him
soundly, sir: well, was it fit for a servant to use his
master so, being perhaps, for aught I see, two-and-
thirty, a pip out?
Whom would to God I had well knock'd at first,
Then had not Grumio come by the worst.

PETRUCHIO

A senseless villain! Good Hortensio,
I bade the rascal knock upon your gate
And could not get him for my heart to do it.

GRUMIO

Knock at the gate! O heavens! Spake you not these
words plain, 'Sirrah, knock me here, rap me here,
knock me well, and knock me soundly'? And come
you now with, 'knocking at the gate'?

PETRUCHIO

Sirrah, be gone, or talk not, I advise you.

HORTENSIO

Petruchio, patience; I am Grumio's pledge:
Why, this's a heavy chance 'twixt him and you,
Your ancient, trusty, pleasant servant Grumio.
And tell me now, sweet friend, what happy gale
Blows you to Padua here from old Verona?

PETRUCHIO

Such wind as scatters young men through the
    world,
To seek their fortunes farther than at home,
Where small experience grows. But in a few,
Signior Hortensio, thus it stands with me:
Antonio, my father, is deceased;
And I have thrust myself into this maze,
Haply to wive and thrive as best I may:
Crowns in my purse I have and goods at home,
And so am come abroad to see the world.

HORTENSIO

Petruchio, shall I then come roundly to thee,
And wish thee to a shrewd ill-favour'd wife?
Thou'ldst thank me but a little for my counsel:
And yet I'll promise thee she shall be rich,
And very rich: but thou'rt too much my friend,
And I'll not wish thee to her.

PETRUCHIO

Signior Hortensio, 'twixt such friends as we
Few words suffice; and therefore, if thou know
One rich enough to be Petruchio's wife,
As wealth is burden of my wooing dance,
Be she as foul as was Florentius' love.
As old as Sibyl, and as curst and shrewd
As Socrates' Xanthippe, or a worse,
She moves me not, or not removes, at least,
Affection's edge in me, were she as rough
As are the swelling Adriatic seas:
I come to wive it wealthily in Padua;
If wealthily, then happily in Padua.

GRUMIO

Nay, look you, sir, he tells you flatly what his mind
is: why, give him gold enough and marry him to a
puppet or an aglet-baby; or an old trot with ne'er a
tooth in her head, though she have as many diseases
as two and fifty horses: why, nothing comes amiss,
so money comes withal.

HORTENSIO

Petruchio, since we are stepp'd thus far in,
I will continue that I broach'd in jest.
I can, Petruchio, help thee to a wife
With wealth enough and young and beauteous,
Brought up as best becomes a gentlewoman:
Her only fault, and that is faults enough,
Is that she is intolerable curst
And shrewd and froward, so beyond all measure,
That, were my state far worser than it is,
I would not wed her for a mine of gold.

PETRUCHIO

Hortensio, peace! thou know'st not gold's effect:
Tell me her father's name and 'tis enough;
For I will board her, though she chide as loud
As thunder when the clouds in autumn crack.

HORTENSIO

Her father is Baptista Minola,
An affable and courteous gentleman:
Her name is Katharina Minola,
Renown'd in Padua for her scolding tongue.

PETRUCHIO

I know her father, though I know not her;
And he knew my deceased father well.
I will not sleep, Hortensio, till I see her;
And therefore let me be thus bold with you
To give you over at this first encounter,
Unless you will accompany me thither.

GRUMIO

I pray you, sir, let him go while the humour lasts.
O' my word, an she knew him as well as I do, she
would think scolding would do little good upon
him: she may perhaps call him half a score knaves
or so: why, that's nothing; an he begin once, he'll
rail in his rope-tricks. I'll tell you what, sir, an she
stand him but a little, he will throw a figure in her
face and so disfigure her with it that she shall have
no more eyes to see withal than a cat. You know
him not, sir.

HORTENSIO

Tarry, Petruchio, I must go with thee;
For in Baptista's keep my treasure is:
He hath the jewel of my life in hold,
His youngest daughter, beautiful Bianca;
And her withholds from me and other more,
Suitors to her and rivals in my love;
Supposing it a thing impossible,
For those defects I have before rehearsed,
That ever Katharina will be woo'd;
Therefore this order hath Baptista ta'en,
That none shall have access unto Bianca
Till Katharine the curst have got a husband.

GRUMIO

Katharine the curst!
A title for a maid of all titles the worst.

HORTENSIO

Now shall my friend Petruchio do me grace;
And offer me disguised in sober robes
To old Baptista as a schoolmaster
Well seen in music, to instruct Bianca;
That so I may, by this device, at least
Have leave and leisure to make love to her,
And unsuspected court her by herself.

GRUMIO

Here's no knavery! See, to beguile the old folks,
how the young folks lay their heads together!
        Enter GREMIO, *and* LUCENTIO *disguised*
Master, master, look about you: who goes there, ha?

HORTENSIO

Peace, Grumio! it is the rival of my love.
Petruchio, stand by a while.

GRUMIO

A proper stripling and an amorous!

GREMIO

O, very well; I have perused the note.
Hark you, sir; I'll have them very fairly bound:
All books of love, see that at any hand;
And see you read no other lectures to her:
You understand me: over and beside
Signior Baptista's liberality,
I'll mend it with a largess. Take your paper too,

And let me have them very well perfumed:
For she is sweeter than perfume itself
To whom they go to. What will you read to her?

LUCENTIO

Whate'er I read to her, I'll plead for you
As for my patron, stand you so assured,
As firmly as yourself were still in place:
Yea, and perhaps with more successful words
Than you, unless you were a scholar, sir:

GREMIO

O this learning, what a thing it is!

GRUMIO

O this woodcock, what an ass it is!

PETRUCHIO

Peace, sirrah!

HORTENSIO

Grumio, mum! God save you, Signior Gremio.

GREMIO

And you are well met, Signior Hortensio.
Trow you whither I am going? To Baptista Minola.
I promised to inquire carefully
About a schoolmaster for the fair Bianca:
And by good fortune I have lighted well
On this young man, for learning and behaviour
Fit for her turn, well read in poetry
And other books, good ones, I warrant ye.

HORTENSIO

'Tis well; and I have met a gentleman
Hath promised me to help me to another,
A fine musician to instruct our mistress;
So shall I no whit be behind in duty
To fair Bianca, so beloved of me.

GREMIO

Beloved of me; and that my deeds shall prove.

GRUMIO

And that his bags shall prove.

HORTENSIO

Gremio, 'tis now no time to vent our love:
Listen to me, and if you speak me fair,
I'll tell you news indifferent good for either.
Here is a gentleman whom by chance I met,
Upon agreement from us to his liking,
Will undertake to woo curst Katharine,
Yea, and to marry her, if her dowry please.

GREMIO

So said, so done, is well.
Hortensio, have you told him all her faults?

PETRUCHIO

I know she is an irksome brawling scold:
If that be all, masters, I hear no harm.

GREMIO

No, say'st me so, friend? What countryman?

PETRUCHIO

Born in Verona, old Antonio's son:
My father dead, my fortune lives for me;
And I do hope good days and long to see.

GREMIO

O sir, such a life, with such a wife, were strange!
But if you have a stomach, to't i' God's name:

You shall have me assisting you in all.
But will you woo this wild-cat?

PETRUCHIO

Will I live?

GRUMIO

Will he woo her? ay, or I'll hang her.

PETRUCHIO

Why came I hither but to that intent?
Think you a little din can daunt mine ears?
Have I not in my time heard lions roar?
Have I not heard the sea puff'd up with winds
Rage like an angry boar chafed with sweat?
Have I not heard great ordnance in the field,
And heaven's artillery thunder in the skies?
Have I not in a pitched battle heard
Loud 'larums, neighing steeds, and trumpets' clang?
And do you tell me of a woman's tongue,
That gives not half so great a blow to hear
As will a chestnut in a farmer's fire?
Tush, tush! fear boys with bugs.

GRUMIO

For he fears none.

GREMIO

Hortensio, hark:
This gentleman is happily arrived,
My mind presumes, for his own good and ours.

HORTENSIO

I promised we would be contributors
And bear his charge of wooing, whatsoe'er.

GREMIO

And so we will, provided that he win her.

GRUMIO

I would I were as sure of a good dinner.

Enter TRANIO *brave, and* BIONDELLO

TRANIO

Gentlemen, God save you. If I may be bold,
Tell me, I beseech you, which is the readiest way
To the house of Signior Baptista Minola?

BIONDELLO

He that has the two fair daughters: is't he you mean?

TRANIO

Even he, Biondello.

GREMIO

Hark you, sir; you mean not her to—

TRANIO

Perhaps, him and her, sir: what have you to do?

PETRUCHIO

Not her that chides, sir, at any hand, I pray.

TRANIO

I love no chiders, sir. Biondello, let's away.

LUCENTIO

Well begun, Tranio.

HORTENSIO

Sir, a word ere you go;
Are you a suitor to the maid you talk of, yea or no?

TRANIO

And if I be, sir, is it any offence?

GREMIO

No; if without more words you will get you hence.

TRANIO

Why, sir, I pray, are not the streets as free
For me as for you?

GREMIO

But so is not she.

TRANIO

For what reason, I beseech you?

GREMIO

For this reason, if you'll know,
That she's the choice love of Signior Gremio.

HORTENSIO

That she's the chosen of Signior Hortensio.

TRANIO

Softly, my masters! if you be gentlemen,
Do me this right; hear me with patience.
Baptista is a noble gentleman,
To whom my father is not all unknown;
And were his daughter fairer than she is,
She may more suitors have and me for one.
Fair Leda's daughter had a thousand wooers;
Then well one more may fair Bianca have:
And so she shall; Lucentio shall make one,
Though Paris came in hope to speed alone.

GREMIO

What, this gentleman will out-talk us all!

LUCENTIO

Sir, give him head: I know he'll prove a jade.

PETRUCHIO

Hortensio, to what end are all these words?

HORTENSIO

Sir, let me be so bold as ask you,
Did you yet ever see Baptista's daughter?

TRANIO

No, sir; but hear I do that he hath two,
The one as famous for a scolding tongue
As is the other for beauteous modesty.

PETRUCHIO

Sir, sir, the first's for me; let her go by.

GREMIO

Yea, leave that labour to great Hercules;
And let it be more than Alcides' twelve.

PETRUCHIO

Sir, understand you this of me in sooth:
The youngest daughter whom you hearken for
Her father keeps from all access of suitors;
And will not promise her to any man
Until the elder sister first be wed:
The younger then is free and not before.

TRANIO

If it be so, sir, that you are the man
Must stead us all and me amongst the rest;
And if you break the ice and do this feat,
Achieve the elder, set the younger free
For our access, whose hap shall be to have her
Will not so graceless be to be ingrate.

HORTENSIO

Sir, you say well and well you do conceive;
And since you do profess to be a suitor,
You must, as we do, gratify this gentleman,
To whom we all rest generally beholding.

TRANIO

Sir, I shall not be slack: in sign whereof,
Please ye we may contrive this afternoon,
And quaff carouses to our mistress' health,
And do as adversaries do in law,
Strive mightily, but eat and drink as friends.

GRUMIO, BIONDELLO

O excellent motion! Fellows, let's be gone.

HORTENSIO

The motion's good indeed and be it so,
Petruchio, I shall be your ben venuto.   [Exeunt

ACT II

SCENE I. *Padua. A room in* BAPTISTA'S *house*

Enter KATHARINA *and* BIANCA

BIANCA

Good sister, wrong me not, nor wrong yourself,
To make a bondmaid and a slave of me;
That I disdain: but for these other gawds,
Unbind my hands, I'll pull them off myself,
Yea, all my raiment, to my petticoat;
Or what you will command me will I do,
So well I know my duty to my elders.

KATHARINA

Of all thy suitors, here I charge thee, tell
Whom thou lovest best: see thou dissemble not.

BIANCA

Believe me, sister, of all the men alive
I never yet beheld that special face
Which I could fancy more than any other.

KATHARINA

Minion, thou liest. Is't not Hortensio?

BIANCA

If you affect him, sister, here I swear
I'll plead for you myself, but you shall have him.

KATHARINA

O then, belike, you fancy riches more:
You will have Gremio to keep you fair.

BIANCA

Is it for him you do envy me so?
Nay then you jest, and now I well perceive
You have but jested with me all this while:
I prithee, sister Kate, untie my hands.

KATHARINA

If that be jest, then all the rest was so.   [*Strikes her*
Enter BAPTISTA

BAPTISTA

Why, how now, dame! whence grows this insolence?
Bianca, stand aside. Poor girl! she weeps.
Go ply thy needle; meddle not with her.
For shame, thou hilding of a devilish spirit,
Why dost thou wrong her that did ne'er wrong thee?
When did she cross thee with a bitter word?

KATHARINA

Her silence flouts me, and I'll be revenged.
[*Flies after* BIANCA

[224]

BAPTISTA

What, in my sight? Bianca, get thee in. [*Exit* BIANCA

KATHARINA

What, will you not suffer me? Nay, now I see
She is your treasure, she must have a husband;
I must dance bare-foot on her wedding day
And for your love to her lead apes in hell.
Talk not to me: I will go sit and weep
Till I can find occasion of revenge.   [*Exit*

BAPTISTA

Was ever gentleman thus grieved as I?
But who comes here?
Enter GREMIO, LUCENTIO *in the habit of a mean man;*
PETRUCHIO, *with* HORTENSIO *as a musician; and* TRANIO,
    with BIONDELLO *bearing a lute and books*

GREMIO

Good morrow, neighbour Baptista.

BAPTISTA

Good morrow, neighbour Gremio. God save you,
gentlemen!

PETRUCHIO

And you, good sir; Pray have you not a daughter
Call'd Katharina, fair and virtuous?

BAPTISTA

I have a daughter, sir, called Katharina.

GREMIO

You are too blunt: go to it orderly.

PETRUCHIO

You wrong me, Signior Gremio: give me leave.
I am a gentleman of Verona, sir,
That, hearing of her beauty and her wit,
Her affability and bashful modesty,
Her wondrous qualities and mild behaviour,
Am bold to show myself a forward guest
Within your house, to make mine eye the witness
Of that report which I so oft have heard.
And, for an entrance to my entertainment,
I do present you with a man of mine,
                    [*Presenting* HORTENSIO
Cunning in music and the mathematics,
To instruct her fully in those sciences,
Whereof I know she is not ignorant:
Accept of him, or else you do me wrong:
His name is Licio, born in Mantua.

BAPTISTA

You're welcome, sir; and he, for your good sake.
But for my daughter Katharine, this I know,
She is not for your turn, the more my grief.

PETRUCHIO

I see you do not mean to part with her,
Or else you like not of my company.

BAPTISTA

Mistake me not; I speak but as I find.
Whence are you, sir? what may I call your name?

PETRUCHIO

Petruchio is my name; Antonio's son,
A man well known throughout all Italy.

BAPTISTA

I know him well: you are welcome for his sake.

GREMIO

Saving your tale, Petruchio, I pray,
Let us, that are poor petitioners, speak too:
Baccare! you are marvellous forward.

PETRUCHIO

O, pardon me, Signior Gremio; I would fain be
    doing.

GREMIO

I doubt it not, sir; but you will curse your wooing.
Neighbour, this is a gift very grateful, I am sure of
it. To express the like kindness, myself, that have
been more kindly beholding to you than any, freely
give unto you this young scholar [*presenting* LU-
CENTIO], that hath been long studying at Rheims;
as cunning in Greek, Latin, and other languages, as
the other in music and mathematics: his name is
Cambio; pray, accept his service.

BAPTISTA

A thousand thanks, Signior Gremio. Welcome,
good Cambio. But, gentle sir [*to* TRANIO], methinks
you walk like a stranger: may I be so bold to know
the cause of your coming?

TRANIO

Pardon me, sir, the boldness is mine own;
That, being a stranger in this city here,
Do make myself a suitor to your daughter,
Unto Bianca, fair and virtuous.
Nor is your firm resolve unknown to me,
In the preferment of the eldest sister.
This liberty is all that I request,
That, upon knowledge of my parentage,
I may have welcome 'mongst the rest that woo
And free access and favour as the rest:
And, toward the education of your daughters,
I here bestow a simple instrument,
And this small packet of Greek and Latin books:
If you accept them, then their worth is great.

BAPTISTA

Lucentio is your name; of whence, I pray?

TRANIO

Of Pisa, sir; son to Vincentio.

BAPTISTA

A mighty man of Pisa; by report
I know him well: you are very welcome, sir.
Take you the lute, and you the set of books;
You shall go see your pupils presently.
Holla, within!

Enter a SERVANT

                    Sirrah, lead these gentlemen
To my daughters; and tell them both,
These are their tutors: bid them use them well.
[*Exit* SERVANT, *with* LUCENTIO *and* HORTENSIO, BION-
                                        DELLO *following*
We will go walk a little in the orchard,
And then to dinner. You are passing welcome,
And so I pray you all to think yourselves.

PETRUCHIO

Signior Baptista, my business asketh haste,
And every day I cannot come to woo.
You knew my father well, and in him me,

Left solely heir to all his lands and goods,
Which I have better'd rather than decreased:
Then tell me, if I get your daughter's love,
What dowry shall I have with her to wife?

BAPTISTA

After my death the one half of my lands,
And in possession twenty thousand crowns.

PETRUCHIO

And, for that dowry, I'll assure her of
Her widowhood, be it that she survive me,
In all my lands and leases whatsoever:
Let specialties be therefore drawn between us,
That covenants may be kept on either hand.

BAPTISTA

Ay, when the special thing is well obtain'd,
That is, her love; for that is all in all.

PETRUCHIO

Why, that is nothing; for I tell you, father,
I am as peremptory as she proud-minded;
And where two raging fires meet together
They do consume the thing that feeds their fury:
Though little fire grows great with little wind,
Yet extreme gusts will blow out fire and all:
So I to her and so she yields to me;
For I am rough and woo not like a babe.

BAPTISTA

Well mayst thou woo, and happy be thy speed!
But be thou arm'd for some unhappy words.

PETRUCHIO

Ay, to the proof; as mountains are for winds,
That shake not, though they blow perpetually.

Re-enter HORTENSIO, *with his head broke*

BAPTISTA

How now, my friend! why dost thou look so pale?

HORTENSIO

For fear, I promise you, if I look pale.

BAPTISTA

What, will my daughter prove a good musician?

HORTENSIO

I think she'll sooner prove a soldier:
Iron may hold with her, but never lutes.

BAPTISTA

Why, then thou canst not break her to the lute?

HORTENSIO

Why, no; for she hath broke the lute to me.
I did but tell her she mistook her frets,
And bow'd her hand to teach her fingering;
When, with a most impatient devilish spirit,
'Frets, call you these?' quoth she; 'I'll fume with
    them:'
And, with that word, she struck me on the head,
And through the instrument my pate made way;
And there I stood amazed for a while,
As on a pillory, looking through the lute;
While she did call me rascal fiddler
And twangling Jack; with twenty such vile terms,
As had she studied to misuse me so.

PETRUCHIO

Now, by the world, it is a lusty wench;

I love her ten times more than e'er I did:
O, how I long to have some chat with her!

BAPTISTA

Well, go with me and be not so discomfited:
Proceed in practice with my younger daughter;
She's apt to learn and thankful for good turns.
Signior Petruchio, will you go with us,
Or shall I send my daughter Kate to you?

PETRUCHIO

I pray you do; I will attend her here,
[*Exeunt* BAPTISTA, GREMIO, TRANIO, *and* HORTENSIO
And woo her with some spirit when she comes.
Say that she rail: why then I'll tell her plain
She sings as sweetly as a nightingale:
Say that she frown; I'll say she looks as clear
As morning roses newly wash'd with dew:
Say she be mute and will not speak a word;
Then I'll commend her volubility,
And say she uttereth piercing eloquence:
If she do bid me pack, I'll give her thanks,
As though she bid me stay by her a week:
If she deny to wed, I'll crave the day
When I shall ask the banns, and when be married.
But here she comes; and now, Petruchio, speak.

Enter KATHARINA

Good morrow, Kate; for that's your name, I hear.

KATHARINA

Well have you heard, but something hard of hear-
    ing:
They call me Katharine that do talk of me.

PETRUCHIO

You lie, in faith; for you are call'd plain Kate,
And bonny Kate, and sometimes Kate the curst;
But Kate, the prettiest Kate in Christendom,
Kate of Kate-Hall, my super-dainty Kate,
For dainties are all Kates, and therefore, Kate,
Take this of me, Kate of my consolation;
Hearing thy mildness praised in every town,
Thy virtues spoke of, and thy beauty sounded,
Yet not so deeply as to thee belongs,
Myself am moved to woo thee for my wife.

KATHARINA

Moved! in good time: let him that moved you
    hither
Remove you hence: I knew you at the first
You were a moveable.

PETRUCHIO

                    Why, what's a moveable?

KATHARINA

A join'd-stool.

PETRUCHIO

                Thou hast hit it: come, sit on me.

KATHARINA

Asses are made to bear, and so are you.

PETRUCHIO

Women are made to bear, and so are you.

KATHARINA

No such jade as you, if me you mean.

PETRUCHIO

Alas, good Kate, I will not burden thee!
For, knowing thee to be but young and light,—

KATHARINA

Too light for such a swain as you to catch;
And yet as heavy as my weight should be.

PETRUCHIO

Should be! should—buzz!

KATHARINA

          Well ta'en, and like a buzzard.

PETRUCHIO

O slow-wing'd turtle! shall a buzzard take thee?

KATHARINA

Ay, for a turtle, as he takes a buzzard.

PETRUCHIO

Come, come, you wasp; i' faith, you are too angry.

KATHARINA

If I be waspish, best beware my sting.

PETRUCHIO

My remedy is then, to pluck it out.

KATHARINA

Ay, if the fool could find it where it lies.

PETRUCHIO

Who knows not where a wasp does wear his sting?
In his tail.

KATHARINA

    In his tongue.

PETRUCHIO

        Whose tongue?

KATHARINA

Yours, if you talk of tails: and so farewell.

PETRUCHIO

What, with my tongue in your tail? nay, come
again,
Good Kate; I am a gentleman.

KATHARINA

          That I'll try.
[She strikes him

PETRUCHIO

I swear I'll cuff you, if you strike again.

KATHARINA

So may you lose your arms:
If you strike me, you are no gentleman;
And if no gentleman, why then no arms.

PETRUCHIO

A herald, Kate? O, put me in thy books!

KATHARINA

What is your crest? a coxcomb?

PETRUCHIO

A combless cock, so Kate will be my hen.

KATHARINA

No cock of mine; you crow too like a craven.

PETRUCHIO

Nay, come, Kate, come; you must not look so sour.

KATHARINA

It is my fashion, when I see a crab.

PETRUCHIO

Why, here's no crab; and therefore look not sour.

KATHARINA

There is, there is.

PETRUCHIO

Then show it me.

KATHARINA

          Had I a glass, I would.

PETRUCHIO

What, you mean my face?

KATHARINA

          Well aim'd of such a young one.

PETRUCHIO

Now, by Saint George, I am too young for you.

KATHARINA

Yet you are wither'd.

PETRUCHIO

          'Tis with cares.

KATHARINA

               I care not.

PETRUCHIO

Nay, hear you, Kate: in sooth you scape not so.

KATHARINA

I chafe you, if I tarry: let me go.

PETRUCHIO

No, not a whit: I find you passing gentle.
'Twas told me you were rough and coy and sullen,
And now I find report a very liar;
For thou art pleasant, gamesome, passing courteous,
But slow in speech, yet sweet as spring-time flowers:
Thou canst not frown, thou canst not look askance,
Nor bite the lip, as angry wenches will,
Nor hast thou pleasure to be cross in talk,
But thou with mildness entertain'st thy wooers,
With gentle conference, soft and affable.
Why does the world report that Kate doth limp?
O slanderous world! Kate like the hazel-twig
Is straight and slender, and as brown in hue
As hazel-nuts and sweeter than the kernels.
O, let me see thee walk: thou dost not halt.

KATHARINA

Go, fool, and whom thou keep'st command.

PETRUCHIO

Did ever Dian so become a grove
As Kate this chamber with her princely gait?
O, be thou Dian, and let her be Kate;
And then let Kate be chaste and Dian sportful!

KATHARINA

Where did you study all this goodly speech?

PETRUCHIO

It is extempore, from my mother-wit.

KATHARINA

A witty mother! witless else her son.

PETRUCHIO

Am I not wise?

KATHARINA

          Yes; keep you warm.

PETRUCHIO

Marry, so I mean, sweet Katharine, in thy bed:
And therefore, setting all this chat aside,
Thus in plain terms: your father hath consented
That you shall be my wife; your dowry 'greed on;
And, will you, nill you, I will marry you.

Now, Kate, I am a husband for your turn;
For, by this light, whereby I see thy beauty,
Thy beauty, that doth make me like thee well,
Thou must be married to no man but me;
For I am he am born to tame you Kate,
And bring you from a wild Kate to a Kate
Conformable as other household Kates.
Here comes your father: never make denial;
I must and will have Katharine to my wife.

     Re-enter BAPTISTA, GREMIO, *and* TRANIO

BAPTISTA

Now, Signior Petruchio, how speed you with my
    daughter?

PETRUCHIO

How but well, sir? how but well?
It were impossible I should speed amiss.

BAPTISTA

Why, how now, daughter Katharine! in your
    dumps?

KATHARINA

Call you me daughter? now, I promise you
You have show'd a tender fatherly regard,
To wish me wed to one half lunatic;
A mad-cap ruffian and a swearing Jack,
That thinks with oaths to face the matter out.

PETRUCHIO

Father, 'tis thus: yourself and all the world,
That talk'd of her, have talk'd amiss of her:
If she be curst, it is for policy,
For she's not froward, but modest as the dove;
She is not hot, but temperate as the morn;
For patience she will prove a second Grissel,
And Roman Lucrece for her chastity:
And to conclude, we have 'greed so well together,
That upon Sunday is the wedding-day.

KATHARINA

I'll see thee hang'd on Sunday first.

GREMIO

Hark, Petruchio; she says she'll see thee hang'd first.

TRANIO

Is this your speeding? nay, then, good night our
    part!

PETRUCHIO

Be patient, gentlemen; I choose her for myself:
If she and I be pleased, what's that to you?
'Tis bargain'd 'twixt us twain, being alone,
That she shall still be curst in company.
I tell you, 'tis incredible to believe
How much she loves me: O, the kindest Kate!
She hung about my neck; and kiss on kiss
She vied so fast, protesting oath on oath,
That in a twink she won me to her love.
O, you are novices! 'tis a world to see,
How tame, when men and women are alone,
A meacock wretch can make the curstest shrew.
Give me thy hand, Kate: I will unto Venice,
To buy apparel 'gainst the wedding-day.
Provide the feast, father, and bid the guests;
I will be sure my Katharine shall be fine.

BAPTISTA

I know not what to say: but give me your hands;
God send you joy, Petruchio! 'tis a match.

GREMIO, TRANIO

Amen, say we: we will be witnesses.

PETRUCHIO

Father, and wife, and gentlemen, adieu;
I will to Venice; Sunday comes apace:
We will have rings, and things, and fine array;
And, kiss me, Kate, we will be married o' Sunday.

     [*Exeunt* PETRUCHIO *and* KATHARINA *severally*

GREMIO

Was ever match clapp'd up so suddenly?

BAPTISTA

Faith, gentlemen, now I play a merchant's part,
And venture madly on a desperate mart.

TRANIO

'Twas a commodity lay fretting by you:
'Twill bring you gain, or perish on the seas.

BAPTISTA

The gain I seek is, quiet in the match.

GREMIO

No doubt but he hath got a quiet catch.
But now, Baptista, to your younger daughter:
Now is the day we long have looked for:
I am your neighbour, and was suitor first.

TRANIO

And I am one that love Bianca more
Than words can witness, or your thoughts can guess.

GREMIO

Youngling, thou canst not love so dear as I.

TRANIO

Greybeard, thy love doth freeze.

GREMIO

           But thine doth fry.
Skipper, stand back: 'tis age that nourisheth.

TRANIO

But youth in ladies' eyes that flourisheth.

BAPTISTA

Content you, gentlemen: I will compound this
    strife:
'Tis deeds must win the prize; and he, of both,
That can assure my daughter greatest dower
Shall have my Bianca's love.
Say, Signior Gremio, what can you assure her?

GREMIO

First, as you know, my house within the city
Is richly furnished with plate and gold;
Basins and ewers to lave her dainty hands;
My hangings all of Tyrian tapestry;
In ivory coffers I have stuff'd my crowns;
In cypress chests my arras counterpoints,
Costly apparel, tents, and canopies,
Fine linen, Turkey cushions boss'd with pearl,
Valance of Venice gold in needlework,
Pewter and brass and all things that belong
To house or housekeeping: then, at my farm
I have a hundred milch-kine to the pail,
Sixscore fat oxen standing in my stalls,
And all things answerable to this portion.

Myself am struck in years, I must confess;
And if I die to-morrow, this is hers,
If whilst I live she will be only mine.

TRANIO

That 'only' came well in. Sir, list to me:
I am my father's heir and only son:
If I may have your daughter to my wife,
I'll leave her houses three or four as good,
Within rich Pisa walls, as any one
Old Signior Gremio has in Padua;
Besides two thousand ducats by the year
Of fruitful land, all which shall be her jointure.
What, have I pinch'd you, Signior Gremio?

GREMIO

Two thousand ducats by the year of land!
My land amounts not to so much in all:
That she shall have; besides an argosy
That now is lying in Marseilles' road.
What, have I choked you with an argosy?

TRANIO

Gremio, 'tis known my father hath no less
Than three great argosies; besides two galliasses,
And twelve tight galleys: these I will assure her,
And twice as much, whate'er thou offer'st next.

GREMIO

Nay, I have offer'd all, I have no more;
And she can have no more than all I have:
If you like me, she shall have me and mine.

TRANIO

Why, then the maid is mine from all the world,
By your firm promise: Gremio is out-vied.

BAPTISTA

I must confess your offer is the best;
And, let your father make her the assurance,
She is your own; else, you must pardon me,
If you should die before him, where's her dower?

TRANIO

That's but a cavil: he is old, I young.

GREMIO

And may not young men die, as well as old?

BAPTISTA

Well, gentlemen,
I am thus resolved: on Sunday next you know
My daughter Katharine is to be married:
Now, on the Sunday following, shall Bianca
Be bride to you, if you make this assurance;
If not, to Signior Gremio:
And so, I take my leave, and thank you both.

GREMIO

Adieu, good neighbour.   [*Exit* BAPTISTA
    Now I fear thee not:
Sirrah young gamester, your father were a fool
To give thee all, and in his waning age
Set foot under thy table: tut, a toy!
An old Italian fox is not so kind, my boy.   [*Exit*

TRANIO

A vengeance on your crafty wither'd hide!
Yet I have faced it with a card of ten.
'Tis in my head to do my master good:
I see no reason but supposed Lucentio

Must get a father, call'd—supposed Vincentio;
And that's a wonder: fathers commonly
Do get their children; but in this case of wooing,
A child shall get a sire, if I fail not of my cunning.
                           [*Exit*

ACT III

SCENE I. *Padua.* BAPTISTA's *house*

Enter LUCENTIO, HORTENSIO, *and* BIANCA

LUCENTIO

Fiddler, forbear; you grow too forward, sir;
Have you so soon forgot the entertainment
Her sister Katharine welcomed you withal?

HORTENSIO

But, wrangling pedant, this is
The patroness of heavenly harmony:
Then give me leave to have prerogative;
And when in music we have spent an hour,
Your lecture shall have leisure for as much.

LUCENTIO

Preposterous ass, that never read so far
To know the cause why music was ordain'd!
Was it not to refresh the mind of man
After his studies or his usual pain?
Then give me leave to read philosophy,
And while I pause, serve in your harmony.

HORTENSIO

Sirrah, I will not bear these braves of thine.

BIANCA

Why, gentlemen, you do me double wrong,
To strive for that which resteth in my choice:
I am no breeching scholar in the schools;
I'll not be tied to hours nor 'pointed times,
But learn my lessons as I please myself.
And, to cut off all strife, here sit we down:
Take you your instrument, play you the whiles;
His lecture will be done ere you have tuned.

HORTENSIO

You'll leave his lecture when I am in tune?

LUCENTIO

That will be never: tune your instrument.

BIANCA

Where left we last?

LUCENTIO

Here, madam:
   'Hic ibat Simois; hic est Sigeia tellus;
     Hic steterat Priami regia celsa senis.'

BIANCA

Construe them.

LUCENTIO

'Hic ibat,' as I told you before,—'Simois,' I am
Lucentio,—'hic est,' son unto Vincentio of Pisa,—
'Sigeia tellus,' disguised thus to get your love;—'Hic
steterat,' and that Lucentio that comes a-wooing,—
'Priami,' is my man Tranio,—'regia,' bearing my
port,—'celsa senis,' that we might beguile the old
pantaloon.

HORTENSIO
Madam, my instrument's in tune.

Let's hear. O fie! the treble jars.

LUCENTIO
Spit in the hole, man, and tune again.

BIANCA
Now let me see if I can construe it:
'Hic ibat Simois,' I know you not,—'hic est Sigeia
tellus,' I trust you not,—'Hic steterat Priami,' take
heed he hear us not,—'regia,' presume not,—'celsa
senis,' despair not.

HORTENSIO
Madam, 'tis now in tune.

LUCENTIO
            All but the base.

HORTENSIO
The base is right; 'tis the base knave that jars.
[Aside] How fiery and forward our pedant is!
Now, for my life, the knave doth court my love:
Pedascule, I'll watch you better yet.

BIANCA
In time I may believe, yet I mistrust.

LUCENTIO
Mistrust it not; for, sure, Æacides
Was Ajax, call'd so from his grandfather.

BIANCA
I must believe my master; else, I promise you,
I should be arguing still upon that doubt:
But let it rest. Now, Licio, to you:
Good masters, take it not unkindly, pray,
That I have been thus pleasant with you both.

HORTENSIO
You may go walk, and give me leave a while:
My lessons make no music in three parts.

LUCENTIO
Are you so formal, sir? well, I must wait,
[Aside] And watch withal; for, but I be deceived,
Our fine musician groweth amorous.

HORTENSIO
Madam, before you touch the instrument,
To learn the order of my fingering,
I must begin with rudiments of art;
To teach you gamut in a briefer sort,
More pleasant, pithy, and effectual,
Than hath been taught by any of my trade:
And there it is in writing, fairly drawn.

BIANCA
Why, I am past my gamut long ago.

HORTENSIO
Yet read the gamut of Hortensio.

BIANCA
[Reads]   "'Gamut' I am, the ground of all accord,
      'A re,' to plead Hortensio's passion;
     'B mi,' Bianca, take him for thy lord,
      'C fa ut,' that loves with all affection:
     'D sol re,' one clef, two notes have I:
     'E la mi,' show pity, or I die."
Call you this gamut? tut, I like it not:
Old fashions please me best; I am not so nice,
To change true rules for old inventions.

Enter a SERVANT

SERVANT
Mistress, your father prays you leave your books,
And help to dress your sister's chamber up:
You know to-morrow is the wedding-day.

BIANCA
Farewell, sweet masters both; I must be gone.
        [Exeunt BIANCA and SERVANT

LUCENTIO
Faith, mistress, then I have no cause to stay.   [Exit

HORTENSIO
But I have cause to pry into this pedant:
Methinks he looks as though he were in love:
Yet if thy thoughts, Bianca, be so humble,
To cast thy wandering eyes on every stale,
Seize thee that list: if once I find thee ranging,
Hortensio will be quit with thee by changing. [Exit

SCENE II. *Padua. Before* BAPTISTA'S *house*

Enter BAPTISTA, GREMIO, TRANIO, KATHARINA,
BIANCA, LUCENTIO, *and others,* ATTENDANTS

BAPTISTA
Signior Lucentio [To TRANIO], this is the 'pointed
    day.
That Katharine and Petruchio should be married,
And yet we hear not of our son-in-law.
What will be said? what mockery will it be,
To want the bridegroom when the priest attends
To speak the ceremonial rites of marriage!
What says Lucentio to this shame of ours?

KATHARINA
No shame but mine: I must, forsooth, be forced
To give my hand, opposed against my heart,
Unto a mad-brain rudesby, full of spleen;
Who woo'd in haste, and means to wed at leisure.
I told you, I, he was a frantic fool,
Hiding his bitter jests in blunt behaviour:
And, to be noted for a merry man,
He'll woo a thousand, 'point the day of marriage,
Make friends, invite, and proclaim the banns;
Yet never means to wed where he hath woo'd.
Now must the world point at poor Katharine,
And say, 'Lo, there is mad Petruchio's wife,
If it would please him come and marry her!'

TRANIO
Patience, good Katharine, and Baptista too.
Upon my life, Petruchio means but well,
Whatever fortune stays him from his word:
Though he be blunt, I know him passing wise;
Though he be merry, yet withal he's honest.

KATHARINA
Would Katharine had never seen him though!
      [Exit weeping, followed by BIANCA and others

BAPTISTA
Go, girl; I cannot blame thee now to weep;
For such an injury would vex a very saint,
Much more a shrew of thy impatient humour.

Enter BIONDELLO

BIONDELLO

Master, master! news, old news, and such news as you never heard of!

BAPTISTA

Is it new and old too? how may that be?

BIONDELLO

Why, is it not news, to hear of Petruchio's coming?

BAPTISTA

Is he come?

BIONDELLO

Why, no, sir.

BAPTISTA

What then?

BIONDELLO

He is coming.

BAPTISTA

When will he be here?

BIONDELLO

When he stands where I am and sees you there.

TRANIO

But say, what to thine old news?

BIONDELLO

Why, Petruchio is coming in a new hat and an old jerkin, a pair of old breeches thrice turned, a pair of boots that have been candle-cases, one buckled, another laced, an old rusty sword ta'en out of the town-armoury, with a broken hilt, and chapeless; with two broken points: his horse hipped with an old mothy saddle and stirrups of no kindred; besides, possessed with the glanders and like to mose in the chine; troubled with the lampass, infected with the fashions, full of windgalls, sped with spavins, rayed with the yellows, past cure of the fives, stark spoiled with the staggers, begnawn with the bots, swayed in the back and shoulder-shotten; near-legged before and with a half-cheeked bit and a head-stall of sheep's leather which, being restrained to keep him from stumbling, hath been often burst and now repaired with knots; one girth six times pieced and a woman's crupper of velure, which hath two letters for her name fairly set down in studs, and here and there pieced with packthread.

BAPTISTA

Who comes with him?

BIONDELLO

O, sir, his lackey, for all the world caparisoned like the horse; with a linen stock on one leg, and a kersey boot-hose on the other, gartered with a red and blue list; an old hat, and 'the humour of forty fancies' pricked in 't for a feather: a monster, a very monster in apparel, and not like a Christian footboy or a gentleman's lackey.

TRANIO

'Tis some odd humour pricks him to this fashion;
Yet oftentimes he goes but mean-apparell'd.

BAPTISTA

I am glad he's come, howsoe'er he comes.

BIONDELLO

Why, sir, he comes not.

BAPTISTA

Didst thou not say he comes?

BIONDELLO

Who? that Petruchio came?

BAPTISTA

Ay, that Petruchio came.

BIONDELLO

No, sir; I say his horse comes, with him on his back.

BAPTISTA

Why, that's all one.

BIONDELLO

Nay, by Saint Jamy,
I hold you a penny,
A horse and a man
Is more than one,
And yet not many.

Enter PETRUCHIO *and* GRUMIO

PETRUCHIO

Come, where be these gallants? who's at home?

BAPTISTA

You are welcome, sir.

PETRUCHIO

And yet I come not well.

BAPTISTA

And yet you halt not.

TRANIO

Not so well apparell'd
As I wish you were.

PETRUCHIO

Were it better, I should rush in thus.
But where is Kate? where is my lovely bride?
How does my father? Gentles, methinks you frown:
And wherefore gaze this goodly company,
As if they saw some wondrous monument,
Some comet or unusual prodigy?

BAPTISTA

Why, sir, you know this is your wedding-day:
First were we sad, fearing you would not come;
Now sadder, that you come so unprovided.
Fie, doff this habit, shame to your estate,
An eye-sore to our solemn festival!

TRANIO

And tell us, what occasion of import
Hath all so long detain'd you from your wife,
And sent you hither so unlike yourself?

PETRUCHIO

Tedious it were to tell, and harsh to hear:
Sufficeth, I am come to keep my word,
Though in some part enforced to digress;
Which, at more leisure, I will so excuse
As you shall well be satisfied withal.
But where is Kate? I stay too long from her:
The morning wears, 'tis time we were at church.

TRANIO

See not your bride in these unreverent robes:
Go to my chamber; put on clothes of mine.

PETRUCHIO

Not I, believe me: thus I'll visit her.

BAPTISTA

But thus, I trust, you will not marry her.

PETRUCHIO

Good sooth, even thus; therefore ha' done with
    words:
To me she's married, not unto my clothes:
Could I repair what she will wear in me,
As I can change these poor accoutrements,
'Twere well for Kate and better for myself.
But what a fool am I to chat with you,
When I should bid good morrow to my bride,
And seal the title with a lovely kiss!

      [*Exeunt* PETRUCHIO *and* GRUMIO

TRANIO

He hath some meaning in his mad attire:
We will persuade him, be it possible,
To put on better ere he go to church.

BAPTISTA

I'll after him, and see the event of this.

      [*Exeunt* BAPTISTA, GREMIO, *and* ATTENDANTS

TRANIO

But to her love concerneth us to add
Her father's liking: which to bring to pass,
As I before imparted to your worship,
I am to get a man,—whate'er he be,
It skills not much, we'll fit him to our turn,—
And he shall be Vincentio of Pisa;
And make assurance here in Padua
Of greater sums than I have promised.
So shall you quietly enjoy your hope,
And marry sweet Bianca with consent.

LUCENTIO

Were it not that my fellow-schoolmaster
Doth watch Bianca's steps so narrowly,
'Twere good, methinks, to steal our marriage;
Which once perform'd, let all the world say no,
I'll keep mine own, despite of all the world.

TRANIO

That by degrees we mean to look into,
And watch our vantage in this business:
We'll over-reach the greybeard, Gremio,
The narrow-prying father, Minola,
The quaint musician, amorous Licio;
All for my master's sake, Lucentio.

Re-enter GREMIO

Signior Gremio, came you from the church?

GREMIO

As willingly as e'er I came from school.

TRANIO

And is the bride and bridegroom coming home?

GREMIO

A bridegroom say you? 'tis a groom indeed,
A grumbling groom, and that the girl shall find.

TRANIO

Curster than she? why, 'tis impossible.

GREMIO

Why, he's a devil, a devil, a very fiend.

TRANIO

Why, she's a devil, a devil, the devil's dam.

GREMIO

Tut, she's a lamb, a dove, a fool to him!
I'll tell you, Sir Lucentio: when the priest
Should ask, if Katharine should be his wife,
'Ay, by gogs-wouns,' quoth he; and swore so loud,
That, all amazed, the priest let fall the book;
And, as he stoop'd again to take it up,
This mad-brain'd bridegroom took him such a cuff,
That down fell priest and book, and book and priest:
'Now take them up,' quoth he, 'if any list.'

TRANIO

What said the wench when he rose again?

GREMIO

Trembled and shook; for why he stamp'd and
    swore,
As if the vicar meant to cozen him.
But after many ceremonies done,
He calls for wine: 'A health!' quoth he; as if
He had been aboard, carousing to his mates
After a storm: quaff'd off the muscadel,
And threw the sops all in the sexton's face;
Having no other reason
But that his beard grew thin and hungerly
And seem'd to ask him sops as he was drinking.
This done, he took the bride about the neck
And kiss'd her lips with such a clamorous smack
That at the parting all the church did echo:
And I seeing this came thence for very shame;
And after me, I know, the rout is coming.
Such a mad marriage never was before:
Hark, hark! I hear the minstrels play.   [*Music*

Re-enter PETRUCHIO, KATHARINA, BIANCA, BAPTISTA,
    HORTENSIO, GRUMIO, *and* TRAIN

PETRUCHIO

Gentlemen and friends, I thank you for your pains:
I know you think to dine with me to-day,
And have prepared great store of wedding cheer;
But so it is, my haste doth call me hence,
And therefore here I mean to take my leave.

BAPTISTA

Is't possible you will away to-night?

PETRUCHIO

I must away to-day, before night come:
Make it no wonder; if you knew my business,
You would entreat me rather go than stay.
And, honest company, I thank you all,
That have beheld me give away myself
To this most patient, sweet, and virtuous wife:
Dine with my father, drink a health to me;
For I must hence; and farewell to you all.

TRANIO

Let us entreat you stay till after dinner.

PETRUCHIO

It may not be.

GREMIO

Let me entreat you.

PETRUCHIO

It cannot be.

KATHARINA

Let me entreat you.

PETRUCHIO
I am content.

KATHARINA
Are you content to stay?

PETRUCHIO
I am content you shall entreat me stay;
But yet not stay, entreat me how you can.

KATHARINA
Now, if you love me, stay.

PETRUCHIO
Grumio, my horse.

GRUMIO
Ay, sir, they be ready: the oats have eaten the
horses.

KATHARINA
Nay, then,
Do what thou canst, I will not go to-day;
No, nor to-morrow, not till I please myself.
The door is open, sir; there lies your way;
You may be jogging whiles your boots are green;
For me, I'll not be gone till I please myself:
'Tis like you'll prove a jolly surly groom,
That take it on you at the first so roundly.

PETRUCHIO
O Kate, content thee; prithee, be not angry.

KATHARINA
I will be angry: what hast thou to do?
Father, be quiet: he shall stay my leisure.

GREMIO
Ay, marry, sir, now it begins to work.

KATHARINA
Gentlemen, forward to the bridal dinner:
I see a woman may be made a fool,
If she had not a spirit to resist.

PETRUCHIO
They shall go forward, Kate, at thy command.
Obey the bride, you that attend on her;
Go to the feast, revel and domineer,
Carouse full measure to her maidenhead,
Be mad and merry, or go hang yourselves:
But for my bonny Kate, she must with me.
Nay, look not big, nor stamp, nor stare, nor fret;
I will be master of what is mine own:
She is my goods, my chattels; she is my house,
My household stuff, my field, my barn,
My horse, my ox, my ass, my any thing;
And here she stands, touch her whoever dare;
I'll bring mine action on the proudest he
That stops my way in Padua. Grumio,
Draw forth thy weapon, we are beset with thieves;
Rescue thy mistress, if thou be a man.
Fear not, sweet wench, they shall not touch thee,
    Kate:
I'll buckler thee against a million.
    [Exeunt PETRUCHIO, KATHARINA, and GRUMIO

BAPTISTA
Nay, let them go, a couple of quiet ones.

GREMIO
Went they not quickly, I should die with laughing.

TRANIO
Of all mad matches never was the like.

LUCENTIO
Mistress, what's your opinion of your sister?

BIANCA
That, being mad herself, she's madly mated.

GREMIO
I warrant him, Petruchio is Kated.

BAPTISTA
Neighbours and friends, though bride and bride-
    groom wants
For to supply the places at the table,
You know there wants no junkets at the feast.
Lucentio, you shall supply the bridegroom's place;
And let Bianca take her sister's room.

TRANIO
Shall sweet Bianca practise how to bride it?

BAPTISTA
She shall, Lucentio. Come, gentlemen, let's go.
    [Exeunt

ACT IV

SCENE I. PETRUCHIO's *country house*
Enter GRUMIO

GRUMIO
Fie, fie on all tired jades, on all mad masters, and
all foul ways! Was ever man so beaten? was ever
man so rayed? was ever man so weary? I am sent
before to make a fire, and they are coming after to
warm them. Now, were not I a little pot, and soon
hot, my very lips might freeze to my teeth, my
tongue to the roof of my mouth, my heart in my
belly, ere I should come by a fire to thaw me: but I,
with blowing the fire, shall warm myself; for, considering the weather, a taller man than I will take
cold. Holla, ho! Curtis!

Enter CURTIS

CURTIS
Who is that calls so coldly?

GRUMIO
A piece of ice: if thou doubt it, thou mayst slide
from my shoulder to my heel with no greater a run
but my head and my neck. A fire, good Curtis.

CURTIS
Is my master and his wife coming, Grumio?

GRUMIO
O, ay, Curtis, ay: and therefore fire, fire; cast on no
water.

CURTIS
Is she so hot a shrew as she's reported?

GRUMIO
She was, good Curtis, before this frost: but, thou
knowest, winter tames man, woman, and beast; for
it hath tamed my old master, and my new mistress,
and myself, fellow Curtis.

CURTIS
Away, you three-inch fool! I am no beast

GRUMIO

Am I but three inches? why, thy horn is a foot; and
so long am I at the least. But wilt thou make a fire,
or shall I complain on thee to our mistress, whose
hand, she being now at hand, thou shalt soon feel,
to thy cold comfort, for being slow in thy hot office?

CURTIS

I prithee, good Grumio, tell me, how goes the
world?

GRUMIO

A cold world, Curtis, in every office but thine; and
therefore fire: do thy duty, and have thy duty; for
my master and mistress are almost frozen to death.

CURTIS

There's fire ready; and therefore, good Grumio, the
news.

GRUMIO

Why, 'Jack, boy! ho! boy!' and as much news as
thou wilt.

CURTIS

Come, you are so full of cony-catching!

GRUMIO

Why, therefore fire; for I have caught extreme cold.
Where's the cook? is supper ready, the house
trimmed, rushes strewed, cobwebs swept; the
serving-men in their new fustian, their white stockings, and every officer his wedding-garment on? Be
the jacks fair within, the jills fair without, the car-
pets laid, and every thing in order?

CURTIS

All ready; and therefore, I pray thee, news.

GRUMIO

First, know, my horse is tired; my master and mistress fallen out.

CURTIS

How?

GRUMIO

Out of their saddles into the dirt; and thereby
hangs a tale.

CURTIS

Let's ha't, good Grumio.

GRUMIO

Lend thine ear.

CURTIS

Here.

GRUMIO

There.   [Strikes him.

CURTIS

This is to feel a tale, not to hear a tale.

GRUMIO

And therefore 'tis called a sensible tale: and this
cuff was but to knock at your ear, and beseech listening. Now I begin: Imprimis, we came down a foul
hill, my master riding behind my mistress,—

CURTIS

Both of one horse?

GRUMIO

What's that to thee?

CURTIS

Why, a horse.

GRUMIO

Tell thou the tale: but hadst thou not crossed me,
thou shouldst have heard how her horse fell and she
under her horse; thou shouldst have heard in how
miry a place, how she was bemoiled, how he left
her with the horse upon her, how he beat me because her horse stumbled, how she waded through
the dirt to pluck him off me, how he swore, how she
prayed, that never prayed before, how I cried, how
the horses ran away, how her bridle was burst, how
I lost my crupper, with many things of worthy
memory, which now shall die in oblivion and thou
return unexperienced to thy grave.

CURTIS

By this reckoning he is more shrew than she.

GRUMIO

Ay; and that thou and the proudest of you all shall
find when he comes home. But what talk I of this?
Call forth Nathaniel, Joseph, Nicholas, Philip,
Walter, Sugarsop and the rest: let their heads be
sleekly combed, their blue coats brushed, and their
garters of an indifferent knit: let them curtsy with
their left legs, and not presume to touch a hair of
my master's horse-tail till they kiss their hands. Are
they all ready?

CURTIS

They are.

GRUMIO

Call them forth.

CURTIS

Do you hear, ho? you must meet my master to
countenance my mistress!

GRUMIO

Why, she hath a face of her own.

CURTIS

Who knows not that?

GRUMIO

Thou, it seems, that calls for company to countenance her.

CURTIS

I call them forth to credit her.

GRUMIO

Why, she comes to borrow nothing of them.

Enter four or five SERVING-MEN

NATHANIEL

Welcome home, Grumio!

PHILIP

How now, Grumio!

JOSEPH

What, Grumio!

NICHOLAS

Fellow Grumio!

NATHANIEL

How now, old lad?

GRUMIO

Welcome, you;—how now, you;—what, you;—
fellow, you;—and thus much for greeting. Now, my
spruce companions, is all ready, and all things neat?

NATHANIEL

All things is ready. How near is our master?

[234]

GRUMIO

E'en at hand, alighted by this; and therefore be not
—Cock's passion, silence! I hear my master.

Enter PETRUCHIO *and* KATHARINA

PETRUCHIO

Where be these knaves? What, no man at door
To hold my stirrup nor to take my horse!
Where is Nathaniel, Gregory, Philip?

ALL SERVANTS

Here, here, sir; here, sir.

PETRUCHIO

Here, sir! here, sir! here, sir! here, sir!
You logger-headed and unpolish'd grooms!
What, no attendance? no regard? no duty?
Where is the foolish knave I sent before?

GRUMIO

Here, sir; as foolish as I was before.

PETRUCHIO

You peasant swain! you whoreson malt-horse
     drudge!
Did I not bid thee meet me in the park,
And bring along these rascal knaves with thee?

GRUMIO

Nathaniel's coat, sir, was not fully made,
And Gabriel's pumps were all unpink'd i' the heel;
There was no link to colour Peter's hat,
And Walter's dagger was not come from sheathing:
There were none fine but Adam, Ralph, and Greg-
     ory;
The rest were ragged, old, and beggarly;
Yet, as they are, here are they come to meet you.

PETRUCHIO

Go, rascals, go, and fetch my supper in.

[*Exeunt* SERVANTS

[*Singing*]   Where is the life that late I led—
Where are those—Sit down, Kate, and welcome.—
Soud, soud, soud, soud!

Re-enter SERVANTS *with supper*

Why, when, I say? Nay, good sweet Kate, be merry.
Off with my boots, you rogues! you villains, when?

[*Sings*]   It was the friar of orders grey,
                         As he forth walked on his way:—

Out, you rogue! you pluck my foot awry:
Take that, and mend the plucking off the other.

[*Strikes him*

Be merry, Kate. Some water, here; what, ho!
Where's my spaniel Troilus? Sirrah, get you hence,
And bid my cousin Ferdinand come hither:
One, Kate, that you must kiss, and be acquainted
     with.
Where are my slippers? Shall I have some water?

Enter one with water

Come, Kate, and wash, and welcome heartily.
You whoreson villain! will you let it fall? [*Strikes him*

KATHARINA

Patience, I pray you; 'twas a fault unwilling.

PETRUCHIO

A whoreson beetle-headed, flap-ear'd knave!
Come, Kate, sit down; I know you have a stomach.

Will you give thanks, sweet Kate; or else shall I?
What's this? mutton?

FIRST SERVANT

Ay.

PETRUCHIO

Who brought it?

PETER

I.

PETRUCHIO

'Tis burnt; and so is all the meat.
What dogs are these! where is the rascal cook?
How durst you, villains, bring it from the dresser,
And serve it thus to me that love it not?
There, take it to you, trenchers, cups, and all:

[*Throws the meat, &c. about the stage*

You heedless joltheads and unmanner'd slaves!
What, do you grumble? I'll be with you straight.

KATHARINA

I pray you, husband, be not so disquiet:
The meat was well, if you were so contented.

PETRUCHIO

I tell thee, Kate, 'twas burnt and dried away;
And I expressly am forbid to touch it,
For it engenders choler, planteth anger;
And better 'twere that both of us did fast,
Since, of ourselves, ourselves are choleric,
Than feed it with such over-roasted flesh.
Be patient; to-morrow 't shall be mended,
And, for this night, we'll fast for company:
Come, I will bring thee to thy bridal chamber.

[*Exeunt*

Re-enter SERVANTS *severally*

NATHANIEL

Peter, didst ever see the like?

PETER

He kills her in her own humour.

Re-enter CURTIS

GRUMIO

Where is he?

CURTIS

In her chamber, making a sermon of continency to
her;
And rails, and swears, and rates, that she, poor soul,
Knows not which way to stand, to look, to speak,
And sits as one new-risen from a dream.
Away, away! for he is coming hither.   [*Exeunt*

Re-enter PETRUCHIO

PETRUCHIO

Thus have I politicly begun my reign,
And 'tis my hope to end successfully.
My falcon now is sharp and passing empty;
And till she stoop she must not be full-gorged,
For then she never looks upon her lure.
Another way I have to man my haggard,
To make her come and know her keeper's call,
That is, to watch her, as we watch these kites
That bate and beat and will not be obedient.
She eat no meat to-day, nor none shall eat;
Last night she slept not, nor to-night she shall not;
As with the meat, some undeserved fault

[235]

I'll find about the making of the bed;
And here I'll fling the pillow, there the bolster,
This way the coverlet, another way the sheets:
Ay, and amid this hurly I intend
That all is done in reverend care of her;
And in conclusion she shall watch all night:
And if she chance to nod, I'll rail and brawl,
And with the clamour keep her still awake.
This is a way to kill a wife with kindness;
And thus I'll curb her mad and headstrong humour.
He that knows better how to tame a shrew,
Now let him speak: 'tis charity to show.   [*Exit*

Scene II. *Padua. Before* BAPTISTA'S *house*

Enter TRANIO *and* HORTENSIO

TRANIO

Is't possible, friend Licio, that Mistress Bianca
Doth fancy any other but Lucentio?
I tell you, sir, she bears me fair in hand.

HORTENSIO

Sir, to satisfy you in what I have said,
Stand by and mark the manner of his teaching.

Enter BIANCA *and* LUCENTIO

LUCENTIO

Now, mistress, profit you in what you read?

BIANCA

What, master, read you? first resolve me that.

LUCENTIO

I read that I profess, the Art to Love.

BIANCA

And may you prove, sir, master of your art!

LUCENTIO

While you, sweet dear, prove mistress of my heart!

HORTENSIO

Quick proceeders, marry! Now, tell me, I pray,
You that durst swear that your mistress Bianca
Loved none in the world so well as Lucentio.

TRANIO

O despiteful love! unconstant womankind!
I tell thee, Licio, this is wonderful.

HORTENSIO

Mistake no more: I am not Licio,
Nor a musician, as I seem to be;
But one that scorn to live in this disguise,
For such a one as leaves a gentleman,
And makes a god of such a cullion:
Know, sir, that I am call'd Hortensio.

TRANIO

Signior Hortensio, I have often heard
Of your entire affection to Bianca;
And since mine eyes are witness of her lightness,
I will with you, if you be so contented,
Forswear Bianca and her love for ever.

HORTENSIO

See, how they kiss and court! Signior Lucentio,
Here is my hand, and here I firmly vow
Never to woo her more, but do forswear her,

As one unworthy all the former favours
That I have fondly flatter'd her withal.

TRANIO

And here I take the like unfeigned oath,
Never to marry with her though she would entreat:
Fie on her! see, how beastly she doth court him!

HORTENSIO

Would all the world but he had quite forsworn!
For me, that I may surely keep mine oath,
I will be married to a wealthy widow,
Ere three days pass, which hath as long loved me
As I have loved this proud disdainful haggard.
And so farewell, Signior Lucentio.
Kindness in women, not their beauteous looks,
Shall win my love: and so I take my leave,
In resolution as I swore before.   [*Exit*

TRANIO

Mistress Bianca, bless you with such grace
As 'longeth to a lover's blessed case!
Nay, I have ta'en you napping, gentle love,
And have forsworn you with Hortensio.

BIANCA

Tranio, you jest: but have you both forsworn me?

TRANIO

Mistress, we have.

LUCENTIO

                 Then we are rid of Licio.

TRANIO

I'faith, he'll have a lusty widow now,
That shall be woo'd and wedded in a day.

BIANCA

God give him joy!

TRANIO

Ay, and he'll tame her.

BIANCA

                 He says so, Tranio.

TRANIO

Faith, he is gone unto the taming-school.

BIANCA

The taming-school! what, is there such a place?

TRANIO

Ay, mistress, and Petruchio is the master;
That teacheth tricks eleven and twenty long,
To tame a shrew and charm her chattering tongue.

Enter BIONDELLO

BIONDELLO

O master, master, I have watch'd so long
That I am dog-weary! but at last I spied
An ancient angel coming down the hill,
Will serve the turn.

TRANIO

                 What is he, Biondello?

BIONDELLO

Master, a mercatante, or a pedant,
I know not what; but formal in apparel,
In gait and countenance surely like a father.

LUCENTIO

And what of him, Tranio?

TRANIO

If he be credulous and trust my tale,

I'll make him glad to seem Vincentio,
And give assurance to Baptista Minola,
As if he were the right Vincentio.
Take in your love, and then let me alone.

[Exeunt LUCENTIO *and* BIANCA

Enter a PEDANT

PEDANT

God save you, sir!

TRANIO

                    And you, sir! you are welcome.
Travel you far on, or are you at the farthest?

PEDANT

Sir, at the farthest for a week or two:
But then up farther, and as far as Rome;
And so to Tripoli, if God lend me life.

TRANIO

What countryman, I pray?

PEDANT

                    Of Mantua.

TRANIO

Of Mantua, sir? marry, God forbid!
And come to Padua, careless of your life?

PEDANT

My life, sir! how, I pray? for that goes hard.

TRANIO

'Tis death for any one in Mantua
To come to Padua. Know you not the cause?
Your ships are stay'd at Venice; and the Duke,
For private quarrel 'twixt your duke and him,
Hath publish'd and proclaim'd it openly:
'Tis marvel, but that you are but newly come,
You might have heard it else proclaim'd about.

PEDANT

Alas, sir, it is worse for me than so!
For I have bills for money by exchange
From Florence, and must here deliver them.

TRANIO

Well, sir, to do you courtesy,
This will I do, and this I will advise you:
First, tell me, have you ever been at Pisa?

PEDANT

Ay, sir, in Pisa have I often been;
Pisa renowned for grave citizens.

TRANIO

Among them know you one Vincentio?

PEDANT

I know him not, but I have heard of him;
A merchant of incomparable wealth.

TRANIO

He is my father, sir; and, sooth to say,
In countenance somewhat doth resemble you.

BIONDELLO

As much as an apple doth an oyster, and all one.

[Aside

TRANIO

To save your life in this extremity,
This favour will I do you for his sake;
And think it not the worst of all your fortunes
That you are like to Sir Vincentio.
His name and credit shall you undertake,

And in my house you shall be friendly lodged:
Look that you take upon you as you should;
You understand me, sir: so shall you stay
Till you have done your business in the city:
If this be courtesy, sir, accept of it.

PEDANT

O sir, I do; and will repute you ever
The patron of my life and liberty.

TRANIO

Then go with me to make the matter good.
This, by the way, I let you understand;
My father is here look'd for every day,
To pass assurance of a dower in marriage
'Twixt me and one Baptista's daughter here:
In all these circumstances I'll instruct you:
Go with me to clothe you as becomes you.   *[Exeunt*

SCENE III. *A room in* PETRUCHIO'S *house*

Enter KATHARINA *and* GRUMIO

GRUMIO

No, no, forsooth; I dare not for my life.

KATHARINA

The more my wrong, the more his spite appears:
What, did he marry me to famish me?
Beggars, that come unto my father's door,
Upon entreaty have a present alms;
If not, elsewhere they meet with charity:
But I, who never knew how to entreat,
Nor never needed that I should entreat,
Am starved for meat, giddy for lack of sleep;
With oaths kept waking, and with brawling fed:
And that which spites me more than all these wants,
He does it under name of perfect love;
As who should say, if I should sleep or eat,
'Twere deadly sickness or else present death.
I prithee go and get me some repast;
I care not what, so it be wholesome food.

GRUMIO

What say you to a neat's foot?

KATHARINA

'Tis passing good: I prithee let me have it.

GRUMIO

I fear it is too choleric a meat.
How say you to a fat tripe finely broil'd?

KATHARINA

I like it well: good Grumio, fetch it me.

GRUMIO

I cannot tell; I fear 'tis choleric.
What say you to a piece of beef and mustard?

KATHARINA

A dish that I do love to feed upon.

GRUMIO

Ay, but the mustard is too hot a little.

KATHARINA

Why then, the beef, and let the mustard rest.

GRUMIO

Nay then, I will not: you shall have the mustard,
Or else you get no beef of Grumio.

KATHARINA

Then both, or one, or any thing thou wilt.

GRUMIO

Why then, the mustard without the beef.

KATHARINA

Go, get thee gone, thou false deluding slave,
                                              [Beats him
That feed'st me with the very name of meat:
Sorrow on thee and all the pack of you
That triumph thus upon my misery!
Go, get thee gone, I say.

Enter PETRUCHIO and HORTENSIO with meat

PETRUCHIO

How fares my Kate? What, sweeting, all amort?

HORTENSIO

Mistress, what cheer?

KATHARINA

                Faith, as cold as can be.

PETRUCHIO

Pluck up thy spirits; look cheerfully upon me.
Here, love; thou see'st how diligent I am
To dress thy meat myself and bring it thee:
I am sure, sweet Kate, this kindness merits thanks.
What, not a word? Nay, then thou lovest it not;
And all my pains is sorted to no proof.
Here, take away this dish.

KATHARINA

                I pray you, let it stand.

PETRUCHIO

The poorest service is repaid with thanks;
And so shall mine, before you touch the meat.

KATHARINA

I thank you, sir.

HORTENSIO

Signior Petruchio, fie! you are to blame.
Come, Mistress Kate, I'll bear you company.

PETRUCHIO

Eat it up all, Hortensio, if thou lovest me.   [Aside
Much good do it unto thy gentle heart!
Kate, eat apace: and now, my honey love,
Will we return unto thy father's house,
And revel it as bravely as the best,
With silken coats and caps and golden rings,
With ruffs and cuffs and fardingales and things;
With scarfs and fans and double change of bravery,
With amber bracelets, beads and all this knavery.
What, hast thou dined? The tailor stays thy leisure
To deck thy body with his ruffling treasure.

Enter TAILOR

Come, tailor, let us see these ornaments;
Lay forth the gown.

Enter HABERDASHER

                What news with you, sir?

HABERDASHER

Here is the cap your worship did bespeak.

PETRUCHIO

Why, this was moulded on a porringer;
A velvet dish: fie, fie! 'tis lewd and filthy:
Why, 'tis a cockle or a walnut-shell,

A knack, a toy, a trick, a baby's cap:
Away with it! come, let me have a bigger.

KATHARINA

I'll have no bigger: this doth fit the time,
And gentlewomen wear such caps as these.

PETRUCHIO

When you are gentle, you shall have one too,
And not till then.

HORTENSIO

                That will not be in haste.   [Aside

KATHARINA

Why, sir, I trust I may have leave to speak;
And speak I will; I am no child, no babe:
Your betters have endured me say my mind,
And if you cannot, best you stop your ears.
My tongue will tell the anger of my heart,
Or else my heart concealing it will break;
And rather than it shall, I will be free
Even to the uttermost, as I please, in words.

PETRUCHIO

Why, thou say'st true; it is a paltry cap,
A custard-coffin, a bauble, a silken pie:
I love thee well, in that thou likest it not.

KATHARINA

Love me or love me not, I like the cap;
And it I will have, or I will have none.
                                        [Exit HABERDASHER

PETRUCHIO

Thy gown? why, ay: come, tailor, let us see't.
O mercy, God! what masquing stuff is here?
What's this? a sleeve? 'tis like a demi-cannon:
What, up and down, carved like an apple-tart?
Here's snip and nip and cut and slish and slash,
Like to a censer in a barber's shop:
Why, what, i' devil's name, tailor, call'st thou this?

HORTENSIO

I see she's like to have neither cap nor gown. [Aside

TAILOR

You bid me make it orderly and well,
According to the fashion and the time.

PETRUCHIO

Marry, and did; but if you be remember'd,
I did not bid you mar it to the time.
Go, hop me over every kennel home,
For you shall hop without my custom, sir:
I'll none of it: hence! make your best of it.

KATHARINA

I never saw a better-fashion'd gown,
More quaint, more pleasing, nor more commendable:
Belike you mean to make a puppet of me.

PETRUCHIO

Why, true; he means to make a puppet of thee.

TAILOR

She says your worship means to make a puppet of
her.

PETRUCHIO

O monstrous arrogance! Thou liest, thou thread,
thou thimble,
Thou yard, three-quarters, half-yard, quarter, nail!

Thou flea, thou nit, thou winter-cricket thou!
Braved in mine own house with a skein of thread?
Away, thou rag, thou quantity, thou remnant;
Or I shall so be-mete thee with thy yard,
As thou shalt think on prating whilst thou livest!
I tell thee, I, that thou hast marr'd her gown.

TAILOR

Your worship is deceived; the gown is made
Just as my master had direction:
Grumio gave order how it should be done.

GRUMIO

I gave him no order; I gave him the stuff.

TAILOR

But how did you desire it should be made?

GRUMIO

Marry, sir, with needle and thread.

TAILOR

But did you not request to have it cut?

GRUMIO

Thou hast faced many things.

TAILOR

I have.

GRUMIO

Face not me: thou hast braved many men; brave
not me; I will neither be faced nor braved. I say
unto thee, I bid thy master cut out the gown; but I
did not bid him cut it to pieces: ergo, thou liest.

TAILOR

Why, here is the note of the fashion to testify.

PETRUCHIO

Read it.

GRUMIO

The note lies in's throat, if he say I said so.

TAILOR

[Reads] 'Imprimis, a loose-bodied gown:'

GRUMIO

Master, if ever I said loose-bodied gown, sew me in
the skirts of it, and beat me to death with a bottom
of brown thread: I said a gown.

PETRUCHIO

Proceed.

TAILOR

[Reads] 'With a small compassed cape:'

GRUMIO

I confess the cape.

TAILOR

[Reads] 'With a trunk sleeve:'

GRUMIO

I confess two sleeves.

TAILOR

[Reads] 'The sleeves curiously cut.'

PETRUCHIO

Ay, there's the villany.

GRUMIO

Error i' the bill, sir; error i' the bill. I commanded
the sleeves should be cut out, and sewed up again;
and that I'll prove upon thee, though thy little
finger be armed in a thimble.

TAILOR

This is true that I say: an I had thee in place where,
thou shouldst know it.

GRUMIO

I am for thee straight: take thou the bill, give me
thy mete-yard, and spare not me.

HORTENSIO

God-a-mercy, Grumio! then he shall have no odds.

PETRUCHIO

Well, sir, in brief, the gown is not for me.

GRUMIO

You are i' the right, sir: 'tis for my mistress.

PETRUCHIO

Go, take it up unto thy master's use.

GRUMIO

Villain, not for thy life: take up my mistress' gown
for thy master's use!

PETRUCHIO

Why, sir, what's your conceit in that?

GRUMIO

O, sir, the conceit is deeper than you think for:
Take up my mistress' gown to his master's use!
O, fie, fie, fie!

PETRUCHIO

Hortensio, say thou wilt see the tailor paid.   [Aside
Go take it hence; be gone, and say no more.

HORTENSIO

Tailor, I'll pay thee for thy gown to-morrow:
Take no unkindness of his hasty words:
Away! I say; commend me to thy master.

[Exit TAILOR

PETRUCHIO

Well, come, my Kate; we will unto your father's
Even in these honest mean habiliments:
Our purses shall be proud, our garments poor;
For 'tis the mind that makes the body rich;
And as the sun breaks through the darkest clouds,
So honour peereth in the meanest habit.
What is the jay more precious than the lark,
Because his feathers are more beautiful?
Or is the adder better than the eel,
Because his painted skin contents the eye?
O, no, good Kate; neither art thou the worse
For this poor furniture and mean array.
If thou account'st it shame, lay it on me;
And therefore frolic: we will hence forthwith,
To feast and sport us at thy father's house.
Go, call my men, and let us straight to him;
And bring our horses unto Long-lane end;
There will we mount, and thither walk on foot.
Let's see; I think 'tis now some seven o'clock,
And well we may come there by dinner-time.

KATHARINA

I dare assure you, sir, 'tis almost two;
And 'twill be supper-time ere you come there.

PETRUCHIO

It shall be seven ere I go to horse:
Look, what I speak, or do, or think to do,
You are still crossing it. Sirs, let 't alone:

I will not go to-day; and ere I do,
It shall be what o'clock I say it is.

HORTENSIO

Why, so this gallant will command the sun. [Exeunt

SCENE IV. *Padua. Before* BAPTISTA's *house*

Enter TRANIO, *and the* PEDANT *dressed like* VINCENTIO

TRANIO

Sir, this is the house: please it you that I call?

PEDANT

Ay, what else? and but I be deceived
Signior Baptista may remember me,
Near twenty years ago, in Genoa,
Where we were lodgers at the Pegasus.

TRANIO

'Tis well; and hold your own, in any case,
With such austerity as 'longeth to a father.

PEDANT

I warrant you.

Enter BIONDELLO

But, sir, here comes your boy;
'Twere good he were school'd.

TRANIO

Fear you not him. Sirrah Biondello,
Now do your duty throughly, I advise you:
Imagine 'twere the right Vincentio.

BIONDELLO

Tut, fear not me.

TRANIO

But hast thou done thy errand to Baptista?

BIONDELLO

I told him that your father was at Venice;
And that you look'd for him this day in Padua.

TRANIO

Thou'rt a tall fellow: hold thee that to drink.
Here comes Baptista: set your countenance, sir.

Enter BAPTISTA *and* LUCENTIO

Signior Baptista, you are happily met.
[To the PEDANT] Sir, this is the gentleman I told you
of:
I pray you, stand good father to me now,
Give me Bianca for my patrimony.

PEDANT

Soft, son!
Sir, by your leave: having come to Padua
To gather in some debts, my son Lucentio
Made me acquainted with a weighty cause
Of love between your daughter and himself:
And, for the good report I hear of you,
And for the love he beareth to your daughter,
And she to him, to stay him not too long,
I am content, in a good father's care,
To have him match'd; and, if you please to like
No worse than I, upon some agreement
Me shall you find ready and willing
With one consent to have her so bestow'd;
For curious I cannot be with you,
Signior Baptista, of whom I hear so well.

BAPTISTA

Sir, pardon me in what I have to say:
Your plainness and your shortness, please me well.
Right true it is, your son Lucentio here
Doth love my daughter, and she loveth him,
Or both dissemble deeply their affections:
And therefore, if you say no more than this,
That like a father you will deal with him,
And pass my daughter a sufficient dower,
The match is made, and all is done:
Your son shall have my daughter with consent.

TRANIO

I thank you, sir. Where then do you know best
We be affied and such assurance ta'en
As shall with either part's agreement stand?

BAPTISTA

Not in my house, Lucentio; for, you know,
Pitchers have ears, and I have many servants:
Besides, old Gremio is hearkening still;
And happily we might be interrupted.

TRANIO

Then at my lodging, an it like you:
There doth my father lie; and there, this night,
We'll pass the business privately and well.
Send for your daughter by your servant here;
My boy shall fetch the scrivener presently.
The worst is this, that, at so slender warning,
You are like to have a thin and slender pittance.

BAPTISTA

It likes me well. Cambio, hie you home,
And bid Bianca make her ready straight;
And, if you will, tell what hath happened,
Lucentio's father is arrived in Padua,
And how she's like to be Lucentio's wife.

BIONDELLO

I pray the gods she may with all my heart!

TRANIO

Dally not with the gods, but get thee gone.
[Exit BIONDELLO
Signior Baptista, shall I lead the way?
Welcome! one mess is like to be your cheer:
Come, sir; we will better it in Pisa.

BAPTISTA

I follow you. [Exeunt TRANIO, PEDANT *and* BAPTISTA
Re-enter BIONDELLO

BIONDELLO

Cambio.

LUCENTIO

What sayest thou, Biondello?

BIONDELLO

You saw my master wink and laugh upon you?

LUCENTIO

Biondello, what of that?

BIONDELLO

Faith, nothing; but has left me here behind, to expound the meaning or moral of his signs and tokens.

LUCENTIO

I pray thee, moralize them.

BIONDELLO

Then thus. Baptista is safe, talking with the deceiving father of a deceitful son.

LUCENTIO

And what of him?

BIONDELLO

His daughter is to be brought by you to the supper.

LUCENTIO

And then?

BIONDELLO

The old priest at Saint Luke's church is at your
command at all hours.

LUCENTIO

And what of all this?

BIONDELLO

I cannot tell; expect they are busied about a counterfeit assurance: take you assurance of her, 'cum
privilegio ad imprimendum solum:' to the church;
take the priest, clerk, and some sufficient honest
witnesses:
If this be not that you look for, I have no more to
say,
But bid Bianca farewell for ever and a day.

LUCENTIO

Hearest thou, Biondello?

BIONDELLO

I cannot tarry: I knew a wench married in an afternoon as she went to the garden for parsley to stuff a
rabbit; and so may you, sir: and so, adieu, sir. My
master hath appointed me to go to Saint Luke's, to
bid the priest be ready to come against you come
with your appendix.   [Exit

LUCENTIO

I may, and will, if she be so contented:
She will be pleased; then wherefore should I doubt?
Hap what hap may, I'll roundly go about her:
It shall go hard if Cambio go without her.   [Exit

SCENE V. *A public road*

Enter PETRUCHIO, KATHARINA, HORTENSIO *and*
SERVANTS

PETRUCHIO

Come on, i' God's name; once more toward our
father's.
Good Lord, how bright and goodly shines the moon!

KATHARINA

The moon! the sun: it is not moonlight now.

PETRUCHIO

I say it is the moon that shines so bright.

KATHARINA

I know it is the sun that shines so bright.

PETRUCHIO

Now, by my mother's son, and that's myself,
It shall be moon, or star, or what I list,
Or ere I journey to your father's house.
Go on, and fetch our horses back again.
Evermore cross'd and cross'd; nothing but cross'd!

HORTENSIO

Say as he says, or we shall never go.

KATHARINA

Forward, I pray, since we have come so far,
And be it moon, or sun, or what you please:
An if you please to call it a rush-candle,
Henceforth I vow it shall be so for me.

PETRUCHIO

I say it is the moon.

KATHARINA

I know it is the moon.

PETRUCHIO

Nay, then you lie: it is the blessed sun.

KATHARINA

Then, God be bless'd, it is the blessed sun:
But sun it is not, when you say it is not;
And the moon changes even as your mind.
What you will have it named, even that it is;
And so it shall be so for Katharine.

HORTENSIO

Petruchio, go thy ways; the field is won.

PETRUCHIO

Well, forward, forward! thus the bowl should run,
And not unluckily against the bias.
But, soft! company is coming here.

Enter VINCENTIO

[*To* VINCENTIO] Good morrow, gentle mistress:
    where away?
Tell me, sweet Kate, and tell me truly too,
Hast thou beheld a fresher gentlewoman?
Such war of white and red within her cheeks!
What stars do spangle heaven with such beauty,
As those two eyes become that heavenly face?
Fair lovely maid, once more good day to thee.
Sweet Kate, embrace her for her beauty's sake.

HORTENSIO

A' will make the man mad, to make a woman of
him.

KATHARINA

Young budding virgin, fair and fresh and sweet,
Whither away, or where is thy abode?
Happy the parents of so fair a child;
Happier the man, whom favourable stars
Allot thee for his lovely bed-fellow!

PETRUCHIO

Why, how now, Kate! I hope thou art not mad:
This is a man, old, wrinkled, faded, wither'd;
And not a maiden, as thou say'st he is.

KATHARINA

Pardon, old father, my mistaking eyes,
That have been so bedazzled with the sun,
That every thing I look on seemeth green:
Now I perceive thou art a reverend father;
Pardon, I pray thee, for my mad mistaking.

PETRUCHIO

Do, good old grandsire; and withal make known
Which way thou travellest: if along with us,
We shall be joyful of thy company.

VINCENTIO

Fair sir, and you my merry mistress,

That with your strange encounter much amazed
  me,
My name is call'd Vincentio; my dwelling Pisa;
And bound I am to Padua; there to visit
A son of mine, which long I have not seen.

PETRUCHIO

What is his name?

VINCENTIO

Lucentio, gentle sir.

PETRUCHIO

Happily met; the happier for thy son.
And now by law, as well as reverend age,
I may entitle thee my loving father:
The sister to my wife, this gentlewoman,
Thy son by this hath married. Wonder not,
Nor be not grieved: she is of good esteem,
Her dowry wealthy, and of worthy birth;
Beside, so qualified as may beseem
The spouse of any noble gentleman.
Let me embrace with old Vincentio,
And wander we to see thy honest son,
Who will of thy arrival be full joyous.

VINCENTIO

But is this true? or is it else your pleasure,
Like pleasant travellers, to break a jest
Upon the company you overtake?

HORTENSIO

I do assure thee, father, so it is.

PETRUCHIO

Come, go along, and see the truth hereof;
For our first merriment hath made thee jealous.
                        [Exeunt all but HORTENSIO

HORTENSIO

Well, Petruchio, this has put me in heart.
Have to my widow! and if she be froward,
Then hast thou taught Hortensio to be untoward.
                                [Exit

ACT V

SCENE I. *Padua. Before* LUCENTIO's *house*

GREMIO *discovered. Enter behind* BIONDELLO, LUCENTIO,
and BIANCA

BIONDELLO

Softly and swiftly, sir; for the priest is ready.

LUCENTIO

I fly, Biondello: but they may chance to need thee
at home; therefore leave us.

BIONDELLO

Nay, faith, I'll see the church o' your back; and
then come back to my master's as soon as I can.
            [Exeunt LUCENTIO, BIANCA, *and* BIONDELLO

GREMIO

I marvel Cambio comes not all this while.

Enter PETRUCHIO, KATHARINA, VINCENTIO, GRUMIO,
with ATTENDANTS

PETRUCHIO

Sir, here's the door, this is Lucentio's house:

My father's bears more toward the market-place;
Thither must I, and here I leave you, sir.

VINCENTIO

You shall not choose but drink before you go:
I think I shall command your welcome here,
And, by all likelihood, some cheer is toward.
                                     [Knock

GREMIO

They're busy within; you were best knock louder.
          PEDANT *looks out of the window*

PEDANT

What's he that knocks as he would beat down th
gate?

VINCENTIO

Is Signior Lucentio within, sir?

PEDANT

He's within, sir, but not to be spoken withal.

VINCENTIO

What if a man bring him a hundred pound or two
to make merry withal?

PEDANT

Keep your hundred pounds to yourself: he shal
need none, so long as I live.

PETRUCHIO

Nay, I told you your son was well beloved i
Padua. Do you hear, sir?—to leave frivolous cir
cumstances,—I pray you, tell Signior Lucentio
that his father is come from Pisa, and is here at the
door to speak with him.

PEDANT

Thou liest: his father has come from Padua, and
here looking out at the window.

VINCENTIO

Art thou his father?

PEDANT

Ay, sir; so his mother says, if I may believe her.

PETRUCHIO

[To VINCENTIO] Why, how now, gentleman! why
this is flat knavery, to take upon you another man'
name.

PEDANT

Lay hands on the villain: I believe a' means t
cozen somebody in this city under my countenance
                 Re-enter BIONDELLO

BIONDELLO

I have seen them in the church together: God send
'em good shipping! But who is here? mine old mas
ter Vincentio! now we are undone, and brought t
nothing.

VINCENTIO

[Seeing BIONDELLO] Come hither, crack-hemp.

BIONDELLO

I hope I may choose, sir.

VINCENTIO

Come hither, you rogue. What, have you forgot me

BIONDELLO

Forgot you! no, sir: I could not forget you, for
never saw you before in all my life.

VINCENTIO
What, you notorious villain, didst thou never see
thy master's father, Vincentio?

BIONDELLO
What, my old worshipful old master? yes, marry,
sir: see where he looks out of the window.

VINCENTIO
Is't so, indeed?　　　　　　　　　*[Beats* BIONDELLO

BIONDELLO
Help, help, help! here's a madman will murder me.
　　　　　　　　　　　　　　　　[Exit

PEDANT
Help, son! help, Signior Baptista!　*[Exit from above*

PETRUCHIO
Prithee, Kate, let's stand aside, and see the end of
this controversy.　　　　　　　　*[They retire*

Re-enter PEDANT *below;* TRANIO, BAPTISTA,
and SERVANTS

TRANIO
Sir, what are you, that offer to beat my servant?

VINCENTIO
What am I, sir! nay, what are you, sir? O immortal
gods! O fine villain! A silken doublet! a velvet hose!
a scarlet cloak! and a copatain hat! O, I am undone! I am undone! while I play the good husband
at home, my son and my servant spend all at the
university.

TRANIO
How now! what's the matter?

BAPTISTA
What, is the man lunatic?

TRANIO
Sir, you seem a sober ancient gentleman by your
habit, but your words show you a madman. Why,
sir, what 'cerns it you if I wear pearl and gold? I
thank my good father, I am able to maintain it.

VINCENTIO
Thy father! O villain! he is a sail-maker in Ber-
gamo.

BAPTISTA
You mistake, sir, you mistake, sir. Pray, what do
you think is his name?

VINCENTIO
His name! as if I knew not his name: I have brought
him up ever since he was three years old, and his
name is Tranio.

PEDANT
Away, away, mad ass! his name is Lucentio; and he
is mine only son, and heir to the lands of me,
Signior Vincentio.

VINCENTIO
Lucentio! O, he hath murdered his master! Lay
hold on him, I charge you, in the Duke's name. O,
my son, my son! Tell me, thou villain, where is my
son Lucentio?

TRANIO
Call forth an officer.
　　　　Enter one with an Officer
Carry this mad knave to the gaol. Father Baptista, I
charge you see that he be forthcoming.

VINCENTIO
Carry me to the gaol!

GREMIO
Stay, officer: he shall not go to prison.

BAPTISTA
Talk not, Signior Gremio: I say he shall go to
prison.

GREMIO
Take heed, Signior Baptista, lest you be cony-
catched in this business: I dare swear this is the
right Vincentio.

PEDANT
Swear, if thou darest.

GREMIO
Nay, I dare not swear it.

TRANIO
Then thou wert best say that I am not Lucentio.

GREMIO
Yes, I know thee to be Signior Lucentio.

BAPTISTA
Away with the dotard! to the gaol with him!

VINCENTIO
Thus strangers may be haled and abused:
O monstrous villain!

Re-enter BIONDELLO, *with* LUCENTIO *and* BIANCA

BIONDELLO
O, we are spoiled! and—yonder he is: deny him,
forswear him, or else we are all undone.

LUCENTIO
Pardon, sweet father.　　　　　　*[Kneeling*

VINCENTIO
　　　　　Lives my sweet son?
[Exeunt BIONDELLO, TRANIO, *and* PEDANT, *as fast as
　　　　　　　　　　　　　　　　　may be*

BIANCA
Pardon, dear father.

BAPTISTA
　　　　　　　　How hast thou offended?
Where is Lucentio?

LUCENTIO
　　　　　　　　Here's Lucentio,
Right son to the right Vincentio;
That have by marriage made thy daughter mine,
While counterfeit supposes blear'd thine eyne.

GREMIO
Here's packing, with a witness, to deceive us all!

VINCENTIO
Where is that damned villain Tranio,
That faced and braved me in this matter so?

BAPTISTA
Why, tell me, is not this my Cambio?

BIANCA
Cambio is changed into Lucentio.

LUCENTIO
Love wrought these miracles. Bianca's love
Made me exchange my state with Tranio,
While he did bear my countenance in the town;
And happily I have arrived at the last
Unto the wished haven of my bliss.

What Tranio did, myself enforced him to;
Then pardon him, sweet father, for my sake.
VINCENTIO
I'll slit the villain's nose, that would have sent me to
the gaol.
BAPTISTA
But do you hear, sir? have you married my daugh-
ter without asking my good will?
VINCENTIO
Fear not, Baptista; we will content you, go to: but I
will in, to be revenged for this villany.   [*Exit*
BAPTISTA
And I, to sound the depth of this knavery.   [*Exit*
LUCENTIO
Look not pale, Bianca; thy father will not frown.
          [*Exeunt* LUCENTIO *and* BIANCA
GREMIO
My cake is dough: but I'll in among the rest;
Out of hope of all, but my share of the feast.   [*Exit*
KATHARINA
Husband, let's follow, to see the end of this ado.
PETRUCHIO
First kiss me, Kate, and we will.
KATHARINA
What, in the midst of the street?
PETRUCHIO
What, art thou ashamed of me?
KATHARINA
No, sir, God forbid; but ashamed to kiss.
PETRUCHIO
Why, then let's home again. Come, sirrah, let's
away.
KATHARINA
Nay, I will give thee a kiss: now pray thee, love,
stay.
PETRUCHIO
Is not this well? Come, my sweet Kate:
Better once than never, for never too late.   [*Exeunt*

SCENE II. *Padua.* LUCENTIO's *house*

Enter BAPTISTA, VINCENTIO, GREMIO, *the* PEDANT,
LUCENTIO, BIANCA, PETRUCHIO, KATHARINA, HOR-
TENSIO, *and* WIDOW, TRANIO, BIONDELLO, *and* GRUMIO:
the SERVING-MEN *with* TRANIO *bringing in a banquet*
LUCENTIO
At last, though long, our jarring notes agree:
And time it is, when raging war is done,
To smile at scapes and perils overblown.
My fair Bianca, bid my father welcome,
While I with self-same kindness welcome thine.
Brother Petruchio, sister Katharina,
And thou, Hortensio, with thy loving widow,
Feast with the best, and welcome to my house:
My banquet is to close our stomachs up,
After our great good cheer. Pray you, sit down;
For now we sit to chat, as well as eat.
PETRUCHIO
Nothing but sit and sit, and eat and eat!

BAPTISTA
Padua affords this kindness, son Petruchio.
PETRUCHIO
Padua affords nothing but what is kind.
HORTENSIO
For both our sakes, I would that word were true.
PETRUCHIO
Now, for my life, Hortensio fears his widow.
WIDOW
Then never trust me, if I be afeard.
PETRUCHIO
You are very sensible, and yet you miss my sense:
I mean, Hortensio is afeard of you.
WIDOW
He that is giddy thinks the world turns round.
PETRUCHIO
Roundly replied.
KATHARINA
          Mistress, how mean you that?
WIDOW
Thus I conceive by him.
PETRUCHIO
Conceives by me! How likes Hortensio that?
HORTENSIO
My widow says, thus she conceives her tale.
PETRUCHIO
Very well mended. Kiss him for that, good widow.
KATHARINA
'He that is giddy thinks the world turns round:'
I pray you, tell me what you meant by that.
WIDOW
Your husband, being troubled with a shrew,
Measures my husband's sorrow by his woe:
And now you know my meaning.
KATHARINA
A very mean meaning.
WIDOW
          Right, I mean you.
KATHARINA
And I am mean, indeed, respecting you.
PETRUCHIO
To her, Kate!
HORTENSIO
To her, widow!
PETRUCHIO
A hundred marks, my Kate does put her down.
HORTENSIO
That's my office.
PETRUCHIO
Spoke like an officer: ha' to thee, lad.
          [*Drinks to* HORTENSIO
BAPTISTA
How likes Gremio these quick-witted folks?
GREMIO
Believe me, sir, they butt together well.
BIANCA
Head, and butt! an hasty-witted body
Would say your head and butt were head and horn.
VINCENTIO
Ay, mistress bride, hath that awaken'd you?

BIANCA

Ay, but not frighted me; therefore I'll sleep again.

PETRUCHIO

Nay, that you shall not: since you have begun,
Have at you for a bitter jest or two!

BIANCA

Am I your bird? I mean to shift my bush;
And then pursue me as you draw your bow.
You are welcome all.

[_Exeunt_ BIANCA, KATHARINA, _and_ WIDOW

PETRUCHIO

She hath prevented me. Here, Signior Tranio,
This bird you aim'd at, though you hit her not;
Therefore a health to all that shot and miss'd.

TRANIO

O, sir, Lucentio slipp'd me like his greyhound,
Which runs himself, and catches for his master.

PETRUCHIO

A good swift simile, but something currish.

TRANIO

'Tis well, sir, that you hunted for yourself:
'Tis thought your deer does hold you at a bay.

BAPTISTA

O ho, Petruchio! Tranio hits you now.

LUCENTIO

I thank thee for that gird, good Tranio.

HORTENSIO

Confess, confess, hath he not hit you here?

PETRUCHIO

A' has a little gall'd me, I confess;
And, as the jest did glance away from me,
'Tis ten to one it maim'd you two outright.

BAPTISTA

Now, in good sadness, son Petruchio,
I think thou hast the veriest shrew of all.

PETRUCHIO

Well, I say no: and therefore for assurance
Let's each one send unto his wife;
And he whose wife is most obedient,
To come at first when he doth send for her,
Shall win the wager which we will propose.

HORTENSIO

Content. What is the wager?

LUCENTIO

Twenty crowns.

PETRUCHIO

Twenty crowns!
I'll venture so much of my hawk or hound,
But twenty times so much upon my wife.

LUCENTIO

A hundred then.

HORTENSIO

Content.

PETRUCHIO

A match! 'tis done.

HORTENSIO

Who shall begin?

LUCENTIO

That will I.
Go, Biondello, bid your mistress come to me.

BIONDELLO

I go.   [_Exit_

BAPTISTA

Son, I'll be your half, Bianca comes.

LUCENTIO

I'll have no halves; I'll bear it all myself.

Re-enter BIONDELLO

How now! what news?

BIONDELLO

Sir, my mistress sends you word
That she is busy, and she cannot come.

PETRUCHIO

How! she is busy, and she cannot come!
Is that an answer?

GREMIO

Ay, and a kind one too:
Pray God, sir, your wife send you not a worse.

PETRUCHIO

I hope, better.

HORTENSIO

Sirrah Biondello, go and entreat my wife
To come to me forthwith.   [_Exit_ BIONDELLO

PETRUCHIO

O, ho! entreat her!
Nay, then she must needs come.

HORTENSIO

I am afraid, sir,
Do what you can, yours will not be entreated.

Re-enter BIONDELLO

Now, where's my wife?

BIONDELLO

She says you have some goodly jest in hand:
She will not come; she bids you come to her.

PETRUCHIO

Worse and worse; she will not come! O vile,
Intolerable, not to be endured!
Sirrah Grumio, go to your mistress;
Say, I command her come to me.   [_Exit_ GRUMIO

HORTENSIO

I know her answer.

PETRUCHIO

What?

HORTENSIO

She will not.

PETRUCHIO

The fouler fortune mine, and there an end.

BAPTISTA

Now, by my holidame, here comes Katharina!

Re-enter KATHARINA

KATHARINA

What is your will, sir, that you send for me?

PETRUCHIO

Where is your sister, and Hortensio's wife?

KATHARINA

They sit conferring by the parlour fire.

PETRUCHIO

Go, fetch them hither: if they deny to come,
Swinge me them soundly forth unto their husbands:
Away, I say, and bring them hither straight.

[_Exit_ KATHARINA

LUCENTIO

Here is a wonder, if you talk of a wonder.

HORTENSIO

And so it is: I wonder what it bodes.

PETRUCHIO

Marry, peace it bodes, and love, and quiet life,
An awful rule, and right supremacy;
And, to be short, what not, that's sweet and happy?

BAPTISTA

Now, fair befal thee, good Petruchio!
The wager thou hast won; and I will add
Unto their losses twenty thousand crowns;
Another dowry to another daughter,
For she is changed, as she had never been.

PETRUCHIO

Nay, I will win my wager better yet,
And show more sign of her obedience,
Her new-built virtue and obedience.
See where she comes and brings your froward wives
As prisoners to her womanly persuasion.

Re-enter KATHARINA, *with* BIANCA *and* WIDOW

Katharine, that cap of yours becomes you not:
Off with that bauble, throw it under-foot.

WIDOW

Lord, let me never have a cause to sigh,
Till I be brought to such a silly pass!

BIANCA

Fie, what a foolish duty call you this?

LUCENTIO

I would your duty were as foolish too:
The wisdom of your duty, fair Bianca,
Hath cost me an hundred crowns since supper-time.

BIANCA

The more fool you, for laying on my duty.

PETRUCHIO

Katharine, I charge thee, tell these headstrong
women
What duty they do owe their lords and husbands.

WIDOW

Come, come, you're mocking: we will have no telling.

PETRUCHIO

Come on, I say; and first begin with her.

WIDOW

She shall not.

PETRUCHIO

I say she shall: and first begin with her.

KATHARINA

Fie, fie! unknit that threatening unkind brow;
And dart not scornful glances from those eyes,
To wound thy lord, thy king, thy governor:
It blots thy beauty as frosts do bite the meads,
Confounds thy fame as whirlwinds shake fair buds,
And in no sense is meet or amiable.
A woman moved is like a fountain troubled,
Muddy, ill-seeming, thick, bereft of beauty;

And while it is so, none so dry or thirsty
Will deign to sip or touch one drop of it.
Thy husband is thy lord, thy life, thy keeper,
Thy head, thy sovereign; one that cares for thee,
And for thy maintenance commits his body
To painful labour both by sea and land,
To watch the night in storms, the day in cold,
Whilst thou liest warm at home, secure and safe;
And craves no other tribute at thy hands
But love, fair looks and true obedience;
Too little payment for so great a debt.
Such duty as the subject owes the prince
Even such a woman oweth to her husband;
And when she is froward, peevish, sullen, sour,
And not obedient to his honest will,
What is she but a foul contending rebel,
And graceless traitor to her loving lord?
I am ashamed that women are so simple
To offer war where they should kneel for peace;
Or seek for rule, supremacy and sway,
When they are bound to serve, love and obey.
Why are our bodies soft and weak and smooth,
Unapt to toil and trouble in the world,
But that our soft conditions and our hearts
Should well agree with our external parts?
Come, come, you froward and unable worms!
My mind hath been as big as one of yours,
My heart as great, my reason haply more,
To bandy word for word and frown for frown;
But now I see our lances are but straws,
Our strength as weak, our weakness past compare,
That seeming to be most which we indeed least are.
Then vail your stomachs, for it is no boot,
And place your hands below your husband's foot:
In token of which duty, if he please,
My hand is ready, may it do him ease.

PETRUCHIO

Why, there's a wench! Come on, and kiss me, Kate.

LUCENTIO

Well, go thy ways, old lad; for thou shalt ha't.

VINCENTIO

'Tis a good hearing, when children are toward.

LUCENTIO

But a harsh hearing, when women are froward.

PETRUCHIO

Come, Kate, we'll to bed.
We three are married, but you two are sped.
'Twas I won the wager, though you hit the white;
                              [*To* LUCENTIO
And, being a winner, God give you good night!
          [*Exeunt* PETRUCHIO *and* KATHARINA

HORTENSIO

Now, go thy ways; thou hast tamed a curst shrew.

LUCENTIO

'Tis a wonder, by your leave, she will be tamed so.
                                        [*Exeunt*

THE TWO GENTLEMEN OF VERONA

SYNOPSIS

Two young men of noble Veronese families, Proteus and Valentine, have grown up together from childhood and each one is apparently devoted to the other, but Valentine is by nature capable of loving to a high pitch of loyalty, while Proteus, though gifted with all the graces of feature and mind, is deceitful and inconstant.

Valentine leaves Verona to seek his fortune at the Emperor's court in Milan, and Proteus, desiring to win the love of his adored Julia, is content to remain at home, but his ambitious father, Antonio, who knows nothing of his son's love affair, orders him to follow Valentine to court. Now privately betrothed to Julia, Proteus exchanges rings with her, makes elaborate protestations of his faithfulness and kisses her good-bye, at the same time looking forward to the not unpleasant prospect of the change. Upon reaching the court, he is joyously received by his friend and at once presented to Silvia, the exquisite daughter of the Duke of Milan, with whom Valentine is deeply in love.

To make her lover understand that there is mutual affection between them, the sprightly Silvia commissions him to write some love letters, presumably to one of her suitors, then she returns them, audaciously telling him to write more fervently and keep the letters for himself. They pledge their love to each other in secret, well knowing they are about to face the opposition of the determined old Duke, who, planning to marry Silvia to her wealthy suitor Thurio and having noticed Valentine's devotion, safeguards his daughter from possible elopement by removing her sleeping quarters to a high tower to which he keeps the key. Together they devise a means of outwitting the Duke, and Valentine has a rope ladder made with strong hooks for scaling the wall and carrying Silvia away.

But unfortunately, the eager lover confides with his usual frankness and trust in his friend Proteus who had fallen in love with Silvia at first sight, and, despite his vows to Julia and his professed loyalty to Valentine, is determined to win the girl for himself. He at once reveals the plot to her father who intercepts Valentine that evening as he is hastening away, tricks him into explaining the use of rope ladders, discloses one under his cloak together with a note telling Silvia she will soon be freed, and orders the young man speedily to leave his dukedom on the pain of death.

The way is now clear for Proteus to get the Duke's consent to visit Silvia very often on the pretext of promoting the lovesuit of the stupid Thurio, whose interests he plans soon to sidetrack for his own. Just at this time Julia, who cannot live without the sight of Proteus, arrives in Milan disguised as a page, and the good-natured host of the inn where she stops takes her to the court of the palace so that she may see the gentleman of whom she has inquired. Here she listens to a serenade to the Duke's daughter given by the befooled Thurio's musicians who depart after Silvia thanks them graciously from her window, and in the darkness, the innkeeper dropping asleep beside her, the miserable girl overhears Proteus making ardent love to the lady in the tower above him who turns on him in calm scorn, and scathingly sums up his conduct as a disloyal friend to Valentine and a false lover to his Julia. On the next day the supposed page asks Proteus for employment, and as his messenger is sent to Silvia with the very ring she gave him when they parted in Verona. Silvia returns the ring in angry contempt and when she tells Julia that she recognizes it as a love-token of which Proteus had often spoken, the little page speaks so feelingly of the deserted sweetheart's sorrow that Silvia gives him her purse.

Meanwhile, Valentine has been captured in a forest near Mantua by a band of outlaws who, being gentlemen that have been banished for political reasons, attracted by the young man's manner and bearing ask him to live with them as their chief. Hearing that her lover is in Mantua, Silvia implores her chivalrous suitor, Sir Eglamour, to help her reach him, meets the knight at Friar Patrick's cell where she had intended to confess, and they escape together. Silvia is recognized in spite of her mask, the Duke is informed of her flight and starts off with Thurio, Proteus and his page in pursuit of the runaways. The outlaws seize Silvia but as they are taking her to their chief, Proteus and Julia arrive, disperse the bandits, and free the captive.

Taking full advantage of the situation, Proteus threatens to force Silvia to yield to him, but at her cry of terror Valentine, who has heard everything from his hiding place near by, confronts his false friend, who confesses his guilt and begs for forgiveness so humbly that Valentine readily grants it. To show his sincerity Valentine offers to relinquish Silvia to his friend, but at his words the little page faints, Proteus discovers from his ring on her finger that she is actually Julia, and they are reunited. The Duke and Thurio are now brought in by the outlaws, but her lover refuses to give up Silvia to this suitor who will not fight for her, and the Duke, relenting, gladly bestows her hand on Valentine whom he forgives freely and at whose request he also pardons the bandits.

HISTORICAL DATA

The story of *The Two Gentlemen of Verona* is probably derived from the story of the shepherdess Felismena in the Spanish pastoral romance *Diana Enamorada*, by Jorge de Montemayor, published in 1560. Although no printed English edition of this famous book appeared until the translation by Bartholomew Yonge in 1598, it is known that it was in circulation in manuscript form many years prior to that. A play based on this translation, entitled *The History of Felix and Philiomena*, was performed at Greenwich as early as 1584. From these sources Shakespeare undoubtedly obtained his plot.

Some of the incidents in the comedy may have come from Bandello's novel *Apolonius and Silla* (taken from Cinthio's *Hecatommithi*) which Barnabe Rich translated in 1581. Passages in Sir Philip Sidney's *Arcadia* may have suggested Valentine's consent to lead the robber band.

The date of the composition of the comedy cannot be definitely fixed, but from the style, notably the doggerel lines, the alternately rhymed verses and the sonnets, critics conclude that the play belongs in the earliest group, general opinion placing it between 1590 and 1595.

"Come, come,
Be patient; we must bring you to our captain."
THE TWO GENTLEMEN OF VERONA

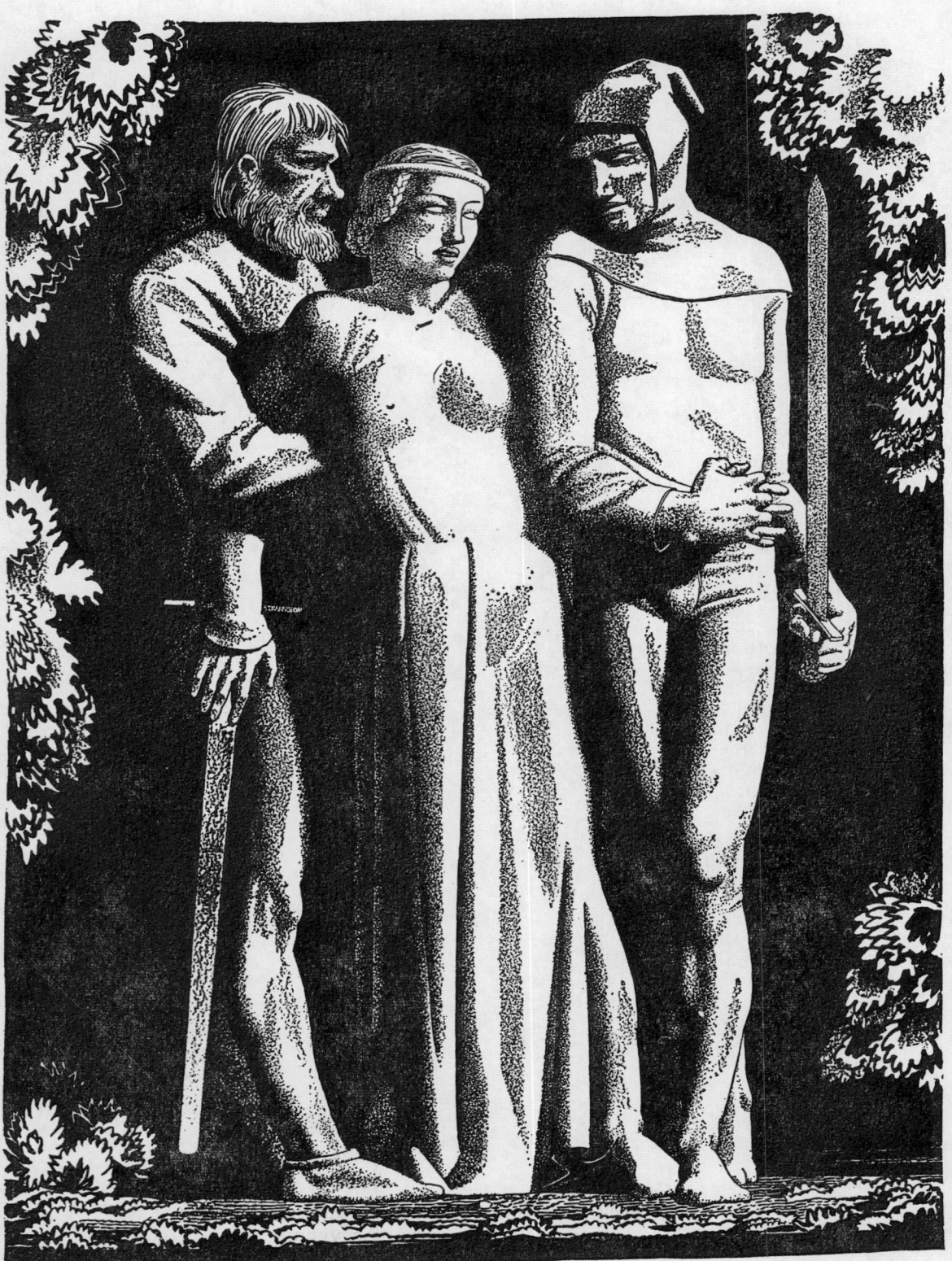

THE TWO GENTLEMEN OF VERONA

DRAMATIS PERSONÆ

DUKE OF MILAN, *father to Silvia.*
VALENTINE,
PROTEUS, } *the two gentlemen.*
ANTONIO, *father to Proteus.*
THURIO, *a foolish rival to Valentine.*
EGLAMOUR, *agent for Silvia in her escape.*
HOST, *where Julia lodges.*
OUTLAWS, *with Valentine.*
SPEED, *a clownish servant to Valentine.*

LAUNCE, *the like to Proteus.*
PANTHINO, *servant to Antonio.*

JULIA, *beloved of Proteus.*
SILVIA, *beloved of Valentine.*
LUCETTA, *waiting-woman to Julia.*

SERVANTS, MUSICIANS.

SCENE—*Verona; Milan; the frontiers of Mantua.*

ACT I

SCENE I. *Verona. An open place.*

Enter VALENTINE *and* PROTEUS

VALENTINE

CEASE to persuade, my loving Proteus:
Home-keeping youth have ever homely wits.
Were't not affection chains thy tender days
To the sweet glances of thy honour'd love,
I rather would entreat thy company
To see the wonders of the world abroad,
Than, living dully sluggardized at home,
Wear out thy youth with shapeless idleness.
But since thou lovest, love still, and thrive therein,
Even as I would, when I to love begin.

PROTEUS

Wilt thou be gone? Sweet Valentine, adieu!
Think on thy Proteus, when thou haply seest
Some rare note-worthy object in thy travel:
Wish me partaker in thy happiness,
When thou dost meet good hap; and in thy danger,
If ever danger do environ thee,
Commend thy grievance to my holy prayers,
For I will be thy beadsman, Valentine.

VALENTINE

And on a love-book pray for my success?

PROTEUS

Upon some book I love I'll pray for thee.

VALENTINE

That's on some shallow story of deep love:
How young Leander cross'd the Hellespont.

PROTEUS

That's a deep story of a deeper love;
For he was more than over shoes in love.

VALENTINE

'Tis true; for you are over boots in love,
And yet you never swum the Hellespont.

PROTEUS

Over the boots? nay, give me not the boots.

VALENTINE

No, I will not, for it boots thee not.

PROTEUS

What?

VALENTINE

To be in love, where scorn is bought with groans;
Coy looks with heart-sore sighs; one fading moment's
   mirth
With twenty watchful, weary, tedious nights:
If haply won, perhaps a hapless gain;
If lost, why then a grievous labour won;
However, but a folly bought with wit,
Or else a wit by folly vanquished.

PROTEUS

So, by your circumstance, you call me fool.

VALENTINE

So, by your circumstance, I fear you'll prove.

PROTEUS

'Tis love you cavil at: I am not Love.

VALENTINE

Love is your master, for he masters you:
And he that is so yoked by a fool,
Methinks, should not be chronicled for wise.

PROTEUS

Yet writers say, as in the sweetest bud
The eating canker dwells, so eating love
Inhabits in the finest wits of all.

VALENTINE

And writers say, as the most forward bud
Is eaten by the canker ere it blow,
Even so by love the young and tender wit
Is turn'd to folly; blasting in the bud,
Losing his verdure even in the prime,
And all the fair effects of future hopes.
But wherefore waste I time to counsel thee,
That art a votary to fond desire?
Once more adieu! my father at the road
Expects my coming, there to see me shipp'd.

PROTEUS

And thither will I bring thee, Valentine.

VALENTINE

Sweet Proteus, no; now let us take our leave.
To Milan let me hear from thee by letters
Of thy success in love, and what news else
Betideth here in absence of thy friend;
And I likewise will visit thee with mine.

PROTEUS

All happiness bechance to thee in Milan!

VALENTINE

As much to you at home! and so, farewell.   [*Exit*

PROTEUS

He after honour hunts, I after love:
He leaves his friends to dignify them more;
I leave myself, my friends, and all, for love.
Thou, Julia, thou hast metamorphosed me,
Made me neglect my studies, lose my time,
War with good counsel, set the world at nought;
Made wit with musing weak, heart sick with thought.

Enter SPEED

SPEED

Sir Proteus, save you! Saw you my master?

PROTEUS

But now he parted hence, to embark for Milan.

SPEED

Twenty to one, then, he is shipp'd already,
And I have play'd the sheep in losing him.

PROTEUS

Indeed, a sheep doth very often stray,
An if the shepherd be awhile away.

SPEED

You conclude that my master is a shepherd, then,
and I a sheep?

PROTEUS

I do.

SPEED

Why then, my horns are his horns, whether I wake
or sleep.

PROTEUS

A silly answer, and fitting well a sheep.

SPEED

This proves me still a sheep.

PROTEUS

True; and thy master a shepherd.

SPEED

Nay, that I can deny by a circumstance.

PROTEUS

It shall go hard but I'll prove it by another.

SPEED

The shepherd seeks the sheep, and not the sheep the
shepherd; but I seek my master, and my master seeks
not me: therefore I am no sheep.

PROTEUS

The sheep for fodder follow the shepherd; the shepherd for food follows not the sheep: thou for wages
followest thy master; thy master for wages follows not
thee: therefore thou art a sheep.

SPEED

Such another proof will make me cry 'baa.'

PROTEUS

But, dost thou hear? gavest thou my letter to Julia?

SPEED

Ay, sir: I, a lost mutton, gave your letter to her, a
laced mutton, and she, a laced mutton, gave me, a
lost mutton, nothing for my labour.

PROTEUS

Here's too small a pasture for such store of muttons.

SPEED

If the ground be overcharged, you were best stick her.

PROTEUS

Nay: in that you are astray, 'twere best pound you.

SPEED

Nay, sir, less than a pound shall serve me for carrying your letter.

PROTEUS

You mistake; I mean the pound,—a pinfold.

SPEED

From a pound to a pin? fold it over and over,
'Tis threefold too little for carrying a letter to your
lover.

PROTEUS

But what said she?

SPEED

[*First nodding*] Ay.

PROTEUS

Nod—Ay—why, that's noddy.

SPEED

You mistook, sir; I say, she did nod: and you ask me
if she did nod; and I say, 'Ay.'

PROTEUS

And that set together is noddy.

SPEED

Now you have taken the pains to set it together, take
it for your pains.

PROTEUS

No, no; you shall have it for bearing the letter.

SPEED

Well, I perceive I must be fain to bear with you.

PROTEUS

Why, sir, how do you bear with me?

SPEED

Marry, sir, the letter, very orderly; having nothing
but the word 'noddy' for my pains.

PROTEUS

Beshrew me, but you have a quick wit.

SPEED

And yet it cannot overtake your slow purse.

PROTEUS

Come, come, open the matter in brief: what said she?

SPEED

Open your purse, that the money and the matter may
be both at once delivered.

PROTEUS

Well, sir, here is for your pains. What said she?

SPEED

Truly, sir, I think you'll hardly win her.

PROTEUS

Why, couldst thou perceive so much from her?

SPEED

Sir, I could perceive nothing at all from her; no, not
so much as a ducat for delivering your letter: and
being so hard to me that brought your mind, I fear
she'll prove as hard to you in telling your mind. Give
her no token but stones; for she's as hard as steel.

PROTEUS

What said she? nothing?

SPEED

No, not so much as 'Take this for thy pains.' To testify
your bounty, I thank you, you have testerned me; in
requital whereof, henceforth carry your letters yourself: and so, sir, I'll commend you to my master.

PROTEUS

Go, go, be gone, to save your ship from wreck,
Which cannot perish having thee aboard,
Being destined to a drier death on shore. [*Exit* SPEED
I must go send some better messenger:
I fear my Julia would not deign my lines,
Receiving them from such a worthless post.   [*Exit*

SCENE II. *The same. Garden of* JULIA's *house*

Enter JULIA *and* LUCETTA

JULIA

But say, Lucetta, now we are alone,
Wouldst thou, then, counsel me to fall in love?

LUCETTA

Ay, madam; so you stumble not unheedfully.

JULIA

Of all the fair resort of gentlemen
That every day with parle encounter me,
In thy opinion which is worthiest love?

LUCETTA

Please you repeat their names, I'll show my mind
According to my shallow simple skill.

JULIA

What think'st thou of the fair Sir Eglamour?

LUCETTA

As of a knight well-spoken, neat and fine;
But, were I you, he never should be mine.

JULIA

What think'st thou of the rich Mercatio?

LUCETTA

Well of his wealth; but of himself, so so.

JULIA

What think'st thou of the gentle Proteus?

LUCETTA

Lord, Lord! to see what folly reigns in us!

JULIA

How now! what means this passion at his name?

LUCETTA

Pardon, dear madam: 'tis a passing shame
That I, unworthy body as I am,
Should censure thus on lovely gentlemen.

JULIA

Why not on Proteus, as of all the rest?

LUCETTA

Then thus,—of many good I think him best.

JULIA

Your reason?

LUCETTA

I have no other but a woman's reason;
I think him so, because I think him so.

JULIA

And wouldst thou have me cast my love on him?

LUCETTA

Ay, if you thought your love not cast away.

JULIA

Why, he, of all the rest, hath never moved me.

LUCETTA

Yet he, of all the rest, I think, best loves ye.

JULIA

His little speaking shows his love but small.

LUCETTA

Fire that's closest kept burns most of all.

JULIA

They do not love that do not show their love.

LUCETTA

O, they love least that let men know their love.

JULIA

I would I knew his mind.

LUCETTA

Peruse this paper, madam.

JULIA

'To Julia.'—Say, from whom?

LUCETTA

That the contents will show.

JULIA

Say, say, who gave it thee?

LUCETTA

Sir Valentine's page; and sent, I think, from Proteus.
He would have given it you; but I, being in the way,
Did in your name receive it: pardon the fault, I pray.

JULIA

Now, by my modesty, a goodly broker!
Dare you presume to harbour wanton lines?
To whisper and conspire against my youth?
Now, trust me, 'tis an office of great worth,
And you an officer fit for the place.
There, take the paper: see it be return'd;
Or else return no more into my sight.

LUCETTA

To plead for love deserves more fee than hate.

JULIA

Will ye be gone?

LUCETTA

That you may ruminate.   [*Exit*

JULIA

And yet I would I had o'erlook'd the letter:
It were a shame to call her back again,
And pray her to a fault for which I chid her.
What fool is she, that knows I am a maid,
And would not force the letter to my view!
Since maids, in modesty, say 'no' to that
Which they would have the profferer construe 'ay.'
Fie, fie, how wayward is this foolish love,
That, like a testy babe, will scratch the nurse,
And presently, all humbled, kiss the rod!
How churlishly I chid Lucetta hence,
When willingly I would have had her here!
How angerly I taught my brow to frown,
When inward joy enforced my heart to smile!
My penance is, to call Lucetta back,
And ask remission for my folly past.
What, ho! Lucetta!

Re-enter LUCETTA

LUCETTA
What would your ladyship?

JULIA
Is't near dinner-time?

LUCETTA
I would it were;
That you might kill your stomach on your meat,
And not upon your maid.

JULIA
What is't that you took up so gingerly?

LUCETTA
Nothing.

JULIA
Why didst thou stoop, then?

LUCETTA
To take a paper up that I let fall.

JULIA
And is that paper nothing?

LUCETTA
Nothing concerning me.

JULIA
Then let it lie for those that it concerns.

LUCETTA
Madam, it will not lie where it concerns,
Unless it have a false interpreter.

JULIA
Some love of yours hath writ to you in rhyme.

LUCETTA
That I might sing it, madam, to a tune.
Give me a note: your ladyship can set.

JULIA
As little by such toys as may be possible.
Best sing it to the tune of 'Light o' love.'

LUCETTA
It is too heavy for so light a tune.

JULIA
Heavy! belike it hath some burden, then?

LUCETTA
Ay; and melodious were it, would you sing it.

JULIA
And why not you?

LUCETTA
I cannot reach so high.

JULIA
Let's see your song. How now, minion!

LUCETTA
Keep tune there still, so you will sing it out:
And yet methinks I do not like this tune.

JULIA
You do not?

LUCETTA
No, madam; it is too sharp.

JULIA
You, minion, are too saucy.

LUCETTA
Nay, now you are too flat,
And mar the concord with too harsh a descant:
There wanteth but a mean to fill your song.

JULIA
The mean is drown'd with your unruly bass.

LUCETTA
Indeed, I bid the base for Proteus.

JULIA
This babble shall not henceforth trouble me.
Here is a coil with protestation!   [*Tears the letter*
Go get you gone, and let the papers lie:
You would be fingering them, to anger me.

LUCETTA
She makes it strange; but she would be best pleased
To be so anger'd with another letter.   [*Exit*

JULIA
Nay, would I were so anger'd with the same!
O hateful hands, to tear such loving words!
Injurious wasps, to feed on such sweet honey,
And kill the bees, that yield it, with your stings!
I'll kiss each several paper for amends.
Look, here is writ 'kind Julia.' Unkind Julia!
As in revenge of thy ingratitude,
I throw thy name against the bruising stones,
Trampling contemptuously on thy disdain.
And here is writ 'love-wounded Proteus.'
Poor wounded name! my bosom, as a bed,
Shall lodge thee, till thy wound be throughly heal'd;
And thus I search it with a sovereign kiss.
But twice or thrice was 'Proteus' written down.
Be calm, good wind, blow not a word away,
Till I have found each letter in the letter,
Except mine own name: that some whirlwind bear
Unto a ragged, fearful-hanging rock,
And throw it thence into the raging sea!
Lo, here in one line is his name twice writ,
'Poor forlorn Proteus, passionate Proteus,
To the sweet Julia':—that I'll tear away.—
And yet I will not, sith so prettily
He couples it to his complaining names.
Thus will I fold them one upon another:
Now kiss, embrace, contend, do what you will.

Re-enter LUCETTA

LUCETTA
Madam,
Dinner is ready, and your father stays.

JULIA
Well, let us go.

LUCETTA
What, shall these papers lie like tell-tales here?

JULIA
If you respect them, best to take them up.

LUCETTA
Nay, I was taken up for laying them down:
Yet here they shall not lie, for catching cold.

JULIA
I see you have a month's mind to them.

LUCETTA
Ay, madam, you may say what sights you see;
I see things too, although you judge I wink.

JULIA
Come, come; will't please you go?   [*Exeunt*

Scene III. *The same.* Antonio's *house*

Enter Antonio *and* Panthino

ANTONIO
Tell me, Panthino, what sad talk was that
Wherewith my brother held you in the cloister?

PANTHINO
'Twas of his nephew Proteus, your son.

ANTONIO
Why, what of him?

PANTHINO
                        He wonder'd that your lordship
Would suffer him to spend his youth at home,
While other men, of slender reputation,
Put forth their sons to seek preferment out:
Some to the wars, to try their fortune there;
Some to discover islands far away;
Some to the studious universities.
For any, or for all these exercises,
He said that Proteus your son was meet;
And did request me to importune you
To let him spend his time no more at home,
Which would be great impeachment to his age,
In having known no travel in his youth.

ANTONIO
Nor need'st thou much importune me to that
Whereon this month I have been hammering.
I have consider'd well his loss of time,
And how he cannot be a perfect man,
Not being tried and tutor'd in the world:
Experience is by industry achieved,
And perfected by the swift course of time.
Then, tell me, whither were I best to send him?

PANTHINO
I think your lordship is not ignorant
How his companion, youthful Valentine,
Attends the emperor in his royal court.

ANTONIO
I know it well.

PANTHINO
'Twere good, I think, your lordship sent him thither:
There shall he practise tilts and tournaments,
Hear sweet discourse, converse with noblemen,
And be in eye of every exercise
Worthy his youth and nobleness of birth.

ANTONIO
I like thy counsel; well hast thou advised:
And that thou mayst perceive how well I like it
The execution of it shall make known.
Even with the speediest expedition
I will dispatch him to the emperor's court.

PANTHINO
To-morrow, may it please you, Don Alphonso,
With other gentlemen of good esteem,
Are journeying to salute the emperor,
And to commend their service to his will.

ANTONIO
Good company; with them shall Proteus go:
And, in good time! now will we break with him.

Enter PROTEUS

PROTEUS
Sweet love! sweet lines! sweet life!
Here is her hand, the agent of her heart;
Here is her oath for love, her honour's pawn.
O, that our fathers would applaud our loves,
To seal our happiness with their consents!
O heavenly Julia!

ANTONIO
How now! what letter are you reading there?

PROTEUS
May't please your lordship, 'tis a word or two
Of commendations sent from Valentine,
Deliver'd by a friend that came from him.

ANTONIO
Lend me the letter; let me see what news.

PROTEUS
There is no news, my lord; but that he writes
How happily he lives, how well beloved,
And daily graced by the emperor;
Wishing me with him, partner of his fortune.

ANTONIO
And how stand you affected to his wish?

PROTEUS
As one relying on your lordship's will,
And not depending on his friendly wish.

ANTONIO
My will is something sorted with his wish.
Muse not that I thus suddenly proceed;
For what I will, I will, and there an end.
I am resolved that thou shalt spend some time
With Valentinus in the emperor's court:
What maintenance he from his friends receives,
Like exhibition thou shalt have from me.
To-morrow be in readiness to go:
Excuse it not, for I am peremptory.

PROTEUS
My lord, I cannot be so soon provided:
Please you, deliberate a day or two.

ANTONIO
Look, what thou want'st shall be sent after thee:
No more of stay! to-morrow thou must go.
Come on, Panthino: you shall be employ'd
To hasten on his expedition.

[*Exeunt* ANTONIO *and* PANTHINO

PROTEUS
Thus have I shunn'd the fire for fear of burning,
And drench'd me in the sea, where I am drown'd.
I fear'd to show my father Julia's letter,
Lest he should take exceptions to my love;
And with the vantage of mine own excuse
Hath he excepted most against my love.
O, how this spring of love resembleth
The uncertain glory of an April day,
Which now shows all the beauty of the sun,
And by and by a cloud takes all away!

Re-enter PANTHINO

PANTHINO
Sir Proteus, your father calls for you:
He is in haste; therefore, I pray you, go.

PROTEUS

Why, this it is: my heart accords thereto,
And yet a thousand times it answers 'no.'   [*Exeunt*

ACT II

SCENE I. *Milan. The* DUKE's *palace*

Enter VALENTINE *and* SPEED

SPEED

Sir, your glove.

VALENTINE

Not mine; my gloves are on.

SPEED

Why, then, this may be yours, for this is but one.

VALENTINE

Ha! let me see: ay, give it me, it's mine:
Sweet ornament that decks a thing divine!
Ah, Silvia, Silvia!

SPEED

Madam Silvia! Madam Silvia!

VALENTINE

How now, sirrah?

SPEED

She is not within hearing, sir.

VALENTINE

Why, sir, who bade you call her?

SPEED

Your worship, sir; or else I mistook.

VALENTINE

Well, you'll still be too forward.

SPEED

And yet I was last chidden for being too slow.

VALENTINE

Go to, sir: tell me, do you know Madam Silvia?

SPEED

She that your worship loves?

VALENTINE

Why, how know you that I am in love?

SPEED

Marry, by these special marks: first, you have learned,
like Sir Proteus, to wreathe your arms, like a male-
content; to relish a love-song, like a robin-redbreast;
to walk alone, like one that had the pestilence; to
sigh, like a school-boy that had lost his A B C; to
weep, like a young wench that had buried her grandam; to fast, like one that takes diet; to watch, like
one that fears robbing; to speak puling, like a beggar
at Hallowmas. You were wont, when you laughed, to
crow like a cock; when you walked, to walk like one
of the lions; when you fasted, it was presently after
dinner; when you looked sadly, it was for want of
money: and now you are metamorphosed with a
mistress, that, when I look on you, I can hardly
think you my master.

VALENTINE

Are all these things perceived in me?

SPEED

They are all perceived without ye.

VALENTINE

Without me? they cannot.

SPEED

Without you? nay, that's certain, for, without you
were so simple, none else would: but you are so without these follies, that these follies are within you, and
shine through you like the water in an urinal, that
not an eye that sees you but is a physician to comment on your malady.

VALENTINE

But tell me, dost thou know my lady Silvia?

SPEED

She that you gaze on so as she sits at supper?

VALENTINE

Hast thou observed that? even she, I mean.

SPEED

Why, sir, I know her not.

VALENTINE

Dost thou know her by my gazing on her, and yet
knowest her not?

SPEED

Is she not hard-favoured, sir?

VALENTINE

Not so fair, boy, as well-favoured.

SPEED

Sir, I know that well enough.

VALENTINE

What dost thou know?

SPEED

That she is not so fair as, of you, well favoured.

VALENTINE

I mean that her beauty is exquisite, but her favour
infinite.

SPEED

That's because the one is painted, and the other out
of all count.

VALENTINE

How painted? and how out of count?

SPEED

Marry, sir, so painted, to make her fair, that no man
counts of her beauty.

VALENTINE

How esteemest thou me? I account of her beauty.

SPEED

You never saw her since she was deformed.

VALENTINE

How long hath she been deformed?

SPEED

Ever since you loved her.

VALENTINE

I have loved her ever since I saw her; and still I see
her beautiful.

SPEED

If you love her, you cannot see her.

VALENTINE

Why?

SPEED

Because Love is blind. O, that you had mine eyes;

or your own eyes had the lights they were wont to
have when you chid at Sir Proteus for going ungartered!

VALENTINE

What should I see then?

SPEED

Your own present folly, and her passing deformity:
for he, being in love, could not see to garter his hose;
and you, being in love, cannot see to put on your
hose.

VALENTINE

Belike, boy, then, you are in love; for last morning
you could not see to wipe my shoes.

SPEED

True, sir; I was in love with my bed: I thank you,
you swinged me for my love, which makes me the
bolder to chide you for yours.

VALENTINE

In conclusion, I stand affected to her.

SPEED

I would you were set, so your affection would cease.

VALENTINE

Last night she enjoined me to write some lines to one
she loves.

SPEED

And have you?

VALENTINE

I have.

SPEED

Are they not lamely writ?

VALENTINE

No, boy, but as well as I can do them. Peace! here
she comes.

SPEED

[Aside] O excellent motion! O exceeding puppet!
Now will he interpret to her.

Enter SILVIA

VALENTINE

Madam and mistress, a thousand good-morrows.

SPEED

[Aside] O, give ye good even! here's a million of manners.

SILVIA

Sir Valentine and servant, to you two thousand.

SPEED

[Aside] He should give her interest, and she gives it
him.

VALENTINE

As you enjoin'd me, I have writ your letter
Unto the secret nameless friend of yours;
Which I was much unwilling to proceed in,
But for my duty to your ladyship.

SILVIA

I thank you, gentle servant: 'tis very clerkly done.

VALENTINE

Now trust me, madam, it came hardly off;
For, being ignorant to whom it goes,
I writ at random, very doubtfully.

SILVIA

Perchance you think too much of so much pains?

VALENTINE

No, madam; so it stead you, I will write,
Please you command, a thousand times as much;
And yet—

SILVIA

A pretty period! Well, I guess the sequel;
And yet I will not name it;—and yet I care not;—
And yet take this again:—and yet I thank you;
Meaning henceforth to trouble you no more.

SPEED

[Aside] And yet you will; and yet another 'yet.'

VALENTINE

What means your ladyship? do you not like it?

SILVIA

Yes, yes: the lines are very quaintly writ;
But since unwillingly, take them again.
Nay, take them.

VALENTINE

Madam, they are for you.

SILVIA

Ay, ay: you writ them, sir, at my request;
But I will none of them; they are for you;
I would have had them writ more movingly.

VALENTINE

Please you, I'll write your ladyship another.

SILVIA

And when it's writ, for my sake read it over,
And if it please you, so; if not, why, so.

VALENTINE

If it please me, madam, what then?

SILVIA

Why, if it please you, take it for your labour:
And so, good morrow, servant.   [Exit

SPEED

O jest unseen, inscrutable, invisible,
As a nose on a man's face, or a weathercock on a
steeple!
My master sues to her; and she hath taught her suitor,
He being her pupil, to become her tutor.
O excellent device! was there ever heard a better,
That my master, being scribe, to himself should write
the letter?

VALENTINE

How now, sir? what are you reasoning with yourself?

SPEED

Nay, I was rhyming: 'tis you that have the reason.

VALENTINE

To do what?

SPEED

To be a spokesman from Madam Silvia.

VALENTINE

To whom?

SPEED

To yourself: why, she wooes you by a figure.

VALENTINE

What figure?

SPEED

By a letter, I should say.

VALENTINE

Why, she hath not writ to me?

SPEED

What need she, when she hath made you write to yourself? Why, do you not perceive the jest?

VALENTINE

No, believe me.

SPEED

No believing you, indeed, sir. But did you perceive her earnest?

VALENTINE

She gave me none, except an angry word.

SPEED

Why, she hath given you a letter.

VALENTINE

That's the letter I writ to her friend.

SPEED

And that letter hath she delivered, and there an end.

VALENTINE

I would it were no worse.

SPEED

I'll warrant you, 'tis as well:
For often have you writ to her; and she, in modesty,
Or else for want of idle time, could not again reply;
Or fearing else some messenger, that might her mind discover,
Herself hath taught her love himself to write unto her lover.
All this I speak in print, for in print I found it.
Why muse you, sir? 'tis dinner-time.

VALENTINE

I have dined.

SPEED

Ay, but hearken, sir; though the chameleon Love can feed on the air, I am one that am nourished by my victuals, and would fain have meat. O, be not like your mistress; be moved, be moved.   [Exeunt

SCENE II. *Verona.* JULIA'S *house*

Enter PROTEUS *and* JULIA

PROTEUS

Have patience, gentle Julia.

JULIA

I must, where is no remedy.

PROTEUS

When possibly I can, I will return.

JULIA

If you turn not, you will return the sooner.
Keep this remembrance for thy Julia's sake.

[*Giving a ring*

PROTEUS

Why, then, we'll make exchange; here, take you this.

JULIA

And seal the bargain with a holy kiss.

PROTEUS

Here is my hand for my true constancy;
And when that hour o'erslips me in the day
Wherein I sigh not, Julia, for thy sake,
The next ensuing hour some foul mischance
Torment me for my love's forgetfulness!
My father stays my coming; answer not;

The tide is now:—nay, not thy tide of tears;
That tide will stay me longer than I should.
Julia, farewell!   [*Exit* JULIA
            What, gone without a word?
Ay, so true love should do: it cannot speak;
For truth hath better deeds than words to grace it.

Enter PANTHINO

PANTHINO

Sir Proteus, you are stay'd for.

PROTEUS

Go; I come, I come.
Alas! this parting strikes poor lovers dumb.   [*Exeunt*

SCENE III. *The same. A street*

Enter LAUNCE, *leading a dog*

LAUNCE

Nay, 'twill be this hour ere I have done weeping; all the kind of the Launces have this very fault. I have received my proportion, like the prodigious son, and am going with Sir Proteus to the Imperial's court. I think Crab my dog be the sourest-natured dog that lives: my mother weeping, my father wailing, my sister crying, our maid howling, our cat wringing her hands, and all our house in a great perplexity, yet did not this cruel-hearted cur shed one tear: he is a stone, a very pebble stone, and has no more pity in him than a dog: a Jew would have wept to have seen our parting; why, my grandam, having no eyes, look you, wept herself blind at my parting. Nay, I'll show you the manner of it. This shoe is my father: no, this left shoe is my father: no, no, this left shoe is my mother: nay, that cannot be so neither: yes, it is so, it is so, it hath the worser sole. This shoe, with the hole in it, is my mother, and this my father; a vengeance on't! there 'tis: now, sir, this staff is my sister, for, look you, she is as white as a lily, and as small as a wand: this hat is Nan, our maid: I am the dog: no, the dog is himself, and I am the dog,—Oh! the dog is me, and I am myself; ay, so, so. Now come I to my father; Father, your blessing: now should not the shoe speak a word for weeping: now should I kiss my father; well, he weeps on. Now come I to my mother: Oh, that she could speak now like a wood woman! Well, I kiss her, why, there 'tis; here's my mother's breath up and down. Now come I to my sister; mark the moan she makes. Now the dog all this while sheds not a tear, nor speaks a word; but see how I lay the dust with my tears.

Enter PANTHINO

PANTHINO

Launce, away, away, aboard! thy master is shipped, and thou art to post after with oars. What's the matter? why weepest thou, man? Away, ass! you'll lose the tide, if you tarry any longer.

LAUNCE

It is no matter if the tied were lost; for it is the unkindest tied that ever an*y* man tied.

PANTHINO
What's the unkindest tide?

LAUNCE
Why, he that's tied here, Crab, my dog.

PANTHINO
Tut, man, I mean thou'lt lose the flood: and, in
losing the flood, lose thy voyage, and, in losing thy
voyage, lose thy master, and, in losing thy master,
lose thy service, and, in losing thy service,—Why
dost thou stop my mouth?

LAUNCE
For fear thou shouldst lose thy tongue.

PANTHINO
Where should I lose my tongue?

LAUNCE
In thy tale.

PANTHINO
In thy tail!

LAUNCE
Lose the tide, and the voyage, and the master, and
the service, and the tied! Why, man, if the river were
dry, I am able to fill it with my tears; if the wind
were down, I could drive the boat with my sighs.

PANTHINO
Come, come away, man; I was sent to call thee.

LAUNCE
Sir, call me what thou darest.

PANTHINO
Wilt thou go?

LAUNCE
Well, I will go.   [Exeunt

SCENE IV. Milan. The DUKE's palace

Enter SILVIA, VALENTINE, THURIO, and SPEED

SILVIA
Servant!

VALENTINE
Mistress?

SPEED
Master, Sir Thurio frowns on you.

VALENTINE
Ay, boy, it's for love.

SPEED
Not of you.

VALENTINE
Of my mistress, then.

SPEED
'Twere good you knocked him.   [Exit

SILVIA
Servant, you are sad.

VALENTINE
Indeed, madam, I seem so.

THURIO
Seem you that you are not?

VALENTINE
Haply I do.

THURIO
So do counterfeits.

VALENTINE
So do you.

THURIO
What seem I that I am not?

VALENTINE
Wise.

THURIO
What instance of the contrary?

VALENTINE
Your folly.

THURIO
And how quote you my folly?

VALENTINE
I quote it in your jerkin.

THURIO
My jerkin is a doublet.

VALENTINE
Well, then, I'll double your folly.

THURIO
How?

SILVIA
What, angry, Sir Thurio! do you change colour?

VALENTINE
Give him leave, madam; he is a kind of chameleon.

THURIO
That hath more mind to feed on your blood than
live in your air.

VALENTINE
You have said, sir.

THURIO
Ay, sir, and done too, for this time.

VALENTINE
I know it well, sir; you always end ere you begin.

SILVIA
A fine volley of words, gentlemen, and quickly shot
off.

VALENTINE
'Tis indeed, madam; we thank the giver.

SILVIA
Who is that, servant?

VALENTINE
Yourself, sweet lady; for you gave the fire. Sir Thurio
borrows his wit from your ladyship's looks, and spends
what he borrows kindly in your company.

THURIO
Sir, if you spend word for word with me, I shall
make your wit bankrupt.

VALENTINE
I know it well, sir; you have an exchequer of words,
and, I think, no other treasure to give your followers, for it appears, by their bare liveries, that they
live by your bare words.

SILVIA
No more, gentlemen, no more:—here comes my
father.

Enter DUKE

DUKE OF MILAN
Now, daughter Silvia, you are hard beset.
Sir Valentine, your father's in good health

What say you to a letter from your friends
Of much good news?

DUKE OF MILAN
        My lord, I will be thankful
To any happy messenger from thence.

DUKE OF MILAN
Know ye Don Antonio, your countryman?

VALENTINE
Ay, my good lord, I know the gentleman
To be of worth, and worthy estimation,
And not without desert so well reputed.

DUKE OF MILAN
Hath he not a son?

VALENTINE
Ay, my good lord; a son that well deserves
The honour and regard of such a father.

DUKE OF MILAN
You know him well?

VALENTINE
I know him as myself; for from our infancy
We have conversed and spent our hours together:
And though myself have been an idle truant,
Omitting the sweet benefit of time
To clothe mine age with angel-like perfection,
Yet hath Sir Proteus, for that's his name,
Made use and fair advantage of his days;
His years but young, but his experience old;
His head unmellow'd, but his judgement ripe;
And, in a word, for far behind his worth
Comes all the praises that I now bestow,
He is complete in feature and in mind
With all good grace to grace a gentleman.

DUKE OF MILAN
Beshrew me, sir, but if he make this good,
He is as worthy for an empress' love
As meet to be an emperor's counsellor.
Well, sir, this gentleman is come to me,
With commendation from great potentates;
And here he means to spend his time awhile:
I think 'tis no unwelcome news to you.

VALENTINE
Should I have wish'd a thing, it had been he.

DUKE OF MILAN
Welcome him, then, according to his worth.
Silvia, I speak to you, and you, Sir Thurio,
For Valentine, I need not cite him to it:
I will send him hither to you presently.   [*Exit*

VALENTINE
This is the gentleman I told your ladyship
Had come along with me, but that his mistress
Did hold his eyes lock'd in her crystal looks.

Belike that now she hath enfranchised them,
Upon some other pawn for fealty.

VALENTINE
Nay, sure, I think she holds them prisoners still.

SILVIA
Nay, then, he should be blind; and, being blind,
How could he see his way to seek out you?

VALENTINE
Why, lady, Love hath twenty pair of eyes.

THURIO
They say that Love hath not an eye at all.

VALENTINE
To see such lovers, Thurio, as yourself:
Upon a homely object Love can wink.

SILVIA
Have done, have done; here comes the gentleman.

Enter PROTEUS

VALENTINE
Welcome, dear Proteus! Mistress, I beseech you,
Confirm his welcome with some special favour.

SILVIA
His worth is warrant for his welcome hither,
If this be he you oft have wish'd to hear from.

VALENTINE
Mistress, it is: sweet lady, entertain him
To be my fellow-servant to your ladyship.

SILVIA
Too low a mistress for so high a servant.

PROTEUS
Not so, sweet lady: but too mean a servant
To have a look of such a worthy mistress.

VALENTINE
Leave off discourse of disability:
Sweet lady, entertain him for your servant.

PROTEUS
My duty will I boast of; nothing else.

SILVIA
And duty never yet did want his meed:
Servant, you are welcome to a worthless mistress.

PROTEUS
I'll die on him that says so but yourself.

SILVIA
That you are welcome?

PROTEUS
        That you are worthless.

Enter SERVANT

SERVANT
Madam, my lord your father would speak with you.

SILVIA
I wait upon his pleasure. [*Exit* SERVANT] Come, Sir
   Thurio,
Go with me. Once more, new servant, welcome:
I'll leave you to confer of home affairs;
When you have done, we look to hear from you.

PROTEUS
We'll both attend upon your ladyship.

        [*Exeunt* SILVIA *and* THURIO

VALENTINE
Now, tell me, how do all from whence you came?

PROTEUS
Your friends are well, and have them much commended.

VALENTINE
And how do yours?

PROTEUS
        I left them all in health.

VALENTINE

How does your lady? and how thrives your love?

PROTEUS

My tales of love were wont to weary you;
I know you joy not in a love-discourse.

VALENTINE

Ay, Proteus, but that life is alter'd now:
I have done penance for contemning Love,
Whose high imperious thoughts have punish'd me
With bitter fasts, with penitential groans,
With nightly tears, and daily heart-sore sighs;
For, in revenge of my contempt of love,
Love hath chased sleep from my enthralled eyes,
And made them watchers of mine own heart's sor-
    row.
O gentle Proteus, Love's a mighty lord,
And hath so humbled me, as I confess
There is no woe to his correction,
Nor to his service no such joy on earth.
Now no discourse, except it be of love;
Now can I break my fast, dine, sup and sleep,
Upon the very naked name of love.

PROTEUS

Enough; I read your fortune in your eye.
Was this the idol that you worship so?

VALENTINE

Even she; and is she not a heavenly saint?

PROTEUS

No; but she is an earthly paragon.

VALENTINE

Call her divine.

PROTEUS

            I will not flatter her.

VALENTINE

O, flatter me; for love delights in praises.

PROTEUS

When I was sick, you gave me bitter pills;
And I must minister the like to you.

VALENTINE

Then speak the truth by her; if not divine,
Yet let her be a principality,
Sovereign to all the creatures on the earth.

PROTEUS

Except my mistress.

VALENTINE

            Sweet, except not any;
Except thou wilt except against my love.

PROTEUS

Have I not reason to prefer mine own?

VALENTINE

And I will help thee to prefer her too:
She shall be dignified with this high honour,—
To bear my lady's train, lest the base earth
Should from her vesture chance to steal a kiss,
And, of so great a favour growing proud,
Disdain to root the summer-swelling flower,
And make rough winter everlastingly.

PROTEUS

Why, Valentine, what braggardism is this?

VALENTINE

Pardon me, Proteus: all I can is nothing
To her, whose worth makes other worthies nothing;
She is alone.

PROTEUS

        Then let her alone.

VALENTINE

Not for the world: why, man, she is mine own;
And I as rich in having such a jewel
As twenty seas, if all their sand were pearl,
The water nectar, and the rocks pure gold.
Forgive me, that I do not dream on thee,
Because thou see'st me dote upon my love.
My foolish rival, that her father likes
Only for his possessions are so huge,
Is gone with her along; and I must after,
For love, thou know'st, is full of jealousy.

PROTEUS

But she loves you?

VALENTINE

Ay, and we are betroth'd: nay, more, our marriage-
    hour,
With all the cunning manner of our flight,
Determined of; how I must climb her window;
The ladder made of cords; and all the means
Plotted and 'greed on for my happiness.
Good Proteus, go with me to my chamber,
In these affairs to aid me with thy counsel.

PROTEUS

Go on before; I shall inquire you forth.
I must unto the road, to disembark
Some necessaries that I needs must use;
And then I'll presently attend you.

VALENTINE

Will you make haste?

PROTEUS

I will.   [Exit VALENTINE
Even as one heat another heat expels,
Or as one nail by strength drives out another,
So the remembrance of my former love
Is by a newer object quite forgotten.
Is it mine, or Valentine's praise,
Her true perfection, or my false transgression,
That makes me reasonless to reason thus?
She is fair; and so is Julia, that I love,—
That I did love, for now my love is thaw'd;
Which, like a waxen image 'gainst a fire,
Bears no impression of the thing it was.
Methinks my zeal to Valentine is cold,
And that I love him not as I was wont.
O, but I love his lady too too much!
And that's the reason I love him so little.
How shall I dote on her with more advice,
That thus without advice begin to love her!
'Tis but her picture I have yet beheld,
And that hath dazzled my reason's light;
But when I look on her perfections,
There is no reason but I shall be blind.
If I can check my erring love, I will;
If not, to compass her I'll use my skill.   [Exit

SCENE V. *The same. A street*

Enter SPEED *and* LAUNCE *severally*

SPEED
Launce! by mine honesty, welcome to Padua!

LAUNCE
Forswear not thyself, sweet youth; for I am not welcome. I reckon this always—that a man is never undone till he be hanged; nor never welcome to a place till some certain shot be paid, and the hostess say 'Welcome!'

SPEED
Come on, you madcap, I'll to the alehouse with you presently; where, for one shot of five pence, thou shalt have five thousand welcomes. But, sirrah, how did thy master part with Madam Julia?

LAUNCE
Marry, after they closed in earnest, they parted very fairly in jest.

SPEED
But shall she marry him?

LAUNCE
No.

SPEED
How, then? shall he marry her?

LAUNCE
No, neither.

SPEED
What, are they broken?

LAUNCE
No, they are both as whole as a fish.

SPEED
Why, then, how stands the matter with them?

LAUNCE
Marry, thus; when it stands well with him, it stands well with her.

SPEED
What an ass art thou! I understand thee not.

LAUNCE
What a block art thou, that thou canst not!
My staff understands me.

SPEED
What thou sayest?

LAUNCE
Ay, and what I do too: look thee, I'll but lean, and my staff understands me.

SPEED
It stands under thee, indeed.

LAUNCE
Why, stand-under and under-stand is all one.

SPEED
But tell me true, will't be a match?

LAUNCE
Ask my dog: if he say ay, it will; if he say, no, it will; if he shake his tail and say nothing, it will.

SPEED
The conclusion is, then, that it will.

LAUNCE
Thou shalt never get such a secret from me but by a parable.

SPEED
'Tis well that I get it so. But, Launce, how sayest thou, that my master is become a notable lover?

LAUNCE
I never knew him otherwise.

SPEED
Than how?

LAUNCE
A notable lubber, as thou reportest him to be.

SPEED
Why, thou whoreson ass, thou mistakest me.

LAUNCE
Why fool, I meant not thee; I meant thy master.

SPEED
I tell thee, my master is become a hot lover.

LAUNCE
Why, I tell thee, I care not though he burn himself in love. If thou wilt, go with me to the alehouse; if not, thou art an Hebrew, a Jew, and not worth the name of a Christian.

SPEED
Why?

LAUNCE
Because thou hast not so much charity in thee as to go to the ale with a Christian. Wilt thou go?

SPEED
At thy service.   [*Exeunt*

SCENE VI. *The same. The* DUKE's *palace*

Enter PROTEUS

PROTEUS
To leave my Julia, shall I be forsworn;
To love fair Silvia, shall I be forsworn;
To wrong my friend, I shall be much forsworn;
And even that power, which gave me first my oath,
Provokes me to this threefold perjury;
Love bade me swear, and Love bids me forswear.
O sweet-suggesting Love, if thou hast sinn'd,
Teach me, thy tempted subject, to excuse it!
At first I did adore a twinkling star,
But now I worship a celestial sun.
Unheedful vows may heedfully be broken;
And he wants wit that wants resolved will
To learn his wit to exchange the bad for better.
Fie, fie, unreverend tongue! to call her bad,
Whose sovereignty so oft thou hast preferr'd
With twenty thousand soul-confirming oaths.
I cannot leave to love, and yet I do;
But there I leave to love where I should love.
Julia I lose, and Valentine I lose:
If I keep them, I needs must lose myself;
If I lose them, thus find I by their loss
For Valentine, myself, for Julia, Silvia.
I to myself am dearer than a friend,
For love is still most precious in itself;
And Silvia—witness Heaven, that made her fair!—
Shows Julia but a swarthy Ethiope.
I will forget that Julia is alive,

Remembering that my love to her is dead;
And Valentine I'll hold an enemy,
Aiming at Silvia as a sweeter friend.
I cannot now prove constant to myself,
Without some treachery used to Valentine.
This night he meaneth with a corded ladder
To climb celestial Silvia's chamber-window;
Myself in counsel, his competitor.
Now presently I'll give her father notice
Of their disguising and pretended flight;
Who, all enraged, will banish Valentine;
For Thurio, he intends, shall wed his daughter;
But, Valentine being gone, I'll quickly cross
By some sly trick blunt Thurio's dull proceeding.
Love, lend me wings to make my purpose swift,
As thou hast lent me wit to plot this drift!   [Exit

SCENE VII. *Verona.* JULIA's *house*

Enter JULIA *and* LUCETTA

JULIA

Counsel, Lucetta; gentle girl, assist me;
And, even in kind love, I do conjure thee,
Who art the table wherein all my thoughts
Are visibly character'd and engraved,
To lesson me; and tell me some good mean,
How, with my honour, I may undertake
A journey to my loving Proteus.

LUCETTA

Alas, the way is wearisome and long!

JULIA

A true-devoted pilgrim is not weary
To measure kingdoms with his feeble steps;
Much less shall she that hath Love's wings to fly,
And when the flight is made to one so dear,
Of such divine perfection, as Sir Proteus.

LUCETTA

Better forbear till Proteus make return.

JULIA

O, know'st thou not, his looks are my soul's food?
Pity the dearth that I have pined in,
By longing for that food so long a time.
Didst thou but know the inly touch of love,
Thou wouldst as soon go kindle fire with snow
As seek to quench the fire of love with words.

LUCETTA

I do not seek to quench your love's hot fire,
But qualify the fire's extreme rage,
Lest it should burn above the bounds of reason.

JULIA

The more thou damm'st it up, the more it burns.
The current that with gentle murmur glides,
Thou know'st, being stopp'd, impatiently doth rage;
But when his fair course is not hindered,
He makes sweet music with the enamell'd stones,
Giving a gentle kiss to every sedge
He overtaketh in his pilgrimage:
And so by many winding nooks he strays,
With willing sport, to the wild ocean.

Then let me go, and hinder not my course:
I'll be as patient as a gentle stream,
And make a pastime of each weary step,
Till the last step have brought me to my love;
And there I'll rest, as after much turmoil
A blessed soul doth in Elysium.

LUCETTA

But in what habit will you go along?

JULIA

Not like a woman; for I would prevent
The loose encounters of lascivious men:
Gentle Lucetta, fit me with such weeds
As may beseem some well-reputed page.

LUCETTA

Why, then, your ladyship must cut your hair.

JULIA

No, girl; I'll knit it up in silken strings
With twenty odd-conceited true-love knots.
To be fantastic may become a youth
Of greater time than I shall show to be.

LUCETTA

What fashion, madam, shall I make your breeches?

JULIA

That fits as well as, 'Tell me, good my lord,
What compass will you wear your farthingale?'
Why even what fashion thou best likest, Lucetta.

LUCETTA

You must needs have them with a codpiece, madam.

JULIA

Out, out, Lucetta! that will be ill-favour'd.

LUCETTA

A round hose, madam, now's not worth a pin,
Unless you have a codpiece to stick pins on.

JULIA

Lucetta, as thou lovest me, let me have
What thou think'st meet, and is most mannerly.
But tell me, wench, how will the world repute me
For undertaking so unstaid a journey?
I fear me, it will make me scandalized.

LUCETTA

If you think so, then stay at home, and go not.

JULIA

Nay, that I will not.

LUCETTA

Then never dream on infamy, but go.
If Proteus like your journey when you come,
No matter who's displeased when you are gone:
I fear me, he will scarce be pleased withal.

JULIA

That is the least, Lucetta, of my fear:
A thousand oaths, an ocean of his tears,
And instances of infinite of love,
Warrant me welcome to my Proteus.

LUCETTA

All these are servants to deceitful men.

JULIA

Base men, that use them to so base effect!
But truer stars did govern Proteus' birth:
His words are bonds, his oaths are oracles;
His love sincere, his thoughts immaculate;

His tears pure messengers sent from his heart;
His heart as far from fraud as heaven from earth.

LUCETTA

Pray heaven he prove so, when you come to him!

JULIA

Now, as thou lovest me, do him not that wrong,
To bear a hard opinion of his truth:
Only deserve my love by loving him;
And presently go with me to my chamber,
To take a note of what I stand in need of,
To furnish me upon my longing journey.
All that is mine I leave at thy dispose,
My goods, my lands, my reputation;
Only, in lieu thereof, dispatch me hence.
Come, answer not, but to it presently!
I am impatient of my tarriance.   [Exeunt

ACT III

SCENE I. *Milan. Ante-room in the* DUKE's *palace*

Enter DUKE, THURIO, *and* PROTEUS

DUKE OF MILAN

Sir Thurio, give us leave, I pray, awhile;
We have some secrets to confer about. [*Exit* THURIO
Now, tell me, Proteus, what's your will with me?

PROTEUS

My gracious lord, that which I would discover
The law of friendship bids me to conceal;
But when I call to mind your gracious favours
Done to me, undeserving as I am,
My duty pricks me on to utter that
Which else no worldly good should draw from me.
Know, worthy prince, Sir Valentine, my friend,
This night intends to steal away your daughter:
Myself am one made privy to the plot.
I know you have determined to bestow her
On Thurio, whom your gentle daughter hates;
And should she thus be stol'n away from you,
It would be much vexation to your age.
Thus, for my duty's sake, I rather chose
To cross my friend in his intended drift
Than, by concealing it, heap on your head
A pack of sorrows, which would press you down,
Being unprevented, to your timeless grave.

DUKE OF MILAN

Proteus, I thank thee for thine honest care;
Which to requite, command me while I live.
This love of theirs myself have often seen,
Haply when they have judged me fast asleep;
And oftentimes have purposed to forbid
Sir Valentine her company and my court:
But, fearing lest my jealous aim might err,
And so, unworthily disgrace the man,
A rashness that I ever yet have shunn'd,
I gave him gentle looks; thereby to find
That which thyself hast now disclosed to me.
And, that thou mayst perceive my fear of this,

Knowing that tender youth is soon suggested,
I nightly lodge her in an upper tower,
The key whereof myself have ever kept;
And thence she cannot be convey'd away.

PROTEUS

Know, noble lord, they have devised a mean
How he her chamber-window will ascend,
And with a corded ladder fetch her down;
For which the youthful lover now is gone,
And this way comes he with it presently;
Where, if it please you, you may intercept him.
But, good my Lord, do it so cunningly
That my discovery be not aimed at;
For, love of you, not hate unto my friend,
Hath made me publisher of this pretence.

DUKE OF MILAN

Upon mine honour, he shall never know
That I had any light from thee of this.

PROTEUS

Adieu, my Lord; Sir Valentine is coming.   [*Exit*

Enter VALENTINE

DUKE OF MILAN

Sir Valentine, whither away so fast?

VALENTINE

Please it your grace, there is a messenger
That stays to bear my letters to my friends,
And I am going to deliver them.

DUKE OF MILAN

Be they of much import?

VALENTINE

The tenour of them doth but signify
My health and happy being at your court.

DUKE OF MILAN

Nay then, no matter; stay with me awhile;
I am to break with thee of some affairs
That touch me near, wherein thou must be secret.
'Tis not unknown to thee that I have sought
To match my friend Sir Thurio to my daughter.

VALENTINE

I know it well, my Lord; and, sure, the match
Were rich and honourable; besides, the gentleman
Is full of virtue, bounty, worth and qualities
Beseeming such a wife as your fair daughter:
Cannot your Grace win her to fancy him?

DUKE OF MILAN

No, trust me; she is peevish, sullen, froward,
Proud, disobedient, stubborn, lacking duty;
Neither regarding that she is my child,
Nor fearing me as if I were her father:
And, may I say to thee, this pride of hers,
Upon advice, hath drawn my love from her;
And, where I thought the remnant of mine age
Should have been cherish'd by her child-like duty,
I now am full resolved to take a wife,
And turn her out to who will take her in:
Then let her beauty be her wedding-dower;
For me and my possessions she esteems not.

VALENTINE

What would your Grace have me to do in this?

DUKE OF MILAN

There is a lady in Verona here
Whom I affect; but she is nice and coy,
And nought esteems my aged eloquence:
Now, therefore, would I have thee to my tutor,—
For long agone I have forgot to court;
Besides, the fashion of the time is changed,—
How and which way I may bestow myself,
To be regarded in her sun-bright eye.

VALENTINE

Win her with gifts, if she respect not words:
Dumb jewels often in their silent kind
More than quick words do move a woman's mind.

DUKE OF MILAN

But she did scorn a present that I sent her.

VALENTINE

A woman sometime scorns what best contents her.
Send her another; never give her o'er;
For scorn at first makes after-love the more.
If she do frown, 'tis not in hate of you,
But rather to beget more love in you:
If she do chide, 'tis not to have you gone;
For why, the fools are mad, if left alone.
Take no repulse, whatever she doth say;
For 'get you gone,' she doth not mean 'away!'
Flatter and praise, commend, extol their graces;
Though ne'er so black, say they have angels' faces.
That man that hath a tongue, I say, is no man,
If with his tongue he cannot win a woman.

DUKE OF MILAN

But she I mean is promised by her friends
Unto a youthful gentleman of worth;
And kept severely from resort of men,
That no man hath access by day to her.

VALENTINE

Why, then, I would resort to her by night.

DUKE OF MILAN

Ay, but the doors be lock'd, and keys kept safe,
That no man hath recourse to her by night.

VALENTINE

What lets but one may enter at her window?

DUKE OF MILAN

Her chamber is aloft, far from the ground,
And built so shelving, that one cannot climb it
Without apparent hazard of his life.

VALENTINE

Why, then, a ladder, quaintly made of cords,
To cast up, with a pair of anchoring hooks,
Would serve to scale another Hero's tower,
So bold Leander would adventure it.

DUKE OF MILAN

Now, as thou art a gentleman of blood,
Advise me where I may have such a ladder.

VALENTINE

When would you use it? pray, sir, tell me that.

DUKE OF MILAN

This very night; for Love is like a child,
That longs for every thing that he can come by.

VALENTINE

By seven o'clock I'll get you such a ladder.

DUKE OF MILAN

But, hark thee; I will go to her alone:
How shall I best convey the ladder thither?

VALENTINE

It will be light, my lord, that you may bear it
Under a cloak that is of any length.

DUKE OF MILAN

A cloak as long as thine will serve the turn?

VALENTINE

Ay, my good lord.

DUKE OF MILAN

Then let me see thy cloak:
I'll get me one of such another length.

VALENTINE

Why, any cloak will serve the turn, my lord.

DUKE OF MILAN

How shall I fashion me to wear a cloak?
I pray thee, let me feel thy cloak upon me.
What letter is this same? What's here? 'To Silvia'
And here an engine fit for my proceeding.
I'll be so bold to break the seal for once.   [Reads

'My thoughts do harbour with my Silvia nightly;
   And slaves they are to me, that send them flying:
O, could their master come and go as lightly,
   Himself would lodge where senseless they are lying!
My herald thoughts in thy pure bosom rest them;
   While I, their king, that thither them importune,
Do curse the grace that with such grace hath bless'd them,
   Because myself do want my servants' fortune:
I curse myself, for they are sent by me,
That they should harbour where their lord would be.'

What's here?

'Silvia, this night I will enfranchise thee.'

'Tis so; and here's the ladder for the purpose.
Why, Phaethon,—for thou art Merops' son,—
Wilt thou aspire to guide the heavenly car,
And with thy daring folly burn the world?
Wilt thou reach stars, because they shine on thee?
Go, base intruder! overweening slave!
Bestow thy fawning smiles on equal mates;
And think my patience, more than thy desert,
Is privilege for thy departure hence:
Thank me for this more than for all the favours,
Which all too much I have bestow'd on thee.
But if thou linger in my territories
Longer than swiftest expedition
Will give thee time to leave our royal court,
By heaven! my wrath shall far exceed the love
I ever bore my daughter or thyself.
Be gone! I will not hear thy vain excuse;
But, as thou lovest thy life, make speed from hence.
                             [Exit

VALENTINE

And why not death rather than living torment?
To die is to be banish'd from myself;
And Silvia is myself: banish'd from her,
Is self from self: a deadly banishment!
What light is light, if Silvia be not seen?
What joy is joy, if Silvia be not by?
Unless it be to think that she is by,

And feed upon the shadow of perfection.
Except I be by Silvia in the night,
There is no music in the nightingale;
Unless I look on Silvia in the day,
There is no day for me to look upon:
She is my essence; and I leave to be,
If I be not by her fair influence
Foster'd, illumined, cherish'd, kept alive.
I fly not death, to fly his deadly doom:
Tarry I here, I but attend on death:
But, fly I hence, I fly away from life.

Enter PROTEUS *and* LAUNCE

PROTEUS
Run, boy, run, run, and seek him out.

LAUNCE
Soho, soho!

PROTEUS
What seest thou?

LAUNCE
Him we go to find: there's not a hair on's head but
'tis a Valentine.

PROTEUS
Valentine?

VALENTINE
No.

PROTEUS
Who then? his spirit?

VALENTINE
Neither.

PROTEUS
What then?

VALENTINE
Nothing.

LAUNCE
Can nothing speak? Master, shall I strike?

PROTEUS
Who wouldst thou strike?

LAUNCE
Nothing.

PROTEUS
Villain, forbear.

LAUNCE
Why, sir, I'll strike nothing: I pray you,—

PROTEUS
Sirrah, I say, forbear. Friend Valentine, a word.

VALENTINE
My ears are stopt, and cannot hear good news,
So much of bad already hath possess'd them.

PROTEUS
Then in dumb silence will I bury mine,
For they are harsh, untuneable, and bad.

VALENTINE
Is Silvia dead?

PROTEUS
No, Valentine.

VALENTINE
No Valentine, indeed, for sacred Silvia.
Hath she forsworn me?

PROTEUS
No, Valentine.

VALENTINE
No Valentine, if Silvia have forsworn me.
What is your news?

LAUNCE
Sir, there is a proclamation that you are vanished.

PROTEUS
That thou art banished—O, that's the news!—
From hence, from Silvia, and from me thy friend.

VALENTINE
O, I have fed upon this woe already,
And now excess of it will make me surfeit.
Doth Silvia know that I am banished?

PROTEUS
Ay, ay; and she hath offer'd to the doom—
Which, unreversed, stands in effectual force—
A sea of melting pearl, which some call tears:
Those at her father's churlish feet she tender'd;
With them, upon her knees, her humble self;
Wringing her hands, whose whiteness so became them
As if but now they waxed pale for woe:
But neither bended knees, pure hands held up,
Sad sighs, deep groans, nor silver-shedding tears,
Could penetrate her uncompassionate sire;
But Valentine, if he be ta'en, must die.
Besides, her intercession chafed him so,
When she for thy repeal was suppliant,
That to close prison he commanded her,
With many bitter threats of biding there.

VALENTINE
No more; unless the next word that thou speak'st
Have some malignant power upon my life:
If so, I pray thee, breathe it in mine ear,
As ending anthem of my endless dolour.

PROTEUS
Cease to lament for that thou canst not help,
And study help for that which thou lament'st.
Time is the nurse and breeder of all good.
Here if thou stay, thou canst not see thy love;
Besides, thy staying will abridge thy life.
Hope is a lover's staff; walk hence with that,
And manage it against despairing thoughts.
Thy letters may be here, though thou art hence;
Which, being writ to me, shall be deliver'd
Even in the milk-white bosom of thy love.
The time now serves not to expostulate:
Come, I'll convey thee through the city-gate;
And, ere I part with thee, confer at large
Of all that may concern thy love-affairs.
As thou lovest Silvia, though not for thyself,
Regard thy danger, and along with me!

VALENTINE
I pray thee, Launce, an if thou seest my boy,
Bid him make haste, and meet me at the North-gate.

PROTEUS
Go, sirrah, find him out. Come, Valentine.

VALENTINE
O my dear Sylvia! Hapless Valentine!

[*Exeunt* VALENTINE *and* PROTEUS

LAUNCE
I am but a fool, look you; and yet I have the wit to

think my master is a kind of a knave: but that's all one, if he be but one knave. He lives not now that knows me to be in love; yet I am in love; but a team of horse shall not pluck that from me; nor who 'tis I love; and yet 'tis a woman; but what woman, I will not tell myself; and yet 'tis a milkmaid; yet 'tis not a maid, for she hath had gossips; yet 'tis a maid, for she is her master's maid, and serves for wages. She hath more qualities than a water-spaniel,—which is much in a bare Christian. [*Pulling out a paper*] Here is the cate-log of her condition. 'Imprimis: She can fetch and carry.' Why, a horse can do no more: nay, a horse cannot fetch, but only carry; therefore is she better than a jade. 'Item: She can milk;' look you, a sweet virtue in a maid with clean hands.

Enter SPEED

SPEED

How now, Signior Launce! what news with your mastership?

LAUNCE

With my master's ship? why, it is at sea.

SPEED

Well, your old vice still; mistake the word. What news, then, in your paper?

LAUNCE

The blackest news that ever thou heardest.

SPEED

Why, man, how black?

LAUNCE

Why, as black as ink.

SPEED

Let me read them.

LAUNCE

Fie on thee, jolt-head! thou canst not read.

SPEED

Thou liest; I can.

LAUNCE

I will try thee. Tell me this: who begot thee?

SPEED

Marry, the son of my grandfather.

LAUNCE

O illiterate loiterer! it was the son of thy grand-mother: this proves that thou canst not read.

SPEED

Come, fool, come; try me in thy paper.

LAUNCE

There; and Saint Nicholas be thy speed!

SPEED

[*Reads*] 'Imprimis: She can milk.'

LAUNCE

Ay, that she can.

SPEED

'Item: She brews good ale.'

LAUNCE

And thereof comes the proverb: 'Blessing of your heart, you brew good ale.'

SPEED

'Item: She can sew.'

LAUNCE

That's as much as to say, Can she so?

SPEED

'Item: She can knit.'

LAUNCE

What need a man care for a stock with a wench, when she can knit him a stock?

SPEED

'Item: She can wash and scour.'

LAUNCE

A special virtue; for then she need not be washed and scoured.

SPEED

'Item: She can spin.'

LAUNCE

Then may I set the world on wheels, when she can spin for her living.

SPEED

'Item: She hath many nameless virtues.'

LAUNCE

That's as much as to say, bastard virtues; that, in-deed, know not their fathers, and therefore have no names.

SPEED

'Here follow her vices.'

LAUNCE

Close at the heels of her virtues.

SPEED

'Item: She is not to be kissed fasting, in respect of her breath.'

LAUNCE

Well, that fault may be mended with a breakfast. Read on.

SPEED

'Item: She hath a sweet mouth.'

LAUNCE

That makes amends for her sour breath.

SPEED

'Item: She doth talk in her sleep.'

LAUNCE

It's no matter for that, so she sleep not in her talk.

SPEED

'Item: She is slow in words.'

LAUNCE

O villain, that set this down among her vices! To be slow in words is a woman's only virtue: I pray thee, out with 't, and place it for her chief virtue.

SPEED

'Item: She is proud.'

LAUNCE

Out with that too; it was Eve's legacy, and cannot be ta'en from her.

SPEED

'Item: She hath no teeth.'

LAUNCE

I care not for that neither, because I love crusts.

SPEED

'Item: She is curst.'

LAUNCE

Well, the best is, she hath no teeth to bite.

SPEED

'Item: She will often praise her liquor.'

LAUNCE

If her liquor be good, she shall: if she will not, I will; for good things should be praised.

SPEED

'Item: She is too liberal.'

LAUNCE

Of her tongue she cannot, for that's writ down she is slow of; of her purse she shall not, for that I'll keep shut: now, of another thing she may, and that cannot I help. Well, proceed.

SPEED

'Item: She hath more hair than wit, and more faults than hairs, and more wealth than faults.'

LAUNCE

Stop there; I'll have her: she was mine, and not mine, twice or thrice in that last article. Rehearse that once more.

SPEED

'Item: She hath more hair than wit,'—

LAUNCE

More hair than wit? It may be; I'll prove it. The cover of the salt hides the salt, and therefore it is more than the salt; the hair that covers the wit is more than the wit, for the greater hides the less. What's next?

SPEED

'And more faults than hairs,'—

LAUNCE

That's monstrous: O, that that were out!

SPEED

'And more wealth than faults.'

LAUNCE

Why, that word makes the faults gracious. Well, I'll have her: and if it be a match, as nothing is impossible,—

SPEED

What then?

LAUNCE

Why, then will I tell thee—that thy master stays for thee at the North-gate?

SPEED

For me?

LAUNCE

For thee! ay, who art thou? he hath stayed for a better man than thee.

SPEED

And must I go to him?

LAUNCE

Thou must run to him, for thou hast stayed so long, that going will scarce serve the turn.

SPEED

Why didst not tell me sooner? pox of your love-letters!   [Exit

LAUNCE

Now will he be swinged for reading my letter,—an unmannerly slave, that will thrust himself into secrets! I'll after, to rejoice in the boy's correction.
                                                        [Exit

SCENE II. *The same. The* DUKE'S *palace*

Enter DUKE *and* THURIO

DUKE OF MILAN

Sir Thurio, fear not but that she will love you,
Now Valentine is banish'd from her sight.

THURIO

Since his exile she hath despised me most,
Forsworn my company, and rail'd at me,
That I am desperate of obtaining her.

DUKE OF MILAN

This weak impress of love is as a figure
Trenched in ice, which with an hour's heat
Dissolves to water, and doth lose his form.
A little time will melt her frozen thoughts,
And worthless Valentine shall be forgot.

Enter PROTEUS

How now, Sir Proteus! Is your countryman,
According to our proclamation, gone?

PROTEUS

Gone, my good lord.

DUKE OF MILAN

My daughter takes his going grievously.

PROTEUS

A little time, my lord, will kill that grief.

DUKE OF MILAN

So I believe; but Thurio thinks not so.
Proteus, the good conceit I hold of thee—
For thou hast shown some sign of good desert—
Makes me the better to confer with thee.

PROTEUS

Longer than I prove loyal to your Grace
Let me not live to look upon your Grace.

DUKE OF MILAN

Thou know'st how willingly I would effect
The match between Sir Thurio and my daughter.

PROTEUS

I do, my lord.

DUKE OF MILAN

And also, I think, thou art not ignorant
How she opposes her against my will.

PROTEUS

She did, my lord, when Valentine was here.

DUKE OF MILAN

Ay, and perversely she persevers so.
What might we do to make the girl forget
The love of Valentine, and love Sir Thurio?

PROTEUS

The best way is to slander Valentine
With falsehood, cowardice and poor descent,
Three things that women highly hold in hate.

DUKE OF MILAN

Ay, but she'll think that it is spoke in hate.

PROTEUS

Ay, if his enemy deliver it:
Therefore it must with circumstance be spoken
By one whom she esteemeth as his friend.

DUKE OF MILAN

Then you must undertake to slander him.

[266]

PROTEUS

And that, my lord, I shall be loath to do:
'Tis an ill office for a gentleman,
Especially against his very friend.

DUKE OF MILAN

Where your good word cannot advantage him,
Your slander never can endamage him;
Therefore the office is indifferent,
Being entreated to it by your friend.

PROTEUS

You have prevail'd, my lord: if I can do it
By aught that I can speak in his dispraise,
She shall not long continue love to him.
But say this weed her love from Valentine,
It follows not that she will love Sir Thurio.

THURIO

Therefore, as you unwind her love from him,
Lest it should ravel and be good to none,
You must provide to bottom it on me;
Which must be done by praising me as much
As you in worth dispraise Sir Valentine.

DUKE OF MILAN

And, Proteus, we dare trust you in this kind,
Because we know, on Valentine's report,
You are already Love's firm votary,
And cannot soon revolt and change your mind.
Upon this warrant shall you have access
Where you with Silvia may confer at large;
For she is lumpish, heavy, melancholy,
And, for your friend's sake, will be glad of you;
Where you may temper her by your persuasion
To hate young Valentine and love my friend.

PROTEUS

As much as I can do, I will effect.
But you, Sir Thurio, are not sharp enough;
You must lay lime to tangle her desires
By wailful sonnets, whose composed rhymes
Should be full-fraught with serviceable vows.

DUKE OF MILAN

Ay,
Much is the force of heaven-bred poesy.

PROTEUS

Say that upon the altar of her beauty
You sacrifice your tears, your sighs, your heart:
Write till your ink be dry, and with your tears
Moist it again; and frame some feeling line
That may discover such integrity:
For Orpheus' lute was strung with poets' sinews;
Whose golden touch could soften steel and stones,
Make tigers tame, and huge leviathans
Forsake unsounded deeps to dance on sands.
After your dire-lamenting elegies,
Visit by night your lady's chamber-window
With some sweet consort; to their instruments
Tune a deploring dump: the night's dead silence
Will well become such sweet-complaining grievance.
This, or else nothing, will inherit her.

DUKE OF MILAN

This discipline shows thou hast been in love.

THURIO

And thy advice this night I'll put in practice.
Therefore, sweet Proteus, my direction-giver,
Let us into the city presently
To sort some gentlemen well skill'd in music.
I have a sonnet that will serve the turn
To give the onset to thy good advice.

DUKE OF MILAN

About it, gentlemen!

PROTEUS

We'll wait upon your Grace till after supper,
And afterward determine our proceedings.

DUKE OF MILAN

Even now about it! I will pardon you.   [*Exeunt*

ACT IV

SCENE I. *The frontiers of Mantua. A forest*

Enter certain OUTLAWS

FIRST OUTLAW

Fellows, stand fast; I see a passenger.

SECOND OUTLAW

If there be ten, shrink not, but down with 'em.

Enter VALENTINE *and* SPEED

THIRD OUTLAW

Stand, sir, and throw us that you have about ye:
If not, we'll make you sit, and rifle you.

SPEED

Sir, we are undone; these are the villains
That all the travellers do fear so much.

VALENTINE

My friends,—

FIRST OUTLAW

That's not so, sir: we are your enemies.

SECOND OUTLAW

Peace! we'll hear him.

THIRD OUTLAW

Ay, by my beard, will we, for he's a proper man.

VALENTINE

Then know that I have little wealth to lose:
A man I am cross'd with adversity;
My riches are these poor habiliments,
Of which if you should here disfurnish me,
You take the sum and substance that I have.

SECOND OUTLAW

Whither travel you?

VALENTINE

To Verona.

FIRST OUTLAW

Whence came you?

VALENTINE

From Milan.

THIRD OUTLAW

Have you long sojourned there?

VALENTINE

Some sixteen months, and longer might have stay'd,
If crooked fortune had not thwarted me.

FIRST OUTLAW
What, were you banish'd thence?
VALENTINE
I was.
SECOND OUTLAW
For what offence?
VALENTINE
For that which now torments me to rehearse:
I kill'd a man, whose death I much repent;
But yet I slew him manfully in fight,
Without false vantage or base treachery.
FIRST OUTLAW
Why, ne'er repent it, if it were done so.
But were you banish'd for so small a fault?
VALENTINE
I was, and held me glad of such a doom.
SECOND OUTLAW
Have you the tongues?
VALENTINE
My youthful travel therein made me happy,
Or else I often had been miserable.
THIRD OUTLAW
By the bare scalp of Robin Hood's fat friar,
This fellow were a king for our wild faction!
FIRST OUTLAW
We'll have him. Sirs, a word.
SPEED
Master, be one of them; it's an honourable kind of
thievery.
VALENTINE
Peace, villain!
SECOND OUTLAW
Tell us this: have you any thing to take to?
VALENTINE
Nothing but my fortune.
THIRD OUTLAW
Know, then, that some of us are gentlemen,
Such as the fury of ungovern'd youth
Thrust from the company of awful men:
Myself was from Verona banished
For practising to steal away a lady,
An heir, and near allied unto the duke.
SECOND OUTLAW
And I from Mantua, for a gentleman,
Who, in my mood, I stabb'd unto the heart.
FIRST OUTLAW
And I for such like petty crimes as these.
But to the purpose,—for we cite our faults,
That they may hold excused our lawless lives;
And partly, seeing you are beautified
With goodly shape, and by your own report
A linguist, and a man of such perfection
As we do in our quality much want,—
SECOND OUTLAW
Indeed, because you are a banish'd man,
Therefore, above the rest, we parley to you:
Are you content to be our general?
To make a virtue of necessity,
And live, as we do, in this wilderness?

THIRD OUTLAW
What say'st thou? wilt thou be of our consort?
Say ay, and be the captain of us all:
We'll do thee homage and be ruled by thee,
Love thee as our commander and our king.
FIRST OUTLAW
But if thou scorn our courtesy, thou diest.
SECOND OUTLAW
Thou shalt not live to brag what we have offer'd.
VALENTINE
I take your offer, and will live with you,
Provided that you do no outrages
On silly women or poor passengers.
THIRD OUTLAW
No, we detest such vile base practices.
Come, go with us, we'll bring thee to our crews,
And show thee all the treasure we have got;
Which, with ourselves, all rest at thy dispose.
[*Exeunt*

SCENE II. *Milan. Outside the* DUKE's *palace, under*
SILVIA's *chamber*

Enter PROTEUS
PROTEUS
Already have I been false to Valentine,
And now I must be as unjust to Thurio.
Under the colour of commending him,
I have access my own love to prefer:
But Silvia is too fair, too true, too holy,
To be corrupted with my worthless gifts.
When I protest true loyalty to her,
She twits me with my falsehood to my friend;
When to her beauty I commend my vows,
She bids me think how I have been forsworn
In breaking faith with Julia whom I loved:
And notwithstanding all her sudden quips,
The least whereof would quell a lover's hope,
Yet, spaniel-like, the more she spurns my love,
The more it grows, and fawneth on her still.
But here comes Thurio: now must we to her window,
And give some evening music to her ear.
Enter THURIO *and* MUSICIANS
THURIO
How now, Sir Proteus, are you crept before us?
PROTEUS
Ay, gentle Thurio; for you know that love
Will creep in service where it cannot go.
THURIO
Ay, but I hope, sir, that you love not here.
PROTEUS
Sir, but I do; or else I would be hence.
THURIO
Who? Silvia?
PROTEUS
Ay, Silvia; for your sake.
THURIO
I thank you for your own. Now, gentlemen,
Let's tune, and to it lustily awhile.

Enter, at a distance, HOST, *and* JULIA *in boy's clothes*

HOST

Now, my young guest, methinks you're ally-cholly:
I pray you, why is it?

JULIA

Marry, mine host, because I cannot be merry.

HOST

Come, we'll have you merry: I'll bring you where
you shall hear music, and see the gentleman that
you asked for.

JULIA

But shall I hear him speak?

HOST

Ay, that you shall.

JULIA

That will be music.   [*Music plays*

HOST

Hark, hark!

JULIA

Is he among these?

HOST

Ay: but, peace! let's hear 'em.

SONG.

Who is Silvia? what is she,
    That all our swains commend her?
Holy, fair, and wise is she;
    The heaven such grace did lend her,
That she might admired be.

Is she kind as she is fair?
    For beauty lives with kindness.
Love doth to her eyes repair,
    To help him of his blindness,
And, being help'd, inhabits there.

Then to Silvia let us sing,
    That Silvia is excelling;
She excels each mortal thing
    Upon the dull earth dwelling:
To her let us garlands bring.

HOST

How now! are you sadder than you were before?
How do you, man? the music likes you not.

JULIA

You mistake; the musician likes me not.

HOST

Why, my pretty youth?

JULIA

He plays false, father.

HOST

How? out of tune on the strings?

JULIA

Not so; but yet so false that he grieves my very heart-
strings.

HOST

You have a quick ear.

JULIA

Ay, I would I were deaf; it makes me have a slow
heart.

HOST

I perceive you delight not in music.

JULIA

Not a whit, when it jars so.

HOST

Hark, what fine change is in the music!

JULIA

Ay, that change is the spite.

HOST

You would have them always play but one thing?

I would always have one play but one thing.
But, host, doth this Sir Proteus that we talk on
Often resort unto this gentlewoman?

HOST

I tell you what Launce, his man, told me,—he loved
her out of all nick.

JULIA

Where is Launce?

HOST

Gone to seek his dog; which to-morrow, by his
master's command, he must carry for a present to
his lady.

JULIA

Peace! stand aside: the company parts.

PROTEUS

Sir Thurio, fear not you: I will so plead,
That you shall say my cunning drift excels.

THURIO

Where meet we?

PROTEUS

        At Saint Gregory's well.

THURIO

                       Farewell.
        [*Exeunt* THURIO *and* MUSICIANS
        Enter SILVIA *above*

PROTEUS

Madam, good even to your ladyship.

SILVIA

I thank you for your music, gentlemen.
Who is that that spake?

PROTEUS

One, lady, if you knew his pure heart's truth,
You would quickly learn to know him by his voice.

SILVIA

Sir Proteus, as I take it.

PROTEUS

Sir Proteus, gentle lady, and your servant.

SILVIA

What's your will?

PROTEUS

        That I may compass yours.

SILVIA

You have your wish; my will is even this:
That presently you hie you home to bed.
Thou subtle, perjured, false, disloyal man!
Think'st thou I am so shallow, so conceitless,
To be seduced by thy flattery,
That hast deceived so many with thy vows?
Return, return, and make thy love amends.
For me,—by this pale queen of night I swear,
I am so far from granting thy request,

That I despise thee for thy wrongful suit;
And by and by intend to chide myself
Even for this time I spend in talking to thee.

PROTEUS
I grant, sweet love, that I did love a lady;
But she is dead.

JULIA
[Aside] 'Twere false, if I should speak it;
For I am sure she is not buried.

SILVIA
Say that she be; yet Valentine thy friend
Survives; to whom, thyself art witness,
I am betroth'd: and art thou not ashamed
To wrong him with thy importunacy?

PROTEUS
I likewise hear that Valentine is dead.

SILVIA
And so suppose am I; for in his grave
Assure thyself my love is buried.

PROTEUS
Sweet lady, let me rake it from the earth.

SILVIA
Go to thy lady's grave, and call hers thence;
Or, at the least, in hers sepulchre thine.

JULIA
[Aside] He heard not that.

PROTEUS
Madam, if your heart be so obdurate,
Vouchsafe me yet your picture for my love,
The picture that is hanging in your chamber;
To that I'll speak, to that I'll sigh and weep:
For since the substance of your perfect self
Is else devoted, I am but a shadow;
And to your shadow will I make true love.

JULIA
[Aside] If 'twere a substance, you would, sure, deceive it,
And make it but a shadow, as I am.

SILVIA
I am very loath to be your idol, sir;
But since your falsehood shall become you well
To worship shadows and adore false shapes,
Send to me in the morning, and I'll send it:
And so, good rest.

PROTEUS
As wretches have o'ernight
That wait for execution in the morn.

[Exeunt PROTEUS and SILVIA severally

JULIA
Host, will you go?

HOST
By my halidom, I was fast asleep.

JULIA
Pray you, where lies Sir Proteus?

HOST
Marry, at my house. Trust me, I think 'tis almost day.

JULIA
Not so; but it hath been the longest night
That e'er I watch'd, and the most heaviest. [Exeunt

SCENE III. *The same*

Enter EGLAMOUR

EGLAMOUR
This is the hour that Madam Silvia
Entreated me to call and know her mind:
There's some great matter she'ld employ me in.
Madam, madam!

Enter SILVIA *above*

SILVIA
Who calls?

EGLAMOUR
Your servant and your friend;
One that attends your ladyship's command.

SILVIA
Sir Eglamour, a thousand times good morrow.

EGLAMOUR
As many, worthy lady, to yourself:
According to your ladyship's impose,
I am thus early come to know what service
It is your pleasure to command me in.

SILVIA
O Eglamour, thou art a gentleman,—
Think not I flatter, for I swear I do not,—
Valiant, wise, remorseful, well accomplish'd:
Thou art not ignorant what dear good will
I bear unto the banish'd Valentine;
Nor how my father would enforce me marry
Vain Thurio, whom my very soul abhors.
Thyself hast loved; and I have heard thee say
No grief did ever come so near thy heart
As when thy lady and thy true love died,
Upon whose grave thou vow'dst pure chastity.
Sir Eglamour, I would to Valentine,
To Mantua, where I hear he makes abode;
And, for the ways are dangerous to pass,
I do desire thy worthy company,
Upon whose faith and honour I repose.
Urge not my father's anger, Eglamour,
But think upon my grief, a lady's grief,
And on the justice of my flying hence,
To keep me from a most unholy match,
Which heaven and fortune still rewards with plagues.
I do desire thee, even from a heart
As full of sorrows as the sea of sands,
To bear me company, and go with me:
If not, to hide what I have said to thee,
That I may venture to depart alone.

EGLAMOUR
Madam, I pity much your grievances;
Which since I know they virtuously are placed,
I give consent to go along with you;
Recking as little what betideth me
As much I wish all good befortune you.
When will you go?

SILVIA
This evening coming.

EGLAMOUR
Where shall I meet you?

SILVIA
            At Friar Patrick's cell,
Where I intend holy confession.

EGLAMOUR
I will not fail your ladyship. Good morrow, gentle
lady.

SILVIA
Good morrow, kind Sir Eglamour.   [Exeunt severally

SCENE IV. The same

Enter LAUNCE, with his dog

LAUNCE
When a man's servant shall play the cur with him,
look you, it goes hard: one that I brought up of a
puppy; one that I saved from drowning, when three
or four of his blind brothers and sisters went to it! I
have taught him, even as one would say precisely,
'thus I would teach a dog.' I was sent to deliver him
as a present to Mistress Silvia from my master; and
I came no sooner into the dining-chamber, but he
steps me to her trencher, and steals her capon's leg:
O, 'tis a foul thing when a cur cannot keep himself
in all companies! I would have, as one should say,
one that takes upon him to be a dog indeed, to be,
as it were, a dog at all things. If I had not had more
wit than he, to take a fault upon me that he did, I
think verily he had been hanged for't; sure as I live,
he had suffered for't: you shall judge. He thrusts me
himself into the company of three or four gentleman-
like dogs, under the duke's table: he had not been
there—bless the mark!—a pissing while, but all the
chamber smelt him. 'Out with the dog!' says one:
'What cur is that?' says another: 'Whip him out,'
says the third: 'Hang him up,' says the duke. I, having been acquainted with the smell before, knew it
was Crab, and goes me to the fellow that whips the
dogs: 'Friend,' quoth I, 'you mean to whip the
dog?' 'Ay, marry, do I,' quoth he. 'You do him the
more wrong,' quoth I; ''twas I did the thing you
wot of.' He makes me no more ado, but whips me
out of the chamber. How many masters would do
this for his servant? Nay, I'll be sworn, I have sat in
the stocks for puddings he hath stolen, otherwise he
had been executed; I have stood on the pillory for
geese he hath killed, otherwise he had suffered for't.
Thou thinkest not of this now. Nay, I remember the
trick you served me when I took my leave of Madam
Silvia: did not I bid thee still mark me, and do as I
do? when didst thou see me heave up my leg, and
make water against a gentlewoman's farthingale?
didst thou ever see me do such a trick?

Enter PROTEUS and JULIA

PROTEUS
Sebastian is thy name? I like thee well,
And will employ thee in some service presently.

JULIA
In what you please: I'll do what I can.

PROTEUS
I hope thou wilt. [To LAUNCE] How now, you whore-
son peasant!
Where have you been these two days loitering?

LAUNCE
Marry, sir, I carried Mistress Silvia the dog you bade
me.

PROTEUS
And what says she to my little jewel?

LAUNCE
Marry, she says your dog was a cur, and tells you
currish thanks is good enough for such a present.

PROTEUS
But she received my dog?

LAUNCE
No, indeed, did she not: here have I brought him
back again.

PROTEUS
What, didst thou offer her this from me?

LAUNCE
Ay, sir; the other squirrel was stolen from me by the
hangman boys in the market-place: and then I offered
her mine own, who is a dog as big as ten of yours,
and therefore the gift the greater.

PROTEUS
Go get thee hence, and find my dog again,
Or ne'er return again into my sight.
Away, I say! stay'st thou to vex me here?
                                    [Exit LAUNCE
A slave, that still an end turns me to shame!
Sebastian, I have entertained thee,
Partly that I have need of such a youth,
That can with some discretion do my business,
For 'tis no trusting to yond foolish lout;
But chiefly for thy face and thy behaviour,
Which, if my augury deceive me not,
Witness good bringing up, fortune, and truth:
Therefore know thou, for this I entertain thee.
Go presently, and take this ring with thee,
Deliver it to Madam Silvia:
She loved me well deliver'd it to me.

JULIA
It seems you loved not her, to leave her token.
She is dead, belike?

PROTEUS
                    Not so; I think she lives.

JULIA
Alas!

PROTEUS
Why dost thou cry, 'alas'?

JULIA
                            I cannot choose
But pity her.

PROTEUS
Wherefore shouldst thou pity her?

JULIA
Because methinks that she loved you as well
As you do love your lady Silvia:
She dreams on him that has forgot her love;
You dote on her that cares not for your love.

'Tis pity love should be so contrary;
And thinking on it makes me cry, 'alas!'
PROTEUS
Well, give her that ring, and therewithal
This letter. That's her chamber. Tell my lady
I claim the promise for her heavenly picture.
Your message done, hie home unto my chamber,
Where thou shalt find me, sad and solitary.   [Exit
JULIA
How many women would do such a message?
Alas, poor Proteus! thou hast entertain'd
A fox to be the shepherd of thy lambs.
Alas, poor fool! why do I pity him
That with his very heart despiseth me?
Because he loves her, he despiseth me;
Because I love him, I must pity him.
This ring I gave him when he parted from me,
To bind him to remember my good will;
And now am I, unhappy messenger,
To plead for that which I would not obtain,
To carry that which I would have refused,
To praise his faith which I would have dispraised.
I am my master's true-confirmed love;
But cannot be true servant to my master,
Unless I prove false traitor to myself.
Yet will I woo for him, but yet so coldly,
As, heaven it knows, I would not have him speed.
Enter SILVIA, *attended*
Gentlewoman, good day! I pray you, be my mean
To bring me where to speak with Madam Silvia.
SILVIA
What would you with her, if that I be she?
JULIA
If you be she, I do entreat your patience
To hear me speak the message I am sent on.
SILVIA
From whom?
JULIA
From my master, Sir Proteus, madam.
SILVIA
O, he sends you for a picture.
JULIA
Ay, madam.
SILVIA
Ursula, bring my picture there.
Go give your master this: tell him, from me,
One Julia, that his changing thoughts forget,
Would better fit his chamber than this shadow.
JULIA
Madam, please you peruse this letter.—
Pardon me, madam; I have unadvised
Deliver'd you a paper that I should not:
This is the letter to your ladyship.
SILVIA
I pray thee, let me look on that again.
JULIA
It may not be; good madam, pardon me.
SILVIA
There, hold!

I will not look upon your master's lines:
I know they are stuff'd with protestations,
And full of new-found oaths; which he will break
As easily as I do tear his paper.
JULIA
Madam, he sends your ladyship this ring.
SILVIA
The more shame for him that he sends it me;
For I have heard him say a thousand times
His Julia gave it him at his departure.
Though his false finger have profaned the ring,
Mine shall not do his Julia so much wrong.
JULIA
She thanks you.
SILVIA
What say'st thou?
JULIA
I thank you, madam, that you tender her.
Poor gentlewoman! my master wrongs her much.
SILVIA
Dost thou know her?
JULIA
Almost as well as I do know myself:
To think upon her woes I do protest
That I have wept a hundred several times.
SILVIA
Belike she thinks that Proteus hath forsook her.
JULIA
I think she doth; and that's her cause of sorrow.
SILVIA
Is she not passing fair?
JULIA
She hath been fairer, madam, than she is:
When she did think my master loved her well,
She, in my judgement, was as fair as you;
But since she did neglect her looking-glass,
And threw her sun-expelling mask away,
The air hath starved the roses in her cheeks,
And pinch'd the lily-tincture of her face,
That now she is become as black as I.
SILVIA
How tall was she?
JULIA
About my stature: for, at Pentecost,
When all our pageants of delight were play'd,
Our youth got me to play the woman's part,
And I was trimm'd in Madam Julia's gown;
Which served me as fit, by all men's judgements,
As if the garment had been made for me:
Therefore I know she is about my height.
And at that time I made her weep agood,
For I did play a lamentable part:
Madam, 'twas Ariadne passioning
For Theseus' perjury and unjust flight;
Which I so lively acted with my tears,
That my poor mistress, moved therewithal,
Wept bitterly; and, would I might be dead,
If I in thought felt not her very sorrow!

SILVIA
She is beholding to thee, gentle youth.
Alas, poor lady, desolate and left!
I weep myself to think upon thy words.
Here, youth, there is my purse: I give thee this
For thy sweet mistress' sake, because thou lovest her.
Farewell.   [*Exit* SILVIA, *with attendants*

JULIA
And she shall thank you for't, if e'er you know her.
A virtuous gentlewoman, mild and beautiful!
I hope my master's suit will be but cold,
Since she respects my mistress' love so much.
Alas, how love can trifle with itself!
Here is her picture: let me see; I think,
If I had such a tire, this face of mine
Were full as lovely as is this of hers:
And yet the painter flatter'd her a little,
Unless I flatter with myself too much.
Her hair is auburn, mine is perfect yellow:
If that be all the difference in his love,
I'll get me such a colour'd periwig.
Her eyes are grey as glass; and so are mine:
Ay, but her forehead's low, and mine's as high.
What should it be that he respects in her,
But I can make respective in myself,
If this fond Love were not a blinded god?
Come, shadow, come, and take this shadow up,
For 'tis thy rival. O thou senseless form,
Thou shalt be worshipp'd, kiss'd, loved, and adored!
And, were there sense in his idolatry,
My substance should be statue in thy stead.
I'll use thee kindly for thy mistress' sake,
That used me so; or else, by Jove I vow,
I should have scratch'd out your unseeing eyes,
To make my master out of love with thee!   [*Exit*

ACT V
SCENE I. *Milan. An abbey*

Enter EGLAMOUR
EGLAMOUR
The sun begins to gild the western sky;
And now it is about the very hour
That Silvia, at Friar Patrick's cell, should meet me.
She will not fail, for lovers break not hours,
Unless it be to come before their time;
So much they spur their expedition.
See where she comes.
                Enter SILVIA
Lady, a happy evening!
SILVIA
Amen, amen! Go on, good Eglamour,
Out at the postern by the abbey-wall:
I fear I am attended by some spies.
EGLAMOUR
Fear not: the forest is not three leagues off;
If we recover that, we are sure enough.   [*Exeunt*

SCENE II. *The same. The* DUKE'S *palace*

Enter THURIO, PROTEUS, *and* JULIA
THURIO
Sir Proteus, what says Silvia to my suit?
PROTEUS
O, sir, I find her milder than she was;
And yet she takes exceptions at your person.
THURIO
What, that my leg is too long?
PROTEUS
No; that it is too little.
THURIO
I'll wear a boot, to make it somewhat rounder.
JULIA
[*Aside*] But love will not be spurr'd to what it loathes.
THURIO
What says she to my face?
PROTEUS
She says it is a fair one.
THURIO
Nay then, the wanton lies; my face is black.
PROTEUS
But pearls are fair; and the old saying is,
Black men are pearls in beauteous ladies' eyes.
JULIA
[*Aside*] 'Tis true, such pearls as put out ladies' eyes;
For I had rather wink than look on them.
THURIO
How likes she my discourse?
PROTEUS
Ill, when you talk of war.
THURIO
But well, when I discourse of love and peace?
JULIA
[*Aside*] But better, indeed, when you hold your peace.
THURIO
What says she to my valour?
PROTEUS
O, sir, she makes no doubt of that.
JULIA
[*Aside*] She needs not, when she knows it cowardice.
THURIO
What says she to my birth?
PROTEUS
That you are well derived.
JULIA
[*Aside*] True; from a gentleman to a fool.
THURIO
Considers she my possessions?
PROTEUS
O, ay; and pities them.
THURIO
Wherefore?
JULIA
[*Aside*] That such an ass should owe them.
PROTEUS
That they are out by lease.

JULIA

Here comes the duke.

Enter DUKE OF MILAN

DUKE OF MILAN

How now, Sir Proteus! how now, Thurio!
Which of you saw Sir Eglamour of late?

THURIO

Not I.

PROTEUS

Nor I.

DUKE OF MILAN

Saw you my daughter?

PROTEUS

Neither.

DUKE OF MILAN

Why then,
She's fled unto that peasant Valentine;
And Eglamour is in her company.
'Tis true; for Friar Laurence met them both,
As he in penance wander'd through the forest;
Him he knew well, and guess'd that it was she,
But, being mask'd, he was not sure of it;
Besides, she did intend confession
At Patrick's cell this even; and there she was not;
These likelihoods confirm her flight from hence.
Therefore, I pray you, stand not to discourse,
But mount you presently, and meet with me
Upon the rising of the mountain-foot
That leads toward Mantua, whither they are fled:
Dispatch, sweet gentlemen, and follow me.   [*Exit*

THURIO

Why, this it is to be a peevish girl,
That flies her fortune when it follows her.
I'll after, more to be revenged on Eglamour
Than for the love of reckless Silvia.   [*Exit*

PROTEUS

And I will follow, more for Silvia's love
Than hate of Eglamour, that goes with her.   [*Exit*

JULIA

And I will follow, more to cross that love
Than hate for Silvia, that is gone for love.   [*Exit*

SCENE III. *The frontiers of Mantua. The forest*

Enter OUTLAWS *with* SILVIA

FIRST OUTLAW

Come, come,
Be patient; we must bring you to our captain.

SILVIA

A thousand more mischances than this one
Have learn'd me how to brook this patiently.

SECOND OUTLAW

Come, bring her away.

FIRST OUTLAW

Where is the gentleman that was with her?

THIRD OUTLAW

Being nimble-footed, he hath outrun us,
But Moses and Valerius follow him.
Go thou with her to the west end of the wood;

There is our captain: we'll follow him that's fled;
The thicket is beset; he cannot 'scape.

FIRST OUTLAW

Come, I must bring you to our captain's cave:
Fear not; he bears an honourable mind,
And will not use a woman lawlessly.

SILVIA

O Valentine, this I endure for thee!   [*Exeunt*

SCENE IV. *Another part of the forest*

Enter VALENTINE

VALENTINE

How use doth breed a habit in a man!
This shadowy desert, unfrequented woods,
I better brook than flourishing peopled towns:
Here can I sit alone, unseen of any,
And to the nightingale's complaining notes
Tune my distresses and record my woes.
O thou that dost inhabit in my breast,
Leave not the mansion so long tenantless,
Lest, growing ruinous, the building fall,
And leave no memory of what it was!
Repair me with thy presence, Silvia;
Thou gentle nymph, cherish thy forlorn swain!
What halloing and what stir is this to-day?
These are my mates, that make their wills their law,
Have some unhappy passenger in chase.
They love me well; yet I have much to do
To keep them from uncivil outrages.
Withdraw thee, Valentine: who's this comes here?

Enter PROTEUS, SILVIA, *and* JULIA

PROTEUS

Madam, this service I have done for you,
Though you respect not aught your servant doth,
To hazard life, and rescue you from him
That would have forced your honour and your love;
Vouchsafe me, for my meed, but one fair look;
A smaller boon than this I cannot beg,
And less than this, I am sure, you cannot give.

VALENTINE

[*Aside*] How like a dream is this I see and hear!
Love, lend me patience to forbear awhile.

SILVIA

O miserable, unhappy that I am!

PROTEUS

Unhappy were you, madam, ere I came;
But by my coming I have made you happy.

SILVIA

By thy approach thou makest me most unhappy.

JULIA

[*Aside*] And me, when he approacheth to your presence.

SILVIA

Had I been seized by a hungry lion,
I would have been a breakfast to the beast,
Rather than have false Proteus rescue me.
O, Heaven be judge how I love Valentine
Whose life's as tender to me as my soul!

And full as much, for more there cannot be,
I do detest false perjured Proteus.
Therefore be gone; solicit me no more.

PROTEUS

What dangerous action, stood it next to death,
Would I not undergo for one calm look!
O, 'tis the curse in love, and still approved,
When women cannot love where they're beloved!

SILVIA

When Proteus cannot love where he's beloved.
Read over Julia's heart, thy first, best love,
For whose dear sake thou didst then rend thy faith
Into a thousand oaths; and all those oaths
Descended into perjury, to love me.
Thou hast no faith left now, unless thou'dst two,
And that's far worse than none; better have none
Than plural faith which is too much by one:
Thou counterfeit to thy true friend!

PROTEUS

                    In love
Who respects friend?

SILVIA

            All men but Proteus.

PROTEUS

Nay, if the gentle spirit of moving words
Can no way change you to a milder form,
I'll woo you like a soldier, at arms' end,
And love you 'gainst the nature of love,—force ye.

SILVIA

O heaven!

PROTEUS

        I'll force thee yield to my desire.

VALENTINE

Ruffian, let go that rude uncivil touch,
Thou friend of an ill fashion!

PROTEUS

                Valentine!

VALENTINE

Thou common friend, that's without faith or love,
For such is a friend now; treacherous man!
Thou hast beguiled my hopes; nought but mine eye
Could have persuaded me: now I dare not say
I have one friend alive; thou wouldst disprove me.
Who should be trusted now, when one's right hand
Is perjured to the bosom? Proteus,
I am sorry I must never trust thee more,
But count the world a stranger for thy sake.
The private wound is deepest: O time most accurst,
'Mongst all foes that a friend should be the worst!

PROTEUS

My shame and guilt confounds me.
Forgive me, Valentine: if hearty sorrow
Be a sufficient ransom for offence,
I tender 't here; I do as truly suffer
As e'er I did commit.

VALENTINE

            Then I am paid;
And once again I do receive thee honest.
Who by repentance is not satisfied

Is nor of heaven nor earth, for these are pleased.
By penitence the Eternal's wrath's appeased:
And, that my love may appear plain and free,
All that was mine in Silvia I give thee.

JULIA

O me unhappy!   [Swoons

PROTEUS

Look to the boy.

VALENTINE

Why, boy! why, wag! how now! what's the matter?
Look up; speak.

JULIA

O good sir, my master charged me to deliver a ring
to Madam Silvia, which, out of my neglect, was never
done.

PROTEUS

Where is that ring, boy?

JULIA

            Here 'tis; this is it.

PROTEUS

How! let me see:
Why, this is the ring I gave to Julia.

JULIA

O, cry you mercy, sir, I have mistook:
This is the ring you sent to Silvia.

PROTEUS

But how camest thou by this ring? At my depart
I gave this unto Julia.

JULIA

And Julia herself did give it me;
And Julia herself hath brought it hither.

PROTEUS

How! Julia!

JULIA

Behold her that gave aim to all thy oaths,
And entertain'd 'em deeply in her heart.
How oft hast thou with perjury cleft the root!
O Proteus, let this habit make thee blush!
Be thou ashamed that I have took upon me
Such an immodest raiment, if shame live
In a disguise of love:
It is the lesser blot, modesty finds,
Women to change their shapes than men their minds.

PROTEUS

Than men their minds! 'tis true. O heaven, were man
But constant, he were perfect! That one error
Fills him with faults; makes him run through all the
    sins:
Inconstancy falls off ere it begins.
What is in Silvia's face, but I may spy
More fresh in Julia's with a constant eye?

VALENTINE

Come, come, a hand from either:
Let me be blest to make this happy close;
'Twere pity two such friends should be long foes.

PROTEUS

Bear witness, Heaven, I have my wish for ever.

JULIA

And I mine.

Enter OUTLAWS, *with* DUKE OF MILAN *and* THURIO
OUTLAWS
A prize, a prize, a prize!
VALENTINE
Forbear, forbear, I say! it is my lord the duke.
Your Grace is welcome to a man disgraced,
Banished Valentine.
DUKE OF MILAN
Sir Valentine!
THURIO
Yonder is Silvia; and Silvia's mine.
VALENTINE
Thurio, give back, or else embrace thy death;
Come not within the measure of my wrath;
Do not name Silvia thine; if once again,
Verona shall not hold thee. Here she stands:
Take but possession of her with a touch:
I dare thee but to breathe upon my love.
THURIO
Sir Valentine, I care not for her, I:
I hold him but a fool that will endanger
His body for a girl that loves him not:
I claim her not, and therefore she is thine.
DUKE OF MILAN
The more degenerate and base art thou,
To make such means for her as thou hast done,
And leave her on such slight conditions.
Now, by the honour of my ancestry,
I do applaud thy spirit, Valentine,
And think thee worthy of an empress' love:
Know, then, I here forget all former griefs,
Cancel all grudge, repeal thee home again,
Plead a new state in thy unrival'd merit,
To which I thus subscribe: Sir Valentine,
Thou art a gentleman, and well derived;
Take thou thy Silvia, for thou hast deserved her.

VALENTINE
I thank your Grace; the gift hath made me happy.
I now beseech you, for your daughter's sake,
To grant one boon that I shall ask of you.
DUKE OF MILAN
I grant it, for thine own, whate'er it be.
VALENTINE
These banish'd men that I have kept withal
Are men endued with worthy qualities:
Forgive them what they have committed here,
And let them be recall'd from their exile:
They are reformed, civil, full of good,
And fit for great employment, worthy lord.
DUKE OF MILAN
Thou hast prevail'd; I pardon them and thee:
Dispose of them as thou know'st their deserts.
Come, let us go: we will include all jars
With triumphs, mirth, and rare solemnity.
VALENTINE
And, as we walk along, I dare be bold
With our discourse to make your Grace to smile.
What think you of this page, my lord?
DUKE OF MILAN
I think the boy hath grace in him; he blushes.
VALENTINE
I warrant you, my lord, more grace than boy.
DUKE OF MILAN
What mean you by that saying?
VALENTINE
Please you, I'll tell you as we pass along,
That you will wonder what hath fortuned.
Come, Proteus; 'tis your penance but to hear
The story of your loves discovered:
That done, our day of marriage shall be yours;
One feast, one house, one mutual happiness.
[*Exeunt*

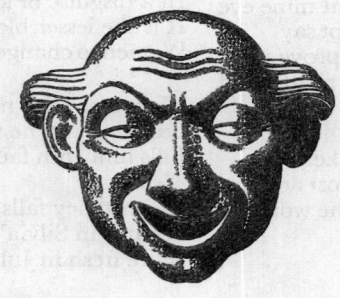

LOVE'S LABOUR'S LOST

SYNOPSIS

KING FERDINAND of Navarre and his gentlemen, instead of following the customary round of court functions and frivolities, resolve to make Navarre a little academy of learning, and enter into a compact for three years, under severe penalty, to live a life of seclusion in which food and sleep are to be placed under precise regulation and women's society is positively prohibited. The only recreation that is provided is the conversation of Costard, a natural clown, and Don Armado, a pompous, fantastical Spaniard. When it comes to signing the articles of their agreement, Biron, though declaring his readiness to take the oath, is more doubtful than his two madcap companions, Longaville and Dumain, who ordinarily are much given to wit and mockery. With malicious promptness, he points out to the King the imminent necessity of breaking their vows because of the visit to the court of the Princess of France which the King had completely overlooked.

When the Princess arrives on the mission of diplomacy she has undertaken for her old bed-ridden father, the King is unable because of his recent vows to entertain her in his palace, and he is compelled to house both her and her train in tents in the park outside his gates. During the conduct of their business, the King is greatly attracted to the Princess, and his lords manifest a lively interest in renewing their previous acquaintances with her vivacious ladies, Rosaline, Maria and Katherine.

Meanwhile the first violation of the edict of retirement is made when the clown, Costard, is found in the company of Jaquenetta, a country girl to whom Don Armado, also smitten, secretly writes love verses. Costard, for punishment, is placed in the Spaniard's custody for a week's fasting on bran and water, but he is released from jail to deliver a love-letter of Armado's to Jaquenetta. At the same time Biron gives Costard a note to Rosaline, and the clown gets the letters mixed, so that Armado's absurd effusion is placed in Rosaline's hands, causing the ladies great amusement, while Biron's poetry reaches Jaquenetta who, unable to read it, seeks the aid of the village school-master, Holofernes.

Love, however, has gradually turned all the votaries of wisdom to the furtive occupation of sonnet-writing. Biron, with his own verses, hides in a tree as the King passes reading aloud some lines to the Princess; both overhear Longaville reading a sonnet to Maria; and the three listen to Dumain's ode to Katherine. One by one, they reveal themselves, Longaville reproving Dumain, and the King, Longaville, with Biron finally accusing all his companions of inconstancy and broken vows. Just then Costard and Jaquenetta arrive with Biron's letter which the schoolmaster had dispatched to the King, recognizing it as the composition of one of the court lords. Confessing his guilt, Biron staunchly argues that since love gives knowledge, it is one of the many means besides study to gain power to live more abundantly, and the King, agreeing, unites with his gentlemen in promoting revels, masques and dances wherewith to woo their loves. They send favors and love verses to their sweethearts, and set out, disguised as Russians, to visit the Princess and her suite, one of whom, however, has overheard and reported their plans to the ladies, who mask and exchange presents, so that each is wooed by the wrong gentleman. Unmercifully taunted, the lords admit the joke when they return in their usual apparel.

The schoolmaster and the curate now ask permission to present a pageant of the Nine Worthies which they have prepared in honor of the Princess with the assistance of Costard, Armado and his page Moth, and a riot of merriment is provided to the sophisticated ladies and courtiers over the successive appearance of Pompey, Alexander, Judas, Hercules and Hector.

In the midst of the jesting and laughter, news is brought to the Princess that her father is dead and she is obliged to return home with all possible speed. This sudden turn of events induces the King and his lords to make open avowals of their love, but the Princess declares the time is too short for a marriage contract, and each lady assigns a suitable penance to her forsworn lover for breaking his vow, while postponing their answers for a year and a day.

HISTORICAL DATA

The source of the slender plot of this comedy is unknown, and many authorities credit it to the imagination of Shakespeare, unaided by the work of others. It is essentially a satire on the manners and modes of the day, burlesquing fads and affectations as manifested in the Euphuistic era of Lyly.

French history undoubtedly contributed much to the formation of the plot. Biron and Longaville were two well-known adherents of Henry of Navarre, and the name Dumain appears to be an anglicized form of that of the Duc de Mayenne, another prominent figure in the contemporary civil wars in France.

The comedy shows evidence of the author's knowledge of the Spanish romances of chivalry, and there is a marked resemblance between Armado and Holofernes and the Italian comic characters of the braggart and the pedant in *Gl' Ingannati*.

It appears in the list of Shakespeare's comedies in Meres's *Palladis Tamia* (1598) and is mentioned in Tofte's *Alba or Month's Mind of a Melancholy Lover* published the same year.

Critics agree from the character and style of its writing that it is one of the early plays. Coleridge speaks of it as "a juvenile drama" and as the author's "earliest dramatic attempt" which suggests a date about 1590. It was first published in quarto form in 1598 and Shakespeare's name appeared on the title page for the first time in print as the author of a play.

"*So sweet a kiss the golden sun gives not*"
LOVE'S LABOUR'S LOST

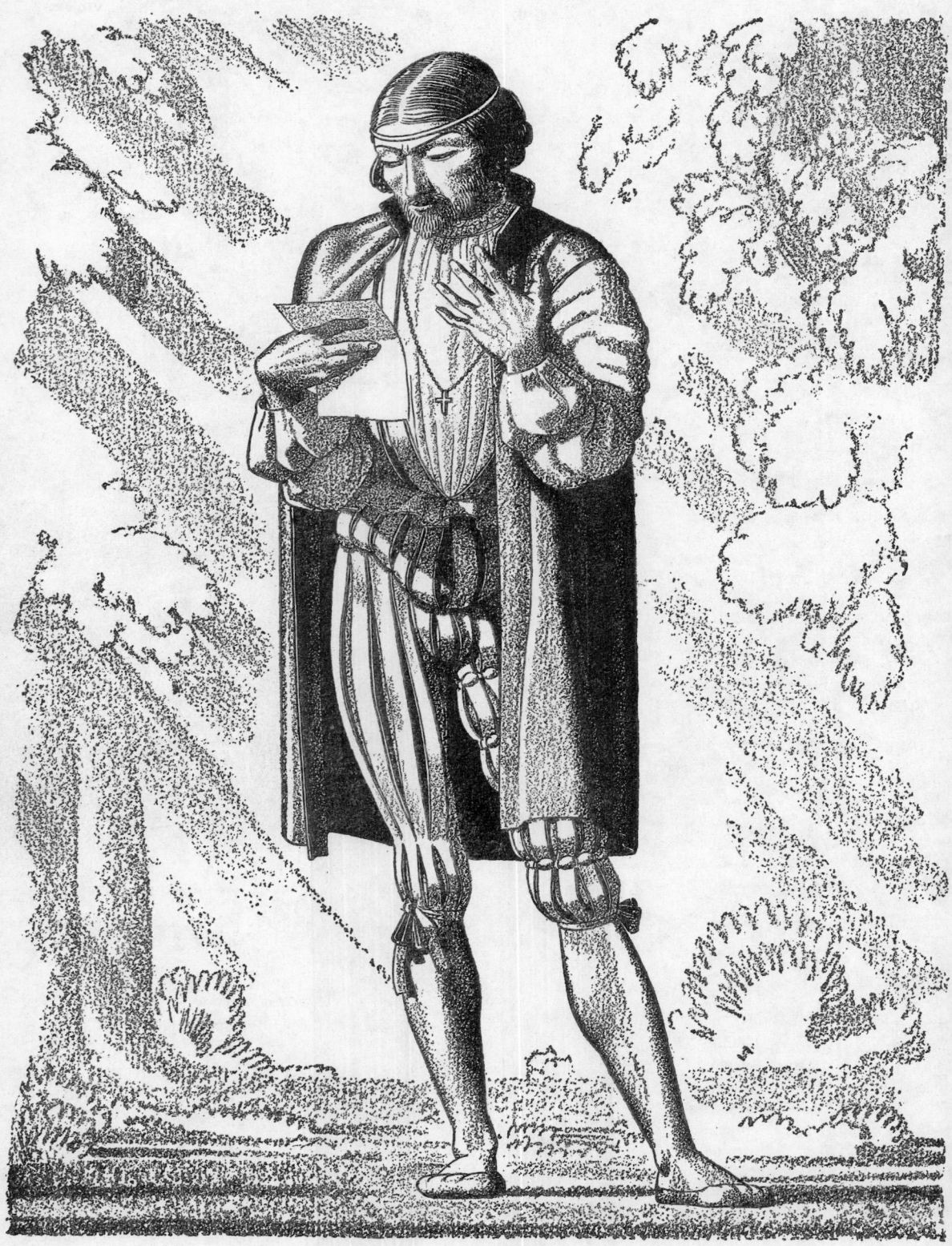

LOVE'S LABOUR'S LOST

DRAMATIS PERSONÆ

FERDINAND, *King of Navarre.*
BIRON,
LONGAVILLE, } *lords attending on the King.*
DUMAIN,
BOYET,
MERCADE, } *lords attending on the Princess of France*
DON ADRIANO DE ARMADO, *a fantastical Spaniard.*
SIR NATHANIEL, *a curate.*
HOLOFERNES, *a schoolmaster.*
DULL, *a constable.*
COSTARD, *a clown.*

MOTH, *page to Armado.*
A FORESTER.

THE PRINCESS *of France.*
ROSALINE,
MARIA, } *ladies attending on the Princess.*
KATHARINE,
JAQUENETTA, *a country wench.*

LORDS, ATTENDANTS, &c.

SCENE—*Navarre.*

ACT I

SCENE I. *The King of Navarre's park*

Enter FERDINAND, *King of Navarre,* BIRON,
LONGAVILLE, *and* DUMAIN

KING

LET fame, that all hunt after in their lives,
Live register'd upon our brazen tombs,
And then grace us in the disgrace of death;
When, spite of cormorant devouring Time,
The endeavour of this present breath may buy
That honour which shall bate his scythe's keen edge,
And make us heirs of all eternity.
Therefore, brave conquerors,—for so you are,
That war against your own affections
And the huge army of the world's desires,—
Our late edict shall strongly stand in force:
Navarre shall be the wonder of the world;
Our court shall be a little Academe,
Still and contemplative in living art.
You three, Biron, Dumain, and Longaville,
Have sworn for three years' term to live with me
My fellow-scholars, and to keep those statutes
That are recorded in this schedule here:
Your oaths are pass'd; and now subscribe your names,
That his own hand may strike his honour down
That violates the smallest branch herein:
If you are arm'd to do as sworn to do,
Subscribe to your deep oaths, and keep it too.

LONGAVILLE

I am resolved; 'tis but a three years' fast:
The mind shall banquet, though the body pine:
Fat paunches have lean pates; and dainty bits
Make rich the ribs, but bankrupt quite the wits.

DUMAIN

My loving lord, Dumain is mortified:
The grosser manner of these world's delights
He throws upon the gross world's baser slaves:
To love, to wealth, to pomp, I pine and die;
With all these living in philosophy.

BIRON

I can but say their protestation over;
So much, dear liege, I have already sworn,
That is, to live and study here three years.
But there are other strict observances;
As, not to see a woman in that term,
Which I hope well is not enrolled there;
And one day in a week to touch no food,
And but one meal on every day beside,
The which I hope is not enrolled there;
And then, to sleep but three hours in the night,
And not be seen to wink of all the day,—
When I was wont to think no harm all night,
And make a dark night too of half the day,—
Which I hope well is not enrolled there:
O, these are barren tasks, too hard to keep,
Not to see ladies, study, fast, not sleep!

KING

Your oath is pass'd to pass away from these.

BIRON

Let me say no, my liege, an if you please:
I only swore to study with your grace,
And stay here in your court for three years' space.

LONGAVILLE

You swore to that, Biron, and to the rest.

BIRON

By yea and nay, sir, then I swore in jest.
What is the end of study? let me know.

KING

Why, that to know, which else we should not know.

BIRON

Things hid and barr'd, you mean, from common sense?

KING

Ay, that is study's god-like recompence.

BIRON

Come on, then; I will swear to study so,
To know the thing I am forbid to know:
As thus,—to study where I well may dine,
When I to feast expressly am forbid;

[279]

Or study where to meet some mistress fine,
  When mistresses from common sense are hid;
Or, having sworn too hard a keeping oath,
Study to break it, and not break my troth.
If study's gain be thus, and this be so,
Study knows that which yet it doth not know:
Swear me to this, and I will ne'er say no.

KING

These be the stops that hinder study quite,
And train our intellects to vain delight.

BIRON

Why, all delights are vain; but that most vain,
Which, with pain purchased, doth inherit pain:
As, painfully to pore upon a book
  To seek the light of truth; while truth the while
Doth falsely blind the eyesight of his look:
  Light, seeking light, doth light of light beguile:
So, ere you find where light in darkness lies,
Your light grows dark by losing of your eyes.
Study me how to please the eye indeed,
  By fixing it upon a fairer eye;
Who dazzling so, that eye shall be his heed,
  And give him light that it was blinded by.
Study is like the heaven's glorious sun,
  That will not be deep-search'd with saucy looks:
Small have continual plodders ever won,
  Save base authority from others' books.
These earthly godfathers of heaven's lights,
  That give a name to every fixed star,
Have no more profit of their shining nights
  Than those that walk and wot not what they are.
Too much to know, is to know nought but fame;
And every godfather can give a name.

KING

How well he's read, to reason against reading!

DUMAIN

Proceeded well, to stop all good proceeding!

LONGAVILLE

He weeds the corn, and still lets grow the weeding.

BIRON

The spring is near, when green geese are a-breeding.

DUMAIN

How follows that?

BIRON

      Fit in his place and time.

DUMAIN

In reason nothing.

BIRON

      Something, then, in rhyme.

KING

Biron is like an envious sneaping frost,
  That bites the first-born infants of the spring.

BIRON

Well, say I am; why should proud summer boast,
  Before the birds have any cause to sing?
Why should I joy in any abortive birth?
At Christmas I no more desire a rose
Than wish a snow in May's new-fangled shows;
But like of each thing that in season grows.

So you, to study now it is too late,
Climb o'er the house to unlock the little gate.

KING

Well, sit you out: go home, Biron: adieu.

BIRON

No, my good lord; I have sworn to stay with you:
And though I have for barbarism spoke more
  Than for that angel knowledge you can say,
Yet confident I'll keep what I have swore,
  And bide the penance of each three years' day.
Give me the paper; let me read the same;
And to the strict'st decrees I'll write my name.

KING

How well this yielding rescues thee from shame!

BIRON

[Reads] 'Item, That no woman shall come within a mile of my court,'—

Hath this been proclaimed?

LONGAVILLE

Four days ago.

BIRON

Let's see the penalty.

[Reads] 'on pain of losing her tongue.'

Who devised this penalty?

LONGAVILLE

Marry, that did I.

BIRON

Sweet lord, and why?

LONGAVILLE

To fright them hence with that dread penalty.

BIRON

A dangerous law against gentility!

[Reads] 'Item, If any man be seen to talk with a woman within the term of three years, he shall endure such public shame as the rest of the court can possibly devise.'

This article, my liege, yourself must break;
  For well you know here comes in embassy
The French king's daughter with yourself to speak,—
  A maid of grace and complete majesty,—
About surrender up of Aquitaine
  To her decrepit, sick, and bedrid father:
Therefore this article is made in vain,
  Or vainly comes the admired princess hither.

KING

What say you, lords? why, this was quite forgot.

BIRON

So study evermore is overshot:
While it doth study to nave what it would,
It doth forget to do the thing it should;
And when it hath the thing it hunteth most,
'Tis won as towns with fire, so won, so lost.

KING

We must of force dispense with this decree;
She must lie here on mere necessity.

BIRON

Necessity will make us all forsworn
  Three thousand times within this three years'
    space;

For every man with his affects is born,
  Not by might master'd, but by special grace:
If I break faith, this word shall speak for me,
I am forsworn on 'mere necessity.'
So to the laws at large I write my name: [*Subscribes*
  And he that breaks them in the least degree
Stands in attainder of eternal shame:
  Suggestions are to other as to me;
But I believe, although I seem so loth,
I am the last that will last keep his oath.
But is there no quick recreation granted?

KING

Ay, that there is. Our court, you know, is haunted
  With a refined traveller of Spain;
A man in all the world's new fashion planted,
  That hath a mint of phrases in his brain;
One whom the music of his own vain tongue
  Doth ravish like enchanting harmony;
A man of complements, whom right and wrong
  Have chose as umpire of their mutiny:
This child of fancy, that Armado hight,
  For interim to our studies, shall relate,
In high-born words, the worth of many a knight
  From tawny Spain, lost in the world's debate.
How you delight, my lords, I know not, I;
But, I protest, I love to hear him lie,
And I will use him for my minstrelsy.

BIRON

Armado is a most illustrious wight,
A man of fire-new words, fashion's own knight.

LONGAVILLE

Costard the swain and he shall be our sport;
And, so to study, three years is but short.

Enter DULL *with a letter, and* COSTARD

DULL

Which is the Duke's own person?

BIRON

This, fellow: what wouldst?

DULL

I myself reprehend his own person, for I am his
Grace's tharborough: but I would see his own person in flesh and blood.

BIRON

This is he.

DULL

Signior Arme—Arme—commends you. There's villany abroad: this letter will tell you more.

COSTARD

Sir, the contempts thereof are as touching me.

KING

A letter from the magnificent Armado.

BIRON

How low soever the matter, I hope in God for high
words.

LONGAVILLE

A high hope for a low heaven: God grant us patience!

BIRON

To hear? or forbear laughing?

LONGAVILLE

To hear meekly, sir, and to laugh moderately; or to
forbear both.

BIRON

Well, sir, be it as the style shall give us cause to
climb in the merriness.

COSTARD

The matter is to me, sir, as concerning Jaquenetta.
The matter of it is, I was taken with the manner.

BIRON

In what manner?

COSTARD

In manner and form following, sir; all those three:
I was seen with her in the manor-house, sitting with
her upon the form, and taken following her into the
park; which, put together, is in manner and form
following. Now, sir, for the manner,—it is the manner of a man to speak to a woman: for the form,—
in some form.

BIRON

For the following, sir?

COSTARD

As it shall follow in my correction: and God defend
the right!

KING

Will you hear this letter with attention?

BIRON

As we would hear an oracle.

COSTARD

Such is the simplicity of man to hearken after the
flesh.

KING

[*Reads*] 'Great deputy, the welkin's vicegerent, and sole dominator of Navarre, my soul's earth's god, and body's fostering
patron.'—

COSTARD

Not a word of Costard yet.

KING

[*Reads*] 'So it is,'—

COSTARD

It may be so: but if he say it is so, he is, in telling
true, but so.

KING

Peace!

COSTARD

Be to me, and every man that dares not fight!

KING

No words!

COSTARD

Of other men's secrets, I beseech you.

KING

[*Reads*] 'So it is, besieged with sable-coloured melancholy, I
did commend the black-oppressing humour to the most wholesome physic of thy health-giving air; and, as I am a gentleman, betook myself to walk. The time when? About the sixth
hour; when beasts most graze, birds best peck, and men sit
down to that nourishment which is called supper: so much for
the time when. Now for the ground which; which, I mean, I
walked upon: it is ycleped thy park. Then for the place where;
where, I mean, I did encounter that obscene and most preposterous event, that draweth from my snow-white pen the
ebon-coloured ink, which here thou viewest, beholdest, sur-

veyest, or seest: but to the place where,—it standeth north-north-east and by east from the west corner of thy curious-knotted garden: there did I see that low-spirited swain, that base minnow of thy mirth,'—

COSTARD

Me?

KING

[*Reads*] 'that unlettered small-knowing soul,'—

COSTARD

Me?

KING

[*Reads*] 'that shallow vassal,'—

COSTARD

Still me?

KING

[*Reads*] 'which, as I remember, hight Costard,'—

COSTARD

O, me!

KING

[*Reads*] 'sorted and consorted, contrary to thy established proclaimed edict and continent canon, which with,—O, with—but with this I passion to say wherewith,'—

COSTARD

With a wench.

KING

[*Reads*] 'with a child of our grandmother Eve, a female; or, for thy more sweet understanding, a woman. Him I, as my ever-esteemed duty pricks me on, have sent to thee, to receive the meed of punishment, by thy sweet Grace's officer, Anthony Dull; a man of good repute, carriage, bearing, and estimation.'

DULL

Me, an't shall please you: I am Anthony Dull.

KING

[*Reads*] 'For Jaquenetta,—so is the weaker vessel called which I apprehended with the aforesaid swain,—I keep her as a vessel of thy law's fury; and shall, at the least of thy sweet notice, bring her to trial. Thine, in all compliments of devoted and heart-burning heat of duty.   DON ADRIANO DE ARMADO.'

BIRON

This is not so well as I looked for, but the best that ever I heard.

KING

Ay, the best for the worst. But, sirrah, what say you to this?

COSTARD

Sir, I confess the wench.

KING

Did you hear the proclamation?

COSTARD

I do confess much of the hearing it, but little of the marking of it.

KING

It was proclaimed a year's imprisonment, to be taken with a wench.

COSTARD

I was taken with none, sir: I was taken with a damsel.

KING

Well, it was proclaimed damsel.

COSTARD

This was no damsel neither, sir; she was a virgin.

KING

It is so varied too; for it was proclaimed virgin.

COSTARD

If it were, I deny her virginity: I was taken with a maid.

KING

This maid will not serve your turn, sir.

COSTARD

This maid will serve my turn, sir.

KING

Sir, I will pronounce your sentence: you shall fast a week with bran and water.

COSTARD

I had rather pray a month with mutton and porridge.

KING

And Don Armado shall be your keeper.
My Lord Biron, see him deliver'd o'er;
And go we, lords, to put in practice that
   Which each to other hath so strongly sworn.
      [*Exeunt* KING, LONGAVILLE, *and* DUMAIN

BIRON

I'll lay my head to any good man's hat,
   These oaths and laws will prove an idle scorn.
Sirrah, come on.

COSTARD

I suffer for the truth, sir; for true it is, I was taken with Jaquenetta, and Jaquenetta is a true girl; and, therefore, welcome the sour cup of prosperity! Affliction may one day smile again; and till then, sit thee down, sorrow!   [*Exeunt*

SCENE II. *The same*

Enter ARMADO *and* MOTH *his page*

ARMADO

Boy, what sign is it when a man of great spirit grows melancholy?

MOTH

A great sign, sir, that he will look sad.

ARMADO

Why, sadness is one and the self-same thing, dear imp.

MOTH

No, no; O Lord, sir, no.

ARMADO

How canst thou part sadness and melancholy, my tender juvenal?

MOTH

By a familiar demonstration of the working, my tough senior.

ARMADO

Why tough senior? why tough senior?

MOTH

Why tender juvenal? why tender juvenal?

ARMADO

I spoke it, tender juvenal, as a congruent epitheton

appertaining to thy young days, which we may nominate tender.

MOTH

And I, tough senior, as an appertinent title to your old time, which we may name tough.

ARMADO

Pretty and apt.

MOTH

How mean you, sir? I pretty, and my saying apt? or I apt, and my saying pretty?

ARMADO

Thou pretty, because little.

MOTH

Little pretty, because little. Wherefore apt?

ARMADO

And therefore apt, because quick.

MOTH

Speak you this in my praise, master?

ARMADO

In thy condign praise.

MOTH

I will praise an eel with the same praise.

ARMADO

What, that an eel is ingenious?

MOTH

That an eel is quick.

ARMADO

I do say thou art quick in answers: thou heatest my blood.

MOTH

I am answered, sir.

ARMADO

I love not to be crossed.

MOTH

[Aside] He speaks the mere contrary; crosses love not him.

ARMADO

I have promised to study three years with the Duke.

MOTH

You may do it in an hour, sir.

ARMADO

Impossible.

MOTH

How many is one thrice told?

ARMADO

I am ill at reckoning; it fitteth the spirit of a tapster.

MOTH

You are a gentleman and a gamester, sir.

ARMADO

I confess both: they are both the varnish of a complete man.

MOTH

Then, I am sure, you know how much the gross sum of deuce-ace amounts to.

ARMADO

It doth amount to one more than two.

MOTH

Which the base vulgar do call three.

ARMADO

True.

MOTH

Why, sir, is this such a piece of study? Now here is three studied, ere ye'll thrice wink: and how easy it is to put years to the word three, and study three years in two words, the dancing horse will tell you.

ARMADO

A most fine figure!

MOTH

To prove you a cipher.

ARMADO

I will hereupon confess I am in love: and as it is base for a soldier to love, so am I in love with a base wench. If drawing my sword against the humour of affection would deliver me from the reprobate thought of it, I would take Desire prisoner, and ransom him to any French courtier for a new-devised courtesy. I think scorn to sigh: methinks I should outswear Cupid. Comfort me, boy: what great men have been in love?

MOTH

Hercules, master.

ARMADO

Most sweet Hercules! More authority, dear boy, name more; and, sweet my child, let them be men of good repute and carriage.

MOTH

Samson, master: he was a man of good carriage, great carriage, for he carried the town-gates on his back like a porter: and he was in love.

ARMADO

O well-knit Samson! strong-jointed Samson! I do excel thee in my rapier as much as thou didst me in carrying gates. I am in love too. Who was Samson's love, my dear Moth?

MOTH

A woman, master.

ARMADO

Of what complexion?

MOTH

Of all the four, or the three, or the two, or one of the four.

ARMADO

Tell me precisely of what complexion.

MOTH

Of the sea-water green, sir.

ARMADO

Is that one of the four complexions?

MOTH

As I have read, sir; and the best of them too.

ARMADO

Green, indeed, is the colour of lovers; but to have a love of that colour, methinks Samson had small reason for it. He surely affected her for her wit.

MOTH

It was so, sir; for she had a green wit.

ARMADO

My love is most immaculate white and red.

MOTH

Most maculate thoughts, master, are masked under such colours.

ARMADO

Define, define, well-educated infant.

MOTH

My father's wit, and my mother's tongue, assist me!

ARMADO

Sweet invocation of a child; most pretty and pathetical!

MOTH

If she be made of white and red,
　Her faults will ne'er be known;
For blushing cheeks by faults are bred,
　And fears by pale white shown:
Then if she fear, or be to blame,
　By this you shall not know;
For still her cheeks possess the same
　Which native she doth owe.

A dangerous rhyme, master, against the reason of white and red.

ARMADO

Is there not a ballad, boy, of the King and the Beggar?

MOTH

The world was very guilty of such a ballad some three ages since: but, I think, now 'tis not to be found; or, if it were, it would neither serve for the writing nor the tune.

ARMADO

I will have that subject newly writ o'er, that I may example my digression by some mighty precedent. Boy, I do love that country girl that I took in the park with the rational hind Costard: she deserves well.

MOTH

[Aside] To be whipped; and yet a better love than my master.

ARMADO

Sing, boy; my spirit grows heavy in love.

MOTH

And that's great marvel, loving a light wench.

ARMADO

I say, sing.

MOTH

Forbear till this company be past.

Enter DULL, COSTARD, *and* JAQUENETTA

DULL

Sir, the duke's pleasure is, that you keep Costard safe: and you must suffer him to take no delight nor no penance; but a' must fast three days a week. For this damsel, I must keep her at the park: she is allowed for the day-woman. Fare you well.

ARMADO

I do betray myself with blushing. Maid.

JAQUENETTA

Man.

ARMADO

I will visit thee at the lodge.

JAQUENETTA

That's hereby.

ARMADO

I know where it is situate.

JAQUENETTA

Lord, how wise you are!

ARMADO

I will tell thee wonders.

JAQUENETTA

With that face?

ARMADO

I love thee.

JAQUENETTA

So I heard you say.

ARMADO

And so, farewell.

JAQUENETTA

Fair weather after you!

DULL

Come, Jaquenetta, away!

[*Exeunt* DULL *and* JAQUENETTA

ARMADO

Villain, thou shalt fast for thy offences ere thou be pardoned.

COSTARD

Well, sir, I hope, when I do it, I shall do it on a full stomach.

ARMADO

Thou shalt be heavily punished.

COSTARD

I am more bound to you than your fellows, for they are but lightly rewarded.

ARMADO

Take away this villain; shut him up.

MOTH

Come, you transgressing slave; away!

COSTARD

Let me not be pent up, sir: I will fast, being loose.

MOTH

No, sir; that were fast and loose: thou shalt to prison.

COSTARD

Well, if ever I do see the merry days of desolation that I have seen, some shall see.

MOTH

What shall some see?

COSTARD

Nay, nothing, Master Moth, but what they look upon. It is not for prisoners to be too silent in their words; and therefore I will say nothing: I thank God I have as little patience as another man; and therefore I can be quiet. [*Exeunt* MOTH *and* COSTARD

ARMADO

I do affect the very ground, which is base, where her shoe, which is baser, guided by her foot, which is basest, doth tread. I shall be forsworn, which is a great argument of falsehood, if I love. And how can that be true love which is falsely attempted? Love is a familiar; Love is a devil: there is no evil angel but Love. Yet was Samson so tempted, and he had an excellent strength; yet was Solomon so seduced, and he had a very good wit. Cupid's butt-shaft is too hard for Hercules' club; and therefore too much odds for a Spaniard's rapier. The first and second cause will not serve my turn; the passado he respects

not, the duello he regards not: his disgrace is to be **ca**lled boy; but his glory is to subdue men. Adieu, valour! rust, rapier! be still, drum! for your manager is in love; yea, he loveth. Assist me some extemporal god of rhyme, for I am sure I shall turn sonnet. Devise, wit; write, pen; for I am for whole volumes in folio.   [*Exit*

ACT II
Scene I. *The same*

Enter the PRINCESS OF FRANCE, ROSALINE, MARIA, KATHARINE, BOYET, LORDS, *and other* ATTENDANTS

BOYET
Now, madam, summon up your dearest spirits:
Consider who the king your father sends;
To whom he sends; and what's his embassy:
Yourself, held precious in the world's esteem,
To parley with the sole inheritor
Of all perfections that a man may owe,
Matchless Navarre; the plea of no less weight
Than Aquitaine, a dowry for a queen.
Be now as prodigal of all dear grace,
As Nature was in making graces dear,
When she did starve the general world beside,
And prodigally gave them all to you.

PRINCESS
Good Lord Boyet, my beauty, though but mean,
Needs not the painted flourish of your praise:
Beauty is bought by judgement of the eye,
Not utter'd by base sale of chapmen's tongues:
I am less proud to hear you tell my worth
Than you much willing to be counted wise
In spending your wit in the praise of mine.
But now to task the tasker: good Boyet,
You are not ignorant, all-telling fame
Doth noise abroad, Navarre hath made a vow,
Till painful study shall outwear three years,
No woman may approach his silent court:
Therefore to's seemeth it a needful course,
Before we enter his forbidden gates,
To know his pleasure; and in that behalf,
Bold of your worthiness, we single you
As our best-moving fair solicitor.
Tell him, the daughter of the King of France,
On serious business craving quick dispatch,
Importunes personal conference with his Grace:
Haste, signify so much; while we attend,
Like humble-visaged suitors, his high will.

BOYET
Proud of employment, willingly I go.

PRINCESS
All pride is willing pride, and yours is so.
                                                    [*Exit* BOYET
Who are the votaries, my loving lords,
That are vow-fellows with this virtuous duke?

FIRST LORD
Lord Longaville is one.

PRINCESS
          Know you the man?

MARIA
I know him, madam: at a marriage-feast,
Between Lord Perigort and the beauteous heir
Of Jaques Falconbridge, solemnized
In Normandy, saw I this Longaville:
A man of sovereign parts he is esteem'd;
Well fitted in arts, glorious in arms:
Nothing becomes him ill that he would well.
The only soil of his fair virtue's gloss,
If virtue's gloss will stain with any soil,
Is a sharp wit match'd with too blunt a will;
Whose edge hath power to cut, whose will still wills
It should none spare that come within his power.

PRINCESS
Some merry mocking lord, belike; is't so?

MARIA
They say so most that most his humours know.

PRINCESS
Such short-lived wits do wither as they grow.
Who are the rest?

KATHARINE
The young Dumain, a well-accomplish'd youth,
Of all that virtue love for virtue loved:
Most power to do most harm, least knowing ill;
For he hath wit to make an ill shape good,
And shape to win grace, though he had no wit.
I saw him at the Duke Alençon's once;
And much too little of that good I saw
Is my report to his great worthiness.

ROSALINE
Another of these students at that time
Was there with him, if I have heard a truth.
Biron they call him; but a merrier man,
Within the limit of becoming mirth,
I never spent an hour's talk withal:
His eye begets occasion for his wit;
For every object that the one doth catch,
The other turns to a mirth-moving jest,
Which his fair tongue, conceit's expositor,
Delivers in such apt and gracious words,
That aged ears play truant at his tales,
And younger hearings are quite ravished;
So sweet and voluble is his discourse.

PRINCESS
God bless my ladies! are they all in love,
That every one her own hath garnished
With such bedecking ornaments of praise?

FIRST LORD
Here comes Boyet.

                    Re-enter BOYET

PRINCESS
          Now, what admittance, lord?

BOYET
Navarre had notice of your fair approach;
And he and his competitors in oath
Were all address'd to meet you, gentle lady,
Before I came. Marry, thus much I have learnt:
He rather means to lodge you in the field,

Like one that comes here to besiege his court,
Than seek a dispensation for his oath,
To let you enter his unpeeled house.
Here comes Navarre.

Enter KING, LONGAVILLE, DUMAIN, BIRON, *and*
ATTENDANTS

KING

Fair princess, welcome to the court of Navarre.

PRINCESS

'Fair' I give you back again; and 'welcome' I have
not yet: the roof of this court is too high to be yours;
and welcome to the wide fields too base to be mine.

KING

You shall be welcome, madam, to my court.

PRINCESS

I will be welcome, then: conduct me thither.

KING

Hear me, dear lady; I have sworn an oath.

PRINCESS

Our Lady help my lord! he'll be forsworn.

KING

Not for the world, fair madam, by my will.

PRINCESS

Why, will shall break it; will, and nothing else.

KING

Your ladyship is ignorant what it is.

PRINCESS

Were my lord so, his ignorance were wise,
Where now his knowledge must prove ignorance.
I hear your grace hath sworn out house-keeping:
'Tis deadly sin to keep that oath, my lord,
And sin to break it.
But pardon me, I am too sudden-bold:
To teach a teacher ill beseemeth me.
Vouchsafe to read the purpose of my coming,
And suddenly resolve me in my suit.

KING

Madam, I will, if suddenly I may.

PRINCESS

You will the sooner, that I were away;
For you'll prove perjured, if you make me stay.

BIRON

Did not I dance with you in Brabant once?

ROSALINE

Did not I dance with you in Brabant once?

BIRON

I know you did.

ROSALINE

How needless was it, then, to ask the question!

BIRON

You must not be so quick.

ROSALINE

'Tis 'long of you that spur me with such questions.

BIRON

Your wit's too hot, it speeds too fast, 'twill tire.

ROSALINE

Not till it leave the rider in the mire.

BIRON

What time o' day?

ROSALINE

The hour that fools should ask.

BIRON

Now fair befall your mask!

ROSALINE

Fair fall the face it covers!

BIRON

And send you many lovers!

ROSALINE

Amen, so you be none.

BIRON

Nay, then will I be gone.

KING

Madam, your father here doth intimate
The payment of a hundred thousand crowns;
Being but the one half of an entire sum
Disbursed by my father in his wars.
But say that he or we, as neither have,
Received that sum, yet there remains unpaid
A hundred thousand more; in surety of the which,
One part of Aquitaine is bound to us,
Although not valued to the money's worth.
If, then, the king your father will restore
But that one-half which is unsatisfied,
We will give up our right in Aquitaine,
And hold fair friendship with his Majesty.
But that, it seems, he little purposeth,
For here he doth demand to have repaid
A hundred thousand crowns; and not demands,
On payment of a hundred thousand crowns,
To have his title live in Aquitaine;
Which we much rather had depart withal,
And have the money by our father lent,
Than Aquitaine so gelded as it is.
Dear princess, were not his requests so far
From reason's yielding, your fair self should make
A yielding, 'gainst some reason, in my breast,
And go well satisfied to France again.

PRINCESS

You do the king my father too much wrong,
And wrong the reputation of your name,
In so unseeming to confess receipt
Of that which hath so faithfully been paid.

KING

I do protest I never heard of it;
And if you prove it, I'll repay it back,
Or yield up Aquitaine.

PRINCESS

           We arrest your word.
Boyet, you can produce acquittances
For such a sum from special officers
Of Charles his father.

KING

           Satisfy me so.

BOYET

So please your Grace, the packet is not come,
Where that and other specialties are bound:
To-morrow you shall have a sight of them.

KING

It shall suffice me: at which interview

All liberal reason I will yield unto.
Meantime receive such welcome at my hand
As honour, without breach of honour, may
Make tender of to thy true worthiness:
You may not come, fair princess, in my gates;
But here without you shall be so received
As you shall deem yourself lodged in my heart,
Though so denied fair harbour in my house.
Your own good thoughts excuse me, and farewell:
To-morrow shall we visit you again.

PRINCESS
Sweet health and fair desires consort your Grace!

KING
Thy own wish wish I thee in every place!   [Exit

BIRON
Lady, I will commend you to mine own heart.

ROSALINE
Pray you, do my commendations; I would be glad
to see it.

BIRON
I would you heard it groan.

ROSALINE
Is the fool sick?

BIRON
Sick at the heart.

ROSALINE
Alack, let it blood.

BIRON
Would that do it good?

ROSALINE
My physic says 'ay'.

BIRON
Will you prick't with your eye?

ROSALINE
No point, with my knife.

BIRON
Now, God save thy life!

ROSALINE
And yours from long living!

BIRON
I cannot stay thanksgiving.   [Retiring

DUMAIN
Sir, I pray you, a word: what lady is that same?

BOYET
The heir of Alençon, Katharine her name.

DUMAIN
A gallant lady. Monsieur, fare you well.   [Exit

LONGAVILLE
I beseech you a word: what is she in the white?

BOYET
A woman sometimes, an you saw her in the light.

LONGAVILLE
Perchance light in the light. I desire her name.

BOYET
She hath but one for herself, to desire that were a
shame.

LONGAVILLE
Pray you, sir, whose daughter?

BOYET
Her mother's I have heard.

LONGAVILLE
God's blessing on your beard!

BOYET
Good sir, be not offended.
She is an heir of Falconbridge.

LONGAVILLE
Nay, my choler is ended.
She is a most sweet lady.

BOYET
Not unlike, sir, that may be.   [Exit LONGAVILLE

BIRON
What's her name in the cap?

BOYET
Rosaline, by good hap.

BIRON
Is she wedded or no?

BOYET
To her will, sir, or so.

BIRON
You are welcome, sir: adieu.

BOYET
Farewell to me, sir, and welcome to you.
        [Exit BIRON

MARIA
That last is Biron, the merry mad-cap lord:
Not a word with him but a jest.

BOYET
        And every jest but a word.

PRINCESS
It was well done of you to take him at his word.

BOYET
I was as willing to grapple as he was to board.

MARIA
Two hot sheeps, marry.

BOYET
        And wherefore not ships?
No sheep, sweet lamb, unless we feed on your lips.

MARIA
You sheep, and I pasture: shall that finish the jest?

BOYET
So you grant pasture for me.   [Offering to kiss her

MARIA
        Not so, gentle beast:
My lips are no common, though several they be.

BOYET
Belonging to whom?

MARIA
        To my fortunes and me.

PRINCESS
Good wits will be jangling; but, gentles, agree:
This civil war of wits were much better used
On Navarre and his book-men; for here 'tis abused.

BOYET
If my observation, which very seldom lies,
By the heart's still rhetoric disclosed with eyes,
Deceive me not now, Navarre is infected.

PRINCESS
With what?

BOYET
With that which we lovers entitle affected.

PRINCESS

Your reason?

BOYET

Why, all his behaviours did make their retire
To the court of his eye, peeping thorough desire:
His heart, like an agate, with your print impress'd,
Proud with his form, in his eye pride express'd:
His tongue, all impatient to speak and not see,
Did stumble with haste in his eyesight to be;
All senses to that sense did make their repair,
To feel only looking on fairest of fair:
Methought all his senses were lock'd in his eye,
As jewels in crystal for some prince to buy;
Who, tendering their own worth from where they
      were glass'd,
Did point you to buy them, along as you pass'd:
His face's own margent did quote such amazes,
That all eyes saw his eyes enchanted with gazes.
I'll give you Aquitaine, and all that is his,
An you give him for my sake but one loving kiss.

PRINCESS

Come to our pavilion: Boyet is disposed.

BOYET

But to speak that in words which his eye hath dis-
    closed.
I only have made a mouth of his eye,
By adding a tongue which I know will not lie.

ROSALINE

Thou art an old love-monger, and speakest skilfully.

MARIA

He is Cupid's grandfather, and learns news of him.

ROSALINE

Then was Venus like her mother; for her father is
    but grim.

BOYET

Do you hear, my mad wenches?

MARIA

          No.

BOYET

          What then, do you see?

ROSALINE

Ay, our way to be gone.

BOYET

          You are too hard for me.
                              [Exeunt

ACT III

Scene I. The same

Enter ARMADO *and* MOTH

ARMADO

Warble, child; make passionate my sense of hearing.

MOTH

Concolinel.   [Singing

ARMADO

Sweet air! Go, tenderness of years; take this key,
give enlargement to the swain, bring him festinately
hither: I must employ him in a letter to my love.

MOTH

Master, will you win your love with a French brawl?

ARMADO

How meanest thou? brawling in French?

MOTH

No, my complete master: but to jig off a tune at the
tongue's end, canary to it with your feet, humour it
with turning up your eyelids, sigh a note and sing a
note, sometime through the throat, as if you swallowed love with singing love, sometime through the
nose, as if you snuffed up love by smelling love; with
your hat penthouse-like o'er the shop of your eyes;
with your arms crossed on your thin-belly doublet,
like a rabbit on a spit; or your hands in your pocket,
like a man after the old painting; and keep not too
long in one tune, but a snip and away. These are
complements, these are humours; these betray nice
wenches, that would be betrayed without these; and
make them men of note—do you note me?—that
most are affected to these.

ARMADO

How hast thou purchased this experience?

MOTH

By my penny of observation.

ARMADO

But O,—but O,—

MOTH

'The hobby-horse is forgot.'

ARMADO

Callest thou my love 'hobby-horse'?

MOTH

No, master; the hobby-horse is but a colt, and your
love perhaps a hackney. But have you forgot your
love?

ARMADO

Almost I had.

MOTH

Negligent student! learn her by heart.

ARMADO

By heart and in heart, boy.

MOTH

And out of heart, master: all those three I will prove.

ARMADO

What wilt thou prove?

MOTH

A man, if I live; and this, by, in, and without, upon
the instant: by heart you love her, because your
heart cannot come by her; in heart you love her,
because your heart is in love with her; and out of
heart you love her, being out of heart that you cannot enjoy her.

ARMADO

I am all these three.

MOTH

And three times as much more, and yet nothing at
all.

ARMADO

Fetch hither the swain: he must carry me a letter.

MOTH

A message well sympathized; a horse to be ambassador for an ass.

ARMADO

Ha, ha! what sayest thou?

MOTH

Marry, sir, you must send the ass upon the horse, for he is very slow-gaited. But I go.

ARMADO

The way is but short: away!

MOTH

As swift as lead, sir.

ARMADO

The meaning, pretty ingenious?
Is not lead a metal heavy, dull, and slow?

MOTH

Minimè, honest master; or rather, master, no.

ARMADO

I say lead is slow.

MOTH

       You are too swift, sir, to say so:
Is that lead slow which is fired from a gun?

ARMADO

Sweet smoke of rhetoric!
He reputes me a cannon; and the bullet, that's he:
I shoot thee at the swain.

MOTH

       Thump, then, and I flee.
                            [*Exit*

ARMADO

A most acute juvenal; volable and free of grace!
By thy favour, sweet welkin, I must sigh in thy face:
Most rude melancholy, valour gives thee place.
My herald is return'd.

Re-enter MOTH *with* COSTARD

MOTH

A wonder, master! here's a Costard broken in a shin.

ARMADO

Some enigma, some riddle: come, thy l'envoy; begin.

COSTARD

No egma, no riddle, no l'envoy; no salve in the mail, sir: O, sir, plantain, a plain plantain! no l'envoy, no l'envoy; no salve, sir, but a plantain!

ARMADO

By virtue, thou enforcest laughter; thy silly thought my spleen; the heaving of my lungs provokes me to ridiculous smiling. O, pardon me, my stars! Doth the inconsiderate take salve for l'envoy, and the word l'envoy for a salve?

MOTH

Do the wise think them other? is not l'envoy a salve?

ARMADO

No, page: it is an epilogue or discourse, to make plain
Some obscure precedence that hath tofore been sain.
I will example it:
The fox, the ape, and the humble-bee,
Were still at odds, being but three.
There's the moral. Now the l'envoy.

MOTH

I will add the l'envoy. Say the moral again.

ARMADO

The fox, the ape, the humble-bee,
Were still at odds, being but three.

MOTH

Until the goose came out of door,
And stay'd the odds by adding four.
Now will I begin your moral, and do you follow with my l'envoy.
The fox, the ape, and the humble-bee,
Were still at odds, being but three.

ARMADO

Until the goose came out of door,
Staying the odds by adding four.

MOTH

A good l'envoy, ending in the goose: would you desire more?

COSTARD

The boy hath sold him a bargain, a goose, that's flat.
Sir, your pennyworth is good, an your goose be fat.
To sell a bargain well is as cunning as fast and loose:
Let me see; a fat l'envoy; ay, that's a fat goose.

ARMADO

Come hither, come hither. How did this argument begin?

MOTH

By saying that a Costard was broken in a shin.
Then call'd you for the l'envoy.

COSTARD

True, and I for a plantain: thus came your argument in;
Then the boy's fat l'envoy, the goose that you bought;
And he ended the market.

ARMADO

But tell me; how was there a Costard broken in a shin?

MOTH

I will tell you sensibly.

COSTARD

Thou hast no feeling of it, Moth: I will speak that l'envoy:
I Costard, running out, that was safely within,
Fell over the threshold, and broke my shin.

ARMADO

We will talk no more of this matter.

COSTARD

Till there be more matter in the shin.

ARMADO

Sirrah Costard, I will enfranchise thee.

COSTARD

O, marry me to one Frances: I smell some l'envoy, some goose, in this.

ARMADO

By my sweet soul, I mean setting thee at liberty, enfreedoming thy person: thou wert immured, restrained, captivated, bound.

COSTARD

True, true; and now you will be my purgation, and let me loose.

ARMADO

I give thee thy liberty, set thee from durance; and, in lieu thereof, impose on thee nothing but this: bear this significant [*giving a letter*] to the country maid Jaquenetta: there is remuneration; for the best ward of mine honour is rewarding my dependents. Moth, follow.   [*Exit*

MOTH

Like the sequel, I. Signior Costard, adieu.

COSTARD

My sweet ounce of man's flesh! my incony Jew!
                      [*Exit* MOTH

Now will I look to his remuneration. Remuneration! O, that's the Latin word for three farthings: three farthings—remuneration.—'What's the price of this inkle?'—'One penny.'—'No, I'll give you a remuneration:' why, it carries it. Remuneration! why, it is a fairer name than French crown. I will never buy and sell out of this word.

Enter BIRON

BIRON

O, my good knave Costard! exceedingly well met.

COSTARD

Pray you, sir, how much carnation ribbon may a man buy for a remuneration?

BIRON

What is a remuneration?

COSTARD

Marry, sir, halfpenny farthing.

BIRON

Why, then, three-farthing worth of silk.

COSTARD

I thank your worship: God be wi' you!

BIRON

Stay, slave; I must employ thee:
As thou wilt win my favour, good my knave,
Do one thing for me that I shall entreat.

COSTARD

When would you have it done, sir?

BIRON

This afternoon.

COSTARD

Well, I will do it, sir: fare you well.

BIRON

Thou knowest not what it is.

COSTARD

I shall know, sir, when I have done it.

BIRON

Why, villain, thou must know first.

COSTARD

I will come to your worship to-morrow morning.

BIRON

It must be done this afternoon. Hark, slave, it is but this:
The princess comes to hunt here in the park,
And in her train there is a gentle lady;

When tongues speak sweetly, then they name her name,
And Rosaline they call her: ask for her;
And to her white hand see thou do commend
This seal'd-up counsel. There's thy guerdon; go.
             [*Giving him a shilling*

COSTARD

Gardon, O sweet gardon! better than remuneration, a 'leven-pence farthing better: most sweet gardon! I will do it, sir, in print. Gardon! Remuneration!
                          [*Exit*

BIRON

And I, forsooth, in love! I, that have been love's whip;
A very beadle to a humorous sigh;
A critic, nay, a night-watch constable;
A domineering pedant o'er the boy;
Than whom no mortal so magnificent!
This wimpled, whining, purblind, wayward boy;
This senior-junior, giant-dwarf, Dan Cupid;
Regent of love-rhymes, lord of folded arms,
The anointed sovereign of sighs and groans,
Liege of all loiterers and malcontents,
Dread prince of plackets, king of codpieces,
Sole imperator and great general
Of trotting 'paritors:—O my little heart!—
And I to be a corporal of his field,
And wear his colours like a tumbler's hoop!
What! I love! I sue! I seek a wife!
A woman, that is like a German clock,
Still a-repairing, ever out of frame,
And never going aright, being a watch,
But being watch'd that it may still go right!
Nay, to be perjured, which is worst of all;
And, among three, to love the worst of all;
A whitely wanton with a velvet brow,
With two pitch-balls stuck in her face for eyes;
Ay, and, by heaven, one that will do the deed,
Though Argus were her eunuch and her guard:
And I to sigh for her! to watch for her!
To pray for her! Go to; it is a plague
That Cupid will impose for my neglect
Of his almighty dreadful little might.
Well, I will love, write, sigh, pray, sue and groan:
Some men must love my lady, and some Joan. [*Exit*

ACT IV

SCENE I. *The same*

Enter the PRINCESS, *and her* TRAIN, *a* FORESTER,
BOYET, ROSALINE, MARIA, *and* KATHARINE

PRINCESS

Was that the king, that spurr'd his horse so hard
Against the steep uprising of the hill?

BOYET

I know not; but I think it was not he.

PRINCESS

Whoe'er a' was, a' showed a mounting mind.
Well, lords, to-day we shall have our dispatch:
On Saturday we will return to France.
Then, forester, my friend, where is the bush
That we must stand and play the murderer in?

FORESTER

Hereby, upon the edge of yonder coppice;
A stand where you may make the fairest shoot.

PRINCESS

I thank my beauty, I am fair that shoot,
And thereupon thou speak'st the fairest shoot.

FORESTER

Pardon me, madam, for I meant not so.

PRINCESS

What, what? first praise me, and again say no?
O short-lived pride! Not fair? alack for woe!

FORESTER

Yes, madam, fair.

PRINCESS

            Nay, never paint me now:
Where fair is not, praise cannot mend the brow.
Here, good my glass, take this for telling true:
Fair payment for foul words is more than due.

FORESTER

Nothing but fair is that which you inherit.

PRINCESS

See, see, my beauty will be saved by merit!
O heresy in fair, fit for these days!
A giving hand, though foul, shall have fair praise.
But come, the bow: now mercy goes to kill,
And shooting well is then accounted ill.
Thus will I save my credit in the shoot:
Not wounding, pity would not let me do't;
If wounding, then it was to show my skill,
That more for praise than purpose meant to kill.
And, out of question, so it is sometimes,
Glory grows guilty of detested crimes,
When, for fame's sake, for praise, an outward part,
We bend to that the working of the heart;
As I for praise alone now seek to spill
The poor deer's blood, that my heart means no ill.

BOYET

Do not curst wives hold that self-sovereignty
Only for praise sake, when they strive to be
Lords o'er their lords?

PRINCESS

Only for praise: and praise we may afford
To any lady that subdues a lord.

BOYET

Here comes a member of the commonwealth.

Enter COSTARD

COSTARD

God dig-you-den all! Pray you, which is the head
lady?

PRINCESS

Thou shalt know her, fellow, by the rest that have
no heads.

COSTARD

Which is the greatest lady, the highest?

PRINCESS

The thickest and the tallest.

COSTARD

The thickest and the tallest! it is so; truth is truth.
An your waist, mistress, were as slender as my wit,
One o' these maids' girdles for your waist should be
fit.
Are not you the chief woman? you are the thickest
here.

PRINCESS

What's your will, sir? what's your will?

COSTARD

I have a letter from Monsieur Biron to one Lady
Rosaline.

PRINCESS

O, thy letter, thy letter! he's a good friend of mine:
Stand aside, good bearer. Boyet, you can carve;
Break up this capon.

BOYET

            I am bound to serve.
This letter is mistook, it importeth none here;
It is writ to Jaquenetta.

PRINCESS

            We will read it, I swear.
Break the neck of the wax, and every one give ear.

BOYET

[*Reads*] By heaven, that thou art fair, is most infallible; true,
that thou art beauteous; truth itself, that thou art lovely. More
fairer than fair, beautiful than beauteous, truer than truth itself, have commiseration on thy heroical vassal! The magnanimous and most illustrate king Cophetua set eye upon the pernicious and indubitate beggar Zenelophon; and he it was that
might rightly say, Veni, vidi, vici; which to annothanize in
the vulgar,—O base and obscure vulgar!—videlicet, He came,
saw, and overcame: he came, one; saw, two; overcame, three.
Who came? the king: why did he come? to see: why did he see?
to overcome: to whom came he? to the beggar: what saw he?
the beggar: who overcame he? the beggar. The conclusion is
victory: on whose side? the king's. The captive is enriched: on
whose side? the beggar's. The catastrophe is a nuptial: on
whose side? the king's: no, on both in one, or one in both. I
am the king; for so stands the comparison: thou the beggar;
for so witnesseth thy lowliness. Shall I command thy love? I
may: shall I enforce thy love? I could: shall I entreat thy love?
I will. What shalt thou exchange for rags? robes; for tittles?
titles; for thyself? me. Thus, expecting thy reply, I profane my
lips on thy foot, my eyes on thy picture, and my heart on thy
every part. Thine, in the dearest design of industry,
                                        DON ADRIANO DE ARMADO.

    Thus dost thou hear the Nemean lion roar
      'Gainst thee, thou lamb, that standest as his prey.
    Submissive fall his princely feet before,
      And he from forage will incline to play:
    But if thou strive, poor soul, what art thou then?
    Food for his rage, repasture for his den.

PRINCESS

What plume of feathers is he that indited this letter?
What vane? what weathercock? did you ever hear
better?

BOYET

I am much deceived but I remember the style.

PRINCESS

Else your memory is bad, going o'er it erewhile.

BOYET

This Armado is a Spaniard, that keeps here in court;
A phantasime, a Monarcho, and one that makes
    sport
To the prince and his bookmates.

PRINCESS
                  Thou fellow, a word:
Who gave thee this letter?

COSTARD
           I told you; my lord.

PRINCESS
To whom shouldst thou give it?

COSTARD
             From my lord to my lady.

PRINCESS
From which lord to which lady?

COSTARD
From my lord Biron, a good master of mine,
To a lady of France that he call'd Rosaline.

PRINCESS
Thou hast mistaken his letter. Come, lords, away.
[To ROSALINE] Here, sweet, put up this: 'twill be
    thine another day.   [Exeunt PRINCESS and TRAIN

BOYET
Who is the suitor? who is the suitor?

ROSALINE
             Shall I teach you to know?

BOYET
Ay, my continent of beauty.

ROSALINE
             Why, she that bears the bow.
Finely put off!

BOYET
My lady goes to kill horns; but, if thou marry,
Hang me by the neck, if horns that year miscarry.
Finely put on!

ROSALINE
Well, then, I am the shooter.

BOYET
            And who is your deer?

ROSALINE
If we choose by the horns, yourself come not near.
Finely put on, indeed!

MARIA
You still wrangle with her, Boyet, and she strikes at
    the brow.

BOYET
But she herself is hit lower: have I hit her now?

ROSALINE
Shall I come upon thee with an old saying, that was
a man when King Pepin of France was a little boy,
as touching the hit it?

BOYET
So I may answer thee with one as old, that was a
woman when Queen Guinover of Britain was a
little wench, as touching the hit it.

ROSALINE
    Thou canst not hit it, hit it, hit it,
    Thou canst not hit it, my good man.

BOYET
    An I cannot, cannot, cannot,
    An I cannot, another can.
           [Exeunt ROSALINE and KATHARINE

COSTARD
By my troth, most pleasant: how both did fit it!

MARIA
A mark marvellous well shot, for they both did hit
it.

BOYET
A mark! O, mark but that mark! A mark, says my
lady!
Let the mark have a prick in't, to mete at, if it may
be.

MARIA
Wide o' the bow-hand! i' faith, your hand is out.

COSTARD
Indeed, a' must shoot nearer, or he'll ne'er hit the
clout.

BOYET
An if my hand be out, then belike your hand is in.

COSTARD
Then will she get the upshoot by cleaving the pin.

MARIA
Come, come, you talk greasily; your lips grow foul.

COSTARD
She's too hard for you at pricks, sir: challenge her to
bowl.

BOYET
I fear too much rubbing. Good night, my good owl.
           [Exeunt BOYET and MARIA

COSTARD
By my soul, a swain! a most simple clown!
Lord, Lord, how the ladies and I have put him
down!
O' my troth, most sweet jests! most incony vulgar
wit!
When it comes so smoothly off, so obscenely, as it
were, so fit.
Armado o' th' one side,—O, a most dainty man!
To see him walk before a lady and to bear her fan!
To see him kiss his hand! and how most sweetly a'
will swear!
And his page o' t' other side, that handful of wit!
Ah, heavens, it is a most pathetical nit!
Sola, sola!
           [Shout within
           [Exit COSTARD, running

SCENE II. *The same*

Enter HOLOFERNES, SIR NATHANIEL, *and* DULL

NATHANIEL
Very reverend sport, truly; and done in the testimony of a good conscience.

HOLOFERNES
The deer was, as you know, sanguis, in blood; ripe
as the pomewater, who now hangeth like a jewel in
the ear of caelo, the sky, the welkin, the heaven; and

anon falleth like a crab on the face of terra, the soil, the land, the earth.

NATHANIEL

Truly, Master Holofernes, the epithets are sweetly varied, like a scholar at the least: but, sir, I assure ye, it was a buck of the first head.

HOLOFERNES

Sir Nathaniel, haud credo.

DULL

'Twas not a haud credo; 'twas a pricket.

HOLOFERNES

Most barbarous intimation! yet a kind of insinuation, as it were, in via, in way, of explication; facere, as it were, replication, or, rather, ostentare, to show, as it were, his inclination, after his undressed, unpolished, uneducated, unpruned, untrained, or, rather, unlettered, or, ratherest, unconfirmed fashion, to insert again my haud credo for a deer.

DULL

I said the deer was not a haud credo; 'twas a pricket.

HOLOFERNES

Twice-sod simplicity, bis coctus!
O thou monster Ignorance, how deformed dost thou look!

NATHANIEL

Sir, he hath never fed of the dainties that are bred in a book;
he hath not eat paper, as it were; he hath not drunk ink: his intellect is not replenished; he is only an animal, only sensible in the duller parts:
And such barren plants are set before us, that we thankful should be,
Which we of taste and feeling are, for those parts that do fructify in us more than he.
For as it would ill become me to be vain, indiscreet, or a fool,
So were there a patch set on learning, to see him in a school:
But omne bene, say I; being of an old father's mind,
Many can brook the weather that love not the wind.

DULL

You two are book-men: can you tell me by your wit
What was a month old at Cain's birth, that's not five weeks old as yet?

HOLOFERNES

Dictynna, goodman Dull; Dictynna, goodman Dull.

DULL

What is Dictynna?

NATHANIEL

A title to Phœbe, to Luna, to the moon.

HOLOFERNES

The moon was a month old when Adam was no more,
And raught not to five weeks when he came to five-score.
The allusion holds in the exchange.

DULL

'Tis true indeed; the collusion holds in the exchange.

HOLOFERNES

God comfort thy capacity! I say, the allusion holds in the exchange.

DULL

And I say, the pollusion holds in the exchange; for the moon is never but a month old: and I say beside that, 'twas a pricket that the princess killed.

HOLOFERNES

Sir Nathaniel, will you hear an extemporal epitaph on the death of the deer? And, to humour the ignorant, call I the deer the princess killed a pricket.

NATHANIEL

Perge, good Master Holofernes, perge; so it shall please you to abrogate scurrility.

HOLOFERNES

I will something affect the letter, for it argues facility.

The preyful princess pierced and prick'd a pretty pleasing pricket;
  Some say a sore; but not a sore, till now made sore with shooting.
The dogs did yell: put L to sore, then sorel jumps from thicket;
  Or pricket sore, or else sorel; the people fall a-hooting.
If sore be sore, then L to sore makes fifty sores one sorel.
Of one sore I an hundred make by adding but one more L.

NATHANIEL

A rare talent!

DULL

[Aside] If a talent be a claw, look how he claws him with a talent.

HOLOFERNES

This is a gift that I have, simple, simple; a foolish extravagant spirit, full of forms, figures, shapes, objects, ideas, apprehensions, motions, revolutions: these are begot in the ventricle of memory, nourished in the womb of pia mater, and delivered upon the mellowing of occasion. But the gift is good in those in whom it is acute, and I am thankful for it.

NATHANIEL

Sir, I praise the Lord for you: and so may my parishioners; for their sons are well tutored by you, and their daughters profit very greatly under you: you are a good member of the commonwealth.

HOLOFERNES

Mehercle, if their sons be ingenuous, they shall want no instruction; if their daughters be capable, I will put it to them: but vir sapit qui pauca loquitur; a soul feminine saluteth us.

Enter JAQUENETTA and COSTARD

JAQUENETTA

God give you good morrow, master Parson.

HOLOFERNES

Master Parson, quasi pers-on. And if one should be pierced, which is the one?

COSTARD

Marry, master schoolmaster, he that is likest to a hogshead.

HOLOFERNES

Piercing a hogshead! a good lustre of conceit in a turf of earth; fire enough for a flint, pearl enough for a swine: 'tis pretty; it is well.

JAQUENETTA

Good master Parson, be so good as read me this letter: it was given me by Costard, and sent me from Don Armado: I beseech you, read it.

HOLOFERNES

Fauste, precor gelida quando pecus omne sub umbra Ruminat,—and so forth. Ah, good old Mantuan! I may speak of thee as the traveller doth of Venice;

Venetia, Venetia,

Chi non ti vede non ti pretia.

Old Mantuan, old Mantuan! who understandeth thee not, loves thee not. Ut, re, sol, la, mi, fa. Under pardon, sir, what are the contents? or rather, as Horace says in his— What, my soul, verses?

NATHANIEL

Ay, sir, and very learned.

HOLOFERNES

Let me hear a staff, a stanze, a verse; lege, domine.

NATHANIEL

[Reads]

If love make me forsworn, how shall I swear to love?
  Ah, never faith could hold, if not to beauty vow'd!
Though to myself forsworn, to thee I'll faithful prove;
  Those thoughts to me were oaks, to thee like osiers bow'd.
Study his bias leaves, and makes his book thine eyes,
  Where all those pleasures live that art would comprehend:
If knowledge be the mark, to know thee shall suffice;
  Well learned is that tongue that well can thee commend;
All ignorant that soul that sees thee without wonder;
  Which is to me some praise that I thy parts admire:
Thy eye Jove's lightning bears, thy voice his dreadful thunder,
  Which, not to anger bent, is music and sweet fire.
Celestial as thou art, O, pardon love this wrong,
That sings heaven's praise with such an earthly tongue.

HOLOFERNES

You find not the apostrophas, and so miss the accent: let me supervise the canzonet. Here are only numbers ratified; but, for the elegancy, facility, and golden cadence of poesy, caret. Ovidius Naso was the man: and why, indeed, Naso, but for smelling out the odoriferous flowers of fancy, the jerks of invention? Imitari is nothing: so doth the hound his master, the ape his keeper, the tired horse his rider. But, damosella virgin, was this directed to you?

JAQUENETTA

Ay, sir, from one Monsieur Biron, one of the strange queen's lords.

HOLOFERNES

I will overglance the superscript:

'To the snow-white hand of the most beauteous Lady Rosaline.'

I will look again on the intellect of the letter, for the nomination of the party writing to the person written unto:

'Your ladyship's in all desired employment, BIRON.'

Sir Nathaniel, this Biron is one of the votaries with the king; and here he hath framed a letter to a sequent of the stranger queen's, which accidentally, or by the way of progression, hath miscarried. Trip and go, my sweet; deliver this paper into the royal hand of the king: it may concern much. Stay not thy compliment; I forgive thy duty: adieu.

JAQUENETTA

Good Costard, go with me. Sir, God save your life!

COSTARD

Have with thee, my girl.

[Exeunt COSTARD and JAQUENETTA

NATHANIEL

Sir, you have done this in the fear of God, very religiously; and, as a certain father saith,—

HOLOFERNES

Sir, tell not me of the father; I do fear colourable colours. But to return to the verses: did they please you, Sir Nathaniel?

NATHANIEL

Marvellous well for the pen.

HOLOFERNES

I do dine to-day at the father's of a certain pupil of mine; where, if, before repast, it shall please you to gratify the table with a grace, I will, on my privilege I have with the parents of the foresaid child or pupil, undertake your ben venuto; where I will prove those verses to be very unlearned, neither savouring of poetry, wit, nor invention: I beseech your society.

NATHANIEL

And thank you too; for society, saith the text, is the happiness of life.

HOLOFERNES

And, certes, the text most infallibly concludes it. [To DULL] Sir, I do invite you too; you shall not say me nay: pauca verba. Away! the gentles are at their game, and we will to our recreation.   [Exeunt

SCENE III. The same

Enter BIRON, with a paper

BIRON

The king he is hunting the deer; I am coursing myself: they have pitched a toil; I am toiling in a pitch,—pitch that defiles: defile! a foul word. Well, set thee down, sorrow! for so they say the fool said, and so say I, and I the fool: well proved, wit! By the Lord, this love is as mad as Ajax: it kills sheep; it kills me, I a sheep: well proved again o' my side! I will not love: if I do, hang me; i' faith, I will not. O, but her eye,—by this light, but for her eye, I would not love her; yes, for her two eyes. Well, I do nothing in the world but lie, and lie in my throat. By heaven, I do love: and it hath taught me to rhyme, and to be melancholy; and here is part of my rhyme, and here my melancholy. Well, she hath one o' my sonnets already: the clown bore it, the fool sent it, and the lady hath it: sweet clown, sweeter fool, sweetest lady! By the world, I would not care a pin, if the other three were in. Here comes one with a paper: God give him grace to groan! [Stands aside

Enter the KING, with a paper

KING

Ay me!

BIRON

[*Aside*] Shot, by heaven! Proceed, sweet Cupid: thou hast thumped him with thy bird-bolt under the left pap. In faith, secrets!

KING

[*Reads*]

So sweet a kiss the golden sun gives not
  To those fresh morning drops upon the rose,
As thy eye-beams, when their fresh rays have smote
  The night of dew that on my cheeks down flows:
Nor shines the silver moon one half so bright
  Through the transparent bosom of the deep,
As doth thy face through tears of mine give light;
  Thou shinest in every tear that I do weep:
No drop but as a coach doth carry thee;
  So ridest thou triumphing in my woe.
Do but behold the tears that swell in me,
  And they thy glory through my grief will show:
But do not love thyself; then thou wilt keep
My tears for glasses, and still make me weep.
O queen of queens! how far dost thou excel,
No thought can think, nor tongue of mortal tell.

How shall she know my griefs? I'll drop the paper:—
Sweet leaves, shade folly. Who is he comes here?
                                        [*Steps aside*
What, Longaville! and reading! listen, ear.

BIRON

Now, in thy likeness, one more fool appear!
    Enter LONGAVILLE, *with a paper*

LONGAVILLE

Ay me, I am forsworn!

BIRON

Why, he comes in like a perjure, wearing papers.

KING

In love, I hope: sweet fellowship in shame!

BIRON

One drunkard loves another of the name.

LONGAVILLE

Am I the first that have been perjured so?

BIRON

I could put thee in comfort. Not by two that I know:
Thou makest the triumviry, the corner-cap of society,
The shape of Love's Tyburn that hangs up simplicity.

LONGAVILLE

I fear these stubborn lines lack power to move.
O sweet Maria, empress of my love!
These numbers will I tear, and write in prose.

BIRON

O, rhymes are guards on wanton Cupid's hose:
Disfigure not his slop.

LONGAVILLE

                    This same shall go.   [*Reads*

Did not the heavenly rhetoric of thine eye,
  'Gainst whom the world cannot hold argument,
Persuade my heart to this false perjury?
  Vows for thee broke deserve not punishment.
A woman I foreswore; but I will prove,
  Thou being a goddess, I foreswore not thee:
My vow was earthly, thou a heavenly love;
  Thy grace being gain'd cures all disgrace in me.

Vows are but breath, and breath a vapour is:
  Then thou, fair sun, which on my earth dost shine,
Exhalest this vapour-vow; in thee it is:
  If broken then, it is no fault of mine:
If by me broke, what fool is not so wise
To lose an oath to win a paradise?

BIRON

This is the liver-vein, which makes flesh a deity,
A green goose a goddess: pure, pure idolatry.
God amend us, God amend! we are much out o' the way.

LONGAVILLE

By whom shall I send this?—Company! stay.
                                        [*Steps aside*

BIRON

All hid, all hid, an old infant play.
Like a demigod here sit I in the sky,
And wretched fools' secrets heedfully o'er-eye.
More sacks to the mill! O heavens, I have my wish!
    Enter DUMAIN *with a paper*
Dumain transform'd! four woodcocks in a dish!

DUMAIN

O most divine Kate!

BIRON

O most profane coxcomb!

DUMAIN

By heaven, the wonder in a mortal eye!

BIRON

By earth, she is not, corporal, there you lie.

DUMAIN

Her amber hairs for foul hath amber quoted.

BIRON

An amber-colour'd raven was well noted.

DUMAIN

As upright as the cedar.

BIRON

                    Stoop, I say;
Her shoulder is with child.

DUMAIN

                    As fair as day.

BIRON

Ay, as some days; but then no sun must shine.

DUMAIN

O that I had my wish!

LONGAVILLE

                    And I had mine!

KING

And I mine too, good Lord!

BIRON

Amen, so I had mine: is not that a good word?

DUMAIN

I would forget her; but a fever she
Reigns in my blood, and will remember'd be.

BIRON

A fever in your blood! why, then incision
Would let her out in saucers: sweet misprision!

DUMAIN

Once more I'll read the ode that I have writ.

BIRON

Once more I'll mark how love can vary wit.

[295]

DUMAIN

[Reads]

On a day—alack the day!—
Love, whose month is ever May,
Spied a blossom passing fair
Playing in the wanton air:
Through the velvet leaves the wind,
All unseen, can passage find;
That the lover, sick to death,
Wish himself the heaven's breath.
Air, quoth he, thy cheeks may blow;
Air, would I might triumph so!
But, alack, my hand is sworn
Ne'er to pluck thee from thy thorn;
Vow, alack, for youth unmeet,
Youth so apt to pluck a sweet!
Do not call it sin in me,
That I am forsworn for thee;
Thou for whom Jove would swear
Juno but an Ethiope were;
And deny himself for Jove,
Turning mortal for thy love.

This will I send and something else more plain,
That shall express my true love's fasting pain.
O, would the king, Biron, and Longaville,
Were lovers too! Ill, to example ill,
Would from my forehead wipe a perjured note;
For none offend where all alike do dote.

LONGAVILLE

[Advancing] Dumain, thy love is far from charity,
That in love's grief desirest society:
You may look pale, but I should blush, I know,
To be o'erheard and taken napping so.

KING

[Advancing] Come, sir, you blush; as his your case is
    such;
You chide at him, offending twice as much;
You do not love Maria; Longaville
Did never sonnet for her sake compile,
Nor never lay his wreathed arms athwart
His loving bosom, to keep down his heart.
I have been closely shrouded in this bush
And mark'd you both and for you both did blush:
I heard your guilty rhymes, observed your fashion,
Saw sighs reek from you, noted well your passion:
Ay me! says one; O Jove! the other cries;
One, her hairs were gold, crystal the other's eyes:
You would for paradise break faith and troth;
                [To LONGAVILLE
And Jove, for your love, would infringe an oath.
                [To DUMAIN
What will Biron say when that he shall hear
Faith infringed, which such zeal did swear?
How will he scorn! how will he spend his wit!
How will he triumph, leap and laugh at it!
For all the wealth that ever I did see,
I would not have him know so much by me.

BIRON

Now step I forth to whip hypocrisy.   [Advancing
Ah, good my liege, I pray thee, pardon me!
Good heart, what grace hast thou, thus to reprove
These worms for loving, that art most in love?
Your eyes do make no coaches; in your tears

There is no certain princess that appears;
You'll not be perjured, 'tis a hateful thing;
Tush, none but minstrels like of sonneting!
But are you not ashamed? nay, are you not,
All three of you, to be thus much o'ershot?
You found his mote; the king your mote did see;
But I a beam do find in each of three.
O, what a scene of foolery have I seen,
Of sighs, of groans, of sorrow and of teen!
O me, with what strict patience have I sat,
To see a king transformed to a gnat!
To see great Hercules whipping a gig,
And profound Solomon to tune a jig,
And Nestor play at push-pin with the boys,
And critic Timon laugh at idle toys!
Where lies thy grief, O, tell me, good Dumain?
And, gentle Longaville, where lies thy pain?
And where my liege's? all about the breast:
A caudle, ho!

KING

           Too bitter is thy jest.
Are we betray'd thus to thy over-view?

BIRON

Not you to me, but I betray'd by you:
I, that am honest; I, that hold it sin
To break the vow I am engaged in;
I am betray'd, by keeping company
With men like you, men of inconstancy.
When shall you see me write a thing in rhyme?
Or groan for love? or spend a minute's time
In pruning me? When shall you hear that I
Will praise a hand, a foot, a face, an eye,
A gait, a state, a brow, a breast, a waist,
A leg, a limb?—

KING

           Soft! whither away so fast?
A true man or a thief that gallops so?

BIRON

I post from love: good lover, let me go.
        Enter JAQUENETTA and COSTARD

JAQUENETTA

God bless the king!

KING

           What present hast thou there?

COSTARD

Some certain treason.

KING

           What makes treason here?

COSTARD

Nay, it makes nothing, sir.

KING

           If it mar nothing neither,
The treason and you go in peace away together.

JAQUENETTA

I beseech your Grace, let this letter be read:
Our parson misdoubts it; 'twas treason, he said.

KING

Biron, read it over.   [Giving him the paper
Where hadst thou it?

JAQUENETTA
Of Costard.

KING
Where hadst thou it?

COSTARD
Of Dun Adramadio, Dun Adramadio.
[BIRON *tears the letter*

KING
How now! what is in you? why dost thou tear it?

BIRON
A toy, my liege, a toy: your Grace needs not fear it.

LONGAVILLE
It did move him to passion, and therefore let's hear
it.

DUMAIN
It is Biron's writing, and here is his name.
[*Gathering up the pieces*

BIRON
[*To* COSTARD] Ah, you whoreson loggerhead! you
were born to do me shame.
Guilty, my lord, guilty! I confess, I confess.

KING
What?

BIRON
That you three fools lack'd me fool to make up the
mess:
He, he, and you, and you, my liege, and I,
Are pick-purses in love, and we deserve to die.
O, dismiss this audience, and I shall tell you more.

DUMAIN
Now the number is even.

BIRON
True, true; we are four.
Will these turtles be gone?

KING
Hence, sirs; away!

COSTARD
Walk aside the true folk, and let the traitors stay.
[*Exeunt* COSTARD *and* JAQUENETTA

BIRON
Sweet lords, sweet lovers, O, let us embrace!
As true we are as flesh and blood can be:
The sea will ebb and flow, heaven show his face;
Young blood doth not obey an old decree:
We cannot cross the cause why we were born;
Therefore of all hands must we be forsworn.

KING
What, did these rent lines show some love of thine?

BIRON
Did they, quoth you? Who sees the heavenly Rosa-
line,
That, like a rude and savage man of Inde,
At the first opening of the gorgeous east,
Bows not his vassal head and strucken blind
Kisses the base ground with obedient breast?
What peremptory eagle-sighted eye
Dares look upon the heaven of her brow,
That is not blinded by her majesty?

KING
What zeal, what fury hath inspired thee now?

My love, her mistress, is a gracious moon;
She an attending star, scarce seen a light.

BIRON
My eyes are then no eyes, nor I Biron:
O, but for my love, day would turn to night!
Of all complexions the cull'd sovereignty
Do meet, as at a fair, in her fair cheek;
Where several worthies make one dignity,
Where nothing wants that want itself doth seek.
Lend me the flourish of all gentle tongues,—
Fie, painted rhetoric! O, she needs it not:
To things of sale a seller's praise belongs,
She passes praise; then praise too short doth blot.
A wither'd hermit, five-score winters worn,
Might shake off fifty, looking in her eye:
Beauty doth varnish age, as if new-born
And gives the crutch the cradle's infancy:
O, 'tis the sun that maketh all things shine.

KING
By heaven, thy love is black as ebony.

BIRON
Is ebony like her? O wood divine!
A wife of such wood were felicity.
O, who can give an oath? where is a book?
That I may swear beauty doth beauty lack,
If that she learn not of her eye to look:
No face is fair that is not full so black.

KING
O paradox! Black is the badge of hell,
The hue of dungeons and the school of night;
And beauty's crest becomes the heavens well.

BIRON
Devils soonest tempt, resembling spirits of light.
O, if in black my lady's brows be deck'd,
It mourns that painting and usurping hair
Should ravish doters with a false aspect;
And therefore is she born to make black fair.
Her favour turns the fashion of the days,
For native blood is counted painting now;
And therefore red, that would avoid dispraise,
Paints itself black, to imitate her brow.

DUMAIN
To look like her are chimney-sweepers black.

LONGAVILLE
And since her time are colliers counted bright.

KING
And Ethiopes of their sweet complexion crack.

DUMAIN
Dark needs no candles now, for dark is light.

BIRON
Your mistresses dare never come in rain,
For fear their colours should be wash'd away.

KING
'Twere good, yours did; for, sir, to tell you plain,
I'll find a fairer face not wash'd to-day.

BIRON
I'll prove her fair, or talk till doomsday here.

KING
No devil will fright thee then so much as she.

DUMAIN

I never knew man hold vile stuff so dear.

LONGAVILLE

Look, here's thy love: my foot and her face see.

BIRON

O, if the streets were paved with thine eyes,
Her feet were much too dainty for such tread!

DUMAIN

O vile! then, as she goes, what upward lies
The street should see as she walk'd overhead.

KING

But what of this? are we not all in love?

BIRON

Nothing so sure; and thereby all forsworn.

KING

Then leave this chat; and, good Biron, now prove
Our loving lawful, and our faith not torn.

DUMAIN

Ay, marry, there; some flattery for this evil.

LONGAVILLE

O, some authority how to proceed;
Some tricks, some quillets, how to cheat the devil.

DUMAIN

Some salve for perjury.

BIRON

'Tis more than need.

Have at you, then, affection's men at arms.
Consider what you first did swear unto,
To fast, to study, and to see no woman;
Flat treason 'gainst the kingly state of youth.
Say, can you fast? your stomachs are too young;
And abstinence engenders maladies.
And where that you have vow'd to study, lords,
In that each of you have forsworn his book,
Can you still dream and pore and thereon look?
For when would you, my Lord, or you, or you,
Have found the ground of study's excellence
Without the beauty of a woman's face?
From women's eyes this doctrine I derive;
They are the ground, the books, the academes
From whence doth spring the true Promethean fire.
Why, universal plodding prisons up
The nimble spirits in the arteries,
As motion and long-during action tires
The sinewy vigour of the traveller.
Now, for not looking on a woman's face,
You have in that forsworn the use of eyes
And study too, the causer of your vow;
For where is any author in the world
Teaches such beauty as a woman's eye?
Learning is but an adjunct to ourself,
And where we are our learning likewise is,
Then when ourselves we see in ladies' eyes,
Do we not likewise see our learning there?
O, we have made a vow to study, lords,
And in that vow we have forsworn our books.
For when would you, my liege, or you, or you,
In leaden contemplation have found out
Such fiery numbers as the prompting eyes
Of beauty's tutors have enrich'd you with?

Other slow arts entirely keep the brain;
And therefore, finding barren practisers,
Scarce show a harvest of their heavy toil:
But love, first learned in a lady's eyes,
Lives not alone immured in the brain;
But, with the motion of all elements,
Courses as swift as thought in every power,
And gives to every power a double power,
Above their functions and their offices.
It adds a precious seeing to the eye;
A lover's eyes will gaze an eagle blind;
A lover's ear will hear the lowest sound,
When the suspicious head of theft is stopp'd:
Love's feeling is more soft and sensible
Than are the tender horns of cockled snails;
Love's tongue proves dainty Bacchus gross in taste:
For valour, is not Love a Hercules,
Still climbing trees in the Hesperides?
Subtle as Sphinx; as sweet and musical
As bright Apollo's lute, strung with his hair;
And when Love speaks, the voice of all the gods
Make heaven drowsy with the harmony.
Never durst poet touch a pen to write
Until his ink were temper'd with Love's sighs;
O, then his lines would ravish savage ears,
And plant in tyrants mild humility.
From women's eyes this doctrine I derive:
They sparkle still the right Promethean fire;
They are the books, the arts, the academes,
That show, contain and nourish all the world:
Else none at all in aught proves excellent.
Then fools you were these women to forswear;
Or keeping what is sworn, you will prove fools.
For wisdom's sake, a word that all men love;
Or for love's sake, a word that loves all men;
Or for men's sake, the authors of these women;
Or women's sake, by whom we men are men;
Let us once lose our oaths to find ourselves,
Or else we lose ourselves to keep our oaths.
It is religion to be thus forsworn,
For charity itself fulfils the law,
And who can sever love from charity?

KING

Saint Cupid, then! and, soldiers, to the field!

BIRON

Advance your standards, and upon them, lords;
Pell-mell, down with them! but be first advised,
In conflict that you get the sun of them.

LONGAVILLE

Now to plain-dealing; lay these glozes by:
Shall we resolve to woo these girls of France?

KING

And win them too: therefore let us devise
Some entertainment for them in their tents.

BIRON

First, from the park let us conduct them thither;
Then homeward every man attach the hand
Of his fair mistress: in the afternoon
We will with some strange pastime solace them,
Such as the shortness of the time can shape;

For revels, dances, masks and merry hours
Forerun fair Love, strewing her way with flowers.

KING

Away, away! no time shall be omitted
That will betime, and may by us be fitted.

BIRON

Allons! allons! Sow'd cockle reap'd no corn;
  And justice always whirls in equal measure:
Light wenches may prove plagues to men forsworn;
  If so, our copper buys no better treasure. [*Exeunt*

ACT V

SCENE I. *The same*

Enter HOLOFERNES, SIR NATHANIEL, *and* DULL

HOLOFERNES

Satis quod sufficit.

NATHANIEL

I praise God for you, sir: your reasons at dinner
have been sharp and sententious; pleasant without
scurrility, witty without affection, audacious without
impudency, learned without opinion, and strange
without heresy. I did converse this quondam day
with a companion of the king's, who is intituled,
nominated, or called, Don Adriano de Armado.

HOLOFERNES

Novi hominem tanquam te: his humour is lofty, his
discourse peremptory, his tongue filed, his eye ambitious, his gait majestical, and his general behaviour vain, ridiculous, and thrasonical. He is too
picked, too spruce, too affected, too odd, as it were,
too peregrinate, as I may call it.

NATHANIEL

A most singular and choice epithet.
                    [*Draws out his table-book*

HOLOFERNES

He draweth out the thread of his verbosity finer
than the staple of his argument. I abhor such fanat-
ical phantasimes, such insociable and point-devise
companions; such rackers of orthography, as to
speak dout, fine, when he should say doubt; det,
when he should pronounce debt,—d, e, b, t, not
d, e, t: he clepeth a calf, cauf; half, hauf; neighbour
vocatur nebour; neigh abbreviated ne. This is ab-
hominable,—which he would call abbominable: it
insinuateth me of insanie: ne intelligis, domine? to
make frantic, lunatic.

NATHANIEL

Laus Deo, bene intelligo.

HOLOFERNES

Bon, bon, fort bon! Priscian a little scratched; 'twill
serve.

NATHANIEL

Videsne quis venit?

HOLOFERNES

Video, et gaudeo.

Enter ARMADO, MOTH, *and* COSTARD

ARMADO

Chirrah!   [*To* MOTH

HOLOFERNES

Quare chirrah, not sirrah?

ARMADO

Men of peace, well encountered.

HOLOFERNES

Most military sir, salutation.

MOTH

[*Aside to* COSTARD] They have been at a great feast of
languages, and stolen the scraps.

COSTARD

O, they have lived long on the alms-basket of words.
I marvel thy master hath not eaten thee for a word;
for thou art not so long by the head as honorificabi-
litudinitatibus: thou art easier swallowed than a
flap-dragon.

MOTH

Peace! the peal begins.

ARMADO

[*To* HOLOFERNES] Monsieur, are you not lettered?

MOTH

Yes, yes; he teaches boys the horn-book.
What is a, b, spelt backward, with the horn on his
head?

HOLOFERNES

Ba, pueritia, with a horn added.

MOTH

Ba, most silly sheep with a horn. You hear his learning.

HOLOFERNES

Quis, quis, thou consonant?

MOTH

The third of the five vowels, if you repeat them; or
the fifth, if I.

HOLOFERNES

I will repeat them,—a, e, i,—

MOTH

The sheep: the other two concludes it,—o, u.

ARMADO

Now, by the salt wave of the Mediterraneum, a
sweet touch, a quick venue of wit,—snip, snap,
quick and home! it rejoiceth my intellect: true wit!

MOTH

Offered by a child to an old man; which is wit-old.

HOLOFERNES

What is the figure? what is the figure?

MOTH

Horns.

HOLOFERNES

Thou disputest like an infant: go, whip thy gig.

MOTH

Lend me your horn to make one, and I will whip
about your infamy circum circa,—a gig of a cuckold's horn.

COSTARD

An I had but one penny in the world, thou shouldst
have it to buy gingerbread: hold, there is the very

remuneration I had of thy master, thou halfpenny purse of wit, thou pigeon-egg of discretion. O, an the heavens were so pleased that thou wert but my bastard, what a joyful father wouldst thou make me! Go to; thou hast it ad dunghill, at the finger's ends, as they say.

HOLOFERNES

O, I smell false Latin; dunghill for unguem.

ARMADO

Arts-man, preambulate, we will be singuled from the barbarous. Do you not educate youth at the charge-house on the top of the mountain?

HOLOFERNES

Or mons, the hill.

ARMADO

At your sweet pleasure, for the mountain.

HOLOFERNES

I do, sans question.

ARMADO

Sir, it is the king's most sweet pleasure and affection to congratulate the princess at her pavilion in the posteriors of this day, which the rude multitude call the afternoon.

HOLOFERNES

The posterior of the day, most generous sir, is liable, congruent and measurable for the afternoon: the word is well culled, chose, sweet and apt, I do assure you, sir, I do assure.

ARMADO

Sir, the king is a noble gentleman, and my familiar, I do assure ye, very good friend: for what is inward between us, let it pass. I do beseech thee, remember thy courtesy; I beseech thee, apparel thy head: and among other important and most serious designs, and of great import indeed, too, but let that pass: for I must tell thee, it will please his Grace, by the world, sometime to lean upon my poor shoulder, and with his royal finger, thus, dally with my excrement, with my mustachio; but, sweet heart, let that pass. By the world, I recount no fable: some certain special honours it pleaseth his greatness to impart to Armado, a soldier, a man of travel, that hath seen the world; but let that pass. The very all of all is,—but, sweet heart, I do implore secrecy,— that the king would have me present the princess, sweet chuck, with some delightful ostentation, or show, or pageant, or antique, or firework. Now, understanding that the curate and your sweet self are good at such eruptions and sudden breaking out of mirth, as it were, I have acquainted you withal, to the end to crave your assistance.

HOLOFERNES

Sir, you shall present before her the Nine Worthies. Sir, as concerning some entertainment of time, some show in the posterior of this day, to be rendered by our assistants, at the king's command, and this most gallant, illustrate, and learned gentleman, before the princess; I say none so fit as to present the Nine Worthies.

NATHANIEL

Where will you find men worthy enough to present them?

HOLOFERNES

Joshua, yourself; myself and this gallant gentleman, Judas Maccabæus; this swain, because of his great limb or joint, shall pass Pompey the Great; the page, Hercules,—

ARMADO

Pardon, sir; error: he is not quantity enough for that Worthy's thumb: he is not so big as the end of his club.

HOLOFERNES

Shall I have audience? he shall present Hercules in minority: his enter and exit shall be strangling a snake; and I will have an apology for that purpose.

MOTH

An excellent device! so, if any of the audience hiss, you may cry, 'Well done, Hercules! now thou crushest the snake!' that is the way to make an offence gracious, though few have the grace to do it.

ARMADO

For the rest of the Worthies?—

HOLOFERNES

I will play three myself.

MOTH

Thrice-worthy gentleman!

ARMADO

Shall I tell you a thing?

HOLOFERNES

We attend.

ARMADO

We will have, if this fadge not, an antique. I beseech you, follow.

HOLOFERNES

Via, goodman Dull! thou hast spoken no word all this while.

DULL

Nor understood none neither, sir.

HOLOFERNES

Allons! we will employ thee.

DULL

I'll make one in a dance, or so; or I will play
On the tabor to the Worthies, and let them dance
　the hay.

HOLOFERNES

Most dull, honest Dull! To our sport, away!

[*Exeunt*

SCENE II. *The same*

Enter the PRINCESS, KATHARINE, ROSALINE, *and* MARIA

PRINCESS

Sweet hearts, we shall be rich ere we depart,
If fairings come thus plentifully in:
A lady wall'd about with diamonds!
Look you what I have from the loving king.

ROSALINE

Madam, came nothing else along with that?

PRINCESS

Nothing but this! yes, as much love in rhyme
As would be cramm'd up in a sheet of paper,
Writ o' both sides the leaf, margent and all,
That he was fain to seal on Cupid's name.

ROSALINE

That was the way to make his godhead wax,
For he hath been five thousand years a boy.

KATHARINE

Ay, and a shrewd unhappy gallows too.

ROSALINE

You'll ne'er be friends with him; a' kill'd your sister.

KATHARINE

He made her melancholy, sad, and heavy;
And so she died: had she been light, like you,
Of such a merry, nimble, stirring spirit,
She might ha' been a grandam ere she died:
And so may you; for a light heart lives long.

ROSALINE

What's your dark meaning, mouse, of this light
    word?

KATHARINE

A light condition in a beauty dark.

ROSALINE

We need more light to find your meaning out.

KATHARINE

You'll mar the light by taking it in snuff;
Therefore I'll darkly end the argument.

ROSALINE

Look, what you do, you do it still i' th' dark.

KATHARINE

So do not you, for you are a light wench.

ROSALINE

Indeed I weigh not you, and therefore light.

KATHARINE

You weigh me not?—O, that's you care not for me.

ROSALINE

Great reason; for 'past cure is still past care.'

PRINCESS

Well bandied both; a set of wit well play'd.
But, Rosaline, you have a favour too:
Who sent it? and what is it?

ROSALINE

               I would you knew:
And if my face were but as fair as yours,
My favour were as great; be witness this.
Nay, I have verses too, I thank Biron:
The numbers true; and, were the numbering too,
I were the fairest goddess on the ground:
I am compared to twenty thousand fairs.
O, he hath drawn my picture in his letter!

PRINCESS

Any thing like?

ROSALINE

Much in the letters; nothing in the praise.

PRINCESS

Beauteous as ink; a good conclusion.

KATHARINE

Fair as a text B in a copy-book.

ROSALINE

'Ware pencils, ho! let me not die your debtor,
My red dominical, my golden letter:
O that your face were not so full of O's!

KATHARINE

A pox of that jest! and I beshrew all shrows.

PRINCESS

But, Katharine, what was sent to you from fair
    Dumain?

KATHARINE

Madam, this glove.

PRINCESS

           Did he not send you twain?

KATHARINE

Yes, madam, and, moreover,
Some thousand verses of a faithful lover,
A huge translation of hypocrisy,
Vilely compiled, profound simplicity.

MARIA

This and these pearls to me sent Longaville:
The letter is too long by half a mile.

PRINCESS

I think no less. Dost thou not wish in heart
The chain were longer and the letter short?

MARIA

Ay, or I would these hands might never part.

PRINCESS

We are wise girls to mock our lovers so.

ROSALINE

They are worse fools to purchase mocking so.
That same Biron I'll torture ere I go:
O that I knew he were but in by the week!
How I would make him fawn, and beg, and seek,
And wait the season, and observe the times,
And spend his prodigal wits in bootless rhymes,
And shape his service wholly to my hests,
And make him proud to make me proud that jests
So perttaunt-like would I o'ersway his state,
That he should be my fool, and I his fate.

PRINCESS

None are so surely caught, when they are catch'd,
As wit turn'd fool: folly, in wisdom hatch'd,
Hath wisdom's warrant and the help of school,
And wit's own grace to grace a learned fool.

ROSALINE

The blood of youth burns not with such excess
As gravity's revolt to wantonness.

MARIA

Folly in fools bears not so strong a note
As foolery in the wise, when wit doth dote;
Since all the power thereof it doth apply
To prove, by wit, worth in simplicity.

PRINCESS

Here comes Boyet, and mirth is in his face.

Enter BOYET

BOYET

O, I am stabb'd with laughter! Where's her Grace?

PRINCESS

Thy news, Boyet?

BOYET

Prepare, madam, prepare!
Arm, wenches, arm! encounters mounted are
Against your peace: Love doth approach disguised,
Armed in arguments; you'll be surprised:
Muster your wits; stand in your own defence;
Or hide your heads like cowards, and fly hence.

PRINCESS

Saint Denis to Saint Cupid! What are they
That charge their breath against us? say, scout, say.

BOYET

Under the cool shade of a sycamore
I thought to close mine eyes some half an hour;
When, lo! to interrupt my purposed rest,
Toward that shade I might behold addrest
The king and his companions: warily
I stole into a neighbour thicket by,
And overheard what you shall overhear;
That, by and by, disguised they will be here.
Their herald is a pretty knavish page,
That well by heart hath conn'd his embassage:
Action and accent did they teach him there;
'Thus must thou speak,' and 'thus thy body bear:'
And ever and anon they made a doubt
Presence majestical would put him out;
'For,' quoth the king, 'an angel shalt thou see;
Yet fear not thou, but speak audaciously.'
The boy replied, 'An angel is not evil;
I should have fear'd her, had she been a devil.'
With that, all laugh'd, and clapped him on the
    shoulder,
Making the bold wag by their praises bolder:
One rubb'd his elbow thus, and fleer'd and swore
A better speech was never spoke before;
Another, with his finger and his thumb,
Cried, 'Via! we will do't, come what will come;'
The third he caper'd, and cried, 'All goes well;'
The fourth turn'd on the toe, and down he fell.
With that, they all did tumble on the ground,
With such a zealous laughter, so profound,
That in this spleen ridiculous appears,
To check their folly, passion's solemn tears.

PRINCESS

But what, but what, come they to visit us?

BOYET

They do, they do; and are apparell'd thus,
Like Muscovites or Russians, as I guess.
Their purpose is to parle, to court and dance;
And every one his love-feat will advance
Unto his several mistress, which they'll know
By favours several which they did bestow.

PRINCESS

And will they so? the gallants shall be task'd;
For, ladies, we will every one be mask'd;
And not a man of them shall have the grace,
Despite of suit, to see a lady's face.
Hold, Rosaline, this favour thou shalt wear,
And then the king will court thee for his dear;
Hold, take thou this, my sweet, and give me thine,
So shall Biron take me for Rosaline.

And change you favours too; so shall your loves
Woo contrary, deceived by these removes.

ROSALINE

Come on, then; wear the favours most in sight.

KATHARINE

But in this changing what is your intent?

PRINCESS

The effect of my intent is to cross theirs:
They do it but in mocking merriment;
And mock for mock is only my intent.
Their several counsels they unbosom shall
To loves mistook, and so be mock'd withal
Upon the next occasion that we meet,
With visages display'd, to talk and greet.

ROSALINE

But shall we dance, if they desire us to't?

PRINCESS

No, to the death, we will not move a foot:
Nor to their penn'd speech render we no grace;
But while 'tis spoke each turn away her face.

BOYET

Why, that contempt will kill the speaker's heart,
And quite divorce his memory from his part.

PRINCESS

Therefore I do it; and I make no doubt
The rest will ne'er come in, if he be out.
There's no such sport as sport by sport o'erthrown;
To make theirs ours, and ours none but our own:
So shall we stay, mocking intended game,
And they, well mock'd, depart away with shame.

[Trumpets sound within

BOYET

The trumpet sounds: be mask'd; the maskers come.

[The LADIES mask

Enter BLACKAMOORS with music; MOTH; the KING,
BIRON, LONGAVILLE, and DUMAIN, in Russian habits,
and masked

MOTH

All hail, the richest beauties on the earth!—

BOYET

Beauties no richer than rich taffeta.

MOTH

A holy parcel of the fairest dames

[The LADIES turn their backs to him.

That ever turn'd their—backs—to mortal views!

BIRON

[Aside to MOTH] Their eyes, villain, their eyes.

MOTH

That ever turn'd their eyes to mortal views!—
Out—

BOYET

True; out indeed.

MOTH

Out of your favours, heavenly spirits, vouchsafe
Not to behold—

BIRON

[Aside to MOTH] Once to behold, rogue.

MOTH

Once to behold with your sun-beamed eyes,
——with your sun-beamed eyes—

BOYET

They will not answer to that epithet;
You were best call it 'daughter-beamed eyes.'

MOTH

They do not mark me, and that brings me out.

BIRON

Is this your perfectness? be gone, you rogue!

[*Exit* MOTH

ROSALINE

What would these strangers? know their minds,
    Boyet:
If they do speak our language, 'tis our will
That some plain man recount their purposes:
Know what they would.

BOYET

What would you with the princess?

BIRON

Nothing but peace and gentle visitation.

ROSALINE

What would they, say they?

BOYET

Nothing but peace and gentle visitation.

ROSALINE

Why, that they have; and bid them so be gone.

BOYET

She says, you have it, and you may be gone.

KING

Say to her, we have measured many miles
To tread a measure with her on this grass.

BOYET

They say, that they have measured many a mile
To tread a measure with you on this grass.

ROSALINE

It is not so. Ask them how many inches
Is in one mile: if they have measured many,
The measure then of one is easily told.

BOYET

If to come hither you have measured miles,
And many miles, the princess bids you tell
How many inches doth fill up one mile.

BIRON

Tell her, we measure them by weary steps.

BOYET

She hears herself.

ROSALINE

                    How many weary steps,
Of many weary miles you have o'ergone,
Are number'd in the travel of one mile?

BIRON

We number nothing that we spend for you:
Our duty is so rich, so infinite,
That we may do it still without accompt.
Vouchsafe to show the sunshine of your face,
That we, like savages, may worship it.

ROSALINE

My face is but a moon, and clouded too.

KING

Blessed are clouds, to do as such clouds do!
Vouchsafe, bright moon, and these thy stars, to
    shine,
Those clouds removed, upon our watery eyne.

ROSALINE

O vain petitioner! beg a greater matter;
Thou now request'st but moonshine in the water.

KING

Then, in our measure do but vouchsafe one change.
Thou bid'st me beg: this begging is not strange.

ROSALINE

Play, music, then! Nay, you must do it soon.

[*Music plays*

Not yet! no dance! Thus change I like the moon.

KING

Will you not dance? How come you thus estranged?

ROSALINE

You took the moon at full, but now she's changed.

KING

Yet still she is the moon, and I the man.
The music plays; vouchsafe some motion to it.

ROSALINE

Our ears vouchsafe it.

KING

                        But your legs should do it.

ROSALINE

Since you are strangers, and come here by chance,
We'll not be nice: take hands. We will not dance.

KING

Why take we hands, then?

ROSALINE

                        Only to part friends:
Curtsey, sweet hearts; and so the measure ends.

KING

More measure of this measure; be not nice.

ROSALINE

We can afford no more at such a price.

KING

Prize you yourselves: what buys your company?

ROSALINE

Your absence only.

KING

                    That can never be.

ROSALINE

Then cannot we be bought: and so, adieu;
Twice to your visor, and half once to you.

KING

If you deny to dance, let's hold more chat.

ROSALINE

In private, then.

KING

                    I am best pleased with that.

[*They converse apart*

BIRON

White-handed mistress, one sweet word with thee.

PRINCESS

Honey, and milk, and sugar; there is three.

BIRON

Nay then, two treys, an if you grow so nice,

[303]

Metheglin, wort, and malmsey: well run, dice!
There's half-a-dozen sweets.

PRINCESS

            Seventh sweet, adieu:
Since you can cog, I'll play no more with you.

BIRON

One word in secret.

PRINCESS

            Let it not be sweet.

BIRON

Thou grievest my gall.

PRINCESS

            Gall! bitter.

BIRON

                Therefore meet.
[They converse apart

DUMAIN

Will you vouchsafe with me to change a word?

MARIA

Name it.

DUMAIN

      Fair lady,—

MARIA

           Say you so? Fair lord,—
Take that for your fair lady.

DUMAIN

            Please it you,
As much in private, and I'll bid adieu.
[They converse apart

KATHARINE

What, was your vizard made without a tongue?

LONGAVILLE

I know the reason, lady, why you ask.

KATHARINE

O for your reason! quickly, sir; I long.

LONGAVILLE

You have a double tongue within your mask,
And would afford my speechless vizard half.

KATHARINE

Veal, quoth the Dutchman. Is not 'veal' a calf?

LONGAVILLE

A calf, fair lady!

KATHARINE

      No, a fair lord calf.

LONGAVILLE

Let's part the word.

KATHARINE

      No, I'll not be your half:
Take all, and wean it; it may prove an ox.

LONGAVILLE

Look, how you butt yourself in these sharp mocks!
Will you give horns, chaste lady? do not so.

KATHARINE

Then die a calf, before your horns do grow.

LONGAVILLE

One word in private with you, ere I die.

KATHARINE

Bleat softly, then; the butcher hears you cry.
[They converse apart

BOYET

The tongues of mocking wenches are as keen
  As is the razor's edge invisible,
Cutting a smaller hair than may be seen;
  Above the sense of sense; so sensible
Seemeth their conference; their conceits have wings
Fleeter than arrows, bullets, wind, thought, swifter
    things.

ROSALINE

Not one word more, my maids; break off, break off.

BIRON

By heaven, all dry-beaten with pure scoff!

KING

Farewell, mad wenches; you have simple wits.

PRINCESS

Twenty adieus, my frozen Muscovits.
[Exeunts KING, LORDS, *and* BLACKAMOORS
Are these the breed of wits so wonder'd at?

BOYET

Tapers they are, with your sweet breaths puff'd out.

ROSALINE

Well-liking wits they have; gross, gross; fat, fat.

PRINCESS

O poverty in wit, kingly-poor flout!
Will they not, think you, hang themselves to-night?
  Or ever, but in vizards, show their faces?
This pert Biron was out of countenance quite.

ROSALINE

O, they were all in lamentable cases!
The king was weeping-ripe for a good word.

PRINCESS

Biron did swear himself out of all suit.

MARIA

Dumain was at my service, and his sword:
No point, quoth I; my servant straight was mute.

KATHARINE

Lord Longaville said, I came o'er his heart;
And trow you what he call'd me?

PRINCESS

            Qualm, perhaps.

KATHARINE

Yes, in good faith.

PRINCESS

         Go, sickness as thou art!

ROSALINE

Well, better wits have worn plain statute-caps.
But will you hear? the king is my love sworn.

PRINCESS

And quick Biron hath plighted faith to me.

KATHARINE

And Longaville was for my service born.

MARIA

Dumain is mine, as sure as bark on tree.

BOYET

Madam, and pretty mistresses, give ear:
Immediately they will again be here
In their own shapes; for it can never be
They will digest this harsh indignity.

PRINCESS

Will they return?

BOYET

They will, they will, God knows,
And leap for joy, though they are lame with blows:
Therefore change favours; and, when they repair,
Blow like sweet roses in this summer air.

PRINCESS

How blow? how blow? speak to be understood.

BOYET

Fair ladies mask'd are roses in their bud;
Dismask'd, their damask sweet commixture shown,
Are angels vailing clouds, or roses blown.

PRINCESS

Avaunt, perplexity! What shall we do,
If they return in their own shapes to woo?

ROSALINE

Good madam, if by me you'll be advised,
Let's mock them still, as well known as disguised:
Let us complain to them what fools were here,
Disguised like Muscovites, in shapeless gear;
And wonder what they were and to what end
Their shallow shows and prologue vilely penn'd,
And their rough carriage so ridiculous,
Should be presented at our tent to us.

BOYET

Ladies, withdraw: the gallants are at hand.

PRINCESS

Whip to our tents, as roes run o'er land.
[*Exeunt* PRINCESS, ROSALINE, KATHARINE, *and* MARIA
Re-enter the KING, BIRON, LONGAVILLE, *and* DUMAIN, *in
their proper habits*

KING

Fair sir, God save you! Where's the princess?

BOYET

Gone to her tent. Please it your Majesty
Command me any service to her thither?

KING

That she vouchsafe me audience for one word.

BOYET

I will; and so will she, I know, my lord.   [*Exit*

BIRON

This fellow pecks up wit as pigeons pease,
And utters it again when God doth please:
He is wit's pedler, and retails his wares
At wakes and wassails, meetings, markets, fairs;
And we that sell by gross, the Lord doth know,
Have not the grace to grace it with such show.
This gallant pins the wenches on his sleeve;
Had he been Adam, he had tempted Eve;
A' can carve too, and lisp: why, this is he
That kiss'd his hand away in courtesy;
This is the ape of form, monsieur the nice,
That, when he plays at tables, chides the dice
In honourable terms: nay, he can sing
A mean most meanly; and in ushering,
Mend him who can: the ladies call him sweet;
The stairs, as he treads on them, kiss his feet:
This is the flower that smiles on every one,
To show his teeth as white as whale's bone;
And consciences, that will not die in debt,
Pay him the due of honey-tongued Boyet.

KING

A blister on his sweet tongue, with my heart,
That put Armado's page out of his part!

BIRON

See where it comes! Behaviour, what wert thou
Till this madman show'd thee? and what art thou
  now?
Re-enter the PRINCESS, *ushered by* BOYET; ROSALINE,
MARIA, *and* KATHARINE

KING

All hail, sweet madam, and fair time of day!

PRINCESS

'Fair' in 'all hail' is foul, as I conceive.

KING

Construe my speeches better, if you may.

PRINCESS

Then wish me better; I will give you leave.

KING

We came to visit you, and purpose now
To lead you to our court; vouchsafe it then.

PRINCESS

This field shall hold me; and so hold your vow:
Nor God, nor I, delights in perjured men.

KING

Rebuke me not for that which you provoke:
The virtue of your eye must break my oath.

PRINCESS

You nickname virtue; vice you should have spoke;
  For virtue's office never breaks men's troth.
Now by my maiden honour yet as pure
  As the unsullied lily I protest,
A world of torments though I should endure,
  I would not yield to be your house's guest;
So much I hate a breaking cause to be
Of heavenly oaths, vow'd with integrity.

KING

O, you have lived in desolation here,
  Unseen, unvisited, much to our shame.

PRINCESS

Not so, my lord; it is not so, I swear;
  We have had pastimes here and pleasant game:
A mess of Russians left us but of late.

KING

How, madam! Russians!

PRINCESS

                    Ay, in truth, my lord;
Trim gallants, full of courtship and of state.

ROSALINE

Madam, speak true. It is not so, my lord:
My lady, to the manner of the days,
In courtesy gives undeserving praise.
We four indeed confronted were with four
In Russian habit: here they stay'd an hour,
And talk'd apace; and in that hour, my lord,
They did not bless us with one happy word.
I dare not call them fools; but this I think,
When they are thirsty, fools would fain have drink.

BIRON

This jest is dry to me. Fair gentle sweet,
Your wit makes wise things foolish: when we greet,

With eyes best seeing, heaven's fiery eye,
By light we lose light: your capacity
Is of that nature that to your huge store
Wise things seem foolish and rich things but poor.
ROSALINE
This proves you wise and rich, for in my eye,—
BIRON
I am a fool, and full of poverty.
ROSALINE
But that you take what doth to you belong,
It were a fault to snatch words from my tongue.
BIRON
O, I am yours, and all that I possess!
ROSALINE
All the fool mine?
BIRON
I cannot give you less.
ROSALINE
Which of the vizards was it that you wore?
BIRON
Where? when? what vizard? why demand you this?
ROSALINE
There, then, that vizard; that superfluous case
That hid the worse, and show'd the better face.
KING
We are descried; they'll mock us now downright.
DUMAIN
Let us confess, and turn it to a jest.
PRINCESS
Amazed, my lord? why looks your highness sad?
ROSALINE
Help, hold his brows! he'll swound! Why look you
pale?
Sea-sick, I think, coming from Muscovy.
BIRON
Thus pour the stars down plagues for perjury.
Can any face of brass hold longer out?
Here stand I: lady, dart thy skill at me;
Bruise me with scorn, confound me with a flout;
Thrust thy sharp wit quite through my ignorance;
Cut me to pieces with thy keen conceit;
And I will wish thee never more to dance,
Nor never more in Russian habit wait.
O, never will I trust to speeches penn'd,
Nor to the motion of a schoolboy's tongue,
Nor never come in vizard to my friend;
Nor woo in rhyme, like a blind harper's song!
Taffeta phrases, silken terms precise,
Three-piled hyperboles, spruce affectation,
Figures pedantical; these summer-flies
Have blown me full of maggot ostentation:
I do forswear them; and I here protest,
By this white glove,—how white the hand, God
knows!—
Henceforth my wooing mind shall be express'd
In russet yeas, and honest kersey noes:
And, to begin, wench,—so God help me, la!—
My love to thee is sound, sans crack or flaw.
ROSALINE
Sans sans, I pray you.

BIRON
Yet I have a trick
Of the old rage:—bear with me, I am sick;
I'll leave it by degrees. Soft, let us see:
Write, 'Lord have mercy on us' on those three;
They are infected; in their hearts it lies;
They have the plague, and caught it of your eyes;
These lords are visited; you are not free,
For the Lord's tokens on you do I see.
PRINCESS
No, they are free that gave these tokens to us.
BIRON
Our states are forfeit: seek not to undo us.
ROSALINE
It is not so; for how can this be true,
That you stand forfeit, being those that sue?
BIRON
Peace! for I will not have to do with you.
ROSALINE
Nor shall not, if I do as I intend.
BIRON
Speak for yourselves; my wit is at an end.
KING
Teach us, sweet madam, for our rude transgression
Some fair excuse.
PRINCESS
The fairest is confession.
Were not you here but even now disguised?
KING
Madam, I was.
PRINCESS
And were you well advised?
KING
I was, fair madam.
PRINCESS
When you then were here.
What did you whisper in your lady's ear?
KING
That more than all the world I did respect her.
PRINCESS
When she shall challenge this, you will reject her.
KING
Upon mine honour, no.
PRINCESS
Peace, peace! forbear:
Your oath once broke, you force not to forswear.
KING
Despise me, when I break this oath of mine.
PRINCESS
I will: and therefore keep it. Rosaline,
What did the Russian whisper in your ear?
ROSALINE
Madam, he swore that he did hold me dear
As precious eyesight, and did value me
Above this world; adding thereto, moreover,
That he would wed me, or else die my lover.
PRINCESS
God give thee joy of him! the noble lord
Most honourably doth uphold his word.

KING

What mean you, madam? by my life, my troth,
I never swore this lady such an oath.

ROSALINE

By heaven, you did; and to confirm it plain,
You gave me this: but take it, sir, again.

KING

My faith and this the princess I did give:
I knew her by this jewel on her sleeve.

PRINCESS

Pardon me, sir, this jewel did she wear;
And Lord Biron, I thank him, is my dear.
What, will you have me, or your pearl again?

BIRON

Neither of either; I remit both twain.
I see the trick on't: here was a consent,
Knowing aforehand of our merriment,
To dash it like a Christmas comedy:
Some carry-tale, some please-man, some slight zany,
Some mumble-news, some trencher-knight, some
  Dick,
That smiles his cheek in years, and knows the trick
To make my lady laugh when she's disposed,
Told our intents before; which once disclosed,
The ladies did change favours; and then we,
Following the signs, woo'd but the sign of she.
Now, to our perjury to add more terror,
We are again forsworn, in will and error.
Much upon this it is: and might not you [To BOYET
Forestall our sport, to make us thus untrue?
Do not you know my lady's foot by the squier,
  And laugh upon the apple of her eye?
And stand between her back, sir, and the fire,
  Holding a trencher, jesting merrily?
You put our page out: go, you are allow'd;
Die when you will, a smock shall be your shroud.
You leer upon me, do you? there's an eye
Wounds like a leaden sword.

BOYET

          Full merrily
Hath this brave manage, this career, been run.

BIRON

Lo, he is tilting straight! Peace! I have done.
          Enter COSTARD
Welcome, pure wit! thou part'st a fair fray.

COSTARD

O Lord, sir, they would know
Whether the three Worthies shall come in or no.

BIRON

What, are there but three?

COSTARD

          No, sir; but it is vara fine,
For every one pursents three.

BIRON

          And three times thrice is nine.

COSTARD

Not so, sir; under correction, sir; I hope it is not so.
You cannot beg us, sir, I can assure you, sir; we
  know what we know:
I hope, sir, three times thrice, sir,—

BIRON

Is not nine.

COSTARD

Under correction, sir, we know whereuntil it doth
amount.

BIRON

By Jove, I always took three threes for nine.

COSTARD

O Lord, sir, it were pity you should get your living
by reckoning, sir.

BIRON

How much is it?

COSTARD

O Lord, sir, the parties themselves, the actors, sir,
will show whereuntil it doth amount: for mine own
part, I am, as they say, but to parfect one man in
one poor man,
Pompion the Great, sir.

BIRON

Art thou one of the Worthies?

COSTARD

It pleased them to think me worthy of Pompion the
Great: for mine own part, I know not the degree of
the Worthy, but I am to stand for him.

BIRON

Go, bid them prepare.

COSTARD

We will turn it finely off, sir; we will take some care.
          [*Exit*

KING

Biron, they will shame us: let them not approach.

BIRON

We are shame-proof, my lord: and 'tis some policy
To have one show worse than the king's and his
  company.

KING

I say they shall not come.

PRINCESS

Nay, my good lord, let me o'errule you now:
That sport best pleases that doth least know how:
Where zeal strives to content, and the contents
Dies in the zeal of that which it presents:
Their form confounded makes most form in mirth,
When great things labouring perish in their birth.

BIRON

A right description of our sport, my lord.
          Enter ARMADO

ARMADO

Anointed, I implore so much expense of thy royal
sweet breath as will utter a brace of words.
[*Converses apart with the* KING, *and delivers him a paper*

PRINCESS

Doth this man serve God?

BIRON

Why ask you?

PRINCESS

He speaks not like a man of God's making.

ARMADO

That is all one, my fair, sweet, honey monarch; for,
I protest, the schoolmaster is exceeding fantastical;

too too vain, too too vain: but we will put it, as they
say, to fortuna de la guerra. I wish you the peace of
mind, most royal couplement!   [*Exit*

KING

Here is like to be a good presence of Worthies.
He presents Hector of Troy; the swain, Pompey the
Great; the parish curate, Alexander; Armado's
page, Hercules; the pedant, Judas Maccabæus:
And if these four Worthies in their first show thrive,
These four will change habits, and present the other
   five.

BIRON

There is five in the first show.

KING

You are deceived; 'tis not so.

BIRON

The pedant, the braggart, the hedge-priest, the fool
and the boy:—
Abate throw at novum, and the whole world again
Cannot pick out five such, take each one in his vein.

KING

The ship is under sail, and here she comes amain.
          Enter COSTARD, *for* POMPEY

COSTARD

I Pompey am,—

BOYET

You lie, you are not he.

COSTARD

I Pompey am,—

BOYET

With libbard's head on knee.

BIRON

Well said, old mocker: I must needs be friends with
   thee.

COSTARD

I Pompey am, Pompey surnamed the Big,—

DUMAIN

The great.

COSTARD

It is, 'Great,' sir:—
          Pompey surnamed the Great;
That oft in field, with targe and shield, did make my foe to
   sweat:
And travelling along this coast, I here am come by chance,
And lay my arms before the legs of this sweet lass of France.

If your ladyship would say, 'Thanks, Pompey,' I
   had done.

PRINCESS

Great thanks, Great Pompey.

COSTARD

'Tis not so much worth; but I hope I was perfect:
I made a little fault in 'Great.'

BIRON

My hat to a halfpenny, Pompey proves the best
Worthy.
          Enter SIR NATHANIEL, *for* ALEXANDER

NATHANIEL

When in the world I lived, I was the world's commander;
By east, west, north, and south, I spread my conquering might:
My scutcheon plain declares that I am Alisander,—

BOYET

Your nose says, no, you are not; for it stands too
   right.

BIRON

Your nose smells 'no' in this, most tender-smelling
   knight.

PRINCESS

The conqueror is dismay'd. Proceed, good Alexander.

NATHANIEL

When in the world I lived, I was the world's commander,—

BOYET

Most true, 'tis right; you were so, Alisander.

BIRON

Pompey the Great,—

COSTARD

Your servant, and Costard.

BIRON

Take away the conqueror, take away Alisander.

COSTARD

[*To* SIR NATHANIEL] O, sir, you have overthrown
Alisander the conqueror! You will be scraped out of
the painted cloth for this: your lion, that holds his
poll-axe sitting on a close-stool, will be given to
Ajax: he will be the ninth Worthy. A conqueror,
and afeared to speak! run away for shame, Alisander.
[NATHANIEL *retires*] There, an't shall please you; a
foolish mild man; an honest man, look you, and
soon dashed. He is a marvellous good neighbour,
faith, and a very good bowler: but, for Alisander,—
alas, you see how 'tis,—a little o'erparted. But there
are Worthies a-coming will speak their mind in
some other sort.

PRINCESS

Stand aside, good Pompey.
Enter HOLOFERNES, *for* JUDAS; *and* MOTH, *for* HERCULES

HOLOFERNES

   Great Hercules is presented by this imp,
      Whose club kill'd Cerberus, that three-headed canis;
   And when he was a babe, a child, a shrimp,
      Thus did he strangle serpents in his manus.
   Quoniam he seemeth in minority,
   Ergo I come with this apology.

Keep some state in thy exit, and vanish.
          [MOTH *retires*

Judas I am,—

DUMAIN

A Judas!

HOLOFERNES

Not Iscariot, sir.
Judas I am, ycliped Maccabæus.

DUMAIN

Judas Maccabæus clipt is plain Judas.

BIRON

A kissing traitor. How art thou proved Judas?

HOLOFERNES

Judas I am,—

DUMAIN

The more shame for you, Judas.

HOLOFERNES

What mean you, sir?

BOYET

To make Judas hang himself.

HOLOFERNES

Begin, sir; you are my elder.

BIRON

Well followed: Judas was hanged on an elder.

HOLOFERNES

I will not be put out of countenance.

BIRON

Because thou hast no face.

HOLOFERNES

What is this?

BOYET

A cittern-head.

DUMAIN

The head of a bodkin.

BIRON

A Death's face in a ring.

LONGAVILLE

The face of an old Roman coin, scarce seen.

BOYET

The pommel of Cæsar's falchion.

DUMAIN

The carved-bone face on a flask.

BIRON

Saint George's half-cheek in a brooch.

DUMAIN

Ay, and in a brooch of lead.

BIRON

Ay, and worn in the cap of a tooth-drawer.
And now forward; for we have put thee in countenance.

HOLOFERNES

You have put me out of countenance.

BIRON

False: we have given thee faces.

HOLOFERNES

But you have out-faced them all.

BIRON

An thou wert a lion, we would do so.

BOYET

Therefore, as he is an ass, let him go.
And so adieu, sweet Jude! nay, why dost thou stay?

DUMAIN

For the latter end of his name.

BIRON

For the ass to the Jude; give it him:—Jud-as, away!

HOLOFERNES

This is not generous, not gentle, not humble.

BOYET

A light for Monsieur Judas! it grows dark, he may
stumble.   [HOLOFERNES retires

PRINCESS

Alas, poor Maccabæus, how hath he been baited!
Enter ARMADO, *for* HECTOR

BIRON

Hide thy head, Achilles: here comes Hector in arms.

DUMAIN

Though my mocks come home by me, I will now be
merry.

KING

Hector was but a Troyan in respect of this.

BOYET

But is this Hector?

KING

I think Hector was not so clean-timbered.

LONGAVILLE

His leg is too big for Hector's.

DUMAIN

More calf, certain.

BOYET

No; he is best indued in the small.

BIRON

This cannot be Hector.

DUMAIN

He's a god or a painter; for he makes faces.

ARMADO

The armipotent Mars, of lances the almighty,
   Gave Hector a gift,—

DUMAIN

A gilt nutmeg.

BIRON

A lemon.

LONGAVILLE

Stuck with cloves.

DUMAIN

No, cloven.

ARMADO

Peace!—
   The armipotent Mars, of lances the almighty,
     Gave Hector a gift, the heir of Ilion;
   A man so breathed, that certain he would fight ye,
     From morn till night, out of his pavilion.
   I am that flower,—

DUMAIN

        That mint.

LONGAVILLE

        That columbine.

ARMADO

Sweet Lord Longaville, rein thy tongue.

LONGAVILLE

I must rather give it the rein, for it runs against
Hector.

DUMAIN

Ay, and Hector's a greyhound.

ARMADO

The sweet war-man is dead and rotten; sweet
chucks, beat not the bones of the buried: when he
breathed, he was a man. But I will forward with my
device. [*To the* PRINCESS] Sweet royalty, bestow on
me the sense of hearing.

PRINCESS

Speak, brave Hector: we are much delighted.

ARMADO

I do adore thy sweet Grace's slipper.

BOYET

[*Aside to* DUMAIN] Loves her by the foot.

DUMAIN
[*Aside to* BOYET] He may not by the yard.

ARMADO
This Hector far surmounted Hannibal,—

COSTARD
The party is gone, fellow Hector, she is gone; she is two months on her way.

ARMADO
What meanest thou?

COSTARD
Faith, unless you play the honest Troyan, the poor wench is cast away: she's quick; the child brags in her belly already: 'tis yours.

ARMADO
Dost thou infamonize me among potentates? thou shalt die.

COSTARD
Then shall Hector be whipped for Jaquenetta that is quick by him, and hanged for Pompey that is dead by him.

DUMAIN
Most rare Pompey!

BOYET
Renowned Pompey!

BIRON
Greater than great, great, great, great Pompey! Pompey the Huge!

DUMAIN
Hector trembles.

BIRON
Pompey is moved. More Ates, more Ates! stir them on! stir them on!

DUMAIN
Hector will challenge him.

BIRON
Ay, if a' have no more man's blood in's belly than will sup a flea.

ARMADO
By the north pole, I do challenge thee.

COSTARD
I will not fight with a pole, like a northern man: I'll slash; I'll do it by the sword. I bepray you, let me borrow my arms again.

DUMAIN
Room for the incensed Worthies!

COSTARD
I'll do it in my shirt.

DUMAIN
Most resolute Pompey!

MOTH
Master, let me take you a button-hole lower. Do you not see Pompey is uncasing for the combat? What mean you? You will lose your reputation.

ARMADO
Gentlemen and soldiers, pardon me; I will not combat in my shirt.

DUMAIN
You may not deny it: Pompey hath made the challenge.

ARMADO
Sweet bloods, I both may and will.

BIRON
What reason have you for't?

ARMADO
The naked truth of it is, I have no shirt; I go woolward for penance.

BOYET
True, and it was enjoined him in Rome for want of linen: since when, I'll be sworn, he wore none but a dish-clout of Jaquenetta's, and that a' wears next his heart for a favour.

Enter MERCADE

MERCADE
God save you, madam!

PRINCESS
Welcome, Mercade;
But that thou interrupt'st our merriment.

MERCADE
I am sorry, madam; for the news I bring
Is heavy in my tongue. The king your father—

PRINCESS
Dead, for my life!

MERCADE
Even so; my tale is told.

BIRON
Worthies, away! the scene begins to cloud.

ARMADO
For mine own part, I breathe free breath. I have seen the day of wrong through the little hole of discretion, and I will right myself like a soldier.
[*Exeunt* WORTHIES

KING
How fares your majesty?

PRINCESS
Boyet, prepare; I will away to-night.

KING
Madam, not so; I do beseech you, stay.

PRINCESS
Prepare, I say. I thank you, gracious lords,
For all your fair endeavours; and entreat,
Out of a new-sad soul, that you vouchsafe
In your rich wisdom to excuse, or hide,
The liberal opposition of our spirits,
If over-boldly we have borne ourselves
In the converse of breath: your gentleness
Was guilty of it. Farewell, worthy lord!
A heavy heart bears not a nimble tongue:
Excuse me so, coming too short of thanks
For my great suit so easily obtain'd.

KING
The extreme parts of time extremely forms
All causes to the purpose of his speed;
And often, at his very loose, decides
That which long process could not arbitrate:
And though the mourning brow of progeny
Forbid the smiling courtesy of love
The holy suit which fain it would convince;
Yet, since love's argument was first on foot,
Let not the cloud of sorrow justle it

From what it purposed; since, to wail friends lost
Is not by much so wholesome-profitable
As to rejoice at friends but newly found.

PRINCESS

I understand you not: my griefs are double.

BIRON

Honest plain words best pierce the ear of grief;
And by these badges understand the king.
For your fair sakes have we neglected time,
Play'd foul play with our oaths: your beauty, ladies,
Hath much deform'd us, fashioning our humours
Even to the opposed end of our intents:
And what in us hath seem'd ridiculous,—
As love is full of unbefitting strains;
All wanton as a child, skipping, and vain;
Form'd by the eye, and therefore, like the eye,
Full of strange shapes, of habits and of forms,
Varying in subjects as the eye doth roll
To every varied object in his glance:
Which parti-coated presence of loose love
Put on by us, if, in your heavenly eyes,
Have misbecomed our oaths and gravities,
Those heavenly eyes, that look into these faults,
Suggested us to make. Therefore, ladies,
Our love being yours, the error that love makes
Is likewise yours: we to ourselves prove false,
By being once false for ever to be true
To those that make us both,—fair ladies, you:
And even that falsehood, in itself a sin,
Thus purifies itself, and turns to grace.

PRINCESS

We have received your letters full of love;
Your favours, the ambassadors of love;
And, in our maiden council, rated them
At courtship, pleasant jest and courtesy,
As bombast and as lining to the time:
But more devout than this in our respects
Have we not been; and therefore met your loves
In their own fashion, like a merriment.

DUMAIN

Our letters, madam, show'd much more than jest.

LONGAVILLE

So did our looks.

ROSALINE

We did not quote them so.

KING

Now, at the latest minute of the hour,
Grant us your loves.

PRINCESS

A time, methinks, too short
To make a world-without-end bargain in.
No, no, my lord, your grace is perjured much,
Full of dear guiltiness; and therefore this:—
If for my love, as there is no such cause,
You will do aught, this shall you do for me:
Your oath I will not trust; but go with speed
To some forlorn and naked hermitage,
Remote from all the pleasures of the world;
There stay until the twelve celestial signs
Have brought about the annual reckoning.

If this austere insociable life
Change not your offer made in heat of blood;
If frosts and fasts, hard lodging and thin weeds
Nip not the gaudy blossoms of your love,
But that it bear this trial, and last love;
Then, at the expiration of the year,
Come challenge me, challenge me by these deserts.
And, by this virgin palm now kissing thine,
I will be thine; and till that instant shut
My woeful self up in a mourning house,
Raining the tears of lamentation
For the remembrance of my father's death.
If this thou do deny, let our hands part,
Neither intitled in the other's heart.

KING

If this, or more than this, I would deny,
To flatter up these powers of mine with rest,
The sudden hand of death close up mine eye!
Hence ever then my heart is in thy breast.

BIRON

And what to me, my love? and what to me?

ROSALINE

You must be purged too, your sins are rack'd,
You are attaint with faults and perjury:
Therefore if you my favour mean to get,
A twelvemonth shall you spend, and never rest,
But seek the weary beds of people sick.

DUMAIN

But what to me, my love? but what to me?
A wife?

KATHARINE

A beard, fair health, and honesty;
With three-fold love I wish you all these three.

DUMAIN

O, shall I say, I thank you, gentle wife?

KATHARINE

Not so, my lord; a twelvemonth and a day
I'll mark no words that smooth-faced wooers say:
Come when the king doth to my lady come;
Then, if I have much love, I'll give you some.

DUMAIN

I'll serve thee true and faithfully till then.

KATHARINE

Yet swear not, lest ye be forsworn again.

LONGAVILLE

What says Maria?

MARIA

At the twelvemonth's end
I'll change my black gown for a faithful friend.

LONGAVILLE

I'll stay with patience; but the time is long.

MARIA

The liker you; few taller are so young.

BIRON

Studies my lady? mistress, look on me;
Behold the window of my heart, mine eye,
What humble suit attends thy answer there:
Impose some service on me for thy love.

ROSALINE

Oft have I heard of you, my Lord Biron,

[311]

Before I saw you; and the world's large tongue
Proclaims you for a man replete with mocks,
Full of comparisons and wounding flouts,
Which you on all estates will execute
That lie within the mercy of your wit.
To weed this wormwood from your fruitful brain,
And therewithal to win me, if you please,
Without the which I am not to be won,
You shall this twelvemonth term from day to day
Visit the speechless sick, and still converse
With groaning wretches; and your task shall be,
With all the fierce endeavour of your wit
To enforce the pained impotent to smile.

BIRON

To move wild laughter in the throat of death?
It cannot be; it is impossible:
Mirth cannot move a soul in agony.

ROSALINE

Why, that's the way to choke a gibing spirit,
Whose influence is begot of that loose grace
Which shallow laughing hearers give to fools:
A jest's prosperity lies in the ear
Of him that hears it, never in the tongue
Of him that makes it: then, if sickly ears,
Deaf'd with the clamours of their own dear groans,
Will hear your idle scorns, continue then,
And I will have you and that fault withal;
But if they will not, throw away that spirit,
And I shall find you empty of that fault,
Right joyful of your reformation.

BIRON

A twelvemonth! well; befall what will befall,
I'll jest a twelvemonth in an hospital.

PRINCESS

[To the KING] Ay, sweet my Lord; and so I take my
leave.

KING

No, madam; we will bring you on your way.

BIRON

Our wooing doth not end like an old play;
Jack hath not Jill: these ladies' courtesy
Might well have made our sport a comedy.

KING

Come, sir, it wants a twelvemonth and a day,
And then 'twill end.

BIRON

That's too long for a play.
Re-enter ARMADO

ARMADO

Sweet Majesty, vouchsafe me,—

PRINCESS

Was not that Hector?

DUMAIN

The worthy knight of Troy.

ARMADO

I will kiss thy royal finger, and take leave. I am a
votary; I have vowed to Jaquenetta to hold the
plough for her sweet love three years. But, most
esteemed greatness, will you hear the dialogue that
the two learned men have compiled in praise of the
owl and the cuckoo? it should have followed in the
end of our show.

KING

Call them forth quickly; we will do so.

ARMADO

Holla! approach.
Re-enter HOLOFERNES, NATHANIEL, MOTH, COSTARD,
and others
This side is Hiems, Winter, this Ver, the Spring; the
one maintained by the owl, the other by the cuckoo.
Ver, begin.

THE SONG

SPRING.   When daisies pied and violets blue
       And lady-smocks all silver-white
   And cuckoo-buds of yellow hue
       Do paint the meadows with delight,
   The cuckoo then, on every tree,
   Mocks married men; for thus sings he,
       Cuckoo;
   Cuckoo, cuckoo: O word of fear,
   Unpleasing to a married ear!

   When shepherds pipe on oaten straws,
       And merry larks are ploughmen's clocks,
   When turtles tread, and rooks, and daws,
       And maidens bleach their summer smocks,
   The cuckoo then, on every tree,
   Mocks married men; for thus sings he,
       Cuckoo;
   Cuckoo, cuckoo: O word of fear,
   Unpleasing to a married ear!

WINTER.   When icicles hang by the wall,
       And Dick the shepherd blows his nail,
   And Tom bears logs into the hall,
       And milk comes frozen home in pail,
   When blood is nipp'd and ways be foul,
   Then nightly sings the staring owl,
       Tu-whit;
   Tu-who, a merry note,
   While greasy Joan doth keel the pot.

   When all aloud the wind doth blow,
       And coughing drowns the parson's saw,
   And birds sit brooding in the snow,
       And Marian's nose looks red and raw,
   When roasted crabs hiss in the bowl,
   Then nightly sings the staring owl,
       Tu-whit;
   Tu-who, a merry note,
   While greasy Joan doth keel the pot.

ARMADO

The words of Mercury are harsh after the songs of
Apollo. You that way,—we this way.   [*Exeunt*

THE TRAGEDY OF ROMEO AND JULIET

SYNOPSIS

Caught in the deadly grip of an insensate hatred emanating from old family feuds, the members of the two distinguished Veronese houses of Capulet and Montague, from highest relative to lowest servant, become continually embroiled in bickerings, fierce quarrels, and occasional bloodshed when they encounter each other in the quiet streets of the town. The Prince of Verona, together with the citizenry, resent these disturbances, and the Prince finally declares the lives of the next offenders to be forfeited.

Passionate hatred flares out, however, when the Capulets discover that Romeo, heir of the Montagues, has come, uninvited and disguised, to the great banquet given by old Lord Capulet to his intimate friends.

Unknown to the others, Juliet, heiress of the Capulets, is approached after the dance by the handsome Romeo, who is charmed by her beauty and grace. A hasty, inconsiderate passion seizes both. That night, Juliet, having learned Romeo's name, appears on her balcony to mourn her secret to the moon and stars. Risking his life, Romeo has gained access to the orchard and is listening to her words. He makes himself known, and after many confessions and avowals, the lovers resolve to act secretly and speedily. They are married the next morning in the cell of the good Friar Laurence, who can deny nothing to his friend Romeo, and who devoutly hopes that the marriage will help to end the old family quarrel.

Juliet hastens home, and at noonday Romeo joins some companions in the streets who are contending with the furious Tybalt, nephew of Lady Capulet, still fuming over Romeo's intrusion at last night's ball. A devastating fight now occurs. Tybalt kills Romeo's friend, Mercutio. Romeo fights and kills Tybalt. A crowd gathers, including the heads of both houses; then the Prince of Verona himself arrives and immediately banishes Romeo from the land.

Juliet's father, knowing nothing of her secret marriage, decides that she shall marry the young Count Paris who loves her dearly, and arranges for early ceremonies. The despairing girl beseeches Friar Laurence to help her, and relies utterly upon the plan he suggests. She consents to the marriage, but on the morning of her wedding day drinks a potion prepared for her by the Friar which gives her every appearance of death. Heart-broken parents, sorrowing lover, distracted nurse, mourn her as dead, and she is carried to the ancient tomb of the Capulets.

Before Friar Laurence's letter of explanation can reach him, the exiled Romeo is informed by a fleet messenger of Juliet's death. He persuades a poverty-stricken apothecary to sell him enough poison to despatch twenty men to quick death, and sets out for the Capulet tomb.

Count Paris has come that night to strew Juliet's grave with tears and flowers, and intercepts Romeo brusquely as he is forcing the tomb open with wrenching irons. In his desperation Romeo fails to understand why Paris will not go away and leave him with his beloved dead. They fight, and Paris dies, pleading with his last breath to be laid near Juliet in death.

With gradually clearing vision, Romeo accedes and drags the dead body of Paris into Juliet's vault, whose dark horror seems to him to be filled with the radiance of her presence. He forgives his enemies, and makes to his Juliet his last protestations of undying affection. Raising the cup of poison to his lips, he drinks to his love, and dies.

Friar Laurence comes to the grave at the time when he knows Juliet will wake up. He finds bloody swords and the dead bodies of the two men, and quickly suggests to Juliet as she asks her first question that she escape at once from the tomb and find shelter with some sisterhood of holy nuns. She refuses the Friar's plea. Her only wish is to continue their perfect love by following her husband through death. She plunges Romeo's dagger into her heart, and falls across his body, dead.

Like wild fire, the news of these consummating tragedies flies through the town. The Prince of Verona and his attendants, with the households of the two warring factions, quickly gather at the Capulet tomb where Friar Laurence tells the entire story. The Prince points out the dreadful scourge which hate has brought upon these families, and Montague and Capulet join hands in peace over the poor sacrifices of their enmity.

HISTORICAL DATA

Although the Veronese give historical verity to this story of unhappy lovers by fixing the date of the tragedy as 1303, similar stories have been traced back as far as the second-century Greek romance *Anthia and Abrocomas*, by Xenophon Ephesius. In Italian literature it appears in the *Novellino* of Massuccio Salernitano (1476) and is retold by Luigi da Porto, who uses for the first time the names of Romeo and Giulietta, children of rival Veronese families. Bandello adapts the story in his *Novelle* (1554) which version was translated into French by Pierre Boisteau de Launay, and appeared in the *Histoires Tragiques* of his collaborator François de Belleforest (1559). From this source Arthur Brooke rendered it into English verse in his *Romeus and Juliet* (1562) and William Paynter translated it into English prose in his *Palace of Pleasure* (1567).

Shakespeare closely followed Brooke's metrical version, but as Brooke speaks of having seen "the same argument lately set forth on the stage" there is a possibility that Shakespeare also made use of an earlier non-extant English play, or possibly *La Hadriana*, a tragedy by an Italian actor-poet Luigi Proto (1578).

Basing their opinion largely on the Nurse's reference to the earthquake of eleven years before (Act I, Scene iii), which probably refers to the quake of 1580, many authorities fix the date of at least the first version of the play as 1591, but this is largely a matter of conjecture. It is known to have been played by "Lord Hunsdon's Servants" in 1596–7 and appeared in quarto form in the latter year.

"Good-night, good-night"
ROMEO AND JULIET

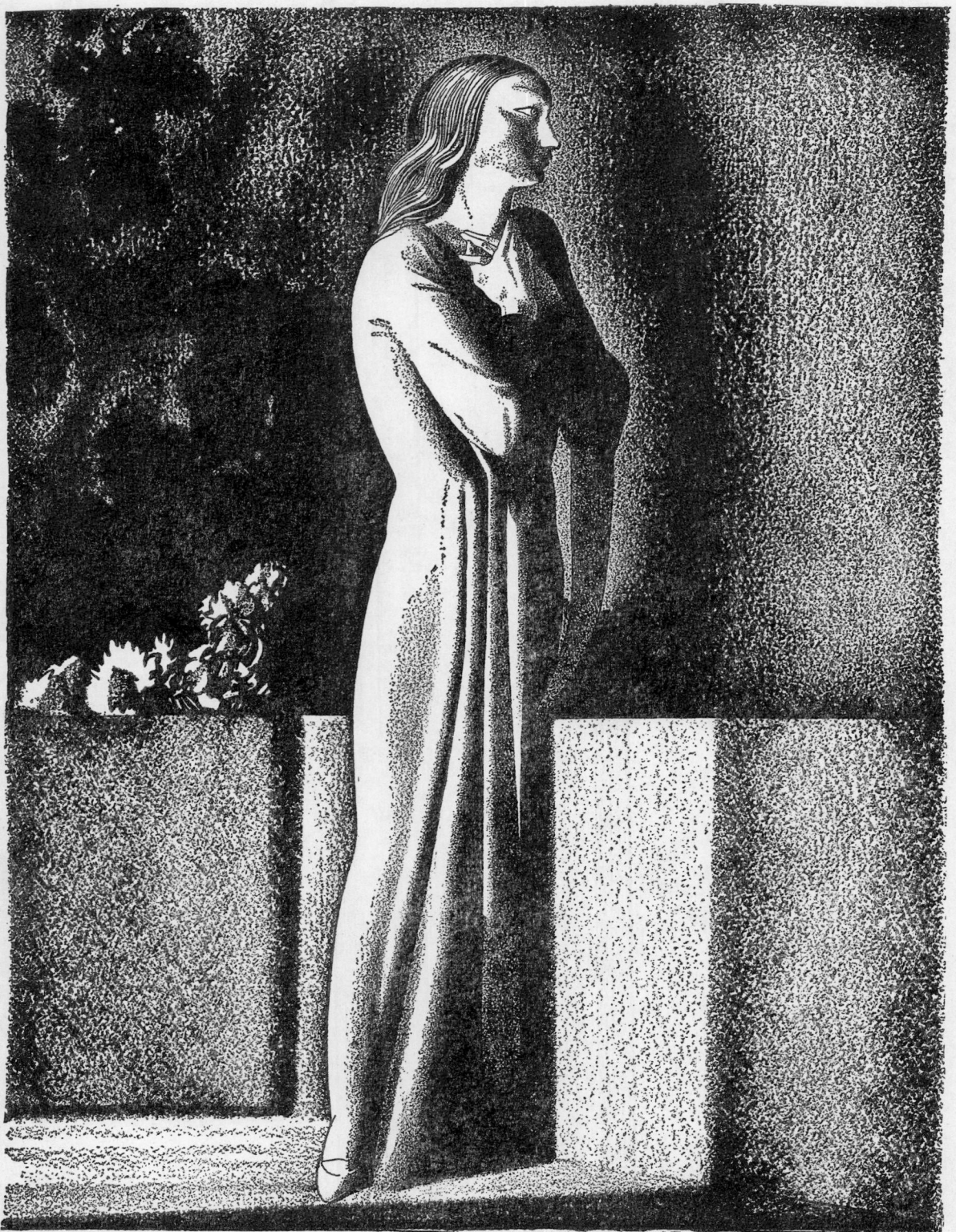

THE TRAGEDY OF ROMEO AND JULIET

DRAMATIS PERSONÆ

ESCALUS, *Prince of Verona.*
PARIS, *a young nobleman, kinsman to the Prince.*
MONTAGUE, } *heads of two houses at variance with*
CAPULET, } *each other.*
AN OLD MAN, *of the Capulet family.*
ROMEO, *son to Montague.*
MERCUTIO, *kinsman to the Prince, and friend to Romeo.*
BENVOLIO, *nephew to Montague, and friend to Romeo.*
TYBALT, *nephew to Lady Capulet.*
FRIAR LAURENCE, *a Franciscan.*
FRIAR JOHN, *of the same order.*
BALTHASAR, *servant to Romeo.*
SAMPSON, } *servants to Capulet.*
GREGORY, }
PETER, *servant to Juliet's nurse.*

ABRAHAM, *servant to Montague.*
AN APOTHECARY.
THREE MUSICIANS.
PAGE *to Paris; another* PAGE; *an* OFFICER.

LADY MONTAGUE, *wife to Montague.*
LADY CAPULET, *wife to Capulet.*
JULIET, *daughter to Capulet.*
NURSE *to Juliet.*

CITIZENS *of Verona:* KINSFOLK *of both houses;* MASKERS, GUARDS, WATCHMEN, *and* ATTENDANTS.

CHORUS

SCENE— *Verona; Mantua.*

PROLOGUE

Enter CHORUS
CHORUS

Two households, both alike in dignity,
  In fair Verona, where we lay our scene,
From ancient grudge break to new mutiny,
  Where civil blood makes civil hands unclean.
From forth the fatal loins of these two foes
  A pair of star-cross'd lovers take their life;
Whose misadventured piteous overthrows
  Do with their death bury their parents' strife.
The fearful passage of their death-mark'd love,
  And the continuance of their parents' rage,
Which, but their children's end, nought could remove,
  Is now the two hours traffic of our stage;
The which if you with patient ears attend,
What here shall miss, our toil shall strive to mend.

ACT I
SCENE I. *Verona. A public place*

Enter SAMPSON *and* GREGORY, *of the house of Capulet, with swords and bucklers*
SAMPSON
Gregory, on my word, we'll not carry coals.
GREGORY
No, for then we should be colliers.
SAMPSON
I mean, an we be in choler, we'll draw.

GREGORY
Ay, while you live, draw your neck out o' the collar.
SAMPSON
I strike quickly, being moved.
GREGORY
But thou art not quickly moved to strike.
SAMPSON
A dog of the house of Montague moves me.
GREGORY
To move is to stir, and to be valiant is to stand: therefore, if thou art moved, thou runn'st away.
SAMPSON
A dog of that house shall move me to stand: I will take the wall of any man or maid of Montague's.
GREGORY
That shows thee a weak slave; for the weakest goes to the wall.
SAMPSON
'Tis true; and therefore women, being the weaker vessels, are ever thrust to the wall: therefore I will push Montague's men from the wall and thrust his maids to the wall.
GREGORY
The quarrel is between our masters and us their men.
SAMPSON
'Tis all one, I will show myself a tyrant: when I have fought with the men, I will be cruel with the maids; I will cut off their heads.
GREGORY
The heads of the maids?
SAMPSON
Ay, the heads of the maids, or their maiden-heads; take it in what sense thou wilt.

[315]

GREGORY
They must take it in sense that feel it.

SAMPSON
Me they shall feel while I am able to stand: and 'tis known I am a pretty piece of flesh.

GREGORY
'Tis well thou art not fish; if thou hadst, thou hadst been poor John. Draw thy tool; here comes two of the house of Montagues.

Enter ABRAHAM *and* BALTHASAR

SAMPSON
My naked weapon is out: quarrel; I will back thee.

GREGORY
How! turn thy back and run?

SAMPSON
Fear me not.

GREGORY
No, marry; I fear thee!

SAMPSON
Let us take the law of our sides; let them begin.

GREGORY
I will frown as I pass by, and let them take it as they list.

SAMPSON
Nay, as they dare. I will bite my thumb at them; which is a disgrace to them, if they bear it.

ABRAHAM
Do you bite your thumb at us, sir?

SAMPSON
I do bite my thumb, sir.

ABRAHAM
Do you bite your thumb at us, sir?

SAMPSON
[*Aside to* GREGORY] Is the law of our side, if I say ay?

GREGORY
No.

SAMPSON
No, sir, I do not bite my thumb at you, sir; but I bite my thumb, sir.

GREGORY
Do you quarrel, sir?

ABRAHAM
Quarrel, sir! no, sir.

SAMPSON
But if you do, sir, I am for you: I serve as good a man as you.

ABRAHAM
No better.

SAMPSON
Well, sir.

Enter BENVOLIO

GREGORY
[*Aside to* SAMPSON] Say 'better': here comes one of my master's kinsmen.

SAMPSON
Yes, better, sir.

ABRAHAM
You lie.

SAMPSON
Draw, if you be men. Gregory, remember thy swashing blow.   [*They fight*

BENVOLIO
Part, fools!   [*Beating down their weapons*
Put up your swords; you know not what you do.

Enter TYBALT

TYBALT
What, art thou drawn among these heartless hinds?
Turn thee, Benvolio, look upon thy death.

BENVOLIO
I do but keep the peace: put up thy sword,
Or manage it to part these men with me.

TYBALT
What, drawn, and talk of peace! I hate the word,
As I hate hell, all Montagues, and thee:
Have at thee, coward!   [*They fight*

Enter several of both houses, who join the fray; then enter CITIZENS *and* PEACE-OFFICERS, *with clubs*

FIRST OFFICER
Clubs, bills, and partisans! strike! beat them down!
Down with the Capulets! down with the Montagues!

Enter old CAPULET *in his gown, and* LADY CAPULET

CAPULET
What noise is this? Give me my long sword, ho!

LADY CAPULET
A crutch, a crutch! why call you for a sword?

CAPULET
My sword, I say! Old Montague is come,
And flourishes his blade in spite of me.

Enter old MONTAGUE *and* LADY MONTAGUE

MONTAGUE
Thou villain Capulet!—Hold me not, let me go.

LADY MONTAGUE
Thou shalt not stir one foot to seek a foe.

Enter PRINCE ESCALUS, *with his train*

PRINCE
Rebellious subjects, enemies to peace,
Profaners of this neighbour-stained steel,—
Will they not hear? What, ho! you men, you beasts,
That quench the fire of your pernicious rage
With purple fountains issuing from your veins,
On pain of torture, from those bloody hands
Throw your mistemper'd weapons to the ground,
And hear the sentence of your moved prince.
Three civil brawls, bred of an airy word,
By thee, old Capulet, and Montague,
Have thrice disturb'd the quiet of our streets,
And made Verona's ancient citizens
Cast by their grave beseeming ornaments,
To wield old partisans, in hands as old,
Canker'd with peace, to part your canker'd hate:
If ever you disturb our streets again,
Your lives shall pay the forfeit of the peace.
For this time, all the rest depart away:
You, Capulet, shall go along with me;
And, Montague, come you this afternoon,
To know our father pleasure in this case,

To old Free-town, our common judgement-place.
Once more, on pain of death, all men depart.

[Exeunt all but MONTAGUE, LADY
MONTAGUE, *and* BENVOLIO

MONTAGUE

Who set this ancient quarrel new abroach?
Speak, nephew, were you by when it began?

BENVOLIO

Here were the servants of your adversary
And yours close fighting ere I did approach:
I drew to part them: in the instant came
The fiery Tybalt, with his sword prepared;
Which, as he breathed defiance to my ears,
He swung about his head, and cut the winds,
Who, nothing hurt withal, hiss'd him in scorn:
While we were interchanging thrusts and blows,
Came more and more, and fought on part and part,
Till the prince came, who parted either part.

LADY MONTAGUE

O, where is Romeo? saw you him to-day?
Right glad I am he was not at this fray.

BENVOLIO

Madam, an hour before the worshipp'd sun
Peer'd forth the golden window of the east,
A troubled mind drave me to walk abroad;
Where, underneath the grove of sycamore
That westward rooteth from the city's side,
So early walking did I see your son:
Towards him I made; but he was ware of me,
And stole into the covert of the wood:
I, measuring his affections by my own,
Which then most sought where most might not be
    found,
Being one too many by my weary self,
Pursued my humour, not pursuing his,
And gladly shunn'd who gladly fled from me.

MONTAGUE

Many a morning hath he there been seen,
With tears augmenting the fresh morning's dew,
Adding to clouds more clouds with his deep sighs:
But all so soon as the all-cheering sun
Should in the farthest east begin to draw
The shady curtains from Aurora's bed,
Away from light steals home my heavy son,
And private in his chamber pens himself,
Shuts up his windows, locks fair daylight out,
And makes himself an artificial night:
Black and portentous must this humour prove,
Unless good counsel may the cause remove.

BENVOLIO

My noble uncle, do you know the cause?

MONTAGUE

I neither know it nor can learn of him.

BENVOLIO

Have you importuned him by any means?

MONTAGUE

Both by myself and many other friends:
But he, his own affections' counsellor,
Is to himself—I will not say how true—

But to himself so secret and so close,
So far from sounding and discovery,
As is the bud bit with an envious worm,
Ere he can spread his sweet leaves to the air,
Or dedicate his beauty to the sun.
Could we but learn from whence his sorrows grow,
We would as willingly give cure as know.

Enter ROMEO

BENVOLIO

See, where he comes: so please you step aside,
I'll know his grievance, or be much denied.

MONTAGUE

I would thou wert so happy by thy stay,
To hear true shrift. Come, madam, let's away.

[Exeunt MONTAGUE *and* LADY

BENVOLIO

Good morrow, cousin.

ROMEO

         Is the day so young?

BENVOLIO

But new struck nine.

ROMEO

         Ay me! sad hours seem long.
Was that my father that went hence so fast?

BENVOLIO

It was. What sadness lengthens Romeo's hours?

ROMEO

Not having that which, having, makes them short.

BENVOLIO

In love?

ROMEO

Out—

BENVOLIO

Of love?

ROMEO

Out of her favour, where I am in love.

BENVOLIO

Alas, that love, so gentle in his view,
Should be so tyrannous and rough in proof!

ROMEO

Alas, that love, whose view is muffled still,
Should without eyes see pathways to his will!
Where shall we dine? O me! What fray was here?
Yet tell me not, for I have heard it all.
Here's much to do with hate, but more with love:
Why, then, O brawling love! O loving hate!
O any thing, of nothing first create!
O heavy lightness! serious vanity!
Mis-shapen chaos of well-seeming forms!
Feather of lead, bright smoke, cold fire, sick health!
Still-waking sleep, that is not what it is!
This love feel I, that feel no love in this.
Dost thou not laugh?

BENVOLIO

         No, coz, I rather weep.

ROMEO

Good heart, at what?

BENVOLIO

         At thy good heart's oppression.

ROMEO

Why, such is love's transgression.
Griefs of mine own lie heavy in my breast;
Which thou wilt propagate, to have it prest
With more of thine: this love that thou hast shown
Doth add more grief to too much of mine own.
Love is a smoke raised with the fume of sighs;
Being purged, a fire sparkling in lovers' eyes;
Being vex'd, a sea nourish'd with lovers' tears:
What is it else? a madness most discreet,
A choking gall and a preserving sweet.
Farewell, my coz.

BENVOLIO

Soft! I will go along:
And if you leave me so, you do me wrong.

ROMEO

Tut, I have lost myself; I am not here;
This is not Romeo, he's some other where.

BENVOLIO

Tell me in sadness, who is that you love?

ROMEO

What, shall I groan and tell thee?

BENVOLIO

Groan! why, no;
But sadly tell me who.

ROMEO

Bid a sick man in sadness make his will:
Ah, word ill urged to one that is so ill!
In sadness, cousin, I do love a woman.

BENVOLIO

I aim'd so near when I supposed you loved.

ROMEO

A right good mark-man! And she's fair I love.

BENVOLIO

A right fair mark, fair coz, is soonest hit.

ROMEO

Well, in that hit you miss: she'll not be hit
With Cupid's arrow; she hath Dian's wit,
And in strong proof of chastity well arm'd,
From love's weak childish bow she lives unharm'd.
She will not stay the siege of loving terms,
Nor bide the encounter of assailing eyes,
Nor ope her lap to saint-seducing gold:
O, she is rich in beauty, only poor
That, when she dies, with beauty dies her store.

BENVOLIO

Then she hath sworn that she will still live chaste?

ROMEO

She hath, and in that sparing makes huge waste;
For beauty, starved with her severity,
Cuts beauty off from all posterity.
She is too fair, too wise, wisely too fair,
To merit bliss by making me despair:
She hath forsworn to love; and in that vow
Do I live dead, that live to tell it now.

BENVOLIO

Be ruled by me, forget to think of her.

ROMEO

O, teach me how I should forget to think.

BENVOLIO

By giving liberty unto thine eyes;
Examine other beauties.

ROMEO

'Tis the way
To call hers, exquisite, in question more:
These happy masks that kiss fair ladies' brows,
Being black, put us in mind they hide the fair;
He that is strucken blind cannot forget
The precious treasure of his eyesight lost:
Show me a mistress that is passing fair,
What doth her beauty serve but as a note
Where I may read who pass'd that passing fair?
Farewell: thou canst not teach me to forget.

BENVOLIO

I'll pay that doctrine, or else die in debt.   [*Exeunt*

Scene II. *A street*

Enter CAPULET, PARIS, *and* SERVANT

CAPULET

But Montague is bound as well as I,
In penalty alike; and 'tis not hard, I think,
For men so old as we to keep the peace.

PARIS

Of honourable reckoning are you both;
And pity 'tis you lived at odds so long.
But now, my lord, what say you to my suit?

CAPULET

But saying o'er what I have said before:
My child is yet a stranger in the world;
She hath not seen the change of fourteen years:
Let two more summers wither in their pride
Ere we may think her ripe to be a bride.

PARIS

Younger than she are happy mothers made.

CAPULET

And too soon marr'd are those so early made.
The earth hath swallow'd all my hopes but she,
She is the hopeful lady of my earth:
But woo her, gentle Paris, get her heart;
My will to her consent is but a part;
An she agree, within her scope of choice
Lies my consent and fair according voice.
This night I hold an old accustom'd feast,
Whereto I have invited many a guest,
Such as I love; and you among the store,
One more, most welcome, makes my number more.
At my poor house look to behold this night
Earth-treading stars that make dark heaven light:
Such comfort as do lusty young men feel
When well-apparell'd April on the heel
Of limping winter treads, even such delight
Among fresh female buds shall you this night
Inherit at my house; hear all, all see,
And like her most whose merit most shall be:
Which on more view, of many mine being one
May stand in number, though in reckoning none.
Come, go with me. Go, sirrah, trudge about

Through fair Verona; find those persons out
Whose names are written there, and to them say,
My house and welcome on their pleasure stay.
                              [*Exeunt* CAPULET *and* PARIS
SERVANT
Find them out whose names are written here!
It is written that the shoemaker should meddle with
his yard and the tailor with his last, the fisher with
his pencil and the painter with his nets; but I am
sent to find those persons whose names are here writ,
and can never find what names the writing person
hath here writ. I must to the learned. In good time.

Enter BENVOLIO *and* ROMEO
BENVOLIO
Tut, man, one fire burns out another's burning.
  One pain is lessen'd by another's anguish;
Turn giddy, and be holp by backward turning;
  One desperate grief cures with another's languish:
Take thou some new infection to thy eye,
And the rank poison of the old will die.
ROMEO
Your plantain-leaf is excellent for that.
BENVOLIO
For what, I pray thee?
ROMEO
                              For your broken shin.
BENVOLIO
Why, Romeo, art thou mad?
ROMEO
Not mad, but bound more than a madman is;
Shut up in prison, kept without my food,
Whipt and tormented and—God-den, good fellow.
SERVANT
God gi' god-den. I pray, sir, can you read?
ROMEO
Ay, mine own fortune in my misery.
SERVANT
Perhaps you have learned it without book: but,
I pray, can you read any thing you see?
ROMEO
Ay, if I know the letters and the language.
SERVANT
Ye say honestly: rest you merry!
ROMEO
Stay, fellow; I can read.   [*Reads*
'Signior Martino and his wife and daughters;
County Anselme and his beauteous sisters; the lady
widow of Vitruvio; Signior Placentio and his lovely
nieces; Mercutio and his brother Valentine; mine
uncle Capulet, his wife, and daughters; my fair niece
Rosaline; Livia; Signior Valentio and his cousin
Tybalt; Lucio and the lively Helena.'
A fair assembly: whither should they come?
SERVANT
Up.
ROMEO
Whither?
SERVANT
To supper; to our house.

ROMEO
Whose house?
SERVANT
My master's.
ROMEO
Indeed, I should have ask'd you that before.
SERVANT
Now I'll tell you without asking: my master is the
great rich Capulet; and if you be not of the house of
Montagues, I pray, come and crush a cup of wine.
Rest you merry!   [*Exit*
BENVOLIO
At this same ancient feast of Capulet's
Sups the fair Rosaline whom thou so lovest,
With all the admired beauties of Verona:
Go thither, and with unattainted eye
Compare her face with some that I shall show,
And I will make thee think thy swan a crow.
ROMEO
When the devout religion of mine eye
Maintains such falsehood, then turn tears to fires;
And these, who, often drown'd, could never die,
    Transparent heretics, be burnt for liars!
One fairer than my love! the all-seeing sun
Ne'er saw her match since first the world begun.
BENVOLIO
Tut, you saw her fair, none else being by,
Herself poised with herself in either eye:
But in that crystal scales let there be weigh'd
Your lady's love against some other maid,
That I will show you shining at this feast,
And she shall scant show well that now seems best.
ROMEO
I'll go along, no such sight to be shown,
But to rejoice in splendour of mine own.   [*Exeunt*

SCENE III. *A room in* CAPULET'S *house*

Enter LADY CAPULET *and* NURSE
LADY CAPULET
Nurse, where's my daughter? call her forth to me.
NURSE
Now, by my maidenhead at twelve year old,
I bade her come. What, lamb! what, lady-bird!—
God forbid!—Where's this girl? What, Juliet!
Enter JULIET
JULIET
How now! who calls?
NURSE
Your mother.
JULIET
Madam, I am here. What is your will?
LADY CAPULET
This is the matter. Nurse, give leave awhile,
We must talk in secret:—nurse, come back again;
I have remember'd me, thou's hear our counsel.
Thou know'st my daughter's of a pretty age.
NURSE
Faith, I can tell her age unto an hour.

LADY CAPULET

She's not fourteen.

NURSE

I'll lay fourteen of my teeth,—
And yet, to my teen be it spoken, I have but four,—
She is not fourteen. How long is it now
To Lammas-tide?

LADY CAPULET

A fortnight and odd days.

NURSE

Even or odd, of all days in the year,
Come Lammas-eve at night shall she be fourteen.
Susan and she—God rest all Christian souls!—
Were of an age: well, Susan is with God;
She was too good for me:—but, as I said,
On Lammas-eve at night shall she be fourteen;
That shall she, marry; I remember it well.
'Tis since the earthquake now eleven years;
And she was wean'd,—I never shall forget it—
Of all the days of the year, upon that day:
For I had then laid wormwood to my dug,
Sitting in the sun under the dove-house wall;
My lord and you were then at Mantua:—
Nay, I do bear a brain:—but, as I said,
When it did taste the wormwood on the nipple
Of my dug, and felt it bitter, pretty fool,
To see it tetchy, and fall out with the dug!
Shake, quoth the dove-house: 'twas no need, I trow,
To bid me trudge.
And since that time it is eleven years;
For then she could stand high-lone; nay, by the
     rood,
She could have run and waddled all about;
For even the day before, she broke her brow:
And then my husband,—God be with his soul!
A' was a merry man—took up the child:
'Yea,' quoth he, 'dost thou fall upon thy face?
Thou wilt fall backward when thou hast more wit;
Wilt thou not, Jule?' and, by my holidame,
The pretty wretch left crying, and said 'Ay.'
To see now how a jest shall come about!
I warrant, an I should live a thousand years,
I never should forget it: 'Wilt thou not, Jule?' quoth
     he;
And, pretty fool, it stinted, and said 'Ay.'

LADY CAPULET

Enough of this; I pray thee, hold thy peace.

NURSE

Yes, madam: yet I cannot choose but laugh,
To think it should leave crying, and say 'Ay:'
And yet, I warrant, it had upon it brow
A bump as big as a young cockerel's stone;
A perilous knock; and it cried bitterly:
'Yea,' quoth my husband, 'fall'st upon thy face?
Thou wilt fall backward when thou comest to age;
Wilt thou not, Jule?' it stinted, and said 'Ay.'

JULIET

And stint thou too, I pray thee, nurse, say I.

NURSE

Peace, I have done. God mark thee to his grace!

Thou wast the prettiest babe that e'er I nursed:
An I might live to see thee married once,
I have my wish.

LADY CAPULET

Marry, that 'marry' is the very theme
I came to talk of. Tell me, daughter Juliet,
How stands your disposition to be married?

JULIET

It is an honour that I dream not of.

NURSE

An honour! were not I thine only nurse,
I would say thou hadst suck'd wisdom from thy teat.

LADY CAPULET

Well, think of marriage now; younger than you
Here in Verona, ladies of esteem,
Are made already mothers. By my count,
I was your mother much upon these years
That you are now a maid. Thus then in brief;
The valiant Paris seeks you for his love.

NURSE

A man, young lady! lady, such a man
As all the world—why, he's a man of wax.

LADY CAPULET

Verona's summer hath not such a flower.

NURSE

Nay, he's a flower; in faith, a very flower.

LADY CAPULET

What say you? can you love the gentleman?
This night you shall behold him at our feast:
Read o'er the volume of young Paris' face,
And find delight writ there with beauty's pen;
Examine every married lineament,
And see how one another lends content;
And what obscured in this fair volume lies
Find written in the margent of his eyes.
This precious book of love, this unbound lover,
To beautify him, only lacks a cover:
The fish lives in the sea; and 'tis much pride
For fair without the fair within to hide:
That book in many's eyes doth share the glory,
That in gold clasps locks in the golden story:
So shall you share all that he doth possess,
By having him making yourself no less.

NURSE

No less! nay, bigger: women grow by men.

LADY CAPULET

Speak briefly, can you like of Paris' love?

JULIET

I'll look to like, if looking liking move:
But no more deep will I endart mine eye
Than your consent gives strength to make it fly.

Enter a SERVINGMAN

SERVINGMAN

Madam, the guests are come, supper served up, you
called, my young lady asked for, the nurse cursed in
the pantry, and every thing in extremity. I must
hence to wait; I beseech you, follow straight.

LADY CAPULET

We follow thee. [*Exit* SERVINGMAN] Juliet, the
county stays.

NURSE

Go, girl, seek happy nights to happy days. [*Exeunt*

SCENE IV. *A street*

Enter ROMEO, MERCUTIO, BENVOLIO, *with five or six other* MASKERS, *and* TORCH-BEARERS

ROMEO

What, shall this speech be spoke for our excuse?
Or shall we on without apology?

BENVOLIO

The date is out of such prolixity:
We'll have no Cupid hoodwink'd with a scarf,
Bearing a Tartar's painted bow of lath,
Scaring the ladies like a crow-keeper;
Nor no without-book prologue, faintly spoke
After the prompter, for our entrance:
But, let them measure us by what they will,
We'll measure them a measure, and be gone.

ROMEO

Give me a torch: I am not for this ambling;
Being but heavy, I will bear the light.

MERCUTIO

Nay, gentle Romeo, we must have you dance.

ROMEO

Not I, believe me: you have dancing shoes
With n mble soles: I have a soul of lead
So stakes me to the ground, I cannot move.

MERCUTIO

You are a lover; borrow Cupid's wings,
And soar with them above a common bound.

ROMEO

I am too sore enpierced with his shaft
To soar with his light feathers, and so bound,
I cannot bound a pitch above dull woe:
Under love's heavy burthen do I sink.

MERCUTIO

And, to sink in it, should you burthen love;
Too great oppression for a tender thing.

ROMEO

Is love a tender thing? it is too rough,
Too rude, too boisterous, and it pricks like thorn.

MERCUTIO

If love be rough with you, be rough with love;
Prick love for pricking, and you beat love down.
Give me a case to put my visage in:
A visor for a visor! what care I
What curious eye doth quote deformities?
Here are the beetle-brows shall blush for me.

BENVOLIO

Come, knock and enter, and no sooner in
But every man betake him to his legs.

ROMEO

A torch for me: let wantons light of heart
Tickle the senseless rushes with their heels;
For I am proverb'd with a grandsire phrase;
I'll be a candle-holder, and look on.
The game was ne'er so fair, and I am done.

MERCUTIO

Tut, dun's the mouse, the constable's own word:
If thou art dun, we'll draw thee from the mire
Of this sir-reverence love, wherein thou stick'st
Up to the ears. Come, we burn daylight, ho.

ROMEO

Nay, that's not so.

MERCUTIO

I mean, sir, in delay
We waste our lights in vain, like lamps by day.
Take our good meaning, for our judgement sits
Five times in that ere once in our five wits.

ROMEO

And we mean well, in going to this mask;
But 'tis no wit to go.

MERCUTIO

Why, may one ask?

ROMEO

I dreamt a dream to-night.

MERCUTIO

And so did I.

ROMEO

Well, what was yours?

MERCUTIO

That dreamers often lie.

ROMEO

In bed asleep, while they do dream things true.

MERCUTIO

O, then, I see Queen Mab hath been with you.
She is the fairies' midwife, and she comes
In shape no bigger than an agate-stone
On the fore-finger of an alderman,
Drawn with a team of little atomies
Athwart men's noses as they lie asleep:
Her waggon-spokes made of long spinners' legs;
The cover, of the wings of grasshoppers;
Her traces, of the smallest spider's web;
Her collars, of the moonshine's watery beams;
Her whip, of cricket's bone; the lash, of film;
Her waggoner, a small grey-coated gnat,
Not half so big as a round little worm
Prick'd from the lazy finger of a maid:
Her chariot is an empty hazel-nut,
Made by the joiner squirrel or old grub,
Time out o' mind the fairies' coachmakers.
And in this state she gallops night by night
Through lovers' brains, and then they dream of love;
O'er courtiers' knees, that dream on court'sies straight;
O'er lawyers' fingers, who straight dream on fees;
O'er ladies' lips, who straight on kisses dream,
Which oft the angry Mab with blisters plagues,
Because their breaths with sweetmeats tainted are:
Sometime she gallops o'er a courtier's nose,
And then dreams he of smelling out a suit;
And sometime comes she with a tithe-pig's tail
Tickling a parson's nose as a' lies asleep,
Then dreams he of another benefice:
Sometime she driveth o'er a soldier's neck,
And then dreams he of cutting foreign throats,

Of breaches, ambuscadoes, Spanish blades,
Of healths five fathom deep; and then anon
Drums in his ear, at which he starts and wakes,
And being thus frighted swears a prayer or two,
And sleeps again. This is that very Mab
That plats the manes of horses in the night,
And bakes the elf-locks in foul sluttish hairs,
Which once untangled much misfortune bodes:
This is the hag, when maids lie on their backs,
That presses them and learns them first to bear,
Making them women of good carriage:
This is she—

ROMEO
       Peace, peace, Mercutio, peace!
Thou talk'st of nothing.

MERCUTIO
         True, I talk of dreams;
Which are the children of an idle brain,
Begot of nothing but vain fantasy,
Which is as thin of substance as the air,
And more inconstant than the wind, who wooes
Even now the frozen bosom of the north,
And, being anger'd, puffs away from thence,
Turning his face to the dew-dropping south.

BENVOLIO
This wind you talk of blows us from ourselves;
Supper is done, and we shall come too late.

ROMEO
I fear, too early: for my mind misgives
Some consequence, yet hanging in the stars,
Shall bitterly begin his fearful date
With this night's revels, and expire the term
Of a despised life closed in my breast,
By some vile forfeit of untimely death:
But He, that hath the steerage of my course,
Direct my sail! On, lusty gentlemen.

BENVOLIO
Strike, drum.   [*Exeunt*

SCENE V. *A hall in* CAPULET's *house*

MUSICIANS *waiting. Enter* SERVINGMEN, *with napkins*
FIRST SERVINGMAN
Where's Potpan, that he helps not to take away? he
shift a trencher! he scrape a trencher!

SECOND SERVINGMAN
When good manners shall lie all in one or two men's
hands, and they unwashed too, 'tis a foul thing.

FIRST SERVINGMAN
Away with the joint-stools, remove the court-
cupboard, look to the plate. Good thou, save me a
piece of marchpane; and, as thou lovest me, let the
porter let in Susan Grindstone and Nell. Antony,
and Potpan!

SECOND SERVINGMAN
Ay, boy, ready.

FIRST SERVINGMAN
You are looked for and called for, asked for and
sought for, in the great chamber.

THIRD SERVINGMAN
We cannot be here and there too. Cheerly, boys; be
brisk a while, and the longer liver take all.
                       [*They retire behind*
Enter CAPULET, *with* JULIET *and others of his house,*
         meeting the GUESTS *and* MASKERS
CAPULET
Welcome, gentlemen! ladies that have their toes
Unplagued with corns will have a bout with you:
Ah ha, my mistresses! which of you all
Will now deny to dance? she that makes dainty,
She, I'll swear, hath corns; am I come near ye now?
Welcome, gentlemen! I have seen the day
That I have worn a visor, and could tell
A whispering tale in a fair lady's ear,
Such as would please: 'tis gone, 'tis gone, 'tis gone:
You are welcome, gentlemen! Come, musicians,
  play.
A hall, a hall! give room! and foot it, girls.
               [*Music plays, and they dance*
More light, you knaves; and turn the tables up,
And quench the fire, the room is grown too hot.
Ah, sirrah, this unlook'd-for sport comes well.
Nay, sit, nay, sit, good cousin Capulet;
For you and I are past our dancing days:
How long is 't now since last yourself and I
Were in a mask?

SECOND CAPULET
       By 'r lady, thirty years.

CAPULET
What, man! 'tis not so much, 'tis not so much:
'Tis since the nuptial of Lucentio,
Come Pentecost as quickly as it will,
Some five and twenty years; and then we mask'd.

SECOND CAPULET
'Tis more, 'tis more: his son is elder, sir;
His son is thirty.

CAPULET
       Will you tell me that?
His son was but a ward two years ago.

ROMEO
[*To a* SERVINGMAN] What lady's that, which doth
  enrich the hand
Of yonder knight?

SERVINGMAN
I know not, sir.

ROMEO
O, she doth teach the torches to burn bright!
It seems she hangs upon the cheek of night
Like a rich jewel in an Ethiop's ear;
Beauty too rich for use, for earth too dear!
So shows a snowy dove trooping with crows,
As yonder lady o'er her fellows shows.
The measure done, I'll watch her place of stand,
And, touching hers, make blessed my rude hand.
Did my heart love till now? forswear it, sight!
For I ne'er saw true beauty till this night.

TYBALT
This, by his voice, should be a Montague
Fetch me my rapier, boy. What dares the slave

Come hither, cover'd with an antic face,
To fleer and scorn at our solemnity?
Now, by the stock and honour of my kin,
To strike him dead I hold it not a sin.

CAPULET

Why, how now, kinsman! wherefore storm you so?

TYBALT

Uncle, this is a Montague, our foe;
A villain, that is hither come in spite,
To scorn at our solemnity this night.

CAPULET

Young Romeo is it?

TYBALT

        'Tis he, that villain Romeo.

CAPULET

Content thee, gentle coz, let him alone,
He bears him like a portly gentleman;
And, to say truth, Verona brags of him
To be a virtuous and well-govern'd youth:
I would not for the wealth of all this town
Here in my house do him disparagement:
Therefore be patient, take no note of him:
It is my will, the which if thou respect,
Show a fair presence and put off these frowns,
An ill-beseeming semblance for a feast.

TYBALT

It fits, when such a villain is a guest:
I'll not endure him.

CAPULET

        He shall be endured:
What, goodman boy! I say, he shall: go to;
Am I the master here, or you? go to.
You'll not endure him! God shall mend my soul,
You'll make a mutiny among my guests!
You will set cock-a-hoop! you'll be the man!

TYBALT

Why, uncle, 'tis a shame.

CAPULET

        Go to, go to;
You are a saucy boy: is 't so, indeed?
This trick may chance to scathe you, I know what:
You must contrary me! marry, 'tis time.
Well said, my hearts! You are a princox; go:
Be quiet, or— More light, more light! For shame!
I'll make you quiet. What, cheerly, my hearts!

TYBALT

Patience perforce with wilful choler meeting
Makes my flesh tremble in their different greeting.
I will withdraw: but this intrusion shall,
Now seeming sweet, convert to bitterest gall. [Exit

ROMEO

[To JULIET] If I profane with my unworthiest hand
  This holy shrine, the gentle fine is this,
My lips, two blushing pilgrims, ready stand
  To smooth that rough touch with a tender kiss.

JULIET

Good pilgrim, you do wrong your hand too much,
  Which mannerly devotion shows in this;
For saints have hands that pilgrims' hands do touch,
  And palm to palm is holy palmers' kiss.

ROMEO

Have not saints lips, and holy palmers too?

JULIET

Ay, pilgrim, lips that they must use in prayer.

ROMEO

O, then, dear saint, let lips do what hands do;
  They pray, grant thou, lest faith turn to despair.

JULIET

Saints do not move, though grant for prayers' sake.

ROMEO

Then move not, while my prayer's effect I take.
Thus from my lips by thine my sin is purged.
                [Kissing her

JULIET

Then have my lips the sin that they have took.

ROMEO

Sin from my lips? O trespass sweetly urged!
  Give me my sin again.

JULIET

        You kiss by the book.

NURSE

Madam, your mother craves a word with you.

ROMEO

What is her mother?

NURSE

        Marry, bachelor,
Her mother is the lady of the house,
And a good lady, and a wise and virtuous:
I nursed her daughter, that you talk'd withal;
I tell you, he that can lay hold of her
Shall have the chinks.

ROMEO

        Is she a Capulet?
O dear account! my life is my foe's debt.

BENVOLIO

Away, be gone; the sport is at the best.

ROMEO

Ay, so I fear; the more is my unrest.

CAPULET

Nay, gentlemen, prepare not to be gone;
We have a trifling foolish banquet towards.
Is it e'en so? why, then, I thank you all;
I thank you, honest gentlemen; good night.
More torches here! Come on then, let's to bed.
Ah, sirrah, by my fay, it waxes late:
I'll to my rest.   [Exeunt all but JULIET and NURSE

JULIET

Come hither, nurse. What is yond gentleman?

NURSE

The son and heir of old Tiberio.

JULIET

What's he that now is going out of door?

NURSE

Marry, that, I think, be young Petruchio.

JULIET

What's he that follows there, that would not dance?

NURSE

I know not.

JULIET

Go ask his name. If he be married,
My grave is like to be my wedding bed.

NURSE

His name is Romeo, and a Montague,
The only son of your great enemy.

JULIET

My only love sprung from my only hate!
Too early seen unknown, and known too late!
Prodigious birth of love it is to me,
That I must love a loathed enemy.

NURSE

What's this? what's this?

JULIET

A rhyme I learn'd even now
Of one I danced withal.　　　[*One calls within 'Juliet'*

NURSE

Anon, anon!

Come, let's away; the strangers all are gone. [*Exeunt*

ACT II

PROLOGUE

Enter CHORUS

CHORUS

Now old desire doth in his death-bed lie,
　　And young affection gapes to be his heir;
That fair for which love groan'd for and would die,
　　With tender Juliet match'd, is now not fair.
Now Romeo is beloved and loves again,
　　Alike bewitched by the charm of looks,
But to his foe supposed he must complain,
　　And she steal love's sweet bait from fearful hooks:
Being held a foe, he may not have access
　　To breathe such vows as lovers use to swear;
And she as much in love, her means much less
　　To meet her new beloved any where:
But passion lends them power, time means, to meet,
Tempering extremities with extreme sweet.　　[*Exit*

SCENE I. *A lane by the wall of* CAPULET'S *orchard*

Enter ROMEO, *alone*

ROMEO

Can I go forward when my heart is here?
Turn back, dull earth, and find thy centre out.
　　[*He climbs the wall, and leaps down within it*
Enter BENVOLIO *with* MERCUTIO

BENVOLIO

Romeo! my cousin Romeo!

MERCUTIO

He is wise;
And, on my life, hath stol'n him home to bed.

BENVOLIO

He ran this way, and leap'd this orchard wall:
Call, good Mercutio.

MERCUTIO

Nay, I'll conjure too.
Romeo! humours! madman! passion! lover!
Appear thou in the likeness of a sigh:
Speak but one rhyme, and I am satisfied;
Cry but 'ay me!' pronounce but 'love' and 'dove;'
Speak to my gossip Venus one fair word,
One nick-name for her purblind son and heir,
Young Adam Cupid, he that shot so trim
When King Cophetua loved the beggar-maid!
He heareth not, he stirreth not, he moveth not;
The ape is dead, and I must conjure him.
I conjure thee by Rosaline's bright eyes,
By her high forehead and her scarlet lip,
By her fine foot, straight leg and quivering thigh,
And the demesnes that there adjacent lie,
That in thy likeness thou appear to us!

BENVOLIO

An if he hear thee, thou wilt anger him.

MERCUTIO

This cannot anger him: 'twould anger him
To raise a spirit in his mistress' circle
Of some strange nature, letting it there stand
Till she had laid it and conjured it down;
That were some spite: my invocation
Is fair and honest, and in his mistress' name
I conjure only but to raise up him.

BENVOLIO

Come, he hath hid himself among these trees,
To be consorted with the humorous night:
Blind is his love, and best befits the dark.

MERCUTIO

If love be blind, love cannot hit the mark.
Now will he sit under a medlar-tree,
And wish his mistress were that kind of fruit
As maids call medlars when they laugh alone.
O, Romeo, that she were, O, that she were
An open et cetera, thou a poperin pear!
Romeo, good night: I'll to my truckle-bed;
This field-bed is too cold for me to sleep:
Come, shall we go?

BENVOLIO

Go then, for 'tis in vain
To seek him here that means not to be found.
　　　　　　　　　　　　　　　　　　[*Exeunt*

SCENE II. CAPULET'S *orchard*

Enter ROMEO

ROMEO

He jests at scars that never felt a wound.
　　[JULIET *appears above at a window*
But, soft! what light through yonder window
　　breaks?
It is the east, and Juliet is the sun!
Arise, fair sun, and kill the envious moon,
Who is already sick and pale with grief,
That thou her maid art far more fair than she:
Be not her maid, since she is envious;
Her vestal livery is but sick and green,

And none but fools do wear it; cast it off.
It is my lady; O, it is my love!
O, that she knew she were!
She speaks, yet she says nothing: what of that?
Her eye discourses, I will answer it.
I am too bold, 'tis not to me she speaks:
Two of the fairest stars in all the heaven,
Having some business, do intreat her eyes
To twinkle in their spheres till they return.
What if her eyes were there, they in her head?
The brightness of her cheek would shame those stars,
As daylight doth a lamp; her eyes in heaven
Would through the airy region stream so bright
That birds would sing and think it were not night.
See, how she leans her cheek upon her hand!
O, that I were a glove upon that hand,
That I might touch that cheek!

JULIET

Ay me!

ROMEO

She speaks:

O, speak again, bright angel! for thou art
As glorious to this night, being o'er my head,
As is a winged messenger of heaven
Unto the white-upturned wondering eyes
Of mortals that fall back to gaze on him,
When he bestrides the lazy-pacing clouds
And sails upon the bosom of the air.

JULIET

O Romeo, Romeo! wherefore art thou Romeo?
Deny thy father and refuse thy name;
Or, if thou wilt not, be but sworn my love
And I'll no longer be a Capulet.

ROMEO

[Aside] Shall I hear more, or shall I speak at this?

JULIET

'Tis but thy name that is my enemy;
Thou art thyself, though not a Montague.
What's Montague? it is nor hand, nor foot,
Nor arm, nor face, nor any other part
Belonging to a man. O, be some other name!
What's in a name? that which we call a rose
By any other name would smell as sweet;
So Romeo would, were he not Romeo call'd,
Retain that dear perfection which he owes
Without that title. Romeo, doff thy name,
And for thy name, which is no part of thee,
Take all myself.

ROMEO

I take thee at thy word:
Call me but love, and I'll be new baptized;
Henceforth I never will be Romeo.

JULIET

What man art thou, that, thus bescreen'd in night,
So stumblest on my counsel?

ROMEO

By a name
I know not how to tell thee who I am:
My name, dear saint, is hateful to myself,

Because it is an enemy to thee;
Had I it written, I would tear the word.

JULIET

My ears have yet not drunk a hundred words
Of thy tongue's uttering, yet I know the sound:
Art thou not Romeo, and a Montague?

ROMEO

Neither, fair maid, if either thee dislike.

JULIET

How camest thou hither, tell me, and wherefore?
The orchard walls are high and hard to climb,
And the place death, considering who thou art,
If any of my kinsmen find thee here.

ROMEO

With love's light wings did I o'er-perch these walls,
For stony limits cannot hold love out:
And what love can do, that dares love attempt;
Therefore thy kinsmen are no let to me.

JULIET

If they do see thee, they will murder thee.

ROMEO

Alack, there lies more peril in thine eye
Than twenty of their swords: look thou but sweet,
And I am proof against their enmity.

JULIET

I would not for the world they saw thee here.

ROMEO

I have night's cloak to hide me from their eyes;
And but thou love me, let them find me here:
My life were better ended by their hate,
Than death prorogued, wanting of thy love.

JULIET

By whose direction found'st thou out this place?

ROMEO

By love, that first did prompt me to inquire;
He lent me counsel, and I lent him eyes.
I am no pilot; yet, wert thou as far
As that vast shore wash'd with the farthest sea,
I would adventure for such merchandise.

JULIET

Thou know'st the mask of night is on my face,
Else would a maiden blush bepaint my cheek
For that which thou hast heard me speak to-night.
Fain would I dwell on form, fain, fain deny
What I have spoke: but farewell compliment!
Dost thou love me? I know thou wilt say 'Ay,'
And I will take thy word: yet, if thou swear'st,
Thou mayst prove false: at lovers' perjuries,
They say, Jove laughs. O gentle Romeo,
If thou dost love, pronounce it faithfully:
Or if thou think'st I am too quickly won,
I'll frown and be perverse and say thee nay,
So thou wilt woo; but else, not for the world.
In truth, fair Montague, I am too fond;
And therefore thou mayst think my 'haviour light:
But trust me, gentleman, I'll prove more true
Than those that have more cunning to be strange.
I should have been more strange, I must confess,
But that thou overheard'st, ere I was ware,
My true love's passion: therefore pardon me,

And not impute this yielding to light love,
Which the dark night hath so discovered.

ROMEO
Lady, by yonder blessed moon I swear,
That tips with silver all these fruit-tree tops,—

JULIET
O, swear not by the moon, th' inconstant moon,
That monthly changes in her circled orb,
Lest that thy love prove likewise variable.

ROMEO
What shall I swear by?

JULIET
Do not swear at all;
Or, if thou wilt, swear by thy gracious self,
Which is the god of my idolatry,
And I'll believe thee.

ROMEO
If my heart's dear love—

JULIET
Well, do not swear: although I joy in thee,
I have no joy of this contract to-night:
It is too rash, too unadvised, too sudden,
Too like the lightning, which doth cease to be
Ere one can say 'It lightens.' Sweet, good night!
This bud of love, by summer's ripening breath,
May prove a beauteous flower when next we meet.
Good night, good night! as sweet repose and rest
Come to thy heart as that within my breast!

ROMEO
O, wilt thou leave me so unsatisfied?

JULIET
What satisfaction canst thou have to-night?

ROMEO
The exchange of thy love's faithful vow for mine.

JULIET
I gave thee mine before thou didst request it:
And yet I would it were to give again.

ROMEO
Wouldst thou withdraw it? for what purpose, love?

JULIET
But to be frank, and give it thee again.
And yet I wish but for the thing I have:
My bounty is as boundless as the sea,
My love as deep; the more I give to thee,
The more I have, for both are infinite.
I hear some noise within; dear love, adieu!

[NURSE calls within
Anon, good nurse! Sweet Montague, be true.
Stay but a little, I will come again.   [Exit

ROMEO
O blessed, blessed night! I am afeard,
Being in night, all this is but a dream,
Too flattering-sweet to be substantial.

Re-enter JULIET, above

JULIET
Three words, dear Romeo, and good night indeed.
If that thy bent of love be honourable,
Thy purpose marriage, send me word to-morrow,
By one that I'll procure to come to thee,
Where and what time thou wilt perform the rite,

And all my fortunes at thy foot I'll lay,
And follow thee my lord throughout the world.

NURSE
[Within] Madam!

JULIET
I come, anon.—But if thou mean'st not well, I do
beseech thee—

NURSE
[Within] Madam!

JULIET
By and by, I come:—
To cease thy suit, and leave me to my grief:
To-morrow will I send.

ROMEO
So thrive my soul,—

JULIET
A thousand times good night!   [Exit

ROMEO
A thousand times the worse, to want thy light.
Love goes toward love, as schoolboys from their
books,
But love from love, toward school with heavy looks.
[Retiring slowly

Re-enter JULIET, above

JULIET
Hist! Romeo, hist!—O, for a falconer's voice,
To lure this tassel-gentle back again!
Bondage is hoarse, and may not speak aloud;
Else would I tear the cave where Echo lies,
And make her airy tongue more hoarse than mine,
With repetition of my Romeo's name.
Romeo!

ROMEO
It is my soul that calls upon my name:
How silver-sweet sound lovers' tongues by night,
Like softest music to attending ears!

JULIET
Romeo!

ROMEO
My dear?

JULIET
At what o'clock to-morrow
Shall I send to thee?

ROMEO
At the hour of nine.

JULIET
I will not fail: 'tis twenty years till then.
I have forgot why I did call thee back.

ROMEO
Let me stand here till thou remember it.

JULIET
I shall forget, to have thee still stand there,
Remembering how I love thy company.

ROMEO
And I'll still stay, to have thee still forget,
Forgetting any other home but this.

JULIET
'Tis almost morning; I would have thee gone:
And yet no farther than a wanton's bird,
Who lets it hop a little from her hand,

[326]

Like a poor prisoner in his twisted gyves,
And with a silk thread plucks it back again,
So loving-jealous of his liberty.

ROMEO

I would I were thy bird.

JULIET

Sweet, so would I:
Yet I should kill thee with much cherishing.
Good night, good night! parting is such sweet
    sorrow
That I shall say good night till it be morrow. [Exit

ROMEO

Sleep dwell upon thine eyes, peace in thy breast!
Would I were sleep and peace, so sweet to rest!
Hence will I to my ghostly father's cell,
His help to crave and my dear hap to tell.   [Exit

SCENE III. FRIAR LAURENCE'S cell

Enter FRIAR LAURENCE, with a basket

FRIAR LAURENCE

The grey-eyed morn smiles on the frowning night,
Chequering the eastern clouds with streaks of light;
And flecked darkness like a drunkard reels
From forth day's path and Titan's fiery wheels:
Now, ere the sun advance his burning eye,
The day to cheer and night's dank dew to dry,
I must up-fill this osier cage of ours
With baleful weeds and precious-juiced flowers.
The earth that's nature's mother is her tomb;
What is her burying grave, that is her womb:
And from her womb children of divers kind
We sucking on her natural bosom find,
Many for many virtues excellent,
None but for some, and yet all different.
O, mickle is the powerful grace that lies
In herbs, plants, stones, and their true qualities:
For nought so vile that on the earth doth live,
But to the earth some special good doth give;
Nor aught so good, but, strain'd from that fair use,
Revolts from true birth, stumbling on abuse:
Virtue itself turns vice, being misapplied,
And vice sometime's by action dignified.
Within the infant rind of this small flower
Poison hath residence, and medicine power:
For this, being smelt, with that part cheers each
    part,
Being tasted, slays all senses with the heart.
Two such opposed kings encamp them still
In man as well as herbs, grace and rude will;
And where the worser is predominant,
Full soon the canker death eats up that plant.

Enter ROMEO

ROMEO

Good morrow, father.

FRIAR LAURENCE

Benedicite!
What early tongue so sweet saluteth me?
Young son, it argues a distemper'd head

So soon to bid good morrow to thy bed:
Care keeps his watch in every old man's eye,
And where care lodges, sleep will never lie;
But where unbruised youth with unstuff'd brain
Doth couch his limbs, there golden sleep doth reign:
Therefore thy earliness doth me assure
Thou art up-roused by some distemperature;
Or if not so, then here I hit it right,
Our Romeo hath not been in bed to-night.

ROMEO

That last is true; the sweeter rest was mine.

FRIAR LAURENCE

God pardon sin! wast thou with Rosaline?

ROMEO

With Rosaline, my ghostly father? no;
I have forgot that name and that name's woe.

FRIAR LAURENCE

That's my good son: but where hast thou been then?

ROMEO

I'll tell thee ere thou ask it me again.
I have been feasting with mine enemy;
Where on a sudden one hath wounded me,
That's by me wounded: both our remedies
Within thy help and holy physic lies:
I bear no hatred, blessed man, for, lo,
My intercession likewise steads my foe.

FRIAR LAURENCE

Be plain, good son, and homely in thy drift;
Riddling confession finds but riddling shrift.

ROMEO

Then plainly know my heart's dear love is set
On the fair daughter of rich Capulet:
As mine on hers, so hers is set on mine;
And all combined, save what thou must combine
By holy marriage: when, and where, and how,
We met, we woo'd and made exchange of vow,
I'll tell thee as we pass; but this I pray,
That thou consent to marry us to-day.

FRIAR LAURENCE

Holy Saint Francis, what a change is here!
Is Rosaline, that thou didst love so dear,
So soon forsaken? young men's love then lies
Not truly in their hearts, but in their eyes.
Jesu Maria, what a deal of brine
Hath wash'd thy sallow cheeks for Rosaline!
How much salt water thrown away in waste,
To season love, that of it doth not taste!
The sun not yet thy sighs from heaven clears,
Thy old groans ring yet in mine ancient ears;
Lo, here upon thy cheek the stain doth sit
Of an old tear that is not wash'd off yet:
If e'er thou wast thyself and these woes thine,
Thou and these woes were all for Rosaline:
And art thou changed? pronounce this sentence
    then:
Women may fall when there's no strength in men.

ROMEO

Thou chid'st me oft for loving Rosaline.

FRIAR LAURENCE

For doting, not for loving, pupil mine.

ROMEO

And bad'st me bury love.

FRIAR LAURENCE

　　　　Not in a grave,

To lay one in, another out to have.

ROMEO

I pray thee, chide not: she whom I love now

Doth grace for grace and love for love allow;

The other did not so.

FRIAR LAURENCE

　　　　O, she knew well

Thy love did read by rote and could not spell.

But come, young waverer, come, go with me,

In one respect I'll thy assistant be;

For this alliance may so happy prove,

To turn your households' rancour to pure love.

ROMEO

O, let us hence; I stand on sudden haste.

FRIAR LAURENCE

Wisely and slow; they stumble that run fast.

　　　　　　　　　　　　　　　[Exeunt

SCENE IV. *A street*

Enter BENVOLIO AND MERCUTIO

MERCUTIO

Where the devil should this Romeo be? Came he not
home to-night?

BENVOLIO

Not to his father's; I spoke with his man.

MERCUTIO

Ah, that same pale hard-hearted wench, that
　　Rosaline,

Torments him so that he will sure run mad.

BENVOLIO

Tybalt, the kinsman to old Capulet,

Hath sent a letter to his father's house.

MERCUTIO

A challenge, on my life.

BENVOLIO

Romeo will answer it.

MERCUTIO

Any man that can write may answer a letter.

BENVOLIO

Nay, he will answer the letter's master, how he
dares, being dared.

MERCUTIO

Alas, poor Romeo, he is already dead! stabbed with
a white wench's black eye; shot thorough the ear
with a love-song; the very pin of his heart cleft with
the blind bow-boy's butt-shaft: and is he a man to
encounter Tybalt?

BENVOLIO

Why, what is Tybalt?

MERCUTIO

More than prince of cats, I can tell you. O, he's the
courageous captain of compliments. He fights as
you sing prick-song, keeps time, distance and proportion; rests me his minim rest, one, two, and the
third in your bosom: the very butcher of a silk but-

ton, a duellist, a duellist; a gentleman of the very
first house, of the first and second cause: ah, the
immortal passado! the punto reverso! the hai!

BENVOLIO

The what?

MERCUTIO

The pox of such antic, lisping, affecting fantasti-
coes; these new tuners of accents! 'By Jesu, a very
good blade! a very tall man! a very good whore!'
Why, is not this a lamentable thing, grandsire, that
we should be thus afflicted with these strange flies,
these fashion-mongers, these perdona-mi's, who
stand so much on the new form that they cannot
sit at ease on the old bench? O, their bones, their
bones!

Enter ROMEO

BENVOLIO

Here comes Romeo, here comes Romeo.

MERCUTIO

Without his roe, like a dried herring: O flesh, flesh,
how art thou fishified! Now is he for the numbers
that Petrarch flowed in: Laura to his lady was but a
kitchen-wench; marry, she had a better love to be-
rhyme her; Dido, a dowdy; Cleopatra, a gipsy;
Helen and Hero, hildings and harlots; Thisbe, a
grey eye or so, but not to the purpose. Signior Romeo, bon jour! there's a French salutation to your
French slop. You gave us the counterfeit fairly last
night.

ROMEO

Good morrow to you both. What counterfeit did I
give you?

MERCUTIO

The slip, sir, the slip; can you not conceive?

ROMEO

Pardon, good Mercutio, my business was great; and
in such a case as mine a man may strain courtesy.

MERCUTIO

That's as much as to say, Such a case as yours constrains a man to bow in the hams.

ROMEO

Meaning, to court'sy.

MERCUTIO

Thou hast most kindly hit it.

ROMEO

A most courteous exposition.

MERCUTIO

Nay, I am the very pink of courtesy.

ROMEO

Pink for flower.

MERCUTIO

Right.

ROMEO

Why, then is my pump well flowered.

MERCUTIO

Well said: follow me this jest now, till thou hast
worn out thy pump, that, when the single sole of it
is worn, the jest may remain, after the wearing,
solely singular.

ROMEO

O single-soled jest, solely singular for the singleness!

MERCUTIO

Come between us, good Benvolio; my wits faint.

ROMEO

Switch and spurs, switch and spurs; or I'll cry a match.

MERCUTIO

Nay, if thy wits run the wild-goose chase, I have done; for thou hast more of the wild-goose in one of thy wits than, I am sure, I have in my whole five: was I with you there for the goose?

ROMEO

Thou wast never with me for any thing when thou wast not there for the goose.

MERCUTIO

I will bite thee by the ear for that jest.

ROMEO

Nay, good goose, bite not.

MERCUTIO

Thy wit is a very bitter sweeting; it is a most sharp sauce.

ROMEO

And is it not well served in to a sweet goose?

MERCUTIO

O, here's a wit of cheveril, that stretches from an inch narrow to an ell broad!

ROMEO

I stretch it out for that word 'broad;' which added to the goose, proves thee far and wide a broad goose.

MERCUTIO

Why, is not this better now than groaning for love? now art thou sociable, now art thou Romeo; now art thou what thou art, by art as well as by nature: for this drivelling love is like a great natural, that runs lolling up and down to hide his bauble in a hole.

BENVOLIO

Stop there, stop there.

MERCUTIO

Thou desirest me to stop in my tale against the hair.

BENVOLIO

Thou wouldst else have made thy tale large.

MERCUTIO

O, thou art deceived; I would have made it short: for I was come to the whole depth of my tale, and meant indeed to occupy the argument no longer.

ROMEO

Here's goodly gear!

Enter NURSE *and* PETER

MERCUTIO

A sail, a sail!

BENVOLIO

Two, two; a shirt and a smock.

NURSE

Peter!

PETER

Anon?

NURSE

My fan, Peter.

MERCUTIO

Good Peter, to hide her face; for her fan's the fairer of the two.

NURSE

God ye good morrow, gentlemen.

MERCUTIO

God ye good den, fair gentlewoman.

NURSE

Is it good den?

MERCUTIO

'Tis no less, I tell you; for the bawdy hand of the dial is now upon the prick of noon.

NURSE

Out upon you! what a man are you!

ROMEO

One, gentlewoman, that God hath made himself to mar.

NURSE

By my troth, it is well said; 'for himself to mar,' quoth a'? Gentlemen, can any of you tell me where I may find the young Romeo?

ROMEO

I can tell you; but young Romeo will be older when you have found him than he was when you sought him: I am the youngest of that name, for fault of a worse.

NURSE

You say well.

MERCUTIO

Yea, is the worst well? very well took, i' faith; wisely, wisely.

NURSE

If you be he, sir, I desire some confidence with you.

BENVOLIO

She will indite him to some supper.

MERCUTIO

A bawd, a bawd, a bawd! So ho!

ROMEO

What hast thou found?

MERCUTIO

No hare, sir; unless a hare, sir, in a lenten pie, that is something stale and hoar ere it be spent.   [*Sings*

An old hare hoar,
And an old hare hoar,
Is very good meat in lent:
But a hare that is hoar,
Is too much for a score,
When it hoars ere it be spent.

Romeo, will you come to your father's? we'll to dinner thither.

ROMEO

I will follow you.

MERCUTIO

Farewell, ancient lady; farewell, [*singing*] 'lady, lady, lady.'   [*Exeunt* MERCUTIO *and* BENVOLIO

NURSE

Marry, farewell! I pray you, sir, what saucy merchant was this, that was so full of his ropery?

ROMEO

A gentleman, nurse, that loves to hear himself talk, and will speak more in a minute than he will stand to in a month.

NURSE

An a' speak any thing against me, I'll take him down, an a' were lustier than he is, and twenty such Jacks; and if I cannot, I'll find those that shall. Scurvy knave! I am none of his flirt-gills; I am none of his skains-mates. [*Turning to* PETER] And thou must stand by too, and suffer every knave to use me at his pleasure?

PETER

I saw no man use you at his pleasure; if I had, my weapon should quickly have been out, I warrant you: I dare draw as soon as another man, if I see occasion in a good quarrel and the law on my side.

NURSE

Now, afore God, I am so vexed that every part about me quivers. Scurvy knave! Pray you, sir, a word: and as I told you, my young lady bade me inquire you out; what she bade me say, I will keep to myself: but first let me tell ye, if ye should lead her into a fool's paradise, as they say, it were a very gross kind of behaviour, as they say: for the gentlewoman is young, and therefore, if you should deal double with her, truly it were an ill thing to be offered to any gentlewoman, and very weak dealing.

ROMEO

Nurse, commend me to thy lady and mistress. I protest unto thee—

NURSE

Good heart, and, i' faith, I will tell her as much: Lord, Lord, she will be a joyful woman.

ROMEO

What wilt thou tell her, nurse? thou dost not mark me.

NURSE

I will tell her, sir, that you do protest; which, as I take it, is a gentlemanlike offer.

ROMEO

Bid her devise
Some means to come to shrift this afternoon;
And there she shall at Friar Laurence' cell
Be shrived and married. Here is for thy pains.

NURSE

No, truly, sir; not a penny.

ROMEO

Go to; I say you shall.

NURSE

This afternoon, sir? well, she shall be there.

ROMEO

And stay, good nurse, behind the abbey-wall:
Within this hour my man shall be with thee,
And bring thee cords made like a tackled stair;
Which to the high top-gallant of my joy
Must be my convoy in the secret night.
Farewell; be trusty, and I'll quit thy pains:
Farewell: commend me to thy mistress.

NURSE

Now God in heaven bless thee! Hark you, sir.

ROMEO

What say'st thou, my dear nurse?

NURSE

Is your man secret? Did you ne'er hear say,
Two may keep counsel, putting one away?

ROMEO

I warrant thee, my man's as true as steel.

NURSE

Well, sir; my mistress is the sweetest lady—Lord, Lord! when 'twas a little prating thing—O, there is a nobleman in town, one Paris, that would fain lay knife aboard; but she, good soul, had as lieve see a toad, a very toad, as see him. I anger her sometimes, and tell her that Paris is the properer man; but, I'll warrant you, when I say so, she looks as pale as any clout in the versal world. Doth not rosemary and Romeo begin both with a letter?

ROMEO

Ay, nurse; what of that? both with an R.

NURSE

Ah, mocker! that's the dog's name; R is for the—No; I know it begins with some other letter—and she hath the prettiest sententious of it, of you and rosemary, that it would do you good to hear it.

ROMEO

Commend me to thy lady.

NURSE

Ay, a thousand times. [*Exit* ROMEO] Peter!

PETER

Anon?

NURSE

Peter, take my fan, and go before, and apace.

[*Exeunt*

SCENE V. CAPULET'S *orchard*

Enter JULIET

JULIET

The clock struck nine when I did send the nurse;
In half an hour she promised to return.
Perchance she cannot meet him: that's not so.
O, she is lame! love's heralds should be thoughts,
Which ten times faster glide than the sun's beams,
Driving back shadows over louring hills:
Therefore do nimble-pinion'd doves draw love,
And therefore hath the wind-swift Cupid wings.
Now is the sun upon the highmost hill
Of this day's journey, and from nine till twelve
Is three long hours; yet she is not come.
Had she affections and warm youthful blood,
She would be as swift in motion as a ball;
My words would bandy her to my sweet love,
And his to me:
But old folks, many feign as they were dead;
Unwieldy, slow, heavy and pale as lead.

Enter NURSE, *with* PETER

O God, she comes! O honey nurse, what news?
Hast thou met with him? Send thy man away.

NURSE

Peter, stay at the gate.   [*Exit* PETER

JULIET

Now, good sweet nurse,—O Lord, why look'st thou
          sad?
Though news be sad, yet tell them merrily;
If good, thou shamest the music of sweet news
By playing it to me with so sour a face.

NURSE

I am a-weary; give me leave a while.
Fie, how my bones ache! what a jaunce have I had!

JULIET

I would thou hadst my bones and I thy news:
Nay, come, I pray thee, speak; good, good nurse,
          speak.

NURSE

Jesu, what haste? can you not stay a while?
Do you not see that I am out of breath?

JULIET

How art thou out of breath, when thou hast breath
To say to me that thou art out of breath?
The excuse that thou dost make in this delay
Is longer than the tale thou dost excuse.
Is thy news good, or bad? answer to that;
Say either, and I'll stay the circumstance:
Let me be satisfied, is 't good or bad?

NURSE

Well, you have made a simple choice; you know not
how to choose a man: Romeo! no, not he; though
his face be better than any man's, yet his leg excels
all men's; and for a hand, and a foot, and a body,
though they be not to be talked on, yet they are past
compare: he is not the flower of courtesy, but, I'll
warrant him, as gentle as a lamb. Go thy ways,
wench; serve God. What, have you dined at home?

JULIET

No, no: but all this did I know before.
What says he of our marriage? what of that?

NURSE

Lord, how my head aches! what a head have I!
It beats as it would fall in twenty pieces.
My back o' t' other side,—ah, my back, my back!
Beshrew your heart for sending me about,
To catch my death with jauncing up and down!

JULIET

I' faith, I am sorry that thou art not well.
Sweet, sweet, sweet nurse, tell me, what says my
          love?

NURSE

Your love says, like an honest gentleman, and a
courteous, and a kind, and a handsome, and, I warrant, a virtuous,— Where is your mother?

JULIET

Where is my mother! why, she is within;
Where should she be? How oddly thou repliest!
'Your love says, like an honest gentleman,
Where is your mother?'

NURSE

          O God's lady dear!
Are you so hot? marry, come up, I trow;

Is this the poultice for my aching bones?
Henceforward do your messages yourself.

JULIET

Here's such a coil! come, what says Romeo?

NURSE

Have you got leave to go to shrift to-day?

JULIET

I have.

NURSE

Then hie you hence to Friar Laurence' cell;
There stays a husband to make you a wife:
Now comes the wanton blood up in your cheeks,
They'll be in scarlet straight at any news.
Hie you to church; I must another way,
To fetch a ladder, by the which your love
Must climb a bird's nest soon when it is dark;
I am the drudge, and toil in your delight;
But you shall bear the burthen soon at night.
Go; I'll to dinner; hie you to the cell.

JULIET

Hie to high fortune! Honest nurse, farewell.

          [*Exeunt*

SCENE VI. FRIAR LAURENCE's *cell*

Enter FRIAR LAURENCE *and* ROMEO

FRIAR LAURENCE

So smile the heavens upon this holy act
That after-hours with sorrow chide us not!

ROMEO

Amen, amen! but come what sorrow can,
It cannot countervail the exchange of joy
That one short minute gives me in her sight:
Do thou but close our hands with holy words,
Then love-devouring death do what he dare,
It is enough I may but call her mine.

FRIAR LAURENCE

These violent delights have violent ends,
And in their triumph die; like fire and powder
Which as they kiss consume: the sweetest honey
Is loathsome in his own deliciousness,
And in the taste confounds the appetite:
Therefore, love moderately; long love doth so;
Too swift arrives as tardy as too slow.

Enter JULIET

Here comes the lady. O, so light a foot
Will ne'er wear out the everlasting flint.
A lover may bestride the gossamer
That idles in the wanton summer air,
And yet not fall; so light is vanity.

JULIET

Good even to my ghostly confessor.

FRIAR LAURENCE

Romeo shall thank thee, daughter, for us both.

JULIET

As much to him, else is his thanks too much.

ROMEO

Ah, Juliet, if the measure of thy joy
Be heap'd like mine, and that thy skill be more
To blazon it, then sweeten with thy breath

This neighbour air, and let rich music's tongue
Unfold the imagined happiness that both
Receive in either by this dear encounter.

JULIET

Conceit, more rich in matter than in words,
Brags of his substance, not of ornament:
They are but beggars that can count their worth;
But my true love is grown to such excess,
I cannot sum up sum of half my wealth.

FRIAR LAURENCE

Come, come with me, and we will make short work;
For, by your leaves, you shall not stay alone
Till holy church incorporate two in one.   [Exeunt

ACT III
SCENE I. *A public place*

Enter MERCUTIO, BENVOLIO, PAGE, *and* SERVANTS

BENVOLIO

I pray thee, good Mercutio, let's retire:
The day is hot, the Capulets abroad,
And, if we meet, we shall not 'scape a brawl;
For now these hot days is the mad blood stirring.

MERCUTIO

Thou art like one of those fellows that when he enters the confines of a tavern claps me his sword upon
the table, and says 'God send me no need of thee!'
and by the operation of the second cup draws it on
the drawer, when indeed there is no need.

BENVOLIO

Am I like such a fellow?

MERCUTIO

Come, come, thou art as hot a Jack in thy mood as
any in Italy, and as soon moved to be moody, and
as soon moody to be moved.

BENVOLIO

And what to?

MERCUTIO

Nay, an there were two such, we should have none
shortly, for one would kill the other. Thou! why,
thou wilt quarrel with a man that hath a hair more,
or a hair less, in his beard than thou hast: thou wilt
quarrel with a man for cracking nuts, having no
other reason but because thou hast hazel eyes; what
eye, but such an eye, would spy out such a quarrel?
thy head is as full of quarrels as an egg is full of meat,
and yet thy head hath been beaten as addle as an
egg for quarrelling: thou hast quarrelled with a
man for coughing in the street, because he hath
wakened thy dog that hath lain asleep in the sun:
didst thou not fall out with a tailor for wearing his
new doublet before Easter? with another, for tying
his new shoes with old riband? and yet thou wilt
tutor me from quarrelling!

BENVOLIO

An I were so apt to quarrel as thou art, any man

should buy the fee-simple of my life for an hour and
a quarter.

MERCUTIO

The fee-simple! O simple!

Enter TYBALT *and others*

BENVOLIO

By my head, here come the Capulets.

MERCUTIO

By my heel, I care not.

TYBALT

Follow me close, for I will speak to them.
Gentlemen, good den: a word with one of you.

MERCUTIO

And but one word with one of us? couple it with
something; make it a word and a blow.

TYBALT

You shall find me apt enough to that, sir, an you
will give me occasion.

MERCUTIO

Could you not take some occasion without giving?

TYBALT

Mercutio, thou consort'st with Romeo,—

MERCUTIO

Consort! what, dost thou make us minstrels? an
thou make minstrels of us, look to hear nothing but
discords: here's my fiddlestick; here's that shall
make you dance. 'Zounds, consort!

BENVOLIO

We talk here in the public haunt of men:
Either withdraw unto some private place,
Or reason coldly of your grievances,
Or else depart; here all eyes gaze on us.

MERCUTIO

Men's eyes were made to look, and let them gaze;
I will not budge for no man's pleasure, I.

Enter ROMEO

TYBALT

Well, peace be with you, sir: here comes my man.

MERCUTIO

But I'll be hang'd, sir, if he wear your livery:
Marry, go before to field, he'll be your follower;
Your worship in that sense may call him man.

TYBALT

Romeo, the love I bear thee can afford
No better term than this,—thou art a villain.

ROMEO

Tybalt, the reason that I have to love thee
Doth much excuse the appertaining rage
To such a greeting: villain am I none;
Therefore farewell; I see thou know'st me not.

TYBALT

Boy, this shall not excuse the injuries
That thou hast done me; therefore turn and draw.

ROMEO

I do protest, I never injured thee,
But love thee better than thou canst devise
Till thou shalt know the reason of my love:
And so, good Capulet,—which name I tender
As dearly as mine own,—be satisfied.

MERCUTIO

O calm, dishonourable, vile submission!
Alla stoccata carries it away.   [*Draws*
Tybalt, you rat-catcher, will you walk?

TYBALT

What wouldst thou have with me?

MERCUTIO

Good king of cats, nothing but one of your nine
lives, that I mean to make bold withal, and, as you
shall use me hereafter, dry-beat the rest of the eight.
Will you pluck your sword out of his pilcher by the
ears? make haste, lest mine be about your ears ere
it be out.

TYBALT

I am for you.   [*Drawing*

ROMEO

Gentle Mercutio, put thy rapier up.

MERCUTIO

Come, sir, your passado.   [*They fight*

ROMEO

Draw, Benvolio; beat down their weapons.
Gentlemen, for shame, forbear this outrage!
Tybalt, Mercutio, the prince expressly hath
Forbid this bandying in Verona streets:
Hold, Tybalt! good Mercutio!   [TYBALT *under*
ROMEO's *arm stabs* MERCUTIO *and flies with his followers*

MERCUTIO

                I am hurt;
A plague o' both your houses! I am sped:
Is he gone, and hath nothing?

BENVOLIO

              What, art thou hurt?

MERCUTIO

Ay, ay, a scratch, a scratch; marry, 'tis enough.
Where is my page? Go, villain, fetch a surgeon.
                      [*Exit* PAGE

ROMEO

Courage, man; the hurt cannot be much.

MERCUTIO

No, 'tis not so deep as a well, nor so wide as a
church-door; but 'tis enough, 'twill serve: ask for
me to-morrow, and you shall find me a grave man.
I am peppered, I warrant, for this world. A plague
o' both your houses! 'Zounds, a dog, a rat, a mouse,
a cat, to scratch a man to death! a braggart, a rogue,
a villain, that fights by the book of arithmetic! Why
the devil came you between us? I was hurt under
your arm.

ROMEO

I thought all for the best.

MERCUTIO

Help me into some house, Benvolio,
Or I shall faint. A plague o' both your houses!
They have made worms' meat of me: I have it,
And soundly too: your houses!
               [*Exeunt* MERCUTIO *and* BENVOLIO

ROMEO

This gentleman, the prince's near ally,
My very friend, hath got this mortal hurt
In my behalf; my reputation stain'd

With Tybalt's slander,—Tybalt, that an hour
Hath been my kinsman: O sweet Juliet,
Thy beauty hath made me effeminate,
And in my temper soften'd valour's steel!

Re-enter BENVOLIO

BENVOLIO

O Romeo, Romeo, brave Mercutio's dead!
That gallant spirit hath aspired the clouds,
Which too untimely here did scorn the earth.

ROMEO

This day's black fate on more days doth depend;
This but begins the woe others must end.

Re-enter TYBALT

BENVOLIO

Here comes the furious Tybalt back again.

ROMEO

Alive, in triumph! and Mercutio slain!
Away to heaven, respective lenity,
And fire-eyed fury be my conduct now!
Now, Tybalt, take the 'villain' back again
That late thou gavest me; for Mercutio's soul
Is but a little way above our heads,
Staying for thine to keep him company:
Either thou, or I, or both, must go with him.

TYBALT

Thou, wretched boy, that didst consort him here,
Shalt with him hence.

ROMEO

           This shall determine that.
           [*They fight;* TYBALT *falls*

BENVOLIO

Romeo, away, be gone!
The citizens are up, and Tybalt slain:
Stand not amazed: the prince will doom thee death
If thou art taken: hence, be gone, away!

ROMEO

O, I am fortune's fool!

BENVOLIO

           Why dost thou stay? [*Exit* ROMEO
         Enter CITIZENS, *&c.*

FIRST CITIZEN

Which way ran he that kill'd Mercutio?
Tybalt, that murderer, which way ran he?

BENVOLIO

There lies that Tybalt.

FIRST CITIZEN

           Up, sir, go with me;
I charge thee in the prince's name, obey.
 Enter PRINCE, *attended;* MONTAGUE, CAPULET, *their*
              WIVES, *and others*

PRINCE

Where are the vile beginners of this fray?

BENVOLIO

O noble prince, I can discover all
The unlucky manage of this fatal brawl:
There lies the man, slain by young Romeo,
That slew thy kinsman, brave Mercutio.

LADY CAPULET

Tybalt, my cousin! O my brother's child!
O prince! O cousin! husband! O, the blood is spilt

Of my dear kinsman! Prince, as thou art true,
For blood of ours, shed blood of Montague.
O cousin, cousin!

PRINCE

Benvolio, who began this bloody fray?

BENVOLIO

Tybalt, here slain, whom Romeo's hand did slay;
Romeo that spoke him fair, bid him bethink
How nice the quarrel was, and urged withal
Your high displeasure: all this uttered
With gentle breath, calm look, knees humbly bow'd
Could not take truce with the unruly spleen
Of Tybalt deaf to peace, but that he tilts
With piercing steel at bold Mercutio's breast;
Who, all as hot, turns deadly point to point,
And, with a martial scorn, with one hand beats
Cold death aside, and with the other sends
It back to Tybalt, whose dexterity
Retorts it: Romeo he cries aloud,
'Hold, friends! friends, part!' and, swifter than his
     tongue,
His agile arm beats down their fatal points,
And 'twixt them rushes; underneath whose arm
An envious thrust from Tybalt hit the life
Of stout Mercutio, and then Tybalt fled:
But by and by comes back to Romeo,
Who had but newly entertain'd revenge,
And to 't they go like lightning: for, ere I
Could draw to part them, was stout Tybalt slain;
And, as he fell, did Romeo turn and fly;
This is the truth, or let Benvolio die.

LADY CAPULET

He is a kinsman to the Montague,
Affection makes him false, he speaks not true:
Some twenty of them fought in this black strife,
And all those twenty could but kill one life.
I beg for justice, which thou, prince, must give;
Romeo slew Tybalt, Romeo must not live.

PRINCE

Romeo slew him, he slew Mercutio;
Who now the price of his dear blood doth owe?

MONTAGUE

Not Romeo, prince, he was Mercutio's friend;
His fault concludes but what the law should end,
The life of Tybalt.

PRINCE

                    And for that offence
Immediately we do exile him hence:
I have an interest in your hate's proceeding,
My blood for your rude brawls doth lie a-bleeding;
But I'll amerce you with so strong a fine,
That you shall all repent the loss of mine:
I will be deaf to pleading and excuses:
Nor tears nor prayers shall purchase out abuses:
Therefore use none: let Romeo hence in haste,
Else, when he's found, that hour is his last.
Bear hence this body, and attend our will:
Mercy but murders, pardoning those that kill.

                                        [Exeunt

SCENE II. CAPULET'S *orchard*

Enter JULIET

JULIET

Gallop apace, you fiery-footed steeds,
Towards Phœbus' lodging: such a waggoner
As Phaethon would whip you to the west,
And bring in cloudy night immediately.
Spread thy close curtain, love-performing night,
That runaways' eyes may wink, and Romeo
Leap to these arms, untalk'd of and unseen.
Lovers can see to do their amorous rites
By their own beauties; or, if love be blind,
It best agrees with night. Come, civil night,
Thou sober-suited matron, all in black,
And learn me how to lose a winning match,
Play'd for a pair of stainless maidenhoods:
Hood my unmann'd blood bating in my cheeks
With thy black mantle, till strange love grown bold
Think true love acted simple modesty.
Come, night, come, Romeo, come, thou day in
     night;
For thou wilt lie upon the wings of night
Whiter than new snow on a raven's back.
Come, gentle night, come, loving, black-brow'd
     night,
Give me my Romeo; and, when he shall die,
Take him and cut him out in little stars,
And he will make the face of heaven so fine,
That all the world will be in love with night,
And pay no worship to the garish sun.
O, I have bought the mansion of a love,
But not possess'd it, and, though I am sold,
Not yet enjoy'd; so tedious is this day
As is the night before some festival
To an impatient child that hath new robes
And may not wear them. O, here comes my nurse,
And she brings news, and every tongue that speaks
But Romeo's name speaks heavenly eloquence.

Enter NURSE, *with cords*

Now, nurse, what news? What hast thou there? the
     cords
That Romeo bid thee fetch?

NURSE

                    Ay, ay, the cords. [*Throws them down*

JULIET

Ay me! what news? why dost thou wring thy hands?

NURSE

Ah, well-a-day! he's dead, he's dead, he's dead.
We are undone, lady, we are undone.
Alack the day! he's gone, he's kill'd, he's dead.

JULIET

Can heaven be so envious?

NURSE

                    Romeo can,
Though heaven cannot. O Romeo, Romeo!
Who ever would have thought it? Romeo!

JULIET

What devil art thou that dost torment me thus?
This torture should be roar'd in dismal hell.

Hath Romeo slain himself? say thou but 'I,'
And that bare vowel 'I' shall poison more
Than the death-darting eye of cockatrice:
I am not I, if there be such an I,
Or those eyes shut, that make thee answer 'I.'
If he be slain, say 'I;' or if not, no:
Brief sounds determine of my weal or woe.

NURSE

I saw the wound, I saw it with mine eyes—
God save the mark!—here on his manly breast:
A piteous corse, a bloody piteous corse;
Pale, pale as ashes, all bedaub'd in blood,
All in gore blood: I swounded at the sight.

JULIET

O, break, my heart! poor bankrupt, break at once!
To prison, eyes, ne'er look on liberty!
Vile earth, to earth resign, end motion here,
And thou and Romeo press one heavy bier!

NURSE

O Tybalt, Tybalt, the best friend I had!
O courteous Tybalt! honest gentleman!
That ever I should live to see thee dead!

JULIET

What storm is this that blows so contrary?
Is Romeo slaughter'd, and is Tybalt dead?
My dear-loved cousin, and my dearer lord?
Then, dreadful trumpet, sound the general doom!
For who is living, if those two are gone?

NURSE

Tybalt is gone, and Romeo banished;
Romeo that kill'd him, he is banished.

JULIET

O God! did Romeo's hand shed Tybalt's blood?

NURSE

It did, it did; alas the day, it did!

JULIET

O serpent heart, hid with a flowering face!
Did ever dragon keep so fair a cave?
Beautiful tyrant! fiend angelical!
Dove-feather'd raven! wolvish-ravening lamb!
Despised substance of divinest show!
Just opposite to what thou justly seem'st,
A damned saint, an honourable villain!
O nature, what hadst thou to do in hell,
When thou didst bower the spirit of a fiend
In mortal paradise of such sweet flesh?
Was ever book containing such vile matter
So fairly bound? O, that deceit should dwell
In such a gorgeous palace!

NURSE

There's no trust,
No faith, no honesty in men; all perjured,
All forsworn, all naught, all dissemblers.
Ah, where's my man? give me some aqua vitæ:
These griefs, these woes, these sorrows make me old.
Shame come to Romeo!

JULIET

Blister'd be thy tongue
For such a wish! he was not born to shame:

Upon his brow shame is ashamed to sit;
For 'tis a throne where honour may be crown'd
Sole monarch of the universal earth.
O, what a beast was I to chide at him!

NURSE

Will you speak well of him that kill'd your cousin?

JULIET

Shall I speak ill of him that is my husband?
Ah, poor my lord, what tongue shall smooth thy
name,
When I, thy three-hours wife, have mangled it?
But wherefore, villain, didst thou kill my cousin?
That villain cousin would have kill'd my husband:
Back, foolish tears, back to your native spring;
Your tributary drops belong to woe,
Which you mistaking offer up to joy.
My husband lives, that Tybalt would have slain;
And Tybalt's dead, that would have slain my hus-
band:
All this is comfort; wherefore weep I then?
Some word there was, worser than Tybalt's death,
That murder'd me: I would forget it fain;
But, O, it presses to my memory,
Like damned guilty deeds to sinners' minds:
'Tybalt is dead, and Romeo banished;'
That 'banished,' that one word 'banished,'
Hath slain ten thousand Tybalts. Tybalt's death
Was woe enough, if it had ended there:
Or, if sour woe delights in fellowship,
And needly will be rank'd with other griefs,
Why follow'd not, when she said 'Tybalt's dead,'
Thy father, or thy mother, nay, or both,
Which modern lamentation might have moved?
But with a rear-ward following Tybalt's death,
'Romeo is banished:' to speak that word,
Is father, mother, Tybalt, Romeo, Juliet,
All slain, all dead. 'Romeo is banished.'
There is no end, no limit, measure, bound,
In that word's death; no words can that woe sound.
Where is my father, and my mother, nurse?

NURSE

Weeping and wailing over Tybalt's corse:
Will you go to them? I will bring you thither.

JULIET

Wash they his wounds with tears: mine shall be
spent,
When theirs are dry, for Romeo's banishment.
Take up those cords: poor ropes, you are beguiled,
Both you and I; for Romeo is exiled:
He made you for a highway to my bed;
But I, a maid, die maiden-widowed.
Come, cords; come, nurse; I'll to my wedding-bed;
And death, not Romeo, take my maidenhead!

NURSE

Hie to your chamber: I'll find Romeo
To comfort you: I wot well where he is.
Hark ye, your Romeo will be here at night:
I'll to him; he is hid at Laurence' cell.

JULIET

O, find him! give this ring to my true knight,
And bid him come to take his last farewell. [*Exeunt*

SCENE III. FRIAR LAURENCE's *cell*

Enter FRIAR LAURENCE

FRIAR LAURENCE

Romeo, come forth; come forth, thou fearful man:
Affliction is enamour'd of thy parts,
And thou art wedded to calamity.

Enter ROMEO

ROMEO

Father, what news? what is the prince's doom?
What sorrow craves acquaintance at my hand,
That I yet know not?

FRIAR LAURENCE

Too familiar
Is my dear son with such sour company:
I bring thee tidings of the prince's doom.

ROMEO

What less than dooms-day is the prince's doom?

FRIAR LAURENCE

A gentler judgement vanish'd from his lips,
Not body's death, but body's banishment.

ROMEO

Ha, banishment! be merciful, say 'death;'
For exile hath more terror in his look,
Much more than death: do not say 'banishment.'

FRIAR LAURENCE

Here from Verona art thou banished:
Be patient, for the world is broad and wide.

ROMEO

There is no world without Verona walls,
But purgatory, torture, hell itself.
Hence banished is banish'd from the world,
And world's exile is death: then 'banished'
Is death mis-term'd: calling death 'banished,'
Thou cut'st my head off with a golden axe,
And smilest upon the stroke that murders me.

FRIAR LAURENCE

O deadly sin! O rude unthankfulness!
Thy fault our law calls death; but the kind prince,
Taking thy part, hath rush'd aside the law,
And turn'd that black word death to banishment:
This is dear mercy, and thou seest it not.

ROMEO

'Tis torture, and not mercy: heaven is here,
Where Juliet lives; and every cat and dog
And little mouse, every unworthy thing,
Live here in heaven and may look on her,
But Romeo may not: more validity,
More honourable state, more courtship lives
In carrion-flies than Romeo: they may seize
On the white wonder of dear Juliet's hand,
And steal immortal blessing from her lips;
Who, even in pure and vestal modesty,
Still blush, as thinking their own kisses sin;

But Romeo may not; he is banished:
This may flies do, but I from this must fly:
They are free men, but I am banished:
And say'st thou yet, that exile is not death?
Hadst thou no poison mix'd, no sharp-ground knife,
No sudden mean of death, though ne'er so mean,
But 'banished' to kill me?—'Banished'?
O friar, the damned use that word in hell;
Howling attends it: how hast thou the heart,
Being a divine, a ghostly confessor,
A sin-absolver, and my friend profess'd,
To mangle me with that word 'banished'?

FRIAR LAURENCE

Thou fond mad man, hear me but speak a word.

ROMEO

O, thou wilt speak again of banishment.

FRIAR LAURENCE

I'll give thee armour to keep off that word;
Adversity's sweet milk, philosophy,
To comfort thee, though thou art banished.

ROMEO

Yet 'banished'? Hang up philosophy!
Unless philosophy can make a Juliet,
Displant a town, reverse a prince's doom,
It helps not, it prevails not: talk no more.

FRIAR LAURENCE

O, then I see that madmen have no ears.

ROMEO

How should they, when that wise men have no eyes?

FRIAR LAURENCE

Let me dispute with thee of thy estate.

ROMEO

Thou canst not speak of that thou dost not feel:
Wert thou as young as I, Juliet thy love,
An hour but married, Tybalt murdered,
Doting like me, and like me banished,
Then mightst thou speak, then mightst thou tear
    thy hair,
And fall upon the ground, as I do now,
Taking the measure of an unmade grave.

[*Knocking within*

FRIAR LAURENCE

Arise; one knocks; good Romeo, hide thyself.

ROMEO

Not I; unless the breath of heart-sick groans
Mist-like infold me from the search of eyes. [*Knocking*

FRIAR LAURENCE

Hark, how they knock! Who's there? Romeo, arise;
Thou wilt be taken.—Stay awhile!—Stand up;

[*Knocking*

Run to my study.—By and by!—God's will,
What simpleness is this!—I come, I come! [*Knocking*
Who knocks so hard? whence come you? what's
    your will?

NURSE

[*Within*] Let me come in, and you shall know my er-
    rand;
I come from Lady Juliet.

FRIAR LAURENCE

Welcome, then.

Enter NURSE

NURSE

O holy friar, O, tell me, holy friar,
Where is my lady's lord, where's Romeo?

FRIAR LAURENCE

There on the ground, with his own tears made
     drunk.

NURSE

O, he is even in my mistress' case,
Just in her case!

FRIAR LAURENCE

               O woeful sympathy!
Piteous predicament!

NURSE

               Even so lies she,
Blubbering and weeping, weeping and blubbering.
Stand up, stand up; stand, an you be a man:
For Juliet's sake, for her sake, rise and stand;
Why should you fall into so deep an O?

ROMEO

Nurse!

NURSE

Ah sir! ah sir! Well, death's the end of all.

ROMEO

Spakest thou of Juliet? how is it with her?
Doth she not think me an old murderer,
Now I have stain'd the childhood of our joy
With blood removed but little from her own?
Where is she? and how doth she? and what says
My conceal'd lady to our cancell'd love?

NURSE

O, she says nothing, sir, but weeps and weeps;
And now falls on her bed; and then starts up,
And Tybalt calls; and then on Romeo cries,
And then down falls again.

ROMEO

               As if that name,
Shot from the deadly level of a gun,
Did murder her, as that name's cursed hand
Murder'd her kinsman. O, tell me, friar, tell me,
In what vile part of this anatomy
Doth my name lodge? tell me, that I may sack
The hateful mansion.   [*Drawing his sword*

FRIAR LAURENCE

               Hold thy desperate hand:
Art thou a man? thy form cries out thou art:
Thy tears are womanish; thy wild acts denote
The unreasonable fury of a beast:
Unseemly woman in a seeming man!
Or ill-beseeming beast in seeming both!
Thou hast amazed me: by my holy order,
I thought thy disposition better temper'd.
Hast thou slain Tybalt? wilt thou slay thyself?
And slay thy lady that in thy life lives,
By doing damned hate upon thyself?
Why rail'st thou on thy birth, the heaven and earth?
Since birth and heaven and earth, all three do meet
In thee at once, which thou at once wouldst lose.
Fie, fie, thou shamest thy shape, thy love, thy wit;

Which, like a usurer, abound'st in all,
And usest none in that true use indeed
Which should bedeck thy shape, thy love, thy wit:
Thy noble shape is but a form of wax,
Digressing from the valour of a man;
Thy dear love sworn, but hollow perjury,
Killing that love which thou hast vow'd to cherish;
Thy wit, that ornament to shape and love,
Mis-shapen in the conduct of them both,
Like powder in a skilless soldier's flask,
Is set a-fire by thine own ignorance,
And thou dismember'd with thine own defence.
What, rouse thee, man! thy Juliet is alive,
For whose dear sake thou wast but lately dead;
There art thou happy: Tybalt would kill thee,
But thou slew'st Tybalt; there art thou happy too:
The law, that threaten'd death, becomes thy friend,
And turns it to exile; there art thou happy:
A pack of blessings lights upon thy back;
Happiness courts thee in her best array;
But, like a misbehaved and sullen wench,
Thou pout'st upon thy fortune and thy love:
Take heed, take heed, for such die miserable.
Go, get thee to thy love, as was decreed,
Ascend her chamber, hence and comfort her:
But look thou stay not till the watch be set,
For then thou canst not pass to Mantua;
Where thou shalt live till we can find a time
To blaze your marriage, reconcile your friends,
Beg pardon of the prince, and call thee back
With twenty hundred thousand times more joy
Than thou went'st forth in lamentation.
Go before, nurse: commend me to thy lady,
And bid her hasten all the house to bed,
Which heavy sorrow makes them apt unto:
Romeo is coming.

NURSE

O Lord, I could have stay'd here all the night
To hear good counsel: O, what learning is!
My lord, I'll tell my lady you will come.

ROMEO

Do so, and bid my sweet prepare to chide.

NURSE

Here, sir, a ring she bid me give you, sir:
Hie you, make haste, for it grows very late.   [*Exit*

ROMEO

How well my comfort is revived by this!

FRIAR LAURENCE

Go hence; good night; and here stands all your
     state:
Either be gone before the watch be set,
Or by the break of day disguised from hence:
Sojourn in Mantua; I'll find out your man,
And he shall signify from time to time
Every good hap to you that chances here:
Give me thy hand; 'tis late: farewell; good night.

ROMEO

But that a joy past joy calls out on me,
It were a grief, so brief to part with thee:
Farewell.   [*Exeunt*

SCENE IV. *A room in* CAPULET'S *house*

Enter CAPULET, LADY CAPULET, *and* PARIS

CAPULET

'Things have fall'n out, sir, so unluckily,
That we have had no time to move our daughter.
Look you, she loved her kinsman Tybalt dearly,
And so did I. Well, we were born to die.
'Tis very late; she'll not come down to-night:
I promise you, but for your company,
I would have been a-bed an hour ago.

PARIS

These times of woe afford no time to woo.
Madam, good night: commend me to your daughter.

LADY CAPULET

I will, and know her mind early to-morrow;
To-night she's mew'd up to her heaviness.

CAPULET

Sir Paris, I will make a desperate tender
Of my child's love: I think she will be ruled
In all respects by me; nay more, I doubt it not.
Wife, go you to her ere you go to bed;
Acquaint her here of my son Paris' love;
And bid her, mark you me, on Wednesday next—
But, soft! what day is this?

PARIS

Monday, my lord.

CAPULET

Monday! ha, ha! Well, Wednesday is too soon;
O' Thursday let it be: o' Thursday, tell her,
She shall be married to this noble earl.
Will you be ready? do you like this haste?
We'll keep no great ado; a friend or two;
For, hark you, Tybalt being slain so late,
It may be thought we held him carelessly,
Being our kinsman, if we revel much:
Therefore we'll have some half-a-dozen friends,
And there an end. But what say you to Thursday?

PARIS

My lord, I would that Thursday were to-morrow.

CAPULET

Well, get you gone: o' Thursday be it then.
Go you to Juliet ere you go to bed,
Prepare her, wife, against this wedding-day.
Farewell, my lord. Light to my chamber, ho!
Afore me, it is so very very late,
That we may call it early by and by:
Good night.   [*Exeunt*

SCENE V. CAPULET'S *orchard*

Enter ROMEO *and* JULIET, *above, at the window*

JULIET

Wilt thou be gone? it is not yet near day:
It was the nightingale, and not the lark,
That pierced the fearful hollow of thine ear;
Nightly she sings on yond pomegranate-tree:
Believe me, love, it was the nightingale.

ROMEO

It was the lark, the herald of the morn,
No nightingale: look, love, what envious streaks
Do lace the severing clouds in yonder east:
Night's candles are burnt out, and jocund day
Stands tiptoe on the misty mountain tops:
I must be gone and live, or stay and die.

JULIET

Yond light is not day-light, I know it, I:
It is some meteor that the sun exhales,
To be to thee this night a torch-bearer,
And light thee on thy way to Mantua:
Therefore stay yet; thou need'st not to be gone.

ROMEO

Let me be ta'en, let me be put to death;
I am content, so thou wilt have it so.
I'll say yon grey is not the morning's eye,
'Tis but the pale reflex of Cynthia's brow;
Nor that is not the lark, whose notes do beat
The vaulty heaven so high above our heads:
I have more care to stay than will to go:
Come, death, and welcome! Juliet wills it so.
How is 't, my soul? let's talk: it is not day.

JULIET

It is, it is: hie hence, be gone, away!
It is the lark that sings so out of tune,
Straining harsh discords and unpleasing sharps.
Some say the lark makes sweet division;
This doth not so, for she divideth us:
Some say the lark and loathed toad change eyes;
O, now I would they had changed voices too!
Since arm from arm that voice doth us affray,
Hunting thee hence with hunts-up to the day.
O, now be gone; more light and light it grows.

ROMEO

More light and light: more dark and dark our woes!

Enter NURSE, *to the chamber*

NURSE

Madam!

JULIET

Nurse?

NURSE

Your lady mother is coming to your chamber:
The day is broke; be wary, look about.   [*Exit*

JULIET

Then, window, let day in, and let life out.

ROMEO

Farewell, farewell! one kiss, and I'll descend.
                                        [*Descends*

JULIET

Art thou gone so? my lord, my love, my friend!
I must hear from thee every day in the hour,
For in a minute there are many days:
O, by this count I shall be much in years
Ere I again behold my Romeo!

ROMEO

Farewell!
I will omit no opportunity
That may convey my greetings, love, to thee.

JULIET

O, think'st thou we shall ever meet again?

ROMEO

I doubt it not; and all these woes shall serve
For sweet discourses in our time to come.

JULIET

O God! I have an ill-divining soul.
Methinks I see thee, now thou art below,
As one dead in the bottom of a tomb:
Either my eyesight fails or thou look'st pale.

ROMEO

And trust me, love, in my eye so do you:
Dry sorrow drinks our blood. Adieu, adieu!   [Exit

JULIET

O fortune, fortune; all men call thee fickle:
If thou art fickle, what dost thou with him
That is renown'd for faith? Be fickle, fortune;
For then, I hope, thou wilt not keep him long,
But send him back.

LADY CAPULET

[Within] Ho, daughter! are you up?

JULIET

Who is 't that calls? it is my lady mother!
Is she not down so late, or up so early?
What unaccustom'd cause procures her hither?

Enter LADY CAPULET

LADY CAPULET

Why, how now, Juliet!

JULIET

               Madam, I am not well.

LADY CAPULET

Evermore weeping for your cousin's death?
What, wilt thou wash him from his grave with tears?
And if thou couldst, thou couldst not make him live;
Therefore have done: some grief shows much of love,
But much of grief shows still some want of wit.

JULIET

Yet let me weep for such a feeling loss.

LADY CAPULET

So shall you feel the loss, but not the friend
Which you weep for.

JULIET

               Feeling so the loss,
I cannot choose but ever weep the friend.

LADY CAPULET

Well, girl, thou weep'st not so much for his death
As that the villain lives which slaughter'd him.

JULIET

What villain, madam?

LADY CAPULET

               That same villain, Romeo.

JULIET

[Aside] Villain and he be many miles asunder.
God pardon him! I do, with all my heart;
And yet no man like he doth grieve my heart.

LADY CAPULET

That is because the traitor murderer lives.

JULIET

Ay, madam, from the reach of these my hands:
Would none but I might venge my cousin's death!

LADY CAPULET

We will have vengeance for it, fear thou not:
Then weep no more. I'll send to one in Mantua,
Where that same banish'd runagate doth live,
Shall give him such an unaccustom'd dram
That he shall soon keep Tybalt company:
And then, I hope, thou wilt be satisfied.

JULIET

Indeed, I never shall be satisfied
With Romeo, till I behold him—dead—
Is my poor heart so for a kinsman vex'd.
Madam if you could find out but a man
To bear a poison, I would temper it,
That Romeo should, upon receipt thereof,
Soon sleep in quiet. O, how my heart abhors
To hear him named, and cannot come to him,
To wreak the love I bore my cousin
Upon his body that hath slaughter'd him!

LADY CAPULET

Find thou the means, and I'll find such a man.
But now I'll tell thee joyful tidings, girl.

JULIET

And joy comes well in such a needy time:
What are they, I beseech your ladyship?

LADY CAPULET

Well, well, thou hast a careful father, child;
One who, to put thee from thy heaviness,
Hath sorted out a sudden day of joy,
That thou expect'st not, nor I look'd not for.

JULIET

Madam, in happy time, what day is that?

LADY CAPULET

Marry, my child, early next Thursday morn,
The gallant, young, and noble gentleman,
The County Paris, at Saint Peter's Church,
Shall happily make thee there a joyful bride.

JULIET

Now, by Saint Peter's Church, and Peter too,
He shall not make me there a joyful bride.
I wonder at this haste; that I must wed
Ere he that should be husband comes to woo.
I pray you, tell my lord and father, madam,
I will not marry yet; and, when I do, I swear,
It shall be Romeo, whom you know I hate,
Rather than Paris. These are news indeed!

LADY CAPULET

Here comes your father; tell him so yourself,
And see how he will take it at your hands.

Enter CAPULET and NURSE

CAPULET

When the sun sets, the air doth drizzle dew;
But for the sunset of my brother's son
It rains downright.
How now! a conduit, girl? what, still in tears?
Evermore showering? In one little body
Thou counterfeit'st a bark, a sea, a wind:
For still thy eyes, which I may call the sea,
Do ebb and flow with tears; the bark thy body is,
Sailing in this salt flood; the winds, thy sighs;
Who raging with thy tears, and they with them,

Without a sudden calm will overset
Thy tempest-tossed body. How now, wife!
Have you deliver'd to her our decree?

LADY CAPULET

Ay, sir; but she will none, she gives you thanks.
I would the fool were married to her grave!

CAPULET

Soft! take me with you, take me with you, wife.
How! will she none? doth she not give us thanks?
Is she not proud? doth she not count her blest,
Unworthy as she is, that we have wrought
So worthy a gentleman to be her bridegroom?

JULIET

Not proud, you have, but thankful that you have:
Proud can I never be of what I hate;
But thankful even for hate that is meant love.

CAPULET

How, how! how, how! chop-logic! What is this?
'Proud,' and 'I thank you,' and 'I thank you not;'
And yet 'not proud:' mistress minion, you,
Thank me no thankings, nor proud me no prouds,
But fettle your fine joints 'gainst Thursday next,
To go with Paris to Saint Peter's Church,
Or I will drag thee on a hurdle thither.
Out, you green-sickness carrion! out, you baggage!
You tallow-face!

LADY CAPULET

Fie, fie! what, are you mad?

JULIET

Good father, I beseech you on my knees,
Hear me with patience but to speak a word.

CAPULET

Hang thee, young baggage! disobedient wretch!
I tell thee what: get thee to church o' Thursday,
Or never after look me in the face:
Speak not, reply not, do not answer me;
My fingers itch. Wife, we scarce thought us blest
That God had lent us but this only child;
But now I see this one is one too much,
And that we have a curse in having her:
Out on her, hilding!

NURSE

God in heaven bless her!
You are to blame, my lord, to rate her so.

CAPULET

And why, my lady wisdom? hold your tongue,
Good prudence; smatter with your gossips, go.

NURSE

I speak no treason.

CAPULET

O, God ye god-den.

NURSE

May not one speak?

CAPULET

Peace, you mumbling fool!
Utter your gravity o'er a gossip's bowl;
For here we need it not.

LADY CAPULET

You are too hot.

CAPULET

God's bread! it makes me mad:
Day, night, hour, tide, time, work, play,
Alone, in company, still my care hath been
To have her match'd: and having now provided
A gentleman of noble parentage,
Of fair demesnes, youthful, and nobly train'd,
Stuff'd, as they say, with honourable parts,
Proportion'd as one's thought would wish a man;
And then to have a wretched puling fool,
A whining mammet, in her fortune's tender,
To answer 'I'll not wed; I cannot love,
I am too young; I pray you, pardon me.'
But, an you will not wed, I'll pardon you:
Graze where you will, you shall not house with me:
Look to 't, think on 't, I do not use to jest.
Thursday is near; lay hand on heart, advise:
An you be mine, I'll give you to my friend;
An you be not, hang, beg, starve, die in the streets,
For, by my soul, I'll ne'er acknowledge thee,
Nor what is mine shall never do thee good:
Trust to 't, bethink you; I'll not be forsworn. [Exit

JULIET

Is there no pity sitting in the clouds,
That sees into the bottom of my grief?
O, sweet my mother, cast me not away!
Delay this marriage for a month, a week;
Or, if you do not, make the bridal bed
In that dim monument where Tybalt lies.

LADY CAPULET

Talk not to me, for I'll not speak a word:
Do as thou wilt, for I have done with thee. [Exit

JULIET

O God!—O nurse, how shall this be prevented?
My husband is on earth, my faith in heaven;
How shall that faith return again to earth,
Unless that husband send it me from heaven
By leaving earth? comfort me, counsel me.
Alack, alack, that heaven should practise stratagems
Upon so soft a subject as myself!
What say'st thou? hast thou not a word of joy?
Some comfort, nurse.

NURSE

Faith, here it is.
Romeo is banish'd, and all the world to nothing,
That he dares ne'er come back to challenge you;
Or, if he do, it needs must be by stealth.
Then, since the case so stands as now it doth,
I think it best you married with the county.
O, he's a lovely gentleman!
Romeo's a dishclout to him: an eagle, madam,
Hath not so green, so quick, so fair an eye
As Paris hath. Beshrew my very heart,
I think you are happy in this second match,
For it excels your first: or if it did not,
Your first is dead, or 'twere as good he were
As living here and you no use of him.

JULIET

Speakest thou from thy heart?

NURSE

And from my soul too; else beshrew them both.

JULIET

Amen!

NURSE

What?

JULIET

Well, thou hast comforted me marvellous much.
Go in, and tell my lady I am gone,
Having displeased my father, to Laurence' cell,
To make confession and to be absolved.

NURSE

Marry, I will, and this is wisely done.   [*Exit*

JULIET

Ancient damnation! O most wicked fiend!
Is it more sin to wish me thus forsworn,
Or to dispraise my lord with that same tongue
Which she hath praised him with above compare
So many thousand times? Go, counsellor;
Thou and my bosom henceforth shall be twain.
I'll to the friar, to know his remedy:
If all else fail, myself have power to die.   [*Exit*

ACT IV

SCENE I. FRIAR LAURENCE'S *cell*

Enter FRIAR LAURENCE *and* PARIS

FRIAR LAURENCE

On Thursday, sir? the time is very short.

PARIS

My father Capulet will have it so;
And I am nothing slow to slack his haste.

FRIAR LAURENCE

You say you do not know the lady's mind:
Uneven is the course; I like it not.

PARIS

Immoderately she weeps for Tybalt's death,
And therefore have I little talk'd of love,
For Venus smiles not in a house of tears.
Now, sir, her father counts it dangerous
That she doth give her sorrow so much sway,
And in his wisdom hastes our marriage,
To stop the inundation of her tears,
Which, too much minded by herself alone,
May be put from her by society:
Now do you know the reason of this haste.

FRIAR LAURENCE

[*Aside*] I would I knew not why it should be slow'd.
Look, sir, here comes the lady toward my cell.

Enter JULIET

PARIS

Happily met, my lady and my wife!

JULIET

That may be, sir, when I may be a wife.

PARIS

That may be must be, love, on Thursday next.

JULIET

What must be shall be.

FRIAR LAURENCE

That's a certain text.

PARIS

Come you to make confession to this father?

JULIET

To answer that, I should confess to you.

PARIS

Do not deny to him that you love me.

JULIET

I will confess to you that I love him.

PARIS

So will ye, I am sure, that you love me.

JULIET

If I do so, it will be of more price,
Being spoke behind your back, than to your face.

PARIS

Poor soul, thy face is much abused with tears.

JULIET

The tears have got small victory by that;
For it was bad enough before their spite.

PARIS

Thou wrong'st it more than tears with that report.

JULIET

That is no slander, sir, which is a truth,
And what I spake, I spake it to my face.

PARIS

Thy face is mine, and thou hast slander'd it.

JULIET

It may be so, for it is not mine own.
Are you at leisure, holy father, now;
Or shall I come to you at evening mass?

FRIAR LAURENCE

My leisure serves me, pensive daughter, now.
My lord, we must entreat the time alone.

PARIS

God shield I should disturb devotion!
Juliet, on Thursday early will I rouse ye:
Till then, adieu, and keep this holy kiss.   [*Exit*

JULIET

O, shut the door, and when thou hast done so,
Come weep with me; past hope, past cure, past help!

FRIAR LAURENCE

Ah, Juliet, I already know thy grief;
It strains me past the compass of my wits:
I hear thou must, and nothing may prorogue it,
On Thursday next be married to this county.

JULIET

Tell me not, friar, that thou hear'st of this,
Unless thou tell me how I may prevent it:
If in thy wisdom thou canst give no help,
Do thou but call my resolution wise,
And with this knife I'll help it presently.
God join'd my heart and Romeo's, thou our hands;
And ere this hand, by thee to Romeo's seal'd,
Shall be the label to another deed,
Or my true heart with treacherous revolt
Turn to another, this shall slay them both:
Therefore, out of thy long-experienced time,

[341]

Give me some present counsel; or, behold,
'Twixt my extremes and me this bloody knife
Shall play the umpire, arbitrating that
Which the commission of thy years and art
Could to no issue of true honour bring.
Be not so long to speak; I long to die,
If what thou speak'st speak not of remedy.

FRIAR LAURENCE

Hold, daughter: I do spy a kind of hope,
Which craves as desperate an execution
As that is desperate which we would prevent.
If, rather than to marry County Paris,
Thou hast the strength of will to slay thyself,
Then is it likely thou wilt undertake
A thing like death to chide away this shame,
That copest with death himself to 'scape from it;
And, if thou darest, I'll give thee remedy.

JULIET

O, bid me leap, rather than marry Paris,
From off the battlements of yonder tower;
Or walk in thievish ways; or bid me lurk
Where serpents are; chain me with roaring bears;
Or shut me nightly in a charnel-house,
O'er-cover'd quite with dead men's rattling bones,
With reeky shanks and yellow chapless skulls;
Or bid me go into a new-made grave,
And hide me with a dead man in his shroud;
Things that to hear them told, have made me
    tremble;
And I will do it without fear or doubt,
To live an unstain'd wife to my sweet love.

FRIAR LAURENCE

Hold, then; go home, be merry, give consent
To marry Paris: Wednesday is to-morrow;
To-morrow night look that thou lie alone,
Let not thy nurse lie with thee in thy chamber:
Take thou this vial, being then in bed,
And this distilled liquor drink thou off:
When presently through all thy veins shall run
A cold and drowsy humour; for no pulse
Shall keep his native progress, but surcease:
No warmth, no breath, shall testify thou livest;
The roses in thy lips and cheeks shall fade
To paly ashes; thy eyes' windows fall,
Like death, when he shuts up the day of life;
Each part, deprived of supple government,
Shall, stiff and stark and cold, appear like death:
And in this borrow'd likeness of shrunk death
Thou shalt continue two and forty hours,
And then awake as from a pleasant sleep.
Now, when the bridegroom in the morning comes
To rouse thee from thy bed, there art thou dead:
Then, as the manner of our country is,
In thy best robes uncover'd on the bier
Thou shalt be borne to that same ancient vault
Where all the kindred of the Capulets lie.
In the mean time, against thou shalt awake,
Shall Romeo by my letters know our drift;
And hither shall he come: and he and I
Will watch thy waking, and that very night

Shall Romeo bear thee hence to Mantua.
And this shall free thee from this present shame,
If no inconstant toy nor womanish fear
Abate thy valour in the acting it.

JULIET

Give me, give me! O, tell not me of fear!

FRIAR LAURENCE

Hold; get you gone, be strong and prosperous
In this resolve: I'll send a friar with speed
To Mantua, with my letters to thy lord.

JULIET

Love give me strength! and strength shall help
    afford.
Farewell, dear father!   [Exeunt

SCENE II. *Hall in* CAPULET'S *house*

Enter CAPULET, LADY CAPULET, NURSE, *and two*
SERVINGMEN

CAPULET

So many guests invite as here are writ.
                              [*Exit* FIRST SERVANT
Sirrah, go hire me twenty cunning cooks.

SECOND SERVINGMAN

You shall have none ill, sir, for I'll try if they can
lick their fingers.

CAPULET

How canst thou try them so?

SECOND SERVINGMAN

Marry, sir, 'tis an ill cook that cannot lick his own
fingers: therefore he that cannot lick his fingers goes
not with me.

CAPULET

Go, be gone.   [*Exit* SECOND SERVANT
We shall be much unfurnish'd for this time.
What, is my daughter gone to Friar Laurence?

NURSE

Ay, forsooth.

CAPULET

Well, he may chance to do some good on her:
A peevish self-will'd harlotry it is.

Enter JULIET

NURSE

See where she comes from shrift with merry look.

CAPULET

How now, my headstrong! where have you been
    gadding?

JULIET

Where I have learn'd me to repent the sin
Of disobedient opposition
To you and your behests, and am enjoin'd
By holy Laurence to fall prostrate here,
To beg your pardon: pardon, I beseech you!
Henceforward I am ever ruled by you.

CAPULET

Send for the county; go tell him of this:
I'll have this knot knit up to-morrow morning.

JULIET

I met the youthful lord at Laurence' cell,

And gave him what becomed love I might,
Not stepping o'er the bounds of modesty.
                    CAPULET
Why, I am glad on 't; this is well: stand up:
This is as 't should be. Let me see the county;
Ay, marry, go, I say, and fetch him hither.
Now, afore God, this reverend holy friar,
All our whole city is much bound to him.
                    JULIET
Nurse, will you go with me into my closet,
To help me sort such needful ornaments
As you think fit to furnish me to-morrow?
                 LADY CAPULET
No, not till Thursday; there is time enough.
                    CAPULET
Go, nurse, go with her: we'll to church to-morrow.
                 [Exeunt JULIET and NURSE
                 LADY CAPULET
We shall be short in our provision:
'Tis now near night.
                    CAPULET
            Tush, I will stir about,
And all things shall be well, I warrant thee, wife:
Go thou to Juliet, help to deck up her;
I'll not to bed to-night; let me alone;
I'll play the housewife for this once. What, ho!
They are all forth: well, I will walk myself
To County Paris, to prepare him up
Against to-morrow: my heart is wondrous light,
Since this same wayward girl is so reclaim'd. [Exeunt

SCENE III. JULIET'S *chamber*

Enter JULIET *and* NURSE
                    JULIET
Ay, those attires are best: but, gentle nurse,
I pray thee, leave me to myself to-night;
For I have need of many orisons
To move the heavens to smile upon my state,
Which, well thou know'st, is cross and full of sin.
                Enter LADY CAPULET
                 LADY CAPULET
What, are you busy, ho? need you my help?
                    JULIET
No, madam; we have cull'd such necessaries
As are behoveful for our state to-morrow:
So please you, let me now be left alone,
And let the nurse this night sit up with you,
For I am sure you have your hands full all
In this so sudden business.
                 LADY CAPULET
            Good night:
Get thee to bed and rest, for thou hast need.
                 [Exeunt LADY CAPULET and NURSE
                    JULIET
Farewell! God knows when we shall meet again.
I have a faint cold fear thrills through my veins,
That almost freezes up the heat of life:

I'll call them back again to comfort me.
Nurse!—What should she do here?
My dismal scene I needs must act alone.
Come, vial.
What if this mixture do not work at all?
Shall I be married then to-morrow morning?
No, no: this shall forbid it. Lie thou there.
                 [Laying down a dagger
What if it be a poison, which the friar
Subtly hath minister'd to have me dead,
Lest in this marriage he should be dishonour'd,
Because he married me before to Romeo?
I fear it is: and yet, methinks, it should not,
For he hath still been tried a holy man.
How if, when I am laid into the tomb,
I wake before the time that Romeo
Come to redeem me? there's a fearful point.
Shall I not then be stifled in the vault,
To whose foul mouth no healthsome air breathes in,
And there die strangled ere my Romeo comes?
Or, if I live, is it not very like,
The horrible conceit of death and night,
Together with the terror of the place,
As in a vault, an ancient receptacle,
Where for this many hundred years the bones
Of all my buried ancestors are pack'd;
Where bloody Tybalt, yet but green in earth,
Lies festering in his shroud; where, as they say,
At some hours in the night spirits resort;
Alack, alack, is it not like that I
So early waking, what with loathsome smells
And shrieks like mandrakes' torn out of the earth,
That living mortals hearing them run mad:
O, if I wake, shall I not be distraught,
Environed with all these hideous fears?
And madly play with my forefathers' joints?
And pluck the mangled Tybalt from his shroud?
And, in this rage, with some great kinsman's bone,
As with a club, dash out my desperate brains?
O, look! methinks I see my cousin's ghost
Seeking out Romeo, that did spit his body
Upon a rapier's point: stay, Tybalt, stay!
Romeo, I come! this do I drink to thee.
                 [She falls upon her bed, within the curtains

SCENE IV. *Hall in* CAPULET'S *house*

Enter LADY CAPULET *and* NURSE
                 LADY CAPULET
Hold, take these keys, and fetch more spices, nurse.
                    NURSE
They call for dates and quinces in the pastry.
                Enter CAPULET
                    CAPULET
Come, stir, stir, stir! the second cock hath crow'd,
The curfew-bell hath rung, 'tis three o'clock:
Look to the baked meats, good Angelica:
Spare not for cost.

[343]

NURSE

Go, you cot-quean, go,
Get you to bed; faith, you'll be sick to-morrow
For this night's watching.

CAPULET

No, not a whit: what! I have watch'd ere now
All night for lesser cause, and ne'er been sick.

LADY CAPULET

Ay, you have been a mouse-hunt in your time;
But I will watch you from such watching now.
            [Exeunt LADY CAPULET and NURSE

CAPULET

A jealous-hood, a jealous-hood!
Enter three or four SERVINGMEN, with spits, and logs, and
            baskets
                              Now, fellow,
What's there?

FIRST SERVINGMAN

Things for the cook, sir, but I know not what.

CAPULET

Make haste, make haste. [Exit FIRST SERVINGMAN
Sirrah, fetch drier logs:
Call Peter, he will show thee where they are.

SECOND SERVINGMAN

I have a head, sir, that will find out logs,
And never trouble Peter for the matter.

CAPULET

Mass, and well said; a merry whoreson, ha!
Thou shalt be logger-head. [Exit SECOND SERVING-
MAN] Good faith, 'tis day:
The county will be here with music straight,
For so he said he would. [Music within] I hear him
near.
Nurse! Wife! What, ho! What, nurse, I say!
            Re-enter NURSE
Go waken Juliet, go and trim her up;
I'll go and chat with Paris: hie, make haste,
Make haste: the bridegroom he is come already:
Make haste, I say.   [Exeunt

SCENE V. JULIET'S chamber
            Enter NURSE
NURSE

Mistress! what, mistress! Juliet! fast, I warrant her,
she:
Why, lamb! why, lady! fie, you slug-a-bed!
Why, love, I say! madam! sweet-heart! why, bride!
What, not a word? you take your pennyworths now;
Sleep for a week; for the next night, I warrant,
The County Paris hath set up his rest
That you shall rest but little. God forgive me,
Marry, and amen, how sound is she asleep!
I needs must wake her. Madam, madam, madam!
Ay, let the county take you in your bed;
He'll fright you up, i' faith. Will it not be?
                              [Undraws the curtains
What, dress'd! and in your clothes! and down
again!
I must needs wake you. Lady! lady! lady!

Alas, alas! Help, help! my lady's dead!
O, well-a-day, that ever I was born!
Some aqua-vitæ, ho! My lord! my lady!
            Enter LADY CAPULET
LADY CAPULET

What noise is here?

NURSE

O lamentable day!

LADY CAPULET

What is the matter?

NURSE

Look, look! O heavy day!

LADY CAPULET

O me, O me! My child, my only life,
Revive, look up, or I will die with thee.
Help, help! call help.
            Enter CAPULET
CAPULET

For shame, bring Juliet forth; her lord is come.

NURSE

She's dead, deceased, she's dead; alack the day!

LADY CAPULET

Alack the day, she's dead, she's dead, she's dead!

CAPULET

Ha! let me see her. Out, alas! she's cold;
Her blood is settled and her joints are stiff;
Life and these lips have long been separated.
Death lies on her like an untimely frost
Upon the sweetest flower of all the field.

NURSE

O lamentable day!

LADY CAPULET

O woeful time!

CAPULET

Death, that hath ta'en her hence to make me wail,
Ties up my tongue and will not let me speak.
            Enter FRIAR LAURENCE and PARIS, with MUSICIANS
FRIAR LAURENCE

Come, is the bride ready to go to church?

CAPULET

Ready to go, but never to return.
O son, the night before thy wedding-day
Hath death lain with thy wife: see, there she lies,
Flower as she was, deflowered by him.
Death is my son-in-law, death is my heir;
My daughter he hath wedded: I will die,
And leave him all; life, living, all is Death's.

PARIS

Have I thought long to see this morning's face,
And doth it give me such a sight as this?

LADY CAPULET

Accurst, unhappy, wretched, hateful day!
Most miserable hour that e'er time saw
In lasting labour of his pilgrimage!
But one, poor one, one poor and loving child,
But one thing to rejoice and solace in,
And cruel death hath catch'd it from my sight!

NURSE

O woe! O woeful, woeful, woeful day!

Most lamentable day, most woeful day,
That ever, ever, I did yet behold!
O day! O day! O day! O hateful day!
Never was seen so black a day as this:
O woeful day, O woeful day!

PARIS

Beguiled, divorced, wronged, spited, slain!
Most detestable death, by thee beguiled,
By cruel cruel thee quite overthrown!
O love! O life! not life, but love in death!

CAPULET

Despised, distressed, hated, martyr'd, kill'd!
Uncomfortable time, why camest thou now
To murder, murder our solemnity?
O child! O child! my soul, and not my child!
Dead art thou! Alack, my child is dead;
And with my child my joys are buried!

FRIAR LAURENCE

Peace, ho, for shame! confusion's cure lives not
In these confusions. Heaven and yourself
Had part in this fair maid; now heaven hath all,
And all the better is it for the maid:
Your part in her you could not keep from death;
But heaven keeps his part in eternal life.
The most you sought was her promotion,
For 'twas your heaven she should be advanced:
And weep ye now, seeing she is advanced
Above the clouds, as high as heaven itself?
O, in this love, you love your child so ill,
That you run mad, seeing that she is well:
She's not well married that lives married long,
But she's best married that dies married young.
Dry up your tears, and stick your rosemary
On this fair corse, and, as the custom is,
In all her best array bear her to church:
For though fond nature bids us all lament,
Yet nature's tears are reason's merriment.

CAPULET

All things that we ordained festival,
Turn from their office to black funeral:
Our instruments to melancholy bells;
Our wedding cheer to a sad burial feast;
Our solemn hymns to sullen dirges change;
Our bridal flowers serve for a buried corse,
And all things change them to the contrary.

FRIAR LAURENCE

Sir, go you in; and, madam, go with him;
And go, Sir Paris; every one prepare
To follow this fair corse unto her grave:
The heavens do lour upon you for some ill;
Move them no more by crossing their high will.
[Exeunt CAPULET, LADY CAPULET, PARIS, and FRIAR

FIRST MUSICIAN

Faith, we may put up our pipes, and be gone.

NURSE

Honest good fellows, ah, put up, put up;
For, well you know, this is a pitiful case.　　[Exit

FIRST MUSICIAN

Ay, by my troth, the case may be amended.

Enter PETER

PETER

Musicians, O, musicians, 'Heart's ease, Heart's ease:'
O, an you will have me live, play 'Heart's ease.'

FIRST MUSICIAN

Why 'Heart's ease'?

PETER

O, musicians, because my heart itself plays 'My
heart is full of woe:' O, play me some merry dump,
to comfort me.

FIRST MUSICIAN

Not a dump we; 'tis no time to play now.

PETER

You will not then?

FIRST MUSICIAN

No.

PETER

I will then give it you soundly.

FIRST MUSICIAN

What will you give us?

PETER

No money, on my faith, but the gleek; I will give
you the minstrel.

FIRST MUSICIAN

Then will I give you the serving-creature.

PETER

Then will I lay the serving-creature's dagger on
your pate. I will carry no crotchets: I'll re you, I'll
fa you; do you note me?

FIRST MUSICIAN

An you re us and fa us, you note us.

SECOND MUSICIAN

Pray you, put up your dagger, and put out your wit.

PETER

Then have at you with my wit! I will dry-beat you
with an iron wit, and put up my iron dagger. Answer me like men:

'When griping grief the heart doth wound
And doleful dumps the mind oppress,
Then music with her silver sound'—

why 'silver sound'? why 'music with her silver
sound'?—
What say you, Simon Catling?

FIRST MUSICIAN

Marry, sir, because silver hath a sweet sound.

PETER

Pretty! What say you, Hugh Rebeck?

SECOND MUSICIAN

I say, 'silver sound,' because musicians sound for
silver.

PETER

Pretty too! What say you, James Soundpost?

THIRD MUSICIAN

Faith, I know not what to say.

PETER

O, I cry you mercy; you are the singer: I will say for
you. It is 'music with her silver sound,' because
musicians have no gold for sounding:

'Then music with her silver sound
With speedy help doth lend redress.'　　[Exit

FIRST MUSICIAN

What a pestilent knave is this same!

SECOND MUSICIAN

Hang him, Jack! Come, we'll in here; tarry for the mourners, and stay dinner.   [*Exeunt*

ACT V

SCENE I. *Mantua. A street*

Enter ROMEO

ROMEO

If I may trust the flattering truth of sleep,
My dreams presage some joyful news at hand:
My bosom's lord sits lightly in his throne,
And all this day an unaccustom'd spirit
Lifts me above the ground with cheerful thoughts.
I dreamt my lady came and found me dead—
Strange dream, that gives a dead man leave to
    think!—
And breathed such life with kisses in my lips,
That I revived and was an emperor.
Ah me! how sweet is love itself possess'd,
When but love's shadows are so rich in joy!

Enter BALTHASAR, *booted*

News from Verona! How now, Balthasar!
Dost thou not bring me letters from the friar?
How doth my lady? Is my father well?
How fares my Juliet? that I ask again;
For nothing can be ill, if she be well.

BALTHASAR

Then she is well, and nothing can be ill:
Her body sleeps in Capels' monument,
And her immortal part with angels lives.
I saw her laid low in her kindred's vault,
And presently took post to tell it you:
O, pardon me for bringing these ill news,
Since you did leave it for my office, sir.

ROMEO

Is it e'en so? then I defy you, stars!
Thou know'st my lodging: get me ink and paper,
And hire post-horses; I will hence to-night.

BALTHASAR

I do beseech you, sir, have patience:
Your looks are pale and wild, and do import
Some misadventure.

ROMEO

        Tush, thou art deceived:
Leave me, and do the thing I bid thee do.
Hast thou no letters to me from the friar?

BALTHASAR

No, my good lord.

ROMEO

        No matter: get thee gone,
And hire those horses; I'll be with thee straight.

        [*Exit* BALTHASAR

Well, Juliet, I will lie with thee to-night.
Let's see for means:—O mischief, thou art swift

To enter in the thoughts of desperate men!
I do remember an apothecary,
And hereabouts a' dwells, which late I noted
In tatter'd weeds, with overwhelming brows,
Culling of simples; meagre were his looks;
Sharp misery had worn him to the bones:
And in his needy shop a tortoise hung,
An alligator stuff'd and other skins
Of ill-shaped fishes; and about his shelves
A beggarly account of empty boxes,
Green earthen pots, bladders and musty seeds,
Remnants of packthread and old cakes of roses,
Were thinly scatter'd, to make up a show.
Noting this penury, to myself I said,
An if a man did need a poison now,
Whose sale is present death in Mantua,
Here lives a caitiff wretch would sell it him.
O, this same thought did but forerun my need,
And this same needy man must sell it me.
As I remember, this should be the house:
Being holiday, the beggar's shop is shut.
What, ho! apothecary!

Enter APOTHECARY

APOTHECARY

        Who calls so loud?

ROMEO

Come hither, man. I see that thou art poor;
Hold, there is forty ducats: let me have
A dram of poison; such soon-speeding gear
As will disperse itself through all the veins,
That the life-weary taker may fall dead,
And that the trunk may be discharged of breath
As violently as hasty powder fired
Doth hurry from the fatal cannon's womb.

APOTHECARY

Such mortal drugs I have; but Mantua's law
Is death to any he that utters them.

ROMEO

Art thou so bare and full of wretchedness,
And fear'st to die? famine is in thy cheeks,
Need and oppression starveth in thy eyes,
Contempt and beggary hangs upon thy back,
The world is not thy friend, nor the world's law:
The world affords no law to make thee rich;
Then be not poor, but break it, and take this.

APOTHECARY

My poverty, but not my will, consents.

ROMEO

I pay thy poverty and not thy will.

APOTHECARY

Put this in any liquid thing you will,
And drink it off; and, if you had the strength
Of twenty men, it would dispatch you straight.

ROMEO

There is thy gold, worse poison to men's souls,
Doing more murder in this loathsome world,
Than these poor compounds that thou mayst not
    sell:
I sell thee poison, thou hast sold me none.
Farewell: buy food, and get thyself in flesh.

[346]

Come, cordial and not poison, go with me
To Juliet's grave; for there must I use thee. [*Exeunt*

SCENE II. FRIAR LAURENCE's *cell*

Enter FRIAR JOHN
FRIAR JOHN
Holy Franciscan friar! brother, ho!
Enter FRIAR LAURENCE
FRIAR LAURENCE
This same should be the voice of Friar John.
Welcome from Mantua: what says Romeo?
Or, if his mind be writ, give me his letter.
FRIAR JOHN
Going to find a bare-foot brother out,
One of our order, to associate me,
Here in this city visiting the sick,
And finding him, the searchers of the town,
Suspecting that we both were in a house
Where the infectious pestilence did reign,
Seal'd up the doors and would not let us forth;
So that my speed to Mantua there was stay'd.
FRIAR LAURENCE
Who bare my letter then to Romeo?
FRIAR JOHN
I could not send it,—here it is again,—
Nor get a messenger to bring it thee,
So fearful were they of infection.
FRIAR LAURENCE
Unhappy fortune! by my brotherhood,
The letter was not nice, but full of charge
Of dear import, and the neglecting it
May do much danger. Friar John, go hence;
Get me an iron crow and bring it straight
Unto my cell.
FRIAR JOHN
Brother, I'll go and bring it thee. [*Exit*
FRIAR LAURENCE
Now must I to the monument alone;
Within this three hours will fair Juliet wake:
She will beshrew me much that Romeo
Hath had no notice of these accidents;
But I will write again to Mantua,
And keep her at my cell till Romeo come:
Poor living corse, closed in a dead man's tomb! [*Exit*

SCENE III. *A churchyard; in it a monument belonging to the* CAPULETS

Enter PARIS *and his* PAGE, *bearing flowers and a torch*
PARIS
Give me thy torch, boy: hence, and stand aloof:
Yet put it out, for I would not be seen.
Under yond yew-trees lay thee all along,
Holding thine ear close to the hollow ground;
So shall no foot upon the churchyard tread,
Being loose, unfirm, with digging up of graves,
But thou shalt hear it: whistle then to me,

As signal that thou hear'st something approach.
Give me those flowers. Do as I bid thee, go.
PAGE
[*Aside*] I am almost afraid to stand alone
Here in the churchyard; yet I will adventure.
[*Retires*
PARIS
Sweet flower, with flowers thy bridal bed I strew,—
O woe! thy canopy is dust and stones;—
Which with sweet water nightly I will dew,
Or, wanting that, with tears distill'd by moans:
The obsequies that I for thee will keep
Nightly shall be to strew thy grave and weep.
[*The* PAGE *whistles*
The boy gives warning something doth approach.
What cursed foot wanders this way to-night,
To cross my obsequies and true love's rite?
What, with a torch! Muffle me, night, a while.
[*Retires*
Enter ROMEO *and* BALTHASAR, *with a torch, mattock, &c.*
ROMEO
Give me that mattock and the wrenching iron.
Hold, take this letter; early in the morning
See thou deliver it to my lord and father.
Give me the light: upon thy life, I charge thee,
Whate'er thou hear'st or seest, stand all aloof,
And do not interrupt me in my course.
Why I descend into this bed of death
Is partly to behold my lady's face,
But chiefly to take thence from her dead finger
A precious ring, a ring that I must use
In dear employment: therefore hence, be gone:
But if thou, jealous, dost return to pry
In what I farther shall intend to do,
By heaven, I will tear thee joint by joint
And strew this hungry churchyard with thy limbs:
The time and my intents are savage-wild,
More fierce and more inexorable far
Than empty tigers or the roaring sea.
BALTHASAR
I will be gone, sir, and not trouble you.
ROMEO
So shalt thou show me friendship. Take thou that:
Live, and be prosperous: and farewell, good fellow.
BALTHASAR
[*Aside*] For all this same, I'll hide me hereabout:
His looks I fear, and his intents I doubt. [*Retires*
ROMEO
Thou detestable maw, thou womb of death,
Gorged with the dearest morsel of the earth,
Thus I enforce thy rotten jaws to open,
And in despite I'll cram thee with more food.
[*Opens the tomb*
PARIS
This is that banish'd haughty Montague
That murder'd my love's cousin, with which grief,
It is supposed, the fair creature died,
And here is come to do some villanous shame
To the dead bodies: I will apprehend him.
[*Comes forward*

Stop thy unhallow'd toil, vile Montague!
Can vengeance be pursued further than death?
Condemned villain, I do apprehend thee:
Obey, and go with me; for thou must die.

ROMEO

I must indeed, and therefore came I hither.
Good gentle youth, tempt not a desperate man;
Fly hence and leave me: think upon these gone;
Let them affright thee. I beseech thee, youth,
Put not another sin upon my head,
By urging me to fury: O, be gone!
By heaven, I love thee better than myself,
For I come hither arm'd against myself:
Stay not, be gone: live, and hereafter say,
A madman's mercy bid thee run away.

PARIS

I do defy thy conjurations
And apprehend thee for a felon here.

ROMEO

Wilt thou provoke me? then have at thee, boy!
[They fight

PAGE

O Lord, they fight! I will go call the watch. [Exit

PARIS

O, I am slain! [Falls] If thou be merciful,
Open the tomb, lay me with Juliet. [Dies

ROMEO

In faith, I will. Let me peruse this face:
Mercutio's kinsman, noble County Paris!
What said my man, when my betossed soul
Did not attend him as we rode? I think
He told me Paris should have married Juliet:
Said he not so? or did I dream it so?
Or am I mad, hearing him talk of Juliet,
To think it was so? O, give me thy hand,
One writ with me in sour misfortune's book!
I'll bury thee in a triumphant grave;
A grave? O, no, a lantern, slaughter'd youth;
For here lies Juliet, and her beauty makes
This vault a feasting presence full of light.
Death, lie thou there, by a dead man interr'd.
[Laying PARIS in the monument
How oft when men are at the point of death
Have they been merry! which their keepers call
A lightning before death: O, how may I
Call this a lightning? O my love! my wife!
Death, that hath suck'd the honey of thy breath,
Hath had no power yet upon thy beauty:
Thou art not conquer'd; beauty's ensign yet
Is crimson in thy lips and in thy cheeks,
And death's pale flag is not advanced there.
Tybalt, liest thou there in thy bloody sheet?
O, what more favour can I do to thee
Than with that hand that cut thy youth in twain
To sunder his that was thine enemy?
Forgive me, cousin! Ah, dear Juliet,
Why art thou yet so fair? shall I believe
That unsubstantial death is amorous,
And that the lean abhorred monster keeps
Thee here in dark to be his paramour?

For fear of that, I still will stay with thee,
And never from this palace of dim night
Depart again: here, here will I remain
With worms that are thy chamber-maids; O, here
Will I set up my everlasting rest,
And shake the yoke of inauspicious stars
From this world-wearied flesh. Eyes, look your last!
Arms, take your last embrace! and, lips, O you
The doors of breath, seal with a righteous kiss
A dateless bargain to engrossing death!
Come, bitter conduct, come, unsavoury guide!
Thou desperate pilot, now at once run on
The dashing rocks thy sea-sick weary bark.
Here's to my love! [Drinks] O true apothecary!
Thy drugs are quick. Thus with a kiss I die. [Dies
Enter, at the other end of the churchyard, FRIAR LAURENCE,
with a lantern, crow, and spade

FRIAR LAURENCE

Saint Francis be my speed! how oft to-night
Have my old feet stumbled at graves! Who's there?

BALTHASAR

Here's one, a friend, and one that knows you well.

FRIAR LAURENCE

Bliss be upon you! Tell me, good my friend,
What torch is yond that vainly lends his light
To grubs and eyeless skulls? as I discern,
It burneth in the Capel's monument.

BALTHASAR

It doth so, holy sir; and there's my master,
One that you love.

FRIAR LAURENCE

Who is it?

BALTHASAR

Romeo.

FRIAR LAURENCE

How long hath he been there?

BALTHASAR

Full half an hour.

FRIAR LAURENCE

Go with me to the vault.

BALTHASAR

I dare not, sir:
My master knows not but I am gone hence;
And fearfully did menace me with death,
If I did stay to look on his intents.

FRIAR LAURENCE

Stay, then; I'll go alone: fear comes upon me;
O, much I fear some ill unlucky thing.

BALTHASAR

As I did sleep under this yew-tree here,
I dreamt my master and another fought,
And that my master slew him.

FRIAR LAURENCE

Romeo! [Advances
Alack, alack, what blood is this, which stains
The stony entrance of this sepulchre?
What mean these masterless and gory swords
To lie discolour'd by this place of peace?
[Enters the tomb
Romeo! O, pale! Who else? what, Paris too?

And steep'd in blood? Ah, what an unkind hour
Is guilty of this lamentable chance!
The lady stirs.   [JULIET *wakes*

JULIET

O comfortable friar! where is my lord?
I do remember well where I should be,
And there I am: where is my Romeo? [*Noise within*

FRIAR LAURENCE

I hear some noise. Lady, come from that nest
Of death, contagion and unnatural sleep:
A greater power than we can contradict
Hath thwarted our intents: come, come away:
Thy husband in thy bosom there lies dead;
And Paris too: come, I'll dispose of thee
Among a sisterhood of holy nuns:
Stay not to question, for the watch is coming;
Come, go, good Juliet; I dare no longer stay.

JULIET

Go, get thee hence, for I will not away.
                    [*Exit* FRIAR LAURENCE
What's here? a cup, closed in my true love's hand?
Poison, I see, hath been his timeless end:
O churl! drunk all, and left no friendly drop
To help me after? I will kiss thy lips;
Haply some poison yet doth hang on them,
To make me die with a restorative. [*Kisses him*
Thy lips are warm.

FIRST WATCHMAN

[*Within*] Lead, boy: which way?

JULIET

Yea, noise? then I'll be brief. O happy dagger!
                    [*Snatching* ROMEO's *dagger*
This is thy sheath [*Stabs herself*]; there rust, and let
    me die.   [*Falls on* ROMEO's *body, and dies*
        Enter WATCH, *with the* PAGE *of* PARIS

PAGE

This is the place; there, where the torch doth burn.

FIRST WATCHMAN

The ground is bloody; search about the churchyard:
Go, some of you, whoe'er you find attach.
Pitiful sight! here lies the county slain;
And Juliet bleeding, warm, and newly dead,
Who here hath lain this two days buried.
Go, tell the prince: run to the Capulets:
Raise up the Montagues: some others search:
We see the ground whereon these woes do lie;
But the true ground of all these piteous woes
We cannot without circumstance descry.
        Re-enter some of the WATCH, *with* BALTHASAR

SECOND WATCHMAN

Here's Romeo's man; we found him in the churchyard.

FIRST WATCHMAN

Hold him in safety, till the prince come hither.
    Re-enter FRIAR LAURENCE, *and another* WATCHMAN

THIRD WATCHMAN

Here is a friar, that trembles, sighs and weeps:
We took this mattock and this spade from him,
As he was coming from this churchyard's side.

FIRST WATCHMAN

A great suspicion: stay the friar too.
        Enter the PRINCE *and* ATTENDANTS

PRINCE

What misadventure is so early up,
That calls our person from our morning rest?
        Enter CAPULET, LADY CAPULET, *and others*

CAPULET

What should it be that they so shriek abroad?

LADY CAPULET

The people in the street cry Romeo,
Some Juliet, and some Paris, and all run
With open outcry toward our monument.

PRINCE

What fear is this which startles in our ears?

FIRST WATCHMAN

Sovereign, here lies the County Paris slain;
And Romeo dead; and Juliet, dead before,
Warm and new kill'd.

PRINCE

Search, seek, and know how this foul murder comes.

FIRST WATCHMAN

Here is a friar, and slaughter'd Romeo's man,
With instruments upon them fit to open
These dead men's tombs.

CAPULET

O heavens! O wife, look how our daughter bleeds!
This dagger hath mista'en, for, lo, his house
Is empty on the back of Montague,
And it mis-sheathed in my daughter's bosom!

LADY CAPULET

O me! this sight of death is as a bell
That warns my old age to a sepulchre.
        Enter MONTAGUE *and others*

PRINCE

Come, Montague; for thou art early up,
To see thy son and heir more early down.

MONTAGUE

Alas, my liege, my wife is dead to-night;
Grief of my son's exile hath stopp'd her breath:
What further woe conspires against mine age?

PRINCE

Look, and thou shalt see.

MONTAGUE

O thou untaught! what manners is in this,
To press before thy father to a grave?

PRINCE

Seal up the mouth of outrage for a while,
Till we can clear these ambiguities,
And know their spring, their head, their true de-
    scent;
And then will I be general of your woes,
And lead you even to death: meantime forbear,
And let mischance be slave to patience.
Bring forth the parties of suspicion.

FRIAR LAURENCE

I am the greatest, able to do least,
Yet most suspected, as the time and place
Doth make against me, of this direful murder;

And here I stand, both to impeach and purge
Myself condemned and myself excused.

PRINCE

Then say at once what thou dost know in this.

FRIAR LAURENCE

I will be brief, for my short date of breath
Is not so long as is a tedious tale.
Romeo, there dead, was husband to that Juliet;
And she, there dead, that Romeo's faithful wife:
I married them; and their stol'n marriage-day
Was Tybalt's dooms-day, whose untimely death
Banish'd the new-made bridegroom from this city;
For whom, and not for Tybalt, Juliet pined.
You, to remove that siege of grief from her,
Betroth'd and would have married her perforce
To County Paris: then comes she to me,
And with wild looks bid me devise some mean
To rid her from this second marriage,
Or in my cell there would she kill herself.
Then gave I her, so tutor'd by my art,
A sleeping potion; which so took effect
As I intended, for it wrought on her
The form of death: meantime I writ to Romeo,
That he should hither come as this dire night,
To help to take her from her borrow'd grave,
Being the time the potion's force should cease.
But he which bore my letter, Friar John,
Was stay'd by accident, and yesternight
Return'd my letter back. Then all alone
At the prefixed hour of her waking
Came I to take her from her kindred's vault,
Meaning to keep her closely at my cell
Till I conveniently could send to Romeo:
But when I came, some minute ere the time
Of her awaking, here untimely lay
The noble Paris and true Romeo dead.
She wakes, and I entreated her come forth,
And bear this work of heaven with patience:
But then a noise did scare me from the tomb,
And she too desperate would not go with me,
But, as it seems, did violence on herself.
All this I know; and to the marriage
Her nurse is privy: and, if aught in this
Miscarried by my fault, let my old life
Be sacrificed some hour before his time
Unto the rigour of severest law.

PRINCE

We still have known thee for a holy man.
Where's Romeo's man? what can he say in this?

BALTHASAR

I brought my master news of Juliet's death,
And then in post he came from Mantua
To this same place, to this same monument.
This letter he early bid me give his father,
And threaten'd me with death, going in the vault,
If I departed not and left him there.

PRINCE

Give me the letter; I will look on it.
Where is the county's page, that raised the watch?
Sirrah, what made your master in this place?

PAGE

He came with flowers to strew his lady's grave;
And bid me stand aloof, and so I did:
Anon comes one with light to ope the tomb;
And by and by my master drew on him;
And then I ran away to call the watch.

PRINCE

This letter doth make good the friar's words,
Their course of love, the tidings of her death:
And here he writes that he did buy a poison
Of a poor 'pothecary, and therewithal
Came to this vault to die and lie with Juliet.
Where be these enemies? Capulet! Montague!
See, what a scourge is laid upon your hate,
That heaven finds means to kill your joys with love!
And I, for winking at your discords too,
Have lost a brace of kinsmen: all are punish'd.

CAPULET

O brother Montague, give me thy hand:
This is my daughter's jointure, for no more
Can I demand.

MONTAGUE

      But I can give thee more:
For I will raise her statue in pure gold;
That whiles Verona by that name is known,
There shall no figure at such rate be set
As that of true and faithful Juliet.

CAPULET

As rich shall Romeo's by his lady's lie;
Poor sacrifices of our enmity!

PRINCE

A glooming peace this morning with it brings;
   The sun for sorrow will not show his head:
Go hence, to have more talk of these sad things;
   Some shall be pardon'd and some punished:
For never was a story of more woe
Than this of Juliet and her Romeo.   [Exeunt

THE TRAGEDY OF KING RICHARD II

SYNOPSIS

Henry, surnamed Bolingbroke, eldest son of John of Gaunt, Duke of Lancaster, who is Richard II's uncle, is summoned into the King's presence to make public his charges against Thomas Mowbray, Duke of Norfolk, of misappropriating military funds and plotting the death of the late Duke of Gloucester, another uncle of the King. Richard gives the two adversaries permission to settle their dispute by combat in the lists at Coventry, but as they face each other in full armor, lances in hand, and the marshal sounds the trumpet for the charge, the fickle King stops the contest, banishes Norfolk for life, Bolingbroke for six years, and, with his usual suspicious foreboding, requires both to swear never to plot against him. With diplomatic cunning, Bolingbroke urges his opponent to confess his treason before leaving England, but Norfolk, refusing, warns the King against his enemy.

Shortly after his son's banishment, John of Gaunt falls ill, and sending for Richard from his deathbed reproaches him for his selfish extravagance and the mortgaging of his realm, bitterly prophesying that the kingdom would suffer for his sins, but no sooner has the Duke died than the King, brushing aside the protests of his honest old uncle, the Duke of York, seizes the Lancaster estates to raise money for his Irish wars. This high-handed act quickly brings the reprisals York had feared. Bolingbroke makes capital of it as an excuse for ending his exile in order to protect his title and rights as Duke of Lancaster, lands in the north of England with ships and men supplied by the Duke of Brittany, and is soon joined by the Earl of Northumberland, his son, Henry Percy, called Hotspur, Ross, Willoughby and other estranged noblemen.

Meanwhile the King has gone to Ireland, leaving the feeble Duke of York in charge of his almost bankrupt kingdom but confidently expecting to find his Welsh army of twelve thousand men awaiting him when he returns. He arrives with a small train to hear that upon rumors of his death his Welshmen have disbanded, many of them having joined the forces of Bolingbroke who has prevailed upon the vacillating York to help him regain his title and estates, and has executed the King's influential court favorites, Bushy, Green and the Earl of Wiltshire.

The forsaken King in deep dejection takes refuge in Flint Castle where Bolingbroke seeks him out with an effective showing of obeisance, and under the pretext of claiming nothing but his family rights takes Richard to London a virtual prisoner. Capable only of sentimentalizing on his fate, the King yields up his crown to Bolingbroke, who, aided by the cold, unfeeling Northumberland, forces Richard to sign a confession of his crimes against the state and a complete abdication, commits him to imprisonment in the Tower, and proclaims himself the successor to the throne.

Well supported by documents, Bolingbroke proceeds in confidence to his coronation as Henry IV, but the Bishop of Carlisle makes a dire prophecy on the result of his acts and calls him a traitor to his country's best interests. Together with the incensed Abbot of Westminster and Carlisle, Aumerle, son of the Duke of York and a former favorite of King Richard's, plots to murder Henry at the Oxford tournaments, but the old York discovers the intrigue, and, although grieving over Richard's downfall, goes loyally to his new sovereign, demanding that his son be executed for treason. His Duchess, having contended in vain against her husband's decision, urges Aumerle to outdistance his father and confess his crime to Henry before the old man reaches the palace. She herself follows, and gaining admittance to the royal presence sues with stubborn insistence until she wins her son's pardon.

The new ruler, already feeling his insecurity, vows vengeance on the other conspirators, orders Northumberland to remove the deposed King to the dungeons of Pomfret Castle, and the sorrowing young Queen to her native France. Before he leaves, Richard warns the curt Northumberland that the fact of his having been the ladder by which Bolingbroke mounted the throne will remind the distrustful Henry that he knows how to make usurpers kings.

Subtly Henry conveys to the mind of a devoted courtier, Sir Pierce Exton, his desire to be rid of the imprisoned King Richard, and the knight loses no time in reaching Pomfret Castle and attacking Richard who kills one of Exton's servants before he is struck down himself. In the royal castle at Windsor, Henry is telling the old Duke of York of a sudden rebellion among his subjects in the north, and receiving reports of Northumberland and his other followers on the execution of several disaffected noblemen and churchmen, when Exton arrives with attendants bearing the coffin of King Richard. Henry affects astonishment and righteous indignation at the murder, and protesting to his lords that his soul is full of woe he announces that he will do penance by making a journey to the Holy Land.

HISTORICAL DATA

The historical material for *Richard II* is largely derived from Holinshed's *Chronicles of England, Scotland and Ireland*, and apparently from the second edition of that work, as only from this later edition could Shakespeare have obtained the omen of the withered bay trees (Act II, Scene iv). The account of the Duke of Norfolk's sojourn in the Holy Land probably has origin in Stowe's *Annals* (1580) as Holinshed makes no mention of this.

The female characters in the play are wholly the creation of Shakespeare, there being no historical accuracy in the depiction of the Queen in particular, as actually she was but eleven years old at the time of Richard's deposition.

In style and treatment of the subject Shakespeare closely followed Marlowe, although this play is more divorced from the influence of the latter's *Edward II* than is *Richard III*. The frequency of rhyme and the absence of prose indicate that this is one of the early plays and the date assigned to it is generally 1593–4.

Two quarto editions were published in 1597 in which lines relating to the deposition of Richard II (Act IV, Scene i), were omitted, presumably because of the sensitiveness of Queen Elizabeth on the subject. As "new additions," however, the lines were restored in the Third Quarto in 1608.

"*I have been studying how I may compare*
This prison where I live unto the world."
RICHARD II

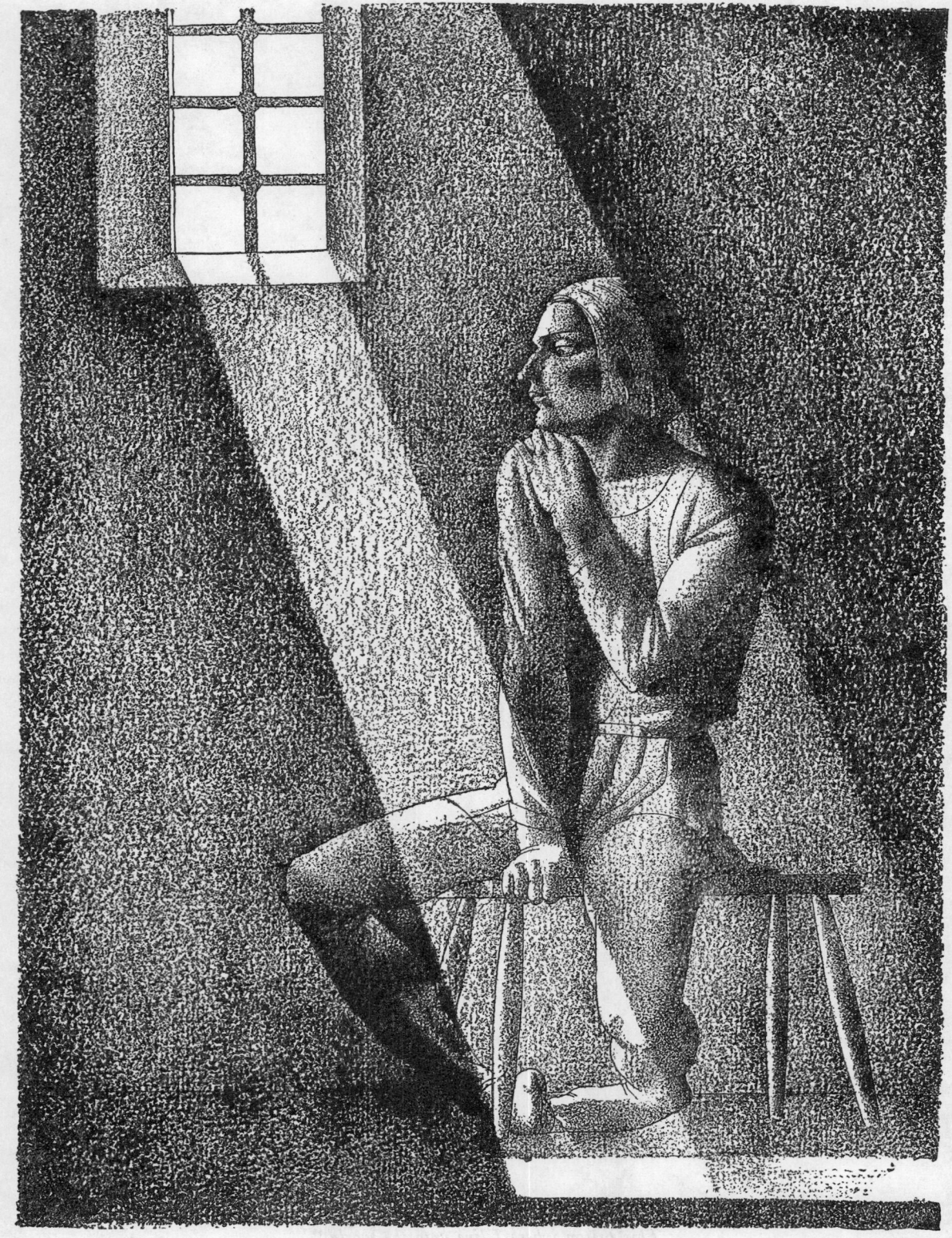

THE TRAGEDY OF KING RICHARD II

DRAMATIS PERSONÆ

KING RICHARD *the Second.*
JOHN OF GAUNT, *Duke of Lancaster,* } *uncles to the*
EDMUND OF LANGLEY, *Duke of York,* } *King.*
HENRY, *surnamed* BOLINGBROKE, *Duke of Here-*
ford, son to John of Gaunt; afterwards KING
HENRY IV.
DUKE OF AUMERLE, *son to the Duke of York.*
THOMAS MOWBRAY, *Duke of Norfolk.*
DUKE OF SURREY.
EARL OF SALISBURY.
LORD BERKELEY.
BUSHY, }
BAGOT, } *servants to King Richard.*
GREEN, }
EARL OF NORTHUMBERLAND.
HENRY PERCY, *surnamed* Hotspur, *his son.*
LORD ROSS.

LORD WILLOUGHBY.
LORD FITZWATER.
BISHOP *of Carlisle.*
ABBOT *of Westminster.*
LORD MARSHAL.
SIR STEPHEN SCROOP.
SIR PIERCE OF EXTON.
CAPTAIN *of a band of Welshmen.*
QUEEN *to King Richard.*
DUCHESS OF YORK.
DUCHESS OF GLOUCESTER.
LADY *attending on the Queen.*

LORDS, HERALDS, OFFICERS, SOLDIERS, *two* GAR-
DENERS, KEEPER, MESSENGER, GROOM, *and other*
ATTENDANTS.

SCENE—*England and Wales.*

ACT I

SCENE I. *London.* KING RICHARD's *palace*

Enter KING RICHARD, JOHN OF GAUNT, *with other*
NOBLES *and* ATTENDANTS

KING RICHARD

OLD John of Gaunt, time-honour'd Lancaster,
Hast thou, according to thy oath and band,
Brought hither Henry Hereford thy bold son,
Here to make good the boisterous late appeal,
Which then our leisure would not let us hear,
Against the Duke of Norfolk, Thomas Mowbray?

GAUNT

I have, my liege.

KING RICHARD

Tell me, moreover, hast thou sounded him,
If he appeal the duke on ancient malice;
Or worthily, as a good subject should,
On some known ground of treachery in him?

GAUNT

As near as I could sift him on that argument,
On some apparent danger seen in him
Aim'd at your highness, no inveterate malice.

KING RICHARD

Then call them to our presence; face to face,
And frowning brow to brow, ourselves will hear
The accuser and the accused freely speak:
High-stomach'd are they both, and full of ire,
In rage deaf as the sea, hasty as fire.

Enter BOLINGBROKE *and* MOWBRAY

BOLINGBROKE

Many years of happy days befal
My gracious sovereign, my most loving liege!

MOWBRAY

Each day still better other's happiness;
Until the heavens, envying earth's good hap,
Add an immortal title to your crown!

KING RICHARD

We thank you both: yet one but flatters us,
As well appeareth by the cause you come;
Namely, to appeal each other of high treason.
Cousin of Hereford, what dost thou object
Against the Duke of Norfolk, Thomas Mowbray?

BOLINGBROKE

First, heaven be the record of my speech!
In the devotion of a subject's love,
Tendering the precious safety of my prince,
And free from other misbegotten hate,
Come I appellant to this princely presence.
Now, Thomas Mowbray, do I turn to thee,
And mark my greeting well; for what I speak
My body shall make good upon this earth,
Or my divine soul answer it in heaven.
Thou art a traitor and a miscreant,
Too good to be so, and too bad to live,
Since the more fair and crystal is the sky,
The uglier seem the clouds that in it fly.
Once more, the more to aggravate the note,
With a foul traitor's name stuff I thy throat;
And wish, so please my sovereign, ere I move,
What my tongue speaks my right drawn sword may
    prove.

MOWBRAY

Let not my cold words here accuse my zeal:
'Tis not the trial of a woman's war,
The bitter clamour of two eager tongues,
Can arbitrate this cause betwixt us twain;

[353]

The blood is hot that must be cool'd for this:
Yet can I not of such tame patience boast
As to be hush'd and nought at all to say:
First, the fair reverence of your highness curbs me
From giving reins and spurs to my free speech;
Which else would post until it had return'd
These terms of treason doubled down his throat.
Setting aside his high blood's royalty,
And let him be no kinsman to my liege,
I do defy him, and I spit at him;
Call him a slanderous coward and a villain:
Which to maintain I would allow him odds,
And meet him, were I tied to run afoot
Even to the frozen ridges of the Alps,
Or any other ground inhabitable,
Where ever Englishman durst set his foot.
Mean time let this defend my loyalty,
By all my hopes, most falsely doth he lie.

BOLINGBROKE

Pale trembling coward, there I throw my gage,
Disclaiming here the kindred of the king;
And lay aside my high blood's royalty,
Which fear, not reverence, makes thee to except.
If guilty dread have left thee so much strength
As to take up mine honour's pawn, then stoop:
By that and all the rites of knighthood else,
Will I make good against thee, arm to arm,
What I have spoke, or thou canst worse devise.

MOWBRAY

I take it up; and by that sword I swear,
Which gently laid my knighthood on my shoulder,
I'll answer thee in any fair degree,
Or chivalrous design of knightly trial:
And when I mount, alive may I not light,
If I be traitor or unjustly fight!

KING RICHARD

What doth our cousin lay to Mowbray's charge?
It must be great that can inherit us
So much as of a thought of ill in him.

BOLINGBROKE

Look, what I speak, my life shall prove it true;
That Mowbray hath received eight thousand nobles
In name of lendings for your highness' soldiers,
The which he hath detain'd for lewd employments,
Like a false traitor and injurious villain.
Besides I say and will in battle prove,
Or here or elsewhere to the furthest verge
That ever was survey'd by English eye,
That all the treasons for these eighteen years
Complotted and contrived in this land
Fetch from false Mowbray their first head and
    spring.
Further I say, and further will maintain
Upon his bad life to make all this good,
That he did plot the Duke of Gloucester's death,
Suggest his soon-believing adversaries,
And consequently, like a traitor coward,
Sluiced out his innocent soul through streams of
    blood:
Which blood, like sacrificing Abel's, cries,

Even from the tongueless caverns of the earth,
To me for justice and rough chastisement;
And, by the glorious worth of my descent,
This arm shall do it, or this life be spent.

KING RICHARD

How high a pitch his resolution soars!
Thomas of Norfolk, what say'st thou to this?

MOWBRAY

O, let my sovereign turn away his face,
And bid his ears a little while be deaf,
Till I have told this slander of his blood,
How God and good men hate so foul a liar.

KING RICHARD

Mowbray, impartial are our eyes and ears:
Were he my brother, nay, my kingdom's heir,
As he is but my father's brother's son,
Now, by my sceptre's awe, I make a vow,
Such neighbour nearness to our sacred blood
Should nothing privilege him, nor partialize
The unstooping firmness of my upright soul:
He is our subject, Mowbray; so art thou:
Free speech and fearless I to thee allow.

MOWBRAY

Then, Bolingbroke, as low as to thy heart,
Through the false passage of thy throat, thou liest.
Three parts of that receipt I had for Calais
Disbursed I duly to his highness' soldiers;
The other part reserved I by consent,
For that my sovereign liege was in my debt
Upon remainder of a dear account,
Since last I went to France to fetch his queen:
Now swallow down that lie. For Gloucester's death,
I slew him not; but to my own disgrace
Neglected my sworn duty in that case.
For you, my noble Lord of Lancaster,
The honourable father to my foe,
Once did I lay an ambush for your life,
A trespass that doth vex my grieved soul;
But ere I last received the sacrament
I did confess it, and exactly begg'd
Your grace's pardon, and I hope I had it.
This is my fault: as for the rest appeal'd,
It issues from the rancour of a villain,
A recreant and most degenerate traitor:
Which in myself I boldly will defend;
And interchangeably hurl down my gage
Upon this overweening traitor's foot,
To prove myself a loyal gentleman
Even in the best blood chamber'd in his bosom.
In haste whereof, most heartily I pray
Your highness to assign our trial day.

KING RICHARD

Wrath-kindled gentlemen, be ruled by me;
Let's purge this choler without letting blood:
This we prescribe, though no physician;
Deep malice makes too deep incision:
Forget, forgive; conclude and be agreed;
Our doctors say this is no month to bleed.
Good uncle, let this end where it begun;
We'll calm the Duke of Norfolk, you your son.

GAUNT

To be a make-peace shall become my age:
Throw down, my son, the Duke of Norfolk's gage.

KING RICHARD

And, Norfolk, throw down his.

GAUNT

           When, Harry, when?
Obedience bids I should not bid again.

KING RICHARD

Norfolk, throw down, we bid; there is no boot.

MOWBRAY

Myself I throw, dread sovereign, at thy foot.
My life thou shalt command, but not my shame:
The one my duty owes; but my fair name,
Despite of death that lives upon my grave,
To dark dishonour's use thou shalt not have.
I am disgraced, impeach'd and baffled here;
Pierced to the soul with slander's venom'd spear,
The which no balm can cure but his heart-blood
Which breathed this poison.

KING RICHARD

           Rage must be withstood:
Give me his gage: lions make leopards tame.

MOWBRAY

Yea, but not change his spots: take but my shame,
And I resign my gage. My dear dear lord,
The purest treasure mortal times afford
Is spotless reputation: that away,
Men are but gilded loam or painted clay.
A jewel in a ten-times-barr'd-up chest
Is a bold spirit in a loyal breast.
Mine honour is my life; both grow in one;
Take honour from me, and my life is done:
Then, dear my liege, mine honour let me try;
In that I live and for that will I die.

KING RICHARD

Cousin, throw up your gage; do you begin.

BOLINGBROKE

O, God defend my soul from such deep sin!
Shall I seem crest-fallen in my father's sight?
Or with pale beggar-fear impeach my height
Before this out-dared dastard? Ere my tongue
Shall wound my honour with such feeble wrong,
Or sound so base a parle, my teeth shall tear
The slavish motive of recanting fear,
And spit it bleeding in his high disgrace,
Where shame doth harbour, even in Mowbray's
    face.   [*Exit* GAUNT

KING RICHARD

We were not born to sue, but to command;
Which since we cannot do to make you friends,
Be ready, as your lives shall answer it,
At Coventry, upon Saint Lambert's day:
There shall your swords and lances arbitrate
The swelling difference of your settled hate:
Since we can not atone you, we shall see
Justice design the victor's chivalry.
Lord marshal, command our officers at arms
Be ready to direct these home alarms.   [*Exeunt*

SCENE II. *The* DUKE OF LANCASTER'S *palace*

Enter JOHN OF GAUNT *with the* DUCHESS OF GLOUCESTER

GAUNT

Alas, the part I had in Woodstock's blood
Doth more solicit me than your exclaims,
To stir against the butchers of his life!
But since correction lieth in those hands
Which made the fault that we cannot correct,
Put we our quarrel to the will of heaven;
Who, when they see the hours ripe on earth,
Will rain hot vengeance on offenders' heads.

DUCHESS OF GLOUCESTER

Finds brotherhood in thee no sharper spur?
Hath love in thy old blood no living fire?
Edward's seven sons, whereof thyself art one,
Were as seven vials of his sacred blood,
Or seven fair branches springing from one root:
Some of those seven are dried by nature's course,
Some of those branches by the Destinies cut;
But Thomas, my dear lord, my life, my Gloucester,
One vial full of Edward's sacred blood,
One flourishing branch of his most royal root,
Is crack'd, and all the precious liquor spilt,
Is hack'd down, and his summer leaves all faded,
By envy's hand and murder's bloody axe.
Ah, Gaunt, his blood was thine! that bed, that
    womb,
That metal, that self-mould, that fashion'd thee
Made him a man; and though thou livest and
    breathest,
Yet art thou slain in him: thou dost consent
In some large measure to thy father's death,
In that thou seest thy wretched brother die,
Who was the model of thy father's life.
Call it not patience, Gaunt; it is despair:
In suffering thus thy brother to be slaughter'd,
Thou showest the naked pathway to thy life,
Teaching stern murder how to butcher thee:
That which in mean men we intitle patience
Is pale cold cowardice in noble breasts.
What shall I say? to safeguard thine own life,
The best way is to venge my Gloucester's death.

GAUNT

God's is the quarrel; for God's substitute,
His deputy anointed in His sight,
Hath caused his death: the which if wrongfully,
Let heaven revenge; for I may never lift
An angry arm against His minister.

DUCHESS OF GLOUCESTER

Where then, alas, may I complain myself?

GAUNT

To God, the widow's champion and defence.

DUCHESS OF GLOUCESTER

Why, then, I will. Farewell, old Gaunt.
Thou goest to Coventry, there to behold
Our cousin Hereford and fell Mowbray fight:
O, sit my husband's wrongs on Hereford's spear,
That it may enter butcher Mowbray's breast!
Or, if misfortune miss the first career,

Be Mowbray's sins so heavy in his bosom,
That they may break his foaming courser's back,
And throw the rider headlong in the lists,
A caitiff recreant to my cousin Hereford!
Farewell, old Gaunt: thy sometimes brother's wife
With her companion grief must end her life.

GAUNT

Sister, farewell; I must to Coventry:
As much good stay with thee as go with me!

DUCHESS OF GLOUCESTER

Yet one word more: grief boundeth where it falls,
Not with the empty hollowness, but weight:
I take my leave before I have begun,
For sorrow ends not when it seemeth done.
Commend me to thy brother, Edmund York.
Lo, this is all:—nay, yet depart not so;
Though this be all, do not so quickly go;
I shall remember more. Bid him—ah, what?—
With all good speed at Plashy visit me.
Alack, and what shall good old York there see
But empty lodgings and unfurnish'd walls,
Unpeopled offices, untrodden stones?
And what hear there for welcome but my groans?
Therefore commend me; let him not come there,
To seek out sorrow that dwells every where.
Desolate, desolate, will I hence and die:
The last leave of thee takes my weeping eye. [*Exeunt*

SCENE III. *The lists at Coventry*

Enter the LORD MARSHAL *and the* DUKE OF AUMERLE

MARSHAL

My Lord Aumerle, is Harry Hereford arm'd?

AUMERLE

Yea, at all points; and longs to enter in.

MARSHAL

The Duke of Norfolk, sprightfully and bold,
Stays but the summons of the appellant's trumpet.

AUMERLE

Why, then, the champions are prepared, and stay
For nothing but his majesty's approach.

The trumpets sound, and the KING *enters with his nobles,*
GAUNT, BUSHY, BAGOT, GREEN, *and others. When they
are set, enter* MOWBRAY *in arms, defendant, with a*
HERALD

KING RICHARD

Marshal, demand of yonder champion
The cause of his arrival here in arms:
Ask him his name, and orderly proceed
To swear him in the justice of his cause.

MARSHAL

In God's name and the king's, say who thou art,
And why thou comest thus knightly clad in arms;
Against what man thou comest, and what thy
   quarrel:
Speak truly, on thy knighthood and thy oath;
As so defend thee heaven and thy valour!

MOWBRAY

My name is Thomas Mowbray, Duke of Norfolk;

Who hither come engaged by my oath—
Which God defend a knight should violate!—
Both to defend my loyalty and truth
To God, my king, and my succeeding issue,
Against the Duke of Hereford that appeals me;
And, by the grace of God and this mine arm,
To prove him, in defending of myself,
A traitor to my God, my king, and me:
And as I truly fight, defend me heaven!

The trumpets sound. Enter BOLINGBROKE, *appellant, in
armour, with a* HERALD

KING RICHARD

Marshal, ask yonder knight in arms,
Both who he is, and why he cometh hither
Thus plated in habiliments of war;
And formally, according to our law,
Depose him in the justice of his cause.

MARSHAL

What is thy name? and wherefore comest thou
   hither,
Before King Richard in his royal lists?
Against whom comest thou? and what's thy quarrel?
Speak like a true knight, so defend thee heaven!

BOLINGBROKE

Harry of Hereford, Lancaster and Derby,
Am I; who ready here do stand in arms,
To prove, by God's grace and my body's valour,
In lists, on Thomas Mowbray, Duke of Norfolk,
That he is a traitor, foul and dangerous,
To God of heaven, King Richard and to me;
And as I truly fight, defend me heaven!

MARSHAL

On pain of death, no person be so bold
Or daring-hardy as to touch the lists,
Except the marshal and such officers
Appointed to direct these fair designs.

BOLINGBROKE

Lord marshal, let me kiss my sovereign's hand,
And bow my knee before his majesty:
For Mowbray and myself are like two men
That vow a long and weary pilgrimage;
Then let us take a ceremonious leave
And loving farewell of our several friends.

MARSHAL

The appellant in all duty greets your highness,
And craves to kiss your hand and take his leave.

KING RICHARD

We will descend and fold him in our arms.
Cousin of Hereford, as thy cause is right,
So be thy fortune in this royal fight!
Farewell, my blood; which if to-day thou shed,
Lament we may, but not revenge thee dead.

BOLINGBROKE

O, let no noble eye profane a tear
For me, if I be gored with Mowbray's spear:
As confident as is the falcon's flight
Against a bird, do I with Mowbray fight.
My loving lord, I take my leave of you;
Of you, my noble cousin, Lord Aumerle;
Not sick, although I have to do with death,

But lusty, young, and cheerly drawing breath.
Lo, as at English feasts, so I regreet
The daintiest last, to make the end most sweet:
O thou, the earthly author of my blood,
Whose youthful spirit, in me regenerate,
Doth with a twofold vigour lift me up
To reach at victory above my head,
Add proof unto mine armour with thy prayers;
And with thy blessings steel my lance's point,
That it may enter Mowbray's waxen coat,
And furbish new the name of John a Gaunt,
Even in the lusty haviour of his son.

GAUNT
God in thy good cause make thee prosperous!
Be swift like lightning in the execution;
And let thy blows, doubly redoubled,
Fall like amazing thunder on the casque
Of thy adverse pernicious enemy:
Rouse up thy youthful blood, be valiant and live.

BOLINGBROKE
Mine innocency and Saint George to thrive!

MOWBRAY
However God or fortune cast my lot,
There lives or dies, true to King Richard's throne,
A loyal, just and upright gentleman:
Never did captive with a freer heart
Cast off his chains of bondage, and embrace
His golden uncontroll'd enfranchisement,
More than my dancing soul doth celebrate
This feast of battle with mine adversary.
Most mighty liege, and my companion peers,
Take from my mouth the wish of happy years:
As gentle and as jocund as to jest
Go I to fight: truth hath a quiet breast.

KING RICHARD
Farewell, my lord: securely I espy
Virtue with valour couched in thine eye.
Order the trial, marshal, and begin.

MARSHAL
Harry of Hereford, Lancaster and Derby,
Receive thy lance; and God defend the right!

BOLINGBROKE
Strong as a tower in hope, I cry amen.

MARSHAL
Go bear this lance to Thomas, Duke of Norfolk.

FIRST HERALD
Harry of Hereford, Lancaster and Derby,
Stands here for God, his sovereign and himself,
On pain to be found false and recreant,
To prove the Duke of Norfolk, Thomas Mowbray,
A traitor to his God, his king and him;
And dares him to set forward to the fight.

SECOND HERALD
Here standeth Thomas Mowbray, Duke of Norfolk,
On pain to be found false and recreant,
Both to defend himself and to approve
Henry of Hereford, Lancaster and Derby,
To God, his sovereign and to him disloyal;
Courageously and with a free desire
Attending but the signal to begin.

MARSHAL
Sound, trumpets; and set forward, combatants.

[*A charge sounded*

Stay, the king hath thrown his warder down.

KING RICHARD
Let them lay by their helmets and their spears,
And both return back to their chairs again:
Withdraw with us: and let the trumpets sound
While we return these dukes what we decree.

[*A long flourish*

Draw near,
And list what with our council we have done.
For that our kingdom's earth should not be soil'd
With that dear blood which it hath fostered;
And for our eyes do hate the dire aspect
Of civil wounds plough'd up with neighbours'
     sword;
And for we think the eagle-winged pride
Of sky-aspiring and ambitious thoughts,
With rival-hating envy, set on you
To wake our peace, which in our country's cradle
Draws the sweet infant breath of gentle sleep;
Which so roused up with boisterous untuned drums,
With harsh-resounding trumpets' dreadful bray,
And grating shock of wrathful iron arms,
Might from our quiet confines fright fair peace,
And make us wade even in our kindred's blood;
Therefore, we banish you our territories:
You, cousin Hereford, upon pain of life,
Till twice five summers have enrich'd our fields
Shall not regreet our fair dominions,
But tread the stranger paths of banishment.

BOLINGBROKE
Your will be done: this must my comfort be,
That sun that warms you here shall shine on me;
And those his golden beams to you here lent
Shall point on me and gild my banishment.

KING RICHARD
Norfolk, for thee remains a heavier doom,
Which I with some unwillingness pronounce:
The sly slow hours shall not determinate
The dateless limit of thy dear exile;
The hopeless word of 'never to return'
Breathe I against thee, upon pain of life.

MOWBRAY
A heavy sentence, my most sovereign liege,
And all unlook'd for from your highness' mouth:
A dearer merit, not so deep a maim
As to be cast forth in the common air,
Have I deserved at your highness' hands.
The language I have learn'd these forty years,
My native English, now I must forgo:
And now my tongue's use is to me no more
Than an unstringed viol or a harp;
Or like a cunning instrument cased up,
Or, being open, put into his hands
That knows no touch to tune the harmony:
Within my mouth you have engaol'd my tongue,
Doubly portcullis'd with my teeth and lips;
And dull unfeeling barren ignorance

Is made my gaoler to attend on me.
I am too old to fawn upon a nurse,
Too far in years to be a pupil now:
What is thy sentence then but speechless death,
Which robs my tongue from breathing native breath?

KING RICHARD

It boots thee not to be compassionate:
After our sentence plaining comes too late.

MOWBRAY

Then thus I turn me from my country's light,
To dwell in solemn shades of endless night.

KING RICHARD

Return again, and take an oath with thee.
Lay on our royal sword your banish'd hands;
Swear by the duty that you owe to God—
Our part therein we banish with yourselves—
To keep the oath that we administer:
You never shall, so help you truth and God!
Embrace each other's love in banishment;
Nor never look upon each other's face;
Nor never write, regreet, nor reconcile
This louring tempest of your home-bred hate;
Nor never by advised purpose meet
To plot, contrive, or complot any ill
'Gainst us, our state, our subjects, or our land.

BOLINGBROKE

I swear.

MOWBRAY

And I, to keep all this.

BOLINGBROKE

Norfolk, so far as to mine enemy:—
By this time, had the king permitted us,
One of our souls had wander'd in the air,
Banish'd this frail sepulchre of our flesh,
As now our flesh is banish'd from this land:
Confess thy treasons ere thou fly the realm;
Since thou hast far to go, bear not along
The clogging burthen of a guilty soul.

MOWBRAY

No, Bolingbroke: if ever I were traitor,
My name be blotted from the book of life,
And I from heaven banish'd as from hence!
But what thou art, God, thou, and I do know;
And all too soon, I fear, the king shall rue.
Farewell, my liege. Now no way can I stray;
Save back to England, all the world's my way. [Exit

KING RICHARD

Uncle, even in the glasses of thine eyes
I see thy grieved heart: thy sad aspect
Hath from the number of his banish'd years
Pluck'd four away. [To BOLINGBROKE] Six frozen winters spent,
Return with welcome home from banishment.

BOLINGBROKE

How long a time lies in one little word!
Four lagging winters and four wanton springs
End in a word: such is the breath of kings.

GAUNT

I thank my liege, that in regard of me

He shortens four years of my son's exile:
But little vantage shall I reap thereby;
For, ere the six years that he hath to spend
Can change their moons and bring their times about,
My oil-dried lamp and time-bewasted light
Shall be extinct with age and endless night;
My inch of taper will be burnt and done,
And blindfold death not let me see my son.

KING RICHARD

Why, uncle, thou hast many years to live.

GAUNT

But not a minute, king, that thou canst give:
Shorten my days thou canst with sullen sorrow,
And pluck nights from me, but not lend a morrow;
Thou canst help time to furrow me with age,
But stop no wrinkle in his pilgrimage;
Thy word is current with him for my death,
But dead, thy kingdom cannot buy my breath.

KING RICHARD

Thy son is banish'd upon good advice,
Whereto thy tongue a party-verdict gave:
Why at our justice seem'st thou then to lour?

GAUNT

Things sweet to taste prove in digestion sour.
You urged me as a judge; but I had rather
You would have bid me argue like a father.
O, had it been a stranger, not my child,
To smooth his fault I should have been more mild:
A partial slander sought I to avoid,
And in the sentence my own life destroy'd.
Alas, I look'd when some of you should say,
I was too strict to make mine own away;
But you gave leave to my unwilling tongue
Against my will to do myself this wrong.

KING RICHARD

Cousin, farewell; and, uncle, bid him so:
Six years we banish him, and he shall go.
          [Flourish. Exeunt KING RICHARD and TRAIN

AUMERLE

Cousin, farewell: what presence must not know,
From where you do remain let paper show.

MARSHAL

My lord, no leave take I; for I will ride,
As far as land will let me, by your side.

GAUNT

O, to what purpose dost thou hoard thy words,
That thou return'st no greeting to thy friends?

BOLINGBROKE

I have too few to take my leave of you,
When the tongue's office should be prodigal
To breathe the abundant dolour of the heart.

GAUNT

Thy grief is but thy absence for a time.

BOLINGBROKE

Joy absent, grief is present for that time.

GAUNT

What is six winters? they are quickly gone.

BOLINGBROKE

To men in joy; but grief makes one hour ten.

GAUNT

Call it a travel that thou takest for pleasure.

BOLINGBROKE

My heart will sigh when I miscall it so,
Which finds it an inforced pilgrimage.

GAUNT

The sullen passage of thy weary steps
Esteem as foil wherein thou art to set
The precious jewel of thy home return.

BOLINGBROKE

Nay, rather, every tedious stride I make
Will but remember me what a deal of world
I wander from the jewels that I love.
Must I not serve a long apprenticehood
To foreign passages, and in the end,
Having my freedom, boast of nothing else
But that I was a journeyman to grief?

GAUNT

All places that the eye of heaven visits
Are to a wise man ports and happy havens.
Teach thy necessity to reason thus;
There is no virtue like necessity.
Think not the king did banish thee,
But thou the king. Woe doth the heavier sit,
Where it perceives it is but faintly borne.
Go, say I sent thee forth to purchase honour
And not the king exiled thee; or suppose
Devouring pestilence hangs in our air
And thou art flying to a fresher clime:
Look, what thy soul holds dear, imagine it
To lie that way thou go'st, not whence thou comest:
Suppose the singing birds musicians,
The grass whereon thou tread'st the presence
　　strew'd,
The flowers fair ladies, and thy steps no more
Than a delightful measure or a dance;
For gnarling sorrow hath less power to bite
The man that mocks at it and sets it light.

BOLINGBROKE

O, who can hold a fire in his hand
By thinking on the frosty Caucasus?
Or cloy the hungry edge of appetite
By bare imagination of a feast?
Or wallow naked in December snow
By thinking on fantastic summer's heat?
O, no! the apprehension of the good
Gives but the greater feeling to the worse:
Fell sorrow's tooth doth never rankle more
Than when he bites, but lanceth not the sore.

GAUNT

Come, come, my son, I'll bring thee on thy way:
Had I thy youth and cause, I would not stay.

BOLINGBROKE

Then, England's ground, farewell; sweet soil, adieu;
My mother, and my nurse, that bears me yet!
Where'er I wander, boast of this I can,
Though banish'd, yet a trueborn Englishman.

[Exeunt

SCENE IV. *The court*

Enter the KING, *with* BAGOT *and* GREEN *at one door; and
the* DUKE OF AUMERLE *at another*

KING RICHARD

We did observe. Cousin Aumerle,
How far brought you high Hereford on his way?

AUMERLE

I brought high Hereford, if you call him so,
But to the next highway, and there I left him.

KING RICHARD

And say, what store of parting tears were shed?

AUMERLE

Faith, none for me; except the north-east wind,
Which then blew bitterly against our faces,
Awaked the sleeping rheum, and so by chance
Did grace our hollow parting with a tear.

KING RICHARD

What said our cousin when you parted with him?

AUMERLE

'Farewell:'
And, for my heart disdained that my tongue
Should so profane the word, that taught me craft
To counterfeit oppression of such grief,
That words seem'd buried in my sorrow's grave.
Marry, would the word 'farewell' have lengthen'd
　　hours
And added years to his short banishment,
He should have had a volume of farewells;
But since it would not, he had none of me.

KING RICHARD

He is our cousin, cousin; but 'tis doubt,
When time shall call him home from banishment,
Whether our kinsman come to see his friends.
Ourself and Bushy, Bagot here and Green
Observed his courtship to the common people;
How he did seem to dive into their hearts
With humble and familiar courtesy,
What reverence he did throw away on slaves,
Wooing poor craftsmen with the craft of smiles
And patient underbearing of his fortune,
As 'twere to banish their affects with him.
Off goes his bonnet to an oyster-wench;
A brace of draymen bid God speed him well
And had the tribute of his supple knee,
With 'Thanks, my countrymen, my loving friends;'
As were our England in reversion his,
And he our subjects' next degree in hope.

GREEN

Well, he is gone; and with him go these thoughts.
Now for the rebels which stand out in Ireland,
Expedient manage must be made, my liege,
Ere further leisure yield them further means
For their advantage and your highness' loss.

KING RICHARD

We will ourself in person to this war:
And, for our coffers, with too great a court
And liberal largess, are grown somewhat light,
We are inforced to farm our royal realm;
The revenue whereof shall furnish us

For our affairs in hand: if that come short,
Our substitutes at home shall have blank charters;
Whereto, when they shall know what men are rich,
They shall subscribe them for large sums of gold
And send them after to supply our wants;
For we will make for Ireland presently.

Enter BUSHY

Bushy, what news?

BUSHY

Old John of Gaunt is grievous sick, my lord,
Suddenly taken; and hath sent post haste
To entreat your majesty to visit him.

KING RICHARD

Where lies he?

BUSHY

At Ely House.

KING RICHARD

Now put it, God, in the physician's mind
To help him to his grave immediately!
The lining of his coffers shall make coats
To deck our soldiers for these Irish wars.
Come, gentlemen, let's all go visit him:
Pray God we may make haste, and come too late!

ALL

Amen.   [*Exeunt*

ACT II

Scene I. *Ely House*

Enter JOHN OF GAUNT *sick, with the* DUKE OF YORK, *&c.*

GAUNT

Will the king come, that I may breathe my last
In wholesome counsel to his unstaid youth?

YORK

Vex not yourself, nor strive not with your breath;
For all in vain comes counsel to his ear.

GAUNT

O, but they say the tongues of dying men
Enforce attention like deep harmony:
Where words are scarce, they are seldom spent in
 vain,
For they breathe truth that breathe their words in
 pain.
He that no more must say is listen'd more
 Than they whom youth and ease have taught to
  glose;
More are men's ends mark'd than their lives before:
 The setting sun, and music at the close,
As the last taste of sweets, is sweetest last,
Writ in remembrance more than things long past:
Though Richard my life's counsel would not hear,
My death's sad tale may yet undeaf his ear.

YORK

No; it is stopp'd with other flattering sounds,
As praises, of whose taste the wise are fond,
Lascivious metres, to whose venom sound
The open ear of youth doth always listen;

Report of fashions in proud Italy,
Whose manners still our tardy apish nation
Limps after in base imitation.
Where doth the world thrust forth a vanity—
So it be new, there's no respect how vile—
That is not quickly buzz'd into his ears?
Then all too late comes counsel to be heard,
Where will doth mutiny with wit's regard.
Direct not him whose way himself will choose:
'Tis breath thou lack'st, and that breath wilt thou
 lose.

GAUNT

Methinks I am a prophet new inspired
And thus expiring do foretell of him:
His rash fierce blaze of riot cannot last,
For violent fires soon burn out themselves;
Small showers last long, but sudden storms are short;
He tires betimes that spurs too fast betimes;
With eager feeding food doth choke the feeder:
Light vanity, insatiate cormorant,
Consuming means, soon preys upon itself.
This royal throne of kings, this scepter'd isle,
This earth of majesty, this seat of Mars,
This other Eden, demi-paradise;
This fortress built by Nature for herself
Against infection and the hand of war;
This happy breed of men, this little world,
This precious stone set in the silver sea,
Which serves it in the office of a wall,
Or as a moat defensive to a house,
Against the envy of less happier lands;
This blessed plot, this earth, this realm, this Eng-
 land,
This nurse, this teeming womb of royal kings,
Fear'd by their breed and famous by their birth,
Renowned for their deeds as far from home,
For Christian service and true chivalry,
As is the sepulchre in stubborn Jewry
Of the world's ransom, blessed Mary's Son;
This land of such dear souls, this dear dear land,
Dear for her reputation through the world,
Is now leased out, I die pronouncing it,
Like to a tenement or pelting farm:
England, bound in with the triumphant sea,
Whose rocky shore beats back the envious siege
Of watery Neptune, is now bound in with shame,
With inky blots and rotten parchment bonds:
That England, that was wont to conquer others,
Hath made a shameful conquest of itself.
Ah, would the scandal vanish with my life,
How happy then were my ensuing death!

Enter KING RICHARD *and* QUEEN, AUMERLE, BUSHY,
 GREEN, BAGOT, ROSS, *and* WILLOUGHBY

YORK

The king is come: deal mildly with his youth;
For young hot colts being raged do rage the more.

QUEEN

How fares our noble uncle, Lancaster?

KING RICHARD

What comfort, man? how is't with aged Gaunt?

GAUNT

O, how that name befits my composition!
Old Gaunt indeed, and gaunt in being old:
Within me grief hath kept a tedious fast;
And who abstains from meat that is not gaunt?
For sleeping England long time have I watch'd;
Watching breeds leanness, leanness is all gaunt:
The pleasure that some fathers feed upon,
Is my strict fast; I mean, my children's looks;
And therein fasting, hast thou made me gaunt:
Gaunt am I for the grave, gaunt as a grave,
Whose hollow womb inherits nought but bones.

KING RICHARD

Can sick men play so nicely with their names?

GAUNT

No, misery makes sport to mock itself:
Since thou dost seek to kill my name in me,
I mock my name, great king, to flatter thee.

KING RICHARD

Should dying men flatter with those that live?

GAUNT

No, no, men living flatter those that die.

KING RICHARD

Thou, now a-dying, say'st thou flatterest me.

GAUNT

O, no! thou diest, though I the sicker be.

KING RICHARD

I am in health, I breathe, and see thee ill.

GAUNT

Now, He that made me knows I see thee ill;
Ill in myself to see, and in thee seeing ill.
Thy death-bed is no lesser than thy land,
Wherein thou liest in reputation sick;
And thou, too careless patient as thou art,
Commit'st thy anointed body to the cure
Of those physicians that first wounded thee:
A thousand flatterers sit within thy crown,
Whose compass is no bigger than thy head;
And yet, incaged in so small a verge,
The waste is no whit lesser than thy land.
O, had thy grandsire with a prophet's eye
Seen how his son's son should destroy his sons,
From forth thy reach he would have laid thy shame,
Deposing thee before thou wert possess'd,
Which art possess'd now to depose thyself.
Why, cousin, wert thou regent of the world,
It were a shame to let this land by lease;
But, for thy world enjoying but this land,
Is it not more than shame to shame it so?
Landlord of England art thou now, not king:
Thy state of law is bondslave to the law;
And thou—

KING RICHARD

A lunatic lean-witted fool,
Presuming on an ague's privilege,
Darest with thy frozen admonition
Make pale our cheek, chasing the royal blood
With fury from his native residence.
Now, by my seat's right royal majesty,
Wert thou not brother to great Edward's son,

This tongue that runs so roundly in thy head
Should run thy head from thy unreverent shoulders.

GAUNT

O, spare me not, my brother Edward's son,
For that I was his father Edward's son;
That blood already, like the pelican,
Hast thou tapp'd out and drunkenly caroused:
My brother Gloucester, plain well-meaning soul,
Whom fair befal in heaven 'mongst happy souls!
May be a precedent and witness good
That thou respect'st not spilling Edward's blood:
Join with the present sickness that I have;
And thy unkindness be like crooked age,
To crop at once a too long wither'd flower.
Live in thy shame, but die not shame with thee!
These words hereafter thy tormentors be!
Convey me to my bed, then to my grave:
Love they to live that love and honour have.

[Exit, borne off by his ATTENDANTS

KING RICHARD

And let them die that age and sullens have;
For both hast thou, and both become the grave.

YORK

I do beseech your majesty, impute his words
To wayward sickliness and age in him:
He loves you, on my life, and holds you dear
As Harry Duke of Hereford, were he here.

KING RICHARD

Right, you say true: as Hereford's love, so his;
As theirs, so mine; and all be as it is.

Enter NORTHUMBERLAND

NORTHUMBERLAND

My liege, old Gaunt commends him to your majesty.

KING RICHARD

What says he?

NORTHUMBERLAND

     Nay, nothing; all is said:
His tongue is now a stringless instrument;
Words, life and all, old Lancaster hath spent.

YORK

Be York the next that must be bankrupt so!
Though death be poor, it ends a mortal woe.

KING RICHARD

The ripest fruit first falls, and so doth he;
His time is spent, our pilgrimage must be.
So much for that. Now for our Irish wars:
We must supplant those rough rug-headed kerns,
Which live like venom where no venom else
But only they have privilege to live.
And for these great affairs do ask some charge,
Towards our assistance we do seize to us
The plate, coin, revenues and moveables,
Whereof our uncle Gaunt did stand possess'd.

YORK

How long shall I be patient? ah, how long
Shall tender duty make me suffer wrong?
Not Gloucester's death, nor Hereford's banishment,
Not Gaunt's rebukes, nor England's private wrongs,
Nor the prevention of poor Bolingbroke

About his marriage, nor my own disgrace,
Have ever made me sour my patient cheek,
Or bend one wrinkle on my sovereign's face.
I am the last of noble Edward's sons,
Of whom thy father, Prince of Wales, was first:
In war was never lion raged more fierce,
In peace was never gentle lamb more mild,
Than was that young and princely gentleman.
His face thou hast, for even so look'd he,
Accomplish'd with the number of thy hours;
But when he frown'd, it was against the French
And not against his friends; his noble hand
Did win what he did spend, and spent not that
Which his triumphant father's hand had won;
His hands were guilty of no kindred blood,
But bloody with the enemies of his kin.
O Richard! York is too far gone with grief,
Or else he never would compare between.

KING RICHARD
Why, uncle, what's the matter?

YORK
                O my liege,
Pardon me, if you please; if not, I, pleased
Not to be pardon'd, am content withal.
Seek you to seize and gripe into your hands
The royalties and rights of banish'd Hereford?
Is not Gaunt dead, and doth not Hereford live?
Was not Gaunt just, and is not Harry true?
Did not the one deserve to have an heir?
Is not his heir a well-deserving son?
Take Hereford's rights away, and take from time
His charters and his customary rights;
Let not to-morrow then ensue to-day;
Be not thyself; for how art thou a king
But by fair sequence and succession?
Now, afore God—God forbid I say true!—
If you do wrongfully seize Hereford's rights,
Call in the letters patents that he hath
By his attorneys-general to sue
His livery, and deny his offer'd homage,
You pluck a thousand dangers on your head,
You lose a thousand well-disposed hearts,
And prick my tender patience to those thoughts
Which honour and allegiance cannot think.

KING RICHARD
Think what you will, we seize into our hands
His plate, his goods, his money and his lands.

YORK
I'll not be by the while: my liege, farewell:
What will ensue hereof, there's none can tell;
But by bad courses may be understood
That their events can never fall out good.   [Exit

KING RICHARD
Go, Bushy, to the Earl of Wiltshire straight:
Bid him repair to us to Ely House
To see this business. To-morrow next
We will for Ireland; and 'tis time, I trow:
And we create, in absence of ourself,
Our uncle York lord governor of England;
For he is just and always loved us well.

Come on, our queen: to-morrow must we part;
Be merry, for our time of stay is short.
       [Flourish. Exeunt KING, QUEEN, AUMERLE,
                  BUSHY, GREEN, and BAGOT

NORTHUMBERLAND
Well, lords, the Duke of Lancaster is dead.

ROSS
And living too; for now his son is duke.

WILLOUGHBY
Barely in title, not in revenues.

NORTHUMBERLAND
Richly in both, if justice had her right.

ROSS
My heart is great; but it must break with silence,
Ere't be disburden'd with a liberal tongue.

NORTHUMBERLAND
Nay, speak thy mind; and let him ne'er speak more
That speaks thy words again to do thee harm!

WILLOUGHBY
Tends that thou wouldst speak to the Duke of Here-
    ford?
If it be so, out with it boldly, man;
Quick is mine ear to hear of good towards him.

ROSS
No good at all that I can do for him;
Unless you call it good to pity him,
Bereft and gelded of his patrimony.

NORTHUMBERLAND
Now, afore God, 'tis shame such wrongs are borne
In him a royal prince and many moe
Of noble blood in this declining land.
The king is not himself, but basely led
By flatterers; and what they will inform,
Merely in hate, 'gainst any of us all,
That will the king severely prosecute
'Gainst us, our lives, our children, and our heirs.

ROSS
The commons hath he pill'd with grievous taxes,
And quite lost their hearts: the nobles hath he fined
For ancient quarrels, and quite lost their hearts.

WILLOUGHBY
And daily new exactions are devised,
As blanks, benevolences, and I wot not what:
But what, o' God's name, doth become of this?

NORTHUMBERLAND
Wars have not wasted it, for warr'd he hath not,
But basely yielded upon compromise
That which his noble ancestors achieved with blows:
More hath he spent in peace than they in wars.

ROSS
The Earl of Wiltshire hath the realm in farm.

WILLOUGHBY
The king's grown bankrupt, like a broken man.

NORTHUMBERLAND
Reproach and dissolution hangeth over him.

ROSS
He hath not money for these Irish wars,
His burthenous taxations notwithstanding,
But by the robbing of the banish'd duke.

NORTHUMBERLAND

His noble kinsman: most degenerate king!
But, lords, we hear this fearful tempest sing,
Yet seek no shelter to avoid the storm;
We see the wind sit sore upon our sails,
And yet we strike not, but securely perish.

ROSS

We see the very wreck that we must suffer;
And unavoided is the danger now,
For suffering so the causes of our wreck.

NORTHUMBERLAND

Not so; even through the hollow eyes of death
I spy life peering; but I dare not say
How near the tidings of our comfort is.

WILLOUGHBY

Nay, let us share thy thoughts, as thou dost ours.

ROSS

Be confident to speak, Northumberland:
We three are but thyself; and, speaking so,
Thy words are but as thoughts; therefore, be bold.

NORTHUMBERLAND

Then thus: I have from le Port Blanc, a bay
In Brittany, received intelligence
That Harry Duke of Hereford, Rainold Lord Cob-
     ham,

. . . .

That late broke from the Duke of Exeter,
His brother, Archbishop late of Canterbury,
Sir Thomas Erpingham, Sir John Ramston,
Sir John Norbery, Sir Robert Waterton and Francis
     Quoint,
All these well furnish'd by the Duke of Bretagne
With eight tall ships, three thousand men of war,
Are making hither with all due expedience
And shortly mean to touch our northern shore:
Perhaps they had ere this, but that they stay
The first departing of the king for Ireland.
If then we shall shake off our slavish yoke,
Imp out our drooping country's broken wing,
Redeem from broking pawn the blemish'd crown,
Wipe off the dust that hides our sceptre's gilt,
And make high majesty look like itself,
Away with me in post to Ravenspurgh;
But if you faint, as fearing to do so,
Stay and be secret, and myself will go.

ROSS

To horse, to horse! urge doubts to them that fear.

WILLOUGHBY

Hold out my horse, and I will first be there. [Exeunt

SCENE II. Windsor Castle

Enter QUEEN, BUSHY, and BAGOT

BUSHY

Madam, your majesty is too much sad:
You promised, when you parted with the king,
To lay aside life-harming heaviness,
And entertain a cheerful disposition.

QUEEN

To please the king I did; to please myself
I cannot do it; yet I know no cause
Why I should welcome such a guest as grief,
Save bidding farewell to so sweet a guest
As my sweet Richard: yet again, methinks,
Some unborn sorrow, ripe in fortune's womb,
Is coming towards me, and my inward soul
With nothing trembles: at some thing it grieves,
More than with parting from my lord the king.

BUSHY

Each substance of a grief hath twenty shadows,
Which shows like grief itself, but is not so;
For sorrow's eye, glazed with blinding tears,
Divides one thing entire to many objects;
Like perspectives, which, rightly gazed upon,
Show nothing but confusion, eyed awry,
Distinguish form: so your sweet majesty,
Looking awry upon your lord's departure,
Find shapes of grief, more than himself, to wail;
Which, look'd on as it is, is nought but shadows
Of what it is not. Then, thrice-gracious queen,
More than your lord's departure weep not: more's
     not seen;
Or if it be, 'tis with false sorrow's eye,
Which for things true weeps things imaginary.

QUEEN

It may be so; but yet my inward soul
Persuades me it is otherwise: howe'er it be,
I cannot but be sad; so heavy sad,
As, though on thinking on no thought I think,
Makes me with heavy nothing faint and shrink.

BUSHY

'Tis nothing but conceit, my gracious lady.

QUEEN

'Tis nothing less: conceit is still derived
From some forefather grief; mine is not so,
For nothing hath begot my something grief;
Or something hath the nothing that I grieve:
'Tis in reversion that I do possess;
But what it is, that is not yet known; what
I cannot name; 'tis nameless woe, I wot.

Enter GREEN

GREEN

God save your majesty! and well met, gentlemen:
I hope the king is not yet shipp'd for Ireland.

QUEEN

Why hopest thou so? 'tis better hope he is;
For his designs crave haste, his haste good hope:
Then wherefore dost thou hope he is not shipp'd?

GREEN

That he, our hope, might have retired his power,
And driven into despair an enemy's hope,
Who strongly hath set footing in this land:
The banish'd Bolingbroke repeals himself,
And with uplifted arms is safe arrived
At Ravenspurgh.

QUEEN

Now God in heaven forbid!

GREEN

Ah madam, 'tis too true: and that is worse,
The Lord Northumberland, his son young Henry
    Percy,
The Lords of Ross, Beaumond, and Willoughby,
With all their powerful friends, are fled to him.

BUSHY

Why have you not proclaim'd Northumberland
And all the rest revolted faction traitors?

GREEN

We have: whereupon the Earl of Worcester
Hath broke his staff, resign'd his stewardship,
And all the household servants fled with him
To Bolingbroke.

QUEEN

So, Green, thou art the midwife to my woe,
And Bolingbroke my sorrow's dismal heir:
Now hath my soul brought forth her prodigy,
And I, a gasping new-deliver'd mother,
Have woe to woe, sorrow to sorrow join'd.

BUSHY

Despair not, madam.

QUEEN

                    Who shall hinder me?
I will despair, and be at enmity
With cozening hope: he is a flatterer,
A parasite, a keeper back of death,
Who gently would dissolve the bands of life,
Which false hope lingers in extremity.

Enter YORK

GREEN

Here comes the Duke of York.

QUEEN

With signs of war about his aged neck;
O, full of careful business are his looks!
Uncle, for God's sake, speak comfortable words.

YORK

Should I do so, I should belie my thoughts:
Comfort's in heaven; and we are on the earth,
Where nothing lives but crosses, cares and grief.
Your husband, he is gone to save far off,
Whilst others come to make him lose at home:
Here am I left to underprop his land,
Who, weak with age, cannot support myself:
Now comes the sick hour that his surfeit made;
Now shall he try his friends that flatter'd him.

Enter a SERVANT

SERVANT

My lord, your son was gone before I came.

YORK

He was? Why, so! go all which way it will!
The nobles they are fled, the commons they are cold,
And will, I fear, revolt on Hereford's side.
Sirrah, get thee to Plashy, to my sister Gloucester;
Bid her send me presently a thousand pound:
Hold, take my ring.

SERVANT

My lord, I had forgot to tell your lordship,
To-day, as I came by, I called there;
But I shall grieve you to report the rest.

YORK

What is't, knave?

SERVANT

An hour before I came, the duchess died.

YORK

God for his mercy! what a tide of woes
Comes rushing on this woeful land at once!
I know not what to do: I would to God,
So my untruth had not provoked him to it,
The king had cut off my head with my brother's.
What, are there no posts dispatch'd for Ireland?
How shall we do for money for these wars?
Come, sister,—cousin, I would say,—pray, pardon
    me.
Go, fellow, get thee home, provide some carts
And bring away the armour that is there.
                                    [*Exit* SERVANT
Gentlemen, will you go muster men?
If I know how or which way to order these affairs
Thus thrust disorderly into my hands,
Never believe me. Both are my kinsmen:
The one is my sovereign, whom both my oath
And duty bids defend; the other again
Is my kinsman, whom the king hath wrong'd,
Whom conscience and my kindred bids to right.
Well, somewhat we must do. Come, cousin, I'll
Dispose of you.
Gentlemen, go, muster up your men,
And meet me presently at Berkeley.
I should to Plashy too;
But time will not permit: all is uneven,
And everything is left at six and seven.
                          [*Exeunt* YORK *and* QUEEN

BUSHY

The wind sits fair for news to go to Ireland,
But none returns. For us to levy power
Proportionable to the enemy
Is all unpossible.

GREEN

Besides, our nearness to the king in love
Is near the hate of those love not the king.

BAGOT

And that's the wavering commons: for their love
Lies in their purses, and whoso empties them
By so much fills their hearts with deadly hate.

BUSHY

Wherein the king stands generally condemn'd.

BAGOT

If judgement lie in them, then so do we,
Because we ever have been near the king.

GREEN

Well, I will for refuge straight to Bristol castle:
The Earl of Wiltshire is already there.

BUSHY

Thither will I with you; for little office
The hateful commons will perform for us,
Except like curs to tear us all to pieces.
Will you go along with us?

BAGOT

No; I will to Ireland to his majesty.

Farewell: if heart's presages be not vain,
We three here part that ne'er shall meet again.

BUSHY

That's as York thrives to beat back Bolingbroke.

GREEN

Alas, poor duke! the task he undertakes
Is numbering sands and drinking oceans dry:
Where one on his side fights, thousands will fly.
Farewell at once, for once, for all, and ever.

BUSHY

Well, we may meet again.

BAGOT

        I fear me, never. [*Exeunt*

SCENE III. *Wilds in Gloucestershire*

Enter BOLINGBROKE *and* NORTHUMBERLAND,
with Forces

BOLINGBROKE

How far is it, my lord, to Berkeley now?

NORTHUMBERLAND

Believe me, noble lord,
I am a stranger here in Gloucestershire:
These high wild hills and rough uneven ways
Draws out our miles, and makes them wearisome;
And yet your fair discourse hath been as sugar,
Making the hard way sweet and delectable.
But I bethink me what a weary way
From Ravenspurgh to Cotswold will be found
In Ross and Willoughby, wanting your company,
Which, I protest, hath very much beguiled
The tediousness and process of my travel:
But theirs is sweetened with the hope to have
The present benefit which I possess;
And hope to joy is little less in joy
Than hope enjoy'd: by this the weary lords
Shall make their way seem short, as mine hath done
By sight of what I have, your noble company.

BOLINGBROKE

Of much less value is my company
Than your good words. But who comes here?

Enter HENRY PERCY

NORTHUMBERLAND

It is my son, young Harry Percy,
Sent from my brother Worcester, whencesoever.
Harry, how fares your uncle?

HENRY PERCY

I had thought, my lord, to have learn'd his health of
you.

NORTHUMBERLAND

Why, is he not with the queen?

HENRY PERCY

No, my good lord; he hath forsook the court,
Broken his staff of office and dispersed
The household of the king.

NORTHUMBERLAND

        What was his reason?
He was not so resolved when last we spake together.

HENRY PERCY

Because your lordship was proclaimed traitor.
But he, my lord, is gone to Ravenspurgh,
To offer service to the Duke of Hereford,
And sent me over by Berkeley, to discover
What power the Duke of York had levied there;
Then with directions to repair to Ravenspurgh.

NORTHUMBERLAND

Have you forgot the Duke of Hereford, boy?

HENRY PERCY

No, my good lord, for that is not forgot
Which ne'er I did remember: to my knowledge,
I never in my life did look on him.

NORTHUMBERLAND

Then learn to know him now; this is the duke.

HENRY PERCY

My gracious lord, I tender you my service,
Such as it is, being tender, raw and young;
Which elder days shall ripen and confirm
To more approved service and desert.

BOLINGBROKE

I thank thee, gentle Percy; and be sure
I count myself in nothing else so happy
As in a soul remembering my good friends;
And, as my fortune ripens with thy love,
It shall be still thy true love's recompense:
My heart this covenant makes, my hand thus seals it.

NORTHUMBERLAND

How far is it to Berkeley? and what stir
Keeps good old York there with his men of war?

HENRY PERCY

There stands the castle, by yon tuft of trees,
Mann'd with three hundred men, as I have heard;
And in it are the Lords of York, Berkeley, and
   Seymour;
None else of name and noble estimate.

Enter ROSS *and* WILLOUGHBY

NORTHUMBERLAND

Here come the Lords of Ross and Willoughby,
Bloody with spurring, fiery-red with haste.

BOLINGBROKE

Welcome, my lords. I wot your love pursues
A banish'd traitor: all my treasury
Is yet but unfelt thanks, which more enrich'd
Shall be your love and labour's recompense.

ROSS

Your presence makes us rich, most noble lord.

WILLOUGHBY

And far surmounts our labour to attain it.

BOLINGBROKE

Evermore thanks, the exchequer of the poor;
Which, till my infant fortune comes to years,
Stands for my bounty. But who comes here?

Enter BERKELEY

NORTHUMBERLAND

It is my Lord of Berkeley, as I guess.

BERKELEY

My Lord of Hereford, my message is to you.

BOLINGBROKE

My lord, my answer is—to Lancaster;

[365]

And I am come to seek that name in England;
And I must find that title in your tongue,
Before I make reply to aught you say.

BERKELEY

Mistake me not, my lord; 'tis not my meaning
To raze one title of your honour out:
To you, my lord, I come, what lord you will,
From the most gracious regent of this land,
The Duke of York, to know what pricks you on
To take advantage of the absent time
And fright our native peace with self-born arms.

Enter YORK *attended*

BOLINGBROKE

I shall not need transport my words by you;
Here comes his grace in person.
               My noble uncle!
                        [*Kneels*

YORK

Show me thy humble heart, and not thy knee,
Whose duty is deceiveable and false.

BOLINGBROKE

My gracious uncle!

YORK

Tut, tut!
Grace me no grace, nor uncle me no uncle:
I am no traitor's uncle; and that word 'grace'
In an ungracious mouth is but profane.
Why have those banish'd and forbidden legs
Dared once to touch a dust of England's ground?
But then more 'why?' why have they dared to march
So many miles upon her peaceful bosom,
Frighting her pale-faced villages with war
And ostentation of despised arms?
Comest thou because the anointed king is hence?
Why, foolish boy, the king is left behind,
And in my loyal bosom lies his power.
Were I but now the lord of such hot youth
As when brave Gaunt, thy father, and myself
Rescued the Black Prince, that young Mars of men,
From forth the ranks of many thousand French,
O, then how quickly should this arm of mine,
Now prisoner to the palsy, chastise thee
And minister correction to thy fault!

BOLINGBROKE

My gracious uncle, let me know my fault:
On what condition stands it and wherein?

YORK

Even in condition of the worst degree,
In gross rebellion and detested treason:
Thou art a banish'd man, and here art come
Before the expiration of thy time,
In braving arms against thy sovereign.

BOLINGBROKE

As I was banish'd, I was banish'd Hereford;
But as I come, I come for Lancaster.
And, noble uncle, I beseech your grace
Look on my wrongs with an indifferent eye:
You are my father, for methinks in you
I see old Gaunt alive; O, then, my father,

Will you permit that I shall stand condemn'd
A wandering vagabond; my rights and royalties
Pluck'd from my arms perforce and given away
To upstart unthrifts? Wherefore was I born?
If that my cousin king be King of England,
It must be granted I am Duke of Lancaster.
You have a son, Aumerle, my noble cousin;
Had you first died, and he been thus trod down,
He should have found his uncle Gaunt a father,
To rouse his wrongs and chase them to the bay.
I am denied to sue my livery here,
And yet my letters-patents give me leave:
My father's goods are all distrain'd and sold;
And these and all are all amiss employ'd.
What would you have me do? I am a subject,
And I challenge law: attorneys are denied me;
And therefore personally I lay my claim
To my inheritance of free descent.

NORTHUMBERLAND

The noble duke hath been too much abused.

ROSS

It stands your grace upon to do him right.

WILLOUGHBY

Base men by his endowments are made great.

YORK

My lords of England, let me tell you this:
I have had feeling of my cousin's wrongs
And labour'd all I could to do him right;
But in this kind to come, in braving arms,
Be his own carver and cut out his way,
To find out right with wrong, it may not be;
And you that do abet him in this kind
Cherish rebellion and are rebels all.

NORTHUMBERLAND

The noble duke hath sworn his coming is
But for his own; and for the right of that
We all have strongly sworn to give him aid;
And let him ne'er see joy that breaks that oath!

YORK

Well, well, I see the issue of these arms:
I cannot mend it, I must needs confess,
Because my power is weak and all ill left:
But if I could, by Him that gave me life,
I would attach you all and make you stoop
Unto the sovereign mercy of the king;
But since I cannot, be it known to you
I do remain as neuter. So, fare you well;
Unless you please to enter in the castle
And there repose you for this night.

BOLINGBROKE

An offer, uncle, that we will accept:
But we must win your grace to go with us
To Bristol castle, which they say is held
By Bushy, Bagot and their complices,
The caterpillars of the commonwealth,
Which I have sworn to weed and pluck away.

YORK

It may be I will go with you: but yet I'll pause;
For I am loath to break our country's laws.

Nor friends nor foes, to me welcome you are:
Things past redress are now with me past care.   [*Exeunt*

Scene IV. *A camp in Wales*

Enter SALISBURY *and a Welsh* CAPTAIN
CAPTAIN
My Lord of Salisbury, we have stay'd ten days,
And hardly kept our countrymen together,
And yet we hear no tidings from the king;
Therefore we will disperse ourselves: farewell.
SALISBURY
Stay yet another day, thou trusty Welshman:
The king reposeth all his confidence in thee.
CAPTAIN
'Tis thought the king is dead; we will not stay.
The bay-trees in our country are all wither'd,
And meteors fright the fixed stars of heaven;
The pale-faced moon looks bloody on the earth,
And lean-look'd prophets whisper fearful change;
Rich men look sad and ruffians dance and leap,
The one in fear to lose what they enjoy,
The other to enjoy by rage and war:
These signs forerun the death or fall of kings.
Farewell: our countrymen are gone and fled,
As well assured Richard their king is dead.   [*Exit*
SALISBURY
Ah, Richard, with the eyes of heavy mind
I see thy glory like a shooting star
Fall to the base earth from the firmament.
Thy sun sets weeping in the lowly west,
Witnessing storms to come, woe and unrest:
Thy friends are fled to wait upon thy foes,
And crossly to thy good all fortune goes.   [*Exit*

ACT III

Scene I. *Bristol. Before the castle*

Enter BOLINGBROKE, YORK, NORTHUMBERLAND, ROSS,
PERCY, WILLOUGHBY, *with* BUSHY *and* GREEN, *prisoners*
BOLINGBROKE
Bring forth these men.
Bushy and Green, I will not vex your souls—
Since presently your souls must part your bodies—
With too much urging your pernicious lives,
For 'twere no charity; yet, to wash your blood
From off my hands, here in the view of men
I will unfold some causes of your deaths.
You have misled a prince, a royal king,
A happy gentleman in blood and lineaments,
By you unhappied and disfigured clean:
You have in manner with your sinful hours
Made a divorce betwixt his queen and him,
Broke the possession of a royal bed
And stain'd the beauty of a fair queen's cheeks
With tears drawn from her eyes by your foul wrongs.

Myself, a prince by fortune of my birth,
Near to the king in blood, and near in love
Till you did make him misinterpret me,
Have stoop'd my neck under your injuries,
And sigh'd my English breath in foreign clouds,
Eating the bitter bread of banishment;
Whilst you have fed upon my signories,
Dispark'd my parks and fell'd my forest woods,
From my own windows torn my household coat,
Razed out my imprese, leaving me no sign,
Save men's opinions and my living blood,
To show the world I am a gentleman.
This and much more, much more than twice all this,
Condemns you to the death. See them deliver'd over
To execution and the hand of death.
BUSHY
More welcome is the stroke of death to me
Than Bolingbroke to England. Lords, farewell.
GREEN
My comfort is that heaven will take our souls
And plague injustice with the pains of hell.
BOLINGBROKE
My Lord Northumberland, see them dispatch'd.
[*Exeunt* NORTHUMBERLAND *and others, with the prisoners*
Uncle, you say the queen is at your house;
For God's sake, fairly let her be entreated:
Tell her I send to her my kind commends;
Take special care my greetings be deliver'd.
YORK
A gentleman of mine I have dispatch'd
With letters of your love to her at large.
BOLINGBROKE
Thanks, gentle uncle. Come, lords, away,
To fight with Glendower and his complices:
Awhile to work, and after holiday.   [*Exeunt*

Scene II. *The coast of Wales. A castle in view*

Drums: flourish and colours. Enter KING RICHARD, *the*
BISHOP OF CARLISLE, AUMERLE, *and Soldiers*
KING RICHARD
Barkloughly castle call they this at hand?
AUMERLE
Yea, my lord. How brooks your grace the air,
After your late tossing on the breaking seas?
KING RICHARD
Needs must I like it well: I weep for joy
To stand upon my kingdom once again.
Dear earth, I do salute thee with my hand,
Though rebels wound thee with their horses' hoofs:
As a long-parted mother with her child
Plays fondly with her tears and smiles in meeting,
So, weeping, smiling, greet I thee, my earth,
And do thee favours with my royal hands.
Feed not thy sovereign's foe, my gentle earth,
Nor with thy sweets comfort his ravenous sense;
But let thy spiders, that suck up thy venom,
And heavy-gaited toads lie in their way,
Doing annoyance to the treacherous feet

Which with usurping steps do trample thee:
Yield stinging nettles to mine enemies;
And when they from thy bosom pluck a flower,
Guard it, I pray thee, with a lurking adder,
Whose double tongue may with a mortal touch
Throw death upon thy sovereign's enemies.
Mock not my senseless conjuration, lords:
This earth shall have a feeling and these stones
Prove armed soldiers, ere her native king
Shall falter under foul rebellion's arms.

CARLISLE

Fear not, my lord: that Power that made you king
Hath power to keep you king in spite of all.
The means that heaven yields must be embraced,
And not neglected; else, if heaven would,
And we will not, heaven's offer we refuse,
The proffer'd means of succour and redress.

AUMERLE

He means, my lord, that we are too remiss;
Whilst Bolingbroke, through our security,
Grows strong and great in substance and in power.

KING RICHARD

Discomfortable cousin! know'st thou not
That when the searching eye of heaven is hid,
Behind the globe, that lights the lower world,
Then thieves and robbers range abroad unseen
In murders and in outrage, boldly here;
But when from under this terrestrial ball
He fires the proud tops of the eastern pines
And darts his light through every guilty hole,
Then murders, treasons and detested sins,
The cloak of night being pluck'd from off their
    backs,
Stand bare and naked, trembling at themselves?
So when this thief, this traitor, Bolingbroke,
Who all this while hath revell'd in the night,
Whilst we were wandering with the antipodes,
Shall see us rising in our throne, the east,
His treasons will sit blushing in his face,
Not able to endure the sight of day,
But self-affrighted tremble at his sin.
Not all the water in the rough rude sea
Can wash the balm off from an anointed king;
The breath of worldly men cannot depose
The deputy elected by the Lord:
For every man that Bolingbroke hath press'd
To lift shrewd steel against our golden crown,
God for his Richard hath in heavenly pay
A glorious angel: then, if angels fight,
Weak men must fall, for heaven still guards the right.

Enter SALISBURY

Welcome, my lord: how far off lies your power?

SALISBURY

Nor near nor farther off, my gracious lord,
Than this weak arm: discomfort guides my tongue
And bids me speak of nothing but despair.
One day too late, I fear me, noble lord,
Hath clouded all thy happy days on earth:
O, call back yesterday, bid time return,
And thou shalt have twelve thousand fighting men!

To-day, to-day, unhappy day, too late,
O'erthrows thy joys, friends, fortune and thy state:
For all the Welshmen, hearing thou wert dead,
Are gone to Bolingbroke, dispersed and fled.

AUMERLE

Comfort, my liege: why looks your grace so pale?

KING RICHARD

But now the blood of twenty thousand men
Did triumph in my face, and they are fled;
And, till so much blood thither come again,
Have I not reason to look pale and dead?
All souls that will be safe, fly from my side,
For time hath set a blot upon my pride.

AUMERLE

Comfort, my liege; remember who you are.

KING RICHARD

I had forgot myself: am I not king?
Awake, thou coward majesty! thou sleepest.
Is not the king's name twenty thousand names?
Arm, arm, my name! a puny subject strikes
At thy great glory. Look not to the ground,
Ye favourites of a king: are we not high?
High be our thoughts: I know my uncle York
Hath power enough to serve our turn. But who
    comes here?

Enter SCROOP

SCROOP

More health and happiness betide my liege
Than can my care-tuned tongue deliver him!

KING RICHARD

Mine ear is open and my heart prepared:
The worst is worldly loss thou canst unfold.
Say, is my kingdom lost? why, 'twas my care;
And what loss is it to be rid of care?
Strives Bolingbroke to be as great as we?
Greater he shall not be; if he serve God,
We'll serve Him too and be his fellow so:
Revolt our subjects? that we cannot mend;
They break their faith to God as well as us:
Cry woe, destruction, ruin and decay;
The worst is death, and death will have his day.

SCROOP

Glad am I that your highness is so arm'd
To bear the tidings of calamity.
Like an unseasonable stormy day,
Which makes the silver rivers drown their shores,
As if the world were all dissolved to tears,
So high above his limits swells the rage
Of Bolingbroke, covering your fearful land
With hard bright steel and hearts harder than steel.
White-beards have arm'd their thin and hairless
    scalps
Against thy majesty; boys, with women's voices,
Strive to speak big and clap their female joints
In stiff unwieldy arms against thy crown:
Thy very beadsmen learn to bend their bows
Of double-fatal yew against thy state;
Yea, distaff-women manage rusty bills
Against thy seat: both young and old rebel,
And all goes worse than I have power to tell.

KING RICHARD

Too well, too well thou tell'st a tale so ill.
Where is the Earl of Wiltshire? where is Bagot?
What is become of Bushy? where is Green?
That they have let the dangerous enemy
Measure our confines with such peaceful steps?
If we prevail, their heads shall pay for it:
I warrant they have made peace with Bolingbroke.

SCROOP

Peace have they made with him indeed, my lord.

KING RICHARD

O villains, vipers, damn'd without redemption!
Dogs, easily won to fawn on any man!
Snakes, in my heart-blood warm'd, that sting my
    heart!
Three Judases, each one thrice worse than Judas!
Would they make peace? terrible hell make war
Upon their spotted souls for this offence!

SCROOP

Sweet love, I see, changing his property,
Turns to the sourest and most deadly hate:
Again uncurse their souls; their peace is made
With heads, and not with hands: those whom you
    curse
Have felt the worst of death's destroying wound,
And lie full low, graved in the hollow ground.

AUMERLE

Is Bushy, Green and the Earl of Wiltshire dead?

SCROOP

Ay, all of them at Bristol lost their heads.

AUMERLE

Where is the duke my father with his power?

KING RICHARD

No matter where; of comfort no man speak:
Let's talk of graves, of worms and epitaphs;
Make dust our paper and with rainy eyes
Write sorrow on the bosom of the earth.
Let's choose executors and talk of wills:
And yet not so, for what can we bequeath
Save our deposed bodies to the ground?
Our lands, our lives and all are Bolingbroke's,
And nothing can we call our own but death,
And that small model of the barren earth
Which serves as paste and cover to our bones.
For God's sake, let us sit upon the ground
And tell sad stories of the death of kings:
How some have been deposed; some slain in war;
Some haunted by the ghosts they have deposed;
Some poison'd by their wives; some sleeping kill'd;
All murder'd: for within the hollow crown
That rounds the mortal temples of a king
Keeps Death his court, and there the antic sits,
Scoffing his state and grinning at his pomp,
Allowing him a breath, a little scene,
To monarchize, be fear'd and kill with looks,
Infusing him with self and vain conceit,
As if this flesh which walls about our life
Were brass impregnable, and humour'd thus
Comes at the last and with a little pin
Bores through his castle wall, and farewel' king!

Cover your heads and mock not flesh and blood
With solemn reverence: throw away respect,
Tradition, form and ceremonious duty,
For you have but mistook me all this while:
I live with bread like you, feel want,
Taste grief, need friends: subjected thus,
How can you say to me, I am a king?

CARLISLE

My lord, wise men ne'er sit and wail their woes,
But presently prevent the ways to wail.
To fear the foe, since fear oppresseth strength,
Gives in your weakness strength unto your foe,
And so your follies fight against yourself.
Fear, and be slain; no worse can come to fight:
And fight and die is death destroying death;
Where fearing dying pays death servile breath.

AUMERLE

My father hath a power; inquire of him,
And learn to make a body of a limb.

KING RICHARD

Thou chidest me well: proud Bolingbroke, I come
To change blows with thee for our day of doom.
This ague fit of fear is over-blown;
An easy task it is to win our own.
Say, Scroop, where lies our uncle with his power?
Speak sweetly, man, although thy looks be sour.

SCROOP

Men judge by the complexion of the sky
    The state and inclination of the day:
So may you by my dull and heavy eye,
    My tongue hath but a heavier tale to say.
I play the torturer, by small and small
To lengthen out the worst that must be spoken:
Your uncle York is join'd with Bolingbroke,
And all your northern castles yielded up,
And all your southern gentlemen in arms
Upon his party.

KING RICHARD

Thou hast said enough.
Beshrew thee, cousin, which didst lead me forth
                                    [To AUMERLE
Of that sweet way I was in to despair!
What say you now? what comfort have we now?
By heaven, I'll hate him everlastingly
That bids me be of comfort any more.
Go to Flint castle: there I'll pine away;
A king, woe's slave, shall kingly woe obey.
That power I have, discharge; and let them go
To ear the land that hath some hope to grow,
For I have none: let no man speak again
To alter this, for counsel is but vain.

AUMERLE

My liege, one word.

KING RICHARD

                    He does me double wrong
That wounds me with the flatteries of his tongue.
Discharge my followers: let them hence away,
From Richard's night to Bolingbroke's fair day.
                                         [Exeunt

SCENE III. *Wales. Before Flint castle*

Enter, with drum and colours, BOLINGBROKE, YORK,
NORTHUMBERLAND, *Attendants, and forces*

BOLINGBROKE
So that by this intelligence we learn
The Welshmen are dispersed; and Salisbury
Is gone to meet the king, who lately landed
With some few private friends upon this coast.

NORTHUMBERLAND
The news is very fair and good, my lord:
Richard not far from hence hath hid his head.

YORK
It would beseem the Lord Northumberland
To say 'King Richard': alack the heavy day
When such a sacred king should hide his head.

NORTHUMBERLAND
Your grace mistakes; only to be brief,
Left I his title out.

YORK
          The time hath been,
Would you have been so brief with him, he would
Have been so brief with you, to shorten you,
For taking so the head, your whole head's length.

BOLINGBROKE
Mistake not, uncle, further than you should.

YORK
Take not, good cousin, further than you should,
Lest you mistake the heavens are o'er our heads.

BOLINGBROKE
I know it, uncle, and oppose not myself
Against their will. But who comes here?

Enter HENRY PERCY

Welcome, Harry: what, will not this castle yield?

HENRY PERCY
The castle royally is mann'd, my lord,
Against thy entrance.

BOLINGBROKE
Royally!
Why, it contains no king?

HENRY PERCY
          Yes, my good lord,
It doth contain a king; King Richard lies
Within the limits of yon lime and stone:
And with him are the Lord Aumerle, Lord Salisbury,
Sir Stephen Scroop, besides a clergyman
Of holy reverence; who, I cannot learn.

NORTHUMBERLAND
O, belike it is the Bishop of Carlisle.

BOLINGBROKE
Noble lords,
Go to the rude ribs of that ancient castle;
Through brazen trumpet send the breath of parley
Into his ruin'd ears, and thus deliver:
Henry Bolingbroke
On both his knees doth kiss King Richard's hand
And sends allegiance and true faith of heart
To his most royal person; hither come
Even at his feet to lay my arms and power,
Provided that my banishment repeal'd

And lands restored again be freely granted:
If not, I'll use the advantage of my power
And lay the summer's dust with showers of blood
Rain'd from the wounds of slaughter'd Englishmen:
The which, how far off from the mind of Boling-
  broke
It is, such crimson tempest should bedrench
The fresh green lap of fair King Richard's land,
My stooping duty tenderly shall show.
Go, signify as much, while here we march
Upon the grassy carpet of this plain.
Let's march without the noise of threatening drum,
That from this castle's tatter'd battlements
Our fair appointments may be well perused.
Methinks King Richard and myself should meet
With no less terror than the elements
Of fire and water, when their thundering shock
At meeting tears the cloudy cheeks of heaven.
Be he the fire, I'll be the yielding water:
The rage be his, whilst on the earth I rain
My waters; on the earth, and not on him.
March on, and mark King Richard how he looks.

*Parle without, and answer within. Then a flourish. Enter
on the walls,* KING RICHARD, *the* BISHOP OF CARLISLE,
  AUMERLE, SCROOP, *and* SALISBURY

See, see, King Richard doth himself appear,
As doth the blushing discontented sun
From out the fiery portal of the east,
When he perceives the envious clouds are bent
To dim his glory and to stain the track
Of his bright passage to the occident.

YORK
Yet looks he like a king: behold, his eye,
As bright as is the eagle's, lightens forth
Controlling majesty: alack, alack, for woe,
That any harm should stain so fair a show!

KING RICHARD
We are amazed; and thus long have we stood
To watch the fearful bending of thy knee,
               [*To* NORTHUMBERLAND
Because we thought ourself thy lawful king:
And if we be, how dare thy joints forget
To pay their awful duty to our presence?
If we be not, show us the hand of God
That hath dismiss'd us from our stewardship;
For well we know, no hand of blood and bone
Can gripe the sacred handle of our sceptre,
Unless he do profane, steal, or usurp.
And though you think that all, as you have done,
Have torn their souls by turning them from us,
And we are barren and bereft of friends;
Yet know, my master, God omnipotent,
Is mustering in his clouds on our behalf
Armies of pestilence; and they shall strike
Your children yet unborn and unbegot,
That lift your vassal hands against my head,
And threat the glory of my precious crown.
Tell Bolingbroke—for yond methinks he stands—
That every stride he makes upon my land
Is dangerous treason: he is come to open

The purple testament of bleeding war;
But ere the crown he looks for live in peace,
Ten thousand bloody crowns of mothers' sons
Shall ill become the flower of England's face,
Change the complexion of her maid-pale peace
To scarlet indignation, and bedew
Her pastures' grass with faithful English blood.

NORTHUMBERLAND

The king of heaven forbid our lord the king
Should so with civil and uncivil arms
Be rush'd upon! Thy thrice noble cousin
Harry Bolingbroke doth humbly kiss thy hand;
And by the honourable tomb he swears,
That stands upon your royal grandsire's bones,
And by the royalties of both your bloods,
Currents that spring from one most gracious head,
And by the buried hand of warlike Gaunt,
And by the worth and honour of himself,
Comprising all that may be sworn or said,
His coming hither hath no further scope
Than for his lineal royalties, and to beg
Enfranchisement immediate on his knees:
Which on thy royal party granted once,
His glittering arms he will commend to rust,
His barbed steeds to stables, and his heart
To faithful service of your majesty.
This swears he, as he is a prince, is just;
And, as I am a gentleman, I credit him.

KING RICHARD

Northumberland, say thus the king returns:
His noble cousin is right welcome hither;
And all the number of his fair demands
Shall be accomplish'd without contradiction:
With all the gracious utterance thou hast,
Speak to his gentle hearing kind commends.
We do debase ourselves, cousin, do we not,
                                    [To AUMERLE
To look so poorly and to speak so fair?
Shall we call back Northumberland, and send
Defiance to the traitor, and so die?

AUMERLE

No, good my lord; let's fight with gentle words,
Till time lend friends and friends their helpful
    swords.

KING RICHARD

O God, O God! that e'er this tongue of mine,
That laid the sentence of dread banishment
On yon proud man, should take it off again
With words of sooth! O that I were as great
As is my grief, or lesser than my name!
Or that I could forget what I have been,
Or not remember what I must be now!
Swell'st thou, proud heart? I'll give thee scope to
    beat,
Since foes have scope to beat both thee and me.

AUMERLE

Northumberland comes back from Bolingbroke.

KING RICHARD

What must the king do now? must he submit?
The king shall do it: must he be deposed?

The king shall be contented: must he lose
The name of king? o' God's name, let it go:
I'll give my jewels for a set of beads,
My gorgeous palace for a hermitage,
My gay apparel for an almsman's gown,
My figured goblets for a dish of wood,
My sceptre for a palmer's walking-staff,
My subjects for a pair of carved saints,
And my large kingdom for a little grave,
A little little grave, an obscure grave;
Or I'll be buried in the king's highway,
Some way of common trade, where subjects' feet
May hourly trample on their sovereign's head;
For on my heart they tread now whilst I live;
And buried once, why not upon my head?
Aumerle, thou weep'st, my tender-hearted cousin!
We'll make foul weather with despised tears;
Our sighs and they shall lodge the summer corn,
And make a dearth in this revolting land.
Or shall we play the wantons with our woes,
And make some pretty match with shedding tears?
As thus, to drop them still upon one place,
Till they have fretted us a pair of graves
Within the earth; and, therein laid,—there lies
Two kinsmen digg'd their graves with weeping eyes.
Would not this ill do well? Well, well, I see
I talk but idly, and you laugh at me.
Most mighty prince, my Lord Northumberland,
What says King Bolingbroke? will his majesty
Give Richard leave to live till Richard die?
You make a leg, and Bolingbroke says ay.

NORTHUMBERLAND

My lord, in the base court he doth attend
To speak with you; may it please you to come down.

KING RICHARD

Down, down I come; like glistering Phaeton,
Wanting the manage of unruly jades.
In the base court? Base court, where kings grow
    base,
To come at traitors' calls and do them grace.
In the base court? Come down? Down, court! down,
    king!
For night-owls shriek where mounting larks should
    sing.   [Exeunt from above

BOLINGBROKE

What says his majesty?

NORTHUMBERLAND

                        Sorrow and grief of heart
Makes him speak fondly, like a frantic man:
Yet he is come.

        Enter KING RICHARD and his attendants below

BOLINGBROKE

Stand all apart,
And show fair duty to his majesty.   [He kneels down
My gracious lord,—

KING RICHARD

Fair cousin, you debase your princely knee
To make the base earth proud with kissing it:
Me rather had my heart might feel your love
Than my unpleased eye see your courtesy.

Up, cousin, up; your heart is up, I know,
Thus high at least, although your knee be low.
BOLINGBROKE
My gracious lord, I come but for mine own.
KING RICHARD
Your own is yours, and I am yours, and all.
BOLINGBROKE
So far be mine, my most redoubted lord,
As my true service shall deserve your love.
KING RICHARD
Well you deserve: they well deserve to have,
That know the strong'st and surest way to get.
Uncle, give me your hands: nay, dry your eyes;
Tears show their love, but want their remedies.
Cousin, I am too young to be your father,
Though you are old enough to be my heir.
What you will have, I'll give, and willing too;
For do we must what force will have us do.
Set on towards London, cousin, is it so?
BOLINGBROKE
Yea, my good lord.
KING RICHARD
Then I must not say no.   [*Flourish. Exeunt*

SCENE IV. *Langley. The* DUKE OF YORK'S *garden*

Enter the QUEEN *and two* LADIES
QUEEN
What sport shall we devise here in this garden,
To drive away the heavy thought of care?
LADY
Madam, we'll play at bowls.
QUEEN
'Twill make me think the world is full of rubs,
And that my fortune runs against the bias.
LADY
Madam, we'll dance.
QUEEN
My legs can keep no measure in delight,
When my poor heart no measure keeps in grief:
Therefore, no dancing, girl; some other sport.
LADY
Madam, we'll tell tales.
QUEEN
Of sorrow or of joy?
LADY
Of either, madam.
QUEEN
Of neither, girl:
For if of joy, being altogether wanting,
It doth remember me the more of sorrow;
Or if of grief, being altogether had,
It adds more sorrow to my want of joy:
For what I have I need not to repeat;
And what I want it boots not to complain.
LADY
Madam, I'll sing.
QUEEN
'Tis well that thou hast cause;

But thou shouldst please me better, wouldst thou
weep.
LADY
I could weep, madam, would it do you good.
QUEEN
And I could sing, would weeping do me good,
And never borrow any tear of thee.
Enter a GARDENER, *and two* SERVANTS
But stay, here come the gardeners:
Let's step into the shadow of these trees.
My wretchedness unto a row of pins,
They'll talk of state; for every one doth so
Against a change; woe is forerun with woe.
[QUEEN *and* LADIES *retire*
GARDENER
Go, bind thou up yon dangling apricocks,
Which, like unruly children, make their sire
Stoop with oppression of their prodigal weight:
Give some supportance to the bending twigs.
Go thou, and like an executioner,
Cut off the heads of too fast growing sprays,
That look too lofty in our commonwealth:
All must be even in our government.
You thus employ'd, I will go root away
The noisome weeds, which without profit suck
The soil's fertility from wholesome flowers.
SERVANT
Why should we in the compass of a pale
Keep law and form and due proportion,
Showing, as in a model, our firm estate,
When our sea-walled garden, the whole land,
Is full of weeds; her fairest flowers choked up,
Her fruit-trees all unpruned, her hedges ruin'd,
Her knots disorder'd, and her wholesome herbs
Swarming with caterpillars?
GARDENER
                      Hold thy peace:
He that hath suffer'd this disorder'd spring
Hath now himself met with the fall of leaf:
The weeds which his broad-spreading leaves did
shelter,
That seem'd in eating him to hold him up,
Are pluck'd up root and all by Bolingbroke:
I mean the Earl of Wiltshire, Bushy, Green.
SERVANT
What, are they dead?
GARDENER
                      They are; and Bolingbroke
Hath seized the wasteful king. O, what pity is it
That he had not so trimm'd and dress'd his land
As we this garden! We at time of year
Do wound the bark, the skin of our fruit-trees,
Lest, being over-proud in sap and blood,
With too much riches it confound itself:
Had he done so to great and growing men,
They might have lived to bear and he to taste
Their fruits of duty: superfluous branches
We lop away, that bearing boughs may live:
Had he done so, himself had borne the crown,
Which waste of idle hours hath quite thrown down.

SERVANT
What, think you then the king shall be deposed?
GARDENER
Depress'd he is already, and deposed
'Tis doubt he will be: letters came last night
To a dear friend of the good Duke of York's,
That tell black tidings.
QUEEN
O, I am press'd to death through want of speaking!
    [*Coming forward*
Thou, old Adam's likeness, set to dress this garden,
How dares thy harsh rude tongue sound this un-
    pleasing news?
What Eve, what serpent, hath suggested thee
To make a second fall of cursed man?
Why dost thou say King Richard is deposed?
Darest thou, thou little better thing than earth,
Divine his downfal? Say, where, when, and how,
Camest thou by this ill tidings? speak, thou wretch.
GARDENER
Pardon me, madam: little joy have I
To breathe this news; yet what I say is true.
King Richard, he is in the mighty hold
Of Bolingbroke: their fortunes both are weigh'd:
In your lord's scale is nothing but himself,
And some few vanities that make him light;
But in the balance of great Bolingbroke,
Besides himself, are all the English peers,
And with that odds he weighs King Richard down.
Post you to London, and you will find it so;
I speak no more than every one doth know.
QUEEN
Nimble mischance, that art so light of foot,
Doth not thy embassage belong to me,
And am I last that knows it? O, thou think'st
To serve me last, that I may longest keep
Thy sorrow in my breast. Come, ladies, go,
To meet at London London's king in woe.
What, was I born to this, that my sad look
Should grace the triumph of great Bolingbroke?
Gardener, for telling me these news of woe,
Pray God the plants thou graft'st may never grow.
    [*Exeunt* QUEEN *and* LADIES
GARDENER
Poor queen! so that thy state might be no worse,
I would my skill were subject to thy curse.
Here did she fall a tear; here in this place
I'll set a bank of rue, sour herb of grace:
Rue, even for ruth, here shortly shall be seen,
In the remembrance of a weeping queen.   [*Exeunt*

ACT IV
SCENE I. *Westminster Hall*

Enter as to the Parliament, BOLINGBROKE, AUMERLE,
NORTHUMBERLAND, PERCY, FITZWATER, SURREY, *the*
BISHOP OF CARLISLE, *the* ABBOT OF WESTMINISTER, *and*
another LORD, HERALD, OFFICERS, *and* BAGOT

BOLINGBROKE
Call forth Bagot.
Now, Bagot, freely speak thy mind;
What thou dost know of noble Gloucester's death;
Who wrought it with the king, and who perform'd
The bloody office of his timeless end.
BAGOT
Then set before my face the Lord Aumerle.
BOLINGBROKE
Cousin, stand forth, and look upon that man.
BAGOT
My Lord Aumerle, I know your daring tongue
Scorns to unsay what once it hath deliver'd.
In that dead time when Gloucester's death was
    plotted,
I heard you say, 'Is not my arm of length,
That reacheth from the restful English court
As far as Calais, to mine uncle's head?'
Amongst much other talk, that very time,
I heard you say that you had rather refuse
The offer of an hundred thousand crowns
Than Bolingbroke's return to England;
Adding withal, how blest this land would be
In this your cousin's death.
AUMERLE
                Princes and noble lords,
What answer shall I make to this base man?
Shall I so much dishonour my fair stars,
On equal terms to give him chastisement?
Either I must, or have mine honour soil'd
With the attainder of his slanderous lips.
There is my gage, the manual seal of death,
That marks thee out for hell: I say, thou liest,
And will maintain what thou hast said is false
In thy heart-blood, though being all too base
To stain the temper of my knightly sword.
BOLINGBROKE
Bagot, forbear; thou shalt not take it up.
AUMERLE
Excepting one, I would he were the best
In all this presence that hath moved me so.
FITZWATER
If that thy valour stand on sympathy,
There is my gage, Aumerle, in gage to thine:
By that fair sun which shows me where thou stand'st,
I heard thee say, and vauntingly thou spakest it,
That thou wert cause of noble Gloucester's death.
If thou deny'st it twenty times, thou liest;
And I will turn thy falsehood to thy heart,
Where it was forged, with my rapier's point.
AUMERLE
Thou darest not, coward, live to see that day.
FITZWATER
Now, by my soul, I would it were this hour.
AUMERLE
Fitzwater, thou art damn'd to hell for this.
HENRY PERCY
Aumerle, thou liest; his honour is as true
In this appeal as thou art all unjust;
And that thou art so, there I throw my gage,

To prove it on thee to the extremest point
Of mortal breathing: seize it, if thou darest.
AUMERLE
An if I do not, may my hands rot off,
And never brandish more revengeful steel
Over the glittering helmet of my foe!
ANOTHER LORD
I task the earth to the like, forsworn Aumerle;
And spur thee on with full as many lies
As may be holloa'd in thy treacherous ear
From sun to sun: there is my honour's pawn;
Engage it to the trial, if thou darest.
AUMERLE
Who sets me else? by heaven, I'll throw at all:
I have a thousand spirits in one breast,
To answer twenty thousand such as you.
SURREY
My Lord Fitzwater, I do remember well
The very time Aumerle and you did talk.
FITZWATER
'Tis very true: you were in presence then;
And you can witness with me this is true.
SURREY
As false, by heaven, as heaven itself is true.
FITZWATER
Surrey, thou liest.
SURREY
Dishonourable boy!
That lie shall lie so heavy on my sword,
That it shall render vengeance and revenge,
Till thou the lie-giver and that lie do lie
In earth as quiet as thy father's skull:
In proof whereof, there is my honour's pawn;
Engage it to the trial, if thou darest.
FITZWATER
How fondly dost thou spur a forward horse!
If I dare eat, or drink, or breathe, or live,
I dare meet Surrey in a wilderness,
And spit upon him, whilst I say he lies,
And lies, and lies: there is my bond of faith,
To tie thee to my strong correction.
As I intend to thrive in this new world,
Aumerle is guilty of my true appeal:
Besides, I heard the banish'd Norfolk say,
That thou, Aumerle, didst send two of thy men
To execute the noble duke at Calais.
AUMERLE
Some honest Christian trust me with a gage,
That Norfolk lies: here do I throw down this,
If he may be repeal'd, to try his honour.
BOLINGBROKE
These differences shall all rest under gage
Till Norfolk be repeal'd: repeal'd he shall be,
And, though mine enemy, restored again
To all his lands and signories: when he's return'd,
Against Aumerle we will enforce his trial.
CARLISLE
That honourable day shall ne'er be seen.
Many a time hath banish'd Norfolk fought
For Jesu Christ in glorious Christian field,

Streaming the ensign of the Christian cross
Against black pagans, Turks, and Saracens;
And toil'd with works of war, retired himself
To Italy; and there at Venice gave
His body to that pleasant country's earth,
And his pure soul unto his captain Christ,
Under whose colours he had fought so long.
BOLINGBROKE
Why, bishop, is Norfolk dead?
CARLISLE
As surely as I live, my lord.
BOLINGBROKE
Sweet peace conduct his sweet soul to the bosom
Of good old Abraham! Lords appellants,
Your differences shall all rest under gage
Till we assign you to your days of trial.
Enter YORK, *attended*
YORK
Great Duke of Lancaster, I come to thee
From plume-pluck'd Richard; who with willing soul
Adopts thee heir, and his high sceptre yields
To the possession of thy royal hand:
Ascend his throne, descending now from him;
And long live Henry, fourth of that name!
BOLINGBROKE
In God's name, I'll ascend the regal throne.
CARLISLE
Marry, God forbid!
Worst in this royal presence may I speak,
Yet best beseeming me to speak the truth.
Would God that any in this noble presence
Were enough noble to be upright judge
Of noble Richard! then true noblesse would
Learn him forbearance from so foul a wrong.
What subject can give sentence on his king?
And who sits here that is not Richard's subject?
Thieves are not judged but they are by to hear,
Although apparent guilt be seen in them;
And shall the figure of God's majesty,
His captain, steward, deputy elect,
Anointed, crowned, planted many years,
Be judged by subject and inferior breath,
And he himself not present? O, forfend it, God,
That in a Christian climate souls refined
Should show so heinous, black, obscene a deed!
I speak to subjects, and a subject speaks,
Stirr'd up by God, thus boldly for his king.
My Lord of Hereford here, whom you call king,
Is a foul traitor to proud Hereford's king:
And if you crown him, let me prophesy;
The blood of English shall manure the ground,
And future ages groan for this foul act;
Peace shall go sleep with Turks and infidels,
And in this seat of peace tumultuous wars
Shall kin with kin and kind with kind confound;
Disorder, horror, fear and mutiny
Shall here inhabit, and this land be call'd
The field of Golgotha and dead men's skulls.
O, if you raise this house against this house,
It will the woefullest division prove

That ever fell upon this cursed earth.
Prevent it, resist it, let it not be so,
Lest child, child's children, cry against you 'woe!'

NORTHUMBERLAND

Well have you argued, sir; and, for your pains,
Of capital treason we arrest you here.
My Lord of Westminster, be it your charge
To keep him safely till his day of trial.
May it please you, lords, to grant the commons'
    suit?

BOLINGBROKE

Fetch hither Richard, that in common view
He may surrender; so we shall proceed
Without suspicion.

YORK

              I will be his conduct.   [*Exit*

BOLINGBROKE

Lords, you that here are under our arrest,
Procure your sureties for your days of answer.
Little are we beholding to your love,
And little look'd for at your helping hands.

Re-enter YORK, *with* RICHARD, *and* OFFICERS *bearing the*
regalia

KING RICHARD

Alack, why am I sent for to a king,
Before I have shook off the regal thoughts
Wherewith I reign'd? I hardly yet have learn'd
To insinuate, flatter, bow, and bend my limbs:
Give sorrow leave awhile to tutor me
To this submission. Yet I well remember
The favours of these men: were they not mine?
Did they not sometime cry 'all hail!' to me?
So Judas did to Christ: but he, in twelve,
Found truth in all but one; I, in twelve thousand,
    none.
God save the king! Will no man say amen?
Am I both priest and clerk? well then, amen.
God save the king! although I be not he;
And yet, amen, if heaven do think him me.
To do what service am I sent for hither?

YORK

To do that office of thine own good will
Which tired majesty did make thee offer,
The resignation of thy state and crown
To Henry Bolingbroke.

KING RICHARD

Give me the crown. Here, cousin, seize the crown;
Here cousin;
On this side my hand, and on that side yours.
Now is this golden crown like a deep well
That owes two buckets, filling one another,
The emptier ever dancing in the air,
The other down, unseen and full of water:
That bucket down and full of tears am I,
Drinking my griefs, whilst you mount up on high.

BOLINGBROKE

I thought you had been willing to resign.

KING RICHARD

My crown I am; but still my griefs are mine:

You may my glories and my state depose.
But not my griefs; still am I king of those.

BOLINGBROKE

Part of your cares you give me with your crown.

KING RICHARD

Your cares set up do not pluck my cares down.
My care is loss of care, by old care done;
Your care is gain of care, by new care won:
The cares I give, I have, though given away;
They tend the crown, yet still with me they stay.

BOLINGBROKE

Are you contented to resign the crown?

KING RICHARD

Ay, no; no, ay; for I must nothing be;
Therefore no no, for I resign to thee.
Now mark me, how I will undo myself:
I give this heavy weight from off my head
And this unwieldy sceptre from my hand,
The pride of kingly sway from out my heart;
With mine own tears I wash away my balm,
With mine own hands I give away my crown,
With mine own tongue deny my sacred state,
With mine own breath release all duty's rites:
All pomp and majesty I do forswear;
My manors, rents, revenues I forgo;
My acts, decrees, and statutes I deny:
God pardon all oaths that are broke to me!
God keep all vows unbroke that swear to thee!
Make me, that nothing have, with nothing grieved,
And thou with all pleased, that hast all achieved!
Long mayst thou live in Richard's seat to sit,
And soon lie Richard in an earthy pit!
God save King Harry, unking'd Richard says,
And send him many years of sunshine days!
What more remains?

NORTHUMBERLAND

              No more, but that you read
These accusations and these grievous crimes,
Committed by your person and your followers
Against the state and profit of this land;
That, by confessing them, the souls of men
May deem that you are worthily deposed.

KING RICHARD

Must I do so? and must I ravel out
My weaved-up folly? Gentle Northumberland,
If thy offences were upon record,
Would it not shame thee in so fair a troop
To read a lecture of them? If thou wouldst,
There shouldst thou find one heinous article,
Containing the deposing of a king
And cracking the strong warrant of an oath,
Mark'd with a blot, damn'd in the book of heaven:
Nay, all of you that stand and look upon,
Whilst that my wretchedness doth bait myself,
Though some of you with Pilate wash your hands,
Showing an outward pity; yet you Pilates
Have here deliver'd me to my sour cross,
And water cannot wash away your sin.

NORTHUMBERLAND

My lord, dispatch; read o'er these articles.

KING RICHARD
Mine eyes are full of tears, I cannot see:
And yet salt water blinds them not so much
But they can see a sort of traitors here.
Nay, if I turn mine eyes upon myself,
I find myself a traitor with the rest;
For I have given here my soul's consent
To undeck the pompous body of a king;
Made glory base and sovereignty a slave,
Proud majesty a subject, state a peasant.

NORTHUMBERLAND
My lord,—

KING RICHARD
No lord of thine, thou haught insulting man,
Nor no man's lord; I have no name, no title,
No, not that name was given me at the font,
But 'tis usurp'd: alack the heavy day,
That I have worn so many winters out,
And know not now what name to call myself!
O that I were a mockery king of snow,
Standing before the sun of Bolingbroke,
To melt myself away in water-drops!
Good king, great king, and yet not greatly good,
An if my word be sterling yet in England,
Let it command a mirror hither straight,
That it may show me what a face I have,
Since it is bankrupt of his majesty.

BOLINGBROKE
Go some of you and fetch a looking-glass.
                              [Exit an ATTENDANT

NORTHUMBERLAND
Read o'er this paper while the glass doth come.

KING RICHARD
Fiend, thou torment'st me ere I come to hell!

BOLINGBROKE
Urge it no more, my Lord Northumberland.

NORTHUMBERLAND
The commons will not then be satisfied.

KING RICHARD
They shall be satisfied: I'll read enough,
When I do see the very book indeed
Where all my sins are writ, and that's myself.
        Re-enter ATTENDANT, with a glass
Give me the glass, and therein will I read.
No deeper wrinkles yet? hath sorrow struck
So many blows upon this face of mine,
And made no deeper wounds? O flattering glass,
Like to my followers in prosperity,
Thou dost beguile me! Was this face the face
That every day under his household roof
Did keep ten thousand men? was this the face
That, like the sun, did make beholders wink?
Was this the face that faced so many follies,
And was at last out-faced by Bolingbroke?
A brittle glory shineth in this face:
As brittle as the glory is the face;
        [Dashes the glass against the ground
For there it is, crack'd in a hundred shivers.
Mark, silent king, the moral of this sport,
How soon my sorrow hath destroy'd my face.

BOLINGBROKE
The shadow of your sorrow hath destroy'd
The shadow of your face.

KING RICHARD
                    Say that again.
The shadow of my sorrow! ha! let's see:
'Tis very true, my grief lies all within;
And these external manners of laments
Are merely shadows to the unseen grief,
That swells with silence in the tortured soul;
There lies the substance: and I thank thee, king,
For thy great bounty, that not only givest
Me cause to wail, but teachest me the way
How to lament the cause. I'll beg one boon,
And then be gone and trouble you no more.
Shall I obtain it?

BOLINGBROKE
        Name it, fair cousin.

KING RICHARD
'Fair cousin'? I am greater than a king:
For when I was a king, my flatterers
Were then but subjects; being now a subject,
I have a king here to my flatterer.
Being so great, I have no need to beg.

BOLINGBROKE
Yet ask.

KING RICHARD
And shall I have?

BOLINGBROKE
You shall.

KING RICHARD
Then give me leave to go.

BOLINGBROKE
Whither?

KING RICHARD
Whither you will, so I were from your sights.

BOLINGBROKE
Go, some of you convey him to the Tower.

KING RICHARD
O, good! convey? conveyers are you all,
That rise thus nimbly by a true king's fall.
    [Exeunt KING RICHARD, some LORDS, and a GUARD

BOLINGBROKE
On Wednesday next we solemnly set down
Our coronation: lords, prepare yourselves.
    [Exeunt all except the BISHOP OF CARLISLE,
    the ABBOT OF WESTMINSTER, and AUMERLE

ABBOT
A woeful pageant have we here beheld.

CARLISLE
The woe's to come; the children yet unborn
Shall feel this day as sharp to them as thorn.

AUMERLE
You holy clergymen, is there no plot
To rid the realm of this pernicious blot?

ABBOT
My lord,
Before I freely speak my mind herein,
You shall not only take the sacrament
To bury mine intents, but also to effect

Whatever I shall happen to devise.
I see your brows are full of discontent,
Your hearts of sorrow and your eyes of tears:
Come home with me to supper; and I'll lay
A plot shall show us all a merry day.   [*Exeunt*

ACT V

SCENE I. *London. A street leading to the Tower*

Enter QUEEN *and* LADIES

QUEEN

This way the king will come; this is the way
To Julius Cæsar's ill-erected tower,
To whose flint bosom my condemned lord
Is doom'd a prisoner by proud Bolingbroke:
Here let us rest, if this rebellious earth
Have any resting for her true king's queen.

Enter RICHARD *and* GUARD

But soft, but see, or rather do not see,
My fair rose wither: yet look up, behold,
That you in pity may dissolve to dew,
And wash him fresh again with true-love tears.
Ah, thou, the model where old Troy did stand,
Thou map of honour, thou King Richard's tomb,
And not King Richard; thou most beauteous inn,
Why should hard-favour'd grief be lodged in thee,
When triumph is become an alehouse guest?

KING RICHARD

Join not with grief, fair woman, do not so,
To make my end too sudden: learn, good soul,
To think our former state a happy dream;
From which awaked, the truth of what we are
Shows us but this: I am sworn brother, sweet,
To grim Necessity, and he and I
Will keep a league till death. Hie thee to France
And cloister thee in some religious house:
Our holy lives must win a new world's crown,
Which our profane hours here have stricken down.

QUEEN

What, is my Richard both in shape and mind
Transform'd and weaken'd? hath Bolingbroke de-
          posed
Thine intellect? hath he been in thy heart?
The lion dying thrusteth forth his paw,
And wounds the earth, if nothing else, with rage
To be o'erpower'd; and wilt thou, pupil-like,
Take thy correction mildly, kiss the rod,
And fawn on rage with base humility,
Which art a lion and a king of beasts?

KING RICHARD

A king of beasts, indeed; if aught but beasts,
I had been still a happy king of men.
Good sometime queen, prepare thee hence for France:
Think I am dead, and that even here thou takest,
As from my death-bed, thy last living leave.
In winter's tedious nights sit by the fire
With good old folks, and let them tell thee tales

Of woeful ages long ago betid;
And ere thou bid good night, to quit their griefs,
Tell thou the lamentable tale of me,
And send the hearers weeping to their beds:
For why, the senseless brands will sympathize
The heavy accent of thy moving tongue,
And in compassion weep the fire out;
And some will mourn in ashes, some coal-black,
For the deposing of a rightful king.

Enter NORTHUMBERLAND *and others*

NORTHUMBERLAND

My lord, the mind of Bolingbroke is changed;
You must to Pomfret, not unto the Tower.
And, madam, there is order ta'en for you;
With all swift speed you must away to France.

KING RICHARD

Northumberland, thou ladder wherewithal
The mounting Bolingbroke ascends my throne,
The time shall not be many hours of age
More than it is, ere foul sin gathering head
Shall break into corruption: thou shalt think,
Though he divide the realm, and give thee half,
It is too little, helping him to all;
And he shall think that thou, which know'st the way
To plant unrightful kings, wilt know again,
Being ne'er so little urged, another way
To pluck him headlong from the usurped throne.
The love of wicked men converts to fear;
That fear to hate, and hate turns one or both
To worthy danger and deserved death.

NORTHUMBERLAND

My guilt be on my head, and there an end.
Take leave and part; for you must part forthwith.

KING RICHARD

Doubly divorced! Bad men, you violate
A twofold marriage; 'twixt my crown and me,
And then betwixt me and my married wife.
Let me unkiss the oath 'twixt thee and me;
And yet not so, for with a kiss 'twas made.
Part us, Northumberland; I towards the north,
Where shivering cold and sickness pines the clime;
My wife to France: from whence, set forth in pomp,
She came adorned hither like sweet May,
Sent back like Hallowmas or short'st of day.

QUEEN

And must we be divided? must we part?

KING RICHARD

Ay, hand from hand, my love, and heart from heart.

QUEEN

Banish us both and send the king with me.

NORTHUMBERLAND

That were some love but little policy.

QUEEN

Then whither he goes, thither let me go.

KING RICHARD

So two, together weeping, make one woe.
Weep thou for me in France, I for thee here;
Better far off than near, be ne'er the near.
Go, count thy way with sighs; I mine with groans.

QUEEN

So longest way shall have the longest moans.

KING RICHARD

Twice for one step I'll groan, the way being short,
And piece the way out with a heavy heart.
Come, come, in wooing sorrow let's be brief,
Since, wedding it, there is such length in grief:
One kiss shall stop our mouths, and dumbly part;
Thus give I mine, and thus take I thy heart.

QUEEN

Give me mine own again; 'twere no good part
To take on me to keep and kill thy heart.
So, now I have mine own again, be gone,
That I may strive to kill it with a groan.

KING RICHARD

We make woe wanton with this fond delay:
Once more, adieu; the rest let sorrow say.　　[Exeunt

SCENE II. *The* DUKE OF YORK'S *palace*

Enter YORK *and his* DUCHESS

DUCHESS OF YORK

My lord, you told me you would tell the rest,
When weeping made you break the story off
Of our two cousins coming into London.

YORK

Where did I leave?

DUCHESS OF YORK

　　　　　　At that sad stop, my lord,
Where rude misgovern'd hands from windows' tops
Threw dust and rubbish on King Richard's head.

YORK

Then, as I said, the duke, great Bolingbroke,
Mounted upon a hot and fiery steed,
Which his aspiring rider seem'd to know,
With slow but stately pace kept on his course,
Whilst all tongues cried 'God save thee, Boling-
　broke!'
You would have thought the very windows spake,
So many greedy looks of young and old
Through casements darted their desiring eyes
Upon his visage, and that all the walls
With painted imagery had said at once
'Jesu preserve thee! welcome, Bolingbroke!'
Whilst he, from the one side to the other turning,
Bareheaded, lower than his proud steed's neck,
Bespake them thus; 'I thank you, countrymen:'
And thus still doing, thus he pass'd along.

DUCHESS OF YORK

Alack, poor Richard! where rode he the whilst?

YORK

As in a theatre, the eyes of men,
After a well-graced actor leaves the stage,
Are idly bent on him that enters next,
Thinking his prattle to be tedious;
Even so, or with much more contempt, men's eyes
Did scowl on gentle Richard; no man cried 'God
　save him!'
No joyful tongue gave him his welcome home:

But dust was thrown upon his sacred head;
Which with such gentle sorrow he shook off,
His face still combating with tears and smiles,
The badges of his grief and patience,
That had not God, for some strong purpose, steel'd
The hearts of men, they must perforce have melted,
And barbarism itself have pitied him.
But heaven hath a hand in these events,
To whose high will we bound our calm contents.
To Bolingbroke are we sworn subjects now,
Whose state and honour I for aye allow.

DUCHESS OF YORK

Here comes my son Aumerle.

YORK

　　　　　　　Aumerle that was;
But that is lost for being Richard's friend,
And, madam, you must call him Rutland now:
I am in parliament pledge for his truth
And lasting fealty to the new made king.

Enter AUMERLE

DUCHESS OF YORK

Welcome, my son: who are the violets now
That strew the green lap of the new come spring?

AUMERLE

Madam, I know not, nor I greatly care not:
God knows I had as lief be none as one.

YORK

Well, bear you well in this new spring of time,
Lest you be cropp'd before you come to prime.
What news from Oxford? hold those justs and tri-
　umphs?

AUMERLE

For aught I know, my lord, they do.

YORK

You will be there, I know.

AUMERLE

If God prevent not, I purpose so.

YORK

What seal is that, that hangs without thy bosom?
Yea, look'st thou pale? let me see the writing.

AUMERLE

My lord, 'tis nothing.

YORK

　　　　　　No matter, then, who see it:
I will be satisfied; let me see the writing.

AUMERLE

I do beseech your grace to pardon me:
It is a matter of small consequence,
Which for some reasons I would not have seen.

YORK

Which for some reasons, sir, I mean to see.
I fear, I fear,—

DUCHESS OF YORK

　　　　　What should you fear?
'Tis nothing but some band, that he is enter'd into
For gay apparel 'gainst the triumph day.

YORK

Bound to himself! what doth he with a bond
That he is bound to? Wife, thou art a fool.
Boy, let me see the writing.

AUMERLE
I do beseech you, pardon me; I may not show it.
YORK
I will be satisfied; let me see it, I say.
[*He plucks it out of his bosom and reads it*
Treason! foul treason! Villain! traitor! slave!
DUCHESS OF YORK
What is the matter, my lord?
YORK
Ho! who is within there?
Enter a SERVANT
Saddle my horse.
God for his mercy, what treachery is here!
DUCHESS OF YORK
Why, what is it, my lord?
YORK
Give me my boots, I say; saddle my horse.
[*Exit* SERVANT
Now, by mine honour, by my life, by my troth,
I will appeach the villain.
DUCHESS OF YORK
What is the matter?
YORK
Peace, foolish woman.
DUCHESS OF YORK
I will not peace. What is the matter, Aumerle?
AUMERLE
Good mother, be content; it is no more
Than my poor life must answer.
DUCHESS OF YORK
Thy life answer!
YORK
Bring me my boots: I will unto the king.
Re-enter SERVANT *with boots*
DUCHESS OF YORK
Strike him, Aumerle. Poor boy, thou art amazed.
Hence, villain! never more come in my sight.
YORK
Give me my boots, I say.
DUCHESS OF YORK
Why, York, what wilt thou do?
Wilt thou not hide the trespass of thine own?
Have we more sons? or are we like to have?
Is not my teeming date drunk up with time?
And wilt thou pluck my fair son from mine age,
And rob me of a happy mother's name?
Is he not like thee? is he not thine own?
YORK
Thou fond mad woman,
Wilt thou conceal this dark conspiracy?
A dozen of them here have ta'en the sacrament,
And interchangeably set down their hands,
To kill the king at Oxford.
DUCHESS OF YORK
He shall be none;
We'll keep him here: then what is that to him?
YORK
Away, fond woman! were he twenty times my son,
I would appeach him.

DUCHESS OF YORK
Hadst thou groan'd for him
As I have done, thou wouldst be more pitiful.
But now I know thy mind; thou dost suspect
That I have been disloyal to thy bed,
And that he is a bastard, not thy son:
Sweet York, sweet husband, be not of that mind:
He is as like thee as a man may be,
Not like to me, or any of my kin,
And yet I love him.
YORK
Make way, unruly woman!   [*Exit*
DUCHESS OF YORK
After, Aumerle! mount thee upon his horse;
Spur post, and get before him to the king,
And beg thy pardon ere he do accuse thee.
I'll not be long behind; though I be old,
I doubt not but to ride as fast as York:
And never will I rise up from the ground
Till Bolingbroke have pardon'd thee. Away, be
gone!   [*Exeunt*

SCENE III. *Windsor Castle*

Enter BOLINGBROKE, HENRY PERCY, *and other* LORDS
BOLINGBROKE
Can no man tell me of my unthrifty son?
'Tis full three months since I did see him last:
If any plague hang over us, 'tis he.
I would to God, my lords, he might be found:
Inquire at London, 'mongst the taverns there,
For there, they say, he daily doth frequent,
With unrestrained loose companions,
Even such, they say, as stand in narrow lanes,
And beat our watch, and rob our passengers;
Which he, young wanton and effeminate boy,
Takes on the point of honour to support
So dissolute a crew.
HENRY PERCY
My lord, some two days since I saw the prince,
And told him of those triumphs held at Oxford.
BOLINGBROKE
And what said the gallant?
HENRY PERCY
His answer was, he would unto the stews,
And from the common'st creature pluck a glove,
And wear it as a favour; and with that
He would unhorse the lustiest challenger.
BOLINGBROKE
As dissolute as desperate; yet through both
I see some sparks of better hope, which elder years
May happily bring forth. But who comes here?
Enter AUMERLE
AUMERLE
Where is the king?
BOLINGBROKE
What means our cousin, that he stares and looks
So wildly?

[379]

AUMERLE

God save your grace! I do beseech your majesty,
To have some conference with your grace alone.

BOLINGBROKE

Withdraw yourselves, and leave us here alone.
                [Exeunt PERCY *and* LORDS
What is the matter with our cousin now?

AUMERLE

For ever may my knees grow to the earth,
My tongue cleave to my roof within my mouth,
Unless a pardon ere I rise or speak.

BOLINGBROKE

Intended or committed was this fault?
If on the first, how heinous e'er it be,
To win thy after-love I pardon thee.

AUMERLE

Then give me leave that I may turn the key,
That no man enter till my tale be done.

BOLINGBROKE

Have thy desire.

YORK

[Within] My liege, beware; look to thyself;
Thou hast a traitor in thy presence there.

BOLINGBROKE

Villain, I'll make thee safe.   *[Drawing*

AUMERLE

Stay thy revengeful hand; thou hast no cause to fear.

YORK

[Within] Open the door, secure, foolhardy king:
Shall I for love speak treason to thy face?
Open the door, or I will break it open.
                Enter YORK

BOLINGBROKE

What is the matter, uncle? speak;
Recover breath; tell us how near is danger,
That we may arm us to encounter it.

YORK

Peruse this writing here, and thou shalt know
The treason that my haste forbids me show.

AUMERLE

Remember, as thou read'st, thy promise pass'd:
I do repent me; read not my name there;
My heart is not confederate with my hand.

YORK

It was, villain, ere thy hand did set it down.
I tore it from the traitor's bosom, king;
Fear, and not love, begets his penitence:
Forget to pity him, lest thy pity prove
A serpent that will sting thee to the heart.

BOLINGBROKE

O heinous, strong and bold conspiracy!
O loyal father of a treacherous son!
Thou sheer, immaculate and silver fountain,
From whence this stream through muddy passages
Hath held his current and defiled himself!
Thy overflow of good converts to bad,
And thy abundant goodness shall excuse
This deadly blot in thy digressing son.

YORK

So shall my virtue be his vice's bawd;
And he shall spend mine honour with his shame,
As thriftless sons their scraping fathers' gold.
Mine honour lives when his dishonour dies,
Or my shamed life in his dishonour lies:
Thou kill'st me in his life; giving him breath,
The traitor lives, the true man's put to death.

DUCHESS OF YORK

[Within] What ho, my liege! for God's sake, let me
in.

BOLINGBROKE

What shrill-voiced suppliant makes this eager cry?

DUCHESS OF YORK

A woman, and thy aunt, great king; 'tis I.
Speak with me, pity me, open the door:
A beggar begs that never begg'd before.

BOLINGBROKE

Our scene is alter'd from a serious thing,
And now changed to 'The Beggar and the King.'
My dangerous cousin, let your mother in:
I know she is come to pray for your foul sin.

YORK

If thou do pardon, whosoever pray,
More sins for this forgiveness prosper may.
This fester'd joint cut off, the rest rest sound;
This let alone will all the rest confound.
           Enter DUCHESS OF YORK

DUCHESS OF YORK

O king, believe not this hard-hearted man!
Love loving not itself none other can.

YORK

Thou frantic woman, what dost thou make here?
Shall thy old dugs once more a traitor rear?

DUCHESS OF YORK

Sweet York, be patient. Hear me, gentle liege.
                        [Kneels

BOLINGBROKE

Rise up, good aunt.

DUCHESS OF YORK

            Not yet, I thee beseech:
For ever will I walk upon my knees,
And never see day that the happy sees,
Till thou give joy; until thou bid me joy,
By pardoning Rutland, my transgressing boy.

AUMERLE

Unto my mother's prayers I bend my knee.   *[Kneels*

YORK

Against them both my true joints bended be.
                        [Kneels
Ill mayst thou thrive, if thou grant any grace!

DUCHESS OF YORK

Pleads he in earnest? look upon his face;
His eyes do drop no tears, his prayers are in jest;
His words come from his mouth, ours from our
breast:
He prays but faintly and would be denied;
We pray with heart and soul and all beside:

His weary joints would gladly rise, I know;
Our knees shall kneel till to the ground they grow:
His prayers are full of false hypocrisy;
Ours of true zeal and deep integrity.
Our prayers do out-pray his; then let them have
That mercy which true prayer ought to have.

BOLINGBROKE

Good aunt, stand up.

DUCHESS OF YORK

           Nay, do not say, 'stand up;'
Say 'pardon' first, and afterwards 'stand up.'
An if I were thy nurse, thy tongue to teach,
'Pardon' should be the first word of thy speech.
I never long'd to hear a word till now;
Say 'pardon,' king; let pity teach thee how:
The word is short, but not so short as sweet;
No word like 'pardon' for kings' mouths so meet.

YORK

Speak it in French, king; say, 'pardonne moi.'

DUCHESS OF YORK

Dost thou teach pardon pardon to destroy?
Ah, my sour husband, my hard-hearted lord,
That set'st the word itself against the word!
Speak 'pardon' as 'tis current in our land;
The chopping French we do not understand.
Thine eye begins to speak, set thy tongue there:
Or in thy piteous heart plant thou thine ear;
That hearing how our plaints and prayers do pierce,
Pity may move thee 'pardon' to rehearse.

BOLINGBROKE

Good aunt, stand up.

DUCHESS OF YORK

           I do not sue to stand;
Pardon is all the suit I have in hand.

BOLINGBROKE

I pardon him, as God shall pardon me.

DUCHESS OF YORK

O happy vantage of a kneeling knee!
Yet am I sick for fear: speak it again;
Twice saying 'pardon' doth not pardon twain,
But makes one pardon strong.

BOLINGBROKE

                With all my heart
I pardon him.

DUCHESS OF YORK

A god on earth thou art.

BOLINGBROKE

But for our trusty brother-in-law, and the abbot,
With all the rest of that consorted crew,
Destruction straight shall dog them at the heels.
Good uncle, help to order several powers
To Oxford, or where'er these traitors are:
They shall not live within this world, I swear,
But I will have them, if I once know where.
Uncle, farewell: and, cousin too, adieu:
Your mother well hath pray'd, and prove you true.

DUCHESS OF YORK

Come, my old son: I pray God make thee new.

                            [*Exeunt*

SCENE IV. *The same*

Enter EXTON *and* SERVANT

EXTON

Didst thou not mark the king, what words he spake,
'Have I no friend will rid me of this living fear?'
Was it not so?

SERVANT

           These were his very words.

EXTON

'Have I no friend?' quoth he: he spake it twice,
And urged it twice together, did he not?

SERVANT

He did.

EXTON

And speaking it, he wistly look'd on me;
As who should say, 'I would thou wert the man
That would divorce this terror from my heart;'
Meaning the king at Pomfret. Come, let's go:
I am the king's friend, and will rid his foe.   [*Exeunt*

SCENE V. *Pomfret Castle*

Enter KING RICHARD

KING RICHARD

I have been studying how I may compare
This prison where I live unto the world:
And for because the world is populous,
And here is not a creature but myself,
I cannot do it; yet I'll hammer it out.
My brain I'll prove the female to my soul,
My soul the father; and these two beget
A generation of still-breeding thoughts,
And these same thoughts people this little world,
In humours like the people of this world,
For no thought is contented. The better sort,
As thoughts of things divine, are intermix'd
With scruples, and do set the word itself
Against the word:
As thus, 'Come, little ones,' and then again,
'It is as hard to come as for a camel
To thread the postern of a small needle's eye.'
Thoughts tending to ambition, they do plot
Unlikely wonders; how these vain weak nails
May tear a passage through the flinty ribs
Of this hard world, my ragged prison walls,
And, for they cannot, die in their own pride,
Thoughts tending to content flatter themselves
That they are not the first of fortune's slaves,
Nor shall not be the last; like silly beggars
Who sitting in the stocks refuge their shame,
That many have and others must sit there;
And in this thought they find a kind of ease,
Bearing their own misfortunes on the back
Of such as have before endured the like.
Thus play I in one person many people,
And none contented: sometimes am I king;
Then treasons make me wish myself a beggar,
And so I am: then crushing penury

Persuades me I was better when a king;
Then am I king'd again: and by and by
Think that I am unking'd by Bolingbroke,
And straight am nothing: but whate'er I be,
Nor I nor any man that but man is
With nothing shall be pleased, till he be eased
With being nothing. Music do I hear?   [*Music*
Ha, ha! keep time: how sour sweet music is,
When time is broke and no proportion kept!
So is it in the music of men's lives.
And here have I the daintiness of ear
To check time broke in a disorder'd string;
But for the concord of my state and time
Had not an ear to hear my true time broke.
I wasted time, and now doth time waste me;
For now hath time made me his numbering clock:
My thoughts are minutes; and with sighs they jar
Their watches on unto mine eyes, the outward
     watch,
Whereto my finger, like a dial's point,
Is pointing still, in cleansing them from tears.
Now sir, the sound that tells what hour it is
Are clamorous groans, which strike upon my heart,
Which is the bell: so sighs and tears and groans
Show minutes, times, and hours: but my time
Runs posting on in Bolingbroke's proud joy,
While I stand fooling here, his Jack o' the clock.
This music mads me; let it sound no more;
For though it have holp madmen to their wits,
In me it seems it will make wise men mad.
Yet blessing on his heart that gives it me!
For 'tis a sign of love; and love to Richard
Is a strange brooch in this all-hating world.

Enter a GROOM OF THE STABLE

GROOM

Hail, royal prince!

KING RICHARD

Thanks, noble peer;
The cheapest of us is ten groats too dear.
What art thou? and how comest thou hither,
Where no man never comes, but that sad dog
That brings me food to make misfortune live?

GROOM

I was a poor groom of thy stable, king,
When thou wert king; who, travelling towards York,
With much ado at length have gotten leave
To look upon my sometimes royal master's face.
O, how it yearn'd my heart when I beheld
In London streets, that coronation-day,
When Bolingbroke rode on roan Barbary,
That horse that thou so often hast bestrid,
That horse that I so carefully have dress'd!

KING RICHARD

Rode he on Barbary? Tell me, gentle friend,
How went he under him?

GROOM

So proudly as if he disdain'd the ground.

KING RICHARD

So proud that Bolingbroke was on his back!
That jade hath eat bread from my royal hand;

This hand hath made him proud with clapping him
Would he not stumble? would he not fall down,
Since pride must have a fall, and break the neck
Of that proud man that did usurp his back?
Forgiveness, horse! why do I rail on thee,
Since thou, created to be awed by man,
Wast born to bear? I was not made a horse;
And yet I bear a burthen like an ass,
Spurr'd, gall'd and tired by jauncing Bolingbroke.

Enter KEEPER, *with a dish*

KEEPER

Fellow, give place; here is no longer stay.

KING RICHARD

If thou love me, 'tis time thou wert away.

GROOM

What my tongue dares not, that my heart shall say.
                                              [*Exit*

KEEPER

My lord, will't please you to fall to?

KING RICHARD

Taste of it first, as thou art wont to do.

KEEPER

My lord, I dare not: sir Pierce of Exton, who lately
came from the king, commands the contrary.

KING RICHARD

The devil take Henry of Lancaster and thee!
Patience is stale, and I am weary of it.
                                  [*Beats the* KEEPER

KEEPER

Help, help, help!

Enter EXTON *and* SERVANTS, *armed*

KING RICHARD

How now! what means death in this rude assault?
Villain, thy own hand yields thy death's instrument.
     [*Snatching an axe from a* SERVANT *and killing him*
Go thou, and fill another room in hell.
     [*He kills another. Then* EXTON *strikes him down*
That hand shall burn in never-quenching fire
That staggers thus my person. Exton, thy fierce
     hand
Hath with the king's blood stain'd the king's own
     land.
Mount, mount, my soul! thy seat is up on high;
Whilst my gross flesh sinks downward, here to die.
                                              [*Dies*

EXTON

As full of valour as of royal blood:
Both have I spill'd; O would the deed were good!
For now the devil, that told me I did well,
Says that this deed is chronicled in hell.
This dead king to the living king I'll bear:
Take hence the rest, and give them burial here.
                                            [*Exeunt*

SCENE VI. *Windsor Castle*

Flourish. Enter BOLINGBROKE, YORK, *with other* LORDS,
     and ATTENDANTS

BOLINGBROKE

Kind uncle York, the latest news we hear

Is that the rebels have consumed with fire
Our town of Cicester in Gloucestershire;
But whether they be ta'en or slain we hear not.
Enter NORTHUMBERLAND
Welcome, my lord: what is the news?
NORTHUMBERLAND
First, to thy sacred state wish I all happiness.
The next news is, I have to London sent
The heads of Oxford, Salisbury, Blunt, and Kent:
The manner of their taking may appear
At large discoursed in this paper here.
BOLINGBROKE
We thank thee, gentle Percy, for thy pains;
And to thy worth will add right worthy gains.
Enter FITZWATER
FITZWATER
My lord, I have from Oxford sent to London
The heads of Brocas and Sir Bennet Seely,
Two of the dangerous consorted traitors
That sought at Oxford thy dire overthrow.
BOLINGBROKE
Thy pains, Fitzwater, shall not be forgot;
Right noble is thy merit, well I wot.
Enter HENRY PERCY, *and the* BISHOP OF CARLISLE
HENRY PERCY
The grand conspirator, Abbot of Westminster,
With clog of conscience and sour melancholy
Hath yielded up his body to the grave;
But here is Carlisle living, to abide
Thy kingly doom and sentence of his pride.
BOLINGBROKE
Carlisle, this is your doom:
Choose out some secret place, some reverend room,

More than thou hast, and with it joy thy life;
So as thou livest in peace, die free from strife:
For though mine enemy thou hast ever been,
High sparks of honour in thee have I seen.
Enter EXTON, *with persons bearing a coffin*
EXTON
Great king, within this coffin I present
Thy buried fear: herein all breathless lies
The mightiest of thy greatest enemies,
Richard of Bordeaux, by me hither brought.
BOLINGBROKE
Exton, I thank thee not; for thou hast wrought
A deed of slander, with thy fatal hand,
Upon my head and all this famous land.
EXTON
From your own mouth, my lord, did I this deed.
BOLINGBROKE
They love not poison that do poison need,
Nor do I thee: though I did wish him dead,
I hate the murderer, love him murdered.
The guilt of conscience take thou for thy labour,
But neither my good word nor princely favour:
With Cain go wander thorough shades of night,
And never show thy head by day nor light.
Lords, I protest, my soul is full of woe,
That blood should sprinkle me to make me grow:
Come, mourn with me for that I do lament,
And put on sullen black incontinent:
I'll make a voyage to the Holy Land,
To wash this blood off from my guilty hand:
March sadly after; grace my mournings here;
In weeping after this untimely bier.   [*Exeunt*

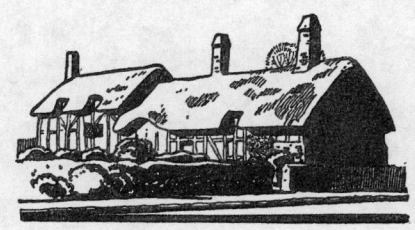

A MIDSUMMER-NIGHT'S DREAM

SYNOPSIS

THE marriage of the heroic Theseus, Duke of Athens, to Hippolyta, Queen of the Amazons, is to take place at the next new moon, and he requests his master of ceremonies, Philostrate, to urge the Athenian youths to participate in the fortnight's revels that will follow the wedding.

A group of simple, untutored craftsmen, anxious to entertain the royal couple, meet to select parts in a play which is their own version of the story of Pyramus and Thisbe, and plan to hold a rehearsal in the woods at the Duke's oak. Just at this time, the Duke is called upon by a prominent citizen, Egeus, to evoke the old Athenian law which will force his daughter Hermia to marry the man of her father's choice, Demetrius, or accept the alternative of death or life in a convent. The Duke upholding the law, Hermia and Lysander, the man she loves, arrange in desperation to meet in the wood the following night and escape to the home of the youth's aunt where they will be married. They make the mistake, however, of confiding in Hermia's friend Helena who, in love with Demetrius, warns him of the elopement in a foolish endeavor to win his favor and in order to follow him in his chase after the runaway pair.

The wood which is the destination of both the lovers and the craftsmen is filled with fairies who have come from India to wish joy and prosperity to Theseus and Hippolyta, but at the present moment they are seriously disturbed by a quarrel between Oberon, the King, and his Queen Titania, over the custody of a little changeling boy whom the Queen insists upon rearing, while the King wants him for his henchman. Oberon suddenly recalls having seen Cupid aim at a fair vestal with one of his swift arrows which, missing fire, fell on a little milk-white flower, turning it purple. He sends his hobgoblin, Puck, on a hasty search of the world for the flower, the juice of which when dropped on the eyelids of any sleeper will make the victim dote foolishly on the first creature he sees when awakening, and he plans to embarrass Titania by causing her to fall in love with some monstrosity while he gains possession of the changeling.

Demetrius now appears, seeking for the eloping lovers, with Helena closely following, and the fairy king, perceiving the young man's scorn for the girl, instructs Puck upon his return a little later to squeeze the fatal juice into the youth's eyes, whom the hobgoblin is to recognize by his Athenian clothes. Through Puck's error, Lysander, sleeping on the ground near Hermia, is anointed, awakens to see Helena still in pursuit of Demetrius, makes violent love to her, and follows her into the wood. Hermia wakes up and goes in search of Lysander, only to meet Demetrius whom she accuses of murdering her lover. After a while Demetrius, exhausted, lies down to sleep, and Oberon, having learned of Puck's mistake, sends his messenger to fetch Helena while he drops the love-potion into Demetrius' eyes. As Helena comes to the spot, quarreling with Lysander, the noise awakens Demetrius who falls in love with the girl in rivalry with Lysander, and when Hermia arrives, the confusion deepens and bitter words are exchanged on all sides, with the young men rushing out at length to fight a duel. Puck sets things straight, however, by intercepting the duellists, causing the four lovers to fall asleep, and removing the spell from Lysander's eyes with the juice of another flower.

Meanwhile the craftsmen meet in the wood near the fairy queen's abode, and the knavish Puck gleefully watches his chance to slip an ass's head upon the foolish Nick Bottom's shoulders. The rest of the company flee in terror at the sight and Titania wakes up, falls violently in love with the absurd monster, adorns his head with musk-roses, orders her fairies to wait upon him and fetch him fairy food, and falls asleep in his arms. Oberon, having achieved his purpose in carrying off the changeling boy, cures her enchantment and orders Puck to release the ass's head as Bottom wakes up, stretches himself and thinks it all a rare dream.

At the break of day Theseus, Hippolyta and their train come to the wood to hunt and awaken the lovers with their horns. When the Duke finds that Demetrius, being in love with Helena, willingly gives up Hermia to Lysander, he is so pleased that he invites the lovers to be married in the same ceremony with himself and Hippolyta. Festivities hold full sway in Athens for two weeks after the wedding, and one night the list of revels includes the craftsmen's play against which Philostrate, master of ceremonies, protests saying it is laughably crude. The Duke reminds him that when duty and simpleness tender anything it is never amiss, and he graciously requests the performance of Pyramus and Thisbe.

Leaving nothing to the imagination, the craftsmen present an actor to represent the lion, another the moonshine, and yet another the wall which holds up its fingers to allow Pyramus to peer through at Thisbe. The craftsmen close their entertainment with a dance and leave well pleased with themselves and their reception. At midnight Oberon and Titania with their fairy train sweep through the palace, dancing and singing, and when they have blessed the sleepers they vanish.

HISTORICAL DATA

A variety of sources supplied Shakespeare with the material which he blended together in the harmonious and original world of faery in *A Midsummer-Night's Dream*. North's translation of Plutarch's *Lives* and Chaucer's *Knight's Tale* furnished the chief suggestions for Theseus and Hippolyta and their marriage. Golding's translation of Ovid's *Metamorphoses* and Chaucer's *Wife of Bath's Tale* gave him his characterization of Titania, which name was also one of Ovid's variants of Diana. Oberon appears in mediæval romances such as *Huon of Bordeaux* (1534), Greene's *James IV*, in the *Faerie Queen*, and elsewhere. Chaucer's *Merchant's Tale* probably was the source of the Fairy King and Queen's quarrel, while Montemayor's *Diana Enamorada* may have suggested the love-potion flower. The story of Pyramis and Thisbe is found both in Chaucer and in Ovid.

The comedy may have been written in celebration of the marriage of some nobleman (sometimes identified as the Earl of Derby who espoused Elizabeth Vere at the Court at Greenwich in 1594) but a reasonable opinion indicates that it was probably written for a performance on the festival of St. John, "Midsummer's Night," just as *Twelfth Night* was prepared for performance on that Winter festival.

From Titania's description of the cold summer (of 1594) authorities are inclined to the year 1594 as the probable date of the comedy. It is included by Meres in his compilation of 1598 and was first published in quarto edition in 1600.

"—and let me rest."
A MIDSUMMER-NIGHT'S DREAM

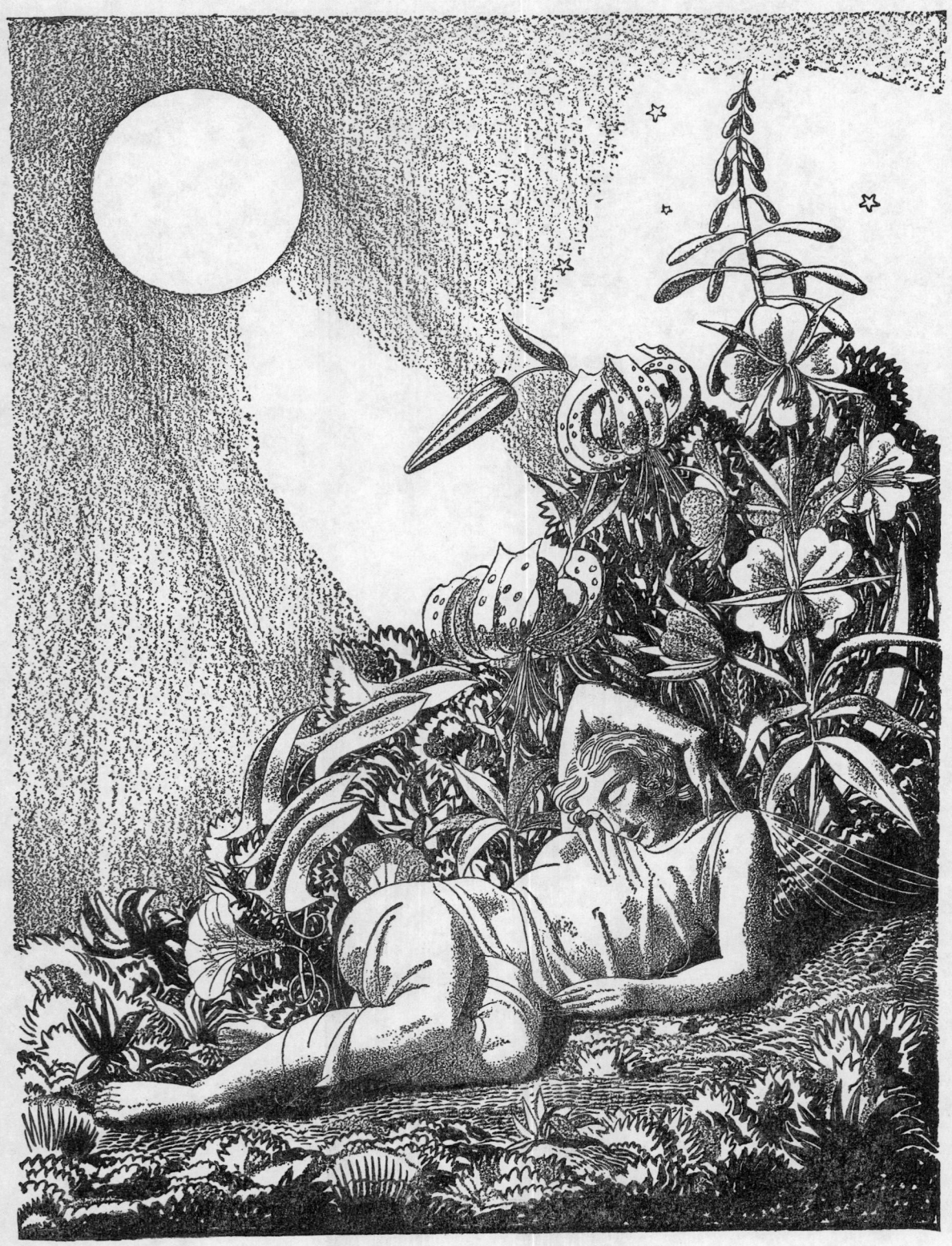

A MIDSUMMER-NIGHT'S DREAM

DRAMATIS PERSONÆ

THESEUS, *Duke of Athens.*
EGEUS, *father to Hermia.*
LYSANDER,
DEMETRIUS, } *in love with Hermia.*
PHILOSTRATE, *master of the revels to Theseus.*
QUINCE, *a carpenter.*
SNUG, *a joiner.*
BOTTOM, *a weaver.*
FLUTE, *a bellows-mender.*
SNOUT, *a tinker.*
STARVELING, *a tailor.*

HIPPOLYTA, *queen of the Amazons, betrothed to Theseus.*

HERMIA, *daughter to Egeus, in love with Lysander.*
HELENA, *in love with Demetrius.*

OBERON, *king of the fairies.*
TITANIA, *queen of the fairies.*
PUCK, *or Robin Goodfellow.*
PEASEBLOSSOM,
COBWEB,
MOTH, } *fairies.*
MUSTARDSEED,
OTHER FAIRIES *attending their King and Queen.
Attendants on Theseus and Hippolyta.*

SCENE—*Athens, and a wood near it.*

ACT I

SCENE I. *Athens. The palace of* THESEUS

Enter THESEUS, HIPPOLYTA, PHILOSTRATE, *and Attendants*

THESEUS

Now, fair Hippolyta, our nuptial hour
Draws on apace; four happy days bring in
Another moon: but, O, methinks, how slow
This old moon wanes! she lingers my desires,
Like to a step-dame, or a dowager,
Long withering out a young man's revenue.

HIPPOLYTA

Four days will quickly steep themselves in night;
Four nights will quickly dream away the time;
And then the moon, like to a silver bow
New-bent in heaven, shall behold the night
Of our solemnities.

THESEUS

Go, Philostrate,
Stir up the Athenian youth to merriments;
Awake the pert and nimble spirit of mirth:
Turn melancholy forth to funerals;
The pale companion is not for our pomp.
                                [*Exit* PHILOSTRATE
Hippolyta, I woo'd thee with my sword,
And won thy love, doing thee injuries;
But I will wed thee in another key,
With pomp, with triumph and with revelling.

Enter EGEUS, HERMIA, LYSANDER, *and* DEMETRIUS

EGEUS

Happy be Theseus, our renowned duke!

THESEUS

Thanks, good Egeus: what's the news with thee?

EGEUS

Full of vexation come I, with complaint
Against my child, my daughter Hermia.

Stand forth, Demetrius. My noble lord,
This man hath my consent to marry her.
Stand forth, Lysander: and, my gracious duke,
This man hath bewitch'd the bosom of my child:
Thou, thou, Lysander, thou hast given her rhymes,
And interchanged love-tokens with my child:
Thou hast by moonlight at her window sung,
With feigning voice, verses of feigning love;
And stolen the impression of her fantasy
With bracelets of thy hair, rings, gawds, conceits,
Knacks, trifles, nosegays, sweetmeats, messengers
Of strong prevailment in unharden'd youth:
With cunning hast thou filch'd my daughter's heart;
Turn'd her obedience, which is due to me,
To stubborn harshness: and, my gracious duke,
Be it so she will not here before your Grace
Consent to marry with Demetrius,
I beg the ancient privilege of Athens,
As she is mine, I may dispose of her:
Which shall be either to this gentleman
Or to her death, according to our law
Immediately provided in that case.

THESEUS

What say you, Hermia? be advised, fair maid:
To you your father should be as a god;
One that composed your beauties; yea, and one
To whom you are but as a form in wax
By him imprinted and within his power
To leave the figure or disfigure it.
Demetrius is a worthy gentleman.

HERMIA

So is Lysander.

THESEUS

In himself he is;
But in this kind, wanting your father's voice,
The other must be held the worthier.

HERMIA

I would my father look'd but with my eyes.

THESEUS
Rather your eyes must with his judgement look.
HERMIA
I do entreat your Grace to pardon me.
I know not by what power I am made bold,
Nor how it may concern my modesty,
In such a presence here to plead my thoughts;
But I beseech your Grace that I may know
The worst that may befall me in this case,
If I refuse to wed Demetrius.
THESEUS
Either to die the death, or to abjure
For ever the society of men.
Therefore, fair Hermia, question your desires;
Know of your youth, examine well your blood,
Whether, if you yield not to your father's choice,
You can endure the livery of a nun;
For aye to be in shady cloister mew'd,
To live a barren sister all your life,
Chanting faint hymns to the cold fruitless moon.
Thrice-blessed they that master so their blood,
To undergo such maiden pilgrimage;
But earthlier happy is the rose distill'd,
Than that which, withering on the virgin thorn,
Grows, lives, and dies in single blessedness.
HERMIA
So will I grow, so live, so die, my lord,
Ere I will yield my virgin patent up
Unto his lordship, whose unwished yoke
My soul consents not to give sovereignty.
THESEUS
Take time to pause; and, by the next new moon,—
The sealing-day betwixt my love and me,
For everlasting bond of fellowship,—
Upon that day either prepare to die
For disobedience to your father's will,
Or else to wed Demetrius, as he would;
Or on Diana's altar to protest
For aye austerity and single life.
DEMETRIUS
Relent, sweet Hermia: and, Lysander, yield
Thy crazed title to my certain right.
LYSANDER
You have her father's love, Demetrius;
Let me have Hermia's: do you marry him.
EGEUS
Scornful Lysander! true, he hath my love,
And what is mine my love shall render him.
And she is mine, and all my right of her
I do estate unto Demetrius.
LYSANDER
I am, my lord, as well derived as he,
As well possess'd; my love is more than his;
My fortunes every way as fairly rank'd,
If not with vantage, as Demetrius';
And, which is more than all these boasts can be,
I am beloved of beauteous Hermia:
Why should not I then prosecute my right?
Demetrius, I'll avouch it to his head,
Made love to Nedar's daughter, Helena,

And won her soul; and she, sweet lady, dotes,
Devoutly dotes, dotes in idolatry,
Upon this spotted and inconstant man.
THESEUS
I must confess that I have heard so much,
And with Demetrius thought to have spoke thereof;
But, being over-full of self-affairs,
My mind did lose it. But, Demetrius, come;
And come, Egeus; you shall go with me,
I have some private schooling for you both.
For you, fair Hermia, look you arm yourself
To fit your fancies to your father's will;
Or else the law of Athens yields you up,—
Which by no means we may extenuate,—
To death, or to a vow of single life.
Come, my Hippolyta: what cheer, my love?
Demetrius and Egeus, go along:
I must employ you in some business
Against our nuptial, and confer with you
Of something nearly that concerns yourselves.
EGEUS
With duty and desire we follow you.
[Exeunt all but LYSANDER and HERMIA
LYSANDER
How now, my love! why is your cheek so pale?
How chance the roses there do fade so fast?
HERMIA
Belike for want of rain, which I could well
Beteem them from the tempest of my eyes.
LYSANDER
Ay me! for aught that I could ever read,
Could ever hear by tale or history,
The course of true love never did run smooth;
But, either it was different in blood,—
HERMIA
O cross! too high to be enthrall'd to low.
LYSANDER
Or else misgraffed in respect of years,—
HERMIA
O spite! too old to be engaged to young.
LYSANDER
Or else it stood upon the choice of friends,—
HERMIA
O hell! to choose love by another's eyes.
LYSANDER
Or, if there were a sympathy in choice,
War, death, or sickness did lay siege to it,
Making it momentany as a sound,
Swift as a shadow, short as any dream;
Brief as the lightning in the collied night,
That, in a spleen, unfolds both heaven and earth,
And ere a man hath power to say 'Behold!'
The jaws of darkness do devour it up:
So quick bright things come to confusion.
HERMIA
If then true lovers have been ever cross'd,
It stands as an edict in destiny:
Then let us teach our trial patience,
Because it is a customary cross,

As due to love as thoughts and dreams and sighs,
Wishes and tears, poor fancy's followers.

LYSANDER

A good persuasion: therefore, hear me, Hermia.
I have a widow aunt, a dowager
Of great revenue, and she hath no child:
From Athens is her house remote seven leagues;
And she respects me as her only son.
There, gentle Hermia, may I marry thee;
And to that place the sharp Athenian law
Cannot pursue us. If thou lovest me, then,
Steal forth thy father's house to-morrow night;
And in the wood, a league without the town,
Where I did meet thee once with Helena,
To do observance to a morn of May,
There will I stay for thee.

HERMIA
                My good Lysander!
I swear to thee, by Cupid's strongest bow,
By his best arrow with the golden head,
By the simplicity of Venus' doves,
By that which knitteth souls and prospers loves,
And by that fire which burn'd the Carthage queen,
When the false Troyan under sail was seen,
By all the vows that ever men have broke,
In number more than ever women spoke,
In that same place thou hast appointed me,
To-morrow truly will I meet with thee.

LYSANDER

Keep promise, love. Look, here comes Helena.

Enter HELENA

HERMIA

God speed fair Helena! whither away?

HELENA

Call you me fair? that fair again unsay.
Demetrius loves your fair: O happy fair!
Your eyes are lode-stars; and your tongue's sweet
    air
More tuneable than lark to shepherd's ear,
When wheat is green, when hawthorn buds appear.
Sickness is catching: O, were favour so,
Yours would I catch, fair Hermia, ere I go;
My ear should catch your voice, my eye your eye,
My tongue should catch your tongue's sweet mel-
    ody.
Were the world mine, Demetrius being bated,
The rest I'ld give to be to you translated.
O, teach me how you look; and with what art
You sway the motion of Demetrius' heart!

HERMIA

I frown upon him, yet he loves me still.

HELENA

O that your frowns would teach my smiles such skill!

HERMIA

I give him curses, yet he gives me love.

HELENA

O that my prayers could such affection move!

HERMIA

The more I hate, the more he follows me.

HELENA

The more I love, the more he hateth me.

HERMIA

His folly, Helena, is no fault of mine.

HELENA

None, but your beauty: would that fault were mine!

HERMIA

Take comfort: he no more shall see my face;
Lysander and myself will fly this place.
Before the time I did Lysander see,
Seem'd Athens as a paradise to me:
O, then, what graces in my love do dwell,
That he hath turn'd a heaven unto a hell!

LYSANDER

Helen, to you our minds we will unfold:
To-morrow night, when Phœbe doth behold
Her silver visage in the watery glass,
Decking with liquid pearl the bladed grass,
A time that lovers' flights doth still conceal,
Through Athens' gates have we devised to steal.

HERMIA

And in the wood, where often you and I
Upon faint primrose-beds were wont to lie,
Emptying our bosoms of their counsel sweet,
There my Lysander and myself shall meet;
And thence from Athens turn away our eyes,
To seek new friends and stranger companies.
Farewell, sweet playfellow: pray thou for us;
And good luck grant thee thy Demetrius!
Keep word, Lysander: we must starve our sight
From lovers' food till morrow deep midnight.

LYSANDER

I will, my Hermia.   [*Exit* HERMIA
            Helena, adieu:
As you on him, Demetrius dote on you!   [*Exit*

HELENA

How happy some o'er other some can be!
Through Athens I am thought as fair as she.
But what of that? Demetrius thinks not so;
He will not know what all but he do know:
And as he errs, doting on Hermia's eyes,
So I, admiring of his qualities:
Things base and vile, holding no quantity,
Love can transpose to form and dignity:
Love looks not with the eyes, but with the mind;
And therefore is wing'd Cupid painted blind:
Nor hath Love's mind of any judgement taste;
Wings, and no eyes, figure unheedy haste:
And therefore is Love said to be a child,
Because in choice he is so oft beguiled.
As waggish boys in game themselves forswear,
So the boy Love is perjured everywhere:
For ere Demetrius look'd on Hermia's eyne,
He hail'd down oaths that he was only mine;
And when this hail some heat from Hermia felt,
So he dissolved, and showers of oaths did melt.
I will go tell him of fair Hermia's flight:
Then to the wood will he to-morrow night
Pursue her; and for this intelligence
If I have thanks, it is a dear expense:

But herein mean I to enrich my pain,
To have his sight thither and back again.   [*Exit*

SCENE II. *The same.* QUINCE'*s house*

Enter QUINCE, SNUG, BOTTOM, FLUTE, SNOUT,
and STARVELING

QUINCE
Is all our company here?

BOTTOM
You were best to call them generally, man by man,
according to the scrip.

QUINCE
Here is the scroll of every man's name, which is
thought fit, through all Athens, to play in our interlude before the duke and the duchess, on his
wedding-day at night.

BOTTOM
First, good Peter Quince, say what the play treats
on; then read the names of the actors; and so grow
to a point.

QUINCE
Marry, our play is, The most lamentable comedy,
and most cruel death of Pyramus and Thisby.

BOTTOM
A very good piece of work, I assure you, and a
merry. Now, good Peter Quince, call forth your actors by the scroll. Masters, spread yourselves.

QUINCE
Answer as I call you. Nick Bottom, the weaver.

BOTTOM
Ready. Name what part I am for, and proceed.

QUINCE
You, Nick Bottom, are set down for Pyramus.

BOTTOM
What is Pyramus? a lover, or a tyrant?

QUINCE
A lover, that kills himself most gallant for love.

BOTTOM
That will ask some tears in the true performing of it:
if I do it, let the audience look to their eyes; I will
move storms, I will condole in some measure. To
the rest: yet my chief humour is for a tyrant: I could
play Ercles rarely, or a part to tear a cat in, to make
all split.

> The raging rocks
> And shivering shocks
> Shall break the locks
>   Of prison-gates;
> And Phibbus' car
> Shall shine from far,
> And make and mar
>   The foolish Fates.

This was lofty! Now name the rest of the players.
This is Ercles' vein, a tyrant's vein; a lover is more
condoling.

QUINCE
Francis Flute, the bellows-mender.

FLUTE
Here, Peter Quince.

QUINCE
Flute, you must take Thisby on you.

FLUTE
What is Thisby? a wandering knight?

QUINCE
It is the lady that Pyramus must love.

FLUTE
Nay, faith, let not me play a woman; I have a beard
coming.

QUINCE
That's all one: you shall play it in a mask, and you
may speak as small as you will.

BOTTOM
An I may hide my face, let me play Thisby too, I'll
speak in a monstrous little voice, 'Thisne, Thisne;'
'Ah Pyramus, my lover dear! thy Thisby dear, and
lady dear!'

QUINCE
No, no; you must play Pyramus: and, Flute, you
Thisby.

BOTTOM
Well, proceed.

QUINCE
Robin Starveling, the tailor.

STARVELING
Here, Peter Quince.

QUINCE
Robin Starveling, you must play Thisby's mother.
Tom Snout, the tinker.

SNOUT
Here, Peter Quince.

QUINCE
You, Pyramus' father: myself, Thisby's father:
Snug, the joiner; you, the lion's part: and, I hope,
here is a play fitted.

SNUG
Have you the lion's part written? pray you, if it be,
give it me, for I am slow of study.

QUINCE
You may do it extempore, for it is nothing but roaring.

BOTTOM
Let me play the lion too: I will roar, that I will do
any man's heart good to hear me; I will roar, that I
will make the duke say, 'Let him roar again, let him
roar again.'

QUINCE
An you should do it too terribly, you would fright
the duchess and the ladies, that they would shriek;
and that were enough to hang us all.

ALL
That would hang us, every mother's son.

BOTTOM
I grant you, friends, if you should fright the ladies
out of their wits, they would have no more discretion but to hang us: but I will aggravate my voice
so, that I will roar you as gently as any sucking
dove; I will roar you an 'twere any nightingale.

QUINCE
You can play no part but Pyramus; for Pyramus is

a sweet-faced man; a proper man, as one shall see in a summer's day; a most lovely, gentleman-like man: therefore you must needs play Pyramus.

BOTTOM

Well, I will undertake it. What beard were I best to play it in?

QUINCE

Why, what you will.

BOTTOM

I will discharge it in either your straw colour beard, your orange-tawny beard, your purple-in-grain beard, or your French crown colour beard, your perfect yellow.

QUINCE

Some of your French crowns have no hair at all, and then you will play barefaced. But, masters, here are your parts: and I am to entreat you, request you, and desire you, to con them by to-morrow night; and meet me in the palace wood, a mile without the town, by moonlight; there will we rehearse, for if we meet in the city, we shall be dogged with company, and our devices known. In the mean time I will draw a bill of properties, such as our play wants. I pray you, fail me not.

BOTTOM

We will meet; and there we may rehearse most obscenely and courageously. Take pains; be perfect: adieu.

QUINCE

At the duke's oak we meet.

BOTTOM

Enough; hold or cut bow-strings.   [*Exeunt*

ACT II

SCENE I. *A wood near Athens.*

Enter, from opposite sides, a FAIRY, *and* PUCK

PUCK

How now, spirit! whither wander you?

FAIRY

Over hill, over dale,
  Thorough bush, thorough brier,
Over park, over pale,
  Thorough flood, thorough fire,
I do wander every where,
Swifter than the moon's sphere;
And I serve the fairy queen,
To dew her orbs upon the green.
The cowslips tall her pensioners be:
In their gold coats spots you see;
Those be rubies, fairy favours,
In those freckles live their savours:
I must go seek some dewdrops here,
And hang a pearl in every cowslip's ear.
Farewell, thou lob of spirits; I'll be gone:
Our queen and all her elves come here anon.

PUCK

The king doth keep his revels here to-night:
Take heed the queen come not within his sight;
For Oberon is passing fell and wrath,
Because that she as her attendant hath
A lovely boy, stolen from an Indian king;
She never had so sweet a changeling:
And jealous Oberon would have the child
Knight of his train, to trace the forests wild;
But she perforce withholds the loved boy,
Crowns him with flowers, and makes him all her joy:
And now they never meet in grove or green,
By fountain clear, or spangled starlight sheen,
But they do square, that all their elves for fear
Creep into acorn cups and hide them there.

FAIRY

Either I mistake your shape and making quite,
Or else you are that shrewd and knavish sprite
Call'd Robin Goodfellow: are not you he
That frights the maidens of the villagery;
Skim milk, and sometimes labour in the quern,
And bootless make the breathless housewife churn;
And sometime make the drink to bear no barm;
Mislead night-wanderers, laughing at their harm?
Those that Hobgoblin call you, and sweet Puck,
You do their work, and they shall have good luck:
Are not you he?

PUCK

Thou speak'st aright;
I am that merry wanderer of the night.
I jest to Oberon, and make him smile,
When I a fat and bean-fed horse beguile,
Neighing in likeness of a filly foal:
And sometime lurk I in a gossip's bowl,
In very likeness of a roasted crab;
And when she drinks, against her lips I bob
And on her withered dewlap pour the ale.
The wisest aunt, telling the saddest tale,
Sometime for three-foot stool mistaketh me;
Then slip I from her bum, down topples she,
And 'tailor' cries, and falls into a cough;
And then the whole quire hold their hips and laugh;
And waxen in their mirth, and neeze, and swear
A merrier hour was never wasted there.
But, room, fairy! here comes Oberon.

FAIRY

And here my mistress. Would that he were gone!
Enter, from one side, OBERON, *with his train; from the other,* TITANIA, *with hers*

OBERON

Ill met by moonlight, proud Titania.

TITANIA

What, jealous Oberon! Fairies, skip hence: I have forsworn his bed and company.

OBERON

Tarry, rash wanton: am not I thy lord?

TITANIA

Then I must be thy lady: but I know
When thou hast stolen away from fairy land,

And in the shape of Corin sat all day,
Playing on pipes of corn, and versing love
To amorous Phillida. Why art thou here,
Come from the farthest steppe of India?
But that, forsooth, the bouncing Amazon,
Your buskin'd mistress and your warrior love,
To Theseus must be wedded, and you come
To give their bed joy and prosperity.

OBERON

How canst thou thus for shame, Titania,
Glance at my credit with Hippolyta,
Knowing I know thy love to Theseus?
Didst thou not lead him through the glimmering
    night
From Perigenia, whom he ravished?
And make him with fair Ægle break his faith,
With Ariadne and Antiopa?

TITANIA

These are the forgeries of jealousy:
And never, since the middle summer's spring,
Met we on hill, in dale, forest, or mead,
By paved fountain or by rushy brook,
Or in the beached margent of the sea,
To dance our ringlets to the whistling wind,
But with thy brawls thou hast disturb'd our sport.
Therefore the winds, piping to us in vain,
As in revenge, have suck'd up from the sea
Contagious fogs; which, falling in the land,
Have every pelting river made so proud,
That they have overborne their continents:
The ox hath therefore stretch'd his yoke in vain,
The ploughman lost his sweat; and the green corn
Hath rotted ere his youth attain'd a beard:
The fold stands empty in the drowned field,
And crows are fatted with the murrion flock;
The nine men's morris is fill'd up with mud,
And the quaint mazes in the wanton green,
For lack of tread, are undistinguishable:
The human mortals want their winter here;
No night is now with hymn or carol blest:
Therefore the moon, the governess of floods,
Pale in her anger, washes all the air,
That rheumatic diseases do abound:
And thorough this distemperature we see
The seasons alter: hoary-headed frosts
Fall in the fresh lap of the crimson rose;
And on old Hiems' thin and icy crown
An odorous chaplet of sweet summer buds
Is, as in mockery, set: the spring, the summer,
The childing autumn, angry winter, change
Their wonted liveries; and the mazed world,
By their increase, now knows not which is which:
And this same progeny of evils comes
From our debate, from our dissension;
We are their parents and original.

OBERON

Do you amend it, then; it lies in you:
Why should Titania cross her Oberon?
I do but beg a little changeling boy,
To be my henchman.

TITANIA

Set your heart at rest:
The fairy land buys not the child of me.
His mother was a votaress of my order:
And, in the spiced Indian air, by night,
Full often hath she gossip'd by my side;
And sat with me on Neptune's yellow sands,
Marking the embarked traders on the flood;
When we have laugh'd to see the sails conceive
And grow big-bellied with the wanton wind;
Which she, with pretty and with swimming gait
Following,—her womb then rich with my young
    squire,—
Would imitate, and sail upon the land,
To fetch me trifles, and return again,
As from a voyage, rich with merchandise.
But she, being mortal, of that boy did die;
And for her sake do I rear up her boy;
And for her sake I will not part with him.

OBERON

How long within this wood intend you stay?

TITANIA

Perchance till after Theseus' wedding-day.
If you will patiently dance in our round,
And see our moonlight revels, go with us;
If not, shun me, and I will spare your haunts.

OBERON

Give me that boy, and I will go with thee.

TITANIA

Not for thy fairy kingdom. Fairies, away!
We shall chide downright, if I longer stay.
    [Exit TITANIA with her train

OBERON

Well, go thy way: thou shalt not from this grove
Till I torment thee for this injury.
My gentle Puck, come hither. Thou rememberest
Since once I sat upon a promontory,
And heard a mermaid, on a dolphin's back,
Uttering such dulcet and harmonious breath,
That the rude sea grew civil at her song,
And certain stars shot madly from their spheres,
To hear the sea-maid's music.

PUCK

I remember.

OBERON

That very time I saw, but thou couldst not,
Flying between the cold moon and the earth,
Cupid all arm'd: a certain aim he took
At a fair vestal throned by the west,
And loosed his love-shaft smartly from his bow,
As it should pierce a hundred thousand hearts:
But I might see young Cupid's fiery shaft
Quench'd in the chaste beams of the watery moon,
And the imperial votaress passed on,
In maiden meditation, fancy-free.
Yet mark'd I where the bolt of Cupid fell:
It fell upon a little western flower,
Before milk-white, now purple with love's wound,
And maidens call it love-in-idleness.
Fetch me that flower; the herb I shew'd thee once:

The juice of it on sleeping eye-lids laid
Will make or man or woman madly dote
Upon the next live creature that it sees.
Fetch me this herb; and be thou here again
Ere the leviathan can swim a league.

PUCK

I'll put a girdle round about the earth
In forty minutes.

OBERON

Having once this juice,
I'll watch Titania when she is asleep,
And drop the liquor of it in her eyes.
The next thing then she waking looks upon,
Be it on lion, bear, or wolf, or bull,
On meddling monkey, or on busy ape,
She shall pursue it with the soul of love:
And ere I take this charm from off her sight,
As I can take it with another herb,
I'll make her render up her page to me.
But who comes here? I am invisible;
And I will overhear their conference.

Enter DEMETRIUS, HELENA *following him*

DEMETRIUS

I love thee not, therefore pursue me not.
Where is Lysander and fair Hermia?
The one I'll slay, the other slayeth me.
Thou told'st me they were stolen unto this wood;
And here am I, and wode within this wood,
Because I cannot meet my Hermia.
Hence, get thee gone, and follow me no more.

HELENA

You draw me, you hard-hearted adamant;
But yet you draw not iron, for my heart
Is true as steel: leave you your power to draw,
And I shall have no power to follow you.

DEMETRIUS

Do I entice you? do I speak you fair?
Or, rather, do I not in plainest truth
Tell you, I do not nor I cannot love you?

HELENA

And even for that do I love you the more.
I am your spaniel; and, Demetrius,
The more you beat me, I will fawn on you:
Use me but as your spaniel, spurn me, strike me,
Neglect me, lose me; only give me leave,
Unworthy as I am, to follow you.
What worser place can I beg in your love,—
And yet a place of high respect with me,—
Than to be used as you use your dog?

DEMETRIUS

Tempt not too much the hatred of my spirit;
For I am sick when I do look on thee.

HELENA

And I am sick when I look not on you.

DEMETRIUS

You do impeach your modesty too much,
To leave the city, and commit yourself
Into the hands of one that loves you not;
To trust the opportunity of night

And the ill counsel of a desert place
With the rich worth of your virginity.

HELENA

Your virtue is my privilege: for that
It is not night when I do see your face,
Therefore I think I am not in the night;
Nor doth this wood lack worlds of company,
For you in my respect are all the world:
Then how can it be said I am alone,
When all the world is here to look on me?

DEMETRIUS

I'll run from thee and hide me in the brakes,
And leave thee to the mercy of wild beasts.

HELENA

The wildest hath not such a heart as you.
Run when you will, the story shall be changed:
Apollo flies, and Daphne holds the chase;
The dove pursues the griffin; the mild hind
Makes speed to catch the tiger; bootless speed,
When cowardice pursues, and valour flies.

DEMETRIUS

I will not stay thy questions; let me go:
Or, if thou follow me, do not believe
But I shall do thee mischief in the wood.

HELENA

Ay, in the temple, in the town, the field,
You do me mischief. Fie, Demetrius!
Your wrongs do set a scandal on my sex:
We cannot fight for love, as men may do;
We should be woo'd, and were not made to woo.
                              [*Exit* DEMETRIUS

I'll follow thee, and make a heaven of hell,
To die upon the hand I love so well.   [*Exit*

OBERON

Fare thee well, nymph: ere he do leave this grove,
Thou shalt fly him, and he shall seek thy love.

Re-enter PUCK

Hast thou the flower there? Welcome, wanderer.

PUCK

Ay, there it is.

OBERON

I pray thee, give it me.
I know a bank where the wild thyme blows,
Where oxlips and the nodding violet grows;
Quite over-canopied with luscious woodbine,
With sweet musk-roses, and with eglantine:
There sleeps Titania sometime of the night,
Lull'd in these flowers with dances and delight;
And there the snake throws her enamell'd skin,
Weed wide enough to wrap a fairy in:
And with the juice of this I'll streak her eyes,
And make her full of hateful fantasies.
Take thou some of it, and seek through this grove:
A sweet Athenian lady is in love
With a disdainful youth: anoint his eyes;
But do it when the next thing he espies
May be the lady: thou shalt know the man
By the Athenian garments he hath on.
Effect it with some care that he may prove

More fond on her than she upon her love:
And look thou meet me ere the first cock crow.

PUCK

Fear not, my lord, your servant shall do so.

[Exeunt

SCENE II. *Another part of the wood*

Enter TITANIA, *with her train*

TITANIA

Come, now a roundel and a fairy song;
Then, for the third part of a minute, hence;
Some to kill cankers in the musk-rose buds;
Some war with rere-mice for their leathern wings,
To make my small elves coats; and some keep back
The clamorous owl, that nightly hoots and wonders
At our quaint spirits. Sing me now asleep;
Then to your offices, and let me rest.

SONG

FIRST FAIRY

You spotted snakes with double tongue,
  Thorny hedgehogs, be not seen;
Newts and blind-worms, do no wrong,
  Come not near our fairy queen.

CHORUS

Philomel, with melody
  Sing in our sweet lullaby;
Lulla, lulla, lullaby, lulla, lulla, lullaby:
    Never harm,
    Nor spell, nor charm,
Come our lovely lady nigh;
So, good night, with lullaby.

FIRST FAIRY

Weaving spiders, come not here;
  Hence, you long-legg'd spinners, hence!
Beetles black, approach not near;
  Worm nor snail, do no offence.

CHORUS

Philomel, with melody, &c.

SECOND FAIRY

Hence, away! now all is well:
One aloof stand sentinel.

[Exeunt FAIRIES. TITANIA *sleeps*
Enter OBERON, *and squeezes the flower on*
TITANIA'S *eyelids*

OBERON

What thou seest when thou dost wake,
Do it for thy true-love take;
Love and languish for his sake:
Be it ounce, or cat, or bear,
Pard, or boar with bristled hair,
In thy eye that shall appear
When thou wakest, it is thy dear:
Wake when some vile thing is near. *[Exit*

Enter LYSANDER *and* HERMIA

LYSANDER

Fair love, you faint with wandering in the wood;
And to speak troth, I have forgot our way:
We'll rest us, Hermia, if you think it good,
  And tarry for the comfort of the day.

HERMIA

Be it so, Lysander: find you out a bed;
For I upon this bank will rest my head.

LYSANDER

One turf shall serve as pillow for us both;
One heart, one bed, two bosoms, and one troth.

HERMIA

Nay, good Lysander; for my sake, my dear,
Lie further off yet, do not lie so near.

LYSANDER

O, take the sense, sweet, of my innocence!
Love takes the meaning in love's conference.
I mean, that my heart unto yours is knit,
So that but one heart we can make of it:
Two bosoms interchained with an oath;
So then two bosoms and a single troth.
Then by your side no bed-room me deny;
For lying so, Hermia, I do not lie.

HERMIA

Lysander riddles very prettily:
Now much beshrew my manners and my pride,
If Hermia meant to say Lysander lied.
But, gentle friend, for love and courtesy
Lie further off; in human modesty,
Such separation as may well be said
Becomes a virtuous bachelor and a maid,
So far be distant; and, good night, sweet friend:
Thy love ne'er alter till thy sweet life end!

LYSANDER

Amen, amen, to that fair prayer, say I;
And then end life when I end loyalty!
Here is my bed: sleep give thee all his rest!

HERMIA

With half that wish the wisher's eyes be press'd!

[They sleep

Enter PUCK

PUCK

Through the forest have I gone,
But Athenian found I none,
On whose eyes I might approve
This flower's force in stirring love.
Night and silence.—Who is here?
Weeds of Athens he doth wear:
This is he, my master said,
Despised the Athenian maid;
And here the maiden, sleeping sound,
On the dank and dirty ground.
Pretty soul! she durst not lie
Near this lack-love, this kill-courtesy.
Churl, upon thy eyes I throw
All the power this charm doth owe.
When thou wakest, let love forbid
Sleep his seat on thy eyelid:
So awake when I am gone;
For I must now to Oberon. *[Exit*

Enter DEMETRIUS *and* HELENA, *running*

HELENA

Stay, though thou kill me, sweet Demetrius.

DEMETRIUS

I charge thee, hence, and do not haunt me thus.

HELENA

O, wilt thou darkling leave me? do not so.

DEMETRIUS

Stay, on thy peril: I alone will go.   [*Exit*

HELENA

O, I am out of breath in this fond chase!
The more my prayer, the lesser is my grace.
Happy is Hermia, wheresoe'er she lies;
For she hath blessed and attractive eyes.
How came her eyes so bright? Not with salt tears:
If so, my eyes are oftener wash'd than hers.
No, no, I am as ugly as a bear;
For beasts that meet me run away for fear:
Therefore no marvel though Demetrius
Do, as a monster, fly my presence thus.
What wicked and dissembling glass of mine
Made me compare with Hermia's sphery eyne?
But who is here? Lysander! on the ground!
Dead? or asleep? I see no blood, no wound.
Lysander, if you live, good sir, awake.

LYSANDER

[*Awaking*] And run through fire I will for thy sweet
    sake.
Transparent Helena! Nature shews art,
That through thy bosom makes me see thy heart.
Where is Demetrius? O, how fit a word
Is that vile name to perish on my sword!

HELENA

Do not say so, Lysander; say not so.
What though he love your Hermia? Lord, what
    though?
Yet Hermia still loves you: then be content.

LYSANDER

Content with Hermia! No; I do repent
The tedious minutes I with her have spent.
Not Hermia but Helena I love:
Who will not change a raven for a dove?
The will of man is by his reason sway'd
And reason says you are the worthier maid.
Things growing are not ripe until their season:
So I, being young, till now ripe not to reason;
And touching now the point of human skill,
Reason becomes the marshal to my will,
And leads me to your eyes; where I o'erlook
Love's stories, written in love's richest book.

HELENA

Wherefore was I to this keen mockery born?
When at your hands did I deserve this scorn?
Is't not enough, is't not enough, young man,
That I did never, no, nor never can,
Deserve a sweet look from Demetrius' eye,
But you must flout my insufficiency?
Good troth, you do me wrong, good sooth, you do,
In such disdainful manner me to woo.
But fare you well: perforce I must confess
I thought you lord of more true gentleness.
O, that a lady, of one man refused,
Should of another therefore be abused!   [*Exit*

LYSANDER

She sees not Hermia. Hermia, sleep thou there:

And never mayst thou come Lysander near!
For as a surfeit of the sweetest things
The deepest loathing to the stomach brings,
Or as the heresies that men do leave
Are hated most of those they did deceive,
So thou, my surfeit and my heresy,
Of all be hated, but the most of me!
And, all my powers, address your love and might
To honour Helen and to be her knight!   [*Exit*

HERMIA

[*Awaking*] Help me, Lysander, help me! do thy best
To pluck this crawling serpent from my breast!
Ay me, for pity! what a dream was here!
Lysander, look how I do quake with fear:
Methought a serpent eat my heart away,
And you sat smiling at his cruel prey.
Lysander! what, removed? Lysander! lord!
What, out of hearing? gone? no sound, no word?
Alack, where are you? speak, an if you hear;
Speak, of all loves! I swoon almost with fear.
No? then I well perceive you are not nigh:
Either death or you I'll find immediately.   [*Exit*

ACT III

SCENE I. *The wood.* TITANIA *lying asleep*

Enter QUINCE, SNUG, BOTTOM, FLUTE, SNOUT, *and*
STARVELING

BOTTOM

Are we all met?

QUINCE

Pat, pat; and here's a marvellous convenient place
for our rehearsal. This green plot shall be our stage,
this hawthorn-brake our tiring-house; and we will
do it in action as we will do it before the duke.

BOTTOM

Peter Quince,—

QUINCE

What sayest thou, bully Bottom?

BOTTOM

There are things in this comedy of Pyramus and
Thisby that will never please. First, Pyramus must
draw a sword to kill himself; which the ladies cannot abide. How answer you that?

SNOUT

By'r lakin, a parlous fear.

STARVELING

I believe we must leave the killing out, when all is
done.

BOTTOM

Not a whit: I have a device to make all well. Write
me a prologue; and let the prologue seem to say,
we will do no harm with our swords, and that Pyramus is not killed indeed; and, for the more better
assurance, tell them that I Pyramus am not Pyramus, but Bottom the weaver: this will put them out
of fear.

QUINCE

Well, we will have such a prologue; and it shall be written in eight and six.

BOTTOM

No, make it two more; let it be written in eight and eight.

SNOUT

Will not the ladies be afeard of the lion?

STARVELING

I fear it, I promise you.

BOTTOM

Masters, you ought to consider with yourselves: to bring in,—God shield us!—a lion among ladies, is a most dreadful thing; for there is not a more fearful wild-fowl than your lion living: and we ought to look to 't.

SNOUT

Therefore another prologue must tell he is not a lion.

BOTTOM

Nay, you must name his name, and half his face must be seen through the lion's neck; and he himself must speak through, saying thus, or to the same defect,—'Ladies,'—or, 'Fair ladies,—I would wish you,'—or, 'I would request you,'—or, 'I would entreat you,—not to fear, not to tremble: my life for yours. If you think I come hither as a lion, it were pity of my life: no, I am no such thing; I am a man as other men are:' and there indeed let him name his name, and tell them plainly, he is Snug the joiner.

QUINCE

Well, it shall be so. But there is two hard things; that is, to bring the moonlight into a chamber; for, you know, Pyramus and Thisby meet by moonlight.

SNOUT

Doth the moon shine that night we play our play?

BOTTOM

A calendar, a calendar! look in the almanac; find out moonshine, find out moonshine.

QUINCE

Yes, it doth shine that night.

BOTTOM

Why, then may you leave a casement of the great chamber window, where we play, open, and the moon may shine in at the casement.

QUINCE

Ay; or else one must come in with a bush of thorns and a lantern, and say he comes to disfigure, or to present, the person of moonshine. Then, there is another thing: we must have a wall in the great chamber; for Pyramus and Thisby, says the story, did talk through the chink of a wall.

SNOUT

You can never bring in a wall. What say you, Bottom?

BOTTOM

Some man or other must present wall: and let him have some plaster, or some loam, or some rough-cast about him, to signify wall; and let him hold his fingers thus, and through that cranny shall Pyramus and Thisby whisper.

QUINCE

If that may be, then all is well. Come, sit down, every mother's son, and rehearse your parts. Pyramus, you begin: when you have spoken your speech, enter into that brake: and so every one according to his cue.

Enter PUCK *behind*

PUCK

What hempen home-spuns have we swaggering here,
So near the cradle of the fairy queen?
What, a play toward! I'll be an auditor;
An actor too perhaps, if I see cause.

QUINCE

Speak, Pyramus. Thisby, stand forth.

BOTTOM

Thisby, the flowers of odious savours sweet,—

QUINCE

Odours, odours.

BOTTOM

——odours savours sweet:
So hath thy breath, my dearest Thisby dear.
But hark, a voice! stay thou but here awhile,
And by and by I will to thee appear.   [*Exit*

PUCK

A stranger Pyramus than e'er play'd here.   [*Exit*

FLUTE

Must I speak now?

QUINCE

Ay, marry, must you; for you must understand he goes but to see a noise that he heard, and is to come again.

FLUTE

Most radiant Pyramus, most lily-white of hue,
  Of colour like the red rose on triumphant brier,
Most brisky juvenal, and eke most lovely Jew,
  As true as truest horse, that yet would never tire,
I'll meet thee, Pyramus, at Ninny's tomb.

QUINCE

'Ninus' tomb,' man: why, you must not speak that yet; that you answer to Pyramus: you speak all your part at once, cues and all. Pyramus enter: your cue is past; it is, 'never tire.'

FLUTE

O,—As true as truest horse, that yet would never tire.

Re-enter PUCK, *and* BOTTOM *with an ass's head*

BOTTOM

If I were fair, Thisby, I were only thine.

QUINCE

O monstrous! O strange! we are haunted. Pray, masters! fly, masters! Help!
[*Exeunt* QUINCE, SNUG, FLUTE, SNOUT, *and* STARVELING

PUCK

I'll follow you, I'll lead you about a round,
  Through bog, through bush, through brake, through brier:

Sometime a horse I'll be, sometime a hound,
  A hog, a headless bear, sometime a fire;
And neigh, and bark, and grunt, and roar, and burn,
Like horse, hound, hog, bear, fire, at every turn.
                      [*Exit*

BOTTOM

Why do they run away? this is a knavery of them to make me afeard.

Re-enter SNOUT

SNOUT

O Bottom, thou art changed! what do I see on thee?

BOTTOM

What do you see? you see an ass-head of your own, do you?   [*Exit* SNOUT

Re-enter QUINCE

QUINCE

Bless thee, Bottom! bless thee! thou art translated.
                      [*Exit*

BOTTOM

I see their knavery: this is to make an ass of me; to fright me, if they could. But I will not stir from this place, do what they can: I will walk up and down here, and I will sing, that they shall hear I am not afraid.   [*Sings*

    The ousel cock so black of hue,
      With orange-tawny bill,
    The throstle with his note so true,
      The wren with little quill;

TITANIA

[*Awaking*] What angel wakes me from my flowery bed?

BOTTOM

[*Sings*]

    The finch, the sparrow, and the lark,
      The plain-song cuckoo gray,
    Whose note full many a man doth mark,
      And dares not answer nay;—

for, indeed, who would set his wit to so foolish a bird? who would give a bird the lie, though he cry 'cuckoo' never so?

TITANIA

I pray thee, gentle mortal, sing again:
Mine ear is much enamour'd of thy note;
So is mine eye enthralled to thy shape;
And thy fair virtue's force perforce doth move me
On the first view to say, to swear, I love thee.

BOTTOM

Methinks, mistress, you should have little reason for that: and yet, to say the truth, reason and love keep little company together now-a-days; the more the pity, that some honest neighbours will not make them friends. Nay, I can gleek upon occasion.

TITANIA

Thou art as wise as thou art beautiful.

BOTTOM

Not so, neither: but if I had wit enough to get out of this wood, I have enough to serve mine own turn.

TITANIA

Out of this wood do not desire to go:

Thou shalt remain here, whether thou wilt or no.
I am a spirit of no common rate:
The summer still doth tend upon my state;
And I do love thee: therefore, go with me;
I'll give thee fairies to attend on thee;
And they shall fetch thee jewels from the deep,
And sing, while thou on pressed flowers dost sleep:
And I will purge thy mortal grossness so,
That thou shalt like an airy spirit go.
Peaseblossom! Cobweb! Moth! and Mustardseed!

    Enter PEASEBLOSSOM, COBWEB, MOTH, *and*
                MUSTARDSEED

FIRST FAIRY

Ready.

SECOND FAIRY

    And I.

THIRD FAIRY

      And I.

FOURTH FAIRY

        And I.

ALL

           Where shall we go?

TITANIA

Be kind and courteous to this gentleman;
Hop in his walks, and gambol in his eyes;
Feed him with apricocks and dewberries,
With purple grapes, green figs, and mulberries;
The honey-bags steal from the humble-bees,
And for night-tapers crop their waxen thighs,
And light them at the fiery glow-worm's eyes,
To have my love to bed and to arise;
And pluck the wings from painted butterflies,
To fan the moonbeams from his sleeping eyes:
Nod to him, elves, and do him courtesies.

FIRST FAIRY

Hail, mortal!

SECOND FAIRY

Hail!

THIRD FAIRY

Hail!

FOURTH FAIRY

Hail!

BOTTOM

I cry your worship's mercy, heartily: I beseech your worship's name.

COBWEB

Cobweb.

BOTTOM

I shall desire you of more acquaintance, good Master Cobweb: if I cut my finger, I shall make bold with you. Your name, honest gentleman?

PEASEBLOSSOM

Peaseblossom.

BOTTOM

I pray you, commend me to Mistress Squash, your mother, and to Master Peascod, your father. Good Master Peaseblossom, I shall desire you of more acquaintance too. Your name, I beseech you, sir?

MUSTARDSEED

Mustardseed.

BOTTOM

Good Master Mustardseed, I know your patience
well: that same cowardly, giant-like ox-beef hath
devoured many a gentleman of your house: I
promise you your kindred hath made my eyes water
ere now. I desire your more acquaintance, good
Master Mustardseed.

TITANIA

Come, wait upon him; lead him to my bower.
    The moon methinks looks with a watery eye;
And when she weeps, weeps every little flower,
    Lamenting some enforced chastity.
    Tie up my love's tongue, bring him silently.
                                        [*Exeunt*

SCENE II. *Another part of the wood*

Enter OBERON

OBERON

I wonder if Titania be awaked;
Then, what it was that next came in her eye,
Which she must dote on in extremity.

Enter PUCK

Here comes my messenger.
                    How now, mad spirit!
What night-rule now about this haunted grove?

PUCK

My mistress with a monster is in love.
Near to her close and consecrated bower,
While she was in her dull and sleeping hour,
A crew of patches, rude mechanicals,
That work for bread upon Athenian stalls,
Were met together to rehearse a play,
Intended for great Theseus' nuptial-day.
The shallowest thick-skin of that barren sort,
Who Pyramus presented, in their sport
Forsook his scene, and enter'd in a brake:
When I did him at this advantage take,
An ass's nole I fixed on his head:
Anon his Thisbe must be answered,
And forth my mimic comes. When they him spy,
As wild geese that the creeping fowler eye,
Or russet-pated choughs, many in sort,
Rising and cawing at the gun's report,
Sever themselves and madly sweep the sky,
So, at his sight, away his fellows fly;
And, at our stamp, here o'er and o'er one falls;
He murder cries, and help from Athens calls.
Their sense thus weak, lost with their fears thus
    strong,
Made senseless things begin to do them wrong;
For briers and thorns at their apparel snatch;
Some sleeves, some hats, from yielders all things
    catch.
I led them on in this distracted fear,
And left sweet Pyramus translated there:
When in that moment, so it came to pass,
Titania waked, and straightway loved an ass.

OBERON

This falls out better than I could devise.

But hast thou yet latch'd the Athenian's eyes
With the love-juice, as I did bid thee do?

PUCK

I took him sleeping,—that is finish'd too,—
And the Athenian woman by his side;
That, when he waked, of force she must be eyed.

Enter HERMIA *and* DEMETRIUS

OBERON

Stand close: this is the same Athenian.

PUCK

This is the woman, but not this the man.

DEMETRIUS

O, why rebuke you him that loves you so?
Lay breath so bitter on your bitter foe.

HERMIA

Now I but chide; but I should use thee worse,
For thou, I fear, hast given me cause to curse.
If thou hast slain Lysander in his sleep,
Being o'er shoes in blood, plunge in the deep,
And kill me too.
The sun was not so true unto the day
As he to me: would he have stolen away
From sleeping Hermia? I'll believe as soon
This whole earth may be bored, and that the moon
May through the centre creep, and so displease
Her brother's noontide with the Antipodes.
It cannot be but thou hast murder'd him;
So should a murderer look, so dead, so grim.

DEMETRIUS

So should the murder'd look; and so should I,
Pierced through the heart with your stern cruelty:
Yet you, the murderer, look as bright, as clear,
As yonder Venus in her glimmering sphere.

HERMIA

What's this to my Lysander? where is he?
Ah, good Demetrius, wilt thou give him me?

DEMETRIUS

I had rather give his carcass to my hounds.

HERMIA

Out, dog! out, cur! thou drivest me past the bounds
Of maiden's patience. Hast thou slain him, then?
Henceforth be never number'd among men!
O, once tell true, tell true, even for my sake!
Durst thou have look'd upon him being awake,
And hast thou kill'd him sleeping? O brave touch!
Could not a worm, an adder, do so much?
An adder did it; for with doubler tongue
Than thine, thou serpent, never adder stung.

DEMETRIUS

You spend your passion on a mispris'd mood:
I am not guilty of Lysander's blood;
Nor is he dead, for aught that I can tell.

HERMIA

I pray thee, tell me then that he is well.

DEMETRIUS

An if I could, what should I get therefore?

HERMIA

A privilege, never to see me more.
And from thy hated presence part I so:
See me no more, whether he be dead or no.   [*Exit*

[398]

DEMETRIUS

There is no following her in this fierce vein:
Here therefore for a while I will remain.
So sorrow's heaviness doth heavier grow
For debt that bankrupt sleep doth sorrow owe;
Which now in some slight measure it will pay,
If for his tender here I make some stay.

[*Lies down and sleeps*

OBERON

What hast thou done? thou hast mistaken quite,
And laid the love-juice on some true-love's sight:
Of thy misprision must perforce ensue
Some true love turn'd, and not a false turn'd true.

PUCK

Then fate o'er-rules, that, one man holding troth,
A million fail, confounding oath on oath.

OBERON

About the wood go swifter than the wind,
And Helena of Athens look thou find:
All fancy-sick she is and pale of cheer,
With sighs of love, that costs the fresh blood dear:
By some illusion see thou bring her here:
I'll charm his eyes against she do appear.

PUCK

I go, I go; look how I go,
Swifter than arrow from the Tartar's bow.   [*Exit*

OBERON

Flower of this purple dye,
Hit with Cupid's archery,
Sink in apple of his eye.
When his love he doth espy,
Let her shine as gloriously
As the Venus of the sky.
When thou wakest, if she be by,
Beg of her for remedy.

Re-enter PUCK

PUCK

Captain of our fairy band,
Helena is here at hand;
And the youth, mistook by me,
Pleading for a lover's fee.
Shall we their fond pageant see?
Lord, what fools these mortals be!

OBERON

Stand aside: the noise they make
Will cause Demetrius to awake.

PUCK

Then will two at once woo one;
That must needs be sport alone;
And those things do best please me
That befal preposterously.

Enter LYSANDER *and* HELENA

LYSANDER

Why should you think that I should woo in scorn?
 Scorn and derision never come in tears:
Look, when I vow, I weep; and vows so born,
 In their nativity all truth appears.
How can these things in me seem scorn to you,
Bearing the badge of faith, to prove them true?

HELENA

You do advance your cunning more and more.
 When truth kills truth, O devilish-holy fray!
These vows are Hermia's: will you give her o'er?
 Weigh oath with oath, and you will nothing
  weigh:
Your vows to her and me, put in two scales,
Will even weigh; and both as light as tales.

LYSANDER

I had no judgement when to her I swore.

HELENA

Nor none, in my mind, now you give her o'er.

LYSANDER

Demetrius loves her, and he loves not you.

DEMETRIUS

[*Awaking*] O Helen, goddess, nymph, perfect, di-
 vine!
To what, my love, shall I compare thine eyne?
Crystal is muddy. O, how ripe in show
Thy lips, those kissing cherries, tempting grow!
That pure congealed white, high Taurus' snow,
Fann'd with the eastern wind, turns to a crow
When thou hold'st up thy hand: O, let me kiss
This princess of pure white, this seal of bliss!

HELENA

O spite! O hell! I see you all are bent
To set against me for your merriment:
If you were civil and knew courtesy,
You would not do me thus much injury.
Can you not hate me, as I know you do,
But you must join in souls to mock me too?
If you were men, as men you are in show,
You would not use a gentle lady so;
To vow, and swear, and superpraise my parts,
When I am sure you hate me with your hearts.
You both are rivals, and love Hermia;
And now both rivals, to mock Helena:
A trim exploit, a manly enterprise,
To conjure tears up in a poor maid's eyes
With your derision! none of noble sort
Would so offend a virgin, and extort
A poor soul's patience, all to make you sport.

LYSANDER

You are unkind, Demetrius; be not so;
For you love Hermia; this you know I know:
And here, with all good will, with all my heart,
In Hermia's love I yield you up my part;
And yours of Helena to me bequeath,
Whom I do love, and will do till my death.

HELENA

Never did mockers waste more idle breath.

DEMETRIUS

Lysander, keep thy Hermia; I will none:
If e'er I loved her, all that love is gone.
My heart to her but as guest-wise sojourn'd,
And now to Helen is it home return'd,
There to remain.

LYSANDER

Helen, it is not so.

DEMETRIUS

Disparage not the faith thou dost not know,
Lest, to thy peril, thou aby it dear.
Look, where thy love comes; yonder is thy dear.

Re-enter HERMIA

HERMIA

Dark night, that from the eye his function takes,
The ear more quick of apprehension makes;
Wherein it doth impair the seeing sense,
It pays the hearing double recompence.
Thou art not by mine eye, Lysander, found;
Mine ear, I thank it, brought me to thy sound.
But why unkindly didst thou leave me so?

LYSANDER

Why should he stay, whom love doth press to go?

HERMIA

What love could press Lysander from my side?

LYSANDER

Lysander's love, that would not let him bide,
Fair Helena, who more engilds the night
Than all yon fiery oes and eyes of light.
Why seek'st thou me? could not this make thee
    know,
The hate I bare thee made me leave thee so?

HERMIA

You speak not as you think: it cannot be.

HELENA

Lo, she is one of this confederacy!
Now I perceive they have conjoin'd all three
To fashion this false sport, in spite of me.
Injurious Hermia! most ungrateful maid!
Have you conspired, have you with these contrived
To bait me with this foul derision?
Is all the counsel that we two have shared,
The sister's vows, the hours that we have spent,
When we have chid the hasty-footed time
For parting us,—O, is all forgot?
All school-days' friendship, childhood innocence?
We, Hermia, like two artificial gods,
Have with our needles created both one flower,
Both on one sampler, sitting on one cushion,
Both warbling of one song, both in one key;
As if our hands, our sides, voices, and minds,
Had been incorporate. So we grew together,
Like to a double cherry, seeming parted,
But yet an union in partition;
Two lovely berries moulded on one stem;
So, with two seeming bodies, but one heart;
Two of the first, like coats in heraldry,
Due but to one, and crowned with one crest.
And will you rent our ancient love asunder,
To join with men in scorning your poor friend?
It is not friendly, 'tis not maidenly:
Our sex, as well as I, may chide you for it,
Though I alone do feel the injury.

HERMIA

I am amazed at your passionate words.
I scorn you not: it seems that you scorn me.

HELENA

Have you not set Lysander, as in scorn,

To follow me and praise my eyes and face?
And made your other love, Demetrius,
Who even but now did spurn me with his foot,
To call me goddess, nymph, divine and rare,
Precious, celestial? Wherefore speaks he this
To her he hates? and wherefore doth Lysander
Deny your love, so rich within his soul,
And tender me, forsooth, affection,
But by your setting on, by your consent?
What though I be not so in grace as you,
So hung upon with love, so fortunate,
But miserable most, to love unloved?
This you should pity rather than despise.

HERMIA

I understand not what you mean by this.

HELENA

Ay, do, persever, counterfeit sad looks,
Make mouths upon me when I turn my back;
Wink each at other; hold the sweet jest up:
This sport, well carried, shall be chronicled.
If you have any pity, grace, or manners,
You would not make me such an argument.
But fare ye well: 'tis partly mine own fault;
Which death or absence soon shall remedy.

LYSANDER

Stay, gentle Helena; hear my excuse:
My love, my life, my soul, fair Helena!

HELENA

O excellent!

HERMIA

            Sweet, do not scorn her so.

DEMETRIUS

If she cannot entreat, I can compel.

LYSANDER

Thou canst compel no more than she entreat:
Thy threats have no more strength than her weak
    prayers.
Helen, I love thee; by my life, I do:
I swear by that which I will lose for thee,
To prove him false that says I love thee not.

DEMETRIUS

I say I love thee more than he can do.

LYSANDER

If thou say so, withdraw, and prove it too.

DEMETRIUS

Quick, come!

HERMIA

            Lysander, whereto tends all this?

LYSANDER

Away, you Ethiope!

DEMETRIUS

            No, no; he'll . . .
Seem to break loose; take on as you would follow,
But yet come not: you are a tame man, go!

LYSANDER

Hang off, thou cat, thou burr! vile thing, let loose,
Or I will shake thee from me like a serpent!

HERMIA

Why are you grown so rude? what change is this?
Sweet love,—

LYSANDER
Thy love! out, tawny Tartar, out!
Out, loathed medicine! hated potion, hence!

HERMIA
Do you not jest?

HELENA
Yes, sooth; and so do you.

LYSANDER
Demetrius, I will keep my word with thee.

DEMETRIUS
I would I had your bond, for I perceive
A weak bond holds you: I'll not trust your word.

LYSANDER
What, should I hurt her, strike her, kill her dead?
Although I hate her, I'll not harm her so.

HERMIA
What, can you do me greater harm than hate?
Hate me! wherefore? O me! what news, my love!
Am not I Hermia? are not you Lysander?
I am as fair now as I was erewhile.
Since night you loved me; yet since night you left
     me:
Why, then you left me,—O, the gods forbid!—
In earnest, shall I say?

LYSANDER
Ay, by my life;
And never did desire to see thee more.
Therefore be out of hope, of question, of doubt;
Be certain, nothing truer; 'tis no jest
That I do hate thee, and love Helena.

HERMIA
O me! you juggler! you canker-blossom!
You thief of love! what, have you come by night
And stolen my love's heart from him?

HELENA
Fine, i'faith!
Have you no modesty, no maiden shame,
No touch of bashfulness? What, will you tear
Impatient answers from my gentle tongue?
Fie, fie! you counterfeit, you puppet, you!

HERMIA
Puppet? why so? ay, that way goes the game.
Now I perceive that she hath made compare
Between our statures; she hath urged her height;
And with her personage, her tall personage,
Her height, forsooth, she hath prevail'd with him.
And are you grown so high in his esteem,
Because I am so dwarfish and so low?
How low am I, thou painted maypole? speak;
How low am I? I am not yet so low
But that my nails can reach unto thine eyes.

HELENA
I pray you, though you mock me, gentlemen,
Let her not hurt me: I was never curst;
I have no gift at all in shrewishness;
I am a right maid for my cowardice:
Let her not strike me. You perhaps may think,
Because she is something lower than myself,
That I can match her.

HERMIA
Lower! hark, again.

HELENA
Good Hermia, do not be so bitter with me.
I ever more did love you, Hermia,
Did ever keep your counsels, never wrong'd you;
Save that, in love unto Demetrius,
I told him of your stealth unto this wood.
He follow'd you; for love I follow'd him;
But he hath chid me hence, and threaten'd me
To strike me, spurn me, nay, to kill me too:
And now, so you will let me quiet go,
To Athens will I bear my folly back,
And follow you no further: let me go:
You see how simple and how fond I am.

HERMIA
Why, get you gone: who is't that hinders you?

HELENA
A foolish heart, that I leave here behind.

HERMIA
What, with Lysander?

HELENA
With Demetrius.

LYSANDER
Be not afraid; she shall not harm thee, Helena.

DEMETRIUS
No, sir, she shall not, though you take her part.

HELENA
O, when she's angry, she is keen and shrewd!
She was a vixen when she went to school;
And though she be but little, she is fierce.

HERMIA
Little again! nothing but low and little!
Why will you suffer her to flout me thus?
Let me come to her.

LYSANDER
Get you gone, you dwarf;
You minimus, of hindering knot-grass made;
You bead, you acorn.

DEMETRIUS
You are too officious
In her behalf that scorns your services.
Let her alone: speak not of Helena;
Take not her part; for, if thou dost intend
Never so little show of love to her,
Thou shalt aby it.

LYSANDER
Now she holds me not;
Now follow, if thou darest, to try whose right,
Of thine or mine, is most in Helena.

DEMETRIUS
Follow! nay, I'll go with thee, cheek by jole.
[Exeunt LYSANDER and DEMETRIUS

HERMIA
You, mistress, all this coil is 'long of you:
Nay, go not back.

HELENA
I will not trust you, I,
Nor longer stay in your curst company.

Your hands than mine are quicker for a fray,
My legs are longer though, to run away.   [*Exit*

HERMIA

I am amazed, and know not what to say.   [*Exit*

OBERON

This is thy negligence: still thou mistakest,
Or else committ'st thy knaveries wilfully.

PUCK

Believe me, king of shadows, I mistook.
Did not you tell me I should know the man
By the Athenian garments he had on?
And so far blameless proves my enterprise,
That I have 'nointed an Athenian's eyes;
And so far am I glad it so did sort,
As this their jangling I esteem a sport.

OBERON

Thou see'st these lovers seek a place to fight:
Hie therefore, Robin, overcast the night;
The starry welkin cover thou anon
With drooping fog, as black as Acheron;
And lead these testy rivals so astray,
As one come not within another's way.
Like to Lysander sometime frame thy tongue,
Then stir Demetrius up with bitter wrong;
And sometime rail thou like Demetrius;
And from each other look thou lead them thus,
Till o'er their brows death-counterfeiting sleep
With leaden legs and batty wings doth creep:
Then crush this herb into Lysander's eye;
Whose liquor hath this virtuous property,
To take from thence all error with his might,
And make his eyeballs roll with wonted sight.
When they next awake, all this derision
Shall seem a dream and fruitless vision;
And back to Athens shall the lovers wend,
With league whose date till death shall never end.
Whiles I in this affair do thee employ,
I'll to my queen and beg her Indian boy;
And then I will her charmed eye release
From monster's view, and all things shall be peace.

PUCK

My fairy lord, this must be done with haste,
For night's swift dragons cut the clouds full fast,
And yonder shines Aurora's harbinger;
At whose approach, ghosts, wandering here and
     there,
Troop home to churchyards: damned spirits all,
That in crossways and floods have burial,
Already to their wormy beds are gone;
For fear lest day should look their shames upon,
They wilfully themselves exile from light,
And must for aye consort with black-brow'd night.

OBERON

But we are spirits of another sort:
I with the morning's love have oft made sport;
And, like a forester, the groves may tread,
Even till the eastern gate, all fiery-red,
Opening on Neptune with fair blessed beams,
Turns into yellow gold his salt green streams.

But, notwithstanding, haste; make no delay:
We may effect this business yet ere day.   [*Exit*

PUCK

Up and down, up and down,
I will lead them up and down:
I am fear'd in field and town:
Goblin, lead them up and down.
Here comes one.

Re-enter LYSANDER

LYSANDER

Where art thou, proud Demetrius? speak thou now.

PUCK

Here, villain; drawn and ready. Where art thou?

LYSANDER

I will be with thee straight.

PUCK

                              Follow me, then,
To plainer ground.
     [*Exit* LYSANDER, *as following the voice.*
Re-enter DEMETRIUS

DEMETRIUS

                         Lysander! speak again:
Thou runaway, thou coward, art thou fled?
Speak! In some bush? Where dost thou hide thy
     head?

PUCK

Thou coward, art thou bragging to the stars,
Telling the bushes that thou look'st for wars,
And wilt not come? Come, recreant; come, thou
     child;
I'll whip thee with a rod: he is defiled
That draws a sword on thee.

DEMETRIUS

                              Yea, art thou there?

PUCK

Follow my voice: we'll try no manhood here.
                                        [*Exeunt*

Re-enter LYSANDER

LYSANDER

He goes before me and still dares me on:
When I come where he calls, then he is gone.
The villain is much lighter-heel'd than I:
I follow'd fast, but faster he did fly;
That fallen am I in dark uneven way,
And here will rest me. [*Lies down*] Come, thou
     gentle day!
For if but once thou show me thy grey light,
I'll find Demetrius, and revenge this spite.   [*Sleeps*

Re-enter PUCK *and* DEMETRIUS

PUCK

Ho, ho, ho! Coward, why comest thou not?

DEMETRIUS

Abide me, if thou darest; for well I wot
Thou runn'st before me, shifting every place,
And darest not stand, nor look me in the face
Where art thou now?

PUCK

                    Come hither: I am here.

DEMETRIUS

Nay, then, thou mock'st me. Thou shalt buy this
  dear,
If ever I thy face by daylight see:
Now, go thy way. Faintness constraineth me
To measure out my length on this cold bed.
By day's approach look to be visited.

[Lies down and sleeps

Re-enter HELENA

HELENA

O weary night, O long and tedious night,
  Abate thy hours! Shine comforts from the east,
That I may back to Athens by daylight,
  From these that my poor company detest:
And sleep, that sometimes shuts up sorrow's eye,
Steal me awhile from mine own company.

[Lies down and sleeps

PUCK

Yet but three? Come one more;
Two of both kinds makes up four.
Here she comes, curst and sad:
Cupid is a knavish lad,
Thus to make poor females mad.

Re-enter HERMIA

HERMIA

Never so weary, never so in woe;
  Bedabbled with the dew, and torn with briers;
I can no further crawl, no further go;
  My legs can keep no pace with my desires.
Here will I rest me till the break of day.
Heavens shield Lysander, if they mean a fray!

[Lies down and sleeps

PUCK

On the ground
Sleep sound:
I'll apply
To your eye,
Gentle lover, remedy.

[Squeezing the juice on LYSANDER'S *eye*

When thou wakest,
Thou takest
True delight
In the sight
Of thy former lady's eye:
And the country proverb known,
That every man should take his own,
In your waking shall be shown:
Jack shall have Jill;
Nought shall go ill;
The man shall have his mare again, and all shall be
  well.

[Exit

ACT IV

SCENE I. *The same.* LYSANDER, DEMETRIUS, HELENA,
and HERMIA, *lying asleep*

Enter TITANIA *and* BOTTOM; PEASEBLOSSOM, COBWEB,
MOTH, MUSTARDSEED, *and other* FAIRIES *attending*;
OBERON *behind unseen*

TITANIA

Come, sit thee down upon this flowery bed,
  While I thy amiable cheeks do coy,
And stick musk-roses in thy sleek smooth head,
  And kiss thy fair large ears, my gentle joy.

BOTTOM

Where's Peaseblossom?

PEASEBLOSSOM

Ready.

BOTTOM

Scratch my head, Peaseblossom. Where's Mounsieur Cobweb?

COBWEB

Ready.

BOTTOM

Mounsieur, Cobweb, good mounsieur, get you your
weapons in your hand, and kill me a red-hipped
humble-bee on the top of a thistle; and, good mounsieur, bring me the honey-bag. Do not fret yourself
too much in the action, mounsieur; and, good
mounsieur, have a care the honey-bag break not; I
would be loth to have you overflown with a honey-
bag, signior. Where's Mounsieur Mustardseed.

MUSTARDSEED

Ready.

BOTTOM

Give me your neaf, Mounsieur Mustardseed. Pray
you, leave your courtesy, good mounsieur.

MUSTARDSEED

What's your will?

BOTTOM

Nothing, good mounsieur, but to help Cavalery
Cobweb to scratch. I must to the barber's, mounsieur; for methinks I am marvellous hairy about the
face; and I am such a tender ass, if my hair do but
tickle me, I must scratch.

TITANIA

What, wilt thou hear some music, my sweet love?

BOTTOM

I have a reasonable good ear in music. Let's have
the tongs and the bones.

TITANIA

Or say, sweet love, what thou desirest to eat.

BOTTOM

Truly, a peck of provender: I could munch your
good dry oats. Methinks I have a great desire to a
bottle of hay: good hay, sweet hay, hath no fellow.

TITANIA

I have a venturous fairy that shall seek
The squirrel's hoard, and fetch thee new nuts.

BOTTOM

I had rather have a handful or two of dried peas.
But, I pray you, let none of your people stir me: I
have an exposition of sleep come upon me.

TITANIA

Sleep thou, and I will wind thee in my arms.
Fairies, be gone, and be all ways away.

[Exeunt FAIRIES

So doth the woodbine the sweet honeysuckle
Gently entwist; the female ivy so

Enrings the barky fingers of the elm.
O, how I love thee! how I dote on thee! [*They sleep*
Enter PUCK

OBERON

[*Advancing*] Welcome, good Robin. See'st thou this
    sweet sight?
Her dotage now I do begin to pity:
For, meeting her of late behind the wood,
Seeking sweet favours for this hateful fool,
I did upbraid her, and fall out with her;
For she his hairy temples then had rounded
With coronet of fresh and fragrant flowers;
And that same dew, which sometime on the buds
Was wont to swell, like round and orient pearls,
Stood now within the pretty flowerets' eyes,
Like tears, that did their own disgrace bewail.
When I had at my pleasure taunted her,
And she in mild terms begg'd my patience,
I then did ask of her her changeling child;
Which straight she gave me, and her fairy sent
To bear him to my bower in fairy land.
And now I have the boy, I will undo
This hateful imperfection of her eyes:
And, gentle Puck, take this transformed scalp
From off the head of this Athenian swain;
That, he awaking when the other do,
May all to Athens back again repair,
And think no more of this night's accidents,
But as the fierce vexation of a dream.
But first I will release the fairy queen.
    Be as thou wast wont to be;
    See as thou wast wont to see:
    Dian's bud o'er Cupid's flower
    Hath such force and blessed power.
Now, my Titania; wake you, my sweet queen.

TITANIA

My Oberon! what visions have I seen!
Methought I was enamour'd of an ass.

OBERON

There lies your love.

TITANIA

              How came these things to pass?
O, how mine eyes do loathe his visage now!

OBERON

Silence awhile. Robin, take off this head.
Titania, music call; and strike more dead
Than common sleep of all these five the sense.

TITANIA

Music, ho! music, such as charmeth sleep!
                          [*Music, still*

PUCK

Now, when thou wakest, with thine own fool's eyes
    peep.

OBERON

Sound, music! Come, my queen, take hands with
    me,
And rock the ground whereon these sleepers be.
Now thou and I are new in amity,
And will to-morrow midnight solemnly
Dance in Duke Theseus' house triumphantly,

And bless it to all fair prosperity:
There shall the pairs of faithful lovers be
Wedded, with Theseus, all in jollity.

PUCK

Fairy king, attend, and mark:
I do hear the morning lark.

OBERON

Then, my queen, in silence sad,
Trip we after night's shade:
We the globe can compass soon,
Swifter than the wandering moon.

TITANIA

Come, my lord; and in our flight,
Tell me how it came this night,
That I sleeping here was found
With these mortals on the ground.   [*Exeunt*
                         [*Horns winded within*
Enter THESEUS, HIPPOLYTA, EGEUS, *and train*

THESEUS

Go, one of you, find out the forester;
For now our observation is perform'd;
And since we have the vaward of the day,
My love shall hear the music of my hounds.
Uncouple in the western valley; let them go:
Dispatch, I say, and find the forester.
                        [*Exit an* ATTENDANT
We will, fair queen, up to the mountain's top,
And mark the musical confusion
Of hounds and echo in conjunction.

HIPPOLYTA

I was with Hercules and Cadmus once,
When in a wood of Crete they bay'd the bear
With hounds of Sparta: never did I hear
Such gallant chiding; for, besides the groves,
The skies, the fountains, every region near
Seem'd all one mutual cry: I never heard
So musical a discord, such sweet thunder.

THESEUS

My hounds are bred out of the Spartan kind,
So flew'd, so sanded; and their heads are hung
With ears that sweep away the morning dew;
Crook-knee'd, and dew-lapp'd like Thessalian bulls;
Slow in pursuit, but match'd in mouth like bells,
Each under each. A cry more tuneable
Was never holla'd to, nor cheer'd with horn,
In Crete, in Sparta, nor in Thessaly:
Judge when you hear. But, soft! what nymphs are
    these?

EGEUS

My lord, this is my daughter here asleep;
And this, Lysander; this Demetrius is;
This Helena, old Nedar's Helena:
I wonder of their being here together.

THESEUS

No doubt they rose up early to observe
The rite of May; and, hearing our intent,
Came here in grace of our solemnity.
But speak, Egeus; is not this the day
That Hermia should give answer of her choice?

EGEUS

It is, my lord.

THESEUS

Go, bid the huntsmen wake them with their horns.
[Horns and shout within. LYSANDER,
DEMETRIUS, HELENA, and HERMIA, wake and start up
Good morrow, friends. Saint Valentine is past:
Begin these wood-birds but to couple now?

LYSANDER

Pardon, my lord.

THESEUS

                    I pray you all, stand up.
I know you two are rival enemies:
How comes this gentle concord in the world,
That hatred is so far from jealousy,
To sleep by hate, and fear no enmity?

LYSANDER

My lord, I shall reply amazedly,
Half sleep, half waking: but as yet, I swear,
I cannot truly say how I came here;
But, as I think,—for truly would I speak,
And now I do bethink me, so it is,—
I came with Hermia hither: our intent
Was to be gone from Athens, where we might,
Without the peril of the Athenian law.

EGEUS

Enough, enough, my lord; you have enough:
I beg the law, the law, upon his head.
They would have stolen away; they would, Deme-
trius,
Thereby to have defeated you and me,
You of your wife and me of my consent,
Of my consent that she should be your wife.

DEMETRIUS

My lord, fair Helen told me of their stealth,
Of this their purpose hither to this wood;
And I in fury hither follow'd them,
Fair Helena in fancy following me.
But, my good lord, I wot not by what power,—
But by some power it is,—my love to Hermia,
Melted as the snow, seems to me now
As the remembrance of an idle gaud,
Which in my childhood I did dote upon;
And all the faith, the virtue of my heart,
The object and the pleasure of mine eye,
Is only Helena. To her, my lord,
Was I betroth'd ere I saw Hermia:
But, like in sickness, did I loathe this food;
But, as in health, come to my natural taste,
Now I do wish it, love it, long for it,
And will for evermore be true to it.

THESEUS

Fair lovers, you are fortunately met:
Of this discourse we more will hear anon.
Egeus, I will overbear your will;
For in the temple, by and by, with us
These couples shall eternally be knit:
And, for the morning now is something worn,
Our purposed hunting shall be set aside.

Away with us to Athens! three and three,
We'll hold a feast in great solemnity.
Come, Hippolyta.
[Exeunt THESEUS, HIPPOLYTA, EGEUS, and train

DEMETRIUS

These things seem small and undistinguishable,
Like far-off mountains turned into clouds.

HERMIA

Methinks I see these things with parted eye,
When every thing seems double.

HELENA

                                      So methinks:
And I have found Demetrius like a jewel,
Mine own, and not mine own.

DEMETRIUS

                                      Are you sure
That we are awake? It seems to me
That yet we sleep, we dream. Do not you think
The Duke was here, and bid us follow him?

HERMIA

Yea; and my father.

HELENA

                    And Hippolyta.

LYSANDER

And he did bid us follow to the temple.

DEMETRIUS

Why, then, we are awake: let's follow him;
And by the way let us recount our dreams. [Exeunt

BOTTOM

[Awaking] When my cue comes, call me, and I will
answer: my next is, 'Most fair Pyramus.' Heigh-ho!
Peter Quince! Flute, the bellows-mender! Snout,
the tinker! Starveling! God's my life, stolen hence,
and left me asleep! I have had a most rare vision. I
have had a dream, past the wit of man to say what
dream it was: man is but an ass, if he go about to expound this dream. Methought I was—there is no
man can tell what. Methought I was,—and methought I had,—but man is but a patched fool, if he
will offer to say what methought I had. The eye of
man hath not heard, the ear of man hath not seen,
man's hand is not able to taste, his tongue to conceive, nor his heart to report, what my dream was.
I will get Peter Quince to write a ballad of this
dream: it shall be called Bottom's Dream, because
it hath no bottom; and I will sing it in the latter end
of a play, before the Duke: peradventure, to make
it the more gracious, I shall sing it at her death.
[Exit

SCENE II. Athens. QUINCE's house

Enter QUINCE, FLUTE, SNOUT, and STARVELING

QUINCE

Have you sent to Bottom's house? is he come home
yet?

STARVELING

He cannot be heard of. Out of doubt he is transported.

FLUTE

If he come not, then the play is marred: it goes not forward, doth it?

QUINCE

It is not possible: you have not a man in all Athens able to discharge Pyramus but he.

FLUTE

No, he hath simply the best wit of any handicraft man in Athens.

QUINCE

Yea, and the best person too; and he is a very paramour for a sweet voice.

FLUTE

You must say 'paragon': a paramour is, God bless us, a thing of naught.

Enter SNUG

SNUG

Masters, the Duke is coming from the temple, and there is two or three lords and ladies more married: if our sport had gone forward, we had all been made men.

FLUTE

O sweet bully Bottom! Thus hath he lost sixpence a day during his life; he could not have scaped sixpence a day: an the Duke had not given him sixpence a day for playing Pyramus, I'll be hanged; he would have deserved it: sixpence a day in Pyramus, or nothing.

Enter BOTTOM

BOTTOM

Where are these lads? where are these hearts?

QUINCE

Bottom! O most courageous day! O most happy hour!

BOTTOM

Masters, I am to discourse wonders: but ask me not what; for if I tell you, I am no true Athenian. I will tell you every thing, right as it fell out.

QUINCE

Let us hear, sweet Bottom.

BOTTOM

Not a word of me. All that I will tell you is, that the Duke hath dined. Get your apparel together, good strings to your beards, new ribbons to your pumps; meet presently at the palace; every man look o'er his part; for the short and the long is, our play is preferred. In any case, let Thisby have clean linen; and let not him that plays the lion pare his nails, for they shall hang out for the lion's claws. And, most dear actors, eat no onions nor garlic, for we are to utter sweet breath; and I do not doubt but to hear them say, it is a sweet comedy. No more words: away! go, away!   [*Exeunt*

ACT V

SCENE I. *Athens. The palace of* THESEUS

Enter THESEUS, HIPPOLYTA, PHILOSTRATE, LORDS,
and ATTENDANTS

HIPPOLYTA

'Tis strange, my Theseus, that these lovers speak of.

THESEUS

More strange than true: I never may believe
These antique fables, nor these fairy toys.
Lovers and madmen have such seething brains,
Such shaping fantasies, that apprehend
More than cool reason ever comprehends.
The lunatic, the lover and the poet
Are of imagination all compact:
One sees more devils than vast hell can hold,
That is, the madman: the lover, all as frantic,
Sees Helen's beauty in a brow of Egypt:
The poet's eye, in a fine frenzy rolling,
Doth glance from heaven to earth, from earth to
    heaven;
And as imagination bodies forth
The forms of things unknown, the poet's pen
Turns them to shapes, and gives to airy nothing
A local habitation and a name.
Such tricks hath strong imagination,
That, if it would but apprehend some joy,
It comprehends some bringer of that joy;
Or in the night, imagining some fear,
How easy is a bush supposed a bear!

HIPPOLYTA

But all the story of the night told over,
And all their minds transfigured so together,
More witnesseth than fancy's images,
And grows to something of great constancy;
But, howsoever, strange and admirable.

THESEUS

Here come the lovers, full of joy and mirth.
    Enter LYSANDER, DEMETRIUS, HERMIA, *and* HELENA
Joy, gentle friends! joy and fresh days of love
Accompany your hearts!

LYSANDER

          More than to us
Wait in your royal walks, your board, your bed!

THESEUS

Come now; what masques, what dances shall we
    have,
To wear away this long age of three hours
Between our after-supper and bed-time?
Where is our usual manager of mirth?
What revels are in hand? Is there no play,
To ease the anguish of a torturing hour?
Call Philostrate.

PHILOSTRATE

          Here, mighty Theseus.

THESEUS

Say, what abridgement have you for this evening?
What masque? what music? How shall we beguile
The lazy time, if not with some delight?

PHILOSTRATE

There is a brief how many sports are ripe:
Make choice of which your highness will see first.
                                        [*Giving a paper.*

THESEUS

[*Reads*]   The battle with the Centaurs, to be sung
              By an Athenian eunuch to the harp.

We'll none of that: that have I told my love,
In glory of my kinsman Hercules.

[*Reads*]   The riot of the tipsy Bacchanals,
              Tearing the Thracian singer in their rage.

That is an old device; and it was play'd
When I from Thebes came last a conqueror.

[*Reads*]   The thrice three Muses mourning for the death
              Of Learning, late deceased in beggary.

That is some satire, keen and critical,
Not sorting with a nuptial ceremony.

[*Reads*]   A tedious brief scene of young Pyramus
              And his love Thisbe; very tragical mirth.

Merry and tragical! tedious and brief!
That is, hot ice and wondrous strange snow.
How shall we find the concord of this discord?

PHILOSTRATE

A play there is, my lord, some ten words long,
Which is as brief as I have known a play;
But by ten words, my lord, it is too long,
Which makes it tedious; for in all the play
There is not one word apt, one player fitted:
And tragical, my noble lord, it is;
For Pyramus therein doth kill himself.
Which, when I saw rehearsed, I must confess,
Made mine eyes water; but more merry tears
The passion of loud laughter never shed.

THESEUS

What are they that do play it?

PHILOSTRATE

Hard-handed men, that work in Athens here,
Which never labour'd in their minds till now;
And now have toil'd their unbreathed memories
With this same play, against your nuptial.

THESEUS

And we will hear it.

PHILOSTRATE

                    No, my noble lord;
It is not for you: I have heard it over,
And it is nothing, nothing in the world;
Unless you can find sport in their intents,
Extremely stretch'd and conn'd with cruel pain,
To do you service.

THESEUS

              I will hear that play;
For never any thing can be amiss,
When simpleness and duty tender it.
Go, bring them in: and take your places, ladies.
                            [*Exit* PHILOSTRATE

HIPPOLYTA

I love not to see wretchedness o'ercharged,
And duty in his service perishing.

THESEUS

Why, gentle sweet, you shall see no such thing.

HIPPOLYTA

He says they can do nothing in this kind.

THESEUS

The kinder we, to give them thanks for nothing.
Our sport shall be to take what they mistake:
And what poor duty cannot do, noble respect
Takes it in might, not merit.
Where I have come, great clerks have purposed
To greet me with premeditated welcomes;
Where I have seen them shiver and look pale,
Make periods in the midst of sentences,
Throttle their practised accent in their fears,
And, in conclusion, dumbly have broke off,
Not paying me a welcome. Trust me, sweet,
Out of this silence yet I picked a welcome;
And in the modesty of fearful duty
I read as much as from the rattling tongue
Of saucy and audacious eloquence.
Love, therefore, and tongue-tied simplicity
In least speak most, to my capacity.

                    Re-enter PHILOSTRATE

PHILOSTRATE

So please your Grace, the Prologue is address'd.

THESEUS

Let him approach.   [*Flourish of trumpets*
              Enter QUINCE *for the* PROLOGUE

PROLOGUE

If we offend, it is with our good will.
    That you should think, we come not to offend,
But with good will. To show our simple skill,
    That is the true beginning of our end.
Consider, then, we come but in despite.
    We do not come, as minding to content you,
Our true intent is. All for your delight,
    We are not here. That you should here repent you,
The actors are at hand; and, by their show,
You shall know all, that you are like to know.

THESEUS

This fellow doth not stand upon points.

LYSANDER

He hath rid his prologue like a rough colt; he knows
not the stop. A good moral, my lord: it is not
enough to speak, but to speak true.

HIPPOLYTA

Indeed he hath played on his prologue like a child
on a recorder; a sound, but not in government.

THESEUS

His speech was like a tangled chain; nothing im-
paired, but all disordered. Who is next?
    Enter PYRAMUS *and* THISBE, WALL, MOONSHINE, *and*
                        LION

PROLOGUE

Gentles, perchance you wonder at this show;
    But wonder on, till truth make all things plain.
This man is Pyramus, if you would know;
    This beauteous lady Thisby is certain.
This man, with lime and rough-cast, doth present
    Wall, that vile Wall which did these lovers sunder;
And through Wall's chink, poor souls, they are content
    To whisper. At the which let no man wonder.

This man, with lanthorn, dog, and bush of thorn,
  Presenteth Moonshine; for, if you will know,
By moonshine did these lovers think no scorn
  To meet at Ninus' tomb, there, there to woo.
This grisly beast, which Lion hight by name,
The trusty Thisby, coming first by night,
Did scare away, or rather did affright;
And, as she fled, her mantle she did fall,
  Which Lion vile with bloody mouth did stain.
Anon comes Pyramus, sweet youth and tall,
  And finds his trusty Thisby's mantle slain:
Whereat, with blade, with bloody blameful blade,
  He bravely broach'd his boiling bloody breast;
And Thisby, tarrying in mulberry shade,
  His dagger drew, and died. For all the rest,
Let Lion, Moonshine, Wall, and lovers twain
  At large discourse, while here they do remain.

[*Exeunt* PROLOGUE, PYRAMUS, THISBE,
LION, *and* MOONSHINE

THESEUS

I wonder if the lion be to speak.

DEMETRIUS

No wonder, my lord: one lion may, when many asses do.

WALL

In this same interlude it doth befall
That I, one Snout by name, present a wall;
And such a wall, as I would have you think,
That had in it a crannied hole or chink,
Through which the lovers, Pyramus and Thisby,
Did whisper often very secretly.
This loam, this rough-cast, and this stone, doth show
That I am that same wall; the truth is so:
And this the cranny is, right and sinister,
Through which the fearful lovers are to whisper.

THESEUS

Would you desire lime and hair to speak better?

DEMETRIUS

It is the wittiest partition that ever I heard discourse, my lord.

THESEUS

Pyramus draws near the wall: silence!

Re-enter PYRAMUS

PYRAMUS

O grim-look'd night! O night with hue so black!
  O night, which ever art when day is not!
O night, O night! alack, alack, alack,
  I fear my Thisby's promise is forgot!
And thou, O wall, O sweet, O lovely wall,
  That stand'st between her father's ground and mine!
Thou wall, O wall, O sweet and lovely wall,
  Show me thy chink, to blink through with mine eyne!

[WALL *holds up his fingers*

Thanks, courteous wall: Jove shield thee well for this!
  But what see I? No Thisby do I see.
O wicked wall, through whom I see no bliss!
  Cursed be thy stones for thus deceiving me!

THESEUS

The wall, methinks, being sensible, should curse again.

PYRAMUS

No, in truth, sir, he should not. 'Deceiving me' is Thisby's cue: she is to enter now, and I am to spy her through the wall. You shall see, it will fall pat as I told you. Yonder she comes.

Re-enter THISBE

THISBE

O wall, full often hast thou heard my moans,
  For parting my fair Pyramus and me!
My cherry lips have often kiss'd thy stones,
  Thy stones with lime and hair knit up in thee.

PYRAMUS

I see a voice: now will I to the chink,
  To spy an I can hear my Thisby's face.
Thisby!

THISBE

My love thou art, my love I think.

PYRAMUS

Think what thou wilt, I am thy lover's grace;
And, like Limander, am I trusty still.

THISBE

And I like Helen, till the Fates me kill.

PYRAMUS

Not Shafalus to Procrus was so true.

THISBE

As Shafalus to Procrus, I to you.

PYRAMUS

O, kiss me through the hole of this vile wall!

THISBE

I kiss the wall's hole, not your lips at all.

PYRAMUS

Wilt thou at Ninny's tomb meet me straightway?

THISBE

'Tide life, 'tide death, I come without delay.

[*Exeunt* PYRAMUS *and* THISBE

WALL

Thus have I, wall, my part discharged so;
And, being done, thus wall away doth go.

[*Exit*

THESEUS

Now is the mural down between the two neighbours.

DEMETRIUS

No remedy, my lord, when walls are so wilful to hear without warning.

HIPPOLYTA

This is the silliest stuff that ever I heard.

THESEUS

The best in this kind are but shadows; and the worst are no worse, if imagination amend them.

HIPPOLYTA

It must be your imagination then, and not theirs.

THESEUS

If we imagine no worse of them than they of themselves, they may pass for excellent men. Here come two noble beasts in, a man and a lion.

Re-enter LION *and* MOONSHINE

LION

You, ladies, you, whose gentle hearts do fear
  The smallest monstrous mouse that creeps on floor,
May now perchance both quake and tremble here,
  When lion rough in wildest rage doth roar.

Then know that I, one Snug the joiner, am
A lion-fell, nor else no lion's dam;
For, if I should as lion come in strife
Into this place, 'twere pity on my life.

THESEUS

A very gentle beast, and of a good conscience.

DEMETRIUS

The very best at a beast, my lord, that e'er I saw.

LYSANDER

This lion is a very fox for his valour.

THESEUS

True; and a goose for his discretion.

DEMETRIUS

Not so, my lord; for his valour cannot carry his discretion; and the fox carries the goose.

THESEUS

His discretion, I am sure, cannot carry his valour;
for the goose carries not the fox. It is well: leave it to
his discretion, and let us listen to the moon.

MOONSHINE

This lanthorn doth the horned moon present;—

DEMETRIUS

He should have worn the horns on his head.

THESEUS

He is no crescent, and his horns are invisible within
the circumference.

MOONSHINE

This lanthorn doth the horned moon present;
Myself the man i' the moon do seem to be.

THESEUS

This is the greatest error of all the rest: the man
should be put into the lantern. How is it else the
man i' the moon?

DEMETRIUS

He dares not come there for the candle; for, you
see, it is already in snuff.

HIPPOLYTA

I am aweary of this moon: would he would change!

THESEUS

It appears, by his small light of discretion, that he is
in the wane; but yet, in courtesy, in all reason, we
must stay the time.

LYSANDER

Proceed, Moon.

MOONSHINE

All that I have to say, is, to tell you that the lanthorn is the moon; I, the man i' the moon; this
thorn-bush, my thorn-bush; and this dog, my dog.

DEMETRIUS

Why, all these should be in the lantern; for all these
are in the moon. But, silence! here comes Thisbe.

Re-enter THISBE

THISBE

This is old Ninny's tomb. Where is my love?

LION

[Roaring]   Oh——   [THISBE *runs off*

DEMETRIUS

Well roared, Lion.

THESEUS

Well run, Thisbe.

HIPPOLYTA

Well shone, Moon. Truly, the moon shines with a
good grace. [*The* LION *shakes* THISBE's *mantle, and exit*

THESEUS

Well moused, Lion.

DEMETRIUS

And then came Pyramus.

LYSANDER

And so the lion vanished.

Re-enter PYRAMUS

PYRAMUS

Sweet Moon, I thank thee for thy sunny beams;
I thank thee, Moon, for shining now so bright;
For, by thy gracious, golden, glittering gleams,
  I trust to take of truest Thisby sight.
      But stay, O spite!
      But mark, poor knight,
  What dreadful dole is here!
      Eyes, do you see?
      How can it be?
  O dainty duck! O dear!
      Thy mantle good,
  What, stain'd with blood!
  Approach, ye Furies fell!
      O Fates, come, come,
      Cut thread and thrum;
  Quail, crush, conclude, and quell!

THESEUS

This passion, and the death of a dear friend, would
go near to make a man look sad.

HIPPOLYTA

Beshrew my heart, but I pity the man.

PYRAMUS

O wherefore, Nature, didst thou lions frame?
  Since lion vile hath here deflower'd my dear:
Which is—no, no—which was the fairest dame
  That lived, that loved, that liked, that look'd with cheer.
      Come, tears, confound;
      Out, sword, and wound
  The pap of Pyramus;
      Ay, that left pap,
      Where heart doth hop: [*Stabs himself*
  Thus die I, thus, thus, thus.
      Now am I dead,
      Now am I fled;
  My soul is in the sky:
      Tongue, lose thy light;
      Moon, take thy flight: [*Exit* MOONSHINE
  Now die, die, die, die, die.   [*Dies*

DEMETRIUS

No die, but an ace, for him; for he is but one.

LYSANDER

Less than an ace, man; for he is dead; he is nothing.

THESEUS

With the help of a surgeon he might yet recover,
and prove an ass.

HIPPOLYTA

How chance Moonshine is gone before Thisbe comes
back and finds her lover?

[409]

THESEUS

She will find him by starlight. Here she comes; and
her passion ends the play.

Re-enter THISBE

HIPPOLYTA

Methinks she should not use a long one for such a
Pyramus: I hope she will be brief.

DEMETRIUS

A mote will turn the balance, which Pyramus,
which Thisbe, is the better; he for a man, God warrant us; she for a woman, God bless us.

LYSANDER

She hath spied him already with those sweet eyes.

DEMETRIUS

And thus she means, videlicet:—

THISBE

Asleep, my love?
　　What, dead, my dove?
O Pyramus, arise!
　　Speak, speak. Quite dumb?
　　Dead, dead? A tomb
Must cover thy sweet eyes.
　　These lily lips,
　　This cherry nose,
These yellow cowslip cheeks,
　　Are gone, are gone:
Lovers, make moan:
His eyes were green as leeks.
　　O Sisters Three,
　　Come, come to me,
With hands as pale as milk;
　　Lay them in gore,
　　Since you have shore
With shears his thread of silk.
　　Tongue, not a word:
　　Come, trusty sword;
Come, blade, my breast imbrue: [*Stabs herself*
　　And, farewell, friends;
　　Thus Thisby ends:
Adieu, adieu, adieu.　　　　　　　　[*Dies*

THESEUS

Moonshine and Lion are left to bury the dead.

DEMETRIUS

Ay, and Wall too.

BOTTOM

[*Starting up*] No, I assure you; the wall is down that
parted their fathers. Will it please you to see the
epilogue, or to hear a Bergomask dance between
two of our company?

THESEUS

No epilogue, I pray you; for your play needs no excuse. Never excuse; for when the players are all
dead, there need none to be blamed. Marry, if he
that writ it had played Pyramus and hanged himself in Thisbe's garter, it would have been a fine
tragedy: and so it is, truly; and very notably discharged. But, come, your Bergomask: let your epilogue alone.　　　　　　　　　　　[*A dance*
The iron tongue of midnight hath told twelve:
Lovers, to bed; 'tis almost fairy time.
I fear we shall out-sleep the coming morn,
As much as we this night have overwatch'd.

This palpable-gross play hath well beguiled
The heavy gait of night. Sweet friends, to bed.
A fortnight hold we this solemnity,
In nightly revels and new jollity.　　　　　[*Exeunt*

Enter PUCK

PUCK

Now the hungry lion roars,
　　And the wolf behowls the moon;
Whilst the heavy ploughman snores,
　　All with weary task fordone.
Now the wasted brands do glow,
　　Whilst the screech-owl, screeching loud,
Puts the wretch that lies in woe
　　In remembrance of a shroud.
Now it is the time of night,
　　That the graves, all gaping wide,
Every one lets forth his sprite,
　　In the church-way paths to glide:
And we fairies, that do run
　　By the triple Hecate's team,
From the presence of the sun,
　　Following darkness like a dream,
Now are frolic: not a mouse
Shall disturb this hallow'd house:
I am sent with broom before,
To sweep the dust behind the door.

Enter OBERON *and* TITANIA *with their train*

OBERON

Through the house give glimmering light,
　　By the dead and drowsy fire:
Every elf and fairy sprite
　　Hop as light as bird from brier;
And this ditty, after me,
Sing, and dance it trippingly.

TITANIA

First, rehearse your song by rote,
To each word a warbling note:
Hand in hand, with fairy grace,
Will we sing, and bless this place. [*Song and dance*

OBERON

Now, until the break of day,
Through this house each fairy stray.
To the best bride-bed will we,
Which by us shall blessed be;
And the issue there create
Ever shall be fortunate.
So shall all the couples three
Ever true in loving be;
And the blots of Nature's hand
Shall not in their issue stand;
Never mole, hare lip, nor scar,
Nor mark prodigious, such as are
Despised in nativity,
Shall upon their children be.
With this field-dew consecrate,
Every fairy take his gait;
And each several chamber bless,
Through this palace, with sweet peace,
Ever shall in safety rest,
And the owner of it blest.

Trip away; make no stay;
Meet me all by break of day.

     [*Exeunt* OBERON, TITANIA, *and train*
        PUCK

If we shadows have offended,
Think but this, and all is mended,
That you have but slumber'd here,
While these visions did appear.
And this weak and idle theme,
No more yielding but a dream,

Gentles, do not reprehend:
If you pardon, we will mend.
And, as I am an honest Puck,
If we have unearned luck
Now to scape the serpent's tongue,
We will make amends ere long;
Else the Puck a liar call:
So, good night unto you all.
Give me your hands, if we be friends,
And Robin shall restore amends.   [*Exit*

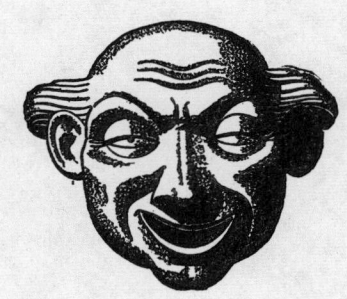

THE LIFE AND DEATH OF KING JOHN

SYNOPSIS

WHEN King Richard Cœur-de-lion died, the rightful heir in the line of succession to the English throne was the son of his deceased brother Geoffrey, the little Arthur, but the crown was seized by Richard's younger brother, the weak, treacherous John, with the able help of the queen-mother Elinor, his strongest ally and counsellor.

King Philip of France, upholding the claim of young Arthur and his French mother, Constance, sends an ambassador to King John to demand the surrender of his crown to his nephew, and John, angrily refusing, at once prepares to invade French territory. At this moment, both the King and Queen Elinor are strongly attracted by the big, impetuous Philip Faulconbridge who is revealed to them as the bastard son of Cœur-de-lion, and to settle the legal controversy between this headstrong, forthright young giant and his feeble half-brother, the legitimate heir to his father's title and lands, John dubs the bastard "Sir Richard Plantagenet," and appoints him as a leader in the expedition to France.

The English army opposes that of the French King and his ally, the Duke of Austria, before the town of Angiers whose inhabitants, while acknowledging English rule, will not open their gates until a decisive battle is fought to decide whether John or Arthur is England's king. After a bloody but indecisive skirmish, the Bastard suggests that both sides unite their forces for the time being to destroy the town, but the citizens prevail upon the two Kings to make peace through the marriage of Lewis, Dauphin of France, and the Lady Blanch of Spain, John's niece. The cold Queen Elinor sees in the proposal a direct means of checkmating Constance's plans for her young son, and advises King John to give the Lady Blanch, in addition to a dowry of thirty thousand marks in English gold, the five English provinces in France which Philip has claimed for Arthur.

This falsely created peace, despised by the Bastard and railed against by Constance in a torrent of denunciation, does not last long, for Cardinal Pandulph, the Pope's legate, upon John's refusal to accept Stephen Langton as the archbishop of Canterbury, not only curses and excommunicates the King but orders Philip and Lewis to break the new treaty and continue war on England. A battle takes place near Angiers, in which the French are defeated, the Duke of Austria is killed by the Bastard, and little Arthur is carried off by his uncle. Feeling certain that John will have the boy murdered, and afraid of the English people becoming estranged from Rome through the King's quarrel and the Bastard's ransacking of the churches and abbeys for funds, Pandulph persuades the Dauphin to invade England and claim the throne in his wife's right.

Meanwhile, in confinement in England, Arthur succeeds in softening the heart of the King's chamberlain, Hubert de Burgh, who is ordered by John to burn out the boy's eyes, and he is spared this cruelty, but in an attempt to escape from his prison by leaping from the walls, he is killed on the stones below.

Three English noblemen, Pembroke, Bigot, and Salisbury, are moved to go in search of the Prince, and notwithstanding their suspicions of the King's evil designs they are so horrified at the sight of the little crushed body beneath the castle walls and so convinced that John has ordered the murder that, despite the Bastard's advice to remain loyal, they resolve to join the Dauphin who has just landed large forces in England. The cowardly King, harassed by the news of the foreign army, the defection of his nobles, and the general disturbances throughout the country, is now utterly crushed by the tidings of his mother's death and seeks Rome's help against the French. He surrenders his authority to Cardinal Pandulph in exchange for his promise to turn back the French, and as a matter of form, delivers up his crown on Ascension Day and receives it back again, so that a prophecy be fulfilled that on that day he would give up his crown.

The Dauphin, however, will not be dissuaded from his purpose, and with the English traitors who have joined them, the French fight John's army led by the Bastard. The French have lost great supplies in a wreck on the Goodwin Sands and this engagement is indecisive, but the wounded Count Melun of France, whose mother was English, warns the revolting noblemen that the Dauphin is perjured and purposes to have them executed after he has gained his ends with their help. They return to King John whom they find wretchedly dying in the orchard of Swinstead Abbey where he has been carried for air to alleviate the burning of the poison inside him, supposedly administered by a monk.

The Bastard, devoted, voluble, blusters in with his last bit of bad news for his liege lord. The Dauphin is preparing to advance, and the best part of the English forces have been lost at night in the tide, while crossing the Wash. As the words fall on the King's dead ears, Salisbury announces that a lasting peace has been arranged by Pandulph between France and England, and with Pembroke, Bigot, and the Bastard he pledges allegiance to Prince Henry, John's son.

HISTORICAL DATA

King John is an adaptation of an older play in two parts, *The Troublesome Raigne of John, King of England*, which was published in 1591. Shakespeare does not appear to have gone further for his source material in this instance and as a result the play is less historically accurate than any of its fellows. No mention even is made of Magna Carta, certainly the most familiar and important contribution of John to his country's history.

While closely following the older play, Shakespeare condensed the ten acts of the original to five, omitting the coarse scenes of comic complexion from his adaption. He both elaborated and condensed episodes but added almost nothing to the action. He did recreate and elevate several of the main characters.

King John is, as it were, a prologue to the ten historical plays of Shakespeare which cover English history from the reign of Richard II through that of Richard III, with Henry VIII as an epilogue. It is the only undoubtedly Shakespearean play not entered in the Stationers' Register, nor is there any trace of its having been printed prior to its appearance in the First Folio in 1623. It is mentioned, however, in Meres's *Palladis Tamia*, and its date of composition is generally agreed to be 1594–5.

"*Heaven take my soul, and England keep my bones!*"
KING JOHN

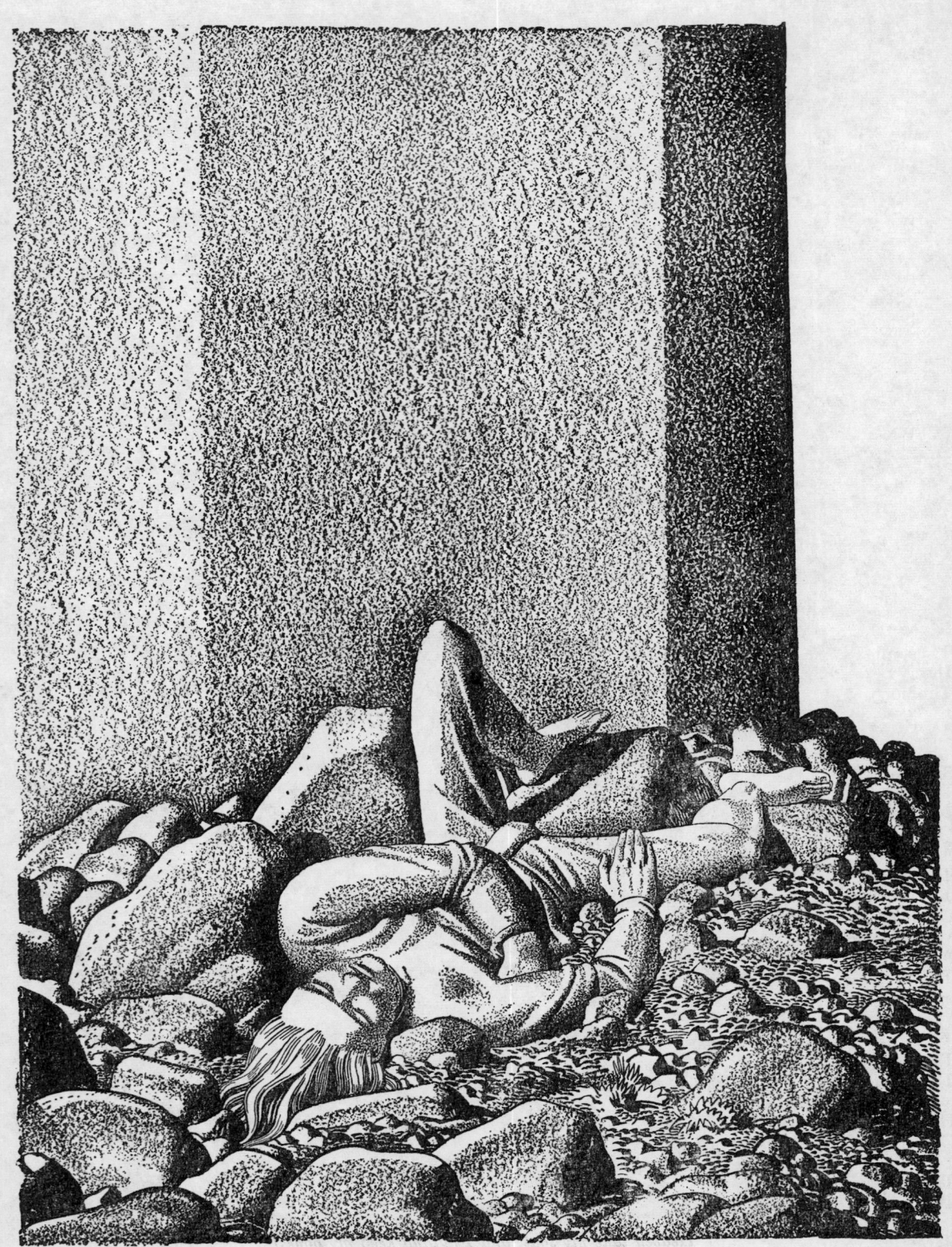

THE LIFE AND DEATH OF KING JOHN

DRAMATIS PERSONÆ

KING JOHN.
PRINCE HENRY, *son to the King.*
ARTHUR, *Duke of Bretagne, nephew to the King.*
THE EARL OF PEMBROKE.
THE EARL OF ESSEX.
THE EARL OF SALISBURY.
THE LORD BIGOT.
HUBERT DE BURGH.
ROBERT FAULCONBRIDGE, *son to Sir Robert Faulconbridge.*
PHILIP THE BASTARD, *his half-brother.*
JAMES GURNEY, *servant to Lady Faulconbridge.*
PETER OF POMFRET, *a prophet.*
PHILIP, *King of France.*

LEWIS, *the Dauphin.*
LYMOGES, *Duke of Austria.*
CARDINAL PANDULPH, *the Pope's legate.*
MELUN, *a French lord.*
CHATILLON, *ambassador from France to King John.*

QUEEN ELINOR, *mother to King John.*
CONSTANCE, *mother to Arthur.*
BLANCH *of Spain, niece to King John.*
LADY FAULCONBRIDGE.

LORDS, CITIZENS *of Angiers,* SHERIFF, HERALDS, OFFICERS, SOLDIERS, MESSENGERS, *and other* ATTENDANTS.

SCENE—*Partly in England, and partly in France.*

ACT I

SCENE I. KING JOHN's *palace*

Enter KING JOHN, QUEEN ELINOR, PEMBROKE, ESSEX, SALISBURY, *and others, with* CHATILLON

KING JOHN
Now, say, Chatillon, what would France with us?

CHATILLON
Thus, after greeting, speaks the King of France
In my behaviour to the majesty,
The borrowed majesty, of England here.

ELINOR
A strange beginning: 'borrowed majesty!'

KING JOHN
Silence, good mother; hear the embassy.

CHATILLON
Philip of France, in right and true behalf
Of thy deceased brother Geffrey's son,
Arthur Plantagenet, lays most lawful claim
To this fair island and the territories,
To Ireland, Poictiers, Anjou, Touraine, Maine,
Desiring thee to lay aside the sword
Which sways usurpingly these several titles,
And put the same into young Arthur's hand,
Thy nephew and right royal sovereign.

KING JOHN
What follows if we disallow of this?

CHATILLON
The proud control of fierce and bloody war,
To enforce these rights so forcibly withheld.

KING JOHN
Here have we war for war and blood for blood,
Controlment for controlment: so answer France.

CHATILLON
Then take my king's defiance from my mouth,
The farthest limit of my embassy.

KING JOHN
Bear mine to him, and so depart in peace:

Be thou as lightning in the eyes of France;
For ere thou canst report I will be there,
The thunder of my cannon shall be heard:
So hence! Be thou the trumpet of our wrath
And sullen presage of your own decay.
An honourable conduct let him have.
Pembroke, look to't. Farewell, Chatillon.
                    [*Exeunt* CHATILLON *and* PEMBROKE

ELINOR
What now, my son! have I not ever said
How that ambitious Constance would not cease
Till she had kindled France and all the world,
Upon the right and party of her son?
This might have been prevented and made whole
With very easy arguments of love,
Which now the manage of two kingdoms must
With fearful bloody issue arbitrate.

KING JOHN
Our strong possession and our right for us.

ELINOR
Your strong possession much more than your right,
Or else it must go wrong with you and me:
So much my conscience whispers in your ear,
Which none but heaven and you and I shall hear.

Enter a SHERIFF

ESSEX
My liege, here is the strangest controversy
Come from the country to be judged by you,
That e'er I heard: shall I produce the men?

KING JOHN
Let them approach.
Our abbeys and our priories shall pay
This expedition's charge.

Enter ROBERT FAULCONBRIDGE, *and* PHILIP *his bastard brother*

                    What men are you?

BASTARD
Your faithful subject I, a gentleman

[415]

Born in Northamptonshire, and eldest son,
As I suppose, to Robert Faulconbridge,
A soldier, by the honour-giving hand
Of Cœur-de-lion knighted in the field.

KING JOHN

What art thou?

ROBERT FAULCONBRIDGE

The son and heir to that same Faulconbridge.

KING JOHN

Is that the elder, and art thou the heir?
You came not of one mother then, it seems.

BASTARD

Most certain of one mother, mighty king;
That is well known; and, as I think, one father:
But for the certain knowledge of that truth
I put you o'er to heaven and to my mother:
Of that I doubt, as all men's children may.

ELINOR

Out on thee, rude man! thou dost shame thy
    mother
And wound her honour with this diffidence.

BASTARD

I, madam? no, I have no reason for it;
That is my brother's plea and none of mine;
The which if he can prove, a' pops me out
At least from fair five hundred pound a year:
Heaven guard my mother's honour and my land!

KING JOHN

A good blunt fellow. Why, being younger born,
Doth he lay claim to thine inheritance?

BASTARD

I know not why, except to get the land.
But once he slander'd me with bastardy:
But whether I be as true begot or no,
That still I lay upon my mother's head;
But that I am as well begot, my liege,—
Fair fall the bones that took the pains for me!—
Compare our faces and be judge yourself.
If old Sir Robert did beget us both
And were our father and this son like him,
O old Sir Robert, father, on my knee
I give heaven thanks I was not like to thee!

KING JOHN

Why, what a madcap hath heaven lent us here!

ELINOR

He hath a trick of Cœur-de-lion's face;
The accent of his tongue affecteth him.
Do you not read some tokens of my son
In the large composition of this man?

KING JOHN

Mine eye hath well examined his parts
And finds them perfect Richard. Sirrah, speak,
What doth move you to claim your brother's land?

BASTARD

Because he hath a half-face, like my father.
With half that face would he have all my land:
A half-faced groat five hundred pound a year!

ROBERT FAULCONBRIDGE

My gracious liege, when that my father lived,
Your brother did employ my father much,—

BASTARD

Well, sir, by this you cannot get my land:
Your tale must be how he employ'd my mother.

ROBERT FAULCONBRIDGE

And once dispatch'd him in an embassy
To Germany, there with the emperor
To treat of high affairs touching that time.
The advantage of his absence took the king
And in the mean time sojourn'd at my father's;
Where how he did prevail I shame to speak,
But truth is truth: large lengths of seas and shores
Between my father and my mother lay,
As I have heard my father speak himself,
When this same lusty gentleman was got.
Upon his death-bed he by will bequeath'd
His lands to me, and took it on his death
That this my mother's son was none of his;
And if he were, he came into the world
Full fourteen weeks before the course of time.
Then, good my liege, let me have what is mine,
My father's land, as was my father's will.

KING JOHN

Sirrah, your brother is legitimate;
Your father's wife did after wedlock bear him,
And if she did play false, the fault was hers;
Which fault lies on the hazards of all husbands
That marry wives. Tell me, how if my brother,
Who, as you say, took pains to get this son,
Had of your father claim'd this son for his?
In sooth, good friend, your father might have kept
This calf, bred from his cow, from all the world;
In sooth he might; then, if he were my brother's,
My brother might not claim him; nor your father,
Being none of his, refuse him: this concludes;
My mother's son did get your father's heir;
Your father's heir must have your father's land.

ROBERT FAULCONBRIDGE

Shall then my father's will be of no force
To dispossess that child which is not his?

BASTARD

Of no more force to dispossess me, sir,
Than was his will to get me, as I think.

ELINOR

Whether hadst thou rather be a Faulconbridge,
And like thy brother, to enjoy thy land,
Or the reputed son of Cœur-de-lion,
Lord of thy presence and no land beside?

BASTARD

Madam, an if my brother had my shape,
And I had his, sir Robert's his, like him;
And if my legs were two such riding-rods,
My arms such eel-skins stuff'd, my face so thin
That in mine ear I durst not stick a rose
Lest men should say 'Look, where three-farthings
    goes!'
And, to his shape, were heir to all this land,
Would I might never stir from off this place,
I would give it every foot to have this face;
I would not be sir Nob in any case.

ELINOR

I like thee well: wilt thou forsake thy fortune,
Bequeath thy land to him and follow me?
I am a soldier and now bound to France.

BASTARD

Brother, take you my land, I'll take my chance.
Your face hath got five hundred pound a year,
Yet sell your face for five pence and 'tis dear.
Madam, I'll follow you unto the death.

ELINOR

Nay, I would have you go before me thither.

BASTARD

Our country manners give our betters way.

KING JOHN

What is thy name?

BASTARD

Philip, my liege, so is my name begun;
Philip, good old sir Robert's wife's eldest son.

KING JOHN

From henceforth bear his name whose form thou
    bear'st:
Kneel thou down Philip, but rise more great,
Arise sir Richard and Plantagenet.

BASTARD

Brother by the mother's side, give me your hand:
My father gave me honour, yours gave land.
Now blessed be the hour, by night or day,
When I was got, sir Robert was away!

ELINOR

The very spirit of Plantagenet!
I am thy grandam, Richard; call me so.

BASTARD

Madam, by chance but not by truth; what though?
Something about, a little from the right,
In at the window, or else o'er the hatch:
Who dares not stir by day must walk by night,
And have is have, however men do catch:
Near or far off, well won is still well shot,
And I am I, howe'er I was begot.

KING JOHN

Go, Faulconbridge: now hast thou thy desire;
A landless knight makes thee a landed squire.
Come, madam, and come, Richard, we must speed
For France, for France, for it is more than need.

BASTARD

Brother, adieu: good fortune come to thee!
For thou wast got i' the way of honesty.
                [Exeunt all but BASTARD
A foot of honour better than I was;
But many a many foot of land the worse.
Well, now can I make any Joan a lady.
'Good den, sir Richard!'—'God-a-mercy, fellow!'—
And if his name be George, I'll call him Peter;
For new-made honour doth forget men's names;
'Tis too respective and too sociable
For your conversion. Now your traveller,
He and his toothpick at my worship's mess,
And when my knightly stomach is sufficed,
Why then I suck my teeth and catechize

My picked man of countries: 'My dear sir,'
Thus, leaning on mine elbow, I begin,
'I shall beseech you'—that is question now;
And then comes answer like an Absey book:
'O sir,' says answer, 'at your best command;
At your employment; at your service, sir:'
'No, sir,' says question, 'I, sweet sir, at yours:'
And so, ere answer knows what question would,
Saving in dialogue of compliment,
And talking of the Alps and Apennines,
The Pyrenean and the river Po,
It draws toward supper in conclusion so.
But this is worshipful society,
And fits the mounting spirit like myself;
For he is but a bastard to the time
That doth not smack of observation;
And so am I, whether I smack or no;
And not alone in habit and device,
Exterior form, outward accoutrement,
But from the inward motion to deliver
Sweet, sweet, sweet poison for the age's tooth:
Which, though I will not practise to deceive,
Yet, to avoid deceit, I mean to learn;
For it shall strew the footsteps of my rising.
But who comes in such haste in riding-robes?
What woman-post is this? hath she no husband
That will take pains to blow a horn before her?
    Enter LADY FAULCONBRIDGE *and* JAMES GURNEY
O me! it is my mother. How now, good lady?
What brings you here to court so hastily?

LADY FAULCONBRIDGE

Where is that slave, thy brother? where is he,
That holds in chase mine honour up and down?

BASTARD

My brother Robert? old sir Robert's son?
Colbrand the giant, that same mighty man?
Is it sir Robert's son that you seek so?

LADY FAULCONBRIDGE

Sir Robert's son! Ay, thou unreverend boy,
Sir Robert's son: why scorn'st thou at sir Robert?
He is sir Robert's son, and so art thou.

BASTARD

James Gurney, wilt thou give us leave awhile?

JAMES GURNEY

Good leave, good Philip.

BASTARD

              Philip! sparrow: James,
There's toys abroad: anon I'll tell thee more.
                      [Exit GURNEY
Madam, I was not old sir Robert's son:
Sir Robert might have eat his part in me
Upon Good-Friday and ne'er broke his fast:
Sir Robert could do well: marry, to confess,
Could he get me? Sir Robert could not do it:
We know his handiwork: therefore, good mother,
To whom am I beholding for these limbs?
Sir Robert never holp to make this leg.

LADY FAULCONBRIDGE

Hast thou conspired with thy brother too,

That for thine own gain shouldst defend mine
    honour?
What means this scorn, thou most untoward knave?

BASTARD

Knight, knight, good mother, Basilisco-like.
What! I am dubb'd! I have it on my shoulder.
But, mother, I am not sir Robert's son;
I have disclaim'd sir Robert and my land;
Legitimation, name and all is gone:
Then, good my mother, let me know my father;
Some proper man, I hope: who was it, mother?

LADY FAULCONBRIDGE

Hast thou denied thyself a Faulconbridge?

BASTARD

As faithfully as I deny the devil.

LADY FAULCONBRIDGE

King Richard Cœur-de-lion was thy father:
By long and vehement suit I was seduced
To make room for him in my husband's bed:
Heaven lay not my transgression to my charge!
Thou art the issue of my dear offence,
Which was so strongly urged past my defence.

BASTARD

Now, by this light, were I to get again,
Madam, I would not wish a better father.
Some sins do bear their privilege on earth,
And so doth yours; your fault was not your folly:
Needs must you lay your heart at his dispose,
Subjected tribute to commanding love,
Against whose fury and unmatched force
The aweless lion could not wage the fight,
Nor keep his princely heart from Richard's hand.
He that perforce robs lions of their hearts
May easily win a woman's. Ay, my mother,
With all my heart I thank thee for my father!
Who lives and dares but say thou didst not well
When I was got, I'll send his soul to hell.
Come, lady, I will show thee to my kin;
    And they shall say, when Richard me begot,
If thou hadst said him nay, it had been sin:
    Who says it was, he lies; I say 'twas not. [Exeunt

ACT II

Scene I. France. Before Angiers

Enter AUSTRIA *and forces, drums, etc. on one side: on the
other* KING PHILIP *of France and his power;* LEWIS,
ARTHUR, CONSTANCE *and* ATTENDANTS

LEWIS

Before Angiers well met, brave Austria.
Arthur, that great forerunner of thy blood,
Richard, that robb'd the lion of his heart
And fought the holy wars in Palestine,
By this brave duke came early to his grave:
And for amends to his posterity,
At our importance hither is he come,
To spread his colours, boy, in thy behalf,

And to rebuke the usurpation
Of thy unnatural uncle, English John:
Embrace him, love him, give him welcome hither.

ARTHUR

God shall forgive you Cœur-de-lion's death
The rather that you give his offspring life,
Shadowing their right under your wings of war:
I give you welcome with a powerless hand,
But with a heart full of unstained love:
Welcome before the gates of Angiers, duke.

LEWIS

A noble boy! Who would not do thee right?

AUSTRIA

Upon thy cheek lay I this zealous kiss,
As seal to this indenture of my love,
That to my home I will no more return,
Till Angiers and the right thou hast in France,
Together with that pale, that white-faced shore,
Whose foot spurns back the ocean's roaring tides
And coops from other lands her islanders,
Even till that England, hedged in with the main,
That water-walled bulwark, still secure
And confident from foreign purposes,
Even till that utmost corner of the west
Salute thee for her king: till then, fair boy,
Will I not think of home, but follow arms.

CONSTANCE

O, take his mother's thanks, a widow's thanks,
Till your strong hand shall help to give him strength
To make a more requital to your love!

AUSTRIA

The peace of heaven is theirs that lift their swords
In such a just and charitable war.

KING PHILIP

Well then, to work: our cannon shall be bent
Against the brows of this resisting town.
Call for our chiefest men of discipline,
To cull the plots of best advantages:
We'll lay before this town our royal bones,
Wade to the market-place in Frenchmen's blood,
But we will make it subject to this boy.

CONSTANCE

Stay for an answer to your embassy,
Lest unadvised you stain your swords with blood:
My Lord Chatillon may from England bring
That right in peace which here we urge in war,
And then we shall repent each drop of blood
That hot rash haste so indirectly shed.

Enter CHATILLON

KING PHILIP

A wonder, lady! lo, upon thy wish,
Our messenger Chatillon is arrived!
What England says, say briefly, gentle lord;
We coldly pause for thee; Chatillon, speak.

CHATILLON

Then turn your forces from this paltry siege
And stir them up against a mightier task.
England, impatient of your just demands,
Hath put himself in arms: the adverse winds,

Whose leisure I have stay'd, have given him time
To land his legions all as soon as I;
His marches are expedient to this town,
His forces strong, his soldiers confident.
With him along is come the mother-queen,
An Ate, stirring him to blood and strife;
With her her niece, the Lady Blanch of Spain;
With them a bastard of the king's deceased;
And all the unsettled humours of the land,
Rash, inconsiderate, fiery voluntaries,
With ladies' faces and fierce dragons' spleens,
Have sold their fortunes at their native homes,
Bearing their birthrights proudly on their backs,
To make a hazard of new fortunes here:
In brief, a braver choice of dauntless spirits
Than now the English bottoms have waft o'er
Did never float upon the swelling tide,
To do offence and scath in Christendom.
          [*Drum beats*
The interruption of their churlish drums
Cuts off more circumstance: they are at hand,
To parley or to fight; therefore prepare.
      KING PHILIP
How much unlook'd for is this expedition!
      AUSTRIA
By how much unexpected, by so much
We must awake endeavour for defence;
For courage mounteth with occasion:
Let them be welcome then; we are prepared.
Enter KING JOHN, ELINOR, BLANCH, *the* BASTARD,
    LORDS, *and* FORCES
      KING JOHN
Peace be to France, if France in peace permit
Our just and lineal entrance to our own;
If not, bleed France, and peace ascend to heaven,
Whiles we, God's wrathful agent, do correct
Their proud contempt that beats His peace to
  heaven.
      KING PHILIP
Peace be to England, if that war return
From France to England, there to live in peace.
England we love; and for that England's sake
With burden of our armour here we sweat.
This toil of ours should be a work of thine;
But thou from loving England art so far,
That thou hast under-wrought his lawful king,
Cut off the sequence of posterity,
Out-faced infant state and done a rape
Upon the maiden virtue of the crown.
Look here upon thy brother Geffrey's face;
These eyes, these brows, were moulded out of his:
This little abstract doth contain that large
Which died in Geffrey, and the hand of time
Shall draw this brief into as huge a volume.
That Geffrey was thy elder brother born,
And this his son; England was Geffrey's right,
And this is Geffrey's: in the name of God
How comes it then that thou art call'd a king,
When living blood doth in these temples beat,
Which owe the crown that thou o'ermasterest?

      KING JOHN
From whom hast thou this great commission,
  France,
To draw my answer from thy articles?
      KING PHILIP
From that supernal judge, that stirs good thoughts
In any breast of strong authority,
To look into the blots and stains of right:
That judge hath made me guardian to this boy:
Under whose warrant I impeach thy wrong,
And by whose help I mean to chastise it.
      KING JOHN
Alack, thou dost usurp authority.
      KING PHILIP
Excuse; it is to beat usurping down.
      ELINOR
Who is it thou dost call usurper, France?
      CONSTANCE
Let me make answer; thy usurping son.
      ELINOR
Out, insolent! thy bastard shall be king,
That thou mayst be a queen, and check the world!
      CONSTANCE
My bed was ever to thy son as true
As thine was to thy husband; and this boy
Liker in feature to his father Geffrey
Than thou and John in manners; being as like
As rain to water, or devil to his dam.
My boy a bastard! By my soul, I think
His father never was so true begot:
It cannot be, an if thou wert his mother.
      ELINOR
There's a good mother, boy, that blots thy father.
      CONSTANCE
There's a good grandam, boy, that would blot thee.
      AUSTRIA
Peace!
      BASTARD
  Hear the crier.
      AUSTRIA
     What the devil art thou?
      BASTARD
One that will play the devil, sir, with you,
An a' may catch your hide and you alone:
You are the hare of whom the proverb goes,
Whose valour plucks dead lions by the beard:
I'll smoke your skin-coat, an I catch you right;
Sirrah, look to 't; i' faith, I will, i' faith.
      BLANCH
O, well did he become that lion's robe
That did disrobe the lion of that robe!
      BASTARD
It lies as sightly on the back of him
As great Alcides' shows upon an ass:
But, ass, I'll take that burthen from your back,
Or lay on that shall make your shoulders crack.
      AUSTRIA
What cracker is this same that deafs our ears
With this abundance of superfluous breath?
King Philip, determine what we shall do straight.

KING PHILIP

Women and fools, break off your conference.
King John, this is the very sum of all;
England and Ireland, Anjou, Touraine, Maine,
In right of Arthur do I claim of thee:
Wilt thou resign them and lay down thy arms?

KING JOHN

My life as soon: I do defy thee, France.
Arthur of Bretagne, yield thee to my hand;
And out of my dear love I'll give thee more
Than e'er the coward hand of France can win:
Submit thee, boy.

ELINOR

        Come to thy grandam, child.

CONSTANCE

Do, child, go to it grandam, child;
Give grandam kingdom, and it grandam will
Give it a plum, a cherry, and a fig:
There's a good grandam.

ARTHUR

        Good my mother, peace!
I would that I were low laid in my grave:
I am not worth this coil that's made for me.

ELINOR

His mother shames him so, poor boy, he weeps.

CONSTANCE

Now shame upon him, whether she does or no!
His grandam's wrongs, and not his mother's shames,
Draws those heaven-moving pearls from his poor
    eyes,
Which heaven shall take in nature of a fee;
Ay, with these crystal beads heaven shall be bribed
To do him justice and revenge on you.

ELINOR

Thou monstrous slanderer of heaven and earth!

CONSTANCE

Thou monstrous injurer of heaven and earth!
Call not me slanderer; thou and thine usurp
The dominations, royalties and rights
Of this oppressed boy: this is thy eld'st son's son,
Infortunate in nothing but in thee:
Thy sins are visited in this poor child;
The canon of the law is laid on him,
Being but the second generation
Removed from thy sin-conceiving womb.

KING JOHN

Bedlam, have done.

CONSTANCE

        I have but this to say,
That he is not only plagued for her sin,
But God hath made her sin and her the plague
On this removed issue, plagued for her
And with her plague; her sin his injury,
Her injury the beadle to her sin,
All punish'd in the person of this child,
And all for her; a plague upon her!

ELINOR

Thou unadvised scold, I can produce
A will that bars the title of thy son.

CONSTANCE

Ay, who doubts that? a will! a wicked will;
A woman's will; a canker'd grandam's will!

KING PHILIP

Peace, lady! pause, or be more temperate:
It ill beseems this presence to cry aim
To these ill-tuned repetitions.
Some trumpet summon hither to the walls
These men of Angiers: let us hear them speak
Whose title they admit, Arthur's or John's.

Trumpet sounds. Enter certain CITIZENS *upon the walls*

FIRST CITIZEN

Who is it that hath warn'd us to the walls?

KING PHILIP

'Tis France, for England.

KING JOHN

        England, for itself.
You men of Angiers, and my loving subjects,—

KING PHILIP

You loving men of Angiers, Arthur's subjects,
Our trumpet call'd you to this gentle parle,—

KING JOHN

For our advantage; therefore hear us first.
These flags of France, that are advanced here
Before the eye and prospect of your town,
Have hither march'd to your endamagement:
The cannons have their bowels full of wrath,
And ready mounted are they to spit forth
Their iron indignation 'gainst your walls:
All preparation for a bloody siege
And merciless proceeding by these French
Confronts your city's eyes, your winking gates;
And but for our approach those sleeping stones,
That as a waist doth girdle you about,
By the compulsion of their ordinance
By this time from their fixed beds of lime
Had been dishabited, and wide havoc made
For bloody power to rush upon your peace.
But on the sight of us your lawful king,
Who painfully with much expedient march
Have brought a countercheck before your gates,
To save unscratch'd your city's threatened cheeks,
Behold, the French amazed vouchsafe a parle;
And now, instead of bullets wrapp'd in fire,
To make a shaking fever in your walls,
They shoot but calm words folded up in smoke,
To make a faithless error in your ears:
Which trust accordingly, kind citizens,
And let us in, your king, whose labour'd spirits,
Forwearied in this action of swift speed,
Crave harbourage within your city walls.

KING PHILIP

When I have said, make answer to us both.
Lo, in this right hand, whose protection
Is most divinely vow'd upon the right
Of him it holds, stands young Plantagenet,
Son to the elder brother of this man,
And king o'er him and all that he enjoys:
For this down-trodden equity, we tread
In warlike march these greens before your town,

Being no further enemy to you
Than the constraint of hospitable zeal
In the relief of this oppressed child
Religiously provokes. Be pleased then
To pay that duty which you truly owe
To him that owes it, namely this young prince:
And then our arms, like to a muzzled bear,
Save in aspect, hath all offence seal'd up;
Our cannons' malice vainly shall be spent
Against the invulnerable clouds of heaven;
And with a blessed and unvex'd retire,
With unhack'd swords and helmets all unbruised,
We will bear home that lusty blood again
Which here we came to spout against your town,
And leave your children, wives and you in peace.
But if you fondly pass our proffer'd offer,
'Tis not the roundure of your old-faced walls
Can hide you from our messengers of war,
Though all these English and their discipline
Were harbour'd in their rude circumference.
Then tell us, shall your city call us lord,
In that behalf which we have challenged it?
Or shall we give the signal to our rage
And stalk in blood to our possession?

FIRST CITIZEN
In brief, we are the king of England's subjects:
For him, and in his right, we hold this town.

KING JOHN
Acknowledge then the king, and let me in.

FIRST CITIZEN
That can we not; but he that proves the king,
To him will we prove loyal: till that time
Have we ramm'd up our gates against the world.

KING JOHN
Doth not the crown of England prove the king?
And if not that, I bring you witnesses,
Twice fifteen thousand hearts of England's breed,—

BASTARD
Bastards, and else.

KING JOHN
To verify our title with their lives.

KING PHILIP
As many and as well-born bloods as those—

BASTARD
Some bastards too.

KING PHILIP
Stand in his face to contradict his claim.

FIRST CITIZEN
Till you compound whose right is worthiest,
We for the worthiest hold the right from both.

KING JOHN
Then God forgive the sin of all those souls
That to their everlasting residence,
Before the dew of evening fall, shall fleet,
In dreadful trial of our kingdom's king!

KING PHILIP
Amen, amen! Mount, chevaliers! to arms!

BASTARD
Saint George, that swinged the dragon, and e'er
since

Sits on his horse back at mine hostess' door,
Teach us some fence! [*To* AUSTRIA] Sirrah, were I at
home,
At your den, sirrah, with your lioness,
I would set an ox-head to your lion's hide,
And make a monster of you.

AUSTRIA
           Peace! no more.

BASTARD
O, tremble, for you hear the lion roar.

KING JOHN
Up higher to the plain; where we'll set forth
In best appointment all our regiments.

BASTARD
Speed then, to take advantage of the field.

KING PHILIP
It shall be so; and at the other hill
Command the rest to stand. God and our right!
[*Exeunt*
Here after excursions, enter the HERALD *of France, with
trumpets, to the gates*

FRENCH HERALD
You men of Angiers, open wide your gates,
And let young Arthur, Duke of Bretagne, in,
Who by the hand of France this day hath made
Much work for tears in many an English mother,
Whose sons lie scattered on the bleeding ground:
Many a widow's husband grovelling lies,
Coldly embracing the discoloured earth;
And victory, with little loss, doth play
Upon the dancing banners of the French,
Who are at hand, triumphantly display'd,
To enter conquerors, and to proclaim
Arthur of Bretagne England's king and yours.
Enter ENGLISH HERALD, *with trumpet*

ENGLISH HERALD
Rejoice, you men of Angiers, ring your bells;
King John, your king and England's, doth ap-
proach,
Commander of this hot malicious day:
Their armours, that march'd hence so silver-bright,
Hither return all gilt with Frenchmen's blood;
There stuck no plume in any English crest
That is removed by a staff of France;
Our colours do return in those same hands
That did display them when we first march'd forth:
And, like a jolly troop of huntsmen, come
Our lusty English, all with purpled hands,
Dyed in the dying slaughter of their foes:
Open your gates and give the victors way.

FIRST CITIZEN
Heralds, from off our towers we might behold,
From first to last, the onset and retire
Of both your armies; whose equality
By our best eyes cannot be censured:
Blood hath bought blood and blows have answered
blows;
Strength match'd with strength, and power con-
fronted power:
Both are alike; and both alike we like.

One must prove greatest: while they weigh so even,
We hold our town for neither, yet for both.
    Re-enter the two KINGS, *with their powers, severally*

KING JOHN

France, hast thou yet more blood to cast away?
Say, shall the current of our right run on?
Whose passage, vex'd with thy impediment,
Shall leave his native channel, and o'erswell
With course disturb'd even thy confining shores,
Unless thou let his silver water keep
A peaceful progress to the ocean.

KING PHILIP

England, thou hast not saved one drop of blood,
In this hot trial, more than we of France;
Rather, lost more. And by this hand I swear,
That sways the earth this climate overlooks,
Before we will lay down our just-borne arms,
We'll put thee down, 'gainst whom these arms we
    bear,
Or add a royal number to the dead,
Gracing the scroll that tells of this war's loss
With slaughter coupled to the name of kings.

BASTARD

Ha, majesty! how high thy glory towers,
When the rich blood of kings is set on fire!
O, now doth Death line his dead chaps with steel;
The swords of soldiers are his teeth, his fangs;
And now he feasts, mousing the flesh of men,
In undetermined differences of kings.
Why stand these royal fronts amazed thus?
Cry 'havoc!' kings; back to the stained field,
You equal potents, fiery kindled spirits!
Then let confusion of one part confirm
The other's peace; till then, blows, blood, and
    death!

KING JOHN

Whose party do the townsmen yet admit?

KING PHILIP

Speak, citizens, for England; who's your king?

FIRST CITIZEN

The king of England, when we know the king.

KING PHILIP

Know him in us, that here hold up his right.

KING JOHN

In us, that are our own great deputy,
And bear possession of our person here,
Lord of our presence, Angiers, and of you.

FIRST CITIZEN

A greater power than we denies all this;
And till it be undoubted, we do lock
Our former scruple in our strong-barr'd gates;
King'd of our fears, until our fears, resolved,
Be by some certain king purged and deposed.

BASTARD

By heaven, these scroyles of Angiers flout you, kings,
And stand securely on their battlements,
As in a theatre, whence they gape and point
At your industrious scenes and acts of death.
Your royal presences be ruled by me:
Do like the mutines of Jerusalem,

Be friends awhile and both conjointly bend
Your sharpest deeds of malice on this town:
By east and west let France and England mount
Their battering cannon charged to the mouths,
Till their soul-fearing clamours have brawl'd down
The flinty ribs of this contemptuous city:
I'ld play incessantly upon these jades,
Even till unfenced desolation
Leave them as naked as the vulgar air.
That done, dissever your united strengths,
And part your mingled colours once again;
Turn face to face and bloody point to point;
Then, in a moment, Fortune shall cull forth
Out of one side her happy minion,
To whom in favour she shall give the day,
And kiss him with a glorious victory.
How like you this wild counsel, mighty states?
Smacks it not something of the policy?

KING JOHN

Now, by the sky that hangs above our heads,
I like it well. France, shall we knit our powers
And lay this Angiers even with the ground;
Then after fight who shall be king of it?

BASTARD

An if thou hast the mettle of a king,
Being wrong'd as we are by this peevish town,
Turn thou the mouth of thy artillery,
As we will ours, against these saucy walls;
And when that we have dash'd them to the ground,
Why then defy each other, and pell-mell
Make work upon ourselves, for heaven or hell.

KING PHILIP

Let it be so. Say, where will you assault?

KING JOHN

We from the west will send destruction
Into this city's bosom.

AUSTRIA

I from the north.

KING PHILIP

    Our thunder from the south
Shall rain their drift of bullets on this town.

BASTARD

O prudent discipline! From north to south:
Austria and France shoot in each other's mouth:
I'll stir them to it. Come, away, away!

FIRST CITIZEN

Hear us, great kings: vouchsafe awhile to stay,
And I shall show you peace and fair-faced league;
Win you this city without stroke or wound;
Rescue those breathing lives to die in beds,
That here come sacrifices for the field:
Persever not, but hear me, mighty kings.

KING JOHN

Speak on with favour; we are bent to hear.

FIRST CITIZEN

That daughter there of Spain, the Lady Blanch,
Is niece to England: look upon the years
Of Lewis the Dauphin and that lovely maid:
If lusty love should go in quest of beauty,
Where should he find it fairer than in Blanch?

If zealous love should go in search of virtue,
Where should he find it purer than in Blanch?
If love ambitious sought a match of birth,
Whose veins bound richer blood than Lady Blanch?
Such as she is, in beauty, virtue, birth,
Is the young Dauphin every way complete:
If not complete of, say he is not she;
And she again wants nothing, to name want,
If want it be not that she is not he:
He is the half part of a blessed man,
Left to be finished by such as she;
And she a fair divided excellence,
Whose fulness of perfection lies in him.
O, two such silver currents, when they join,
Do glorify the banks that bound them in;
And two such shores to two such streams made one,
Two such controlling bounds shall you be, kings,
To these two princes, if you marry them.
This union shall do more than battery can
To our fast-closed gates; for at this match,
With swifter spleen than powder can enforce,
The mouth of passage shall we fling wide ope,
And give you entrance: but without this match,
The sea enraged is not half so deaf,
Lions more confident, mountains and rocks
More free from motion, no, not Death himself
In mortal fury half so peremptory,
As we to keep this city.

BASTARD

           Here's a stay
That shakes the rotten carcass of old Death
Out of his rags! Here's a large mouth, indeed,
That spits forth death and mountains, rocks and
    seas,
Talks as familiarly of roaring lions
As maids of thirteen do of puppy-dogs!
What cannoneer begot this lusty blood?
He speaks plain cannon fire, and smoke and bounce;
He gives the bastinado with his tongue:
Our ears are cudgell'd; not a word of his
But buffets better than a fist of France:
Zounds! I was never so bethump'd with words
Since I first call'd my brother's father dad.

ELINOR

Son, list to this conjunction, make this match;
Give with our niece a dowry large enough:
For by this knot thou shalt so surely tie
Thy now unsured assurance to the crown,
That yon green boy shall have no sun to ripe
The bloom that promiseth a mighty fruit.
I see a yielding in the looks of France;
Mark, how they whisper: urge them while their
    souls
Are capable of this ambition,
Lest zeal, now melted by the windy breath
Of soft petitions, pity and remorse,
Cool and congeal again to what it was.

FIRST CITIZEN

Why answer not the double majesties
This friendly treaty of our threaten'd town?

KING PHILIP

Speak England first, that hath been forward first
To speak unto this city: what say you?

KING JOHN

If that the Dauphin there, thy princely son,
Can in this book of beauty read 'I love,'
Her dowry shall weigh equal with a queen:
For Anjou, and fair Touraine, Maine, Poictiers,
And all that we upon this side the sea,
Except this city now by us besieged,
Find liable to our crown and dignity,
Shall gild her bridal bed, and make her rich
In titles, honours and promotions,
As she in beauty, education, blood,
Holds hand with any princess of the world.

KING PHILIP

What say'st thou, boy? look in the lady's face.

LEWIS

I do, my lord; and in her eye I find
A wonder, or a wondrous miracle,
The shadow of myself form'd in her eye;
Which, being but the shadow of your son,
Becomes a sun and makes your son a shadow:
I do protest I never loved myself
Till now infixed I beheld myself
Drawn in the flattering table of her eye.

[Whispers with BLANCH

BASTARD

Drawn in the flattering table of her eye!
  Hang'd in the frowning wrinkle of her brow!
And quarter'd in her heart! he doth espy
  Himself love's traitor: this is pity now,
That, hang'd and drawn and quarter'd, there
    should be
In such a love so vile a lout as he.

BLANCH

My uncle's will in this respect is mine:
If he see aught in you that makes him like,
That any thing he sees, which moves his liking,
I can with ease translate it to my will;
Or if you will, to speak more properly,
I will enforce it easily to my love.
Further I will not flatter you, my lord,
That all I see in you is worthy love,
Than this; that nothing do I see in you,
Though churlish thoughts themselves should be
    your judge,
That I can find should merit any hate.

KING JOHN

What say these young ones? What say you, my niece?

BLANCH

That she is bound in honour still to do
What you in wisdom still vouchsafe to say.

KING JOHN

Speak then, prince Dauphin; can you love this lady?

LEWIS

Nay, ask me if I can refrain from love;
For I do love her most unfeignedly.

KING JOHN

Then do I give Volquessen, Touraine, Maine,

Poictiers, and Anjou, these five provinces,
With her to thee; and this addition more,
Full thirty thousand marks of English coin.
Philip of France, if thou be pleased withal,
Command thy son and daughter to join hands.

KING PHILIP

It likes us well; young princes, close your hands.

AUSTRIA

And your lips too; for I am well assured
That I did so when I was first assured.

KING PHILIP

Now, citizens of Angiers, ope your gates,
Let in that amity which you have made;
For at Saint Mary's chapel presently
The rites of marriage shall be solemnized.
Is not the Lady Constance in this troop?
I know she is not, for this match made up
Her presence would have interrupted much:
Where is she and her son? tell me, who knows.

LEWIS

She is sad and passionate at your highness' tent.

KING PHILIP

And, by my faith, this league that we have made
Will give her sadness very little cure.
Brother of England, how may we content
This widow lady? In her right we came;
Which we, God knows, have turn'd another way,
To our own vantage.

KING JOHN

We will heal up all;
For we'll create young Arthur Duke of Bretagne
And Earl of Richmond; and this rich fair town
We make him lord of. Call the Lady Constance;
Some speedy messenger bid her repair
To our solemnity: I trust we shall,
If not fill·up the measure of her will,
Yet in some measure satisfy her so
That we shall stop her exclamation.
Go we, as well as haste will suffer us,
To this unlook'd for, unprepared pomp.

[Exeunt all but the BASTARD

BASTARD

Mad world! mad kings! mad composition!
John, to stop Arthur's title in the whole,
Hath willingly departed with a part:
And France, whose armour conscience buckled on,
Whom zeal and charity brought to the field
As God's own soldier, rounded in the ear
With that same purpose-changer, that sly devil,
That broker, that still breaks the pate of faith,
That daily break-vow, he that wins of all,
Of kings, of beggars, old men, young men, maids,
Who, having no external thing to lose
But the word 'maid,' cheats the poor maid of that,
That smooth-faced gentleman, tickling Commodity,
Commodity, the bias of the world,
The world, who of itself is peised well.
Made to run even upon even ground,
Till this advantage, this vile-drawing bias,

This sway of motion, this Commodity,
Makes it take head from all indifferency,
From all direction, purpose, course, intent:
And this same bias, this Commodity,
This bawd, this broker, this all-changing word,
Clapp'd on the outward eye of fickle France,
Hath drawn him from his own determined aid,
From a resolved and honourable war,
To a most base and vile-concluded peace.
And why rail I on this Commodity?
But for because he hath not woo'd me yet:
Not that I have the power to clutch my hand,
When his fair angels would salute my palm;
But for my hand, as unattempted yet,
Like a poor beggar, raileth on the rich.
Well, whiles I am a beggar, I will rail
And say there is no sin but to be rich;
And being rich, my virtue then shall be
To say there is no vice but beggary.
Since kings break faith upon commodity,
Gain, be my lord, for I will worship thee.   [Exit

ACT III

SCENE I. *The French* KING'S *pavilion*

Enter CONSTANCE, ARTHUR, *and* SALISBURY

CONSTANCE

Gone to be married! gone to swear a peace!
False blood to false blood join'd! gone to be friends!
Shall Lewis have Blanch, and Blanch those provinces?
It is not so; thou hast misspoke, misheard;
Be well advised, tell o'er thy tale again:
It cannot be; thou dost but say 'tis so:
I trust I may not trust thee; for thy word
Is but the vain breath of a common man:
Believe me, I do not believe thee, man;
I have a king's oath to the contrary.
Thou shalt be punish'd for thus frighting me,
For I am sick and capable of fears,
Oppress'd with wrongs and therefore full of fears,
A widow, husbandless, subject to fears,
A woman, naturally born to fears;
And though thou now confess thou didst but jest,
With my vex'd spirits I cannot take a truce,
But they will quake and tremble all this day.
What dost thou mean by shaking of thy head?
Why dost thou look so sadly on my son?
What means that hand upon that breast of thine?
Why holds thine eye that lamentable rheum,
Like a proud river peering o'er his bounds?
Be these sad signs confirmers of thy words?
Then speak again; not all thy former tale,
But this one word, whether thy tale be true.

SALISBURY

As true as I believe you think them false
That give you cause to prove my saying true.

[424]

CONSTANCE

O, if thou teach me to believe this sorrow,
Teach thou this sorrow how to make me die,
And let belief and life encounter so
As doth the fury of two desperate men
Which in the very meeting fall and die.
Lewis marry Blanch! O boy, then where art thou?
France friend with England, what becomes of me?
Fellow, be gone: I cannot brook thy sight:
This news hath made thee a most ugly man.

SALISBURY

What other harm have I, good lady, done,
But spoke the harm that is by others done?

CONSTANCE

Which harm within itself so heinous is
As it makes harmful all that speak of it.

ARTHUR

I do beseech you, madam, be content.

CONSTANCE

If thou, that bid'st me be content, wert grim,
Ugly and slanderous to thy mother's womb,
Full of unpleasing blots and sightless stains,
Lame, foolish, crooked, swart, prodigious,
Patch'd with foul moles and eye-offending marks,
I would not care, I then would be content,
For then I should not love thee, no, nor thou
Become thy great birth nor deserve a crown.
But thou art fair, and at thy birth, dear boy,
Nature and Fortune join'd to make thee great:
Of Nature's gifts thou mayst with lilies boast
And with the half-blown rose. But Fortune O,
She is corrupted, changed and won from thee;
She adulterates hourly with thine uncle John,
And with her golden hand hath pluck'd on France
To tread down fair respect of sovereignty,
And made his majesty the bawd to theirs.
France is a bawd to Fortune and King John,
That strumpet Fortune, that usurping John!
Tell me, thou fellow, is not France forsworn?
Envenom him with words, or get thee gone,
And leave those woes alone which I alone
Am bound to under-bear.

SALISBURY

Pardon me, madam,
I may not go without you to the kings.

CONSTANCE

Thou mayst, thou shalt; I will not go with thee:
I will instruct my sorrows to be proud;
For grief is proud and makes his owner stoop.
To me and to the state of my great grief
Let kings assemble; for my grief's so great
That no supporter but the huge firm earth
Can hold it up: here I and sorrows sit;
Here is my throne, bid kings come bow to it.

[Seats herself on the ground

Enter KING JOHN, KING PHILIP, LEWIS, BLANCH,
ELINOR, the BASTARD, AUSTRIA, and ATTENDANTS

KING PHILIP

'Tis true, fair daughter; and this blessed day
Ever in France shall be kept festival:

To solemnize this day the glorious sun
Stays in his course and plays the alchemist,
Turning with splendour of his precious eye
The meagre cloddy earth to glittering gold:
The yearly course that brings this day about
Shall never see it but a holiday.

CONSTANCE

A wicked day, and not a holy day!   [Rising
What hath this day deserved? what hath it done,
That it in golden letters should be set
Among the high tides in the calendar?
Nay, rather turn this day out of the week,
This day of shame, oppression, perjury.
Or, if it must stand still, let wives with child
Pray that their burthens may not fall this day,
Lest that their hopes prodigiously be cross'd:
But on this day let seamen fear no wreck;
No bargains break that are not this day made:
This day, all things begun come to ill end,
Yea, faith itself to hollow falsehood change!

KING PHILIP

By heaven, lady, you shall have no cause
To curse the fair proceedings of this day:
Have I not pawn'd to you my majesty?

CONSTANCE

You have beguiled me with a counterfeit
Resembling majesty, which, being touch'd and
tried,
Proves valueless: you are forsworn, forsworn;
You came in arms to spill mine enemies' blood,
But now in arms you strengthen it with yours:
The grappling vigour and rough frown of war
Is cold in amity and painted peace,
And our oppression hath made up this league.
Arm, arm, you heavens, against these perjured
kings!
A widow cries; be husband to me, heavens!
Let not the hours of this ungodly day
Wear out the day in peace; but, ere sunset,
Set armed discord 'twixt these perjured kings!
Hear me, O, hear me!

AUSTRIA

Lady Constance, peace!

CONSTANCE

War! war! no peace! peace is to me a war.
O Lymoges! O Austria! thou dost shame
That bloody spoil: thou slave, thou wretch, thou
coward!
Thou little valiant, great in villany!
Thou ever strong upon the stronger side!
Thou Fortune's champion, that dost never fight
But when her humorous ladyship is by
To teach thee safety! thou art perjured too,
And soothest up greatness. What a fool art thou,
A ramping fool, to brag and stamp and swear
Upon my party! Thou cold-blooded slave,
Hast thou not spoke like thunder on my side,
Been sworn my soldier, bidding me depend
Upon thy stars, thy fortune and thy strength,
And dost thou now fall over to my foes?

Thou wear a lion's hide! doff it for shame,
And hang a calf's-skin on those recreant limbs.

AUSTRIA

O, that a man should speak those words to me!

BASTARD

And hang a calf's-skin on those recreant limbs.

AUSTRIA

Thou darest not say so, villain, for thy life.

BASTARD

And hang a calf's-skin on those recreant limbs.

KING JOHN

We like not this; thou dost forget thyself.

Enter PANDULPH

KING PHILIP

Here comes the holy legate of the pope.

PANDULPH

Hail, you anointed deputies of heaven!
To thee, King John, my holy errand is.
I Pandulph, of fair Milan cardinal,
And from Pope Innocent the legate here,
Do in his name religiously demand
Why thou against the church, our holy mother,
So wilfully dost spurn; and force perforce
Keep Stephen Langton, chosen archbishop
Of Canterbury, from that holy see:
This, in our aforesaid holy father's name,
Pope Innocent, I do demand of thee.

KING JOHN

What earthy name to interrogatories
Can task the free breath of a sacred king?
Thou canst not, cardinal, devise a name
So slight, unworthy and ridiculous,
To charge me to an answer, as the pope.
Tell him this tale; and from the mouth of England
Add thus much more, that no Italian priest
Shall tithe or toll in our dominions;
But as we, under heaven, are supreme head,
So under Him that great supremacy,
Where we do reign, we will alone uphold,
Without the assistance of a mortal hand.
So tell the pope, all reverence set apart
To him and his usurp'd authority.

KING PHILIP

Brother of England, you blaspheme in this.

KING JOHN

Though you and all the kings of Christendom
Are led so grossly by this meddling priest,
Dreading the curse that money may buy out;
And by the merit of vile gold, dross, dust,
Purchase corrupted pardon of a man,
Who in that sale sells pardon from himself,
Though you and all the rest so grossly led
This juggling witchcraft with revenue cherish,
Yet I alone, alone do me oppose
Against the pope and count his friends my foes.

PANDULPH

Then, by the lawful power that I have,
Thou shalt stand cursed and excommunicate:
And blessed shall he be that doth revolt
From his allegiance to an heretic;

And meritorious shall that hand be call'd,
Canonized and worshipp'd as a saint,
That takes away by any secret course
Thy hateful life.

CONSTANCE

O, lawful let it be
That I have room with Rome to curse awhile!
Good father cardinal, cry thou amen
To my keen curses; for without my wrong
There is no tongue hath power to curse him right.

PANDULPH

There's law and warrant, lady, for my curse.

CONSTANCE

And for mine too: when law can do no right,
Let it be lawful that law bar no wrong:
Law cannot give my child his kingdom here,
For he that holds his kingdom holds the law;
Therefore, since law itself is perfect wrong,
How can the law forbid my tongue to curse?

PANDULPH

Philip of France, on peril of a curse,
Let go the hand of that arch-heretic;
And raise the power of France upon his head,
Unless he do submit himself to Rome.

ELINOR

Look'st thou pale, France? do not let go thy hand.

CONSTANCE

Look to that, devil; lest that France repent,
And by disjoining hands, hell lose a soul.

AUSTRIA

King Philip, listen to the cardinal.

BASTARD

And hang a calf's-skin on his recreant limbs.

AUSTRIA

Well, ruffian, I must pocket up these wrongs,
Because—

BASTARD

Your breeches best may carry them.

KING JOHN

Philip, what say'st thou to the cardinal?

CONSTANCE

What should he say, but as the cardinal?

LEWIS

Bethink you, father; for the difference
Is purchase of a heavy curse from Rome,
Or the light loss of England for a friend:
Forgo the easier.

BLANCH

That's the curse of Rome.

CONSTANCE

O Lewis, stand fast! the devil tempts thee here
In likeness of a new untrimmed bride.

BLANCH

The Lady Constance speaks not from her faith,
But from her need.

CONSTANCE

O, if thou grant my need,
Which only lives but by the death of faith,
That need must needs infer this principle,
That faith would live again by death of need.

O then, tread down my need, and faith mounts up;
Keep my need up, and faith is trodden down!

KING JOHN

The king is moved, and answers not to this.

CONSTANCE

O, be removed from him, and answer well!

AUSTRIA

Do so, King Philip; hang no more in doubt.

BASTARD

Hang nothing but a calf's-skin, most sweet lout.

KING PHILIP

I am perplex'd, and know not what to say.

PANDULPH

What canst thou say but will perplex thee more,
If thou stand excommunicate and cursed?

KING PHILIP

Good reverend father, make my person yours,
And tell me how you would bestow yourself.
This royal hand and mine are newly knit,
And the conjunction of our inward souls
Married in league, coupled and link'd together
With all religious strength of sacred vows;
The latest breath that gave the sound of words
Was deep-sworn faith, peace, amity, true love
Between our kingdoms and our royal selves,
And even before this truce, but new before,
No longer than we well could wash our hands
To clap this royal bargain up of peace,
Heaven knows, they were besmear'd and overstain'd
With slaughter's pencil, where revenge did paint
The fearful difference of incensed kings:
And shall these hands, so lately purged of blood,
So newly join'd in love, so strong in both,
Unyoke this seizure and this kind regreet?
Play fast and loose with faith? so jest with heaven,
Make such unconstant children of ourselves,
As now again to snatch our palm from palm,
Unswear faith sworn, and on the marriage-bed
Of smiling peace to march a bloody host,
And make a riot on the gentle brow
Of true sincerity? O, holy sir,
My reverend father, let it not be so!
Out of your grace, devise, ordain, impose
Some gentle order; and then we shall be blest
To do your pleasure and continue friends.

PANDULPH

All form is formless, order orderless,
Save what is opposite to England's love.
Therefore to arms! be champion of our church,
Or let the church, our mother, breathe her curse,
A mother's curse, on her revolting son.
France, thou mayst hold a serpent by the tongue,
A chafed lion by the mortal paw,
A fasting tiger safer by the tooth,
Than keep in peace that hand which thou dost hold.

KING PHILIP

I may disjoin my hand, but not my faith.

PANDULPH

So makest thou faith an enemy to faith;
And like a civil war set'st oath to oath,

Thy tongue against thy tongue. O, let thy vow
First made to heaven, first be to heaven perform'd,
That is, to be the champion of our church.
What since thou sworest is sworn against thyself
And may not be performed by thyself,
For that which thou hast sworn to do amiss
Is not amiss when it is truly done,
And being not done, where doing tends to ill,
The truth is then most done not doing it:
The better act of purposes mistook
Is to mistake again; though indirect,
Yet indirection thereby grows direct,
And falsehood falsehood cures, as fire cools fire
Within the scorched veins of one new-burn'd.
It is religion that doth make vows kept;
But thou hast sworn against religion,
By what thou swear'st against the thing thou
      swear'st,
And makest an oath the surety for thy truth
Against an oath: the truth thou art unsure
To swear, swears only not to be forsworn;
Else what a mockery should it be to swear!
But thou dost swear only to be forsworn;
And most forsworn, to keep what thou dost swear.
Therefore thy later vows against thy first
Is in thyself rebellion to thyself;
And better conquest never canst thou make
Than arm thy constant and thy nobler parts
Against these giddy loose suggestions:
Upon which better part our prayers come in,
If thou vouchsafe them. But if not, then know
The peril of our curses light on thee
So heavy as thou shalt not shake them off,
But in despair die under their black weight.

AUSTRIA

Rebellion, flat rebellion!

BASTARD

                    Will't not be?
Will not a calf's-skin stop that mouth of thine?

LEWIS

Father, to arms!

BLANCH

                    Upon thy wedding-day?
Against the blood that thou hast married?
What, shall our feast be kept with slaughtered men?
Shall braying trumpets and loud churlish drums,
Clamours of hell, be measures to our pomp?
O husband, hear me! ay, alack, how new
Is husband in my mouth! even for that name,
Which till this time my tongue did ne'er pronounce,
Upon my knee I beg, go not to arms
Against mine uncle.

CONSTANCE

                    O, upon my knee,
Made hard with kneeling, I do pray to thee,
Thou virtuous Dauphin, alter not the doom
Forethought by heaven!

BLANCH

Now shall I see thy love: what motive may
Be stronger with thee than the name of wife?

CONSTANCE

That which upholdeth him that thee upholds,
His honour: O, thine honour, Lewis, thine honour!

LEWIS

I muse your majesty doth seem so cold,
When such profound respects do pull you on.

PANDULPH

I will denounce a curse upon his head.

KING PHILIP

Thou shalt not need. England, I will fall from thee.

CONSTANCE

O fair return of banish'd majesty!

ELINOR

O foul revolt of French inconstancy!

KING JOHN

France, thou shalt rue this hour within this hour.

BASTARD

Old Time the clock-setter, that bald sexton Time,
Is it as he will? well then, France shall rue.

BLANCH

The sun's o'ercast with blood: fair day, adieu!
Which is the side that I must go withal?
I am with both: each army hath a hand;
And in their rage, I having hold of both,
They whirl asunder and dismember me.
Husband, I cannot pray that thou mayst win;
Uncle, I needs must pray that thou mayst lose;
Father, I may not wish the fortune thine;
Grandam, I will not wish thy wishes thrive:
Whoever wins, on that side shall I lose;
Assured loss before the match be play'd.

LEWIS

Lady, with me, with me thy fortune lies.

BLANCH

There where my fortune lives, there my life dies.

KING JOHN

Cousin, go draw our puissance together.
                                        [Exit BASTARD
France, I am burn'd up with inflaming wrath;
A rage whose heat hath this condition,
That nothing can allay, nothing but blood,
The blood, and dearest-valued blood, of France.

KING PHILIP

Thy rage shall burn thee up, and thou shalt turn
To ashes, ere our blood shall quench that fire:
Look to thyself, thou art in jeopardy.

KING JOHN

No more than he that threats. To arms let's hie!
                                        [Exeunt

SCENE II. *The same. Plains near Angiers*

Alarums, excursions. Enter the BASTARD, *with* AUSTRIA'S *head*

BASTARD

Now, by my life, this day grows wondrous hot;
Some airy devil hovers in the sky,
And pours down mischief. Austria's head lie there,
While Philip breathes.

Enter KING JOHN, ARTHUR, *and* HUBERT

KING JOHN

Hubert, keep this boy. Philip, make up:
My mother is assailed in our tent,
And ta'en, I fear.

BASTARD

                My lord, I rescued her;
Her highness is in safety, fear you not:
But on, my liege; for very little pains
Will bring this labour to an happy end.   [*Exeunt*

SCENE III. *The same*

Alarums, excursions, retreat. Enter KING JOHN, ELINOR,
ARTHUR, *the* BASTARD, HUBERT, *and* LORDS

KING JOHN

[*To* ELINOR] So shall it be; your grace shall stay be-
     hind
So strongly guarded. [*To* ARTHUR] Cousin, look not
     sad:
Thy grandam loves thee; and thy uncle will
As dear be to thee as thy father was.

ARTHUR

O, this will make my mother die with grief!

KING JOHN

[*To the* BASTARD] Cousin, away for England! haste
     before:
And, ere our coming, see thou shake the bags
Of hoarding abbots; imprisoned angels
Set at liberty: the fat ribs of peace
Must by the hungry now be fed upon:
Use our commission in his utmost force.

BASTARD

Bell, book, and candle shall not drive me back,
When gold and silver becks me to come on.
' leave your highness. Grandam, I will pray,
If ever I remember to be holy,
For your fair safety; so, I kiss your hand.

ELINOR

Farewell, gentle cousin.

KING JOHN

                Coz, farewell.
                                        [*Exit* BASTARD

ELINOR

Come hither, little kinsman; hark, a word.

KING JOHN

Come hither, Hubert. O my gentle Hubert,
We owe thee much! within this wall of flesh
There is a soul counts thee her creditor,
And with advantage means to pay thy love:
And, my good friend, thy voluntary oath
Lives in this bosom, dearly cherished.
Give me thy hand. I had a thing to say,
But I will fit it with some better time.
By heaven, Hubert, I am almost ashamed
To say what good respect I have of thee.

HUBERT

I am much bounden to your majesty.

KING JOHN

Good friend, thou hast no cause to say so yet,
But thou shalt have; and creep time ne'er so slow,
Yet it shall come for me to do thee good.
I had a thing to say, but let it go:
The sun is in the heaven, and the proud day,
Attended with the pleasures of the world,
Is all too wanton and too full of gawds
To give me audience: if the midnight bell
Did, with his iron tongue and brazen mouth,
Sound on into the drowsy ear of night;
If this same were a churchyard where we stand,
And thou possessed with a thousand wrongs;
Or if that surly spirit, melancholy,
Had baked thy blood and made it heavy-thick,
Which else runs tickling up and down the veins,
Making that idiot, laughter, keep men's eyes
And strain their cheeks to idle merriment,
A passion hateful to my purposes;
Or if that thou couldst see me without eyes,
Hear me without thine ears, and make reply
Without a tongue, using conceit alone,
Without eyes, ears and harmful sound of words;
Then, in despite of brooded watchful day,
I would into thy bosom pour my thoughts:
But, ah, I will not! yet I love thee well;
And, by my troth, I think thou lovest me well.

HUBERT

So well, that what you bid me undertake,
Though that my death were adjunct to my act,
By heaven, I would do it.

KING JOHN

          Do not I know thou wouldst?
Good Hubert, Hubert, Hubert, throw thine eye
On yon young boy: I'll tell thee what, my friend,
He is a very serpent in my way;
And wheresoe'er this foot of mine doth tread,
He lies before me: dost thou understand me?
Thou art his keeper.

HUBERT

          And I'll keep him so,
That he shall not offend your majesty.

KING JOHN

                 Death.

HUBERT

My lord?

KING JOHN

  A grave.

HUBERT

      He shall not live.

KING JOHN

             Enough.
I could be merry now. Hubert, I love thee;
Well, I'll not say what I intend for thee:
Remember. Madam, fare you well:
I'll send those powers o'er to your majesty.

ELINOR

My blessing go with thee!

KING JOHN

          For England, cousin, go:

Hubert shall be your man, attend on you
With all true duty. On toward Calais, ho! [*Exeunt*

SCENE IV. *The same. The* FRENCH KING'S *tent*

Enter KING PHILIP, LEWIS, PANDULPH, *and*
ATTENDANTS

KING PHILIP

So, by a roaring tempest on the flood,
A whole armado of convicted sail
Is scattered and disjoin'd from fellowship.

PANDULPH

Courage and comfort! all shall yet go well.

KING PHILIP

What can go well, when we have run so ill?
Are we not beaten? Is not Angiers lost?
Arthur ta'en prisoner? divers dear friends slain?
And bloody England into England gone,
O'erbearing interruption, spite of France?

LEWIS

What he hath won, that hath he fortified:
So hot a speed with such advice disposed,
Such temperate order in so fierce a cause,
Doth want example: who hath read or heard
Of any kindred action like to this?

KING PHILIP

Well could I bear that England had this praise,
So we could find some pattern of our shame.

Enter CONSTANCE

Look, who comes here! a grave unto a soul;
Holding the eternal spirit, against her will,
In the vile prison of afflicted breath.
I prithee, lady, go away with me.

CONSTANCE

Lo, now! now see the issue of your peace.

KING PHILIP

Patience, good lady! comfort, gentle Constance!

CONSTANCE

No, I defy all counsel, all redress,
But that which ends all counsel, true redress,
Death, death; O amiable lovely death!
Thou odoriferous stench! sound rottenness!
Arise forth from the couch of lasting night,
Thou hate and terror to prosperity,
And I will kiss thy detestable bones
And put my eyeballs in thy vaulty brows
And ring these fingers with thy household worms
And stop this gap of breath with fulsome dust
And be a carrion monster like thyself:
Come, grin on me, and I will think thou smilest,
And buss thee as thy wife. Misery's love,
O, come to me!

KING PHILIP

        O fair affliction, peace!

CONSTANCE

No, no, I will not, having breath to cry:
O, that my tongue were in the thunder's mouth!
Then with a passion would I shake the world;
And rouse from sleep that fell anatomy

Which cannot hear a lady's feeble voice,
Which scorns a modern invocation.

PANDULPH

Lady, you utter madness, and not sorrow.

CONSTANCE

Thou art not holy to belie me so;
I am not mad: this hair I tear is mine;
My name is Constance; I was Geffrey's wife;
Young Arthur is my son, and he is lost:
I am not mad: I would to heaven I were!
For then, 'tis like I should forget myself:
O, if I could, what grief should I forget!
Preach some philosophy to make me mad,
And thou shalt be canonized, cardinal;
For, being not mad but sensible of grief,
My reasonable part produces reason
How I may be deliver'd of these woes,
And teaches me to kill or hang myself:
If I were mad, I should forget my son,
Or madly think a babe of clouts were he:
I am not mad; too well, too well I feel
The different plague of each calamity.

KING PHILIP

Bind up those tresses. O, what love I note
In the fair multitude of those her hairs!
Where but by chance a silver drop hath fallen,
Even to that drop ten thousand wiry friends
Do glue themselves in sociable grief,
Like true, inseparable, faithful loves,
Sticking together in calamity.

CONSTANCE

To England, if you will.

KING PHILIP

Bind up your hairs.

CONSTANCE

Yes, that I will; and wherefore will I do it?
I tore them from their bonds and cried aloud,
'O that these hands could so redeem my son,
As they have given these hairs their liberty!'
But now I envy at their liberty,
And will again commit them to their bonds,
Because my poor child is a prisoner.
And, father cardinal, I have heard you say
That we shall see and know our friends in heaven:
If that be true, I shall see my boy again;
For since the birth of Cain, the first male child,
To him that did but yesterday suspire,
There was not such a gracious creature born.
But now will canker sorrow eat my bud
And chase the native beauty from his cheek
And he will look as hollow as a ghost,
As dim and meagre as an ague's fit,
And so he'll die; and, rising so again,
When I shall meet him in the court of heaven
I shall not know him: therefore never, never
Must I behold my pretty Arthur more.

PANDULPH

You hold too heinous a respect of grief.

CONSTANCE

He talks to me that never had a son.

KING PHILIP

You are as fond of grief as of your child.

CONSTANCE

Grief fills the room up of my absent child,
Lies in his bed, walks up and down with me,
Puts on his pretty looks, repeats his words,
Remembers me of all his gracious parts,
Stuffs out his vacant garments with his form;
Then have I reason to be fond of grief.
Fare you well: had you such a loss as I,
I could give better comfort than you do.
I will not keep this form upon my head,
When there is such disorder in my wit.
O Lord! my boy, my Arthur, my fair son!
My life, my joy, my food, my all the world!
My widow-comfort, and my sorrows' cure! [Exit

KING PHILIP

I fear some outrage, and I'll follow her. [Exit

LEWIS

There's nothing in this world can make me joy:
Life is as tedious as a twice-told tale
Vexing the dull ear of a drowsy man;
And bitter shame hath spoil'd the sweet world's
　　taste,
That it yields nought but shame and bitterness.

PANDULPH

Before the curing of a strong disease,
Even in the instant of repair and health,
The fit is strongest; evils that take leave,
On their departure most of all show evil:
What have you lost by losing of this day?

LEWIS

All days of glory, joy and happiness.

PANDULPH

If you had won it, certainly you had.
No, no; when Fortune means to men most good,
She looks upon them with a threatening eye.
'Tis strange to think how much King John hath
　　lost
In this which he accounts so clearly won:
Are not you grieved that Arthur is his prisoner?

LEWIS

As heartily as he is glad he hath him.

PANDULPH

Your mind is all as youthful as your blood.
Now hear me speak with a prophetic spirit;
For even the breath of what I mean to speak
Shall blow each dust, each straw, each little rub,
Out of the path which shall directly lead
Thy foot to England's throne; and therefore mark.
John hath seized Arthur; and it cannot be
That, whiles warm life plays in that infant's veins,
The misplaced John should entertain an hour,
One minute, nay, one quiet breath of rest.
A sceptre snatch'd with an unruly hand
Must be as boisterously maintain'd as gain'd;
And he that stands upon a slippery place
Makes nice of no vile hold to stay him up:
That John may stand, then Arthur needs must fall;
So be it, for it cannot be but so.

LEWIS

But what shall I gain by young Arthur's fall?

PANDULPH

You, in the right of Lady Blanch your wife,
May then make all the claim that Arthur did.

LEWIS

And lose it, life and all, as Arthur did.

PANDULPH

How green you are and fresh in this old world!
John lays you plots; the times conspire with you;
For he that steeps his safety in true blood
Shall find but bloody safety and untrue.
This act so evilly born shall cool the hearts
Of all his people and freeze up their zeal,
That none so small advantage shall step forth
To check his reign, but they will cherish it;
No natural exhalation in the sky,
No scope of nature, no distemper'd day,
No common wind, no customed event,
But they will pluck away his natural cause
And call them meteors, prodigies and signs,
Abortives, presages and tongues of heaven,
Plainly denouncing vengeance upon John.

LEWIS

May be he will not touch young Arthur's life,
But hold himself safe in his prisonment.

PANDULPH

O, sir, when he shall hear of your approach,
If that young Arthur be not gone already,
Even at that news he dies; and then the hearts
Of all his people shall revolt from him,
And kiss the lips of unacquainted change,
And pick strong matter of revolt and wrath
Out of the bloody fingers' ends of John.
Methinks I see this hurly all on foot:
And, O, what better matter breeds for you
Than I have named! The bastard Faulconbridge
Is now in England, ransacking the church,
Offending charity: if but a dozen French
Were there in arms, they would be as a call
To train ten thousand English to their side,
Or as a little snow, tumbled about,
Anon becomes a mountain. O noble Dauphin,
Go with me to the king: 'tis wonderful
What may be wrought out of their discontent,
Now that their souls are topful of offence.
For England go: I will whet on the king.

LEWIS

Strong reasons make strong actions: let us go:
If you say ay, the king will not say no.   [Exeunt

ACT IV

SCENE I. *A room in a castle*

Enter HUBERT *and* EXECUTIONERS

HUBERT

Heat me these irons hot; and look thou stand

Within the arras: when I strike my foot
Upon the bosom of the ground, rush forth,
And bind the boy which you shall find with me
Fast to the chair: be heedful: hence, and watch.

FIRST EXECUTIONER

I hope your warrant will bear out the deed.

HUBERT

Uncleanly scruples! fear not you: look to 't.
    [*Exeunt* EXECUTIONERS
Young lad, come forth; I have to say with you.
    Enter ARTHUR

ARTHUR

Good morrow, Hubert.

HUBERT

    Good morrow, little prince.

ARTHUR

As little prince, having so great a title
To be more prince, as may be. You are sad.

HUBERT

Indeed, I have been merrier.

ARTHUR

    Mercy on me!
Methinks no body should be sad but I:
Yet, I remember, when I was in France,
Young gentlemen would be as sad as night,
Only for wantonness. By my christendom,
So I were out of prison and kept sheep,
I should be as merry as the day is long;
And so I would be here, but that I doubt
My uncle practises more harm to me:
He is afraid of me and I of him:
Is it my fault that I was Geffrey's son?
No, indeed, is't not; and I would to heaven
I were your son, so you would love me, Hubert.

HUBERT

[*Aside*] If I talk to him, with his innocent prate
He will awake my mercy which lies dead:
Therefore I will be sudden and dispatch.

ARTHUR

Are you sick, Hubert? you look pale to-day:
In sooth, I would you were a little sick,
That I might sit all night and watch with you:
I warrant I love you more than you do me.

HUBERT

[*Aside*] His words do take possession of my bosom.
Read here, young Arthur.   [*Showing a paper*
    [*Aside*] How now, foolish rheum!
Turning dispiteous torture out of door!
I must be brief, lest resolution drop
Out at mine eyes in tender womanish tears.
Can you not read it? is it not fair writ?

ARTHUR

Too fairly, Hubert, for so foul effect:
Must you with hot irons burn out both mine eyes?

HUBERT

Young boy, I must.

ARTHUR

    And will you?

HUBERT

    And I will.

ARTHUR

Have you the heart? When your head did but ache,
I knit my handkercher about your brows,
The best I had, a princess wrought it me,
And I did never ask it you again;
And with my hand at midnight held your head,
And like the watchful minutes to the hour,
Still and anon cheer'd up the heavy time,
Saying, 'What lack you?' and 'Where lies your
    grief?'
Or 'What good love may I perform for you?'
Many a poor man's son would have lien still
And ne'er have spoke a loving word to you;
But you at your sick service had a prince.
Nay, you may think my love was crafty love,
And call it cunning: do, an if you will:
If heaven be pleased that you must use me ill,
Why then you must. Will you put out mine eyes?
These eyes that never did nor never shall
So much as frown on you.

HUBERT

                    I have sworn to do it;
And with hot irons must I burn them out.

ARTHUR

Ah, none but in this iron age would do it!
The iron of itself, though heat red-hot,
Approaching near these eyes, would drink my tears
And quench his fiery indignation
Even in the matter of mine innocence;
Nay, after that, consume away in rust,
But for containing fire to harm mine eye.
Are you more stubborn-hard than hammer'd iron?
An if an angel should have come to me
And told me Hubert should put out mine eyes,
I would not have believed him,—no tongue but
    Hubert's.

HUBERT

Come forth.   [Stamps
    Re-enter EXECUTIONERS, with a cord, irons, &c.
Do as I bid you do.

ARTHUR

O, save me, Hubert, save me! my eyes are out
Even with the fierce looks of these bloody men.

HUBERT

Give me the iron, I say, and bind him here.

ARTHUR

Alas, what need you be so boisterous-rough?
I will not struggle, I will stand stone-still.
For heaven sake, Hubert, let me not be bound!
Nay, hear me, Hubert, drive these men away,
And I will sit as quiet as a lamb;
I will not stir, nor wince, nor speak a word,
Nor look upon the iron angerly:
Thrust but these men away, and I'll forgive you,
Whatever torment you do put me to.

HUBERT

Go, stand within; let me alone with him.

FIRST EXECUTIONER

I am best pleased to be from such a deed.
                    [Exeunt EXECUTIONERS

ARTHUR

Alas, I then have chid away my friend!
He hath a stern look, but a gentle heart:
Let him come back, that his compassion may
Give life to yours.

HUBERT

            Come, boy, prepare yourself.

ARTHUR

Is there no remedy?

HUBERT

                None, but to lose your eyes.

ARTHUR

O heaven, that there were but a mote in yours,
A grain, a dust, a gnat, a wandering hair,
Any annoyance in that precious sense!
Then, feeling what small things are boisterous there,
Your vile intent must needs seem horrible.

HUBERT

Is this your promise? go to, hold your tongue.

ARTHUR

Hubert, the utterance of a brace of tongues
Must needs want pleading for a pair of eyes:
Let me not hold my tongue, let me not, Hubert;
Or, Hubert, if you will, cut out my tongue,
So I may keep mine eyes: O, spare mine eyes,
Though to no use but still to look on you!
Lo, by my troth, the instrument is cold
And would not harm me.

HUBERT

                I can heat it, boy.

ARTHUR

No, in good sooth; the fire is dead with grief,
Being create for comfort, to be used
In undeserved extremes: see else yourself;
There is no malice in this burning coal;
The breath of heaven hath blown his spirit out
And strew'd repentant ashes on his head.

HUBERT

But with my breath I can revive it, boy.

ARTHUR

An if you do, you will but make it blush
And glow with shame of your proceedings, Hubert:
Nay, it perchance will sparkle in your eyes;
And like a dog that is compell'd to fight,
Snatch at his master that doth tarre him on.
All things that you should use to do me wrong
Deny their office: only you do lack
That mercy which fierce fire and iron extends,
Creatures of note for mercy-lacking uses.

HUBERT

Well, see to live; I will not touch thine eye
For all the treasure that thine uncle owes:
Yet am I sworn and I did purpose, boy,
With this same very iron to burn them out.

ARTHUR

O, now you look like Hubert! all this while
You were disguised.

HUBERT

            Peace; no more. Adieu.
Your uncle must not know but you are dead;

I'll fill these dogged spies with false reports:
And, pretty child, sleep doubtless and secure,
That Hubert, for the wealth of all the world,
Will not offend thee.

ARTHUR

O heaven! I thank you, Hubert.

HUBERT

Silence; no more: go closely in with me:
Much danger do I undergo for thee.   [*Exeunt*

SCENE II. KING JOHN's *palace*

Enter KING JOHN, PEMBROKE, SALISBURY, *and other*
LORDS

KING JOHN

Here once again we sit, once again crown'd,
And look'd upon, I hope, with cheerful eyes.

PEMBROKE

This 'once again,' but that your highness pleased,
Was once superfluous: you were crown'd before,
And that high royalty was ne'er pluck'd off,
The faiths of men ne'er stained with revolt;
Fresh expectation troubled not the land
With any long'd-for change or better state.

SALISBURY

Therefore, to be possess'd with double pomp,
To guard a title that was rich before,
To gild refined gold, to paint the lily,
To throw a perfume on the violet,
To smooth the ice, or add another hue
Unto the rainbow, or with taper-light
To seek the beauteous eye of heaven to garnish,
Is wasteful and ridiculous excess.

PEMBROKE

But that your royal pleasure must be done,
This act is as an ancient tale new told,
And in the last repeating troublesome,
Being urged at a time unseasonable.

SALISBURY

In this the antique and well noted face
Of plain old form is much disfigured;
And, like a shifted wind unto a sail,
It makes the course of thoughts to fetch about,
Startles and frights consideration,
Makes sound opinion sick and truth suspected,
For putting on so new a fashion'd robe.

PEMBROKE

When workmen strive to do better than well,
They do confound their skill in covetousness;
And oftentimes excusing of a fault
Doth make the fault the worse by the excuse,
As patches set upon a little breach
Discredit more in hiding of the fault
Than did the fault before it was so patch'd.

SALISBURY

To this effect, before you were new crown'd,
We breathed our counsel: but it pleased your highness

To overbear it, and we are all well pleased,
Since all and every part of what we would
Doth make a stand at what your highness will.

KING JOHN

Some reasons of this double coronation
I have possess'd you with and think them strong;
And more, more strong, then lesser is my fear,
I shall indue you with: meantime but ask
What you would have reform'd that is not well,
And well shall you perceive how willingly
I will both hear and grant you your requests.

PEMBROKE

Then I, as one that am the tongue of these,
To sound the purposes of all their hearts,
Both for myself and them, but, chief of all,
Your safety, for the which myself and them
Bend their best studies, heartily request
The enfranchisement of Arthur; whose restraint
Doth move the murmuring lips of discontent
To break into this dangerous argument,—
If what in rest you have in right you hold,
Why then your fears, which as they say, attend
The steps of wrong, should move you to mew up
Your tender kinsman, and to choke his days
With barbarous ignorance, and deny his youth
The rich advantage of good exercise.
That the time's enemies may not have this
To grace occasions, let it be our suit
That you have bid us ask his liberty;
Which for our goods we do no further ask
Than whereupon our weal, on you depending,
Counts it your weal he have his liberty.

Enter HUBERT

KING JOHN

Let it be so: I do commit his youth
To your direction. Hubert, what news with you?
     [*Taking him apart*

PEMBROKE

This is the man should do the bloody deed;
He show'd his warrant to a friend of mine:
The image of a wicked heinous fault
Lives in his eye; that close aspect of his
Does show the mood of a much troubled breast;
And I do fearfully believe 'tis done,
What we so fear'd he had a charge to do.

SALISBURY

The colour of the king doth come and go
Between his purpose and his conscience,
Like heralds 'twixt two dreadful battles set:
His passion is so ripe, it needs must break.

PEMBROKE

And when it breaks, I fear will issue thence
The foul corruption of a sweet child's death.

KING JOHN

We cannot hold mortality's strong hand:
Good lords, although my will to give is living,
The suit which you demand is gone and dead:
He tells us Arthur is deceased to-night.

SALISBURY
Indeed we fear'd his sickness was past cure.

PEMBROKE
Indeed we heard how near his death he was,
Before the child himself felt he was sick:
This must be answer'd either here or hence.

KING JOHN
Why do you bend such solemn brows on me?
Think you I bear the shears of destiny?
Have I commandment on the pulse of life?

SALISBURY
It is apparent foul-play; and 'tis shame
That greatness should so grossly offer it:
So thrive it in your game! and so, farewell.

PEMBROKE
Stay yet, Lord Salisbury; I'll go with thee,
And find the inheritance of this poor child,
His little kingdom of a forced grave.
That blood which owed the breadth of all this isle,
Three foot of it doth hold: bad world the while!
This must not be thus borne: this will break out
To all our sorrows, and ere long I doubt.
                              [Exeunt LORDS

KING JOHN
They burn in indignation. I repent:
There is no sure foundation set on blood,
No certain life achieved by others' death.
              Enter a MESSENGER
A fearful eye thou hast: where is that blood
That I have seen inhabit in those cheeks?
So foul a sky clears not without a storm:
Pour down thy weather: how goes all in France?

MESSENGER
From France to England. Never such a power
For any foreign preparation
Was levied in the body of a land.
The copy of your speed is learn'd by them;
For when you should be told they do prepare,
The tidings comes that they are all arrived.

KING JOHN
O, where hath our intelligence been drunk?
Where hath it slept? Where is my mother's care,
That such an army could be drawn in France,
And she not hear of it?

MESSENGER
                    My liege, her ear
Is stopp'd with dust; the first of April died
Your noble mother: and, as I hear, my lord,
The Lady Constance in a frenzy died
Three days before: but this from rumour's tongue
I idly heard; if true or false I know not.

KING JOHN
Withhold thy speed, dreadful occasion!
O, make a league with me, till I have pleased
My discontented peers! What! mother dead!
How wildly then walks my estate in France!
Under whose conduct came those powers of France
That thou for truth givest out are landed here?

MESSENGER
Under the Dauphin.

KING JOHN
                Thou hast made me giddy
With these ill tidings.
        Enter the BASTARD and PETER of Pomfret
                    Now, what says the world
To your proceedings? do not seek to stuff
My head with more ill news, for it is full.

BASTARD
But if you be afeard to hear the worst,
Then let the worst unheard fall on your head.

KING JOHN
Bear with me, cousin; for I was amazed
Under the tide: but now I breathe again
Aloft the flood, and can give audience
To any tongue, speak it of what it will.

BASTARD
How I have sped among the clergy-men,
The sums I have collected shall express.
But as I travell'd hither through the land,
I find the people strangely fantasied;
Possess'd with rumours, full of idle dreams,
Not knowing what they fear, but full of fear:
And here's a prophet, that I brought with me
From forth the streets of Pomfret, whom I found
With many hundreds treading on his heels;
To whom he sung, in rude harsh-sounding rhymes,
That, ere the next Ascension-day at noon,
Your highness should deliver up your crown.

KING JOHN
Thou idle dreamer, wherefore didst thou so?

PETER
Foreknowing that the truth will fall out so.

KING JOHN
Hubert, away with him; imprison him;
And on that day at noon, whereon he says
I shall yield up my crown, let him be hang'd.
Deliver him to safety; and return,
For I must use thee.   [Exit HUBERT with PETER
                O my gentle cousin,
Hear'st thou the news abroad, who are arrived?

BASTARD
The French, my lord; men's mouths are full of it:
Besides, I met Lord Bigot and Lord Salisbury,
With eyes as red as new-enkindled fire,
And others more, going to seek the grave
Of Arthur, whom they say is kill'd to-night
On your suggestion.

KING JOHN
              Gentle kinsman, go,
And thrust thyself into their companies:
I have a way to win their loves again;
Bring them before me.

BASTARD
        I will seek them out.

KING JOHN
Nay, but make haste; the better foot before.

O, let me have no subject enemies,
When adverse foreigners affright my towns
With dreadful pomp of stout invasion!
Be Mercury, set feathers to thy heels,
And fly like thought from them to me again.

BASTARD
The spirit of the time shall teach me speed.   [*Exit*

KING JOHN
Spoke like a sprightful noble gentleman.
Go after him; for he perhaps shall need
Some messenger betwixt me and the peers;
And be thou he.

MESSENGER
      With all my heart, my liege.   [*Exit*

KING JOHN
My mother dead!

Re-enter HUBERT

HUBERT
My lord, they say five moons were seen to-night;
Four fixed, and the fifth did whirl about
The other four in wondrous motion.

KING JOHN
Five moons!

HUBERT
      Old men and beldams in the streets
Do prophesy upon it dangerously:
Young Arthur's death is common in their mouths:
And when they talk of him, they shake their heads
And whisper one another in the ear;
And he that speaks doth gripe the hearer's wrist,
Whilst he that hears makes fearful action,
With wrinkled brows, with nods, with rolling eyes.
I saw a smith stand with his hammer, thus,
The whilst his iron did on the anvil cool,
With open mouth swallowing a tailor's news;
Who, with his shears and measure in his hand,
Standing on slippers, which his nimble haste
Had falsely thrust upon contrary feet,
Told of a many thousand warlike French
That were embattailed and rank'd in Kent:
Another lean unwash'd artificer
Cuts off his tale and talks of Arthur's death.

KING JOHN
Why seek'st thou to possess me with these fears?
Why urgest thou so oft young Arthur's death?
Thy hand hath murder'd him: I had a mighty cause
To wish him dead, but thou hadst none to kill him.

HUBERT
No had, my lord! why, did you not provoke me?

KING JOHN
It is the curse of kings to be attended
By slaves that take their humours for a warrant
To break within the bloody house of life,
And on the winking of authority
To understand a law, to know the meaning
Of dangerous majesty, when perchance it frowns
More upon humour than advised respect.

HUBERT
Here is your hand and seal for what I did.

KING JOHN
O, when the last account 'twixt heaven and earth
Is to be made, then shall this hand and seal
Witness against us to damnation!
How oft the sight of means to do ill deeds
Make deeds ill done! Hadst not thou been by,
A fellow by the hand of nature mark'd,
Quoted and sign'd to do a deed of shame,
This murder had not come into my mind:
But taking note of thy abhorr'd aspect,
Finding thee fit for bloody villany,
Apt, liable to be employ'd in danger,
I faintly broke with thee of Arthur's death;
And thou, to be endeared to a king,
Made it no conscience to destroy a prince.

HUBERT
My lord,—

KING JOHN
Hadst thou but shook thy head or made a pause
When I spake darkly what I purposed,
Or turn'd an eye of doubt upon my face,
As bid me tell my tale in express words,
Deep shame had struck me dumb, made me break
     off,
And those thy fears might have wrought fears in me:
But thou didst understand me by my signs
And didst in signs again parley with sin;
Yea, without stop, didst let thy heart consent,
And consequently thy rude hand to act
The deed, which both our tongues held vile to name.
Out of my sight, and never see me more!
My nobles leave me; and my state is braved,
Even at my gates, with ranks of foreign powers:
Nay, in the body of this fleshly land,
This kingdom, this confine of blood and breath,
Hostility and civil tumult reigns
Between my conscience and my cousin's death.

HUBERT
Arm you against your other enemies,
I'll make a peace between your soul and you.
Young Arthur is alive: this hand of mine
Is yet a maiden and an innocent hand,
Not painted with the crimson spots of blood.
Within this bosom never enter'd yet
The dreadful motion of a murderous thought;
And you have slander'd nature in my form,
Which, howsoever rude exteriorly,
Is yet the cover of a fairer mind
Than to be butcher of an innocent child.

KING JOHN
Doth Arthur live? O, haste thee to the peers,
Throw this report on their incensed rage,
And make them tame to their obedience!
Forgive the comment that my passion made
Upon thy feature; for my rage was blind,
And foul imaginary eyes of blood
Presented thee more hideous than thou art.
O, answer not, but to my closet bring
The angry lords with all expedient haste.
I conjure thee but slowly; run more fast.   [*Exeunt*

SCENE III. *Before the castle*

Enter ARTHUR, *on the walls*

ARTHUR
The wall is high, and yet will I leap down:
Good ground, be pitiful and hurt me not!
There's few or none do know me: if they did,
This ship-boy's semblance hath disguised me quite.
I am afraid; and yet I'll venture it.
If I get down, and do not break my limbs,
I'll find a thousand shifts to get away:
As good to die and go, as die and stay.   [*Leaps down*
O me! my uncle's spirit is in these stones:
Heaven take my soul, and England keep my bones!
                                          [*Dies*

Enter PEMBROKE, SALISBURY, *and* BIGOT

SALISBURY
Lords, I will meet him at Saint Edmundsbury:
It is our safety, and we must embrace
This gentle offer of the perilous time.

PEMBROKE
Who brought that letter from the cardinal?

SALISBURY
The Count Melun, a noble lord of France;
Whose private with me of the Dauphin's love
Is much more general than these lines import.

BIGOT
To-morrow morning let us meet him then.

SALISBURY
Or rather then set forward; for 'twill be
Two long days' journey, lords, or ere we meet.

Enter the BASTARD

BASTARD
Once more to-day well met, distemper'd lords!
The king by me requests your presence straight.

SALISBURY
The king hath dispossess'd himself of us:
We will not line his thin bestained cloak
With our pure honours, nor attend the foot
That leaves the print of blood where'er it walks.
Return and tell him so: we know the worst.

BASTARD
Whate'er you think, good words, I think, were best.

SALISBURY
Our griefs, and not our manners, reason now.

BASTARD
But there is little reason in your grief;
Therefore 'twere reason you had manners now.

PEMBROKE
Sir, sir, impatience hath his privilege.

BASTARD
'Tis true, to hurt his master, no man else.

SALISBURY
This is the prison. What is he lies here?
                                  [*Seeing* ARTHUR

PEMBROKE
O death, made proud with pure and princely
    beauty!
The earth had not a hole to hide this deed.

SALISBURY
Murder, as hating what himself hath done,
Doth lay it open to urge on revenge.

BIGOT
Or, when he doom'd this beauty to a grave,
Found it too precious-princely for a grave.

SALISBURY
Sir Richard, what think you? have you beheld,
Or have you read or heard? or could you think?
Or do you almost think, although you see,
That you do see? could thought, without this object,
Form such another? This is the very top,
The height, the crest, or crest unto the crest,
Of murder's arms: this is the bloodiest shame,
The wildest savagery, the vilest stroke,
That ever wall-eyed wrath or staring rage
Presented to the tears of soft remorse.

PEMBROKE
All murders past do stand excused in this:
And this, so sole and so unmatchable,
Shall give a holiness, a purity,
To the yet unbegotten sin of times;
And prove a deadly bloodshed but a jest,
Exampled by this heinous spectacle.

BASTARD
It is a damned and a bloody work;
The graceless action of a heavy hand,
If that it be the work of any hand.

SALISBURY
If that it be the work of any hand!
We had a kind of light what would ensue:
It is the shameful work of Hubert's hand;
The practice and the purpose of the king:
From whose obedience I forbid my soul,
Kneeling before this ruin of sweet life,
And breathing to his breathless excellence
The incense of a vow, a holy vow,
Never to taste the pleasures of the world,
Never to be infected with delight,
Nor conversant with ease and idleness,
Till I have set a glory to this hand,
By giving it the worship of revenge.

PEMBROKE *and* BIGOT
Our souls religiously confirm thy words.

Enter HUBERT

HUBERT
Lords, I am hot with haste in seeking you:
Arthur doth live; the king hath sent for you.

SALISBURY
O, he is bold and blushes not at death.
Avaunt, thou hateful villain, get thee gone!

HUBERT
I am no villain.

SALISBURY
Must I rob the law?
                          [*Drawing his sword*

BASTARD
Your sword is bright, sir; put it up again.

SALISBURY
Not till I sheathe it in a murderer's skin

HUBERT

Stand back, Lord Salisbury, stand back, I say;
By heaven, I think my sword's as sharp as yours:
I would not have you, lord, forget yourself,
Nor tempt the danger of my true defence;
Lest I, by marking of your rage, forget
Your worth, your greatness and nobility.

BIGOT

Out, dunghill! darest thou brave a nobleman?

HUBERT

Not for my life: but yet I dare defend
My innocent life against an emperor.

SALISBURY

Thou art a murderer.

HUBERT

     Do not prove me so;
Yet I am none: whose tongue soe'er speaks false,
Not truly speaks; who speaks not truly, lies.

PEMBROKE

Cut him to pieces.

BASTARD

     Keep the peace, I say.

SALISBURY

Stand by, or I shall gall you, Faulconbridge.

BASTARD

Thou wert better gall the devil, Salisbury:
If thou but frown on me, or stir thy foot,
Or teach thy hasty spleen to do me shame,
I'll strike thee dead. Put up thy sword betime;
Or I'll so maul you and your toasting-iron,
That you shall think the devil is come from hell.

BIGOT

What wilt thou do, renowned Faulconbridge?
Second a villain and a murderer?

HUBERT

Lord Bigot, I am none.

BIGOT

     Who kill'd this prince?

HUBERT

'Tis not an hour since I left him well:
I honour'd him, I loved him, and will weep
My date of life out for his sweet life's loss.

SALISBURY

Trust not those cunning waters of his eyes,
For villany is not without such rheum;
And he, long traded in it, makes it seem
Like rivers of remorse and innocency.
Away with me, all you whose souls abhor
The uncleanly savours of a slaughter-house;
For I am stifled with this smell of sin.

BIGOT

Away toward Bury, to the Dauphin there!

PEMBROKE

There tell the king he may inquire us out.
     [*Exeunt* LORDS

BASTARD

Here's a good world! Knew you of this fair work?
Beyond the infinite and boundless reach
Of mercy, if thou didst this deed of death,
Art thou damn'd, Hubert.

HUBERT

     Do but hear me, sir.

BASTARD

Ha! I'll tell thee what;
Thou'rt damn'd as black—nay, nothing is so black;
Thou art more deep damn'd than Prince Lucifer:
There is not yet so ugly a fiend of hell
As thou shalt be, if thou didst kill this child.

HUBERT

Upon my soul—

BASTARD

     If thou didst but consent
To this most cruel act, do but despair;
And if thou want'st a cord, the smallest thread
That ever spider twisted from her womb
Will serve to strangle thee; a rush will be a beam
To hang thee on; or wouldst thou drown thyself,
Put but a little water in a spoon,
And it shall be as all the ocean,
Enough to stifle such a villain up.
I do suspect thee very grievously.

HUBERT

If I in act, consent, or sin of thought,
Be guilty of the stealing that sweet breath
Which was embounded in this beauteous clay,
Let hell want pains enough to torture me.
I left him well.

BASTARD

     Go, bear him in thine arms.
I am amazed, methinks, and lose my way
Among the thorns and dangers of this world.
How easy dost thou take all England up!
From forth this morsel of dead royalty,
The life, the right and truth of all this realm
Is fled to heaven; and England now is left
To tug and scamble and to part by the teeth
The unowed interest of proud-swelling state.
Now for the bare-pick'd bone of majesty
Doth dogged war bristle his angry crest
And snarleth in the gentle eyes of peace:
Now powers from home and discontents at home
Meet in one line; and vast confusion waits,
As doth a raven on a sick-fallen beast,
The imminent decay of wrested pomp.
Now happy he whose cloak and cincture can
Hold out this tempest. Bear away that child
And follow me with speed: I'll to the king:
A thousand businesses are brief in hand,
And heaven itself doth frown upon the land. [*Exeunt*

ACT V

SCENE I. KING JOHN'S *palace*

Enter KING JOHN, PANDULPH, *and* ATTENDANTS

KING JOHN

Thus have I yielded up into your hand
The circle of my glory.   [*Giving the crown*

PANDULPH
Take again
From this my hand, as holding of the pope
Your sovereign greatness and authority.

KING JOHN
Now keep your holy word: go meet the French,
And from his holiness use all your power
To stop their marches 'fore we are inflamed.
Our discontented counties do revolt;
Our people quarrel with obedience,
Swearing allegiance and the love of soul
To stranger blood, to foreign royalty.
This inundation of mistempered humour
Rests by you only to be qualified:
Then pause not; for the present time's so sick,
That present medicine must be minister'd,
Or overthrow incurable ensues.

PANDULPH
It was my breath that blew this tempest up,
Upon your stubborn usage of the pope;
But since you are a gentle convertite,
My tongue shall hush again this storm of war,
And make fair weather in your blustering land.
On this Ascension-day, remember well,
Upon your oath of service to the pope,
Go I to make the French lay down their arms. [Exit

KING JOHN
Is this Ascension-day? Did not the prophet
Say that before Ascension-day at noon
My crown I should give off? Even so I have:
I did suppose it should be on constraint;
But, heaven be thank'd, it is but voluntary.
                    Enter the BASTARD
BASTARD
All Kent hath yielded; nothing there holds out
But Dover Castle: London hath received,
Like a kind host, the Dauphin and his powers:
Your nobles will not hear you, but are gone
To offer service to your enemy,
And wild amazement hurries up and down
The little number of your doubtful friends.

KING JOHN
Would not my lords return to me again,
After they heard young Arthur was alive?

BASTARD
They found him dead and cast into the streets,
An empty casket, where the jewel of life
By some damn'd hand was robb'd and ta'en away.

KING JOHN
That villain Hubert told me he did live.

BASTARD
So, on my soul, he did, for aught he knew.
But wherefore do you droop? why look you sad?
Be great in act, as you have been in thought;
Let not the world see fear and sad distrust
Govern the motion of a kingly eye:
Be stirring as the time; be fire with fire;
Threaten the threatener, and outface the brow
Of bragging horror: so shall inferior eyes,

That borrow their behaviours from the great,
Grow great by your example and put on
The dauntless spirit of resolution.
Away, and glister like the god of war,
When he intendeth to become the field:
Show boldness and aspiring confidence.
What, shall they seek the lion in his den,
And fright him there? and make him tremble there?
O, let it not be said: forage, and run
To meet displeasure farther from the doors,
And grapple with him ere he come so nigh.

KING JOHN
The legate of the pope hath been with me,
And I have made a happy peace with him;
And he hath promised to dismiss the powers
Led by the Dauphin.

BASTARD
O inglorious league!
Shall we, upon the footing of our land,
Send fair-play orders and make compromise,
Insinuation, parley and base truce
To arms invasive? shall a beardless boy,
A cocker'd silken wanton, brave our fields,
And flesh his spirit in a warlike soil,
Mocking the air with colours idly spread,
And find no check? Let us, my liege, to arms:
Perchance the cardinal cannot make your peace;
Or if he do, let it at least be said
They saw we had a purpose of defence.

KING JOHN
Have thou the ordering of this present time.

BASTARD
Away, then, with good courage! yet, I know,
Our party may well meet a prouder foe.   [Exeunt

SCENE II. The DAUPHIN'S camp at St. Edmundsbury

Enter, in arms, LEWIS, SALISBURY, MELUN, PEMBROKE,
                    BIGOT, and SOLDIERS
LEWIS
My Lord Melun, let this be copied out,
And keep it safe for our remembrance:
Return the precedent to these lords again;
That, having our fair order written down,
Both they and we, perusing o'er these notes,
May know wherefore we took the sacrament
And keep our faiths firm and inviolable.

SALISBURY
Upon our sides it never shall be broken.
And, noble Dauphin, albeit we swear
A voluntary zeal and an unurged faith
To your proceedings; yet believe me, prince,
I am not glad that such a sore of time
Should seek a plaster by contemn'd revolt,
And heal the inveterate canker of one wound
By making many. O, it grieves my soul,
That I must draw this metal from my side
To be a widow-maker! O, and there

Where honourable rescue and defence
Cries out upon the name of Salisbury!
But such is the infection of the time,
That, for the health and physic of our right,
We cannot deal but with the very hand
Of stern injustice and confused wrong.
And is't not pity, O my grieved friends,
That we, the sons and children of this isle,
Were born to see so sad an hour as this;
Wherein we step after a stranger, march
Upon her gentle bosom, and fill up
Her enemies' ranks,—I must withdraw and weep
Upon the spot of this enforced cause,—
To grace the gentry of a land remote,
And follow unacquainted colours here?
What, here? O nation, that thou couldst remove!
That Neptune's arms, who clippeth thee about,
Would bear thee from the knowledge of thyself,
And grapple thee unto a pagan shore;
Where these two Christian armies might combine
The blood of malice in a vein of league,
And not to spend it so unneighbourly!

LEWIS

A noble temper dost thou show in this;
And great affections wrestling in thy bosom
Doth make an earthquake of nobility.
O, what a noble combat hast thou fought
Between compulsion and a brave respect!
Let me wipe off this honourable dew,
That silvery doth progress on thy cheeks:
My heart hath melted at a lady's tears,
Being an ordinary inundation;
But this effusion of such manly drops,
This shower, blown up by tempest of the soul,
Startles mine eyes, and makes me more amazed
Than had I seen the vaulty top of heaven
Figured quite o'er with burning meteors.
Lift up thy brow, renowned Salisbury,
And with a great heart heave away this storm:
Commend these waters to those baby eyes
That never saw the giant world enraged;
Nor met with fortune other than at feasts,
Full of warm blood, of mirth, of gossiping.
Come, come; for thou shalt thrust thy hand as deep
Into the purse of rich prosperity
As Lewis himself: so, nobles, shall you all,
That knit your sinews to the strength of mine.
And even there, methinks, an angel spake:

Enter PANDULPH

Look, where the holy legate comes apace,
To give us warrant from the hand of heaven,
And on our actions set the name of right
With holy breath.

PANDULPH

      Hail, noble prince of France!
The next is this, King John hath reconciled
Himself to Rome; his spirit is come in,
That so stood out against the holy church,
The great metropolis and see of Rome:
Therefore thy threatening colours now wind up;

And tame the savage spirit of wild war,
That, like a lion foster'd up at hand,
It may lie gently at the foot of peace,
And be no further harmful than in show.

LEWIS

Your grace shall pardon me, I will not back:
I am too high-born to be propertied,
To be a secondary at control,
Or useful serving-man and instrument
To any sovereign state throughout the world.
Your breath first kindled the dead coal of wars
Between this chastised kingdom and myself,
And brought in matter that should feed this fire;
And now 'tis far too huge to be blown out
With that same weak wind which enkindled it.
You taught me how to know the face of right,
Acquainted me with interest to this land,
Yea, thrust this enterprise into my heart;
And come ye now to tell me John hath made
His peace with Rome? What is that peace to me?
I, by the honour of my marriage-bed,
After young Arthur, claim this land for mine;
And, now it is half-conquer'd, must I back
Because that John hath made his peace with Rome?
Am I Rome's slave? What penny hath Rome borne,
What men provided, what munition sent,
To underprop this action? Is 't not I
That undergo this charge? who else but I,
And such as to my claim are liable,
Sweat in this business and maintain this war?
Have I not heard these islanders shout out
'Vive le roi!' as I have bank'd their towns?
Have I not here the best cards for the game,
To win this easy match play'd for a crown?
And shall I now give o'er the yielded set?
No, no, on my soul, it never shall be said.

PANDULPH

You look but on the outside of this work.

LEWIS

Outside or inside, I will not return
Till my attempt so much be glorified
As to my ample hope was promised
Before I drew this gallant head of war,
And cull'd these fiery spirits from the world,
To outlook conquest and to win renown
Even in the jaws of danger and of death.

      [*Trumpet sounds*

What lusty trumpet thus doth summon us?

Enter the BASTARD, *attended*

BASTARD

According to the fair-play of the world,
Let me have audience; I am sent to speak:
My holy lord of Milan, from the king
I come, to learn how you have dealt for him;
And, as you answer, I do know the scope
And warrant limited unto my tongue.

PANDULPH

The Dauphin is too wilful-opposite,
And will not temporize with my entreaties;
He flatly says he'll not lay down his arms.

BASTARD

By all the blood that ever fury breathed,
The youth says well. Now hear our English king;
For thus his royalty doth speak in me.
He is prepared, and reason too he should:
This apish and unmannerly approach,
This harness'd masque and unadvised revel,
This unhair'd sauciness and boyish troops,
The king doth smile at; and is well prepared
To whip this dwarfish war, these pigmy arms,
From out the circle of his territories.
That hand which had the strength, even at your
    door,
To cudgel you and make you take the hatch,
To dive like buckets in concealed wells,
To crouch in litter of your stable planks,
To lie like pawns lock'd up in chests and trunks,
To hug with swine, to seek sweet safety out
In vaults and prisons, and to thrill and shake
Even at the crying of your nation's crow,
Thinking his voice an armed Englishman;
Shall that victorious hand be feebled here,
That in your chambers gave you chastisement?
No: know the gallant monarch is in arms
And like an eagle o'er his aery towers,
To souse annoyance that comes near his nest.
And you denegerate, you ingrate revolts,
You bloody Neroes, ripping up the womb
Of your dear mother England, blush for shame;
For your own ladies and pale-visaged maids
Like Amazons come tripping after drums,
Their thimbles into armed gauntlets change,
Their needles to lances, and their gentle hearts
To fierce and bloody inclination.

LEWIS

There end thy brave, and turn thy face in peace;
We grant thou canst outscold us: fare thee well;
We hold our time too precious to be spent
With such a brabbler.

PANDULPH
      Give me leave to speak.

BASTARD

No, I will speak.

LEWIS
      We will attend to neither.
Strike up the drums; and let the tongue of war
Plead for our interest and our being here.

BASTARD

Indeed, your drums, being beaten, will cry out;
And so shall you, being beaten: do but start
An echo with the clamour of thy drum,
And even at hand a drum is ready braced
That shall reverberate all as loud as thine;
Sound but another, and another shall
As loud as thine rattle the welkin's ear
And mock the deep-mouth'd thunder: for at hand,
Not trusting to this halting legate here,
Whom he hath used rather for sport than need,
Is warlike John; and in his forehead sits

A bare-ribb'd death, whose office is this day
To feast upon whole thousands of the French.

LEWIS

Strike up our drums, to find this danger out.

BASTARD

And thou shalt find it, Dauphin, do not doubt.
                           [Exeunt

SCENE III. *The field of battle*

Alarums. Enter KING JOHN *and* HUBERT
KING JOHN

How goes the day with us? O, tell me, Hubert.

HUBERT

Badly, I fear. How fares your majesty?

KING JOHN

This fever, that hath troubled me so long,
Lies heavy on me; O, my heart is sick!
       Enter a MESSENGER

MESSENGER

My lord, your valiant kinsman, Faulconbridge,
Desires your majesty to leave the field
And send him word by me which way you go.

KING JOHN

Tell him, toward Swinstead, to the abbey there.

MESSENGER

Be of good comfort; for the great supply
That was expected by the Dauphin here,
Are wreck'd three nights ago on Goodwin Sands.
This news was brought to Richard but even now:
The French fight coldly, and retire themselves.

KING JOHN

Ay me! this tyrant fever burns me up,
And will not let me welcome this good news.
Set on toward Swinstead: to my litter straight;
Weakness possesseth me, and I am faint.   *[Exeunt*

SCENE IV. *Another part of the field*

Enter SALISBURY, PEMBROKE, *and* BIGOT
SALISBURY

I did not think the king so stored with friends.

PEMBROKE

Up once again; put spirit in the French:
If they miscarry, we miscarry too.

SALISBURY

That misbegotten devil, Faulconbridge,
In spite of spite, alone upholds the day.

PEMBROKE

They say King John sore sick hath left the field.
       Enter MELUN, *wounded*

MELUN

Lead me to the revolts of England here.

SALISBURY

When we were happy we had other names.

PEMBROKE

It is the Count Melun.

SALISBURY

Wounded to death.

MELUN

Fly, noble English, you are bought and sold;
Unthread the rude eye of rebellion
And welcome home again discarded faith.
Seek out King John and fall before his feet;
For if the French be lords of this loud day,
He means to recompense the pains you take
By cutting off your heads: thus hath he sworn
And I with him, and many moe with me,
Upon the altar at Saint Edmundsbury;
Even on that altar where we swore to you
Dear amity and everlasting love.

SALISBURY

May this be possible? may this be true?

MELUN

Have I not hideous death within my view,
Retaining but a quantity of life,
Which bleeds away, even as a form of wax
Resolveth from his figure 'gainst the fire?
What in the world should make me now deceive,
Since I must lose the use of all deceit?
Why should I then be false, since it is true
That I must die here and live hence by truth?
I say again, if Lewis do win the day,
He is forsworn, if e'er those eyes of yours
Behold another day break in the east:
But even this night, whose black contagious breath
Already smokes about the burning crest
Of the old, feeble and day-wearied sun,
Even this ill night, your breathing shall expire,
Paying the fine of rated treachery
Even with a treacherous fine of all your lives,
If Lewis by your assistance win the day.
Commend me to one Hubert with your king:
The love of him, and this respect besides,
For that my grandsire was an Englishman,
Awakes my conscience to confess all this.
In lieu whereof, I pray you, bear me hence
From forth the noise and rumour of the field,
Where I may think the remnant of my thoughts
In peace, and part this body and my soul
With contemplation and devout desires.

SALISBURY

We do believe thee: and beshrew my soul
But I do love the favour and the form
Of this most fair occasion, by the which
We will untread the steps of damned flight,
And like a bated and retired flood,
Leaving our rankness and irregular course,
Stoop low within those bounds we have o'erlook'd,
And calmly run on in obedience
Even to our ocean, to our great King John.
My arm shall give thee help to bear thee hence;
For I do see the cruel pangs of death
Right in thine eye. Away, my friends! New flight;
And happy newness, that intends old right.

[Exeunt, leading off MELUN

SCENE V. *The French camp*

Enter LEWIS *and his train*

LEWIS

The sun of heaven methought was loath to set,
But stay'd, and made the western welkin blush,
When English measure backward their own ground
In faint retire. O, bravely came we off,
When with a volley of our needless shot,
After such bloody toil, we bid good night;
And wound our tottering colours clearly up,
Last in the field, and almost lords of it!

Enter a MESSENGER

MESSENGER

Where is my prince, the Dauphin?

LEWIS

Here: what news?

MESSENGER

The Count Melun is slain; the English lords
By his persuasion are again fall'n off,
And your supply, which you have wish'd so long,
Are cast away and sunk on Goodwin Sands.

LEWIS

Ah, foul shrewd news! beshrew thy very heart!
I did not think to be so sad to-night
As this hath made me. Who was he that said
King John did fly an hour or two before
The stumbling night did part our weary powers?

MESSENGER

Whoever spoke it, it is true, my lord.

LEWIS

Well; keep good quarter and good care to-night:
The day shall not be up so soon as I,
To try the fair adventure of to-morrow.   [Exeunt

SCENE VI. *An open place in the neighbourhood
of Swinstead Abbey*

Enter the BASTARD *and* HUBERT, *severally*

HUBERT

Who's there? speak, ho! speak quickly, or I shoot.

BASTARD

A friend. What art thou?

HUBERT

Of the part of England.

BASTARD

Whither dost thou go?

HUBERT

What's that to thee? why may not I demand
Of thine affairs, as well as thou of mine?

BASTARD

Hubert, I think.

HUBERT

Thou hast a perfect thought:
I will upon all hazards well believe
Thou art my friend, that know'st my tongue so well.
Who art thou?

BASTARD

Who thou wilt: and if thou please,

Thou mayst befriend me so much as to think
I come one way of the Plantagenets.
HUBERT
Unkind remembrance! thou and eyeless night
Have done me shame: brave soldier, pardon me,
That any accent breaking from thy tongue
Should 'scape the true acquaintance of mine ear.
BASTARD
Come, come; sans compliment, what news abroad?
HUBERT
Why, here walk I in the black brow of night,
To find you out.
BASTARD
               Brief, then; and what's the news?
HUBERT
O, my sweet sir, news fitting to the night,
Black, fearful, comfortless and horrible.
BASTARD
Show me the very wound of this ill news:
I am no woman, I'll not swoon at it.
HUBERT
The king, I fear, is poison'd by a monk:
I left him almost speechless; and broke out
To acquaint you with this evil, that you might
The better arm you to the sudden time,
Than if you had at leisure known of this.
BASTARD
How did he take it? who did taste to him?
HUBERT
A monk, I tell you; a resolved villain,
Whose bowels suddenly burst out: the king
Yet speaks and peradventure may recover.
BASTARD
Who didst thou leave to tend his majesty?
HUBERT
Why, know you not? the lords are all come back,
And brought Prince Henry in their company;
At whose request the king hath pardon'd them,
And they are all about his majesty.
BASTARD
Withhold thine indignation, mighty heaven,
And tempt us not to bear above our power!
I'll tell thee, Hubert, half my power this night,
Passing these flats, are taken by the tide;
These Lincoln Washes have devoured them;
Myself, well mounted, hardly have escaped.
Away before: conduct me to the king;
I doubt he will be dead or ere I come.   [Exeunt

SCENE VII. *The orchard at Swinstead Abbey*

Enter PRINCE HENRY, SALISBURY, *and* BIGOT
PRINCE HENRY
It is too late: the life of all his blood
Is touch'd corruptibly, and his pure brain,
Which some suppose the soul's frail dwelling-house,
Doth by the idle comments that it makes
Foretell the ending of mortality.

Enter PEMBROKE
PEMBROKE
His highness yet doth speak, and holds belief
That, being brought into the open air,
It would allay the burning quality
Of that fell poison which assaileth him.
PRINCE HENRY
Let him be brought into the orchard here.
Doth he still rage?   [Exit BIGOT
PEMBROKE
        He is more patient
Than when you left him; even now he sung.
PRINCE HENRY
O vanity of sickness! fierce extremes
In their continuance will not feel themselves.
Death, having prey'd upon the outward parts,
Leaves them invisible, and his siege is now
Against the mind, the which he pricks and wounds
With many legions of strange fantasies,
Which, in their throng and press to that last hold,
Confound themselves. 'Tis strange that death
    should sing.
I am the cygnet to this pale faint swan,
Who chants a doleful hymn to his own death,
And from the organ-pipe of frailty sings
His soul and body to their lasting rest.
SALISBURY
Be of good comfort, prince; for you are born
To set a form upon that indigest
Which he hath left so shapeless and so rude.
Enter ATTENDANTS, *and* BIGOT, *carrying* KING JOHN *in a
    chair*
KING JOHN
Ay, marry, now my soul hath elbow-room;
It would not out at windows nor at doors.
There is so hot a summer in my bosom,
That all my bowels crumble up to dust:
I am a scribbled form, drawn with a pen
Upon a parchment, and against this fire
Do I shrink up.
PRINCE HENRY
        How fares your majesty?
KING JOHN
Poison'd,—ill fare—dead, forsook, cast off:
And none of you will bid the winter come
To thrust his icy fingers in my maw,
Nor let my kingdom's rivers take their course
Through my burn'd bosom, nor entreat the north
To make his bleak winds kiss my parched lips
And comfort me with cold. I do not ask you much,
I beg cold comfort; and you are so strait
And so ingrateful, you deny me that.
PRINCE HENRY
O that there were some virtue in my tears,
That might relieve you!
KING JOHN
           The salt in them is hot.
Within me is a hell; and there the poison
Is as a fiend confined to tyrannize
On unreprieveable condemned blood.

Enter the BASTARD

BASTARD

O, I am scalded with my violent motion,
And spleen of speed to see your majesty!

KING JOHN

O cousin, thou art come to set mine eye:
The tackle of my heart is crack'd and burn'd,
And all the shrouds wherewith my life should sail
Are turned to one thread, one little hair:
My heart hath one poor string to stay it by,
Which holds but till thy news be uttered;
And then all this thou seest is but a clod
And module of confounded royalty.

BASTARD

The Dauphin is preparing hitherward,
Where heaven He knows how we shall answer him;
For in a night the best part of my power,
As I upon advantage did remove,
Were in the Washes all unwarily
Devoured by the unexpected flood.   [*The* KING *dies*

SALISBURY

You breathe these dead news in as dead an ear.
My liege! my lord! but now a king, now thus.

PRINCE HENRY

Even so must I run on, and even so stop.
What surety of the world, what hope, what stay,
When this was now a king, and now is clay?

BASTARD

Art thou gone so? I do but stay behind
To do the office for thee of revenge,
And then my soul shall wait on thee to heaven,
As it on earth hath been thy servant still.
Now, now, you stars that move in your right spheres,
Where be your powers? show now your mended
     faiths,
And instantly return with me again,
To push destruction and perpetual shame
Out of the weak door of our fainting land.
Straight let us seek, or straight we shall be sought;
The Dauphin rages at our very heels.

SALISBURY

It seems you know not, then, so much as we:
The Cardinal Pandulph is within at rest,
Who half an hour since came from the Dauphin,

And brings from him such offers of our peace
As we with honour and respect may take,
With purpose presently to leave this war.

BASTARD

He will the rather do it when he sees
Ourselves well sinewed to our defence.

SALISBURY

Nay, it is in a manner done already;
For many carriages he hath dispatch'd
To the sea-side, and put his cause and quarrel
To the disposing of the cardinal:
With whom yourself, myself and other lords,
If you think meet, this afternoon will post
To consummate this business happily.

BASTARD

Let it be so: and you, my noble prince,
With other princes that may best be spared,
Shall wait upon your father's funeral.

PRINCE HENRY

At Worcester must his body be interr'd;
For so he will'd it.

BASTARD

       Thither shall it then:
And happily may your sweet self put on
The lineal state and glory of the land!
To whom, with all submission, on my knee
I do bequeath my faithful services
And true subjection everlastingly.

SALISBURY

And the like tender of our love we make,
To rest without a spot for evermore.

PRINCE HENRY

I have a kind soul that would give you thanks
And knows not how to do it but with tears.

BASTARD

O, let us pay the time but needful woe,
Since it hath been beforehand with our griefs.
This England never did, nor never shall,
Lie at the proud foot of a conqueror,
But when it first did help to wound itself.
Now these her princes are come home again,
Come the three corners of the world in arms,
And we shall shock them. Nought shall make us rue,
If England to itself do rest but true.   [*Exeunt*

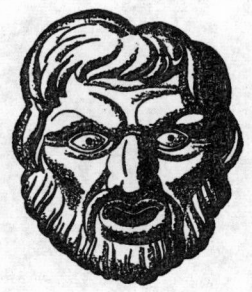

THE MERCHANT OF VENICE

SYNOPSIS

Bassanio, a gay, improvident young gentleman of Venice, is very much in love with the beautiful Portia of Belmont, heiress to a princely name and such a colossal fortune that distinguished men from all parts of the world come to court her. Knowing he has no chance of winning her without sufficient funds to defray his expenses, Bassanio turns as usual to his good friend Antonio, a wealthy merchant, regretting his previous heedlessly contracted debts and suggesting that a little present assistance might help him eventually to return all the borrowed money.

The generous, lovable Antonio seems sad, as though vaguely apprehensive of coming distress, but responds immediately to his young friend's request for a loan of three thousand ducats for three months. Antonio's entire wealth at the time happens to be tied up in his merchandise-laden ships at sea, but he breaks his custom of never lending or borrowing on interest and asks Shylock, a rich Jewish money-lender, for the required sum.

The Jew, brooding over insults and injuries and hating the Christian merchant for despising his usurious habits, at once foresees an opportunity for revenge by one desperate act, and blandly agrees to lend the money without interest, provided that Antonio sign a bond, by way of a jest, stipulating that the forfeit be one pound of flesh cut from any part of the body that he, Shylock, may designate. Bassanio protests against taking the loan on such terms, but Antonio dismisses the matter lightly in his confidence that his ships will be back within the next two months, and the gay-hearted lover with his friend, the sportive Gratiano, sets out for Belmont to woo the heiress.

Meanwhile, in her palatial home, Portia is carrying out the terms of her father's will by having each suitor make his choice of three caskets, gold, silver, and lead, the lucky aspirant being the one who will choose the casket containing her picture. With stately ceremony, the Prince of Morocco is led to the caskets and chooses the golden one, only to be disappointed by the picture of a skull. The haughty Prince of Aragon opens the silver one and finds the portrait of an idiot. Then, to Portia's great joy, comes news of Bassanio's arrival, and she orders a song sung during his trial that hints the proper choice. He selects the leaden casket and finding Portia's picture at once claims his bride, who gives him a ring which he vows always to keep.

His friend Gratiano has made love successfully to Portia's confidential companion, the pensive but practical Nerissa, and now another pair appears on the scene, Lorenzo, an artist-friend of Bassanio's, with his bride Jessica, Shylock's pretty daughter, who, bored with the seclusion of her father's house, has eloped with her Christian lover, taking with her in her flight bags of ducats and jewels. They had met Salerio, a messenger, who asked for their company to Belmont where he was ordered to deliver an important letter from Antonio, telling Bassanio that all his ships are lost and he is ruined, that Shylock's forfeit of the pound of flesh from his breast must be paid, and that he greatly desires to see his friend before he dies.

Bassanio is appalled by the tragic news which he explains to Portia, and Salerio adds to his distress by describing the utterly futile efforts that have been made by twenty merchants, the Duke, and prominent Venetian noblemen, to dissuade the Jew from his purpose, even the payment of ten times the amount of the overdue loan having been refused. Hurrying Bassanio through a marriage ceremony, likewise Gratiano and Nerissa, and dispatching the two men to Venice with enough gold to pay Antonio's debt many times over, the level-headed Portia appeals for help to her cousin, a distinguished lawyer, and leaving her household in charge of Lorenzo and Jessica she proceeds to the court in Venice, introduced and disguised as the learned young Doctor Balthasar of Rome, with Nerissa dressed as a lawyer's clerk.

As judge in the case, Portia upholds the law in favor of the Jew who fawns upon her admiringly, but when she makes an eloquent appeal to him to be merciful, Shylock, doubly hardened by the loss of his daughter, his money and jewels, defends himself well and firmly demands the full penalty of the law. This the court awards, but in his moment of triumph as he faces his enemy with whetted knife, the Jew is suddenly warned by Portia, on the pain of death, not to shed a drop of blood or take even a fraction more or less of flesh than the law allows. Adhering strictly to the letter of the law, the young judge then informs the astounded Shylock that, having refused payment of the debt in open court, nothing is due him but his legal forfeiture, and because of his evident plot against the life of a Venetian citizen half of his possessions go to Antonio, the other half to the state, and his life itself lies at the mercy of the Duke alone.

The Duke pardons the broken old man before he can ask, and Antonio requests, while refusing his share, that the Jew make a will leaving his estate at death to his daughter Jessica and her husband. Portia waves aside the fee offered her, but both Nerissa and she ask for the rings, their own bridal gifts, which Bassanio and Gratiano are wearing. At home again in Belmont, they tease and banter merrily about these trinkets until it is revealed to the amazed men that Portia was the acute doctor of laws and Nerissa her clerk, and Portia hands Antonio a letter telling him of the safe arrival of three of his most valued ships.

HISTORICAL DATA

The two romantic stories forming the main plot of *The Merchant of Venice* have appeared separately in the literature of many countries. The story of the caskets is found as early as 800 in the Greek romance *Barlaam and Josaphat* by Joannes Damascenus, and variations are given by the English poet Gower and the Italian novelist Boccaccio. The *Gesta Romanorum*, in the English version by Richard Robinson, *Records of Ancyent Historyes* (1577), contains both this story and that of the pound of flesh. Shakespeare, however, followed more closely the version as presented in *Il Pecorone* by Ser Giovanni Fiorentino (1558) in which not only are both stories combined but "Belmont" is named as the lady's residence.

A play entitled *The Jew*, described by Stephen Gosson in his *School of Abuse* (1579) seems to have combined both plots and another, *The Three Ladies of London* by Robert Wilson (1584), may have suggested the scenes between Antonio and Shylock. Marlowe's *Jew of Malta* is generally conceded to have been of some influence in connection with the relationship of father and daughter.

The play may well have been written in 1594 to take advantage of popular feeling against the Jews stirred up by the conviction of Roderigo Lopez, a Spanish Jew who was physician to Queen Elizabeth and was hanged for plotting her death and that of Antonio Perez, the Portuguese pretender. Some corroboration of this theory may be found in the occurrence of the name Antonio as that of the intended victim in both history and drama. Scholars are inclined to feel, however, that the maturity and workmanship of the play indicate a later date, and that probably 1596 is the earliest that it was written. Henslowe in his *Diary*, on the other hand, notes the performance of a new play, *The Venesyon Comedy* in 1594, which some commentators insist is the earliest version of *The Merchant*.

In any case the play is listed by Meres in 1598 and entered on the Stationers' Register in that year. Two quarto editions appeared in 1600.

"Shed thou no blood; nor cut thou less nor more,"
THE MERCHANT OF VENICE

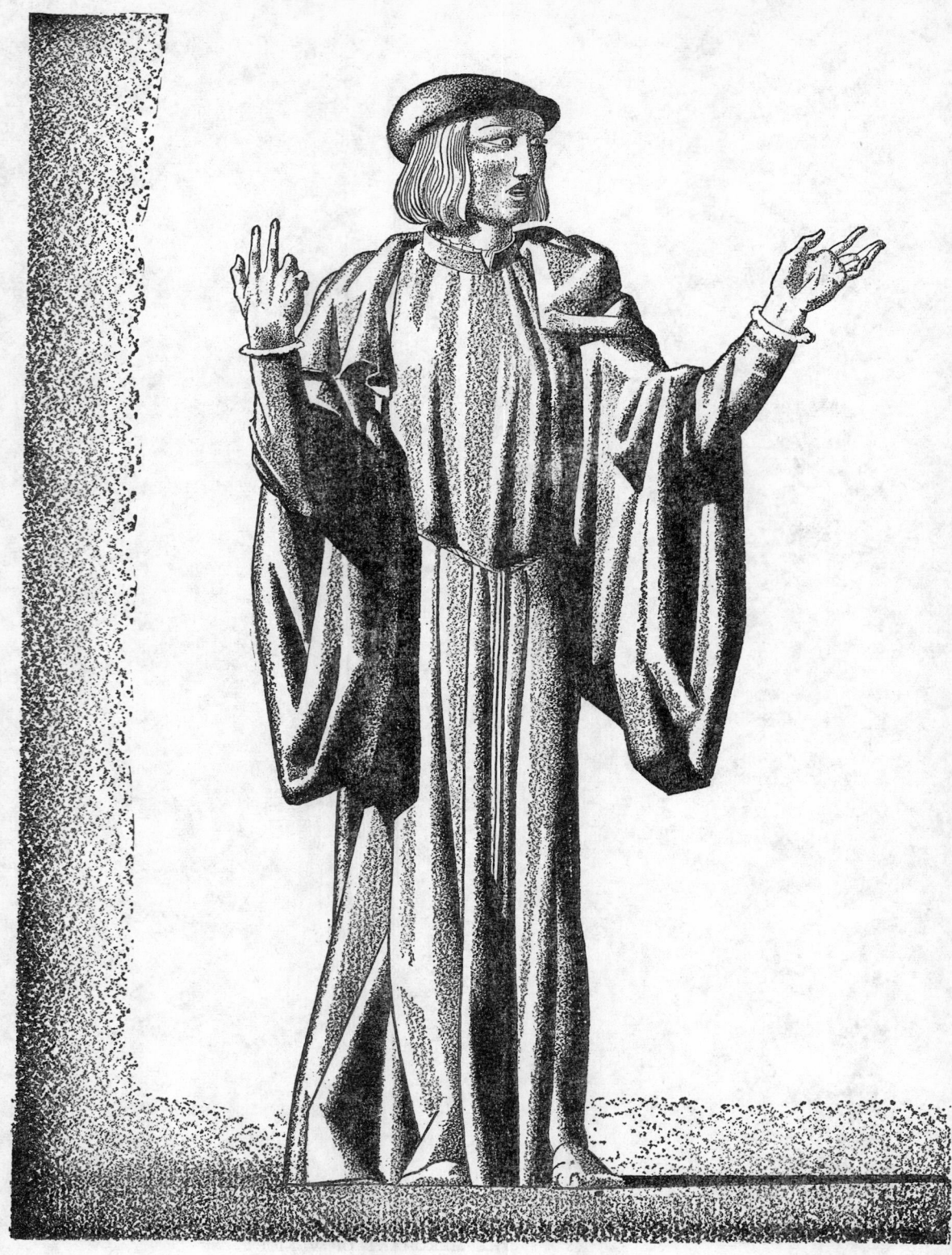

THE MERCHANT OF VENICE

DRAMATIS PERSONÆ

THE DUKE OF VENICE,
THE PRINCE OF MOROCCO, } *suitors to Portia.*
THE PRINCE OF ARRAGON,
ANTONIO, *a merchant of Venice.*
BASSANIO, *his friend, suitor likewise to Portia.*
SALANIO,
SALARINO, } *friends to Antonio and Bassanio.*
GRATIANO,
SALERIO,
LORENZO, *in love with Jessica.*
SHYLOCK, *a rich Jew.*
TUBAL, *a Jew, his friend.*
LAUNCELOT GOBBO, *the clown, servant to Shylock.*
OLD GOBBO, *father to Launcelot.*

LEONARDO, *servant to Bassanio.*
BALTHASAR, } *servants to Portia.*
STEPHANO,

PORTIA, *a rich heiress.*
NERISSA, *her waiting-maid.*
JESSICA, *daughter to Shylock.*

MAGNIFICOES *of Venice,* OFFICERS *of the Court of Justice,* GAOLER, SERVANTS *to Portia, and other* ATTENDANTS.

SCENE—*Partly at Venice, and partly at Belmont, the seat of Portia, on the Continent.*

ACT I
SCENE I. *Venice. A street*

Enter ANTONIO, SALARINO, *and* SALANIO

ANTONIO

IN SOOTH, I know not why I am so sad:
It wearies me; you say it wearies you;
But how I caught it, found it, or came by it,
What stuff 'tis made of, whereof it is born,
I am to learn;
And such a want-wit sadness makes of me,
That I have much ado to know myself.

SALARINO

Your mind is tossing on the ocean;
There, where your argosies with portly sail,
Like signiors and rich burghers on the flood,
Or, as it were, the pageants of the sea,
Do overpeer the petty traffickers,
That curt'sy to them, do them reverence,
As they fly by them with their woven wings.

SALANIO

Believe me, sir, had I such venture forth,
The better part of my affections would
Be with my hopes abroad. I should be still
Plucking the grass, to know where sits the wind;
Peering in maps for ports, and piers, and roads;
And every object, that might make me fear
Misfortune to my ventures, out of doubt
Would make me sad.

SALARINO
              My wind, cooling my broth,
Would blow me to an ague, when I thought
What harm a wind too great at sea might do.
I should not see the sandy hour-glass run,
But I should think of shallows and of flats,
And see my wealthy Andrew dock'd in sand
Vailing her high top lower than her ribs

To kiss her burial. Should I go to church
And see the holy edifice of stone,
And not bethink me straight of dangerous rocks,
Which touching but my gentle vessel's side
Would scatter all her spices on the stream,
Enrobe the roaring waters with my silks;
And, in a word, but even now worth this,
And now worth nothing? Shall I have the thought
To think on this; and shall I lack the thought,
That such a thing bechanced would make me sad?
But tell not me; I know, Antonio
Is sad to think upon his merchandise.

ANTONIO

Believe me, no: I thank my fortune for it,
My ventures are not in one bottom trusted,
Nor to one place; nor is my whole estate
Upon the fortune of this present year:
Therefore my merchandise makes me not sad.

SALARINO

Why, then you are in love.

ANTONIO
                    Fie, fie!

SALARINO

Not in love neither? Then let us say you are sad,
Because you are not merry: and 'twere as easy
For you to laugh, and leap, and say you are merry,
Because you are not sad. Now, by two-headed Janus,
Nature hath framed strange fellows in her time:
Some that will evermore peep through their eyes,
And laugh like parrots at a bag-piper;
And other of such vinegar aspect,
That they'll not show their teeth in way of smile,
Though Nestor swear the jest be laughable.

Enter BASSANIO, LORENZO, *and* GRATIANO

SALANIO

Here comes Bassanio, your most noble kinsman,
Gratiano, and Lorenzo. Fare ye well:
We leave you now with better company.

[447]

SALARINO

I would have stay'd till I had made you merry,
If worthier friends had not prevented me.

ANTONIO

Your worth is very dear in my regard.
I take it, your own business calls on you,
And you embrace the occasion to depart.

SALARINO

Good morrow, my good lords.

BASSANIO

Good signiors both, when shall we laugh? say, when?
You grow exceeding strange: must it be so?

SALARINO

We'll make our leisures to attend on yours.
[Exeunt SALARINO and SALANIO

LORENZO

My Lord Bassanio, since you have found Antonio,
We two will leave you: but, at dinner-time,
I pray you, have in mind where we must meet.

BASSANIO

I will not fail you.

GRATIANO

You look not well, Signior Antonio;
You have too much respect upon the world:
They lose it that do buy it with much care:
Believe me, you are marvellously changed.

ANTONIO

I hold the world but as the world, Gratiano;
A stage, where every man must play a part,
And mine a sad one.

GRATIANO

Let me play the fool:
With mirth and laughter let old wrinkles come;
And let my liver rather heat with wine
Than my heart cool with mortifying groans.
Why should a man, whose blood is warm within,
Sit like his grandsire cut in alabaster?
Sleep when he wakes, and creep into the jaundice
By being peevish? I tell thee what, Antonio—
I love thee, and it is my love that speaks,—
There are a sort of men, whose visages
Do cream and mantle like a standing pond;
And do a wilful stillness entertain,
With purpose to be dress'd in an opinion
Of wisdom, gravity, profound conceit;
As who should say, 'I am Sir Oracle,
And, when I ope my lips, let no dog bark!'
O my Antonio, I do know of these,
That therefore only are reputed wise
For saying nothing; when, I am very sure,
If they should speak, would almost damn those ears,
Which, hearing them, would call their brothers fools.
I'll tell thee more of this another time:
But fish not, with this melancholy bait,
For this fool gudgeon, this opinion.
Come, good Lorenzo. Fare ye well awhile:
I'll end my exhortation after dinner.

LORENZO

Well, we will leave you, then, till dinner-time:

I must be one of these same dumb wise men,
For Gratiano never lets me speak.

GRATIANO

Well, keep me company but two years moe,
Thou shalt not know the sound of thine own tongue.

ANTONIO

Farewell: I'll grow a talker for this gear.

GRATIANO

Thanks, i'faith; for silence is only commendable
In a neat's tongue dried, and a maid not vendible.
[Exeunt GRATIANO and LORENZO

ANTONIO

Is that any thing now?

BASSANIO

Gratiano speaks an infinite deal of nothing, more
than any man in all Venice. His reasons are as two
grains of wheat hid in two bushels of chaff: you shall
seek all day ere you find them: and when you have
them, they are not worth the search.

ANTONIO

Well, tell me now, what lady is the same
To whom you swore a secret pilgrimage,
That you to-day promised to tell me of?

BASSANIO

'Tis not unknown to you, Antonio,
How much I have disabled mine estate,
By something showing a more swelling port
Than my faint means would grant continuance:
Nor do I now make moan to be abridged
From such a noble rate; but my chief care
Is, to come fairly off from the great debts,
Wherein my time, something too prodigal,
Hath left me gaged. To you, Antonio,
I owe the most, in money and in love;
And from your love I have a warranty
To unburthen all my plots and purposes
How to get clear of all the debts I owe.

ANTONIO

I pray you, good Bassanio, let me know it;
And if it stand, as you yourself still do,
Within the eye of honour, be assured,
My purse, my person, my extremest means,
Lie all unlock'd to your occasions.

BASSANIO

In my school-days, when I had lost one shaft,
I shot his fellow of the self-same flight
The self-same way with more advised watch,
To find the other forth; and by adventuring both,
I oft found both: I urge this childhood proof,
Because what follows is pure innocence.
I owe you much; and, like a wilful youth,
That which I owe is lost: but if you please
To shoot another arrow that self way
Which you did shoot the first, I do not doubt,
As I will watch the aim, or to find both,
Or bring your latter hazard back again,
And thankfully rest debtor for the first.

ANTONIO

You know me well; and herein spend but time
To wind about my love with circumstance;

And out of doubt you do me now more wrong
In making question of my uttermost,
Than if you had made waste of all I have:
Then do but say to me what I should do,
That in your knowledge may by me be done,
And I am prest unto it: therefore, speak.

BASSANIO

In Belmont is a lady richly left;
And she is fair, and, fairer than that word,
Of wondrous virtues: sometimes from her eyes
I did receive fair speechless messages:
Her name is Portia; nothing undervalued
To Cato's daughter, Brutus' Portia:
Nor is the wide world ignorant of her worth;
For the four winds blow in from every coast
Renowned suitors: and her sunny locks
Hang on her temples like a golden fleece;
Which makes her seat of Belmont Colchos' strond,
And many Jasons come in quest of her.
O my Antonio, had I but the means
To hold a rival place with one of them,
I have a mind presages me such thrift,
That I should questionless be fortunate!

ANTONIO

Thou know'st that all my fortunes are at sea;
Neither have I money, nor commodity
To raise a present sum: therefore go forth;
Try what my credit can in Venice do:
That shall be rack'd, even to the uttermost,
To furnish thee to Belmont, to fair Portia.
Go, presently inquire, and so will I,
Where money is; and I no question make,
To have it of my trust, or for my sake.   [Exeunt

SCENE II. *Belmont. A room in* PORTIA'S *house*

Enter PORTIA *and* NERISSA

PORTIA

By my troth, Nerissa, my little body is aweary o
this great world.

NERISSA

You would be, sweet madam, if your miseries were
in the same abundance as your good fortunes are:
and yet, for aught I see, they are as sick that surfeit
with too much, as they that starve with nothing. It
is no mean happiness, therefore, to be seated in the
mean: superfluity comes sooner by white hairs; but
competency lives longer.

PORTIA

Good sentences, and well pronounced.

NERISSA

They would be better, if well followed.

PORTIA

If to do were as easy as to know what were good to
do, chapels had been churches, and poor men's cottages princes' palaces. It is a good divine that follows his own instructions: I can easier teach twenty
what were good to be done, than be one of the
twenty to follow mine own teaching. The brain

may devise laws for the blood; but a hot temper
leaps o'er a cold decree: such a hare is madness the
youth, to skip o'er the meshes of good counsel the
cripple. But this reasoning is not in the fashion to
choose me a husband. O me, the word 'choose'! I
may neither choose whom I would, nor refuse whom
I dislike; so is the will of a living daughter curbed
by the will of a dead father. Is it not hard, Nerissa,
that I cannot choose one, nor refuse none?

NERISSA

Your father was ever virtuous; and holy men, at
their death, have good inspirations: therefore, the
lottery, that he hath devised in these three chests of
gold, silver, and lead,—whereof who chooses his
meaning chooses you,—will, no doubt, never be
chosen by any rightly, but one who shall rightly
love. But what warmth is there in your affection
towards any of these princely suitors that are already come?

PORTIA

I pray thee, over-name them; and as thou namest
them, I will describe them; and, according to my
description, level at my affection.

NERISSA

First, there is the Neapolitan prince.

PORTIA

Ay, that's a colt indeed, for he doth nothing but
talk of his horse; and he makes it a great appropria-
tion to his own good parts, that he can shoe him
himself. I am much afeard my lady his mother
played false with a smith.

NERISSA

Then there is the County Palatine.

PORTIA

He doth nothing but frown; as who should say, 'if
you will not have me, choose:' he hears merry tales,
and smiles not: I fear he will prove the weeping
philosopher when he grows old, being so full of unmannerly sadness in his youth. I had rather be married to a death's-head with a bone in his mouth
than to either of these. God defend me from these
two!

NERISSA

How say you by the French lord, Monsieur Le Bon?

PORTIA

God made him, and therefore let him pass for a
man. In truth, I know it is a sin to be a mocker: but,
he!—why, he hath a horse better than the Neapolitan's; a better bad habit of frowning than the Count
Palatine: he is every man in no man; if a throstle
sing, he falls straight a capering: he will fence with
his own shadow: if I should marry him, I should
marry twenty husbands. If he would despise me, I
would forgive him; for if he love me to madness, I
shall never requite him.

NERISSA

What say you, then, to Falconbridge, the young
baron of England?

PORTIA

You know I say nothing to him; for he understands

not me, nor I him: he hath neither Latin, French, nor Italian; and you will come into the court and swear that I have a poor pennyworth in the English. He is a proper man's picture; but, alas, who can converse with a dumb-show? How oddly he is suited! I think he bought his doublet in Italy, his round hose in France, his bonnet in Germany, and his behaviour every where.

NERISSA

What think you of the Scottish lord, his neighbour?

PORTIA

That he hath a neighbourly charity in him; for he borrowed a box of the ear of the Englishman, and swore he would pay him again when he was able: I think the Frenchman became his surety, and sealed under for another.

NERISSA

How like you the young German, the Duke of Saxony's nephew?

PORTIA

Very vilely in the morning, when he is sober; and most vilely in the afternoon, when he is drunk: when he is best, he is a little worse than a man; and when he is worst, he is little better than a beast: an the worst fall that ever fell, I hope I shall make shift to go without him.

NERISSA

If he should offer to choose, and choose the right casket, you should refuse to perform your father's will, if you should refuse to accept him.

PORTIA

Therefore, for fear of the worst, I pray thee, set a deep glass of Rhenish wine on the contrary casket; for, if the devil be within and that temptation without, I know he will choose it. I will do any thing, Nerissa, ere I'll be married to a sponge.

NERISSA

You need not fear, lady, the having any of these lords: they have acquainted me with their determinations; which is, indeed, to return to their home, and to trouble you with no more suit, unless you may be won by some other sort than your father's imposition, depending on the caskets.

PORTIA

If I live to be as old as Sibylla, I will die as chaste as Diana, unless I be obtained by the manner of my father's will. I am glad this parcel of wooers are so reasonable; for there is not one among them but I dote on his very absence; and I pray God grant them a fair departure.

NERISSA

Do you not remember, lady, in your father's time, a Venetian, a scholar, and a soldier, that came hither in company of the Marquis of Montferrat?

PORTIA

Yes, yes, it was Bassanio; as I think he was so called.

NERISSA

True, madam: he, of all the men that ever my foolish eyes looked upon, was the best deserving a fair lady.

PORTIA

I remember him well; and I remember him worthy of thy praise.

Enter a SERVING-MAN

How now! what news?

SERVANT

The four strangers seek for you, madam, to take their leave: and there is a forerunner come from a fifth, the Prince of Morocco; who brings word, the prince his master will be here to-night.

PORTIA

If I could bid the fifth welcome with so good a heart as I can bid the other four farewell, I should be glad of his approach: if he have the condition of a saint and the complexion of a devil, I had rather he should shrive me than wive me.

Come, Nerissa. Sirrah, go before.

Whiles we shut the gates upon one wooer, another knocks at the door.   [Exeunt

SCENE III. Venice. A public place

Enter BASSANIO and SHYLOCK

SHYLOCK

Three thousand ducats; well.

BASSANIO

Ay, sir, for three months.

SHYLOCK

For three months; well.

BASSANIO

For the which, as I told you, Antonio shall be bound.

SHYLOCK

Antonio shall become bound; well.

BASSANIO

May you stead me? will you pleasure me? shall I know your answer?

SHYLOCK

Three thousand ducats for three months, and Antonio bound.

BASSANIO

Your answer to that.

SHYLOCK

Antonio is a good man.

BASSANIO

Have you heard any imputation to the contrary?

SHYLOCK

Ho, no, no, no, no: my meaning, in saying he is a good man, is to have you understand me, that he is sufficient. Yet his means are in supposition: he hath an argosy bound to Tripolis, another to the Indies; I understand, moreover, upon the Rialto, he hath a third at Mexico, a fourth for England, and other ventures he hath, squandered abroad. But ships are but boards, sailors but men: there be land-rats and water-rats, water-thieves and land-thieves, I mean pirates; and then there is the peril of waters, winds, and rocks. The man is, notwithstanding, sufficient. Three thousand ducats; I think I may take his bond.

BASSANIO

Be assured you may.

SHYLOCK

I will be assured I may; and, that I may be assured,
I will bethink me. May I speak with Antonio?

BASSANIO

If it please you to dine with us.

SHYLOCK

Yes, to smell pork; to eat of the habitation which
your prophet the Nazarite conjured the devil into.
I will buy with you, sell with you, talk with you,
walk with you, and so following; but I will not eat
with you, drink with you, nor pray with you. What
news on the Rialto? Who is he comes here?

Enter ANTONIO

BASSANIO

This is Signior Antonio.

SHYLOCK

[*Aside*] How like a fawning publican he looks!
I hate him for he is a Christian;
But more for that in low simplicity
He lends out money gratis and brings down
The rate of usance here with us in Venice.
If I can catch him once upon the hip,
I will feed fat the ancient grudge I bear him.
He hates our sacred nation; and he rails,
Even there where merchants most do congregate,
On me, my bargains, and my well-won thrift,
Which he calls interest. Cursed be my tribe,
If I forgive him!

BASSANIO

Shylock, do you hear?

SHYLOCK

I am debating of my present store;
And, by the near guess of my memory,
I cannot instantly raise up the gross
Of full three thousand ducats. What of that?
Tubal, a wealthy Hebrew of my tribe,
Will furnish me. But soft! how many months
Do you desire? [*To* ANTONIO] Rest you fair, good
  signior;
Your worship was the last man in our mouths.

ANTONIO

Shylock, although I neither lend nor borrow,
By taking nor by giving of excess,
Yet, to supply the ripe wants of my friend,
I'll break a custom. Is he yet possess'd
How much ye would?

SHYLOCK

Ay, ay, three thousand ducats.

ANTONIO

And for three months.

SHYLOCK

I had forgot; three months, you told me so.
Well then, your bond; and let me see; but hear you;
Methought you said you neither lend nor borrow
Upon advantage.

ANTONIO

I do never use it.

SHYLOCK

When Jacob grazed his uncle Laban's sheep,—
This Jacob from our holy Abram was,
As his wise mother wrought in his behalf,
The third possessor; ay, he was the third,—

ANTONIO

And what of him? did he take interest?

SHYLOCK

No, not take interest; not, as you would say,
Directly interest: mark what Jacob did.
When Laban and himself were compromised
That all the eanlings which were streak'd and pied
Should fall as Jacob's hire, the ewes, being rank,
In the end of Autumn turned to the rams;
And when the work of generation was
Between these woolly breeders in the act,
The skilful shepherd peel'd me certain wands,
And, in the doing of the deed of kind,
He stuck them up before the fulsome ewes,
Who, then conceiving, did in eaning time
Fall parti-colour'd lambs, and those were Jacob's.
This was a way to thrive, and he was blest:
And thrift is blessing, if men steal it not.

ANTONIO

This was a venture, sir, that Jacob served for;
A thing not in his power to bring to pass,
But sway'd and fashion'd by the hand of heaven.
Was this inserted to make interest good?
Or is your gold and silver ewes and rams?

SHYLOCK

I cannot tell; I make it breed as fast:
But note me, signior.

ANTONIO

Mark you this, Bassanio,
The devil can cite Scripture for his purpose.
An evil soul, producing holy witness,
Is like a villain with a smiling cheek;
A goodly apple rotten at the heart:
O, what a goodly outside falsehood hath!

SHYLOCK

Three thousand ducats; 'tis a good round sum.
Three months from twelve; then, let me see; the
  rate—

ANTONIO

Well, Shylock, shall we be beholding to you?

SHYLOCK

Signior Antonio, many a time and oft
In the Rialto you have rated me
About my moneys and my usances:
Still have I borne it with a patient shrug;
For sufferance is the badge of all our tribe.
You call me misbeliever, cut-throat dog,
And spit upon my Jewish gaberdine,
And all for use of that which is mine own.
Well then, it now appears you need my help:
Go to, then; you come to me, and you say
'Shylock, we would have moneys:' you say so;
You, that did void your rheum upon my beard,
And foot me as you spurn a stranger cur
Over your threshold: moneys is your suit.

What should I say to you? Should I not say
'Hath a dog money? is it possible
A cur can lend three thousand ducats?' or
Shall I bend low and in a bondman's key,
With bated breath and whispering humbleness,
Say this,—
'Fair sir, you spit on me on Wednesday last;
You spurn'd me such a day; another time
You call'd me dog; and for these courtesies
I'll lend you thus much moneys'?

ANTONIO

I am as like to call thee so again,
To spit on thee again, to spurn thee too.
If thou wilt lend this money, lend it not
As to thy friends; for when did friendship take
A breed for barren metal of his friend?
But lend it rather to thine enemy;
Who if he break, thou mayst with better face
Exact the penalty.

SHYLOCK

Why, look you, how you storm!
I would be friends with you, and have your love,
Forget the shames that you have stain'd me with,
Supply your present wants, and take no doit
Of usance for my moneys, and you'll not hear me:
This is kind I offer.

BASSANIO

This were kindness.

SHYLOCK

This kindness will I show.
Go with me to a notary, seal me there
Your single bond; and, in a merry sport,
If you repay me not on such a day,
In such a place, such sum or sums as are
Express'd in the condition, let the forfeit
Be nominated for an equal pound
Of your fair flesh, to be cut off and taken
In what part of your body pleaseth me.

ANTONIO

Content, i' faith: I'll seal to such a bond,
And say there is much kindness in the Jew.

BASSANIO

You shall not seal to such a bond for me:
I'll rather dwell in my necessity.

ANTONIO

Why, fear not, man; I will not forfeit it:
Within these two months, that's a month before
This bond expires, I do expect return
Of thrice three times the value of this bond.

SHYLOCK

O father Abram, what these Christians are,
Whose own hard dealings teaches them suspect
The thoughts of others! Pray you, tell me this;
If he should break his day, what should I gain
By the exaction of the forfeiture?
A pound of man's flesh taken from a man
Is not so estimable, profitable neither,
As flesh of muttons, beefs, or goats. I say,
To buy his favour, I extend this friendship:

If he will take it, so; if not, adieu;
And, for my love, I pray you wrong me not.

ANTONIO

Yes, Shylock, I will seal unto this bond.

SHYLOCK

Then meet me forthwith at the notary's;
Give him direction for this merry bond;
And I will go and purse the ducats straight;
See to my house, left in the fearful guard
Of an unthrifty knave; and presently
I will be with you.

ANTONIO

Hie thee, gentle Jew. [*Exit* SHYLOCK
The Hebrew will turn Christian: he grows kind.

BASSANIO

I like not fair terms and a villain's mind.

ANTONIO

Come on: in this there can be no dismay;
My ships come home a month before the day.

[*Exeunt*

ACT II

SCENE I. *Belmont. A room in* PORTIA'S *house*

Flourish of cornets. Enter the PRINCE OF MOROCCO *and
his train;* PORTIA, NERISSA, *and others attending*

MOROCCO

Mislike me not for my complexion,
The shadow'd livery of the burnish'd sun,
To whom I am a neighbour and near bred.
Bring me the fairest creature northward born,
Where Phœbus' fire scarce thaws the icicles,
And let us make incision for your love,
To prove whose blood is reddest, his or mine.
I tell thee, lady, this aspect of mine
Hath fear'd the valiant: by my love, I swear
The best-regarded virgins of our clime
Have loved it too: I would not change this hue,
Except to steal your thoughts, my gentle queen.

PORTIA

In terms of choice I am not solely led
By nice direction of a maiden's eyes;
Besides, the lottery of my destiny
Bars me the right of voluntary choosing:
But if my father had not scanted me
And hedged me by his wit, to yield myself
His wife who wins me by that means I told you,
Yourself, renowned prince, then stood as fair
As any comer I have look'd on yet
For my affection.

MOROCCO

Even for that I thank you:
Therefore, I pray you, lead me to the caskets,
To try my fortune. By this scimitar
That slew the Sophy and a Persian prince
That won three fields of Sultan Solyman,
I would outstare the sternest eyes that look,
Outbrave the heart most daring on the earth,

Pluck the young sucking cubs from the she-bear,
Yea, mock the lion when he roars for prey,
To win thee, lady. But, alas the while!
If Hercules and Lichas play at dice
Which is the better man, the greater throw
May turn by fortune from the weaker hand:
So is Alcides beaten by his page;
And so may I, blind fortune leading me,
Miss that which one unworthier may attain,
And die with grieving.

PORTIA
                    You must take your chance;
And either not attempt to choose at all,
Or swear before you choose, if you choose wrong,
Never to speak to lady afterward
In way of marriage: therefore be advised.

MOROCCO
Nor will not. Come, bring me unto my chance.

PORTIA
First, forward to the temple: after dinner
Your hazard shall be made.

MOROCCO
                    Good fortune then!
To make me blest or cursed'st among men.
                              [*Cornets, and exeunt*

SCENE II. *Venice. A street*

Enter LAUNCELOT GOBBO

LAUNCELOT GOBBO
Certainly my conscience will serve me to run from
this Jew my master. The fiend is at mine elbow, and
tempts me, saying to me, 'Gobbo, Launcelot Gobbo,
good Launcelot,' or 'good Gobbo,' or 'good Launcelot Gobbo, use your legs, take the start, run away.'
My conscience says, 'No; take heed, honest Launcelot; take heed, honest Gobbo,' or, as aforesaid,
'honest Launcelot Gobbo; do not run; scorn running with thy heels.' Well, the most courageous
fiend bids me pack: 'Via!' says the fiend; 'away!'
says the fiend; 'for the heavens, rouse up a brave
mind,' says the fiend, 'and run.' Well, my conscience, hanging about the neck of my heart, says
very wisely to me, 'My honest friend Launcelot, being an honest man's son,'—or rather an honest
woman's son;—for, indeed, my father did something smack, something grow to, he had a kind of
taste;—well, my conscience says, 'Launcelot, budge
not.' 'Budge,' says the fiend. 'Budge not,' says my
conscience. 'Conscience,' say I, 'you counsel well;'
'Fiend,' say I, 'you counsel well:' to be ruled by my
conscience, I should stay with the Jew my master,
who, God bless the mark, is a kind of devil; and, to
run away from the Jew, I should be ruled by the
fiend, who, saving your reverence, is the devil himself. Certainly the Jew is the very devil incarnal;
and, in my conscience, my conscience is but a kind
of hard conscience, to offer to counsel me to stay
with the Jew. The fiend gives the more friendly

counsel: I will run, fiend; my heels are at your command; I will run.

Enter OLD GOBBO, *with a basket*

OLD GOBBO
Master young man, you, I pray you, which is the
way to master Jew's?

LAUNCELOT GOBBO
[*Aside*] O heavens, this is my true-begotten father!
who, being more than sand-blind, high-gravel
blind, knows me not: I will try confusions with him.

OLD GOBBO
Master young gentleman, I pray you, which is the
way to master Jew's?

LAUNCELOT GOBBO
Turn up on your right hand at the next turning,
but, at the next turning of all, on your left; marry,
at the very next turning, turn of no hand, but turn
down indirectly to the Jew's house.

OLD GOBBO
By God's sonties, 'twill be a hard way to hit. Can
you tell me whether one Launcelot, that dwells with
him, dwell with him or no?

LAUNCELOT GOBBO
Talk you of young Master Launcelot? [*Aside*] Mark
me now; now will I raise the waters. Talk you of
young Master Launcelot?

OLD GOBBO
No master, sir, but a poor man's son: his father,
though I say it, is an honest exceeding poor man,
and, God be thanked, well to live.

LAUNCELOT GOBBO
Well, let his father be what a' will, we talk of young
Master Launcelot.

OLD GOBBO
Your worship's friend, and Launcelot, sir.

LAUNCELOT GOBBO
But I pray you, ergo, old man, ergo, I beseech you,
talk you of young Master Launcelot?

OLD GOBBO
Of Launcelot, an't please your mastership.

LAUNCELOT GOBBO
Ergo, Master Launcelot. Talk not of Master Launcelot, father; for the young gentleman, according to
Fates and Destinies and such odd sayings, the Sisters Three and such branches of learning, is indeed
deceased; or, as you would say in plain terms, gone
to heaven.

OLD GOBBO
Marry, God forbid! the boy was the very staff of my
age, my very prop.

LAUNCELOT GOBBO
Do I look like a cudgel or a hovel-post, a staff or a
prop? Do you know me, father?

OLD GOBBO
Alack the day, I know you not, young gentleman:
but, I pray you, tell me, is my boy, God rest his
soul, alive or dead?

LAUNCELOT GOBBO
Do you not know me, father?

OLD GOBBO

Alack, sir, I am sand-blind; I know you not.

LAUNCELOT GOBBO

Nay, indeed, if you had your eyes, you might fail of the knowing me: it is a wise father that knows his own child. Well, old man, I will tell you news of your son: give me your blessing: truth will come to light; murder cannot be hid long; a man's son may; but, at the length, truth will out.

OLD GOBBO

Pray you, sir, stand up: I am sure you are not Launcelot, my boy.

LAUNCELOT GOBBO

Pray you, let's have no more fooling about it, but give me your blessing: I am Launcelot, your boy that was, your son that is, your child that shall be.

OLD GOBBO

I cannot think you are my son.

LAUNCELOT GOBBO

I know not what I shall think of that: but I am Launcelot, the Jew's man; and I am sure Margery your wife is my mother.

OLD GOBBO

Her name is Margery, indeed: I'll be sworn, if thou be Launcelot, thou art mine own flesh and blood. Lord worshipped might he be! what a beard hast thou got! thou hast got more hair on thy chin than Dobbin my fill-horse has on his tail.

LAUNCELOT GOBBO

It should seem, then, that Dobbin's tail grows backward: I am sure he had more hair of his tail than I have of my face when I last saw him.

OLD GOBBO

Lord, how art thou changed! How dost thou and thy master agree? I have brought him a present. How 'gree you now?

LAUNCELOT GOBBO

Well, well: but, for mine own part, as I have set up my rest to run away, so I will not rest till I have run some ground. My master's a very Jew: give him a present! give him a halter: I am famished in his service; you may tell every finger I have with my ribs. Father, I am glad you are come: give me your present to one Master Bassanio, who, indeed, gives rare new liveries: if I serve not him, I will run as far as God has any ground. O rare fortune! here comes the man: to him, father; for I am a Jew, if I serve the Jew any longer.

Enter BASSANIO, *with* LEONARDO *and other followers*

BASSANIO

You may do so; but let it be so hasted, that supper be ready at the farthest by five of the clock. See these letters delivered; put the liveries to making; and desire Gratiano to come anon to my lodging.

[*Exit a* SERVANT

LAUNCELOT GOBBO

To him, father.

OLD GOBBO

God bless your worship!

BASSANIO

Gramercy! wouldst thou aught with me?

OLD GOBBO

Here's my son, sir, a poor boy,—

LAUNCELOT GOBBO

Not a poor boy, sir, but the rich Jew's man; that would, sir,—as my father shall specify,—

OLD GOBBO

He hath a great infection, sir, as one would say, to serve—

LAUNCELOT GOBBO

Indeed, the short and the long is, I serve the Jew, and have a desire,—as my father shall specify,—

OLD GOBBO

His master and he, saving your worship's reverence, are scarce cater-cousins,—

LAUNCELOT GOBBO

To be brief, the very truth is that the Jew, having done me wrong, doth cause me,—as my father, being, I hope, an old man, shall frutify unto you,—

OLD GOBBO

I have here a dish of doves that I would bestow upon your worship, and my suit is,—

LAUNCELOT GOBBO

In very brief, the suit is impertinent to myself, as your worship shall know by this honest old man; and, though I say it, though old man, yet poor man, my father.

BASSANIO

One speak for both. What would you?

LAUNCELOT GOBBO

Serve you, sir.

OLD GOBBO

That is the very defect of the matter, sir.

BASSANIO

I know thee well; thou hast obtain'd thy suit:
Shylock thy master spoke with me this day,
And hath preferr'd thee, if it be preferment
To leave a rich Jew's service, to become
The follower of so poor a gentleman.

LAUNCELOT GOBBO

The old proverb is very well parted between my master Shylock and you, sir: you have the grace of God, sir, and he hath enough.

BASSANIO

Thou speak'st it well. Go, father, with thy son.
Take leave of thy old master and inquire
My lodging out. Give him a livery
More guarded than his fellows': see it done.

LAUNCELOT GOBBO

Father, in. I cannot get a service, no; I have ne'er a tongue in my head. Well, if any man in Italy have a fairer table which doth offer to swear upon a book, I shall have good fortune. Go to, here's a simple line of life: here's a small trifle of wives: alas, fifteen wives is nothing! a'leven widows and nine maids is a simple coming-in for one man: and then to 'scape drowning thrice, and to be in peril of my life with the edge of a feather-bed; here are simple scapes. Well, if Fortune be a woman she's a good

wench for this gear. Father, come; I'll take my leave
of the Jew in the twinkling of an eye.

[*Exeunt* LAUNCELOT *and* OLD GOBBO

BASSANIO

I pray thee, good Leonardo, think on this:
These things being bought and orderly bestow'd,
Return in haste, for I do feast to-night
My best-esteem'd acquaintance: hie thee, go.

LEONARDO

My best endeavours shall be done herein.

Enter GRATIANO

GRATIANO

Where is your master?

LEONARDO

Yonder, sir, he walks.   [*Exit*

GRATIANO

Signior Bassanio,—

BASSANIO

Gratiano!

GRATIANO

I have a suit to you.

BASSANIO

You have obtain'd it.

GRATIANO

You must not deny me: I must go with you to Belmont.

BASSANIO

Why, then you must. But hear thee, Gratiano:
Thou art too wild, too rude, and bold of voice;
Parts that become thee happily enough,
And in such eyes as ours appear not faults;
But where thou art not known, why there they show
Something too liberal. Pray thee, take pain
To allay with some cold drops of modesty
Thy skipping spirit; lest, through thy wild behav-
iour,
I be misconstrued in the place I go to,
And lose my hopes.

GRATIANO

Signior Bassanio, hear me:
If I do not put on a sober habit,
Talk with respect, and swear but now and then,
Wear prayer-books in my pocket, look demurely;
Nay more, while grace is saying, hood mine eyes
Thus with my hat, and sigh, and say 'amen;'
Use all the observance of civility,
Like one well studied in a sad ostent
To please his grandam, never trust me more.

BASSANIO

Well, we shall see your bearing.

GRATIANO

Nay, but I bar to-night: you shall not gauge me
By what we do to-night.

BASSANIO

No, that were pity:
I would entreat you rather to put on
Your boldest suit of mirth, for we have friends
That purpose merriment. But fare you well:
I have some business.

GRATIANO

And I must to Lorenzo and the rest:
But we will visit you at supper-time.   [*Exeunt*

SCENE III. *The same. A room in* SHYLOCK'S *house*

Enter JESSICA *and* LAUNCELOT GOBBO

JESSICA

I am sorry thou wilt leave my father so:
Our house is hell; and thou, a merry devil,
Didst rob it of some taste of tediousness.
But fare thee well; there is a ducat for thee:
And, Launcelot, soon at supper shalt thou see
Lorenzo, who is thy new master's guest:
Give him this letter; do it secretly;
And so farewell: I would not have my father
See me in talk with thee.

LAUNCELOT GOBBO

Adieu! tears exhibit my tongue. Most beautiful
pagan, most sweet Jew! if a Christian did not play
the knave, and get thee, I am much deceived. But,
adieu: these foolish drops do something drown my
manly spirit: adieu.

JESSICA

Farewell, good Launcelot. [*Exit* LAUNCELOT GOBBO
Alack, what heinous sin is it in me
To be ashamed to be my father's child!
But though I am a daughter to his blood,
I am not to his manners. O Lorenzo,
If thou keep promise, I shall end this strife,
Become a Christian, and thy loving wife.   [*Exit*

SCENE IV. *The same. A street*

Enter GRATIANO, LORENZO, SALARINO, *and* SALANIO

LORENZO

Nay, we will slink away in supper-time,
Disguise us at my lodging, and return
All in an hour.

GRATIANO

We have not made good preparation.

SALARINO

We have not spoke us yet of torch-bearers.

SALANIO

'Tis vile, unless it may be quaintly order'd,
And better in my mind not undertook.

LORENZO

'Tis now but four o'clock: we have two hours
To furnish us.

Enter LAUNCELOT GOBBO, *with a letter*
Friend Launcelot, what's the news?

LAUNCELOT GOBBO

An it shall please you to break up this, it shall seem
to signify.

LORENZO

I know the hand: in faith, 'tis a fair hand;

And whiter than the paper it writ on
Is the fair hand that writ.

GRATIANO

Love-news, in faith.

LAUNCELOT GOBBO

By your leave, sir.

LORENZO

Whither goest thou?

LAUNCELOT GOBBO

Marry, sir, to bid my old master the Jew to sup to-
night with my new master the Christian.

LORENZO

Hold here, take this: tell gentle Jessica
I will not fail her; speak it privately.
Go, gentlemen,   [*Exit* LAUNCELOT GOBBO
Will you prepare you for this masque to-night?
I am provided of a torch-bearer.

SALARINO

Ay, marry, I'll be gone about it straight.

SALANIO

And so will I.

LORENZO

Meet me and Gratiano
At Gratiano's lodging some hour hence.

SALARINO

'Tis good we do so.   [*Exeunt* SALARINO *and* SALANIO

GRATIANO

Was not that letter from fair Jessica?

LORENZO

I must needs tell thee all. She hath directed
How I shall take her from her father's house;
What gold and jewels she is furnish'd with;
What page's suit she hath in readiness.
If e'er the Jew her father come to heaven,
It will be for his gentle daughter's sake:
And never dare misfortune cross her foot,
Unless she do it under this excuse,
That she is issue to a faithless Jew.
Come, go with me; peruse this as thou goest:
Fair Jessica shall be my torch-bearer.   [*Exeunt*

SCENE V. *The same. Before* SHYLOCK'S *house*

Enter SHYLOCK *and* LAUNCELOT GOBBO

SHYLOCK

Well, thou shalt see, thy eyes shall be thy judge,
The difference of old Shylock and Bassanio:—
What, Jessica!—thou shalt not gormandise,
As thou hast done with me:—What, Jessica!—
And sleep and snore, and rend apparel out;—
Why, Jessica, I say!

LAUNCELOT GOBBO

Why, Jessica!

SHYLOCK

Who bids thee call? I do not bid thee call.

LAUNCELOT GOBBO

Your worship was wont to tell me that I could do
nothing without bidding.

Enter JESSICA

JESSICA

Call you? what is your will?

SHYLOCK

I am bid forth to supper, Jessica:
There are my keys. But wherefore should I go?
I am not bid for love; they flatter me:
But yet I'll go in hate, to feed upon
The prodigal Christian. Jessica, my girl,
Look to my house. I am right loath to go:
There is some ill a-brewing towards my rest,
For I did dream of money-bags to-night.

LAUNCELOT GOBBO

I beseech you, sir, go: my young master doth expect
your reproach.

SHYLOCK

So do I his.

LAUNCELOT GOBBO

And they have conspired together, I will not say
you shall see a masque; but if you do, then it was
not for nothing that my nose fell a-bleeding on
Black-Monday last at six o'clock i' the morning,
falling out that year on Ash-Wednesday was four
year, in the afternoon.

SHYLOCK

What, are there masques? Hear you me, Jessica:
Lock up my doors; and when you hear the drum,
and the vile squealing of the wry-neck'd fife,
Clamber not you up to the casements then,
Nor thrust your head into the public street
To gaze on Christian fools with varnish'd faces;
But stop my house's ears, I mean my casements:
Let not the sound of shallow foppery enter
My sober house. By Jacob's staff, I swear
I have no mind of feasting forth to-night:
But I will go. Go you before me, sirrah;
Say I will come.

LAUNCELOT GOBBO

I will go before, sir. Mistress, look out at window,
for all this;
There will come a Christian by,
Will be worth a Jewess' eye.   [*Exit*

SHYLOCK

What says that fool of Hagar's offspring, ha?

JESSICA

His words were, 'Farewell, mistress;' nothing else

SHYLOCK

The patch is kind enough, but a huge feeder;
Snail-slow in profit, and he sleeps by day
More than the wild-cat: drones hive not with me;
Therefore I part with him; and part with him
To one that I would have him help to waste
His borrow'd purse. Well, Jessica, go in:
Perhaps I will return immediately:
Do as I bid you; shut doors after you:
Fast bind, fast find,
A proverb never stale in thrifty mind.   [*Exit*

JESSICA

Farewell; and if my fortune be not crost,
I have a father, you a daughter, lost.   [*Exit*

SCENE VI. *The same*

Enter GRATIANO *and* SALARINO, *masqued*

GRATIANO
This is the pent-house under which Lorenzo
Desired us to make stand.

SALARINO
                              His hour is almost past.

GRATIANO
And it is marvel he out-dwells his hour,
For lovers ever run before the clock.

SALARINO
O, ten times faster Venus' pigeons fly
To seal love's bonds new-made, than they are wont
To keep obliged faith unforfeited!

GRATIANO
That ever holds: who riseth from a feast
With that keen appetite that he sits down?
Where is the horse that doth untread again
His tedious measures with the unbated fire
That he did pace them first? All things that are,
Are with more spirit chased than enjoy'd.
How like a younker or a prodigal
The scarfed bark puts from her native bay,
Hugg'd and embraced by the strumpet wind!
How like the prodigal doth she return,
With over-weather'd ribs and ragged sails,
Lean, rent, and beggar'd by the strumpet wind!

SALARINO
Here comes Lorenzo: more of this hereafter.

Enter LORENZO

LORENZO
Sweet friends, your patience for my long abode;
Not I, but my affairs, have made you wait:
When you shall please to play the thieves for wives,
I'll watch as long for you then. Approach;
Here dwells my father Jew. Ho! who's within?

Enter JESSICA, *above, in boy's clothes*

JESSICA
Who are you? Tell me, for more certainty,
Albeit I'll swear that I do know your tongue.

LORENZO
Lorenzo, and thy love.

JESSICA
Lorenzo, certain; and my love, indeed,
For who love I so much? And now who knows
But you, Lorenzo, whether I am yours?

LORENZO
Heaven and thy thoughts are witness that thou art.

JESSICA
Here, catch this casket; it is worth the pains.
I am glad 'tis night, you do not look on me,
For I am much ashamed of my exchange:
But love is blind, and lovers cannot see
The pretty follies that themselves commit;
For if they could, Cupid himself would blush
To see me thus transformed to a boy.

LORENZO
Descend, for you must be my torch-bearer.

JESSICA
What, must I hold a candle to my shames?
They in themselves, good sooth, are too too light.
Why, 'tis an office of discovery, love;
And I should be obscured.

LORENZO
                              So are you, sweet,
Even in the lovely garnish of a boy.
But come at once;
For the close night doth play the runaway,
And we are stay'd for at Bassanio's feast.

JESSICA
I will make fast the doors, and gild myself
With some mo ducats, and be with you straight.
                                        [*Exit above*

GRATIANO
Now, by my hood, a Gentile, and no Jew.

LORENZO
Beshrew me but I love her heartily;
For she is wise, if I can judge of her;
And fair she is, if that mine eyes be true;
And true she is, as she hath proved herself;
And therefore, like herself, wise, fair, and true,
Shall she be placed in my constant soul.

Enter JESSICA, *below*

What, art thou come? On, gentlemen; away!
Our masquing mates by this time for us stay.
                    [*Exit with* JESSICA *and* SALARINO

Enter ANTONIO

ANTONIO
Who's there?

GRATIANO
Signior Antonio!

ANTONIO
Fie, fie, Gratiano; where are all the rest?
'Tis nine o'clock: our friends all stay for you.
No masque to-night: the wind is come about;
Bassanio presently will go aboard:
I have sent twenty out to seek for you.

GRATIANO
I am glad on't: I desire no more delight
Than to be under sail and gone to-night.   [*Exeunt*

SCENE VII. *Belmont. A room in* PORTIA'S *house*

Flourish of cornets. Enter PORTIA, *with the* PRINCE OF
MOROCCO, *and their trains*

PORTIA
Go draw aside the curtains, and discover
The several caskets to this noble prince.
Now make your choice.

MOROCCO
The first, of gold, who this inscription bears,
'Who chooseth me shall gain what many men de-
    sire;'
The second, silver, which this promise carries,
'Who chooseth me shall get as much as he deserves;'
This third, dull lead, with warning all as blunt,

'Who chooseth me must give and hazard all he
    hath.'
How shall I know if I do choose the right?
              PORTIA
The one of them contains my picture, prince:
If you choose that, then I am yours withal.
            MOROCCO
Some god direct my judgement! Let me see;
I will survey the inscriptions back again.
What says this leaden casket?
'Who chooseth me must give and hazard all he
    hath.'
Must give,—for what? for lead? hazard for lead?
This casket threatens. Men that hazard all
Do it in hope of fair advantages:
A golden mind stoops not to shows of dross;
I'll then nor give nor hazard aught for lead.
What says the silver with her virgin hue?
'Who chooseth me shall get as much as he deserves.'
As much as he deserves! Pause there, Morocco,
And weigh thy value with an even hand:
If thou be'st rated by thy estimation,
Thou dost deserve enough; and yet enough
May not extend so far as to the lady:
And yet to be afeard of my deserving
Were but a weak disabling of myself.
As much as I deserve! Why, that's the lady:
I do in birth deserve her, and in fortunes,
In graces and in qualities of breeding;
But more than these, in love I do deserve.
What if I stray'd no further, but chose here?
Let's see once more this saying graved in gold;
'Who chooseth me shall gain what many men de-
    sire.'
Why, that's the lady; all the world desires her;
From the four corners of the earth they come,
To kiss this shrine, this mortal-breathing saint:
The Hyrcanian deserts and the vasty wilds
Of wide Arabia are as throughfares now
For princes to come view fair Portia:
The watery kingdom, whose ambitious head
Spits in the face of heaven, is no bar
To stop the foreign spirits; but they come,
As o'er a brook, to see fair Portia.
One of these three contains her heavenly picture.
Is't like that lead contains her? 'Twere damnation
To think so base a thought: it were too gross
To rib her cerecloth in the obscure grave.
Or shall I think in silver she's immured,
Being ten times undervalued to tried gold?
O sinful thought! Never so rich a gem
Was set in worse than gold. They have in England
A coin that bears the figure of an angel
Stamped in gold, but that's insculp'd upon;
But here an angel in a golden bed
Lies all within. Deliver me the key:
Here do I choose, and thrive I as I may!
            PORTIA
There, take it, prince; and if my form lie there,
Then I am yours.   *[He unlocks the golden casket*

           MOROCCO
      O hell! what have we here?
A carrion Death, within whose empty eye
There is a written scroll! I'll read the writing. *[Reads*

    All that glisters is not gold;
    Often have you heard that told:
    Many a man his life hath sold
    But my outside to behold:
    Gilded tombs do worms infold.
    Had you been as wise as bold,
    Young in limbs, in judgement old,
    Your answer had not been inscroll'd:
    Fare you well; your suit is cold.

Cold, indeed; and labour lost:
Then, farewell, heat, and welcome, frost!
Portia, adieu. I have too grieved a heart
To take a tedious leave: thus losers part.
       [Exit with his train. Flourish of cornets
            PORTIA
A gentle riddance. Draw the curtains, go.
Let all of his complexion choose me so.   *[Exeunt*

SCENE VIII. *Venice. A street*

Enter SALARINO *and* SALANIO
          SALARINO
Why, man, I saw Bassanio under sail:
With him is Gratiano gone along;
And in their ship I am sure Lorenzo is not.
          SALANIO
The villain Jew with outcries raised the Duke,
Who went with him to search Bassanio's ship.
          SALARINO
He came too late, the ship was under sail:
But there the Duke was given to understand
That in a gondola were seen together
Lorenzo and his amorous Jessica:
Besides, Antonio certified the Duke
They were not with Bassanio in his ship.
          SALANIO
I never heard a passion so confused,
So strange, outrageous, and so variable,
As the dog Jew did utter in the streets:
'My daughter! O my ducats! O my daughter!
Fled with a Christian! O my Christian ducats!
Justice! the law! my ducats, and my daughter!
A sealed bag, two sealed bags of ducats,
Of double ducats, stolen from me by my daughter!
And jewels, two stones, two rich and precious stones,
Stolen by my daughter! Justice! find the girl!
She hath the stones upon her, and the ducats!'
          SALARINO
Why, all the boys in Venice follow him,
Crying, his stones, his daughter, and his ducats.
          SALANIO
Let good Antonio look he keep his day,
Or he shall pay for this.
          SALARINO
          Marry, well remember'd.
I reason'd with a Frenchman yesterday,

Who told me, in the narrow seas that part
The French and English, there miscarried
A vessel of our country richly fraught:
I thought upon Antonio when he told me;
And wish'd in silence that it were not his.

SALANIO
You were best to tell Antonio what you hear;
Yet do not suddenly, for it may grieve him.

SALARINO
A kinder gentleman treads not the earth.
I saw Bassanio and Antonio part:
Bassanio told him he would make some speed
Of his return: he answer'd, 'Do not so;
Slubber not business for my sake, Bassanio,
But stay the very riping of the time;
And for the Jew's bond which he hath of me,
Let it not enter in your mind of love:
Be merry; and employ your chiefest thoughts
To courtship, and such fair ostents of love
As shall conveniently become you there:'
And even there, his eye being big with tears,
Turning his face, he put his hand behind him,
And with affection wondrous sensible
He wrung Bassanio's hand; and so they parted.

SALANIO
I think he only loves the world for him.
I pray thee, let us go and find him out,
And quicken his embraced heaviness
With some delight or other.

SALARINO
            Do we so.   [Exeunt

SCENE IX. Belmont. A room in PORTIA's house

Enter NERISSA and a SERVITOR
NERISSA
Quick, quick, I pray thee: draw the curtain straight:
The Prince of Arragon hath ta'en his oath,
And comes to his election presently.
Flourish of cornets. Enter the PRINCE OF ARRAGON,
PORTIA, and their trains

PORTIA
Behold, there stand the caskets, noble prince:
If you choose that wherein I am contain'd,
Straight shall our nuptial rites be solemnized:
But if you fail, without more speech, my lord,
You must be gone from hence immediately.

ARRAGON
I am enjoin'd by oath to observe three things:
First, never to unfold to any one
Which casket 'twas I chose; next, if I fail
Of the right casket, never in my life
To woo a maid in way of marriage:
Lastly,
If I do fail in fortune of my choice,
Immediately to leave you and be gone.

PORTIA
To these injunctions every one doth swear
That comes to hazard for my worthless self.

ARRAGON
And so have I address'd me. Fortune now
To my heart's hope! Gold; silver; and base lead.
'Who chooseth me must give and hazard all he
   hath.'
You shall look fairer, ere I give or hazard.
What says the golden chest? ha! let me see:
'Who chooseth me shall gain what many men de-
   sire.'
What many men desire! that 'many' may be meant
By the fool multitude, that choose by show,
Not learning more than the fond eye doth teach;
Which pries not to the interior, but, like the martlet,
Builds in the weather on the outward wall,
Even in the force and road of casualty.
I will not choose what many men desire,
Because I will not jump with common spirits,
And rank me with the barbarous multitudes.
Why, then to thee, thou silver treasure-house;
Tell me once more what title thou dost bear:
'Who chooseth me shall get as much as he deserves:'
And well said too; for who shall go about
To cozen fortune, and be honourable
Without the stamp of merit? Let none presume
To wear an undeserved dignity.
O, that estates, degrees and offices
Were not derived corruptly, and that clear honour
Were purchased by the merit of the wearer!
How many then should cover that stand bare!
How many be commanded that command!
How much low peasantry would then be glean'd
From the true seed of honour! and how much hon-
   our
Pick'd from the chaff and ruin of the times,
To be new-varnish'd! Well, but to my choice:
'Who chooseth me shall get as much as he deserves.'
I will assume desert. Give me a key for this,
And instantly unlock my fortunes here.
                              [He opens the silver casket

PORTIA
[Aside] Too long a pause for that which you find
   there.

ARRAGON
What's here? the portrait of a blinking idiot,
Presenting me a schedule! I will read it.
How much unlike art thou to Portia!
How much unlike my hopes and my deservings!
'Who chooseth me shall have as much as he de-
   serves.'
Did I deserve no more than a fool's head?
Is that my prize? are my deserts no better?

PORTIA
To offend, and judge, are distinct offices,
And of opposed natures.

ARRAGON
            What is here?

[Reads]   The fire seven times tried this:
            Seven times tried that judgement is,
            That did never choose amiss.
            Some there be that shadows kiss;

Such have but a shadow's bliss:
There be fools alive, I wis,
Silver'd o'er; and so was this.
Take what wife you will to bed,
I will ever be your head:
So be gone: you are sped.

Still more fool I shall appear
By the time I linger here:
With one fool's head I came to woo,
But I go away with two.
Sweet, adieu. I'll keep my oath,
Patiently to bear my wroth.

[*Exeunt* ARRAGON *and train*

PORTIA
Thus hath the candle singed the moth.
O, these deliberate fools! when they do choose,
They have the wisdom by their wit to lose.

NERISSA
The ancient saying is no heresy,
Hanging and wiving goes by destiny.

PORTIA
Come, draw the curtain, Nerissa.

Enter a SERVANT

SERVANT
Where is my lady?

PORTIA
Here: what would my lord?

SERVANT
Madam, there is alighted at your gate
A young Venetian, one that comes before
To signify the approaching of his lord;
From whom he bringeth sensible regreets,
To wit, besides commends and courteous breath,
Gifts of rich value. Yet I have not seen
So likely an ambassador of love:
A day in April never came so sweet,
To show how costly summer was at hand,
As this fore-spurrer comes before his lord.

PORTIA
No more, I pray thee: I am half afeard
Thou wilt say anon he is some kin to thee,
Thou spend'st such high-day wit in praising him.
Come, come, Nerissa; for I long to see
Quick Cupid's post that comes so mannerly.

NERISSA
Bassanio, lord Love, if thy will it be!   [*Exeunt*

ACT III

Scene I. *Venice. A street*

Enter SALANIO *and* SALARINO

SALANIO
Now, what news on the Rialto?

SALARINO
Why, yet it lives there unchecked, that Antonio
hath a ship of rich lading wrecked on the narrow
seas; the Goodwins, I think they call the place; a
very dangerous flat and fatal, where the carcases of
many a tall ship lie buried, as they say, if my gossip
Report be an honest woman of her word.

SALANIO
I would she were as lying a gossip in that as ever
knapped ginger, or made her neighbours believe
she wept for the death of a third husband. But it is
true, without any slips of prolixity, or crossing the
plain highway of talk, that the good Antonio, the
honest Antonio,—O that I had a title good enough
to keep his name company!—

SALARINO
Come, the full stop.

SALANIO
Ha! what sayest thou? Why, the end is, he hath lost
a ship.

SALARINO
I would it might prove the end of his losses.

SALANIO
Let me say 'amen' betimes, lest the devil cross my
prayer, for here he comes in the likeness of a Jew.

Enter SHYLOCK

How now, Shylock! what news among the merchants?

SHYLOCK
You knew, none so well, none so well as you, of my
daughter's flight.

SALARINO
That's certain: I, for my part, knew the tailor that
made the wings she flew withal.

SALANIO
And Shylock, for his own part, knew the bird was
fledged; and then it is the complexion of them all to
leave the dam.

SHYLOCK
She is damned for it.

SALARINO
That's certain, if the devil may be her judge.

SHYLOCK
My own flesh and blood to rebel!

SALANIO
Out upon it, old carrion! rebels it at these years?

SHYLOCK
I say, my daughter is my flesh and blood.

SALARINO
There is more difference between thy flesh and hers
than between jet and ivory; more between your
bloods than there is between red wine and rhenish.
But tell us, do you hear whether Antonio have had
any loss at sea or no?

SHYLOCK
There I have another bad match: a bankrupt, a
prodigal, who dare scarce show his head on the
Rialto; a beggar, that was used to come so smug
upon the mart; let him look to his bond: he was
wont to call me usurer; let him look to his bond: he
was wont to lend money for a Christian courtesy;
let him look to his bond.

SALARINO
Why, I am sure, if he forfeit, thou wilt not take his
flesh: what's that good for?

SHYLOCK

To bait fish withal: if it will feed nothing else, it will feed my revenge. He hath disgraced me, and hindered me half a million; laughed at my losses, mocked at my gains, scorned my nation, thwarted my bargains, cooled my friends, heated mine enemies; and what's his reason? I am a Jew. Hath not a Jew eyes? hath not a Jew hands, organs, dimensions, senses, affections, passions? fed with the same food, hurt with the same weapons, subject to the same diseases, healed by the same means, warmed and cooled by the same winter and summer, as a Christian is? If you prick us, do we not bleed? if you tickle us, do we not laugh? if you poison us, do we not die? and if you wrong us, shall we not revenge? if we are like you in the rest, we will resemble you in that. If a Jew wrong a Christian, what is his humility? Revenge. If a Christian wrong a Jew, what should his sufferance be by Christian example? Why, revenge. The villany you teach me, I will execute; and it shall go hard but I will better the instruction.

Enter a SERVANT

SERVANT

Gentlemen, my master Antonio is at his house, and desires to speak with you both.

SALARINO

We have been up and down to seek him.

Enter TUBAL

SALANIO

Here comes another of the tribe: a third cannot be matched, unless the devil himself turn Jew.

[*Exeunt* SALANIO, SALARINO, *and* SERVANT

SHYLOCK

How now, Tubal! what news from Genoa? hast thou found my daughter?

TUBAL

I often came where I did hear of her, but cannot find her.

SHYLOCK

Why, there, there, there, there! a diamond gone, cost me two thousand ducats in Frankfort! The curse never fell upon our nation till now; I never felt it till now: two thousand ducats in that; and other precious, precious jewels. I would my daughter were dead at my foot, and the jewels in her ear! would she were hearsed at my foot, and the ducats in her coffin! No news of them? Why, so:—and I know not what's spent in the search: why, thou loss upon loss! the thief gone with so much, and so much to find the thief; and no satisfaction, no revenge: nor no ill luck stirring but what lights on my shoulders; no sighs but of my breathing; no tears but of my shedding.

TUBAL

Yes, other men have ill luck too: Antonio, as I heard in Genoa,—

SHYLOCK

What, what, what? ill luck, ill luck?

TUBAL

Hath an argosy cast away, coming from Tripolis.

SHYLOCK

I thank God, I thank God! Is't true, is't true?

TUBAL

I spoke with some of the sailors that escaped the wreck.

SHYLOCK

I thank thee, good Tubal: good news, good news! ha, ha! where? in Genoa?

TUBAL

Your daughter spent in Genoa, as I heard, in one night fourscore ducats.

SHYLOCK

Thou stick'st a dagger in me: I shall never see my gold again: fourscore ducats at a sitting! fourscore ducats!

TUBAL

There came divers of Antonio's creditors in my company to Venice, that swear he cannot choose but break.

SHYLOCK

I am very glad of it: I'll plague him; I'll torture him: I am glad of it.

TUBAL

One of them showed me a ring that he had of your daughter for a monkey.

SHYLOCK

Out upon her! Thou torturest me, Tubal: it was my turquoise; I had it of Leah when I was a bachelor: I would not have given it for a wilderness of monkeys.

TUBAL

But Antonio is certainly undone.

SHYLOCK

Nay, that's true, that's very true. Go, Tubal, fee me an officer; bespeak him a fortnight before. I will have the heart of him, if he forfeit; for, were he out of Venice, I can make what merchandise I will. Go, go, Tubal, and meet me at our synagogue; go, good Tubal; at our synagogue, Tubal.   [*Exeunt*

SCENE II. *Belmont. A room in* PORTIA'S *house*

Enter BASSANIO, PORTIA, GRATIANO, NERISSA, *and*
ATTENDANTS

PORTIA

I pray you, tarry: pause a day or two
Before you hazard; for, in choosing wrong,
I lose your company: therefore forbear awhile.
There's something tells me, but it is not love,
I would not lose you; and you know yourself,
Hate counsels not in such a quality.
But lest you should not understand me well,—
And yet a maiden hath no tongue but thought,—
I would detain you here some month or two
Before you venture for me. I could teach you
How to choose right, but I am then forsworn:
So will I never be: so may you miss me;

But if you do, you'll make me wish a sin,
That I had been forsworn. Beshrew your eyes,
They have o'er-look'd me, and divided me;
One half of me is yours, the other half yours,
Mine own, I would say; but if mine, then yours,
And so all yours! O, these naughty times
Put bars between the owners and their rights!
And so, though yours, not yours. Prove it so,
Let fortune go to hell for it, not I.
I speak too long; but 'tis to peize the time,
To eke it and to draw it out in length,
To stay you from election.

BASSANIO
                    Let me choose;
For as I am, I live upon the rack.

PORTIA
Upon the rack, Bassanio! then confess
What treason there is mingled with your love.

BASSANIO
None but that ugly treason of mistrust,
Which makes me fear the enjoying of my love:
There may as well be amity and life
'Tween snow and fire, as treason and my love.

PORTIA
Ay, but I fear you speak upon the rack,
Where men enforced do speak any thing.

BASSANIO
Promise me life, and I'll confess the truth.

PORTIA
Well then, confess and live.

BASSANIO
                    'Confess,' and 'love,'
Had been the very sum of my confession:
O happy torment, when my torturer
Doth teach me answers for deliverance!
But let me to my fortune and the caskets.

PORTIA
Away, then! I am lock'd in one of them:
If you do love me, you will find me out.
Nerissa and the rest, stand all aloof.
Let music sound while he doth make his choice;
Then, if he lose, he makes a swan-like end,
Fading in music: that the comparison
May stand more proper, my eye shall be the stream,
And watery death-bed for him. He may win;
And what is music then? Then music is
Even as the flourish when true subjects bow
To a new-crowned monarch: such it is
As are those dulcet sounds in break of day
That creep into the dreaming bridegroom's ear,
And summon him to marriage. Now he goes,
With no less presence, but with much more love,
Than young Alcides, when he did redeem
The virgin tribute paid by howling Troy
To the sea-monster: I stand for sacrifice;
The rest aloof are the Dardanian wives,
With bleared visages, come forth to view
The issue of the exploit. Go, Hercules!
Live thou, I live: with much much more dismay
I view the fight than thou that makest the fray.

Music, whilst BASSANIO *comments on the caskets to himself*

SONG

Tell me where is fancy bred,
Or in the heart or in the head?
How begot, how nourished?
        Reply, reply.
It is engender'd in the eyes,
With gazing fed; and fancy dies
In the cradle where it lies.
        Let us all ring fancy's knell;
        I'll begin it,—Ding, dong, bell.

ALL
Ding, dong, bell.

BASSANIO
So may the outward shows be least themselves:
The world is still deceived with ornament.
In law, what plea so tainted and corrupt,
But, being season'd with a gracious voice,
Obscures the show of evil? In religion,
What damned error, but some sober brow
Will bless it, and approve it with a text,
Hiding the grossness with fair ornament?
There is no vice so simple, but assumes
Some mark of virtue on his outward parts:
How many cowards, whose hearts are all as false
As stairs of sand, wear yet upon their chins
The beards of Hercules and frowning Mars;
Who, inward search'd, have livers white as milk;
And these assume but valour's excrement
To render them redoubted! Look on beauty,
And you shall see 'tis purchased by the weight;
Which therein works a miracle in nature,
Making them lightest that wear most of it:
So are those crisped snaky golden locks
Which make such wanton gambols with the wind,
Upon supposed fairness, often known
To be the dowry of a second head,
The skull that bred them in the sepulchre.
Thus ornament is but the guiled shore
To a most dangerous sea; the beauteous scarf
Veiling an Indian beauty; in a word,
The seeming truth which cunning times put on
To entrap the wisest. Therefore, thou gaudy gold,
Hard food for Midas, I will none of thee;
Nor none of thee, thou pale and common drudge
'Tween man and man: but thou, thou meagre lead,
Which rather threatenest than dost promise aught,
Thy paleness moves me more than eloquence;
And here choose I: joy be the consequence!

PORTIA
[*Aside*] How all the other passions fleet to air,
As doubtful thoughts, and rash-embraced despair,
And shuddering fear, and green-eyed jealousy!
O love, be moderate; allay thy ecstasy;
In measure rain thy joy; scant this excess!
I feel too much thy blessing: make it less,
For fear I surfeit!

BASSANIO
What find I here?
                    [*Opening the leaden casket*

Fair Portia's counterfeit! What demi-god
Hath come so near creation? Move these eyes?
Or whether, riding on the balls of mine,
Seem they in motion? Here are sever'd lips,
Parted with sugar breath: so sweet a bar
Should sunder such sweet friends. Here in her hairs
The painter plays the spider, and hath woven
A golden mesh to entrap the hearts of men,
Faster than gnats in cobwebs: but her eyes,—
How could he see to do them? having made one,
Methinks it should have power to steal both his
And leave itself unfurnish'd. Yet look, how far
The substance of my praise doth wrong this shadow
In underprizing it, so far this shadow
Doth limp behind the substance. Here's the scroll,
The continent and summary of my fortune.

[Reads]   You that choose not by the view,
       Chance as fair, and choose as true!
       Since this fortune falls to you,
       Be content and seek no new.
       If you be well pleased with this,
       And hold your fortune for your bliss,
       Turn you where your lady is,
       And claim her with a loving kiss.

A gentle scroll. Fair lady, by your leave;
I come by note, to give and to receive.
Like one of two contending in a prize,
That thinks he hath done well in people's eyes,
Hearing applause and universal shout,
Giddy in spirit, still gazing in a doubt
Whether those peals of praise be his or no;
So, thrice-fair lady, stand I, even so;
As doubtful whether what I see be true,
Until confirm'd, sign'd, ratified by you.

PORTIA
You see me, Lord Bassanio, where I stand,
Such as I am: though for myself alone
I would not be ambitious in my wish,
To wish myself much better; yet, for you
I would be trebled twenty times myself;
A thousand times more fair, ten thousand times
More rich;
That only to stand high in your account,
I might in virtues, beauties, livings, friends,
Exceed account; but the full sum of me
Is sum of something, which, to term in gross,
Is an unlesson'd girl, unschool'd, unpractised;
Happy in this, she is not yet so old
But she may learn; happier than this,
She is not bred so dull but she can learn;
Happiest of all is that her gentle spirit
Commits itself to yours to be directed,
As from her lord, her governor, her king.
Myself and what is mine to you and yours
Is now converted: but now I was the lord
Of this fair mansion, master of my servants,
Queen o'er myself; and even now, but now,
This house, these servants, and this same myself,
Are yours, my lord: I give them with this ring;
Which when you part from, lose, or give away,

Let it presage the ruin of your love,
And be my vantage to exclaim on you.

BASSANIO
Madam, you have bereft me of all words,
Only my blood speaks to you in my veins;
And there is such confusion in my powers,
As, after some oration fairly spoke
By a beloved prince, there doth appear
Among the buzzing pleased multitude;
Where every something, being blent together,
Turns to a wild of nothing, save of joy,
Express'd and not express'd. But when this ring
Parts from this finger, then parts life from hence:
O, then be bold to say Bassanio's dead!

NERISSA
My lord and lady, it is now our time,
That have stood by and seen our wishes prosper,
To cry, good joy: good joy, my lord and lady!

GRATIANO
My Lord Bassanio and my gentle lady,
I wish you all the joy that you can wish;
For I am sure you can wish none from me:
And when your honours mean to solemnize
The bargain of your faith, I do beseech you,
Even at that time I may be married too.

BASSANIO
With all my heart, so thou canst get a wife.

GRATIANO
I thank your lordship, you have got me one.
My eyes, my lord, can look as swift as yours:
You saw the mistress, I beheld the maid;
You loved, I loved for intermission.
No more pertains to me, my lord, than you.
Your fortune stood upon the casket there,
And so did mine too, as the matter falls;
For wooing here until I sweat again,
And swearing till my very roof was dry
With oaths of love, at last, if promise last,
I got a promise of this fair one here
To have her love, provided that your fortune
Achieved her mistress.

PORTIA
       Is this true, Nerissa?

NERISSA
Madam, it is, so you stand pleased withal.

BASSANIO
And do you, Gratiano, mean good faith?

GRATIANO
Yes, faith, my lord.

BASSANIO
Our feast shall be much honoured in your marriage.

GRATIANO
We'll play with them the first boy for a thousand
ducats.

NERISSA
What, and stake down?

GRATIANO
No; we shall ne'er win at that sport, and stake down.
But who comes here? Lorenzo and his infidel?
What, and my old Venetian friend Salerio?

Enter LORENZO, JESSICA, *and* SALERIO, *a messenger
from Venice*

BASSANIO

Lorenzo and Salerio, welcome hither;
If that the youth of my new interest here
Have power to bid you welcome. By your leave,
I bid my very friends and countrymen,
Sweet Portia, welcome.

PORTIA

So do I, my lord:
They are entirely welcome.

LORENZO

I thank your honour. For my part, my lord,
My purpose was not to have seen you here;
But meeting with Salerio by the way,
He did entreat me, past all saying nay,
To come with him along.

SALERIO

I did, my lord;
And I have reason for it. Signior Antonio
Commends him to you.   [*Gives* BASSANIO *a letter*

BASSANIO

Ere I ope this letter,
I pray you, tell me how my good friend doth.

SALERIO

Not sick, my lord, unless it be in mind;
Nor well, unless in mind: his letter there
Will show you his estate.

GRATIANO

Nerissa, cheer yon stranger; bid her welcome.
Your hand, Salerio: what's the news from Venice?
How doth that royal merchant, good Antonio?
I know he will be glad of our success;
We are the Jasons, we have won the fleece.

SALERIO

I would you had won the fleece that he hath lost.

PORTIA

There are some shrewd contents in yon same paper,
That steals the colour from Bassanio's cheek:
Some dear friend dead; else nothing in the world
Could turn so much the constitution
Of any constant man. What, worse and worse!
With leave, Bassanio; I am half yourself,
And I must freely have the half of anything
That this same paper brings you.

BASSANIO

O sweet Portia,
Here are a few of the unpleasant'st words
That ever blotted paper! Gentle lady,
When I did first impart my love to you,
I freely told you, all the wealth I had
Ran in my veins, I was a gentleman;
And then I told you true: and yet, dear lady,
Rating myself at nothing, you shall see
How much I was a braggart. When I told you
My state was nothing, I should then have told you
That I was worse than nothing; for, indeed,
I have engaged myself to a dear friend,
Engaged my friend to his mere enemy,
To feed my means. Here is a letter, lady;

The paper as the body of my friend,
And every word in it a gaping wound,
Issuing life-blood. But is it true, Salerio?
Have all his ventures fail'd? What, not one hit?
From Tripolis, from Mexico, and England,
From Lisbon, Barbary, and India?
And not one vessel scape the dreadful touch
Of merchant-marring rocks?

SALERIO

Not one, my lord.
Besides, it should appear, that if he had
The present money to discharge the Jew,
He would not take it. Never did I know
A creature, that did bear the shape of man,
So keen and greedy to confound a man:
He plies the Duke at morning and at night;
And doth impeach the freedom of the state,
If they deny him justice: twenty merchants,
The Duke himself, and the magnificoes
Of greatest port, have all persuaded with him;
But none can drive him from the envious plea
Of forfeiture, of justice, and his bond.

JESSICA

When I was with him I have heard him swear
To Tubal and to Chus, his countrymen,
That he would rather have Antonio's flesh
Than twenty times the value of the sum
That he did owe him: and I know, my lord,
If law, authority and power deny not,
It will go hard with poor Antonio.

PORTIA

Is it your dear friend that is thus in trouble?

BASSANIO

The dearest friend to me, the kindest man,
The best-condition'd and unwearied spirit
In doing courtesies; and one in whom
The ancient Roman honour more appears
Than any that draws breath in Italy.

PORTIA

What sum owes he the Jew?

BASSANIO

For me three thousand ducats.

PORTIA

What, no more?
Pay him six thousand, and deface the bond;
Double six thousand, and then treble that,
Before a friend of this description
Shall lose a hair through Bassanio's fault.
First go with me to church and call me wife,
And then away to Venice to your friend;
For never shall you lie by Portia's side
With an unquiet soul. You shall have gold
To pay the petty debt twenty times over:
When it is paid, bring your true friend along.
My maid Nerissa and myself meantime
Will live as maids and widows. Come, away!
For you shall hence upon your wedding-day:
Bid your friends welcome, show a merry cheer:
Since you are dear bought, I will love you dear.
But let me hear the letter of your friend.

BASSANIO

[*Reads*] Sweet Bassanio, my ships have all miscarried, my creditors grow cruel, my estate is very low, my bond to the Jew is forfeit; and since in paying it, it is impossible I should live, all debts are cleared between you and I, if I might but see you at my death. Notwithstanding, use your pleasure: if your love do not persuade you to come, let not my letter.

PORTIA

O love, dispatch all business, and be gone!

BASSANIO

Since I have your good leave to go away,
    I will make haste: but, till I come again,
No bed shall e'er be guilty of my stay,
    No rest be interposer 'twixt us twain.   [*Exeunt*

SCENE III. *Venice. A street*

Enter SHYLOCK, SALARINO, ANTONIO, *and* GAOLER

SHYLOCK

Gaoler, look to him: tell not me of mercy;
This is the fool that lent out money gratis:
Gaoler, look to him.

ANTONIO

                    Hear me yet, good Shylock.

SHYLOCK

I'll have my bond; speak not against my bond:
I have sworn an oath that I will have my bond.
Thou call'dst me dog before thou hadst a cause;
But, since I am a dog, beware my fangs:
The Duke shall grant me justice. I do wonder,
Thou naughty gaoler, that thou art so fond
To come abroad with him at his request.

ANTONIO

I pray thee, hear me speak.

SHYLOCK

I'll have my bond; I will not hear thee speak:
I'll have my bond; and therefore speak no more.
I'll not be made a soft and dull-eyed fool,
To shake the head, relent, and sigh, and yield
To Christian intercessors. Follow not;
I'll have no speaking: I will have my bond.   [*Exit*

SALARINO

It is the most impenetrable cur
That ever kept with men.

ANTONIO

                    Let him alone:
I'll follow him no more with bootless prayers.
He seeks my life; his reason well I know:
I oft deliver'd from his forfeitures
Many that have at times made moan to me;
Therefore he hates me.

SALARINO

                    I am sure the Duke
Will never grant this forfeiture to hold.

ANTONIO

The Duke cannot deny the course of law:
For the commodity that strangers have
With us in Venice, if it be denied,

Will much impeach the justice of his state;
Since that the trade and profit of the city
Consisteth of all nations. Therefore, go:
These griefs and losses have so bated me,
That I shall hardly spare a pound of flesh
To-morrow to my bloody creditor.
Well, gaoler, on. Pray God, Bassanio come
To see me pay his debt, and then I care not! [*Exeunt*

SCENE IV. *Belmont. A room in* PORTIA'S *house*

Enter PORTIA, NERISSA, LORENZO, JESSICA, *and*
BALTHASAR

LORENZO

Madam, although I speak it in your presence,
You have a noble and a true conceit
Of god-like amity; which appears most strongly
In bearing thus the absence of your lord.
But if you knew to whom you show this honour,
How true a gentleman you send relief,
How dear a lover of my lord your husband,
I know you would be prouder of the work
Than customary bounty can enforce you.

PORTIA

I never did repent for doing good,
Nor shall not now: for in companions
That do converse and waste the time together,
Whose souls do bear an equal yoke of love,
There must be needs a like proportion
Of lineaments, of manners and of spirit;
Which makes me think that this Antonio,
Being the bosom lover of my lord,
Must needs be like my lord. If it be so,
How little is the cost I have bestow'd
In purchasing the semblance of my soul
From out the state of hellish misery!
This comes too near the praising of myself;
Therefore no more of it: hear other things.
Lorenzo, I commit into your hands
The husbandry and manage of my house
Until my lord's return: for mine own part,
I have toward heaven breathed a secret vow
To live in prayer and contemplation,
Only attended by Nerissa here,
Until her husband and my lord's return:
There is a monastery two miles off;
And there will we abide. I do desire you
Not to deny this imposition;
The which my love and some necessity
Now lays upon you.

LORENZO

                    Madam, with all my heart;
I shall obey you in all fair commands.

PORTIA

My people do already know my mind,
And will acknowledge you and Jessica
In place of Lord Bassanio and myself.
And so farewell, till we shall meet again.

LORENZO

Fair thoughts and happy hours attend on you!

JESSICA

I wish your ladyship all heart's content.

PORTIA

I thank you for your wish, and am well pleased
To wish it back on you: fare you well, Jessica.

[*Exeunt* JESSICA *and* LORENZO

Now, Balthasar,
As I have ever found thee honest-true,
So let me find thee still. Take this same letter,
And use thou all the endeavour of a man
In speed to Padua: see thou render this
Into my cousin's hand, Doctor Bellario;
And, look, what notes and garments he doth give
thee,
Bring them, I pray thee, with imagined speed
Unto the tranect, to the common ferry
Which trades to Venice. Waste no time in words,
But get thee gone: I shall be there before thee.

BALTHASAR

Madam, I go with all convenient speed.   [*Exit*

PORTIA

Come on, Nerissa; I have work in hand
That you yet know not of; we'll see our husbands
Before they think of us.

NERISSA

                         Shall they see us?

PORTIA

They shall, Nerissa; but in such a habit,
That they shall think we are accomplished
With that we lack. I'll hold thee any wager,
When we are both accoutred like young men,
I'll prove the prettier fellow of the two,
And wear my dagger with the braver grace,
And speak between the change of man and boy
With a reed voice, and turn two mincing steps
Into a manly stride, and speak of frays
Like a fine bragging youth; and tell quaint lies,
How honourable ladies sought my love,
Which I denying, they fell sick and died;
I could not do withal: then I'll repent,
And wish, for all that, that I had not kill'd them;
And twenty of these puny lies I'll tell,
That men shall swear I have discontinued school
Above a twelvemonth. I have within my mind
A thousand raw tricks of these bragging Jacks,
Which I will practise.

NERISSA

                      Why, shall we turn to men?

PORTIA

Fie, what a question's that,
If thou wert near a lewd interpreter!
But come, I'll tell thee all my whole device
When I am in my coach, which stays for us
At the park-gate; and therefore haste away,
For we must measure twenty miles to-day.   [*Exeunt*

SCENE V. *The same. A garden*

Enter LAUNCELOT GOBBO *and* JESSICA

LAUNCELOT GOBBO

Yes, truly; for, look you, the sins of the father are to
be laid upon the children: therefore, I promise ye,
I fear you. I was always plain with you, and so now
I speak my agitation of the matter: therefore be of
good cheer; for, truly, I think you are damned.
There is but one hope in it that can do you any
good; and that is but a kind of bastard hope neither.

JESSICA

And what hope is that, I pray thee?

LAUNCELOT GOBBO

Marry, you may partly hope that your father got
you not, that you are not the Jew's daughter.

JESSICA

That were a kind of bastard hope, indeed: so the
sins of my mother should be visited upon me.

LAUNCELOT GOBBO

Truly then I fear you are damned both by father
and mother: thus when I shun Scylla, your father,
I fall into Charybdis, your mother: well, you are
gone both ways.

JESSICA

I shall be saved by my husband; he hath made me
a Christian.

LAUNCELOT GOBBO

Truly, the more to blame he: we were Christians
enow before; e'en as many as could well live, one by
another. This making of Christians will raise the
price of hogs: if we grow all to be pork-eaters, we
shall not shortly have a rasher on the coals for
money.

Enter LORENZO

JESSICA

I'll tell my husband, Launcelot, what you say: here
he comes.

LORENZO

I shall grow jealous of you shortly, Launcelot, if you
thus get my wife into corners.

JESSICA

Nay, you need not fear us, Lorenzo: Launcelot and
I are out. He tells me flatly, there is no mercy for me
in heaven, because I am a Jew's daughter: and he
says, you are no good member of the commonwealth; for, in converting Jews to Christians, you
raise the price of pork.

LORENZO

I shall answer that better to the commonwealth
than you can the getting up of the negro's belly: the
Moor is with child by you, Launcelot.

LAUNCELOT GOBBO

It is much that the Moor should be more than reason: but if she be less than an honest woman, she is
indeed more than I took her for.

LORENZO

How every fool can play upon the word! I think the
best grace of wit will shortly turn into silence; and

discourse grow commendable in none only but parrots. Go in, sirrah; bid them prepare for dinner.

LAUNCELOT GOBBO

That is done, sir; they have all stomachs.

LORENZO

Goodly Lord, what a wit-snapper are you! then bid
them prepare dinner.

LAUNCELOT GOBBO

That is done too, sir; only 'cover' is the word.

LORENZO

Will you cover, then, sir?

LAUNCELOT GOBBO

Not so, sir, neither; I know my duty.

LORENZO

Yet more quarrelling with occasion! Wilt thou show
the whole wealth of thy wit in an instant? I pray
thee, understand a plain man in his plain meaning:
go to thy fellows; bid them cover the table, serve in
the meat, and we will come in to dinner.

LAUNCELOT GOBBO

For the table, sir, it shall be served in; for the meat,
sir, it shall be covered; for your coming in to dinner,
sir, why, let it be as humours and conceits shall
govern.   [Exit

LORENZO

O dear discretion, how his words are suited!
The fool hath planted in his memory
An army of good words; and I do know
A many fools, that stand in better place,
Garnish'd like him, that for a tricksy word
Defy the matter. How cheer'st thou, Jessica?
And now, good sweet, say thy opinion,
How dost thou like the Lord Bassanio's wife?

JESSICA

Past all expressing. It is very meet
The Lord Bassanio live an upright life;
For, having such a blessing in his lady,
He finds the joys of heaven here on earth;
And if on earth he do not mean it, then
In reason he should never come to heaven.
Why, if two gods should play some heavenly match
And on the wager lay two earthly women,
And Portia one, there must be something else
Pawn'd with the other; for the poor rude world
Hath not her fellow.

LORENZO

Even such a husband
Hast thou of me as she is for a wife.

JESSICA

Nay, but ask my opinion too of that.

LORENZO

I will anon: first, let us go to dinner.

JESSICA

Nay, let me praise you while I have a stomach.

LORENZO

No, pray thee, let it serve for table-talk;
Then, howsoe'er thou speak'st, 'mong other things
I shall digest it.

JESSICA

Well, I'll set you forth.   [Exeunt

ACT IV

Scene I. *Venice. A court of justice*

Enter the DUKE, *the* MAGNIFICOES, ANTONIO,
BASSANIO, GRATIANO, SALERIO, *and others*

DUKE

What, is Antonio here?

ANTONIO

Ready, so please your Grace.

DUKE

I am sorry for thee: thou art come to answer
A stony adversary, an inhuman wretch
Uncapable of pity, void and empty
From any dram of mercy.

ANTONIO

I have heard
Your Grace hath ta'en great pains to qualify
His rigorous course; but since he stands obdurate,
And that no lawful means can carry me
Out of his envy's reach, I do oppose
My patience to his fury; and am arm'd
To suffer, with a quietness of spirit,
The very tyranny and rage of his.

DUKE

Go one, and call the Jew into the court.

SALERIO

He is ready at the door: he comes, my lord.

Enter SHYLOCK

DUKE

Make room, and let him stand before our face.
Shylock, the world thinks, and I think so too,
That thou but lead'st this fashion of thy malice
To the last hour of act; and then 'tis thought
Thou'lt show thy mercy and remorse more strange
Than is thy strange apparent cruelty;
And where thou now exact'st the penalty,
Which is a pound of this poor merchant's flesh,
Thou wilt not only loose the forfeiture,
But, touch'd with human gentleness and love,
Forgive a moiety of the principal;
Glancing an eye of pity on his losses,
That have of late so huddled on his back,
Enow to press a royal merchant down,
And pluck commiseration of his state
From brassy bosoms and rough hearts of flint,
From stubborn Turks and Tartars, never train'd
To offices of tender courtesy.
We all expect a gentle answer, Jew.

SHYLOCK

I have possess'd your Grace of what I purpose;
And by our holy Sabbath have I sworn
To have the due and forfeit of my bond:
If you deny it, let the danger light
Upon your charter and your city's freedom.
You'll ask me, why I rather choose to have
A weight of carrion-flesh than to receive
Three thousand ducats: I'll not answer that:
But, say, it is my humour: is it answer'd?
What if my house be troubled with a rat,

And I be pleased to give ten thousand ducats
To have it baned? What, are you answer'd yet?
Some men there are love not a gaping pig;
Some, that are mad if they behold a cat;
And others, when the bagpipe sings i' the nose,
Cannot contain their urine: for affection,
Mistress of passion, sways it to the mood
Of what it likes or loathes. Now, for your answer:
As there is no firm reason to be render'd,
Why he cannot abide a gaping pig;
Why he, a harmless necessary cat;
Why he, a woollen bag-pipe; but of force
Must yield to such inevitable shame
As to offend, himself being offended;
So can I give no reason, nor I will not,
More than a lodged hate and a certain loathing
I bear Antonio, that I follow thus
A losing suit against him. Are you answer'd?

BASSANIO

This is no answer, thou unfeeling man,
To excuse the current of thy cruelty.

SHYLOCK

I am not bound to please thee with my answer.

BASSANIO

Do all men kill the things they do not love?

SHYLOCK

Hates any man the thing he would not kill?

BASSANIO

Every offence is not a hate at first.

SHYLOCK

What, wouldst thou have a serpent sting thee twice?

ANTONIO

I pray you, think you question with the Jew:
You may as well go stand upon the beach,
And bid the main flood bate his usual height;
You may as well use question with the wolf,
Why he hath made the ewe bleat for the lamb;
You may as well forbid the mountain pines
To wag their high tops, and to make no noise,
When they are fretten with the gusts of heaven;
You may as well do any thing most hard,
As seek to soften that—than which what's harder?—
His Jewish heart: therefore, I do beseech you,
Make no more offers, use no farther means,
But with all brief and plain conveniency
Let me have judgement and the Jew his will.

BASSANIO

For thy three thousand ducats here is six.

SHYLOCK

If every ducat in six thousand ducats
Were in six parts and every part a ducat,
I would not draw them; I would have my bond.

DUKE

How shalt thou hope for mercy, rendering none?

SHYLOCK

What judgement shall I dread, doing no wrong?
You have among you many a purchased slave,
Which, like your asses and your dogs and mules,
You use in abject and in slavish parts,
Because you bought them: shall I say to you,

Let them be free, marry them to your heirs?
Why sweat they under burthens? let their beds
Be made as soft as yours, and let their palates
Be season'd with such viands? You will answer
'The slaves are ours:' so do I answer you:
The pound of flesh, which I demand of him,
Is dearly bought; 'tis mine and I will have it.
If you deny me, fie upon your law!
There is no force in the decrees of Venice.
I stand for judgement: answer; shall I have it?

DUKE

Upon my power I may dismiss this court,
Unless Bellario, a learned doctor,
Whom I have sent for to determine this,
Come here to-day.

SALERIO

　　　　　My lord, here stays without
A messenger with letters from the doctor,
New come from Padua.

DUKE

Bring us the letters; call the messenger.

BASSANIO

Good cheer, Antonio! What, man, courage yet!
The Jew shall have my flesh, blood, bones, and all,
Ere thou shalt lose for me one drop of blood.

ANTONIO

I am a tainted wether of the flock,
Meetest for death: the weakest kind of fruit
Drops earliest to the ground; and so let me:
You cannot better be employ'd, Bassanio,
Than to live still, and write mine epitaph.

　　　Enter NERISSA, dressed like a lawyer's clerk

DUKE

Came you from Padua, from Bellario?

NERISSA

From both, my lord. Bellario greets your Grace.
　　　　　　　　　　　　　　　[Presenting a letter

BASSANIO

Why dost thou whet thy knife so earnestly?

SHYLOCK

To cut the forfeiture from that bankrupt there.

GRATIANO

Not on thy sole, but on thy soul, harsh Jew,
Thou makest thy knife keen; but no metal can,
No, not the hangman's axe, bear half the keenness
Of thy sharp envy. Can no prayers pierce thee?

SHYLOCK

No, none that thou hast wit enough to make.

GRATIANO

O, be thou damn'd, inexecrable dog!
And for thy life let justice be accused.
Thou almost makest me waver in my faith,
To hold opinion with Pythagoras,
That souls of animals infuse themselves
Into the trunks of men: thy currish spirit
Govern'd a wolf, who hang'd for human slaughter,
Even from the gallows did his fell soul fleet,
And, whilst thou lay'st in thy unhallow'd dam,
Infused itself in thee; for thy desires
Are wolvish, bloody, starved and ravenous.

SHYLOCK

Till thou canst rail the seal from off my bond,
Thou but offend'st thy lungs to speak so loud:
Repair thy wit, good youth, or it will fall
To cureless ruin. I stand here for law.

DUKE

This letter from Bellario doth commend
A young and learned doctor to our court.
Where is he?

NERISSA

He attendeth here hard by,
To know your answer, whether you'll admit him.

DUKE

With all my heart. Some three or four of you
Go give him courteous conduct to this place.
Meantime the court shall hear Bellario's letter.

CLERK

[Reads] Your Grace shall understand that at the receipt of your letter I am very sick: but in the instant that your messenger came, in loving visitation was with me a young doctor of Rome; his name is Balthasar. I acquainted him with the cause in controversy between the Jew and Antonio the merchant: we turned o'er many books together: he is furnished with my opinion; which, bettered with his own learning,—the greatness whereof I cannot enough commend,—comes with him, at my importunity, to fill up your Grace's request in my stead. I beseech you, let his lack of years be no impediment to let him lack a reverend estimation; for I never knew so young a body with so old a head. I leave him to your gracious acceptance, whose trial shall better publish his commendation.

DUKE

You hear the learn'd Bellario, what he writes:
And here, I take it, is the doctor come.
        Enter PORTIA *for* BALTHASAR
Give me your hand. Come you from old Bellario?

PORTIA

I did, my lord.

DUKE

You are welcome: take your place.
Are you acquainted with the difference
That holds this present question in the court?

PORTIA

I am informed throughly of the cause.
Which is the merchant here, and which the Jew?

DUKE

Antonio and old Shylock, both stand forth.

PORTIA

Is your name Shylock?

SHYLOCK

Shylock is my name.

PORTIA

Of a strange nature is the suit you follow;
Yet in such rule that the Venetian law
Cannot impugn you as you do proceed.
You stand within his danger, do you not?

ANTONIO

Ay, so he says.

PORTIA

Do you confess the bond?

ANTONIO

I do.

PORTIA

Then must the Jew be merciful.

SHYLOCK

On what compulsion must I? tell me that.

PORTIA

The quality of mercy is not strain'd,
It droppeth as the gentle rain from heaven
Upon the place beneath: it is twice blest;
It blesseth him that gives, and him that takes:
'Tis mightiest in the mightiest: it becomes
The throned monarch better than his crown;
His sceptre shows the force of temporal power,
The attribute to awe and majesty,
Wherein doth sit the dread and fear of kings;
But mercy is above this sceptred sway;
It is enthroned in the hearts of kings,
It is an attribute to God himself;
And earthly power doth then show likest God's
When mercy seasons justice. Therefore, Jew,
Though justice be thy plea, consider this,
That, in the course of justice, none of us
Should see salvation: we do pray for mercy;
And that same prayer doth teach us all to render
The deeds of mercy. I have spoke thus much
To mitigate the justice of thy plea;
Which if thou follow, this strict court of Venice
Must needs give sentence 'gainst the merchant there.

SHYLOCK

My deeds upon my head! I crave the law,
The penalty and forfeit of my bond.

PORTIA

Is he not able to discharge the money?

BASSANIO

Yes, here I tender it for him in the court;
Yea, twice the sum: if that will not suffice,
I will be bound to pay it ten times o'er,
On forfeit of my hands, my head, my heart:
If this will not suffice, it must appear
That malice bears down truth. And I beseech you,
Wrest once the law to your authority:
To do a great right, do a little wrong,
And curb this cruel devil of his will.

PORTIA

It must not be; there is no power in Venice
Can alter a decree established:
'Twill be recorded for a precedent,
And many an error, by the same example,
Will rush into the state: it cannot be.

SHYLOCK

A Daniel come to judgement! yea, a Daniel!
O wise young judge, how I do honour thee!

PORTIA

I pray you, let me look upon the bond.

SHYLOCK

Here 'tis, most reverend doctor, here it is.

PORTIA

Shylock, there's thrice thy money offer'd thee.

SHYLOCK

An oath, an oath, I have an oath in heaven:

Shall I lay perjury upon my soul?
No, not for Venice.

PORTIA

Why, this bond is forfeit;
And lawfully by this the Jew may claim
A pound of flesh, to be by him cut off
Nearest the merchant's heart. Be merciful:
Take thrice thy money; bid me tear the bond.

SHYLOCK

When it is paid according to the tenour.
It doth appear you are a worthy judge;
You know the law, your exposition
Hath been most sound: I charge you by the law,
Whereof you are a well-deserving pillar,
Proceed to judgement: by my soul I swear
There is no power in the tongue of man
To alter me: I stay here on my bond.

ANTONIO

Most heartily I do beseech the court
To give the judgement.

PORTIA

Why then, thus it is:
You must prepare your bosom for his knife.

SHYLOCK

O noble judge! O excellent young man!

PORTIA

For the intent and purpose of the law
Hath full relation to the penalty,
Which here appeareth due upon the bond.

SHYLOCK

'Tis very true: O wise and upright judge!
How much more elder art thou than thy looks!

PORTIA

Therefore lay bare your bosom.

SHYLOCK

Ay, his breast:
So says the bond:—doth it not, noble judge?—
'Nearest his heart:' those are the very words.

PORTIA

It is so. Are there balance here to weigh
The flesh?

SHYLOCK

I have them ready.

PORTIA

Have by some surgeon, Shylock, on your charge,
To stop his wounds, lest he do bleed to death.

SHYLOCK

Is it so nominated in the bond?

PORTIA

It is not so express'd: but what of that?
'Twere good you do so much for charity.

SHYLOCK

I cannot find it; 'tis not in the bond.

PORTIA

You, merchant, have you any thing to say?

ANTONIO

But little: I am arm'd and well prepared.
Give me your hand, Bassanio: fare you well!
Grieve not that I am fallen to this for you;
For herein Fortune shows herself more kind

Than is her custom: it is still her use
To let the wretched man outlive his wealth,
To view with hollow eye and wrinkled brow
An age of poverty; from which lingering penance
Of such misery doth she cut me off.
Commend me to your honourable wife:
Tell her the process of Antonio's end;
Say how I loved you, speak me fair in death;
And, when the tale is told, bid her be judge
Whether Bassanio had not once a love.
Repent but you that you shall lose your friend,
And he repents not that he pays your debt;
For if the Jew do cut but deep enough,
I'll pay it presently with all my heart.

BASSANIO

Antonio, I am married to a wife
Which is as dear to me as life itself;
But life itself, my wife, and all the world,
Are not with me esteem'd above thy life:
I would lose all, ay, sacrifice them all
Here to this devil, to deliver you.

PORTIA

Your wife would give you little thanks for that,
If she were by, to hear you make the offer.

GRATIANO

I have a wife, whom, I protest, I love:
I would she were in heaven, so she could
Entreat some power to change this currish Jew.

NERISSA

'Tis well you offer it behind her back;
The wish would make else an unquiet house.

SHYLOCK

These be the Christian husbands. I have a daughter;
Would any of the stock of Barrabas
Had been her husband rather than a Christian!
                                        [Aside
We trifle time: I pray thee, pursue sentence.

PORTIA

A pound of that same merchant's flesh is thine:
The court awards it, and the law doth give it.

SHYLOCK

Most rightful judge!

PORTIA

And you must cut this flesh from off his breast:
The law allows it, and the court awards it.

SHYLOCK

Most learned judge! A sentence! Come, prepare!

PORTIA

Tarry a little; there is something else.
This bond doth give thee here no jot of blood;
The words expressly are 'a pound of flesh:'
Take then thy bond, take thou thy pound of flesh;
But, in the cutting it, if thou dost shed
One drop of Christian blood, thy lands and goods
Are, by the laws of Venice, confiscate
Unto the state of Venice.

GRATIANO

O upright judge! Mark, Jew: O learned judge!

SHYLOCK

Is that the law?

PORTIA
Thyself shalt see the act:
For, as thou urgest justice, be assured
Thou shalt have justice, more than thou desirest.

GRATIANO
O learned judge! Mark, Jew: a learned judge!

SHYLOCK
I take this offer, then; pay the bond thrice,
And let the Christian go.

BASSANIO
Here is the money.

PORTIA
Soft!
The Jew shall have all justice; soft! no haste:
He shall have nothing but the penalty.

GRATIANO
O Jew! an upright judge, a learned judge!

PORTIA
Therefore prepare thee to cut off the flesh.
Shed thou no blood; nor cut thou less nor more
But just a pound of flesh: if thou cut'st more
Or less than a just pound, be it but so much
As makes it light or heavy in the substance,
Or the division of the twentieth part
Of one poor scruple, nay, if the scale do turn
But in the estimation of a hair,
Thou diest and all thy goods are confiscate.

GRATIANO
A second Daniel, a Daniel, Jew!
Now, infidel, I have you on the hip.

PORTIA
Why doth the Jew pause? take thy forfeiture.

SHYLOCK
Give me my principal, and let me go.

BASSANIO
I have it ready for thee; here it is.

PORTIA
He hath refused it in the open court:
He shall have merely justice and his bond.

GRATIANO
A Daniel, still say I, a second Daniel!
I thank thee, Jew, for teaching me that word.

SHYLOCK
Shall I not have barely my principal?

PORTIA
Thou shalt have nothing but the forfeiture,
To be so taken at thy peril, Jew.

SHYLOCK
Why, then the devil give him good of it!
I'll stay no longer question.

PORTIA
Tarry, Jew:
The law hath yet another hold on you.
It is enacted in the laws of Venice,
If it be proved against an alien
That by direct or indirect attempts
He seek the life of any citizen,
The party 'gainst the which he doth contrive
Shall seize one half his goods; the other half
Comes to the privy coffer of the state;

And the offender's life lies in the mercy
Of the Duke only, 'gainst all other voice.
In which predicament, I say, thou stand'st;
For it appears, by manifest proceeding,
That indirectly, and directly too,
Thou hast contrived against the very life
Of the defendant; and thou hast incurr'd
The danger formerly by me rehearsed.
Down, therefore, and beg mercy of the Duke.

GRATIANO
Beg that thou mayst have leave to hang thyself:
And yet, thy wealth being forfeit to the state,
Thou hast not left the value of a cord;
Therefore thou must be hang'd at the state's charge.

DUKE
That thou shalt see the difference of our spirits,
I pardon thee thy life before thou ask it:
For half thy wealth, it is Antonio's;
The other half comes to the general state,
Which humbleness may drive unto a fine.

PORTIA
Ay, for the state, not for Antonio.

SHYLOCK
Nay, take my life and all; pardon not that:
You take my house, when you do take the prop
That doth sustain my house; you take my life,
When you do take the means whereby I live.

PORTIA
What mercy can you render him, Antonio?

GRATIANO
A halter gratis; nothing else, for God's sake.

ANTONIO
So please my lord the Duke and all the court
To quit the fine for one half of his goods,
I am content; so he will let me have
The other half in use, to render it,
Upon his death, unto the gentleman
That lately stole his daughter:
Two things provided more, that, for this favour,
He presently become a Christian;
The other, that he do record a gift,
Here in the court, of all he dies possess'd,
Unto his son Lorenzo and his daughter.

DUKE
He shall do this, or else I do recant
The pardon that I late pronounced here.

PORTIA
Art thou contented, Jew? what dost thou say?

SHYLOCK
I am content.

PORTIA
Clerk, draw a deed of gift.

SHYLOCK
I pray you, give me leave to go from hence;
I am not well: send the deed after me,
And I will sign it.

DUKE
Get thee gone, but do it.

GRATIANO
In christening shalt thou have two godfathers:

Had I been judge, thou shouldst have had ten more,
To bring thee to the gallows, not the font.
                                        [*Exit* SHYLOCK
DUKE
Sir, I entreat you home with me to dinner.
PORTIA
I humbly do desire your Grace of pardon:
I must away this night toward Padua,
And it is meet I presently set forth.
DUKE
I am sorry that your leisure serves you not.
Antonio, gratify this gentleman,
For, in my mind, you are much bound to him.
                            [*Exeunt* DUKE *and his train*
BASSANIO
Most worthy gentleman, I and my friend
Have by your wisdom been this day acquitted
Of grievous penalties; in lieu whereof,
Three thousand ducats, due unto the Jew,
We freely cope your courteous pains withal.
ANTONIO
And stand indebted, over and above,
In love and service to you evermore.
PORTIA
He is well paid that is well satisfied;
And I, delivering you, am satisfied,
And therein do account myself well paid:
My mind was never yet more mercenary.
I pray you, know me when we meet again:
I wish you well, and so I take my leave.
BASSANIO
Dear sir, of force I must attempt you further:
Take some remembrance of us, as a tribute,
Not as a fee: grant me two things, I pray you,
Not to deny me, and to pardon me.
PORTIA
You press me far, and therefore I will yield.
Give me your gloves, I'll wear them for your sake;
                                        [*To* ANTONIO
And, for your love, I'll take this ring from you:
                                        [*To* BASSANIO
Do not draw back your hand; I'll take no more;
And you in love shall not deny me this.
BASSANIO
This ring, good sir, alas, it is a trifle!
I will not shame myself to give you this.
PORTIA
I will have nothing else but only this;
And now methinks I have a mind to it.
BASSANIO
There's more depends on this than on the value.
The dearest ring in Venice will I give you,
And find it out by proclamation:
Only for this, I pray you, pardon me.
PORTIA
I see, sir, you are liberal in offers:
You taught me first to beg; and now methinks
You teach me how a beggar should be answer'd.
BASSANIO
Good sir, this ring was given me by my wife;

And when she put it on, she made me vow
That I should neither sell nor give nor lose it.
PORTIA
That 'scuse serves many men to save their gifts.
An if your wife be not a mad-woman,
And know how well I have deserved the ring,
She would not hold out enemy for ever,
For giving it to me. Well, peace be with you!
                            [*Exeunt* PORTIA *and* NERISSA
ANTONIO
My Lord Bassanio, let him have the ring:
Let his deservings and my love withal
Be valued 'gainst your wife's commandment.
BASSANIO
Go, Gratiano, run and overtake him;
Give him the ring; and bring him, if thou canst,
Unto Antonio's house: away! make haste.
                                        [*Exit* GRATIANO
Come, you and I will thither presently;
And in the morning early will we both
Fly toward Belmont: come, Antonio.   [*Exeunt*

SCENE II. *The same. A street*

Enter PORTIA *and* NERISSA
PORTIA
Inquire the Jew's house out, give him this deed
And let him sign it: we'll away to-night
And be a day before our husbands home:
This deed will be well welcome to Lorenzo.
Enter GRATIANO
GRATIANO
Fair sir, you are well o'erta'en:
My Lord Bassanio upon more advice
Hath sent you here this ring, and doth entreat
Your company at dinner.
PORTIA
                        That cannot be:
His ring I do accept most thankfully:
And so, I pray you, tell him: furthermore,
I pray you, show my youth old Shylock's house.
GRATIANO
That will I do.
NERISSA
                    Sir, I would speak with you.
I'll see if I can get my husband's ring,
                                        [*Aside to* PORTIA
Which I did make him swear to keep for ever.
PORTIA
[*Aside to* NERISSA] Thou mayst, I warrant. We shall
    have old swearing
That they did give the rings away to men;
But we'll outface them, and outswear them too.
[*Aloud*] Away! make haste: thou know'st where I
    will tarry.
NERISSA
Come, good sir, will you show me to this house?
                                        [*Exeunt*

ACT V

Scene I. *Belmont. Avenue to* PORTIA's *house*

Enter LORENZO *and* JESSICA

LORENZO

The moon shines bright: in such a night as this,
When the sweet wind did gently kiss the trees
And they did make no noise, in such a night
Troilus methinks mounted the Troyan walls,
And sigh'd his soul toward the Grecian tents,
Where Cressid lay that night.

JESSICA

                    In such a night
Did Thisbe fearfully o'ertrip the dew,
And saw the lion's shadow ere himself,
And ran dismay'd away.

LORENZO

                    In such a night
Stood Dido with a willow in her hand
Upon the wild sea banks, and waft her love
To come again to Carthage.

JESSICA

                    In such a night
Medea gather'd the enchanted herbs
That did renew old Æson.

LORENZO

                    In such a night
Did Jessica steal from the wealthy Jew,
And with an unthrift love did run from Venice
As far as Belmont.

JESSICA

In such a night
Did young Lorenzo swear he loved her well,
Stealing her soul with many vows of faith
And ne'er a true one.

LORENZO

                    In such a night
Did pretty Jessica, like a little shrew,
Slander her love, and he forgave it her.

JESSICA

I would out-night you, did no body come;
But, hark, I hear the footing of a man.

Enter STEPHANO

LORENZO

Who comes so fast in silence of the night?

STEPHANO

A friend.

LORENZO

A friend! what friend? your name, I pray you,
friend?

STEPHANO

Stephano is my name; and I bring word
My mistress will before the break of day
Be here at Belmont: she doth stray about
By holy crosses, where she kneels and prays
For happy wedlock hours.

LORENZO

                    Who comes with her?

STEPHANO

None but a holy hermit and her maid.
I pray you, is my master yet return'd?

LORENZO

He is not, nor we have not heard from him.
But go we in, I pray thee, Jessica,
And ceremoniously let us prepare
Some welcome for the mistress of the house.

Enter LAUNCELOT GOBBO

LAUNCELOT GOBBO

Sola, sola! wo ha, ho! sola, sola!

LORENZO

Who calls?

LAUNCELOT GOBBO

Sola! did you see Master Lorenzo? Master Lorenzo,
sola, sola!

LORENZO

Leave hollaing, man: here.

LAUNCELOT GOBBO

Sola! where? where?

LORENZO

Here.

LAUNCELOT GOBBO

Tell him there's a post come from my master, with
his horn full of good news: my master will be here
ere morning.   [*Exit*

LORENZO

Sweet soul, let's in, and there expect their coming.
And yet no matter: why should we go in?
My friend Stephano, signify, I pray you,
Within the house, your mistress is at hand;
And bring your music forth into the air.
                                    [*Exit* STEPHANO
How sweet the moonlight sleeps upon this bank!
Here will we sit, and let the sounds of music
Creep in our ears: soft stillness and the night
Become the touches of sweet harmony.
Sit, Jessica. Look how the floor of heaven
Is thick inlaid with patines of bright gold:
There's not the smallest orb which thou behold'st
But in his motion like an angel sings,
Still quiring to the young-eyed cherubins;
Such harmony is in immortal souls;
But whilst this muddy vesture of decay
Doth grossly close it in, we cannot hear it.

Enter MUSICIANS

Come, ho, and wake Diana with a hymn!
With sweetest touches pierce your mistress' ear,
And draw her home with music.   [*Music*

JESSICA

I am never merry when I hear sweet music.

LORENZO

The reason is, your spirits are attentive:
For do but note a wild and wanton herd,
Or race of youthful and unhandled colts,
Fetching mad bounds, bellowing and neighing loud,
Which is the hot condition of their blood;
If they but hear perchance a trumpet sound,
Or any air of music touch their ears,
You shall perceive them make a mutual stand,

Their savage eyes turn'd to a modest gaze
By the sweet power of music: therefore the poet
Did feign that Orpheus drew trees, stones and floods;
Since nought so stockish, hard and full of rage,
But music for the time doth change his nature.
The man that hath no music in himself,
Nor is not moved with concord of sweet sounds,
Is fit for treasons, stratagems and spoils;
The motions of his spirit are dull as night,
And his affections dark as Erebus:
Let no such man be trusted. Mark the music.

Enter PORTIA *and* NERISSA

PORTIA
That light we see is burning in my hall.
How far that little candle throws his beams!
So shines a good deed in a naughty world.

NERISSA
When the moon shone, we did not see the candle.

PORTIA
So doth the greater glory dim the less:
A substitute shines brightly as a king,
Until a king be by; and then his state
Empties itself, as doth an inland brook
Into the main of waters. Music! hark!

NERISSA
It is your music, madam, of the house.

PORTIA
Nothing is good, I see, without respect:
Methinks it sounds much sweeter than by day.

NERISSA
Silence bestows that virtue on it, madam.

PORTIA
The crow doth sing as sweetly as the lark,
When neither is attended; and I think
The nightingale, if she should sing by day,
When every goose is cackling, would be thought
No better a musician than the wren.
How many things by season season'd are
To their right praise and true perfection!
Peace, ho! the moon sleeps with Endymion,
And would not be awaked.   [*Music ceases*

LORENZO
                    That is the voice,
Or I am much deceived, of Portia.

PORTIA
He knows me as the blind man knows the cuckoo,
By the bad voice.

LORENZO
          Dear lady, welcome home.

PORTIA
We have been praying for our husbands' healths,
Which speed, we hope, the better for our words.
Are they return'd?

LORENZO
          Madam, they are not yet;
But there is come a messenger before,
To signify their coming.

PORTIA
          Go in, Nerissa;
Give order to my servants that they take

No note at all of our being absent hence;
Nor you, Lorenzo; Jessica, nor you. [*A tucket sounds*

LORENZO
Your husband is at hand; I hear his trumpet:
We are no tell-tales, madam; fear you not.

PORTIA
This night methinks is but the daylight sick;
It looks a little paler: 'tis a day,
Such as the day is when the sun is hid.

Enter BASSANIO, ANTONIO, GRATIANO, *and their*
                    followers

BASSANIO
We should hold day with the Antipodes,
If you would walk in absence of the sun.

PORTIA
Let me give light, but let me not be light;
For a light wife doth make a heavy husband,
And never be Bassanio so for me:
But God sort all! You are welcome home, my lord.

BASSANIO
I thank you, madam. Give welcome to my friend.
This is the man, this is Antonio,
To whom I am so infinitely bound.

PORTIA
You should in all sense be much bound to him,
For, as I hear, he was much bound for you.

ANTONIO
No more than I am well acquitted of.

PORTIA
Sir, you are very welcome to our house:
It must appear in other ways than words,
Therefore I scant this breathing courtesy.

GRATIANO
[*To* NERISSA] By yonder moon 1 swear you do me
          wrong;
In faith, I gave it to the judge's clerk:
Would he were gelt that had it, for my part,
Since you do take it, love, so much at heart.

PORTIA
A quarrel, ho, already! what's the matter?

GRATIANO
About a hoop of gold, a paltry ring
That she did give me, whose posy was
For all the world like cutler's poetry
Upon a knife, 'Love me, and leave me not.'

NERISSA
What talk you of the posy or the value?
You swore to me, when I did give it you,
That you would wear it till your hour of death,
And that it should lie with you in your grave:
Though not for me, yet for your vehement oaths,
You should have been respective, and have kept it.
Gave it a judge's clerk! no, God's my judge,
The clerk will ne'er wear hair on's face that had it.

GRATIANO
He will, an if he live to be a man.

NERISSA
Ay, if a woman live to be a man.

GRATIANO
Now, by this hand, I gave it to a youth,

[474]

A kind of boy, a little scrubbed boy,
No higher than thyself, the judge's clerk,
A prating boy, that begg'd it as a fee:
I could not for my heart deny it him.

PORTIA

You were to blame, I must be plain with you,
To part so slightly with your wife's first gift;
A thing stuck on with oaths upon your finger
And so riveted with faith unto your flesh.
I gave my love a ring, and made him swear
Never to part with it; and here he stands;
I dare be sworn for him he would not leave it
Nor pluck it from his finger, for the wealth
That the world masters. Now, in faith, Gratiano,
You give your wife too unkind a cause of grief:
An 'twere to me, I should be mad at it.

BASSANIO

[Aside] Why, I were best to cut my left hand off,
And swear I lost the ring defending it.

GRATIANO

My Lord Bassanio gave his ring away
Unto the judge that begg'd it, and indeed
Deserved it too; and then the boy, his clerk,
That took some pains in writing, he begg'd mine;
And neither man nor master would take aught
But the two rings.

PORTIA

                    What ring gave you, my lord?
Not that, I hope, which you received of me.

BASSANIO

If I could add a lie unto a fault,
I would deny it; but you see my finger
Hath not the ring upon it, it is gone.

PORTIA

Even so void is your false heart of truth.
By heaven, I will ne'er come in your bed
Until I see the ring.

NERISSA

                    Nor I in yours
Till I again see mine.

BASSANIO

                    Sweet Portia,
If you did know to whom I gave the ring,
If you did know for whom I gave the ring,
And would conceive for what I gave the ring,
And how unwillingly I left the ring,
When nought would be accepted but the ring,
You would abate the strength of your displeasure.

PORTIA

If you had known the virtue of the ring,
Or half her worthiness that gave the ring,
Or your own honour to contain the ring,
You would not then have parted with the ring.
What man is there so much unreasonable,
If you had pleased to have defended it
With any terms of zeal, wanted the modesty
To urge the thing held as a ceremony?
Nerissa teaches me what to believe:
I'll die for't but some woman had the ring.

BASSANIO

No, by my honour, madam, by my soul,
No woman had it, but a civil doctor,
Which did refuse three thousand ducats of me,
And begg'd the ring; the which I did deny him,
And suffer'd him to go displeased away;
Even he that did uphold the very life
Of my dear friend. What should I say, sweet lady?
I was enforced to send it after him;
I was beset with shame and courtesy;
My honour would not let ingratitude
So much besmear it. Pardon me, good lady;
For, by these blessed candles of the night,
Had you been there, I think you would have begg'd
The ring of me to give the worthy doctor.

PORTIA

Let not that doctor e'er come near my house:
Since he hath got the jewel that I loved,
And that which you did swear to keep for me,
I will become as liberal as you;
I'll not deny him any thing I have,
No, not my body nor my husband's bed:
Know him I shall, I am well sure of it:
Lie not a night from home; watch me like Argus:
If you do not, if I be left alone,
Now, by mine honour, which is yet mine own,
I'll have that doctor for my bedfellow.

NERISSA

And I his clerk; therefore be well advised
How you do leave me to mine own protection.

GRATIANO

Well, do you so: let not me take him, then;
For if I do, I'll mar the young clerk's pen.

ANTONIO

I am the unhappy subject of these quarrels.

PORTIA

Sir, grieve not you; you are welcome notwithstanding.

BASSANIO

Portia, forgive me this enforced wrong;
And, in the hearing of these many friends,
I swear to thee, even by thine own fair eyes,
Wherein I see myself,—

PORTIA

                    Mark you but that!
In both my eyes he doubly sees himself;
In each eye, one: swear by your double self,
And there's an oath of credit.

BASSANIO

                    Nay, but hear me:
Pardon this fault, and by my soul I swear
I never more will break an oath with thee.

ANTONIO

I once did lend my body for his wealth;
Which, but for him that had your husband's ring,
Had quite miscarried: I dare be bound again,
My soul upon the forfeit, that your lord
Will never more break faith advisedly.

[475]

PORTIA

Then you shall be his surety. Give him this,
And bid him keep it better than the other.

ANTONIO

Here, Lord Bassanio; swear to keep this ring.

BASSANIO

By heaven, it is the same I gave the doctor!

PORTIA

I had it of him: pardon me, Bassanio;
For, by this ring, the doctor lay with me.

NERISSA

And pardon me, my gentle Gratiano;
For that same scrubbed boy, the doctor's clerk,
In lieu of this last night did lie with me.

GRATIANO

Why, this is like the mending of highways
In summer, where the ways are fair enough:
What, are we cuckolds ere we have deserved it?

PORTIA

Speak not so grossly. You are all amazed:
Here is a letter; read it at your leisure;
It comes from Padua, from Bellario:
There you shall find that Portia was the doctor,
Nerissa there her clerk: Lorenzo here
Shall witness I set forth as soon as you,
And even but now return'd; I have not yet
Enter'd my house. Antonio, you are welcome;
And I have better news in store for you
Than you expect: unseal this letter soon;
There you shall find three of your argosies
Are richly come to harbour suddenly:
You shall not know by what strange accident
I chanced on this letter.

ANTONIO

I am dumb.

BASSANIO

Were you the doctor and I knew you not?

GRATIANO

Were you the clerk that is to make me cuckold?

NERISSA

Ay, but the clerk that never means to do it,
Unless he live until he be a man.

BASSANIO

Sweet doctor, you shall be my bedfellow:
When I am absent, then lie with my wife.

ANTONIO

Sweet lady, you have given me life and living;
For here I read for certain that my ships
Are safely come to road.

PORTIA

How now, Lorenzo!
My clerk hath some good comforts too for you.

NERISSA

Ay, and I'll give them him without a fee.
There do I give to you and Jessica,
From the rich Jew, a special deed of gift,
After his death, of all he dies possess'd of.

LORENZO

Fair ladies, you drop manna in the way
Of starved people.

PORTIA

It is almost morning,
And yet I am sure you are not satisfied
Of these events at full. Let us go in;
And charge us there upon inter'gatories,
And we will answer all things faithfully.

GRATIANO

Let it be so: the first inter'gatory
That my Nerissa shall be sworn on is,
Whether till the next night she had rather stay,
Or go to bed now, being two hours to day:
But were the day come, I should wish it dark,
That I were couching with the doctor's clerk.
Well, while I live I'll fear no other thing
So sore as keeping safe Nerissa's ring.   [*Exeunt*

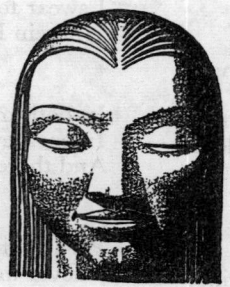

THE FIRST PART OF KING HENRY IV

SYNOPSIS

Henry IV quickly drops his plan to lead an expedition to the Holy Land as an act of penance for the death of Richard II when complete information reaches him of the uprisings and battles in Wales and Scotland. He hears with elation of the conquest of the Scotch army under the command of the Earl of Douglas by Henry Percy, nicknamed Hotspur, son of the Earl of Northumberland, but is greatly annoyed when Hotspur sends word that he will not give up the Scottish prisoners he has captured until Henry ransoms Lady Percy's brother, Edmund Mortimer, who was captured by the Welsh warrior, Owen Glendower, while leading an English expedition against him.

Summoned by the King, the three Percys come to London, the cold, impassive Northumberland, his brother, the suspicious insubordinate Worcester, and his son, the sincere, impulsive Hotspur, each of whom was instrumental in placing Henry on the throne. The King again demands the Scottish prisoners, refuses to ransom Mortimer, whom the late King Richard had named as his rightful heir, calls him a traitor because he has recently married Glendower's daughter, scoffs at Hotspur's staunch defence of his brother-in-law's nobility and valor as a fighter, and peremptorily orders no further mention of his name.

Fuming with angry resentment, Hotspur, his father and uncle return home and plan a rebellion against Henry by combining their forces with those of the Welsh rebel, Glendower; his new son-in-law, Mortimer, claimant to the throne; the Archbishop of York, whose brother, a loyal adherent of King Richard's, was executed by the present King; and Malcolm of Scotland, whose aid they purpose to secure by the release of the Scottish prisoners.

When the King hears of the revolt, he is forcibly reminded of the Bishop of Carlisle's prophecy that kindred should be set against kindred as the result of King Richard's deposition, and he bitterly contrasts the devotion and energy of young Hotspur with the carefree recklessness of his own son, the fun-loving Prince of Wales, whom he has not seen for three months. Just at this time, the madcap Prince is planning a wild escapade with his boon companion, the corpulent Sir John Falstaff, and a few of his disreputable associates. After Falstaff and the others have attacked and robbed some travellers at Gadshill near London, they are put to a comical flight by the Prince and Ned Poins in disguises of buckram. Later, in the Boar's-Head Tavern in Eastcheap, Prince Hal's favorite resort, the irrepressible Falstaff tells of a hand-to-hand fight with eleven men in buckram and is not at all embarrassed when the Prince discloses the real facts.

In the midst of their riotous fun, a messenger from the King arrives with news of the northern rebellion and summoning his son to the palace, whereupon Falstaff seats himself on a chair with impressive dignity, his dagger in his hand for a scepter, and a cushion on his head for a crown, and practices Prince Hal in his answers to his father's questions on his recent doings and companions. Once the Prince of Wales has aroused himself to a full sense of his responsibilities, he pledges the King that he will be worthy of his title and is given command of part of the royal forces, with Falstaff in charge of a company of foot soldiers.

Meanwhile, in the north of Wales, the rebels confer on the plan of campaign against Henry's army and confidently divide the map of England and Wales into three parts for Mortimer, Glendower, and Hotspur. Later, in their camp at Shrewsbury, these plans are disarranged by the desertion of Northumberland himself, who pleads illness, and by Glendower, who sends word that his forces cannot be drawn upon for fourteen days, but in spite of their diminished numbers Hotspur and Douglas are determined to meet the superior royal army advancing to meet them under the command of the Earl of Westmoreland, the Prince of Wales, and his brother, Prince John of Lancaster.

In the parley before battle, the King assures the enemy generals, the Earl of Worcester and Sir Richard Vernon, that he will grant full pardon to the rebels if they will disperse, but Worcester's suspicions of Henry's motives are so deeply rooted that instead of conveying the terms of surrender to Hotspur, or telling him of the Prince of Wales' offer to decide the issue in a personal combat, he delivers a challenge to immediate battle. Douglas, ranging over the field, fights anyone attired like the King and at length encounters Henry himself who is saved at a critical moment by the Prince Hal whose skillful fighting forces Douglas to flight.

The Prince soon afterwards meets the valiant Hotspur whom he fights and kills. Worcester and Vernon are captured and ordered by Henry to execution. As the rebel forces are scattered in utter defeat, Douglas is seized but released through the generosity of the Prince of Wales, Prince John of Lancaster and Westmoreland are dispatched to meet the forces of Northumberland and the Archbishop of York, while the King and the Prince depart for Wales to fight Glendower and Mortimer, Earl of March.

HISTORICAL DATA

Holinshed and, to a lesser extent, Halle provide the outline of events covered in this play, which deals with the period of English history from the battle of Holmedon Hill in 1402 to the battle of Shrewsbury in 1403. As usual, Shakespeare elaborated the merest suggestions of fact into dramatic situations, but in general he followed history in this play fairly closely. For the sake of dramatic contrast Prince Hal and Hotspur are made the same age, and the character development is almost altogether Shakespeare's own contribution.

For the comedy elements in the play an older drama, performed as early as 1588, was freely drawn upon. This was called *The Famous Victories of Henry the Fifth* and presented in crude form various episodes at the Tavern in Eastcheap, the robbery at Gadshill, Hal's relationships with his boon companions and the Chief Justice, and a number of other details of which Shakespeare made excellent use.

Falstaff, although based upon Sir John Oldcastle in *The Famous Victories*, is very largely Shakespeare's own creation. The new name may have been suggested by the historical Sir John Fastolfe, who appears in Part One of *Henry VI*.

Contemporary events of 1596 are referred to and the play was entered in the Stationers' Register in 1598, so that 1597 is reasonably well established as the date of its writing.

"*Fare thee well, great heart!*"
HENRY IV, PART I

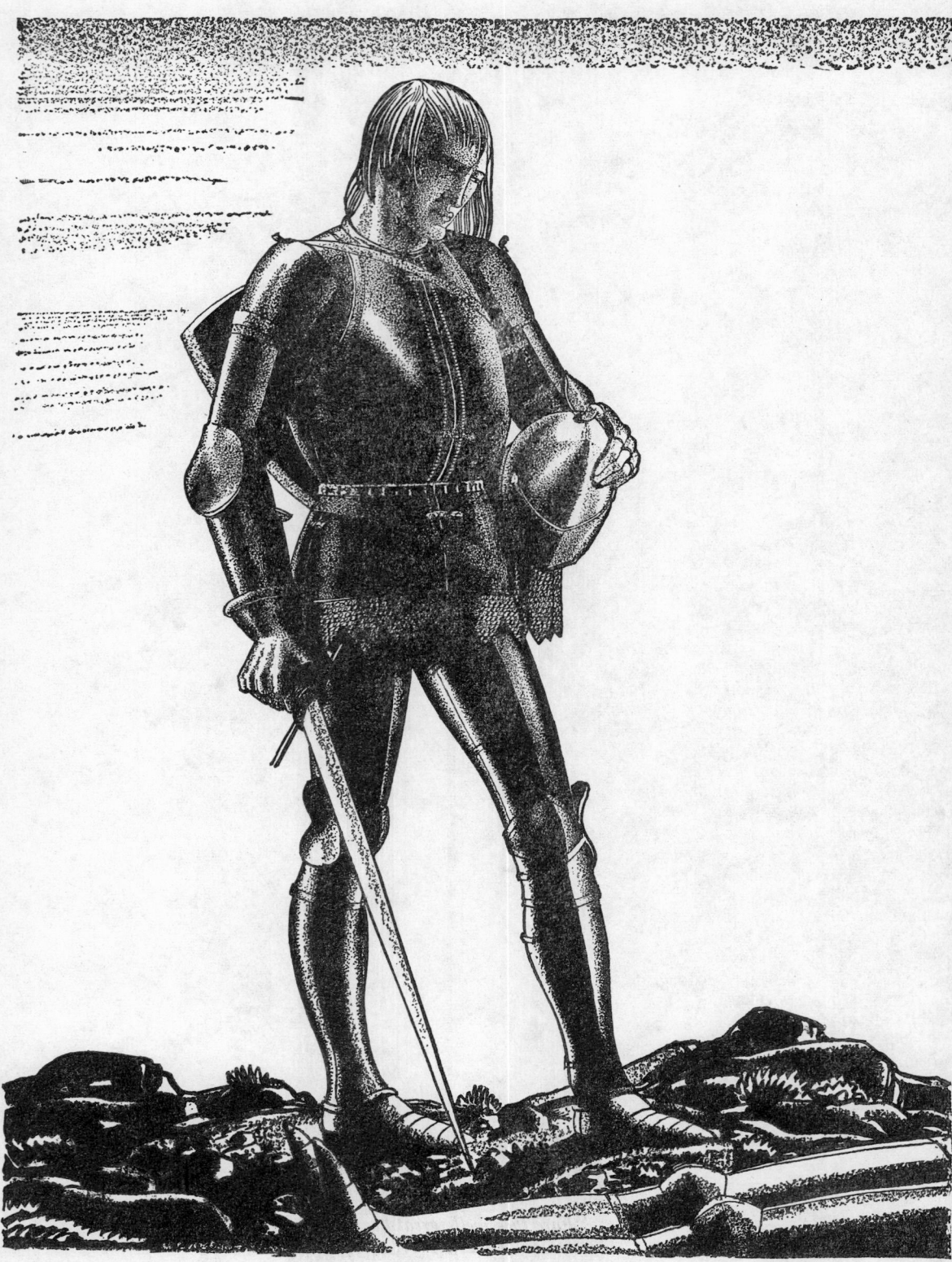

THE FIRST PART OF KING HENRY IV

DRAMATIS PERSONÆ

KING HENRY *the Fourth.*
HENRY, *Prince of Wales,*
JOHN *of Lancaster,* } *sons to the King.*
EARL OF WESTMORELAND.
SIR WALTER BLUNT.
THOMAS PERCY, *Earl of Worcester.*
HENRY PERCY, *Earl of Northumberland.*
HENRY PERCY, *surnamed* HOTSPUR, *his son.*
EDMUND MORTIMER, *Earl of March.*
RICHARD SCROOP, *Archbishop of York.*
ARCHIBALD, *Earl of Douglas.*
OWEN GLENDOWER.
SIR RICHARD VERNON.
SIR JOHN FALSTAFF.
SIR MICHAEL, *a friend to the Archbishop of York.*
POINS.

GADSHILL.
PETO.
BARDOLPH.

LADY PERCY, *wife to Hotspur, and sister to Mortimer.*
LADY MORTIMER, *daughter to Glendower, and wife to Mortimer.*
MISTRESS QUICKLY, *hostess of a tavern in Eastcheap.*

LORDS, OFFICERS, SHERIFF, VINTNER, CHAMBER-LAIN, DRAWERS, *two* CARRIERS, TRAVELLERS, *and* ATTENDANTS.

SCENE—*England and Wales.*

ACT I

SCENE I. *London. The palace*

Enter KING HENRY, LORD JOHN OF LANCASTER, *the* EARL OF WESTMORELAND, SIR WALTER BLUNT, *and others*

KING

So SHAKEN as we are, so wan with care,
Find we a time for frighted peace to pant,
And breathe short-winded accents of new broils
To be commenced in strongs afar remote.
No more the thirsty entrance of this soil
Shall daub her lips with her own children's blood;
No more shall trenching war channel her fields,
Nor bruise her flowerets with the armed hoofs
Of hostile paces: those opposed eyes,
Which, like the meteors of a troubled heaven,
All of one nature, of one substance bred,
Did lately meet in the intestine shock
And furious close of civil butchery,
Shall now, in mutual well-beseeming ranks,
March all one way, and be no more opposed
Against acquaintance, kindred and allies:
The edge of war, like an ill-sheathed knife,
No more shall cut his master. Therefore, friends,
As far as to the sepulchre of Christ,
Whose soldier now, under whose blessed cross
We are impressed and engaged to fight,
Forthwith a power of English shall we levy;
Whose arms were moulded in their mothers' womb
To chase these pagans in those holy fields
Over whose acres walk'd those blessed feet,
Which fourteen hundred years ago were nail'd
For our advantage on the bitter cross.
But this our purpose now is twelve month old,
And bootless 'tis to tell you we will go:
Therefore we meet not now. Then let me hear

Of you, my gentle cousin Westmoreland,
What yesternight our council did decree
In forwarding this dear expedience.

WESTMORELAND

My liege, this haste was hot in question,
And many limits of the charge set down
But yesternight: when all athwart there came
A post from Wales loaden with heavy news;
Whose worst was, that the noble Mortimer,
Leading the men of Herefordshire to fight
Against the irregular and wild Glendower,
Was by the rude hands of that Welshman taken,
A thousand of his people butchered;
Upon whose dead corpse there was such misuse,
Such beastly shameless transformation,
By those Welshwomen done, as may not be
Without much shame retold or spoken of.

KING

It seems then that the tidings of this broil
Brake off our business for the Holy Land.

WESTMORELAND

This match'd with other did, my gracious lord;
For more uneven and unwelcome news
Came from the north and thus it did import:
On Holy-rood day, the gallant Hotspur there,
Young Harry Percy, and brave Archibald,
That ever-valiant and approved Scot,
At Holmedon met,
Where they did spend a sad and bloody hour;
As by discharge of their artillery,
And shape of likelihood, the news was told;
For he that brought them, in the very heat
And pride of their contention did take horse,
Uncertain of the issue any way.

KING

Here is a dear, a true industrious friend,
Sir Walter Blunt, new lighted from his horse,

[479]

Stain'd with the variation of each soil
Betwixt that Holmedon and this seat of ours;
And he hath brought us smooth and welcome news.
The Earl of Douglas is discomfited:
Ten thousand bold Scots, two and twenty knights,
Balk'd in their own blood did Sir Walter see
On Holmedon's plains. Of prisoners, Hotspur took
Mordake the Earl of Fife, and eldest son
To beaten Douglas; and the Earl of Athol,
Of Murray, Angus, and Menteith:
And is not this an honourable spoil?
A gallant prize? ha, cousin, is it not?

WESTMORELAND

In faith,
It is a conquest for a prince to boast of.

KING

Yea, there thou makest me sad and makest me sin
In envy that my Lord Northumberland
Should be the father to so blest a son,
A son who is the theme of honour's tongue;
Amongst a grove, the very straightest plant;
Who is sweet Fortune's minion and her pride:
Whilst I, by looking on the praise of him,
See riot and dishonour stain the brow
Of my young Harry. O that it could be proved
That some night-tripping fairy had exchanged
In cradle-clothes our children where they lay,
And call'd mine Percy, his Plantagenet!
Then would I have his Harry, and he mine.
But let him from my thoughts. What think you, coz,
Of this young Percy's pride? the prisoners,
Which he in this adventure hath surprised,
To his own use he keeps; and sends me word,
I shall have none but Mordake Earl of Fife.

WESTMORELAND

This is his uncle's teaching: this is Worcester,
Malevolent to you in all aspects;
Which makes him prune himself, and bristle up
The crest of youth against your dignity.

KING

But I have sent for him to answer this;
And for this cause awhile we must neglect
Our holy purpose to Jerusalem.
Cousin, on Wednesday next our council we
Will hold at Windsor; so inform the lords:
But come yourself with speed to us again;
For more is to be said and to be done
Than out of anger can be uttered.

WESTMORELAND

I will, my liege.   [Exeunt

SCENE II. London. An apartment of the PRINCE'S

Enter the PRINCE OF WALES and FALSTAFF

FALSTAFF

Now, Hal, what time of day is it, lad?

PRINCE

Thou art so fat-witted, with drinking of old sack
and unbuttoning thee after supper and sleeping
upon benches after noon, that thou hast forgotten
to demand that truly which thou wouldst truly
know. What a devil hast thou to do with the time of
the day? Unless hours were cups of sack, and minutes capons, and clocks the tongues of bawds, and
dials the signs of leaping-houses, and the blessed sun
himself a fair hot wench in flame-coloured taffeta,
I see no reason why thou shouldst be so superfluous
to demand the time of the day.

FALSTAFF

Indeed, you come near me now, Hal; for we that
take purses go by the moon and the seven stars, and
not by Phœbus, he, 'that wandering knight so fair.'
And, I prithee, sweet wag, when thou art king, as,
God save thy grace,—majesty I should say, for
grace thou wilt have none,—

PRINCE

What, none?

FALSTAFF

No, by my troth, not so much as will serve to be
prologue to an egg and butter.

PRINCE

Well, how then? come, roundly, roundly.

FALSTAFF

Marry, then, sweet wag, when thou art king, let not
us that are squires of the night's body be called
thieves of the day's beauty: let us be Diana's foresters, gentlemen of the shade, minions of the moon;
and let men say we be men of good government, being governed, as the sea is, by our noble and chaste
mistress the moon, under whose countenance we
steal.

PRINCE

Thou sayest well, and it holds well too; for the fortune of us that are the moon's men doth ebb and
flow like the sea, being governed, as the sea is, by
the moon. As, for proof, now: a purse of gold most
resolutely snatched on Monday night and most dissolutely spent on Tuesday morning; got with swearing 'Lay by' and spent with crying 'Bring in;' now
in as low an ebb as the foot of the ladder, and by
and by in as high a flow as the ridge of the gallows.

FALSTAFF

By the Lord, thou sayest true, lad. And is not my
hostess of the tavern a most sweet wench?

PRINCE

As the honey of Hybla, my old lad of the castle. And
is not a buff jerkin a most sweet robe of durance?

FALSTAFF

How now, how now, mad wag! what, in thy quips
and thy quiddities? what a plague have I to do with
a buff jerkin?

PRINCE

Why, what a pox have I to do with my hostess of the
tavern?

FALSTAFF

Well, thou hast called her to a reckoning many a
time and oft.

PRINCE

Did I ever call for thee to pay thy part?

FALSTAFF

No; I'll give thee thy due, thou hast paid all there.

PRINCE

Yea, and elsewhere, so far as my coin would stretch; and where it would not, I have used my credit.

FALSTAFF

Yea, and so used it that, were it not here apparent that thou art heir apparent—But, I prithee, sweet wag, shall there be gallows standing in England when thou art king? and resolution thus fobbed as it is with the rusty curb of old father antic the law? Do not thou, when thou art king, hang a thief.

PRINCE

No; thou shalt.

FALSTAFF

Shall I? O rare! By the Lord, I'll be a brave judge.

PRINCE

Thou judgest false already: I mean, thou shalt have the hanging of the thieves and so become a rare hangman.

FALSTAFF

Well, Hal, well; and in some sort it jumps with my humour as well as waiting in the court, I can tell you.

PRINCE

For obtaining of suits?

FALSTAFF

Yea, for obtaining of suits, whereof the hangman hath no lean wardrobe. 'Sblood, I am as melancholy as a gib cat or a lugged bear.

PRINCE

Or an old lion, or a lover's lute.

FALSTAFF

Yea, or the drone of a Lincolnshire bagpipe.

PRINCE

What sayest thou to a hare, or the melancholy of Moor-ditch?

FALSTAFF

Thou hast the most unsavoury similes, and art indeed the most comparative, rascalliest, sweet young prince. But, Hal, I prithee, trouble me no more with vanity. I would to God thou and I knew where a commodity of good names were to be bought. An old lord of the council rated me the other day in the street about you, sir, but I marked him not; and yet he talked very wisely, but I regarded him not; and yet he talked wisely, and in the street too.

PRINCE

Thou didst well; for wisdom cries out in the streets, and no man regards it.

FALSTAFF

O, thou hast damnable iteration, and art indeed able to corrupt a saint. Thou hast done much harm upon me, Hal; God forgive thee for it! Before I knew thee, Hal, I knew nothing; and now am I, if a man should speak truly, little better than one of the wicked. I must give over this life, and I will give it over: by the Lord, an I do not, I am a villain: I'll be damned for never a king's son in Christendom.

PRINCE

Where shall we take a purse to-morrow, Jack?

FALSTAFF

'Zounds, where thou wilt, lad; I'll make one; an I do not, call me villain and baffle me.

PRINCE

I see a good amendment of life in thee; from praying to purse-taking.

FALSTAFF

Why, Hal, 'tis my vocation, Hal; 'tis no sin for a man to labour in his vocation.

Enter POINS

Poins! Now shall we know if Gadshill have set a match.
O, if men were to be saved by merit, what hole in hell were hot enough for him? This is the most omnipotent villain that ever cried 'Stand' to a true man.

PRINCE

Good morrow, Ned.

POINS

Good morrow, sweet Hal. What says Monsieur Remorse? what says Sir John Sack and Sugar? Jack! how agrees the devil and thee about thy soul, that thou soldest him on Good Friday last for a cup of Madeira and a cold capon's leg?

PRINCE

Sir John stands to his word, the devil shall have his bargain; for he was never yet a breaker of proverbs: he will give the devil his due.

POINS

Then art thou damned for keeping thy word with the devil.

PRINCE

Else he had been damned for cozening the devil.

POINS

But, my lads, my lads, to-morrow morning, by four o'clock, early at Gadshill! there are pilgrims going to Canterbury with rich offerings, and traders riding to London with fat purses: I have vizards for you all; you have horses for yourselves: Gadshill lies to-night in Rochester: I have bespoke supper to-morrow night in Eastcheap: we may do it as secure as sleep. If you will go, I will stuff your purses full of crowns; if you will not, tarry at home and be hanged.

FALSTAFF

Hear ye, Yedward; if I tarry at home and go not, I'll hang you for going.

POINS

You will, chops?

FALSTAFF

Hal, wilt thou make one?

PRINCE

Who, I rob? I a thief? not I, by my faith.

FALSTAFF

There's neither honesty, manhood, nor good fellowship in thee, nor thou camest not of the blood royal, if thou darest not stand for ten shillings.

PRINCE

Well then, once in my days I'll be a madcap.

FALSTAFF
Why, that's well said.

PRINCE
Well, come what will, I'll tarry at home.

FALSTAFF
By the Lord, I'll be a traitor then, when thou art king.

PRINCE
I care not.

POINS
Sir John, I prithee, leave the prince and me alone: I will lay him down such reasons for this adventure that he shall go.

FALSTAFF
Well, God give thee the spirit of persuasion and him the ears of profiting, that what thou speakest may move and what he hears may be believed, that the true prince may, for recreation sake, prove a false thief; for the poor abuses of the time want countenance. Farewell: you shall find me in Eastcheap.

PRINCE
Farewell, thou latter spring! farewell, All-hallown summer!   [Exit FALSTAFF

POINS
Now, my good sweet honey lord, ride with us to-morrow: I have a jest to execute that I cannot manage alone. Falstaff, Bardolph, Peto and Gadshill shall rob those men that we have already waylaid; yourself and I will not be there; and when they have the booty, if you and I do not rob them, cut this head off from my shoulders.

PRINCE
How shall we part with them in setting forth?

POINS
Why, we will set forth before or after them, and appoint them a place of meeting, wherein it is at our pleasure to fail, and then will they adventure upon the exploit themselves; which they shall have no sooner achieved, but we'll set upon them.

PRINCE
Yea, but 'tis like that they will know us by our horses, by our habits, and by every other appointment, to be ourselves.

POINS
Tut! our horses they shall not see; I'll tie them in the wood; our vizards we will change after we leave them: and, sirrah, I have cases of buckram for the nonce, to immask our noted outward garments.

PRINCE
Yea, but I doubt they will be too hard for us.

POINS
Well, for two of them, I know them to be as true-bred cowards as ever turned back; and for the third, if he fight longer than he sees reason, I'll forswear arms. The virtue of this jest will be, the incomprehensible lies that this same fat rogue will tell us when we meet at supper: how thirty, at least, he fought with; what wards, what blows, what extremities he endured; and in the reproof of this lies the jest.

PRINCE
Well, I'll go with thee: provide us all things necessary and meet me to-morrow night in Eastcheap; there I'll sup. Farewell.

POINS
Farewell, my lord.   [Exit

PRINCE
I know you all, and will a while uphold
The unyoked humour of your idleness:
Yet herein will I imitate the sun,
Who doth permit the base contagious clouds
To smother up his beauty from the world,
That, when he please again to be himself,
Being wanted, he may be more wonder'd at,
By breaking through the foul and ugly mists
Of vapours that did seem to strangle him.
If all the year were playing holidays,
To sport would be as tedious as to work;
But when they seldom come, they wish'd for come,
And nothing pleaseth but rare accidents.
So, when this loose behaviour I throw off
And pay the debt I never promised,
By how much better than my word I am,
By so much shall I falsify men's hopes;
And like bright metal on a sullen ground,
My reformation, glittering o'er my fault,
Shall show more goodly and attract more eyes
Than that which hath no foil to set it off.
I'll so offend, to make offence a skill;
Redeeming time when men think least I will. [Exit

SCENE III. London. The palace

Enter the KING, NORTHUMBERLAND, WORCESTER,
HOTSPUR, SIR WALTER BLUNT, with others

KING
My blood hath been too cold and temperate,
Unapt to stir at these indignities,
And you have found me; for accordingly
You tread upon my patience: but be sure
I will from henceforth rather be myself,
Mighty and to be fear'd, than my condition;
Which hath been smooth as oil, soft as young down,
And therefore lost that title of respect
Which the proud soul ne'er pays but to the proud.

WORCESTER
Our house, my sovereign liege, little deserves
The scourge of greatness to be used on it;
And that same greatness too which our own hands
Have holp to make so portly.

NORTHUMBERLAND
My lord,—

KING
Worcester, get thee gone; for I do see
Danger and disobedience in thine eye:
O, sir, your presence is too bold and peremptory,
And majesty might never yet endure
The moody frontier of a servant brow.
You have good leave to leave us: when we need

Your use and counsel, we shall send for you.
                    [*Exit* WORCESTER
You were about to speak.   [*To* NORTHUMBERLAND
                NORTHUMBERLAND
            Yea, my good lord.
Those prisoners in your highness' name demanded,
Which Harry Percy here at Holmedon took,
Were, as he says, not with such strength denied
As is deliver'd to your majesty:
Either envy, therefore, or misprision
Is guilty of this fault and not my son.
                HOTSPUR
My liege, I did deny no prisoners.
But I remember, when the fight was done,
When I was dry with rage and extreme toil,
Breathless and faint, leaning upon my sword,
Came there a certain lord, neat, and trimly dress'd,
Fresh as a bridegroom; and his chin new reap'd
Show'd like a stubble-land at harvest-home;
He was perfumed like a milliner;
And 'twixt his finger and his thumb he held
A pouncet-box, which ever and anon
He gave his nose and took 't away again;
Who therewith angry, when it next came there,
Took it in snuff; and still he smiled and talk'd,
And as the soldiers bore dead bodies by,
He call'd them untaught knaves, unmannerly,
To bring a slovenly unhandsome corse
Betwixt the wind and his nobility.
With many holiday and lady terms
He question'd me; amongst the rest, demanded
My prisoners in your majesty's behalf.
I then, all smarting with my wounds being cold,
To be so pester'd with a popinjay,
Out of my grief and my impatience,
Answer'd neglectingly I know not what,
He should, or he should not; for he made me mad
To see him shine so brisk, and smell so sweet,
And talk so like a waiting-gentlewoman
Of guns and drums and wounds,—God save the
    mark!—
And telling me the sovereign'st thing on earth
Was parmaceti for an inward bruise;
And that it was great pity, so it was,
This villanous salt-petre should be digg'd
Out of the bowels of the harmless earth,
Which many a good tall fellow had destroy'd
So cowardly; and but for these vile guns,
He would himself have been a soldier.
This bald unjointed chat of his, my lord,
I answer'd indirectly, as I said;
And I beseech you, let not his report
Come current for an accusation
Betwixt my love and your high majesty.
                BLUNT
The circumstance consider'd, good my lord,
Whate'er Lord Harry Percy then had said
To such a person and in such a place,
At such a time, with all the rest re-told,
May reasonably die and never rise

To do him wrong, or any way impeach
What then he said, so he unsay it now.
                KING
Why, yet he doth deny his prisoners,
But with proviso and exception,
That we at our own charge shall ransom straight
His brother-in-law, the foolish Mortimer;
Who, on my soul, hath wilfully betray'd
The lives of those that he did lead to fight
Against that great magician, damn'd Glendower,
Whose daughter, as we hear, the Earl of March
Hath lately married. Shall our coffers, then,
Be emptied to redeem a traitor home?
Shall we buy treason? and indent with fears,
When they have lost and forfeited themselves?
No, on the barren mountains let him starve;
For I shall never hold that man my friend
Whose tongue shall ask me for one penny cost
To ransom home revolted Mortimer.
                HOTSPUR
Revolted Mortimer!
He never did fall off, my sovereign liege,
But by the chance of war: to prove that true
Needs no more but one tongue for all those wounds,
Those mouthed wounds, which valiantly he took,
When on the gentle Severn's sedgy bank,
In single opposition, hand to hand,
He did confound the best part of an hour
In changing hardiment with great Glendower:
Three times they breathed and three times did they
    drink,
Upon agreement, of swift Severn's flood;
Who then, affrighted with their bloody looks,
Ran fearfully among the trembling reeds,
And hid his crisp head in the hollow bank
Bloodstained with these valiant combatants.
Never did base and rotten policy
Colour her working with such deadly wounds;
Nor never could the noble Mortimer
Receive so many, and all willingly:
Then let not him be slander'd with revolt.
                KING
Thou dost belie him, Percy, thou dost belie him;
He never did encounter with Glendower:
I tell thee,
He durst as well have met the devil alone
As Owen Glendower for an enemy.
Art thou not ashamed? But, sirrah, henceforth
Let me not hear you speak of Mortimer:
Send me your prisoners with the speediest means,
Or you shall hear in such a kind from me
As will displease you. My Lord Northumberland,
We license your departure with your son.
Send us your prisoners, or you will hear of it.
              [*Exeunt* KING HENRY, BLUNT, *and train*
                HOTSPUR
An if the devil come and roar for them,
I will not send them: I will after straight
And tell him so; for I will ease my hear
Albeit I make a hazard of my head.

NORTHUMBERLAND

What, drunk with choler? stay and pause a while:
Here comes your uncle.

Re-enter WORCESTER

HOTSPUR

          Speak of Mortimer!
'Zounds, I will speak of him; and let my soul
Want mercy, if I do not join with him:
Yea, on his part I'll empty all these veins,
And shed my dear blood drop by drop in the dust,
But I will lift the down-trod Mortimer
As high in the air as this unthankful king,
As this ingrate and canker'd Bolingbroke.

NORTHUMBERLAND

Brother, the king hath made your nephew mad.

WORCESTER

Who struck this heat up after I was gone?

HOTSPUR

He will, forsooth, have all my prisoners;
And when I urged the ransom once again
Of my wife's brother, then his cheek look'd pale,
And on my face he turn'd an eye of death,
Trembling even at the name of Mortimer.

WORCESTER

I cannot blame him: was not he proclaim'd
By Richard that dead is the next of blood?

NORTHUMBERLAND

He was; I heard the proclamation:
And then it was when the unhappy king,—
Whose wrongs in us God pardon!—did set forth
Upon his Irish expedition;
From whence he intercepted did return
To be deposed and shortly murdered.

WORCESTER

And for whose death we in the world's wide mouth
Live scandalized and foully spoken of.

HOTSPUR

But, soft, I pray you; did King Richard then
Proclaim my brother Edmund Mortimer
Heir to the crown?

NORTHUMBERLAND

          He did; myself did hear it.

HOTSPUR

Nay, then I cannot blame his cousin king,
That wish'd him on the barren mountains starve.
But shall it be, that you, that set the crown
Upon the head of this forgetful man,
And for his sake wear the detested blot
Of murderous subornation, shall it be,
That you a world of curses undergo,
Being the agents, or base second means,
The cords, the ladder, or the hangman rather?
O, pardon me that I descend so low,
To show the line and the predicament
Wherein you range under this subtle king;
Shall it for shame be spoken in these days,
Or fill up chronicles in time to come,
That men of your nobility and power
Did gage them both in an unjust behalf,
As both of you—God pardon it!—have done,

To put down Richard, that sweet lovely rose,
And plant this thorn, this canker, Bolingbroke?
And shall it in more shame be further spoken,
That you are fool'd, discarded and shook off
By him for whom these shames ye underwent?
No; yet time serves wherein you may redeem
Your banish'd honours, and restore yourselves
Into the good thoughts of the world again,
Revenge the jeering and disdain'd contempt
Of this proud king, who studies day and night
To answer all the debt he owes to you
Even with the bloody payment of your deaths:
Therefore, I say,—

WORCESTER

          Peace, cousin, say no more:
And now I will unclasp a secret book,
And to your quick-conceiving discontents
I'll read you matter deep and dangerous,
As full of peril and adventurous spirit
As to o'er-walk a current roaring loud
On the unsteadfast footing of a spear.

HOTSPUR

If he fall in, good night! or sink or swim:
Send danger from the east unto the west,
So honour cross it from the north to south,
And let them grapple: O, the blood more stirs
To rouse a lion than to start a hare!

NORTHUMBERLAND

Imagination of some great exploit
Drives him beyond the bounds of patience.

HOTSPUR

By heaven, methinks it were an easy leap,
To pluck bright honour from the pale-faced moon,
Or dive into the bottom of the deep,
Where fathom-line could never touch the ground,
And pluck up drowned honour by the locks;
So he that doth redeem her thence might wear
Without corrival all her dignities:
But out upon this half-faced fellowship!

WORCESTER

He apprehends a world of figures here,
But not the form of what he should attend.
Good cousin, give me audience for a while.

HOTSPUR

I cry you mercy.

WORCESTER

          Those same noble Scots
That are your prisoners,—

HOTSPUR

          I'll keep them all;
By God, he shall not have a Scot of them;
No, if a Scot would save his soul, he shall not:
I'll keep them, by this hand.

WORCESTER

          You start away
And lend no ear unto my purposes.
Those prisoners you shall keep.

HOTSPUR

          Nay, I will; that's flat:
He said he would not ransom Mortimer;

Forbad my tongue to speak of Mortimer;
But I will find him when he lies asleep,
And in his ear I'll holla 'Mortimer!'
Nay,
I'll have a starling shall be taught to speak
Nothing but 'Mortimer,' and give it him,
To keep his anger still in motion.

WORCESTER

Hear you, cousin; a word.

HOTSPUR

All studies here I solemnly defy,
Save how to gall and pinch this Bolingbroke:
And that same sword-and-buckler Prince of Wales,
But that I think his father loves him not
And would be glad he met with some mischance,
I would have him poison'd with a pot of ale.

WORCESTER

Farewell, kinsman: I'll talk to you
When you are better temper'd to attend.

NORTHUMBERLAND

Why, what a wasp-stung and impatient fool
Art thou to break into this woman's mood,
Tying thine ear to no tongue but thine own!

HOTSPUR

Why, look you, I am whipp'd and scourged with
    rods,
Nettled, and stung with pismires, when I hear
Of this vile politician, Bolingbroke.
In Richard's time,—what do you call the place?—
A plague upon it, it is in Gloucestershire;
'Twas where the madcap duke his uncle kept,
His uncle York; where I first bow'd my knee
Unto this king of smiles, this Bolingbroke,—
'Sblood!—
When you and he came back from Ravenspurgh.

NORTHUMBERLAND

At Berkley-castle.

HOTSPUR

You say true:
Why, what a candy deal of courtesy
This fawning greyhound then did proffer me!
Look, 'when his infant fortune came to age,'
And 'gentle Harry Percy,' and 'kind cousin;'
O, the devil take such cozeners! God forgive me!
Good uncle, tell your tale; I have done.

WORCESTER

Nay, if you have not, to it again;
We will stay your leisure.

HOTSPUR

                    I have done, i' faith.

WORCESTER

Then once more to your Scottish prisoners.
Deliver them up without their ransom straight,
And make the Douglas' son your only mean
For powers in Scotland; which, for divers reasons
Which I shall send you written, be assured,
Will easily be granted. You, my lord,
                    [To NORTHUMBERLAND
Your son in Scotland being thus employ'd,
Shall secretly into the bosom creep

Of that same noble prelate, well beloved,
The archbishop.

HOTSPUR

Of York, is it not?

WORCESTER

True; who bears hard
His brother's death at Bristol, the Lord Scroop.
I speak not this in estimation,
As what I think might be, but what I know
Is ruminated, plotted and set down,
And only stays but to behold the face
Of that occasion that shall bring it on.

HOTSPUR

I smell it: upon my life, it will do well.

NORTHUMBERLAND

Before the game is a-foot, thou still let'st slip.

HOTSPUR

Why, it cannot choose but be a noble plot:
And then the power of Scotland and of York,
To join with Mortimer, ha?

WORCESTER

                    And so they shall.

HOTSPUR

In faith, it is exeedingly well aim'd.

WORCESTER

And 'tis no little reason bids us speed,
To save our heads by raising of a head;
For, bear ourselves as even as we can,
The king will always think him in our debt,
And think we think ourselves unsatisfied,
Till he hath found a time to pay us home:
And see already how he doth begin
To make us strangers to his looks of love.

HOTSPUR

He does, he does: we'll be revenged on him.

WORCESTER

Cousin, farewell: no further go in this
Than I by letters shall direct your course.
When time is ripe, which will be suddenly,
I'll steal to Glendower and Lord Mortimer;
Where you and Douglas and our powers at once,
As I will fashion it, shall happily meet,
To bear our fortunes in our own strong arms,
Which now we hold at much uncertainty.

NORTHUMBERLAND

Farewell, good brother: we shall thrive, I trust.

HOTSPUR

Uncle, adieu: O, let the hours be short
Till fields and blows and groans applaud our sport!
                    [Exeunt

ACT II

SCENE I. *Rochester. An inn yard*

Enter a CARRIER with a lantern in his hand

FIRST CARRIER

Heigh-ho! an it be not four by the day, I'll be
hanged: Charles' wain is over the new chimney,
and yet our horse not packed. What, ostler!

OSTLER

[*Within*] Anon, anon.

FIRST CARRIER

I prithee, Tom, beat Cut's saddle, put a few flocks in the point; poor jade, is wrung in the withers out of all cess.

Enter another CARRIER

SECOND CARRIER

Peas and beans are as dank here as a dog, and that is the next way to give poor jades the bots: this house is turned upside down since Robin Ostler died.

FIRST CARRIER

Poor fellow, never joyed since the price of oats rose; it was the death of him.

SECOND CARRIER

I think this be the most villanous house in all London road for fleas: I am stung like a tench.

FIRST CARRIER

Like a tench! by the mass, there is ne'er a king christen could be better bit than I have been since the first cock.

SECOND CARRIER

Why, they will allow us ne'er a jordan, and then we leak in your chimney; and your chamber-lie breeds fleas like a loach.

FIRST CARRIER

What, ostler! come away and be hanged! come away.

SECOND CARRIER

I have a gammon of bacon and two razes of ginger, to be delivered as far as Charing-cross.

FIRST CARRIER

God's body! the turkeys in my pannier are quite starved. What, ostler! A plague on thee! hast thou never an eye in thy head? canst not hear? An 'twere not as good deed as drink, to break the pate on thee, I am a very villain. Come, and be hanged! hast no faith in thee?

Enter GADSHILL

GADSHILL

Good morrow, carriers. What's o'clock?

FIRST CARRIER

I think it be two o'clock.

GADSHILL

I prithee, lend me thy lantern, to see my gelding in the stable.

FIRST CARRIER

Nay, by God, soft; I know a trick worth two of that, i' faith.

GADSHILL

I pray thee, lend me thine.

SECOND CARRIER

Ay, when? canst tell? Lend me thy lantern, quoth he? marry, I'll see thee hanged first.

GADSHILL

Sirrah carrier, what time do you mean to come to London?

SECOND CARRIER

Time enough to go to bed with a candle, I warrant thee. Come, neighbour Mugs, we'll call up the gentlemen: they will along with company, for they have great charge.   [*Exeunt* CARRIERS

GADSHILL

What, ho! chamberlain!

CHAMBERLAIN

[*Within*] At hand, quoth pick-purse.

GADSHILL

That's even as fair as—at hand, quoth the chamberlain; for thou variest no more from picking of purses than giving direction doth from labouring; thou layest the plot how.

Enter CHAMBERLAIN

CHAMBERLAIN

Good morrow, Master Gadshill. It holds current that I told you yesternight: there's a franklin in the wild of Kent hath brought three hundred marks with him in gold: I heard him tell it to one of his company last night at supper; a kind of auditor; one that hath abundance of charge too, God knows what. They are up already, and call for eggs and butter: they will away presently.

GADSHILL

Sirrah, if they meet not with Saint Nicholas' clerks, I'll give thee this neck.

CHAMBERLAIN

No, I'll none of it: I pray thee, keep that for the hangman; for I know thou worshippest Saint Nicholas as truly as a man of falsehood may.

GADSHILL

What talkest thou to me of the hangman? if I hang, I'll make a fat pair of gallows; for if I hang, old Sir John hangs with me, and thou knowest he is no starveling. Tut! there are other Trojans that thou dreamest not of, the which for sport sake are content to do the profession some grace; that would, if matters should be looked into, for their own credit sake, make all whole. I am joined with no foot landrakers, no long-staff sixpenny strikers, none of these mad mustachio purple-hued malt-worms; but with nobility and tranquillity, burgomasters and great oneyers, such as can hold in, such as will strike sooner than speak, and speak sooner than drink, and drink sooner than pray: and yet, 'zounds, I lie; for they pray continually to their saint, the commonwealth; or rather, not pray to her, but prey on her, for they ride up and down on her and make her their boots.

CHAMBERLAIN

What, the commonwealth their boots? will she hold out water in foul way?

GADSHILL

She will, she will; justice hath liquored her. We steal as in a castle, cock-sure; we have the receipt of fern-seed, we walk invisible.

CHAMBERLAIN

Nay, by my faith, I think you are more beholding to the night than to fern-seed for your walking invisible.

GADSHILL

Give me thy hand: thou shalt have a share in our purchase, as I am a true man.

CHAMBERLAIN

Nay, rather let me have it, as you are a false thief.

GADSHILL

Go to; 'homo' is a common name to all men. Bid the ostler bring my gelding out of the stable. Farewell, you muddy knave.   [*Exeunt*

SCENE II. *The highway, near* GADSHILL

Enter PRINCE HENRY *and* POINS

POINS

Come, shelter, shelter: I have removed Falstaff's horse, and he frets like a gummed velvet.

PRINCE

Stand close.

Enter FALSTAFF

FALSTAFF

Poins! Poins, and be hanged! Poins!

PRINCE

Peace, ye fat-kidneyed rascal! what a brawling dost thou keep!

FALSTAFF

Where's Poins, Hal?

PRINCE

He is walked up to the top of the hill: I'll go seek him.

FALSTAFF

I am accursed to rob in that thief's company: the rascal hath removed my horse, and tied him I know not where. If I travel but four foot by the squier further afoot, I shall break my wind. Well, I doubt not but to die a fair death for all this, if I 'scape hanging for killing that rogue. I have forsworn his company hourly any time this two and twenty years, and yet I am bewitched with the rogue's company. If the rascal have not given me medicines to make me love him, I'll be hanged; it could not be else; I have drunk medicines. Poins! Hal! a plague upon you both! Bardolph! Peto! I'll starve ere I'll rob a foot further. An 'twere not as good a deed as drink, to turn true man and to leave these rogues, I am the veriest varlet that ever chewed with a tooth. Eight yards of uneven ground is threescore and ten miles afoot with me; and the stony-hearted villains know it well enough: a plague upon it when thieves cannot be true one to another! [*They whistle*] Whew! A plague upon you all! Give me my horse, you rogues; give me my horse, and be hanged!

PRINCE

Peace, ye fat-guts! lie down; lay thine ear close to the ground and list if thou canst hear the tread of travellers.

FALSTAFF

Have you any levers to lift me up again, being down? 'Sblood, I'll not bear mine own flesh so far afoot again for all the coin in thy father's exchequer. What a plague mean ye to colt me thus?

PRINCE

Thou liest; thou art not colted, thou art uncolted.

FALSTAFF

I prithee, good Prince Hal, help me to my horse, good king's son.

PRINCE

Out, ye rogue! shall I be your ostler?

FALSTAFF

Go hang thyself in thine own heir-apparent garters! If I be ta'en, I'll peach for this. An I have not ballads made on you all and sung to filthy tunes, let a cup of sack be my poison: when a jest is so forward, and afoot too! I hate it.

Enter GADSHILL, BARDOLPH *and* PETO *with him*

GADSHILL

Stand.

FALSTAFF

So I do, against my will.

POINS

O, 'tis our setter: I know his voice. Bardolph, what news?

BARDOLPH

Case ye, case ye; on with your vizards: there's money of the king's coming down the hill; 'tis going to the king's exchequer.

FALSTAFF

You lie, ye rogue; 'tis going to the king's tavern.

GADSHILL

There's enough to make us all.

FALSTAFF

To be hanged.

PRINCE

Sirs, you four shall front them in the narrow lane; Ned Poins and I will walk lower: if they 'scape from your encounter, then they light on us.

PETO

How many be there of them?

GADSHILL

Some eight or ten.

FALSTAFF

'Zounds, will they not rob us?

PRINCE

What, a coward, Sir John Paunch?

FALSTAFF

Indeed, I am not John of Gaunt, your grandfather; but yet no coward, Hal.

PRINCE

Well, we leave that to the proof.

POINS

Sirrah Jack, thy horse stands behind the hedge: when thou needest him, there thou shalt find him. Farewell, and stand fast.

FALSTAFF

Now cannot I strike him, if I should be hanged.

PRINCE

Ned, where are our disguises?

POINS

Here, hard by: stand close.

[*Exeunt* PRINCE *and* POINS

FALSTAFF

Now, my masters, happy man be his dole, say I: every man to his business.

Enter the TRAVELLERS

FIRST TRAVELLER

Come, neighbour: the boy shall lead our horses down the hill; we'll walk afoot awhile, and ease our legs.

THIEVES

Stand!

TRAVELLERS

Jesus bless us!

FALSTAFF

Strike; down with them; cut the villains' throats: ah! whoreson caterpillars! bacon-fed knaves! they hate us youth: down with them; fleece them.

TRAVELLERS

O, we are undone, both we and ours for ever!

FALSTAFF

Hang ye, gorbellied knaves, are ye undone? No, ye fat chuffs; I would your store were here! On, bacons, on! What, ye knaves! young men must live. You are grandjurors, are ye? we'll jure ye, 'faith.

[*Here they rob them and bind them. Exeunt*
Re-enter PRINCE HENRY *and* POINS *disguised*

PRINCE

The thieves have bound the true men. Now could thou and I rob the thieves and go merrily to London, it would be argument for a week, laughter for a month and a good jest for ever.

POINS

Stand close; I hear them coming.

Enter the THIEVES *again*

FALSTAFF

Come, my masters, let us share, and then to horse before day. An the Prince and Poins be not two arrant cowards, there's no equity stirring: there's no more valour in that Poins than in a wild-duck.

PRINCE

Your money!

POINS

Villains! [*As they are sharing, the* PRINCE *and* POINS *set upon them; they all run away; and* FALSTAFF, *after a blow or two, runs away too, leaving the booty behind them*]

PRINCE

Got with much ease. Now merrily to horse:
The thieves are all scatter'd and possess'd with fear
So strongly that they dare not meet each other;
Each takes his fellow for an officer.
Away, good Ned. Falstaff sweats to death,
And lards the lean earth as he walks along:
Were't not for laughing, I should pity him.

POINS

How the rogue roar'd!

[*Exeunt*

SCENE III. *Warkworth Castle*

Enter HOTSPUR *solus, reading a letter*

HOTSPUR

'But, for mine own part, my lord, I could be well contented to be there, in respect of the love I bear your house.' He could be contented: why is he not, then? In respect of the love he bears our house: he shows in this, he loves his own barn better than he loves our house. Let me see some more. 'The purpose you undertake is dangerous;'— why, that's certain: 'tis dangerous to take a cold, to sleep, to drink; but I tell you, my lord fool, out of this nettle, danger, we pluck this flower, safety. 'The purpose you undertake is dangerous; the friends you have named uncertain; the time itself unsorted; and your whole plot too light for the counterpoise of so great an opposition.' Say you so, say you so? I say unto you again, you are a shallow cowardly hind, and you lie. What a lack-brain is this! By the Lord, our plot is a good plot as ever was laid; our friends true and constant: a good plot, good friends, and full of expectation; an excellent plot, very good friends. What a frosty-spirited rogue is this! Why, my lord of York commends the plot and the general course of the action. 'Zounds, an I were now by this rascal, I could brain him with his lady's fan. Is there not my father, my uncle, and myself? lord Edmund Mortimer, my lord of York, and Owen Glendower? is there not besides the Douglas? have I not all their letters to meet me in arms by the ninth of the next month? and are they not some of them set forward already? What a pagan rascal is this! an infidel! Ha! you shall see now in very sincerity of fear and cold heart, will he to the king, and lay open all our proceedings. O, I could divide myself, and go to buffets, for moving such a dish of skim milk with so honourable an action! Hang him! let him tell the king: we are prepared. I will set forward to-night.

Enter LADY PERCY

How now, Kate! I must leave you within these two hours.

LADY PERCY

O, my good lord, why are you thus alone?
For what offence have I this fortnight been
A banish'd woman from my Harry's bed?
Tell me, sweet lord, what is't that takes from thee
Thy stomach, pleasure, and thy golden sleep?
Why dost thou bend thine eyes upon the earth,
And start so often when thou sit'st alone?
Why hast thou lost the fresh blood in thy cheeks,
And given my treasures and my rights of thee
To thick-eyed musing and cursed melancholy?
In thy faint slumbers I by thee have watch'd,
And heard thee murmur tales of iron wars;
Speak terms of manage to thy bounding steed;
Cry 'Courage! to the field!' And thou hast talk'd
Of sallies and retires, of trenches, tents,
Of palisadoes, frontiers, parapets,
Of basilisks, of cannon, culverin,
Of prisoners' ransom, and of soldiers slain,

And all the currents of a heady fight.
Thy spirit within thee hath been so at war
And thus hath so bestirr'd thee in thy sleep,
That beads of sweat have stood upon thy brow,
Like bubbles in a late-disturbed stream;
And in thy face strange motions have appear'd,
Such as we see when men restrain their breath
On some great sudden hest. O, what portents are
    these?
Some heavy business hath my lord in hand,
And I must know it, else he loves me not.

HOTSPUR

What, ho!

Enter SERVANT

Is Gilliams with the packet gone?

SERVANT

He is, my lord, an hour ago.

HOTSPUR

Hath Butler brought those horses from the sheriff?

SERVANT

One horse, my lord, he brought even now.

HOTSPUR

What horse? a roan, a crop-ear, is it not?

SERVANT

It is, my lord.

HOTSPUR

    That roan shall be my throne.
Well, I will back him straight: O esperance!
Bid Butler lead him forth into the park.

[*Exit* SERVANT

LADY PERCY

But hear you, my lord.

HOTSPUR

What say'st thou, my lady?

LADY PERCY

What is it carries you away?

HOTSPUR

Why, my horse, my love, my horse.

LADY PERCY

Out, you mad-headed ape!
A weasel hath not such a deal of spleen
As you are toss'd with. In faith,
I'll know your business, Harry, that I will.
I fear my brother Mortimer doth stir
About his title, and hath sent for you
To line his enterprize: but if you go—

HOTSPUR

So far afoot, I shall be weary, love.

LADY PERCY

Come, come, you paraquito, answer me
Directly unto this question that I ask:
In faith, I'll break thy little finger, Harry,
And if thou wilt not tell me all things true.

HOTSPUR

Away,
Away, you trifler! Love! I love thee not,
I care not for thee, Kate: this is no world
To play with mammets and to tilt with lips:
We must have bloody noses and crack'd crowns,
And pass them current too. God's me, my horse!

What say'st thou, Kate? what wouldst thou have
    with me?

LADY PERCY

Do you not love me? do you not, indeed?
Well, do not then; for since you love me not,
I will not love myself. Do you not love me?
Nay, tell me if you speak in jest or no.

HOTSPUR

Come, wilt thou see me ride?
And when I am o' horseback, I will swear
I love thee infinitely. But hark you, Kate;
I must not have you henceforth question me
Whither I go, nor reason whereabout:
Whither I must, I must; and, to conclude,
This evening must I leave you, gentle Kate.
I know you wise, but yet no farther wise
Than Harry Percy's wife: constant you are,
But yet a woman: and for secrecy,
No lady closer; for I well believe
Thou wilt not utter what thou dost not know;
And so far will I trust thee, gentle Kate.

LADY PERCY

How! so far?

HOTSPUR

Not an inch further. But hark you, Kate:
Whither I go, thither shall you go too;
To-day will I set forth, to-morrow you.
Will this content you, Kate?

LADY PERCY

    It must of force. [*Exeunt*

SCENE IV. *The Boar's-Head Tavern in Eastcheap*

Enter the PRINCE, *and* POINS

PRINCE

Ned, prithee, come out of that fat room, and lend
me thy hand to laugh a little.

POINS

Where hast been, Hal?

PRINCE

With three or four loggerheads amongst three or
fourscore hogsheads. I have sounded the very base-
string of humility. Sirrah, I am sworn brother to a
leash of drawers; and can call them all by their
christen names, as Tom, Dick, and Francis. They
take it already upon their salvation, that though I
be but Prince of Wales, yet I am the king of courtesy; and tell me flatly I am no proud Jack, like
Falstaff, but a Corinthian, a lad of mettle, a good
boy, by the Lord, so they call me, and when I am
king of England, I shall command all the good lads
in Eastcheap. They call drinking deep, dyeing scarlet; and when you breathe in your watering, they
cry 'hem!' and bid you play it off. To conclude, I
am so good a proficient in one quarter of an hour,
that I can drink with any tinker in his own language
during my life. I tell thee, Ned, thou hast lost much
honour, that thou wert not with me in this action.
But, sweet Ned,—to sweeten which name of Ned, I

give thee this pennyworth of sugar, clapped even now into my hand by an under-skinker, one that never spake other English in his life than 'Eight shillings and sixpence,' and 'You are welcome,' with this shrill addition, 'Anon, anon, sir! Score a pint of bastard in the Half-moon,' or so. But, Ned, to drive away the time till Falstaff come, I prithee, do thou stand in some by-room, while I question my puny drawer to what end he gave me the sugar; and do thou never leave calling 'Francis,' that his tale to me may be nothing but 'Anon.' Step aside, and I'll show thee a precedent.

POINS

Francis!

PRINCE

Thou art perfect.

POINS

Francis!   [Exit POINS

Enter FRANCIS

FRANCIS

Anon, anon, sir. Look down into the Pomgarnet, Ralph.

PRINCE

Come hither, Francis.

FRANCIS

My lord?

PRINCE

How long hast thou to serve, Francis?

FRANCIS

Forsooth, five years, and as much as to—

POINS

[Within] Francis!

FRANCIS

Anon, anon, sir.

PRINCE

Five year! by'r lady, a long lease for the clinking of pewter. But, Francis, darest thou be so valiant as to play the coward with thy indenture and show it a fair pair of heels and run from it?

FRANCIS

O Lord, sir, I'll be sworn upon all the books in England, I could find in my heart.

POINS

[Within] Francis!

FRANCIS

Anon, sir.

PRINCE

How old art thou, Francis?

FRANCIS

Let me see—about Michaelmas next I shall be—

POINS

[Within] Francis!

FRANCIS

Anon, sir. Pray stay a little, my lord.

PRINCE

Nay, but hark you, Francis: for the sugar thou gavest me, 'twas a pennyworth, was't not?

FRANCIS

O Lord ¹ would it had been two!

PRINCE

I will give thee for it a thousand pound: ask me when thou wilt, and thou shalt have it.

POINS

[Within] Francis!

FRANCIS

Anon, anon.

PRINCE

Anon, Francis? No, Francis; but to-morrow, Francis; or Francis, o' Thursday; or indeed, Francis, when thou wilt. But, Francis!

FRANCIS

My lord?

PRINCE

Wilt thou rob this leathern jerkin, crystal-button, not-pated, agate-ring, puke-stocking, caddis-garter, smooth-tongue, Spanish-pouch,—

FRANCIS

O lord, sir, who do you mean?

PRINCE

Why, then, your brown bastard is your only drink; for look you, Francis, your white canvas doublet will sully: in Barbary, sir, it cannot come to so much.

FRANCIS

What, sir?

POINS

[Within] Francis!

PRINCE

Away, you rogue! dost thou not hear them call?
[Here they both call him; the DRAWER stands amazed, not knowing which way to go

Enter VINTNER

VINTNER

What, standest thou still, and hearest such a calling? Look to the guests within. [Exit FRANCIS] My lord, old Sir John, with half-a-dozen more, are at the door: shall I let them in?

PRINCE

Let them alone awhile, and then open the door. [Exit VINTNER] Poins!

Re-enter POINS

POINS

Anon, anon, sir.

PRINCE

Sirrah, Falstaff and the rest of the thieves are at the door: shall we be merry?

POINS

As merry as crickets, my lad. But hark ye; what cunning match have you made with this jest of the drawer? come, what's the issue?

PRINCE

I am now of all humours that have showed themselves humours since the old days of goodman Adam to the pupil age of this present twelve o'clock at midnight.

Re-enter FRANCIS

What's o'clock, Francis?

FRANCIS

Anon, anon, sir.   [Exit

PRINCE

That ever this fellow should have fewer words than a parrot, and yet the son of a woman! His industry is up-stairs and down-stairs; his eloquence the parcel of a reckoning. I am not yet of Percy's mind, the Hotspur of the north; he that kills me some six or seven dozen of Scots at a breakfast, washes his hands, and says to his wife 'Fie upon this quiet life! I want work.' 'O my sweet Harry,' says she, 'how many hast thou killed to-day?' 'Give my roan horse a drench,' says he; and answers 'Some fourteen,' an hour after; 'a trifle, a trifle.' I prithee, call in Falstaff: I'll play Percy, and that damned brawn shall play Dame Mortimer his wife. 'Rivo!' says the drunkard. Call in ribs, call in tallow.

Enter FALSTAFF, GADSHILL, BARDOLPH, *and* PETO; FRANCIS *following with wine*

POINS

Welcome, Jack: where hast thou been?

FALSTAFF

A plague of all cowards, I say, and a vengeance too! marry, and amen! Give me a cup of sack, boy. Ere I lead this life long, I'll sew nether stocks and mend them and foot them too. A plague of all cowards! Give me a cup of sack, rogue. Is there no virtue extant?   [*He drinks*

PRINCE

Didst thou never see Titan kiss a dish of butter? pitiful-hearted Titan, that melted at the sweet tale of the sun's! if thou didst, then behold that compound.

FALSTAFF

You rogue, here's lime in this sack too: there is nothing but roguery to be found in villanous man: yet a coward is worse than a cup of sack with lime in it. A villanous coward! Go thy ways, old Jack; die when thou wilt, if manhood, good manhood, be not forgot upon the face of the earth, then am I a shotten herring. There lives not three good men unhanged in England; and one of them is fat, and grows old: God help the while! a bad world, I say. I would I were a weaver; I could sing psalms or any thing. A plague of all cowards, I say still.

PRINCE

How now, wool-sack! what mutter you?

FALSTAFF

A king's son! If I do not beat thee out of thy kingdom with a dagger of lath, and drive all thy subjects afore thee like a flock of wild-geese, I'll never wear hair on my face more. You Prince of Wales!

PRINCE

Why, you whoreson round man, what's the matter?

FALSTAFF

Are not you a coward? answer me to that: and Poins there?

POINS

'Zounds, ye fat paunch, an ye call me coward, by the Lord, I'll stab thee.

FALSTAFF

I call thee coward! I'll see thee damned ere I call

thee coward: but I would give a thousand pound I could run as fast as thou canst. You are straight enough in the shoulders, you care not who sees your back: call you that backing of your friends? A plague upon such backing! give me them that will face me. Give me a cup of sack: I am a rogue, if I drunk to-day.

PRINCE

O villain! thy lips are scarce wiped since thou drunkest last.

FALSTAFF

All's one for that. [*He drinks*] A plague of all cowards, still say I.

PRINCE

What's the matter?

FALSTAFF

What's the matter! there be four of us here have ta'en a thousand pound this day morning.

PRINCE

Where is it, Jack? where is it?

FALSTAFF

Where is it! taken from us it is: a hundred upon poor four of us.

PRINCE

What, a hundred, man?

FALSTAFF

I am a rogue, if I were not at half-sword with a dozen of them two hours together. I have 'scaped by miracle. I am eight times thrust through the doublet, four through the hose; my buckler cut through and through; my sword hacked like a hand-saw— ecce signum! I never dealt better since I was a man: all would not do. A plague of all cowards! Let them speak: if they speak more or less than truth, they are villains and the sons of darkness.

PRINCE

Speak, sirs; how was it?

GADSHILL

We four set upon some dozen—

FALSTAFF

Sixteen at least, my lord.

GADSHILL

And bound them.

PETO

No, no, they were not bound.

FALSTAFF

You rogue, they were bound, every man of them; or I am a Jew else, an Ebrew Jew.

GADSHILL

As we were sharing, some six or seven fresh men set upon us—

FALSTAFF

And unbound the rest, and then come in the other.

PRINCE

What, fought you with them all?

FALSTAFF

All! I know not what you call all; but if I fought not with fifty of them, I am a bunch of radish: if there were not two or three and fifty upon poor old Jack, then am I no two-legged creature.

PRINCE

Pray God you have not murdered some of them.

FALSTAFF

Nay, that's past praying for: I have peppered two of them; two I am sure I have paid, two rogues in buckram suits. I tell thee what, Hal, if I tell thee a lie, spit in my face, call me horse. Thou knowest my old ward; here I lay, and thus I bore my point. Four rogues in buckram let drive at me—

PRINCE

What, four? thou saidst but two even now.

FALSTAFF

Four, Hal; I told thee four.

POINS

Ay, ay, he said four.

FALSTAFF

These four came all a-front, and mainly thrust at me. I made me no more ado but took all their seven points in my target, thus.

PRINCE

Seven? why, there were but four even now.

FALSTAFF

In buckram?

POINS

Ay, four, in buckram suits.

FALSTAFF

Seven, by these hilts, or I am a villain else.

PRINCE

Prithee, let him alone; we shall have more anon.

FALSTAFF

Dost thou hear me, Hal?

PRINCE

Ay, and mark thee too, Jack.

FALSTAFF

Do so, for it is worth the listening to. These nine in buckram that I told thee of,—

PRINCE

So, two more already.

FALSTAFF

Their points being broken,—

POINS

Down fell their hose.

FALSTAFF

Began to give me ground: but I followed me close, came in foot and hand; and with a thought seven of the eleven I paid.

PRINCE

O monstrous! eleven buckram men grown out of two!

FALSTAFF

But, as the devil would have it, three misbegotten knaves in Kendal green came at my back and let drive at me; for it was so dark, Hal, that thou couldst not see thy hand.

PRINCE

These lies are like their father that begets them; gross as a mountain, open, palpable. Why, thou clay-brained guts, thou knotty-pated fool, thou whoreson, obscene, greasy tallow-catch,—

FALSTAFF

What, art thou mad? art thou mad? is not the truth the truth?

PRINCE

Why, how couldst thou know these men in Kendal green, when it was so dark thou couldst not see thy hand? come, tell us thy reason: what sayest thou to this?

POINS

Come, your reason, Jack, your reason.

FALSTAFF

What, upon compulsion? 'Zounds, an I were at the strappado, or all the racks in the world, I would not tell you on compulsion. Give you a reason on compulsion! if reasons were as plentiful as blackberries, I would give no man a reason upon compulsion, I.

PRINCE

I'll be no longer guilty of this sin; this sanguine coward, this bed-presser, this horse-back-breaker, this huge hill of flesh,—

FALSTAFF

'Sblood, you starveling, you elf-skin, you dried neat's tongue, you bull's pizzle, you stock-fish! O for breath to utter what is like thee! you tailor's-yard, you sheath, you bow-case, you vile standing tuck,—

PRINCE

Well, breathe a while, and then to it again: and when thou hast tired thyself in base comparisons, hear me speak but this.

POINS

Mark, Jack.

PRINCE

We two saw you four set on four and bound them, and were masters of their wealth. Mark now, how a plain tale shall put you down. Then did we two set on you four; and, with a word, out-faced you from your prize, and have it; yea, and can show it you here in the house: and, Falstaff, you carried your guts away as nimbly, with as quick dexterity, and roared for mercy, and still run and roared, as ever I heard bull-calf. What a slave art thou, to hack thy sword as thou hast done, and then say it was in fight! What trick, what device, what starting-hole, canst thou now find out to hide thee from this open and apparent shame?

POINS

Come, let's hear, Jack; what trick hast thou now?

FALSTAFF

By the Lord, I knew ye as well as he that made ye. Why, hear you, my masters: was it for me to kill the heir-apparent? should I turn upon the true prince? why, thou knowest I am as valiant as Hercules: but beware instinct; the lion will not touch the true prince. Instinct is a great matter; I was now a coward on instinct. I shall think the better of myself and thee during my life; I for a valiant lion, and thou for a true prince. But, by the Lord, lads, I am glad you have the money. Hostess, clap to the doors: watch to-night, pray to-morrow. Gallants, lads, boys, hearts of gold, all the titles of good fellowship come to you! What, shall we be merry? shall we have a play extempore?

PRINCE

Content; and the argument shall be thy running away.

FALSTAFF

Ah, no more of that, Hal, an thou lovest me!

Enter HOSTESS

HOSTESS

O Jesu, my lord the prince!

PRINCE

How now, my lady the hostess! what sayest thou to me?

HOSTESS

Marry, my lord, there is a nobleman of the court at door would speak with you: he says he comes from your father.

PRINCE

Give him as much as will make him a royal man, and send him back again to my mother.

FALSTAFF

What manner of man is he?

HOSTESS

An old man.

FALSTAFF

What doth gravity out of his bed at midnight? Shall I give him his answer?

PRINCE

Prithee, do, Jack.

FALSTAFF

Faith, and I'll send him packing.　　　[*Exit*

PRINCE

Now, sirs: by'r lady, you fought fair; so did you, Peto; so did you, Bardolph: you are lions too, you ran away upon instinct, you will not touch the true prince; no, fie!

BARDOLPH

Faith, I ran when I saw others run.

PRINCE

Faith, tell me now in earnest, how came Falstaff's sword so hacked?

PETO

Why, he hacked it with his dagger, and said he would swear truth out of England but he would make you believe it was done in fight, and persuaded us to do the like.

BARDOLPH

Yea, and to tickle our noses with spear-grass to make them bleed, and then to beslubber our garments with it and swear it was the blood of true men. I did that I did not this seven year before, I blushed to hear his monstrous devices.

PRINCE

O villain, thou stolest a cup of sack eighteen years ago, and wert taken with the manner, and ever since thou hast blushed extempore. Thou hadst fire and sword on thy side, and yet thou rannest away: what instinct hadst thou for it?

BARDOLPH

My lord, do you see these meteors? do you behold these exhalations?

PRINCE

I do.

BARDOLPH

What think you they portend?

PRINCE

Hot livers and cold purses.

BARDOLPH

Choler, my lord, if rightly taken.

PRINCE

No, if rightly taken, halter.

Re-enter FALSTAFF

Here comes lean Jack, here comes bare-bone. How now, my sweet creature of bombast! How long is't ago, Jack, since thou sawest thine own knee?

FALSTAFF

My own knee! when I was about thy years, Hal, I was not an eagle's talon in the waist; I could have crept into any alderman's thumb-ring: a plague of sighing and grief! it blows a man up like a bladder. There's villanous news abroad: here was Sir John Bracy from your father; you must to the court in the morning. That same mad fellow of the north, Percy, and he of Wales, that gave Amamon the bastinado, and made Lucifer cuckold, and swore the devil his true liegeman upon the cross of a Welsh hook— what a plague call you him?

POINS

O, Glendower.

FALSTAFF

Owen, Owen, the same; and his son-in-law Mortimer, and old Northumberland, and that sprightly Scot of Scots, Douglas, that runs o' horseback up a hill perpendicular,—

PRINCE

He that rides at high speed and with his pistol kills a sparrow flying.

FALSTAFF

You have hit it.

PRINCE

So did he never the sparrow.

FALSTAFF

Well, that rascal hath good mettle in him; he will not run.

PRINCE

Why, what a rascal art thou then, to praise him so for running!

FALSTAFF

O' horseback, ye cuckoo; but afoot he will not budge a foot.

PRINCE

Yes, Jack, upon instinct.

FALSTAFF

I grant ye, upon instinct. Well, he is there too, and one Mordake, and a thousand blue-caps more: Worcester is stolen away to-night; thy father's beard is turned white with the news: you may buy land now as cheap as stinking mackerel.

PRINCE

Why, then, it is like, if there come a hot June and this civil buffeting hold, we shall buy maidenheads as they buy hob-nails, by the hundreds.

FALSTAFF

By the mass, lad, thou sayest true; it is like we shall have good trading that way. But tell me, Hal, art not thou horrible afeard? thou being heir-apparent, could the world pick thee out three such enemies again as that fiend Douglas, that spirit Percy, and that devil Glendower? art thou not horribly afraid? doth not thy blood thrill at it?

PRINCE

Not a whit, i' faith; I lack some of thy instinct.

FALSTAFF

Well, thou wilt be horribly chid to-morrow when thou comest to thy father: if thou love me, practise an answer.

PRINCE

Do thou stand for my father, and examine me upon the particulars of my life.

FALSTAFF

Shall I? content: this chair shall be my state, this dagger my sceptre, and this cushion my crown.

PRINCE

Thy state is taken for a joined-stool, thy golden sceptre for a leaden dagger, and thy precious rich crown for a pitiful bald crown!

FALSTAFF

Well, an the fire of grace be not quite out of thee, now shalt thou be moved. Give me a cup of sack to make my eyes look red, that it may be thought I have wept; for I must speak in passion, and I will do it in King Cambyses' vein.

PRINCE

Well, here is my leg.

FALSTAFF

And here is my speech. Stand aside, nobility.

HOSTESS

O Jesu, this is excellent sport, i' faith!

FALSTAFF

Weep not, sweet queen; for trickling tears are vain.

HOSTESS

O, the father, how he holds his countenance!

FALSTAFF

For God's sake, lords, convey my tristful queen;
For tears do stop the flood-gates of her eyes.

HOSTESS

O Jesu, he doth it as like one of these harlotry players as ever I see!

FALSTAFF

Peace, good pint-pot; peace, good tickle-brain. Harry, I do not only marvel where thou spendest thy time, but also how thou art accompanied: for though the camomile, the more it is trodden on the faster it grows, yet youth, the more it is wasted the sooner it wears. That thou art my son, I have partly thy mother's word, partly my own opinion, but chiefly a villanous trick of thine eye, and a foolish hanging of thy nether lip, that doth warrant me.

If then thou be son to me, here lies the point; why, being son to me, art thou so pointed at? Shall the blessed sun of heaven prove a micher and eat blackberries? a question not to be asked. Shall the son of England prove a thief and take purses? a question to be asked. There is a thing, Harry, which thou hast often heard of, and it is known to many in our land by the name of pitch: this pitch, as ancient writers do report, doth defile; so doth the company thou keepest: for, Harry, now I do not speak to thee in drink but in tears, not in pleasure but in passion, not in words only, but in woes also: and yet there is a virtuous man whom I have often noted in thy company, but I know not his name.

PRINCE

What manner of man, an it like your majesty?

FALSTAFF

A goodly portly man, i' faith, and a corpulent; of a cheerful look, a pleasing eye, and a most noble carriage; and, as I think, his age some fifty, or, by'r lady, inclining to three score; and now I remember me, his name is Falstaff: if that man should be lewdly given, he deceiveth me; for, Harry, I see virtue in his looks. If then the tree may be known by the fruit, as the fruit by the tree, then, peremptorily I speak it, there is virtue in that Falstaff: him keep with, the rest banish. And tell me now, thou naughty varlet, tell me, where hast thou been this month?

PRINCE

Dost thou speak like a king? Do thou stand for me, and I'll play my father.

FALSTAFF

Depose me? if thou dost it half so gravely, so majestically, both in word and matter, hang me up by the heels for a rabbit-sucker or a poulter's hare.

PRINCE

Well, here I am set.

FALSTAFF

And here I stand: judge, my masters.

PRINCE

Now, Harry, whence come you?

FALSTAFF

My noble lord, from Eastcheap.

PRINCE

The complaints I hear of thee are grievous.

FALSTAFF

'Sblood, my lord, they are false: nay, I'll tickle ye for a young prince, i' faith.

PRINCE

Swearest thou, ungracious boy? henceforth ne'er look on me. Thou art violently carried away from grace: there is a devil haunts thee in the likeness of an old fat man; a tun of man is thy companion. Why dost thou converse with that trunk of humours, that bolting-hutch of beastliness, that swollen parcel of dropsies, that huge bombard of sack, that stuffed cloak-bag of guts, that roasted Manningtree ox with the pudding in his belly, that reverend vice, that grey iniquity, that father ruffian, that vanity in years? Wherein is he good, but to taste sack and drink it? wherein neat and cleanly, but to carve a capon and eat it? wherein cunning, but in craft? wherein crafty, but in villany? wherein villanous, but in all things? wherein worthy, but in nothing?

FALSTAFF

I would your grace would take me with you: whom means your grace?

PRINCE

That villanous abominable misleader of youth, Falstaff, that old white-bearded Satan.

FALSTAFF

My lord, the man I know.

PRINCE

I know thou dost.

FALSTAFF

But to say I know more harm in him than in myself, were to say more than I know. That he is old, the more the pity, his white hairs do witness it; but that he is, saving your reverence, a whoremaster, that I utterly deny. If sack and sugar be a fault, God help the wicked! if to be old and merry be a sin, then many an old host that I know is damned: if to be fat be to be hated, then Pharaoh's lean kine are to be loved. No, my good lord; banish Peto, banish Bardolph, banish Poins: but for sweet Jack Falstaff, kind Jack Falstaff, true Jack Falstaff, valiant Jack Falstaff, and therefore more valiant, being, as he is, old Jack Falstaff, banish not him thy Harry's company, banish not him thy Harry's company: banish plump Jack, and banish all the world.

PRINCE

I do, I will.

[A knocking heard
[Exeunt HOSTESS, FRANCIS, and BARDOLPH
Re-enter BARDOLPH, running

BARDOLPH

O, my lord, my lord! the sheriff with a most monstrous watch is at the door.

FALSTAFF

Out, ye rogue! Play out the play: I have much to say in the behalf of that Falstaff.

Re-enter the HOSTESS

HOSTESS

O Jesu, my lord, my lord!—

PRINCE

Heigh, heigh! the devil rides upon a fiddlestick: what's the matter?

HOSTESS

The sheriff and all the watch are at the door: they are come to search the house. Shall I let them in?

FALSTAFF

Dost thou hear, Hal? never call a true piece of gold a counterfeit: thou art essentially mad, without seeming so.

PRINCE

And thou a natural coward, without instinct.

FALSTAFF

I deny your major: if you will deny the sheriff, so; if not, let him enter: if I become not a cart as well as another man, a plague on my bringing up! I hope I shall as soon be strangled with a halter as another.

PRINCE

Go, hide thee behind the arras: the rest walk up above. Now, my masters, for a true face and good conscience.

FALSTAFF

Both which I have had: but their date is out, and therefore I'll hide me.

PRINCE

Call in the sheriff.

[Exeunt all except the PRINCE and PETO
Enter SHERIFF and the CARRIER

Now, master sheriff, what is your will with me?

SHERIFF

First, pardon me, my lord. A hue and cry
Hath follow'd certain men unto this house.

PRINCE

What men?

SHERIFF

One of them is well known, my gracious lord,
A gross fat man.

CARRIER

As fat as butter.

PRINCE

The man, I do assure you, is not here;
For I myself at this time have employ'd him.
And, sheriff, I will engage my word to thee
That I will, by to-morrow dinner-time,
Send him to answer thee, or any man,
For any thing he shall be charged withal:
And so let me entreat you leave the house.

SHERIFF

I will, my lord. There are two gentlemen
Have in this robbery lost three hundred marks.

PRINCE

It may be so: if he have robb'd these men,
He shall be answerable; and so farewell.

SHERIFF

Good night, my noble lord.

PRINCE

I think it is good morrow, is it not?

SHERIFF

Indeed, my lord, I think it be two o'clock.

[Exeunt SHERIFF and CARRIER

PRINCE

This oily rascal is known as well as Paul's.
Go, call him forth.

PETO

Falstaff!—Fast asleep behind the arras, and snorting like a horse.

PRINCE

Hark, how hard he fetches breath. Search his pockets. [He searcheth his pockets, and findeth certain papers]
What hast thou found?

PETO

Nothing but papers, my lord.

PRINCE

Let's see what they be: read them.

PETO

[*Reads*] Item, A capon, ...   2s. 2d.
Item, Sauce, ...   4d.
Item, Sack, two gallons, ...   5s. 8d.
Item, Anchovies and sack after supper,   2s. 6d.
Item, Bread, ...   ob.

PRINCE

O monstrous! but one half-pennyworth of bread to
this intolerable deal of sack! What there is else, keep
close; we'll read it at more advantage: there let him
sleep till day. I'll to the court in the morning. We
must all to the wars, and thy place shall be honourable. I'll procure this fat rogue a charge of foot; and
I know his death will be a march of twelve-score.
The money shall be paid back again with advantage. Be with me betimes in the morning; and so,
good morrow, Peto.

PETO

Good morrow, good my lord.   [*Exeunt*

ACT III

Scene I. *Bangor. The* Archdeacon's *house*

Enter Hotspur, Worcester, Mortimer, *and*
Glendower

MORTIMER

These promises are fair, the parties sure.
And our induction full of prosperous hope.

HOTSPUR

Lord Mortimer, and cousin Glendower,
Will you sit down?
And uncle Worcester: a plague upon it!
I have forgot the map.

GLENDOWER

No, here it is.
Sit, cousin Percy; sit, good cousin Hotspur,
For by that name as oft as Lancaster
Doth speak of you, his cheek looks pale, and with
A rising sigh he wisheth you in heaven.

HOTSPUR

And you in hell, as oft as he hears Owen Glendower
spoke of.

GLENDOWER

I cannot blame him: at my nativity
The front of heaven was full of fiery shapes,
Of burning cressets; and at my birth
The frame and huge foundation of the earth
Shaked like a coward.

HOTSPUR

Why, so it would have done at the same season, if
your mother's cat had but kittened, though yourself
had never been born.

GLENDOWER

I say the earth did shake when I was born.

HOTSPUR

And I say the earth was not of my mind,
If you suppose as fearing you it shook.

GLENDOWER

The heavens were all on fire, the earth did tremble.

HOTSPUR

O, then the earth shook to see the heavens on fire,
And not in fear of your nativity.
Diseased nature oftentimes breaks forth
In strange eruptions; oft the teeming earth
Is with a kind of colic pinch'd and vex'd
By the imprisoning of unruly wind.
Within her womb; which, for enlargement striving,
Shakes the old beldam earth and topples down
Steeples and moss-grown towers. At your birth
Our grandam earth, having this distemperature,
In passion shook.

GLENDOWER

Cousin, of many men
I do not bear these crossings. Give me leave
To tell you once again that at my birth
The front of heaven was full of fiery shapes,
The goats ran from the mountains, and the herds
Were strangely clamorous to the frighted fields.
These signs have mark'd me extraordinary;
And all the courses of my life do show
I am not in the roll of common men.
Where is he living, clipp'd in with the sea
That chides the banks of England, Scotland, Wales,
Which calls me pupil, or hath read to me?
And bring him out that is but woman's son
Can trace me in the tedious ways of art,
And hold me pace in deep experiments.

HOTSPUR

I think there's no man speaks better Welsh.
I'll to dinner.

MORTIMER

Peace, cousin Percy; you will make him mad.

GLENDOWER

I can call spirits from the vasty deep.

HOTSPUR

Why, so can I, or so can any man;
But will they come when you do call for them?

GLENDOWER

Why, I can teach you, cousin, to command
The devil.

HOTSPUR

And I can teach thee, coz, to shame the devil
By telling truth: tell truth, and shame the devil.
If thou have power to raise him, bring him hither,
And I'll be sworn I have power to shame him
hence.
O, while you live, tell truth, and shame the devil!

MORTIMER

Come, come, no more of this unprofitable chat.

GLENDOWER

Three times hath Henry Bolingbroke made head
Against my power; thrice from the banks of Wye
And sandy-bottom'd Severn have I sent him
Bootless home and weather-beaten back.

HOTSPUR

Home without boots, and in foul weather too!
How 'scapes he agues, in the devil's name?

GLENDOWER

Come, here's the map: shall we divide our right
According to our threefold order ta'en?

MORTIMER

The archdeacon hath divided it
Into three limits very equally:
England, from Trent and Severn hitherto,
By south and east is to my part assign'd:
All westward, Wales beyond the Severn shore,
And all the fertile land within that bound,
To Owen Glendower: and, dear coz, to you
The remnant northward, lying off from Trent.
And our indentures tripartite are drawn;
Which being sealed interchangeably,
A business that this night may execute,
To-morrow, cousin Percy, you and I
And my good Lord of Worcester will set forth
To meet your father and the Scottish power,
As is appointed us, at Shrewsbury.
My father Glendower is not ready yet,
Nor shall we need his help these fourteen days.
Within that space you may have drawn together
Your tenants, friends, and neighbouring gentlemen.

GLENDOWER

A shorter time shall send me to you, lords:
And in my conduct shall your ladies come;
From whom you now must steal and take no leave,
For there will be a world of water shed
Upon the parting of your wives and you.

HOTSPUR

Methinks my moiety, north from Burton here,
In quantity equals not one of yours:
See how this river comes me cranking in,
And cuts me from the best of all my land
A huge half-moon, a monstrous cantle out.
I'll have the current in this place damm'd up;
And here the smug and silver Trent shall run
In a new channel, fair and evenly;
It shall not wind with such a deep indent,
To rob me of so rich a bottom here.

GLENDOWER

Not wind? it shall, it must; you see it doth.

MORTIMER

Yea, but
Mark how he bears his course, and runs me up
With like advantage on the other side;
Gelding the opposed continent as much
As on the other side it takes from you.

WORCESTER

Yea, but a little charge will trench him here,
And on this north side win this cape of land;
And then he runs straight and even.

HOTSPUR

I'll have it so: a little charge will do it.

GLENDOWER

I'll not have it alter'd.

HOTSPUR

Will not you?

GLENDOWER

No, nor you shall not.

HOTSPUR

Who shall say me nay?

GLENDOWER

Why, that will I.

HOTSPUR

Let me not understand you, then; speak it in Welsh.

GLENDOWER

I can speak English, lord, as well as you;
For I was train'd up in the English court;
Where, being but young, I framed to the harp
Many an English ditty lovely well,
And gave the tongue a helpful ornament,
A virtue that was never seen in you.

HOTSPUR

Marry,
And I am glad of it with all my heart:
I had rather be a kitten and cry mew
Than one of these same metre ballad-mongers;
I had rather hear a brazen canstick turn'd,
Or a dry wheel grate on the axle-tree;
And that would set my teeth nothing on edge,
Nothing so much as mincing poetry:
'Tis like the forced gait of a shuffling nag.

GLENDOWER

Come, you shall have Trent turn'd.

HOTSPUR

I do not care: I'll give thrice so much land
To any well-deserving friend;
But in the way of bargain, mark ye me,
I'll cavil on the ninth part of a hair.
Are the indentures drawn? shall we be gone?

GLENDOWER

The moon shines fair; you may away by night:
I'll haste the writer, and withal
Break with your wives of your departure hence:
I am afraid my daughter will run mad,
So much she doteth on her Mortimer.   [Exit

MORTIMER

Fie, cousin Percy! how you cross my father!

HOTSPUR

I cannot choose: sometime he angers me
With telling me of the moldwarp and the ant,
Of the dreamer Merlin and his prophecies,
And of a dragon and a finless fish,
A clip-wing'd griffin and a moulten raven,
A couching lion and a ramping cat,
And such a deal of skimble-skamble stuff
As puts me from my faith. I tell you what,—
He held me last night at least nine hours
In reckoning up the several devils' names
That were his lackeys: I cried 'hum,' and 'well, go
    to,'
But mark'd him not a word. O, he is as tedious
As a tired horse, a railing wife;
Worse than a smoky house: I had rather live
With cheese and garlic in a windmill, far,
Than feed on cates and have him talk to me
In any summer-house in Christendom.

MORTIMER

In faith, he is a worthy gentleman,
Exceedingly well read, and profited
In strange concealments; valiant as a lion,
And wondrous affable, and as bountiful
As mines of India. Shall I tell you, cousin?
He holds your temper in a high respect,
And curbs himself even of his natural scope
When you come 'cross his humour; faith, he does:
I warrant you, that man is not alive
Might so have tempted him as you have done,
Without the taste of danger and reproof:
But do not use it oft, let me entreat you.

WORCESTER

In faith, my lord, you are too wilful-blame;
And since your coming hither have done enough
To put him quite beside his patience.
You must needs learn, lord, to amend this fault:
Though sometimes it show greatness, courage,
    blood,—
And that's the dearest grace it renders you,—
Yet oftentimes it doth present harsh rage,
Defect of manners, want of government,
Pride, haughtiness, opinion and disdain:
The least of which haunting a nobleman
Loseth men's hearts, and leaves behind a stain
Upon the beauty of all parts besides,
Beguiling them of commendation.

HOTSPUR

Well, I am school'd: good manners be your speed!
Here come our wives, and let us take our leave.

      Re-enter GLENDOWER *with the* LADIES

MORTIMER

This is the deadly spite that angers me;
My wife can speak no English, I no Welsh.

GLENDOWER

My daughter weeps: she will not part with you;
She'll be a soldier too, she'll to the wars.

MORTIMER

Good father, tell her that she and my aunt Percy
Shall follow in your conduct speedily. [GLENDOWER
speaks to her in Welsh, and she answers him in the same

GLENDOWER

She is desperate here; a peevish self-will'd harlotry,
one that no persuasion can do good upon.

            [*The* LADY *speaks in Welsh*

MORTIMER

I understand thy looks: that pretty Welsh
Which thou pour'st down from these swelling
    heavens
I am too perfect in; and, but for shame,
In such a parley should I answer thee.

            [*The* LADY *speaks again in Welsh*

I understand thy kisses and thou mine,
And that's a feeling disputation:
But I will never be a truant, love,
Till I have learn'd thy language; for thy tongue
Makes Welsh as sweet as ditties highly penn'd,
Sung by a fair queen in a summer's bower,
With ravishing division, to her lute.

GLENDOWER

Nay, if you melt, then will she run mad.

            [*The* LADY *speaks again in Welsh*

MORTIMER

O, I am ignorance itself in this!

GLENDOWER

She bids you on the wanton rushes lay you down
And rest your gentle head upon her lap,
And she will sing the song that pleaseth you,
And on your eyelids crown the god of sleep,
Charming your blood with pleasing heaviness,
Making such difference 'twixt wake and sleep
As is the difference betwixt day and night
The hour before the heavenly-harness'd team
Begins his golden progress in the east.

MORTIMER

With all my heart I'll sit and hear her sing:
By that time will our book, I think, be drawn.

GLENDOWER

Do so;
And those musicians that shall play to you
Hang in the air a thousand leagues from hence,
And straight they shall be here: sit, and attend.

HOTSPUR

Come, Kate, thou art perfect in lying down: come,
quick, quick, that I may lay my head in thy lap.

LADY PERCY

Go, ye giddy goose.   [*The music plays*

HOTSPUR

Now I perceive the devil understands Welsh;
And 'tis no marvel he is so humorous.
By'r lady, he is a good musician.

LADY PERCY

Then should you be nothing but musical, for you
are altogether governed by humours. Lie still, ye
thief, and hear the lady sing in Welsh.

HOTSPUR

I had rather hear Lady, my brach, howl in Irish.

LADY PERCY

Wouldst thou have thy head broken?

HOTSPUR

No.

LADY PERCY

Then be still.

HOTSPUR

Neither; 'tis a woman's fault.

LADY PERCY

Now God help thee!

HOTSPUR

To the Welsh lady's bed.

LADY PERCY

What's that?

HOTSPUR

Peace! she sings.

            [*Here the* LADY *sings a Welsh song*

HOTSPUR

Come, Kate, I'll have your song too.

LADY PERCY

Not mine, in good sooth.

HOTSPUR

Not yours, in good sooth! Heart! you swear like a
comfit-maker's wife. 'Not you, in good sooth,' and
'as true as I live,' and 'as God shall mend me,' and
'as sure as day,'
And givest such sarcenet surety for thy oaths,
As if thou never walk'st further than Finsbury.
Swear me, Kate, like a lady as thou art,
A good mouth-filling oath, and leave 'in sooth,'
And such protest of pepper-gingerbread,
To velvet-guards and Sunday-citizens.
Come, sing.

LADY PERCY

I will not sing.

HOTSPUR

'Tis the next way to turn tailor, or be red-breast
teacher. An the indentures be drawn, I'll away
within these two hours; and so, come in when ye
will.   [Exit

GLENDOWER

Come, come, Lord Mortimer; you are as slow
As hot Lord Percy is on fire to go.
But this our book is drawn; we'll but seal,
And then to horse immediately.

MORTIMER

With all my heart.
[Exeunt

SCENE II. London. The palace

Enter the KING, PRINCE OF WALES, and others

KING

Lords, give us leave; the Prince of Wales and I
Must have some private conference: but be near at
hand,
For we shall presently have need of you.
[Exeunt LORDS
I know not whether God will have it so,
For some displeasing service I have done,
That, in his secret doom, out of my blood
He'll breed revengement and a scourge for me;
But thou dost in thy passages of life
Make me believe that thou art only mark'd
For the hot vengeance and the rod of heaven
To punish my mistreadings. Tell me else,
Could such inordinate and low desires,
Such poor, such bare, such lewd, such mean at-
tempts,
Such barren pleasures, rude society,
As thou art match'd withal and grafted to,
Accompany the greatness of thy blood,
And hold their level with thy princely heart?

PRINCE

So please your majesty, I would I could
Quit all offences with as clear excuse
As well as I am doubtless I can purge
Myself of many I am charged withal:
Yet such extenuation let me beg,
As, in reproof of many tales devised,
Which oft the ear of greatness needs must hear,

By smiling pick-thanks and base newsmongers,
I may, for some things true, wherein my youth
Hath faulty wander'd and irregular,
Find pardon on my true submission.

KING

God pardon thee! yet let me wonder, Harry,
At thy affections, which do hold a wing
Quite from the flight of all thy ancestors.
Thy place in council thou hast rudely lost,
Which by thy younger brother is supplied,
And art almost an alien to the hearts
Of all the court and princes of my blood:
The hope and expectation of thy time
Is ruin'd, and the soul of every man
Prophetically doth forethink thy fall.
Had I so lavish of my presence been,
So common-hackney'd in the eyes of men,
So stale and cheap to vulgar company,
Opinion, that did help me to the crown,
Had still kept loyal to possession,
And left me in reputeless banishment,
A fellow of no mark nor likelihood.
By being seldom seen, I could not stir
But like a comet I was wonder'd at;
That men would tell their children 'This is he;'
Others would say 'Where, which is Bolingbroke?'
And then I stole all courtesy from heaven,
And dress'd myself in such humility
That I did pluck allegiance from men's hearts,
Loud shouts and salutations from their mouths,
Even in the presence of the crowned king.
Thus did I keep my person fresh and new;
My presence, like a robe pontifical,
Ne'er seen but wonder'd at: and so my state,
Seldom but sumptuous, showed like a feast,
And wan by rareness such solemnity.
The skipping king, he ambled up and down,
With shallow jesters and rash bavin wits,
Soon kindled and soon burnt; carded his state,
Mingled his royalty with capering fools,
Had his great name profaned with their scorns,
And gave his countenance, against his name,
To laugh at gibing boys, and stand the push
Of every beardless vain comparative,
Grew a companion to the common streets,
Enfeoff'd himself to popularity;
That, being daily swallow'd by men's eyes,
They surfeited with honey and began
To loathe the taste of sweetness, whereof a little
More than a little is by much too much.
So when he had occasion to be seen,
He was but as the cuckoo is in June,
Heard, not regarded; seen, but with such eyes
As, sick and blunted with community,
Afford no extraordinary gaze,
Such as is bent on sun-like majesty
When it shines seldom in admiring eyes;
But rather drowzed and hung their eyelids down,
Slept in his face and render'd such aspect
As cloudy men use to their adversaries,

Being with his presence glutted, gorged and full.
And in that very line, Harry, standest thou;
For thou hast lost thy princely privilege
With vile participation: not an eye
But is a-weary of thy common sight,
Save mine, which hath desired to see thee more;
Which now doth that I would not have it do,
Make blind itself with foolish tenderness.

PRINCE
I shall hereafter, my thrice gracious lord,
Be more myself.

KING
          For all the world
As thou art to this hour was Richard then
When I from France set foot at Ravenspurgh,
And even as I was then is Percy now.
Now, by my sceptre and my soul to boot,
He hath more worthy interest to the state
Than thou the shadow of succession;
For of no right, nor colour like to right,
He doth fill fields with harness in the realm,
Turns head against the lion's armed jaws,
And, being no more in debt to years than thou,
Leads ancient lords and reverend bishops on
To bloody battles and to bruising arms.
What never-dying honour hath he got
Against renowned Douglas! whose high deeds,
Whose hot incursions and great name in arms
Holds from all soldiers chief majority
And military title capital
Through all the kingdoms that acknowledge Christ:
Thrice hath this Hotspur, Mars in swathling clothes,
This infant warrior, in his enterprizes
Discomfited great Douglas, ta'en him once,
Enlarged him and made a friend of him,
To fill the mouth of deep defiance up,
And shake the peace and safety of our throne.
And what say you to this? Percy, Northumberland,
The Archibishop's grace of York, Douglas, Morti-
     mer,
Capitulate against us and are up.
But wherefore do I tell these news to thee?
Why, Harry, do I tell thee of my foes,
Which art my near'st and dearest enemy?
Thou that art like enough, through vassal fear,
Base inclination and the start of spleen,
To fight against me under Percy's pay,
To dog his heels and curtsy at his frowns,
To show how much thou art degenerate.

PRINCE
Do not think so; you shall not find it so:
And God forgive them that so much have sway'd
Your majesty's good thoughts away from me!
I will redeem all this on Percy's head,
And in the closing of some glorious day
Be bold to tell you that I am your son;
When I will wear a garment all of blood,
And stain my favours in a bloody mask,
Which, wash'd away, shall scour my shame with it:
And that shall be the day, whene'er it lights,

That this same child of honour and renown,
This gallant Hotspur, this all-praised knight,
And your unthought-of Harry chance to meet.
For every honour sitting on his helm,
Would they were multitudes, and on my head
My shames redoubled! for the time will come,
That I shall make this northern youth exchange
His glorious deeds for my indignities.
Percy is but my factor, good my lord,
To engross up glorious deeds on my behalf;
And I will call him to so strict account,
That he shall render every glory up,
Yea, even the slightest worship of his time,
Or I will tear the reckoning from his heart.
This, in the name of God, I promise here:
The which if He be pleased I shall perform,
I do beseech your majesty may salve
The long-grown wounds of my intemperance:
If not, the end of life cancels all bands;
And I will die a hundred thousand deaths
Ere break the smallest parcel of this vow.

KING
A hundred thousand rebels die in this:
Thou shalt have charge and sovereign trust herein.

Enter BLUNT
How now, good Blunt? thy looks are full of speed.

BLUNT
So hath the business that I come to speak of.
Lord Mortimer of Scotland hath sent word
That Douglas and the English rebels met
The eleventh of this month at Shrewsbury:
A mighty and a fearful head they are,
If promises be kept on every hand,
As ever offer'd foul play in a state.

KING
The Earl of Westmoreland set forth to-day;
With him my son, Lord John of Lancaster;
For this advertisement is five days old:
On Wednesday next, Harry, you shall set forward;
On Thursday we ourselves will march: our meeting
Is Bridgenorth: and, Harry, you shall march
Through Gloucestershire; by which account,
Our business valued, some twelve days hence
Our general forces at Bridgenorth shall meet.
Our hands are full of business: let's away;
Advantage feeds him fat, while men delay. [*Exeunt*

SCENE III. *Boar's-Head Tavern in Eastcheap*

Enter FALSTAFF *and* BARDOLPH
FALSTAFF
Bardolph, am I not fallen away vilely since this last
action? do I not bate? do I not dwindle? Why, my
skin hangs about me like an old lady's loose gown;
I am withered like an old apple-john. Well, I'll repent, and that suddenly, while I am in some liking;
I shall be out of heart shortly, and then I shall have
no strength to repent. An I have not forgotten what
the inside of a church is made of, I am a pepper-

corn, a brewer's horse: the inside of a church! Company, villanous company, hath been the spoil of me.

BARDOLPH

Sir John, you are so fretful, you cannot live long.

FALSTAFF

Why, there is it: come sing me a bawdy song; make me merry. I was as virtuously given as a gentleman need to be; virtuous enough; swore little; diced not above seven times a week; went to a bawdy-house not above once in a quarter—of an hour; paid money that I borrowed, three or four times; lived well, and in good compass: and now I live out of all order, out of all compass.

BARDOLPH

Why, you are so fat, Sir John, that you must needs be out of all compass, out of all reasonable compass, Sir John.

FALSTAFF

Do thou amend thy face, and I'll amend my life: thou art our admiral, thou bearest the lantern in the poop, but 'tis in the nose of thee; thou art the Knight of the Burning Lamp.

BARDOLPH

Why, Sir John, my face does you no harm.

FALSTAFF

No, I'll be sworn; I make as good use of it as many a man doth of a Death's-head or a memento mori: I never see thy face but I think upon hell-fire, and Dives that lived in purple; for there he is in his robes, burning, burning. If thou wert any way given to virtue, I would swear by thy face; my oath should be, 'By this fire, that's God's angel:' but thou art altogether given over; and wert indeed, but for the light in thy face, the son of utter darkness. When thou rannest up Gadshill in the night to catch my horse, if I did not think thou hadst been an ignis fatuus or a ball of wildfire, there's no purchase in money. O, thou art a perpetual triumph, an everlasting bonfire-light! Thou hast saved me a thousand marks in links and torches, walking with thee in the night betwixt tavern and tavern: but the sack that thou hast drunk me would have bought me lights as good cheap at the dearest chandler's in Europe. I have maintained that salamander of yours with fire any time this two and thirty years; God reward me for it!

BARDOLPH

'Sblood, I would my face were in your belly!

FALSTAFF

God-a-mercy! so should I be sure to be heart burned.

Enter HOSTESS

How now, Dame Partlet the hen! have you inquired yet who picked my pocket?

HOSTESS

Why, Sir John, what do you think, Sir John? do you think I keep thieves in my house? I have searched, I have inquired, so has my husband, man by man, boy by boy, servant by servant: the tithe of a hair was never lost in my house before.

FALSTAFF

Ye lie, hostess: Bardolph was shaved, and lost many a hair; and I'll be sworn my pocket was picked. Go to, you are a woman, go.

HOSTESS

Who, I? no; I defy thee: God's light, I was never called so in mine own house before.

FALSTAFF

Go to, I know you well enough.

HOSTESS

No, Sir John; you do not know me, Sir John. I know you, Sir John: you owe me money, Sir John; and now you pick a quarrel to beguile me of it: I bought you a dozen of shirts to your back.

FALSTAFF

Dowlas, filthy dowlas: I have given them away to bakers' wives, and they have made bolters of them.

HOSTESS

Now, as I am a true woman, holland of eight shillings an ell. You owe money here besides, Sir John, for your diet and by-drinkings, and money lent you, four and twenty pound.

FALSTAFF

He had his part of it; let him pay.

HOSTESS

He? alas, he is poor; he hath nothing.

FALSTAFF

How! poor? look upon his face; what call you rich? let them coin his nose, let them coin his cheeks: I'll not pay a denier. What, will you make a younker of me? shall I not take mine ease in mine inn but I shall have my pocket picked? I have lost a seal-ring of my grandfather's worth forty mark.

HOSTESS

O Jesu, I have heard the prince tell him, I know not how oft, that that ring was copper!

FALSTAFF

How! the prince is a Jack, a sneak-cup: 'sblood, an he were here, I would cudgel him like a dog, if he would say so.

Enter the PRINCE *and* PETO, *marching, and* FALSTAFF *meets them playing on his truncheon like a fife*

How now, lad! is the wind in that door, i' faith? must we all march?

BARDOLPH

Yea, two and two, Newgate fashion.

HOSTESS

My lord, I pray you, hear me.

PRINCE

What sayest thou, Mistress Quickly? How doth thy husband? I love him well; he is an honest man.

HOSTESS

Good my lord, hear me.

FALSTAFF

Prithee, let her alone, and list to me.

PRINCE

What sayest thou, Jack?

FALSTAFF

The other night I fell asleep here behind the arras,

and had my pocket picked: this house is turned bawdy-house; they pick pockets.

PRINCE

What didst thou lose, Jack?

FALSTAFF

Wilt thou believe me, Hal? three or four bonds of forty pound a-piece, and a seal-ring of my grandfather's.

PRINCE

A trifle, some eight-penny matter.

HOSTESS

So I told him, my lord; and I said I heard your grace say so: and, my lord, he speaks most vilely of you, like a foul-mouthed man as he is; and said he would cudgel you.

PRINCE

What! he did not?

HOSTESS

There's neither faith, truth, nor womanhood in me else.

FALSTAFF

There's no more faith in thee than in a stewed prune; nor no more truth in thee than in a drawn fox; and for womanhood, Maid Marian may be the deputy's wife of the ward to thee. Go, you thing, go.

HOSTESS

Say, what thing? what thing?

FALSTAFF

What thing! why, a thing to thank God on.

HOSTESS

I am no thing to thank God on, I would thou shouldst know it; I am an honest man's wife: and, setting thy knighthood aside, thou art a knave to call me so.

FALSTAFF

Setting thy womanhood aside, thou art a beast to say otherwise.

HOSTESS

Say, what beast, thou knave, thou?

FALSTAFF

What beast! why, an otter.

PRINCE

An otter, Sir John! why an otter?

FALSTAFF

Why, she's neither fish nor flesh; a man knows not where to have her.

HOSTESS

Thou art an unjust man in saying so: thou or any man knows where to have me, thou knave, thou!

PRINCE

Thou sayest true, hostess; and he slanders thee most grossly.

HOSTESS

So he doth you, my lord; and said this other day you ought him a thousand pound.

PRINCE

Sirrah, do I owe you a thousand pound?

FALSTAFF

A thousand pound, Hal! a million: thy love is worth a million: thou owest me thy love.

HOSTESS

Nay, my lord, he called you Jack, and said he would cudgel you.

FALSTAFF

Did I, Bardolph?

BARDOLPH

Indeed, Sir John, you said so.

FALSTAFF

Yea, if he said my ring was copper.

PRINCE

I say 'tis copper: darest thou be as good as thy word now?

FALSTAFF

Why, Hal, thou knowest, as thou art but man, I dare: but as thou art prince, I fear thee as I fear the roaring of the lion's whelp.

PRINCE

And why not as the lion?

FALSTAFF

The king himself is to be feared as the lion: dost thou think I'll fear thee as I fear thy father? nay, an I do, I pray God my girdle break.

PRINCE

O, if it should, how would thy guts fall about thy knees! But, sirrah, there's no room for faith, truth, nor honesty in this bosom of thine; it is all filled up with guts and midriff. Charge an honest woman with picking thy pocket! why, thou whoreson, impudent, embossed rascal, if there were anything in thy pocket but tavern-reckonings, memorandums of bawdy-houses, and one poor penny-worth of sugar-candy to make thee long-winded, if thy pocket were enriched with any other injuries but these, I am a villain: and yet you will stand to it; you will not pocket up wrong: art thou not ashamed?

FALSTAFF

Dost thou hear, Hal? thou knowest in the state of innocency Adam fell; and what should poor Jack Falstaff do in the days of villany? Thou seest I have more flesh than another man; and therefore more frailty. You confess then, you picked my pocket?

PRINCE

It appears so by the story.

FALSTAFF

Hostess, I forgive thee: go, make ready breakfast; love thy husband, look to thy servants, cherish thy guests: thou shalt find me tractable to any honest reason: thou seest I am pacified still. Nay, prithee, be gone. [Exit HOSTESS] Now, Hal, to the news at court: for the robbery, lad, how is that answered?

PRINCE

O, my sweet beef, I must still be good angel to thee: the money is paid back again.

FALSTAFF

O, I do not like that paying back; 'tis a double labour.

PRINCE

I am good friends with my father, and may do any thing.

FALSTAFF

Rob me the exchequer the first thing thou doest,
and do it with unwashed hands too.

BARDOLPH

Do, my lord.

PRINCE

I have procured thee, Jack, a charge of foot.

FALSTAFF

I would it had been of horse. Where shall I find one
that can steal well? O for a fine thief, of the age of
two and twenty or thereabouts! I am heinously unprovided. Well, God be thanked for these rebels,
they offend none but the virtuous: I laud them, I
praise them.

PRINCE

Bardolph!

BARDOLPH

My lord?

PRINCE

Go bear this letter to Lord John of Lancaster, to my
brother John; this to my Lord of Westmoreland.
[Exit BARDOLPH] Go, Peto, to horse, to horse; for
thou and I have thirty miles to ride yet ere dinner
time. [Exit PETO] Jack, meet me to-morrow in the
Temple hall at two o'clock in the afternoon.
There shalt thou know thy charge, and there receive
Money and order for their furniture.
The land is burning; Percy stands on high;
And either we or they must lower lie.   [Exit

FALSTAFF

Rare words! brave world! Hostess, my breakfast,
    come!
O, I could wish this tavern were my drum!   [Exit

ACT IV

SCENE I. *The rebel camp near Shrewsbury*

Enter HOTSPUR, WORCESTER, *and* DOUGLAS

HOTSPUR

Well said, my noble Scot: if speaking truth
In this fine age were not thought flattery,
Such attribution should the Douglas have,
As not a soldier of this season's stamp
Should go so general current through the world.
By God, I cannot flatter; I do defy
The tongues of soothers; but a braver place
In my heart's love hath no man than yourself:
Nay, task me to my word; approve me, lord.

DOUGLAS

Thou art the king of honour:
No man so potent breathes upon the ground
But I will beard him.

HOTSPUR

Do so, and 'tis well.

Enter a MESSENGER *with letters*

What letters hast thou there?—I can but thank you.

MESSENGER

These letters come from your father.

HOTSPUR

Letters from him! why comes he not himself?

MESSENGER

He cannot come, my lord; he is grievous sick.

HOTSPUR

'Zounds! how has he the leisure to be sick
In such a justling time? Who leads his power?
Under whose government come they along?

MESSENGER

His letters bear his mind, not I, my lord.

WORCESTER

I prithee, tell me, doth he keep his bed?

MESSENGER

He did, my lord, four days ere I set forth;
And at the time of my departure thence
He was much fear'd by his physicians.

WORCESTER

I would the state of time had first been whole,
Ere he by sickness had been visited:
His health was never better worth than now.

HOTSPUR

Sick now! droop now! this sickness doth infect
The very life-blood of our enterprise;
'Tis catching hither, even to our camp.
He writes me here, that inward sickness—
And that his friends by deputation could not
So soon be drawn, nor did he think it meet
To lay so dangerous and dear a trust
On any soul removed but on his own.
Yet doth he give us bold advertisement,
That with our small conjunction we should on,
To see how fortune is disposed to us;
For, as he writes, there is no quailing now,
Because the king is certainly possess'd
Of all our purposes. What say you to it?

WORCESTER

Your father's sickness is a maim to us.

HOTSPUR

A perilous gash, a very limb lopp'd off:
And yet, in faith, it is not; his present want
Seems more than we shall find it: were it good
To set the exact wealth of all our states
All at one cast? to set so rich a main
On the nice hazard of one doubtful hour?
It were not good; for therein should we read
The very bottom and the soul of hope,
The very list, the very utmost bound
Of all our fortunes.

DOUGLAS

Faith, and so we should;
Where now remains a sweet reversion:
We may boldly spend upon the hope of what
Is to come in:
A comfort of retirement lives in this.

HOTSPUR

A rendezvous, a home to fly unto,
If that the devil and mischance look big
Upon the maidenhead of our affairs.

WORCESTER

But yet I would your father had been here.
The quality and hair of our attempt
Brooks no division: it will be thought
By some, that know not why he is away,
That wisdom, loyalty and mere dislike
Of our proceedings kept the earl from hence:
And think how such an apprehension
May turn the tide of fearful faction,
And breed a kind of question in our cause;
For well you know we of the offering side
Must keep aloof from strict arbitrement,
And stop all sight-holes, every loop from whence
The eye of reason may pry in upon us:
This absence of your father's draws a curtain,
That shows the ignorant a kind of fear
Before not dreamt of.

HOTSPUR
          You strain too far.
I rather of his absence make this use:
It lends a lustre and more great opinion,
A larger dare to our great enterprise,
Than if the earl were here; for men must think,
If we without his help can make a head
To push against a kingdom, with his help
We shall o'erturn it topsy-turvy down.
Yet all goes well, yet all our joints are whole.

DOUGLAS

As heart can think: there is not such a word
Spoke of in Scotland as this term of fear.

Enter SIR RICHARD VERNON

HOTSPUR

My cousin Vernon! welcome, by my soul.

VERNON

Pray God my news be worth a welcome, lord.
The Earl of Westmoreland, seven thousand strong,
Is marching hitherwards; with him Prince John.

HOTSPUR

No harm: what more?

VERNON
        And further, I have learn'd,
The king himself in person is set forth,
Or hitherwards intended speedily,
With strong and mighty preparation.

HOTSPUR

He shall be welcome too. Where is his son,
The nimble-footed madcap Prince of Wales,
And his comrades, that daff'd the world aside,
And bid it pass?

VERNON
         All furnish'd, all in arms;
All plumed like estridges that with the wind
Baited like eagles having lately bathed;
Glittering in golden coats, like images;
As full of spirit as the month of May,
And gorgeous as the sun at midsummer;
Wanton as youthful goats, wild as young bulls.
I saw young Harry, with his beaver on,
His cuisses on his thighs, gallantly arm'd,
Rise from the ground like feather'd Mercury,

And vaulted with such ease into his seat,
As if an angel dropp'd down from the clouds,
To turn and wind a fiery Pegasus,
And witch the world with noble horsemanship.

HOTSPUR

No more, no more: worse than the sun in March,
This praise doth nourish agues. Let them come;
They come like sacrifices in their trim,
And to the fire-eyed maid of smoky war
All hot and bleeding will we offer them:
The mailed Mars shall on his altar sit
Up to the ears in blood. I am on fire
To hear this rich reprisal is so nigh
And yet not ours. Come, let me taste my horse,
Who is to bear me like a thunderbolt
Against the bosom of the Prince of Wales:
Harry to Harry shall, hot horse to horse,
Meet and ne'er part till one drop down a corse.
O that Glendower were come!

VERNON
           There is more news:
I learn'd in Worcester, as I rode along,
He cannot draw his power this fourteen days.

DOUGLAS

That's the worst tidings that I hear of yet.

WORCESTER

Ay, by my faith, that bears a frosty sound.

HOTSPUR

What may the king's whole battle reach unto?

VERNON

To thirty thousand.

HOTSPUR
         Forty let it be:
My father and Glendower being both away,
The powers of us may serve so great a day.
Come, let us take a muster speedily:
Doomsday is near; die all, die merrily.

DOUGLAS

Talk not of dying: I am out of fear
Of death or death's hand for this one half year.

[*Exeunt*

SCENE II. *A public road near Coventry*

Enter FALSTAFF *and* BARDOLPH

FALSTAFF

Bardolph, get thee before to Coventry; fill me a bottle of sack: our soldiers shall march through; we'll
to Sutton Co'fil' to-night.

BARDOLPH

Will you give me money, captain?

FALSTAFF

Lay out, lay out.

BARDOLPH

This bottle makes an angel.

FALSTAFF

An if it do, take it for thy labour; and if it make
twenty, take them all; I'll answer the coinage. Bid
my lieutenant Peto meet me at town's end.

BARDOLPH

I will, captain: farewell.   [*Exit*

FALSTAFF

If I be not ashamed of my soldiers, I am a soused gurnet. I have misused the king's press damnably. I have got, in exchange of a hundred and fifty soldiers, three hundred and odd pounds. I press me none but good householders, yeomen's sons; inquire me out contracted bachelors, such as had been asked twice on the banns; such a commodity of warm slaves, as had as lieve hear the devil as a drum; such as fear the report of a caliver worse than a struck fowl or a hurt wild-duck. I pressed me none but such toasts-and-butter, with hearts in their bellies no bigger than pins'-heads, and they have bought out their services; and now my whole charge consists of ancients, corporals, lieutenants, gentlemen of companies, slaves as ragged as Lazarus in the painted cloth, where the glutton's dogs licked his sores; and such as indeed were never soldiers, but discarded unjust serving-men, younger sons to younger brothers, revolted tapsters, and ostlers trade-fallen; the cankers of a calm world and a long peace, ten times more dishonourable ragged than an old faced ancient: and such have I, to fill up the rooms of them that have bought out their services, that you would think that I had a hundred and fifty tattered prodigals lately come from swine-keeping, from eating draff and husks. A mad fellow met me on the way and told me I had unloaded all the gibbets and pressed the dead bodies. No eye hath seen such scarecrows. I'll not march through Coventry with them, that's flat: nay, and the villains march wide betwixt the legs, as if they had gyves on; for indeed I had the most of them out of prison. There's but a shirt and a half in all my company; and the half shirt is two napkins tacked together and thrown over the shoulders like a herald's coat without sleeves; and the shirt, to say the truth, stolen from my host at Saint Alban's, or the red-nose innkeeper of Daventry. But that's all one; they'll find linen enough on every hedge.

Enter the PRINCE *and* WESTMORELAND

PRINCE

How now, blown Jack! how now, quilt!

FALSTAFF

What, Hal! how now, mad wag! what a devil dost thou in Warwickshire? My good Lord of Westmoreland, I cry you mercy: I thought your honour had already been at Shrewsbury.

WESTMORELAND

Faith, Sir John, 'tis more than time that I were there, and you too; but my powers are there already. The king, I can tell you, looks for us all: we must away all night.

FALSTAFF

Tut, never fear me: I am as vigilant as a cat to steal cream.

PRINCE

I think, to steal cream indeed, for thy theft hath already made thee butter. But tell me, Jack, whose fellows are these that come after?

FALSTAFF

Mine, Hal, mine.

PRINCE

I did never see such pitiful rascals.

FALSTAFF

Tut, tut; good enough to toss; food for powder, food for powder; they'll fill a pit as well as better: tush, man, mortal men, mortal men.

WESTMORELAND

Ay, but, Sir John, methinks they are exceeding poor and bare, too beggarly.

FALSTAFF

Faith, for their poverty, I know not where they had that; and for their bareness, I am sure they never learned that of me.

PRINCE

No, I'll be sworn; unless you call three fingers on the ribs bare. But, sirrah, make haste: Percy is already in the field.

FALSTAFF

What, is the king encamped?

WESTMORELAND

He is, Sir John: I fear we shall stay too long.

FALSTAFF

Well,

To the latter end of a fray and the beginning of a feast

Fits a dull fighter and a keen guest.   [*Exeunt*

SCENE III. *The rebel camp near Shrewsbury*

Enter HOTSPUR, WORCESTER, DOUGLAS, *and* VERNON

HOTSPUR

We'll fight with him to-night.

WORCESTER

It may not be.

DOUGLAS

You give him then advantage.

VERNON

Not a whit.

HOTSPUR

Why say you so? looks he not for supply?

VERNON

So do we.

HOTSPUR

His is certain, ours is doubtful.

WORCESTER

Good cousin, be advised; stir not to-night.

VERNON

Do not, my lord.

DOUGLAS

You do not counsel well:

You speak it out of fear and cold heart.

VERNON

Do me no slander, Douglas: by my life,

And I dare well maintain it with my life,

If well-respected honour bid me on,

I hold as little counsel with weak fear
As you, my lord, or any Scot that this day lives:
Let it be seen to-morrow in the battle
Which of us fears.

DOUGLAS
Yea, or to-night.

VERNON
Content.

HOTSPUR
To-night, say I.

VERNON
Come, come, it may not be. I wonder much,
Being men of such great leading as you are,
That you foresee not what impediments
Drag back our expedition: certain horse
Of my cousin Vernon's are not yet come up:
Your uncle Worcester's horse came but to-day;
And now their pride and mettle is asleep,
Their courage with hard labour tame and dull,
That not a horse is half the half of himself.

HOTSPUR
So are the horses of the enemy
In general, journey-bated and brought low:
The better part of ours are full of rest.

WORCESTER
The number of the king exceedeth ours:
For God's sake, cousin, stay till all come in.

[*The trumpet sounds a parley*

Enter SIR WALTER BLUNT

BLUNT
I come with gracious offers from the king,
If you vouchsafe me hearing and respect.

HOTSPUR
Welcome, Sir Walter Blunt; and would to God
You were of our determination!
Some of us love you well; and even those some
Envy your great deservings and good name,
Because you are not of our quality,
But stand against us like an enemy.

BLUNT
And God defend but still I should stand so,
So long as out of limit and true rule
You stand against anointed majesty.
But to my charge. The king hath sent to know
The nature of your griefs, and whereupon
You conjure from the breast of civil peace
Such bold hostility, teaching his duteous land
Audacious cruelty. If that the king
Have any way your good deserts forgot,
Which he confesseth to be manifold,
He bids you name your griefs; and with all speed
You shall have your desires with interest,
And pardon absolute for yourself and these
Herein misled by your suggestion.

HOTSPUR
The king is kind; and well we know the king
Knows at what time to promise, when to pay.
My father and my uncle and myself
Did give him that same royalty he wears;
And when he was not six and twenty strong,

Sick in the world's regard, wretched and low,
A poor unminded outlaw sneaking home,
My father gave him welcome to the shore;
And when he heard him swear and vow to God
He came but to be Duke of Lancaster,
To sue his livery and beg his peace,
With tears of innocency and terms of zeal,
My father, in kind heart and pity moved,
Swore him assistance and perform'd it too.
Now when the lords and barons of the realm
Perceived Northumberland did lean to him,
The more and less came in with cap and knee;
Met him in boroughs, cities, villages,
Attended him on bridges, stood in lanes,
Laid gifts before him, proffer'd him their oaths,
Gave him their heirs, as pages follow'd him
Even at the heels in golden multitudes.
He presently, as greatness knows itself,
Steps me a little higher than his vow
Made to my father, while his blood was poor,
Upon the naked shore at Ravenspurgh;
And now, forsooth, takes on him to reform
Some certain edicts and some strait decrees
That lie too heavy on the commonwealth,
Cries out upon abuses, seems to weep
Over his country's wrongs; and by this face,
This seeming brow of justice, did he win
The hearts of all that he did angle for;
Proceeded further; cut me off the heads
Of all the favourites that the absent king
In deputation left behind him here,
When he was personal in the Irish war.

BLUNT
Tut, I came not to hear this.

HOTSPUR
Then to the point.
In short time after, he deposed the king;
Soon after that, deprived him of his life;
And in the neck of that, task'd the whole state;
To make that worse, suffer'd his kinsman March,
Who is, if every owner were well placed,
Indeed his king, to be engaged in Wales,
There without ransom to lie forfeited;
Disgraced me in my happy victories,
Sought to entrap me by intelligence;
Rated mine uncle from the council-board;
In rage dismiss'd my father from the court;
Broke oath on oath, committed wrong on wrong,
And in conclusion drove us to seek out
This head of safety, and withal to pry
Into his title, the which we find
Too indirect for long continuance.

BLUNT
Shall I return this answer to the king?

HOTSPUR
Not so, Sir Walter: we'll withdraw a while.
Go to the king; and let there be impawn'd
Some surety for a safe return again,
And in the morning early shall mine uncle
Bring him our purposes: and so farewell.

BLUNT

I would you would accept of grace and love.

HOTSPUR

And may be so we shall.

BLUNT

Pray God you do. [*Exeunt*

SCENE IV. *York. The* ARCHBISHOP'S *palace*

Enter the ARCHBISHOP OF YORK *and* SIR MICHAEL

ARCHBISHOP

Hie, good Sir Michael; bear this sealed brief
With winged haste to the lord marshal;
This to my cousin Scroop, and all the rest
To whom they are directed. If you knew
How much they do import, you would make haste.

SIR MICHAEL

My good lord,
I guess their tenour.

ARCHBISHOP

Like enough you do.
To-morrow, good Sir Michael, is a day
Wherein the fortune of ten thousand men
Must bide the touch; for, sir, at Shrewsbury,
As I am truly given to understand,
The king with mighty and quick-raised power
Meets with Lord Harry: and, I fear, Sir Michael,
What with the sickness of Northumberland,
Whose power was in the first proportion,
And what with Owen Glendower's absence thence,
Who with them was a rated sinew too
And comes not in, o'er-ruled by prophecies,
I fear the power of Percy is too weak
To wage an instant trial with the king.

SIR MICHAEL

Why, my good lord, you need not fear;
There is Douglas and Lord Mortimer.

ARCHBISHOP

No, Mortimer is not there.

SIR MICHAEL

But there is Mordake, Vernon, Lord Harry Percy,
And there is my Lord of Worcester and a head
Of gallant warriors, noble gentlemen.

ARCHBISHOP

And so there is: but yet the king hath drawn
The special head of all the land together:
The Prince of Wales, Lord John of Lancaster,
The noble Westmoreland and warlike Blunt;
And many mo corrivals and dear men
Of estimation and command in arms.

SIR MICHAEL

Doubt not, my lord, they shall be well opposed.

ARCHBISHOP

I hope no less, yet needful 'tis to fear;
And, to prevent the worst, Sir Michael, speed:
For if Lord Percy thrive not, ere the king
Dismiss his power, he means to visit us,
For he hath heard of our confederacy,

And 'tis but wisdom to make strong against him:
Therefore make haste. I must go write again
To other friends; and so farewell, Sir Michael.

[*Exeunt*

ACT V

SCENE I. *The* KING'S *camp near Shrewsbury*

Enter the KING, PRINCE OF WALES, LORD JOHN OF
LANCASTER, SIR WALTER BLUNT, *and* FALSTAFF

KING

How bloodily the sun begins to peer
Above yon busky hill! the day looks pale
At his distemperature.

PRINCE

The southern wind
Doth play the trumpet to his purposes,
And by his hollow whistling in the leaves
Foretells a tempest and a blustering day.

KING

Then with the losers let it sympathise,
For nothing can seem foul to those that win.

[*The trumpet sounds*

Enter WORCESTER *and* VERNON

How now, my Lord of Worcester! 'tis not well
That you and I should meet upon such terms
As now we meet. You have deceived our trust,
And made us doff our easy robes of peace,
To crush our old limbs in ungentle steel:
This is not well, my lord, this is not well.
What say you to it? will you again unknit
This churlish knot of all-abhorred war?
And move in that obedient orb again
Where you did give a fair and natural light,
And be no more an exhaled meteor,
A prodigy of fear, and a portent
Of broached mischief to the unborn times?

WORCESTER

Hear me, my liege:
For mine own part, I could be well content
To entertain the lag-end of my life
With quiet hours; for, I do protest,
I have not sought the day of this dislike.

KING

You have not sought it! how comes it, then?

FALSTAFF

Rebellion lay in his way, and he found it.

PRINCE

Peace, chewet, peace!

WORCESTER

It pleased your majesty to turn your looks
Of favour from myself and all our house;
And yet I must remember you, my lord,
We were the first and dearest of your friends.
For you my staff of office did I break
In Richard's time; and posted day and night

To meet you on the way, and kiss your hand,
When yet you were in place and in account
Nothing so strong and fortunate as I.
It was myself, my brother, and his son,
That brought you home, and boldly did outdare
The dangers of the time. You swore to us,
And you did swear that oath at Doncaster,
That you did nothing purpose 'gainst the state;
Nor claim no further than your new-fall'n right,
The seat of Gaunt, dukedom of Lancaster:
To this we swore our aid. But in short space
It rain'd down fortune showering on your head;
And such a flood of greatness fell on you,
What with our help, what with the absent king,
What with the injuries of a wanton time,
The seeming sufferances that you had borne,
And the contrarious winds that held the king
So long in his unlucky Irish wars
That all in England did repute him dead:
And from this swarm of fair advantages
You took occasion to be quickly woo'd
To gripe the general sway into your hand;
Forgot your oath to us at Doncaster;
And being fed by us you used us so
As that ungentle gull, the cuckoo's bird,
Useth the sparrow; did oppress our nest;
Grew by our feeding to so great a bulk
That even our love durst not come near your sight
For fear of swallowing; but with nimble wing
We were enforced, for safety sake, to fly
Out of your sight and raise this present head;
Whereby we stand opposed by such means
As you yourself have forged against yourself,
By unkind usage, dangerous countenance,
And violation of all faith and troth
Sworn to us in your younger enterprise.

KING

These things indeed you have articulate,
Proclaim'd at market-crosses, read in churches,
To face the garment of rebellion
With some fine colour that may please the eye
Of fickle changelings and poor discontents,
Which gape and rub the elbow at the news
Of hurlyburly innovation:
And never yet did insurrection want
Such water-colours to impaint his cause;
Nor moody beggars, starving for a time
Of pellmell havoc and confusion.

PRINCE

In both your armies there is many a soul
Shall pay full dearly for this encounter,
If once they join in trial. Tell your nephew,
The Prince of Wales doth join with all the world
In praise of Henry Percy: by my hopes,
This present enterprise set off his head,
I do not think a braver gentleman,
More active-valiant or more valiant-young,
More daring or more bold, is now alive
To grace this latter age with noble deeds.
For my part, I may speak it to my shame,

I have a truant been to chivalry;
And so I hear he doth account me too;
Yet this before my father's majesty—
I am content that he shall take the odds
Of his great name and estimation,
And will, to save the blood on either side,
Try fortune with him in a single fight.

KING

And, Prince of Wales, so dare we venture thee,
Albeit considerations infinite
Do make against it. No, good Worcester, no,
We love our people well; even those we love
That are misled upon your cousin's part;
And, will they take the offer of our grace,
Both he and they and you, yea, every man
Shall be my friend again and I'll be his:
So tell your cousin, and bring me word
What he will do: but if he will not yield,
Rebuke and dread correction wait on us
And they shall do their office. So, be gone;
We will not now be troubled with reply:
We offer fair; take it advisedly.

                          [Exeunt WORCESTER and VERNON

PRINCE

It will not be accepted, on my life:
The Douglas and the Hotspur both together
Are confident against the world in arms.

KING

Hence, therefore, every leader to his charge;
For, on their answer, will we set on them:
And God befriend us, as our cause is just!

         [Exeunt all but the PRINCE OF WALES and FALSTAFF

FALSTAFF

Hal, if thou see me down in the battle, and bestride
me, so; 'tis a point of friendship.

PRINCE

Nothing but a colossus can do thee that friendship.
Say thy prayers, and farewell.

FALSTAFF

I would 'twere bed-time, Hal, and all well.

PRINCE

Why, thou owest God a death.   [Exit

FALSTAFF

'Tis not due yet; I would be loath to pay him before
his day. What need I be so forward with him that
calls not on me? Well, 'tis no matter; honour pricks
me on. Yea, but how if honour prick me off when I
come on? how then? Can honour set to a leg? no:
or an arm? no: or take away the grief of a wound?
no. Honour hath no skill in surgery, then? no. What
is honour? a word. What is in that word honour?
what is that honour? air. A trim reckoning! Who
hath it? he that died o' Wednesday. Doth he feel it?
no. Doth he hear it? no. 'Tis insensible, then? yea,
to the dead. But will it not live with the living? no.
Why? detraction will not suffer it. Therefore I'll
none of it. Honour is a mere scutcheon: and so ends
my catechism.   [Exit

SCENE II. *The rebel camp*

Enter WORCESTER *and* VERNON

WORCESTER

O, no, my nephew must not know, Sir Richard,
The liberal and kind offer of the king.

VERNON

'Twere best he did.

WORCESTER
　　　　　　　Then are we all undone.
It is not possible, it cannot be,
The king should keep his word in loving us·
He will suspect us still, and find a time
To punish this offence in other faults:
Suspicion all our lives shall be stuck full of eyes;
For treason is but trusted like the fox,
Who, ne'er so tame, so cherish'd and lock'd up,
Will have a wild trick of his ancestors.
Look how we can, or sad or merrily,
Interpretation will misquote our looks,
And we shall feed like oxen at a stall,
The better cherish'd, still the nearer death.
My nephew's trespass may be well forgot;
It hath the excuse of youth and heat of blood;
And an adopted name of privilege,
A hare-brain'd Hotspur, govern'd by a spleen:
All his offences live upon my head
And on his father's; we did train him on,
And, his corruption being ta'en from us,
We, as the spring of all, shall pay for all.
Therefore, good cousin, let not Harry know,
In any case, the offer of the king.

VERNON

Deliver what you will; I'll say 'tis so.
Here comes your cousin.

Enter HOTSPUR *and* DOUGLAS

HOTSPUR

My uncle is return'd:
Deliver up my Lord of Westmoreland.
Uncle, what news?

WORCESTER

The king will bid you battle presently.

DOUGLAS

Defy him by the Lord of Westmoreland.

HOTSPUR

Lord Douglas, go you and tell him so.

DOUGLAS

Marry, and shall, and very willingly.　　　　[*Exit*

WORCESTER

There is no seeming mercy in the king.

HOTSPUR

Did you beg any? God forbid!

WORCESTER

I told him gently of our grievances,
Of his oath-breaking; which he mended thus,
By now forswearing that he is forsworn:
He calls us rebels, traitors; and will scourge
With haughty arms this hateful name in us.

Re-enter DOUGLAS

DOUGLAS

Arm, gentlemen; to arms! for I have thrown
A brave defiance in King Henry's teeth,
And Westmoreland, that was engaged, did bear it;
Which cannot choose but bring him quickly on.

WORCESTER

The Prince of Wales stepp'd forth before the king,
And, nephew, challenged you to single fight.

HOTSPUR

O, would the quarrel lay upon our heads,
And that no man might draw short breath to-day
But I and Harry Monmouth! Tell me, tell me,
How show'd his tasking? seem'd it in contempt?

VERNON

No, by my soul; I never in my life
Did hear a challenge urged more modestly,
Unless a brother should a brother dare
To gentle exercise and proof of arms.
He gave you all the duties of a man;
Trimm'd up your praises with a princely tongue,
Spoke your deservings like a chronicle,
Making you ever better than his praise
By still dispraising praise valued with you;
And, which became him like a prince indeed,
He made a blushing cital of himself;
And chid his truant youth with such a grace
As if he master'd there a double spirit
Of teaching and of learning instantly.
There did he pause: but let me tell the world,
If he outlive the envy of this day,
England did never owe so sweet a hope,
So much misconstrued in his wantonness.

HOTSPUR

Cousin, I think thou art enamoured
On his follies: never did I hear
Of any prince so wild a libertine.
But be he as he will, yet once ere night
I will embrace him with a soldier's arm,
That he shall shrink under my courtesy.
Arm, arm with speed: and, fellows, soldiers, friends,
Better consider what you have to do
Than I, that have not well the gift of tongue,
Can lift your blood up with persuasion.

Enter a MESSENGER

MESSENGER

My lord, here are letters for you.

HOTSPUR

I cannot read them now.
O gentlemen, the time of life is short!
To spend that shortness basely were too long,
If life did ride upon a dial's point,
Still ending at the arrival of an hour.
An if we live, we live to tread on kings;
If die, brave death, when princes die with us!
Now, for our consciences, the arms are fair,
When the intent of bearing them is just.

Enter another MESSENGER

MESSENGER

My lord, prepare; the king comes on apace.

HOTSPUR

I thank him, that he cuts me from my tale,
For I profess not talking; only this—
Let each man do his best: and here draw I
A sword, whose temper I intend to stain
With the best blood that I can meet withal
In the adventure of this perilous day.
Now, Esperance! Percy! and set on.
Sound all the lofty instruments of war,
And by that music let us all embrace;
For, heaven to earth, some of us never shall
A second time do such a courtesy.
[The trumpets sound. They embrace, and exeunt

SCENE III. *Plain between the camps*

The KING *enters with his power. Alarum to the battle.
Then enter* DOUGLAS *and* SIR WALTER BLUNT
BLUNT

What is thy name, that in the battle thus
Thou crossest me? what honour dost thou seek
Upon my head?

DOUGLAS

Know then, my name is Douglas;
And I do haunt thee in the battle thus,
Because some tell me that thou art a king.

BLUNT

They tell thee true.

DOUGLAS

The Lord of Stafford dear to-day hath bought
Thy likeness; for instead of thee, King Harry,
This sword hath ended him: so shall it thee,
Unless thou yield thee as my prisoner.

BLUNT

I was not born a yielder, thou proud Scot;
And thou shalt find a king that will revenge
Lord Stafford's death.
[They fight. DOUGLAS *kills* BLUNT
Enter HOTSPUR
HOTSPUR

O Douglas, hadst thou fought at Holmedon thus,
I never had triumph'd upon a Scot.

DOUGLAS

All's done, all's won; here breathless lies the king.

HOTSPUR

Where?

DOUGLAS

Here.

HOTSPUR

This, Douglas? no: I know this face full well:
A gallant knight he was, his name was Blunt;
Semblably furnish'd like the king himself.

DOUGLAS

A fool go with thy soul, whither it goes!
A borrow'd title hast thou bought too dear:
Why didst thou tell me that thou wert a king?

HOTSPUR

The king hath many marching in his coats.

DOUGLAS

Now, by my sword, I will kill all his coats;

I'll murder all his wardrobe, piece by piece,
Until I meet the king.

HOTSPUR

Up, and away!
Our soldiers stand full fairly for the day.   *[Exeunt*
Alarum. Enter FALSTAFF, *solus*
FALSTAFF

Though I could 'scape shot-free at London, I fear
the shot here; here's no scoring but upon the pate.
Soft! who are you? Sir Walter Blunt: there's honour
for you! here's no vanity! I am as hot as molten
lead, and as heavy too: God keep lead out of me! I
need no more weight than mine own bowels. I have
led my ragamuffins where they are peppered: there's
not three of my hundred and fifty left alive; and
they are for the town's end, to beg during life. But
who comes here?

Enter the PRINCE
PRINCE

What, stand'st thou idle here? lend me thy sword:
Many a nobleman lies stark and stiff
Under the hoofs of vaunting enemies,
Whose deaths are yet unrevenged: I prithee, lend
me thy sword.

FALSTAFF

O Hal, I prithee, give me leave to breathe a while.
Turk Gregory never did such deeds in arms as I
have done this day. I have paid Percy, I have made
him sure.

PRINCE

He is, indeed; and living to kill thee. I prithee, lend
me thy sword.

FALSTAFF

Nay, before God, Hal, if Percy be alive, thou get'st
not my sword; but take my pistol, if thou wilt.

PRINCE

Give it me: what, is it in the case?

FALSTAFF

Ay, Hal; 'tis hot, 'tis hot; there's that will sack a
city.
[The PRINCE *draws it out, and finds it to be a bottle of sack*
PRINCE

What, is it a time to jest and dally now?
[He throws the bottle at him. Exit
FALSTAFF

Well, if Percy be alive, I'll pierce him. If he do come
in my way, so: if he do not, if I come in his willingly,
let him make a carbonado of me. I like not such
grinning honour as Sir Walter hath: give me life:
which if I can save, so; if not, honour comes un-
looked for, and there's an end.   *[Exit*

SCENE IV. *Another part of the field*

Alarum. Excursions. Enter the KING, *the* PRINCE, LORD
JOHN OF LANCASTER, *and* EARL OF WESTMORELAND
KING

I prithee,
Harry, withdraw thyself; thou bleed'st too much.
Lord John of Lancaster, go you with him.

LANCASTER

Not I, my lord, unless I did bleed too.

PRINCE

I beseech your majesty, make up,
Lest your retirement do amaze your friends.

KING

I will do so.
My Lord of Westmoreland, lead him to his tent.

WESTMORELAND

Come, my lord, I'll lead you to your tent.

PRINCE

Lead me, my lord? I do not need your help:
And God forbid a shallow scratch should drive
The Prince of Wales from such a field as this,
Where stain'd nobility lies trodden on,
And rebels' arms triumph in massacres!

LANCASTER

We breathe too long: come, cousin Westmoreland,
Our duty this way lies; for God's sake, come.

[*Exeunt* PRINCE JOHN *and* WESTMORELAND

PRINCE

By God, thou hast deceived me, Lancaster;
I did not think thee lord of such a spirit:
Before, I loved thee as a brother, John;
But now, I do respect thee as my soul.

KING

I saw him hold Lord Percy at the point,
With lustier maintenance than I did look for
Of such an ungrown warrior.

PRINCE

                    O, this boy
Lends mettle to us all!   [*Exit*

Enter DOUGLAS

DOUGLAS

Another king! they grow like Hydra's heads:
I am the Douglas, fatal to all those
That wear those colours on them: what art thou,
That counterfeit'st the person of a king?

KING

The king himself; who, Douglas, grieves at heart
So many of his shadows thou hast met
And not the very king. I have two boys
Seek Percy and thyself about the field:
But, seeing thou fall'st on me so luckily,
I will assay thee: so, defend thyself.

DOUGLAS

I fear thou art another counterfeit;
And yet, in faith, thou bear'st thee like a king:
But mine I am sure thou art, whoe'er thou be,
And thus I win thee.

[*They fight; the* KING *being in danger, re-enter* PRINCE
OF WALES

PRINCE

Hold up thy head, vile Scot, or thou art like
Never to hold it up again! the spirits
Of valiant Shirley, Stafford, Blunt, are in my arms:
It is the Prince of Wales that threatens thee;
Who never promiseth but he means to pay.

[*They fight:* DOUGLAS *flies*

Cheerly, my lord: how fares your grace?

Sir Nicholas Gawsey hath for succour sent,
And so hath Clifton: I'll to Clifton straight.

KING

Stay, and breathe a while:
Thou hast redeem'd thy lost opinion,
And show'd thou makest some tender of my life,
In this fair rescue thou hast brought to me.

PRINCE

O God! they did me too much injury
That ever said I hearken'd for your death.
If it were so, I might have let alone
The insulting hand of Douglas over you,
Which would have been as speedy in your end
As all the poisonous potions in the world,
And saved the treacherous labour of your son.

KING

Make up to Clifton: I'll to Sir Nicholas Gawsey.

[*Exit*

Enter HOTSPUR

HOTSPUR

If I mistake not, thou art Harry Monmouth.

PRINCE

Thou speak'st as if I would deny my name.

HOTSPUR

My name is Harry Percy.

PRINCE

                    Why, then I see
A very valiant rebel of the name.
I am the Prince of Wales; and think not, Percy,
To share with me in glory any more:
Two stars keep not their motion in one sphere;
Nor can one England brook a double reign,
Of Harry Percy and the Prince of Wales.

HOTSPUR

Nor shall it, Harry; for the hour is come
To end the one of us; and would to God
Thy name in arms were now as great as mine!

PRINCE

I'll make it greater ere I part from thee;
And all the budding honours on thy crest
I'll crop, to make a garland for my head.

HOTSPUR

I can no longer brook thy vanities.   [*They fight*

Enter FALSTAFF

FALSTAFF

Well said, Hal! to it, Hal! Nay, you shall find no
boy's play here, I can tell you.
Re-enter DOUGLAS; *he fights with* FALSTAFF, *who falls
down as if he were dead, and exit* DOUGLAS. HOTSPUR
is wounded, and falls

HOTSPUR

O, Harry, thou hast robb'd me of my youth!
I better brook the loss of brittle life
Than those proud titles thou hast won of me;
They wound my thoughts worse than thy sword mv
flesh:
But thought's the slave of life, and life time's fool;
And time, that takes survey of all the world,
Must have a stop. O, I could prophesy,
But that the earthy and cold hand of death

[511]

Lies on my tongue: no, Percy, thou art dust,
And food for—   [*Dies*

PRINCE

For worms, brave Percy: fare thee well, great heart!
Ill-weaved ambition, how much art thou shrunk!
When that this body did contain a spirit,
A kingdom for it was too small a bound;
But now two paces of the vilest earth
Is room enough: this earth that bears thee dead
Bears not alive so stout a gentleman.
If thou wert sensible of courtesy,
I should not make so dear a show of zeal:
But let my favours hide thy mangled face;
And, even in thy behalf, I'll thank myself
For doing these fair rites of tenderness.
Adieu, and take thy praise with thee to heaven!
Thy ignominy sleep with thee in the grave,
But not remember'd in thy epitaph!
                    [*He spieth* FALSTAFF *on the ground*
What, old acquaintance! could not all this flesh
Keep in a little life? Poor Jack, farewell!
I could have better spared a better man:
O, I should have a heavy miss of thee,
If I were much in love with vanity!
Death hath not struck so fat a deer to-day,
Though many dearer, in this bloody fray.
Embowell'd will I see thee by and by:
Till then in blood by noble Percy lie.   [*Exit*

FALSTAFF

[*Rising up*] Embowelled! if thou embowel me to-day,
I'll give you leave to powder me and eat me too to-
morrow. 'Sblood, 'twas time to counterfeit, or that
hot termagant Scot had paid me scot and lot too.
Counterfeit? I lie, I am no counterfeit: to die, is to
be a counterfeit; for he is but the counterfeit of a
man who hath not the life of a man: but to counterfeit dying, when a man thereby liveth, is to be no
counterfeit, but the true and perfect image of life
indeed. The better part of valour is discretion; in
the which better part I have saved my life. 'Zounds,
I am afraid of this gunpowder Percy, though he be
dead: how, if he should counterfeit too, and rise? by
my faith, I am afraid he would prove the better
counterfeit. Therefore I'll make him sure; yea, and
I'll swear I killed him. Why may he not rise as well
as I? Nothing confutes me but eyes, and nobody
sees me. Therefore, sirrah [*stabbing him*], with a new
wound in your thigh, come you along with me.
                    [*Takes up* HOTSPUR *on his back*
Re-enter the PRINCE OF WALES *and* LORD JOHN OF
LANCASTER

PRINCE

Come, brother John; full bravely hast thou flesh'd
Thy maiden sword.

LANCASTER

                    But, soft! whom have we here?
Did you not tell me this fat man was dead?

PRINCE

I did; I saw him dead,

Breathless and bleeding on the ground. Art thou
alive?
Or is it fantasy that plays upon our eyesight?
I prithee, speak; we will not trust our eyes
Without our ears: thou art not what thou seem'st.

FALSTAFF

No, that's certain; I am not a double man: but if I
be not Jack Falstaff, then am I a Jack. There is
Percy [*throwing the body down*]: if your father will do
me any honour, so; if not, let him kill the next Percy
himself. I look to be either earl or duke, I can assure
you.

PRINCE

Why, Percy I killed myself, and saw thee dead.

FALSTAFF

Didst thou? Lord, Lord, how this world is given to
lying! I grant you I was down and out of breath;
and so was he: but we rose both at an instant, and
fought a long hour by Shrewsbury clock. If I may
be believed, so; if not, let them that should reward
valour bear the sin upon their own heads. I'll take it
upon my death, I gave him this wound in the thigh:
if the man were alive, and would deny it, 'zounds, I
would make him eat a piece of my sword.

LANCASTER

This is the strangest tale that ever I heard.

PRINCE

This is the strangest fellow, brother John.
Come, bring your luggage nobly on your back:
For my part, if a lie may do thee grace,
I'll gild it with the happiest terms I have.
                    [*A retreat is sounded*
The trumpet sounds retreat; the day is ours.
Come, brother, let us to the highest of the field,
To see what friends are living, who are dead.
          [*Exeunt* PRINCE OF WALES *and* LANCASTER

FALSTAFF

I'll follow, as they say, for reward. He that rewards
me, God reward him! If I do grow great, I'll grow
less; for I'll purge, and leave sack, and live cleanly
as a nobleman should do.   [*Exit*

SCENE V. *Another part of the field*

The trumpets sound. Enter the KING, PRINCE OF WALES,
LORD JOHN OF LANCASTER, EARL OF WESTMORELAND,
with WORCESTER *and* VERNON *prisoners*

KING

Thus ever did rebellion find rebuke.
Ill-spirited Worcester! did not we send grace,
Pardon and terms of love to all of you?
And wouldst thou turn our offers contrary?
Misuse the tenour of thy kinsman's trust?
Three knights upon our party slain to-day,
A noble earl and many a creature else
Had been alive this hour,
If like a Christian thou hadst truly borne
Betwixt our armies true intelligence.

WORCESTER

What I have done my safety urged me to;

And I embrace this fortune patiently,
Since not to be avoided it falls on me.
KING
Bear Worcester to the death, and Vernon too:
Other offenders we will pause upon.
[*Exeunt* WORCESTER *and* VERNON, *guarded*
How goes the field?
PRINCE
The noble Scot, Lord Douglas, when he saw
The fortune of the day quite turn'd from him,
The noble Percy slain, and all his men
Upon the foot of fear, fled with the rest;
And falling from a hill, he was so bruised
That the pursuers took him. At my tent
The Douglas is; and I beseech your grace
I may dispose of him.
KING
With all my heart.
PRINCE
Then, brother John of Lancaster, to you
This honourable bounty shall belong:

Go to the Douglas, and deliver him
Up to his pleasure, ransomless and free:
His valour shown upon our crests to-day
Hath taught us how to cherish such high deeds
Even in the bosom of our adversaries.
LANCASTER
I thank your grace for this high courtesy,
Which I shall give away immediately.
KING
Then this remains, that we divide our power.
You, son John, and my cousin Westmoreland
Towards York shall bend you with your dearest
     speed,
To meet Northumberland and the prelate Scroop,
Who, as we hear, are busily in arms:
Myself and you, son Harry, will towards Wales,
To fight with Glendower and the Earl of March.
Rebellion in this land shall lose his sway,
Meeting the check of such another day:
And since this business so fair is done,
Let us not leave till all our own be won.   [*Exeunt*

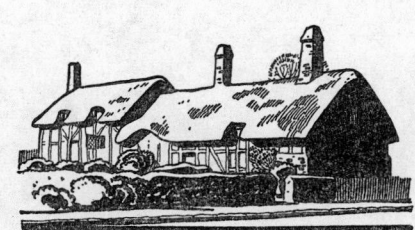

THE SECOND PART OF KING HENRY IV

SYNOPSIS

THE first reports from the Shrewsbury field of battle which come to the Earl of Northumberland are of the entire success of the rebellion against King Henry, but he finally hears the sad truth of the death of his son Hotspur at the hands of the Prince of Wales and the complete defeat of the insurgent forces, together with the tidings that the King has ordered an army under Prince John of Lancaster and the Earl of Westmoreland to proceed against the Archbishop of York and himself.

In a towering rage which his retainers strive to calm, Northumberland makes plans to join his forces with those of the Archbishop, and the prelate, warned by Hotspur's recklessness, ponders the chances of battle with his followers, Hastings and Mowbray, son of the King's old enemy, the banished Duke of Norfolk, but determines to oppose the royal army in Yorkshire, in view of Henry's forces being divided on three fronts, against the French, the Welsh and the rebels, and in confident expectation of reinforcements from Northumberland.

The Earl's wife and daughter-in-law, Hotspur's widow, urge him, however, to let his allies prove their own strength, and at length prevail upon him to take refuge for a time in Scotland from his enemies, while King Henry, ill both in body and soul, gives up the Welsh campaign and returns with the Prince of Wales to London after dispatching a large additional force against the rebels.

Meanwhile, Sir John Falstaff, commissioned by the King to enlist soldiers on his way north to join Prince John's army, is lingering in London with his old associates at the Boar's-Head Tavern. He barely escapes arrest for debt at the instance of the Hostess, Mistress Quickly, but with his usual effrontery capitalizes on his present employment and borrows still more money from the stupid woman to continue his drunken roistering in which the Prince and his companion Poins join, disguised as waiters upon Falstaff's table. Messengers arriving from Westminster with news of important dispatches from the north quickly restore the Prince to his sense of duty, and he hurries away to be in attendance on his sick father. Falstaff is haled to his job by army officers, and journeying to Gloucestershire to the home of his friend, Justice Shallow, the fat rascal fills his purse by allowing the able-bodied recruits he has selected for the northern army to buy themselves off, while he retains the weaklings for the King's service.

In the rebel camp in Yorkshire, the Archbishop of York, Mowbray and Hastings receive the cold regrets of Northumberland that he cannot join them, but feeling that they are sufficiently strong they prepare for battle as the royal forces approach. Instead of hazarding an engagement, Prince John sends the Earl of Westmoreland to parley with the insurgents in Gaultree Forest, and asks for a presentation of their alleged grievances which the Prince later promises on his sacred word of honor to have redressed upon the immediate disbandment of both armies. The rebels take him at his word and dismiss their forces, whereupon the cold-blooded, perjured Prince arrests for high treason and condemns to death the Archbishop and his associates, with the dastardly assertion that he had pledged nothing but the redress of grievances, and, having given secret instructions to his own army to remain intact, he orders them to pursue and slaughter the scattered insurgents.

At Westminster, Henry's counsellor, the Earl of Warwick, endeavors to ease the mind of the sleepless, conscience-stricken King by assuring him of the ultimate success of his armies, and of the death of his enemy Glendower, the powerful Welsh warrior, but the monarch's sick thoughts travel back to Richard's deposition and to the days of his old friendship with Northumberland. Apathetically, he receives the tidings the messengers bring, one by one, of the overthrow of Northumberland by the Sheriff of Yorkshire and the routing of the Archbishop of York's rebel army. Past hope and comfort, the King falls into a deep stupor which deceives the Prince of Wales watching alone at his bedside, and, thinking his father dead, he carries the crown to an adjoining room where he may mourn in solitude. Awakening and finding his crown gone, Henry accuses his son of desiring his death, and it is only through the pleading of the Prince, coupled with Warwick's testimony of his genuine grief, that the two are reconciled. The dying King advises his son to avert further domestic rebellions by engaging in foreign wars, and is carried to breathe his last in the Jerusalem Chamber at Westminster and thus fulfil a prophecy that he would die in Jerusalem.

Again sponging on his friends in Gloucestershire, Falstaff hears of the King's death, calls for his horse and proceeds posthaste to London for the coronation of his old friend, Prince Hal, promising all his companions knighthoods, dignities and riches, and to Justice Shallow any office in the land that he may choose. But the onetime wastrel Prince, already approved as a level-headed, efficient soldier, and now putting duty to the state before all other considerations, rebukes Falstaff publicly and orders his arrest and banishment, at the same time arranging for his maintenance for life. He appoints as one of his advisers the same Lord Chief-Justice who once committed him to jail when as Prince Hal he struck the judge in the face for sentencing to imprisonment one of his riotous companions. And, crowned King as Henry V, he calls Parliament to discuss the invasion of France.

HISTORICAL DATA

The Second Part of *Henry IV* continues history from 1403 to the King's death and the accession of Henry V in 1413. Its sources are the same as those from which Part One was derived, Shakespeare, in this instance, leaning rather more heavily upon *The Famous Victories of Henry the Fifth* for episodes in his narrative.

As was the case in the Induction to *The Taming of the Shrew*, Part Two contains many references to familiar places and persons with whom the dramatist was acquainted. The character of Falstaff is further developed, and a touch of pathos added in the contrast of his old age with his riotous manner

of living. Shallow and Silence, the country justices, appear to have been invented solely as foils for Sir John.

As no reference is made on the title page of the first quarto edition of the First Part to any sequel, it seems evident that Part Two, which is an epilogue to *The Historie of Henry IV*, was not written until after the publication of the first part. Ben Jonson mentions "Justice Silence" in his *Every Man out of his Humor*, acted in 1599, so the date of composition of this play may be fixed with reasonable certainty as 1598.

"*As good a man as he, sir, whoe'er I am*"
HENRY IV, PART II

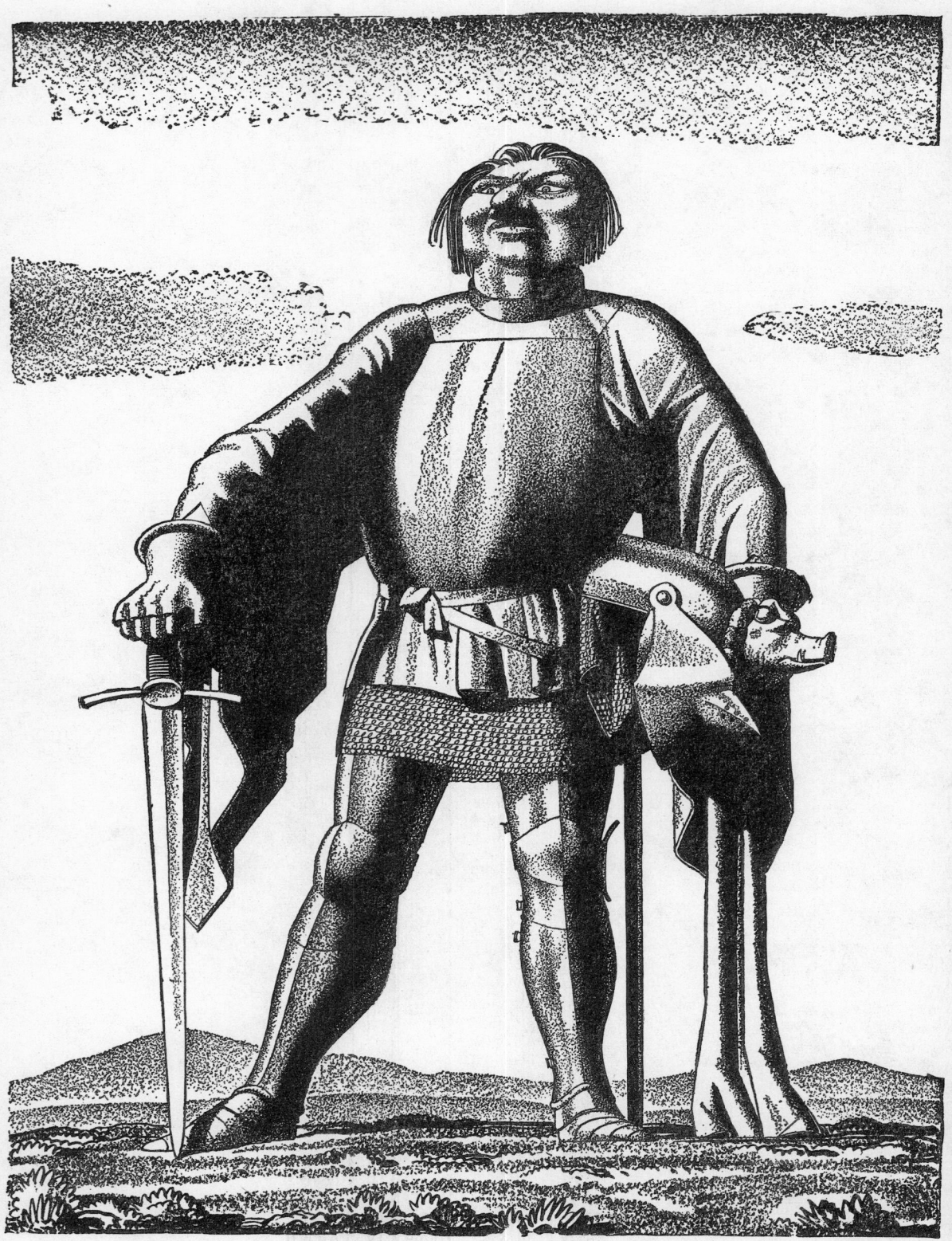

THE SECOND PART OF KING HENRY IV

DRAMATIS PERSONÆ

RUMOUR, the Presenter.
KING HENRY the Fourth.
HENRY, PRINCE OF WALES, after-
    wards King Henry V.,
THOMAS, DUKE OF CLARENCE,   } his sons.
PRINCE JOHN OF LANCASTER,
PRINCE HUMPHREY OF GLOUCESTER,
EARL OF WARWICK.
EARL OF WESTMORELAND.
EARL OF SURREY.
GOWER.
HARCOURT.
BLUNT.
LORD CHIEF JUSTICE of the King's Bench.
A SERVANT of the Chief Justice.
EARL OF NORTHUMBERLAND.
SCROOP, Archbishop of York.
LORD MOWBRAY.
LORD HASTINGS.
LORD BARDOLPH.
SIR JOHN COLEVILE.
TRAVERS and MORTON, retainers of Northumber-
    land.

SIR JOHN FALSTAFF.
HIS PAGE.
BARDOLPH.
PISTOL.
POINS.
PETO.
SHALLOW,   } country justices.
SILENCE,
DAVY, servant to Shallow.
MOULDY, SHADOW, WART, FEEBLE, and BULL-
    CALF, recruits.
FANG and SNARE, sheriff's officers.

LADY NORTHUMBERLAND.
LADY PERCY.
MISTRESS QUICKLY, hostess of a tavern in Eastcheap.
DOLL TEARSHEET.

LORDS and ATTENDANTS; PORTER, DRAWERS,
    BEADLES, GROOMS, &c. A DANCER, speaker of
    the epilogue.

SCENE—England.

INDUCTION

Warkworth. Before the castle

Enter RUMOUR, painted full of tongues

RUMOUR

OPEN your ears; for which of you will stop
The vent of hearing when loud Rumour speaks?
I, from the orient to the drooping west,
Making the wind my post-horse, still unfold
The acts commenced on this ball of earth:
Upon my tongues continual slanders ride,
The which in every language I pronounce,
Stuffing the ears of men with false reports.
I speak of peace, while covert enmity
Under the smile of safety wounds the world:
And who but Rumour, who but only I,
Make fearful musters and prepared defence,
Whiles the big year, swoln with some other grief,
Is thought with child by the stern tyrant war,
And no such matter? Rumour is a pipe
Blown by surmises, jealousies, conjectures,
And of so easy and so plain a stop
That the blunt monster with uncounted heads,
The still-discordant wavering multitude,
Can play upon it. But what need I thus
My well-known body to anatomize
Among my household? Why is Rumour here?
I run before King Harry's victory;
Who in a bloody field by Shrewsbury

Hath beaten down young Hotspur and his troops,
Quenching the flame of bold rebellion
Even with the rebels' blood. But what mean I
To speak so true at first? my office is
To noise abroad that Harry Monmouth fell
Under the wrath of noble Hotspur's sword,
And that the king before the Douglas' rage
Stoop'd his anointed head as low as death.
This have I rumour'd through the peasant towns
Between that royal field of Shrewsbury
And this worm-eaten hold of ragged stone,
Where Hotspur's father, old Northumberland,
Lies crafty-sick: the posts come tiring on,
And not a man of them brings other news
Than they have learn'd of me: from Rumour's
    tongues
They bring smooth comforts false, worse than true
    wrongs.   *[Exit*

ACT I

SCENE I. The same

Enter LORD BARDOLPH

LORD BARDOLPH

Who keeps the gate here, ho?

The PORTER opens the gate

    Where is the earl?

PORTER

What shall I say you are?

LORD BARDOLPH

            Tell thou the earl

That the Lord Bardolph doth attend him here.

PORTER

His lordship is walk'd forth into the orchard:

Please it your honour, knock but at the gate,

And he himself will answer.

Enter NORTHUMBERLAND

LORD BARDOLPH

            Here comes the earl.

                    [*Exit* PORTER

NORTHUMBERLAND

What news, Lord Bardolph? every minute now

Should be the father of some stratagem:

The times are wild; contention, like a horse

Full of high feeding, madly hath broke loose

And bears down all before him.

LORD BARDOLPH

            Noble earl,

I bring you certain news from Shrewsbury.

NORTHUMBERLAND

Good, an God will!

LORD BARDOLPH

            As good as heart can wish:

The king is almost wounded to the death;

And, in the fortune of my lord your son,

Prince Harry slain outright; and both the Blunts

Kill'd by the hand of Douglas; young Prince John

And Westmoreland and Stafford fled the field;

And Harry Monmouth's brawn, the hulk Sir John,

Is prisoner to your son: O, such a day,

So fought, so follow'd and so fairly won,

Came not till now to dignify the times,

Since Cæsar's fortunes!

NORTHUMBERLAND

            How is this derived?

Saw you the field? came you from Shrewsbury?

LORD BARDOLPH

I spake with one, my lord, that came from thence,

A gentleman well bred and of good name,

That freely render'd me these news for true.

NORTHUMBERLAND

Here comes my servant Travers, whom I sent

On Tuesday last to listen after news.

Enter TRAVERS

LORD BARDOLPH

My lord, I over-rode him on the way;

And he is furnish'd with no certainties

More than he haply may retail from me.

NORTHUMBERLAND

Now, Travers, what good tidings comes with you?

TRAVERS

My lord, Sir John Umfrevile turn'd me back

With joyful tidings; and, being better horsed,

Out-rode me. After him came spurring hard

A gentleman, almost forspent with speed,

That stopp'd by me to breathe his bloodied horse.

He ask'd the way to Chester; and of him

I did demand what news from Shrewsbury:

He told me that rebellion had bad luck,

And that young Harry Percy's spur was cold.

With that, he gave his able horse the head,

And bending forward struck his armed heels

Against the panting sides of his poor jade

Up to the rowel-head, and starting so

He seem'd in running to devour the way,

Staying no longer question.

NORTHUMBERLAND

            Ha! Again:

Said he young Harry Percy's spur was cold?

Of Hotspur Coldspur? that rebellion

Had met ill luck?

LORD BARDOLPH

            My lord, I'll tell you what;

If my young lord your son have not the day,

Upon mine honour, for a silken point

I'll give my barony: never talk of it.

NORTHUMBERLAND

Why should that gentleman that rode by Travers

Give then such instances of loss?

LORD BARDOLPH

            Who, he?

He was some hilding fellow that had stolen

The horse he rode on, and, upon my life,

Spoke at a venture. Look, here comes more news.

Enter MORTON

NORTHUMBERLAND

Yea, this man's brow, like to a title-leaf,

Foretells the nature of a tragic volume:

So looks the strond whereon the imperious flood

Hath left a witness'd usurpation.

Say, Morton, didst thou come from Shrewsbury?

MORTON

I ran from Shrewsbury, my noble lord;

Where hateful death put on his ugliest mask

To fright our party.

NORTHUMBERLAND

            How doth my son and brother?

Thou tremblest; and the whiteness in thy cheek

Is apter than thy tongue to tell thy errand.

Even such a man, so faint, so spiritless,

So dull, so dead in look, so woe-begone,

Drew Priam's curtain in the dead of night,

And would have told him half his Troy was burnt;

But Priam found the fire ere he his tongue,

And I my Percy's death ere thou report'st it.

This thou wouldst say, 'Your son did thus and thus;

Your brother thus: so fought the noble Douglas:'

Stopping my greedy ear with their bold deeds:

But in the end, to stop my ear indeed,

Thou hast a sigh to blow away this praise,

Ending with 'Brother, son, and all are dead.'

MORTON

Douglas is living, and your brother, yet;

But, for my lord your son,—

NORTHUMBERLAND

            Why, he is dead.

See what a ready tongue suspicion hath!

He that but fears the thing he would not know
Hath by instinct knowledge from others' eyes
That what he fear'd is chanced. Yet speak, Morton;
Tell thou an earl his divination lies,
And I will take it as a sweet disgrace,
And make thee rich for doing me such wrong.

MORTON

You are too great to be by me gainsaid:
Your spirit is too true, your fears too certain.

NORTHUMBERLAND

Yet, for all this, say not that Percy's dead.
I see a strange confession in thine eye:
Thou shakest thy head, and hold'st it fear or sin
To speak a truth. If he be slain, say so;
The tongue offends not that reports his death:
And he doth sin that doth belie the dead,
Not he which says the dead is not alive.
Yet the first bringer of unwelcome news
Hath but a losing office, and his tongue
Sounds ever after as a sullen bell,
Remember'd tolling a departing friend.

LORD BARDOLPH

I cannot think, my lord, your son is dead.

MORTON

I am sorry I should force you to believe
That which I would to God I had not seen;
But these mine eyes saw him in bloody state,
Rendering faint quittance, wearied and out-
      breathed,
To Harry Monmouth; whose swift wrath beat down
The never-daunted Percy to the earth,
From whence with life he never more sprung up.
In few, his death, whose spirit lent a fire
Even to the dullest peasant in his camp,
Being bruited once, took fire and heat away
From the best-temper'd courage in his troops;
For from his metal was his party steel'd;
Which once in him abated, all the rest
Turn'd on themselves, like dull and heavy lead:
And as the thing that's heavy in itself,
Upon enforcement flies with greatest speed,
So did our men, heavy in Hotspur's loss,
Lend to this weight such lightness with their fear
That arrows fled not swifter toward their aim
Than did our soldiers, aiming at their safety,
Fly from the field. Then was that noble Worcester
Too soon ta'en prisoner; and that furious Scot,
The bloody Douglas, whose well-labouring sword
Had three times slain the appearance of the king,
'Gan vail his stomach and did grace the shame
Of those that turn'd their backs, and in his flight,
Stumbling in fear, was took. The sum of all
Is that the king hath won, and hath sent out
A speedy power to encounter you, my lord,
Under the conduct of young Lancaster
And Westmoreland. This is the news at full.

NORTHUMBERLAND

For this I shall have time enough to mourn.
In poison there is physic; and these news,
Having been well, that would have made me sick,

Being sick, have in some measure made me well:
And as the wretch, whose fever-weaken'd joints,
Like strengthless hinges, buckle under life,
Impatient of his fit, breaks like a fire
Out of his keeper's arms, even so my limbs,
Weaken'd with grief, being now enraged with grief,
Are thrice themselves. Hence, therefore, thou nice
      crutch!
A scaly gauntlet now with joints of steel
Must glove this hand: and hence, thou sickly quoif!
Thou art a guard too wanton for the head
Which princes, flesh'd with conquest, aim to hit.
Now bind my brows with iron; and approach
The ragged'st hour that time and spite dare bring
To frown upon the enraged Northumberland!
Let heaven kiss earth! now let not Nature's hand
Keep the wild flood confined! let order die!
And let this world no longer be a stage
To feed contention in a lingering act;
But let one spirit of the first-born Cain
Reign in all bosoms, that, each heart being set
On bloody courses, the rude scene may end,
And darkness be the burier of the dead!

TRAVERS

This strained passion doth you wrong, my lord.

LORD BARDOLPH

Sweet earl, divorce not wisdom from your honour.

MORTON

The lives of all your loving complices
Lean on your health; the which, if you give o'er
To stormy passion, must perforce decay.
You cast the event of war, my noble lord,
And summ'd the account of chance, before you said
'Let us make head.' It was your presurmise,
That, in the dole of blows, your son might drop:
You knew he walk'd o'er perils, on an edge,
More likely to fall in than to get o'er;
You were advised his flesh was capable
Of wounds and scars, and that his forward spirit
Would lift him where most trade of danger ranged:
Yet did you say 'Go forth;' and none of this,
Though strongly apprehended, could restrain
The stiff-borne action: what hath then befallen,
Or what hath this bold enterprise brought forth,
More than that being which was like to be?

LORD BARDOLPH

We all that are engaged to this loss
Knew that we ventured on such dangerous seas
That if we wrought out life 'twas ten to one;
And yet we ventured, for the gain proposed
Choked the respect of likely peril fear'd;
And since we are o'erset, venture again.
Come, we will all put forth, body and goods.

MORTON

'Tis more than time: and, my most noble lord,
I hear for certain, and do speak the truth,
The gentle Archbishop of York is up
With well-appointed powers: he is a man
Who with a double surety binds his followers.
My lord your son had only but the corpse.

But shadows and the shows of men, to fight;
For that same word, rebellion, did divide
The action of their bodies from their souls;
And they did fight with queasiness, constrain'd,
As men drink potions, that their weapons only
Seem'd on our side; but, for their spirits and souls,
This word, rebellion, it had froze them up,
As fish are in a pond. But now the bishop
Turns insurrection to religion:
Supposed sincere and holy in his thoughts,
He's followed both with body and with mind;
And doth enlarge his rising with the blood
Of fair King Richard, scraped from Pomfret stones;
Derives from heaven his quarrel and his cause;
Tells them he doth bestride a bleeding land,
Gasping for life under great Bolingbroke;
And more and less do flock to follow him.

NORTHUMBERLAND

I knew of this before; but, to speak truth,
This present grief had wiped it from my mind.
Go in with me; and counsel every man
The aptest way for safety and revenge:
Get posts and letters, and make friends with speed:
Never so few, and never yet more need.   [*Exeunt*

SCENE II. *London. A street*

Enter FALSTAFF, *with his* PAGE *bearing his
sword and buckler*

FALSTAFF

Sirrah, you giant, what says the doctor to my water?

PAGE

He said, sir, the water itself was a good healthy
water; but, for the party that owed it, he might have
moe diseases than he knew for.

FALSTAFF

Men of all sorts take a pride to gird at me: the brain
of this foolish-compounded clay, man, is not able to
invent any thing that tends to laughter, more than I
invent or is invented on me: I am not only witty in
myself, but the cause that wit is in other men. I do
here walk before thee like a sow that hath overwhelmed all her litter but one. If the prince put thee
into my service for any other reason than to set me
off, why then I have no judgement. Thou whoreson
mandrake, thou art fitter to be worn in my cap than
to wait at my heels. I was never manned with an
agate till now: but I will inset you neither in gold
nor silver, but in vile apparel, and send you back
again to your master, for a jewel,—the juvenal, the
prince your master, whose chin is not yet fledged. I
will sooner have a beard grow in the palm of my
hand than he shall get one on his cheek; and yet he
will not stick to say his face is a face-royal: God may
finish it when he will, 'tis not a hair amiss yet: he
may keep it still at a face-royal, for a barber shall
never earn sixpence out of it; and yet he'll be crowing as if he had writ man ever since his father was a
bachelor. He may keep his own grace, but he's al-

most out of mine, I can assure him. What said
Master Dombledon about the satin for my short
cloak and my slops?

PAGE

He said, sir, you should procure him better assurance than Bardolph: he would not take his band
and yours; he liked not the security.

FALSTAFF

Let him be damned, like the glutton! pray God his
tongue be hotter! A whoreson Achitophel! a rascally
yea-forsooth knave! to bear a gentleman in hand,
and then stand upon security! The whoreson
smooth-pates do now wear nothing but high shoes,
and bunches of keys at their girdles; and if a man is
through with them in honest taking up, then they
must stand upon security. I had as lief they would
put ratsbane in my mouth as offer to stop it with
security. I looked a' should have sent me two and
twenty yards of satin, as I am a true knight, and he
sends me security. Well, he may sleep in security;
for he hath the horn of abundance, and the lightness of his wife shines through it: and yet cannot he
see, though he have his own lanthorn to light him.
Where's Bardolph?

PAGE

He's gone into Smithfield to buy your worship a
horse.

FALSTAFF

I bought him in Paul's, and he'll buy me a horse in
Smithfield: an I could get me but a wife in the
stews, I were manned, horsed, and wived.

Enter the LORD CHIEF JUSTICE *and* SERVANT

PAGE

Sir, here comes the nobleman that committed the
prince for striking him about Bardolph.

FALSTAFF

Wait close; I will not see him.

CHIEF JUSTICE

What's he that goes there?

SERVANT

Falstaff, an't please your lordship.

CHIEF JUSTICE

He that was in question for the robbery?

SERVANT

He, my lord: but he hath since done good service at
Shrewsbury; and, as I hear, is now going with some
charge to the Lord John of Lancaster.

CHIEF JUSTICE

What, to York? Call him back again.

SERVANT

Sir John Falstaff!

FALSTAFF

Boy, tell him I am deaf.

PAGE

You must speak louder; my master is deaf.

CHIEF JUSTICE

I am sure he is, to the hearing of any thing good.
Go, pluck him by the elbow; I must speak with him.

SERVANT

Sir John!

FALSTAFF

What! a young knave, and begging! Is there not wars? is there not employment? doth not the king lack subjects? do not the rebels need soldiers? Though it be a shame to be on any side but one, it is worse shame to beg than to be on the worst side, were it worse than the name of rebellion can tell how to make it.

SERVANT

You mistake me, sir.

FALSTAFF

Why, sir, did I say you were an honest man? setting my knighthood and my soldiership aside, I had lied in my throat, if I had said so.

SERVANT

I pray you, sir, then set your knighthood and your soldiership aside; and give me leave to tell you, you lie in your throat, if you say I am any other than an honest man.

FALSTAFF

I give thee leave to tell me so! I lay aside that which grows to me! If thou gettest any leave of me, hang me; if thou takest leave, thou wert better be hanged. You hunt counter: hence! avaunt!

SERVANT

Sir, my lord would speak with you.

CHIEF JUSTICE

Sir John Falstaff, a word with you.

FALSTAFF

My good lord! God give your lordship good time of day. I am glad to see your lordship abroad: I heard say your lordship was sick: I hope your lordship goes abroad by advice. Your lordship, though not clean past your youth, hath yet some smack of age in you, some relish of the saltness of time; and I most humbly beseech your lordship to have a reverend care of your health.

CHIEF JUSTICE

Sir John, I sent for you before your expedition to Shrewsbury.

FALSTAFF

An't please your lordship, I hear his majesty is returned with some discomfort from Wales.

CHIEF JUSTICE

I talk not of his majesty: you would not come when I sent for you.

FALSTAFF

And I hear, moreover, his highness is fallen into this same whoreson apoplexy.

CHIEF JUSTICE

Well, God mend him! I pray you, let me speak with you.

FALSTAFF

This apoplexy is, as I take it, a kind of lethargy, an't please your lordship; a kind of sleeping in the blood, a whoreson tingling.

CHIEF JUSTICE

What tell you me of it? be it as it is.

FALSTAFF

It hath it original from much grief, from study and

perturbation of the brain: I have read the cause of his effects in Galen: it is a kind of deafness.

CHIEF JUSTICE

I think you are fallen into the disease; for you hear not what I say to you.

FALSTAFF

Very well, my lord, very well: rather, an 't please you, it is the disease of not listening, the malady of not marking, that I am troubled withal.

CHIEF JUSTICE

To punish you by the heels would amend the attention of your ears; and I care not if I do become your physician.

FALSTAFF

I am as poor as Job, my lord, but not so patient: your lordship may minister the potion of imprisonment to me in respect of poverty; but how I should be your patient to follow your prescriptions, the wise may make some dram of a scruple, or indeed a scruple itself.

CHIEF JUSTICE

I sent for you, when there were matters against you for your life, to come speak with me.

FALSTAFF

As I was then advised by my learned counsel in the laws of this land-service, I did not come.

CHIEF JUSTICE

Well, the truth is, Sir John, you live in great infamy.

FALSTAFF

He that buckles him in my belt cannot live in less.

CHIEF JUSTICE

Your means are very slender, and your waste is great.

FALSTAFF

I would it were otherwise; I would my means were greater, and my waist slenderer.

CHIEF JUSTICE

You have misled the youthful prince.

FALSTAFF

The young prince hath misled me: I am the fellow with the great belly, and he my dog.

CHIEF JUSTICE

Well, I am loath to gall a new-healed wound: your day's service at Shrewsbury hath a little gilded over your night's exploit on Gadshill: you may thank the unquiet time for your quiet o'er-posting that action.

FALSTAFF

My lord?

CHIEF JUSTICE

But since all is well, keep it so: wake not a sleeping wolf.

FALSTAFF

To wake a wolf is as bad as to smell a fox.

CHIEF JUSTICE

What! you are as a candle, the better part burnt out.

FALSTAFF

A wassail candle, my lord, all tallow: if I did say of wax, my growth would approve the truth.

CHIEF JUSTICE

There is not a white hair on your face but should have his effect of gravity.

FALSTAFF

His effect of gravy, gravy, gravy.

CHIEF JUSTICE

You follow the young prince up and down, like his ill angel.

FALSTAFF

Not so, my lord; your ill angel is light; but I hope he that looks upon me will take me without weighing: and yet, in some respects, I grant, I cannot go: I cannot tell. Virtue is of so little regard in these costermonger times that true valour is turned bearherd: pregnancy is made a tapster, and hath his quick wit wasted in giving reckonings: all the other gifts appertinent to man, as the malice of this age shapes them, are not worth a gooseberry. You that are old consider not the capacities of us that are young; you do measure the heat of our livers with the bitterness of your galls: and we that are in the vaward of our youth, I must confess, are wags too.

CHIEF JUSTICE

Do you set down your name in the scroll of youth, that are written down old with all the characters of age? Have you not a moist eye? a dry hand? a yellow cheek? a white beard? a decreasing leg? an increasing belly? is not your voice broken? your wind short? your chin double? your wit single? and every part about you blasted with antiquity? and will you yet call yourself young? Fie, fie, fie, Sir John!

FALSTAFF

My lord, I was born about three of the clock in the afternoon, with a white head and something a round belly. For my voice, I have lost it with halloing and singing of anthems. To approve my youth further, I will not: the truth is, I am only old in judgement and understanding; and he that will caper with me for a thousand marks, let him lend me the money, and have at him. For the box of the ear that the prince gave you, he gave it like a rude prince, and you took it like a sensible lord. I have checked him for it, and the young lion repents; marry, not in ashes and sackcloth, but in new silk and old sack.

CHIEF JUSTICE

Well, God send the prince a better companion!

FALSTAFF

God send the companion a better prince! I cannot rid my hands of him.

CHIEF JUSTICE

Well, the king hath severed you and Prince Harry: I hear you are going with Lord John of Lancaster against the Archbishop and the Earl of Northumberland.

FALSTAFF

Yea; I thank your pretty sweet wit for it. But look you pray, all you that kiss my lady Peace at home, that our armies join not in a hot day; for, by the

Lord, I take but two shirts out with me, and I mean not to sweat extraordinarily: if it be a hot day, and I brandish any thing but a bottle, I would I might never spit white again. There is not a dangerous action can peep out his head, but I am thrust upon it: well, I cannot last ever: but it was alway yet the trick of our English nation, if they have a good thing, to make it too common. If ye will needs say I am an old man, you should give me rest. I would to God my name were not so terrible to the enemy as it is: I were better to be eaten to death with a rust than to be scoured to nothing with perpetual motion.

CHIEF JUSTICE

Well, be honest, be honest; and God bless your expedition!

FALSTAFF

Will your lordship lend me a thousand pound to furnish me forth?

CHIEF JUSTICE

Not a penny, not a penny; you are too impatient to bear crosses. Fare you well: commend me to my cousin Westmoreland.

[Exeunt CHIEF JUSTICE and SERVANT

FALSTAFF

If I do, fillip me with a three-man beetle. A man can no more separate age and covetousness than a' can part young limbs and lechery: but the gout galls the one, and the pox pinches the other; and so both the degrees prevent my curses. Boy!

PAGE

Sir?

FALSTAFF

What money is in my purse?

PAGE

Seven groats and two pence.

FALSTAFF

I can get no remedy against this consumption of the purse: borrowing only lingers and lingers it out, but the disease is incurable. Go bear this letter to my Lord of Lancaster; this to the prince; this to the Earl of Westmoreland; and this to old Mistress Ursula, whom I have weekly sworn to marry since I perceived the first white hair on my chin. About it: you know where to find me. [Exit PAGE] A pox of this gout! or, a gout of this pox! for the one or the other plays the rogue with my great toe. 'Tis no matter if I do halt; I have the wars for my colour, and my pension shall seem the more reasonable. A good wit will make use of any thing: I will turn diseases to commodity.

[Exit

SCENE III. *York. The* ARCHBISHOP's *palace*

Enter the ARCHBISHOP, *the* LORDS HASTINGS, MOWBRAY, *and* BARDOLPH

ARCHBISHOP

Thus have you heard our cause and known our means;

And, my most noble friends, I pray you all,
Speak plainly your opinions of our hopes:
And first, lord marshal, what say you to it?

MOWBRAY

I well allow the occasion of our arms;
But gladly would be better satisfied
How in our means we should advance ourselves
To look with forehead bold and big enough
Upon the power and puissance of the king.

HASTINGS

Our present musters grow upon the file
To five and twenty thousand men of choice;
And our supplies live largely in the hope
Of great Northumberland, whose bosom burns
With an incensed fire of injuries.

LORD BARDOLPH

The question then, Lord Hastings, standeth thus;
Whether our present five and twenty thousand
May hold up head without Northumberland?

HASTINGS

With him, we may.

LORD BARDOLPH

           Yea, marry, there's the point:
But if without him we be thought too feeble,
My judgement is, we should not step too far
Till we had his assistance by the hand;
For in a theme so bloody-faced as this
Conjecture, expectation, and surmise
Of aids incertain should not be admitted.

ARCHBISHOP

'Tis very true, Lord Bardolph; for indeed
It was young Hotspur's case at Shrewsbury.

LORD BARDOLPH

It was, my lord; who lined himself with hope,
Eating the air on promise of supply,
Flattering himself in project of a power
Much smaller than the smallest of his thoughts:
And so, with great imagination
Proper to madmen, led his powers to death,
And winking leap'd into destruction.

HASTINGS

But, by your leave, it never yet did hurt
To lay down likelihoods and forms of hope.

LORD BARDOLPH

Yes, if this present quality of war,
Indeed the instant action: a cause on foot,
Lives so in hope, as in an early spring
We see the appearing buds; which to prove fruit,
Hope gives not so much warrant as despair
That frosts will bite them. When we mean to build,
We first survey the plot, then draw the model;
And when we see the figure of the house,
Then must we rate the cost of the erection;
Which if we find outweighs ability,
What do we then but draw anew the model
In fewer offices, or at least desist
To build at all? Much more, in this great work,
Which is almost to pluck a kingdom down
And set another up, should we survey
The plot of situation and the model,

Consent upon a sure foundation,
Question surveyors, know our own estate,
How able such a work to undergo,
To weigh against his opposite; or else
We fortify in paper and in figures,
Using the names of men instead of men:
Like one that draws the model of a house
Beyond his power to build it; who, half through,
Gives o'er and leaves his part-created cost
A naked subject to the weeping clouds,
And waste for churlish winter's tyranny.

HASTINGS

Grant that our hopes, yet likely of fair birth,
Should be still-born, and that we now possess'd
The utmost man of expectation,
I think we are a body strong enough,
Even as we are, to equal with the king.

LORD BARDOLPH

What, is the king but five and twenty thousand?

HASTINGS

To us no more; nay, not so much, Lord Bardolph.
For his divisions, as the times do brawl,
Are in three heads: one power against the French,
And one against Glendower; perforce a third
Must take up us: so is the unfirm king
In three divided; and his coffers sound
With hollow poverty and emptiness.

ARCHBISHOP

That he should draw his several strengths together
And come against us in full puissance,
Need not be dreaded.

HASTINGS

           If he should do so,
He leaves his back unarm'd, the French and Welsh
Baying him at the heels: never fear that.

LORD BARDOLPH

Who is it like should lead his forces hither?

HASTINGS

The Duke of Lancaster and Westmoreland;
Against the Welsh, himself and Harry Monmouth:
But who is substituted 'gainst the French,
I have no certain notice.

ARCHBISHOP

           Let us on,
And publish the occasion of our arms.
The commonwealth is sick of their own choice;
Their over-greedy love hath surfeited:
An habitation giddy and unsure
Hath he that buildeth on the vulgar heart.
O thou fond many, with what loud applause
Didst thou beat heaven with blessing Bolingbroke,
Before he was what thou wouldst have him be!
And being now trimm'd in thine own desires,
Thou, beastly feeder, art so full of him,
That thou provokest thyself to cast him up.
So, so, thou common dog, didst thou disgorge
Thy glutton bosom of the royal Richard;
And now thou wouldst eat thy dead vomit up,
And howl'st to find it. What trust is in these times?

They that, when Richard lived, would have him
   die,
Are now become enamour'd on his grave:
Thou, that threw'st dust upon his goodly head
When through proud London he came sighing on
After the admired heels of Bolingbroke,
Criest now 'O earth, yield us that king again,
And take thou this!' O thoughts of men accursed!
Past and to come seems best; things present, worst.

MOWBRAY

Shall we go draw our numbers, and set on?

HASTINGS

We are time's subjects, and time bids be gone.

                                     [Exeunt

ACT II

SCENE I. *London. A street*

Enter HOSTESS, FANG *and his* BOY *with her, and*
           SNARE *following*

HOSTESS

Master Fang, have you entered the action?

FANG

It is entered.

HOSTESS

Where's your yeoman? Is 't a lusty yeoman? will a'
stand to 't?

FANG

Sirrah, where's Snare?

HOSTESS

O Lord, ay! good Master Snare.

SNARE

Here, here.

FANG

Snare, we must arrest Sir John Falstaff.

HOSTESS

Yea, good Master Snare; I have entered him and
all.

SNARE

It may chance cost some of us our lives, for he will
stab.

HOSTESS

Alas the day! take heed of him; he stabbed me in
mine own house, and that most beastly: in good
faith, he cares not what mischief he does, if his
weapon be out: he will foin like any devil; he will
spare neither man, woman, nor child.

FANG

If I can close with him, I care not for his thrust.

HOSTESS

No, nor I neither: I'll be at your elbow.

FANG

An I but fist him once; an a' come but within my
vice,—

HOSTESS

I am undone by his going; I warrant you, he's an
infinitive thing upon my score. Good Master Fang,
hold him sure: good Master Snare, let him not

'scape. A' comes continually to Pie-corner—saving
your manhoods—to buy a saddle; and he is indited
to dinner to the Lubber's-head in Lumbert street,
to Master Smooth's the silkman: I pray ye, since my
exion is entered and my case so openly known to the
world, let him be brought in to his answer. A hundred mark is a long one for a poor lone woman to
bear: and I have borne, and borne, and borne; and
have been fubbed off, and fubbed off, and fubbed
off, from this day to that day, that it is a shame to
be thought on. There is no honesty in such dealing;
unless a woman should be made an ass and a beast,
to bear every knave's wrong. Yonder he comes; and
that arrant malmsey-nose knave, Bardolph, with
him. Do your offices, do your offices: Master Fang
and Master Snare, do me, do me, do me your
offices.

Enter FALSTAFF, PAGE, *and* BARDOLPH

FALSTAFF

How now! whose mare's dead? what's the matter?

FANG

Sir John, I arrest you at the suit of Mistress Quickly.

FALSTAFF

Away, varlets! Draw, Bardolph: cut me off the villain's head: throw the quean in the channel.

HOSTESS

Throw me in the channel! I'll throw thee in the
channel. Wilt thou? wilt thou? thou bastardly
rogue! Murder, murder! Ah, thou honey-suckle villain! wilt thou kill God's officers and the king's? Ah,
thou honey-seed rogue! thou art a honey-seed, a
man-queller, and a woman-queller.

FALSTAFF

Keep them off, Bardolph.

FANG

A rescue! a rescue!

HOSTESS

Good people, bring a rescue or two. Thou wo't,
wo't thou? thou wo't, wo't ta? do, do, thou rogue!
do, thou hemp-seed!

PAGE

Away, you scullion! you rampallian! you fustilar-
ian! I'll tickle your catastrophe.

Enter the LORD CHIEF JUSTICE, *and his men*

CHIEF JUSTICE

What is the matter? keep the peace here, ho!

HOSTESS

Good my lord, be good to me. I beseech you, stand
to me.

CHIEF JUSTICE

How now, Sir John! what are you brawling here?
Doth this become your place, your time and busi-
   ness?
You should have been well on your way to York.
Stand from him, fellow: wherefore hang'st upon
   him?

HOSTESS

O my most worshipful lord, an 't please your grace,
I am a poor widow of Eastcheap, and he is arrested
at my suit.

CHIEF JUSTICE

For what sum?

HOSTESS

It is more than for some, my lord; it is for all, all I have. He hath eaten me out of house and home; he hath put all my substance into that fat belly of his: but I will have some of it out again, or I will ride thee o' nights like the mare.

FALSTAFF

I think I am as like to ride the mare, if I have any vantage of ground to get up.

CHIEF JUSTICE

How comes this, Sir John? Fie! what man of good temper would endure this tempest of exclamation? Are you not ashamed to enforce a poor widow to so rough a course to come by her own?

FALSTAFF

What is the gross sum that I owe thee?

HOSTESS

Marry, if thou wert an honest man, thyself and the money too. Thou didst swear to me upon a parcel-gilt goblet, sitting in my Dolphin-chamber, at the round table, by a sea-coal fire, upon Wednesday in Wheeson week, when the prince broke thy head for liking his father to a singing-man of Windsor, thou didst swear to me then, as I was washing thy wound, to marry me and make me my lady thy wife. Canst thou deny it? Did not goodwife Keech, the butcher's wife, come in then and call me gossip Quickly? coming in to borrow a mess of vinegar; telling us she had a good dish of prawns; whereby thou didst desire to eat some; whereby I told thee they were ill for a green wound? And didst thou not, when she was gone down stairs, desire me to be no more so familiarity with such poor people; saying that ere long they should call me madam? And didst thou not kiss me and bid me fetch thee thirty shillings? I put thee now to thy book-oath: deny it, if thou canst.

FALSTAFF

My lord, this is a poor mad soul; and she says up and down the town that her eldest son is like you: she hath been in good case, and the truth is, poverty hath distracted her. But for these foolish officers, I beseech you I may have redress against them.

CHIEF JUSTICE

Sir John, Sir John, I am well acquainted with your manner of wrenching the true cause the false way. It is not a confident brow, nor the throng of words that come with such more than impudent sauciness from you, can thrust me from a level consideration: you have, as it appears to me, practised upon the easy-yielding spirit of this woman, and made her serve your uses both in purse and in person.

HOSTESS

Yea, in truth, my lord.

CHIEF JUSTICE

Pray thee, peace. Pay her the debt you owe her, and unpay the villany you have done her: the one you may do with sterling money, and the other with current repentance.

FALSTAFF

My lord, I will not undergo this sneap without reply. You call honourable boldness impudent sauciness: if a man will make courtesy and say nothing, he is virtuous: no, my lord, my humble duty remembered, I will not be your suitor. I say to you, I do desire deliverance from these officers, being upon hasty employment in the king's affairs.

CHIEF JUSTICE

You speak as having power to do wrong: but answer in the effect of your reputation, and satisfy the poor woman.

FALSTAFF

Come hither, hostess.

Enter GOWER

CHIEF JUSTICE

Now, Master Gower, what news?

GOWER

The king, my lord, and Harry Prince of Wales
Are near at hand: the rest the paper tells.

FALSTAFF

As I am a gentleman.

HOSTESS

Faith, you said so before.

FALSTAFF

As I am a gentleman. Come, no more words of it.

HOSTESS

By this heavenly ground I tread on, I must be fain to pawn both my plate and the tapestry of my dining-chambers.

FALSTAFF

Glasses, glasses, is the only drinking: and for thy walls, a pretty slight drollery, or the story of the Prodigal, or the German hunting in water-work, is worth a thousand of these bed-hangings and these fly-bitten tapestries. Let it be ten pound, if thou canst. Come, an 'twere not for thy humours, there's not a better wench in England. Go, wash thy face, and draw the action. Come, thou must not be in this humour with me; dost not know me? come, come, I know thou wast set on to this.

HOSTESS

Pray thee, Sir John, let it be but twenty nobles: i' faith, I am loath to pawn my plate, so God save me, la!

FALSTAFF

Let it alone; I'll make other shift: you'll be a fool still.

HOSTESS

Well, you shall have it, though I pawn my gown. I hope you'll come to supper. You'll pay me all together?

FALSTAFF

Will I live? [*To* BARDOLPH] Go, with her, with her; hook on, hook on.

HOSTESS

Will you have Doll Tearsheet meet you at supper?

FALSTAFF

No more words; let's have her.

[*Exeunt* HOSTESS, BARDOLPH, OFFICERS, *and* BOY

CHIEF JUSTICE

I have heard better news.

FALSTAFF

What's the news, my lord?

CHIEF JUSTICE

Where lay the king last night?

GOWER

At Basingstoke, my lord.

FALSTAFF

I hope, my lord, all's well: what is the news, my lord?

CHIEF JUSTICE

Come all his forces back?

GOWER

No; fifteen hundred foot, five hundred horse,
Are march'd up to my Lord of Lancaster,
Against Northumberland and the Archbishop.

FALSTAFF

Comes the king back from Wales, my noble lord?

CHIEF JUSTICE

You shall have letters of me presently:
Come, go along with me, good Master Gower.

FALSTAFF

My lord!

CHIEF JUSTICE

What's the matter?

FALSTAFF

Master Gower, shall I entreat you with me to dinner?

GOWER

I must wait upon my good lord here; I thank you, good Sir John.

CHIEF JUSTICE

Sir John, you loiter here too long, being you are to take soldiers up in counties as you go.

FALSTAFF

Will you sup with me, Master Gower?

CHIEF JUSTICE

What foolish master taught you these manners, Sir John?

FALSTAFF

Master Gower, if they become me not, he was a fool that taught them me. This is the right fencing grace, my lord; tap for tap, and so part fair.

CHIEF JUSTICE

Now the Lord lighten thee! thou art a great fool.

[*Exeunt*

SCENE II. *London. Another street*

Enter PRINCE HENRY *and* POINS

PRINCE

Before God, I am exceeding weary.

POINS

Is 't come to that? I had thought weariness durst not have attached one of so high blood.

PRINCE

Faith, it does me; though it discolours the complexion of my greatness to acknowledge it. Doth it not show vilely in me to desire small beer?

POINS

Why, a prince should not be so loosely studied as to remember so weak a composition.

PRINCE

Belike then my appetite was not princely got; for, by my troth, I do now remember the poor creature, small beer. But, indeed, these humble considerations make me out of love with my greatness. What a disgrace is it to me to remember thy name! or to know thy face to-morrow! or to take note how many pair of silk stockings thou hast, viz. these, and those that were thy peach-coloured ones! or to bear the inventory of thy shirts; as, one for superfluity, and another for use! But that the tennis-court-keeper knows better than I; for it is a low ebb of linen with thee when thou keepest not racket there; as thou hast not done a great while, because the rest of thy low countries have made a shift to eat up thy holland: and God knows, whether those that bawl out the ruins of thy linen shall inherit his kingdom: but the midwives say the children are not in the fault; whereupon the world increases, and kindreds are mightily strengthened.

POINS

How ill it follows, after you have laboured so hard, you should talk so idly! Tell me, how many good young princes would do so, their fathers being so sick as yours at this time is?

PRINCE

Shall I tell thee one thing, Poins?

POINS

Yes, faith; and let it be an excellent good thing.

PRINCE

It shall serve among wits of no higher breeding than thine.

POINS

Go to; I stand the push of your one thing that you will tell.

PRINCE

Marry, I tell thee, it is not meet that I should be sad, now my father is sick: albeit I could tell to thee, as to one it pleases me, for fault of a better, to call my friend, I could be sad, and sad indeed too.

POINS

Very hardly upon such a subject.

PRINCE

By this hand, thou thinkest me as far in the devil's book as thou and Falstaff for obduracy and persistency: let the end try the man. But I tell thee, my heart bleeds inwardly that my father is so sick: and keeping such vile company as thou art hath in reason taken from me all ostentation of sorrow.

POINS

The reason?

PRINCE

What wouldst thou think of me, if I should weep?

POINS

I would think thee a most princely hypocrite.

PRINCE

It would be every man's thought; and thou art a blessed fellow to think as every man thinks: never a man's thought in the world keeps the road-way better than thine: every man would think me an hypocrite indeed. And what accites your most worshipful thought to think so?

POINS

Why, because you have been so lewd, and so much engraffed to Falstaff.

PRINCE

And to thee.

POINS

By this light, I am well spoke on; I can hear it with mine own ears: the worst that they can say of me is that I am a second brother, and that I am a proper fellow of my hands; and those two things, I confess, I cannot help. By the mass, here comes Bardolph.

Enter BARDOLPH *and* PAGE

PRINCE

And the boy that I gave Falstaff: a' had him from me Christian; and look, if the fat villain have not transformed him ape.

BARDOLPH

God save your grace!

PRINCE

And yours, most noble Bardolph!

BARDOLPH

Come, you virtuous ass, you bashful fool, must you be blushing? wherefore blush you now? What a maidenly man-at-arms are you become! Is 't such a matter to get a pottle-pot's maidenhead?

PAGE

A' calls me e'en now, my lord, through a red lattice, and I could discern no part of his face from the window: at last I spied his eyes; and methought he had made two holes in the ale-wife's new petticoat and so peeped through.

PRINCE

Has not the boy profited?

BARDOLPH

Away, you whoreson upright rabbit, away!

PAGE

Away, you rascally Althæa's dream, away!

PRINCE

Instruct us, boy; what dream, boy?

Marry, my lord, Althæa dreamed she was delivered of a fire-brand; and therefore I call him her dream.

PRINCE

A crown's worth of good interpretation: there 'tis, boy.

POINS

O, that this good blossom could ke kept from cankers! Well, there is sixpence to preserve thee.

BARDOLPH

An you do not make him hanged among you, the gallows shall have wrong.

PRINCE

And how doth thy master, Bardolph?

BARDOLPH

Well, my lord. He heard of your grace's coming to town: there's a letter for you.

POINS

Delivered with good respect. And how doth the martlemas, your master?

BARDOLPH

In bodily health, sir.

POINS

Marry, the immortal part needs a physician; but that moves not him: though that be sick, it dies not.

PRINCE

I do allow this wen to be as familiar with me as my dog; and he holds his place; for look you how he writes.

POINS

[*Reads*] 'John Falstaff, knight,'—every man must know that, as oft as he has occasion to name himself: even like those that are kin to the king; for they never prick their finger but they say, 'There's some of the king's blood spilt.' 'How comes that?' says he, that takes upon him not to conceive. The answer is as ready as a borrower's cap, 'I am the king's poor cousin, sir.'

PRINCE

Nay, they will be kin to us, or they will fetch it from Japhet. But to the letter:

POINS

[*Reads*] 'Sir John Falstaff, knight, to the son of the king, nearest his father, Harry Prince of Wales, greeting.' Why, this is a certificate.

PRINCE

Peace!

POINS

[*Reads*] 'I will imitate the honourable Romans in brevity:' he sure means brevity in breath, short-winded. 'I commend me to thee, I commend thee, and I leave thee. Be not too familiar with Poins; for he misuses thy favours so much, that he swears thou art to marry his sister Nell. Repent at idle times as thou mayest; and so, farewell.

'Thine, by yea and no, which is as much as to say, as thou usest him, JACK FALSTAFF with my familiars, JOHN with my brothers and sisters, and SIR JOHN with all Europe.'

My lord, I'll steep this letter in sack, and make him eat it.

PRINCE

That's to make him eat twenty of his words. But do you use me thus, Ned? must I marry your sister?

POINS

God send the wench no worse fortune! But I never said so.

PRINCE

Well, thus we play the fools with the time; and the spirits of the wise sit in the clouds and mock us. Is your master here in London?

BARDOLPH

Yea, my lord.

PRINCE

Where sups he? doth the old boar feed in the old frank?

BARDOLPH

At the old place, my lord, in Eastcheap.

PRINCE

What company?

PAGE

Ephesians, my lord, of the old church.

PRINCE

Sup any women with him?

PAGE

None, my lord, but old Mistress Quickly and Mistress Doll Tearsheet.

PRINCE

What pagan may that be?

PAGE

A proper gentlewoman, sir, and a kinswoman of my master's.

PRINCE

Even such kin as the parish heifers are to the town bull. Shall we steal upon them, Ned, at supper?

POINS

I am your shadow, my lord; I'll follow you.

PRINCE

Sirrah, you boy, and Bardolph, no word to your master that I am yet come to town: there's for your silence.

BARDOLPH

I have no tongue, sir.

PAGE

And for mine, sir, I will govern it.

PRINCE

Fare you well; go.   [Exeunt BARDOLPH and PAGE
This Doll Tearsheet should be some road.

POINS

I warrant you, as common as the way between Saint Alban's and London.

PRINCE

How might we see Falstaff bestow himself to-night in his true colours, and not ourselves be seen?

POINS

Put on two leathern jerkins and aprons, and wait upon him at his table as drawers.

PRINCE

From a god to a bull? a heavy descension! it was Jove's case. From a prince to a prentice? a low transformation! that shall be mine; for in every thing the purpose must weigh with the folly. Follow me, Ned.   [Exeunt

SCENE III. Warkworth. Before the castle

Enter NORTHUMBERLAND, LADY NORTHUMBERLAND,
and LADY PERCY

NORTHUMBERLAND

I pray thee, loving wife, and gentle daughter,
Give even way unto my rough affairs:
Put not you on the visage of the times,
And be like them to Percy troublesome.

LADY NORTHUMBERLAND

I have given over, I will speak no more:
Do what you will; your wisdom be your guide.

NORTHUMBERLAND

Alas, sweet wife, my honour is at pawn;
And, but my going, nothing can redeem it.

LADY PERCY

O yet, for God's sake, go not to these wars!
The time was, father, that you broke your word,
When you were more endear'd to it than now;
When your own Percy, when my heart's dear Harry,
Threw many a northward look to see his father
Bring up his powers; but he did long in vain.
Who then persuaded you to stay at home?
There were two honours lost, yours and your son's.
For yours, the God of heaven brighten it!
For his, it stuck upon him as the sun
In the grey vault of heaven, and by his light
Did all the chivalry of England move
To do brave acts: he was indeed the glass
Wherein the noble youth did dress themselves:
He had no legs that practised not his gait;
And speaking thick, which nature made his blemish,
Became the accents of the valiant;
For those that could speak low and tardily
Would turn their own perfection to abuse,
To seem like him: so that in speech, in gait,
In diet, in affections of delight,
In military rules, humours of blood,
He was the mark and glass, copy and book,
That fashion'd others. And him, O wondrous him!
O miracle of men! him did you leave,
Second to none, unseconded by you,
To look upon the hideous god of war
In disadvantage; to abide a field
Where nothing but the sound of Hotspur's name
Did seem defensible: so you left him.
Never, O never, do his ghost the wrong
To hold your honour more precise and nice
With others than with him! let them alone:
The marshal and the archbishop are strong:
Had my sweet Harry had but half their numbers,
To-day might I, hanging on Hotspur's neck,
Have talk'd of Monmouth's grave.

NORTHUMBERLAND

                                    Beshrew your heart,
Fair daughter, you do draw my spirits from me
With new lamenting ancient oversights.
But I must go and meet with danger there,
Or it will seek me in another place
And find me worse provided.

LADY NORTHUMBERLAND

                          O, fly to Scotland,
Till that the nobles and the armed commons
Have of their puissance made a little taste.

LADY PERCY

If they get ground and vantage of the king,
Then join you with them, like a rib of steel,
To make strength stronger; but, for all our loves,

First let them try themselves. So did your son;
He was so suffer'd: so came I a widow;
And never shall have length of life enough
To rain upon remembrance with mine eyes,
That it may grow and sprout as high as heaven,
For recordation to my noble husband.

NORTHUMBERLAND

Come, come, go in with me. 'Tis with my mind
As with the tide swell'd up unto his height,
That makes a still-stand, running neither way:
Fain would I go to meet the archbishop,
But many thousand reasons hold me back.
I will resolve for Scotland: there am I,
Till time and vantage crave my company. [*Exeunt*

SCENE IV. *London. The Boar's-Head Tavern
in Eastcheap*

Enter two DRAWERS

FIRST DRAWER

What the devil hast thou brought there? apple-
johns? thou knowest Sir John cannot endure an
apple-john.

SECOND DRAWER

Mass, thou sayest true. The prince once set a dish of
apple-johns before him, and told him there were
five more Sir Johns; and, putting off his hat, said,
'I will now take my leave of these six dry, round,
old, withered knights.' It angered him to the heart:
but he hath forgot that.

FIRST DRAWER

Why, then, cover, and set them down: and see if
thou canst find out Sneak's noise; Mistress Tearsheet would fain hear some music. Dispatch: the
room where they supped is too hot; they'll come in
straight.

SECOND DRAWER

Sirrah, here will be the prince and Master Poins
anon; and they will put on two of our jerkins and
aprons; and Sir John must not know of it: Bardolph
hath brought word.

FIRST DRAWER

By the mass, here will be old utis: it will be an excellent stratagem.

SECOND DRAWER

I'll see if I can find out Sneak. [*Exit*

Enter HOSTESS *and* DOLL TEARSHEET

HOSTESS

I' faith, sweetheart, methinks now you are in an
excellent good temperality: your pulsidge beats as
extraordinarily as heart would desire; and your
colour, I warrant you, is as red as any rose, in good
truth, la! But, i' faith, you have drunk too much
canaries; and that's a marvellous searching wine,
and it perfumes the blood ere one can say 'What's
this?' How do you now?

DOLL

Better than I was: hem!

HOSTESS

Why, that's well said; a good heart's worth gold.
Lo, here comes Sir John.

Enter FALSTAFF

FALSTAFF

[*Singing*] 'When Arthur first in court'
—Empty the jordan.　　　[*Exit* FIRST DRAWER]—
[*Singing*] 'And was a worthy king.'
How now, Mistress Doll!

HOSTESS

Sick of a calm; yea, good faith.

FALSTAFF

So is all her sect; an they be once in a calm, they
are sick.

DOLL

You muddy rascal, is that all the comfort you give
me?

FALSTAFF

You make fat rascals, Mistress Doll.

DOLL

I make them! gluttony and diseases make them; I
make them not.

FALSTAFF

If the cook help to make the gluttony, you help to
make the diseases, Doll: we catch of you, Doll, we
catch of you; grant that, my poor virtue, grant that.

DOLL

Yea, joy, our chains and our jewels.

FALSTAFF

'Your brooches, pearls, and ouches:' for to serve
bravely is to come halting off, you know; to come
off the breach with his pike bent bravely, and to
surgery bravely; to venture upon the charged
chambers bravely,—

DOLL

Hang yourself, you muddy conger, hang yourself!

HOSTESS

By my troth, this is the old fashion; you two never
meet but you fall to some discord: you are both, i'
good truth, as rheumatic as two dry toasts; you cannot one bear with another's confirmities. What the
good-year! one must bear, and that must be you:
you are the weaker vessel, as they say, the emptier
vessel.

DOLL

Can a weak empty vessel bear such a huge full hogshead? there's a whole merchant's venture of Bourdeaux stuff in him; you have not seen a hulk better
stuffed in the hold. Come, I'll be friends with thee,
Jack: thou art going to the wars; and whether I
shall ever see thee again or no, there is nobody
cares.

Re-enter FIRST DRAWER

FIRST DRAWER

Sir, Ancient Pistol's below, and would speak with
you.

DOLL

Hang him, swaggering rascal! let him not come
hither: it is the foul-mouthedst rogue in England.

HOSTESS

If he swagger, let him not come here: no, by my faith; I must live among my neighbours; I'll no swaggerers: I am in good name and fame with the very best: shut the door; there comes no swaggerers here: I have not lived all this while, to have swaggering now: shut the door, I pray you.

FALSTAFF

Dost thou hear, hostess?

HOSTESS

Pray ye, pacify yourself, Sir John: there comes no swaggerers here.

FALSTAFF

Dost thou hear? it is mine ancient.

HOSTESS

Tilly-fally, Sir John, ne'er tell me: your ancient swaggerer comes not in my doors. I was before Master Tisick, the debuty, t' other day; and, as he said to me, 'twas no longer ago than Wednesday last, 'I' good faith, neighbour Quickly,' says he; Master Dumbe, our minister, was by then; 'neighbour Quickly,' says he, 'receive those that are civil; for,' said he, 'you are in an ill name:' now a' said so, I can tell whereupon; 'for,' says he, 'you are an honest woman, and well thought on; therefore take heed what guests you receive: receive,' says he, 'no swaggering companions.' There comes none here: you would bless you to hear what he said: no, I'll no swaggerers.

FALSTAFF

He's no swaggerer, hostess; a tame cheater, i' faith; you may stroke him as gently as a puppy greyhound: he'll not swagger with a Barbary hen, if her feathers turn back in any show of resistance. Call him up, drawer.   [Exit FIRST DRAWER

HOSTESS

Cheater, call you him? I will bar no honest man my house, nor no cheater: but I do not love swaggering, by my troth; I am the worse, when one says swagger: feel, masters, how I shake; look you, I warrant you.

DOLL

So you do, hostess.

HOSTESS

Do I? yea, in very truth, do I, an 'twere an aspen leaf: I cannot abide swaggerers.

Enter PISTOL, BARDOLPH, *and* PAGE

PISTOL

God save you, Sir John!

FALSTAFF

Welcome, Ancient Pistol. Here, Pistol, I charge you with a cup of sack: do you discharge upon mine hostess.

PISTOL

I will discharge upon her, Sir John, with two bullets.

FALSTAFF

She is pistol-proof, sir; you shall hardly offend her.

HOSTESS

Come, I'll drink no proofs nor no bullets: I'll drink

no more than will do me good, for no man's pleasure, I.

PISTOL

Then to you, Mistress Dorothy; I will charge you.

DOLL

Charge me! I scorn you, scurvy companion. What! you poor, base, rascally, cheating, lack-linen mate! Away, you mouldy rogue, away! I am meat for your master.

PISTOL

I know you, Mistress Dorothy.

DOLL

Away, you cut-purse rascal! you filthy bung, away! by this wine, I'll thrust my knife in your mouldy chaps, an you play the saucy cuttle with me. Away, you bottle-ale rascal! you basket-hilt stale juggler, you! Since when, I pray you, sir? God's light, with two points on your shoulder? much!

PISTOL

God let me not live, but I will murder your ruff for this.

FALSTAFF

No more, Pistol; I would not have you go off here: discharge yourself of our company, Pistol.

HOSTESS

No, good Captain Pistol; not here, sweet captain.

DOLL

Captain! thou abominable damned cheater, art thou not ashamed to be called captain? An captains were of my mind, they would truncheon you out, for taking their names upon you before you have earned them. You a captain! you slave, for what? for tearing a poor whore's ruff in a bawdy-house? He a captain! hang him, rogue! he lives upon mouldy stewed prunes and dried cakes. A captain! God's light, these villains will make the word as odious as the word 'occupy;' which was an excellent good word before it was ill sorted; therefore captains had need look to 't.

BARDOLPH

Pray thee, go down, good ancient.

FALSTAFF

Hark thee hither, Mistress Doll.

PISTOL

Not I: I tell thee what, Corporal Bardolph, I could tear her: I'll be revenged of her.

PAGE

Pray thee, go down.

PISTOL

I'll see her damned first; to Pluto's damned lake, by this hand, to the infernal deep, with Erebus and tortures vile also. Hold hook and line, say I. Down, down, dogs! down, faitors! Have we not Hiren here?

HOSTESS

Good Captain Peesel, be quiet; 'tis very late, i' faith: I beseek you now, aggravate your choler.

PISTOL

These be good humours, indeed! Shall pack-horses, And hollow pamper'd jades of Asia, Which cannot go but thirty mile a day,

[530]

Compare with Cæsars, and with Cannibals,
And Trojan Greeks? nay, rather damn them with
King Cerberus; and let the welkin roar.
Shall we fall foul for toys?

HOSTESS

By my troth, captain, these are very bitter words.

BARDOLPH

Be gone, good ancient: this will grow to a brawl
anon.

PISTOL

Die men like dogs! give crowns like pins! Have we
not Hiren here?

HOSTESS

O' my word, captain, there's none such here. What
the good-year! do you think I would deny her? For
God's sake, be quiet.

PISTOL

Then feed, and be fat, my fair Calipolis. Come,
give's some sack.
'Si fortune me tormente, sperato me contento.'
Fear we broadsides? no, let the fiend give fire:
Give me some sack: and, sweetheart, lie thou there.
[Laying down his sword
Come we to full points here; and are etceteras noth-
ing?

FALSTAFF

Pistol, I would be quiet.

PISTOL

Sweet knight, I kiss thy neaf: what! we have seen
the seven stars.

DOLL

For God's sake, thrust him down stairs: I cannot
endure such a fustian rascal.

PISTOL

Thrust him down stairs! know we not Galloway
nags?

FALSTAFF

Quoit him down, Bardolph, like a shove-groat shilling: nay, an a' do nothing but speak nothing, a'
shall be nothing here.

BARDOLPH

Come, get you down stairs.

PISTOL

What! shall we have incision? shall we imbrue?
[Snatching up his sword
Then death rock me asleep, abridge my doleful
days!
Why, then, let grievous, ghastly, gaping wounds
Untwine the Sisters Three! Come, Atropos, I say!

HOSTESS

Here's goodly stuff toward!

FALSTAFF

Give me my rapier, boy.

DOLL

I pray thee, Jack, I pray thee, do not draw.

FALSTAFF

Get you down stairs. [Drawing, and driving PISTOL out

HOSTESS

Here's a goodly tumult! I'll forswear keeping house,
afore I'll be in these tirrits and frights. So; murder,

I warrant now. Alas, alas! put up your naked
weapons, put up your naked weapons.
[Exeunt PISTOL and BARDOLPH

DOLL

I pray thee, Jack, be quiet; the rascal's gone. Ah,
you whoreson little valiant villain, you!

HOSTESS

Are you not hurt i' the groin? methought a' made a
shrewd thrust at your belly.

Re-enter BARDOLPH

FALSTAFF

Have you turned him out o' doors?

BARDOLPH

Yea, sir. The rascal's drunk: you have hurt him, sir,
i' the shoulder.

FALSTAFF

A rascal! to brave me!

DOLL

Ah, you sweet little rogue, you! Alas, poor ape, how
thou sweatest! come, let me wipe thy face; come on,
you whoreson chops: ah, rogue! i' faith, I love thee:
thou art as valorous as Hector of Troy, worth five of
Agamemnon, and ten times better than the Nine
Worthies: ah, villain!

FALSTAFF

A rascally slave! I will toss the rogue in a blanket.

DOLL

Do, an thou darest for thy heart: an thou dost, I'll
canvass thee between a pair of sheets.

Enter Music

PAGE

The music is come, sir.

FALSTAFF

Let them play. Play, sirs. Sit on my knee, Doll. A
rascal bragging slave! the rogue fled from me like
quicksilver.

DOLL

I' faith, and thou followedst him like a church.
Thou whoreson little tidy Bartholomew boar-pig,
when wilt thou leave fighting o' days and foining o'
nights, and begin to patch up thine old body for
heaven?

Enter, behind, PRINCE HENRY and POINS, disguised

FALSTAFF

Peace, good Doll! do not speak like a death's-head;
do not bid me remember mine end.

DOLL

Sirrah, what humour's the prince of?

FALSTAFF

A good shallow young fellow: a' would have made
a good pantler, a' would ha' chipped bread well.

DOLL

They say Poins has a good wit.

FALSTAFF

He a good wit? hang him, baboon! his wit's as thick
as Tewksbury mustard; there's no more conceit in
him than is in a mallet.

DOLL

Why does the prince love him so, then?

FALSTAFF

Because their legs are both of a bigness; and a' plays at quoits well; and eats conger and fennel; and drinks off candles' ends for flap-dragons; and rides the wild-mare with the boys; and jumps upon joined-stools; and swears with a good grace; and wears his boots very smooth, like unto the sign of the leg; and breeds no bate with telling of discreet stories; and such other gambol faculties a' has, that show a weak mind and an able body, for the which the prince admits him: for the prince himself is such another; the weight of a hair will turn the scales between their avoirdupois.

PRINCE

Would not this nave of a wheel have his ears cut off?

POINS

Let's beat him before his whore.

PRINCE

Look, whether the withered elder hath not his poll clawed like a parrot.

POINS

Is it not strange that desire should so many years outlive performance?

FALSTAFF

Kiss me, Doll.

PRINCE

Saturn and Venus this year in conjunction! what says the almanac to that?

POINS

And, look, whether the fiery Trigon, his man, be not lisping to his master's old tables, his note-book, his counsel-keeper.

FALSTAFF

Thou dost give me flattering busses.

DOLL

By my troth, I kiss thee with a most constant heart.

FALSTAFF

I am old, I am old.

DOLL

I love thee better than I love e'er a scurvy young boy of them all.

FALSTAFF

What stuff wilt have a kirtle of? I shall receive money o' Thursday: shalt have a cap to-morrow. A merry song, come: it grows late; we'll to bed. Thou 'lt forget me when I am gone.

DOLL

By my troth, thou 'lt set me a-weeping, an thou sayest so: prove that ever I dress myself handsome till thy return: well, hearken at the end.

FALSTAFF

Some sack, Francis.

PRINCE and POINS

Anon, anon, sir.   [Coming forward

FALSTAFF

Ha! a bastard son of the king's? And art not thou Poins his brother?

PRINCE

Why, thou globe of sinful continents, what a life dost thou lead!

FALSTAFF

A better than thou: I am a gentleman; thou art a drawer.

PRINCE

Very true, sir; and I come to draw you out by the ears.

HOSTESS

O, the Lord preserve thy good grace! by my troth, welcome to London. Now, the Lord bless that sweet face of thine! O Jesu, are you come from Wales?

FALSTAFF

Thou whoreson mad compound of majesty, by this light flesh and corrupt blood, thou art welcome.

DOLL

How, you fat fool! I scorn you.

POINS

My lord, he will drive you out of your revenge and turn all to a merriment, if you take not the heat.

PRINCE

You whoreson candle-mine, you, how vilely did you speak of me even now before this honest, virtuous, civil gentlewoman!

HOSTESS

God's blessing of your good heart! and so she is, by my troth.

FALSTAFF

Didst thou hear me?

PRINCE

Yea, and you knew me, as you did when you ran away by Gadshill: you knew I was at your back, and spoke it on purpose to try my patience.

FALSTAFF

No, no, no; not so; I did not think thou wast within hearing.

PRINCE

I shall drive you then to confess the wilful abuse; and then I know how to handle you.

FALSTAFF

No abuse, Hal, o' mine honour; no abuse.

PRINCE

Not to dispraise me, and call me pantler and bread-chipper and I know not what?

FALSTAFF

No abuse, Hal.

POINS

No abuse?

FALSTAFF

No abuse, Ned, i' the world; honest Ned, none. I dispraised him before the wicked, that the wicked might not fall in love with him; in which doing, I have done the part of a careful friend and a true subject, and thy father is to give me thanks for it. No abuse, Hal: none, Ned, none: no, faith, boys, none.

PRINCE

See now, whether pure fear and entire cowardice doth not make thee wrong this virtuous gentle-woman to close with us. Is she of the wicked? is thine hostess here of the wicked? or is thy boy of the wicked? or honest Bardolph, whose zeal burns in his nose, of the wicked?

POINS

Answer, thou dead elm, answer.

FALSTAFF

The fiend hath pricked down Bardolph irrecoverable; and his face is Lucifer's privy-kitchen, where he doth nothing but roast malt-worms. For the boy, there is a good angel about him; but the devil outbids him too.

PRINCE

For the women?

FALSTAFF

For one of them, she is in hell already, and burns poor souls. For the other, I owe her money; and whether she be damned for that, I know not.

HOSTESS

No, I warrant you.

FALSTAFF

No, I think thou art not; I think thou art quit for that. Marry, there is another indictment upon thee, for suffering flesh to be eaten in thy house, contrary to the law; for the which I think thou wilt howl.

HOSTESS

All victuallers do so: what's a joint of mutton or two in a whole Lent?

PRINCE

You, gentlewoman,—

DOLL

What says your grace?

FALSTAFF

His grace says that which his flesh rebels against.

[Knocking within

HOSTESS

Who knocks so loud at door? Look to the door there, Francis.

Enter PETO

PRINCE

Peto, how now! what news?

PETO

The king your father is at Westminster;
And there are twenty weak and wearied posts
Come from the north: and, as I came along,
I met and overtook a dozen captains,
Bare-headed, sweating, knocking at the taverns,
And asking every one for Sir John Falstaff.

PRINCE

By heaven, Poins, I feel me much to blame,
So idly to profane the precious time;
When tempest of commotion, like the south
Borne with black vapour, doth begin to melt,
And drop upon our bare unarmed heads.
Give me my sword and cloak. Falstaff, good night.

[Exeunt PRINCE HENRY, POINS, PETO, and BARDOLPH

FALSTAFF

Now comes in the sweetest morsel of the night, and we must hence, and leave it unpicked. [Knocking within] More knocking at the door!

Re-enter BARDOLPH

How now! what's the matter?

BARDOLPH

You must away to court, sir, presently;
A dozen captains stay at door for you.

FALSTAFF

[To the PAGE] Pay the musicians, sirrah. Farewell, hostess; farewell, Doll. You see, my good wenches, how men of merit are sought after: the undeserver may sleep, when the man of action is called on. Farewell, good wenches: if I be not sent away post, I will see you again ere I go.

DOLL

I cannot speak; if my heart be not ready to burst,— well, sweet Jack, have a care of thyself.

FALSTAFF

Farewell, farewell. [Exeunt FALSTAFF and BARDOLPH

HOSTESS

Well, fare thee well: I have known thee these twenty nine years, come peascod-time; but an honester and truer-hearted man,—well, fare thee well.

BARDOLPH

[Within] Mistress Tearsheet!

HOSTESS

What's the matter?

BARDOLPH

[Within] Bid Mistress Tearsheet come to my master.

HOSTESS

O, run, Doll, run; run, good Doll: come. [She comes blubbered] Yea, will you come, Doll? [Exeunt

ACT III

Scene I. Westminster. The palace

Enter the KING in his nightgown, with a PAGE

KING

Go call the Earls of Surrey and of Warwick;
But, ere they come, bid them o'er-read these letters,
And well consider of them: make good speed.

[Exit PAGE

How many thousand of my poorest subjects
Are at this hour asleep! O sleep, O gentle sleep,
Nature's soft nurse, how have I frighted thee,
That thou no more wilt weigh my eyelids down,
And steep my senses in forgetfulness?
Why rather, sleep, liest thou in smoky cribs,
Upon uneasy pallets stretching thee,
And hush'd with buzzing night-flies to thy slumber,
Than in the perfumed chambers of the great,
Under the canopies of costly state,
And lull'd with sound of sweetest melody?
O thou dull god, why liest thou with the vile
In loathsome beds, and leavest the kingly couch
A watch-case or a common 'larum-bell?
Wilt thou upon the high and giddy mast
Seal up the ship-boy's eyes, and rock his brains
In cradle of the rude imperious surge,
And in the visitation of the winds,
Who take the ruffian billows by the top,

Curling their monstrous heads, and hanging them
With deafening clamour in the slippery clouds,
That, with the hurly, death itself awakes?
Canst thou, O partial sleep, give thy repose
To the wet sea-boy in an hour so rude;
And in the calmest and most stillest night,
With all appliances and means to boot,
Deny it to a king? Then happy low, lie down!
Uneasy lies the head that wears a crown.

Enter WARWICK *and* SURREY

WARWICK
Many good morrows to your majesty!

KING
Is it good morrow, lords?

WARWICK
'Tis one o'clock, and past.

KING
Why, then, good morrow to you all, my lords.
Have you read o'er the letters that I sent you?

WARWICK
We have, my liege.

KING
Then you perceive the body of our kingdom
How foul it is; what rank diseases grow,
And with what danger, near the heart of it.

WARWICK
It is but as a body yet distemper'd;
Which to his former strength may be restored
With good advice and little medicine:
My Lord Northumberland will soon be cool'd.

KING
O God! that one might read the book of fate,
And see the revolution of the times
Make mountains level, and the continent,
Weary of solid firmness, melt itself
Into the sea! and, other times, to see
The beachy girdle of the ocean
Too wide for Neptune's hips; how chances mock,
And changes fill the cup of alteration
With divers liquors! O, if this were seen,
The happiest youth, viewing his progress through,
What perils past, what crosses to ensue,
Would shut the book, and sit him down and die.
'Tis not ten years gone
Since Richard and Northumberland, great friends,
Did feast together, and in two years after
Were they at wars: it is but eight years since
This Percy was the man nearest my soul;
Who like a brother toil'd in my affairs,
And laid his love and life under my foot;
Yea, for my sake, even to the eyes of Richard
Gave him defiance. But which of you was by—
You, cousin Nevil, as I may remember—
                                    [*To* WARWICK
When Richard, with his eye brimful of tears,
Then check'd and rated by Northumberland,
Did speak these words, now proved a prophecy?
'Northumberland, thou ladder by the which
My cousin Bolingbroke ascends my throne;'
Though then, God knows, I had no such intent,

But that necessity so bow'd the state,
That I and greatness were compell'd to kiss:
'The time shall come,' thus did he follow it,
'The time will come, that foul sin, gathering head,
Shall break into corruption:' so went on,
Foretelling this same time's condition,
And the division of our amity.

WARWICK
There is a history in all men's lives,
Figuring the nature of the times decreased;
The which observed, a man may prophesy,
With a near aim, of the main chance of things
As yet not come to life, which in their seeds
And weak beginnings lie intreasured.
Such things become the hatch and brood of time;
And by the necessary form of this
King Richard might create a perfect guess
That great Northumberland, then false to him,
Would of that seed grow to a greater falseness;
Which should not find a ground to root upon,
Unless on you.

KING
          Are these things then necessities?
Then let us meet them like necessities:
And that same word even now cries out on us:
They say the bishop and Northumberland
Are fifty thousand strong.

WARWICK
                    It cannot be, my lord;
Rumour doth double, like the voice and echo,
The numbers of the fear'd. Please it your grace
To go to bed. Upon my soul, my lord,
The powers that you already have sent forth
Shall bring this prize in very easily.
To comfort you the more, I have received
A certain instance that Glendower is dead.
Your majesty hath been this fortnight ill;
And these unseason'd hours perforce must add
Unto your sickness.

KING
          I will take your counsel:
And were these inward wars once out of hand,
We would, dear lords, unto the Holy Land. [*Exeunt*

SCENE II. *Gloucestershire. Before* JUSTICE
SHALLOW'S *house*

Enter SHALLOW *and* SILENCE, *meeting*; MOULDY,
SHADOW, WART, FEEBLE, BULLCALF, *a* SERVANT *or two*
with them

SHALLOW
Come on, come on, come on, sir; give me your
hand, sir, give me your hand, sir: an early stirrer,
by the rood! And how doth my good cousin Silence?

SILENCE
Good morrow, good cousin Shallow.

SHALLOW
And how doth my cousin, your bedfellow? and your
fairest daughter and mine, my god-daughter Ellen?

SILENCE

Alas, a black ousel, cousin Shallow!

SHALLOW

By yea and nay, sir, I dare say my cousin William is become a good scholar: he is at Oxford still, is he not?

SILENCE

Indeed, sir, to my cost.

SHALLOW

A' must, then, to the inns o' court shortly: I was once of Clement's Inn, where I think they will talk of mad Shallow yet.

SILENCE

You were called 'lusty Shallow' then, cousin.

SHALLOW

By the mass, I was called any thing; and I would have done any thing indeed too, and roundly too. There was I, and little John Doit of Staffordshire, and black George Barnes, and Francis Pickbone, and Will Squele, a Cotswold man; you had not four such swinge-bucklers in all the inns o' court again: and I may say to you, we knew where the bona-robas were, and had the best of them all at commandment. Then was Jack Falstaff, now Sir John, a boy, and page to Thomas Mowbray, Duke of Norfolk.

SILENCE

This Sir John, cousin, that comes hither anon about soldiers?

SHALLOW

The same Sir John, the very same. I see him break Skogan's head at the court-gate, when a' was a crack not thus high: and the very same day did I fight with one Sampson Stockfish, a fruiterer, behind Gray's Inn. Jesu, Jesu, the mad days that I have spent! and to see how many of my old acquaintance are dead!

SILENCE

We shall all follow, cousin.

SHALLOW

Certain, 'tis certain; very sure, very sure: death, as the Psalmist saith, is certain to all; all shall die. How a good yoke of bullocks at Stamford fair?

SILENCE

By my troth, I was not there.

SHALLOW

Death is certain. Is old Double of your town living yet?

SILENCE

Dead, sir.

SHALLOW

Jesu, Jesu, dead! a' drew a good bow; and dead! a' shot a fine shoot: John a Gaunt loved him well, and betted much money on his head. Dead! a' would have clapped i' the clout at twelve score; and carried you a forehand shaft a fourteen and fourteen and a half, that it would have done a man's heart good to see. How a score of ewes now?

SILENCE

Thereafter as they be: a score of good ewes may be worth ten pounds.

SHALLOW

And is old Double dead?

SILENCE

Here come two of Sir John Falstaff's men, as I think.

Enter BARDOLPH, *and one with him*

BARDOLPH

Good morrow, honest gentlemen: I beseech you, which is Justice Shallow?

SHALLOW

I am Robert Shallow, sir; a poor esquire of this county, and one of the king's justices of the peace: what is your good pleasure with me?

BARDOLPH

My captain, sir, commends him to you; my captain, Sir John Falstaff, a tall gentleman, by heaven, and a most gallant leader.

SHALLOW

He greets me well, sir. I knew him a good back-sword man. How doth the good knight? may I ask how my lady his wife doth?

BARDOLPH

Sir, pardon; a soldier is better accommodated than with a wife.

SHALLOW

It is well said, in faith, sir; and it is well said indeed too. Better accommodated! it is good; yea, indeed, is it: good phrases are surely, and ever were, very commendable. Accommodated! it comes of 'accommodo:' very good; a good phrase.

BARDOLPH

Pardon me, sir; I have heard the word. Phrase call you it? by this good day, I know not the phrase; but I will maintain the word with my sword to be a soldier-like word, and a word of exceeding good command, by heaven. Accommodated; that is, when a man is, as they say, accommodated; or when a man is, being, whereby a' may be thought to be accommodated; which is an excellent thing.

SHALLOW

It is very just.

Enter FALSTAFF

Look, here comes good Sir John. Give me your good hand, give me your worship's good hand: by my troth, you like well and bear your years very well: welcome, good Sir John.

FALSTAFF

I am glad to see you well, good Master Robert Shallow: Master Surecard, as I think?

SHALLOW

No, Sir John; it is my cousin Silence, in commission with me.

FALSTAFF

Good Master Silence, it well befits you should be of the peace.

SILENCE

Your good worship is welcome.

FALSTAFF

Fie! this is hot weather, gentlemen. Have you provided me here half a dozen sufficient men?

SHALLOW

Marry, have we, sir. Will you sit?

FALSTAFF

Let me see them, I beseech you.

SHALLOW

Where's the roll? where's the roll? where's the roll? Let me see, let me see, let me see. So, so, so, so, so, so, so: yea, marry, sir: Ralph Mouldy! Let them appear as I call; let them do so, let them do so. Let me see; where is Mouldy?

MOULDY

Here, an 't please you.

SHALLOW

What think you, Sir John? a good-limbed fellow; young, strong, and of good friends.

FALSTAFF

Is thy name Mouldy?

MOULDY

Yea, an 't please you.

FALSTAFF

'Tis the more time thou wert used.

SHALLOW

Ha, ha, ha! most excellent, i' faith! things that are mouldy lack use: very singular good! in faith, well said, Sir John; very well said.

FALSTAFF

Prick him.

MOULDY

I was pricked well enough before, an you could have let me alone: my old dame will be undone now, for one to do her husbandry and her drudgery: you need not to have pricked me; there are other men fitter to go out than I.

FALSTAFF

Go to: peace, Mouldy; you shall go. Mouldy, it is time you were spent.

MOULDY

Spent!

SHALLOW

Peace, fellow, peace; stand aside: know you where you are? For the other, Sir John: let me see: Simon Shadow!

FALSTAFF

Yea, marry, let me have him to sit under: he's like to be a cold soldier.

SHALLOW

Where's Shadow?

SHADOW

Here, sir.

FALSTAFF

Shadow, whose son art thou?

SHADOW

My mother's son, sir.

FALSTAFF

Thy mother's son! like enough, and thy father's shadow: so the son of the female is the shadow of the male: it is often so, indeed; but much of the father's substance!

SHALLOW

Do you like him, Sir John?

FALSTAFF

Shadow will serve for summer; prick him, for we have a number of shadows to fill up the muster-book.

SHALLOW

Thomas Wart!

FALSTAFF

Where's he?

WART

Here, sir.

FALSTAFF

Is thy name Wart?

WART

Yea, sir.

FALSTAFF

Thou art a very ragged wart.

SHALLOW

Shall I prick him down, Sir John?

FALSTAFF

It were superfluous; for his apparel is built upon his back, and the whole frame stands upon pins: prick him no more.

SHALLOW

Ha, ha, ha! you can do it, sir; you can do it: I commend you well. Francis Feeble!

FEEBLE

Here, sir.

SHALLOW

What trade art thou, Feeble?

FEEBLE

A woman's tailor, sir.

SHALLOW

Shall I prick him, sir?

FALSTAFF

You may: but if he had been a man's tailor, he'ld ha' pricked you. Wilt thou make as many holes in an enemy's battle as thou hast done in a woman's petticoat?

FEEBLE

I will do my good will, sir: you can have no more.

FALSTAFF

Well said, good woman's tailor! well said, courageous Feeble! thou wilt be as valiant as the wrathful dove or most magnanimous mouse. Prick the woman's tailor: well, Master Shallow; deep, Master Shallow.

FEEBLE

I would Wart might have gone, sir.

FALSTAFF

I would thou wert a man's tailor, that thou mightst mend him and make him fit to go. I cannot put him to a private soldier, that is the leader of so many thousands: let that suffice, most forcible Feeble.

FEEBLE

It shall suffice, sir.

FALSTAFF

I am bound to thee, reverend Feeble. Who is next?

SHALLOW

Peter Bullcalf o' the green!

FALSTAFF

Yea, marry, let's see Bullcalf.

BULLCALF

Here, sir.

FALSTAFF

'Fore God, a likely fellow! Come, prick me Bullcalf till he roar again.

BULLCALF

O Lord! good my lord captain,—

FALSTAFF

What, dost thou roar before thou art pricked?

BULLCALF

O Lord, sir! I am a diseased man.

FALSTAFF

What disease hast thou?

BULLCALF

A whoreson cold, sir, a cough, sir, which I caught with ringing in the king's affairs upon his coronation-day, sir.

FALSTAFF

Come, thou shalt go to the wars in a gown; we will have away thy cold; and I will take such order that thy friends shall ring for thee. Is here all?

SHALLOW

Here is two more called than your number; you must have but four here, sir: and so, I pray you, go in with me to dinner.

FALSTAFF

Come, I will go drink with you, but I cannot tarry dinner. I am glad to see you, by my troth, Master Shallow.

SHALLOW

O, Sir John, do you remember since we lay all night in the windmill in Saint George's field?

FALSTAFF

No more of that, good Master Shallow, no more of that.

SHALLOW

Ha! 'twas a merry night. And is Jane Nightwork alive?

FALSTAFF

She lives, Master Shallow.

SHALLOW

She never could away with me.

FALSTAFF

Never, never; she would always say she could not abide Master Shallow.

SHALLOW

By the mass, I could anger her to the heart. She was then a bona-roba. Doth she hold her own well?

FALSTAFF

Old, old, Master Shallow.

SHALLOW

Nay, she must be old; she cannot choose but be old; certain she's old; and had Robin Nightwork by old Nightwork before I came to Clement's Inn.

SILENCE

That's fifty five year ago.

SHALLOW

Ha, cousin Silence, that thou hadst seen that that this knight and I have seen! Ha, Sir John, said I well?

FALSTAFF

We have heard the chimes at midnight, Master Shallow.

SHALLOW

That we have, that we have, that we have; in faith, Sir John, we have: our watch-word was 'Hem boys!' Come, let's to dinner; come, let's to dinner: Jesus, the days that we have seen! Come, come.

[Exeunt FALSTAFF and the JUSTICES

BULLCALF

Good master corporate Bardolph, stand my friend; and here's four Harry ten shillings in French crowns for you. In very truth, sir, I had as lief be hanged, sir, as go: and yet, for mine own part, sir, I do not care; but rather, because I am unwilling, and, for mine own part, have a desire to stay with my friends; else, sir, I did not care, for mine own part, so much.

BARDOLPH

Go to; stand aside.

MOULDY

And, good master corporal captain, for my old dame's sake, stand my friend: she has nobody to do any thing about her when I am gone; and she is old, and cannot help herself: you shall have forty, sir.

BARDOLPH

Go to; stand aside.

FEEBLE

By my troth, I care not; a man can die but once: we owe God a death: I'll ne'er bear a base mind: an 't be my destiny, so; an 't be not, so: no man's too good to serve 's prince; and let it go which way it will, he that dies this year is quit for the next.

BARDOLPH

Well said; thou 'rt a good fellow.

FEEBLE

Faith, I'll bear no base mind.

Re-enter FALSTAFF and the JUSTICES

FALSTAFF

Come, sir, which men shall I have?

SHALLOW

Four of which you please.

BARDOLPH

Sir, a word with you: I have three pound to free Mouldy and Bullcalf.

FALSTAFF

Go to; well.

SHALLOW

Come, Sir John, which four will you have?

FALSTAFF

Do you choose for me.

SHALLOW

Marry, then, Mouldy, Bullcalf, Feeble and Shadow.

FALSTAFF

Mouldy and Bullcalf: for you, Mouldy, stay at home till you are past service: and for your part, Bullcalf, grow till you come unto it: I will none of you.

SHALLOW

Sir John, Sir John, do not yourself wrong: they are your likeliest men, and I would have you served with the best.

FALSTAFF

Will you tell me, Master Shallow, how to choose a man? Care I for the limb, the thewes, the stature, bulk, and big assemblance of a man! Give me the spirit, Master Shallow. Here's Wart; you see what a ragged appearance it is: a' shall charge you and discharge you with the motion of a pewterer's hammer, come off and on swifter than he that gibbets on the brewer's bucket. And this same half-faced fellow, Shadow: give me this man: he presents no mark to the enemy; the foeman may with as great aim level at the edge of a penknife. And for a retreat; how swiftly will this Feeble the woman's tailor run off! O, give me the spare men, and spare me the great ones. Put me a caliver into Wart's hand, Bardolph.

BARDOLPH

Hold, Wart, traverse; thus, thus, thus.

FALSTAFF

Come, manage me your caliver. So: very well: go to: very good, exceeding good. O, give me always a little, lean, old, chapt, bald shot. Well said, i' faith, Wart; thou 'rt a good scab: hold, there's a tester for thee.

SHALLOW

He is not his craft's-master; he doth not do it right. I remember at Mile-end Green, when I lay at Clement's Inn,—I was then Sir Dagonet in Arthur's show,—there was a little quiver fellow, and a' would manage you his piece thus; and a' would about and about, and come you in and come you in: 'rah, tah, tah,' would a' say; 'bounce' would a' say; and away again would a' go, and again would a' come: I shall ne'er see such a fellow.

FALSTAFF

These fellows will do well, Master Shallow. God keep you, Master Silence: I will not use many words with you. Fare you well, gentlemen both: I thank you: I must a dozen mile to-night. Bardolph, give the soldiers coats.

SHALLOW

Sir John, the Lord bless you! God prosper your affairs! God send us peace! At your return visit our house; let our old acquaintance be renewed: peradventure I will with ye to the court.

FALSTAFF

'Fore God, I would you would, Master Shallow.

SHALLOW

Go to; I have spoke at a word. God keep you.

FALSTAFF

Fare you well, gentle gentlemen. [*Exeunt* JUSTICES] On, Bardolph; lead the men away. [*Exeunt* BAR-

DOLPH, RECRUITS, &c.] As I return, I will fetch off these justices: I do see the bottom of Justice Shallow. Lord, Lord, how subject we old men are to this vice of lying! This same starved justice hath done nothing but prate to me of the wildness of his youth, and the feats he hath done about Turnbull Street; and every third word a lie, duer paid to the hearer than the Turk's tribute. I do remember him at Clement's Inn like a man made after supper of a cheese-paring: when a' was naked, he was, for all the world, like a forked radish, with a head fantastically carved upon it with a knife: a' was so forlorn, that his dimensions to any thick sight were invisible: a' was the very genius of famine; yet lecherous as a monkey, and the whores called him mandrake: a' came ever in the rearward of the fashion, and sung those tunes to the overscutched huswives that he heard the carmen whistle, and sware they were his fancies or his good-nights. And now is this Vice's dagger become a squire, and talks as familiarly of John a Gaunt as if he had been sworn brother to him; and I'll be sworn a' ne'er saw him but once in the Tilt-yard; and then he burst his head for crowding among the marshal's men. I saw it, and told John a Gaunt he beat his own name; for you might have thrust him and all his apparel into an eel-skin; the case of a treble hautboy was a mansion for him, a court: and now has he land and beefs. Well, I'll be acquainted with him, if I return; and it shall go hard but I will make him a philosopher's two stones to me: if the young dace be a bait for the old pike, I see no reason in the law of nature but I may snap at him. Let time shape, and there an end.

[*Exit*

ACT IV

SCENE I. *Yorkshire. Gaultree Forest*

Enter the ARCHBISHOP OF YORK, MOWBRAY, HASTINGS, *and others*

ARCHBISHOP

What is this forest call'd?

HASTINGS

'Tis Gaultree Forest, an 't shall please your grace.

ARCHBISHOP

Here stand, my lords; and send discoverers forth To know the numbers of our enemies.

HASTINGS

We have sent forth already.

ARCHBISHOP

'Tis well done. My friends and brethren in these great affairs, I must acquaint you that I have received New-dated letters from Northumberland; Their cold intent, tenour and substance, thus: Here doth he wish his person, with such powers As might hold sortance with his quality, The which he could not levy; whereupon

He is retired, to ripe his growing fortunes,
To Scotland: and concludes in hearty prayers
That your attempts may overlive the hazard
And fearful meeting of their opposite.

MOWBRAY

Thus do the hopes we have in him touch ground
And dash themselves to pieces.

Enter a MESSENGER

HASTINGS

Now, what news?

MESSENGER

West of this forest, scarcely off a mile,
In goodly form comes on the enemy;
And, by the ground they hide, I judge their number
Upon or near the rate of thirty thousand.

MOWBRAY

The just proportion that we gave them out.
Let us sway on and face them in the field.

ARCHBISHOP

What well-appointed leader fronts us here?

Enter WESTMORELAND

MOWBRAY

I think it is my Lord of Westmoreland.

WESTMORELAND

Health and fair greeting from our general,
The prince, Lord John and Duke of Lancaster.

ARCHBISHOP

Say on, my Lord of Westmoreland, in peace:
What doth concern your coming?

WESTMORELAND

Then, my lord,
Unto your grace do I in chief address
The substance of my speech. If that rebellion
Came like itself, in base and abject routs,
Led on by bloody youth, guarded with rags,
And countenanced by boys and beggary;
I say, if damn'd commotion so appear'd,
In his true, native and most proper shape,
You, reverend father, and these noble lords
Had not been here, to dress the ugly form
Of base and bloody insurrection
With your fair honours. You, lord Archbishop,
Whose see is by a civil peace maintain'd,
Whose beard the silver hand of peace hath touch'd,
Whose learning and good letters peace hath tutor'd,
Whose white investments figure innocence,
The dove and very blessed spirit of peace,
Wherefore do you so ill translate yourself
Out of the speech of peace that bears such grace,
Into the harsh and boisterous tongue of war;
Turning your books to graves, your ink to blood,
Your pens to lances, and your tongue divine
To a loud trumpet and a point of war?

ARCHBISHOP

Wherefore do I this? so the question stands.
Briefly to this end: we are all diseased,
And with our surfeiting and wanton hours
Have brought ourselves into a burning fever,
And we must bleed for it; of which disease

Our late king, Richard, being infected, died.
But, my most noble Lord of Westmoreland,
I take not on me here as a physician,
Nor do I as an enemy to peace
Troop in the throngs of military men;
But rather show a while like fearful war,
To diet rank minds sick of happiness,
And purge the obstructions which begin to stop
Our very veins of life. Hear me more plainly.
I have in equal balance justly weigh'd
What wrongs our arms may do, what wrongs we
          suffer,
And find our griefs heavier than our offences.
We see which way the stream of time doth run,
And are enforced from our most quiet there
By the rough torrent of occasion;
And have the summary of all our griefs,
When time shall serve, to show in articles;
Which long ere this we offer'd to the king,
And might by no suit gain our audience:
When we are wrong'd and would unfold our griefs,
We are denied access unto his person
Even by those men that most have done us wrong.
The dangers of the days but newly gone,
Whose memory is written on the earth
With yet appearing blood, and the examples
Of every minute's instance, present now,
Hath put us in these ill-beseeming arms,
Not to break peace or any branch of it,
But to establish here a peace indeed,
Concurring both in name and quality.

WESTMORELAND

When ever yet was your appeal denied?
Wherein have you been galled by the king?
What peer hath been suborn'd to grate on you,
That you should seal this lawless bloody book
Of forged rebellion with a seal divine,
And consecrate commotion's bitter edge?

ARCHBISHOP

My brother general, the commonwealth,
To brother born an household cruelty,
I make my quarrel in particular.

WESTMORELAND

There is no need of any such redress;
Or if there were, it not belongs to you.

MOWBRAY

Why not to him in part, and to us all
That feel the bruises of the days before,
And suffer the condition of these times
To lay a heavy and unequal hand
Upon our honours?

WESTMORELAND

O, my good Lord Mowbray,
Construe the times to their necessities,
And you shall say indeed, it is the time,
And not the king, that doth you injuries.
Yet for your part, it not appears to me
Either from the king or in the present time
That you should have an inch of any ground
To build a grief on: were you not restored

To all the Duke of Norfolk's signories,
Your noble and right well remember'd father's?
                MOWBRAY
What thing, in honour, had my father lost,
That need to be revived and breathed in me?
The king that loved him, as the state stood then,
Was force perforce compell'd to banish him:
And then that Henry Bolingbroke and he,
Being mounted and both roused in their seats,
Their neighing coursers daring of the spur,
Their armed staves in charge, their beavers down,
Their eyes of fire sparkling through sights of steel
And the loud trumpet blowing them together,
Then, then, when there was nothing could have stay'd
My father from the breast of Bolingbroke,
O, when the king did throw his warder down,
His own life hung upon the staff he threw;
Then threw he down himself and all their lives
That by indictment and by dint of sword
Have since miscarried under Bolingbroke.
             WESTMORELAND
You speak, Lord Mowbray, now you know not what.
The Earl of Hereford was reputed then
In England the most valiant gentleman:
Who knows on whom fortune would then have smiled?
But if your father had been victor there,
He ne'er had borne it out of Coventry:
For all the country in a general voice
Cried hate upon him; and all their prayers and love
Were set on Hereford, whom they doted on
And bless'd and graced indeed, more than the king.
But this is mere digression from my purpose.
Here come I from our princely general
To know your griefs; to tell you from his grace
That he will give you audience; and wherein
It shall appear that your demands are just,
You shall enjoy them, every thing set off
That might so much as think you enemies.
                MOWBRAY
But he hath forced us to compel this offer;
And it proceeds from policy, not love.
             WESTMORELAND
Mowbray, you overween to take it so;
This offer comes from mercy, not from fear:
For, lo! within a ken our army lies,
Upon mine honour, all too confident
To give admittance to a thought of fear.
Our battle is more full of names than yours,
Our men more perfect in the use of arms,
Our armour all as strong, our cause the best;
Then reason will our hearts should be as good:
Say you not then our offer is compell'd.
                MOWBRAY
Well, by my will we shall admit no parley.
             WESTMORELAND
That argues but the shame of your offence:
A rotten case abides no handling.

                HASTINGS
Hath the Prince John a full commission,
In very ample virtue of his father,
To hear and absolutely to determine
Of what conditions we shall stand upon?
             WESTMORELAND
That is intended in the general's name:
I muse you make so slight a question.
              ARCHBISHOP
Then take, my Lord of Westmoreland, this schedule,
For this contains our general grievances:
Each several article herein redress'd,
All members of our cause, both here and hence,
That are insinewed to this action,
Acquitted by a true substantial form,
And present execution of our wills
To us and to our purposes confined,
We come within our awful banks again,
And knit our powers to the arm of peace.
             WESTMORELAND
This will I show the general. Please you, lords,
In sight of both our battles we may meet;
And either end in peace, which God so frame!
Or to the place of difference call the swords
Which must decide it.
              ARCHBISHOP
         My lord, we will do so.
               [Exit WESTMORELAND
                MOWBRAY
There is a thing within my bosom tells me
That no conditions of our peace can stand.
                HASTINGS
Fear you not that: if we can make our peace
Upon such large terms and so absolute
As our conditions shall consist upon,
Our peace shall stand as firm as rocky mountains.
                MOWBRAY
Yea, but our valuation shall be such
That every slight and false-derived cause,
Yea, every idle, nice and wanton reason
Shall to the king taste of this action;
That, were our royal faiths martyrs in love,
We shall be winnow'd with so rough a wind
That even our corn shall seem as light as chaff
And good from bad find no partition.
              ARCHBISHOP
No, no, my lord. Note this; the king is weary
Of dainty and such picking grievances:
For he hath found to end one doubt by death
Revives two greater in the heirs of life,
And therefore will he wipe his tables clean,
And keep no tell-tale to his memory
That may repeat and history his loss
To new remembrance; for full well he knows
He cannot so precisely weed this land
As his misdoubts present occasion:
His foes are so enrooted with his friends
That, plucking to unfix an enemy,
He doth unfasten so and shake a friend.
So that this land, like an offensive wife

That hath enraged him on to offer strokes,
As he is striking, holds his infant up,
And hangs resolved correction in the arm
That was uprear'd to execution.

HASTINGS

Besides, the king hath wasted all his rods
On late offenders, that he now doth lack
The very instruments of chastisement:
So that his power, like to a fangless lion,
May offer, but not hold.

ARCHBISHOP
'Tis very true:
And therefore be assured, my good lord marshal,
If we do now make our atonement well,
Our peace will, like a broken limb united,
Grow stronger for the breaking.

MOWBRAY
Be it so.
Here is return'd my Lord of Westmoreland.

Re-enter WESTMORELAND

WESTMORELAND

The prince is here at hand: pleaseth your lordship
To meet his grace just distance 'tween our armies.

MOWBRAY

Your grace of York, in God's name, then, set forward.

ARCHBISHOP

Before, and greet his grace: my lord, we come.
[*Exeunt*

SCENE II. *Another part of the forest*

Enter, from one side, MOWBRAY, *attended; afterwards, the*
ARCHBISHOP, HASTINGS, *and others; from the other side,*
PRINCE JOHN OF LANCASTER, *and* WESTMORELAND;
OFFICERS, *and others with them*

LANCASTER

You are well encounter'd here, my cousin Mow-
bray:
Good day to you, gentle lord archbishop;
And so to you, Lord Hastings, and to all.
My Lord of York, it better show'd with you
When that your flock, assembled by the bell,
Encircled you to hear with reverence
Your exposition on the holy text,
Than now to see you here an iron man,
Cheering a rout of rebels with your drum,
Turning the word to sword and life to death.
That man that sits within a monarch's heart,
And ripens in the sunshine of his favour,
Would he abuse the countenance of the king,
Alack, what mischiefs might he set abroach
In shadow of such greatness! With you, lord bishop,
It is even so. Who hath not heard it spoken
How deep you were within the books of God?
To us the speaker in his parliament;
To us the imagined voice of God himself;
The very opener and intelligencer
Between the grace, the sanctities of heaven

And our dull workings. O, who shall believe
But you misuse the reverence of your place,
Employ the countenance and grace of heaven,
As a false favourite doth his prince's name,
In deeds dishonourable? You have ta'en up,
Under the counterfeited zeal of God,
The subjects of his substitute, my father,
And both against the peace of heaven and him
Have here up-swarm'd them.

ARCHBISHOP
Good my Lord of Lancaster,
I am not here against your father's peace;
But, as I told my Lord of Westmoreland,
The time misorder'd doth, in common sense,
Crowd us and crush us to this monstrous form,
To hold our safety up. I sent your grace
The parcels and particulars of our grief,
The which hath been with scorn shoved from the
court,
Whereon this Hydra son of war is born;
Whose dangerous eyes may well be charm'd asleep
With grant of our most just and right desires,
And true obedience, of this madness cured,
Stoop tamely to the foot of majesty.

MOWBRAY

If not, we ready are to try our fortunes
To the last man.

HASTINGS
And though we here fall down,
We have supplies to second our attempt:
If they miscarry, theirs shall second them;
And so success of mischief shall be born,
And heir from heir shall hold this quarrel up,
Whiles England shall have generation.

LANCASTER

You are too shallow, Hastings, much too shallow,
To sound the bottom of the after-times.

WESTMORELAND

Pleaseth your grace to answer them directly
How far forth you do like their articles.

LANCASTER

I like them all, and do allow them well;
And swear here, by the honour of my blood,
My father's purposes have been mistook;
And some about him have too lavishly
Wrested his meaning and authority.
My lord, these griefs shall be with speed redress'd;
Upon my soul, they shall. If this may please you,
Discharge your powers unto their several counties,
As we will ours: and here between the armies
Let's drink together friendly and embrace,
That all their eyes may bear those tokens home
Of our restored love and amity.

ARCHBISHOP

I take your princely word for these redresses.

LANCASTER

I give it you, and will maintain my word:
And thereupon I drink unto your grace.

HASTINGS

Go, captain, and deliver to the army

This news of peace: let them have pay, and part:
I know it will well please them. Hie thee, captain.

[*Exit* OFFICER

ARCHBISHOP

To you, my noble Lord of Westmoreland.

WESTMORELAND

I pledge your grace; and, if you knew what pains
I have bestow'd to breed this present peace,
You would drink freely: but my love to ye
Shall show itself more openly hereafter.

ARCHBISHOP

I do not doubt you.

WESTMORELAND

        I am glad of it.
Health to my lord and gentle cousin, Mowbray.

MOWBRAY

You wish me health in very happy season;
For I am, on the sudden, something ill.

ARCHBISHOP

Against ill chances men are ever merry;
But heaviness foreruns the good event.

WESTMORELAND

Therefore be merry, coz; since sudden sorrow
Serves to say thus, 'some good thing comes to-
    morrow.'

ARCHBISHOP

Believe me, I am passing light in spirit.

MOWBRAY

So much the worse, if your own rule be true.

[*Shouts within*

LANCASTER

The word of peace is render'd: hark, how they
    shout!

MOWBRAY

This had been cheerful after victory.

ARCHBISHOP

A peace is of the nature of a conquest;
For then both parties nobly are subdued,
And neither party loser.

LANCASTER

        Go, my lord,
And let our army be discharged too.

[*Exit* WESTMORELAND

And, good my lord, so please you, let our trains
March by us, that we may peruse the men
We should have coped withal.

ARCHBISHOP

        Go, good Lord Hastings,
And, ere they be dismiss'd, let them march by.

[*Exit* HASTINGS

LANCASTER

I trust, lords, we shall lie to-night together.

Re-enter WESTMORELAND

Now, cousin, wherefore stands our army still?

WESTMORELAND

The leaders, having charge from you to stand,
Will not go off until they hear you speak.

LANCASTER

They know their duties.

Re-enter HASTINGS

HASTINGS

My lord, our army is dispersed already:
Like youthful steers unyoked, they take their courses
East, west, north, south; or, like a school broke up,
Each hurries toward his home and sporting-place.

WESTMORELAND

Good tidings, my Lord Hastings; for the which
I do arrest thee, traitor, of high treason:
And you, lord archbishop, and you, Lord Mowbray,
Of capital treason I attach you both.

MOWBRAY

Is this proceeding just and honourable?

WESTMORELAND

Is your assembly so?

ARCHBISHOP

Will you thus break your faith?

LANCASTER

        I pawn'd thee none:
I promised you redress of these same grievances
Whereof you did complain; which, by mine honour,
I will perform with a most Christian care.
But for you, rebels, look to taste the due
Meet for rebellion and such acts as yours.
Most shallowly did you these arms commence,
Fondly brought here and foolishly sent hence.
Strike up our drums, pursue the scatter'd stray:
God, and not we, hath safely fought to-day.
Some guard these traitors to the block of death,
Treason's true bed and yielder up of breath. [*Exeunt*

SCENE III. *Another part of the forest*

Alarum. Excursions. Enter FALSTAFF *and* COLEVILE,
meeting

FALSTAFF

What's your name, sir? of what condition are you,
and of what place, I pray?

COLEVILE

I am a knight, sir; and my name is Colevile of the
dale.

FALSTAFF

Well, then, Colevile is your name, a knight is your
degree, and your place the dale: Colevile shall be
still your name, a traitor your degree, and the dungeon your place, a place deep enough; so shall you
be still Colevile of the dale.

COLEVILE

Are not you Sir John Falstaff?

FALSTAFF

As good a man as he, sir, whoe'er I am. Do ye yield,
sir? or shall I sweat for you? If I do sweat, they are
the drops of thy lovers, and they weep for thy death:
therefore rouse up fear and trembling, and do observance to my mercy.

COLEVILE

I think you are Sir John Falstaff, and in that
thought yield me.

FALSTAFF

I have a whole school of tongues in this belly of mine, and not a tongue of them all speaks any other word but my name. An I had but a belly of any indifferency, I were simply the most active fellow in Europe: my womb, my womb, my womb, undoes me. Here comes our general.

Enter PRINCE JOHN OF LANCASTER, WESTMORELAND, BLUNT, *and others*

LANCASTER

The heat is past; follow no further now: Call in the powers, good cousin Westmoreland.

[*Exit* WESTMORELAND

Now, Falstaff, where have you been all this while? When every thing is ended, then you come: These tardy tricks of yours will, on my life, One time or other break some gallows' back.

FALSTAFF

I would be sorry, my lord, but it should be thus: I never knew yet but rebuke and check was the reward of valour. Do you think me a swallow, an arrow, or a bullet? have I, in my poor and old motion, the expedition of thought? I have speeded hither with the very extremest inch of possibility; I have foundered nine score and odd posts: and here, travel-tainted as I am, have, in my pure and immaculate valour, taken Sir John Colevile of the dale, a most furious knight and valorous enemy. But what of that? he saw me, and yielded; that I may justly say, with the hook-nosed fellow of Rome, 'I came, saw, and overcame.'

LANCASTER

It was more of his courtesy than your deserving.

FALSTAFF

I know not: here he is, and here I yield him: and I beseech your grace, let it be booked with the rest of this day's deeds; or, by the Lord, I will have it in a particular ballad else, with mine own picture on the ever top on 't, Colevile kissing my foot: to the which course if I be enforced, if you do not all show like gilt two-pences to me, and I in the clear sky of fame o'ershine you as much as the full moon doth the cinders of the element, which show like pins' heads to her, believe not the word of the noble: therefore let me have right, and let desert mount.

LANCASTER

Thine's too heavy to mount.

FALSTAFF

Let it shine, then.

LANCASTER

Thine's too thick to shine.

FALSTAFF

Let it do something, my good lord, that may do me good, and call it what you will.

LANCASTER

Is thy name Colevile?

COLEVILE

It is, my lord.

LANCASTER

A famous rebel art thou, Colevile.

FALSTAFF

And a famous true subject took him.

COLEVILE

I am, my lord, but as my betters are That led me hither: had they been ruled by me, You should have won them dearer than you have.

FALSTAFF

I know not how they sold themselves: but thou, like a kind fellow, gavest thyself away gratis; and I thank thee for thee.

Re-enter WESTMORELAND

LANCASTER

Now, have you left pursuit?

WESTMORELAND

Retreat is made and execution stay'd.

LANCASTER

Send Colevile with his confederates To York, to present execution: Blunt, lead him hence; and see you guard him sure.

[*Exeunt* BLUNT *and others with* COLEVILE

And now dispatch we toward the court, my lords: I hear the king my father is sore sick: Our news shall go before us to his majesty, Which, cousin, you shall bear to comfort him; And we with sober speed will follow you.

FALSTAFF

My lord, I beseech you, give me leave to go Through Gloucestershire: and, when you come to court, Stand my good lord, pray, in your good report.

LANCASTER

Fare you well, Falstaff: I, in my condition, Shall better speak of you than you deserve.

[*Exeunt all except* FALSTAFF

FALSTAFF

I would you had but the wit: 'twere better than your dukedom. Good faith, this same young sober-blooded boy doth not love me; nor a man cannot make him laugh; but that's no marvel, he drinks no wine. There's never none of these demure boys come to any proof; for thin drink doth so over-cool their blood, and making many fish-meals, that they fall into a kind of male green-sickness; and then, when they marry, they get wenches: they are generally fools and cowards; which some of us should be too, but for inflammation. A good sherris-sack hath a two-fold operation in it. It ascends me into the brain; dries me there all the foolish and dull and crudy vapours which environ it; makes it apprehensive, quick, forgetive, full of nimble, fiery and delectable shapes; which, delivered o'er to the voice, the tongue, which is the birth, becomes excellent wit. The second property of your excellent sherris is, the warming of the blood; which, before cold and settled, left the liver white and pale, which is the badge of pusillanimity and cowardice; but the sherris warms it and makes it course from the inwards to the parts extreme: it illumineth the face, which as a beacon gives warning to all the rest of this little kingdom, man, to arm; and then the vital

commoners and inland petty spirits muster me all
to their captain, the heart, who, great and puffed
up with this retinue, doth any deed of courage; and
this valour comes of sherris. So that skill in the
weapon is nothing without sack, for that sets it
a-work; and learning a mere hoard of gold kept by
a devil, till sack commences it and sets it in act and
use. Hereof comes it that Prince Harry is valiant;
for the cold blood he did naturally inherit of his
father, he hath, like lean sterile and bare land, manured, husbanded and tilled with excellent endeavour of drinking good and good store of fertile
sherris, that he is become very hot and valiant. If I
had a thousand sons, the first humane principle I
would teach them should be, to forswear thin potations, and to addict themselves to sack.

Enter BARDOLPH

How now, Bardolph?

BARDOLPH

The army is discharged all and gone.

FALSTAFF

Let them go. I'll through Gloucestershire; and there
will I visit Master Robert Shallow, esquire: I have
him already tempering between my finger and my
thumb, and shortly will I seal with him. Come
away.   [*Exeunt*

SCENE IV. *Westminster. The Jerusalem Chamber*

Enter the KING, *the* PRINCES THOMAS OF CLARENCE *and*
HUMPHREY OF GLOUCESTER, WARWICK, *and others*

KING

Now, lords, if God doth give successful end
To this debate that bleedeth at our doors,
We will our youth lead on to higher fields
And draw no swords but what are sanctified.
Our navy is address'd, our power collected,
Our substitutes in absence well invested,
And every thing lies level to our wish:
Only, we want a little personal strength;
And pause us, till these rebels, now afoot,
Come underneath the yoke of government.

WARWICK

Both which we doubt not but your majesty
Shall soon enjoy.

KING

                    Humphrey, my son of Gloucester,
Where is the prince your brother?

GLOUCESTER

I think he's gone to hunt, my lord, at Windsor.

KING

And how accompanied?

GLOUCESTER

                    I do not know, my lord.

KING

Is not his brother, Thomas of Clarence, with him?

GLOUCESTER

No, my good lord; he is in presence here.

CLARENCE

What would my lord and father?

KING

Nothing but well to thee, Thomas of Clarence.
How chance thou art not with the prince thy
    brother?
He loves thee, and thou dost neglect him, Thomas;
Thou hast a better place in his affection
Than all thy brothers: cherish it, my boy,
And noble offices thou mayst effect
Of mediation, after I am dead,
Between his greatness and thy other brethren:
Therefore omit him not; blunt not his love,
Nor lose the good advantage of his grace
By seeming cold or careless of his will;
For he is gracious, if he be observed:
He hath a tear for pity, and a hand
Open as day for melting charity:
Yet notwithstanding, being incensed, he's flint,
As humorous as winter, and as sudden
As flaws congealed in the spring of day.
His temper, therefore, must be well observed:
Chide him for faults, and do it reverently,
When you perceive his blood inclined to mirth;
But, being moody, give him line and scope,
Till that his passions, like a whale on ground,
Confound themselves with working. Learn this,
    Thomas,
And thou shalt prove a shelter to thy friends,
A hoop of gold to bind thy brothers in,
That the united vessel of their blood,
Mingled with venom of suggestion—
As, force perforce, the age will pour it in—
Shall never leak, though it do work as strong
As aconitum or rash gunpowder.

CLARENCE

I shall observe him with all care and love.

KING

Why art thou not at Windsor with him, Thomas?

CLARENCE

He is not there to-day; he dines in London.

KING

And how accompanied? canst thou tell that?

CLARENCE

With Poins, and other his continual followers.

KING

Most subject is the fattest soil to weeds;
And he, the noble image of my youth,
Is overspread with them: therefore my grief
Stretches itself beyond the hour of death:
The blood weeps from my heart when I do shape,
In forms imaginary, the unguided days
And rotten times that you shall look upon,
When I am sleeping with my ancestors.
For when his headstrong riot hath no curb,
When rage and hot blood are his counsellors,
When means and lavish manners meet together,
O, with what wings shall his affections fly
Towards fronting peril and opposed decay!

WARWICK

My gracious lord, you look beyond him quite:
The prince but studies his companions
Like a strange tongue, wherein, to gain the lan-
    guage,
'Tis needful that the most immodest word
Be look'd upon and learn'd; which once attain'd,
Your highness knows, comes to no further use
But to be known and hated. So, like gross terms,
The prince will in the perfectness of time
Cast off his followers; and their memory
Shall as a pattern or a measure live,
By which his grace must mete the lives of others,
Turning past evils to advantages.

KING

'Tis seldom when the bee doth leave her comb
In the dead carrion.

Enter WESTMORELAND
    Who's here? Westmoreland?

WESTMORELAND

Health to my sovereign, and new happiness
Added to that that I am to deliver!
Prince John your son doth kiss your grace's hand:
Mowbray, the Bishop Scroop, Hastings and all
Are brought to the correction of your law;
There is not now a rebel's sword unsheathed,
But Peace puts forth her olive every where.
The manner how this action hath been borne
Here at more leisure may your highness read,
With every course in his particular.

KING

O Westmoreland, thou art a summer bird,
Which ever in the haunch of winter sings
The lifting up of day.

Enter HARCOURT
    Look, here's more news.

HARCOURT

From enemies heaven keep your majesty;
And, when they stand against you, may they fall
As those that I am come to tell you of!
The Earl Northumberland and the Lord Bardolph,
With a great power of English and of Scots,
Are by the sheriff of Yorkshire overthrown:
The manner and true order of the fight,
This packet, please it you, contains at large.

KING

And wherefore should these good news make me
    sick?
Will Fortune never come with both hands full,
But write her fair words still in foulest letters?
She either gives a stomach and no food;
Such are the poor, in health; or else a feast
And takes away the stomach; such are the rich,
That have abundance and enjoy it not.
I should rejoice now at this happy news;
And now my sight fails, and my brain is giddy:
O me! come near me; now I am much ill.

GLOUCESTER

Comfort, your majesty!

CLARENCE

    O my royal father!

WESTMORELAND

My sovereign lord, cheer up yourself, look up.

WARWICK

Be patient, princes; you do know, these fits
Are with his highness very ordinary.
Stand from him, give him air; he'll straight be well.

CLARENCE

No, no, he cannot long hold out these pangs:
The incessant care and labour of his mind
Hath wrought the mure, that should confine it in,
So thin that life looks through and will break out.

GLOUCESTER

The people fear me; for they do observe
Unfather'd heirs and loathly births of nature:
The seasons change their manners, as the year
Had found some months asleep and leap'd them
    over.

CLARENCE

The river hath thrice flow'd, no ebb between;
And the old folk, time's doting chronicles,
Say it did so a little time before
That our great-grandsire, Edward, sick'd and died.

WARWICK

Speak lower, princes, for the king recovers.

GLOUCESTER

This apoplexy will certain be his end.

KING

I pray you, take me up, and bear me hence
Into some other chamber: softly, pray.   [*Exeunt*

SCENE V. *Another chamber*

The KING *lying on a bed:* CLARENCE, GLOUCESTER,
WARWICK, *and others in attendance*

KING

Let there be no noise made, my gentle friends;
Unless some dull and favourable hand
Will whisper music to my weary spirit.

WARWICK

Call for the music in the other room.

KING

Set me the crown upon my pillow here.

CLARENCE

His eye is hollow, and he changes much.

WARWICK

Less noise, less noise!

Enter PRINCE HENRY

PRINCE

    Who saw the Duke of Clarence?

CLARENCE

I am here, brother, full of heaviness.

PRINCE

How now! rain within doors, and none abroad!
How doth the king?

GLOUCESTER

Exceeding ill.

PRINCE

Heard he the good news yet?
Tell it him.

GLOUCESTER

He alter'd much upon the hearing it.

PRINCE

If he be sick with joy, he'll recover without physic.

WARWICK

Not so much noise, my lords: sweet prince, speak
    low;
The king your father is disposed to sleep.

CLARENCE

Let us withdraw into the other room.

WARWICK

Will 't please your grace to go along with us?

PRINCE

No; I will sit and watch here by the king.
                    [Exeunt all except the PRINCE
Why doth the crown lie there upon his pillow,
Being so troublesome a bedfellow?
O polish'd perturbation! golden care!
That keep'st the ports of slumber open wide
To many a watchful night! sleep with it now!
Yet not so sound and half so deeply sweet
As he whose brow with homely biggen bound
Snores out the watch of night. O majesty!
When thou dost pinch thy bearer, thou dost sit
Like a rich armour worn in heat of day,
That scalds with safety. By his gates of breath
There lies a downy feather which stirs not:
Did he suspire, that light and weightless down
Perforce must move. My gracious lord! my father!
This sleep is sound indeed; this is a sleep,
That from this golden rigol hath divorced
So many English kings. Thy due from me
Is tears and heavy sorrows of the blood,
Which nature, love, and filial tenderness,
Shall, O dear father, pay thee plenteously:
My due from thee is this imperial crown,
Which, as immediate from thy place and blood,
Derives itself to me. Lo, here it sits,
Which God shall guard: and put the world's whole
    strength
Into one giant arm, it shall not force
This lineal honour from me: this from thee
Will I to mine leave, as 'tis left to me.   [Exit

KING

Warwick! Gloucester! Clarence!
    Re-enter WARWICK, GLOUCESTER, CLARENCE,
                   and the rest

CLARENCE

Doth the king call?

WARWICK

What would your majesty? How fares your grace?

KING

Why did you leave me here alone, my lords?

CLARENCE

We left the prince my brother here, my liege,
Who undertook to sit and watch by you.

KING

The Prince of Wales! Where is he? let me see him:
He is not here.

WARWICK

This door is open; he is gone this way.

GLOUCESTER

He came not through the chamber where we stay'd.

KING

Where is the crown? who took it from my pillow?

WARWICK

When we withdrew, my liege, we left it here.

KING

The prince hath ta'en it hence: go, seek him out.
Is he so hasty that he doth suppose
My sleep my death?
Find him, my Lord of Warwick; chide him hither.
                        [Exit WARWICK
This part of his conjoins with my disease,
And helps to end me. See, sons, what things you
    are!
How quickly nature falls into revolt
When gold becomes her object!
For this the foolish over-careful fathers
Have broke their sleep with thoughts, their brains
    with care,
Their bones with industry;
For this they have engrossed and piled up
The canker'd heaps of strange-achieved gold;
For this they have been thoughtful to invest
Their sons with arts and martial exercises:
When, like the bee, culling from every flower
The virtuous sweets,
Our thighs pack'd with wax, our mouths with
    honey,
We bring it to the hive; and, like the bees,
Are murder'd for our pains. This bitter taste
Yield his engrossments to the ending father.
                Re-enter WARWICK
Now, where is he that will not stay so long
Till his friend sickness hath determined me?

WARWICK

My lord, I found the prince in the next room,
Washing with kindly tears his gentle cheeks,
With such a deep demeanour in great sorrow,
That tyranny, which never quaff'd but blood,
Would, by beholding him, have wash'd his knife
With gentle eye-drops. He is coming hither.

KING

But wherefore did he take away the crown?
                Re-enter PRINCE HENRY
Lo, where he comes. Come hither to me, Harry.
Depart the chamber, leave us here alone.
              [Exeunt WARWICK and the rest

PRINCE

I never thought to hear you speak again.

KING

Thy wish was father, Harry, to that thought:
I stay too long by thee, I weary thee.
Dost thou so hunger for mine empty chair
That thou wilt needs invest thee with my honours

[546]

Before thy hour be ripe? O foolish youth!
Thou seek'st the greatness that will overwhelm thee.
Stay but a little; for my cloud of dignity
Is held from falling with so weak a wind
That it will quickly drop: my day is dim.
Thou hast stolen that which after some few hours
Were thine without offence; and at my death
Thou hast seal'd up my expectation:
Thy life did manifest thou lovedst me not,
And thou wilt have me die assured of it.
Thou hidest a thousand daggers in thy thoughts,
Which thou hast whetted on thy stony heart,
To stab at half an hour of my life.
What! canst thou not forbear me half an hour?
Then get thee gone and dig my grave thyself,
And bid the merry bells ring to thine ear
That thou art crowned, not that I am dead.
Let all the tears that should bedew my hearse
Be drops of balm to sanctify thy head:
Only compound me with forgotten dust;
Give that which gave thee life unto the worms.
Pluck down my officers, break my decrees;
For now a time is come to mock at form:
Harry the fifth is crown'd: up, vanity!
Down, royal state! all you sage counsellors, hence!
And to the English court assemble now,
From every region, apes of idleness!
Now, neighbour confines, purge you of your scum:
Have you a ruffian that will swear, drink, dance,
Revel the night, rob, murder, and commit
The oldest sins the newest kind of ways?
Be happy, he will trouble you no more;
England shall double gild his treble guilt,
England shall give him office, honour, might;
For the fifth Harry from curb'd license plucks
The muzzle of restraint, and the wild dog
Shall flesh his tooth on every innocent.
O my poor kingdom, sick with civil blows!
When that my care could not withhold thy riots,
What wilt thou do when riot is thy care?
O, thou wilt be a wilderness again,
Peopled with wolves, thy old inhabitants!

PRINCE

O, pardon me, my liege! but for my tears,
The moist impediments unto my speech,
I had forestall'd this dear and deep rebuke,
Ere you with grief had spoke and I had heard
The course of it so far. There is your crown;
And He that wears the crown immortally
Long guard it yours! If I affect it more
Than as your honour and as your renown,
Let me no more from this obedience rise,
Which my most inward true and duteous spirit
Teacheth, this prostrate and exterior bending.
God witness with me, when I here came in,
And found no course of breath within your majesty,
How cold it struck my heart! If I do feign,
O, let me in my present wildness die,
And never live to show the incredulous world
The noble change that I have purposed!

Coming to look on you, thinking you dead,
And dead almost, my liege, to think you were,
I spake unto this crown as having sense,
And thus upbraided it: 'The care on thee depending
Hath fed upon the body of my father;
Therefore, thou best of gold art worst of gold:
Other, less fine in carat, is more precious,
Preserving life in medicine potable;
But thou, most fine, most honour'd, most renown'd,
Hast eat thy bearer up.' Thus, my most royal liege,
Accusing it, I put it on my head,
To try with it, as with an enemy
That had before my face murder'd my father,
The quarrel of a true inheritor.
But if it did infect my blood with joy,
Or swell my thoughts to any strain of pride;
If any rebel or vain spirit of mine
Did with the least affection of a welcome
Give entertainment to the might of it,
Let God for ever keep it from my head,
And make me as the poorest vassal is,
That doth with awe and terror kneel to it!

KING

O my son,
God put it in thy mind to take it hence,
That thou mightst win the more thy father's love,
Pleading so wisely in excuse of it!
Come hither, Harry, sit thou by my bed;
And hear, I think, the very latest counsel
That ever I shall breathe. God knows, my son,
By what by-paths and indirect crook'd ways
I met this crown; and I myself know well
How troublesome it sat upon my head.
To thee it shall descend with better quiet,
Better opinion, better confirmation;
For all the soil of the achievement goes
With me into the earth. It seem'd in me
But as an honour snatch'd with boisterous hand,
And I had many living to upbraid
My gain of it by their assistances;
Which daily grew to quarrel and to bloodshed,
Wounding supposed peace: all these bold fears
Thou see'st with peril I have answered;
For all my reign hath been but as a scene
Acting that argument: and now my death
Changes the mode; for what in me was purchased,
Falls upon thee in a more fairer sort;
So thou the garland wear'st successively.
Yet, though thou stand'st more sure than I could do,
Thou art not firm enough, since griefs are green;
And all my friends, which thou must make thy friends,
Have but their stings and teeth newly ta'en out;
By whose fell working I was first advanced
And by whose power I well might lodge a fear
To be again displaced: which to avoid,
I cut them off; and had a purpose now
To lead out many to the Holy Land,
Lest rest and lying still might make them look

Too near unto my state. Therefore, my Harry,
Be it thy course to busy giddy minds
With foreign quarrels; that action, hence borne out,
May waste the memory of the former days.
More would I, but my lungs are wasted so
That strength of speech is utterly denied me.
How I came by the crown, O God forgive;
And grant it may with thee in true peace live!

PRINCE

My gracious liege,
You won it, wore it, kept it, gave it me;
Then plain and right must my possession be:
Which I with more than with a common pain
'Gainst all the world will rightfully maintain.

Enter LORD JOHN OF LANCASTER

KING

Look, look, here comes my John of Lancaster.

LANCASTER

Health, peace, and happiness to my royal father!

KING

Thou bring'st me happiness and peace, son John;
But health, alack, with youthful wings is flown
From this bare wither'd trunk: upon thy sight
My worldly business makes a period.
Where is my Lord of Warwick?

PRINCE

My Lord of Warwick!

Re-enter WARWICK, *and others*

KING

Doth any name particular belong
Unto the lodging where I first did swoon?

WARWICK

'Tis call'd Jerusalem, my noble lord.

KING

Laud be to God! even there my life must end.
It hath been prophesied to me many years,
I should not die but in Jerusalem;
Which vainly I supposed the Holy Land:
But bear me to that chamber; there I'll lie;
In that Jerusalem shall Harry die.　　[*Exeunt*

ACT V

SCENE I. *Gloucestershire.* SHALLOW's *house*

Enter SHALLOW, FALSTAFF, BARDOLPH, *and* PAGE

SHALLOW

By cock and pie, sir, you shall not away tonight.
What, Davy, I say!

FALSTAFF

You must excuse me, Master Robert Shallow.

SHALLOW

I will not excuse you; you shall not be excused; excuses shall not be admitted; there is no excuse shall
serve; you shall not be excused. Why, Davy!

Enter DAVY

DAVY

Here, sir.

SHALLOW

Davy, Davy, Davy, Davy, let me see, Davy; let me
see, Davy; let me see: yea, marry, William cook, bid
him come hither. Sir John, you shall not be excused.

DAVY

Marry, sir, thus; those precepts cannot be served:
and, again, sir, shall we sow the headland with
wheat?

SHALLOW

With red wheat, Davy. But for William cook: are
there no young pigeons?

DAVY

Yes, sir. Here is now the smith's note for shoeing
and plough-irons.

SHALLOW

Let it be cast and paid. Sir John, you shall not be
excused.

DAVY

Now, sir, a new link to the bucket must needs be
had: and, sir, do you mean to stop any of William's
wages, about the sack he lost the other day at
Hinckley fair?

SHALLOW

A' shall answer it. Some pigeons, Davy, a couple of
short-legged hens, a joint of mutton, and any pretty
little tiny kickshaws, tell William cook.

DAVY

Doth the man of war stay all night, sir?

SHALLOW

Yea, Davy. I will use him well: a friend i' the court
is better than a penny in purse. Use his men well,
Davy; for they are arrant knaves, and will backbite.

DAVY

No worse than they are backbitten, sir; for they
have marvellous foul linen.

SHALLOW

Well conceited, Davy: about thy business, Davy.

DAVY

I beseech you, sir, to countenance William Visor
of Woncot against Clement Perkes o' the hill.

SHALLOW

There is many complaints, Davy, against that Visor: that Visor is an arrant knave, on my knowledge.

DAVY

I grant your worship that he is a knave, sir; but yet,
God forbid, sir, but a knave should have some
countenance at his friend's request. An honest man,
sir, is able to speak for himself, when a knave is not.
I have served your worship truly, sir, this eight
years; and if I cannot once or twice in a quarter
bear out a knave against an honest man, I have but
a very little credit with your worship. The knave is
mine honest friend, sir; therefore, I beseech your
worship, let him be countenanced.

SHALLOW

Go to; I say he shall have no wrong. Look about,
Davy. [*Exit* DAVY] Where are you, Sir John? Come,
come, come, off with your boots. Give me your
hand, Master Bardolph.

[548]

BARDOLPH

I am glad to see your worship.

SHALLOW

I thank thee with all my heart, kind Master Bardolph: and welcome, my tall fellow [*to the* PAGE]. Come, Sir John.

FALSTAFF

I'll follow you, good Master Robert Shallow. [*Exit* SHALLOW] Bardolph, look to our horses. [*Exeunt* BARDOLPH *and* PAGE] If I were sawed into quantities, I should make four dozen of such bearded hermits' staves as Master Shallow. It is a wonderful thing to see the semblable coherence of his men's spirits and his: they, by observing of him, do bear themselves like foolish justices; he, by conversing with them, is turned into a justice-like serving-man: their spirits are so married in conjunction with the participation of society that they flock together in consent, like so many wild-geese. If I had a suit to Master Shallow, I would humour his men with the imputation of being near their master: if to his men, I would curry with Master Shallow that no man could better command his servants. It is certain that either wise bearing or ignorant carriage is caught, as men take diseases, one of another: therefore let men take heed of their company. I will devise matter enough out of this Shallow to keep Prince Harry in continual laughter the wearing out of six fashions, which is four terms, or two actions, and a' shall laugh without intervallums. O, it is much that a lie with a slight oath and a jest with a sad brow will do with a fellow that never had the ache in his shoulders! O, you shall see him laugh till his face be like a wet cloak ill laid up!

SHALLOW

[*Within*] Sir John!

FALSTAFF

I come, Master Shallow; I come, Master Shallow.
[*Exit*

SCENE II. *Westminster. The palace*

Enter WARWICK *and the* LORD CHIEF JUSTICE, *meeting*

WARWICK

How now, my lord chief justice! whither away?

CHIEF JUSTICE

How doth the king?

WARWICK

Exceeding well; his cares are now all ended.

CHIEF JUSTICE

I hope, not dead.

WARWICK

He's walk'd the way of nature;
And to our purposes he lives no more.

CHIEF JUSTICE

I would his majesty had call'd me with him:
The service that I truly did his life
Hath left me open to all injuries.

WARWICK

Indeed I think the young king loves you not.

CHIEF JUSTICE

I know he doth not, and do arm myself
To welcome the condition of the time,
Which cannot look more hideously upon me
Than I have drawn it in my fantasy.

Enter LANCASTER, CLARENCE, GLOUCESTER,
WESTMORELAND, *and others*

WARWICK

Here come the heavy issue of dead Harry:
O that the living Harry had the temper
Of him, the worst of these three gentlemen!
How many nobles then should hold their places,
That must strike sail to spirits of vile sort!

CHIEF JUSTICE

O God, I fear all will be overturn'd!

LANCASTER

Good morrow, cousin Warwick, good morrow.

GLOUCESTER *and* **CLARENCE**

Good morrow, cousin.

LANCASTER

We meet like men that had forgot to speak.

WARWICK

We do remember; but our argument
Is all too heavy to admit much talk.

LANCASTER

Well, peace be with him that hath made us heavy!

CHIEF JUSTICE

Peace be with us, lest we be heavier!

GLOUCESTER

O, good my lord, you have lost a friend indeed;
And I dare swear you borrow not that face
Of seeming sorrow, it is sure your own.

LANCASTER

Though no man be assured what grace to find,
You stand in coldest expectation:
I am the sorrier; would 'twere otherwise.

CLARENCE

Well, you must now speak Sir John Falstaff fair;
Which swims against your stream of quality.

CHIEF JUSTICE

Sweet princes, what I did, I did in honour,
Led by the impartial conduct of my soul;
And never shall you see that I will beg
A ragged and forestall'd remission.
If truth and upright innocency fail me,
I'll to the king my master that is dead,
And tell him who hath sent me after him.

WARWICK

Here comes the prince.

Enter KING HENRY *the Fifth, attended*

CHIEF JUSTICE

Good morrow, and God save your majesty!

KING

This new and gorgeous garment, majesty,
Sits not so easy on me as you think.
Brothers, you mix your sadness with some fear:
This is the English, not the Turkish court;
Not Amurath an Amurath succeeds,
But Harry Harry. Yet be sad, good brothers,

For, by my faith, it very well becomes you:
Sorrow so royally in you appears
That I will deeply put the fashion on,
And wear it in my heart: why then, be sad;
But entertain no more of it, good brothers,
Than a joint burden laid upon us all.
For me, by heaven, I bid you be assured,
I'll be your father and your brother too;
Let me but bear your love, I'll bear your cares:
Yet weep that Harry's dead; and so will I;
But Harry lives, that shall convert those tears
By number into hours of happiness.

PRINCES

We hope no other from your majesty.

KING

You all look strangely on me: and you most;
You are, I think, assured I love you not.

CHIEF JUSTICE

I am assured, if I be measured rightly,
Your majesty hath no just cause to hate me.

KING

No!
How might a prince of my great hopes forget
So great indignities you laid upon me?
What! rate, rebuke, and roughly send to prison
The immediate heir of England! Was this easy?
May this be wash'd in Lethe, and forgotten?

CHIEF JUSTICE

I then did use the person of your father;
The image of his power lay then in me:
And, in the administration of his law,
Whiles I was busy for the commonwealth,
Your highness pleased to forget my place,
The majesty and power of law and justice,
The image of the king whom I presented,
And struck me in my very seat of judgement;
Whereon, as an offender to your father,
I gave bold way to my authority,
And did commit you. If the deed were ill,
Be you contented, wearing now the garland,
To have a son set your decrees at nought,
To pluck down justice from your awful bench,
To trip the course of law and blunt the sword
That guards the peace and safety of your person;
Nay, more, to spurn at your most royal image
And mock your workings in a second body.
Question your royal thoughts, make the case yours;
Be now the father and propose a son,
Hear your own dignity so much profaned,
See your most dreadful laws so loosely slighted,
Behold yourself so by a son disdain'd;
And then imagine me taking your part,
And in your power soft silencing your son:
After this cold considerance, sentence me;
And, as you are a king, speak in your state
What I have done that misbecame my place,
My person, or my liege's sovereignty.

KING

You are right, justice, and you weigh this well;
Therefore still bear the balance and the sword:

And I do wish your honours may increase,
Till you do live to see a son of mine
Offend you, and obey you, as I did.
So shall I live to speak my father's words:
'Happy am I, that have a man so bold,
That dares do justice on my proper son;
And not less happy, having such a son,
That would deliver up his greatness so
Into the hands of justice.' You did commit me:
For which, I do commit into your hand
The unstained sword that you have used to bear;
With this remembrance, that you use the same
With the like bold, just, and impartial spirit
As you have done 'gainst me. There is my hand.
You shall be as a father to my youth:
My voice shall sound as you do prompt mine ear,
And I will stoop and humble my intents
To your well-practised wise directions.
And, princes all, believe me, I beseech you;
My father is gone wild into his grave,
For in his tomb lie my affections;
And with his spirit sadly I survive,
To mock the expectation of the world,
To frustrate prophecies, and to raze out
Rotten opinion, who hath writ me down
After my seeming. The tide of blood in me
Hath proudly flow'd in vanity till now:
Now doth it turn and ebb back to the sea,
Where it shall mingle with the state of floods,
And flow henceforth in formal majesty.
Now call we our high court of parliament:
And let us choose such limbs of noble counsel,
That the great body of our state may go
In equal rank with the best govern'd nation;
That war, or peace, or both at once, may be
As things acquainted and familiar to us;
In which you, father, shall have foremost hand.
Our coronation done, we will accite,
As I before remember'd, all our state:
And, God consigning to my good intents,
No prince nor peer shall have just cause to say,
God shorten Harry's happy life one day!   [Exeunt

SCENE III. *Gloucestershire.* SHALLOW's *orchard*

Enter FALSTAFF, SHALLOW, SILENCE, DAVY, BAR-
DOLPH, *and the* PAGE

SHALLOW

Nay, you shall see my orchard, where, in an arbour,
we will eat a last year's pippin of my own graffing,
with a dish of caraways, and so forth: come, cousin
Silence: and then to bed.

FALSTAFF

'Fore God, you have here a goodly dwelling and
a rich.

SHALLOW

Barren, barren, barren; beggars all, beggars all,
Sir John: marry, good air. Spread, Davy; spread,
Davy: well said, Davy.

FALSTAFF

This Davy serves you for good uses; he is your serving-man and your husband.

SHALLOW

A good varlet, a good varlet, a very good varlet, Sir John: by the mass, I have drunk too much sack at supper: a good varlet. Now sit down, now sit down: come, cousin.

SILENCE

Ah, sirrah! quoth-a, we shall

> Do nothing but eat, and make good cheer,   [*Singing*
> And praise God for the merry year;
> When flesh is cheap and females dear,
> And lusty lads roam here and there
>   So merrily,
> And ever among so merrily.

FALSTAFF

There's a merry heart! Good Master Silence, I'll give you a health for that anon.

SHALLOW

Give Master Bardolph some wine, Davy.

DAVY

Sweet sir, sit; I'll be with you anon; most sweet sir, sit. Master page, good master page, sit. Proface! What you want in meat, we'll have in drink: but you must bear; the heart's all.   [*Exit*

SHALLOW

Be merry, Master Bardolph; and, my little soldier there, be merry.

SILENCE

> Be merry, be merry, my wife has all;   [*Singing*
> For women are shrews, both short and tall:
> 'Tis merry in hall when beards wag all,
>   And welcome merry Shrove-tide.
> Be merry, be merry.

FALSTAFF

I did not think Master Silence had been a man of this mettle.

SILENCE

Who, I? I have been merry twice and once ere now.
Re-enter DAVY

DAVY

There's a dish of leather-coats for you.
                [*To* BARDOLPH

SHALLOW

Davy!

DAVY

Your worship! I'll be with you straight [*to* BAR-DOLPH]. A cup of wine, sir?

SILENCE

> A cup of wine that's brisk and fine,   [*Singing*
> And drink unto the leman mine;
> And a merry heart lives long-a.

FALSTAFF

Well said, Master Silence.

SILENCE

An we shall be merry, now comes in the sweet o' the night.

FALSTAFF

Health and long life to you, Master Silence.

SILENCE

Fill the cup, and let it come;   [*Singing*
I'll pledge you a mile to the bottom.

SHALLOW

Honest Bardolph, welcome: if thou wantest any thing, and wilt not call, beshrew thy heart. Welcome, my little tiny thief [*to the* PAGE], and welcome indeed too. I'll drink to Master Bardolph, and to all the cavaleros about London.

DAVY

I hope to see London once ere I die.

BARDOLPH

An I might see you there, Davy,—

SHALLOW

By the mass, you'll crack a quart together, ha! will you not, Master Bardolph?

BARDOLPH

Yea, sir, in a pottle-pot.

SHALLOW

By God's liggens, I thank thee: the knave will stick by thee, I can assure thee that. A' will not out; he is true bred.

BARDOLPH

And I'll stick by him, sir.

SHALLOW

Why, there spoke a king. Lack nothing: be merry. [*Knocking within*] Look who's at door there, ho! who knocks?   [*Exit* DAVY

FALSTAFF

Why, now you have done me right.
    [*To* SILENCE, *seeing him take off a bumper*

SILENCE

Do me right,   [*Singing*
And dub me knight:
  Samingo.

Is 't not so?

FALSTAFF

'Tis so.

SILENCE

Is 't so? Why then, say an old man can do somewhat.
Re-enter DAVY

DAVY

An 't please your worship, there's one Pistol come from the court with news.

FALSTAFF

From the court! let him come in.
Enter PISTOL

How now, Pistol!

PISTOL

Sir John, God save you!

FALSTAFF

What wind blew you hither, Pistol?

PISTOL

Not the ill wind which blows no man to good. Sweet knight, thou art now one of the greatest men in this realm.

SILENCE

By 'r lady, I think a' be, but goodman Puff of Barson.

PISTOL

Puff!
Puff in thy teeth, most recreant coward base!
Sir John, I am thy Pistol and thy friend,
And helter-skelter have I rode to thee,
And tidings do I bring and lucky joys
And golden times and happy news of price.

FALSTAFF

I pray thee now, deliver them like a man of this
world.

PISTOL

A foutre for the world and worldlings base!
I speak of Africa and golden joys.

FALSTAFF

O base Assyrian knight, what is thy news?
Let King Cophetua know the truth thereof.

SILENCE

And Robin Hood, Scarlet, and John.   [Singing

PISTOL

Shall dunghill curs confront the Helicons?
And shall good news be baffled?
Then, Pistol, lay thy head in Furies' lap.

SHALLOW

Honest gentleman, I know not your breeding.

PISTOL

Why then, lament therefore.

SHALLOW

Give me pardon, sir: if, sir, you come with news
from the court, I take it there's but two ways, either
to utter them, or to conceal them. I am, sir, under
the king, in some authority.

PISTOL

Under which king, Besonian? speak, or die.

SHALLOW

Under King Harry.

PISTOL

Harry the fourth? or fifth?

SHALLOW

Harry the fourth.

PISTOL

A foutre for thine office!
Sir John, thy tender lambkin now is king;
Harry the fifth's the man. I speak the truth:
When Pistol lies, do this; and fig me, like
The bragging Spaniard.

FALSTAFF

What, is the old king dead?

PISTOL

As nail in door: the things I speak are just.

FALSTAFF

Away, Bardolph! saddle my horse. Master Robert
Shallow, choose what office thou wilt in the land,
'tis thine. Pistol, I will double-charge thee with
dignities.

BARDOLPH

O joyful day!
I would not take a knighthood for my fortune.

PISTOL

What! I do bring good news.

FALSTAFF

Carry Master Silence to bed. Master Shallow, my
Lord Shallow,—be what thou wilt; I am fortune's
steward—get on thy boots: we'll ride all night. O
sweet Pistol! Away, Bardolph! [Exit BARDOLPH]
Come, Pistol, utter more to me; and withal devise
something to do thyself good. Boot, boot, Master
Shallow! I know the young king is sick for me. Let
us take any man's horses; the laws of England are
at my commandment. Blessed are they that have
been my friends; and woe to my lord chief justice!

PISTOL

Let vultures vile seize on his lungs also!
'Where is the life that late I led?' say they:
Why, here it is; welcome these pleasant days!
[Exeunt

SCENE IV. London. A street

Enter BEADLES, dragging in HOSTESS QUICKLY and
DOLL TEARSHEET

HOSTESS

No, thou arrant knave; I would to God that I might
die, that I might have thee hanged: thou hast
drawn my shoulder out of joint.

FIRST BEADLE

The constables have delivered her over to me; and
she shall have whipping-cheer enough, I warrant
her: there hath been a man or two lately killed
about her.

DOLL

Nut-hook, nut-hook, you lie. Come on; I'll tell thee
what, thou damned tripe-visaged rascal, an the
child I now go with do miscarry, thou wert better
thou hadst struck thy mother, thou paper-faced
villain.

HOSTESS

O the Lord, that Sir John were come! he would
make this a bloody day to somebody. But I pray
God the fruit of her womb miscarry!

FIRST BEADLE

If it do, you shall have a dozen of cushions again;
you have but eleven now. Come, I charge you both
go with me; for the man is dead that you and Pistol
beat amongst you.

DOLL

I'll tell you what, you thin man in a censer, I will
have you as soundly swinged for this,—you blue-
bottle rogue, you filthy famished correctioner, if
you be not swinged, I'll forswear half-kirtles.

FIRST BEADLE

Come, come, you she knight-errant, come.

HOSTESS

O God, that right should thus overcome might!
Well, of sufferance comes ease.

DOLL

Come, you rogue, come; bring me to a justice.

HOSTESS

Ay, come, you starved blood-hound.

DOLL

Goodman death, goodman bones!

HOSTESS

Thou atomy, thou!

DOLL

Come, you thin thing; come, you rascal.

FIRST BEADLE

Very well.　　　　　　　　　　　　　　[*Exeunt*

SCENE V. *A public place near Westminster Abbey*

Enter two GROOMS, *strewing rushes*

FIRST GROOM

More rushes, more rushes.

SECOND GROOM

The trumpets have sounded twice.

FIRST GROOM

'Twill be two o'clock ere they come from the coronation: dispatch, dispatch.　　　　　　[*Exeunt*

Enter FALSTAFF, SHALLOW, PISTOL, BARDOLPH, *and*
PAGE

FALSTAFF

Stand here by me, Master Robert Shallow; I will make the king do you grace: I will leer upon him as a' comes by; and do but mark the countenance that he will give me.

PISTOL

God bless thy lungs, good knight.

FALSTAFF

Come here, Pistol; stand behind me. O, if I had had time to have made new liveries, I would have bestowed the thousand pound I borrowed of you. But 'tis no matter; this poor show doth better: this doth infer the zeal I had to see him.

SHALLOW

It doth so.

FALSTAFF

It shows my earnestness of affection,—

SHALLOW

It doth so.

FALSTAFF

My devotion,—

SHALLOW

It doth, it doth, it doth.

FALSTAFF

As it were, to ride day and night; and not to deliberate, not to remember, not to have patience to shift me,—

SHALLOW

It is best, certain.

FALSTAFF

But to stand stained with travel, and sweating with desire to see him; thinking of nothing else, putting all affairs else in oblivion, as if there were nothing else to be done but to see him.

PISTOL

'Tis 'semper idem,' for 'obsque hoc nihil est:' 'tis all in every part.

SHALLOW

'Tis so, indeed.

PISTOL

My knight, I will inflame thy noble liver,
And make thee rage.
Thy Doll, and Helen of thy noble thoughts,
Is in base durance and contagious prison;
Haled thither
By most mechanical and dirty hand:
Rouse up revenge from ebon den with fell Alecto's snake,
For Doll is in. Pistol speaks nought but truth.

FALSTAFF

I will deliver her

[*Shouts within, and the trumpets sound*

PISTOL

There roar'd the sea, and trumpet-clangor sounds.

Enter the KING *and his train, the* LORD CHIEF JUSTICE
among them

FALSTAFF

God save thy grace, King Hal! my royal Hal!

PISTOL

The heavens thee guard and keep, most royal imp of fame!

FALSTAFF

God save thee, my sweet boy!

KING

My lord chief justice, speak to that vain man.

CHIEF JUSTICE

Have you your wits? know you what 'tis you speak?

FALSTAFF

My king! my Jove! I speak to thee, my heart!

KING

I know thee not, old man: fall to thy prayers;
How ill white hairs become a fool and jester!
I have long dream'd of such a kind of man,
So surfeit-swell'd, so old, and so profane;
But, being awaked, I do despise my dream.
Make less thy body hence, and more thy grace;
Leave gormandizing; know the grave doth gape
For thee thrice wider than for other men.
Reply not to me with a fool-born jest:
Presume not that I am the thing I was;
For God doth know, so shall the world perceive,
That I have turn'd away my former self;
So will I those that kept me company.
When thou dost hear I am as I have been,
Approach me, and thou shalt be as thou wast,
The tutor and the feeder of my riots:
Till then, I banish thee, on pain of death,
As I have done the rest of my misleaders,
Not to come near our person by ten mile.
For competence of life I will allow you,
That lack of means enforce you not to evil:
And, as we hear you do reform yourselves,
We will, according to your strengths and qualities,
Give you advancement. Be it your charge, my lord,
To see perform'd the tenour of our word.
Set on.　　　　　　　　　　　[*Exeunt* KING, *&c.*

FALSTAFF

Master Shallow, I owe you a thousand pound.

SHALLOW

Yea, marry, Sir John; which I beseech you to let me have home with me.

FALSTAFF

That can hardly be, Master Shallow. Do not you grieve at this; I shall be sent for in private to him: look you, he must seem thus to the world: fear not your advancements; I will be the man yet that shall make you great.

SHALLOW

I cannot well perceive how, unless you should give me your doublet, and stuff me out with straw. I beseech you, good Sir John, let me have five hundred of my thousand.

FALSTAFF

Sir, I will be as good as my word: this that you heard was but a colour.

SHALLOW

A colour that I fear you will die in, Sir John.

FALSTAFF

Fear no colours: go with me to dinner: come, Lieutenant Pistol; come, Bardolph: I shall be sent for soon at night.

Re-enter PRINCE JOHN, and the LORD CHIEF JUSTICE; OFFICERS with them

CHIEF JUSTICE

Go, carry Sir John Falstaff to the Fleet:
Take all his company along with him.

FALSTAFF

My lord, my lord,—

CHIEF JUSTICE

I cannot now speak: I will hear you soon.
Take them away.

PISTOL

Si fortuna me tormenta, spero contenta.

[Exeunt all but PRINCE JOHN and the CHIEF JUSTICE

LANCASTER

I like this fair proceeding of the king's:
He hath intent his wonted followers
Shall all be very well provided for;
But all are banish'd till their conversations
Appear more wise and modest to the world.

CHIEF JUSTICE

And so they are.

LANCASTER

The king hath call'd his parliament, my lord.

CHIEF JUSTICE

He hath.

LANCASTER

I will lay odds that, ere this year expire,
We bear our civil swords and native fire
As far as France: I heard a bird so sing,
Whose music, to my thinking, pleased the king.
Come, will you hence?　　　　　　　　　[Exeunt

EPILOGUE

Spoken by a DANCER

First my fear; then my courtesy; last my speech. My fear is, your displeasure; my courtesy, my duty; and my speech, to beg your pardons. If you look for a good speech now, you undo me: for what I have to say is of mine own making; and what indeed I should say will, I doubt, prove mine own marring. But to the purpose, and so to the venture. Be it known to you, as it is very well, I was lately here in the end of a displeasing play, to pray your patience for it and to promise you a better. I meant indeed to pay you with this; which, if like an ill venture it come unluckily home, I break, and you, my gentle creditors, lose. Here I promised you I would be, and here I commit my body to your mercies: bate me some, and I will pay you some, and, as most debtors do, promise you infinitely.

If my tongue cannot entreat you to acquit me, will you command me to use my legs? and yet that were but light payment, to dance out of your debt. But a good conscience will make any possible satisfaction, and so would I. All the gentlewomen here have forgiven me: if the gentlemen will not, then the gentlemen do not agree with the gentlewomen, which was never seen before in such an assembly.

One word more, I beseech you. If you be not too much cloyed with fat meat, our humble author will continue the story, with Sir John in it, and make you merry with fair Katharine of France: where, for any thing I know, Falstaff shall die of a sweat, unless already a' be killed with your hard opinions; for Oldcastle died a martyr, and this is not the man. My tongue is weary; when my legs are too, I will bid you good night: and so kneel down before you; but, indeed, to pray for the queen.

THE LIFE OF KING HENRY V

SYNOPSIS

The memory of his sad father prompts Henry V to expiate the late King's sins by having the body of Richard II reinterred and wept over, masses being continually sung in the two chantries the King has built for this purpose, and prayers for the repose of the murdered King's soul offered twice a day by the five hundred poor to whom Henry gives yearly maintenance. Remembering also his father's advice to keep domestic rebellions subdued by turning people's thoughts to foreign wars, and wishing to know if he can rightfully lay claim to the French throne, the King invites the opinion of some leading churchmen on the subject.

It so happens that the prelates are greatly disturbed by a bill that has recently been recommended in Parliament, by which the state will collect a large share of the money left by devout persons to the Church. Partly to divert the King's attention from the passage of this law, the astute Archbishop of Canterbury gives a learned, politic discourse in which he declares that through a misapplication of the ancient Salic law the French are depriving the King of the rights to their crown secured by his great-grandfather, Edward III of England, and he prevails upon Henry to invade France.

Just at that moment, in answer to his demand already sent for certain French dukedoms, the King receives a contemptuous message from the Dauphin who considers him nothing but a madcap to the effect that revelling will not gain dukedoms, together with an insulting gift of Paris tennis balls, presented by the ambassadors, as being better suited to Henry's purposes. Angrily retorting that after he has found tennis rackets to match the balls, he will play a set in France with the French crown as the wager, the King speeds up preparations for war, and inspires his followers to bend every thought and energy to the task.

A large army is soon levied and ready to embark from Southampton, where the apprehensive French, in order to check the invasion, plot to have the King murdered by three English noblemen of high standing in his councils, the Earl of Cambridge, Lord Scroop and Sir Thomas Grey. With papers in his hand revealing the plot, the King fearlessly faces the traitors as he enters his council-chamber at Southampton, and delivers such a terrible indictment of their proposed crime that they beg for forgiveness and death.

Meanwhile, at the Boar's-Head Tavern in London, cared for by Mistress Quickly, Falstaff, who cannot fathom the change in his Prince Hal, dies presumably of a broken heart, and his cronies, Pistol, Nym and Bardolph decide to follow the King to France, where Nym and Bardolph are hung for their thefts in the army, while the swaggering Pistol escapes by returning to England.

At the royal court of France, the King and Dauphin answer the English ruler's demand for their crown and kingdom by offering him the hand of the Princess Katharine, together with some petty dukedoms. But, as the charming Katharine reviews her newly-acquired stock of English words, Henry replies by pressing the siege of the city of Harfleur, which, failing to receive support from the Dauphin, yields to the English who fortify it against the French. Sickness and privation make serious inroads on the English army, but the King notwithstanding marches to Calais and then crosses the Somme, to find himself faced at Agincourt with a well-equipped French force outnumbering his own five to one. So confident of victory are the French that their noblemen, sneering at the poverty of the English troops, cast dice for the prisoners they anticipate, and the Constable of France sends a scornful message to King Henry telling him to bid his soldiers to repentance, as they all will soon meet death.

On the English side all is preparation and watchfulness, as the King demonstrates his ability as a born manipulator of men, uniting in his service the loyalties of soldiers of such diverse sentiments as Captain Fluellen, a Welshman, Captain Jamy, a Scot, and Captain Macmorris, an Irishman. On the night before battle, disguised and alone, he goes through his camp learning the temper of his rank and file, even indulging in a practical joke with one of the men, while his staff officers worry over his absence. Meeting the enemy at daybreak, the English army, though vastly inferior to the French in numbers and equipment, inflicts an overwhelming, disgraceful defeat upon the badly-generalled forces of the Dauphin. The field of Agincourt is strewn with the dead bodies of thousands of common soldiers and great numbers of French princes and noblemen, while the English losses are light. The French, forced to sue for peace, negotiate with the English King through the friendly offices of the Duke of Burgundy who paves the way successfully for the acceptance of Henry's terms.

Though very much in love with the coy, fascinating Princess Katharine, Henry remains inflexible in his demands as a conqueror and insists on their proposed marriage being the seal of his succession to the French throne. The French King finally yields, and, signing away his own son's birthright, acknowledges Henry as his heir. Henry marries Katharine, by whom, as the chorus of the Epilogue announces, he has a son, crowned as an infant, Henry VI, King of France and England.

HISTORICAL DATA

In *Henry V* Shakespeare continued the history of "Prince Hal," now King of England, from the opening of Parliament in 1414 to his betrothal to Katharine six years later. The material for the play was taken, as was usually the case in his historical dramas, directly from Holinshed's *Chronicles*, although some part may have been derived from a crude French play entitled *The Famous Victories of Henry the Fifth*. In general it is more historically accurate than any of the series.

The scenes in which Pistol and his fellows appear, and the conversations of the Welsh, Scotch and English captains are of course wholly Shakespearean, as are many of the minor episodes and incidents of character development.

Although not included in Meres's *Palladis Tamia* in 1598 the play was entered on the Stationers' Register in 1600 and published in a quarto (probably pirated) that same year. It is accordingly fairly definitely fixed as having been written in 1599, a theory borne out by clear references to the return of Essex from the rebellion in Ireland (1599) in the Chorus prefixed to Act V, and by a further reference in the Prologue to the Globe Theatre built by Burbage in 1599.

"Then I will kiss your lips, Kate."
HENRY V

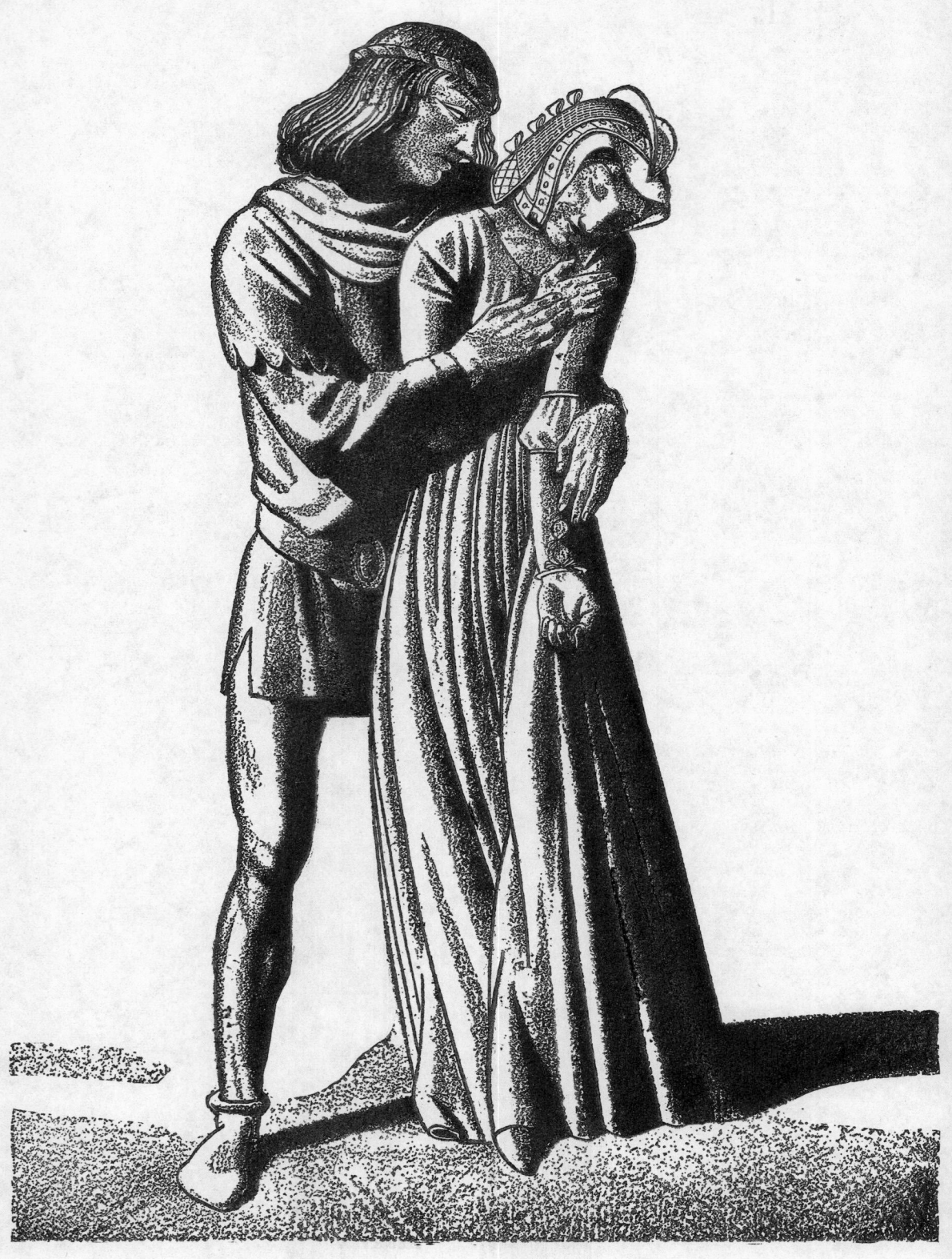

THE LIFE OF KING HENRY V

DRAMATIS PERSONÆ

KING HENRY the Fifth.
DUKE OF GLOUCESTER, } brothers to the King.
DUKE OF BEDFORD,
DUKE OF EXETER, uncle to the King.
DUKE OF YORK, cousin to the King.
EARLS OF SALISBURY, WESTMORELAND, and
    WARWICK.
ARCHBISHOP OF CANTERBURY.
BISHOP OF ELY.
EARL OF CAMBRIDGE.
LORD SCROOP.
SIR THOMAS GREY.
SIR THOMAS ERPINGHAM, GOWER, FLUELLEN,
    MACMORRIS, JAMY, officers in King Henry's army.
BATES, COURT, WILLIAMS, soldiers in the same.
PISTOL, NYM, BARDOLPH.
BOY.
A HERALD.

CHARLES the Sixth, King of France.
LEWIS, the Dauphin.
DUKES OF BURGUNDY, ORLEANS, and BOURBON.
THE CONSTABLE of France.
RAMBURES and GRANDPRE, French Lords.
GOVERNOR of Harfleur.
MONTJOY, a French Herald.
AMBASSADORS to the King of England.

ISABEL, Queen of France.
KATHARINE, daughter to Charles and Isabel.
ALICE, a lady attending on her.
HOSTESS of a tavern in Eastcheap, formerly Mistress
    Quickly, and now married to Pistol.
LORDS, LADIES, OFFICERS, SOLDIERS, CITIZENS,
    MESSENGERS, and ATTENDANTS.
CHORUS.

SCENE—England; afterwards France.

PROLOGUE

Enter CHORUS

CHORUS

O FOR a Muse of fire, that would ascend
The brightest heaven of invention,
A kingdom for a stage, princes to act
And monarchs to behold the swelling scene!
Then should the warlike Harry, like himself,
Assume the port of Mars; and at his heels,
Leash'd in like hounds, should famine, sword and
    fire
Crouch for employment. But pardon, gentles all,
The flat unraised spirits that have dared
On this unworthy scaffold to bring forth
So great an object: can this cockpit hold
The vasty fields of France? or may we cram
Within this wooden O the very casques
That did affright the air at Agincourt?
O, pardon! since a crooked figure may
Attest in little place a million;
And let us, ciphers to this great accompt,
On your imaginary forces work.
Suppose within the girdle of these walls
Are now confined two mighty monarchies,
Whose high upreared and abutting fronts
The perilous narrow ocean parts asunder:
Piece out our imperfections with your thoughts;
Into a thousand parts divide one man,
And make imaginary puissance;
Think, when we talk of horses, that you see them
Printing their proud hoofs i' the receiving earth;
For 'tis your thoughts that now must deck our kings,
Carry them here and there; jumping o'er times,

Turning the accomplishment of many years
Into an hour-glass: for the which supply,
Admit me Chorus to this history;
Who prologue-like your humble patience pray,
Gently to hear, kindly to judge, our play.   [Exit

ACT I

SCENE I. London. An ante-chamber in the KING's palace

ENTER the ARCHBISHOP OF CANTERBURY, and the
BISHOP OF ELY

CANTERBURY

My lord, I'll tell you; that self bill is urged,
Which in the eleventh year of the last king's reign
Was like, and had indeed against us pass'd,
But that the scambling and unquiet time
Did push it out of farther question.

ELY

But how, my lord, shall we resist it now?

CANTERBURY

It must be thought on. If it pass against us,
We lose the better half of our possession:
For all the temporal lands, which men devout
By testament have given to the church,
Would they strip from us; being valued thus:
As much as would maintain, to the king's honour,
Full fifteen earls and fifteen hundred knights,
Six thousand and two hundred good esquires;
And, to relief of lazars and weak age,
Of indigent faint souls past corporal toil,
A hundred almshouses right well supplied;

And to the coffers of the king beside,
A thousand pounds by the year: thus runs the bill.

ELY
This would drink deep.

CANTERBURY
        'Twould drink the cup and all.

ELY
But what prevention?

CANTERBURY
The king is full of grace and fair regard.

ELY
And a true lover of the holy church.

CANTERBURY
The courses of his youth promised it not.
The breath no sooner left his father's body,
But that his wildness, mortified in him,
Seem'd to die too; yea, at that very moment,
Consideration like an angel came
And whipp'd the offending Adam out of him,
Leaving his body as a paradise,
To envelope and contain celestial spirits.
Never was such a sudden scholar made;
Never came reformation in a flood,
With such a heady currance, scouring faults;
Nor never Hydra-headed wilfulness
So soon did lose his seat, and all at once,
As in this king.

ELY
        We are blessed in the change.

CANTERBURY
Hear him but reason in divinity,
And all-admiring with an inward wish
You would desire the king were made a prelate:
Hear him debate of commonwealth affairs,
You would say it hath been all in all his study:
List his discourse of war, and you shall hear
A fearful battle render'd you in music:
Turn him to any cause of policy,
The Gordian knot of it he will unloose,
Familiar as his garter: that, when he speaks,
The air, a charter'd libertine, is still,
And the mute wonder lurketh in men's ears,
To steal his sweet and honey'd sentences;
So that the art and practic part of life
Must be the mistress to this theoric:
Which is a wonder how his grace should glean it,
Since his addiction was to courses vain,
His companies unletter'd, rude and shallow,
His hours fill'd up with riots, banquets, sports,
And never noted in him any study,
Any retirement, any sequestration
From open haunts and popularity.

ELY
The strawberry grows underneath the nettle,
And wholesome berries thrive and ripen best
Neighbour'd by fruit of baser quality:
And so the prince obscured his contemplation
Under the veil of wildness; which, no doubt,
Grew like the summer grass, fastest by night,
Unseen, yet crescive in his faculty.

CANTERBURY
It must be so; for miracles are ceased;
And therefore we must needs admit the means
How things are perfected.

ELY
        But, my good lord,
How now for mitigation of this bill
Urged by the commons? Doth his majesty
Incline to it, or no?

CANTERBURY
        He seems indifferent,
Or rather swaying more upon our part
Than cherishing the exhibiters against us;
For I have made an offer to his majesty,
Upon our spiritual convocation
And in regard of causes now in hand,
Which I have open'd to his grace at large,
As touching France, to give a greater sum
Than ever at one time the clergy yet
Did to his predecessors part withal.

ELY
How did this offer seem received, my lord?

CANTERBURY
With good acceptance of his majesty;
Save that there was not time enough to hear,
As I perceived his grace would fain have done,
The severals and unhidden passages
Of his true titles to some certain dukedoms,
And generally to the crown and seat of France,
Derived from Edward, his great-grandfather.

ELY
What was the impediment that broke this off?

CANTERBURY
The French ambassador upon that instant
Craved audience; and the hour, I think, is come
To give him hearing: is it four o'clock?

ELY
It is.

CANTERBURY
Then go we in, to know his embassy;
Which I could with a ready guess declare,
Before the Frenchman speak a word of it.

ELY
I'll wait upon you, and I long to hear it. [Exeunt

SCENE II. *The same. The Presence chamber*

Enter KING HENRY, GLOUCESTER, BEDFORD, EXETER,
WARWICK, WESTMORELAND, *and* ATTENDANTS

KING
Where is my gracious Lord of Canterbury?

EXETER
Not here in presence.

KING
        Send for him, good uncle.

WESTMORELAND
Shall we call in the ambassador, my liege?

KING

Not yet, my cousin: we would be resolved,
Before we hear him, of some things of weight
That task our thoughts, concerning us and France.
Enter the ARCHBISHOP OF CANTERBURY *and the* BISHOP
OF ELY

CANTERBURY

God and his angels guard your sacred throne,
And make you long become it!

KING

Sure, we thank you.
My learned lord, we pray you to proceed
And justly and religiously unfold
Why the law Salique that they have in France
Or should, or should not, bar us in our claim:
And God forbid, my dear and faithful lord,
That you should fashion, wrest, or bow your read-
ing,
Or nicely charge your understanding soul
With opening titles miscreate, whose right
Suits not in native colours with the truth;
For God doth know how many now in health
Shall drop their blood in approbation
Of what your reverence shall incite us to.
Therefore take heed how you impawn our person,
How you awake our sleeping sword of war:
We charge you, in the name of God, take heed;
For never two such kingdoms did contend
Without much fall of blood; whose guiltless drops
Are every one a woe, a sore complaint
'Gainst him whose wrongs give edge unto the
swords
That make such waste in brief mortality.
Under this conjuration speak, my lord;
For we will hear, note and believe in heart
That what you speak is in your conscience wash'd
As pure as sin with baptism.

CANTERBURY

Then hear me, gracious sovereign, and you peers,
That owe yourselves, your lives and services
To this imperial throne. There is no bar
To make against your highness' claim to France
But this, which they produce from Pharamond,
'In terram Salicam mulieres ne succedant:'
'No woman shall succeed in Salique land:'
Which Salique land the French unjustly gloze
To be the realm of France, and Pharamond
The founder of this law and female bar.
Yet their own authors faithfully affirm
That the land Salique is in Germany,
Between the floods of Sala and of Elbe;
Where Charles the Great, having subdued the
Saxons,
There left behind and settled certain French,
Who, holding in disdain the German women
For some dishonest manners of their life,
Establish'd then this law; to wit, no female
Should be inheritrix in Salique land:
Which Salique, as I said, 'twixt Elbe and Sala,
Is at this day in Germany call'd Meisen.

Then doth it well appear the Salique law
Was not devised for the realm of France;
Nor did the French possess the Salique land
Until four hundred one and twenty years
After defunction of King Pharamond,
Idly supposed the founder of this law;
Who died within the year of our redemption
Four hundred twenty-six; and Charles the Great
Subdued the Saxons, and did seat the French
Beyond the river Sala, in the year
Eight hundred five. Besides, their writers say,
King Pepin, which deposed Childeric,
Did, as heir general, being descended
Of Blithild, which was daughter to King Clothair,
Make claim and title to the crown of France.
Hugh Capet also, who usurp'd the crown
Of Charles the duke of Lorraine, sole heir male
Of the true line and stock of Charles the Great,
To find his title with some shows of truth,
Though, in pure truth, it was corrupt and naught,
Convey'd himself as heir to the Lady Lingare,
Daughter to Charlemain, who was the son
To Lewis the emperor, and Lewis the son
Of Charles the Great. Also King Lewis the tenth,
Who was sole heir to the usurper Capet,
Could not keep quiet in his conscience,
Wearing the crown of France, till satisfied
That fair Queen Isabel, his grandmother,
Was lineal of the Lady Ermengare,
Daughter to Charles the foresaid duke of Lorraine:
By the which marriage the line of Charles the Great
Was re-united to the crown of France.
So that, as clear as is the summer's sun,
King Pepin's title and Hugh Capet's claim,
King Lewis his satisfaction, all appear
To hold in right and title of the female:
So do the kings of France unto this day;
Howbeit they would hold up this Salique law
To bar your highness claiming from the female,
And rather choose to hide them in a net
Than amply to imbar their crooked titles
Usurp'd from you and your progenitors.

KING

May I with right and conscience make this claim?

CANTERBURY

The sin upon my head, dread sovereign!
For in the book of Numbers is it writ,
When the man dies, let the inheritance
Descend unto the daughter. Gracious lord,
Stand for your own; unwind your bloody flag;
Look back into your mighty ancestors:
Go, my dread lord, to your great-grandsire's tomb,
From whom you claim; invoke his warlike spirit,
And your great-uncle's, Edward the Black Prince,
Who on the French ground play'd a tragedy,
Making defeat on the full power of France,
Whiles his most mighty father on a hill
Stood smiling to behold his lion's whelp
Forage in blood of French nobility.
O noble English, that could entertain

With half their forces the full pride of France
And let another half stand laughing by,
All out of work and cold for action!

ELY

Awake remembrance of these valiant dead,
And with your puissant arm renew their feats:
You are their heir; you sit upon their throne;
The blood and courage that renowned them
Runs in your veins; and my thrice-puissant liege
Is in the very May-morn of his youth,
Ripe for exploits and mighty enterprises.

EXETER

Your brother kings and monarchs of the earth
Do all expect that you should rouse yourself,
As did the former lions of your blood.

WESTMORELAND

They know your grace hath cause and means and
   might;
So hath your highness; never king of England
Had nobles richer and more loyal subjects,
Whose hearts have left their bodies here in England
And lie pavilion'd in the fields of France.

CANTERBURY

O, let their bodies follow, my dear liege,
With blood and sword and fire to win your right;
In aid whereof we of the spiritualty
Will raise your highness such a mighty sum
As never did the clergy at one time
Bring in to any of your ancestors.

KING

We must not only arm to invade the French,
But lay down our proportions to defend
Against the Scot, who will make road upon us
With all advantages.

CANTERBURY

They of those marches, gracious sovereign,
Shall be a wall sufficient to defend
Our inland from the pilfering borderers.

KING

We do not mean the coursing snatchers only,
But fear the main intendment of the Scot,
Who hath been still a giddy neighbour to us;
For you shall read that my great-grandfather
Never went with his forces into France,
But that the Scot on his unfurnish'd kingdom
Came pouring, like the tide into a breach,
With ample and brim fulness of his force,
Galling the gleaned land with hot assays,
Girding with grievous siege castles and towns;
That England, being empty of defence,
Hath shook and trembled at the ill neighbourhood.

CANTERBURY

She hath been then more fear'd than harm'd, my
   liege;
For hear her but exampled by herself:
When all her chivalry hath been in France,
And she a mourning widow of her nobles,
She hath herself not only well defended,
But taken and impounded as a stray
The King of Scots; whom she did send to France,

To fill King Edward's fame with prisoner kings,
And make her chronicle as rich with praise,
As is the ooze and bottom of the sea
With sunken wreck and sumless treasuries.

WESTMORELAND

But there's a saying very old and true,
  'If that you will France win,
    Then with Scotland first begin:'
For once the eagle England being in prey,
To her unguarded nest the weasel Scot
Comes sneaking and so sucks her princely eggs,
Playing the mouse in absence of the cat,
To tear and havoc more than she can eat.

EXETER

It follows then the cat must stay at home:
Yet that is but a crush'd necessity,
Since we have locks to safeguard necessaries,
And pretty traps to catch the petty thieves.
While that the armed hand doth fight abroad,
The advised head defends itself at home;
For government, though high and low and lower,
Put into parts, doth keep in one consent,
Congreeing in a full and natural close,
Like music.

CANTERBURY

      Therefore doth heaven divide
The state of man in divers functions,
Setting endeavour in continual motion;
To which is fixed, as an aim or butt,
Obedience: for so work the honey-bees,
Creatures that by a rule in nature teach
The act of order to a peopled kingdom.
They have a king and officers of sorts;
Where some, like magistrates, correct at home,
Others, like merchants, venture trade abroad,
Others, like soldiers, armed in their stings,
Make boot upon the summer's velvet buds,
Which pillage they with merry march bring home
To the tent-royal of their emperor;
Who, busied in his majesty, surveys
The singing masons building roofs of gold,
The civil citizens kneading up the honey,
The poor mechanic porters crowding in
Their heavy burdens at his narrow gate,
The sad-eyed justice, with his surly hum,
Delivering o'er to executors pale
The lazy yawning drone. I this infer,
That many things, having full reference
To one consent, may work contrariously:
As many arrows, loosed several ways,
Come to one mark; as many ways meet in one
   town;
As many fresh streams meet in one salt sea;
As many lines close in the dial's centre;
So may a thousand actions, once afoot,
End in one purpose, and be all well borne
Without defeat. Therefore to France, my liege.
Divide your happy England into four;
Whereof take you one quarter into France,
And you withal shall make all Gallia shake.

If we, with thrice such powers left at home,
Cannot defend our own doors from the dog,
Let us be worried and our nation lose
The name of hardiness and policy.

KING

Call in the messengers sent from the Dauphin.

[*Exeunt some* ATTENDANTS

Now are we well resolved; and, by God's help,
And yours, the noble sinews of our power,
France being ours, we'll bend it to our awe,
Or break it all to pieces: or there we'll sit,
Ruling in large and ample empery
O'er France and all her almost kingly dukedoms,
Or lay these bones in an unworthy urn,
Tombless, with no remembrance over them:
Either our history shall with full mouth
Speak freely of our acts, or else our grave,
Like Turkish mute, shall have a tongueless mouth,
Not worshipp'd with a waxen epitaph.

Enter AMBASSADORS *of France*

Now are we well prepared to know the pleasure
Of our fair cousin Dauphin; for we hear
Your greeting is from him, not from the king.

FIRST AMBASSADOR

May't please your majesty to give us leave
Freely to render what we have in charge;
Or shall we sparingly show you far off
The Dauphin's meaning and our embassy?

KING

We are no tyrant, but a Christian king;
Unto whose grace our passion is as subject
As are our wretches fetter'd in our prisons:
Therefore with frank and with uncurbed plainness
Tell us the Dauphin's mind.

FIRST AMBASSADOR

Thus, then, in few.
Your highness, lately sending into France,
Did claim some certain dukedoms, in the right
Of your great predecessor, King Edward the third.
In answer of which claim, the prince our master
Says that you savour too much of your youth,
And bids you be advised there's nought in France
That can be with a nimble galliard won;
You cannot revel into dukedoms there.
He therefore sends you, meeter for your spirit,
This tun of treasure; and, in lieu of this,
Desires you let the dukedoms that you claim
Hear no more of you. This the Dauphin speaks.

KING

What treasure, uncle?

EXETER

Tennis-balls, my liege.

KING

We are glad the Dauphin is so pleasant with us;
His present and your pains we thank you for:
When we have match'd our rackets to these balls,
We will, in France, by God's grace, play a set
Shall strike his father's crown into the hazard.
Tell him he hath made a match with such a wran-
gler

That all the courts of France will be disturb'd
With chaces. And we understand him well,
How he comes o'er us with our wilder days,
Not measuring what use we made of them.
We never valued this poor seat of England;
And therefore, living hence, did give ourself
To barbarous license; as 'tis ever common
That men are merriest when they are from home.
But tell the Dauphin I will keep my state,
Be like a king and show my sail of greatness
When I do rouse me in my throne of France:
For that I have laid by my majesty,
And plodded like a man for working-days;
But I will rise there with so full a glory
That I will dazzle all the eyes of France,
Yea, strike the Dauphin blind to look on us.
And tell the pleasant prince this mock of his
Hath turn'd his balls to gun-stones; and his soul
Shall stand sore charged for the wasteful vengeance
That shall fly with them: for many a thousand wid-
ows
Shall this his mock mock out of their dear husbands;
Mock mothers from their sons, mock castles down;
And some are yet ungotten and unborn
That shall have cause to curse the Dauphin's scorn.
But this lies all within the will of God,
To whom I do appeal; and in whose name
Tell you the Dauphin I am coming on,
To venge me as I may and to put forth
My rightful hand in a well-hallow'd cause.
So get you hence in peace; and tell the Dauphin
His jest will savour but of shallow wit,
When thousands weep more than did laugh at it.
Convey them with safe conduct. Fare you well.

[*Exeunt* AMBASSADORS

EXETER

This was a merry message.

KING

We hope to make the sender blush at it.
Therefore, my lords, omit no happy hour
That may give furtherance to our expedition;
For we have now no thought in us but France,
Save those to God, that run before our business.
Therefore let our proportions for these wars
Be soon collected, and all things thought upon
That may with reasonable swiftness add
More feathers to our wings; for, God before,
We'll chide this Dauphin at his father's door.
Therefore let every man now task his thought,
That this fair action may on foot be brought.

[*Exeunt. Flourish*

ACT II

PROLOGUE

Enter CHORUS

CHORUS

Now all the youth of England are on fire,
And silken dalliance in the wardrobe lies:

[561]

Now thrive the armorers, and honour's thought
Reigns solely in the breast of every man:
They sell the pasture now to buy the horse,
Following the mirror of all Christian kings,
With winged heels, as English Mercuries.
For now sits Expectation in the air,
And hides a sword from hilts unto the point
With crowns imperial, crowns and coronets,
Promised to Harry and his followers.
The French, advised by good intelligence
Of this most dreadful preparation,
Shake in their fear and with pale policy
Seek to divert the English purposes.
O England! model to thy inward greatness,
Like little body with a mighty heart,
What mightst thou do, that honour would thee do,
Were all thy children kind and natural!
But see thy fault! France hath in thee found out
A nest of hollow bosoms, which he fills
With treacherous crowns; and three corrupted men,
One, Richard Earl of Cambridge, and the second,
Henry Lord Scroop of Masham, and the third,
Sir Thomas Grey, knight, of Northumberland,
Have, for the gilt of France,—O guilt indeed!—
Confirm'd conspiracy with fearful France;
And by their hands this grace of kings must die,
If hell and treason hold their promises,
Ere he take ship for France, and in Southampton.
Linger your patience on; and we'll digest
The abuse of distance; force a play.
The sum is paid; the traitors are agreed;
The king is set from London; and the scene
Is now transported, gentles, to Southampton;
There is the playhouse now, there must you sit:
And thence to France shall we convey you safe,
And bring you back, charming the narrow seas
To give you gentle pass; for, if we may,
We'll not offend one stomach with our play.
But, till the king come forth, and not till then,
Unto Southampton do we shift our scene.   [*Exit*

SCENE I. *London. A street*

Enter CORPORAL NYM *and* LIEUTENANT BARDOLPH
BARDOLPH
Well met, Corporal Nym.
NYM
Good morrow, Lieutenant Bardolph.
BARDOLPH
What, are Ancient Pistol and you friends yet?
NYM
For my part, I care not: I say little; but when time
shall serve, there shall be smiles; but that shall be as
it may. I dare not fight; but I will wink and hold
out mine iron: it is a simple one; but what though?
it will toast cheese, and it will endure cold as
another man's sword will: and there's an end.
BARDOLPH
I will bestow a breakfast to make you friends; and

we'll be all three sworn brothers to France: let it be
so, good Corporal Nym.
NYM
Faith, I will live so long as I may, that's the certain
of it; and when I cannot live any longer, I will do as
I may: that is my rest, that is the rendezvous of it.
BARDOLPH
It is certain, corporal, that he is married to Nell
Quickly: and, certainly, she did you wrong; for you
were troth-plight to her.
NYM
I cannot tell: things must be as they may: men may
sleep, and they may have their throats about them
at that time; and some say knives have edges. It
must be as it may: though patience be a tired mare,
yet she will plod. There must be conclusions. Well, I
cannot tell.

Enter PISTOL *and* HOSTESS
BARDOLPH
Here comes Ancient Pistol and his wife: good cor-
poral, be patient here. How now, mine host Pistol!
PISTOL
Base tike, call'st thou me host?
Now, by this hand, I swear, I scorn the term;
Nor shall my Nell keep lodgers.
HOSTESS
No, by my troth, not long; for we cannot lodge and
board a dozen or fourteen gentlewomen that live
honestly by the prick of their needles, but it will be
thought we keep a bawdy house straight. [NYM *and*
PISTOL *draw.*] O well a day. Lady, if he be not
drawn now! we shall see wilful adultery and murder
committed.
BARDOLPH
Good lieutenant! good corporal! offer nothing here.
NYM
Pish!
PISTOL
Pish for thee, Iceland dog! thou prick-ear'd cur of
Iceland!
HOSTESS
Good Corporal Nym, show thy valour, and put up
your sword.
NYM
Will you shog off? I would have you solus.
PISTOL
'Solus,' egregious dog? O viper vile!
The 'solus' in thy most mervailous face;
The 'solus' in thy teeth, and in thy throat,
And in thy hateful lungs, yea, in thy maw, perdy,
And, which is worse, within thy nasty mouth!
I do retort the 'solus' in thy bowels;
For I can take, and Pistol's cock is up,
And flashing fire will follow.
NYM
I am not Barbason; you cannot conjure me. I have
an humour to knock you indifferently well. If you
grow foul with me, Pistol, I will scour you with my
rapier, as I may, in fair terms: if you would walk

off, I would prick your guts a little, in good terms,
as I may: and that's the humour of it.

PISTOL

O braggart vile, and damned furious wight!
The grave doth gape, and doting death is near;
Therefore exhale.

BARDOLPH

Hear me, hear me what I say: he that strikes the
first stroke, I'll run him up to the hilts, as I am a
soldier.   [*Draws*

PISTOL

An oath of mickle might; and fury shall abate.
Give me thy fist, thy fore-foot to me give:
Thy spirits are most tall.

NYM

I will cut thy throat, one time or other, in fair
terms: that is the humour of it.

PISTOL

'Couple a gorge!'
That is the word. I thee defy again.
O hound of Crete, think'st thou my spouse to get?
No; to the spital go,
And from the powdering-tub of infamy
Fetch forth the lazar kite of Cressid's kind,
Doll Tearsheet she by name, and her espouse:
I have, and I will hold, the quondam Quickly
For the only she; and—pauca, there's enough.
Go to.

Enter the BOY

BOY

Mine host Pistol, you must come to my master, and
you, hostess: he is very sick, and would to bed. Good
Bardolph, put thy face between his sheets, and do
the office of a warming-pan. Faith, he's very ill.

BARDOLPH

Away, you rogue!

HOSTESS

By my troth, he'll yield the crow a pudding one of
these days. The king has killed his heart. Good husband, come home presently. [*Exeunt* HOSTESS *and* BOY

BARDOLPH

Come, shall I make you two friends? We must to
France together: why the devil should we keep
knives to cut one another's throats?

PISTOL

Let floods o'erswell, and fiends for food howl on!

NYM

You'll pay me the eight shillings I won of you at
betting?

PISTOL

Base is the slave that pays.

NYM

That now I will have: that's the humour of it.

PISTOL

As manhood shall compound: push home.
     [*They draw*

BARDOLPH

By this sword, he that makes the first thrust, I'll kill
him; by this sword, I will.

PISTOL

Sword is an oath, and oaths must have their course.

BARDOLPH

Corporal Nym, an thou wilt be friends, be friends:
an thou wilt not, why, then, be enemies with me
too. Prithee, put up.

NYM

I shall have my eight shillings I won of you at
betting?

PISTOL

A noble shalt thou have, and present pay;
And liquor likewise will I give to thee,
And friendship shall combine, and brotherhood:
I'll live by Nym, and Nym shall live by me;
Is not this just? for I shall sutler be
Unto the camp, and profits will accrue.
Give me thy hand.

NYM

I shall have my noble?

PISTOL

In cash most justly paid.

NYM

Well, then, that's the humour of 't.
     Re-enter HOSTESS

HOSTESS

As ever you came of women, come in quickly to Sir
John. Ah, poor heart! he is so shaked of a burning
quotidian tertian, that it is most lamentable to behold. Sweet men, come to him.

NYM

The king hath run bad humours on the knight;
that's the even of it.

PISTOL

Nym, thou hast spoke the right;
His heart is fracted and corroborate.

NYM

The king is a good king: but it must be as it may; he
passes some humours and careers.

PISTOL

Let us condole the knight; for, lambkins, we will
live.

SCENE II. *Southampton. A council-chamber*

Enter EXETER, BEDFORD, *and* WESTMORELAND

BEDFORD

'Fore God, his grace is bold, to trust these traitors.

EXETER

They shall be apprehended by and by.

WESTMORELAND

How smooth and even they do bear themselves!
As if allegiance in their bosoms sat,
Crowned with faith and constant loyalty.

BEDFORD

The king hath note of all that they intend,
By interception which they dream not of.

EXETER

Nay, but the man that was his bedfellow,
Whom he hath dull'd and cloy'd with gracious
     favours,

That he should, for a foreign purse, so sell
His sovereign's life to death and treachery.
Trumpets sound. Enter KING HENRY, SCROOP, CAM-
BRIDGE, GREY, *and* ATTENDANTS
KING
Now sits the wind fair, and we will aboard.
My Lord of Cambridge, and my kind Lord of Ma-
sham,
And you, my gentle knight, give me your thoughts:
Think you not that the powers we bear with us
Will cut their passage through the force of France,
Doing the execution and the act
For which we have in head assembled them?
SCROOP
No doubt, my liege, if each man do his best.
KING
I doubt not that; since we are well persuaded
We carry not a heart with us from hence
That grows not in a fair consent with ours,
Nor leave not one behind that doth not wish
Success and conquest to attend on us.
CAMBRIDGE
Never was monarch better fear'd and loved
Than is your majesty: there's not, I think, a subject
That sits in heart-grief and uneasiness
Under the sweet shade of your government.
GREY
True: those that were your father's enemies
Have steep'd their galls in honey, and do serve you
With hearts create of duty and of zeal.
KING
We therefore have great cause of thankfulness;
And shall forget the office of our hand,
Sooner than quittance of desert and merit
According to the weight and worthiness.
SCROOP
So service shall with steeled sinews toil,
And labour shall refresh itself with hope,
To do your grace incessant services.
KING
We judge no less. Uncle of Exeter,
Enlarge the man committed yesterday,
That rail'd against our person: we consider
It was excess of wine that set him on;
And on his more advice we pardon him.
SCROOP
That's mercy, but too much security:
Let him be punish'd, sovereign, lest example
Breed, by his sufferance, more of such a kind.
KING
O, let us yet be merciful.
CAMBRIDGE
So may your highness, and yet punish too.
GREY
Sir,
You show great mercy, if you give him life,
After the taste of much correction.
KING
Alas, your too much love and care of me
Are heavy orisons 'gainst this poor wretch!

If little faults, proceeding on distemper,
Shall not be wink'd at, how shall we stretch our eye
When capital crimes, chew'd, swallow'd and di-
gested,
Appear before us? We'll yet enlarge that man,
Though Cambridge, Scroop and Grey, in their dear
care
And tender preservation of our person,
Would have him punish'd. And now to our French
causes:
Who are the late commissioners?
CAMBRIDGE
I one, my lord:
Your highness bade me ask for it to-day.
SCROOP
So did you me, my liege.
GREY
And I, my royal sovereign.
KING
Then, Richard Earl of Cambridge, there is yours;
There yours, Lord Scroop of Masham; and, sir
knight,
Grey of Northumberland, this same is yours:
Read them; and know, I know your worthiness.
My Lord of Westmoreland, and uncle Exeter,
We will aboard to night. Why, how now, gentlemen!
What see you in those papers that you lose
So much complexion? Look ye, how they change!
Their cheeks are paper. Why, what read you there,
That hath so cowarded and chased your blood
Out of appearance?
CAMBRIDGE
I do confess my fault;
And do submit me to your highness' mercy.
GREY *and* SCROOP
To which we all appeal.
KING
The mercy that was quick in us but late,
By your own counsel is suppress'd and kill'd:
You must not dare, for shame, to talk of mercy;
For your own reasons turn into your bosoms,
As dogs upon their masters, worrying you.
See you, my princes and my noble peers,
These English monsters! My Lord of Cambridge
here,
You know how apt our love was to accord
To furnish him with all appertinents
Belonging to his honour; and this man
Hath, for a few light crowns, lightly conspired,
And sworn unto the practices of France,
To kill us here in Hampton: to the which
This knight, no less for bounty bound to us
Than Cambridge is, hath likewise sworn. But, O,
What shall I say to thee, Lord Scroop? thou cruel,
Ingrateful, savage and inhuman creature!
Thou that didst bear the key of all my counsels,
That knew'st the very bottom of my soul,
That almost mightst have coin'd me into gold,
Wouldst thou have practised on me for thy use,
May it be possible, that foreign hire

[564]

Could out of thee extract one spark of evil
That might annoy my finger? 'tis so strange,
That, though the truth of it stands off as gross
As black and white, my eye will scarcely see it.
Treason and murder ever kept together,
As two yoke-devils sworn to either's purpose,
Working so grossly in a natural cause,
That admiration did not hoop at them:
But thou, 'gainst all proportion, didst bring in
Wonder to wait on treason and on murder:
And whatsoever cunning fiend it was
That wrought upon thee so preposterously
Hath got the voice in hell for excellence:
All other devils that suggest by treasons
Do botch and bungle up damnation
With patches, colours, and with forms being fetch'd
From glistering semblances of piety;
But he that temper'd thee bade thee stand up,
Gave thee no instance why thou shouldst do trea-
    son,
Unless to dub thee with the name of traitor.
If that same demon that hath gull'd thee thus
Should with his lion gait walk the whole world,
He might return to vasty Tartar back,
And tell the legions 'I can never win
A soul so easy as that Englishman's.'
O, how hast thou with jealousy infected
The sweetness of affiance! Show men dutiful?
Why, so didst thou: seem they grave and learned?
Why, so didst thou: come they of noble family?
Why, so didst thou: seem they religious?
Why, so didst thou: or are they spare in diet,
Free from gross passion or of mirth or anger,
Constant in spirit, not swerving with the blood,
Garnish'd and deck'd in modest complement,
Not working with the eye without the ear,
And but in purged judgement trusting neither?
Such and so finely bolted didst thou seem:
And thus thy fall hath left a kind of blot,
To mark the full-fraught man and best indued
With some suspicion. I will weep for thee;
For this revolt of thine, methinks, is like
Another fall of man. Their faults are open:
Arrest them to the answer of the law;
And God acquit them of their practices!

EXETER

I arrest thee of high treason, by the name of Rich-
ard Earl of Cambridge.
I arrest thee of high treason, by the name of Henry
Lord Scroop of Masham.
I arrest thee of high treason, by the name of Thomas
Grey, knight, of Northumberland.

SCROOP

Our purposes God justly hath discover'd;
And I repent my fault more than my death;
Which I beseech your highness to forgive,
Although my body pay the price of it.

CAMBRIDGE

For me, the gold of France did not seduce;
Although I did admit it as a motive

The sooner to effect what I intended:
But God be thanked for prevention;
Which I in sufferance heartily will rejoice,
Beseeching God and you to pardon me.

GREY

Never did faithful subject more rejoice
At the discovery of most dangerous treason
Than I do at this hour joy o'er myself,
Prevented from a damned enterprise:
My fault, but not my body, pardon, sovereign.

KING

God quit you in his mercy! Hear your sentence.
You have conspired against our royal person,
Join'd with an enemy proclaim'd, and from his cof-
    fers
Received the golden earnest of our death;
Wherein you would have sold your king to slaugh-
    ter,
His princes and his peers to servitude,
His subjects to oppression and contempt,
And his whole kingdom into desolation.
Touching our person seek we no revenge;
But we our kingdom's safety must so tender,
Whose ruin you have sought, that to her laws
We do deliver you. Get you therefore hence,
Poor miserable wretches, to your death:
The taste whereof, God of his mercy give
You patience to endure, and true repentance
Of all your dear offences! Bear them hence.
    [Exeunt CAMBRIDGE, SCROOP, and GREY, guarded
Now, lords, for France; the enterprise whereof
Shall be to you, as us, like glorious.
We doubt not of a fair and lucky war,
Since God so graciously hath brought to light
This dangerous treason lurking in our way
To hinder our beginnings. We doubt not now
But every rub is smoothed on our way.
Then forth, dear countrymen: let us deliver
Our puissance into the hand of God,
Putting it straight in expedition.
Cheerly to sea; the signs of war advance:
No king of England, if not king of France.   [Exeunt

SCENE III. *London. Before a tavern*

Enter PISTOL, HOSTESS, NYM, BARDOLPH, *and* BOY

HOSTESS

Prithee, honey-sweet husband, let me bring thee to
Staines.

PISTOL

No; for my manly heart doth yearn.
Bardolph, be blithe: Nym, rouse thy vaunting veins:
Boy, bristle thy courage up; for Falstaff he is dead,
And we must yearn therefore.

BARDOLPH

Would I were with him, wheresome'er he is, either
in heaven or in hell!

HOSTESS

Nay, sure, he's not in hell: he's in Arthur's bosom,

if ever man went to Arthur's bosom. A' made a finer
end and went away an it had been any christom
child; a' parted even just between twelve and one,
even at the turning o' the tide: for after I saw him
fumble with the sheets, and play with flowers, and
smile upon his fingers' ends, I knew there was but
one way; for his nose was as sharp as a pen, and a'
babbled of green fields. 'How now, Sir John!' quoth
I: 'what, man! be o' good cheer.' So a' cried out
'God, God, God!' three or four times. Now I, to
comfort him, bid him a' should not think of God; I
hoped there was no need to trouble himself with
any such thoughts yet. So a' bade me lay more
clothes on his feet: I put my hand into the bed and
felt them, and they were as cold as any stone; then I
felt to his knees, and they were as cold as any stone,
and so upward and upward, and all was as cold as
any stone.

NYM

They say he cried out of sack.

HOSTESS

Ay, that a' did.

BARDOLPH

And of women.

HOSTESS

Nay, that a' did not.

BOY

Yes, that a' did; and said they were devils incarnate.

HOSTESS

A' could never abide carnation; 'twas a colour he
never liked.

BOY

A' said once, the devil would have him about
women.

HOSTESS

A' did in some sort, indeed, handle women; but
then he was rheumatic, and talked of the whore of
Babylon.

BOY

Do you not remember, a' saw a flea stick upon
Bardolph's nose, and a' said it was a black soul
burning in hell-fire?

BARDOLPH

Well, the fuel is gone that maintained that fire:
that's all the riches I got in his service.

NYM

Shall we shog? the king will be gone from Southampton.

PISTOL

Come, let's away. My love, give me thy lips.
Look to my chattels and my movables:
Let senses rule; the word is 'Pitch and Pay:'
Trust none;
For oaths are straws, men's faiths are wafer-cakes,
And hold-fast is the only dog, my duck:
Therefore, Caveto be thy counsellor.
Go, clear thy crystals. Yoke-fellows in arms,
Let us to France; like horse-leeches, my boys,
To suck, to suck, the very blood to suck!

BOY

And that's but unwholesome food, they say.

PISTOL

Touch her soft mouth, and march.

BARDOLPH

Farewell, hostess.   [*Kissing her*

NYM

I cannot kiss, that is the humour of it; but, adieu.

PISTOL

Let housewifery appear: keep close, I thee command.

HOSTESS

Farewell; adieu.   [*Exeunt*

SCENE IV. *France. The* KING'S *palace*

Flourish. Enter the FRENCH KING, *the* DAUPHIN, *the*
DUKES OF BERRI *and* BRETAGNE, *the* CONSTABLE, *and*
others

FRENCH KING

Thus comes the English with full power upon us;
And more than carefully it us concerns
To answer royally in our defences.
Therefore the Dukes of Berri and of Bretagne,
Of Brabant and of Orleans, shall make forth,
And you, Prince Dauphin, with all swift dispatch,
To line and new repair our towns of war
With men of courage and with means defendant;
For England his approaches makes as fierce
As waters to the sucking of a gulf.
It fits us then to be as provident
As fear may teach us out of late examples
Left by the fatal and neglected English
Upon our fields.

DAUPHIN

      My most redoubted father,
It is most meet we arm us 'gainst the foe;
For peace itself should not so dull a kingdom,
Though war nor no known quarrel were in question,
But that defences, musters, preparations,
Should be maintain'd, assembled and collected,
As were a war in expectation.
Therefore, I say 'tis meet we all go forth
To view the sick and feeble parts of France:
And let us do it with no show of fear;
No, with no more than if we heard that England
Were busied with a Whitsun morris-dance:
For, my good liege, she is so idly king'd,
Her sceptre so fantastically borne
By a vain, giddy, shallow, humorous youth,
That fear attends her not.

CONSTABLE

      O peace, Prince Dauphin!
You are too much mistaken in this king:
Question your grace the late ambassadors,
With what great state he heard their embassy,
How well supplied with noble counsellors,
How modest in exception, and withal
How terrible in constant resolution,

And you shall find his vanities forespent
Were but the outside of the Roman Brutus,
Covering discretion with a coat of folly,
As gardeners do with ordure hide those roots
That shall first spring and be most delicate.

DAUPHIN

Well, 'tis not so, my lord high constable;
But though we think it so, it is no matter:
In cases of defence 'tis best to weigh
The enemy more mighty than he seems:
So the proportions of defence are fill'd;
Which of a weak and niggardly projection
Doth, like a miser, spoil his coat with scanting
A little cloth.

FRENCH KING

Think we King Harry strong;
And, princes, look you strongly arm to meet him.
The kindred of him hath been flesh'd upon us;
And he is bred out of that bloody strain
That haunted us in our familiar paths:
Witness our too much memorable shame
When Cressy battle fatally was struck,
And all our princes captived by the hand
Of that black name, Edward, Black Prince of Wales;
Whiles that his mountain sire, on mountain stand-
ing,
Up in the air, crown'd with the golden sun,
Saw his heroical seed, and smiled to see him,
Mangle the work of nature, and deface
The patterns that by God and by French fathers
Had twenty years been made. This is a stem
Of that victorious stock; and let us fear
The native mightiness and fate of him.

Enter a MESSENGER

MESSENGER

Ambassadors from Harry King of England
Do crave admittance to your majesty.

FRENCH KING

We'll give them present audience. Go, and bring
them.   [*Exeunt* MESSENGER *and certain* LORDS
You see this chase is hotly follow'd, friends.

DAUPHIN

Turn head, and stop pursuit; for coward dogs
Most spend their mouths when what they seem to
threaten
Runs far before them. Good my sovereign,
Take up the English short, and let them know
Of what a monarchy you are the head:
Self-love, my liege, is not so vile a sin
As self-neglecting.

Re-enter LORDS, *with* EXETER *and train*

FRENCH KING

From our brother England?

EXETER

From him; and thus he greets your majesty.
He wills you, in the name of God Almighty,
That you divest yourself, and lay apart
The borrow'd glories that by gift of heaven,
By law of nature and of nations, 'long
To him and to his heirs; namely, the crown

And all wide-stretched honours that pertain
By custom and the ordinance of times
Unto the crown of France. That you may know
'Tis no sinister nor no awkward claim,
Pick'd from the worm-holes of long-vanish'd days,
Nor from the dust of old oblivion raked,
He sends you this most memorable line,
In every branch truly demonstrative;
Willing you overlook this pedigree:
And when you find him evenly derived
From his most famed of famous ancestors,
Edward the third, he bids you then resign
Your crown and kingdom, indirectly held
From him the native and true challenger.

FRENCH KING

Or else what follows?

EXETER

Bloody constraint; for if you hide the crown
Even in your hearts, there will he rake for it:
Therefore in fierce tempest is he coming,
In thunder and in earthquake, like a Jove,
That, if requiring fail, he will compel;
And bids you, in the bowels of the Lord,
Deliver up the crown, and to take mercy
On the poor souls for whom this hungry war
Opens his vasty jaws; and on your head
Turning the widows' tears, the orphans' cries,
The dead men's blood, the pining maidens' groans,
For husbands, fathers and betrothed lovers,
That shall be swallow'd in this controversy.
This is his claim, his threatening, and my message;
Unless the Dauphin be in presence here,
To whom expressly I bring greeting too.

FRENCH KING

For us, we will consider of this further:
To-morrow shall you bear our full intent
Back to our brother England.

DAUPHIN

For the Dauphin,
I stand here for him: what to him from England?

EXETER

Scorn and defiance; slight regard, contempt,
And any thing that may not misbecome
The mighty sender, doth he prize you at.
Thus says my king; an if your father's highness
Do not, in grant of all demands at large,
Sweeten the bitter mock you sent his majesty,
He'll call you to so hot an answer of it,
That caves and womby vaultages of France
Shall chide your trespass, and return your mock
In second accent of his ordnance.

DAUPHIN

Say, if my father render fair return,
It is against my will; for I desire
Nothing but odds with England: to that end,
As matching to his youth and vanity,
I did present him with the Paris balls.

EXETER

He'll make your Paris Louvre shake for it,
Were it the mistress-court of mighty Europe:

And, be assured, you'll find a difference,
As we his subjects have in wonder found,
Between the promise of his greener days
And these he masters now: now he weighs time
Even to the utmost grain: that you shall read
In your own losses, if he stay in France.
FRENCH KING
To-morrow shall you know our mind at full.
EXETER
Dispatch us with all speed, lest that our king
Come here himself to question our delay;
For he is footed in this land already.
FRENCH KING
You shall be soon dispatch'd with fair conditions:
A night is but small breath and little pause
To answer matters of this consequence.
[Flourish. Exeunt

ACT III

PROLOGUE

Enter CHORUS
CHORUS
Thus with imagined wing our swift scene flies
In motion of no less celerity
Than that of thought. Suppose that you have seen
The well-appointed king at Hampton pier
Embark his royalty; and his brave fleet
With silken streamers the young Phœbus fanning:
Play with your fancies, and in them behold
Upon the hempen tackle ship-boys climbing;
Hear the shrill whistle which doth order give
To sounds confused; behold the threaden sails,
Borne with the invisible and creeping wind,
Draw the huge bottoms through the furrow'd sea,
Breasting the lofty surge: O, do but think
You stand upon the rivage and behold
A city on the inconstant billows dancing;
For so appears this fleet majestical,
Holding due course to Harfleur. Follow, follow:
Grapple your minds to sternage of this navy,
And leave your England, as dead midnight still,
Guarded with grandsires, babies and old women,
Either past or not arrived to pith and puissance;
For who is he, whose chin is but enrich'd
With one appearing hair, that will not follow
These cull'd and choice-drawn cavaliers to France?
Work, work your thoughts, and therein see a siege;
Behold the ordnance on their carriages,
With fatal mouths gaping on girded Harfleur.
Suppose the ambassador from the French comes
    back;
Tells Harry that the king doth offer him
Katharine his daughter, and with her, to dowry,
Some petty and unprofitable dukedoms.
The offer likes not: and the nimble gunner
With linstock now the devilish cannon touches,
[Alarum, and chambers go off

And down goes all before them. Still be kind,
And eke out our performance with your mind. [Exit

SCENE I. *France. Before Harfleur*

Alarum. Enter KING HENRY, EXETER, BEDFORD,
GLOUCESTER, *and* SOLDIERS, *with scaling-ladders*
KING
Once more unto the breach, dear friends, once
    more;
Or close the wall up with our English dead.
In peace there's nothing so becomes a man
As modest stillness and humility:
But when the blast of war blows in our ears,
Then imitate the action of the tiger;
Stiffen the sinews, summon up the blood,
Disguise fair nature with hard-favour'd rage;
Then lend the eye a terrible aspect;
Let it pry through the portage of the head
Like the brass cannon; let the brow o'erwhelm it
As fearfully as doth a galled rock
O'erhang and jutty his confounded base,
Swill'd with the wild and wasteful ocean.
Now set the teeth and stretch the nostril wide,
Hold hard the breath and bend up every spirit
To his full height. On, on, you noblest English,
Whose blood is fet from fathers of war-proof!
Fathers that, like so many Alexanders,
Have in these parts from morn till even fought,
And sheathed their swords for lack of argument:
Dishonour not your mothers; now attest
That those whom you call'd fathers did beget you.
Be copy now to men of grosser blood,
And teach them how to war. And you, good yeo-
    men,
Whose limbs were made in England, show us here
The mettle of your pasture; let us swear
That you are worth your breeding; which I doubt
    not;
For there is none of you so mean and base,
That hath not noble lustre in your eyes.
I see you stand like greyhounds in the slips,
Straining upon the start. The game's afoot:
Follow your spirit, and upon this charge
Cry 'God for Harry, England, and Saint George!'
[Exeunt. Alarum, and chambers go off

SCENE II. *The same*

Enter NYM, BARDOLPH, PISTOL, *and* BOY
BARDOLPH
On, on, on, on, on! to the breach, to the breach!
NYM
Pray thee, corporal, stay: the knocks are too hot;
and, for mine own part, I have not a case of lives:
the humour of it is too hot, that is the very plain-
song of it.

PISTOL

The plain-song is most just; for humours do abound:

Knocks go and come; God's vassals drop and die;
　And sword and shield,
　　In bloody field,
　Doth win immortal fame.

BOY

Would I were in an alehouse in London! I would give all my fame for a pot of ale and safety.

PISTOL

And I:

If wishes would prevail with me,
My purpose should not fail with me,
　But thither would I hie.

BOY

As duly, but not as truly,
As bird doth sing on bough.

Enter FLUELLEN

FLUELLEN

Up to the breach, you dogs! avaunt, you cullions!

[Driving them forward

PISTOL

Be merciful, great duke, to men of mould.
Abate thy rage, abate thy manly rage,
Abate thy rage, great duke!
Good bawcock, bate thy rage; use lenity, sweet chuck!

NYM

These be good humours! your honour wins bad humours.　　　*[Exeunt all but* BOY

BOY

As young as I am, I have observed these three swashers. I am boy to them all three: but all they three, though they would serve me, could not be man to me; for indeed three such antics do not amount to a man. For Bardolph, he is white-livered and red-faced; by the means whereof a' faces it out, but fights not. For Pistol, he hath a killing tongue and a quiet sword; by the means whereof a' breaks words, and keeps whole weapons. For Nym, he hath heard that men of few words are the best men; and therefore he scorns to say his prayers, lest a' should be thought a coward: but his few bad words are matched with as few good deeds; for a' never broke any man's head but his own, and that was against a post when he was drunk. They will steal any thing, and call it purchase. Bardolph stole a lute-case, bore it twelve leagues, and sold it for three half-pence. Nym and Bardolph are sworn brothers in filching, and in Calais they stole a fire-shovel: I knew by that piece of service the men would carry coals. They would have me as familiar with men's pockets as their gloves or their handker-chers: which makes much against my manhood, if I should take from another's pocket to put into mine; for it is plain pocketing up of wrongs. I must leave them, and seek some better service: their villany goes against my weak stomach, and therefore I must cast it up.　　　*[Exit*

Re-enter FLUELLEN, GOWER *following*

GOWER

Captain Fluellen, you must come presently to the mines; the Duke of Gloucester would speak with you.

FLUELLEN

To the mines! tell you the duke, it is not so good to come to the mines; for, look you, the mines is not according to the disciplines of the war: the concavi-ties of it is not sufficient; for, look you, th' athver-sary, you may discuss unto the duke, look you, is digt himself four yard under the countermines: by Cheshu, I think a' will plow up all, if there is not better directions.

GOWER

The Duke of Gloucester, to whom the order of the siege is given, is altogether directed by an Irishman, a very valiant gentleman, i' faith.

FLUELLEN

It is Captain Macmorris, is it not?

GOWER

I think it be.

FLUELLEN

By Cheshu, he is an ass, as in the world: I will verify as much in his beard: he has no more directions in the true disciplines of the wars, look you, of the Roman disciplines, than is a puppy-dog.

Enter MACMORRIS *and* CAPTAIN JAMY

GOWER

Here a' comes; and the Scots captain, Captain Jamy, with him.

FLUELLEN

Captain Jamy is a marvellous falorous gentleman, that is certain; and of great expedition and knowl-edge in th' aunchient wars, upon my particular knowledge of his directions: by Cheshu, he will maintain his argument as well as any military man in the world, in the disciplines of the pristine wars of the Romans.

JAMY

I say gud-day, Captain Fluellen.

FLUELLEN

God-den to your worship, good Captain James.

GOWER

How now, Captain Macmorris! have you quit the mines? have the pioners given o'er?

MACMORRIS

By Chrish, la! tish ill done: the work ish give over, the trompet sound the retreat. By my hand, I swear, and my father's soul, the work ish ill done; it ish give over: I would have blowed up the town, so Chrish save me, la! in an hour: O, tish ill done, tish ill done; by my hand, tish ill done!

FLUELLEN

Captain Macmorris, I beseech you now, will you voutsafe me, look you, a few disputations with you, as partly touching or concerning the disciplines of the war, the Roman wars, in the way of argument, look you, and friendly communication; partly to satisfy my opinion, and partly for the satisfaction,

look you, of my mind, as touching the direction of
the military discipline; that is the point.

JAMY

It sall be vary gud, gud feith, gud captains bath:
and I sall quit you with gud leve, as I may pick occasion; that sall I, marry.

MACMORRIS

It is no time to discourse, so Chrish save me: the day
is hot, and the weather, and the wars, and the king,
and the dukes: it is no time to discourse. The town
is beseeched, and the trumpet call us to the breach;
and we talk, and, be Chrish, do nothing: 'tis shame
for us all: so God sa' me, 'tis shame to stand still; it
is shame, by my hand: and there is throats to be cut,
and works to be done; and there ish nothing done,
so Chrish sa' me, la!

JAMY

By the mess, ere theise eyes of mine take themselves
to slomber, ay'll de gud service, or ay'll lig i' the
grund for it; ay, or go to death; and ay'll pay 't as
valorously as I may, that sall I suerly do, that is the
breff and the long. Marry, I wad full fain hear some
question 'tween you tway.

FLUELLEN

Captain Macmorris, I think, look you, under your
correction, there is not many of your nation—

MACMORRIS

Of my nation! What ish my nation? Ish a villain,
and a bastard, and a knave, and a rascal. What ish
my nation? Who talks of my nation?

FLUELLEN

Look you, if you take the matter otherwise than is
meant, Captain Macmorris, peradventure I shall
think you do not use me with that affability as in
discretion you ought to use me, look you; being as
good a man as yourself, both in the disciplines of
war, and in the derivation of my birth, and in other
particularities.

MACMORRIS

I do not know you so good a man as myself: so
Chrish save me, I will cut off your head.

GOWER

Gentlemen both, you will mistake each other.

JAMY

A! that's a foul fault.   [A parley sounded

GOWER

The town sounds a parley.

FLUELLEN

Captain Macmorris, when there is more better opportunity to be required, look you, I will be so bold
as to tell you I know the disciplines of war; and
there is an end.   [Exeunt

SCENE III. *The same. Before the gates*

The GOVERNOR *and some* CITIZENS *on the walls; the
English forces below. Enter* KING HENRY *and his train*

KING

How yet resolves the governor of the town?

This is the latest parle we will admit:
Therefore to our best mercy give yourselves;
Or like to men proud of destruction
Defy us to our worst: for, as I am a soldier,
A name that in my thoughts becomes me best,
If I begin the battery once again,
I will not leave the half-achieved Harfleur
Till in her ashes she lie buried.
The gates of mercy shall be all shut up,
And the flesh'd soldier, rough and hard of heart,
In liberty of bloody hand shall range
With conscience wide as hell, mowing like grass
Your fresh-fair virgins and your flowering infants.
What is it then to me, if impious war,
Array'd in flames like to the prince of fiends,
Do, with his smirch'd complexion, all fell feats
Enlink'd to waste and desolation?
What is 't to me, when you yourselves are cause,
If your pure maidens fall into the hand
Of hot and forcing violation?
What rein can hold licentious wickedness
When down the hill he holds his fierce career?
We may as bootless spend our vain command
Upon the enraged soldiers in their spoil
As send precepts to the leviathan
To come ashore. Therefore, you men of Harfleur,
Take pity of your town and of your people,
Whiles yet my soldiers are in my command;
Whiles yet the cool and temperate wind of grace
O'erblows the filthy and contagious clouds
Of heady murder, spoil and villany.
If not, why, in a moment look to see
The blind and bloody soldier with foul hand
Defile the locks of your shrill-shrieking daughters;
Your fathers taken by the silver beards,
And their most reverend heads dash'd to the walls,
Your naked infants spitted upon pikes,
Whiles the mad mothers with their howls confused
Do break the clouds, as did the wives of Jewry
At Herod's bloody-hunting slaughtermen.
What say you? will you yield, and this avoid,
Or, guilty in defence, be thus destroy'd?

GOVERNOR

Our expectation hath this day an end:
The Dauphin, whom of succours we entreated,
Returns us that his powers are yet not ready
To raise so great a siege. Therefore, great king,
We yield our town and lives to thy soft mercy.
Enter our gates; dispose of us and ours;
For we no longer are defensible.

KING

Open your gates. Come, uncle Exeter,
Go you and enter Harfleur; there remain,
And fortify it strongly 'gainst the French:
Use mercy to them all. For us, dear uncle,
The winter coming on, and sickness growing
Upon our soldiers, we will retire to Calais.
To-night in Harfleur will we be your guest;
To-morrow for the march are we addrest.
      [*Flourish. The* KING *and his train enter the town*

SCENE IV. *The* FRENCH KING'S *palace*

Enter KATHARINE *and* ALICE

KATHARINE
Alice, tu as été en Angleterre, et tu parles bien le langage.

ALICE
Un peu, madame.

KATHARINE
Je te prie, m'enseignez; il faut que j'apprenne à parler. Comment appelez-vous la main en Anglois?

ALICE
La main? elle est appelée de hand.

KATHARINE
De hand. Et les doigts?

ALICE
Les doigts? ma foi, j'oublie les doigts; mais je me souviendrai. Les doigts? je pense qu'ils sont appelés de fingres; oui, de fingres.

KATHARINE
La main, de hand; les doigts, de fingres. Je pense que je suis le bon écolier; j'ai gagné deux mots d'Anglois vîtement. Comment appelez-vous les ongles?

ALICE
Les ongles? nous les appelons de nails.

KATHARINE
De nails. Ecoutez; dites-moi, si je parle bien: de hand, de fingres, et de nails.

ALICE
C'est bien dit, madame; il est fort bon Anglois.

KATHARINE
Dites-moi l'Anglois pour le bras.

ALICE
De arm, madame.

KATHARINE
Et le coude.

ALICE
De elbow.

KATHARINE
De elbow. Je m'en fais la répétition de tous les mots que vous m'avez appris dès à présent.

ALICE
Il est trop difficile, madame, comme je pense.

KATHARINE
Excusez-moi, Alice; écoutez: de hand, de fingres, de nails, de arma, de bilbow.

ALICE
De elbow, madame.

KATHARINE
O Seigneur Dieu, je m'en oublie! de elbow. Comment appelez-vous le col?

ALICE
De neck, madame.

KATHARINE
De nick. Et le menton?

ALICE
De chin.

KATHARINE
De sin. Le col, de nick; le menton, de sin.

ALICE
Oui. Sauf votre honneur, en vérité, vous prononcez les mots aussi droit que les natifs d'Angleterre.

KATHARINE
Je ne doute point d'apprendre, par la grace de Dieu, et en peu de temps.

ALICE
N'avez vous pas déjà oublié ce que je vous ai enseigné?

KATHARINE
Non, je reciterai à vous promptement: de hand, de fingres, de mails,—

ALICE
De nails, madame.

KATHARINE
De nails, de arm, de ilbow.

ALICE
Sauf votre honneur, de elbow.

KATHARINE
Ainsi dis-je; de elbow, de nick, et de sin. Comment appelez-vous le pied et la robe?

ALICE
De foot, madame; et de coun.

KATHARINE
De foot et de coun! O Seigneur Dieu! ce sont mots de son mauvais, corruptible, gros, et impudique, et non pour les dames d'honneur d'user: je ne voudrais prononcer ces mots devant les seigneurs de France pour tout le monde. Foh! le foot et le coun! Néanmoins, je reciterai une autre fois ma leçon ensemble: de hand, de fingres, de nails, de arm, de elbow, de nick, de sin, de foot, de coun.

ALICE
Excellent, madame!

KATHARINE
C'est assez pour une fois: allons-nous à dîner.

[*Exeunt*

SCENE V. *The same*

Enter the KING OF FRANCE, *the* DAUPHIN, *the* DUKE OF BOURBON, *the* CONSTABLE OF FRANCE, *and others*

FRENCH KING
'Tis certain he hath pass'd the river Somme.

CONSTABLE
And if he be not fought withal, my lord,
Let us not live in France; let us quit all,
And give our vineyards to a barbarous people.

DAUPHIN
O Dieu vivant! shall a few sprays of us,
The emptying of our fathers' luxury,
Our scions, put in wild and savage stock,
Spirt up so suddenly into the clouds,
And overlook their grafters?

BOURBON
Normans, but bastard Normans, Norman bastards!
Mort de ma vie! if they march along
Unfought withal, but I will sell my dukedom,
To buy a slobbery and a dirty farm
In that nook-shotten isle of Albion.

CONSTABLE

Dieu de batailles! where have they this mettle?
Is not their climate foggy, raw and dull,
On whom, as in despite, the sun looks pale,
Killing their fruit with frowns? Can sodden water,
A drench for sur-rein'd jades, their barley-broth,
Decoct their cold blood to such valiant heat?
And shall our quick blood, spirited with wine,
Seem frosty? O, for honour of our land,
Let us not hang like roping icicles
Upon our houses' thatch, whiles a more frosty people
Sweat drops of gallant youth in our rich fields!—
Poor we may call them in their native lords.

DAUPHIN

By faith and honour,
Our madams mock at us, and plainly say
Our mettle is bred out, and they will give
Their bodies to the lust of English youth,
To new-store France with bastard warriors.

BOURBON

They bid us to the English dancing-schools,
And teach lavoltas high and swift corantos;
Saying our grace is only in our heels,
And that we are most lofty runaways.

FRENCH KING

Where is Montjoy the herald? speed him hence:
Let him greet England with our sharp defiance.
Up, princes! and, with spirit of honour edged
More sharper than your swords, hie to the field:
Charles Delabreth, high constable of France;
You Dukes of Orleans, Bourbon, and of Berri,
Alençon, Brabant, Bar, and Burgundy;
Jaques Chatillon, Rambures, Vaudemont,
Beaumont, Grandpré, Roussi, and Fauconberg,
Foix, Lestrale, Bouciqualt, and Charolois;
High dukes, great princes, barons, lords and knights,
For your great seats now quit you of great shames.
Bar Harry England, that sweeps through our land
With pennons painted in the blood of Harfleur:
Rush on his host, as doth the melted snow
Upon the valleys, whose low vassal seat
The Alps doth spit and void his rheum upon:
Go down upon him, you have power enough,
And in a captive chariot into Rouen
Bring him our prisoner.

CONSTABLE

This becomes the great.
Sorry am I his numbers are so few,
His soldiers sick and famish'd in their march,
For I am sure, when he shall see our army,
He'll drop his heart into the sink of fear
And for achievement offer us his ransom.

FRENCH KING

Therefore, lord constable, haste on Montjoy,
And let him say to England that we send
To know what willing ransom he will give.
Prince Dauphin, you shall stay with us in Rouen.

DAUPHIN

Not so, I do beseech your majesty.

FRENCH KING

Be patient, for you shall remain with us.
Now forth, lord constable and princes all,
And quickly bring us word of England's fall. [Exeunt

SCENE VI. *The English camp in Picardy*

Enter GOWER *and* FLUELLEN, *meeting*

GOWER

How now, Captain Fluellen! come you from the
bridge?

FLUELLEN

I assure you, there is very excellent services committed at the bridge.

GOWER

Is the Duke of Exeter safe?

FLUELLEN

The Duke of Exeter is as magnanimous as Agamemnon; and a man that I love and honour with
my soul, and my heart, and my duty, and my life,
and my living, and my uttermost power: he is not—
God be praised and blessed!—any hurt in the world;
but keeps the bridge most valiantly, with excellent
discipline. There is an aunchient lieutenant there
at the pridge, I think in my very conscience he is as
valiant a man as Mark Antony; and he is a man of
no estimation in the world; but I did see him do as
gallant service.

GOWER

What do you call him?

FLUELLEN

He is called Aunchient Pistol.

GOWER

I know him not.

Enter PISTOL

FLUELLEN

Here is the man.

PISTOL

Captain, I thee beseech to do me favours:
The Duke of Exeter doth love thee well.

FLUELLEN

Ay, I praise God; and I have merited some love at
his hands.

PISTOL

Bardolph, a soldier, firm and sound of heart,
And of buxom valour, hath, by cruel fate,
And giddy Fortune's furious fickle wheel,
That goddess blind,
That stands upon the rolling restless stone—

FLUELLEN

By your patience, Aunchient Pistol. Fortune is
painted blind, with a muffler afore her eyes, to
signify to you that Fortune is blind; and she is
painted also with a wheel, to signify to you, which is
the moral of it, that she is turning, and inconstant,
and mutability, and variation: and her foot, look
you, is fixed upon a spherical stone, which rolls, and
rolls, and rolls: in good truth, the poet makes a

most excellent description of it: Fortune is an excellent moral.

PISTOL

Fortune is Bardolph's foe, and frowns on him;
For he hath stolen a pax, and hanged must a' be:
A damned death!
Let gallows gape for dog; let man go free
And let not hemp his wind-pipe suffocate:
But Exeter hath given the doom of death
For pax of little price.
Therefore, go speak; the duke will hear thy voice;
And let not Bardolph's vital thread be cut
With edge of penny cord and vile reproach:
Speak, captain, for his life, and I will thee requite.

FLUELLEN

Aunchient Pistol, I do partly understand your meaning.

PISTOL

Why then, rejoice therefore.

FLUELLEN

Certainly, aunchient, it is not a thing to rejoice at: for if, look you, he were my brother, I would desire the duke to use his good pleasure, and put him to execution; for discipline ought to be used.

PISTOL

Die and be damn'd! and figo for thy friendship!

FLUELLEN

It is well.

PISTOL

The fig of Spain!   [Exit

FLUELLEN

Very good.

GOWER

Why, this is an arrant counterfeit rascal; I remember him now; a bawd, a cutpurse.

FLUELLEN

I'll assure you, a' uttered as prave words at the pridge as you shall see in a summer's day. But it is very well; what he has spoke to me, that is well, I warrant you, when time is serve.

GOWER

Why, 'tis a gull, a fool, a rogue, that now and then goes to the wars, to grace himself at his return into London under the form of a soldier. And such fellows are perfect in the great commanders' names: and they will learn you by rote where services were done; at such and such a sconce, at such a breach, at such a convoy; who came off bravely, who was shot, who disgraced, what terms the enemy stood on; and this they con perfectly in the phrase of war, which they trick up with new-tuned oaths: and what a beard of the general's cut and a horrid suit of the camp will do among foaming bottles and ale-washed wits, is wonderful to be thought on. But you must learn to know such slanders of the age, or else you may be marvellously mistook.

FLUELLEN

I tell you what, Captain Gower; I do perceive he is not the man that he would gladly make show to the world he is: if I find a hole in his coat, I will tell him

my mind. [Drum heard] Hark you, the king is coming, and I must speak with him from the pridge.

Drum and Colours. Enter KING HENRY, GLOUCESTER, and SOLDIERS

God pless your majesty!

KING

How now, Fluellen! camest thou from the bridge?

FLUELLEN

Ay, so please your majesty. The Duke of Exeter has very gallantly maintained the pridge: the French is gone off, look you; and there is gallant and most prave passages: marry, th' athversary was have possession of the pridge; but he is enforced to retire, and the Duke of Exeter is master of the pridge: I can tell your majesty, the duke is a prave man.

KING

What men have you lost, Fluellen?

FLUELLEN

The perdition of th' athversary hath been very great, reasonable great: marry, for my part, I think the duke hath lost never a man, but one that is like to be executed for robbing a church, one Bardolph, if your majesty know the man: his face is all bu-bukles, and whelks, and knobs, and flames o' fire: and his lips blows at his nose, and it is like a coal of fire, sometimes plue and sometimes red; but his nose is executed, and his fire's out.

KING

We would have all such offenders so cut off: and we give express charge, that in our marches through the country, there be nothing compelled from the villages, nothing taken but paid for, none of the French upbraided or abused in disdainful language; for when lenity and cruelty play for a kingdom, the gentler gamester is the soonest winner.

Tucket. Enter MONTJOY

MONTJOY

You know me by my habit.

KING

Well then I know thee: what shall I know of thee?

MONTJOY

My master's mind.

KING

Unfold it.

MONTJOY

Thus says my king: Say thou to Harry of England: Though we seemed dead, we did but sleep: advantage is a better soldier than rashness. Tell him we could have rebuked him at Harfleur, but that we thought not good to bruise an injury till it were full ripe: now we speak upon our cue, and our voice is imperial: England shall repent his folly, see his weakness, and admire our sufferance. Bid him therefore consider of his ransom; which must proportion the losses we have borne, the subjects we have lost, the disgrace we have digested; which in weight to re-answer, his pettiness would bow under. For our losses, his exchequer is too poor; for the effusion of our blood, the muster of his kingdom too faint a number; and for our disgrace, his own per-

son, kneeling at our feet, but a weak and worthless
satisfaction. To this add defiance: and tell him, for
conclusion, he hath betrayed his followers, whose
condemnation is pronounced. So far my king and
master; so much my office.

KING

What is thy name? I know thy quality.

MONTJOY

Montjoy.

KING

Thou dost thy office fairly. Turn thee back,
And tell thy king I do not seek him now;
But could be willing to march on to Calais
Without impeachment: for, to say the sooth,
Though 'tis no wisdom to confess so much
Unto an enemy of craft and vantage,
My people are with sickness much enfeebled,
My numbers lessen'd, and those few I have
Almost no better than so many French;
Who when they were in health, I tell thee, herald,
I thought upon one pair of English legs
Did march three Frenchmen. Yet, forgive me, God,
That I do brag thus! This your air of France
Hath blown that vice in me; I must repent.
Go therefore, tell thy master here I am;
My ransom is this frail and worthless trunk,
My army but a weak and sickly guard;
Yet, God before, tell him we will come on,
Though France himself and such another neigh-
    bour
Stand in our way. There's for thy labour, Montjoy.
Go, bid thy master well advise himself:
If we may pass, we will; if we be hinder'd,
We shall your tawny ground with your red blood
Discolour: and so, Montjoy, fare you well.
The sum of all our answer is but this:
We would not seek a battle, as we are;
Nor, as we are, we say we will not shun it:
So tell your master.

MONTJOY

I shall deliver so. Thanks to your highness.   [Exit

GLOUCESTER

I hope they will not come upon us now.

KING

We are in God's hand, brother, not in theirs.
March to the bridge; it now draws toward night:
Beyond the river we'll encamp ourselves,
And on to-morrow bid them march away.   [Exeunt

SCENE VII. *The French camp, near Agincourt*

Enter the CONSTABLE *of France, the* LORD RAMBURES,
ORLEANS, DAUPHIN, *with others*

CONSTABLE

Tut! I have the best armour of the world. Would it
were day!

ORLEANS

You have an excellent armour; but let my horse
have his due.

CONSTABLE

It is the best horse of Europe.

ORLEANS

Will it never be morning?

DAUPHIN

My Lord of Orleans, and my lord high constable,
you talk of horse and armour?

ORLEANS

You are as well provided of both as any prince in
the world.

DAUPHIN

What a long night is this! I will not change my horse
with any that treads but on four pasterns. Ça, ha! he
bounds from the earth, as if his entrails were hairs;
le cheval volant, the Pegasus, chez les narines de
feu! When I bestride him, I soar, I am a hawk: he
trots the air; the earth sings when he touches it; the
basest horn of his hoof is more musical than the pipe
of Hermes.

ORLEANS

He's of the colour of the nutmeg.

DAUPHIN

And of the heat of the ginger. It is a beast for Perseus: he is pure air and fire; and the dull elements
of earth and water never appear in him, but only in
patient stillness while his rider mounts him: he is
indeed a horse; and all other jades you may call
beasts.

CONSTABLE

Indeed, my lord, it is a most absolute and excellent
horse.

DAUPHIN

It is the prince of palfreys; his neigh is like the bidding of a monarch, and his countenance enforces
homage.

ORLEANS

No more, cousin.

DAUPHIN

Nay, the man hath no wit that cannot, from the
rising of the lark to the lodging of the lamb, vary
deserved praise on my palfrey: it is a theme as
fluent as the sea: turn the sands into eloquent
tongues, and my horse is argument for them all: 'tis
a subject for a sovereign to reason on, and for a
sovereign's sovereign to ride on; and for the world,
familiar to us and unknown, to lay apart their particular functions and wonder at him. I once writ a
sonnet in his praise, and began thus: 'Wonder of
nature,'—

ORLEANS

I have heard a sonnet begin so to one's mistress.

DAUPHIN

Then did they imitate that which I composed to my
courser, for my horse is my mistress.

ORLEANS

Your mistress bears well.

DAUPHIN

Me well; which is the prescript praise and perfection of a good and particular mistress.

CONSTABLE
Nay, for methought yesterday your mistress shrewdly shook your back.

DAUPHIN
So perhaps did yours.

CONSTABLE
Mine was not bridled.

DAUPHIN
O then belike she was old and gentle; and you rode, like a kern of Ireland, your French hose off, and in your strait strossers.

CONSTABLE
You have good judgement in horsemanship.

DAUPHIN
Be warned by me, then: they that ride so, and ride not warily, fall into foul bogs. I had rather have my horse to my mistress.

CONSTABLE
I had as lief have my mistress a jade.

DAUPHIN
I tell thee, constable, my mistress wears his own hair.

CONSTABLE
I could make as true a boast as that, if I had a sow to my mistress.

DAUPHIN
'Le chien est retourné à son propre vomissement, et la truie lavée au bourbier:' thou makest use of any thing.

CONSTABLE
Yet do I not use my horse for my mistress, or any such proverb so little kin to the purpose.

RAMBURES
My lord constable, the armour that I saw in your tent to-night, are those stars or suns upon it?

CONSTABLE
Stars, my lord.

DAUPHIN
Some of them will fall to-morrow, I hope.

CONSTABLE
And yet my sky shall not want.

DAUPHIN
That may be, for you bear a many superfluously, and 'twere more honour some were away.

CONSTABLE
Even as your horse bears your praises; who would trot as well, were some of your brags dismounted.

DAUPHIN
Would I were able to load him with his desert! Will it never be day? I will trot to-morrow a mile, and my way shall be paved with English faces.

CONSTABLE
I will not say so, for fear I should be faced out of my way: but I would it were morning; for I would fain be about the ears of the English.

RUMBURES
Who will go to hazard with me for twenty prisoners?

CONSTABLE
You must first go yourself to hazard, ere you have them.

DAUPHIN
'Tis midnight; I'll go arm myself.   [Exit

ORLEANS
The Dauphin longs for morning.

RAMBURES
He longs to eat the English.

CONSTABLE
I think he will eat all he kills.

ORLEANS
By the white hand of my lady, he's a gallant prince.

CONSTABLE
Swear by her foot, that she may tread out the oath.

ORLEANS
He is simply the most active gentleman of France.

CONSTABLE
Doing his activity; and he will still be doing.

ORLEANS
He never did harm, that I heard of.

CONSTABLE
Nor will do none to-morrow: he will keep that good name still.

ORLEANS
I know him to be valiant.

CONSTABLE
I was told that by one that knows him better than you.

ORLEANS
What's he?

CONSTABLE
Marry, he told me so himself; and he said he cared not who knew it.

ORLEANS
He needs not; it is no hidden virtue in him.

CONSTABLE
By my faith, sir, but it is; never any body saw it but his lackey: 'tis a hooded valour; and when it appears, it will bate.

ORLEANS
Ill will never said well.

CONSTABLE
I will cap that proverb with 'There is flattery in friendship.'

ORLEANS
And I will take up that with 'Give the devil his due.'

CONSTABLE
Well placed: there stands your friend for the devil: have at the very eye of that proverb with 'A pox of the devil.'

ORLEANS
You are the better at proverbs, by how much 'A fool's bolt is soon shot.'

CONSTABLE
You have shot over.

ORLEANS
'Tis not the first time you were overshot.

Enter a MESSENGER
MESSENGER

My lord high constable, the English lie within
fifteen hundred paces of your tents.

CONSTABLE

Who hath measured the ground?

MESSENGER

The Lord Grandpré.

CONSTABLE

A valiant and most expert gentleman. Would it
were day! Alas, poor Harry of England! he longs
not for the dawning as we do.

ORLEANS

What a wretched and peevish fellow is this King of
England, to mope with his fat-brained followers so
far out of his knowledge!

CONSTABLE

If the English had any apprehension, they would
run away.

ORLEANS

That they lack; for if their heads had any intellectual armour, they could never wear such heavy
headpieces.

RAMBURES

That island of England breeds very valiant creatures; their mastiffs are of unmatchable courage.

ORLEANS

Foolish curs, that run winking into the mouth of a
Russian bear and have their heads crushed like rotten apples! You may as well say, that's a valiant flea
that dare eat his breakfast on the lip of a lion.

CONSTABLE

Just, just; and the men do sympathize with the
mastiffs in robustious and rough coming on, leaving
their wits with their wives: and then give them great
meals of beef, and iron and steel, they will eat like
wolves, and fight like devils.

ORLEANS

Ay, but these English are shrewdly out of beef.

CONSTABLE

Then shall we find to-morrow they have only
stomachs to eat and none to fight. Now is it time to
arm: come, shall we about it?

ORLEANS

It is now two o'clock: but, let me see, by ten
We shall have each a hundred Englishmen. [*Exeunt*

ACT IV

PROLOGUE

Enter CHORUS
CHORUS

Now entertain conjecture of a time
When creeping murmur and the poring dark
Fills the wide vessel of the universe.
From camp to camp through the foul womb of
    night

The hum of either army stilly sounds,
That the fix'd sentinels almost receive
The secret whispers of each other's watch:
Fire answers fire, and through their paly flames
Each battle sees the other's umber'd face;
Steed threatens steed, in high and boastful neighs
Piercing the night's dull ear; and from the tents
The armourers, accomplishing the knights,
With busy hammers closing rivets up,
Give dreadful note of preparation:
The country cocks do crow, the clocks do toll,
And the third hour of drowsy morning name.
Proud of their numbers and secure in soul,
The confident and over-lusty French
Do the low-rated English play at dice;
And chide the cripple tardy-gaited night
Who, like a foul and ugly witch, doth limp
So tediously away. The poor condemned English,
Like sacrifices, by their watchful fires
Sit patiently and inly ruminate
The morning's danger, and their gesture sad
Investing lank-lean cheeks and war-worn coats
Presenteth them unto the gazing moon
So many horrid ghosts. O now, who will behold
The royal captain of this ruin'd band
Walking from watch to watch, from tent to tent,
Let him cry 'Praise and glory on his head!'
For forth he goes and visits all his host,
Bids them good morrow with a modest smile,
And calls them brothers, friends and countrymen.
Upon his royal face there is no note
How dread an army hath enrounded him;
Nor doth he dedicate one jot of colour
Unto the weary and all-watched night,
But freshly looks and over-bears attaint
With cheerful semblance and sweet majesty;
That every wretch, pining and pale before,
Beholding him, plucks comfort from his looks:
A largess universal like the sun
His liberal eye doth give to every one,
Thawing cold fear, that mean and gentle all
Behold, as may unworthiness define,
A little touch of Harry in the night.
And so our scene must to the battle fly;
Where—O for pity!—we shall much disgrace
With four or five most vile and ragged foils,
Right ill-disposed in brawl ridiculous,
The name of Agincourt. Yet sit and see,
Minding true things by what their mockeries be.
                                                            [*Exit*

SCENE I. *The English camp at Agincourt*

Enter KING HENRY, BEDFORD, *and* GLOUCESTER
KING

Gloucester, 'tis true that we are in great danger;
The greater therefore should our courage be.
Good morrow, brother Bedford. God Almighty!
There is some soul of goodness in things evil,
Would men observingly distil it out.

For our bad neighbour makes us early stirrers,
Which is both healthful and good husbandry:
Besides, they are our outward consciences,
And preachers to us all, admonishing
That we should dress us fairly for our end.
Thus may we gather honey from the weed,
And make a moral of the devil himself.

Enter ERPINGHAM

Good morrow, old Sir Thomas Erpingham:
A good soft pillow for that good white head
Were better than a churlish turf of France.

ERPINGHAM

Not so, my liege: this lodging likes me better,
Since I may say 'Now lie I like a king.'

KING

'Tis good for men to love their present pains
Upon example; so the spirit is eased:
And when the mind is quicken'd, out of doubt,
The organs, though defunct and dead before,
Break up their drowsy grave and newly move,
With casted slough and fresh legerity.
Lend me thy cloak, Sir Thomas. Brothers both,
Commend me to the princes in our camp;
Do my good morrow to them, and anon
Desire them all to my pavilion.

GLOUCESTER

We shall, my liege.

ERPINGHAM

Shall I attend your grace?

KING

           No, my good knight;
Go with my brothers to my lords of England:
I and my bosom must debate a while,
And then I would no other company.

ERPINGHAM

The Lord in heaven bless thee, noble Harry!

[*Exeunt all but* KING

KING

God-a-mercy, old heart! thou speak'st cheerfully.

Enter PISTOL

PISTOL

Qui va là?

KING

A friend.

PISTOL

Discuss unto me; art thou officer?
Or art thou base, common, and popular?

KING

I am a gentleman of a company.

PISTOL

Trail'st thou the puissant pike?

KING

Even so. What are you?

PISTOL

As good a gentleman as the emperor.

KING

Then you are a better than the king.

PISTOL

The king's a bawcock, and a heart of gold,
A lad of life, an imp of fame;

Of parents good, of fist most valiant:
I kiss his dirty shoe, and from heart-string
I love the lovely bully. What is thy name?

KING

Harry le Roy.

PISTOL

Le Roy! a Cornish name: art thou of Cornish crew?

KING

No, I am a Welshman.

PISTOL

Know'st thou Fluellen?

KING

Yes.

PISTOL

Tell him, I'll knock his leek about his pate
Upon Saint Davy's day.

KING

Do not you wear your dagger in your cap that day,
lest he knock that about yours.

PISTOL

Art thou his friend?

KING

And his kinsman too.

PISTOL

The figo for thee, then!

KING

I thank you: God be with you!

PISTOL

My name is Pistol call'd.   [*Exit*

KING

It sorts well with your fierceness.

Enter FLUELLEN *and* GOWER

GOWER

Captain Fluellen!

FLUELLEN

So! in the name of Jesu Christ, speak lower. It is the
greatest admiration in the universal world, when
the true and aunchient prerogatifes and laws of the
wars is not kept: if you would take the pains but to
examine the wars of Pompey the Great, you shall
find, I warrant you, that there is no tiddle taddle
nor pibble pabble in Pompey's camp; I warrant
you, you shall find the ceremonies of the wars, and
the cares of it, and the forms of it, and the sobriety
of it, and the modesty of it, to be otherwise.

GOWER

Why, the enemy is loud; you hear him all night.

FLUELLEN

If the enemy is an ass and a fool and a prating coxcomb, is it meet, think you, that we should also,
look you, be an ass and a fool and a prating coxcomb? in your own conscience, now?

GOWER

I will speak lower.

FLUELLEN

I pray you and beseech you that you will.

[*Exeunt* GOWER *and* FLUELLEN

KING

Though it appear a little out of fashion,
There is much care and valour in this Welshman.

Enter three soldiers, JOHN BATES, ALEXANDER COURT, *and* MICHAEL WILLIAMS

COURT

Brother John Bates, is not that the morning which breaks yonder?

BATES

I think it be: but we have no great cause to desire the approach of day.

WILLIAMS

We see yonder the beginning of the day, but I think we shall never see the end of it. Who goes there?

KING

A friend.

WILLIAMS

Under what captain serve you?

KING

Under Sir Thomas Erpingham.

WILLIAMS

A good old commander and a most kind gentleman: I pray you, what thinks he of our estate?

KING

Even as men wrecked upon a sand, that look to be washed off the next tide.

BATES

He hath not told his thought to the king?

KING

No; nor it is not meet he should. For, though I speak it to you, I think the king is but a man, as I am: the violet smells to him as it doth to me; the element shows to him as it doth to me; all his senses have but human conditions: his ceremonies laid by, in his nakedness he appears but a man; and though his affections are higher mounted than ours, yet, when they stoop, they stoop with the like wing. Therefore when he sees reason of fears, as we do, his fears, out of doubt, be of the same relish as ours are: yet, in reason, no man should possess him with any appearance of fear, lest he, by showing it, should dishearten his army.

BATES

He may show what outward courage he will; but I believe, as cold a night as 'tis, he could wish himself in Thames up to the neck; and so I would he were, and I by him, at all adventures, so we were quit here.

KING

By my troth, I will speak my conscience of the king: I think he would not wish himself any where but where he is.

BATES

Then I would he were here alone; so should he be sure to be ransomed, and a many poor men's lives saved.

KING

I dare say you love him not so ill, to wish him here alone, howsoever you speak this to feel other men's minds: methinks I could not die any where so contented as in the king's company; his cause being just and his quarrel honourable.

WILLIAMS

That's more than we know.

BATES

Ay, or more than we should seek after; for we know enough, if we know we are the king's subjects: if his cause be wrong, our obedience to the king wipes the crime of it out of us.

WILLIAMS

But if the cause be not good, the king himself hath a heavy reckoning to make, when all those legs and arms and heads, chopped off in a battle, shall join together at the latter day and cry all 'We died at such a place;' some swearing, some crying for a surgeon, some upon their wives left poor behind them, some upon the debts they owe, some upon their children rawly left. I am afeard there are few die well that die in a battle; for how can they charitably dispose of any thing, when blood is their argument? Now, if these men do not die well, it will be a black matter for the king that led them to it; whom to disobey were against all proportion of subjection.

KING

So, if a son that is by his father sent about merchandise do sinfully miscarry upon the sea, the imputation of his wickedness, by your rule, should be imposed upon his father that sent him: or if a servant, under his master's command transporting a sum of money, be assailed by robbers and die in many irreconciled iniquities, you may call the business of the master the author of the servant's damnation: but this is not so: the king is not bound to answer the particular endings of his soldiers, the father of his son, nor the master of his servant; for they purpose not their death, when they purpose their services. Besides, there is no king, be his cause never so spotless, if it come to the arbitrement of swords, can try it out with all unspotted soldiers: some peradventure have on them the guilt of premeditated and contrived murder; some, of beguiling virgins with the broken seals of perjury; some, making the wars their bulwark, that have before gored the gentle bosom of peace with pillage and robbery. Now, if these men have defeated the law and outrun native punishment, though they can outstrip men, they have no wings to fly from God: war is His beadle, war is His vengeance; so that here men are punished for before-breach of the king's laws in now the king's quarrel: where they feared the death, they have borne life away; and where they would be safe, they perish: then if they die unprovided, no more is the king guilty of their damnation than he was before guilty of those impieties for the which they are now visited. Every subject's duty is the king's; but every subject's soul is his own. Therefore should every soldier in the wars do as every sick man in his bed, wash every mote out of his conscience: and dying so, death is to him advantage; or not dying, the time was blessedly lost wherein such preparation was gained: and in him that escapes, it were not sin to think that, making God so free an offer, He let him outlive that day to see His greatness and to teach others how they should prepare.

WILLIAMS

'Tis certain, every man that dies ill, the ill upon his own head, the king is not to answer it.

BATES

I do not desire he should answer for me; and yet I determine to fight lustily for him.

KING

I myself heard the king say he would not be ransomed.

WILLIAMS

Ay, he said so, to make us fight cheerfully: but when our throats are cut, he may be ransomed, and we ne'er the wiser.

KING

If I live to see it, I will never trust his word after.

WILLIAMS

You pay him then. That's a perilous shot out of an elder-gun, that a poor and a private displeasure can do against a monarch! you may as well go about to turn the sun to ice with fanning in his face with a peacock's feather. You'll never trust his word after! come, 'tis a foolish saying.

KING

Your reproof is something too round: I should be angry with you, if the time were convenient.

WILLIAMS

Let it be a quarrel between us, if you live.

KING

I embrace it.

WILLIAMS

How shall I know thee again?

KING

Give me any gage of thine, and I will wear it in my bonnet: then, if ever thou darest acknowledge it, I will make it my quarrel.

WILLIAMS

Here's my glove: give me another of thine.

KING

There.

WILLIAMS

This will I also wear in my cap: if ever thou come to me and say, after to-morrow, 'This is my glove,' by this hand, I will take thee a box on the ear.

KING

If ever I live to see it, I will challenge it.

WILLIAMS

Thou darest as well be hanged.

KING

Well, I will do it, though I take thee in the king's company.

WILLIAMS

Keep thy word: fare thee well.

BATES

Be friends, you English fools, be friends: we have French quarrels enow, if you could tell how to reckon.

KING

Indeed, the French may lay twenty French crowns to one, they will beat us; for they bear them on their shoulders: but it is no English treason to cut French crowns, and to-morrow the king himself will be a clipper.　　　　　　　[Exeunt SOLDIERS

Upon the king! let us our lives, our souls,
Our debts, our careful wives,
Our children and our sins lay on the king!
We must bear all. O hard condition,
Twin-born with greatness, subject to the breath
Of every fool, whose sense no more can feel
But his own wringing! What infinite heart's-ease
Must kings neglect, that private men enjoy!
And what have kings, that privates have not too,
Save ceremony, save general ceremony?
And what art thou, thou idol ceremony?
What kind of god art thou, that suffer'st more
Of mortal griefs than do thy worshippers?
What are thy rents? what are thy comings in?
O ceremony, show me but thy worth!
What is thy soul of adoration?
Art thou aught else but place, degree and form,
Creating awe and fear in other men?
Wherein thou art less happy being fear'd
Than they in fearing.
What drink'st thou oft, instead of homage sweet,
But poison'd flattery? O, be sick, great greatness,
And bid thy ceremony give thee cure!
Think'st thou the fiery fever will go out
With titles blown from adulation?
Will it give place to flexure and low bending?
Canst thou, when thou command'st the beggar's knee,
Command the health of it? No, thou proud dream,
That play'st so subtly with a king's repose;
I am a king that find thee, and I know
'Tis not the balm, the sceptre and the ball,
The sword, the mace, the crown imperial,
The intertissued robe of gold and pearl,
The farced title running 'fore the king,
The throne he sits on, nor the tide of pomp
That beats upon the high shore of this world,
No, not all these, thrice-gorgeous ceremony,
Not all these, laid in bed majestical,
Can sleep so soundly as the wretched slave,
Who with a body fill'd and vacant mind
Gets him to rest, cramm'd with distressful bread;
Never sees horrid night, the child of hell,
But, like a lackey, from the rise to set
Sweats in the eye of Phœbus and all night
Sleeps in Elysium; next day after dawn,
Doth rise and help Hyperion to his horse,
And follows so the ever-running year,
With profitable labour, to his grave:
And, but for ceremony, such a wretch,
Winding up days with toil and nights with sleep,
Had the fore-hand and vantage of a king.
The slave, a member of the country's peace,
Enjoys it; but in gross brain little wots

What watch the king keeps to maintain the peace,
Whose hours the peasant best advantages.

Re-enter ERPINGHAM

ERPINGHAM

My lord, your nobles, jealous of your absence,
Seek through your camp to find you.

KING

      Good old knight,
Collect them all together at my tent:
I'll be before thee.

ERPINGHAM

    I shall do 't, my lord.   [*Exit*

KING

O God of battles! steel my soldiers' hearts;
Possess them not with fear; take from them now
The sense of reckoning, if the opposed numbers
Pluck their hearts from them. Not to-day, O Lord,
O, not to-day, think not upon the fault
My father made in compassing the crown!
I Richard's body have interred new;
And on it have bestow'd more contrite tears
Than from it issued forced drops of blood:
Five hundred poor I have in yearly pay,
Who twice a-day their wither'd hands hold up
Toward heaven, to pardon blood; and I have built
Two chantries, where the sad and solemn priests
Sing still for Richard's soul. More will I do;
Though all that I can do is nothing worth,
Since that my penitence comes after all,
Imploring pardon.

Re-enter GLOUCESTER

GLOUCESTER

My liege!

KING

   My brother Gloucester's voice? Ay;
I know thy errand, I will go with thee:
The day, my friends and all things stay for me.

           [*Exeunt*

SCENE II. *The French camp*

Enter the DAUPHIN, ORLEANS, RAMBURES, *and others*

ORLEANS

The sun doth gild our armour; up, my lords!

DAUPHIN

Montez à cheval! My horse! varlet! laquais! ha!

ORLEANS

O brave spirit!

DAUPHIN

Via! les eaux et la terre.

ORLEANS

Rien puis? l'air et le feu.

DAUPHIN

Ciel, cousin Orleans.

Enter CONSTABLE

Now, my lord constable!

CONSTABLE

Hark, how our steeds for present service neigh!

DAUPHIN

Mount them, and make incision in their hides,

That their hot blood may spin in English eyes,
And dout them with superfluous courage, ha!

RAMBURES

What, will you have them weep our horses' blood?
How shall we then behold their natural tears?

Enter MESSENGER

MESSENGER

The English are embattled, you French peers.

CONSTABLE

To horse, you gallant princes! straight to horse!
Do but behold yon poor and starved band,
And your fair show shall suck away their souls,
Leaving them but the shales and husks of men.
There is not work enough for all our hands;
Scarce blood enough in all their sickly veins
To give each naked curtle-axe a stain,
That our French gallants shall to-day draw out,
And sheathe for lack of sport: let us but blow on
 them,
The vapour of our valour will o'erturn them.
'Tis positive 'gainst all exceptions, lords,
That our superfluous lackeys and our peasants,
Who in unnecessary action swarm
About our squares of battle, were enow
To purge this field of such a hilding foe,
Though we upon this mountain's basis by
Took stand for idle speculation:
But that our honours must not. What's to say?
A very little little let us do,
And all is done. Then let the trumpets sound
The tucket sonance and the note to mount;
For our approach shall so much dare the field
That England shall couch down in fear and yield.

Enter GRANDPRÉ

GRANDPRÉ

Why do you stay so long, my lords of France?
Yon island carrions, desperate of their bones,
Ill-favouredly become the morning field:
Their ragged curtains poorly are let loose,
And our air shakes them passing scornfully:
Big Mars seems bankrupt in their beggar'd host
And faintly through a rusty beaver peeps:
The horsemen sit like fixed candlesticks,
With torch-staves in their hand; and their poor
 jades
Lob down their heads, dropping the hides and hips,
The gum down-roping from their pale-dead eyes,
And in their pale dull mouths the gimmal bit
Lies foul with chew'd grass, still and motionless;
And their executors, the knavish crows,
Fly o'er them, all impatient for their hour.
Description cannot suit itself in words
To demonstrate the life of such a battle
In life so lifeless as it shows itself.

CONSTABLE

They have said their prayers, and they stay for
 death.

DAUPHIN

Shall we go send them dinners and fresh suits

And give their fasting horses provender,
And after fight with them?
CONSTABLE
I stay but for my guidon: to the field!
I will the banner from a trumpet take,
And use it for my haste. Come, come, away!
The sun is high, and we outwear the day. [Exeunt

SCENE III. *The English camp*

Enter GLOUCESTER, BEDFORD, EXETER, ERPINGHAM,
with all his host: SALISBURY *and* WESTMORELAND
GLOUCESTER
Where is the king?
BEDFORD
The king himself is rode to view their battle.
WESTMORELAND
Of fighting men they have full three score thousand.
EXETER
There's five to one; besides, they all are fresh.
SALISBURY
God's arm strike with us! 'tis a fearful odds.
God be wi' you, princes all; I'll to my charge:
If we no more meet till we meet in heaven,
Then, joyfully, my noble Lord of Bedford,
My dear Lord Gloucester, and my good Lord
Exeter,
And my kind kinsman, warriors all, adieu!
BEDFORD
Farewell, good Salisbury; and good luck go with
thee!
EXETER
Farewell, kind lord; fight valiantly to-day:
And yet I do thee wrong to mind thee of it,
For thou art framed of the firm truth of valour.
[*Exit* SALISBURY
BEDFORD
He is as full of valour as of kindness;
Princely in both.
Enter the KING
WESTMORELAND
O that we now had here
But one ten thousand of those men in England
That do no work to-day!
KING
What's he that wishes so?
My cousin Westmoreland? No, my fair cousin:
If we are mark'd to die, we are enow
To do our country loss; and if to live,
The fewer men, the greater share of honour.
God's will! I pray thee, wish not one man more.
By Jove, I am not covetous for gold,
Nor care I who doth feed upon my cost;
It yearns me not if men my garments wear;
Such outward things dwell not in my desires:
But if it be a sin to covet honour,
I am the most offending soul alive.
No, faith, my coz, wish not a man from England:
God's peace! I would not lose so great an honour

As one man more, methinks, would share from me
For the best hope I have. O, do not wish one more!
Rather proclaim it, Westmoreland, through my
host,
That he which hath no stomach to this fight,
Let him depart; his passport shall be made
And crowns for convoy put into his purse:
We would not die in that man's company
That fears his fellowship to die with us.
This day is call'd the feast of Crispian:
He that outlives this day, and comes safe home,
Will stand a tip-toe when this day is named,
And rouse him at the name of Crispian.
He that shall live this day, and see old age,
Will yearly on the vigil feast his neighbours,
And say, 'To-morrow is Saint Crispian:'
Then will he strip his sleeve and show his scars,
And say, 'These wounds I had on Crispin's day.'
Old men forget; yet all shall be forgot,
But he'll remember with advantages
What feats he did that day: then shall our names,
Familiar in his mouth as household words,
Harry the king, Bedford and Exeter,
Warwick and Talbot, Salisbury and Gloucester,
Be in their flowing cups freshly remember'd.
This story shall the good man teach his son;
And Crispin Crispian shall ne'er go by,
From this day to the ending of the world,
But we in it shall be remembered;
We few, we happy few, we band of brothers;
For he to-day that sheds his blood with me
Shall be my brother; be he ne'er so vile,
This day shall gentle his condition:
And gentlemen in England now a-bed
Shall think themselves accursed they were not here,
And hold their manhoods cheap whiles any speaks
That fought with us upon Saint Crispin's day.
Re-enter SALISBURY
SALISBURY
My sovereign lord, bestow yourself with speed:
The French are bravely in their battles set,
And will with all expedience charge on us.
KING
All things are ready, if our minds be so.
WESTMORELAND
Perish the man whose mind is backward now!
KING
Thou dost not wish more help from England, coz?
WESTMORELAND
God's will! my liege, would you and I alone,
Without more help, could fight this royal battle!
KING
Why, now thou hast unwish'd five thousand men;
Which likes me better than to wish us one.
You know your places: God be with you all!
Tucket. Enter MONTJOY
MONTJOY
Once more I come to know of thee, King Harry,
If for thy ransom thou wilt now compound,
Before thy most assured overthrow:

For certainly thou art so near the gulf,
Thou needs must be englutted. Besides, in mercy,
The constable desires thee thou wilt mind
Thy followers of repentance; that their souls
May make a peaceful and a sweet retire
From off these fields, where, wretches, their poor
    bodies
Must lie and fester.

KING
Who hath sent thee now?

MONTJOY
The Constable of France.

KING
I pray thee, bear my former answer back:
Bid them achieve me and then sell my bones.
Good God! why should they mock poor fellows thus?
The man that once did sell the lion's skin
While the beast lived, was killed with hunting him.
A many of our bodies shall no doubt
Find native graves; upon the which, I trust,
Shall witness live in brass of this day's work:
And those that leave their valiant bones in France,
Dying like men, though buried in your dunghills,
They shall be famed; for there the sun shall greet
    them,
And draw their honours reeking up to heaven;
Leaving their earthly parts to choke your clime,
The smell whereof shall breed a plague in France.
Mark then abounding valour in our English,
That being dead, like to the bullet's grazing,
Break out into a second course of mischief,
Killing in relapse of mortality.
Let me speak proudly: tell the constable
We are but warriors for the working-day;
Our gayness and our gilt are all besmirch'd
With rainy marching in the painful field;
There's not a piece of feather in our host—
Good argument, I hope, we will not fly—
And time hath worn us into slovenry:
But, by the mass, our hearts are in the trim;
And my poor soldiers tell me, yet ere night
They'll be in fresher robes, or they will pluck
The gay new coats o'er the French soldiers' heads
And turn them out of service. If they do this,—
As, if God please, they shall,—my ransom then
Will soon be levied. Herald, save thou thy labour;
Come thou no more for ransom, gentle herald:
They shall have none, I swear, but these my joints;
Which if they have as I will leave 'em them,
Shall yield them little, tell the constable.

MONTJOY
I shall, King Harry. And so fare thee well:
Thou never shalt hear herald any more.   [Exit

KING
I fear thou'lt once more come again for ransom.

Enter YORK

YORK
My lord, most humbly on my knee I beg
The leading of the vaward.

KING
Take it, brave York. Now, soldiers, march away:
And how thou pleasest, God, dispose the day!
     [Exeunt

SCENE IV. *The field of battle*

Alarum. Excursions. Enter PISTOL, FRENCH SOLDIER,
and BOY

PISTOL
Yield, cur!

FRENCH SOLDIER
Je pense que vous êtes gentilhomme de bonne
qualité.

PISTOL
Qualtitie calmie custure me! Art thou a gentleman?
what is thy name? Discuss.

FRENCH SOLDIER
O Seigneur Dieu!

PISTOL
O, Signieur Dew should be a gentleman:
Perpend my words, O Signieur Dew, and mark;
O Signieur Dew, thou diest on point of fox,
Except, O signieur, thou do give to me
Egregious ransom.

FRENCH SOLDIER
O, prenez miséricorde! ayez pitié de moi!

PISTOL
Moy shall not serve; I will have forty moys;
Or I will fetch thy rim out at thy throat
In drops of crimson blood.

FRENCH SOLDIER
Est-il impossible d'échapper la force de ton bras?

PISTOL
Brass, cur!
Thou damned and luxurious mountain goat,
Offer'st me brass?

FRENCH SOLDIER
O pardonnez moi!

PISTOL
Say'st thou me so? is that a ton of moys?
Come hither, boy: ask me this slave in French
What is his name.

BOY
Écoutez: comment êtes-vous appelé?

FRENCH SOLDIER
Monsieur le Fer.

BOY
He says his name is Master Fer.

PISTOL
Master Fer! I'll fer him, and firk him, and ferret
him: discuss the same in French unto him.

BOY
I do not know the French for fer, and ferret, and
firk.

PISTOL
Bid him prepare; for I will cut his throat.

FRENCH SOLDIER

Que dit-il, monsieur?

BOY

Il me commande de vous dire que vous faites vous
prêt; car ce soldat ici est disposé tout à cette heure
de couper votre gorge.

PISTOL

Owy, cuppele gorge, permafoy,
Peasant, unless thou give me crowns, brave crowns;
Or mangled shalt thou be by this my sword.

FRENCH SOLDIER

O, je vous supplie, pour l'amour de Dieu, me pardonner! Je suis gentilhomme de bonne maison:
gardez ma vie, et je vous donnerai deux cents écus.

PISTOL

What are his words?

BOY

He prays you to save his life: he is a gentleman of a
good house; and for his ransom he will give you two
hundred crowns.

PISTOL

Tell him my fury shall abate, and I
The crowns will take.

FRENCH SOLDIER

Petit monsieur, que dit-il?

BOY

Encore qu'il est contre son jurement de pardonner
aucun prisonnier, néanmoins, pour les écus que
vous l'avez promis, il est content de vous donner la
liberté, le franchisement.

FRENCH SOLDIER

Sur mes genoux je vous donne mille remercîmens;
et je m'estime heureux que je suis tombé entre les
mains d'un chevalier, je pense, le plus brave, vail-
lant, et très distingué seigneur d'Angleterre.

PISTOL

Expound unto me, boy.

BOY

He gives you, upon his knees, a thousand thanks;
and he esteems himself happy that he hath fallen
into the hands of one, as he thinks, the most brave,
valorous, and thrice-worthy signieur of England.

PISTOL

As I suck blood, I will some mercy show.
Follow me!

BOY

Suivez-vous le grand capitaine. [*Exeunt* PISTOL, *and*
FRENCH SOLDIER] I did never know so full a voice
issue from so empty a heart: but the saying is true,
'The empty vessel makes the greatest sound.' Bardolph and Nym had ten times more valour than this
roaring devil i' the old play, that every one may
pare his nails with a wooden dagger; and they are
both hanged; and so would this be, if he durst steal
any thing adventurously. I must stay with the
lackeys, with the luggage of our camp: the French
might have a good prey of us, if he knew of it; for
there is none to guard it but boys. [*Exit*

SCENE V. *Another part of the field*

Enter CONSTABLE, ORLEANS, BOURBON, DAUPHIN, *and*
RAMBURES

CONSTABLE

O diable!

ORLEANS

O Seigneur! le jour est perdu, tout est perdu!

DAUPHIN

Mort de ma vie! all is confounded, all!
Reproach and everlasting shame
Sits mocking in our plumes. O méchante fortune!
Do not run away. [*A short alarum*

CONSTABLE

       Why, all our ranks are broke.

DAUPHIN

O perdurable shame! let's stab ourselves.
Be these the wretches that we play'd at dice for?

ORLEANS

Is this the king we sent to for his ransom?

BOURBON

Shame and eternal shame, nothing but shame!
Let us die in honour: once more back again;
And he that will not follow Bourbon now,
Let him go hence, and with his cap in hand,
Like a base pandar, hold the chamber-door
Whilst by a slave, no gentler than my dog,
His fairest daughter is contaminated.

CONSTABLE

Disorder, that hath spoil'd us, friend us now!
Let us on heaps go offer up our lives.

ORLEANS

We are enow yet living in the field
To smother up the English in our throngs,
If any order might be thought upon.

BOURBON

The devil take order now! I'll to the throng:
Let life be short; else shame will be too long. [*Exeunt*

SCENE VI. *Another part of the field*

Alarum. Enter KING HENRY *and forces*, EXETER, *and*
others

KING

Well have we done, thrice valiant countrymen:
But all's not done; yet keep the French the field.

EXETER

The Duke of York commends him to your majesty

KING

Lives he, good uncle? thrice within this hour
I saw him down; thrice up again, and fighting;
From helmet to the spur all blood he was.

EXETER

In which array, brave soldier, doth he lie,
Larding the plain; and by his bloody side,
Yoke-fellow to his honour-owing wounds,
The noble Earl of Suffolk also lies.
Suffolk first died: and York, all haggled over,
Comes to him, where in gore he lay insteep'd,

And takes him by the beard; kisses the gashes
That bloodily did yawn upon his face;
And cries aloud 'Tarry, dear cousin Suffolk!
My soul shall thine keep company to heaven;
Tarry, sweet soul, for mine, then fly abreast,
As in this glorious and well-foughten field
We kept together in our chivalry!'
Upon these words I came and cheer'd him up:
He smiled me in the face, raught me his hand,
And, with a feeble gripe, says 'Dear my lord,
Commend my service to my sovereign.'
So did he turn, and over Suffolk's neck
He threw his wounded arm and kiss'd his lips;
And so espoused to death, with blood he seal'd
A testament of noble-ending love.
The pretty and sweet manner of it forced
Those waters from me which I would have stopp'd,
But I had not so much of man in me,
And all my mother came into mine eyes
And gave me up to tears.

KING
                    I blame you not;
For, hearing this, I must perforce compound
With mistful eyes, or they will issue too.   [Alarum
But, hark! what new alarum is this same?
The French have reinforced their scatter'd men:
Then every soldier kill his prisoners;
Give the word through.   [Exeunt

SCENE VII. *Another part of the field*

Enter FLUELLEN *and* GOWER
FLUELLEN
Kill the poys and the luggage! 'tis expressly against
the law of arms: 'tis as arrant a piece of knavery,
mark you now, as can be offer't; in your conscience,
now, is it not?

GOWER
'Tis certain there's not a boy left alive; and the
cowardly rascals that ran from the battle ha' done
this slaughter: besides, they have burned and
carried away all that was in the king's tent; wherefore the king, most worthily, hath caused every
soldier to cut his prisoner's throat. O, 'tis a gallant
king!

FLUELLEN
Ay, he was porn at Monmouth, Captain Gower.
What call you the town's name where Alexander
the Pig was born?

GOWER
Alexander the Great.

FLUELLEN
Why, I pray you, is not pig great? the pig, or the
great, or the mighty, or the huge, or the magnanimous, are all one reckonings, save the phrase is a
little variations.

GOWER
I think Alexander the Great was born in Macedon:
his father was called Philip of Macedon, as I take it.

FLUELLEN
I think it is in Macedon where Alexander is porn.
I tell you, captain, if you look in the maps of the
'orld, I warrant you sall find, in the comparisons between Macedon and Monmouth, that the situations, look you, is both alike. There is a river in
Macedon; and there is also moreover a river at
Monmouth: it is called Wye at Monmouth; but it is
out of my prains what is the name of the other river;
but 'tis all one, 'tis alike as my fingers is to my
fingers, and there is salmons in both. If you mark
Alexander's life well, Harry of Monmouth's life is
come after it indifferent well; for there is figures in
all things. Alexander, God knows, and you know, in
his rages, and his furies, and his wraths, and his
cholers, and his moods, and his displeasures, and his
indignations, and also being a little intoxicates in
his prains, did, in his ales and his angers, look you,
kill his best friend, Cleitus.

GOWER
Our king is not like him in that: he never killed any
of his friends.

FLUELLEN
It is not well done, mark you now, to take the tales
out of my mouth, ere it is made and finished. I
speak but in the figures and comparisons of it: as
Alexander killed his friend Cleitus, being in his ales
and his cups; so also Harry Monmouth, being in his
right wits and his good judgements, turned away
the fat knight with the great-belly doublet: he was
full of jests, and gipes, and knaveries, and mocks; I
have forgot his name.

GOWER
Sir John Falstaff.

FLUELLEN
That is he: I'll tell you there is good men porn at
Monmouth.

GOWER
Here comes his majesty.
Alarum. Enter KING HENRY *and forces;* WARWICK,
GLOUCESTER, EXETER, *and others*

KING
I was not angry since I came to France
Until this instant. Take a trumpet, herald;
Ride thou unto the horsemen on yon hill:
If they will fight with us, bid them come down,
Or void the field; they do offend our sight:
If they'll do neither, we will come to them,
And make them skirr away, as swift as stones
Enforced from the old Assyrian slings:
Besides, we'll cut the throats of those we have,
And not a man of them that we shall take
Shall taste our mercy. Go and tell them so.
Enter MONTJOY

EXETER
Here comes the herald of the French, my liege.

GLOUCESTER
His eyes are humbler than they used to be.

[584]

KING

How now! what means this, herald? know'st thou
not
That I have fined these bones of mine for ransom?
Comest thou again for ransom?

MONTJOY

No, great king:
I come to thee for charitable license,
That we may wander o'er this bloody field
To book our dead, and then to bury them;
To sort our nobles from our common men.
For many of our princes—woe the while!—
Lie drown'd and soak'd in mercenary blood;
So do our vulgar drench their peasant limbs
In blood of princes; and their wounded steeds
Fret fetlock deep in gore, and with wild rage
Yerk out their armed heels at their dead masters,
Killing them twice. O, give us leave, great king,
To view the field in safety and dispose
Of their dead bodies!

KING

I tell thee truly, herald,
I know not if the day be ours or no;
For yet a many of your horsemen peer
And gallop o'er the field.

MONTJOY

The day is yours.

KING

Praised be God, and not our strength, for it!
What is this castle call'd that stands hard by?

MONTJOY

They call it Agincourt.

KING

Then call we this the field of Agincourt,
Fought on the day of Crispin Crispianus.

FLUELLEN

Your grandfather of famous memory, an 't please
your majesty, and your great-uncle Edward the
Plack Prince of Wales, as I have read in the chronicles, fought a most prave pattle here in France.

KING

They did, Fluellen.

FLUELLEN

Your majesty says very true: if your majesties is
remembered of it, the Welshmen did good service in
a garden where leeks did grow, wearing leeks in
their Monmouth caps; which, your majesty know,
to this hour is an honourable badge of the service;
and I do believe your majesty takes no scorn to wear
the leek upon Saint Tavy's day.

KING

I wear it for a memorable honour;
For I am Welsh, you know, good countryman.

FLUELLEN

All the water in Wye cannot wash your majesty's
Welsh plood out of your pody, I can tell you that:
God pless it and preserve it, as long as it pleases his
grace, and his majesty too!

KING

Thanks, good my countryman.

FLUELLEN

By Jeshu, I am your majesty's countryman, I care
not who know it; I will confess it to all the 'orld:
I need not to be ashamed of your majesty, praised
be God, so long as your majesty is an honest man.

KING

God keep me so! Our heralds go with him:
Bring me just notice of the numbers dead
On both our parts. Call yonder fellow hither.

[Points to WILLIAMS. Exeunt HERALDS with MONTJOY

EXETER

Soldier, you must come to the king.

KING

Soldier, why wearest thou that glove in thy cap?

WILLIAMS

An 't please your majesty, 'tis the gage of one that I
should fight withal, if he be alive.

KING

An Englishman?

WILLIAMS

An 't please your majesty, a rascal that swaggered
with me last night; who, if alive and ever dare to
challenge this glove, I have sworn to take him a box
o' th' ear: or if I can see my glove in his cap, which
he swore, as he was a soldier, he would wear if alive,
I will strike it out soundly.

KING

What think you, Captain Fluellen? is it fit this
soldier keep his oath?

FLUELLEN

He is a craven and a villain else, an 't please your
majesty, in my conscience.

KING

It may be his enemy is a gentleman of great sort,
quite from the answer of his degree.

FLUELLEN

Though he be as good a gentleman as the devil is,
as Lucifer and Belzebub himself, it is necessary, look
your grace, that he keep his vow and his oath: if he
be perjured, see you now, his reputation is as arrant
a villain and a Jacksauce, as ever his black shoe trod
upon God's ground and his earth, in my conscience,
la!

KING

Then keep thy vow, sirrah, when thou meetest the
fellow.

WILLIAMS

So I will, my liege, as I live.

KING

Who servest thou under?

WILLIAMS

Under Captain Gower, my liege.

FLUELLEN

Gower is a good captain, and is good knowledge
and literatured in the wars.

KING

Call him hither to me, soldier.

WILLIAMS

I will, my liege.   [Exit

KING

Here, Fluellen; wear thou this favour for me and
stick it in thy cap: when Alençon and myself were
down together, I plucked this glove from his helm:
if any man challenge this, he is a friend to Alençon,
and an enemy to our person; if thou encounter any
such, apprehend him, an thou dost me love.

FLUELLEN

Your grace doo's me as great honours as can be
desired in the hearts of his subjects: I would fain see
the man, that has but two legs, that shall find himself aggriefed at this glove; that is all; but I would
fain see it once, an 't please God of his grace that I
might see.

KING

Knowest thou Gower?

FLUELLEN

He is my dear friend, an 't please you.

KING

Pray thee, go seek him, and bring him to my tent.

FLUELLEN

I will fetch him.   [*Exit*

KING

My Lord of Warwick, and my brother Gloucester,
Follow Fluellen closely at the heels:
The glove which I have given him for a favour
May haply purchase him a box o' th' ear;
It is the soldier's; I by bargain should
Wear it myself. Follow, good cousin Warwick:
If that the soldier strike him, as I judge
By his blunt bearing he will keep his word,
Some sudden mischief may arise of it;
For I do know Fluellen valiant,
And, touch'd with choler, hot as gunpowder,
And quickly will return an injury:
Follow, and see there be no harm between them.
Go you with me, uncle of Exeter.   [*Exeunt*

SCENE VIII. *Before* KING HENRY's *pavilion*

Enter GOWER *and* WILLIAMS

WILLIAMS

I warrant it is to knight you, captain.

Enter FLUELLEN

FLUELLEN

God's will and his pleasure, captain, I beseech you
now, come apace to the king: there is more good
toward you peradventure than is in your knowledge
to dream of.

WILLIAMS

Sir, know you this glove?

FLUELLEN

Know the glove! I know the glove is a glove.

WILLIAMS

I know this; and thus I challenge it.   [*Strikes him*

FLUELLEN

'Sblood! an arrant traitor as any is in the universal
world, or in France, or in England!

GOWER

How now, sir! you villain!

WILLIAMS

Do you think I'll be forsworn?

FLUELLEN

Stand away, Captain Gower; I will give treason his
payment into plows, I warrant you.

WILLIAMS

I am no traitor.

FLUELLEN

That's a lie in thy throat. I charge you in his majesty's name, apprehend him: he's a friend of the
Duke Alençon's.

Enter WARWICK *and* GLOUCESTER

WARWICK

How now, how now! what's the matter?

FLUELLEN

My Lord of Warwick, here is—praised be God for
it!—a most contagious treason come to light, look
you, as you shall desire in a summer's day. Here is
his majesty.

Enter KING HENRY *and* EXETER

KING

How now! what's the matter?

FLUELLEN

My liege, here is a villain and a traitor, that, look
your grace, has struck the glove which your majesty
is take out of the helmet of Alençon.

WILLIAMS

My liege, this was my glove; here is the fellow of it;
and he that I gave it to in change promised to wear
it in his cap: I promised to strike him, if he did: I
met this man with my glove in his cap, and I have
been as good as my word.

FLUELLEN

Your majesty hear now, saving your majesty's
manhood, what an arrant, rascally, beggarly, lousy
knave it is: I hope your majesty is pear me testimony
and witness, and will avouchment, that this is the
glove of Alençon, that your majesty is give me; in
your conscience, now.

KING

Give me thy glove, soldier: look, here is the fellow of
it.
'Twas I, indeed, thou promised'st to strike;
And thou hast given me most bitter terms.

FLUELLEN

And please your majesty, let his neck answer for it,
if there is any martial law in the world.

KING

How canst thou make me satisfaction?

WILLIAMS

All offences, my lord, come from the heart: never
came any from mine that might offend your majesty.

KING

It was ourself thou didst abuse.

WILLIAMS

Your majesty came not like yourself: you appeared
to me but as a common man; witness the night, your

garments, your lowliness; and what your highness suffered under that shape, I beseech you to take it for your own fault and not mine: for had you been as I took you for, I made no offence; therefore, I beseech your highness, pardon me.

KING

Here, uncle Exeter, fill this glove with crowns,
And give it to this fellow. Keep it, fellow;
And wear it for an honour in thy cap
Till I do challenge it. Give him the crowns:
And, captain, you must needs be friends with him.

FLUELLEN

By this day and this light, the fellow has mettle enough in his belly. Hold, there is twelve pence for you; and I pray you to serve God, and keep you out of prawls, and prabbles, and quarrels, and dissensions, and, I warrant you, it is the better for you.

WILLIAMS

I will none of your money.

FLUELLEN

It is with a good will; I can tell you, it will serve you to mend your shoes: come, wherefore should you be so pashful? your shoes is not so good: 'tis a good silling, I warrant you, or I will change it.

Enter an ENGLISH HERALD

KING

Now, herald, are the dead number'd?

HERALD

Here is the number of the slaughter'd French.

KING

What prisoners of good sort are taken, uncle?

EXETER

Charles Duke of Orleans, nephew to the king;
John Duke of Bourbon, and Lord Boucicqualt:
Of other lords and barons, knights and squires,
Full fifteen hundred, besides common men.

KING

This note doth tell me of ten thousand French
That in the field lie slain: of princes, in this number,
And nobles bearing banners, there lie dead
One hundred twenty six: added to these,
Of knights, esquires, and gallant gentlemen,
Eight thousand and four hundred; of the which,
Five hundred were but yesterday dubb'd knights:
So that, in these ten thousand they have lost,
There are but sixteen hundred mercenaries;
The rest are princes, barons, lords, knights, squires,
And gentlemen of blood and quality.
The names of those their nobles that lie dead:
Charles Delabreth, high constable of France;
Jaques of Chatillon, admiral of France;
The master of the cross-bows, Lord Rambures;
Great Master of France, the brave Sir Guichard
  Dolphin,
John Duke of Alençon, Anthony Duke of Brabant,
The brother to the Duke of Burgundy,
And Edward Duke of Bar: of lusty earls,
Grandpré and Roussi, Fauconberg and Foix,
Beaumont and Marle, Vaudemont and Lestrale.

Here was a royal fellowship of death!
Where is the number of our English dead?

[HERALD *shews him another paper*

Edward the Duke of York, the Earl of Suffolk,
Sir Richard Ketly, Davy Gam, esquire:
None else of name; and of all other men
But five and twenty. O God, thy arm was here;
And not to us, but to thy arm alone,
Ascribe we all! When, without stratagem,
But in plain shock and even play of battle,
Was ever known so great and little loss
On one part and on th' other? Take it, God,
For it is none but thine!

EXETER

'Tis wonderful!

KING

Come, go we in procession to the village:
And be it death proclaimed through our host
To boast of this or take that praise from God
Which is his only.

FLUELLEN

Is it not lawful, an 't please your majesty, to tell how many is killed?

KING

Yes, captain; but with this acknowledgement,
That God fought for us.

FLUELLEN

Yes, my conscience, he did us great good.

KING

Do we all holy rites;
Let there be sung 'Non nobis' and 'Te Deum;'
The dead with charity enclosed in clay:
And then to Calais; and to England then;
Where ne'er from France arrived more happy men.

[*Exeunt*

ACT V

PROLOGUE

Enter CHORUS

CHORUS

Vouchsafe to those that have not read the story,
That I may prompt them: and of such as have,
I humbly pray them to admit the excuse
Of time, of numbers and due course of things,
Which cannot in their huge and proper life
Be here presented. Now we bear the king
Toward Calais: grant him there; there seen,
Heave him away upon your winged thoughts
Athwart the sea. Behold, the English beach
Pales in the flood with men, with wives and boys,
Whose shouts and claps out-voice the deep-mouth'd
  sea,
Which like a mighty whiffler 'fore the king
Seems to prepare his way: so let him land,
And solemnly see him set on to London.
So swift a pace hath thought, that even now
You may imagine him upon Blackheath;

Where that his lords desire him to have borne
His bruised helmet and his bended sword
Before him through the city: he forbids it,
Being free from vainness and self-glorious pride;
Giving full trophy, signal and ostent
Quite from himself to God. But now behold,
In the quick forge and working-house of thought,
How London doth pour out her citizens!
The mayor and all his brethren in best sort,
Like to the senators of the antique Rome,
With the plebeians swarming at their heels,
Go forth and fetch their conquering Cæsar in:
As, by a lower but loving likelihood,
Were now the general of our gracious empress,
As in good time he may, from Ireland coming,
Bringing rebellion broached on his sword,
How many would the peaceful city quit,
To welcome him! much more, and much more
    cause,
Did they this Harry. Now in London place him;
As yet the lamentation of the French
Invites the King of England's stay at home;
The emperor's coming in behalf of France,
To order peace between them; and omit
All the occurrences, whatever chanced,
Till Harry's back return again to France:
There must we bring him; and myself have play'd
The interim, by remembering you 'tis past.
Then brook abridgement, and your eyes advance,
After your thoughts, straight back again to France.
                             [*Exit*

Scene I. *France. The English camp*

Enter FLUELLEN *and* GOWER

GOWER

Nay, that's right; but why wear you your leek to-day? Saint Davy's day is past.

FLUELLEN

There is occasions and causes why and wherefore in all things: I will tell you, asse my friend, Captain Gower: the rascally, scauld, beggarly, lousy, pragging knave, Pistol, which you and yourself and all the world know to be no petter than a fellow, look you now, of no merits, he is come to me and prings me pread and salt yesterday, look you, and bid me eat my leek: it was in a place where I could not breed no contention with him; but I will be so bold as to wear it in my cap till I see him once again, and then I will tell him a little piece of my desires.

Enter PISTOL

GOWER

Why, here he comes, swelling like a turkey-cock.

FLUELLEN

'Tis no matter for his swellings nor his turkey-cocks. God pless you, Aunchient Pistol! you scurvy, lousy knave, God pless you.

PISTOL

Ha! art thou bedlam? dost thou thirst, base Trojan,

To have me fold up Parca's fatal web?
Hence! I am qualmish at the smell of leek.

FLUELLEN

I peseech you heartily, scurvy, lousy knave, at my desires, and my requests, and my petitions, to eat, look you, this leek: because, look you, you do not love it, nor your affections and your appetites and your disgestions doo's not agree with it, I would desire you to eat it.

PISTOL

Not for Cadwallader and all his goats.

FLUELLEN

There is one goat for you. [*Strikes him*] Will you be so good, scauld knave, as eat it?

PISTOL

Base Trojan, thou shalt die.

FLUELLEN

You say very true, scauld knave, when God's will is: I will desire you to live in the mean time, and eat your victuals: come, there is sauce for it. [*Strikes him*] You called me yesterday mountain-squire; but I will make you to-day a squire of low degree. I pray you, fall to: if you can mock a leek, you can eat a leek.

GOWER

Enough, captain: you have astonished him.

FLUELLEN

I say, I will make him eat some part of my leek, or I will peat his pate four days. Bite, I pray you; it is good for your green wound and your ploody coxcomb.

PISTOL

Must I bite?

FLUELLEN

Yes, certainly, and out of doubt and out of question too, and ambiguities.

PISTOL

By this leek, I will most horribly revenge: I eat and eat, I swear—

FLUELLEN

Eat, I pray you: will you have some more sauce to your leek? there is not enough leek to swear by.

PISTOL

Quiet thy cudgel; thou dost see I eat.

FLUELLEN

Much good do you, scauld knave, heartily. Nay, pray you, throw none away; the skin is good for your broken coxcomb. When you take occasions to see leeks hereafter, I pray you, mock at 'em; that is all.

PISTOL

Good.

FLUELLEN

Ay, leeks is good: hold you, there is a groat to heal your pate.

PISTOL

Me a groat!

FLUELLEN

Yes, verily and in truth, you shall take it; or I have another leek in my pocket, which you shall eat.

PISTOL

I take thy groat in earnest of revenge.

FLUELLEN

If I owe you any thing, I will pay you in cudgels:
you shall be a woodmonger, and buy nothing of me
but cudgels. God b' wi' you, and keep you, and heal
your pate.   [*Exit*

PISTOL

All hell shall stir for this.

GOWER

Go, go; you are a counterfeit cowardly knave. Will
you mock at an ancient tradition, begun upon an
honourable respect, and worn as a memorable
trophy of predeceased valour, and dare not avouch
in your deeds any of your words? I have seen you
gleeking and galling at this gentleman twice or
thrice. You thought, because he could not speak
English in the native garb, he could not therefore
handle an English cudgel: you find it otherwise;
and henceforth let a Welsh correction teach you a
good English condition. Fare ye well.   [*Exit*

PISTOL

Doth Fortune play the huswife with me now?
News have I, that my Doll is dead i' the spital
Of malady of France;
And there my rendezvous is quite cut off.
Old I do wax; and from my weary limbs
Honour is cudgelled. Well, bawd I'll turn,
And something lean to cutpurse of quick hand.
To England will I steal, and there I'll steal:
And patches will I get unto these cudgell'd scars,
And swear I got them in the Gallia wars.   [*Exit*

SCENE II. *France. A royal palace*

Enter, at one door, KING HENRY, EXETER, BEDFORD,
GLOUCESTER, WARWICK, WESTMORELAND, *and other*
LORDS; *at another, the* FRENCH KING, QUEEN ISABEL, *the*
PRINCESS KATHARINE, ALICE *and other* LADIES; *the* DUKE
OF BURGUNDY, *and his train*

KING

Peace to this meeting, wherefore we are met!
Unto our brother France, and to our sister,
Health and fair time of day; joy and good wishes
To our most fair and princely cousin Katharine;
And, as a branch and member of this royalty,
By whom this great assembly is contrived,
We do salute you, Duke of Burgundy;
And, princes French, and peers, health to you all!

FRENCH KING

Right joyous are we to behold your face,
Most worthy brother England; fairly met:
So are you, princes English, every one.

QUEEN

So happy be the issue, brother England,
Of this good day and of this gracious meeting,
As we are now glad to behold your eyes;
Your eyes, which hitherto have borne in them
Against the French, that met them in their bent,

The fatal balls of murdering basilisks:
The venom of such looks, we fairly hope,
Have lost their quality, and that this day
Shall change all griefs and quarrels into love.

KING

To cry amen to that, thus we appear.

QUEEN

You English princes all, I do salute you.

BURGUNDY

My duty to you both, on equal love,
Great Kings of France and England! That I have
   labour'd,
With all my wits, my pains and strong endeavours,
To bring your most imperial majesties
Unto this bar and royal interview,
Your mightiness on both parts best can witness.
Since then my office hath so far prevail'd
That, face to face and royal eye to eye,
You have congreeted, let it not disgrace me,
If I demand, before this royal view,
What rub or what impediment there is,
Why that the naked, poor and mangled Peace,
Dear nurse of arts, plenties and joyful births,
Should not in this best garden of the world,
Our fertile France, put up her lovely visage?
Alas, she hath from France too long been chased,
And all her husbandry doth lie on heaps,
Corrupting in it own fertility.
Her vine, the merry cheerer of the heart,
Unpruned dies; her hedges even-pleach'd,
Like prisoners wildly overgrown with hair,
Put forth disorder'd twigs; her fallow leas
The darnel, hemlock and rank fumitory
Doth root upon, while that the coulter rusts
That should deracinate such savagery;
The even mead, that erst brought sweetly forth
The freckled cowslip, burnet and green clover,
Wanting the scythe, all uncorrected, rank,
Conceives by idleness, and nothing teems
But hateful docks, rough thistles, kecksies, burs,
Losing both beauty and utility.
And as our vineyards, fallows, meads and hedges,
Defective in their natures, grow to wildness,
Even so our houses and ourselves and children
Have lost, or do not learn for want of time,
The sciences that should become our country;
But grow like savages,—as soldiers will
That nothing do but meditate on blood,—
To swearing and stern looks, diffused attire
And every thing that seems unnatural.
Which to reduce into our former favour
You are assembled: and my speech entreats
That I may know the let, why gentle Peace
Should not expel these inconveniences
And bless us with her former qualities.

KING

If, Duke of Burgundy, you would the peace,
Whose want gives growth to the imperfections
Which you have cited, you must buy that peace
With full accord to all our just demands;

Whose tenours and particular effects
You have enscheduled briefly in your hands.

BURGUNDY

The king hath heard them; to the which as yet
There is no answer made.

KING

Well then the peace,
Which you before so urged, lies in his answer.

FRENCH KING

I have but with a cursorary eye
O'erglanced the articles: pleaseth your grace
To appoint some of your council presently
To sit with us once more, with better heed
To re-survey them, we will suddenly
Pass our accept and peremptory answer.

KING

Brother, we shall. Go, uncle Exeter,
And brother Clarence, and you, brother Gloucester,
Warwick and Huntingdon, go with the king;
And take with you free power to ratify,
Augment, or alter, as your wisdoms best
Shall see advantageable for our dignity,
Any thing in or out of our demands;
And we'll consign thereto. Will you, fair sister,
Go with the princes, or stay here with us?

QUEEN

Our gracious brother, I will go with them:
Haply a woman's voice may do some good,
When articles too nicely urged be stood on.

KING

Yet leave our cousin Katharine here with us:
She is our capital demand, comprised
Within the fore-rank of our articles.

QUEEN

She hath good leave.

[*Exeunt all except* HENRY, KATHARINE, *and* ALICE

KING

Fair Katharine, and most fair,
Will you vouchsafe to teach a soldier terms
Such as will enter at a lady's ear
And plead his love-suit to her gentle heart?

KATHARINE

Your majesty shall mock at me; I cannot speak your
England.

KING

O fair Katharine, if you will love me soundly with
your French heart, I will be glad to hear you confess it brokenly with your English tongue. Do you
like me, Kate?

KATHARINE

Pardonnez-moi, I cannot tell vat is 'like me.'

KING

An angel is like you, Kate, and you are like an
angel.

KATHARINE

Que dit-il? que je suis semblable à les anges?

ALICE

Oui, vraiment, sauf votre grace, ainsi dit-il.

KING

I said so, dear Katharine; and I must not blush to
affirm it.

KATHARINE

O bon Dieu! les langues des hommes sont pleines de
tromperies.

KING

What says she, fair one? that the tongues of men are
full of deceits?

ALICE

Oui, dat de tongues of de mans is be full of deceits:
dat is de princess.

KING

The princess is the better Englishwoman. I' faith,
Kate, my wooing is fit for thy understanding: I am
glad thou canst speak no better English; for, if thou
couldst, thou wouldst find me such a plain king that
thou wouldst think I had sold my farm to buy my
crown. I know no ways to mince it in love, but directly to say 'I love you:' then if you urge me
farther than to say 'Do you in faith?' I wear out my
suit. Give me your answer; i' faith, do: and so clap
hands and a bargain: how say you, lady?

KATHARINE

Sauf votre honneur, me understand vell.

KING

Marry, if you would put me to verses or to dance for
your sake, Kate, why you undid me: for the one, I
have neither words nor measure, and for the other,
I have no strength in measure, yet a reasonable
measure in strength. If I could win a lady at leap-
frog, or by vaulting into my saddle with my armour
on my back, under the correction of bragging be it
spoken, I should quickly leap into a wife. Or if I
might buffet for my love, or bound my horse for her
favours, I could lay on like a butcher and sit like a
jack-an-apes, never off. But, before God, Kate, I
cannot look greenly nor gasp out my eloquence, nor
I have no cunning in protestation; only downright
oaths, which I never use till urged, nor never break
for urging. If thou canst love a fellow of this temper,
Kate, whose face is not worth sun-burning, that
never looks in his glass for love of any thing he sees
there, let thine eye be thy cook. I speak to thee plain
soldier: if thou canst love me for this, take me; if
not, to say to thee that I shall die, is true; but for
thy love, by the Lord, no; yet I love thee too. And
while thou livest, dear Kate, take a fellow of plain
and uncoined constancy; for he perforce must do
thee right, because he hath not the gift to woo in
other places: for these fellows of infinite tongue,
that can rhyme themselves into ladies' favours, they
do always reason themselves out again. What! a
speaker is but a prater; a rhyme is but a ballad. A
good leg will fall; a straight back will stoop; a black
beard will turn white; a curled pate will grow bald;
a fair face will wither; a full eye will wax hollow:
but a good heart, Kate, is the sun and the moon; or,
rather, the sun, and not the moon; for it shines
bright and never changes, but keeps his course

truly. If thou would have such a one, take me; and take me, take a soldier; take a soldier, take a king. And what sayest thou then to my love? speak, my fair, and fairly, I pray thee.

KATHARINE

Is it possible dat I sould love de enemy of France?

KING

No; it is not possible you should love the enemy of France, Kate: but, in loving me, you should love the friend of France; for I love France so well that I will not part with a village of it; I will have it all mine: and, Kate, when France is mine and I am yours, then yours is France and you are mine.

KATHARINE

I cannot tell vat is dat.

KING

No, Kate? I will tell thee in French; which I am sure will hang upon my tongue like a new-married wife about her husband's neck, hardly to be shook off. Je quand sur le possession de France, et quand vous avez le possession de moi,—let me see, what then? Saint Denis be my speed!—donc votre est France et vous êtes mienne. It is as easy for me, Kate, to conquer the kingdom as to speak so much more French: I shall never move thee in French, unless it be to laugh at me.

KATHARINE

Sauf votre honneur, le François que vous parlez, il est meilleur que l'Anglois lequel je parle.

KING

No, faith, is 't not, Kate: but thy speaking of my tongue, and I thine, most truly-falsely, must needs be granted to be much at one. But, Kate, dost thou understand thus much English, canst thou love me?

KATHARINE

I cannot tell.

KING

Can any of your neighbours tell, Kate? I'll ask them. Come, I know thou lovest me: and at night, when you come into your closet, you'll question this gentlewoman about me; and I know, Kate, you will to her dispraise those parts in me that you love with your heart: but, good Kate, mock me mercifully; the rather, gentle princess, because I love thee cruelly. If ever thou beest mine, Kate, as I have a saving faith within me tells me thou shalt, I get thee with scambling, and thou must therefore needs prove a good soldier-breeder: shall not thou and I, between Saint Denis and Saint George, compound a boy, half French, half English, that shall go to Constantinople and take the Turk by the beard? shall we not? what sayest thou, my fair flower-de-luce?

KATHARINE

I do not know dat.

KING

No; 'tis hereafter to know, but now to promise: do but now promise, Kate, you will endeavour for your French part of such a boy; and for my English moiety take the word of a king and a bachelor. How answer you, la plus belle Katharine du monde, mon très cher et devin déesse?

KATHARINE

Your majestee ave fausse French enough to deceive de most sage demoiselle dat is en France.

KING

Now, fie upon my false French! By mine honour, in true English, I love thee, Kate: by which honour I dare not swear thou lovest me; yet my blood begins to flatter me that thou dost, notwithstanding the poor and untempering effect of my visage. Now, beshrew my father's ambition! he was thinking of civil wars when he got me: therefore was I created with a stubborn outside, with an aspect of iron, that, when I come to woo ladies, I fright them. But, in faith, Kate, the elder I wax, the better I shall appear: my comfort is, that old age, that ill layer up of beauty, can do no more spoil upon my face: thou hast me, if thou hast me, at the worst; and thou shalt wear me, if thou wear me, better and better: and therefore tell me, most fair Katharine, will you have me? Put off your maiden blushes; avouch the thoughts of your heart with the looks of an empress; take me by the hand, and say 'Harry of England, I am thine:' which word thou shalt no sooner bless mine ear withal, but I will tell thee aloud 'England is thine, Ireland is thine, France is thine, and Henry Plantagenet is thine;' who, though I speak it before his face, if he be not fellow with the best king, thou shalt find the best king of good fellows. Come, your answer in broken music; for thy voice is music and thy English broken; therefore, queen of all, Katharine, break thy mind to me in broken English, wilt thou have me?

KATHARINE

Dat is as it sall please de roi mon père.

KING

Nay, it will please him well, Kate; it shall please him, Kate.

KATHARINE

Den it sall also content me.

KING

Upon that I kiss your hand, and I call you my queen.

KATHARINE

Laissez, mon seigneur, laissez, laissez: ma foi, je ne veux point que vous abaissiez votre grandeur en baisant la main d'une de votre seigneurie indigne serviteur; excusez-moi, je vous supplie, mon trèspuissant seigneur.

KING

Then I will kiss your lips, Kate.

KATHARINE

Les dames et demoiselles pour être baisées devant leur noces, il n'est pas la coutume de France.

KING

Madam my interpreter, what says she?

ALICE

Dat it is not be de fashion pour les ladies of France, —I cannot tell vat is baiser en Anglish.

KING

To kiss.

ALICE

Your majesty entendre bettre que moi.

KING

It is not a fashion for the maids in France to kiss before they are married, would she say?

ALICE

Oui, vraiment.

KING

O Kate, nice customs courtesy to great kings. Dear Kate, you and I cannot be confined within the weak list of a country's fashion: we are the makers of manners, Kate; and the liberty that follows our places stops the mouth of all find-faults; as I will do yours, for upholding the nice fashion of your country in denying me a kiss: therefore, patiently and yielding. [*Kissing her*] You have witchcraft in your lips, Kate: there is more eloquence in a sugar touch of them than in the tongues of the French council; and they should sooner persuade Harry of England than a general petition of monarchs. Here comes your father.

Re-enter the FRENCH KING *and his* QUEEN, BURGUNDY, *and other* LORDS

BURGUNDY

God save your majesty! my royal cousin, teach you our princess English?

KING

I would have her learn, my fair cousin, how perfectly I love her; and that is good English.

BURGUNDY

Is she not apt?

KING

Our tongue is rough, coz, and my condition is not smooth; so that, having neither the voice nor the heart of flattery about me, I cannot so conjure up the spirit of love in her, that he will appear in his true likeness.

BURGUNDY

Pardon the frankness of my mirth, if I answer you for that. If you would conjure in her, you must make a circle; if conjure up love in her in his true likeness, he must appear naked and blind. Can you blame her then, being a maid yet rosed over with the virgin crimson of modesty, if she deny the appearance of a naked blind boy in her naked seeing self? It were, my lord, a hard condition for a maid to consign to.

KING

Yet they do wink and yield, as love is blind and enforces.

BURGUNDY

They are then excused, my lord, when they see not what they do.

KING

Then, good my lord, teach your cousin to consent winking.

BURGUNDY

I will wink on her to consent, my lord, if you will

teach her to know my meaning: for maids, well summered and warm kept, are like flies at Bartholomewtide, blind, though they have their eyes; and then they will endure handling, which before would not abide looking on.

KING

This moral ties me over to time and a hot summer; and so I shall catch the fly, your cousin, in the latter end, and she must be blind too.

BURGUNDY

As love is, my lord, before it loves.

KING

It is so: and you may, some of you, thank love for my blindness, who cannot see many a fair French city for one fair French maid that stands in my way.

FRENCH KING

Yes, my lord, you see them perspectively, the cities turned into a maid; for they are all girdled with maiden walls that war hath never entered.

KING

Shall Kate be my wife?

FRENCH KING

So please you.

KING

I am content; so the maiden cities you talk of may wait on her: so the maid that stood in the way for my wish shall show me the way to my will.

FRENCH KING

We have consented to all terms of reason.

KING

Is 't so, my lords of England?

WESTMORELAND

The king hath granted every article:
His daughter first, and then in sequel all,
According to their firm proposed natures.

EXETER

Only he hath not yet subscribed this:
Where your majesty demands, that the King of France, having any occasion to write for matter of grant, shall name your highness in this form and with this addition, in French, Notre très-cher fils Henri, Roi d'Angleterre, Héritier de France; and thus in Latin, Præclarissimus filius noster Henricus, Rex Angliæ, et Hæres Franciæ.

FRENCH KING

Nor this I have not, brother, so denied,
But your request shall make me let it pass.

KING

I pray you then, in love and dear alliance,
Let that one article rank with the rest;
And thereupon give me your daughter.

FRENCH KING

Take her, fair son, and from her blood raise up
Issue to me; that the contending kingdoms
Of France and England, whose very shores look
    pale
With envy of each other's happiness,
May cease their hatred, and this dear conjunction

Plant neighbourhood and Christian-like accord
In their sweet bosoms, that never war advance
His bleeding sword 'twixt England and fair France.
ALL
Amen!
KING
Now, welcome, Kate: and bear me witness all,
That here I kiss her as my sovereign queen. [*Flourish*
QUEEN
God, the best maker of all marriages,
Combine your hearts in one, your realms in one!
As man and wife, being two, are one in love,
So be there 'twixt your kingdoms such a spousal,
That never may ill office, or fell jealousy,
Which troubles oft the bed of blessed marriage,
Thrust in between the paction of these kingdoms,
To make divorce of their incorporate league;
That English may as French, French Englishmen,
Receive each other. God speak this Amen!
ALL
Amen!
KING
Prepare we for our marriage: on which day,
My Lord of Burgundy, we'll take your oath,
And all the peers', for surety of our leagues.

Then shall I swear to Kate, and you to me;
And may our oaths well kept and prosperous be!
[*Sennet. Exeunt*

EPILOGUE

Enter CHORUS
CHORUS
Thus far, with rough and all-unable pen,
  Our bending author hath pursued the story,
In little room confining mighty men,
  Mangling by starts the full course of their glory.
Small time, but in that small most greatly lived
  This star of England: Fortune made his sword;
By which the world's best garden he achieved,
  And of it left his son imperial lord.
Henry the Sixth, in infant bands crown'd King
  Of France and England, did this king succeed;
Whose state so many had the managing,
  That they lost France and made his England
    bleed:
Which oft our stage hath shown; and, for their sake,
In your fair minds let this acceptance take.   [*Exit*

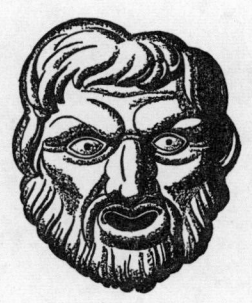

MUCH ADO ABOUT NOTHING

SYNOPSIS

THE genial Don Pedro, Prince of Arragon, has not only forgiven the intrigues of his evil bastard brother Don John, who recently led an unsuccessful rebellion against him, but he includes him in his train as he goes to visit Leonato, governor of Messina, together with two young noblemen, Benedick and Claudio, who have served him with great distinction in his wars.

Both of these young men are already acquainted with Leonato's quiet, charming daughter Hero, and his spirited, talkative niece Beatrice, and whenever Benedick and Beatrice have met there has always been a series of witty bantering and scornful repartee, which is now renewed in full force. Claudio is again attracted to the gentle Hero, and tells Don Pedro of his love. The Prince offers to help in getting Leonato's consent, and also by personally wooing the girl for her lover by impersonating him at a masked ball that evening. This plan is overheard by two servants, through one of whom Leonato hears that Don Pedro is in love with Hero, while the other gives the actual facts to the dour brooding Don John who, under his masquerading disguise, insinuates to the touchy Claudio that Don Pedro is faithlessly making love on his own account. This suspicion quickly evaporates, however, when the Prince and Hero appear with Leonato who consents to the young soldier's suit and arranges for a wedding in a week's time.

Don Pedro, an inveterate matchmaker, jovially proposes to Leonato and Claudio that in the interim they undertake to make the lively Benedick and Beatrice fall in love with each other, in spite of their denunciations of marriage. Apparently on a leisurely stroll through the garden, these friendly conspirators stop at a secluded spot where Benedick sits reading to talk among themselves of Beatrice's love for him which she conceals under a showing of combative temper, and, after perceiving that the young man's emotions are aroused, they apply the same method successfully to the scornful lady.

Meanwhile, Don John's malicious mind has turned upon the impending marriage as an opportunity to bring humiliation on his brother who has defeated him and Claudio who has gained military glory through his overthrow. Realizing how easily he can play upon Claudio's self-centered, impetuous nature, he lays a plot whereby he brings Don Pedro and his friend to Hero's bedroom window in the darkness of the night before her wedding day and reveals to them a secret meeting, obviously between Hero and some lover, while in reality her innocent unwitting gentlewoman is talking to a follower of Don John's, Borachio, who addresses the woman by her mistress' name. In his fury, Claudio determines to be revenged in public for his damaged dignity, and the heart-

[595]

sickened Don Pedro consents to accompany him to the church where, as the ceremony begins, he harshly repudiates Hero before the assembled guests. The bewildered girl stammers her protests of innocence as Don Pedro and Don John bear witness to the midnight tryst, and her half-dazed father cries in despair for a dagger to end his life, then she drops in a dead faint into Beatrice's arms whose cry of angry pity brings Benedick to her side as the others leave.

The level-headed Friar Francis strongly suspects Don John of villainy and suggests that Leonato give out the report that his daughter has died, and await developments. In the tense moments that follow, Benedick and Beatrice confess their love for each other, but the soldier in Benedick at first recoils in horror when Beatrice commands him to kill Claudio, his old comrade and constant companion, but, with his fine understanding, he soon arrives at Beatrice's point of view that the man who broke the heart and smirched the honor of the innocent Hero must die, and seeking him out he challenges his amazed friend to a duel.

At this juncture, the sexton of the church, knowing of Hero's public disgrace, solves the whole problem by producing Dogberry, the local constable, who had been discouraged in his clumsy effort to gain Leonato's attention while hastening to Hero's wedding with an involved story of his watchman having arrested Borachio and Conrade, Don John's henchmen. Don Pedro recognizes the men, and Borachio verifies the story of Don John's vicious plot which the watchman overheard him tell Conrade while drunk. Claudio, genuinely distressed, offers to make amends through any penance Hero's father may prescribe, and accedes at once to Leonato's request that he publicly demonstrate his belief in his dead love's innocence by hanging an epitaph on her tomb in a ceremony of song which he vows to repeat yearly, and by marrying the old governor's niece and heir who exactly resembles his lost daughter.

When Claudio is married the next day, he joyfully discovers his veiled bride to be Hero herself. Benedick, who has just asked the good friar to marry him to Beatrice, all but loses her through a sudden tiff, but love poems written by each of them are produced which cannot be denied, and they finally declare they are marrying out of sheer pity for one another. Gaily swinging the party into a dance, Benedick bids his Prince, Don Pedro, to get himself a wife, and put off until the morrow all thought of the punishment of Don John who has just been captured in his flight from Messina.

HISTORICAL DATA

The more serious part of the plot of *Much Ado About Nothing*, the story of Claudio and Hero, is distinctly similar to the story of Ariodante and Ginevra in Ariosto's *Orlando Furioso*. The tale appears in one of Bandello's *Novelle* and was translated by Belleforest in his *Histoires Tragiques* (1582). A dramatization of Ariosto's story was performed before Queen Elizabeth in 1582, and translations of the book were published by Beverly in 1565 and later by Sir John Harington in 1591, the latter, in the opinion of some authorities, being the direct source of the plot.

The comedy portion of the play appears to be entirely Shakespeare's own invention. The characters of Beatrice and Benedick, although some effort has been made to connect them with a contemporary(?) play called *Benedicke and Betteris*, are probably wholly original creations. Certainly Dogberry and Verges are without prototypes.

The play is not mentioned by Meres (unless credence is given to the suggestion that it be identified with the unknown play listed as *Love's Labour's Won*) and was first published in a quarto edition in 1600. Authorities generally assign it to the year 1599.

"But know that I have tonight wooed Margaret,—"
MUCH ADO ABOUT NOTHING

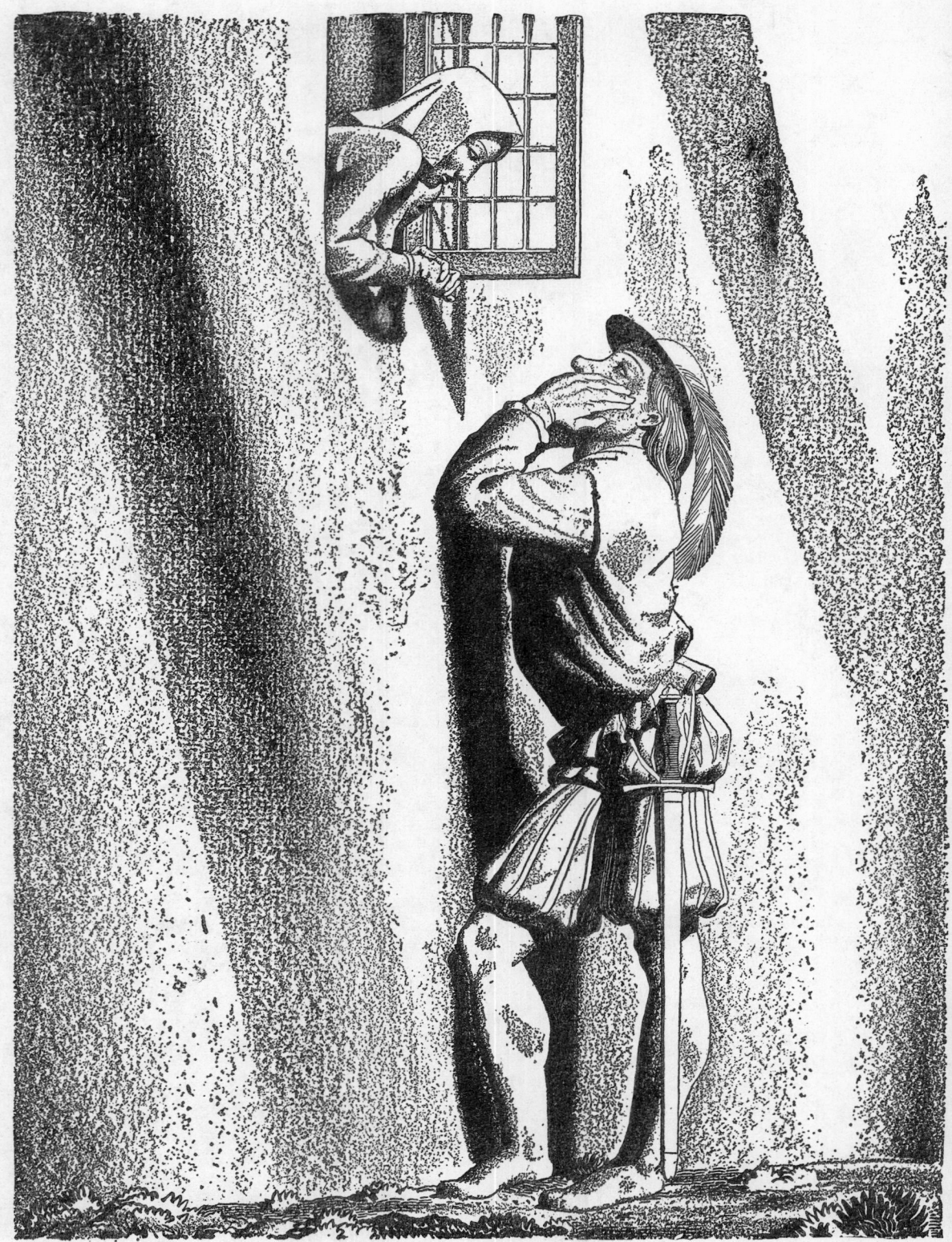

MUCH ADO ABOUT NOTHING

DRAMATIS PERSONÆ

DON PEDRO, *prince of Arragon.*
DON JOHN, *his bastard brother.*
CLAUDIO, *a young lord of Florence.*
BENEDICK, *a young lord of Padua.*
LEONATO, *governor of Messina.*
ANTONIO, *his brother.*
BALTHASAR, *attendant on Don Pedro.*
CONRADE, } *followers of Don John.*
BORACHIO, }
FRIAR FRANCIS.
DOGBERRY, *a constable.*

VERGES, *a headborough.*
A SEXTON.
A BOY.

HERO, *daughter to Leonato.*
BEATRICE, *niece to Leonato.*
MARGARET, } *gentlewomen attending on Hero.*
URSULA, }

MESSENGERS, WATCH, ATTENDANTS, &c.

SCENE—*Messina.*

ACT I

SCENE I. *Before* LEONATO's *house*

Enter LEONATO, HERO, *and* BEATRICE, *with a*
MESSENGER

LEONATO

I LEARN in this letter that Don Pedro of Arragon comes this night to Messina.

MESSENGER

He is very near by this: he was not three leagues off when I left him.

LEONATO

How many gentlemen have you lost in this action?

MESSENGER

But few of any sort, and none of name.

LEONATO

A victory is twice itself when the achiever brings home full numbers. I find here that Don Pedro hath bestowed much honour on a young Florentine called Claudio.

MESSENGER

Much deserved on his part, and equally remembered by Don Pedro: he hath borne himself beyond the promise of his age; doing, in the figure of a lamb, the feats of a lion: he hath indeed better bettered expectation than you must expect of me to tell you how.

LEONATO

He hath an uncle here in Messina will be very much glad of it.

MESSENGER

I have already delivered him letters, and there appears much joy in him; even so much, that joy could not show itself modest enough without a badge of bitterness.

LEONATO

Did he break out into tears?

MESSENGER

In great measure.

LEONATO

A kind overflow of kindness: there are no faces truer than those that are so washed. How much better is it to weep at joy than to joy at weeping!

BEATRICE

I pray you, is Signior Mountanto returned from the wars or no?

MESSENGER

I know none of that name, lady: there was none such in the army of any sort.

LEONATO

What is he that you ask for, niece?

HERO

My cousin means Signior Benedick of Padua.

MESSENGER

O, he's returned; and as pleasant as ever he was.

BEATRICE

He set up his bills here in Messina and challenged Cupid at the flight; and my uncle's fool, reading the challenge, subscribed for Cupid, and challenged him at the bird-bolt. I pray you, how many hath he killed and eaten in these wars? But how many hath he killed? for, indeed, I promised to eat all of his killing.

LEONATO

Faith, niece, you tax Signior Benedick too much; but he'll be meet with you, I doubt it not.

MESSENGER

He hath done good service, lady, in these wars.

BEATRICE

You had musty victual, and he hath holp to eat it: he is a very valiant trencher-man; he hath an excellent stomach.

MESSENGER

And a good soldier too, lady.

BEATRICE

And a good soldier to a lady; but what is he to a lord?

MESSENGER

A lord to a lord, a man to a man; stuffed with all honourable virtues.

[597]

BEATRICE

It is so, indeed; he is no less than a stuffed man: but for the stuffing,—well, we are all mortal.

LEONATO

You must not, sir, mistake my niece. There is a kind of merry war betwixt Signior Benedick and her: they never meet but there's a skirmish of wit between them.

BEATRICE

Alas! he gets nothing by that. In our last conflict four of his five wits went halting off, and now is the whole man governed with one: so that if he have wit enough to keep himself warm, let him bear it for a difference between himself and his horse; for it is all the wealth that he hath left, to be known a reasonable creature. Who is his companion now? He hath every month a new sworn brother.

MESSENGER

Is't possible?

BEATRICE

Very easily possible: he wears his faith but as the fashion of his hat; it ever changes with the next block.

MESSENGER

I see, lady, the gentleman is not in your books.

BEATRICE

No; an he were, I would burn my study. But, I pray you, who is his companion? Is there no young squarer now that will make a voyage with him to the devil?

MESSENGER

He is most in the company of the right noble Claudio.

BEATRICE

O Lord, he will hang upon him like a disease: he is sooner caught than the pestilence, and the taker runs presently mad. God help the noble Claudio! if he have caught the Benedick, it will cost him a thousand pound ere a' be cured.

MESSENGER

I will hold friends with you, lady.

BEATRICE

Do, good friend.

LEONATO

You will never run mad, niece.

BEATRICE

No, not till a hot January.

MESSENGER

Don Pedro is approached.

Enter DON PEDRO, DON JOHN, CLAUDIO, BENEDICK, *and* BALTHASAR

DON PEDRO

Good Signior Leonato, you are come to meet your trouble: the fashion of the world is to avoid cost, and you encounter it.

LEONATO

Never came trouble to my house in the likeness of your Grace: for trouble being gone, comfort should remain; but when you depart from me, sorrow abides, and happiness takes his leave.

DON PEDRO

You embrace your charge too willingly. I think this is your daughter.

LEONATO

Her mother hath many times told me so.

BENEDICK

Were you in doubt, sir, that you asked her?

LEONATO

Signior Benedick, no; for then were you a child.

DON PEDRO

You have it full, Benedick: we may guess by this what you are, being a man. Truly, the lady fathers herself. Be happy, lady; for you are like an honourable father.

BENEDICK

If Signior Leonato be her father, she would not have his head on her shoulders for all Messina, as like him as she is.

BEATRICE

I wonder that you will still be talking, Signior Benedick: nobody marks you.

BENEDICK

What, my dear Lady Disdain! are you yet living?

BEATRICE

Is it possible disdain should die while she hath such meet food to feed it, as Signior Benedick? Courtesy itself must convert to disdain, if you come in her presence.

BENEDICK

Then is courtesy a turncoat. But it is certain I am loved of all ladies, only you excepted: and I would I could find in my heart that I had not a hard heart; for, truly, I love none.

BEATRICE

A dear happiness to women: they would else have been troubled with a pernicious suitor. I thank God and my cold blood, I am of your humour for that: I had rather hear my dog bark at a crow than a man swear he loves me.

BENEDICK

God keep your ladyship still in that mind! so some gentleman or other shall 'scape a predestinate scratched face.

BEATRICE

Scratching could not make it worse, an 'twere such a face as yours were.

BENEDICT

Well, you are a rare parrot-teacher.

BEATRICE

A bird of my tongue is better than a beast of yours.

BENEDICK

I would my horse had the speed of your tongue, and so good a continuer. But keep your way, i' God's name; I have done.

BEATRICE

You always end with a jade's trick: I know you of old.

DON PEDRO

That is the sum of all, Leonato. Signior Claudio and Signior Benedick, my dear friend Leonato hath invited you all. I tell him we shall stay here at the least a month; and he heartily prays some occasion may detain us longer. I dare swear he is no hypocrite, but prays from his heart.

LEONATO

If you swear, my lord, you shall not be forsworn. [*To* DON JOHN] Let me bid you welcome, my lord: being reconciled to the prince your brother, I owe you all duty.

DON JOHN

I thank you: I am not of many words, but I thank you.

LEONATO

Please it your Grace lead on?

DON PEDRO

Your hand, Leonato; we will go together.

[*Exeunt all except* BENEDICK *and* CLAUDIO

CLAUDIO

Benedick, didst thou note the daughter of Signior Leonato?

BENEDICK

I noted her not; but I looked on her.

CLAUDIO

Is she not a modest young lady?

BENEDICK

Do you question me, as an honest man should do, for my simple true judgement? or would you have me speak after my custom, as being a professed tyrant to their sex?

CLAUDIO

No; I pray thee speak in sober judgement.

BENEDICK

Why, i'faith, methinks she's too low for a high praise, too brown for a fair praise, and too little for a great praise: only this commendation I can afford her, that were she other than she is, she were unhandsome; and being no other but as she is, I do not like her.

CLAUDIO

Thou thinkest I am in sport: I pray thee tell me truly how thou likest her.

BENEDICK

Would you buy her, that you inquire after her?

CLAUDIO

Can the world buy such a jewel?

BENEDICK

Yea, and a case to put it into. But speak you this with a sad brow? or do you play the flouting Jack, to tell us Cupid is a good hare-finder, and Vulcan a rare carpenter? Come, in what key shall a man take you, to go in the song?

CLAUDIO

In mine eye she is the sweetest lady that ever I looked on.

BENEDICK

I can see yet without spectacles, and I see no such matter: there's her cousin, an she were not possessed with a fury, exceeds her as much in beauty as the first of May doth the last of December. But I hope you have no intent to turn husband, have you?

CLAUDIO

I would scarce trust myself, though I had sworn the contrary, if Hero would be my wife.

BENEDICK

Is't come to this? In faith, hath not the world one man but he will wear his cap with suspicion? Shall I never see a bachelor of threescore again? Go to, i'faith; an thou wilt needs thrust thy neck into a yoke, wear the print of it, and sigh away Sundays. Look; Don Pedro is returned to seek you.

Re-enter DON PEDRO

DON PEDRO

What secret hath held you here, that you followed not to Leonato's?

BENEDICK

I would your Grace would constrain me to tell.

DON PEDRO

I charge thee on thy allegiance.

BENEDICK

You hear, Count Claudio: I can be secret as a dumb man; I would have you think so; but, on my allegiance, mark you this, on my allegiance. He is in love. With who? now that is your Grace's part. Mark how short his answer is;—With Hero, Leonato's short daughter.

CLAUDIO

If this were so, so were it uttered.

BENEDICK

Like the old tale, my lord: 'it is not so, nor 'twas not so, but, indeed, God forbid it should be so.'

CLAUDIO

If my passion change not shortly, God forbid it should be otherwise.

DON PEDRO

Amen, if you love her; for the lady is very well worthy.

CLAUDIO

You speak this to fetch me in, my lord.

DON PEDRO

By my troth, I speak my thought.

CLAUDIO

And, in faith, my lord, I spoke mine.

BENEDICK

And, by my two faiths and troths, my lord, I spoke mine.

CLAUDIO

That I love her, I feel.

DON PEDRO

That she is worthy, I know.

BENEDICK

That I neither feel how she should be loved, nor know how she should be worthy, is the opinion that fire cannot melt out of me: I will die in it at the stake.

DON PEDRO

Thou wast ever an obstinate heretic in the despite of beauty.

CLAUDIO

And never could maintain his part but in the force of his will.

BENEDICK

That a woman conceived me, I thank her; that she brought me up, I likewise give her most humble thanks: but that I will have a recheat winded in my forehead, or hang my bugle in an invisible baldrick, all women shall pardon me. Because I will not do them the wrong to mistrust any, I will do myself the right to trust none; and the fine is, for the which I may go the finer, I will live a bachelor.

DON PEDRO

I shall see thee, ere I die, look pale with love.

BENEDICK

With anger, with sickness, or with hunger, my lord; not with love: prove that ever I lose more blood with love than I will get again with drinking, pick out mine eyes with a ballad-maker's pen, and hang me up at the door of a brothel-house for the sign of blind Cupid.

DON PEDRO

Well, if ever thou dost fall from this faith, thou wilt prove a notable argument.

BENEDICK

If I do, hang me in a bottle like a cat, and shoot at me; and he that hits me, let him be clapped on the shoulder and called Adam.

DON PEDRO

Well, as time shall try:
'In time the savage bull doth bear the yoke.'

BENEDICK

The savage bull may; but if ever the sensible Benedick bear it, pluck off the bull's horns, and set them in my forehead: and let me be vilely painted; and in such great letters as they write 'Here is good horse to hire,' let them signify under my sign 'Here you may see Benedick the married man.'

CLAUDIO

If this should ever happen, thou wouldst be horn-mad.

DON PEDRO

Nay, if Cupid have not spent all his quiver in Venice, thou wilt quake for this shortly.

BENEDICK

I look for an earthquake too, then.

DON PEDRO

Well, you will temporize with the hours. In the meantime, good Signior Benedick, repair to Leonato's: commend me to him, and tell him I will not fail him at supper; for indeed he hath made great preparation.

BENEDICK

I have almost matter enough in me for such an embassage; and so I commit you—

CLAUDIO

To the tuition of God: From my house, if I had it,—

DON PEDRO

The sixth of July: Your loving friend, Benedick.

BENEDICK

Nay, mock not, mock not. The body of your discourse is sometime guarded with fragments, and the guards are but slightly basted on neither: ere you

flout old ends any further, examine your conscience: and so I leave you.   [*Exit*

CLAUDIO

My liege, your highness now may do me good.

DON PEDRO

My love is thine to teach: teach it but how,
And thou shalt see how apt it is to learn
Any hard lesson that may do thee good.

CLAUDIO

Hath Leonato any son, my lord?

DON PEDRO

No child but Hero; she's his only heir.
Dost thou affect her, Claudio?

CLAUDIO

                              O, my lord,
When you went onward on this ended action,
I look'd upon her with a soldier's eye,
That liked, but had a rougher task in hand
Than to drive liking to the name of love:
But now I am return'd and that war-thoughts
Have left their places vacant, in their rooms
Come thronging soft and delicate desires,
All prompting me how fair young Hero is,
Saying, I liked her ere I went to wars.

DON PEDRO

Thou wilt be like a lover presently,
And tire the hearer with a book of words.
If thou dost love fair Hero, cherish it;
And I will break with her and with her father,
And thou shalt have her. Was't not to this end
That thou began'st to twist so fine a story?

CLAUDIO

How sweetly you do minister to love,
That know love's grief by his complexion!
But lest my liking might too sudden seem,
I would have salved it with a longer treatise.

DON PEDRO

What need the bridge much broader than the flood?
The fairest grant is the necessity.
Look, what will serve is fit: 'tis once, thou lovest,
And I will fit thee with the remedy.
I know we shall have revelling to-night:
I will assume thy part in some disguise,
And tell fair Hero I am Claudio;
And in her bosom I'll unclasp my heart,
And take her hearing prisoner with the force
And strong encounter of my amorous tale:
Then after to her father will I break;
And the conclusion is, she shall be thine.
In practice let us put it presently.   [*Exeunt*

SCENE II. *A room in* LEONATO'S *house*

Enter LEONATO *and* ANTONIO, *meeting*

LEONATO

How now, brother! Where is my cousin, your son?
hath he provided this music?

ANTONIO

He is very busy about it. But, brother, I can tell you strange news, that you yet dreamt not of.

LEONATO

Are they good?

ANTONIO

As the event stamps them: but they have a good cover; they show well outward. The prince and Count Claudio, walking in a thick-pleached alley in mine orchard, were thus much overheard by a man of mine: the prince discovered to Claudio that he loved my niece your daughter, and meant to acknowledge it this night in a dance; and if he found her accordant, he meant to take the present time by the top, and instantly break with you of it.

LEONATO

Hath the fellow any wit that told you this?

ANTONIO

A good sharp fellow: I will send for him; and question him yourself.

LEONATO

No, no; we will hold it as a dream till it appear itself: but I will acquaint my daughter withal, that she may be the better prepared for an answer, if peradventure this be true. Go you and tell her of it. [Enter ATTENDANTS] Cousins, you know what you have to do. O, I cry you mercy, friend; go you with me, and I will use your skill. Good cousin, have a care this busy time.   [Exeunt

SCENE III. *The same*

Enter DON JOHN *and* CONRADE

CONRADE

What the good-year, my lord! why are you thus out of measure sad?

DON JOHN

There is no measure in the occasion that breeds; therefore the sadness is without limit.

CONRADE

You should hear reason.

DON JOHN

And when I have heard it, what blessing brings it?

CONRADE

If not a present remedy, at least a patient sufferance.

DON JOHN

I wonder that thou, being (as thou sayest thou art) born under Saturn, goest about to apply a moral medicine to a mortifying mischief. I cannot hide what I am: I must be sad when I have cause, and smile at no man's jests; eat when I have stomach, and wait for no man's leisure; sleep when I am drowsy, and tend on no man's business; laugh when I am merry, and claw no man in his humour.

CONRADE

Yea, but you must not make the full show of this till you may do it without controlment. You have of late stood out against your brother, and he hath

ta'en you newly into his grace; where it is impossible you should take true root but by the fair weather that you make yourself: it is needful that you frame the season for your own harvest.

DON JOHN

I had rather be a canker in a hedge than a rose in his grace; and it better fits my blood to be disdained of all than to fashion a carriage to rob love from any: in this, though I cannot be said to be a flattering honest man, it must not be denied but I am a plain-dealing villain. I am trusted with a muzzle, and enfranchised with a clog; therefore I have decreed not to sing in my cage. If I had my mouth, I would bite; if I had my liberty, I would do my liking: in the meantime let me be that I am, and seek not to alter me.

CONRADE

Can you make no use of your discontent?

DON JOHN

I make all use of it, for I use it only. Who comes here?

Enter BORACHIO

What news, Borachio?

BORACHIO

I came yonder from a great supper: the prince your brother is royally entertained by Leonato; and I can give you intelligence of an intended marriage.

DON JOHN

Will it serve for any model to build mischief on? What is he for a fool that betroths himself to unquietness?

BORACHIO

Marry, it is your brother's right hand.

DON JOHN

Who? the most exquisite Claudio?

BORACHIO

Even he.

DON JOHN

A proper squire! And who, and who? which way looks he?

BORACHIO

Marry, on Hero, the daughter and heir of Leonato.

DON JOHN

A very forward March-chick! How came you to this?

BORACHIO

Being entertained for a perfumer, as I was smoking a musty room, comes me the prince and Claudio, hand in hand, in sad conference: I whipt me behind the arras; and there heard it agreed upon, that the prince should woo Hero for himself, and having obtained her, give her to Count Claudio.

DON JOHN

Come, come, let us thither: this may prove food to my displeasure. That young start-up hath all the glory of my overthrow: if I can cross him any way, I bless myself every way. You are both sure, and will assist me?

CONRADE

To the death, my lord.

DON JOHN

Let us to the great supper: their cheer is the greater
that I am subdued. Would the cook were of my
mind! Shall we go prove what's to be done?

BORACHIO

We'll wait upon your lordship.   [Exeunt

ACT II

SCENE I. A hall in LEONATO's house

Enter LEONATO, ANTONIO, HERO, BEATRICE, and others

LEONATO

Was not Count John here at supper?

ANTONIO

I saw him not.

BEATRICE

How tartly that gentleman looks! I never can see
him but I am heart-burned an hour after.

HERO

He is of a very melancholy disposition.

BEATRICE

He were an excellent man that were made just in
the midway between him and Benedick: the one is
too like an image and says nothing, and the other too
like my lady's eldest son, evermore tattling.

LEONATO

Then half Signior Benedick's tongue in Count
John's mouth, and half Count John's melancholy
in Signior Benedick's face,—

BEATRICE

With a good leg and a good foot, uncle, and money
enough in his purse, such a man would win any
woman in the world, if a' could get her good-will.

LEONATO

By my troth, niece, thou wilt never get thee a husband, if thou be so shrewd of thy tongue.

ANTONIO

In faith, she's too curst.

BEATRICE

Too curst is more than curst: I shall lessen God's
sending that way; for it is said, 'God sends a curst
cow short horns;' but to a cow too curst he sends
none.

LEONATO

So, by being too curst, God will send you no horns.

BEATRICE

Just, if he send me no husband; for the which blessing I am at him upon my knees every morning and
evening. Lord, I could not endure a husband with a
beard on his face: I had rather lie in the woollen.

LEONATO

You may light on a husband that hath no beard.

BEATRICE

What should I do with him? dress him in my apparel, and make him my waiting-gentlewoman? He
that hath a beard is more than a youth; and he that
hath no beard is less than a man: and he that is less
more than a youth is not for me; and he that is less

than a man, I am not for him: therefore I will even
take sixpence in earnest of the bear-ward, and lead
his apes into hell.

LEONATO

Well, then, go you into hell?

BEATRICE

No, but to the gate; and there will the devil meet
me, like an old cuckold, with horns on his head, and
say 'Get you to heaven, Beatrice, get you to heaven;
here's no place for you maids:' so deliver I up my
apes, and away to Saint Peter for the heavens; he
shows me where the bachelors sit, and there live we
as merry as the day is long.

ANTONIO

[To HERO] Well, niece, I trust you will be ruled by
your father.

BEATRICE

Yes, faith; it is my cousin's duty to make courtesy,
and say, 'Father, as it please you.' But yet for all
that, cousin, let him be a handsome fellow, or else
make another courtesy, and say, 'Father, as it
please me.'

LEONATO

Well, niece, I hope to see you one day fitted with a
husband.

BEATRICE

Not till God make men of some other metal than
earth. Would it not grieve a woman to be overmas-
tered with a piece of valiant dust? to make an account of her life to a clod of wayward marl? No,
uncle, I'll none: Adam's sons are my brethren; and,
truly, I hold it a sin to match in my kindred.

LEONATO

Daughter, remember what I told you: if the prince
do solicit you in that kind, you know your answer.

BEATRICE

The fault will be in the music, cousin, if you be not
wooed in good time: if the prince be too important,
tell him there is measure in every thing, and so
dance out the answer. For, hear me, Hero: wooing,
wedding, and repenting, is as a Scotch jig, a measure, and a cinque pace: the first suit is hot and
hasty, like a Scotch jig, and full as fantastical; the
wedding, mannerly-modest, as a measure, full of
state and ancientry; and then comes repentance,
and, with his bad legs, falls into the cinque pace
faster and faster, till he sink into his grave.

LEONATO

Cousin, you apprehend passing shrewdly.

BEATRICE

I have a good eye, uncle; I can see a church by daylight.

LEONATO

The revellers are entering, brother: make good
room.   [All put on their masks

Enter DON PEDRO, CLAUDIO, BENEDICK, BALTHASAR,
DON JOHN, BORACHIO, MARGARET, URSULA, and
others, masked

DON PEDRO

Lady, will you walk about with your friend?

HERO

So you walk softly, and look sweetly, and say nothing, I am yours for the walk; and especially when I walk away.

DON PEDRO

With me in your company?

HERO

I may say so, when I please.

DON PEDRO

And when please you to say so?

HERO

When I like your favour; for God defend the lute should be like the case!

DON PEDRO

My visor is Philemon's roof; within the house is Jove.

HERO

Why, then, your visor should be thatched.

DON PEDRO

Speak low, if you speak love.   [Drawing her aside

BALTHASAR

Well, I would you did like me.

MARGARET

So would not I, for your own sake; for I have many ill qualities.

BALTHASAR

Which is one?

MARGARET

I say my prayers aloud.

BALTHASAR

I love you the better: the hearers may cry, Amen.

MARGARET

God match me with a good dancer!

BALTHASAR

Amen.

MARGARET

And God keep him out of my sight when the dance is done! Answer, clerk.

BALTHASAR

No more words: the clerk is answered.

URSULA

I know you well enough; you are Signior Antonio.

ANTONIO

At a word, I am not.

URSULA

I know you by the waggling of your head.

ANTONIO

To tell you true, I counterfeit him.

URSULA

You could never do him so ill-well, unless you were the very man. Here's his dry hand up and down: you are he, you are he.

ANTONIO

At a word, I am not.

URSULA

Come, come, do you think I do not know you by your excellent wit? can virtue hide itself? Go to, mum, you are he: graces will appear, and there's an end.

BEATRICE

Will you not tell me who told you so?

BENEDICK

No, you shall pardon me.

BEATRICE

Nor will you not tell me who you are?

BENEDICK

Not now.

BEATRICE

That I was disdainful, and that I had my good wit out of the 'Hundred Merry Tales':—well, this was Signior Benedick that said so.

BENEDICK

What's he?

BEATRICE

I am sure you know him well enough.

BENEDICK

Not I, believe me.

BEATRICE

Did he never make you laugh?

BENEDICK

I pray you, what is he?

BEATRICE

Why, he is the prince's jester: a very dull fool; only his gift is in devising impossible slanders: none but libertines delight in him; and the commendation is not in his wit, but in his villany; for he both pleases men and angers them, and then they laugh at him and beat him. I am sure he is in the fleet: I would he had boarded me.

BENEDICK

When I know the gentleman, I'll tell him what you say.

BEATRICE

Do, do: he'll but break a comparison or two on me; which, peradventure not marked or not laughed at, strikes him into melancholy; and then there's a partridge wing saved, for the fool will eat no supper that night. [Music] We must follow the leaders.

BENEDICK

In every good thing.

BEATRICE

Nay, if they lead to any ill, I will leave them at the next turning.   [Dance. Then exeunt all except DON JOHN, BORACHIO, and CLAUDIO

DON JOHN

Sure my brother is amorous on Hero, and hath withdrawn her father to break with him about it. The ladies follow her, and but one visor remains.

BORACHIO

And that is Claudio: I know him by his bearing.

DON JOHN

Are not you Signior Benedick?

CLAUDIO

You know me well; I am he.

DON JOHN

Signior, you are very near my brother in his love: he is enamoured on Hero; I pray you, dissuade him from her: she is no equal for his birth: you may do the part of an honest man in it.

CLAUDIO

How know you he loves her?

DON JOHN

I heard him swear his affection.

BORACHIO

So did I too; and he swore he would marry her to-night.

DON JOHN

Come, let us to the banquet.

[*Exeunt* DON JOHN *and* BORACHIO

CLAUDIO

Thus answer I in name of Benedick,
But hear these ill news with the ears of Claudio.
'Tis certain so; the prince wooes for himself.
Friendship is constant in all other things
Save in the office and affairs of love:
Therefore all hearts in love use their own tongues;
Let every eye negotiate for itself,
And trust no agent; for beauty is a witch,
Against whose charms faith melteth into blood.
This is an accident of hourly proof,
Which I mistrusted not. Farewell, therefore, Hero!

Re-enter BENEDICK

BENEDICK

Count Claudio?

CLAUDIO

Yea, the same.

BENEDICK

Come, will you go with me?

CLAUDIO

Whither?

BENEDICK

Even to the next willow, about your own business, county. What fashion will you wear the garland of? about your neck, like an usurer's chain? or under your arm, like a lieutenant's scarf? You must wear it one way, for the prince hath got your Hero.

CLAUDIO

I wish him joy of her.

BENEDICK

Why, that's spoken like an honest drovier; so they sell bullocks. But did you think the prince would have served you thus?

CLAUDIO

I pray you, leave me.

BENEDICK

Ho! now you strike like the blind man; 'twas the boy that stole your meat, and you'll beat the post.

CLAUDIO

If it will not be, I'll leave you. [*Exit*

BENEDICK

Alas, poor hurt fowl! now will he creep into sedges. But, that my Lady Beatrice should know me, and not know me! The prince's fool! Ha? It may be I go under that title because I am merry. Yea, but so I am apt to do myself wrong; I am not so reputed: it is the base, though bitter, disposition of Beatrice that puts the world into her person, and so gives me out. Well, I'll be revenged as I may.

Re-enter DON PEDRO

DON PEDRO

Now, signior, where's the count? did you see him?

BENEDICK

Troth, my lord, I have played the part of Lady Fame. I found him here as melancholy as a lodge in a warren: I told him, and I think I told him true, that your grace had got the good will of this young lady; and I offered him my company to a willow-tree, either to make him a garland, as being forsaken, or to bind him up a rod, as being worthy to be whipped.

DON PEDRO

To be whipped! What's his fault?

BENEDICK

The flat transgression of a school-boy, who, being overjoyed with finding a birds' nest, shows it his companion, and he steals it.

DON PEDRO

Wilt thou make a trust a trangression? The transgression is in the stealer.

BENEDICK

Yet it had not been amiss the rod had been made, and the garland too; for the garland he might have worn himself, and the rod he might have bestowed on you, who, as I take it, have stolen his birds' nest.

DON PEDRO

I will but teach them to sing, and restore them to the owner.

BENEDICK

If their singing answer your saying, by my faith, you say honestly.

DON PEDRO

The Lady Beatrice hath a quarrel to you: the gentleman that danced with her told her she is much wronged by you.

BENEDICK

O, she misused me past the endurance of a block! an oak but with one green leaf on it would have answered her; my very visor began to assume life and scold with her. She told me, not thinking I had been myself, that I was the prince's jester, that I was duller than a great thaw; huddling jest upon jest, with such impossible conveyance, upon me, that I stood like a man at a mark, with a whole army shooting at me. She speaks poniards, and every word stabs: if her breath were as terrible as her terminations, there were no living near her; she would infect to the north star. I would not marry her, though she were endowed with all that Adam had left him before he transgressed: she would have made Hercules have turned spit, yea, and have cleft his club to make the fire too. Come, talk not of her: you shall find her the infernal Ate in good apparel. I would to God some scholar would conjure her; for certainly, while she is here, a man may live as quiet in hell as in a sanctuary; and people sin upon purpose, because they would go thither; so, indeed, all disquiet, horror, and perturbation follows her.

DON PEDRO

Look, here she comes.

Re-enter CLAUDIO, BEATRICE, HERO, *and* LEONATO

BENEDICK

Will your grace command me any service to the world's end? I will go on the slightest errand now to the Antipodes that you can devise to send me on; I will fetch you a toothpicker now from the furthest inch of Asia; bring you the length of Prester John's foot; fetch you a hair off the great Cham's beard; do you any embassage to the Pigmies; rather than hold three words' conference with this harpy. You have no employment for me?

DON PEDRO

None, but to desire your good company.

BENEDICK

O God, sir, here's a dish I love not: I cannot endure my Lady Tongue.   [*Exit*

DON PEDRO

Come, lady, come; you have lost the heart of Signior Benedick.

BEATRICE

Indeed, my lord, he lent it me awhile; and I gave him use for it, a double heart for his single one: marry, once before he won it of me with false dice, therefore your Grace may well say I have lost it.

DON PEDRO

You have put him down, lady, you have put him down.

BEATRICE

So I would not he should do me, my lord, lest I should prove the mother of fools. I have brought Count Claudio, whom you sent me to seek.

DON PEDRO

Why, how now, count! wherefore are you sad?

CLAUDIO

Not sad, my lord.

DON PEDRO

How then? sick?

CLAUDIO

Neither, my lord.

BEATRICE

The count is neither sad, nor sick, nor merry, nor well; but civil count, civil as an orange, and something of that jealous complexion.

DON PEDRO

I' faith, lady, I think your blazon to be true; though, I'll be sworn, if he be so, his conceit is false. Here, Claudio, I have wooed in thy name, and fair Hero is won: I have broke with her father, and his good will obtained: name the day of marriage, and God give thee joy!

LEONATO

Count, take of me my daughter, and with her my fortunes: his Grace hath made the match, and all grace say Amen to it.

BEATRICE

Speak, count, 'tis your cue.

CLAUDIO

Silence is the perfectest herald of joy: I were but little happy, if I could say how much. Lady, as you are mine, I am yours: I give away myself for you, and dote upon the exchange.

BEATRICE

Speak, cousin; or, if you cannot, stop his mouth with a kiss, and let not him speak neither.

DON PEDRO

In faith, lady, you have a merry heart.

BEATRICE

Yea, my lord; I thank it, poor fool, it keeps on the windy side of care. My cousin tells him in his ear that he is in her heart.

CLAUDIO

And so she doth, cousin.

BEATRICE

Good Lord, for alliance! Thus goes every one to the world but I, and I am sun-burnt; I may sit in a corner, and cry heigh-ho for a husband!

DON PEDRO

Lady Beatrice, I will get you one.

BEATRICE

I would rather have one of your father's getting. Hath your Grace ne'er a brother like you? Your father got excellent husbands, if a maid could come by them.

DON PEDRO

Will you have me, lady?

BEATRICE

No, my lord, unless I might have another for working-days: your Grace is too costly to wear every day. But, I beseech your Grace, pardon me: I was born to speak all mirth and no matter.

DON PEDRO

Your silence most offends me, and to be merry best becomes you; for, out of question, you were born in a merry hour.

BEATRICE

No, sure, my lord, my mother cried; but then there was a star danced, and under that was I born. Cousins, God give you joy!

LEONATO

Niece, will you look to those things I told you of?

BEATRICE

I cry you mercy, uncle. By your Grace's pardon.

    [*Exit*

DON PEDRO

By my troth, a pleasant-spirited lady.

LEONATO

There's little of the melancholy element in her, my lord: she is never sad but when she sleeps; and not ever sad then; for I have heard my daughter say, she hath often dreamed of unhappiness, and waked herself with laughing.

DON PEDRO

She cannot endure to hear tell of a husband.

LEONATO

O, by no means: she mocks all her wooers out of suit.

DON PEDRO

She were an excellent wife for Benedick.

LEONATO

O Lord, my lord, if they were but a week married, they would talk themselves mad.

DON PEDRO

County Claudio, when mean you to go to church?

CLAUDIO

To-morrow, my lord: time goes on crutches till love have all his rites.

LEONATO

Not till Monday, my dear son, which is hence a just seven-night; and a time too brief, too, to have all things answer my mind.

DON PEDRO

Come, you shake the head at so long a breathing: but, I warrant thee, Claudio, the time shall not go dully by us. I will, in the interim, undertake one of Hercules' labours; which is, to bring Signior Benedick and the Lady Beatrice into a mountain of affection the one with the other. I would fain have it a match; and I doubt not but to fashion it, if you three will but minister such assistance as I shall give you direction.

LEONATO

My lord, I am for you, though it cost me ten nights' watchings.

CLAUDIO

And I, my lord.

DON PEDRO

And you too, gentle Hero?

HERO

I will do any modest office, my lord, to help my cousin to a good husband.

DON PEDRO

And Benedick is not the unhopefullest husband that I know. Thus far can I praise him; he is of a noble strain, of approved valour, and confirmed honesty. I will teach you how to humour your cousin, that she shall fall in love with Benedick; and I, with your two helps, will so practise on Benedick, that, in despite of his quick wit and his queasy stomach, he shall fall in love with Beatrice. If we can do this, Cupid is no longer an archer: his glory shall be ours, for we are the only love-gods. Go in with me, and I will tell you my drift.   [*Exeunt*

SCENE II. *The same*

Enter DON JOHN *and* BORACHIO

DON JOHN

It is so; the Count Claudio shall marry the daughter of Leonato.

BORACHIO

Yea, my lord; but I can cross it.

DON JOHN

Any bar, any cross, any impediment will be medicinable to me: I am sick in displeasure to him; and whatsoever comes athwart his affection ranges evenly with mine. How canst thou cross this marriage?

BORACHIO

Not honestly, my lord; but so covertly that no dishonesty shall appear in me.

DON JOHN

Show me briefly how.

BORACHIO

I think I told your lordship, a year since, how much I am in the favour of Margaret, the waiting gentlewoman to Hero.

DON JOHN

I remember.

BORACHIO

I can, at any unseasonable instant of the night, appoint her to look out at her lady's chamber window.

DON JOHN

What life is in that, to be the death of this marriage?

BORACHIO

The poison of that lies in you to temper. Go you to the prince your brother; spare not to tell him that he hath wronged his honour in marrying the renowned Claudio—whose estimation do you mightily hold up—to a contaminated stale, such a one as Hero.

DON JOHN

What proof shall I make of that?

BORACHIO

Proof enough to misuse the prince, to vex Claudio, to undo Hero, and kill Leonato. Look you for any other issue?

DON JOHN

Only to despite them I will endeavour any thing.

BORACHIO

Go, then; find me a meet hour to draw Don Pedro and the Count Claudio alone: tell them that you know that Hero loves me; intend a kind of zeal both to the prince and Claudio, as,—in love of your brother's honour, who hath made this match, and his friend's reputation, who is thus like to be cozened with the semblance of a maid,—that you have discovered thus. They will scarcely believe this without trial: offer them instances; which shall bear no less likelihood than to see me at her chamber-window; hear me call Margaret, Hero; hear Margaret term me Claudio; and bring them to see this the very night before the intended wedding,—for in the meantime I will so fashion the matter that Hero shall be absent,—and there shall appear such seeming truth of Hero's disloyalty, that jealousy shall be called assurance and all the preparation overthrown.

DON JOHN

Grow this to what adverse issue it can, I will put it in practice. Be cunning in the working this, and thy fee is a thousand ducats.

BORACHIO

Be you constant in the accusation, and my cunning shall not shame me.

DON JOHN

I will presently go learn their day of marriage.
     [*Exeunt*

SCENE III. LEONATO's *orchard*

Enter BENEDICK

BENEDICK

Boy!

Enter BOY

BOY

Signior?

BENEDICK

In my chamber-window lies a book: bring it hither to me in the orchard.

BOY

I am here already, sir.

BENEDICK

I know that; but I would have thee hence, and here again. [*Exit* BOY] I do much wonder that one man, seeing how much another man is a fool when he dedicates his behaviours to love, will, after he hath laughed at such shallow follies in others, become the argument of his own scorn by falling in love: and such a man is Claudio. I have known when there was no music with him but the drum and the fife; and now had he rather hear the tabor and the pipe: I have known when he would have walked ten mile a-foot to see a good armour; and now will he lie ten nights awake, carving the fashion of a new doublet. He was wont to speak plain and to the purpose, like an honest man and a soldier; and now is he turned orthography; his words are a very fantastical banquet,—just so many strange dishes. May I be so converted, and see with these eyes? I cannot tell; I think not: I will not be sworn but love may transform me to an oyster; but I'll take my oath on it, till he have made an oyster of me, he shall never make me such a fool. One woman is fair, yet I am well; another is wise, yet I am well; another virtuous, yet I am well: but till all graces be in one woman, one woman shall not come in my grace. Rich she shall be, that's certain; wise, or I'll none; virtuous, or I'll never cheapen her; fair, or I'll never look on her; mild, or come not near me; noble, or not I for an angel; of good discourse, an excellent musician, and her hair shall be of what colour it please God. Ha! the prince and Monsieur Love! I will hide me in the arbour.   [*Withdraws*

Enter DON PEDRO, CLAUDIO, *and* LEONATO

DON PEDRO

Come, shall we hear this music?

CLAUDIO

Yea, my good lord. How still the evening is,
As hush'd on purpose to grace harmony!

DON PEDRO

See you where Benedick hath hid himself?

CLAUDIO

O, very well, my lord: the music ended,
We'll fit the kid-fox with a pennyworth.

Enter BALTHASAR *with Music*

DON PEDRO

Come, Balthasar, we'll hear that song again.

BALTHASAR

O, good my lord, tax not so bad a voice
To slander music any more than once.

DON PEDRO

It is the witness still of excellency
To put a strange face on his own perfection.
I pray thee, sing, and let me woo no more.

BALTHASAR

Because you talk of wooing, I will sing;
Since many a wooer doth commence his suit
To her he thinks not worthy, yet he wooes,
Yet will he swear he loves.

DON PEDRO

           Nay, pray thee, come;
Or, if thou wilt hold longer argument,
Do it in notes.

BALTHASAR

           Note this before my notes;
There's not a note of mine that's worth the noting.

DON PEDRO

Why, these are very crotchets that he speaks;
Note, notes, forsooth, and nothing.   [*Air*

BENEDICK

Now, divine air! now is his soul ravished! Is it not strange that sheeps' guts should hale souls out of men's bodies? Well, a horn for my money, when all's done.

THE SONG

BALTHASAR

Sigh no more, ladies, sigh no more,
   Men were deceivers ever,
One foot in sea and one on shore,
   To one thing constant never:
Then sigh not so, but let them go,
   And be you blithe and bonny,
Converting all your sounds of woe
   Into Hey nonny, nonny.

Sing no more ditties, sing no moe,
   Of dumps so dull and heavy;
The fraud of men was ever so,
   Since summer first was leavy:
   Then sigh not so, &c.

DON PEDRO

By my troth, a good song.

BALTHASAR

And an ill singer, my lord.

DON PEDRO

Ha, no, no, faith; thou singest well enough for a shift.

BENEDICK

An he had been a dog that should have howled thus, they would have hanged him: and I pray God his bad voice bode no mischief. I had as lief have heard the night-raven, come what plague could have come after it.

DON PEDRO

Yea, marry, dost thou hear, Balthasar? I pray thee, get us some excellent music; for to-morrow night we would have it at the Lady Hero's chamber-window.

BALTHASAR

The best I can, my lord.

DON PEDRO

Do so: farewell. [*Exit* BALTHASAR] Come hither, Leonato. What was it you told me of to-day, that your niece Beatrice was in love with Signior Benedick?

CLAUDIO

O, ay: stalk on, stalk on; the fowl sits. I did never think that lady would have loved any man.

LEONATO

No, nor I neither; but most wonderful that she should so dote on Signior Benedick, whom she hath in all outward behaviours seemed ever to abhor.

BENEDICK

Is't possible? Sits the wind in that corner?

LEONATO

By my troth, my lord, I cannot tell what to think of it, but that she loves him with an enraged affection; it is past the infinite of thought.

DON PEDRO

May be she doth but counterfeit.

CLAUDIO

Faith, like enough.

LEONATO

O God, counterfeit! There was never counterfeit of passion came so near the life of passion as she discovers it.

DON PEDRO

Why, what effects of passion shows she?

CLAUDIO

Bait the hook well; this fish will bite.

LEONATO

What effects, my lord? She will sit you, you heard my daughter tell you how.

CLAUDIO

She did, indeed.

DON PEDRO

How, how, I pray you? You amaze me: I would have thought her spirit had been invincible against all assaults of affection.

LEONATO

I would have sworn it had, my lord; especially against Benedick.

BENEDICK

I should think this a gull, but that the white-bearded fellow speaks it: knavery cannot, sure, hide himself in such reverence.

CLAUDIO

He hath ta'en the infection: hold it up.

DON PEDRO

Hath she made her affection known to Benedick?

LEONATO

No; and swears she never will: that's her torment.

CLAUDIO

'Tis true, indeed; so your daughter says: 'Shall I,' says she, 'that have so oft encountered him with scorn, write to him that I love him?'

LEONATO

This says she now when she is beginning to write to him; for she'll be up twenty times a night; and

there will she sit in her smock till she have writ a sheet of paper: my daughter tells us all.

CLAUDIO

Now you talk of a sheet of paper, I remember a pretty jest your daughter told us of.

LEONATO

O, when she had writ it, and was reading it over, she found Benedick and Beatrice between the sheet?

CLAUDIO

That.

LEONATO

O, she tore the letter into a thousand halfpence; railed at herself, that she should be so immodest to write to one that she knew would flout her; 'I measure him,' says she, 'by my own spirit; for I should flout him, if he writ to me; yea, though I love him, I should.'

CLAUDIO

Then down upon her knees she falls, weeps, sobs, beats her heart, tears her hair, prays, curses; 'O sweet Benedick! God give me patience!'

LEONATO

She doth indeed; my daughter says so: and the ecstasy hath so much overborne her, that my daughter is sometime afeard she will do a desperate outrage to herself: it is very true.

DON PEDRO

It were good that Benedick knew of it by some other, if she will not discover it.

CLAUDIO

To what end? He would make but a sport of it, and torment the poor lady worse.

DON PEDRO

An he should, it were an alms to hang him. She's an excellent sweet lady; and, out of all suspicion, she is virtuous.

CLAUDIO

And she is exceeding wise.

DON PEDRO

In every thing but in loving Benedick.

LEONATO

O, my lord, wisdom and blood combating in so tender a body, we have ten proofs to one that blood hath the victory. I am sorry for her, as I have just cause, being her uncle and her guardian.

DON PEDRO

I would she had bestowed this dotage on me: I would have daffed all other respects, and made her half myself. I pray you, tell Benedick of it, and hear what a' will say.

LEONATO

Were it good, think you?

CLAUDIO

Hero thinks surely she will die; for she says she will die, if he love her not; and she will die, ere she make her love known; and she will die, if he woo her, rather than she will bate one breath of her accustomed crossness.

DON PEDRO

She doth well: if she should make tender of her love,

'tis very possible he'll scorn it; for the man, as you know all, hath a contemptible spirit.

CLAUDIO

He is a very proper man.

DON PEDRO

He hath indeed a good outward happiness.

CLAUDIO

Before God! and in my mind, very wise.

DON PEDRO

He doth indeed show some sparks that are like wit.

CLAUDIO

And I take him to be valiant.

DON PEDRO

As Hector, I assure you: and in the managing of quarrels you may say he is wise; for either he avoids them with great discretion, or undertakes them with a most Christian-like fear.

LEONATO

If he do fear God, a' must necessarily keep peace: if he break the peace, he ought to enter into a quarrel with fear and trembling.

DON PEDRO

And so will he do; for the man doth fear God, howsoever it seems not in him by some large jests he will make. Well, I am sorry for your niece. Shall we go seek Benedick, and tell him of her love?

CLAUDIO

Never tell him, my lord: let her wear it out with good counsel.

LEONATO

Nay, that's impossible: she may wear her heart out first.

DON PEDRO

Well, we will hear further of it by your daughter: let it cool the while. I love Benedick well; and I could wish he would modestly examine himself, to see how much he is unworthy so good a lady.

LEONATO

My lord, will you walk? dinner is ready.

CLAUDIO

If he do not dote on her upon this, I will never trust my expectation.

DON PEDRO

Let there be the same net spread for her; and that must your daughter and her gentlewomen carry. The sport will be, when they hold one an opinion of another's dotage, and no such matter: that's the scene that I would see, which will be merely a dumb-show. Let us send her to call him in to dinner.

[*Exeunt* DON PEDRO, CLAUDIO, *and* LEONATO

BENEDICK

[*Coming forward*] This can be no trick: the conference was sadly borne. They have the truth of this from Hero. They seem to pity the lady: it seems her affections have their full bent. Love me! why, it must be requited. I hear how I am censured: they say I will bear myself proudly, if I perceive the love come from her; they say too that she will rather die than give any sign of affection. I did never think to marry: I must not seem proud: happy are they that

hear their detractions, and can put them to mending. They say the lady is fair,—'tis a truth, I can bear them witness; and virtuous,—'tis so, I cannot reprove it; and wise, but for loving me,—by my troth, it is no addition to her wit, nor no great argument of her folly, for I will be horribly in love with her. I may chance have some odd quirks and remnants of wit broken on me, because I have railed so long against marriage: but doth not the appetite alter? a man loves the meat in his youth that he cannot endure in his age. Shall quips and sentences and these paper bullets of the brain awe a man from the career of his humour? No, the world must be peopled. When I said I would die a bachelor, I did not think I should live till I were married. Here comes Beatrice. By this day! she's a fair lady: I do spy some marks of love in her.

Enter BEATRICE

BEATRICE

Against my will I am sent to bid you come in to dinner.

BENEDICK

Fair Beatrice, I thank you for your pains.

BEATRICE

I took no more pains for those thanks than you take pains to thank me: if it had been painful, I would not have come.

BENEDICK

You take pleasure, then, in the message?

BEATRICE

Yea, just so much as you may take upon a knife's point, and choke a daw withal. You have no stomach, signior: fare you well.   [*Exit*

BENEDICK

Ha! 'Against my will I am sent to bid you come in to dinner;' there's a double meaning in that. 'I took no more pains for those thanks than you took pains to thank me;' that's as much as to say, Any pains that I take for you is as easy as thanks. If I do not take pity of her, I am a villain; if I do not love her, I am a Jew. I will go get her picture.   [*Exit*

ACT III

SCENE I. LEONATO's *orchard*

Enter HERO, MARGARET, *and* URSULA

HERO

Good Margaret, run thee to the parlour;
There shalt thou find my cousin Beatrice
Proposing with the prince and Claudio:
Whisper her ear, and tell her, I and Ursula
Walk in the orchard, and our whole discourse
Is all of her; say that thou overheard'st us;
And bid her steal into the pleached bower,
Where honeysuckles, ripen'd by the sun,
Forbid the sun to enter; like favourites,
Made proud by princes, that advance their pride

Against that power that bred it: there will she hide
  her,
To listen our propose. This is thy office;
Bear thee well in it, and leave us alone.

MARGARET

I'll make her come, I warrant you, presently. [*Exit*

HERO

Now, Ursula, when Beatrice doth come,
As we do trace this alley up and down,
Our talk must only be of Benedick.
When I do name him, let it be thy part
To praise him more than ever man did merit:
My talk to thee must be, how Benedick
Is sick in love with Beatrice. Of this matter
Is little Cupid's crafty arrow made,
That only wounds by hearsay.

Enter BEATRICE, *behind*
                          Now begin;
For look where Beatrice, like a lapwing, runs
Close by the ground, to hear our conference.

URSULA

The pleasant'st angling is to see the fish
Cut with her golden oars the silver stream,
And greedily devour the treacherous bait:
So angle we for Beatrice; who even now
Is couched in the woodbine coverture.
Fear you not my part of the dialogue.

HERO

Then go we near her, that her ear lose nothing
Of the false sweet bait that we lay for it.
                        [*Approaching the bower*
No, truly, Ursula, she is too disdainful;
I know her spirits are as coy and wild
As haggards of the rock.

URSULA

              But are you sure
That Benedick loves Beatrice so entirely?

HERO

So says the prince and my new-trothed lord.

URSULA

And did they bid you tell her of it, madam?

HERO

They did entreat me to acquaint her of it;
But I persuaded them, if they loved Benedick,
To wish him wrestle with affection,
And never to let Beatrice know of it.

URSULA

Why did you so? Doth not the gentleman
Deserve as full as fortunate a bed
As ever Beatrice shall couch upon?

HERO

O god of love! I know he doth deserve
As much as may be yielded to a man:
But Nature never framed a woman's heart
Of prouder stuff than that of Beatrice;
Disdain and scorn ride sparkling in her eyes,
Misprising what they look on; and her wit
Values itself so highly, that to her
All matter else seems weak: she cannot love,

Nor take no shape nor project of affection,
She is so self-endeared.

URSULA

            Sure, I think so;
And therefore certainly it were not good
She knew his love, lest she make sport at it.

HERO

Why, you speak truth. I never yet saw man,
How wise, how noble, young, how rarely featured,
But she would spell him backward: if fair-faced,
She would swear the gentleman should be her sister;
If black, why, Nature, drawing of an antique,
Made a fowl blot; if tall, a lance ill-headed;
If low, an agate very vilely cut;
If speaking, why, a vane blown with all winds;
If silent, why, a block moved with none.
So turns she every man the wrong side out;
And never gives to truth and virtue that
Which simpleness and merit purchaseth.

URSULA

Sure, sure, such carping is not commendable.

HERO

No, not to be so odd, and from all fashions,
As Beatrice is, cannot be commendable:
But who dare tell her so? If I should speak,
She would mock me into air; O, she would laugh
  me
Out of myself, press me to death with wit!
Therefore let Benedick, like cover'd fire,
Consume away in sighs, waste inwardly:
It were a better death than die with mocks,
Which is as bad as die with tickling.

URSULA

Yet tell her of it: hear what she will say.

HERO

No; rather I will go to Benedick,
And counsel him to fight against his passion.
And, truly, I'll devise some honest slanders
To stain my cousin with: one doth not know
How much an ill word may empoison liking.

URSULA

O, do not do your cousin such a wrong!
She cannot be so much without true judgement,—
Having so swift and excellent a wit
As she is prized to have,—as to refuse
So rare a gentleman as Signior Benedick.

HERO

He is the only man of Italy,
Always excepted my dear Claudio.

URSULA

I pray you, be not angry with me, madam,
Speaking my fancy: Signior Benedick,
For shape, for bearing, argument and valour
Goes foremost in report through Italy.

HERO

Indeed, he hath an excellent good name.

URSULA

His excellence did earn it, ere he had it.
When are you married, madam?

HERO

Why, every day, to-morrow. Come, go in:
I'll show thee some attires; and have thy counsel
Which is the best to furnish me to-morrow.

URSULA

She's limed, I warrant you: we have caught her,
    madam.

HERO

If it prove so, then loving goes by haps:
Some Cupid kills with arrows, some with traps.
                              [Exeunt HERO and URSULA

BEATRICE

[Coming forward] What fire is in mine ears? Can this
    be true?
    Stand I condemn'd for pride and scorn so much?
Contempt, farewell! and maiden pride, adieu!
    No glory lives behind the back of such.
And, Benedick, love on; I will requite thee,
    Taming my wild heart to thy loving hand:
If thou dost love, my kindness shall incite thee
    To bind our loves up in a holy band;
For others say thou dost deserve, and I
Believe it better than reportingly.   [Exit

SCENE II. A room in LEONATO's house

Enter DON PEDRO, CLAUDIO, BENEDICK, and LEONATO

DON PEDRO

I do but stay till your marriage be consummate,
and then go I toward Arragon.

CLAUDIO

I'll bring you thither, my lord, if you'll vouchsafe
me.

Nay, that would be as great a soil in the new gloss
of your marriage, as to show a child his new coat
and forbid him to wear it. I will only be bold with
Benedick for his company; for, from the crown of
his head to the sole of his foot, he is all mirth: he
hath twice or thrice cut Cupid's bow-string, and the
little hangman dare not shoot at him; he hath a
heart as sound as a bell, and his tongue is the clap-
per, for what his heart thinks his tongue speaks.

BENEDICK

Gallants, I am not as I have been.

LEONATO

So say I: methinks you are sadder.

CLAUDIO

I hope he be in love.

DON PEDRO

Hang him, truant! there's no true drop of blood in
him, to be truly touched with love; if he be sad, he
wants money.

BENEDICK

I have the toothache.

DON PEDRO

Draw it.

BENEDICK

Hang it!

CLAUDIO

You must hang it first, and draw it afterwards.

DON PEDRO

What! sigh for the toothache?

LEONATO

Where is but a humour or a worm.

BENEDICK

Well, every one can master a grief but he that has it.

CLAUDIO

Yet say I, he is in love.

DON PEDRO

There is no appearance of fancy in him, unless it be
a fancy that he hath to strange disguises; as, to be a
Dutchman to-day, a Frenchman to-morrow; or in
the shape of two countries at once, as, a German
from the waist downward, all slops, and a Spaniard
from the hip upward, no doublet. Unless he have a
fancy to this foolery, as it appears he hath, he is no
fool for fancy, as you would have it appear he is.

CLAUDIO

If he be not in love with some woman, there is no
believing old signs: a' brushes his hat o' mornings;
what should that bode?

DON PEDRO

Hath any man seen him at the barber's?

CLAUDIO

No, but the barber's man hath been seen with him;
and the old ornament of his cheek hath already
stuffed tennis-balls.

LEONATO

Indeed, he looks younger than he did, by the loss of
a beard.

DON PEDRO

Nay, a' rubs himself with civet: can you smell him
out by that?

CLAUDIO

That's as much as to say, the sweet youth's in love.

DON PEDRO

The greatest note of it is his melancholy.

CLAUDIO

And when was he wont to wash his face?

DON PEDRO

Yea, or to paint himself? for the which, I hear what
they say of him.

CLAUDIO

Nay, but his jesting spirit; which is now crept into a
lute-string, and now governed by stops.

DON PEDRO

Indeed, that tells a heavy tale for him: conclude,
conclude he is in love.

CLAUDIO

Nay, but I know who loves him.

DON PEDRO

That would I know too: I warrant, one that knows
him not.

CLAUDIO

Yes, and his ill conditions; and, in despite of all,
dies for him.

DON PEDRO

She shall be buried with her face upwards.

BENEDICK

Yet is this no charm for the toothache. Old signior, walk aside with me: I have studied eight or nine wise words to speak to you, which these hobby-horses must not hear. [*Exeunt* BENEDICK *and* LEONATO

DON PEDRO

For my life, to break with him about Beatrice.

CLAUDIO

'Tis even so. Hero and Margaret have by this played their parts with Beatrice; and then the two bears will not bite one another when they meet.

Enter DON JOHN

DON JOHN

My lord and brother, God save you!

DON PEDRO

Good den, brother.

DON JOHN

If your leisure served, I would speak with you.

DON PEDRO

In private?

DON JOHN

If it please you: yet Count Claudio may hear; for what I would speak of concerns him.

DON PEDRO

What's the matter?

DON JOHN

[*To* CLAUDIO] Means your lordship to be married to-morrow?

DON PEDRO

You know he does.

DON JOHN

I know not that, when he knows what I know.

CLAUDIO

If there be any impediment, I pray you discover it.

DON JOHN

You may think I love you not: let that appear here-after, and aim better at me by that I now will manifest. For my brother, I think he holds you well, and in dearness of heart hath help to effect your ensuing marriage,—surely suit ill spent and labour ill bestowed.

DON PEDRO

Why, what's the matter?

DON JOHN

I came hither to tell you; and, circumstances short-ened, for she has been too long a talking of, the lady is disloyal.

CLAUDIO

Who, Hero?

DON JOHN

Even she; Leonato's Hero, your Hero, every man's Hero.

CLAUDIO

Disloyal?

DON JOHN

The word is too good to paint out her wickedness; I could say she were worse: think you of a worse title, and I will fit her to it. Wonder not till further warrant: go but with me to-night, you shall see her

chamber-window entered, even the night before her wedding-day: if you love her then, to-morrow wed her; but it would better fit your honour to change your mind.

CLAUDIO

May this be so?

DON PEDRO

I will not think it.

DON JOHN

If you dare not trust that you see, confess not that you know: if you will follow me, I will show you enough; and when you have seen more, and heard more, proceed accordingly.

CLAUDIO

If I see any thing to-night why I should not marry her to-morrow, in the congregation, where I should wed, there will I shame her.

DON PEDRO

And, as I wooed for thee to obtain her, I will join with thee to disgrace her.

DON JOHN

I will disparage her no farther till you are my witnesses: bear it coldly but till midnight, and let the issue show itself.

DON PEDRO

O day untowardly turned!

CLAUDIO

O mischief strangely thwarting!

DON JOHN

O plague right well prevented! so will you say when you have seen the sequel. [*Exeunt*

SCENE III. *A street*

Enter DOGBERRY *and* VERGES *with the* WATCH

DOGBERRY

Are you good men and true?

VERGES

Yea, or else it were pity but they should suffer salvation, body and soul.

DOGBERRY

Nay, there were a punishment too good for them, if they should have any allegiance in them, being chosen for the prince's watch.

VERGES

Well, give them their charge, neighbour Dogberry.

DOGBERRY

First, who think you the most desartless man to be constable?

FIRST WATCH

Hugh Otecake, sir, or George Seacole; for they can write and read.

DOGBERRY

Come hither, neighbour Seacole. God hath blessed you with a good name: to be a well-favoured man is the gift of fortune; but to write and read comes by nature.

SECOND WATCH

Both which, master constable,—

DOGBERRY

You have: I knew it would be your answer. Well, for your favour, sir, why, give God thanks, and make no boast of it; and for your writing and reading, let that appear when there is no need of such vanity. You are thought here to be the most senseless and fit man for the constable of the watch; therefore bear you the lantern. This is your charge: you shall comprehend all vagrom men; you are to bid any man stand, in the prince's name.

SECOND WATCH

How if a' will not stand?

DOGBERRY

Why, then, take no note of him, but let him go; and presently call the rest of the watch together, and thank God you are rid of a knave.

VERGES

If he will not stand when he is bidden, he is none of the prince's subjects.

DOGBERRY

True, and they are to meddle with none but the prince's subjects. You shall also make no noise in the streets; for for the watch to babble and to talk is most tolerable and not to be endured.

WATCH

We will rather sleep than talk: we know what belongs to a watch.

DOGBERRY

Why, you speak like an ancient and most quiet watchman; for I cannot see how sleeping should offend: only, have a care that your bills be not stolen. Well, you are to call at all the ale-houses, and bid those that are drunk get them to bed.

WATCH

How if they will not?

DOGBERRY

Why, then, let them alone till they are sober: if they make you not then the better answer, you may say they are not the men you took them for.

WATCH

Well, sir.

DOGBERRY

If you meet a thief, you may suspect him, by virtue of your office, to be no true man; and, for such kind of men, the less you meddle or make with them, why, the more is for your honesty.

WATCH

If we know him to be a thief, shall we not lay hands on him?

DOGBERRY

Truly, by your office, you may; but I think they that touch pitch will be defiled: the most peaceable way for you, if you do take a thief, is to let him show himself what he is, and steal out of your company.

VERGES

You have been always called a merciful man, partner.

DOGBERRY

Truly, I would not hang a dog by my will, much more a man who hath any honesty in him.

VERGES

If you hear a child cry in the night, you must call to the nurse and bid her still it.

WATCH

How if the nurse be asleep and will not hear us?

DOGBERRY

Why, then, depart in peace, and let the child wake her with crying; for the ewe that will not hear her lamb when it baes will never answer a calf when he bleats.

VERGES

'Tis very true.

DOGBERRY

This is the end of the charge:—you, constable, are to present the prince's own person: if you meet the prince in the night, you may stay him.

VERGES

Nay, by'r lady, that I think a' cannot.

DOGBERRY

Five shillings to one on't, with any man that knows the statues, he may stay him: marry, not without the prince be willing; for, indeed, the watch ought to offend no man; and it is an offence to stay a man against his will.

VERGES

By'r lady, I think it be so.

DOGBERRY

Ha, ah, ha! Well, masters, good night: an there be any matter of weight chances, call up me: keep your fellows' counsels and your own; and good night. Come, neighbour.

WATCH

Well, masters, we hear our charge: let us go sit here upon the church-bench till two, and then all to bed.

DOGBERRY

One word more, honest neighbours. I pray you, watch about Signior Leonato's door; for the wedding being there to-morrow, there is a great coil tonight. Adieu: be vigitant, I beseech you.

[Exeunt DOGBERRY and VERGES

Enter BORACHIO and CONRADE

BORACHIO

What, Conrade!

WATCH

[Aside] Peace! stir not.

BORACHIO

Conrade, I say!

CONRADE

Here, man; I am at thy elbow.

BORACHIO

Mass, and my elbow itched; I thought there would a scab follow.

CONRADE

I will owe thee an answer for that: and now forward with thy tale.

BORACHIO

Stand thee close, then, under this pent-house, for it drizzles rain; and I will, like a true drunkard, utter all to thee.

WATCH

[*Aside*] Some treason, masters: yet stand close.

BORACHIO

Therefore know I have earned of Don John a thousand ducats.

CONRADE

Is it possible that any villany should be so dear?

BORACHIO

Thou shouldst rather ask, if it were possible any villany should be so rich; for when rich villains have need of poor ones, poor ones may make what price they will.

CONRADE

I wonder at it.

BORACHIO

That shows thou art unconfirmed. Thou knowest that the fashion of a doublet, or a hat, or a cloak, is nothing to a man.

CONRADE

Yes, it is apparel.

BORACHIO

I mean, the fashion.

CONRADE

Yes, the fashion is the fashion.

BORACHIO

Tush! I may as well say the fool's the fool. But seest thou not what a deformed thief this fashion is?

WATCH

[*Aside*] I know that Deformed; a' has been a vile thief this seven year; a' goes up and down like a gentleman: I remember his name.

BORACHIO

Didst thou not hear somebody?

CONRADE

No; 'twas the vane on the house.

BORACHIO

Seest thou not, I say, what a deformed thief this fashion is? how giddily a' turns about all the hot bloods between fourteen and five-and-thirty? sometimes fashioning them like Pharaoh's soldiers in the reechy painting, sometime like god Bel's priests in the old church-window, sometime like the shaven Hercules in the smirched worm-eaten tapestry, where his codpiece seems as massy as his club?

CONRADE

All this I see; and I see that the fashion wears out more apparel than the man. But art not thou thyself giddy with the fashion too, that thou hast shifted out of thy tale into telling me of the fashion?

BORACHIO

Not so, neither: but know that I have to-night wooed Margaret, the Lady Hero's gentlewoman, by the name of Hero: she leans me out at her mistress' chamber-window, bids me a thousand times good night,—I tell this tale vilely:—I should first tell thee how the prince, Claudio and my master, planted and placed and possessed by my master Don John, saw afar off in the orchard this amiable encounter.

CONRADE

And thought they Margaret was Hero?

BORACHIO

Two of them did, the prince and Claudio; but the devil my master knew she was Margaret; and partly by his oaths, which first possessed them, partly by the dark night, which did deceive them, but chiefly by my villany, which did confirm any slander that Don John had made, away went Claudio enraged; swore he would meet her, as he was appointed, next morning at the temple, and there, before the whole congregation, shame her with what he saw o'er night, and send her home again without a husband.

FIRST WATCH

We charge you, in the prince's name, stand!

SECOND WATCH

Call up the right master constable. We have here recovered the most dangerous piece of lechery that ever was known in the commonwealth.

FIRST WATCH

And one Deformed is one of them: I know him; a' wears a lock.

CONRADE

Masters, masters,—

SECOND WATCH

You'll be made bring Deformed forth, I warrant you.

CONRADE

Masters,—

FIRST WATCH

Never speak: we charge you let us obey you to go with us.

BORACHIO

We are like to prove a goodly commodity, being taken up of these men's bills.

CONRADE

A commodity in question, I warrant you. Come, we'll obey you.   [*Exeunt*

Scene IV. HERO's *apartment*

Enter HERO, MARGARET, *and* URSULA

HERO

Good Ursula, wake my cousin Beatrice, and desire her to rise.

URSULA

I will, lady.

HERO

And bid her come hither.

URSULA

Well.   [*Exit*

MARGARET

Troth, I think your other rabato were better.

HERO

No, pray thee, good Meg, I'll wear this.

MARGARET

By my troth's not so good; and I warrant your cousin will say so.

HERO

My cousin's a fool, and thou art another: I'll wear none but this.

MARGARET

I like the new tire within excellently, if the hair were a thought browner; and your gown's a most rare fashion, i' faith. I saw the Duchess of Milan's gown that they praise so.

HERO

O, that exceeds, they say.

MARGARET

By my troth's but a night-gown in respect of yours, —cloth o' gold, and cuts, and laced with silver, set with pearls, down sleeves, side sleeves, and skirts, round underborne with a bluish tinsel: but for a fine, quaint, graceful and excellent fashion, yours is worth ten on't.

HERO

God give me joy to wear it! for my heart is exceeding heavy.

MARGARET

'Twill be heavier soon by the weight of a man.

HERO

Fie upon thee! art not ashamed?

MARGARET

Of what, lady? of speaking honourably? Is not marriage honourable in a beggar? Is not your lord honourable without marriage? I think you would have me say, 'saving your reverence, a husband:' an bad thinking do not wrest true speaking, I'll offend nobody: is there any harm in 'the heavier for a husband'? None, I think, an it be the right husband and the right wife; otherwise 'tis light, and not heavy: ask my Lady Beatrice else; here she comes.

Enter BEATRICE

HERO

Good morrow, coz.

BEATRICE

Good morrow, sweet Hero.

HERO

Why, how now? do you speak in the sick tune?

BEATRICE

I am out of all other tune, methinks.

MARGARET

Clap's into 'Light o' love;' that goes without a burden: do you sing it, and I'll dance it.

BEATRICE

Ye light o' love, with your heels! then, if your husband have stables enough, you'll see he shall lack no barns.

MARGARET

O illegitimate construction! I scorn that with my heels.

BEATRICE

'Tis almost five o'clock, cousin; 'tis time you were ready. By my troth, I am exceeding ill: heigh-ho!

MARGARET

For a hawk, a horse, or a husband?

BEATRICE

For the letter that begins them all, H.

MARGARET

Well, an you be not turned Turk, there's no more sailing by the star.

BEATRICE

What means the fool, trow?

MARGARET

Nothing I; but God send every one their heart's desire!

HERO

These gloves the count sent me; they are an excellent perfume.

BEATRICE

I am stuffed, cousin; I cannot smell.

MARGARET

A maid, and stuffed! there's goodly catching of cold.

BEATRICE

O, God help me! God help me! how long have you professed apprehension?

MARGARET

Ever since you left it. Doth not my wit become me rarely?

BEATRICE

It is not seen enough, you should wear it in your cap. By my troth, I am sick.

MARGARET

Get you some of this distilled Carduus Benedictus, and lay it to your heart: it is the only thing for a qualm.

HERO

There thou prickest her with a thistle.

BEATRICE

Benedictus! why Benedictus? you have some moral in this Benedictus.

MARGARET

Moral! no, by my troth, I have no moral meaning; I meant, plain holy-thistle. You may think perchance that I think you are in love: nay, by'r lady, I am not such a fool to think what I list; nor I list not to think what I can; nor, indeed, I cannot think, if I would think my heart out of thinking, that you are in love, or that you will be in love, or that you can be in love. Yet Benedick was such another, and now is he become a man: he swore he would never marry; and yet now, in despite of his heart, he eats his meat without grudging: and how you may be converted, I know not; but methinks you look with your eyes as other women do.

BEATRICE

What pace is this that thy tongue keeps?

MARGARET

Not a false gallop.

Re-enter URSULA

URSULA

Madam, withdraw: the prince, the count, Signior Benedick, Don John, and all the gallants of the town, are come to fetch you to church.

HERO

Help to dress me, good coz, good Meg, good Ursula.

[*Exeunt*

SCENE V. *Another room in* LEONATO'*s house*

Enter LEONATO, *with* DOGBERRY *and* VERGES

LEONATO

What would you with me, honest neighbour?

DOGBERRY

Marry, sir, I would have some confidence with you
that decerns you nearly.

LEONATO

Brief, I pray you; for you see it is a busy time with
me.

DOGBERRY

Marry, this it is, sir.

VERGES

Yes, in truth it is, sir.

LEONATO

What is it, my good friends?

DOGBERRY

Goodman Verges, sir, speaks a little off the matter:
an old man, sir, and his wits are not so blunt as,
God help, I would desire they were; but, in faith,
honest as the skin between his brows.

VERGES

Yes, I thank God I am as honest as any man living
that is an old man and no honester than I.

DOGBERRY

Comparisons are odorous: palabras, neighbour
Verges.

LEONATO

Neighbours, you are tedious.

DOGBERRY

It pleases your worship to say so, but we are the
poor duke's officers; but truly, for mine own part,
if I were as tedious as a king, I could find in my
heart to bestow it all of your worship.

LEONATO

All thy tediousness on me, ah?

DOGBERRY

Yea, an 'twere a thousand pound more than 'tis; for
I hear as good exclamation on your worship as of
any man in the city; and though I be but a poor
man, I am glad to hear it.

VERGES

And so am I.

LEONATO

I would fain know what you have to say.

VERGES

Marry, sir, our watch to-night, excepting your worship's presence, ha' ta'en a couple of as arrant
knaves as any in Messina.

DOGBERRY

A good old man, sir; he will be talking: as they say,
When the age is in, the wit is out: God help us! it is
a world to see. Well said, i' faith, neighbour Verges:
well, God's a good man; an two men ride of a
horse, one must ride behind. An honest soul, i'
faith, sir; by my troth he is, as ever broke bread;
but God is to be worshipped; all men are not alike;
alas, good neighbour!

LEONATO

Indeed, neighbour, he comes too short of you.

DOGBERRY

Gifts that God gives.

LEONATO

I must leave you.

DOGBERRY

One word, sir: our watch, sir, have indeed compre-
hended two aspicious persons, and we would have
them this morning examined before your worship.

LEONATO

Take their examination yourself, and bring it me: I
am now in great haste, as it may appear unto you.

DOGBERRY

It shall be suffigance.

LEONATO

Drink some wine ere you go: fare you well.

Enter a MESSENGER

MESSENGER

My lord, they stay for you to give your daughter to
her husband.

LEONATO

I'll wait upon them: I am ready.

[*Exeunt* LEONATO *and* MESSENGER

DOGBERRY

Go, good partner, go, get you to Francis Seacole;
bid him bring his pen and inkhorn to the gaol: we
are now to examination these men.

VERGES

And we must do it wisely.

DOGBERRY

We will spare for no wit, I warrant you; here's that
shall drive some of them to a noncome: only get the
learned writer to set down our excommunication,
and meet me at the gaol.   [*Exeunt*

ACT IV

SCENE I. *A church*

Enter DON PEDRO, DON JOHN, LEONATO, FRIAR
FRANCIS, CLAUDIO, BENEDICK, HERO, BEATRICE,
and attendants

LEONATO

Come, Friar Francis, be brief; only to the plain form
of marriage, and you shall recount their particular
duties afterwards.

FRIAR FRANCIS

You come hither, my lord, to marry this lady.

CLAUDIO

No.

LEONATO

To be married to her: friar, you come to marry her

FRIAR FRANCIS

Lady, you come hither to be married to this count.

HERO

I do.

FRIAR FRANCIS
If either of you know any inward impediment why
you should not be conjoined, I charge you, on your
souls, to utter it.

CLAUDIO
Know you any, Hero?

HERO
None, my lord.

FRIAR FRANCIS
Know you any, count?

LEONATO
I dare make his answer, none.

CLAUDIO
O, what men dare do! what men may do! what men
daily do, not knowing what they do!

BENEDICK
How now! interjections? Why, then, some be of
laughing, as, ah, ha, he!

CLAUDIO
Stand thee by, friar. Father, by your leave:
Will you with free and unconstrained soul
Give me this maid, your daughter?

LEONATO
As freely, son, as God did give her me.

CLAUDIO
And what have I to give you back, whose worth
May counterpoise this rich and precious gift?

DON PEDRO
Nothing, unless you render her again.

CLAUDIO
Sweet prince, you learn me noble thankfulness.
There, Leonato, take her back again:
Give not this rotten orange to your friend;
She's but the sign and semblance of her honour.
Behold how like a maid she blushes here!
O, what authority and show of truth
Can cunning sin cover itself withal!
Comes not that blood as modest evidence
To witness simple virtue? Would you not swear,
All you that see her, that she were a maid,
By these exterior shows? But she is none:
She knows the heat of a luxurious bed;
Her blush is guiltiness, not modesty.

LEONATO
What do you mean, my lord?

CLAUDIO
                                    Not to be married,
Not to knit my soul to an approved wanton.

LEONATO
Dear my lord, if you, in your own proof,
Have vanquish'd the resistance of her youth,
And made defeat of her virginity,—

CLAUDIO
I know what you would say: if I have known her,
You will say she did embrace me as a husband,
And so extenuate the 'forehand sin:
No, Leonato,
I never tempted her with word too large;
But, as a brother to his sister, show'd
Bashful sincerity and comely love.

HERO
And seem'd I ever otherwise to you?

CLAUDIO
Out on thee! Seeming! I will write against it:
You seem to me as Dian in her orb,
As chaste as is the bud ere it be blown;
But you are more intemperate in your blood
Than Venus, or those pamper'd animals
That rage in savage sensuality.

HERO
Is my lord well, that he doth speak so wide?

LEONATO
Sweet prince, why speak not you?

DON PEDRO
                                    What should I speak?
I stand dishonour'd, that have gone about
To link my dear friend to a common stale.

LEONATO
Are these things spoken, or do I but dream?

DON JOHN
Sir, they are spoken, and these things are true.

BENEDICK
This looks not like a nuptial.

HERO
                                    True! O God!

CLAUDIO
Leonato, stand I here?
Is this the prince? is this the prince's brother?
Is this face Hero's? are our eyes our own?

LEONATO
All this is so: but what of this, my lord?

CLAUDIO
Let me but move one question to your daughter;
And, by that fatherly and kindly power
That you have in her, bid her answer truly.

LEONATO
I charge thee do so, as thou art my child.

HERO
O, God defend me! how am I beset!
What kind of catechising call you this?

CLAUDIO
To make you answer truly to your name.

HERO
Is it not Hero? Who can blot that name
With any just reproach?

CLAUDIO
                                    Marry, that can Hero;
Hero itself can blot out Hero's virtue.
What man was he talk'd with you yesternight
Out at your window betwixt twelve and one?
Now, if you are a maid, answer to this.

HERO
I talk'd with no man at that hour, my lord.

DON PEDRO
Why, then are you no maiden. Leonato,
I am sorry you must hear: upon mine honour,
Myself, my brother, and this grieved count
Did see her, hear her, at that hour last night
Talk with a ruffian at her chamber-window;
Who hath indeed, most like a liberal villain.

Confess'd the vile encounters they have had
A thousand times in secret.

DON JOHN

Fie, fie! they are not to be named, my lord,
Not to be spoke of;
There is not chastity enough in language,
Without offence to utter them. Thus, pretty lady,
I am sorry for thy much misgovernment.

CLAUDIO

O Hero, what a Hero hadst thou been,
If half thy outward graces had been placed
About thy thoughts and counsels of thy heart!
But fare thee well, most foul, most fair! farewell,
Thou pure impiety and impious purity!
For thee I'll lock up all the gates of love,
And on my eyelids shall conjecture hang,
To turn all beauty into thoughts of harm,
And never shall it more be gracious.

LEONATO

Hath no man's dagger here a point for me?

[HERO *swoons*

BEATRICE

Why, how now, cousin! wherefore sink you down?

DON JOHN

Come, let us go. These things, come thus to light,
Smother her spirits up.

[*Exeunt* DON PEDRO, DON JOHN, *and* CLAUDIO

BENEDICK

How doth the lady?

BEATRICE

Dead, I think. Help, uncle!
Hero! why, Hero! Uncle! Signior Benedick! Friar!

LEONATO

O Fate! take not away thy heavy hand.
Death is the fairest cover for her shame
That may be wish'd for.

BEATRICE

How now, cousin Hero!

FRIAR FRANCIS

Have comfort, lady.

LEONATO

Dost thou look up?

FRIAR FRANCIS

Yea, wherefore should she not?

LEONATO

Wherefore! Why, doth not every earthly thing
Cry shame upon her? Could she here deny
The story that is printed in her blood?
Do not live, Hero; do not ope thine eyes:
For, did I think thou wouldst not quickly die,
Thought I thy spirits were stronger than thy shames,
Myself would, on the rearward of reproaches,
Strike at thy life. Grieved I, I had but one?
Chid I for that at frugal nature's frame?
O, one too much by thee! Why had I one?
Why ever wast thou lovely in my eyes?
Why had I not with charitable hand
Took up a beggar's issue at my gates,
Who smirched thus and mired with infamy,
I might have said, 'No part of it is mine;

This shame derives itself from unknown loins'?
But mine, and mine I loved, and mine I praised,
And mine that I was proud on, mine so much
That I myself was to myself not mine,
Valuing of her,—why, she, O, she is fallen
Into a pit of ink, that the wide sea
Hath drops too few to wash her clean again,
And salt too little which may season give
To her foul-tainted flesh!

BENEDICK

Sir, sir, be patient.
For my part, I am so attired in wonder,
I know not what to say.

BEATRICE

O, on my soul, my cousin is belied!

BENEDICK

Lady, were you her bedfellow last night?

BEATRICE

No, truly, not; although, until last night,
I have this twelvemonth been her bedfellow.

LEONATO

Confirm'd, confirm'd! O, that is stronger made
Which was before barr'd up with ribs of iron!
Would the two princes lie, and Claudio lie,
Who loved her so, that, speaking of her foulness,
Wash'd it with tears? Hence from her! let her die.

FRIAR FRANCIS

Hear me a little;
For I have only been silent so long,
And given way unto this course of fortune,
By noting of the lady: I have mark'd
A thousand blushing apparitions
To start into her face; a thousand innocent shames
In angel whiteness beat away those blushes;
And in her eye there hath appear'd a fire,
To burn the errors that these princes hold
Against her maiden truth. Call me a fool;
Trust not my reading nor my observations,
Which with experimental seal doth warrant
The tenour of my book; trust not my age,
My reverence, calling, nor divinity,
If this sweet lady lie not guiltless here
Under some biting error.

LEONATO

Friar, it cannot be.
Thou seest that all the grace that she hath left
Is that she will not add to her damnation
A sin of perjury; she not denies it:
Why seek'st thou, then, to cover with excuse
That which appears in proper nakedness?

FRIAR FRANCIS

Lady, what man is he you are accused of?

HERO

They know that do accuse me; I know none:
If I know more of any man alive
Than that which maiden modesty doth warrant,
Let all my sins lack mercy! O my father,
Prove you that any man with me conversed
At hours unmeet, or that I yesternight

Maintain'd the change of words with any creature,
Refuse me, hate me, torture me to death!

FRIAR FRANCIS

There is some strange misprision in the princes.

BENEDICK

Two of them have the very bent of honour;
And if their wisdoms be misled in this,
The practice of it lives in John the bastard,
Whose spirits toil in frame of villanies.

LEONATO

I know not. If they speak but truth of her,
These hands shall tear her; if they wrong her hon-
        our,
The proudest of them shall well hear of it.
Time hath not yet so dried this blood of mine,
Nor age so eat up my invention,
Nor fortune made such havoc of my means,
Nor my bad life reft me so much of friends,
But they shall find, awaked in such a kind,
Both strength of limb and policy of mind,
Ability in means and choice of friends,
To quit me of them throughly.

FRIAR FRANCIS
                    Pause awhile,
And let my counsel sway you in this case.
Your daughter here the princes left for dead:
Let her awhile be secretly kept in,
And publish it that she is dead indeed;
Maintain a mourning ostentation,
And on your family's old monument
Hang mournful epitaphs, and do all rites
That appertain unto a burial.

LEONATO

What shall become of this? what will this do?

FRIAR FRANCIS

Marry, this, well carried, shall on her behalf
Change slander to remorse; that is some good:
But not for that dream I on this strange course,
But on this travail look for greater birth.
She dying, as it must be so maintain'd,
Upon the instant that she was accused,
Shall be lamented, pitied, and excused
Of every hearer: for it so falls out,
That what we have we prize not to the worth
Whiles we enjoy it; but being lack'd and lost,
Why, then we rack the value, then we find
The virtue that possession would not show us
Whiles it was ours. So will it fare with Claudio:
When he shall hear she died upon his words,
The idea of her life shall sweetly creep
Into his study of imagination;
And every lovely organ of her life
Shall come apparell'd in more precious habit,
More moving-delicate and full of life,
Into the eye and prospect of his soul,
Than when she lived indeed; then shall he mourn,
If ever love had interest in his liver,
And wish he had not so accused her,
No, though he thought his accusation true.
Let this be so, and doubt not but success

Will fashion the event in better shape
Than I can lay it down in likelihood.
But if all aim but this be levell'd false,
The supposition of the lady's death
Will quench the wonder of her infamy:
And if it sort not well, you may conceal her,
As best befits her wounded reputation,
In some reclusive and religious life,
Out of all eyes, tongues, minds, and injuries.

BENEDICK

Signior Leonato, let the friar advise you:
And though you know my inwardness and love
Is very much unto the prince and Claudio,
Yet, by mine honour, I will deal in this
As secretly and justly as your soul
Should with your body.

LEONATO
                Being that I flow in grief,
The smallest twine may lead me.

FRIAR FRANCIS

'Tis well consented: presently away;
    For to strange sores strangely they strain the cure.
Come, lady, die to live: this wedding day
    Perhaps is but prolong'd: have patience and en-
dure.   [*Exeunt all but* BENEDICK *and* BEATRICE

BENEDICK

Lady Beatrice, have you wept all this while?

BEATRICE

Yea, and I will weep a while longer.

BENEDICK

I will not desire that.

BEATRICE

You have no reason; I do it freely.

BENEDICK

Surely I do believe your fair cousin is wronged.

BEATRICE

Ah, how much might the man deserve of me that
would right her!

BENEDICK

Is there any way to show such friendship?

BEATRICE

A very even way, but no such friend.

BENEDICK

May a man do it?

BEATRICE

It is a man's office, but not yours.

BENEDICK

I do love nothing in the world so well as you: is not
that strange?

BEATRICE

As strange as the thing I know not. It were as possible for me to say I loved nothing so well as you:
but believe me not; and yet I lie not; I confess nothing, nor I deny nothing. I am sorry for my cousin.

BENEDICK

By my sword, Beatrice, thou lovest me.

BEATRICE

Do not swear, and eat it.

BENEDICK

I will swear by it that you love me; and I will make him eat it that says I love not you.

BEATRICE

Will you not eat your word?

BENEDICK

With no sauce that can be devised to it. I protest I love thee.

BEATRICE

Why, then, God forgive me!

BENEDICK

What offence, sweet Beatrice?

BEATRICE

You have stayed me in a happy hour: I was about to protest I loved you.

BENEDICK

And do it with all thy heart.

BEATRICE

I love you with so much of my heart, that none is left to protest.

BENEDICK

Come, bid me do any thing for thee.

BEATRICE

Kill Claudio.

BENEDICK

Ha! not for the wide world.

BEATRICE

You kill me to deny it. Farewell.

BENEDICK

Tarry, sweet Beatrice.

BEATRICE

I am gone, though I am here: there is no love in you: nay, I pray you, let me go.

BENEDICK

Beatrice,—

BEATRICE

In faith, I will go.

BENEDICK

We'll be friends first.

BEATRICE

You dare easier be friends with me than fight with mine enemy.

BENEDICK

Is Claudio thine enemy?

BEATRICE

Is he not approved in the height a villain, that hath slandered, scorned, dishonoured my kinswoman? O that I were a man! What, bear her in hand until they come to take hands; and then, with public accusation, uncovered slander, unmitigated rancour,—O God, that I were a man! I would eat his heart in the market-place.

BENEDICK

Hear me, Beatrice,—

BEATRICE

Talk with a man out at a window! A proper saying!

BENEDICK

Nay, but, Beatrice,—

BEATRICE

Sweet Hero! She is wronged, she is slandered, she is undone.

BENEDICK

Beat—

BEATRICE

Princes and counties! Surely, a princely testimony, a goodly count, Count Comfect; a sweet gallant, surely! O that I were a man for his sake! or that I had any friend would be a man for my sake! But manhood is melted into courtesies, valour into compliment, and men are only turned into tongue, and trim ones too: he is now as valiant as Hercules that only tells a lie, and swears it. I cannot be a man with wishing, therefore I will die a woman with grieving.

BENEDICK

Tarry, good Beatrice. By this hand, I love thee.

BEATRICE

Use it for my love some other way than swearing by it.

BENEDICK

Think you in your soul the Count Claudio hath wronged Hero?

BEATRICE

Yea, as sure as I have a thought or a soul.

BENEDICK

Enough, I am engaged; I will challenge him. I will kiss your hand, and so I leave you. By this hand, Claudio shall render me a dear account. As you hear of me, so think of me. Go, comfort your cousin: I must say she is dead: and so, farewell.   [Exeunt

SCENE II. *A prison*

Enter DOGBERRY, VERGES, *and* SEXTON, *in gowns; and the* WATCH, *with* CONRADE *and* BORACHIO

DOGBERRY

Is our whole dissembly appeared?

VERGES

O, a stool and a cushion for the sexton.

SEXTON

Which be the malefactors?

DOGBERRY

Marry, that am I and my partner.

VERGES

Nay, that's certain; we have the exhibition to examine.

SEXTON

But which are the offenders that are to be examined? let them come before master constable.

DOGBERRY

Yea, marry, let them come before me. What is your name, friend?

BORACHIO

Borachio.

DOGBERRY

Pray, write down, Borachio. Yours, sirrah?

CONRADE

I am a gentleman, sir, and my name is Conrade.

DOGBERRY

Write down, master gentleman Conrade. Masters, do you serve God?

CONRADE *and* BORACHIO

Yea, sir, we hope.

DOGBERRY

Write down, that they hope they serve God: and write God first; for God defend but God should go before such villains! Masters, it is proved already that you are little better than false knaves; and it will go near to be thought so shortly. How answer you for yourselves?

CONRADE

Marry, sir, we say we are none.

DOGBERRY

A marvellous witty fellow, I assure you; but I will go about with him. Come you hither, sirrah; a word in your ear: sir, I say to you, it is thought you are false knaves.

BORACHIO

Sir, I say to you we are none.

DOGBERRY

Well, stand aside. 'Fore God, they are both in a tale. Have you writ down, that they are none?

SEXTON

Master constable, you go not the way to examine: you must call forth the watch that are their accusers.

DOGBERRY

Yea, marry, that's the eftest way. Let the watch come forth. Masters, I charge you, in the prince's name, accuse these men.

FIRST WATCH

This man said, sir, that Don John, the prince's brother, was a villain.

DOGBERRY

Write down, Prince John a villain. Why, this is flat perjury, to call a prince's brother villain.

BORACHIO

Master, constable,—

DOGBERRY

Pray thee, fellow, peace: I do not like thy look, I promise thee.

SEXTON

What heard you him say else?

SECOND WATCH

Marry, that he had received a thousand ducats of Don John for accusing the Lady Hero wrongfully.

DOGBERRY

Flat burglary as ever was committed.

VERGES

Yea, by mass, that it is.

SEXTON

What else, fellow?

FIRST WATCH

And that Count Claudio did mean, upon his words, to disgrace Hero before the whole assembly, and not marry her.

DOGBERRY

O villain! thou wilt be condemned into everlasting redemption for this.

SEXTON

What else?

WATCH

This is all.

SEXTON

And this is more, masters, than you can deny. Prince John is this morning secretly stolen away; Hero was in this manner accused, in this very manner refused, and upon the grief of this suddenly died. Master constable, let these men be bound, and brought to Leonato's: I will go before and show him their examination. [*Exit*

DOGBERRY

Come, let them be opinioned.

VERGES

Let them be in the hands—

CONRADE

Off, coxcomb!

DOGBERRY

God's my life, where's the sexton? let him write down, the prince's officer, coxcomb. Come, bind them. Thou naughty varlet!

CONRADE

Away! you are an ass, you are an ass.

DOGBERRY

Dost thou not suspect my place? dost thou not suspect my years? O that he were here to write me down an ass! But, masters, remember that I am an ass; though it be not written down, yet forget not that I am an ass. No, thou villain, thou art full of piety, as shall be proved upon thee by good witness. I am a wise fellow; and, which is more, an officer; and, which is more, a householder; and, which is more, as pretty a piece of flesh as any is in Messina; and one that knows the law, go to; and a rich fellow enough, go to; and a fellow that hath had losses; and one that hath two gowns, and every thing handsome about him. Bring him away. O that I had been writ down an ass! [*Exeunt*

ACT V

SCENE I. *Before* LEONATO'S *house*

Enter LEONATO *and* ANTONIO

ANTONIO

If you go on thus, you will kill yourself;
And 'tis not wisdom thus to second grief
Against yourself.

LEONATO

I pray thee, cease thy counsel,
Which falls into mine ears as profitless
As water in a sieve: give not me counsel;
Nor let no comforter delight mine ear
But such a one whose wrcngs do suit with mine.

Bring me a father that so loved his child,
Whose joy of her is overwhelm'd like mine,
And bid him speak of patience:
Measure his woe the length and breadth of mine,
And let it answer every strain for strain,
As thus for thus, and such a grief for such,
In every lineament, branch, shape, and form:
If such a one will smile, and stroke his beard,
Bid sorrow wag, cry 'hem!' when he should groan,
Patch grief with proverbs, make misfortune drunk
With candle-wasters; bring him yet to me,
And I of him will gather patience.
But there is no such man: for, brother, men
Can counsel and speak comfort to that grief
Which they themselves not feel; but, tasting it,
Their counsel turns to passion, which before
Would give preceptial medicine to rage,
Fetter strong madness in a silken thread,
Charm ache with air, and agony with words:
No, no; 'tis all men's office to speak patience
To those that wring under the load of sorrow,
But no man's virtue nor sufficiency,
To be so moral when he shall endure
The like himself. Therefore give me no counsel:
My griefs cry louder than advertisement.

ANTONIO
Therein do men from children nothing differ.

LEONATO
I pray thee, peace. I will be flesh and blood;
For there was never yet philosopher
That could endure the toothache patiently,
However they have writ the style of gods,
And made a push at chance and sufferance.

ANTONIO
Yet bend not all the harm upon yourself;
Make those that do offend you suffer too.

LEONATO
There thou speak'st reason: nay, I will do so.
My soul doth tell me Hero is belied;
And that shall Claudio know; so shall the prince,
And all of them that thus dishonour her.

ANTONIO
Here comes the prince and Chaudio hastily.

Enter DON PEDRO *and* CLAUDIO

DON PEDRO
Good den, good den.

CLAUDIO
Good day to both of you.

LEONATO
Hear you, my lords,—

DON PEDRO
We have some haste, Leonato.

LEONATO
Some haste, my lord! well, fare you well, my lord:
Are you so hasty now? well, all is one.

DON PEDRO
Nay, do not quarrel with us, good old man.

ANTONIO
If he could right himself with quarrelling,
Some of us would lie low.

CLAUDIO
Who wrongs him?

LEONATO
Marry, thou dost wrong me, thou dissembler, thou:—
Nay, never lay thy hand upon thy sword;
I fear thee not.

CLAUDIO
Marry, beshrew my hand,
If it should give your age such cause of fear:
In faith, my hand meant nothing to my sword.

LEONATO
Tush, tush, man; never fleer and jest at me:
I speak not like a dotard nor a fool,
As, under privilege of age, to brag
What I have done being young, or what would do,
Were I not old. Know, Claudio, to thy head,
Thou hast so wrong'd mine innocent child and me,
That I am forced to lay my reverence by,
And, with grey hairs and bruise of many days,
Do challenge thee to trial of a man.
I say thou hast belied mine innocent child;
Thy slander hath gone through and through her
heart,
And she lies buried with her ancestors;
O, in a tomb where never scandal slept,
Save this of hers, framed by thy villany!

CLAUDIO
My villany?

LEONATO
Thine, Claudio; thine, I say.

DON PEDRO
You say not right, old man.

LEONATO
My lord, my lord,
I'll prove it on his body, if he dare,
Despite his nice fence and his active practice,
His May of youth and bloom of lustihood.

CLAUDIO
Away! I will not have to do with you.

LEONATO
Canst thou so daff me? Thou hast kill'd my child:
If thou kill'st me, boy, thou shalt kill a man.

ANTONIO
He shall kill two of us, and men indeed:
But that's no matter; let him kill one first;
Win me and wear me; let him answer me.
Come, follow me, boy; come, sir boy, come, follow
me:
Sir boy, I'll whip you from your foining fence;
Nay, as I am a gentleman, I will.

LEONATO
Brother,—

ANTONIO
Content yourself. God knows I loved my niece;
And she is dead, slander'd to death by villains,
That dare as well answer a man indeed
As I dare take a serpent by the tongue:
Boys, apes, braggarts, Jacks, milksops!

LEONATO
Brother, Antony,—

ANTONIO

Hold you content. What, man! I know them, yea,
And what they weigh, even to the utmost scruple,—
Scambling, out-facing, fashion-monging boys,
That lie, and cog, and flout, deprave, and slander,
Go antiquely, and show outward hideousness,
And speak off half a dozen dangerous words,
How they might hurt their enemies, if they durst;
And this is all.

LEONATO

But, brother Antony,—

ANTONIO

Come, 'tis no matter:
Do not you meddle; let me deal in this.

DON PEDRO

Gentlemen both, we will not wake your patience.
My heart is sorry for your daughter's death:
But, on my honour, she was charged with nothing
But what was true, and very full of proof.

LEONATO

My lord, my lord,—

DON PEDRO

I will not hear you.

LEONATO

No? Come, brother; away! I will be heard.

ANTONIO

And shall, or some of us will smart for it.

[Exeunt LEONATO and ANTONIO

DON PEDRO

See, see; here comes the man we went to seek.

Enter BENEDICK

CLAUDIO

Now, signior, what news?

BENEDICK

Good day, my lord.

DON PEDRO

Welcome, signior: you are almost come to part almost a fray.

CLAUDIO

We had like to have had our two noses snapped off
with two old men without teeth.

DON PEDRO

Leonato and his brother. What thinkest thou? Had
we fought, I doubt we should have been too young
for them.

BENEDICK

In a false quarrel there is no true valour. I came to
seek you both.

CLAUDIO

We have been up and down to seek thee; for we are
high-proof melancholy, and would fain have it
beaten away. Wilt thou use thy wit?

BENEDICK

It is in my scabbard: shall I draw it?

DON PEDRO

Dost thou wear thy wit by thy side?

CLAUDIO

Never any did so, though very many have been beside their wit. I will bid thee draw, as we do the
minstrels; draw, to pleasure us.

DON PEDRO

As I am an honest man, he looks pale. Art thou sick,
or angry?

CLAUDIO

What, courage, man! What though care killed a
cat, thou hast mettle enough in thee to kill care.

BENEDICK

Sir, I shall meet your wit in the career, an you
charge it against me. I pray you choose another
subject.

CLAUDIO

Nay, then, give him another staff: this last was
broke cross.

DON PEDRO

By this light, he changes more and more: I think he
be angry indeed.

CLAUDIO

If he be, he knows how to turn his girdle.

BENEDICK

Shall I speak a word in your ear?

CLAUDIO

God bless me from a challenge!

BENEDICK

[Aside to CLAUDIO] You are a villain; I jest not: I
will make it good how you dare, with what you
dare, and when you dare. Do me right, or I will
protest your cowardice. You have killed a sweet
lady, and her death shall fall heavy on you. Let me
hear from you.

CLAUDIO

Well, I will meet you, so I may have good cheer.

DON PEDRO

What, a feast, a feast?

CLAUDIO

I'faith, I thank him; he hath bid me to a calf's-head
and a capon; the which if I do not carve most curiously, say my knife's naught. Shall I not find a
woodcock too?

BENEDICK

Sir, your wit ambles well; it goes easily.

DON PEDRO

I'll tell thee how Beatrice praised thy wit the other
day. I said, thou hadst a fine wit: 'True,' said she, 'a
fine little one.' 'No,' said I, 'a great wit:' 'Right,'
says she, 'a great gross one.' 'Nay,' said I, 'a good
wit:' 'Just,' said she, 'it hurts nobody.' 'Nay,' said I,
'the gentleman is wise:' 'Certain,' said she, 'a wise
gentleman.' 'Nay,' said I, 'he hath the tongues:'
'That I believe,' said she, 'for he swore a thing to
me on Monday night, which he forswore on Tuesday morning; there's a double tongue; there's two
tongues.' Thus did she, an hour together, transshape thy particular virtues: yet at last she concluded with a sigh, thou wast the properest man in
Italy.

CLAUDIO

For the which she wept heartily, and said she cared
not.

DON PEDRO

Yea, that she did; but yet, for all that, an if she did

not hate him deadly, she would love him dearly: the old man's daughter told us all.

CLAUDIO

All, all; and, moreover, God saw him when he was hid in the garden.

DON PEDRO

But when shall we set the savage bull's horns on the sensible Benedick's head?

CLAUDIO

Yea, and text underneath, 'Here dwells Benedick the married man'?

BENEDICK

Fare you well, boy: you know my mind. I will leave you now to your gossip-like humour: you break jests as braggarts do their blades, which, God be thanked, hurt not. My lord, for your many courtesies I thank you: I must discontinue your company: your brother the bastard is fled from Messina: you have among you killed a sweet and innocent lady. For my Lord Lackbeard there, he and I shall meet: and till then peace be with him.   [Exit

DON PEDRO

He is in earnest.

CLAUDIO

In most profound earnest; and, I'll warrant you, for the love of Beatrice.

DON PEDRO

And hath challenged thee.

CLAUDIO

Most sincerely.

DON PEDRO

What a pretty thing man is when he goes in his doublet and hose, and leaves off his wit!

CLAUDIO

He is then a giant to an ape: but then is an ape a doctor to such a man.

DON PEDRO

But, soft you, let me be: pluck up, my heart, and be sad. Did he not say, my brother was fled?

Enter DOGBERRY, VERGES, and the WATCH, with CON-RADE and BORACHIO

DOGBERRY

Come, you, sir: if justice cannot tame you, she shall ne'er weigh more reasons in her balance: nay, an you be a cursing hypocrite once, you must be looked to.

DON PEDRO

How now? two of my brother's men bound! Borachio one!

CLAUDIO

Hearken after their offence, my lord.

DON PEDRO

Officers, what offence have these men done?

DOGBERRY

Marry, sir, they have committed false report; moreover, they have spoken untruths; secondarily, they are slanders; sixth and lastly, they have belied a lady; thirdly, they have verified unjust things; and, to conclude, they are lying knaves.

DON PEDRO

First, I ask thee what they have done; thirdly, I ask

thee what's their offence; sixth and lastly, why they are committed; and, to conclude, what you lay to their charge.

CLAUDIO

Rightly reasoned, and in his own division; and, by my troth, there's one meaning well suited.

DON PEDRO

Who have you offended, masters, that you are thus bound to your answer? this learned constable is too cunning to be understood: what's your offence?

BORACHIO

Sweet prince, let me go no farther to mine answer: do you hear me, and let this count kill me. I have deceived even your very eyes: what your wisdoms could not discover, these shallow fools have brought to light; who, in the night, overheard me confessing to this man, how Don John your brother incensed me to slander the Lady Hero; how you were brought into the orchard, and saw me court Margaret in Hero's garments: how you disgraced her, when you should marry her: my villany they have upon record; which I had rather seal with my death than repeat over to my shame. The lady is dead upon mine and my master's false accusation; and, briefly, I desire nothing but the reward of a villain.

DON PEDRO

Runs not this speech like iron through your blood?

CLAUDIO

I have drunk poison whiles he utter'd it.

DON PEDRO

But did my brother set thee on to this?

BORACHIO

Yea, and paid me richly for the practice of it.

DON PEDRO

He is composed and framed of treachery:
And fled he is upon this villany.

CLAUDIO

Sweet Hero! now thy image doth appear
In the rare semblance that I loved it first.

DOGBERRY

Come, bring away the plaintiffs: by this time our sexton hath reformed Signior Leonato of the matter: and, masters, do not forget to specify, when time and place shall serve, that I am an ass.

VERGES

Here, here comes master Signior Leonato, and the sexton too.

Re-enter LEONATO and ANTONIO, with the SEXTON

LEONATO

Which is the villain? let me see his eyes,
That, when I note another man like him,
I may avoid him: which of these is he?

BORACHIO

If you would know your wronger, look on me.

LEONATO

Art thou the slave that with thy breath hast kill'd
Mine innocent child?

BORACHIO

Yea, even I alone.

LEONATO

No, not so, villain; thou beliest thyself:
Here stand a pair of honourable men;
A third is fled, that had a hand in it.
I thank you, princes, for my daughter's death:
Record it with your high and worthy deeds:
'Twas bravely done, if you bethink you of it.

CLAUDIO

I know not how to pray your patience;
Yet I must speak. Choose your revenge yourself;
Impose me to what penance your invention
Can lay upon my sin: yet sinn'd I not
But in mistaking.

DON PEDRO

          By my soul, nor I:
And yet, to satisfy this good old man,
I would bend under any heavy weight
That he'll enjoin me to.

LEONATO

I cannot bid you bid my daughter live;
That were impossible: but, I pray you both,
Possess the people in Messina here
How innocent she died; and if your love
Can labour aught in sad invention,
Hang her an epitaph upon her tomb,
And sing it to her bones, sing it to-night:
To-morrow morning come you to my house;
And since you could not be my son-in-law,
Be yet my nephew: my brother hath a daughter,
Almost the copy of my child that's dead,
And she alone is heir to both of us:
Give her the right you should have given her cousin,
And so dies my revenge.

CLAUDIO

          O noble sir,
Your over-kindness doth wring tears from me!
I do embrace your offer; and dispose
For henceforth of poor Claudio.

LEONATO

To-morrow, then, I will expect your coming;
To-night I take my leave. This naughty man
Shall face to face be brought to Margaret,
Who I believe was pack'd in all this wrong,
Hired to it by your brother.

BORACHIO

          No, by my soul, she was not;
Nor knew not what she did when she spoke to me;
But always hath been just and virtuous
In any thing that I do know by her.

DOGBERRY

Moreover, sir, which indeed is not under white and
black, this plaintiff here, the offender, did call me
ass: I beseech you, let it be remembered in his punishment. And also, the watch heard them talk of one
Deformed: they say he wears a key in his ear, and a
lock hanging by it; and borrows money in God's
name, the which he hath used so long and never
paid, that now men grow hard-hearted, and will
lend nothing for God's sake: pray you, examine him
upon that point.

LEONATO

I thank thee for thy care and honest pains.

DOGBERRY

Your worship speaks like a most thankful and reverend youth; and I praise God for you.

LEONATO

There's for thy pains.

DOGBERRY

God save the foundation!

LEONATO

Go, I discharge thee of thy prisoner, and I thank
thee.

DOGBERRY

I leave an arrant knave with your worship; which
I beseech your worship to correct yourself, for the
example of others. God keep your worship! I wish
your worship well; God restore you to health! I
humbly give you leave to depart; and if a merry
meeting may be wished, God prohibit it! Come,
neighbour.   [Exeunt DOGBERRY and VERGES

LEONATO

Until to-morrow morning, lords, farewell.

ANTONIO

Farewell, my lords: we look for you to-morrow.

DON PEDRO

We will not fail.

CLAUDIO

To-night I'll mourn with Hero.

LEONATO

[To the WATCH] Bring you these fellows on. We'll
    talk with Margaret,
How her acquaintance grew with this lewd fellow.
                  [Exeunt, severally

Scene II. LEONATO's garden

Enter BENEDICK *and* MARGARET, *meeting*

BENEDICK

Pray thee, sweet Mistress Margaret, deserve well at
my hands by helping me to the speech of Beatrice.

MARGARET

Will you, then, write me a sonnet in praise of my
beauty?

BENEDICK

In so high a style Margaret, that no man living
shall come over it; for, in most comely truth, thou
deservest it.

MARGARET

To have no man come over me! why, shall I always
keep below stairs?

BENEDICK

Thy wit is as quick as the greyhound's mouth; it
catches.

MARGARET

And yours as blunt as the fencer's foils, which hit,
but hurt not.

BENEDICK

A most manly wit, Margaret; it will not hurt a
woman: and so, I pray thee, call Beatrice: I give
thee the bucklers.

MARGARET

Give us the swords; we have bucklers of our own.

BENEDICK

If you use them, Margaret, you must put in the pikes with a vice; and they are dangerous weapons for maids.

MARGARET

Well, I will call Beatrice to you, who I think hath legs.

BENEDICK

And therefore will come.　　　　[*Exit* MARGARET

[*Sings*]　　　　The god of love,
　　　　　　　That sits above,
　　　And knows me, and knows me,
　　　　How pitiful I deserve,—

I mean in singing; but in loving, Leander the good swimmer, Troilus the first employer of pandars, and a whole bookful of these quondam carpet-mongers, whose names yet run smoothly in the even road of a blank verse, why, they were never so truly turned over and over as my poor self in love. Marry, I cannot show it in rhyme; I have tried: I can find out no rhyme to 'lady' but 'baby,' an innocent rhyme; for 'scorn,' 'horn,' a hard rhyme; for 'school,' 'fool,' a babbling rhyme; very ominous endings: no, I was not born under a rhyming planet, nor I cannot woo in festival terms.

Enter BEATRICE

Sweet Beatrice, wouldst thou come when I called thee?

BEATRICE

Yea, signior, and depart when you bid me.

BENEDICK

O, stay but till then!

BEATRICE

'Then' is spoken; fare you well now: and yet, ere I go, let me go with that I came; which is, with knowing what hath passed between you and Claudio.

BENEDICK

Only foul words; and thereupon I will kiss thee.

BEATRICE

Foul words is but foul wind, and foul wind is but foul breath, and foul breath is noisome; therefore I will depart unkissed.

BENEDICK

Thou hast frighted the word out of his right sense, so forcible is thy wit. But I must tell thee plainly, Claudio undergoes my challenge; and either I must shortly hear from him, or I will subscribe him a coward. And, I pray thee now, tell me for which of my bad parts didst thou first fall in love with me?

BEATRICE

For them all together; which maintained so politic a state of evil, that they will not admit any good part to intermingle with them. But for which of my good parts did you first suffer love for me?

BENEDICK

Suffer love,—a good epithet! I do suffer love indeed, for I love thee against my will.

BEATRICE

In spite of your heart, I think; alas, poor heart! If you spite it for my sake, I will spite it for yours; for I will never love that which my friend hates.

BENEDICK

Thou and I are too wise to woo peaceably.

BEATRICE

It appears not in this confession: there's not one wise man among twenty that will praise himself.

BENEDICK

An old, an old instance, Beatrice, that lived in the time of good neighbours. If a man do not erect in this age his own tomb ere he dies, he shall live no longer in monument than the bell rings and the widow weeps.

BEATRICE

And how long is that, think you?

BENEDICK

Question: why, an hour in clamour, and a quarter in rheum: therefore is it most expedient for the wise, if Don Worm, his conscience, find no impediment to the contrary, to be the trumpet of his own virtues, as I am to myself. So much for praising myself, who, I myself will bear witness, is praiseworthy: and now tell me, how doth your cousin?

BEATRICE

Very ill.

BENEDICK

And how do you?

BEATRICE

Very ill too.

BENEDICK

Serve God, love me, and mend. There will I leave you too, for here comes one in haste.

Enter URSULA

URSULA

Madam, you must come to your uncle. Yonder's old coil at home: it is proved my Lady Hero hath been falsely accused, the prince and Claudio mightily abused; and Don John is the author of all, who is fled and gone. Will you come presently?

BEATRICE

Will you go hear this news, signior?

BENEDICK

I will live in thy heart, die in thy lap, and be buried in thy eyes; and moreover I will go with thee to thy uncle's.　　　　　　　　　　　　[*Exeunt*

SCENE III. *A church*

Enter DON PEDRO, CLAUDIO, *and three or four with tapers*

CLAUDIO

Is this the monument of Leonato?

A LORD

It is, my lord.

CLAUDIO

[*Reading out of a scroll*]

　　Done to death by slanderous tongues
　　　Was the Hero that here lies:
　　Death, in guerdon of her wrongs,
　　　Gives her fame which never dies.

So the life that died with shame
Lives in death with glorious fame.

Hang thou there upon the tomb,
Praising her when I am dumb.
Now, music, sound, and sing your solemn hymn.

SONG

Pardon, goddess of the night,
Those that slew thy virgin knight;
For the which, with songs of woe,
Round about her tomb they go.
     Midnight, assist our moan;
     Help us to sigh and groan,
          Heavily, heavily:
     Graves, yawn, and yield your dead,
     Till death be uttered,
          Heavily, heavily.

CLAUDIO

Now, unto thy bones good night!
Yearly will I do this rite.

DON PEDRO

Good morrow, masters; put your torches out:
     The wolves have prey'd; and look, the gentle day,
Before the wheels of Phœbus, round about
     Dapples the drowsy east with spots of grey.
Thanks to you all, and leave us: fare you well.

CLAUDIO

Good morrow, masters: each his several way.

DON PEDRO

Come, let us hence, and put on other weeds;
     And then to Leonato's we will go.

CLAUDIO

And Hymen now with luckier issue speed's
     Than this for whom we render'd up this woe.
                                        [Exeunt

SCENE IV. *A room in* LEONATO'S *house*

Enter LEONATO, ANTONIO, BENEDICK, BEATRICE,
MARGARET, URSULA, FRIAR FRANCIS, *and* HERO

FRIAR FRANCIS

Did I not tell you she was innocent?

LEONATO

So are the prince and Claudio, who accused her
Upon the error that you heard debated:
But Margaret was in some fault for this,
Although against her will, as it appears
In the true course of all the question.

ANTONIO

Well, I am glad that all things sort so well.

BENEDICK

And so am I, being else by faith enforced
To call young Claudio to a reckoning for it.

LEONATO

Well, daughter, and you gentlewomen all,
Withdraw into a chamber by yourselves,
And when I send for you, come hither mask'd.
                                        [Exeunt LADIES
The prince and Claudio promised by this hour
To visit me. You know your office, brother:
You must be father to your brother's daughter,
And give her to young Claudio.

ANTONIO

Which I will do with confirm'd countenance.

BENEDICK

Friar, I must entreat your pains, I think.

FRIAR FRANCIS

To do what, signior?

BENEDICK

To bind me, or undo me; one of them.
Signior Leonato, truth it is, good signior,
Your niece regards me with an eye of favour.

LEONATO

That eye my daughter lent her: 'tis most true.

BENEDICK

And I do with an eye of love requite her.

LEONATO

The sight whereof I think you had from me,
From Claudio, and the prince: but what's your will?

BENEDICK

Your answer, sir, is enigmatical:
But, for my will, my will is, your good will
May stand with ours, this day to be conjoin'd
In the state of honourable marriage:
In which, good friar, I shall desire your help.

LEONATO

My heart is with your liking

FRIAR FRANCIS

                              And my help.
Here comes the prince and Claudio.
Enter DON PEDRO *and* CLAUDIO, *and two or three others*

DON PEDRO

Good morrow to this fair assembly.

LEONATO

Good morrow, prince; good morrow, Claudio:
We here attend you. Are you yet determined
To-day to marry with my brother's daughter?

CLAUDIO

I'll hold my mind, were she an Ethiope.

LEONATO

Call her forth, brother; here's the friar ready.
                                        [Exit ANTONIO

DON PEDRO

Good morrow, Benedick. Why, what's the matter,
That you have such a February face,
So full of frost, of storm, and cloudiness?

CLAUDIO

I think he thinks upon the savage bull.
Tush, fear not, man; we'll tip thy horns with gold,
And all Europa shall rejoice at thee;
As once Europa did at lusty Jove,
When he would play the noble beast in love.

BENEDICK

Bull Jove, sir, had an amiable low;
And some such strange bull leap'd your father's
     cow,
And got a calf in that same noble feat
Much like to you, for you have just his bleat.

CLAUDIO

For this I owe you: here comes other reckonings.
     Re-enter ANTONIO, *with the* LADIES *masked*
Which is the lady I must seize upon?

ANTONIO
This same is she, and I do give you her.

CLAUDIO
Why, then she's mine. Sweet, let me see your face.

LEONATO
No, that you shall not, till you take her hand
Before this friar, and swear to marry her.

CLAUDIO
Give me your hand: before this holy friar,
I am your husband, if you like of me.

HERO
And when I lived, I was your other wife:
[Unmasking
And when you loved, you were my other husband.

CLAUDIO
Another Hero!

HERO
Nothing certainer:
One Hero died defiled; but I do live,
And surely as I live, I am a maid.

DON PEDRO
The former Hero! Hero that is dead!

LEONATO
She died, my lord, but whiles her slander lived.

FRIAR FRANCIS
All this amazement can I qualify;
When after that the holy rites are ended,
I'll tell you largely of fair Hero's death:
Meantime let wonder seem familiar,
And to the chapel let us presently.

BENEDICK
Soft and fair, friar. Which is Beatrice?

BEATRICE
[Unmasking] I answer to that name. What is your
will?

BENEDICK
Do not you love me?

BEATRICE
Why, no; no more than reason.

BENEDICK
Why, then your uncle, and the prince, and Claudio
Have been deceived; they swore you did.

BEATRICE
Do not you love me?

BENEDICK
Troth, no; no more than reason.

BEATRICE
Why, then my cousin, Margaret, and Ursula
Are much deceived; for they did swear you did.

BENEDICK
They swore that you were almost sick for me.

BEATRICE
They swore that you were well-nigh dead for me.

BENEDICK
'Tis no such matter. Then you do not love me?

BEATRICE
No, truly, but in friendly recompence.

LEONATO
Come, cousin, I am sure you love the gentleman.

CLAUDIO
And I'll be sworn upon't that he loves her;
For here's a paper, written in his hand,
A halting sonnet of his own pure brain,
Fashion'd to Beatrice.

HERO
And here's another,
Writ in my cousin's hand, stolen from her pocket,
Containing her affection unto Benedick.

BENEDICK
A miracle! here's our own hands against our hearts.
Come, I will have thee; but, by this light, I take
thee for pity.

BEATRICE
I would not deny you; but, by this good day, I yield
upon great persuasion; and partly to save your life,
for I was told you were in a consumption.

BENEDICK
Peace! I will stop your mouth.   *[Kissing her*

DON PEDRO
How dost thou, Benedick, the married man?

BENEDICK
I'll tell thee what, prince; a college of wit-crackers
cannot flout me out of my humour. Dost thou think
I care for a satire or an epigram? No: if a man will
be beaten with brains, a' shall wear nothing handsome about him. In brief, since I do purpose to
marry, I will think nothing to any purpose that the
world can say against it; and therefore never flout
at me for what I have said against it; for man is a
giddy thing, and this is my conclusion. For thy part,
Claudio, I did think to have beaten thee; but in
that thou art like to be my kinsman, live unbruised,
and love my cousin.

CLAUDIO
I had well hoped thou wouldst have denied Beatrice, that I might have cudgelled thee out of thy
single life, to make thee a double-dealer; which, out
of question, thou wilt be, if my cousin do not look
exceeding narrowly to thee.

BENEDICK
Come, come, we are friends: let's have a dance ere
we are married, that we may lighten our own hearts
and our wives' heels.

LEONATO
We'll have dancing afterward.

BENEDICK
First, of my word; therefore play, music. Prince,
thou art sad; get thee a wife, get thee a wife: there
is no staff more reverend than one tipped with horn.

Enter a MESSENGER

MESSENGER
My lord, your brother John is ta'en in flight,
And brought with armed men back to Messina.

BENEDICK
Think not on him till to-morrow: I'll devise thee
brave punishments for him. Strike up, pipers.
*[Dance
*[Exeunt

THE TRAGEDY OF JULIUS CÆSAR

SYNOPSIS

IT IS the feast of the Lupercalia, and Roman citizens are taking advantage of the holiday to celebrate Caesar's recent victories, but under the seemingly universal rejoicing hidden fires are burning. Two tribunes tear down Caesar's trophies and urge people to return to their homes. Prominent noblemen stand aside and speak of Caesar's arrogance and growing ambition. A soothsayer, gaining the dictator's attention as he passes in triumph, warns him to beware of the Ides of March. Mark Antony, Caesar's henchman, considers the occasion auspicious, however, and three times offers the crown to Caesar who each time refuses it, to the great plaudits of the multitude.

The envious Cassius, the leading intriguer against Caesar, greatly desires to win to the support of his party the high-minded Brutus, whose unassailable character will lend it prestige. He arranges for papers to be thrown within Brutus' reach, designed to show a widespread public alarm over the threat to Roman freedom of Caesar's domination. Brutus is gradually convinced, against his better nature, that Caesar's life must be sacrificed for the common good, but he refuses to consent to the assassination of Mark Antony, whose influence Cassius fears.

The fatal deed is planned for March the fifteenth, but the night before all nature is strangely disturbed and Calpurnia, Caesar's wife, had ill-omened dreams. In the morning the augurers advise and Calpurnia implores Caesar not to leave his house that day. But a tricky conspirator reinterprets the dreams to the dictator's entire satisfaction, and the others, anticipating his hesitancy, call at his house to conduct him to the Capitol. The soothsayer again warns Caesar that the Ides of March are not yet gone, and a friend puts into his hand a scroll revealing the plot which he carries unopened to his death.

In the Senate chamber, Mark Antony is enticed away, and the conspirators crowd around Caesar as though to second a petition which one of them is presenting. Upon Caesar's refusal, first Casca, then the others stab him, and he falls with twenty-three bleeding wounds.

After his own personal safety is assured, the wily Antony affects a willingness to concede the conspirators' point of view, but obtains from the unsuspecting Brutus, against Cassius' advice, permission to follow him in making an address at Caesar's funeral. The crowd, once swayed by Brutus, is now held spellbound by the eloquent Antony who craftily fans their passions to such vows of vengeance and destruction that the conspirators flee the city. Two opposing factions arise. A new triumvirate, composed of Mark Antony, Octavius and Lepidus, joins forces against Cassius and Brutus, and sets out for the conspirators' camp at Sardis.

Meanwhile Brutus and Cassius quarrel violently over mutual grievances until Brutus informs his fellow general that his wife, the noble and beloved Portia—sister to Cassius—has killed herself in her distraction over the strength of Antony and Octavius. Cassius is so overcome with grief and shock that he yields to Brutus on a vital point of strategy against his own better judgment as a soldier, and their army leaves the safety of the hills around Sardis to meet the advancing enemy on the plains of Philippi. In his tent that night the sleepless Brutus sees the ghost of Caesar who tells him they will meet at Philippi.

When the battle begins, Brutus overthrows Octavius' forces, but Antony forces back those of Cassius. Hard pressed, Cassius sends Titinius, one of his followers, to ascertain whether some far-off troops which he sees are friend or enemy, and, watching eagerly from a hill with his servant, Pindarus, catches sight of Titinius being pulled from his horse. Then they hear a shout of joy. Without waiting for the report, which would have told him of Brutus' success, Cassius orders Pindarus to kill him. When Titinius returns with some of Brutus' victorious soldiers and finds his general dead, he kills himself. The saddened and dispirited forces charge again under the leadership of Brutus, but are driven back by the enemy. His friends having refused his appeal for death, Brutus turns to his faithful servant, asks him to hold his sword and turn his face away. Brutus falls upon it and dies.

HISTORICAL DATA

The historical material for the plot of this tragedy is taken from the account of the lives of Julius Caesar, Marcus Brutus and Marcus Antonius as found in Sir Thomas North's translation of Plutarch's *Lives of the Noble Grecians and Romans*, published in 1579. Shakespeare followed North closely, a large portion of the play consisting merely of the latter's language couched in blank verse. Suggestions for the speeches of Brutus and Antony may have been derived from the English translation (1578) of Appian's *History of the Roman Wars*.

The subject of Julius Caesar was popular among the early Elizabethan dramatists. Among these plays mention is made by Machya in his *Diary* in 1562 of a play *Julyus Sesar*, and by Stephen Gossen in 1582 of a contemporary play entitled *Caesar and Pompey*. A Latin play on Caesar's death was presented at Oxford that same year.

There is no clear authority for fixing the date of the play, but since it was not included in the list in *Palladis Tamia* in 1598 and is alluded to in John Weever's *Mirror of Martyrs* in 1601, the presumption that it was composed some time between the two dates seems reasonable.

"*Farewell, good Strato—Cæsar, now be still;*"
JULIUS CÆSAR

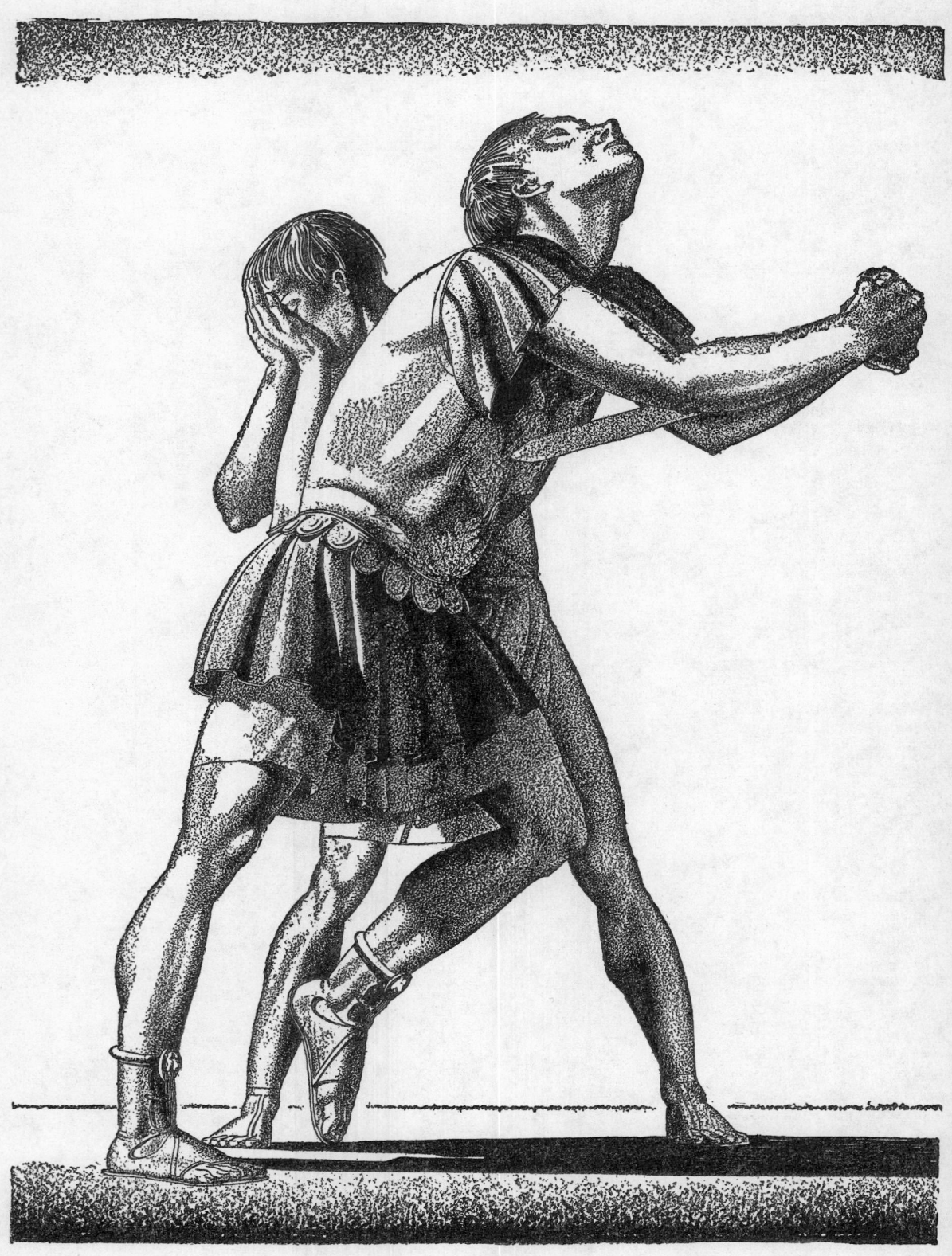

THE TRAGEDY OF JULIUS CÆSAR

DRAMATIS PERSONÆ

JULIUS CÆSAR.

OCTAVIUS CÆSAR,
MARCUS ANTONIUS,
M. ÆMIL. LEPIDUS,
} *triumvirs after the death of Julius Cæsar.*

CICERO,
PUBLIUS,
POPILIUS LENA,
} *senators.*

MARCUS BRUTUS,
CASSIUS,
CASCA,
TREBONIUS,
LIGARIUS,
DECIUS BRUTUS,
METELLUS CIMBER,
CINNA,
} *conspirators against Julius Cæsar.*

FLAVIUS *and* MARULLUS, *tribunes.*
ARTEMIDORUS *of Cnidos, a teacher of Rhetoric.*
A SOOTHSAYER.
CINNA, *a poet.*
ANOTHER POET.

LUCILIUS,
TITINIUS,
MESSALA,
YOUNG CATO,
VOLUMNIUS,
} *friends to Brutus and Cassius.*

VARRO,
CLITUS,
CLAUDIUS,
STRATO,
LUCIUS,
DARDANIUS,
} *servants to Brutus.*

PINDARUS, *servant to Cassius.*

CALPURNIA, *wife to Cæsar.*
PORTIA, *wife to Brutus.*

SENATORS, CITIZENS, GUARDS, ATTENDANTS, &c.

SCENE—*Rome; the neighbourhood of Sardis; the neighbourhood of Philippi.*

ACT I

SCENE I. *Rome. A street*

Enter FLAVIUS, MARULLUS, *and certain* COMMONERS

FLAVIUS

Hence! home, you idle creatures, get you home:
Is this a holiday? what! know you not,
Being mechanical, you ought not walk
Upon a labouring day without the sign
Of your profession? Speak, what trade art thou?

FIRST COMMONER

Why, sir, a carpenter.

MARULLUS

Where is thy leather apron and thy rule?
What dost thou with thy best apparel on?
You, sir, what trade are you?

SECOND COMMONER

Truly, sir, in respect of a fine workman, I am but,
as you would say, a cobbler.

MARULLUS

But what trade art thou? answer me directly.

SECOND COMMONER

A trade, sir, that, I hope, I may use with a safe conscience; which is indeed, sir, a mender of bad soles.

MARULLUS

What trade, thou knave? thou naughty knave, what
trade?

SECOND COMMONER

Nay, I beseech you, sir, be not out with me: yet, if
you be out, sir, I can mend you.

MARULLUS

What mean'st thou by that? mend me, thou saucy
fellow!

SECOND COMMONER

Why, sir, cobble you.

FLAVIUS

Thou art a cobbler, art thou?

SECOND COMMONER

Truly, sir, all that I live by is with the awl: I meddle
with no tradesman's matters, nor women's matters,
but with awl. I am indeed, sir, a surgeon to old
shoes; when they are in great danger, I re-cover
them. As proper men as ever trod upon neats-
leather have gone upon my handiwork.

FLAVIUS

But wherefore art not in thy shop to-day?
Why dost thou lead these men about the streets?

SECOND COMMONER

Truly, sir, to wear out their shoes, to get myself into
more work. But indeed, sir, we make holiday, to see
Cæsar and to rejoice in his triumph.

MARULLUS

Wherefore rejoice? What conquest brings he home?
What tributaries follow him to Rome,
To grace in captive bonds his chariot-wheels?
You blocks, you stones, you worse than senseless
things!
O you hard hearts, you cruel men of Rome,
Knew you not Pompey? Many a time and oft
Have you climb'd up to walls and battlements,
To towers and windows, yea, to chimney-tops,
Your infants in your arms, and there have sat

[631]

The live-long day with patient expectation
To see great Pompey pass the streets of Rome:
And when you saw his chariot but appear,
Have you not made an universal shout,
That Tiber trembled underneath her banks
To hear the replication of your sounds
Made in her concave shores?
And do you now put on your best attire?
And do you now cull out a holiday?
And do you now strew flowers in his way
That comes in triumph over Pompey's blood?
Be gone!
Run to your houses, fall upon your knees,
Pray to the gods to intermit the plague
That needs must light on this ingratitude.

FLAVIUS
Go, go, good countrymen, and, for this fault,
Assemble all the poor men of your sort;
Draw them to Tiber banks and weep your tears
Into the channel, till the lowest stream
Do kiss the most exalted shores of all.
　　　　　　　　[Exeunt all the COMMONERS
See, whether their basest metal be not moved;
They vanish tongue-tied in their guiltiness.
Go you down that way towards the Capitol;
This way will I: disrobe the images,
If you do find them deck'd with ceremonies.

MARULLUS
May we do so?
You know it is the feast of Lupercal.

FLAVIUS
It is no matter; let no images
Be hung with Cæsar's trophies. I'll about,
And drive away the vulgar from the streets:
So do you too, where you perceive them thick.
These growing feathers pluck'd from Cæsar's wing
Will make him fly an ordinary pitch,
Who else would soar above the view of men
And keep us all in servile fearfulness.　　　[Exeunt

SCENE II. *A public place*

Flourish. Enter CÆSAR; ANTONY, *for the course;* CAL-
PURNIA, PORTIA, DECIUS, CICERO, BRUTUS, CASSIUS,
and CASCA; *a great crowd following, among them a*
SOOTHSAYER

CÆSAR
Calpurnia!

CASCA
　　　Peace, ho! Cæsar speaks.　　[Music ceases

CÆSAR
　　　　　　　　　　Calpurnia!

CALPURNIA
Here, my lord.

CÆSAR
Stand you directly in Antonius' way,
When he doth run his course. Antonius!

ANTONY
Cæsar, my lord?

CÆSAR
Forget not, in your speed, Antonius,
To touch Calpurnia; for our elders say,
The barren, touched in this holy chase,
Shake off their sterile curse.

ANTONY
　　　　　　　I shall remember:
When Cæsar says 'do this,' it is perform'd.

CÆSAR
Set on, and leave no ceremony out.　　[Flourish

SOOTHSAYER
Cæsar!

CÆSAR
Ha! who calls?

CASCA
Bid every noise be still: peace yet again!

CÆSAR
Who is it in the press that calls on me?
I hear a tongue, shriller than all the music,
Cry 'Cæsar.' Speak; Cæsar is turn'd to hear.

SOOTHSAYER
Beware the ides of March.

CÆSAR
　　　　　　　What man is that?

BRUTUS
A soothsayer bids you beware the ides of March.

CÆSAR
Set him before me; let me see his face.

CASSIUS
Fellow, come from the throng; look upon Cæsar.

CÆSAR
What say'st thou to me now? speak once again.

SOOTHSAYER
Beware the ides of March.

CÆSAR
He is a dreamer; let us leave him: pass.
　　　　　　[Sennet. Exeunt all but BRUTUS and CASSIUS

CASSIUS
Will you go see the order of the course?

BRUTUS
Not I.

CASSIUS
I pray you, do.

BRUTUS
I am not gamesome: I do lack some part
Of that quick spirit that is in Antony.
Let me not hinder, Cassius, your desires;
I'll leave you.

CASSIUS
Brutus, I do observe you now of late:
I have not from your eyes that gentleness
And show of love as I was wont to have:
You bear too stubborn and too strange a hand
Over your friend that loves you.

BRUTUS
　　　　　　　　Cassius,
Be not deceived: if I have veil'd my look,
I turn the trouble of my countenance
Merely upon myself. Vexed I am
Of late with passions of some difference,

Conceptions only proper to myself,
Which give some soil perhaps to my behaviours;
But let not therefore my good friends be grieved—
Among which number, Cassius, be you one—
Nor construe any further my neglect
Than that poor Brutus with himself at war
Forgets the shows of love to other men.

CASSIUS

Then, Brutus, I have much mistook your passion;
By means whereof this breast of mine hath buried
Thoughts of great value, worthy cogitations.
Tell me, good Brutus, can you see your face?

BRUTUS

No, Cassius; for the eye sees not itself
But by reflection, by some other things.

CASSIUS

'Tis just:
And it is very much lamented, Brutus,
That you have no such mirrors as will turn
Your hidden worthiness into your eye,
That you might see your shadow. I have heard
Where many of the best respect in Rome,
Except immortal Cæsar, speaking of Brutus,
And groaning underneath this age's yoke,
Have wish'd that noble Brutus had his eyes.

BRUTUS

Into what dangers would you lead me, Cassius,
That you would have me seek into myself
For that which is not in me?

CASSIUS

Therefore, good Brutus, be prepared to hear:
And since you know you cannot see yourself
So well as by reflection, I your glass
Will modestly discover to yourself
That of yourself which you yet know not of.
And be not jealous on me, gentle Brutus:
Were I a common laughter, or did use
To stale with ordinary oaths my love
To every new protester; if you know
That I do fawn on men and hug them hard,
And after scandal them; or if you know
That I profess myself in banqueting
To all the rout, then hold me dangerous.
          [Flourish and shout

BRUTUS

What means this shouting? I do fear, the people
Choose Cæsar for their king.

CASSIUS

      Ay, do you fear it?
Then must I think you would not have it so.

BRUTUS

I would not, Cassius, yet I love him well.
But wherefore do you hold me here so long?
What is it that you would impart to me?
If it be aught toward the general good,
Set honour in one eye and death i' the other,
And I will look on both indifferently:
For let the gods so speed me as I love
The name of honour more than I fear death.

CASSIUS

I know that virtue to be in you, Brutus,
As well as I do know your outward favour.
Well, honour is the subject of my story.
I cannot tell what you and other men
Think of this life, but, for my single self,
I had as lief not be as live to be
In awe of such a thing as I myself.
I was born free as Cæsar; so were you:
We both have fed as well, and we can both
Endure the winter's cold as well as he:
For once, upon a raw and gusty day,
The troubled Tiber chafing with her shores,
Cæsar said to me 'Darest thou, Cassius, now
Leap in with me into this angry flood,
And swim to yonder point?' Upon the word,
Accoutred as I was, I plunged in
And bade him follow: so indeed he did.
The torrent roar'd, and we did buffet it
With lusty sinews, throwing it aside
And stemming it with hearts of controversy;
But ere we could arrive the point proposed,
Cæsar cried 'Help me, Cassius, or I sink!'
I, as Æneas our great ancestor
Did from the flames of Troy upon his shoulder
The old Anchises bear, so from the waves of Tiber
Did I the tired Cæsar: and this man
Is now become a god, and Cassius is
A wretched creature, and must bend his body
If Cæsar carelessly but nod on him.
He had a fever when he was in Spain,
And when the fit was on him, I did mark
How he did shake: 'tis true, this god did shake;
His coward lips did from their colour fly,
And that same eye whose bend doth awe the world
Did lose his lustre: I did hear him groan:
Ay, and that tongue of his that bade the Romans
Mark him and write his speeches in their books,
Alas, it cried, 'Give me some drink, Titinius,'
As a sick girl. Ye gods! it doth amaze me
A man of such a feeble temper should
So get the start of the majestic world
And bear the palm alone.   *[Shout. Flourish*

BRUTUS

Another general shout!
I do believe that these applauses are
For some new honours that are heap'd on Cæsar.

CASSIUS

Why, man, he doth bestride the narrow world
Like a Colossus, and we petty men
Walk under his huge legs and peep about
To find ourselves dishonourable graves.
Men at some time are masters of their fates:
The fault, dear Brutus, is not in our stars,
But in ourselves, that we are underlings.
Brutus, and Cæsar: what should be in that Cæsar?
Why should that name be sounded more than yours?
Write them together, yours is as fair a name;
Sound them, it doth become the mouth as well;
Weigh them, it is as heavy; conjure with 'em.

Brutus will start a spirit as soon as Cæsar.
Now, in the names of all the gods at once,
Upon what meat doth this our Cæsar feed,
That he is grown so great? Age, thou art shamed!
Rome, thou hast lost the breed of noble bloods!
When went there by an age, since the great flood,
But it was famed with more than with one man?
When could they say till now that talk'd of Rome
That her wide walls encompass'd but one man?
Now is it Rome indeed, and room enough,
When there is in it but one only man.
O, you and I have heard our fathers say
There was a Brutus once that would have brook'd
The eternal devil to keep his state in Rome
As easily as a king.

BRUTUS

That you do love me, I am nothing jealous;
What you would work me to, I have some aim:
How I have thought of this and of these times,
I shall recount hereafter; for this present,
I would not, so with love I might entreat you,
Be any further moved. What you have said
I will consider; what you have to say
I will with patience hear, and find a time
Both meet to hear and answer such high things.
Till then, my noble friend, chew upon this:
Brutus had rather be a villager
Than to repute himself a son of Rome
Under these hard conditions as this time
Is like to lay upon us.

CASSIUS

I am glad that my weak words
Have struck but thus much show of fire from Brutus.

BRUTUS

The games are done, and Cæsar is returning.

CASSIUS

As they pass by, pluck Casca by the sleeve;
And he will, after his sour fashion, tell you
What hath proceeded worthy note to-day.
Re-enter CÆSAR *and his train*

BRUTUS

I will do so: but, look you, Cassius,
The angry spot doth glow on Cæsar's brow,
And all the rest look like a chidden train:
Calpurnia's cheek is pale, and Cicero
Looks with such ferret and such fiery eyes
As we have seen him in the Capitol,
Being cross'd in conference by some senators.

CASSIUS

Casca will tell us what the matter is.

CÆSAR

Antonius!

ANTONY

Cæsar?

CÆSAR

Let me have men about me that are fat,
Sleek-headed men, and such as sleep o' nights:
Yond Cassius has a lean and hungry look;
He thinks too much: such men are dangerous.

ANTONY

Fear him not, Cæsar; he's not dangerous;
He is a noble Roman, and well given.

CÆSAR

Would he were fatter! but I fear him not:
Yet if my name were liable to fear,
I do not know the man I should avoid
So soon as that spare Cassius. He reads much;
He is a great observer, and he looks
Quite through the deeds of men: he loves no plays,
As thou dost, Antony; he hears no music:
Seldom he smiles, and smiles in such a sort
As if he mock'd himself, and scorn'd his spirit
That could be moved to smile at any thing.
Such men as he be never at heart's ease
Whiles they behold a greater than themselves,
And therefore are they very dangerous.
I rather tell thee what is to be fear'd
Than what I fear; for always I am Cæsar.
Come on my right hand, for this ear is deaf,
And tell me truly what thou think'st of him.
　　　　[*Sennet. Exeunt* CÆSAR *and all his train but* CASCA

CASCA

You pull'd me by the cloak; would you speak with
　me?

BRUTUS

Ay, Casca; tell us what hath chanced to-day,
That Cæsar looks so sad.

CASCA

Why, you were with him, were you not?

BRUTUS

I should not then ask Casca what had chanced.

CASCA

Why, there was a crown offered him: and being
offered him, he put it by with the back of his hand,
thus: and then the people fell a-shouting.

BRUTUS

What was the second noise for?

CASCA

Why, for that too.

CASSIUS

They shouted thrice: what was the last cry for?

CASCA

Why, for that too.

BRUTUS

Was the crown offered him thrice?

CASCA

Ay, marry, was 't, and he put it by thrice, every time
gentler than other; and at every putting by mine
honest neighbours shouted.

CASSIUS

Who offered him the crown?

CASCA

Why, Antony.

BRUTUS

Tell us the manner of it, gentle Casca.

CASCA

I can as well be hang'd as tell the manner of it: it
was mere foolery; I did not mark it. I saw Mark
Antony offer him a crown: yet 'twas not a crown

neither, 'twas one of these coronets: and, as I told you, he put it by once: but for all that, to my thinking, he would fain have had it. Then he offered it to him again; then he put it by again: but, to my thinking, he was very loath to lay his fingers off it. And then he offered it the third time; he put it the third time by: and still as he refused it, the rabblement hooted and clapped their chopped hands and threw up their sweaty night-caps and uttered such a deal of stinking breath because Cæsar refused the crown, that it had almost choked Cæsar; for he swounded and fell down at it: and for mine own part, I durst not laugh, for fear of opening my lips and receiving the bad air.

CASSIUS
But, soft, I pray you: what, did Cæsar swound?

CASCA
He fell down in the market-place and foamed at mouth and was speechless.

BRUTUS
'Tis very like: he hath the falling-sickness.

CASSIUS
No, Cæsar hath it not: but you, and I,
And honest Casca, we have the falling-sickness.

CASCA
I know not what you mean by that, but I am sure Cæsar fell down. If the tag-rag people did not clap him and hiss him according as he pleased and displeased them, as they use to do the players in the theatre, I am no true man.

BRUTUS
What said he when he came unto himself?

CASCA
Marry, before he fell down, when he perceived the common herd was glad he refused the crown, he plucked me ope his doublet and offered them his throat to cut. An I had been a man of any occupation, if I would not have taken him at a word, I would I might go to hell among the rogues. And so he fell. When he came to himself again, he said, if he had done or said any thing amiss, he desired their worships to think it was his infirmity. Three or four wenches, where I stood, cried 'Alas, good soul!' and forgave him with all their hearts: but there's no heed to be taken of them; if Cæsar had stabbed their mothers, they would have done no less.

BRUTUS
And after that, he came, thus sad, away?

CASCA
Ay.

CASSIUS
Did Cicero say any thing?

CASCA
Ay, he spoke Greek.

CASSIUS
To what effect?

CASCA
Nay, an I tell you that, I'll ne'er look you i' the face again: but those that understood him smiled at one another and shook their heads; but for mine own

part, it was Greek to me. I could tell you more news too: Marullus and Flavius, for pulling scarfs off Cæsar's images, are put to silence. Fare you well. There was more foolery yet, if I could remember it.

CASSIUS
Will you sup with me to-night, Casca?

CASCA
No, I am promised forth.

CASSIUS
Will you dine with me to-morrow?

CASCA
Ay, if I be alive, and your mind hold, and your dinner worth the eating.

CASSIUS
Good; I will expect you.

CASCA
Do so: farewell, both. [Exit

BRUTUS
What a blunt fellow is this grown to be!
He was quick mettle when he went to school.

CASSIUS
So is he now in execution
Of any bold or noble enterprise,
However he puts on this tardy form.
This rudeness is a sauce to his good wit,
Which gives men stomach to digest his words
With better appetite.

BRUTUS
And so it is. For this time I will leave you:
To-morrow, if you please to speak with me,
I will come home to you, or, if you will,
Come home to me and I will wait for you.

CASSIUS
I will do so: till then, think of the world.

[Exit BRUTUS

Well, Brutus, thou art noble; yet, I see,
Thy honourable metal may be wrought
From that it is disposed: therefore it is meet
That noble minds keep ever with their likes;
For who so firm that cannot be seduced?
Cæsar doth bear me hard; but he loves Brutus:
If I were Brutus now and he were Cassius,
He should not humour me. I will this night,
In several hands, in at his windows throw,
As if they came from several citizens,
Writings, all tending to the great opinion
That Rome holds of his name, wherein obscurely
Cæsar's ambition shall be glanced at:
And after this let Cæsar seat him sure;
For we will shake him, or worse days endure. [Exit

SCENE III. A street

Thunder and lightning. Enter, from opposite sides, CASCA, with his sword drawn, and CICERO

CICERO
Good even, Casca: brought you Cæsar home?
Why are you breathless? and why stare you so?

CASCA

Are not you moved, when all the sway of earth
Shakes like a thing unfirm? O Cicero,
I have seen tempests, when the scolding winds
Have rived the knotty oaks, and I have seen
The ambitious ocean swell and rage and foam,
To be exalted with the threatening clouds;
But never till to-night, never till now,
Did I go through a tempest dropping fire.
Either there is a civil strife in heaven,
Or else the world too saucy with the gods
Incenses them to send destruction.

CICERO

Why, saw you any thing more wonderful?

CASCA

A common slave—you know him well by sight—
Held up his left hand, which did flame and burn
Like twenty torches join'd, and yet his hand
Not sensible of fire remain'd unscorch'd.
Besides—I ha' not since put up my sword—
Against the Capitol I met a lion,
Who glazed upon me and went surly by
Without annoying me: and there were drawn
Upon a heap a hundred ghastly women
Transformed with their fear, who swore they saw
Men all in fire walk up and down the streets.
And yesterday the bird of night did sit
Even at noon-day upon the market-place,
Hooting and shrieking. When these prodigies
Do so conjointly meet, let not men say
'These are their reasons: they are natural:'
For, I believe, they are portentous things
Unto the climate that they point upon.

CICERO

Indeed, it is a strange-disposed time:
But men may construe things after their fashion,
Clean from the purpose of the things themselves.
Comes Cæsar to the Capitol to-morrow?

CASCA

He doth; for he did bid Antonius
Send word to you he would be there to-morrow.

CICERO

Good night then, Casca: this disturbed sky
Is not to walk in.

CASCA

         Farewell, Cicero.   [*Exit* CICERO
        Enter CASSIUS

CASSIUS

Who's there?

CASCA

     A Roman.

CASSIUS

         Casca, by your voice.

CASCA

Your ear is good. Cassius, what night is this!

CASSIUS

A very pleasing night to honest men.

CASCA

Who ever knew the heavens menace so?

CASSIUS

Those that have known the earth so full of faults.
For my part, I have walk'd about the streets,
Submitting me unto the perilous night,
And thus unbraced, Casca, as you see,
Have bared my bosom to the thunder-stone;
And when the cross blue lightning seem'd to open
The breast of heaven, I did present myself
Even in the aim and very flash of it.

CASCA

But wherefore did you so much tempt the heavens?
It is the part of men to fear and tremble
When the most mighty gods by tokens send
Such dreadful heralds to astonish us.

CASSIUS

You are dull, Casca, and those sparks of life
That should be in a Roman you do want,
Or else you use not. You look pale and gaze
And put on fear and cast yourself in wonder,
To see the strange impatience of the heavens:
But if you would consider the true cause
Why all these fires, why all these gliding ghosts,
Why birds and beasts from quality and kind,
Why old men fool and children calculate,
Why all these things change from their ordinance,
Their natures and preformed faculties,
To monstrous quality, why, you shall find
That heaven hath infused them with these spirits
To make them instruments of fear and warning
Unto some monstrous state.
Now could I, Casca, name to thee a man
Most like this dreadful night,
That thunders, lightens, opens graves, and roars
As doth the lion in the Capitol,
A man no mightier than thyself or me
In personal action, yet prodigious grown
And fearful, as these strange eruptions are.

CASCA

'Tis Cæsar that you mean; is it not, Cassius?

CASSIUS

Let it be who it is: for Romans now
Have thews and limbs like to their ancestors;
But, woe the while! our fathers' minds are dead,
And we are govern'd with our mothers' spirits;
Our yoke and sufferance show us womanish.

CASCA

Indeed they say the senators to-morrow
Mean to establish Cæsar as a king;
And he shall wear his crown by sea and land,
In every place save here in Italy.

CASSIUS

I know where I will wear this dagger then:
Cassius from bondage will deliver Cassius.
Therein, ye gods, you make the weak most strong;
Therein, ye gods, you tyrants do defeat:
Nor stony tower, nor walls of beaten brass,
Nor airless dungeon, nor strong links of iron,
Can be retentive to the strength of spirit;
But life, being weary of these worldly bars,
Never lacks power to dismiss itself.

If I know this, know all the world besides,
That part of tyranny that I do bear
I can shake off at pleasure.   [*Thunder still*

CASCA

           So can I:
So every bondman in his own hand bears
The power to cancel his captivity.

CASSIUS

And why should Cæsar be a tyrant then?
Poor man! I know he would not be a wolf
But that he sees the Romans are but sheep:
He were no lion, were not Romans hinds.
Those that with haste will make a mighty fire
Begin it with weak straws: what trash is Rome,
What rubbish and what offal, when it serves
For the base matter to illuminate
So vile a thing as Cæsar! But, O grief,
Where hast thou led me? I perhaps speak this
Before a willing bondman; then I know
My answer must be made. But I am arm'd,
And dangers are to me indifferent.

CASCA

You speak to Casca, and to such a man
That is no fleering tell-tale. Hold, my hand:
Be factious for redress of all these griefs,
And I will set this foot of mine as far
As who goes farthest.

CASSIUS

           There's a bargain made.
Now know you, Casca, I have moved already
Some certain of the noblest-minded Romans
To undergo with me an enterprise
Of honourable-dangerous consequence;
And I do know, by this they stay for me
In Pompey's porch: for now, this fearful night,
There is no stir or walking in the streets,
And the complexion of the element
In favour's like the work we have in hand,
Most bloody, fiery, and most terrible.

Enter CINNA

CASCA

Stand close awhile, for here comes one in haste.

CASSIUS

'Tis Cinna; I do know him by his gait;
He is a friend. Cinna, where haste you so?

CINNA

To find out you. Who's that? Metellus Cimber?

CASSIUS

No, it is Casca; one incorporate
To our attempts. Am I not stay'd for, Cinna?

CINNA

I am glad on 't. What a fearful night is this!
There's two or three of us have seen strange sights.

CASSIUS

Am I not stay'd for? tell me.

CINNA

           Yes, you are.
O Cassius, if you could
But win the noble Brutus to our party—

CASSIUS

Be you content: good Cinna, take this paper,
And look you lay it in the prætor's chair,
Where Brutus may but find it, and throw this
In at his window; set this up with wax
Upon old Brutus' statue: all this done,
Repair to Pompey's porch, where you shall find us.
Is Decius Brutus and Trebonius there?

CINNA

All but Metellus Cimber; and he's gone
To seek you at your house. Well, I will hie,
And so bestow these papers as you bade me.

CASSIUS

That done, repair to Pompey's theatre. [*Exit* CINNA
Come, Casca, you and I will yet ere day
See Brutus at his house: three parts of him
Is ours already, and the man entire
Upon the next encounter yields him ours.

CASCA

O, he sits high in all the people's hearts;
And that which would appear offence in us
His countenance, like richest alchemy,
Will change to virtue and to worthiness.

CASSIUS

Him and his worth and our great need of him
You have right well conceited. Let us go,
For it is after midnight, and ere day
We will awake him and be sure of him.   [*Exeunt*

ACT II

SCENE I. *Rome.* BRUTUS'S *orchard*

Enter BRUTUS

BRUTUS

What, Lucius, ho!
I cannot, by the progress of the stars,
Give guess how near to day. Lucius, I say!
I would it were my fault to sleep so soundly.
When, Lucius, when? awake, I say! what, Lucius!

Enter LUCIUS

LUCIUS

Call'd you, my lord?

BRUTUS

Get me a taper in my study, Lucius:
When it is lighted, come and call me here.

LUCIUS

I will, my lord.   [*Exit*

BRUTUS

It must be by his death: and, for my part,
I know no personal cause to spurn at him,
But for the general. He would be crown'd:
How that might change his nature, there's the question:
It is the bright day that brings forth the adder;
And that craves wary walking. Crown him?—
that;—
And then, I grant, we put a sting in him,

That at his will he may do danger with.
The abuse of greatness is when it disjoins
Remorse from power: and, to speak truth of Cæsar,
I have not known when his affections sway'd
More than his reason. But 'tis a common proof,
That lowliness is young ambition's ladder,
Whereto the climber-upward turns his face;
But when he once attains the upmost round,
He then unto the ladder turns his back,
Looks in the clouds, scorning the base degrees
By which he did ascend: so Cæsar may;
Then, lest he may, prevent. And, since the quarrel
Will bear no colour for the thing he is,
Fashion it thus; that what he is, augmented,
Would run to these and these extremities:
And therefore think him as a serpent's egg
Which hatch'd would as his kind grow mischievous,
And kill him in the shell.

Re-enter LUCIUS

LUCIUS
The taper burneth in your closet, sir.
Searching the window for a flint I found
This paper thus seal'd up, and I am sure
It did not lie there when I went to bed.
              [*Gives him the letter*

BRUTUS
Get you to bed again; it is not day.
Is not to-morrow, boy, the ides of March?

LUCIUS
I know not, sir.

BRUTUS
Look in the calendar and bring me word.

LUCIUS
I will, sir.   [*Exit*

BRUTUS
The exhalations whizzing in the air
Give so much light that I may read by them.
              [*Opens the letter and reads*

    'Brutus, thou sleep'st: awake and see thyself.
    Shall Rome, &c. Speak, strike, redress.
    Brutus, thou sleep'st: awake.'

Such instigations have been often dropp'd
Where I have took them up.
'Shall Rome, &c.' Thus must I piece it out:
Shall Rome stand under one man's awe? What,
    Rome?
My ancestors did from the streets of Rome
The Tarquin drive, when he was call'd a king.
'Speak, strike, redress.' Am I entreated
To speak and strike? O Rome, I make thee promise,
If the redress will follow, thou receivest
Thy full petition at the hand of Brutus!

Re-enter LUCIUS

LUCIUS
Sir, March is wasted fifteen days.   [*Knocking within*

BRUTUS
'Tis good. Go to the gate; somebody knocks.
                    [*Exit* LUCIUS
Since Cassius first did whet me against Cæsar
I have not slept.

Between the acting of a dreadful thing
And the first motion, all the interim is
Like a phantasma or a hideous dream:
The Genius and the mortal instruments
Are then in council, and the state of man,
Like to a little kingdom, suffers then
The nature of an insurrection.

Re-enter LUCIUS

LUCIUS
Sir, 'tis your brother Cassius at the door,
Who doth desire to see you.

BRUTUS
             Is he alone?

LUCIUS
No, sir, there are moe with him.

BRUTUS
               Do you know them?

LUCIUS
No, sir; their hats are pluck'd about their ears,
And half their faces buried in their cloaks,
That by no means I may discover them
By any mark of favour.

BRUTUS
             Let 'em enter.   [*Exit* LUCIUS
They are the faction. O conspiracy,
Shamest thou to show thy dangerous brow by night,
When evils are most free? O, then, by day
Where wilt thou find a cavern dark enough
To mask thy monstrous visage? Seek none, con-
    spiracy;
Hide it in smiles and affability:
For if thou path, thy native semblance on,
Not Erebus itself were dim enough
To hide thee from prevention.

Enter the conspirators, CASSIUS, CASCA, DECIUS, CINNA,
       METELLUS CIMBER, *and* TREBONIUS

CASSIUS
I think we are too bold upon your rest:
Good morrow, Brutus; do we trouble you?

BRUTUS
I have been up this hour, awake all night.
Know I these men that come along with you?

CASSIUS
Yes, every man of them; and no man here
But honours you; and every one doth wish
You had but that opinion of yourself
Which every noble Roman bears of you.
This is Trebonius.

BRUTUS
       He is welcome hither.

CASSIUS
This, Decius Brutus.

BRUTUS
       He is welcome too.

CASSIUS
This, Casca; this, Cinna; and this, Metellus Cimber.

BRUTUS
They are all welcome.
What watchful cares do interpose themselves
Betwixt your eyes and night?

CASSIUS

Shall I entreat a word?   [*They whisper*

DECIUS

Here lies the east: doth not the day break here?

CASCA

No.

CINNA

O, pardon, sir, it doth, and yon grey lines
That fret the clouds are messengers of day.

CASCA

You shall confess that you are both deceived.
Here, as I point my sword, the sun arises;
Which is a great way growing on the south,
Weighing the youthful season of the year.
Some two months hence up higher toward the north
He first presents his fire, and the high east
Stands as the Capitol, directly here.

BRUTUS

Give me your hands all over, one by one.

CASSIUS

And let us swear our resolution.

BRUTUS

No, not an oath: if not the face of men,
The sufferance of our souls, the time's abuse,—
If these be motives weak, break off betimes,
And every man hence to his idle bed;
So let high-sighted tyranny range on
Till each man drop by lottery. But if these,
As I am sure they do, bear fire enough
To kindle cowards and to steel with valour
The melting spirits of women, then, countrymen,
What need we any spur but our own cause
To prick us to redress? what other bond
Than secret Romans that have spoke the word,
And will not palter? and what other oath
Than honesty to honesty engaged
That this shall be or we will fall for it?
Swear priests and cowards and men cautelous,
Old feeble carrions and such suffering souls
That welcome wrongs; unto bad causes swear
Such creatures as men doubt: but do not stain
The even virtue of our enterprise,
Nor the insuppressive mettle of our spirits,
To think that or our cause or our performance
Did need an oath; when every drop of blood
That every Roman bears, and nobly bears,
Is guilty of a several bastardy
If he do break the smallest particle
Of any promise that hath pass'd from him.

CASSIUS

But what of Cicero? shall we sound him?
I think he will stand very strong with us.

CASCA

Let us not leave him out.

CINNA

       No, by no means.

METELLUS

O, let us have him, for his silver hairs
Will purchase us a good opinion,
And buy men's voices to commend our deeds:

It shall be said his judgement ruled our hands;
Our youths and wildness shall no whit appear,
But all be buried in his gravity.

BRUTUS

O, name him not: let us not break with him,
For he will never follow any thing
That other men begin.

CASSIUS

       Then leave him out.

CASCA

Indeed he is not fit.

DECIUS

Shall no man else be touch'd but only Cæsar?

CASSIUS

Decius, well urged: I think it is not meet
Mark Antony, so well beloved of Cæsar,
Should outlive Cæsar: we shall find of him
A shrewd contriver; and you know his means,
If he improve them, may well stretch so far
As to annoy us all: which to prevent,
Let Antony and Cæsar fall together.

BRUTUS

Our course will seem too bloody, Caius Cassius,
To cut the head off and then hack the limbs,
Like wrath in death and envy afterwards;
For Antony is but a limb of Cæsar:
Let us be sacrificers, but not butchers, Caius.
We all stand up against the spirit of Cæsar,
And in the spirit of men there is no blood:
O, that we then could come by Cæsar's spirit,
And not dismember Cæsar! But, alas,
Cæsar must bleed for it! And, gentle friends,
Let's kill him boldly, but not wrathfully;
Let's carve him as a dish fit for the gods,
Not hew him as a carcass fit for hounds:
And let our hearts, as subtle masters do,
Stir up their servants to an act of rage
And after seem to chide 'em. This shall make
Our purpose necessary and not envious:
Which so appearing to the common eyes,
We shall be call'd purgers, not murderers.
And for Mark Antony, think not of him;
For he can do no more than Cæsar's arm
When Cæsar's head is off.

CASSIUS

       Yet I fear him,
For in the ingrafted love he bears to Cæsar—

BRUTUS

Alas, good Cassius, do not think of him:
If he love Cæsar, all that he can do
Is to himself, take thought and die for Cæsar:
And that were much he should, for he is given
To sports, to wildness and much company.

TREBONIUS

There is no fear in him; let him not die;
For he will live and laugh at this hereafter.

       [*Clock strikes*

BRUTUS

Peace! count the clock.

CASSIUS
The clock hath stricken three.

TREBONIUS
'Tis time to part.

CASSIUS
But it is doubtful yet
Whether Cæsar will come forth to-day or no;
For he is superstitious grown of late,
Quite from the main opinion he held once
Of fantasy, of dreams and ceremonies:
It may be these apparent prodigies,
The unaccustom'd terror of this night
And the persuasion of his augurers,
May hold him from the Capitol to-day.

DECIUS
Never fear that: if he be so resolved,
I can o'ersway him; for he loves to hear
That unicorns may be betray'd with trees
And bears with glasses, elephants with holes,
Lions with toils and men with flatterers:
But when I tell him he hates flatterers,
He says he does, being then most flattered.
Let me work;
For I can give his humour the true bent,
And I will bring him to the Capitol.

CASSIUS
Nay, we will all of us be there to fetch him.

BRUTUS
By the eighth hour: is that the uttermost?

CINNA
Be that the uttermost, and fail not then.

METELLUS
Caius Ligarius doth bear Cæsar hard,
Who rated him for speaking well of Pompey:
I wonder none of you have thought of him.

BRUTUS
Now, good Metellus, go along by him:
He loves me well, and I have given him reasons;
Send him but hither, and I'll fashion him.

CASSIUS
The morning comes upon 's: we'll leave you, Brutus:
And, friends, disperse yourselves: but all remember
What you have said and show yourselves true
    Romans.

BRUTUS
Good gentlemen, look fresh and merrily;
Let not our looks put on our purposes;
But bear it as our Roman actors do,
With untired spirits and formal constancy:
And so, good morrow to you every one.
            [*Exeunt all but* BRUTUS
Boy! Lucius! Fast asleep! It is no matter;
Enjoy the honey-heavy dew of slumber:
Thou hast no figures nor no fantasies,
Which busy care draws in the brains of men;
Therefore thou sleep'st so sound.
        Enter PORTIA

PORTIA
Brutus, my lord!

BRUTUS
Portia, what mean you? wherefore rise you now?
It is not for your health thus to commit
Your weak condition to the raw cold morning.

PORTIA
Nor for yours neither. You've ungently, Brutus,
Stole from my bed: and yesternight at supper
You suddenly arose and walk'd about,
Musing and sighing, with your arms across;
And when I ask'd you what the matter was,
You stared upon me with ungentle looks:
I urged you further; then you scratch'd your head,
And too impatiently stamp'd with your foot:
Yet I insisted, yet you answer'd not,
But with an angry wafture of your hand
Gave sign for me to leave you: so I did,
Fearing to strengthen that impatience
Which seem'd too much enkindled, and withal
Hoping it was but an effect of humour,
Which sometime hath his hour with every man.
It will not let you eat, nor talk, nor sleep,
And, could it work so much upon your shape
As it hath much prevail'd on your condition,
I should not know you, Brutus. Dear my lord,
Make me acquainted with your cause of grief.

BRUTUS
I am not well in health, and that is all.

PORTIA
Brutus is wise, and, were he not in health,
He would embrace the means to come by it.

BRUTUS
Why, so I do: good Portia, go to bed.

PORTIA
Is Brutus sick, and is it physical
To walk unbraced and suck up the humours
Of the dank morning? What, is Brutus sick,
And will he steal out of his wholesome bed,
To dare the vile contagion of the night,
And tempt the rheumy and unpurged air
To add unto his sickness? No, my Brutus;
You have some sick offence within your mind,
Which by the right and virtue of my place
I ought to know of: and, upon my knees,
I charm you, by my once commended beauty,
By all your vows of love and that great vow
Which did incorporate and make us one,
That you unfold to me, yourself, your half,
Why you are heavy, and what men to-night
Have had resort to you; for here have been
Some six or seven, who did hide their faces
Even from darkness.

BRUTUS
Kneel not, gentle Portia.

PORTIA
I should not need, if you were gentle Brutus.
Within the bond of marriage, tell me, Brutus,
Is it excepted I should know no secrets
That appertain to you? Am I yourself
But, as it were, in sort or limitation,
To keep with you at meals, comfort your bed,

And talk to you sometimes? Dwell I but in the sub-
　　urbs
Of your good pleasure? If it be no more,
Portia is Brutus' harlot, not his wife.

BRUTUS

You are my true and honourable wife,
As dear to me as are the ruddy drops
That visit my sad heart.

PORTIA

If this were true, then should I know this secret.
I grant I am a woman, but withal
A woman that Lord Brutus took to wife:
I grant I am a woman, but withal
A woman well reputed, Cato's daughter.
Think you I am no stronger than my sex,
Being so father'd and so husbanded?
Tell me your counsels, I will not disclose 'em:
I have made strong proof of my constancy,
Giving myself a voluntary wound
Here in the thigh: can I bear that with patience
And not my husband's secrets?

BRUTUS

　　　　　　　O ye gods,
Render me worthy of this noble wife!
　　　　　　　　　　[Knocking within
Hark, hark! one knocks: Portia, go in a while;
And by and by thy bosom shall partake
The secrets of my heart:
All my engagements I will construe to thee,
All the charactery of my sad brows.
Leave me with haste. [Exit PORTIA] Lucius, who's
　　that knocks?

Re-enter LUCIUS with LIGARIUS

LUCIUS

Here is a sick man that would speak with you.

BRUTUS

Caius Ligarius, that Metellus spake of.
Boy, stand aside. Caius Ligarius! how?

LIGARIUS

Vouchsafe good morrow from a feeble tongue.

BRUTUS

O, what a time have you chose out, brave Caius,
To wear a kerchief! Would you were not sick!

LIGARIUS

I am not sick, if Brutus have in hand
Any exploit worthy the name of honour.

BRUTUS

Such an exploit have I in hand, Ligarius,
Had you a healthful ear to hear of it.

LIGARIUS

By all the gods that Romans bow before,
I here discard my sickness! Soul of Rome!
Brave son, derived from honourable loins!
Thou, like an exorcist, hast conjured up
My mortified spirit. Now bid me run,
And I will strive with things impossible,
Yea, get the better of them. What's to do?

BRUTUS

A piece of work that will make sick men whole.

LIGARIUS

But are not some whole that we must make sick?

BRUTUS

That must we also. What it is, my Caius,
I shall unfold to thee, as we are going
To whom it must be done.

LIGARIUS

　　　　　　　Set on your foot,
And with a heart new-fired I follow you,
To do I know not what: but it sufficeth
That Brutus leads me on.

BRUTUS

　　　　　　　Follow me then.　　[Exeunt

SCENE II. CÆSAR'S house

Thunder and lightning. Enter CÆSAR, in his night-gown

CÆSAR

Nor heaven nor earth have been at peace to-night:
Thrice hath Calpurnia in her sleep cried out,
'Help, ho! they murder Cæsar!' Who's within?

Enter a SERVANT

SERVANT

My lord?

CÆSAR

Go bid the priests do present sacrifice,
And bring me their opinions of success.

SERVANT

I will, my lord.　　　　　　　　　　[Exit

Enter CALPURNIA

CALPURNIA

What mean you, Cæsar? think you to walk forth?
You shall not stir out of your house to-day.

CÆSAR

Cæsar shall forth: the things that threaten'd me
Ne'er look'd but on my back; when they shall see
The face of Cæsar, they are vanished.

CALPURNIA

Cæsar, I never stood on ceremonies,
Yet now they fright me. There is one within,
Besides the things that we have heard and seen,
Recounts most horrid sights seen by the watch.
A lioness hath whelped in the streets;
And graves have yawn'd, and yielded up their dead;
Fierce fiery warriors fight upon the clouds,
In ranks and squadrons and right form of war,
Which drizzled blood upon the Capitol;
The noise of battle hurtled in the air,
Horses did neigh and dying men did groan,
And ghosts did shriek and squeal about the streets
O Cæsar! these things are beyond all use,
And I do fear them.

CÆSAR

　　　　　　　What can be avoided
Whose end is purposed by the mighty gods?
Yet Cæsar shall go forth; for these predictions
Are to the world in general as to Cæsar.

CALPURNIA

When beggars die, there are no comets seen;

[641]

The heavens themselves blaze forth the death of
　　princes.

CÆSAR

Cowards die many times before their deaths;
The valiant never taste of death but once.
Of all the wonders that I yet have heard,
It seems to me most strange that men should fear;
Seeing that death, a necessary end,
Will come when it will come.

Re-enter SERVANT

　　　　　　　　What say the augurers?

SERVANT

They would not have you to stir forth to-day.
Plucking the entrails of an offering forth,
They could not find a heart within the beast.

CÆSAR

The gods do this in shame of cowardice:
Cæsar should be a beast without a heart
If he should stay at home to-day for fear.
No, Cæsar shall not: danger knows full well
That Cæsar is more dangerous than he:
We are two lions litter'd in one day,
And I the elder and more terrible:
And Cæsar shall go forth.

CALPURNIA

　　　　　　　　Alas, my lord,
Your wisdom is consumed in confidence.
Do not go forth to-day: call it my fear
That keeps you in the house and not your own.
We'll send Mark Antony to the senate-house,
And he shall say you are not well to-day:
Let me, upon my knee, prevail in this.

CÆSAR

Mark Antony shall say I am not well,
And, for thy humour, I will stay at home.

Enter DECIUS

Here's Decius Brutus, he shall tell them so.

DECIUS

Cæsar, all hail! good morrow, worthy Cæsar:
I come to fetch you to the senate-house.

CÆSAR

And you are come in very happy time,
To bear my greeting to the senators
And tell them that I will not come to-day:
Cannot, is false, and that I dare not, falser:
I will not come to-day: tell them so, Decius.

CALPURNIA

Say he is sick.

CÆSAR

　　　　　Shall Cæsar send a lie?
Have I in conquest stretch'd mine arm so far,
To be afeard to tell graybeards the truth?
Decius, go tell them Cæsar will not come.

DECIUS

Most mighty Cæsar, let me know some cause,
Lest I be laugh'd at when I tell them so.

CÆSAR

The cause is in my will: I will not come;
That is enough to satisfy the senate.
But, for your private satisfaction,

Because I love you, I will let you know.
Calpurnia here, my wife, stays me at home:
She dreamt to-night she saw my statuë,
Which like a fountain with an hundred spouts
Did run pure blood, and many lusty Romans
Came smiling and did bathe their hands in it:
And these does she apply for warnings and portents
And evils imminent, and on her knee
Hath begg'd that I will stay at home to-day.

DECIUS

This dream is all amiss interpreted;
It was a vision fair and fortunate:
Your statue spouting blood in many pipes,
In which so many smiling Romans bathed,
Signifies that from you great Rome shall suck
Reviving blood, and that great men shall press
For tinctures, stains, relics and cognizance.
This by Calpurnia's dream is signified.

CÆSAR

And this way have you well expounded it.

DECIUS

I have, when you have heard what I can say:
And know it now: the senate have concluded
To give this day a crown to mighty Cæsar.
If you shall send them word you will not come,
Their minds may change. Besides, it were a mock
Apt to be render'd, for some one to say
'Break up the senate till another time,
When Cæsar's wife shall meet with better dreams.'
If Cæsar hide himself, shall they not whisper
'Lo, Cæsar is afraid'?
Pardon me, Cæsar, for my dear dear love
To your proceeding bids me tell you this,
And reason to my love is liable.

CÆSAR

How foolish do your fears seem now, Calpurnia!
I am ashamed I did yield to them.
Give me my robe, for I will go.

Enter PUBLIUS, BRUTUS, LIGARIUS, METELLUS, CASCA,
　　　　　　TREBONIUS, *and* CINNA

And look where Publius is come to fetch me.

PUBLIUS

Good morrow, Cæsar.

CÆSAR

　　　　　　Welcome, Publius.
What, Brutus, are you stirr'd so early too?
Good morrow, Casca. Caius Ligarius,
Cæsar was ne'er so much your enemy
As that same ague which hath made you lean.
What is 't o'clock?

BRUTUS

　　　　　Cæsar, 'tis strucken eight.

CÆSAR

I thank you for your pains and courtesy.

Enter ANTONY

See! Antony, that revels long o' nights,
Is notwithstanding up. Good morrow, Antony.

ANTONY

So to most noble Cæsar.

CÆSAR

Bid them prepare within:
I am to blame to be thus waited for.
Now, Cinna: now, Metellus: what, Trebonius!
I have an hour's talk in store for you;
Remember that you call on me to-day:
Be near me, that I may remember you.

TREBONIUS

Cæsar, I will. [*Aside*] And so near will I be,
That your best friends shall wish I had been further.

CÆSAR

Good friends, go in and taste some wine with me;
And we like friends will straightway go together.

BRUTUS

[*Aside*] That every like is not the same, O Cæsar,
The heart of Brutus yearns to think upon!   [*Exeunt*

SCENE III. *A street near the Capitol*

Enter ARTEMIDORUS, *reading a paper*

ARTEMIDORUS

'Cæsar, beware of Brutus; take heed of Cassius; come not near
Casca; have an eye to Cinna; trust not Trebonius; mark well
Metellus Cimber: Decius Brutus loves thee not: thou hast
wronged Caius Ligarius. There is but one mind in all these
men, and it is bent against Cæsar. If thou beest not immortal,
look about you: security gives way to conspiracy. The mighty
gods defend thee!

Thy lover, ARTEMIDORUS.'

Here will I stand till Cæsar pass along,
And as a suitor will I give him this.
My heart laments that virtue cannot live
Out of the teeth of emulation.
If thou read this, O Cæsar, thou mayst live;
If not, the Fates with traitors do contrive.   [*Exit*

SCENE IV. *Another part of the same street, before the house
of* BRUTUS

Enter PORTIA *and* LUCIUS

PORTIA

I prithee, boy, run to the senate-house;
Stay not to answer me, but get thee gone.
Why dost thou stay?

LUCIUS

To know my errand, madam.

PORTIA

I would have had thee there, and here again,
Ere I can tell thee what thou shouldst do there.
O constancy, be strong upon my side!
Set a huge mountain 'tween my heart and tongue!
I have a man's mind, but a woman's might.
How hard it is for women to keep counsel!
Art thou here yet?

LUCIUS

Madam, what should I do?

Run to the Capitol, and nothing else?
And so return to you, and nothing else?

PORTIA

Yes, bring me word, boy, if thy lord look well,
For he went sickly forth: and take good note
What Cæsar doth, what suitors press to him.
Hark, boy! what noise is that?

LUCIUS

I hear none, madam.

PORTIA

Prithee, listen well:
I heard a bustling rumour like a fray,
And the wind brings it from the Capitol.

LUCIUS

Sooth, madam, I hear nothing.

Enter the SOOTHSAYER

PORTIA

Come hither, fellow:
Which way hast thou been?

SOOTHSAYER

At mine own house, good lady.

PORTIA

What is 't o'clock?

SOOTHSAYER

About the ninth hour, lady.

PORTIA

Is Cæsar yet gone to the Capitol?

SOOTHSAYER

Madam, not yet: I go to take my stand,
To see him pass on to the Capitol.

PORTIA

Thou hast some suit to Cæsar, hast thou not?

SOOTHSAYER

That I have, lady: if it will please Cæsar
To be so good to Cæsar as to hear me,
I shall beseech him to befriend himself.

PORTIA

Why, know'st thou any harm's intended towards
him?

SOOTHSAYER

None that I know will be, much that I fear may
chance.
Good morrow to you. Here the street is narrow:
The throng that follows Cæsar at the heels,
Of senators, of prætors, common suitors,
Will crowd a feeble man almost to death:
I'll get me to a place more void and there
Speak to great Cæsar as he comes along.   [*Exit*

PORTIA

I must go in. Ay me, how weak a thing
The heart of woman is! O Brutus,
The heavens speed thee in thine enterprise!
Sure, the boy heard me. Brutus hath a suit
That Cæsar will not grant. O, I grow faint.
Run, Lucius, and commend me to my lord;
Say I am merry: come to me again,
And bring me word what he doth say to thee.

[*Exeunt severally*

ACT III

SCENE I. *Rome. Before the Capitol; the Senate sitting above*

A crowd of people; among them ARTEMIDORUS *and the* SOOTHSAYER. *Flourish. Enter* CÆSAR, BRUTUS, CASSIUS, CASCA, DECIUS, METELLUS, TREBONIUS, CINNA, ANTONY, LEPIDUS, POPILIUS, PUBLIUS, *and others*

CÆSAR

The ides of March are come.

SOOTHSAYER

Ay, Cæsar; but not gone.

ARTEMIDORUS

Hail, Cæsar! read this schedule.

DECIUS

Trebonius doth desire you to o'er-read,
At your best leisure, this his humble suit.

ARTEMIDORUS

O Cæsar, read mine first; for mine's a suit
That touches Cæsar nearer: read it, great Cæsar.

CÆSAR

What touches us ourself shall be last served.

ARTEMIDORUS

Delay not, Cæsar; read it instantly.

CÆSAR

What, is the fellow mad?

PUBLIUS

           Sirrah, give place.

CASSIUS

What, urge you your petitions in the street?
Come to the Capitol.

CÆSAR goes up to the Senate-house, the rest following

POPILIUS

I wish your enterprise to-day may thrive.

CASSIUS

What enterprise, Popilius?

POPILIUS

           Fare you well.

[*Advances to* CÆSAR

BRUTUS

What said Popilius Lena?

CASSIUS

He wish'd to-day our enterprise might thrive.
I fear our purpose is discovered.

BRUTUS

Look, how he makes to Cæsar: mark him.

CASSIUS

           Casca,
Be sudden, for we fear prevention.
Brutus, what shall be done? If this be known,
Cassius or Cæsar never shall turn back,
For I will slay myself.

BRUTUS

           Cassius, be constant:
Popilius Lena speaks not of our purposes;
For, look, he smiles, and Cæsar doth not change.

CASSIUS

Trebonius knows his time; for, look you, Brutus,
He draws Mark Antony out of the way.

[*Exeunt* ANTONY *and* TREBONIUS

DECIUS

Where is Metellus Cimber? Let him go,
And presently prefer his suit to Cæsar.

BRUTUS

He is address'd: press near and second him.

CINNA

Casca, you are the first that rears your hand.

CÆSAR

Are we all ready? What is now amiss
That Cæsar and his senate must redress?

METELLUS

Most high, most mighty and most puissant Cæsar,
Metellus Cimber throws before thy seat
An humble heart:—   [*Kneeling*

CÆSAR

           I must prevent thee, Cimber.
These couchings and these lowly courtesies
Might fire the blood of ordinary men,
And turn pre-ordinance and first decree
Into the law of children. Be not fond,
To think that Cæsar bears such rebel blood
That will be thaw'd from the true quality
With that which melteth fools, I mean, sweet words,
Low-crooked court'sies and base spaniel-fawning.
Thy brother by decree is banished:
If thou dost bend and pray and fawn for him,
I spurn thee like a cur out of my way.
Know, Cæsar doth not wrong, nor without cause
Will he be satisfied.

METELLUS

Is there no voice more worthy than my own,
To sound more sweetly in great Cæsar's ear
For the repealing of my banish'd brother?

BRUTUS

I kiss thy hand, but not in flattery, Cæsar,
Desiring thee that Publius Cimber may
Have an immediate freedom of repeal.

CÆSAR

What, Brutus!

CASSIUS

           Pardon, Cæsar; Cæsar, pardon:
As low as to thy foot doth Cassius fall,
To beg enfranchisement for Publius Cimber.

CÆSAR

I could be well moved, if I were as you;
If I could pray to move, prayers would move me:
But I am constant as the northern star,
Of whose true-fix'd and resting quality
There is no fellow in the firmament.
The skies are painted with unnumber'd sparks;
They are all fire and every one doth shine;
But there's but one in all doth hold his place:
So in the world; 'tis furnish'd well with men,
And men are flesh and blood, and apprehensive:
Yet in the number I do know but one
That unassailable holds on his rank,
Unshaked of motion: and that I am he,
Let me a little show it, even in this;
That I was constant Cimber should be banish'd,
And constant do remain to keep him so.

CINNA

O Cæsar,—

CÆSAR

Hence! wilt thou lift up Olympus?

DECIUS

Great Cæsar,—

CÆSAR

Doth not Brutus bootless kneel?

CASCA

Speak, hands, for me!   [CASCA *first, then the
other Conspirators and* MARCUS BRUTUS *stab* CÆSAR

CÆSAR

Et tu, Brute? Then fall, Cæsar!   [*Dies*

CINNA

Liberty! freedom! Tyranny is dead!
Run hence, proclaim, cry it about the streets.

CASSIUS

Some to the common pulpits, and cry out
'Liberty, freedom and enfranchisement!'

BRUTUS

People, and senators, be not affrighted;
Fly not; stand still: ambition's debt is paid.

CASCA

Go to the pulpit, Brutus.

DECIUS

And Cassius too.

BRUTUS

Where's Publius?

CINNA

Here, quite confounded with this mutiny.

METELLUS

Stand fast together, lest some friend of Cæsar's
Should chance—

BRUTUS

Talk not of standing. Publius, good cheer;
There is no harm intended to your person,
Nor to no Roman else: so tell them, Publius.

CASSIUS

And leave us, Publius; lest that the people
Rushing on us should do your age some mischief.

BRUTUS

Do so: and let no man abide this deed
But we the doers.

Re-enter TREBONIUS

CASSIUS

Where is Antony?

TREBONIUS

Fled to his house amazed:
Men, wives and children stare, cry out and run
As it were doomsday.

BRUTUS

Fates, we will know your pleasures:
That we shall die, we know; 'tis but the time,
And drawing days out, that men stand upon.

CASSIUS

Why, he that cuts off twenty years of life
Cuts off so many years of fearing death.

BRUTUS

Grant that, and then is death a benefit:
So are we Cæsar's friends, that have abridged

His time of fearing death. Stoop, Romans, stoop,
And let us bathe our hands in Cæsar's blood
Up to the elbows, and besmear our swords:
Then walk we forth, even to the market-place,
And waving our red weapons o'er our heads,
Let's all cry 'Peace, freedom and liberty!'

CASSIUS

Stoop then, and wash. How many ages hence
Shall this our lofty scene be acted over
In states unborn and accents yet unknown!

BRUTUS

How many times shall Cæsar bleed in sport,
That now on Pompey's basis lies along
No worthier than the dust!

CASSIUS

So oft as that shall be,
So often shall the knot of us be call'd
The men that gave their country liberty.

DECIUS

What, shall we forth?

CASSIUS

Ay, every man away:
Brutus shall lead, and we will grace his heels
With the most boldest and best hearts of Rome.

Enter a SERVANT

BRUTUS

Soft! who comes here? A friend of Antony's.

SERVANT

Thus, Brutus, did my master bid me kneel;
Thus did Mark Antony bid me fall down;
And, being prostrate, thus he bade me say:
Brutus is noble, wise, valiant and honest;
Cæsar was mighty, bold, royal and loving:
Say I love Brutus and I honour him;
Say I fear'd Cæsar, honour'd him and loved him.
If Brutus will vouchsafe that Antony
May safely come to him and be resolved
How Cæsar hath deserved to lie in death,
Mark Antony shall not love Cæsar dead
So well as Brutus living, but will follow
The fortunes and affairs of noble Brutus
Thorough the hazards of this untrod state
With all true faith. So says my master Antony.

BRUTUS

Thy master is a wise and valiant Roman;
I never thought him worse.
Tell him, so please him come unto this place,
He shall be satisfied and, by my honour,
Depart untouch'd.

SERVANT

I'll fetch him presently.   [*Exit*

BRUTUS

I know that we shall have him well to friend.

CASSIUS

I wish we may: but yet have I a mind
That fears him much, and my misgiving still
Falls shrewdly to the purpose.

Re-enter ANTONY

BRUTUS

But here comes Antony. Welcome, Mark Antony.

ANTONY

O mighty Cæsar! dost thou lie so low?
Are all thy conquests, glories, triumphs, spoils,
Shrunk to this little measure? Fare thee well.
I know not, gentlemen, what you intend,
Who else must be let blood, who else is rank:
If I myself, there is no hour so fit
As Cæsar's death's hour, nor no instrument
Of half that worth as those your swords, made rich
With the most noble blood of all this world.
I do beseech ye, if you bear me hard,
Now, whilst your purpled hands do reek and smoke,
Fulfil your pleasure. Live a thousand years,
I shall not find myself so apt to die:
No place will please me so, no mean of death,
As here by Cæsar, and by you cut off,
The choice and master spirits of this age.

BRUTUS

O Antony, beg not your death of us.
Though now we must appear bloody and cruel,
As, by our hands and this our present act,
You see we do; yet see you but our hands
And this the bleeding business they have done:
Our hearts you see not; they are pitiful;
And pity to the general wrong of Rome—
As fire drives out fire, so pity pity—
Hath done this deed on Cæsar. For your part,
To you our swords have leaden points, Mark Antony:
Our arms in strength of malice, and our hearts
Of brothers' temper, do receive you in
With all kind love, good thoughts and reverence.

CASSIUS

Your voice shall be as strong as any man's
In the disposing of new dignities.

BRUTUS

Only be patient till we have appeased
The multitude, beside themselves with fear,
And then we will deliver you the cause
Why I, that did love Cæsar when I struck him,
Have thus proceeded.

ANTONY

                    I doubt not of your wisdom.
Let each man render me his bloody hand:
First, Marcus Brutus, will I shake with you;
Next, Caius Cassius, do I take your hand;
Now, Decius Brutus, yours; now yours, Metellus;
Yours, Cinna; and, my valiant Casca, yours;
Though last, not least in love, yours, good Trebonius.
Gentlemen all,—alas, what shall I say?
My credit now stands on such slippery ground,
That one of two bad ways you must conceit me,
Either a coward or a flatterer.
That I did love thee, Cæsar, O, 'tis true:
If then thy spirit look upon us now,
Shall it not grieve thee dearer than thy death,
To see thy Antony making his peace,
Shaking the bloody fingers of thy foes,
Most noble! in the presence of thy corse?

Had I as many eyes as thou hast wounds,
Weeping as fast as they stream forth thy blood,
It would become me better than to close
In terms of friendship with thine enemies.
Pardon me, Julius! Here wast thou bay'd, brave hart;
Here didst thou fall, and here thy hunters stand,
Sign'd in thy spoil and crimson'd in thy lethe.
O world, thou wast the forest to this hart;
And this, indeed, O world, the heart of thee.
How like a deer strucken by many princes
Dost thou here lie!

CASSIUS

Mark Antony,—

ANTONY

                    Pardon me, Caius Cassius:
The enemies of Cæsar shall say this;
Then, in a friend, it is cold modesty.

CASSIUS

I blame you not for praising Cæsar so;
But what compact mean you to have with us?
Will you be prick'd in number of our friends,
Or shall we on, and not depend on you?

ANTONY

Therefore I took your hands, but was indeed
Sway'd from the point by looking down on Cæsar.
Friends am I with you all and love you all,
Upon this hope that you shall give me reasons
Why and wherein Cæsar was dangerous.

BRUTUS

Or else were this a savage spectacle:
Our reasons are so full of good regard
That were you, Antony, the son of Cæsar,
You should be satisfied.

ANTONY

                    That's all I seek:
And am moreover suitor that I may
Produce his body to the market-place,
And in the pulpit, as becomes a friend,
Speak in the order of his funeral.

BRUTUS

You shall, Mark Antony.

CASSIUS

                    Brutus, a word with you.
[Aside to BRUTUS] You know not what you do: do not consent
That Antony speak in his funeral:
Know you how much the people may be moved
By that which he will utter?

BRUTUS

                    By your pardon:
I will myself into the pulpit first,
And show the reason of our Cæsar's death:
What Antony shall speak, I will protest
He speaks by leave and by permission,
And that we are contented Cæsar shall
Have all true rites and lawful ceremonies.
It shall advantage more than do us wrong.

CASSIUS

I know not what may fall; I like it not.

BRUTUS

Mark Antony, here, take you Cæsar's body.
You shall not in your funeral speech blame us,
But speak all good you can devise of Cæsar,
And say you do 't by our permission;
Else shall you not have any hand at all
About his funeral: and you shall speak
In the same pulpit whereto I am going,
After my speech is ended.

ANTONY
　　　　　　　　Be it so;
I do desire no more.

BRUTUS

Prepare the body then, and follow us.
　　　　　　　　　[Exeunt all but ANTONY

ANTONY

O, pardon me, thou bleeding piece of earth,
That I am meek and gentle with these butchers!
Thou art the ruins of the noblest man
That ever lived in the tide of times.
Woe to the hand that shed this costly blood!
Over thy wounds now do I prophesy,
Which like dumb mouths do ope their ruby lips
To beg the voice and utterance of my tongue,
A curse shall light upon the limbs of men;
Domestic fury and fierce civil strife
Shall cumber all the parts of Italy;
Blood and destruction shall be so in use,
And dreadful objects so familiar,
That mothers shall but smile when they behold
Their infants quarter'd with the hands of war;
All pity choked with custom of fell deeds:
And Cæsar's spirit ranging for revenge,
With Ate by his side come hot from hell,
Shall in these confines with a monarch's voice
Cry 'Havoc,' and let slip the dogs of war;
That this foul deed shall smell above the earth
With carrion men, groaning for burial.

Enter a SERVANT

You serve Octavius Cæsar, do you not?

SERVANT

I do, Mark Antony.

ANTONY

Cæsar did write for him to come to Rome.

SERVANT

He did receive his letters, and is coming;
And bid me say to you by word of mouth—
O Cæsar!　　　　　　　[Seeing the body

ANTONY

Thy heart is big; get thee apart and weep.
Passion, I see, is catching, for mine eyes,
Seeing those beads of sorrow stand in thine,
Began to water. Is thy master coming?

SERVANT

He lies to-night within seven leagues of Rome.

ANTONY

Post back with speed, and tell him what hath
　　chanced:
Here is a mourning Rome, a dangerous Rome,
No Rome of safety for Octavius yet;

Hie hence, and tell him so. Yet stay awhile;
Thou shalt not back till I have borne this corse
Into the market-place: there shall I try,
In my oration, how the people take
The cruel issue of these bloody men;
According to the which, thou shalt discourse
To young Octavius of the state of things.
Lend me your hand.　　　[Exeunt with CÆSAR's body

SCENE II. The Forum

Enter BRUTUS and CASSIUS, and a throng of CITIZENS

CITIZENS

We will be satisfied; let us be satisfied.

BRUTUS

Then follow me, and give me audience, friends.
Cassius, go you into the other street,
And part the numbers.
Those that will hear me speak, let 'em stay here;
Those that will follow Cassius, go with him;
And public reasons shall be rendered
Of Cæsar's death.

FIRST CITIZEN
　　　　　I will hear Brutus speak.

SECOND CITIZEN

I will hear Cassius; and compare their reasons,
When severally we hear them rendered.
　　　　[Exit CASSIUS, with some of the CITIZENS.
　　　　　　BRUTUS goes into the pulpit

THIRD CITIZEN

The noble Brutus is ascended: silence!

BRUTUS

Be patient till the last.
Romans, countrymen, and lovers! hear me for my
cause, and be silent, that you may hear: believe me
for mine honour, and have respect to mine honour,
that you may believe: censure me in your wisdom,
and awake your senses, that you may the better
judge. If there be any in this assembly, any dear
friend of Cæsar's, to him I say that Brutus' love to
Cæsar was no less than his. If then that friend demand why Brutus rose against Cæsar, this is my
answer: not that I loved Cæsar less, but that I loved
Rome more. Had you rather Cæsar were living, and
die all slaves, than that Cæsar were dead, to live all
freemen? As Cæsar loved me, I weep for him; as he
was fortunate, I rejoice at it; as he was valiant, I
honour him; but as he was ambitious, I slew him.
There is tears for his love; joy for his fortune; honour for his valour; and death for his ambition. Who
is here so base that would be a bondman? If any,
speak; for him have I offended. Who is here so rude
that would not be a Roman? If any, speak; for him
have I offended. Who is here so vile that will not
love his country? If any, speak; for him have I
offended. I pause for a reply.

ALL

None, Brutus, none.

BRUTUS

Then none have I offended. I have done no more to
Cæsar than you shall do to Brutus. The question of
his death is enrolled in the Capitol; his glory not
extenuated, wherein he was worthy, nor his offences
enforced, for which he suffered death.

Enter ANTONY *and others, with* CÆSAR's *body*

Here comes his body, mourned by Mark Antony:
who, though he had no hand in his death, shall receive the benefit of his dying, a place in the commonwealth; as which of you shall not? With this I
depart,—that, as I slew my best lover for the good
of Rome, I have the same dagger for myself, when
it shall please my country to need my death.

ALL

Live, Brutus! live, live!

FIRST CITIZEN

Bring him with triumph home unto his house.

SECOND CITIZEN

Give him a statue with his ancestors.

THIRD CITIZEN

Let him be Cæsar.

FOURTH CITIZEN

Cæsar's better parts

Shall be crown'd in Brutus.

FIRST CITIZEN

We'll bring him to his house with shouts and
clamours.

BRUTUS

My countrymen,—

SECOND CITIZEN

Peace! silence! Brutus speaks.

FIRST CITIZEN

Peace, ho!

BRUTUS

Good countrymen, let me depart alone,
And, for my sake, stay here with Antony:
Do grace to Cæsar's corpse, and grace his speech
Tending to Cæsar's glories, which Mark Antony
By our permission is allow'd to make.
I do entreat you, not a man depart,
Save I alone, till Antony have spoke.   [*Exit*

FIRST CITIZEN

Stay, ho! and let us hear Mark Antony.

THIRD CITIZEN

Let him go up into the public chair;
We'll hear him. Noble Antony, go up.

ANTONY

For Brutus' sake, I am beholding to you.
          [*Goes into the pulpit*

FOURTH CITIZEN

What does he say of Brutus?

THIRD CITIZEN

He says, for Brutus' sake,

He finds himself beholding to us all.

FOURTH CITIZEN

'Twere best he speak no harm of Brutus here.

FIRST CITIZEN

This Cæsar was a tyrant.

THIRD CITIZEN

Nay, that's certain:

We are blest that Rome is rid of him.

SECOND CITIZEN

Peace! let us hear what Antony can say.

ANTONY

You gentle Romans,—

ALL

Peace, ho! let us hear him.

ANTONY

Friends, Romans, countrymen, lend me your ears;
I come to bury Cæsar, not to praise him.
The evil that men do lives after them;
The good is oft interred with their bones;
So let it be with Cæsar. The noble Brutus
Hath told you Cæsar was ambitious:
If it were so, it was a grievous fault,
And grievously hath Cæsar answer'd it.
Here, under leave of Brutus and the rest,—
For Brutus is an honourable man;
So are they all, all honourable men,—
Come I to speak in Cæsar's funeral.
He was my friend, faithful and just to me:
But Brutus says he was ambitious;
And Brutus is an honourable man.
He hath brought many captives home to Rome,
Whose ransoms did the general coffers fill:
Did this in Cæsar seem ambitious?
When that the poor have cried, Cæsar hath wept:
Ambition should be made of sterner stuff:
Yet Brutus says he was ambitious;
And Brutus is an honourable man.
You all did see that on the Lupercal
I thrice presented him a kingly crown,
Which he did thrice refuse: was this ambition?
Yet Brutus says he was ambitious;
And, sure, he is an honourable man.
I speak not to disprove what Brutus spoke,
But here I am to speak what I do know.
You all did love him once, not without cause:
What cause withholds you then to mourn for him?
O judgement! thou art fled to brutish beasts,
And men have lost their reason. Bear with me;
My heart is in the coffin there with Cæsar,
And I must pause till it come back to me.

FIRST CITIZEN

Methinks there is much reason in his sayings.

SECOND CITIZEN

If thou consider rightly of the matter,
Cæsar has had great wrong.

THIRD CITIZEN

Has he, masters?

I fear there will a worse come in his place.

FOURTH CITIZEN

Mark'd ye his words? He would not take the crown;
Therefore 'tis certain he was not ambitious.

FIRST CITIZEN

If it be found so, some will dear abide it.

SECOND CITIZEN

Poor soul! his eyes are red as fire with weeping.

THIRD CITIZEN
There's not a nobler man in Rome than Antony.

FOURTH CITIZEN
Now mark him, he begins again to speak.

ANTONY
But yesterday the word of Cæsar might
Have stood against the world: now lies he there,
And none so poor to do him reverence.
O masters, if I were disposed to stir
Your hearts and minds to mutiny and rage,
I should do Brutus wrong and Cassius wrong,
Who, you all know, are honourable men:
I will not do them wrong; I rather choose
To wrong the dead, to wrong myself and you,
Than I will wrong such honourable men.
But here's a parchment with the seal of Cæsar;
I found it in his closet; 'tis his will:
Let but the commons hear this testament—
Which, pardon me, I do not mean to read—
And they would go and kiss dead Cæsar's wounds
And dip their napkins in his sacred blood,
Yea, beg a hair of him for memory,
And, dying, mention it within their wills,
Bequeathing it as a rich legacy
Unto their issue.

FOURTH CITIZEN
We'll hear the will: read it, Mark Antony.

ALL
The will, the will! we will hear Cæsar's will.

ANTONY
Have patience, gentle friends, I must not read it;
It is not meet you know how Cæsar loved you.
You are not wood, you are not stones, but men;
And, being men, hearing the will of Cæsar,
It will inflame you, it will make you mad:
'Tis good you know not that you are his heirs;
For if you should, O, what would come of it!

FOURTH CITIZEN
Read the will; we'll hear it, Antony;
You shall read us the will, Cæsar's will.

ANTONY
Will you be patient? will you stay awhile?
I have o'ershot myself to tell you of it:
I fear I wrong the honourable men
Whose daggers have stabb'd Cæsar; I do fear it.

FOURTH CITIZEN
They were traitors: honourable men!

ALL
The will! the testament!

SECOND CITIZEN
They were villains, murderers: the will! read the
will.

ANTONY
You will compel me then to read the will?
Then make a ring about the corpse of Cæsar,
And let me show you him that made the will.
Shall I descend? and will you give me leave?

ALL
Come down.

SECOND CITIZEN
Descend.   [He comes down from the pulpit

THIRD CITIZEN
You shall have leave.

FOURTH CITIZEN
A ring; stand round.

FIRST CITIZEN
Stand from the hearse, stand from the body.

SECOND CITIZEN
Room for Antony, most noble Antony.

ANTONY
Nay, press not so upon me; stand far off.

ALL
Stand back. Room! Bear back.

ANTONY
If you have tears, prepare to shed them now.
You all do know this mantle: I remember
The first time ever Cæsar put it on;
'Twas on a summer's evening, in his tent,
That day he overcame the Nervii:
Look, in this place ran Cassius' dagger through:
See what a rent the envious Casca made:
Through this the well-beloved Brutus stabb'd;
And as he pluck'd his cursed steel away,
Mark how the blood of Cæsar follow'd it,
As rushing out of doors, to be resolved
If Brutus so unkindly knock'd, or no:
For Brutus, as you know, was Cæsar's angel:
Judge, O you gods, how dearly Cæsar loved him!
This was the most unkindest cut of all;
For when the noble Cæsar saw him stab,
Ingratitude, more strong than traitors' arms,
Quite vanquish'd him: then burst his mighty heart;
And, in his mantle muffling up his face,
Even at the base of Pompey's statuë,
Which all the while ran blood, great Cæsar fell.
O, what a fall was there, my countrymen!
Then I, and you, and all of us fell down,
Whilst bloody treason flourish'd over us.
O, now you weep, and I perceive you feel
The dint of pity: these are gracious drops.
Kind souls, what weep you when you but behold
Our Cæsar's vesture wounded? Look you here,
Here is himself, marr'd, as you see, with traitors.

FIRST CITIZEN
O piteous spectacle!

SECOND CITIZEN
O noble Cæsar!

THIRD CITIZEN
O woful day!

FOURTH CITIZEN
O traitors, villains!

FIRST CITIZEN
O most bloody sight!

SECOND CITIZEN
We will be revenged.

ALL
Revenge! About! Seek! Burn! Fire! Kill! Slay!
Let not a traitor live!

ANTONY

Stay, countrymen.

FIRST CITIZEN

Peace there! hear the noble Antony.

SECOND CITIZEN

We'll hear him, we'll follow him, we'll die with him.

ANTONY

Good friends, sweet friends, let me not stir you up
To such a sudden flood of mutiny.
They that have done this deed are honourable;
What private griefs they have, alas, I know not,
That made them do it: they are wise and honour-
    able,
And will, no doubt, with reasons answer you.
I come not, friends, to steal away your hearts:
I am no orator, as Brutus is;
But, as you know me all, a plain blunt man,
That love my friend; and that they know full well
That gave me public leave to speak of him:
For I have neither wit, nor words, nor worth,
Action, nor utterance, nor the power of speech,
To stir men's blood: I only speak right on;
I tell you that which you yourselves do know;
Show you sweet Cæsar's wounds, poor poor dumb
    mouths,
And bid them speak for me: but were I Brutus,
And Brutus Antony, there were an Antony
Would ruffle up your spirits, and put a tongue
In every wound of Cæsar, that should move
The stones of Rome to rise and mutiny.

ALL

We'll mutiny.

FIRST CITIZEN

We'll burn the house of Brutus.

THIRD CITIZEN

Away, then! come, seek the conspirators.

ANTONY

Yet hear me, countrymen; yet hear me speak.

ALL

Peace, ho! Hear Antony. Most noble Antony!

ANTONY

Why, friends, you go to do you know not what:
Wherein hath Cæsar thus deserved your loves?
Alas, you know not; I must tell you then:
You have forgot the will I told you of.

ALL

Most true: the will! Let's stay and hear the will.

ANTONY

Here is the will, and under Cæsar's seal.
To every Roman citizen he gives,
To every several man, seventy five drachmas.

SECOND CITIZEN

Most noble Cæsar! we'll revenge his death.

THIRD CITIZEN

O royal Cæsar!

ANTONY

Hear me with patience.

ALL

Peace, ho!

ANTONY

Moreover, he hath left you all his walks,
His private arbours and new-planted orchards,
On this side Tiber; he hath left them you,
And to your heirs for ever; common pleasures,
To walk abroad and recreate yourselves.
Here was a Cæsar! when comes such another?

FIRST CITIZEN

Never, never. Come, away, away!
We'll burn his body in the holy place,
And with the brands fire the traitors' houses.
Take up the body.

SECOND CITIZEN

Go fetch fire.

THIRD CITIZEN

Pluck down benches.

FOURTH CITIZEN

Pluck down forms, windows, any thing.

[Exeunt CITIZENS with the body

ANTONY

Now let it work. Mischief, thou art afoot,
Take thou what course thou wilt.

Enter a SERVANT

                              How now, fellow!

SERVANT

Sir, Octavius is already come to Rome.

ANTONY

Where is he?

SERVANT

He and Lepidus are at Cæsar's house.

ANTONY

And thither will I straight to visit him:
He comes upon a wish. Fortune is merry,
And in this mood will give us any thing.

SERVANT

I heard him say, Brutus and Cassius
Are rid like madmen through the gates of Rome.

ANTONY

Belike they had some notice of the people,
How I had moved them. Bring me to Octavius.

[Exeunt

SCENE III. A street

Enter CINNA the poet

CINNA

I dreamt to-night that I did feast with Cæsar,
And things unluckily charge my fantasy:
I have no will to wander forth of doors,
Yet something leads me forth.

Enter CITIZENS

FIRST CITIZEN

What is your name?

SECOND CITIZEN

Whither are you going?

THIRD CITIZEN

Where do you dwell?

FOURTH CITIZEN

Are you a married man or a bachelor?

SECOND CITIZEN
Answer every man directly.

FIRST CITIZEN
Ay, and briefly.

FOURTH CITIZEN
Ay, and wisely.

THIRD CITIZEN
Ay, and truly, you were best.

CINNA
What is my name? Whither am I going? Where do
I dwell? Am I a married man or a bachelor? Then,
to answer every man directly and briefly, wisely
and truly: wisely I say, I am a bachelor.

SECOND CITIZEN
That's as much as to say, they are fools that marry:
you'll bear me a bang for that, I fear. Proceed;
directly.

CINNA
Directly, I am going to Cæsar's funeral.

FIRST CITIZEN
As a friend or an enemy?

CINNA
As a friend.

SECOND CITIZEN
That matter is answered directly.

FOURTH CITIZEN
For your dwelling, briefly.

CINNA
Briefly, I dwell by the Capitol.

THIRD CITIZEN
Your name, sir, truly.

CINNA
Truly, my name is Cinna.

FIRST CITIZEN
Tear him to pieces; he's a conspirator.

CINNA
I am Cinna the poet, I am Cinna the poet.

FOURTH CITIZEN
Tear him for his bad verses, tear him for his bad
verses.

CINNA
I am not Cinna the conspirator.

FOURTH CITIZEN
It is no matter, his name's Cinna; pluck but his
name out of his heart, and turn him going.

THIRD CITIZEN
Tear him, tear him! Come, brands, ho! fire-brands:
to Brutus', to Cassius'; burn all: some to Decius'
house, and some to Casca's; some to Ligarius':
away, go!   [*Exeunt*

ACT IV

SCENE I. *A house in Rome*

ANTONY, OCTAVIUS, *and* LEPIDUS, *seated at a table*

ANTONY
These many then shall die; their names are prick'd.

OCTAVIUS
Your brother too must die; consent you, Lepidus?

LEPIDUS
I do consent—

OCTAVIUS
Prick him down, Antony.

LEPIDUS
Upon condition Publius shall not live,
Who is your sister's son, Mark Antony.

ANTONY
He shall not live; look, with a spot I damn him.
But, Lepidus, go you to Cæsar's house;
Fetch the will hither, and we shall determine
How to cut off some charge in legacies.

LEPIDUS
What, shall I find you here?

OCTAVIUS
Or here, or at the Capitol.   [*Exit* LEPIDUS

ANTONY
This is a slight unmeritable man,
Meet to be sent on errands: is it fit,
The three-fold world divided, he should stand
One of the three to share it?

OCTAVIUS
So you thought him,
And took his voice who should be prick'd to die
In our black sentence and proscription.

ANTONY
Octavius, I have seen more days than you:
And though we lay these honours on this man,
To ease ourselves of divers slanderous loads,
He shall but bear them as the ass bears gold,
To groan and sweat under the business,
Either led or driven, as we point the way;
And having brought our treasure where we will,
Then take we down his load and turn him off,
Like to the empty ass, to shake his ears
And graze in commons.

OCTAVIUS
You may do your will:
But he's a tried and valiant soldier.

ANTONY
So is my horse, Octavius, and for that
I do appoint him store of provender:
It is a creature that I teach to fight,
To wind, to stop, to run directly on,
His corporal motion govern'd by my spirit.
And, in some taste, is Lepidus but so;
He must be taught, and train'd, and bid go forth;
A barren-spirited fellow; one that feeds
On abjects, orts and imitations,
Which, out of use and staled by other men,
Begin his fashion: do not talk of him
But as a property. And now, Octavius,
Listen great things: Brutus and Cassius
Are levying powers: we must straight make head:
Therefore let our alliance be combined,
Our best friends made, our means stretch'd;
And let us presently go sit in council,

How covert matters may be best disclosed,
And open perils surest answered.

OCTAVIUS

Let us do so: for we are at the stake,
And bay'd about with many enemies;
And some that smile have in their hearts, I fear,
Millions of mischiefs.   [*Exeunt*

SCENE II. *Camp near Sardis. Before* BRUTUS's *tent*

Drum. Enter BRUTUS, LUCILIUS, LUCIUS, *and* SOLDIERS;
TITANIUS *and* PINDARUS *meet them*

BRUTUS

Stand, ho!

LUCILIUS

Give the word, ho! and stand.

BRUTUS

What now, Lucilius! is Cassius near?

LUCILIUS

He is at hand; and Pindarus is come
To do you salutation from his master.

BRUTUS

He greets me well. Your master, Pindarus,
In his own change, or by ill officers,
Hath given me some worthy cause to wish
Things done undone: but if he be at hand,
I shall be satisfied.

PINDARUS

I do not doubt
But that my noble master will appear
Such as he is, full of regard and honour.

BRUTUS

He is not doubted. A word, Lucilius,
How he received you: let me be resolved.

LUCILIUS

With courtesy and with respect enough;
But not with such familiar instances,
Nor with such free and friendly conference,
As he hath used of old.

BRUTUS

Thou hast described
A hot friend cooling: ever note, Lucilius,
When love begins to sicken and decay,
It useth an enforced ceremony.
There are no tricks in plain and simple faith:
But hollow men, like horses hot at hand,
Make gallant show and promise of their mettle;
But when they should endure the bloody spur,
They fall their crests and like deceitful jades
Sink in the trial. Comes his army on?

LUCILIUS

They mean this night in Sardis to be quarter'd;
The greater part, the horse in general,
Are come with Cassius.   [*Low march within*

BRUTUS

Hark! he is arrived:
March gently on to meet him.

Enter CASSIUS *and his powers*

CASSIUS

Stand, ho!

BRUTUS

Stand, ho! Speak the word along.

FIRST SOLDIER

Stand!

SECOND SOLDIER

Stand!

THIRD SOLDIER

Stand!

CASSIUS

Most noble brother, you have done me wrong.

BRUTUS

Judge me, you gods! wrong I mine enemies?
And, if not so, how should I wrong a brother?

CASSIUS

Brutus, this sober form of yours hides wrongs;
And when you do them—

BRUTUS

Cassius, be content;
Speak your griefs softly: I do know you well.
Before the eyes of both our armies here,
Which should perceive nothing but love from us,
Let us not wrangle: bid them move away;
Then in my tent, Cassius, enlarge your griefs,
And I will give you audience.

CASSIUS

Pindarus,
Bid our commanders lead their charges off
A little from this ground.

BRUTUS

Lucilius, do you the like, and let no man
Come to our tent till we have done our conference.
Let Lucius and Titinius guard our door.   [*Exeunt*

SCENE III. BRUTUS's *tent*

Enter BRUTUS *and* CASSIUS

CASSIUS

That you have wrong'd me doth appear in this:
You have condemn'd and noted Lucius Pella
For taking bribes here of the Sardians;
Wherein my letters, praying on his side,
Because I knew the man, were slighted off.

BRUTUS

You wrong'd yourself to write in such a case.

CASSIUS

In such a time as this it is not meet
That every nice offence should bear his comment.

BRUTUS

Let me tell you, Cassius, you yourself
Are much condemn'd to have an itching palm,
To sell and mart your offices for gold
To undeservers.

CASSIUS

I an itching palm!
You know that you are Brutus that speaks this,
Or, by the gods, this speech were else your last.

BRUTUS

The name of Cassius honours this corruption,
And chastisement doth therefore hide his head.

CASSIUS

Chastisement!

BRUTUS

Remember March, the ides of March remember:
Did not great Julius bleed for justice' sake?
What villain touch'd his body, that did stab,
And not for justice? What, shall one of us,
That struck the foremost man of all this world
But for supporting robbers, shall we now
Contaminate our fingers with base bribes,
And sell the mighty space of our large honours
For so much trash as may be grasped thus?
I had rather be a dog, and bay the moon,
Than such a Roman.

CASSIUS

         Brutus, bait not me;
I'll not endure it: you forget yourself,
To hedge me in; I am a soldier, I,
Older in practice, abler than yourself
To make conditions.

BRUTUS

         Go to; you are not, Cassius.

CASSIUS

I am.

BRUTUS

I say you are not.

CASSIUS

Urge me no more, I shall forget myself;
Have mind upon your health, tempt me no farther.

BRUTUS

Away, slight man!

CASSIUS

Is 't possible?

BRUTUS

         Hear me, for I will speak.
Must I give way and room to your rash choler?
Shall I be frighted when a madman stares?

CASSIUS

O ye gods, ye gods! must I endure all this?

BRUTUS

All this! ay, more: fret till your proud heart break;
Go show your slaves how choleric you are,
And make your bondmen tremble. Must I budge?
Must I observe you? must I stand and crouch
Under your testy humour? By the gods,
You shall digest the venom of your spleen,
Though it do split you; for, from this day forth,
I'll use you for my mirth, yea, for my laughter,
When you are waspish.

CASSIUS

         Is it come to this?

BRUTUS

You say you are a better soldier:
Let it appear so; make your vaunting true,
And it shall please me well: for mine own part,
I shall be glad to learn of noble men.

CASSIUS

You wrong me every way; you wrong me, Brutus;
I said, an elder soldier, not a better:
Did I say, better?

BRUTUS

         If you did, I care not.

CASSIUS

When Cæsar lived, he durst not thus have moved
me.

BRUTUS

Peace, peace! you durst not so have tempted him.

CASSIUS

I durst not!

BRUTUS

No.

CASSIUS

What, durst not tempt him!

BRUTUS

         For your life you durst not.

CASSIUS

Do not presume too much upon my love;
I may do that I shall be sorry for.

BRUTUS

You have done that you should be sorry for.
There is no terror, Cassius, in your threats;
For I am arm'd so strong in honesty,
That they pass by me as the idle wind
Which I respect not. I did send to you
For certain sums of gold, which you denied me:
For I can raise no money by vile means:
By heaven, I had rather coin my heart,
And drop my blood for drachmas, than to wring
From the hard hands of peasants their vile trash
By any indirection. I did send
To you for gold to pay my legions,
Which you denied me: was that done like Cassius?
Should I have answer'd Caius Cassius so?
When Marcus Brutus grows so covetous,
To lock such rascal counters from his friends,
Be ready, gods, with all your thunderbolts,
Dash him to pieces!

CASSIUS

         I denied you not.

BRUTUS

You did.

CASSIUS

         I did not: he was but a fool
That brought my answer back. Brutus hath rived
my heart:
A friend should bear his friend's infirmities,
But Brutus makes mine greater than they are.

BRUTUS

I do not, till you practise them on me.

CASSIUS

You love me not.

BRUTUS

         I do not like your faults.

CASSIUS

A friendly eye could never see such faults.

BRUTUS

A flatterer's would not, though they do appear
As huge as high Olympus.

CASSIUS

Come, Antony, and young Octavius, come,
Revenge yourselves alone on Cassius,
For Cassius is aweary of the world;
Hated by one he loves; braved by his brother;
Check'd like a bondman; all his faults observed,
Set in a note-book, learn'd and conn'd by rote,
To cast into my teeth. O, I could weep
My spirit from mine eyes! There is my dagger,
And here my naked breast; within, a heart
Dearer than Plutus' mine, richer than gold:
If that thou be'st a Roman, take it forth;
I, that denied thee gold, will give my heart:
Strike, as thou didst at Cæsar; for I know,
When thou didst hate him worst, thou lovedst him better
Than ever thou lovedst Cassius.

BRUTUS

          Sheathe your dagger:
Be angry when you will, it shall have scope;
Do what you will, dishonour shall be humour.
O Cassius, you are yoked with a lamb,
That carries anger as the flint bears fire,
Who, much enforced, shows a hasty spark
And straight is cold again.

CASSIUS

          Hath Cassius lived
To be but mirth and laughter to his Brutus,
When grief and blood ill-temper'd vexeth him?

BRUTUS

When I spoke that, I was ill-temper'd too.

CASSIUS

Do you confess so much? Give me your hand.

BRUTUS

And my heart too.

CASSIUS

          O Brutus!

BRUTUS

          What's the matter?

CASSIUS

Have not you love enough to bear with me,
When that rash humour which my mother gave me
Makes me forgetful?

BRUTUS

          Yes, Cassius, and from henceforth,
When you are over-earnest with your Brutus,
He'll think your mother chides, and leave you so.

POET

[Within] Let me go in to see the generals;
There is some grudge between 'em; 'tis not meet
They be alone.

LUCILIUS

[Within] You shall not come to them.

POET

[Within] Nothing but death shall stay me.
Enter POET, followed by LUCILIUS, TITINIUS, and LUCIUS

CASSIUS

How now! what's the matter?

POET

For shame, you generals! what do you mean?
Love, and be friends, as two such men should be;
For I have seen more years, I'm sure, than ye.

CASSIUS

Ha, ha! how vilely doth this cynic rhyme!

BRUTUS

Get you hence, sirrah; saucy fellow, hence!

CASSIUS

Bear with him, Brutus; 'tis his fashion.

BRUTUS

I'll know his humour when he knows his time:
What should the wars do with these jigging fools?
Companion, hence!

CASSIUS

          Away, away, be gone!
[Exit POET

BRUTUS

Lucilius and Titinius, bid the commanders
Prepare to lodge their companies to-night.

CASSIUS

And come yourselves, and bring Messala with you
Immediately to us.   [Exeunt LUCILIUS and TITINIUS

BRUTUS

         Lucius, a bowl of wine!
[Exit LUCIUS

CASSIUS

I did not think you could have been so angry.

BRUTUS

O Cassius, I am sick of many griefs.

CASSIUS

Of your philosophy you make no use,
If you give place to accidental evils.

BRUTUS

No man bears sorrow better: Portia is dead.

CASSIUS

Ha! Portia!

BRUTUS

She is dead.

CASSIUS

How 'scaped I killing when I cross'd you so?
O insupportable and touching loss!
Upon what sickness?

BRUTUS

         Impatient of my absence,
And grief that young Octavius with Mark Antony
Have made themselves so strong: for with her death
That tidings came: with this she fell distract,
And, her attendants absent, swallow'd fire.

CASSIUS

And died so?

BRUTUS

         Even so.

CASSIUS

         O ye immortal gods!

Re-enter LUCIUS, *with wine and taper*

BRUTUS

Speak no more of her. Give me a bowl of wine

In this I bury all unkindness, Cassius.   [*Drinks*

CASSIUS

My heart is thirsty for that noble pledge.

Fill, Lucius, till the wine o'erswell the cup;

I cannot drink too much of Brutus' love.   [*Drinks*

BRUTUS

Come in, Titinius!   [*Exit* LUCIUS

Re-enter TITINIUS, *with* MESSALA

Welcome, good Messala.

Now sit we close about this taper here,

And call in question our necessities.

CASSIUS

Portia, art thou gone?

BRUTUS

No more, I pray you.

Messala, I have here received letters,

That young Octavius and Mark Antony

Come down upon us with a mighty power,

Bending their expedition toward Philippi.

MESSALA

Myself have letters of the selfsame tenour.

BRUTUS

With what addition?

MESSALA

That by proscription and bills of outlawry

Octavius, Antony and Lepidus,

Have put to death an hundred senators.

BRUTUS

Therein our letters do not well agree;

Mine speak of seventy senators that died

By their proscriptions, Cicero being one.

CASSIUS

Cicero one!

MESSALA

Cicero is dead,

And by that order of proscription.

Had you your letters from your wife, my lord?

BRUTUS

No, Messala.

MESSALA

Nor nothing in your letters writ of her?

BRUTUS

Nothing, Messala.

MESSALA

That, methinks, is strange.

BRUTUS

Why ask you? hear you aught of her in yours?

MESSALA

No, my lord.

BRUTUS

Now, as you are a Roman, tell me true.

MESSALA

Then like a Roman bear the truth I tell:

For certain she is dead, and by strange manner.

BRUTUS

Why, farewell, Portia. We must die, Messala:

With meditating that she must die once

I have the patience to endure it now.

MESSALA

Even so great men great losses should endure.

CASSIUS

I have as much of this in art as you,

But yet my nature could not bear it so.

BRUTUS

Well, to our work alive. What do you think

Of marching to Philippi presently?

CASSIUS

I do not think it good.

BRUTUS

Your reason?

CASSIUS

This it is:

'Tis better that the enemy seek us:

So shall he waste his means, weary his soldiers,

Doing himself offence; whilst we lying still

Are full of rest, defence and nimbleness.

BRUTUS

Good reasons must of force give place to better.

The people 'twixt Philippi and this ground

Do stand but in a forced affection,

For they have grudged us contribution:

The enemy, marching along by them,

By them shall make a fuller number up,

Come on refresh'd, new-added and encouraged;

From which advantage shall we cut him off

If at Philippi we do face him there,

These people at our back.

CASSIUS

Hear me, good brother.

BRUTUS

Under your pardon. You must note beside

That we have tried the utmost of our friends,

Our legions are brim-full, our cause is ripe:

The enemy increaseth every day;

We, at the height, are ready to decline.

There is a tide in the affairs of men

Which taken at the flood leads on to fortune;

Omitted, all the voyage of their life

Is bound in shallows and in miseries.

On such a full sea are we now afloat,

And we must take the current when it serves,

Or lose our ventures.

CASSIUS

Then, with your will, go on,

We'll along ourselves and meet them at Philippi.

BRUTUS

The deep of night is crept upon our talk,

And nature must obey necessity;

Which we will niggard with a little rest.

There is no more to say?

CASSIUS

No more. Good night:

Early to-morrow will we rise and hence.

BRUTUS

Lucius! [*Re-enter* LUCIUS] My gown.   [*Exit* LUCIUS

Farewell, good Messala:

Good night, Titinius: noble, noble Cassius,
Good night, and good repose.

CASSIUS

          O my dear brother!
This was an ill beginning of the night:
Never come such division 'tween our souls!
Let it not, Brutus.

BRUTUS

          Every thing is well.

CASSIUS

Good night, my lord.

BRUTUS

          Good night, good brother.

TITINIUS and MESSALA

Good night, Lord Brutus.

BRUTUS

          Farewell, every one.
          [Exeunt all but BRUTUS
  Re-enter LUCIUS, with the gown
Give me the gown. Where is thy instrument?

LUCIUS

Here in the tent.

BRUTUS

          What, thou speak'st drowsily?
Poor knave, I blame thee not; thou art o'er-watch'd.
Call Claudius and some other of my men;
I'll have them sleep on cushions in my tent.

LUCIUS

Varro and Claudius!
    Enter VARRO and CLAUDIUS

VARRO

Calls my lord?

BRUTUS

I pray you, sirs, lie in my tent and sleep;
It may be I shall raise you by and by
On business to my brother Cassius.

VARRO

So please you, we will stand and watch your
   pleasure.

BRUTUS

I will not have it so: lie down, good sirs;
It may be I shall otherwise bethink me.
Look, Lucius, here's the book I sought for so;
I put it in the pocket of my gown.
      [VARRO and CLAUDIUS lie down

LUCIUS

I was sure your lordship did not give it me.

BRUTUS

Bear with me, good boy, I am much forgetful.
Canst thou hold up thy heavy eyes awhile,
And touch thy instrument a strain or two?

LUCIUS

Ay, my lord, an 't please you.

BRUTUS

          It does, my boy:
I trouble thee too much, but thou art willing.

LUCIUS

It is my duty, sir.

I should not urge thy duty past thy might;
I know young bloods look for a time of rest.

LUCIUS

I have slept, my lord, already.

BRUTUS

It was well done; and thou shalt sleep again;
I will not hold thee long: if I do live,
I will be good to thee.   [Music, and a song
This is a sleepy tune. O murderous slumber,
Lay'st thou thy leaden mace upon my boy,
That plays thee music? Gentle knave, good night;
I will not do thee so much wrong to wake thee:
If thou dost nod, thou break'st thy instrument;
I'll take it from thee; and, good boy, good night.
Let me see, let me see; is not the leaf turn'd down
Where I left reading? Here it is, I think.   [Sits down
     Enter the GHOST OF CÆSAR
How ill this taper burns! Ha! who comes here?
I think it is the weakness of mine eyes
That shapes this monstrous apparition.
It comes upon me. Art thou any thing?
Art thou some god, some angel, or some devil,
That makest my blood cold, and my hair to stare?
Speak to me what thou art.

GHOST

Thy evil spirit, Brutus.

BRUTUS

          Why comest thou?

GHOST

To tell thee thou shalt see me at Philippi.

BRUTUS

Well; then I shall see thee again?

GHOST

Ay, at Philippi.

BRUTUS

Why, I will see thee at Philippi then.   [Exit GHOST
Now I have taken heart thou vanishest.
Ill spirit, I would hold more talk with thee.
Boy, Lucius! Varro! Claudius! Sirs, awake!
Claudius!

LUCIUS

The strings, my lord, are false.

BRUTUS

He thinks he still is at his instrument.
Lucius, awake!

LUCIUS

My lord?

BRUTUS

Didst thou dream, Lucius, that thou so criedst out?

LUCIUS

My lord, I do not know that I did cry.

BRUTUS

Yes, that thou didst: didst thou see any thing?

LUCIUS

Nothing, my lord.

BRUTUS

Sleep again, Lucius. Sirrah Claudius!
[To VARRO] Fellow thou, awake!

VARRO

My lord?

CLAUDIUS

My lord?

BRUTUS

Why did you so cry out, sirs, in your sleep?

VARRO *and* CLAUDIUS

Did we, my lord?

BRUTUS

　　　　　Ay: saw you any thing?

VARRO

No, my lord, I saw nothing.

CLAUDIUS

　　　　　Nor I, my lord.

BRUTUS

Go and commend me to my brother Cassius;
Bid him set on his powers betimes before,
And we will follow.

VARRO *and* CLAUDIUS

　　　　It shall be done, my lord.

　　　　　　　　　　　　　　　　[*Exeunt*

ACT V

SCENE I. *The plains of Philippi*

Enter OCTAVIUS, ANTONY, *and their* ARMY

OCTAVIUS

Now, Antony, our hopes are answered:
You said the enemy would not come down,
But keep the hills and upper regions;
It proves not so: their battles are at hand;
They mean to warn us at Philippi here,
Answering before we do demand of them.

ANTONY

Tut, I am in their bosoms, and I know
Wherefore they do it: they could be content
To visit other places; and come down
With fearful bravery, thinking by this face
To fasten in our thoughts that they have courage;
But 'tis not so.

Enter a MESSENGER

MESSENGER

　　　　Prepare you, generals:
The enemy comes on in gallant show;
Their bloody sign of battle is hung out,
And something to be done immediately.

ANTONY

Octavius, lead your battle softly on,
Upon the left hand of the even field.

OCTAVIUS

Upon the right hand I; keep thou the left.

ANTONY

Why do you cross me in this exigent?

OCTAVIUS

I do not cross you; but I will do so. 　[*March*
Drum. Enter BRUTUS, CASSIUS, *and their* ARMY; LUCILIUS,
TITINIUS, MESSALA, *and others*

BRUTUS

They stand, and would have parley.

CASSIUS

Stand fast, Titinius: we must out and talk.

OCTAVIUS

Mark Antony, shall we give sign of battle?

ANTONY

No, Cæsar, we will answer on their charge.
Make forth; the generals would have some words.

OCTAVIUS

Stir not until the signal.

BRUTUS

Words before blows: is it so, countrymen?

OCTAVIUS

Not that we love words better, as you do.

BRUTUS

Good words are better than bad strokes, Octavius.

ANTONY

In your bad strokes, Brutus, you give good words:
Witness the hole you made in Cæsar's heart,
Crying 'Long live! hail, Cæsar!'

CASSIUS

　　　　　　　　Antony,
The posture of your blows are yet unknown;
But for your words, they rob the Hybla bees,
And leave them honeyless.

ANTONY

　　　　　　　　Not stingless too.

BRUTUS

O, yes, and soundless too;
For you have stol'n their buzzing, Antony,
And very wisely threat before you sting.

ANTONY

Villains, you did not so, when your vile daggers
Hack'd one another in the sides of Cæsar:
You show'd your teeth like apes, and fawn'd like
　　hounds,
And bow'd like bondmen, kissing Cæsar's feet;
Whilst damned Casca, like a cur, behind
Struck Cæsar on the neck. O you flatterers!

CASSIUS

Flatterers! Now, Brutus, thank yourself:
This tongue had not offended so to-day,
If Cassius might have ruled.

OCTAVIUS

Come, come, the cause: if arguing make us sweat,
The proof of it will turn to redder drops.
Look;
I draw a sword against conspirators;
When think you that the sword goes up again?
Never, till Cæsar's three and thirty wounds
Be well avenged, or till another Cæsar
Have added slaughter to the sword of traitors.

BRUTUS

Cæsar, thou canst not die by traitors' hands,
Unless thou bring'st them with thee.

OCTAVIUS

　　　　　　　　　　　　So I hope;
I was not born to die on Brutus' sword.

BRUTUS

O, if thou wert the noblest of thy strain,
Young man, thou couldst not die more honourable.

[657]

CASSIUS

A peevish schoolboy, worthless of such honour,
Join'd with a masker and a reveller!

ANTONY

Old Cassius still!

OCTAVIUS

Come, Antony; away!
Defiance, traitors, hurl we in your teeth;
If you dare fight to-day, come to the field:
If not when you have stomachs.

[Exeunt OCTAVIUS, ANTONY, and their ARMY

CASSIUS

Why, now, blow wind, swell billow, and swim bark!
The storm is up, and all is on the hazard.

BRUTUS

Ho, Lucilius! hark, a word with you.

LUCILIUS

[Standing forth] My lord?

[BRUTUS and LUCILIUS converse apart

CASSIUS

Messala!

MESSALA

[Standing forth] What says my general?

CASSIUS

Messala,
This is my birth-day; as this very day
Was Cassius born. Give me thy hand, Messala:
Be thou my witness that, against my will,
As Pompey was, am I compell'd to set
Upon one battle all our liberties.
You know that I held Epicurus strong,
And his opinion: now I change my mind,
And partly credit things that do presage.
Coming from Sardis, on our former ensign
Two mighty eagles fell, and there they perch'd,
Gorging and feeding from our soldiers' hands;
Who to Philippi here consorted us:
This morning are they fled away and gone;
And in their steads do ravens, crows and kites
Fly o'er our heads and downward look on us,
As we were sickly prey: their shadows seem
A canopy most fatal, under which
Our army lies, ready to give up the ghost.

MESSALA

Believe not so.

CASSIUS

I but believe it partly,
For I am fresh of spirit and resolved
To meet all perils very constantly.

BRUTUS

Even so, Lucilius.

CASSIUS

Now, most noble Brutus,
The gods to-day stand friendly, that we may,
Lovers in peace, lead on our days to age!
But, since the affairs of men rest still incertain,
Let's reason with the worst that may befall.
If we do lose this battle, then is this
The very last time we shall speak together:
What are you then determined to do?

BRUTUS

Even by the rule of that philosophy
By which I did blame Cato for the death
Which he did give himself: I know not how,
But I do find it cowardly and vile,
For fear of what might fall, so to prevent
The time of life: arming myself with patience
To stay the providence of some high powers
That govern us below.

CASSIUS

Then, if we lose this battle,
You are contented to be led in triumph
Thorough the streets of Rome?

BRUTUS

No, Cassius, no: think not, thou noble Roman,
That ever Brutus will go bound to Rome;
He bears too great a mind. But this same day
Must end that work the ides of March begun;
And whether we shall meet again I know not.
Therefore our everlasting farewell take.
For ever, and for ever, farewell, Cassius!
If we do meet again, why, we shall smile;
If not, why then this parting was well made.

CASSIUS

For ever and for ever farewell, Brutus!
If we do meet again, we'll smile indeed;
If not, 'tis true this parting was well made.

BRUTUS

Why then, lead on. O, that a man might know
The end of this day's business ere it come!
But it sufficeth that the day will end,
And then the end is known. Come, ho! away!

[Exeunt

SCENE II. The field of battle

Alarum. Enter BRUTUS and MESSALA

BRUTUS

Ride, ride, Messala, ride, and give these bills
Unto the legions on the other side: [Loud alarum
Let them set on at once; for I perceive
But cold demeanour in Octavius' wing,
And sudden push gives them the overthrow.
Ride, ride, Messala: let them all come down.

[Exeunt

SCENE III. Another part of the field

Alarums. Enter CASSIUS and TITINIUS

CASSIUS

O, look, Titinius, look, the villains fly!
Myself have to mine own turn'd enemy:
This ensign here of mine was turning back;
I slew the coward, and did take it from him.

TITINIUS

O Cassius, Brutus gave the word too early;
Who, having some advantage on Octavius,
Took it too eagerly: his soldiers fell to spoil,
Whilst we by Antony are all enclosed.

Enter PINDARUS

PINDARUS

Fly further off, my lord, fly further off;
Mark Antony is in your tents, my lord:
Fly, therefore, noble Cassius, fly far off.

CASSIUS

This hill is far enough. Look, look, Titinius;
Are those my tents where I perceive the fire?

TITINIUS

They are, my lord.

CASSIUS

        Titinius, if thou lovest me,
Mount thou my horse and hide thy spurs in him,
Till he have brought thee up to yonder troops
And here again; that I may rest assured
Whether yond troops are friend or enemy.

TITINIUS

I will be here again, even with a thought.   [*Exit*

CASSIUS

Go, Pindarus, get higher on that hill;
My sight was ever thick; regard Titinius,
And tell me what thou notest about the field.
                 [PINDARUS *ascends the hill*
This day I breathed first: time is come round,
And where I did begin, there shall I end;
My life is run his compass. Sirrah, what news?

PINDARUS

[*Above*] O my lord!

CASSIUS

What news?

PINDARUS

[*Above*] Titinius is enclosed round about
With horsemen, that make to him on the spur;
Yet he spurs on. Now they are almost on him.
Now, Titinius! Now some light. O, he lights too.
He's ta'en. [*Shout*] And, hark! they shout for joy.

CASSIUS

Come down; behold no more.
O, coward that I am, to live so long,
To see my best friend ta'en before my face!

PINDARUS *descends*

Come hither, sirrah:
In Parthia did I take thee prisoner;
And then I swore thee, saving of thy life,
That whatsoever I did bid thee do,
Thou shouldst attempt it. Come now, keep thine
    oath;
Now be a freeman; and with this good sword,
That ran through Cæsar's bowels, search this bosom.
Stand not to answer: here, take thou the hilts;
And when my face is cover'd, as 'tis now,
Guide thou the sword. [PINDARUS *stabs him*] Cæsar,
    thou art revenged,
Even with the sword that kill'd thee.   [*Dies*

PINDARUS

So, I am free; yet would not so have been,
Durst I have done my will. O Cassius!
Far from this country Pindarus shall run,
Where never Roman shall take note of him.   [*Exit*

Re-enter TITINIUS *with* MESSALA

MESSALA

It is but change, Titinius; for Octavius
Is overthrown by noble Brutus' power,
As Cassius' legions are by Antony.

TITINIUS

These tidings will well comfort Cassius.

MESSALA

Where did you leave him?

TITINIUS

            All disconsolate,
With Pindarus his bondman, on this hill.

MESSALA

Is not that he that lies upon the ground?

TITINIUS

He lies not like the living. O my heart!

MESSALA

Is not that he?

TITINIUS

        No, this was he, Messala,
But Cassius is no more. O setting sun,
As in thy red rays thou dost sink to night,
So in his red blood Cassius' day is set,
The sun of Rome is set! Our day is gone;
Clouds, dews and dangers come; our deeds are
    done!
Mistrust of my success hath done this deed.

MESSALA

Mistrust of good success hath done this deed.
O hateful error, melancholy's child,
Why dost thou show to the apt thoughts of men
The things that are not? O error, soon conceived,
Thou never comest unto a happy birth,
But kill'st the mother that engender'd thee!

TITINIUS

What, Pindarus! where art thou, Pindarus?

MESSALA

Seek him, Titinius, whilst I go to meet
The noble Brutus, thrusting this report
Into his ears: I may say 'thrusting' it,
For piercing steel and darts envenomed
Shall be as welcome to the ears of Brutus
As tidings of this sight.

TITINIUS

          Hie you, Messala,
And I will seek for Pindarus the while.
                  [*Exit* MESSALA
Why didst thou send me forth, brave Cassius?
Did I not meet thy friends? and did not they
Put on my brows this wreath of victory,
And bid me give it thee? Didst thou not hear their
    shouts?
Alas, thou hast misconstrued every thing!
But, hold thee, take this garland on thy brow;
Thy Brutus bid me give it thee, and I
Will do his bidding. Brutus, come apace,
And see how I regarded Caius Cassius.
By your leave, gods: this is a Roman's part:
Come, Cassius' sword, and find Titinius' heart.
                  [*Kills himself*

Alarum. Re-enter MESSALA, *with* BRUTUS, *young* CATO, *and others*

BRUTUS
Where, where, Messala, doth his body lie?

MESSALA
Lo, yonder, and Titinius mourning it.

BRUTUS
Titinius' face is upward.

CATO
     He is slain.

BRUTUS
O Julius Cæsar, thou art mighty yet!
Thy spirit walks abroad, and turns our swords
In our own proper entrails.   [*Low alarums*

CATO
     Brave Titinius!
Look, whether he have not crown'd dead Cassius!

BRUTUS
Are yet two Romans living such as these?
The last of all the Romans, fare thee well!
It is impossible that ever Rome
Should breed thy fellow. Friends I owe moe tears
To this dead man than you shall see me pay.
I shall find time, Cassius, I shall find time.
Come therefore, and to Thasos send his body:
His funerals shall not be in our camp,
Lest it discomfort us. Lucilius, come,
And come, young Cato: let us to the field.
Labeo and Flavius, set our battles on.
'Tis three o'clock; and, Romans, yet ere night
We shall try fortune in a second fight.   [*Exeunt*

SCENE IV. *Another part of the field*

Alarum. Enter, fighting, SOLDIERS *of both armies; then*
BRUTUS, *young* CATO, LUCILIUS, *and others*

BRUTUS
Yet, countrymen, O, yet hold up your heads!

CATO
What bastard doth not? Who will go with me?
I will proclaim my name about the field.
I am the son of Marcus Cato, ho!
A foe to tyrants, and my country's friend;
I am the son of Marcus Cato, ho!

BRUTUS
And I am Brutus, Marcus Brutus, I;
Brutus, my country's friend; know me for Brutus!
     [*Exit*

LUCILIUS
O young and noble Cato, art thou down?
Why, now thou diest as bravely as Titinius,
And mayst be honour'd, being Cato's son.

FIRST SOLDIER
Yield, or thou diest.

LUCILIUS
     Only I yield to die:
[*Offering money*] There is so much that thou wilt kill
   me straight;
Kill Brutus, and be honour'd in his death.

FIRST SOLDIER
We must not. A noble prisoner!

SECOND SOLDIER
Room, ho! Tell Antony, Brutus is ta'en.

FIRST SOLDIER
I'll tell the news. Here comes the general.
Enter ANTONY
Brutus is ta'en, Brutus is ta'en, my lord.

ANTONY
Where is he?

LUCILIUS
Safe, Antony; Brutus is safe enough:
I dare assure thee that no enemy
Shall ever take alive the noble Brutus:
The gods defend him from so great a shame!
When you do find him, or alive or dead,
He will be found like Brutus, like himself.

ANTONY
This is not Brutus, friend, but, I assure you,
A prize no less in worth: keep this man safe,
Give him all kindness: I had rather have
Such men my friends than enemies. Go on,
And see whether Brutus be alive or dead,
And bring us word unto Octavius' tent
How every thing is chanced.   [*Exeunt*

SCENE V. *Another part of the field*

Enter BRUTUS, DARDANIUS, CLITUS, STRATO, *and*
VOLUMNIUS

BRUTUS
Come, poor remains of friends, rest on this rock.

CLITUS
Statilius show'd the torch-light, but, my lord,
He came not back: he is or ta'en or slain.

BRUTUS
Sit thee down, Clitus: slaying is the word;
It is a deed in fashion. Hark thee, Clitus.
     [*Whispering*

CLITUS
What, I, my lord? No, not for all the world.

BRUTUS
Peace then, no words.

CLITUS
     I'll rather kill myself.

BRUTUS
Hark thee, Dardanius.   [*Whispering*

DARDANIUS
     Shall I do such a deed?

CLITUS
O Dardanius!

DARDANIUS
O Clitus!

CLITUS
What ill request did Brutus make to thee?

DARDANIUS
To kill him, Clitus. Look, he meditates.

CLITUS

Now is that noble vessel full of grief,
That it runs over even at his eyes.

BRUTUS

Come hither, good Volumnius; list a word.

VOLUMNIUS

What says my lord?

BRUTUS

　　　　　Why, this, Volumnius:
The ghost of Cæsar hath appear'd to me
Two several times by night; at Sardis once,
And this last night here in Philippi fields:
I know my hour is come.

VOLUMNIUS

　　　　　Not so, my lord.

BRUTUS

Nay, I am sure it is, Volumnius.
Thou seest the world, Volumnius, how it goes;
Our enemies have beat us to the pit:　　[Low alarums
It is more worthy to leap in ourselves
Than tarry till they push us. Good Volumnius,
Thou know'st that we two went to school together:
Even for that our love of old, I prithee,
Hold thou my sword-hilts, whilst I run on it.

VOLUMNIUS

That's not an office for a friend, my lord.
　　　　　　　　　　　　　[Alarum still

CLITUS

Fly, fly, my lord; there is no tarrying here.

BRUTUS

Farewell to you; and you; and you, Volumnius.
Strato, thou hast been all this while asleep;
Farewell to thee too, Strato. Countrymen,
My heart doth joy that yet in all my life
I found no man but he was true to me.
I shall have glory by this losing day,
More than Octavius and Mark Antony
By this vile conquest shall attain unto.
So, fare you well at once; for Brutus' tongue
Hath almost ended his life's history:
Night hangs upon mine eyes; my bones would rest,
That have but labour'd to attain this hour.
　　　　　[Alarum. Cry within, 'Fly, fly, fly!'

CLITUS

Fly, my lord, fly.

BRUTUS

　　　　　Hence! I will follow.
　　[Exeunt CLITUS, DARDANIUS, and VOLUMNIUS
I prithee, Strato, stay thou by thy lord:
Thou art a fellow of a good respect;
Thy life hath had some smatch of honour in it:

Hold then my sword, and turn away thy face,
While I do run upon it. Wilt thou, Strato?

STRATO

Give me your hand first: fare you well, my lord.

BRUTUS

Farewell, good Strato. [Runs on his sword] Cæsar,
　　now be still:
I kill'd not thee with half so good a will.　　[Dies
Alarum. Retreat. Enter OCTAVIUS, ANTONY, MESSALA,
　　　　　LUCILIUS, and the ARMY

OCTAVIUS

What man is that?

MESSALA

My master's man. Strato, where is thy master?

STRATO

Free from the bondage you are in, Messala:
The conquerors can but make a fire of him;
For Brutus only overcame himself,
And no man else hath honour by his death.

LUCILIUS

So Brutus should be found. I thank thee, Brutus,
That thou hast proved Lucilius' saying true.

OCTAVIUS

All that served Brutus, I will entertain them.
Fellow, wilt thou bestow thy time with me?

STRATO

Ay, if Messala will prefer me to you.

OCTAVIUS

Do so, good Messala.

MESSALA

How died my master, Strato?

STRATO

I held the sword, and he did run on it.

MESSALA

Octavius, then take him to follow thee,
That did the latest service to my master.

ANTONY

This was the noblest Roman of them all:
All the conspirators, save only he,
Did that they did in envy of great Cæsar;
He only, in a general honest thought
And common good to all, made one of them.
His life was gentle, and the elements
So mix'd in him that Nature might stand up
And say to all the world 'This was a man!'

OCTAVIUS

According to his virtue let us use him,
With all respect and rites of burial.
Within my tent his bones to-night shall lie,
Most like a soldier, order'd honourably.
So call the field to rest, and let's away,
To part the glories of this happy day.　　[Exeunt

BRUTUS
Now is that noble vessel full of grief,
That it runs over even at his eyes.

BRUTUS
Come hither, good Volumnius: list a word.

VOLUMNIUS
What says my lord?

BRUTUS
Why, this, Volumnius:
The ghost of Caesar hath appear'd to me
Two several times by night; at Sardis once,
And this last night here in Philippi fields:
I know my hour is come.

VOLUMNIUS
Not so, my lord.

BRUTUS
Nay, I am sure it is, Volumnius.
Thou seest the world, Volumnius, how it goes;
Our enemies have beat us to the pit: [Low alarums]
It is more worthy to leap in ourselves,
Than tarry till they push us. Good Volumnius,
Thou know'st that we two went to school together:
Even for that our love of old, I prithee,
Hold thou my sword-hilts, whilst I run on it.

VOLUMNIUS
That's not an office for a friend, my lord.
[Alarum still]

CLITUS
Fly, fly, my lord; there is no tarrying here.

BRUTUS
Farewell to you; and you; and you, Volumnius.
Strato, thou hast been all this while asleep;
Farewell to thee too, Strato. Countrymen,
My heart doth joy that yet in all my life
I found no man but he was true to me.
I shall have glory by this losing day,
More than Octavius and Mark Antony
By this vile conquest shall attain unto.
So, fare you well at once; for Brutus' tongue
Hath almost ended his life's history:
Night hangs upon mine eyes; my bones would rest,
That have but labour'd to attain this hour.
[Alarum. Cry within, 'Fly, fly, fly!']

CLITUS
Fly, my lord, fly.

BRUTUS
Hence! I will follow.
[Exeunt CLITUS, DARDANIUS, and VOLUMNIUS]
I prithee, Strato, stay thou by thy lord:
Thou art a fellow of a good respect;
Thy life hath had some smatch of honour in it:

Hold then my sword, and turn away thy face,
While I do run upon it. Wilt thou, Strato?

STRATO
Give me your hand first. Fare you well, my lord.

BRUTUS
Farewell, good Strato. [Runs on his sword] Caesar,
now be still:
I kill'd not thee with half so good a will. [Dies]
[Alarum. Retreat. Enter OCTAVIUS, ANTONY, MESSALA,
LUCILIUS, and the army]

OCTAVIUS
What man is that?

MESSALA
My master's man. Strato, where is thy master?

STRATO
Free from the bondage you are in, Messala:
The conquerors can but make a fire of him;
For Brutus only overcame himself,
And no man else hath honour by his death.

LUCILIUS
So Brutus should be found. I thank thee, Brutus,
That thou hast proved Lucilius' saying true.

OCTAVIUS
All that served Brutus, I will entertain them.
Fellow, wilt thou bestow thy time with me?

STRATO
Ay, if Messala will prefer me to you.

OCTAVIUS
Do so, good Messala.

MESSALA
How died my master, Strato?

STRATO
I held the sword, and he did run on it.

MESSALA
Octavius, then take him to follow thee,
That did the latest service to my master.

ANTONY
This was the noblest Roman of them all:
All the conspirators save only he
Did that they did in envy of great Caesar;
He only, in a general honest thought
And common good to all, made one of them.
His life was gentle, and the elements
So mix'd in him that Nature might stand up
And say to all the world 'This was a man!'

OCTAVIUS
According to his virtue let us use him,
With all respect and rites of burial.
Within my tent his bones to-night shall lie,
Most like a soldier, order'd honourably.
So call the field to rest; and let's away,
To part the glories of this happy day. [Exeunt]

AS YOU LIKE IT

SYNOPSIS

DUKE FREDERICK is a usurper reigning over one of the great dukedoms of France from which he has dispossessed and banished his elder brother, the lawful Duke, who, with a band of loyal friends, takes refuge in the Forest of Arden where they live a carefree, rustic life like that of old Robin Hood of England.

Each brother has a daughter who is his only heir, and these girls, brought up together from infancy, are devoted to each other. Duke Frederick retains Rosalind, his niece, at his court as companion to his daughter Celia. One day they happen to see a wrestling match between the Duke's champion and an extremely young, inexperienced lad, named Orlando, who comes off victor. Duke Frederick is greatly pleased with the youth's bravery and skill until he learns that he is the son of a close friend of the former Duke, the late Sir Rowland de Boys. Rosalind, however, is delighted. She has been talking to Orlando, and a romantic attachment between the two has already developed.

Duke Frederick hears that more young noblemen are daily joining the exiles in the forest, and finding the respite from court pomp and intrigue very agreeable. His envy and malice vents itself upon his niece, because she is popular with the people who pity her. He orders her to quit the court, but Celia refuses to be left behind, so they disguise themselves and leave the palace with Touchstone, the court clown. Rosalind, who is tall, appears as a sturdy young countryman and takes the name of Ganymede, while Celia is dressed as a village maiden and is called Aliena. Having taken sufficient money, they at last reach their destination, the Forest of Arden, where they buy the house and sheep of a shepherd and establish themselves contentedly until they can locate Rosalind's father, the senior Duke.

After the wrestling match, Orlando is warned by their old family servant, Adam, that his eldest brother, who has always been cruel and unjust to him, is planning to kill him. Orlando is penniless and friendless, but Adam gives him the five hundred crowns he has saved in his long years of servitude, and begs the young man to flee with him as companion. They wander about uncertainly, finally reaching the Forest of Arden. Orlando starts off in frantic search for food for the exhausted old Adam, and, coming across the senior Duke and his company at dinner under the trees, brusquely demands some of their fare. The kindly Duke, upon learning that Orlando is the son of his beloved friend, welcomes both the travellers very heartily.

Orlando, continually pining for Rosalind, writes poems on her charms which he fastens on trees where he carves her name, to bear witness to his love. Rosalind finds these poems, and, when she meets Orlando, is dismayed because of her manly disguise, but she quickly invents a plan whereby she may see him often and test his affection. Talking to him in an arch, boyish manner, she tells him that love is merely a madness and offers to cure him. Orlando readily accepts her invitation to visit the cottage daily and talk to her as though she were really his dear Rosalind. She, on her part, seems bent only on proving to him how whimsical and shallow women are, so as to make him ashamed of his love.

One morning, Orlando finds a sleeping man in the forest and recognizes his cruel brother Oliver, whom Duke Frederick has sent out to find Orlando and bring him back. Orlando rescues him from attack by a large snake, and from a lioness, but the beast tears his arm badly. Oliver, awakening, sees his brother's struggle for his life, and is overwhelmed with shame and remorse. With tears he beseeches Orlando's forgiveness which is readily granted. Orlando is too weak from his wound to proceed to the cottage, so he sends Oliver with the news of his accident, at which Rosalind faints. Oliver and Celia fall in love with each other at first sight and Orlando arranges with the Duke for a speedy marriage, but he confesses to Rosalind how bitterly he resents his own unhappy state. Rosalind, satisfied that his devotion is strong and lasting, goes, still in her disguise as a shepherd, to the Duke, her father, and assures him that she will produce Rosalind by her secret magic on the day of the wedding, if he will consent to her marriage to Orlando. Clad again in the rich garments of her rank, she appears before her delighted father and lover, then kneels to ask the Duke's blessing.

It is a gay, eventful time for others than these two young couples, because with them are also married two pairs, Touchstone, the court clown, and a country maid, together with a young shepherd and shepherdess. As the dancing is about to start, a breathless messenger breaks in upon the party with the exciting news that Duke Frederick, while on his way with an army to exterminate the Forest of Arden colony, had met an old religious hermit who had succeeded in turning him from his purpose. Stricken with remorse, he becomes a recluse, leaving the dukedom to the rightful Duke and his followers.

HISTORICAL DATA

The plot of *As You Like It* is an adaptation of the romantic novel of Thomas Lodge, *Rosalynde, Euphues' Golden Legacie*, published in 1590, which in turn derived from the old *Tale of Gamelyn* of unknown authorship, although sometimes wrongly ascribed to Chaucer's *Cook's Tale*. In the introduction to his novel Lodge suggested the title used by Shakespeare.

Shakespeare introduced finer motives and raised the chief characters to a much higher spiritual level than appeared in the source material. In addition he created many new characters, among them "the melancholy Jaques," Audrey and Touchstone, whom Jane Lee characterizes as "the most carefully elaborated of all Shakespeare's fools."

Probably the most famous passage in the play, known as "The Seven Ages of Man," is met under various presentations in Hebrew, Greek and Roman literature.

The comedy, not included in *Palladis Tamia*, is entered on the Stationers' Register in 1600.

A line from Marlowe's *Hero and Leander* (1598) is quoted in Act III, Scene v, and on this evidence, despite the fact that Shakespeare may well have seen the line in manuscript, the date of *As You Like It* is generally considered to be 1599.

"*O Rosalind! these trees shall be my books,*"
AS YOU LIKE IT

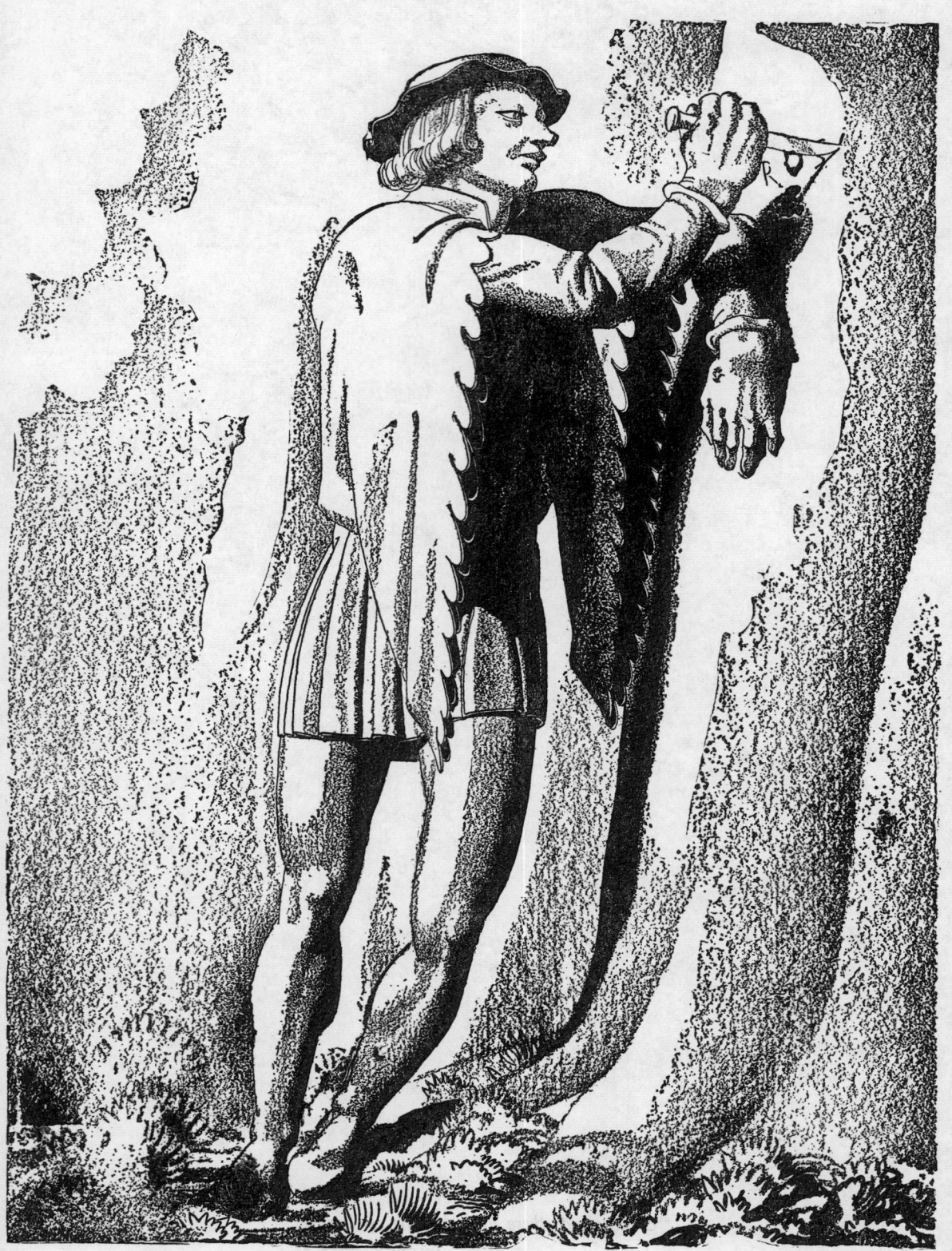

AS YOU LIKE IT

DRAMATIS PERSONÆ

DUKE, *living in banishment.*
FREDERICK, *his brother, and usurper of his dominions.*
AMIENS,
JAQUES, } *lords attending on the banished Duke.*
LE BEAU, *a courtier attending upon Frederick.*
CHARLES, *wrestler to Frederick.*
OLIVER,
JAQUES, } *sons of Sir Rowland de Boys.*
ORLANDO,
ADAM,
DENNIS, } *servants to Oliver.*
TOUCHSTONE, *a clown.*
SIR OLIVER MARTEXT, *a vicar.*

CORIN,
SILVIUS, } *shepherds.*
WILLIAM, *a country fellow, in love with Audrey.*
A person representing Hymen.

ROSALIND, *daughter to the banished Duke.*
CELIA, *daughter to Frederick.*
PHEBE, *a shepherdess.*
AUDREY, *a country wench.*

LORDS, PAGES, *and* ATTENDANTS, &c.

SCENE—*Oliver's house; Duke Frederick's court; and the Forest of Arden*

ACT I

SCENE I. *Orchard of* OLIVER's *house*

Enter ORLANDO *and* ADAM

ORLANDO

As I remember it, Adam, it was upon this fashion: bequeathed me by will but poor a thousand crowns, and, as thou sayest, charged my brother, on his blessing, to breed me well: and there begins my sadness. My brother Jaques he keeps at school, and report speaks goldenly of his profit: for my part, he keeps me rustically at home, or, to speak more properly, stays me here at home unkept; for call you that keeping for a gentleman of my birth, that differs not from the stalling of an ox? His horses are bred better; for, besides that they are fair with their feeding, they are taught their manage, and to that end riders dearly hired: but I, his brother, gain nothing under him but growth; for the which his animals on his dunghills are as much bound to him as I. Besides this nothing that he so plentifully gives me, the something that nature gave me his countenance seems to take from me: he lets me feed with his hinds, bars me the place of a brother, and, as much as in him lies, mines my gentility with my education. This is it, Adam, that grieves me; and the spirit of my father, which I think is within me, begins to mutiny against this servitude: I will no longer endure it, though yet I know no wise remedy how to avoid it.

ADAM

Yonder comes my master, your brother.

ORLANDO

Go apart, Adam, and thou shalt hear how he will shake me up.

Enter OLIVER

OLIVER

Now, sir! what make you here?

ORLANDO

Nothing: I am not taught to make any thing.

OLIVER

What mar you then, sir?

ORLANDO

Marry, sir, I am helping you to mar that which God made, a poor unworthy brother of yours, with idleness.

OLIVER

Marry, sir, be better employed, and be naught awhile.

ORLANDO

Shall I keep your hogs and eat husks with them? What prodigal portion have I spent, that I should come to such penury?

OLIVER

Know you where you are, sir?

ORLANDO

O, sir, very well; here in your orchard.

OLIVER

Know you before whom, sir?

ORLANDO

Ay, better than him I am before knows me. I know you are my eldest brother; and, in the gentle condition of blood, you should so know me. The courtesy of nations allows you my better, in that you are the first-born; but the same tradition takes not away my blood, were there twenty brothers betwixt us: I have as much of my father in me as you; albeit, I confess, your coming before me is nearer to his reverence.

OLIVER

What, boy!

ORLANDO

Come, come, elder brother, you are too young in this.

OLIVER

Wilt thou lay hands on me, villain?

ORLANDO

I am no villain; I am the youngest son of Sir Rowland de Boys; he was my father, and he is thrice a villain that says such a father begot villains. Wert thou not my brother, I would not take this hand from thy throat till this other had pulled out thy tongue for saying so: thou hast railed on thyself.

ADAM

Sweet masters, be patient: for your father's remembrance, be at accord.

OLIVER

Let me go, I say.

ORLANDO

I will not, till I please: you shall hear me. My father charged you in his will to give me good education: you have trained me like a peasant, obscuring and hiding from me all gentleman-like qualities. The spirit of my father grows strong in me, and I will no longer endure it: therefore allow me such exercises as may become a gentleman, or give me the poor allottery my father left me by testament; with that I will go buy my fortunes.

OLIVER

And what wilt thou do? beg, when that is spent? Well, sir, get you in: I will not long be troubled with you; you shall have some part of your will: I pray you, leave me.

ORLANDO

I will no further offend you than becomes me for my good.

OLIVER

Get you with him, you old dog.

ADAM

Is 'old dog' my reward? Most true, I have lost my teeth in your service. God be with my old master! he would not have spoke such a word.

[*Exeunt* ORLANDO *and* ADAM

OLIVER

Is it even so? begin you to grow upon me? I will physic your rankness, and yet give no thousand crowns neither. Holla, Dennis!

Enter DENNIS

DENNIS

Calls your worship?

OLIVER

Was not Charles, the Duke's wrestler, here to speak with me?

DENNIS

So please you, he is here at the door and importunes access to you.

OLIVER

Call him in. [*Exit* DENNIS] 'Twill be a good way; and to-morrow the wrestling is.

Enter CHARLES

CHARLES

Good morrow to your worship.

OLIVER

Good Monsieur Charles, what's the new news at the new court?

CHARLES

There's no news at the court, sir, but the old news: that is, the old Duke is banished by his younger brother the new Duke; and three or four loving lords have put themselves into voluntary exile with him, whose lands and revenues enrich the new Duke; therefore he gives them good leave to wander.

OLIVER

Can you tell if Rosalind, the Duke's daughter, be vanished with her father?

CHARLES

O, no; for the Duke's daughter, her cousin, so loves her, being ever from their cradles bred together, that she would have followed her exile, or have died to stay behind her. She is at the court, and no less beloved of her uncle than his own daughter; and never two ladies loved as they do.

OLIVER

Where will the old Duke live?

CHARLES

They say he is already in the forest of Arden, and a many merry men with him; and there they live like the old Robin Hood of England: they say many young gentlemen flock to him every day, and fleet the time carelessly, as they did in the golden world.

OLIVER

What, you wrestle to-morrow before the new Duke?

CHARLES

Marry, do I, sir; and I came to acquaint you with a matter. I am given, sir, secretly to understand that your younger brother, Orlando, hath a disposition to come in disguised against me to try a fall. To-morrow, sir, I wrestle for my credit; and he that escapes me without some broken limb shall acquit him well. Your brother is but young and tender; and, for your love, I would be loath to foil him, as I must, for my own honour, if he come in: therefore, out of my love to you, I came hither to acquaint you withal; that either you might stay him from his intendment, or brook such disgrace well as he shall run into; in that it is a thing of his own search, and altogether against my will.

OLIVER

Charles, I thank thee for thy love to me, which thou shalt find I will most kindly requite. I had myself notice of my brother's purpose herein, and have by underhand means laboured to dissuade him from it, but he is resolute. I'll tell thee, Charles:—it is the stubbornest young fellow of France; full of ambition, an envious emulator of every man's good parts, a secret and villanous contriver against me his natural brother: therefore use thy discretion; I had as lief thou didst break his neck as his finger. And thou wert best look to't; for if thou dost him any slight disgrace, or if he do not mightily grace himself on thee, he will practise against thee by poison, entrap thee by some treacherous device, and never leave thee till he hath ta'en thy life by some indirect means or other; for, I assure thee, and almost with tears I speak it, there is not one so young and so villanous this day living. I speak but brotherly of him; but should I anatomize him to thee as he is, I must blush and weep, and thou must look pale and wonder.

CHARLES

I am heartily glad I came hither to you. If he come to-morrow, I'll give him his payment: if ever he go alone again, I'll never wrestle for prize more: and so, God keep your worship!

OLIVER

Farewell, good Charles. [*Exit* CHARLES] Now will I stir this gamester: I hope I shall see an end of him; for my soul, yet I know not why, hates nothing more than he. Yet he's gentle; never schooled, and yet learned; full of noble device; of all sorts enchantingly beloved; and indeed so much in the heart of the world, and especially of my own people, who best know him, that I am altogether misprised: but it shall not be so long; this wrestler shall clear all: nothing remains but that I kindle the boy thither; which now I'll go about.   [*Exit*

SCENE II. *Lawn before the* DUKE'S *palace*

Enter ROSALIND *and* CELIA

CELIA

I pray thee, Rosalind, sweet my coz, be merry.

ROSALIND

Dear Celia, I show more mirth than I am mistress of; and would you yet I were merrier? Unless you could teach me to forget a vanished father, you must not learn me how to remember any extraordinary pleasure.

CELIA

Herein I see thou lovest me not with the full weight that I love thee. If my uncle, thy vanished father, had banished thy uncle, the Duke my father, so thou hadst been still with me, I could have taught my love to take thy father for mine: so wouldst thou, if the truth of thy love to me were so righteously tempered as mine is to thee.

ROSALIND

Well, I will forget the condition of my estate, to rejoice in yours.

CELIA

You know my father hath no child but I, nor none is like to have: and, truly, when he dies, thou shalt be his heir; for what he hath taken away from thy father perforce, I will render thee again in affection; by mine honour, I will; and when I break that oath, let me turn monster: therefore, my sweet Rose, my dear Rose, be merry.

ROSALIND

From henceforth I will, coz, and devise sports. Let me see; what think you of falling in love?

CELIA

Marry, I prithee, do, to make sport withal: but love no man in good earnest; nor no further in sport

neither, than with safety of a pure blush thou mayst in honour come off again.

ROSALIND

What shall be our sport, then?

CELIA

Let us sit and mock the good housewife Fortune from her wheel, that her gifts may henceforth be bestowed equally.

ROSALIND

I would we could do so; for her benefits are mightily misplaced; and the bountiful blind woman doth most mistake in her gifts to women.

CELIA

'Tis true; for those that she makes fair she scarce makes honest; and those that she makes honest she makes very ill-favouredly.

ROSALIND

Nay, now thou goest from Fortune's office to Nature's: Fortune reigns in gifts of the world, not in the lineaments of Nature.

Enter TOUCHSTONE

CELIA

No? when Nature hath made a fair creature, may she not by Fortune fall into the fire? Though Nature hath given us wit to flout at Fortune, hath not Fortune sent in this fool to cut off the argument?

ROSALIND

Indeed, there is Fortune too hard for Nature, when Fortune makes Nature's natural the cutter-off of Nature's wit.

CELIA

Peradventure this is not Fortune's work neither, but Nature's; who perceiveth our natural wits too dull to reason of such goddesses, and hath sent this natural for our whetstone; for always the dulness of the fool is the whetstone of the wits. How now, wit! whither wander you?

TOUCHSTONE

Mistress, you must come away to your father.

CELIA

Were you made the messenger?

TOUCHSTONE

No, by mine honour, but I was bid to come for you.

ROSALIND

Where learned you that oath, fool?

TOUCHSTONE

Of a certain knight that swore by his honour they were good pancakes, and swore by his honour the mustard was naught; now I'll stand to it, the pancakes were naught and the mustard was good, and yet was not the knight forsworn.

CELIA

How prove you that, in the great heap of your knowledge?

ROSALIND

Ay, marry, now unmuzzle your wisdom.

TOUCHSTONE

Stand you both forth now: stroke your chins, and swear by your beards that I am a knave.

CELIA

By our beards, if we had them, thou art.

TOUCHSTONE

By my knavery, if I had it, then I were; but if you swear by that that is not, you are not forsworn: no more was this knight, swearing by his honour, for he never had any; or if he had, he had sworn it away before ever he saw those pancakes or that mustard.

CELIA

Prithee, who is't that thou meanest?

TOUCHSTONE

One that old Frederick, your father, loves.

CELIA

My father's love is enough to honour him: enough! speak no more of him; you'll be whipped for taxation one of these days.

TOUCHSTONE

The more pity, that fools may not speak wisely what wise men do foolishly.

CELIA

By my troth, thou sayest true; for since the little wit that fools have was silenced, the little foolery that wise men have makes a great show. Here comes Monsieur Le Beau.

ROSALIND

With his mouth full of news.

CELIA

Which he will put on us, as pigeons feed their young.

ROSALIND

Then shall we be news-crammed.

CELIA

All the better; we shall be the more marketable.

Enter LE BEAU

Bon jour, Monsieur Le Beau: what's the news?

LE BEAU

Fair princess, you have lost much good sport.

CELIA

Sport! of what colour?

LE BEAU

What colour, madam! how shall I answer you?

ROSALIND

As wit and fortune will.

TOUCHSTONE

Or as the Destinies decrees.

CELIA

Well said: that was laid on with a trowel.

TOUCHSTONE

Nay, if I keep not my rank,—

ROSALIND

Thou losest thy old smell.

LE BEAU

You amaze me, ladies: I would have told you of good wrestling, which you have lost the sight of.

ROSALIND

Yet tell us the manner of the wrestling.

LE BEAU

I will tell you the beginning; and, if it please your ladyships, you may see the end; for the best is yet to do; and here, where you are, they are coming to perform it.

CELIA

Well, the beginning, that is dead and buried.

LE BEAU

There comes an old man and his three sons,—

CELIA

I could match this beginning with an old tale.

LE BEAU

Three proper young men, of excellent growth and presence.

ROSALIND

With bills on their necks, 'Be it known unto all men by these presents.'

LE BEAU

The eldest of the three wrestled with Charles, the Duke's wrestler; which Charles in a moment threw him, and broke three of his ribs, that there is little hope of life in him: so he served the second, and so the third. Yonder they lie; the poor old man, their father, making such pitiful dole over them that all the beholders take his part with weeping.

ROSALIND

Alas!

TOUCHSTONE

But what is the sport, monsieur, that the ladies have lost?

LE BEAU

Why, this that I speak of.

TOUCHSTONE

Thus men may grow wiser every day: it is the first time that ever I heard breaking of ribs was sport for ladies.

CELIA

Or I, I promise thee.

ROSALIND

But is there any else longs to see this broken music in his sides? is there yet another dotes upon rib-breaking? Shall we see this wrestling, cousin?

LE BEAU

You must, if you stay here; for here is the place appointed for the wrestling, and they are ready to perform it.

CELIA

Yonder, sure, they are coming: let us now stay and see it.

Flourish. Enter DUKE FREDERICK, LORDS, ORLANDO, CHARLES, *and* ATTENDANTS

DUKE FREDERICK

Come on: since the youth will not be entreated, his own peril on his forwardness.

ROSALIND

Is yonder the man?

LE BEAU

Even he, madam.

CELIA

Alas, he is too young! yet he looks successfully.

DUKE FREDERICK

How now, daughter and cousin! are you crept hither to see the wrestling?

ROSALIND

Ay, my liege, so please you give us leave.

DUKE FREDERICK

You will take little delight in it, I can tell you, there is such odds in the man. In pity of the challenger's youth I would fain dissuade him, but he will not be entreated. Speak to him, ladies; see if you can move him.

CELIA

Call him hither, good Monsieur Le Beau.

DUKE FREDERICK

Do so: I'll not be by.

LE BEAU

Monsieur the challenger, the princess calls for you.

ORLANDO

I attend them with all respect and duty.

ROSALIND

Young man, have you challenged Charles the wrestler?

ORLANDO

No, fair princess; he is the general challenger: I come but in, as others do, to try with him the strength of my youth.

CELIA

Young gentleman, your spirits are too bold for your years. You have seen cruel proof of this man's strength: if you saw yourself with your eyes, or knew yourself with your judgement, the fear of your adventure would counsel you to a more equal enterprise. We pray you, for your own sake, to embrace your own safety, and give over this attempt.

ROSALIND

Do, young sir; your reputation shall not therefore be misprised: we will make it our suit to the Duke that the wrestling might not go forward.

ORLANDO

I beseech you, punish me not with your hard thoughts; wherein I confess me much guilty, to deny so fair and excellent ladies any thing. But let your fair eyes and gentle wishes go with me to my trial: wherein if I be foiled, there is but one shamed that was never gracious; if killed, but one dead that is willing to be so: I shall do my friends no wrong, for I have none to lament me; the world no injury, for in it I have nothing: only in the world I fill up a place, which may be better supplied when I have made it empty.

ROSALIND

The little strength that I have, I would it were with you.

CELIA

And mine, to eke out hers.

ROSALIND

Fare you well: pray heaven I be deceived in you!

CELIA

Your heart's desires be with you!

CHARLES

Come, where is this young gallant that is so desirous to lie with his mother earth?

ORLANDO

Ready, sir; but his will hath in it a more modest working.

DUKE FREDERICK

You shall try but one fall.

CHARLES

No, I warrant your Grace, you shall not entreat him to a second, that have so mightily persuaded him from a first.

ORLANDO

You mean to mock me after; you should not have mocked me before: but come your ways.

ROSALIND

Now Hercules be thy speed, young man!

CELIA

I would I were invisible, to catch the strong fellow by the leg.   [They wrestle

ROSALIND

O excellent young man!

CELIA

If I had a thunderbolt in mine eye, I can tell who should down.   [Shout. CHARLES is thrown

DUKE FREDERICK

No more, no more.

ORLANDO

Yes, I beseech your Grace: I am not yet well breathed.

DUKE FREDERICK

How dost thou, Charles?

LE BEAU

He cannot speak, my lord.

DUKE FREDERICK

Bear him away. What is thy name, young man?

ORLANDO

Orlando, my liege; the youngest son of Sir Rowland de Boys.

DUKE FREDERICK

I would thou hadst been son to some man else:
The world esteem'd thy father honourable,
But I did find him still mine enemy:
Thou shouldst have better pleased me with this deed,
Hadst thou descended from another house.
But fare thee well; thou art a gallant youth:
I would thou hadst told me of another father.

[Exeunt DUKE FREDERICK, train, and LE BEAU

CELIA

Were I my father, coz, would I do this?

ORLANDO

I am more proud to be Sir Rowland's son,
His youngest son; and would not change that calling,
To be adopted heir to Frederick.

ROSALIND

My father loved Sir Rowland as his soul,
And all the world was of my father's mind:
Had I before known this young man his son,
I should have given him tears unto entreaties,
Ere he should thus have ventured.

CELIA
                              Gentle cousin,
Let us go thank him and encourage him:
My father's rough and envious disposition
Sticks me at heart. Sir, you have well deserved:
If you do keep your promises in love
But justly, as you have exceeded all promise,
Your mistress shall be happy.

ROSALIND
                              Gentleman,
[*Giving him a chain from her neck*
Wear this for me, one out of suits with fortune,
That could give more, but that her hand lacks
    means.
Shall we go, coz?

CELIA
                    Ay. Fare you well, fair gentleman.

ORLANDO
Can I not say, I thank you? My better parts
Are all thrown down, and that which here stands up
Is but a quintain, a mere lifeless block.

ROSALIND
He calls us back: my pride fell with my fortunes;
I'll ask him what he would. Did you call, sir?
Sir, you have wrestled well and overthrown
More than your enemies.

CELIA
                    Will you go, coz?

ROSALIND
Have with you. Fare you well.
                    [*Exeunt* ROSALIND *and* CELIA

ORLANDO
What passion hangs these weights upon my tongue?
I cannot speak to her, yet she urged conference.
O poor Orlando, thou art overthrown!
Or Charles or something weaker masters thee.

Re-enter LE BEAU

LE BEAU
Good sir, I do in friendship counsel you
To leave this place. Albeit you have deserved
High commendation, true applause, and love,
Yet such is now the Duke's condition,
That he misconstrues all that you have done.
The Duke is humorous: what he is, indeed,
More suits you to conceive than I to speak of.

ORLANDO
I thank you, sir: and, pray you, tell me this;
Which of the two was daughter of the Duke,
That here was at the wrestling?

LE BEAU
Neither his daughter, if we judge by manners;
But yet, indeed, the taller is his daughter:
The other is daughter to the banish'd Duke,
And here detain'd by her usurping uncle,
To keep his daughter company; whose loves
Are dearer than the natural bond of sisters.
But I can tell you that of late this Duke
Hath ta'en displeasure 'gainst his gentle niece,
Grounded upon no other argument
But that the people praise her for her virtues,

And pity her for her good father's sake;
And, on my life, his malice 'gainst the lady
Will suddenly break forth. Sir, fare you well.
Hereafter, in a better world than this,
I shall desire more love and knowledge of you.

ORLANDO
I rest much bounden to you: fare you well.
                    [*Exit* LE BEAU
Thus must I from the smoke into the smother;
From tyrant Duke unto a tyrant brother:
But heavenly Rosalind!   [*Exit*

SCENE III. *A room in the palace*

Enter CELIA *and* ROSALIND

CELIA
Why, cousin! why, Rosalind! Cupid have mercy!
not a word?

ROSALIND
Not one to throw at a dog.

CELIA
No, thy words are too precious to be cast away upon
curs; throw some of them at me; come, lame me
with reasons.

ROSALIND
Then there were two cousins laid up; when the one
should be lamed with reasons and the other mad
without any.

CELIA
But is all this for your father?

ROSALIND
No, some of it is for my child's father. O, how full of
briers is this working-day world!

CELIA
They are but burs, cousin, thrown upon thee in
holiday foolery: if we walk not in the trodden paths,
our very petticoats will catch them.

ROSALIND
I could shake them off my coat: these burs are in my
heart.

CELIA
Hem them away.

ROSALIND
I would try, if I could cry hem and have him.

CELIA
Come, come, wrestle with thy affections.

ROSALIND
O, they take the part of a better wrestler than myself!

CELIA
O, a good wish upon you! you will try in time, in
despite of a fall. But, turning these jests out of service, let us talk in good earnest: is it possible, on
such a sudden, you should fall into so strong a liking
with old Sir Rowland's youngest son?

ROSALIND
The Duke my father loved his father dearly.

CELIA
Doth it therefore ensue that you should love his son

dearly? By this kind of chase, I should hate him, for my father hated his father dearly; yet I hate not Orlando.

ROSALIND

No, faith, hate him not, for my sake.

CELIA

Why should I not? doth he not deserve well?

ROSALIND

Let me love him for that, and do you love him because I do. Look, here comes the Duke.

CELIA

With his eyes full of anger.

Enter DUKE FREDERICK, *with* LORDS

DUKE FREDERICK

Mistress, dispatch you with your safest haste
And get you from our court.

ROSALIND

Me, uncle?

DUKE FREDERICK

You, cousin:
Within these ten days if that thou be'st found
So near our public court as twenty miles,
Thou diest for it.

ROSALIND

I do beseech your Grace,
Let me the knowledge of my fault bear with me:
If with myself I hold intelligence,
Or have acquaintance with mine own desires;
If that I do not dream, or be not frantic,—
As I do trust I am not,—then, dear uncle,
Never so much as in a thought unborn
Did I offend your Highness.

DUKE FREDERICK

Thus do all traitors:
If their purgation did consist in words,
They are as innocent as grace itself:
Let it suffice thee that I trust thee not.

ROSALIND

Yet your mistrust cannot make me a traitor:
Tell me whereon the likelihood depends.

DUKE FREDERICK

Thou art thy father's daughter; there's enough.

ROSALIND

So was I when your Highness took his dukedom;
So was I when your Highness banish'd him:
Treason is not inherited, my lord;
Or, if we did derive it from our friends,
What's that to me? my father was no traitor:
Then, good my liege, mistake me not so much
To think my poverty is treacherous.

CELIA

Dear sovereign, hear me speak.

DUKE FREDERICK

Ay, Celia; we stay'd her for your sake,
Else had she with her father ranged along.

CELIA

I did not then entreat to have her stay;
It was your pleasure and your own remorse:
I was too young that time to value her;

But now I know her: if she be a traitor,
Why so am I; we still have slept together,
Rose at an instant, learn'd, play'd, eat together,
And wheresoe'er we went, like Juno's swans,
Still we went coupled and inseparable.

DUKE FREDERICK

She is too subtle for thee; and her smoothness,
Her very silence and her patience
Speak to the people, and they pity her.
Thou art a fool: she robs thee of thy name;
And thou wilt show more bright and seem more virtuous
When she is gone. Then open not thy lips:
Firm and irrevocable is my doom
Which I have pass'd upon her; she is vanish'd.

CELIA

Pronounce that sentence then on me, my liege:
I cannot live out of her company.

DUKE FREDERICK

You are a fool. You, niece, provide yourself:
If you outstay the time, upon mine honour,
And in the greatness of my word, you die.

[*Exeunt* DUKE FREDERICK *and* LORDS

CELIA

O my poor Rosalind, whither wilt thou go?
Wilt thou change fathers? I will give thee mine.
I charge thee, be not thou more grieved than I am.

ROSALIND

I have more cause.

CELIA

Thou hast not, cousin;
Prithee, be cheerful: know'st thou not, the Duke
Hath banish'd me, his daughter?

ROSALIND

That he hath not.

CELIA

No, hath not? Rosalind lacks then the love
Which teacheth thee that thou and I am one:
Shall we be sunder'd? shall we part, sweet girl?
No: let my father seek another heir.
Therefore devise with me how we may fly,
Whither to go and what to bear with us;
And do not seek to take your change upon you,
To bear your griefs yourself and leave me out;
For, by this heaven, now at our sorrows pale,
Say what thou canst, I'll go along with thee.

ROSALIND

Why, whither shall we go?

CELIA

To seek my uncle in the forest of Arden.

ROSALIND

Alas, what danger will it be to us,
Maids as we are, to travel forth so far!
Beauty provoketh thieves sooner than gold.

CELIA

I'll put myself in poor and mean attire
And with a kind of umber smirch my face;
The like do you: so shall we pass along
And never stir assailants.

ROSALIND

Were it not better,
Because that I am more than common tall,
That I did suit me all points like a man?
A gallant curtle-axe upon my thigh,
A boar-spear in my hand; and—in my heart
Lie there what hidden woman's fear there will—
We'll have a swashing and a martial outside,
As many other mannish cowards have
That do outface it with their semblances.

CELIA

What shall I call thee when thou art a man?

ROSALIND

I'll have no worse a name than Jove's own page;
And therefore look you call me Ganymede.
But what will you be call'd?

CELIA

Something that hath a reference to my state;
No longer Celia, but Aliena.

ROSALIND

But, cousin, what if we assay'd to steal
The clownish fool out of your father's court?
Would he not be a comfort to our travel?

CELIA

He'll go along o'er the wide world with me;
Leave me alone to woo him. Let's away,
And get our jewels and our wealth together;
Devise the fittest time and safest way
To hide us from pursuit that will be made
After my flight. Now go we in content
To liberty and not to banishment.   [Exeunt

ACT II

SCENE I. *The Forest of Arden*

Enter DUKE *senior,* AMIENS, *and two or three* LORDS, *like foresters*

DUKE

Now, my co-mates and brothers in exile,
Hath not old custom made this life more sweet
Than that of painted pomp? Are not these woods
More free from peril than the envious court?
Here feel we but the penalty of Adam,
The seasons' difference; as the icy fang
And churlish chiding of the winter's wind,
Which, when it bites and blows upon my body,
Even till I shrink with cold, I smile and say
'This is no flattery: these are counsellors
That feelingly persuade me what I am.'
Sweet are the uses of adversity;
Which, like the toad, ugly and venomous,
Wears yet a precious jewel in his head:
And this our life exempt from public haunt
Finds tongues in trees, books in the running brooks,
Sermons in stones and good in every thing.
I would not change it.

AMIENS

Happy is your Grace,
That can translate the stubbornness of fortune
Into so quiet and so sweet a style.

DUKE

Come, shall we go and kill us venison?
And yet it irks me the poor dappled fools,
Being native burghers of this desert city,
Should in their own confines with forked heads
Have their round haunches gored.

FIRST LORD

Indeed, my lord,
The melancholy Jaques grieves at that,
And, in that kind, swears you do more usurp
Than doth your brother that hath banish'd you.
To-day my Lord of Amiens and myself
Did steal behind him as he lay along
Under an oak whose antique root peeps out
Upon the brook that brawls along this wood:
To the which place a poor sequester'd stag,
That from the hunter's aim had ta'en a hurt,
Did come to languish, and indeed, my lord,
The wretched animal heaved forth such groans,
That their discharge did stretch his leathern coat
Almost to bursting, and the big round tears
Coursed one another down his innocent nose
In piteous chase; and thus the hairy fool,
Much marked of the melancholy Jaques,
Stood on the extremest verge of the swift brook,
Augmenting it with tears.

DUKE

But what said Jaques?
Did he not moralize this spectacle?

FIRST LORD

O, yes, into a thousand similes.
First, for his weeping into the needless stream;
'Poor deer,' quoth he, 'thou makest a testament
As worldlings do, giving thy sum of more
To that which had too much:' then, being there
    alone,
Left and abandon'd of his velvet friends;
''Tis right,' quoth he; 'thus misery doth part
The flux of company:' anon a careless herd,
Full of the pasture, jumps along by him
And never stays to greet him; 'Ay,' quoth Jaques,
'Sweep on, you fat and greasy citizens;
'Tis just the fashion: wherefore do you look
Upon that poor and broken bankrupt there?'
Thus most invectively he pierceth through
The body of the country, city, court,
Yea, and of this our life; swearing that we
Are mere usurpers, tyrants and what's worse,
To fright the animals and to kill them up
In their assign'd and native dwelling-place.

DUKE

And did you leave him in this contemplation?

SECOND LORD

We did, my lord, weeping and commenting
Upon the sobbing deer.

DUKE

Show me the place:
I love to cope him in these sullen fits,
For then he's full of matter.

FIRST LORD

I'll bring you to him straight.   [*Exeunt*

SCENE II. *A room in the palace*

Enter DUKE FREDERICK, *with* LORDS

DUKE FREDERICK

Can it be possible that no man saw them?
It cannot be: some villains of my court
Are of consent and sufferance in this.

FIRST LORD

I cannot hear of any that did see her.
The ladies, her attendants of her chamber,
Saw her a-bed, and in the morning early
They found the bed untreasured of their mistress.

SECOND LORD

My lord, the roynish clown, at whom so oft
Your Grace was wont to laugh, is also missing.
Hisperia, the princess' gentlewoman,
Confesses that she secretly o'erheard
Your daughter and her cousin much commend
The parts and graces of the wrestler
That did but lately foil the sinewy Charles;
And she believes, wherever they are gone,
That youth is surely in their company.

DUKE FREDERICK

Send to his brother; fetch that gallant hither;
If he be absent, bring his brother to me;
I'll make him find him: do this suddenly,
And let not search and inquisition quail
To bring again these foolish runaways.   [*Exeunt*

SCENE III. *Before* OLIVER'S *house*

Enter ORLANDO *and* ADAM, *meeting*

ORLANDO

Who's there?

ADAM

What, my young master? O my gentle master!
O my sweet master! O you memory
Of old Sir Rowland! why, what make you here?
Why are you virtuous? why do people love you?
And wherefore are you gentle, strong and valiant?
Why would you be so fond to overcome
The bonny priser of the humorous Duke?
Your praise is come too swiftly home before you.
Know you not, master, to some kind of men
Their graces serve them but as enemies?
No more do yours: your virtues, gentle master,
Are sanctified and holy traitors to you.
O, what a world is this, when what is comely
Envenoms him that bears it!

ORLANDO

Why, what's the matter?

ADAM

O unhappy youth!
Come not within these doors; within this roof
The enemy of all your graces lives:
Your brother—no, no brother; yet the son—
Yet not the son, I will not call him son,
Of him I was about to call his father,—
Hath heard your praises, and this night he means
To burn the lodging where you use to lie
And you within it: if he fail of that,
He will have other means to cut you off.
I overheard him and his practices.
This is no place; this house is but a butchery:
Abhor it, fear it, do not enter it.

ORLANDO

Why, whither, Adam, wouldst thou have me go?

ADAM

No matter whither, so you come not here.

ORLANDO

What, wouldst thou have me go and beg my food?
Or with a base and boisterous sword enforce
A thievish living on the common road?
This I must do, or know not what to do:
Yet this I will not do, do how I can;
I rather will subject me to the malice
Of a diverted blood and bloody brother.

ADAM

But do not so. I have five hundred crowns,
The thrifty hire I saved under your father,
Which I did store to be my foster-nurse
When service should in my old limbs lie lame,
And unregarded age in corners thrown:
Take that, and He that doth the ravens feed
Yea, providently caters for the sparrow,
Be comfort to my age! Here is the gold;
All this I give you. Let me be your servant:
Though I look old, yet I am strong and lusty;
For in my youth I never did apply
Hot and rebellious liquors in my blood,
Nor did not with unbashful forehead woo
The means of weakness and debility;
Therefore my age is as a lusty winter,
Frosty, but kindly: let me go with you;
I'll do the service of a younger man
In all your business and necessities.

ORLANDO

O good old man, how well in thee appears
The constant service of the antique world,
When service sweat for duty, not for meed!
Thou art not for the fashion of these times,
Where none will sweat but for promotion,
And having that do choke their service up
Even with the having: it is not so with thee.
But, poor old man, thou prunest a rotten tree,
That cannot so much as a blossom yield
In lieu of all thy pains and husbandry.
But come thy ways; we'll go along together,
And ere we have thy youthful wages spent,
We'll light upon some settled low content.

ADAM

Master, go on, and I will follow thee,
To the last gasp, with truth and loyalty.
From seventeen years till now almost fourscore
Here lived I, but now live here no more.
At seventeen years many their fortunes seek;
But at fourscore it is too late a week:
Yet fortune cannot recompense me better
Than to die well and not my master's debtor.

[Exeunt

SCENE IV. *The Forest of Arden*

Enter ROSALIND *for* GANYMEDE, CELIA *for* ALIENA, *and*
TOUCHSTONE

ROSALIND

O Jupiter, how weary are my spirits!

TOUCHSTONE

I care not for my spirits, if my legs were not weary.

ROSALIND

I could find in my heart to disgrace my man's apparel and to cry like a woman; but I must comfort the weaker vessel, as doublet and hose ought to show itself courageous to petticoat: therefore, courage, good Aliena.

CELIA

I pray you, bear with me; I cannot go no further.

TOUCHSTONE

For my part, I had rather bear with you than bear you: yet I should bear no cross, if I did bear you; for I think you have no money in your purse.

ROSALIND

Well, this is the forest of Arden.

TOUCHSTONE

Ay, now am I in Arden; the more fool I; when I was at home, I was in a better place: but travellers must be content.

ROSALIND

Ay, be so, good Touchstone.

Enter CORIN *and* SILVIUS

Look you, who comes here; a young man and an old in solemn talk.

CORIN

That is the way to make her scorn you still.

SILVIUS

O Corin, that thou knew'st how I do love her!

CORIN

I partly guess; for I have loved ere now.

SILVIUS

No, Corin, being old, thou canst not guess,
Though in thy youth thou wast as true a lover
As ever sigh'd upon a midnight pillow:
But if thy love were ever like to mine,—
As sure I think did never man love so,—
How many actions most ridiculous
Hast thou been drawn to by thy fantasy?

CORIN

Into a thousand that I have forgotten.

SILVIUS

O, thou didst then ne'er love so heartily!

If thou remember'st not the slightest folly
That ever love did make thee run into,
Thou hast not loved:
Or if thou hast not sat as I do now,
Wearing thy hearer in thy mistress' praise,
Thou hast not loved:
Or if thou hast not broke from company
Abruptly, as my passion now makes me,
Thou hast not loved.
O Phebe, Phebe, Phebe!   [*Exit*

ROSALIND

Alas, poor shepherd! searching of thy wound,
I have by hard adventure found mine own.

TOUCHSTONE

And I mine. I remember, when I was in love I broke my sword upon a stone and bid him take that for coming a-night to Jane Smile: and I remember the kissing of her batlet and the cow's dugs that her pretty chopt hands had milked: and I remember the wooing of a peascod instead of her; from whom I took two cods and, giving her them again, said with weeping tears 'Wear these for my sake.' We that are true lovers run into strange capers; but as all is mortal in nature, so is all nature in love mortal in folly.

ROSALIND

Thou speakest wiser than thou art ware of.

TOUCHSTONE

Nay, I shall ne'er be ware of mine own wit till I break my shins against it.

ROSALIND

Jove, Jove! this shepherd's passion
Is much upon my fashion.

TOUCHSTONE

And mine; but it grows something stale with me.

CELIA

I pray you, one of you question yon man
If he for gold will give us any food:
I faint almost to death.

TOUCHSTONE

Holla, you clown!

ROSALIND

Peace, fool: he's not thy kinsman.

CORIN

Who calls?

TOUCHSTONE

Your betters, sir.

CORIN

Else are they very wretched.

ROSALIND

Peace, I say. Good even to you, friend.

CORIN

And to you, gentle sir, and to you all.

ROSALIND

I prithee, shepherd, if that love or gold
Can in this desert place buy entertainment,
Bring us where we may rest ourselves and feed:
Here's a young maid with travel much oppress'd
And faints for succour.

CORIN

Fair sir, I pity her

And wish, for her sake more than for mine own,
My fortunes were more able to relieve her;
But I am shepherd to another man
And do not shear the fleeces that I graze:
My master is of churlish disposition
And little recks to find the way to heaven
By doing deeds of hospitality:
Besides, his cote, his flocks and bounds of feed
Are now on sale, and at our sheepcote now,
By reason of his absence, there is nothing
That you will feed on; but what is, come see,
And in my voice most welcome shall you be.

ROSALIND

What is he that shall buy his flock and pasture?

CORIN

That young swain that you saw here but erewhile,
That little cares for buying any thing.

ROSALIND

I pray thee, if it stand with honesty,
Buy thou the cottage, pasture and the flock,
And thou shalt have to pay for it of us.

CELIA

And we will mend thy wages. I like this place,
And willingly could waste my time in it.

CORIN

Assuredly the thing is to be sold:
Go with me: if you like upon report
The soil, the profit and this kind of life,
I will your very faithful feeder be
And buy it with your gold right suddenly. [Exeunt

SCENE V. *The forest*

Enter AMIENS, JAQUES, *and others*

AMIENS

SONG

Under the greenwood tree
Who loves to lie with me,
And turn his merry note
Unto the sweet bird's throat,
Come hither, come hither, come hither:
   Here shall he see
   No enemy
But winter and rough weather.

JAQUES

More, more, I prithee, more.

AMIENS

It will make you melancholy, Monsieur Jaques.

JAQUES

I thank it. More, I prithee, more. I can suck melancholy out of a song, as a weasel sucks eggs. More, I prithee, more.

AMIENS

My voice is ragged: I know I cannot please you.

JAQUES

I do not desire you to please me; I do desire you to sing. Come, more; another stanzo: call you 'em stanzos?

AMIENS

What you will, Monsieur Jaques.

JAQUES

Nay, I care not for their names; they owe me nothing. Will you sing?

AMIENS

More at your request than to please myself.

JAQUES

Well then, if ever I thank any man, I'll thank you; but that they call compliment is like the encounter of two dog-apes, and when a man thanks me heartily, methinks I have given him a penny and he renders me the beggarly thanks. Come, sing; and you that will not, hold your tongues.

AMIENS

Well, I'll end the song. Sirs, cover the while; the Duke will drink under this tree. He hath been all this day to look you.

JAQUES

And I have been all this day to avoid him. He is too disputable for my company: I think of as many matters as he; but I give heaven thanks, and make no boast of them. Come, warble, come.

SONG

Who doth ambition shun,   [*All together here*
And loves to live i' the sun,
Seeking the food he eats,
And pleased with what he gets,
Come hither, come hither, come hither:
   Here shall he see
   No enemy
But winter and rough weather.

JAQUES

I'll give you a verse to this note, that I made yesterday in despite of my invention.

AMIENS

And I'll sing it.

JAQUES

Thus it goes:—

If it do come to pass
That any man turn ass,
Leaving his wealth and ease
A stubborn will to please,
Ducdame, ducdame, ducdame:
   Here shall he see
   Gross fools as he,
And if he will come to me.

AMIENS

What's that 'ducdame'?

JAQUES

'Tis a Greek invocation, to call fools into a circle. I'll go sleep, if I can; if I cannot, I'll rail against all the first-born of Egypt.

AMIENS

And I'll go seek the Duke: his banquet is prepared.
[*Exeunt severally*

SCENE VI. *The forest*

Enter ORLANDO *and* ADAM

ADAM

Dear master, I can go no further; O, I die for food!

Here lie I down, and measure out my grave. Farewell, kind master.

ORLANDO

Why, how now, Adam! no greater heart in thee?
Live a little; comfort a little; cheer thyself a little. If
this uncouth forest yield any thing savage, I will
either be food for it or bring it for food to thee. Thy
conceit is nearer death than thy powers. For my
sake be comfortable; hold death awhile at the arm's
end: I will here be with thee presently; and if I
bring thee not something to eat, I will give thee
leave to die: but if thou diest before I come, thou
art a mocker of my labour. Well said! thou lookest
cheerly, and I'll be with thee quickly. Yet thou liest
in the bleak air: come, I will bear thee to some shelter; and thou shalt not die for lack of a dinner, if
there live any thing in this desert. Cheerly, good
Adam!   [Exeunt

SCENE VII. *The forest*

A table set out. Enter DUKE senior, AMIENS, *and* LORDS
like outlaws

DUKE

I think he be transform'd into a beast;
For I can no where find him like a man.

FIRST LORD

My lord, he is but even now gone hence:
Here was he merry, hearing of a song.

DUKE

If he, compact of jars, grow musical,
We shall have shortly discord in the spheres.
Go, seek him: tell him I would speak with him.

Enter JAQUES

FIRST LORD

He saves my labour by his own approach.

DUKE

Why, how now, monsieur! what a life is this,
That your poor friends must woo your company?
What, you look merrily!

JAQUES

A fool, a fool! I met a fool i' the forest,
A motley fool; a miserable world!
As I do live by food, I met a fool;
Who laid him down and bask'd him in the sun,
And rail'd on Lady Fortune in good terms,
In good set terms, and yet a motley fool.
'Good morrow, fool,' quoth I. 'No, sir,' quoth he,
'Call me not fool till heaven hath sent me fortune:'
And then he drew a dial from his poke,
And, looking on it with lack-lustre eye,
Says very wisely, 'It is ten o'clock:
Thus we may see,' quoth he, 'how the world wags:
'Tis but an hour ago since it was nine;
And after one hour more 'twill be eleven;
And so, from hour to hour, we ripe and ripe,
And then, from hour to hour, we rot and rot;
And thereby hangs a tale.' When I did hear
The motley fool thus moral on the time,
My lungs began to crow like chanticleer,

That fools should be so deep-contemplative;
And I did laugh sans intermission
An hour by his dial. O noble fool!
A worthy fool! Motley's the only wear.

DUKE

What fool is this?

JAQUES

O worthy fool! One that hath been a courtier,
And says, if ladies be but young and fair,
They have the gift to know it: and in his brain,
Which is as dry as the remainder biscuit
After a voyage, he hath strange places cramm'd
With observation, the which he vents
In mangled forms. O that I were a fool!
I am ambitious for a motley coat.

DUKE

Thou shalt have one.

JAQUES

                   It is my only suit;
Provided that you weed your better judgements
Of all opinion that grows rank in them
That I am wise. I must have liberty
Withal, as large a charter as the wind,
To blow on whom I please; for so fools have;
And they that are most galled with my folly,
They most must laugh. And why, sir, must they so?
The 'why' is plain as way to parish church:
He that a fool doth very wisely hit
Doth very foolishly, although he smart,
Not to seem senseless of the bob: if not,
The wise man's folly is anatomized
Even by the squandering glances of the fool.
Invest me in my motley; give me leave
To speak my mind, and I will through and through
Cleanse the foul body of the infected world,
If they will patiently receive my medicine.

DUKE

Fie on thee! I can tell what thou wouldst do.

JAQUES

What, for a counter, would I do but good?

DUKE

Most mischievous foul sin, in chiding sin:
For thou thyself hast been a libertine,
As sensual as the brutish sting itself;
And all the embossed sores and headed evils,
That thou with license of free foot hast caught,
Wouldst thou disgorge into the general world.

JAQUES

Why, who cries out on pride,
That can therein tax any private party?
Doth it not flow as hugely as the sea,
Till that the weary very means do ebb?
What woman in the city do I name,
When that I say the city-woman bears
The cost of princes on unworthy shoulders?
Who can come in and say that I mean her,
When such a one as she such is her neighbour?
Or what is he of basest function,
That says his bravery is not on my cost,
Thinking that I mean him, but therein suits

His folly to the mettle of my speech?
There then; how then? what then? Let me see
  wherein
My tongue hath wrong'd him: if it do him right,
Then he hath wrong'd himself; if he be free,
Why then my taxing like a wild-goose flies,
Unclaim'd of any man. But who comes here?

Enter ORLANDO, *with his sword drawn*

ORLANDO

Forbear, and eat no more.

JAQUES

              Why, I have eat none yet.

ORLANDO

Nor shalt not, till necessity be served.

JAQUES

Of what kind should this cock come of?

DUKE

Art thou thus bolden'd, man, by thy distress?
Or else a rude despiser of good manners,
That in civility thou seem'st so empty?

ORLANDO

You touch'd my vein at first: the thorny point
Of bare distress hath ta'en from me the show
Of smooth civility: yet am I inland bred
And know some nurture. But forbear, I say:
He dies that touches any of this fruit
Till I and my affairs are answered.

JAQUES

An you will not be answered with reason, I must
die.

DUKE

What would you have? Your gentleness shall force,
More than your force move us to gentleness.

ORLANDO

I almost die for food; and let me have it.

DUKE

Sit down and feed, and welcome to our table.

ORLANDO

Speak you so gently? Pardon me, I pray you:
I thought that all things had been savage here;
And therefore put I on the countenance
Of stern commandment. But whate'er you are
That in this desert inaccessible,
Under the shade of melancholy boughs,
Lose and neglect the creeping hours of time;
If ever you have look'd on better days,
If ever been where bells have knoll'd to church,
If ever sat at any good man's feast,
If ever from your eyelids wiped a tear
And know what 'tis to pity and be pitied,
Let gentleness my strong enforcement be:
In the which hope I blush, and hide my sword.

DUKE

True is it that we have seen better days,
And have with holy bell been knoll'd to church,
And sat at good men's feasts, and wiped our eyes
Of drops that sacred pity hath engender'd:
And therefore sit you down in gentleness
And take upon command what help we have
That to your wanting may be minister'd.

ORLANDO

Then but forbear your food a little while,
Whiles, like a doe, I go to find my fawn
And give it food. There is an old poor man,
Who after me hath many a weary step
Limp'd in pure love: till he be first sufficed,
Oppress'd with two weak evils, age and hunger,
I will not touch a bit.

DUKE

           Go find him out,
And we will nothing waste till you return.

ORLANDO

I thank ye; and be blest for your good comfort!

                          [*Exit*

DUKE

Thou seest we are not all alone unhappy:
This wide and universal theatre
Presents more woeful pageants than the scene
Wherein we play in.

JAQUES

           All the world's a stage,
And all the men and women merely players:
They have their exits and their entrances;
And one man in his time plays many parts,
His acts being seven ages. At first the infant,
Mewling and puking in the nurse's arms.
Then the whining school-boy, with his satchel
And shining morning face, creeping like snail
Unwillingly to school. And then the lover,
Sighing like furnace, with a woeful ballad
Made to his mistress' eyebrow. Then a soldier,
Full of strange oaths, and bearded like the pard,
Jealous in honour, sudden and quick in quarrel,
Seeking the bubble reputation
Even in the cannon's mouth. And then the justice,
In fair round belly with good capon lined,
With eyes severe and beard of formal cut,
Full of wise saws and modern instances;
And so he plays his part. The sixth age shifts
Into the lean and slipper'd pantaloon,
With spectacles on nose and pouch on side,
His youthful hose, well saved, a world too wide
For his shrunk shank; and his big manly voice,
Turning again toward childish treble, pipes
And whistles in his sound. Last scene of all,
That ends this strange eventful history,
Is second childishness and mere oblivion,
Sans teeth, sans eyes, sans taste, sans every thing.

Re-enter ORLANDO, *with* ADAM

DUKE

Welcome. Set down your venerable burthen,
And let him feed.

ORLANDO

I thank you most for him.

ADAM

              So had you need:
I scarce can speak to thank you for myself.

DUKE

Welcome; fall to: I will not trouble you

As yet, to question you about your fortunes.
Give us some music; and, good cousin, sing.

AMIENS

SONG

Blow, blow, thou winter wind,
Thou art not so unkind
As man's ingratitude;
Thy tooth is not so keen,
Because thou art not seen,
Although thy breath be rude.
Heigh-ho! sing, heigh-ho! unto the green holly:
Most friendship is feigning, most loving mere folly:
Then, heigh-ho, the holly!
This life is most jolly.

Freeze, freeze, thou bitter sky,
That dost not bite so nigh
As benefits forgot:
Though thou the waters warp,
Thy sting is not so sharp
As friend remember'd not.
Heigh-ho! sing, &c.

DUKE

If that you were the good Sir Rowland's son,
As you have whisper'd faithfully you were,
And as mine eye doth his effigies witness
Most truly limn'd and living in your face,
Be truly welcome hither: I am the Duke
That loved your father: the residue of your fortune,
Go to my cave and tell me. Good old man,
Thou art right welcome as thy master is.
Support him by the arm. Give me your hand,
And let me all your fortunes understand.   [Exeunt

ACT III

SCENE I. *A room in the palace*

Enter DUKE FREDERICK, LORDS, *and* OLIVER

DUKE FREDERICK

Not see him since? Sir, sir, that cannot be:
But were I not the better part made mercy,
I should not seek an absent argument
Of my revenge, thou present. But look to it:
Find out thy brother, wheresoe'er he is;
Seek him with candle; bring him dead or living
Within this twelvemonth, or turn thou no more
To seek a living in our territory.
Thy lands and all things that thou dost call thine
Worth seizure do we seize into our hands,
Till thou canst quit thee by thy brother's mouth
Of what we think against thee.

OLIVER

O that your Highness knew my heart in this!
I never loved my brother in my life.

DUKE FREDERICK

More villain thou. Well, push him out of doors;
And let my officers of such a nature
Make an extent upon his house and lands:
Do this expediently and turn him going.   [Exeunt

SCENE II. *The forest*

Enter ORLANDO, *with a paper*

ORLANDO

Hang there, my verse, in witness of my love:
And thou, thrice-crowned queen of night, survey
With thy chaste eye, from thy pale sphere above,
Thy huntress' name that my full life doth sway.
O Rosalind! these trees shall be my books
And in their barks my thoughts I'll character;
That every eye which in this forest looks
Shall see thy virtue witness'd every where.
Run, run, Orlando; carve on every tree
The fair, the chaste and unexpressive she.   [Exit

Enter CORIN *and* TOUCHSTONE

CORIN

And how like you this shepherd's life, Master
Touchstone?

TOUCHSTONE

Truly, shepherd, in respect of itself, it is a good life;
but in respect that it is a shepherd's life, it is naught.
In respect that it is solitary, I like it very well; but
in respect that it is private, it is a very vile life.
Now, in respect it is in the fields, it pleaseth me well;
but in respect it is not in the court, it is tedious. As it
is a spare life, look you, it fits my humour well; but as
there is no more plenty in it, it goes much against
my stomach. Hast any philosophy in thee, shepherd?

CORIN

No more but that I know the more one sickens the
worse at ease he is; and that he that wants money,
means and content is without three good friends;
that the property of rain is to wet and fire to burn;
that good pasture makes fat sheep, and that a great
cause of the night is lack of the sun; that he that
hath learned no wit by nature nor art may complain of good breeding or comes of a very dull kindred.

TOUCHSTONE

Such a one is a natural philosopher. Wast ever in
court, shepherd?

CORIN

No, truly.

TOUCHSTONE

Then thou art damned.

CORIN

Nay, I hope.

TOUCHSTONE

Truly, thou art damned, like an ill-roasted egg all
on one side.

CORIN

For not being at court? Your reason.

TOUCHSTONE

Why, if thou never wast at court, thou never sawest
good manners; if thou never sawest good manners,
then thy manners must be wicked; and wickedness
is sin, and sin is damnation. Thou art in a parlous
state, shepherd.

CORIN

Not a whit, Touchstone: those that are good manners at the court are as ridiculous in the country as the behaviour of the country is most mockable at the court. You told me you salute not at the court, but you kiss your hands: that courtesy would be uncleanly, if courtiers were shepherds.

TOUCHSTONE

Instance, briefly; come, instance.

CORIN

Why, we are still handling our ewes, and their fells, you know, are greasy.

TOUCHSTONE

Why, do not your courtier's hands sweat? and is not the grease of a mutton as wholesome as the sweat of a man? Shallow, shallow. A better instance, I say; come.

CORIN

Besides, our hands are hard.

TOUCHSTONE

Your lips will feel them the sooner. Shallow again. A more sounder instance, come.

CORIN

And they are often tarred over with the surgery of our sheep; and would you have us kiss tar? The courtier's hands are perfumed with civet.

TOUCHSTONE

Most shallow man! thou worms-meat, in respect of a good piece of flesh indeed! Learn of the wise, and perpend: civet is of a baser birth than tar, the very uncleanly flux of a cat. Mend the instance, shepherd.

CORIN

You have too courtly a wit for me: I'll rest.

TOUCHSTONE

Wilt thou rest damned? God help thee, shallow man! God make incision in thee! thou art raw.

CORIN

Sir, I am a true labourer: I earn that I eat, get that I wear, owe no man hate, envy no man's happiness, glad of other men's good, content with my harm, and the greatest of my pride is to see my ewes graze and my lambs suck.

TOUCHSTONE

That is another simple sin in you, to bring the ewes and the rams together and to offer to get your living by the copulation of cattle; to be bawd to a bell-wether, and to betray a she-lamb of a twelvemonth to a crooked-pated, old, cuckoldy ram, out of all reasonable match. If thou beest not damned for this, the devil himself will have no shepherds; I cannot see else how thou shouldst 'scape.

CORIN

Here comes young Master Ganymede, my new mistress's brother.

Enter ROSALIND, *with a paper, reading*

ROSALIND

From the east to western Ind,
No jewel is like Rosalind.
Her worth, being mounted on the wind,

Through all the world bears Rosalind.
All the pictures fairest lined
Are but black to Rosalind.
Let no face be kept in mind
But the fair of Rosalind.

TOUCHSTONE

I'll rhyme you so eight years together, dinners and suppers and sleeping-hours excepted: it is the right butter-women's rank to market.

ROSALIND

Out, fool!

TOUCHSTONE

For a taste:

 If a hart do lack a hind,
 Let him seek out Rosalind.
 If the cat will after kind,
 So be sure will Rosalind.
 Winter garments must be lined,
 So must slender Rosalind.
 They that reap must sheaf and bind;
 Then to cart with Rosalind.
 Sweetest nut hath sourest rind,
 Such a nut is Rosalind.
 He that sweetest rose will find,
 Must find love's prick and Rosalind.

This is the very false gallop of verses: why do you infect yourself with them?

ROSALIND

Peace, you dull fool! I found them on a tree.

TOUCHSTONE

Truly, the tree yields bad fruit.

ROSALIND

I'll graff it with you, and then I shall graff it with a medlar: then it will be the earliest fruit i' the country; for you'll be rotten ere you be half ripe, and that's the right virtue of the medlar.

TOUCHSTONE

You have said; but whether wisely or no, let the forest judge.

Enter CELIA, *with a writing*

ROSALIND

Peace!
Here comes my sister, reading: stand aside.

CELIA

[*Reads*]

 Why should this a desert be?
  For it is unpeopled? No;
 Tongues I'll hang on every tree,
  That shall civil sayings show:
 Some, how brief the life of man
  Runs his erring pilgrimage,
 That the stretching of a span
  Buckles in his sum of age;
 Some, of violated vows
  'Twixt the souls of friend and friend:
 But upon the fairest boughs,
  Or at every sentence end,
 Will I Rosalinda write,
  Teaching all that read to know
 The quintessence of every sprite
  Heaven would in little show.
 Therefore Heaven Nature charged
  That one body should be fill'd
 With all graces wide-enlarged:
  Nature presently distill'd

    Helen's cheek, but not her heart,
      Cleopatra's majesty,
    Atalanta's better part,
      Sad Lucretia's modesty.
    Thus Rosalind of many parts
      By heavenly synod was devised;
    Of many faces, eyes and hearts,
      To have the touches dearest prized.
Heaven would that she these gifts should have,
And I to live and die her slave.

ROSALIND

O most gentle pulpiter! what tedious homily of love have you wearied your parishioners withal, and never cried 'Have patience, good people'!

CELIA

How now! back, friends! Shepherd, go off a little. Go with him, sirrah.

TOUCHSTONE

Come, shepherd, let us make an honourable retreat; though not with bag and baggage, yet with scrip and scrippage. [*Exeunt* CORIN *and* TOUCHSTONE

CELIA

Didst thou hear these verses?

ROSALIND

O, yes, I heard them all, and more too; for some of them had in them more feet than the verses would bear.

CELIA

That's no matter: the feet might bear the verses.

ROSALIND

Ay, but the feet were lame and could not bear themselves without the verse and therefore stood lamely in the verse.

CELIA

But didst thou hear without wondering how thy name should be hanged and carved upon these trees?

ROSALIND

I was seven of the nine days out of the wonder before you came; for look here what I found on a palm-tree. I was never so be-rhymed since Pythagoras' time, that I was an Irish rat, which I can hardly remember.

CELIA

Trow you who hath done this?

ROSALIND

Is it a man?

CELIA

And a chain, that you once wore, about his neck. Change you colour?

ROSALIND

I prithee, who?

CELIA

O Lord, Lord! it is a hard matter for friends to meet; but mountains may be removed with earthquakes and so encounter.

ROSALIND

Nay, but who is it?

CELIA

Is it possible?

ROSALIND

Nay, I prithee now with most petitionary vehemence, tell me who it is.

CELIA

O wonderful, wonderful, and most wonderful wonderful! and yet again wonderful, and after that, out of all hooping!

ROSALIND

Good my complexion! dost thou think, though I am caparisoned like a man, I have a doublet and hose in my disposition? One inch of delay more is a South-sea of discovery; I prithee, tell me who is it quickly, and speak apace. I would thou couldst stammer, that thou mightst pour this concealed man out of thy mouth, as wine comes out of a narrow-mouthed bottle, either too much at once, or none at all. I prithee, take the cork out of thy mouth that I may drink thy tidings.

CELIA

So you may put a man in your belly.

ROSALIND

Is he of God's making? What manner of man? Is his head worth a hat? or his chin worth a beard?

CELIA

Nay, he hath but a little beard.

ROSALIND

Why, God will send more, if the man will be thankful: let me stay the growth of his beard, if thou delay me not the knowledge of his chin.

CELIA

It is young Orlando, that tripped up the wrestler's heels and your heart both in an instant.

ROSALIND

Nay, but the devil take mocking: speak sad brow and true maid.

CELIA

I'faith, coz, 'tis he.

ROSALIND

Orlando?

CELIA

Orlando.

ROSALIND

Alas the day! what shall I do with my doublet and hose? What did he when thou sawest him? What said he? How looked he? Wherein went he? What makes he here? Did he ask for me? Where remains he? How parted he with thee? and when shalt thou see him again? Answer me in one word.

CELIA

You must borrow me Gargantua's mouth first: 'tis a word too great for any mouth of this age's size. To say ay and no to these particulars is more than to answer in a catechism.

ROSALIND

But doth he know that I am in this forest and in man's apparel? Looks he as freshly as he did the day he wrestled?

CELIA

It is as easy to count atomies as to resolve the propositions of a lover; but take a taste of my finding

him, and relish it with good observance. I found
him under a tree, like a dropped acorn.

ROSALIND

It may well be called Jove's tree, when it drops forth
such fruit.

CELIA

Give me audience, good madam.

ROSALIND

Proceed.

CELIA

There lay he, stretched along, like a wounded
knight.

ROSALIND

Though it be pity to see such a sight, it well becomes the ground.

CELIA

Cry 'holla' to thy tongue, I prithee; it curvets unseasonably. He was furnished like a hunter.

ROSALIND

O, ominous! he comes to kill my heart.

CELIA

I would sing my song without a burden: thou bringest me out of tune.

ROSALIND

Do you not know I am a woman? when I think, I
must speak. Sweet, say on.

CELIA

You bring me out. Soft! comes he not here?

Enter ORLANDO *and* JAQUES

ROSALIND

'Tis he: slink by, and note him.

JAQUES

I thank you for your company; but, good faith, I
had as lief have been myself alone.

ORLANDO

And so had I; but yet, for fashion sake, I thank you
too for your society.

JAQUES

God buy you: let's meet as little as we can.

ORLANDO

I do desire we may be better strangers.

JAQUES

I pray you, mar no more trees with writing love-
songs in their barks.

ORLANDO

I pray you, mar no moe of my verses with reading
them ill-favouredly.

JAQUES

Rosalind is your love's name?

ORLANDO

Yes, just.

JAQUES

I do not like her name.

ORLANDO

There was no thought of pleasing you when she was
christened.

JAQUES

What stature is she of?

ORLANDO

Just as high as my heart.

JAQUES

You are full of pretty answers. Have you not been
acquainted with goldsmiths' wives, and conned
them out of rings?

ORLANDO

Not so; but I answer you right painted cloth, from
whence you have studied your questions.

JAQUES

You have a nimble wit: I think 'twas made of Ata-
lanta's heels. Will you sit down with me? and we
two will rail against our mistress the world, and all
our misery.

ORLANDO

I will chide no breather in the world but myself,
against whom I know most faults.

JAQUES

The worst fault you have is to be in love.

ORLANDO

'Tis a fault I will not change for your best virtue.
I am weary of you.

JAQUES

By my troth, I was seeking for a fool when I found
you.

ORLANDO

He is drowned in the brook: look but in, and you
shall see him.

JAQUES

There I shall see mine own figure.

ORLANDO

Which I take to be either a fool or a cipher.

JAQUES

I'll tarry no longer with you: farewell, good Signior
Love.

ORLANDO

I am glad of your departure: adieu, good Monsieur
Melancholy.　　　　　　　　　　　[*Exit* JAQUES

ROSALIND

[*Aside to* CELIA] I will speak to him like a saucy
lackey, and under that habit play the knave with
him. Do you hear, forester?

ORLANDO

Very well: what would you?

ROSALIND

I pray you, what is't o' clock?

ORLANDO

You should ask me what time o' day: there's no
clock in the forest.

ROSALIND

Then there is no true lover in the forest; else sighing
every minute and groaning every hour would detect the lazy foot of Time as well as a clock.

ORLANDO

And why not the swift foot of Time? had not that
been as proper?

ROSALIND

By no means, sir: Time travels in divers paces with
divers persons. I'll tell you who Time ambles withal,
who Time trots withal, who Time gallops withal
and who he stands still withal.

ORLANDO

I prithee, who doth he trot withal?

ROSALIND

Marry, he trots hard with a young maid between the contract of her marriage and the day it is solemnized: if the interim be but a se'nnight, Time's pace is so hard that it seems the length of seven year.

ORLANDO

Who ambles Time withal?

ROSALIND

With a priest that lacks Latin, and a rich man that hath not the gout; for the one sleeps easily because he cannot study, and the other lives merrily because he feels no pain; the one lacking the burden of lean and wasteful learning, the other knowing no burden of heavy tedious penury: these Time ambles withal.

ORLANDO

Who doth he gallop withal?

ROSALIND

With a thief to the gallows; for though he go as softly as foot can fall, he thinks himself too soon there.

ORLANDO

Who stays it still withal?

ROSALIND

With lawyers in the vacation; for they sleep between term and term and then they perceive not how Time moves.

ORLANDO

Where dwell you, pretty youth?

ROSALIND

With this shepherdess, my sister: here in the skirts of the forest, like fringe upon a petticoat.

ORLANDO

Are you native of this place?

ROSALIND

As the cony that you see dwell where she is kindled.

ORLANDO

Your accent is something finer than you could purchase in so removed a dwelling.

ROSALIND

I have been told so of many: but indeed an old religious uncle of mine taught me to speak, who was in his youth an inland man; one that knew courtship too well, for there he fell in love. I have heard him read many lectures against it, and I thank God I am not a woman, to be touched with so many giddy offences as he hath generally taxed their whole sex withal.

ORLANDO

Can you remember any of the principal evils that he laid to the charge of women?

ROSALIND

There were none principal; they were all like one another as half-pence are, every one fault seeming monstrous till his fellow-fault came to match it.

ORLANDO

I prithee, recount some of them.

ROSALIND

No, I will not cast away my physic but on those that

are sick. There is a man haunts the forest, that abuses our young plants with carving Rosalind on their barks; hangs odes upon hawthorns and elegies on brambles; all, forsooth, deifying the name of Rosalind: if I could meet that fancy-monger, I would give him some good counsel, for he seems to have the quotidian of love upon him.

ORLANDO

I am he that is so love-shaked: I pray you, tell me your remedy.

ROSALIND

There is none of my uncle's marks upon you: he taught me how to know a man in love; in which cage of rushes I am sure you are not prisoner.

ORLANDO

What were his marks?

ROSALIND

A lean cheek, which you have not; a blue eye and sunken, which you have not; an unquestionable spirit, which you have not; a beard neglected, which you have not; but I pardon you for that, for simply your having in beard is a younger brother's revenue: then your hose should be ungartered, your bonnet unbanded, your sleeve unbuttoned, your shoe untied and every thing about you demonstrating a careless desolation; but you are no such man; you are rather point-device in your accoutrements, as loving yourself than seeming the lover of any other.

ORLANDO

Fair youth, I would I could make thee believe I love.

ROSALIND

Me believe it! you may as soon make her that you love believe it; which, I warrant, she is apter to do than to confess she does: that is one of the points in the which women still give the lie to their consciences. But, in good sooth, are you he that hangs the verses on the trees, wherein Rosalind is so admired?

ORLANDO

I swear to thee, youth, by the white hand of Rosalind, I am that he, that unfortunate he.

ROSALIND

But are you so much in love as your rhymes speak?

ORLANDO

Neither rhyme nor reason can express how much.

ROSALIND

Love is merely a madness; and, I tell you, deserves as well a dark house and a whip as madmen do: and the reason why they are not so punished and cured is, that the lunacy is so ordinary that the whippers are in love too. Yet I profess curing it by counsel.

ORLANDO

Did you ever cure any so?

ROSALIND

Yes, one, and in this manner. He was to imagine me his love, his mistress; and I set him every day to woo me: at which time would I, being but a moonish youth, grieve, be effeminate, changeable, longing and liking; proud, fantastical, apish, shallow, inconstant, full of tears, full of smiles; for every passion something and for no passion truly any thing, as boys and women are for the most part cattle of this colour: would now like him, now loathe him; then entertain him, then forswear him; now weep for him, then spit at him; that I drave my suitor from his mad humour of love to a living humour of madness; which was, to forswear the full stream of the world and to live in a nook merely monastic. And thus I cured him; and this way will I take upon me to wash your liver as clean as a sound sheep's heart, that there shall not be one spot of love in't.

ORLANDO
I would not be cured, youth.

ROSALIND
I would cure you, if you would but call me Rosalind and come every day to my cote and woo me.

ORLANDO
Now, by the faith of my love, I will: tell me where it is.

ROSALIND
Go with me to it and I'll show it you: and by the way you shall tell me where in the forest you live. Will you go?

ORLANDO
With all my heart, good youth.

ROSALIND
Nay, you must call me Rosalind. Come, sister, will you go?   [Exeunt

SCENE III. *The forest*

Enter TOUCHSTONE *and* AUDREY; JAQUES *behind*

TOUCHSTONE
Come apace, good Audrey: I will fetch up your goats, Audrey. And how, Audrey? am I the man yet? doth my simple feature content you?

AUDREY
Your features! Lord warrant us! what features?

TOUCHSTONE
I am here with thee and thy goats, as the most capricious poet, honest Ovid, was among the Goths.

JAQUES
[*Aside*] O knowledge ill-inhabited, worse than Jove in a thatched house!

TOUCHSTONE
When a man's verses cannot be understood, nor a man's good wit seconded with the forward child, understanding, it strikes a man more dead than a great reckoning in a little room. Truly, I would the gods had made thee poetical.

AUDREY
I do not know what 'poetical' is: is it honest in deed and word? is it a true thing?

TOUCHSTONE
No, truly; for the truest poetry is the most feigning; and lovers are given to poetry, and what they swear in poetry may be said as lovers they do feign.

AUDREY
Do you wish then that the gods had made me poetical?

TOUCHSTONE
I do, truly; for thou swearest to me thou art honest: now, if thou wert a poet, I might have some hope thou didst feign.

AUDREY
Would you not have me honest?

TOUCHSTONE
No, truly, unless thou wert hard-favoured; for honesty coupled to beauty is to have honey a sauce to sugar.

JAQUES
[*Aside*] A material fool!

AUDREY
Well, I am not fair; and therefore I pray the gods make me honest.

TOUCHSTONE
Truly, and to cast away honesty upon a foul slut were to put good meat into an unclean dish.

AUDREY
I am not a slut, though I thank the gods I am foul.

TOUCHSTONE
Well, praised be the gods for thy foulness! sluttishness may come hereafter. But be it as it may be, I will marry thee, and to that end I have been with Sir Oliver Martext the vicar of the next village, who hath promised to meet me in this place of the forest and to couple us.

JAQUES
[*Aside*] I would fain see this meeting.

AUDREY
Well, the gods give us joy!

TOUCHSTONE
Amen. A man may, if he were of a fearful heart, stagger in this attempt; for here we have no temple but the wood, no assembly but horn-beasts. But what though? Courage! As horns are odious, they are necessary. It is said, 'many a man knows no end of his goods:' right; many a man has good horns, and knows no end of them. Well, that is the dowry of his wife; 'tis none of his own getting. Horns?—even so:—poor men alone? No, no; the noblest deer hath them as huge as the rascal. Is the single man therefore blessed? No: as a walled town is more worthier than a village, so is the forehead of a married man more honourable than the bare brow of a bachelor; and by how much defence is better than no skill, by so much is a horn more precious than to want. Here comes Sir Oliver.

Enter SIR OLIVER MARTEXT

Sir Oliver Martext, you are well met: will you dispatch us here under this tree, or shall we go with you to your chapel?

SIR OLIVER
Is there none here to give the woman?

TOUCHSTONE
I will not take her on gift of any man.

SIR OLIVER

Truly, she must be given, or the marriage is not lawful.

JAQUES

Proceed, proceed: I'll give her.

TOUCHSTONE

Good even, good Master What-ye-call't: how do you, sir? You are very well met: God 'ild you for your last company: I am very glad to see you: even a toy in hand here, sir: nay, pray be covered.

JAQUES

Will you be married, motley?

TOUCHSTONE

As the ox hath his bow, sir, the horse his curb and the falcon her bells, so man hath his desires; and as pigeons bill, so wedlock would be nibbling.

JAQUES

And will you, being a man of your breeding, be married under a bush like a beggar? Get you to church, and have a good priest that can tell you what marriage is: this fellow will but join you together as they join wainscot; then one of you will prove a shrunk panel, and like green timber warp, warp.

TOUCHSTONE

[Aside] I am not in the mind but I were better to be married of him than of another: for he is not like to marry me well; and not being well married, it will be a good excuse for me hereafter to leave my wife.

JAQUES

Go thou with me, and let me counsel thee.

TOUCHSTONE

Come, sweet Audrey:
We must be married, or we must live in bawdry.
Farewell, good Master Oliver: not,—

    O sweet Oliver,
    O brave Oliver,
    Leave me not behind thee:

but,—

    Wind away,
    Begone, I say,
    I will not to wedding with thee.

[*Exeunt* JAQUES, TOUCHSTONE *and* AUDREY

SIR OLIVER

'Tis no matter: ne'er a fantastical knave of them all shall flout me out of my calling.   [*Exit*

SCENE IV. *The forest*

Enter ROSALIND *and* CELIA

ROSALIND

Never talk to me; I will weep.

CELIA

Do, I prithee; but yet have the grace to consider that tears do not become a man.

ROSALIND

But have I not cause to weep?

CELIA

As good cause as one would desire; therefore weep.

ROSALIND

His very hair is of the dissembling colour.

CELIA

Something browner than Judas's: marry, his kisses are Judas's own children.

ROSALIND

I'faith, his hair is of a good colour.

CELIA

An excellent colour: your chestnut was ever the only colour.

ROSALIND

And his kissing is as full of sanctity as the touch of holy bread.

CELIA

He hath bought a pair of cast lips of Diana: a nun of winter's sisterhood kisses not more religiously; the very ice of chastity is in them.

ROSALIND

But why did he swear he would come this morning, and comes not?

CELIA

Nay, certainly, there is no truth in him.

ROSALIND

Do you think so?

CELIA

Yes; I think he is not a pick-purse nor a horse-stealer; but for his verity in love, I do think him as concave as a covered goblet or a worm-eaten nut.

ROSALIND

Not true in love?

CELIA

Yes, when he is in; but I think he is not in.

ROSALIND

You have heard him swear downright he was.

CELIA

'Was' is not 'is': besides, the oath of a lover is no stronger than the word of a tapster; they are both the confirmer of false reckonings. He attends here in the forest on the Duke your father.

ROSALIND

I met the Duke yesterday and had much question with him: he asked me of what parentage I was; I told him, of as good as he; so he laughed and let me go. But what talk we of fathers, when there is such a man as Orlando?

CELIA

O, that's a brave man! he writes brave verses, speaks brave words, swears brave oaths and breaks them bravely, quite traverse, athwart the heart of his lover; as a puisny tilter, that spurs his horse but on one side, breaks his staff like a noble goose: but all's brave that youth mounts and folly guides. Who comes here?

Enter CORIN

CORIN

Mistress and master, you have oft inquired
After the shepherd that complain'd of love,
Who you saw sitting by me on the turf,
Praising the proud disdainful shepherdess
That was his mistress.

CELIA

Well, and what of him?

CORIN

If you will see a pageant truly play'd,
Between the pale complexion of true love
And the red glow of scorn and proud disdain,
Go hence a little and I shall conduct you,
If you will mark it.

ROSALIND

O, come, let us remove:
The sight of lovers feedeth those in love.
Bring us to this sight, and you shall say
I'll prove a busy actor in their play.   [*Exeunt*

SCENE V. *Another part of the forest*

Enter SILVIUS *and* PHEBE

SILVIUS

Sweet Phebe, do not scorn me; do not, Phebe;
Say that you love me not, but say not so
In bitterness. The common executioner,
Whose heart the accustom'd sight of death makes
    hard,
Falls not the axe upon the humbled neck
But first begs pardon: will you sterner be
Than he that dies and lives by bloody drops?

Enter ROSALIND, CELIA, *and* CORIN, *behind*

PHEBE

I would not be thy executioner:
I fly thee, for I would not injure thee.
Thou tell'st me there is murder in mine eye:
'Tis pretty, sure, and very probable,
That eyes, that are the frail'st and softest things,
Who shut their coward gates on atomies,
Should be call'd tyrants, butchers, murderers!
Now I do frown on thee with all my heart;
And if mine eyes can wound, now let them kill thee:
Now counterfeit to swoon; why now fall down;
Or if thou canst not, O, for shame, for shame,
Lie not, to say mine eyes are murderers!
Now show the wound mine eye hath made in thee:
Scratch thee but with a pin, and there remains
Some scar of it; lean but upon a rush,
The cicatrice and capable impressure
Thy palm some moment keeps; but now mine eyes,
Which I have darted at thee, hurt thee not,
Nor, I am sure, there is no force in eyes
That can do hurt.

SILVIUS

O dear Phebe,
If ever,—as that ever may be near,—
You meet in some fresh cheek the power of fancy,
Then shall you know the wounds invisible
That love's keen arrows make.

PHEBE

But till that time
Come not thou near me: and when that time comes,
Afflict me with thy mocks, pity me not;
As till that time I shall not pity thee.

ROSALIND

And why, I pray you? Who might be your mother,
That you insult, exult, and all at once,
Over the wretched? What though you have no
    beauty,—
As, by my faith, I see no more in you
Than without candle may go dark to bed,—
Must you be therefore proud and pitiless?
Why, what means this? Why do you look on me?
I see no more in you than in the ordinary
Of nature's sale-work. 'Od's my little life,
I think she means to tangle my eyes too!
No, faith, proud mistress, hope not after it:
'Tis not your inky brows, your black silk hair,
Your bugle eyeballs, nor your cheek of cream,
That can entame my spirits to your worship.
You foolish shepherd, wherefore do you follow her,
Like foggy south, puffing with wind and rain?
You are a thousand times a properer man
Than she a woman: 'tis such fools as you
That makes the world full of ill-favour'd children:
'Tis not her glass, but you, that flatters her;
And out of you she sees herself more proper
Than any of her lineaments can show her.
But, mistress, know yourself: down on your knees,
And thank heaven, fasting, for a good man's love:
For I must tell you friendly in your ear,
Sell when you can: you are not for all markets:
Cry the man mercy; love him; take his offer:
Foul is most foul, being foul to be a scoffer.
So take her to thee, shepherd: fare you well.

PHEBE

Sweet youth, I pray you, chide a year together:
I had rather hear you chide than this man woo.

ROSALIND

He's fallen in love with your foulness and she'll fall
in love with my anger. If it be so, as fast as she answers thee with frowning looks, I'll sauce her with
bitter words. Why look you so upon me?

PHEBE

For no ill will I bear you.

ROSALIND

I pray you, do not fall in love with me,
For I am falser than vows made in wine:
Besides, I like you not. If you will know my house,
'Tis at the tuft of olives here hard by.
Will you go, sister? Shepherd, ply her hard.
Come, sister. Shepherdess, look on him better,
And be not proud: though all the world could see,
None could be so abused in sight as he.
Come, to our flock.

    [*Exeunt* ROSALIND, CELIA *and* CORIN

PHEBE

Dead shepherd, now I find thy saw of might,
'Who ever loved that loved not at first sight?'

SILVIUS

Sweet Phebe,—

PHEBE

Ha, what say'st thou, Silvius?

[685]

SILVIUS

Sweet Phebe, pity me.

PHEBE

Why, I am sorry for thee, gentle Silvius.

SILVIUS

Wherever sorrow is, relief would be:
If you do sorrow at my grief in love,
By giving love your sorrow and my grief
Were both extermined.

PHEBE

Thou hast my love: is not that neighbourly?

SILVIUS

I would have you.

PHEBE

Why, that were covetousness.
Silvius, the time was that I hated thee,
And yet it is not that I bear thee love;
But since that thou canst talk of love so well,
Thy company, which erst was irksome to me,
I will endure, and I'll employ thee too:
But do not look for further recompense
Than thine own gladness that thou art employ'd.

SILVIUS

So holy and so perfect is my love,
And I in such a poverty of grace,
That I shall think it a most plenteous crop
To glean the broken ears after the man
That the main harvest reaps: loose now and then
A scatter'd smile, and that I'll live upon.

PHEBE

Know'st thou the youth that spoke to me ere-while?

SILVIUS

Not very well, but I have met him oft;
And he hath bought the cottage and the bounds
That the old carlot once was master of.

PHEBE

Think not I love him, though I ask for him;
'Tis but a peevish boy; yet he talks well;
But what care I for words? yet words do well
When he that speaks them pleases those that hear.
It is a pretty youth: not very pretty:
But, sure, he's proud, and yet his pride becomes
 him:
He'll make a proper man: the best thing in him
Is his complexion; and faster than his tongue
Did make offence his eye did heal it up.
He is not very tall; yet for his years he's tall:
His leg is but so so; and yet 'tis well:
There was a pretty redness in his lip,
A little riper and more lusty red
Than that mix'd in his cheek; 'twas just the differ-
 ence
Betwixt the constant red and mingled damask.
There be some women, Silvius, had they mark'd
 him
In parcels as I did, would have gone near
To fall in love with him: but, for my part,
I love him not nor hate him not; and yet
I have more cause to hate him than to love him:
For what had he to do to chide at me?

He said mine eyes were black and my hair black;
And, now I am remember'd, scorn'd at me:
I marvel why I answer'd not again:
But that's all one; omittance is no quittance.
I'll write to him a very taunting letter,
And thou shalt bear it: wilt thou, Silvius?

SILVIUS

Phebe, with all my heart.

PHEBE

    I'll write it straight;
The matter's in my head and in my heart:
I will be bitter with him and passing short.
Go with me, Silvius.   [Exeunt

ACT IV

SCENE I. *The forest*

Enter ROSALIND, CELIA, *and* JAQUES

JAQUES

I prithee, pretty youth, let me be better acquainted
with thee.

ROSALIND

They say you are a melancholy fellow.

JAQUES

I am so; I do love it better than laughing.

ROSALIND

Those that are in extremity of either are abominable fellows, and betray themselves to every modern censure worse than drunkards.

JAQUES

Why, 'tis good to be sad and say nothing.

ROSALIND

Why then, 'tis good to be a post.

JAQUES

I have neither the scholar's melancholy, which is
emulation; nor the musician's, which is fantastical;
nor the courtier's, which is proud; nor the soldier's,
which is ambitious; nor the lawyer's, which is politic; nor the lady's, which is nice; nor the lover's,
which is all these: but it is a melancholy of mine
own, compounded of many simples, extracted from
many objects; and indeed the sundry contemplation
of my travels, in which my often rumination wraps
me in a most humorous sadness.

ROSALIND

A traveller! By my faith, you have great reason to
be sad: I fear you have sold your own lands to see
other men's; then, to have seen much, and to have
nothing, is to have rich eyes and poor hands.

JAQUES

Yes, I have gained my experience.

ROSALIND

And your experience makes you sad: I had rather
have a fool to make me merry than experience to
make me sad; and to travel for it too!

Enter ORLANDO

ORLANDO

Good day and happiness, dear Rosalind!

JAQUES
Nay, then, God buy you, an you talk in blank verse.
[*Exit*

ROSALIND
Farewell, Monsieur Traveller: look you lisp and wear strange suits; disable all the benefits of your own country; be out of love with your nativity and almost chide God for making you that countenance you are; or I will scarce think you have swam in a gondola. Why, how now, Orlando! where have you been all this while? You a lover! An you serve me such another trick, never come in my sight more.

ORLANDO
My fair Rosalind, I come within an hour of my promise.

ROSALIND
Break an hour's promise in love! He that will divide a minute into a thousand parts, and break but a part of the thousandth part of a minute in the affairs of love, it may be said of him that Cupid hath clapped him o' the shoulder, but I'll warrant him heart-whole.

ORLANDO
Pardon me, dear Rosalind.

ROSALIND
Nay, an you be so tardy, come no more in my sight: I had as lief be wooed of a snail.

ORLANDO
Of a snail?

ROSALIND
Ay, of a snail; for though he comes slowly, he carries his house on his head; a better jointure, I think, than you make a woman: besides, he brings his destiny with him.

ORLANDO
What's that?

ROSALIND
Why, horns, which such as you are fain to be beholding to your wives for: but he comes armed in his fortune and prevents the slander of his wife.

ORLANDO
Virtue is no horn-maker; and my Rosalind is virtuous.

ROSALIND
And I am your Rosalind.

CELIA
It pleases him to call you so; but he hath a Rosalind of a better leer than you.

ROSALIND
Come, woo me, woo me; for now I am in a holiday humour and like enough to consent. What would you say to me now, an I were your very very Rosalind?

ORLANDO
I would kiss before I spoke.

ROSALIND
Nay, you were better speak first; and when you were gravelled for lack of matter, you might take occasion to kiss. Very good orators, when they are

out, they will spit; and for lovers lacking—God warn us!—matter, the cleanliest shift is to kiss.

ORLANDO
How if the kiss be denied?

ROSALIND
Then she puts you to entreaty and there begins new matter.

ORLANDO
Who could be out, being before his beloved mistress?

ROSALIND
Marry, that should you, if I were your mistress, or I should think my honesty ranker than my wit.

ORLANDO
What, of my suit?

ROSALIND
Not out of your apparel, and yet out of your suit. Am not I your Rosalind?

ORLANDO
I take some joy to say you are, because I would be talking of her.

ROSALIND
Well, in her person, I say I will not have you.

ORLANDO
Then in mine own person I die.

ROSALIND
No, faith, die by attorney. The poor world is almost six thousand years old, and in all this time there was not any man died in his own person, videlicet, in a love-cause. Troilus had his brains dashed out with a Grecian club; yet he did what he could to die before, and he is one of the patterns of love. Leander, he would have lived many a fair year, though Hero had turned nun, if it had not been for a hot midsummer night; for, good youth, he went but forth to wash him in the Hellespont and being taken with the cramp was drowned: and the foolish chroniclers of that age found it was 'Hero of Sestos.' But these are all lies: men have died from time to time and worms have eaten them, but not for love.

ORLANDO
I would not have my right Rosalind of this mind; for, I protest, her frown might kill me.

ROSALIND
By this hand, it will not kill a fly. But come, now I will be your Rosalind in a more coming-on disposition, and ask me what you will, I will grant it.

ORLANDO
Then love me, Rosalind.

ROSALIND
Yes, faith, will I, Fridays and Saturdays and all.

ORLANDO
And wilt thou have me?

ROSALIND
Ay, and twenty such.

ORLANDO
What sayest thou?

ROSALIND
Are you not good?

ORLANDO

I hope so.

ROSALIND

Why then, can one desire too much of a good thing? Come, sister, you shall be the priest and marry us. Give me your hand, Orlando. What do you say, sister?

ORLANDO

Pray thee, marry us.

CELIA

I cannot say the words.

ROSALIND

You must begin, 'Will you, Orlando—'

CELIA

Go to. Will you, Orlando, have to wife this Rosalind?

ORLANDO

I will.

ROSALIND

Ay, but when?

ORLANDO

Why now; as fast as she can marry us.

ROSALIND

Then you must say 'I take thee, Rosalind, for wife.'

ORLANDO

I take thee, Rosalind, for wife.

ROSALIND

I might ask you for your commission; but I do take thee, Orlando, for my husband: there's a girl goes before the priest; and certainly a woman's thought runs before her actions.

ORLANDO

So do all thoughts; they are winged.

ROSALIND

Now tell me how long you would have her after you have possessed her.

ORLANDO

For ever and a day.

ROSALIND

Say 'a day', without the 'ever'. No, no, Orlando; men are April when they woo, December when they wed: maids are May when they are maids, but the sky changes when they are wives. I will be more jealous of thee than a Barbary cock-pigeon over his hen, more clamorous than a parrot against rain, more new-fangled than an ape, more giddy in my desires than a monkey: I will weep for nothing, like Diana in the fountain, and I will do that when you are disposed to be merry; I will laugh like a hyen, and that when thou art inclined to sleep.

ORLANDO

But will my Rosalind do so?

ROSALIND

By my life, she will do as I do.

ORLANDO

O, but she is wise.

ROSALIND

Or else she could not have the wit to do this: the wiser, the waywarder: make the doors upon a woman's wit and it will out at the casement; shut that and 'twill out at the key-hole; stop that, 'twill fly with the smoke out at the chimney.

ORLANDO

A man that had a wife with such a wit, he might say 'Wit, whither wilt?'

ROSALIND

Nay, you might keep that check for it till you met your wife's wit going to your neighbour's bed.

ORLANDO

And what wit could wit have to excuse that?

ROSALIND

Marry, to say she came to seek you there. You shall never take her without her answer, unless you take her without her tongue. O, that woman that cannot make her fault her husband's occasion, let her never nurse her child herself, for she will breed it like a fool!

ORLANDO

For these two hours, Rosalind, I will leave thee.

ROSALIND

Alas, dear love, I cannot lack thee two hours!

ORLANDO

I must attend the Duke at dinner: by two o'clock I will be with thee again.

ROSALIND

Ay, go your ways, go your ways; I knew what you would prove: my friends told me as much, and I thought no less: that flattering tongue of yours won me: 'tis but one cast away, and so, come, death! Two o'clock is your hour?

ORLANDO

Ay, sweet Rosalind.

ROSALIND

By my troth, and in good earnest, and so God mend me, and by all pretty oaths that are not dangerous, if you break one jot of your promise or come one minute behind your hour, I will think you the most pathetical break-promise, and the most hollow lover, and the most unworthy of her you call Rosalind, that may be chosen out of the gross band of the unfaithful: therefore beware my censure and keep your promise.

ORLANDO

With no less religion than if thou wert indeed my Rosalind: so adieu.

ROSALIND

Well, Time is the old justice that examines all such offenders, and let Time try: adieu. [*Exit* ORLANDO

CELIA

You have simply misused our sex in your love-prate: we must have your doublet and hose plucked over your head, and show the world what the bird hath done to her own nest.

ROSALIND

O coz, coz, coz, my pretty little coz, that thou didst know how many fathom deep I am in love! But it cannot be sounded: my affection hath an unknown bottom, like the bay of Portugal.

CELIA

Or rather, bottomless; that as fast as you pour affection in, it runs out.

ROSALIND

No, that same wicked bastard of Venus that was begot of thought, conceived of spleen, and born of madness, that blind rascally boy that abuses every one's eyes because his own are out, let him be judge how deep I am in love. I'll tell thee, Aliena, I cannot be out of the sight of Orlando: I'll go find a shadow and sigh till he come.

CELIA

And I'll sleep.　　　　　　　　　　　[*Exeunt*

SCENE II. *The forest*

Enter JAQUES, LORDS, *and* FORESTERS

JAQUES

Which is he that killed the deer?

A LORD

Sir, it was I.

JAQUES

Let's present him to the Duke, like a Roman conqueror; and it would do well to set the deer's horns upon his head, for a branch of victory. Have you no song, forester, for this purpose?

FORESTER

Yes, sir.

JAQUES

Sing it: 'tis no matter how it be in tune, so it make noise enough.

FORESTER

SONG

What shall he have that kill'd the deer?
His leather skin and horns to wear.
　　Then sing him home:
　　　　　[*The rest shall bear this burden*
Take thou no scorn to wear the horn;
It was a crest ere thou wast born:
　　Thy father's father wore it,
　　And thy father bore it:
The horn, the horn, the lusty horn
Is not a thing to laugh to scorn.

　　　　　　　　　　　[*Exeunt*

SCENE III. *The forest*

Enter ROSALIND *and* CELIA

ROSALIND

How say you now? Is it not past two o'clock? and here much Orlando!

CELIA

I warrant you, with pure love and troubled brain, he hath ta'en his bow and arrows and is gone forth to sleep. Look, who comes here.

Enter SILVIUS

SILVIUS

My errand is to you, fair youth;
My gentle Phebe bid me give you this:
I know not the contents; but, as I guess

By the stern brow and waspish action
Which she did use as she was writing of it,
It bears an angry tenour: pardon me;
I am but as a guiltless messenger.

ROSALIND

Patience herself would startle at this letter
And play the swaggerer; bear this, bear all:
She says I am not fair, that I lack manners;
She calls me proud, and that she could not love me,
Were man as rare as phœnix. 'Od's my will!
Her love is not the hare that I do hunt:
Why writes she so to me? Well, shepherd, well,
This is a letter of your own device.

SILVIUS

No, I protest, I know not the contents:
Phebe did write it.

ROSALIND

　　　　　　　Come, come, you are a fool,
And turn'd into the extremity of love.
I saw her hand: she has a leathern hand,
A freestone-colour'd hand; I verily did think
That her old gloves were on, but 'twas her hands:
She has a huswife's hand; but that's no matter:
I say she never did invent this letter;
This is a man's invention and his hand.

SILVIUS

Sure, it is hers.

ROSALIND

Why, 'tis a boisterous and a cruel style,
A style for challengers; why, she defies me,
Like Turk to Christian: women's gentle brain
Could not drop forth such giant-rude invention,
Such Ethiope words, blacker in their effect
Than in their countenance. Will you hear the letter?

SILVIUS

So please you, for I never heard it yet;
Yet heard too much of Phebe's cruelty.

ROSALIND

She Phebes me: mark how the tyrant writes.

[*Reads*]　　　Art thou god to shepherd turn'd,
　　　　　　That a maiden's heart hath burn'd?

Can a woman rail thus?

SILVIUS

Call you this railing?

ROSALIND

[*Reads*]　　　Why, thy godhead laid apart,
　　　　　　Warr'st thou with a woman's heart?

Did you ever hear such railing?

　　　　Whiles the eye of man did woo me,
　　　　That could do no vengeance to me.

Meaning me a beast.

　　　　If the scorn of your bright eyne
　　　　Have power to raise such love in mine,
　　　　Alack, in me what strange effect
　　　　Would they work in mild aspect!
　　　　Whiles you chid me, I did love;
　　　　How then might your prayers move!
　　　　He that brings this love to thee
　　　　Little knows this love in me:
　　　　And by him seal up thy mind;
　　　　Whether that thy youth and kind

Will the faithful offer take
Of me and all that I can make;
Or else by him my love deny,
And then I'll study how to die.

SILVIUS

Call you this chiding?

CELIA

Alas, poor shepherd!

ROSALIND

Do you pity him? no, he deserves no pity. Wilt thou
love such a woman? What, to make thee an instrument and play false strains upon thee! not to be endured! Well, go your way to her, for I see love hath
made thee a tame snake, and say this to her: that if
she love me, I charge her to love thee; if she will not,
I will never have her unless thou entreat for her. If
you be a true lover, hence, and not a word; for here
comes more company.   [Exit SILVIUS

Enter OLIVER

OLIVER

Good morrow, fair ones: pray you, if you know,
Where in the purlieus of this forest stands
A sheep-cote fenced about with olive-trees?

CELIA

West of this place, down in the neighbour bottom:
The rank of osiers by the murmuring stream
Left on your right hand brings you to the place.
But at this hour the house doth keep itself;
There's none within.

OLIVER

If that an eye may profit by a tongue,
Then should I know you by description;
Such garments and such years: 'The boy is fair,
Of female favour, and bestows himself
Like a ripe sister: the woman low,
And browner than her brother.' Are not you
The owner of the house I did inquire for?

CELIA

It is no boast, being ask'd, to say we are.

OLIVER

Orlando doth commend him to you both,
And to that youth he calls his Rosalind
He sends this bloody napkin. Are you he?

ROSALIND

I am: what must we understand by this?

OLIVER

Some of my shame; if you will know of me
What man I am, and how, and why, and where
This handkercher was stain'd.

CELIA

I pray you, tell it.

OLIVER

When last the young Orlando parted from you
He left a promise to return again
Within an hour, and pacing through the forest,
Chewing the food of sweet and bitter fancy,
Lo, what befel! he threw his eye aside,
And mark what object did present itself:
Under an oak, whose boughs were moss'd with age

And high top bald with dry antiquity,
A wretched ragged man, o'ergrown with hair,
Lay sleeping on his back: about his neck
A green and gilded snake had wreathed itself,
Who with her head nimble in threats approach'd
The opening of his mouth; but suddenly,
Seeing Orlando, it unlink'd itself,
And with indented glides did slip away
Into a bush: under which bush's shade
A lioness, with udders all drawn dry,
Lay couching, head on ground, with catlike watch,
When that the sleeping man should stir; for 'tis
The royal disposition of that beast
To prey on nothing that doth seem as dead:
This seen, Orlando did approach the man
And found it was his brother, his elder brother.

CELIA

O, I have heard him speak of that same brother;
And he did render him the most unnatural
That lived amongst men.

OLIVER

And well he might so do,
For well I know he was unnatural.

ROSALIND

But, to Orlando: did he leave him there,
Food to the suck'd and hungry lioness?

OLIVER

Twice did he turn his back and purposed so;
But kindness, nobler ever than revenge,
And nature, stronger than his just occasion,
Made him give battle to the lioness,
Who quickly fell before him: in which hurtling
From miserable slumber I awaked.

CELIA

Are you his brother?

ROSALIND

Was't you he rescued?

CELIA

Was't you that did so oft contrive to kill him?

OLIVER

'Twas I; but 'tis not I: I do not shame
To tell you what I was, since my conversion
So sweetly tastes, being the thing I am.

ROSALIND

But, for the bloody napkin?

OLIVER

By and by.
When from the first to last betwixt us two
Tears our recountments had most kindly bathed,
As how I came into that desert place;
In brief, he led me to the gentle Duke,
Who gave me fresh array and entertainment,
Committing me unto my brother's love;
Who led me instantly unto his cave,
There stripp'd himself, and here upon his arm
The lioness had torn some flesh away,
Which all this while had bled; and now he fainted
And cried, in fainting, upon Rosalind.
Brief, I recover'd him, bound up his wound;
And, after some small space, being strong at heart,

He sent me hither, stranger as I am,
To tell this story, that you might excuse
His broken promise, and to give this napkin,
Dyed in his blood, unto the shepherd youth
That he in sport doth call his Rosalind.

        [ROSALIND *swoons*

CELIA

Why, how now, Ganymede! sweet Ganymede!

OLIVER

Many will swoon when they do look on blood.

CELIA

There is more in it. Cousin Ganymede!

OLIVER

Look, he recovers.

ROSALIND

I would I were at home.

CELIA

     We'll lead you thither.
I pray you, will you take him by the arm?

OLIVER

Be of good cheer, youth: you a man! you lack a
man's heart.

ROSALIND

I do so, I confess it. Ah, sirrah, a body would think
this was well counterfeited! I pray you, tell your
brother how well I counterfeited. Heigh-ho!

OLIVER

This was not counterfeit: there is too great testimony in your complexion that it was a passion of
earnest.

ROSALIND

Counterfeit, I assure you.

OLIVER

Well then, take a good heart and counterfeit to be a
man.

ROSALIND

So I do: but, i'faith, I should have been a woman
by right.

CELIA

Come, you look paler and paler: pray you, draw
homewards. Good sir, go with us.

OLIVER

That will I, for I must bear answer back
How you excuse my brother, Rosalind.

ROSALIND

I shall devise something: but, I pray you, commend
my counterfeiting to him. Will you go? [*Exeunt*

ACT V

SCENE I. *The forest*

Enter TOUCHSTONE *and* AUDREY

TOUCHSTONE

We shall find a time, Audrey; patience, gentle
Audrey.

AUDREY

Faith, the priest was good enough, for all the old
gentleman's saying.

TOUCHSTONE

A most wicked Sir Oliver, Audrey, a most vile Martext. But, Audrey, there is a youth here in the forest
lays claim to you.

AUDREY

Ay, I know who 'tis: he hath no interest in me in
the world: here comes the man you mean.

TOUCHSTONE

It is meat and drink to me to see a clown: by my
troth, we that have good wits have much to answer
for; we shall be flouting; we cannot hold.

Enter WILLIAM

WILLIAM

Good even, Audrey.

AUDREY

God ye good even, William.

WILLIAM

And good even to you, sir.

TOUCHSTONE

Good even, gentle friend. Cover thy head, cover thy
head; nay, prithee, be covered. How old are you,
friend?

WILLIAM

Five and twenty, sir.

TOUCHSTONE

A ripe age. Is thy name William?

WILLIAM

William, sir.

TOUCHSTONE

A fair name. Wast born i' the forest here?

WILLIAM

Ay, sir, I thank God.

TOUCHSTONE

'Thank God;' a good answer. Art rich?

WILLIAM

Faith, sir, so so.

TOUCHSTONE

'So so' is good, very good, very excellent good; and
yet it is not; it is but so so. Art thou wise?

WILLIAM

Ay, sir, I have a pretty wit.

TOUCHSTONE

Why, thou sayest well. I do now remember a saying,
'The fool doth think he is wise, but the wise man
knows himself to be a fool.' The heathen philosopher, when he had a desire to eat a grape, would
open his lips when he put it into his mouth; meaning thereby that grapes were made to eat and lips
to open. You do love this maid?

WILLIAM

I do, sir.

TOUCHSTONE

Give me your hand. Art thou learned?

WILLIAM

No, sir.

TOUCHSTONE

Then learn this of me: to have, is to have; for it is a
figure in rhetoric that drink, being poured out of a
cup into a glass, by filling the one doth empty the

other; for all your writers do consent that ipse is he: now, you are not ipse, for I am he.

WILLIAM

Which he, sir?

TOUCHSTONE

He, sir, that must marry this woman. Therefore, you clown, abandon,—which is in the vulgar leave, —the society,—which in the boorish is company,— of this female,—which in the common is woman; which together is, abandon the society of this fe- male, or, clown, thou perishest; or, to thy better understanding, diest; or, to wit, I kill thee, make thee away, translate thy life into death, thy liberty into bondage: I will deal in poison with thee, or in bastinado, or in steel; I will bandy with thee in fac- tion; I will o'er-run thee with policy; I will kill thee a hundred and fifty ways: therefore tremble, and depart.

AUDREY

Do, good William.

WILLIAM

God rest you merry, sir.   [*Exit*

Enter CORIN

CORIN

Our master and mistress seeks you; come, away, away!

TOUCHSTONE

Trip, Audrey! trip, Audrey! I attend, I attend.

         [*Exeunt*

SCENE II. *The forest*

Enter ORLANDO *and* OLIVER

ORLANDO

Is't possible that on so little acquaintance you should like her? that but seeing you should love her? and loving woo? and, wooing, she should grant? and will you persever to enjoy her?

OLIVER

Neither call the giddiness of it in question, the poverty of her, the small acquaintance, my sudden wooing, nor her sudden consenting; but say with me, I love Aliena; say with her that she loves me; consent with both that we may enjoy each other: it shall be to your good; for my father's house and all the revenue that was old Sir Rowland's will I estate upon you, and here live and die a shepherd.

ORLANDO

You have my consent. Let your wedding be to- morrow: thither will I invite the Duke and all's con- tented followers. Go you and prepare Aliena; for look you, here comes my Rosalind.

Enter ROSALIND

ROSALIND

God save you, brother.

OLIVER

And you, fair sister.   [*Exit*

ROSALIND

O, my dear Orlando, how it grieves me to see thee wear thy heart in a scarf!

ORLANDO

It is my arm.

ROSALIND

I thought thy heart had been wounded with the claws of a lion.

ORLANDO

Wounded it is, but with the eyes of a lady.

ROSALIND

Did your brother tell you how I counterfeited to swoon when he showed me your handkercher?

ORLANDO

Ay, and greater wonders than that.

ROSALIND

O, I know where you are: nay, 'tis true: there was never any thing so sudden but the fight of two rams, and Cæsar's thrasonical brag of 'I came, saw, and overcame:' for your brother and my sister no sooner met but they looked; no sooner looked but they loved; no sooner loved but they sighed; no sooner sighed but they asked one another the reason; no sooner knew the reason but they sought the remedy: and in these degrees have they made a pair of stairs to marriage which they will climb incontinent, or else be incontinent before marriage: they are in the very wrath of love and they will together; clubs can- not part them.

ORLANDO

They shall be married to-morrow, and I will bid the Duke to the nuptial. But, O, how bitter a thing it is to look into happiness through another man's eyes! By so much the more shall I to-morrow be at the height of heart-heaviness, by how much I shall think my brother happy in having what he wishes for.

ROSALIND

Why then, to-morrow I cannot serve your turn for Rosalind?

ORLANDO

I can live no longer by thinking.

ROSALIND

I will weary you then no longer with idle talking. Know of me then, for now I speak to some purpose, that I know you are a gentleman of good conceit: I speak not this that you should bear a good opinion of my knowledge, insomuch I say I know you are; neither do I labour for a greater esteem than may in some little measure draw a belief from you, to do yourself good and not to grace me. Believe then, if you please, that I can do strange things: I have, since I was three year old, conversed with a magi- cian, most profound in his art and yet not damn- able. If you do love Rosalind so near the heart as your gesture cries it out, when your brother marries Aliena, shall you marry her: I know into what straits of fortune she is driven; and it is not impossi- ble to me, if it appear not inconvenient to you, to set her before your eyes to-morrow human as she is and without any danger.

ORLANDO

Speakest thou in sober meanings?

ROSALIND

By my life, I do; which I tender dearly, though I
say I am a magician. Therefore, put you in your
best array; bid your friends; for if you will be married to-morrow, you shall; and to Rosalind, if you
will.

Enter SILVIUS *and* PHEBE

Look, here comes a lover of mine and a lover of
hers.

PHEBE

Youth, you have done me much ungentleness,
To show the letter that I writ to you.

ROSALIND

I care not if I have: it is my study
To seem despiteful and ungentle to you:
You are there followed by a faithful shepherd;
Look upon him, love him; he worships you.

PHEBE

Good shepherd, tell this youth what 'tis to love.

SILVIUS

It is to be all made of sighs and tears;
And so am I for Phebe.

PHEBE

And I for Ganymede.

ORLANDO

And I for Rosalind.

ROSALIND

And I for no woman.

SILVIUS

It is to be all made of faith and service;
And so am I for Phebe.

PHEBE

And I for Ganymede.

ORLANDO

And I for Rosalind.

ROSALIND

And I for no woman.

SILVIUS

It is to be all made of fantasy,
All made of passion, and all made of wishes;
All adoration, duty, and observance,
All humbleness, all patience, and impatience,
All purity, all trial, all observance;
And so am I for Phebe.

PHEBE

And so am I for Ganymede.

ORLANDO

And so am I for Rosalind.

ROSALIND

And so am I for no woman.

PHEBE

If this be so, why blame you me to love you?

SILVIUS

If this be so, why blame you me to love you?

ORLANDO

If this be so, why blame you me to love you?

ROSALIND

Why do you speak too, 'Why blame you me to love
you?'

ORLANDO

To her that is not here, nor doth not hear.

ROSALIND

Pray you, no more of this; 'tis like the howling of
Irish wolves against the moon. [*To* SILVIUS] I will
help you, if I can: [*To* PHEBE] I would love you, if
I could. To-morrow meet me all together. [*To*
PHEBE] I will marry you, if ever I marry woman,
and I'll be married to-morrow: [*To* ORLANDO] I will
satisfy you, if ever I satisfied man, and you shall be
married to-morrow: [*To* SILVIUS] I will content you,
if what pleases you contents you, and you shall be
married to-morrow. [*To* ORLANDO] As you love
Rosalind, meet: [*To* SILVIUS] as you love Phebe,
meet: and as I love no woman, I'll meet. So, fare
you well: I have left you commands.

SILVIUS

I'll not fail, if I live.

PHEBE

Nor I.

ORLANDO

Nor I.　　　　　　　　　　　　　　　　　　[*Exeunt*

SCENE III. *The forest*

Enter TOUCHSTONE *and* AUDREY

TOUCHSTONE

To-morrow is the joyful day, Audrey; to-morrow
will we be married.

AUDREY

I do desire it with all my heart; and I hope it is no
dishonest desire to desire to be a woman of the
world. Here come two of the banished Duke's
pages.

Enter two PAGES

FIRST PAGE

Well met, honest gentleman.

TOUCHSTONE

By my troth, well met. Come, sit, sit, and a song.

SECOND PAGE

We are for you: sit i' the middle.

FIRST PAGE

Shall we clap into't roundly, without hawking or
spitting or saying we are hoarse, which are the only
prologues to a bad voice?

SECOND PAGE

I'faith, i'faith; and both in a tune, like two gipsies
on a horse.

SONG

It was a lover and his lass,
　With a hey, and a ho, and a hey nonino,
That o'er the green corn-field did pass
　In the spring time, the only pretty ring time,
When birds do sing, hey ding a ding, ding:
Sweet lovers love the spring.

Between the acres of the rye,
　With a hey, and a ho, and a hey nonino,
These pretty country folks would lie,
　In spring time, &c.

This carol they began that hour,
  With a hey, and a ho, and a hey nonino,
How that a life was but a flower
  In spring time, &c.

And therefore take the present time,
  With a hey, and a ho, and a hey nonino;
For love is crowned with the prime
  In spring time, &c.

TOUCHSTONE

Truly, young gentlemen, though there was no great matter in the ditty, yet the note was very untuneable.

FIRST PAGE

You are deceived, sir: we kept time, we lost not our time.

TOUCHSTONE

By my troth, yes; I count it but time lost to hear such a foolish song. God buy you; and God mend your voices! Come, Audrey.   [Exeunt

SCENE IV. *The forest*

Enter DUKE senior, AMIENS, JAQUES, ORLANDO, OLIVER, *and* CELIA

DUKE

Dost thou believe, Orlando, that the boy
Can do all this that he hath promised?

ORLANDO

I sometimes do believe, and sometimes do not;
As those that fear they hope, and know they fear.

Enter ROSALIND, SILVIUS, *and* PHEBE

ROSALIND

Patience once more, whiles our compact is urged:
You say, if I bring in your Rosalind,
You will bestow her on Orlando here?

DUKE

That would I, had I kingdoms to give with her.

ROSALIND

And you say, you will have her, when I bring her?

ORLANDO

That would I, were I of all kingdoms king.

ROSALIND

You say, you'll marry me, if I be willing?

PHEBE

That will I, should I die the hour after.

ROSALIND

But if you do refuse to marry me,
You'll give yourself to this most faithful shepherd?

PHEBE

So is the bargain.

ROSALIND

You say, that you'll have Phebe, if she will?

SILVIUS

Though to have her and death were both one thing.

ROSALIND

I have promised to make all this matter even.
Keep you your word, O Duke, to give your daughter;

You yours, Orlando, to receive his daughter:
Keep your word, Phebe, that you'll marry me,
Or else refusing me, to wed this shepherd:
Keep your word, Silvius, that you'll marry her,
If she refuse me: and from hence I go,
To make these doubts all even.

          [*Exeunt* ROSALIND *and* CELIA

DUKE

I do remember in this shepherd boy
Some lively touches of my daughter's favour.

ORLANDO

My lord, the first time that I ever saw him
Methought he was a brother to your daughter:
But, my good lord, this boy is forest-born,
And hath been tutor'd in the rudiments
Of many desperate studies by his uncle,
Whom he reports to be a great magician,
Obscured in the circle of this forest.

Enter TOUCHSTONE *and* AUDREY

JAQUES

There is, sure, another flood toward, and these couples are coming to the ark. Here comes a pair of very strange beasts, which in all tongues are called fools.

TOUCHSTONE

Salutation and greeting to you all!

JAQUES

Good my lord, bid him welcome: this is the motley-minded gentleman that I have so often met in the forest: he hath been a courtier, he swears.

TOUCHSTONE

If any man doubt that, let him put me to my purgation. I have trod a measure; I have flattered a lady; I have been politic with my friend, smooth with mine enemy; I have undone three tailors; I have had four quarrels, and like to have fought one.

JAQUES

And how was that ta'en up?

TOUCHSTONE

Faith, we met, and found the quarrel was upon the seventh cause.

JAQUES

How seventh cause? Good my lord, like this fellow.

DUKE

I like him very well.

TOUCHSTONE

God 'ild you, sir; I desire you of the like. I press in here, sir, amongst the rest of the country copulatives, to swear and to forswear; according as marriage binds and blood breaks: a poor virgin, sir, an ill-favoured thing, sir, but mine own; a poor humour of mine, sir, to take that that no man else will: rich honesty dwells like a miser, sir, in a poor house; as your pearl in your foul oyster.

DUKE

By my faith, he is very swift and sententious.

TOUCHSTONE

According to the fool's bolt, sir, and such dulcet diseases.

JAQUES

But, for the seventh cause; how did you find the quarrel on the seventh cause?

TOUCHSTONE

Upon a lie seven times removed:—bear your body more seeming, Audrey:—as thus, sir. I did dislike the cut of a certain courtier's beard: he sent me word, if I said his beard was not cut well, he was in the mind it was: this is called the Retort Courteous. If I sent him word again 'it was not well cut,' he would send me word, he cut it to please himself: this is called the Quip Modest. If again 'it was not well cut,' he disabled my judgement: this is called the Reply Churlish. If again 'it was not well cut,' he would answer, I spake not true: this is called the Reproof Valiant. If again 'it was not well cut,' he would say, I lie: this is called the Countercheck Quarrelsome: and so to the Lie Circumstantial and the Lie Direct.

JAQUES

And how oft did you say his beard was not well cut?

TOUCHSTONE

I durst go no further than the Lie Circumstantial, nor he durst not give me the Lie Direct; and so we measured swords and parted.

JAQUES

Can you nominate in order now the degrees of the lie?

TOUCHSTONE

O sir, we quarrel in print, by the book; as you have books for good manners: I will name you the degrees. The first, the Retort Courteous; the second, the Quip Modest; the third, the Reply Churlish; the fourth, the Reproof Valiant; the fifth, the Countercheck Quarrelsome; the sixth, the Lie with Circumstance; the seventh, the Lie Direct. All these you may avoid but the Lie Direct; and you may avoid that too, with an If. I knew when seven justices could not take up a quarrel, but when the parties were met themselves, one of them thought but of an If, as, 'If you said so, then I said so;' and they shook hands and swore brothers. Your If is the only peace-maker; much virtue in If.

JAQUES

Is not this a rare fellow, my lord? he's as good at any thing and yet a fool.

DUKE

He uses his folly like a stalking-horse and under the presentation of that he shoots his wit.

Enter HYMEN, ROSALIND, *and* CELIA

Still music

HYMEN

Then is there mirth in heaven,
When earthly things made even
  Atone together.
Good Duke, receive thy daughter:
Hymen from heaven brought her,
  Yea, brought her hither,
That thou mightst join her hand with his
Whose heart within his bosom is.

ROSALIND

To you I give myself, for I am yours.
To you I give myself, for I am yours.

DUKE

If there be truth in sight, you are my daughter.

ORLANDO

If there be truth in sight, you are my Rosalind.

PHEBE

If sight and shape be true,
  Why then, my love adieu!

ROSALIND

I'll have no father, if you be not he:
I'll have no husband, if you be not he:
Nor ne'er wed woman, if you be not she.

HYMEN

Peace, ho! I bar confusion:
'Tis I must make conclusion
  Of these most strange events:
Here's eight that must take hands
To join in Hymen's bands,
  If truth holds true contents.
You and you no cross shall part:
You and you are heart in heart:
You to his love must accord,
Or have a woman to your lord:
You and you are sure together,
As the winter to foul weather.
Whiles a wedlock-hymn we sing,
Feed yourselves with questioning;
That reason wonder may diminish,
How thus we met, and these things finish.

SONG

Wedding is great Juno's crown:
  O blessed bond of board and bed!
'Tis Hymen peoples every town;
  High wedlock then be honoured:
Honour, high honour and renown,
To Hymen, god of every town!

DUKE

O my dear niece, welcome thou art to me!
Even daughter, welcome, in no less degree.

PHEBE

I will not eat my word, now thou art mine;
Thy faith my fancy to thee doth combine.

Enter JAQUES DE BOYS

JAQUES DE BOYS

Let me have audience for a word or two:
I am the second son of old Sir Rowland,
That bring these tidings to this fair assembly.
Duke Frederick, hearing how that every day
Men of great worth resorted to this forest,
Address'd a mighty power; which were on foot,
In his own conduct, purposely to take
His brother here and put him to the sword:
And to the skirts of this wild wood he came;
Where meeting with an old religious man,
After some question with him, was converted
Both from his enterprise and from the world;
His crown bequeathing to his banish'd brother,
And all their lands restored to them again

That were with him exiled. This to be true,
I do engage my life.

DUKE

Welcome, young man;
Thou offer'st fairly to thy brothers' wedding:
To one his lands withheld; and to the other
A land itself at large, a potent dukedom.
First, in this forest let us do those ends
That here were well begun and well begot:
And after, every of this happy number,
That have endured shrewd days and nights with us,
Shall share the good of our returned fortune,
According to the measure of their states.
Meantime, forget this new-fallen dignity,
And fall into our rustic revelry.
Play, music! And you, brides and bridegrooms all,
With measure heap'd in joy, to the measures fall.

JAQUES

Sir, by your patience. If I heard you rightly,
The Duke hath put on a religious life
And thrown into neglect the pompous court?

JAQUES DE BOYS

He hath.

JAQUES

To him will I: out of these convertites
There is much matter to be heard and learn'd.
[*To* DUKE] You to your former honour I bequeath;
Your patience and your virtue well deserves it:
[*To* ORLANDO] You to a love, that your true faith
    doth merit:
[*To* OLIVER] You to your land, and love, and great
    allies:
[*To* SILVIUS] You to a long and well-deserved bed:
[*To* TOUCHSTONE] And you to wrangling; for thy
    loving voyage
Is but for two months victuall'd. So, to your pleas-
    ures:
I am for other than for dancing measures.

DUKE

Stay, Jaques, stay.

JAQUES

To see no pastime I: what you would have
I'll stay to know at your abandon'd cave.   [*Exit*

DUKE

Proceed, proceed: we will begin these rites,
As we do trust they'll end, in true delights. [*A dance*

EPILOGUE

ROSALIND

It is not the fashion to see the lady the epilogue; but
it is no more unhandsome than to see the lord the
prologue. If it be true that good wine needs no bush,
'tis true that a good play needs no epilogue: yet to
good wine they do use good bushes; and good plays
prove the better by the help of good epilogues.
What a case am I in then, that am neither a good
epilogue, nor cannot insinuate with you in the behalf of a good play! I am not furnished like a beggar, therefore to beg will not become me: my way is
to conjure you; and I'll begin with the women. I
charge you, O women, for the love you bear to men,
to like as much of this play as please you: and I
charge you, O men, for the love you bear to
women,—as I perceive by your simpering, none of
you hates them,—that between you and the women
the play may please. If I were a woman I would
kiss as many of you as had beards that pleased me,
complexions that liked me and breaths that I defied
not: and, I am sure, as many as have good beards
or good faces or sweet breaths will, for my kind offer, when I make curtsy, bid me farewell.   [*Exeunt*

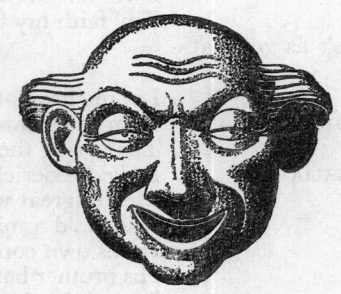

TWELFTH NIGHT; OR, WHAT YOU WILL

SYNOPSIS

Viola, a charming, high-born girl, is separated by shipwreck from her twin brother Sebastian whom she exactly resembles, and each thinks the other dead. Finding herself cast ashore on the coast of Illyria, in need of protection, she learns from the captain of their vessel that there is no chance of entering the service of the wealthy, beautiful Countess Olivia, because she refuses to grant interviews, being in mourning for her brother. With the captain's help, Viola disguises herself as a boy and is employed by the Duke Orsino who soon advances her as his special envoy to press his lovesuit with Olivia. Viola, herself in love with the sentimental Duke, manages to gain admittance to the Countess who falls passionately in love with the graceful youth speaking so eloquently of his master's devotion, and to intrigue Cesario, as Viola is called, sends her steward Malvolio after the page with a ring.

This Malvolio, a sour superior individual, has been so arrogant toward the members of Olivia's household, including her irresponsible uncle, Sir Toby Belch, who pursues his drinking, riotous habits under her roof, that Maria, the Countess' witty, audacious gentlewoman, plots with the others to get the officious steward out of the way. She places within his reach a letter written apparently by Olivia telling him of her love and begging him, if he returns her affection, to wear yellow stockings, go cross-gartered, and smile perpetually while in her presence. These suggestions stimulate Malvio to such a degree that the Countess thinks him mad, and the rollicking conspirators have him committed to a dark room.

When Olivia sees Cesario again, she makes love to him so openly that she arouses the jealousy of Sir Andrew Aguecheek, a wealthy but brainless man, who keeps Sir Toby supplied with money as compensation for his pretended help in the knight's courtship of the Countess. With Malvolio locked up, Sir Tobby blithely arranges a duel between Sir Andrew and Cesario, neither of whom wishes to fight.

In the meantime, the shipwrecked Sebastian, lashed firmly to a mast, has been rescued and cared for by a sea-captain, the good Antonio, and the two men become devoted friends. When Sebastian leaves to seek out Duke Orsino's court at Illyria, the sea-captain accompanies him although he realizes he will be in danger, having once fought against the Duke. The friends separating for a while, Antonio gives Sebastian his purse, and soon comes across the trumped-up duel between Sir Andrew and Cesario. Rushing to the defence of his supposed friend Sebastian, he is arrested by an officer who recognizes him as an old enemy of the state, and, to his amazement and grief, Cesario, to whom he turns for money in his hour of need, still thinking him to be Sebastian, denies that he ever saw him.

Sir Andrew, noting Cesario's timidity in fighting, and egged on by Sir Toby, speeds after Cesario to complete the duel and encounters Sebastian who wounds them both. Olivia now interferes and takes Sebastian to her home, where, having sent for a priest, she secretly marries the unresisting but surprised young man.

The Duke Orsino, with his page, the disguised Viola, and other attendants, comes to Olivia's house just as his officers appear with Antonio whom the Duke recognizes. He demands to know why such a valiant fighter should be implicated in a common street brawl, and of all places in a city full of his enemies! The sea-captain tells how his love for the lad he rescued from an angry sea three months before had induced him to follow Sebastian that very day to Illyria, even at the risk of his life, and, pointing to the Duke's page, he accuses him of ingratitude and lack of principle in keeping his purse.

The Duke is disparaging Antonio's story when Olivia comes upon the scene and addresses Cesario as her husband, calling upon the priest to confirm her words. Orsino turns savagely upon the page, calling him a dissembler, when he is again interrupted by the entrance of the bleeding Sir Andrew and Sir Toby in a search of a doctor. Sir Andrew, espying Cesario, blames him for their injuries, but Olivia sends them packing just as Sebastian arrives, all love and apologies to the Countess for hurting her guests, and the Duke exclaims in amazement at his resemblance to the page. Sebastian joyfully greets his friend Antonio, then stares in bewilderment at the boy in a page's clothes but with his sister's face.

Viola clears up the mystery, and the brother and sister are fondly united, while the Duke, realizing that he loves the girl, asks her to dress again as a maiden, but she explains that the good sea-captain who helped to disguise her and is holding her clothes for safekeeping is in prison on some pretext of Malvolio's. Just then Olivia's clown, who through some prank of Maria's and Sir Toby's has visited the incarcerated Malvolio in the garb of a curate in order to torment him, but had a change of heart, comes to the Countess with a letter from the steward which shows that he is rational and has been badly treated. The conspirators confess their plot, Maria marries Sir Toby, and Malvolio, now freed to liberate the captain, vows vengeance on them all.

HISTORICAL DATA

There is considerable obscurity as to the exact source of the plot of this play, five different predecessors on the stage and three novels all being in part accredited with a contribution to its origin. An Italian play, *Gl' Ingannati*, produced in Siena in 1531, is probably the earliest source. Bendello's novel *Nicuola* (1538), translated into French by Belleforest and thence into English by Barnabe Riche with the title *Apolonius and Silla* in his book *Barnabe Riche his Farewell to Militarie Profession* (1581), has substantially the same plot.

Mention is made of a performance of *Twelfth Night or What You Will*, under the date of February 2, 1601–2, in the *Diary* of John Manningham, which describes it in terms that identify it as Shakespeare's.

The play, however, is not listed in Meres's *Palladis Tamia*, so that a date of composition between 1598 and 1602 is indicated. Some, not altogether convincing, evidence is at hand in the reference to the "new map with the augmentation of the Indies" (Act III, Scene ii) which is generally taken to refer to that in Hakluyt's *Voyages* published in 1600. In any case, the probable date of composition is 1601–2.

The title of the comedy, which has no bearing on the story, is probably due to its performance on the festival of "Twelfth Night."

It does not appear in print prior to the First Folio in 1623.

"Fortune forbid my outside have not charm'd her"
TWELFTH NIGHT

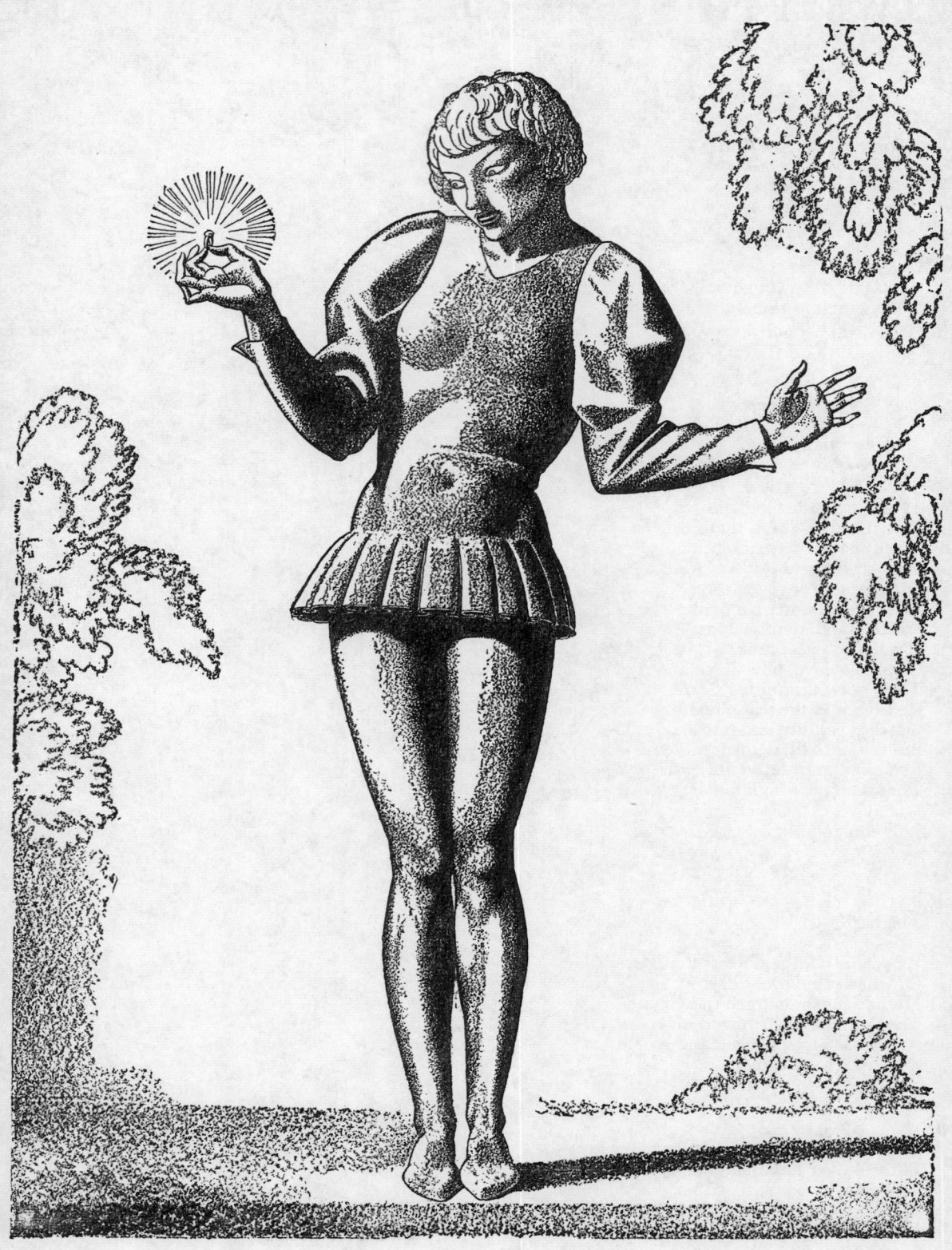

TWELFTH NIGHT; OR, WHAT YOU WILL

DRAMATIS PERSONÆ

ORSINO, *Duke of Illyria.*
SEBASTIAN, *brother to Viola.*
ANTONIO, *a sea captain, friend to Sebastian.*
A SEA CAPTAIN, *friend to Viola.*
VALENTINE,
CURIO, } *gentlemen attending on the Duke.*
SIR TOBY BELCH, *uncle to Olivia.*
SIR ANDREW AGUECHEEK.
MALVOLIO, *steward to Olivia.*

FABIAN,
FESTE, *a clown,* } *servants to Olivia.*
OLIVIA.
VIOLA.
MARIA, *Olivia's woman.*

LORDS, PRIESTS, SAILORS, OFFICERS, MUSICIANS,
   and other ATTENDANTS.

SCENE—*A city in Illyria, and the sea-coast near it.*

ACT I

SCENE I. *An apartment in the* DUKE's *palace*

Enter DUKE, CURIO, *and other* LORDS; MUSICIANS
attending

DUKE

IF MUSIC be the food of love, play on;
Give me excess of it, that, surfeiting,
The appetite may sicken, and so die.
That strain again! it had a dying fall:
O, it came o'er my ear like the sweet sound,
That breathes upon a bank of violets,
Stealing and giving odour! Enough; no more:
'Tis not so sweet now as it was before.
O spirit of love, how quick and fresh art thou!
That, notwithstanding thy capacity
Receiveth as the sea, nought enters there,
Of what validity and pitch soe'er,
But falls into abatement and low price,
Even in a minute! so full of shapes is fancy,
That it alone is high fantastical.

CURIO

Will you go hunt, my lord?

DUKE

       What, Curio?

CURIO

The hart.

DUKE

Why, so I do, the noblest that I have:
O, when mine eyes did see Olivia first,
Methought she purged the air of pestilence!
That instant was I turn'd into a hart;
And my desires, like fell and cruel hounds,
E'er since pursue me.

Enter VALENTINE

       How now! what news from her?

VALENTINE

So please my lord, I might not be admitted;
But from her handmaid do return this answer:
The element itself, till seven years' heat,
Shall not behold her face at ample view;
But, like a cloistress, she will veiled walk

And water once a day her chamber round
With eye-offending brine: all this to season
A brother's dead love, which she would keep fresh
And lasting in her sad remembrance.

DUKE

O, she that hath a heart of that fine frame
To pay this debt of love but to a brother,
How will she love, when the rich golden shaft
Hath kill'd the flock of all affections else
That live in her; when liver, brain and heart,
These sovereign thrones, are all supplied, and fill'd
Her sweet perfections with one self king!
Away before me to sweet beds of flowers:
Love-thoughts lie rich when canopied with bowers.

[*Exeunt*

SCENE II. *The sea-coast*

Enter VIOLA, *a* CAPTAIN, *and* SAILORS

VIOLA

What country, friends, is this?

CAPTAIN

This is Illyria, lady.

VIOLA

And what should I do in Illyria?
My brother he is in Elysium.
Perchance he is not drown'd: what think you, sailors?

CAPTAIN

It is perchance that you yourself were saved.

VIOLA

O my poor brother! and so perchance may he be.

CAPTAIN

True, madam: and, to comfort you with chance,
Assure yourself, after our ship did split,
When you and those poor number saved with you
Hung on our driving boat, I saw your brother,
Most provident in peril, bind himself,
Courage and hope both teaching him the practice,
To a strong mast that lived upon the sea;
Where, like Arion on the dolphin's back,
I saw him hold acquaintance with the waves
So long as I could see.

VIOLA

For saying so, there's gold:
Mine own escape unfoldeth to my hope,
Whereto thy speech serves for authority,
The like of him. Know'st thou this country?

CAPTAIN

Ay, madam, well; for I was bred and born
Not three hours' travel from this very place.

VIOLA

Who governs here?

CAPTAIN

A noble Duke, in nature as in name.

VIOLA

What is his name?

CAPTAIN

Orsino.

VIOLA

Orsino! I have heard my father name him:
He was a bachelor then.

CAPTAIN

And so is now, or was so very late;
For but a month ago I went from hence,
And then 'twas fresh in murmur,—as, you know,
What great ones do the less will prattle of,—
That he did seek the love of fair Olivia.

VIOLA

What's she?

CAPTAIN

A virtuous maid, the daughter of a count
That died some twelvemonth since; then leaving
    her
In the protection of his son, her brother,
Who shortly also died: for whose dear love,
They say, she hath abjured the company
And sight of men.

VIOLA

                    O that I served that lady,
And might not be delivered to the world,
Till I had made mine own occasion mellow,
What my estate is!

CAPTAIN

                    That were hard to compass;
Because she will admit no kind of suit,
No, not the Duke's.

VIOLA

There is a fair behaviour in thee, captain;
And though that nature with a beauteous wall
Doth oft close in pollution, yet of thee
I will believe thou hast a mind that suits
With this thy fair and outward character.
I prithee, and I'll pay thee bounteously,
Conceal me what I am, and be my aid
For such disguise as haply shall become
The form of my intent. I'll serve this Duke:
Thou shalt present me as an eunuch to him:
It may be worth thy pains; for I can sing,
And speak to him in many sorts of music,
That will allow me very worth his service.
What else may hap to time I will commit;
Only shape thou thy silence to my wit.

CAPTAIN

Be you his eunuch, and your mute I'll be:
When my tongue blabs, then let mine eyes not see.

VIOLA

I thank thee: lead me on.   [Exeunt

SCENE III. OLIVIA'S house

Enter SIR TOBY BELCH and MARIA

SIR TOBY

What a plague means my niece, to take the death of
her brother thus? I am sure care's an enemy to life.

MARIA

By my troth, Sir Toby, you must come in earlier o'
nights: your cousin, my lady, takes great exceptions
to your ill hours.

SIR TOBY

Why, let her except, before excepted.

MARIA

Ay, but you must confine yourself within the modest
limits of order.

SIR TOBY

Confine! I'll confine myself no finer than I am:
these clothes are good enough to drink in; and so be
these boots too: an they be not, let them hang themselves in their own straps.

MARIA

That quaffing and drinking will undo you: I heard
my lady talk of it yesterday; and of a foolish knight
that you brought in one night here to be her wooer.

SIR TOBY

Who, Sir Andrew Aguecheek?

MARIA

Ay, he.

SIR TOBY

He's as tall a man as any 's in Illyria.

MARIA

What's that to the purpose?

SIR TOBY

Why, he has three thousand ducats a year.

MARIA

Ay, but he'll have but a year in all these ducats: he's
a very fool and a prodigal.

SIR TOBY

Fie, that you'll say so! he plays o' the viol-de-gam-
boys, and speaks three or four languages word for
word without book, and hath all the good gifts of
nature.

MARIA

He hath indeed, almost natural: for besides that
he's a fool, he's a great quarreller; and but that he
hath the gift of a coward to allay the gust he hath in
quarrelling, 'tis thought among the prudent he
would quickly have the gift of a grave.

SIR TOBY

By this hand, they are scoundrels and substractors
that say so of him. Who are they?

MARIA

They that add, moreover, he's drunk nightly in your company.

SIR TOBY

With drinking healths to my niece: I'll drink to her as long as there is a passage in my throat and drink in Illyria: he's a coward and a coystrill that will not drink to my niece till his brains turn o' the toe like a parish-top. What, wench! Castiliano vulgo; for here comes Sir Andrew Agueface.

Enter SIR ANDREW AGUECHEEK

SIR ANDREW

Sir Toby Belch! how now, Sir Toby Belch!

SIR TOBY

Sweet Sir Andrew!

SIR ANDREW

Bless you, fair shrew.

MARIA

And you too, sir.

SIR TOBY

Accost, Sir Andrew, accost.

SIR ANDREW

What's that?

SIR TOBY

My niece's chambermaid.

SIR ANDREW

Good Mistress Accost, I desire better acquaintance.

MARIA

My name is Mary, sir.

SIR ANDREW

Good Mistress Mary Accost,—

SIR TOBY

You mistake, knight: 'accost' is front her, board her, woo her, assail her.

SIR ANDREW

By my troth, I would not undertake her in this company. Is that the meaning of 'accost'?

MARIA

Fare you well, gentlemen.

SIR TOBY

An thou let part so, Sir Andrew, would thou mightst never draw sword again.

SIR ANDREW

An you part so, mistress, I would I might never draw sword again. Fair lady, do you think you have fools in hand?

MARIA

Sir, I have not you by the hand.

SIR ANDREW

Marry, but you shall have; and here's my hand.

MARIA

Now, sir, 'thought is free': I pray you, bring your hand to the buttery-bar and let it drink.

SIR ANDREW

Wherefore, sweet-heart? what's your metaphor?

MARIA

It's dry, sir.

SIR ANDREW

Why, I think so: I am not such an ass but I can keep my hand dry. But what's your jest?

MARIA

A dry jest, sir.

SIR ANDREW

Are you full of them?

MARIA

Ay, sir, I have them at my fingers' ends: marry, now I let go your hand, I am barren.   [*Exit*

SIR TOBY

O knight, thou lackest a cup of canary: when did I see thee so put down?

SIR ANDREW

Never in your life, I think; unless you see canary put me down. Methinks sometimes I have no more wit than a Christian or an ordinary man has: but I am a great eater of beef and I believe that does harm to my wit.

SIR TOBY

No question.

SIR ANDREW

An I thought that, I 'ld forswear it. I'll ride home to-morrow, Sir Toby.

SIR TOBY

Pourquoi, my dear knight?

SIR ANDREW

What is 'pourquoi'? do or not do? I would I had bestowed that time in the tongues that I have in fencing, dancing and bear-baiting: O, had I but followed the arts!

SIR TOBY

Then hadst thou had an excellent head of hair.

SIR ANDREW

Why, would that have mended my hair?

SIR TOBY

Past question; for thou seest it will not curl by nature.

SIR ANDREW

But it becomes me well enough, does 't not?

SIR TOBY

Excellent; it hangs like flax on a distaff; and I hope to see a housewife take thee between her legs and spin it off.

SIR ANDREW

Faith, I'll home to-morrow, Sir Toby: your niece will not be seen; or if she be, it's four to one she'll none of me: the count himself here hard by woos her.

SIR TOBY

She'll none o' the count: she'll not match above her degree, neither in estate, years, nor wit; I have heard her swear 't. Tut, there's life in 't, man.

SIR ANDREW

I'll stay a month longer. I am a fellow o' the strangest mind i' the world; I delight in masques and revels sometimes altogether.

SIR TOBY

Art thou good at these kickshawses, knight?

SIR ANDREW

As any man in Illyria, whatsoever he be, under the degree of my betters; and yet I will not compare with an old man.

SIR TOBY

What is thy excellence in a galliard, knight?

SIR ANDREW

Faith, I can cut a caper.

SIR TOBY

And I can cut the mutton to 't.

SIR ANDREW

And I think I have the back-trick simply as strong
as any man in Illyria.

SIR TOBY

Wherefore are these things hid? wherefore have
these gifts a curtain before 'em? are they like to take
dust, like Mistress Mall's picture? why dost thou
not go to church in a galliard and come home in a
coranto? My very walk should be a jig; I would not
so much as make water but in a sink-a-pace. What
dost thou mean? Is it a world to hide virtues in? I
did think, by the excellent constitution of thy leg,
it was formed under the star of a galliard.

SIR ANDREW

Ay, 'tis strong, and it does indifferent well in a
flame-coloured stock. Shall we set about some revels?

SIR TOBY

What shall we do else? were we not born under
Taurus?

SIR ANDREW

Taurus! That's sides and heart.

SIR TOBY

No, sir; it is legs and thighs. Let me see thee caper:
ha! higher: ha, ha! excellent!   [Exeunt

SCENE IV. The DUKE's palace

Enter VALENTINE, and VIOLA in man's attire

VALENTINE

If the Duke continue these favours towards you,
Cesario, you are like to be much advanced: he hath
known you but three days, and already you are no
stranger.

VIOLA

You either fear his humour or my negligence, that
you call in question the continuance of his love: is
he inconstant, sir, in his favours?

VALENTINE

No, believe me.

VIOLA

I thank you. Here comes the count.

Enter DUKE, CURIO, and ATTENDANTS

DUKE

Who saw Cesario, ho?

VIOLA

On your attendance, my lord; here.

DUKE

Stand you a while aloof. Cesario,
Thou know'st no less but all; I have unclasp'd
To thee the book even of my secret soul:
Therefore. good youth, address thy gait unto her;

Be not denied access, stand at her doors,
And tell them, there thy fixed foot shall grow
Till thou have audience.

VIOLA

Sure, my noble lord,
If she be so abandon'd to her sorrow
As it is spoke, she never will admit me.

DUKE

Be clamorous and leap all civil bounds
Rather than make unprofited return.

VIOLA

Say I do speak with her, my lord, what then?

DUKE

O, then unfold the passion of my love,
Surprise her with discourse of my dear faith:
It shall become thee well to act my woes;
She will attend it better in thy youth
Than in a nuncio's of more grave aspect.

VIOLA

I think not so, my lord.

DUKE

Dear lad, believe it;
For they shall yet belie thy happy years,
That say thou art a man: Diana's lip
Is not more smooth and rubious; thy small pipe
Is as the maiden's organ, shrill and sound;
And all is semblative a woman's part.
I know thy constellation is right apt
For this affair. Some four or five attend him;
All, if you will; for I myself am best
When least in company. Prosper well in this,
And thou shalt live as freely as thy lord,
To call his fortunes thine.

VIOLA

I'll do my best
To woo your lady: [Aside] yet, a barful strife!
Whoe'er I woo, myself would be his wife.   [Exeunt

SCENE V. OLIVIA's house

Enter MARIA and CLOWN

MARIA

Nay, either tell me where thou hast been, or I will
not open my lips so wide as a bristle may enter in
way of thy excuse: my lady will hang thee for thy
absence.

CLOWN

Let her hang me: he that is well hanged in this
world needs to fear no colours.

MARIA

Make that good.

CLOWN

He shall see none to fear.

MARIA

A good lenten answer: I can tell thee where that
saying was born, of 'I fear no colours.'

CLOWN

Where, good Mistress Mary?

MARIA

In the wars; and that may you be bold to say in your foolery.

CLOWN

Well, God give them wisdom that have it; and those that are fools, let them use their talents.

MARIA

Yet you will be hanged for being so long absent; or, to be turned away, is not that as good as a hanging to you?

CLOWN

Many a good hanging prevents a bad marriage; and, for turning away, let summer bear it out.

MARIA

You are resolute, then?

CLOWN

Not so, neither; but I am resolved on two points.

MARIA

That if one break, the other will hold; or, if both break, your gaskins fall.

CLOWN

Apt, in good faith; very apt. Well, go thy way; if Sir Toby would leave drinking, thou wert as witty a piece of Eve's flesh as any in Illyria.

MARIA

Peace, you rogue, no more o' that. Here comes my lady: make your excuse wisely, you were best. [*Exit*

CLOWN

Wit, an 't be thy will, put me into good fooling! Those wits, that think they have thee, do very oft prove fools; and I, that am sure I lack thee, may pass for a wise man: for what says Quinapalus? 'Better a witty fool than a foolish wit.'

Enter LADY OLIVIA *with* MALVOLIO

God bless thee, lady!

OLIVIA

Take the fool away.

CLOWN

Do you not hear, fellows? Take away the lady.

OLIVIA

Go to, you're a dry fool; I'll no more of you: besides, you grow dishonest.

CLOWN

Two faults, madonna, that drink and good counsel will amend: for give the dry fool drink, then is the fool not dry: bid the dishonest man mend himself; if he mend, he is no longer dishonest; if he cannot, let the botcher mend him. Any thing that's mended is but patched: virtue that transgresses is but patched with sin; and sin that amends is but patched with virtue. If that this simple syllogism will serve, so; if it will not, what remedy? As there is no true cuckold but calamity, so beauty's a flower. The lady bade take away the fool; therefore, I say again, take her away.

OLIVIA

Sir, I bade them take away you.

CLOWN

Misprision in the highest degree! Lady, cucullus

non facit monachum; that's as much to say as I wear not motley in my brain. Good madonna, give me leave to prove you a fool.

OLIVIA

Can you do it?

CLOWN

Dexteriously, good madonna.

OLIVIA

Make your proof.

CLOWN

I must catechize you for it, madonna: good my mouse of virtue, answer me.

OLIVIA

Well, sir, for want of other idleness, I'll bide your proof.

CLOWN

Good madonna, why mournest thou?

OLIVIA

Good fool, for my brother's death.

CLOWN

I think his soul is in hell, madonna.

OLIVIA

I know his soul is in heaven, fool.

CLOWN

The more fool, madonna, to mourn for your brother's soul being in heaven. Take away the fool, gentlemen.

OLIVIA

What think you of this fool, Malvolio? doth he not mend?

MALVOLIO

Yes, and shall do till the pangs of death shake him: infirmity, that decays the wise, doth ever make the better fool.

CLOWN

God send you, sir, a speedy infirmity, for the better increasing your folly! Sir Toby will be sworn that I am no fox; but he will not pass his word for two pence that you are no fool.

OLIVIA

How say you to that, Malvolio?

MALVOLIO

I marvel your ladyship takes delight in such a barren rascal: I saw him put down the other day with an ordinary fool that has no more brain than a stone. Look you now, he's out of his guard already; unless you laugh and minister occasion to him, he is gagged. I protest, I take these wise men, that crow so at these set kind of fools, no better than the fools' zanies.

OLIVIA

O, you are sick of self-love, Malvolio, and taste with a distempered appetite. To be generous, guiltless and of free disposition, is to take those things for bird-bolts that you deem cannon-bullets: there is no slander in an allowed fool, though he do nothing but rail; nor no railing in a known discreet man, though he do nothing but reprove.

CLOWN

Now Mercury endue thee with leasing, for thou speakest well of fools!

Re-enter MARIA

MARIA

Madam, there is at the gate a young gentleman much desires to speak with you.

OLIVIA

From the Count Orsino, is it?

MARIA

I know not, madam: 'tis a fair young man, and well attended.

OLIVIA

Who of my people hold him in delay?

MARIA

Sir Toby, madam, your kinsman.

OLIVIA

Fetch him off, I pray you; he speaks nothing but madman: fie on him! [*Exit* MARIA] Go you, Malvolio: if it be a suit from the count, I am sick, or not at home; what you will, to dismiss it. [*Exit* MAL-VOLIO] Now you see, sir, how your fooling grows old, and people dislike it.

CLOWN

Thou hast spoke for us, madonna, as if thy eldest son should be a fool; whose skull Jove cram with brains! for,—here he comes,—one of thy kin has a most weak pia mater.

Enter SIR TOBY

OLIVIA

By mine honour, half drunk. What is he at the gate, cousin?

SIR TOBY

A gentleman.

OLIVIA

A gentleman! what gentleman?

SIR TOBY

'Tis a gentleman here—a plague o' these pickle-herring! How now, sot!

CLOWN

Good Sir Toby!

OLIVIA

Cousin, cousin, how have you come so early by this lethargy?

SIR TOBY

Lechery! I defy lechery. There's one at the gate.

OLIVIA

Ay, marry, what is he?

SIR TOBY

Let him be the devil, an he will, I care not: give me faith, say I. Well, it's all one.   [*Exit*

OLIVIA

What's a drunken man like, fool?

CLOWN

Like a drowned man, a fool and a mad man: one draught above heat makes him a fool; the second mads him; and a third drowns him.

OLIVIA

Go thou and seek the crowner, and let him sit o'

my coz; for he's in the third degree of drink, he's drowned: go look after him.

CLOWN

He is but mad yet, madonna; and the fool shall look to the madman.   [*Exit*

Re-enter MALVOLIO

MALVOLIO

Madam, yond young fellow swears he will speak with you. I told him you were sick; he takes on him to understand so much, and therefore comes to speak with you. I told him you were asleep; he seems to have a foreknowledge of that too, and therefore comes to speak with you. What is to be said to him, lady? he's fortified against any denial.

OLIVIA

Tell him he shall not speak with me.

MALVOLIO

Has been told so; and he says, he'll stand at your door like a sheriff's post, and be the supporter to a bench, but he'll speak with you.

OLIVIA

What kind o' man is he?

MALVOLIO

Why, of mankind.

OLIVIA

What manner of man?

MALVOLIO

Of very ill manner; he'll speak with you, will you or no.

OLIVIA

Of what personage and years is he?

MALVOLIO

Not yet old enough for a man, nor young enough for a boy; as a squash is before 'tis a peascod, or a cod-ling when 'tis almost an apple: 'tis with him in standing water, between boy and man. He is very well-favoured and he speaks very shrewishly; one would think his mother's milk were scarce out of him.

OLIVIA

Let him approach: call in my gentlewoman.

MALVOLIO

Gentlewoman, my lady calls.   [*Exit*

Re-enter MARIA

OLIVIA

Give me my veil: come, throw it o'er my face. We'll once more hear Orsino's embassy.

Enter VIOLA, *and* ATTENDANTS

VIOLA

The honourable lady of the house, which is she?

OLIVIA

Speak to me; I shall answer for her. Your will?

VIOLA

Most radiant, exquisite and unmatchable beauty,— I pray you, tell me if this be the lady of the house, for I never saw her: I would be loath to cast away my speech, for besides that it is excellently well penned, I have taken great pains to con it. Good beauties, let me sustain no scorn; I am very compti-ble, even to the least sinister usage.

OLIVIA

Whence came you, sir?

VIOLA

I can say little more than I have studied, and that question's out of my part. Good gentle one, give me modest assurance if you be the lady of the house, that I may proceed in my speech.

OLIVIA

Are you a comedian?

VIOLA

No, my profound heart: and yet, by the very fangs of malice I swear, I am not that I play. Are you the lady of the house?

OLIVIA

If I do not usurp myself, I am.

VIOLA

Most certain, if you are she, you do usurp yourself; for what is yours to bestow is not yours to reserve. But this is from my commission: I will on with my speech in your praise, and then show you the heart of my message.

OLIVIA

Come to what is important in 't: I forgive you the praise.

VIOLA

Alas, I took great pains to study it, and 'tis poetical.

OLIVIA

It is the more like to be feigned: I pray you, keep it in. I heard you were saucy at my gates, and allowed your approach rather to wonder at you than to hear you. If you be not mad, be gone; if you have reason, be brief: 'tis not that time of moon with me to make one in so skipping a dialogue.

MARIA

Will you hoist sail, sir? here lies your way.

VIOLA

No, good swabber; I am to hull here a little longer. Some mollification for your giant, sweet lady. Tell me your mind: I am a messenger.

OLIVIA

Sure, you have some hideous matter to deliver, when the courtesy of it is so fearful. Speak your office.

VIOLA

It alone concerns your ear. I bring no overture of war, no taxation of homage: I hold the olive in my hand; my words are as full of peace as matter.

OLIVIA

Yet you began rudely. What are you? what would you?

VIOLA

The rudeness that hath appeared in me have I learned from my entertainment. What I am, and what I would, are as secret as maidenhead; to your ears, divinity, to any other's, profanation.

OLIVIA

Give us the place alone: we will hear this divinity. [Exeunt MARIA and ATTENDANTS] Now, sir, what is your text?

VIOLA

Most sweet lady,—

OLIVIA

A comfortable doctrine, and much may be said of it. Where lies your text?

VIOLA

In Orsino's bosom.

OLIVIA

In his bosom! In what chapter of his bosom?

VIOLA

To answer by the method, in the first of his heart.

OLIVIA

O, I have read it: it is heresy. Have you no more to say?

VIOLA

Good madam, let me see your face.

OLIVIA

Have you any commission from your lord to negotiate with my face? You are now out of your text: but we will draw the curtain and show you the picture. Look you, sir, such a one I was this present. is't not well done?   [Unveiling

VIOLA

Excellently done, if God did all.

OLIVIA

'Tis in grain, sir; 'twill endure wind and weather.

VIOLA

'Tis beauty truly blent, whose red and white Nature's own sweet and cunning hand laid on:
Lady, you are the cruell'st she alive,
If you will lead these graces to the grave
And leave the world no copy.

OLIVIA

O, sir, I will not be so hard-hearted; I will give out divers schedules of my beauty: it shall be inventoried, and every particle and utensil labelled to my will: as, item, two lips, indifferent red; item, two grey eyes, with lids to them; item, one neck, one chin, and so forth. Were you sent hither to praise me?

VIOLA

I see what you are, you are too proud;
But, if you were the devil, you are fair.
My lord and master loves you: O, such love
Could be but recompensed, though you were crown'd
The nonpareil of beauty!

OLIVIA

How does he love me?

VIOLA

With adorations, fertile tears,
With groans that thunder love, with sighs of fire.

OLIVIA

Your lord does know my mind; I cannot love him:
Yet I suppose him virtuous, know him noble,
Of great estate, of fresh and stainless youth;
In voices well divulged, free, learn'd and valiant;
And in dimension and the shape of nature
A gracious person: but yet I cannot love him;
He might have took his answer long ago.

VIOLA

If I did love you in my master's flame,
With such a suffering, such a deadly life,
In your denial I would find no sense;
I would not understand it.

OLIVIA
           Why, what would you?

VIOLA

Make me a willow cabin at your gate,
And call upon my soul within the house;
Write loyal cantons of contemned love
And sing them loud even in the dead of night;
Halloo your name to the reverberate hills,
And make the babbling gossip of the air
Cry out 'Olivia!' O, you should not rest
Between the elements of air and earth,
But you should pity me!

OLIVIA
           You might do much.
What is your parentage?

VIOLA

Above my fortunes, yet my state is well:
I am a gentleman.

OLIVIA
           Get you to your lord;
I cannot love him: let him send no more;
Unless, perchance, you come to me again,
To tell me how he takes it. Fare you well:
I thank you for your pains: spend this for me.

VIOLA

I am no fee'd post, lady; keep your purse:
My master, not myself, lacks recompense.
Love make his heart of flint that you shall love;
And let your fervour, like my master's, be
Placed in contempt! Farewell, fair cruelty.   [Exit

OLIVIA

'What is your parentage?'
'Above my fortunes, yet my state is well:
I am a gentleman.' I'll be sworn thou art;
Thy tongue, thy face, thy limbs, actions, and spirit,
Do give thee five-fold blazon: not too fast: soft, soft!
Unless the master were the man. How now!
Even so quickly may one catch the plague?
Methinks I feel this youth's perfections
With an invisible and subtle stealth
To creep in at mine eyes. Well, let it be.
What ho, Malvolio!

Re-enter MALVOLIO

MALVOLIO
          Here, madam, at your service.

OLIVIA

Run after that same peevish messenger,
The county's man: he left this ring behind him,
Would I or not: tell him I'll none of it.
Desire him not to flatter with his lord,
Nor hold him up with hopes; I am not for him:
If that the youth will come this way to-morrow,
I'll give him reasons for't: hie thee, Malvolio.

MALVOLIO
Madam, I will.   [Exit

OLIVIA

I do I know not what, and fear to find
Mine eye too great a flatterer for my mind.
Fate, show thy force: ourselves we do not owe;
What is decreed must be, and be this so.   [Exit

ACT II

SCENE I. *The sea-coast*

Enter ANTONIO *and* SEBASTIAN

ANTONIO
Will you stay no longer? nor will you not that I go
with you?

SEBASTIAN
By your patience, no. My stars shine darkly over
me: the malignancy of my fate might perhaps distemper yours; therefore I shall crave of you your
leave that I may bear my evils alone: it were a bad
recompense for your love, to lay any of them on
you.

ANTONIO
Let me yet know of you whither you are bound.

SEBASTIAN
No, sooth, sir: my determinate voyage is mere ex-
travagancy. But I perceive in you so excellent a
touch of modesty, that you will not extort from me
what I am willing to keep in; therefore it charges
me in manners the rather to express myself. You
must know of me then, Antonio, my name is Sebastian, which I called Roderigo. My father was
that Sebastian of Messaline, whom I know you
have heard of. He left behind him myself and a
sister, both born in an hour: if the heavens had been
pleased, would we had so ended! but you, sir,
altered that; for some hour before you took me
from the breach of the sea was my sister drowned.

ANTONIO
Alas the day!

SEBASTIAN
A lady, sir, though it was said she much resembled
me, was yet of many accounted beautiful: but,
though I could not with such estimable wonder
overfar believe that, yet thus far I will boldly publish her; she bore a mind that envy could not but
call fair. She is drowned already, sir, with salt
water, though I seem to drown her remembrance
again with more.

ANTONIO
Pardon me, sir, your bad entertainment.

SEBASTIAN
O good Antonio, forgive me your trouble.

ANTONIO
If you will not murder me for my love, let me be
your servant.

SEBASTIAN
If you will not undo what you have done, that is,
kill him whom you have recovered, desire it not.

Fare ye well at once: my bosom is full of kindness,
and I am yet so near the manners of my mother,
that upon the least occasion more mine eyes will
tell tales of me. I am bound to the Count Orsino's
court: farewell.　　　　　　　　　　　　　[*Exit*

ANTONIO

The gentleness of all the gods go with thee!
I have many enemies in Orsino's court,
Else would I very shortly see thee there.
But, come what may, I do adore thee so,
That danger shall seem sport, and I will go. 　[*Exit*

SCENE II. *A street*

Enter VIOLA, MALVOLIO *following*

MALVOLIO

Were not you even now with the Countess Olivia?

VIOLA

Even now, sir; on a moderate pace I have since
arrived but hither.

MALVOLIO

She returns this ring to you, sir: you might have
saved me my pains, to have taken it away yourself.
She adds, moreover, that you should put your lord
into a desperate assurance she will none of him: and
one thing more, that you be never so hardy to come
again in his affairs, unless it be to report your lord's
taking of this. Receive it so.

VIOLA

She took the ring of me: I'll none of it.

MALVOLIO

Come, sir, you peevishly threw it to her; and her
will is, it should be so returned: if it be worth stooping for, there it lies in your eye; if not, be it his that
finds it.　　　　　　　　　　　　　　　　[*Exit*

VIOLA

I left no ring with her: what means this lady?
Fortune forbid my outside have not charm'd her!
She made good view of me; indeed, so much,
That methought her eyes had lost her tongue,
For she did speak in starts distractedly.
She loves me, sure; the cunning of her passion
Invites me in this churlish messenger.
None of my lord's ring! why, he sent her none.
I am the man: if it be so, as 'tis,
Poor lady, she were better love a dream.
Disguise, I see, thou art a wickedness,
Wherein the pregnant enemy does much.
How easy is it for the proper-false
In women's waxen hearts to set their forms!
Alas, our frailty is the cause, not we!
For such as we are made of, such we be.
How will this fadge? my master loves her dearly;
And I, poor monster, fond as much on him;
And she, mistaken, seems to dote on me.
What will become of this? As I am man,
My state is desperate for my master's love;
As I am woman,—now alas the day!—
What thriftless sighs shall poor Olivia breathe!

O time! thou must untangle this, not I;
It is too hard a knot for me to untie! 　　　　[*Exit*

SCENE III. OLIVIA'S *house*

Enter SIR TOBY *and* SIR ANDREW

SIR TOBY

Approach, Sir Andrew: not to be a-bed after midnight is to be upbetimes; and 'diluculo surgere,'
thou know'st,—

SIR ANDREW

Nay, by my troth, I know not: but I know, to be up
late is to be up late.

SIR TOBY

A false conclusion: I hate it as an unfilled can. To
be up after midnight and to go to bed then, is early:
so that to go to bed after midnight is to go to bed
betimes. Does not our life consist of the four elements?

SIR ANDREW

Faith, so they say; but I think it rather consists of
eating and drinking.

SIR TOBY

Thou'rt a scholar; let us therefore eat and drink.
Marian, I say! a stoup of wine!

Enter CLOWN

SIR ANDREW

Here comes the fool, i' faith.

CLOWN

How now, my hearts! did you never see the picture
of 'we three'?

SIR TOBY

Welcome, ass. Now let's have a catch.

SIR ANDREW

By my troth, the fool has an excellent breast. I had
rather than forty shillings I had such a leg, and so
sweet a breath to sing, as the fool has. In sooth, thou
wast in very gracious fooling last night, when thou
spokest of Pigrogromitus, of the Vapians passing the
equinoctial of Queubus: 'twas very good, i' faith. I
sent thee sixpence for thy leman: hadst it?

CLOWN

I did impeticos thy gratillity; for Malvolio's nose is
no whipstock: my lady has a white hand, and the
Myrmidons are no bottle-ale houses.

SIR ANDREW

Excellent! why, this is the best fooling, when all is
done. Now, a song.

SIR TOBY

Come on; there is sixpence for you: let's have a
song.

SIR ANDREW

There's a testril of me too: if one knight give a—

CLOWN

Would you have a love-song, or a song of good life?

SIR TOBY

A love-song, a love-song.

SIR ANDREW

Ay, ay: I care not for good life.

CLOWN

[*Sings*]   O mistress mine, where are you roaming?
       O, stay and hear; your true love's coming,
         That can sing both high and low:
       Trip no further, pretty sweeting;
       Journeys end in lovers meeting,
         Every wise man's son doth know.

SIR ANDREW

Excellent good, i' faith.

SIR TOBY

Good, good.

CLOWN

[*Sings*]   What is love? 'tis not hereafter;
       Present mirth hath present laughter;
         What's to come is still unsure:
       In delay there lies no plenty;
       Then come kiss me, sweet and twenty,
         Youth's a stuff will not endure.

SIR ANDREW

A mellifluous voice, as I am a true knight.

SIR TOBY

A contagious breath.

SIR ANDREW

Very sweet and contagious, i' faith.

SIR TOBY

To hear by the nose, it is dulcet in contagion. But
shall we make the welkin dance indeed? shall we
rouse the night-owl in a catch that will draw three
souls out of one weaver? shall we do that?

SIR ANDREW

An you love me, let's do't: I am dog at a catch.

CLOWN

By'r lady, sir, and some dogs will catch well.

SIR ANDREW

Most certain. Let our catch be, 'Thou knave.'

CLOWN

'Hold thy peace, thou knave,' knight? I shall be
constrained in't to call thee knave, knight.

SIR ANDREW

'Tis not the first time I have constrained one to call
me knave. Begin, fool: it begins 'Hold thy peace.'

CLOWN

I shall never begin if I hold my peace.

SIR ANDREW

Good, i'faith. Come, begin.   [*Catch sung*

Enter MARIA

MARIA

What a caterwauling do you keep here! If my lady
have not called up her steward Malvolio and bid
him turn you out of doors, never trust me.

SIR TOBY

My lady's a Cataian, we are politicians, Malvolio's
a Peg-a-Ramsey, and 'Three merry men be we.'
Am not I consanguineous? am I not of her blood?
Tillyvally. Lady! [*Sings*] 'There dwelt a man in
Babylon, lady, lady!'

CLOWN

Beshrew me, the knight's in admirable fooling.

SIR ANDREW

Ay, he does well enough if he be disposed, and so do

I too: he does it with a better grace, but I do it more
natural.

SIR TOBY

[*Sings*] 'O, the twelfth day of December',—

MARIA

For the love o' God, peace!

Enter MALVOLIO

MALVOLIO

My masters, are you mad? or what are you? Have
you no wit, manners, nor honesty, but to gabble like
tinkers at this time of night? Do ye make an alehouse of my lady's house, that ye squeak out your
coziers' catches without any mitigation or remorse
of voice? Is there no respect of place, persons, nor
time in you?

SIR TOBY

We did keep time, sir, in our catches. Sneck up!

MALVOLIO

Sir Toby, I must be round with you. My lady bade
me tell you, that, though she harbours you as her
kinsman, she's nothing allied to your disorders. If
you can separate yourself and your misdemeanours,
you are welcome to the house; if not, an it would
please you to take leave of her, she is very willing to
bid you farewell.

SIR TOBY

'Farewell, dear heart, since I must needs be gone.'

MARIA

Nay, good Sir Toby.

CLOWN

'His eyes do show his days are almost done.'

MALVOLIO

Is't even so?

SIR TOBY

'But I will never die.'

CLOWN

Sir Toby, there you lie.

MALVOLIO

This is much credit to you.

SIR TOBY

'Shall I bid him go?'

CLOWN

'What an if you do?'

SIR TOBY

'Shall I bid him go, and spare not?'

CLOWN

'O no, no, no, no, you dare not.'

SIR TOBY

Out o' tune, sir: ye lie. Art any more than a steward? Dost thou think, because thou art virtuous,
there shall be no more cakes and ale?

CLOWN

Yes, by Saint Anne, and ginger shall be hot i' the
mouth too.

SIR TOBY

Thou 'rt i' the right. Go, sir, rub your chain with
crums. A stoup of wine, Maria!

MALVOLIO

Mistress Mary, if you prized my lady's favour at
any thing more than contempt, you would not give

means for this uncivil rule: she shall know of it, by this hand.   [*Exit*

MARIA

Go shake your ears.

SIR ANDREW

'Twere as good a deed as to drink when a man's a-hungry, to challenge him the field, and then to break promise with him and make a fool of him.

SIR TOBY

Do't, knight: I'll write thee a challenge; or I'll deliver thy indignation to him by word of mouth.

MARIA

Sweet Sir Toby, be patient for to-night: since the youth of the count's was to-day with my lady, she is much out of quiet. For Monsieur Malvolio, let me alone with him: if I do not gull him into a nayword, and make him a common recreation, do not think I have wit enough to lie straight in my bed: I know I can do it.

SIR TOBY

Possess us, possess us; tell us something of him.

MARIA

Marry, sir, sometimes he is a kind of puritan.

SIR ANDREW

O, if I thought that, I'ld beat him like a dog!

SIR TOBY

What, for being a puritan? thy exquisite reason, dear knight?

SIR ANDREW

I have no exquisite reason for't, but I have reason good enough.

MARIA

The devil a puritan that he is, or any thing constantly, but a time-pleaser; an affectioned ass, that cons state without book and utters it by great swarths: the best persuaded of himself, so crammed, as he thinks, with excellencies, that it is his grounds of faith that all that look on him love him; and on that vice in him will my revenge find notable cause to work.

SIR TOBY

What wilt thou do?

MARIA

I will drop in his way some obscure epistles of love; wherein, by the colour of his beard, the shape of his leg, the manner of his gait, the expressure of his eye, forehead, and complexion, he shall find himself most feelingly personated. I can write very like my lady your niece: on a forgotten matter we can hardly make distinction of our hands.

SIR TOBY

Excellent! I smell a device.

SIR ANDREW

I have't in my nose too.

SIR TOBY

He shall think, by the letters that thou wilt drop, that they come from my niece, and that she's in love with him.

MARIA

My purpose is, indeed, a horse of that colour.

SIR ANDREW

And your horse now would make him an ass.

MARIA

Ass, I doubt not.

SIR ANDREW

O, 'twill be admirable!

MARIA

Sport royal, I warrant you: I know my physic will work with him. I will plant you two, and let the fool make a third, where he shall find the letter: observe his construction of it. For this night, to bed, and dream on the event. Farewell.   [*Exit*

SIR TOBY

Good night, Penthesilea.

SIR ANDREW

Before me, she's a good wench.

SIR TOBY

She's a beagle, true-bred, and one that adores me: what o' that?

SIR ANDREW

I was adored once too.

SIR TOBY

Let's to bed, knight. Thou hadst need send for more money.

SIR ANDREW

If I cannot recover your niece, I am a foul way out.

SIR TOBY

Send for money, knight: if thou hast her not i' the end, call me cut.

SIR ANDREW

If I do not, never trust me, take it how you will.

SIR TOBY

Come, come, I'll go burn some sack; 'tis too late to go to bed now: come, knight; come, knight.
                                                       [*Exeunt*

SCENE IV. *The* DUKE's *palace*

Enter DUKE, VIOLA, CURIO, *and others*

DUKE

Give me some music. Now, good morrow, friends.
Now, good Cesario, but that piece of song,
That old and antique song we heard last night:
Methought it did relieve my passion much,
More than light airs and recollected terms
Of these most brisk and giddy-paced times:
Come, but one verse.

CURIO

He is not here, so please your lordship, that should sing it.

DUKE

Who was it?

CURIO

Feste, the jester, my lord; a fool that the lady Olivia's father took much delight in. He is about the house.

DUKE

Seek him out, and play the tune the while.
                              [*Exit* CURIO. *Music plays*
Come hither, boy: if ever thou shalt love,

In the sweet pangs of it remember me;
For such as I am all true lovers are,
Unstaid and skittish in all motions else,
Save in the constant image of the creature
That is beloved. How dost thou like this tune?

VIOLA

It gives a very echo to the seat
Where Love is throned.

DUKE

　　　　　Thou dost speak masterly:
My life upon't, young though thou art, thine eye
Hath stay'd upon some favour that it loves:
Hath it not, boy?

VIOLA

　　　A little, by your favour.

DUKE

What kind of woman is't?

VIOLA

　　　Of your complexion.

DUKE

She is not worth thee, then. What years, i'faith?

VIOLA

About your years, my lord.

DUKE

Too old, by heaven: let still the woman take
An elder than herself; so wears she to him,
So sways she level in her husband's heart:
For, boy, however we do praise ourselves,
Our fancies are more giddy and unfirm,
More longing, wavering, sooner lost and worn,
Than women's are.

VIOLA

　　　I think it well, my lord.

DUKE

Then let thy love be younger than thyself,
Or thy affection cannot hold the bent;
For women are as roses, whose fair flower
Being once display'd, doth fall that very hour.

VIOLA

And so they are: alas, that they are so;
To die, even when they to perfection grow!

Re-enter CURIO *and* CLOWN

DUKE

O, fellow, come, the song we had last night.
Mark it, Cesario, it is old and plain;
The spinsters and the knitters in the sun
And the free maids that weave their thread with
　　　　bones
Do use to chant it: it is silly sooth,
And dallies with the innocence of love,
Like the old age.

CLOWN

Are you ready, sir?

DUKE

Ay; prithee, sing.　　　　　　　　　　　[*Music*

CLOWN

SONG

Come away, come away, death,
　And in sad cypress let me be laid;

Fly away, fly away, breath;
　I am slain by a fair cruel maid.
My shroud of white, stuck all with yew,
　　　O, prepare it!
My part of death, no one so true
　　　Did share it.

Not a flower, not a flower sweet,
　On my black coffin let there be strown;
Not a friend, not a friend greet
　My poor corpse, where my bones shall be thrown:
A thousand thousand sighs to save,
　　　Lay me, O, where
Sad true lover never find my grave,
　　　To weep there!

DUKE

There's for thy pains.

CLOWN

No pains, sir; I take pleasure in singing, sir.

DUKE

I'll pay thy pleasure then.

CLOWN

Truly, sir, and pleasure will be paid, one time or
another.

DUKE

Give me now leave to leave thee.

CLOWN

Now, the melancholy god protect thee; and the
tailor make thy doublet of changeable taffeta, for
thy mind is a very opal. I would have men of such
constancy put to sea, that their business might be
every thing and their intent every where; for that's
it that always makes a good voyage of nothing.
Farewell.　　　　　　　　　　　　　　[*Exit*

DUKE

Let all the rest give place.

[CURIO *and* ATTENDANTS *retire*
　　　　Once more, Cesario,
Get thee to yond same sovereign cruelty:
Tell her, my love, more noble than the world,
Prizes not quantity of dirty lands;
The parts that fortune hath bestow'd upon her,
Tell her, I hold as giddily as fortune;
But 'tis that miracle and queen of gems
That nature pranks her in attracts my soul.

VIOLA

But if she cannot love you, sir?

DUKE

I cannot be so answer'd.

VIOLA

　　　Sooth, but you must.
Say that some lady, as perhaps there is,
Hath for your love as great a pang of heart
As you have for Olivia: you cannot love her;
You tell her so; must she not then be answer'd?

DUKE

There is no woman's sides
Can bide the beating of so strong a passion
As love doth give my heart; no woman's heart
So big, to hold so much; they lack retention.
Alas, their love may be call'd appetite,—
No motion of the liver, but the palate,—

That suffer surfeit, cloyment and revolt;
But mine is all as hungry as the sea,
And can digest as much: make no compare
Between that love a woman can bear me
And that I owe Olivia.

VIOLA
　　　　　Ay, but I know,—

DUKE
What dost thou know?

VIOLA
Too well what love women to men may owe:
In faith, they are as true of heart as we.
My father had a daughter loved a man,
As it might be, perhaps, were I a woman,
I should your lordship.

DUKE
　　　　　And what's her history?

VIOLA
A blank, my lord. She never told her love,
But let concealment, like a worm i' the bud,
Feed on her damask cheek: she pined in thought;
And with a green and yellow melancholy
She sat like patience on a monument,
Smiling at grief. Was not this love indeed?
We men may say more, swear more: but indeed
Our shows are more than will; for still we prove
Much in our vows, but little in our love.

DUKE
But died thy sister of her love, my boy?

VIOLA
I am all the daughters of my father's house,
And all the brothers too: and yet I know not.
Sir, shall I to this lady?

DUKE
　　　　　Ay, that's the theme.
To her in haste; give her this jewel; say,
My love can give no place, bide no denay. [Exeunt

SCENE V. OLIVIA's garden

Enter SIR TOBY, SIR ANDREW, and FABIAN

SIR TOBY
Come thy ways, Signior Fabian.

FABIAN
Nay, I'll come: if I lose a scruple of this sport, let
me be boiled to death with melancholy.

SIR TOBY
Wouldst thou not be glad to have the niggardly
rascally sheep-biter come by some notable shame?

FABIAN
I would exult, man: you know, he brought me out
o' favour with my lady about a bear-baiting here.

SIR TOBY
To anger him we'll have the bear again; and we will
fool him black and blue: shall we not, Sir Andrew?

SIR ANDREW
An we do not, it is pity of our lives.

SIR TOBY
Here comes the little villain.

Enter MARIA

How now, my metal of India!

MARIA
Get ye all three into the box-tree: Malvolio's coming down this walk: he has been yonder i' the sun
practising behaviour to his own shadow this half
hour: observe him, for the love of mockery; for I
know this letter will make a contemplative idiot of
him. Close, in the name of jesting! Lie thou there
[throws down a letter]; for here comes the trout that
must be caught with tickling. [Exit

Enter MALVOLIO

MALVOLIO
'Tis but fortune; all is fortune. Maria once told me
she did affect me: and I have heard herself come
thus near, that, should she fancy, it should be one of
my complexion. Besides, she uses me with a more
exalted respect than any one else that follows her.
What should I think on't?

SIR TOBY
Here's an overweening rogue!

FABIAN
O, peace! Contemplation makes a rare turkey-cock
of him: how he jets under his advanced plumes!

SIR ANDREW
'Slight, I could so beat the rogue!

SIR TOBY
Peace, I say.

MALVOLIO
To be Count Malvolio!

SIR TOBY
Ah, rogue!

SIR ANDREW
Pistol him, pistol him.

SIR TOBY
Peace, peace!

MALVOLIO
There is example for't; the lady of the Strachy
married the yeoman of the wardrobe.

SIR ANDREW
Fie on him Jezebel!

FABIAN
O, peace! now he's deeply in: look how imagination
blows him.

MALVOLIO
Having been three months married to her, sitting in
my state,—

SIR TOBY
O, for a stone-bow, to hit him in the eye!

MALVOLIO
Calling my officers about me, in my branched velvet gown; having come from a day-bed, where I
have left Olivia sleeping,—

SIR TOBY
Fire and brimstone!

FABIAN
O, peace, peace!

MALVOLIO
And then to have the humour of state; and after a
demure travel of regard, telling them I know my

place as I would they should do theirs, to ask for my kinsman Toby,—

SIR TOBY

Bolts and shackles!

FABIAN

O, peace, peace, peace! now, now.

MALVOLIO

Seven of my people, with an obedient start, make out for him: I frown the while; and perchance wind up my watch, or play with my—some rich jewel. Toby approaches; courtesies there to me,—

SIR TOBY

Shall this fellow live?

FABIAN

Though our silence be drawn from us with cars, yet peace.

MALVOLIO

I extend my hand to him thus, quenching my familiar smile with an austere regard of control,—

SIR TOBY

And does not Toby take you a blow o' the lips then?

MALVOLIO

Saying, 'Cousin Toby, my fortunes having cast me on your niece give me this prerogative of speech,'—

SIR TOBY

What, what?

MALVOLIO

'You must amend your drunkenness.'

SIR TOBY

Out, scab!

FABIAN

Nay, patience, or we break the sinews of our plot.

MALVOLIO

'Besides, you waste the treasure of your time with a foolish knight,'—

SIR ANDREW

That's me, I warrant you.

MALVOLIO

'One Sir Andrew,'—

SIR ANDREW

I knew 'twas I; for many do call me fool.

MALVOLIO

What employment have we here?

[Taking up the letter

FABIAN

Now is the woodcock near the gin.

SIR TOBY

O, peace! and the spirit of humours intimate reading aloud to him!

MALVOLIO

By my life, this is my lady's hand: these be her very C's, her U's, and her T's; and thus makes she her great P's. It is, in contempt of question, her hand.

SIR ANDREW

Her C's, her U's and her T's: why that?

MALVOLIO

[Reads] To the unknown beloved, this, and my good wishes:— her very phrases! By your leave, wax. Soft! and the

impressure her Lucrece, with which she uses to seal: 'tis my lady. To whom should this be?

FABIAN

This wins, him, liver and all.

MALVOLIO

[Reads] Jove knows I love:
         But who?
         Lips, do not move;
         No man must know.

'No man must know.' What follows? the numbers altered!
'No man must know:' if this should be thee, Malvolio?

SIR TOBY

Marry, hang thee, brock!

MALVOLIO

[Reads] I may command where I adore;
         But silence, like a Lucrece knife,
         With bloodless stroke my heart doth gore:
         M, O, A, I, doth sway my life.

FABIAN

A fustian riddle!

SIR TOBY

Excellent wench, say I.

MALVOLIO

'M, O, A, I, doth sway my life.' Nay, but first, let me see, let me see, let me see.

FABIAN

What dish o' poison has she dressed him!

SIR TOBY

And with what wing the staniel checks at it!

MALVOLIO

'I may command where I adore.' Why, she may command me: I serve her; she is my lady. Why, this is evident to any formal capacity; there is no obstruction in this: and the end,—what should that alphabetical position portend? If I could make that resemble something in me,—Softly! M, O, A, I,—

SIR TOBY

O, ay, make up that: he is now at a cold scent.

FABIAN

Sowter will cry upon't for all this, though it be as rank as a fox.

MALVOLIO

M,—Malvolio; M,—why, that begins my name.

FABIAN

Did not I say he would work it out? the cur is excellent at faults.

MALVOLIO

M,—but then there is no consonancy in the sequel; that suffers under probation: A should follow, but O does.

FABIAN

And O shall end, I hope.

SIR TOBY

Ay, or I'll cudgel him, and make him cry O!

MALVOLIO

And then I comes behind.

FABIAN

Ay, an you had any eye behind you, you might see

more detraction at your heels than fortunes before you.

MALVOLIO

M, O, A, I; this simulation is not as the former: and yet, to crush this a little, it would bow to me, for every one of these letters are in my name. Soft! here follows prose.

[*Reads*] If this fall into thy hand, revolve. In my stars I am above thee; but be not afraid of greatness: some are born great, some achieve greatness, and some have greatness thrust upon 'em. Thy Fates open their hands; let thy blood and spirit embrace them; and, to inure thyself to what thou art like to be, cast thy humble slough and appear fresh. Be opposite with a kinsman, surly with servants; let thy tongue tang arguments of state; put thyself into the trick of singularity: she thus advises thee that sighs for thee. Remember who commended thy yellow stockings, and wished to see thee ever cross-gartered: I say, remember. Go to, thou art made, if thou desirest to be so; if not, let me see thee a steward still, the fellow of servants, and not worthy to touch Fortune's fingers. Farewell. She that would alter services with thee,

                       THE FORTUNATE-UNHAPPY.

Daylight and champain discovers not more: this is open. I will be proud, I will read politic authors, I will baffle Sir Toby, I will wash off gross acquaintance, I will be point-devise the very man. I do not now fool myself, to let imagination jade me; for every reason excites to this, that my lady loves me. She did commend my yellow stockings of late, she did praise my leg being cross-gartered; and in this she manifests herself to my love, and with a kind of injunction drives me to these habits of her liking. I thank my stars I am happy. I will be strange, stout, in yellow stockings, and cross-gartered, even with the swiftness of putting on. Jove and my stars be praised! Here is yet a postscript.

[*Reads*] Thou canst not choose but know who I am. If thou entertainest my love, let it appear in thy smiling; thy smiles become thee well; therefore in my presence still smile, dear my sweet, I prithee.

Jove, I thank thee: I will smile; I will do every thing that thou wilt have me.   [*Exit*

FABIAN

I will not give my part of this sport for a pension of thousands to be paid from the Sophy.

SIR TOBY

I could marry this wench for this device,—

SIR ANDREW

So could I too.

SIR TOBY

And ask no other dowry with her but such another jest.

SIR ANDREW

Nor I neither.

FABIAN

Here comes my noble gull-catcher.

Re-enter MARIA

SIR TOBY

Wilt thou set thy foot o' my neck?

SIR ANDREW

Or o' mine either?

SIR TOBY

Shall I play my freedom at tray-trip, and become thy bond-slave?

SIR ANDREW

I' faith, or I either?

SIR TOBY

Why, thou hast put him in such a dream, that when the image of it leaves him he must run mad.

MARIA

Nay, but say true; does it work upon him?

SIR TOBY

Like aqua-vitæ with a midwife.

MARIA

If you will then see the fruits of the sport, mark his first approach before my lady: he will come to her in yellow stockings, and 'tis a colour she abhors, and cross-gartered, a fashion she detests; and he will smile upon her, which will now be so unsuitable to her disposition, being addicted to a melancholy as she is, that it cannot but turn him into a notable contempt. If you will see it, follow me.

SIR TOBY

To the gates of Tartar, thou most excellent devil of wit!

SIR ANDREW

I'll make one too.   [*Exeunt*

ACT III

SCENE I. OLIVIA'S *garden*

Enter VIOLA, *and* CLOWN *with a tabor*

VIOLA

Save thee, friend, and thy music: dost thou live by thy tabor?

CLOWN

No, sir, I live by the church.

VIOLA

Art thou a churchman?

CLOWN

No such matter, sir: I do live by the church; for I do live at my house, and my house doth stand by the church.

VIOLA

So thou mayst say, the king lies by a beggar, if a beggar dwell near him; or, the church stands by thy tabor, if thy tabor stand by the church.

CLOWN

You have said, sir. To see this age! A sentence is but a cheveril glove to a good wit: how quickly the wrong side may be turned outward!

VIOLA

Nay, that's certain; they that dally nicely with words may quickly make them wanton.

CLOWN

I would, therefore, my sister had had no name, sir.

VIOLA

Why, man?

CLOWN

Why, sir, her name's a word; and to dally with that word might make my sister wanton. But indeed words are very rascals since bonds disgraced them.

VIOLA

Thy reason, man?

CLOWN

Troth, sir, I can yield you none without words; and words are grown so false, I am loath to prove reason with them.

VIOLA

I warrant thou art a merry fellow and carest for nothing.

CLOWN

Not so, sir, I do care for something; but in my conscience, sir, I do not care for you: if that be to care for nothing, sir, I would it would make you invisible.

VIOLA

Art not thou the Lady Olivia's fool?

CLOWN

No, indeed, sir; the Lady Olivia has no folly: she will keep no fool, sir, till she be married; and fools are as like husbands as pilchards are to herrings; the husband's the bigger: I am indeed not her fool, but her corrupter of words.

VIOLA

I saw thee late at the Count Orsino's.

CLOWN

Foolery, sir, does walk about the orb like the sun, it shines every where. I would be sorry, sir, but the fool should be as oft with your master as with my mistress: I think I saw your wisdom there.

VIOLA

Nay, an thou pass upon me, I'll no more with thee. Hold, there's expenses for thee.

CLOWN

Now Jove, in his next commodity of hair, send thee a beard!

VIOLA

By my troth, I'll tell thee, I am almost sick for one; [Aside] though I would not have it grow on my chin. Is thy lady within?

CLOWN

Would not a pair of these have bred, sir?

VIOLA

Yes, being kept together and put to use.

CLOWN

I would play Lord Pandarus of Phrygia, sir, to bring a Cressida to this Troilus.

VIOLA

I understand you, sir; 'tis well begged.

CLOWN

The matter, I hope, is not great, sir, begging but a beggar: Cressida was a beggar. My lady is within, sir. I will construe to them whence you come; who you are and what you would are out of my welkin, I might say 'element,' but the word is over-worn.

[Exit

VIOLA

This fellow is wise enough to play the fool;
And to do that well craves a kind of wit:
He must observe their mood on whom he jests,
The quality of persons, and the time,
And, like the haggard, check at every feather
That comes before his eye. This is a practice
As full of labour as a wise man's art:
For folly that he wisely shows is fit;
But wise men, folly-fall'n, quite taint their wit.

Enter SIR TOBY, *and* SIR ANDREW

SIR TOBY

Save you, gentleman.

VIOLA

And you, sir.

SIR ANDREW

Dieu vous garde, monsieur.

VIOLA

Et vous aussi; votre serviteur.

SIR ANDREW

I hope, sir, you are; and I am yours.

SIR TOBY

Will you encounter the house? my niece is desirous you should enter, if your trade be to her.

VIOLA

I am bound to your niece, sir; I mean, she is the list of my voyage.

SIR TOBY

Taste your legs, sir; put them to motion.

VIOLA

My legs do better understand me, sir, than I understand what you mean by bidding me taste my legs.

SIR TOBY

I mean, to go, sir, to enter.

VIOLA

I will answer you with gait and entrance. But we are prevented.

Enter OLIVIA *and* MARIA

Most excellent accomplished lady, the heavens rain odours on you!

SIR ANDREW

That youth's a rare courtier: 'Rain odours;' well.

VIOLA

My matter hath no voice, lady, but to your own most pregnant and vouchsafed ear.

SIR ANDREW

'Odours,' 'pregnant,' and 'vouchsafed': I'll get 'em all three all ready.

OLIVIA

Let the garden door be shut, and leave me to my hearing. [*Exeunt* SIR TOBY, SIR ANDREW, *and* MARIA] Give me your hand, sir.

VIOLA

My duty, madam, and most humble service.

OLIVIA

What is your name?

VIOLA

Cesario is your servant's name, fair princess.

OLIVIA

My servant, sir! 'Twas never merry world

Since lowly feigning was call'd compliment:
You're servant to the Count Orsino, youth.

VIOLA

And he is yours, and his must needs be yours:
Your servant's servant is your servant, madam.

OLIVIA

For him, I think not on him: for his thoughts,
Would they were blanks, rather than fill'd with me!

VIOLA

Madam, I come to whet your gentle thoughts
On his behalf.

OLIVIA

         O, by your leave, I pray you;
I bade you never speak again of him:
But, would you undertake another suit,
I had rather hear you to solicit that
Than music from the spheres.

VIOLA

         Dear lady,—

OLIVIA

Give me leave, beseech you. I did send,
After the last enchantment you did here,
A ring in chase of you: so did I abuse
Myself, my servant and, I fear me, you:
Under your hard construction must I sit,
To force that on you, in a shameful cunning,
Which you knew none of yours: what might you
    think?
Have you not set mine honour at the stake
And baited it with all the unmuzzled thoughts
That tyrannous heart can think? To one of your re-
    ceiving
Enough is shown: a cypress, not a bosom,
Hides my heart. So, let me hear you speak.

VIOLA

I pity you.

OLIVIA

         That's a degree to love.

VIOLA

No, not a grize; for 'tis a vulgar proof,
That very oft we pity enemies.

OLIVIA

Why, then, methinks 'tis time to smile again.
O world, how apt the poor are to be proud!
If one should be a prey, how much the better
To fall before the lion than the wolf!   [Clock strikes
The clock upbraids me with the waste of time.
Be not afraid, good youth, I will not have you:
And yet, when wit and youth is come to harvest,
Your wife is like to reap a proper man:
There lies your way, due west.

VIOLA

         Then westward-ho!
Grace and good disposition attend your ladyship!
You'll nothing, madam, to my lord by me?

OLIVIA

Stay:
I prithee, tell me what thou think'st of me.

VIOLA

That you do think you are not what you are.

OLIVIA

If I think so, I think the same of you.

VIOLA

Then think you right: I am not what I am.

OLIVIA

I would you were as I would have you be!

VIOLA

Would it be better, madam, than I am?
I wish it might, for now I am your fool.

OLIVIA

O, what a deal of scorn looks beautiful
In the contempt and anger of his lip!
A murderous guilt shows not itself more soon
Than love that would seem hid: love's night is noon
Cesario, by the roses of the spring,
By maidhood, honour, truth and every thing,
I love thee so, that, maugre all thy pride,
Nor wit nor reason can my passion hide.
Do not extort thy reasons from this clause,
For that I woo, thou therefore hast no cause;
But rather reason thus with reason fetter,
Love sought is good, but given unsought is better.

VIOLA

By innocence I swear, and by my youth,
I have one heart, one bosom and one truth,
And that no woman has; nor never none
Shall mistress be of it, save I alone.
And so adieu, good madam: never more
Will I my master's tears to you deplore.

OLIVIA

Yet come again; for thou perhaps mayst move
That heart, which now abhors, to like his love.

                           [Exeunt

SCENE II. OLIVIA'S house

Enter SIR TOBY, SIR ANDREW, and FABIAN

SIR ANDREW

No, faith, I'll not stay a jot longer.

SIR TOBY

Thy reason, dear venom, give thy reason.

FABIAN

You must needs yield your reason, Sir Andrew.

SIR ANDREW

Marry, I saw your niece do more favours to the
count's serving-man than ever she bestowed upon
me; I saw 't i' the orchard.

SIR TOBY

Did she see thee the while, old boy? tell me that.

SIR ANDREW

As plain as I see you now.

FABIAN

This was a great argument of love in her toward
you.

SIR ANDREW

'Slight, will you make an ass o' me?

FABIAN

I will prove it legitimate, sir, upon the oaths of
judgement and reason.

SIR TOBY

And they have been grand-jurymen since before Noah was a sailor.

FABIAN

She did show favour to the youth in your sight only to exasperate you, to awake your dormouse valour, to put fire in your heart, and brimstone in your liver. You should then have accosted her; and with some excellent jests, fire-new from the mint, you should have banged the youth into dumbness. This was looked for at your hand, and this was balked: the double gilt of this opportunity you let time wash off, and you are now sailed into the north of my lady's opinion; where you will hang like an icicle on a Dutchman's beard, unless you do redeem it by some laudable attempt either of valour or policy.

SIR ANDREW

An't be any way, it must be with valour; for policy I hate: I had as lief be a Brownist as a politician.

SIR TOBY

Why, then, build me thy fortunes upon the basis of valour. Challenge me the count's youth to fight with him; hurt him in eleven places: my niece shall take note of it; and assure thyself, there is no love-broker in the world can more prevail in man's commendation with woman than report of valour.

FABIAN

There is no way but this, Sir Andrew.

SIR ANDREW

Will either of you bear me a challenge to him?

SIR TOBY

Go, write it in a martial hand; be curst and brief; it is no matter how witty, so it be eloquent and full of invention: taunt him with the license of ink: if thou thou'st him some thrice, it shall not be amiss; and as many lies as will lie in thy sheet of paper, although the sheet were big enough for the bed of Ware in England, set 'em down: go, about it. Let there be gall enough in thy ink, though thou write with a goose-pen, no matter: about it.

SIR ANDREW

Where shall I find you?

SIR TOBY

We'll call thee at the cubiculo: go.

[Exit SIR ANDREW

FABIAN

This is a dear manakin to you, Sir Toby.

SIR TOBY

I have been dear to him, lad, some two thousand strong, or so.

FABIAN

We shall have a rare letter from him: but you'll not deliver't?

SIR TOBY

Never trust me, then; and by all means stir on the youth to an answer. I think oxen and wainropes cannot hale them together. For Andrew, if he were opened, and you find so much blood in his liver as will clog the foot of a flea, I'll eat the rest of the anatomy.

FABIAN

And his opposite, the youth, bears in his visage no great presage of cruelty.

Enter MARIA

SIR TOBY

Look, where the youngest wren of nine comes.

MARIA

If you desire the spleen, and will laugh yourself into stitches, follow me. Yond gull Malvolio is turned heathen, a very renegado; for there is no Christian, that means to be saved by believing rightly, can ever believe such impossible passages of grossness. He's in yellow stockings.

SIR TOBY

And cross-gartered?

MARIA

Most villanously; like a pedant that keeps a school i' the church. I have dogged him, like his murderer. He does obey every point of the letter that I dropped to betray him: he does smile his face into more lines than is in the new map with the augmentation of the Indies: you have not seen such a thing as 'tis. I can hardly forbear hurling things at him. I know my lady will strike him: if she do, he'll smile and take 't for a great favour.

SIR TOBY

Come, bring us, bring us where he is. [Exeunt

SCENE III. A street

Enter SEBASTIAN and ANTONIO

SEBASTIAN

I would not by my will have troubled you;
But, since you make your pleasure of your pains,
I will no further chide you.

ANTONIO

I could not stay behind you: my desire,
More sharp than filed steel, did spur me forth;
And not all love to see you, though so much
As might have drawn one to a longer voyage,
But jealousy what might befall your travel,
Being skilless in these parts; which to a stranger,
Unguided and unfriended, often prove
Rough and unhospitable: my willing love,
The rather by these arguments of fear,
Set forth in your pursuit.

SEBASTIAN

My kind Antonio,
I can no other answer make but thanks,
And thanks; and ever . . . oft good turns
Are shuffled off with such uncurrent pay:
But, were my worth as is my conscience firm,
You should find better dealing. What's to do?
Shall we go see the reliques of this town?

ANTONIO

To-morrow, sir: best first go see your lodging.

SEBASTIAN

I am not weary, and 'tis long to night:
I pray you, let us satisfy our eyes

With the memorials and the things of fame
That do renown this city.

ANTONIO

         Would you'ld pardon me;
I do not without danger walk these streets:
Once, in a sea-fight, 'gainst the count his galleys
I did some service; of such note indeed,
That were I ta'en here it would scarce be answer'd.

SEBASTIAN

Belike you slew great number of his people.

ANTONIO

The offence is not of such a bloody nature;
Albeit the quality of the time and quarrel
Might well have given us bloody argument.
It might have since been answer'd in repaying
What we took from them; which, for traffic's sake,
Most of our city did: only myself stood out;
For which, if I be lapsed in this place,
I shall pay dear.

SEBASTIAN

      Do not then walk too open.

ANTONIO

It doth not fit me. Hold, sir, here's my purse.
In the south suburbs, at the Elephant,
Is best to lodge: I will bespeak our diet,
Whiles you beguile the time and feed your knowl-
    edge
With viewing of the town: there shall you have me.

SEBASTIAN

Why I your purse?

ANTONIO

Haply your eye shall light upon some toy
You have desire to purchase; and your store,
I think, is not for idle markets, sir.

SEBASTIAN

I'll be your purse-bearer and leave you
For an hour.

ANTONIO

    To the Elephant.

SEBASTIAN

        I do remember.

[*Exeunt*

SCENE IV. OLIVIA's *garden*

Enter OLIVIA *and* MARIA

OLIVIA

I have sent after him: he says he'll come;
How shall I feast him? what bestow of him?
For youth is bought more oft than begg'd or bor-
    row'd.
I speak too loud.
Where is Malvolio? he is sad and civil,
And suits well for a servant with my fortunes:
Where is Malvolio?

MARIA

He's coming, madam; but in very strange manner.
He is, sure, possessed, madam.

OLIVIA

Why, what's the matter? does he rave?

MARIA

No, madam, he does nothing but smile: your ladyship were best to have some guard about you, if he
come; for, sure, the man is tainted in 's wits.

OLIVIA

Go call him hither. [*Exit* MARIA] I am as mad as he,
If sad and merry madness equal be.

Re-enter MARIA, *with* MALVOLIO

How now, Malvolio!

MALVOLIO

Sweet lady, ho, ho.

OLIVIA

Smilest thou?
I sent for thee upon a sad occasion.

MALVOLIO

Sad, lady? I could be sad: this does make some obstruction in the blood, this cross-gartering; but what
of that? if it please the eye of one, it is with me as the
very true sonnet is, 'Please one, and please all.'

OLIVIA

Why, how dost thou, man? what is the matter with
thee?

MALVOLIO

Not black in my mind, though yellow in my legs. It
did come to his hands, and commands shall be
executed: I think we do know the sweet Roman
hand.

OLIVIA

Wilt thou go to bed, Malvolio?

MALVOLIO

To bed! ay, sweet-heart, and I'll come to thee.

OLIVIA

God comfort thee! Why dost thou smile so and kiss
thy hand so oft?

MARIA

How do you, Malvolio?

MALVOLIO

At your request! yes; nightingales answer daws.

MARIA

Why appear you with this ridiculous boldness before my lady?

MALVOLIO

'Be not afraid of greatness:' 'twas well writ.

OLIVIA

What meanest thou by that, Malvolio?

MALVOLIO

'Some are born great,'—

OLIVIA

Ha!

MALVOLIO

'Some achieve greatness,'—

OLIVIA

What sayest thou?

MALVOLIO

'And some have greatness thrust upon them.'

OLIVIA

Heaven restore thee!

MALVOLIO

'Remember who commended thy yellow stockings,'—

OLIVIA

Thy yellow stockings!

MALVOLIO

'And wished to see thee cross-gartered.'

OLIVIA

Cross-gartered!

MALVOLIO

'Go to, thou art made, if thou desirest to be so;'—

OLIVIA

Am I made?

MALVOLIO

'If not, let me see thee a servant still.'

OLIVIA

Why, this is very midsummer madness.

Enter SERVANT

SERVANT

Madam, the young gentleman of the Count Orsino's is returned: I could hardly entreat him back: he attends your ladyship's pleasure.

OLIVIA

I'll come to him. [*Exit* SERVANT] Good Maria, let this fellow be looked to. Where's my cousin Toby? Let some of my people have a special care of him: I would not have him miscarry for the half of my dowry.   [*Exeunt* OLIVIA *and* MARIA

MALVOLIO

O, ho! do you come near me now? no worse man than Sir Toby to look to me! This concurs directly with the letter: she sends him on purpose, that I may appear stubborn to him; for she incites me to that in the letter. 'Cast thy humble slough,' says she; 'be opposite with a kinsman, surly with servants; let thy tongue tang with arguments of state; put thyself into the trick of singularity;' and consequently sets down the manner how; as, a sad face, a reverend carriage, a slow tongue, in the habit of some sir of note, and so forth. I have limed her; but it is Jove's doing, and Jove make me thankful! And when she went away now, 'Let this fellow be looked to:' fellow! not Malvolio, nor after my degree, but fellow. Why, every thing adheres together, that no dram of a scruple, no scruple of a scruple, no obstacle, no incredulous or unsafe circumstance— What can be said? Nothing that can be can come between me and the full prospect of my hopes. Well, Jove, not I, is the doer of this, and he is to be thanked.

Re-enter MARIA, *with* SIR TOBY *and* FABIAN

SIR TOBY

Which way is he, in the name of sanctity? If all the devils of hell be drawn in little, and Legion himself possessed him, yet I'll speak to him.

FABIAN

Here he is, here he is. How is 't with you, sir? how is 't with you, man?

MALVOLIO

Go off; I discard you: let me enjoy my private: go off.

MARIA

Lo, how hollow the fiend speaks within him! did not I tell you? Sir Toby, my lady prays you to have a care of him.

MALVOLIO

Ah, ha! does she so?

SIR TOBY

Go to, go to; peace, peace; we must deal gently with him: let me alone. How do you, Malvolio? how is 't with you? What man! defy the devil: consider, he 's an enemy to mankind.

MALVOLIO

Do you know what you say?

MARIA

La you, an you speak ill of the devil, how he takes it at heart! Pray God, he be not bewitched!

FABIAN

Carry his water to the wise woman.

MARIA

Marry, and it shall be done to-morrow morning, if I live. My lady would not lose him for more than I'll say.

MALVOLIO

How now, mistress!

MARIA

O Lord!

SIR TOBY

Prithee, hold thy peace; this is not the way: do you not see you move him? let me alone with him.

FABIAN

No way but gentleness; gently, gently: the fiend is rough, and will not be roughly used.

SIR TOBY

Why, how now, my bawcock! how dost thou, chuck?

MALVOLIO

Sir!

SIR TOBY

Ay, Biddy, come with me. What, man! 'tis not for gravity to play at cherry-pit with Satan: hang him, foul collier!

MARIA

Get him to say his prayers, good Sir Toby, get him to pray.

MALVOLIO

My prayers, minx!

MARIA

No, I warrant you, he will not hear of godliness.

MALVOLIO

Go, hang yourselves all! you are idle shallow things: I am not of your element: you shall know more hereafter.   [*Exit*

SIR TOBY

Is 't possible?

FABIAN

If this were played upon a stage now, I could condemn it as an improbable fiction.

SIR TOBY

His very genius hath taken the infection of the device, man.

MARIA

Nay, pursue him now, lest the device take air and taint.

FABIAN

Why, we shall make him mad indeed.

MARIA

The house will be the quieter.

SIR TOBY

Come, we'll have him in a dark room and bound. My niece is already in the belief that he's mad: we may carry it thus, for our pleasure and his penance, till our very pastime, tired out of breath, prompt us to have mercy on him: at which time we will bring the device to the bar and crown thee for a finder of madmen. But see, but see.

Enter SIR ANDREW

FABIAN

More matter for a May morning.

SIR ANDREW

Here's the challenge, read it: I warrant there's vinegar and pepper in 't.

FABIAN

Is 't so saucy?

SIR ANDREW

Ay, is 't, I warrant him: do but read.

SIR TOBY

Give me.

[*Reads*] Youth, whatsoever thou art, thou art but a scurvy fellow.

FABIAN

Good, and valiant.

SIR TOBY

[*Reads*] Wonder not, nor admire not in thy mind, why I do call thee so, for I will show thee no reason for 't.

FABIAN

A good note; that keeps you from the blow of the law.

SIR TOBY

[*Reads*] Thou comest to the lady Olivia, and in my sight she uses thee kindly: but thou liest in thy throat; that is not the matter I challenge thee for.

FABIAN

Very brief, and to exceeding good sense—less.

SIR TOBY

[*Reads*] I will waylay thee going home; where if it be thy chance to kill me,—

FABIAN

Good.

SIR TOBY

[*Reads*] Thou killest me like a rogue and a villain.

FABIAN

Still you keep o' the windy side of the law: good.

SIR TOBY

[*Reads*] Fare thee well; and God have mercy upon one of our souls! He may have mercy upon mine; but my hope is better, and so look to thyself. Thy friend, as thou usest him, and thy sworn enemy,   ANDREW AGUECHEEK.

If this letter move him not, his legs cannot: I'll give 't him.

MARIA

You may have very fit occasion for 't: he is now in some commerce with my lady, and will by and by depart.

SIR TOBY

Go, Sir Andrew; scout me for him at the corner of the orchard like a bum-baily: so soon as ever thou seest him, draw; and, as thou drawest, swear horrible; for it comes to pass oft that a terrible oath, with a swaggering accent sharply twanged off, gives manhood more approbation than ever proof itself would have earned him. Away!

SIR ANDREW

Nay, let me alone for swearing.   [*Exit*

SIR TOBY

Now will not I deliver his letter: for the behaviour of the young gentleman gives him out to be of good capacity and breeding; his employment between his lord and my niece confirms no less: therefore this letter, being so excellently ignorant, will breed no terror in the youth: he will find it comes from a clodpole. But, sir, I will deliver his challenge by word of mouth; set upon Aguecheek a notable report of valour; and drive the gentleman, as I know his youth will aptly receive it, into a most hideous opinion of his rage, skill, fury and impetuosity. This will so fright them both, that they will kill one another by the look, like cockatrices.

Re-enter OLIVIA, *with* VIOLA

FABIAN

Here he comes with your niece: give them way till he take leave, and presently after him.

SIR TOBY

I will meditate the while upon some horrid message for a challenge. [*Exeunt* SIR TOBY, FABIAN, *and* MARIA

OLIVIA

I have said too much unto a heart of stone,
And laid mine honour too unchary out:
There's something in me that reproves my fault;
But such a headstrong potent fault it is,
That it but mocks reproof.

VIOLA

With the same 'haviour that your passion bears
Goes on my master's grief.

OLIVIA

Here, wear this jewel for me, 'tis my picture;
Refuse it not; it hath no tongue to vex you;
And I beseech you come again to-morrow.
What shall you ask of me that I'll deny,
That honour saved may upon asking give?

VIOLA

Nothing but this;—your true love for my master.

OLIVIA

How with mine honour may I give him that
Which I have given to you?

VIOLA

     I will acquit you.

OLIVIA

Well, come again to-morrow: fare thee well:
A fiend like thee might bear my soul to hell. [*Exit*

Re-enter SIR TOBY *and* FABIAN

SIR TOBY

Gentleman, God save thee.

VIOLA

And you, sir.

SIR TOBY

That defence thou hast, betake thee to 't: of what nature the wrongs are thou hast done him, I know not; but thy intercepter, full of despite, bloody as the hunter, attends thee at the orchard-end: dismount thy tuck, be yare in thy preparation, for thy assailant is quick, skilful and deadly.

VIOLA

You mistake, sir; I am sure no man hath any quarrel to me: my remembrance is very free and clear from any image of offence done to any man.

SIR TOBY

You'll find it otherwise, I assure you: therefore, if you hold your life at any price, betake you to your guard; for your opposite hath in him what youth, strength, skill and wrath can furnish man withal.

VIOLA

I pray you, sir, what is he?

SIR TOBY

He is knight, dubbed with unhatched rapier and on carpet consideration; but he is a devil in private brawl: souls and bodies hath he divorced three; and his incensement at this moment is so implacable, that satisfaction can be none but by pangs of death and sepulchre. Hob, nob, is his word; give 't or take 't.

VIOLA

I will return again into the house and desire some conduct of the lady. I am no fighter. I have heard of some kind of men that put quarrels purposely on others, to taste their valour: belike this is a man of that quirk.

SIR TOBY

Sir, no; his indignation derives itself out of a very competent injury: therefore, get you on and give him his desire. Back you shall not to the house, unless you undertake that with me which with as much safety you might answer him: therefore, on, or strip your sword stark naked; for meddle you must, that's certain, or forswear to wear iron about you.

VIOLA

This is as uncivil as strange. I beseech you, do me this courteous office, as to know of the knight what my offence to him is: it is something of my negligence, nothing of my purpose.

SIR TOBY

I will do so. Signior Fabian, stay you by this gentleman till my return.   [*Exit*

VIOLA

Pray you, sir, do you know of this matter?

FABIAN

I know the knight is incensed against you, even to a mortal arbitrement; but nothing of the circumstance more.

VIOLA

I beseech you, what manner of man is he?

FABIAN

Nothing of that wonderful promise, to read him by his form, as you are like to find him in the proof of his valour. He is, indeed, sir, the most skilful, bloody and fatal opposite that you could possibly have found in any part of Illyria. Will you walk towards him? I will make your peace with him if I can.

VIOLA

I shall be much bound to you for 't: I am one that had rather go with sir priest than sir knight: I care not who knows so much of my mettle. [*Exeunt*

Re-enter SIR TOBY, *with* SIR ANDREW

SIR TOBY

Why, man, he's a very devil; I have not seen such a firago. I had a pass with him, rapier, scabbard and all, and he gives me the stuck in with such a mortal motion, that it is inevitable; and on the answer, he pays you as surely as your feet hit the ground they step on. They say he has been fencer to the Sophy.

SIR ANDREW

Pox on 't, I'll not meddle with him.

SIR TOBY

Ay, but he will not now be pacified: Fabian can scarce hold him yonder.

SIR ANDREW

Plague on 't, an I thought he had been valiant and so cunning in fence, I 'ld have seen him damned ere I 'ld have challenged him. Let him let the matter slip, and I'll give him my horse, grey Capilet.

SIR TOBY

I'll make the motion: stand here, make a good show on 't: this shall end without the perdition of souls. [*Aside*] Marry, I'll ride your horse as well as I ride you.

Re-enter FABIAN *and* VIOLA

[*To* FABIAN] I have his horse to take up the quarrel: I have persuaded him the youth's a devil.

FABIAN

He is as horribly conceited of him; and pants and looks pale, as if a bear were at his heels.

SIR TOBY

[*To* VIOLA] There's no remedy, sir; he will fight with you for's oath sake: marry, he hath better bethought him of his quarrel, and he finds that now scarce to be worth talking of: therefore draw, for the supportance of his vow; he protests he will not hurt you.

VIOLA

[*Aside*] Pray God defend me! A little thing would make me tell them how much I lack of a man.

FABIAN

Give ground, if you see him furious.

SIR TOBY

Come, Sir Andrew, there's no remedy; the gentleman will, for his honour's sake, have one bout with you; he cannot by the duello avoid it: but he has promised me, as he is a gentleman and a soldier, he will not hurt you. Come on; to 't.

SIR ANDREW
Pray God, he keep his oath!

VIOLA
I do assure you, 'tis against my will.   [*They draw*

Enter ANTONIO

ANTONIO
Put up your sword. If this young gentleman
Have done offence, I take the fault on me:
If you offend him, I for him defy you.

SIR TOBY
You, sir! why, what are you?

ANTONIO
One, sir, that for his love dares yet do more
Than you have heard him brag to you he will.

SIR TOBY
Nay, if you be an undertaker, I am for you.
          [*They draw*

Enter OFFICERS

FABIAN
O good Sir Toby, hold! here come the officers.

SIR TOBY
I'll be with you anon.

VIOLA
Pray, sir, put your sword up, if you please.

SIR ANDREW
Marry, will I, sir; and, for that I promised you, I'll
be as good as my word: he will bear you easily and
reins well.

FIRST OFFICER
This is the man; do thy office.

SECOND OFFICER
Antonio, I arrest thee at the suit of Count Orsino.

ANTONIO
You do mistake me, sir.

FIRST OFFICER
No, sir, no jot; I know your favour well,
Though now you have no sea-cap on your head.
Take him away: he knows I know him well.

ANTONIO
I must obey. [*To* VIOLA] This comes with seeking
          you:
But there's no remedy; I shall answer it.
What will you do, now my necessity
Makes me to ask you for my purse? It grieves me
Much more for what I cannot do for you
Than what befalls myself. You stand amazed;
But be of comfort.

SECOND OFFICER
Come, sir, away.

ANTONIO
I must entreat of you some of that money.

VIOLA
What money, sir?
For the fair kindness you have show'd me here,
And, part, being prompted by your present trouble,
Out of my lean and low ability
I'll lend you something: my having is not much;
I'll make division of my present with you:
Hold, there's half my coffer.

ANTONIO
          Will you deny me now?
Is 't possible that my deserts to you
Can lack persuasion? Do not tempt my misery,
Lest that it make me so unsound a man
As to upbraid you with those kindnesses
That I have done for you.

VIOLA
          I know of none;
Nor know I you by voice or any feature:
I hate ingratitude more in a man
Than lying vainness, babbling drunkenness,
Or any taint of vice whose strong corruption
Inhabits our frail blood.

ANTONIO
          O heavens themselves!

SECOND OFFICER
Come, sir, I pray you, go.

ANTONIO
Let me speak a little. This youth that you see here
I snatch'd one half out of the jaws of death;
Relieved him with such sanctity of love;
And to his image, which methought did promise
Most venerable worth, did I devotion.

FIRST OFFICER
What's that to us? The time goes by: away!

ANTONIO
But O how vile an idol proves this god!
Thou hast, Sebastian, done good feature shame.
In nature there's no blemish but the mind;
None can be call'd deform'd but the unkind:
Virtue is beauty; but the beauteous evil
Are empty trunks, o'erflourish'd by the devil.

FIRST OFFICER
The man grows mad: away with him! Come, come,
          sir.

ANTONIO
Lead me on.   [*Exit with* OFFICERS

VIOLA
Methinks his words do from such passion fly,
That he believes himself: so do not I.
Prove true, imagination, O prove true,
That I, dear brother, be now ta'en for you!

SIR TOBY
Come hither, knight; come hither, Fabian: we'll
whisper o'er a couplet or two of most sage saws.

VIOLA
He named Sebastian: I my brother know
Yet living in my glass; even such and so
In favour was my brother, and he went
Still in this fashion, colour, ornament,
For him I imitate: O, if it prove,
Tempests are kind and salt waves fresh in love!
          [*Exit*

SIR TOBY
A very dishonest paltry boy, and more a coward
than a hare: his dishonesty appears in leaving his
friend here in necessity and denying him; and for
his cowardship, ask Fabian.

FABIAN

A coward, a most devout coward, religious in it.

SIR ANDREW

'Slid, I'll after him again and beat him.

SIR TOBY

Do; cuff him soundly, but never draw thy sword.

SIR ANDREW

An I do not,— [Exit

FABIAN

Come, let's see the event.

SIR TOBY

I dare lay any money 'twill be nothing yet. [Exeunt

ACT IV

SCENE I. *Before* OLIVIA'S *house*

Enter SEBASTIAN *and* CLOWN

CLOWN

Will you make me believe that I am not sent for you?

SEBASTIAN

Go to, go to, thou art a foolish fellow:
Let me be clear of thee.

CLOWN

Well held out, i' faith! No, I do not know you; nor I am not sent to you by my lady, to bid you come speak with her; nor your name is not Master Cesario; nor this is not my nose neither. Nothing that is so is so.

SEBASTIAN

I prithee, vent thy folly somewhere else:
Thou know'st not me.

CLOWN

Vent my folly! he has heard that word of some great man and now applies it to a fool. Vent my folly! I am afraid this great lubber, the world, will prove a cockney. I prithee now, ungird thy strangeness and tell me what I shall vent to my lady: shall I vent to her that thou art coming?

SEBASTIAN

I prithee, foolish Greek, depart from me:
There's money for thee: if you tarry longer,
I shall give worse payment.

CLOWN

By my troth, thou hast an open hand. These wise men that give fools money get themselves a good report—after fourteen years' purchase.

Enter SIR ANDREW, SIR TOBY, *and* FABIAN

SIR ANDREW

Now, sir, have I met you again? there's for you.

SEBASTIAN

Why, there's for thee, and there, and there. Are all the people mad?

SIR TOBY

Hold, sir, or I'll throw your dagger o'er the house.

CLOWN

This will I tell my lady straight: I would not be in some of your coats for two pence. [Exit

SIR TOBY

Come on, sir; hold.

SIR ANDREW

Nay, let him alone: I'll go another way to work with him; I'll have an action of battery against him, if there be any law in Illyria: though I struck him first, yet it's no matter for that.

SEBASTIAN

Let go thy hand.

SIR TOBY

Come, sir, I will not let you go. Come, my young soldier, put up your iron: you are well fleshed; come on.

SEBASTIAN

I will be free from thee. What wouldst thou now?
If thou darest tempt me further, draw thy sword.

SIR TOBY

What, what? Nay, then I must have an ounce or two of this malapert blood from you.

Enter OLIVIA

OLIVIA

Hold, Toby; on thy life, I charge thee, hold!

SIR TOBY

Madam!

OLIVIA

Will it be ever thus? Ungracious wretch,
Fit for the mountains and the barbarous caves,
Where manners ne'er were preach'd! out of my
   sight!
Be not offended, dear Cesario.
Rudesby, be gone!
      [*Exeunt* SIR TOBY, SIR ANDREW, *and* FABIAN
            I prithee, gentle friend,
Let thy fair wisdom, not thy passion, sway
In this uncivil and unjust extent
Against thy peace. Go with me to my house;
And hear thou there how many fruitless pranks
This ruffian hath botch'd up, that thou thereby
Mayst smile at this: thou shalt not choose but go:
Do not deny. Beshrew his soul for me,
He started one poor heart of mine in thee.

SEBASTIAN

What relish is in this? how runs the stream?
Or I am mad, or else this is a dream:
Let fancy still my sense in Lethe steep;
If it be thus to dream, still let me sleep!

OLIVIA

Nay, come, I prithee: would thou 'ldst be ruled by me!

SEBASTIAN

Madam, I will.

OLIVIA

O, say so, and so be! [*Exeunt*

SCENE II. OLIVIA'S *house*

Enter MARIA *and* CLOWN

MARIA

Nay, I prithee, put on this gown and this beard;

make him believe thou art Sir Topas the curate: do it quickly; I'll call Sir Toby the whilst.   [*Exit*

CLOWN

Well, I'll put it on, and I will dissemble myself in 't; and I would I were the first that ever dissembled in such a gown. I am not tall enough to become the function well, nor lean enough to be thought a good student; but to be said an honest man and a good housekeeper goes as fairly as to say a careful man and a great scholar. The competitors enter.

Enter SIR TOBY *and* MARIA

SIR TOBY

Jove bless thee, master Parson.

CLOWN

Bonos dies, Sir Toby: for, as the old hermit of Prague, that never saw pen and ink, very wittily said to a niece of King Gorboduc, 'That that is is;' so I, being master Parson, am master Parson; for, what is 'that' but 'that,' and 'is' but 'is'?

SIR TOBY

To him, Sir Topas.

CLOWN

What, ho, I say! peace in this prison!

SIR TOBY

The knave counterfeits well; a good knave.

MALVOLIO

[*Within*] Who calls there?

CLOWN

Sir Topas the curate, who comes to visit Malvolio the lunatic.

MALVOLIO

Sir Topas, Sir Topas, good Sir Topas, go to my lady.

CLOWN

Out, hyperbolical fiend! how vexest thou this man! talkest thou nothing but of ladies?

SIR TOBY

Well said, master Parson.

MALVOLIO

Sir Topas, never was man thus wronged: good Sir Topas, do not think I am mad: they have laid me here in hideous darkness.

CLOWN

Fie, thou dishonest Satan! I call thee by the most modest terms; for I am one of those gentle ones that will use the devil himself with courtesy: sayest thou that house is dark?

MALVOLIO

As hell, Sir Topas.

CLOWN

Why, it hath bay windows transparent as barricadoes, and the clearstories toward the south north are as lustrous as ebony; and yet complainest thou of obstruction?

MALVOLIO

I am not mad, Sir Topas: I say to vou, this house is dark.

CLOWN

Madman, thou errest: I say, there is no darkness

but ignorance; in which thou art more puzzled than the Egyptians in their fog.

MALVOLIO

I say, this house is as dark as ignorance, though ignorance were as dark as hell; and I say, there was never man thus abused. I am no more mad than you are: make the trial of it in any constant question.

CLOWN

What is the opinion of Pythagoras concerning wild fowl?

MALVOLIO

That the soul of our grandam might haply inhabit a bird.

CLOWN

What thinkest thou of his opinion?

MALVOLIO

I think nobly of the soul, and no way approve his opinion.

CLOWN

Fare thee well. Remain thou still in darkness: thou shalt hold the opinion of Pythagoras ere I will allow of thy wits; and fear to kill a woodcock, lest thou dispossess the soul of thy grandam. Fare thee well.

MALVOLIO

Sir Topas, Sir Topas!

SIR TOBY

My most exquisite Sir Topas!

CLOWN

Nay, I am for all waters.

MARIA

Thou mightst have done this without thy beard and gown: he sees thee not.

SIR TOBY

To him in thine own voice, and bring me word how thou findest him: I would we were well rid of this knavery. If he may be conveniently delivered, I would he were; for I am now so far in offence with my niece, that I cannot pursue with any safety this sport to the upshot. Come by and by to my chamber.   [*Exeunt* SIR TOBY *and* MARIA

CLOWN

[*Singing*]   Hey, Robin, jolly Robin,
                      Tell me how thy lady does.

MALVOLIO

Fool,—

CLOWN

My lady is unkind, perdy.

MALVOLIO

Fool,—

CLOWN

Alas, why is she so?

MALVOLIO

Fool, I say,—

CLOWN

She loves another—

                                 Who calls, ha?

MALVOLIO

Good fool, as ever thou wilt deserve well at my hand, help me to a candle, and pen, ink and paper: as I am a gentleman, I will live to be thankful to thee for 't.

CLOWN

Master Malvolio!

MALVOLIO

Ay, good fool.

CLOWN

Alas, sir, how fell you besides your five wits?

MALVOLIO

Fool, there was never man so notoriously abused: I am as well in my wits, fool, as thou art.

CLOWN

But as well? then you are mad indeed, if you be no better in your wits than a fool.

MALVOLIO

They have here propertied me; keep me in darkness, send ministers to me, asses, and do all they can to face me out of my wits.

CLOWN

Advise you what you say; the minister is here. Malvolio, Malvolio, thy wits the heavens restore! endeavour thyself to sleep, and leave thy vain bibble babble.

MALVOLIO

Sir Topas,—

CLOWN

Maintain no words with him, good fellow. Who, I, sir? not I, sir. God be wi' you, good Sir Topas. Marry, amen. I will, sir, I will.

MALVOLIO

Fool, fool, fool, I say,—

CLOWN

Alas, sir, be patient. What say you, sir? I am shent for speaking to you.

MALVOLIO

Good fool, help me to some light and some paper: I tell thee, I am as well in my wits as any man in Illyria.

CLOWN

Well-a-day that you were, sir!

MALVOLIO

By this hand, I am. Good fool, some ink, paper and light; and convey what I will set down to my lady: it shall advantage thee more than ever the bearing of letter did.

CLOWN

I will help you to 't. But tell me true, are you not mad indeed? or do you but counterfeit?

MALVOLIO

Believe me, I am not; I tell thee true.

CLOWN

Nay, I'll ne'er believe a madman till I see his brains. I will fetch you light and paper and ink.

MALVOLIO

Fool, I'll requite it in the highest degree: I prithee, be gone.

CLOWN

[Singing]　　I am gone, sir,
　　　　And anon, sir,
　　I'll be with you again,
　　　　In a trice,
　　　　Like to the old vice,
　　Your need to sustain;
　　Who, with dagger of lath,
　　In his rage and his wrath,
　　　　Cries, ah, ha! to the devil:
　　Like a mad lad,
　　Pare thy nails, dad;
　　　　Adieu, goodman devil.　　[Exit

SCENE III. OLIVIA's *garden*

Enter SEBASTIAN

SEBASTIAN

This is the air; that is the glorious sun;
This pearl she gave me, I do feel 't and see 't;
And though 'tis wonder that enwraps me thus,
Yet 'tis not madness. Where's Antonio, then?
I could not find him at the Elephant:
Yet there he was; and there I found this credit,
That he did range the town to seek me out.
His counsel now might do me golden service;
For though my soul disputes well with my sense,
That this may be some error, but no madness,
Yet doth this accident and flood of fortune
So far exceed all instance, all discourse,
That I am ready to distrust mine eyes
And wrangle with my reason, that persuades me
To any other trust but that I am mad,
Or else the lady's mad; yet, if 'twere so,
She could not sway her house, command her followers,
Take and give back affairs and their dispatch
With such a smooth, discreet, and stable bearing
As I perceive she does: there's something in 't
That is deceivable. But here the lady comes.

Enter OLIVIA *and* PRIEST

OLIVIA

Blame not this haste of mine. If you mean well,
Now go with me and with this holy man
Into the chantry by: there, before him,
And underneath that consecrated roof,
Plight me the full assurance of your faith;
That my most jealous and too doubtful soul
May live at peace. He shall conceal it
Whiles you are willing it shall come to note,
What time we will our celebration keep
According to my birth. What do you say?

SEBASTIAN

I'll follow this good man, and go with you;
And, having sworn truth, ever will be true.

OLIVIA

Then lead the way, good father; and heavens so shine,
That they may fairly note this act of mine!　[*Exeunt*

ACT V

SCENE I. *Before* OLIVIA'S *house*

Enter CLOWN *and* FABIAN

FABIAN

Now, as thou lovest me, let me see his letter.

CLOWN

Good Master Fabian, grant me another request.

FABIAN

Any thing.

CLOWN

Do not desire to see this letter.

FABIAN

This is, to give a dog, and in recompense desire my dog again.

Enter DUKE, VIOLA, CURIO, *and* LORDS

DUKE

Belong you to the Lady Olivia, friends?

CLOWN

Ay, sir; we are some of her trappings.

DUKE

I know thee well: how dost thou, my good fellow?

CLOWN

Truly, sir, the better for my foes and the worse for my friends.

DUKE

Just the contrary; the better for thy friends.

CLOWN

No, sir, the worse.

DUKE

How can that be?

CLOWN

Marry, sir, they praise me and make an ass of me; now my foes tell me plainly I am an ass: so that by my foes, sir, I profit in the knowledge of myself; and by my friends I am abused: so that, conclusions to be as kisses, if your four negatives make your two affirmatives, why then, the worse for my friends, and the better for my foes.

DUKE

Why, this is excellent.

CLOWN

By my troth, sir, no; though it please you to be one of my friends.

DUKE

Thou shalt not be the worse for me: there's gold.

CLOWN

But that it would be double-dealing, sir, I would you could make it another.

DUKE

O, you give me ill counsel.

CLOWN

Put your grace in your pocket, sir, for this once, and let your flesh and blood obey it.

DUKE

Well, I will be so much a sinner, to be a double-dealer: there's another.

CLOWN

Primo, secundo, tertio, is a good play; and the old

saying is, the third pays for all: the triplex, sir, is a good tripping measure; or the bells of Saint Bennet, sir, may put you in mind; one, two, three.

DUKE

You can fool no more money out of me at this throw: if you will let your lady know I am here to speak with her, and bring her along with you, it may awake my bounty further.

CLOWN

Marry, sir, lullaby to your bounty till I come again. I go, sir; but I would not have you to think that my desire of having is the sin of covetousness: but, as you say, sir, let your bounty take a nap, I will awake it anon.   [*Exit*

VIOLA

Here comes the man, sir, that did rescue me.

Enter ANTONIO *and* OFFICERS

DUKE

That face of his I do remember well;
Yet, when I saw it last, it was besmear'd
As black as Vulcan in the smoke of war:
A bawbling vessel was he captain of,
For shallow draught and bulk unprizable;
With which such scathful grapple did he make
With the most noble bottom of our fleet,
That very envy and the tongue of loss
Cried fame and honour on him. What's the matter?

FIRST OFFICER

Orsino, this is that Antonio
That took the Phœnix and her fraught from Candy;
And this is he that did the Tiger board,
When your young nephew Titus lost his leg:
Here in the streets, desperate of shame and state,
In private brabble did we apprehend him.

VIOLA

He did me kindness, sir, drew on my side;
But in conclusion put strange speech upon me:
I know not what 'twas but distraction.

DUKE

Notable pirate! thou salt-water thief!
What foolish boldness brought thee to their mercies,
Whom thou, in terms so bloody and so dear,
Hast made thine enemies?

ANTONIO

Orsino, noble sir,
Be pleased that I shake off these names you give me:
Antonio never yet was thief or pirate,
Though I confess, on base and ground enough,
Orsino's enemy. A witchcraft drew me hither:
That most ingrateful boy there by your side,
From the rude sea's enraged and foamy mouth
Did I redeem; a wreck past hope he was:
His life I gave him and did thereto add
My love, without retention or restraint,
All his in dedication; for his sake
Did I expose myself, pure for his love,
Into the danger of this adverse town;
Drew to defend him when he was beset:
Where being apprehended, his false cunning,
Not meaning to partake with me in danger,

Taught him to face me out of his acquaintance,
And grew a twenty years removed thing
While one would wink; denied me mine own purse,
Which I had recommended to his use
Not half an hour before.

VIOLA
How can this be?

DUKE
When came he to this town?

ANTONIO
To-day, my lord; and for three months before,
No interim, not a minute's vacancy,
Both day and night did we keep company.

Enter OLIVIA *and* ATTENDANTS

DUKE
Here comes the countess: now heaven walks on earth.
But for thee, fellow; fellow, thy words are madness:
Three months this youth hath tended upon me;
But more of that anon. Take him aside.

OLIVIA
What would my lord, but that he may not have,
Wherein Olivia may seem serviceable?
Cesario, you do not keep promise with me.

VIOLA
Madam!

DUKE
Gracious Olivia,—

OLIVIA
What do you say, Cesario? Good my lord,—

VIOLA
My lord would speak; my duty hushes me.

OLIVIA
If it be aught to the old tune, my lord,
It is as fat and fulsome to mine ear
As howling after music.

DUKE
Still so cruel?

OLIVIA
Still so constant, lord.

DUKE
What, to perverseness? you uncivil lady,
To whose ingrate and unauspicious altars
My soul the faithfull'st offerings hath breathed out
That e'er devotion tender'd! What shall I do?

OLIVIA
Even what it please my lord, that shall become him.

DUKE
Why should I not, had I the heart to do it,
Like to the Egyptian thief at point of death,
Kill what I love?—a savage jealousy
That sometime savours nobly. But hear me this:
Since you to non-regardance cast my faith,
And that I partly know the instrument
That screws me from my true place in your favour,
Live you the marble-breasted tyrant still;
But this your minion, whom I know you love,
And whom, by heaven I swear, I tender dearly,
Him will I tear out of that cruel eye,
Where he sits crowned in his master's spite.

Come, boy, with me; my thoughts are ripe in mischief:
I'll sacrifice the lamb that I do love,
To spite a raven's heart within a dove.

VIOLA
And I, most jocund, apt and willingly,
To do you rest, a thousand deaths would die.

OLIVIA
Where goes Cesario?

VIOLA
After him I love
More than I love these eyes, more than my life,
More, by all mores, than e'er I shall love wife.
If I do feign, you witnesses above
Punish my life for tainting of my love!

OLIVIA
Ay me, detested! how am I beguiled!

VIOLA
Who does beguile you? who does do you wrong?

OLIVIA
Hast thou forgot thyself? is it so long?
Call forth the holy father.

DUKE
Come, away!

OLIVIA
Whither, my lord? Cesario, husband, stay.

DUKE
Husband!

OLIVIA
Ay, husband: can he that deny?

DUKE
Her husband, sirrah!

VIOLA
No, my lord, not I.

OLIVIA
Alas, it is the baseness of thy fear
That makes thee strangle thy propriety:
Fear not, Cesario; take thy fortunes up;
Be that thou know'st thou art, and then thou art
As great as that thou fear'st.

Enter PRIEST

O, welcome, father!
Father, I charge thee, by thy reverence,
Here to unfold, though lately we intended
To keep in darkness what occasion now
Reveals before 'tis ripe, what thou dost know
Hath newly pass'd between this youth and me.

PRIEST
A contract of eternal bond of love,
Confirm'd by mutual joinder of your hands,
Attested by the holy close of lips,
Strengthen'd by interchangement of your rings;
And all the ceremony of this compact
Seal'd in my function, by my testimony:
Since when, my watch hath told me, toward my grave
I have travell'd but two hours.

DUKE
O thou dissembling cub! what wilt thou be
When time hath sow'd a grizzle on thy case?

Or will not else thy craft so quickly grow,
That thine own trip shall be thine overthrow?
Farewell, and take her; but direct thy feet
Where thou and I henceforth may never meet.

VIOLA

My lord, I do protest—

OLIVIA

O, do not swear!
Hold little faith, though thou hast too much fear.

Enter SIR ANDREW

SIR ANDREW

For the love of God, a surgeon! Send one presently
to Sir Toby.

OLIVIA

What's the matter?

SIR ANDREW

He has broke my head across and has given Sir
Toby a bloody coxcomb too: for the love of God,
your help! I had rather than forty pound I were
at home.

OLIVIA

Who has done this, Sir Andrew?

SIR ANDREW

The count's gentleman, one Cesario: we took him
for a coward, but he's the very devil incardinate.

DUKE

My gentleman, Cesario?

SIR ANDREW

'Od's lifelings, here he is! You broke my head for
nothing; and that that I did, I was set on to do 't by
Sir Toby.

VIOLA

Why do you speak to me? I never hurt you:
You drew your sword upon me without cause;
But I bespake you fair, and hurt you not.

SIR ANDREW

If a bloody coxcomb be a hurt, you have hurt me:
I think you set nothing by a bloody coxcomb.

Enter SIR TOBY *and* CLOWN

Here comes Sir Toby halting; you shall hear more:
but if he had not been in drink, he would have
tickled you othergates than he did.

DUKE

How now, gentleman! how is 't with you?

SIR TOBY

That's all one: has hurt me, and there's the end
on 't. Sot, didst see Dick surgeon, sot?

CLOWN

O, he's drunk, Sir Toby, an hour agone; his eyes
were set at eight i' the morning.

SIR TOBY

Then he's a rogue, and a passy measures pavin: I
hate a drunken rogue.

OLIVIA

Away with him! Who hath made this havoc with
them?

SIR ANDREW

I'll help you, Sir Toby, because we'll be dressed together.

SIR TOBY

Will you help? an ass-head and a coxcomb and a
knave, a thin-faced knave, a gull!

OLIVIA

Get him to bed, and let his hurt be look'd to.

[*Exeunt* CLOWN, FABIAN, SIR TOBY, *and* SIR ANDREW

Enter SEBASTIAN

SEBASTIAN

I am sorry, madam, I have hurt your kinsman;
But, had it been the brother of my blood,
I must have done no less with wit and safety.
You throw a strange regard upon me, and by that
I do perceive it hath offended you:
Pardon me, sweet one, even for the vows
We made each other but so late ago.

DUKE

One face, one voice, one habit, and two persons,
A natural perspective, that is and is not!

SEBASTIAN

Antonio, O my dear Antonio!
How have the hours rack'd and tortured me,
Since I have lost thee!

ANTONIO

Sebastian are you?

SEBASTIAN

Fear'st thou that, Antonio?

ANTONIO

How have you made division of yourself?
An apple, cleft in two, is not more twin
Than these two creatures. Which is Sebastian?

OLIVIA

Most wonderful!

SEBASTIAN

Do I stand there? I never had a brother;
Nor can there be that deity in my nature,
Of here and every where. I had a sister,
Whom the blind waves and surges have devour'd.
Of charity, what kin are you to me?
What countryman? what name? what parentage?

VIOLA

Of Messaline: Sebastian was my father;
Such a Sebastian was my brother too,
So went he suited to his watery tomb:
If spirits can assume both form and suit,
You come to fright us.

SEBASTIAN

A spirit I am indeed;
But am in that dimension grossly clad
Which from the womb I did participate.
Were you a woman, as the rest goes even,
I should my tears let fall upon your cheek,
And say 'Thrice-welcome, drowned Viola!'

VIOLA

My father had a mole upon his brow.

SEBASTIAN

And so had mine.

VIOLA

And died that day when Viola from her birth
Had number'd thirteen years.

SEBASTIAN

O, that record is lively in my soul!
He finished indeed his mortal act
That day that made my sister thirteen years.

VIOLA

If nothing lets to make us happy both
But this my masculine usurp'd attire,
Do not embrace me till each circumstance
Of place, time, fortune, do cohere and jump
That I am Viola: which to confirm,
I'll bring you to a captain in this town,
Where lie my maiden weeds; by whose gentle help
I was preserved to serve this noble count.
All the occurrence of my fortune since
Hath been between this lady and this lord.

SEBASTIAN

[To OLIVIA] So comes it, lady, you have been mistook:
But nature to her bias drew in that.
You would have been contracted to a maid;
Nor are you therein, by my life, deceived,
You are betroth'd both to a maid and man.

DUKE

Be not amazed; right noble is his blood.
If this be so, as yet the glass seems true,
I shall have share in this most happy wreck.
[To VIOLA] Boy, thou hast said to me a thousand times
Thou never shouldst love woman like to me.

VIOLA

And all those sayings will I over-swear;
And all those swearings keep as true in soul
As doth that orbed continent the fire
That severs day from night.

DUKE

             Give me thy hand;
And let me see thee in thy woman's weeds.

VIOLA

The captain that did bring me first on shore
Hath my maid's garments: he upon some action
Is now in durance, at Malvolio's suit,
A gentleman, and follower of my lady's.

OLIVIA

He shall enlarge him: fetch Malvolio hither:
And yet, alas, now I remember me,
They say, poor gentleman, he's much distract.
Re-enter CLOWN *with a letter, and* FABIAN
A most extracting frenzy of mine own
From my remembrance clearly banish'd his.
How does he, sirrah?

CLOWN

Truly, madam, he holds Belzebub at the stave's end
as well as a man in his case may do: has here writ
a letter to you; I should have given 't you to-day
morning, but as a madman's epistles are no gospels,
so it skills not much when they are delivered.

OLIVIA

Open 't, and read it.

CLOWN

Look then to be well edified when the fool delivers
the madman. [*Reads*]   By the Lord, madam,—

OLIVIA

How now! art thou mad?

CLOWN

No, madam, I do but read madness: an your ladyship will have it as it ought to be, you must allow
Vox.

OLIVIA

Prithee, read i' thy right wits.

CLOWN

So I do, madonna; but to read his right wits is to
read thus: therefore perpend, my princess, and give
ear.

OLIVIA

Read it you, sirrah.   [*To* FABIAN

FABIAN

[*Reads*] By the Lord, madam, you wrong me, and the world
shall know it: though you have put me into darkness and given
your drunken cousin rule over me, yet have I the benefit of my
senses as well as your ladyship. I have your own letter that induced me to the semblance I put on; with the which I doubt
not but to do myself much right, or you much shame. Think of
me as you please. I leave my duty a little unthought of, and
speak out of my injury.

           THE MADLY-USED MALVOLIO.

OLIVIA

Did he write this?

CLOWN

Ay, madam.

DUKE

This savours not much of distraction.

OLIVIA

See him deliver'd, Fabian; bring him hither.
           [*Exit* FABIAN
My lord, so please you, these things further thought on,
To think me as well a sister as a wife,
One day shall crown the alliance on 't, so please you,
Here at my house and at my proper cost.

DUKE

Madam, I am most apt to embrace your offer.
[*To* VIOLA] Your master quits you; and for your
    service done him,
So much against the mettle of your sex,
So far beneath your soft and tender breeding,
And since you call'd me master for so long,
Here is my hand: you shall from this time be
Your master's mistress.

OLIVIA

           A sister! you are she.
Re-enter FABIAN, *with* MALVOLIO

DUKE

Is this the madman?

OLIVIA

           Ay, my lord, this same.
How now, Malvolio!

MALVOLIO

Madam, you have done me wrong,
Notorious wrong.

OLIVIA

Have I, Malvolio? no.

MALVOLIO

Lady, you have. Pray you, peruse that letter.
You must not now deny it is your hand:
Write from it, if you can, in hand or phrase;
Or say 'tis not your seal, not your invention:
You can say none of this: well, grant it then
And tell me, in the modesty of honour,
Why you have given me such clear lights of favour,
Bade me come smiling and cross-garter'd to you,
To put on yellow stockings and to frown
Upon Sir Toby and the lighter people;
And, acting this in an obedient hope,
Why have you suffer'd me to be imprison'd,
Kept in a dark house, visited by the priest,
And made the most notorious geck and gull
That e'er invention play'd on? tell me why.

OLIVIA

Alas, Malvolio, this is not my writing,
Though, I confess, much like the character:
But out of question 'tis Maria's hand.
And now I do bethink me, it was she
First told me thou wast mad; then camest in smil-
    ing,
And in such forms which here were presupposed
Upon thee in the letter. Prithee, be content:
This practice hath most shrewdly pass'd upon thee;
But when we know the grounds and authors of it,
Thou shalt be both the plaintiff and the judge
Of thine own cause.

FABIAN

Good madam, hear me speak,
And let no quarrel nor no brawl to come
Taint the condition of this present hour,
Which I have wonder'd at. In hope it shall not,
Most freely I confess, myself and Toby
Set this device against Malvolio here,
Upon some stubborn and uncourteous parts
We had conceived against him: Maria writ
The letter at Sir Toby's great importance;
In recompense whereof he hath married her.
How with a sportful malice it was follow'd
May rather pluck on laughter than revenge;

If that the injuries be justly weigh'd
That have on both sides pass'd.

OLIVIA

Alas, poor fool, how have they baffled thee!

CLOWN

Why, 'some are born great, some achieve greatness,
and some have greatness thrown upon them.' I was
one, sir, in this interlude; one Sir Topas, sir; but
that's all one. 'By the Lord, fool, I am not mad.'
But do you remember? 'Madam, why laugh you at
such a barren rascal? an you smile not, he's gagged:'
and thus the whirligig of time brings in his revenges.

MALVOLIO

I'll be revenged on the whole pack of you.   [Exit

OLIVIA

He hath been most notoriously abused.

DUKE

Pursue him, and entreat him to a peace:
He hath not told us of the captain yet:
When that is known, and golden time convents,
A solemn combination shall be made
Of our dear souls. Meantime, sweet sister,
We will not part from hence. Cesario, come;
For so you shall be, while you are a man;
But when in other habits you are seen,
Orsino's mistress and his fancy's queen.

[Exeunt all, except CLOWN

CLOWN

[Sings] When that I was and a little tiny boy,
    With hey, ho, the wind and the rain,
A foolish thing was but a toy,
    For the rain it raineth every day.

But when I came to man's estate,
    With hey, ho, &c.
'Gainst knaves and thieves men shut their gate,
    For the rain, &c.

But when I came, alas! to wive,
    With hey, ho, &c.
By swaggering could I never thrive,
    For the rain, &c.

But when I came unto my beds,
    With hey, ho, &c.
With toss-pots still had drunken heads,
    For the rain, &c.

A great while ago the world begun,
    With hey, ho, &c.
But that's all one, our play is done,
    And we'll strive to please you every day.   [Exit

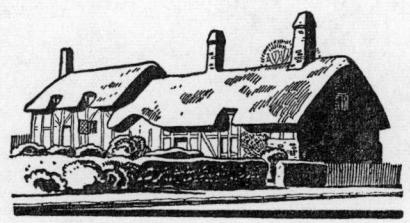

THE TRAGEDY OF HAMLET, PRINCE OF DENMARK

SYNOPSIS

THE golden days in the life of Prince Hamlet of Denmark, when as a scholarly idealist he studied at his beloved University of Wittenberg, ended abruptly and forever upon the death of his reverenced kingly father. He is now obliged to remain at the hard-drinking, shallow Danish court at Elsinore under the furtive eye of his uncle Claudius who has seized the throne, prevented the invasion of the Norwegian prince Fortinbras to recover lost territory, and, after two months' court mourning, married Hamlet's mother, the placid, weak-willed Queen Gertrude, to the great distress of the proud sorrowing Prince.

From his sordid environment, Hamlet turns for solace and love to the pretty modest Ophelia, daughter of the lord chamberlain Polonius, who returns his affection in her simple way but is utterly incapable of understanding him. Her companionship is soon lost to him, however, because her father and her worldly brother Laertes insist on her discouraging the Prince's attentions in view of his superior rank.

Horatio, his one true friend, tells him that he and two others have seen the late King's ghost stalking the gloomy castle battlements, and in a terrifying encounter Hamlet learns from the spectre that his father was murdered by his brother, the present King. Strictly bidden to vengeance by the ghost, the distracted Prince affects an erratic manner and speech as a cover for overwrought emotions and sick nerves, under which he may brood over his misery and plot retribution. Polonius is certain that Hamlet has gone mad for the love of Ophelia, but the shifty, uneasy King is not so sure and straightway sends for two disloyal college friends of the Prince, Rosencrantz and Guildenstern, to spy upon him and learn the truth.

These men have brought with them a company of strolling players, and under Hamlet's direction they present an Italian tragedy in which several episodes so strongly resemble those of the actual killing of the former King that Claudius rises, panic-stricken, from his seat and hastily breaks up the performance. Completely convinced of his uncle's guilt, Hamlet is on the point of killing him when finding him alone at prayer, but his undecided, philosophical nature prevents him from acting. When the Queen in her own room upbraids the Prince for his conduct, he turns on her in such a fury of denunciation that she utters a cry which is repeated by someone hiding near by. Thinking the King is spying, Hamlet runs his rapier through a screen and kills the listening Polonius.

Meanwhile, his father's ghost reappears to urge the Prince to his purpose, bidding him at the

[731]

same time to be gentle with his mother. The King speeds his plans for Rosencrantz and Guildenstern to accompany his nephew to England, but Hamlet shrewdly guesses their errand, and, securing on the journey the King's order for his death by the English authorities, he substitutes another command for the death of the two spies, escapes by boarding a pirate vessel that challenges their ship, and reaches Denmark safely, sending letters of his arrival to his friend Horatio and the King.

In Elsinore, the death and secret burial of her father Polonius, who has been the centre of her life, coupled with her grieving over Hamlet's strange behavior, break Ophelia's gentle mind, and, wandering about piteously in her madness, she is drowned in a brook with her flowers floating around her. Her rash, hot-headed brother Laertes, summoned home from the University of Paris by his father's death, invades the King's castle with a mob demanding vengeance, but Claudius, who has just learned of Hamlet's return to Denmark, craftily turns the young man's fury upon the Prince and together they plot his destruction in a duel in which Laertes will use a poisoned foil.

As Hamlet arrives home, accompanied by Horatio, they pass a churchyard where a burial is taking place, and the Prince, hearing in great anguish that it is Ophelia's, leaps wildly into her grave to dispute with Laertes the privilege of being chief mourner. The two grapple, but are separated upon entreaties from the King and Queen. Although he is not in training, Hamlet accepts Laertes' challenge to a friendly duel in the presence of the court, but studiously declines the cup of poisoned wine which the King has prepared for him. Laertes wounds Hamlet with the fatal foil, but in their scufflings weapons are dropped and inadvertently exchanged so that Hamlet finally wounds Laertes with his own foil. The Queen, wishing to drink to her son's success, unwittingly swallows the poisoned wine, and dies, exposing the King's guilt. Laertes, dying, confesses the plot of Claudius and himself against Hamlet's life, and the Prince now kills the evil King.

As he sees his friend about to die, Horatio in his grief seizes the poisoned cup but Hamlet snatches it from him, begging him to live to clear his name. Hamlet expires as the English ambassadors arrive to report the death of the two spies, and Fortinbras, marching through Denmark on his way to Norway, comes in time to bury the dead. As the great ordnance guns boom the royal salute, the cool-headed Norwegian prince claims the empty throne.

HISTORICAL DATA

The story of *The Tragedy of Hamlet* is probably taken from an English prose version of Belleforest's *Histoires Tragiques*, which adapted the tale from the old story of *Amleth* in the *Historia Danica*, written in Latin by a twelfth-century Danish historian, Saxo Grammaticus. The story was popular among earlier dramatists and Thomas Nash in his "Epistle" prefacing Greene's *Menaphon* (1589) and Lodge in his *Wit's Miserie and the World's Madnesse* (1596) refer to an earlier play of *Hamlet*, non-extant, generally attributed to Thomas Kyd. Similarities in structure and style tend to support the conjecture that the author of *The Spanish Tragedy* contributed to the *Hamlet* of Shakespeare, and it is reasonable to suppose that this earlier work of Kyd's materially aided in the composition of its illustrious successor.

The date of this play is generally fixed as 1602, based on the evidence of references in certain lines to the "inhibition" due to the limitation of theatres about London (1600–1) and the "innovation" of having children act in the theatre (Act II, Scene ii). Further light is thrown by the several references to the play *Julius Caesar* and the entry on the Stationers' Register in 1602. A garbled, probably shorthand, version appeared in quarto form in 1603, and subsequent quartos differed radically from this edition. Surviving texts are generally based on the First Folio and Second Quarto versions.

"Alas! poor Yorick."
HAMLET

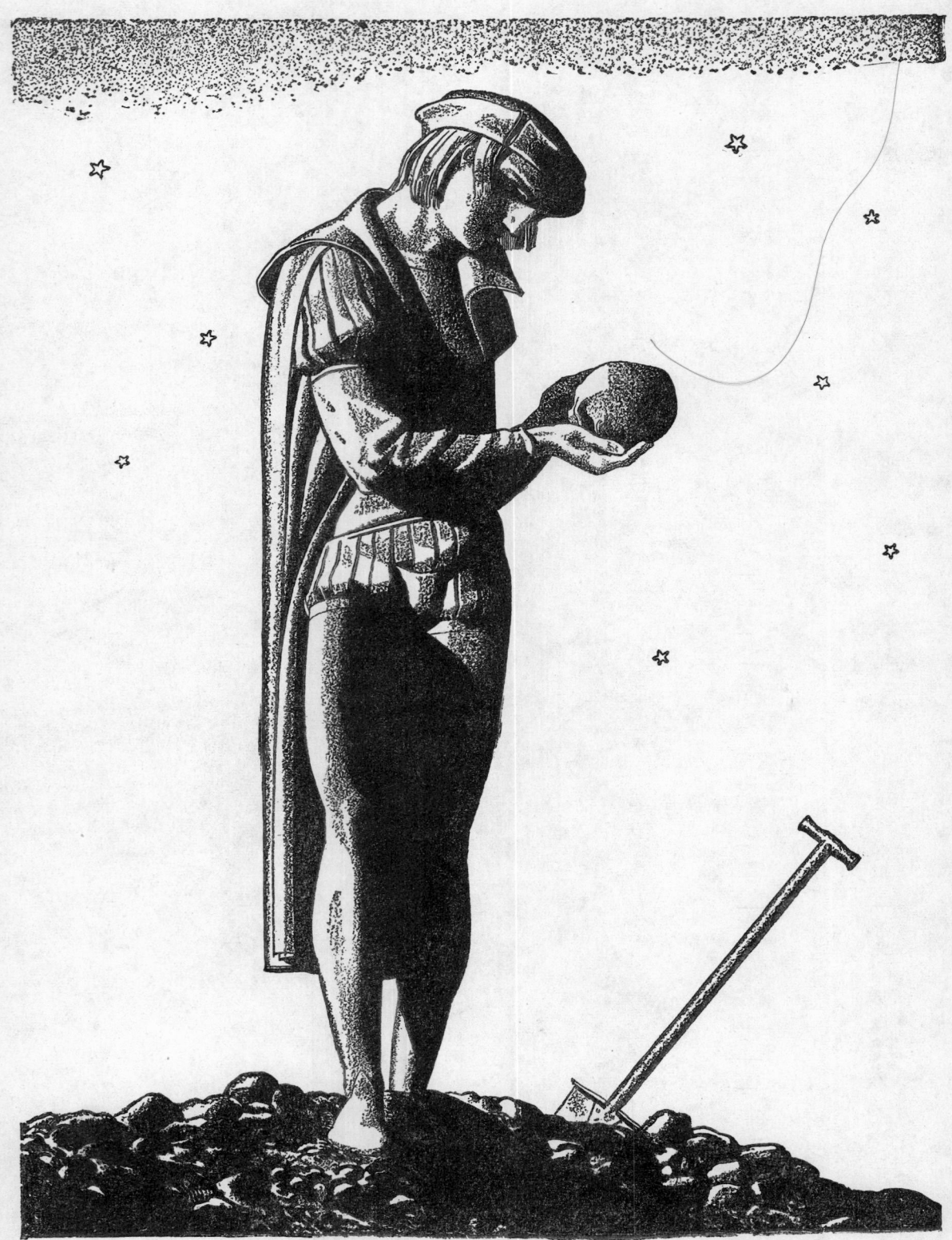

THE TRAGEDY OF HAMLET, PRINCE OF DENMARK

DRAMATIS PERSONÆ

CLAUDIUS, *king of Denmark.*
HAMLET, *son to the late, and nephew to the present king.*
POLONIUS, *lord chamberlain.*
HORATIO, *friend to Hamlet.*
LAERTES, *son to Polonius.*
VOLTIMAND,
CORNELIUS,
ROSENCRANTZ,
GUILDENSTERN, } *courtiers.*
OSRIC,
A GENTLEMAN,
A PRIEST.
MARCELLUS,
BERNARDO, } *officers.*
FRANCISCO, *a soldier.*

REYNALDO, *servant to Polonius.*
PLAYERS.
TWO CLOWNS, *grave-diggers.*
FORTINBRAS, *prince of Norway.*
A CAPTAIN.
ENGLISH AMBASSADORS.

GERTRUDE, *queen of Denmark, and mother to Hamlet.*
OPHELIA, *daughter to Polonius.*

LORDS, LADIES, OFFICERS, SOLDIERS, SAILORS, MESSENGERS, *and other* ATTENDANTS

GHOST *of Hamlet's Father.*

SCENE—*Denmark.*

ACT I

SCENE I. *Elsinore. A platform before the castle*

FRANCISCO *at his post. Enter to him* BERNARDO

BERNARDO
Who's there?

FRANCISCO
Nay, answer me: stand, and unfold yourself.

BERNARDO
Long live the king!

FRANCISCO
Bernardo?

BERNARDO
He.

FRANCISCO
You come most carefully upon your hour.

BERNARDO
'Tis now struck twelve; get thee to bed, Francisco.

FRANCISCO
For this relief much thanks: 'tis bitter cold,
And I am sick at heart.

BERNARDO
Have you had quiet guard?

FRANCISCO
Not a mouse stirring.

BERNARDO
Well, good night.
If you do meet Horatio and Marcellus,
The rivals of my watch, bid them make haste.

FRANCISCO
I think I hear them. Stand, ho! Who is there?

Enter HORATIO *and* MARCELLUS

HORATIO
Friends to this ground.

MARCELLUS
And liegemen to the Dane.

FRANCISCO
Give you good night.

MARCELLUS
O, farewell, honest soldier:
Who hath relieved you?

FRANCISCO
Bernardo hath my place.
Give you good night. [*Exit*

MARCELLUS
Holla! Bernardo!

BERNARDO
Say,
What, is Horatio there?

HORATIO
A piece of him.

BERNARDO
Welcome, Horatio; welcome, good Marcellus.

MARCELLUS
What, has this thing appear'd again to-night?

BERNARDO
I have seen nothing.

MARCELLUS
Horatio says 'tis but our fantasy,
And will not let belief take hold of him
Touching this dreaded sight, twice seen of us:
Therefore I have entreated him along
With us to watch the minutes of this night,
That if again this apparition come,
He may approve our eyes and speak to it.

HORATIO

Tush, tush, 'twill not appear.

BERNARDO

                Sit down a while;

And let us once again assail your ears,

That are so fortified against our story,

What we have two nights seen.

HORATIO

                Well, sit we down,

And let us hear Bernardo speak of this.

BERNARDO

Last night of all,

When yond same star that's westward from the pole

Had made his course to illume that part of heaven

Where now it burns, Marcellus and myself,

The bell then beating one,—

Enter GHOST

MARCELLUS

Peace, break thee off; look, where it comes again!

BERNARDO

In the same figure, like the king that's dead.

MARCELLUS

Thou art a scholar; speak to it, Horatio.

BERNARDO

Looks it not like the king? mark it, Horatio.

HORATIO

Most like: it harrows me with fear and wonder.

BERNARDO

It would be spoke to.

MARCELLUS

                Question it, Horatio.

HORATIO

What art thou, that usurp'st this time of night,

Together with that fair and warlike form

In which the majesty of buried Denmark

Did sometimes march? by heaven I charge thee,

    speak!

MARCELLUS

It is offended.

BERNARDO

             See, it stalks away!

HORATIO

Stay! speak, speak! I charge thee, speak! [*Exit* GHOST

MARCELLUS

'Tis gone, and will not answer.

BERNARDO

How now, Horatio! you tremble and look pale:

Is not this something more than fantasy?

What think you on 't?

HORATIO

Before my God, I might not this believe

Without the sensible and true avouch

Of mine own eyes.

MARCELLUS

             Is it not like the king?

HORATIO

As thou art to thyself:

Such was the very armour he had on

When he the ambitious Norway combated;

So frown'd he once, when, in an angry parle,

He smote the sledded Polacks on the ice.

'Tis strange.

MARCELLUS

Thus twice before, and jump at this dead hour,

With martial stalk hath he gone by our watch.

HORATIO

In what particular thought to work I know not;

But, in the gross and scope of my opinion,

This bodes some strange eruption to our state.

MARCELLUS

Good now, sit down, and tell me, he that knows,

Why this same strict and most observant watch

So nightly toils the subject of the land,

And why such daily cast of brazen cannon,

And foreign mart for implements of war;

Why such impress of shipwrights, whose sore task

Does not divide the Sunday from the week;

What might be toward, that this sweaty haste

Doth make the night joint-labourer with the day:

Who is 't that can inform me?

HORATIO

                That can I;

At least the whisper goes so. Our last king,

Whose image even but now appear'd to us,

Was, as you know, by Fortinbras of Norway,

Thereto prick'd on by a most emulate pride,

Dared to the combat; in which our valiant Hamlet—

For so this side of our known world esteem'd him—

Did slay this Fortinbras; who by a seal'd compact,

Well ratified by law and heraldry,

Did forfeit, with his life, all those his lands

Which he stood seized of, to the conqueror:

Against the which, a moiety competent

Was gaged by our king; which had return'd

To the inheritance of Fortinbras,

Had he been vanquisher; as, by the same covenant

And carriage of the article design'd,

His fell to Hamlet. Now, sir, young Fortinbras,

Of unimproved metal hot and full,

Hath in the skirts of Norway here and there

Shark'd up a list of lawless resolutes,

For food and diet, to some enterprise

That hath a stomach in 't: which is no other—

As it doth well appear unto our state—

But to recover of us, by strong hand

And terms compulsatory, those foresaid lands

So by his father lost: and this, I take it,

Is the main motive of our preparations,

The source of this our watch and the chief head

Of this post-haste and romage in the land.

BERNARDO

I think it be no other but e'en so:

Well may it sort, that this portentous figure

Comes armed through our watch, so like the king

That was and is the question of these wars.

HORATIO

A mote it is to trouble the mind's eye.

In the most high and palmy state of Rome,

A little ere the mightiest Julius fell,

The graves stood tenantless, and the sheeted dead
Did squeak and gibber in the Roman streets:

. . . .

As stars with trains of fire and dews of blood,
Disasters in the sun; and the moist star,
Upon whose influence Neptune's empire stands,
Was sick almost to doomsday with eclipse:
And even the like precurse of fierce events,
As harbingers preceding still the fates
And prologue to the omen coming on,
Have heaven and earth together demonstrated
Unto our climatures and countrymen.

Re-enter GHOST

But soft, behold! lo, where it comes again!
I'll cross it, though it blast me. Stay, illusion!
If thou hast any sound, or use of voice,
Speak to me:
If there be any good thing to be done,
That may to thee do ease and grace to me,
Speak to me:
If thou art privy to thy country's fate,
Which, happily, foreknowing may avoid,
O, speak!
Or if thou hast uphoarded in thy life
Extorted treasure in the womb of earth,
For which, they say, you spirits oft walk in death,
Speak of it: stay, and speak! [*The cock crows*] Stop it,
  Marcellus.

MARCELLUS
Shall I strike at it with my partisan?

HORATIO
Do, if it will not stand.

BERNARDO
'Tis here!

HORATIO
                'Tis here!

MARCELLUS
'Tis gone!   [*Exit* GHOST
We do it wrong, being so majestical,
To offer it the show of violence;
For it is, as the air, invulnerable,
And our vain blows malicious mockery.

BERNARDO
It was about to speak, when the cock crew.

HORATIO
And then it started like a guilty thing
Upon a fearful summons. I have heard,
The cock, that is the trumpet to the morn,
Doth with his lofty and shrill-sounding throat
Awake the god of day, and at his warning,
Whether in sea or fire, in earth or air,
The extravagant and erring spirit hies
To his confine: and of the truth herein
This present object made probation.

MARCELLUS
It faded on the crowing of the cock.
Some say that ever 'gainst that season comes
Wherein our Saviour's birth is celebrated,
The bird of dawning singeth all night long:

And then, they say, no spirit dare stir abroad,
The nights are wholesome, then no planets strike,
No fairy takes nor witch hath power to charm,
So hallow'd and so gracious is the time.

HORATIO
So have I heard and do in part believe it.
But look, the morn, in russet mantle clad,
Walks o'er the dew of yon high eastward hill:
Break we our watch up; and by my advice,
Let us impart what we have seen to-night
Unto young Hamlet; for, upon my life,
This spirit, dumb to us, will speak to him:
Do you consent we shall acquaint him with it,
As needful in our loves, fitting our duty?

MARCELLUS
Let's do 't, I pray; and I this morning know
Where we shall find him most conveniently. [*Exeunt*

SCENE II. *A room of state in the castle*

Flourish. Enter the KING, QUEEN, HAMLET, POLONIUS,
LAERTES, VOLTIMAND, CORNELIUS, LORDS, *and*
ATTENDANTS

KING
Though yet of Hamlet our dear brother's death
The memory be green, and that it us befitted
To bear our hearts in grief and our whole kingdom
To be contracted in one brow of woe,
Yet so far hath discretion fought with nature
That we with wisest sorrow think on him,
Together with remembrance of ourselves.
Therefore our sometime sister, now our queen,
The imperial jointress to this warlike state,
Have we, as 'twere with a defeated joy,—
With an auspicious and a dropping eye,
With mirth in funeral and with dirge in marriage,
In equal scale weighing delight and dole,—
Taken to wife: nor have we herein barr'd
Your better wisdoms, which have freely gone
With this affair along. For all, our thanks.
Now follows, that you know, young Fortinbras,
Holding a weak supposal of our worth,
Or thinking by our late dear brother's death
Our state to be disjoint and out of frame,
Colleagued with this dream of his advantage,
He hath not fail'd to pester us with message,
Importing the surrender of those lands
Lost by his father, with all bonds of law,
To our most valiant brother. So much for him.
Now for ourself, and for this time of meeting:
Thus much the business is: we have here writ
To Norway, uncle of young Fortinbras,—
Who, impotent and bed-rid, scarcely hears
Of this his nephew's purpose,—to suppress
His further gait herein; in that the levies,
The lists and full proportions, are all made
Out of his subject: and we here dispatch
You, good Cornelius, and you, Voltimand,
For bearers of this greeting to old Norway,

Giving to you no further personal power
To business with the king more than the scope
Of these delated articles allow.
Farewell, and let your haste commend your duty.

CORNELIUS *and* VOLTIMAND

In that and all things will we show our duty.

KING

We doubt it nothing: heartily farewell.

[*Exeunt* VOLTIMAND *and* CORNELIUS

And now, Laertes, what's the news with you?
You told us of some suit; what is 't, Laertes?
You cannot speak of reason to the Dane,
And lose your voice: what wouldst thou beg, Laertes,
That shall not be my offer, not thy asking?
The head is not more native to the heart,
The hand more instrumental to the mouth,
Than is the throne of Denmark to thy father.
What wouldst thou have, Laertes?

LAERTES

            My dread lord,
Your leave and favour to return to France,
From whence though willingly I came to Denmark,
To show my duty in your coronation,
Yet now, I must confess, that duty done,
My thoughts and wishes bend again toward France
And bow them to your gracious leave and pardon.

KING

Have you your father's leave? What says Polonius?

POLONIUS

He hath, my lord, wrung from me my slow leave
By laboursome petition, and at last
Upon his will I seal'd my hard consent:
I do beseech you, give him leave to go.

KING

Take thy fair hour, Laertes; time be thine,
And thy best graces spend it at thy will!
But now, my cousin Hamlet, and my son,—

HAMLET

[*Aside*] A little more than kin, and less than kind.

KING

How is it that the clouds still hang on you?

HAMLET

Not so, my lord; I am too much i' the sun.

QUEEN

Good Hamlet, cast thy nighted colour off,
And let thine eye look like a friend on Denmark.
Do not for ever with thy vailed lids
Seek for thy noble father in the dust:
Thou know'st 'tis common; all that lives must die,
Passing through nature to eternity.

HAMLET

Ay, madam, it is common.

QUEEN

        If it be,
Why seems it so particular with thee?

HAMLET

Seems, madam! nay, it is; I know not 'seems.'
'Tis not alone my inky cloak, good mother,
Nor customary suits of solemn black,

Nor windy suspiration of forced breath,
No, nor the fruitful river in the eye,
Nor the dejected haviour of the visage,
Together with all forms, moods, shapes of grief,
That can denote me truly: these indeed seem,
For they are actions that a man might play:
But I have that within which passeth show;
These but the trappings and the suits of woe.

KING

'Tis sweet and commendable in your nature, Hamlet,
To give these mourning duties to your father:
But, you must know, your father lost a father,
That father lost, lost his, and the survivor bound
In filial obligation for some term
To do obsequious sorrow: but to persever
In obstinate condolement is a course
Of impious stubbornness; 'tis unmanly grief:
It shows a will most incorrect to heaven,
A heart unfortified, a mind impatient,
An understanding simple and unschool'd:
For what we know must be and is as common
As any the most vulgar thing to sense,
Why should we in our peevish opposition
Take it to heart? Fie! 'tis a fault to heaven,
A fault against the dead, a fault to nature,
To reason most absurd, whose common theme
Is death of fathers, and who still hath cried,
From the first corse till he that died to-day,
'This must be so.' We pray you, throw to earth
This unprevailing woe, and think of us
As of a father: for let the world take note,
You are the most immediate to our throne,
And with no less nobility of love
Than that which dearest father bears his son
Do I impart toward you. For your intent
In going back to school in Wittenberg,
It is most retrograde to our desire:
And we beseech you, bend you to remain
Here in the cheer and comfort of our eye,
Our chiefest courtier, cousin and our son.

QUEEN

Let not thy mother lose her prayers, Hamlet:
I pray thee, stay with us; go not to Wittenberg.

HAMLET

I shall in all my best obey you, madam.

KING

Why, 'tis a loving and a fair reply:
Be as ourself in Denmark. Madam, come;
This gentle and unforced accord of Hamlet
Sits smiling to my heart: in grace whereof,
No jocund health that Denmark drinks to-day,
But the great cannon to the clouds shall tell,
And the king's rouse the heaven shall bruit again,
Re-speaking earthly thunder. Come away.

[*Flourish. Exeunt all but* HAMLET

HAMLET

O, that this too too solid flesh would melt
Thaw and resolve itself into a dew!
Or that the Everlasting had not fix'd

His canon 'gainst self-slaughter! O God! God!
How weary, stale, flat and unprofitable
Seem to me all the uses of this world!
Fie on 't! ah fie! 'tis an unweeded garden,
That grows to seed; things rank and gross in nature
Possess it merely. That it should come to this!
But two months dead! nay, not so much, not two:
So excellent a king; that was, to this,
Hyperion to a satyr: so loving to my mother,
That he might not beteem the winds of heaven
Visit her face too roughly. Heaven and earth!
Must I remember? why, she would hang on him,
As if increase of appetite had grown
By what it fed on: and yet, within a month—
Let me not think on 't—Frailty, thy name is
    woman!—
A little month, or ere those shoes were old
With which she follow'd my poor father's body,
Like Niobe, all tears:—why she, even she,—
O God! a beast that wants discourse of reason
Would have mourn'd longer,—married with my
    uncle,
My father's brother, but no more like my father
Than I to Hercules: within a month;
Ere yet the salt of most unrighteous tears
Had left the flushing in her galled eyes,
She married. O, most wicked speed, to post
With such dexterity to incestuous sheets!
It is not, nor it cannot come to good:
But break, my heart, for I must hold my tongue!

    Enter HORATIO, MARCELLUS, *and* BERNARDO

HORATIO

Hail to your lordship!

HAMLET

           I am glad to see you well:
Horatio,—or I do forget myself.

HORATIO

The same, my lord, and your poor servant ever.

HAMLET

Sir, my good friend; I'll change that name with you:
And what make you from Wittenberg, Horatio?
Marcellus?

MARCELLUS

My good lord?

HAMLET

I am very glad to see you. [*To* BERNARDO] Good
    even, sir.
But what, in faith, make you from Wittenberg?

HORATIO

A truant disposition, good my lord.

HAMLET

I would not hear your enemy say so,
Nor shall you do my ear that violence,
To make it truster of your own report
Against yourself: I know you are no truant.
But what is your affair in Elsinore?
We'll teach you to drink deep ere you depart.

HORATIO

My lord, I came to see your father's funeral.

HAMLET

I pray thee, do not mock me, fellow-student;
I think it was to see my mother's wedding.

HORATIO

Indeed, my lord, it follow'd hard upon.

HAMLET

Thrift, thrift, Horatio! the funeral baked-meats
Did coldly furnish forth the marriage tables.
Would I had met my dearest foe in heaven
Or ever I had seen that day, Horatio!
My father!—methinks I see my father.

HORATIO

O where, my lord?

HAMLET

          In my mind's eye, Horatio.

HORATIO

I saw him once; he was a goodly king.

HAMLET

He was a man, take him for all in all,
I shall not look upon his like again.

HORATIO

My lord, I think I saw him yesternight.

HAMLET

Saw? who?

HORATIO

My lord, the king your father.

HAMLET

             The king my father!

HORATIO

Season your admiration for a while
With an attent ear, till I may deliver,
Upon the witness of these gentlemen,
This marvel to you.

HAMLET

          For God's love, let me hear.

HORATIO

Two nights together had these gentlemen,
Marcellus and Bernardo, on their watch,
In the dead vast and middle of the night,
Been thus encounter'd. A figure like your father,
Armed at point exactly, cap-a-pe,
Appears before them, and with solemn march
Goes slow and stately by them: thrice he walk'd
By their oppress'd and fear-surprised eyes,
Within his truncheon's length; whilst they, distill'd
Almost to jelly with the act of fear,
Stand dumb, and speak not to him. This to me
In dreadful secrecy impart they did;
And I with them the third night kept the watch:
Where, as they had deliver'd, both in time,
Form of the thing, each word made true and good,
The apparition comes: I knew your father;
These hands are not more like.

HAMLET

              But where was this?

MARCELLUS

My lord, upon the platform where we watch'd.

HAMLET

Did you not speak to it?

HORATIO

My lord, I did,
But answer made it none: yet once methought
It lifted up it head and did address
Itself to motion, like as it would speak:
But even then the morning cock crew loud,
And at the sound it shrunk in haste away
And vanish'd from our sight.

HAMLET

'Tis very strange.

HORATIO

As I do live, my honour'd lord, 'tis true,
And we did think it writ down in our duty
To let you know of it.

HAMLET

Indeed, indeed, sirs, but this troubles me.
Hold you the watch to-night?

MARCELLUS and BERNARDO

We do, my lord.

HAMLET

Arm'd, say you?

MARCELLUS and BERNARDO

Arm'd, my lord.

HAMLET

From top to toe?

MARCELLUS and BERNARDO

My lord, from head to foot.

HAMLET

Then saw you not his face?

HORATIO

O, yes, my lord; he wore his beaver up.

HAMLET

What, look'd he frowningly?

HORATIO

A countenance more in sorrow than in anger.

HAMLET

Pale, or red?

HORATIO

Nay, very pale.

HAMLET

And fix'd his eyes upon you?

HORATIO

Most constantly.

HAMLET

I would I had been there.

HORATIO

It would have much amazed you.

HAMLET

Very like, very like. Stay'd it long?

HORATIO

While one with moderate haste might tell a hundred.

MARCELLUS and BERNARDO

Longer, longer.

HORATIO

Not when I saw 't.

HAMLET

His beard was grizzled? no?

HORATIO

It was, as I have seen it in his life,
A sable silver'd.

HAMLET

I will watch to-night;
Perchance 'twill walk again.

HORATIO

I warrant it will.

HAMLET

If it assume my noble father's person,
I'll speak to it, though hell itself should gape
And bid me hold my peace. I pray you all,
If you have hitherto conceal'd this sight,
Let it be tenable in your silence still,
And whatsoever else shall hap to-night,
Give it an understanding, but no tongue:
I will requite your loves. So fare you well:
Upon the platform, 'twixt eleven and twelve,
I'll visit you.

ALL

Our duty to your honour.

HAMLET

Your loves, as mine to you: farewell.
          [Exeunt all but HAMLET
My father's spirit in arms! all is not well;
I doubt some foul play: would the night were come!
Till then sit still, my soul: foul deeds will rise,
Though all the earth o'erwhelm them, to men's
    eyes.   [Exit

SCENE III. A room in POLONIUS'S house

Enter LAERTES and OPHELIA

LAERTES

My necessaries are embark'd: farewell:
And, sister, as the winds give benefit
And convoy is assistant, do not sleep,
But let me hear from you.

OPHELIA

Do you doubt that?

LAERTES

For Hamlet, and the trifling of his favour,
Hold it a fashion, and a toy in blood,
A violet in the youth of primy nature,
Forward, not permanent, sweet, not lasting,
The perfume and suppliance of a minute;
No more.

OPHELIA

No more but so?

LAERTES

Think it no more:
For nature crescent does not grow alone
In thews and bulk; but, as this temple waxes,
The inward service of the mind and soul
Grows wide withal. Perhaps he loves you now;
And now no soil nor cautel doth besmirch
The virtue of his will: but you must fear,
His greatness weigh'd, his will is not his own;
For he himself is subject to his birth:
He may not, as unvalued persons do,
Carve for himself, for on his choice depends
The safety and health of this whole state,

And therefore must his choice be circumscribed
Unto the voice and yielding of that body
Whereof he is the head. Then if he says he loves you,
It fits your wisdom so far to believe it
As he in his particular act and place
May give his saying deed; which is no further
Than the main voice of Denmark goes withal.
Then weigh what loss your honour may sustain,
If with too credent ear you list his songs,
Or lose your heart, or your chaste treasure open
To his unmaster'd importunity.
Fear it, Ophelia, fear it, my dear sister,
And keep you in the rear of your affection,
Out of the shot and danger of desire.
The chariest maid is prodigal enough,
If she unmask her beauty to the moon:
Virtue itself 'scapes not calumnious strokes:
The canker galls the infants of the spring
Too oft before their buttons be disclosed,
And in the morn and liquid dew of youth
Contagious blastments are most imminent.
Be wary then; best safety lies in fear:
Youth to itself rebels, though none else near.

OPHELIA

I shall the effect of this good lesson keep,
As watchman to my heart. But, good my brother,
Do not, as some ungracious pastors do,
Show me the steep and thorny way to heaven,
Whilst, like a puff'd and reckless libertine,
Himself the primrose path of dalliance treads
And recks not his own rede.

LAERTES

                 O, fear me not.
I stay too long: but here my father comes.

Enter POLONIUS

A double blessing is a double grace;
Occasion smiles upon a second leave.

POLONIUS

Yet here, Laertes! Aboard, aboard, for shame!
The wind sits in the shoulder of your sail,
And you are stay'd for. There; my blessing with
    thee!
And these few precepts in thy memory
Look thou character. Give thy thoughts no tongue,
Nor any unproportion'd thought his act.
Be thou familiar, but by no means vulgar.
Those friends thou hast, and their adoption tried,
Grapple them to thy soul with hoops of steel,
But do not dull thy palm with entertainment
Of each new-hatch'd unfledged comrade. Beware
Of entrance to a quarrel; but being in,
Bear 't, that the opposed may beware of thee.
Give every man thy ear, but few thy voice:
Take each man's censure, but reserve thy judge-
    ment.
Costly thy habit as thy purse can buy,
But not express'd in fancy; rich, not gaudy:
For the apparel oft proclaims the man;
And they in France of the best rank and station
Are of a most select and generous chief in that.

Neither a borrower nor a lender be:
For loan oft loses both itself and friend,
And borrowing dulls the edge of husbandry.
This above all: to thine own self be true,
And it must follow, as the night the day,
Thou canst not then be false to any man.
Farewell: my blessing season this in thee!

LAERTES

Most humbly do I take my leave, my lord.

POLONIUS

The time invites you; go, your servants tend.

LAERTES

Farewell, Ophelia, and remember well
What I have said to you.

OPHELIA

             'Tis in my memory lock'd,
And you yourself shall keep the key of it.

LAERTES

Farewell.   [*Exit*

POLONIUS

What is 't, Ophelia, he hath said to you?

OPHELIA

So please you, something touching the Lord Hamlet.

POLONIUS

Marry, well bethought:
'Tis told me, he hath very oft of late
Given private time to you, and you yourself
Have of your audience been most free and bounte-
    ous:
If it be so—as so 'tis put on me,
And that in way of caution—I must tell you,
You do not understand yourself so clearly
As it behoves my daughter and your honour.
What is between you? give me up the truth.

OPHELIA

He hath, my lord, of late made many tenders
Of his affection to me.

POLONIUS

Affection! pooh! you speak like a green girl,
Unsifted in such perilous circumstance.
Do you believe his tenders, as you call them?

OPHELIA

I do not know, my lord, what I should think.

POLONIUS

Marry, I'll teach you: think yourself a baby,
That you have ta'en these tenders for true pay,
Which are not sterling. Tender yourself more dearly;
Or—not to crack the wind of the poor phrase,
Running it thus—you'll tender me a fool.

OPHELIA

My lord, he hath importuned me with love
In honourable fashion.

POLONIUS

Ay, fashion you may call it; go to, go to.

OPHELIA

And hath given countenance to his speech, my lord,
With almost all the holy vows of heaven.

POLONIUS

Ay, springes to catch woodcocks. I do know,
When the blood burns, how prodigal the soul

Lends the tongue vows: these blazes, daughter,
Giving more light than heat, extinct in both,
Even in their promise, as it is a-making,
You must not take for fire. From this time
Be something scanter of your maiden presence;
Set your entreatments at a higher rate
Than a command to parley. For Lord Hamlet,
Believe so much in him, that he is young,
And with a larger tether may he walk
Than may be given you: in few, Ophelia,
Do not believe his vows; for they are brokers,
Not of that dye which their investments show,
But mere implorators of unholy suits,
Breathing like sanctified and pious bawds,
The better to beguile. This is for all:
I would not, in plain terms, from this time forth,
Have you so slander any moment leisure,
As to give words or talk with the Lord Hamlet.
Look to 't, I charge you: come your ways.

OPHELIA

I shall obey, my lord.　　　　　　　　[Exeunt

SCENE IV. *The platform*

Enter HAMLET, HORATIO, *and* MARCELLUS

HAMLET

The air bites shrewdly; it is very cold.

HORATIO

It is a nipping and an eager air.

HAMLET

What hour now?

HORATIO

　　　　　I think it lacks of twelve.

MARCELLUS

No, it is struck.

HORATIO

Indeed? I heard it not: it then draws near the season
Wherein the spirit held his wont to walk.
　　　[*A flourish of trumpets, and ordnance shot off within*
What doth this mean, my lord?

HAMLET

The king doth wake to-night and takes his rouse,
Keeps wassail, and the swaggering up-spring reels;
And as he drains his draughts of Rhenish down,
The kettle-drum and trumpet thus bray out
The triumph of his pledge.

HORATIO

　　　　　　Is it a custom?

HAMLET

Ay, marry, is 't:
But to my mind, though I am native here
And to the manner born, it is a custom
More honour'd in the breach than the observance.
This heavy-headed revel east and west
Makes us traduced and tax'd of other nations:
They clepe us drunkards, and with swinish phrase
Soil our addition; and indeed it takes
From our achievements, though perform'd at
　　height,

The pith and marrow of our attribute.
So, oft it chances in particular men,
That for some vicious mole of nature in them,
As, in their birth,—wherein they are not guilty,
Since nature cannot choose his origin,—
By the o'ergrowth of some complexion,
Oft breaking down the pales and forts of reason,
Or by some habit that too much o'er-leavens
The form of plausive manners, that these men,—
Carrying, I say, the stamp of one defect,
Being nature's livery, or fortune's star,—
Their virtues else—be they as pure as grace,
As infinite as man may undergo—
Shall in the general censure take corruption
From that particular fault: the dram of eale
Doth all the noble substance of a doubt
To his own scandal.

Enter GHOST

HORATIO

　　　　Look, my lord, it comes!

HAMLET

Angels and ministers of grace defend us!
Be thou a spirit of health or goblin damn'd,
Bring with thee airs from heaven or blasts from hell,
Be thy intents wicked or charitable,
Thou comest in such a questionable shape
That I will speak to thee: I'll call thee Hamlet,
King, father, royal Dane: O, answer me!
Let me not burst in ignorance; but tell
Why thy canonized bones, hearsed in death,
Have burst their cerements; why the sepulchre,
Wherein we saw thee quietly inurn'd,
Hath oped his ponderous and marble jaws,
To cast thee up again. What may this mean,
That thou, dead corse, again, in complete steel,
Revisit'st thus the glimpses of the moon,
Making night hideous; and we fools of nature
So horridly to shake our disposition
With thoughts beyond the reaches of our souls?
Say, why is this? wherefore? what should we do?
　　　　　　　　[GHOST *beckons* HAMLET

HORATIO

It beckons you to go away with it,
As if it some impartment did desire
To you alone.

MARCELLUS

　　　Look, with what courteous action
It waves you to a more removed ground:
But do not go with it.

HORATIO

　　　　No, by no means.

HAMLET

It will not speak; then I will follow it.

HORATIO

Do not, my lord.

HAMLET

　　　　Why, what should be the fear?
I do not set my life at a pin's fee;
And for my soul, what can it do to that,

Being a thing immortal as itself?
It waves me forth again: I'll follow it.

HORATIO

What if it tempt you toward the flood, my lord,
Or to the dreadful summit of the cliff
That beetles o'er his base into the sea,
And there assume some other horrible form,
Which might deprive your sovereignty of reason
And draw you into madness? think of it:
The very place puts toys of desperation,
Without more motive, into every brain
That looks so many fathoms to the sea
And hears it roar beneath.

HAMLET

           It waves me still.
Go on; I'll follow thee.

MARCELLUS

You shall not go, my lord.

HAMLET

           Hold off your hands.

HORATIO

Be ruled; you shall not go.

HAMLET

           My fate cries out,
And makes each petty artery in this body
As hardy as the Nemean lion's nerve.
Still am I call'd: unhand me, gentlemen;
By heaven, I'll make a ghost of him that lets me:
I say, away! Go on; I'll follow thee.

[Exeunt GHOST and HAMLET

HORATIO

He waxes desperate with imagination.

MARCELLUS

Let's follow; 'tis not fit thus to obey him.

HORATIO

Have after. To what issue will this come?

MARCELLUS

Something is rotten in the state of Denmark.

HORATIO

Heaven will direct it.

MARCELLUS

           Nay, let's follow him. [Exeunt

SCENE V. Another part of the platform

Enter GHOST and HAMLET

HAMLET

Whither wilt thou lead me? speak; I'll go no fur-
    ther.

GHOST

Mark me.

HAMLET

    I will.

GHOST

           My hour is almost come,
When I to sulphurous and tormenting flames
Must render up myself.

HAMLET

           Alas, poor ghost!

GHOST

Pity me not, but lend thy serious hearing
To what I shall unfold.

HAMLET

           Speak; I am bound to hear.

GHOST

So art thou to revenge, when thou shalt hear.

HAMLET

What?

GHOST

I am thy father's spirit;
Doom'd for a certain term to walk the night,
And for the day confined to fast in fires,
Till the foul crimes done in my days of nature
Are burnt and purged away. But that I am forbid
To tell the secrets of my prison-house,
I could a tale unfold whose lightest word
Would harrow up thy soul, freeze thy young blood,
Make thy two eyes, like stars, start from their
    spheres,
Thy knotted and combined locks to part
And each particular hair to stand an end,
Like quills upon the fretful porpentine:
But this eternal blazon must not be
To ears of flesh and blood. List, list, O, list!
If thou didst ever thy dear father love—

HAMLET

O God!

GHOST

Revenge his foul and most unnatural murder.

HAMLET

Murder!

GHOST

Murder most foul, as in the best it is,
But this most foul, strange, and unnatural.

HAMLET

Haste me to know 't, that I, with wings as swift
As meditation or the thoughts of love,
May sweep to my revenge.

GHOST

           I find thee apt;
And duller shouldst thou be than the fat weed
That roots itself in ease on Lethe wharf,
Wouldst thou not stir in this. Now, Hamlet, hear:
'Tis given out that, sleeping in my orchard,
A serpent stung me; so the whole ear of Denmark
Is by a forged process of my death
Rankly abused: but know, thou noble youth,
The serpent that did sting thy father's life
Now wears his crown.

HAMLET

           O my prophetic soul!
My uncle!

GHOST

Ay, that incestuous, that adulterate beast,
With witchcraft of his wit, with traitorous gifts,—
O wicked wit and gifts, that have the power
So to seduce!—won to his shameful lust
The will of my most seeming-virtuous queen:
O Hamlet, what a falling-off was there!

From me, whose love was of that dignity
That it went hand in hand even with the vow
I made to her in marriage; and to decline
Upon a wretch, whose natural gifts were poor
To those of mine!
But virtue, as it never will be moved,
Though lewdness court it in a shape of heaven,
So lust, though to a radiant angel link'd,
Will sate itself in a celestial bed
And prey on garbage.
But, soft! methinks I scent the morning air;
Brief let me be. Sleeping within my orchard,
My custom always of the afternoon,
Upon my secure hour thy uncle stole,
With juice of cursed hebenon in a vial,
And in the porches of my ears did pour
The leperous distilment; whose effect
Holds such an enmity with blood of man
That swift as quicksilver it courses through
The natural gates and alleys of the body;
And with a sudden vigour it doth posset
And curd, like eager droppings into milk,
The thin and wholesome blood: so did it mine;
And a most instant tetter bark'd about,
Most lazar-like, with vile and loathsome crust,
All my smooth body.
Thus was I, sleeping, by a brother's hand
Of life, of crown, of queen, at once dispatch'd:
Cut off even in the blossoms of my sin,
Unhousel'd, disappointed, unaneled;
No reckoning made, but sent to my account
With all my imperfections on my head:
O, horrible! O, horrible! most horrible!
If thou hast nature in thee, bear it not;
Let not the royal bed of Denmark be
A couch for luxury and damned incest.
But, howsoever thou pursuest this act,
Taint not thy mind, nor let thy soul contrive
Against thy mother aught: leave her to heaven,
And to those thorns that in her bosom lodge,
To prick and sting her. Fare thee well at once!
The glow-worm shows the matin to be near,
And 'gins to pale his uneffectual fire:
Adieu, adieu, adieu! remember me.   [*Exit*

HAMLET

O all you host of heaven! O earth! what else?
And shall I couple hell? O, fie! Hold, hold, my
  heart;
And you, my sinews, grow not instant old,
But bear me stiffly up. Remember thee!
Ay, thou poor ghost, while memory holds a seat
In this distracted globe. Remember thee!
Yea, from the table of my memory
I'll wipe away all trivial fond records,
All saws of books, all forms, all pressures past,
That youth and observation copied there;
And thy commandment all alone shall live
Within the book and volume of my brain,
Unmix'd with baser matter: yes, by heaven!
O most pernicious woman!

O villain, villain, smiling, damned villain!
My tables,—meet it is I set it down,
That one may smile, and smile, and be a villain;
At least I'm sure it may be so in Denmark. [*Writing*
So, uncle, there you are. Now to my word;
It is 'Adieu, adieu! remember me.'
I have sworn 't.

HORATIO *and* MARCELLUS

[*Within*] My lord, my lord!

Enter HORATIO *and* MARCELLUS

MARCELLUS

                    Lord Hamlet!

HORATIO

                    Heaven secure him!

HAMLET

So be it!

MARCELLUS

Illo, ho, ho, my lord!

HAMLET

Hillo, ho, ho, boy! come, bird, come.

MARCELLUS

How is 't, my noble lord?

HORATIO

                    What news, my lord?

HAMLET

O, wonderful!

HORATIO

Good my lord, tell it.

HAMLET

                    No; you will reveal it.

HORATIO

Not I, my lord, by heaven.

MARCELLUS

                    Nor I, my lord.

HAMLET

How say you, then; would heart of man once think
  it?
But you'll be secret?

HORATIO *and* MARCELLUS

                    Ay, by heaven, my lord.

HAMLET

There's ne'er a villain dwelling in all Denmark
But he's an arrant knave.

HORATIO

There needs no ghost, my lord, come from the grave
To tell us this.

HAMLET

                    Why, right; you are i' the right;
And so, without more circumstance at all,
I hold it fit that we shake hands and part:
You, as your business and desire shall point you;
For every man hath business and desire,
Such as it is; and for my own poor part,
Look you, I'll go pray.

HORATIO

These are but wild and whirling words, my lord.

HAMLET

I'm sorry they offend you, heartily;
Yes, faith, heartily.

HORATIO

There's no offence, my lord.

HAMLET

Yes, by Saint Patrick, but there is, Horatio,
And much offence too. Touching this vision here,
It is an honest ghost, that let me tell you:
For your desire to know what is between us,
O'ermaster 't as you may. And now, good friends,
As you are friends, scholars and soldiers,
Give me one poor request.

HORATIO

What is 't, my lord? we will.

HAMLET

Never make known what you have seen tonight.

HORATIO *and* MARCELLUS

My lord, we will not.

HAMLET

Nay, but swear 't.

HORATIO

In faith,
My lord, not I.

MARCELLUS

Nor I, my lord, in faith.

HAMLET

Upon my sword.

MARCELLUS

We have sworn, my lord, already.

HAMLET

Indeed, upon my sword, indeed.

GHOST

[*Beneath*] Swear.

HAMLET

Ah, ha, boy! say'st thou so? art thou there, true-
penny?
Come on: you hear this fellow in the cellarage:
Consent to swear.

HORATIO

Propose the oath, my lord.

HAMLET

Never to speak of this that you have seen,
Swear by my sword.

GHOST

[*Beneath*] Swear.

HAMLET

Hic et ubique? then we'll shift our ground.
Come hither, gentlemen,
And lay your hands again upon my sword:
Never to speak of this that you have heard,
Swear by my sword.

GHOST

[*Beneath*] Swear.

HAMLET

Well said, old mole! canst work i' the earth so fast?
A worthy pioner! Once more remove, good friends.

HORATIO

O day and night, but this is wondrous strange!

HAMLET

And therefore as a stranger give it welcome.
There are more things in heaven and earth, Horatio,
Than are dreamt of in your philosophy.

But come;
Here, as before, never, so help you mercy,
How strange or odd soe'er I bear myself,
As I perchance hereafter shall think meet
To put an antic disposition on,
That you, at such times seeing me, never shall,
With arms encumber'd thus, or this head-shake,
Or by pronouncing of some doubtful phrase,
As 'Well, well, we know,' or 'We could, an if we
would,'
Or 'If we list to speak,' or 'There be, an if they
might,'
Or such ambiguous giving out, to note
That you know aught of me: this not to do,
So grace and mercy at your most need help you,
Swear.

GHOST

[*Beneath*] Swear.

HAMLET

Rest, rest, perturbed spirit! [*They swear*] So, gentle-
men,
With all my love I do commend me to you:
And what so poor a man as Hamlet is
May do, to express his love and friending to you,
God willing, shall not lack. Let us go in together;
And still your fingers on your lips, I pray.
The time is out of joint: O cursed spite,
That ever I was born to set it right!
Nay, come, let's go together.　　　　　[*Exeunt*

ACT II

SCENE I. *A room in* POLONIUS'S *house*

Enter POLONIUS *and* REYNALDO

POLONIUS

Give him this money and these notes, Reynaldo.

REYNALDO

I will, my lord.

POLONIUS

You shall do marvellous wisely, good Reynaldo,
Before you visit him, to make inquire
Of his behaviour.

REYNALDO

My lord, I did intend it.

POLONIUS

Marry, well said, very well said. Look you, sir,
Inquire me first what Danskers are in Paris,
And how, and who, what means, and where they
keep,
What company, at what expense, and finding
By this encompassment and drift of question
That they do know my son, come you more nearer
Than your particular demands will touch it:
Take you, as 'twere, some distant knowledge of him,
As thus, 'I know his father and his friends,
And in part him:' do you mark this, Reynaldo?

REYNALDO

Ay, very well, my lord.

POLONIUS

'And in part him; but,' you may say, 'not well:
But if 't be he I mean, he's very wild,
Addicted so and so;' and there put on him
What forgeries you please; marry, none so rank
As may dishonour him; take heed of that;
But, sir, such wanton, wild and usual slips
As are companions noted and most known
To youth and liberty.

REYNALDO

As gaming, my lord.

POLONIUS

Ay, or drinking, fencing, swearing, quarrelling,
Drabbing: you may go so far.

REYNALDO

My lord, that would dishonour him.

POLONIUS

Faith, no; as you may season it in the charge.
You must not put another scandal on him,
That he is open to incontinency;
That's not my meaning: but breathe his faults so
    quaintly
That they may seem the taints of liberty,
The flash and outbreak of a fiery mind,
A savageness in unreclaimed blood,
Of general assault.

REYNALDO

But, my good lord,—

POLONIUS

Wherefore should you do this?

REYNALDO

Ay, my lord,
I would know that.

POLONIUS

Marry, sir, here's my drift,
And I believe it is a fetch of warrant:
You laying these slight sullies on my son,
As 'twere a thing a little soil'd i' the working,
Mark you,
Your party in converse, him you would sound,
Having ever seen in the prenominate crimes
The youth you breathe of guilty, be assured
He closes with you in this consequence;
'Good sir,' or so, or 'friend,' or 'gentleman,'
According to the phrase or the addition
Of man and country.

REYNALDO

Very good, my lord.

POLONIUS

And then, sir, does he this—he does—what was I
about to say? By the mass, I was about to say something: where did I leave?

REYNALDO

At 'closes in the consequence,' at 'friend or so,' and
'gentleman.'

POLONIUS

At 'closes in the consequence,' ay, marry;
He closes with you thus: 'I know the gentleman;

I saw him yesterday, or t'other day,
Or then, or then, with such, or such, and, as you say,
There was a' gaming, there o'ertook in 's rouse,
There falling out at tennis:' or perchance,
'I saw him enter such a house of sale,'
Videlicet, a brothel, or so forth.
See you now;
Your bait of falsehood takes this carp of truth:
And thus do we of wisdom and of reach,
With windlasses and with assays of bias,
By indirections find directions out:
So, by my former lecture and advice,
Shall you my son. You have me, have you not?

REYNALDO

My lord, I have.

POLONIUS

God be wi' ye; fare ye well.

REYNALDO

Good my lord!

POLONIUS

Observe his inclination in yourself.

REYNALDO

I shall, my lord.

POLONIUS

And let him ply his music.

REYNALDO

Well, my lord.

POLONIUS

Farewell!   [Exit REYNALDO

Enter OPHELIA

How now, Ophelia! what's the matter?

OPHELIA

O, my lord, my lord, I have been so affrighted!

POLONIUS

With what, i' the name of God?

OPHELIA

My lord, as I was sewing in my closet,
Lord Hamlet, with his doublet all unbraced,
No hat upon his head, his stockings foul'd,
Ungarter'd and down-gyved to his ancle;
Pale as his shirt, his knees knocking each other,
And with a look so piteous in purport
As if he had been loosed out of hell
To speak of horrors, he comes before me.

POLONIUS

Mad for thy love?

OPHELIA

My lord, I do not know,
But truly I do fear it.

POLONIUS

What said he?

OPHELIA

He took me by the wrist and held me hard;
Then goes he to the length of all his arm,
And with his other hand thus o'er his brow,
He falls to such perusal of my face
As he would draw it. Long stay'd he so;
At last, a little shaking of mine arm
And thrice his head thus waving up and down,
He raised a sigh so piteous and profound

As it did seem to shatter all his bulk
And end his being: that done, he lets me go:
And with his head over his shoulder turn'd,
He seem'd to find his way without his eyes;
For out o' doors he went without their helps,
And to the last bended their light on me.

POLONIUS

Come, go with me: I will go seek the king.
This is the very ecstasy of love;
Whose violent property fordoes itself
And leads the will to desperate undertakings
As oft as any passion under heaven
That does afflict our natures. I am sorry.
What, have you given him any hard words of late?

OPHELIA

No, my good lord, but, as you did command,
I did repel his letters and denied
His access to me.

POLONIUS

             That hath made him mad.
I am sorry that with better heed and judgement
I had not quoted him: I fear'd he did but trifle
And meant to wreck thee; but beshrew my jealousy!
By heaven, it is as proper to our age
To cast beyond ourselves in our opinions
As it is common for the younger sort
To lack discretion. Come, go we to the king:
This must be known; which, being kept close, might
     move
More grief to hide than hate to utter love.
Come.   [Exeunt

SCENE II. *A room in the castle*

Flourish. Enter KING, QUEEN, ROSENCRANTZ,
GUILDENSTERN, *and* ATTENDANTS

KING

Welcome, dear Rosencrantz and Guildenstern!
Moreover that we much did long to see you,
The need we have to use you did provoke
Our hasty sending. Something have you heard
Of Hamlet's transformation; so call it,
Sith nor the exterior nor the inward man
Resembles that it was. What it should be,
More than his father's death, that thus hath put him
So much from the understanding of himself,
I cannot dream of: I entreat you both,
That, being of so young days brought up with him
And sith so neighbour'd to his youth and haviour,
That you vouchsafe your rest here in our court
Some little time: so by your companies
To draw him on to pleasures, and to gather
So much as from occasion you may glean,
Whether aught to us unknown afflicts him thus,
That open'd lies within our remedy.

QUEEN

Good gentlemen, he hath much talk'd of you,
And sure I am two men there are not living
To whom he more adheres. If it will please you

To show us so much gentry and good will
As to expend your time with us a while
For the supply and profit of our hope,
Your visitation shall receive such thanks
As fits a king's remembrance.

ROSENCRANTZ

                Both your majesties
Might, by the sovereign power you have of us,
Put your dread pleasures more into command
Than to entreaty.

GUILDENSTERN

               But we both obey,
And here give up ourselves, in the full bent
To lay our service freely at your feet,
To be commanded.

KING

Thanks, Rosencrantz and gentle Guildenstern.

QUEEN

Thanks, Guildenstern and gentle Rosencrantz:
And I beseech you instantly to visit
My too much changed son. Go, some of you,
And bring these gentlemen where Hamlet is.

GUILDENSTERN

Heavens make our presence and our practices
Pleasant and helpful to him!

QUEEN

               Ay, amen!   [*Exeunt*
ROSENCRANTZ, GUILDENSTERN, *and some* ATTENDANTS
Enter POLONIUS

POLONIUS

The ambassadors from Norway, my good lord,
Are joyfully return'd.

KING

Thou still hast been the father of good news.

POLONIUS

Have I, my lord? I assure my good liege,
I hold my duty as I hold my soul,
Both to my God and to my gracious king:
And I do think, or else this brain of mine
Hunts not the trail of policy so sure
As it hath used to do, that I have found
The very cause of Hamlet's lunacy.

KING

O, speak of that; that do I long to hear.

POLONIUS

Give first admittance to the ambassadors;
My news shall be the fruit to that great feast.

KING

Thyself do grace to them, and bring them in.
                        [*Exit* POLONIUS
He tells me, my dear Gertrude, he hath found
The head and source of all your son's distemper.

QUEEN

I doubt it is no other but the main;
His father's death and our o'erhasty marriage.

KING

Well, we shall sift him.
Re-enter POLONIUS, *with* VOLTIMAND *and* CORNELIUS
              Welcome, my good friends!
Say, Voltimand, what from our brother Norway?

VOLTIMAND

Most fair return of greetings and desires.
Upon our first, he sent out to suppress
His nephew's levies, which to him appear'd
To be a preparation 'gainst the Polack,
But better look'd into, he truly found
It was against your highness: whereat grieved,
That so his sickness, age and impotence
Was falsely borne in hand, sends out arrests
On Fortinbras; which he, in brief, obeys,
Receives rebuke from Norway, and in fine
Makes vow before his uncle never more
To give the assay of arms against your majesty.
Whereon old Norway, overcome with joy,
Gives him three thousand crowns in annual fee
And his commission to employ those soldiers,
So levied as before, against the Polack:
With an entreaty, herein further shown,

[Giving a paper

That it might please you to give quiet pass
Through your dominions for this enterprise,
On such regards of safety and allowance
As therein are set down.

KING

It likes us well,
And at our more consider'd time we'll read,
Answer, and think upon this business.
Meantime we thank you for your well-took labour:
Go to your rest; at night we'll feast together:
Most welcome home!

[Exeunt VOLTIMAND *and* CORNELIUS

POLONIUS

This business is well ended.
My liege, and madam, to expostulate
What majesty should be, what duty is,
Why day is day, night night, and time is time,
Were nothing but to waste night, day and time.
Therefore, since brevity is the soul of wit
And tediousness the limbs and outward flourishes,
I will be brief. Your noble son is mad:
Mad call I it; for, to define true madness,
What is 't but to be nothing else but mad?
But let that go.

QUEEN

More matter, with less art.

POLONIUS

Madam, I swear I use no art at all.
That he is mad, 'tis true: 'tis true 'tis pity,
And pity 'tis 'tis true: a foolish figure;
But farewell it, for I will use no art.
Mad let us grant him then: and now remains
That we find out the cause of this effect,
Or rather say, the cause of this defect,
For this effect defective comes by cause:
Thus it remains and the remainder thus.
Perpend.
I have a daughter,—have while she is mine,—
Who in her duty and obedience, mark,
Hath given me this: now gather and surmise. *[Reads*

'To the celestial, and my soul's idol, the most beautified
　Ophelia,'—

That's an ill phrase, a vile phrase; 'beautified' is a
vile phrase: but you shall hear. Thus:　　*[Reads*

'In her excellent white bosom, these,' &c.

QUEEN

Came this from Hamlet to her?

POLONIUS

Good madam, stay awhile; I will be faithful. *[Reads*

'Doubt thou the stars are fire;
　　Doubt that the sun doth move;
　　Doubt truth to be a liar;
　　But never doubt I love.

'O dear Ophelia, I am ill at these numbers; I have not art to
reckon my groans: but that I love thee best, O most best, believe it. Adieu.

'Thine evermore, most dear lady, whilst this
　　　　machine is to him, HAMLET.'

This in obedience hath my daughter shown me;
And more above, hath his solicitings,
As they fell out by time, by means and place,
All given to mine ear.

KING

But how hath she
Received his love?

POLONIUS

What do you think of me?

KING

As of a man faithful and honourable.

POLONIUS

I would fain prove so. But what might you think,
When I had seen this hot love on the wing,—
As I perceived it, I must tell you that,
Before my daughter told me,—what might you,
Or my dear majesty your queen here, think,
If I had play'd the desk or table-book,
Or given my heart a winking, mute and dumb,
Or look'd upon this love with idle sight;
What might you think? No, I went round to work,
And my young mistress thus I did bespeak:
'Lord Hamlet is a prince, out of thy star;
This must not be:' and then I prescripts gave her,
That she should lock herself from his resort,
Admit no messengers, receive no tokens.
Which done, she took the fruits of my advice;
And he repulsed, a short tale to make,
Fell into a sadness, then into a fast,
Thence to a watch, thence into a weakness,
Thence to a lightness, and by this declension
Into the madness wherein now he raves
And all we mourn for.

KING

Do you think this?

QUEEN

It may be, very like.

POLONIUS

Hath there been such a time, I'ld fain know that,
That I have positively said ''tis so,'
When it proved otherwise?

KING
Not that I know.
POLONIUS
[*Pointing to his head and shoulder*] Take this from this,
    if this be otherwise:
If circumstances lead me, I will find
Where truth is hid, though it were hid indeed
Within the centre.
KING
How may we try it further?
POLONIUS
You know, sometimes he walks four hours together
Here in the lobby.
QUEEN
So he does, indeed.
POLONIUS
At such a time I'll loose my daughter to him:
Be you and I behind an arras then;
Mark the encounter: if he love her not,
And be not from his reason fall'n thereon,
Let me be no assistant for a state,
But keep a farm and carters.
KING
We will try it.
QUEEN
But look where sadly the poor wretch comes reading.
POLONIUS
Away, I do beseech you, both away:
I'll board him presently.
        [*Exeunt* KING, QUEEN, *and* ATTENDANTS
        Enter HAMLET, *reading*
O, give me leave: how does my good Lord Hamlet?
HAMLET
Well, God-a-mercy.
POLONIUS
Do you know me, my lord?
HAMLET
Excellent well; you are a fishmonger.
POLONIUS
Not I, my lord.
HAMLET
Then I would you were so honest a man.
POLONIUS
Honest, my lord!
HAMLET
Ay, sir; to be honest, as this world goes, is to be one
man picked out of ten thousand.
POLONIUS
That's very true, my lord.
HAMLET
For if the sun breed maggots in a dead dog, being a
god kissing carrion—Have you a daughter?
POLONIUS
I have, my lord.
HAMLET
Let her not walk i' the sun: conception is a blessing;
but as your daughter may conceive,—friend, look
to 't.
POLONIUS
[*Aside*] How say you by that? Still harping on my

daughter: yet he knew me not at first; he said I was
a fishmonger: he is far gone: and truly in my youth
I suffered much extremity for love; very near this.
I'll speak to him again.—What do you read, my
lord?
HAMLET
Words, words, words.
POLONIUS
What is the matter, my lord?
HAMLET
Between who?
POLONIUS
I mean, the matter that you read, my lord.
HAMLET
Slanders, sir: for the satirical rogue says here that
old men have grey beards, that their faces are wrin-
kled, their eyes purging thick amber and plum-tree
gum, and that they have a plentiful lack of wit, to-
gether with most weak hams: all which, sir, though
I most powerfully and potently believe, yet I hold it
not honesty to have it thus set down; for yourself,
sir, shall grow old as I am, if like a crab you could
go backward.
POLONIUS
[*Aside*] Though this be madness, yet there is method
in 't.—Will you walk out of the air, my lord?
HAMLET
Into my grave.
POLONIUS
Indeed, that's out of the air. [*Aside*] How pregnant
sometimes his replies are! a happiness that often
madness hits on, which reason and sanity could not
so prosperously be delivered of. I will leave him,
and suddenly contrive the means of meeting be-
tween him and my daughter.—My honourable lord,
I will most humbly take my leave of you.
HAMLET
You cannot, sir, take from me any thing that I will
more willingly part withal: except my life, except
my life, except my life.
POLONIUS
Fare you well, my lord.
HAMLET
These tedious old fools!
    Enter ROSENCRANTZ *and* GUILDENSTERN
POLONIUS
You go to seek the Lord Hamlet; there he is.
ROSENCRANTZ
[*To* POLONIUS] God save you, sir!   [*Exit* POLONIUS
GUILDENSTERN
My honoured lord!
ROSENCRANTZ
My most dear lord!
HAMLET
My excellent good friends! How dost thou, Guilden-
stern? Ah, Rosencrantz! Good lads, how do you
both?
ROSENCRANTZ
As the indifferent children of the earth.

GUILDENSTERN

Happy, in that we are not over-happy;
On Fortune's cap we are not the very button.

HAMLET

Nor the soles of her shoe?

ROSENCRANTZ

Neither, my lord.

HAMLET

Then you live about her waist, or in the middle of her favours?

GUILDENSTERN

Faith, her privates we.

HAMLET

In the secret parts of Fortune? O, most true; she is a strumpet. What's the news?

ROSENCRANTZ

None, my lord, but that the world's grown honest.

HAMLET

Then is doomsday near: but your news is not true. Let me question more in particular: what have you, my good friends, deserved at the hands of Fortune, that she sends you to prison hither?

GUILDENSTERN

Prison, my lord!

HAMLET

Denmark's a prison.

ROSENCRANTZ

Then is the world one.

HAMLET

A goodly one; in which there are many confines, wards and dungeons, Denmark being one o' the worst.

ROSENCRANTZ

We think not so, my lord.

HAMLET

Why, then 'tis none to you; for there is nothing either good or bad, but thinking makes it so: to me it is a prison.

ROSENCRANTZ

Why, then your ambition makes it one; 'tis too narrow for your mind.

HAMLET

O God, I could be bounded in a nut-shell and count myself a king of infinite space, were it not that I have bad dreams.

GUILDENSTERN

Which dreams indeed are ambition; for the very substance of the ambitious is merely the shadow of a dream.

HAMLET

A dream itself is but a shadow.

ROSENCRANTZ

Truly, and I hold ambition of so airy and light a quality that it is but a shadow's shadow.

HAMLET

Then are our beggars bodies, and our monarchs and outstretched heroes the beggars' shadows. Shall we to the court? for, by my fay, I cannot reason.

ROSENCRANTZ and GUILDENSTERN

We'll wait upon you.

HAMLET

No such matter: I will not sort you with the rest of my servants; for, to speak to you like an honest man, I am most dreadfully attended. But, in the beaten way of friendship, what make you at Elsinore?

ROSENCRANTZ

To visit you, my lord; no other occasion.

HAMLET

Beggar that I am, I am even poor in thanks; but I thank you: and sure, dear friends, my thanks are too dear a halfpenny. Were you not sent for? Is it your own inclining? Is it a free visitation? Come, deal justly with me: come, come; nay, speak.

GUILDENSTERN

What should we say, my lord?

HAMLET

Why, any thing, but to the purpose. You were sent for; and there is a kind of confession in your looks, which your modesties have not craft enough to colour: I know the good king and queen have sent for you.

ROSENCRANTZ

To what end, my lord?

HAMLET

That you must teach me. But let me conjure you, by the rights of our fellowship, by the consonancy of our youth, by the obligation of our ever-preserved love, and by what more dear a better proposer could charge you withal, be even and direct with me, whether you were sent for, or no.

ROSENCRANTZ

[Aside to GUILDENSTERN] What say you?

HAMLET

[Aside] Nay then, I have an eye of you.—If you love me, hold not off.

GUILDENSTERN

My lord, we were sent for.

HAMLET

I will tell you why; so shall my anticipation prevent your discovery, and your secrecy to the king and queen moult no feather. I have of late—but wherefore I know not—lost all my mirth, forgone all custom of exercises; and indeed it goes so heavily with my disposition that this goodly frame, the earth, seems to me a sterile promontory; this most excellent canopy, the air, look you, this brave o'erhanging firmament, this majestical roof fretted with golden fire, why, it appears no other thing to me than a foul and pestilent congregation of vapours. What a piece of work is a man! how noble in reason! how infinite in faculty! in form and moving how express and admirable! in action how like an angel! in apprehension how like a god! the beauty of the world! the paragon of animals! and yet, to me, what is this quintessence of dust? man delights not me; no, nor woman neither, though by your smiling you seem to say so.

ROSENCRANTZ

My lord, there was no such stuff in my thoughts.

HAMLET

Why did you laugh then, when I said 'man delights not me'?

ROSENCRANTZ

To think, my lord, if you delight not in man, what lenten entertainment the players shall receive from you: we coted them on the way; and hither are they coming, to offer you service.

HAMLET

He that plays the king shall be welcome; his majesty shall have tribute of me; the adventurous knight shall use his foil and target; the lover shall not sigh gratis; the humorous man shall end his part in peace; the clown shall make those laugh whose lungs are tickle o' the sere, and the lady shall say her mind freely, or the blank verse shall halt for 't. What players are they?

ROSENCRANTZ

Even those you were wont to take such delight in, the tragedians of the city.

HAMLET

How chances it they travel? their residence, both in reputation and profit, was better both ways.

ROSENCRANTZ

I think their inhibition comes by the means of the late innovation.

HAMLET

Do they hold the same estimation they did when I was in the city? are they so followed?

ROSENCRANTZ

No, indeed, are they not.

HAMLET

How comes it? do they grow rusty?

ROSENCRANTZ

Nay, their endeavour keeps in the wonted pace: but there is, sir, an eyrie of children, little eyases, that cry out on the top of question and are most tyranically clapped for 't: these are now the fashion, and so be-rattle the common stages—so they call them—that many wearing rapiers are afraid of goose-quills, and dare scarce come thither.

HAMLET

What, are they children? who maintains 'em? how are they escoted? Will they pursue the quality no longer than they can sing? will they not say after-wards, if they should grow themselves to common players,—as it is most like, if their means are no better,—their writers do them wrong, to make them exclaim against their own succession?

ROSENCRANTZ

Faith, there has been much to do on both sides, and the nation holds it no sin to tarre them to contro-versy: there was for a while no money bid for argu-ment unless the poet and the player went to cuffs in the question.

HAMLET

Is 't possible?

GUILDENSTERN

O, there has been much throwing about of brains.

HAMLET

Do the boys carry it away?

ROSENCRANTZ

Ay, that they do, my lord; Hercules and his load too.

HAMLET

It is not very strange; for my uncle is king of Den-mark, and those that would make mows at him while my father lived, give twenty, forty, fifty, a hundred ducats a-piece, for his picture in little. 'Sblood, there is something in this more than nat-ural, if philosophy could find it out.

[*Flourish of trumpets within*

GUILDENSTERN

There are the players.

HAMLET

Gentlemen, you are welcome to Elsinore. Your hands, come then: the appurtenance of welcome is fashion and ceremony: let me comply with you in this garb, lest my extent to the players, which, I tell you, must show fairly outwards, should more ap-pear like entertainment than yours. You are wel-come: but my uncle-father and aunt-mother are deceived.

GUILDENSTERN

In what, my dear lord?

HAMLET

I am but mad north-north-west: when the wind is southerly I know a hawk from a handsaw.

Re-enter POLONIUS

POLONIUS

Well be with you, gentlemen!

HAMLET

Hark you, Guildenstern; and you too: at each ear a hearer: that great baby you see there is not yet out of his swaddling clouts.

ROSENCRANTZ

Happily he's the second time come to them; for they say an old man is twice a child.

HAMLET

I will prophesy he comes to tell me of the players; mark it. You say right, sir: o' Monday morning; 'twas so, indeed.

POLONIUS

My lord, I have news to tell you.

HAMLET

My lord, I have news to tell you. When Roscius was an actor in Rome,—

POLONIUS

The actors are come hither, my lord.

HAMLET

Buz, buz!

POLONIUS

Upon my honour,—

HAMLET

Then came each actor on his ass,—

POLONIUS

The best actors in the world, either for trag-edy, comedy, history, pastoral, pastoral-comical, historical-pastoral, tragical-historical, tragical-comical-historical-pastoral, scene individable, or poem unlimited: Seneca cannot be too heavy, nor Plautus too light. For the law of writ and the liberty, these are the only men.

HAMLET

O Jephthah, judge of Israel, what a treasure hadst thou!

POLONIUS

What a treasure had he, my lord?

HAMLET

Why,

'One fair daughter, and no more,
The which he loved passing well.'

POLONIUS

[Aside] Still on my daughter.

HAMLET

Am I not i' the right, old Jephthah?

POLONIUS

If you call me Jephthah, my lord, I have a daughter that I love passing well.

HAMLET

Nay, that follows not.

POLONIUS

What follows, then, my lord?

HAMLET

Why,

'As by lot, God wot,'

and then you know,

'It came to pass, as most like it was,'—

the first row of the pious chanson will show you more; for look, where my abridgement comes.

Enter four or five PLAYERS

You are welcome, masters; welcome, all. I am glad to see thee well. Welcome, good friends. O, my old friend! Why thy face is valanced since I saw thee last; comest thou to beard me in Denmark? What, my young lady and mistress! By 'r lady, your ladyship is nearer to heaven than when I saw you last, by the altitude of a chopine. Pray God, your voice, like a piece of uncurrent gold, be not cracked within the ring. Masters, you are all welcome. We'll e'en to 't like French falconers, fly at any thing we see: we'll have a speech straight: come, give us a taste of your quality; come, a passionate speech.

FIRST PLAYER

What speech, my good lord?

HAMLET

I heard thee speak me a speech once, but it was never acted; or, if it was, not above once; for the play, I remember, pleased not the million; 'twas caviare to the general: but it was—as I received it, and others, whose judgements in such matters cried in the top of mine—an excellent play, well digested in the scenes, set down with as much modesty as cunning. I remember, one said there were no sallets in the lines to make the matter savoury, nor no matter in the phrase that might indict the author of affection; but called it an honest method, as wholesome as sweet, and by very much more handsome

than fine. One speech in it I chiefly loved: 'twas Æneas' tale to Dido; and thereabout of it especially, where he speaks of Priam's slaughter: if it live in your memory, begin at this line; let me see, let me see;

'The rugged Pyrrhus, like th' Hyrcanian beast,'—

It is not so: it begins with 'Pyrrhus.'

'The rugged Pyrrhus, he whose sable arms,
Black as his purpose, did the night resemble
When he lay couched in the ominous horse,
Hath now this dread and black complexion smear'd
With heraldry more dismal: head to foot
Now is he total gules; horridly trick'd
With blood of fathers, mothers, daughters, sons,
Baked and impasted with the parching streets,
That lend a tyrannous and a damned light
To their lord's murder: roasted in wrath and fire,
And thus o'er-sized with coagulate gore,
With eyes like carbuncles, the hellish Pyrrhus
Old grandsire Priam seeks.'

So, proceed you.

POLONIUS

'Fore God, my lord, well spoken, with good accent and good discretion.

FIRST PLAYER

'Anon he finds him
Striking too short at Greeks; his antique sword,
Rebellious to his arm, lies where it falls,
Repugnant to command: unequal match'd,
Pyrrhus at Priam drives; in rage strikes wide;
But with the whiff and wind of his fell sword
The unnerved father falls. Then senseless Ilium,
Seeming to feel this blow, with flaming top
Stoops to his base, and with a hideous crash
Takes prisoner Pyrrhus' ear: for, lo! his sword,
Which was declining on the milky head
Of reverend Priam, seem'd i' the air to stick:
So, as a painted tyrant, Pyrrhus stood,
And like a neutral to his will and matter,
Did nothing.
But as we often see, against some storm,
A silence in the heavens, the rack stand still,
The bold winds speechless and the orb below
As hush as death, anon the dreadful thunder
Doth rend the region, so after Pyrrhus' pause
Aroused vengeance sets him new a-work;
And never did the Cyclops' hammers fall
On Mars's armour, forged for proof eterne,
With less remorse than Pyrrhus' bleeding sword
Now falls on Priam.
Out, out, thou strumpet, Fortune! All you gods,
In general synod take away her power,
Break all the spokes and fellies from her wheel,
And bowl the round nave down the hill of heaven
As low as to the fiends!'

POLONIUS

This is too long.

HAMLET

It shall to the barber's, with your beard. Prithee, say on: he's for a jig or a tale of bawdry, or he sleeps: say on: come to Hecuba.

FIRST PLAYER

'But who, O, who had seen the mobled queen—'

HAMLET

'The mobled queen?'

POLONIUS

That's good; 'mobled queen' is good.

FIRST PLAYER

'Run barefoot up and down, threatening the flames
With bisson rheum; a clout upon that head
Where late the diadem stood; and for a robe,
About her lank and all o'er-teemed loins,
A blanket, in the alarm of fear caught up:
Who this had seen, with tongue in venom steep'd
'Gainst Fortune's state would treason have pronounced:
But if the gods themselves did see her then,
When she saw Pyrrhus make malicious sport
In mincing with his sword her husband's limbs,
The instant burst of clamour that she made,
Unless things mortal move them not at all,
Would have made milch the burning eyes of heaven
And passion in the gods.'

POLONIUS

Look, whether he has not turned his colour and has
tears in 's eyes. Prithee, no more.

HAMLET

'Tis well; I'll have thee speak out the rest of this
soon. Good my lord, will you see the players well
bestowed? Do you hear, let them be well used, for
they are the abstract and brief chronicles of the
time: after your death you were better have a bad
epitaph than their ill report while you live.

POLONIUS

My lord, I will use them according to their desert.

HAMLET

God's bodykins, man, much better: use every man
after his desert, and who shall 'scape whipping? Use
them after your own honour and dignity: the less
they deserve, the more merit is in your bounty.
Take them in.

POLONIUS

Come, sirs.

HAMLET

Follow him, friends: we'll hear a play to-morrow.
[Exit POLONIUS with all the PLAYERS but the FIRST
Dost thou hear me, old friend; can you play the
Murder of Gonzago?

FIRST PLAYER

Ay, my lord.

HAMLET

We'll ha 't to-morrow night. You could, for a need,
study a speech of some dozen or sixteen lines, which
I would set down and insert in 't, could you not?

FIRST PLAYER

Ay, my lord.

HAMLET

Very well. Follow that lord; and look you mock him
not. [Exit FIRST PLAYER] My good friends, I'll leave
you till night: you are welcome to Elsinore.

ROSENCRANTZ

Good my lord!

HAMLET

Ay, so, God be wi' ye! [Exeunt ROSENCRANTZ and
GUILDENSTERN] Now I am alone.

O, what a rogue and peasant slave am I!
Is it not monstrous that this player here,
But in a fiction, in a dream of passion,
Could force his soul so to his own conceit
That from her working all his visage wann'd;
Tears in his eyes, distraction in 's aspect,
A broken voice, and his whole function suiting
With forms to his conceit? and all for nothing!
For Hecuba!
What's Hecuba to him, or he to Hecuba,
That he should weep for her? What would he do,
Had he the motive and the cue for passion
That I have? He would drown the stage with tears
And cleave the general ear with horrid speech,
Make mad the guilty and appal the free,
Confound the ignorant, and amaze indeed
The very faculties of eyes and ears.
Yet I,
A dull and muddy-mettled rascal, peak,
Like John-a-dreams, unpregnant of my cause,
And can say nothing; no, not for a king,
Upon whose property and most dear life
A damn'd defeat was made. Am I a coward?
Who calls me villain? breaks my pate across?
Plucks off my beard, and blows it in my face?
Tweaks me by the nose? gives me the lie i' the throat,
As deep as to the lungs? who does me this?
Ha!
'Swounds, I should take it: for it cannot be
But I am pigeon-liver'd and lack gall
To make oppression bitter, or ere this
I should have fatted all the region kites
With this slave's offal: bloody, bawdy villain!
Remorseless, treacherous, lecherous, kindless villain!
O, vengeance!
Why, what an ass am I! This is most brave,
That I, the son of a dear father murder'd,
Prompted to my revenge by heaven and hell,
Must, like a whore, unpack my heart with words,
And fall a-cursing, like a very drab,
A scullion!
Fie upon 't! foh! About, my brain! Hum, I have
    heard
That guilty creatures, sitting at a play,
Have by the very cunning of the scene
Been struck so to the soul that presently
They have proclaim'd their malefactions;
For murder, though it have no tongue, will speak
With most miraculous organ. I'll have these players
Play something like the murder of my father
Before mine uncle: I'll observe his looks;
I'll tent him to the quick: if he but blench,
I know my course. The spirit that I have seen
May be the devil; and the devil hath power
To assume a pleasing shape; yea, and perhaps
Out of my weakness and my melancholy,
As he is very potent with such spirits,
Abuses me to damn me. I'll have grounds
More relative than this. The play's the thing
Wherein I'll catch the conscience of the king. [Exit

ACT III

SCENE I. *A room in the castle*

Enter KING, QUEEN, POLONIUS, OPHELIA, ROSENCRANTZ,
and GUILDENSTERN

KING

And can you, by no drift of circumstance,
Get from him why he puts on this confusion,
Grating so harshly all his days of quiet
With turbulent and dangerous lunacy?

ROSENCRANTZ

He does confess he feels himself distracted,
But from what cause he will by no means speak.

GUILDENSTERN

Nor do we find him forward to be sounded;
But, with a crafty madness, keeps aloof,
When we would bring him on to some confession
Of his true state.

QUEEN

Did he receive you well?

ROSENCRANTZ

Most like a gentleman.

GUILDENSTERN

But with much forcing of his disposition.

ROSENCRANTZ

Niggard of question, but of our demands
Most free in his reply.

QUEEN

Did you assay him

To any pastime?

ROSENCRANTZ

Madam, it so fell out that certain players
We o'er-raught on the way: of these we told him,
And there did seem in him a kind of joy
To hear of it: they are about the court,
And, as I think, they have already order
This night to play before him.

POLONIUS

'Tis most true:

And he beseech'd me to entreat your majesties
To hear and see the matter.

KING

With all my heart; and it doth much content me
To hear him so inclined.
Good gentlemen, give him a further edge,
And drive his purpose on to these delights.

ROSENCRANTZ

We shall, my lord.

[*Exeunt* ROSENCRANTZ *and* GUILDENSTERN

KING

Sweet Gertrude, leave us too;
For we have closely sent for Hamlet hither,
That he, as 'twere by accident, may here
Affront Ophelia:
Her father and myself, lawful espials,
Will so bestow ourselves that, seeing unseen,
We may of their encounter frankly judge,
And gather by him, as he is behaved,
If 't be the affliction of his love or no
That thus he suffers for.

QUEEN

I shall obey you:

And for your part, Ophelia, I do wish
That your good beauties be the happy cause
Of Hamlet's wildness: so shall I hope your virtues
Will bring him to his wonted way again,
To both your honours.

OPHELIA

Madam, I wish it may. [*Exit* QUEEN

POLONIUS

Ophelia, walk you here. Gracious, so please you,
We will bestow ourselves. [*To* OPHELIA] Read on
  this book;
That show of such an exercise may colour
Your loneliness. We are oft to blame in this,—
'Tis too much proved—that with devotion's visage
And pious action we do sugar o'er
The devil himself.

KING

[*Aside*] O, 'tis too true!

How smart a lash that speech doth give my con-
  science!
The harlot's cheek, beautied with plastering art,
Is not more ugly to the thing that helps it
Than is my deed to my most painted word:
O heavy burthen!

POLONIUS

I hear him coming: let's withdraw, my lord.

[*Exeunt* KING *and* POLONIUS

Enter HAMLET

HAMLET

To be, or not to be: that is the question:
Whether 'tis nobler in the mind to suffer
The slings and arrows of outrageous fortune,
Or to take arms against a sea of troubles,
And by opposing end them. To die: to sleep;
No more; and by a sleep to say we end
The heart-ache, and the thousand natural shocks
That flesh is heir to, 'tis a consummation
Devoutly to be wish'd. To die, to sleep;
To sleep: perchance to dream: ay, there's the rub;
For in that sleep of death what dreams may come,
When we have shuffled off this mortal coil,
Must give us pause: there's the respect
That makes calamity of so long life;
For who would bear the whips and scorns of time,
The oppressor's wrong, the proud man's contumely,
The pangs of despised love, the law's delay,
The insolence of office, and the spurns
That patient merit of the unworthy takes,
When he himself might his quietus make
With a bare bodkin? who would fardels bear,
To grunt and sweat under a weary life,
But that the dread of something after death,
The undiscover'd country from whose bourn
No traveller returns, puzzles the will,
And makes us rather bear those ills we have
Than fly to others that we know not of?
Thus conscience does make cowards of us all,
And thus the native hue of resolution

Is sicklied o'er with the pale cast of thought,
And enterprises of great pitch and moment
With this regard their currents turn awry
And lose the name of action. Soft you now!
The fair Ophelia! Nymph, in thy orisons
Be all my sins remember'd.

OPHELIA

        Good my lord,
How does your honour for this many a day?

HAMLET

I humbly thank you: well, well, well.

OPHELIA

My lord, I have remembrances of yours,
That I have longed long to re-deliver;
I pray you, now receive them.

HAMLET

        No, not I;
I never gave you aught.

OPHELIA

My honour'd lord, you know right well you did;
And with them words of so sweet breath composed
As made the things more rich: their perfume lost,
Take these again; for to the noble mind
Rich gifts wax poor when givers prove unkind.
There, my lord.

HAMLET

Ha, ha! are you honest?

OPHELIA

My lord?

HAMLET

Are you fair?

OPHELIA

What means your lordship?

HAMLET

That if you be honest and fair, your honesty should
admit no discourse to your beauty.

OPHELIA

Could beauty, my lord, have better commerce than
with honesty?

HAMLET

Ay, truly; for the power of beauty will sooner transform honesty from what it is to a bawd than the
force of honesty can translate beauty into his likeness: this was sometime a paradox, but now the
time gives it proof. I did love you once.

OPHELIA

Indeed, my lord, you made me believe so.

HAMLET

You should not have believed me; for virtue cannot
so inoculate our old stock but we shall relish of it:
I loved you not.

OPHELIA

I was the more deceived.

HAMLET

Get thee to a nunnery: why wouldst thou be a
breeder of sinners? I am myself indifferent honest;
but yet I could accuse me of such things that it were
better my mother had not borne me: I am very
proud, revengeful, ambitious; with more offences at
my beck than I have thoughts to put them in, imagination to give them shape, or time to act them
in. What should such fellows as I do crawling between heaven and earth? We are arrant knaves all;
believe none of us. Go thy ways to a nunnery.
Where's your father?

OPHELIA

At home, my lord.

HAMLET

Let the doors be shut upon him, that he may play
the fool no where but in 's own house. Farewell.

OPHELIA

O, help him, you sweet heavens!

HAMLET

If thou dost marry, I'll give thee this plague for thy
dowry: be thou as chaste as ice, as pure as snow,
thou shalt not escape calumny. Get thee to a nunnery, go: farewell. Or, if thou wilt needs marry,
marry a fool; for wise men know well enough what
monsters you make of them. To a nunnery, go; and
quickly too. Farewell.

OPHELIA

O heavenly powers, restore him!

HAMLET

I have heard of your paintings too, well enough;
God hath given you one face, and you make yourselves another: you jig, you amble, and you lisp, and
nick-name God's creatures, and make your wantonness your ignorance. Go to, I'll no more on 't; it
hath made me mad. I say, we will have no more
marriages: those that are married already, all but
one, shall live; the rest shall keep as they are. To a
nunnery, go.   [Exit

OPHELIA

O, what a noble mind is here o'erthrown!
The courtier's, soldier's, scholar's, eye, tongue,
        sword:
The expectancy and rose of the fair state,
The glass of fashion and the mould of form,
The observed of all observers, quite, quite down!
And I, of ladies most deject and wretched,
That suck'd the honey of his music vows,
Now see that noble and most sovereign reason,
Like sweet bells jangled, out of tune and harsh;
That unmatch'd form and feature of blown youth
Blasted with ecstasy: O, woe is me,
To have seen what I have seen, see what I see!

Re-enter KING and POLONIUS

KING

Love! his affections do not that way tend;
Nor what he spake, though it lack'd form a little,
Was not like madness. There's something in his soul
O'er which his melancholy sits on brood,
And I do doubt the hatch and the disclose
Will be some danger: which for to prevent,
I have in quick determination
Thus set it down:—he shall with speed to England,
For the demand of our neglected tribute:
Haply the seas and countries different
With variable objects shall expel
This something-settled matter in his heart,

Whereon his brains still beating puts him thus
From fashion of himself. What think you on 't?

POLONIUS

It shall do well: but yet do I believe
The origin and commencement of his grief
Sprung from neglected love. How now, Ophelia!
You need not tell us what Lord Hamlet said;
We heard it all. My lord, do as you please;
But, if you hold it fit, after the play,
Let his queen mother all alone entreat him
To show his grief: let her be round with him;
And I'll be placed, so please you, in the ear
Of all their conference. If she find him not,
To England send him, or confine him where
Your wisdom best shall think.

KING

               It shall be so:
Madness in great ones must not unwatch'd go.
                                    [*Exeunt*

SCENE II. *A hall in the castle*

Enter HAMLET *and* PLAYERS

HAMLET

Speak the speech, I pray you, as I pronounced it to
you, trippingly on the tongue: but if you mouth it,
as many of your players do, I had as lief the town-
crier spoke my lines. Nor do not saw the air too
much with your hand, thus; but use all gently: for
in the very torrent, tempest, and, as I may say,
whirlwind of your passion, you must acquire and
beget a temperance that may give it smoothness. O,
it offends me to the soul to hear a robustious periwig-
pated fellow tear a passion to tatters, to very rags,
to split the ears of the groundlings, who, for the
most part, are capable of nothing but inexplicable
dumb-shows and noise: I would have such a fellow
whipped for o'erdoing Termagant; it out-herods
Herod: pray you, avoid it.

FIRST PLAYER

I warrant your honour.

HAMLET

Be not too tame neither, but let your own discretion
be your tutor: suit the action to the word, the word
to the action; with this special observance, that you
o'erstep not the modesty of nature: for anything so
overdone is from the purpose of playing, whose end,
both at the first and now, was and is, to hold, as
'twere, the mirror up to nature; to show virtue her
own feature, scorn her own image, and the very age
and body of the time his form and pressure. Now
this overdone or come tardy off, though it make the
unskilful laugh, cannot but make the judicious
grieve; the censure of the which one must in your
allowance o'erweigh a whole theatre of others. O,
there be players that I have seen play, and heard
others praise, and that highly, not to speak it pro-
fanely, that neither having the accent of Christians
nor the gait of Christian, pagan, nor man, have so
strutted and bellowed, that I have thought some of

nature's journeymen had made men, and not made
them well, they imitated humanity so abominably.

FIRST PLAYER

I hope we have reformed that indifferently with us,
sir.

HAMLET

O, reform it altogether. And let those that play
your clowns speak no more than is set down for
them: for there be of them that will themselves
laugh, to set on some quantity of barren spectators
to laugh too, though in the mean time some necessary question of the play be then to be considered:
that's villanous, and shows a most pitiful ambition
in the fool that uses it. Go, make you ready.
                            [*Exeunt* PLAYERS

Enter POLONIUS, ROSENCRANTZ, *and* GUILDENSTERN

How now, my lord! will the king hear this piece of
  work?

POLONIUS

And the queen too, and that presently.

HAMLET

Bid the players make haste.   [*Exit* POLONIUS
Will you two help to hasten them?

ROSENCRANTZ *and* GUILDENSTERN

We will, my lord.
          [*Exeunt* ROSENCRANTZ *and* GUILDENSTERN

HAMLET

What ho! Horatio!

Enter HORATIO

HORATIO

Here, sweet lord, at your service.

HAMLET

Horatio, thou art e'en as just a man
As e'er my conversation coped withal.

HORATIO

O, my dear lord,—

HAMLET

               Nay, do not think I flatter;
For what advancement may I hope from thee,
That no revenue hast but thy good spirits,
To feed and clothe thee? Why should the poor be
  flatter'd?
No, let the candied tongue lick absurd pomp,
And crook the pregnant hinges of the knee
Where thrift may follow fawning. Dost thou hear?
Since my dear soul was mistress of her choice,
And could of men distinguish, her election
Hath seal'd thee for herself: for thou hast been
As one, in suffering all, that suffers nothing;
A man that fortune's buffets and rewards
Hast ta'en with equal thanks: and blest are those
Whose blood and judgement are so well commingle
That they are not a pipe for fortune's finger
To sound what stop she please. Give me that man
That is not passion's slave, and I will wear him
In my heart's core, ay, in my heart of heart,
As I do thee. Something too much of this.
There is a play to-night before the king;
One scene of it comes near the circumstance
Which I have told thee of my father's death:

I prithee, when thou seest that act a-foot,
Even with the very comment of thy soul
Observe my uncle: if his occulted guilt
Do not itself unkennel in one speech,
It is a damned ghost that we have seen,
And my imaginations are as foul
As Vulcan's stithy. Give him heedful note;
For I mine eyes will rivet to his face,
And after we will both our judgements join
In censure of his seeming.

HORATIO
                    Well, my lord:
If he steal aught the whilst this play is playing,
And 'scape detecting, I will pay the theft.

HAMLET
They are coming to the play: I must be idle:
Get you a place.

Danish march. A flourish. Enter KING, QUEEN, POLONIUS,
OPHELIA, ROSENCRANTZ, GUILDENSTERN, *and other*
LORDS *attendant, with the* GUARD *carrying torches*

KING
How fares our cousin Hamlet?

HAMLET
Excellent, i' faith; of the chameleon's dish: I eat the
air, promise-crammed: you cannot feed capons so.

KING
I have nothing with this answer, Hamlet; these
words are not mine.

HAMLET
No, nor mine now. [*To* POLONIUS] My lord, you
played once i' the university, you say?

POLONIUS
That did I, my lord, and was accounted a good
actor.

HAMLET
What did you enact?

POLONIUS
I did enact Julius Cæsar: I was killed i' the Capitol;
Brutus killed me.

HAMLET
It was a brute part of him to kill so capital a calf
there. Be the players ready?

ROSENCRANTZ
Ay, my lord; they stay upon your patience.

QUEEN
Come hither, my dear Hamlet, sit by me.

HAMLET
No, good mother, here's metal more attractive.

POLONIUS
[*To the* KING] O, ho! do you mark that?

HAMLET
Lady, shall I lie in your lap?
                    [*Lying down at* OPHELIA's *feet*

OPHELIA
No, my lord.

HAMLET
I mean, my head upon your lap?

OPHELIA
Ay, my lord.

HAMLET
Do you think I meant country matters?

OPHELIA
I think nothing, my lord.

HAMLET
That's a fair thought to lie between maids' legs.

OPHELIA
What is, my lord?

HAMLET
Nothing.

OPHELIA
You are merry, my lord.

HAMLET
Who, I?

OPHELIA
Ay, my lord.

HAMLET
O God, your only jig-maker. What should a man do
but be merry? for, look you, how cheerfully my
mother looks, and my father died within 's two
hours.

OPHELIA
Nay, 'tis twice two months, my lord.

HAMLET
So long? Nay then, let the devil wear black, for I'll
have a suit of sables. O heavens! die two months
ago, and not forgotten yet? Then there's hope a
great man's memory may outlive his life half a year:
but, by 'r lady, he must build churches then; or else
shall he suffer not thinking on, with the hobby-
horse, whose epitaph is, 'For, O, for, O, the hobby-
horse is forgot.'

Hautboys play. The dumb-show enters
Enter a KING *and a* QUEEN *very lovingly; the* QUEEN
embracing him, and he her. She kneels, and makes show of
protestation unto him. He takes her up, and declines his
head upon her neck: lays him down upon a bank of flowers:
she, seeing him asleep, leaves him. Anon comes in a fellow,
takes off his crown, kisses it, and pours poison in the
KING's *ears, and exit. The* QUEEN *returns; finds the* KING
dead, and makes passionate action. The Poisoner, with
some two or three Mutes, comes in again, seeming to
lament with her. The dead body is carried away. The
Poisoner wooes the QUEEN *with gifts: she seems loath and*
unwilling awhile, but in the end accepts his love [*Exeunt*

OPHELIA
What means this, my lord?

HAMLET
Marry, this is miching mallecho; it means mischief.

OPHELIA
Belike this show imports the argument of the play.

Enter PROLOGUE

HAMLET
We shall know by this fellow: the players cannot
keep counsel; they'll tell all.

OPHELIA
Will he tell us what this show meant?

HAMLET
Ay, or any show that you'll show him: be not you

ashamed to show, he'll not shame to tell you what it means.

OPHELIA

You are naught, you are naught: I'll mark the play.

PROLOGUE

For us, and for our tragedy,
Here stooping to your clemency,
We beg your hearing patiently.

HAMLET

Is this a prologue, or the posy of a ring?

OPHELIA

'Tis brief, my lord.

HAMLET

As woman's love.

Enter two PLAYERS, KING *and* QUEEN

PLAYER KING

Full thirty times hath Phœbus' cart gone round
Neptune's salt wash and Tellus' orbed ground,
And thirty dozen moons with borrowed sheen
About the world have times twelve thirties been,
Since love our hearts and Hymen did our hands
Unite commutual in most sacred bands.

PLAYER QUEEN

So many journeys may the sun and moon
Make us again count o'er ere love be done!
But, woe is me, you are so sick of late,
So far from cheer and from your former state,
That I distrust you. Yet, though I distrust,
Discomfort you, my lord, it nothing must:
For women's fear and love holds quantity,
In neither aught, or in extremity.
Now, what my love is, proof hath made you know,
And as my love is sized, my fear is so:
Where love is great, the littlest doubts are fear,
Where little fears grow great, great love grows there.

PLAYER KING

Faith, I must leave thee, love, and shortly too;
My operant powers their functions leave to do:
And thou shalt live in this fair world behind,
Honour'd, beloved; and haply one as kind
For husband shalt thou—

PLAYER QUEEN

O, confound the rest!
Such love must needs be treason in my breast:
In second husband let me be accurst!
None wed the second but who kill'd the first.

HAMLET

Aside] Wormwood, wormwood.

PLAYER QUEEN

The instances that second marriage move
Are base respects of thrift, but none of love:
A second time I kill my husband dead,
When second husband kisses me in bed.

PLAYER KING

I do believe you think what now you speak,
But what we do determine oft we break.
Purpose is but the slave to memory,
Of violent birth but poor validity:
Which now, like fruit unripe, sticks on the tree,
But fall unshaken when they mellow be.
Most necessary 'tis that we forget
To pay ourselves what to ourselves is debt:

What to ourselves in passion we propose,
The passion ending, doth the purpose lose.
The violence of either grief or joy
Their own enactures with themselves destroy:
Where joy most revels, grief doth most lament;
Grief joys, joy grieves, on slender accident.
This world is not for aye, nor 'tis not strange
That even our loves should with our fortunes change.
For 'tis a question left us yet to prove,
Whether love lead fortune or else fortune love.
The great man down, you mark his favourite flies;
The poor advanced makes friends of enemies:
And hitherto doth love on fortune tend;
For who not needs shall never lack a friend,
And who in want a hollow friend doth try
Directly seasons him his enemy.
But, orderly to end where I begun,
Our wills and fates do so contrary run,
That our devices still are overthrown,
Our thoughts are ours, their ends none of our own:
So think thou wilt no second husband wed,
But die thy thoughts when thy first lord is dead.

PLAYER QUEEN

Nor earth to me give food nor heaven light!
Sport and repose lock from me day and night!
To desperation turn my trust and hope!
An anchor's cheer in prison be my scope!
Each opposite, that blanks the face of joy,
Meet what I would have well and it destroy!
Both here and hence pursue me lasting strife,
If, once a widow, ever I be wife!

HAMLET

If she should break it now!

PLAYER KING

'Tis deeply sworn. Sweet, leave me here a while;
My spirits grow dull, and fain I would beguile
The tedious day with sleep.   [*Sleeps*

PLAYER QUEEN

Sleep rock thy brain;
And never come mischance between us twain!   [*Exit*

HAMLET

Madam, how like you this play?

QUEEN

The lady doth protest too much, methinks.

HAMLET

O, but she'll keep her word.

KING

Have you heard the argument? Is there no offence in 't?

HAMLET

No, no, they do but jest, poison in jest; no offence i' the world.

KING

What do you call the play?

HAMLET

The Mouse-trap. Marry, how? Tropically. This play is the image of a murder done in Vienna: Gonzago is the duke's name; his wife, Baptista: you shall see anon; 'tis a knavish piece of work: but what o' that? your majesty, and we that have free souls, it touches us not: let the galled jade wince, our withers are unwrung.

Enter LUCIANUS

This is one Lucianus, nephew to the king.

OPHELIA

You are as good as a chorus, my lord.

HAMLET

I could interpret between you and your love, if I could see the puppets dallying.

OPHELIA

You are keen, my lord, you are keen.

HAMLET

It would cost you a groaning to take off my edge.

OPHELIA

Still better, and worse.

HAMLET

So you must take your husbands. Begin, murderer; pox, leave thy damnable faces, and begin. Come: the croaking raven doth bellow for revenge.

LUCIANUS

Thoughts black, hands apt, drugs fit, and time agreeing;
Confederate season, else no creature seeing;
Thou mixture rank, of midnight weeds collected,
With Hecate's ban thrice blasted, thrice infected,
Thy natural magic and dire property,
On wholesome life usurp immediately.

[*Pours the poison into the sleeper's ear*

HAMLET

He poisons him i' the garden for his estate. His name's Gonzago: the story is extant, and written in very choice Italian: you shall see anon how the murderer gets the love of Gonzago's wife.

OPHELIA

The king rises.

HAMLET

What, frighted with false fire!

QUEEN

How fares my lord?

POLONIUS

Give o'er the play.

KING

Give me some light. Away!

POLONIUS

Lights, lights, lights!

[*Exeunt all but* HAMLET *and* HORATIO

HAMLET

Why, let the stricken deer go weep,
　The hart ungalled play;
For some must watch, while some must sleep:
　Thus runs the world away.

Would not this, sir, and a forest of feathers—if the rest of my fortunes turn Turk with me—with two Provincial roses on my razed shoes, get me a fellow-ship in a cry of players, sir?

HORATIO

Half a share.

HAMLET

A whole one, I.

For thou dost know, O Damon dear,
　This realm dismantled was
Of Jove himself; and now reigns here
　A very, very—pajock.

HORATIO

You might have rhymed.

HAMLET

O good Horatio, I'll take the ghost's word for a thousand pound. Didst perceive?

HORATIO

Very well, my lord.

HAMLET

Upon the talk of the poisoning?

HORATIO

I did very well note him.

HAMLET

Ah, ha! Come, some music! come, the recorders!

For if the king like not the comedy,
　Why then, belike, he likes it not, perdy.

Come, some music!

Re-enter ROSENCRANTZ *and* GUILDENSTERN

GUILDENSTERN

Good my lord, vouchsafe me a word with you.

HAMLET

Sir, a whole history.

GUILDENSTERN

The king, sir,—

HAMLET

Ay, sir, what of him?

GUILDENSTERN

Is in his retirement marvellous distempered.

HAMLET

With drink, sir?

GUILDENSTERN

No, my lord, rather with choler.

HAMLET

Your wisdom should show itself more richer to signify this to the doctor; for, for me to put him to his purgation would perhaps plunge him into far more choler.

GUILDENSTERN

Good my lord, put your discourse into some frame, and start not so wildly from my affair.

HAMLET

I am tame, sir: pronounce.

GUILDENSTERN

The queen, your mother, in most great affliction of spirit, hath sent me to you.

HAMLET

You are welcome.

GUILDENSTERN

Nay, good my lord, this courtesy is not of the right breed. If it shall please you to make me a whole-some answer, I will do your mother's command-ment: if not, your pardon and my return shall be the end of my business.

HAMLET

Sir, I cannot.

GUILDENSTERN

What, my lord?

HAMLET

Make you a wholesome answer; my wit's diseased: but, sir, such answer as I can make, you shall com-mand; or rather, as you say, my mother: therefore no more, but to the matter: my mother, you say,—

ROSENCRANTZ

Then thus she says; your behaviour hath struck her
into amazement and admiration.

HAMLET

O wonderful son, that can so astonish a mother!
But is there no sequel at the heels of this mother's
admiration? Impart.

ROSENCRANTZ

She desires to speak with you in her closet, ere you
go to bed.

HAMLET

We shall obey, were she ten times our mother.
Have you any further trade with us?

ROSENCRANTZ

My lord, you once did love me.

HAMLET

So I do still, by these pickers and stealers.

ROSENCRANTZ

Good my lord, what is your cause of distemper? you
do surely bar the door upon your own liberty, if
you deny your griefs to your friend.

HAMLET

Sir, I lack advancement.

ROSENCRANTZ

How can that be, when you have the voice of the
king himself for your succession in Denmark?

HAMLET

Ay, sir, but 'while the grass grows,'—the proverb is
something musty.

Re-enter PLAYERS *with recorders*

O, the recorders! let me see one. To withdraw with
you:—why do you go about to recover the wind of
me, as if you would drive me into a toil?

GUILDENSTERN

O, my lord, if my duty be too bold, my love is too
unmannerly.

HAMLET

I do not well understand that. Will you play upon
this pipe?

GUILDENSTERN

My lord, I cannot.

HAMLET

I pray you.

GUILDENSTERN

Believe me, I cannot.

HAMLET

I do beseech you.

GUILDENSTERN

I know no touch of it, my lord.

HAMLET

It is as easy as lying: govern these ventages with
your fingers and thumb, give it breath with your
mouth, and it will discourse most eloquent music.
Look you, these are the stops.

GUILDENSTERN

But these cannot I command to any utterance of
harmony; I have not the skill.

HAMLET

Why, look you now, how unworthy a thing you
make of me! You would play upon me; you would

seem to know my stops; you would pluck out the
heart of my mystery; you would sound me from my
lowest note to the top of my compass: and there is
much music, excellent voice, in this little organ; yet
cannot you make it speak. 'Sblood, do you think I
am easier to be played on than a pipe? Call me what
instrument you will, though you can fret me, yet
you cannot play upon me.

Re-enter POLONIUS

God bless you, sir!

POLONIUS

My lord, the queen would speak with you, and
presently.

HAMLET

Do you see yonder cloud that's almost in shape of a
camel?

POLONIUS

By the mass, and 'tis like a camel, indeed.

HAMLET

Methinks it is like a weasel.

POLONIUS

It is backed like a weasel.

HAMLET

Or like a whale?

POLONIUS

Very like a whale.

HAMLET

Then I will come to my mother by and by.
They fool me to the top of my bent. I will come by
and by.

POLONIUS

I will say so.　　　　　　　　　　　　[*Exit* POLONIUS

HAMLET

'By and by' is easily said. Leave me, friends.

[*Exeunt all but* HAMLET

'Tis now the very witching time of night,
When churchyards yawn, and hell itself breathes
　out
Contagion to this world: now could I drink hot
　blood,
And do such bitter business as the day
Would quake to look on. Soft! now to my mother.
O heart, lose not thy nature; let not ever
The soul of Nero enter this firm bosom:
Let me be cruel, not unnatural:
I will speak daggers to her, but use none;
My tongue and soul in this be hypocrites;
How in my words soever she be shent,
To give them seals never, my soul, consent! [*Exit*

SCENE III. *A room in the castle*

Enter KING, ROSENCRANTZ, *and* GUILDENSTERN

KING

I like him not, nor stands it safe with us
To let his madness range. Therefore prepare you;
I your commission will forthwith dispatch,
And he to England shall along with you:
The terms of our estate may not endure

Hazard so near us as doth hourly grow
Out of his lunacies.
                    GUILDENSTERN
                              We will ourselves provide:
Most holy and religious fear it is
To keep those many many bodies safe
That live and feed upon your majesty.
                    ROSENCRANTZ
The single and peculiar life is bound
With all the strength and armour of the mind
To keep itself from noyance; but much more
That spirit upon whose weal depends and rests
The lives of many. The cease of majesty
Dies not alone, but like a gulf doth draw
What's near it with it: it is a massy wheel,
Fix'd on the summit of the highest mount,
To whose huge spokes ten thousand lesser things
Are mortised and adjoin'd; which, when it falls,
Each small annexment, petty consequence,
Attends the boisterous ruin. Never alone
Did the king sigh, but with a general groan.
                    KING
Arm you, I pray you, to this speedy voyage,
For we will fetters put about this fear,
Which now goes too free-footed.
                    ROSENCRANTZ and GUILDENSTERN
                                        We will haste us.
            [Exeunt ROSENCRANTZ and GUILDENSTERN
                    Enter POLONIUS
                    POLONIUS
My lord, he's going to his mother's closet:
Behind the arras I'll convey myself,
To hear the process; I'll warrant she'll tax him
    home:
And, as you said, and wisely was it said,
'Tis meet that some more audience than a mother,
Since nature makes them partial, should o'erhear
The speech, of vantage. Fare you well, my liege:
I'll call upon you ere you go to bed,
And tell you what I know.
                    KING
                        Thanks, dear my lord.
                                    [Exit POLONIUS
O, my offence is rank, it smells to heaven;
It hath the primal eldest curse upon 't,
A brother's murder. Pray can I not,
Though inclination be as sharp as will:
My stronger guilt defeats my strong intent,
And like a man to double business bound,
I stand in pause where I shall first begin,
And both neglect. What if this cursed hand
Were thicker than itself with brother's blood,
Is there not rain enough in the sweet heavens
To wash it white as snow? Whereto serves mercy
But to confront the visage of offence?
And what's in prayer but this twofold force,
To be forestalled ere we come to fall,
Or pardon'd being down? Then I'll look up;
My fault is past. But O, what form of prayer
Can serve my turn? 'Forgive me my foul murder?'

That cannot be, since I am still possess'd
Of those effects for which I did the murder,
My crown, mine own ambition and my queen.
May one be pardon'd and retain the offence?
In the corrupted currents of this world
Offence's gilded hand may shove by justice,
And oft 'tis seen the wicked prize itself
Buys out the law: but 'tis not so above;
There is no shuffling, there the action lies
In his true nature, and we ourselves compell'd
Even to the teeth and forehead of our faults
To give in evidence. What then? what rests?
Try what repentance can: what can it not?
Yet what can it when one can not repent?
O wretched state! O bosom black as death!
O limed soul, that struggling to be free
Art more engaged! Help, angels! make asssay!
Bow, stubborn knees, and, heart with strings of steel,
Be soft as sinews of the new-born babe!
All may be well.   [Retires and kneels
                    Enter HAMLET
Now might I do it pat, now he is praying;
And now I'll do 't: and so he goes to heaven:
And so am I revenged. That would be scann'd:
A villain kills my father; and for that,
I, his sole son, do this same villain send
To heaven.
O, this is hire and salary, not revenge,
He took my father grossly, full of bread,
With all his crimes broad blown, as flush as May;
And how his audit stands who knows save heaven?
But in our circumstance and course of thought,
'Tis heavy with him: and am I then revenged,
To take him in the purging of his soul,
When he is fit and season'd for his passage?
No.
Up, sword, and know thou a more horrid hent:
When he is drunk asleep, or in his rage,
Or in the incestuous pleasure of his bed;
At game, a-swearing, or about some act
That has no relish of salvation in 't;
Then trip him, that his heels may kick at heaven
And that his soul may be as damn'd and black
As hell, whereto it goes. My mother stays:
This physic but prolongs thy sickly days.   [Exit
                    KING
[Rising] My words fly up, my thoughts remain be-
    low:
Words without thoughts never to heaven go.   [Exit

                SCENE IV. The QUEEN's closet

                Enter QUEEN and POLONIUS
                    POLONIUS
He will come straight. Look you lay home to him:
Tell him his pranks have been too broad to bear
    with,
And that your grace hath screen'd and stood be-
    tween

Much heat and him. I'll sconce me even here.
Pray you, be round with him.

HAMLET

[*Within*] Mother, mother, mother!

QUEEN

I'll warrant you; fear me not. Withdraw, I hear him
coming.   [POLONIUS *hides behind the arras*

Enter HAMLET

HAMLET

Now, mother, what's the matter?

QUEEN

Hamlet, thou hast thy father much offended.

HAMLET

Mother, you have my father much offended.

QUEEN

Come, come, you answer with an idle tongue.

HAMLET

Go, go, you question with a wicked tongue.

QUEEN

Why, how now, Hamlet!

HAMLET

     What's the matter now?

QUEEN

Have you forgot me?

HAMLET

     No, by the rood, not so:
You are the queen, your husband's brother's wife;
And—would it were not so!—you are my mother.

QUEEN

Nay, then, I'll set those to you that can speak.

HAMLET

Come, come, and sit you down; you shall not budge;
You go not till I set you up a glass
Where you may see the inmost part of you.

QUEEN

What wilt thou do? thou wilt not murder me?
Help, help, ho!

POLONIUS

[*Behind*] What, ho! help, help, help!

HAMLET

[*Drawing*] How now! a rat? Dead, for a ducat, dead!
     [*Makes a pass through the arras*

POLONIUS

[*Behind*] O, I am slain!   [*Falls and dies*

QUEEN

     O me, what hast thou done?

HAMLET

Nay, I know not: is it the king?

QUEEN

O, what a rash and bloody deed is this!

HAMLET

A bloody deed! almost as bad, good mother,
As kill a king, and marry with his brother.

QUEEN

As kill a king!

HAMLET

     Ay, lady, 'twas my word.
     [*Lifts up the arras and discovers* POLONIUS
Thou wretched, rash, intruding fool, farewell!
I took thee for thy better: take thy fortune;

Thou find'st to be too busy is some danger.
Leave wringing of your hands: peace! sit you down,
And let me wring your heart: for so I shall,
If it be made of penetrable stuff;
If damned custom have not brass'd it so,
That it be proof and bulwark against sense.

QUEEN

What have I done, that thou darest wag thy tongue
In noise so rude against me?

HAMLET

     Such an act
That blurs the grace and blush of modesty,
Calls virtue hypocrite, takes off the rose
From the fair forehead of an innocent love,
And sets a blister there; makes marriage vows
As false as dicers' oaths: O, such a deed
As from the body of contraction plucks
The very soul, and sweet religion makes
A rhapsody of words: heaven's face doth glow;
Yea, this solidity and compound mass,
With tristful visage, as against the doom,
Is thought-sick at the act.

QUEEN

     Ay me, what act,
That roars so loud and thunders in the index?

HAMLET

Look here, upon this picture, and on this,
The counterfeit presentment of two brothers.
See what a grace was seated on this brow;
Hyperion's curls, the front of Jove himself,
An eye like Mars, to threaten and command;
A station like the herald Mercury
New-lighted on a heaven-kissing hill;
A combination and a form indeed,
Where every god did seem to set his seal
To give the world assurance of a man:
This was your husband. Look you now, what fol-
     lows:
Here is your husband; like a mildew'd ear,
Blasting his wholesome brother. Have you eyes?
Could you on this fair mountain leave to feed,
And batten on this moor? Ha! have you eyes?
You cannot call it love, for at your age
The hey-day in the blood is tame, it's humble,
And waits upon the judgement: and what judge-
     ment
Would step from this to this? Sense sure you have,
Else could you not have motion: but sure that sense
Is apoplex'd: for madness would not err,
Nor sense to ecstasy was ne'er so thrall'd
But it reserved some quantity of choice,
To serve in such a difference. What devil was 't
That thus hath cozen'd you at hoodman-blind?
Eyes without feeling, feeling without sight,
Ears without hands or eyes, smelling sans all,
Or but a sickly part of one true sense
Could not so mope.
O shame! where is thy blush? Rebellious hell,
If thou canst mutine in a matron's bones,
To flaming youth let virtue be as wax

And melt in her own fire: proclaim no shame
When the compulsive ardour gives the charge,
Since frost itself as actively doth burn,
And reason pandars will.

QUEEN
         O Hamlet, speak no more:
Thou turn'st mine eyes into my very soul,
And there I see such black and grainèd spots
As will not leave their tinct.

HAMLET
         Nay, but to live
In the rank sweat of an enseamèd bed,
Stew'd in corruption, honeying and making love
Over the nasty sty,—

QUEEN
         O, speak to me no more;
These words like daggers enter in my ears;
No more, sweet Hamlet!

HAMLET
         A murderer and a villain;
A slave that is not twentieth part the tithe
Of your precedent lord; a vice of kings;
A cutpurse of the empire and the rule,
That from a shelf the precious diadem stole
And put it in his pocket!

QUEEN
         No more!

HAMLET
A king of shreds and patches—
         Enter GHOST
Save me, and hover o'er me with your wings,
You heavenly guards! What would your gracious
    figure?

QUEEN
Alas, he's mad!

HAMLET
Do you not come your tardy son to chide,
That, lapsed in time and passion, lets go by
The important acting of your dread command?
O, say!

GHOST
Do not forget: this visitation
Is but to whet thy almost blunted purpose.
But look, amazement on thy mother sits:
O, step between her and her fighting soul:
Conceit in weakest bodies strongest works:
Speak to her, Hamlet.

HAMLET
         How is it with you, lady?

QUEEN
Alas, how is 't with you,
That you do bend your eye on vacancy
And with the incorporal air do hold discourse?
Forth at your eyes your spirits wildly peep;
And, as the sleeping soldiers in the alarm,
Your bedded hairs, like life in excrements,
Start up and stand an end. O gentle son,
Upon the heat and flame of thy distemper
Sprinkle cool patience. Whereon do you look?

HAMLET
On him, on him! Look you how pale he glares!
His form and cause conjoin'd, preaching to stones,
Would make them capable. Do not look upon me,
Lest with this piteous action you convert
My stern effects: then what I have to do
Will want true colour; tears perchance for blood.

QUEEN
To whom do you speak this?

HAMLET
         Do you see nothing there?

QUEEN
Nothing at all; yet all that is I see.

HAMLET
Nor did you nothing hear?

QUEEN
         No, nothing but ourselves.

HAMLET
Why, look you there! look, how it steals away!
My father, in his habit as he lived!
Look, where he goes, even now, out at the portal!
         [Exit GHOST

QUEEN
This is the very coinage of your brain:
This bodiless creation ecstasy
Is very cunning in.

HAMLET
         Ecstasy!
My pulse, as yours, doth temperately keep time,
And makes as healthful music: it is not madness
That I have utter'd: bring me to the test,
And I the matter will re-word, which madness
Would gambol from. Mother, for love of grace,
Lay not that flattering unction to your soul,
That not your trespass but my madness speaks:
It will but skin and film the ulcerous place,
Whiles rank corruption, mining all within,
Infects unseen. Confess yourself to heaven;
Repent what's past, avoid what is to come,
And do not spread the compost on the weeds,
To make them ranker. Forgive me this my virtue,
For in the fatness of these pursy times
Virtue itself of vice must pardon beg,
Yea, curb and woo for leave to do him good.

QUEEN
O Hamlet, thou hast cleft my heart in twain.

HAMLET
O, throw away the worser part of it,
And live the purer with the other half.
Good night: but go not to my uncle's bed;
Assume a virtue, if you have it not.
That monster, custom, who all sense doth eat,
Of habits devil, is angel yet in this,
That to the use of actions fair and good
He likewise gives a frock or livery,
That aptly is put on. Refrain to-night,
And that shall lend a kind of easiness
To the next abstinence; the next more easy;
For use almost can change the stamp of nature,

And either . . . the devil, or throw him out
With wondrous potency. Once more, good night:
And when you are desirous to be blest,
I'll blessing beg of you. For this same lord,
　　　　　　　　　　[*Pointing to* POLONIUS
I do repent: but heaven hath pleased it so,
To punish me with this, and this with me,
That I must be their scourge and minister.
I will bestow him, and will answer well
The death I gave him. So, again, good night.
I must be cruel, only to be kind:
Thus bad begins, and worse remains behind.
One word more, good lady.

　　　　　　　QUEEN
　　　　　　　　　　What shall I do?

　　　　　　　HAMLET
Not this, by no means, that I bid you do:
Let the bloat king tempt you again to bed;
Pinch wanton on your cheek, call you his mouse;
And let him, for a pair of reechy kisses,
Or paddling in your neck with his damn'd fingers,
Make you to ravel all this matter out,
That I essentially am not in madness,
But mad in craft. 'Twere good you let him know;
For who, that's but a queen, fair, sober, wise,
Would from a paddock, from a bat, a gib,
Such dear concernings hide? who would do so?
No, in despite of sense and secrecy,
Unpeg the basket on the house's top,
Let the birds fly, and like the famous ape,
To try conclusions, in the basket creep
And break your own neck down.

　　　　　　　QUEEN
Be thou assured, if words be made of breath
And breath of life, I have no life to breathe
What thou hast said to me.

　　　　　　　HAMLET
I must to England; you know that?

　　　　　　　QUEEN
　　　　　　　　　　Alack,
I had forgot: 'tis so concluded on.

　　　　　　　HAMLET
There's letters seal'd: and my two schoolfellows,
Whom I will trust as I will adders fang'd,
They bear the mandate; they must sweep my way,
And marshal me to knavery. Let it work;
For 'tis the sport to have the enginer
Hoist with his own petar: and 't shall go hard
But I will delve one yard below their mines,
And blow them at the moon: O, 'tis most sweet
When in one line two crafts directly meet.
This man shall set me packing:
I'll lug the guts into the neighbour room.
Mother, good night. Indeed this counsellor
Is now most still, most secret and most grave,
Who was in life a foolish prating knave.
Come, sir, to draw toward an end with you.
Good night, mother.

　　[*Exeunt severally;* HAMLET *dragging in* POLONIUS

ACT IV
SCENE I. *A room in the castle*

Enter KING, QUEEN, ROSENCRANTZ, *and* GUILDENSTERN

　　　　　　　KING
There's matter in these sighs, these profound heaves:
You must translate: 'tis fit we understand them.
Where is your son?

　　　　　　　QUEEN
Bestow this place on us a little while.
　　　　　[*Exeunt* ROSENCRANTZ *and* GUILDENSTERN
Ah, mine own lord, what have I seen to-night!

　　　　　　　KING
What, Gertrude? How does Hamlet?

　　　　　　　QUEEN
Mad as the sea and wind, when both contend
Which is the mightier: in his lawless fit,
Behind the arras hearing something stir,
Whips out his rapier, cries 'A rat, a rat!'
And in this brainish apprehension kills
The unseen good old man.

　　　　　　　KING
　　　　　　　　　　O heavy deed!
It had been so with us, had we been there:
His liberty is full of threats to all,
To you yourself, to us, to every one.
Alas, how shall this bloody deed be answer'd?
It will be laid to us, whose providence
Should have kept short, restrain'd and out of haunt,
This mad young man: but so much was our love,
We would not understand what was most fit,
But, like the owner of a foul disease,
To keep it from divulging, let it feed
Even on the pith of life. Where is he gone?

　　　　　　　QUEEN
To draw apart the body he hath kill'd:
O'er whom his very madness, like some ore
Among a mineral of metals base,
Shows itself pure; he weeps for what is done.

　　　　　　　KING
O Gertrude, come away!
The sun no sooner shall the mountains touch,
But we will ship him hence: and this vile deed
We must, with all our majesty and skill,
Both countenance and excuse. Ho, Guildenstern!

　　Re-enter ROSENCRANTZ *and* GUILDENSTERN
Friends both, go join you with some further aid:
Hamlet in madness hath Polonius slain,
And from his mother's closet hath he dragg'd him:
Go seek him out; speak fair, and bring the body
Into the chapel. I pray you, haste in this.
　　　　　[*Exeunt* ROSENCRANTZ *and* GUILDENSTERN
Come, Gertrude, we'll call up our wisest friends;
And let them know, both what we mean to do,
And what's untimely done. . . .
Whose whisper o'er the world's diameter
As level as the cannon to his blank
Transports his poison'd shot, may miss our name
And hit the woundless air. O, come away!
My soul is full of discord and dismay.　　　[*Exeunt*

SCENE II. *Another room in the castle*

Enter HAMLET

HAMLET

Safely stowed.

ROSENCRANTZ *and* GUILDENSTERN

[*Within*] Hamlet! Lord Hamlet!

HAMLET

But soft, what noise? who calls on Hamlet?
O, here they come.

Enter ROSENCRANTZ *and* GUILDENSTERN

ROSENCRANTZ

What have you done, my lord, with the dead body?

HAMLET

Compounded it with dust, whereto 'tis kin.

ROSENCRANTZ

Tell us where 'tis, that we may take it thence
And bear it to the chapel.

HAMLET

Do not believe it.

ROSENCRANTZ

Believe what?

HAMLET

That I can keep your counsel and not mine own.
Besides, to be demanded of a sponge! what replication should be made by the son of a king?

ROSENCRANTZ

Take you me for a sponge, my lord?

HAMLET

Ay, sir; that soaks up the king's countenance, his rewards, his authorities. But such officers do the king
best service in the end: he keeps them, like an ape,
in the corner of his jaw; first mouthed, to be last
swallowed: when he needs what you have gleaned,
it is but squeezing you, and, sponge, you shall be
dry again.

ROSENCRANTZ

I understand you not, my lord.

HAMLET

I am glad of it: a knavish speech sleeps in a foolish
ear.

ROSENCRANTZ

My lord, you must tell us where the body is, and go
with us to the king.

HAMLET

The body is with the king, but the king is not with
the body. The king is a thing—

GUILDENSTERN

A thing, my lord?

HAMLET

Of nothing: bring me to him. Hide fox, and all
after.　　　　　　　　　　　　　　　　[*Exeunt*

SCENE III. *Another room in the castle*

Enter KING, *attended*

KING

I have sent to seek him, and to find the body.
How dangerous is it that this man goes loose!
Yet must not we put the strong law on him:

He's loved of the distracted multitude,
Who like not in their judgement, but their eyes;
And where 'tis so, the offender's scourge is weigh'd,
But never the offence. To bear all smooth and even,
This sudden sending him away must seem
Deliberate pause: diseases desperate grown
By desperate appliance are relieved,
Or not at all.

Enter ROSENCRANTZ

　　　　　　　　　How now! what hath befall'n?

ROSENCRANTZ

Where the dead body is bestow'd, my lord,
We cannot get from him.

KING

　　　　　　　　　But where is he?

ROSENCRANTZ

Without, my lord; guarded, to know your pleasure.

KING

Bring him before us.

ROSENCRANTZ

Ho, Guildenstern! bring in my lord.

Enter HAMLET *and* GUILDENSTERN

KING

Now, Hamlet, where's Polonius?

HAMLET

At supper.

KING

At supper! where?

HAMLET

Not where he eats, but where he is eaten: a certain
convocation of politic worms are e'en at him. Your
worm is your only emperor for diet: we fat all creatures else to fat us, and we fat ourselves for maggots:
your fat king and your lean beggar is but variable
service, two dishes, but to one table: that's the end.

KING

Alas, alas!

HAMLET

A man may fish with the worm that hath eat of a
king, and eat of the fish that hath fed of that worm.

KING

What dost thou mean by this?

HAMLET

Nothing but to show you how a king may go a progress through the guts of a beggar.

KING

Where is Polonius?

HAMLET

In heaven; send thither to see: if your messenger
find him not there, seek him i' the other place yourself. But indeed, if you find him not within this
month, you shall nose him as you go up the stairs
into the lobby.

KING

Go seek him there.　　　　　　　　[*To some* ATTENDANTS

HAMLET

He will stay till you come.　　　　[*Exeunt* ATTENDANTS

KING

Hamlet, this deed, for thine especial safety,
Which we do tender, as we dearly grieve

For that which thou hast done, must send thee
  hence
With fiery quickness: therefore prepare thyself;
The bark is ready and the wind at help,
The associates tend, and every thing is bent
For England.

HAMLET

For England?

KING

Ay, Hamlet.

HAMLET

Good.

KING

So is it, if thou knew'st our purposes.

HAMLET

I see a cherub that sees them. But, come; for England! Farewell, dear mother.

KING

Thy loving father, Hamlet.

HAMLET

My mother: father and mother is man and wife;
man and wife is one flesh, and so, my mother.
Come, for England!   [Exit

KING

Follow him at foot; tempt him with speed aboard;
Delay it not; I'll have him hence to-night:
Away! for every thing is seal'd and done
That else leans on the affair: pray you, make haste.
        [Exeunt ROSENCRANTZ and GUILDENSTERN
And, England, if my love thou hold'st at aught—
As my great power thereof may give thee sense,
Since yet thy cicatrice looks raw and red
After the Danish sword, and thy free awe
Pays homage to us—thou mayst not coldly set
Our sovereign process; which imports at full,
By letters congruing to that effect,
The present death of Hamlet. Do it, England;
For like the hectic in my blood he rages,
And thou must cure me: till I know 'tis done,
Howe'er my haps, my joys were ne'er begun. [Exit

SCENE IV. A plain in Denmark

Enter FORTINBRAS, a CAPTAIN and SOLDIERS, marching

FORTINBRAS

Go, captain, from me greet the Danish king;
Tell him that by his license Fortinbras
Craves the conveyance of a promised march
Over his kingdom. You know the rendezvous.
If that his majesty would aught with us,
We shall express our duty in his eye;
And let him know so.

CAPTAIN

I will do 't, my lord.

FORTINBRAS

Go softly on.   [Exeunt FORTINBRAS and SOLDIERS
Enter HAMLET, ROSENCRANTZ, GUILDENSTERN, and
                        others

HAMLET

Good sir, whose powers are these?

CAPTAIN

They are of Norway, sir.

HAMLET

How purposed, sir, I pray you?

CAPTAIN

Against some part of Poland.

HAMLET

Who commands them, sir?

CAPTAIN

The nephew to old Norway, Fortinbras.

HAMLET

Goes it against the main of Poland, sir,
Or for some frontier?

CAPTAIN

Truly to speak, and with no addition,
We go to gain a little patch of ground
That hath in it no profit but the name.
To pay five ducats, five, I would not farm it;
Nor will it yield to Norway or the Pole
A ranker rate, should it be sold in fee.

HAMLET

Why, then the Polack never will defend it.

CAPTAIN

Yes, it is already garrison'd.

HAMLET

Two thousand souls and twenty thousand ducats
Will not debate the question of this straw:
This is the imposthume of much wealth and peace,
That inward breaks, and shows no cause without
Why the man dies. I humbly thank you, sir.

CAPTAIN

God be wi' you, sir.   [Exit

ROSENCRANTZ

Will 't please you go, my lord?

HAMLET

I'll be with you straight. Go a little before.
                [Exeunt all but HAMLET
How all occasions do inform against me,
And spur my dull revenge! What is a man,
If his chief good and market of his time
Be but to sleep and feed? a beast, no more.
Sure, he that made us with such large discourse,
Looking before and after, gave us not
That capability and god-like reason
To fust in us unused. Now, whether it be
Bestial oblivion, or some craven scruple
Of thinking too precisely on the event,—
A thought which, quarter'd, hath but one part wis-
  dom
And ever three parts coward,—I do not know
Why yet I live to say 'this thing's to do,'
Sith I have cause, and will, and strength, and
  means,
To do 't. Examples gross as earth exhort me:
Witness this army, of such mass and charge,
Led by a delicate and tender prince,
Whose spirit with divine ambition puff'd
Makes mouths at the invisible event,

Exposing what is mortal and unsure
To all that fortune, death and danger dare,
Even for an egg-shell. Rightly to be great
Is not to stir without great argument,
But greatly to find quarrel in a straw
When honour's at the stake. How stand I then,
That have a father kill'd, a mother stain'd,
Excitements of my reason and my blood,
And let all sleep, while to my shame I see
The imminent death of twenty thousand men,
That for a fantasy and trick of fame
Go to their graves like beds, fight for a plot
Whereon the numbers cannot try the cause,
Which is not tomb enough and continent
To hide the slain? O, from this time forth,
My thoughts be bloody, or be nothing worth! [*Exit*

SCENE V. *Elsinore. A room in the castle*

Enter QUEEN, HORATIO, *and a* GENTLEMAN
QUEEN
I will not speak with her.
GENTLEMAN
She is importunate, indeed distract:
Her mood will needs be pitied.
QUEEN
           What would she have?
GENTLEMAN
She speaks much of her father, says she hears
There's tricks i' the world, and hems and beats her
     heart,
Spurns enviously at straws; speaks things in doubt,
That carry but half sense: her speech is nothing,
Yet the unshaped use of it doth move
The hearers to collection; they aim at it,
And botch the words up fit to their own thoughts;
Which, as her winks and nods and gestures yield
     them,
Indeed would make one think there might be
     thought,
Though nothing sure, yet much unhappily.
HORATIO
'Twere good she were spoken with, for she may
     strew
Dangerous conjectures in ill-breeding minds.
QUEEN
Let her come in.   [*Exit* GENTLEMAN
[*Aside*] To my sick soul, as sin's true nature is,
Each toy seems prologue to some great amiss:
So full of artless jealousy is guilt,
It spills itself in fearing to be spilt.
Re-enter GENTLEMAN, *with* OPHELIA
OPHELIA
Where is the beauteous majesty of Denmark?
QUEEN
How now, Ophelia!
OPHELIA
[*Sings*] How should I your true love know
            From another one?

           By his cockle hat and staff
           And his sandal shoon.
QUEEN
Alas, sweet lady, what imports this song?
OPHELIA
Say you? nay, pray you, mark.
    [*Sings*] He is dead and gone, lady,
           He is dead and gone;
           At his head a grass-green turf,
           At his heels a stone.
Oh, oh!
QUEEN
     Nay, but, Ophelia,—
OPHELIA
                Pray you, mark.
[*Sings*] White his shroud as the mountain snow,—
Enter KING
QUEEN
Alas, look here, my lord.
OPHELIA
   [*Sings*]   Larded with sweet flowers;
           Which bewept to the grave did go
           With true-love showers.
KING
How do you, pretty lady?
OPHELIA
Well, God 'ild you! They say the owl was a baker's
daughter. Lord, we know what we are, but know
not what we may be. God be at your table!
KING
Conceit upon her father.
OPHELIA
Pray you, let's have no words of this; but when they
ask you what it means, say you this:
   [*Sings*] To-morrow is Saint Valentine's day,
           All in the morning betime,
           And I a maid at your window,
           To be your Valentine.

           Then up he rose, and donn'd his clothes,
           And dupp'd the chamber-door;
           Let in the maid, that out a maid
           Never departed more.
KING
Pretty Ophelia!
OPHELIA
Indeed, la, without an oath, I'll make an end on 't:
   [*Sings*] By Gis and by Saint Charity,
           Alack, and fie for shame!
           Young men will do 't, if they come to 't;
           By cock, they are to blame.
           Quoth she, before you tumbled me,
           You promised me to wed.
He answers:
           So would I ha' done, by yonder sun,
           An thou hadst not come to my bed.
KING
How long hath she been thus?
OPHELIA
I hope all will be well. We must be patient: but I

[765]

cannot choose but weep, to think they should lay
him i' the cold ground. My brother shall know of it:
and so I thank you for your good counsel. Come,
my coach! Good night, ladies; good night, sweet
ladies; good night, good night.   [*Exit*

KING

Follow her close; give her good watch, I pray you.
                                        [*Exit* HORATIO

O, this is the poison of deep grief; it springs
All from her father's death. O Gertrude, Gertrude,
When sorrows come, they come not single spies,
But in battalions! First, her father slain:
Next, your son gone; and he most violent author
Of his own just remove: the people muddied,
Thick and unwholesome in their thoughts and
    whispers,
For good Polonius' death; and we have done but
    greenly,
In hugger-mugger to inter him: poor Ophelia
Divided from herself and her fair judgement,
Without the which we are pictures, or mere beasts:
Last, and as much containing as all these,
Her brother is in secret come from France,
Feeds on his wonder, keeps himself in clouds,
And wants not buzzers to infect his ear
With pestilent speeches of his father's death;
Wherein necessity, of matter beggar'd,
Will nothing stick our person to arraign
In ear and ear. O my dear Gertrude, this,
Like to a murdering-piece, in many places
Gives me superfluous death.   [*A noise within*

QUEEN
                    Alack, what noise is this?

KING

Where are my Switzers? Let them guard the door.
                    Enter another GENTLEMAN
What is the matter?

GENTLEMAN
                    Save yourself, my lord:
The ocean, overpeering of his list,
Eats not the flats with more impetuous haste
Than young Laertes, in a riotous head,
O'erbears your officers. The rabble call him lord;
And, as the world were now but to begin,
Antiquity forgot, custom not known,
The ratifiers and props of every word,
They cry 'Choose we; Laertes shall be king!'
Caps, hands and tongues applaud it to the clouds,
'Laertes shall be king, Laertes king!'

QUEEN

How cheerfully on the false trail they cry!
O, this is counter, you false Danish dogs!
                                        [*Noise within*

KING

The doors are broke.
          Enter LAERTES, *armed;* DANES *following*

LAERTES

Where is this king? Sirs, stand you all without.

DANES

No, let's come in.

LAERTES
          I pray you, give me leave.

DANES

We will, we will.   [*They retire without the door.*

LAERTES

I thank you: keep the door. O thou vile king,
Give me my father!

QUEEN
                    Calmly, good Laertes.

LAERTES

That drop of blood that's calm proclaims me bas-
    tard;
Cries cuckold to my father; brands the harlot
Even here, between the chaste unsmirched brows
Of my true mother.

KING
                    What is the cause, Laertes,
That thy rebellion looks so giant-like?
Let him go, Gertrude; do not fear our person:
There's such divinity doth hedge a king,
That treason can but peep to what it would,
Acts little of his will. Tell me, Laertes,
Why thou art thus incensed: let him go, Gertrude:
Speak, man.

LAERTES

Where is my father?

KING
                    Dead.

QUEEN
                    But not by him.

KING

Let him demand his fill.

LAERTES

How came he dead? I'll not be juggled with:
To hell, allegiance! vows, to the blackest devil!
Conscience and grace, to the profoundest pit!
I dare damnation: to this point I stand,
That both the worlds I give to negligence,
Let come what comes; only I'll be revenged
Most throughly for my father.

KING
                    Who shall stay you?

LAERTES

My will, not all the world:
And for my means, I'll husband them so well,
They shall go far with little.

KING
                    Good Laertes,
If you desire to know the certainty
Of your dear father's death, is 't writ in your re-
    venge
That, swoopstake, you will draw both friend and
    foe,
Winner and loser?

LAERTES

None but his enemies.

KING
                    Will you know them then?

LAERTES

To his good friends thus wide I'll ope my arms;

And, like the kind life-rendering pelican,
Repast them with my blood.

KING

　　　　　　　　Why, now you speak
Like a good child and a true gentleman.
That I am guiltless of your father's death,
And am most sensibly in grief for it,
It shall as level to your judgement pierce
As day does to your eye.

DANES

[Within] Let her come in.

LAERTES

How now! what noise is that?

Re-enter OPHELIA

O heat, dry up my brains! tears seven times salt,
Burn out the sense and virtue of mine eye!
By heaven, thy madness shall be paid with weight,
Till our scale turn the beam. O rose of May!
Dear maid, kind sister, sweet Ophelia!
O heavens! is 't possible a young maid's wits
Should be as mortal as an old man's life?
Nature is fine in love, and where 'tis fine
It sends some precious instance of itself
After the thing it loves.

OPHELIA

[*Sings*] They bore him barefaced on the bier;
　　　　Hey non nonny, nonny, hey nonny:
　　　　And in his grave rain'd many a tear,—

Fare you well, my dove!

LAERTES

Hadst thou thy wits, and didst persuade revenge,
It could not move thus.

OPHELIA

[*Sings*] You must sing down a-down,
　　　　An you call him a-down-a.

O, how the wheel becomes it! It is the false steward,
that stole his master's daughter.

LAERTES

This nothing's more than matter.

OPHELIA

There's rosemary, that's for remembrance: pray
you, love, remember: and there is pansies, that's for
thoughts.

LAERTES

A document in madness; thoughts and remembrance fitted.

OPHELIA

There's fennel for you, and columbines: there's rue
for you; and here's some for me: we may call it herb
of grace o' Sundays: O, you must wear your rue
with a difference. There's a daisy: I would give you
some violets, but they withered all when my father
died: they say a' made a good end,—

[*Sings*] For bonny sweet Robin is all my joy.

LAERTES

Thought and affliction, passion, hell itself,
She turns to favour and to prettiness.

OPHELIA

[*Sings*] And will a' not come again?
　　　　And will a' not come again?
　　　　　No, no, he is dead,
　　　　　Go to thy death-bed,
　　　　He never will come again.

　　　　His beard was as white as snow,
　　　　All flaxen was his poll:
　　　　　He is gone, he is gone,
　　　　　And we cast away moan:
　　　　God ha' mercy on his soul!

And of all Christian souls, I pray God. God be wi'
you.　　　　　　　　　　　　　　　　　[*Exit*

LAERTES

Do you see this, O God?

KING

Laertes, I must commune with your grief,
Or you deny me right. Go but apart,
Make choice of whom your wisest friends you will,
And they shall hear and judge 'twixt you and me:
If by direct or by collateral hand
They find us touch'd, we will our kingdom give,
Our crown, our life, and all that we call ours,
To you in satisfaction; but if not,
Be you content to lend your patience to us,
And we shall jointly labour with your soul
To give it due content.

LAERTES

　　　　　　　Let this be so;
His means of death, his obscure funeral,
No trophy, sword, nor hatchment o'er his bones,
No noble rite nor formal ostentation,
Cry to be heard, as 'twere from heaven to earth,
That I must call 't in question.

KING

　　　　　　　　　　So you shall;
And where the offence is let the great axe fall.
I pray you, go with me.　　　　　　　　[*Exeunt*

SCENE VI. *Another room in the castle*

Enter HORATIO *and a* SERVANT

HORATIO

What are they that would speak with me?

SERVANT

Sea-faring men, sir: they say they have letters for
you.

HORATIO

Let them come in.　　　　　　　[*Exit* SERVANT
I do not know from what part of the world
I should be greeted, if not from Lord Hamlet.

Enter SAILORS

FIRST SAILOR

God bless you, sir.

HORATIO

Let him bless thee too.

FIRST SAILOR

He shall, sir, an 't please him. There's a letter for
you, sir; it comes from the ambassador that was

bound for England; if your name be Horatio, as I
am let to know it is.

HORATIO

[*Reads*] 'Horatio, when thou shalt have overlooked this, give
these fellows some means to the king: they have letters for him.
Ere we were two days old at sea, a pirate of very warlike appointment gave us chase. Finding ourselves too slow of sail, we
put on a compelled valour, and in the grapple I boarded them:
on the instant they got clear of our ship; so I alone became
their prisoner. They have dealt with me like thieves of mercy:
but they knew what they did; I am to do a good turn for them.
Let the king have the letters I have sent; and repair thou to
me with as much speed as thou wouldest fly death. I have
words to speak in thine ear will make thee dumb; yet are they
much too light for the bore of the matter. These good fellows
will bring thee where I am. Rosencrantz and Guildenstern
hold their course for England: of them I have much to tell
thee. Farewell.

       'He that thou knowest thine, HAMLET.'

Come, I will make you way for these your letters;
And do 't the speedier, that you may direct me
To him from whom you brought them.   [*Exeunt*

SCENE VII. *Another room in the castle*

Enter KING *and* LAERTES

KING

Now must your conscience my acquittance seal,
And you must put me in your heart for friend,
Sith you have heard, and with a knowing ear,
That he which hath your noble father slain
Pursued my life.

LAERTES

       It well appears: but tell me
Why you proceeded not against these feats,
So crimeful and so capital in nature,
As by your safety, wisdom, all things else,
You mainly were stirr'd up.

KING

       O, for two special reasons,
Which may to you perhaps seem much unsinew'd,
But yet to me they're strong. The queen his mother
Lives almost by his looks; and for myself—
My virtue or my plague, be it either which—
She's so conjunctive to my life and soul,
That, as the star moves not but in his sphere,
I could not but by her. The other motive,
Why to a public count I might not go,
Is the great love the general gender bear him;
Who, dipping all his faults in their affection,
Would, like the spring that turneth wood to stone,
Convert his gyves to graces; so that my arrows,
Too slightly timber'd for so loud a wind,
Would have reverted to my bow again
And not where I had aim'd them.

LAERTES

And so have I a noble father lost;
A sister driven into desperate terms,
Whose worth, if praises may go back again,
Stood challenger on mount of all the age
For her perfections: but my revenge will come.

KING

Break not your sleeps for that: you must not think
That we are made of stuff so flat and dull
That we can let our beard be shook with danger
And think it pastime. You shortly shall hear more:
I loved your father, and we love ourself;
And that, I hope, will teach you to imagine—

    Enter a MESSENGER, *with letters*
How now! what news?

MESSENGER

       Letters, my lord, from Hamlet:
This to your majesty; this to the queen.

KING

From Hamlet! who brought them?

MESSENGER

Sailors, my lord, they say; I saw them not:
They were given me by Claudio; he received them
Of him that brought them.

KING

       Laertes, you shall hear them.
Leave us.   [*Exit* MESSENGER

[*Reads*] 'High and mighty, You shall know I am set naked on your
kingdom. To-morrow shall I beg leave to see your kingly eyes:
when I shall, first asking your pardon thereunto, recount the
occasion of my sudden and more strange return.

       'HAMLET.'

What should this mean? Are all the rest come back?
Or is it some abuse, and no such thing?

LAERTES

Know you the hand?

KING

'Tis Hamlet's character. 'Naked'!
And in a postscript here, he says 'alone'.
Can you advise me?

LAERTES

I'm lost in it, my lord. But let him come;
It warms the very sickness in my heart,
That I shall live and tell him to his teeth,
'Thus didest thou.'

KING

       If it be so, Laertes,—
As how should it be so? how otherwise?—
Will you be ruled by me?

LAERTES

       Ay, my lord;
So you will not o'errule me to a peace.

KING

To thine own peace. If he be now return'd,
As checking at his voyage, and that he means
No more to undertake it, I will work him
To an exploit now ripe in my device,
Under the which he shall not choose but fall:
And for his death no wind of blame shall breathe;
But even his mother shall uncharge the practice,
And call it accident.

LAERTES

       My lord, I will be ruled;
The rather, if you could devise it so
That I might be the organ.

KING
It falls right.
You have been talk'd of since your travel much,
And that in Hamlet's hearing, for a quality
Wherein, they say, you shine: your sum of parts
Did not together pluck such envy from him,
As did that one, and that in my regard
Of the unworthiest siege.

LAERTES
What part is that, my lord?

KING
A very riband in the cap of youth,
Yet needful too; for youth no less becomes
The light and careless livery that it wears
Than settled age his sables and his weeds,
Importing health and graveness. Two months since,
Here was a gentleman of Normandy:—
I've seen myself, and served against, the French,
And they can well on horseback: but this gallant
Had witchcraft in 't; he grew unto his seat,
And to such wondrous doing brought his horse
As had he been incorpsed and demi-natured
With the brave beast: so far he topp'd my thought
That I, in forgery of shapes and tricks,
Come short of what he did.

LAERTES
A Norman was 't?

KING
A Norman.

LAERTES
Upon my life, Lamond.

KING
The very same.

LAERTES
I know him well: he is the brooch indeed
And gem of all the nation.

KING
He made confession of you,
And gave you such a masterly report,
For art and exercise in your defence,
And for your rapier most especial,
That he cried out, 'twould be a sight indeed
If one could match you: the scrimers of their nation,
He swore, had neither motion, guard, nor eye,
If you opposed them. Sir, this report of his
Did Hamlet so envenom with his envy
That he could nothing do but wish and beg
Your sudden coming o'er, to play with him.
Now, out of this—

LAERTES
What out of this, my lord?

KING
Laertes, was your father dear to you?
Or are you like the painting of a sorrow,
A face without a heart?

LAERTES
Why ask you this?

KING
Not that I think you did not love your father,
But that I know love is begun by time,

And that I see, in passages of proof,
Time qualifies the spark and fire of it.
There lives within the very flame of love
A kind of wick or snuff that will abate it;
And nothing is at a like goodness still,
For goodness, growing to a plurisy,
Dies in his own too much: that we would do
We should do when we would; for this 'would'
changes
And hath abatements and delays as many
As there are tongues, are hands, are accidents,
And then this 'should' is like a spendthrift sigh,
That hurts by easing. But, to the quick o' the ulcer:
Hamlet comes back: what would you undertake,
To show yourself your father's son in deed
More than in words?

LAERTES
To cut his throat i' the church.

KING
No place indeed should murder sanctuarize;
Revenge should have no bounds. But, good Laertes,
Will you do this, keep close within your chamber.
Hamlet return'd shall know you are come home:
We'll put on those shall praise your excellence
And set a double varnish on the fame
The Frenchman gave you; bring you in fine together
And wager on your heads: he, being remiss,
Most generous and free from all contriving,
Will not peruse the foils, so that with ease,
Or with a little shuffling, you may choose
A sword unbated, and in a pass of practice
Requite him for your father.

LAERTES
I will do 't;
And for that purpose I'll anoint my sword.
I bought an unction of a mountebank,
So mortal that but dip a knife in it,
Where it draws blood no cataplasm so rare,
Collected from all simples that have virtue
Under the moon, can save the thing from death
That is but scratch'd withal: I'll touch my point
With this contagion, that, if I gall him slightly,
It may be death.

KING
Let's further think of this;
Weigh what convenience both of time and means
May fit us to our shape: if this should fail,
And that our drift look through our bad perform-
ance,
'Twere better not assay'd: therefore this project
Should have a back or second, that might hold
If this did blast in proof. Soft! let me see:
We'll make a solemn wager on your cunnings:
I ha 't:
When in your motion you are hot and dry—
As make your bouts more violent to that end—
And that he calls for drink, I'll have prepared him
A chalice for the nonce; whereon but sipping,
If he by chance escape your venom'd stuck,
Our purpose may hold there. But stay, what noise?

Enter QUEEN

How now, sweet queen!

QUEEN

One woe doth tread upon another's heel,
So fast they follow: your sister's drown'd, Laertes.

LAERTES

Drown'd! O, where?

QUEEN

There is a willow grows aslant a brook,
That shows his hoar leaves in the glassy stream;
There with fantastic garlands did she come
Of crow-flowers, nettles, daisies, and long purples,
That liberal shepherds give a grosser name,
But our cold maids do dead men's fingers call them:
There, on the pendent boughs her coronet weeds
Clambering to hang, an envious sliver broke;
When down her weedy trophies and herself
Fell in the weeping brook. Her clothes spread wide,
And mermaid-like a while they bore her up:
Which time she chanted snatches of old tunes,
As one incapable of her own distress,
Or like a creature native and indued
Unto that element: but long it could not be
Till that her garments, heavy with their drink,
Pull'd the poor wretch from her melodious lay
To muddy death.

LAERTES

Alas, then she is drown'd!

QUEEN

Drown'd, drown'd.

LAERTES

Too much of water hast thou, poor Ophelia,
And therefore I forbid my tears: but yet
It is our trick; nature her custom holds,
Let shame say what it will: when these are gone,
The woman will be out. Adieu, my lord:
I have a speech of fire that fain would blaze,
But that this folly douts it.   [*Exit*

KING

Let's follow, Gertrude:
How much I had to do to calm his rage!
Now fear I this will give it start again;
Therefore let's follow.   [*Exeunt*

ACT V

SCENE I. *A churchyard*

Enter two CLOWNS, *with spades, &c.*

FIRST CLOWN

Is she to be buried in Christian burial that wilfully
seeks her own salvation?

SECOND CLOWN

I tell thee she is; and therefore make her grave
straight: the crowner hath sat on her, and finds it
Christian burial.

FIRST CLOWN

How can that be, unless she drowned herself in her
own defence?

SECOND CLOWN

Why, 'tis found so.

FIRST CLOWN

It must be 'se offendendo;' it cannot be else. For
here lies the point: if I drown myself wittingly, it
argues an act: and an act hath three branches; it is,
to act, to do, and to perform: argal, she drowned
herself wittingly.

SECOND CLOWN

Nay, but hear you, goodman delver.

FIRST CLOWN

Give me leave. Here lies the water; good: here stands
the man; good: if the man go to this water and
drown himself, it is, will he, nill he, he goes; mark
you that; but if the water come to him and drown
him, he drowns not himself: argal, he that is not
guilty of his own death shortens not his own life.

SECOND CLOWN

But is this law?

FIRST CLOWN

Ay, marry, is 't; crowner's quest law.

SECOND CLOWN

Will you ha' the truth on 't? If this had not been a
gentlewoman, she should have been buried out o'
Christian burial.

FIRST CLOWN

Why, there thou say'st: and the more pity that great
folk should have countenance in this world to drown
or hang themselves, more than their even Christian.
Come, my spade. There is no ancient gentlemen but
gardeners, ditchers and grave-makers: they hold up
Adam's profession.

SECOND CLOWN

Was he a gentleman?

FIRST CLOWN

A' was the first that ever bore arms.

SECOND CLOWN

Why, he had none.

FIRST CLOWN

What, art a heathen? How dost thou understand
the Scripture? The Scripture says Adam digged:
could he dig without arms? I'll put another question
to thee: if thou answerest me not to the purpose,
confess thyself—

SECOND CLOWN

Go to.

FIRST CLOWN

What is he that builds stronger than either the
mason, the shipwright, or the carpenter?

SECOND CLOWN

The gallows-maker; for that frame outlives a thousand tenants.

FIRST CLOWN

I like thy wit well, in good faith: the gallows does
well; but how does it well? it does well to those that
do ill: how, thou dost ill to say the gallows is built

stronger than the church: argal, the gallows may do well to thee. To 't again, come.

SECOND CLOWN

'Who builds stronger than a mason, a shipwright, or a carpenter?'

FIRST CLOWN

Ay, tell me that, and unyoke.

SECOND CLOWN

Marry, now I can tell.

FIRST CLOWN

To 't.

SECOND CLOWN

Mass, I cannot tell.

Enter HAMLET *and* HORATIO, *afar off*

FIRST CLOWN

Cudgel thy brains no more about it, for your dull ass will not mend his pace with beating, and when you are asked this question next, say 'a grave-maker:' the houses that he makes last till doomsday. Go, get thee to Yaughan; fetch me a stoup of liquor.

[*Exit* SECOND CLOWN

[*He digs, and sings*

In youth, when I did love, did love,
　Methought it was very sweet,
To contract, O, the time, for-a my behove,
　O, methought, there-a was nothing-a meet.

HAMLET

Has this fellow no feeling of his business, that he sings at grave-making?

HORATIO

Custom hath made it in him a property of easiness.

HAMLET

'Tis e'en so: the hand of little employment hath the daintier sense.

FIRST CLOWN

[*Sings*]　But age, with his stealing steps,
　Hath claw'd me in his clutch,
And hath shipped me intil the land,
　As if I had never been such.

[*Throws up a skull*

HAMLET

That skull had a tongue in it, and could sing once: how the knave jowls it to the ground, as if it were Cain's jaw-bone, that did the first murder! It might be the pate of a politician, which this ass now o'er-reaches; one that would circumvent God, might it not?

HORATIO

It might, my lord.

HAMLET

Or of a courtier, which could say 'Good morrow, sweet lord! How dost thou, sweet lord?' This might be my lord such-a-one, that praised my lord such-a-one's horse, when he meant to beg it; might it not?

HORATIO

Ay, my lord.

HAMLET

Why, e'en so: and now my Lady Worm's; chapless, and knocked about the mazzard with a sexton's spade: here's fine revolution, an we had the trick to see 't. Did these bones cost no more the breeding, but to play at loggats with 'em? mine ache to think on 't.

FIRST CLOWN

[*Sings*] A pick-axe, and a spade, a spade,
　For and a shrouding sheet:
O, a pit of clay for to be made
　For such a guest is meet.

[*Throws up another skull*

HAMLET

There's another: why may not that be the skull of a lawyer? Where be his quiddities now, his quillets, his cases, his tenures, and his tricks? why does he suffer this rude knave now to knock him about the sconce with a dirty shovel, and will not tell him of his action of battery? Hum! This fellow might be in 's time a great buyer of land, with his statutes, his recognizances, his fines, his double vouchers, his re-coveries: is this the fine of his fines and the recovery of his recoveries, to have his fine pate full of fine dirt? will his vouchers vouch him no more of his purchases, and double ones too, than the length and breadth of a pair of indentures? The very convey-ances of his lands will hardly lie in this box; and must the inheritor himself have no more, ha?

HORATIO

Not a jot more, my lord.

HAMLET

Is not parchment made of sheep-skins?

HORATIO

Ay, my lord, and of calf-skins too.

HAMLET

They are sheep and calves which seek out assurance in that. I will speak to this fellow. Whose grave's this, sirrah?

FIRST CLOWN

Mine, sir.

[*Sings*] O, a pit of clay for to be made
　For such a guest is meet.

HAMLET

I think it be thine indeed, for thou liest in 't.

FIRST CLOWN

You lie out on 't, sir, and therefore 'tis not yours: for my part, I do not lie in 't, and yet it is mine.

HAMLET

Thou dost lie in 't, to be in 't and say it is thine: 'tis for the dead, not for the quick; therefore thou liest.

FIRST CLOWN

'Tis a quick lie, sir; 'twill away again, from me to you.

HAMLET

What man dost thou dig it for?

FIRST CLOWN

For no man, sir.

HAMLET

What woman then?

FIRST CLOWN

For none, neither.

HAMLET

Who is to be buried in 't?

FIRST CLOWN

One that was a woman, sir; but, rest her soul, she's dead.

HAMLET

How absolute the knave is! we must speak by the card, or equivocation will undo us. By the Lord, Horatio, this three years I have taken note of it; the age is grown so picked that the toe of the peasant comes so near the heel of the courtier, he galls his kibe. How long hast thou been a grave-maker?

FIRST CLOWN

Of all the days i' the year, I came to 't that day that our last king Hamlet o'ercame Fortinbras.

HAMLET

How long is that since?

FIRST CLOWN

Cannot you tell that? every fool can tell that: it was that very day that young Hamlet was born; he that is mad, and sent into England.

HAMLET

Ay, marry, why was he sent into England?

FIRST CLOWN

Why, because a' was mad: a' shall recover his wits there; or, if a' do not, 'tis no great matter there.

HAMLET

Why?

FIRST CLOWN

'Twill not be seen in him there; there the men are as mad as he.

HAMLET

How came he mad?

FIRST CLOWN

Very strangely, they say.

HAMLET

How 'strangely'?

FIRST CLOWN

Faith, e'en with losing his wits.

HAMLET

Upon what ground?

FIRST CLOWN

Why, here in Denmark: I have been sexton here, man and boy, thirty years.

HAMLET

How long will a man lie i' the earth ere he rot?

FIRST CLOWN

I' faith, if a' be not rotten before a' die—as we have many pocky corses now-a-days, that will scarce hold the laying in—a' will last you some eight year or nine year: a tanner will last you nine year.

HAMLET

Why he more than another?

FIRST CLOWN

Why, sir, his hide is so tanned with his trade that a' will keep out water a great while; and your water is a sore decayer of your whoreson dead body. Here's a skull now: this skull has lain in the earth three and twenty years.

HAMLET

Whose was it?

FIRST CLOWN

A whoreson mad fellow's it was: whose do you think it was?

HAMLET

Nay, I know not.

FIRST CLOWN

A pestilence on him for a mad rogue! a' poured a flagon of Rhenish on my head once. This same skull, sir, was Yorick's skull, the king's jester.

HAMLET

This?

FIRST CLOWN

E'en that.

HAMLET

Let me see. [Takes the skull] Alas, poor Yorick! I knew him, Horatio: a fellow of infinite jest, of most excellent fancy: he hath borne me on his back a thousand times; and now how abhorred in my imagination it is! my gorge rises at it. Here hung those lips that I have kissed I know not how oft. Where be your gibes now? your gambols? your songs? your flashes of merriment, that were wont to set the table on a roar? Not one now, to mock your own grinning? quite chop-fallen? Now get you to my lady's chamber, and tell her, let her paint an inch thick, to this favour she must come; make her laugh at that. Prithee, Horatio, tell me one thing.

HORATIO

What's that, my lord?

HAMLET

Dost thou think Alexander looked o' this fashion i' the earth?

HORATIO

E'en so.

HAMLET

And smelt so? pah!   [Puts down the skull

HORATIO

E'en so, my lord.

HAMLET

To what base uses we may return, Horatio! Why may not imagination trace the noble dust of Alexander, till he find it stopping a bung-hole?

HORATIO

'Twere to consider too curiously, to consider so.

HAMLET

No, faith, not a jot; but to follow him thither with modesty enough and likelihood to lead it: as thus: Alexander died, Alexander was buried, Alexander returneth into dust; the dust is earth; of earth we make loam; and why of that loam, whereto he was converted, might they not stop a beer-barrel?

Imperious Cæsar, dead and turn'd to clay,
Might stop a hole to keep the wind away:
O, that that earth, which kept the world in awe,
Should patch a wall to expel the winter's flaw!

But soft! but soft! aside: here comes the king.
Enter PRIESTS, &c. in procession; the Corpse of Ophelia, LAERTES and MOURNERS following; KING, QUEEN, their trains, &c.
The queen, the courtiers: who is this they follow?

And with such maimed rites? This doth betoken
The corse they follow did with desperate hand
Fordo its own life: 'twas of some estate.
Couch we awhile, and mark.

                [Retiring with HORATIO

LAERTES

What ceremony else?

HAMLET

That is Laertes, a very noble youth: mark.

LAERTES

What ceremony else?

FIRST PRIEST

Her obsequies have been as far enlarged
As we have warranty: her death was doubtful;
And, but that great command o'ersways the order,
She should in ground unsanctified have lodged
Till the last trumpet; for charitable prayers,
Shards, flints and pebbles should be thrown on her:
Yet here she is allow'd her virgin crants,
Her maiden strewments and the bringing home
Of bell and burial.

LAERTES

Must there no more be done?

FIRST PRIEST

              No more be done:
We should profane the service of the dead
To sing a requiem and such rest to her
As to peace-parted souls.

LAERTES

             Lay her i' the earth:
And from her fair and unpolluted flesh
May violets spring! I tell thee, churlish priest,
A ministering angel shall my sister be,
When thou liest howling.

HAMLET

             What, the fair Ophelia!

QUEEN

[Scattering flowers] Sweets to the sweet: farewell!
I hoped thou shouldst have been my Hamlet's wife;
I thought thy bride-bed to have deck'd, sweet maid,
And not have strew'd thy grave.

LAERTES

             O, treble woe
Fall ten times treble on that cursed head
Whose wicked deed thy most ingenious sense
Deprived thee of! Hold off the earth a while,
Till I have caught her once more in mine arms:

                [Leaps into the grave
Now pile your dust upon the quick and dead,
Till of this flat a mountain you have made
To o'ertop old Pelion or the skyish head
Of blue Olympus.

HAMLET

[Advancing] What is he whose grief
Bears such an emphasis? whose phrase of sorrow
Conjures the wandering stars and makes them stand
Like wonder-wounded hearers? This is I,
Hamlet the Dane.   *[Leaps into the grave*

LAERTES

The devil take thy soul!   *[Grappling with him*

HAMLET

             Thou pray'st not well.
I prithee, take thy fingers from my throat;
For, though I am not splenitive and rash,
Yet have I in me something dangerous,
Which let thy wisdom fear. Hold off thy hand.

KING

Pluck them asunder.

QUEEN

             Hamlet, Hamlet!

ALL

                Gentlemen,—

HORATIO

Good my lord, be quiet.

[The ATTENDANTS *part them, and they come out of the grave*

HAMLET

Why, I will fight with him upon this theme
Until my eyelids will no longer wag.

QUEEN

O my son, what theme?

HAMLET

I loved Ophelia: forty thousand brothers
Could not, with all their quantity of love,
Make up my sum. What wilt thou do for her?

KING

O, he is mad, Laertes.

QUEEN

For love of God, forbear him.

HAMLET

'Swounds, show me what thou 'lt do:
Woo 't weep? woo 't fight? woo 't fast? woo 't tear
    thyself?
Woo 't drink up eisel? eat a crocodile?
I'll do 't. Dost thou come here to whine?
To outface me with leaping in her grave?
Be buried quick with her, and so will I:
And, if thou prate of mountains, let them throw
Millions of acres on us, till our ground,
Singeing his pate against the burning zone,
Make Ossa like a wart! Nay, an thou 'lt mouth,
I'll rant as well as thou.

QUEEN

             This is mere madness:
And thus a while the fit will work on him;
Anon, as patient as the female dove
When that her golden couplets are disclosed,
His silence will sit drooping.

HAMLET

             Hear you, sir;
What is the reason that you use me thus?
I loved you ever: but it is no matter;
Let Hercules himself do what he may,
The cat will mew, and dog will have his day. *[Exit*

KING

I pray thee, good Horatio, wait upon him.

                [Exit HORATIO
[To LAERTES] Strengthen your patience in our last
    night's speech;
We'll put the matter to the present push.

Good Gertrude, set some watch over your son.
This grave shall have a living monument:
An hour of quiet shortly shall we see;
Till then, in patience our proceeding be.　　[*Exeunt*

SCENE II. *A hall in the castle*

Enter HAMLET *and* HORATIO

HAMLET
So much for this, sir: now shall you see the other;
You do remember all the circumstance?

HORATIO
Remember it, my lord!

HAMLET
Sir, in my heart there was a kind of fighting,
That would not let me sleep: methought I lay
Worse than the mutines in the bilboes. Rashly,
And praised be rashness for it, let us know,
Our indiscretion sometime serves us well
When our deep plots do pall; and that should learn
　　us
There's a divinity that shapes our ends,
Rough-hew them how we will.

HORATIO
　　　　　　　　　That is most certain.

HAMLET
Up from my cabin,
My sea-gown scarf'd about me, in the dark
Groped I to find out them; had my desire,
Finger'd their packet, and in fine withdrew
To mine own room again; making so bold,
My fears forgetting manners, to unseal
Their grand commission; where I found, Horatio,—
O royal knavery!—an exact command,
Larded with many several sorts of reasons,
Importing Denmark's health and England's too,
With, ho! such bugs and goblins in my life,
That, on the supervise, no leisure bated,
No, not to stay the grinding of the axe,
My head should be struck off.

HORATIO
　　　　　　　　　Is 't possible?

HAMLET
Here's the commission: read it at more leisure.
But wilt thou hear now how I did proceed?

HORATIO
I beseech you.

HAMLET
Being thus be-netted round with villanies,—
Or I could make a prologue to my brains,
They had begun the play,—I sat me down;
Devised a new commission; wrote it fair:
I once did hold it, as our statists do,
A baseness to write fair, and labour'd much
How to forget that learning; but, sir, now
It did me yeoman's service: wilt thou know
The effect of what I wrote?

HORATIO
　　　　　　　　　Ay, good my lord.

HAMLET
An earnest conjuration from the king,
As England was his faithful tributary,
As love between them like the palm might flourish,
As peace should still her wheaten garland wear
And stand a comma 'tween their amities,
And many such-like 'As' es of great charge,
That, on the view and knowing of these contents,
Without debatement further, more or less,
He should the bearers put to sudden death,
Not shriving-time allow'd.

HORATIO
　　　　　　　　　How was this seal'd?

HAMLET
Why, even in that was heaven ordinant.
I had my father's signet in my purse,
Which was the model of that Danish seal:
Folded the writ up in the form of the other;
Subscribed it; gave 't the impression; placed it
　　safely,
The changeling never known. Now, the next day
Was our sea-fight; and what to this was sequent
Thou know'st already.

HORATIO
So Guildenstern and Rosencrantz go to 't.

HAMLET
Why, man, they did make love to this employment;
They are not near my conscience; their defeat
Does by their own insinuation grow:
'Tis dangerous when the baser nature comes
Between the pass and fell incensed points
Of mighty opposites.

HORATIO
　　　　　　　　　Why, what a king is this!

HAMLET
Does it not, thinks 't thee, stand me now upon—
He that hath kill'd my king, and whored my
　　mother;
Popp'd in between the election and my hopes;
Thrown out his angle for my proper life,
And with such cozenage—is 't not perfect con-
　　science,
To quit him with this arm? and is 't not to be
　　damn'd,
To let this canker of our nature come
In further evil?

HORATIO
It must be shortly known to him from England
What is the issue of the business there.

HAMLET
It will be short: the interim is mine;
And a man's life's no more than to say 'One.'
But I am very sorry, good Horatio,
That to Laertes I forgot myself;
For, by the image of my cause, I see
The portraiture of his: I'll court his favours:
But, sure, the bravery of his grief did put me
Into a towering passion.

HORATIO
　　　　　　　　　Peace! who comes here?

Enter OSRIC

OSRIC

Your lordship is right welcome back to Denmark.

HAMLET

I humbly thank you, sir. Dost know this water-fly?

HORATIO

No, my good lord.

HAMLET

Thy state is the more gracious, for 'tis a vice to know him. He hath much land, and fertile: let a beast be lord of beasts, and his crib shall stand at the king's mess: 'tis a chough, but, as I say, spacious in the possession of dirt.

OSRIC

Sweet lord, if your lordship were at leisure, I should impart a thing to you from his majesty.

HAMLET

I will receive it, sir, with all diligence of spirit. Put your bonnet to his right use; 'tis for the head.

OSRIC

I thank your lordship, it is very hot.

HAMLET

No, believe me, 'tis very cold; the wind is northerly.

OSRIC

It is indifferent cold, my lord, indeed.

HAMLET

But yet methinks it is very sultry and hot, or my complexion—

OSRIC

Exceedingly, my lord; it is very sultry, as 'twere, —I cannot tell how. But, my lord, his majesty bade me signify to you that he has laid a great wager on your head: sir, this is the matter—

HAMLET

I beseech you, remember—

[HAMLET *moves him to put on his hat*

OSRIC

Nay, good my lord; for mine ease, in good faith. Sir, here is newly come to court Laertes; believe me, an absolute gentleman, full of most excellent differences, of very soft society and great showing: indeed, to speak feelingly of him, he is the card or calendar of gentry, for you shall find in him the continent of what part a gentleman would see.

HAMLET

Sir, his definement suffers no perdition in you; though, I know, to divide him inventorially would dizzy the arithmetic of memory, and yet but yaw neither, in respect of his quick sail. But in the verity of extolment, I take him to be a soul of great article, and his infusion of such dearth and rareness, as, to make true diction of him, his semblable is his mirror, and who else would trace him, his umbrage, nothing more.

OSRIC

Your lordship speaks most infallibly of him.

HAMLET

The concernancy, sir? why do we wrap the gentleman in our more rawer breath?

OSRIC

Sir?

HORATIO

Is 't not possible to understand in another tongue? You will do 't, sir, really.

HAMLET

What imports the nomination of this gentleman?

OSRIC

Of Laertes?

HORATIO

His purse is empty already; all's golden words are spent.

HAMLET

Of him, sir.

OSRIC

I know you are not ignorant—

HAMLET

I would you did, sir; yet, in faith, if you did, it would not much approve me. Well, sir?

OSRIC

You are not ignorant of what excellence Laertes is—

HAMLET

I dare not confess that, lest I should compare with him in excellence; but, to know a man well, were to know himself.

OSRIC

I mean, sir, for his weapon; but in the imputation laid on him by them, in his meed he's unfellowed.

HAMLET

What's his weapon?

OSRIC

Rapier and dagger.

HAMLET

That's two of his weapons: but, well.

OSRIC

The king, sir, hath wagered with him six Barbary horses: against the which he has imponed, as I take it, six French rapiers and poniards, with their assigns, as girdle, hanger, and so: three of the carriages, in faith, are very dear to fancy, very responsive to the hilts, most delicate carriages, and of very liberal conceit.

HAMLET

What call you the carriages?

HORATIO

I knew you must be edified by the margent ere you had done.

OSRIC

The carriages, sir, are the hangers.

HAMLET

The phrase would be more germane to the matter if we could carry a cannon by our sides: I would it might be hangers till then. But, on: six Barbary horses against six French swords, their assigns, and three liberal-conceited carriages; that's the French bet against the Danish. Why is this 'imponed,' as you call it?

OSRIC

The king, sir, hath laid, sir, that in a dozen passes between yourself and him, he shall not exceed you three hits: he hath laid on twelve for nine; and it would come to immediate trial, if your lordship would vouchsafe the answer.

HAMLET
How if I answer 'no'?

OSRIC
I mean, my lord, the opposition of your person in trial.

HAMLET
Sir, I will walk here in the hall: if it please his majesty, it is the breathing time of day with me; let the foils be brought, the gentleman willing, and the king hold his purpose, I will win for him an I can; if not, I will gain nothing but my shame and the odd hits.

OSRIC
Shall I redeliver you e'en so?

HAMLET
To this effect, sir, after what flourish your nature will.

OSRIC
I commend my duty to your lordship.

HAMLET
Yours, yours. [Exit OSRIC] He does well to commend it himself; there are no tongues else for 's turn.

HORATIO
This lapwing runs away with the shell on his head.

HAMLET
He did comply with his dug before he sucked it. Thus has he—and many more of the same breed that I know the drossy age dotes on—only got the tune of the time and outward habit of encounter; a kind of yesty collection, which carries them through and through the most fond and winnowed opinions; and do but blow them to their trial, the bubbles are out.

Enter a LORD

LORD
My lord, his majesty commended him to you by young Osric, who brings back to him, that you attend him in the hall: he sends to know if your pleasure hold to play with Laertes, or that you will take longer time.

HAMLET
I am constant to my purposes; they follow the king's pleasure: if his fitness speaks, mine is ready; now or whensoever, provided I be so able as now.

LORD
The king and queen and all are coming down.

HAMLET
In happy time.

LORD
The queen desires you to use some gentle entertainment to Laertes before you fall to play.

HAMLET
She well instructs me.　　　　　　　[Exit LORD

HORATIO
You will lose this wager, my lord.

HAMLET
I do not think so; since he went into France, I have been in continual practice; I shall win at the odds. But thou wouldst not think how ill all's here about my heart: but it is no matter.

HORATIO
Nay, good my lord,—

HAMLET
It is but foolery; but it is such a kind of gain-giving as would perhaps trouble a woman.

HORATIO
If your mind dislike any thing, obey it. I will forestal their repair hither, and say you are not fit.

HAMLET
Not a whit; we defy augury: there is special providence in the fall of a sparrow. If it be now, 'tis not to come; if it be not to come, it will be now; if it be not now, yet it will come: the readiness is all; since no man has aught of what he leaves, what is 't to leave betimes? Let be.

Enter KING, QUEEN, LAERTES, and LORDS, OSRIC and other ATTENDANTS with foils and gauntlets; a table and flagons of wine on it

KING
Come, Hamlet, come, and take this hand from me.
　　　[The KING puts LAERTES' hand into HAMLET'S

HAMLET
Give me your pardon, sir: I've done you wrong;
But pardon 't, as you are a gentleman.
This presence knows,
And you must needs have heard, how I am punish'd
With sore distraction. What I have done,
That might your nature, honour and exception
Roughly awake, I here proclaim was madness.
Was 't Hamlet wrong'd Laertes? Never Hamlet:
If Hamlet from himself be ta'en away,
And when he's not himself does wrong Laertes,
Then Hamlet does it not, Hamlet denies it.
Who does it then? His madness: if 't be so,
Hamlet is of the faction that is wrong'd;
His madness is poor Hamlet's enemy.
Sir, in this audience,
Let my disclaiming from a purposed evil
Free me so far in your most generous thoughts,
That I have shot mine arrow o'er the house,
And hurt my brother.

LAERTES
　　　　　I am satisfied in nature,
Whose motive, in this case, should stir me most
To my revenge: but in my terms of honour
I stand aloof, and will no reconcilement,
Till by some elder masters of known honour
I have a voice and precedent of peace,
To keep my name ungored. But till that time
I do receive your offer'd love like love
And will not wrong it.

HAMLET
　　　　　　I embrace it freely,
And will this brother's wager frankly play.
Give us the foils. Come on.

LAERTES

Come, one for me.

HAMLET

I'll be your foil, Laertes: in mine ignorance
Your skill shall, like a star i' the darkest night,
Stick fiery off indeed.

LAERTES

You mock me, sir.

HAMLET

No, by this hand.

KING

Give them the foils, young Osric. Cousin Hamlet,
You know the wager?

HAMLET

Very well, my lord;
Your grace has laid the odds o' the weaker side.

KING

I do not fear it; I have seen you both:
But since he is better'd, we have therefore odds.

LAERTES

This is too heavy; let me see another.

HAMLET

This likes me well. These foils have all a length?
[They prepare to play

OSRIC

Ay, my good lord.

KING

Set me the stoups of wine upon that table.
If Hamlet give the first or second hit,
Or quit in answer of the third exchange,
Let all the battlements their ordnance fire;
The king shall drink to Hamlet's better breath;
And in the cup an union shall he throw,
Richer than that which four successive kings
In Denmark's crown have worn. Give me the cups;
And let the kettle to the trumpet speak,
The trumpet to the cannoneer without,
The cannons to the heavens, the heaven to earth,
'Now the king drinks to Hamlet.' Come, begin;
And you, the judges, bear a wary eye.

HAMLET

Come on, sir.

LAERTES

Come, my lord. [They play

HAMLET

One.

LAERTES

No.

HAMLET

Judgement.

OSRIC

A hit, a very palpable hit.

LAERTES

Well; again.

KING

Stay; give me drink. Hamlet, this pearl is thine;
Here's to thy health.
[Trumpets sound, and cannon shot off within
Give him the cup.

HAMLET

I'll play this bout first; set it by a while.
Come. [They play] Another hit; what say you?

LAERTES

A touch, a touch, I do confess.

KING

Our son shall win.

QUEEN

He's fat and scant of breath.
Here, Hamlet, take my napkin, rub thy brows:
The queen carouses to thy fortune, Hamlet.

HAMLET

Good madam!

KING

Gertrude, do not drink.

QUEEN

I will, my lord; I pray you, pardon me.

KING

[Aside] It is the poison'd cup; it is too late.

HAMLET

I dare not drink yet, madam; by and by.

QUEEN

Come, let me wipe thy face.

LAERTES

My lord, I'll hit him now.

KING

I do not think 't.

LAERTES

[Aside] And yet it is almost against my conscience.

HAMLET

Come, for the third, Laertes: you but dally;
I pray you, pass with your best violence;
I am afeard you make a wanton of me.

LAERTES

Say you so? come on. [They play

OSRIC

Nothing, neither way.

LAERTES

Have at you now!
[LAERTES wounds HAMLET; then, in scuffling, they change
rapiers, and HAMLET wounds LAERTES

KING

Part them; they are incensed.

HAMLET

Nay, come, again. [The QUEEN falls

OSRIC

Look to the queen there, ho!

HORATIO

They bleed on both sides. How is it, my lord?

OSRIC

How is 't, Laertes?

LAERTES

Why, as a woodcock to mine own springe, Osric;
I am justly kill'd with mine own treachery.

HAMLET

How does the queen?

KING

She swounds to see them bleed.

QUEEN

No, no, the drink, the drink,—O my dear Hamlet,—
The drink, the drink! I am poison'd.　　　　[Dies

HAMLET

O villany! Ho! let the door be lock'd:
Treachery! seek it out.　　　　[LAERTES falls

LAERTES

It is here, Hamlet: Hamlet, thou art slain;
No medicine in the world can do thee good,
In thee there is not half an hour of life;
The treacherous instrument is in thy hand,
Unbated and envenom'd: the foul practice
Hath turn'd itself on me; lo, here I lie,
Never to rise again: thy mother's poison'd:
I can no more: the king, the king's to blame.

HAMLET

The point envenom'd too!
Then, venom, to thy work.　　　　[Stabs the KING

ALL

Treason! treason!

KING

O, yet defend me, friends; I am but hurt.

HAMLET

Here, thou incestuous, murderous, damned Dane,
Drink off this potion: is thy union here?
Follow my mother.　　　　[KING dies

LAERTES

He is justly served;
It is a poison temper'd by himself.
Exchange forgiveness with me, noble Hamlet:
Mine and my father's death come not upon thee,
Nor thine on me!　　　　[Dies

HAMLET

Heaven make thee free of it! I follow thee.
I am dead, Horatio. Wretched queen, adieu!
You that look pale and tremble at this chance,
That are but mutes or audience to this act,
Had I but time—as this fell sergeant, death,
Is strict in his arrest—O, I could tell you—
But let it be. Horatio, I am dead;
Thou livest; report me and my cause aright
To the unsatisfied.

HORATIO

Never believe it:
I am more an antique Roman than a Dane:
Here's yet some liquor left.

HAMLET

As thou 'rt a man,
Give me the cup: let go; by heaven, I'll have 't.
O good Horatio, what a wounded name,
Things standing thus unknown, shall live behind
me!
If thou didst ever hold me in thy heart,
Absent thee from felicity a while,
And in this harsh world draw thy breath in pain,
To tell my story.　　　　[March afar off, and shot within
What warlike noise is this?

OSRIC

Young Fortinbras, with conquest come from Poland,
To the ambassadors of England gives
This warlike volley.

HAMLET

O, I die, Horatio;
The potent poison quite o'er-crows my spirit:
I cannot live to hear the news from England;
But I do prophesy the election lights
On Fortinbras: he has my dying voice;
So tell him, with the occurrents, more and less,
Which have solicited. The rest is silence.　　　　[Dies

HORATIO

Now cracks a noble heart. Good night, sweet prince,
And flights of angels sing thee to thy rest!
　　　　[March within
Why does the drum come hither?
Enter FORTINBRAS, and the ENGLISH AMBASSADORS, with
drum, colours, and ATTENDANTS

FORTINBRAS

Where is this sight?

HORATIO

What is it you would see?
If aught of woe or wonder, cease your search.

FORTINBRAS

This quarry cries on havoc. O proud death,
What feast is toward in thine eternal cell,
That thou so many princes at a shot
So bloodily hast struck?

FIRST AMBASSADOR

The sight is dismal;
And our affairs from England come too late:
The ears are senseless that should give us hearing,
To tell him his commandment is fulfill'd,
That Rosencrantz and Guildenstern are dead:
Where should we have our thanks?

HORATIO

Not from his mouth
Had it the ability of life to thank you:
He never gave commandment for their death.
But since, so jump upon this bloody question,
You from the Polack wars, and you from England,
Are here arrived, give order that these bodies
High on a stage be placed to the view;
And let me speak to the yet unknowing world
How these things came about: so shall you hear
Of carnal, bloody and unnatural acts,
Of accidental judgements, casual slaughters,
Of deaths put on by cunning and forced cause,
And, in this upshot, purposes mistook
Fall'n on the inventors' heads: all this can I
Truly deliver.

FORTINBRAS

Let us haste to hear it,
And call the noblest to the audience.
For me, with sorrow I embrace my fortune:
I have some rights of memory in this kingdom,
Which now to claim my vantage doth invite me.

HORATIO

Of that I shall have also cause to speak,

And from his mouth whose voice will draw on
    more:
But let this same be presently perform'd,
Even while men's minds are wild; lest more mis-
    chance
On plots and errors happen.
             FORTINBRAS
                Let four captains
Bear Hamlet, like a soldier, to the stage;

For he was likely, had he been put on,
To have proved most royally: and, for his passage,
The soldiers' music and the rites of war
Speak loudly for him.
Take up the bodies: such a sight as this
Becomes the field, but here shows much amiss.
Go, bid the soldiers shoot.
[*A dead march. Exeunt, bearing off the bodies: after which*
                    a peal of ordnance is shot off

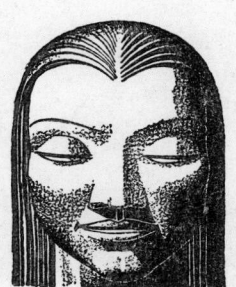

THE MERRY WIVES OF WINDSOR

SYNOPSIS

Sir John Falstaff and his thieving followers, Bardolph, Nym and Pistol, have been poaching in the vicinity of Windsor, and three good citizens, Justice Shallow, his cousin Slender, and Sir Hugh Evans, a Welsh parson, call at Master Page's house when Sir John happens to be there to make a vigorous protest against these actions, but Page persuades them to forget all unkindnesses in a neighborly bowl of wine and some hot venison pie.

This social gathering gives Falstaff an opportunity to meet Mistress Page and her friend Mistress Ford, and the fat rogue thinks he has made a great impression on both of these spirited, buxom ladies. He then hears that each has control of her husband's purse and being very low in funds, he plans to woo the smitten dames to his own financial profit. Writing love-letters in duplicate, he orders Pistol and Nym to deliver them to the Mistresses Page and Ford, and when they refuse to be go-betweens in such business he discharges them and sends the letters by his little page Robin.

Pistol and Nym revenge themselves by informing the two husbands of Falstaff's intentions. The bluff, kindly Page declares his perfect faith in his wife, but Ford's suspicious nature leads him to remark that a man can be over-confident, and, disguised as Master Brook, he sends Falstaff a sack of wine and then visits him to sound him out, telling him that he is in love with Mistress Ford and asking his aid as a go-between. Falstaff roughly admits that he is after Ford's gold, and will be glad to help Brook win the wife.

When the two ladies read and compare Falstaff's letters, they are convulsed with laughter, but resentful of the knight's impudence they determine to be thoroughly revenged. With the help of the artful Dame Quickly, they send him appreciative, encouraging messages and it is arranged for Falstaff to visit Mistress Ford one day between ten and eleven when her husband will be away from his home, whereas Mistress Page, through the same medium, asks to have Robin, the little page, sent to her to carry messages between them.

In the meantime, three suitors are pressing for Anne Page's hand. The cocksure Slender, tongue-tied and bashful in Anne's presence, is supported by Shallow and Sir Hugh, the parson, and is Master Page's choice; Dr. Caius, a French doctor who dreadfully abuses the King's English, is Mistress Page's selection; while Fenton, a gentleman of charming manner, is the man Anne loves. Each lover confides in Dame Quickly, and through her gossip and love letters are exchanged and delivered.

When Falstaff keeps his engagement with Mistress Ford, he makes good progress with his lovemaking until it is cut short by the entrance of Mistress Page with the disconcerting news that Ford is on his way to the house with officers of the law. Falstaff, who had quickly hidden himself, now reappears to find a means of escape, and with Robin's help the women get him into a large clothes hamper, and, piling the dirty linen on top of him, send the servants to dump him in the river where the clothes are to be washed. Ford's vain search of his house makes his jealousy seem ridiculous, but Falstaff, when telling him what has happened, bids him keep up hope because another tryst with Mistress Ford has been arranged by Dame Quickly. This time Ford again surprises them, and frantically searches the clothes hamper, but Falstaff flees in the dress of the aunt of Mistress Ford's maid, the fat woman of Brainford, whom Ford calls an evil witch and beats unmercifully on her way out of the house.

The two ladies now tell their husbands the whole story of the plot to humiliate Falstaff, and everyone joins in his final undoing. Dame Quickly beguiles him into meeting the merry wives at night in Windsor Park, disguised as Herne, the hunter, and wearing a buck's head. The ladies meet him with words of endearment, then suddenly depart, leaving him to the mercy of a band of satyrs, hobgoblins and fairies in green and white, led by Anne Page as the Fairy Queen, who pinch the knight and burn him with their tapers as they dance around him.

This is also the night when the elopement plans of each of Anne Page's three suitors are to materialize. Her father commands her to wear a white dress and elope with Slender, while her mother orders her to wear green and run off with Dr. Caius, and the girl consents to each parent. But while the fairies dance around the prostrate Falstaff, Slender seizes and runs off with a fairy in white who gives him the correct password, and the doctor carries away a fairy in green, both finding later to their utter dismay that they have eloped with clumsy boys. In the midst of their rollicking fun when Ford, Page and their wives reveal the jest to Falstaff, the indignant lovers appear with their stories of frustration, followed by Anne Page herself and Fenton who had slipped away during the dance, and with the good help of Mine Host of the Garter Inn had been married by the vicar. Cordial feelings are restored all around, and Falstaff goes home with the Pages to dinner.

HISTORICAL DATA

A tradition, first recorded by John Dennis in 1702, represents this comedy as having been written in a fortnight at the request of Queen Elizabeth, who professed a desire to see Falstaff in love. This theory is in part substantiated by the choice of Windsor as the scene of action, the complimentary references to the Court, and the abundance of prose which would suggest a hasty composition.

It appears undoubtedly to have followed *Henry IV* and, perhaps, *Henry V*, although there is dispute on the latter point. In any event, it was entered on the Stationers' Register in January 1602, and was probably written in 1599 or 1600.

The source of the play roots from *Le Tredici Piacevoli Notte* by Straparola, which was available to Shakespeare in an English version entitled *The Tale of the Two Lovers of Pisa* in Tarlton's *Newes out of Purgatorie* (1590). It is of particular interest in that it is virtually the only play of Shakespeare's in which attention is given to the portrayal of middle-class life in the English country.

"He's too big to go in there. What shall I do?"
THE MERRY WIVES OF WINDSOR

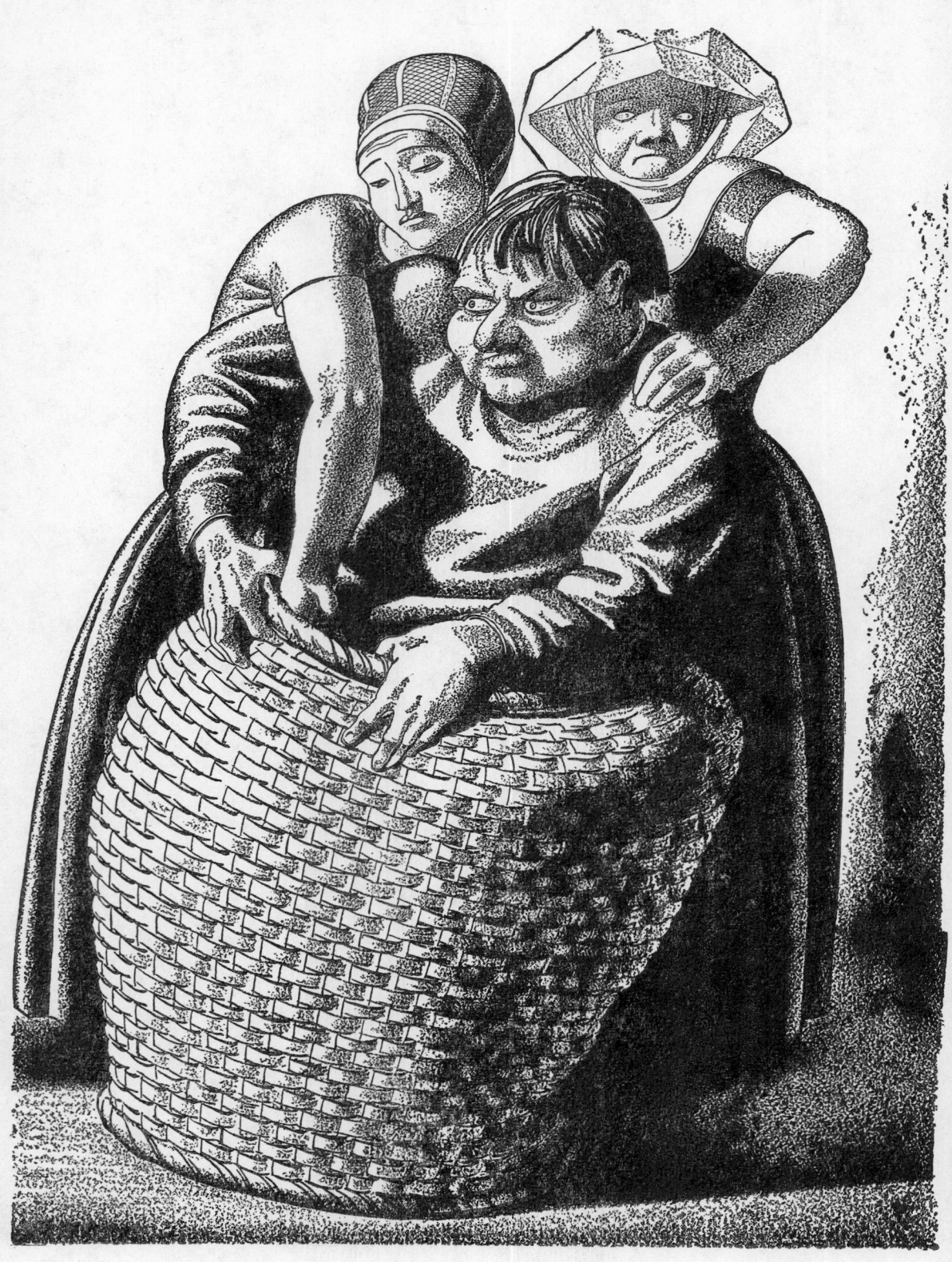

THE MERRY WIVES OF WINDSOR

DRAMATIS PERSONÆ

SIR JOHN FALSTAFF.
FENTON, *a gentleman.*
SHALLOW, *a country justice.*
SLENDER, *cousin to Shallow.*
FORD,⎱ *two gentlemen dwelling at Windsor.*
PAGE,⎰
WILLIAM PAGE, *a boy, son to Page.*
SIR HUGH EVANS, *a Welsh parson.*
DOCTOR CAIUS, *a French physician.*
HOST *of the Garter Inn.*
BARDOLPH,⎱
PISTOL, ⎰ *sharpers attending on Falstaff.*
NYM,

ROBIN, *page to Falstaff.*
SIMPLE, *servant to Slender.*
RUGBY, *servant to Doctor Caius.*

MISTRESS FORD.
MISTRESS PAGE.
ANNE PAGE, *her daughter.*
MISTRESS QUICKLY, *servant to Doctor Caius.*

SERVANTS *to Page, Ford, &c.*

SCENE—*Windsor, and the neighbourhood.*

ACT I

SCENE I. *Windsor. Before* PAGE'S *house*

Enter JUSTICE SHALLOW, SLENDER, *and* SIR HUGH EVANS

SHALLOW

SIR HUGH, persuade me not; I will make a Star-chamber matter of it: if he were twenty Sir John Falstaffs, he shall not abuse Robert Shallow, esquire.

SLENDER

In the county of Gloucester, justice of peace and 'Coram.'

SHALLOW

Ay, cousin Slender, and 'Custalorum.'

SLENDER

Ay, and 'Rato-lorum' too; and a gentleman born, master parson; who writes himself 'Armigero,' in any bill, warrant, quittance, or obligation, 'Armi-gero.'

SHALLOW

Ay, that I do; and have done any time these three hundred years.

SLENDER

All his successors gone before him hath done't; and all his ancestors that come after him may: they may give the dozen white luces in their coat.

SHALLOW

It is an old coat.

SIR HUGH EVANS

The dozen white louses do become an old coat well; it agrees well, passant; it is a familiar beast to man, and signifies love.

SHALLOW

The luce is the fresh fish; the salt fish is an old coat.

SLENDER

I may quarter, coz.

SHALLOW

You may, by marrying.

SIR HUGH EVANS

It is marring indeed, if he quarter it.

SHALLOW

Not a whit.

SIR HUGH EVANS

Yes, py'r lady; if he has a quarter of your coat, there is but three skirts for yourself, in my simple conjectures: but that is all one. If Sir John Falstaff have committed disparagements unto you, I am of the church, and will be glad to do my benevolence to make atonements and comprimises between you.

SHALLOW

The council shall hear it; it is a riot.

SIR HUGH EVANS

It is not meet the council hear a riot; there is no fear of Got in a riot: the council, look you, shall desire to hear the fear of Got, and not to hear a riot; take your vizaments in that.

SHALLOW

Ha! o' my life, if I were young again, the sword should end it.

SIR HUGH EVANS

It is petter that friends is the sword, and end it: and there is also another device in my prain, which per-adventure prings goot discretions with it:—there is Anne Page, which is daughter to Master Thomas Page, which is pretty virginity.

SLENDER

Mistress Anne Page? She has brown hair, and speaks small like a woman.

SIR HUGH EVANS

It is that fery person for all the orld, as just as you will desire; and seven hundred pounds of moneys, and gold and silver, is her grandsire upon his death's-bed (Got deliver to a joyful resurrections!) give, when she is able to overtake seventeen years old: it were a goot motion if we leave our pribbles and prabbles, and desire a marriage between Master Abraham and Mistress Anne Page.

SLENDER

Did her grandsire leave her seven hundred pound?

SIR HUGH EVANS

Ay, and her father is make her a petter penny.

SLENDER

I know the young gentlewoman; she has good gifts.

SIR HUGH EVANS

Seven hundred pounds and possibilities is goot gifts.

SHALLOW

Well, let us see honest Master Page. Is Falstaff there?

SIR HUGH EVANS

Shall I tell you a lie? I do despise a liar as I do despise one that is false, or as I despise one that is not true. The knight, Sir John, is there; and, I beseech you, be ruled by your well-willers. I will peat the door for Master Page. [Knocks] What, hoa! Got pless your house here!

PAGE

[Within] Who's there?

Enter PAGE

SIR HUGH EVANS

Here is Got's plessing, and your friend, and Justice Shallow; and here young Master Slender, that peradventures shall tell you another tale, if matters grow to your likings.

PAGE

I am glad to see your worships well. I thank you for my venison, Master Shallow.

SHALLOW

Master Page, I am glad to see you: much good do it your good heart! I wished your venison better; it was ill killed. How doth good Mistress Page?—and I thank you always with my heart, la! with my heart.

PAGE

Sir, I thank you.

SHALLOW

Sir, I thank you; by yea and no, I do.

PAGE

I am glad to see you, good Master Slender.

SLENDER

How does your fallow greyhound, sir? I heard say he was outrun on Cotsall.

PAGE

It could not be judged, sir.

SLENDER

You'll not confess, you'll not confess.

SHALLOW

That he will not. 'Tis your fault, 'tis your fault; 'tis a good dog.

PAGE

A cur, sir.

SHALLOW

Sir, he's a good dog, and a fair dog: can there be more said? he is good and fair. Is Sir John Falstaff here?

PAGE

Sir, he is within; and I would I could do a good office between you.

SIR HUGH EVANS

It is spoke as a Christians ought to speak.

SHALLOW

He hath wronged me, Master Page.

PAGE

Sir, he doth in some sort confess it.

SHALLOW

If it be confessed, it is not redressed: is not that so, Master Page? He hath wronged me; indeed he hath; at a word, he hath, believe me: Robert Shallow, esquire, saith, he is wronged.

PAGE

Here comes Sir John.

Enter SIR JOHN FALSTAFF, BARDOLPH, NYM, and PISTOL

SIR JOHN FALSTAFF

Now, Master Shallow, you'll complain of me to the king?

SHALLOW

Knight, you have beaten my men, killed my deer, and broke open my lodge.

SIR JOHN FALSTAFF

But not kissed your keeper's daughter?

SHALLOW

Tut, a pin! this shall be answered.

SIR JOHN FALSTAFF

I will answer it straight; I have done all this. That is now answered.

SHALLOW

The council shall know this.

SIR JOHN FALSTAFF

'Twere better for you if it were known in counsel: you'll be laughed at.

SIR HUGH EVANS

Pauca verba, Sir John; goot worts.

SIR JOHN FALSTAFF

Good worts! good cabbage. Slender, I broke your head: what matter have you against me?

SLENDER

Marry, sir, I have matter in my head against you; and against your cony-catching rascals, Bardolph, Nym, and Pistol.

BARDOLPH

You Banbury cheese!

SLENDER

Ay, it is no matter.

PISTOL

How now, Mephostophilus!

SLENDER

Ay, it is no matter.

NYM

Slice, I say! pauca, pauca: slice! that's my humour.

SLENDER

Where's Simple, my man? Can you tell, cousin?

SIR HUGH EVANS

Peace, I pray you. Now let us understand. There is three umpires in this matter, as I understand; that is, Master Page, fidelicet Master Page; and there is myself, fidelicet myself; and the three party is, lastly and finally, mine host of the Garter.

PAGE

We three, to hear it and end it between them.

SIR HUGH EVANS

Fery goot: I will make a prief of it in my note-book;

and we will afterwards ork upon the cause with as great discreetly as we can.

SIR JOHN FALSTAFF

Pistol!

PISTOL

He hears with ears.

SIR HUGH EVANS

The tevil and his tam! what phrase is this, 'He hears with ear'? why, it is affectations.

SIR JOHN FALSTAFF

Pistol, did you pick Master Slender's purse?

SLENDER

Ay, by these gloves, did he, or I would I might never come in mine own great chamber again else, of seven groats in mill-sixpences, and two Edward shovel-boards, that cost me two shilling and two pence a-piece of Yead Miller, by these gloves.

SIR JOHN FALSTAFF

Is this true, Pistol?

SIR HUGH EVANS

No; it is false, if it is a pick-purse.

PISTOL

Ha, thou mountain-foreigner! Sir John and master mine,
I combat challenge of this latten bilbo.
Word of denial in thy labras here!
Word of denial: froth and scum, thou liest!

SLENDER

By these gloves, then, 'twas he.

NYM

Be advised, sir, and pass good humours: I will say 'marry trap' with you, if you run the nuthook's humour on me; that is the very note of it.

SLENDER

By this hat, then, he in the red face had it; for though I cannot remember what I did when you made me drunk, yet I am not altogether an ass.

SIR JOHN FALSTAFF

What say you, Scarlet and John?

BARDOLPH

Why, sir, for my part, I say the gentleman had drunk himself out of his five sentences.

SIR HUGH EVANS

It is his five senses: fie, what the ignorance is!

BARDOLPH

And being fap, sir, was, as they say, cashiered; and so conclusions passed the careires.

SLENDER

Ay, you spake in Latin then too; but 'tis no matter: I'll ne'er be drunk whilst I live again, but in honest, civil, godly company, for this trick: if I be drunk, I'll be drunk with those that have the fear of God, and not with drunken knaves.

SIR HUGH EVANS

So Got udge me, that is a virtuous mind.

SIR JOHN FALSTAFF

You hear all these matters denied, gentlemen; you hear it.

Enter ANNE PAGE, *with wine;* MISTRESS FORD *and* MISTRESS PAGE, *following*

PAGE

Nay, daughter, carry the wine in; we'll drink within.
[*Exit* ANNE PAGE

SLENDER

O heaven! this is Mistress Anne Page.

PAGE

How now, Mistress Ford!

SIR JOHN FALSTAFF

Mistress Ford, by my troth, you are very well met: by your leave, good mistress.　　[*Kisses her*

PAGE

Wife, bid these gentlemen welcome. Come, we have a hot venison pasty to dinner: come, gentlemen, I hope we shall drink down all unkindness.
[*Exeunt all except* SHALLOW, SLENDER, *and* EVANS

SLENDER

I had rather than forty shillings I had my Book of Songs and Sonnets here.

Enter SIMPLE

How now, Simple! where have you been? I must wait on myself, must I? You have not the Book of Riddles about you, have you?

SIMPLE

Book of Riddles! why, did you not lend it to Alice Shortcake upon All-hallowmass last, a fortnight afore Michaelmas?

SHALLOW

Come, coz; come, coz; we stay for you. A word with you, coz; marry, this, coz: there is, as 'twere, a tender, a kind of tender, made afar off by Sir Hugh here. Do you understand me?

SLENDER

Ay, sir, you shall find me reasonable; if it be so, I shall do that that is reason.

SHALLOW

Nay, but understand me.

SLENDER

So I do, sir.

SIR HUGH EVANS

Give ear to his motions, Master Slender: I will description the matter to you, if you be capacity of it.

SLENDER

Nay, I will do as my cousin Shallow says: I pray you, pardon me; he's a justice of peace in his country, simple though I stand here.

SIR HUGH EVANS

But that is not the question: the question is concerning your marriage.

SHALLOW

Ay, there's the point, sir.

SIR HUGH EVANS

Marry, is it; the very point of it; to Mistress Anne Page.

SLENDER

Why, if it be so, I will marry her upon any reasonable demands.

SIR HUGH EVANS

But can you affection the 'oman? Let us command

to know that of your mouth or of your lips; for divers philosophers hold that the lips is parcel of the mouth. Therefore, precisely, can you carry your good will to the maid?

SHALLOW

Cousin Abraham Slender, can you love her?

SLENDER

I hope, sir, I will do as it shall become one that would do reason.

SIR HUGH EVANS

Nay, Got's lords and his ladies! you must speak possitable, if you can carry her your desires towards her.

SHALLOW

That you must. Will you, upon good dowry, marry her?

SLENDER

I will do a greater thing than that, upon your request, cousin, in any reason.

SHALLOW

Nay, conceive me, conceive me, sweet coz: what I do is to pleasure you, coz. Can you love the maid?

SLENDER

I will marry her, sir, at your request: but if there be no great love in the beginning, yet heaven may decrease it upon better acquaintance, when we are married and have more occasion to know one another; I hope, upon familiarity will grow more contempt: but if you say, 'Marry her,' I will marry her; that I am freely dissolved, and dissolutely.

SIR HUGH EVANS

It is a fery discretion answer; save the fall is in the ort 'dissolutely:' the ort is, according to our meaning, 'resolutely:' his meaning is good.

SHALLOW

Ay, I think my cousin meant well.

SLENDER

Ay, or else I would I might be hanged, la!

SHALLOW

Here comes fair Mistress Anne.

Re-enter ANNE PAGE

Would I were young for your sake, Mistress Anne!

ANNE PAGE

The dinner is on the table; my father desires your worships' company.

SHALLOW

I will wait on him, fair Mistress Anne.

SIR HUGH EVANS

Od's plessed will! I will not be absence at the grace.

[*Exeunt* SHALLOW *and* EVANS

ANNE PAGE

Will't please your worship to come in, sir?

SLENDER

No, I thank you, forsooth, heartily; I am very well.

ANNE PAGE

The dinner attends you, sir.

SLENDER

I am not a-hungry, I thank you, forsooth. Go, sirrah, for all you are my man, go wait upon my cousin Shallow. [*Exit* SIMPLE] A justice of peace sometime

may be beholding to his friend for a man. I keep but three men and a boy yet, till my mother be dead: but what though? yet I live like a poor gentleman born.

ANNE PAGE

I may not go in without your worship: they will not sit till you come.

SLENDER

I' faith, I'll eat nothing; I thank you as much as though I did.

ANNE PAGE

I pray you, sir, walk in.

SLENDER

I had rather walk here, I thank you. I bruised my shin th' other day with playing at sword and dagger with a master of fence; three veneys for a dish of stewed prunes; and, by my troth, I cannot abide the smell of hot meat since. Why do your dogs bark so? be there bears i' the town?

ANNE PAGE

I think there are, sir; I heard them talked of.

SLENDER

I love the sport well; but I shall as soon quarrel at it as any man in England. You are afraid, if you see the bear loose, are you not?

ANNE PAGE

Ay, indeed, sir.

SLENDER

That's meat and drink to me, now. I have seen Sackerson loose twenty times, and have taken him by the chain; but, I warrant you, the women have so cried and shrieked at it, that it passed: but women, indeed, cannot abide 'em; they are very ill-favoured rough things.

Re-enter PAGE

PAGE

Come, gentle Master Slender, come; we stay for you.

SLENDER

I'll eat nothing, I thank you, sir.

PAGE

By cock and pie, you shall not choose, sir! come, come.

SLENDER

Nay, pray you, lead the way.

PAGE

Come on, sir.

SLENDER

Mistress Anne, yourself shall go first.

ANNE PAGE

Not I, sir; pray you, keep on.

SLENDER

Truly, I will not go first; truly, la! I will not do you that wrong.

ANNE PAGE

I pray you, sir.

SLENDER

I'll rather be unmannerly than troublesome. You do yourself wrong, indeed, la!   [*Exeunt*

SCENE II. *The same*

Enter SIR HUGH EVANS *and* SIMPLE

SIR HUGH EVANS

Go your ways, and ask of Doctor Caius' house which is the way: and there dwells one Mistress Quickly, which is in the manner of his nurse, or his dry nurse, or his cook, or his laundry, his washer, and his wringer.

SIMPLE

Well, sir.

SIR HUGH EVANS

Nay, it is petter yet. Give her this letter; for it is a 'oman that altogether's acquaintance with Mistress Anne Page: and the letter is, to desire and require her to solicit your master's desires to Mistress Anne Page. I pray you, be gone: I will make an end of my dinner; there's pippins and cheese to come.

[*Exeunt*

SCENE III. *A room in the Garter Inn*

Enter SIR JOHN FALSTAFF, HOST, BARDOLPH, NYM,
PISTOL, *and* ROBIN

SIR JOHN FALSTAFF

Mine host of the Garter!

HOST

What says my bully-rook? speak scholarly and wisely.

SIR JOHN FALSTAFF

Truly, mine host, I must turn away some of my followers.

HOST

Discard, bully Hercules; cashier: let them wag; trot, trot.

SIR JOHN FALSTAFF

I sit at ten pounds a week.

HOST

Thou'rt an emperor, Cæsar, Keisar, and Pheezar. I will entertain Bardolph; he shall draw, he shall tap: said I well, bully Hector?

SIR JOHN FALSTAFF

Do so, good mine host.

HOST

I have spoke; let him follow. [*To* BARDOLPH] Let me see thee froth and lime: I am at a word; follow.

[*Exit*

SIR JOHN FALSTAFF

Bardolph, follow him. A tapster is a good trade: an old cloak makes a new jerkin; a withered serving-man a fresh tapster. Go; adieu.

BARDOLPH

It is a life that I have desired: I will thrive.

PISTOL

O base Hungarian wight! wilt thou the spigot wield?

[*Exit* BARDOLPH

NYM

He was gotten in drink: is not the humour conceited?

SIR JOHN FALSTAFF

I am glad I am so acquit of this tinder-box: his

thefts were too open; his filching was like an unskilful singer; he kept not time.

NYM

The good humour is to steal at a minute's rest.

PISTOL

'Convey,' the wise it call. 'Steal!' foh! a fico for the phrase!

SIR JOHN FALSTAFF

Well, sirs, I am almost out at heels.

PISTOL

Why, then, let kibes ensue.

SIR JOHN FALSTAFF

There is no remedy; I must cony-catch; I must shift.

PISTOL

Young ravens must have food.

SIR JOHN FALSTAFF

Which of you know Ford of this town?

PISTOL

I ken the wight: he is of substance good.

SIR JOHN FALSTAFF

My honest lads, I will tell you what I am about.

PISTOL

Two yards, and more.

SIR JOHN FALSTAFF

No quips now, Pistol! Indeed, I am in the waist two yards about; but I am now about no waste; I am about thrift. Briefly, I do mean to make love to Ford's wife: I spy entertainment in her; she discourses, she carves, she gives the leer of invitation: I can construe the action of her familiar style; and the hardest voice of her behaviour, to be Englished rightly, is, 'I am Sir John Falstaff's.'

PISTOL

He hath studied her will, and translated her will, out of honesty into English.

NYM

The anchor is deep: will that humour pass?

SIR JOHN FALSTAFF

Now, the report goes she has all the rule of her husband's purse: he hath a legion of angels.

PISTOL

As many devils entertain; and 'To her, boy,' say I.

NYM

The humour rises; it is good: humour me the angels.

SIR JOHN FALSTAFF

I have writ me here a letter to her: and here another to Page's wife, who even now gave me good eyes too, examined my parts with most judicious œillades; sometimes the beam of her view gilded my foot, sometimes my portly belly.

PISTOL

Then did the sun on dunghill shine.

NYM

I thank thee for that humour.

SIR JOHN FALSTAFF

O, she did so course o'er my exteriors with such a greedy intention, that the appetite of her eye did seem to scorch me up like a burning-glass! Here's another letter to her: she bears the purse too; she is a region in Guiana, all gold and bounty. I will be cheaters to them both, and they shall be exchequers to me; they shall be my East and West Indies, and I will trade to them both. Go bear thou this letter to Mistress Page; and thou this to Mistress Ford: we will thrive, lads, we will thrive.

PISTOL

Shall I Sir Pandarus of Troy become,
And by my side wear steel? then, Lucifer take all!

NYM

I will run no base humour: here, take the humour-letter: I will keep the haviour of reputation.

SIR JOHN FALSTAFF

[To ROBIN] Hold, sirrah, bear you these letters tightly;
Sail like my pinnace to these golden shores.
Rogues, hence, avaunt! vanish like hailstones, go;
Trudge, plod away o' the hoof; seek shelter, pack!
Falstaff will learn the humour of the age,
French thrift, you rogues; myself and skirted page.
[Exeunt SIR JOHN FALSTAFF and ROBIN

PISTOL

Let vultures gripe thy guts! for gourd and fullam holds,
And high and low beguiles the rich and poor:
Tester I'll have in pouch when thou shalt lack,
Base Phrygian Turk!

NYM

I have operations which be humours of revenge.

PISTOL

Wilt thou revenge?

NYM

By welkin and her star!

PISTOL

With wit or steel?

NYM

With both the humours, I:
I will discuss the humour of this love to Page.

PISTOL

And I to Ford shall eke unfold
How Falstaff, varlet vile,
His dove will prove, his gold will hold,
And his soft couch defile.

NYM

My humour shall not cool: I will incense Page to deal with poison; I will possess him with yellowness, for the revolt of mine is dangerous: that is my true humour.

PISTOL

Thou art the Mars of malecontents: I second thee;
troop on.   [Exeunt

SCENE IV. A room in DOCTOR CAIUS's house

Enter MISTRESS QUICKLY, SIMPLE, and RUGBY

MISTRESS QUICKLY

What, John Rugby! I pray thee, go to the casement, and see if you can see my master, Master Doctor Caius, coming. If he do, i' faith, and find any body in the house, here will be an old abusing of God's patience and the king's English.

RUGBY

I'll go watch.

MISTRESS QUICKLY

Go; and we'll have a posset for 't soon at night, in faith, at the latter end of a sea-coal fire. [Exit RUGBY] An honest, willing, kind fellow, as ever servant shall come in house withal; and, I warrant you, no tell-tale nor no breed-bate: his worst fault is, that he is given to prayer; he is something peevish that way: but nobody but has his fault; but let that pass. Peter Simple, you say your name is?

SIMPLE

Ay, for fault of a better.

MISTRESS QUICKLY

And Master Slender's your master?

SIMPLE

Ay, forsooth.

MISTRESS QUICKLY

Does he not wear a great round beard, like a glover's paring-knife?

SIMPLE

No, forsooth: he hath but a little wee face, with a little yellow beard,—a Cain-coloured beard.

MISTRESS QUICKLY

A softly-sprighted man, is he not?

SIMPLE

Ay, forsooth: but he is as tall a man of his hands as any is between this and his head; he hath fought with a warrener.

MISTRESS QUICKLY

How say you?—O, I should remember him: does he not hold up his head, as it were, and strut in his gait?

SIMPLE

Yes, indeed, does he.

MISTRESS QUICKLY

Well, heaven send Anne Page no worse fortune! Tell Master Parson Evans I will do what I can for your master: Anne is a good girl, and I wish—

Re-enter RUGBY

RUGBY

Out, alas! here comes my master.

MISTRESS QUICKLY

We shall all be shent. Run in here, good young man; go into this closet: he will not stay long. [Shuts SIMPLE in the closet] What, John Rugby! John! what, John, I say! Go, John, go inquire for my master; I doubt he be not well, that he comes not home.

[Singing] And down, down, adown-a, &c.

Enter DOCTOR CAIUS

DOCTOR CAIUS

Vat is you sing? I do not like des toys. Pray you, go and vetch me in my closet un boitier vert,—a box, a green-a box: do intend vat I speak? a green-a box.

MISTRESS QUICKLY

Ay, forsooth; I'll fetch it you. [Aside] I am glad he went not in himself: if he had found the young man, he would have been horn-mad.

DOCTOR CAIUS

Fe, fe, fe, fe! ma foi, il fait fort chaud. Je m'en vais à la cour,—la grande affaire.

MISTRESS QUICKLY

Is it this, sir?

DOCTOR CAIUS

Oui; mette le au mon pocket: dépêche, quickly. Vere is dat knave Rugby?

MISTRESS QUICKLY

What, John Rugby! John!

RUGBY

Here, Sir!

DOCTOR CAIUS

You are John Rugby, and you **are Jack** Rugby. Come, take-a your rapier, and **come after my** heel to the court.

RUGBY

'Tis ready, sir, here in the porch.

DOCTOR CAIUS

By my trot, I tarry too long. Od's **me! Qu'ai-j'**oublié! dere is some simples in my closet, **dat I** vill not for the varld I shall leave behind.

MISTRESS QUICKLY

Ay me, he'll find the young man **there, and** be mad!

DOCTOR CAIUS

O diable, diable! vat is in my closet? **Villain! larron!** [*Pulling* SIMPLE *out*] Rugby, my rapier!

MISTRESS QUICKLY

Good master, be content.

DOCTOR CAIUS

Wherefore shall I be content-a?

MISTRESS QUICKLY

The young man is an honest man.

DOCTOR CAIUS

What shall de honest man do in my closet? dere is no honest man dat shall come in my closet.

MISTRESS QUICKLY

I beseech you, be not so phlegmatic. Hear the truth of it: he came of an errand to me from Parson Hugh.

DOCTOR CAIUS

Vell.

SIMPLE

Ay, forsooth; to desire her to—

MISTRESS QUICKLY

Peace, I pray you.

DOCTOR CAIUS

Peace-a your tongue. Speak-a your tale.

SIMPLE

To desire this honest gentlewoman, your maid, to speak a good word to Mistress Anne Page for my master in the way of marriage

MISTRESS QUICKLY

This is all, indeed, la! but I'll ne'er put my finger in the fire, and need not.

DOCTOR CAIUS

Sir Hugh send-a you? Rugby, baille me some paper. Tarry you a little-a while.   [*Writes*

MISTRESS QUICKLY

[*Aside to* SIMPLE] I am glad he is so quiet: if he had been throughly moved, you should have heard him so loud and so melancholy. But notwithstanding, man, I'll do you your master what good I can: and the very yea and the no is, the French doctor, my master,—I may call him my master, look you, for I keep his house; and I wash, wring, brew, bake, scour, dress meat and drink, make the beds, and do all myself,—

SIMPLE

[*Aside to* MISTRESS QUICKLY] 'Tis a great charge to come under one body's hand.

MISTRESS QUICKLY

[*Aside to* SIMPLE] Are you avised o' that? you shall find it a great charge: and to be up early and down late;—but notwithstanding,—to tell you in your ear; I would have no words of it,—my master himself is in love with Mistress Anne Page: but notwithstanding that, I know Anne's mind,—that's neither here nor there.

DOCTOR CAIUS

You jack'nape, give-a this letter to Sir Hugh; by gar, it is a shallenge: I will cut his troat in de park; and I will teach a scurvy jack-a-nape priest to meddle or make. You may be gone; it is not good you tarry here.—By gar, I will cut all his two stones; by gar, he shall not have a stone to throw at his dog.

[*Exit* SIMPLE

MISTRESS QUICKLY

Alas, he speaks but for his friend.

DOCTOR CAIUS

It is no matter-a ver dat:—do not you tell-a me dat I shall have Anne Page for myself?—By gar, I vill kill de Jack priest; and I have appointed mine host of de Jarteer to measure our weapon.—By gar, I will myself have Anne Page.

MISTRESS QUICKLY

Sir, the maid loves you, and all shall be well. We must give folks leave to prate: what, the good-jer!

DOCTOR CAIUS

Rugby, come to the court with me. By gar, if I have not Anne Page, I shall turn your head out of my door. Follow my heels, Rugby.

[*Exeunt* DOCTOR CAIUS *and* RUGBY

MISTRESS QUICKLY

You shall have An fool's-head of your own. No, I know Anne's mind for that: never a woman in Windsor knows more of Anne's mind than I do; nor can do more than I do with her, I thank heaven.

FENTON

[*Within*] Who's within there? ho!

MISTRESS QUICKLY

Who's there, I trow? Come near the house, I pray you.

Enter FENTON

FENTON

How now, good woman! how dost thou?

MISTRESS QUICKLY

The better that it pleases your good worship to ask.

FENTON

What news? how does pretty Mistress Anne?

MISTRESS QUICKLY

In truth, sir, and she is pretty, and honest, and gentle; and one that is your friend, I can tell you that by the way; I praise heaven for it.

FENTON

Shall I do any good, think'st thou? shall I not lose my suit?

MISTRESS QUICKLY

Troth, sir, all is in his hands above: but notwithstanding, Master Fenton, I'll be sworn on a book, she loves you. Have not your worship a wart above your eye?

FENTON

Yes, marry, have I; what of that?

MISTRESS QUICKLY

Well, thereby hangs a tale:—good faith, it is such another Nan; but, I detest, an honest maid as ever broke bread:—we had an hour's talk of that wart. —I shall never laugh but in that maid's company!— But, indeed, she is given too much to allicholy and musing: but for you—well, go to.

FENTON

Well, I shall see her to-day. Hold, there's money for thee; let me have thy voice in my behalf: if thou seest her before me, commend me.

MISTRESS QUICKLY

Will I? i' faith, that we will; and I will tell your worship more of the wart the next time we have confidence; and of other wooers.

FENTON

Well, farewell; I am in great haste now.

MISTRESS QUICKLY

Farewell to your worship. [*Exit* FENTON] Truly, an honest gentleman: but Anne loves him not; for I know Anne's mind as well as another does.—Out upon 't! what have I forgot?   [*Exit*

ACT II

SCENE I. *Before* PAGE's *house*

Enter MISTRESS PAGE, *with a letter*

MISTRESS PAGE

What, have I scaped love-letters in the holiday-time of my beauty, and am I now a subject for them? Let me see.   [*Reads*

'Ask me no reason why I love you; for though Love use Reason for his physician, he admits him not for his counsellor. You are not young, no more am I; go to, then, there's sympathy: you are merry, so am I; ha, ha! then there's more sympathy: you love sack, and so do I; would you desire better sympathy? Let it suffice thee, Mistress Page,—at the least, if the love of soldier can suffice,—that I love thee. I will not say, pity me,—'tis not a soldier-like phrase; but I say, love me. By me,

Thine own true knight,
By day or night,
Or any kind of light,
With all his might
For thee to fight,   JOHN FALSTAFF.'

What a Herod of Jewry is this! O wicked, wicked world! One that is well-nigh worn to pieces with age to show himself a young gallant! What an unweighed behaviour hath this Flemish drunkard picked—with the devil's name!—out of my conversation, that he dares in this manner assay me? Why, he hath not been thrice in my company! What should I say to him? I was then frugal of my mirth: Heaven forgive me! Why, I'll exhibit a bill in the parliament for the putting down of men. How shall I be revenged on him? for revenged I will be, as sure as his guts are made of puddings.

Enter MISTRESS FORD

MISTRESS FORD

Mistress Page! trust me, I was going to your house.

MISTRESS PAGE

And, trust me, I was coming to you. You look very ill.

MISTRESS FORD

Nay, I'll ne'er believe that; I have to show to the contrary.

MISTRESS PAGE

Faith, but you do, in my mind.

MISTRESS FORD

Well, I do, then; yet, I say, I could show you to the contrary. O Mistress Page, give me some counsel!

MISTRESS PAGE

What's the matter, woman?

MISTRESS FORD

O woman, if it were not for one trifling respect, I could come to such honour!

MISTRESS PAGE

Hang the trifle, woman! take the honour. What is it?—dispense with trifles;—what is it?

MISTRESS FORD

If I would but go to hell for an eternal moment or so, I could be knighted.

MISTRESS PAGE

What? thou liest! Sir Alice Ford! These knights will hack; and so thou shouldst not alter the article of thy gentry.

MISTRESS FORD

We burn daylight:—here, read, read; perceive how I might be knighted. I shall think the worse of fat men, as long as I have an eye to make difference of men's liking: and yet he would not swear; praised women's modesty; and gave such orderly and well-behaved reproof to all uncomeliness, that I would have sworn his disposition would have gone to the truth of his words; but they do no more adhere and keep place together than the Hundredth Psalm to the tune of 'Green Sleeves.' What tempest, I trow, threw this whale, with so many tuns of oil in his belly, ashore at Windsor? How shall I be revenged on him? I think the best way were to entertain him with hope, till the wicked fire of lust have melted him in his own grease. Did you ever hear the like?

MISTRESS PAGE

Letter for letter, but that the name of Page and Ford differs! To thy great comfort in this mystery of ill opinions, here's the twin-brother of thy letter: but let thine inherit first; for, I protest, mine never shall. I warrant he hath a thousand of these letters, writ with blank space for different names,—sure, more, —and these are of the second edition: he will print them, out of doubt; for he cares not what he puts into the press, when he would put us two. I had rather be a giantess, and lie under Mount Pelion. Well, I will find you twenty lascivious turtles ere one chaste man.

MISTRESS FORD

Why, this is the very same; the very hand, the very words. What doth he think of us?

MISTRESS PAGE

Nay, I know not: it makes me almost ready to wrangle with mine own honesty. I'll entertain myself like one that I am not acquainted withal; for, sure, unless he know some strain in me, that I know not myself, he would never have boarded me in this fury.

MISTRESS FORD

'Boarding,' call you it? I'll be sure to keep him above deck.

MISTRESS PAGE

So will I: if he come under my hatches, I'll never to sea again. Let's be revenged on him: let's appoint him a meeting; give him a show of comfort in his suit, and lead him on with a fine-baited delay, till he hath pawned his horses to mine host of the Garter.

MISTRESS FORD

Nay, I will consent to act any villany against him, that may not sully the chariness of our honesty. O, that my husband saw this letter! it would give eternal food to his jealousy.

MISTRESS PAGE

Why, look where he comes; and my good man too: he's as far from jealousy as I am from giving him cause; and that, I hope, is an unmeasurable distance.

MISTRESS FORD

You are the happier woman.

MISTRESS PAGE

Let's consult together against this greasy knight. Come hither.   [*They retire*
Enter FORD, *with* PISTOL, *and* PAGE, *with* NYM

FORD

Well, I hope it be not so.

PISTOL

Hope is a curtal dog in some affairs:
Sir John affects thy wife.

FORD

Why, sir, my wife is not young.

PISTOL

He wooes both high and low, both rich and poor,
Both young and old, one with another, Ford;
He loves the gallimaufry: Ford, perpend.

FORD

Love my wife!

PISTOL

With liver burning hot. Prevent, or go thou,

Like Sir Actæon he, with Ringwood at thy heels:
O, odious is the name!

FORD

What name, sir?

PISTOL

The horn, I say. Farewell.
Take heed; have open eye; for thieves do foot by night:
Take heed, ere summer comes, or cuckoo-birds do sing.
Away, Sir Corporal Nym!—
Believe it, Page; he speaks sense.   [*Exit*

FORD

[*Aside*] I will be patient; I will find out this.

NYM

[*To* PAGE] And this is true; I like not the humour of lying. He hath wronged me in some humours: I should have borne the humoured letter to her; but I have a sword, and it shall bite upon my necessity. He loves your wife; there's the short and the long. My name is Corporal Nym; I speak, and I avouch; 'tis true: my name is Nym, and Falstaff loves your wife. Adieu. I love not the humour of bread and cheese; and there's the humour of it. Adieu.   [*Exit*

PAGE

'The humour of it,' quoth 'a! here's a fellow frights English out of his wits.

FORD

I will seek out Falstaff.

PAGE

I never heard such a drawling, affecting rogue.

FORD

If I do find it:—well.

PAGE

I will not believe such a Cataian, though the priest o' the town commended him for a true man.

FORD

'Twas a good sensible fellow:—well.

PAGE

How now, Meg!
      [MISTRESS PAGE *and* MISTRESS FORD *come forward*

MISTRESS PAGE

Whither go you, George? Hark you.

MISTRESS FORD

How now, sweet Frank! why art thou melancholy?

FORD

I melancholy! I am not melancholy. Get you home, go.

MISTRESS FORD

Faith, thou hast some crotchets in thy head. Now, will you go, Mistress Page?

MISTRESS PAGE

Have with you. You'll come to dinner, George? [*Aside to* MISTRESS FORD] Look who comes yonder: she shall be our messenger to this paltry knight.

MISTRESS FORD

[*Aside to* MISTRESS PAGE] Trust me, I thought on her: she'll fit it.

Enter MISTRESS QUICKLY

MISTRESS PAGE

You are come to see my daughter Anne?

MISTRESS QUICKLY

Ay, forsooth; and, I pray, how does good Mistress Anne?

MISTRESS PAGE

Go in with us and see: we have an hour's talk with you. [*Exeunt* MISTRESS PAGE, MISTRESS FORD, *and* MISTRESS QUICKLY

PAGE

How now, Master Ford!

FORD

You heard what this knave told me, did you not?

PAGE

Yes: and you heard what the other told me?

FORD

Do you think there is truth in them?

PAGE

Hang 'em, slaves! I do not think the knight would offer it: but these that accuse him in his intent towards our wives are a yoke of his discarded men; very rogues, now they be out of service.

FORD

Were they his men?

PAGE

Marry, were they.

FORD

I like it never the better for that. Does he lie at the Garter?

PAGE

Ay, marry, does he. If he should intend this voyage toward my wife, I would turn her loose to him; and what he gets more of her than sharp words, let it lie on my head.

FORD

I do not misdoubt my wife; but I would be loath to turn them together. A man may be too confident: I would have nothing lie on my head: I cannot be thus satisfied.

PAGE

Look where my ranting host of the Garter comes: there is either liquor in his pate, or money in his purse, when he looks so merrily.

Enter HOST

How now, mine host!

HOST

How now, bully-rook! thou'rt a gentleman. Cavaleiro-justice, I say!

Enter SHALLOW

SHALLOW

I follow, mine host, I follow. Good even and twenty, good Master Page! Master Page, will you go with us? we have sport in hand.

HOST

Tell him, cavaleiro-justice; tell him, bully-rook.

SHALLOW

Sir, there is a fray to be fought between Sir Hugh the Welsh priest and Caius the French doctor.

FORD

Good mine host o' the Garter, a word with you. [*Drawing him aside*

HOST

What say'st thou, my bully-rook?

SHALLOW

[*To* PAGE] Will you go with us to behold it? My merry host hath had the measuring of their weapons; and, I think, hath appointed them contrary places; for, believe me, I hear the parson is no jester. Hark, I will tell you what our sport shall be. [*They converse apart*

HOST

Hast thou no suit against my knight, my guest-cavaleire?

FORD

None, I protest: but I'll give you a pottle of burnt sack to give me recourse to him, and tell him my name is Brook; only for a jest.

HOST

My hand, bully; thou shalt have egress and regress; —said I well?—and thy name shall be Brook. It is a merry knight. Will you go, An-haires?

SHALLOW

Have with you, mine host.

PAGE

I have heard the Frenchman hath good skill in his rapier.

SHALLOW

Tut, sir, I could have told you more. In these times you stand on distance, your passes, stoccadoes, and I know not what: 'tis the heart, Master Page; 'tis here, 'tis here. I have seen the time, with my long sword I would have made you four tall fellows skip like rats.

HOST

Here, boys, here, here! shall we wag?

PAGE

Have with you. I had rather hear them scold than fight. [*Exeunt* HOST, SHALLOW, *and* PAGE

FORD

Though Page be a secure fool, and stands so firmly on his wife's frailty, yet I cannot put off my opinion so easily: she was in his company at Page's house; and what they made there, I know not. Well, I will look further into't: and I have a disguise to sound Falstaff. If I find her honest, I lose not my labour; if she be otherwise, 'tis labour well bestowed. [*Exit*

SCENE II. *A room in the Garter Inn*

Enter SIR JOHN FALSTAFF *and* PISTOL

SIR JOHN FALSTAFF

I will not lend thee a penny.

PISTOL

Why, then the world's mine oyster,
Which I with sword will open.

SIR JOHN FALSTAFF

Not a penny. I have been content, sir, you should

lay my countenance to pawn: I have grated upon my good friends for three reprieves for you and your coach-fellow Nym; or else you had looked through the grate, like a geminy of baboons. I am damned in hell for swearing to gentlemen my friends, you were good soldiers and tall fellows; and when Mistress Bridget lost the handle of her fan, I took't upon mine honour thou hadst it not.

PISTOL

Didst not thou share? hadst thou not fifteen pence?

SIR JOHN FALSTAFF

Reason, you rogue, reason: think'st thou I'll endanger my soul gratis? At a word, hang no more about me, I am no gibbet for you. Go. A short knife and a throng!—To your manor of Pickt-hatch! Go. You'll not bear a letter for me, you rogue! you stand upon your honour! Why, thou unconfinable baseness, it is as much as I can do to keep the terms of my honour precise: I, I, I myself sometimes, leaving the fear of God on the left hand, and hiding mine honour in my necessity, am fain to shuffle, to hedge, and to lurch; and yet you, rogue, will ensconce your rags, your cat-a-mountain looks, your red-lattice phrases, and your bold-beating oaths, under the shelter of your honour! You will not do it, you!

PISTOL

I do relent: what would thou more of man?

Enter ROBIN

ROBIN

Sir, here's a woman would speak with you.

SIR JOHN FALSTAFF

Let her approach.

Enter MISTRESS QUICKLY

MISTRESS QUICKLY

Give your worship good morrow.

SIR JOHN FALSTAFF

Good morrow, good wife.

MISTRESS QUICKLY

Not so, an't please your worship.

SIR JOHN FALSTAFF

Good maid, then.

MISTRESS QUICKLY

I'll be sworn;
As my mother was, the first hour I was born.

SIR JOHN FALSTAFF

I do believe the swearer. What with me?

MISTRESS QUICKLY

Shall I vouchsafe your worship a word or two?

SIR JOHN FALSTAFF

Two thousand, fair woman: and I'll vouchsafe thee the hearing.

MISTRESS QUICKLY

There is one Mistress Ford, sir:—I pray, come a little nearer this ways:—I myself dwell with Master Doctor Caius,—

SIR JOHN FALSTAFF

Well, on: Mistress Ford, you say,—

MISTRESS QUICKLY

Your worship says very true:—I pray your worship, come a little nearer this ways.

SIR JOHN FALSTAFF

I warrant thee, nobody hears;—mine own people, mine own people.

MISTRESS QUICKLY

Are they so? God bless them, and make them his servants!

SIR JOHN FALSTAFF

Well, Mistress Ford;—what of her?

MISTRESS QUICKLY

Why, sir, she's a good creature.—Lord, Lord! your worship's a wanton! Well, heaven forgive you and all of us, I pray!

SIR JOHN FALSTAFF

Mistress Ford;—come, Mistress Ford,—

MISTRESS QUICKLY

Marry, this is the short and the long of it; you have brought her into such a canaries as 'tis wonderful. The best courtier of them all, when the court lay at Windsor, could never have brought her to such a canary. Yet there has been knights, and lords, and gentlemen, with their coaches; I warrant you, coach after coach, letter after letter, gift after gift; smelling so sweetly, all musk, and so rushling, I warrant you, in silk and gold; and in such alligant terms; and in such wine and sugar of the best and the fairest, that would have won any woman's heart; and, I warrant you, they could never get an eye-wink of her: I had myself twenty angels given me this morning; but I defy all angels—in any such sort, as they say—but in the way of honesty: and, I warrant you, they could never get her so much as sip on a cup with the proudest of them all: and yet there has been earls, nay, which is more, pensioners; but, I warrant you, all is one with her.

SIR JOHN FALSTAFF

But what says she to me? be brief, my good she-Mercury.

MISTRESS QUICKLY

Marry, she hath received your letter; for the which she thanks you a thousand times; and she gives you to notify, that her husband will be absence from his house between ten and eleven.

SIR JOHN FALSTAFF

Ten and eleven.

MISTRESS QUICKLY

Ay, forsooth; and then you may come and see the picture, she says, that you wot of: Master Ford, her husband, will be from home. Alas, the sweet woman leads an ill life with him! he's a very jealousy man: she leads a very frampold life with him, good heart.

SIR JOHN FALSTAFF

Ten and eleven. Woman, commend me to her; I will not fail her.

MISTRESS QUICKLY

Why, you say well. But I have another messenger to your worship. Mistress Page hath her hearty commendations to you, too: and let me tell you in your ear, she's as fartuous a civil modest wife, and one, I tell you, that will not miss you morning nor evening prayer, as any is in Windsor, whoe'er be the other:

and she bade me tell your worship that her husband is seldom from home; but, she hopes, there will come a time. I never knew a woman so dote upon a man: surely, I think you have charms, la; yes, in truth.

SIR JOHN FALSTAFF

Not I, I assure thee: setting the attraction of my good parts aside, I have no other charms.

MISTRESS QUICKLY

Blessing on your heart for't!

SIR JOHN FALSTAFF

But, I pray thee, tell me this: has Ford's wife and Page's wife acquainted each other how they love me?

MISTRESS QUICKLY

That were a jest indeed! they have not so little grace, I hope: that were a trick indeed! But Mistress Page would desire you to send her your little page, of all loves: her husband has a marvellous infection to the little page; and, truly, Master Page is an honest man. Never a wife in Windsor leads a better life than she does: do what she will, say what she will, take all, pay all, go to bed when she list, rise when she list, all is as she will: and, truly, she deserves it; for if there be a kind woman in Windsor, she is one. You must send her your page; no remedy.

SIR JOHN FALSTAFF

Why, I will.

MISTRESS QUICKLY

Nay, but do so, then: and, look you, he may come and go between you both; and, in any case, have a nay-word, that you may know one another's mind, and the boy never need to understand any thing; for 'tis not good that children should know any wickedness: old folks, you know, have discretion, as they say, and know the world.

SIR JOHN FALSTAFF

Fare thee well: commend me to them both: there's my purse; I am yet thy debtor. Boy, go along with this woman. [*Exeunt* MISTRESS QUICKLY *and* ROBIN] This news distracts me!

PISTOL

This punk is one of Cupid's carriers:
Clap on more sails; pursue; up with your fights:
Give fire: she is my prize, or ocean whelm them all!
[*Exit*

SIR JOHN FALSTAFF

Say'st thou so, old Jack? go thy ways; I'll make more of thy old body than I have done. Will they yet look after thee? Wilt thou, after the expense of so much money, be now a gainer? Good body, I thank thee. Let them say 'tis grossly done; so it be fairly done, no matter.

Enter BARDOLPH

BARDOLPH

Sir John, there's one Master Brook below would fain speak with you, and be acquainted with you; and hath sent your worship a morning's draught of sack.

SIR JOHN FALSTAFF

Brook is his name?

BARDOLPH

Ay, sir.

SIR JOHN FALSTAFF

Call him in. [*Exit* BARDOLPH] Such Brooks are welcome to me, that o'erflow such liquor. Ah, ha! Mistress Ford and Mistress Page, have I encompassed you? go to; via!

Re-enter BARDOLPH, *with* FORD *disguised*

FORD

Bless you, sir!

SIR JOHN FALSTAFF

And you, sir! Would you speak with me?

FORD

I make bold to press with so little preparation upon you.

SIR JOHN FALSTAFF

You're welcome. What's your will?—Give us leave, drawer.   [*Exit* BARDOLPH

FORD

Sir, I am a gentleman that have spent much; my name is Brook.

SIR JOHN FALSTAFF

Good Master Brook, I desire more acquaintance of you.

FORD

Good Sir John, I sue for yours: not to charge you; for I must let you understand I think myself in better plight for a lender than you are: the which hath something emboldened me to this unseasoned intrusion; for they say, if money go before, all ways do lie open.

SIR JOHN FALSTAFF

Money is a good soldier, sir, and will on.

FORD

Troth, and I have a bag of money here troubles me: if you will help to bear it, Sir John, take all, or half, for easing me of the carriage.

SIR JOHN FALSTAFF

Sir, I know not how I may deserve to be your porter.

FORD

I will tell you, sir, if you will give me the hearing.

FALSTAFF

Speak, good Master Brook: I shall be glad to be your servant.

FORD

Sir, I hear you are a scholar,—I will be brief with you,—and you have been a man long known to me, though I had never so good means, as desire, to make myself acquainted with you. I shall discover a thing to you, wherein I must very much lay open mine own imperfection: but, good Sir John, as you have one eye upon my follies, as you hear them unfolded, turn another into the register of your own; that I may pass with a reproof the easier, sith you yourself know how easy it is to be such an offender.

SIR JOHN FALSTAFF

Very well, sir; proceed.

FORD

There is a gentlewoman in this town; her husband's name is Ford.

SIR JOHN FALSTAFF

Well, sir.

FORD

I have long loved her, and, I protest to you, bestowed much on her; followed her with a doting observance; engrossed opportunities to meet her; fee'd every slight occasion that could but niggardly give me sight of her; not only bought many presents to give her, but have given largely to many to know what she would have given; briefly, I have pursued her as love hath pursued me; which hath been on the wing of all occasions. But whatsoever I have merited, either in my mind or in my means, meed, I am sure, I have received none; unless experience be a jewel that I have purchased at an infinite rate, and that hath taught me to say this:

'Love like a shadow flies when substance love pursues;
Pursuing that that flies, and flying what pursues.'

SIR JOHN FALSTAFF

Have you received no promise of satisfaction at her hands?

FORD

Never.

SIR JOHN FALSTAFF

Have you importuned her to such a purpose?

FORD

Never.

SIR JOHN FALSTAFF

Of what quality was your love, then?

FORD

Like a fair house built on another man's ground; so that I have lost my edifice by mistaking the place where I erected it.

SIR JOHN FALSTAFF

To what purpose have you unfolded this to me?

FORD

When I have told you that, I have told you all. Some say, that though she appear honest to me, yet in other places she enlargeth her mirth so far that there is shrewd construction made of her. Now, Sir John, here is the heart of my purpose: you are a gentleman of excellent breeding, admirable discourse, of great admittance, authentic in your place and person, generally allowed for your many warlike, court-like, and learned preparations.

SIR JOHN FALSTAFF

O, sir!

FORD

Believe it, for you know it. There is money; spend it, spend it; spend more; spend all I have; only give me so much of your time in exchange of it, as to lay an amiable siege to the honesty of this Ford's wife: use your art of wooing; win her to consent to you: if any man may, you may as soon as any.

SIR JOHN FALSTAFF

Would it apply well to the vehemency of your affection, that I should win what you would enjoy? Methinks you prescribe to yourself very preposterously.

FORD

O, understand my drift. She dwells so securely on the excellency of her honour, that the folly of my soul dares not present itself: she is too bright to be looked against. Now, could I come to her with any detection in my hand, my desires had instance and argument to commend themselves: I could drive her then from the ward of her purity, her reputation, her marriage-vow, and a thousand other her defences, which now are too too strongly embattled against me. What say you to't, Sir John?

SIR JOHN FALSTAFF

Master Brook, I will first make bold with your money; next, give me your hand; and last, as I am a gentleman, you shall, if you will, enjoy Ford's wife.

FORD

O good sir!

SIR JOHN FALSTAFF

I say you shall.

FORD

Want no money, Sir John; you shall want none.

SIR JOHN FALSTAFF

Want no Mistress Ford, Master Brook; you shall want none. I shall be with her, I may tell you, by her own appointment; even as you came in to me, her assistant, or go-between, parted from me: I say I shall be with her between ten and eleven; for at that time the jealous rascally knave her husband will be forth. Come you to me at night; you shall know how I speed.

FORD

I am blest in your acquaintance. Do you know Ford, sir?

SIR JOHN FALSTAFF

Hang him, poor cuckoldly knave! I know him not: —yet I wrong him to call him poor; they say the jealous wittolly knave hath masses of money; for the which his wife seems to me well-favoured. I will use her as the key of the cuckoldly rogue's coffer; and there's my harvest-home.

FORD

I would you knew Ford, sir, that you might avoid him, if you saw him.

SIR JOHN FALSTAFF

Hang him, mechanical salt-butter rogue! I will stare him out of his wits; I will awe him with my cudgel: it shall hang like a meteor o'er the cuckold's horns. Master Brook, thou shalt know I will predominate over the peasant, and thou shalt lie with his wife. Come to me soon at night. Ford's a knave, and I will aggravate his style; thou, Master Brook, shalt know him for knave and cuckold. Come to me soon at night. [Exit

FORD

What a damned Epicurean rascal is this! My heart is ready to crack with impatience. Who says this is improvident jealousy? my wife hath sent to him; the hour is fixed; the match is made. Would any man have thought this? See the hell of having a false woman! My bed shall be abused, my coffers ransacked, my reputation gnawn at; and I shall not only receive this villanous wrong, but stand under the adoption of abominable terms, and by him that does me this wrong. Terms! names!—Amaimon sounds well; Lucifer, well; Barbason, well; yet they are devils' additions, the names of fiends: but Cuckold! Wittol!—Cuckold! the devil himself hath not such a name. Page is an ass, a secure ass: he will trust his wife; he will not be jealous. I will rather trust a Fleming with my butter, Parson Hugh the Welshman with my cheese, an Irishman with my aqua-vitæ bottle, or a thief to walk my ambling gelding, than my wife with herself: then she plots, then she ruminates, then she devises; and what they think in their hearts they may effect, they will break their hearts but they will effect. God be praised for my jealousy!—Eleven o'clock the hour. I will prevent this, detect my wife, be revenged on Falstaff, and laugh at Page. I will about it; better three hours too soon than a minute too late. Fie, fie, fie! cuckold! cuckold! cuckold!   [Exit

SCENE III. *A field near Windsor*

Enter DOCTOR CAIUS *and* RUGBY
DOCTOR CAIUS
Jack Rugby!
RUGBY
Sir?
DOCTOR CAIUS
Vat is de clock, Jack?
RUGBY
'Tis past the hour, sir, that Sir Hugh promised to meet.
DOCTOR CAIUS
By gar, he has save his soul, dat he is no come; he has pray his Pible well, dat he is no come: by gar, Jack Rugby, he is dead already, if he be come.
RUGBY
He is wise, sir; he knew your worship would kill him, if he came.
DOCTOR CAIUS
By gar, de herring is no dead so as I vill kill him. Take your rapier, Jack; I vill tell you how I vill kill him.
RUGBY
Alas, sir, I cannot fence.
DOCTOR CAIUS
Villainy, take your rapier.
RUGBY
Forbear; here's company.
Enter HOST, SHALLOW, SLENDER, *and* PAGE
HOST
Bless thee, bully doctor!
SHALLOW
Save you, Master Doctor Caius!
PAGE
Now, good master doctor!
SLENDER
Give you good morrow, sir.

DOCTOR CAIUS
Vat be all you, one, two, tree, four, come for?
HOST
To see thee fight, to see thee foin, to see thee traverse; to see thee here, to see thee there; to see thee pass thy punto, thy stock, thy reverse, thy distance, thy montant. Is he dead, my Ethiopian? is he dead, my Francisco? ha, bully! What says my Æsculapius? my Galen? my heart of elder? ha! is he dead, bully-stale? is he dead?
DOCTOR CAIUS
By gar, he is de coward Jack priest of de vorld; he is not show his face.
HOST
Thou art a Castalion-King-Urinal. Hector of Greece, my boy!
DOCTOR CAIUS
I pray you, bear vitness that me have stay six or seven, two, tree hours for him, and he is no come.
SHALLOW
He is the wiser man, master doctor: he is a curer of souls, and you a curer of bodies; if you should fight, you go against the hair of your professions. Is it not true, Master Page?
PAGE
Master Shallow, you have yourself been a great fighter, though now a man of peace.
SHALLOW
Bodykins, Master Page, though I now be old, and of the peace, if I see a sword out, my finger itches to make one. Though we are justices, and doctors, and churchmen, Master Page, we have some salt of our youth in us; we are the sons of women, Master Page.
PAGE
'Tis true, Master Shallow.
SHALLOW
It will be found so, Master Page. Master Doctor Caius, I am come to fetch you home. I am sworn of the peace: you have shewed yourself a wise physician, and Sir Hugh hath shewn himself a wise and patient churchman. You must go with me, master doctor.
HOST
Pardon, guest-justice.—A word, Mounseur Mock-water.
DOCTOR CAIUS
Mock-vater! vat is dat?
HOST
Mock-water, in our English tongue, is valour, bully.
DOCTOR CAIUS
By gar, den, I have as much mock-vater as de Englishman.—Scurvy jack-dog priest! by gar, me vill cut his ears.
HOST
He will clapper-claw thee tightly, bully.
DOCTOR CAIUS
Clapper-de-claw! vat is dat?
HOST
That is, he will make thee amends.

DOCTOR CAIUS

By gar, me do look he shall clapper-de-claw me; for, by gar, me vill have it.

HOST

And I will provoke him to't, or let him wag.

DOCTOR CAIUS

Me tank you for dat.

HOST

And, moreover, bully,—But first, master guest, and Master Page, and eke Cavaleiro Slender, go you through the town to Frogmore. [*Aside to them*

PAGE

Sir Hugh is there, is he?

HOST

He is there: see what humour he is in; and I will bring the doctor about by the fields. Will it do well?

SHALLOW

We will do it.

PAGE, SHALLOW, *and* SLENDER

Adieu, good master doctor.

[*Exeunt* PAGE, SHALLOW, *and* SLENDER

DOCTOR CAIUS

By gar, me vill kill de priest; for he speak for a jack-an-ape to Anne Page.

HOST

Let him die: sheathe thy impatience, throw cold water on thy choler: go about the fields with me through Frogmore: I will bring thee where Mistress Anne Page is, at a farm-house a-feasting; and thou shalt woo her. Cried I aim? said I well?

DOCTOR CAIUS

By gar, me dank you vor dat: by gar, I love you; and I shall procure-a you de good guest, de earl, de knight, de lords, de gentlemen, my patients.

HOST

For the which I will be thy adversary toward Anne Page. Said I well?

DOCTOR CAIUS

By gar, 'tis good; vell said.

HOST

Let us wag, then.

DOCTOR CAIUS

Come at my heels, Jack Rugby. [*Exeunt*

ACT III

Scene I. *A field near Frogmore*

Enter SIR HUGH EVANS *and* SIMPLE

SIR HUGH EVANS

I pray you now, good Master Slender's serving-man, and friend Simple by your name, which way have you looked for Master Caius, that calls himself doc-'tor of physic?

SIMPLE

Marry, sir, the pittie-ward, the park-ward, every way; old Windsor way, and every way but the town way.

SIR HUGH EVANS

I most fehemently desire you you will also look that way.

SIMPLE

I will, sir. [*Exit*

SIR HUGH EVANS

Pless my soul, how full of chollors I am, and trempling of mind!—I shall be glad if he have deceived me.—How melancholies I am!—I will knog his urinals about his knave's costard when I have goot opportunities for the ork.—Pless my soul!— [*Sings*

> To shallow rivers, to whose falls
> Melodious birds sings madrigals;
> There will we make our peds of roses,
> And a thousand fragrant posies.
> To shallow—

Mercy on me! I have a great dispositions to cry.

[*Sings*

> Melodious birds sing madrigals—
> Whenas I sat in Pabylon—
> And a thousand vagram posies.
> To shallow &c.

Re-enter SIMPLE

SIMPLE

Yonder he is coming, this way, Sir Hugh.

SIR HUGH EVANS

He's welcome.— [*Sings*

> To shallow rivers, to whose falls—

Heaven prosper the right!—What weapons is he?

SIMPLE

No weapons, sir. There comes my master, Master Shallow, and another gentleman, from Frogmore, over the stile, this way.

SIR HUGH EVANS

Pray you, give me my gown; or else keep it in your arms.

Enter PAGE, SHALLOW, *and* SLENDER

SHALLOW

How now, master parson! Good morrow, good Sir Hugh. Keep a gamester from the dice, and a good student from his book, and it is wonderful.

SLENDER

[*Aside*] Ah, sweet Anne Page!

PAGE

Save you, good Sir Hugh!

SIR HUGH EVANS

Pless you from his mercy sake, all of you!

SHALLOW

What, the sword and the word! do you study them both, master parson?

PAGE

And youthful still! in your doublet and hose this raw rheumatic day!

SIR HUGH EVANS

There is reasons and causes for it.

PAGE

We are come to you to do a good office, master parson.

SIR HUGH EVANS

Fery well: what is it?

PAGE

Yonder is a most reverend gentleman, who, belike having received wrong by some person, is at most odds with his own gravity and patience that ever you saw.

SHALLOW

I have lived fourscore years and upward; I never heard a man of his place, gravity, and learning, so wide of his own respect.

SIR HUGH EVANS

What is he?

PAGE

I think you know him; Master Doctor Caius, the renowned French physician.

SIR HUGH EVANS

Got's will, and his passion of my heart! I had as lief you would tell me of a mess of porridge.

PAGE

Why?

SIR HUGH EVANS

He has no more knowledge in Hibocrates and Galen, —and he is a knave besides; a cowardly knave as you would desires to be acquainted withal.

PAGE

I warrant you, he's the man should fight with him.

SLENDER

[Aside] O sweet Anne Page!

SHALLOW

It appears so, by his weapons. Keep them asunder: here comes Doctor Caius.

Enter HOST, DOCTOR CAIUS, and RUGBY

PAGE

Nay, good master parson, keep in your weapon.

SHALLOW

So do you, good master doctor.

HOST

Disarm them, and let them question: let them keep their limbs whole, and hack our English.

DOCTOR CAIUS

I pray you, let-a me speak a word with your ear. Verefore vill you not meet-a me?

SIR HUGH EVANS

[Aside to DOCTOR CAIUS] Pray you, use your patience: in good time.

DOCTOR CAIUS

By gar, you are de coward, de Jack dog, John ape.

SIR HUGH EVANS

[Aside to DOCTOR CAIUS] Pray you, let us not be laughing-stocks to other men's humours; I desire you in friendship, and I will one way or other make you amends. [Aloud] I will knog your urinals about your knave's cogscomb for missing your meetings and appointments.

DOCTOR CAIUS

Diable!—Jack Rugby,—mine host de Jarteer,—have I not stay for him to kill him? have I not, at de place I did appoint?

SIR HUGH EVANS

As I am a Christians soul, now, look you, this is the

place appointed: I'll be judgement by mine host of the Garter.

HOST

Peace, I say, Gallia and Gaul, French and Welsh, soul-curer and body-curer!

DOCTOR CAIUS

Ay, dat is very good; excellent.

HOST

Peace, I say! hear mine host of the Garter. Am I politic? am I subtle? am I a Machiavel? Shall I lose my doctor? no; he gives me the potions and the motions. Shall I lose my parson, my priest, my Sir Hugh? no; he gives me the proverbs and the no-verbs. Give me thy hand, terrestrial; so. Give me thy hand, celestial; so. Boys of art, I have deceived you both; I have directed you to wrong places: your hearts are mighty, your skins are whole, and let burnt sack be the issue. Come, lay their swords to pawn. Follow me, lads of peace; follow, follow, follow.

SHALLOW

Trust me, a mad host. Follow, gentlemen, follow.

SLENDER

[Aside] O sweet Anne Page!

[Exeunt SHALLOW, SLENDER, PAGE, and HOST

DOCTOR CAIUS

Ha, do I perceive dat? have you make-a de sot of us, ha, ha?

SIR HUGH EVANS

This is well; he has made us his vlouting-stog.—I desire you that we may be friends; and let us knog our prains together to be revenge on this same scall, scurvy, cogging companion, the host of the Garter.

DOCTOR CAIUS

By gar, with all my heart. He promise to bring me where is Anne Page; by gar, he deceive me too.

SIR HUGH EVANS

Well, I will smite his noddles. Pray you, follow.

[Exeunt

SCENE II. The street, in Windsor

Enter MISTRESS PAGE and ROBIN

MISTRESS PAGE

Nay, keep your way, little gallant; you were wont to be a follower, but now you are a leader. Whether had you rather lead mine eyes, or eye your master's heels?

ROBIN

I had rather, forsooth, go before you like a man than follow him like a dwarf.

MISTRESS PAGE

O, you are a flattering boy: now I see you'll be a courtier.

Enter FORD

FORD

Well met, Mistress Page. Whither go you?

MISTRESS PAGE

Truly, sir, to see your wife. Is she at home?

FORD

Ay; and as idle as she may hang together, for want

of company. I think, if your husbands were dead,
you two would marry.

MISTRESS PAGE

Be sure of that,—two other husbands.

FORD

Where had you this pretty weathercock?

MISTRESS PAGE

I cannot tell what the dickens his name is my husband had him of.—What do you call your knight's
name, sirrah?

ROBIN

Sir John Falstaff.

FORD

Sir John Falstaff!

MISTRESS PAGE

He, he; I can never hit on's name. There is such a
league between my good man and he!—Is your wife
at home indeed?

FORD

Indeed she is.

MISTRESS PAGE

By your leave, sir: I am sick till I see her.

[*Exeunt* MISTRESS PAGE *and* ROBIN

FORD

Has Page any brains? hath he any eyes? hath he any
thinking? Sure, they sleep; he hath no use of them.
Why, this boy will carry a letter twenty mile, as easy
as a cannon will shoot point-blank twelve score. He
pieces out his wife's inclination; he gives her folly
motion and advantage: and now she's going to my
wife, and Falstaff's boy with her. A man may hear
this shower sing in the wind. And Falstaff's boy with
her! Good plots, they are laid; and our revolted
wives share damnation together. Well; I will take
him, then torture my wife, pluck the borrowed veil
of modesty from the so seeming Mistress Page, di-
vulge Page himself for a secure and wilful Actæon;
and to these violent proceedings all my neighbours
shall cry aim. [*Clock heard*] The clock gives me my
cue, and my assurance bids me search: there I shall
find Falstaff: I shall be rather praised for this than
mocked; for it is as positive as the earth is firm that
Falstaff is there: I will go.

Enter PAGE, SHALLOW, SLENDER, HOST, SIR HUGH EVANS,
DOCTOR CAIUS, *and* RUGBY

SHALLOW, PAGE, &c.

Well met, Master Ford.

FORD

Trust me, a good knot: I have good cheer at home;
and I pray you all go with me.

SHALLOW

I must excuse myself, Master Ford.

SLENDER

And so must I, sir: we have appointed to dine with
Mistress Anne, and I would not break with her for
more money than I'll speak of.

SHALLOW

We have lingered about a match between Anne Page
and my cousin Slender, and this day we shall have
our answer.

SLENDER

I hope I have your good will, father Page.

PAGE

You have, Master Slender; I stand wholly for you:
—but my wife, master doctor, is for you altogether.

DOCTOR CAIUS

Ay, be-gar; and de maid is love-a me: my nursh-a
Quickly tell me so mush.

HOST

What say you to young Master Fenton? he capers,
he dances, he has eyes of youth, he writes verses, he
speaks holiday, he smells April and May: he will
carry't, he will carry't; 'tis in his buttons; he will
carry't.

PAGE

Not by my consent, I promise you. The gentleman
is of no having: he kept company with the wild prince
and Poins; he is of too high a region; he knows too
much. No, he shall not knit a knot in his fortunes
with the finger of my substance: if he take her, let
him take her simply; the wealth I have waits on my
consent, and my consent goes not that way.

FORD

I beseech you heartily, some of you go home with
me to dinner: besides your cheer, you shall have
sport; I will show you a monster. Master doctor,
you shall go; so shall you, Master Page; and you,
Sir Hugh.

SHALLOW

Well, fare you well: we shall have the freer wooing
at Master Page's.   [*Exeunt* SHALLOW *and* SLENDER

DOCTOR CAIUS

Go home, John Rugby; I come anon. [*Exit* RUGBY

HOST

Farewell, my hearts: I will to my honest knight Falstaff, and drink canary with him.   [*Exit*

FORD

[*Aside*] I think I shall drink in pipe-wine first with
him; I'll make him dance. Will you go, gentles?

ALL

Have with you to see this monster.   [*Exeunt*

SCENE III. *A room in* FORD'S *house*

Enter MISTRESS FORD *and* MISTRESS PAGE

MISTRESS FORD

What, John! What, Robert!

MISTRESS PAGE

Quickly, quickly!—is the buck-basket—

MISTRESS FORD

I warrant. What, Robin, I say!

Enter SERVANTS *with a basket*

MISTRESS PAGE

Come, come, come.

MISTRESS FORD

Here, set it down.

MISTRESS PAGE

Give your men the charge; we must be brief.

MISTRESS FORD

Marry, as I told you before, John and Robert, be ready here hard by in the brew-house; and when I suddenly call you, come forth, and, without any pause or staggering, take this basket on your shoulders: that done, trudge with it in all haste, and carry it among the whitsters in Datchet-mead, and there empty it in the muddy ditch close by the Thames side.

MISTRESS PAGE

You will do it?

MISTRESS FORD

I ha' told them over and over; they lack no direction. Be gone, and come when you are called.

[*Exeunt* SERVANTS

MISTRESS PAGE

Here comes little Robin.

Enter ROBIN

MISTRESS FORD

How now, my eyas-musket! what news with you?

ROBIN

My master, Sir John, is come in at your back-door, Mistress Ford, and requests your company.

MISTRESS PAGE

You little Jack-a-Lent, have you been true to us?

ROBIN

Ay, I'll be sworn. My master knows not of your being here, and hath threatened to put me into everlasting liberty, if I tell you of it; for he swears he'll turn me away.

MISTRESS PAGE

Thou'rt a good boy: this secrecy of thine shall be a tailor to thee, and shall make thee a new doublet and hose. I'll go hide me.

MISTRESS FORD

Do so. Go tell thy master I am alone. [*Exit* ROBIN] Mistress Page, remember you your cue.

MISTRESS PAGE

I warrant thee; if I do not act it, hiss me.   [*Exit*

MISTRESS FORD

Go to, then: we'll use this unwholesome humidity, this gross watery pumpion; we'll teach him to know turtles from jays.

Enter SIR JOHN FALSTAFF

SIR JOHN FALSTAFF

'Have I caught' thee, 'my heavenly jewel?' Why, now let me die, for I have lived long enough: this is the period of my ambition: O this blessed hour!

MISTRESS FORD

O sweet Sir John!

SIR JOHN FALSTAFF

Mistress Ford, I cannot cog, I cannot prate, Mistress Ford. Now shall I sin in my wish: I would thy husband were dead: I'll speak it before the best lord; I would make thee my lady.

MISTRESS FORD

I your lady, Sir John! alas, I should be a pitiful lady!

SIR JOHN FALSTAFF

Let the court of France show me such another. I see how thine eye would emulate the diamond: thou

hast the right arched beauty of the brow that becomes the ship-tire, the tire-valiant, or any tire of Venetian admittance.

MISTRESS FORD

A plain kerchief, Sir John: my brows become nothing else; nor that well neither.

SIR JOHN FALSTAFF

By the Lord, thou art a traitor to say so: thou wouldst make an absolute courtier; and the firm fixture of thy foot would give an excellent motion to thy gait in a semi-circled farthingale. I see what thou wert, if Fortune thy foe were not, Nature thy friend. Come, thou canst not hide it.

MISTRESS FORD

Believe me, there's no such thing in me.

SIR JOHN FALSTAFF

What made me love thee? let that persuade thee there's something extraordinary in thee. Come, I cannot cog, and say thou art this and that, like a many of these lisping hawthorn-buds, that come like women in men's apparel, and smell like Bucklersbury in simple time; I cannot: but I love thee; none but thee; and thou deservest it.

MISTRESS FORD

Do not betray me, sir. I fear you love Mistress Page.

SIR JOHN FALSTAFF

Thou mightst as well say I love to walk by the Counter-gate, which is as hateful to me as the reek of a lime-kiln.

MISTRESS FORD

Well, heaven knows how I love you; and you shall one day find it.

SIR JOHN FALSTAFF

Keep in that mind; I'll deserve it.

MISTRESS FORD

Nay, I must tell you, so you do; or else I could not be in that mind.

ROBIN

[*Within*] Mistress Ford, Mistress Ford! here's Mistress Page at the door, sweating, and blowing, and looking wildly, and would needs speak with you presently.

SIR JOHN FALSTAFF

She shall not see me: I will ensconce me behind the arras.

MISTRESS FORD

Pray you, do so: she's a very tattling woman.

[FALSTAFF *hides himself*

Re-enter MISTRESS PAGE *and* ROBIN

What's the matter? how now!

MISTRESS PAGE

O Mistress Ford, what have you done? You're shamed, you're overthrown, you're undone for ever!

MISTRESS FORD

What's the matter, good Mistress Page?

MISTRESS PAGE

O well-a-day, Mistress Ford! having an honest man to your husband, to give him such cause of suspicion!

MISTRESS FORD

What cause of suspicion?

MISTRESS PAGE

What cause of suspicion! Out upon you! how am I mistook in you!

MISTRESS FORD

Why, alas, what's the matter?

MISTRESS PAGE

Your husband's coming hither, woman, with all the officers in Windsor, to search for a gentleman that he says is here now in the house, by your consent, to take an ill advantage of his absence: you are undone.

MISTRESS FORD

'Tis not so, I hope.

MISTRESS PAGE

Pray heaven it be not so, that you have such a man here! but 'tis most certain your husband's coming, with half Windsor at his heels, to search for such a one. I come before to tell you. If you know yourself clear, why, I am glad of it; but if you have a friend here, convey, convey him out. Be not amazed; call all your senses to you; defend your reputation, or bid farewell to your good life for ever.

MISTRESS FORD

What shall I do? There is a gentleman my dear friend; and I fear not mine own shame so much as his peril: I had rather than a thousand pound he were out of the house.

MISTRESS PAGE

For shame! never stand 'you had rather' and 'you had rather:' your husband's here at hand; bethink you of some conveyance: in the house you cannot hide him. O, how have you deceived me! Look, here here is a basket: if he be of any reasonable stature, he may creep in here; and throw foul linen upon him, as if it were going to bucking: or,—it is whiting-time,—send him by your two men to Datchet-mead.

MISTRESS FORD

He's too big to go in there. What shall I do?

SIR JOHN FALSTAFF

[Coming forward] Let me see't, let me see't, O, let me see't!—I'll in, I'll in.—Follow your friend's counsel. —I'll in.

MISTRESS PAGE

What, Sir John Falstaff! Are these your letters, knight?

SIR JOHN FALSTAFF

I love thee.—Help me away.—Let me creep in here. —I'll never—

[Gets into the basket; they cover him with foul linen

MISTRESS PAGE

Help to cover your master, boy.—Call your men, Mistress Ford.—You dissembling knight!

MISTRESS FORD

What, John! Robert! John!   [Exit ROBIN

Re-enter SERVANTS

Go take up these clothes here quickly.—Where's the cowl-staff? look, how you drumble!—Carry them to the laundress in Datchet-mead; quickly, come.

Enter FORD, PAGE, DOCTOR CAIUS, and SIR HUGH EVANS

FORD

Pray you, come near: if I suspect without cause, why

then make sport at me; then let me be your jest; I deserve it.—How now! whither bear you this?

SERVANT

To the laundress, forsooth.

MISTRESS FORD

Why, what have you to do whither they bear it? You were best meddle with buck-washing.

FORD

Buck!—I would I could wash myself of the buck!— Buck, buck, buck! Ay, buck; I warrant you, buck; and of the season too, it shall appear. [Exeunt SERV-ANTS with the basket] Gentlemen, I have dreamed to-night; I'll tell you my dream. Here, here, here be my keys: ascend my chambers; search, seek, find out: I'll warrant we'll unkennel the fox. Let me stop this way first. [Locking the door] So, now uncape.

PAGE

Good Master Ford, be contented: you wrong your-self too much.

FORD

True, Master Page. Up, gentlemen; you shall see sport anon: follow me, gentlemen.   [Exit

SIR HUGH EVANS

This is fery fantastical humours and jealousies.

DOCTOR CAIUS

By gar, 'tis no the fashion of France; it is not jealous in France.

PAGE

Nay, follow him, gentlemen; see the issue of his search.   [Exeunt PAGE, DOCTOR CAIUS, and EVANS

MISTRESS PAGE

Is there not a double excellency in this?

MISTRESS FORD

I know not which pleases me better, that my hus-band is deceived, or Sir John.

MISTRESS PAGE

What a taking was he in when your husband asked who was in the basket!

MISTRESS FORD

I am half afraid he will have need of washing; so throwing him into the water will do him a benefit.

MISTRESS PAGE

Hang him, dishonest rascal! I would all of the same strain were in the same distress.

MISTRESS FORD

I think my husband hath some special suspicion of Falstaff's being here; for I never saw him so gross in his jealousy till now.

MISTRESS PAGE

I will lay a plot to try that; and we will yet have more tricks with Falstaff: his dissolute disease will scarce obey this medicine.

MISTRESS FORD

Shall we send that foolish carrion, Mistress Quickly, to him, and excuse his throwing into the water; and give him another hope, to betray him to another punishment?

MISTRESS PAGE

We will do it: let him be sent for to-morrow, eight o'clock, to have amends.

Re-enter FORD, PAGE, DOCTOR CAIUS, *and* SIR HUGH EVANS

FORD

I cannot find him: may be the knave bragged of that
he could not compass.

MISTRESS PAGE

[*Aside to* MISTRESS FORD] Heard you that?

MISTRESS FORD

You use me well, Master Ford, do you?

FORD

Ay, I do so.

MISTRESS FORD

Heaven make you better than your thoughts!

FORD

Amen!

MISTRESS PAGE

You do yourself mighty wrong, Master Ford.

FORD

Ay, ay; I must bear it.

SIR HUGH EVANS

If there be any pody in the house, and in the chambers, and in the coffers, and in the presses, heaven
forgive my sins at the day of judgement!

DOCTOR CAIUS

By gar, nor I too: there is no bodies.

PAGE

Fie, fie, Master Ford! are you not ashamed? What
spirit, what devil suggests this imagination? I would
not ha' your distemper in this kind for the wealth of
Windsor Castle.

FORD

'Tis my fault, Master Page: I suffer for it.

SIR HUGH EVANS

You suffer for a pad conscience: your wife is as honest a 'omans as I will desires among five thousand,
and five hundred too.

DOCTOR CAIUS

By gar, I see 'tis an honest woman.

FORD

Well, I promised you a dinner.—Come, come, walk
in the Park: I pray you, pardon me; I will hereafter
make known to you why I have done this.—Come,
wife; come, Mistress Page.—I pray you, pardon me;
pray heartily pardon me.

PAGE

Let's go in, gentlemen; but, trust me, we'll mock
him. I do invite you to-morrow morning to my
house to breakfast: after, we'll a-birding together; I
have a fine hawk for the bush. Shall it be so?

FORD

Any thing.

SIR HUGH EVANS

If there is one, I shall make two in the company.

DOCTOR CAIUS

If there be one or two, I shall make-a the turd.

FORD

Pray you, go, Master Page.

SIR HUGH EVANS

I pray you now, remembrance to-morrow on the
lousy knave, mine host.

DOCTOR CAIUS

Dat is good; by gar, with all my heart!

SIR HUGH EVANS

A lousy knave, to have his gibes and his mockeries!

[*Exeunt*

SCENE IV. *A room in* PAGE'S *house*

Enter FENTON *and* ANNE PAGE

FENTON

I see I cannot get thy father's love;
Therefore no more turn me to him, sweet Nan.

ANNE PAGE

Alas, how then?

FENTON

Why, thou must be thyself.
He doth object I am too great of birth;
And that, my state being gall'd with my expense,
I seek to heal it only by his wealth:
Besides these, other bars he lays before me,—
My riots past, my wild societies;
And tells me 'tis a thing impossible
I should love thee but as a property.

ANNE PAGE

May be he tells you true.

FENTON

No, heaven so speed me in my time to come!
Albeit I will confess thy father's wealth
Was the first motive that I woo'd thee, Anne:
Yet, wooing thee, I found thee of more value
Than stamps in gold or sums in sealed bags;
And 'tis the very riches of thyself
That now I aim at.

ANNE PAGE

Gentle Master Fenton,
Yet seek my father's love; still seek it, sir:
If opportunity and humblest suit
Cannot attain it, why, then,—hark you hither!

[*They converse apart*

Enter SHALLOW, SLENDER, *and* MISTRESS QUICKLY

SHALLOW

Break their talk, Mistress Quickly: my kinsman shall
speak for himself.

SLENDER

I'll make a shaft or a bolt on't: 'slid, 'tis but venturing.

SHALLOW

Be not dismayed.

SLENDER

No, she shall not dismay me: I care not for that, but
that I am afeard.

MISTRESS QUICKLY

Hark ye; Master Slender would speak a word with
you.

ANNE PAGE

I come to him. [*Aside*] This is my father's choice.
O, what a world of vile ill-favour'd faults
Looks handsome in three hundred pounds a-year!

MISTRESS QUICKLY

And how does good Master Fenton? Pray you, a
word with you.

SHALLOW

She's coming; to her, coz. O boy, thou hadst a father!

SLENDER

I had a father, Mistress Anne; my uncle can tell you good jests of him. Pray you, uncle, tell Mistress Anne the jest, how my father stole two geese out of a pen, good uncle.

SHALLOW

Mistress Anne, my cousin loves you.

SLENDER

Ay, that I do; as well as I love any woman in Gloucestershire.

SHALLOW

He will maintain you like a gentlewoman.

SLENDER

Ay, that I will, come cut and long-tail, under the degree of a squire.

SHALLOW

He will make you a hundred and fifty pounds join-ture.

ANNE PAGE

Good Master Shallow, let him woo for himself.

SHALLOW

Marry, I thank you for it; I thank you for that good comfort. She calls you, coz: I'll leave you.

ANNE PAGE

Now, Master Slender,—

SLENDER

Now, good Mistress Anne,—

ANNE PAGE

What is your will?

SLENDER

My will! od's heartlings, that's a pretty jest indeed! I ne'er made my will yet, I thank heaven; I am not such a sickly creature, I give heaven praise.

ANNE PAGE

I mean, Master Slender, what would you with me?

SLENDER

Truly, for mine own part, I would little or nothing with you. Your father and my uncle hath made mo-tions: if it be my luck, so; if not, happy man be his dole! They can tell you how things go better than I can: you may ask your father; here he comes.

Enter PAGE *and* MISTRESS PAGE

PAGE

Now, Master Slender: love him, daughter Anne.— Why, how now! what does Master Fenton here? You wrong me, sir, thus still to haunt my house: I told you, sir, my daughter is disposed of.

FENTON

Nay, Master Page, be not impatient.

MISTRESS PAGE

Good Master Fenton, come not to my child.

PAGE

She is no match for you.

FENTON

Sir, will you hear me?

PAGE

No, good Master Fenton.

Come, Master Shallow; come, son Slender, in. Knowing my mind, you wrong me, Master Fenton.

[*Exeunt* PAGE, SHALLOW, *and* SLENDER

MISTRESS QUICKLY

Speak to Mistress Page.

FENTON

Good Mistress Page, for that I love your daughter In such a righteous fashion as I do, Perforce, against all checks, rebukes and manners, I must advance the colours of my love, And not retire: let me have your good will.

ANNE PAGE

Good mother, do not marry me to yond fool.

MISTRESS PAGE

I mean it not; I seek you a better husband.

MISTRESS QUICKLY

That's my master, master doctor.

ANNE PAGE

Alas, I had rather be set quick i' the earth, And bowl'd to death with turnips!

MISTRESS PAGE

Come, trouble not yourself. Good Master Fenton, I will not be your friend nor enemy: My daughter will I question how she loves you, And as I find her, so am I affected. Till then farewell, sir: she must needs go in; Her father will be angry.

FENTON

Farewell, gentle mistress: farewell, Nan.

[*Exeunt* MISTRESS PAGE *and* ANNE PAGE

MISTRESS QUICKLY

This is my doing now: 'Nay,' said I, 'will you cast away your child on a fool, and a physician? Look on Master Fenton:' this is my doing.

FENTON

I thank thee; and I pray thee, once to-night Give my sweet Nan this ring: there's for thy pains.

MISTRESS QUICKLY

Now heaven send thee good fortune! [*Exit* FENTON] A kind heart he hath: a woman would run through fire and water for such a kind heart. But yet I would my master had Mistress Anne; or I would Master Slender had her; or, in sooth, I would Master Fen-ton had her: I will do what I can for them all three; for so I have promised, and I'll be as good as my word; but speciously for Master Fenton. Well, I must of another errand to Sir John Falstaff from my two mistresses: what a beast am I to slack it! [*Exit*

SCENE V. *A room in the Garter Inn*

Enter SIR JOHN FALSTAFF *and* BARDOLPH

SIR JOHN FALSTAFF

Bardolph, I say,—

BARDOLPH

Here, sir.

SIR JOHN FALSTAFF

Go fetch me a quart of sack; put a toast in't. [*Exit* BARDOLPH] Have I lived to be carried in a basket, like a barrow of butcher's offal, and to be thrown in the Thames? Well, if I be served such another trick, I'll have my brains ta'en out, and buttered, and give them to a dog for a new-year's gift. The rogues slighted me into the river with as little remorse as they would have drowned a blind bitch's puppies, fifteen i' the litter: and you may know by my size that I have a kind of alacrity in sinking; if the bottom were as deep as hell, I should down. I had been drowned, but that the shore was shelvy and shallow, —a death that I abhor; for the water swells a man; and what a thing should I have been when I had been swelled! I should have been a mountain of mummy.

Re-enter BARDOLPH *with sack*

BARDOLPH

Here's Mistress Quickly, sir, to speak with you.

SIR JOHN FALSTAFF

Come, let me pour in some sack to the Thames water; for my belly's as cold as if I had swallowed snowballs for pills to cool the reins. Call her in.

BARDOLPH

Come in, woman!

Enter MISTRESS QUICKLY

MISTRESS QUICKLY

By your leave; I cry you mercy: give your worship good morrow.

SIR JOHN FALSTAFF

Take away these chalices. Go brew me a pottle of sack finely.

BARDOLPH

With eggs, sir?

SIR JOHN FALSTAFF

Simple of itself; I'll no pullet-sperm in my brewage. [*Exit* BARDOLPH] How now!

MISTRESS QUICKLY

Marry, sir, I come to your worship from Mistress Ford.

SIR JOHN FALSTAFF

Mistress Ford! I have had ford enough; I was thrown into the ford; I have my belly full of ford.

MISTRESS QUICKLY

Alas the day! good heart, that was not her fault: she does so take on with her men; they mistook their erection.

SIR JOHN FALSTAFF

So did I mine, to build upon a foolish woman's promise.

MISTRESS QUICKLY

Well, she laments, sir, for it, that it would yearn your heart to see it. Her husband goes this morning a-birding; she desires you once more to come to her between eight and nine: I must carry her word quickly: she'll make you amends, I warrant you.

SIR JOHN FALSTAFF

Well, I will visit her: tell her so; and bid her think what a man is: let her consider his frailty, and then judge of my merit.

MISTRESS QUICKLY

I will tell her.

SIR JOHN FALSTAFF

Do so. Between nine and ten, sayest thou?

MISTRESS QUICKLY

Eight and nine, sir.

SIR JOHN FALSTAFF

Well, be gone: I will not miss her.

MISTRESS QUICKLY

Peace be with you, sir.   [*Exit*

SIR JOHN FALSTAFF

I marvel I hear not of Master Brook; he sent me word to stay within: I like his money well.—O, here he comes.

Enter FORD

FORD

Bless you, sir!

SIR JOHN FALSTAFF

Now, Master Brook,—you come to know what hath passed between me and Ford's wife?

FORD

That, indeed, Sir John, is my business.

SIR JOHN FALSTAFF

Master Brook, I will not lie to you: I was at her house the hour she appointed me.

FORD

And sped you, sir?

SIR JOHN FALSTAFF

Very ill-favouredly, Master Brook.

FORD

How so, sir? Did she change her determination?

SIR JOHN FALSTAFF

No, Master Brook; but the peaking Cornuto her husband, Master Brook, dwelling in a continual 'larum of jealousy, comes me in the instant of our encounter, after we had embraced, kissed, protested, and, as it were, spoke the prologue of our comedy; and at his heels a rabble of his companions, thither provoked and instigated by his distemper, and, forsooth, to search his house for his wife's love.

FORD

What, while you were there?

SIR JOHN FALSTAFF

While I was there.

FORD

And did he search for you, and could not find you?

SIR JOHN FALSTAFF

You shall hear. As good luck would have it, comes in one Mistress Page; gives intelligence of Ford's approach; and, in her invention and Ford's wife's distraction, they conveyed me into a buck-basket.

FORD

A buck-basket!

SIR JOHN FALSTAFF

By the Lord, a buck-basket!—rammed me in with foul shirts and smocks, socks, foul stockings, greasy napkins; that, Master Brook, there was the rankest compound of villanous smell that ever offended nostril.

FORD

And how long lay you there?

SIR JOHN FALSTAFF

Nay, you shall hear, Master Brook, what I have suffered to bring this woman to evil for your good. Being thus crammed in the basket, a couple of Ford's knaves, his hinds, were called forth by their mistress to carry me in the name of foul clothes to Datchet-lane: they took me on their shoulders; met the jealous knave their master in the door, who asked them once or twice what they had in their basket: I quaked for fear, lest the lunatic knave would have searched it; but fate, ordaining he should be a cuckold, held his hand. Well: on went he for a search, and away went I for foul clothes. But mark the sequel, Master Brook: I suffered the pangs of three several deaths; first, an intolerable fright, to be detected with a jealous rotten bell-wether; next, to be compassed, like a good bilbo, in the circumference of a peck, hilt to point, heel to head; and then, to be stopped in, like a strong distillation, with stinking clothes that fretted in their own grease: think of that,—a man of my kidney,—think of that, —that am as subject to heat as butter; a man of continual dissolution and thaw: it was a miracle to 'scape suffocation. And in the height of this bath, when I was more than half stewed in grease, like a Dutch dish, to be thrown into the Thames, and cooled, glowing hot, in that surge, like a horse-shoe; think of that,—hissing hot,—think of that, Master Brook.

FORD

In good sadness, sir, I am sorry that for my sake you have suffered all this. My suit, then, is desperate; you'll undertake her no more?

SIR JOHN FALSTAFF

Master Brook, I will be thrown into Etna, as I have been into Thames, ere I will leave her thus. Her husband is this morning gone a-birding: I have received from her another embassy of meeting; 'twixt eight and nine is the hour, Master Brook.

FORD

'Tis past eight already, sir.

SIR JOHN FALSTAFF

Is it? I will then address me to my appointment. Come to me at your convenient leisure, and you shall know how I speed; and the conclusion shall be crowned with your enjoying her. Adieu. You shall have her, Master Brook; Master Brook, you shall cuckold Ford.   [Exit

FORD

Hum! ha! is this a vision? is this a dream? do I sleep? Master Ford, awake! awake, Master Ford! there's a hole made in your best coat, Master Ford. This 'tis to be married! this 'tis to have linen and buck-baskets! Well, I will proclaim myself what I am: I will now take the lecher; he is at my house; he cannot 'scape me; 'tis impossible he should; he cannot creep into a halfpenny purse, nor into a pepper-box: but, lest the devil that guides him should aid him, I will search impossible places. Though what I am I cannot avoid, yet to be what I would not shall not

make me tame: if I have horns to make one mad, let the proverb go with me,—I'll be horn-mad.
                                                          [Exit

ACT IV
Scene I. *A street*

Enter MISTRESS PAGE, MISTRESS QUICKLY, *and*
WILLIAM PAGE

MISTRESS PAGE

Is he at Master Ford's already, think'st thou?

MISTRESS QUICKLY

Sure he is by this, or will be presently: but, truly, he is very courageous mad about his throwing into the water. Mistress Ford desires you to come suddenly.

MISTRESS PAGE

I'll be with her by and by; I'll but bring my young man here to school. Look, where his master comes; 'tis a playing-day, I see.

Enter SIR HUGH EVANS

How now, Sir Hugh! no school to-day?

SIR HUGH EVANS

No; Master Slender is let the boys leave to play.

MISTRESS QUICKLY

Blessing of his heart!

MISTRESS PAGE

Sir Hugh, my husband says my son profits nothing in the world at his book. I pray you, ask him some questions in his accidence.

SIR HUGH EVANS

Come hither, William; hold up your head; come.

MISTRESS PAGE

Come on, sirrah; hold up your head; answer your master, be not afraid.

SIR HUGH EVANS

William, how many numbers is in nouns?

WILLIAM PAGE

Two.

MISTRESS QUICKLY

Truly, I thought there had been one number more, because they say, 'Od's nouns.'

SIR HUGH EVANS

Peace your tattlings! What is 'fair,' William?

WILLIAM PAGE

Pulcher.

MISTRESS QUICKLY

Polecats! there are fairer things than polecats, sure.

SIR HUGH EVANS

You are a very simplicity 'oman: I pray you, peace. —What is 'lapis,' William?

WILLIAM PAGE

A stone.

SIR HUGH EVANS

And what is 'a stone,' William?

WILLIAM PAGE

A pebble.

SIR HUGH EVANS

No, it is 'lapis': I pray you, remember in your prain-

WILLIAM PAGE

Lapis.

SIR HUGH EVANS

That is a good William. What is he, William, that
does lend articles?

WILLIAM PAGE

Articles are borrowed of the pronoun, and be thus
declined, Singulariter, nominativo, hic, hæc, hoc.

SIR HUGH EVANS

Nominativo, hig, hag, hog; pray you, mark: geni-
tivo, hujus. Well, what is your accusative case?

WILLIAM PAGE

Accusativo, hinc.

SIR HUGH EVANS

I pray you, have your remembrance, child; accusativo, hung, hang, hog.

MISTRESS QUICKLY

'Hang-hog' is Latin for bacon, I warrant you.

SIR HUGH EVANS

Leave your prabbles, 'oman.—What is the focative
case, William?

WILLIAM PAGE

O,—vocativo, O.

SIR HUGH EVANS

Remember, William; focative is caret.

MISTRESS QUICKLY

And that's a good root.

SIR HUGH EVANS

'Oman, forbear.

MISTRESS PAGE

Peace!

SIR HUGH EVANS

What is your genitive case plural, William?

WILLIAM PAGE

Genitive case!

SIR HUGH EVANS

Ay.

WILLIAM PAGE

Genitive,—horum, harum, horum.

MISTRESS QUICKLY

Vengeance of Jenny's case! fie on her! never name
her, child, if she be a whore.

SIR HUGH EVANS

For shame, 'oman.

MISTRESS QUICKLY

You do ill to teach the child such words:—he teaches
him to hick and to hack, which they'll do fast enough
of themselves, and to call 'horum':—fie upon you!

SIR HUGH EVANS

'Oman, art thou lunatics? hast thou no understand-
ings for thy cases, and the numbers of the genders?
Thou art as foolish Christian creatures as I would
desires.

MISTRESS PAGE

Prithee, hold thy peace.

SIR HUGH EVANS

Show me now, William, some declensions of your
pronouns.

WILLIAM PAGE

Forsooth, I have forgot.

SIR HUGH EVANS

It is qui, quæ, quod: if you forget your 'quies,' your
'quæs,' and your 'quods,' you must be preeches. Go
your ways, and play; go.

MISTRESS PAGE

He is a better scholar than I thought he was.

SIR HUGH EVANS

He is a good sprag memory. Farewell, Mistress Page.

MISTRESS PAGE

Adieu, good Sir Hugh.   [*Exit* SIR HUGH
Get you home, boy. Come, we stay too long. [*Exeunt*

SCENE II. *A room in* FORD'S *house*

Enter SIR JOHN FALSTAFF *and* MISTRESS FORD

SIR JOHN FALSTAFF

Mistress Ford, your sorrow hath eaten up my sufferance. I see you are obsequious in your love, and I
profess requital to a hair's breadth; not only, Mistress Ford, in the simple office of love, but in all the
accoutrement, complement, and ceremony of it. But
are you sure of your husband now?

MISTRESS FORD

He's a-birding, sweet Sir John.

MISTRESS PAGE

[*Within*] What, ho, gossip Ford! what, ho!

MISTRESS FORD

Step into the chamber, Sir John.

[*Exit* SIR JOHN FALSTAFF

Enter MISTRESS PAGE

MISTRESS PAGE

How now, sweetheart! who's at home besides yourself?

MISTRESS FORD

Why, none but mine own people.

MISTRESS PAGE

Indeed!

MISTRESS FORD

No, certainly. [*Aside to her*] Speak louder.

MISTRESS PAGE

Truly, I am so glad you have nobody here.

MISTRESS FORD

Why?

MISTRESS PAGE

Why, woman, your husband is in his old lunes again:
he so takes on yonder with my husband; so rails
against all married mankind; so curses all Eve's
daughters, of what complexion soever; and so buffets
himself on the forehead, crying, 'Peer out, peer out!'
that any madness I ever yet beheld seemed but
tameness, civility, and patience, to this his distemper
he is in now: I am glad the fat knight is not here.

MISTRESS FORD

Why, does he talk of him?

MISTRESS PAGE

Of none but him; and swears he was carried out, the
last time he searched for him, in a basket; protests to
my husband he is now here; and hath drawn him
and the rest of their company from their sport, to

make another experiment of his suspicion: but I am glad the knight is not here; now he shall see his own foolery.

MISTRESS FORD

How near is he, Mistress Page?

MISTRESS PAGE

Hard by, at street end; he will be here anon.

MISTRESS FORD

I am undone!—the knight is here.

MISTRESS PAGE

Why, then, you are utterly shamed, and he's but a dead man. What a woman are you!—Away with him, away with him! better shame than murder.

MISTRESS FORD

Which way should he go? how should I bestow him? Shall I put him into the basket again?

Re-enter SIR JOHN FALSTAFF

SIR JOHN FALSTAFF

No, I'll come no more i' the basket. May I not go out ere he come?

MISTRESS PAGE

Alas, three of Master Ford's brothers watch the door with pistols, that none shall issue out; otherwise you might slip away ere he came. But what make you here?

SIR JOHN FALSTAFF

What shall I do?—I'll creep up into the chimney.

MISTRESS FORD

There they always use to discharge their birding-pieces. Creep into the kiln-hole.

SIR JOHN FALSTAFF

Where is it?

MISTRESS FORD

He will seek there, on my word. Neither press, coffer, chest, trunk, well, vault, but he hath an abstract for the remembrance of such places, and goes to them by his note: there is no hiding you in the house.

SIR JOHN FALSTAFF

I'll go out, then.

MISTRESS PAGE

If you go out in your own semblance, you die, Sir John. Unless you go out disguised,—

MISTRESS FORD

How might we disguise him?

MISTRESS PAGE

Alas the day, I know not! There is no woman's gown big enough for him; otherwise he might put on a hat, a muffler, and a kerchief, and so escape.

SIR JOHN FALSTAFF

Good hearts, devise something: any extremity rather than a mischief.

MISTRESS FORD

My maid's aunt, the fat woman of Brentford, has a gown above.

MISTRESS PAGE

On my word, it will serve him; she's as big as he is: and there's her thrummed hat, and her muffler too. Run up, Sir John.

MISTRESS FORD

Go, go, sweet Sir John: Mistress Page and I will look some linen for your head.

MISTRESS PAGE

Quick, quick! we'll come dress you straight: put on the gown the while.   [*Exit* SIR JOHN FALSTAFF

MISTRESS FORD

I would my husband would meet him in this shape: he cannot abide the old woman of Brentford; he swears she's a witch; forbade her my house, and hath threatened to beat her.

MISTRESS PAGE

Heaven guide him to thy husband's cudgel, and the devil guide his cudgel afterwards!

MISTRESS FORD

But is my husband coming?

MISTRESS PAGE

Ay, in good sadness, is he; and talks of the basket too, howsoever he hath had intelligence.

MISTRESS FORD

We'll try that; for I'll appoint my men to carry the basket again, to meet him at the door with it, as they did last time.

MISTRESS PAGE

Nay, but he'll be here presently: let's go dress him like the witch of Brentford.

MISTRESS FORD

I'll first direct my men what they shall do with the basket. Go up; I'll bring linen for him straight.
            [*Exit*

MISTRESS PAGE

Hang him, dishonest varlet! we cannot misuse him enough.
We'll leave a proof, by that which we will do,
Wives may be merry, and yet honest too:
We do not act that often jest and laugh;
'Tis old, but true,—Still swine eats all the draff.
            [*Exit*

Re-enter MISTRESS FORD *with two* SERVANTS

MISTRESS FORD

Go, sirs, take the basket again on your shoulders: your master is hard at door; if he bid you set it down, obey him: quickly, dispatch.   [*Exit*

FIRST SERVANT

Come, come, take it up.

SECOND SERVANT

Pray heaven it be not full of knight again.

FIRST SERVANT

I hope not; I had as lief bear so much lead.

Enter FORD, PAGE, SHALLOW, DOCTOR CAIUS, *and*
SIR HUGH EVANS

FORD

Ay, but if it prove true, Master Page, have you any way then to unfool me again? Set down the basket, villain! Somebody call my wife. Youth in a basket! —O you pandarly rascals! there's a knot, a ging, a pack, a conspiracy against me: now shall the devil be shamed.—What, wife, I say!—Come, come forth! Behold what honest clothes you send forth to bleaching!

PAGE

Why, this passes, Master Ford; you are not to go loose any longer; you must be pinioned.

SIR HUGH EVANS

Why, this is lunatics! this is mad as a mad dog!

SHALLOW

Indeed, Master Ford, this is not well, indeed.

FORD

So say I too, sir.

Re-enter MISTRESS FORD

Come hither, Mistress Ford; Mistress Ford, the honest woman, the modest wife, the virtuous creature, that hath the jealous fool to her husband! I suspect without cause, mistress, do I?

MISTRESS FORD

Heaven be my witness you do, if you suspect me in any dishonesty.

FORD

Well said, brazen-face! hold it out. Come forth, sirrah!   [*Pulling clothes out of the basket*

PAGE

This passes!

MISTRESS FORD

Are you not ashamed? let the clothes alone.

FORD

I shall find you anon.

SIR HUGH EVANS

'Tis unreasonable! Will you take up your wife's clothes? Come away.

FORD

Empty the basket, I say!

MISTRESS FORD

Why, man, why?

FORD

Master Page, as I am a man, there was one conveyed out of my house yesterday in this basket: why may not he be there again? In my house I am sure he is: my intelligence is true; my jealousy is reasonable. Pluck me out all the linen.

MISTRESS FORD

If you find a man there, he shall die a flea's death.

PAGE

Here's no man.

SHALLOW

By my fidelity, this is not well, Master Ford; this wrongs you.

SIR HUGH EVANS

Master Ford, you must pray, and not follow the imaginations of your own heart: this is jealousies.

FORD

Well, he's not here I seek for.

PAGE

No, nor nowhere else but in your brain.

FORD

Help to search my house this one time. If I find not what I seek, show no colour for my extremity; let me for ever be your table-sport; let them say of me, 'As jealous as Ford, that searched a hollow walnut for his wife's leman.' Satisfy me once more; once more search with me.

MISTRESS FORD

What, ho, Mistress Page! come you and the old woman down; my husband will come into the chamber.

FORD

Old woman! what old woman's that?

MISTRESS FORD

Why, it is my maid's aunt of Brentford.

FORD

A witch, a quean, an old cozening quean! Have I not forbid her my house? She comes of errands, does she? We are simple men; we do not know what's brought to pass under the profession of fortune-telling. She works by charms, by spells, by the figure, and such daubery as this is, beyond our element: we know nothing. Come down, you witch, you hag, you; come down, I say!

MISTRESS FORD

Nay, good, sweet husband!—Good gentlemen, let him not strike the old woman.

Re-enter SIR JOHN FALSTAFF *in woman's clothes, and*

MISTRESS PAGE

MISTRESS PAGE

Come, Mother Prat; come, give me your hand.

FORD

I'll prat her. [*Beating him*] Out of my door, you witch, you hag, you baggage, you polecat, you ronyon! out, out! I'll conjure you, I'll fortune-tell you.

[*Exit* SIR JOHN FALSTAFF

MISTRESS PAGE

Are you not ashamed? I think you have killed the poor woman.

MISTRESS FORD

Nay, he will do it. 'Tis a goodly credit for you.

FORD

Hang her, witch!

SIR HUGH EVANS

By yea and no, I think the 'oman is a witch indeed: I like not when a 'oman has a great peard; I spy a great peard under his muffler.

FORD

Will you follow, gentlemen? I beseech you, follow; see but the issue of my jealousy: if I cry out thus upon no trail, never trust me when I open again.

PAGE

Let's obey his humour a little further: come, gentlemen. [*Exeunt* FORD, PAGE, SHALLOW, DOCTOR CAIUS, *and* SIR HUGH EVANS

MISTRESS PAGE

Trust me, he beat him most pitifully.

MISTRESS FORD

Nay, by the mass, that he did not; he beat him most unpitifully methought.

MISTRESS PAGE

I'll have the cudgel hallowed and hung o'er the altar; it hath done meritorious service.

MISTRESS FORD

What think you? may we, with the warrant of womanhood and the witness of a good conscience, pursue him with any further revenge?

MISTRESS PAGE

The spirit of wantonness is, sure, scared out of him:
if the devil have him not in fee-simple, with fine and
recovery, he will never, I think, in the way of waste,
attempt us again.

MISTRESS FORD

Shall we tell our husbands how we have served him?

MISTRESS PAGE

Yes, by all means; if it be but to scrape the figures
out of your husband's brains. If they can find in their
hearts the poor unvirtuous fat knight shall be any
further afflicted, we two will still be the ministers.

MISTRESS FORD

I'll warrant they'll have him publicly shamed: and
methinks there would be no period to the jest, should
he not be publicly shamed.

MISTRESS PAGE

Come, to the forge with it, then; shape it: I would
not have things cool.   [Exeunt

SCENE III. *A room in the Garter Inn*

Enter HOST *and* BARDOLPH

BARDOLPH

Sir, the Germans desire to have three of your horses:
the duke himself will be to-morrow at court, and
they are going to meet him.

HOST

What duke should that be comes so secretly? I hear
not of him in the court. Let me speak with the gentlemen: they speak English?

BARDOLPH

Ay, sir; I'll call them to you.

HOST

They shall have my horses; but I'll make them pay;
I'll sauce them: they have had my house a week at
command; I have turned away my other guests:
they must come off; I'll sauce them. Come. [Exeunt

SCENE IV. *A room in* FORD'S *house*

Enter PAGE, FORD, MISTRESS PAGE, MISTRESS FORD, *and*
SIR HUGH EVANS

SIR HUGH EVANS

'Tis one of the best discretions of a 'oman as ever I
did look upon.

PAGE

And did he send you both these letters at an instant?

MISTRESS PAGE

Within a quarter of an hour.

FORD

Pardon me, wife. Henceforth do what thou wilt;
I rather will suspect the sun with cold
Than thee with wantonness: now doth thy honour
    stand,
In him that was of late an heretic,
As firm as faith.

PAGE

'Tis well, 'tis well; no more:
Be not as extreme in submission
As in offence.
But let our plot go forward: let our wives
Yet once again, to make us public sport,
Appoint a meeting with this old fat fellow,
Where we may take him, and disgrace him for it.

FORD

There is no better way than that they spoke of.

PAGE

How? to send him word they'll meet him in the Park
at midnight? Fie, fie! he'll never come.

SIR HUGH EVANS

You say he has been thrown in the rivers, and has
been grievously peaten, as an old 'oman: methinks
there should be terrors in him that he should not
come; methinks his flesh is punished, he shall have
no desires.

PAGE

So think I too.

MISTRESS FORD

Devise but how you'll use him when he comes,
And let us two devise to bring him thither.

MISTRESS PAGE

There is an old tale goes that Herne the hunter,
Sometime a keeper here in Windsor forest,
Doth all the winter-time, at still midnight,
Walk round about an oak, with great ragg'd horns;
And there he blasts the tree, and takes the cattle,
And makes milch-kine yield blood, and shakes a
    chain
In a most hideous and dreadful manner:
You have heard of such a spirit; and well you know
The superstitious idle-headed eld
Received, and did deliver to our age,
This tale of Herne the hunter for a truth.

PAGE

Why, yet there want not many that do fear
In deep of night to walk by this Herne's oak:
But what of this?

MISTRESS FORD

Marry, this is our device;
That Falstaff at that oak shall meet with us.

PAGE

Well, let it not be doubted but he'll come:
And in this shape when you have brought him thither,
What shall be done with him? what is your plot?

MISTRESS PAGE

That likewise have we thought upon, and thus:
Nan Page my daughter and my little son
And three or four more of their growth we'll dress
Like urchins, ouphes and fairies, green and white,
With rounds of waxen tapers on their heads,
And rattles in their hands: upon a sudden,
As Falstaff, she, and I, are newly met,
Let them from forth a sawpit rush at once
With some diffused song: upon their sight,
We two in great amazedness will fly:
Then let them all encircle him about,

And, fairy-like, to pinch the unclean knight;
And ask him why, that hour of fairy revel,
In their so sacred paths he dares to tread
In shape profane.

MISTRESS FORD
                    And till he tell the truth,
Let the supposed fairies pinch him sound,
And burn him with their tapers.

MISTRESS PAGE
                              The truth being known,
We'll all present ourselves, dis-horn the spirit,
And mock him home to Windsor.

FORD
                              The children must
Be practised well to this, or they'll ne'er do't.

SIR HUGH EVANS
I will teach the children their behaviours; and I will
be like a jack-an-apes also, to burn the knight with
my taber.

FORD
That will be excellent. I'll go buy them vizards.

MISTRESS PAGE
My Nan shall be the queen of all the fairies,
Finely attired in a robe of white.

PAGE
That silk will I go buy. [Aside] And in that time
Shall Master Slender steal my Nan away,
And marry her at Eton. Go send to Falstaff straight.

FORD
Nay, I'll to him again in name of Brook:
He'll tell me all his purpose: sure, he'll come.

MISTRESS PAGE
Fear not you that. Go get us properties
And tricking for our fairies.

SIR HUGH EVANS
Let us about it: it is admirable pleasures and fery
honest knaveries.
              [Exeunt PAGE, FORD, and SIR HUGH EVANS

MISTRESS PAGE
Go, Mistress Ford,
Send quickly to Sir John, to know his mind.
                              [Exit MISTRESS FORD
I'll to the doctor: he hath my good will,
And none but he, to marry with Nan Page.
That Slender, though well landed, is an idiot;
And he my husband best of all affects.
The doctor is well money'd, and his friends
Potent at court: he, none but he, shall have her,
Though twenty thousand worthier come to crave
    her.   [Exit

SCENE V. A room in the Garter Inn

Enter HOST and SIMPLE

HOST
What wouldst thou have, boor? what, thick-skin?
speak, breathe, discuss; brief, short, quick, snap.

SIMPLE
Marry, sir, I come to speak with Sir John Falstaff
from Master Slender.

HOST
There's his chamber, his house, his castle, his
standing-bed, and truckle-bed; 'tis painted about
with the story of the Prodigal, fresh and new. Go
knock and call; he'll speak like an Anthropophagi-
nian unto thee: knock, I say.

SIMPLE
There's an old woman, a fat woman, gone up into
his chamber: I'll be so bold as stay, sir, till she come
down; I come to speak with her, indeed.

HOST
Ha! a fat woman! the knight may be robbed: I'll
call.—Bully knight! bully Sir John! speak from thy
lungs military: art thou there? it is thine host, thine
Ephesian, calls.

SIR JOHN FALSTAFF
[Above] How now, mine host!

HOST
Here's a Bohemian-Tartar tarries the coming down
of thy fat woman. Let her descend, bully, let her descend; my chambers are honourable: fie! privacy?
fie!

Enter SIR JOHN FALSTAFF

SIR JOHN FALSTAFF
There was, mine host, an old fat woman even now
with me; but she's gone.

SIMPLE
Pray you, sir, was't not the wise woman of Brentford?

SIR JOHN FALSTAFF
Ay, marry, was it, muscle-shell: what would you
with her?

SIMPLE
My master, sir, Master Slender, sent to her, seeing
her go thorough the streets, to know, sir, whether
one Nym, sir, that beguiled him of a chain, had the
chain or no.

SIR JOHN FALSTAFF
I spake with the old woman about it.

SIMPLE
And what says she, I pray, sir?

SIR JOHN FALSTAFF
Marry, she says that the very same man that beguiled Master Slender of his chain cozened him of it.

SIMPLE
I would I could have spoken with the woman herself; I had other things to have spoken with her too
from him.

SIR JOHN FALSTAFF
What are they? let us know.

HOST
Ay, come; quick.

SIMPLE
I may not conceal them, sir.

HOST
Conceal them, or thou diest.

SIMPLE

Why, sir, they were nothing but about Mistress Anne Page; to know if it were my master's fortune to have her or no.

SIR JOHN FALSTAFF

'Tis, 'tis his fortune.

SIMPLE

What, sir?

SIR JOHN FALSTAFF

To have her, or no. Go; say the woman told me so.

SIMPLE

May I be bold to say so, sir?

SIR JOHN FALSTAFF

Ay, sir; like who more bold.

SIMPLE

I thank your worship: I shall make my master glad with these tidings.   [Exit

HOST

Thou art clerkly, thou art clerkly, Sir John. Was there a wise woman with thee?

SIR JOHN FALSTAFF

Ay, that there was, mine host; one that hath taught me more wit than ever I learned before in my life; and I paid nothing for it neither, but was paid for my learning.

Enter BARDOLPH

BARDOLPH

Out, alas, sir! cozenage, mere cozenage!

HOST

Where be my horses? speak well of them, varletto.

BARDOLPH

Run away with the cozeners: for so soon as I came beyond Eton, they threw me off, from behind one of them, in a slough of mire; and set spurs and away, like three German devils, three Doctor Faustuses.

HOST

They are gone but to meet the duke, villain: do not say they be fled; Germans are honest men.

Enter SIR HUGH EVANS

SIR HUGH EVANS

Where is mine host?

HOST

What is the matter, sir?

SIR HUGH EVANS

Have a care of your entertainments: there is a friend of mine come to town, tells me there is three cozengermans that has cozened all the hosts of Readins, of Maidenhead, of Colebrook, of horses and money. I tell you for good will, look you: you are wise, and full of gibes and vlouting-stocks, and 'tis not convenient you should be cozened. Fare you well.   [Exit

Enter DOCTOR CAIUS

DOCTOR CAIUS

Vere is mine host de Jarteer?

HOST

Here, master doctor, in perplexity and doubtful dilemma.

DOCTOR CAIUS

I cannot tell vat is dat: but it is tell-a me dat you make grand preparation for a duke de Jamany: by my trot, dere is no duke dat the court is know to come. I tell you for good vill: adieu.   [Exit

HOST

Hue and cry, villain, go!—Assist me, knight.—I am undone!—Fly, run, hue and cry, villain!—I am undone!   [Exeunt HOST and BARDOLPH

SIR JOHN FALSTAFF

I would all the world might be cozened; for I have been cozened and beaten too. If it should come to the ear of the court, how I have been transformed, and how my transformation hath been washed and cudgelled, they would melt me out of my fat drop by drop, and liquor fishermen's boots with me: I warrant they would whip me with their fine wits till I were as crest-fallen as a dried pear. I never prospered since I forswore myself at primero. Well, if my wind were but long enough to say my prayers, I would repent.

Enter MISTRESS QUICKLY

Now, whence come you?

MISTRESS QUICKLY

From the two parties, forsooth.

SIR JOHN FALSTAFF

The devil take one party, and his dam the other! and so they shall be both bestowed. I have suffered more for their sakes, more than the villanous inconstancy of man's disposition is able to bear.

MISTRESS QUICKLY

And have not they suffered? Yes, I warrant; speciously one of them; Mistress Ford, good heart, is beaten black and blue, that you cannot see a white spot about her.

SIR JOHN FALSTAFF

What tell'st thou me of black and blue? I was beaten myself into all the colours of the rainbow; and I was like to be apprehended for the witch of Brentford: but that my admirable dexterity of wit, my counterfeiting the action of an old woman, delivered me, the knave constable had set me i' the stocks, i' the common stocks, for a witch.

MISTRESS QUICKLY

Sir, let me speak with you in your chamber: you shall hear how things go; and, I warrant, to your content. Here is a letter will say somewhat. Good hearts, what ado here is to bring you together! Sure, one of you does not serve heaven well, that you are so crossed.

SIR JOHN FALSTAFF

Come up into my chamber.   [Exeunt

SCENE VI. *The same. Another room in the Garter Inn*

Enter FENTON and HOST

HOST

Master Fenton, talk not to me; my mind is heavy: I will give over all.

FENTON

Yet hear me speak. Assist me in my purpose,
And, as I am a gentleman, I'll give thee
A hundred pound in gold more than your loss.

HOST

I will hear you, Master Fenton; and I will at the
least keep your counsel.

FENTON

From time to time I have acquainted you
With the dear love I bear to fair Anne Page;
Who mutually hath answer'd my affection,
So far forth as herself might be her chooser,
Even to my wish: I have a letter from her
Of such contents as you will wonder at;
The mirth whereof so larded with my matter,
That neither singly can be manifested,
Without the show of both; fat Falstaff
Hath a great scene: the image of the jest
I'll show you here at large. Hark, good mine host.
To-night at Herne's oak, just 'twixt twelve and one,
Must my sweet Nan present the Fairy Queen;
The purpose why, is here: in which disguise,
While other jests are something rank on foot,
Her father hath commanded her to slip
Away with Slender, and with him at Eton
Immediately to marry: she hath consented:
Now, sir,
Her mother, even strong against that match,
And firm for Doctor Caius, hath appointed
That he shall likewise shuffle her away,
While other sports are tasking of their minds,
And at the deanery, where a priest attends,
Straight marry her: to this her mother's plot
She seemingly obedient likewise hath
Made promise to the doctor. Now, thus it rests:
Her father means she shall be all in white;
And in that habit, when Slender sees his time
To take her by the hand and bid her go,
She shall go with him: her mother hath intended,
The better to denote her to the doctor,—
For they must all be mask'd and vizarded,—
That quaint in green she shall be loose enrobed,
With ribands pendent, flaring, 'bout her head;
And when the doctor spies his vantage ripe,
To pinch her by the hand, and, on that token,
The maid hath given consent to go with him.

HOST

Which means she to deceive, father or mother?

FENTON

Both, my good host, to go along with me:
And here it rests,—that you'll procure the vicar
To stay for me at church 'twixt twelve and one,
And, in the lawful name of marrying,
To give our hearts united ceremony.

HOST

Well, husband your device; I'll to the vicar:
Bring you the maid, you shall not lack a priest.

FENTON

So shall I evermore be bound to thee;
Besides, I'll make a present recompence.   [Exeunt

ACT V

SCENE I. A room in the Garter Inn

Enter SIR JOHN FALSTAFF *and* MISTRESS QUICKLY

SIR JOHN FALSTAFF

Prithee, no more prattling; go. I'll hold. This is the
third time; I hope good luck lies in odd numbers.
Away! go. They say there is divinity in odd numbers,
either in nativity, chance, or death. Away!

MISTRESS QUICKLY

I'll provide you a chain; and I'll do what I can to
get you a pair of horns.

SIR JOHN FALSTAFF

Away, I say; time wears: hold up your head, and
mince.   [Exit MISTRESS QUICKLY

Enter FORD

How now, Master Brook! Master Brook, the matter
will be known to-night, or never. Be you in the Park
about midnight, at Herne's oak, and you shall see
wonders.

FORD

Went you not to her yesterday, sir, as you told me
you had appointed?

SIR JOHN FALSTAFF

I went to her, Master Brook, as you see, like a poor
old man: but I came from her, Master Brook, like a
poor old woman. That same knave Ford, her husband, hath the finest mad devil of jealousy in him,
Master Brook, that ever governed frenzy. I will tell
you:—he beat me grievously, in the shape of a
woman; for in the shape of man, Master Brook, I
fear not Goliath with a weaver's beam; because I
know also life is a shuttle. I am in haste; go along
with me: I'll tell you all, Master Brook. Since I
plucked geese, played truant, and whipped top, I
knew not what 'twas to be beaten till lately. Follow
me: I'll tell you strange things of this knave Ford,
on whom to-night I will be revenged, and I will deliver his wife into your hand. Follow. Strange things
in hand, Master Brook! Follow.   [Exeunt

SCENE II. Windsor Park

Enter PAGE, SHALLOW, *and* SLENDER

PAGE

Come, come; we'll couch i' the castle-ditch till we
see the light of our fairies. Remember, son Slender,
my daughter.

SLENDER

Ay, forsooth; I have spoke with her, and we have a
nay-word how to know one another: I come to her
in white, and cry, 'mum;' she cries 'budget;' and by
that we know one another.

SHALLOW

That's good too: but what needs either your 'mum'
or her 'budget?' the white will decipher her well
enough. It hath struck ten o'clock.

PAGE

The night is dark; light and spirits will become it

well. Heaven prosper our sport! No man means evil but the devil, and we shall know him by his horns. Let's away; follow me.   [*Exeunt*

SCENE III. *A street leading to the Park*

Enter MISTRESS PAGE, MISTRESS FORD, *and* DOCTOR CAIUS

MISTRESS PAGE

Master Doctor, my daughter is in green: when you see your time, take her by the hand, away with her to the deanery, and dispatch it quickly. Go before into the Park: we two must go together.

DOCTOR CAIUS

I know vat I have to do. Adieu.

MISTRESS PAGE

Fare you well, sir. [*Exit* DOCTOR CAIUS] My husband will not rejoice so much at the abuse of Falstaff as he will chafe at the doctor's marrying my daughter: but 'tis no matter; better a little chiding than a great deal of heart-break.

MISTRESS FORD

Where is Nan now and her troop of fairies, and the Welsh devil Hugh?

MISTRESS PAGE

They are all couched in a pit hard by Herne's oak, with obscured lights; which, at the very instant of Falstaff's and our meeting, they will at once display to the night.

MISTRESS FORD

That cannot choose but amaze him.

MISTRESS PAGE

If he be not amazed, he will be mocked; if he be amazed, he will every way be mocked.

MISTRESS FORD

We'll betray him finely.

MISTRESS PAGE

Against such lewdsters and their lechery
Those that betray them do no treachery.

MISTRESS FORD

The hour draws on. To the oak, to the oak! [*Exeunt*

SCENE IV. *Windsor Park*

Enter SIR HUGH EVANS *disguised, with others as Fairies*

SIR HUGH EVANS

Trib, trib, fairies; come; and remember your parts: be pold, I pray you; follow me into the pit; and when I give the watch-'ords, do as I pid you: come, come; trib, trib.   [*Exeunt*

SCENE V. *Another part of the Park*

Enter SIR JOHN FALSTAFF *disguised as Herne*

SIR JOHN FALSTAFF

The Windsor bell hath struck twelve; the minute draws on. Now, the hot-blooded gods assist me! Re-member, Jove, thou wast a bull for thy Europa; love set on thy horns. O powerful love! that, in some re-spects, makes a beast a man; in some other, a man a beast. You were also, Jupiter, a swan for the love of Leda. O omnipotent Love! how near the god drew to the complexion of a goose! A fault done first in the form of a beast;—O Jove, a beastly fault! And then another fault in the semblance of a fowl;—think on't, Jove; a foul fault! When gods have hot backs, what shall poor men do? For me, I am here a Windsor stag; and the fattest, I think, i' the forest. Send me a cool rut-time, Jove, or who can blame me to piss my tallow?—Who comes here? my doe?

Enter MISTRESS FORD *and* MISTRESS PAGE

MISTRESS FORD

Sir John! art thou there, my deer? my male deer?

SIR JOHN FALSTAFF

My doe with the black scut! Let the sky rain pota-toes; let it thunder to the tune of Green Sleeves, hail kissing-comfits, and snow eringoes; let there come a tempest of provocation, I will shelter me here.

MISTRESS FORD

Mistress Page is come with me, sweetheart.

SIR JOHN FALSTAFF

Divide me like a bribe buck, each a haunch: I will keep my sides to myself, my shoulders for the fellow of this walk, and my horns I bequeath your hus-bands. Am I a woodman, ha? Speak I like Herne the hunter? Why, now is Cupid a child of conscience; he makes restitution. As I am a true spirit, welcome!
                [*Noise within*

MISTRESS PAGE

Alas, what noise?

MISTRESS FORD

Heaven forgive our sins!

SIR JOHN FALSTAFF

What should this be?

MISTRESS FORD *and* MISTRESS PAGE

Away, away!   [*They run off*

SIR JOHN FALSTAFF

I think the devil will not have me damned, lest the oil that's in me should set hell on fire; he would never else cross me thus.

Enter SIR HUGH EVANS, *disguised as before;* PISTOL, *as* Hobgoblin; MISTRESS QUICKLY, ANNE PAGE, *and others, as Fairies, with tapers*

MISTRESS QUICKLY

Fairies, black, grey, green, and white,
You moonshine revellers, and shades of night,
You orphan heirs of fixed destiny,
Attend your office and your quality.
Crier Hobgoblin, make the fairy oyes.

PISTOL

Elves, list your names; silence, you airy toys.
Cricket, to Windsor chimneys shalt thou leap:
Where fires thou find'st unraked and hearths un-swept,
There pinch the maids as blue as bilberry:
Our radiant queen hates sluts and sluttery.

SIR JOHN FALSTAFF

They are fairies; he that speaks to them shall die:
I'll wink and couch: no man their works must eye.
[*Lies down upon his face*

SIR HUGH EVANS

Where's Bede? Go you, and where you find a maid
That, ere she sleep, has thrice her prayers said,
Raise up the organs of her fantasy;
Sleep she as sound as careless infancy:
But those as sleep and think not on their sins,
Pinch them, arms, legs, backs, shoulders, sides, and
  shins.

MISTRESS QUICKLY

About, about;
Search Windsor Castle, elves, within and out:
Strew good luck, ouphes, on every sacred room;
That it may stand till the perpetual doom,
In state as wholesome as in state 'tis fit,
Worthy the owner, and the owner it.
The several chairs of order look you scour
With juice of balm and every precious flower:
Each fair instalment, coat, and several crest,
With loyal blazon, evermore be blest!
And nightly, meadow-fairies, look you sing,
Like to the Garter's compass, in a ring:
Th' expressure that it bears, green let it be,
More fertile-fresh than all the field to see;
And *Honi soit qui mal y pense* write
In emerald tufts, flowers purple, blue, and white;
Like sapphire, pearl, and rich embroidery,
Buckled below fair knighthood's bending knee:
Fairies use flowers for their charactery.
Away; disperse: but till 'tis one o'clock,
Our dance of custom round about the oak
Of Herne the hunter, let us not forget.

SIR HUGH EVANS

Pray you, lock hand in hand; yourselves in order set;
And twenty glow-worms shall our lanterns be,
To guide our measure round about the tree.
But, stay; I smell a man of middle-earth.

SIR JOHN FALSTAFF

Heavens defend me from that Welsh fairy, lest he
transform me to a piece of cheese!

PISTOL

Vile worm, thou wast o'erlook'd even in thy birth.

MISTRESS QUICKLY

With trial-fire touch me his finger-end:
If he be chaste, the flame will back descend,
And turn him to no pain; but if he start,
It is the flesh of a corrupted heart.

PISTOL

A trial, come.

SIR HUGH EVANS

Come, will this wood take fire?
[*They burn him with their tapers*

SIR JOHN FALSTAFF

Oh, Oh, Oh!

MISTRESS QUICKLY

Corrupt, corrupt, and tainted in desire!

About him, fairies; sing a scornful rhyme:
And, as you trip, still pinch him to your time.

SONG

Fie on sinful fantasy!
Fie on lust and luxury!
Lust is but a bloody fire,
Kindled with unchaste desire,
Fed in heart, whose flames aspire,
As thoughts do blow them, higher and higher.
Pinch him, fairies, mutually;
Pinch him for his villany;
Pinch him, and burn him, and turn him about,
Till candles and starlight and moonshine be out.

During this song they pinch SIR JOHN FALSTAFF. DOCTOR
CAIUS *comes one way, and steals away a boy in green;*
SLENDER *another way, and takes off a boy in white; and*
FENTON *comes, and steals away* MISTRESS ANNE PAGE. *A
noise of hunting is heard within. All the Fairies run away.*
SIR JOHN FALSTAFF *pulls off his buck's head, and rises.*

Enter PAGE, FORD, MISTRESS PAGE *and* MISTRESS FORD

PAGE

Nay, do not fly; I think we have watch'd you now:
Will none but Herne the hunter serve your turn?

MISTRESS PAGE

I pray you, come, hold up the jest no higher.
Now, good Sir John, how like you Windsor wives?
See you these, husband? do not these fair yokes
Become the forest better than the town?

FORD

Now, sir, who's a cuckold now? Master Brook, Falstaff's a knave, a cuckoldly knave; here are his horns,
Master Brook: and, Master Brook, he hath enjoyed
nothing of Ford's but his buck-basket, his cudgel,
and twenty pounds of money, which must be paid
to Master Brook; his horses are arrested for it, Master Brook.

MISTRESS FORD

Sir John, we have had ill luck; we could never meet.
I will never take you for my love again; but I will
always count you my deer.

SIR JOHN FALSTAFF

I do begin to perceive that I am made an ass.

FORD

Ay, and an ox too: both the proofs are extant.

SIR JOHN FALSTAFF

And these are not fairies? I was three or four times
in the thought they were not fairies: and yet the
guiltiness of my mind, the sudden surprise of my
powers, drove the grossness of the foppery into a received belief, in despite of the teeth of all rhyme and
reason, that they were fairies. See now how wit may
be made a Jack-a-Lent, when 'tis upon ill employment!

SIR HUGH EVANS

Sir John Falstaff, serve Got, and leave your desires,
and fairies will not pinse you.

FORD

Well said, fairy Hugh.

SIR HUGH EVANS

And leave you your jealousies too, I pray you.

FORD

I will never mistrust my wife again, till thou art able to woo her in good English.

SIR JOHN FALSTAFF

Have I laid my brain in the sun and dried it, that it wants matter to prevent so gross o'erreaching as this? Am I ridden with a Welsh goat too? shall I have a coxcomb of frize? 'Tis time I were choked with a piece of toasted cheese.

SIR HUGH EVANS

Seese is not good to give putter; your pelly is all putter.

SIR JOHN FALSTAFF

'Seese' and 'putter'? Have I lived to stand at the taunt of one that makes fritters of English? This is enough to be the decay of lust and late-walking through the realm.

MISTRESS PAGE

Why, Sir John, do you think, though we would have thrust virtue out of our hearts by the head and shoulders, and have given ourselves without scruple to hell, that ever the devil could have made you our delight?

FORD

What, a hodge-pudding? a bag of flax?

MISTRESS PAGE

A puffed man?

PAGE

Old, cold, withered, and of intolerable entrails?

FORD

And one that is as slanderous as Satan?

PAGE

And as poor as Job?

FORD

And as wicked as his wife?

SIR HUGH EVANS

And given to fornications, and to taverns, and sack, and wine, and metheglins, and to drinkings, and swearings, and starings, pribbles and prabbles?

SIR JOHN FALSTAFF

Well, I am your theme: you have the start of me; I am dejected; I am not able to answer the Welsh flannel: ignorance itself is a plummet o'er me: use me as you will.

FORD

Marry, sir, we'll bring you to Windsor, to one Master Brook, that you have cozened of money, to whom you should have been a pandar: over and above that you have suffered, I think to repay that money will be a biting affliction.

PAGE

Yet be cheerful, knight: thou shalt eat a posset to-night at my house; where I will desire thee to laugh at my wife, that now laughs at thee: tell her Master Slender hath married her daughter.

MISTRESS PAGE

[Aside] Doctors doubt that: if Anne Page be my daughter, she is, by this, Doctor Caius' wife.

Enter SLENDER

SLENDER

Whoa, ho! ho, father Page!

PAGE

Son, how now! how now, son! have you dispatched?

SLENDER

Dispatched! I'll make the best in Gloucestershire know on't; would I were hanged, la, else!

PAGE

Of what, son?

SLENDER

I came yonder at Eton to marry Mistress Anne Page, and she's a great lubberly boy. If it had not been i' the church, I would have swinged him, or he should have swinged me. If I did not think it had been Anne Page, would I might never stir!—and 'tis a postmaster's boy.

PAGE

Upon my life, then, you took the wrong.

SLENDER

What need you tell me that? I think so, when I took a boy for a girl. If I had been married to him, for all he was in woman's apparel, I would not have had him.

PAGE

Why, this is your own folly. Did not I tell you how you should know my daughter by her garments?

SLENDER

I went to her in white, and cried 'mum,' and she cried 'budget,' as Anne and I had appointed; and yet it was not Anne, but a postmaster's boy.

MISTRESS PAGE

Good George, be not angry: I knew of your purpose; turned my daughter into green; and, indeed, she is now with the doctor at the deanery, and there married.

Enter DOCTOR CAIUS

DOCTOR CAIUS

Vere is Mistress Page? By gar, I am cozened: I ha' married un garçon, a boy; un paysan, by gar, a boy; it is not Anne Page: by gar, I am cozened.

MISTRESS PAGE

Why, did you take her in green?

DOCTOR CAIUS

Ay, by gar, and 'tis a boy: by gar, I'll raise all Windsor.   [Exit

FORD

This is strange. Who hath got the right Anne?

PAGE

My heart misgives me:—here comes Master Fenton.

Enter FENTON *and* ANNE PAGE

How now, Master Fenton!

ANNE PAGE

Pardon, good father! good my mother, pardon!

PAGE

Now, mistress, how chance you went not with Master Slender?

MISTRESS PAGE

Why went you not with master doctor, maid?

FENTON

You do amaze her: hear the truth of it.
You would have married her most shamefully,
Where there was no proportion held in love.
The truth is, she and I, long since contracted,
Are now so sure that nothing can dissolve us.
The offence is holy that she hath committed;
And this deceit loses the name of craft,
Of disobedience, or unduteous title;
Since therein she doth evitate and shun
A thousand irreligious cursed hours,
Which forced marriage would have brought upon
    her.

FORD

Stand not amazed; here is no remedy:
In love the heavens themselves do guide the
    state;
Money buys lands, and wives are sold by fate.

SIR JOHN FALSTAFF

I am glad, though you have ta'en a special stand to
strike at me, that your arrow hath glanced.

PAGE

Well, what remedy? Fenton, heaven give thee joy!
What cannot be eschew'd must be embraced.

SIR JOHN FALSTAFF

When night-dogs run, all sorts of deer are chased.

MISTRESS PAGE

Well, I will muse no further. Master Fenton,
Heaven give you many, many merry days!
Good husband, let us every one go home,
And laugh this sport o'er by a country fire;
Sir John and all.

FORD

Let it be so. Sir John,
To Master Brook you yet shall hold your word;
For he to-night shall lie with Mistress Ford. [*Exeunt*

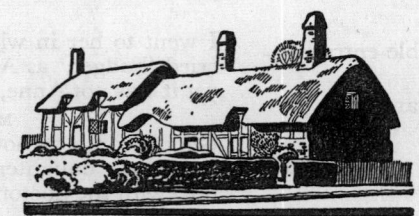

TROILUS AND CRESSIDA

SYNOPSIS

I͟T ͟I͟S the eighth year of the siege of Troy, with King Priam's youngest son, the gallant Troilus, madly in love with Cressida, a beautiful Trojan girl, and asking her uncle Pandarus to intercede for him, as the Grecian camp during a truce discusses the futility of its efforts, and the Trojan leaders in council wonder if the stolen Helen is worth all she has cost.

Hector is in favor of returning her and paying the indemnity included in the Greeks' conditions of peace, but his younger brothers, Paris, Troilus and Helenus, present their more romantic arguments to offset his, and it is decided, in spite of the woeful prophecies of their sister Cassandra, to keep up the fight for honor and glory, with Hector himself announcing that he has sent a challenge to any Greek who will meet him in personal combat, hoping thereby to cope with their great champion Achilles. The Grecian generals, particularly the wise Ulysses, realize that their army's morale is being undermined by the influence of the insubordinate Achilles, who, proudly resting upon his laurels, lolls in his tent with his friend Patroclus, and scornfully evades all orders from his superior officers.

When the Trojan Æneas brings Hector's challenge, Agamemnon and the other generals plan to spite Achilles by selecting their protagonist by lot and contriving to have the dull-witted Ajax chosen for the duel. Achilles, by pretending to be ill and declining to receive a deputation of the staff officers, strengthens them in their resolution and they encourage Ajax by their flattery to fight with Hector, while they continue their strategy by snubbing the champion until he consults Ulysses about it and is told that an effeminate man is loathed in time of action, and that only perseverance keeps honor bright. Beginning at last to understand that he is endangering his reputation, Achilles sends a messenger to Ajax asking him to invite Hector and his Trojan followers to a feast in his tent after the duel, and to arrange with Agamemnon for their safe conduct.

Meanwhile, the Lord Pandarus arranges an assignation for Troilus and Cressida, who has purposely appeared hard to win, and they pledge eternal faith to each other, not knowing that her father, Calchas, a Trojan priest serving in the Grecian army, had already secured her exchange for a Trojan prisoner, Antenor. The despairing lovers part at dawn, Troilus passionately vowing to bribe the Grecian sentries and visit her nightly, and, noticing the intense admiration of the Greek, Diomedes, who is sent to conduct Cressida to the enemy camp, he threatens him with death if she is not well used.

The generals in Agamemnon's tent gaily request kisses when welcoming the fair Trojan, which the recently heart-broken girl as lightly gives, and Ulysses passes a shrewd remark on her wanton spirit and glib tongue. The fight between the champions begins at this moment, but ends unexpectedly with Hector's refusal to strive against Ajax who is his kinsman, and both Greeks and Trojans adjourn in friendliness to the feast in Achilles' tent.

Troilus inquires the location of Calchas' tent and Ulysses offers his guidance to a place of vantage where, hidden from view and almost doubting the evidence of his own eyes and ears, the eager deluded boy witnesses the betrayal of his faith as Cressida returns the love of the ardent Diomedes and gives him her former lover's favor.

The next day, Hector's wife Andromache, who has had ominous dreams, and his sister Cassandra, who prophesies disaster and death, labor to dissuade him from the field of battle, and the old King Priam begs his son to remain at home for that one day. But Hector refuses, reminding them that it is his duty to keep faith with the Greeks with whom he is engaged to fight.

In the fierce fighting, Troilus engages Diomedes and Menelaus, Paris, but without decisive results. Hector, fighting like a thousand men, as it seems to Agamemnon, mows down the Grecian ranks and finally kills Patroclus, Achilles' intimate friend. Achilles' anger is aroused but he will not fight Hector single-handed, and waits until the great Trojan warrior has taken his armor off and is resting in his tent when, in defiance of all rules of honor in warfare, he cowardly sets his Myrmidons on him, afterwards dragging the dead body around the city tied to his horse's tail. Æneas sorrowfully leads the Trojan troops homewards, while Troilus lingers with a wild cry of defiance to the gods and the Greeks.

HISTORICAL DATA

The extraordinary vogue of the story of Troy in the literature of many nations makes the identification of the true source of Shakespeare's play extremely difficult. It is presumable that the playwright used several accounts in preparing his material. Chief among these were Chaucer's poem of the same name and Caxton's *Recuyell of the Historyes of Troye*. Certain passages also undoubtedly derive from Chapman's translation of Homer.

It is possible that the suggestion of the subject came from an earlier play which Henslowe commissioned Dekker and Chettle to write in 1599. On the Stationers' Register, under date of February 7, 1602–3, was entered for James Roberts "The Booke of Troilus and Cressida, as yt is acted by My Lo. Chamberlen's men. When he hathe gotten sufficient aucthority for yt." Apparently the "aucthority" was not forthcoming, but this entry helps fix the date of the play. There seems to be an allusion in the Prologue to Ben Jonson's *Poetaster*, produced in 1601, and the inference is that this play must have been written in or about 1602. Authorities differ, however, and the exact date cannot be established with certainty, although the years 1599–1603 would seem to fix the extreme limits of its composition.

"'Tis Troilus! there's a man!"
TROILUS AND CRESSIDA

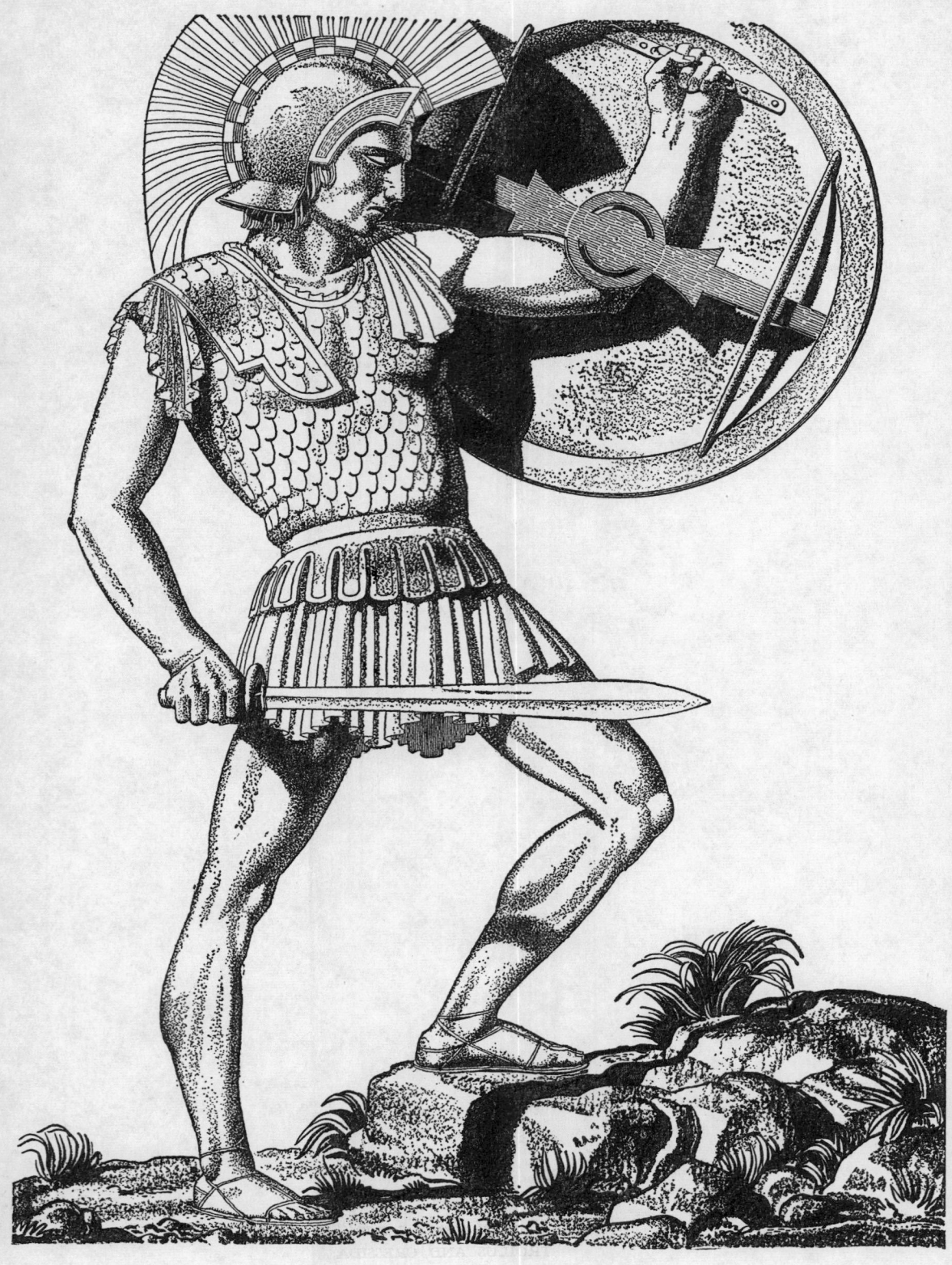

TROILUS AND CRESSIDA

DRAMATIS PERSONÆ

PRIAM, *king of Troy.*
HECTOR, }
TROILUS,
PARIS, } *his sons.*
DEIPHOBUS,
HELENUS, }
MARGARELON, *a bastard son of Priam.*
ÆNEAS, } *Trojan commanders.*
ANTENOR,
CALCHAS, *a Trojan priest, taking part with the Greeks.*
PANDARUS, *uncle to Cressida.*
AGAMEMNON, *the Grecian general.*
MENELAUS, *his brother.*
THERSITES, *a deformed and scurrilous Grecian.*
ALEXANDER, *servant to Cressida.*
SERVANT *to Troilus.*

ACHILLES, }
AJAX,
ULYSSES, }
NESTOR, } *Grecian commanders.*
DIOMEDES,
PATROCLUS, }
SERVANT *to Paris.*
SERVANT *to Diomedes.*

HELEN, *wife to Menelaus.*
ANDROMACHE, *wife to Hector.*
CASSANDRA, *daughter to Priam; a prophetess.*
CRESSIDA, *daughter to Calchas.*

TROJAN *and* GREEK SOLDIERS, *and* ATTENDANTS.

SCENE—*Troy, and the Grecian camp.*

THE PROLOGUE

IN TROY there lies the scene. From isles of Greece
The princes orgulous, their high blood chafed,
Have to the port of Athens sent their ships,
Fraught with the ministers and instruments
Of cruel war: sixty and nine, that wore
Their crownets regal, from the Athenian bay
Put forth toward Phrygia, and their vow is made
To ransack Troy, within whose strong immures
The ravish'd Helen, Menelaus' queen,
With wanton Paris sleeps; and that's the quarrel.
To Tenedos they come;
And the deep-drawing barks do there disgorge
Their warlike fraughtage: now on Dardan plains
The fresh and yet unbruised Greeks do pitch
Their brave pavilions: Priam's six-gated city,
Dardan, and Timbria, Helias, Chetas, Troien,
And Antenorides, with massy staples,
And corresponsive and fulfilling bolts,
Sperr up the sons of Troy.
Now expectation, tickling skittish spirits,
On one and other side, Trojan and Greek,
Sets all on hazard: and hither am I come
A prologue arm'd, but not in confidence
Of author's pen or actor's voice, but suited
In like conditions as our argument,
To tell you, fair beholders, that our play
Leaps o'er the vaunt and firstlings of those broils,
Beginning in the middle; starting thence away
To what may be digested in a play.
Like, or find fault; do as your pleasures are:
Now good or bad, 'tis but the chance of war.

ACT I

SCENE I. *Troy. Before* PRIAM'S *palace*

Enter PANDARUS *and* TROILUS

TROILUS

Call here my varlet; I'll unarm again:
Why should I war without the walls of Troy,
That find such cruel battle here within?
Each Trojan that is master of his heart,
Let him to field; Troilus, alas, hath none!

PANDARUS

Will this gear ne'er be mended?

TROILUS

The Greeks are strong and skilful to their strength,
Fierce to their skill and to their fierceness valiant,
But I am weaker than a woman's tear,
Tamer than sleep, fonder than ignorance,
Less valiant than the virgin in the night,
And skilless as unpractised infancy.

PANDARUS

Well, I have told you enough of this: for my part,
I'll not meddle nor make no farther. He that will
have a cake out of the wheat must needs tarry the
grinding.

TROILUS

Have I not tarried?

PANDARUS

Ay, the grinding; but you must tarry the bolting.

TROILUS

Have I not tarried?

PANDARUS

Ay, the bolting; but you must tarry the leavening.

[819]

TROILUS

Still have I tarried.

PANDARUS

Ay, to the leavening; but here's yet in the word
'hereafter,' the kneading, the making of the cake, the
heating of the oven, and the baking; nay, you must
stay the cooling too, or you may chance to burn
your lips.

TROILUS

Patience herself, what goddess e'er she be,
Doth lesser blench at sufferance than I do.
At Priam's royal table do I sit;
And when fair Cressid comes into my thoughts,—
So, traitor!—'When she comes!'—When is she
    thence?

PANDARUS

Well, she looked yesternight fairer than ever I saw
her look, or any woman else.

TROILUS

I was about to tell thee:—when my heart,
As wedged with a sigh, would rive in twain,
Lest Hector or my father should perceive me,
I have, as when the sun doth light a storm,
Buried this sigh in wrinkle of a smile:
But sorrow, that is couch'd in seeming gladness,
Is like that mirth fate turns to sudden sadness.

PANDARUS

An her hair were not somewhat darker than Helen's
—well, go to—there were no more comparison between the women: but, for my part, she is my kinswoman; I would not, as they term it, praise her: but
I would somebody had heard her talk yesterday, as
I did. I will not dispraise your sister Cassandra's
wit, but—

TROILUS

O Pandarus! I tell thee, Pandarus,—
When I do tell thee, there my hopes lie drown'd,
Reply not in how many fathoms deep
They lie indrench'd. I tell thee, I am mad
In Cressid's love: thou answer'st 'she is fair;'
Pour'st in the open ulcer of my heart
Her eyes, her hair, her cheek, her gait, her voice,
Handlest in thy discourse, O, that her hand,
In whose comparison all whites are ink
Writing their own reproach, to whose soft seizure
The cygnet's down is harsh, and spirit of sense
Hard as the palm of ploughman: this thou tell'st me,
As true thou tell'st me, when I say I love her;
But, saying thus, instead of oil and balm,
Thou lay'st in every gash that love hath given me
The knife that made it.

PANDARUS

I speak no more than truth.

TROILUS

Thou dost not speak so much.

PANDARUS

Faith, I'll not meddle in 't. Let her be as she is: if
she be fair, 'tis the better for her; an she be not, she
has the mends in her own hands.

TROILUS

Good Pandarus, how now, Pandarus!

PANDARUS

I have had my labour for my travail; ill-thought on
of her, and ill-thought on of you: gone between and
between, but small thanks for my labour.

TROILUS

What, art thou angry, Pandarus? what, with me?

PANDARUS

Because she's kin to me, therefore she's not so fair as
Helen: an she were not kin to me, she would be as
fair on Friday as Helen is on Sunday. But what care
I? I care not an she were a black-a-moor; 'tis all one
to me.

TROILUS

Say I she is not fair?

PANDARUS

I do not care whether you do or no. She's a fool to
stay behind her father; let her to the Greeks; and so
I'll tell her the next time I see her: for my part, I'll
meddle nor make no more i' the matter.

TROILUS

Pandarus,—

PANDARUS

Not I.

TROILUS

Sweet Pandarus,—

PANDARUS

Pray you, speak no more to me: I will leave all as I
found it, and there an end.   [Exit. An alarum

TROILUS

Peace, you ungracious clamours! peace, rude
    sounds!
Fools on both sides! Helen must needs be fair,
When with your blood you daily paint her thus.
I cannot fight upon this argument;
It is too starved a subject for my sword.
But Pandarus—O gods, how do you plague me!
I cannot come to Cressid but by Pandar;
And he's as tetchy to be woo'd to woo
As she is stubborn-chaste against all suit.
Tell me, Apollo, for thy Daphne's love,
What Cressid is, what Pandar, and what we.
Her bed is India; there she lies, a pearl:
Between our Ilium and where she resides,
Let it be call'd the wild and wandering flood,
Ourself the merchant, and this sailing Pandar
Our doubtful hope, our convoy and our bark.

Alarum. Enter ÆNEAS

ÆNEAS

How now, Prince Troilus! wherefore not afield?

TROILUS

Because not there: this woman's answer sorts,
For womanish it is to be from thence.
What news, Æneas, from the field to-day?

ÆNEAS

That Paris is returned home, and hurt.

TROILUS

By whom, Æneas?

ÆNEAS
Troilus, by Menelaus.

TROILUS
Let Paris bleed: 'tis but a scar to scorn;
Paris is gored with Menelaus' horn. 　　　　[*Alarum*

ÆNEAS
Hark, what good sport is out of town to-day!

TROILUS
Better at home, if 'would I might' were 'may.'
But to the sport abroad: are you bound thither?

ÆNEAS
In all swift haste.

TROILUS
Come, go we then together.
　　　　　　　　　　　　　　　　　[*Exeunt*

SCENE II. *The same. A street*

Enter CRESSIDA *and* ALEXANDER *her man*

CRESSIDA
Who were those went by?

ALEXANDER
Queen Hecuba and Helen.

CRESSIDA
And whither go they?

ALEXANDER
Up to the eastern tower,
Whose height commands as subject all the vale,
To see the battle. Hector, whose patience
Is as a virtue fix'd, to-day was moved:
He chid Andromache and struck his armourer;
And, like as there were husbandry in war,
Before the sun rose he was harness'd light,
And to the field goes he; where every flower
Did, as a prophet, weep what it foresaw
In Hector's wrath.

CRESSIDA
What was his cause of anger?

ALEXANDER
The noise goes, this: there is among the Greeks
A lord of Trojan blood, nephew to Hector;
They call him Ajax.

CRESSIDA
Good; and what of him?

ALEXANDER
They say he is a very man per se,
And stands alone.

CRESSIDA
So do all men, unless they are drunk, sick, or have
no legs.

ALEXANDER
This man, lady, hath robbed many beasts of their
particular additions; he is as valiant as the lion,
churlish as the bear, slow as the elephant: a man
into whom nature hath so crowded humours that
his valour is crushed into folly, his folly sauced with
discretion: there is no man hath a virtue that he
hath not a glimpse of, nor any man an attaint but
he carries some stain of it: he is melancholy without
cause and merry against the hair: he hath the joints

of every thing; but every thing so out of joint that
he is a gouty Briareus, many hands and no use, or
purblind Argus, all eyes and no sight.

CRESSIDA
But how should this man, that makes me smile,
make Hector angry?

ALEXANDER
They say he yesterday coped Hector in the battle
and struck him down, the disdain and shame
whereof hath ever since kept Hector fasting and
waking.

Enter PANDARUS

CRESSIDA
Who comes here?

ALEXANDER
Madam, your uncle Pandarus.

CRESSIDA
Hector's a gallant man.

ALEXANDER
As may be in the world, lady.

PANDARUS
What's that? what's that?

CRESSIDA
Good morrow, uncle Pandarus.

PANDARUS
Good morrow, cousin Cressid: what do you talk of?
Good morrow, Alexander. How do you, cousin?
When were you at Ilium?

CRESSIDA
This morning, uncle.

PANDARUS
What were you talking of when I came? Was Hector armed and gone ere you came to Ilium? Helen
was not up, was she?

CRESSIDA
Hector was gone; but Helen was not up.

PANDARUS
E'en so: Hector was stirring early.

CRESSIDA
That were we talking of, and of his anger.

PANDARUS
Was he angry?

CRESSIDA
So he says here.

PANDARUS
True, he was so; I know the cause too; he'll lay
about him to-day, I can tell them that: and there's
Troilus will not come far behind him; let them take
heed of Troilus, I can tell them that too.

CRESSIDA
What, is he angry too?

PANDARUS
Who, Troilus? Troilus is the better man of the two.

CRESSIDA
O Jupiter! there's no comparison.

PANDARUS
What, not between Troilus and Hector? Do you
know a man if you see him?

CRESSIDA
Ay, if I ever saw him before and knew him.

PANDARUS

Well, I say Troilus is Troilus.

CRESSIDA

Then you say as I say; for, I am sure, he is not Hector.

PANDARUS

No, nor Hector is not Troilus in some degrees.

CRESSIDA

'Tis just to each of them; he is himself.

PANDARUS

Himself! Alas, poor Troilus! I would he were.

CRESSIDA

So he is.

PANDARUS

Condition, I had gone barefoot to India.

CRESSIDA

He is not Hector.

PANDARUS

Himself! no, he's not himself: would a' were himself! Well, the gods are above; time must friend or end: well, Troilus, well, I would my heart were in her body! No, Hector is not a better man than Troilus.

CRESSIDA

Excuse me.

PANDARUS

He is elder.

CRESSIDA

Pardon me, pardon me.

PANDARUS

Th' other's not come to 't; you shall tell me another tale, when th' other's come to 't. Hector shall not have his wit this year.

CRESSIDA

He shall not need it, if he have his own.

PANDARUS

Nor his qualities.

CRESSIDA

No matter.

PANDARUS

Nor his beauty.

CRESSIDA

'Twould not become him; his own's better.

PANDARUS

You have no judgement, niece: Helen herself swore th' other day, that Troilus, for a brown favour—for so 'tis, I must confess,—not brown neither,—

CRESSIDA

No, but brown.

PANDARUS

Faith, to say truth, brown and not brown.

CRESSIDA

To say the truth, true and not true.

PANDARUS

She praised his complexion above Paris.

CRESSIDA

Why, Paris hath colour enough.

PANDARUS

So he has.

CRESSIDA

Then Troilus should have too much: if she praised him above, his complexion is higher than his; he having colour enough, and the other higher, is too flaming a praise for a good complexion. I had as lief Helen's golden tongue had commended Troilus for a copper nose.

PANDARUS

I swear to you, I think Helen loves him better than Paris.

CRESSIDA

Then she's a merry Greek indeed.

PANDARUS

Nay, I am sure she does. She came to him th' other day into the compassed window,—and, you know, he has not past three or four hairs on his chin,—

CRESSIDA

Indeed, a tapster's arithmetic may soon bring his particulars therein to a total.

PANDARUS

Why, he is very young: and yet will he, within three pound, lift as much as his brother Hector.

CRESSIDA

Is he so young a man and so old a lifter?

PANDARUS

But, to prove to you that Helen loves him: she came and puts me her white hand to his cloven chin,—

CRESSIDA

Juno have mercy! how came it cloven?

PANDARUS

Why, you know, 'tis dimpled: I think his smiling becomes him better than any man in all Phrygia.

CRESSIDA

O, he smiles valiantly.

PANDARUS

Does he not?

CRESSIDA

O yes, an 'twere a cloud in autumn.

PANDARUS

Why, go to, then: but to prove to you that Helen loves Troilus,—

CRESSIDA

Troilus will stand to the proof, if you'll prove it so.

PANDARUS

Troilus! why, he esteems her no more than I esteem an addle egg.

CRESSIDA

If you love an addle egg as well as you love an idle head, you would eat chickens i' the shell.

PANDARUS

I cannot choose but laugh, to think how she tickled his chin; indeed, she has a marvellous white hand, I must needs confess,—

CRESSIDA

Without the rack.

PANDARUS

And she takes upon her to spy a white hair on his chin.

CRESSIDA

Alas, poor chin! many a wart is richer.

PANDARUS

But there was such laughing! Queen Hecuba laughed, that her eyes ran o'er.

CRESSIDA

With mill-stones.

PANDARUS

And Cassandra laughed.

CRESSIDA

But there was more temperate fire under the pot of her eyes: did her eyes run o'er too?

PANDARUS

And Hector laughed.

CRESSIDA

At what was all this laughing?

PANDARUS

Marry, at the white hair that Helen spied on Troilus' chin.

CRESSIDA

An 't had been a green hair, I should have laughed too.

PANDARUS

They laughed not so much at the hair as at his pretty answer.

CRESSIDA

What was his answer?

PANDARUS

Quoth she, 'Here's but two and fifty hairs on your chin, and one of them is white.'

CRESSIDA

This is her question.

PANDARUS

That's true; make no question of that. 'Two and fifty hairs,' quoth he, 'and one white: that white hair is my father, and all the rest are his sons.' 'Jupiter!' quoth she, 'which of these hairs is Paris my husband?' 'The forked one,' quoth he, 'pluck 't out, and give it him.' But there was such laughing! and Helen so blushed, and Paris so chafed, and all the rest so laughed, that it passed.

CRESSIDA

So let it now; for it has been a great while going by.

PANDARUS

Well, cousin, I told you a thing yesterday; think on 't.

CRESSIDA

So I do.

PANDARUS

I'll be sworn 'tis true; he will weep you, an 'twere a man born in April.

CRESSIDA

And I'll spring up in his tears, an 'twere a nettle against May.   [A retreat sounded

PANDARUS

Hark! they are coming from the field: shall we stand up here, and see them as they pass toward Ilium? good niece, do, sweet niece Cressida.

CRESSIDA

At your pleasure.

PANDARUS

Here, here, here's an excellent place; here we may see most bravely: I'll tell you them all by their names as they pass by; but mark Troilus above the rest.

ÆNEAS passes

CRESSIDA

Speak not so loud.

PANDARUS

That's Æneas: is not that a brave man? he's one of the flowers of Troy, I can tell you: but mark Troilus; you shall see anon.

CRESSIDA

Who's that?

ANTENOR passes

PANDARUS

That's Antenor: he has a shrewd wit, I can tell you; and he's a man good enough: he's one o' the soundest judgements in Troy, whosoever, and a proper man of person. When comes Troilus? I'll show you Troilus anon: if he see me, you shall see him nod at me.

CRESSIDA

Will he give you the nod?

PANDARUS

You shall see.

CRESSIDA

If he do, the rich shall have more.

HECTOR passes

PANDARUS

That's Hector, that, that, look you, that; there's a fellow! Go thy way, Hector! There's a brave man, niece. O brave Hector! Look how he looks! there's a countenance! is 't not a brave man?

CRESSIDA

O, a brave man!

PANDARUS

Is a' not? it does a man's heart good. Look you what hacks are on his helmet! look you yonder, do you see? look you there: there's no jesting; there's laying on, take 't off who will, as they say: there be hacks!

CRESSIDA

Be those with swords?

PANDARUS

Swords! any thing, he cares not; an the devil come to him, it's all one: by God's lid, it does one's heart good. Yonder comes Paris, yonder comes Paris.

PARIS passes

Look ye yonder, niece; is 't not a gallant man too, is 't not? Why, this is brave now. Who said he came hurt home to-day? he's not hurt: why, this will do Helen's heart good now, ha! Would I could see Troilus now! you shall see Troilus anon.

CRESSIDA

Who's that?

HELENUS passes

PANDARUS

That's Helenus: I marvel where Troilus is. That's Helenus. I think he went not forth to-day. That's Helenus.

CRESSIDA

Can Helenus fight, uncle?

[823]

PANDARUS

Helenus! no; yes, he'll fight indifferent well. I marvel where Troilus is. Hark! do you not hear the people cry 'Troilus'? Helenus is a priest.

CRESSIDA

What sneaking fellow comes yonder?

TROILUS *passes*

PANDARUS

Where? yonder? that's Deiphobus. 'Tis Troilus! there's a man, niece! Hem! Brave Troilus! the prince of chivalry!

CRESSIDA

Peace, for shame, peace!

PANDARUS

Mark him; note him. O brave Troilus! Look well upon him, niece; look you how his sword is bloodied, and his helm more hacked than Hector's; and how he looks, and how he goes! O admirable youth! he never saw three-and-twenty. Go thy way, Troilus, go thy way! Had I a sister were a grace, or a daughter a goddess, he should take his choice. O admirable man! Paris? Paris is dirt to him; and, I warrant, Helen, to change, would give an eye to boot.

COMMON SOLDIERS *pass*

CRESSIDA

Here come more.

PANDARUS

Asses, fools, dolts! chaff and bran, chaff and bran! porridge after meat! I could live and die i' the eyes of Troilus. Ne'er look, ne'er look; the eagles are gone: crows and daws, crows and daws! I had rather be such a man as Troilus than Agamemnon and all Greece.

CRESSIDA

There is among the Greeks Achilles, a better man than Troilus.

PANDARUS

Achilles! a drayman, a porter, a very camel.

CRESSIDA

Well, well.

PANDARUS

Well, well! Why, have you any discretion? have you any eyes? do you know what a man is? Is not birth, beauty, good shape, discourse, manhood, learning, gentleness, virtue, youth, liberality, and such like, the spice and salt that season a man?

CRESSIDA

Ay, a minced man: and then to be baked with no date in the pie, for then the man's date is out.

PANDARUS

You are such a woman! one knows not at what ward you lie.

CRESSIDA

Upon my back, to defend my belly; upon my wit, to defend my wiles; upon my secrecy, to defend mine honesty; my mask, to defend my beauty; and you, to defend all these: and at all these wards I lie, at a thousand watches.

PANDARUS

Say one of your watches.

CRESSIDA

Nay, I'll watch you for that; and that's one of the chiefest of them too: if I cannot ward what I would not have hit, I can watch you for telling how I took the blow; unless it swell past hiding, and then it's past watching.

PANDARUS

You are such another!

Enter TROILUS'S BOY

BOY

Sir, my lord would instantly speak with you.

PANDARUS

Where?

BOY

At your own house; there he unarms him.

PANDARUS

Good boy, tell him I come. [*Exit* BOY] I doubt he be hurt. Fare ye well, good niece.

CRESSIDA

Adieu, uncle.

PANDARUS

I will be with you, niece, by and by.

CRESSIDA

To bring, uncle?

PANDARUS

Ay, a token from Troilus.

CRESSIDA

By the same token, you are a bawd. [*Exit* PANDARUS
Words, vows, gifts, tears, and love's full sacrifice,
He offers in another's enterprise:
But more in Troilus thousand fold I see
Than in the glass of Pandar's praise may be;
Yet hold I off. Women are angels, wooing:
Things won are done; joy's soul lies in the doing:
That she beloved knows nought that knows not this:
Men prize the thing ungain'd more than it is:
That she was never yet that ever knew
Love got so sweet as when desire did sue:
Therefore this maxim out of love I teach:
Achievement is command; ungain'd, beseech.
Then though my heart's content firm love doth bear,
Nothing of that shall from mine eyes appear.
[*Exeunt*

SCENE III. *The Grecian camp. Before* AGAMEMNON'S *tent*

Sennet. Enter AGAMEMNON, NESTOR, ULYSSES, MENELAUS, *with others*

AGAMEMNON

Princes,
What grief hath set the jaundice on your cheeks?
The ample proposition that hope makes
In all designs begun on earth below
Fails in the promised largeness: checks and disasters

Grow in the veins of actions highest rear'd,
As knots, by the conflux of meeting sap,
Infect the sound pine and divert his grain
Tortive and errant from his course of growth.
Nor, princes, is it matter new to us
That we come short of our suppose so far
That after seven years' siege yet Troy walls stand;
Sith every action that hath gone before,
Whereof we have record, trial did draw
Bias and thwart, not answering the aim
And that unbodied figure of the thought
That gave 't surmised shape. Why then, you princes,
Do you with cheeks abash'd behold our works,
And call them shames? which are indeed nought
    else
But the protractive trials of great Jove
To find persistive constancy in men:
The fineness of which metal is not found
In fortune's love; for then the bold and coward,
The wise and fool, the artist and unread,
The hard and soft, seem all affined and kin:
But in the wind and tempest of her frown,
Distinction with a broad and powerful fan,
Puffing at all, winnows the light away,
And what hath mass or matter, by itself
Lies rich in virtue and unmingled.

NESTOR

With due observance of thy godlike seat,
Great Agamemnon, Nestor shall apply
Thy latest words. In the reproof of chance
Lies the true proof of men: the sea being smooth,
How many shallow bauble boats dare sail
Upon her patient breast, making their way
With those of nobler bulk!
But let the ruffian Boreas once enrage
The gentle Thetis, and anon behold
The strong-ribb'd bark through liquid mountains
    cut,
Bounding between the two moist elements,
Like Perseus' horse: where's then the saucy boat,
Whose weak untimber'd sides but even now
Co-rivall'd greatness? either to harbour fled,
Or made a toast for Neptune. Even so
Doth valour's show and valour's worth divide
In storms of fortune: for in her ray and brightness
The herd hath more annoyance by the breese
Than by the tiger; but when the splitting wind
Makes flexible the knees of knotted oaks,
And flies fled under shade, why then the thing of
    courage
As roused with rage with rage doth sympathize,
And with an accent tuned in selfsame key
Retorts to chiding fortune.

ULYSSES
            Agamemnon,
Thou great commander, nerve and bone of Greece,
Heart of our numbers, soul and only spirit,
In whom the tempers and the minds of all
Should be shut up, hear what Ulysses speaks.
Besides the applause and approbation

The which, [To AGAMEMNON] most mighty for thy
    place and sway,
[To NESTOR] And thou most reverend for thy
    stretch'd-out life,
I give to both your speeches, which were such
As Agamemnon and the hand of Greece
Should hold up high in brass, and such again
As venerable Nestor, hatch'd in silver,
Should with a bond of air, strong as the axletree
On which heaven rides, knit all the Greekish ears
To his experienced tongue, yet let it please both,
Thou great, and wise, to hear Ulysses speak.

AGAMEMNON

Speak, Prince of Ithaca; and be 't of less expect
That matter needless, of importless burthen,
Divide thy lips, than we are confident,
When rank Thersites opes his mastic jaws,
We shall hear music, wit and oracle.

ULYSSES

Troy, yet upon his basis, had been down,
And the great Hector's sword had lack'd a master,
But for these instances.
The specialty of rule hath been neglected:
And, look, how many Grecian tents do stand
Hollow upon this plain, so many hollow factions.
When that the general is not like the hive
To whom the foragers shall all repair,
What honey is expected? Degree being vizarded,
The unworthiest shows as fairly in the mask.
The heavens themselves, the planets and this centre,
Observe degree, priority and place,
Insisture, course, proportion, season, form,
Office and custom, in all line of order:
And therefore is the glorious planet Sol
In noble eminence enthroned and sphered
Amidst the other; whose medicinable eye
Corrects the ill aspects of planets evil,
And posts like the commandment of a king,
Sans check to good and bad: but when the planets
In evil mixture to disorder wander,
What plagues and what portents, what mutiny,
What raging of the sea, shaking of earth,
Commotion in the winds, frights, changes, horrors,
Divert and crack, rend and deracinate
The unity and married calm of states
Quite from their fixure! O, when degree is shaked,
Which is the ladder to all high designs,
The enterprise is sick! How could communities,
Degrees in schools and brotherhoods in cities,
Peaceful commerce from dividable shores,
The primogenitive and due of birth,
Prerogative of age, crowns, sceptres, laurels,
But by degree, stand in authentic place?
Take but degree away, untune that string,
And, hark, what discord follows! each thing meets
In mere oppugnancy: the bounded waters
Should lift their bosoms higher than the shores,
And make a sop of all this solid globe:
Strength should be lord of imbecility,
And the rude son should strike his father dead:

Force should be right; or rather, right and wrong,
Between whose endless jar justice resides,
Should lose their names, and so should justice too.
Then every thing includes itself in power,
Power into will, will into appetite;
And appetite, an universal wolf,
So doubly seconded with will and power,
Must make perforce an universal prey,
And last eat up himself. Great Agamemnon,
This chaos, when degree is suffocate,
Follows the choking.
And this neglection of degree it is
That by a pace goes backward, with a purpose
It hath to climb. The general's disdain'd
By him one step below; he by the next;
That next by him beneath: so every step,
Exampled by the first pace that is sick
Of his superior, grows to an envious fever
Of pale and bloodless emulation:
And 'tis this fever that keeps Troy on foot,
Not her own sinews. To end a tale of length,
Troy in our weakness stands, not in her strength.

NESTOR

Most wisely hath Ulysses here discover'd
The fever where of all our power is sick.

AGAMEMNON

The nature of the sickness found, Ulysses,
What is the remedy?

ULYSSES

The great Achilles, whom opinion crowns
The sinew and the forehand of our host,
Having his ear full of his airy fame,
Grows dainty of his worth, and in his tent
Lies mocking our designs: with him, Patroclus,
Upon a lazy bed, the livelong day
Breaks scurril jests;
And with ridiculous and awkward action,
Which, slanderer, he imitation calls,
He pageants us. Sometime, great Agamemnon,
Thy topless deputation he puts on;
And, like a strutting player, whose conceit
Lies in his hamstring, and doth think it rich
To hear the wooden dialogue and sound
'Twixt his stretch'd footing and the scaffoldage,
Such to-be-pitied and o'er-wrested seeming
He acts thy greatness in: and when he speaks,
'Tis like a chime a-mending; with terms unsquared,
Which, from the tongue of roaring Typhon
　　dropp'd,
Would seem hyperboles. At this fusty stuff,
The large Achilles, on his press'd bed lolling,
From his deep chest laughs out a loud applause;
Cries 'Excellent! 'tis Agamemnon just.
Now play me Nestor; hem, and stroke thy beard,
As he being dress'd to some oration.'
That's done; as near as the extremest ends
Of parallels, as like as Vulcan and his wife:
Yet god Achilles still cries 'Excellent!
'Tis Nestor right. Now play him me, Patroclus,
Arming to answer in a night alarm.'

And then, forsooth, the faint defects of age
Must be the scene of mirth; to cough and spit,
And, with a palsy fumbling on his gorget,
Shake in and out the rivet: and at this sport
Sir Valour dies; cries 'O, enough, Patroclus;
Or give me ribs of steel! I shall split all
In pleasure of my spleen.' And in this fashion,
All our abilities, gifts, natures, shapes,
Severals and generals of grace exact,
Achievements, plots, orders, preventions,
Excitements to the field or speech for truce,
Success or loss, what is or is not, serves
As stuff for these two to make paradoxes.

NESTOR

And in the imitation of these twain,
Who, as Ulysses says, opinion crowns
With an imperial voice, many are infect.
Ajax is grown self-will'd, and bears his head
In such a rein, in full as proud a place
As broad Achilles; keeps his tent like him;
Makes factious feasts; rails on our state of war
Bold as an oracle, and sets Thersites,
A slave whose gall coins slanders like a mint,
To match us in comparisons with dirt,
To weaken and discredit our exposure,
How rank soever rounded in with danger.

ULYSSES

They tax our policy and call it cowardice,
Count wisdom as no member of the war,
Forestall prescience, and esteem no act
But that of hand: the still and mental parts
That do contrive how many hands shall strike
When fitness calls them on, and know by measure
Of their observant toil the enemies' weight,—
Why, this hath not a finger's dignity;
They call this bed-work, mappery, closet-war:
So that the ram that batters down the wall,
For the great swing and rudeness of his poise,
They place before his hand that made the engine,
Or those that with the fineness of their souls
By reason guide his execution.

NESTOR

Let this be granted, and Achilles' horse
Makes many Thetis' sons.　　　　　[Tucket

AGAMEMNON

What trumpet? look, Menelaus.

MENELAUS

From Troy.

Enter ÆNEAS

AGAMEMNON

What would you 'fore our tent?

ÆNEAS

Is this great Agamemnon's tent, I pray you?

AGAMEMNON

Even this.

ÆNEAS

May one that is a herald and a prince
Do a fair message to his kingly ears?

AGAMEMNON

With surety stronger than Achilles' arm

'Fore all the Greekish heads, which with one voice
Call Agamemnon head and general.

AGAMEMNON

Fair leave and large security. How may
A stranger to those most imperial looks
Know them from eyes of other mortals?

AGAMEMNON

                                        How!

ÆNEAS

Ay:
I ask, that I might waken reverence,
And bid the cheek be ready with a blush
Modest as morning when she coldly eyes
The youthful Phœbus:
Which is that god in office, guiding men?
Which is the high and mighty Agamemnon?

AGAMEMNON

This Trojan scorns us; or the men of Troy
Are ceremonious courtiers.

ÆNEAS

Courtiers as free, as debonair, unarm'd,
As bending angels; that's their fame in peace:
But when they would seem soldiers, they have galls,
Good arms, strong joints, true swords; and, Jove's
    accord,
Nothing so full of heart. But peace, Æneas,
Peace, Trojan; lay thy finger on thy lips!
The worthiness of praise distains his worth,
If that the praised himself bring the praise forth:
But what the repining enemy commends,
That breath fame blows; that praise, sole pure,
    transcends.

AGAMEMNON

Sir, you of Troy, call you yourself Æneas?

ÆNEAS

Ay, Greek, that is my name.

AGAMEMNON

What's your affair, I pray you?

ÆNEAS

Sir, pardon; 'tis for Agamemnon's ears.

AGAMEMNON

He hears nought privately that comes from Troy.

ÆNEAS

Nor I from Troy come not to whisper him:
I bring a trumpet to awake his ear,
To set his sense on the attentive bent,
And then to speak.

AGAMEMNON

                        Speak frankly as the wind;
It is not Agamemnon's sleeping hour:
That thou shalt know, Trojan, he is awake,
He tells thee so himself.

ÆNEAS

                        Trumpet, blow loud,
Send thy brass voice through all these lazy tents;
And every Greek of mettle, let him know,
What Troy means fairly shall be spoke aloud.

                                [*Trumpet sounds*

We have, great Agamemnon, here in Troy

A prince call'd Hector—Priam is his father—
Who in this dull and long-continued truce
Is rusty grown: he bade me take a trumpet,
And to this purpose speak. Kings, princes, lords!
If there be one among the fair'st of Greece,
That holds his honour higher than his ease,
That seeks his praise more than he fears his peril,
That knows his valour and knows not his fear,
That loves his mistress more than in confession
With truant vows to her own lips he loves,
And dare avow her beauty and her worth
In other arms than hers—to him this challenge.
Hector, in view of Trojans and of Greeks,
Shall make it good, or do his best do it,
He hath a lady, wiser, fairer, truer,
Than ever Greek did compass in his arms;
And will to-morrow with his trumpet call
Midway between your tents and walls of Troy,
To rouse a Grecian that is true in love:
If any come, Hector shall honour him;
If none, he'll say in Troy when he retires,
The Grecian dames are sunburnt and not worth
The splinter of a lance. Even so much.

AGAMEMNON

This shall be told our lovers, Lord Æneas;
If none of them have soul in such a kind,
We left them all at home: but we are soldiers;
And may that soldier a mere recreant prove,
That means not, hath not, or is not in love!
If then one is, or hath, or means to be,
That one meets Hector; if none else, I am he.

NESTOR

Tell him of Nestor, one that was a man
When Hector's grandsire suck'd: he is old now;
But if there be not in our Grecian host
One noble man that hath one spark of fire,
To answer for his love, tell him from me
I'll hide my silver beard in a gold beaver,
And in my vantbrace put this wither'd brawn,
And meeting him will tell him that my lady
Was fairer than his grandam, and as chaste
As may be in the world: his youth in flood,
I'll prove this truth with my three drops of blood.

ÆNEAS

Now heavens forbid such scarcity of youth!

ULYSSES

Amen.

AGAMEMNON

Fair Lord Æneas, let me touch your hand;
To our pavilion shall I lead you, sir.
Achilles shall have word of this intent;
So shall each lord of Greece, from tent to tent:
Yourself shall feast with us before you go,
And find the welcome of a noble foe.

                [*Exeunt all but* ULYSSES *and* NESTOR

ULYSSES

Nestor!

NESTOR

What says Ulysses?

ULYSSES

I have a young conception in my brain;
Be you my time to bring it to some shape.

NESTOR

What is 't?

ULYSSES

This 'tis:
Blunt wedges rive hard knots: the seeded pride
That hath to this maturity blown up
In rank Achilles must or now be cropp'd,
Or, shedding, breed a nursery of like evil,
To overbulk us all.

NESTOR

Well, and how?

ULYSSES

This challenge that the gallant Hector sends,
However it is spread in general name,
Relates in purpose only to Achilles.

NESTOR

The purpose is perspicuous even as substance,
Whose grossness little characters sum up:
And, in the publication, make no strain,
But that Achilles, were his brain as barren
As banks of Libya,—though, Apollo knows,
'Tis dry enough—will, with great speed of judge-
    ment,
Ay, with celerity, find Hector's purpose
Pointing on him.

ULYSSES

And wake him to the answer, think you?

NESTOR

Yes, 'tis most meet: who may you else oppose,
That can from Hector bring his honour off,
If not Achilles? Though 't be a sportful combat,
Yet in this trial much opinion dwells;
For here the Trojans taste our dear'st repute
With their finest palate: and trust to me, Ulysses,
Our imputation shall be oddly poised
In this wild action; for the success,
Although particular, shall give a scantling
Of good or bad unto the general;
And in such indexes, although small pricks
To their subsequent volumes, there is seen
The baby figure of the giant mass
Of things to come at large. It is supposed
He that meets Hector issues from our choice:
And choice, being mutual act of all our souls,
Makes merit her election, and doth boil,
As 'twere from forth us all, a man distill'd
Out of our virtues; who miscarrying,
What heart from hence receives the conquering
    part,
To steel a strong opinion to themselves?
Which entertain'd, limbs are his instruments,
In no less working than are swords and bows
Directive by the limbs.

ULYSSES

Give pardon to my speech;
Therefore 'tis meet Achilles meet not Hector.
Let us, like merchants, show our foulest wares,

And think, perchance, they'll sell; if not,
The lustre of the better yet to show,
Shall show the better. Do not consent
That ever Hector and Achilles meet;
For both our honour and our shame in this
Are dogg'd with two strange followers.

NESTOR

I see them not with my old eyes: what are they?

ULYSSES

What glory our Achilles shares from Hector,
Were he not proud, we all should share with him:
But he already is too insolent;
And we were better parch in Afric sun
Than in the pride and salt scorn of his eyes,
Should he 'scape Hector fair: if he were foil'd,
Why then, we did our main opinion crush
In taint of our best man. No, make a lottery,
And by device let blockish Ajax draw
The sort to fight with Hector: among ourselves
Give him allowance for the better man;
For that will physic the great Myrmidon
Who broils in loud applause, and make him fall
His crest that prouder than blue Iris bends.
If the dull brainless Ajax come safe off,
We'll dress him up in voices: if he fail,
Yet go we under our opinion still
That we have better men. But, hit or miss,
Our project's life this shape of sense assumes,
Ajax employ'd plucks down Achilles' plumes.

NESTOR

Ulysses,
Now I begin to relish thy advice;
And I will give a taste of it forthwith
To Agamemnon: go we to him straight.
Two curs shall tame each other: pride alone
Must tarre the mastiffs on, as 'twere their bone.

[Exeunt

ACT II

SCENE I. The Grecian camp

Enter AJAX and THERSITES

AJAX

Thersites!

THERSITES

Agamemnon—how if he had boils—full, all over,
generally?

AJAX

Thersites!

THERSITES

And those boils did run?—Say so,—did not the
general run then? were not that a botchy core?

AJAX

Dog!

THERSITES

Then would come some matter from him; I see
none now.

AJAX

Thou bitch-wolf's son, canst thou not hear? Feel, then.   [*Strikes him*

THERSITES

The plague of Greece upon thee, thou mongrel beef-witted lord!

AJAX

Speak then, thou vinewed'st leaven, speak: I will beat thee into handsomeness.

THERSITES

I shall sooner rail thee into wit and holiness: but, I think, thy horse will sooner con an oration than thou learn a prayer without book. Thou canst strike, canst thou? a red murrain o' thy jade's tricks!

AJAX

Toadstool, learn me the proclamation.

THERSITES

Dost thou think I have no sense, thou strikest me thus?

AJAX

The proclamation!

THERSITES

Thou art proclaimed a fool, I think.

AJAX

Do not, porpentine, do not; my fingers itch.

THERSITES

I would thou didst itch from head to foot, and I had the scratching of thee; I would make thee the loathsomest scab in Greece. When thou art forth in the incursions, thou strikest as slow as another.

AJAX

I say, the proclamation!

THERSITES

Thou grumblest and railest every hour on Achilles, and thou art as full of envy at his greatness as Cerberus is at Proserpina's beauty, ay, that thou barkest at him.

AJAX

Mistress Thersites!

THERSITES

Thou shouldst strike him.

AJAX

Cobloaf!

THERSITES

He would pun thee into shivers with his fist, as a sailor breaks a biscuit.

AJAX

[*Beating him*] You whoreson cur!

THERSITES

Do, do.

AJAX

Thou stool for a witch!

THERSITES

Ay, do, do; thou sodden-witted lord! thou hast no more brain than I have in mine elbows; an assinego may tutor thee: thou scurvy-valiant ass! thou art here but to thrash Trojans; and thou art bought and sold among those of any wit, like a barbarian

slave. If thou use to beat me, I will begin at thy heel and tell what thou art by inches, thou thing of no bowels, thou!

AJAX

You dog!

THERSITES

You scurvy lord!

AJAX

[*Beating him*] You cur!

THERSITES

Mars his idiot! do, rudeness; do, camel, do, do.

Enter ACHILLES *and* PATROCLUS

ACHILLES

Why, how now, Ajax! wherefore do ye thus? How now, Thersites! what's the matter, man?

THERSITES

You see him there, do you?

ACHILLES

Ay; what's the matter?

THERSITES

Nay, look upon him.

ACHILLES

So I do: what's the matter?

THERSITES

Nay, but regard him well.

ACHILLES

'Well!' why, so I do.

THERSITES

But yet you look not well upon him; for, whosoever you take him to be, he is Ajax.

ACHILLES

I know that, fool.

THERSITES

Ay, but that fool knows not himself.

AJAX

Therefore I beat thee.

THERSITES

Lo, lo, lo, lo, what modicums of wit he utters! his evasions have ears thus long. I have bobbed his brain more than he has beat my bones: I will buy nine sparrows for a penny, and his pia mater is not worth the ninth part of a sparrow. This lord, Achilles, Ajax, who wears his wit in his belly and his guts in his head, I'll tell you what I say of him.

ACHILLES

What?

THERSITES

I say, this Ajax—   [AJAX *offers to strike him*

ACHILLES

Nay, good Ajax.

THERSITES

Has not so much wit—

ACHILLES

Nay, I must hold you.

THERSITES

As will stop the eye of Helen's needle, for whom he comes to fight.

ACHILLES

Peace, fool!

THERSITES

I would have peace and quietness, but the fool will not: he there: that he: look you there!

AJAX

O thou damned cur! I shall—

ACHILLES

Will you set your wit to a fool's?

THERSITES

No, I warrant you; for a fool's will shame it.

PATROCLUS

Good words, Thersites.

ACHILLES

What's the quarrel?

AJAX

I bade the vile owl go learn me the tenour of the proclamation, and he rails upon me.

THERSITES

I serve thee not.

AJAX

Well, go to, go to.

THERSITES

I serve here voluntary.

ACHILLES

Your last service was sufferance, 'twas not voluntary; no man is beaten voluntary: Ajax was here the voluntary, and you as under an impress.

THERSITES

E'en so; a great deal of your wit too lies in your sinews, or else there be liars. Hector shall have a great catch, if he knock out either of your brains: a' were as good crack a fusty nut with no kernel.

ACHILLES

What, with me too, Thersites?

THERSITES

There's Ulysses and old Nestor, whose wit was mouldy ere your grandsires had nails on their toes, yoke you like draught-oxen, and make you plough up the wars.

ACHILLES

What? what?

THERSITES

Yes, good sooth: to, Achilles! to, Ajax! to!

AJAX

I shall cut out your tongue.

THERSITES

'Tis no matter; I shall speak as much as thou afterwards.

PATROCLUS

No more words, Thersites; peace!

THERSITES

I will hold my peace when Achilles' brooch bids me, shall I?

ACHILLES

There's for you, Patroclus.

THERSITES

I will see you hanged, like clotpoles, ere I come any more to your tents: I will keep where there is wit stirring, and leave the faction of fools.   [Exit

PATROCLUS

A good riddance.

ACHILLES

Marry, this, sir, is proclaim'd through all our host:
That Hector, by the fifth hour of the sun,
Will with a trumpet 'twixt our tents and Troy
To-morrow morning call some knight to arms
That hath a stomach, and such a one that dare
Maintain—I know not what: 'tis trash. Farewell.

AJAX

Farewell. Who shall answer him?

ACHILLES

I know not; 'tis put to lottery; otherwise
He knew his man.

AJAX

O, meaning you. I will go learn more of it. [Exeunt

SCENE II. Troy. A room in PRIAM's palace

Enter PRIAM, HECTOR, TROILUS, PARIS, and HELENUS

PRIAM

After so many hours, lives, speeches spent,
Thus once again says Nestor from the Greeks:
'Deliver Helen, and all damage else,
As honour, loss of time, travail, expense,
Wounds, friends, and what else dear that is consumed
In hot digestion of this cormorant war,
Shall be struck off.' Hector, what say you to 't?

HECTOR

Though no man lesser fears the Greeks than I
As far as toucheth my particular,
Yet, dread Priam,
There is no lady of more softer bowels,
More spongy to suck in the sense of fear,
More ready to cry out 'Who knows what follows?'
Than Hector is: the wound of peace is surety,
Surety secure: but modest doubt is call'd
The beacon of the wise, the tent that searches
To the bottom of the worst. Let Helen go.
Since the first sword was drawn about this question,
Every tithe soul, 'mongst many thousand dismes,
Hath been as dear as Helen; I mean, of ours:
If we have lost so many tenths of ours,
To guard a thing not ours, nor worth to us,
Had it our name, the value of one ten,
What merit's in that reason which denies
The yielding of her up?

TROILUS

Fie, fie, my brother!
Weigh you the worth and honour of a king,
So great as our dread father, in a scale
Of common ounces? will you with counters sum
The past proportion of his infinite?
And buckle in a waist most fathomless
With spans and inches so diminutive
As fears and reasons? fie, for godly shame!

HELENUS

No marvel, though you bite so sharp at reasons,
You are so empty of them. Should not our father

Bear the great sway of his affairs with reasons,
Because your speech hath none that tells him so?

TROILUS

You are for dreams and slumbers, brother priest;
You fur your gloves with reason. Here are your
  reasons:
You know an enemy intends you harm;
You know a sword employ'd is perilous,
And reason flies the object of all harm:
Who marvels then, when Helenus beholds
A Grecian and his sword, if he do set
The very wings of reason to his heels,
And fly like chidden Mercury from Jove,
Or like a star disorb'd? Nay, if we talk of reason,
Let's shut our gates, and sleep: manhood and
  honour
Should have hare hearts, would they but fat their
  thoughts
With this cramm'd reason: reason and respect
Make livers pale and lustihood deject.

HECTOR

Brother, she is not worth what she doth cost
The holding.

TROILUS

          What's aught, but as 'tis valued?

HECTOR

But value dwells not in particular will;
It holds his estimate and dignity
As well wherein 'tis precious of itself
As in the prizer: 'tis mad idolatry
To make the service greater than the god;
And the will dotes, that is attributive
To what infectiously itself affects,
Without some image of the affected merit.

TROILUS

I take to-day a wife, and my election
Is led on in the conduct of my will;
My will enkindled by mine eyes and ears,
Two traded pilots 'twixt the dangerous shores
Of will and judgement: how may I avoid,
Although my will distaste what it elected,
The wife I chose? there can be no evasion
To blench from this, and to stand firm by honour.
We turn not back the silks upon the merchant
When we have soil'd them, nor the remainder
  viands
We do not throw in unrespective sieve,
Because we now are full. It was thought meet
Paris should do some vengeance on the Greeks:
Your breath of full consent bellied his sails;
The seas and winds, old wranglers, took a truce,
And did him service: he touch'd the ports desired;
And for an old aunt whom the Greeks held captive
He brought a Grecian queen, whose youth and
  freshness
Wrinkles Apollo's and makes stale the morning.
Why keep we her? the Grecians keep our aunt:
Is she worth keeping? why, she is a pearl,
Whose price hath launch'd above a thousand ships,
And turn'd crown'd kings to merchants.

If you'll avouch 'twas wisdom Paris went,
As you must needs, for you all cried 'Go, go,'
If you'll confess he brought home noble prize,
As you must needs, for you all clapp'd your hands,
And cried 'Inestimable!' why do you now
The issue of your proper wisdoms rate,
And do a deed that Fortune never did,
Beggar the estimation which you prized
Richer than sea and land? O, theft most base,
That we have stol'n what we do fear to keep!
But thieves unworthy of a thing so stol'n,
That in their country did them that disgrace,
We fear to warrant in our native place!

CASSANDRA

[Within] Cry, Trojans, cry!

PRIAM

                What noise? what shriek is this?

TROILUS

'Tis our mad sister, I do know her voice.

CASSANDRA

[Within] Cry, Trojans!

HECTOR

It is Cassandra.
Enter CASSANDRA, raving, with her hair about her ears

CASSANDRA

Cry, Trojans, cry! lend me ten thousand eyes,
And I will fill them with prophetic tears.

HECTOR

Peace, sister, peace!

CASSANDRA

Virgins and boys, mid age and wrinkled eld,
Soft infancy, that nothing canst but cry,
Add to my clamours! let us pay betimes
A moiety of that mass of moan to come.
Cry, Trojans, cry! practise your eyes with tears!
Troy must not be, nor goodly Ilion stand;
Our firebrand brother, Paris, burns us all.
Cry, Trojans, cry! a Helen and a woe:
Cry, cry! Troy burns, or else let Helen go.   [Exit

HECTOR

Now, youthful Troilus, do not these high strains
Of divination in our sister work
Some touches of remorse? or is your blood
So madly hot that no discourse of reason,
Nor fear of bad success in a bad cause,
Can qualify the same?

TROILUS

                Why, brother Hector,
We may not think the justness of each act
Such and no other than event doth form it;
Nor once deject the courage of our minds,
Because Cassandra's mad: her brain-sick raptures
Cannot distaste the goodness of a quarrel
Which hath our several honours all engaged
To make it gracious. For my private part,
I am no more touch'd than all Priam's sons:
And Jove forbid there should be done amongst us
Such things as might offend the weakest spleen
To fight for and maintain!

PARIS

Else might the world convince of levity
As well my undertakings as your counsels:
But I attest the gods, your full consent
Gave wings to my propension, and cut off
All fears attending on so dire a project.
For what, alas, can these my single arms?
What propugnation is in one man's valour,
To stand the push and enmity of those
This quarrel would excite? Yet, I protest,
Were I alone to pass the difficulties,
And had as ample power as I have will,
Paris should ne'er retract what he hath done,
Nor faint in the pursuit.

PRIAM

　　　　　　Paris, you speak
Like one besotted on your sweet delights:
You have the honey still, but these the gall;
So to be valiant is no praise at all.

PARIS

Sir, I propose not merely to myself
The pleasures such a beauty brings with it;
But I would have the soil of her fair rape
Wiped off in honourable keeping her.
What treason were it to the ransack'd queen,
Disgrace to your great worths, and shame to me,
Now to deliver her possession up
On terms of base compulsion! Can it be
That so degenerate a strain as this
Should once set footing in your generous bosoms?
There's not the meanest spirit on our party,
Without a heart to dare, or sword to draw,
When Helen is defended, nor none so noble,
Whose life were ill bestow'd, or death unfamed,
Where Helen is the subject: then, I say,
Well may we fight for her, whom, we know well,
The world's large spaces cannot parallel.

HECTOR

Paris and Troilus, you have both said well;
And on the cause and question now in hand
Have glozed, but superficially; not much
Unlike young men, whom Aristotle thought
Unfit to hear moral philosophy.
The reasons you allege do more conduce
To the hot passion of distemper'd blood,
Than to make up a free determination
'Twixt right and wrong; for pleasure and revenge
Have ears more deaf than adders to the voice
Of any true decision. Nature craves
All dues be render'd to their owners: now,
What nearer debt in all humanity
Than wife is to the husband? If this law
Of nature be corrupted through affection,
And that great minds, of partial indulgence
To their benumbed wills, resist the same,
There is a law in each well-order'd nation
To curb those raging appetites that are
Most disobedient and refractory.
If Helen then be wife to Sparta's king,
As it is known she is, these moral laws

Of nature and of nations speak aloud
To have her back return'd: thus to persist
In doing wrong extenuates not wrong,
But makes it much more heavy. Hector's opinion
Is this in way of truth: yet, ne'ertheless,
My spritely brethren, I propend to you
In resolution to keep Helen still;
For 'tis a cause that hath no mean dependance
Upon our joint and several dignities.

TROILUS

Why, there you touch'd the life of our design:
Were it not glory that we more affected
Than the performance of our heaving spleens,
I would not wish a drop of Trojan blood
Spent more in her defence. But, worthy Hector,
She is a theme of honour and renown;
A spur to valiant and magnanimous deeds,
Whose present courage may beat down our foes,
And fame in time to come canonize us:
For, I presume, brave Hector would not lose
So rich advantage of a promised glory
As smiles upon the forehead of this action
For the wide world's revenue.

HECTOR

　　　　　　　　I am yours,
You valiant offspring of great Priamus.
I have a roisting challenge sent amongst
The dull and factious nobles of the Greeks,
Will strike amazement to their drowsy spirits:
I was advertised their great general slept,
Whilst emulation in the army crept:
This, I presume, will wake him. 　　　[Exeunt

SCENE III. *The Grecian camp. Before the tent of*
ACHILLES

Enter THERSITES, *solus*

THERSITES

How now, Thersites! what, lost in the labyrinth of
thy fury! Shall the elephant Ajax carry it thus? he
beats me, and I rail at him: O, worthy satisfaction!
would it were otherwise; that I could beat him,
whilst he railed at me. 'Sfoot, I'll learn to conjure
and raise devils, but I'll see some issue of my spiteful
execrations. Then there's Achilles, a rare enginer. If
Troy be not taken till these two undermine it, the
walls will stand till they fall of themselves. O thou
great thunder-darter of Olympus, forget that thou
art Jove, the king of gods, and, Mercury, lose all the
serpentine craft of thy caduceus, if ye take not that
little little less than little wit from them that they
have! which short-armed ignorance itself knows is
so abundant scarce, it will not in circumvention deliver a fly from a spider, without drawing their
massy irons and cutting the web. After this, the
vengeance on the whole camp! or, rather, the Neapolitan bone-ache! for that, methinks, is the curse
dependant on those that war for a placket. I have

[832]

said my prayers; and devil Envy say amen. What, ho! my Lord Achilles!

Enter PATROCLUS

PATROCLUS

Who's there? Thersites! Good Thersites, come in and rail.

THERSITES

If I could ha' remembered a gilt counterfeit, thou wouldst not have slipped out of my contemplation: but it is no matter; thyself upon thyself! The common curse of mankind, folly and ignorance, be thine in great revenue! heaven bless thee from a tutor, and discipline come not near thee! Let thy blood be thy direction till thy death! then if she that lays thee out says thou art a fair corse, I'll be sworn and sworn upon 't she never shrouded any but lazars. Amen. Where's Achilles?

PATROCLUS

What, art thou devout? wast thou in prayer?

THERSITES

Ay; the heavens hear me!

PATROCLUS

Amen.

Enter ACHILLES

ACHILLES

Who's there?

PATROCLUS

Thersites, my lord.

ACHILLES

Where, where? Art thou come? why, my cheese, my digestion, why hast thou not served thyself in to my table so many meals? Come, what's Agamemnon?

THERSITES

Thy commander, Achilles: then tell me, Patroclus, what's Achilles?

PATROCLUS

Thy lord, Thersites: then tell me, I pray thee, what's thyself?

THERSITES

Thy knower, Patroclus: then tell me, Patroclus, what art thou?

PATROCLUS

Thou mayst tell that knowest.

ACHILLES

O, tell, tell.

THERSITES

I'll decline the whole question. Agamemnon commands Achilles; Achilles is my lord; I am Patroclus' knower, and Patroclus is a fool.

PATROCLUS

You rascal!

THERSITES

Peace, fool! I have not done.

ACHILLES

He is a privileged man. Proceed, Thersites.

THERSITES

Agamemnon is a fool; Achilles is a fool; Thersites is a fool, and, as aforesaid, Patroclus is a fool.

ACHILLES

Derive this; come.

THERSITES

Agamemnon is a fool to offer to command Achilles; Achilles is a fool to be commanded of Agamemnon; Thersites is a fool to serve such a fool; and Patroclus is a fool positive.

PATROCLUS

Why am I a fool?

THERSITES

Make that demand of the prover. It suffices me thou art. Look you, who comes here?

ACHILLES

Patroclus, I'll speak with nobody. Come in with me, Thersites.   [*Exit*

THERSITES

Here is such patchery, such juggling and such knavery! all the argument is a cuckold and a whore; a good quarrel to draw emulous factions and bleed to death upon. Now, the dry serpigo on the subject! and war and lechery confound all!   [*Exit*

Enter AGAMEMNON, ULYSSES, NESTOR, DIOMEDES, *and* AJAX

AGAMEMNON

Where is Achilles?

PATROCLUS

Within his tent; but ill-disposed, my lord.

AGAMEMNON

Let it be known to him that we are here.
He shent our messengers; and we lay by
Our appertainments, visiting of him:
Let him be told so, lest perchance he think
We dare not move the question of our place,
Or know not what we are.

PATROCLUS

I shall say so to him.   [*Exit*

ULYSSES

We saw him at the opening of his tent:
He is not sick.

AJAX

Yes, lion-sick, sick of proud heart: you may call it melancholy, if you will favour the man; but, by my head, 'tis pride: but why, why? let him show us the cause. A word, my lord.   [*Takes* AGAMEMNON *aside*

NESTOR

What moves Ajax thus to bay at him?

ULYSSES

Achilles hath inveigled his fool from him.

NESTOR

Who, Thersites?

ULYSSES

He.

NESTOR

Then will Ajax lack matter, if he have lost his argument.

ULYSSES

No, you see, he is his argument that has his argument, Achilles.

NESTOR

All the better; their fraction is more our wish than

their faction: but it was a strong composure a fool
could disunite.

ULYSSES

The amity that wisdom knits not, folly may easily
untie.

Re-enter PATROCLUS

Here comes Patroclus.

NESTOR

No Achilles with him.

ULYSSES

The elephant hath joints, but none for courtesy: his
legs are legs for necessity, not for flexure.

PATROCLUS

Achilles bids me say, he is much sorry,
If anything more than your sport and pleasure
Did move your greatness and this noble state
To call upon him; he hopes it is no other
But for your health and your digestion sake,
An after-dinner's breath.

AGAMEMNON

                        Hear you, Patroclus:
We are too well acquainted with these answers:
But his evasion, wing'd thus swift with scorn,
Cannot outfly our apprehensions.
Much attribute he hath, and much the reason
Why we ascribe it to him: yet all his virtues,
Not virtuously on his own part beheld,
Do in our eyes begin to lose their gloss,
Yea, like fair fruit in an unwholesome dish,
Are like to rot untasted. Go and tell him,
We come to speak with him; and you shall not sin,
If you do say we think him over-proud
And under-honest; in self-assumption greater
Than in the note of judgement; and worthier than
    himself
Here tend the savage strangeness he puts on,
Disguise the holy strength of their command,
And underwrite in an observing kind
His humorous predominance; yea, watch
His pettish lunes, his ebbs, his flows, as if
The passage and whole carriage of this action
Rode on his tide. Go tell him this, and add,
That if he overhold his price so much,
We'll none of him, but let him, like an engine
Not portable, lie under this report:
'Bring action hither, this cannot go to war:
A stirring dwarf we do allowance give
Before a sleeping giant:' tell him so.

PATROCLUS

I shall; and bring his answer presently.   [*Exit*

AGAMEMNON

In second voice we'll not be satisfied;
We come to speak with him. Ulysses, enter you.

                                    [*Exit* ULYSSES

AJAX

What is he more than another?

AGAMEMNON

No more than what he thinks he is.

AJAX

Is he so much? Do you not think he thinks himself a
better man than I am?

AGAMEMNON

No question.

AJAX

Will you subscribe his thought and say he is?

AGAMEMNON

No, noble Ajax; you are as strong, as valiant, as wise,
no less noble, much more gentle and altogether
more tractable.

AJAX

Why should a man be proud? How doth pride
grow? I know not what pride is.

AGAMEMNON

Your mind is the clearer, Ajax, and your virtues
the fairer. He that is proud eats up himself: pride
is his own glass, his own trumpet, his own chronicle;
and whatever praises itself but in the deed, devours
the deed in the praise.

AJAX

I do hate a proud man, as I hate the engendering of
toads.

NESTOR

[*Aside*] Yet he loves himself: is 't not strange?

Re-enter ULYSSES

ULYSSES

Achilles will not to the field to-morrow.

AGAMEMNON

What's his excuse?

ULYSSES

                        He doth rely on none,
But carries on the stream of his dispose,
Without observance or respect of any,
In will peculiar and in self-admission.

AGAMEMNON

Why will he not, upon our fair request,
Untent his person, and share the air with us?

ULYSSES

Things small as nothing, for request's sake only
He makes important: possess'd he is with greatness,
And speaks not to himself but with a pride
That quarrels at self-breath: imagined worth
Holds in his blood such swoln and hot discourse
That 'twixt his mental and his active parts
Kingdom'd Achilles in commotion rages
And batters down himself: what should I say?
He is so plaguy proud that the death-tokens of it
Cry 'No recovery.'

AGAMEMNON

                        Let Ajax go to him.
Dear lord, go you and greet him in his tent:
'Tis said he holds you well, and will be led
At your request a little from himself.

ULYSSES

O Agamemnon, let it not be so!
We'll consecrate the steps that Ajax makes
When they go from Achilles. Shall the proud lord
That bastes his arrogance with his own seam,
And never suffers matter of the world

Enter his thoughts, save such as do revolve
And ruminate himself, shall he be worshipp'd
Of that we hold an idol more than he?
No, this thrice worthy and right valiant lord
Must not so stale his palm, nobly acquired,
Nor, by my will, assubjugate his merit,
As amply titled as Achilles is,
By going to Achilles:
That were to enlard his fat-already pride,
And add more coals to Cancer when he burns
With entertaining great Hyperion.
This lord go to him! Jupiter forbid,
And say in thunder 'Achilles go to him.'

NESTOR
[*Aside*] O, this is well; he rubs the vein of him.

DIOMEDES
[*Aside*] And how his silence drinks up this applause!

AJAX
If I go to him, with my armed fist
I'll pash him o'er the face.

AGAMEMNON
O, no, you shall not go.

AJAX
An a' be proud with me, I'll pheeze his pride:
Let me go to him.

ULYSSES
Not for the worth that hangs upon our quarrel.

AJAX
A paltry, insolent fellow!

NESTOR
[*Aside*] How he describes himself!

AJAX
Can he not be sociable?

ULYSSES
[*Aside*] The raven chides blackness.

AJAX
I'll let his humours blood.

AGAMEMNON
[*Aside*] He will be the physician that should be the
patient.

AJAX
An all men were o' my mind,—

ULYSSES
[*Aside*] Wit would be out of fashion.

AJAX
A' should not bear it so, a' should eat swords first:
shall pride carry it?

NESTOR
[*Aside*] An 'twould, you 'ld carry half.

ULYSSES
[*Aside*] A' would have ten shares.

AJAX
I will knead him, I'll make him supple.

NESTOR
[*Aside*] He's not yet through warm: force him with
praises: pour in, pour in; his ambition is dry.

ULYSSES
[*To* AGAMEMNON] My lord, you feed too much on
this dislike.

NESTOR
Our noble general, do not do so.

DIOMEDES
You must prepare to fight without Achilles.

ULYSSES
Why, 'tis this naming of him does him harm.
Here is a man—but 'tis before his face;
I will be silent.

NESTOR
Wherefore should you so?
He is not emulous, as Achilles is.

ULYSSES
Know the whole world, he is as valiant.

AJAX
A whoreson dog, that shall palter thus with us!
Would he were a Trojan!

NESTOR
What a vice were it in Ajax now—

ULYSSES
If he were proud,—

DIOMEDES
Or covetous of praise,—

ULYSSES
Ay, or surly borne,—

DIOMEDES
Or strange, or self-affected!

ULYSSES
Thank the heavens, lord, thou art of sweet com-
posure;
Praise him that got thee, she that gave thee suck:
Famed be thy tutor, and thy parts of nature
Thrice-famed beyond, beyond all erudition:
But he that disciplined thine arms to fight,
Let Mars divide eternity in twain,
And give him half: and, for thy vigour,
Bull-bearing Milo his addition yield
To sinewy Ajax. I will not praise thy wisdom,
Which, like a bourn, a pale, a shore, confines
Thy spacious and dilated parts: here's Nestor,
Instructed by the antiquary times,
He must, he is, he cannot but be wise;
But pardon, father Nestor, were your days
As green as Ajax', and your brain so temper'd,
You should not have the eminence of him,
But be as Ajax.

AJAX
Shall I call you father?

NESTOR
Ay, my good son.

DIOMEDES
Be ruled by him, Lord Ajax.

ULYSSES
There is no tarrying here; the hart Achilles
Keeps thicket. Please it our great general
To call together all his state of war:
Fresh kings are come to Troy: to-morrow
We must with all our main of power stand fast:
And here's a lord, come knights from east to west,
And cull their flower, Ajax shall cope the best.

AGAMEMNON

Go we to council. Let Achilles sleep:
Light boats sail swift, though greater hulks draw
deep.   [*Exeunt*

ACT III

SCENE I. *Troy. A room in* PRIAM'S *palace*

Enter PANDARUS *and a* SERVANT

PANDARUS

Friend, you, pray you, a word: do you not follow
the young Lord Paris?

SERVANT

Ay, sir, when he goes before me.

PANDARUS

You depend upon him, I mean?

SERVANT

Sir, I do depend upon the Lord.

PANDARUS

You depend upon a noble gentleman; I must needs
praise him.

SERVANT

The Lord be praised!

PANDARUS

You know me, do you not?

SERVANT

Faith, sir, superficially.

PANDARUS

Friend, know me better; I am the Lord Pandarus.

SERVANT

I hope I shall know your honour better.

PANDARUS

I do desire it.

SERVANT

You are in the state of grace.

PANDARUS

Grace! not so, friend; honour and lordship are my
titles. [*Music within*] What music is this?

SERVANT

I do but partly know, sir: it is music in parts.

PANDARUS

Know you the musicians?

SERVANT

Wholly, sir.

PANDARUS

Who play they to?

SERVANT

To the hearers, sir.

PANDARUS

At whose pleasure, friend?

SERVANT

At mine, sir, and theirs that love music.

PANDARUS

Command, I mean, friend.

SERVANT

Who shall I command, sir?

PANDARUS

Friend, we understand not one another: I am too
courtly, and thou art too cunning. At whose request
do these men play?

SERVANT

That's to 't, indeed, sir: marry, sir, at the request of
Paris my lord, who is there in person; with him,
the mortal Venus, the heart-blood of beauty, love's
invisible soul.

PANDARUS

Who, my cousin Cressida?

SERVANT

No, sir, Helen: could not you find out that by her
attributes?

PANDARUS

It should seem, fellow, that thou hast not seen the
Lady Cressida. I come to speak with Paris from the
Prince Troilus: I will make a complimental assault
upon him, for my business seethes.

SERVANT

Sodden business! there's a stewed phrase indeed!

Enter PARIS *and* HELEN, *attended*

PANDARUS

Fair be to you, my lord, and to all this fair company! fair desires, in all fair measure, fairly guide
them! especially to you, fair queen! fair thoughts be
your fair pillow!

HELEN

Dear lord, you are full of fair words.

PANDARUS

You speak your fair pleasure, sweet queen. Fair
prince, here is good broken music.

PARIS

You have broke it, cousin: and, by my life, you shall
make it whole again; you shall piece it out with a
piece of your performance. Nell, he is full of harmony.

PANDARUS

Truly, lady, no.

HELEN

O, sir,—

PANDARUS

Rude, in sooth; in good sooth, very rude.

PARIS

Well said, my lord! well, you say so in fits.

PANDARUS

I have business to my lord, dear queen. My lord,
will you vouchsafe me a word?

HELEN

Nay, this shall not hedge us out: we'll hear you sing,
certainly.

PANDARUS

Well, sweet queen, you are pleasant with me. But,
marry, thus, my lord: my dear lord, and most esteemed friend, your brother Troilus—

HELEN

My Lord Pandarus; honey-sweet lord,—

PANDARUS

Go to, sweet queen, go to:—commends himself
most affectionately to you—

HELEN

You shall not bob us out of our melody: if you do, our melancholy upon your head!

PANDARUS

Sweet queen, sweet queen; that's a sweet queen, i' faith.

HELEN

And to make a sweet lady sad is a sour offence.

PANDARUS

Nay, that shall not serve your turn; that shall it not, in truth, la. Nay, I care not for such words; no, no. And, my lord, he desires you, that if the king call for him at supper, you will make his excuse.

HELEN

My Lord Pandarus,—

PANDARUS

What says my sweet queen, my very very sweet queen?

PARIS

What exploit 's in hand? where sups he to-night?

HELEN

Nay, but, my lord,—

PANDARUS

What says my sweet queen? My cousin will fall out with you. You must not know where he sups.

PARIS

I'll lay my life, with my disposer Cressida.

PANDARUS

No, no, no such matter; you are wide: come, your disposer is sick.

PARIS

Well, I'll make excuse.

PANDARUS

Ay, good my lord. Why should you say Cressida? no, your poor disposer's sick.

PARIS

I spy.

PANDARUS

You spy! what do you spy? Come, give me an instrument. Now, sweet queen.

HELEN

Why, this is kindly done.

PANDARUS

My niece is horribly in love with a thing you have, sweet queen.

HELEN

She shall have it, my lord, if it be not my lord Paris.

PANDARUS

He! no, she'll none of him; they two are twain.

HELEN

Falling in, after falling out, may make them three.

PANDARUS

Come, come, I'll hear no more of this; I'll sing you a song now.

HELEN

Ay, ay, prithee now. By my troth, sweet lord, thou hast a fine forehead.

PANDARUS

Ay, you may, you may.

HELEN

Let thy song be love: this love will undo us all. O Cupid, Cupid, Cupid!

PANDARUS

Love! ay, that it shall, i' faith.

PARIS

Ay, good now, love, love, nothing but love.

PANDARUS

In good troth, it begins so.   [Sings

> Love, love, nothing but love, still more!
>   For, O, love's bow
>   Shoots buck and doe;
>   The shaft confounds,
>   Not that it wounds,
> But tickles still the sore.
> These lovers cry Oh! oh! they die:
>   Yet that which seems the wound to kill,
> Doth turn oh! oh! to ha! ha! he!
>   So dying love lives still:
> Oh! oh! a while, but ha! ha! ha!
> Oh! oh! groans out for ha! ha! ha!

Heigh-ho!

HELEN

In love, i' faith, to the very tip of the nose.

PARIS

He eats nothing but doves, love, and that breeds hot blood, and hot blood begets hot thoughts, and hot thoughts beget hot deeds, and hot deeds is love.

PANDARUS

Is this the generation of love? hot blood, hot thoughts and hot deeds? Why, they are vipers: is love a generation of vipers? Sweet lord, who's afield to-day?

PARIS

Hector, Deiphobus, Helenus, Antenor, and all the gallantry of Troy: I would fain have armed to-day, but my Nell would not have it so. How chance my brother Troilus went not?

HELEN

He hangs the lip at something: you know all, Lord Pandarus.

PANDARUS

Not I, honey-sweet queen. I long to hear how they sped to-day. You'll remember your brother's excuse?

PARIS

To a hair.

PANDARUS

Farewell, sweet queen.

HELEN

Commend me to your niece.

PANDARUS

I will, sweet queen.   [Exit
                                    [A retreat sounded

PARIS

They're come from field: let us to Priam's hall,
To greet the warriors. Sweet Helen, I must woo you
To help unarm our Hector: his stubborn buckles,
With these your white enchanting fingers touch'd,
Shall more obey than to the edge of steel
Or force of Greekish sinews; you shall do more
Than all the island kings,—disarm great Hector.

HELEN

'Twill make us proud to be his servant, Paris;
Yea, what he shall receive of us in duty
Gives us more palm in beauty than we have,
Yea, overshines ourself.

PARIS

Sweet, above thought I love thee.   [*Exeunt*

SCENE II. *An orchard to* PANDARUS' *house*

Enter PANDARUS *and* TROILUS' BOY, *meeting*

PANDARUS

How now! where's thy master? at my cousin Cressida's?

BOY

No, sir; he stays for you to conduct him thither.

PANDARUS

O, here he comes.

Enter TROILUS

How now, how now!

TROILUS

Sirrah, walk off.   [*Exit* BOY

PANDARUS

Have you seen my cousin?

TROILUS

No, Pandarus: I stalk about her door,
Like a strange soul upon the Stygian banks
Staying for waftage. O, be thou my Charon,
And give me swift transportance to those fields
Where I may wallow in the lily-beds
Proposed for the deserver! O gentle Pandarus,
From Cupid's shoulder pluck his painted wings,
And fly with me to Cressid!

PANDARUS

Walk here i' the orchard, I'll bring her straight.
    [*Exit*

TROILUS

I am giddy; expectation whirls me round.
The imaginary relish is so sweet
That it enchants my sense: what will it be,
When that the watery palates taste indeed
Love's thrice repured nectar? death, I fear me,
Swounding destruction, or some joy too fine,
Too subtle-potent, tuned too sharp in sweetness,
For the capacity of my ruder powers:
I fear it much, and I do fear besides
That I shall lose distinction in my joys,
As doth a battle, when they charge on heaps
The enemy flying.

Re-enter PANDARUS

PANDARUS

She's making her ready, she'll come straight: you
must be witty now. She does so blush, and fetches
her wind so short, as if she were frayed with a sprite:
I'll fetch her. It is the prettiest villain: she fetches
her breath as short as a new-ta'en sparrow.   [*Exit*

TROILUS

Even such a passion doth embrace my bosom:
My heart beats thicker than a feverous pulse;

And all my powers do their bestowing lose,
Like vassalage at unawares encountering
The eye of majesty.

Re-enter PANDARUS *with* CRESSIDA

PANDARUS

Come, come, what need you blush? shame's a baby.
Here she is now: swear the oaths now to her that
you have sworn to me. What, are you gone again?
you must be watched ere you be made tame, must
you? Come your ways, come your ways; an you
draw backward, we'll put you i' the fills. Why do
you not speak to her? Come, draw this curtain, and
let's see your picture. Alas the day, how loath you
are to offend daylight! an 'twere dark, you 'ld close
sooner. So, so; rub on, and kiss the mistress. How
now! a kiss in fee-farm! build there, carpenter; the
air is sweet. Nay, you shall fight your hearts out ere
I part you. The falcon as the tercel, for all the ducks
i' the river: go to, go to.

TROILUS

You have bereft me of all words, lady.

PANDARUS

Words pay no debts, give her deeds: but she'll
bereave you o' the deeds too, if she call your activity
in question. What, billing again? Here's 'In witness
whereof the parties interchangeably'—Come in,
come in: I'll go get a fire.   [*Exit*

CRESSIDA

Will you walk in, my lord?

TROILUS

O Cressida, how often have I wished me thus!

CRESSIDA

Wished, my lord?—The gods grant—O my lord!

TROILUS

What should they grant? what makes this pretty
abruption? What too curious dreg espies my sweet
lady in the fountain of our love?

CRESSIDA

More dregs than water, if my fears have eyes.

TROILUS

Fears make devils of cherubins; they never see truly.

CRESSIDA

Blind fear, that seeing reason leads, finds safer footing than blind reason stumbling without fear: to
fear the worst oft cures the worse.

TROILUS

O, let my lady apprehend no fear: in all Cupid's
pageant there is presented no monster.

CRESSIDA

Nor nothing monstrous neither?

TROILUS

Nothing, but our undertakings; when we vow to
weep seas, live in fire, eat rocks, tame tigers; thinking it harder for our mistress to devise imposition
enough than for us to undergo any difficulty imposed. This is the monstruosity in love, lady, that
the will is infinite and the execution confined, that
the desire is boundless and the act a slave to limit.

CRESSIDA

They say, all lovers swear more performance than

they are able, and yet reserve an ability that they never perform, vowing more than the perfection of ten, and discharging less than the tenth part of one. They that have the voice of lions and the act of hares, are they not monsters?

TROILUS

Are there such? such are not we: praise us as we are tasted, allow us as we prove; our head shall go bare till merit crown it: no perfection in reversion shall have a praise in present: we will not name desert before his birth, and, being born, his addition shall be humble. Few words to fair faith: Troilus shall be such to Cressid as what envy can say worst shall be a mock for his truth, and what truth can speak truest, not truer than Troilus.

CRESSIDA

Will you walk in, my lord?

Re-enter PANDARUS

PANDARUS

What, blushing still? have you not done talking yet?

CRESSIDA

Well, uncle, what folly I commit, I dedicate to you.

PANDARUS

I thank you for that: if my lord get a boy of you, you'll give him me. Be true to my lord: if he flinch, chide me for it.

TROILUS

You know now your hostages; your uncle's word and my firm faith.

PANDARUS

Nay, I'll give my word for her too: our kindred, though they be long ere they are wooed, they are constant being won: they are burs, I can tell you; they'll stick where they are thrown.

CRESSIDA

Boldness comes to me now, and brings me heart.
Prince Troilus, I have loved you night and day
For many weary months.

TROILUS

Why was my Cressid then so hard to win?

CRESSIDA

Hard to seem won: but I was won, my lord,
With the first glance that ever—pardon me;
If I confess much, you will play the tyrant.
I love you now; but not, till now, so much
But I might master it: in faith, I lie;
My thoughts were like unbridled children, grown
Too headstrong for their mother. See, we fools!
Why have I blabb'd? who shall be true to us,
When we are so unsecret to ourselves?
But, though I loved you well, I woo'd you not;
And yet, good faith, I wish'd myself a man,
Or that we women had men's privilege
Of speaking first. Sweet, bid me hold my tongue;
For in this rapture I shall surely speak
The thing I shall repent. See, see, your silence,
Cunning in dumbness, from my weakness draws
My very soul of counsel! Stop my mouth.

TROILUS

And shall, albeit sweet music issues thence.

PANDARUS

Pretty, i' faith.

CRESSIDA

My lord, I do beseech you, pardon me;
'Twas not my purpose thus to beg a kiss:
I am ashamed; O heavens! what have I done?
For this time will I take my leave, my lord.

TROILUS

Your leave, sweet Cressid?

PANDARUS

Leave! an you take leave till to-morrow morning—

CRESSIDA

Pray you, content you.

TROILUS

What offends you, lady?

CRESSIDA

Sir, mine own company.

TROILUS

You cannot shun yourself.

CRESSIDA

Let me go and try:
I have a kind of self resides with you,
But an unkind self that itself will leave
To be another's fool. I would be gone:
Where is my wit? I know not what I speak.

TROILUS

Well know they what they speak that speak so wisely.

CRESSIDA

Perchance, my lord, I show more craft than love,
And fell so roundly to a large confession
To angle for your thoughts: but you are wise;
Or else you love not, for to be wise and love
Exceeds man's might; that dwells with gods above.

TROILUS

O that I thought it could be in a woman—
As, if it can, I will presume in you—
To feed for aye her lamp and flames of love;
To keep her constancy in plight and youth,
Outliving beauty's outward, with a mind
That doth renew swifter than blood decays!
Or that persuasion could but thus convince me,
That my integrity and truth to you
Might be affronted with the match and weight
Of such a winnowed purity in love;
How were I then uplifted! but, alas!
I am as true as truth's simplicity,
And simpler than the infancy of truth.

CRESSIDA

In that I'll war with you.

TROILUS

O virtuous fight,
When right with right wars who shall be most right!
True swains in love shall in the world to come
Approve their truths by Troilus: when their rhymes,
Full of protest, of oath and big compare,
Want similes, truth tired with iteration,
'As true as steel, as plantage to the moon,
As sun to day, as turtle to her mate,
As iron to adamant, as earth to the centre,'

Yet, after all comparisons of truth,
As truth's authentic author to be cited,
'As true as Troilus' shall crown up the verse
And sanctify the numbers.

CRESSIDA

           Prophet may you be!
If I be false, or swerve a hair from truth,
When time is old and hath forgot itself,
When waterdrops have worn the stones of Troy,
And blind oblivion swallow'd cities up,
And mighty states characterless are grated
To dusty nothing, yet let memory,
From false to false, among false maids in love,
Upbraid my falsehood! when they've said 'as false
As air, as water, wind, or sandy earth,
As fox to lamb, or wolf to heifer's calf,
Pard to the hind, or stepdame to her son,'
'Yea,' let them say, to stick the heart of falsehood,
'As false as Cressid.'

PANDARUS

Go to, a bargain made: seal it, seal it; I'll be the
witness. Here I hold your hand; here my cousin's.
If ever you prove false one to another, since I have
taken such pains to bring you together, let all pitiful
goers-between be called to the world's end after my
name; call them all Pandars; let all constant men
be Troiluses, all false women Cressids, and all
brokers-between Pandars! Say 'amen.'

TROILUS

Amen.

CRESSIDA

Amen.

PANDARUS

Amen. Whereupon I will show you a chamber with
a bed; which bed, because it shall not speak of your
pretty encounters, press it to death: away!

[Exeunt TROILUS and CRESSIDA
And Cupid grant all tongue-tied maidens here
Bed, chamber, Pandar to provide this gear!   [Exit

SCENE III. *The Grecian camp*

Flourish. Enter AGAMEMNON, ULYSSES, DIOMEDES,
NESTOR, AJAX, MENELAUS, *and* CALCHAS

CALCHAS

Now, princes, for the service I have done you,
The advantage of the time prompts me aloud
To call for recompense. Appear it to your mind
That, through the sight I bear in things to love,
I have abandon'd Troy, left my possession,
Incurr'd a traitor's name; exposed myself,
From certain and possess'd conveniences,
To doubtful fortunes; sequestering from me all
That time, acquaintance, custom and condition
Made tame and most familiar to my nature,
And here, to do you service, am become
As new into the world, strange, unacquainted:
I do beseech you, as in way of taste,
To give me now a little benefit,

Out of those many register'd in promise,
Which, you say, live to come in my behalf.

AGAMEMNON

What wouldst thou of us, Trojan? make demand.

CALCHAS

You have a Trojan prisoner, call'd Antenor,
Yesterday took: Troy holds him very dear.
Oft have you—often have you thanks therefore—
Desired my Cressid in right great exchange,
Whom Troy hath still denied: but this Antenor,
I know, is such a wrest in their affairs,
That their negotiations all must slack,
Wanting his manage; and they will almost
Give us a prince of blood, a son of Priam,
In change of him: let him be sent, great princes,
And he shall buy my daughter; and her presence
Shall quite strike off all service I have done,
In most accepted pain.

AGAMEMNON

           Let Diomedes bear him,
And bring us Cressid hither: Calchas shall have
What he requests of us. Good Diomed,
Furnish you fairly for this interchange:
Withal, bring word if Hector will to-morrow
Be answer'd in his challenge: Ajax is ready.

DIOMEDES

This shall I undertake; and 'tis a burthen
Which I am proud to bear.

[*Exeunt* DIOMEDES *and* CALCHAS
Enter ACHILLES *and* PATROCLUS, *before their tent*

ULYSSES

Achilles stands i' the entrance of his tent:
Please it our general pass strangely by him,
As if he were forgot; and, princes all,
Lay negligent and loose regard upon him:
I will come last. 'Tis like he'll question me
Why such unplausive eyes are bent on him:
If so, I have derision medicinable,
To use between your strangeness and his pride,
Which his own will shall have desire to drink.
It may do good: pride hath no other glass
To show itself but pride, for supple knees
Feed arrogance and are the proud man's fees.

AGAMEMNON

We'll execute your purpose and put on
A form of strangeness as we pass along;
So do each lord, and either greet him not
Or else disdainfully, which shall shake him more
Than if not look'd on. I will lead the way.

ACHILLES

What, comes the general to speak with me?
You know my mind; I'll fight no more 'gainst Troy.

AGAMEMNON

What says Achilles? would he aught with us?

NESTOR

Would you, my lord, aught with the general?

ACHILLES

No.

NESTOR

Nothing, my lord.

[840]

AGAMEMNON

The better.   [*Exeunt* AGAMEMNON *and* NESTOR

ACHILLES

Good day, good day.

MENELAUS

How do you? how do you?   [*Exit*

ACHILLES

What, does the cuckold scorn me?

AJAX

How now, Patroclus!

ACHILLES

Good morrow, Ajax.

AJAX

Ha?

ACHILLES

Good morrow.

AJAX

Ay, and good next day too.   [*Exit*

ACHILLES

What mean these fellows? Know they not Achilles?

PATROCLUS

They pass by strangely: they were used to bend,
To send their smiles before them to Achilles,
To come as humbly as they used to creep
To holy altars.

ACHILLES

What, am I poor of late?
'Tis certain, greatness, once fall'n out with fortune,
Must fall out with men too: what the declined is,
He shall as soon read in the eyes of others
As feel in his own fall: for men, like butterflies,
Show not their mealy wings but to the summer;
And not a man, for being simply man,
Hath any honour, but honour for those honours
That are without him, as place, riches, and favour,
Prizes of accident as oft as merit:
Which when they fall, as being slippery standers,
The love that lean'd on them as slippery too,
Do one pluck down another and together
Die in the fall. But 'tis not so with me:
Fortune and I are friends: I do enjoy
At ample point all that I did possess,
Save these men's looks; who do, methinks, find out
Something not worth in me such rich beholding
As they have often given. Here is Ulysses:
I'll interrupt his reading.
How now, Ulysses!

ULYSSES

Now, great Thetis' son!

ACHILLES

What are you reading?

ULYSSES

A strange fellow here
Writes me: 'That man, how dearly ever parted,
How much in having, or without or in,
Cannot make boast to have that which he hath,
Nor feels not what he owes, but by reflection;
As when his virtues shining upon others
Heat them, and they retort that heat again
To the first giver.'

ACHILLES

This is not strange, Ulysses.
The beauty that is borne here in the face
The bearer knows not, but commends itself
To others' eyes: nor doth the eye itself,
That most pure spirit of sense, behold itself,
Not going from itself; but eye to eye opposed
Salutes each other with each other's form:
For speculation turns not to itself,
Till it hath travell'd and is mirror'd there
Where it may see itself. This is not strange at all.

ULYSSES

I do not strain at the position—
It is familiar—but at the author's drift;
Who in his circumstance expressly proves
That no man is the lord of any thing,
Though in and of him there be much consisting,
Till he communicate his parts to others;
Nor doth he of himself know them for aught,
Till he behold them formed in the applause
Where they're extended; who, like an arch, re-
  verberates
The voice again; or, like a gate of steel
Fronting the sun, receives and renders back
His figure and his heat. I was much rapt in this;
And apprehended here immediately
The unknown Ajax.
Heavens, what a man is there! a very horse;
That has he knows not what. Nature, what things
  there are,
Most abject in regard and dear in use!
What things again most dear in the esteem
And poor in worth! Now shall we see to-morrow—
An act that very chance doth throw upon him—
Ajax renown'd. O heavens, what some men do,
While some men leave to do!
How some men creep in skittish fortune's hall,
Whiles others play the idiots in her eyes!
How one man eats into another's pride,
While pride is fasting in his wantonness!
To see these Grecian lords! Why, even already
They clap the lubber Ajax on the shoulder,
As if his foot were on brave Hector's breast
And great Troy shrieking.

ACHILLES

I do believe it; for they pass'd by me
As misers do by beggars, neither gave to me
Good word nor look: what, are my deeds forgot?

ULYSSES

Time hath, my lord, a wallet at his back
Wherein he puts alms for oblivion,
A great-sized monster of ingratitudes:
Those scraps are good deeds past, which are de-
  vour'd
As fast as they are made, forgot as soon
As done: perseverance, dear my lord,
Keeps honour bright: to have done, is to hang
Quite out of fashion, like a rusty mail
In monumental mockery. Take the instant way;
For honour travels in a strait so narrow,

Where one but goes abreast: keep then the path;
For emulation hath a thousand sons
That one by one pursue: if you give way,
Or hedge aside from the direct forthright,
Like to an enter'd tide they all rush by
And leave you hindmost:
Or, like a gallant horse fall'n in first rank,
Lie there for pavement to the abject rear,
O'er-run and trampled on: then what they do in
　　present,
Though less than yours in past, must o'ertop yours;
For time is like a fashionable host
That slightly shakes his parting guest by the hand,
And with his arms outstretch'd, as he would fly,
Grasps in the comer: welcome ever smiles,
And farewell goes out sighing. O, let not virtue seek
Remuneration for the thing it was;
For beauty, wit,
High birth, vigour of bone, desert in service,
Love, friendship, charity, are subjects all
To envious and calumniating time.
One touch of nature makes the whole world kin;
That all with one consent praise new-born gawds,
Though they are made and moulded of things past,
And give to dust that is a little gilt
More laud than gilt o'er-dusted.
The present eye praises the present object:
Then marvel not, thou great and complete man,
That all the Greeks begin to worship Ajax;
Since things in motion sooner catch the eye
Than what not stirs. The cry went once on thee,
And still it might, and yet it may again,
If thou wouldst not entomb thyself alive
And case thy reputation in thy tent,
Whose glorious deeds, but in these fields of late,
Made emulous missions 'mongst the gods them-
　　selves,
And drave great Mars to faction.

ACHILLES
　　　　　　　　　　　Of this my privacy
I have strong reasons.

ULYSSES
　　　　　　　But 'gainst your privacy
The reasons are more potent and heroical:
'Tis known, Achilles, that you are in love
With one of Priam's daughters.

ACHILLES
　　　　　　　　　　Ha! known?

ULYSSES
Is that a wonder?
The providence that's in a watchful state
Knows almost every grain of Plutus' gold,
Finds bottom in the uncomprehensive deeps,
Keeps place with thought, and almost like the gods
Does thoughts unveil in their dumb cradles.
There is a mystery, with whom relation
Durst never meddle, in the soul of state;
Which hath an operation more divine
Than breath or pen can give expressure to:
All the commerce that you have had with Troy

As perfectly is ours as yours, my lord;
And better would it fit Achilles much
To throw down Hector than Polyxena:
But it must grieve young Pyrrhus now at home,
When fame shall in our islands sound her trump;
And all the Greekish girls shall tripping sing
'Great Hector's sister did Achilles win,
But our great Ajax bravely beat down him.'
Farewell, my lord: I as your lover speak;
The fool slides o'er the ice that you should break.
　　　　　　　　　　　　　　　　　　[Exit

PATROCLUS
To this effect, Achilles, have I moved you:
A woman impudent and mannish grown
Is not more loathed than an effeminate man
In time of action. I stand condemn'd for this;
They think my little stomach to the war
And your great love to me restrains you thus:
Sweet, rouse yourself, and the weak wanton Cupid
Shall from your neck unloose his amorous fold,
And, like a dew-drop from the lion's mane,
Be shook to air.

ACHILLES
　　　　　Shall Ajax fight with Hector?

PATROCLUS
Ay, and perhaps receive much honour by him.

ACHILLES
I see my reputation is at stake;
My fame is shrewdly gored.

PATROCLUS
　　　　　　　　　O, then, beware;
Those wounds heal ill that men do give themselves:
Omission to do what is necessary
Seals a commission to a blank of danger;
And danger, like an ague, subtly taints
Even then when we sit idly in the sun.

ACHILLES
Go call Thersites hither, sweet Patroclus:
I'll send the fool to Ajax, and desire him
To invite the Trojan lords after the combat
To see us here unarm'd: I have a woman's longing,
An appetite that I am sick withal,
To see great Hector in his weeds of peace;
To talk with him, and to behold his visage,
Even to my full of view.—A labour saved!

　　　　　　　Enter THERSITES

THERSITES
A wonder!

ACHILLES
What?

THERSITES
Ajax goes up and down the field, asking for himself.

ACHILLES
How so?

THERSITES
He must fight singly to-morrow with Hector, and is
so prophetically proud of an heroical cudgelling
that he raves in saying nothing.

ACHILLES
How can that be?

THERSITES

Why, a' stalks up and down like a peacock,—a stride and a stand: ruminates like an hostess that hath no arithmetic but her brain to set down her reckoning: bites his lip with a politic regard, as who should say 'There were wit in this head, an 'twould out:' and so there is; but it lies as coldly in him as fire in a flint, which will not show without knocking. The man's undone for ever; for if Hector break not his neck i' the combat, he'll break 't himself in vainglory. He knows not me: I said 'Good morrow, Ajax;' and he replies 'Thanks, Agamemnon.' What think you of this man, that takes me for the general? He's grown a very land-fish, languageless, a monster. A plague of opinion! a man may wear it on both sides, like a leather jerkin.

ACHILLES

Thou must be my ambassador to him, Thersites.

THERSITES

Who, I? why, he'll answer nobody; he professes not answering: speaking is for beggars; he wears his tongue in 's arms. I will put on his presence: let Patroclus make demands to me, you shall see the pageant of Ajax.

ACHILLES

To him, Patroclus: tell him I humbly desire the valiant Ajax to invite the most valorous Hector to come unarmed to my tent, and to procure safe-conduct for his person of the magnanimous and most illustrious six-or-seven-times-honoured captain-general of the Grecian army, Agamemnon, et cetera. Do this.

PATROCLUS

Jove bless great Ajax!

THERSITES

Hum!

PATROCLUS

I come from the worthy Achilles,—

THERSITES

Ha!

PATROCLUS

Who most humbly desires you to invite Hector to his tent,—

THERSITES

Hum!

PATROCLUS

And to procure safe-conduct from Agamemnon.

THERSITES

Agamemnon?

PATROCLUS

Ay, my lord.

THERSITES

Ha!

PATROCLUS

What say you to 't?

THERSITES

God be wi' you, with all my heart.

PATROCLUS

Your answer, sir.

THERSITES

If to-morrow be a fair day, by eleven of the clock it will go one way or other: howsoever, he shall pay for me ere he has me.

PATROCLUS

Your answer, sir.

THERSITES

Fare you well, with all my heart.

ACHILLES

Why, but he is not in this tune, is he?

THERSITES

No, but he's out o' tune thus. What music will be in him when Hector has knocked out his brains, I know not; but, I am sure, none, unless the fiddler Apollo get his sinews to make catlings on.

ACHILLES

Come, thou shalt bear a letter to him straight.

THERSITES

Let me bear another to his horse; for that's the more capable creature.

ACHILLES

My mind is troubled like a fountain stirr'd,
And I myself see not the bottom of it.

[*Exeunt* ACHILLES *and* PATROCLUS

THERSITES

Would the fountain of your mind were clear again, that I might water an ass at it! I had rather be a tick in a sheep than such a valiant ignorance. [*Exit*

ACT IV

SCENE I. *Troy. A street*

Enter, at one side, ÆNEAS, *and* SERVANT *with a torch; at the other,* PARIS, DEIPHOBUS, ANTENOR, DIOMEDES, *and others, with torches*

PARIS

See, ho! who is that there?

DEIPHOBUS

It is the Lord Æneas.

ÆNEAS

Is the prince there in person?
Had I so good occasion to lie long
As you, Prince Paris, nothing but heavenly business
Should rob my bed-mate of my company.

DIOMEDES

That's my mind too. Good morrow, Lord Æneas.

PARIS

A valiant Greek, Æneas,—take his hand,—
Witness the process of your speech, wherein
You told how Diomed a whole week by days
Did haunt you in the field.

ÆNEAS

Health to you, valiant sir,
During all question of the gentle truce;
But when I meet you arm'd, as black defiance
As heart can think or courage execute.

DIOMEDES

The one and other Diomed embraces.
Our bloods are now in calm; and, so long, health;
But when contention and occasion meet,
By Jove, I'll play the hunter for thy life
With all my force, pursuit and policy.

ÆNEAS

And thou shalt hunt a lion, that will fly
With his face backward. In humane gentleness,
Welcome to Troy! now, by Anchises' life,
Welcome, indeed! By Venus' hand I swear,
No man alive can love in such a sort
The thing he means to kill more excellently.

DIOMEDES

We sympathise. Jove, let Æneas live,
If to my sword his fate be not the glory,
A thousand complete courses of the sun!
But, in mine emulous honour, let him die,
With every joint a wound, and that to-morrow.

ÆNEAS

We know each other well.

DIOMEDES

We do; and long to know each other worse.

PARIS

This is the most despiteful gentle greeting,
The noblest hateful love, that e'er I heard of.
What business, lord, so early?

ÆNEAS

I was sent for to the king; but why, I know not.

PARIS

His purpose meets you: 'twas to bring this Greek
To Calchas' house; and there to render him,
For the enfreed Antenor, the fair Cressid:
Let's have your company, or, if you please,
Haste there before us. I constantly do think,
Or rather, call my thought a certain knowledge,
My brother Troilus lodges there to-night:
Rouse him and give him note of our approach,
With the whole quality wherefore: I fear
We shall be much unwelcome.

ÆNEAS

That I assure you:
Troilus had rather Troy were borne to Greece
Than Cressid borne from Troy.

PARIS

There is no help;
The bitter disposition of the time
Will have it so. On, lord; we'll follow you.

ÆNEAS

Good morrow, all.　　　　[Exit with SERVANT

PARIS

And tell me, noble Diomed, faith, tell me true,
Even in the soul of sound good-fellowship,
Who, in your thoughts, deserves fair Helen best,
Myself or Menelaus?

DIOMEDES

Both alike:
He merits well to have her that doth seek her,
Not making any scruple of her soilure,
With such a hell of pain and world of charge;

And you as well to keep her, that defend her,
Not palating the taste of her dishonour,
With such a costly loss of wealth and friends:
He, like a puling cuckold, would drink up
The lees and dregs of a flat tamed piece;
You, like a lecher, out of whorish loins
Are pleased to breed out your inheritors:
Both merits poised, each weighs nor less nor more,
But he as he, the heavier for a whore.

PARIS

You are too bitter to your countrywoman.

DIOMEDES

She's bitter to her country: hear me, Paris:
For every false drop in her bawdy veins
A Grecian's life hath sunk; for every scruple
Of her contaminated carrion weight,
A Trojan hath been slain: since she could speak,
She hath not given so many good words breath
As for her Greeks and Trojans suffer'd death.

PARIS

Fair Diomed, you do as chapmen do,
Dispraise the thing that you desire to buy:
But we in silence hold this virtue well,
We'll not commend what we intend to sell.
Here lies our way.　　　　　　　　[Exeunt

SCENE II. Court of PANDARUS' house

Enter TROILUS and CRESSIDA

TROILUS

Dear, trouble not yourself: the morn is cold.

CRESSIDA

Then, sweet my lord, I'll call mine uncle down;
He shall unbolt the gates.

TROILUS

Trouble him not;
To bed, to bed: sleep kill those pretty eyes,
And give as soft attachment to thy senses
As infants' empty of all thought!

CRESSIDA

Good morrow, then.

TROILUS

I prithee now, to bed.

CRESSIDA

Are you a-weary of me?

TROILUS

O Cressida! but that the busy day,
Waked by the lark, hath roused the ribald crows,
And dreaming night will hide our joys no longer,
I would not from thee.

CRESSIDA

Night hath been too brief.

TROILUS

Beshrew the witch! with venomous wights she stays
As tediously as hell, but flies the grasps of love
With wings more momentary-swift than thought.
You will catch cold, and curse me.

CRESSIDA

Prithee, tarry:

You men will never tarry.
O foolish Cressid! I might have still held off,
And then you would have tarried. Hark! there's one
up.

PANDARUS

[*Within*] What, 's all the doors open here?

TROILUS

It is your uncle.

CRESSIDA

A pestilence on him! now will he be mocking:
I shall have such a life!

Enter PANDARUS

PANDARUS

How now, how now! how go maidenheads?
Here, you maid! where's my cousin Cressid?

CRESSIDA

Go hang yourself, you naughty mocking uncle!
You bring me to do—and then you flout me too.

PANDARUS

To do what? to do what? let her say what: what
have I brought you to do?

CRESSIDA

Come, come, beshrew your heart! you'll ne'er be
good, nor suffer others.

PANDARUS

Ha, ha! Alas, poor wretch! a poor capocchia! hast
not slept to-night? would he not, a naughty man,
let it sleep? a bugbear take him!

CRESSIDA

Did not I tell you? would he were knock'd i'
the head!　　　　　　　　　　　　　　[*One knocks*
Who's that at door? good uncle, go and see.
My lord, come you again into my chamber.
You smile and mock me, as if I meant naughtily.

TROILUS

Ha, ha!

CRESSIDA

Come, you are deceived, I think of no such thing.
　　　　　　　　　　　　　　　　[*Knocking*
How earnestly they knock! Pray you, come in:
I would not for half Troy have you seen here.
　　　　　　　　　[*Exeunt* TROILUS *and* CRESSIDA

PANDARUS

Who's there? what's the matter? will you beat down
the door? How now! what's the matter?

Enter ÆNEAS

ÆNEAS

Good morrow, lord, good morrow.

PANDARUS

Who's there? my Lord Æneas! By my troth, I knew
you not: what news with you so early?

ÆNEAS

Is not prince Troilus here?

PANDARUS

Here! what should he do here?

ÆNEAS

Come, he is here, my lord; do not deny him:
It doth import him much to speak with me.

PANDARUS

Is he here, say you? 'tis more than I know, I'll be

sworn: for my own part, I came in late. What
should he do here?

ÆNEAS

Who! nay, then: come, come, you'll do him wrong
ere you are ware: you'll be so true to him, to be
false to him: do not you know of him, but yet go
fetch him hither; go.

Re-enter TROILUS

TROILUS

How now! what's the matter?

ÆNEAS

My lord, I scarce have leisure to salute you,
My matter is so rash: there is at hand
Paris your brother and Deiphobus,
The Grecian Diomed, and our Antenor
Deliver'd to us; and for him forthwith,
Ere the first sacrifice, within this hour,
We must give up to Diomedes' hand
The Lady Cressida.

TROILUS

Is it so concluded?

ÆNEAS

By Priam and the general state of Troy.
They are at hand and ready to effect it.

TROILUS

How my achievements mock me!
I will go meet them: and, my Lord Æneas,
We met by chance; you did not find me here.

ÆNEAS

Good, good, my lord; the secrets of nature
Have not more gift in taciturnity.
　　　　　　　　　　[*Exeunt* TROILUS *and* ÆNEAS

PANDARUS

Is 't possible? no sooner got but lost? The devil take
Antenor! the young prince will go mad: a plague
upon Antenor! I would they had broke 's neck!

Re-enter CRESSIDA

CRESSIDA

How now! what's the matter? who was here?

PANDARUS

Ah, ah!

CRESSIDA

Why sigh you so profoundly? where's my lord?
gone! Tell me, sweet uncle, what's the matter?

PANDARUS

Would I were as deep under the earth as I am
above!

CRESSIDA

O the gods! What's the matter?

PANDARUS

Prithee, get thee in: would thou hadst ne'er been
born! I knew thou wouldst be his death: O, poor
gentleman! A plague upon Antenor!

CRESSIDA

Good uncle, I beseech you, on my knees I beseech
you, what's the matter?

PANDARUS

Thou must be gone, wench, thou must be gone;
thou art changed for Antenor: thou must to thy

father, and be gone from Troilus: 'twill be his
death; 'twill be his bane; he cannot bear it.

CRESSIDA

O you immortal gods! I will not go.

PANDARUS

Thou must.

CRESSIDA

I will not, uncle: I have forgot my father;
I know no touch of consanguinity;
No kin, no love, no blood, no soul so near me
As the sweet Troilus. O you gods divine!
Make Cressid's name the very crown of falsehood,
If ever she leave Troilus! Time, force, and death,
Do to this body what extremes you can;
But the strong base and building of my love
Is as the very centre of the earth,
Drawing all things to it. I'll go in and weep,—

PANDARUS

Do, do.

CRESSIDA

Tear my bright hair and scratch my praised cheeks,
Crack my clear voice with sobs, and break my heart
With sounding Troilus. I will not go from Troy.

[*Exeunt*

SCENE III. *Before* PANDARUS' *house*

Enter PARIS, TROILUS, ÆNEAS, DEIPHOBUS, ANTENOR,
and DIOMEDES

PARIS

It is great morning, and the hour prefix'd
For her delivery to this valiant Greek
Comes fast upon: good my brother Troilus,
Tell you the lady what she is to do,
And haste her to the purpose.

TROILUS

Walk into her house;
I'll bring her to the Grecian presently:
And to his hand when I deliver her,
Think it an altar, and thy brother Troilus
A priest, there offering to it his own heart.   [*Exit*

PARIS

I know what 'tis to love;
And would, as I shall pity, I could help!
Please you walk in, my lords.   [*Exeunt*

SCENE IV. *A room in* PANDARUS' *house*

Enter PANDARUS *and* CRESSIDA

PANDARUS

Be moderate, be moderate.

CRESSIDA

Why tell you me of moderation?
The grief is fine, full, perfect, that I taste,
And violenteth in a sense as strong
As that which causeth it: how can I moderate it?
If I could temporise with my affection,
Or brew it to a weak and colder palate,
The like allayment could I give my grief:

My love admits no qualifying dross;
No more my grief, in such a precious loss.

Enter TROILUS

PANDARUS

Here, here, here he comes. Ah, sweet ducks!

CRESSIDA

O Troilus! Troilus!   [*Embracing him*

PANDARUS

What a pair of spectacles is here! Let me embrace
too. 'O heart,' as the goodly saying is,

'O heart, heavy heart,
Why sigh'st thou without breaking?'

where he answers again,

'Because thou canst not ease thy smart
By friendship nor by speaking.'

There was never a truer rhyme. Let us cast away
nothing, for we may live to have need of such a
verse: we see it, we see it. How now, lambs!

TROILUS

Cressid, I love thee in so strain'd a purity,
That the blest gods, as angry with my fancy,
More bright in zeal than the devotion which
Cold lips blow to their deities, take thee from me.

CRESSIDA

Have the gods envy?

PANDARUS

Ay, ay, ay, ay; 'tis too plain a case.

CRESSIDA

And is it true that I must go from Troy?

TROILUS

A hateful truth.

CRESSIDA

What, and from Troilus too?

TROILUS

From Troy and Troilus.

CRESSIDA

Is it possible?

TROILUS

And suddenly; where injury of chance
Puts back leave-taking, justles roughly by
All time of pause, rudely beguiles our lips
Of all rejoindure, forcibly prevents
Our lock'd embrasures, strangles our dear vows
Even in the birth of our own labouring breath:
We two, that with so many thousand sighs
Did buy each other, must poorly sell ourselves
With the rude brevity and discharge of one.
Injurious time now with a robber's haste
Crams his rich thievery up, he knows not how:
As many farewells as be stars in heaven,
With distinct breath and consign'd kisses to them,
He fumbles up into a loose adieu,
And scants us with a single famish'd kiss,
Distasted with the salt of broken tears.

ÆNEAS

[*Within*] My lord, is the lady ready?

TROILUS

Hark! you are call'd: some say the Genius so

Cries 'Come!' to him that instantly must die.
Bid them have patience; she shall come anon.

PANDARUS

Where are my tears? rain, to lay this wind, or my
heart will be blown up by the root.   [*Exit*

CRESSIDA

I must then to the Grecians?

TROILUS

No remedy.

CRESSIDA

A woeful Cressid 'mongst the merry Greeks!
When shall we see again?

TROILUS

Hear me, my love: be thou but true of heart.

CRESSIDA

I true! how now! what wicked deem is this?

TROILUS

Nay, we must use expostulation kindly,
For it is parting from us:
I speak not 'be thou true,' as fearing thee;
For I will throw my glove to Death himself,
That there's no maculation in thy heart:
But 'be thou true' say I, to fashion in
My sequent protestation; be thou true,
And I will see thee.

CRESSIDA

O, you shall be exposed, my lord, to dangers
As infinite as imminent: but I'll be true.

TROILUS

And I'll grow friend with danger. Wear this sleeve.

CRESSIDA

And you this glove. When shall I see you?

TROILUS

I will corrupt the Grecian sentinels,
To give thee nightly visitation.
But yet, be true.

CRESSIDA

O heavens! 'Be true' again!

TROILUS

Hear why I speak it, love:
The Grecian youths are full of quality;
They're loving, well composed with gifts of nature,
And flowing o'er with arts and exercise:
How novelties may move and parts with person,
Alas, a kind of godly jealousy—
Which, I beseech you, call a virtuous sin—
Makes me afeard.

CRESSIDA

O heavens! you love me not.

TROILUS

Die I a villain then!
In this I do not call your faith in question,
So mainly as my merit: I cannot sing,
Nor heel the high lavolt, nor sweeten talk,
Nor play at subtle games; fair virtues all,
To which the Grecians are most prompt and preg-
    nant:
But I can tell that in each grace of these
There lurks a still and dumb-discoursive devil
That tempts most cunningly: but be not tempted.

CRESSIDA

Do you think I will?

TROILUS

No:
But something may be done that we will not:
And sometimes we are devils to ourselves,
When we will tempt the frailty of our powers,
Presuming on their changeful potency.

ÆNEAS

[*Within*] Nay, good my lord!

TROILUS

Come, kiss; and let us part.

PARIS

[*Within*] Brother Troilus!

TROILUS

Good brother, come you hither;
And bring Æneas and the Grecian with you.

CRESSIDA

My lord, will you be true?

TROILUS

Who, I? alas, it is my vice, my fault:
Whiles others fish with craft for great opinion,
I with great truth catch mere simplicity;
Whilst some with cunning gild their copper crowns,
With truth and plainness I do wear mine bare.
Fear not my truth: the moral of **my wit**
Is 'plain and true'; there's all the reach of it.

Enter ÆNEAS, PARIS, ANTENOR, DEIPHOBUS, *and*
DIOMEDES

Welcome, Sir Diomed! here is the lady
Which for Antenor we deliver you:
At the port, lord, I'll give her to thy hand;
And by the way possess thee what she is.
Entreat her fair; and, by my soul, fair Greek,
If e'er thou stand at mercy of my sword,
Name Cressid, and thy life shall be as safe
As Priam is in Ilion.

DIOMEDES

Fair Lady Cressid,
So please you, save the thanks this prince expects:
The lustre in your eye, heaven in your cheek,
Pleads your fair usage; and to Diomed
You shall be mistress, and command him wholly.

TROILUS

Grecian, thou dost not use me courteously,
To shame the zeal of my petition to thee
In praising her: I tell thee, lord of Greece,
She is as far high-soaring o'er thy praises
As thou unworthy to be call'd her servant.
I charge thee use her well, even for my charge;
For, by the dreadful Pluto, if thou dost not,
Though the great bulk Achilles be thy guard,
I'll cut thy throat.

DIOMEDES

O, be not moved, Prince Troilus:
Let me be privileged by my place and message
To be a speaker free; when I am hence,
I'll answer to my lust: and know you, lord,
I'll nothing do on charge: to her own worth

She shall be prized; but that you say 'Be 't so,'
I'll speak it in my spirit and honour 'No!'

TROILUS

Come, to the port. I'll tell thee, Diomed,
This brave shall oft make thee to hide thy head.
Lady, give me your hand; and, as we walk,
To our own selves bend we our needful talk.

[Exeunt TROILUS, CRESSIDA, *and* DIOMEDES

[A trumpet sounds

PARIS

Hark! Hector's trumpet.

ÆNEAS

　　　　　How have we spent this morning!
The prince must think me tardy and remiss,
That swore to ride before him to the field.

PARIS

'Tis Troilus' fault: come, come, to field with him.

DEIPHOBUS

Let us make ready straight.

ÆNEAS

Yea, with a bridegroom's fresh alacrity,
Let us address to tend on Hector's heels:
The glory of our Troy doth this day lie
On his fair worth and single chivalry.　　　　*[Exeunt*

SCENE V. *The Grecian camp. Lists set out*

Enter AJAX, *armed;* AGAMEMNON, ACHILLES,
PATROCLUS, MENELAUS, ULYSSES, NESTOR, *and others*

AGAMEMNON

Here art thou in appointment fresh and fair,
Anticipating time with starting courage.
Give with thy trumpet a loud note to Troy,
Thou dreadful Ajax, that the appalled air
May pierce the head of the great combatant
And hale him hither.

AJAX

　　　　　Thou, trumpet, there's my purse.
Now crack thy lungs, and split thy brazen pipe:
Blow, villain, till thy sphered bias cheek
Outswell the colic of puff'd Aquilon:
Come, stretch thy chest, and let thy eyes spout
　　blood;
Thou blow'st for Hector.　　　　*[Trumpet sounds*

ULYSSES

No trumpet answers.

ACHILLES

　　　　　'Tis but early days.

AGAMEMNON

Is not yond Diomed, with Calchas' daughter?

ULYSSES

'Tis he, I ken the manner of his gait;
He rises on the toe: that spirit of his
In aspiration lifts him from the earth.

Enter DIOMEDES, *with* CRESSIDA

AGAMEMNON

Is this the Lady Cressid?

DIOMEDES

　　　　　Even she.

AGAMEMNON

Most dearly welcome to the Greeks, sweet lady.

NESTOR

Our general doth salute you with a kiss.

ULYSSES

Yet is the kindness but particular;
'Twere better she were kiss'd in general.

NESTOR

And very courtly counsel: I'll begin.
So much for Nestor.

ACHILLES

I'll take that winter from your lips, fair lady:
Achilles bids you welcome.

MENELAUS

I had good argument for kissing once.

PATROCLUS

But that's no argument for kissing now;
For thus popp'd Paris in his hardiment,
And parted thus you and your argument.

ULYSSES

O deadly gall, and theme of all our scorns!
For which we lose our heads to gild his horns.

PATROCLUS

The first was Menelaus' kiss; this, mine:
Patroclus kisses you.

MENELAUS

　　　　　O, this is trim!

PATROCLUS

Paris and I kiss evermore for him.

MENELAUS

I'll have my kiss, sir. Lady, by your leave.

CRESSIDA

In kissing, do you render or receive?

PATROCLUS

Both take and give.

CRESSIDA

　　　　　I'll make my match to live,
The kiss you take is better than you give;
Therefore no kiss.

MENELAUS

I'll give you boot, I'll give you three for one.

CRESSIDA

You're an odd man; give even, or give none.

MENELAUS

An odd man, lady! every man is odd.

CRESSIDA

No, Paris is not; for, you know, 'tis true,
That you are odd, and he is even with you.

MENELAUS

You fillip me o' the head.

CRESSIDA

　　　　　No, I'll be sworn.

ULYSSES

It were no match, your nail against his horn.
May I, sweet lady, beg a kiss of you?

CRESSIDA

You may.

ULYSSES

　　　　　I do desire it.

CRESSIDA
Why, beg then.
ULYSSES
Why then, for Venus' sake, give me a kiss,
When Helen is a maid again, and his.
CRESSIDA
I am your debtor; claim it when 'tis due.
ULYSSES
Never's my day, and then a kiss of you.
DIOMEDES
Lady, a word: I'll bring you to your father.
                              [*Exit with* CRESSIDA
NESTOR
A woman of quick sense.
ULYSSES
                    Fie, fie upon her!
There's language in her eye, her cheek, her lip,
Nay, her foot speaks; her wanton spirits look out
At every joint and motive of her body.
O, these encounterers, so glib of tongue,
That give accosting welcome ere it comes,
And wide unclasp the tables of their thoughts
To every ticklish reader! set them down
For sluttish spoils of opportunity,
And daughters of the game.   [*Trumpet within*
ALL
The Trojans' trumpet.
AGAMEMNON
                    Yonder comes the troop.
Flourish. Enter HECTOR, *armed;* ÆNEAS, TROILUS, *and
other* TROJANS, *with* ATTENDANTS
ÆNEAS
Hail, all the state of Greece! what shall be done
To him that victory commands? or do you purpose
A victor shall be known? will you the knights
Shall to the edge of all extremity
Pursue each other, or shall they be divided
By any voice or order of the field?
Hector bade ask.
AGAMEMNON
                    Which way would Hector have it?
ÆNEAS
He cares not; he'll obey conditions.
ACHILLES
'Tis done like Hector; but securely done,
A little proudly, and great deal misprizing
The knight opposed.
ÆNEAS
                    If not Achilles, sir,
What is your name?
ACHILLES
                    If not Achilles, nothing.
ÆNEAS
Therefore Achilles: but, whate'er, know this:
In the extremity of great and little,
Valour and pride excel themselves in Hector;
The one almost as infinite as all,
The other blank as nothing. Weigh him well,
And that which looks like pride is courtesy.
This Ajax is half made of Hector's blood:

In love whereof, half Hector stays at home;
Half heart, half hand, half Hector comes to seek
This blended knight, half Trojan and half Greek.
ACHILLES
A maiden battle then? O, I perceive you.
                    Re-enter DIOMEDES
AGAMEMNON
Here is Sir Diomed. Go, gentle knight,
Stand by our Ajax: as you and Lord Æneas
Consent upon the order of their fight,
So be it; either to the uttermost,
Or else a breath: the combatants being kin
Half stints their strife before their strokes begin.
                    [AJAX *and* HECTOR *enter the lists*
ULYSSES
They are opposed already.
AGAMEMNON
What Trojan is that same that looks so heavy?
ULYSSES
The youngest son of Priam, a true knight,
Not yet mature, yet matchless, firm of word,
Speaking in deeds and deedless in his tongue,
Not soon provoked nor being provoked soon calm'd;
His heart and hand both open and both free;
For what he has he gives, what thinks he shows;
Yet gives he not till judgement guide his bounty,
Nor dignifies an impair thought with breath;
Manly as Hector, but more dangerous;
For Hector in his blaze of wrath subscribes
To tender objects, but he in heat of action
Is more vindicative than jealous love:
They call him Troilus, and on him erect
A second hope, as fairly built as Hector.
Thus says Æneas; one that knows the youth
Even to his inches, and with private soul
Did in great Ilion thus translate him to me.
                    [*Alarum.* HECTOR *and* AJAX *fight*
AGAMEMNON
They are in action.
NESTOR
Now, Ajax, hold thine own!
TROILUS
                    Hector, thou sleep'st;
Awake thee!
AGAMEMNON
His blows are well disposed: there, Ajax!
DIOMEDES
You must no more.   [*Trumpets cease*
ÆNEAS
                    Princes, enough, so please you.
AJAX
I am not warm yet; let us fight again.
DIOMEDES
As Hector pleases.
HECTOR
                    Why, then will I no more:
Thou art, great lord, my father's sister son,
A cousin-german to great Priam's seed;
The obligation of our blood forbids
A gory emulation 'twixt us twain:

[849]

Were thy commixtion Greek and Trojan so,
That thou couldst say 'This hand is Grecian all,
And this is Trojan; the sinews of this leg
All Greek, and this all Troy; my mother's blood
Runs on the dexter cheek, and this sinister
Bounds in my father's;' by Jove multipotent,
Thou shouldst not bear from me a Greekish member
Wherein my sword had not impressure made
Of our rank feud: but the just gods gainsay
That any drop thou borrow'dst from thy mother,
My sacred aunt, should by my mortal sword
Be drained! Let me embrace thee, Ajax:
By him that thunders, thou hast lusty arms;
Hector would have them fall upon him thus:
Cousin, all honour to thee!

AJAX
               I thank thee, Hector:
Thou art too gentle and too free a man:
I came to kill thee, cousin, and bear hence
A great addition earned in thy death.

HECTOR
Not Neoptolemus so mirable,
On whose bright crest Fame with her loud'st Oyes
Cries 'This is he,' could promise to himself
A thought of added honour torn from Hector.

ÆNEAS
There is expectance here from both the sides,
What further you will do.

HECTOR
            We'll answer it;
The issue is embracement: Ajax, farewell.

AJAX
If I might in entreaties find success,—
As seld I have the chance—I would desire
My famous cousin to our Grecian tents.

DIOMEDES
'Tis Agamemnon's wish; and great Achilles
Doth long to see unarm'd the valiant Hector.

HECTOR
Æneas, call my brother Troilus to me:
And signify this loving interview
To the expecters of our Trojan part;
Desire them home. Give me thy hand, my cousin;
I will go eat with thee, and see your knights.

AJAX
Great Agamemnon comes to meet us here.

HECTOR
The worthiest of them tell me name by name;
But for Achilles, my own searching eyes
Shall find **him by hi**s large and portly size.

AGAMEMNON
Worthy of arms! as welcome as to one
That would be rid of such an enemy;
But that's no welcome: understand more clear,
What's past and what's to come is strew'd with
    husks
And formless ruin of oblivion;
But in this extant moment, faith and troth,

Strain'd purely from all hollow bias-drawing,
Bids thee, with most divine integrity,
From heart of very heart, great Hector, welcome.

HECTOR
I thank thee, most imperious Agamemnon.

AGAMEMNON
[To TROILUS] My well-famed lord of Troy, no less to
    you.

MENELAUS
Let me confirm my princely brother's greeting;
You brace of warlike brothers, welcome hither.

HECTOR
Who must we answer?

ÆNEAS
              The noble Menelaus.

HECTOR
O, you, my lord! by Mars his gauntlet, thanks!
Mock not, that I affect the untraded oath;
Your quondam wife swears still by Venus' glove:
She's well, but bade me not commend her to you.

MENELAUS
Name her not now, sir; she's a deadly theme.

HECTOR
O, pardon; I offend.

NESTOR
I have, thou gallant Trojan, seen thee oft,
Labouring for destiny, make cruel way
Through ranks of Greekish youth; and I have seen
    thee,
As hot as Perseus, spur thy Phrygian steed,
Despising many forfeits and subduements,
When thou hast hung thy advanced sword i' the air,
Not letting it decline on the declined,
That I have said to some my standers by
'Lo, Jupiter is yonder, dealing life!'
And I have seen thee pause and take thy breath,
When that a ring of Greeks have hemm'd thee in,
Like an Olympian wrestling: this have I seen;
But this thy countenance, still lock'd in steel,
I never saw till now. I knew thy grandsire,
And once fought with him: he was a soldier good;
But, by great Mars the captain of us all,
Never like thee. Let an old man embrace thee;
And, worthy warrior, welcome to our tents.

ÆNEAS
'Tis the old Nestor.

HECTOR
Let me embrace thee, good old chronicle,
That hast so long walk'd hand in hand with time:
Most reverend Nestor, I am glad to clasp thee.

NESTOR
I would my arms could match thee in contention,
As they contend with thee in courtesy.

HECTOR
I would they could.

NESTOR
Ha!
By this white beard, I'ld fight with thee to-morrow:
Well, welcome, welcome!—I have seen the time.

ULYSSES

I wonder now how yonder city stands,
When we have here her base and pillar by us.

HECTOR

I know your favour, Lord Ulysses, well.
Ah, sir, there's many a Greek and Trojan dead,
Since first I saw yourself and Diomed
In Ilion, on your Greekish embassy.

ULYSSES

Sir, I foretold you then what would ensue:
My prophecy is but half his journey yet;
For yonder walls, that pertly front your town,
Yond towers, whose wanton tops do buss the clouds,
Must kiss their own feet.

HECTOR

         I must not believe you:
There they stand yet; and modestly I think,
The fall of every Phrygian stone will cost
A drop of Grecian blood: the end crowns all,
And that old common arbitrator, Time,
Will one day end it.

ULYSSES

         So to him we leave it.
Most gentle and most valiant Hector, welcome:
After the general, I beseech you next
To feast with me and see me at my tent.

ACHILLES

I shall forestall thee, Lord Ulysses, thou!
Now, Hector, I have fed mine eyes on thee;
I have with exact view perused thee, Hector,
And quoted joint by joint.

HECTOR

         Is this Achilles?

ACHILLES

I am Achilles.

HECTOR

Stand fair, I pray thee: let me look on thee.

ACHILLES

Behold thy fill.

HECTOR

         Nay, I have done already.

ACHILLES

Thou art too brief: I will the second time,
As I would buy thee, view thee limb by limb.

HECTOR

O, like a book of sport thou'lt read me o'er;
But there's more in me than thou understand'st.
Why dost thou so oppress me with thine eye?

ACHILLES

Tell me, you heavens, in which part of his body
Shall I destroy him? whether there, or there, or
    there?
That I may give the local wound a name,
And make distinct the very breach whereout
Hector's great spirit flew: answer me, heavens!

HECTOR

It would discredit the blest gods, proud man,
To answer such a question: stand again:
Think'st thou to catch my life so pleasantly,

As to prenominate in nice conjecture
Where thou wilt hit me dead?

ACHILLES

         I tell thee, yea.

HECTOR

Wert thou an oracle to tell me so,
I'ld not believe thee. Henceforth guard thee well;
For I'll not kill thee there, nor there, nor there;
But, by the forge that stithied Mars his helm,
I'll kill thee every where, yea, o'er and o'er.
You wisest Grecians, pardon me this brag;
His insolence draws folly from my lips;
But I'll endeavour deeds to match these words,
Or may I never—

AJAX

         Do not chafe thee, cousin:
And you, Achilles, let these threats alone
Till accident or purpose bring you to 't:
You may have every day enough of Hector,
If you have stomach: the general state, I fear,
Can scarce entreat you to be odd with him.

HECTOR

I pray you, let us see you in the field:
We have had pelting wars since you refused
The Grecians' cause.

ACHILLES

         Dost thou entreat me, Hector?
To-morrow do I meet thee, fell as death;
To-night all friends.

HECTOR

         Thy hand upon that match.

AGAMEMNON

First, all you peers of Greece, go to my tent;
There in the full convive we: afterwards,
As Hector's leisure and your bounties shall
Concur together, severally entreat him.
Beat loud the tabourines, let the trumpets blow,
That this great soldier may his welcome know.

       [*Exeunt all but* TROILUS *and* ULYSSES

TROILUS

My Lord Ulysses, tell me, I beseech you,
In what place of the field doth Calchas keep?

ULYSSES

At Menelaus' tent, most princely Troilus:
There Diomed doth feast with him to-night;
Who neither looks upon the heaven nor earth,
But gives all gaze and bent of amorous view
On the fair Cressid.

TROILUS

Shall I, sweet lord, be bound to you so much,
After we part from Agamemnon's tent,
To bring me thither?

ULYSSES

         You shall command me, sir.
As gentle tell me, of what honour was
This Cressida in Troy? Had she no lover there
That wails her absence?

TROILUS

O, sir, to such as boasting show their scars,
A mock is due. Will you walk on, my lord?

She was beloved, she loved; she is, and doth:
But still sweet love is food for fortune's tooth. [*Exeunt*

ACT V

SCENE I. *The Grecian camp. Before* ACHILLES' *tent*

Enter ACHILLES *and* PATROCLUS

ACHILLES

I'll heat his blood with Greekish wine to-night,
Which with my scimitar I'll cool to-morrow.
Patroclus, let us feast him to the height.

PATROCLUS

Here comes Thersites.

Enter THERSITES

ACHILLES

How now, thou core of envy!
Thou crusty batch of nature, what's the news?

THERSITES

Why, thou picture of what thou seemest, and idol of
idiot-worshippers, here's a letter for thee.

ACHILLES

From whence, fragment?

THERSITES

Why, thou full dish of fool, from Troy.

PATROCLUS

Who keeps the tent now?

THERSITES

The surgeon's box, or the patient's wound.

PATROCLUS

Well said, adversity! and what needs these tricks?

THERSITES

Prithee, be silent, boy; I profit not by thy talk:
thou art thought to be Achilles' male varlet.

PATROCLUS

Male varlet, you rogue! what's that?

THERSITES

Why, his masculine whore. Now, the rotten diseases of the south, the guts-griping, ruptures,
catarrhs, loads o' gravel i' the back, lethargies, cold
palsies, raw eyes, dirt-rotten livers, wheezing
lungs, bladders full of imposthume, sciaticas,
limekilns i' the palm, incurable bone-ache, and the
rivelled fee-simple of the tetter, take and take again
such preposterous discoveries!

PATROCLUS

Why, thou damnable box of envy, thou, what
mean'st thou to curse thus?

THERSITES

Do I curse thee?

PATROCLUS

Why, no, you ruinous butt; you whoreson indis-
tinguishable cur, no.

THERSITES

No! why art thou then exasperate, thou idle immaterial skein of sleave silk, thou green sarcenet flap
for a sore eye, thou tassel of a prodigal's purse, thou?

Ah, how the poor world is pestered with such water-
flies, diminutives of nature!

PATROCLUS

Out, gall!

THERSITES

Finch-egg!

ACHILLES

My sweet Patroclus, I am thwarted quite
From my great purpose in to-morrow's battle.
Here is a letter from Queen Hecuba,
A token from her daughter, my fair love,
Both taxing me and gaging me to keep
An oath that I have sworn. I will not break it:
Fall Greeks; fail fame; honour or go or stay;
My major vow lies here, this I'll obey.
Come, come, Thersites, help to trim my tent:
This night in banqueting must all be spent.
Away, Patroclus! [*Exeunt* ACHILLES *and* PATROCLUS

THERSITES

With too much blood and too little brain, these two
may run mad; but, if with too much brain and too
little blood they do, I'll be a curer of madmen.
Here's Agamemnon, an honest fellow enough and
one that loves quails; but he has not so much brain
as ear-wax: and the goodly transformation of Jupiter
there, his brother, the bull, the primitive statue and
oblique memorial of cuckolds; a thrifty shoeing-
horn in a chain, hanging at his brother's leg,—to
what form but that he is, should wit larded with
malice and malice forced with wit turn him to? To
an ass, were nothing; he is both ass and ox: to an
ox, were nothing; he is both ox and ass. To be a
dog, a mule, a cat, a fitchew, a toad, a lizard, an
owl, a puttock, or a herring without a roe, I would
not care; but to be Menelaus! I would conspire
against destiny. Ask me not what I would be, if I
were not Thersites; for I care not to be the louse of
a lazar, so I were not Menelaus. Hoy-day! spirits
and fires!

Enter HECTOR, TROILUS, AJAX, AGAMEMNON, ULYSSES,
NESTOR, MENELAUS, *and* DIOMEDES, *with lights*

AGAMEMNON

We go wrong, we go wrong.

AJAX

No, yonder 'tis;
There, where we see the lights.

HECTOR

I trouble you.

AJAX

No, not a whit.

Re-enter ACHILLES

ULYSSES

Here comes himself to guide you.

ACHILLES

Welcome, brave Hector; welcome, princes all.

AGAMEMNON

So now, fair Prince of Troy, I bid good night.
Ajax commands the guard to tend on you.

HECTOR

Thanks and good night to the Greeks' general.

MENELAUS
Good night, my lord.

HECTOR
Good night, sweet Lord Menelaus.

THERSITES
Sweet draught: sweet, quoth a'! sweet sink, sweet
sewer.

ACHILLES
Good night and welcome, both at once, to those
That go or tarry.

AGAMEMNON
Good night.   [Exeunt AGAMEMNON and MENELAUS

ACHILLES
Old Nestor tarries; and you too, Diomed,
Keep Hector company an hour or two.

DIOMEDES
I cannot, lord; I have important business,
The tide whereof is now. Good night, great Hector.

HECTOR
Give me your hand.

ULYSSES
[Aside to TROILUS] Follow his torch; he goes to Cal-
chas' tent:
I'll keep you company.

TROILUS
          Sweet sir, you honour me.

HECTOR
And so, good night.
          [Exit DIOMEDES; ULYSSES and TROILUS following

ACHILLES
Come, come, enter my tent.
          [Exeunt ACHILLES, HECTOR, AJAX, and NESTOR

THERSITES
That same Diomed's a false-hearted rogue, a most
unjust knave; I will no more trust him when he
leers than I will a serpent when he hisses: he will
spend his mouth and promise, like Brabbler the
hound; but when he performs, astronomers foretell
it; it is prodigious, there will come some change;
the sun borrows of the moon when Diomed keeps
his word. I will rather leave to see Hector than not
to dog him: they say he keeps a Trojan drab and
uses the traitor Calchas' tent: I'll after. Nothing but
lechery! all incontinent varlets!   [Exit

SCENE II. The same. Before CALCHAS' tent

Enter DIOMEDES

DIOMEDES
What, are you up here, ho? speak.

CALCHAS
[Within] Who calls?

DIOMEDES
Diomed. Calchas, I think. Where's your daughter?

CALCHAS
[Within] She comes to you.
Enter TROILUS and ULYSSES, at a distance; after them,
          THERSITES

ULYSSES
Stand where the torch may not discover us.
          Enter CRESSIDA

TROILUS
Cressid comes forth to him.

DIOMEDES
          How now, my charge!

CRESSIDA
Now, my sweet guardian! Hark, a word with you.
          [Whispers

TROILUS
Yea, so familiar!

ULYSSES
She will sing any man at first sight.

THERSITES
And any man may sing her, if he can take her cliff;
she's noted.

DIOMEDES
Will you remember?

CRESSIDA
Remember! yes.

DIOMEDES
Nay, but do, then;
And let your mind be coupled with your words.

TROILUS
What should she remember?

ULYSSES
List.

CRESSIDA
Sweet honey Greek, tempt me no more to folly.

THERSITES
Roguery!

DIOMEDES
Nay, then,—

CRESSIDA
I'll tell you what,—

DIOMEDES
Foh, foh! come, tell a pin: you are forsworn.

CRESSIDA
In faith, I cannot: what would you have me do?

THERSITES
A juggling trick,—to be secretly open.

DIOMEDES
What did you swear you would bestow on me?

CRESSIDA
I prithee, do not hold me to mine oath;
Bid me do any thing but that, sweet Greek.

DIOMEDES
Good night.

TROILUS
Hold, patience!

ULYSSES
How now, Trojan!

CRESSIDA
Diomed,—

DIOMEDES
No, no, good night: I'll be your fool no more.

TROILUS
Thy better must.

CRESSIDA
Hark, one word in your ear.

TROILUS
O plague and madness!

ULYSSES
You are moved, prince; let us depart, I pray you,
Lest your displeasure should enlarge itself
To wrathful terms: this place is dangerous;
The time right deadly; I beseech you, go.

TROILUS
Behold, I pray you!

ULYSSES
                    Nay, good my lord, go off:
You flow to great distraction; come, my lord.

TROILUS
I pray thee, stay.

ULYSSES
              You have not patience; come.

TROILUS
I pray you, stay; by hell and all hell's torments,
I will not speak a word.

DIOMEDES
                    And so, good night.

CRESSIDA
Nay, but you part in anger.

TROILUS
                    Doth that grieve thee?
O wither'd truth!

ULYSSES
            Why, how now, lord!

TROILUS
                            By Jove,
I will be patient.

CRESSIDA
            Guardian!—why, Greek!

DIOMEDES
Foh, foh! adieu; you palter.

CRESSIDA
In faith, I do not: come hither once again.

ULYSSES
You shake, my lord, at something: will you go?
You will break out.

TROILUS
              She strokes his cheek!

ULYSSES
                            Come, come.

TROILUS
Nay, stay; by Jove, I will not speak a word:
There is between my will and all offences
A guard of patience: stay a little while.

THERSITES
How the devil luxury, with his fat rump and potato-
finger, tickles these together! Fry, lechery, fry!

DIOMEDES
But will you, then?

CRESSIDA
In faith, I will, la; never trust me else.

DIOMEDES
Give me some token for the surety of it.

CRESSIDA
I'll fetch you one.   [Exit

ULYSSES
You have sworn patience.

TROILUS
                    Fear me not, sweet lord;
I will not be myself, nor have cognition
Of what I feel: I am all patience.

Re-enter CRESSIDA

TROILUS
Now the pledge; now, now, now!

CRESSIDA
Here, Diomed, keep this sleeve.

TROILUS
O beauty! where is thy faith?

ULYSSES
                            My lord,—

TROILUS
I will be patient; outwardly I will.

CRESSIDA
You look upon that sleeve; behold it well.
He loved me—O false wench!—Give 't me again.

DIOMEDES
Whose was 't?

CRESSIDA
It is no matter, now I have 't again.
I will not meet with you to-morrow night:
I prithee, Diomed, visit me no more.

THERSITES
Now she sharpens: well said, whetstone!

DIOMEDES
I shall have it.

CRESSIDA
            What, this?

DIOMEDES
                    Ay, that.

CRESSIDA
O, all you gods! O pretty, pretty pledge!
Thy master now lies thinking in his bed
Of thee and me, and sighs, and takes my glove,
And gives memorial dainty kisses to it,
As I kiss thee. Nay, do not snatch it from me;
He that takes that doth take my heart withal.

DIOMEDES
I had your heart before; this follows it.

TROILUS
I did swear patience.

CRESSIDA
You shall not have it, Diomed; faith, you shall not;
I'll give you something else.

DIOMEDES
I will have this: whose was it?

CRESSIDA
                            It is no matter.

DIOMEDES
Come, tell me whose it was.

CRESSIDA
'Twas one's that loved me better than you will.
But, now you have it, take it.

DIOMEDES
Whose was it?
CRESSIDA
By all Diana's waiting-women yond,
And by herself, I will not tell you whose.
DIOMEDES
To-morrow will I wear it on my helm,
And grieve his spirit that dares not challenge it.
TROILUS
Wert thou the devil, and worest it on thy horn,
It should be challenged.
CRESSIDA
Well, well, 'tis done, 'tis past; and yet it is not;
I will not keep my word.
DIOMEDES
Why then, farewell;
Thou never shalt mock Diomed again.
CRESSIDA
You shall not go: one cannot speak a word,
But it straight starts you.
DIOMEDES
I do not like this fooling.
THERSITES
Nor I, by Pluto: but that that likes not you
Pleases me best.
DIOMEDES
What, shall I come? the hour?
CRESSIDA
Ay, come: O Jove! do come: I shall be plagued.
DIOMEDES
Farewell till then.
CRESSIDA
Good night: I prithee, come.
[Exit DIOMEDES
Troilus, farewell! one eye yet looks on thee,
But with my heart the other eye doth see.
Ah, poor our sex! this fault in us I find,
The error of our eye directs our mind:
What error leads must err; O, then conclude
Minds sway'd by eyes are full of turpitude. [Exit
THERSITES
A proof of strength she could not publish more,
Unless she said 'My mind is now turn'd whore.'
ULYSSES
All's done, my lord.
TROILUS
It is.
ULYSSES
Why stay we then?
TROILUS
To make a recordation to my soul
Of every syllable that here was spoke.
But if I tell how these two did co-act,
Shall I not lie in publishing a truth?
Sith yet there is a credence in my heart,
An esperance so obstinately strong,
That doth invert the attest of eyes and ears;
As if those organs had deceptious functions,
Created only to calumniate.
Was Cressid here?

ULYSSES
I cannot conjure, Trojan.
TROILUS
She was not, sure.
ULYSSES
Most sure she was.
TROILUS
Why, my negation hath no taste of madness.
ULYSSES
Nor mine, my lord: Cressid was here but now.
TROILUS
Let it not be believed for womanhood!
Think, we had mothers; do not give advantage
To stubborn critics, apt without a theme
For depravation, to square the general sex
By Cressid's rule: rather think this not Cressid.
ULYSSES
What hath she done, prince, that can soil our
mothers?
TROILUS
Nothing at all, unless that this were she.
THERSITES
Will a' swagger himself out on 's own eyes?
TROILUS
This she? no, this is Diomed's Cressida:
If beauty have a soul, this is not she;
If souls guide vows, if vows be sanctimonies,
If sanctimony be the gods' delight,
If there be rule in unity itself,
This is not she. O madness of discourse,
That cause sets up with and against itself!
Bi-fold authority! where reason can revolt
Without perdition, and loss assume all reason
Without revolt: this is, and is not, Cressid!
Within my soul there doth conduce a fight
Of this strange nature, that a thing inseparate
Divides more wider than the sky and earth;
And yet the spacious breadth of this division
Admits no orifex for a point as subtle
As Ariachne's broken woof to enter.
Instance, O instance! strong as Pluto's gates;
Cressid is mine, tied with the bonds of heaven:
Instance, O instance! strong as heaven itself;
The bonds of heaven are slipp'd, dissolved and
loosed;
And with another knot, five-finger-tied,
The fractions of her faith, orts of her love,
The fragments, scraps, the bits and greasy relics
Of her o'er-eaten faith, are bound to Diomed.
ULYSSES
May worthy Troilus be half attach'd
With that which here his passion doth express?
TROILUS
Ay, Greek; and that shall be divulged well
In characters as red as Mars his heart
Inflamed with Venus: never did young man fancy
With so eternal and so fix'd a soul.
Hark, Greek: as much as I do Cressid love,
So much by weight hate I her Diomed:
That sleeve is mine that he'll bear on his helm:

Were it a casque composed by Vulcan's skill,
My sword should bite it: not the dreadful spout
Which shipmen do the hurricano call,
Constringed in mass by the almighty sun,
Shall dizzy with more clamour Neptune's ear
In his descent, than shall my prompted sword
Falling on Diomed.

THERSITES
He'll tickle it for his concupy.

TROILUS
O Cressid! O false Cressid! false, false, false!
Let all untruths stand by thy stained name,
And they'll seem glorious.

ULYSSES
　　　　　O, contain yourself;
Your passion draws ears hither.

Enter ÆNEAS

ÆNEAS
I have been seeking you this hour, my lord:
Hector by this is arming him in Troy;
Ajax your guard stays to conduct you home.

TROILUS
Have with you, prince. My courteous lord, adieu.
Farewell, revolted fair! and, Diomed,
Stand fast, and wear a castle on thy head!

ULYSSES
I'll bring you to the gates.

TROILUS
Accept distracted thanks.

[Exeunt TROILUS, ÆNEAS, *and* ULYSSES
THERSITES
Would I could meet that rogue Diomed! I would
croak like a raven; I would bode, I would bode.
Patroclus will give me any thing for the intelligence
of this whore: the parrot will not do more for an
almond than he for a commodious drab. Lechery,
lechery! still wars and lechery! nothing else holds
fashion. A burning devil take them!　　　　　*[Exit*

SCENE III. *Troy. Before* PRIAM'S *palace*

Enter HECTOR *and* ANDROMACHE
ANDROMACHE
When was my lord so much ungently temper'd,
To stop his ears against admonishment?
Unarm, unarm, and do not fight to-day.

HECTOR
You train me to offend you; get you in:
By all the everlasting gods, I'll go!

ANDROMACHE
My dreams will, sure, prove ominous to the day.

HECTOR
No more, I say.

Enter CASSANDRA
CASSANDRA
Where is my brother Hector?

ANDROMACHE
Here, sister; arm'd, and bloody in intent.
Consort with me in loud and dear petition;

Pursue we him on knees; for I have dream'd
Of bloody turbulence, and this whole night
Hath nothing been but shapes and forms of slaugh-
ter.

CASSANDRA
O, 'tis true.

HECTOR
Ho! bid my trumpet sound!

CASSANDRA
No notes of sally, for the heavens, sweet brother.

HECTOR
Be gone, I say: the gods have heard me swear.

CASSANDRA
The gods are deaf to hot and peevish vows:
They are polluted offerings, more abhorr'd
Than spotted livers in the sacrifice.

ANDROMACHE
O, be persuaded! do not count it holy
To hurt by being just: it is as lawful,
For we would give much, to use violent thefts
And rob in the behalf of charity.

CASSANDRA
It is the purpose that makes strong the vow;
But vows to every purpose must not hold:
Unarm, sweet Hector.

HECTOR
　　　　　Hold you still, I say;
Mine honour keeps the weather of my fate:
Life every man holds dear; but the dear man
Holds honour far more precious-dear than life.

Enter TROILUS
How now, young man! mean'st thou to fight to-
day?

ANDROMACHE
Cassandra, call my father to persuade.

[Exit CASSANDRA
HECTOR
No, faith, young Troilus; doff thy harness, youth:
I am to-day i' the vein of chivalry:
Let grow thy sinews till their knots be strong,
And tempt not yet the brushes of the war.
Unarm thee, go; and doubt thou not, brave boy,
I'll stand to-day for thee and me and Troy.

Brother, you have a vice of mercy in you,
Which better fits a lion than a man.

HECTOR
What vice is that, good Troilus? chide me for it.

TROILUS
When many times the captive Grecian falls,
Even in the fan and wind of your fair sword,
You bid them rise and live.

HECTOR
O, 'tis fair play.

TROILUS
Fool's play, by heaven, Hector.

HECTOR
How now! how now!

TROILUS
For the love of all the gods,

Let's leave the hermit pity with our mother;
And when we have our armours buckled on,
The venom'd vengeance ride upon our swords,
Spur them to ruthful work, rein them from ruth!

HECTOR

Fie, savage, fie!

TROILUS

Hector, then 'tis wars.

HECTOR

Troilus, I would not have you fight to-day.

TROILUS

Who should withhold me?
Not fate, obedience, nor the hand of Mars
Beckoning with fiery truncheon my retire;
Not Priamus and Hecuba on knees,
Their eyes o'ergalled with recourse of tears;
Nor you, my brother, with your true sword drawn,
Opposed to hinder me, should stop my way,
But by my ruin.

Re-enter CASSANDRA, *with* PRIAM

CASSANDRA

Lay hold upon him, Priam, hold him fast:
He is thy crutch; now if thou lose thy stay,
Thou on him leaning, and all Troy on thee,
Fall all together.

PRIAM

Come, Hector, come, go back:
Thy wife hath dream'd; thy mother hath had visions;
Cassandra doth foresee; and I myself
Am like a prophet suddenly enrapt,
To tell thee that this day is ominous:
Therefore, come back.

HECTOR

Æneas is afield;
And I do stand engaged to many Greeks,
Even in the faith of valour, to appear
This morning to them.

PRIAM

Ay, but thou shalt not go.

HECTOR

I must not break my faith.
You know me dutiful; therefore, dear sir,
Let me not shame respect; but give me leave
To take that course by your consent and voice,
Which you do here forbid me, royal Priam.

CASSANDRA

O Priam, yield not to him!

ANDROMACHE

Do not, dear father.

HECTOR

Andromache, I am offended with you:
Upon the love you bear me, get you in.
[*Exit* ANDROMACHE

TROILUS

This foolish, dreaming, superstitious girl
Makes all these bodements.

CASSANDRA

O, farewell, dear Hector!
Look, how thou diest! look, how thy eye turns pale!

Look, how thy wounds do bleed at many vents!
Hark, how Troy roars! how Hecuba cries out!
How poor Andromache shrills her dolours forth!
Behold, distraction, frenzy and amazement,
Like witless antics, one another meet,
And all cry 'Hector! Hector's dead! O Hector!'

TROILUS

Away! away!

CASSANDRA

Farewell: yet, soft! Hector, I take my leave:
Thou dost thyself and all our Troy deceive.   [*Exit*

HECTOR

You are amazed, my liege, at her exclaim:
Go in and cheer the town: we'll forth and fight,
Do deeds worth praise and tell you them at night.

PRIAM

Farewell: the gods with safety stand about thee!
[*Exeunt severally* PRIAM *and* HECTOR. *Alarum*

TROILUS

They are at it, hark! Proud Diomed, believe,
I come to lose my arm, or win my sleeve.

Enter PANDARUS

PANDARUS

Do you hear, my lord? do you hear?

TROILUS

What now?

PANDARUS

Here's a letter come from yond poor girl.

TROILUS

Let me read.

PANDARUS

A whoreson tisick, a whoreson rascally tisick so
troubles me, and the foolish fortune of this girl; and
what one thing, what another, that I shall leave
you one o' these days: and I have a rheum in mine
eyes too, and such an ache in my bones that, unless
a man were cursed, I cannot tell what to think on 't.
What says she there?

TROILUS

Words, words, mere words, no matter from the
heart;
The effect doth operate another way.
[*Tearing the letter*
Go, wind, to wind, there turn and change together.
My love with words and errors still she feeds,
But edifies another with her deeds. [*Exeunt severally*

SCENE IV. *The field between Troy and the Grecian
camp*

Alarums. Excursions. Enter THERSITES

THERSITES

Now they are clapper-clawing one another; I'll go
look on. That dissembling abominable varlet,
Diomed, has got that same scurvy doting foolish
young knave's sleeve of Troy there in his helm: I
would fain see them meet; that that same young
Trojan ass, that loves the whore there, might send
that Greekish whoremasterly villain, with the

sleeve, back to the dissembling luxurious drab, of a
sleeveless errand. O' the t'other side, the policy of
those crafty swearing rascals, that stale old mouse-
eaten dry cheese, Nestor, and that same dog-fox,
Ulysses, is not proved worth a blackberry. They set
me up in policy that mongrel cur, Ajax, against
that dog of as bad a kind, Achilles: and now is the
cur Ajax prouder than the cur Achilles, and will
not arm to-day; whereupon the Grecians begin to
proclaim barbarism, and policy grows into an ill
opinion.

Enter DIOMEDES *and* TROILUS

Soft! here comes sleeve, and t'other.

TROILUS

Fly not; for shouldst thou take the river Styx,
I would swim after.

DIOMEDES

Thou dost miscall retire:
I do not fly; but advantageous care
Withdrew me from the odds of multitude:
Have at thee!

THERSITES

Hold thy whore, Grecian! Now for thy whore,
Trojan! Now the sleeve, now the sleeve!

[*Exeunt* TROILUS *and* DIOMEDES, *fighting*

Enter HECTOR

HECTOR

What art thou, Greek? art thou for Hector's match?
Art thou of blood and honour?

THERSITES

No, no: I am a rascal; a scurvy railing knave; a very
filthy rogue.

HECTOR

I do believe thee. Live.   [*Exit*

THERSITES

God-a-mercy, that thou wilt believe me; but a
plague break thy neck for frighting me! What's become of the wenching rogues? I think they have
swallowed one another: I would laugh at that
miracle: yet in a sort lechery eats itself. I'll seek
them.   [*Exit*

SCENE V. *Another part of the field*

Enter DIOMEDES *and* SERVANT

DIOMEDES

Go, go, my servant, take thou Troilus' horse;
Present the fair steed to my lady Cressid:
Fellow, commend my service to her beauty;
Tell her I have chastised the amorous Trojan,
And am her knight by proof.

SERVANT

I go, my lord.   [*Exit*

Enter AGAMEMNON

AGAMEMNON

Renew, renew! The fierce Polydamas
Hath beat down Menon: bastard Margarelon
Hath Doreus prisoner,
And stands colossus-wise, waving his beam,
Upon the pashed corses of the kings

Epistrophus and Cedius: Polyxenes is slain;
Amphimachus and Thoas deadly hurt;
Patroclus ta'en or slain; and Palamedes
Sore hurt and bruised: the dreadful sagittary
Appals our numbers: haste we, Diomed,
To reinforcement, or we perish all.

Enter NESTOR

NESTOR

Go, bear Patroclus' body to Achilles,
And bid the snail-paced Ajax arm for shame.
There is a thousand Hectors in the field:
Now here he fights on Galathe his horse,
And there lacks work; anon he's there afoot,
And there they fly or die, like scaled sculls
Before the belching whale; then is he yonder,
And there the strawy Greeks, ripe for his edge,
Fall down before him, like the mower's swath:
Here, there and every where he leaves and takes,
Dexterity so obeying appetite
That what he will he does, and does so much
That proof is call'd impossibility.

Enter ULYSSES

ULYSSES

O, courage, courage, princes! great Achilles
Is arming, weeping, cursing, vowing vengeance:
Patroclus' wounds have roused his drowsy blood,
Together with his mangled Myrmidons,
That noseless, handless, hack'd and chipp'd, come
    to him,
Crying on Hector. Ajax hath lost a friend,
And foams at mouth, and he is arm'd, and at it,
Roaring for Troilus; who hath done to-day
Mad and fantastic execution,
Engaging and redeeming of himself,
With such a careless force and forceless care,
As if that luck, in very spite of cunning,
Bade him win all.

Enter AJAX

AJAX

Troilus! thou coward Troilus!   [*Exit*

DIOMEDES

Ay, there, there.

NESTOR

So, so, we draw together.

Enter ACHILLES

ACHILLES

Where is this Hector?
Come, come, thou boy-queller, show thy face;
Know what it is to meet Achilles angry:
Hector! where's Hector? I will none but Hector.

[*Exeunt*

SCENE VI. *Another part of the field*

Enter AJAX

AJAX

Troilus, thou coward Troilus, show thy head!

Enter DIOMEDES

DIOMEDES

Troilus, I say! where's Troilus?

[858]

AJAX

What wouldst thou?

DIOMEDES

I would correct him.

AJAX

Were I the general, thou shouldst have my office
Ere that correction. Troilus, I say! what, Troilus!

Enter TROILUS

TROILUS

O traitor Diomed! Turn thy false face, thou traitor,
And pay thy life thou owest me for my horse.

DIOMEDES

Ha, art thou there?

AJAX

I'll fight with him alone: stand, Diomed.

DIOMEDES

He is my prize; I will not look upon.

TROILUS

Come both, you cogging Greeks; have at you both!
[Exeunt, fighting

Enter HECTOR

HECTOR

Yea, Troilus? O, well fought, my youngest brother!

Enter ACHILLES

ACHILLES

Now do I see thee; ha! have at thee, Hector!

HECTOR

Pause, if thou wilt.

ACHILLES

I do disdain thy courtesy, proud Trojan:
Be happy that my arms are out of use:
My rest and negligence befriends thee now,
But thou anon shalt hear of me again;
Till when, go seek thy fortune. *[Exit*

HECTOR

Fare thee well:
I would have been much more a fresher man,
Had I expected thee.

Re-enter TROILUS

How now, my brother!

TROILUS

Ajax hath ta'en Æneas: shall it be?
No, by the flame of yonder glorious heaven,
He shall not carry him; I'll be ta'en too,
Or bring him off. Fate, hear me what I say!
I reck not though I end my life to-day. *[Exit*

Enter one in sumptuous armour

HECTOR

Stand, stand, thou Greek; thou art a goodly mark.
No? wilt thou not? I like thy armour well;
I'll frush it, and unlock the rivets all,
But I'll be master of it. Wilt thou not, beast, abide?
Why then, fly on, I'll hunt thee for thy hide. *[Exeunt*

SCENE VII. *Another part of the field*

Enter ACHILLES, *with* MYRMIDONS

ACHILLES

Come here about me, you my Myrmidons;

Mark what I say. Attend me where I wheel:
Strike not a stroke, but keep yourselves in breath:
And when I have the bloody Hector found,
Empale him with your weapons round about;
In fellest manner execute your aims.
Follow me, sirs, and my proceedings eye:
It is decreed Hector the great must die. *[Exeunt*

Enter MENELAUS *and* PARIS, *fighting: then* THERSITES

THERSITES

The cuckold and the cuckold-maker are at it. Now,
bull! now, dog! 'loo, Paris, 'loo! now my double-
henned sparrow! 'loo, Paris, 'loo! The bull has the
game: ware horns, ho! *[Exeunt* PARIS *and* MENELAUS

Enter MARGARELON

MARGARELON

Turn, slave, and fight.

THERSITES

What art thou?

MARGARELON

A bastard son of Priam's.

THERSITES

I am a bastard too; I love bastards: I am a bastard
begot, bastard instructed, bastard in mind, bastard
in valour, in every thing illegitimate. One bear will
not bite another, and wherefore should one bastard?
Take heed, the quarrel's most ominous to us: if the
son of a whore fight for a whore, he tempts judgement: farewell, bastard. *[Exit*

MARGARELON

The devil take thee, coward! *[Exit*

SCENE VIII. *Another part of the field*

Enter HECTOR

HECTOR

Most putrefied core, so fair without,
Thy goodly armour thus hath cost thy life.
Now is my day's work done; I'll take good breath:
Rest, sword; thou hast thy fill of blood and death.
[Puts off his helmet and hangs his shield behind him

Enter ACHILLES *and* MYRMIDONS

ACHILLES

Look, Hector, how the sun begins to set;
How ugly night comes breathing at his heels:
Even with the vail and darking of the sun,
To close the day up, Hector's life is done.

HECTOR

I am unarm'd; forgo this vantage, Greek.

ACHILLES

Strike, fellows, strike; this is the man I seek.
*[HECTOR *falls*

So, Ilion, fall thou next! now, Troy, sink down!
Here lies thy heart, thy sinews, and thy bone.
On, Myrmidons; and cry you all amain,
'Achilles hath the mighty Hector slain.'
[A retreat sounded

Hark! a retire upon our Grecian part.

MYRMIDON

The Trojan trumpets sound the like, my lord.

ACHILLES

The dragon wing of night o'erspreads the earth,
And stickler-like the armies separates.
My half-supp'd sword hat frankly would have fed,
Pleased with this dainty bait, thus goes to bed.
[Sheathes his sword

Come, tie his body to my horse's tail;
Along the field I will the Trojan trail.
[Exeunt. A retreat sounded

SCENE IX. Another part of the field

Enter AGAMEMNON, AJAX, MENELAUS, NESTOR,
DIOMEDES, and the rest, marching. Shouts within

AGAMEMNON

Hark! hark! what shout is that?

NESTOR

Peace, drums!
[Within] 'Achilles! Achilles! Hector's slain! Achilles!'

DIOMEDES

The bruit is, Hector's slain, and by Achilles.

AJAX

If it be so, yet bragless let it be;
Great Hector was a man as good as he.

AGAMEMNON

March patiently along: let one be sent
To pray Achilles see us at our tent.
If in his death the gods have us befriended,
Great Troy is ours, and our sharp wars are ended.
[Exeunt, marching

SCENE X. Another part of the field

Enter ÆNEAS, PARIS, ANTENOR, and DEIPHOBUS

ÆNEAS

Stand, ho! yet are we masters of the field:
Never go home; here starve we out the night.
Enter TROILUS

TROILUS

Hector is slain.

ALL

Hector! The gods forbid!

TROILUS

He's dead; and at the murderer's horse's tail
In beastly sort dragg'd through the shameful field.
Frown on, you heavens, effect your rage with speed!
Sit, gods, upon your thrones, and smile at Troy!
I say, at once let your brief plagues be mercy,
And linger not our sure destructions on!

ÆNEAS

My lord, you do discomfort all the host.

TROILUS

You understand me not that tell me so:
I do not speak of flight, of fear, of death,
But dare all imminence that gods and men
Address their dangers in. Hector is gone:
Who shall tell Priam so, or Hecuba?
Let him that will a screech-owl aye be call'd,
Go in to Troy, and say there 'Hector's dead:'
There is a word will Priam turn to stone,
Make wells and Niobes of the maids and wives,
Cold statues of the youth, and, in a word,
Scare Troy out of itself. But march away:
Hector is dead; there is no more to say.
Stay yet. You vile abominable tents,
Thus proudly pight upon our Phrygian plains,
Let Titan rise as early as he dare,
I'll through and through you! and, thou great-sized coward,
No space of earth shall sunder our two hates:
I'll haunt thee like a wicked conscience still,
That mouldeth goblins swift as frenzy's thoughts.
Strike a free march to Troy! with comfort go:
Hope of revenge shall hide our inward woe.
[Exeunt ÆNEAS and TROJANS

As TROILUS is going out, enter, from the other side,
PANDARUS

PANDARUS

But hear you, hear you!

TROILUS

Hence, broker-lackey! ignomy and shame
Pursue thy life, and live aye with thy name! [Exit

PANDARUS

A goodly medicine for my aching bones!
O world! world! world! thus is the poor agent despised! O traitors and bawds, how earnestly are you set a-work, and how ill requited! why should our endeavour be so loved and the performance so loathed? what verse for it? what instance for it? Let me see:

Full merrily the humble-bee doth sing,
Till he hath lost his honey and his sting;
And being once subdued in armed tail,
Sweet honey and sweet notes together fail.

Good traders in the flesh, set this in your painted cloths:

As many as be here of Pandar's hall,
Your eyes, half out, weep out at Pandar's fall;
Or if you cannot weep, yet give some groans,
Though not for me, yet for your aching bones.
Brethren and sisters of the hold-door trade,
Some two months hence my will shall here be made:
It should be now, but that my fear is this,
Some galled goose of Winchester would hiss:
Till then I'll sweat and seek about for eases,
And at that time bequeath you my diseases. [Exit

ALL'S WELL THAT ENDS WELL

SYNOPSIS

AFTER the death of the distinguished physician, Gerard de Narbon, who was famed for his many medical discoveries, his daughter Helena entered the household of the Countess of Rousillon as gentlewoman. The young Count Bertram leaves his home for service at the court of the French king whose ward he became upon his father's recent death, and Helena's sudden melancholy reveals to the kindly Countess the secret of the girl's love for her handsome son who is entirely oblivious to the charms of his mother's poor, unknown gentlewoman. The Countess, however, loves her beautiful, accomplished charge, treats her as a daughter and encourages her in every way, even when Helena discloses her plan of following Bertram to Paris and attempting to interview the King who is suffering from an affliction the Court physicians pronounce incurable but which Helena knows can be healed by a rare prescription of her father's.

Introduced at court by the good-natured Lafeu, an old lord of the Countess' acquaintance, Helena so impresses the King with her earnest belief in the virtues of the untried medicine, for the efficacy of which she is willing to pledge her own life, that his objections are overcome. In the event of success, Helena is to be granted her request to choose a husband from the King's unmarried courtiers.

In two days' time the King makes a complete recovery to health and cheerfully arranges for an assembly of his young nobles, from whom Helena naturally chooses Bertram, but the young man, resentful at having an unchosen wife thrust on him, refuses to marry her, ungraciously reminding the King that she is beneath him in rank. Helena offers in dismay to relinquish him, but, when Bertram realizes how his public defiance has aroused the King, he submits. Immediately after the marriage ceremony, however, he declares that pressing business affairs force him to leave Paris; he curtly orders his wife home with a bitter letter to his mother; and steals away with his rascally follower and adviser Parolles to join the army of the Duke of Florence, using Helena's dowry from the King to defray his expenses.

As Helena is returning, a gentleman of her escort hands her a letter from Bertram which contains the cruel taunt that she will never call him husband until she can get from his finger a precious ring which six generations of his ancestors have worn and which he never removes, and until she can give him a child to which he is father. He then vows never to return to France while she is his wife. Grieving for having caused him to leave his native land, perhaps to perish in foreign wars, Helena seeks relief from her agonized thoughts in a pilgrimage to St. Jacques le Grand, during which she allows a message to reach the Countess stating that she is dead.

Bertram, in the meantime, has achieved the rank of general in the Italian wars, and is leading his successful troops into Florence as Helena, dressed as a pilgrim, arrives in the city. She later learns from the good widow with whom she takes lodgings that the Count is trying to seduce her pretty clever daughter Diana, whom the evil Parolles has discovered for him, and the idea suggests itself to Helena that use might be made of the situation to fulfil the conditions in Bertram's letter. She reveals herself to the two sympathetic women as the deserted wife of whom they have already heard, promises Diana a large dowry if she will beguile her infatuated lover into giving her his priceless ring, and, by pretending to yield to him, arrange a midnight meeting in her chamber where Helena, unknown to Bertram, will take the girl's place.

The plot works successfully. Diana's intrigue wins the Count's ring as a loan, and she also extracts from him a careless promise of marriage upon his wife's death. Helena takes Diana's place at night, and slips on his finger a ring given her by the King of France in place of his own. Having received a letter from his mother telling him that his wife is dead, Bertram starts for home with high recommendations from the Duke of Florence, but before he goes he is given ample proof from his fellow officers of Parolles' utter worthlessness. Helena gets word of the King being at Marseilles, and sets out to meet him with the widow and her daughter, following him to Rousillon where, in paying a visit to the Countess, he meets her son returning from Florence and forgives him for the sake of his aged mother.

A marriage having been suggested between Bertram and the daughter of the kindly old lord, Lafeu, the King, is about to give his consent when he notices on the Count's finger the ring he had given Helena at court, and, knowing of their estrangement, he accuses Bertram of her death. The Count tries hard to clear himself by telling no more about the ring than is convenient, but Diana appears with her conflicting evidence and talks in riddles that exasperate the King until Helena herself comes, accompanied by the widow, and tells her husband that his conditions are fulfilled for she has his ancestral ring and will be the mother of his child. Bertram declares that her devotion has won his deepest affections, and the joyful Countess again embraces her beloved daughter-in-law.

HISTORICAL DATA

The source of the main plot is the ninth novel of the third day of Boccaccio's *Decameron* which was probably known to Shakespeare in the translation to be found in Paynter's *Palace of Pleasure* (1566). To the original story Shakespeare added the characters of the Countess, Lafeu and the comic characters of Parolles and the clown, Lavache. He further changed the centre of interest of the play and elaborated the character of the heroine, Helena— considered by Coleridge to be Shakespeare's "loveliest creation."

There is considerable confusion as to the date of composition of the play. It is found for the first time in the First Folio and there is very little in the text to aid scholars in establishing contemporary events.

In Meres's *Palladis Tamia* occurs the title *Love's Labour's Won* which many authors consider to be identical with this play. This is borne out in part by an allusion to this older title in Act V, Scene iii of the present play. On the other hand there is much in the play which would indicate a later date for its composition, chiefly the subtlety of the psychology and the general sombreness of tone and the economy of expression, all of which are characteristic of the more mature work of the playwright. It is quite possible that the play was written in an earlier form early in the last decade of the sixteenth century but was probably revised and the present form given it about 1602.

"*But, O strange men!*
That can such sweet use make of what they hate,"
ALL'S WELL THAT ENDS WELL

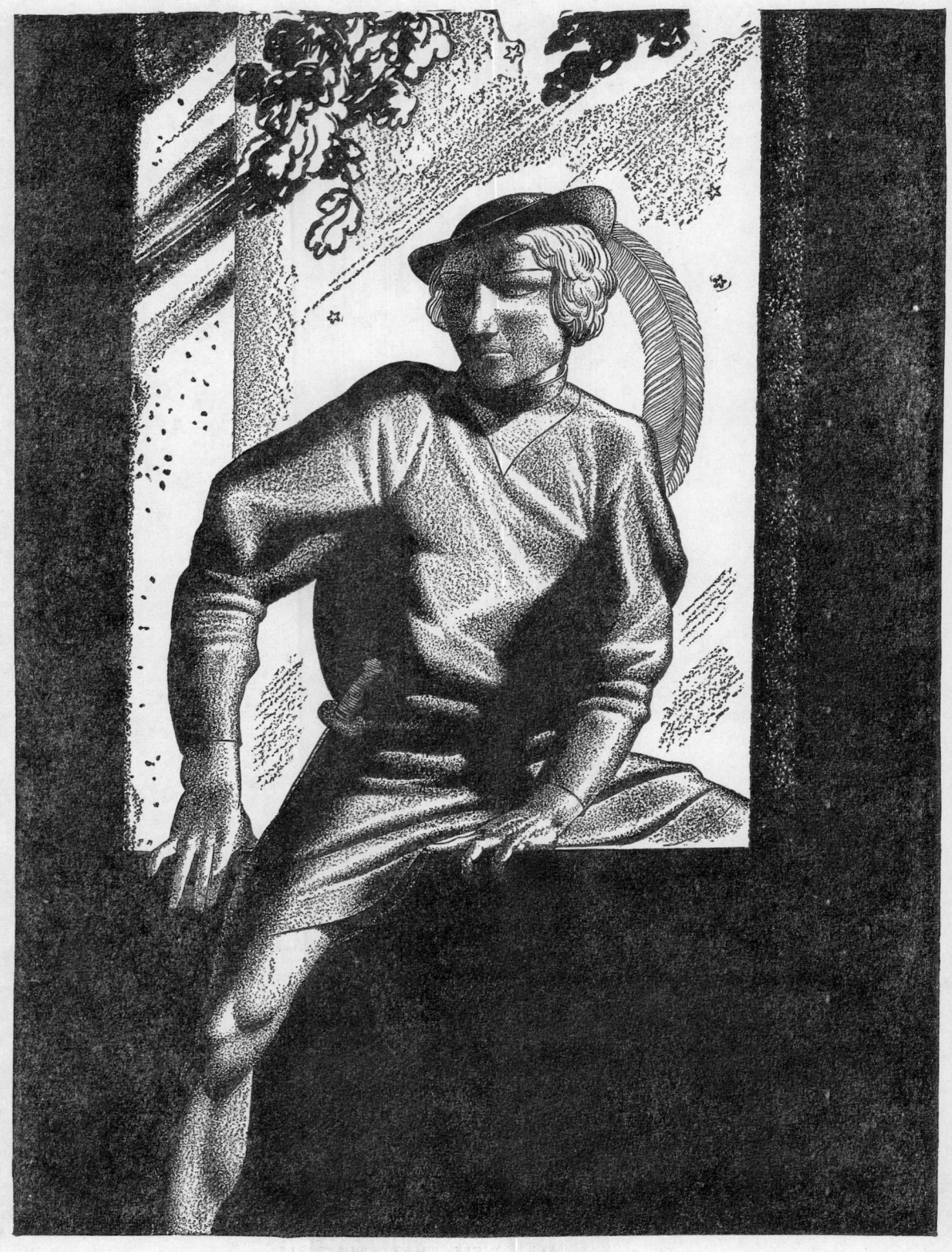

ALL'S WELL THAT ENDS WELL

DRAMATIS PERSONÆ

KING OF FRANCE.
DUKE OF FLORENCE.
BERTRAM, *Count of Rousillon.*
LAFEU, *an old lord.*
PAROLLES, *a follower of Bertram.*
STEWARD, } *servants to the Countess of*
LAVACHE, *a Clown,* } *Rousillon.*
A PAGE.

COUNTESS OF ROUSILLON, *mother to Bertram.*

HELENA, *a gentlewoman protected by the Countess.*
AN OLD WIDOW *of Florence.*
DIANA, *daughter to the Widow.*
VIOLENTA, } *neighbours and friends to the Widow.*
MARIANA, }

LORDS, OFFICERS, SOLDIERS, &c., *French and Florentine.*

SCENE—*Rousillon; Paris; Florence; Marseilles.*

ACT I

SCENE I. *Rousillon. The* COUNT's *palace*

Enter BERTRAM, *the* COUNTESS OF ROUSILLON, HELENA, *and* LAFEU, *all in black*

COUNTESS

In delivering my son from me, I bury a second husband.

BERTRAM

And I in going, madam, weep o'er my father's death anew: but I must attend his majesty's command, to whom I am now in ward, evermore in subjection.

LAFEU

You shall find of the king a husband, madam; you, sir, a father: he that so generally is at all times good, must of necessity hold his virtue to you; whose worthiness would stir it up where it wanted, rather than lack it where there is such abundance.

COUNTESS

What hope is there of his majesty's amendment?

LAFEU

He hath abandoned his physicians, madam; under whose practices he hath persecuted time with hope, and finds no other advantage in the process but only the losing of hope by time.

COUNTESS

This young gentlewoman had a father,—O, that 'had'! how sad a passage 'tis!—whose skill was almost as great as his honesty; had it stretched so far, would have made nature immortal, and death should have play for lack of work. Would, for the king's sake, he were living! I think it would be the death of the king's disease.

LAFEU

How called you the man you speak of, madam?

COUNTESS

He was famous, sir, in his profession, and it was his great right to be so,—Gerard de Narbon.

LAFEU

He was excellent indeed, madam: the king very lately spoke of him admiringly and mourningly: he was skilful enough to have lived still, if knowledge ᵇould be set up against mortality.

BERTRAM

What is it, my good lord, the king languishes of?

LAFEU

A fistula, my lord.

BERTRAM

I heard not of it before.

LAFEU

I would it were not notorious. Was this gentlewoman the daughter of Gerard de Narbon?

COUNTESS

His sole child, my lord; and bequeathed to my overlooking. I have those hopes of her good that her education promises; her dispositions she inherits, which makes fair gifts fairer; for where an unclean mind carries virtuous qualities, there commendations go with pity; they are virtues and traitors too: in her they are the better for their simpleness; she derives her honesty and achieves her goodness.

LAFEU

Your commendations, madam, get from her tears.

COUNTESS

'Tis the best brine a maiden can season her praise in. The remembrance of her father never approaches her heart but the tyranny of her sorrows takes all livelihood from her cheek. No more of this, Helena, go to, no more; lest it be rather thought you affect a sorrow than to have—

HELENA

I do affect a sorrow, indeed, but I have it too.

LAFEU

Moderate lamentation is the right of the dead; excessive grief the enemy to the living.

COUNTESS

If the living be enemy to the grief, the excess makes it soon mortal.

BERTRAM

Madam, I desire your holy wishes.

LAFEU

How understand we that?

COUNTESS

Be thou blest, Bertram, and succeed thy father
In manners, as in shape! thy blood and virtue
Contend for empire in thee, and thy goodness

Share with thy birthright! Love all, trust a few,
Do wrong to none: be able for thine enemy
Rather in power than use; and keep thy friend
Under thy own life's key: be check'd for silence,
But never tax'd for speech. What heaven more will,
That thee may furnish, and my prayers pluck down,
Fall on thy head! Farewell, my lord;
'Tis an unseason'd courtier; good my lord,
Advise him.

LAFEU
      He cannot want the best
That shall attend his love.

COUNTESS
Heaven bless him! Farewell, Bertram.   [*Exit*

BERTRAM
[*To* HELENA] The best wishes that can be forged in
your thoughts be servants to you! Be comfortable to
my mother, your mistress, and make much of her.

LAFEU
Farewell, pretty lady: you must hold the credit of
your father.   [*Exeunt* BERTRAM *and* LAFEU

HELENA
O, were that all! I think not on my father;
And these great tears grace his remembrance more
Than those I shed for him. What was he like?
I have forgot him: my imagination
Carries no favour in 't but Bertram's.
I am undone: there is no living, none,
If Bertram be away. 'Twere all one
That I should love a bright particular star
And think to wed it, he is so above me:
In his bright radiance and collateral light
Must I be comforted, not in his sphere.
The ambition in my love thus plagues itself:
The hind that would be mated by the lion
Must die for love. 'Twas pretty, though a plague,
To see him every hour; to sit and draw
His arched brows, his hawking eye, his curls,
In our heart's table; heart too capable
Of every line and trick of his sweet favour:
But now he's gone, and my idolatrous fancy
Must sanctify his reliques. Who comes here?

Enter PAROLLES

[*Aside*] One that goes with him: I love him for his
  sake;
And yet I know him a notorious liar,
Think him a great way fool, solely a coward;
Yet these fix'd evils sit so fit in him,
That they take place, when virtue's steely bones
Look bleak i' the cold wind: withal, full oft we see
Cold wisdom waiting on superfluous folly.

PAROLLES
Save you, fair queen!

HELENA
And you, monarch!

PAROLLES
No.

HELENA
And no.

PAROLLES
Are you meditating on virginity?

HELENA
Ay. You have some stain of soldier in you: let me
ask you a question. Man is enemy to virginity; how
may we barricado it against him?

PAROLLES
Keep him out.

HELENA
But he assails; and our virginity, though valiant, in
the defence yet is weak: unfold to us some warlike
resistance.

PAROLLES
There is none: man, sitting down before you, will
undermine you and blow you up.

HELENA
Bless our poor virginity from underminers and
blowers up! Is there no military policy, how virgins
might blow up men?

PAROLLES
Virginity being blown down, man will quicklier be
blown up: marry, in blowing him down again, with
the breach yourselves made, you lose your city. It
is not politic in the commonwealth of nature to preserve virginity. Loss of virginity is rational increase,
and there was never virgin got till virginity was first
lost. That you were made of is metal to make virgins. Virginity by being once lost may be ten times
found; by being ever kept, it is ever lost: 'tis too cold
a companion; away with 't!

HELENA
I will stand for 't a little, though therefore I die a
virgin.

PAROLLES
There's little can be said in 't; 'tis against the rule
of nature. To speak on the part of virginity, is to accuse your mothers; which is most infallible disobedience. He that hangs himself is a virgin: virginity
murders itself; and should be buried in highways
out of all sanctified limit, as a desperate offendress
against nature. Virginity breeds mites, much like a
cheese; consumes itself to the very paring, and so
dies with feeding his own stomach. Besides, virginity is peevish, proud, idle, made of self-love, which
is the most inhibited sin in the canon. Keep it not;
you cannot choose but lose by 't: out with 't! within
ten year it will make itself ten, which is a goodly increase; and the principal itself not much the worse:
away with 't!

HELENA
How might one do, sir, to lose it to her own liking?

PAROLLES
Let me see: marry, ill, to like him that ne'er it likes.
'Tis a commodity will lose the gloss with lying; the
longer kept, the less worth: off with 't while 'tis vendible; answer the time of request. Virginity, like an
old courtier, wears her cap out of fashion; richly
suited, but unsuitable: just like the brooch and the
tooth-pick, which wear not now. Your date is better
in your pie and your porridge than in your cheek:

and your virginity, your old virginity, is like one of our French withered pears, it looks ill, it eats drily; marry, 'tis a withered pear; it was formerly better; marry, yet 'tis a withered pear: will you any thing with it?

HELENA

Not my virginity yet......
There shall your master have a thousand loves,
A mother and a mistress and a friend,
A phœnix, captain, and an enemy,
A guide, a goddess, and a sovereign,
A counsellor, a traitress, and a dear;
His humble ambition, proud humility,
His jarring concord, and his discord dulcet,
His faith, his sweet disaster; with a world
Of pretty, fond, adoptious christendoms,
That blinking Cupid gossips. Now shall he—
I know not what he shall. God send him well!
The court's a learning place, and he is one—

PAROLLES

What one, i'faith?

HELENA

That I wish well. 'Tis pity—

PAROLLES

What's pity?

HELENA

That wishing well had not a body in 't,
Which might be felt; that we, the poorer born,
Whose baser stars do shut us up in wishes,
Might with effects of them follow our friends,
And show what we alone must think, which never
Returns us thanks.

Enter PAGE

PAGE

Monsieur Parolles, my lord calls for you.   [*Exit*

PAROLLES

Little Helen, farewell: if I can remember thee, I will think of thee at court.

HELENA

Monsieur Parolles, you were born under a charitable star.

PAROLLES

Under Mars, I.

HELENA

I especially think, under Mars.

PAROLLES

Why under Mars?

HELENA

The wars have so kept you under, that you must needs be born under Mars.

PAROLLES

When he was predominant.

HELENA

When he was retrograde, I think, rather.

PAROLLES

Why think you so?

HELENA

You go so much backward when you fight.

PAROLLES

That's for advantage.

HELENA

So is running away, when fear proposes the safety: but the composition that your valour and fear makes in you is a virtue of a good wing, and I like the wear well.

PAROLLES

I am so full of businesses, I cannot answer thee acutely. I will return perfect courtier; in the which, my instruction shall serve to naturalize thee, so thou wilt be capable of a courtier's counsel, and understand what advice shall thrust upon thee; else thou diest in thine unthankfulness, and thine ignorance makes thee away: farewell. When thou hast leisure, say thy prayers; when thou hast none, remember thy friends: get thee a good husband, and use him as he uses thee: so, farewell.   [*Exit*

HELENA

Our remedies oft in ourselves do lie,
Which we ascribe to heaven: the fated sky
Gives us free scope; only doth backward pull
Our slow designs when we ourselves are dull.
What power is it which mounts my love so high;
That makes me see, and cannot feed mine eye?
The mightiest space in fortune nature brings
To join like likes and kiss like native things.
Impossible be strange attempts to those
That weigh their pains in sense, and do suppose
What hath been cannot be: who ever strove
To show her merit, that did miss her love?
The king's disease—my project may deceive me,
But my intents are fix'd, and will not leave me. [*Exit*

SCENE II. *Paris. The* KING'S *palace*

Flourish of cornets. Enter the KING OF FRANCE *with letters, and divers* ATTENDANTS

KING

The Florentines and Senoys are by the ears;
Have fought with equal fortune, and continue
A braving war.

FIRST LORD

So 'tis reported, sir.

KING

Nay, 'tis most credible; we here receive it
A certainty, vouch'd from our cousin Austria,
With caution, that the Florentine will move us
For speedy aid; wherein our dearest friend
Prejudicates the business, and would seem
To have us make denial.

FIRST LORD

His love and wisdom,
Approved so to your majesty, may plead
For amplest credence.

KING

He hath arm'd our answer,
And Florence is denied before he comes:
Yet, for our gentlemen that mean to see
The Tuscan service, freely have they leave
To stand on either part.

SECOND LORD
It well may serve
A nursery to our gentry, who are sick
For breathing and exploit.

KING
What's he comes here?

Enter BERTRAM, LAFEU, *and* PAROLLES

FIRST LORD
It is the Count Rousillon, my good lord,
Young Bertram.

KING
Youth, thou bear'st thy father's face;
Frank nature, rather curious than in haste,
Hath well composed thee. Thy father's moral parts
Mayst thou inherit too! Welcome to Paris.

BERTRAM
My thanks and duty are your majesty's.

KING
I would I had that corporal soundness now,
As when thy father and myself in friendship
First tried our soldiership! He did look far
Into the service of the time, and was
Discipled of the bravest: he lasted long;
But on us both did haggish age steal on,
And wore us out of act. It much repairs me
To talk of your good father. In his youth
He had the wit, which I can well observe
To-day in our young lords; but they may jest
Till their own scorn return to them unnoted
Ere they can hide their levity in honour:
So like a courtier, contempt nor bitterness
Were in his pride or sharpness; if they were,
His equal had awaked them; and his honour,
Clock to itself, knew the true minute when
Exception bid him speak, and at this time
His tongue obey'd his hand: who were below him
He used as creatures of another place;
And bow'd his eminent top to their low ranks,
Making them proud of his humility,
In their poor praise he humbled. Such a man
Might be a copy to these younger times;
Which, follow'd well, would demonstrate them now
But goers backward.

BERTRAM
His good remembrance, sir,
Lies richer in your thoughts than on his tomb;
So in approof lives not his epitaph
As in your royal speech.

KING
Would I were with him! He would always say—
Methinks I hear him now; his plausive words
He scatter'd not in ears, but grafted them,
To grow there and to bear,—'Let me not live,'—
This his good melancholy oft began,
On the catastrophe and heel of pastime,
When it was out,—'Let me not live,' quoth he,
'After my flame lacks oil, to be the snuff
Of younger spirits, whose apprehensive senses
All but new things disdain; whose judgements are
Mere fathers of their garments; whose constancies

Expire before their fashions.' This he wish'd:
I after him do after him wish too,
Since I nor wax nor honey can bring home,
I quickly were dissolved from my hive,
To give some labourers room.

SECOND LORD
You are loved, sir;
They that least lend it you shall lack you first.

KING
I fill a place, I know't. How long is 't, count,
Since the physician at your father's died?
He was much famed.

BERTRAM
Some six months since, my lord.

KING
If he were living, I would try him yet.
Lend me an arm; the rest have worn me out
With several applications: nature and sickness
Debate it at their leisure. Welcome, count;
My son's no dearer.

BERTRAM
Thank your majesty.

[*Exeunt. Flourish*

SCENE III. *Rousillon. The* COUNT'S *palace*

Enter COUNTESS, STEWARD, *and* CLOWN

COUNTESS
I will now hear; what say you of this gentlewoman?

STEWARD
Madam, the care I have had to even your content,
I wish might be found in the calendar of my past
endeavours; for then we wound our modesty and
make foul the clearness of our deservings, when of
ourselves we publish them.

COUNTESS
What does this knave here? Get you gone, sirrah:
the complaints I have heard of you I do not all believe: 'tis my slowness that I do not; for I know you
lack not folly to commit them, and have ability
enough to make such knaveries yours.

CLOWN
'Tis not unknown to you, madam, I am a poor
fellow.

COUNTESS
Well, sir.

CLOWN
No, madam, 'tis not so well that I am poor, though
many of the rich are damned: but, if I may have
your ladyship's good will to go to the world, Isbel
the woman and I will do as we may.

COUNTESS
Wilt thou needs be a beggar?

CLOWN
I do beg your good will in this case.

COUNTESS
In what case?

CLOWN
In Isbel's case and mine own. Service is no heritage:

and I think I shall never have the blessing of God till I have issue o' my body; for they say barnes are blessings.

COUNTESS

Tell me thy reason why thou wilt marry.

CLOWN

My poor body, madam, requires it: I am driven on by the flesh; and he must needs go that the devil drives.

COUNTESS

Is this all your worship's reason?

CLOWN

Faith, madam, I have other holy reasons, such as they are.

COUNTESS

May the world know them?

CLOWN

I have been, madam, a wicked creature, as you and all flesh and blood are; and, indeed, I do marry that I may repent.

COUNTESS

Thy marriage, sooner than thy wickedness.

CLOWN

I am out o' friends, madam; and I hope to have friends for my wife's sake.

COUNTESS

Such friends are thine enemies, knave.

CLOWN

You're shallow, madam, in great friends; for the knaves come to do that for me, which I am aweary of. He that ears my land spares my team, and gives me leave to in the crop; if I be his cuckold, he's my drudge: he that comforts my wife is the cherisher of my flesh and blood; he that cherishes my flesh and blood loves my flesh and blood; he that loves my flesh and blood is my friend: ergo, he that kisses my wife is my friend. If men could be contented to be what they are, there were no fear in marriage; for young Charbon the puritan and old Poysam the papist, howsome'er their hearts are severed in religion, their heads are both one; they may joul horns together, like any deer i' the herd.

COUNTESS

Wilt thou ever be a foul-mouthed and calumnious knave?

CLOWN

A prophet I, madam; and I speak the truth the next way:

For I the ballad will repeat,
　Which men full true shall find;
Your marriage comes by destiny,
　Your cuckoo sings by kind.

COUNTESS

Get you gone, sir; I'll talk with you more anon.

STEWARD

May it please you, madam, that he bid Helen come to you: of her I am to speak.

COUNTESS

Sirrah, tell my gentlewoman I would speak with her; Helen I mean.

CLOWN

Was this fair face the cause, quoth she,
　Why the Grecians sacked Troy?
Fond done, done fond,
　Was this King Priam's joy?
With that she sighed as she stood,
With that she sighed as she stood,
　And gave this sentence then;
Among nine bad if one be good,
Among nine bad if one be good,
　There's yet one good in ten.

COUNTESS

What, one good in ten? you corrupt the song, sirrah.

CLOWN

One good woman in ten, madam; which is a purifying o' the song: would God would serve the world so all the year! we'd find no fault with the tithewoman, if I were the parson: one in ten, quoth a'! an we might have a good woman born but one every blazing star, or at an earthquake, 'twould mend the lottery well: a man may draw his heart out, ere a' pluck one.

COUNTESS

You'll be gone, sir knave, and do as I command you.

CLOWN

That man should be at woman's command, and yet no hurt done! Though honesty be no puritan, yet it will do no hurt; it will wear the surplice of humility over the black gown of a big heart. I am going, forsooth: the business is for Helen to come hither. [Exit

COUNTESS

Well, now.

STEWARD

I know, madam, you love your gentlewoman entirely.

COUNTESS

Faith, I do: her father bequeathed her to me; and she herself, without other advantage, may lawfully make title to as much love as she finds: there is more owing her than is paid; and more shall be paid her than she'll demand.

STEWARD

Madam, I was very late more near her than I think she wished me: alone she was, and did communicate to herself her own words to her own ears; she thought, I dare vow for her, they touched not any stranger sense. Her matter was, she loved your son: Fortune, she said, was no goddess, that had put such difference betwixt their two estates; Love no god, that would not extend his might, only where qualities were level; ... queen of virgins, that would suffer her poor knight surprised, without rescue in the first assault, or ransom afterward. This she delivered in the most bitter touch of sorrow that e'er I heard virgin exclaim in: which I held my duty speedily to acquaint you withal; sithence, in the loss that may happen, it concerns you something to know it.

COUNTESS

You have discharged this honestly; keep it to yourself: many likelihoods informed me of this before,

which hung so tottering in the balance, that I could
neither believe nor misdoubt. Pray you, leave me:
stall this in your bosom; and I thank you for your
honest care: I will speak with you further anon.

[*Exit* STEWARD

Enter HELENA

Even so it was with me when I was young:
 If ever we are nature's, these are ours; this thorn
Doth to our rose of youth rightly belong;
 Our blood to us, this to our blood is born;
It is the show and seal of nature's truth,
Where love's strong passion is impress'd in youth:
By our remembrances of days foregone,
Such were our faults, or then we thought them none.
Her eye is sick on't: I observe her now.

HELENA

What is your pleasure, madam?

COUNTESS

     You know, Helen,
I am a mother to you.

HELENA

Mine honourable mistress.

COUNTESS

     Nay, a mother:
Why not a mother? When I said 'a mother,'
Methought you saw a serpent: what's in 'mother,'
That you start at it? I say, I am your mother;
And put you in the catalogue of those
That were enwombed mine: 'tis often seen
Adoption strives with nature; and choice breeds
A native slip to us from foreign seeds:
You ne'er oppress'd me with a mother's groan,
Yet I express to you a mother's care:
God's mercy, maiden! does it curd thy blood
To say I am thy mother? What's the matter,
That this distemper'd messenger of wet,
The many-colour'd Iris, rounds thine eye?
Why? that you are my daughter?

HELENA

     That I am not.

COUNTESS

I say, I am your mother.

HELENA

     Pardon, madam;
The Count Rousillon cannot be my brother:
I am from humble, he from honour'd name;
No note upon my parents, his all noble:
My master, my dear lord he is; and I
His servant live, and will his vassal die:
He must not be my brother.

COUNTESS

     Nor I your mother?

HELENA

You are my mother, madam; would you were,—
So that my lord your son were not my brother,—
Indeed my mother! or were you both our mothers,
I care no more for than I do for heaven,
So I were not his sister. Can't no other,
But I your daughter, he must be my brother?

COUNTESS

Yes, Helen, you might be my daughter-in-law:
God shield you mean it not! daughter and mother
So strive upon your pulse. What, pale again?
My fear hath catch'd your fondness: now I see
The mystery of your loneliness, and find
Your salt tears' head: now to all sense 'tis gross
You love my son; invention is ashamed,
Against the proclamation of thy passion,
To say thou dost not: therefore tell me true;
But tell me then, 'tis so; for, look, thy cheeks
Confess it, th'one to th'other; and thine eyes
See it so grossly shown in thy behaviours,
That in their kind they speak it: only sin
And hellish obstinacy tie thy tongue,
That truth should be suspected. Speak, is't so?
If it be so, you have wound a goodly clew;
If it be not, forswear 't: howe'er, I charge thee,
As heaven shall work in me for thine avail,
To tell me truly.

HELENA

     Good madam, pardon me!

COUNTESS

Do you love my son?

HELENA

     Your pardon, noble mistress!

COUNTESS

Love you my son?

HELENA

     Do not you love him, madam?

COUNTESS

Go not about; my love hath in 't a bond,
Whereof the world takes note: come, come, disclose
The state of your affection; for your passions
Have to the full appeach'd.

HELENA

     Then, I confess,
Here on my knee, before high heaven and you,
That before you, and next unto high heaven,
I love your son.
My friends were poor, but honest; so's my love:
Be not offended; for it hurts not him
That he is loved of me: I follow him not
By any token of presumptuous suit;
Nor would I have him till I do deserve him;
Yet never know how that desert should be.
I know I love in vain, strive against hope;
Yet, in this captious and intenible sieve,
I still pour in the waters of my love,
And lack not to lose still: thus, Indian-like,
Religious in mine error, I adore
The sun, that looks upon his worshipper,
But knows of him no more. My dearest madam,
Let not your hate encounter with my love
For loving where you do: but if yourself,
Whose aged honour cites a virtuous youth,
Did ever in so true a flame of liking
Wish chastely and love dearly, that your Dian
Was both herself and love; O, then, give pity
To her, whose state is such, that cannot choose

But lend and give where she is sure to lose;
That seeks not to find that her search implies,
But riddle-like lives sweetly where she dies!

COUNTESS

Had you not lately an intent,—speak truly,—
To go to Paris?

HELENA

Madam, I had.

COUNTESS

Wherefore? tell true.

HELENA

I will tell truth; by grace itself I swear.
You know my father left me some prescriptions
Of rare and proved effects, such as his reading
And manifest experience had collected
For general sovereignty; and that he will'd me
In heedfull'st reservation to bestow them,
As notes, whose faculties inclusive were,
More than they were in note: amongst the rest,
There is a remedy, approved, set down,
To cure the desperate languishings whereof
The king is render'd lost.

COUNTESS

This was your motive
For Paris, was it? speak.

HELENA

My lord your son made me to think of this;
Else Paris, and the medicine, and the king,
Had from the conversation of my thoughts
Haply been absent then.

COUNTESS

But think you, Helen,
If you should tender your supposed aid,
He would receive it? he and his physicians
Are of a mind; he, that they cannot help him,
They, that they cannot help: how shall they credit
A poor unlearned virgin, when the schools,
Embowell'd of their doctrine, have left off
The danger to itself?

HELENA

There's something in 't,
More than my father's skill, which was the great'st
Of his profession, that his good receipt
Shall for my legacy be sanctified
By the luckiest stars in heaven: and, would your
    honour
But give me leave to try success, I'ld venture
The well-lost life of mine on his Grace's cure
By such a day and hour.

COUNTESS

Dost thou believe 't?

HELENA

Ay, madam, knowingly.

COUNTESS

Why, Helen, thou shalt have my leave and love,
Means and attendants, and my loving greetings
To those of mine in court: I'll stay at home
And pray God's blessing into thy attempt:
Be gone to-morrow; and be sure of this,
What I can help thee to, thou shalt not miss. [Exeunt

ACT II

SCENE I. *Paris. The* KING'S *palace*

Flourish of cornets. Enter the KING, *attended with divers
young* LORDS *taking leave for the Florentine war;* BER-
TRAM, *and* PAROLLES

KING

Farewell, young lords; these warlike principles
Do not throw from you: and you, my lords, farewell:
Share the advice betwixt you; if both gain, all
The gift doth stretch itself as 'tis received,
And is enough for both.

FIRST LORD

'Tis our hope, sir,
After well-enter'd soldiers, to return
And find your Grace in health.

KING

No, no, it cannot be; and yet my heart
Will not confess he owes the malady
That doth my life besiege. Farewell, young lords;
Whether I live or die, be you the sons
Of worthy Frenchmen: let higher Italy,—
Those bated that inherit but the fall
Of the last monarchy,—see that you come
Not to woo honour, but to wed it; when
The bravest questant shrinks, find what you seek,
That fame may cry you loud: I say, farewell.

SECOND LORD

Health, at your bidding, serve your majesty!

KING

Those girls of Italy, take heed of them:
They say, our French lack language to deny,
If they demand: beware of being captives,
Before you serve.

BOTH

Our hearts receive your warnings.

KING

Farewell. Come hither to me.   [Exit

FIRST LORD

O my sweet lord, that you will stay behind us!

PAROLLES

'Tis not his fault, the spark.

SECOND LORD

O, 'tis brave wars!

PAROLLES

Most admirable: I have seen those wars.

BERTRAM

I am commanded here, and kept a coil with
'Too young,' and 'the next year,' and ''tis too early.'

PAROLLES

An thy mind stand to 't, boy, steal away bravely.

BERTRAM

I shall stay here the forehorse to a smock,
Creaking my shoes on the plain masonry,
Till honour be bought up, and no sword worn
But one to dance with! By heaven, I'll steal away.

FIRST LORD

There's honour in the theft.

PAROLLES

Commit it, count.

SECOND LORD

I am your accessary; and so, farewell.

BERTRAM

I grow to you, and our parting is a tortured body.

FIRST LORD

Farewell, captain.

SECOND LORD

Sweet Monsieur Parolles!

PAROLLES

Noble heroes, my sword and yours are kin. Good
sparks and lustrous, a word, good metals: you shall
find in the regiment of the Spinii one Captain
Spurio, with his cicatrice, an emblem of war, here
on his sinister cheek; it was this very sword en-
trenched it: say to him, I live; and observe his reports for me.

FIRST LORD

We shall, noble captain.   [Exeunt LORDS

PAROLLES

Mars dote on you for his novices! what will ye do?

BERTRAM

Stay: the king.

Re-enter KING

PAROLLES

[Aside to BERTRAM] Use a more spacious ceremony
to the noble lords; you have restrained yourself
within the list of too cold an adieu: be more expressive to them: for they wear themselves in the cap
of the time, there do muster true gait, eat, speak,
and move under the influence of the most received
star; and though the devil lead the measure, such
are to be followed: after them, and take a more
dilated farewell.

BERTRAM

And I will do so.

PAROLLES

Worthy fellows; and like to prove most sinewy
sword-men.   [Exeunt BERTRAM and PAROLLES
Enter LAFEU

LAFEU

[Kneeling] Pardon, my lord, for me and for my tidings.

KING

I'll fee thee to stand up.

LAFEU

Then here's a man stands, that has brought his
pardon.
I would you had kneel'd, my lord, to ask me mercy;
And that at my bidding you could so stand up.

KING

I would I had; so I had broke thy pate,
And ask'd thee mercy for 't.

LAFEU

Good faith, across: but, my good lord, 'tis thus;
Will you be cured of your infirmity?

KING

No.

LAFEU

O, will you eat no grapes, my royal fox?
Yes, but you will my noble grapes, an if

My royal fox could reach them: I have seen a
medicine
That's able to breathe life into a stone,
Quicken a rock, and make you dance canary
With spritely fire and motion; whose simple touch
Is powerful to araise King Pepin, nay,
To give great Charlemain a pen in 's hand,
And write to her a love-line.

KING

What 'her' is this?

LAFEU

Why, Doctor She: my lord, there's one arrived,
If you will see her: now, by my faith and honour,
If seriously I may convey my thoughts
In this my light deliverance, I have spoke
With one that, in her sex, her years, profession,
Wisdom and constancy, hath amazed me more
Than I dare blame my weakness: will you see her,
For that is her demand, and know her business?
That done, laugh well at me.

KING

Now, good Lafeu,
Bring in the admiration; that we with thee
May spend our wonder too, or take off thine
By wondering how thou took'st it.

LAFEU

Nay, I'll fit you,
And not be all day neither.   [Exit

KING

Thus he his special nothing ever prologues.

Re-enter LAFEU, with HELENA

LAFEU

Nay, come your ways.

KING

This haste hath wings indeed.

LAFEU

Nay, come your ways;
This is his majesty, say your mind to him:
A traitor you do look like; but such traitors
His majesty seldom fears: I am Cressid's uncle,
That dare leave two together; fare you well.   [Exit

KING

Now, fair one, does your business follow us?

HELENA

Ay, my good lord.
Gerard de Narbon was my father;
In what he did profess, well found.

KING

I knew him.

HELENA

The rather will I spare my praises towards him;
Knowing him is enough. On's bed of death
Many receipts he gave me; chiefly one,
Which, as the dearest issue of his practice,
And of his old experience the only darling,
He bade me store up, as a triple eye,
Safer than mine own two, more dear; I have so:
And, hearing your high majesty is touch'd
With that maligant cause, wherein the honour
Of my dear father's gift stands chief in power,

I come to tender it and my appliance,
With all bound humbleness.

KING

We thank you, maiden;
But may not be so credulous of cure,
When our most learned doctors leave us, and
The congregated college have concluded
That labouring art can never ransom nature
From her inaidible estate; I say we must not
So stain our judgement, or corrupt our hope,
To prostitute our past-cure malady
To empirics, or to dissever so
Our great self and our credit, to esteem
A senseless help, when help past sense we deem.

HELENA

My duty, then, shall pay me for my pains:
I will no more enforce mine office on you;
Humbly entreating from your royal thoughts
A modest one, to bear me back again.

KING

I cannot give thee less, to be call'd grateful:
Thou thought'st to help me; and such thanks I give
As one near death to those that wish him live:
But, what at full I know, thou know'st no part;
I knowing all my peril, thou no art.

HELENA

What I can do can do no hurt to try,
Since you set up your rest 'gainst remedy.
He that of greatest works is finisher,
Oft does them by the weakest minister:
So holy writ in babes hath judgement shown,
When judges have been babes; great floods have
    flown
From simple sources; and great seas have dried,
When miracles have by the greatest been denied.
Oft expectation fails, and most oft there
Where most it promises; and oft it hits
Where hope is coldest, and despair most fits.

KING

I must not hear thee; fare thee well, kind maid;
Thy pains not used must by thyself be paid:
Proffers not took reap thanks for their reward.

HELENA

Inspired merit so by breath is barr'd:
It is not so with Him that all things knows,
As 'tis with us that square our guess by shows;
But most it is presumption in us when
The help of heaven we count the act of men.
Dear sir, to my endeavours give consent;
Of heaven, not me, make an experiment.
I am not an impostor, that proclaim
Myself against the level of mine aim;
But know I think, and think I know most sure,
My art is not past power, nor you past cure.

KING

Art thou so confident? within what space
Hopest thou my cure?

HELENA

The great'st grace lending grace,
Ere twice the horses of the sun shall bring
Their fiery torcher his diurnal ring;
Ere twice in murk and occidental damp
Moist Hesperus hath quench'd his sleepy lamp;
Or four and twenty times the pilot's glass
Hath told the thievish minutes how they pass;
What is infirm from your sound parts shall fly,
Health shall live free, and sickness freely die.

KING

Upon thy certainty and confidence
What darest thou venture?

HELENA

Tax of impudence,
A strumpet's boldness, a divulged shame
Traduced by odious ballads: my maiden's name
Sear'd otherwise, ne worse of worst extended,
With vilest torture let my life be ended.

KING

Methinks in thee some blessed spirit doth speak
His powerful sound within an organ weak:
And what impossibility would slay
In common sense, sense saves another way.
Thy life is dear; for all, that life can rate
Worth name of life, in thee hath estimate,
Youth, beauty, wisdom, courage, all
That happiness and prime can happy call:
Thou this to hazard needs must intimate
Skill infinite or monstrous desperate.
Sweet practiser, thy physic I will try,
That ministers thine own death if I die.

HELENA

If I break time, or flinch in property
Of what I spoke, unpitied let me die,
And well deserved: not helping, death's my fee;
But, if I help, what do you promise me?

KING

Make thy demand.

HELENA

But will you make it even?

KING

Ay, by my sceptre and my hopes of heaven.

HELENA

Then shalt thou give me with thy kingly hand
What husband in thy power I will command:
Exempted be from me the arrogance
To choose from forth the royal blood of France,
My low and humble name to propagate
With any branch or image of thy state;
But such a one, thy vassal, whom I know
Is free for me to ask, thee to bestow.

KING

Here is my hand; the premises observed,
Thy will by my performance shall be served:
So make the choice of thy own time; for I,
Thy resolved patient, on thee still rely.
More should I question thee, and more I must,
Though more to know could not be more to trust,
From whence thou camest, how tended on: but rest
Unquestion'd welcome, and undoubted blest.

Give me some help here, ho! If thou proceed
As high as word, my deed shall match thy deed.

[*Flourish. Exeunt*

SCENE II. *Rousillon. The* COUNT'S *palace*

Enter COUNTESS *and* CLOWN

COUNTESS

Come on, sir; I shall now put you to the height of
your breeding.

CLOWN

I will show myself highly fed and lowly taught: I
know my business is but to the court.

COUNTESS

To the court! why, what place make you special,
when you put off that with such contempt? But to
the court!

CLOWN

Truly, madam, if God have lent a man many manners, he may easily put it off at court: he that cannot make a leg, put off 's cap, kiss his hand, and say
nothing, has neither leg, hands, lip, nor cap; and,
indeed, such a fellow, to say precisely, were not for
the court; but for me, I have an answer will serve
all men.

COUNTESS

Marry, that's a bountiful answer that fits all questions.

CLOWN

It is like a barber's chair, that fits all buttocks, the
pin-buttock, the quatch-buttock, the brawn-
buttock, or any buttock.

COUNTESS

Will your answer serve fit to all questions?

CLOWN

As fit as ten groats is for the hand of an attorney, as
your French crown for your taffeta punk, as Tib's
rush for Tom's forefinger, as a pancake for Shrove
Tuesday, a morris for May-day, as the nail to his
hole, the cuckold to his horn, as a scolding quean to
a wrangling knave, as the nun's lip to the friar's
mouth, nay, as the pudding to his skin.

COUNTESS

Have you, I say, an answer of such fitness for all
questions?

CLOWN

From below your duke to beneath your constable,
it will fit any question.

COUNTESS

It must be an answer of most monstrous size that
must fit all demands.

CLOWN

But a trifle neither, in good faith, if the learned
should speak truth of it: here it is, and all that belongs to 't. Ask me if I am a courtier: it shall do you
no harm to learn.

COUNTESS

To be young again, if we could: I will be a fool in
question, hoping to be the wiser by your answer. I
pray you, sir, are you a courtier?

CLOWN

O Lord, sir! There's a simple putting off. More,
more, a hundred of them.

COUNTESS

Sir, I am a poor friend of yours, that loves you.

CLOWN

O Lord, sir! Thick, thick, spare not me.

COUNTESS

I think, sir, you can eat none of this homely meat.

CLOWN

O Lord, sir! Nay, put me to 't, I warrant you.

COUNTESS

You were lately whipped, sir, as I think.

CLOWN

O Lord, sir! spare not me.

COUNTESS

Do you cry, 'O Lord, sir!' at your whipping, and
'spare not me'? Indeed your 'O Lord, sir!' is very
sequent to your whipping: you would answer very
well to a whipping, if you were but bound to 't.

CLOWN

I ne'er had worse luck in my life in my 'O Lord,
sir!' I see things may serve long, but not serve ever.

COUNTESS

I play the noble housewife with the time,
To entertain 't so merrily with a fool.

CLOWN

O Lord, sir! why, there't serves well again.

COUNTESS

An end, sir; to your business. Give Helen this,
And urge her to a present answer back:
Commend me to my kinsmen and my son:
This is not much.

CLOWN

Not much commendation to them.

COUNTESS

Not much employment for you: you understand
me?

CLOWN

Most fruitfully: I am there before my legs.

COUNTESS

Haste you again.   [*Exeunt severally*

SCENE III. *Paris. The* KING'S *palace*

Enter BERTRAM, LAFEU, *and* PAROLLES

LAFEU

They say miracles are past; and we have our philosophical persons, to make modern and familiar,
things supernatural and causeless. Hence is it that
we make trifles of terrors; ensconcing ourselves into
seeming knowledge, when we should submit ourselves to an unknown fear.

PAROLLES

Why, 'tis the rarest argument of wonder that hath
shot out in our latter times.

BERTRAM

And so 'tis.

LAFEU

To be relinquished of the artists,—

PAROLLES

So I say; both of Galen and Paracelsus.

LAFEU

Of all the learned and authentic fellows,—

PAROLLES

Right; so I say.

LAFEU

That gave him out incurable,—

PAROLLES

Why, there 'tis; so say I too.

LAFEU

Not to be helped,—

PAROLLES

Right; as 'twere, a man assured of a—

LAFEU

Uncertain life, and sure death.

PAROLLES

Just, you say well; so would I have said.

LAFEU

I may truly say, it is a novelty to the world.

PAROLLES

It is, indeed: if you will have it in showing, you shall read it in—what do ye call there?

LAFEU

A showing of a heavenly effect in an earthly actor.

PAROLLES

That's it; I would have said the very same.

LAFEU

Why, your dolphin is not lustier: 'fore me, I speak in respect—

PAROLLES

Nay, 'tis strange, 'tis very strange, that is the brief and the tedious of it; and he's of a most facinerious spirit that will not acknowledge it to be the—

LAFEU

Very hand of heaven.

PAROLLES

Ay, so I say.

LAFEU

In a most weak—

PAROLLES

And debile minister, great power, great transcendence: which should, indeed, give us a further use to be made than alone the recovery of the king, as to be—

LAFEU

Generally thankful.

PAROLLES

I would have said it; you say well. Here comes the king.

Enter KING, HELENA, *and* ATTENDANTS

LAFEU

Lustig, as the Dutchman says: I'll like a maid the better, whilst I have a tooth in my head: why, he's able to lead her a coranto.

PAROLLES

Mort du vinaigre! is not this Helen?

LAFEU

'Fore God, I think so.

KING

Go, call before me all the lords in court.
Sit, my preserver, by thy patient's side;
And with this healthful hand, whose banish'd sense
Thou hast repeal'd, a second time receive
The confirmation of my promised gift,
Which but attends thy naming.

Enter three or four LORDS

Fair maid, send forth thine eye: this youthful parcel
Of noble bachelors stand at my bestowing,
O'er whom both sovereign power and father's voice
I have to use: thy frank election make;
Thou hast power to choose, and they none to forsake.

HELENA

To each of you one fair and virtuous mistress
Fall, when Love please! marry, to each, but one!

LAFEU

I'ld give bay Curtal and his furniture,
My mouth no more were broken than these boys',
And writ as little beard.

KING

          Peruse them well:
Not one of those but had a noble father.

HELENA

Gentlemen,
Heaven hath through me restored the king to health.

ALL

We understand it, and thank heaven for you.

HELENA

I am a simple maid; and therein wealthiest,
That I protest I simply am a maid.
Please it your majesty, I have done already:
The blushes in my cheeks thus whisper me:
'We blush that thou shouldst choose; but, be refused,
Let the white death sit on thy cheek for ever;
We'll ne'er come there again.'

KING

          Make choice; and, see,
Who shuns thy love shuns all his love in me.

HELENA

Now, Dian, from thy altar do I fly;
And to imperial Love, that god most high,
Do my sighs stream. Sir, will you hear my suit?

FIRST LORD

And grant it.

HELENA

          Thanks, sir; all the rest is mute.

LAFEU

I had rather be in this choice than throw amesace for my life.

HELENA

The honour, sir, that flames in your fair eyes,
Before I speak, too threateningly replies:
Love make your fortunes twenty times above
Her that so wishes and her humble love!

SECOND LORD

No better, if you please.

HELENA

My wish receive,
Which great Love grant! and so, I take my leave.

LAFEU

Do all they deny her? An they were sons of mine,
I'ld have them whipped; or I would send them to
the Turk, to make eunuchs of.

HELENA

Be not afraid that I your hand should take;
I'll never do you wrong for your own sake:
Blessing upon your vows! and in your bed
Find fairer fortune, if you ever wed!

LAFEU

These boys are boys of ice, they'll none have her:
sure, they are bastards to the English; the French
ne'er got 'em.

HELENA

You are too young, too happy, and too good,
To make yourself a son out of my blood.

FOURTH LORD

Fair one, I think not so.

LAFEU

There's one grape yet; I am sure thy father drunk
wine: but if thou be'st not an ass, I am a youth of
fourteen; I have known thee already.

HELENA

[To BERTRAM] I dare not say I take you; but I give
Me and my service, ever whilst I live,
Into your guiding power. This is the man.

KING

Why, then, young Bertram, take her; she's thy wife.

BERTRAM

My wife, my liege! I shall beseech your highness,
In such a business give me leave to use
The help of mine own eyes.

KING

Know'st thou not, Bertram,
What she has done for me?

BERTRAM

Yes, my good lord;
But never hope to know why I should marry her.

KING

Thou know'st she has raised me from my sickly bed.

BERTRAM

But follows it, my lord, to bring me down
Must answer for your raising? I know her well:
She had her breeding at my father's charge.
A poor physician's daughter my wife! Disdain
Rather corrupt me ever!

KING

'Tis only title thou disdain'st in her, the which
I can build up. Strange is it, that our bloods,
Of colour, weight, and heat, pour'd all together,
Would quite confound distinction, yet stand off
In differences so mighty. If she be
All that is virtuous, save what thou dislikest,
A poor physician's daughter, thou dislikest
Of virtue for the name: but do not so:
From lowest place when virtuous things proceed,
The place is dignified by the doer's deed:

Where great additions swell's, and virtue none,
It is a dropsied honour. Good alone
Is good without a name. Vileness is so:
The property by what it is should go,
Not by the title. She is young, wise, fair;
In these to nature she's immediate heir,
And these breed honour: that is honour's scorn,
Which challenges itself as honour's born,
And is not like the sire: honours thrive,
When rather from our acts we them derive
Than our foregoers: the mere word's a slave
Debosh'd on every tomb, on every grave
A lying trophy; and as oft is dumb
Where dust and damn'd oblivion is the tomb
Of honour'd bones indeed. What should be said?
If thou canst like this creature as a maid,
I can create the rest: virtue and she
Is her own dower; honour and wealth from me.

BERTRAM

I cannot love her, nor will strive to do 't.

KING

Thou wrong'st thyself, if thou shouldst strive to
choose.

HELENA

That you are well restored, my lord, I'm glad:
Let the rest go.

KING

My honour's at the stake; which to defeat,
I must produce my power. Here, take her hand,
Proud scornful boy, unworthy this good gift;
That dost in vile misprision shackle up
My love and her desert; that canst not dream,
We, poising us in her defective scale,
Shall weigh thee to the beam; that wilt not know,
It is in us to plant thine honour where
We please to have it grow. Check thy contempt:
Obey our will, which travails in thy good:
Believe not thy disdain, but presently
Do thine own fortunes that obedient right
Which both thy duty owes and our power claims;
Or I will throw thee from my care for ever
Into the staggers and the careless lapse
Of youth and ignorance; both my revenge and hate
Loosing upon thee, in the name of justice,
Without all terms of pity. Speak; thine answer.

BERTRAM

Pardon, my gracious lord; for I submit
My fancy to your eyes: when I consider
What great creation and what dole of honour
Flies where you bid it, I find that she, which late
Was in my nobler thoughts most base, is now
The praised of the king; who, so ennobled,
Is as't were born so.

KING

Take her by the hand,
And tell her she is thine: to whom I promise
A counterpoise; if not to thy estate,
A balance more replete.

BERTRAM

I take her hand.

KING

Good fortune and the favour of the king
Smile upon this contract; whose ceremony
Shall seem expedient on the now-born brief,
And be perform'd to-night: the solemn feast
Shall more attend upon the coming space,
Expecting absent friends. As thou lovest her,
Thy love's to me religious; else, does err.

[*Exeunt all but* LAFEU *and* PAROLLES

LAFEU

Do you hear, monsieur? a word with you.

PAROLLES

Your pleasure, sir?

LAFEU

Your lord and master did well to make his recantation.

PAROLLES

Recantation! My lord! my master!

LAFEU

Ay; is it not a language I speak?

PAROLLES

A most harsh one, and not to be understood without bloody succeeding. My master!

LAFEU

Are you companion to the Count Rousillon?

PAROLLES

To any count, to all counts, to what is man.

LAFEU

To what is count's man: count's master is of another style.

PAROLLES

You are too old, sir; let it satisfy you, you are too old.

LAFEU

I must tell thee, sirrah, I write man; to which title age cannot bring thee.

PAROLLES

What I dare too well do, I dare not do.

LAFEU

I did think thee, for two ordinaries, to be a pretty wise fellow; thou didst make tolerable vent of thy travel; it might pass: yet the scarfs and the bannerets about thee did manifoldly dissuade me from believing thee a vessel of too great a burthen. I have now found thee; when I lose thee again, I care not: yet art thou good for nothing but taking up; and that thou'rt scarce worth.

PAROLLES

Hadst thou not the privilege of antiquity upon thee,—

LAFEU

Do not plunge thyself too far in anger, lest thou hasten thy trial; which if—Lord have mercy on thee for a hen! So, my good window of lattice, fare thee well: thy casement I need not open, for I look through thee. Give me thy hand.

PAROLLES

My lord, you give me most egregious indignity.

LAFEU

Ay, with all my heart; and thou art worthy of it.

PAROLLES

I have not, my lord, deserved it.

LAFEU

Yes, good faith, every dram of it; and I will not bate thee a scruple.

PAROLLES

Well, I shall be wiser.

LAFEU

Ev'n as soon as thou canst, for thou hast to pull at a smack o' the contrary. If ever thou be'st bound in thy scarf and beaten, thou shalt find what it is to be proud of thy bondage. I have a desire to hold my acquaintance with thee, or rather my knowledge, that I may say in the default, he is a man I know.

PAROLLES

My lord, you do me most insupportable vexation.

LAFEU

I would it were hell-pains for thy sake, and my poor doing eternal: for doing I am past; as I will by thee, in what motion age will give me leave.   [*Exit*

PAROLLES

Well, thou hast a son shall take this disgrace off me; scurvy, old, filthy, scurvy lord! Well, I must be patient; there is no fettering of authority. I'll beat him, by my life, if I can meet him with any convenience, an he were double and double a lord. I'll have no more pity of his age than I would have of—I'll beat him, an if I could but meet him again.

Re-enter LAFEU

LAFEU

Sirrah, your lord and master's married; there's news for you: you have a new mistress.

PAROLLES

I most unfeignedly beseech your lordship to make some reservation of your wrongs: he is my good lord: whom I serve above is my master.

LAFEU

Who? God?

PAROLLES

Ay, sir.

LAFEU

The devil it is that's thy master. Why dost thou garter up thy arms o' this fashion? dost make hose of thy sleeves? do other servants so? Thou wert best set thy lower part where thy nose stands. By mine honour, if I were but two hours younger, I'ld beat thee: methinks't, thou art a general offence, and every man should beat thee: I think thou wast created for men to breathe themselves upon thee.

PAROLLES

This is hard and undeserved measure, my lord.

LAFEU

Go to, sir; you were beaten in Italy for picking a kernel out of a pomegranate; you are a vagabond, and no true traveller: you are more saucy with lords and honourable personages than the commission of your birth and virtue gives you heraldry. You are not worth another word, else I'ld call you knave. I leave you.   [*Exit*

PAROLLES

Good, very good; it is so then: good, very good; let
it be concealed awhile.

Re-enter BERTRAM

BERTRAM

Undone, and forfeited to cares for ever!

PAROLLES

What's the matter, sweet-heart?

BERTRAM

Although before the solemn priest I have sworn, I
will not bed her.

PAROLLES

What, what, sweet-heart?

BERTRAM

O my Parolles, they have married me!
I'll to the Tuscan wars, and never bed her.

PAROLLES

France is a dog-hole, and it no more merits
The tread of a man's foot: to the wars!

BERTRAM

There's letters from my mother: what the import is,
I know not yet.

PAROLLES

Ay, that would be known. To the wars, my boy, to
the wars!
He wears his honour in a box unseen,
That hugs his kicky-wicky here at home,
Spending his manly marrow in her arms,
Which should sustain the bound and high curvet
Of Mars's fiery steed. To other regions
France is a stable; we that dwell in 't jades;
Therefore, to the war!

BERTRAM

It shall be so: I'll send her to my house,
Acquaint my mother with my hate to her,
And wherefore I am fled; write to the king
That which I durst not speak: his present gift
Shall furnish me to those Italian fields,
Where noble fellows strike: war is no strife
To the dark house and the detested wife.

PAROLLES

Will this capriccio hold in thee, art sure?

BERTRAM

Go with me to my chamber, and advise me.
I'll send her straight away: to-morrow
I'll to the wars, she to her single sorrow.

PAROLLES

Why, these balls bound; there's noise in it. 'Tis hard:
A young man married is a man that's marr'd:
Therefore away, and leave her bravely; go:
The king has done you wrong: but, hush, 'tis so.

[*Exeunt*

SCENE IV. *Paris. The* KING'S *palace*

Enter HELENA *and* CLOWN

HELENA

My mother greets me kindly: is she well?

CLOWN

She is not well; but yet she has her health: she's very
merry; but yet she is not well: but thanks be given,
she's very well and wants nothing i' the world; but
yet she is not well.

HELENA

If she be very well, what does she ail, that she's not
very well?

CLOWN

Truly, she's very well indeed, but for two things.

HELENA

What two things?

CLOWN

One, that she's not in heaven, whither God send her
quickly! the other, that she's in earth, from whence
God send her quickly!

Enter PAROLLES

PAROLLES

Bless you, my fortunate lady!

HELENA

I hope, sir, I have your good will to have mine own
good fortunes.

PAROLLES

You had my prayers to lead them on; and to keep
them on, have them still. O, my knave, how does
my old lady?

CLOWN

So that you had her wrinkles, and I her money, I
would she did as you say.

PAROLLES

Why, I say nothing.

CLOWN

Marry, you are the wiser man; for many a man's
tongue shakes out his master's undoing: to say nothing, to do nothing, to know nothing, and to have
nothing, is to be a great part of your title; which is
within a very little of nothing.

PAROLLES

Away! thou'rt a knave.

CLOWN

You should have said, sir, before a knave thou'rt a
knave; that's, before me thou'rt a knave: this had
been truth, sir.

PAROLLES

Go to, thou art a witty fool; I have found thee.

CLOWN

Did you find me in yourself, sir? or were you taught
to find me? The search, sir, was profitable; and
much fool may you find in you, even to the world's
pleasure and the increase of laughter.

PAROLLES

A good knave, i' faith, and well fed.
Madam, my lord will go away to-night;
A very serious business calls on him.
The great prerogative and rite of love,
Which, as your due, time claims, he does acknowl-
edge;
But puts it off to a compell'd restraint;
Whose want, and whose delay, is strew'd with
sweets,
Which they distil now in the curbed time,

To make the coming hour o'erflow with joy,
And pleasure drown the brim.

HELENA

What's his will else?

PAROLLES

That you will take your instant leave o' the king,
And make this haste as your own good proceeding,
Strengthen'd with what apology you think
May make it probable need.

HELENA

What more commands he?

PAROLLES

That, having this obtain'd, you presently
Attend his further pleasure.

HELENA

In every thing I wait upon his will.

PAROLLES

I shall report it so.

HELENA

I pray you. [Exit PAROLLES] Come, sirrah.   [Exeunt

SCENE V. Paris. The KING's palace

Enter LAFEU and BERTRAM

LAFEU

But I hope your lordship thinks not him a soldier.

BERTRAM

Yes, my lord, and of very valiant approof.

LAFEU

You have it from his own deliverance.

BERTRAM

And by other warranted testimony.

LAFEU

Then my dial goes not true: I took this lark for a
bunting.

BERTRAM

I do assure you, my lord, he is very great in knowledge, and accordingly valiant.

LAFEU

I have then sinned against his experience and transgressed against his valour; and my state that way is
dangerous, since I cannot yet find in my heart to repent. Here he comes: I pray you, make us friends; I
will pursue the amity.

Enter PAROLLES

PAROLLES

These things shall be done, sir.   [To BERTRAM

LAFEU

Pray you, sir, who's his tailor?

PAROLLES

Sir?

LAFEU

O, I know him well, I, sir; he, sir, 's a good workman, a very good tailor.

BERTRAM

Is she gone to the king?   [Aside to PAROLLES

PAROLLES

She is.

BERTRAM

Will she away to-night?

PAROLLES

As you'll have her.

BERTRAM

I have writ my letters, casketed my treasure,
Given order for our horses; and to-night,
When I should take possession of the bride,
End ere I do begin.

LAFEU

A good traveller is something at the latter end of a
dinner; but one that lies three thirds, and uses a
known truth to pass a thousand nothings with,
should be once heard, and thrice beaten. God save
you, captain.

BERTRAM

Is there any unkindness between my lord and you,
monsieur?

PAROLLES

I know not how I have deserved to run into my
lord's displeasure.

LAFEU

You have made shift to run into 't, boots and spurs
and all, like him that leaped into the custard; and
out of it you'll run again, rather than suffer question for your residence.

BERTRAM

It may be you have mistaken him, my lord.

LAFEU

And shall do so ever, though I took him at 's prayers. Fare you well, my lord; and believe this of me,
there can be no kernel in this light nut; the soul of
this man is his clothes. Trust him not in matter of
heavy consequence; I have kept of them tame, and
know their natures. Farewell, monsieur: I have
spoken better of you than you have or will to deserve at my hand; but we must do good against evil.
          [Exit

PAROLLES

An idle lord, I swear.

BERTRAM

I think so.

PAROLLES

Why, do you not know him?

BERTRAM

Yes, I do know him well, and common speech
Gives him a worthy pass. Here comes my clog.

Enter HELENA

HELENA

I have, sir, as I was commanded from you,
Spoke with the king, and have procured his leave
For present parting; only he desires
Some private speech with you.

BERTRAM

I shall obey his will.
You must not marvel, Helen, at my course,
Which holds not colour with the time, nor does
The ministration and required office
On my particular. Prepared I was not
For such a business; therefore am I found
So much unsettled: this drives me to entreat you,
That presently you take your way for home,

And rather muse than ask why I entreat you;
For my respects are better than they seem,
And my appointments have in them a need
Greater than shows itself at the first view
To you that know them not. This to my mother:
                         [*Giving a letter*
'Twill be two days ere I shall see you; so,
I leave you to your wisdom.

HELENA
                  Sir, I can nothing say,
But that I am your most obedient servant.

BERTRAM
Come, come, no more of that.

HELENA
                  And ever shall
With true observance seek to eke out that
Wherein toward me my homely stars have fail'd
To equal my great fortune.

BERTRAM
                Let that go:
My haste is very great: farewell; hie home.

HELENA
Pray, sir, your pardon.

BERTRAM
              Well, what would you say?

HELENA
I am not worthy of the wealth I owe;
Nor dare I say 'tis mine, and yet it is;
But, like a timorous thief, most fain would steal
What law does vouch mine own.

BERTRAM
              What would you have?

HELENA
Something; and scarce so much: nothing, indeed.
I would not tell you what I would, my lord: faith,
  yes;
Strangers and foes do sunder, and not kiss.

BERTRAM
I pray you, stay not, but in haste to horse.

HELENA
I shall not break your bidding, good my lord.

BERTRAM
Where are my other men, monsieur? Farewell!
                  [*Exit* HELENA
Go thou toward home; where I will never come,
Whilst I can shake my sword, or hear the drum.
Away, and for our flight.

PAROLLES
          Bravely, coragio! [*Exeunt*

ACT III

SCENE I. *Florence. The* DUKE'S *palace*

Flourish. Enter the DUKE *of Florence, attended; the two
Frenchmen with a troop of soldiers*

DUKE
So that from point to point now have you heard

The fundamental reasons of this war,
Whose great decision hath much blood let forth
And more thirsts after.

FIRST LORD
             Holy seems the quarrel
Upon your Grace's part; black and fearful
On the opposer.

DUKE
Therefore we marvel much our cousin France
Would in so just a business shut his bosom
Against our borrowing prayers.

SECOND LORD
              Good my lord,
The reasons of our state I cannot yield,
But like a common and an outward man,
That the great figure of a council frames
By self-unable motion: therefore dare not
Say what I think of it, since I have found
Myself in my incertain grounds to fail
As often as I guess'd.

DUKE
             Be it his pleasure.

FIRST LORD
But I am sure the younger of our nature,
That surfeit on their ease, will day by day
Come here for physic.

DUKE
             Welcome shall they be;
And all the honours that can fly from us
Shall on them settle. You know your places well;
When better fall, for your avails they fell:
To-morrow to the field. [*Flourish. Exeunt*

SCENE II. *Rousillon. The* COUNT'S *palace*

Enter COUNTESS *and* CLOWN

COUNTESS
It hath happened all as I would have had it, save
that he comes not along with her.

CLOWN
By my troth, I take my young lord to be a very
melancholy man.

COUNTESS
By what observance, I pray you?

CLOWN
Why, he will look upon his boot and sing; mend the
ruff and sing; ask questions and sing; pick his teeth
and sing. I know a man that had this trick of melancholy sold a goodly manor for a song.

COUNTESS
Let me see what he writes, and when he means to
come. [*Opening a letter*

CLOWN
I have no mind to Isbel since I was at court: our old
ling and our Isbels o' the country are nothing like
your old ling and your Isbels o' the court: the brains
of my Cupid's knocked out, and I begin to love, as
an old man loves money, with no stomach.

COUNTESS
What have we here?

CLOWN
E'en that you have there.   [*Exit*

COUNTESS
[*Reads*] I have sent you a daughter-in-law: she hath recovered the king, and undone me. I have wedded her, not bedded her; and sworn to make the 'not' eternal. You shall hear I am run away: know it before the report come. If there be breadth enough in the world, I will hold a long distance. My duty to you.

Your unfortunate son,
BERTRAM.

This is not well, rash and unbridled boy,
To fly the favours of so good a king;
To pluck his indignation on thy head
By the misprising of a maid too virtuous
For the contempt of empire.

Re-enter CLOWN

CLOWN
O madam, yonder is heavy news within between two soldiers and my young lady!

COUNTESS
What is the matter?

CLOWN
Nay, there is some comfort in the news, some comfort; your son will not be killed so soon as I thought he would.

COUNTESS
Why should he be killed?

CLOWN
So say I, madam, if he run away, as I hear he does: the danger is in standing to 't; that's the loss of men, though it be the getting of children. Here they come will tell you more: for my part, I only hear your son was run away.   [*Exit*

Enter HELENA *and two* GENTLEMEN

FIRST GENTLEMAN
Save you, good madam.

HELENA
Madam, my lord is gone, for ever gone.

SECOND GENTLEMAN
Do not say so.

COUNTESS
Think upon patience. Pray you, gentlemen,
I have felt so many quirks of joy and grief,
That the first face of neither, on the start,
Can woman me unto 't: where is my son, I pray you?

SECOND GENTLEMAN
Madam, he's gone to serve the duke of Florence:
We met him thitherward; for thence we came,
And, after some dispatch in hand at court,
Thither we bend again.

HELENA
Look on his letter, madam; here's my passport.

[*Reads*] When thou canst get the ring upon my finger which never shall come off, and show me a child begotten of thy body that I am father to, then call me husband: but in such a 'then' I write a 'never.'

This is a dreadful sentence.

COUNTESS
Brought you this letter, gentlemen?

FIRST GENTLEMAN
Ay, madam;
And for the contents' sake are sorry for our pains.

COUNTESS
I prithee, lady, have a better cheer;
If thou engrossest all the griefs are thine,
Thou robb'st me of a moiety: he was my son;
But I do wash his name out of my blood,
And thou art all my child. Towards Florence is he?

SECOND GENTLEMAN
Ay, madam.

COUNTESS
And to be a soldier?

SECOND GENTLEMAN
Such is his noble purpose; and, believe 't,
The Duke will lay upon him all the honour
That good convenience claims.

COUNTESS
Return you thither?

FIRST GENTLEMAN
Ay, madam, with the swiftest wing of speed.

HELENA
[*Reads*] Till I have no wife, I have nothing in France.
'Tis bitter.

COUNTESS
Find you that there?

HELENA
Ay, madam.

FIRST GENTLEMAN
'Tis but the boldness of his hand, haply, which his heart was not consenting to.

COUNTESS
Nothing in France, until he have no wife!
There's nothing here that is too good for him
But only she; and she deserves a lord
That twenty such rude boys might tend upon
And call her hourly mistress. Who was with him?

FIRST GENTLEMAN
A servant only, and a gentleman
Which I have sometime known.

COUNTESS
Parolles, was it not?

FIRST GENTLEMAN
Ay, my good lady, he.

COUNTESS
A very tainted fellow, and full of wickedness.
My son corrupts a well-derived nature
With his inducement.

FIRST GENTLEMAN
Indeed, good lady,
The fellow has a deal of that too much,
Which holds him much to have.

COUNTESS
Y'are welcome, gentlemen.
I will entreat you, when you see my son,
To tell him that his sword can never win
The honour that he loses: more I'll entreat you
Written to bear along.

SECOND GENTLEMAN
                    We serve you, madam,
In that and all your worthiest affairs.

COUNTESS
Not so, but as we change our courtesies.
Will you draw near?
                    [*Exeunt* COUNTESS *and* GENTLEMEN

HELENA
'Till I have no wife, I have nothing in France.'
Nothing in France, until he has no wife!
Thou shalt have none, Rousillon, none in France;
Then hast thou all again. Poor lord! is 't I
That chase thee from thy country and expose
Those tender limbs of thine to the event
Of the none-sparing war? and is it I
That drive thee from the sportive court, where thou
Wast shot at with fair eyes, to be the mark
Of smoky muskets? O you leaden messengers,
That ride upon the violent speed of fire,
Fly with false aim; move the still-peering air,
That sings with piercing; do not touch my lord.
Whoever shoots at him, I set him there;
Whoever charges on his forward breast,
I am the caitiff that do hold him to 't;
And, though I kill him not, I am the cause
His death was so effected: better 'twere
I met the ravin lion when he roar'd
With sharp constraint of hunger; better 'twere
That all the miseries which nature owes
Were mine at once. No, come thou home, Rousillon,
Whence honour but of danger wins a scar,
As oft it loses all: I will be gone;
My being here it is that holds thee hence:
Shall I stay here to do 't? no, no, although
The air of paradise did fan the house,
And angels officed all: I will be gone,
That pitiful rumour may report my flight,
To consolate thine ear. Come, night; end, day!
For with the dark, poor thief, I'll steal away. [*Exit*

SCENE III. *Florence. Before the* DUKE'S *palace*

Flourish. Enter the DUKE *of Florence,* BERTRAM,
PAROLLES, SOLDIERS, *Drum, and Trumpets*

DUKE
The general of our horse thou art; and we,
Great in our hope, lay our best love and credence
Upon thy promising fortune.

BERTRAM
                    Sir, it is
A charge too heavy for my strength; but yet
We'll strive to bear it for your worthy sake
To the extreme edge of hazard.

DUKE
                    Then go thou forth;
And fortune play upon thy prosperous helm,
As thy auspicious mistress!

BERTRAM
                    This very day,
Great Mars, I put myself into thy file:
Make me but like my thoughts, and I shall prove
A lover of thy drum, hater of love.   [*Exeunt*

SCENE IV. *Rousillon. The* COUNT'S *palace*

Enter COUNTESS *and* STEWARD

COUNTESS
Alas! and would you take the letter of her?
Might you not know she would do as she has done,
By sending me a letter? Read it again.

STEWARD
[*Reads*] I am Saint Jaques' pilgrim, thither gone:
        Ambitious love hath so in me offended,
    That barefoot plod I the cold ground upon,
        With sainted vow my faults to have amended.
    Write, write, that from the bloody course of war
        My dearest master, your dear son, may hie:
    Bless him at home in peace, whilst I from far
        His name with zealous fervour sanctify:
    His taken labours bid him me forgive;
        I, his despiteful Juno, sent him forth
    From courtly friends with camping foes to live,
        Where death and danger dogs the heels of worth:
    He is too good and fair for death and me;
    Whom I myself embrace to set him free.

COUNTESS
Ah, what sharp stings are in her mildest words!
Rinaldo, you did never lack advice so much,
As letting her pass so: had I spoke with her,
I could have well diverted her intents,
Which thus she hath prevented.

STEWARD
                    Pardon me, madam:
If I had given you this at over-night,
She might have been o'erta'en; and yet she writes,
Pursuit would be but vain.

COUNTESS
                    What angel shall
Bless this unworthy husband? he cannot thrive,
Unless her prayers, whom heaven delights to hear
And loves to grant, reprieve him from the wrath
Of greatest justice. Write, write, Rinaldo,
To this unworthy husband of his wife;
Let every word weigh heavy of her worth
That he does weigh too light: my greatest grief,
Though little he do feel it, set down sharply.
Dispatch the most convenient messenger:
When haply he shall hear that she is gone,
He will return; and hope I may that she,
Hearing so much, will speed her foot again,
Led hither by pure love: which of them both
Is dearest to me, I have no skill in sense
To make distinction: provide this messenger:
My heart is heavy and mine age is weak;
Grief would have tears, and sorrow bids me speak.
                                        [*Exeunt*

Scene V. *Florence. Without the walls. A tucket afar off*

Enter an old WIDOW *of Florence,* DIANA, VIOLENTA, *and* MARIANA, *with other* CITIZENS

WIDOW
Nay, come; for if they do approach the city, we shall lose all the sight.

DIANA
They say the French count has done most honourable service.

WIDOW
It is reported that he has taken their greatest commander; and that with his own hand he slew the Duke's brother. [*Tucket*] We have lost our labour; they are gone a contrary way: hark! you may know by their trumpets.

MARIANA
Come, let's return again, and suffice ourselves with the report of it. Well, Diana, take heed of this French earl: the honour of a maid is her name; and no legacy is so rich as honesty.

WIDOW
I have told my neighbour how you have been solicited by a gentleman his companion.

MARIANA
I know that knave; hang him! one Parolles: a filthy officer he is in those suggestions for the young earl. Beware of them, Diana; their promises, enticements, oaths, tokens, and all these engines of lust, are not the things they go under: many a maid hath been seduced by them; and the misery is, example, that so terrible shows in the wreck of maidenhood, cannot for all that dissuade succession, but that they are limed with the twigs that threaten them. I hope I need not to advise you further; but I hope your own grace will keep you where you are, though there were no further danger known but the modesty which is so lost.

DIANA
You shall not need to fear me.

WIDOW
I hope so.
          Enter HELENA, *disguised like a* PILGRIM
Look, here comes a pilgrim: I know she will lie at my house; thither they send one another: I'll question her. God save you, pilgrim! whither are you bound?

HELENA
To Saint Jaques le Grand.
Where do the palmers lodge, I do beseech you?

WIDOW
At the Saint Francis here beside the port.

HELENA
Is this the way?

WIDOW
Ay, marry, is't. [*A march afar*] Hark you! they come this way.
If you will tarry, holy pilgrim,
But till the troops come by,
I will conduct you where you shall be lodged;

The rather, for I think I know your hostess
As ample as myself.

HELENA
Is it yourself?

WIDOW
If you shall please so, pilgrim.

HELENA
I thank you, and will stay upon your leisure.

WIDOW
You came, I think, from France?

HELENA
                              I did so.

WIDOW
Here you shall see a countryman of yours
That has done worthy service.

HELENA
                    His name, I pray you?

DIANA
The Count Rousillon: know you such a one?

HELENA
But by the ear, that hears most nobly of him:
His face I know not.

DIANA
                    Whatsome'er he is,
He's bravely taken here. He stole from France,
As 'tis reported, for the king had married him
Against his liking: think you it is so?

HELENA
Ay, surely, mere the truth: I know his lady.

DIANA
There is a gentleman that serves the count
Reports but coarsely of her.

HELENA
                    What's his name?

DIANA
Monsieur Parolles.

HELENA
                    O, I believe with him,
In argument of praise, or to the worth
Of the great count himself, she is too mean
To have her name repeated: all her deserving
Is a reserved honesty, and that
I have not heard examined.

DIANA
                    Alas, poor lady!
'Tis a hard bondage to become the wife
Of a detesting lord.

WIDOW
I write good creature, wheresoe'er she is,
Her heart weighs sadly: this young maid might do her
A shrewd turn, if she pleased.

HELENA
                    How do you mean?
May be the amorous count solicits her
In the unlawful purpose.

WIDOW
                    He does indeed;
And brokes with all that can in such a suit

Corrupt the tender honour of a maid:
But she is arm'd for him, and keeps her guard
In honestest defence.

MARIANA
The gods forbid else!

WIDOW
So, now they come:
Drum and Colours
Enter BERTRAM, PAROLLES, *and the whole army*
That is Antonio, the Duke's eldest son;
That, Escalus.

HELENA
Which is the Frenchman?

DIANA
He;
That with the plume: 'tis a most gallant fellow.
I would he loved his wife: if he were honester
He were much goodlier: is 't not a handsome gentle-
man?

HELENA
I like him well.

DIANA
'Tis pity he is not honest: yond's that same knave
That leads him to these places: were I his lady,
I would poison that vile rascal.

HELENA
Which is he?

DIANA
That jack-an-apes with scarfs: why is he melancholy?

HELENA
Perchance he's hurt i' the battle.

PAROLLES
Lose our drum! well.

MARIANA
He's shrewdly vexed at something: look, he has
spied us.

WIDOW
Marry, hang you!

MARIANA
And your courtesy, for a ring-carrier!
[*Exeunt* BERTRAM, PAROLLES, *and army*

WIDOW
The troop is past. Come, pilgrim, I will bring you
Where you shall host: of enjoin'd penitents
There's four or five, to great Saint Jaques bound,
Already at my house.

HELENA
I humbly thank you:
Please it this matron and this gentle maid
To eat with us to-night, the charge and thanking
Shall be for me; and, to requite you further,
I will bestow some precepts of this virgin
Worthy the note.

BOTH
We'll take your offer kindly. [*Exeunt*

SCENE VI. *Camp before Florence*

Enter BERTRAM *and the two French* LORDS

SECOND LORD
Nay, good my lord, put him to 't; let him have his
way.

FIRST LORD
If your lordship find him not a hilding, hold me no
more in your respect.

SECOND LORD
On my life, my lord, a bubble.

BERTRAM
Do you think I am so far deceived in him?

SECOND LORD
Believe it, my lord, in mine own direct knowledge,
without any malice, but to speak of him as my kinsman, he's a most notable coward, an infinite and
endless liar, an hourly promise-breaker, the owner
of no one good quality worthy your lordship's entertainment.

FIRST LORD
It were fit you knew him; lest, reposing too far in
his virtue, which he hath not, he might at some
great and trusty business in a main danger fail you.

BERTRAM
I would I knew in what particular action to try him.

FIRST LORD
None better than to let him fetch off his drum,
which you hear him so confidently undertake to do.

SECOND LORD
I, with a troop of Florentines, will suddenly surprise
him; such I will have, whom I am sure he knows
not from the enemy: we will bind and hoodwink
him so, that he shall suppose no other but that he is
carried into the leaguer of the adversaries, when we
bring him to our own tents. Be but your lordship
present at his examination: if he do not, for the
promise of his life and in the highest compulsion of
base fear, offer to betray you and deliver all the intelligence in his power against you, and that with
the divine forfeit of his soul upon oath, never trust
my judgement in any thing.

FIRST LORD
O, for the love of laughter, let him fetch his drum;
he says he has a stratagem for 't: when your lordship
sees the bottom of his success in 't, and to what
metal this counterfeit lump of ore will be melted, if
you give him not John Drum's entertainment, your
inclining cannot be removed. Here he comes.

Enter PAROLLES

SECOND LORD
[*Aside to* BERTRAM] O, for the love of laughter, hinder not the honour of his design: let him fetch off
his drum in any hand.

BERTRAM
How now, monsieur! this drum sticks sorely in your
disposition.

FIRST LORD
A pox on 't, let it go; 'tis but a drum.

PAROLLES

'But a drum'! is 't 'but a drum'? A drum so lost!
There was excellent command,—to charge in with
our horse upon our own wings, and to rend our own
soldiers!

FIRST LORD

That was not to be blamed in the command of the
service: it was a disaster of war that Cæsar himself
could not have prevented, if he had been there to
command.

BERTRAM

Well, we cannot greatly condemn our success: some
dishonour we had in the loss of that drum; but it is
not to be recovered.

PAROLLES

It might have been recovered.

BERTRAM

It might; but it is not now.

PAROLLES

It is to be recovered: but that the merit of service is
seldom attributed to the true and exact performer,
I would have that drum or another, or 'hic jacet.'

BERTRAM

Why, if you have a stomach, to 't, monsieur: if you
think your mystery in stratagem can bring this instrument of honour again into his native quarter, be
magnanimous in the enterprise and go on; I will
grace the attempt for a worthy exploit: if you speed
well in it, the Duke shall both speak of it, and extend to you what further becomes his greatness, even
to the utmost syllable of your worthiness.

PAROLLES

By the hand of a soldier, I will undertake it.

BERTRAM

But you must not now slumber in it.

PAROLLES

I'll about it this evening: and I will presently pen
down my dilemmas, encourage myself in my certainty, put myself into my mortal preparation; and
by midnight look to hear further from me.

BERTRAM

May I be bold to acquaint his Grace you are gone
about it?

PAROLLES

I know not what the success will be, my lord; but
the attempt I vow.

BERTRAM

I know thou'rt valiant; and, to the possibility of thy
soldiership, will subscribe for thee. Farewell.

PAROLLES

I love not many words.   [*Exit*

SECOND LORD

No more than a fish loves water. Is not this a strange
fellow, my lord, that so confidently seems to undertake this business, which he knows is not to be done;
damns himself to do, and dares better be damned
than to do 't?

FIRST LORD

You do not know him, my lord, as we do: certain it
is, that he will steal himself into a man's favour and

for a week escape a great deal of discoveries; but
when you find him out, you have him ever after.

BERTRAM

Why, do you think he will make no deed at all of
this that so seriously he does address himself unto?

SECOND LORD

None in the world; but return with an invention,
and clap upon you two or three probable lies: but
we have almost embossed him; you shall see his fall
to-night; for indeed he is not for your lordship's respect.

FIRST LORD

We'll make you some sport with the fox ere we case
him. He was first smoked by the old lord Lafeu:
when his disguise and he is parted, tell me what a
sprat you shall find him; which you shall see this
very night.

SECOND LORD

I must go look my twigs: he shall be caught.

BERTRAM

Your brother he shall go along with me.

SECOND LORD

As 't please your lordship: I'll leave you.   [*Exit*

BERNARD

Now will I lead you to the house, and show you
The lass I spoke of.

FIRST LORD

                            But you say she's honest.

BERTRAM

That's all the fault: I spoke with her but once
And found her wondrous cold; but I sent to her,
By this same coxcomb that we have i' the wind,
Tokens and letters which she did re-send;
And this is all I have done. She's a fair creature:
Will you go see her?

FIRST LORD

                    With all my heart, my lord. [*Exeunt*

SCENE VII. *Florence. The* WIDOW'*s house*

Enter HELENA *and* WIDOW

HELENA

If you misdoubt me that I am not she,
I know not how I shall assure you further,
But I shall lose the grounds I work upon.

WIDOW

Though my estate be fallen, I was well born,
Nothing acquainted with these businesses;
And would not put my reputation now
In any staining act.

HELENA

                    Nor would I wish you.
First, give me trust, the count he is my husband,
And what to your sworn counsel I have spoken
Is so from word to word; and then you cannot,
By the good aid that I of you shall borrow,
Err in bestowing it.

WIDOW

                    I should believe you;

For you have show'd me that which well approves
You're great in fortune.

HELENA

           Take this purse of gold,
And let me buy your friendly help thus far,
Which I will over-pay and pay again
When I have found it. The count he wooes your
    daughter,
Lays down his wanton siege before her beauty,
Resolved to carry her: let her in fine consent,
As we'll direct her how 'tis best to bear it.
Now his important blood will nought deny
That she'll demand: a ring the county wears,
That downward hath succeeded in his house
From son to son, some four or five descents
Since the first father wore it: this ring he holds
In most rich choice; yet in his idle fire,
To buy his will, it would not seem too dear,
Howe'er repented after.

WIDOW

           Now I see
The bottom of your purpose.

HELENA

You see it lawful, then: it is no more,
But that your daughter, ere she seems as won,
Desires this ring; appoints him an encounter;
In fine, delivers me to fill the time,
Herself most chastely absent: after this,
To marry her, I'll add three thousand crowns
To what is past already.

WIDOW

           I have yielded:
Instruct my daughter how she shall persever,
That time and place with this deceit so lawful
May prove coherent. Every night he comes
With musics of all sorts and songs composed
To her unworthiness: it nothing steads us
To chide him from our eaves; for he persists
As if his life lay on 't.

HELENA

           Why then to-night
Let us assay our plot; which, if it speed,
Is wicked meaning in a lawful deed,
And lawful meaning in a lawful act,
Where both not sin, and yet a sinful fact:
But let's about it.   [Exeunt

ACT IV

SCENE I. *Without the Florentine camp*

Enter SECOND FRENCH LORD, *with five or six other*
SOLDIERS *in ambush*

SECOND LORD

He can come no other way but by this hedge-
corner. When you sally upon him, speak what terrible language you will: though you understand it
not yourselves, no matter; for we must not seem to
understand him, unless some one among us whom
we must produce for an interpreter.

FIRST SOLDIER

Good captain, let me be the interpreter.

SECOND LORD

Art not acquainted with him? knows he not thy
voice?

FIRST SOLDIER

No, sir, I warrant you.

SECOND LORD

But what linsey-woolsey hast thou to speak to us
again?

FIRST SOLDIER

E'en such as you speak to me.

SECOND LORD

He must think us some band of strangers i' the adversary's entertainment. Now he hath a smack of
all neighbouring languages; therefore we must
every one be a man of his own fancy, not to know
what we speak one to another; so we seem to know,
is to know straight our purpose: choughs' language,
gabble enough, and good enough. As for you, interpreter, you must seem very politic. But couch, ho!
here he comes, to beguile two hours in a sleep, and
then to return and swear the lies he forges.

Enter PAROLLES

PAROLLES

Ten o'clock: within these three hours 'twill be time
enough to go home. What shall I say I have done?
It must be a very plausive invention that carries it:
they begin to smoke me; and disgraces have of late
knocked too often at my door. I find my tongue is
too foolhardy; but my heart hath the fear of Mars
before it and of his creatures, not daring the reports
of my tongue.

SECOND LORD

This is the first truth that e'er thine own tongue was
guilty of.

PAROLLES

What the devil should move me to undertake the
recovery of this drum, being not ignorant of the impossibility, and knowing I had no such purpose? I
must give myself some hurts, and say I got them in
exploit: yet slight ones will not carry it; they will
say, 'Came you off with so little?' and great ones I
dare not give. Wherefore, what's the instance?
Tongue, I must put you into a butter-woman's
mouth, and buy myself another of Bajazet's mule, if
you prattle me into these perils.

SECOND LORD

Is it possible he should know what he is, and be that
he is?

PAROLLES

I would the cutting of my garments would serve the
turn, or the breaking of my Spanish sword.

SECOND LORD

We cannot afford you so.

PAROLLES

Or the baring of my beard; and to say it was in
stratagem.

SECOND LORD

'Twould not do.

PAROLLES

Or to drown my clothes, and say I was stripped.

SECOND LORD

Hardly serve.

PAROLLES

Though I swore I leaped from the window of the citadel—

SECOND LORD

How deep?

PAROLLES

Thirty fathom.

SECOND LORD

Three great oaths would scarce make that be believed.

PAROLLES

I would I had any drum of the enemy's: I would swear I recovered it.

SECOND LORD

You shall hear one anon.

PAROLLES

A drum now of the enemy's,—   [Alarum within

SECOND LORD

Throca movousus, cargo, cargo, cargo.

ALL

Cargo, cargo, cargo, villianda par corbo, cargo.

PAROLLES

O, ransom, ransom! do not hide mine eyes.

[They seize and blindfold him

FIRST SOLDIER

Boskos thromuldo boskos.

PAROLLES

I know you are the Muskos' regiment;
And I shall lose my life for want of language:
If there be here German, or Dane, low Dutch,
Italian, or French, let him speak to me; I'll
Discover that which shall undo the Florentine.

FIRST SOLDIER

Boskos vauvado: I understand thee, and can speak
thy tongue. Kerelybonto, sir, betake thee to thy
faith, for seventeen poniards are at thy bosom.

PAROLLES

O!

FIRST SOLDIER

O, pray, pray, pray! Manka revania dulche.

SECOND LORD

Oscorbidulchos volivorco.

FIRST SOLDIER

The general is content to spare thee yet;
And, hoodwink'd as thou art, will lead thee on
To gather from thee: haply thou mayst inform
Something to save thy life.

PAROLLES

O, let me live!
And all the secrets of our camp I'll show,
Their force, their purposes; nay, I'll speak that
Which you will wonder at.

FIRST SOLDIER

But wilt thou faithfully?

PAROLLES

If I do not, damn me.

FIRST SOLDIER

Acordo linta.
Come on; thou art granted space.

[Exit, with PAROLLES guarded. A short alarum within

SECOND LORD

Go, tell the Count Rousillon, and my brother,
We have caught the woodcock, and will keep him
    muffled
Till we do hear from them.

SECOND SOLDIER

Captain, I will.

SECOND LORD

A' will betray us all unto ourselves:
Inform on that.

SECOND SOLDIER

So I will, sir.

SECOND LORD

Till then I'll keep him dark and safely lock'd.

[Exeunt

SCENE II. *Florence. The* WIDOW'S *house*

Enter BERTRAM *and* DIANA

BERTRAM

They told me that your name was Fontibell.

DIANA

No, my good lord, Diana.

BERTRAM

Titled goddess;
And worth it, with addition! But, fair soul,
In your fine frame hath love no quality?
If the quick fire of youth light not your mind,
You are no maiden, but a monument:
When you are dead, you should be such a one
As you are now, for you are cold and stern;
And now you should be as your mother was
When your sweet self was got.

DIANA

She then was honest.

BERTRAM

So should you be.

DIANA

No:
My mother did but duty; such, my lord,
As you owe to your wife.

BERTRAM

No more o' that;
I prithee, do not strive against my vows:
I was compell'd to her; but I love thee
By love's own sweet constraint, and will for ever
Do thee all rights of service.

DIANA

Ay, so you serve us
Till we serve you; but when you have our roses,
You barely leave our thorns to prick ourselves,
And mock us with our bareness.

BERTRAM

How have I sworn!

[885]

DIANA

'Tis not the many oaths that makes the truth,
But the plain single vow that is vow'd true.
What is not holy, that we swear not by,
But take the High'st to witness: then, pray you, tell
    me,
If I should swear by Jove's great attributes,
I loved you dearly, would you believe my oaths,
When I did love you ill? This has no holding,
To swear by him whom I protest to love,
That I will work against him: therefore your oaths
Are words and poor conditions, but unseal'd,
At least in my opinion.

BERTRAM
                        Change it, change it;
Be not so holy-cruel: love is holy;
And my integrity ne'er knew the crafts
That you do charge men with. Stand no more off,
But give thyself unto my sick desires,
Who then recover: say thou art mine, and ever
My love as it begins shall so persever.

DIANA

I see that men make rope's in such a scarre
That we'll forsake ourselves. Give me that ring.

BERTRAM

I'll lend it thee, my dear; but have no power
To give it from me.

DIANA
            Will you not, my lord?

BERTRAM

It is an honour 'longing to our house,
Bequeathed down from many ancestors;
Which were the greatest obloquy i' the world
In me to lose.

DIANA

            Mine honour's such a ring:
My chastity's the jewel of our house,
Bequeathed down from many ancestors;
Which were the greatest obloquy i' the world
In me to lose: thus your own proper wisdom
Brings in the champion Honour on my part,
Against your vain assault.

BERTRAM
                Here, take my ring:
My house, mine honour, yea, my life, be thine,
And I'll be bid by thee.

DIANA

When midnight comes, knock at my chamber-
    window:
I'll order take my mother shall not hear.
Now will I charge you in the band of truth,
When you have conquer'd my yet maiden bed,
Remain there but an hour, nor speak to me:
My reasons are most strong; and you shall know
    them
When back again this ring shall be deliver'd:
And on your finger in the night I'll put
Another ring, that what in time proceeds
May token to the future our past deeds.

Adieu, till then; then, fail not. You have won
A wife of me, though there my hope be done.

BERTRAM

A heaven on earth I have won by wooing thee. [Exit

DIANA

For which live long to thank both heaven and me!
You may so in the end.
My mother told me just how he would woo,
As if she sat in 's heart; she says all men
Have the like oaths: he had sworn to marry me
When his wife's dead; therefore I'll lie with him
When I am buried. Since Frenchmen are so braid,
Marry that will, I live and die a maid:
Only in this disguise I think 't no sin
To cozen him that would unjustly win.   [Exit

SCENE III. *The Florentine camp*

Enter the two French LORDS *and some two or three*
SOLDIERS

FIRST LORD

You have not given him his mother's letter?

SECOND LORD

I have delivered it an hour since: there is something
in 't that stings his nature; for on the reading it he
changed almost into another man.

FIRST LORD

He has much worthy blame laid upon him for shaking off so good a wife and so sweet a lady.

SECOND LORD

Especially he hath incurred the everlasting displeasure of the king, who had even tuned his bounty
to sing happiness to him. I will tell you a thing, but
you shall let it dwell darkly with you.

FIRST LORD

When you have spoken it, 'tis dead, and I am the
grave of it.

SECOND LORD

He hath perverted a young gentlewoman here in
Florence, of a most chaste renown; and this night he
fleshes his will in the spoil of her honour: he hath
given her his monumental ring, and thinks himself
made in the unchaste composition.

FIRST LORD

Now, God delay our rebellion! as we are ourselves,
what things are we!

SECOND LORD

Merely our own traitors. And as in the common
course of all treasons, we still see them reveal themselves, till they attain to their abhorred ends, so he
that in this action contrives against his own nobility, in his proper stream o'erflows himself.

FIRST LORD

Is it not meant damnable in us, to be trumpeters of
our unlawful intents? We shall not then have his
company to-night?

SECOND LORD

Not till after midnight; for he is dieted to his hour.

FIRST LORD

That approaches apace: I would gladly have him

[886]

see his company anatomized, that he might take a measure of his own judgements, wherein so curiously he had set this counterfeit.

SECOND LORD

We will not meddle with him till he come; for his presence must be the whip of the other.

FIRST LORD

In the mean time, what hear you of these wars?

SECOND LORD

I hear there is an overture of peace.

FIRST LORD

Nay, I assure you, a peace concluded.

SECOND LORD

What will Count Rousillon do then? will he travel higher, or return again into France?

FIRST LORD

I perceive, by this demand, you are not altogether of his council.

SECOND LORD

Let it be forbid, sir; so should I be a great deal of his act.

FIRST LORD

Sir, his wife some two months since fled from his house: her pretence is a pilgrimage to Saint Jaques le Grand; which holy undertaking with most austere sanctimony she accomplished; and, there residing, the tenderness of her nature became as a prey to her grief; in fine, made a groan of her last breath, and now she sings in heaven.

SECOND LORD

How is this justified?

FIRST LORD

The stronger part of it by her own letters, which makes her story true, even to the point of her death: her death itself, which could not be her office to say is come, was faithfully confirmed by the rector of the place.

SECOND LORD

Hath the count all this intelligence?

FIRST LORD

Ay, and the particular confirmations, point from point, to the full arming of the verity.

SECOND LORD

I am heartily sorry that he'll be glad of this.

FIRST LORD

How mightily sometimes we make us comforts of our losses!

SECOND LORD

And how mightily some other times we drown our gain in tears! The great dignity that his valour hath here acquired for him shall at home be encountered with a shame as ample.

FIRST LORD

The web of our life is of a mingled yarn, good and ill together: our virtues would be proud, if our faults whipped them not; and our crimes would despair, if they were not cherished by our virtues.

Enter a MESSENGER

How now! where's your master!

SERVANT

He met the Duke in the street, sir, of whom he hath taken a solemn leave: his lordship will next morning for France. The Duke hath offered him letters of commendations to the king.

SECOND LORD

They shall be no more than needful there, if they were more than they can commend.

FIRST LORD

They cannot be too sweet for the king's tartness. Here's his lordship now.

Enter BERTRAM

How now, my lord! is 't not after midnight?

BERTRAM

I have to-night dispatched sixteen businesses, a month's length a-piece, by an abstract of success: I have congied with the Duke, done my adieu with his nearest; buried a wife, mourned for her; writ to my lady mother I am returning; entertained my convoy; and between these main parcels of dispatch effected many nicer needs: the last was the greatest, but that I have not ended yet.

SECOND LORD

If the business be of any difficulty, and this morning your departure hence, it requires haste of your lordship.

BERTRAM

I mean, the business is not ended, as fearing to hear of it hereafter. But shall we have this dialogue between the fool and the soldier? Come, bring forth this counterfeit module, has deceived me, like a double-meaning prophesier.

SECOND LORD

Bring him forth: has sat i' the stocks all night, poor gallant knave.

BERTRAM

No matter; his heels have deserved it, in usurping his spurs so long. How does he carry himself?

SECOND LORD

I have told your lordship already, the stocks carry him. But to answer you as you would be understood; he weeps like a wench that had shed her milk: he hath confessed himself to Morgan, whom he supposes to be a friar, from the time of his remembrance to this very instant disaster of his setting i' the stocks: and what think you he hath confessed?

BERTRAM

Nothing of me, has a'?

SECOND LORD

His confession is taken, and it shall be read to his face: if your lordship be in 't, as I believe you are, you must have the patience to hear it.

Enter PAROLLES *guarded, and* FIRST SOLDIER

BERTRAM

A plague upon him! muffled! he can say nothing of me: hush, hush!

FIRST LORD

Hoodman comes! Portotartarossa.

FIRST SOLDIER

He calls for the tortures: what will you say without
'em?

PAROLLES

I will confess what I know without constraint: if ye
pinch me like a pasty, I can say no more.

FIRST SOLDIER

Bosko chimurcho.

FIRST LORD

Boblibindo chicurmurco.

FIRST SOLDIER

You are a merciful general. Our general bids you
answer to what I shall ask you out of a note.

PAROLLES

And truly, as I hope to live.

FIRST SOLDIER

[Reads] First demand of him how many horse the Duke is strong.

What say you to that?

PAROLLES

Five or six thousand; but very weak and unservice-
able: the troops are all scattered, and the commanders very poor rogues, upon my reputation and credit,
and as I hope to live.

FIRST SOLDIER

Shall I set down your answer so?

PAROLLES

Do: I'll take the sacrament on 't, how and which
way you will.

BERTRAM

All's one to him. What a past-saving slave is this!

FIRST LORD

You're deceived, my lord: this is Monsieur Parolles,
the gallant militarist,—that was his own phrase,—
that had the whole theoric of war in the knot of his
scarf, and the practice in the chape of his dagger.

SECOND LORD

I will never trust a man again for keeping his sword
clean, nor believe he can have every thing in him by
wearing his apparel neatly.

FIRST SOLDIER

Well, that's set down.

PAROLLES

Five or six thousand horse, I said,—I will say true,
—or thereabouts, set down, for I'll speak truth.

FIRST LORD

He's very near the truth in this.

BERTRAM

But I con him no thanks for 't, in the nature he delivers it.

PAROLLES

Poor rogues, I pray you, say.

FIRST SOLDIER

Well, that's set down.

PAROLLES

I humbly thank you, sir: a truth's a truth, the
rogues are marvellous poor.

FIRST SOLDIER

[Reads] Demand of him, of what strength they are a-foot.

What say you to that?

PAROLLES

By my troth, sir, if I were to live this present hour,
I will tell true. Let me see: Spurio, a hundred and
fifty; Sebastian, so many; Corambus, so many;
Jaques, so many; Guiltian, Cosmo, Lodowick, and
Gratii, two hundred and fifty each; mine own company, Chitopher, Vaumond, Bentii, two hundred
and fifty each: so that the muster-file, rotten and
sound, upon my life, amounts not to fifteen thousand poll; half of the which dare not shake the snow
from off their cassocks, lest they shake themselves to
pieces.

BERTRAM

What shall be done to him?

FIRST LORD

Nothing, but let him have thanks. Demand of him
my condition, and what credit I have with the
Duke.

FIRST SOLDIER

Well, that's set down.

[Reads] You shall demand of him, whether one Captain Dumain be i' the camp, a Frenchman; what his reputation is with
the Duke; what his valour, honesty, and expertness in wars; or
whether he thinks it were not possible, with well-weighing
sums of gold, to corrupt him to a revolt.

What say you to this? what do you know of it?

PAROLLES

I beseech you, let me answer to the particular of the
inter'gatories: demand them singly.

FIRST SOLDIER

Do you know this Captain Dumain?

PAROLLES

I know him: a' was a botcher's 'prentice in Paris,
from whence he was whipped for getting the
shrieve's fool with child,—a dumb innocent, that
could not say him nay.

BERTRAM

Nay, by your leave, hold your hands; though I
know his brains are forfeit to the next tile that falls.

FIRST SOLDIER

Well, is this captain in the Duke of Florence's camp?

PAROLLES

Upon my knowledge, he is, and lousy.

FIRST LORD

Nay, look not so upon me; we shall hear of your
lordship anon.

FIRST SOLDIER

What is his reputation with the Duke?

PAROLLES

The Duke knows him for no other but a poor officer
of mine; and writ to me this other day to turn him
out o' the band: I think I have his letter in my
pocket.

FIRST SOLDIER

Marry, we'll search.

PAROLLES

In good sadness, I do not know; either it is there, or
it is upon a file with the Duke's other letters in my
tent.

FIRST SOLDIER

Here 'tis; here's a paper: shall I read it to you?

PAROLLES

I do not know if it be it or no.

BERTRAM

Our interpreter does it well.

FIRST LORD

Excellently.

FIRST SOLDIER

[*Reads*] Dian, the count's a fool, and full of gold,—

PAROLLES

That is not the Duke's letter, sir; that is an advertisement to a proper maid in Florence, one Diana, to take heed of the allurement of one Count Rousillon, a foolish idle boy, but for all that very ruttish: I pray you, sir, put it up again.

FIRST SOLDIER

Nay, I'll read it first, by your favour.

PAROLLES

My meaning in 't, I protest, was very honest in the behalf of the maid; for I knew the young count to be a dangerous and lascivious boy, who is a whale to virginity and devours up all the fry it finds.

BERTRAM

Damnable both-sides rogue!

FIRST SOLDIER

[*Reads*] When he swears oaths, bid him drop gold, and take it;
   After he scores, he never pays the score:
Half won is match well made; match, and well make it,
   He ne'er pays after-debts, take it before;
And say a soldier, Dian, told thee this,
Men are to mell with, boys are not to kiss:
For count of this, the count's a fool, I know it,
Who pays before, but not when he does owe it.

   Thine, as he vowed to thee in thine ear,
                   PAROLLES.

BERTRAM

He shall be whipped through the army with this rhyme in 's forehead.

SECOND LORD

This is your devoted friend, sir, the manifold linguist and the armipotent soldier.

BERTRAM

I could endure any thing before but a cat, and now he's a cat to me.

FIRST SOLDIER

I perceive, sir, by the general's looks, we shall be fain to hang you.

PAROLLES

My life, sir, in any case: not that I am afraid to die; but that, my offences being many, I would repent out the remainder of nature: let me live, sir, in a dungeon, i' the stocks, or any where, so I may live.

We'll see what may be done, so you confess freely; therefore, once more to this Captain Dumain: you have answered to his reputation with the Duke and to his valour: what is his honesty?

PAROLLES

He will steal, sir, an egg out of a cloister: for rapes and ravishments he parallels Nessus: he professes not keeping of oaths; in breaking 'em he is stronger than Hercules: he will lie, sir, with such volubility, that you would think truth were a fool: drunkenness is his best virtue, for he will be swine-drunk; and in his sleep he does little harm, save to his bed-clothes about him; but they know his conditions and lay him in straw. I have but little more to say, sir, of his honesty: he has every thing that an honest man should not have; what an honest man should have, he has nothing.

FIRST LORD

I begin to love him for this.

BERTRAM

For this description of thine honesty? A pox upon him for me, he's more and more a cat.

FIRST SOLDIER

What say you to his expertness in war?

PAROLLES

Faith, sir, has led the drum before the English tragedians; to belie him, I will not, and more of his soldiership I know not; except, in that country he had the honour to be the officer at a place there called Mile-end, to instruct for the doubling of files: I would do the man what honour I can, but of this I am not certain.

FIRST LORD

He hath out-villained villany so far, that the rarity redeems him.

BERTRAM

A pox on him, he's a cat still.

FIRST SOLDIER

His qualities being at this poor price, I need not to ask you if gold will corrupt him to revolt.

PAROLLES

Sir, for a quart d'écu he will sell the fee-simple of his salvation, the inheritance of it; and cut the entail from all remainders, and a perpetual succession for it perpetually.

FIRST SOLDIER

What's his brother, the other Captain Dumain?

SECOND LORD

Why does he ask him of me?

FIRST SOLDIER

What's he?

PAROLLES

E'en a crow o' the same nest; not altogether so great as the first in goodness, but greater a great deal in evil: he excels his brother for a coward, yet his brother is reputed one of the best that is: in a retreat he outruns any lackey; marry, in coming on he has the cramp.

FIRST SOLDIER

If your life be saved, will you undertake to betray the Florentine?

PAROLLES

Ay, and the captain of his horse, Count Rousillon.

FIRST SOLDIER

I'll whisper with the general, and know his pleasure.

PAROLLES

[*Aside*] I'll no more drumming; a plague of all drums! Only to seem to deserve well, and to beguile the supposition of that lascivious young boy the count, have I run into this danger. Yet who would have suspected an ambush where I was taken?

FIRST SOLDIER

There is no remedy, sir, but you must die: the general says, you that have so traitorously discovered the secrets of your army and made such pestiferous reports of men very nobly held, can serve the world for no honest use; therefore you must die. Come, headsman, off with his head.

PAROLLES

O Lord, sir, let me live, or let me see my death!

FIRST SOLDIER

That shall you, and take your leave of all your friends.   [*Unblinding him*

So, look about you: know you any here?

BERTRAM

Good morrow, noble captain.

SECOND LORD

God bless you, Captain Parolles.

FIRST LORD

God save you, noble captain.

SECOND LORD

Captain, what greeting will you to my Lord Lafeu? I am for France.

FIRST LORD

Good captain, will you give me a copy of the sonnet you writ to Diana in behalf of the Count Rousillon? an I were not a very coward, I'd compel it of you: but fare you well.   [*Exeunt* BERTRAM *and* LORDS

FIRST SOLDIER

You are undone, captain, all but your scarf; that has a knot on 't yet.

PAROLLES

Who cannot be crushed with a plot?

FIRST SOLDIER

If you could find out a country where but women were that had received so much shame, you might begin an impudent nation. Fare ye well, sir; I am for France too: we shall speak of you there.

[*Exit, with* SOLDIERS

PAROLLES

Yet am I thankful: if my heart were great,
'Twould burst at this. Captain I'll be no more;
But I will eat and drink, and sleep as soft
As captain shall: simply the thing I am
Shall make me live. Who knows himself a braggart,
Let him fear this, for it will come to pass
That every braggart shall be found an ass.
Rust, sword! cool, blushes! and, Parolles, live
Safest in shame! being fool'd, by foolery thrive!
There's place and means for every man alive.
I'll after them.   [*Exit*

SCENE IV. *Florence. The* WIDOW'S *house*

Enter HELENA, WIDOW, *and* DIANA

HELENA

That you may well perceive I have not wrong'd you,

One of the greatest in the Christian world
Shall be my surety; 'fore whose throne 'tis needful,
Ere I can perfect mine intents, to kneel:
Time was, I did him a desired office,
Dear almost as his life; which gratitude
Through flinty Tartar's bosom would peep forth,
And answer, thanks: I duly am inform'd
His Grace is at Marseilles; to which place
We have convenient convoy. You must know,
I am supposed dead: the army breaking,
My husband hies him home; where, heaven aiding,
And by the leave of my good lord the king,
We'll be before our welcome.

WIDOW

Gentle madam,
You never had a servant to whose trust
Your business was more welcome.

HELENA

Nor you, mistress,
Ever a friend whose thoughts more truly labour
To recompense your love: doubt not but heaven
Hath brought me up to be your daughter's dower,
As it hath fated her to be my motive
And helper to a husband. But, O strange men!
That can such sweet use make of what they hate,
When saucy trusting of the cozen'd thoughts
Defiles the pitchy night: so lust doth play
With what it loathes for that which is away.
But more of this hereafter. You, Diana,
Under my poor instructions yet must suffer
Something in my behalf.

DIANA

Let death and honesty
Go with your impositions, I am yours
Upon your will to suffer.

HELENA

Yet, I pray you:
But with the word the time will bring on summer,
When briers shall have leaves as well as thorns,
And be as sweet as sharp. We must away;
Our waggon is prepared, and time revives us:
ALL'S WELL THAT ENDS WELL: still the fine's the crown;
Whate'er the course, the end is the renown. [*Exeunt*

SCENE V. *Rousillon. The* COUNT'S *palace*

Enter COUNTESS, LAFEU, *and* CLOWN

LAFEU

No, no, no, your son was misled with a snipt-taffeta fellow there, whose villanous saffron would have made all the unbaked and doughy youth of a nation in his colour: your daughter-in-law had been alive at this hour, and your son here at home, more advanced by the king than by that red-tailed humble-bee I speak of.

COUNTESS

I would I had not known him; it was the death of the most virtuous gentlewoman that ever nature had praise for creating. If she had partaken of my flesh, and cost me the dearest groans of a mother, I could not have owed her a more rooted love.

LAFEU

'Twas a good lady, 'twas a good lady: we may pick a thousand salads ere we light on such another herb.

CLOWN

Indeed, sir, she was the sweet-marjoram of the salad, or rather, the herb of grace.

LAFEU

They are not herbs, you knave; they are nose-herbs.

CLOWN

I am no great Nebuchadnezzar, sir; I have not much skill in grass.

LAFEU

Whether dost thou profess thyself, a knave or a fool?

CLOWN

A fool, sir, at a woman's service, and a knave at a man's.

LAFEU

Your distinction?

CLOWN

I would cozen the man of his wife and do his service.

LAFEU

So you were a knave at his service, indeed.

CLOWN

And I would give his wife my bauble, sir, to do her service.

LAFEU

I will subscribe for thee, thou art both knave and fool.

CLOWN

At your service.

LAFEU

No, no, no.

CLOWN

Why, sir, if I cannot serve you, I can serve as great a prince as you are.

LAFEU

Who's that? a Frenchman?

CLOWN

Faith, sir, a' has an English name; but his fisnomy is more hotter in France than there.

LAFEU

What prince is that?

CLOWN

The black prince, sir; alias, the prince of darkness; alias, the devil.

LAFEU

Hold thee, there's my purse: I give thee not this to suggest thee from thy master thou talkest of; serve him still.

CLOWN

I am a woodland fellow, sir, that always loved a great fire; and the master I speak of ever keeps a good fire. But, sure, he is the prince of the world; let his nobility remain in 's court. I am for the house with the narrow gate, which I take to be too little for pomp to enter: some that humble themselves may; but the many will be too chill and tender, and they'll be for the flowery way that leads to the broad gate and the great fire.

LAFEU

Go thy ways, I begin to be aweary of thee; and I tell thee so before, because I would not fall out with thee. Go thy ways: let my horses be well looked to, without any tricks.

CLOWN

If I put any tricks upon 'em, sir, they shall be jades' tricks; which are their own right by the law of nature.   [Exit

LAFEU

A shrewd knave and an unhappy.

COUNTESS

So he is. My lord that's gone made himself much sport out of him: by his authority he remains here, which he thinks is a patent for his sauciness; and, indeed, he has no pace, but runs where he will.

LAFEU

I like him well; 'tis not amiss. And I was about to tell you, since I heard of the good lady's death and that my lord your son was upon his return home, I moved the king my master to speak in the behalf of my daughter; which, in the minority of them both, his majesty, out of a self-gracious remembrance, did first propose: his highness hath promised me to do it: and, to stop up the displeasure he hath conceived against your son, there is no fitter matter. How does your ladyship like it?

COUNTESS

With very much content, my lord; and I wish it happily effected.

LAFEU

His highness comes post from Marseilles, of as able body as when he numbered thirty: he will be here to-morrow, or I am deceived by him that in such intelligence hath seldom failed.

COUNTESS

It rejoices me, that I hope I shall see him ere I die. I have letters that my son will be here to-night: I shall beseech your lordship to remain with me till they meet together.

LAFEU

Madam, I was thinking with what manners I might safely be admitted.

COUNTESS

You need but plead your honourable privilege.

LAFEU

Lady, of that I have made a bold charter; but I thank my God it holds yet.

Re-enter CLOWN

CLOWN

O madam, yonder's my lord your son with a patch of velvet on 's face: whether there be a scar under 't or no, the velvet knows; but 'tis a goodly patch of velvet: his left cheek is a cheek of two pile and a half, but his right cheek is worn bare.

LAFEU

A scar nobly got, or a noble scar, is a good livery of honour; so belike is that.

CLOWN

But it is your carbonadoed face.

LAFEU

Let us go see your son, I pray you: I long to talk with the young noble soldier.

CLOWN

Faith, there's a dozen of 'em, with delicate fine hats and most courteous feathers, which bow the head and nod at every man.   [Exeunt

ACT V

SCENE I. Marseilles. A street

Enter HELENA, WIDOW, *and* DIANA, *with two*
ATTENDANTS

HELENA

But this exceeding posting day and night
Must wear your spirits low; we cannot help it:
But since you have made the days and nights as one,
To wear your gentle limbs in my affairs,
Be bold you do so grow in my requital
As nothing can unroot you. In happy time;

Enter a GENTLEMAN

This man may help me to his majesty's ear,
If he would spend his power. God save you, sir.

GENTLEMAN

And you.

HELENA

Sir, I have seen you in the court of France.

GENTLEMAN

I have been sometimes there.

HELENA

I do presume, sir, that you are not fallen
From the report that goes upon your goodness;
And therefore, goaded with most sharp occasions,
Which lay nice manners by, I put you to
The use of your own virtues, for the which
I shall continue thankful.

GENTLEMAN

What's your will?

HELENA

That it will please you
To give this poor petition to the king,
And aid me with that store of power you have
To come into his presence.

GENTLEMAN

The king's not here.

HELENA

Not here, sir!

GENTLEMAN

Not, indeed:
He hence removed last night and with more haste
Than is his use.

WIDOW

Lord, how we lose our pains!

HELENA

ALL'S WELL THAT ENDS WELL yet,
Though time seem so adverse and means unfit.
I do beseech you, whither is he gone?

GENTLEMAN

Marry, as I take it, to Rousillon;
Whither I am going.

HELENA

I do beseech you, sir,
Since you are like to see the king before me,
Commend the paper to his gracious hand,
Which I presume shall render you no blame
But rather make you thank your pains for it.
I will come after you with what good speed
Our means will make us means.

GENTLEMAN

This I'll do for you.

HELENA

And you shall find yourself to be well thank'd,
Whate'er falls more. We must to horse again.
Go, go, provide.   [Exeunt

SCENE II. Rousillon. Before the COUNT's palace

Enter CLOWN, *and* PAROLLES, *following*

PAROLLES

Good Monsieur Lavache, give my Lord Lafeu this letter: I have ere now, sir, been better known to you, when I have held familiarity with fresher clothes; but I am now, sir, muddied in fortune's mood, and smell somewhat strong of her strong displeasure.

CLOWN

Truly, fortune's displeasure is but sluttish, if it smell so strongly as thou speakest of: I will henceforth eat no fish of fortune's buttering. Prithee, allow the wind.

PAROLLES

Nay, you need not to stop your nose, sir; I spake but by a metaphor.

CLOWN

Indeed, sir, if your metaphor stink, I will stop my nose; or against any man's metaphor. Prithee, get thee further.

PAROLLES

Pray you, sir, deliver me this paper.

CLOWN

Foh! prithee, stand away: a paper from fortune's close-stool to give to a nobleman! Look, here he comes himself.

Enter LAFEU

Here is a purr of fortune's, sir, or of fortune's cat,—but not a musk-cat,—that has fallen into the unclean fishpond of her displeasure, and, as he says, is muddied withal: pray you, sir, use the carp as you may; for he looks like a poor, decayed, ingenious, foolish, rascally knave. I do pity his distress in my similes of comfort and leave him to your lordship.

    [Exit

PAROLLES

My lord, I am a man whom fortune hath cruelly
scratched.

LAFEU

And what would you have me to do? 'Tis too late to
pare her nails now. Wherein have you played the
knave with fortune, that she should scratch you,
who of herself is a good lady and would not have
knaves thrive long under her? There's a quart d'écu
for you: let the justices make you and fortune friends:
I am for other business.

PAROLLES

I beseech your honour to hear me one single word.

LAFEU

You beg a single penny more: come, you shall ha 't;
save your word.

PAROLLES

My name, my good lord, is Parolles.

LAFEU

You beg more than 'word,' then. Cox my passion!
give me your hand. How does your drum?

PAROLLES

O my good lord, you were the first that found me!

LAFEU

Was I, in sooth? and I was the first that lost thee.

PAROLLES

It lies in you, my lord, to bring me in some grace,
for you did bring me out.

LAFEU

Out upon thee, knave! dost thou put upon me at
once both the office of God and the devil? One
brings thee in grace and the other brings thee out.
[Trumpets sound] The king's coming; I know by his
trumpets. Sirrah, inquire further after me; I had talk
of you last night: though you are a fool and a knave,
you shall eat; go to, follow.

PAROLLES

I praise God for you.   [Exeunt

SCENE III. Rousillon. The COUNT's palace

Flourish. Enter KING, COUNTESS, LAFEU, the two
FRENCH LORDS, with ATTENDANTS

KING

We lost a jewel of her; and our esteem
Was made much poorer by it: but your son,
As mad in folly, lack'd the sense to know
Her estimation home.

COUNTESS

             'Tis past, my liege;
And I beseech your majesty to make it
Natural rebellion, done i' the blaze of youth;
When oil and fire, too strong for reason's force,
O'erbears it and burns on.

KING

             My honour'd lady,
I have forgiven and forgotten all;

Though my revenges were high bent upon him,
And watch'd the time to shoot.

LAFEU

             This I must say,
But first I beg my pardon, the young lord
Did to his majesty, his mother and his lady
Offence of mighty note; but to himself
The greatest wrong of all. He lost a wife
Whose beauty did astonish the survey
Of richest eyes, whose words all ears took captive,
Whose dear perfection hearts that scorn'd to serve
Humbly call'd mistress.

KING

             Praising what is lost
Makes the remembrance dear. Well, call him hither;
We are reconciled, and the first view shall kill
All repetition: let him not ask our pardon;
The nature of his great offence is dead,
And deeper than oblivion we do bury
The incensing relics of it: let him approach,
A stranger, no offender; and inform him
So 'tis our will he should.

GENTLEMAN

          I shall, my liege.   [Exit

KING

What says he to your daughter? have you spoke?

LAFEU

All that he is hath reference to your highness.

KING

Then shall we have a match. I have letters sent me
That set him high in fame.

Enter BERTRAM

LAFEU

            He looks well on 't.

KING

I am not a day of season,
For thou mayst see a sunshine and a hail
In me at once: but to the brightest beams
Distracted clouds give way; so stand thou forth;
The time is fair again.

BERTRAM

            My high-repented blames,
Dear sovereign, pardon to me.

KING

            All is whole;
Not one word more of the consumed time.
Let's take the instant by the forward top;
For we are old, and on our quick'st decrees
The inaudible and noiseless foot of Time
Steals ere we can effect them. You remember
The daughter of this lord?

BERTRAM

Admiringly, my liege, at first
I stuck my choice upon her, ere my heart
Durst make too bold a herald of my tongue:
Where the impression of mine eye infixing,
Contempt his scornful perspective did lend me,
Which warp'd the line of every other favour;
Scorn'd a fair colour, or express'd it stolen;
Extended or contracted all proportions

To a most hideous object: thence it came
That she whom all men praised and whom myself,
Since I have lost, have loved, was in mine eye
The dust that did offend it.

KING

     Well excused:
That thou didst love her, strikes some scores away
From the great compt: but love that comes too late,
Like a remorseful pardon slowly carried,
To the great sender turns a sour offence,
Crying 'That's good that's gone.' Our rash faults
Make trivial price of serious things we have,
Not knowing them until we know their grave:
Oft our displeasures, to ourselves unjust,
Destroy our friends and after weep their dust:
Our own love waking cries to see what's done,
While shameful hate sleeps out the afternoon.
Be this sweet Helen's knell, and now forget her.
Send forth your amorous token for fair Maudlin:
The main consents are had; and here we'll stay
To see our widower's second marriage-day.

COUNTESS

Which better than the first, O dear heaven, bless!
Or, ere they meet, in me, O nature, cesse!

LAFEU

Come on, my son, in whom my house's name
Must be digested, give a favour from you
To sparkle in the spirits of my daughter,
That she may quickly come. [BERTRAM *gives a ring*]
  By my old beard,
And every hair that's on 't, Helen, that's dead,
Was a sweet creature: such a ring as this,
The last that e'er I took her leave at court,
I saw upon her finger.

BERTRAM

     Hers it was not.

KING

Now, pray you, let me see it; for mine eye,
While I was speaking, oft was fasten'd to 't.
This ring was mine; and, when I gave it Helen,
I bade her, if her fortunes ever stood
Necessitied to help, that by this token
I would relieve her. Had you that craft, to reave her
Of what should stead her most?

BERTRAM

     My gracious sovereign,
Howe'er it pleases you to take it so,
The ring was never hers.

COUNTESS

     Son, on my life,
I have seen her wear it; and she reckon'd it
At her life's rate.

LAFEU

I am sure I saw her wear it.

BERTRAM

You are deceived, my lord; she never saw it:
In Florence was it from a casement thrown me,
Wrapp'd in a paper, which contain'd the name
Of her that threw it: noble she was, and thought
I stood engaged: but when I had subscribed

To mine own fortune and inform'd her fully
I could not answer in that course of honour
As she had made the overture, she ceased
In heavy satisfaction and would never
Receive the ring again.

KING

     Plutus himself,
That knows the tinct and multiplying medicine,
Hath not in nature's mystery more science
Than I have in this ring: 'twas mine, 'twas Helen's,
Whoever gave it you. Then, if you know
That you are well acquainted with yourself,
Confess 'twas hers, and by what rough enforcement
You got it from her: she call'd the saints to surety
That she would never put it from her finger,
Unless she gave it to yourself in bed,
Where you have never come, or sent it us
Upon her great disaster.

BERTRAM

     She never saw it.

KING

Thou speak'st it falsely, as I love mine honour;
And makest conjectural fears to come into me,
Which I would fain shut out. If it should prove
That thou art so inhuman,—'twill not prove so;—
And yet I know not: thou didst hate her deadly,
And she is dead; which nothing, but to close
Her eyes myself, could win me to believe,
More than to see this ring. Take him away.

[GUARDS *seize* BERTRAM

My fore-past proofs, howe'er the matter fall,
Shall tax my fears of little vanity,
Having vainly fear'd too little. Away with him!
We'll sift this matter further.

BERTRAM

     If you shall prove
This ring was ever hers, you shall as easy
Prove that I husbanded her bed in Florence,
Where yet she never was. [*Exit, guarded*

KING

I am wrapp'd in dismal thinkings.

Enter a GENTLEMAN

GENTLEMAN

     Gracious sovereign,
Whether I have been to blame or no, I know not:
Here's a petition from a Florentine,
Who hath for four or five removes come short
To tender it herself. I undertook it,
Vanquish'd thereto by the fair grace and speech
Of the poor suppliant, who by this I know
Is here attending: her business looks in her
With an importing visage; and she told me,
In a sweet verbal brief, it did concern
Your highness with herself.

KING

[*Reads*] Upon his many protestations to marry me when his
wife was dead, I blush to say it, he won me. Now is the Count
Rousillon a widower: his vows are forfeited to me, and my
honour's paid to him. He stole from Florence, taking no leave,
and I follow him to his country for justice: grant it me, O

king! in you it best lies; otherwise a seducer flourishes, and a
poor maid is undone.

                             DIANA CAPILET.

LAFEU

I will buy me a son-in-law in a fair, and toll for this:
I'll none of him.

KING

The heavens have thought well on thee, Lafeu,
To bring forth this discovery. Seek these suitors:
Go speedily and bring again the count.
I am afeard the life of Helen, lady,
Was foully snatch'd.

COUNTESS

              Now, justice on the doers!

Re-enter BERTRAM, *guarded*

KING

I wonder, sir, sith wives are monsters to you,
And that you fly them as you swear them lordship,
Yet you desire to marry.

Enter WIDOW *and* DIANA

              What woman's that?

DIANA

I am, my lord, a wretched Florentine,
Derived from the ancient Capilet:
My suit, as I do understand, you know,
And therefore know how far I may be pitied.

WIDOW

I am her mother, sir, whose age and honour
Both suffer under this complaint we bring,
And both shall cease, without your remedy.

KING

Come hither, count; do you know these women?

BERTRAM

My lord, I neither can nor will deny
But that I know them: do they charge me further?

DIANA

Why do you look so strange upon your wife?

BERTRAM

She's none of mine, my lord.

DIANA

              If you shall marry,
You give away this hand, and that is mine;
You give away heaven's vows, and those are mine;
You give away myself, which is known mine;
For I by vow am so embodied yours,
That she which marries you must marry me,
Either both or none.

LAFEU

Your reputation comes too short for my daughter;
you are no husband for her.

BERTRAM

My lord, this is a fond and desperate creature,
Whom sometime I have laugh'd with: let your highness
Lay a more noble thought upon mine honour
Than for to think that I would sink it here.

KING

Sir, for my thoughts, you have them ill to friend
Till your deeds gain them: fairer prove your honour
Than in my thought it lies.

DIANA

             Good my lord,
Ask him upon his oath, if he does think
He had not my virginity.

KING

What say'st thou to her?

BERTRAM

             She's impudent, my lord,
And was a common gamester to the camp.

DIANA

He does me wrong, my lord; if I were so,
He might have bought me at a common price:
Do not believe him. O, behold this ring,
Whose high respect and rich validity
Did lack a parallel; yet for all that
He gave it to a commoner o' the camp,
If I be one.

COUNTESS

             He blushes, and 'tis it:
Of six preceding ancestors, that gem,
Conferr'd by testament to the sequent issue,
Hath it been owed and worn. This is his wife;
That ring's a thousand proofs.

KING

             Methought you said
You saw one here in court could witness it.

DIANA

I did, my lord, but loath am to produce
So bad an instrument: his name's Parolles.

LAFEU

I saw the man to-day, if man he be.

KING

Find him, and bring him hither.

                         [Exit an ATTENDANT

BERTRAM

             What of him?
He's quoted for a most perfidious slave,
With all the spots o' the world tax'd and debosh'd;
Whose nature sickens but to speak a truth.
Am I or that or this for what he'll utter,
That will speak any thing?

KING

             She hath that ring of yours.

BERTRAM

I think she has: certain it is I liked her,
And boarded her i' the wanton way of youth:
She knew her distance, and did angle for me,
Madding my eagerness with her restraint,
As all impediments in fancy's course
Are motives of more fancy; and, in fine,
Her infinite cunning, with her modern grace,
Subdued me to her rate: she got the ring;
And I had that which any inferior might
At market-price have bought.

DIANA

             I must be patient:
You, that have turn'd off a first so noble wife,
May justly diet me. I pray you yet,
Since you lack virtue I will lose a husband,

Send for your ring, I will return it home,
And give me mine again.

BERTRAM

I have it not.

KING

What ring was yours, I pray you?

DIANA

Sir, much like
The same upon your finger.

KING

Know you this ring? this ring was his of late.

DIANA

And this was it I gave him, being abed.

KING

The story then goes false, you threw it him
Out of a casement.

DIANA

I have spoke the truth.

Enter PAROLLES

BERTRAM

My lord, I do confess the ring was hers.

KING

You boggle shrewdly, every feather starts you
Is this the man you speak of?

DIANA

Ay, my lord.

KING

Tell me, sirrah, but tell me true, I charge you,
Not fearing the displeasure of your master,
Which on your just proceeding I'll keep off,
By him and by this woman here what know you?

PAROLLES

So please your majesty, my master hath been an
honourable gentleman: tricks he hath had in him,
which gentlemen have.

KING

Come, come, to the purpose: did he love this
woman?

PAROLLES

Faith, sir, he did love her; but how?

KING

How, I pray you?

PAROLLES

He did love her, sir, as a gentleman loves a woman.

KING

How is that?

PAROLLES

He loved her, sir, and loved her not.

KING

As thou art a knave, and no knave. What an equivocal companion is this!

PAROLLES

I am a poor man, and at your majesty's command.

LAFEU

He's a good drum, my lord, but a naughty orator.

DIANA

Do you know he promised me marriage?

PAROLLES

Faith, I know more than I'll speak.

KING

But wilt thou not speak all thou knowest?

PAROLLES

Yes, so please your majesty. I did go between them,
as I said; but more than that, he loved her: for indeed he was mad for her, and talked of Satan, and
of Limbo, and of Furies, and I know not what; yet
I was in that credit with them at that time, that I
knew of their going to bed, and of other motions, as
promising her marriage, and things which would
derive me ill will to speak of; therefore I will not
speak what I know.

KING

Thou hast spoken all already, unless thou canst say
they are married: but thou art too fine in thy evidence; therefore stand aside.
This ring, you say, was yours?

DIANA

Ay, my good lord.

KING

Where did you buy it? or who gave it you?

DIANA

It was not given me, nor I did not buy it.

KING

Who lent it you?

DIANA

It was not lent me neither.

KING

Where did you find it, then?

DIANA

I found it not.

KING

If it were yours by none of all these ways,
How could you give it him?

DIANA

I never gave it him.

LAFEU

This woman's an easy glove, my lord; she goes off
and on at pleasure.

KING

This ring was mine; I gave it his first wife.

DIANA

It might be yours or hers, for aught I know.

KING

Take her away; I do not like her now;
To prison with her: and away with him.
Unless thou tell'st me where thou hadst this ring,
Thou diest within this hour.

DIANA

I'll never tell you.

KING

Take her away.

DIANA

I'll put in bail, my liege.

KING

I think thee now some common customer.

DIANA

By Jove, if ever I knew man, 'twas you.

KING

Wherefore hast thou accused him all this while?

DIANA

Because he's guilty, and he is not guilty:
He knows I am no maid, and he'll swear to 't;
I'll swear I am a maid, and he knows not.
Great king, I am no strumpet, by my life;
I am either maid, or else this old man's wife.

KING

She does abuse our ears: to prison with her.

DIANA

Good mother, fetch my bail. Stay, royal sir:
                                    [*Exit* WIDOW
The jeweller that owes the ring is sent for,
And he shall surety me. But for this lord,
Who hath abused me, as he knows himself,
Though yet he never harm'd me, here I quit him:
He knows himself my bed he hath defiled;
And at that time he got his wife with child:
Dead though she be, she feels her young one kick:
So there's my riddle,—One that's dead is quick:
And now behold the meaning.
            Re-enter WIDOW, *with* HELENA

KING

                        Is there no exorcist
Beguiles the truer office of mine eyes?
Is 't real that I see?

HELENA

              No, my good lord;
'Tis but the shadow of a wife you see,
The name and not the thing.

BERTRAM

                    Both, both. O, pardon!

HELENA

O my good lord, when I was like this maid,
I found you wondrous kind. There is your ring;
And, look you, here's your letter; this it says:
'When from my finger you can get this ring
And are by me with child,' &c. This is done:
Will you be mine, now you are doubly won?

BERTRAM

If she, my liege, can make me know this clearly,
I'll love her dearly, ever, ever dearly.

HELENA

If it appear not plain and prove untrue,
Deadly divorce step between me and you!
O my dear mother, do I see you living?

LAFEU

Mine eyes smell onions; I shall weep anon:
[*To* PAROLLES] Good Tom Drum, lend me a handkercher: so, I thank thee: wait on me home, I'll
make sport with thee: let thy courtesies alone, they
are scurvy ones.

KING

Let us from point to point this story know,
To make the even truth in pleasure flow.
[*To* DIANA] If thou be'st yet a fresh uncropped
    flower,
Choose thou thy husband, and I'll pay thy dower;
For I can guess that by thy honest aid
Thou kept'st a wife herself, thyself a maid.
Of that and all the progress, more and less,
Resolvedly more leisure shall express:
All yet seems well; and if it end so meet,
The bitter past, more welcome is the sweet. [*Flourish*

EPILOGUE

KING

The king's a beggar, now the play is done:
All is well ended, if this suit be won,
That you express content; which we will pay,
With strife to please you, day exceeding day:
Ours be your patience then, and yours our parts;
Your gentle hands lend us, and take our hearts.
                                    [*Exeunt*

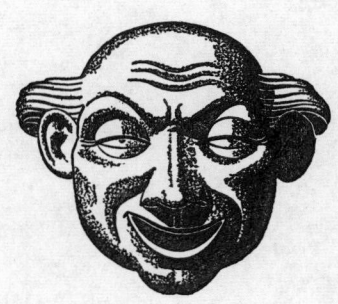

DIANA
Because he's guilty, and he is not guilty:
He knows I am no maid, and he'll swear to 't;
I'll swear I am a maid, and he knows not.
Great king, I am no strumpet, by my life;
I am either maid, or else this old man's wife.

KING
She does abuse our ears: to prison with her.

DIANA
Good mother, fetch my bail. Stay, royal sir:
[Exit Widow]
The jeweller that owes the ring is sent for,
And he shall surety me. But for this lord,
Who hath abused me, as he knows himself,
Though yet he never harm'd me, here I quit him:
He knows himself my bed he hath defiled;
And at that time he got his wife with child:
Dead though she be, she feels her young one kick:
So there's my riddle—one that's dead is quick:
And now behold the meaning.
Re-enter WIDOW, with HELENA

KING
Is there no exorcist
Beguiles the truer office of mine eyes?
Is 't real that I see?

HELENA
No, my good lord;
'Tis but the shadow of a wife you see,
The name and not the thing.

BERTRAM
Both, both. O, pardon!

HELENA
O my good lord, when I was like this maid,
I found you wondrous kind. There is your ring;
And, look you, here's your letter; this it says:
'When from my finger you can get this ring
And are by me with child,' &c. This is done:
Will you be mine, now you are doubly won?

BERTRAM
If she, my liege, can make me know this clearly,
I'll love her dearly, ever, ever dearly.

HELENA
If it appear not plain and prove untrue,
Deadly divorce step between me and you!
O my dear mother, do I see you living?

LAFEU
Mine eyes smell onions; I shall weep anon:
[To Parolles] Good Tom Drum, lend me a hand-kerchief: so, I thank thee: wait on me home, I'll make sport with thee: let thy courtesies alone, they are scurvy ones.

KING
Let us from point to point this story know,
To make the even truth in pleasure flow.
[To Diana] If thou be'st yet a fresh uncropp'd flower,
Choose thou thy husband, and I'll pay thy dower;
For I can guess that by thy honest aid
Thou keep'st a wife herself, thyself a maid.
Of that and all the progress, more and less,
Resolvedly more leisure shall express:
All yet seems well; and if it end so meet,
The bitter past, more welcome is the sweet. [Flourish.

EPILOGUE

KING
The king's a beggar, now the play is done:
All is well ended, if this suit be won,
That you express content; which we will pay,
With strife to please you, day exceeding day:
Ours be your patience then, and yours our parts;
Your gentle hands lend us, and take our hearts. [Exeunt.

MEASURE FOR MEASURE

SYNOPSIS

No one knows better the widespread moral corruption in the private lives of Vienna's citizens than the Duke, the kindly, philosophical Vincentio, but he also knows that he is largely to blame for the existing conditions by allowing corrective laws to become dead letters. He fears, too, that after permitting such laxity for fourteen years, it will seem tyrannical if he himself attempts to revive the disused laws, and he decides to place full control of state affairs and moral reform in the hands of Angelo, an official of well-known austerity and purity of life, with the sober old Escalus as counsellor.

The Duke quietly leaves on an announced visit to Poland, but, desiring to spy unknown on the rule of his deputies, he disguises himself as a friar and returns to Vienna just as Claudio, a young nobleman, is arrested under one of the newly-restored laws, and paraded in disgrace through the streets. Claudio's fiancée Juliet, who is soon to bear him a child, is visited in prison by the friar who learns that the young couple love each other sincerely, were formally betrothed and would have been married, except for some legal difficulties about her dowry. The severity of the new governor gives Claudio's supporters little hope that he will escape the death penalty for his sin, but Escalus and a justice intercede with Angelo, and Lucio, a friend of Claudio's and a professed rake, goes at his request to bring his sister Isabella from the convent where she is a newly-entered novice to plead for his pardon.

Adamant to all petitions for mercy and clemency, Angelo is only moved when his cold nature, supposedly free from common human weaknesses, responds to a sudden passion which the beautiful novice arouses in him. In their second interview, he plainly tells her that her brother's pardon will be gained only at the sacrifice of her own honor, and when with her disgusted refusal she threatens to reveal his true character in public, he remarks calmly that no one will believe her. Hastening to her brother in prison, Isabella despairingly tells him of Angelo's shameful proposal and Claudio at first upholds her decision, but the fear of death quickly overwhelms him and he implores her to yield. Her scornful rejoinder is cut short by the entrance of the supposed friar who has overheard their conversation, and taking Isabella aside suggests another way of saving her brother.

He tells her of the noble lady Mariana, to whom Angelo five years ago was betrothed, but before the wedding could take place the girl's brother had been lost at sea with all her dowry, and Angelo had refused to marry her, hinting at some dishonorable episode in her life. The friar proposes that Isabella pretend to yield to Angelo and arrange to meet him at midnight when his discarded bride Mariana would take her place. Mariana's consent is readily obtained and the plan is carried out successfully, except for Angelo's promise of Claudio's release which he breaks, fearing public exposure, and orders the young nobleman beheaded.

At the friar's instigation, the Provost of the prison puts Claudio in hiding and sends Angelo the head of a prisoner resembling him who had just died a natural death. The friar allows Isabella to think that her brother had been executed, and advises her to appeal for justice to the Duke upon his arrival home the next day.

Letters announcing the Duke's return are received by the Deputy who, accompanied by Escalus and other officials, meets him at the city gates where Isabella, kneeling before him, publicly brands Angelo as a murderer, hypocrite and virgin-violator. The Duke professes anger and has her arrested, leaving Angelo to proceed at once with her trial and to investigate also the claims of the veiled Mariana who says she is the Deputy's wife. He then adds a request that someone be sent for the rascally friar who has been seen lately in the women's company.

Returning shortly as the friar, he makes such fierce accusations against the government that Escalus orders him to prison, while the rakish Lucio, in the crowd, vows that he is the man who slandered the Duke to him and repeats, as the friar's words, the selfsame treasonable speeches that he had once made to the Duke in disguise. Suddenly attacking the supposed friar as a false witness, Lucio pulls off his hood, and the Duke stands revealed. He orders Lucio detained, pardons the old Escalus, and turns to Angelo asking him what he has to say for himself. Stunned by this sudden turn in affairs, Angelo begs the Duke not to try him but to sentence him to death on his own confession.

The Duke orders him first to marry Mariana, then sentences him, telling his wife that with his possessions the state will buy her a better husband, but Mariana, protesting that she loves Angelo in spite of all his wrongs, not only begs herself for his life but asks Isabella to kneel with her in petitioning the Duke. To the great relief of all concerned, Claudio is now produced. The Duke orders him to marry Juliet, pardons Angelo, sends Lucio to prison, and proposes to Isabella.

HISTORICAL DATA

The original story forming the plot of *Measure for Measure* is to be found in a romance in the *Hecatom-mithi* of Giraldi Cinthio (1565), who dramatized the same story in his *Epitia*. From this George Whetstone derived the plot for his double drama *Promos and Cassandra* (1578) and for a prose version which appeared in his *Heptameron of Civil Discourses* in 1582. From Whetstone Shakespeare almost certainly took the sordid story of the perfidy of Angelo.

Shakespeare, however, raised the level of the play enormously, ennobling the heroine and eliminating many of the crudities and brutalities of its proto-type. The character of Mariana appears to be wholly his creation, as is the conception of the Duke's disguise and his final proposal of marriage to Isabella.

In spite of a certain effort to uplift the play, however, it was criticized by Coleridge as being "the most painful" of Shakespeare's plays, and it certainly has always been the least popular.

It was performed at Court in 1604, and allusions to King James (Act I, Scene i and Act II, Scene iv) give evidence that it was written the same year. It first appeared in print in the First Folio in 1623.

*"And did supply thee at thy garden house
In her imagin'd person."*

MEASURE FOR MEASURE

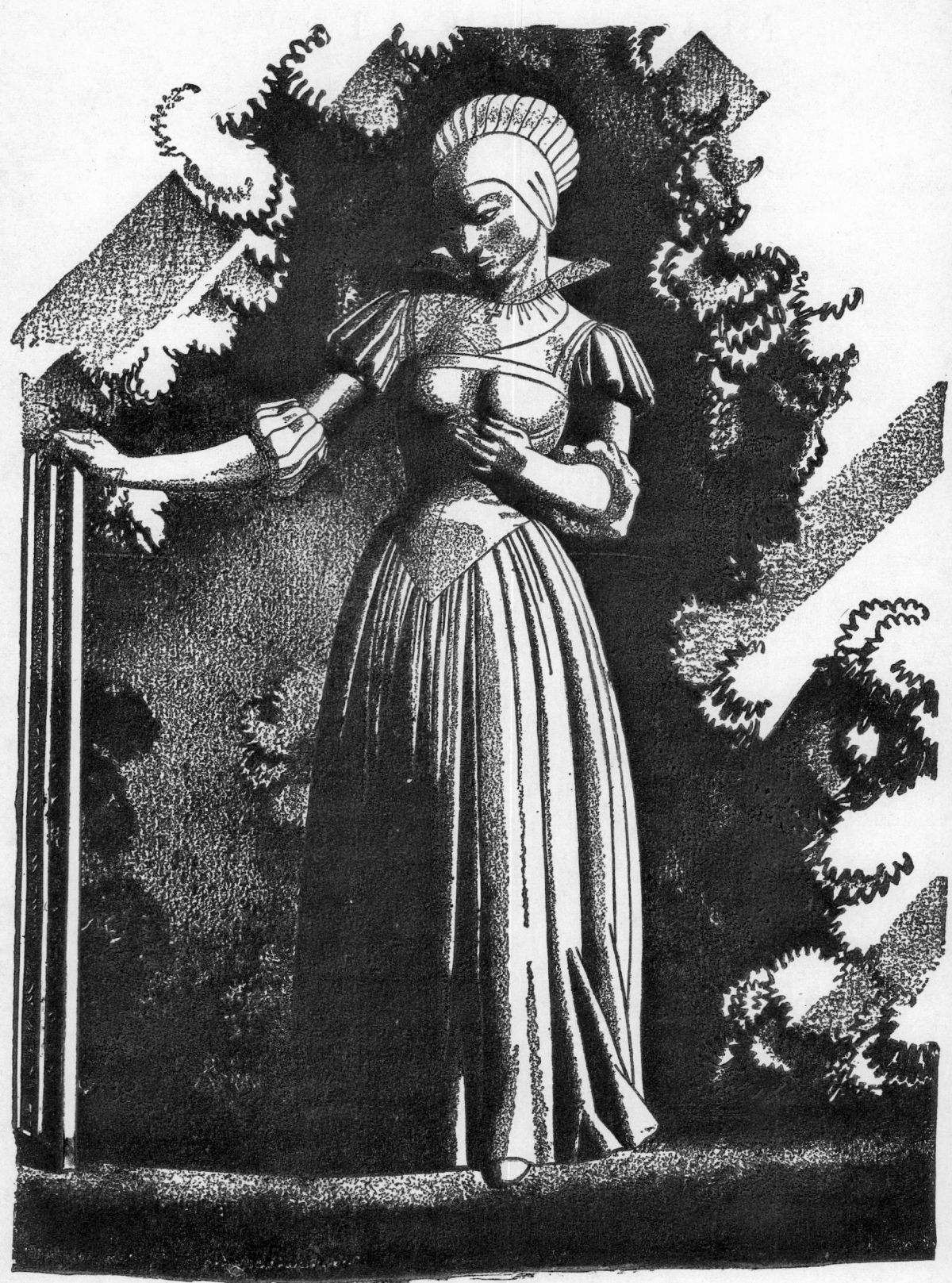

MEASURE FOR MEASURE

DRAMATIS PERSONÆ

VINCENTIO, *the Duke.*
ANGELO, *Deputy.*
ESCALUS, *an ancient Lord.*
CLAUDIO, *a young gentleman.*
LUCIO, *a fantastic.*
TWO OTHER GENTLEMEN.
PROVOST.
THOMAS, } *two friars.*
PETER, }
A JUSTICE.
VARRIUS.
ELBOW, *a simple constable.*

FROTH, *a foolish gentleman.*
POMPEY, *servant to Mistress Overdone.*
ABHORSON, *an executioner.*
BARNARDINE, *a dissolute prisoner.*

ISABELLA, *sister to Claudio.*
MARIANA, *betrothed to Angelo.*
JULIET, *beloved of Claudio.*
FRANCISCA, *a nun.*
MISTRESS OVERDONE, *a bawd.*

LORDS, OFFICERS, CITIZENS, BOY, *and* ATTENDANTS.

SCENE—*Vienna.*

ACT I

SCENE I. *An apartment in the* DUKE's *palace*

Enter DUKE, ESCALUS, LORDS *and* ATTENDANTS

DUKE

Escalus.

ESCALUS

My lord.

DUKE

Of government the properties to unfold,
Would seem in me to affect speech and discourse;
Since I am put to know that your own science
Exceeds, in that, the lists of all advice
My strength can give you: then no more remains,
But that to your sufficiency . . . . . .
. . . . as your worth is able,
And let them work. The nature of our people,
Our city's institutions, and the terms
For common justice, you're as pregnant in
As art and practice hath enriched any
That we remember. There is our commission,
From which we would not have you warp. Call hither,
I say, bid come before us Angelo.
[*Exit an* ATTENDANT
What figure of us think you he will bear?
For you must know, we have with special soul
Elected him our absence to supply;
Lent him our terror, dress'd him with our love,
And given his deputation all the organs
Of our own power: what think you of it?

ESCALUS

If any in Vienna be of worth
To undergo such ample grace and honour,
It is Lord Angelo.

DUKE

Look where he comes.

Enter ANGELO

ANGELO

Always obedient to your Grace's will,
I come to know your pleasure.

DUKE

Angelo,
There is a kind of character in thy life,
That to th' observer doth thy history
Fully unfold. Thyself and thy belongings
Are not thine own so proper, as to waste
Thyself upon thy virtues, they on thee.
Heaven doth with us as we with torches do,
Not light them for themselves; for if our virtues
Did not go forth of us, 'twere all alike
As if we had them not. Spirits are not finely touch'd
But to fine issues; nor Nature never lends
The smallest scruple of her excellence,
But, like a thrifty goddess, she determines
Herself the glory of a creditor,
Both thanks and use. But I do bend my speech
To one that can my part in him advertise;
Hold therefore, Angelo:—
In our remove be thou at full ourself;
Mortality and mercy in Vienna
Live in thy tongue and heart: old Escalus,
Though first in question, is thy secondary.
Take thy commission.

ANGELO

Now, good my lord,
Let there be some more test made of my metal,
Before so noble and so great a figure
Be stamp'd upon it.

DUKE

No more evasion:
We have with a leaven'd and prepared choice
Proceeded to you; therefore take your honours.
Our haste from hence is of so quick condition,
That it prefers itself, and leaves unquestion'd
Matters of needful value. We shall write to you,
As time and our concernings shall importune,
How it goes with us; and do look to know
What doth befall you here. So, fare you well:
To the hopeful execution do I leave you
Of your commissions.

ANGELO

Yet, give leave, my lord,
That we may bring you something on the way.

DUKE

My haste may not admit it;
Nor need you, on mine honour, have to do
With any scruple; your scope is as mine own,
So to enforce or qualify the laws
As to your soul seems good. Give me your hand:
I'll privily away. I love the people,
But do not like to stage me to their eyes:
Though it do well, I do not relish well
Their loud applause and Aves vehement;
Nor do I think the man of safe discretion
That does affect it. Once more, fare you well.

ANGELO

The heavens give safety to your purposes!

ESCALUS

Lead forth and bring you back in happiness!

DUKE

I thank you. Fare you well.   [*Exit*

ESCALUS

I shall desire you, sir, to give me leave
To have free speech with you; and it concerns me
To look into the bottom of my place:
A power I have, but of what strength and nature
I am not yet instructed.

ANGELO

'Tis so with me. Let us withdraw together,
And we may soon our satisfaction have
Touching that point.

ESCALUS

I'll wait upon your honour.
     [*Exeunt*

SCENE II. *A street*

Enter LUCIO *and two* GENTLEMEN

LUCIO

If the Duke, with the other dukes, come not to composition with the King of Hungary, why then all the
dukes fall upon the king.

FIRST GENTLEMAN

Heaven grant us its peace, but not the King of Hungary's!

SECOND GENTLEMAN

Amen.

LUCIO

Thou concludest like the sanctimonious pirate, that
went to sea with the Ten Commandments, but scraped
one out of the table.

SECOND GENTLEMAN

'Thou shalt not steal'?

LUCIO

Ay, that he razed.

FIRST GENTLEMAN

Why, 'twas a commandment to command the captain and all the rest from their functions: they put
forth to steal. There's not a soldier of us all, that, in

the thanksgiving before meat, do relish the petition
well that prays for peace.

SECOND GENTLEMAN

I never heard any soldier dislike it.

LUCIO

I believe thee; for I think thou never wast where
grace was said.

SECOND GENTLEMAN

No? a dozen times at least.

FIRST GENTLEMAN

What, in metre?

LUCIO

In any proportion or in any language.

FIRST GENTLEMAN

I think, or in any religion.

LUCIO

Ay, why not? Grace is grace, despite of all controversy: as, for example, thou thyself art a wicked villain, despite of all grace.

FIRST GENTLEMAN

Well, there went but a pair of shears between us.

LUCIO

I grant; as there may between the lists and the velvet. Thou art the list.

FIRST GENTLEMAN

And thou the velvet: thou art good velvet; thou'rt a
three-piled piece, I warrant thee: I had as lief be a
list of an English kersey, as be piled, as thou art piled,
for a French velvet. Do I speak feelingly now?

LUCIO

I think thou dost; and, indeed, with most painful
feeling of thy speech: I will, out of thine own confession, learn to begin thy health; but, whilst I live,
forget to drink after thee.

FIRST GENTLEMAN

I think I have done myself wrong, have I not?

SECOND GENTLEMAN

Yes, that thou hast, whether thou art tainted or free.

LUCIO

Behold, behold, where Madam Mitigation comes! I
have purchased as many diseases under her roof as
come to—

SECOND GENTLEMAN

To what, I pray?

LUCIO

Judge.

SECOND GENTLEMAN

To three thousand dolours a year.

FIRST GENTLEMAN

Ay, and more.

LUCIO

A French crown more.

FIRST GENTLEMAN

Thou art always figuring diseases in me; but thou
art full of error; I am sound.

LUCIO

Nay, not as one would say, healthy; but so sound as
things that are hollow: thy bones are hollow; impiety has made a feast of thee.

Enter MISTRESS OVERDONE

FIRST GENTLEMAN

How now! which of your hips has the most profound sciatica?

MISTRESS OVERDONE

Well, well; there's one yonder arrested and carried to prison was worth five thousand of you all.

SECOND GENTLEMAN

Who's that, I pray thee?

MISTRESS OVERDONE

Marry, sir, that's Claudio, Signior Claudio.

FIRST GENTLEMAN

Claudio to prison? 'tis not so.

MISTRESS OVERDONE

Nay, but I know 'tis so: I saw him arrested; saw him carried away; and, which is more, within these three days his head to be chopped off.

LUCIO

But, after all this fooling, I would not have it so. Art thou sure of this?

MISTRESS OVERDONE

I am too sure of it: and it is for getting Madam Julietta with child.

LUCIO

Believe me, this may be: he promised to meet me two hours since, and he was ever precise in promise-keeping.

SECOND GENTLEMAN

Besides, you know, it draws something near to the speech we had to such a purpose.

FIRST GENTLEMAN

But, most of all, agreeing with the proclamation.

LUCIO

Away! let's go learn the truth of it.

[*Exeunt* LUCIO *and* GENTLEMEN

MISTRESS OVERDONE

Thus, what with the war, what with the sweat, what with the gallows, and what with poverty, I am custom-shrunk.

Enter POMPEY

How now! what's the news with you?

POMPEY

Yonder man is carried to prison.

MISTRESS OVERDONE

Well; what has he done?

POMPEY

A woman.

MISTRESS OVERDONE

But what's his offence?

POMPEY

Groping for trouts in a peculiar river.

MISTRESS OVERDONE

What, is there a maid with child by him?

POMPEY

No, but there's a woman with maid by him. You have not heard of the proclamation, have you?

MISTRESS OVERDONE

What proclamation, man?

POMPEY

All houses in the suburbs of Vienna must be plucked down.

MISTRESS OVERDONE

And what shall become of those in the city?

POMPEY

They shall stand for seed: they had gone down too, but that a wise burgher put in for them.

MISTRESS OVERDONE

But shall all our houses of resort in the suburbs be pulled down?

POMPEY

To the ground, mistress.

MISTRESS OVERDONE

Why, here's a change indeed in the commonwealth! What shall become of me?

POMPEY

Come; fear not you: good counsellors lack no clients: though you change your place, you need not change your trade; I'll be your tapster still. Courage! there will be pity taken on you: you that have worn your eyes almost out in the service, you will be considered.

MISTRESS OVERDONE

What's to do here, Thomas tapster? let's withdraw.

POMPEY

Here comes Signior Claudio, led by the provost to prison; and there's Madam Juliet.   [*Exeunt*

Enter PROVOST, CLAUDIO, JULIET, *and* OFFICERS

CLAUDIO

Fellow, why dost thou show me thus to the world?
Bear me to prison, where I am committed.

PROVOST

I do it not in evil disposition,
But from Lord Angelo by special charge.

CLAUDIO

Thus can the demigod Authority
Make us pay down for our offence by weight
The words of heaven;—on whom it will, it will;
On whom it will not, so; yet still 'tis just.

Re-enter LUCIO *and two* GENTLEMEN

LUCIO

Why, how now, Claudio! whence comes this restraint?

CLAUDIO

From too much liberty, my Lucio, liberty:
As surfeit is the father of much fast,
So every scope by the immoderate use
Turns to restraint. Our natures do pursue,
Like rats that ravin down their proper bane,
A thirsty evil; and when we drink we die.

LUCIO

If I could speak so wisely under an arrest, I would send for certain of my creditors: and yet, to say the truth, I had as lief have the foppery of freedom as the morality of imprisonment. What's thy offence, Claudio?

CLAUDIO

What but to speak of would offend again.

LUCIO

What, is't murder?

CLAUDIO

No.

LUCIO

Lechery?

CLAUDIO

Call it so.

PROVOST

Away, sir! you must go.

CLAUDIO

One word, good friend. Lucio, a word with you.

LUCIO

A hundred, if they'll do you any good.
Is lechery so look'd after?

CLAUDIO

Thus stands it with me: upon a true contract
I got possession of Julietta's bed:
You know the lady; she is fast my wife,
Save that we do the denunciation lack
Of outward order: this we came not to,
Only for propagation of a dower
Remaining in the coffer of her friends;
From whom we thought it meet to hide our love
Till time had made them for us. But it chances
The stealth of our most mutual entertainment
With character too gross is writ on Juliet.

LUCIO

With child, perhaps?

CLAUDIO

Unhappily, even so.
And the new Deputy now for the Duke,—
Whether it be the fault and glimpse of newness,
Or whether that the body public be
A horse whereon the governor doth ride,
Who, newly in the seat, that it may know
He can command, lets it straight feel the spur;
Whether the tyranny be in his place,
Or in his eminence that fills it up,
I stagger in:—but this new governor
Awakes me all the enrolled penalties
Which have, like unscour'd armour, hung by the wall
So long, that nineteen zodiacs have gone round,
And none of them been worn; and, for a name,
Now puts the drowsy and neglected act
Freshly on me: 'tis surely for a name.

LUCIO

I warrant it is: and thy head stands so tickle on thy
shoulders, that a milkmaid, if she be in love, may
sigh it off. Send after the Duke, and appeal to him.

CLAUDIO

I have done so, but he's not to be found. I prithee,
Lucio, do me this kind service:
This day my sister should the cloister enter
And there receive her approbation:
Acquaint her with the danger of my state;
Implore her, in my voice, that she make friends
To the strict deputy; bid herself assay him:
I have great hope in that; for in her youth
There is a prone and speechless dialect,
Such as move men; beside, she hath prosperous art

When she will play with reason and discourse,
And well she can persuade.

LUCIO

I pray she may; as well for the encouragement of the
like, which else would stand under grievous imposition, as for the enjoying of thy life, who I would be
sorry should be thus foolishly lost at a game of tick-
tack. I'll to her.

CLAUDIO

I thank you, good friend Lucio.

LUCIO

Within two hours.

CLAUDIO

Come, officer, away!   [Exeunt

SCENE III. A monastery

Enter DUKE and FRIAR THOMAS

DUKE

No, holy father; throw away that thought;
Believe not that the dribbling dart of love
Can pierce a complete bosom. Why I desire thee
To give me secret harbour, hath a purpose
More grave and wrinkled than the aims and ends
Of burning youth.

FRIAR THOMAS

May your grace speak of it?

DUKE

My holy sir, none better knows than you
How I have ever loved the life removed,
And held in idle price to haunt assemblies
Where youth, and cost, and witless bravery keeps.
I have deliver'd to Lord Angelo,
A man of stricture and firm abstinence,
My absolute power and place here in Vienna,
And he supposes me travell'd to Poland;
For so I have strew'd it in the common ear,
And so it is received. Now, pious sir,
You will demand of me why I do this.

FRIAR THOMAS

Gladly, my lord.

DUKE

We have strict statutes and most biting laws,
The needful bits and curbs to headstrong weeds,
Which for this fourteen years we have let slip;
Even like an o'ergrown lion in a cave,
That goes not out to prey. Now, as fond fathers,
Having bound up the threatening twigs of birch,
Only to stick it in their children's sight
For terror, not to use, in time the rod
Becomes more mock'd than fear'd; so our decrees,
Dead to infliction, to themselves are dead;
And liberty plucks justice by the nose;
The baby beats the nurse, and quite athwart
Goes all decorum.

FRIAR THOMAS

It rested in your Grace
To unloose this tied-up justice when you pleased:

And it in you more dreadful would have seem'd
Than in Lord Angelo.

DUKE

            I do fear, too dreadful:
Sith 'twas my fault to give the people scope,
'Twould be my tyranny to strike and gall them
For what I bid them do: for we bid this be done,
When evil deeds have their permissive pass,
And not the punishment. Therefore, indeed, my
     father,
I have on Angelo imposed the office;
Who may, in the ambush of my name, strike home,
And yet my nature never in the fight
To do in slander. And to behold his sway,
I will, as 'twere a brother of your order,
Visit both prince and people: therefore, I prithee,
Supply me with the habit, and instruct me
How I may formally in person bear me
Like a true friar. Moe reasons for this action
At our more leisure shall I render you;
Only, this one: Lord Angelo is precise;
Stands at a guard with envy; scarce confesses
That his blood flows, or that his appetite
Is more to bread than stone: hence shall we see,
If power change purpose, what our seemers be.
                                [*Exeunt*

SCENE IV. *A nunnery*

Enter ISABELLA *and* FRANCISCA

ISABELLA

And have you nuns no farther privileges?

FRANCISCA

Are not these large enough?

ISABELLA

Yes, truly: I speak not as desiring more;
But rather wishing a more strict restraint
Upon the sisterhood, the votarists of Saint Clare.

LUCIO

[*Within*] Ho! Peace be in this place!

ISABELLA

                 Who's that which calls?

FRANCISCA

It is a man's voice. Gentle Isabella,
Turn you the key, and know his business of him;
You may, I may not; you are yet unsworn.
When you have vow'd, you must not speak with men
But in the presence of the prioress:
Then, if you speak, you must not show your face;
Or, if you show your face, you must not speak.
He calls again; I pray you, answer him.   [*Exit*

ISABELLA

Peace and prosperity! Who is't that calls?

Enter LUCIO

LUCIO

Hail, virgin, if you be, as those cheek-roses
Proclaim you are no less! Can you so stead me
As bring me to the sight of Isabella,
A novice of this place, and the fair sister
To her unhappy brother Claudio?

ISABELLA

Why, 'her unhappy brother'? let me ask
The rather, for I now must make you know
I am that Isabella and his sister.

LUCIO

Gentle and fair, your brother kindly greets you:
Not to be weary with you, he's in prison.

ISABELLA

Woe me! for what?

LUCIO

For that which, if myself might be his judge,
He should receive his punishment in thanks:
He hath got his friend with child.

ISABELLA

Sir, make me not your story.

LUCIO

               It is true.
I would not—though 'tis my familiar sin
With maids to seem the lapwing, and to jest,
Tongue far from heart—play with all virgins so:
I hold you as a thing ensky'd and sainted;
By your renouncement, an immortal spirit;
And to be talk'd with in sincerity,
As with a saint.

ISABELLA

You do blaspheme the good in mocking me.

LUCIO

Do not believe it. Fewness and truth, 'tis thus:—
Your brother and his lover have embraced:
As those that feed grow full,—as blossoming time,
That from the seedness the bare fallow brings
To teeming foison,—even so her plenteous womb
Expresseth his full tilth and husbandry.

ISABELLA

Some one with child by him?—My cousin Juliet?

LUCIO

Is she your cousin?

ISABELLA

Adoptedly; as school-maids change their names
By vain, though apt, affection.

LUCIO

                  She it is.

ISABELLA

O, let him marry her.

LUCIO

             This is the point.
The duke is very strangely gone from hence;
Bore many gentlemen, myself being one,
In hand, and hope of action: but we do learn
By those that know the very nerves of state,
His givings-out were of an infinite distance
From his true-meant design. Upon his place,
And with full line of his authority,
Governs Lord Angelo; a man whose blood
Is very snow-broth; one who never feels
The wanton stings and motions of the sense,
But doth rebate and blunt his natural edge
With profits of the mind, study and fast.
He—to give fear to use and liberty,
Which have for long run by the hideous law,

As mice by lions—hath pick'd out an act,
Under whose heavy sense your brother's life
Falls into forfeit: he arrests him on it;
And follows close the rigour of the statute,
To make him an example. All hope is gone,
Unless you have the grace by your fair prayer
To soften Angelo: and that's my pith of business
'Twixt you and your poor brother.

ISABELLA
Doth he so seek his life?

LUCIO
                          Has censured him
Already; and, as I hear, the provost hath
A warrant for his execution.

ISABELLA
Alas! what poor ability's in me
To do him good?

LUCIO
          Assay the power you have.

ISABELLA
My power? Alas, I doubt,—

LUCIO
                    Our doubts are traitors,
And make us lose the good we oft might win
By fearing to attempt. Go to Lord Angelo,
And let him learn to know, when maidens sue,
Men give like gods; but when they weep and kneel,
All their petitions are as freely theirs
As they themselves would owe them.

ISABELLA
I'll see what I can do.

LUCIO
                  But speedily.

ISABELLA
I will about it straight;
No longer staying but to give the Mother
Notice of my affair. I humbly thank you:
Commend me to my brother: soon at night
I'll send him certain word of my success.

LUCIO
I take my leave of you.

ISABELLA
              Good sir, adieu.   [*Exeunt*

ACT II

SCENE I. *A hall in* ANGELO's *house*

Enter ANGELO, ESCALUS, *and a* JUSTICE, PROVOST,
OFFICERS, *and other* ATTENDANTS, *behind*

ANGELO
We must not make a scarecrow of the law,
Setting it up to fear the birds of prey,
And let it keep one shape, till custom make it
Their perch, and not their terror.

ESCALUS
                            Ay, but yet
Let us be keen, and rather cut a little,
Than fall, and bruise to death. Alas, this gentleman,

Whom I would save, had a most noble father!
Let but your honour know,
Whom I believe to be most strait in virtue,
That, in the working of your own affections,
Had time cohered with place or place with wishing,
Or that the resolute acting of your blood
Could have attain'd the effect of your own purpose,
Whether you had not sometime in your life
Err'd in this point which now you censure him,
And pull'd the law upon you.

ANGELO
'Tis one thing to be tempted, Escalus,
Another thing to fall. I not deny,
The jury, passing on the prisoner's life,
May in the sworn twelve have a thief or two
Guiltier than him they try. What's open made to
    justice,
That justice seizes: what know the laws
That thieves do pass on thieves? 'Tis very pregnant,
The jewel that we find, we stoop and take't,
Because we see it; but what we do not see
We tread upon, and never think of it.
You may not so extenuate his offence
For I have had such faults; but rather tell me,
When I, that censure him, do so offend,
Let mine own judgement pattern out my death,
And nothing come in partial. Sir, he must die.

ESCALUS
Be it as your wisdom will.

ANGELO
                    Where is the provost?

PROVOST
Here, if it like your honour.

ANGELO
                      See that Claudio
Be executed by nine to-morrow morning:
Bring him his confessor, let him be prepared;
For that's the utmost of his pilgrimage.
                              [*Exit* PROVOST

ESCALUS
[*Aside*] Well, heaven forgive him! and forgive us all!
Some rise by sin, and some by virtue fall:
Some run from brakes of ice, and answer none;
And some condemned for a fault alone.
Enter ELBOW, *and* OFFICERS *with* FROTH *and* POMPEY

ELBOW
Come, bring them away: if these be good people in
a commonweal that do nothing but use their abuses
in common houses, I know no law: bring them away.

ANGELO
How now, sir! What's your name? and what's the
matter?

ELBOW
If it please your honour, I am the poor Duke's constable, and my name is Elbow: I do lean upon justice, sir, and do bring in here before your good honour
two notorious benefactors.

ANGELO
Benefactors? Well; what benefactors are they? are
they not malefactors?

[906]

ELBOW

If it please your honour, I know not well what they are: but precise villains they are, that I am sure of; and void of all profanation in the world that good Christians ought to have.

ESCALUS

This comes off well; here's a wise officer.

ANGELO

Go to: what quality are they of? Elbow is your name? why dost thou not speak, Elbow?

POMPEY

He cannot, sir; he's out at elbow.

ANGELO

What are you, sir?

ELBOW

He, sir! a tapster, sir; parcel-bawd; one that serves a bad woman; whose house, sir, was, as they say, plucked down in the suburbs; and now she professes a hothouse, which, I think, is a very ill house too.

ESCALUS

How know you that?

ELBOW

My wife, sir, whom I detest before heaven and your honour,—

ESCALUS

How? thy wife?

ELBOW

Ay, sir;—whom, I thank heaven, is an honest woman,—

ESCALUS

Dost thou detest her therefore?

ELBOW

I say, sir, I will detest myself also, as well as she, that this house, if it be not a bawd's house, it is pity of her life, for it is a naughty house.

ESCALUS

How dost thou know that, constable?

ELBOW

Marry, sir, by my wife; who, if she had been a woman cardinally given, might have been accused in fornication, adultery, and all uncleanliness there.

ESCALUS

By the woman's means?

ELBOW

Ay, sir, by Mistress Overdone's means: but as she spit in his face, so she defied him.

POMPEY

Sir, if it please your honour, this is not so.

ELBOW

Prove it before these varlets here, thou honourable man; prove it.

ESCALUS

Do you hear how he misplaces?

POMPEY

Sir, she came in great with child; and longing, saving your honour's reverence, for stewed prunes; sir, we had but two in the house, which at that very distant time stood, as it were, in a fruit-dish, a dish of some three-pence; your honours have seen such

dishes; they are not China dishes, but very good dishes,—

ESCALUS

Go to, go to: no matter for the dish, sir.

POMPEY

No, indeed, sir, not of a pin; you are therein in the right: but to the point. As I say, this Mistress Elbow, being, as I say, with child, and being great-bellied, and longing, as I said, for prunes; and having but two in the dish, as I said, Master Froth here, this very man, having eaten the rest, as I said, and, as I say, paying for them very honestly; for, as you know, Master Froth, I could not give you three-pence again.

FROTH

No, indeed.

POMPEY

Very well;—you being then, if you be remembered, cracking the stones of the foresaid prunes,—

FROTH

Ay, so I did indeed.

POMPEY

Why, very well; I telling you then, if you be remembered, that such a one and such a one were past cure of the thing you wot of, unless they kept very good diet, as I told you,—

FROTH

All this is true.

POMPEY

Why, very well, then,—

ESCALUS

Come, you are a tedious fool: to the purpose. What was done to Elbow's wife, that he hath cause to complain of? Come me to what was done to her.

POMPEY

Sir, your honour cannot come to that yet.

ESCALUS

No, sir, nor I mean it not.

POMPEY

Sir, but you shall come to it, by your honour's leave. And, I beseech you, look into Master Froth here, sir; a man of fourscore pound a year; whose father died at Hallowmas:—was't not at Hallowmas, Master Froth?—

FROTH

All-hallond eve.

POMPEY

Why, very well; I hope here be truths. He, sir, sitting, as I say, in a lower chair, sir; 'twas in the Bunch of Grapes, where, indeed, you have a delight to sit, have you not?

FROTH

I have so; because it is an open room, and good for winter.

POMPEY

Why, very well, then; I hope here be truths.

ANGELO

This will last out a night in Russia,
When nights are longest there: I'll take my leave,
And leave you to the hearing of the cause;
Hoping you'll find good cause to whip them all.

ESCALUS

I think no less. Good morrow to your lordship.
[*Exit* ANGELO

Now, sir, come on: what was done to Elbow's wife,
once more?

POMPEY

Once, sir? there was nothing done to her once.

ELBOW

I beseech you, sir, ask him what this man did to my
wife.

POMPEY

I beseech your honour, ask me.

ESCALUS

Well, sir; what did this gentleman to her?

POMPEY

I beseech you, sir, look in this gentleman's face.
Good Master Froth, look upon his honour; 'tis for a
good purpose. Doth your honour mark his face?

ESCALUS

Ay, sir, very well.

POMPEY

Nay, I beseech you, mark it well.

ESCALUS

Well, I do so.

POMPEY

Doth your honour see any harm in his face?

ESCALUS

Why, no.

POMPEY

I'll be supposed upon a book, his face is the worst
thing about him. Good, then; if his face be the worst
thing about him, how could Master Froth do the
constable's wife any harm? I would know that of
your honour.

ESCALUS

He's in the right. Constable, what say you to it?

ELBOW

First, an it like you, the house is a respected house;
next, this is a respected fellow; and his mistress is a
respected woman.

POMPEY

By this hand, sir, his wife is a more respected person
than any of us all.

ELBOW

Varlet, thou liest; thou liest, wicked varlet! the time
is yet to come that she was ever respected with man,
woman, or child.

POMPEY

Sir, she was respected with him before he married
with her.

ESCALUS

Which is the wiser here? Justice or Iniquity? Is this
true?

ELBOW

O thou caitiff! O thou varlet! O thou wicked Hannibal! I respected with her before I was married to
her! If ever I was respected with her, or she with
me, let not your worship think me the poor Duke's
officer. Prove this, thou wicked Hannibal, or I'll
have mine action of battery on thee.

ESCALUS

If he took you a box o' th' ear, you might have your
action of slander too.

ELBOW

Marry, I thank your good worship for it. What is't
your worship's pleasure I shall do with this wicked
caitiff?

ESCALUS

Truly, officer, because he hath some offences in him
that thou wouldst discover if thou couldst, let him
continue in his courses till thou knowest what they
are.

ELBOW

Marry, I thank your worship for it. Thou seest, thou
wicked varlet, now, what's come upon thee: thou art
to continue now, thou varlet; thou art to continue.

ESCALUS

Where were you born, friend?

FROTH

Here in Vienna, sir.

ESCALUS

Are you of fourscore pounds a year?

FROTH

Yes, an 't please you, sir.

ESCALUS

So. What trade are you of, sir?

POMPEY

A tapster; a poor widow's tapster.

ESCALUS

Your mistress' name?

POMPEY

Mistress Overdone.

ESCALUS

Hath she had any more than one husband?

POMPEY

Nine, sir; Overdone by the last.

ESCALUS

Nine! Come hither to me, Master Froth. Master
Froth, I would not have you acquainted with tapsters: they will draw you, Master Froth, and you
will hang them. Get you gone, and let me hear no
more of you.

FROTH

I thank your worship. For mine own part, I never
come into any room in a taphouse, but I am drawn
in.

ESCALUS

Well, no more of it, Master Froth: farewell. [*Exit*
FROTH] Come you hither to me, Master tapster.
What's your name, Master tapster?

POMPEY

Pompey.

ESCALUS

What else?

POMPEY

Bum, sir.

ESCALUS

Troth, and your bum is the greatest thing about you;
so that, in the beastliest sense, you are Pompey the
Great. Pompey, you are partly a bawd, Pompey,

howsoever you colour it in being a tapster, are you not? come, tell me true: it shall be the better for you.

POMPEY

Truly, sir, I am a poor fellow that would live.

ESCALUS

How would you live, Pompey? by being a bawd? What do you think of the trade, Pompey? is it a lawful trade?

POMPEY

If the law would allow it, sir.

ESCALUS

But the law will not allow it, Pompey; nor it shall not be allowed in Vienna.

POMPEY

Does your worship mean to geld and splay all the youth of the city?

ESCALUS

No, Pompey.

POMPEY

Truly, sir, in my poor opinion, they will to't, then. If your worship will take order for the drabs and the knaves, you need not to fear the bawds.

ESCALUS

There are pretty orders beginning, I can tell you: it is but heading and hanging.

POMPEY

If you head and hang all that offend that way but for ten year together, you'll be glad to give out a commission for more heads: if this law hold in Vienna ten year, I'll rent the fairest house in it after threepence a bay: if you live to see this come to pass, say Pompey told you so.

ESCALUS

Thank you, good Pompey; and, in requital of your prophecy, hark you: I advise you, let me not find you before me again upon any complaint whatsoever; no, not for dwelling where you do: if I do, Pompey, I shall beat you to your tent, and prove a shrewd Cæsar to you; in plain dealing, Pompey, I shall have you whipt: so, for this time, Pompey, fare you well.

POMPEY

I thank your worship for your good counsel: [Aside] but I shall follow it as the flesh and fortune shall better determine.

Whip me? No, no; let carman whip his jade:

The valiant heart's not whipt out of his trade.　[Exit

ESCALUS

Come hither to me, Master Elbow; come hither, Master constable. How long have you been in this place of constable?

ELBOW

Seven year and a half, sir.

ESCALUS

I thought, by your readiness in the office, you had continued in it some time. You say, seven years together?

ELBOW

And a half, sir.

ESCALUS

Alas, it hath been great pains to you. They do you

wrong to put you so oft upon 't: are there not men in your ward sufficient to serve it?

ELBOW

Faith, sir, few of any wit in such matters: as they are chosen, they are glad to choose me for them; I do it for some piece of money, and go through with all.

ESCALUS

Look you bring me in the names of some six or seven, the most sufficient of your parish.

ELBOW

To your worship's house, sir?

ESCALUS

To my house. Fare you well. [Exit ELBOW] What's o'clock, think you?

JUSTICE

Eleven, sir.

ESCALUS

I pray you home to dinner with me.

JUSTICE

I humbly thank you.

ESCALUS

It grieves me for the death of Claudio;

But there's no remedy.

JUSTICE

Lord Angelo is severe.

ESCALUS

　　　　　　　　　It is but needful:

Mercy is not itself, that oft looks so;

Pardon is still the nurse of second woe:

But yet,—poor Claudio! There is no remedy.

Come, sir.　　　　　　　　　　　　　[Exeunt

SCENE II. Another room in the same

Enter PROVOST and a SERVANT

SERVANT

He's hearing of a cause; he will come straight:

I'll tell him of you.

PROVOST

　　　　　　Pray you, do. [Exit SERVANT] I'll know

His pleasure; may be he will relent. Alas,

He hath but as offended in a dream!

All sects, all ages smack of this vice; and he

To die for 't!

Enter ANGELO

ANGELO

Now, what's the matter, provost?

PROVOST

Is it your will Claudio shall die to-morrow?

ANGELO

Did not I tell thee yea? hadst thou not order?

Why dost thou ask again?

PROVOST

　　　　　　Lest I might be too rash:

Under your good correction, I have seen,

When, after execution, Judgement hath

Repented o'er his doom.

ANGELO

　　　　　　Go to; let that be mine:

Do you your office, or give up your place,
And you shall well be spared.

PROVOST

          I crave your honour's pardon.
What shall be done, sir, with the groaning Juliet?
She's very near her hour.

ANGELO

          Dispose of her
To some more fitter place, and that with speed.

Re-enter SERVANT

SERVANT

Here is the sister of the man condemn'd
Desires access to you.

ANGELO

          Hath he a sister?

PROVOST

Ay, my good lord; a very virtuous maid
And to be shortly of a sisterhood,
If not already.

ANGELO

          Well, let her be admitted.

[*Exit* SERVANT

See you the fornicatress be removed:
Let her have needful, but not lavish, means;
There shall be order for 't.

Enter ISABELLA *and* LUCIO

PROVOST

          God save your honour!

ANGELO

Stay a little while. [*To* ISABELLA] You're welcome:
  what's your will?

ISABELLA

I am a woeful suitor to your honour,
Please but your honour hear me.

ANGELO

          Well; what's your suit?

ISABELLA

There is a vice that most I do abhor,
And most desire should meet the blow of justice;
For which I would not plead, but that I must;
For which I must not plead, but that I am
At war 'twixt will and will not.

ANGELO

          Well; the matter?

ISABELLA

I have a brother is condemn'd to die:
I do beseech you, let it be his fault,
And not my brother.

PROVOST

          [*Aside*] Heaven give thee moving graces!

ANGELO

Condemn the fault, and not the actor of it?
Why, every fault's condemn'd ere it be done:
Mine were the very cipher of a function,
To fine the faults whose fine stands in record,
And let go by the actor.

ISABELLA

          O just but severe law!
I had a brother, then.—Heaven keep your honour!

LUCIO

[*Aside to* ISABELLA] Give 't not o'er so: to him again,
  entreat him;
Kneel down before him, hang upon his gown:
You are too cold; if you should need a pin,
You could not with more tame a tongue desire it:
To him, I say!

ISABELLA

Must he needs die?

ANGELO

          Maiden, no remedy.

ISABELLA

Yes; I do think that you might pardon him,
And neither heaven nor man grieve at the mercy.

ANGELO

I will not do 't.

ISABELLA

          But can you, if you would?

ANGELO

Look, what I will not, that I cannot do.

ISABELLA

But might you do 't, and do the world no wrong,
If so your heart were touch'd with that remorse
As mine is to him?

ANGELO

          He's sentenced; 'tis too late.

LUCIO

[*Aside to* ISABELLA] You are too cold.

ISABELLA

Too late? why, no; I, that do speak a word,
May call it back again. Well, believe this,
No ceremony that to great ones 'longs,
Not the king's crown, nor the deputed sword,
The marshal's truncheon, nor the judge's robe,
Become them with one half so good a grace
As mercy does.
If he had been as you, and you as he,
You would have slipt like him; but he, like you,
Would not have been so stern.

ANGELO

          Pray you, be gone.

ISABELLA

I would to heaven I had your potency,
And you were Isabel! should it then be thus?
No; I would tell what 'twere to be a judge,
And what a prisoner.

LUCIO

[*Aside to* ISABELLA] Ay, touch him; there's the vein.

ANGELO

Your brother is a forfeit of the law,
And you but waste your words.

ISABELLA

          Alas, alas!
Why, all the souls that were were forfeit once;
And He that might the vantage best have took
Found out the remedy. How would you be,
If He, which is the top of judgement, should
But judge you as you are? O, think on that;

And mercy then will breathe within your lips,
Like man new made.

ANGELO
    Be you content, fair maid;
It is the law, not I condemn your brother:
Were he my kinsman, brother, or my son,
It should be thus with him: he must die to-morrow.

ISABELLA
To-morrow! O, that's sudden! Spare him, spare him!
He's not prepared for death. Even for our kitchens
We kill the fowl of season: shall we serve heaven
With less respect than we do minister
To our gross selves? Good, good my lord, bethink you;
Who is it that hath died for this offence?
There's many have committed it.

LUCIO
   [Aside to ISABELLA] Ay, well said.

ANGELO
The law hath not been dead, though it hath slept:
Those many had not dared to do that evil,
If the first that did the edict infringe
Had answer'd for his deed: now 'tis awake,
Takes note of what is done; and, like a prophet,
Looks in a glass, that shows what future evils,
Either now, or by remissness new-conceived,
And so in progress to be hatch'd and born,
Are now to have no successive degrees,
But, ere they live, to end.

ISABELLA
    Yet show some pity.

ANGELO
I show it most of all when I show justice;
For then I pity those I do not know,
Which a dismiss'd offence would after gall;
And do him right that, answering one foul wrong,
Lives not to act another. Be satisfied;
Your brother dies to-morrow; be content.

ISABELLA
So you must be the first that gives his sentence,
And he, that suffers. O, it is excellent
To have a giant's strength; but it is tyrannous
To use it like a giant.

LUCIO
[Aside to ISABELLA] That's well said.

ISABELLA
Could great men thunder
As Jove himself does, Jove would ne'er be quiet,
For every pelting, petty officer
Would use his heaven for thunder.
Nothing but thunder! Merciful Heaven,
Thou rather with thy sharp and sulphurous bolt
Split'st the unwedgeable and gnarled oak
Than the soft myrtle: but man, proud man,
Drest in a little brief authority,
Most ignorant of what he's most assured,
His glassy essence, like an angry ape,
Plays such fantastic tricks before high heaven
As make the angels weep; who, with our spleens,
Would all themselves laugh mortal.

LUCIO
[Aside to ISABELLA] O, to him, to him, wench! he will
 relent;
He's coming; I perceive 't.

PROVOST
   [Aside] Pray heaven she win him!

ISABELLA
We cannot weigh our brother with ourself:
Great men may jest with saints; 'tis wit in them,
But in the less foul profanation.

LUCIO
Thou'rt i' the right, girl; more o' that.

ISABELLA
That in the captain's but a choleric word,
Which in the soldier is flat blasphemy.

LUCIO
[Aside to ISABELLA] Art avised o' that? more on't.

ANGELO
Why do you put these sayings upon me?

ISABELLA
Because authority, though it err like others,
Hath yet a kind of medicine in itself,
That skins the vice o' the top. Go to your bosom;
Knock there, and ask your heart what it doth know
That's like my brother's fault: if it confess
A natural guiltiness such as is his,
Let it not sound a thought upon your tongue
Against my brother's life.

ANGELO
   [Aside] She speaks, and 'tis
Such sense, that my sense breeds with it. Fare you
 well.

ISABELLA
Gentle my lord, turn back.

ANGELO
I will bethink me: come again to-morrow.

ISABELLA
Hark how I'll bribe you: good my lord, turn back.

ANGELO
How? bribe me?

ISABELLA
Ay, with such gifts that heaven shall share with you.

LUCIO
[Aside to ISABELLA] You had marr'd all else.

ISABELLA
Not with fond sicles of the tested gold,
Or stones whose rates are either rich or poor
As fancy values them; but with true prayers
That shall be up at heaven and enter there
Ere sun-rise, prayers from preserved souls,
From fasting maids whose minds are dedicate
To nothing temporal.

ANGELO
    Well; come to me to-morrow.

LUCIO
[Aside to ISABELLA] Go to; 'tis well; away!

ISABELLA
Heaven keep your honour safe!

ANGELO
    [Aside] Amen:

For I am that way going to temptation,
Where prayers cross.

ISABELLA

           At what hour to-morrow
Shall I attend your lordship?

ANGELO

                At any time 'fore noon.

ISABELLA

'Save your honour!

            [*Exeunt* ISABELLA, LUCIO, *and* PROVOST

ANGELO

           From thee,—even from thy virtue!
What's this, what's this? Is this her fault or mine?
The tempter or the tempted, who sins most?
Ha!
Not she; nor doth she tempt: but it is I
That, lying by the violet in the sun,
Do as the carrion does, not as the flower,
Corrupt with virtuous season. Can it be
That modesty may more betray our sense
Than woman's lightness? Having waste ground
    enough,
Shall we desire to raze the sanctuary,
And pitch our evils there? O, fie, fie, fie!
What dost thou, or what art thou, Angelo?
Dost thou desire her foully for those things
That make her good? O, let her brother live:
Thieves for their robbery have authority
When judges steal themselves. What, do I love her,
That I desire to hear her speak again,
And feast upon her eyes? What is't I dream on?
O cunning enemy, that, to catch a saint,
With saints dost bait thy hook! Most dangerous
Is that temptation that doth goad us on
To sin in loving virtue: never could the strumpet,
With all her double vigour, art and nature,
Once stir my temper; but this virtuous maid
Subdues me quite. Ever till now,
When men were fond, I smiled, and wonder'd how.
                              [*Exit*

SCENE III. *A room in a prison*

Enter, severally, DUKE *disguised as a friar, and* PROVOST

DUKE

Hail to you, provost! so I think you are.

PROVOST

I am the provost. What's your will, good friar?

DUKE

Bound by my charity and my blest order,
I come to visit the afflicted spirits
Here in the prison. Do me the common right
To let me see them, and to make me know
The nature of their crimes, that I may minister
To them accordingly.

PROVOST

I would do more than that, if more were needful.

Enter JULIET

Look, here comes one: a gentlewoman of mine,
Who, falling in the flaws of her own youth,

Hath blister'd her report: she is with child;
And he that got it, sentenced; a young man
More fit to do another such offence
Than die for this.

DUKE

When must he die?

PROVOST

           As I do think, to-morrow.
I have provided for you: stay awhile,   [*To* JULIET
And you shall be conducted.

DUKE

Repent you, fair one, of the sin you carry?

JULIET

I do; and bear the shame most patiently.

DUKE

I'll teach you how you shall arraign your conscience,
And try your penitence, if it be sound,
Or hollowly put on.

JULIET

           I'll gladly learn.

DUKE

Love you the man that wrong'd you?

JULIET

Yes, as I love the woman that wrong'd him.

DUKE

So, then, it seems your most offenceful act
Was mutually committed?

JULIET

              Mutually.

DUKE

Then was your sin of heavier kind than his.

JULIET

I do confess it, and repent it, father.

DUKE

'Tis meet so, daughter: but lest you do repent,
As that the sin hath brought you to this shame,
Which sorrow is always toward ourselves, not heaven,
Showing we would not spare heaven as we love it,
But as we stand in fear,—

JULIET

I do repent me, as it is an evil,
And take the shame with joy.

DUKE

              There rest.
Your partner, as I hear, must die to-morrow,
And I am going with instruction to him.
Grace go with you, *Benedicite!*   [*Exit*

JULIET

Must die to-morrow! O injurious love,
That respites me a life, whose very comfort
Is still a dying horror!

PROVOST

           'Tis pity of him.   [*Exeunt*

SCENE IV. *A room in* ANGELO'S *house*

Enter ANGELO

ANGELO

When I would pray and think, I think and pray

To several subjects. Heaven hath my empty words;
Whilst my invention, hearing not my tongue,
Anchors on Isabel: Heaven in my mouth,
As if I did but only chew his name;
And in my heart the strong and swelling evil
Of my conception. The state, whereon I studied,
Is like a good thing, being often read,
Grown fear'd and tedious; yea, my gravity,
Wherein—let no man hear me—I take pride,
Could I with boot change for an idle plume,
Which the air beats for vain. O place, O form,
How often dost thou with thy case, thy habit,
Wrench awe from fools, and tie the wiser souls
To thy false seeming! Blood, thou art blood:
Let's write good angel on the devil's horn;
'Tis not the devil's crest.

Enter a SERVANT

How now! who's there?

SERVANT

One Isabel, a sister, desires access to you.

ANGELO

Teach her the way. O heavens!
Why does my blood thus muster to my heart,
Making both it unable for itself,
And dispossessing all my other parts
Of necessary fitness?
So play the foolish throngs with one that swoons;
Come all to help him, and so stop the air
By which he should revive: and even so
The general subject to a well-wish'd king
Quit their own part, and in obsequious fondness
Crowd to his presence, where their untaught love
Must needs appear offence.

Enter ISABELLA

How now, fair maid?

ISABELLA

I am come to know your pleasure.

ANGELO

That you might know it, would much better please
    me
Than to demand what 'tis. Your brother cannot live.

ISABELLA

Even so.—Heaven keep your honour!

ANGELO

Yet may he live awhile; and, it may be,
As long as you or I: yet he must die.

ISABELLA

Under your sentence?

ANGELO

Yea.

ISABELLA

When, I beseech you? that in his reprieve,
Longer or shorter, he may be so fitted
That his soul sicken not.

ANGELO

Ha! fie, these filthy vices! It were as good
To pardon him that hath from nature stolen
A man already made, as to remit
Their saucy sweetness that do coin heaven's image
In stamps that are forbid: 'tis all as easy

Falsely to take away a life true made,
As to put metal in restrained means
To make a false one.

ISABELLA

'Tis set down so in heaven, but not in earth.

ANGELO

Say you so? then I shall pose you quickly.
Which had you rather,—that the most just law
Now took your brother's life; or, to redeem him,
Give up your body to such sweet uncleanness
As she that he hath stain'd?

ISABELLA

Sir, believe this,
I had rather give my body than my soul.

ANGELO

I talk not of your soul: our compell'd sins
Stand more for number than for accompt.

ISABELLA

How say you?

ANGELO

Nay, I'll not warrant that; for I can speak
Against the thing I say. Answer to this:—
I, now the voice of the recorded law,
Pronounce a sentence on your brother's life:
Might there not be a charity in sin
To save this brother's life?

ISABELLA

Please you to do't,
I'll take it as a peril to my soul,
It is no sin at all, but charity.

ANGELO

Pleased you to do't at peril of your soul,
Were equal poise of sin and charity.

ISABELLA

That I do beg his life, if it be sin,
Heaven let me bear it! you granting of my suit,
If that be sin, I'll make it my morn prayer
To have it added to the faults of mine,
And nothing of your answer.

ANGELO

Nay, but hear me.
Your sense pursues not mine: either you are ignorant,
Or seem so, craftily; and that's not good.

ISABELLA

Let me be ignorant, and in nothing good,
But graciously to know I am no better.

ANGELO

Thus wisdom wishes to appear most bright
When it doth tax itself; as these black masks
Proclaim an enshield beauty ten times louder
Than beauty could, display'd. But mark me;
To be received plain, I'll speak more gross:
Your brother is to die.

ISABELLA

So.

ANGELO

And his offence is so, as it appears,
Accountant to the law upon that pain.

ISABELLA

True.

ANGELO

Admit no other way to save his life,—
As I subscribe not that, nor any other,
But in the loss of question,—that you, his sister,
Finding yourself desired of such a person,
Whose credit with the judge, or own great place,
Could fetch your brother from the manacles
Of the all-building law; and that there were
No earthly mean to save him, but that either
You must lay down the treasures of your body
To this supposed, or else to let him suffer;
What would you do?

ISABELLA

As much for my poor brother as myself:
That is, were I under the terms of death,
The impression of keen whips I'ld wear as rubies,
And strip myself to death, as to a bed
That longing have been sick for, ere I'ld yield
My body up to shame.

ANGELO

            Then must your brother die.

ISABELLA

And 'twere the cheaper way:
Better it were a brother died at once,
Than that a sister, by redeeming him,
Should die for ever.

ANGELO

Were not you, then, as cruel as the sentence
That you have slander'd so?

ISABELLA

Ignomy in ransom and free pardon
Are of two houses: lawful mercy
Is nothing kin to foul redemption.

ANGELO

You seem'd of late to make the law a tyrant;
And rather proved the sliding of your brother
A merriment than a vice.

ISABELLA

O, pardon me, my lord; it oft falls out,
To have what we would have, we speak not what
   we mean:
I something do excuse the thing I hate,
For his advantage that I dearly love.

ANGELO

We are all frail.

ISABELLA

          Else let my brother die,
If not a feodary, but only he
Owe and succeed thy weakness.

ANGELO

Nay, women are frail too.

ISABELLA

Ay, as the glasses where they view themselves;
Which are as easy broke as they make forms.
Women!—Help Heaven! men their creation mar
In profiting by them. Nay, call us ten times frail;
For we are soft as our complexions are,
And credulous to false prints.

ANGELO

          I think it well:

And from this testimony of your own sex,—
Since, I suppose, we are made to be no stronger
Than faults may shake our frames,—let me be bold;—
I do arrest your words. Be that you are,
That is, a woman; if you be more, you're none;
If you be one,—as you are well express'd
By all external warrants,—show it now,
By putting on the destined livery.

ISABELLA

I have no tongue but one: gentle my lord,
Let me entreat you speak the former language.

ANGELO

Plainly conceive, I love you.

ISABELLA

My brother did love Juliet,
And you tell me that he shall die for it.

ANGELO

He shall not, Isabel, if you give me love.

ISABELLA

I know your virtue hath a license in't,
Which seems a little fouler than it is,
To pluck on others.

ANGELO

          Believe me, on mine honour,
My words express my purpose.

ISABELLA

Ha! little honour to be much believed,
And most pernicious purpose!—Seeming, seeming!—
I will proclaim thee, Angelo; look for't:
Sign me a present pardon for my brother,
Or with an outstretch'd throat I'll tell the world aloud
What man thou art.

ANGELO

          Who will believe thee, Isabel?
My unsoil'd name, the austereness of my life,
My vouch against you, and my place i' the state,
Will so your accusation overweigh,
That you shall stifle in your own report,
And smell of calumny. I have begun;
And now I give my sensual race the rein:
Fit thy consent to my sharp appetite;
Lay by all nicety and prolixious blushes,
That banish what they sue for; redeem thy brother
By yielding up thy body to my will;
Or else he must not only die the death,
But thy unkindness shall his death draw out
To lingering sufferance. Answer me to-morrow,
Or, by the affection that now guides me most,
I'll prove a tyrant to him. As for you,
Say what you can, my false o'erweighs your true.

                             [*Exit*

ISABELLA

To whom should I complain? Did I tell this,
Who would believe me? O perilous mouths,
That bear in them one and the self-same tongue,
Either of condemnation or approof;
Bidding the law make court'sy to their will;
Hooking both right and wrong to the appetite,
To follow as it draws! I'll to my brother:
Though he hath fall'n by prompture of the blood,

Yet hath he in him such a mind of honour,
That, had he twenty heads to tender down
On twenty bloody blocks, he'ld yield them up,
Before his sister should her body stoop
To such abhorr'd pollution.
Then, Isabel, live chaste, and, brother, die:
More than our brother is our chastity.
I'll tell him yet of Angelo's request,
And fit his mind to death, for his soul's rest.   [*Exit*

ACT III
Scene I. *A room in the prison*

Enter DUKE *disguised as before,* CLAUDIO, *and* PROVOST
DUKE
So, then, you hope of pardon from Lord Angelo?
CLAUDIO
The miserable have no other medicine
But only hope:
I've hope to live, and am prepared to die.
DUKE
Be absolute for death; either death or life
Shall thereby be the sweeter. Reason thus with life:
If I do lose thee, I do lose a thing
That none but fools would keep: a breath thou art,
Servile to all the skyey influences,
That dost this habitation, where thou keep'st,
Hourly afflict: merely, thou art death's fool;
For him thou labour'st by thy flight to shun,
And yet runn'st toward him still. Thou art not noble;
For all the accommodations that thou bear'st
Are nursed by baseness. Thou'rt by no means valiant;
For thou dost fear the soft and tender fork
Of a poor worm. Thy best of rest is sleep,
And that thou oft provokest; yet grossly fear'st
Thy death, which is no more. Thou art not thyself;
For thou exist'st on many a thousand grains
That issue out of dust. Happy thou art not;
For what thou hast not, still thou strivest to get,
And what thou hast, forget'st. Thou art not certain;
For thy complexion shifts to strange effects,
After the moon. If thou art rich, thou'rt poor;
For, like an ass whose back with ingots bows,
Thou bear'st thy heavy riches but a journey,
And death unloads thee. Friend hast thou none;
For thine own bowels, which do call thee sire,
The mere effusion of thy proper loins,
Do curse the gout, serpigo, and the rheum,
For ending thee no sooner. Thou hast nor youth nor
      age,
But, as it were, an after-dinner's sleep,
Dreaming on both; for all thy blessed youth
Becomes as aged, and doth beg the alms
Of palsied eld; and when thou art old and rich,
Thou hast neither heat, affection, limb, nor beauty,
To make thy riches pleasant. What's yet in this
That bears the name of life? Yet in this life

Lie hid moe thousand deaths: yet death we fear,
That makes these odds all even.
CLAUDIO
                              I humbly thank you.
To sue to live, I find I seek to die;
And, seeking death, find life: let it come on.
ISABELLA
[*Within*] What, ho! Peace here; grace and good company!
PROVOST
Who's there? come in: the wish deserves a welcome.
DUKE
Dear sir, ere long I'll visit you again.
CLAUDIO
Most holy sir, I thank you.
                    Enter ISABELLA
ISABELLA
My business is a word or two with Claudio.
PROVOST
And very welcome. Look, signior, here's your sister.
DUKE
Provost, a word with you.
PROVOST
As many as you please.
DUKE
Bring me to hear them speak, where I may be concealed.   [*Exeunt* DUKE *and* PROVOST
CLAUDIO
Now, sister, what's the comfort?
ISABELLA
Why,
As all comforts are; most good, most good indeed.
Lord Angelo, having affairs to heaven,
Intends you for his swift ambassador,
Where you shall be an everlasting leiger:
Therefore your best appointment make with speed;
To-morrow you set on.
CLAUDIO
                    Is there no remedy?
ISABELLA
None, but such remedy as, to save a head,
To cleave a heart in twain.
CLAUDIO
                    But is there any?
ISABELLA
Yes, brother, you may live:
There is a devilish mercy in the judge,
If you'll implore it, that will free your life,
But fetter you till death.
CLAUDIO
                    Perpetual durance?
ISABELLA
Ay, just; perpetual durance, a restraint,
Though all the world's vastidity you had.
To a determined scope.
CLAUDIO
                    But in what nature?
ISABELLA
In such a one as, you consenting to't,

Would bark your honour from that trunk you bear,
And leave you naked.

CLAUDIO
Let me know the point.

ISABELLA
O, I do fear thee, Claudio; and I quake,
Lest thou a feverous life shouldst entertain,
And six or seven winters more respect
Than a perpetual honour. Darest thou die?
The sense of death is most in apprehension;
And the poor beetle, that we tread upon,
In corporal sufferance finds a pang as great
As when a giant dies.

CLAUDIO
Why give you me this shame?
Think you I can a resolution fetch
From flowery tenderness? If I must die,
I will encounter darkness as a bride,
And hug it in mine arms.

ISABELLA
There spake my brother; there my father's grave
Did utter forth a voice. Yes, thou must die:
Thou art too noble to conserve a life
In base appliances. This outward-sainted deputy,
Whose settled visage and deliberate word
Nips youth i' the head, and follies doth emmew
As falcon doth the fowl, is yet a devil;
His filth within being cast, he would appear
A pond as deep as hell.

CLAUDIO
The prenzie Angelo!

ISABELLA
O, 'tis the cunning livery of hell,
The damned'st body to invest and cover
In prenzie guards! Dost thou think, Claudio?—
If I would yield him my virginity,
Thou mightst be freed.

CLAUDIO
O heavens! it cannot be.

ISABELLA
Yes, he would give't thee, from this rank offence,
So to offend him still. This night's the time
That I should do what I abhor to name,
Or else thou diest to-morrow.

CLAUDIO
Thou shalt not do't.

ISABELLA
O, were it but my life,
I'ld throw it down for your deliverance
As frankly as a pin.

CLAUDIO
Thanks, dear Isabel.

ISABELLA
Be ready, Claudio, for your death to-morrow.

CLAUDIO
Yes. Has he affections in him,
That thus can make him bite the law by the nose,
When he would force it? Sure, it is no sin;
Or of the deadly seven it is the least.

ISABELLA
Which is the least?

CLAUDIO
If it were damnable, he being so wise,
Why would he for the momentary trick
Be perdurably fined?—O Isabel!

ISABELLA
What says my brother?

CLAUDIO
Death is a fearful thing.

ISABELLA
And shamed life a hateful.

CLAUDIO
Ay, but to die, and go we know not where;
To lie in cold obstruction and to rot;
This sensible warm motion to become
A kneaded clod; and the delighted spirit
To bathe in fiery floods, or to reside
In thrilling region of thick-ribbed ice;
To be imprison'd in the viewless winds,
And blown with restless violence round about
The pendent world; or to be worse than worst
Of those that lawless and incertain thought
Imagine howling:—'tis too horrible!
The weariest and most loathed worldly life
That age, ache, penury, and imprisonment
Can lay on nature is a paradise
To what we fear of death.

ISABELLA
Alas, alas!

CLAUDIO
Sweet sister, let me live:
What sin you do to save a brother's life,
Nature dispenses with the deed so far
That it becomes a virtue.

ISABELLA
O you beast!
O faithless coward! O dishonest wretch!
Wilt thou be made a man out of my vice?
Is't not a kind of incest, to take life
From thine own sister's shame? What should I think?
Heaven shield my mother play'd my father fair!
For such a warped slip of wilderness
Ne'er issued from his blood. Take my defiance!
Die, perish! Might but my bending down
Reprieve thee from thy fate, it should proceed:
I'll pray a thousand prayers for thy death,
No word to save thee.

CLAUDIO
Nay, hear me, Isabel.

ISABELLA
O, fie, fie, fie!
Thy sin's not accidental, but a trade.
Mercy to thee would prove itself a bawd:
'Tis best that thou diest quickly.

CLAUDIO
O, hear me, Isabella!

Re-enter DUKE

DUKE
Vouchsafe a word, young sister, but one word.

ISABELLA

What is your will?

DUKE

Might you dispense with your leisure, I would by and by have some speech with you: the satisfaction I would require is likewise your own benefit.

ISABELLA

I have no superfluous leisure; my stay must be stolen out of other affairs; but I will attend you awhile.

[*Walks apart*

DUKE

Son, I have overheard what hath passed between you and your sister. Angelo had never the purpose to corrupt her; only he hath made an assay of her virtue to practise his judgement with the disposition of natures: she, having the truth of honour in her, hath made him that gracious denial which he is most glad to receive. I am confessor to Angelo, and I know this to be true; therefore prepare yourself to death: do not satisfy your resolution with hopes that are fallible: to-morrow you must die; go to your knees, and make ready.

CLAUDIO

Let me ask my sister pardon. I am so out of love with life, that I will sue to be rid of it.

DUKE

Hold you there: farewell. [*Exit* CLAUDIO] Provost, a word with you!

Re-enter PROVOST

PROVOST

What's your will, father?

DUKE

That now you are come, you will be gone. Leave me awhile with the maid: my mind promises with my habit no loss shall touch her by my company.

PROVOST

In good time.

[*Exit* PROVOST. ISABELLA *comes forward*

DUKE

The hand that hath made you fair hath made you good: the goodness that is cheap in beauty makes beauty brief in goodness; but grace, being the soul of your complexion, shall keep the body of it ever fair. The assault that Angelo hath made to you, fortune hath conveyed to my understanding; and, but that frailty hath examples for his falling, I should wonder at Angelo. How will you do to content this substitute, and to save your brother?

ISABELLA

I am now going to resolve him: I had rather my brother die by the law than my son should be unlawfully born. But, O, how much is the good Duke deceived in Angelo! If ever he return and I can speak to him, I will open my lips in vain, or discover his government.

DUKE

That shall not be much amiss: yet, as the matter now stands, he will avoid your accusation; he made trial of you only. Therefore fasten your ear on my advisings: to the love I have in doing good a remedy presents itself. I do make myself believe that you may most uprighteously do a poor wronged lady a merited benefit; redeem your brother from the angry law; do no stain to your own gracious person; and much please the absent Duke, if peradventure he shall ever return to have hearing of this business.

ISABELLA

Let me hear you speak farther. I have spirit to do any thing that appears not foul in the truth of my spirit.

DUKE

Virtue is bold, and goodness never fearful. Have you not heard speak of Mariana, the sister of Frederick the great soldier who miscarried at sea?

ISABELLA

I have heard of the lady, and good words went with her name.

DUKE

She should this Angelo have married; was affianced to her by oath, and the nuptial appointed: between which time of the contract and limit of the solemnity, her brother Frederick was wrecked at sea, having in that perished vessel the dowry of his sister. But mark how heavily this befell to the poor gentlewoman: there she lost a noble and renowned brother, in his love toward her ever most kind and natural; with him, the portion and sinew of her fortune, her marriage-dowry; with both, her combinate husband, this well-seeming Angelo.

ISABELLA

Can this be so? did Angelo so leave her?

DUKE

Left her in her tears, and dried not one of them with his comfort; swallowed his vows whole, pretending in her discoveries of dishonour: in few, bestowed her on her own lamentation, which she yet wears for his sake; and he, a marble to her tears, is washed with them, but relents not.

ISABELLA

What a merit were it in death to take this poor maid from the world! What corruption in this life, that it will let this man live! But how out of this can she avail?

DUKE

It is a rupture that you may easily heal: and the cure of it not only saves your brother, but keeps you from dishonour in doing it.

ISABELLA

Show me how, good father.

DUKE

This forenamed maid hath yet in her the continuance of her first affection: his unjust unkindness, that in all reason should have quenched her love, hath, like an impediment in the current, made it more violent and unruly. Go you to Angelo; answer his requiring with a plausible obedience; agree with his demands to the point; only refer yourself to this advantage, first, that your stay with him may not be long; that the time may have all shadow and silence in it; and the place answer to convenience. This being granted in course,—and now follows all,—we shall advise this wronged maid to stead up your appointment, go in your place; if the encounter acknowledge itself hereafter, it may compel him to her recompence: and here, by this, is your brother saved, your honour untainted, the poor Mariana advantaged, and the corrupt Deputy scaled. The maid will I frame and make fit for his attempt. If you think well to carry this as you may, the doubleness of the benefit defends the deceit from reproof. What think you of it?

ISABELLA

The image of it gives me content already; and I trust it will grow to a most prosperous perfection.

DUKE

It lies much in your holding up. Haste you speedily to Angelo: if for this night he entreat you to his bed, give him promise of satisfaction. I will presently to Saint Luke's: there, at the moated grange, resides this dejected Mariana. At that place call upon me; and dispatch with Angelo, that it may be quickly.

ISABELLA

I thank you for this comfort. Fare you well, good father.   [Exeunt severally

SCENE II. *The street before the prison*

Enter, on one side, DUKE *disguised as before; on the other,*
ELBOW, *and* OFFICERS *with* POMPEY

ELBOW

Nay, if there be no remedy for it, but that you will needs buy and sell men and women like beasts, we shall have all the world drink brown and white bastard.

DUKE

O heavens! what stuff is here?

POMPEY

'Twas never merry world since, of two usuries, the merriest was put down, and the worser allowed by order of law a furred gown to keep him warm; and furred with fox and lamb-skins too, to signify, that craft, being richer than innocency, stands for the facing.

ELBOW

Come your way, sir. 'Bless you, good father friar.

DUKE

And you, good brother father. What offence hath this man made you, sir?

ELBOW

Marry, sir, he hath offended the law: and, sir, we take him to be a thief too, sir; for we have found upon him, sir, a strange picklock, which we have sent to the Deputy.

DUKE

Fie, sirrah! a bawd, a wicked bawd!
The evil that thou causest to be done,
That is thy means to live. Do thou but think
What 'tis to cram a maw or clothe a back
From such a filthy vice: say to thyself,
From their abominable and beastly touches

I drink, I eat, array myself, and live.
Canst thou believe thy living is a life,
So stinkingly depending? Go mend, go mend.

POMPEY

Indeed, it does stink in some sort, sir; but yet, sir, I would prove—

DUKE

Nay, if the devil have given thee proofs for sin,
Thou wilt prove his. Take him to prison, officer:
Correction and instruction must both work
Ere this rude beast will profit.

ELBOW

He must before the Deputy, sir; he has given him warning: the Deputy cannot abide a whoremaster: if he be a whoremonger, and comes before him, he were as good go a mile on his errand.

DUKE

That we were all, as some would seem to be,
From our faults, as faults from seeming, free!

ELBOW

His neck will come to your waist,—a cord, sir.

POMPEY

I spy comfort; I cry bail. Here's a gentleman and a friend of mine.

Enter LUCIO

LUCIO

How now, noble Pompey! What, at the wheels of Cæsar? art thou led in triumph? What, is there none of Pygmalion's images, newly made woman, to be had now, for putting the hand in the pocket and extracting it clutched? What reply, ha? What sayest thou to this tune, matter and method? Is't not drowned i' the last rain, ha? What sayest thou, Trot? Is the world as it was, man? Which is the way? Is it sad, and few words? or how? The trick of it?

DUKE

Still thus, and thus; still worse!

LUCIO

How doth my dear morsel, thy mistress? Procures she still, ha?

POMPEY

Troth, sir, she hath eaten up all her beef, and she is herself in the tub.

LUCIO

Why, 'tis good; it is the right of it; it must be so: ever your fresh whore and your powdered bawd: an unshunned consequence; it must be so. Art going to prison, Pompey?

POMPEY

Yes, faith, sir.

LUCIO

Why, 'tis not amiss, Pompey. Farewell: go say I sent thee thither. For debt, Pompey? or how?

ELBOW

For being a bawd, for being a bawd.

LUCIO

Well, then, imprison him: if imprisonment be the due of a bawd, why, 'tis his right: bawd is he doubtless, and of antiquity too; bawd-born. Farewell, good Pompey. Commend me to the prison, Pompey: you will turn good husband now, Pompey; you will keep the house.

POMPEY

I hope, sir, your good worship will be my bail.

LUCIO

No, indeed, will I not, Pompey; it is not the wear. I will pray, Pompey, to increase your bondage: if you take it not patiently, why, your mettle is the more. Adieu, trusty Pompey. 'Bless you, friar.

DUKE

And you.

LUCIO

Does Bridget paint still, Pompey, ha?

ELBOW

Come your ways, sir; come.

POMPEY

You will not bail me, then, sir?

LUCIO

Then, Pompey, nor now. What news abroad, friar? what news?

ELBOW

Come your ways, sir; come.

LUCIO

Go to kennel, Pompey; go. [*Exeunt* ELBOW, POMPEY, *and* OFFICERS] What news, friar, of the Duke?

DUKE

I know none. Can you tell me of any?

LUCIO

Some say he is with the Emperor of Russia; other some, he is in Rome: but where is he, think you?

DUKE

I know not where; but wheresoever, I wish him well.

LUCIO

It was a mad fantastical trick of him to steal from the state, and usurp the beggary he was never born to. Lord Angelo dukes it well in his absence; he puts transgression to't.

DUKE

He does well in't.

LUCIO

A little more lenity to lechery would do no harm in him: something too crabbed that way, friar.

DUKE

It is too general a vice, and severity must cure it.

LUCIO

Yes, in good sooth, the vice is of a great kindred; it is well allied: but it is impossible to extirp it quite, friar, till eating and drinking be put down. They say this Angelo was not made by man and woman after this downright way of creation: is it true, think you?

DUKE

How should he be made, then?

LUCIO

Some report a sea-maid spawned him; some, that he was begot between two stock-fishes. But it is certain that, when he makes water, his urine is congealed ice; that I know to be true: and he is a motion generative; that's infallible.

DUKE

You are pleasant, sir, and speak apace.

LUCIO

Why, what a ruthless thing is this in him, for the rebellion of a codpiece to take away the life of a man! Would the Duke that is absent have done this? Ere he would have hanged a man for the getting a hundred bastards, he would have paid for the nursing a thousand: he had some feeling of the sport; he knew the service, and that instructed him to mercy.

DUKE

I never heard the absent Duke much detected for women; he was not inclined that way.

LUCIO

O, sir, you are deceived.

DUKE

'Tis not possible.

LUCIO

Who, not the Duke? yes, your beggar of fifty; and his use was to put a ducat in her clack-dish: the Duke had crotchets in him. He would be drunk too; that let me inform you.

DUKE

You do him wrong, surely.

LUCIO

Sir, I was an inward of his. A shy fellow was the Duke: and I believe I know the cause of his withdrawing.

DUKE

What, I prithee, might be the cause?

LUCIO

No, pardon; 'tis a secret must be locked within the teeth and the lips: but this I can let you understand, the greater file of the subject held the Duke to be wise.

DUKE

Wise! why, no question but he was.

LUCIO

A very superficial, ignorant, unweighing fellow.

DUKE

Either this is envy in you, folly, or mistaking: the very stream of his life and the business he hath helmed must, upon a warranted need, give him a better proclamation. Let him be but testimonied in his own bringings-forth, and he shall appear to the envious a scholar, a statesman and a soldier. Therefore you speak unskilfully; or if your knowledge be more, it is much darkened in your malice.

LUCIO

Sir, I know him, and I love him.

DUKE

Love talks with better knowledge, and knowledge with dearer love.

LUCIO

Come, sir, I know what I know.

DUKE

I can hardly believe that, since you know not what you speak. But, if ever the Duke return, as our prayers are he may, let me desire you to make your answer before him. If it be honest you have spoke, you have courage to maintain it: I am bound to call upon you; and, I pray you, your name?

LUCIO

Sir, my name is Lucio; well known to the Duke.

DUKE

He shall know you better, sir, if I may live to report you.

LUCIO

I fear you not.

DUKE

O, you hope the Duke will return no more; or you imagine me too unhurtful an opposite. But, indeed, I can do you little harm; you'll forswear this again.

LUCIO

I'll be hanged first: thou art deceived in me, friar. But no more of this. Canst thou tell if Claudio die to-morrow or no?

DUKE

Why should he die, sir?

LUCIO

Why? For filling a bottle with a tun-dish. I would the Duke we talk of were returned again: this un-genitured agent will unpeople the province with continency; sparrows must not build in his house-eaves, because they are lecherous. The Duke yet would have dark deeds darkly answered; he would never bring them to light: would he were returned! Marry, this Claudio is condemned for untrussing. Farewell, good friar: I prithee, pray for me. The Duke, I say to thee again, would eat mutton on Fri-days. He's not past it yet, and I say to thee, he would mouth with a beggar, though she smelt brown bread and garlic: say that I said so. Farewell.   [Exit

DUKE

No might nor greatness in mortality
Can censure 'scape; back-wounding calumny
The whitest virtue strikes. What king so strong
Can tie the gall up in the slanderous tongue?
But who comes here?

Enter ESCALUS, PROVOST, and OFFICERS with
MISTRESS OVERDONE

ESCALUS

Go; away with her to prison!

MISTRESS OVERDONE

Good my lord, be good to me; your honour is ac-counted a merciful man; good my lord.

ESCALUS

Double and treble admonition, and still forfeit in the same kind! This would make mercy swear and play the tyrant.

PROVOST

A bawd of eleven years' continuance, may it please your honour.

MISTRESS OVERDONE

My lord, this is one Lucio's information against me. Mistress Kate Keepdown was with child by him in the Duke's time; he promised her marriage: his child is a year and a quarter old, come Philip and Jacob: I have kept it myself; and see how he goes about to abuse me.

ESCALUS

That fellow is a fellow of much license: let him be called before us. Away with her to prison! Go to; no more words. [Exeunt OFFICERS with MISTRESS OVER-DONE] Provost, my brother Angelo will not be altered; Claudio must die to-morrow: let him be furnished with divines, and have all charitable prep-aration. If my brother wrought by my pity, it should not be so with him.

PROVOST

So please you, this friar hath been with him, and advised him for the entertainment of death.

ESCALUS

Good even, good father.

DUKE

Bliss and goodness on you!

ESCALUS

Of whence are you?

DUKE

Not of this country, though my chance is now
To use it for my time: I am a brother
Of gracious order, late come from the See
In special business from his Holiness.

ESCALUS

What news abroad i' the world?

DUKE

None, but that there is so great a fever on goodness, that the dissolution of it must cure it: novelty is only in request; and it is as dangerous to be aged in any kind of course, as it is virtuous to be constant in any undertaking. There is scarce truth enough alive to make societies secure; but security enough to make fellowships accurst:—much upon this riddle runs the wisdom of the world. This news is old enough, yet it is every day's news. I pray you, sir, of what dis-position was the Duke?

ESCALUS

One that, above all other strifes, contended espe-cially to know himself.

DUKE

What pleasure was he given to?

ESCALUS

Rather rejoicing to see another merry, than merry at any thing which professed to make him rejoice: a gentleman of all temperance. But leave we him to his events, with a prayer they may prove prosperous; and let me desire to know how you find Claudio pre-pared. I am made to understand that you have lent him visitation.

DUKE

He professes to have received no sinister measure from his judge, but most willingly humbles himself to the determination of justice: yet had he framed to himself, by the instruction of his frailty, many de-ceiving promises of life; which I, by my good leisure, have discredited to him, and now is he resolved to die.

ESCALUS

You have paid the heavens your function, and the prisoner the very debt of your calling. I have laboured

for the poor gentleman to the extremest shore of my
modesty: but my brother justice have I found so
severe, that he hath forced me to tell him he is indeed Justice.

DUKE

If his own life answer the straitness of his proceeding,
it shall become him well; wherein if he chance to
fail, he hath sentenced himself.

ESCALUS

I am going to visit the prisoner. Fare you well.

DUKE

Peace be with you!   [*Exeunt* ESCALUS *and* PROVOST
He who the sword of heaven will bear
Should be as holy as severe;
Pattern in himself to know,
Grace to stand, and virtue go;
More nor less to others paying
Than by self-offences weighing.
Shame to him whose cruel striking
Kills for faults of his own liking!
Twice treble shame on Angelo,
To weed my vice and let his grow!
O, what may man within him hide,
Though angel on the outward side!
How may likeness made in crimes,
Making practice on the times,
To draw with idle spiders' strings
Most ponderous and substantial things!
Craft against vice I must apply:
With Angelo to-night shall lie
His old betrothed but despised;
So disguise shall, by the disguised,
Pay with falsehood false exacting,
And perform an old contracting.   [*Exit*

ACT IV

SCENE I. *The moated grange at* ST. LUKE'S

Enter MARIANA *and a* BOY

BOY *sings*

Take, O, take those lips away,
    That so sweetly were forsworn;
And those eyes, the break of day,
    Lights that do mislead the morn:
But my kisses bring again, bring again;
Seals of love, but seal'd in vain, seal'd in vain.

MARIANA

Break off thy song, and haste thee quick away:
Here comes a man of comfort, whose advice
Hath often still'd my brawling discontent.
                                        [*Exit* BOY

Enter DUKE *disguised as before*

I cry you mercy, sir; and well could wish
You had not found me here so musical:
Let me excuse me, and believe me so,
My mirth it much displeased, but pleased my woe.

DUKE

'Tis good; though music oft hath such a charm
To make bad good, and good provoke to harm.
I pray you, tell me, hath any body inquired for me
here to-day? much upon this time have I promised
here to meet.

MARIANA

You have not been inquired after: I have sat here
all day.

Enter ISABELLA

DUKE

I do constantly believe you. The time is come even
now. I shall crave your forbearance a little: may be
I will call upon you anon, for some advantage to
yourself.

MARIANA

I am always bound to you.   [*Exit*

DUKE

Very well met, and well come.
What is the news from this good Deputy?

ISABELLA

He hath a garden circummured with brick,
Whose western side is with a vineyard back'd;
And to that vineyard is a planched gate,
That makes his opening with this bigger key:
This other doth command a little door
Which from the vineyard to the garden leads;
There have I made my promise
Upon the heavy middle of the night
To call upon him.

DUKE

But shall you on your knowledge find this way?

ISABELLA

I have ta'en a due and wary note upon 't:
With whispering and most guilty diligence,
In action all of precept, he did show me
The way twice o'er.

DUKE

                    Are there no other tokens
Between you 'greed concerning her observance?

ISABELLA

No, none, but only a repair i' the dark;
And that I have possess'd him my most stay
Can be but brief; for I have made him know
I have a servant comes with me along,
That stays upon me, whose persuasion is
I come about my brother.

DUKE

                    'Tis well borne up.
I have not yet made known to Mariana
A word of this. What, ho! within! come forth!

Re-enter MARIANA

I pray you, be acquainted with this maid;
She comes to do you good.

ISABELLA

                    I do desire the like.

DUKE

Do you persuade yourself that I respect you?

MARIANA

Good friar, I know you do, and have found it.

DUKE

Take, then, this your companion by the hand,
Who hath a story ready for your ear.
I shall attend your leisure: but make haste;
The vaporous night approaches.

MARIANA

Will't please you walk aside?

[Exeunt MARIANA *and* ISABELLA

DUKE

O place and greatness, millions of false eyes
Are stuck upon thee! volumes of report
Run with these false and most contrarious quests
Upon thy doings! thousand escapes of wit
Make thee the father of their idle dreams,
And rack thee in their fancies!

Re-enter MARIANA *and* ISABELLA

Welcome, how agreed?

ISABELLA

She'll take the enterprise upon her, father,
If you advise it.

DUKE

It is not my consent
But my entreaty too.

ISABELLA

Little have you to say
When you depart from him, but, soft and low,
'Remember now my brother.'

MARIANA

Fear me not.

DUKE

Nor, gentle daughter, fear you not at all.
He is your husband on a pre-contract:
To bring you thus together, 'tis no sin,
Sith that the justice of your title to him
Doth flourish the deceit. Come, let us go:
Our corn's to reap, for yet our tithe's to sow.

[Exeunt

SCENE II. *A room in the prison*

Enter PROVOST *and* POMPEY

PROVOST

Come hither, sirrah. Can you cut off a man's head?

POMPEY

If the man be a bachelor, sir, I can; but if he be a
married man, he's his wife's head, and I can never
cut off a woman's head.

PROVOST

Come, sir, leave me your snatches, and yield me a
direct answer. To-morrow morning are to die Claudio
and Barnardine. Here is in our prison a common
executioner, who in his office lacks a helper: if you
will take it on you to assist him, it shall redeem you
from your gyves; if not, you shall have your full
time of imprisonment, and your deliverance with an
unpitied whipping, for you have been a notorious
bawd.

POMPEY

Sir, I have been an unlawful bawd time out of mind;
but yet I will be content to be a lawful hangman. I

would be glad to receive some instruction from my
fellow partner.

PROVOST

What, ho! Abhorson! Where's Abhorson, there?

Enter ABHORSON

ABHORSON

Do you call, sir?

PROVOST

Sirrah, here's a fellow will help you to-morrow in
your execution. If you think it meet, compound
with him by the year, and let him abide here with
you; if not, use him for the present, and dismiss him.
He cannot plead his estimation with you; he hath
been a bawd.

ABHORSON

A bawd, sir? fie upon him! he will discredit our mystery.

PROVOST

Go to, sir; you weigh equally; a feather will turn the
scale.   *[Exit*

POMPEY

Pray, sir, by your good favour,—for surely, sir, a
good favour you have, but that you have a hanging
look,—do you call, sir, your occupation a mystery?

ABHORSON

Ay, sir; a mystery.

POMPEY

Painting, sir, I have heard say, is a mystery; and
your whores, sir, being members of my occupation,
using painting, do prove my occupation a mystery:
but what mystery there should be in hanging, if I
should be hanged, I cannot imagine.

ABHORSON

Sir, it is a mystery.

POMPEY

Proof?

ABHORSON

Every true man's apparel fits your thief: if it be too
little for your thief, your true man thinks it big
enough; if it be too big for your thief, your thief
thinks it little enough: so every true man's apparel
fits your thief.

Re-enter PROVOST

PROVOST

Are you agreed?

POMPEY

Sir, I will serve him; for I do find your hangman is
a more penitent trade than your bawd; he doth
oftener ask forgiveness.

PROVOST

You, sirrah, provide your block and your axe to-
morrow four o'clock.

ABHORSON

Come on, bawd; I will instruct thee in my trade;
follow.

POMPEY

I do desire to learn, sir: and I hope, if you have occasion to use me for your own turn, you shall find
me yare; for, truly, sir, for your kindness I owe you
a good turn.

PROVOST

Call hither Barnardine and Claudio:
                    [*Exeunt* POMPEY *and* ABHORSON
The one has my pity; not a jot the other,
Being a murderer, though he were my brother.
                    Enter CLAUDIO
Look, here's the warrant, Claudio, for thy death:
'Tis now dead midnight, and by eight to-morrow
Thou must be made immortal. Where's Barnardine?

CLAUDIO

As fast lock'd up in sleep as guiltless labour
When it lies starkly in the traveller's bones:
He will not wake.

PROVOST

                    Who can do good on him?
Well, go, prepare yourself. [*Knocking within*] But,
  hark, what noise?—
Heaven give your spirits comfort! [*Exit* CLAUDIO]
  By and by.—
I hope it is some pardon or reprieve
For the most gentle Claudio.
          Enter DUKE *disguised as before*
                              Welcome, father.

DUKE

The best and wholesomest spirits of the night
Envelop you, good Provost! Who call'd here of late?

PROVOST

None, since the curfew rung.

DUKE

Not Isabel?

PROVOST

No.

DUKE

          They will, then, ere't be long.

PROVOST

What comfort is for Claudio?

DUKE

There's some in hope.

PROVOST

It is a bitter deputy.

DUKE

Not so, not so; his life is parallel'd
Even with the stroke and line of his great justice:
He doth with holy abstinence subdue
That in himself which he spurs on his power
To qualify in others: were he meal'd with that
Which he corrects, then were he tyrannous;
But this being so, he's just.   [*Knocking within*
                    Now are they come.
                              [*Exit* PROVOST
This is a gentle provost: seldom when
The steeled gaoler is the friend of men.
                              [*Knocking within*
How now! what noise? That spirit's possess'd with
  haste
That wounds the unsisting postern with these strokes.
          Re-enter PROVOST

PROVOST

There he must stay until the officer
Arise to let him in: he is call'd up.

DUKE

Have you no countermand for Claudio yet,
But he must die to-morrow?

PROVOST

                    None, sir, none.

DUKE

As near the dawning, provost, as it is,
You shall hear more ere morning.

PROVOST

                              Happily
You something know; yet I believe there comes
No countermand; no such example have we:
Besides, upon the very siege of justice
Lord Angelo hath to the public ear
Profess'd the contrary.
                    Enter a MESSENGER
                    This is his lordship's man.

DUKE

And here comes Claudio's pardon.

MESSENGER

[*Giving a paper*] My lord hath sent you this note; and
by me this further charge, that you swerve not from
the smallest article of it, neither in time, matter, or
other circumstance. Good morrow; for, as I take it,
it is almost day.

PROVOST

I shall obey him.   [*Exit* MESSENGER

DUKE

[*Aside*] This is his pardon, purchased by such sin
For which the pardoner himself is in.
Hence hath offence his quick celerity,
When it is borne in high authority:
When vice makes mercy, mercy's so extended,
That for the fault's love is the offender friended.
Now, sir, what news?

PROVOST

I told you. Lord Angelo, belike thinking me remiss
in mine office, awakens me with this unwonted
putting-on; methinks strangely, for he hath not used
it before.

DUKE

Pray you, let's hear.

PROVOST

[*Reads*]

    Whatsoever you may hear to the contrary, let Claudio be
executed by four of the clock; and in the afternoon Barnardine:
for my better satisfaction, let me have Claudio's head sent me
by five. Let this be duly performed; with a thought that more
depends on it than we must yet deliver. Thus fail not to do
your office, as you will answer it at your peril.

What say you to this, sir?

DUKE

What is that Barnardine who is to be executed in
the afternoon?

PROVOST

A Bohemian born, but here nursed up and bred; one
that is a prisoner nine years old.

DUKE

How came it that the absent Duke had not either

delivered him to his liberty or executed him? I have heard it was ever his manner to do so.

PROVOST

His friends still wrought reprieves for him: and, indeed, his fact, till now in the government of Lord Angelo, came not to an undoubtful proof.

DUKE

It is now apparent?

PROVOST

Most manifest, and not denied by himself.

DUKE

Hath he borne himself penitently in prison? how seems he to be touched?

PROVOST

A man that apprehends death no more dreadfully but as a drunken sleep; careless, reckless, and fearless of what's past, present, or to come; insensible of mortality, and desperately mortal.

DUKE

He wants advice.

PROVOST

He will hear none: he hath evermore had the liberty of the prison; give him leave to escape hence, he would not: drunk many times a day, if not many days entirely drunk. We have very oft awaked him, as if to carry him to execution, and showed him a seeming warrant for it: it hath not moved him at all.

DUKE

More of him anon. There is written in your brow, provost, honesty and constancy: if I read it not truly, my ancient skill beguiles me; but, in the boldness of my cunning, I will lay my self in hazard. Claudio, whom here you have warrant to execute, is no greater forfeit to the law than Angelo who hath sentenced him. To make you understand this in a manifested effect, I crave but four days' respite; for the which you are to do me both a present and a dangerous courtesy.

PROVOST

Pray, sir, in what?

DUKE

In the delaying death.

PROVOST

Alack, how may I do it, having the hour limited, and an express command, under penalty, to deliver his head in the view of Angelo? I may make my case as Claudio's, to cross this in the smallest.

DUKE

By the vow of mine order I warrant you, if my instructions may be your guide. Let this Barnardine be this morning executed, and his head borne to Angelo.

PROVOST

Angelo hath seen them both, and will discover the favour.

DUKE

O, death's a great disguiser; and you may add to it. Shave the head, and tie the beard; and say it was the desire of the penitent to be so bared before his death: you know the course is common. If any thing fall to you upon this, more than thanks and good fortune, by the Saint whom I profess, I will plead against it with my life.

PROVOST

Pardon me, good father; it is against my oath.

DUKE

Were you sworn to the Duke, or to the Deputy?

PROVOST

To him, and to his substitutes.

DUKE

You will think you have made no offence, if the Duke avouch the justice of your dealing?

PROVOST

But what likelihood is in that?

DUKE

Not a resemblance, but a certainty. Yet since I see you fearful, that neither my coat, integrity, nor persuasion can with ease attempt you, I will go further than I meant, to pluck all fears out of you. Look you, sir, here is the hand and seal of the Duke: you know the character, I doubt not; and the signet is not strange to you.

PROVOST

I know them both.

DUKE

The contents of this is the return of the Duke: you shall anon over-read it at your pleasure; where you shall find, within these two days he will be here. This is a thing that Angelo knows not; for he this very day receives letters of strange tenour; perchance of the Duke's death; perchance entering into some monastery; but, by chance, nothing of what is writ. Look, the unfolding star calls up the shepherd. Put not yourself into amazement how these things should be: all difficulties are but easy when they are known. Call your executioner, and off with Barnardine's head: I will give him a present shrift and advise him for a better place. Yet you are amazed; but this shall absolutely resolve you. Come away; it is almost clear dawn. [*Exeunt*

SCENE III. *Another room in the same*

Enter POMPEY

POMPEY

I am as well acquainted here as I was in our house of profession: one would think it were Mistress Overdone's own house, for here be many of her old customers. First, here's young Master Rash; he's in for a commodity of brown paper and old ginger, ninescore and seventeen pounds; of which he made five marks, ready money: marry, then ginger was not much in request, for the old women were all dead. Then is there here one Master Caper, at the suit of Master Three-pile the mercer, for some four suits of peach-coloured satin, which now peaches him a beggar. Then have we here young Dizy, and young Master Deep-vow, and Master Copper-spur, and Master Starve-lackey the rapier and dagger man,

and young Drop-heir that killed lusty Pudding, and
Master Forthlight the tilter, and brave Master Shooty
the great traveller, and wild Half-can that stabbed
Pots, and, I think, forty more; all great doers in our
trade, and are now 'for the Lord's sake.'

Enter ABHORSON

ABHORSON
Sirrah, bring Barnardine hither.

POMPEY
Master Barnardine! you must rise and be hanged,
Master Barnardine!

ABHORSON
What, ho, Barnardine!

BARNARDINE
[*Within*] A pox o' your throats! Who makes that noise
there? What are you?

POMPEY
Your friends, sir; the hangman. You must be so good,
sir, to rise and be put to death.

BARNARDINE
[*Within*] Away, you rogue, away! I am sleepy.

ABHORSON
Tell him he must awake, and that quickly too.

POMPEY
Pray, Master Barnardine, awake till you are executed, and sleep afterwards.

ABHORSON
Go in to him, and fetch him out.

POMPEY
He is coming, sir, he is coming; I hear his straw rustle.

ABHORSON
Is the axe upon the block, sirrah?

POMPEY
Very ready, sir.

Enter BARNARDINE

BARNARDINE
How now, Abhorson? what's the news with you?

ABHORSON
Truly, sir, I would desire you to clap into your prayers;
for, look you, the warrant's come.

BARNARDINE
You rogue, I have been drinking all night; I am not
fitted for 't.

POMPEY
O, the better, sir; for he that drinks all night, and
is hanged betimes in the morning, may sleep the
sounder all the next day.

ABHORSON
Look you, sir; here comes your ghostly father: do
we jest now, think you?

Enter DUKE *disguised as before*

DUKE
Sir, induced by my charity, and hearing how hastily
you are to depart, I am come to advise you, comfort you and pray with you.

BARNARDINE
Friar, not I: I have been drinking hard all night,
I will have more time to prepare me, or they shall
beat out my brains with billets: I will not consent to
die this day, that's certain.

DUKE
O, sir, you must: and therefore I beseech you
Look forward on the journey you shall go.

BARNARDINE
I swear I will not die to-day for any man's persuasion.

DUKE
But hear you.

BARNARDINE
Not a word: if you have any thing to say to me, come
to my ward; for thence will not I to-day   [*Exit*

DUKE
Unfit to live or die: O gravel heart!
After him, fellows; bring him to the block.

    [*Exeunt* ABHORSON *and* POMPEY

Enter PROVOST

PROVOST
Now, sir, how do you find the prisoner?

DUKE
A creature unprepared, unmeet for death;
And to transport him in the mind he is
Were damnable.

PROVOST
               Here in the prison, father,
There died this morning of a cruel fever
One Ragozine, a most notorious pirate,
A man of Claudio's years; his beard and head
Just of his colour. What if we do omit
This reprobate till he were well inclined;
And satisfy the Deputy with the visage
Of Ragozine, more like to Claudio?

DUKE
O, 'tis an accident that heaven provides!
Dispatch it presently; the hour draws on
Prefix'd by Angelo: see this be done,
And sent according to command; whiles I
Persuade this rude wretch willingly to die.

PROVOST
This shall be done, good father, presently.
But Barnardine must die this afternoon:
And how shall we continue Claudio,
To save me from the danger that might come
If he were known alive?

DUKE
               Let this be done.
Put them in secret holds, both Barnardine and
   Claudio:
Ere twice the sun hath made his journal greeting
To the under generation, you shall find
Your safety manifested.

PROVOST
I am your free dependant.

DUKE
Quick, dispatch, and send the head to Angelo.

    [*Exit* PROVOST

Now will I write letters to Angelo,—
The provost, he shall bear them,—whose contents
Shall witness to him I am near at home,
And that, by great injunctions, I am bound
To enter publicly: him I'll desire
To meet me at the consecrated fount,

A league below the city; and from thence,
By cold gradation and well-balanced form,
We shall proceed with Angelo.

Re-enter PROVOST

PROVOST
Here is the head; I'll carry it myself.

DUKE
Convenient is it. Make a swift return;
For I would commune with you of such things
That want no ear but yours.

PROVOST
                          I'll make all speed.
                                              [*Exit*

ISABELLA
[*Within*] Peace, ho, be here!

DUKE
The tongue of Isabel. She's come to know
If yet her brother's pardon be come hither:
But I will keep her ignorant of her good,
To make her heavenly comforts of despair,
When it is least expected.

Enter ISABELLA

ISABELLA
                          Ho, by your leave!

DUKE
Good morning to you, fair and gracious daughter.

ISABELLA
The better, given me by so holy a man.
Hath yet the Deputy sent my brother's pardon?

DUKE
He hath released him, Isabel, from the world:
His head is off, and sent to Angelo.

ISABELLA
Nay, but it is not so.

DUKE
It is no other: show your wisdom, daughter,
In your close patience.

ISABELLA
O, I will to him and pluck out his eyes!

DUKE
You shall not be admitted to his sight.

ISABELLA
Unhappy Claudio! wretched Isabel!
Injurious world! most damned Angelo!

DUKE
This nor hurts him nor profits you a jot;
Forbear it therefore; give your cause to heaven.
Mark what I say, which you shall find
By every syllable a faithful verity:
The Duke comes home to-morrow;—nay, dry your
    eyes;
One of our covent, and his confessor,
Gives me this instance: already he hath carried
Notice to Escalus and Angelo;
Who do prepare to meet him at the gates,
There to give up their power. If you can, pace your
    wisdom
In that good path that I would wish it go;
And you shall have your bosom on this wretch,

Grace of the Duke, revenges to your heart,
And general honour.

ISABELLA
I am directed by you.

DUKE
This letter, then, to Friar Peter give;
'Tis that he sent me of the Duke's return:
Say, by this token, I desire his company
At Mariana's house to-night. Her cause and yours
I'll perfect him withal; and he shall bring you
Before the Duke; and to the head of Angelo
Accuse him home and home. For my poor self,
I am combined by a sacred vow,
And shall be absent. Wend you with this letter:
Command these fretting waters from your eyes
With a light heart; trust not my holy order,
If I pervert your course.—Who's here?

Enter LUCIO

LUCIO
Good even. Friar, where's the provost?

DUKE
Not within, sir.

LUCIO
O pretty Isabella, I am pale at mine heart to see
thine eyes so red: thou must be patient. I am fain to
dine and sup with water and bran; I dare not for
my head fill my belly; one fruitful meal would set
me to't. But they say the Duke will be here to-morrow.
By my troth, Isabel, I loved thy brother: if the old
fantastical Duke of dark corners had been at home,
he had lived.   [*Exit* ISABELLA

DUKE
Sir, the Duke is marvellous little beholding to your
reports; but the best is, he lives not in them.

LUCIO
Friar, thou knowest not the Duke so well as I do: he's a
better woodman than thou takest him for.

DUKE
Well, you'll answer this one day. Fare ye well.

LUCIO
Nay, tarry; I'll go along with thee: I can tell thee
pretty tales of the Duke.

DUKE
You have told me too many of him already, sir, if
they be true; if not true, none were enough.

LUCIO
I was once before him for getting a wench with child.

DUKE
Did you such a thing?

LUCIO
Yes, marry, did I: but I was fain to forswear it; they
would else have married me to the rotten medlar.

DUKE
Sir, your company is fairer than honest. Rest you
well.

LUCIO
By my troth, I'll go with thee to the lane's end: if
bawdy talk offend you, we'll have very little of it.
Nay, friar, I am a kind of burr; I shall stick. [*Exeunt*

SCENE IV. *A room in* ANGELO's *house*

Enter ANGELO *and* ESCALUS

ESCALUS

Every letter he hath writ hath disvouched other.

ANGELO

In most uneven and distracted manner. His actions
show much like to madness: pray heaven his wisdom
be not tainted! And why meet him at the gates, and
redeliver our authorities there?

ESCALUS

I guess not.

ANGELO

And why should we proclaim it in an hour before
his entering, that if any crave redress of injustice,
they should exhibit their petitions in the street?

ESCALUS

He shows his reason for that: to have a dispatch of
complaints, and to deliver us from devices hereafter,
which shall then have no power to stand against us.

ANGELO

Well, I beseech you, let it be proclaimed betimes i'
the morn; I'll call you at your house: give notice to
such men of sort and suit as are to meet him.

ESCALUS

I shall, sir. Fare you well.

ANGELO

Good night.   [*Exit* ESCALUS
This deed unshapes me quite, makes me unpregnant,
And dull to all proceedings. A deflower'd maid!
And by an eminent body that enforced
The law against it! But that her tender shame
Will not proclaim against her maiden loss,
How might she tongue me! Yet reason dares her no;
For my authority bears of a credent bulk,
That no particular scandal once can touch
But it confounds the breather. He should have lived,
Save that his riotous youth, with dangerous sense,
Might in the times to come have ta'en revenge,
By so receiving a dishonour'd life
With ransom of such shame. Would yet he had lived!
Alack, when once our grace we have forgot,
Nothing goes right: we would, and we would not.
           [*Exit*

SCENE V. *Fields without the town*

Enter DUKE *in his own habit, and* FRIAR PETER

DUKE

These letters at fit time deliver me: [*Giving letters*
The provost knows our purpose and our plot.
The matter being afoot, keep your instruction,
And hold you ever to our special drift;
Though sometimes you do blench from this to that,
As cause doth minister. Go call at Flavius' house,
And tell him where I stay: give the like notice
To Valentius, Rowland, and to Crassus,
And bid them bring the trumpets to the gate;
But send me Flavius first.

FRIAR PETER

It shall be speeded well.
           [*Exit*

Enter VARRIUS

DUKE

I thank thee, Varrius; thou hast made good haste:
Come, we will walk. There's other of our friends
Will greet us here anon, my gentle Varrius. [*Exeunt*

SCENE VI. *Street near the city-gate*

Enter ISABELLA *and* MARIANA

ISABELLA

To speak so indirectly I am loath:
I would say the truth; but to accuse him so,
That is your part: yet I am advised to do it;
He says, to veil full purpose.

MARIANA

Be ruled by him.

ISABELLA

Besides, he tells me that, if peradventure
He speak against me on the adverse side,
I should not think it strange; for 'tis a physic
That's bitter to sweet end.

MARIANA

I would Friar Peter—

ISABELLA

O, peace! the friar is come.

Enter FRIAR PETER

FRIAR PETER

Come, I have found you out a stand most fit,
Where you may have such vantage on the Duke,
He shall not pass you. Twice have the trumpets
   sounded;
The generous and gravest citizens
Have hent the gates, and very near upon
The Duke is entering: therefore, hence, away!
           [*Exeunt*

ACT V

SCENE I. *The city-gate*

MARIANA *veiled,* ISABELLA, *and* FRIAR PETER, *at their
stand. Enter* DUKE, VARRIUS, LORDS, ANGELO, ESCALUS,
LUCIO, PROVOST, OFFICERS, *and* CITIZENS, *at several doors*

DUKE

My very worthy cousin, fairly met!
Our old and faithful friend, we are glad to see you.

ANGELO *and* ESCALUS

Happy return be to your royal Grace!

DUKE

Many and hearty thankings to you both.
We have made inquiry of you; and we hear
Such goodness of your justice, that our soul
Cannot but yield you forth to public thanks,
Forerunning more requital.

ANGELO

You make my bonds still greater.

DUKE

O, your desert speaks loud; and I should wrong it,
To lock it in the wards of covert bosom,
When it deserves, with characters of brass,
A forted residence 'gainst the tooth of time
And razure of oblivion. Give me your hand,
And let the subject see, to make them know
That outward courtesies would fain proclaim
Favours that keep within. Come, Escalus;
You must walk by us on our other hand:
And good supporters are you.

FRIAR PETER and ISABELLA come forward

FRIAR PETER

Now is your time: speak loud, and kneel before him.

ISABELLA

Justice, O royal Duke! Vail your regard
Upon a wrong'd, I would fain have said, a maid!
O worthy prince, dishonour not your eye
By throwing it on any other object
Till you have heard me in my true complaint,
And given me justice, justice, justice, justice!

DUKE

Relate your wrongs; in what? by whom? be brief.
Here is Lord Angelo shall give you justice:
Reveal yourself to him.

ISABELLA

           O worthy Duke,
You bid me seek redemption of the devil:
Hear me yourself; for that which I must speak
Must either punish me, not being believed,
Or wring redress from you. Hear me, O hear me,
  here!

ANGELO

My lord, her wits, I fear me, are not firm:
She hath been a suitor to me for her brother
Cut off by course of justice,—

ISABELLA

           By course of justice!

ANGELO

And she will speak most bitterly and strange.

ISABELLA

Most strange, but yet most truly, will I speak:
That Angelo's forsworn; is it not strange?
That Angelo's a murderer; is't not strange?
That Angelo is an adulterous thief,
An hypocrite, a virgin-violator;
Is it not strange and strange?

DUKE

           Nay, it is ten times strange.

ISABELLA

It is not truer he is Angelo
Than this is all as true as it is strange:
'Nay, it is ten times true; for truth is truth
'To the end of reckoning.

DUKE

           Away with her!—Poor soul,
She speaks this in the infirmity of sense.

ISABELLA

O prince, I conjure thee, as thou believest

There is another comfort than this world,
That thou neglect me not, with that opinion
That I am touch'd with madness! Make not impossible
That which but seems unlike: 'tis not impossible
But one, the wicked'st caitiff on the ground,
May seem as shy, as grave, as just, as absolute
As Angelo; even so may Angelo,
In all his dressings, characts, titles, forms,
Be an arch-villain; believe it, royal prince:
If he be less, he's nothing; but he's more,
Had I more name for badness.

DUKE

           By mine honesty,
If she be mad,—as I believe no other,—
Her madness hath the oddest frame of sense,
Such a dependency of thing on thing,
As e'er I heard in madness.

ISABELLA

           O gracious Duke,
Harp not on that; nor do not banish reason
For inequality; but let your reason serve
To make the truth appear where it seems hid,
And hide the false seems true.

DUKE

           Many that are not mad
Have, sure, more lack of reason. What would you say?

ISABELLA

I am the sister of one Claudio,
Condemn'd upon the act of fornication
To lose his head; condemn'd by Angelo:
I, in probation of a sisterhood,
Was sent to by my brother; one Lucio
As then the messenger,—

LUCIO

           That's I, an't like your Grace:
I came to her from Claudio, and desired her
To try her gracious fortune with Lord Angelo
For her poor brother's pardon.

ISABELLA

           That's he indeed.

DUKE

You were not bid to speak.

LUCIO

           No, my good lord;
Nor wish'd to hold my peace.

DUKE

           I wish you now, then;
Pray you, take note of it: and when you have
A business for yourself, pray heaven you then
Be perfect.

LUCIO

I warrant your honour.

DUKE

The warrant's for yourself; take heed to't.

ISABELLA

This gentleman told somewhat of my tale,—

LUCIO

Right.

DUKE

It may be right; but you are i' the wrong
To speak before your time. Proceed.

ISABELLA

                    I went
To this pernicious caitiff Deputy,—

DUKE

That's somewhat madly spoken.

ISABELLA

                    Pardon it;
The phrase is to the matter.

DUKE

Mended again. The matter;—proceed.

ISABELLA

In brief,—to set the needless process by,
How I persuaded, how I pray'd, and kneel'd,
How he refell'd me, and how I replied,—
For this was of much length,—the vile conclusion
I now begin with grief and shame to utter:
He would not, but by gift of my chaste body
To his concupiscible intemperate lust,
Release my brother; and, after much debatement,
My sisterly remorse confutes mine honour,
And I did yield to him: but the next morn betimes,
His purpose surfeiting, he sends a warrant
For my poor brother's head.

DUKE

                    This is most likely!

ISABELLA

O, that it were as like as it is true!

DUKE

By heaven, fond wretch, thou know'st not what thou
          speak'st,
Or else thou art suborn'd against his honour
In hateful practice. First, his integrity
Stands without blemish. Next, it imports no reason
That with such vehemency he should pursue
Faults proper to himself: if he had so offended,
He would have weigh'd thy brother by himself,
And not have cut him off. Some one hath set you
          on:
Confess the truth, and say by whose advice
Thou camest here to complain.

ISABELLA

                    And is this all?
Then, O you blessed ministers above,
Keep me in patience, and with ripen'd time
Unfold the evil which is here wrapt up
In countenance!—Heaven shield your Grace from
          woe,
As I, thus wrong'd, hence unbelieved go!

DUKE

I know you'ld fain be gone.—An officer!
To prison with her!—Shall we thus permit
A blasting and a scandalous breath to fall
On him so near us? This needs must be a practice.
Who knew of your intent and coming hither?

ISABELLA

One that I would were here, Friar Lodowick.

DUKE

A ghostly father, belike. Who knows that Lodowick?

LUCIO

My lord, I know him; 'tis a meddling friar;
I do not like the man: had he been lay, my lord,
For certain words he spake against your Grace
In your retirement, I had swinged him soundly.

DUKE

Words against me! this's a good friar, belike!
And to set on this wretched woman here
Against our substitute! Let this friar be found.

LUCIO

But yesternight, my lord, she and that friar,
I saw them at the prison: a saucy friar,
A very scurvy fellow.

FRIAR PETER

Blessed be your royal Grace!
I have stood by, my lord, and I have heard
Your royal ear abused. First, hath this woman
Most wrongfully accused your substitute,
Who is as free from touch or soil with her
As she from one ungot.

DUKE

                    We did believe no less.
Know you that Friar Lodowick that she speaks of?

FRIAR PETER

I know him for a man divine and holy;
Not scurvy, nor a temporary meddler,
As he's reported by this gentleman;
And, on my trust, a man that never yet
Did, as he vouches, misreport your Grace.

LUCIO

My lord, most villanously; believe it.

FRIAR PETER

Well, he in time may come to clear himself;
But at this instant he is sick, my lord,
Of a strange fever. Upon his mere request,—
Being come to knowledge that there was complaint
Intended 'gainst Lord Angelo,—came I hither,
To speak, as from his mouth, what he doth know
Is true and false; and what he with his oath
And all probation will make up full clear,
Whensoever he's convented. First, for this woman,
To justify this worthy nobleman,
So vulgarly and personally accused,
Her shall you hear disproved to her eyes,
Till she herself confess it.

DUKE

                    Good friar, let's hear it.
[ISABELLA *is carried off guarded; and* MARIANA *comes*
                                        forward

Do you not smile at this, Lord Angelo?—
O heaven, the vanity of wretched fools!—
Give us some seats. Come, cousin Angelo;
In this I'll be impartial; be you judge
Of your own cause. Is this the witness, friar?
First, let her show her face, and after speak.

MARIANA

Pardon, my lord; I will not show my face
Until my husband bid me.

DUKE
What, are you married?

MARIANA
No, my lord.

DUKE
Are you a maid?

MARIANA
No, my lord.

DUKE
A widow, then?

MARIANA
Neither, my lord.

DUKE
Why, you are nothing, then:—neither maid, widow,
nor wife?

LUCIO
My lord, she may be a punk; for many of them are
neither maid, widow, nor wife.

DUKE
Silence that fellow: I would he had some cause
To prattle for himself.

LUCIO
Well, my lord.

MARIANA
My lord, I do confess I ne'er was married;
And I confess, besides, I am no maid:
I have known my husband; yet my husband
Knows not that ever he knew me.

LUCIO
He was drunk, then, my lord: it can be no better.

DUKE
For the benefit of silence, would thou wert so too!

LUCIO
Well, my lord.

DUKE
This is no witness for Lord Angelo.

MARIANA
Now I come to't, my lord:
She that accuses him of fornication,
In self-same manner doth accuse my husband;
And charges him, my lord, with such a time
When I'll depose I had him in mine arms
With all the effect of love.

ANGELO
Charges she moe than me?

MARIANA
Not that I know.

DUKE
No? you say your husband.

MARIANA
Why, just, my lord, and that is Angelo,
Who thinks he knows that he ne'er knew my body,
But knows he thinks that he knows Isabel's.

ANGELO
This is a strange abuse. Let's see thy face.

MARIANA
My husband bids me; now I will unmask. [*Unveiling*
This is that face, thou cruel Angelo,
Which once thou sworest was worth the looking on;
This is the hand which, with a vow'd contract,

Was fast belock'd in thine; this is the body
That took away the match from Isabel,
And did supply thee at thy garden-house
In her imagined person.

DUKE
Know you this woman?

LUCIO
Carnally, she says.

DUKE
Sirrah, no more!

LUCIO
Enough, my lord.

ANGELO
My lord, I must confess I know this woman:
And five years since there was some speech of mar-
riage
Betwixt myself and her; which was broke off,
Partly for that her promised proportions
Came short of composition; but in chief,
For that her reputation was disvalued
In levity: since which time of five years
I never spake with her, saw her, nor heard from her,
Upon my faith and honour.

MARIANA
                    Noble prince,
As there comes light from heaven and words from
breath,
As there is sense in truth and truth in virtue,
I am affianced this man's wife as strongly
As words could make up vows: and, my good lord,
But Tuesday night last gone in's garden-house
He knew me as a wife. As this is true,
Let me in safety raise me from my knees;
Or else for ever be confixed here,
A marble monument!

ANGELO
                    I did but smile till now:
Now, good my lord, give me the scope of justice;
My patience here is touch'd. I do perceive
These poor informal women are no more
But instruments of some more mightier member
That sets them on: let me have way, my lord,
To find this practice out.

DUKE
                    Ay, with my heart;
And punish them to your height of pleasure.
Thou foolish friar; and thou pernicious woman,
Compact with her that's gone, think'st thou thy
oaths,
Though they would swear down each particular saint,
Were testimonies against his worth and credit,
That's seal'd in approbation? You, Lord Escalus,
Sit with my cousin; lend him your kind pains
To find out this abuse, whence 'tis derived.
There is another friar that set them on;
Let him be sent for.

FRIAR PETER
Would he were here, my lord! for he, indeed,
Hath set the women on to this complaint:

Your provost knows the place where he abides,
And he may fetch him.

DUKE

　　　　Go, do it instantly. [*Exit* PROVOST
And you, my noble and well-warranted cousin,
Whom it concerns to hear this matter forth,
Do with your injuries as seems you best,
In any chastisement: I for a while will leave you;
But stir not you till you have well determined
Upon these slanderers.

ESCALUS

My lord, we'll do it throughly. [*Exit* DUKE] Signior
Lucio, did not you say you knew that Friar Lodowick to be a dishonest person?

LUCIO

'Cucullus non facit monachum:' honest in nothing
but in his clothes; and one that hath spoke most villanous speeches of the Duke.

ESCALUS

We shall entreat you to abide here till he come, and
enforce them against him: we shall find this friar a
notable fellow.

LUCIO

As any in Vienna, on my word.

ESCALUS

Call that same Isabel here once again: I would
speak with her. [*Exit an* ATTENDANT] Pray you, my
lord, give me leave to question; you shall see how
I'll handle her.

LUCIO

Not better than he, by her own report.

ESCALUS

Say you?

LUCIO

Marry, sir, I think, if you handled her privately, she
would sooner confess: perchance, publicly, she'll be
ashamed.

ESCALUS

I will go darkly to work with her.

LUCIO

That's the way; for women are light at midnight.
Re-enter OFFICERS *with* ISABELLA; *and* PROVOST *with the*
DUKE *in his friar's habit*

ESCALUS

Come on, mistress: here's a gentlewoman denies all
that you have said.

LUCIO

My lord, here comes the rascal I spoke of; here with
the provost.

ESCALUS

In very good time: speak not you to him till we call
upon you.

LUCIO

Mum.

ESCALUS

Come, sir: did you set these women on to slander
Lord Angelo? they have confessed you did.

DUKE

'Tis false.

ESCALUS

How! know you where you are?

DUKE

Respect to your great place! and let the devil
Be sometime honour'd for his burning throne!
Where is the Duke? 'tis he should hear me speak.

ESCALUS

The Duke's in us; and we will hear you speak: Look
you speak justly.

DUKE

Boldly, at least. But, O, poor souls,
Come you to seek the lamb here of the fox?
Good night to your redress! Is the Duke gone?
Then is your cause gone too. The Duke's unjust,
Thus to retort your manifest appeal,
And put your trial in the villain's mouth
Which here you come to accuse.

LUCIO

This is the rascal; this is he I spoke of.

ESCALUS

Why, thou unreverend and unhallow'd friar,
Is't not enough thou hast suborn'd these women
To accuse this worthy man, but, in foul mouth,
And in the witness of his proper ear,
To call him villain? and then to glance from him
To the Duke himself, to tax him with injustice?
Take him hence; to the rack with him! We'll touse
　　you
Joint by joint, but we will know his purpose.
What, 'unjust'!

DUKE

　　　　Be not so hot; the Duke
Dare no more stretch this finger of mine than he
Dare rack his own: his subject am I not,
Nor here provincial. My business in this state
Made me a looker-on here in Vienna,
Where I have seen corruption boil and bubble
Till it o'er-run the stew; laws for all faults,
But faults so countenanced, that the strong statutes
Stand like the forfeits in a barber's shop,
As much in mock as mark.

ESCALUS

Slander to the state! Away with him to prison!

ANGELO

What can you vouch against him, Signior Lucio? Is
this the man that you did tell us of?

LUCIO

'Tis he, my lord. Come hither, goodman baldpate:
do you know me?

DUKE

I remember you, sir, by the sound of your voice: I
met you at the prison, in the absence of the Duke.

LUCIO

O, did you so? And do you remember what you said
of the Duke?

DUKE

Most notedly, sir.

LUCIO

Do you so, sir? And was the Duke a fleshmonger, a
fool, and a coward, as you then reported him to be?

DUKE

You must, sir, change persons with me, ere you make that my report: you, indeed, spoke so of him; and much more, much worse.

LUCIO

O thou damnable fellow! Did not I pluck thee by the nose for thy speeches?

DUKE

I protest I love the Duke as I love myself.

ANGELO

Hark, how the villain would close now, after his treasonable abuses!

ESCALUS

Such a fellow is not to be talked withal. Away with him to prison! Where is the provost? Away with him to prison! lay bolts enough upon him: let him speak no more. Away with those gigglets too, and with the other confederate companion!

DUKE

[To the PROVOST] Stay, sir; stay awhile.

ANGELO

What, resists he? Help him, Lucio.

LUCIO

Come, sir; come, sir; come, sir; foh, sir! Why, you bald-pated, lying rascal, you must be hooded, must you? Show your knave's visage, with a pox to you! show your sheep-biting face, and be hanged an hour! Will't not off?

[Pulls off the friar's hood, and discovers the Duke

DUKE

Thou art the first knave that e'er madest a Duke.

First, provost, let me bail these gentle three.

[To LUCIO] Sneak not away, sir; for the friar and you

Must have a word anon. Lay hold on him.

LUCIO

This may prove worse than hanging.

DUKE

[To ESCALUS] What you have spoke I pardon: sit you down:

We'll borrow place of him. [To ANGELO] Sir, by your leave.

Hast thou or word, or wit, or impudence,

That yet can do thee office? If thou hast,

Rely upon it till my tale be heard,

And hold no longer out.

ANGELO

O my dread lord,

I should be guiltier than my guiltiness,

To think I can be undiscernible,

When I perceive your Grace, like power divine,

Hath look'd upon my passes. Then, good prince,

No longer session hold upon my shame,

But let my trial be mine own confession:

Immediate sentence then, and sequent death,

Is all the grace I beg.

DUKE

Come hither, Mariana.

Say, wast thou e'er contracted to this woman?

ANGELO

I was, my lord.

DUKE

Go take her hence, and marry her instantly.

Do you the office, friar; which consummate,

Return him here again. Go with him, provost.

[Exeunt ANGELO, MARIANA, FRIAR PETER and PROVOST

ESCALUS

My lord, I am more amazed at his dishonour

Than at the strangeness of it.

DUKE

Come hither, Isabel.

Your friar is now your prince: as I was then

Advertising and holy to your business,

Not changing heart with habit, I am still

Attorney'd at your service.

ISABELLA

O, give me pardon,

That I, your vassal, have employ'd and pain'd

Your unknown sovereignty!

DUKE

You are pardon'd, Isabel:

And now, dear maid, be you as free to us.

Your brother's death, I know, sits at your heart;

And you may marvel why I obscured myself,

Labouring to save his life, and would not rather

Make rash remonstrance of my hidden power

Than let him so be lost. O most kind maid,

It was the swift celerity of his death,

Which I did think with slower foot came on,

That brain'd my purpose. But, peace be with him!

That life is better life, past fearing death,

Than that which lives to fear: make it your comfort,

So happy is your brother.

ISABELLA

I do, my lord.

Re-enter ANGELO, MARIANA, FRIAR PETER, and PROVOST

DUKE

For this new-married man, approaching here,

Whose salt imagination yet hath wrong'd

Your well-defended honour, you must pardon

For Mariana's sake: but as he adjudged your brother,—

Being criminal, in double violation

Of sacred chastity, and of promise-breach

Thereon dependent, for your brother's life,—

The very mercy of the law cries out

Most audible, even from his proper tongue,

'An Angelo for Claudio, death for death!'

Haste still pays haste, and leisure answers leisure;

Like doth quit like, and MEASURE still FOR MEASURE.

Then, Angelo, thy fault's thus manifested;

Which, though thou wouldst deny, denies thee vantage.

We do condemn thee to the very block

Where Claudio stoop'd to death, and with like haste.

Away with him!

MARIANA

O my most gracious lord,

I hope you will not mock me with a husband.

DUKE

It is your husband mock'd you with a husband.
Consenting to the safeguard of your honour,
I thought your marriage fit; else imputation,
For that he knew you, might reproach your life,
And choke your good to come: for his possessions,
Although by confiscation they are ours,
We do instate and widow you withal,
To buy you a better husband.

MARIANA

                    O my dear lord,
I crave no other, nor no better man.

DUKE

Never crave him; we are definitive.

MARIANA

Gentle my liege,—   [*Kneeling*

DUKE

                    You do but lose your labour.
Away with him to death! [*To* LUCIO] Now, sir, to
    you.

MARIANA

O my good lord! Sweet Isabel, take my part;
Lend me your knees, and all my life to come
I'll lend you all my life to do you service.

DUKE

Against all sense you do importune her:
Should she kneel down in mercy of this fact,
Her brother's ghost his paved bed would break,
And take her hence in horror.

MARIANA

                    Isabel,
Sweet Isabel, do yet but kneel by me;
Hold up your hands, say nothing, I'll speak all.
They say, best men are moulded out of faults;
And, for the most, become much more the better
For being a little bad: so may my husband.
O Isabel, will you not lend a knee?

DUKE

He dies for Claudio's death.

ISABELLA

                    Most bounteous sir, [*Kneeling*
Look, if it please you, on this man condemn'd,
As if my brother lived: I partly think
A due sincerity govern'd his deeds,
Till he did look on me: since it is so,
Let him not die. My brother had but justice,
In that he did the thing for which he died:
For Angelo,
His act did not o'ertake his bad intent;
And must be buried but as an intent
That perish'd by the way: thoughts are no subjects;
Intents, but merely thoughts.

MARIANA

                    Merely, my lord.

DUKE

Your suit's unprofitable; stand up, I say.
I have bethought me of another fault.
Provost, how came it Claudio was beheaded
At an unusual hour?

PROVOST

                    It was commanded so.

DUKE

Had you a special warrant for the deed?

PROVOST

No, my good lord; it was by private message.

DUKE

For which I do discharge you of your office:
Give up your keys.

PROVOST

                    Pardon me, noble lord:
I thought it was a fault, but knew it not;
Yet did repent me, after more advice:
For testimony whereof, one in the prison,
That should by private order else have died,
I have reserved alive.

DUKE

                    What's he?

PROVOST

                    His name is Barnardine.

DUKE

I would thou hadst done so by Claudio.
Go fetch him hither; let me look upon him.
                                        [*Exit* PROVOST

ESCALUS

I am sorry, one so learned and so wise
As you, Lord Angelo, have still appear'd,
Should slip so grossly, both in the heat of blood,
And lack of temper'd judgement afterward.

ANGELO

I am sorry that such sorrow I procure:
And so deep sticks it in my penitent heart,
That I crave death more willingly than mercy;
'Tis my deserving, and I do entreat it.
    Re-enter PROVOST, *with* BARNARDINE, CLAUDIO
                muffled, and JULIET

DUKE

Which is that Barnardine?

PROVOST

                    This, my lord.

DUKE

There was a friar told me of this man.
Sirrah, thou art said to have a stubborn soul,
That apprehends no further than this world,
And squarest thy life according. Thou'rt condemn'd:
But, for those earthly faults, I quit them all;
And pray thee take this mercy to provide
For better times to come. Friar, advise him;
I leave him to your hand. What muffled fellow's
    that?

PROVOST

This is another prisoner that I saved,
Who should have died when Claudio lost his head;
As like almost to Claudio as himself.
                                    [*Unmuffles* CLAUDIO

DUKE

[*To* ISABELLA] If he be like your brother, for his sake
Is he pardon'd; and, for your lovely sake,
Give me your hand, and say you will be mine,
He is my brother too: but fitter time for that.

By this Lord Angelo perceives he's safe;
Methinks I see a quickening in his eye.
Well, Angelo, your evil quits you well:
Look that you love your wife; her worth worth yours.
I find an apt remission in myself;
And yet here's one in place I cannot pardon.
[*To* LUCIO] You, sirrah, that knew me for a fool, a
    coward,
One all of luxury, an ass, a madman;
Wherein have I so deserved of you,
That you extol me thus?

LUCIO

'Faith, my lord, I spoke it but according to the trick.
If you will hang me for it, you may; but I had rather
it would please you I might be whipt.

DUKE

Whipt first, sir, and hang'd after.
Proclaim it, provost, round about the city,
If any woman wrong'd by this lewd fellow,—
As I have heard him swear himself there's one
Whom he begot with child, let her appear,
And he shall marry her: the nuptial finish'd,
Let him be whipt and hang'd.

LUCIO

I beseech your highness, do not marry me to a
whore. Your highness said even now, I made you a
Duke: good my lord, do not recompense me in making me a cuckold.

DUKE

Upon mine honour, thou shalt marry her.
Thy slanders I forgive; and therewithal
Remit thy other forfeits.—Take him to prison;
And see our pleasure herein executed.

LUCIO

Marrying a punk, my lord, is pressing to death,
whipping, and hanging.

DUKE

Slandering a prince deserves it.
                    [*Exeunt* OFFICERS *with* LUCIO
She, Claudio, that you wrong'd, look you restore.
Joy to you, Mariana! Love her, Angelo:
I have confess'd her, and I know her virtue.
Thanks, good friend Escalus, for thy much goodness:
There's more behind that is more gratulate.
Thanks, provost, for thy care and secrecy:
We shall employ thee in a worthier place.
Forgive him, Angelo, that brought you home
The head of Ragozine for Claudio's:
The offence pardons itself. Dear Isabel,
I have a motion much imports your good;
Whereto if you'll a willing ear incline,
What's mine is yours, and what is yours is mine.
So, bring us to our palace; where we'll show
What's yet behind, that's meet you all should know.
                                        [*Exeunt*

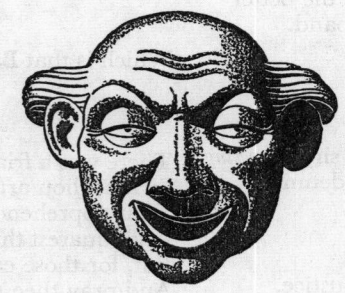

THE TRAGEDY OF OTHELLO, THE MOOR OF VENICE

SYNOPSIS

OTHELLO is a distinguished Moor, a black man, a brave and competent soldier, whose conduct of the Venetian wars against the Turks has raised him to the rank of general. He is now held in high esteem in Venice, and Brabantio, a rich and powerful senator, often invites him to his house, where he meets the fair, much-courted Desdemona, Brabantio's only child, who listens with rapt attention to the Moor's tales of adventures which the senator draws from him.

The strange nobility of this man of simple, commanding action fires the gentle girl's imagination, while her discerning mind so keenly appreciates his fine qualities that the natural barrier of race and color vanishes. With modest frankness, Desdemona shows Othello that she returns his love, and they are secretly married.

Cassio, a young soldier, who has often been the Moor's go-between in his courting, is promoted by Othello to be his chief lieutenant, a position coveted by his ensign, Iago, a crafty villainous man, who vows vengeance on both Othello and Cassio. Aided by Roderigo, a former lover of Desdemona's, he arouses Brabantio one night with a report of the elopement. Brabantio accuses the Moor of using witchcraft upon Desdemona, and orders him before the council which is meeting to discuss some disturbing reports of a large Turkish fleet now off the island of Cyprus, a Venetian stronghold. They had already summoned Othello, but now, when his services are imperatively needed, he stands before the Duke and council charged with a capital crime. The incensed Brabantio is heard respectfully, but his accusations are not always convincing, while Othello's story of his courting is told with such simple eloquence and directness that the Duke, as chief judge, refuses to condemn him, and he is given command of the expedition against the Turks.

Desdemona follows Othello to Cyprus in charge of Iago and his wife, Emilia, who, ignorant of her husband's hatred and schemes, becomes her mistress' devoted friend. A great storm wrecks the Turkish fleet, and Othello proclaims a holiday for rejoicing and for the celebration of his marriage, but he strictly charges Cassio to prevent excessive drinking or brawls among the soldiers which might disgust the people of Cyprus. Through Iago's wiles, the lieutenant himself becomes drunk. Roderigo precipitates a quarrel, rings an alarm bell and creates utmost confusion. Othello dismisses Cassio from his service, Iago urges the despairing young soldier to ask Desdemona to plead with her husband, and an interview is arranged between the lady and Cassio who hastens off when Othello approaches, lured to the spot by Iago who has promised to keep him away. Iago, in whose honesty and wisdom Othello has boundless faith, makes a rather ominous remark on the incident which returns to the Moor's brooding thoughts after he hears Desdemona's heartfelt appeal for Cassio. With consummate skill, Iago continues to drop hints and suggestions into Othello's ear. He speaks of Cassio's help with his courting, and of women's fickleness and ability to deceive, and stealthily torments his victim with insinuations of Cassio's passion for Desdemona.

One day Desdemona drops a beautiful handkerchief, her first gift from her husband who had begged her to guard it closely. It was a magical web, embroidered by a sibyl, which gave its possessor the power to hold her husband's love, and Othello's mother when dying had given it to him for his future wife. Emilia finds it, but Iago takes the handkerchief, and places it in Cassio's room; he then convinces Othello that Desdemona has given it to her lover. Desdemona, afraid to admit the loss of the precious heirloom, makes evasive replies when questioned by her distracted husband, now a ready target for Iago's last villainous shot. With Othello concealed close by, Iago beguiles the gay Cassio into a ribald conversation about his mistress, Bianca, while the Moor thinks his derision is levelled at Desdemona. By a stroke of evil luck, Bianca herself comes upon the scene, and Othello sees this woman of the streets scornfully hand back to Cassio his wife's handkerchief. Blind with rage, Othello orders Iago to kill Cassio. Iago kills Roderigo under cover of a street brawl, because he wants him out of the way, but he only maims Cassio.

Othello has but one thought, the destruction of Desdemona before she can betray other men. He goes to her bedchamber, and smothers his protesting wife to death. Emilia arrives in time to hear her lady breathe a few last words of devotion to her husband, who is now overwhelmed by the woman's testimony, Cassio's explanations, and the evidence of letters in the pockets of the dead Roderigo, proving Iago's villainy and his wife's innocence. Iago kills his wife for revealing his treachery, and is wounded by Othello. In his extreme anguish of soul, Othello falls upon his sword and dies at his wife's side. Cassio is made governor of Cyprus, with instructions from the council to torture and execute Iago under the utmost penalty of the law.

HISTORICAL DATA

The original story of Othello is found in the novel *Il Moro de Venezia* from the *Hecatommithi* of Giraldo Cinthio, published in 1565. A French translation in 1584 was probably the edition with which Shakespeare was familiar. The novel may have been of Oriental origin, as it somewhat resembles the tale of *The Three Apples* in *The Thousand and One Nights*.

Shakespeare, in the main, followed the Italian romance, but reconstructed the catastrophe. He originated the names of all the personages, except that of Desdemona (the only name given by Cinthio), added the character of Roderigo; gave definite significance to Emilia; changed Iago from the conventional criminal of Italian fiction; and

elevated Othello from Cinthio's conception of the savage Moor.

In the words of Sidney Lee, "The whole tragedy displays to magnificent advantage the dramatist's fully matured powers."

Othello was probably written in 1604, as an extract from *The Egerton Papers* notes that it was performed in August of that year at Harefield by Burbage's Players, before Queen Elizabeth, while she was on a visit to Sir Thomas Egerton, Lord Keeper of the Great Seal.

It was first published in quarto form, in 1622, and the following year appeared among "The Tragedies" in the First Folio.

"*It is the cause, it is the cause, my soul;*"
OTHELLO

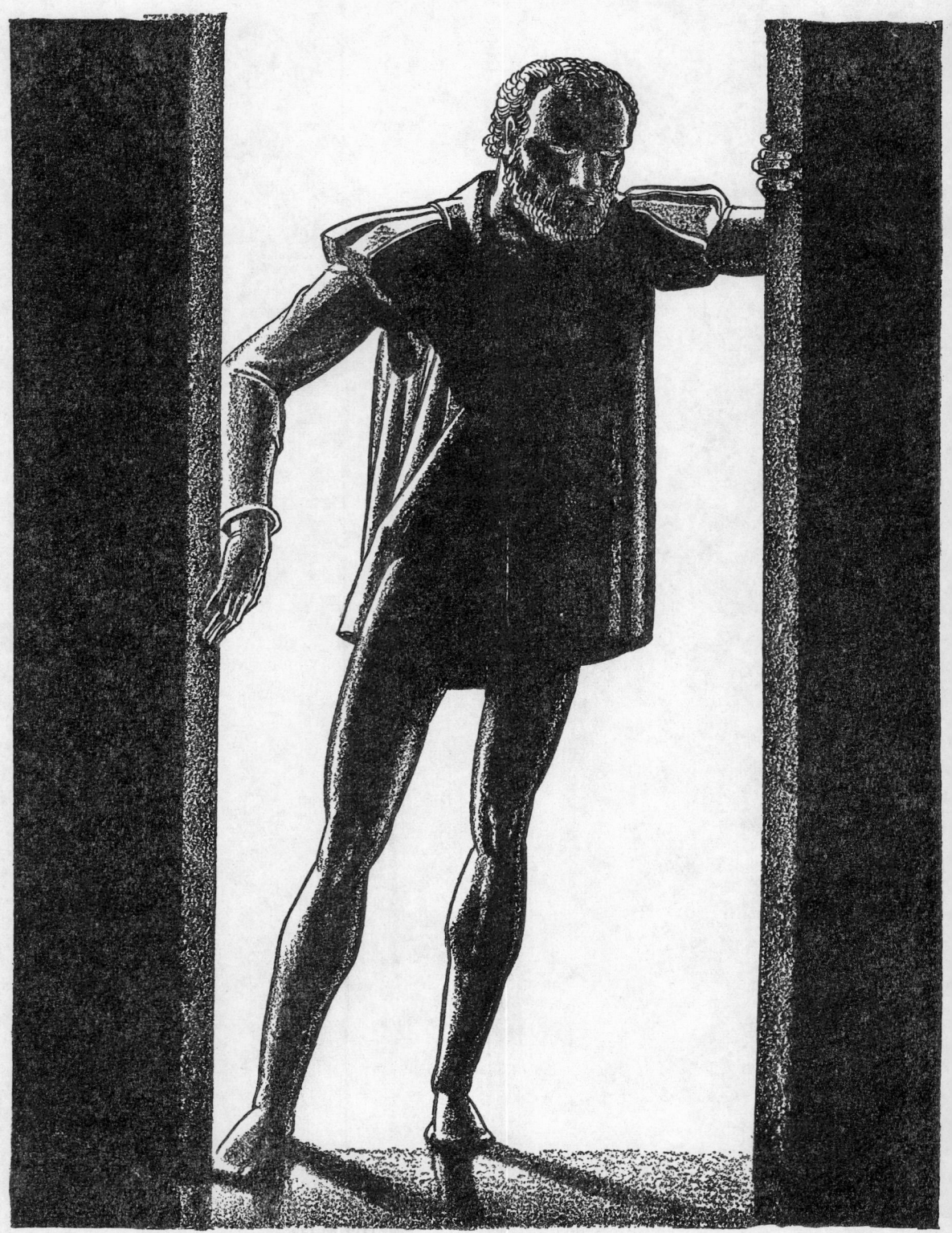

THE TRAGEDY OF OTHELLO, THE MOOR OF VENICE

DRAMATIS PERSONÆ

DUKE OF VENICE.

BRABANTIO, *a senator.*

OTHER SENATORS.

GRATIANO, *brother to Brabantio.*

LODOVICO, *kinsman to Brabantio.*

OTHELLO, *a noble Moor in the service of the Venetian state.*

CASSIO, *his lieutenant.*

IAGO, *his ancient.*

MONTANO, *Othello's predecessor in the government of Cyprus.*

RODERIGO, *a Venetian gentleman.*

CLOWN, *servant to Othello.*

DESDEMONA, *daughter to Brabantio and wife to Othello.*

EMILIA, *wife to Iago.*

BIANCA, *mistress to Cassio.*

SAILOR, MESSENGER, HERALD, OFFICERS, GENTLEMEN, MUSICIANS, *and* ATTENDANTS.

SCENE—*Venice: a seaport in Cyprus.*

ACT I

SCENE I. *Venice. A street*

Enter RODERIGO *and* IAGO

RODERIGO

TUSH, never tell me; I take it much unkindly
That thou, Iago, who hast had my purse
As if the strings were thine, shouldst know of this.

IAGO

'Sblood, but you will not hear me:
If ever I did dream of such a matter,
Abhor me.

RODERIGO

Thou told'st me thou didst hold him in thy hate.

IAGO

Despise me, if I do not. Three great ones of the
city,
In personal suit to make me his lieutenant,
Off-capp'd to him: and, by the faith of man,
I know my price, I am worth no worse a place:
But he, as loving his own pride and purposes,
Evades them, with a bombast circumstance
Horribly stuff'd with epithets of war;
And, in conclusion,
Nonsuits my mediators; for, 'Certes,' says he,
'I have already chose my officer.'
And what was he?
Forsooth, a great arithmetician,
One Michael Cassio, a Florentine,
A fellow almost damn'd in a fair wife;
That never set a squadron in the field,
Nor the division of a battle knows
More than a spinster; unless the bookish theoric,
Wherein the toged consuls can propose
As masterly as he: mere prattle without practice
Is all his soldiership. But he, sir, had the election:
And I, of whom his eyes had seen the proof
At Rhodes, at Cyprus, and on other grounds
Christian and heathen, must be be-lee'd and calm'd

By debitor and creditor: this counter-caster,
He, in good time, must his lieutenant be,
And I—God bless the mark!—his Moorship's ancient.

RODERIGO

By heaven, I rather would have been his hangman.

IAGO

Why, there's no remedy; 'tis the curse of service,
Preferment goes by letter and affection,
And not by old gradation, where each second
Stood heir to the first. Now, sir, be judge yourself
Whether I in any just term am affined
To love the Moor.

RODERIGO

I would not follow him then.

IAGO

O, sir, content you;
I follow him to serve my turn upon him:
We cannot all be masters, nor all masters
Cannot be truly follow'd. You shall mark
Many a duteous and knee-crooking knave,
That doting on his own obsequious bondage
Wears out his time, much like his master's ass,
For nought but provender, and when he's old,
cashier'd:
Whip me such honest knaves. Others there are
Who, trimm'd in forms and visages of duty,
Keep yet their hearts attending on themselves,
And throwing but shows of service on their lords
Do well thrive by them, and when they have lined
their coats
Do themselves homage: these fellows have some
soul,
And such a one do I profess myself.
For, sir,
It is as sure as you are Roderigo,
Were I the Moor, I would not be Iago:
In following him, I follow but myself;
Heaven is my judge, not I for love and duty,

But seeming so, for my peculiar end:
For when my outward action doth demonstrate
The native act and figure of my heart
In compliment extern, 'tis not long after
But I will wear my heart upon my sleeve
For daws to peck at: I am not what I am.

RODERIGO
What a full fortune does the thick-lips owe,
If he can carry 't thus!

IAGO
              Call up her father,
Rouse him: make after him, poison his delight,
Proclaim him in the streets; incense her kinsmen,
And, though he in a fertile climate dwell,
Plague him with flies: though that his joy be joy,
Yet throw such changes of vexation on 't
As it may lose some colour.

RODERIGO
Here is her father's house; I'll call aloud.

IAGO
Do; with like timorous accent and dire yell
As when, by night and negligence, the fire
Is spied in populous cities.

RODERIGO
What, ho, Brabantio! Signior Brabantio, ho!

IAGO
Awake! what, ho, Brabantio! thieves! thieves!
    thieves!
Look to your house, your daughter and your bags!
Thieves! thieves!

     BRABANTIO *appears above, at a window*

BRABANTIO
What is the reason of this terrible summons?
What is the matter there?

RODERIGO
Signior, is all your family within?

IAGO
Are your doors lock'd?

BRABANTIO
          Why, wherefore ask you this?

IAGO
'Zounds, sir, you're robb'd; for shame, put on your
    gown;
Your heart is burst, you have lost half your soul;
Even now, now, very now, an old black ram
Is tupping your white ewe. Arise, arise;
Awake the snorting citizens with the bell,
Or else the devil will make a grandsire of you:
Arise, I say.

BRABANTIO
      What, have you lost your wits?

RODERIGO
Most reverend signior, do you know my voice?

BRABANTIO
Not I: what are you?

RODERIGO
         My name is Roderigo.

BRABANTIO
          The worser welcome:
I have charged thee not to haunt about my doors:

In honest plainness thou hast heard me say
My daughter is not for thee; and now, in madness,
Being full of supper and distempering draughts,
Upon malicious bravery, dost thou come
To start my quiet.

RODERIGO
Sir, sir, sir,—

BRABANTIO
         But thou must needs be sure
My spirit and my place have in them power
To make this bitter to thee.

RODERIGO
            Patience, good sir.

BRABANTIO
What tell'st thou me of robbing? this is Venice;
My house is not a grange.

RODERIGO
           Most grave Brabantio,
In simple and pure soul I come to you.

IAGO
'Zounds, sir, you are one of those that will not
serve God, if the devil bid you. Because we come to
do you service and you think we are ruffians, you'll
have your daughter covered with a Barbary horse;
you'll have your nephews neigh to you; you'll have
coursers for cousins, and gennets for germans.

BRABANTIO
What profane wretch art thou?

IAGO
I am one, sir, that comes to tell you your daughter and the Moor are now making the beast with
two backs.

BRABANTIO
Thou art a villain.

IAGO
        You are—a senator.

BRABANTIO
This thou shalt answer; I know thee, Roderigo.

RODERIGO
Sir, I will answer any thing. But, I beseech you,
If 't be your pleasure and most wise consent,
As partly I find it is, that your fair daughter,
At this odd-even and dull watch o' the night,
Transported with no worse nor better guard
But with a knave of common hire, a gondolier,
To the gross clasps of a lascivious Moor,—
If this be known to you, and your allowance,
We then have done you bold and saucy wrongs;
But if you know not this, my manners tell me
We have your wrong rebuke. Do not believe
That, from the sense of all civility,
I thus would play and trifle with your reverence:
Your daughter, if you have not given her leave,
I say again, hath made a gross revolt,
Tying her duty, beauty, wit and fortunes,
In an extravagant and wheeling stranger
Of here and every where. Straight satisfy yourself:
If she be in her chamber or your house,
Let loose on me the justice of the state
For thus deluding you.

BRABANTIO

Strike on the tinder, ho!
Give me a taper! call up all my people!
This accident is not unlike my dream:
Belief of it oppresses me already.
Light, I say! light!   [*Exit above*

IAGO

Farewell; for I must leave you:
It seems not meet, nor wholesome to my place,
To be produced—as, if I stay, I shall—
Against the Moor: for I do know, the state,
However this may gall him with some check,
Cannot with safety cast him; for he's embark'd
With such loud reason to the Cyprus wars,
Which even now stand in act, that, for their souls,
Another of his fathom they have none
To lead their business: in which regard,
Though I do hate him as I do hell pains,
Yet for necessity of present life,
I must show out a flag and sign of love,
Which is indeed but sign. That you shall surely find
    him,
Lead to the Sagittary the raised search;
And there will I be with him. So farewell.   [*Exit*

Enter, below, BRABANTIO, *in his night-gown, and*
SERVANTS *with torches*

BRABANTIO

It is too true an evil: gone she is;
And what's to come of my despised time
Is nought but bitterness. Now, Roderigo,
Where didst thou see her? O unhappy girl!
With the Moor, say'st thou? Who would be a father!
How didst thou know 'twas she? O, she deceives me
Past thought! What said she to you? Get more
    tapers.
Raise all my kindred. Are they married, think you?

RODERIGO

Truly, I think they are.

BRABANTIO

O heaven! How got she out? O treason of the
    blood!
Fathers, from hence trust not your daughters' minds
By what you see them act. Is there not charms
By which the property of youth and maidhood
May be abused? Have you not read, Roderigo,
Of some such thing?

RODERIGO

Yes, sir, I have indeed.

BRABANTIO

Call up my brother. O, would you had had her!
Some one way, some another. Do you know
Where we may apprehend her and the Moor?

RODERIGO

I think I can discover him, if you please
To get good guard and go along with me.

BRABANTIO

Pray you, lead on. At every house I'll call;
I may command at most. Get weapons, ho!
And raise some special officers of night.
On, good Roderigo; I'll deserve your pains. [*Exeunt*

SCENE II. *Another street*

Enter OTHELLO, IAGO, *and* ATTENDANTS *with torches*

IAGO

Though in the trade of war I have slain men,
Yet do I hold it very stuff o' the conscience
To do no contrived murder: I lack iniquity
Sometimes to do me service: nine or ten times
I had thought to have yerk'd him here under the
    ribs.

OTHELLO

'Tis better as it is.

IAGO

Nay, but he prated
And spoke such scurvy and provoking terms
Against your honour,
That, with the little godliness I have,
I did full hard forbear him. But I pray you, sir,
Are you fast married? Be assured of this,
That the magnifico is much beloved,
And hath in his effect a voice potential
As double as the duke's: he will divorce you,
Or put upon you what restraint and grievance
The law, with all his might to enforce it on,
Will give him cable.

OTHELLO

Let him do his spite:
My services, which I have done the signiory,
Shall out-tongue his complaints. 'Tis yet to know—
Which, when I know that boasting is an honour,
I shall promulgate—I fetch my life and being
From men of royal siege, and my demerits
May speak unbonneted to as proud a fortune
As this that I have reach'd: for know, Iago,
But that I love the gentle Desdemona,
I would not my unhoused free condition
Put into circumscription and confine
For the sea's worth. But, look! what lights come
    yond?

IAGO

Those are the raised father and his friends:
You were best go in.

OTHELLO

Not I; I must be found:
My parts, my title and my perfect soul,
Shall manifest me rightly. Is it they?

IAGO

By Janus, I think no.

Enter CASSIO, *and certain* OFFICERS *with torches*

OTHELLO

The servants of the duke, and my lieutenant.
The goodness of the night upon you, friends!
What is the news?

CASSIO

The duke does greet you, general,
And he requires your haste-post-haste appearance,
Even on the instant.

OTHELLO

What is the matter, think you?

CASSIO
Something from Cyprus, as I may divine:
It is a business of some heat: the galleys
Have sent a dozen sequent messengers
This very night at one another's heels;
And many of the consuls, raised and met,
Are at the duke's already: you have been hotly
　call'd for;
When, being not at your lodging to be found,
The senate hath sent about three several quests
To search you out.

OTHELLO
　　　　'Tis well I am found by you.
I will but spend a word here in the house,
And go with you.　　　　　　　　　　[Exit

CASSIO
　　　Ancient, what makes he here?

IAGO
Faith, he to-night hath boarded a land carack:
If it prove lawful prize, he's made for ever.

CASSIO
I do not understand.

IAGO
　　　He's married.

CASSIO
　　　　　To who?

Re-enter OTHELLO

IAGO
Marry, to—Come, captain, will you go?

OTHELLO
　　　　　Have with you.

CASSIO
Here comes another troop to seek for you.

IAGO
It is Brabantio: general, be advised;
He comes to bad intent.

Enter BRABANTIO, RODERIGO, and OFFICERS with
torches and weapons

OTHELLO
　　　Holla! stand there!

RODERIGO
Signior, it is the Moor.

BRABANTIO
　　　　Down with him, thief!
　　　　　　[They draw on both sides

IAGO
You, Roderigo! come, sir, I am for you.

OTHELLO
Keep up your bright swords, for the dew will rust
　them.
Good signior, you shall more command with years
Than with your weapons.

BRABANTIO
O thou foul thief, where hast thou stow'd my
　daughter?
Damn'd as thou art, thou hast enchanted her;
For I'll refer me to all things of sense,
If she in chains of magic were not bound,
Whether a maid so tender, fair and happy,
So opposite to marriage that she shunn'd

The wealthy curled darlings of our nation,
Would ever have, to incur a general mock,
Run from her guardage to the sooty bosom
Of such a thing as thou, to fear, not to delight.
Judge me the world, if 'tis not gross in sense
That thou hast practised on her with foul charms,
Abused her delicate youth with drugs or minerals
That weaken motion: I'll have 't disputed on;
'Tis probable, and palpable to thinking.
I therefore apprehend and do attach thee
For an abuser of the world, a practiser
Of arts inhibited and out of warrant.
Lay hold upon him: if he do resist,
Subdue him at his peril.

OTHELLO
　　　　Hold your hands,
Both you of my inclining and the rest:
Were it my cue to fight, I should have known it
Without a prompter. Where will you that I go
To answer this your charge?

BRABANTIO
　　　　To prison, till fit time
Of law and course of direct session
Call thee to answer.

OTHELLO
　　　What if I do obey?
How may the duke be therewith satisfied,
Whose messengers are here about my side,
Upon some present business of the state
To bring me to him?

FIRST OFFICER
　　　　'Tis true, most worthy signior;
The duke's in council, and your noble self,
I am sure, is sent for.

BRABANTIO
　　　How! the duke in council!
In this time of the night! Bring him away:
Mine's not an idle cause: the duke himself,
Or any of my brothers of the state,
Cannot but feel this wrong as 'twere their own;
For if such actions may have passage free,
Bond-slaves and pagans shall our statesmen be.
　　　　　　　　　　　　[Exeunt

SCENE III. A council-chamber

The DUKE and SENATORS sitting at a table; OFFICERS
attending

DUKE
There is no composition in these news
That gives them credit.

FIRST SENATOR
　　　Indeed they are disproportion'd;
My letters say a hundred and seven galleys.

DUKE
And mine, a hundred and forty.

SECOND SENATOR
　　　　And mine, two hundred:
But though they jump not on a just account,—
As in these cases, where the aim reports,

'Tis oft with difference,—yet do they all confirm
A Turkish fleet, and bearing up to Cyprus.

DUKE
Nay, it is possible enough to judgement:
I do not so secure me in the error,
But the main article I do approve
In fearful sense.

SAILOR
[*Within*] What, ho! what, ho! what, ho!

FIRST OFFICER
A messenger from the galleys.

Enter SAILOR

DUKE
　　　　　　Now, what's the business?

SAILOR
The Turkish preparation makes for Rhodes;
So was I bid report here to the state
By Signior Angelo.

DUKE
How say you by this change?

FIRST SENATOR
　　　　　　This cannot be,
By no assay of reason: 'tis a pageant
To keep us in false gaze. When we consider
The importancy of Cyprus to the Turk,
And let ourselves again but understand
That as it more concerns the Turk than Rhodes,
So may he with more facile question bear it,
For that it stands not in such warlike brace,
But altogether lacks the abilities
That Rhodes is dress'd in: if we make thought of
this,
We must not think the Turk is so unskilful
To leave that latest which concerns him first,
Neglecting an attempt of ease and gain,
To wake and wage a danger profitless.

DUKE
Nay, in all confidence, he's not for Rhodes.

FIRST OFFICER
Here is more news.

Enter a MESSENGER

MESSENGER
The Ottomites, reverend and gracious,
Steering with due course toward the isle of Rhodes,
Have there injointed them with an after fleet.

FIRST SENATOR
Ay, so I thought. How many, as you guess?

MESSENGER
Of thirty sail: and now they do re-stem
Their backward course, bearing with frank appear-
ance
Their purposes toward Cyprus. Signior Montano,
Your trusty and most valiant servitor,
With his free duty recommends you thus,
And prays you to believe him.

DUKE
'Tis certain then for Cyprus.
Marcus Luccicos, is not he in town?

FIRST SENATOR
He's now in Florence.

DUKE
Write from us to him; post-post-haste dispatch.

FIRST SENATOR
Here comes Brabantio and the valiant Moor.

Enter BRABANTIO, OTHELLO, IAGO, RODERIGO,
　　　and OFFICERS

DUKE
Valiant Othello, we must straight employ you
Against the general enemy Ottoman.
[*To* BRABANTIO] I did not see you; welcome, gentle
signior;
We lack'd your counsel and your help to-night.

BRABANTIO
So did I yours. Good your grace, pardon me;
Neither my place nor aught I heard of business
Hath raised me from my bed, nor doth the general
care
Take hold on me; for my particular grief
Is of so flood-gate and o'erbearing nature
That it engluts and swallows other sorrows,
And it is still itself.

DUKE
　　　　　Why, what's the matter?

BRABANTIO
My daughter! O, my daughter!

ALL
　　　　　　　Dead?

BRABANTIO
　　　　　　　Ay, to me;
She is abused, stol'n from me and corrupted
By spells and medicines bought of mountebanks;
For nature so preposterously to err,
Being not deficient, blind, or lame of sense,
Sans witchcraft could not.

DUKE
Whoe'er he be that in this foul proceeding
Hath thus beguiled your daughter of herself
And you of her, the bloody book of law
You shall yourself read in the bitter letter
After your own sense, yea, though our proper son
Stood in your action.

BRABANTIO
　　　　　Humbly I thank your grace.
Here is the man, this Moor; whom now, it seems,
Your special mandate for the state-affairs
Hath hither brought.

ALL
　　　　We are very sorry for 't.

DUKE
[*To* OTHELLO] What in your own part can you say
to this?

BRABANTIO
Nothing, but this is so.

OTHELLO
Most potent, grave, and reverend signiors,
My very noble and approved good masters,
That I have ta'en away this old man's daughter,
It is most true; true, I have married her:
The very head and front of my offending
Hath this extent, no more. Rude am I in my speech,

And little blest with the soft phrase of peace;
For since these arms of mine had seven years' pith,
Till now some nine moons wasted, they have used
Their dearest action in the tented field;
And little of this great world can I speak,
More than pertains to feats of broil and battle;
And therefore little shall I grace my cause
In speaking for myself. Yet, by your gracious patience,
I will a round unvarnish'd tale deliver
Of my whole course of love; what drugs, what charms,
What conjuration and what mighty magic—
For such proceeding I am charged withal—
I won his daughter.

　　　　　　　BRABANTIO
　　　　　　　　　A maiden never bold;
Of spirit so still and quiet that her motion
Blush'd at herself; and she—in spite of nature,
Of years, of country, credit, every thing—
To fall in love with what she fear'd to look on!
It is a judgement maim'd and most imperfect,
That will confess perfection so could err
Against all rules of nature; and must be driven
To find out practices of cunning hell,
Why this should be. I therefore vouch again,
That with some mixtures powerful o'er the blood,
Or with some dram conjured to this effect,
He wrought upon her.

　　　　　　　DUKE
　　　　　　　　　To vouch this, is no proof,
Without more certain and more overt test
Than these thin habits and poor likelihoods
Of modern seeming do prefer against him.

　　　　　　　FIRST SENATOR
But, Othello, speak:
Did you by indirect and forced courses
Subdue and poison this young maid's affections?
Or came it by request, and such fair question
As soul to soul affordeth?

　　　　　　　OTHELLO
　　　　　　　　　I do beseech you,
Send for the lady to the Sagittary,
And let her speak of me before her father:
If you do find me foul in her report,
The trust, the office I do hold of you,
Not only take away, but let your sentence
Even fall upon my life.

　　　　　　　DUKE
　　　　　　　　　Fetch Desdemona hither.

　　　　　　　OTHELLO
Ancient, conduct them; you best know the place.
　　　　　　　[*Exeunt* IAGO *and* ATTENDANTS
And till she come, as truly as to heaven
I do confess the vices of my blood,
So justly to your grave ears I'll present
How I did thrive in this fair lady's love
And she in mine.

　　　　　　　DUKE
Say it, Othello.

　　　　　　　OTHELLO
Her father loved me, oft invited me,
Still question'd me the story of my life
From year to year, the battles, sieges, fortunes,
That I have pass'd.
I ran it through, even from my boyish days
To the very moment that he bade me tell it:
Wherein I spake of most disastrous chances,
Of moving accidents by flood and field,
Of hair-breadth 'scapes i' the imminent deadly breach,
Of being taken by the insolent foe,
And sold to slavery, of my redemption thence,
And portance in my travels' history:
Wherein of antres vast and deserts idle,
Rough quarries, rocks, and hills whose heads touch heaven,
It was my hint to speak,—such was the process;
And of the Cannibals that each other eat,
The Anthropophagi, and men whose heads
Do grow beneath their shoulders. This to hear
Would Desdemona seriously incline:
But still the house-affairs would draw her thence;
Which ever as she could with haste dispatch,
She'ld come again, and with a greedy ear
Devour up my discourse: which I observing,
Took once a pliant hour, and found good means
To draw from her a prayer of earnest heart
That I would all my pilgrimage dilate,
Whereof by parcels she had something heard,
But not intentively: I did consent,
And often did beguile her of her tears
When I did speak of some distressful stroke
That my youth suffer'd. My story being done,
She gave me for my pains a world of sighs:
She swore, in faith, 'twas strange, 'twas passing strange;
'Twas pitiful, 'twas wondrous pitiful:
She wish'd she had not heard it, yet she wish'd
That heaven had made her such a man: she thank'd me,
And bade me, if I had a friend that loved her,
I should but teach him how to tell my story,
And that would woo her. Upon this hint I spake:
She loved me for the dangers I had pass'd,
And I loved her that she did pity them.
This only is the witchcraft I have used.
Here comes the lady; let her witness it.
　　　Enter DESDEMONA, IAGO, *and* ATTENDANTS

　　　　　　　DUKE
I think this tale would win my daughter too.
Good Brabantio,
Take up this mangled matter at the best:
Men do their broken weapons rather use
Than their bare hands.

　　　　　　　BRABANTIO
　　　　　　　　　I pray you, hear her speak:
If she confess that she was half the wooer,
Destruction on my head, if my bad blame
Light on the man! Come hither, gentle mistress:

Do you perceive in all this noble company
Where most you owe obedience?

DESDEMONA

            My noble father,
I do perceive here a divided duty:
To you I am bound for life and education;
My life and education both do learn me
How to respect you; you are the lord of duty,
I am hitherto your daughter: but here's my husband,
And so much duty as my mother show'd
To you, preferring you before her father,
So much I challenge that I may profess
Due to the Moor my lord.

BRABANTIO

        God be with you! I have done.
Please it your grace, on to the state-affairs:
I had rather to adopt a child than get it.
Come hither, Moor:
I here do give thee that with all my heart,
Which, but thou hast already, with all my heart
I would keep from thee. For your sake, jewel,
I am glad at soul I have no other child;
For thy escape would teach me tyranny,
To hang clogs on them. I have done, my lord.

DUKE

Let me speak like yourself, and lay a sentence
Which, as a grise or step, may help these lovers
Into your favour.
When remedies are past, the griefs are ended
By seeing the worst, which late on hopes depended.
To mourn a mischief that is past and gone
Is the next way to draw new mischief on.
What cannot be preserved when fortune takes,
Patience her injury a mockery makes.
The robb'd that smiles steals something from the thief;
He robs himself that spends a bootless grief.

BRABANTIO

So let the Turk of Cyprus us beguile;
We lose it not so long as we can smile.
He bears the sentence well, that nothing bears
But the free comfort which from thence he hears;
But he bears both the sentence and the sorrow,
That, to pay grief, must of poor patience borrow.
These sentences, to sugar or to gall,
Being strong on both sides, are equivocal:
But words are words; I never yet did hear
That the bruised heart was pierced through the ear.
I humbly beseech you, proceed to the affairs of state.

DUKE

The Turk with a most mighty preparation makes
for Cyprus. Othello, the fortitude of the place is best
known to you; and though we have there a substitute of most allowed sufficiency, yet opinion, a sovereign mistress of effects, throws a more safer voice
on you: you must therefore be content to slubber
the gloss of your new fortunes with this more stubborn and boisterous expedition.

OTHELLO

The tyrant custom, most grave senators,
Hath made the flinty and steel couch of war
My thrice-driven bed of down: I do agnize
A natural and prompt alacrity
I find in hardness; and do undertake
These present wars against the Ottomites.
Most humbly therefore bending to your state,
I crave fit disposition for my wife,
Due reference of place and exhibition,
With such accommodation and besort
As levels with her breeding.

DUKE

            If you please,
Be 't at her father's.

BRABANTIO

        I'll not have it so.

OTHELLO

Nor I.

DESDEMONA

       Nor I, I would not there reside,
To put my father in impatient thoughts
By being in his eye. Most gracious duke,
To my unfolding lend your prosperous ear,
And let me find a charter in your voice
To assist my simpleness.

DUKE

What would you, Desdemona?

DESDEMONA

That I did love the Moor to live with him,
My downright violence and storm of fortunes
May trumpet to the world: my heart's subdued
Even to the very quality of my lord:
I saw Othello's visage in his mind,
And to his honours and his valiant parts
Did I my soul and fortunes consecrate.
So that, dear lords, if I be left behind,
A moth of peace, and he go to the war,
The rites for which I love him are bereft me,
And I a heavy interim shall support
By his dear absence. Let me go with him.

OTHELLO

Let her have your voices.
Vouch with me, heaven, I therefore beg it not,
To please the palate of my appetite;
Nor to comply with heat—the young affects
In me defunct—and proper satisfaction;
But to be free and bounteous to her mind:
And heaven defend your good souls, that you think
I will your serious and great business scant
For she is with me. No, when light-wing'd toys
Of feather'd Cupid seel with wanton dulness
My speculative and officed instruments,
That my disports corrupt and taint my business,
Let housewives make a skillet of my helm,
And all indign and base adversities
Make head against my estimation!

DUKE

Be it as you shall privately determine,

Either for her stay or going: the affair cries haste,
And speed must answer 't; you must hence to-night.

DESDEMONA

To-night, my lord?

DUKE

       This night.

OTHELLO

             With all my heart.

DUKE

At nine i' the morning here we'll meet again.
Othello, leave some officer behind,
And he shall our commission bring to you;
With such things else of quality and respect
As doth import you.

OTHELLO

       So please your grace, my ancient;
A man he is of honesty and trust:
To his conveyance I assign my wife,
With what else needful your good grace shall think
To be sent after me.

DUKE

       Let it be so.
Good night to every one. [To BRABANTIO] And,
    noble signior,
If virtue no delighted beauty lack,
Your son-in-law is far more fair than black.

FIRST SENATOR

Adieu, brave Moor; use Desdemona well.

BRABANTIO

Look to her, Moor, if thou hast eyes to see:
She has deceived her father, and may thee.
       [Exeunt DUKE, SENATORS, OFFICERS, &c.

OTHELLO

My life upon her faith! Honest Iago,
My Desdemona must I leave to thee:
I prithee, let thy wife attend on her;
And bring them after in the best advantage.
Come, Desdemona; I have but an hour
Of love, of worldly matters and direction,
To spend with thee: we must obey the time.
       [Exeunt OTHELLO and DESDEMONA

RODERIGO

Iago!

IAGO

What say'st thou, noble heart?

RODERIGO

What will I do, thinkest thou?

IAGO

Why, go to bed and sleep.

RODERIGO

I will incontinently drown myself.

IAGO

If thou dost, I shall never love thee after.
Why, thou silly gentleman!

RODERIGO

It is silliness to live when to live is torment; and
then have we a prescription to die when death is our
physician.

IAGO

O villanous! I have looked upon the world for

four times seven years; and since I could distinguish
betwixt a benefit and an injury, I never found man
that knew how to love himself. Ere I would say I
would drown myself for the love of a guinea-hen, I
would change my humanity with a baboon.

RODERIGO

What should I do? I confess it is my shame to be so
fond; but it is not in my virtue to amend it.

IAGO

Virtue! a fig! 'tis in ourselves that we are thus or
thus. Our bodies are gardens; to the which our wills
are gardeners: so that if we will plant nettles or sow
lettuce, set hyssop and weed up thyme, supply it
with one gender of herbs or distract it with many,
either to have it sterile with idleness or manured
with industry, why, the power and corrigible authority of this lies in our wills. If the balance of our
lives had not one scale of reason to poise another of
sensuality, the blood and baseness of our natures
would conduct us to most preposterous conclusions:
but we have reason to cool our raging motions, our
carnal stings, our unbitted lusts; whereof I take this,
that you call love, to be a sect or scion.

RODERIGO

It cannot be.

IAGO

It is merely a lust of the blood and a permission of
the will. Come, be a man: drown thyself! drown
cats and blind puppies. I have professed me thy
friend, and I confess me knit to thy deserving with
cables of perdurable toughness: I could never better
stead thee than now. Put money in thy purse; follow
thou the wars; defeat thy favour with an usurped
beard; I say, put money in thy purse. It cannot be
that Desdemona should long continue her love to
the Moor—put money in thy purse—nor he his to
her: it was a violent commencement, and thou shalt
see an answerable sequestration; put but money in
thy purse. These Moors are changeable in their
wills:—fill thy purse with money. The food that to
him now is as luscious as locusts, shall be to him
shortly as bitter as coloquintida. She must change
for youth: when she is sated with his body, she will
find the error of her choice: she must have change,
she must: therefore put money in thy purse. If thou
wilt needs damn thyself, do it a more delicate way
than drowning. Make all the money thou canst: if
sanctimony and a frail vow betwixt an erring barbarian and a supersubtle Venetian be not too hard
for my wits and all the tribe of hell, thou shalt enjoy
her; therefore make money. A pox of drowning thyself! it is clean out of the way: seek thou rather to be
hanged in compassing thy joy than to be drowned
and go without her.

RODERIGO

Wilt thou be fast to my hopes, if I depend on the
issue?

IAGO

Thou art sure of me: go, make money: I have told
thee often, and I re-tell thee again and again, I hate

the Moor: my cause is hearted; thine hath no less
reason. Let us be conjunctive in our revenge against
him: if thou canst cuckold him, thou dost thyself a
pleasure, me a sport. There are many events in the
womb of time, which will be delivered. Traverse;
go; provide thy money. We will have more of this
to-morrow. Adieu.

RODERIGO

Where shall we meet i' the morning?

IAGO

At my lodging.

RODERIGO

I'll be with thee betimes.

IAGO

Go to; farewell. Do you hear, Roderigo?

RODERIGO

What say you?

IAGO

No more of drowning, do you hear?

RODERIGO

I am changed: I'll go sell all my land.   [Exit

IAGO

Thus do I ever make my fool my purse;
For I mine own gain'd knowledge should profane,
If I would time expend with such a snipe
But for my sport and profit. I hate the Moor;
And it is thought abroad that 'twixt my sheets
He has done my office: I know not if 't be true;
But I for mere suspicion in that kind
Will do as if for surety. He holds me well;
The better shall my purpose work on him.
Cassio's a proper man: let me see now;
To get his place, and to plume up my will
In double knavery—How, how?—Let's see:—
After some time, to abuse Othello's ear
That he is too familiar with his wife.
He hath a person and a smooth dispose
To be suspected; framed to make women false.
The Moor is of a free and open nature,
That thinks men honest that but seem to be so;
And will as tenderly be led by the nose
As asses are.
I have 't. It is engender'd. Hell and night
Must bring this monstrous birth to the world's light.
                                                  [Exit

ACT II

SCENE I. *A sea-port in Cyprus. An open place near the
quay*

Enter MONTANO *and two* GENTLEMEN

MONTANO

What from the cape can you discern at sea?

FIRST GENTLEMAN

Nothing at all: it is a high-wrought flood;
I cannot, 'twixt the heaven and the main,
Descry a sail.

MONTANO

Methinks the wind hath spoke aloud at land;
A fuller blast ne'er shook our battlements:
If it hath ruffian'd so upon the sea,
What ribs of oak, when mountains melt on them,
Can hold the mortise? What shall we hear of this?

SECOND GENTLEMAN

A segregation of the Turkish fleet:
For do but stand upon the foaming shore,
The chidden billow seems to pelt the clouds;
The wind-shaked surge, with high and monstrous
mane,
Seems to cast water on the burning bear,
And quench the guards of the ever-fixed pole:
I never did like molestation view
On the enchafed flood.

MONTANO

                    If that the Turkish fleet
Be not enshelter'd and embay'd, they are drown'd;
It is impossible to bear it out.

Enter a THIRD GENTLEMAN

THIRD GENTLEMAN

News, lads! our wars are done.
The desperate tempest hath so bang'd the Turks,
That their designment halts: a noble ship of Venice
Hath seen a grievous wreck and sufferance
On most part of their fleet.

MONTANO

How! is this true?

THIRD GENTLEMAN

                    The ship is here put in,
A Veronesa; Michael Cassio,
Lieutenant to the warlike Moor Othello,
Is come on shore: the Moor himself at sea,
And is in full commission here for Cyprus.

MONTANO

I am glad on 't; 'tis a worthy governor.

THIRD GENTLEMAN

But this same Cassio, though he speak of comfort
Touching the Turkish loss, yet he looks sadly
And prays the Moor be safe; for they were parted
With foul and violent tempest.

MONTANO

                    Pray heavens he be;
For I have served him, and the man commands
Like a full soldier. Let's to the seaside, ho!
As well to see the vessel that's come in
As to throw out our eyes for brave Othello,
Even till we make the main and the aerial blue
An indistinct regard.

THIRD GENTLEMAN

                    Come, let's do so;
For every minute is expectancy
Of more arrivance.

Enter CASSIO

CASSIO

Thanks, you the valiant of this warlike isle,
That so approve the Moor! O, let the heavens
Give him defence against the elements,
For I have lost him on a dangerous sea.

MONTANO

Is he well shipp'd?

CASSIO

His bark is stoutly timber'd, and his pilot
Of very expert and approved allowance;
Therefore my hopes, not surfeited to death,
Stand in bold cure.

[*A cry within: 'A sail, a sail, a sail!'*
Enter a FOURTH GENTLEMAN

CASSIO

What noise?

FOURTH GENTLEMAN

The town is empty; on the brow o' the sea
Stand ranks of people, and they cry 'A sail!'

CASSIO

My hopes do shape him for the governor.

[*Guns heard*

SECOND GENTLEMAN

They do discharge their shot of courtesy:
Our friends at least.

CASSIO

I pray you, sir, go forth,
And give us truth who 'tis that is arrived.

SECOND GENTLEMAN

I shall.   [*Exit*

MONTANO

But, good lieutenant, is your general wived?

CASSIO

Most fortunately: he hath achieved a maid
That paragons description and wild fame;
One that excels the quirks of blazoning pens,
And in the essential vesture of creation
Does tire the ingener.

Re-enter SECOND GENTLEMAN

How now! who has put in?

SECOND GENTLEMAN

'Tis one Iago, ancient to the general.

CASSIO

He has had most favourable and happy speed:
Tempests themselves, high seas, and howling winds,
The gutter'd rocks, and congregated sands,
Traitors ensteep'd to clog the guiltless keel,
As having sense of beauty, do omit
Their mortal natures, letting go safely by
The divine Desdemona.

MONTANO

What is she?'

CASSIO

She that I spake of, our great captain's captain,
Left in the conduct of the bold Iago;
Whose footing here anticipates our thoughts
A se'nnight's speed. Great Jove, Othello guard,
And swell his sail with thine own powerful breath,
That he may bless this bay with his tall ship,
Make love's quick pants in Desdemona's arms,
Give renew'd fire to our extinguish'd spirits,
And bring all Cyprus comfort.

Enter DESDEMONA, EMILIA, IAGO, RODERIGO,
and ATTENDANTS

O, behold,

The riches of the ship is come on shore!
Ye men of Cyprus, let her have your knees.
Hail to thee, lady! and the grace of heaven,
Before, behind thee, and on every hand,
Enwheel thee round!

DESDEMONA

I thank you, valiant Cassio.
What tidings can you tell me of my lord?

CASSIO

He is not yet arrived: nor know I aught
But that he's well and will be shortly here.

DESDEMONA

O, but I fear—How lost you company?

CASSIO

The great contention of the sea and skies
Parted our fellowship—But, hark! a sail.

[*A cry within: 'A sail, a sail!' Guns heard*

SECOND GENTLEMAN

They give their greeting to the citadel:
This likewise is a friend.

CASSIO

See for the news. [*Exit* GENTLEMAN
Good ancient, you are welcome. [*To* EMILIA] Wel-
come, mistress:
Let it not gall your patience, good Iago,
That I extend my manners; 'tis my breeding
That gives me this bold show of courtesy.

[*Kissing her*

IAGO

Sir, would she give you so much of her lips
As of her tongue she oft bestows on me,
You'ld have enough.

DESDEMONA

Alas, she has no speech.

IAGO

In faith, too much;
I find it still when I have list to sleep:
Marry, before your ladyship, I grant,
She puts her tongue a little in her heart
And chides with thinking.

EMILIA

You have little cause to say so.

IAGO

Come on, come on; you are pictures out of doors,
Bells in your parlours, wild-cats in your kitchens,
Saints in your injuries, devils being offended,
Players in your housewifery, and housewives in
your beds.

DESDEMONA

O, fie upon thee, slanderer!

IAGO

Nay, it is true, or else I am a Turk:
You rise to play, and go to bed to work.

EMILIA

You shall not write my praise.

IAGO

No, let me not.

DESDEMONA

What wouldst thou write of me, if thou shouldst
praise me?

IAGO

O gentle lady, do not put me to 't;
For I am nothing if not critical.

DESDEMONA

Come on, assay—There's one gone to the harbour?

IAGO

Ay, madam.

DESDEMONA

I am not merry; but I do beguile
The thing I am by seeming otherwise.
Come, how wouldst thou praise me?

IAGO

I am about it; but indeed my invention
Comes from my pate as birdlime does from frize;
It plucks out brains and all: but my Muse labours,
And thus she is deliver'd.
If she be fair and wise, fairness and wit,
The one's for use, the other useth it.

DESDEMONA

Well praised! How if she be black and witty?

IAGO

If she be black, and thereto have a wit,
She'll find a white that shall her blackness fit.

DESDEMONA

Worse and worse.

EMILIA

How if fair and foolish?

IAGO

She never yet was foolish that was fair;
For even her folly help'd her to an heir.

DESDEMONA

These are old fond paradoxes to make fools laugh
i' the alehouse. What miserable praise hast thou for
her that's foul and foolish?

IAGO

There's none so foul, and foolish thereunto,
But does foul pranks which fair and wise ones do.

DESDEMONA

O heavy ignorance! thou praisest the worst best.
But what praise couldst thou bestow on a deserving
woman indeed, one that in the authority of her
merit did justly put on the vouch of very malice itself?

IAGO

She that was ever fair and never proud,
Had tongue at will and yet was never loud,
Never lack'd gold and yet went never gay,
Fled from her wish and yet said 'Now I may;'
She that, being anger'd, her revenge being nigh,
Bade her wrong stay and her displeasure fly;
She that in wisdom never was so frail
To change the cod's head for the salmon's tail;
She that could think and ne'er disclose her mind,
See suitors following and not look behind;
She was a wight, if ever such wight were,—

DESDEMONA

To do what?

IAGO

To suckle fools and chronicle small beer.

DESDEMONA

O most lame and impotent conclusion! Do not learn
of him, Emilia, though he be thy husband. How say
you, Cassio? is he not a most profane and liberal
counsellor?

CASSIO

He speaks home, madam: you may relish him more
in the soldier than in the scholar.

IAGO

[Aside] He takes her by the palm: ay, well said,
whisper: with as little a web as this will I ensnare as
great a fly as Cassio. Ay, smile upon her, do; I will
gyve thee in thine own courtship. You say true; 'tis
so, indeed: if such tricks as these strip you out of
your lieutenantry, it had been better you had not
kissed your three fingers so oft, which now again you
are most apt to play the sir in. Very good; well
kissed! an excellent courtesy! 'tis so, indeed. Yet
again your fingers to your lips? would they were
clyster-pipes for your sake!—[Trumpet within] The
Moor! I know his trumpet.

CASSIO

'Tis truly so.

DESDEMONA

Let's meet him and receive him.

CASSIO

Lo, where he comes!

Enter OTHELLO *and* ATTENDANTS

OTHELLO

O my fair warrior!

DESDEMONA

My dear Othello!

OTHELLO

It gives me wonder great as my content
To see you here before me. O my soul's joy!
If after every tempest come such calms,
May the winds blow till they have waken'd death!
And let the labouring bark climb hills of seas
Olympus-high, and duck again as low
As hell's from heaven! If it were now to die,
'Twere now to be most happy; for I fear,
My soul hath her content so absolute
That not another comfort like to this
Succeeds in unknown fate.

DESDEMONA

The heavens forbid
But that our loves and comforts should increase,
Even as our days do grow!

OTHELLO

Amen to that, sweet powers!
I cannot speak enough of this content;
It stops me here; it is too much of joy:
And this, and this, the greatest discords be
[Kissing her
That e'er our hearts shall make!

IAGO

[Aside] O, you are well tuned now!
But I'll set down the pegs that make this music,
As honest as I am.

OTHELLO

Come, let us to the castle.
News, friends; our wars are done, the Turks are
    drown'd.
How does my old acquaintance of this isle?
Honey, you shall be well desired in Cyprus;
I have found great love amongst them. O my sweet,
I prattle out of fashion, and I dote
In mine own comforts. I prithee, good Iago,
Go to the bay, and disembark my coffers:
Bring thou the master to the citadel;
He is a good one, and his worthiness
Does challenge much respect. Come, Desdemona,
Once more well met at Cyprus.

    [*Exeunt all but* IAGO *and* RODERIGO

IAGO

Do thou meet me presently at the harbour. Come
hither. If thou be'st valiant—as, they say, base men
being in love have then a nobility in their natures
more than is native to them—list me. The lieutenant to-night watches on the court of guard. First, I
must tell thee this: Desdemona is directly in love
with him.

RODERIGO

With him! why, 'tis not possible.

IAGO

Lay thy finger thus, and let thy soul be instructed.
Mark me with what violence she first loved the
Moor, but for bragging and telling her fantastical
lies: and will she love him still for prating? let not
thy discreet heart think it. Her eye must be fed; and
what delight shall she have to look on the devil?
When the blood is made dull with the act of sport,
there should be, again to inflame it and to give
satiety a fresh appetite, loveliness in favour, sympathy in years, manners and beauties; all which the
Moor is defective in: now, for want of these required
conveniences, her delicate tenderness will find itself
abused, begin to heave the gorge, disrelish and
abhor the Moor; very nature will instruct her in it
and compel her to some second choice. Now, sir,
this granted—as it is a most pregnant and unforced
position—who stands so eminently in the degree of
this fortune as Cassio does? a knave very voluble; no
further conscionable than in putting on the mere
form of civil and humane seeming, for the better
compassing of his salt and most hidden loose affection? why, none; why, none: a slipper and subtle
knave; a finder out of occasions; that has an eye can
stamp and counterfeit advantages, though true advantage never present itself: a devilish knave! Besides, the knave is handsome, young, and hath all
those requisites in him that folly and green minds
look after: a pestilent complete knave; and the
woman hath found him already.

RODERIGO

I cannot believe that in her; she's full of most blest
condition.

IAGO

Blest fig's-end! the wine she drinks is made of
grapes: if she had been blest, she would never have
loved the Moor: blest pudding! Didst thou not see
her paddle with the palm of his hand? didst not
mark that?

RODERIGO

Yes, that I did; but that was but courtesy.

IAGO

Lechery, by this hand; an index and obscure prologue to the history of lust and foul thoughts.
They met so near with their lips that their breaths
embraced together. Villanous thoughts, Roderigo!
when these mutualities so marshal the way, hard at
hand comes the master and main exercise, the incorporate conclusion: pish! But, sir, be you ruled by
me: I have brought you from Venice. Watch you
to-night; for the command, I'll lay 't upon you:
Cassio knows you not: I'll not be far from you: do
you find some occasion to anger Cassio, either by
speaking too loud, or tainting his discipline, or from
what other course you please, which the time shall
more favourably minister.

RODERIGO

Well.

IAGO

Sir, he is rash and very sudden in choler, and
haply may strike at you: provoke him, that he may;
for even out of that will I cause these of Cyprus to
mutiny; whose qualification shall come into no true
taste again but by the displanting of Cassio. So
shall you have a shorter journey to your desires by
the means I shall then have to prefer them, and the
impediment most profitably removed, without the
which there were no expectation of our prosperity.

RODERIGO

I will do this, if I can bring it to any opportunity.

IAGO

I warrant thee. Meet me by and by at the citadel:
I must fetch his necessaries ashore. Farewell.

RODERIGO

Adieu.   [*Exit*

IAGO

That Cassio loves her, I do well believe it;
That she loves him, 'tis apt and of great credit:
The Moor, howbeit that I endure him not,
Is of a constant, loving, noble nature;
And I dare think he'll prove to Desdemona
A most dear husband. Now, I do love her too,
Not out of absolute lust, though peradventure
I stand accountant for as great a sin,
But partly led to diet my revenge,
For that I do suspect the lusty Moor
Hath leap'd into my seat: the thought whereof
Doth like a poisonous mineral gnaw my inwards;
And nothing can or shall content my soul
Till I am even'd with him, wife for wife;
Or failing so, yet that I put the Moor
At least into a jealousy so strong
That judgement cannot cure. Which thing to do,
If this poor trash of Venice, whom I trash
For his quick hunting, stand the putting on,

I'll have our Michael Cassio on the hip,
Abuse him to the Moor in the rank garb;
For I fear Cassio with my night-cap too;
Make the Moor thank me, love me and reward me,
For making him egregiously an ass
And practising upon his peace and quiet
Even to madness. 'Tis here, but yet confused:
Knavery's plain face is never seen till used.   [*Exit*

SCENE II. *A street*

Enter a HERALD *with a proclamation;* PEOPLE *following*
HERALD

It is Othello's pleasure, our noble and valiant
general, that upon certain tidings now arrived, importing the mere perdition of the Turkish fleet,
every man put himself into triumph; some to dance,
some to make bonfires, each man to what sport and
revels his addiction leads him: for, besides these
beneficial news, it is the celebration of his nuptial.
So much was his pleasure should be proclaimed. All
offices are open, and there is full liberty of feasting
from this present hour of five till the bell have told
eleven. Heaven bless the isle of Cyprus and our
noble general Othello!   [*Exeunt*

SCENE III. *A hall in the castle*

Enter OTHELLO, DESDEMONA, CASSIO, *and* ATTENDANTS
OTHELLO

Good Michael, look you to the guard to-night:
Let's teach ourselves that honourable stop,
Not to outsport discretion.

CASSIO

Iago hath direction what to do;
But notwithstanding with my personal eye
Will I look to 't.

OTHELLO

Iago is most honest.
Michael, good night: to-morrow with your earliest
Let me have speech with you. Come, my dear love,
The purchase made, the fruits are to ensue;
That profit's yet to come 'tween me and you.
Good night.
    [*Exeunt* OTHELLO, DESDEMONA, *and* ATTENDANTS
    Enter IAGO

CASSIO

Welcome, Iago; we must to the watch.

IAGO

Not this hour, lieutenant; 'tis not yet ten o' the
clock. Our general cast us thus early for the love
of his Desdemona; who let us not therefore blame:
he hath not yet made wanton the night with her,
and she is sport for Jove.

CASSIO

She's a most exquisite lady.

IAGO

And, I'll warrant her, full of game.

CASSIO

Indeed she's a most fresh and delicate creature.

IAGO

What an eye she has! methinks it sounds a parley
to provocation.

CASSIO

An inviting eye; and yet methinks right modest.

IAGO

And when she speaks, is it not an alarum to love?

CASSIO

She is indeed perfection.

IAGO

Well, happiness to their sheets! Come, lieutenant,
I have a stoup of wine; and here without are a brace
of Cyprus gallants that would fain have a measure
to the health of black Othello.

CASSIO

Not to-night, good Iago: I have very poor and unhappy brains for drinking: I could well wish courtesy would invent some other custom of entertainment.

IAGO

O, they are our friends; but one cup: I'll drink for
you.

CASSIO

I have drunk but one cup to-night, and that was
craftily qualified too, and behold what innovation
it makes here: I am unfortunate in the infirmity,
and dare not task my weakness with any more.

IAGO

What, man! 'tis a night of revels: the gallants desire
it.

CASSIO

Where are they?

IAGO

Here at the door; I pray you, call them in.

CASSIO

I'll do 't; but it dislikes me.   [*Exit*

IAGO

If I can fasten but one cup upon him,
With that which he hath drunk to-night already,
He'll be as full of quarrel and offence
As my young mistress' dog. Now my sick fool Rod-
    erigo,
Whom love hath turn'd almost the wrong side out,
To Desdemona hath to-night caroused
Potations pottle-deep; and he's to watch:
Three lads of Cyprus, noble swelling spirits,
That hold their honours in a wary distance,
The very elements of this warlike isle,
Have I to-night fluster'd with flowing cups,
And they watch too. Now, 'mongst this flock of
    drunkards,
Am I to put our Cassio in some action
That may offend the isle. But here they come:
If consequence do but approve my dream,
My boat sails freely, both with wind and stream.

Re-enter CASSIO; *with him* MONTANO *and* GENTLEMEN;
SERVANTS *following with wine*

CASSIO

'Fore God, they have given me a rouse already.

MONTANO

Good faith, a little one; not past a pint, as I am a
soldier.

IAGO

Some wine, ho!

[*Sings*]   And let me the canakin clink, clink;
And let me the canakin clink:
A soldier's a man;
A life's but a span;
Why then let a soldier drink.

Some wine, boys!

CASSIO

'Fore God, an excellent song.

IAGO

I learned it in England, where indeed they are most
potent in potting: your Dane, your German, and
your swag-bellied Hollander,—Drink, ho!—are
nothing to your English.

CASSIO

Is your Englishman so expert in his drinking?

IAGO

Why, he drinks you with facility your Dane dead
drunk; he sweats not to overthrow your Almain; he
gives your Hollander a vomit ere the next pottle can
be filled.

CASSIO

To the health of our general!

MONTANO

I am for it, lieutenant, and I'll do you justice.

IAGO

O sweet England!

[*Sings*]   King Stephen was a worthy peer,
His breeches cost him but a crown;
He held them sixpence all too dear,
With that he call'd the tailor lown.

He was a wight of high renown,
And thou art but of low degree:
'Tis pride that pulls the country down;
Then take thine auld cloak about thee.

Some wine, ho!

CASSIO

Why, this is a more exquisite song than the other.

IAGO

Will you hear 't again?

CASSIO

No; for I hold him to be unworthy of his place that
does those things. Well: God's above all; and there
be souls must be saved, and there be souls must not
be saved.

IAGO

It's true, good lieutenant.

CASSIO

For mine own part—no offence to the general, nor
any man of quality—I hope to be saved.

IAGO

And so do I too, lieutenant.

CASSIO

Ay, but, by your leave, not before me; the lieutenant is to be saved before the ancient. Let's have no
more of this; let's to our affairs. God forgive us our
sins! Gentlemen, let's look to our business. Do not
think, gentlemen, I am drunk: this is my ancient:
this is my right hand, and this is my left. I am not
drunk now; I can stand well enough, and speak well
enough.

ALL

Excellent well.

CASSIO

Why, very well then; you must not think then that
I am drunk.   [*Exit*

MONTANO

To the platform, masters; come, let's set the watch.

IAGO

You see this fellow that is gone before;
He is a soldier fit to stand by Cæsar
And give direction: and do but see his vice;
'Tis to his virtue a just equinox,
The one as long as the other: 'tis pity of him.
I fear the trust Othello puts him in
On some odd time of his infirmity
Will shake this island.

MONTANO

But is he often thus?

IAGO

'Tis evermore the prologue to his sleep:
He'll watch the horologe a double set,
If drink rock not his cradle.

MONTANO

It were well
The general were put in mind of it.
Perhaps he sees it not, or his good nature
Prizes the virtue that appears in Cassio
And looks not on his evils: is not this true?

Enter RODERIGO

IAGO

[*Aside to him*] How now, Roderigo!
I pray you, after the lieutenant; go. [*Exit* RODERIGO

MONTANO

And 'tis great pity that the noble Moor
Should hazard such a place as his own second
With one of an ingraft infirmity:
It were an honest action to say
So to the Moor.

IAGO

Not I, for this fair island:
I do love Cassio well, and would do much
To cure him of this evil:—But, hark! what noise?
[*A cry within:* 'Help! help!'

Re-enter CASSIO, *driving in* RODERIGO

CASSIO

'Zounds! you rogue! you rascal!

MONTANO

What's the matter, lieutenant?

CASSIO

A knave teach me my duty! But I'll beat the knave
into a wicker bottle.

RODERIGO

Beat me!

CASSIO

Dost thou prate, rogue?   [*Striking* RODERIGO

MONTANO

Nay, good lieutenant; I pray you, sir, hold your hand.

CASSIO

Let me go, sir, or I'll knock you o'er the mazzard.

MONTANO

Come, come, you're drunk.

CASSIO

Drunk!   [*They fight*

IAGO

[*Aside to* RODERIGO] Away, I say; go out, and cry a mutiny.   [*Exit* RODERIGO

Nay, good lieutenant! God's will, gentlemen!

Help, ho!—Lieutenant,—sir,—Montano,—sir;—

Help, masters!—Here's a goodly watch indeed!

                    [*A bell rings*

Who's that that rings the bell?—Diablo, ho!

The town will rise: God's will, lieutenant, hold;

You will be shamed for ever.

      Re-enter OTHELLO *and* ATTENDANTS

OTHELLO

              What is the matter here?

MONTANO

'Zounds, I bleed still; I am hurt to the death.

                    [*Faints*

OTHELLO

Hold, for your lives!

IAGO

Hold, ho! Lieutenant,—sir,—Montano,—gentlemen,—

Have you forgot all sense of place and duty?

Hold! the general speaks to you; hold, hold, for shame!

OTHELLO

Why, how now, ho! from whence ariseth this?

Are we turn'd Turks, and to ourselves do that

Which heaven hath forbid the Ottomites?

For Christian shame, put by this barbarous brawl:

He that stirs next to carve for his own rage

Holds his soul light; he dies upon his motion.

Silence that dreadful bell: it frights the isle

From her propriety. What is the matter, masters?

Honest Iago, that look'st dead with grieving,

Speak, who began this? on thy love, I charge thee.

IAGO

I do not know: friends all but now, even now,

In quarter, and in terms like bride and groom

Devesting them for bed; and then, but now,

As if some planet had unwitted men,

Swords out, and tilting one at other's breast,

In opposition bloody. I cannot speak

Any beginning to this peevish odds;

And would in action glorious I had lost

Those legs that brought me to a part of it!

OTHELLO

How comes it, Michael, you are thus forgot?

CASSIO

I pray you, pardon me; I cannot speak.

OTHELLO

Worthy Montano, you were wont be civil;

The gravity and stillness of your youth

The world hath noted, and your name is great

In mouths of wisest censure: what's the matter,

That you unlace your reputation thus,

And spend your rich opinion for the name

Of a night-brawler? give me answer to it.

MONTANO

Worthy Othello, I am hurt to danger:

Your officer, Iago, can inform you—

While I spare speech, which something now offends me—

Of all that I do know: nor know I aught

By me that's said or done amiss this night;

Unless self-charity be sometimes a vice,

And to defend ourselves it be a sin

When violence assails us.

OTHELLO

              Now, by heaven,

My blood begins my safer guides to rule,

And passion, having my best judgement collied,

Assays to lead the way: if I once stir,

Or do but lift this arm, the best of you

Shall sink in my rebuke. Give me to know

How this foul rout began, who set it on,

And he that is approved in this offence,

Though he had twinn'd with me, both at a birth,

Shall lose me. What! in a town of war,

Yet wild, the people's hearts brimful of fear,

To manage private and domestic quarrel,

In night, and on the court and guard of safety!

'Tis monstrous. Iago, who began 't?

MONTANO

If partially affined, or leagued in office,

Thou dost deliver more or less than truth,

Thou art no soldier.

IAGO

             Touch me not so near:

I had rather have this tongue cut from my mouth

Than it should do offence to Michael Cassio;

Yet, I persuade myself, to speak the truth

Shall nothing wrong him. Thus it is, general.

Montano and myself being in speech,

There comes a fellow crying out for help,

And Cassio following him with determined sword,

To execute upon him. Sir, this gentleman

Steps in to Cassio and entreats his pause:

Myself the crying fellow did pursue,

Lest by his clamour—as it so fell out—

The town might fall in fright: he, swift of foot,

Outran my purpose; and I return'd the rather

For that I heard the clink and fall of swords,

And Cassio high in oath; which till to-night

I ne'er might say before. When I came back—

For this was brief—I found them close together,

At blow and thrust; even as again they were

When you yourself did part them.

More of this matter cannot I report:
But men are men; the best sometimes forget:
Though Cassio did some little wrong to him,
As men in rage strike those that wish them best,
Yet surely Cassio, I believe, received
From him that fled some strange indignity,
Which patience could not pass.

OTHELLO

                 I know, Iago,
Thy honesty and love doth mince this matter,
Making it light to Cassio. Cassio, I love thee;
But never more be officer of mine.

Re-enter DESDEMONA, *attended*

Look, if my gentle love be not raised up!
I'll make thee an example.

DESDEMONA

               What's the matter?

OTHELLO

All's well now, sweeting; come away to bed.
Sir, for your hurts, myself will be your surgeon:
                [*To* MONTANO, *who is led off*
Lead him off.
Iago, look with care about the town,
And silence those whom this vile brawl distracted.
Come, Desdemona: 'tis the soldiers' life
To have their balmy slumbers waked with strife.
          [*Exeunt all but* IAGO *and* CASSIO

IAGO

What, are you hurt, lieutenant?

CASSIO

Ay, past all surgery.

IAGO

Marry, heaven forbid!

CASSIO

Reputation, reputation, reputation! O, I have lost
my reputation! I have lost the immortal part of myself, and what remains is bestial. My reputation,
Iago, my reputation!

IAGO

As I am an honest man, I thought you had received
some bodily wound; there is more sense in that than
in reputation. Reputation is an idle and most false
imposition; oft got without merit and lost without
deserving: you have lost no reputation at all, unless
you repute yourself such a loser. What, man! there
are ways to recover the general again: you are but
now cast in his mood, a punishment more in policy
than in malice; even so as one would beat his of-
fenceless dog to affright an imperious lion: sue to
him again, and he's yours.

CASSIO

I will rather sue to be despised than to deceive so
good a commander with so slight, so drunken, and
so indiscreet an officer. Drunk? and speak parrot?
and squabble? swagger? swear? and discourse fustian with one's own shadow? O thou invisible spirit
of wine, if thou hast no name to be known by, let
us call thee devil!

IAGO

What was he that you followed with your sword?
What had he done to you?

CASSIO

I know not.

IAGO

Is 't possible?

CASSIO

I remember a mass of things, but nothing distinctly;
a quarrel, but nothing wherefore. O God, that men
should put an enemy in their mouths to steal away
their brains! that we should, with joy, pleasance,
revel and applause, transform ourselves into beasts!

IAGO

Why, but you are now well enough: how came you
thus recovered?

CASSIO

It hath pleased the devil drunkenness to give place
to the devil wrath: one unperfectness shows me another, to make me frankly despise myself.

IAGO

Come, you are too severe a moraler: as the time, the
place, and the condition of this country stands, I
could heartily wish this had not befallen; but since it
is as it is, mend it for your own good.

CASSIO

I will ask him for my place again; he shall tell me
I am a drunkard! Had I as many mouths as Hydra,
such an answer would stop them all. To be now a
sensible man, by and by a fool, and presently a
beast! O strange! Every inordinate cup is unblest,
and the ingredient is a devil.

IAGO

Come, come, good wine is a good familiar creature,
if it be well used: exclaim no more against it. And,
good lieutenant, I think you think I love you.

CASSIO

I have well approved it, sir. I drunk!

IAGO

You or any man living may be drunk at some time,
man. I'll tell you what you shall do. Our general's
wife is now the general. I may say so in this respect, for that he hath devoted and given up himself to the contemplation, mark and denotement of
her parts and graces: confess yourself freely to her;
importune her help to put you in your place again:
she is of so free, so kind, so apt, so blessed a disposition, she holds it a vice in her goodness not to do
more than she is requested: this broken joint between you and her husband entreat her to splinter;
and, my fortunes against any lay worth naming,
this crack of your love shall grow stronger than it
was before.

CASSIO

You advise me well.

IAGO

I protest, in the sincerity of love and honest kindness.

CASSIO

I think it freely; and betimes in the morning I will

beseech the virtuous Desdemona to undertake for me: I am desperate of my fortunes if they check me here.

IAGO

You are in the right. Good night, lieutenant; I must to the watch.

CASSIO

Good night, honest Iago.   [*Exit*

IAGO

And what's he then that says I play the villain?
When this advice is free I give and honest,
Probal to thinking, and indeed the course
To win the Moor again? For 'tis most easy
The inclining Desdemona to subdue
In any honest suit. She's framed as fruitful
As the free elements. And then for her
To win the Moor, were 't to renounce his baptism,
All seals and symbols of redeemed sin,
His soul is so enfetter'd to her love,
That she may make, unmake, do what she list,
Even as her appetite shall play the god
With his weak function. How am I then a villain
To counsel Cassio to this parallel course,
Directly to his good? Divinity of hell!
When devils will the blackest sins put on,
They do suggest at first with heavenly shows,
As I do now: for whiles this honest fool
Plies Desdemona to repair his fortunes,
And she for him pleads strongly to the Moor,
I'll pour this pestilence into his ear,
That she repeals him for her body's lust;
And by how much she strives to do him good,
She shall undo her credit with the Moor.
So will I turn her virtue into pitch;
And out of her own goodness make the net
That shall enmesh them all.

Enter RODERIGO

How now, Roderigo!

RODERIGO

I do follow here in the chase, not like a hound that hunts, but one that fills up the cry. My money is almost spent; I have been to-night exceedingly well cudgelled; and I think the issue will be, I shall have so much experience for my pains; and so, with no money at all and a little more wit, return again to Venice.

IAGO

How poor are they that have not patience!
What wound did ever heal but by degrees?
Thou know'st we work by wit and not by witchcraft,
And wit depends on dilatory time.
Does 't not go well? Cassio hath beaten thee,
And thou by that small hurt hast cashier'd Cassio:
Though other things grow fair against the sun,
Yet fruits that blossom first will first be ripe:
Content thyself awhile. By the mass, 'tis morning;
Pleasure and action make the hours seem short.
Retire thee; go where thou art billeted:
Away, I say; thou shalt know more hereafter:

Nay, get thee gone. [*Exit* RODERIGO] Two things are to be done:
My wife must move for Cassio to her mistress;
I'll set her on;
Myself the while to draw the Moor apart,
And bring him jump when he may Cassio find
Soliciting his wife: ay, that's the way;
Dull not device by coldness and delay.   [*Exit*

ACT III

SCENE I. *Before the castle*

Enter CASSIO *and some* MUSICIANS

CASSIO

Masters, play here; I will content your pains;
Something that's brief; and bid 'Good morrow, general.'   [*Music*

Enter CLOWN

CLOWN

Why, masters, have your instruments been in Naples, that they speak i' the nose thus?

FIRST MUSICIAN

How, sir, how?

CLOWN

Are these, I pray you, wind-instruments?

FIRST MUSICIAN

Ay, marry, are they, sir.

CLOWN

O, thereby hangs a tail.

FIRST MUSICIAN

Whereby hangs a tale, sir?

CLOWN

Marry, sir, by many a wind-instrument that I know. But, masters, here's money for you: and the general so likes your music, that he desires you, for love's sake, to make no more noise with it.

FIRST MUSICIAN

Well, sir, we will not.

CLOWN

If you have any music that may not be heard, to 't again: but, as they say, to hear music the general does not greatly care.

FIRST MUSICIAN

We have none such, sir.

CLOWN

Then put up your pipes in your bag, for I'll away: go; vanish into air; away!   [*Exeunt* MUSICIANS

CASSIO

Dost thou hear, my honest friend?

CLOWN

No, I hear not your honest friend; I hear you.

CASSIO

Prithee, keep up thy quillets. There's a poor piece of gold for thee: if the gentlewoman that attends the general's wife be stirring, tell her there's one Cassio entreats her a little favour of speech: wilt thou do this?

CLOWN

She is stirring, sir: if she will stir hither, I shall seem
to notify unto her.

CASSIO

Do, good my friend.   [*Exit* CLOWN

Enter IAGO

In happy time, Iago.

IAGO

You have not been a-bed, then?

CASSIO

Why, no; the day had broke
Before we parted. I have made bold, Iago,
To send in to your wife: my suit to her
Is, that she will to virtuous Desdemona
Procure me some access.

IAGO

I'll send her to you presently;
And I'll devise a mean to draw the Moor
Out of the way, that your converse and business
May be more free.

CASSIO

I humbly thank you for 't. [*Exit* IAGO] I never knew
A Florentine more kind and honest.

Enter EMILIA

EMILIA

Good morrow, good lieutenant: I am sorry
For your displeasure; but all will sure be well.
The general and his wife are talking of it,
And she speaks for you stoutly: the Moor replies,
That he you hurt is of great fame in Cyprus
And great affinity, and that in wholesome wisdom
He might not but refuse you; but he protests he
  loves you,
And needs no other suitor but his likings
To take the safest occasion by the front
To bring you in again.

CASSIO

Yet, I beseech you,
If you think fit, or that it may be done,
Give me advantage of some brief discourse
With Desdemona alone.

EMILIA

Pray you, come in:
I will bestow you where you shall have time
To speak your bosom freely.

CASSIO

I am much bound to you.
     [*Exeunt*

SCENE II. *A room in the castle*

Enter OTHELLO, IAGO, *and* GENTLEMEN

OTHELLO

These letters give, Iago, to the pilot;
And by him do my duties to the senate:
That done, I will be walking on the works;
Repair there to me.

IAGO

Well, my good lord, I'll do 't.

OTHELLO

This fortification, gentlemen, shall we see 't?

GENTLEMAN

We'll wait upon your lordship.   [*Exeunt*

SCENE III. *The garden of the castle*

Enter DESDEMONA, CASSIO, *and* EMILIA

DESDEMONA

Be thou assured, good Cassio, I will do
All my abilities in thy behalf.

EMILIA

Good madam, do: I warrant it grieves my husband
As if the case were his.

DESDEMONA

O, that's an honest fellow. Do not doubt, Cassio,
But I will have my lord and you again
As friendly as you were.

CASSIO

Bounteous madam,
Whatever shall become of Michael Cassio,
He's never any thing but your true servant.

DESDEMONA

I know 't: I thank you. You do love my lord:
You have known him long; and be you well as-
  sured
He shall in strangeness stand no farther off
Than in a politic distance.

CASSIO

Ay, but, lady,
That policy may either last so long,
Or feed upon such nice and waterish diet,
Or breed itself so out of circumstance,
That, I being absent and my place supplied,
My general will forget my love and service.

DESDEMONA

Do not doubt that; before Emilia here
I give thee warrant of thy place: assure thee,
If I do vow a friendship, I'll perform it
To the last article: my lord shall never rest;
I'll watch him tame and talk him out of patience;
His bed shall seem a school, his board a shrift;
I'll intermingle every thing he does
With Cassio's suit: therefore be merry, Cassio;
For thy solicitor shall rather die
Than give thy cause away.

Enter OTHELLO *and* IAGO, *at a distance*

EMILIA

Madam, here comes my lord.

CASSIO

Madam, I'll take my leave.

DESDEMONA

Nay, stay and hear me speak.

CASSIO

Madam, not now: I am very ill at ease,
Unfit for mine own purposes.

DESDEMONA

Well, do your discretion.   [*Exit* CASSIO

IAGO

Ha! I like not that.

OTHELLO

What dost thou say?

IAGO

Nothing, my lord: or if—I know not what.

OTHELLO

Was not that Cassio parted from my wife?

IAGO

Cassio, my lord! No, sure, I cannot think it,
That he would steal away so guilty-like,
Seeing you coming.

OTHELLO

I do believe 'twas he.

DESDEMONA

How now, my lord!
I have been talking with a suitor here,
A man that languishes in your displeasure.

OTHELLO

Who is 't you mean?

DESDEMONA

Why, your lieutenant, Cassio. Good my lord,
If I have any grace or power to move you,
His present reconciliation take;
For if he be not one that truly loves you,
That errs in ignorance and not in cunning,
I have no judgement in an honest face:
I prithee, call him back.

OTHELLO

Went he hence now?

DESDEMONA

Ay, sooth; so humbled,
That he hath left part of his grief with me,
To suffer with him. Good love, call him back.

OTHELLO

Not now, sweet Desdemona; some other time.

DESDEMONA

But shall't be shortly?

OTHELLO

The sooner, sweet, for you.

DESDEMONA

Shall't be to-night at supper?

OTHELLO

No, not to-night.

DESDEMONA

To-morrow dinner then?

OTHELLO

I shall not dine at home;
I meet the captains at the citadel.

DESDEMONA

Why then to-morrow night; or Tuesday morn;
On Tuesday noon, or night; on Wednesday morn:
I prithee, name the time; but let it not
Exceed three days: in faith, he's penitent;
And yet his trespass, in our common reason—
Save that, they say, the wars must make examples
Out of their best—is not almost a fault
To incur a private check. When shall he come?
Tell me, Othello: I wonder in my soul,
What you would ask me, that I should deny,

Or stand so mammering on. What! Michael Cassio,
That came a-wooing with you, and so many a time
When I have spoke of you dispraisingly
Hath ta'en your part; to have so much to do
To bring him in! Trust me, I could do much—

OTHELLO

Prithee, no more: let him come when he will;
I will deny thee nothing.

DESDEMONA

Why, this is not a boon;
'Tis as I should entreat you wear your gloves,
Or feed on nourishing dishes, or keep you warm,
Or sue to you to do a peculiar profit
To your own person: nay, when I have a suit
Wherein I mean to touch your love indeed,
It shall be full of poise and difficult weight,
And fearful to be granted.

OTHELLO

I will deny thee nothing:
Whereon, I do beseech thee, grant me this,
To leave me but a little to myself.

DESDEMONA

Shall I deny you? no: farewell, my lord.

OTHELLO

Farewell, my Desdemona: I'll come to thee straight.

DESDEMONA

Emilia, come. Be as your fancies teach you;
Whate'er you be, I am obedient.

[*Exeunt* DESDEMONA *and* EMILIA

OTHELLO

Excellent wretch! Perdition catch my soul,
But I do love thee! and when I love thee not,
Chaos is come again.

IAGO

My noble lord,—

OTHELLO

What dost thou say, Iago?

IAGO

Did Michael Cassio, when you woo'd my lady,
Know of your love?

OTHELLO

He did, from first to last: why dost thou ask?

IAGO

But for a satisfaction of my thought;
No further harm.

OTHELLO

Why of thy thought, Iago?

IAGO

I did not think he had been acquainted with her.

OTHELLO

O, yes, and went between us very oft.

IAGO

Indeed!

OTHELLO

Indeed! ay, indeed: discern'st thou aught in that?
Is he not honest?

IAGO

Honest, my lord!

OTHELLO

Honest! ay, honest.

IAGO
My lord, for aught I know.

OTHELLO
What dost thou think?

IAGO
Think, my lord!

OTHELLO
Think, my lord! By heaven, he echoes me,
As if there were some monster in his thought
Too hideous to be shown. Thou dost mean some-
thing:
I heard thee say even now, thou likedst not that,
When Cassio left my wife: what didst not like?
And when I told thee he was of my counsel
In my whole course of wooing, thou criedst 'In-
deed!'
And didst contract and purse thy brow together,
As if thou then hadst shut up in thy brain
Some horrible conceit: if thou dost love me,
Show me thy thought.

IAGO
My lord, you know I love you.

OTHELLO
I think thou dost;
And for I know thou'rt full of love and honesty
And weigh'st thy words before thou givest them
breath,
Therefore these stops of thine fright me the more:
For such things in a false disloyal knave
Are tricks of custom; but in a man that's just
They're close delations, working from the heart,
That passion cannot rule.

IAGO
For Michael Cassio,
I dare be sworn I think that he is honest.

OTHELLO
I think so too.

IAGO
Men should be what they seem;
Or those that be not, would they might seem none!

OTHELLO
Certain, men should be what they seem.

IAGO
Why then I think Cassio's an honest man.

OTHELLO
Nay, yet there's more in this:
I prithee, speak to me as to thy thinkings,
As thou dost ruminate, and give thy worst of
thoughts
The worst of words.

IAGO
Good my lord, pardon me:
Though I am bound to every act of duty,
I am not bound to that all slaves are free to.
Utter my thoughts? Why, say they are vile and
false;
As where's that palace whereinto foul things
Sometimes intrude not? who has a breast so pure,
But some uncleanly apprehensions

Keep leets and law-days, and in session sit
With meditations lawful?

OTHELLO
Thou dost conspire against thy friend, Iago,
If thou but think'st him wrong'd and makest his ear
A stranger to thy thoughts.

IAGO
I do beseech you—
Though I perchance am vicious in my guess,
As, I confess, it is my nature's plague
To spy into abuses, and oft my jealousy
Shapes faults that are not—that your wisdom yet,
From one that so imperfectly conceits,
Would take no notice, nor build yourself a trouble
Out of his scattering and unsure observance.
It were not for your quiet nor your good,
Nor for my manhood, honesty, or wisdom,
To let you know my thoughts.

OTHELLO
What dost thou mean?

IAGO
Good name in man and woman, dear my lord,
Is the immediate jewel of their souls:
Who steals my purse steals trash; 'tis something,
nothing;
'Twas mine, 'tis his, and has been slave to thousands
But he that filches from me my good name
Robs me of that which not enriches him
And makes me poor indeed.

OTHELLO
By heaven, I'll know thy thoughts.

IAGO
You cannot, if my heart were in your hand;
Nor shall not, whilst 'tis in my custody.

OTHELLO
Ha!

IAGO
O, beware, my lord, of jealousy;
It is the green-eyed monster, which doth mock
The meat it feeds on: that cuckold lives in bliss
Who, certain of his fate, loves not his wronger;
But, O, what damned minutes tells he o'er
Who dotes, yet doubts, suspects, yet strongly loves!

OTHELLO
O misery!

IAGO
Poor and content is rich, and rich enough;
But riches fineless is as poor as winter
To him that ever fears he shall be poor:
Good heaven, the souls of all my tribe defend
From jealousy!

OTHELLO
Why, why is this?
Think'st thou I'ld make a life of jealousy,
To follow still the changes of the moon
With fresh suspicions? No; to be once in doubt
Is once to be resolved: exchange me for a goat,
When I shall turn the business of my soul
To such exsufflicate and blown surmises,
Matching thy inference. 'Tis not to make me jealous

To say my wife is fair, feeds well, loves company,
Is free of speech, sings, plays and dances well;
Where virtue is, these are more virtuous:
Nor from mine own weak merits will I draw
The smallest fear or doubt of her revolt;
For she had eyes, and chose me. No, Iago;
I'll see before I doubt; when I doubt, prove;
And on the proof, there is no more but this,
Away at once with love or jealousy!

IAGO

I am glad of it; for now I shall have reason
To show the love and duty that I bear you
With franker spirit: therefore, as I am bound,
Receive it from me. I speak not yet of proof.
Look to your wife: observe her well with Cassio;
Wear your eye thus, not jealous nor secure:
I would not have your free and noble nature
Out of self-bounty be abused; look to 't:
I know our country disposition well;
In Venice they do let heaven see the pranks
They dare not show their husbands; their best con-
    science
Is not to leave 't undone, but keep 't unknown.

OTHELLO

Dost thou say so?

IAGO

She did deceive her father, marrying you;
And when she seem'd to shake and fear your looks,
She loved them most.

OTHELLO

And so she did.

IAGO

Why, go to then;
She that so young could give out such a seeming,
To seel her father's eyes up close as oak—
He thought 'twas witchcraft—but I am much to
    blame;
I humbly do beseech you of your pardon
For too much loving you.

OTHELLO

I am bound to thee for ever.

IAGO

I see this hath a little dash'd your spirits.

OTHELLO

Not a jot, not a jot.

IAGO

I' faith, I fear it has.
I hope you will consider what is spoke
Comes from my love; but I do see you're moved:
I am to pray you not to strain my speech
To grosser issues nor to larger reach
Than to suspicion.

OTHELLO

I will not.

IAGO

Should you do so, my lord,
My speech should fall into such vile success
As my thoughts aim not at. Cassio's my worthy
    friend—
My lord, I see you're moved.

OTHELLO

No, not much moved:
I do not think but Desdemona's honest.

IAGO

Long live she so! and long live you to think so!

OTHELLO

And yet, how nature erring from itself—

IAGO

Ay, there's the point: as—to be bold with you—
Not to affect many proposed matches
Of her own clime, complexion and degree,
Whereto we see in all things nature tends—
Foh! one may smell in such a will most rank,
Foul disproportion, thoughts unnatural.
But pardon me: I do not in position
Distinctly speak of her; though I may fear
Her will, recoiling to her better judgement,
May fall to match you with her country forms,
And happily repent.

OTHELLO

Farewell, farewell:
If more thou dost perceive, let me know more;
Set on thy wife to observe: leave me, Iago.

IAGO

[Going] My lord, I take my leave.

OTHELLO

Why did I marry? This honest creature doubtless
Sees and knows more, much more, than he unfolds.

IAGO

[Returning] My lord, I would I might entreat your
    honour
To scan this thing no further; leave it to time:
Though it be fit that Cassio have his place,
For sure he fills it up with great ability,
Yet, if you please to hold him off awhile,
You shall by that perceive him and his means:
Note if your lady strain his entertainment
With any strong or vehement importunity;
Much will be seen in that. In the mean time,
Let me be thought too busy in my fears—
As worthy cause I have to fear I am—
And hold her free, I do beseech your honour.

OTHELLO

Fear not my government.

IAGO

I once more take my leave.   [Exit

OTHELLO

This fellow's of exceeding honesty,
And knows all qualities, with a learned spirit,
Of human dealings. If I do prove her haggard,
Though that her jesses were my dear heart-strings,
I'ld whistle her off and let her down the wind
To prey at fortune. Haply, for I am black
And have not those soft parts of conversation
That chamberers have, or for I am declined
Into the vale of years,—yet that's not much—
She's gone; I am abused, and my relief
Must be to loathe her. O curse of marriage,
That we can call these delicate creatures ours,
And not their appetites! I had rather be a toad,

And live upon the vapour of a dungeon,
Than keep a corner in the thing I love
For others' uses. Yet, 'tis the plague of great ones;
Prerogatived are they less than the base;
'Tis destiny unshunnable, like death:
Even then this forked plague is fated to us
When we do quicken. Desdemona comes:

Re-enter DESDEMONA *and* EMILIA

If she be false, O, then heaven mocks itself!
I'll not believe 't.

DESDEMONA

How now, my dear Othello!
Your dinner, and the generous islanders
By you invited, do attend your presence.

OTHELLO

I am to blame.

DESDEMONA

Why do you speak so faintly?
Are you not well?

OTHELLO

I have a pain upon my forehead here.

DESDEMONA

Faith, that's with watching; 'twill away again:
Let me but bind it hard, within this hour
It will be well.

OTHELLO

Your napkin is too little;
[*He puts the handkerchief from him; and she drops it*
Let it alone. Come, I'll go in with you.

DESDEMONA

I am very sorry that you are not well.
[*Exeunt* OTHELLO *and* DESDEMONA

EMILIA

I am glad I have found this napkin:
This was her first remembrance from the Moor:
My wayward husband hath a hundred times
Woo'd me to steal it; but she so loves the token,
For he conjured her she should ever keep it,
That she reserves it evermore about her
To kiss and talk to. I'll have the work ta'en out,
And give 't Iago: what he will do with it
Heaven knows, not I;
I nothing but to please his fantasy.

Re-enter IAGO

IAGO

How now! what do you here alone?

EMILIA

Do not you chide; I have a thing for you.

IAGO

A thing for me? it is a common thing—

EMILIA

Ha!

IAGO

To have a foolish wife.

EMILIA

O, is that all? What will you give me now
For that same handkerchief?

IAGO

What handkerchief?

EMILIA

What handkerchief!
Why, that the Moor first gave to Desdemona;
That which so often you did bid me steal.

IAGO

Hast stol'n it from her?

EMILIA

No, faith; she let it drop by negligence,
And, to the advantage, I being here took 't up.
Look, here it is.

IAGO

A good wench; give it me.

EMILIA

What will you do with 't, that you have been so
earnest
To have me filch it?

IAGO

[*Snatching it*] Why, what's that to you?

EMILIA

If 't be not for some purpose of import,
Give 't me again: poor lady, she'll run mad
When she shall lack it.

IAGO

Be not acknown on 't; I have use for it.
Go, leave me. [*Exit* EMILIA
I will in Cassio's lodging lose this napkin,
And let him find it. Trifles light as air
Are to the jealous confirmations strong
As proofs of holy writ: this may do something.
The Moor already changes with my poison:
Dangerous conceits are in their natures poisons,
Which at the first are scarce found to distaste,
But with a little act upon the blood
Burn like the mines of sulphur. I did say so:
Look, where he comes!

Re-enter OTHELLO

Not poppy, nor mandragora,
Nor all the drowsy syrups of the world,
Shall ever medicine thee to that sweet sleep
Which thou owedst yesterday.

OTHELLO

Ha! ha! false to me?

IAGO

Why, how now, general! no more of that.

OTHELLO

Avaunt! be gone! thou hast set me on the rack
I swear 'tis better to be much abused
Than but to know 't a little.

IAGO

How now, my lord!

OTHELLO

What sense had I of her stol'n hours of lust?
I saw 't not, thought it not, it harm'd not me:
I slept the next night well, was free and merry;
I found not Cassio's kisses on her lips:
He that is robb'd, not wanting what is stol'n,
Let him not know 't and he's not robb'd at all.

IAGO

I am sorry to hear this.

OTHELLO

I had been happy, if the general camp,
Pioners and all, had tasted her sweet body,
So I had nothing known. O, now for ever
Farewell the tranquil mind! farewell content!
Farewell the plumed troop and the big wars
That make ambition virtue! O, farewell,
Farewell the neighing steed and the shrill trump,
The spirit-stirring drum, the ear-piercing fife,
The royal banner and all quality,
Pride, pomp and circumstance of glorious war!
And, O you mortal engines, whose rude throats
The immortal Jove's dread clamours counterfeit,
Farewell! Othello's occupation's gone!

IAGO

Is 't possible, my lord?

OTHELLO

Villain, be sure thou prove my love a whore;
Be sure of it; give me the ocular proof;
Or, by the worth of man's eternal soul,
Thou hadst been better have been born a dog
Than answer my waked wrath!

IAGO

　　　　　　　　　Is 't come to this?

OTHELLO

Make me to see 't; or at the least so prove it,
That the probation bear no hinge nor loop
To hang a doubt on; or woe upon thy life!

IAGO

My noble lord,—

OTHELLO

If thou dost slander her and torture me,
Never pray more; abandon all remorse;
On horror's head horrors accumulate;
Do deeds to make heaven weep, all earth amazed;
For nothing canst thou to damnation add
Greater than that.

IAGO

　　　　　O grace! O heaven defend me!
Are you a man? have you a soul or sense?
God be wi' you; take mine office. O wretched fool,
That livest to make thine honesty a vice!
O monstrous world! Take note, take note, O world,
To be direct and honest is not safe.
I thank you for this profit, and from hence
I'll love no friend sith love breeds such offence.

OTHELLO

Nay, stay: thou shouldst be honest.

IAGO

I should be wise; for honesty's a fool,
And loses that it works for.

OTHELLO

　　　　　　　　　By the world,
I think my wife be honest, and think she is not;
I think that thou art just, and think thou art not:
I'll have some proof. Her name, that was as fresh
As Dian's visage, is now begrimed and black
As mine own face. If there be cords, or knives,
Poison, or fire, or suffocating streams,
I'll not endure it. Would I were satisfied!

IAGO

I see, sir, you are eaten up with passion:
I do repent me that I put it to you.
You would be satisfied?

OTHELLO

　　　　　　　　　Would! nay, I will.

IAGO

And may: but, how? how satisfied, my lord?
Would you, the supervisor, grossly gape on?
Behold her topp'd?

OTHELLO

　　　　　　　　　Death and damnation! O!

IAGO

It were a tedious difficulty, I think,
To bring them to that prospect: damn them then,
If ever mortal eyes do see them bolster
More than their own! What then? how then?
What shall I say? Where's satisfaction?
It is impossible you should see this,
Were they as prime as goats, as hot as monkeys,
As salt as wolves in pride, and fools as gross
As ignorance made drunk. But yet, I say,
If imputation and strong circumstances,
Which lead directly to the door of truth,
Will give you satisfaction, you may have 't.

OTHELLO

Give me a living reason she's disloyal.

IAGO

I do not like the office:
But sith I am enter'd in this cause so far,
Prick'd to 't by foolish honesty and love,
I will go on. I lay with Cassio lately,
And being troubled with a raging tooth,
I could not sleep.
There are a kind of men so loose of soul,
That in their sleeps will mutter their affairs:
One of this kind is Cassio:
In sleep I heard him say 'Sweet Desdemona,
Let us be wary, let us hide our loves;'
And then, sir, would he gripe and wring my hand,
Cry 'O sweet creature!' and then kiss me hard,
As if he pluck'd up kisses by the roots,
That grew upon my lips: then laid his leg
Over my thigh, and sigh'd and kiss'd, and then
Cried 'Cursed fate that gave thee to the Moor!'

OTHELLO

O monstrous! monstrous!

IAGO

　　　　　　　　　Nay, this was but his dream.

OTHELLO

But this denoted a foregone conclusion:
'Tis a shrewd doubt, though it be but a dream.

IAGO

And this may help to thicken other proofs
That do demonstrate thinly.

OTHELLO

　　　　　　　　　I'll tear her all to pieces.

IAGO

Nay, but be wise: yet we see nothing done;
She may be honest yet. Tell me but this;

Have you not sometimes seen a handkerchief
Spotted with strawberries in your wife's hand?

OTHELLO
I gave her such a one; 'twas my first gift.

IAGO
I know not that: but such a handkerchief—
I am sure it was your wife's—did I to-day
See Cassio wipe his beard with.

OTHELLO
                 If it be that,—

IAGO
If it be that, or any that was hers,
It speaks against her with the other proofs.

OTHELLO
O, that the slave had forty thousand lives!
One is too poor, too weak for my revenge.
Now do I see 'tis true. Look here, Iago;
All my fond love thus do I blow to heaven:
'Tis gone.
Arise, black vengeance, from thy hollow cell!
Yield up, O love, thy crown and hearted throne
To tyrannous hate! Swell, bosom, with thy fraught,
For 'tis of aspics' tongues!

IAGO
              Yet be content.

OTHELLO
O, blood, blood, blood!

IAGO
Patience, I say; your mind perhaps may change.

OTHELLO
Never, Iago. Like to the Pontic sea,
Whose icy current and compulsive course
Ne'er feels retiring ebb, but keeps due on
To the Propontic and the Hellespont;
Even so my bloody thoughts, with violent pace,
Shall ne'er look back, ne'er ebb to humble love,
Till that a capable and wide revenge
Swallow them up. Now, by yond marble heaven,
In the due reverence of a sacred vow   [Kneels
I here engage my words.

IAGO
            Do not rise yet.   [Kneels
Witness, you ever-burning lights above,
You elements that clip us round about,
Witness that here Iago doth give up
The execution of his wit, hands, heart,
To wrong'd Othello's service! Let him command,
And to obey shall be in me remorse,
What bloody business ever.   [They rise

OTHELLO
           I greet thy love,
Not with vain thanks, but with acceptance boun-
    teous,
And will upon the instant put thee to 't:
Within these three days let me hear thee say
That Cassio's not alive.

IAGO
My friend is dead; 'tis done at your request:
But let her live.

OTHELLO
Damn her, lewd minx! O, damn her!
Come, go with me apart; I will withdraw,
To furnish me with some swift means of death
For the fair devil. Now art thou my lieutenant.

IAGO
I am your own for ever.   [Exeunt

SCENE IV. Before the castle

Enter DESDEMONA, EMILIA, and CLOWN

DESDEMONA
Do you know, sirrah, where Lieutenant Cassio lies?

CLOWN
I dare not say he lies any where.

DESDEMONA
Why, man?

CLOWN
He's a soldier; and for one to say a soldier lies, is
stabbing.

DESDEMONA
Go to: where lodges he?

CLOWN
To tell you where he lodges, is to tell you where I
lie.

DESDEMONA
Can any thing be made of this?

CLOWN
I know not where he lodges; and for me to devise a
lodging, and say he lies here or he lies there, were to
lie in mine own throat.

DESDEMONA
Can you inquire him out and be edified by report?

CLOWN
I will catechize the world for him; that is, make
questions and by them answer.

DESDEMONA
Seek him, bid him come hither: tell him I have
moved my lord on his behalf and hope all will be
well.

CLOWN
To do this is within the compass of man's wit, and
therefore I will attempt the doing it.   [Exit

DESDEMONA
Where should I lose that handkerchief, Emilia?

EMILIA
I know not, madam.

DESDEMONA
Believe me, I had rather have lost my purse
Full of crusadoes: and, but my noble Moor
Is true of mind and made of no such baseness
As jealous creatures are, it were enough
To put him to ill thinking.

EMILIA
           Is he not jealous?

DESDEMONA
Who, he? I think the sun where he was born
Drew all such humours from him.

EMILIA
> Look, where he comes.

DESDEMONA
I will not leave him now till Cassio
Be call'd to him.

Enter OTHELLO
> How is 't with you, my lord?

OTHELLO
Well, my good lady. [*Aside*] O, hardness to dis-
semble!
How do you, Desdemona?

DESDEMONA
> Well, my good lord.

OTHELLO
Give me your hand: this hand is moist, my lady.

DESDEMONA
It yet has felt no age nor known no sorrow.

OTHELLO
This argues fruitfulness and liberal heart:
Hot, hot, and moist: this hand of yours requires
A sequester from liberty, fasting and prayer,
Much castigation, exercise devout;
For here's a young and sweating devil here,
That commonly rebels. 'Tis a good hand,
A frank one.

DESDEMONA
> You may, indeed, say so;
For 'twas that hand that gave away my heart.

OTHELLO
A liberal hand: the hearts of old gave hands;
But our new heraldry is hands, not hearts.

DESDEMONA
I cannot speak of this. Come now, your promise.

OTHELLO
What promise, chuck?

DESDEMONA
I have sent to bid Cassio come speak with you.

OTHELLO
I have a salt and sorry rheum offends me;
Lend me thy handkerchief.

DESDEMONA
Here, my lord.

OTHELLO
That which I gave you.

DESDEMONA
I have it not about me.

OTHELLO
Not?

DESDEMONA
No, indeed, my lord.

OTHELLO
That's a fault. That handkerchief
Did an Egyptian to my mother give;
She was a charmer, and could almost read
The thoughts of people: she told her, while she kept
it
'Twould make her amiable and subdue my father
Entirely to her love, but if she lost it
Or made a gift of it, my father's eye
Should hold her loathed and his spirits should hunt

After new fancies: she dying gave it me,
And bid me, when my fate would have me wive,
To give it her. I did so: and take heed on 't;
Make it a darling like your precious eye;
To lose 't or give 't away were such perdition
As nothing else could match.

DESDEMONA
> Is 't possible?

OTHELLO
'Tis true: there's magic in the web of it:
A sibyl, that had number'd in the world
The sun to course two hundred compasses,
In her prophetic fury sew'd the work;
The worms were hallow'd that did breed the silk;
And it was dyed in mummy which the skilful
Conserved of maidens' hearts.

DESDEMONA
> Indeed! is 't true?

OTHELLO
Most veritable; therefore look to 't well.

DESDEMONA
Then would to God that I had never seen 't!

OTHELLO
Ha! wherefore?

DESDEMONA
Why do you speak so startingly and rash?

OTHELLO
Is 't lost? is 't gone? speak, is it out o' the way?

DESDEMONA
Heaven bless us!

OTHELLO
Say you?

DESDEMONA
It is not lost; but what an if it were?

OTHELLO
How!

DESDEMONA
I say, it is not lost.

OTHELLO
Fetch 't, let me see it.

DESDEMONA
Why, so I can, sir, but I will not now.
This is a trick to put me from my suit:
Pray you, let Cassio be received again.

OTHELLO
Fetch me the handkerchief: my mind misgives.

DESDEMONA
Come, come;
You'll never meet a more sufficient man.

OTHELLO
The handkerchief!

DESDEMONA
> I pray, talk me of Cassio.

OTHELLO
The handkerchief!

DESDEMONA
> A man that all his time
Hath founded his good fortunes on your love,
Shared dangers with you,—

OTHELLO

The handkerchief!

DESDEMONA

In sooth, you are to blame.

OTHELLO

Away!   [*Exit*

EMILIA

Is not this man jealous?

DESDEMONA

I ne'er saw this before.
Sure there's some wonder in this handkerchief:
I am most unhappy in the loss of it.

EMILIA

'Tis not a year or two shows us a man:
They are all but stomachs and we all but food;
They eat us hungerly, and when they are full
They belch us. Look you, Cassio and my husband

Enter CASSIO *and* IAGO

IAGO

There is no other way; 'tis she must do 't:
And, lo, the happiness! go and importune her.

DESDEMONA

How now, good Cassio! what's the news with you?

CASSIO

Madam, my former suit: I do beseech you
That by your virtuous means I may again
Exist, and be a member of his love
Whom I with all the office of my heart
Entirely honour: I would not be delay'd.
If my offence be of such mortal kind,
That nor my service past nor present sorrows
Nor purposed merit in futurity
Can ransom me into his love again,
But to know so must be my benefit;
So shall I clothe me in a forced content
And shut myself up in some other course
To fortune's alms.

DESDEMONA

            Alas, thrice-gentle Cassio!
My advocation is not now in tune;
My lord is not my lord, nor should I know him
Were he in favour as in humour alter'd.
So help me every spirit sanctified,
As I have spoken for you all my best
And stood within the blank of his displeasure
For my free speech! You must awhile be patient:
What I can do I will; and more I will
Than for myself I dare: let that suffice you.

IAGO

Is my lord angry?

EMILIA

            He went hence but now,
And certainly in strange unquietness.

IAGO

Can he be angry? I have seen the cannon,
When it hath blown his ranks into the air,
And, like the devil, from his very arm
Puff'd his own brother; and can he be angry?
Something of moment then: I will go meet him:
There's matter in 't indeed if he be angry.

DESDEMONA

I prithee, do so.   [*Exit* IAGO
            Something sure of state,
Either from Venice or some unhatch'd practice
Made demonstrable here in Cyprus to him,
Hath puddled his clear spirit; and in such cases
Men's natures wrangle with inferior things,
Though great ones are their object. 'Tis even so;
For let our finger ache, and it indues
Our other healthful members even to that sense
Of pain: nay, we must think men are not gods,
Nor of them look for such observancy
As fits the bridal. Beshrew me much, Emilia,
I was, unhandsome warrior as I am,
Arraigning his unkindness with my soul;
But now I find I had suborn'd the witness,
And he's indicted falsely.

EMILIA

Pray heaven it be state-matters, as you think,
And no conception nor no jealous toy
Concerning you.

DESDEMONA

Alas the day, I never gave him cause!

EMILIA

But jealous souls will not be answer'd so;
They are not ever jealous for the cause,
But jealous for they are jealous: 'tis a monster
Begot upon itself, born on itself.

DESDEMONA

Heaven keep that monster from Othello's mind!

EMILIA

Lady, amen.

DESDEMONA

I will go seek him. Cassio, walk hereabout:
If I do find him fit, I'll move your suit,
And seek to effect it to my uttermost.

CASSIO

I humbly thank your ladyship.

            [*Exeunt* DESDEMONA *and* EMILIA

Enter BIANCA

BIANCA

Save you, friend Cassio!

CASSIO

            What make you from home?
How is it with you, my most fair Bianca?
I' faith, sweet love, I was coming to your house.

BIANCA

And I was going to your lodging, Cassio.
What, keep a week away? seven days and nights?
Eight score eight hours? and lovers' absent hours,
More tedious than the dial eight score times?
O weary reckoning!

CASSIO

            Pardon me, Bianca:
I have this while with leaden thoughts been press'd;
But I shall in a more continuate time
Strike off this score of absence. Sweet Bianca,

           [*Giving her* DESDEMONA'S *handkerchief*

Take me this work out.

BIANCA
O Cassio, whence came this?
This is some token from a newer friend:
To the felt absence now I feel a cause:
Is 't come to this? Well, well.

CASSIO
Go to, woman!
Throw your vile guesses in the devil's teeth,
From whence you have them. You are jealous now
That this is from some mistress, some remembrance:
No, by my faith, Bianca.

BIANCA
Why, whose is it?

CASSIO
I know not, sweet: I found it in my chamber.
I like the work well: ere it be demanded—
As like enough it will—I'ld have it copied:
Take it, and do 't; and leave me for this time.

BIANCA
Leave you! wherefore?

CASSIO
I do attend here on the general;
And think it no addition, nor my wish,
To have him see me woman'd.

BIANCA
Why, I pray you?

CASSIO
Not that I love you not.

BIANCA
But that you do not love me.
I pray you, bring me on the way a little;
And say if I shall see you soon at night.

CASSIO
'Tis but a little way that I can bring you;
For I attend here: but I'll see you soon.

BIANCA
'Tis very good; I must be circumstanced.

[Exeunt

ACT IV

SCENE I. *Cyprus. Before the castle*

Enter OTHELLO *and* IAGO

IAGO
Will you think so?

OTHELLO
Think so, Iago!

IAGO
What,
To kiss in private?

OTHELLO
An unauthorized kiss.

IAGO
Or to be naked with her friend in bed
An hour or more, not meaning any harm?

OTHELLO
Naked in bed, Iago, and not mean harm!
It is hypocrisy against the devil:

They that mean virtuously and yet do so,
The devil their virtue tempts and they tempt
heaven.

IAGO
So they do nothing, 'tis a venial slip:
But if I give my wife a handkerchief—

OTHELLO
What then?

IAGO
Why, then, 'tis hers, my lord; and being hers,
She may, I think, bestow 't on any man.

OTHELLO
She is protectress of her honour too:
May she give that?

IAGO
Her honour is an essence that's not seen;
They have it very oft that have it not:
But for the handkerchief—

OTHELLO
By heaven, I would most gladly have forgot it:
Thou said'st—O, it comes o'er my memory,
As doth the raven o'er the infected house,
Boding to all—he had my handkerchief.

IAGO
Ay, what of that?

OTHELLO
That's not so good now.

IAGO
What,
If I had said I had seen him do you wrong?
Or heard him say—as knaves be such abroad,
Who having, by their own importunate suit,
Or voluntary dotage of some mistress,
Convinced or supplied them, cannot choose
But they must blab—

OTHELLO
Hath he said any thing?

IAGO
He hath, my lord; but be you well assured,
No more than he'll unswear.

OTHELLO
What hath he said?

IAGO
Faith, that he did—I know not what he did.

OTHELLO
What? what?

IAGO
Lie—

OTHELLO
With her?

IAGO
With her, on her; what you will.

OTHELLO
Lie with her! lie on her!—We say lie on her, when
they belie her.—Lie with her! 'Zounds, that's fulsome! Handkerchief—confessions—handkerchief!—
To confess, and be hanged for his labour; first, to be
hanged, and then to confess. I tremble at it. Nature
would not invest herself in such shadowing passion
without some instruction. It is not words that shakes

[963]

me thus. Pish! Noses, ears and lips. Is 't possible?—
Confess?—Handkerchief?—O devil! [*Falls in a trance*

IAGO

Work on,
My medicine, work! Thus credulous fools are
  caught;
And many worthy and chaste dames even thus,
All guiltless, meet reproach. What, ho! my lord!
My lord, **I say!** Othello!

Enter CASSIO

              How now, Cassio!

CASSIO

What's the matter?

IAGO

My lord is fall'n into an epilepsy:
This is his second fit; he had one yesterday.

CASSIO

Rub him about the temples.

IAGO

              No, forbear;
The lethargy must have his quiet course:
If not, he foams at mouth, and by and by
Breaks out to savage madness. Look, he stirs:
Do you withdraw yourself a little while,
He will recover straight: when he is gone,
I would on great occasion speak with you.
                    [*Exit* CASSIO
How is it, general? have you not hurt your head?

OTHELLO

Dost thou mock me?

IAGO

          I mock you! no, by heaven.
Would you would bear your fortune like a man!

OTHELLO

A horned man's a monster and a beast.

IAGO

There's many a beast then in a populous city,
And many a civil monster.

OTHELLO

Did he confess it?

IAGO

           Good sir, be a man;
Think every bearded fellow that's but yoked
May draw with you: there's millions now alive
That nightly lie in those unproper beds
Which they dare swear peculiar: your case is better.
O, 'tis the spite of hell, the fiend's arch-mock,
To lip a wanton in a secure couch,
And to suppose her chaste! No, let me know;
And knowing what I am, I know what she shall be.

OTHELLO

O, thou art wise; 'tis certain.

IAGO

             Stand you awhile apart;
Confine yourself but in a patient list.
Whilst you were here o'erwhelmed with your grief—
A passion most unsuiting such a man—
Cassio came hither: I shifted him away,
And laid good 'scuse upon your ecstasy;
Bade him anon return and here speak with me;

The which he promised. Do but encave yourself,
And mark the fleers, the gibes and notable scorns,
That dwell in every region of his face;
For I will make him tell the tale anew,
Where, how, how oft, how long ago and when
He hath and is again to cope your wife:
I say, but mark his gesture. Marry, patience;
Or I shall say you are all in all in spleen,
And nothing of a man.

OTHELLO

          Dost thou hear, Iago?
I will be found most cunning in my patience;
But—dost thou hear?—most bloody.

IAGO

              That's not amiss;
But yet keep time in all. Will you withdraw?
                [OTHELLO *retires*
Now will I question Cassio of Bianca,
A housewife that by selling her desires
Buys herself bread and clothes: it is a creature
That dotes on Cassio; as 'tis the strumpet's plague
To beguile many and be beguiled by one.
He, when he hears of her, cannot refrain
From the excess of laughter. Here he comes.
             Re-enter CASSIO
As he shall smile, Othello shall go mad;
And his unbookish jealousy must construe
Poor Cassio's smiles, gestures and light behaviour,
Quite in the wrong. How do you now, lieutenant?

CASSIO

The worser that you give me the addition
Whose want even kills me.

IAGO

Ply Desdemona well, and you are sure on 't.
Now, if this suit lay in Bianca's power,
How quickly should you speed!

CASSIO

             Alas, poor caitiff!

OTHELLO

Look, how he laughs already!

IAGO

I never knew a woman love man so.

CASSIO

Alas, poor rogue! I think, i' faith, she loves me.

OTHELLO

Now he denies it faintly and laughs it out.

IAGO

Do you hear, Cassio?

OTHELLO

             Now he importunes him
To tell it o'er: go to; well said, well said.

IAGO

She gives it out that you shall marry her:
Do you intend it?

CASSIO

Ha, ha, ha!

OTHELLO

Do you triumph, Roman? do you triumph?

CASSIO

I marry her! what, a customer! I prithee, bear some

charity to my wit; do not think it so unwholesome. Ha, ha, ha!

OTHELLO
So, so, so, so: they laugh that win.

IAGO
Faith, the cry goes that you shall marry her.

CASSIO
Prithee, say true.

IAGO
I am a very villain else.

OTHELLO
Have you scored me? Well.

CASSIO
This is the monkey's own giving out: she is persuaded I will marry her, out of her own love and flattery, not out of my promise.

OTHELLO
Iago beckons me; now he begins the story.

CASSIO
She was here even now: she haunts me in every place. I was the other day talking on the sea-bank with certain Venetians; and thither comes the bauble, and, by this hand, she falls me thus about my neck—

OTHELLO
Crying 'O dear Cassio!' as it were: his gesture imports it.

CASSIO
So hangs and lolls and weeps upon me; so hales and pulls me: ha, ha, ha!

OTHELLO
Now he tells how she plucked him to my chamber. O, I see that nose of yours, but not that dog I shall throw it to.

CASSIO
Well, I must leave her company.

IAGO
Before me! look, where she comes.

CASSIO
'Tis such another fitchew! marry, a perfumed one.
Enter BIANCA
What do you mean by this haunting of me?

BIANCA
Let the devil and his dam haunt you! What did you mean by that same handkerchief you gave me even now? I was a fine fool to take it. I must take out the work? A likely piece of work, that you should find it in your chamber, and not know who left it there! This is some minx's token, and I must take out the work? There; give it your hobby-horse: wheresoever you had it, I'll take out no work on 't.

CASSIO
How now, my sweet Bianca! how now! how now!

OTHELLO
By heaven, that should be my handkerchief!

BIANCA
An you'll come to supper to-night, you may; an you will not, come when you are next prepared for.
[*Exit*

IAGO
After her, after her.

CASSIO
Faith, I must; she'll rail i' the street else.

IAGO
Will you sup there?

CASSIO
Faith, I intend so.

IAGO
Well, I may chance to see you; for I would very fain speak with you.

CASSIO
Prithee, come; will you?

IAGO
Go to; say no more.   [*Exit* CASSIO

OTHELLO
[*Advancing*] How shall I murder him, Iago?

IAGO
Did you perceive how he laughed at his vice?

OTHELLO
O Iago!

IAGO
And did you see the handkerchief?

OTHELLO
Was that mine?

IAGO
Yours, by this hand: and to see how he prizes the foolish woman your wife! she gave it him, and he hath given it his whore.

OTHELLO
I would have him nine years a-killing. A fine woman! a fair woman! a sweet woman!

IAGO
Nay, you must forget that.

OTHELLO
Ay, let her rot, and perish, and be damned to-night; for she shall not live: no, my heart is turned to stone; I strike it, and it hurts my hand. O, the world hath not a sweeter creature: she might lie by an emperor's side, and command him tasks.

IAGO
Nay, that's not your way.

OTHELLO
Hang her! I do but say what she is: so delicate with her needle: an admirable musician: O, she will sing the savageness out of a bear: of so high and plenteous wit and invention:—

IAGO
She's the worse for all this.

OTHELLO
O, a thousand thousand times: and then, of so gentle a condition!

IAGO
Ay, too gentle.

OTHELLO
Nay, that's certain: but yet the pity of it, Iago!
O Iago, the pity of it, Iago!

IAGO
If you are so fond over her iniquity, give her patent

to offend; for, if it touch not you, it comes near nobody.

OTHELLO

I will chop her into messes: cuckold me!

IAGO

O, 'tis foul in her.

OTHELLO

With mine officer!

IAGO

That's fouler.

OTHELLO

Get me some poison, Iago; this night. I'll not expostulate with her, lest her body and beauty unprovide my mind again: this night, Iago.

IAGO

Do it not with poison, strangle her in her bed, even the bed she hath contaminated.

OTHELLO

Good, good: the justice of it pleases: very good.

IAGO

And for Cassio, let me be his undertaker: you shall hear more by midnight.

OTHELLO

Excellent good. [A trumpet within] What trumpet is that same?

IAGO

Something from Venice, sure. 'Tis Lodovico
Come from the duke: and, see, your wife is with him.

    Enter LODOVICO, DESDEMONA, and ATTENDANTS

LODOVICO

God save the worthy general!

OTHELLO

                          With all my heart, sir.

LODOVICO

The duke and senators of Venice greet you.

                                  [Gives him a letter

OTHELLO

I kiss the instrument of their pleasures.

                    [Opens the letter, and reads

DESDEMONA

And what's the news, good cousin Lodovico?

IAGO

I am very glad to see you, signior;
Welcome to Cyprus.

LODOVICO

I thank you. How does Lieutenant Cassio?

IAGO

Lives, sir.

DESDEMONA

Cousin, there's fall'n between him and my lord
An unkind breach: but you shall make all well.

OTHELLO

Are you sure of that?

DESDEMONA

My lord?

OTHELLO

[Reads] 'This fail you not to do, as you will—'

LODOVICO

He did not call; he's busy in the paper.
Is there division 'twixt my lord and Cassio?

DESDEMONA

A most unhappy one: I would do much
To atone them, for the love I bear to Cassio.

OTHELLO

Fire and brimstone!

DESDEMONA

My lord?

OTHELLO

Are you wise?

DESDEMONA

What, is he angry?

LODOVICO

                    May be the letter moved him;
For, as I think, they do command him home,
Deputing Cassio in his government.

DESDEMONA

By my troth, I am glad on 't.

OTHELLO

                              Indeed!

DESDEMONA

                                      My lord?

OTHELLO

I am glad to see you mad.

DESDEMONA

                        Why, sweet Othello?

OTHELLO

Devil!   [Striking her

DESDEMONA

I have not deserved this.

LODOVICO

My lord, this would not be believed in Venice,
Though I should swear I saw 't: 'tis very much:
Make her amends; she weeps.

OTHELLO

                    O devil, devil!
If that the earth could teem with woman's tears,
Each drop she falls would prove a crocodile.
Out of my sight!

DESDEMONA

                I will not stay to offend you.

                                          [Going

LODOVICO

Truly, an obedient lady:
I do beseech your lordship, call her back.

OTHELLO

Mistress!

DESDEMONA

My lord?

OTHELLO

What would you with her, sir?

LODOVICO

                              Who, I, my lord?

OTHELLO

Ay; you did wish that I would make her turn:
Sir, she can turn and turn, and yet go on,
And turn again; and she can weep, sir, weep;
And she's obedient, as you say, obedient,
Very obedient. Proceed you in your tears.
Concerning this, sir,—O well-painted passion!—
I am commanded home. Get you away;

I'll send for you anon. Sir, I obey the mandate,
And will return to Venice. Hence, avaunt!
　　　　　　　　　　　[*Exit* DESDEMONA
Cassio shall have my place. And, sir, to-night,
I do entreat that we may sup together:
You are welcome, sir, to Cyprus. Goats and mon-
　　keys!　　　　　　　　　　　[*Exit*

LODOVICO
Is this the noble Moor whom our full senate
Call all in all sufficient? This the nature
Whom passion could not shake? whose solid virtue
The shot of accident nor dart of chance
Could neither graze nor pierce?

IAGO
　　　　　　　　　He is much changed.

LODOVICO
Are his wits safe? is he not light of brain?

IAGO
He's that he is: I may not breathe my censure
What he might be: if what he might he is not,
I would to heaven he were!

LODOVICO
　　　　　　　　What, strike his wife!

IAGO
Faith, that was not so well; yet would I knew
That stroke would prove the worst!

LODOVICO
　　　　　　　　　　Is it his use?
Or did the letters work upon his blood,
And new create this fault?

IAGO
　　　　　　　　Alas, alas!
It is not honesty in me to speak
What I have seen and known. You shall observe
　　him,
And his own courses will denote him so
That I may save my speech: do but go after,
And mark how he continues.

LODOVICO
I am sorry that I am deceived in him.　　[*Exeunt*

SCENE II. *A room in the castle*

Enter OTHELLO *and* EMILIA

OTHELLO
You have seen nothing, then?

EMILIA
Nor ever heard, nor ever did suspect.

OTHELLO
Yes, you have seen Cassio and she together.

EMILIA
But then I saw no harm, and then I heard
Each syllable that breath made up between them.

OTHELLO
What, did they never whisper?

EMILIA
　　　　　　　　　Never, my lord.

OTHELLO
Nor send you out o' the way?

EMILIA
Never.

OTHELLO
To fetch her fan, her gloves, her mask, nor nothing?

EMILIA
Never, my lord.

OTHELLO
That's strange.

EMILIA
I durst, my lord, to wager she is honest,
Lay down my soul at stake: if you think other,
Remove your thought; it doth abuse your bosom.
If any wretch have put this in your head,
Let heaven requite it with the serpent's curse!
For if she be not honest, chaste and true,
There's no man happy; the purest of their wives
Is foul as slander.

OTHELLO
　　　　　　　Bid her come hither: go. [*Exit* EMILIA
She says enough: yet she's a simple bawd
That cannot say as much. This is a subtle whore,
A closet lock and key of villanous secrets:
And yet she'll kneel and pray; I have seen her do 't.

Enter DESDEMONA *with* EMILIA

DESDEMONA
My lord, what is your will?

OTHELLO
　　　　　　　　Pray, chuck, come hither.

DESDEMONA
What is your pleasure?

OTHELLO
　　　　　　　Let me see your eyes;
Look in my face.

DESDEMONA
　　　　　　What horrible fancy's this?

OTHELLO
[*To* EMILIA] Some of your function, mistress,
Leave procreants alone and shut the door;
Cough, or cry hem, if any body come:
Your mystery, your mystery: nay, dispatch.
　　　　　　　　　　　[*Exit* EMILIA

DESDEMONA
Upon my knees, what doth your speech import?
I understand a fury in your words,
But not the words.

OTHELLO
Why, what art thou?

DESDEMONA
Your wife, my lord; your true and loyal wife.

OTHELLO
Come, swear it, damn thyself;
Lest, being like one of heaven, the devils themselves
Should fear to seize thee: therefore be double-
　　damn'd;
Swear thou art honest.

DESDEMONA
　　　　　　　Heaven doth truly know it.

OTHELLO
Heaven truly knows that thou art false as hell.

DESDEMONA

To whom, my lord? with whom? how am I false?

OTHELLO

O Desdemona! Away! away! away!

DESDEMONA

Alas the heavy day! Why do you weep?
Am I the motive of these tears, my lord?
If haply you my father do suspect
An instrument of this your calling back,
Lay not your blame on me: if you have lost him,
Why, I have lost him too.

OTHELLO

           Had it pleased heaven
To try me with affliction; had they rain'd
All kinds of sores and shames on my bare head,
Steep'd me in poverty to the very lips,
Given to captivity me and my utmost hopes,
I should have found in some place of my soul
A drop of patience: but, alas, to make me
A fixed figure for the time of scorn
To point his slow unmoving finger at!
Yet could I bear that too; well, very well:
But there, where I have garner'd up my heart,
Where either I must live or bear no life,
The fountain from the which my current runs,
Or else dries up; to be discarded thence!
Or keep it as a cistern for foul toads
To knot and gender in! Turn thy complexion there,
Patience, thou young and rose-lipp'd cherubin,
Ay, there, look grim as hell!

DESDEMONA

I hope my noble lord esteems me honest.

OTHELLO

O, ay; as summer flies are in the shambles,
That quicken even with blowing. O thou weed,
Who art so lovely fair and smell'st so sweet
That the sense aches at thee, would thou hadst
ne'er been born!

DESDEMONA

Alas, what ignorant sin have I committed?

OTHELLO

Was this fair paper, this most goodly book,
Made to write 'whore' upon? What committed!
Committed! O thou public commoner!
I should make very forges of my cheeks,
That would to cinders burn up modesty,
Did I but speak thy deeds. What committed!
Heaven stops the nose at it, and the moon winks;
The bawdy wind, that kisses all it meets,
Is hush'd within the hollow mine of earth,
And will not hear it. What committed!
Impudent strumpet!

DESDEMONA

        By heaven, you do me wrong.

OTHELLO

Are not you a strumpet?

DESDEMONA

        No, as I am a Christian:
If to preserve this vessel for my lord

From any other foul unlawful touch
Be not to be a strumpet, I am none.

OTHELLO

What, not a whore?

DESDEMONA

        No, as I shall be saved.

OTHELLO

Is 't possible?

DESDEMONA

O, heaven forgive us!

OTHELLO

        I cry you mercy then:
I took you for that cunning whore of Venice
That married with Othello. [*Raising his voice*] You,
mistress,
That have the office opposite to Saint Peter,
And keep the gate of hell!

        Re-enter EMILIA

        You, you, ay, you!
We have done our course; there's money for your
pains:
I pray you, turn the key, and keep our counsel. [*Exit*

EMILIA

Alas, what does this gentleman conceive?
How do you, madam? how do you, my good lady?

DESDEMONA

Faith, half asleep.

EMILIA

Good madam, what's the matter with my lord?

DESDEMONA

With who?

EMILIA

Why, with my lord, madam.

DESDEMONA

Who is thy lord?

EMILIA

        He that is yours, sweet lady.

DESDEMONA

I have none: do not talk to me, Emilia;
I cannot weep, nor answer have I none
But what should go by water. Prithee, to-night
Lay on my bed my wedding sheets: remember;
And call thy husband hither.

EMILIA

        Here's a change indeed! [*Exit*

DESDEMONA

'Tis meet I should be used so, very meet.
How have I been behaved, that he might stick
The small'st opinion on my least misuse?

        Re-enter EMILIA *with* IAGO

IAGO

What is your pleasure, madam? How is 't with you?

DESDEMONA

I cannot tell. Those that do teach young babes
Do it with gentle means and easy tasks:
He might have chid me so; for, in good faith,
I am a child to chiding.

IAGO

        What's the matter, lady?

EMILIA
Alas, Iago, my lord hath so bewhored her,
Thrown such despite and heavy terms upon her,
As true hearts cannot bear.

DESDEMONA
Am I that name, Iago?

IAGO
What name, fair lady?

DESDEMONA
Such as she says my lord did say I was.

EMILIA
He call'd her whore: a beggar in his drink
Could not have laid such terms upon his callet.

IAGO
Why did he so?

DESDEMONA
I do not know; I am sure I am none such.

IAGO
Do not weep, do not weep. Alas the day!

EMILIA
Hath she forsook so many noble matches,
Her father and her country and her friends,
To be call'd whore? would it not make one weep?

DESDEMONA
It is my wretched fortune.

IAGO
Beshrew him for 't!
How comes this trick upon him?

DESDEMONA
Nay, heaven doth know.

EMILIA
I will be hang'd, if some eternal villain,
Some busy and insinuating rogue,
Some cogging, cozening slave, to get some office,
Have not devised this slander; I'll be hang'd else.

IAGO
Fie, there is no such man; it is impossible.

DESDEMONA
If any such there be, heaven pardon him!

EMILIA
A halter pardon him! and hell gnaw his bones!
Why should he call her whore? who keeps her company?
What place? what time? what form? what likelihood?
The Moor's abused by some most villanous knave,
Some base notorious knave, some scurvy fellow.
O heaven, that such companions thou'ldst unfold,
And put in every honest hand a whip
To lash the rascals naked through the world
Even from the east to the west!

IAGO
Speak within door.

EMILIA
O, fie upon them! Some such squire he was
That turn'd your wit the seamy side without,
And made you to suspect me with the Moor.

IAGO
You are a fool; go to.

DESDEMONA
O good Iago,
What shall I do to win my lord again?
Good friend, go to him; for, by this light of heaven,
I know not how I lost him. Here I kneel:
If e'er my will did trespass 'gainst his love
Either in discourse of thought or actual deed,
Or that mine eyes, mine ears, or any sense,
Delighted them in any other form,
Or that I do not yet, and ever did,
And ever will, though he do shake me off
To beggarly divorcement, love him dearly,
Comfort forswear me! Unkindness may do much;
And his unkindness may defeat my life,
But never taint my love. I cannot say 'whore':
It doth abhor me now I speak the word;
To do the act that might the addition earn
Not the world's mass of vanity could make me.

IAGO
I pray you, be content; 'tis but his humour:
The business of the state does him offence,
And he does chide with you.

DESDEMONA
If 'twere no other,—

IAGO
'Tis but so, I warrant. [Trumpets within
Hark, how these instruments summon to supper!
The messengers of Venice stay the meat:
Go in, and weep not; all things shall be well.
[Exeunt DESDEMONA and EMILIA
Enter RODERIGO
How now, Roderigo!

RODERIGO
I do not find that thou dealest justly with me.

IAGO
What in the contrary?

RODERIGO
Every day thou daffest me with some device, Iago;
and rather, as it seems to me now, keepest from me
all conveniency than suppliest me with the least advantage of hope. I will indeed no longer endure it;
nor am I yet persuaded to put up in peace what already I have foolishly suffered.

IAGO
Will you hear me, Roderigo?

RODERIGO
Faith, I have heard too much; for your words and
performances are no kin together.

IAGO
You charge me most unjustly.

RODERIGO
With nought but truth. I have wasted myself out of
my means. The jewels you have had from me to deliver to Desdemona would half have corrupted a
votarist: you have told me she hath received them
and returned me expectations and comforts of sudden respect and acquaintance; but I find none.

IAGO
Well; go to; very well.

RODERIGO

Very well! go to! I cannot go to, man; nor 'tis not very well: by this hand, I say 'tis very scurvy, and begin to find myself fopped in it.

IAGO

Very well.

RODERIGO

I tell you 'tis not very well. I will make myself known to Desdemona: if she will return me my jewels, I will give over my suit and repent my unlawful solicitation; if not, assure yourself I will seek satisfaction of you.

IAGO

You have said now.

RODERIGO

Ay, and said nothing but what I protest intendment of doing.

IAGO

Why, now I see there's mettle in thee; and even from this instant do build on thee a better opinion than ever before. Give me thy hand, Roderigo: thou hast taken against me a most just exception; but yet, I protest, I have dealt most directly in thy affair.

RODERIGO

It hath not appeared.

IAGO

I grant indeed it hath not appeared, and your suspicion is not without wit and judgement. But, Roderigo, if thou hast that in thee indeed, which I have greater reason to believe now than ever, I mean purpose, courage and valour, this night show it: if thou the next night following enjoy not Desdemona, take me from this world with treachery and devise engines for my life.

RODERIGO

Well, what is it? is it within reason and compass?

IAGO

Sir, there is especial commission come from Venice to depute Cassio in Othello's place.

RODERIGO

Is that true? why then Othello and Desdemona return again to Venice.

IAGO

O, no; he goes into Mauritania, and takes away with him the fair Desdemona, unless his abode be lingered here by some accident: wherein none can be so determinate as the removing of Cassio.

RODERIGO

How do you mean, removing of him?

IAGO

Why, by making him uncapable of Othello's place; knocking out his brains.

RODERIGO

And that you would have me to do?

IAGO

Ay, if you dare do yourself a profit and a right. He sups to-night with a harlotry, and thither will I go

to him: he knows not yet of his honourable fortune. If you will watch his going thence, which I will fashion to fall out between twelve and one, you may take him at your pleasure: I will be near to second your attempt, and he shall fall between us. Come, stand not amazed at it, but go along with me; I will show you such a necessity in his death that you shall think yourself bound to put it on him. It is now high supper-time, and the night grows to waste: about it.

RODERIGO

I will hear further reason for this.

IAGO

And you shall be satisfied.   [*Exeunt*

SCENE III. *Another room in the castle*

Enter OTHELLO, LODOVICO, DESDEMONA, EMILIA, *and* ATTENDANTS

LODOVICO

I do beseech you, sir, trouble yourself no further.

OTHELLO

O, pardon me; 'twill do me good to walk.

LODOVICO

Madam, good night; I humbly thank your ladyship.

DESDEMONA

Your honour is most welcome.

OTHELLO

                      Will you walk, sir?
O,—Desdemona,—

DESDEMONA

My lord?

OTHELLO

Get you to bed on the instant; I will be returned forthwith: dismiss your attendant there: look it be done.

DESDEMONA

I will, my lord.
      [*Exeunt* OTHELLO, LODOVICO, *and* ATTENDANTS

EMILIA

How goes it now? he looks gentler than he did.

DESDEMONA

He says he will return incontinent:
He hath commanded me to go to bed,
And bade me to dismiss you.

EMILIA

                   Dismiss me!

DESDEMONA

It was his bidding; therefore, good Emilia,
Give me my nightly wearing, and adieu:
We must not now displease him.

EMILIA

I would you had never seen him!

DESDEMONA

So would not I: my love doth so approve him,
That even his stubbornness, his checks, his frowns,—
Prithee, unpin me,—have grace and favour in them.

EMILIA

I have laid those sheets you bade me on the bed.

DESDEMONA

All's one. Good faith, how foolish are our minds!
If I do die before thee, prithee, shroud me
In one of those same sheets.

EMILIA

         Come, come, you talk.

DESDEMONA

My mother had a maid call'd Barbara:
She was in love; and he she loved proved mad
And did forsake her: she had a song of 'willow;'
An old thing 'twas, but it express'd her fortune,
And she died singing it: that song to-night
Will not go from my mind; I have much to do
But to go hang my head all at one side
And sing it like poor Barbara. Prithee, dispatch.

EMILIA

Shall I go fetch your night-gown?

DESDEMONA

         No, unpin me here.
This Lodovico is a proper man.

EMILIA

A very handsome man.

DESDEMONA

He speaks well.

EMILIA

I know a lady in Venice would have walked bare-
foot to Palestine for a touch of his nether lip.

  [Singing] The poor soul sat sighing by a sycamore tree,
    Sing all a green willow;
  Her hand on her bosom, her head on her knee,
  Sing willow, willow, willow:
  The fresh streams ran by her, and murmur'd her moans;
    Sing willow, willow, willow;
  Her salt tears fell from her, and soften'd the stones;—

Lay by these:—

  [Singing] Sing willow, willow, willow;

Prithee, hie thee; he'll come anon:—

  [Singing] Sing all a green willow must be my garland.
    Let nobody blame him; his scorn I approve,—

Nay, that's not next. Hark! who is 't that knocks?

It's the wind.

DESDEMONA

[Singing] I call'd my love false love; but what said he then?
  Sing willow, willow, willow:
  If I court moe women, you'll couch with moe men.

So get thee gone; good night. Mine eyes do itch;
Doth that bode weeping?

EMILIA

         'Tis neither here nor there.

DESDEMONA

I have heard it said so. O, these men, these men!
Dost thou in conscience think,—tell me, Emilia,—
That there be women do abuse their husbands
In such gross kind?

EMILIA

         There be some such, no question.

DESDEMONA

Wouldst thou do such a deed for all the world?

EMILIA

Why, would not you?

DESDEMONA

         No, by this heavenly light!

EMILIA

Nor I neither by this heavenly light; I might do 't
as well i' the dark.

DESDEMONA

Wouldst thou do such a deed for all the world?

EMILIA

The world's a huge thing: it is a great price
For a small vice.

DESDEMONA

         In troth, I think thou wouldst not.

EMILIA

In troth, I think I should; and undo 't when I had
done. Marry, I would not do such a thing for a joint-
ring, nor for measures of lawn, nor for gowns, petticoats, nor caps, nor any petty exhibition; but, for
the whole world,—why, who would not make her
husband a cuckold to make him a monarch? I
should venture purgatory for 't.

DESDEMONA

Beshrew me, if I would do such a wrong
For the whole world.

EMILIA

Why, the wrong is but a wrong i' the world; and
having the world for your labour, 'tis a wrong in
your own world, and you might quickly make it
right.

DESDEMONA

I do not think there is any such woman.

EMILIA

Yes, a dozen; and as many to the vantage as would
  store the world they played for.
But I do think it is their husbands' faults
If wives do fall: say that they slack their duties
And pour our treasures into foreign laps,
Or else break out in peevish jealousies,
Throwing restraint upon us, or say they strike us,
Or scant our former having in despite,
Why, we have galls, and though we have some
  grace,
Yet have we some revenge. Let husbands know
Their wives have sense like them: they see and smell
And have their palates both for sweet and sour,
As husbands have. What is it that they do
When they change us for others? Is it sport?
I think it is: and doth affection breed it?
I think it doth: is 't frailty that thus errs?
It is so too: and have not we affections,
Desires for sport, and frailty, as men have?
Then let them use us well: else let them know,
The ills we do, their ills instruct us so.

DESDEMONA

Good night, good night: heaven me such uses send,
Not to pick bad from bad, but by bad mend!

                      [Exeunt

ACT V

Scene I. *Cyprus. A street*

Enter IAGO *and* RODERIGO

IAGO

Here, stand behind this bulk; straight will he come:
Wear thy good rapier bare, and put it home:
Quick, quick; fear nothing; I'll be at thy elbow:
It makes us, or it mars us; think on that,
And fix most firm thy resolution.

RODERIGO

Be near at hand; I may miscarry in 't.

IAGO

Here, at thy hand: be bold, and take thy stand.
           [*Retires*

RODERIGO

I have no great devotion to the deed;
And yet he hath given me satisfying reasons;
'Tis but a man gone. Forth, my sword: he dies.

IAGO

I have rubb'd this young quat almost to the sense,
And he grows angry. Now, whether he kill Cassio,
Or Cassio him, or each do kill the other,
Every way makes my gain: live Roderigo,
He calls me to a restitution large
Of gold and jewels that I bobb'd from him,
As gifts to Desdemona:
It must not be: if Cassio do remain,
He hath a daily beauty in his life
That makes me ugly; and besides, the Moor
May unfold me to him; there stand I in much peril:
No, he must die. Be 't so. I hear him coming.

Enter CASSIO

RODERIGO

I know his gait; 'tis he. Villain, thou diest!
           [*Makes a pass at* CASSIO

CASSIO

That thrust had been mine enemy indeed,
But that my coat is better than thou know'st:
I will make proof of thine.
           [*Draws, and wounds* RODERIGO

RODERIGO

           O, I am slain!
[IAGO *from behind wounds* CASSIO *in the leg, and exit*

CASSIO

I am maim'd for ever. Help, ho! murder! murder!
           [*Falls*

Enter OTHELLO

OTHELLO

The voice of Cassio: Iago keeps his word.

RODERIGO

O, villain that I am!

OTHELLO

It is even so.

CASSIO

O, help, ho! light! a surgeon!

OTHELLO

'Tis he. O brave Iago, honest and just,
That hast such noble sense of thy friend's wrong!

Thou teachest me. Minion, your dear lies dead,
And your unblest fate hies: strumpet, I come!
Forth of my heart those charms, thine eyes, are blotted;
Thy bed lust-stain'd shall with lust's blood be spotted.
           [*Exit*

Enter LODOVICO *and* GRATIANO

CASSIO

What, ho! no watch? no passage? murder! murder!

GRATIANO

'Tis some mischance; the cry is very direful.

CASSIO

O, help!

LODOVICO

Hark!

RODERIGO

O wretched villain!

LODOVICO

Two or three groan: it is a heavy night:
These may be counterfeits: let's think 't unsafe
To come in to the cry without more help.

RODERIGO

Nobody come? then shall I bleed to death.

LODOVICO

Hark!

Re-enter IAGO, *with a light*

GRATIANO

Here's one comes in his shirt, with light and weapons.

IAGO

Who's there? whose noise is this that cries on murder?

LODOVICO

We do not know.

IAGO

           Did not you hear a cry?

CASSIO

Here, here! for heaven's sake, help me!

IAGO

           What's the matter?

GRATIANO

This is Othello's ancient, as I take it.

LODOVICO

The same indeed; a very valiant fellow.

IAGO

What are you here that cry so grievously?

CASSIO

Iago? O, I am spoil'd, undone by villains!
Give me some help.

IAGO

O me, lieutenant! what villains have done this?

CASSIO

I think that one of them is hereabout,
And cannot make away.

IAGO

           O treacherous villains!
What are you there? come in and give some help.
           [*To* LODOVICO *and* GRATIANO

RODERIGO

O, help me here!

CASSIO

That's one of them.

IAGO

O murderous slave! O villain!

[Stabs RODERIGO

RODERIGO

O damn'd Iago! O inhuman dog!

IAGO

Kill men i' the dark! Where be these bloody thieves?
How silent is this town! Ho! murder! murder!
What may you be? are you of good or evil?

LODOVICO

As you shall prove us, praise us.

IAGO

Signior Lodovico?

LODOVICO

He, sir.

IAGO

I cry you mercy. Here's Cassio hurt by villains.

GRATIANO

Cassio!

IAGO

How is 't, brother?

CASSIO

My leg is cut in two.

IAGO

Marry, heaven forbid!
Light, gentlemen: I'll bind it with my shirt.

Enter BIANCA

BIANCA

What is the matter, ho? who is 't that cried?

IAGO

Who is 't that cried!

BIANCA

O my dear Cassio! my sweet Cassio! O Cassio,
Cassio, Cassio!

IAGO

O notable strumpet! Cassio, may you suspect
Who they should be that have thus mangled you?

CASSIO

No.

GRATIANO

I am sorry to find you thus: I have been to seek you.

IAGO

Lend me a garter. So. O, for a chair,
To bear him easily hence!

BIANCA

Alas, he faints! O Cassio, Cassio, Cassio!

IAGO

Gentlemen all, I do suspect this trash
To be a party in this injury.
Patience awhile, good Cassio. Come, come;
Lend me a light. Know we this face or no?
Alas, my friend and my dear countryman
Roderigo? no:—yes, sure: O heaven! Roderigo.

GRATIANO

What, of Venice?

IAGO

Even he, sir: did you know him?

GRATIANO

Know him! ay.

IAGO

Signior Gratiano? I cry you gentle pardon;
These bloody accidents must excuse my manners,
That so neglected you.

GRATIANO

I am glad to see you.

IAGO

How do you, Cassio? O, a chair, a chair!

GRATIANO

Roderigo!

IAGO

He, he, 'tis he. [A chair brought in] O, that's well
said; the chair:
Some good man bear him carefully from hence;
I'll fetch the general's surgeon. [To BIANCA] For
you, mistress,
Save you your labour. He that lies slain here, Cassio,
Was my dear friend: what malice was between you?

CASSIO

None in the world; nor do I know the man.

IAGO

[To BIANCA] What, look you pale? O, bear him out
o' the air.   [CASSIO and RODERIGO are borne off
Stay you, good gentlemen. Look you pale, mistress?
Do you perceive the gastness of her eye?
Nay, if you stare, we shall hear more anon.
Behold her well; I pray you, look upon her:
Do you see, gentlemen? nay, guiltiness will speak,
Though tongues were out of use.

Enter EMILIA

EMILIA

'Las, what's the matter? what's the matter, husband?

IAGO

Cassio hath here been set on in the dark
By Roderigo, and fellows that are 'scaped:
He's almost slain, and Roderigo dead.

EMILIA

Alas, good gentleman! alas, good Cassio!

IAGO

This is the fruit of whoring. Prithee, Emilia,
Go know of Cassio where he supp'd to-night.
What, do you shake at that?

BIANCA

He supp'd at my house; but I therefore shake not.

IAGO

O, did he so? I charge you, go with me.

EMILIA

Fie, fie upon thee, strumpet!

BIANCA

I am no strumpet; but of life as honest
As you that thus abuse me.

EMILIA

As I! foh! fie upon thee!

IAGO

Kind gentlemen, let's go see poor Cassio dress'd.
Come, mistress, you must tell 's another tale.
Emilia, run you to the citadel,

And tell my lord and lady what hath happ'd!
Will you go on? I pray. [*Aside*] This is the night
That either makes me or fordoes me quite. [*Exeunt*

SCENE II. *A bedchamber in the castle:* DESDEMONA *in bed
asleep; a light burning*

Enter OTHELLO
OTHELLO
It is the cause, it is the cause, my soul:
Let me not name it to you, you chaste stars!
It is the cause. Yet I'll not shed her blood,
Nor scar that whiter skin of hers than snow
And smooth as monumental alabaster.
Yet she must die, else she'll betray more men.
Put out the light, and then put out the light:
If I quench thee, thou flaming minister,
I can again thy former light restore,
Should I repent me: but once put out thy light,
Thou cunning'st pattern of excelling nature,
I know not where is that Promethean heat
That can thy light relume. When I have pluck'd the
    rose,
I cannot give it vital growth again,
It must needs wither: I'll smell it on the tree.
                                   [*Kissing her*
Ah, balmy breath, that dost almost persuade
Justice to break her sword! One more, one more:
Be thus when thou art dead, and I will kill thee,
And love thee after: one more, and this the last:
So sweet was ne'er so fatal. I must weep,
But they are cruel tears: this sorrow's heavenly;
It strikes where it doth love. She wakes.
DESDEMONA
Who's there? Othello?
OTHELLO
                        Ay, Desdemona.
DESDEMONA
Will you come to bed, my lord?
OTHELLO
Have you pray'd to-night, Desdemona?
DESDEMONA
Ay, my lord.
OTHELLO
If you bethink yourself of any crime
Unreconciled as yet to heaven and grace,
Solicit for it straight.
DESDEMONA
Alas, my lord, what may you mean by that?
OTHELLO
Well, do it, and be brief; I will walk by:
I would not kill thy unprepared spirit;
No; heaven forfend! I would not kill thy soul.
DESDEMONA
Talk you of killing?
OTHELLO
Ay, I do.
DESDEMONA
Then heaven have mercy on me!

OTHELLO
Amen, with all my heart!
DESDEMONA
If you say so, I hope you will not kill me.
OTHELLO
Hum!
DESDEMONA
And yet I fear you; for you are fatal then
When your eyes roll so: why I should fear I know
    not,
Since guiltiness I know not; but yet I feel I fear.
OTHELLO
Think on thy sins.
DESDEMONA
             They are loves I bear to you.
OTHELLO
Ay, and for that thou diest.
DESDEMONA
That death's unnatural that kills for loving.
Alas, why gnaw you so your nether lip?
Some bloody passion shakes your very frame:
These are portents; but yet I hope, I hope,
They do not point on me.
OTHELLO
                   Peace, and be still!
DESDEMONA
I will so. What's the matter?
OTHELLO
That handkerchief which I so loved and gave thee
Thou gavest to Cassio.
DESDEMONA
             No, by my life and soul!
Send for the man, and ask him.
OTHELLO
                   Sweet soul, take heed,
Take heed of perjury; thou art on thy death-bed.
DESDEMONA
Ay, but not yet to die.
OTHELLO
                   Yes, presently:
Therefore confess thee freely of thy sin;
For to deny each article with oath
Cannot remove nor choke the strong conception
That I do groan withal. Thou art to die.
DESDEMONA
Then Lord have mercy on me!
OTHELLO
                        I say, amen.
DESDEMONA
And have you mercy too! I never did
Offend you in my life; never loved Cassio
But with such general warranty of heaven
As I might love: I never gave him token.
OTHELLO
By heaven, I saw my handkerchief in 's hand.
O perjured woman! thou dost stone my heart,
And makest me call what I intend to do
A murder, which I thought a sacrifice:
I saw the handkerchief.

DESDEMONA
He found it then;
I never gave it him: send for him hither;
Let him confess a truth.

OTHELLO
He hath confess'd.

DESDEMONA
What, my lord?

OTHELLO
That he hath used thee.

DESDEMONA
How? unlawfully?

OTHELLO
Ay.

DESDEMONA
He will not say so.

OTHELLO
No, his mouth is stopp'd;
Honest Iago hath ta'en order for 't.

DESDEMONA
O, my fear interprets! what, is he dead?

OTHELLO
Had all his hairs been lives, my great revenge
Had stomach for them all.

DESDEMONA
Alas, he is betray'd, and I undone!

OTHELLO
Out, strumpet! weep'st thou for him to my face?

DESDEMONA
O, banish me, my lord, but kill me not!

OTHELLO
Down, strumpet!

DESDEMONA
Kill me to-morrow; let me live to-night!

OTHELLO
Nay, if you strive,—

DESDEMONA
But half an hour!

OTHELLO
Being done, there is no pause.

DESDEMONA
But while I say one prayer!

OTHELLO
It is too late. [*He stifles her*

EMILIA
[*Within*] My lord, my lord! what, ho! my lord, my
lord!

OTHELLO
What noise is this? Not dead? not yet quite dead?
I that am cruel am yet merciful;
I would not have thee linger in thy pain:
So, so.

EMILIA
[*Within*] What, ho! my lord, my lord!

OTHELLO
Who's there?

EMILIA
[*Within*] O, good my lord, I would speak a word
with you!

OTHELLO
Yes: 'tis Emilia. By and by. She's dead.
'Tis like she comes to speak of Cassio's death.
The noise was here. Ha! no more moving?
Still as the grave. Shall she come in? were 't good?
I think she stirs again. No. What's best to do?
If she come in, she'll sure speak to my wife:
My wife! my wife! what wife? I have no wife.
O, insupportable! O heavy hour!
Methinks it should be now a huge eclipse
Of sun and moon, and that the affrighted globe
Should yawn at alteration.

EMILIA
[*Within*] I do beseech you
That I may speak with you, O, good my lord!

OTHELLO
I had forgot thee: O, come in, Emilia.
Soft; by and by. Let me the curtains draw.
Where art thou? [*Unlocks the door*

Enter EMILIA

What's the matter with thee now?

EMILIA
O, my good lord, yonder's foul murders done!

OTHELLO
What, now?

EMILIA
But now, my lord.

OTHELLO
It is the very error of the moon;
She comes more nearer earth than she was wont
And makes men mad.

EMILIA
Cassio, my lord, hath kill'd a young Venetian
Call'd Roderigo.

OTHELLO
Roderigo kill'd!
And Cassio kill'd!

EMILIA
No, Cassio is not kill'd.

OTHELLO
Not Cassio kill'd! then murder's out of tune,
And sweet revenge grows harsh.

DESDEMONA
O, falsely, falsely murder'd!

EMILIA
Alas, what cry is that?

OTHELLO
That! what?

EMILIA
Out, and alas! that was my lady's voice.
Help! help, ho! help! O lady, speak again!
Sweet Desdemona! O sweet mistress, speak!

DESDEMONA
A guiltless death I die.

EMILIA
O, who hath done this deed?

DESDEMONA
Nobody; I myself. Farewell:
Commend me to my kind lord: O, farewell! [*Dies*

OTHELLO

Why, how should she be murder'd?

EMILIA

　　　　　　　Alas, who knows?

OTHELLO

You heard her say herself, it was not I.

EMILIA

She said so: I must needs report the truth.

OTHELLO

She's like a liar gone to burning hell:
'Twas I that kill'd her.

EMILIA

　　　　　　　O, the more angel she,
And you the blacker devil!

OTHELLO

She turn'd to folly, and she was a whore.

EMILIA

Thou dost belie her, and thou art a devil.

OTHELLO

She was false as water.

EMILIA

　　　　　　Thou art rash as fire, to say
That she was false: O, she was heavenly true!

OTHELLO

Cassio did top her; ask thy husband else.
O, I were damn'd beneath all depth in hell,
But that I did proceed upon just grounds
To this extremity. Thy husband knew it all.

EMILIA

My husband!

OTHELLO

Thy husband.

EMILIA

That she was false to wedlock?

OTHELLO

Ay, with Cassio. Nay, had she been true,
If heaven would make me such another world
Of one entire and perfect chrysolite,
I'ld not have sold her for it.

EMILIA

My husband!

OTHELLO

　　　　　Ay, 'twas he that told me first:
An honest man he is, and hates the slime
That sticks on filthy deeds.

EMILIA

　　　　　My husband!

OTHELLO

What needs this iteration, woman? I say thy husband.

EMILIA

O mistress, villany hath made mocks with love!
My husband say that she was false!

OTHELLO

　　　　　He, woman;
I say thy husband: dost understand the word?
My friend, thy husband, honest, honest Iago.

EMILIA

If he say so, may his pernicious soul

Rot half a grain a day! he lies to the heart:
She was too fond of her most filthy bargain.

OTHELLO

Ha!

EMILIA

Do thy worst:
This deed of thine is no more worthy heaven
Than thou wast worthy her.

OTHELLO

　　　　　　Peace, you were best.

EMILIA

Thou hast not half that power to do me harm
As I have to be hurt. O gull! O dolt!
As ignorant as dirt! thou hast done a deed—
I care not for thy sword; I'll make thee known,
Though I lost twenty lives. Help! help, ho! help!
The Moor hath kill'd my mistress! Murder! murder!

Enter MONTANO, GRATIANO, IAGO, _and others_

MONTANO

What is the matter? How now, general!

EMILIA

O, are you come, Iago? you have done well,
That men must lay their murders on your neck.

GRATIANO

What is the matter?

EMILIA

Disprove this villain, if thou be'st a man:
He says thou told'st him that his wife was false:
I know thou didst not, thou'rt not such a villain.
Speak, for my heart is full.

IAGO

I told him what I thought, and told no more
Than what he found himself was apt and true.

EMILIA

But did you ever tell him she was false?

IAGO

I did.

EMILIA

You told a lie, an odious, damned lie;
Upon my soul, a lie, a wicked lie!
She false with Cassio! Did you say with Cassio?

IAGO

With Cassio, mistress. Go to, charm your tongue.

EMILIA

I will not charm my tongue; I am bound to speak:
My mistress here lies murder'd in her bed,—

ALL

O heavens forfend!

EMILIA

And your reports have set the murder on.

OTHELLO

Nay, stare not, masters: it is true indeed.

GRATIANO

'Tis a strange truth.

MONTANO

O monstrous act!

EMILIA

　　　　　Villany, villany, villany!
I think upon 't: I think: I smell 't: O villany!

I thought so then: I'll kill myself for grief:
O villany, villany!

IAGO

What, are you mad? I charge you, get you home.

EMILIA

Good gentlemen, let me have leave to speak:
'Tis proper I obey him, but not now.
Perchance, Iago, I will ne'er go home.

OTHELLO

O! O! O!　　　　　　　　　*[Falling on the bed*

EMILIA

　　　　Nay, lay thee down and roar;
For thou hast kill'd the sweetest innocent
That e'er did lift up eye.

OTHELLO

　　　　　　[Rising] O, she was foul!
I scarce did know you, uncle: there lies your niece,
Whose breath indeed these hands have newly
　　stopp'd:
I know this act shows horrible and grim.

GRATIANO

Poor Desdemona! I am glad thy father's dead:
Thy match was mortal to him, and pure grief
Shore his old thread in twain: did he live now,
This sight would make him do a desperate turn,
Yea, curse his better angel from his side,
And fall to reprobation.

OTHELLO

'Tis pitiful; but yet Iago knows
That she with Cassio hath the act of shame
A thousand times committed; Cassio confess'd it:
And she did gratify his amorous works
With that recognizance and pledge of love
Which I first gave her; I saw it in his hand:
It was a handkerchief, an antique token
My father gave my mother.

EMILIA

O heaven! O heavenly powers!

IAGO

'Zounds! hold your peace.

EMILIA

　　　　　　　'Twill out, 'twill out. I peace!
No, I will speak as liberal as the north:
Let heaven and men and devils, let them all,
All, all, cry shame against me, yet I'll speak.

IAGO

Be wise, and get you home.

EMILIA

　　　　　　I will not.
　　　[IAGO offers to stab EMILIA

GRATIANO

　　　　　　　　Fie!
Your sword upon a woman!

EMILIA

O thou dull Moor! that handkerchief thou speak'st
　　of
I found by fortune and did give my husband;
For often with a solemn earnestness,
More than indeed belong'd to such a trifle,
He begg'd of me to steal it.

IAGO

　　　　Villanous whore!

EMILIA

She give it Cassio! no, alas, I found it,
And I did give 't my husband.

IAGO

　　　　　　Filth, thou liest!

EMILIA

By heaven, I do not, I do not, gentlemen.
O murderous coxcomb! what should such a fool
Do with so good a wife?

OTHELLO

　　　　　Are there no stones in heaven
But what serve for the thunder? Precious villain!
　　*[He runs at IAGO: IAGO, from behind, stabs
　　　　　　　　EMILIA, and exit*

GRATIANO

The woman falls; sure, he hath kill'd his wife.

EMILIA

Ay, ay: O, lay me by my mistress' side.

GRATIANO

He's gone, but his wife's kill'd.

MONTANO

'Tis a notorious villain. Take you this weapon,
Which I have here recover'd from the Moor:
Come, guard the door without; let him not pass,
But kill him rather. I'll after that same villain,
For 'tis a damned slave.
　　　[Exeunt all but OTHELLO and EMILIA

OTHELLO

　　　　I am not valiant neither.
But every puny whipster gets my sword.
But why should honour outlive honesty?
Let it go all.

EMILIA

　　　What did thy song bode, lady?
Hark, canst thou hear me? I will play the swan,
And die in music.

　　　[Singing] Willow, willow, willow.

Moor, she was chaste; she loved thee, cruel Moor;
So come my soul to bliss, as I speak true;
So speaking as I think, I die, I die.　　*[Dies*

OTHELLO

I have another weapon in this chamber;
It is a sword of Spain, the ice-brook's temper.—
O, here it is. Uncle, I must come forth.

GRATIANO

[Within] If thou attempt it, it will cost thee dear:
Thou hast no weapon, and perforce must suffer.

OTHELLO

Look in upon me then, and speak with me,
Or, naked as I am, I will assault thee.
　　　　Re-enter GRATIANO

GRATIANO

What is the matter?

OTHELLO

　　　　Behold, I have a weapon;
A better never did itself sustain

Upon a soldier's thigh: I have seen the day
That with this little arm and this good sword
I have made my way through more impediments
Than twenty times your stop: but, O vain boast!
Who can control his fate? 'tis not so now.
Be not afraid, though you do see me weapon'd;
Here is my journey's end, here is my butt
And very sea-mark of my utmost sail.
Do you go back dismay'd? 'tis a lost fear:
Man but a rush against Othello's breast,
And he retires. Where should Othello go?
Now, how dost thou look now? O ill-starr'd wench!
Pale as thy smock! when we shall meet at compt,
This look of thine will hurl my soul from heaven,
And fiends will snatch at it. Cold, cold, my girl!
Even like thy chastity. O cursed slave!
Whip me, ye devils,
From the possession of this heavenly sight!
Blow me about in winds! roast me in sulphur!
Wash me in steep-down gulfs of liquid fire!
O Desdemona! Desdemona! dead!
Oh! Oh! Oh!

Enter LODIVICO, MONTANO, CASSIO *carried in a chair,*
and OFFICERS *with* IAGO, *prisoner*

LODOVICO
Where is this rash and most unfortunate man?

OTHELLO
That's he that was Othello: here I am.

LODOVICO
Where is that viper? bring the villain forth.

OTHELLO
I look down towards his feet; but that's a fable.
If that thou be'st a devil, I cannot kill thee.
　　　　　　　　　　　　　　　[*Wounds* IAGO

LODOVICO
Wrench his sword from him.

IAGO
　　　　　I bleed, sir, but not kill'd.

OTHELLO
I am not sorry neither: I'ld have thee live;
For, in my sense, 'tis happiness to die.

LODOVICO
O thou Othello, that wert once so good,
Fall'n in the practice of a damned slave,
What shall be said to thee?

OTHELLO
　　　　　　　　　Why, any thing:
An honourable murderer, if you will;
For nought did I in hate, but all in honour.

LODOVICO
This wretch hath part confess'd his villany:
Did you and he consent in Cassio's death?

OTHELLO
Ay.

CASSIO
Dear general, I never gave you cause.

OTHELLO
I do believe it, and I ask your pardon.

Will you, I pray, demand that demi-devil
Why he hath thus ensnared my soul and body?

IAGO
Demand me nothing; what you know, you know:
From this time forth I never will speak word.

LODOVICO
What, not to pray?

GRATIANO
　　　　　Torments will ope your lips.

OTHELLO
Well, thou dost best.

LODOVICO
Sir, you shall understand what hath befall'n,
Which, as I think, you know not. Here is a letter
Found in the pocket of the slain Roderigo,
And here another: the one of them imports
The death of Cassio to be undertook
By Roderigo.

OTHELLO
O villain!

CASSIO
　　　Most heathenish and most gross!

LODOVICO
Now here's another discontented paper,
Found in his pocket too; and this, it seems,
Roderigo meant to have sent this damned villain:
But that, belike, Iago in the interim
Came in and satisfied him.

OTHELLO
　　　　　　　O the pernicious caitiff!
How came you, Cassio, by that handkerchief
That was my wife's?

CASSIO
　　　　　I found it in my chamber:
And he himself confess'd but even now
That there he dropp'd it for a special purpose
Which wrought to his desire.

OTHELLO
　　　　　　　　　O fool! fool! fool!

CASSIO
There is besides in Roderigo's letter,
How he upbraids Iago, that he made him
Brave me upon the watch; whereon it came
That I was cast: and even but now he spake
After long seeming dead, Iago hurt him,
Iago set him on.

LODOVICO
You must forsake this room, and go with us:
Your power and your command is taken off,
And Cassio rules in Cyprus. For this slave,
If there be any cunning cruelty
That can torment him much and hold him long,
It shall be his. You shall close prisoner rest,
Till that the nature of your fault be known
To the Venetian state. Come, bring away.

OTHELLO
Soft you; a word or two before you go.
I have done the state some service, and they know 't.
No more of that. I pray you, in your letters,

When you shall these unlucky deeds relate,
Speak of me as I am; nothing extenuate,
Nor set down aught in malice: then must you speak
Of one that loved not wisely but too well;
Of one not easily jealous, but, being wrought,
Perplex'd in the extreme; of one whose hand,
Like the base Indian, threw a pearl away
Richer than all his tribe; of one whose subdued eyes,
Albeit unused to the melting mood,
Drop tears as fast as the Arabian trees
Their medicinal gum. Set you down this;
And say besides, that in Aleppo once,
Where a malignant and a turban'd Turk
Beat a Venetian and traduced the state,
I took by the throat the circumcised dog
And smote him, thus.   *[Stabs himself*

LODOVICO

O bloody period!

GRATIANO

    All that's spoke is marr'd.

OTHELLO

I kiss'd thee ere I kill'd thee: no way but this,
Killing myself, to die upon a kiss.

        [Falls on the bed, and dies

This did I fear, but thought he had no weapon;
For he was great of heart.

CASSIO

LODOVICO

        [To IAGO] O Spartan dog,
More fell than anguish, hunger, or the sea!
Look on the tragic loading of this bed;
This is thy work: the object poisons sight;
Let it be hid. Gratiano, keep the house,
And seize upon the fortunes of the Moor,
For they succeed on you. To you, lord governor,
Remains the censure of this hellish villain,
The time, the place, the torture:
O, enforce it!
Myself will straight aboard, and to the state
This heavy act with heavy heart relate.   *[Exeunt*

THE TRAGEDY OF KING LEAR

SYNOPSIS

Lᴇᴀʀ, King of Britain, after many years as ruler, decides to relinquish the reins of government and apportion his kingdom among his three daughters, in whose filial devotion he has complete confidence. Proud of their affection and craving a public expression of it, he makes the rather childish proposal before his assembled court that the actual distribution of his territory will depend upon each daughter's declaration of love for him.

The two eldest, Goneril, wife of the Duke of Albany, and Regan, wife of the Duke of Cornwall, make protestations of devotion that are so obviously insincere and so evidently prompted by greed that the third daughter, the upright, straightforward Cordelia, is disgusted, while their father is highly gratified. He now turns eagerly to his youngest and favorite child, but she can only utter an austerely simple statement of dutiful affection that chills the old King to the heart. Feeling snubbed, insulted, and ridiculous before his court, he gives way to a hot-headed fit of temper that sweeps everything before it. Cordelia is disinherited; her share of the kingdom is divided between her sisters; Lear arranges to live in turn with Goneril and Regan; and the outspoken Earl of Kent who hotly challenges the King's treatment of his youngest daughter is banished forever from his native land, in spite of his long years of service.

Cordelia's genuine worth is apparent to her suitor, the logical courteous King of France, who gladly leads away his dowerless bride, as her sisters plot to subjugate their capricious father and the faithful Kent, instead of going into exile, returns in the disguise of a servant to protect his old master from them. He arrives just as Goneril and her steward Oswald are criticizing and reducing the King's authorized retinue of one hundred knights, whereupon the enraged Lear, cursing his eldest daughter, departs for Regan's home, dispatching Kent in advance, only later to find him insultingly placed in the stocks by Cornwall and his wife who are visiting at the Earl of Gloucester's castle. Regan refuses to harbor her father until he apologizes to her sister who has also arrived, and when Lear realizes that there is nothing but further humiliation in store for him at their hands, he rushes out of the castle, bareheaded and unprotected, into a furious storm that is raging on the heath, accompanied only by his devoted fool.

When Kent joins them, they take refuge in a hovel which is already occupied by Edgar, son and rightful heir of the Earl of Gloucester, who has been deprived of his birthright through the lies and hypocrisy of his evil bastard brother Edmund, and to save his life has adopted the disguise of mad Tom o' Bedlam. Risking the anger of Lear's daughters, the Earl seeks them out and shelters them in a farmhouse on his estate where the King, whose mind has become unbalanced, holds a pitiful mock trial of his daughters with the fool and mad Tom as judges. Gloucester soon returns to tell them that Goneril and Regan are plotting against the King's life, and that he must be hurried to Dover for protection.

Meanwhile, the Earl's destruction is being planned by his bastard son who satisfies Cornwall of his sympathy for the King and proves his knowledge of Cordelia's intended invasion of England to aid her father. Gloucester's eyes are torn out by Cornwall himself, incited by the cruel Regan, but he in turn is wounded by one of his own servants who revolts against his wickedness and is stabbed to death by Regan, Cornwall dying later. Taunted by Regan with Edmund's villainy, and thrown out of his castle, the helpless old Gloucester is found and cared for by his disowned son Edgar, who, without revealing his identity, hears his father's confession of mistaken wrath, becomes his guide, and prevents his suicide.

At Dover, the sad Cordelia finds her poor father wandering about in his madness, fantastically decked with wild flowers, and with the skilful aid of her physician gradually restores him to sanity and happiness in her love and devotion.

Edmund has become commander-in-chief of the English army upon Cornwall's death, and Albany, though despising him for his treacherous betrayal of his old father, joins forces with him to protect England from foreign invasion, and the French are defeated, Lear and Cordelia being sent to prison by Edmund who secretly orders their execution. The jealousy of Goneril and Regan, both of whom are in love with Edmund, results in Regan being poisoned by her sister who afterwards stabs herself when her letter suggesting Edmund's murder of her husband is discovered.

In a formal combat, Edgar fights and wounds Edmund whose repentance when dying comes too late to save Cordelia's life, and she is hanged in prison as Albany's messenger speeds to countermand the order. The old Lear tries to protect her, kills the hangman, and then dies, brokenhearted, as he fails to revive her. Edgar, Kent and Albany are now left with the burden of ruling and sustaining the kingdom.

HISTORICAL DATA

The main plot of *King Lear* finds its origin in the folk-lore of many countries, usually as variants of the Cinderella story. Its oldest extant version in English is in Geoffrey of Monmouth's *Historia Regnum Britanniae* (1147), although it may be found in various forms and under different names in the *Gesta Romanorum*, in the *Romance* of Perceforest, in *The Mirror for Magistrates*, in Spenser's *Faerie Queene* (from whence came the name "Cordelia") and in an abridged version of Holinshed's *Historie of England*. Perhaps the most direct source used by Shakespeare was an older drama, *The True Chronicle of King Leir and his Three Daughters*, an anonymous play apparently presented in 1594.

The sub-plot, the story of Gloucester, is taken from the incident of the blind king of Paphlagonia in Sir Philip Sidney's pastoral romance *Arcadia* (1590).

The pretended madness of Edgar is purely an invention of Shakespeare's, as is the altered ending, which in the traditional story has Lear and his French allies victorious.

The tragedy is generally supposed to have been written in 1605 or 1606, no later, as an entry in the Stationers' Register notes that it was "played before the King's Majesty at Whitehall, St. Stephens Night" (1606).

"Blow, winds, and crack your cheeks! rage! blow!"
KING LEAR

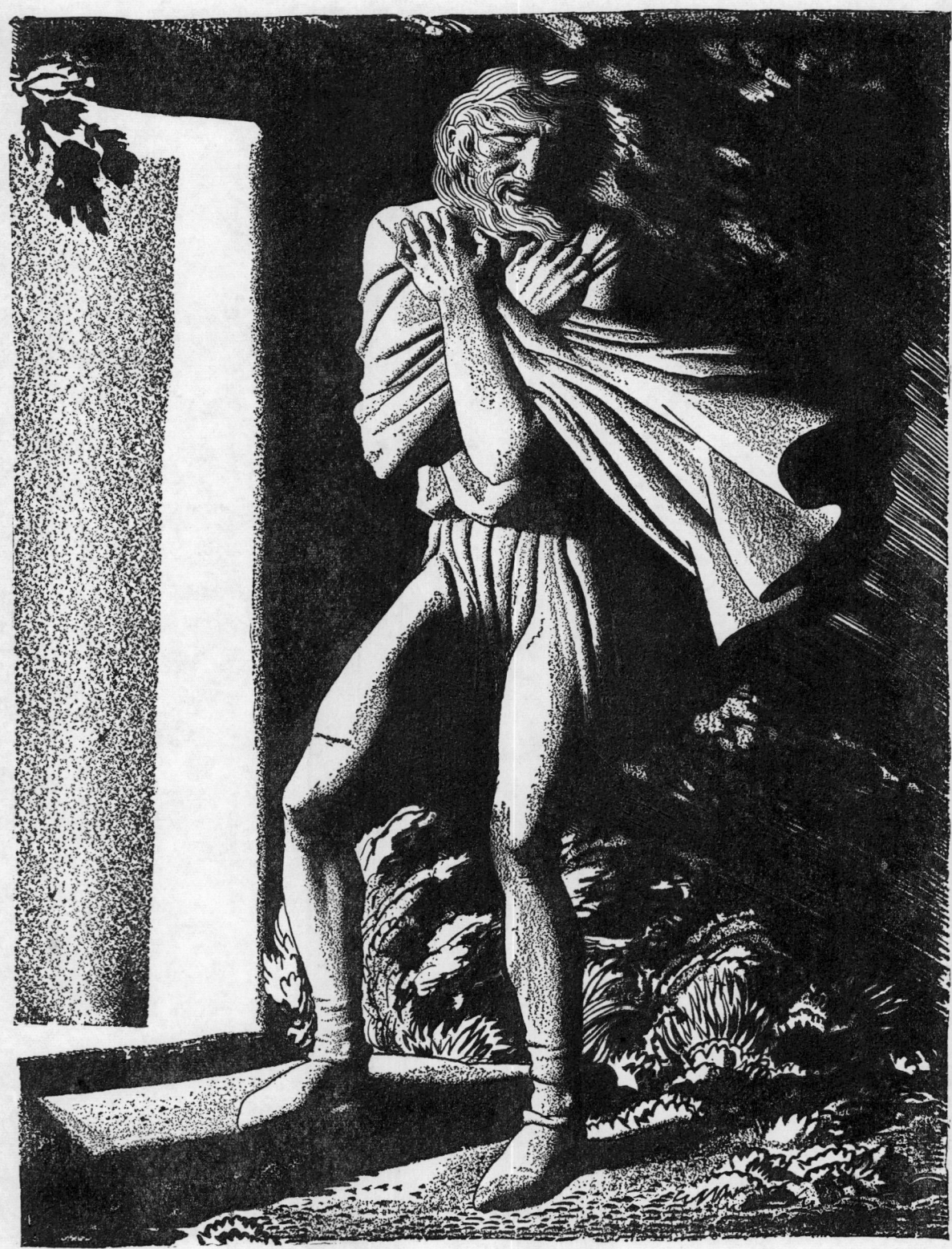

THE TRAGEDY OF KING LEAR

DRAMATIS PERSONÆ

LEAR, *king of Britain.*
KING OF FRANCE.
DUKE OF BURGUNDY.
DUKE OF CORNWALL.
DUKE OF ALBANY.
EARL OF KENT.
EARL OF GLOUCESTER.
EDGAR, *son to Gloucester.*
EDMUND, *bastard son to Gloucester.*
CURAN, *a courtier.*
OLD MAN, *tenant to Gloucester.*
DOCTOR.
FOOL.

OSWALD, *steward to Goneril.*
A CAPTAIN *employed by Edmund.*
GENTLEMAN *attendant on Cordelia.*
HERALD.
SERVANTS *to Cornwall.*

GONERIL,
REGAN, } *daughters to Lear.*
CORDELIA,

KNIGHTS *of Lear's train,* CAPTAINS, MESSENGERS, SOLDIERS, *and* ATTENDANTS.

SCENE—*Britain.*

ACT I

SCENE I. KING LEAR's *palace*

Enter KENT, GLOUCESTER, *and* EDMUND

KENT

I THOUGHT the king had more affected the Duke of Albany than Cornwall.

GLOUCESTER

It did always seem so to us: but now, in the division of the kingdom, it appears not which of the dukes he values most; for equalities are so weighèd that curiosity in neither can make choice of either's moiety.

KENT

Is not this your son, my lord?

GLOUCESTER

His breeding, sir, hath been at my charge: I have so often blushed to acknowledge him that now I am brazed to it.

KENT

I cannot conceive you.

GLOUCESTER

Sir, this young fellow's mother could: whereupon she grew round-wombed, and had indeed, sir, a son for her cradle ere she had a husband for her bed. Do you smell a fault?

KENT

I cannot wish the fault undone, the issue of it being so proper.

GLOUCESTER

But I have, sir, a son by order of law, some year elder than this, who yet is no dearer in my account: though this knave came something saucily into the world before he was sent for, yet was his mother fair; there was good sport at his making, and the whoreson must be acknowledged. Do you know this noble gentleman, Edmund?

EDMUND

No, my lord.

GLOUCESTER

My lord of Kent: remember him hereafter as my honourable friend.

EDMUND

My services to your lordship.

KENT

I must love you, and sue to know you better.

EDMUND

Sir, I shall study deserving.

GLOUCESTER

He hath been out nine years, and away he shall again. The king is coming.

Sennet. Enter one bearing a coronet, KING LEAR, CORN-WALL, ALBANY, GONERIL, REGAN, CORDELIA, *and* ATTENDANTS

LEAR

Attend the lords of France and Burgundy, Gloucester.

GLOUCESTER

I shall, my liege. [*Exeunt* GLOUCESTER *and* EDMUND

LEAR

Meantime we shall express our darker purpose.
Give me the map there. Know we have divided
In three our kingdom: and 'tis our fast intent
To shake all cares and business from our age,
Conferring them on younger strengths, while we
Unburthen'd crawl toward death. Our son of Corn-
  wall,
And you, our no less loving son of Albany,
We have this hour a constant will to publish
Our daughters' several dowers, that future strife
May be prevented now. The princes, France and
  Burgundy,
Great rivals in our youngest daughter's love,
Long in our court have made their amorous so-
  journ,
And here are to be answer'd. Tell me, my daugh-
  ters,
Since now we will divest us both of rule,

[983]

Interest of territory, cares of state,
Which of you shall we say doth love us most?
That we our largest bounty may extend
Where nature doth with merit challenge. Goneril,
Our eldest-born, speak first.

GONERIL

Sir, I love you more than words can wield the
    matter,
Dearer than eye-sight, space and liberty,
Beyond what can be valued, rich or rare,
No less than life, with grace, health, beauty, honour,
As much as child e'er loved or father found;
A love that makes breath poor and speech unable;
Beyond all manner of so much I love you.

CORDELIA

[Aside] What shall Cordelia do? Love, and be silent.

LEAR

Of all these bounds, even from this line to this,
With shadowy forests and with champains rich'd,
With plenteous rivers and wide-skirted meads,
We make thee lady. To thine and Albany's issue
Be this perpetual. What says our second daughter,
Our dearest Regan, wife to Cornwall? Speak.

REGAN

I am made of that self metal as my sister,
And prize me at her worth. In my true heart
I find she names my very deed of love;
Only she comes too short: that I profess
Myself an enemy to all other joys
Which the most precious square of sense possesses,
And find I am alone felicitate
In your dear highness' love.

CORDELIA

[Aside] Then poor Cordelia!
And yet not so, since I am sure my love's
More ponderous than my tongue.

LEAR

To thee and thine hereditary ever
Remain this ample third of our fair kingdom,
No less in space, validity and pleasure,
Than that conferr'd on Goneril. Now, our joy,
Although the last, not least, to whose young love
The vines of France and milk of Burgundy
Strive to be interess'd, what can you say to draw
A third more opulent than your sisters? Speak.

CORDELIA

Nothing, my lord.

LEAR

Nothing!

CORDELIA

Nothing.

LEAR

Nothing will come of nothing: speak again.

CORDELIA

Unhappy that I am, I cannot heave
My heart into my mouth: I love your majesty
According to my bond; nor more nor less.

LEAR

How, how, Cordelia! mend your speech a little,
Lest it may mar your fortunes.

CORDELIA

Good my lord,
You have begot me, bred me, loved me: I
Return those duties back as are right fit,
Obey you, love you, and most honour you.
Why have my sisters husbands, if they say
They love you all? Haply, when I shall wed,
That lord whose hand must take my plight shall
    carry
Half my love with him, half my care and duty:
Sure, I shall never marry like my sisters,
To love my father all.

LEAR

But goes thy heart with this?

CORDELIA

Ay, good my lord.

LEAR

So young, and so untender?

CORDELIA

So young, my lord, and true.

LEAR

Let it be so; thy truth then be thy dower:
For, by the sacred radiance of the sun,
The mysteries of Hecate, and the night;
By all the operation of the orbs
From whom we do exist and cease to be;
Here I disclaim all my paternal care,
Propinquity and property of blood,
And as a stranger to my heart and me
Hold thee from this for ever. The barbarous
    Scythian,
Or he that makes his generation messes
To gorge his appetite, shall to my bosom
Be as well neighbour'd, pitied and relieved,
As thou my sometime daughter.

KENT

Good my liege,—

LEAR

Peace, Kent!
Come not between the dragon and his wrath.
I loved her most, and thought to set my rest
On her kind nursery. Hence, and avoid my sight!
So be my grave my peace, as here I give
Her father's heart from her! Call France. Who stirs?
Call Burgundy. Cornwall and Albany,
With my two daughters' dowers digest this third:
Let pride, which she calls plainness, marry her.
I do invest you jointly with my power,
Pre-eminence and all the large effects
That troop with majesty. Ourself, by monthly
    course,
With reservation of an hundred knights
By you to be sustain'd, shall our abode
Make with you by due turns. Only we still retain
The name and all the additions to a king;
The sway, revenue, execution of the rest,
Beloved sons, be yours: which to confirm,
This coronet part betwixt you.

KENT

Royal Lear,

Whom I have ever honour'd as my king,
Loved as my father, as my master follow'd,
As my great patron thought on in my prayers,—

LEAR

The bow is bent and drawn; make from the shaft.

KENT

Let it fall rather, though the fork invade
The region of my heart: be Kent unmannerly,
When Lear is mad. What wouldst thou do, old man?
Think'st thou that duty shall have dread to speak,
When power to flattery bows? To plainness hon-
    our's bound,
When majesty stoops to folly. Reverse thy doom,
And in thy best consideration check
This hideous rashness: answer my life my judge-
    ment,
Thy youngest daughter does not love thee least;
Nor are those empty-hearted whose low sound
Reverbs no hollowness.

LEAR

    Kent, on thy life, no more.

KENT

My life I never held but as a pawn
To wage against thy enemies, nor fear to lose it,
Thy safety being the motive.

LEAR

    Out of my sight!

KENT

See better, Lear, and let me still remain
The true blank of thine eye.

LEAR

Now, by Apollo,—

KENT

    Now, by Apollo, king.
Thou swear'st thy gods in vain.

LEAR

    O, vassal! miscreant!
    [Laying his hand on his sword

ALBANY and CORNWALL

Dear sir, forbear.

KENT

Do;
Kill thy physician, and the fee bestow
Upon the foul disease. Revoke thy doom;
Or, whilst I can vent clamour from my throat,
I'll tell thee thou dost evil.

LEAR

    Hear me, recreant!
On thy allegiance, hear me!
Since thou hast sought to make us break our vow,
Which we durst never yet, and with strain'd pride
To come between our sentence and our power,
Which nor our nature nor our place can bear,
Our potency made good, take thy reward.
Five days we do allot thee, for provision
To shield thee from diseases of the world,
And on the sixth to turn thy hated back
Upon our kingdom: if on the tenth day following
Thy banish'd trunk be found in our dominions,

The moment is thy death. Away! By Jupiter,
This shall not be revoked.

KENT

Fare thee well, king: sith thus thou wilt appear,
Freedom lives hence, and banishment is here.
[To CORDELIA] The gods to their dear shelter take
    thee, maid,
That justly think'st and hast most rightly said!
[To REGAN and GONERIL] And your large speeches
    may your deeds approve,
That good effects may spring from words of love.
Thus Kent, O princes, bids you all adieu;
He'll shape his old course in a country new.   [Exit

Flourish. Re-enter GLOUCESTER, with FRANCE,
    BURGUNDY, and ATTENDANTS

GLOUCESTER

Here's France and Burgundy, my noble lord.

LEAR

My lord of Burgundy,
We first address towards you, who with this king
Hath rivall'd for our daughter: what, in the least,
Will you require in present dower with her,
Or cease your quest of love?

BURGUNDY

    Most royal majesty,
I crave no more than what your highness offer'd,
Nor will you tender less.

LEAR

    Right noble Burgundy,
When she was dear to us, we did hold her so;
But now her price is fall'n. Sir, there she stands:
If aught within that little seeming substance,
Or all of it, with our displeasure pieced,
And nothing more, may fitly like your grace,
She's there, and she is yours.

BURGUNDY

    I know no answer.

LEAR

Will you, with those infirmities she owes,
Unfriended, new adopted to our hate,
Dower'd with our curse and stranger'd with our
    oath,
Take her, or leave her?

BURGUNDY

    Pardon me, royal sir;
Election makes not up on such conditions.

LEAR

Then leave her, sir; for, by the power that made me,
I tell you all her wealth. [To FRANCE] For you,
    great king,
I would not from your love make such a stray,
To match you where I hate; therefore beseech you
To avert your liking a more worthier way
Than on a wretch whom nature is ashamed
Almost to acknowledge hers.

FRANCE

    This is most strange,
That she, that even but now was your best object,
The argument of your praise, balm of your age,
Most best, most dearest, should in this trice of time

Commit a thing so monstrous, to dismantle
So many folds of favour. Sure, her offence
Must be of such unnatural degree
That monsters it, or your fore-vouch'd affection
Fall'n into taint: which to believe of her,
Must be a faith that reason without miracle
Could never plant in me.

CORDELIA
      I yet beseech your majesty,—
If for I want that glib and oily art,
To speak and purpose not, since what I well intend,
I'll do 't before I speak,—that you make known
It is no vicious blot, murder, or foulness,
No unchaste action, or dishonour'd step,
That hath deprived me of your grace and favour;
But even for want of that for which I am richer,
A still-soliciting eye, and such a tongue
As I am glad I have not, though not to have it
Hath lost me in your liking.

LEAR
      Better thou
Hadst not been born than not to have pleased me
  better.

FRANCE
Is it but this? a tardiness in nature
Which often leaves the history unspoke
That it intends to do? My lord of Burgundy,
What say you to the lady? Love's not love
When it is mingled with regards that stand
Aloof from the entire point. Will you have her?
She is herself a dowry.

BURGUNDY
      Royal Lear,
Give but that portion which yourself proposed,
And here I take Cordelia by the hand,
Duchess of Burgundy.

LEAR
Nothing: I have sworn; I am firm.

BURGUNDY
I am sorry then you have so lost a father
That you must lose a husband.

CORDELIA
      Peace be with Burgundy!
Since that respects of fortune are his love,
I shall not be his wife.

FRANCE
Fairest Cordelia, that art most rich being poor,
Most choice forsaken, and most loved despised,
Thee and thy virtues here I seize upon:
Be it lawful I take up what's cast away.
Gods, gods! 'tis strange that from their cold'st
  neglect
My love should kindle to inflamed respect.
Thy dowerless daughter, king, thrown to my
  chance,
Is queen of us, of ours, and our fair France:
Not all the dukes of waterish Burgundy
Can buy this unprized precious maid of me.
Bid them farewell, Cordelia, though unkind:
Thou losest here, a better where to find.

LEAR
Thou hast her, France: let her be thine, for we
Have no such daughter, nor shall ever see
That face of hers again. Therefore be gone
Without our grace, our love, our benison.
Come, noble Burgundy.   [*Flourish. Exeunt all bu*
    FRANCE, GONERIL, REGAN, *and* CORDELIA

FRANCE
Bid farewell to your sisters.

CORDELIA
The jewels of our father, with wash'd eyes
Cordelia leaves you: I know you what you are;
And, like a sister, am most loath to call
Your faults as they are named. Use well our father:
To your professed bosoms I commit him:
But yet, alas, stood I within his grace,
I would prefer him to a better place.
So farewell to you both.

REGAN
Prescribe not us our duties.

GONERIL
      Let your study
Be to content your lord, who hath received you
At fortune's alms. You have obedience scanted,
And well are worth the want that you have wanted.

CORDELIA
Time shall unfold what plaited cunning hides:
Who cover faults, at last shame them derides.
Well may you prosper!

FRANCE
      Come, my fair Cordelia.
    [*Exeunt* FRANCE *and* CORDELIA

GONERIL
Sister, it is not a little I have to say of what most
nearly appertains to us both. I think our father will
hence to-night.

REGAN
That's most certain, and with you; next month with
us.

GONERIL
You see how full of changes his age is; the observation we have made of it hath not been little: he always loved our sister most; and with what poor
judgement he hath now cast her off appears too
grossly.

REGAN
'Tis the infirmity of his age: yet he hath ever but
slenderly known himself.

GONERIL
The best and soundest of his time hath been but
rash; then must we look to receive from his age, nor
alone the imperfections of long ingrafted condition,
but therewithal the unruly waywardness that infirm
and choleric years bring with them.

REGAN
Such unconstant starts are we like to have from him
as this of Kent's banishment.

GONERIL
There is further compliment of leave-taking between France and him. Pray you, let's hit together:

if our father carry authority with such dispositions as he bears, this last surrender of his will but offend us.

REGAN

We shall further think on 't.

GONERIL

We must do something, and i' the heat.   [*Exeunt*

SCENE II. *The* EARL OF GLOUCESTER'S *castle*

Enter EDMUND, *with a letter*

EDMUND

Thou, nature, art my goddess; to thy law
My services are bound. Wherefore should I
Stand in the plague of custom, and permit
The curiosity of nations to deprive me,
For that I am some twelve or fourteen moonshines
Lag of a brother? Why bastard? wherefore base?
When my dimensions are as well compact,
My mind as generous and my shape as true,
As honest madam's issue? Why brand they us
With base? with baseness? bastardy? base, base?
Who in the lusty stealth of nature take
More composition and fierce quality
Than doth, within a dull, stale, tired bed,
Go to the creating a whole tribe of fops,
Got 'tween asleep and wake? Well then,
Legitimate Edgar, I must have your land:
Our father's love is to the bastard Edmund
As to the legitimate: fine word, 'legitimate'!
Well, my legitimate, if this letter speed
And my invention thrive, Edmund the base
Shall top the legitimate. I grow; I prosper:
Now, gods, stand up for bastards!

Enter GLOUCESTER

GLOUCESTER

Kent banish'd thus! and France in choler parted!
And the king gone to-night! subscribed his power!
Confined to exhibition! All this done
Upon the gad! Edmund, how now! what news?

EDMUND

So please your lordship, none.

        [*Putting up the letter*

GLOUCESTER

Why so earnestly seek you to put up that letter?

EDMUND

I know no news, my lord.

GLOUCESTER

What paper were you reading?

EDMUND

Nothing, my lord.

GLOUCESTER

No? What needed then that terrible dispatch of it into your pocket? the quality of nothing hath not such need to hide itself. Let's see: come, if it be nothing, I shall not need spectacles.

EDMUND

I beseech you, sir, pardon me: it is a letter from my brother, that I have not all o'er-read; and for so

much as I have perused, I find it not fit for your o'er-looking.

GLOUCESTER

Give me the letter, sir.

EDMUND

I shall offend, either to detain or give it. The contents, as in part I understand them, are to blame.

GLOUCESTER

Let's see, let's see.

EDMUND

I hope, for my brother's justification, he wrote this but as an essay or taste of my virtue.

GLOUCESTER

[*Reads*] 'This policy and reverence of age makes the world bitter to the best of our times; keeps our fortunes from us till our oldness cannot relish them. I begin to find an idle and fond bondage in the oppression of aged tyranny; who sways, not as it hath power, but as it is suffered. Come to me, that of this I may speak more. If our father would sleep till I waked him, you should enjoy half his revenue for ever, and live the beloved of your brother,   EDGAR.'

Hum! Conspiracy!—'Sleep till I waked him, you should enjoy half his revenue!'—My son Edgar! Had he a hand to write this? a heart and brain to breed it in? When came this to you? who brought it?

EDMUND

It was not brought me, my lord; there's the cunning of it; I found it thrown in at the casement of my closet.

GLOUCESTER

You know the character to be your brother's?

EDMUND

If the matter were good, my lord, I durst swear it were his; but, in respect of that, I would fain think it were not.

GLOUCESTER

It is his.

EDMUND

It is his hand, my lord; but I hope his heart is not in the contents.

GLOUCESTER

Hath he never heretofore sounded you in this business?

EDMUND

Never, my lord: but I have heard him oft maintain it to be fit, that, sons at perfect age, and fathers declining, the father should be as ward to the son, and the son manage his revenue.

GLOUCESTER

O villain, villain! His very opinion in the letter! Abhorred villain! Unnatural, detested, brutish villain! worse than brutish! Go, sirrah, seek him; ay, apprehend him: abominable villain! Where is he?

EDMUND

I do not well know, my lord. If it shall please you to suspend your indignation against my brother till you can derive from him better testimony of his intent, you should run a certain course; where, if you violently proceed against him, mistaking his purpose, it would make a great gap in your own honour and shake in pieces the heart of his obedience. I dare pawn down my life for him that he hath wrote this to feel my affection to your honour and to no further pretence of danger.

GLOUCESTER

Think you so?

EDMUND

If your honour judge it meet, I will place you where you shall hear us confer of this, and by an auricular assurance have your satisfaction, and that without any further delay than this very evening.

GLOUCESTER

He cannot be such a monster—

EDMUND

Nor is not, sure.

GLOUCESTER

To his father, that so tenderly and entirely loves him. Heaven and earth! Edmund, seek him out; wind me into him, I pray you: frame the business after your own wisdom. I would unstate myself, to be in a due resolution.

EDMUND

I will seek him, sir, presently, convey the business as I shall find means, and acquaint you withal.

GLOUCESTER

These late eclipses in the sun and moon portend no good to us: though the wisdom of nature can reason it thus and thus, yet nature finds itself scourged by the sequent effects: love cools, friendship falls off, brothers divide: in cities, mutinies; in countries, discord; in palaces, treason; and the bond cracked 'twixt son and father. This villain of mine comes under the prediction; there's son against father: the king falls from bias of nature; there's father against child. We have seen the best of our time: machinations, hollowness, treachery and all ruinous disorders follow us disquietly to our graves. Find out this villain, Edmund; it shall lose thee nothing; do it carefully. And the noble and true-hearted Kent banished! his offence, honesty! 'Tis strange.   [Exit

EDMUND

This is the excellent foppery of the world, that when we are sick in fortune—often the surfeit of our own behaviour—we make guilty of our disasters the sun, the moon and the stars: as if we were villains by necessity, fools by heavenly compulsion; knaves, thieves and treachers, by spherical predominance; drunkards, liars and adulterers, by an enforced obedience of planetary influence; and all that we are evil in, by a divine thrusting on: an admirable evasion of whoremaster man, to lay his goatish disposition to the charge of a star! My father compounded with my mother under the dragon's tail, and my nativity was under Ursa major; so that it follows I am rough and lecherous. Tut, I should have been that I am, had the maidenliest star in the firmament twinkled on my bastardizing. Edgar—

Enter EDGAR

And pat he comes like the catastrophe of the old comedy: my cue is villanous melancholy, with a

sigh like Tom o' Bedlam. O, these eclipses do portend these divisions! fa, sol, la, mi.

EDGAR

How now, brother Edmund! what serious contemplation are you in?

EDMUND

I am thinking, brother, of a prediction I read this other day, what should follow these eclipses.

EDGAR

Do you busy yourself about that?

EDMUND

I promise you, the effects he writ of succeed unhappily; as of unnaturalness between the child and the parent; death, dearth, dissolutions of ancient amities; divisions in state, menaces and maledictions against king and nobles; needless diffidences, banishment of friends, dissipation of cohorts, nuptial breaches, and I know not what.

EDGAR

How long have you been a sectary astronomical?

EDMUND

Come, come; when saw you my father last?

EDGAR

Why, the night gone by.

EDMUND

Spake you with him?

EDGAR

Ay, two hours together.

EDMUND

Parted you in good terms? Found you no displeasure in him by word or countenance?

EDGAR

None at all.

EDMUND

Bethink yourself wherein you may have offended him: and at my entreaty forbear his presence till some little time hath qualified the heat of his displeasure, which at this instant so rageth in him that with the mischief of your person it would scarcely allay.

EDGAR

Some villain hath done me wrong.

EDMUND

That's my fear. I pray you, have a continent forbearance till the speed of his rage goes slower, and, as I say, retire with me to my lodging, from whence I will fitly bring you to hear my lord speak: pray ye, go; there's my key: if you do stir abroad, go armed.

EDGAR

Armed, brother!

EDMUND

Brother, I advise you to the best: go armed: I am no honest man if there be any good meaning towards you: I have told you what I have seen and heard; but faintly, nothing like the image and horror of it: pray you, away.

EDGAR

Shall I hear from you anon?

EDMUND

I do serve you in this business.   [Exit EDGAR

A credulous father, and a brother noble,
Whose nature is so far from doing harms
That he suspects none; on whose foolish honesty
My practices ride easy. I see the business.
Let me, if not by birth, have lands by wit:
All with me's meet that I can fashion fit.   [*Exit*

SCENE III. *The* DUKE OF ALBANY'S *palace*

Enter GONERIL *and* OSWALD, *her steward*

GONERIL

Did my father strike my gentleman for chiding of
his fool?

OSWALD

Yes, madam.

GONERIL

By day and night he wrongs me; every hour
He flashes into one gross crime or other,
That sets us all at odds: I'll not endure it:
His knights grow riotous, and himself upbraids us
On every trifle. When he returns from hunting,
I will not speak with him; say I am sick:
If you come slack of former services,
You shall do well; the fault of it I'll answer.

OSWALD

He's coming, madam; I hear him.   [*Horns within*

GONERIL

Put on what weary negligence you please,
You and your fellows; I'ld have it come to ques-
tion:
If he distaste it, let him to our sister,
Whose mind and mine, I know, in that are one,
Not to be over-ruled. Idle old man,
That still would manage those authorities
That he hath given away! Now, by my life,
Old fools are babes again, and must be used
With checks as flatteries, when they are seen abused.
Remember what I tell you.

OSWALD

          Very well, madam.

GONERIL

And let his knights have colder looks among you;
What grows of it, no matter; advice your fellows so:
I would breed from hence occasions, and I shall,
That I may speak: I'll write straight to my sister,
To hold my very course. Prepare for dinner.

          [*Exeunt*

SCENE IV. *A hall in the same*

Enter KENT, *disguised*

KENT

If but as well I other accents borrow,
That can my speech defuse, my good intent
May carry through itself to that full issue
For which I razed my likeness. Now, banish'd Kent,
If thou canst serve where thou dost stand con-
          demn'd,

So may it come, thy master whom thou lovest
Shall find thee full of labours.

Horns within. Enter LEAR, KNIGHTS, *and* ATTENDANTS

LEAR

Let me not stay a jot for dinner; go get it ready.
[*Exit an* ATTENDANT] How now! what art thou?

KENT

A man, sir.

LEAR

What dost thou profess? What wouldst thou with
us?

KENT

I do profess to be no less than I seem; to serve him
truly that will put me in trust; to love him that is
honest; to converse with him that is wise and says
little; to fear judgement; to fight when I cannot
choose, and to eat no fish.

LEAR

What art thou?

KENT

A very honest-hearted fellow, and as poor as the
king.

LEAR

If thou be as poor for a subject as he is for a king,
thou art poor enough. What wouldst thou?

KENT

Service.

LEAR

Who wouldst thou serve?

KENT

You.

LEAR

Dost thou know me, fellow?

KENT

No, sir; but you have that in your countenance
which I would fain call master.

LEAR

What's that?

KENT

Authority.

LEAR

What services canst thou do?

KENT

I can keep honest counsel, ride, run, mar a curious
tale in telling it, and deliver a plain message
bluntly: that which ordinary men are fit for, I am
qualified in, and the best of me is diligence.

LEAR

How old art thou?

KENT

Not so young, sir, to love a woman for singing, nor
so old to dote on her for any thing: I have years on
my back forty eight.

LEAR

Follow me; thou shalt serve me: if I like thee no
worse after dinner, I will not part from thee yet.
Dinner, ho, dinner! Where's my knave? my fool?
Go you, and call my fool hither.

          [*Exit an* ATTENDANT

Enter OSWALD

You, you, sirrah, where's my daughter?

OSWALD

So please you,—   [*Exit*

LEAR

What says the fellow there? Call the clotpoll back. [*Exit a* KNIGHT] Where's my fool, ho? I think the world's asleep.

Re-enter KNIGHT

How now! where's that mongrel?

KNIGHT

He says, my lord, your daughter is not well.

LEAR

Why came not the slave back to me when I called him?

KNIGHT

Sir, he answered me in the roundest manner, he would not.

LEAR

He would not!

KNIGHT

My lord, I know not what the matter is; but, to my judgement, your highness is not entertained with that ceremonious affection as you were wont; there's a great abatement of kindness appears as well in the general dependants as in the duke himself also and your daughter.

LEAR

Ha! sayest thou so?

KNIGHT

I beseech you, pardon me, my lord, if I be mistaken; for my duty cannot be silent when I think your highness wronged.

LEAR

Thou but rememberest me of mine own conception: I have perceived a most faint neglect of late; which I have rather blamed as mine own jealous curiosity than as a very pretence and purpose of unkindness: I will look further into 't. But where's my fool? I have not seen him this two days.

KNIGHT

Since my young lady's going into France, sir, the fool hath much pined away.

LEAR

No more of that; I have noted it well. Go you, and tell my daughter I would speak with her. [*Exit an* ATTENDANT] Go you, call hither my fool.

[*Exit an* ATTENDANT

Re-enter OSWALD

O, you sir, you, come you hither, sir: who am I, sir?

OSWALD

My lady's father.

LEAR

My lady's father! my lord's knave: you whoreson dog! you slave! you cur!

OSWALD

I am none of these, my lord; I beseech your pardon.

LEAR

Do you bandy looks with me, you rascal?

[*Striking him*

OSWALD

I'll not be struck, my lord.

KENT

Nor tripped neither, you base foot-ball player.

[*Tripping up his heels*

LEAR

I thank thee, fellow; thou servest me, and I'll love thee.

KENT

Come, sir, arise, away! I'll teach you differences: away, away! If you will measure your lubber's length again, tarry: but away! go to; have you wisdom? so.   [*Pushes* OSWALD *out*

LEAR

Now, my friendly knave, I thank thee: there's earnest of thy service.   [*Giving* KENT *money*

Enter FOOL

FOOL

Let me hire him too: here's my coxcomb.

[*Offering* KENT *his cap*

LEAR

How now, my pretty knave! how dost thou?

FOOL

Sirrah, you were best take my coxcomb.

KENT

Why, fool?

FOOL

Why, for taking one's part that's out of favour: nay, an thou canst not smile as the wind sits, thou'lt catch cold shortly: there, take my coxcomb: why, this fellow hath banished two on 's daughters, and done the third a blessing against his will; if thou follow him, thou must needs wear my coxcomb. How now, nuncle! Would I had two coxcombs and two daughters!

LEAR

Why, my boy?

FOOL

If I gave them all my living, I'ld keep my coxcombs myself. There's mine; beg another of thy daughters.

LEAR

Take heed, sirrah; the whip.

FOOL

Truth's a dog must to kennel; he must be whipped out, when Lady the brach may stand by the fire and stink.

LEAR

A pestilent gall to me!

FOOL

Sirrah, I'll teach thee a speech.

LEAR

Do.

FOOL

Mark it, nuncle:

> Have more than thou showest,
> Speak less than thou knowest,
> Lend less than thou owest,
> Ride more than thou goest,
> Learn more than thou trowest,
> Set less than thou throwest;

Leave thy drink and thy whore,
And keep in-a-door,
And thou shalt have more
Than two tens to a score.

KENT

This is nothing, fool.

FOOL

Then 'tis like the breath of an unfee'd lawyer, you
gave me nothing for 't. Can you make no use of
nothing, nuncle?

LEAR

Why, no, boy; nothing can be made out of nothing.

FOOL

[To KENT] Prithee, tell him, so much the rent of his
land comes to: he will not believe a fool.

LEAR

A bitter fool!

FOOL

Dost thou know the difference, my boy, between a
bitter fool and a sweet fool?

LEAR

No, lad; teach me.

FOOL

That lord that counsell'd thee
To give away thy land,
Come place him here by me;
Do thou for him stand:
The sweet and bitter fool
Will presently appear;
The one in motley here,
The other found out there.

LEAR

Dost thou call me fool, boy?

FOOL

All thy other titles thou hast given away; that thou
wast born with.

KENT

This is not altogether fool, my lord.

FOOL

No, faith, lords and great men will not let me; if I
had a monopoly out, they would have part on 't:
and ladies too, they will not let me have all the fool
to myself; they'll be snatching. Give me an egg,
nuncle, and I'll give thee two crowns.

LEAR

What two crowns shall they be?

FOOL

Why, after I have cut the egg in the middle and eat
up the meat, the two crowns of the egg. When thou
clovest thy crown i' the middle and gavest away
both parts, thou borest thine ass on thy back o'er
the dirt: thou hadst little wit in thy bald crown
when thou gavest thy golden one away. If I speak
like myself in this, let him be whipped that first
finds it so.

[Singing]   Fools had ne'er less wit in a year;
For wise men are grown foppish,
And know not how their wits to wear,
Their manners are so apish.

LEAR

When were you wont to be so full of songs, sirrah?

FOOL

I have used it, nuncle, ever since thou madest thy
daughters thy mother: for when thou gavest them
the rod and puttest down thine own breeches,

[Singing]   Then they for sudden joy did weep,
And I for sorrow sung,
That such a king should play bo-peep,
And go the fools among.

Prithee, nuncle, keep a schoolmaster that can teach
thy fool to lie: I would fain learn to lie.

LEAR

An you lie, sirrah, we'll have you whipped.

FOOL

I marvel what kin thou and thy daughters are:
they'll have me whipped for speaking true, thou'lt
have me whipped for lying, and sometimes I am
whipped for holding my peace. I had rather be any
kind o' thing than a fool: and yet I would not be
thee, nuncle; thou hast pared thy wit o' both sides
and left nothing i' the middle. Here comes one o'
the parings.

Enter GONERIL

LEAR

How now, daughter! what makes that frontlet on?
Methinks you are too much of late i' the frown.

FOOL

Thou wast a pretty fellow when thou hadst no need
to care for her frowning; now thou art an O without a figure: I am better than thou art now; I am a
fool, thou art nothing. [To GONERIL] Yes, forsooth,
I will hold my tongue; so your face bids me, though
you say nothing.

Mum, mum:
He that keeps nor crust nor crumb,
Weary of all, shall want some.

[Pointing to LEAR] That's a shealed peascod.

GONERIL

Not only, sir, this your all-licensed fool,
But other of your insolent retinue
Do hourly carp and quarrel, breaking forth
In rank and not to be endured riots. Sir,
I had thought, by making this well known unto you,
To have found a safe redress; but now grow fearful,
By what yourself too late have spoke and done,
That you protect this course and put it on
By your allowance; which if you should, the fault
Would not 'scape censure, nor the redresses sleep,
Which, in the tender of a wholesome weal,
Might in their working do you that offence
Which else were shame, that then necessity
Will call discreet proceeding.

FOOL

For, you know, nuncle,

The hedge-sparrow fed the cuckoo so long,
That it had it head bit off by it young.

So out went the candle, and we were left darkling.

LEAR

Are you our daughter?

GONERIL

Come, sir,
I would you would make use of that good wisdom
Whereof I know you are fraught, and put away
These dispositions that of late transform you
From what you rightly are.

FOOL

May not an ass know when the cart draws the
horse? Whoop, Jug! I love thee.

LEAR

Doth any here know me? This is not Lear:
Doth Lear walk thus? speak thus? Where are his
eyes?
Either his notion weakens, his discernings
Are lethargied—Ha! waking? 'tis not so.
Who is it that can tell me who I am?

FOOL

Lear's shadow.

LEAR

I would learn that; for, by the marks of sovereignty,
knowledge and reason, I should be false persuaded
I had daughters.

FOOL

Which they will make an obedient father.

LEAR

Your name, fair gentlewoman?

GONERIL

This admiration, sir, is much o' the savour
Of other your new pranks. I do beseech you
To understand my purposes aright:
As you are old and reverend, you should be wise.
Here do you keep a hundred knights and squires;
Men so disorder'd, so debosh'd and bold,
That this our court, infected with their manners,
Shows like a riotous inn: epicurism and lust
Make it more like a tavern or a brothel
Than a graced palace. The shame itself doth speak
For instant remedy: be then desired
By her that else will take the thing she begs
A little to disquantity your train,
And the remainder that shall still depend,
To be such men as may besort your age,
Which know themselves and you.

LEAR

　　　　　　　　　　Darkness and devils!
Saddle my horses; call my train together.
Degenerate bastard! I'll not trouble thee:
Yet have I left a daughter.

GONERIL

You strike my people, and your disorder'd rabble
Make servants of their betters.

Enter ALBANY

LEAR

Woe, that too late repents,— [*To* ALBANY] O, sir, are
you come?
Is it your will? Speak, sir. Prepare my horses.
Ingratitude, thou marble-hearted fiend,
More hideous when thou show'st thee in a child
Than the sea-monster'

ALBANY

　　　　Pray, sir, be patient.

LEAR

[*To* GONERIL] Detested kite! thou liest.
My train are men of choice and rarest parts,
That all particulars of duty know,
And in the most exact regard support
The worships of their name. O most small fault,
How ugly didst thou in Cordelia show!
That, like an engine, wrench'd my frame of nature
From the fix'd place, drew from my heart all love
And added to the gall. O Lear, Lear, Lear!
Beat at this gate, that let thy folly in [*Striking his head*
And thy dear judgement out! Go, go, my people.

ALBANY

My lord, I am guiltless, as I am ignorant
Of what hath moved you.

LEAR

　　　　　　　　It may be so, my lord.
Hear, nature, hear; dear goddess, hear!
Suspend thy purpose, if thou didst intend
To make this creature fruitful:
Into her womb convey sterility:
Dry up in her the organs of increase,
And from her derogate body never spring
A babe to honour her! If she must teem,
Create her child of spleen, that it may live
And be a thwart disnatured torment to her.
Let it stamp wrinkles in her brow of youth;
With cadent tears fret channels in her cheeks;
Turn all her mother's pains and benefits
To laughter and contempt; that she may feel
How sharper than a serpent's tooth it is
To have a thankless child! Away, away!　　　[*Exit*

ALBANY

Now, gods that we adore, whereof comes this?

GONERIL

Never afflict yourself to know the cause,
But let his disposition have that scope
That dotage gives it.

Re-enter LEAR

LEAR

What, fifty of my followers at a clap!
Within a fortnight!

ALBANY

　　　　What's the matter, sir?

LEAR

I'll tell thee. [*To* GONERIL] Life and death! I am
ashamed
That thou hast power to shake my manhood thus;
That these hot tears, which break from me perforce,
Should make thee worth them. Blasts and fogs upon
thee!
The untented woundings of a father's curse
Pierce every sense about thee! Old fond eyes,
Beweep this cause again, I'll pluck ye out
And cast you with the waters that you lose
To temper clay. Yea, is it come to this?
Let it be so: yet have I left a daughter,
Who, I am sure, is kind and comfortable:

When she shall hear this of thee, with her nails
She'll flay thy wolvish visage. Thou shalt find
That I'll resume the shape which thou dost think
I have cast off for ever: thou shalt, I warrant thee.
            [*Exeunt* LEAR, KENT, *and* ATTENDANTS

GONERIL

Do you mark that, my lord?

ALBANY

I cannot be so partial, Goneril,
To the great love I bear you,—

GONERIL

Pray you, content. What, Oswald, ho!
[*To the* FOOL] You, sir, more knave than fool, after
    your master.

FOOL

Nuncle Lear, nuncle Lear, tarry; take the fool with
thee.

> A fox, when one has caught her,
> And such a daughter,
> Should sure to the slaughter,
> If my cap would buy a halter:
> So the fool follows after.
>   [*Exit*

GONERIL

This man hath had good counsel: a hundred
    knights!
'Tis politic and safe to let him keep
At point a hundred knights: yes, that on every
    dream,
Each buzz, each fancy, each complaint, dislike,
He may enguard his dotage with their powers
And hold our lives in mercy. Oswald, I say!

ALBANY

Well, you may fear too far.

GONERIL

                        Safer than trust too far:
Let me still take away the harms I fear,
Not fear still to be taken: I know his heart.
What he hath utter'd I have writ my sister:
If she sustain him and his hundred knights,
When I have show'd the unfitness,—

Re-enter OSWALD

                        How now, Oswald!
What, have you writ that letter to my sister?

OSWALD

Yes, madam.

GONERIL

Take you some company, and away to horse:
Inform her full of my particular fear,
And thereto add such reasons of your own
As may compact it more. Get you gone;
And hasten your return. [*Exit* OSWALD] No, no, my
    lord,
This milky gentleness and course of yours
Though I condemn not, yet, under pardon,
You are much more attask'd for want of wisdom
Than praised for harmful mildness.

ALBANY

How far your eyes may pierce I cannot tell:
Striving to better, oft we mar what's well.

GONERIL

Nay, then—

ALBANY

Well, well; the event.   [*Exeunt*

SCENE V. *Court before the same*

Enter LEAR, KENT, *and* FOOL

LEAR

Go you before to Gloucester with these letters.
Acquaint my daughter no further with any thing
you know than comes from her demand out of the
letter. If your diligence be not speedy, I shall be
there afore you.

KENT

I will not sleep, my lord, till I have delivered your
letter.   [*Exit*

FOOL

If a man's brains were in 's heels, were 't not in
danger of kibes?

LEAR

Ay, boy.

FOOL

Then, I prithee, be merry; thy wit shall ne'er go
slip-shod.

LEAR

Ha, ha, ha!

FOOL

Shalt see thy other daughter will use thee kindly;
for though she's as like this as a crab's like an apple,
yet I can tell what I can tell.

LEAR

Why, what canst thou tell, my boy?

FOOL

She will taste as like this as a crab does to a crab.
Thou canst tell why one's nose stands i' the middle
on 's face?

LEAR

No.

FOOL

Why, to keep one's eyes of either side 's nose, that
what a man cannot smell out he may spy into.

LEAR

I did her wrong—

FOOL

Canst tell how an oyster makes his shell?

LEAR

No.

FOOL

Nor I neither; but I can tell why a snail has a house.

LEAR

Why?

FOOL

Why, to put 's head in; not to give it away to his
daughters, and leave his horns without a case.

LEAR

I will forget my nature.—So kind a father!—Be my
horses ready?

FOOL

Thy asses are gone about 'em. The reason why the seven stars are no more than seven is a pretty reason.

LEAR

Because they are not eight?

FOOL

Yes, indeed: thou wouldst make a good fool.

LEAR

To take 't again perforce! Monster ingratitude!

FOOL

If thou wert my fool, nuncle, I'ld have thee beaten for being old before thy time.

LEAR

How's that?

FOOL

Thou shouldst not have been old till thou hadst been wise.

LEAR

O, let me not be mad, not mad, sweet heaven! Keep me in temper: I would not be mad!

Enter GENTLEMAN

How now! are the horses ready?

GENTLEMAN

Ready, my lord.

LEAR

Come, boy.

FOOL

She that's a maid now and laughs at my departure Shall not be a maid long, unless things be cut shorter.   [*Exeunt*

ACT II

SCENE I. *The* EARL OF GLOUCESTER'S *castle*

Enter EDMUND *and* CURAN, *meeting*

EDMUND

Save thee, Curan.

CURAN

And you, sir. I have been with your father, and given him notice that the Duke of Cornwall and Regan his duchess will be here with him this night.

EDMUND

How comes that?

CURAN

Nay, I know not. You have heard of the news abroad, I mean the whispered ones, for they are yet but ear-kissing arguments?

EDMUND

Not I: pray you, what are they?

CURAN

Have you heard of no likely wars toward, 'twixt the Dukes of Cornwall and Albany?

EDMUND

Not a word.

CURAN

You may do then in time. Fare you well, sir. [*Exit*

EDMUND

The duke be here to-night? The better! best!

This weaves itself perforce into my business. My father hath set guard to take my brother; And I have one thing, of a queasy question, Which I must act: briefness and fortune, work! Brother, a word; descend: brother, I say!

Enter EDGAR

My father watches: O sir, fly this place; Intelligence is given where you are hid; You have now the good advantage of the night: Have you not spoken 'gainst the Duke of Cornwall? He's coming hither, now, i' the night, i' the haste, And Regan with him: have you nothing said Upon his party 'gainst the Duke of Albany? Advise yourself.

EDGAR

I am sure on 't, not a word.

EDMUND

I hear my father coming: pardon me: In cunning I must draw my sword upon you: Draw: seem to defend yourself: now quit you well. Yield: come before my father. Light, ho, here! Fly, brother. Torches, torches! So farewell.

[*Exit* EDGAR

Some blood drawn on me would beget opinion

[*Wounds his arm*

Of my more fierce endeavour: I have seen drunkards Do more than this in sport. Father, father! Stop, stop! No help?

Enter GLOUCESTER, *and* SERVANTS *with torches*

GLOUCESTER

Now, Edmund, where's the villain?

EDMUND

Here stood he in the dark, his sharp sword out, Mumbling of wicked charms, conjuring the moon To stand 's auspicious mistress.

GLOUCESTER

But where is he?

EDMUND

Look, sir, I bleed.

GLOUCESTER

Where is the villain, Edmund?

EDMUND

Fled this way, sir. When by no means he could—

GLOUCESTER

Pursue him, ho!—Go after. [*Exeunt some* SERVANTS] 'By no means' what?

EDMUND

Persuade me to the murder of your lordship; But that I told him the revenging gods 'Gainst parricides did all their thunders bend, Spoke with how manifold and strong a bond The child was bound to the father; sir, in fine, Seeing how loathly opposite I stood To his unnatural purpose, in fell motion With his prepared sword he charges home My unprovided body, lanced mine arm: But when he saw my best alarum'd spirits Bold in the quarrel's right, roused to the encounter,

Or whether gasted by the noise I made,
Full suddenly he fled.

GLOUCESTER
          Let him fly far:
Not in this land shall he remain uncaught;
And found—dispatch. The noble duke my master,
My worthy arch and patron, comes to-night:
By his authority I will proclaim it,
That he which finds him shall deserve our thanks,
Bringing the murderous caitiff to the stake;
He that conceals him, death.

EDMUND
When I dissuaded him from his intent
And found him pight to do it, with curst speech
I threaten'd to discover him: he replied,
'Thou unpossessing bastard! dost thou think,
If I would stand against thee, could the reposure
Of any trust, virtue, or worth, in thee
Make thy words faith'd? No: what I should deny—
As this I would; ay, though thou didst produce
My very character—I'ld turn it all
To thy suggestion, plot, and damned practice:
And thou must make a dullard of the world,
If they not thought the profits of my death
Were very pregnant and potential spurs
To make thee seek it.'

GLOUCESTER
          Strong and fasten'd villain!
Would he deny his letter? I never got him.
                    [Tucket within
Hark, the duke's trumpets! I know not why he
  comes.
All ports I'll bar; the villain shall not 'scape;
The duke must grant me that: besides, his picture
I will send far and near, that all the kingdom
May have due note of him; and of my land,
Loyal and natural boy, I'll work the means
To make thee capable.

    Enter CORNWALL, REGAN, and ATTENDANTS

CORNWALL
How now, my noble friend! since I came hither,
Which I can call but now, I have heard strange
  news.

REGAN
If it be true, all vengeance comes too short
Which can pursue the offender. How dost, my lord?

GLOUCESTER
O, madam, my old heart is crack'd, is crack'd!

REGAN
What, did my father's godson seek your life?
He whom my father named? your Edgar?

GLOUCESTER
O, lady, lady, shame would have it hid!

REGAN
Was he not companion with the riotous knights
That tend upon my father?

GLOUCESTER
I know not, madam: 'tis too bad, too bad.

EDMUND
Yes, madam, he was of that consort.

REGAN
No marvel then, though he were ill affected:
'Tis they have put him on the old man's death,
To have the waste and spoil of his revenues.
I have this present evening from my sister
Been well inform'd of them, and with such cautions
That if they come to sojourn at my house,
I'll not be there.

CORNWALL
        Nor I, assure thee, Regan.
Edmund, I hear that you have shown your father
A child-like office.

EDMUND
        'Twas my duty, sir.

GLOUCESTER
He did bewray his practice, and received
This hurt you see, striving to apprehend him.

CORNWALL
Is he pursued?

GLOUCESTER
        Ay, my good lord.

CORNWALL
If he be taken, he shall never more
Be fear'd of doing harm: make your own purpose,
How in my strength you please. For you, Edmund,
Whose virtue and obedience doth this instant
So much commend itself, you shall be ours:
Natures of such deep trust we shall much need:
You we first seize on.

EDMUND
        I shall serve you, sir,
Truly, however else.

GLOUCESTER
        For him I thank your grace.

CORNWALL
You know not why we came to visit you,—

REGAN
Thus out of season, threading dark-eyed night:
Occasions, noble Gloucester, of some poise,
Wherein we must have use of your advice:
Our father he hath writ, so hath our sister,
Of differences, which I least thought it fit
To answer from our home; the several messengers
From hence attend dispatch. Our good old friend,
Lay comforts to your bosom, and bestow
Your needful counsel to our business,
Which craves the instant use.

GLOUCESTER
        I serve you, madam:
Your graces are right welcome.   [Flourish. Exeunt

SCENE II. Before GLOUCESTER's castle

Enter KENT and OSWALD, severally

OSWALD
Good dawning to thee, friend: art of this house?

KENT
Ay.

OSWALD

Where may we set our horses?

KENT

I' the mire.

OSWALD

Prithee, if thou lovest me, tell me.

KENT

I love thee not.

OSWALD

Why then I care not for thee.

KENT

If I had thee in Lipsbury pinfold, I would make thee care for me.

OSWALD

Why dost thou use me thus? I know thee not.

KENT

Fellow, I know thee.

OSWALD

What dost thou know me for?

KENT

A knave; a rascal; an eater of broken meats; a base, proud, shallow, beggarly, three-suited, hundred-pound, filthy, worsted-stocking knave; a lily-livered, action-taking knave; a whoreson, glass-gazing, su-perserviceable, finical rogue; one-trunk-inheriting slave; one that wouldst be a bawd in way of good service, and art nothing but the composition of a knave, beggar, coward, pandar, and the son and heir of a mongrel bitch: one whom I will beat into clamorous whining, if thou deniest the least syllable of thy addition.

OSWALD

Why, what a monstrous fellow art thou, thus to rail on one that is neither known of thee nor knows thee!

KENT

What a brazen-faced varlet art thou, to deny thou knowest me! Is it two days ago since I tripped up thy heels and beat thee before the king? Draw, you rogue: for, though it be night, yet the moon shines; I'll make a sop o' the moonshine of you: draw, you whoreson cullionly barber-monger, draw.

[Drawing his sword

OSWALD

Away! I have nothing to do with thee.

KENT

Draw, you rascal: you come with letters against the king, and take vanity the puppet's part against the royalty of her father: draw, you rogue, or I'll so car-bonado your shanks: draw, you rascal; come your ways.

OSWALD

Help, ho! murder! help!

KENT

Strike, you slave; stand, rogue; stand, you neat slave, strike. [Beating him

OSWALD

Help, ho! murder! murder!

Enter EDMUND, with his rapier drawn, CORNWALL, REGAN, GLOUCESTER, and SERVANTS

EDMUND

How now! What's the matter? [Parting them

KENT

With you, goodman boy, an you please: come, I'll flesh you; come on, young master.

GLOUCESTER

Weapons! arms! What's the matter here?

CORNWALL

Keep peace, upon your lives;
He dies that strikes again. What is the matter?

REGAN

The messengers from our sister and the king.

CORNWALL

What is your difference? speak.

OSWALD

I am scarce in breath, my lord.

KENT

No marvel, you have so bestirred your valour. You cowardly rascal, nature disclaims in thee: a tailor made thee.

CORNWALL

Thou art a strange fellow: a tailor make a man?

KENT

Ay, a tailor, sir: a stone-cutter or a painter could not have made him so ill, though he had been but two hours at the trade.

CORNWALL

Speak yet, how grew your quarrel?

OSWALD

This ancient ruffian, sir, whose life I have spared at suit of his gray beard,—

KENT

Thou whoreson zed! thou unnecessary letter! My lord, if you will give me leave, I will tread this un-bolted villain into mortar, and daub the walls of a jakes with him. Spare my gray beard, you wagtail?

CORNWALL

Peace, sirrah!
You beastly knave, know you no reverence?

KENT

Yes, sir; but anger hath a privilege.

CORNWALL

Why art thou angry?

KENT

That such a slave as this should wear a sword,
Who wears no honesty. Such smiling rogues as these,
Like rats, oft bite the holy cords a-twain
Which are too intrinse to unloose; smooth every
    passion
That in the natures of their lords rebel;
Bring oil to fire, snow to their colder moods;
Renege, affirm, and turn their halcyon beaks
With every gale and vary of their masters,
Knowing nought, like dogs, but following.
A plague upon your epileptic visage!
Smile you my speeches, as I were a fool?
Goose, if I had you upon Sarum plain,
I'ld drive ye cackling home to Camelot.

CORNWALL

What, art thou mad, old fellow?

GLOUCESTER

How fell you out? say that.

KENT

No contraries hold more antipathy
Than I and such a knave.

CORNWALL

Why dost thou call him knave? What is his fault?

KENT

His countenance likes me not.

CORNWALL

No more perchance does mine, nor his, nor hers.

KENT

Sir, 'tis my occupation to be plain:
I have seen better faces in my time
Than stands on any shoulder that I see
Before me at this instant.

CORNWALL

              This is some fellow,
Who, having been praised for bluntness, doth affect
A saucy roughness, and constrains the garb
Quite from his nature: he cannot flatter, he,—
An honest mind and plain,—he must speak truth!
An they will take it, so; if not, he's plain.
These kind of knaves I know, which in this plainness
Harbour more craft and more corrupter ends
Than twenty silly ducking observants
That stretch their duties nicely.

KENT

Sir, in good faith, in sincere verity,
Under the allowance of your great aspect,
Whose influence, like the wreath of radiant fire
On flickering Phœbus' front,—

CORNWALL

            What mean'st by this?

KENT

To go out of my dialect, which you discommend so
much. I know, sir, I am no flatterer: he that beguiled you in a plain accent was a plain knave;
which, for my part, I will not be, though I should
win your displeasure to entreat me to 't.

CORNWALL

What was the offence you gave him?

OSWALD

I never gave him any:
It pleased the king his master very late
To strike at me, upon his misconstruction;
When he, conjunct, and flattering his displeasure,
Tripp'd me behind; being down, insulted, rail'd,
And put upon him such a deal of man,
That worthied him, got praises of the king
For him attempting who was self-subdued,
And in the fleshment of this dread exploit
Drew on me here again.

KENT

           None of these rogues and cowards
But Ajax is their fool.

CORNWALL

           Fetch forth the stocks!
You stubborn ancient knave, you reverend braggart,
We'll teach you—

KENT

           Sir, I am too old to learn:
Call not your stocks for me: I serve the king,
On whose employment I was sent to you:
You shall do small respect, show too bold malice
Against the grace and person of my master,
Stocking his messenger.

CORNWALL

Fetch forth the stocks! As I have life and honour,
There shall he sit till noon.

REGAN

Till noon! till night, my lord, and all night too.

KENT

Why, madam, if I were your father's dog,
You should not use me so.

REGAN

           Sir, being his knave, I will.

CORNWALL

This is a fellow of the self-same colour
Our sister speaks of. Come, bring away the stocks!

           [*Stocks brought out*

GLOUCESTER

Let me beseech your grace not to do so:
His fault is much, and the good king his master
Will check him for 't: your purposed low correction
Is such as basest and contemned'st wretches
For pilferings and most common trespasses
Are punish'd with: the king must take it ill,
That he, so slightly valued in his messenger,
Should have him thus restrain'd.

CORNWALL

           I'll answer that.

REGAN

My sister may receive it much more worse,
To have her gentleman abused, assaulted,
For following her affairs. Put in his legs.

           [KENT *is put in the stocks*

Come, my good lord, away.

           [*Exeunt all but* GLOUCESTER *and* KENT

GLOUCESTER

I am sorry for thee, friend; 'tis the duke's pleasure,
Whose disposition, all the world well knows,
Will not be rubb'd nor stopp'd: I'll entreat for thee.

KENT

Pray, do not, sir: I have watch'd and travell'd hard;
Some time I shall sleep out, the rest I'll whistle.
A good man's fortune may grow out at heels:
Give you good morrow!

GLOUCESTER

The duke's to blame in this; 'twill be ill taken.

           [*Exit*

KENT

Good king, that must approve the common saw,
Thou out of heaven's benediction comest
To the warm sun!
Approach, thou beacon to this under globe,
That by thy comfortable beams I may
Peruse this letter! Nothing almost sees miracles
But misery: I know 'tis from Cordelia,
Who hath most fortunately been inform'd

Of my obscured course; and shall find time
From this enormous state, seeking to give
Losses their remedies. All weary and o'er-watch'd,
Take vantage, heavy eyes, not to behold
This shameful lodging.
Fortune, good night: smile once more; turn thy
   wheel!   [*Sleeps*

SCENE III. *A wood*

Enter EDGAR

EDGAR

I heard myself proclaim'd;
And by the happy hollow of a tree
Escaped the hunt. No port is free; no place,
That guard and most unusual vigilance
Does not attend my taking. Whiles I may 'scape
I will preserve myself: and am bethought
To take the basest and most poorest shape
That ever penury in contempt of man
Brought near to beast: my face I'll grime with filth,
Blanket my loins, elf all my hair in knots,
And with presented nakedness out-face
The winds and persecutions of the sky.
The country gives me proof and precedent
Of Bedlam beggars, who with roaring voices
Strike in their numb'd and mortified bare arms
Pins, wooden pricks, nails, sprigs of rosemary;
And with this horrible object, from low farms,
Poor pelting villages, sheep-cotes and mills,
Sometime with lunatic bans, sometime with prayers,
Enforce their charity. Poor Turlygod! poor Tom!
That's something yet: Edgar I nothing am.   [*Exit*

SCENE IV. *Before* GLOUCESTER'S *castle.* KENT *in the stocks*

Enter LEAR, FOOL, *and* GENTLEMAN

LEAR

'Tis strange that they should so depart from home,
And not send back my messenger.

GENTLEMAN

                 As I learn'd,
The night before there was no purpose in them
Of this remove.

KENT

        Hail to thee, noble master!

LEAR

Ha!
Makest thou this shame thy pastime?

KENT

                No, my lord.

FOOL

Ha, ha! he wears cruel garters. Horses are tied by
the heads, dogs and bears by the neck, monkeys by
the loins, and men by the legs: when a man's over-
lusty at legs, then he wears wooden nether-stocks.

LEAR

What's he that hath so much thy place mistook
To set thee here?

KENT

           It is both he and she;
Your son and daughter.

LEAR

No.

KENT

Yes.

LEAR

No, I say.

KENT

I say, yea.

LEAR

No, no, they would not.

KENT

Yes, they have.

LEAR

By Jupiter, I swear, no.

KENT

By Juno, I swear, ay.

LEAR

              They durst not do 't;
They could not, would not do 't; 'tis worse than
   murder,
To do upon respect such violent outrage:
Resolve me with all modest haste which way
Thou mightst deserve, or they impose, this usage,
Coming from us.

KENT

           My lord, when at their home
I did commend your highness' letters to them,
Ere I was risen from the place that show'd
My duty kneeling, came there a reeking post,
Stew'd in his haste, half breathless, panting forth
From Goneril his mistress salutations;
Deliver'd letters, spite of intermission,
Which presently they read: on whose contents
They summon'd up their meiny, straight took horse;
Commanded me to follow and attend
The leisure of their answer; gave me cold looks:
And meeting here the other messenger,
Whose welcome, I perceived, had poison'd mine—
Being the very fellow that of late
Display'd so saucily against your highness—
Having more man than wit about me, drew:
He raised the house with loud and coward cries.
Your son and daughter found this trespass worth
The shame which here it suffers.

FOOL

Winter's not gone yet, if the wild geese fly that way.

     Fathers that wear rags
       Do make their children blind;
     But fathers that bear bags
       Shall see their children kind.
     Fortune, that arrant whore,
     Ne'er turns the key to the poor.

But, for all this, thou shalt have as many dolours for
thy daughters as thou canst tell in a year.

LEAR

O, how this mother swells up toward my heart!
Hysterica passio, down, thou climbing sorrow,
Thy element's below! Where is this daughter?

KENT

With the earl, sir, here within.

LEAR

Follow me not; stay here.　　　　　　　[*Exit*

GENTLEMAN

Made you no more offence but what you speak of?

KENT

None.
How chance the king comes with so small a train?

FOOL

An thou hadst been set i' the stocks for that question, thou hadst well deserved it.

KENT

Why, fool?

FOOL

We'll set thee to school to an ant, to teach thee
there's no labouring i' the winter. All that follow
their noses are led by their eyes but blind men; and
there's not a nose among twenty but can smell him
that's stinking. Let go thy hold when a great wheel
runs down a hill, lest it break thy neck with following it; but the great one that goes up the hill, let him
draw thee after. When a wise man gives thee better
counsel, give me mine again: I would have none but
knaves follow it, since a fool gives it.

> That sir which serves and seeks for gain,
> 　　And follows but for form,
> Will pack when it begins to rain,
> 　　And leave thee in the storm.
>
> But I will tarry; the fool will stay,
> 　　And let the wise man fly:
> The knave turns fool that runs away;
> 　　The fool no knave, perdy.

KENT

Where learned you this, fool?

FOOL

Not i' the stocks, fool.

Re-enter LEAR, *with* GLOUCESTER

LEAR

Deny to speak with me? They are sick? they are
weary?
They have travell'd all the night? Mere fetches;
The images of revolt and flying off.
Fetch me a better answer.

GLOUCESTER

　　　　　　　　My dear lord,
You know the fiery quality of the duke;
How unremoveable and fix'd he is
In his own course.

LEAR

Vengeance! plague! death! confusion!
Fiery? what quality? Why, Gloucester, Gloucester,
I' ld speak with the Duke of Cornwall and his wife.

GLOUCESTER

Well, my good lord, I have inform'd them so.

LEAR

Inform'd them! Dost thou understand me, man?

GLOUCESTER

Ay, my good lord.

LEAR

The king would speak with Cornwall; the dear
father
Would with his daughter speak, commands her
service:
Are they inform'd of this? My breath and blood!
'Fiery'? 'the fiery duke'? Tell the hot duke that—
No, but not yet: may be he is not well:
Infirmity doth still neglect all office
Whereto our health is bound; we are not ourselves
When nature being oppress'd commands the mind
To suffer with the body: I'll forbear;
And am fall'n out with my more headier will,
To take the indisposed and sickly fit
For the sound man. [*Looking on* KENT] Death on my
state! wherefore
Should he sit here? This act persuades me
That this remotion of the duke and her
Is practice only. Give me my servant forth.
Go tell the duke and 's wife I'ld speak with them,
Now, presently: bid them come forth and hear me,
Or at their chamber-door I'll beat the drum
Till it cry sleep to death.

GLOUCESTER

I would have all well betwixt you.　　　[*Exit*

LEAR

O me, my heart, my rising heart! But down!

FOOL

Cry to it, nuncle, as the cockney did to the eels when
she put 'em i' the paste alive; she knapped 'em o'
the coxcombs with a stick, and cried 'Down, wantons, down!' 'Twas her brother that, in pure kindness to his horse, buttered his hay.

Re-enter GLOUCESTER, *with* CORNWALL, REGAN, *and*

SERVANTS

LEAR

Good morrow to you both.

CORNWALL

　　　　　　　　Hail to your grace!
　　　　　　　[KENT *is set at liberty*

REGAN

I am glad to see your highness.

LEAR

Regan, I think you are; I know what reason
I have to think so: if thou shouldst not be glad,
I would divorce me from thy mother's tomb,
Sepulchring an adultress. [*To* KENT] O, are you free?
Some other time for that. Beloved Regan,
Thy sister's naught: O Regan, she hath tied
Sharp-tooth'd unkindness, like a vulture, here:
　　　　　　　　　　　　[*Points to his heart*
I can scarce speak to thee; thou'lt not believe
With how depraved a quality—O Regan!

REGAN

I pray you, sir, take patience: I have hope

You less know how to value her desert
Than she to scant her duty.

LEAR

           Say, how is that?

REGAN

I cannot think my sister in the least
Would fail her obligation: if, sir, perchance
She have restrain'd the riots of your followers,
'Tis on such ground and to such wholesome end
As clears her from all blame.

LEAR

My curses on her!

REGAN

           O, sir, you are old;
Nature in you stands on the very verge
Of her confine: you should be ruled and led
By some discretion that discerns your state
Better than you yourself. Therefore I pray you
That to our sister you do make return;
Say you have wrong'd her, sir.

LEAR

           Ask her forgiveness?
Do you but mark how this becomes the house:
[Kneeling] 'Dear daughter, I confess that I am old;
Age is unnecessary: on my knees I beg
That you'll vouchsafe me raiment, bed and food.'

REGAN

Good sir, no more; these are unsightly tricks:
Return you to my sister.

LEAR

[Rising] Never, Regan:
She hath abated me of half my train;
Look'd black upon me; struck me with her tongue,
Most serpent-like, upon the very heart:
All the stored vengeances of heaven fall
On her ingrateful top! Strike her young bones,
You taking airs, with lameness.

CORNWALL

           Fie, sir, fie!

LEAR

You nimble lightnings, dart your blinding flames
Into her scornful eyes. Infect her beauty,
You fen-suck'd fogs, drawn by the powerful sun
To fall and blast her pride.

REGAN

O the blest gods! so will you wish on me,
When the rash mood is on.

LEAR

No, Regan, thou shalt never have my curse:
Thy tender-hefted nature shall not give
Thee o'er to harshness: her eyes are fierce, but thine
Do comfort and not burn. 'Tis not in thee
To grudge my pleasures, to cut off my train,
To bandy hasty words, to scant my sizes,
And in conclusion to oppose the bolt
Against my coming in: thou better know'st
The offices of nature, bond of childhood,
Effects of courtesy, dues of gratitude;
Thy half o' the kingdom hast thou not forgot,
Wherein I thee endow'd.

REGAN

           Good sir, to the purpose.

LEAR

Who put my man i' the stocks?   [Tucket within

CORNWALL

           What trumpet's that?

REGAN

I know 't; my sister's: this approves her letter,
That she would soon be here.

Enter OSWALD

           Is your lady come?

LEAR

This is a slave whose easy-borrow'd pride
Dwells in the fickle grace of her he follows.
Out, varlet, from my sight!

CORNWALL

           What means your grace?

LEAR

Who stock'd my servant? Regan, I have good hope
Thou didst not know on 't. Who comes here?

Enter GONERIL

           O heavens,
If you do love old men, if your sweet sway
Allow obedience, if yourselves are old,
Make it your cause; send down, and take my part!
[To GONERIL] Art not ashamed to look upon this
   beard?
O Regan, wilt thou take her by the hand?

GONERIL

Why not by the hand, sir? How have I offended?
All's not offence that indiscretion finds
And dotage terms so.

LEAR

           O sides, you are too tough;
Will you yet hold? How came my man i' the stocks?

CORNWALL

I set him there, sir: but his own disorders
Deserved much less advancement.

LEAR

           You! did you?

REGAN

I pray you, father, being weak, seem so.
If, till the expiration of your month,
You will return and sojourn with my sister,
Dismissing half your train, come then to me:
I am now from home and out of that provision
Which shall be needful for your entertainment.

LEAR

Return to her, and fifty men dismiss'd?
No, rather I abjure all roofs, and choose
To wage against the enmity o' the air,
To be a comrade with the wolf and owl,—
Necessity's sharp pinch! Return with her?
Why, the hot-blooded France, that dowerless took
Our youngest born, I could as well be brought
To knee his throne, and, squire-like, pension beg
To keep base life afoot. Return with her?
Persuade me rather to be slave and sumpter
To this detested groom.   [Pointing at OSWALD

GONERIL

At your choice, sir.

LEAR

I prithee, daughter, do not make me mad:
I will not trouble thee, my child; farewell:
We'll no more meet, no more see one another:
But yet thou art my flesh, my blood, my daughter;
Or rather a disease that's in my flesh,
Which I must needs call mine: thou art a boil,
A plague-sore, an embossed carbuncle,
In my corrupted blood. But I'll not chide thee;
Let shame come when it will, I do not call it:
I do not bid the thunder-bearer shoot,
Nor tell tales of thee to high-judging Jove:
Mend when thou canst; be better at thy leisure:
I can be patient; I can stay with Regan,
I and my hundred knights.

REGAN

Not altogether so:
I look'd not for you yet, nor am provided
For your fit welcome. Give ear, sir, to my sister;
For those that mingle reason with your passion
Must be content to think you old, and so—
But she knows what she does.

LEAR

Is this well spoken?

REGAN

I dare avouch it, sir: what, fifty followers?
Is it not well? What should you need of more?
Yea, or so many, sith that both charge and danger
Speak 'gainst so great a number? How in one house
Should many people under two commands
Hold amity? 'Tis hard, almost impossible.

GONERIL

Why might not you, my lord, receive attendance
From those that she calls servants or from mine?

REGAN

Why not, my lord? If then they chanced to slack
    you,
We could control them. If you will come to me,
For now I spy a danger, I entreat you
To bring but five and twenty: to no more
Will I give place or notice.

LEAR

I gave you all—

REGAN

And in good time you gave it.

LEAR

Made you my guardians, my depositaries,
But kept a reservation to be follow'd
With such a number. What, must I come to you
With five and twenty, Regan? said you so?

REGAN

And speak 't again, my lord; no more with me.

LEAR

Those wicked creatures yet do look well-favour'd,
When others are more wicked; not being the worst
Stands in some rank of praise. [To GONERIL] I'll go
    with thee:

Thy fifty yet doth double five and twenty,
And thou art twice her love.

GONERIL

Hear me, my lord:
What need you five and twenty, ten, or five,
To follow in a house where twice so many
Have a command to tend you?

REGAN

What need one?

LEAR

O, reason not the need: our basest beggars
Are in the poorest thing superfluous:
Allow not nature more than nature needs,
Man's life's as cheap as beast's: thou art a lady;
If only to go warm were gorgeous,
Why, nature needs not what thou gorgeous wear'st,
Which scarcely keeps thee warm. But for true need,—
You heavens, give me that patience, patience I need!
You see me here, you gods, a poor old man,
As full of grief as age; wretched in both:
If it be you that stirs these daughters' hearts
Against their father, fool me not so much
To bear it tamely; touch me with noble anger,
And let not women's weapons, water-drops,
Stain my man's cheeks! No, you unnatural hags,
I will have such revenges on you both
That all the world shall—I will do such things,—
What they are, yet I know not, but they shall be
The terrors of the earth. You think I'll weep;
No, I'll not weep:
I have full cause of weeping; but this heart
Shall break into a hundred thousand flaws,
Or ere I'll weep. O fool, I shall go mad!

[Exeunt LEAR, GLOUCESTER, KENT, and FOOL

CORNWALL

Let us withdraw; 'twill be a storm.

[Storm and tempest

REGAN

This house is little: the old man and his people
Cannot be well bestow'd.

GONERIL

'Tis his own blame; hath put himself from rest,
And must needs taste his folly.

REGAN

For his particular, I'll receive him gladly,
But not one follower.

GONERIL

So am I purposed.
Where is my lord of Gloucester?

CORNWALL

Follow'd the old man forth: he is return'd.

Re-enter GLOUCESTER

The king is in high rage.

CORNWALL

Whither is he going?

GLOUCESTER

He calls to horse; but will I know not whither.

CORNWALL

'Tis best to give him way; he leads himself.

GONERIL

My lord, entreat him by no means to stay.

GLOUCESTER

Alack, the night comes on, and the bleak winds
Do sorely ruffle; for many miles about
There's scarce a bush.

REGAN

O, sir, to wilful men
The injuries that they themselves procure
Must be their schoolmasters. Shut up your doors:
He is attended with a desperate train;
And what they may incense him to, being apt
To have his ear abused, wisdom bids fear.

CORNWALL

Shut up your doors, my lord; 'tis a wild night:
My Regan counsels well: come out o' the storm.

[Exeunt

ACT III

Scene I. *A heath*

Storm still. Enter KENT *and a* GENTLEMAN, *meeting*

KENT

Who's there, besides foul weather?

GENTLEMAN

One minded like the weather, most unquietly.

KENT

I know you. Where's the king?

GENTLEMAN

Contending with the fretful elements;
Bids the wind blow the earth into the sea,
Or swell the curled waters 'bove the main,
That things might change or cease; tears his white
hair,
Which the impetuous blasts, with eyeless rage,
Catch in their fury, and make nothing of;
Strives in his little world of man to out-scorn
The to-and-fro-conflicting wind and rain.
This night, wherein the cub-drawn bear would
couch,
The lion and the belly-pinched wolf
Keep their fur dry, unbonneted he runs,
And bids what will take all.

KENT

But who is with him?

GENTLEMAN

None but the fool; who labours to out-jest
His heart-struck injuries.

KENT

Sir, I do know you;
And dare, upon the warrant of my note,
Commend a dear thing to you. There is division,
Although as yet the face of it be cover'd
With mutual cunning, 'twixt Albany and Cornwall;
Who have—as who have not, that their great stars
Throned and set high?—servants, who seem no less,
Which are to France the spies and speculations

Intelligent of our state; what hath been seen,
Either in snuffs and packings of the dukes,
Or the hard rein which both of them have borne
Against the old kind king, or something deeper,
Whereof perchance these are but furnishings,—
But true it is, from France there comes a power
Into this scatter'd kingdom; who already,
Wise in our negligence, have secret feet
In some of our best ports, and are at point
To show their open banner. Now to you:
If on my credit you dare build so far
To make your speed to Dover, you shall find
Some that will thank you, making just report
Of how unnatural and bemadding sorrow
The king hath cause to plain.
I am a gentleman of blood and breeding,
And from some knowledge and assurance offer
This office to you.

GENTLEMAN

I will talk further with you.

KENT

No, do not.
For confirmation that I am much more
Than my out-wall, open this purse and take
What it contains. If you shall see Cordelia,—
As fear not but you shall,—show her this ring,
And she will tell you who your fellow is
That yet you do not know. Fie on this storm!
I will go seek the king.

GENTLEMAN

Give me your hand:
Have you no more to say?

KENT

Few words, but, to effect, more than all yet;
That when we have found the king,—in which your
pain
That way, I'll this,—he that first lights on him
Holla the other.   [Exeunt severally

Scene II. *Another part of the heath. Storm still*

Enter LEAR *and* FOOL

LEAR

Blow, winds, and crack your cheeks! rage! blow!
You cataracts and hurricanoes, spout
Till you have drench'd our steeples, drown'd the
cocks!
You sulphurous and thought-executing fires,
Vaunt-couriers to oak-cleaving thunderbolts,
Singe my white head! And thou, all-shaking thun-
der,
Smite flat the thick rotundity o' the world!
Crack nature's moulds, all germins spill at once
That make ingrateful man!

FOOL

O nuncle, court holy-water in a dry house is better
than this rain-water out o' door. Good nuncle, in,
and ask thy daughters' blessing: here's a night pities
neither wise man nor fool.

LEAR

Rumble thy bellyful! Spit, fire! spout, rain!
Nor rain, wind, thunder, fire, are my daughters:
I tax not you, you elements, with unkindness;
I never gave you kingdom, call'd you children,
You owe me no subscription: then let fall
Your horrible pleasure; here I stand, your slave,
A poor, infirm, weak and despised old man:
But yet I call you servile ministers,
That have with two pernicious daughters join'd
Your high-engender'd battles 'gainst a head
So old and white as this. O! O! 'tis foul!

FOOL

He that has a house to put 's head in has a good
head-piece.

　　　The cod-piece that will house
　　　　　Before the head has any,
　　　The head and he shall louse
　　　　　So beggars marry many.
　　　The man that makes his toe
　　　　　What he his heart should make
　　　Shall of a corn cry woe,
　　　　　And turn his sleep to wake.

For there was never yet fair woman but she made
mouths in a glass.

LEAR

No, I will be the pattern of all patience;
I will say nothing.

Enter KENT

KENT

Who's there?

FOOL

Marry, here's grace and a cod-piece; that's a wise
man and a fool.

KENT

Alas, sir, are you here? things that love night
Love not such nights as these; the wrathful skies
Gallow the very wanderers of the dark,
And make them keep their caves: since I was man,
Such sheets of fire, such bursts of horrid thunder,
Such groans of roaring wind and rain, I never
Remember to have heard: man's nature cannot
　　carry
The affliction nor the fear.

LEAR

　　　　　　Let the great gods,
That keep this dreadful pother o'er our heads,
Find out their enemies now. Tremble, thou wretch,
That hast within thee undivulged crimes,
Unwhipp'd of justice: hide thee, thou bloody hand;
Thou perjured, and thou simular man of virtue
That art incestuous: caitiff, to pieces shake,
That under covert and convenient seeming
Hast practised on man's life: close pent-up guilts,
Rive your concealing continents and cry
These dreadful summoners grace. I am a man
More sinn'd against than sinning.

KENT

　　　　　　　　Alack, bare-headed!
Gracious my lord, hard by here is a hovel;
Some friendship will it lend you 'gainst the tempest:

Repose you there; while I to this hard house—
More harder than the stones whereof 'tis raised;
Which even but now, demanding after you,
Denied me to come in—return, and force
Their scanted courtesy.

LEAR

　　　　　　My wits begin to turn.
Come on, my boy: how dost, my boy? art cold?
I am cold myself. Where is this straw, my fellow?
The art of our necessities is strange,
That can make vile things precious. Come, your
　　hovel.
Poor fool and knave, I have one part in my heart
That's sorry yet for thee.

FOOL

[*Singing*]

　　　He that has and a little tiny wit,—
　　　　With hey, ho, the wind and the rain,—
　　　Must make content with his fortunes fit,
　　　　For the rain it raineth every day.

LEAR

True, my good boy. Come, bring us to this hovel.

[*Exeunt* LEAR *and* KENT

FOOL

This is a brave night to cool a courtezan. I'll speak
a prophecy ere I go:

　　　When priests are more in word than matter;
　　　When brewers mar their malt with water;
　　　When nobles are their tailors' tutors;
　　　No heretics burn'd, but wenches' suitors;
　　　When every case in law is right;
　　　No squire in debt, nor no poor knight;
　　　When slanders do not live in tongues,
　　　Nor cutpurses come not to throngs;
　　　When usurers tell their gold i' the field,
　　　And bawds and whores do churches build;
　　　Then shall the realm of Albion
　　　Come to great confusion:
　　　Then comes the time, who lives to see 't,
　　　That going shall be used with feet.

This prophecy Merlin shall make; for I live before
his time.

[*Exit*

SCENE III. GLOUCESTER's *castle*

Enter GLOUCESTER *and* EDMUND

GLOUCESTER

Alack, alack, Edmund, I like not this unnatural
dealing. When I desired their leave that I might
pity him, they took from me the use of mine own
house; charged me, on pain of their perpetual displeasure, neither to speak of him, entreat for him,
nor any way sustain him.

EDMUND

Most savage and unnatural!

GLOUCESTER

Go to; say you nothing. There's a division betwixt
the dukes, and a worse matter than that: I have received a letter this night; 'tis dangerous to be
spoken; I have locked the letter in my closet: these
injuries the king now bears will be revenged home;
there is part of a power already footed: we must in-

cline to the king. I will seek him and privily relieve him: go you, and maintain talk with the duke, that my charity be not of him perceived: if he ask for me, I am ill and gone to bed. Though I die for it, as no less is threatened me, the king my old master must be relieved. There is some strange thing toward, Edmund; pray you, be careful.　　　　　　[*Exit*

EDMUND

This courtesy, forbid thee, shall the duke
Instantly know, and of that letter too:
This seems a fair deserving, and must draw me
That which my father loses; no less than all:
The younger rises when the old doth fall.　　[*Exit*

SCENE IV. *The heath. Before a hovel*

Enter LEAR, KENT, *and* FOOL

KENT

Here is the place, my lord; good my lord, enter:
The tyranny of the open night's too rough
For nature to endure.　　　　　　　　[*Storm still*

LEAR

Let me alone.

KENT

Good my lord, enter here.

LEAR

Wilt break my heart?

KENT

I had rather break mine own. Good my lord, enter.

LEAR

Thou think'st 'tis much that this contentious storm
Invades us to the skin: so 'tis to thee;
But where the greater malady is fix'd
The lesser is scarce felt. Thou'ldst shun a bear,
But if thy flight lay toward the raging sea
Thou'ldst meet the bear i' the mouth. When the
　mind's free
The body's delicate: the tempest in my mind
Doth from my senses take all feeling else
Save what beats there. Filial ingratitude!
Is it not as this mouth should tear this hand
For lifting food to 't? But I will punish home.
No, I will weep no more. In such a night
To shut me out! Pour on; I will endure.
In such a night as this! O Regan, Goneril!
Your old kind father, whose frank heart gave you
　all,—
O, that way madness lies; let me shun that;
No more of that.

KENT

Good my lord, enter here.

LEAR

Prithee, go in thyself; seek thine own ease:
This tempest will not give me leave to ponder
On things would hurt me more. But I'll go in.
[*To the* FOOL] In, boy; go first. You houseless pov-
　erty,—
Nay, get thee in. I'll pray, and then I'll sleep.
　　　　　　　　　　　　　　　　　[FOOL *goes in*

Poor naked wretches, wheresoe'er you are,
That bide the pelting of this pitiless storm,
How shall your houseless heads and unfed sides,
Your loop'd and window'd raggedness, defend you
From seasons such as these? O, I have ta'en
Too little care of this! Take physic, pomp;
Expose thyself to feel what wretches feel,
That thou mayst shake the superflux to them
And show the heavens more just.

EDGAR

[*Within*] Fathom and half, fathom and half! Poor
Tom!　　　　　[*The* FOOL *runs out from the hovel*

FOOL

Come not in here, nuncle, here's a spirit. Help me, help me!

KENT

Give me thy hand. Who's there?

FOOL

A spirit, a spirit: he says his name's poor Tom.

KENT

What art thou that dost grumble there i' the straw?
Come forth.

Enter EDGAR *disguised as a madman*

EDGAR

Away! the foul fiend follows me!
Through the sharp hawthorn blows the cold wind.
Hum! go to thy cold bed and warm thee.

LEAR

Hast thou given all to thy two daughters? and art
thou come to this?

EDGAR

Who gives any thing to poor Tom? whom the foul fiend hath led through fire and through flame, through ford and whirlpool, o'er bog and quag-mire; that hath laid knives under his pillow and halters in his pew; set ratsbane by his porridge; made him proud of heart, to ride on a bay trotting-horse over four-inched bridges, to course his own shadow for a traitor. Bless thy five wits! Tom's a-cold. O, do de, do de, do de. Bless thee from whirlwinds, star-blasting, and taking! Do poor Tom some charity, whom the foul fiend vexes. There could I have him now, and there, and there again, and there.　　　　　　　　　　　　[*Storm still*

LEAR

What, have his daughters brought him to this pass?
Couldst thou save nothing? Didst thou give them
　all?

FOOL

Nay, he reserved a blanket, else we had been all shamed.

LEAR

Now, all the plagues that in the pendulous air
Hang fated o'er men's faults light on thy daughters!

KENT

He hath no daughters, sir.

LEAR

Death, traitor! nothing could have subdued nature
To such a lowness but his unkind daughters.

[1004]

Is it the fashion that discarded fathers
Should have thus little mercy on their flesh?
Judicious punishment! 'twas this flesh begot
Those pelican daughters.

EDGAR

Pillicock sat on Pillicock-hill:
Halloo, halloo, loo, loo!

FOOL

This cold night will turn us all to fools and madmen.

EDGAR

Take heed o' the foul fiend: obey thy parents; keep
thy word justly; swear not; commit not with man's
sworn spouse; set not thy sweet heart on proud
array. Tom's a-cold.

LEAR

What hast thou been?

EDGAR

A serving-man, proud in heart and mind; that
curled my hair; wore gloves in my cap; served the
lust of my mistress' heart and did the act of darkness with her; swore as many oaths as I spake words
and broke them in the sweet face of heaven: one
that slept in the contriving of lust and waked to do
it: wine loved I deeply, dice dearly, and in woman
out-paramoured the Turk: false of heart, light of
ear, bloody of hand; hog in sloth, fox in stealth,
wolf in greediness, dog in madness, lion in prey.
Let not the creaking of shoes nor the rustling of silks
betray thy poor heart to woman: keep thy foot out
of brothels, thy hand out of plackets, thy pen from
lenders' books, and defy the foul fiend.

'Still through the hawthorn blows the cold wind.'
Says suum, mun, ha, no, nonny.
Dolphin my boy, my boy, sessa! let him trot by.

[Storm still

LEAR

Why, thou wert better in thy grave than to answer
with thy uncovered body this extremity of the skies.
Is man no more than this? Consider him well. Thou
owest the worm no silk, the beast no hide, the sheep
no wool, the cat no perfume. Ha! here's three on 's
are sophisticated. Thou art the thing itself: un-
accommodated man is no more but such a poor,
bare, forked animal as thou art. Off, off, you lendings! come, unbutton here.   [Tearing off his clothes

FOOL

Prithee, nuncle, be contented; 'tis a naughty night
to swim in. Now a little fire in a wild field were like
an old lecher's heart, a small spark, all the rest on 's
body cold. Look, here comes a walking fire.

Enter GLOUCESTER, with a torch

EDGAR

This is the foul fiend Flibbertigibbet: he begins at
curfew and walks till the first cock; he gives the web
and the pin, squints the eye and makes the hare-lip;
mildews the white wheat and hurts the poor creature of earth.

Saint Withold footed thrice the 'old;
He met the night-mare and her nine-fold;

Bid her alight,
And her troth plight,
And aroint thee, witch, aroint thee!

KENT

How fares your grace?

LEAR

What's he?

KENT

Who's there? What is 't you seek?

GLOUCESTER

What are you there? Your names?

EDGAR

Poor Tom, that eats the swimming frog, the toad,
the tadpole, the wall-newt and the water; that in
the fury of his heart, when the foul fiend rages, eats
cow-dung for sallets; swallows the old rat and the
ditch-dog; drinks the green mantle of the standing
pool; who is whipped from tithing to tithing, and
stock-punished, and imprisoned; who hath had
three suits to his back, six shirts to his body, horse
to ride and weapon to wear;

But mice and rats and such small deer
Have been Tom's food for seven long year.

Beware my follower. Peace, Smulkin; peace, thou
fiend!

GLOUCESTER

What, hath your grace no better company?

EDGAR

The prince of darkness is a gentleman: Modo he's
call'd, and Mahu.

GLOUCESTER

Our flesh and blood is grown so vile, my lord,
That it doth hate what gets it.

EDGAR

Poor Tom's a-cold.

GLOUCESTER

Go in with me: my duty cannot suffer
To obey in all your daughters' hard commands:
Though their injunction be to bar my doors
And let this tyrannous night take hold upon you,
Yet have I ventured to come seek you out
And bring you where both fire and food is ready.

LEAR

First let me talk with this philosopher.
What is the cause of thunder?

KENT

Good my lord, take his offer; go into the house.

LEAR

I'll talk a word with this same learned Theban.
What is your study?

EDGAR

How to prevent the fiend and to kill vermin.

LEAR

Let me ask you one word in private.

KENT

Importune him once more to go, my lord;
His wits begin to unsettle.

GLOUCESTER

                     Canst thou blame him?
[Storm still

His daughters seek his death: ah, that good Kent!
He said it would be thus, poor banish'd man!
Thou say'st the king grows mad; I'll tell thee,
    friend,
I am almost mad myself: I had a son,
Now outlaw'd from my blood; he sought my life,
But lately, very late: I loved him, friend,
No father his son dearer: truth to tell thee,
The grief hath crazed my wits. What a night's this!
I do beseech your grace,—

LEAR

              O, cry you mercy, sir.
Noble philosopher, your company.

EDGAR

Tom's a-cold.

GLOUCESTER

In, fellow, there, into the hovel: keep thee warm.

LEAR

Come, let's in all.

KENT

           This way, my lord.

LEAR

                  With him;
I will keep still with my philosopher.

KENT

Good my lord, soothe him; let him take the fellow.

GLOUCESTER

Take him you on.

KENT

Sirrah, come on; go along with us.

LEAR

Come, good Athenian.

GLOUCESTER

No words, no words: hush.

EDGAR

    Child Rowland to the dark tower came:
    His word was still 'Fie, foh, and fum,
    I smell the blood of a British man.'

                         [Exeunt

SCENE V. GLOUCESTER's castle

Enter CORNWALL and EDMUND

CORNWALL

I will have my revenge ere I depart his house.

EDMUND

How, my lord, I may be censured, that nature thus
gives way to loyalty, something fears me to think of.

CORNWALL

I now perceive, it was not altogether your brother's
evil disposition made him seek his death, but a provoking merit, set a-work by a reproveable badness
in himself.

EDMUND

How malicious is my fortune, that I must repent to
be just! This is the letter he spoke of, which approves him an intelligent party to the advantages of
France. O heavens! that this treason were not, or not
I the detector!

CORNWALL

Go with me to the duchess.

EDMUND

If the matter of this paper be certain, you have
mighty business in hand.

CORNWALL

True or false, it hath made thee earl of Gloucester.
Seek out where thy father is, that he may be ready
for our apprehension.

EDMUND

[Aside] If I find him comforting the king, it will stuff
his suspicion more fully.—I will persever in my
course of loyalty, though the conflict be sore between that and my blood.

CORNWALL

I will lay trust upon thee, and thou shalt find a
dearer father in my love.   [Exeunt

SCENE VI. A chamber in a farmhouse adjoining the castle

Enter GLOUCESTER, LEAR, KENT, FOOL, and EDGAR

GLOUCESTER

Here is better than the open air; take it thankfully.
I will piece out the comfort with what addition I
can: I will not be long from you.

KENT

All the power of his wits have given way to his impatience: the gods reward your kindness!

                     [Exit GLOUCESTER

EDGAR

Frateretto calls me, and tells me Nero is an angler
in the lake of darkness. Pray, innocent, and beware
the foul fiend.

FOOL

Prithee, nuncle, tell me whether a madman be a
gentleman or a yeoman.

LEAR

A king, a king!

FOOL

No, he's a yeoman that has a gentleman to his son,
for he's a mad yeoman that sees his son a gentleman
before him.

LEAR

To have a thousand with red burning spits
Come hissing in upon 'em,—

EDGAR

The foul fiend bites my back.

FOOL

He's mad that trusts in the tameness of a wolf, a
horse's health, a boy's love, or a whore's oath.

LEAR

It shall be done; I will arraign them straight.
[To EDGAR] Come, sit thou here, most learned jus-
    ticer;
[To the FOOL] Thou, sapient sir, sit here. Now, you
    she foxes!

EDGAR

Look, where he stands and glares! Wantest thou
eyes at trial, madam?

        Come o'er the bourn, Bessy, to me.

FOOL

Her boat hath a leak,
And she must not speak
Why she dares not come over to thee.

EDGAR

The foul fiend haunts poor Tom in the voice of a
nightingale. Hopdance cries in Tom's belly for two
white herring. Croak not, black angel; I have no
food for thee.

KENT

How do you, sir? Stand you not so amazed:
Will you lie down and rest upon the cushions?

LEAR

I'll see their trial first. Bring in the evidence.
[To EDGAR] Thou robed man of justice, take thy
place;
[To the FOOL] And thou, his yoke-fellow of equity,
Bench by his side. [To KENT] You are o' the com-
mission;
Sit you too.

EDGAR

Let us deal justly.

Sleepest or wakest thou, jolly shepherd?
Thy sheep be in the corn;
And for one blast of thy minikin mouth,
Thy sheep shall take no harm.

Pur! the cat is gray.

LEAR

Arraign her first; 'tis Goneril. I here take my oath
before this honourable assembly, she kicked the
poor king her father.

FOOL

Come hither, mistress. Is your name Goneril?

LEAR

She cannot deny it.

FOOL

Cry you mercy, I took you for a joint-stool.

LEAR

And here's another, whose warp'd looks proclaim
What store her heart is made on. Stop her there!
Arms, arms, sword, fire! Corruption in the place!
False justicer, why hast thou let her 'scape?

EDGAR

Bless thy five wits!

KENT

O pity! Sir, where is the patience now,
That you so oft have boasted to retain?

EDGAR

[Aside] My tears begin to take his part so much,
They'll mar my counterfeiting.

LEAR

The little dogs and all,
Tray, Blanch, and Sweet-heart, see, they bark at
me.

EDGAR

Tom will throw his head at them. Avaunt, you curs!

Be thy mouth or black or white,
Tooth that poisons if it bite;
Mastiff, greyhound, mongrel grim,
Hound or spaniel, brach or lym,

Or bobtail tike or trundle-tail,
Tom will make them weep and wail:
For, with throwing thus my head,
Dogs leap the hatch, and all are fled.

Do de, de, de. Sessa! Come, march to wakes and
fairs and market-towns. Poor Tom, thy horn is dry.

LEAR

Then let them anatomize Regan; see what breeds
about her heart. Is there any cause in nature that
makes these hard hearts? [To EDGAR] You, sir, I
entertain for one of my hundred; only I do not like
the fashion of your garments. You will say they are
Persian attire; but let them be changed.

KENT

Now, good my lord, lie here and rest awhile.

LEAR

Make no noise, make no noise; draw the curtains:
so, so, so. We'll go to supper i' the morning. So, so,
so.

FOOL

And I'll go to bed at noon.

Re-enter GLOUCESTER

GLOUCESTER

Come hither, friend: where is the king my master?

KENT

Here, sir; but trouble him not: his wits are gone.

GLOUCESTER

Good friend, I prithee, take him in thy arms;
I have o'erheard a plot of death upon him:
There is a litter ready; lay him in 't,
And drive toward Dover, friend, where thou shalt
meet
Both welcome and protection. Take up thy master:
If thou shouldst dally half an hour, his life,
With thine and all that offer to defend him,
Stand in assured loss. Take up, take up,
And follow me, that will to some provision
Give thee quick conduct.

KENT

Oppressed nature sleeps.
This rest might yet have balm'd thy broken sinews,
Which, if convenience will not allow,
Stand in hard cure. [To the FOOL] Come, help to
bear thy master;
Thou must not stay behind.

GLOUCESTER

Come, come, away.
[Exeunt all but EDGAR

EDGAR

When we our betters see bearing our woes,
We scarcely think our miseries our foes.
Who alone suffers suffers most i' the mind,
Leaving free things and happy shows behind:
But then the mind much sufferance doth o'erskip,
When grief hath mates, and bearing fellowship.
How light and portable my pain seems now,
When that which makes me bend makes the king
bow,
He childed as I father'd! Tom, away!
Mark the high noises, and thyself bewray

When false opinion, whose wrong thought defiles
thee,
In thy just proof repeals and reconciles thee.
What will hap more to-night, safe 'scape the king!
Lurk, lurk.   [Exit

SCENE VII. GLOUCESTER'S castle

Enter CORNWALL, REGAN, GONERIL, EDMUND, *and*
SERVANTS

CORNWALL

Post speedily to my lord your husband; show him
this letter: the army of France is landed. Seek out
the traitor Gloucester. [*Exeunt some of the* SERVANTS

REGAN

Hang him instantly.

GONERIL

Pluck out his eyes.

CORNWALL

Leave him to my displeasure. Edmund, keep you
our sister company: the revenges we are bound to
take upon your traitorous father are not fit for your
beholding. Advise the duke, where you are going,
to a most festinate preparation: we are bound to the
like. Our posts shall be swift and intelligent betwixt
us. Farewell, dear sister: farewell, my lord of
Gloucester.

Enter OSWALD

How now! where's the king?

OSWALD

My lord of Gloucester hath convey'd him hence:
Some five or six and thirty of his knights,
Hot questrists after him, met him at gate;
Who, with some other of the lords dependants,
Are gone with him toward Dover; where they boast
To have well-armed friends.

CORNWALL

                Get horses for your mistress.

GONERIL

Farewell, sweet lord, and sister.

CORNWALL

Edmund, farewell.

[*Exeunt* GONERIL, EDMUND, *and* OSWALD
Go seek the traitor Gloucester.
Pinion him like a thief, bring him before us.

[*Exeunt other* SERVANTS
Though well we may not pass upon his life
Without the form of justice, yet our power
Shall do a courtesy to our wrath, which men
May blame but not control. Who's there? the
traitor?

Enter GLOUCESTER, *brought in by two or three*

REGAN

Ingrateful fox! 'tis he.

CORNWALL

Bind fast his corky arms.

GLOUCESTER

What mean your graces? Good my friends, consider
You are my guests: do me no foul play, friends.

CORNWALL

Bind him, I say.   [SERVANTS *bind him*

REGAN

        Hard, hard. O filthy traitor!

GLOUCESTER

Unmerciful lady as you are, I'm none.

CORNWALL

To this chair bind him. Villain, thou shalt find—

[REGAN *plucks his beard*

GLOUCESTER

By the kind gods, 'tis most ignobly done
To pluck me by the beard.

REGAN

So white, and such a traitor!

GLOUCESTER

                    Naughty lady,
These hairs which thou dost ravish from my chin
Will quicken and accuse thee: I am your host:
With robbers' hands my hospitable favours
You should not ruffle thus. What will you do?

CORNWALL

Come, sir, what letters had you late from France?

REGAN

Be simple answerer, for we know the truth.

CORNWALL

And what confederacy have you with the traitors
Late footed in the kingdom?

REGAN

To whose hands have you sent the lunatic king?
Speak.

GLOUCESTER

I have a letter guessingly set down,
Which came from one that's of a neutral heart,
And not from one opposed.

CORNWALL

                    Cunning.

REGAN

                        And false.

CORNWALL

Where hast thou sent the king?

GLOUCESTER

                        To Dover.

REGAN

Wherefore to Dover? Wast thou not charged at
peril—

CORNWALL

Wherefore to Dover? Let him first answer that.

GLOUCESTER

I am tied to the stake, and I must stand the course.

REGAN

Wherefore to Dover, sir?

GLOUCESTER

Because I would not see thy cruel nails
Pluck out his poor old eyes, nor thy fierce sister
In his anointed flesh stick boarish fangs.
The sea, with such a storm as his bare head
In hell-black night endured, would have buoy'd up,
And quench'd the stelled fires:
Yet, poor old heart, he holp the heavens to rain.
If wolves had at thy gate howl'd that stern time,

Thou shouldst have said, 'Good porter, turn the
　key,'
All cruels else subscribed: but I shall see
The winged vengeance overtake such children.
CORNWALL
See 't shalt thou never. Fellows, hold the chair.
Upon these eyes of thine I'll set my foot.
GLOUCESTER
He that will think to live till he be old,
Give me some help! O cruel! O you gods!
REGAN
One side will mock another; the other too.
CORNWALL
If you see vengeance—
FIRST SERVANT
　　　　　Hold your hand, my lord:
I have served you ever since I was a child;
But better service have I never done you
Than now to bid you hold.
REGAN
　　　　　　How now, you dog!
FIRST SERVANT
If you did wear a beard upon your chin,
I'd shake it on this quarrel. What do you mean?
CORNWALL
My villain!　　　　　[They draw and fight
FIRST SERVANT
Nay, then, come on, and take the chance of anger.
REGAN
Give me thy sword. A peasant stand up thus!
　　　　[Takes a sword and runs at him behind
FIRST SERVANT
O, I am slain! My lord, you have one eye left
To see some mischief on him. O!　　[Dies
CORNWALL
Lest it see more, prevent it. Out, vile jelly!
Where is thy lustre now?
GLOUCESTER
All dark and comfortless. Where's my son Edmund?
Edmund, enkindle all the sparks of nature,
To quit this horrid act.
REGAN
　　　　　Out, treacherous villain!
Thou call'st on him that hates thee: it was he
That made the overture of thy treasons to us;
Who is too good to pity thee.
GLOUCESTER
O my follies! Then Edgar was abused.
Kind gods, forgive me that, and prosper him!
REGAN
Go thrust him out at gates, and let him smell
His way to Dover. [Exit one with GLOUCESTER] How
　is 't, my lord? how look you?
CORNWALL
I have received a hurt: follow me, lady.
Turn out that eyeless villain: throw this slave
Upon the dunghill. Regan, I bleed apace:
Untimely comes this hurt: give me your arm.
　　　　　[Exit CORNWALL, led by REGAN

SECOND SERVANT
I'll never care what wickedness I do,
If this man come to good.
THIRD SERVANT
　　　　　If she live long,
And in the end meet the old course of death,
Women will all turn monsters.
SECOND SERVANT
Let's follow the old earl, and get the Bedlam
To lead him where he would: his roguish madness
Allows itself to any thing.
THIRD SERVANT
Go thou: I'll fetch some flax and whites of eggs
To apply to his bleeding face. Now, heaven help
　him!　　　　　[Exeunt severally

ACT IV
SCENE I. The heath

Enter EDGAR
EDGAR
Yet better thus, and known to be contemn'd,
Than still contemn'd and flatter'd. To be worst,
The lowest and most dejected thing of fortune,
Stands still in esperance, lives not in fear:
The lamentable change is from the best;
The worst returns to laughter. Welcome then,
Thou unsubstantial air that I embrace!
The wretch that thou hast blown unto the worst
Owes nothing to thy blasts. But who comes here?
　　　Enter GLOUCESTER, led by an OLD MAN
My father, poorly led? World, world, O world!
But that thy strange mutations make us hate thee,
Life would not yield to age.
OLD MAN
O, my good lord, I have been your tenant, and your
father's tenant, these fourscore years.
GLOUCESTER
Away, get thee away; good friend, be gone:
Thy comforts can do me no good at all;
Thee they may hurt.
OLD MAN
Alack, sir, you cannot see your way.
GLOUCESTER
I have no way and therefore want no eyes;
I stumbled when I saw: full oft 'tis seen,
Our means secure us, and our mere defects
Prove our commodities. Ah, dear son Edgar,
The food of thy abused father's wrath!
Might I but live to see thee in my touch,
I'd say I had eyes again!
OLD MAN
　　　　　How now! Who's there?
EDGAR
[Aside] O gods! Who is 't can say 'I am at the
　worst'?
I am worse than e'er I was.

OLD MAN

'Tis poor mad Tom.

EDGAR

[Aside] And worse I may be yet: the worst is not
So long as we can say 'This is the worst.'

OLD MAN

Fellow, where goest?

GLOUCESTER

Is it a beggar-man?

OLD MAN

Madman and beggar too.

GLOUCESTER

He has some reason, else he could not beg.
I' the last night's storm I such a fellow saw,
Which made me think a man a worm: my son
Came then into my mind, and yet my mind
Was then scarce friends with him: I have heard
   more since.
As flies to wanton boys, are we to the gods;
They kill us for their sport.

EDGAR

[Aside] How should this be?
Bad is the trade that must play fool to sorrow,
Angering itself and others. Bless thee, master!

GLOUCESTER

Is that the naked fellow?

OLD MAN

Ay, my lord.

GLOUCESTER

Then, prithee, get thee gone: if for my sake
Thou wilt o'ertake us hence a mile or twain
I' the way toward Dover, do it for ancient love;
And bring some covering for this naked soul,
Who I'll entreat to lead me.

OLD MAN

Alack, sir, he is mad.

GLOUCESTER

'Tis the times' plague, when madmen lead the
   blind.
Do as I bid thee, or rather do thy pleasure;
Above the rest, be gone.

OLD MAN

I'll bring him the best 'parel that I have,
Come on 't what will. [Exit

GLOUCESTER

Sirrah, naked fellow,—

EDGAR

Poor Tom's a-cold. [Aside] I cannot daub it further.

GLOUCESTER

Come hither, fellow.

EDGAR

[Aside] And yet I must.—Bless thy sweet eyes, they
   bleed.

GLOUCESTER

Know'st thou the way to Dover?

EDGAR

Both stile and gate, horse-way and foot-path. Poor
Tom hath been scared out of his good wits. Bless
thee, good man's son, from the foul fiend! Five

fiends have been in poor Tom at once; of lust, as
Obidicut; Hobbididence, prince of dumbness; Mahu, of stealing; Modo, of murder; Flibbertigibbet,
of mopping and mowing; who since possesses cham-
bermaids and waiting-women. So, bless thee, master!

GLOUCESTER

Here, take this purse, thou whom the heavens'
   plagues
Have humbled to all strokes: that I am wretched
Makes thee the happier. Heavens, deal so still!
Let the superfluous and lust-dieted man,
That slaves your ordinance, that will not see
Because he doth not feel, feel your power quickly;
So distribution should undo excess
And each man have enough. Dost thou know
   Dover?

EDGAR

Ay, master.

GLOUCESTER

There is a cliff whose high and bending head
Looks fearfully in the confined deep:
Bring me but to the very brim of it,
And I'll repair the misery thou dost bear
With something rich about me: from that place
I shall no leading need.

EDGAR

Give me thy arm:
Poor Tom shall lead thee. [Exeunt

SCENE II. *Before the* DUKE OF ALBANY's *palace*

Enter GONERIL *and* EDMUND

GONERIL

Welcome, my lord: I marvel our mild husband
Not met us on the way.

Enter OSWALD

Now, where's your master?

OSWALD

Madam, within; but never man so changed.
I told him of the army that was landed;
He smiled at it: I told him you were coming;
His answer was, 'The worse:' of Gloucester's
   treachery
And of the loyal service of his son
When I inform'd him, then he call'd me sot
And told me I had turn'd the wrong side out:
What most he should dislike seems pleasant to him;
What like, offensive.

GONERIL

[To EDMUND] Then shall you go no further.
It is the cowish terror of his spirit,
That dares not undertake: he'll not feel wrongs,
Which tie him to an answer. Our wishes on the way
May prove effects. Back, Edmund, to my brother;
Hasten his musters and conduct his powers:
I must change arms at home and give the distaff
Into my husband's hands. This trusty servant
Shall pass between us: ere long you are like to hear,
If you dare venture in your own behalf,

[1010]

A mistress's command. Wear this; spare speech;

                [*Giving a favour*

Decline your head: this kiss, if it durst speak,
Would stretch thy spirits up into the air:
Conceive, and fare thee well.

EDMUND

Yours in the ranks of death.

GONERIL

         My most dear Gloucester!

                [*Exit* EDMUND

O, the difference of man and man!
To thee a woman's services are due:
My fool usurps my body.

OSWALD

      Madam, here comes my lord.

                [*Exit*

Enter ALBANY

GONERIL

I have been worth the whistle.

ALBANY

           O Goneril!

You are not worth the dust which the rude wind
Blows in your face. I fear your disposition:
That nature which contemns it origin
Cannot be border'd certain in itself;
She that herself will sliver and disbranch
From her material sap, perforce must wither
And come to deadly use.

GONERIL

No more; the text is foolish.

ALBANY

Wisdom and goodness to the vile seem vile:
Filths savour but themselves. What have you done?
Tigers, not daughters, what have you perform'd?
A father, and a gracious aged man,
Whose reverence even the head-lugg'd bear would
     lick,
Most barbarous, most degenerate! have you
     madded.
Could my good brother suffer you to do it?
A man, a prince, by him so benefited!
If that the heavens do not their visible spirits
Send quickly down to tame these vile offences,
It will come,
Humanity must perforce prey on itself,
Like monsters of the deep.

GONERIL

        Milk-liver'd man!

That bear'st a cheek for blows, a head for wrongs;
Who hast not in thy brows an eye discerning
Thine honour from thy suffering; that not know'st
Fools do those villains pity who are punish'd
Ere they have done their mischief. Where's thy
     drum?
France spreads his banners in our noiseless land,
With plumed helm thy state begins to threat,
Whiles thou, a moral fool, sit'st still and criest
'Alack, why does he so?'

ALBANY

        See thyself, devil!

Proper deformity seems not in the fiend
So horrid as in woman.

GONERIL

        O vain fool!

ALBANY

Thou changed and self-cover'd thing, for shame,
Be-monster not thy feature. Were 't my fitness
To let these hands obey my blood,
They are apt enough to dislocate and tear
Thy flesh and bones: howe'er thou art a fiend,
A woman's shape doth shield thee.

GONERIL

Marry, your manhood! mew!

Enter a MESSENGER

ALBANY

What news?

MESSENGER

O, my good lord, the Duke of Cornwall's dead,
Slain by his servant, going to put out
The other eye of Gloucester.

ALBANY

        Gloucester's eyes!

MESSENGER

A servant that he bred, thrill'd with remorse,
Opposed against the act, bending his sword
To his great master; who thereat enraged
Flew on him and amongst them fell'd him dead,
But not without that harmful stroke which since
Hath pluck'd him after.

ALBANY

        This shows you are above,

You justicers, that these our nether crimes
So speedily can venge. But, O poor Gloucester!
Lost he his other eye?

MESSENGER

        Both, both, my lord.

This letter, madam, craves a speedy answer;
'Tis from your sister.

GONERIL

     [*Aside*] One way I like this well;
But being widow, and my Gloucester with her,
May all the building in my fancy pluck
Upon my hateful life: another way,
The news is not so tart.—I'll read, and answer.

                [*Exit*

ALBANY

Where was his son when they did take his eyes?

MESSENGER

Come with my lady hither.

ALBANY

        He is not here.

MESSENGER

No, my good lord; I met him back again.

ALBANY

Knows he the wickedness?

MESSENGER

Ay, my good lord; 'twas he inform'd against him,
And quit the house on purpose, that their punish-
     ment
Might have the freer course.

ALBANY

Gloucester, I live
To thank thee for the love thou show'dst the king,
And to revenge thine eyes. Come hither, friend:
Tell me what more thou know'st.   [*Exeunt*

SCENE III. *The French camp near Dover*

Enter KENT *and a* GENTLEMAN

KENT

Why the King of France is so suddenly gone back
know you the reason?

GENTLEMAN

Something he left imperfect in the state which since
his coming forth is thought of, which imports to the
kingdom so much fear and danger that his personal
return was most required and necessary.

KENT

Who hath he left behind him general?

GENTLEMAN

The Marshal of France, Monsieur La Far.

KENT

Did your letters pierce the queen to any demonstration of grief?

GENTLEMAN

Ay, sir; she took them, read them in my presence,
And now and then an ample tear trill'd down
Her delicate cheek: it seem'd she was a queen
Over her passion, who most rebel-like
Sought to be king o'er her.

KENT

O, then it moved her.

GENTLEMAN

Not to a rage: patience and sorrow strove
Who should express her goodliest. You have seen
Sunshine and rain at once: her smiles and tears
Were like a better way: those happy smilets
That play'd on her ripe lip seem'd not to know
What guests were in her eyes; which parted thence
As pearls from diamonds dropp'd. In brief,
Sorrow would be a rarity most beloved,
If all could so become it.

KENT

Made she no verbal question?

GENTLEMAN

Faith, once or twice she heaved the name of 'father'
Pantingly forth, as if it press'd her heart;
Cried 'Sisters! sisters! Shame of ladies! sisters!
Kent! father! sisters! What, i' the storm? i' the
night?
Let pity not be believed!' There she shook
The holy water from her heavenly eyes,
And clamour moisten'd: then away she started
To deal with grief alone.

KENT

It is the stars,
The stars above us, govern our conditions;
Else one self mate and mate could not beget
Such different issues. You spoke not with her since?

GENTLEMAN

No.

KENT

Was this before the king return'd?

GENTLEMAN

No, since.

KENT

Well, sir, the poor distressed Lear's i' the town;
Who sometime in his better tune remembers
What we are come about, and by no means
Will yield to see his daughter.

GENTLEMAN

Why, good sir?

KENT

A sovereign shame so elbows him: his own unkind-
ness
That stripp'd her from his benediction, turn'd her
To foreign casualties, gave her dear rights
To his dog-hearted daughters: these things sting
His mind so venomously that burning shame
Detains him from Cordelia.

GENTLEMAN

Alack, poor gentleman!

KENT

Of Albany's and Cornwall's powers you heard not?

GENTLEMAN

'Tis so; they are afoot.

KENT

Well, sir, I'll bring you to our master Lear,
And leave you to attend him: some dear cause
Will in concealment wrap me up awhile;
When I am known aright, you shall not grieve
Lending me this acquaintance. I pray you, go
Along with me.   [*Exeunt*

SCENE IV. *The same. A tent*

Enter, with drum and colours, CORDELIA, DOCTOR, *and*
SOLDIERS

CORDELIA

Alack, 'tis he: why, he was met even now
As mad as the vex'd sea; singing aloud;
Crown'd with rank fumiter and furrow-weeds,
With bur-docks, hemlock, nettles, cuckoo-flowers,
Darnel, and all the idle weeds that grow
In our sustaining corn. A century send forth;
Search every acre in the high-grown field,
And bring him to our eye. [*Exit an* OFFICER] What
can man's wisdom
In the restoring his bereaved sense?
He that helps him take all my outward worth.

DOCTOR

There is means, madam:
Our foster-nurse of nature is repose,
The which he lacks: that to provoke in him,
Are many simples operative, whose power
Will close the eye of anguish.

CORDELIA

All blest secrets,

All you unpublish'd virtues of the earth,
Spring with my tears! be aidant and remediate
In the good man's distress! Seek, seek for him;
Lest his ungovern'd rage dissolve the life
That wants the means to lead it.

Enter a MESSENGER

MESSENGER

                News, madam;
The British powers are marching hitherward.

CORDELIA

'Tis known before; our preparation stands
In expectation of them. O dear father,
It is thy business that I go about;
Therefore great France
My mourning and important tears hath pitied.
No blown ambition doth our arms incite,
But love, dear love, and our aged father's right:
Soon may I hear and see him!   [*Exeunt*

SCENE V. GLOUCESTER'S *castle*

Enter REGAN *and* OSWALD

REGAN

But are my brother's powers set forth?

OSWALD

                Ay, madam.

REGAN

Himself in person there?

OSWALD

           Madam, with much ado:
Your sister is the better soldier.

REGAN

Lord Edmund spake not with your lord at home?

OSWALD

No, madam.

REGAN

What might import my sister's letter to him?

OSWALD

I know not, lady.

REGAN

Faith, he is posted hence on serious matter.
It was great ignorance, Gloucester's eyes being out,
To let him live: where he arrives he moves
All hearts against us: Edmund, I think, is gone,
In pity of his misery, to dispatch
His nighted life; moreover, to descry
The strength o' the enemy.

OSWALD

I must needs after him, madam, with my letter.

REGAN

Our troops set forth to-morrow: stay with us;
The ways are dangerous.

OSWALD

           I may not, madam:
My lady charged my duty in this business.

REGAN

Why should she write to Edmund? Might not you
Transport her purposes by word? Belike,

Something—I know not what: I'll love thee much,
Let me unseal the letter.

OSWALD

            Madam, I had rather—

REGAN

I know your lady does not love her husband;
I am sure of that: and at her late being here
She gave strange œillades and most speaking looks
To noble Edmund. I know you are of her bosom.

OSWALD

I, madam?

REGAN

I speak in understanding: you are; I know 't:
Therefore I do advise you, take this note:
My lord is dead; Edmund and I have talk'd;
And more convenient is he for my hand
Than for your lady's: you may gather more.
If you do find him, pray you, give him this;
And when your mistress hears thus much from you,
I pray, desire her call her wisdom to her.
So, fare you well.
If you do chance to hear of that blind traitor,
Preferment falls on him that cuts him off.

OSWALD

Would I could meet him, madam! I should show
What party I do follow.

REGAN

           Fare thee well.   [*Exeunt*

SCENE VI. *Fields near Dover*

Enter GLOUCESTER, *and* EDGAR *dressed like a peasant*

GLOUCESTER

When shall we come to the top of that same hill?

EDGAR

You do climb up it now: look, how we labour.

GLOUCESTER

Methinks the ground is even.

EDGAR

           Horrible steep.
Hark, do you hear the sea?

GLOUCESTER

           No, truly.

EDGAR

Why then your other senses grow imperfect
By your eyes' anguish.

GLOUCESTER

           So may it be indeed:
Methinks thy voice is alter'd, and thou speak'st
In better phrase and matter than thou didst.

EDGAR

You're much deceived: in nothing am I changed
But in my garments.

GLOUCESTER

           Methinks you're better spoken.

EDGAR

Come on, sir; here's the place: stand still. How
   fearful
And dizzy 'tis to cast one's eyes so low!

The crows and choughs that wing the midway air
Show scarce so gross as beetles: half way down
Hangs one that gathers samphire, dreadful trade!
Methinks he seems no bigger than his head:
The fishermen that walk upon the beach
Appear like mice; and yond tall anchoring bark
Diminish'd to her cock; her cock, a buoy
Almost too small for sight: the murmuring surge
That on the unnumber'd idle pebbles chafes
Cannot be heard so high. I'll look no more,
Lest my brain turn and the deficient sight
Topple down headlong.

GLOUCESTER
               Set me where you stand.

EDGAR
Give me your hand: you are now within a foot
Of the extreme verge: for all beneath the moon
Would I not leap upright.

GLOUCESTER
               Let go my hand.
Here, friend, 's another purse; in it a jewel
Well worth a poor man's taking: fairies and gods
Prosper it with thee! Go thou further off;
Bid me farewell, and let me hear thee going.

EDGAR
Now fare you well, good sir.

GLOUCESTER
               With all my heart.

EDGAR
Why I do trifle thus with his despair
Is done to cure it.

GLOUCESTER
[Kneeling] O you mighty gods!
This world I do renounce, and in your sights
Shake patiently my great affliction off:
If I could bear it longer and not fall
To quarrel with your great opposeless wills,
My snuff and loathed part of nature should
Burn itself out. If Edgar live, O bless him!
Now, fellow, fare thee well.   [He falls forward

EDGAR
               Gone, sir: farewell.
And yet I know not how conceit may rob
The treasury of life, when life itself
Yields to the theft: had he been where he thought,
By this had thought been past. Alive or dead?
Ho, you sir! friend! Hear you, sir! speak!
Thus might he pass indeed: yet he revives.
What are you, sir?

GLOUCESTER
               Away, and let me die.

EDGAR
Hadst thou been aught but gossamer, feathers, air,
So many fathom down precipitating,
Thou'dst shiver'd like an egg: but thou dost breathe;
Hast heavy substance; bleed'st not; speak'st; art
    sound.
Ten masts at each make not the altitude
Which thou hast perpendicularly fell:
Thy life's a miracle. Speak yet again.

GLOUCESTER
But have I fall'n, or no?

EDGAR
From the dread summit of this chalky bourn.
Look up a-height; the shrill-gorged lark so far
Cannot be seen or heard: do but look up.

GLOUCESTER
Alack, I have no eyes.
Is wretchedness deprived that benefit,
To end itself by death? 'Twas yet some comfort,
When misery could beguile the tyrant's rage
And frustrate his proud will.

EDGAR
               Give me your arm:
Up: so. How is 't? Feel you your legs? You stand.

GLOUCESTER
Too well, too well.

EDGAR
               This is above all strangeness.
Upon the crown o' the cliff, what thing was that
Which parted from you?

GLOUCESTER
               A poor unfortunate beggar.

EDGAR
As I stood here below, methought his eyes
Were two full moons; he had a thousand noses,
Horns whelk'd and waved like the enridged sea:
It was some fiend; therefore, thou happy father,
Think that the clearest gods, who make them hon-
    ours
Of men's impossibilities, have preserved thee.

GLOUCESTER
I do remember now: henceforth I'll bear
Affliction till it do cry out itself
'Enough, enough,' and die. That thing you speak
    of,
I took it for a man; often 'twould say
'The fiend, the fiend:' he led me to that place.

EDGAR
Bear free and patient thoughts. But who comes
    here?
     Enter LEAR, fantastically dressed with wild flowers
The safer sense will n'er accommodate
His master thus.

LEAR
No, they cannot touch me for coining; I am the
king himself.

EDGAR
O thou side-piercing sight!

LEAR
Nature's above art in that respect. There's your
press-money. That fellow handles his bow like a
crow-keeper; draw me a clothier's yard. Look, look,
a mouse! Peace, peace; this piece of toasted cheese
will do 't. There's my gauntlet; I'll prove it on a
giant. Bring up the brown bills. O, well flown, bird!
i' the clout, i' the clout: hewgh! Give the word.

EDGAR
Sweet marjoram.

Pass.

GLOUCESTER

I know that voice.

LEAR

Ha! Goneril, with a white beard! They flattered me like a dog, and told me I had white hairs in my beard ere the black ones were there. To say 'ay' and 'no' to every thing that I said! 'Ay' and 'no' too was no good divinity. When the rain came to wet me once and the wind to make me chatter; when the thunder would not peace at my bidding; there I found 'em, there I smelt 'em out. Go to, they are not men o' their words: they told me I was every thing; 'tis a lie, I am not ague-proof.

GLOUCESTER

The trick of that voice I do well remember:
Is 't not the king?

LEAR

Ay, every inch a king:
When I do stare, see how the subject quakes.
I pardon that man's life. What was thy cause?
Adultery?
Thou shalt not die: die for adultery! No:
The wren goes to 't, and the small gilded fly
Does lecher in my sight.
Let copulation thrive; for Gloucester's bastard son
Was kinder to his father than my daughters
Got 'tween the lawful sheets.
To 't, luxury, pell-mell! for I lack soldiers.
Behold yond simpering dame,
Whose face between her forks presages snow,
That minces virtue and does shake the head
To hear of pleasure's name;
The fitchew, nor the soiled horse, goes to 't
With a more riotous appetite.
Down from the waist they are Centaurs,
Though women all above:
But to the girdle do the gods inherit,
Beneath is all the fiends';
There's hell, there's darkness, there's the sulphurous
    pit,
Burning, scalding, stench, consumption; fie, fie, fie!
pah, pah! Give me an ounce of civet, good apothe-
cary, to sweeten my imagination: there's money for
thee.

GLOUCESTER

O, let me kiss that hand!

LEAR

Let me wipe it first; it smells of mortality.

GLOUCESTER

O ruin'd piece of nature! This great world
Shall so wear out to nought. Dost thou know me?

LEAR

I remember thine eyes well enough. Dost thou
squiny at me? No, do thy worst, blind Cupid; I'll
not love. Read thou this challenge; mark but the
penning on 't.

GLOUCESTER

Were all the letters suns, I could not see one.

EDGAR

I would not take this from report: it is,
And my heart breaks at it.

LEAR

Read.

GLOUCESTER

What, with the case of eyes?

LEAR

O, ho, are you there with me? No eyes in your head,
nor no money in your purse? Your eyes are in a
heavy case, your purse in a light: yet you see how
this world goes.

GLOUCESTER

I see it feelingly.

LEAR

What, art mad? A man may see how this world goes
with no eyes. Look with thine ears: see how yond
justice rails upon yond simple thief. Hark, in thine
ear: change places, and, handy-dandy, which is the
justice, which is the thief? Thou hast seen a farmer's
dog bark at a beggar?

GLOUCESTER

Ay, sir.

LEAR

And the creature run from the cur? There thou
mightst behold the great image of authority: a dog's
obeyed in office.
Thou rascal beadle, hold thy bloody hand!
Why dost thou lash that whore? Strip thine own
    back;
Thou hotly lust'st to use her in that kind
For which thou whip'st her. The usurer hangs the
    cozener.
Through tatter'd clothes small vices do appear;
Robes and furr'd gowns hide all. Plate sin with gold,
And the strong lance of justice hurtless breaks;
Arm it in rags, a pigmy's straw does pierce it.
None does offend, none, I say, none; I'll able 'em:
Take that of me, my friend, who have the power
To seal the accuser's lips. Get thee glass eyes,
And, like a scurvy politician, seem
To see the things thou dost not.
Now, now, now, now: pull off my boots: harder,
    harder: so.

EDGAR

O, matter and impertinency mix'd!
Reason in madness!

LEAR

If thou wilt weep my fortunes, take my eyes.
I know thee well enough; thy name is Gloucester:
Thou must be patient; we came crying hither·
Thou know'st, the first time that we smell the air,
We wawl and cry. I will preach to thee: mark.

GLOUCESTER

Alack, alack the day!

LEAR

When we are born, we cry that we are come
To this great stage of fools. This 's a good block.
It were a delicate stratagem, to shoe
A troop of horse with felt: I'll put 't in proof;

And when I have stol'n upon these sons-in-law,
Then, kill, kill, kill, kill, kill, kill!

Enter a GENTLEMAN, *with* ATTENDANTS

GENTLEMAN
O, here he is: lay hand upon him. Sir,
Your most dear daughter—

LEAR
No rescue? What, a prisoner? I am even
The natural fool of fortune. Use me well;
You shall have ransom. Let me have a surgeon;
I am cut to the brains.

GENTLEMAN
     You shall have any thing.

LEAR
No seconds? all myself?
Why, this would make a man a man of salt,
To use his eyes for garden water-pots,
Ay, and laying autumn's dust.

GENTLEMAN
Good sir,—

LEAR
I will die bravely, like a smug bridegroom. What!
I will be jovial: come, come; I am a king,
My masters, know you that.

GENTLEMAN
You are a royal one, and we obey you.

LEAR
Then there's life in 't. Nay, an you get it, you shall
get it by running. Sa, sa, sa, sa.

[Exit running; ATTENDANTS *follow*

GENTLEMAN
A sight most pitiful in the meanest wretch,
Past speaking of in a king! Thou hast one daughter,
Who redeems nature from the general curse
Which twain have brought her to.

EDGAR
Hail, gentle sir.

GENTLEMAN
     Sir, speed you: what's your will?

EDGAR
Do you hear aught, sir, of a battle toward?

GENTLEMAN
Most sure and vulgar: every one hears that,
Which can distinguish sound.

EDGAR
     But, by your favour,
How near's the other army?

GENTLEMAN
Near and on speedy foot; the main descry
Stands on the hourly thought.

EDGAR
     I thank you, sir: that's all.

GENTLEMAN
Though that the queen on special cause is here,
Her army is moved on.

EDGAR
     I thank you, sir.

[Exit GENTLEMAN

GLOUCESTER
You ever-gentle gods, take my breath from me;

Let not my worser spirit tempt me again
To die before you please!

EDGAR
     Well pray you, father.

GLOUCESTER
Now, good sir, what are you?

EDGAR
A most poor man, made tame to fortune's blows;
Who, by the art of known and feeling sorrows,
Am pregnant to good pity. Give me your hand,
I'll lead you to some biding.

GLOUCESTER
     Hearty thanks;
The bounty and the benison of heaven
To boot, and boot!

Enter OSWALD

OSWALD
     A proclaim'd prize! Most happy!
That eyeless head of thine was first framed flesh
To raise my fortunes. Thou old unhappy traitor,
Briefly thyself remember: the sword is out
That must destroy thee.

GLOUCESTER
     Now let thy friendly hand
Put strength enough to 't.   *[*EDGAR *interposes*

OSWALD
     Wherefore, bold peasant,
Darest thou support a publish'd traitor? Hence!
Lest that the infection of his fortune take
Like hold on thee. Let go his arm.

EDGAR
Chill not let go, zir, without vurther 'casion.

OSWALD
Let go, slave, or thou diest!

EDGAR
Good gentleman, go your gait, and let poor volk
pass. An chud ha' been zwaggered out of my life,
'twould not ha' been zo long as 'tis by a vortnight.
Nay, come not near th' old man; keep out, che vor
ye, or I'se try whether your costard or my ballow
be the harder: chill be plain with you.

OSWALD
Out, dunghill!   *[They fight*

EDGAR
Chill pick your teeth, zir: come; no matter vor your
foins.   *[*OSWALD *falls*

OSWALD
Slave, thou hast slain me. Villain, take my purse:
If ever thou wilt thrive, bury my body;
And give the letters which thou find'st about me
To Edmund earl of Gloucester; seek him out
Upon the British party. O, untimely death!
Death!   *[Dies*

EDGAR
I know thee well: a serviceable villain,
As duteous to the vices of thy mistress
As badness would desire.

GLOUCESTER
     What, is he dead?

EDGAR

Sit you down, father; rest you.
Let's see these pockets: the letters that he speaks of
May be my friends. He's dead; I am only sorry
He had no other deathsman. Let us see:
Leave, gentle wax; and, manners, blame us not:
To know our enemies' minds, we'ld rip their hearts;
Their papers, is more lawful.

[*Reads*] 'Let our reciprocal vows be remembered. You have
many opportunities to cut him off: if your will want not, time
and place will be fruitfully offered. There is nothing done, if
he return the conqueror: then am I the prisoner, and his bed
my gaol; from the loathed warmth whereof deliver me, and
supply the place for your labour.
    'Your—wife, so I would say—affectionate servant,
                             'GONERIL.'

O undistinguish'd space of woman's will!
A plot upon her virtuous husband's life;
And the exchange my brother! Here, in the sands,
Thee I'll rake up, the post unsanctified
Of murderous lechers; and in the mature time
With this ungracious paper strike the sight
Of the death-practised duke: for him 'tis well
That of thy death and business I can tell.

GLOUCESTER

The king is mad: how stiff is my vile sense,
That I stand up, and have ingenious feeling
Of my huge sorrows! Better I were distract:
So should my thoughts be sever'd from my griefs,
And woes by wrong imaginations lose
The knowledge of themselves.   [*Drum afar off*

EDGAR

                    Give me your hand:
Far off, methinks, I hear the beaten drum:
Come, father, I'll bestow you with a friend. [*Exeunt*

SCENE VII. *A tent in the French camp.* LEAR *on a bed
asleep, soft music playing;* GENTLEMAN, *and others
attending*

Enter CORDELIA, KENT, *and* DOCTOR

CORDELIA

O thou good Kent, how shall I live and work,
To match thy goodness? My life will be too short,
And every measure fail me.

KENT

To be acknowledged, madam, is o'erpaid.
All my reports go with the modest truth,
Nor more nor clipp'd, but so.

CORDELIA

                 Be better suited:
These weeds are memories of those worser hours:
I prithee, put them off.

KENT

             Pardon me, dear madam;
Yet to be known shortens my made intent:
My boon I make it, that you know me not
Till time and I think meet.

CORDELIA

Then be 't so, my good lord. [*To the* DOCTOR] How
  does the king?

DOCTOR

Madam, sleeps still.

CORDELIA

O you kind gods,
Cure this great breach in his abused nature!
The untuned and jarring senses, O, wind up
Of this child-changed father!

DOCTOR

                  So please your majesty
That we may wake the king: he hath slept long.

CORDELIA

Be govern'd by your knowledge, and proceed
I' the sway of your own will. Is he array'd?

GENTLEMAN

Ay, madam; in the heaviness of his sleep
We put fresh garments on him.

DOCTOR

Be by, good madam, when we do awake him;
I doubt not of his temperance.

CORDELIA

                Very well.

DOCTOR

Please you, draw near. Louder the music there!

CORDELIA

O my dear father! Restoration hang
Thy medicine on my lips, and let this kiss
Repair those violent harms that my two sisters
Have in thy reverence made!

KENT

                Kind and dear princess!

CORDELIA

Had you not been their father, these white flakes
Had challenged pity of them. Was this a face
To be opposed against the warring winds?
To stand against the deep dread-bolted thunder?
In the most terrible and nimble stroke
Of quick, cross lightning? to watch—poor perdu!—
With this thin helm? Mine enemy's dog,
Though he had bit me, should have stood that night
Against my fire; and wast thou fain, poor father,
To hovel thee with swine and rogues forlorn,
In short and musty straw? Alack, alack!
'Tis wonder that thy life and wits at once
Had not concluded all. He wakes; speak to him.

DOCTOR

Madam, do you; 'tis fittest.

CORDELIA

How does my royal lord? How fares your majesty?

LEAR

You do me wrong to take me out o' the grave:
Thou art a soul in bliss; but I am bound
Upon a wheel of fire, that mine own tears
Do scald like molten lead.

CORDELIA

                Sir, do you know me?

LEAR

You are a spirit, I know: when did you die?

CORDELIA

Still, still, far wide!

DOCTOR

He's scarce awake: let him alone awhile.

LEAR

Where have I been? Where am I? Fair day-light?
I am mightily abused. I should e'en die with pity,
To see another thus. I know not what to say.
I will not swear these are my hands: let's see;
I feel this pin prick. Would I were assured
Of my condition!

CORDELIA

O, look upon me, sir,
And hold your hands in benediction o'er me.
No, sir, you must not kneel.

LEAR

Pray, do not mock me:
I am a very foolish fond old man,
Fourscore and upward, not an hour more nor less;
And, to deal plainly,
I fear I am not in my perfect mind.
Methinks I should know you and know this man;
Yet I am doubtful; for I am mainly ignorant
What place this is, and all the skill I have
Remembers not these garments, nor I know not
Where I did lodge last night. Do not laugh at me;
For, as I am a man, I think this lady
To be my child Cordelia.

CORDELIA

And so I am, I am.

LEAR

Be your tears wet? yes, faith. I pray, weep not:
If you have poison for me, I will drink it.
I know you do not love me; for your sisters
Have, as I do remember, done me wrong:
You have some cause, they have not.

CORDELIA

No cause, no cause.

LEAR

Am I in France?

KENT

In your own kingdom, sir.

LEAR

Do not abuse me.

DOCTOR

Be comforted, good madam: the great rage,
You see, is kill'd in him: and yet it is danger
To make him even o'er the time he has lost.
Desire him to go in; trouble him no more
Till further settling.

CORDELIA

Will 't please your highness walk?

LEAR

You must bear with me. Pray you now, forget and
forgive: I am old and foolish.

[Exeunt all but KENT and GENTLEMAN

GENTLEMAN

Holds it true, sir, that the Duke of Cornwall was so
slain?

KENT

Most certain, sir.

GENTLEMAN

Who is conductor of his people?

KENT

As 'tis said, the bastard son of Gloucester.

GENTLEMAN

They say Edgar, his banished son, is with the Earl
of Kent in Germany.

KENT

Report is changeable. 'Tis time to look about; the
powers of the kingdom approach apace.

GENTLEMAN

The arbitrement is like to be bloody. Fare you well,
sir.   [Exit

KENT

My point and period will be throughly wrought,
Or well or ill, as this day's battle's fought.   [Exit

ACT V

SCENE I. *The British camp near Dover*

Enter, with drum and colours, EDMUND, REGAN,
GENTLEMEN, *and* SOLDIERS

EDMUND

Know of the duke if his last purpose hold,
Or whether since he is advised by aught
To change the course: he's full of alteration
And self-reproving: bring his constant pleasure.

[*To a* GENTLEMAN, *who goes out*

REGAN

Our sister's man is certainly miscarried.

EDMUND

'Tis to be doubted, madam.

REGAN

Now, sweet lord,
You know the goodness I intend upon you:
Tell me, but truly, but then speak the truth,
Do you not love my sister?

EDMUND

In honour'd love.

REGAN

But have you never found my brother's way
To the forfended place?

EDMUND

That thought abuses you.

REGAN

I am doubtful that you have been conjunct
And bosom'd with her, as far as we call hers.

EDMUND

No, by mine honour, madam.

REGAN

I never shall endure her: dear my lord,
Be not familiar with her.

EDMUND

Fear me not.—
She and the duke her husband!

Enter, with drum and colours, ALBANY, GONERIL, *and*
SOLDIERS

GONERIL

[*Aside*] I had rather lose the battle than that sister
Should loosen him and me.

ALBANY

Our very loving sister, well be-met.
Sir, this I hear; the king is come to his daughter,
With others whom the rigour of our state
Forced to cry out. Where I could not be honest,
I never yet was valiant: for this business,
It toucheth us, as France invades our land,
Not bolds the king, with others, whom, I fear,
Most just and heavy causes make oppose.

EDMUND

Sir, you speak nobly.

REGAN

Why is this reason'd?

GONERIL

Combine together 'gainst the enemy;
For these domestic and particular broils
Are not the question here.

ALBANY

Let's then determine
With the ancient of war on our proceedings.

EDMUND

I shall attend you presently at your tent.

REGAN

Sister, you'll go with us?

GONERIL

No.

REGAN

'Tis most convenient; pray you, go with us.

GONERIL

[*Aside*] O, ho, I know the riddle.—I will go.

As they are going out, enter EDGAR *disguised*

EDGAR

If e'er your grace had speech with man so poor,
Hear me one word.

ALBANY

I'll overtake you. Speak.

[*Exeunt all but* ALBANY *and* EDGAR

EDGAR

Before you fight the battle, ope this letter.
If you have victory, let the trumpet sound
For him that brought it: wretched though I seem,
I can produce a champion that will prove
What is avouched there. If you miscarry,
Your business of the world hath so an end,
And machination ceases. Fortune love you!

ALBANY

Stay till I have read the letter.

EDGAR

I was forbid it.
When time shall serve, let but the herald cry,
And I'll appear again.

ALBANY

Why, fare thee well: I will o'erlook thy paper.

[*Exit* EDGAR

Re-enter EDMUND

EDMUND

The enemy's in view: draw up your powers.
Here is the guess of their true strength and forces
By diligent discovery; but your haste
Is now urged on you.

ALBANY

We will greet the time. [*Exit*

EDMUND

To both these sisters have I sworn my love;
Each jealous of the other, as the stung
Are of the adder. Which of them shall I take?
Both? one? or neither? Neither can be enjoy'd,
If both remain alive: to take the widow
Exasperates, makes mad her sister Goneril;
And hardly shall I carry out my side,
Her husband being alive. Now then we'll use
His countenance for the battle; which being done,
Let her who would be rid of him devise
His speedy taking off. As for the mercy
Which he intends to Lear and to Cordelia,
The battle done, and they within our power,
Shall never see his pardon; for my state
Stands on me to defend, not to debate. [*Exit*

SCENE II. *A field between the two camps*

Alarum within. Enter, with drum and colours, LEAR,
CORDELIA, *and* SOLDIERS, *over the stage; and exeunt*
Enter EDGAR *and* GLOUCESTER

EDGAR

Here, father, take the shadow of this tree
For your good host; pray that the right may thrive:
If ever I return to you again,
I'll bring you comfort.

GLOUCESTER

Grace go with you, sir!

[*Exit* EDGAR

Alarum and retreat within. Re-enter EDGAR

EDGAR

Away, old man; give me thy hand; away!
King Lear hath lost, he and his daughter ta'en:
Give me thy hand; come on.

GLOUCESTER

No further, sir; a man may rot even here.

EDGAR

What, in ill thoughts again? Men must endure
Their going hence, even as their coming hither:
Ripeness is all: come on.

GLOUCESTER

And that's true too.

[*Exeunt*

SCENE III. *The British camp near Dover*

Enter, in conquest, with drum and colours, EDMUND;
LEAR *and* CORDELIA, *as prisoners;* CAPTAIN, SOLDIERS,
&c.

EDMUND

Some officers take them away: good guard,

Until their greater pleasures first be known
That are to censure them.

CORDELIA

           We are not the first
Who with best meaning have incurr'd the worst.
For thee, oppressed king, am I cast down;
Myself could else out-frown false fortune's frown.
Shall we not see these daughters and these sisters?

LEAR

No, no, no, no! Come, let's away to prison:
We two alone will sing like birds i' the cage:
When thou dost ask me blessing, I'll kneel down
And ask of thee forgiveness: so we'll live,
And pray, and sing, and tell old tales, and laugh
At gilded butterflies, and hear poor rogues
Talk of court news; and we'll talk with them too,
Who loses and who wins, who's in, who's out;
And take upon 's the mystery of things,
As if we were God's spies: and we'll wear out,
In a wall'd prison, packs and sects of great ones
That ebb and flow by the moon.

EDMUND

           Take them away.

LEAR

Upon such sacrifices, my Cordelia,
The gods themselves throw incense. Have I caught
    thee?
He that parts us shall bring a brand from heaven,
And fire us hence like foxes. Wipe thine eyes;
The good-years shall devour them, flesh and fell,
Ere they shall make us weep: we'll see 'em starve
    first.
Come.   [*Exeunt* LEAR *and* CORDELIA, *guarded*

EDMUND

Come hither, captain; hark.
Take thou this note: go follow them to prison:
One step I have advanced thee; if thou dost
As this instructs thee, thou dost make thy way
To noble fortunes: know thou this, that men
Are as the time is: to be tender-minded
Does not become a sword: thy great employment
Will not bear question; either say thou'lt do 't,
Or thrive by other means.

CAPTAIN

           I'll do 't, my lord.

EDMUND

About it; and write happy when thou hast done.
Mark; I say, instantly, and carry it so
As I have set it down.

CAPTAIN

I cannot draw a cart, nor eat dried oats;
If it be man's work, I'll do 't.   [*Exit*
    Flourish. Enter ALBANY, GONERIL, REGAN, *another*
        CAPTAIN, *and* SOLDIERS

ALBANY

Sir, you have shown to-day your valiant strain,
And fortune led you well: you have the captives
That were the opposites of this day's strife:
We do require them of you, so to use them

As we shall find their merits and our safety
May equally determine.

EDMUND

           Sir, I thought it fit
To send the old and miserable king
To some retention and appointed guard;
Whose age has charms in it, whose title more,
To pluck the common bosom on his side,
And turn our impress'd lances in our eyes
Which do command them. With him I sent the
    queen:
My reason all the same; and they are ready
To-morrow or at further space to appear
Where you shall hold your session. At this time
We sweat and bleed: the friend hath lost his friend;
And the best quarrels, in the heat, are cursed
By those that feel their sharpness.
The question of Cordelia and her father
Requires a fitter place.

ALBANY

           Sir, by your patience,
I hold you but a subject of this war,
Not as a brother.

REGAN

           That's as we list to grace him.
Methinks our pleasure might have been demanded,
Ere you had spoke so far. He led our powers,
Bore the commission of my place and person;
The which immediacy may well stand up
And call itself your brother.

GONERIL

           Not so hot:
In his own grace he doth exalt himself
More than in your addition.

REGAN

           In my rights,
By me invested, he compeers the best.

GONERIL

That were the most, if he should husband you.

REGAN

Jesters do oft prove prophets.

GONERIL

           Holla, holla!
That eye that told you so look'd but a-squint.

REGAN

Lady, I am not well; else I should answer
From a full-flowing stomach. General,
Take thou my soldiers, prisoners, patrimony;
Dispose of them, of me; the walls are thine:
Witness the world, that I create thee here
My lord and master.

GONERIL

           Mean you to enjoy him?

ALBANY

The let-alone lies not in your good will.

EDMUND

Nor in thine, lord.

ALBANY

           Half-blooded fellow, yes.

REGAN

[*To* EDMUND] Let the drum strike, and prove my title thine.

ALBANY

Stay yet; hear reason. Edmund, I arrest thee
On capital treason; and in thine attaint
This gilded serpent [*pointing to* GONERIL]. For your claim, fair sister,
I bar it in the interest of my wife;
'Tis she is sub-contracted to this lord,
And I, her husband, contradict your bans.
If you will marry, make your loves to me;
My lady is bespoke.

GONERIL

An interlude!

ALBANY

Thou art arm'd, Gloucester: let the trumpet sound:
If none appear to prove upon thy person
Thy heinous, manifest, and many treasons,
There is my pledge [*throwing down a glove*]: I'll prove it on thy heart,
Ere I taste bread, thou art in nothing less
Than I have here proclaim'd thee.

REGAN

Sick, O, sick!

GONERIL

[*Aside*] If not, I'll ne'er trust medicine.

EDMUND

[*Throwing down a glove*] There's my exchange: what in the world he is
That names me traitor, villain-like he lies:
Call by thy trumpet: he that dares approach,
On him, on you,—who not?—I will maintain
My truth and honour firmly.

ALBANY

A herald, ho!

EDMUND

A herald, ho, a herald!

ALBANY

Trust to thy single virtue; for thy soldiers,
All levied in my name, have in my name
Took their discharge.

REGAN

My sickness grows upon me.

ALBANY

She is not well; convey her to my tent.

[*Exit* REGAN, *led*

Enter a HERALD

Come hither, herald,—Let the trumpet sound,—
And read out this.

CAPTAIN

Sound, trumpet!   [*A trumpet sounds*

HERALD

[*Reads*] 'If any man of quality or degree within the lists of the army will maintain upon Edmund, supposed Earl of Gloucester, that he is a manifold traitor, let him appear by the third sound of the trumpet: he is bold in his defence.'

EDMUND

Sound!   [*First trumpet*

HERALD

Again!   [*Second trumpet*

HERALD

Again!   [*Third trumpet*
                        [*Trumpet answers within*

Enter EDGAR, *at the third sound, armed, with a trumpet before him*

ALBANY

Ask him his purposes, why he appears
Upon this call o' the trumpet.

HERALD

What are you?
Your name, your quality? and why you answer
This present summons?

EDGAR

Know, my name is lost;
By treason's tooth bare-gnawn and canker-bit:
Yet am I noble as the adversary
I come to cope.

ALBANY

Which is that adversary?

EDGAR

What's he that speaks for Edmund, Earl of Glouces-ter?

EDMUND

Himself: what say'st thou to him?

EDGAR

Draw thy sword,
That if my speech offend a noble heart,
Thy arm may do thee justice: here is mine.
Behold, it is the privilege of mine honours,
My oath, and my profession: I protest,
Maugre thy strength, youth, place and eminence,
Despite thy victor sword and fire-new fortune,
Thy valour and thy heart, thou art a traitor,
False to thy gods, thy brother and thy father,
Conspirant 'gainst this high illustrious prince,
And from the extremest upward of thy head
To the descent and dust below thy foot,
A most toad-spotted traitor. Say thou 'No,'
This sword, this arm and my best spirits are bent
To prove upon thy heart, whereto I speak,
Thou liest.

EDMUND

In wisdom I should ask thy name,
But since thy outside looks so fair and warlike
And that thy tongue some say of breeding breathes,
What safe and nicely I might well delay
By rule of knighthood, I disdain and spurn:
Back do I toss these treasons to thy head;
With the hell-hated lie o'erwhelm thy heart;
Which for they yet glance by and scarcely bruise,
This sword of mine shall give them instant way,
Where they shall rest for ever. Trumpets, speak!

[*Alarums. They fight.* EDMUND *falls*

ALBANY

Save him, save him!

GONERIL

This is practice, Gloucester:
By the law of arms thou wast not bound to answer

An unknown opposite; thou art not vanquish'd,
But cozen'd and beguiled.

ALBANY

　　　　　Shut your mouth, dame,
Or with this paper shall I stop it. Hold, sir;
Thou worse than any name, read thine own evil.
No tearing, lady; I perceive you know it.

GONERIL

Say, if I do, the laws are mine, not thine:
Who can arraign me for 't?

ALBANY

　　　　　Most monstrous!
Know'st thou this paper?

GONERIL

　　　　　Ask me not what I know.

[Exit

ALBANY

Go after her: she's desperate; govern her.

EDMUND

What you have charged me with, that have I done;
And more, much more; the time will bring it out:
'Tis past, and so am I. But what art thou
That hast this fortune on me? If thou 'rt noble,
I do forgive thee.

EDGAR

　　　　　Let's exchange charity.
I am no less in blood than thou art, Edmund;
If more, the more thou hast wrong'd me.
My name is Edgar, and thy father's son.
The gods are just, and of our pleasant vices
Make instruments to plague us:
The dark and vicious place where thee he got
Cost him his eyes.

EDMUND

　　　　　Thou hast spoken right, 'tis true;
The wheel is come full circle; I am here.

ALBANY

Methought thy very gait did prophesy
A royal nobleness: I must embrace thee:
Let sorrow split my heart, if ever I
Did hate thee or thy father!

EDGAR

　　　　　Worthy prince, I know 't.

ALBANY

Where have you hid yourself?
How have you known the miseries of your father?

EDGAR

By nursing them, my lord. List a brief tale;
And when 'tis told, O, that my heart would burst!
The bloody proclamation to escape
That follow'd me so near,—O, our lives' sweetness!
That we the pain of death would hourly die
Rather than die at once!—taught me to shift
Into a madman's rags, to assume a semblance
That very dogs disdain'd: and in this habit
Met I my father with his bleeding rings,
Their precious stones new lost; became his guide,
Led him, begg'd for him, saved him from despair;
Never—O fault!—reveal'd myself unto him,

Until some half-hour past, when I was arm'd;
Not sure, though hoping, of this good success,
I ask'd his blessing, and from first to last
Told him my pilgrimage: but his flaw'd heart,—
Alack, too weak the conflict to support!—
'Twixt two extremes of passion, joy and grief,
Burst smilingly.

EDMUND

　　　　　This speech of yours hath moved me,
And shall perchance do good: but speak you on;
You look as you had something more to say.

ALBANY

If there be more, more woful, hold it in;
For I am almost ready to dissolve,
Hearing of this.

EDGAR

　　　　　This would have seem'd a period
To such as love not sorrow; but another,
To amplify too much, would make much more,
And top extremity.
Whilst I was big in clamour, came there in a man,
Who, having seen me in my worst estate,
Shunn'd my abhorr'd society; but then, finding
Who 'twas that so endured, with his strong arms
He fasten'd on my neck, and bellow'd out
As he'ld burst heaven; threw him on my father;
Told the most piteous tale of Lear and him
That ever ear received: which in recounting
His grief grew puissant, and the strings of life
Began to crack: twice then the trumpets sounded,
And there I left him tranced.

ALBANY

　　　　　But who was this?

EDGAR

Kent, sir, the banish'd Kent; who in disguise
Follow'd his enemy king, and did him service
Improper for a slave.

Enter a GENTLEMAN, *with a bloody knife*

GENTLEMAN

Help, help, O, help!

EDGAR

What kind of help?

ALBANY

　　　　　Speak, man.

EDGAR

What means this bloody knife?

GENTLEMAN

　　　　　'Tis hot, it smokes;
It came even from the heart of—O, she's dead!

ALBANY

Who dead? speak, man.

GENTLEMAN

Your lady, sir, your lady: and her sister
By her is poisoned; she hath confess'd it.

EDMUND

I was contracted to them both: all three
Now marry in an instant.

EDGAR

　　　　　Here comes Kent.

ALBANY
Produce the bodies, be they alive or dead.
               [*Exit* GENTLEMAN
This judgement of the heavens, that makes us
    tremble,
Touches us not with pity.
            Enter KENT
           O, is this he?
The time will not allow the compliment
Which very manners urges.

KENT
           I am come
To bid my king and master aye good night:
Is he not here?

ALBANY
        Great thing of us forgot!
Speak, Edmund, where's the king? and where's
    Cordelia?
See'st thou this object, Kent?
    [*The bodies of* GONERIL *and* REGAN *are brought in*

KENT
Alack, why thus?

EDMUND
       Yet Edmund was beloved:
The one the other poison'd for my sake,
And after slew herself.

ALBANY
Even so. Cover their faces.

EDMUND
I pant for life: some good I mean to do,
Despite of mine own nature. Quickly send,
Be brief in it, to the castle; for my writ
Is on the life of Lear and on Cordelia:
Nay, send in time.

ALBANY
       Run, run, O, run!

EDGAR
To who, my lord? Who hath the office? send
Thy token of reprieve.

EDMUND
Well thought on: take my sword,
Give it the captain.

ALBANY
       Haste thee, for thy life.
               [*Exit* EDGAR

EDMUND
He hath commission from thy wife and me
To hang Cordelia in the prison, and
To lay the blame upon her own despair,
That she fordid herself.

ALBANY
The gods defend her! Bear him hence awhile.
           [EDMUND *is borne off*
Re-enter LEAR, *with* CORDELIA *dead in his arms;* EDGAR,
    CAPTAIN, *and others following*

LEAR
Howl, howl, howl, howl! O, you are men of stones:
Had I your tongues and eyes, I'ld use them so
That heaven's vault should crack. She's gone for
    ever!

I know when one is dead and when one lives;
She's dead as earth. Lend me a looking-glass;
If that her breath will mist or stain the stone,
Why, then she lives.

KENT
        Is this the promised end?

EDGAR
Or image of that horror?

ALBANY
        Fall and cease.

LEAR
This feather stirs; she lives. If it be so,
It is a chance which does redeem all sorrows
That ever I have felt.

KENT
    [*Kneeling*] O my good master!

LEAR
Prithee, away.

EDGAR
       'Tis noble Kent, your friend.

LEAR
A plague upon you, murderers, traitors all!
I might have saved her; now she's gone for ever!
Cordelia, Cordelia! stay a little. Ha!
What is 't thou say'st? Her voice was ever soft,
Gentle and low, an excellent thing in woman.
I kill'd the slave that was a-hanging thee.

CAPTAIN
'Tis true, my lords, he did.

LEAR
        Did I not, fellow?
I have seen the day, with my good biting falchion
I would have made them skip: I am old now,
And these same crosses spoil me. Who are you?
Mine eyes are not o' the best: I'll tell you straight.

KENT
If fortune brag of two she loved and hated,
One of them we behold.

LEAR
This is a dull sight. Are you not Kent?

KENT
              The same,
Your servant Kent. Where is your servant Caius?

LEAR
He's a good fellow, I can tell you that;
He'll strike, and quickly too: he's dead and rotten.

KENT
No, my good lord; I am the very man—

LEAR
I'll see that straight.

KENT
That from your first of difference and decay
Have follow'd your sad steps.

LEAR
        You are welcome hither.

KENT
Nor no man else: all's cheerless, dark and deadly.
Your eldest daughters have fordone themselves,
And desperately are dead.

LEAR

Ay, so I think.

ALBANY

He knows not what he says, and vain is it
That we present us to him.

EDGAR

Very bootless.

Enter a CAPTAIN

CAPTAIN

Edmund is dead, my lord.

ALBANY

That's but a trifle here.
You lords and noble friends, know our intent.
What comfort to this great decay may come
Shall be applied: for us, we will resign,
During the life of this old majesty,
To him our absolute power: [*To* EDGAR *and* KENT]
  you, to your rights;
With boot, and such addition as your honours
Have more than merited. All friends shall taste
The wages of their virtue, and all foes
The cup of their deservings. O, see, see!

LEAR

And my poor fool is hang'd! No, no, no life!
Why should a dog, a horse, a rat, have life,
And thou no breath at all? Thou'lt come no more,
Never, never, never, never, never!
Pray you, undo this button: thank you, sir.
Do you see this? Look on her, look, her lips,
Look there, look there!   [*Dies*

EDGAR

He faints. My lord, my lord!

KENT

Break, heart; I prithee, break!

EDGAR

Look up, my lord.

KENT

Vex not his ghost: O, let him pass! he hates him
That would upon the rack of this tough world
Stretch him out longer.

EDGAR

He is gone indeed.

KENT

The wonder is he hath endured so long:
He but usurp'd his life.

ALBANY

Bear them from hence. Our present business
Is general woe. [*To* KENT *and* EDGAR] Friends of my
  soul, you twain
Rule in this realm and the gored state sustain.

KENT

I have a journey, sir, shortly to go;
My master calls me, I must not say no.

ALBANY

The weight of this sad time we must obey,
Speak what we feel, not what we ought to say.
The oldest hath borne most: we that are young
Shall never see so much, nor live so long.

          [*Exeunt, with a dead march*

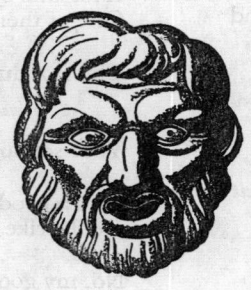

THE TRAGEDY OF MACBETH

SYNOPSIS

I**N THE** midst of thunder and lightning on a barren Scottish heath crouch three uncanny witches in wild attire waiting to intercept the two successful generals, Macbeth and Banquo, on their return from battle where they have just quelled a rebellion led by the traitorous thane of Cawdor against the gentle, unwarlike King Duncan. The witches hail Macbeth first with his own title, thane of Glamis, then as thane of Cawdor, then as "King hereafter." Banquo quickly remarks Macbeth's sudden start at the witches' words, then asks for a prophecy for himself and is told that he will beget kings though he is not one. Macbeth is profoundly stirred when part of the prophecy is fulfilled a few minutes later, two noblemen sent by the King greeting him with the title of the thane of Cawdor who has been put to death. As Duncan's sons are young, Macbeth being the King's cousin had hoped to succeed him in accordance with the Scottish law but the old King announces to his thanes that his eldest son Malcolm will henceforth be known as Duke of Cumberland, heir to the throne.

Macbeth's slumbering ambitions become determined and malignant, and murderous thoughts surge through his brain when Duncan signifies his desire to remain overnight with his sons at Macbeth's castle. Lady Macbeth, as a devoted loving wife, shares her husband's ambitions but, knowing he is not hardened in wickedness, mistrusts his courage and resoluteness, and she herself makes a daring brutal plot against the King's life which she forces her vacillating husband to accept.

The two grooms of the King's bedchamber are soundly drugged, Macbeth stabs the sleeping Duncan to death, and Lady Macbeth finishes the awful night's work by smearing the unconscious grooms with blood and laying their reeking daggers beside them In the morning when the murder is discovered, Macbeth affects great grief and to show his indignation he kills the King's grooms whom he declares are the assassins. The princes, knowing their personal danger and having few doubts as to the real murderer, keep discreet silence and flee the country, Malcolm going to England and Donalbain to Ireland, whereupon Macbeth insinuates that they are the originators of the crime.

Although he now is the crowned King of Scotland, Macbeth remains unsatisfied, knowing that Banquo suspects him of Duncan's murder and galled by the remembrance of the witches' prophecy that another man's children will be kings. No longer wavering and hesitant, he promptly accomplishes the murder of Banquo on the same night when he is giving a formal banquet to his thanes.

While he is praising Banquo and pretending to regret his absence, the murdered man's ghost enters the banquet hall and takes his vacant seat at the table, unseen by all but Macbeth who utters such words of terrified guilt that the noblemen are both confused and suspicious, and Lady Macbeth hurriedly breaks up the gathering.

Frustrated in his plans by the escape of Fleance, Banquo's son, from the murderers, Macbeth visits the witches' cavern, where Hecate, Queen of Evil, has plotted his downfall, and the witches make revelations in which the truth is disguised, mysterious and misleading. They warn him against Macduff, a powerful thane, by showing him an armed head; the apparition of a blood-child bids him be bold and resolute, for no one born of woman will harm him; and a crowned child follows with a tree in his hand, telling him to be lion-hearted and brave for he will never be vanquished until Birnam Wood, near his castle at Dunsinane, moves against him. Although he is afterwards tormented by the sight of eight kings accompanied by Banquo's ghost who smilingly points to them as his progeny, Macbeth pins his faith in the witches' prophecies, places spies in all the thanes' houses to watch their movements, and comes to be feared and hated as a tyrant. When news reaches him of Macduff's flight to England to join Malcolm who is preparing to recover the throne of Scotland, he orders the slaughter of the thane's helpless wife and little children.

Meanwhile in his castle, Lady Macbeth, her mind deranged by its hideous memories, walks and talks piteously in her sleep, revealing their dreadful crimes, and the kindly doctor assures her husband that medicines will not help her. But Macbeth has little time to give her as he is busily preparing to meet the advancing English army under Malcolm and Siward, Lord of Northumberland, who have combined with some rebellious Scottish forces near Birnam Wood. To conceal their numbers, Malcolm orders each soldier to carry before him a leafy branch, with the result that a white-faced, trembling servant rushes into Macbeth's presence with the news that Birnam Wood is moving! At the same time a messenger brings tidings of Lady Macbeth's death.

The desperate, raging King, battling with all his tremendous energy in a losing fight, his soldiers deserting him by scores, encounters young Siward, the English general's son, who fights him upon hearing his hated name, and is killed. Still muttering the prophetic words that no one born of woman will harm him, Macbeth is suddenly faced with Macduff, thirsting for revenge, who scoffs at the witches' charm by saying that he himself was born untimely, and taunts his enemy by declaring that his head will soon be placed on a pole for the public gaze. Macbeth falls fighting and Macduff hails the victorious Malcolm at Dunsinane castle with the tyrant's head.

HISTORICAL DATA

The chief source of the story of *Macbeth* is *The Chronicle of England and Scotland* by Holinshed published in 1577 which in turn was founded largely on the *Scotorum Historia* of Hector Boece (1526). The earliest source of this material probably came from the Scottish historians, John of Fordun (1360) and Andrew of Wyntoun (1420). There is, however, a great deal of purely legendary matter in all of these accounts. The scene is laid in about the year 1040 and recent opinion is indicated that the legendary *Macbeth* was a rather more worthy monarch than the character created by Shakespeare.

Shakespeare added many incidents to the bare details of the earlier accounts. Banquo's ghost, the porter scene, the sleep-walking scene and the famous soliloquies appear to have had no prototype in the earlier works.

There may, perhaps, have been in existence an earlier play on this subject which is not extant, for there was entered for registration in the Stationers' Register in 1596 a ballad or stage play (?) entitled *Macdobeth*.

From political allusions, a reference to the practice of touching for the King's evil which James I was induced to revive, and minor indications in the text, the date of composition of *Macbeth* is generally fixed as 1606. It was first published in the First Folio in 1623.

"Is this a dagger which I see before me?"
MACBETH

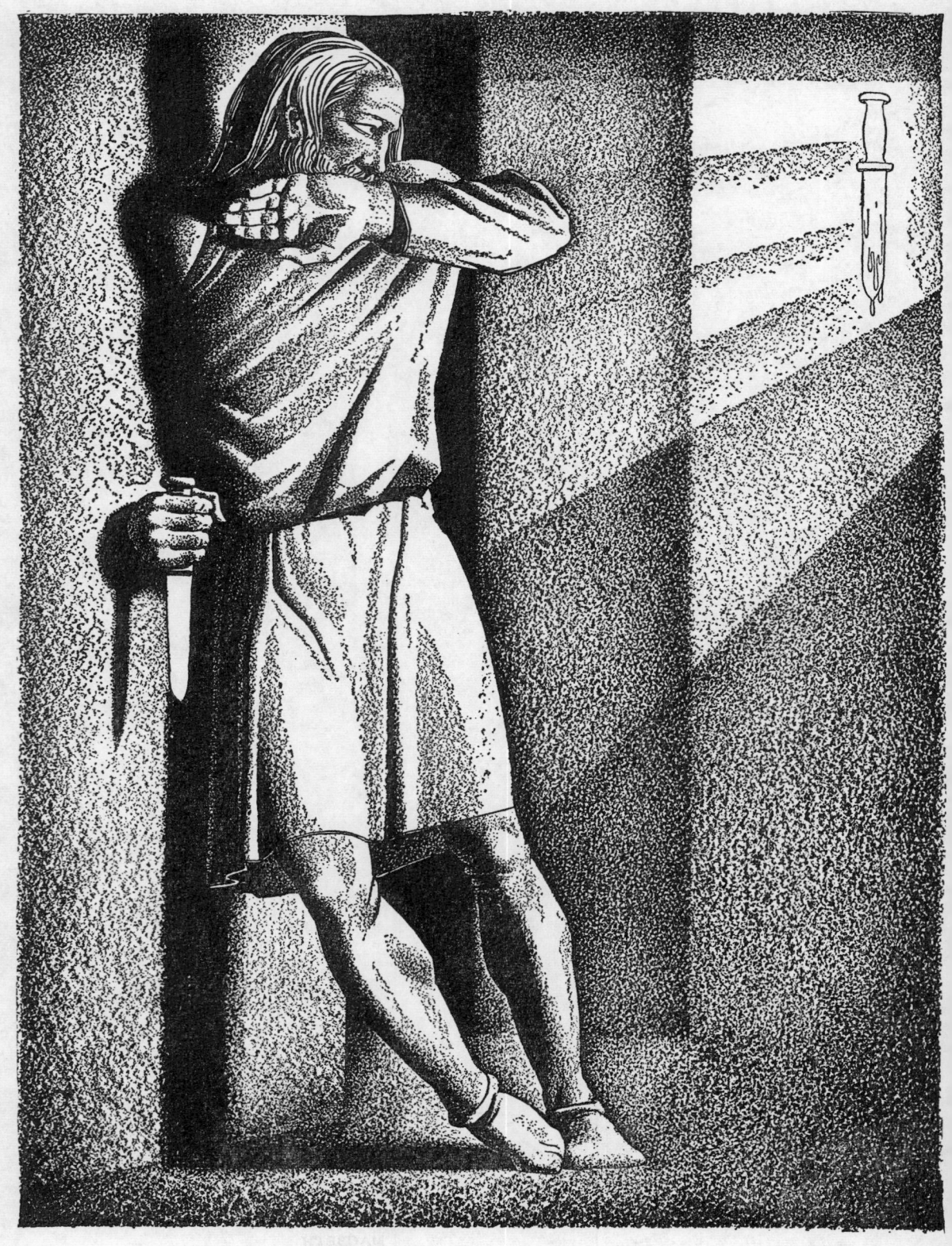

THE TRAGEDY OF MACBETH

DRAMATIS PERSONÆ

DUNCAN, *King of Scotland.*
MALCOLM, } *his sons.*
DONALBAIN, }
MACBETH, } *generals of the King's army.*
BANQUO }
MACDUFF, }
LENNOX, }
ROSS, } *noblemen of Scotland.*
MENTEITH, }
ANGUS, }
CAITHNESS, }
FLEANCE, *son to Banquo.*
SIWARD, *earl of Northumberland, general of the English forces.*
YOUNG SIWARD, *his son.*
SEYTON, *an officer attending on Macbeth.*
BOY, *son to Macduff.*

AN ENGLISH DOCTOR.
A SCOTCH DOCTOR.
A SERGEANT.
A PORTER.
AN OLD MAN.

LADY MACBETH.
LADY MACDUFF.
GENTLEWOMAN *attending on Lady Macbeth.*

HECATE.
THREE WITCHES.
APPARITIONS.
LORDS, GENTLEMEN, OFFICERS, SOLDIERS, MURDERERS, ATTENDANTS, AND MESSENGERS.

SCENE—*Scotland; England.*

ACT I

SCENE I. *A desert place*

Thunder and lightning. Enter THREE WITCHES

FIRST WITCH

WHEN shall we three meet again
In thunder, lightning, or in rain?

SECOND WITCH

When the hurlyburly's done,
When the battle's lost and won.

THIRD WITCH

That will be ere the set of sun.

FIRST WITCH

Where the place?

SECOND WITCH

Upon the heath.

THIRD WITCH

There to meet with Macbeth.

FIRST WITCH

I come, Graymalkin.

ALL

Paddock calls:—anon!
Fair is foul, and foul is fair.
Hover through the fog and filthy air.   [*Exeunt*

SCENE II. *A camp near Forres*

Alarum within. Enter DUNCAN, MALCOLM, DONALBAIN,
LENNOX, *with* ATTENDANTS, *meeting a bleeding*
SERGEANT

DUNCAN

What bloody man is that? He can report,
As seemeth by his plight, of the revolt
The newest state.

MALCOLM

This is the sergeant
Who like a good and hardy soldier fought
'Gainst my captivity. Hail, brave friend!
Say to the king the knowledge of the broil
As thou didst leave it.

SERGEANT

Doubtful it stood;
As two spent swimmers, that do cling together
And choke their art. The merciless Macdonwald—
Worthy to be a rebel, for to that
The multiplying villanies of nature
Do swarm upon him—from the western isles
Of kerns and gallowglasses is supplied;
And fortune, on his damned quarrel smiling,
Show'd like a rebel's whore: but all's too weak:
For brave Macbeth—well he deserves that name—
Disdaining fortune, with his brandish'd steel,
Which smoked with bloody execution,
Like valour's minion carved out his passage
Till he faced the slave;
Which ne'er shook hands, nor bade farewell to him,
Till he unseam'd him from the nave to the chaps,
And fix'd his head upon our battlements.

DUNCAN

O valiant cousin! worthy gentleman!

SERGEANT

As whence the sun 'gins his reflection
Shipwrecking storms and direful thunders break,
So from that spring whence comfort seem'd to come
Discomfort swells. Mark, king of Scotland, mark:
No sooner justice had, with valour arm'd,
Compell'd these skipping kerns to trust their heels,
But the Norweyan lord, surveying vantage,

With furbish'd arms and new supplies of men,
Began a fresh assault.

DUNCAN
　　　　　Dismay'd not this
Our captains, Macbeth and Banquo?

SERGEANT
　　　　　　　　Yes;
As sparrows eagles, or the hare the lion.
If I say sooth, I must report they were
As cannons overcharged with double cracks;
So they
Doubly redoubled strokes upon the foe:
Except they meant to bathe in reeking wounds,
Or memorize another Golgotha,
I cannot tell—
But I am faint; my gashes cry for help.

DUNCAN
So well thy words become thee as thy wounds;
They smack of honour both. Go get him surgeons.
　　　　　　　　[Exit SERGEANT, attended
Who comes here?

Enter ROSS

MALCOLM
　　　The worthy thane of Ross.

LENNOX
What a haste looks through his eyes! So should he
　look
That seems to speak things strange.

ROSS
　　　　　　　God save the king!

DUNCAN
Whence camest thou, worthy thane?

ROSS
　　　　　　　From Fife, great king;
Where the Norweyan banners flout the sky
And fan our people cold.
Norway himself, with terrible numbers,
Assisted by that most disloyal traitor
The thane of Cawdor, began a dismal conflict;
Till that Bellona's bridegroom, lapp'd in proof,
Confronted him with self-comparisons,
Point against point rebellious, arm 'gainst arm,
Curbing his lavish spirit: and, to conclude,
The victory fell on us.

DUNCAN
　　　Great happiness!

ROSS
That now
Sweno, the Norways' king, craves composition;
Nor would we deign him burial of his men
Till he disbursed, at Saint Colme's inch,
Ten thousand dollars to our general use.

DUNCAN
No more that thane of Cawdor shall deceive
Our bosom interest: go pronounce his present death,
And with his former title greet Macbeth.

ROSS
I'll see it done.

DUNCAN
What he hath lost, noble Macbeth hath won.
　　　　　　　　　　　　[Exeunt

SCENE III. A heath

Thunder. Enter the THREE WITCHES

FIRST WITCH
Where hast thou been, sister?

SECOND WITCH
Killing swine.

THIRD WITCH
Sister, where thou?

FIRST WITCH
A sailor's wife had chestnuts in her lap,
And mounch'd, and mounch'd, and mounch'd.
　'Give me,' quoth I:
'Aroint thee, witch!' the rump-fed ronyon cries.
Her husband's to Aleppo gone, master o' the Tiger:
But in a sieve I'll thither sail,
And, like a rat without a tail,
I'll do, I'll do, and I'll do.

SECOND WITCH
I'll give thee a wind.

FIRST WITCH
Thou'rt kind.

THIRD WITCH
And I another.

FIRST WITCH
I myself have all the other;
And the very ports they blow,
All the quarters that they know
I' the shipman's card.
I will drain him dry as hay:
Sleep shall neither night nor day
Hang upon his pent-house lid;
He shall live a man forbid:
Weary se'nnights nine times nine
Shall he dwindle, peak, and pine:
Though his bark cannot be lost,
Yet it shall be tempest-tost.
Look what I have.

SECOND WITCH
Show me, show me.

FIRST WITCH
Here I have a pilot's thumb,
Wreck'd as homeward he did come.　　[Drum within

THIRD WITCH
A drum, a drum!
Macbeth doth come.

ALL
The weird sisters, hand in hand,
Posters of the sea and land,
Thus do go about, about:
Thrice to thine, and thrice to mine,
And thrice again, to make up nine.
Peace! the charm's wound up.

Enter MACBETH and BANQUO

MACBETH
So foul and fair a day I have not seen.

BANQUO

How far is 't call'd to Forres? What are these
So wither'd, and so wild in their attire,
That look not like the inhabitants o' the earth,
And yet are on 't? Live you? or are you aught
That man may question? You seem to understand me,
By each at once her choppy finger laying
Upon her skinny lips: you should be women,
And yet your beards forbid me to interpret
That you are so.

MACBETH

　　　　Speak, if you can: what are you?

FIRST WITCH

All hail, Macbeth! hail to thee, thane of Glamis!

SECOND WITCH

All hail, Macbeth! hail to thee, thane of Cawdor!

THIRD WITCH

All hail, Macbeth, that shalt be king hereafter!

BANQUO

Good sir, why do you start, and seem to fear
Things that do sound so fair? I' the name of truth,
Are ye fantastical, or that indeed
Which outwardly ye show? My noble partner
You greet with present grace and great prediction
Of noble having and of royal hope,
That he seems rapt withal: to me you speak not:
If you can look into the seeds of time,
And say which grain will grow and which will not,
Speak then to me, who neither beg nor fear
Your favours nor your hate.

FIRST WITCH

Hail!

SECOND WITCH

Hail!

THIRD WITCH

Hail!

FIRST WITCH

Lesser than Macbeth, and greater.

SECOND WITCH

Not so happy, yet much happier.

THIRD WITCH

Thou shalt get kings, though thou be none:
So all hail, Macbeth and Banquo!

FIRST WITCH

Banquo and Macbeth, all hail!

MACBETH

Stay, you imperfect speakers, tell me more:
By Sinel's death I know I am thane of Glamis;
But how of Cawdor? the thane of Cawdor lives,
A prosperous gentleman; and to be king
Stands not within the prospect of belief,
No more than to be Cawdor. Say from whence
You owe this strange intelligence? or why
Upon this blasted heath you stop our way
With such prophetic greeting? Speak, I charge you.
　　　　　　　　　　　　[WITCHES vanish

BANQUO

The earth hath bubbles as the water has,
And these are of them: whither are they vanish'd?

MACBETH

Into the air, and what seem'd corporal melted
As breath into the wind. Would they had stay'd!

BANQUO

Were such things here as we do speak about?
Or have we eaten on the insane root
That takes the reason prisoner?

MACBETH

Your children shall be kings.

BANQUO

　　　　　　　　　　You shall be king.

MACBETH

And thane of Cawdor too: went it not so?

BANQUO

To the selfsame tune and words. Who's here?

Enter ROSS *and* ANGUS

ROSS

The king hath happily received, Macbeth,
The news of thy success: and when he reads
Thy personal venture in the rebels' fight,
His wonders and his praises do contend
Which should be thine or his: silenced with that,
In viewing o'er the rest o' the selfsame day,
He finds thee in the stout Norweyan ranks,
Nothing afeard of what thyself didst make,
Strange images of death. As thick as hail
Came post with post, and every one did bear
Thy praises in his kingdom's great defence,
And pour'd them down before him.

ANGUS

　　　　　　　　　　　We are sent
To give thee, from our royal master, thanks;
Only to herald thee into his sight,
Not pay thee.

ROSS

And for an earnest of a greater honour,
He bade me, from him, call thee thane of Cawdor:
In which addition, hail, most worthy thane!
For it is thine.

BANQUO

　　　　　　What, can the devil speak true?

MACBETH

The thane of Cawdor lives: why do you dress me
In borrow'd robes?

ANGUS

　　　　　　　　Who was the thane lives yet,
But under neavy judgement bears that life
Which he deserves to lose. Whether he was combined
With those of Norway, or did line the rebel
With hidden help and vantage, or that with both
He labour'd in his country's wreck, I know not;
But treasons capital, confess'd and proved,
Have overthrown him.

MACBETH

　　　　　　　　[*Aside*] Glamis, and thane of Cawdor:
The greatest is behind.—Thanks for your pains.—
Do you not hope your children shall be kings,
When those that gave the thane of Cawdor to me
Promised no less to them?

BANQUO

                That, trusted home,
Might yet enkindle you unto the crown,
Besides the thane of Cawdor. But 'tis strange:
And oftentimes, to win us to our harm,
The instruments of darkness tell us truths,
Win us with honest trifles, to betray 's
In deepest consequence.
Cousins, a word, I pray you.

MACBETH

                [*Aside*] Two truths are told,
As happy prologues to the swelling act
Of the imperial theme.—I thank you, gentlemen.—
[*Aside*] This supernatural soliciting
Cannot be ill; cannot be good: if ill,
Why hath it given me earnest of success,
Commencing in a truth? I am thane of Cawdor:
If good, why do I yield to that suggestion
Whose horrid image doth unfix my hair
And make my seated heart knock at my ribs,
Against the use of nature? Present fears
Are less than horrible imaginings:
My thought, whose murder yet is but fantastical,
Shakes so my single state of man that function
Is smother'd in surmise, and nothing is
But what is not.

BANQUO

           Look, how our partner's rapt.

MACBETH

[*Aside*] If chance will have me king, why, chance
    may crown me,
Without my stir.

BANQUO

           New honours come upon him,
Like our strange garments, cleave not to their
    mould
But with the aid of use.

MACBETH

           [*Aside*] Come what come may,
Time and the hour runs through the roughest day.

BANQUO

Worthy Macbeth, we stay upon your leisure.

MACBETH

Give me your favour: my dull brain was wrought
With things forgotten. Kind gentlemen, your pains
Are register'd where every day I turn
The leaf to read them. Let us toward the king.
Think upon what hath chanced, and at more time,
The interim having weigh'd it, let us speak
Our free hearts each to other.

BANQUO

                Very gladly.

MACBETH

Till then, enough. Come, friends.   [*Exeunt*

SCENE IV. *Forres. The palace*

Flourish. Enter DUNCAN, MALCOLM, DONALBAIN,
LENNOX, *and* ATTENDANTS

DUNCAN

Is execution done on Cawdor? Are not
Those in commission yet return'd?

MALCOLM

                My liege,
They are not yet come back. But I have spoke
With one that saw him die, who did report
That very frankly he confess'd his treasons,
Implored your highness' pardon and set forth
A deep repentance: nothing in his life
Became him like the leaving it; he died
As one that had been studied in his death,
To throw away the dearest thing he owed
As 'twere a careless trifle.

DUNCAN

              There's no art
To find the mind's construction in the face:
He was a gentleman on whom I built
An absolute trust.

    Enter MACBETH, BANQUO, ROSS, *and* ANGUS
                O worthiest cousin!
The sin of my ingratitude even now
Was heavy on me: thou art so far before,
That swiftest wing of recompense is slow
To overtake thee. Would thou hadst less deserved,
That the proportion both of thanks and payment
Might have been mine! only I have left to say,
More is thy due than more than all can pay.

MACBETH

The service and the loyalty I owe,
In doing it, pays itself. Your highness' part
Is to receive our duties: and our duties
Are to your throne and state children and servants;
Which do but what they should, by doing every
    thing
Safe toward your love and honour.

DUNCAN

              Welcome hither:
I have begun to plant thee, and will labour
To make thee full of growing. Noble Banquo,
That hast no less deserved, nor must be known
No less to have done so: let me infold thee
And hold thee to my heart.

BANQUO

              There if I grow,
The harvest is your own.

DUNCAN

              My plenteous joys,
Wanton in fulness, seek to hide themselves
In drops of sorrow. Sons, kinsmen, thanes,
And you whose places are the nearest, know,
We will establish our estate upon
Our eldest, Malcolm, whom we name hereafter
The Prince of Cumberland: which honour must
Not unaccompanied invest him only,
But signs of nobleness, like stars, shall shine
On all deservers. From hence to Inverness,
And bind us further to you.

MACBETH

The rest is labour, which is not used for you:

I'll be myself the harbinger, and make joyful
The hearing of my wife with your approach;
So humbly take my leave.

DUNCAN

My worthy Cawdor!

MACBETH

[*Aside*] The Prince of Cumberland! that is a step
On which I must fall down, or else o'erleap,
For in my way it lies. Stars, hide your fires;
Let not light see my black and deep desires:
The eye wink at the hand; yet let that be
Which the eye fears, when it is done, to see.   [*Exit*

DUNCAN

True, worthy Banquo; he is full so valiant,
And in his commendations I am fed;
It is a banquet to me. Let's after him,
Whose care is gone before to bid us welcome:
It is a peerless kinsman.   [*Flourish. Exeunt*

SCENE V. *Inverness.* MACBETH'S *castle*

Enter LADY MACBETH, *reading a letter*

LADY MACBETH

'They met me in the day of success; and I have learned by the perfectest report, they have more in them than mortal knowledge. When I burned in desire to question them further, they made themselves air, into which they vanished. Whiles I stood rapt in the wonder of it, came missives from the king, who all-hailed me "Thane of Cawdor;" by which title, before, these weird sisters saluted me, and referred me to the coming on of time, with "Hail, king that shalt be!" This have I thought good to deliver thee, my dearest partner of greatness, that thou mightst not lose the dues of rejoicing, by being ignorant of what greatness is promised thee. Lay it to thy heart, and farewell.'

Glamis thou art, and Cawdor, and shalt be
What thou art promised: yet do I fear thy nature;
It is too full o' the milk of human kindness
To catch the nearest way: thou wouldst be great;
Art not without ambition, but without
The illness should attend it: what thou wouldst
    highly,
That wouldst thou holily; wouldst not play false,
And yet wouldst strongly win: thou'ldst have, great
    Glamis,
That which cries 'Thus thou must do, if thou have
    it;
And that which rather thou dost fear to do
Than wishest should be undone.' Hie thee hither,
That I may pour my spirits in thine ear,
And chastise with the valour of my tongue
All that impedes thee from the golden round,
Which fate and metaphysical aid doth seem
To have thee crown'd withal.

Enter a MESSENGER

What is your tidings?

MESSENGER

The king comes here to-night.

LADY MACBETH

Thou'rt mad to say it:

Is not thy master with him? who, were 't so,
Would have inform'd for preparation.

MESSENGER

So please you, it is true: our thane is coming:
One of my fellows had the speed of him,
Who, almost dead for breath, had scarcely more
Than would make up his message.

LADY MACBETH

Give him tending;
He brings great news.   [*Exit* MESSENGER
The raven himself is hoarse
That croaks the fatal entrance of Duncan
Under my battlements. Come, you spirits
That tend on mortal thoughts, unsex me here,
And fill me, from the crown to the toe, top-full
Of direst cruelty! make thick my blood,
Stop up the access and passage to remorse,
That no compunctious visitings of nature
Shake my fell purpose, nor keep peace between
The effect and it! Come to my woman's breasts,
And take my milk for gall, you murdering ministers,
Wherever in your sightless substances
You wait on nature's mischief! Come, thick night,
And pall thee in the dunnest smoke of hell,
That my keen knife see not the wound it makes,
Nor heaven peep through the blanket of the dark,
To cry 'Hold, hold!'

Enter MACBETH

Great Glamis! worthy Cawdor!
Greater than both, by the all-hail hereafter!
Thy letters have transported me beyond
This ignorant present, and I feel now
The future in the instant.

MACBETH

My dearest love,
Duncan comes here to-night.

LADY MACBETH

And when goes hence?

MACBETH

To-morrow, as he purposes.

LADY MACBETH

O, never
Shall sun that morrow see!
Your face, my thane, is as a book where men
May read strange matters. To beguile the time,
Look like the time; bear welcome in your eye,
Your hand, your tongue: look like the innocent
    flower,
But be the serpent under 't. He that's coming
Must be provided for: and you shall put
This night's great business into my dispatch;
Which shall to all our nights and days to come
Give solely sovereign sway and masterdom.

MACBETH

We will speak further.

LADY MACBETH

Only look up clear;
To alter favour ever is to fear:
Leave all the rest to me.   [*Exeunt*

SCENE VI. *Before* MACBETH's *castle*

Hautboys and torches. Enter DUNCAN, MALCOLM,
DONALBAIN, BANQUO, LENNOX, MACDUFF, ROSS,
ANGUS, *and* ATTENDANTS

DUNCAN

This castle hath a pleasant seat; the air
Nimbly and sweetly recommends itself
Unto our gentle senses.

BANQUO

This guest of summer,
The temple-haunting martlet, does approve
By his loved mansionry that the heaven's breath
Smells wooingly here: no jutty, frieze,
Buttress, nor coign of vantage, but this bird
Hath made his pendent bed and procreant cradle:
Where they most breed and haunt, I have observed
The air is delicate.

Enter LADY MACBETH

DUNCAN

See, see, our honour'd hostess!
The love that follows us sometime is our trouble,
Which still we thank as love. Herein I teach you
How you shall bid God 'ild us for your pains,
And thank us for your trouble.

LADY MACBETH

All our service
In every point twice done, and then done double,
Were poor and single business to contend
Against those honours deep and broad wherewith
Your majesty loads our house: for those of old,
And the late dignities heap'd up to them,
We rest your hermits.

DUNCAN

Where's the thane of Cawdor?
We coursed him at the heels, and had a purpose
To be his purveyor: but he rides well,
And his great love, sharp as his spur, hath holp him
To his home before us. Fair and noble hostess,
We are your guest to-night.

LADY MACBETH

Your servants ever
Have theirs, themselves, and what is theirs, in
  compt,
To make their audit at your highness' pleasure,
Still to return your own.

DUNCAN

Give me your hand;
Conduct me to mine host: we love him highly,
And shall continue our graces towards him.
By your leave, hostess.   [*Exeunt*

SCENE VII. MACBETH's *castle*

Hautboys and torches. Enter a SEWER, *and divers*
SERVANTS *with dishes and service, and pass over
the stage. Then enter* MACBETH

MACBETH

If it were done when 'tis done, then 'twere well

It were done quickly: if the assassination
Could trammel up the consequence, and catch,
With his surcease, success; that but this blow
Might be the be-all and the end-all here,
But here, upon this bank and shoal of time,
We'd jump the life to come. But in these cases
We still have judgement here; that we but teach
Bloody instructions, which being taught return
To plague the inventor: this even-handed justice
Commends the ingredients of our poison'd chalice
To our own lips. He's here in double trust:
First, as I am his kinsman and his subject,
Strong both against the deed; then, as his host,
Who should against his murderer shut the door,
Not bear the knife myself. Besides, this Duncan
Hath borne his faculties so meek, hath been
So clear in his great office, that his virtues
Will plead like angels trumpet-tongued against
The deep damnation of his taking-off;
And pity, like a naked new-born babe,
Striding the blast, or heaven's cherubin horsed
Upon the sightless couriers of the air,
Shall blow the horrid deed in every eye,
That tears shall drown the wind. I have no spur
To prick the sides of my intent, but only
Vaulting ambition, which o'erleaps itself
And falls on the other.

Enter LADY MACBETH

How now! what news?

LADY MACBETH

He has almost supp'd: why have you left the chamber?

MACBETH

Hath he ask'd for me?

LADY MACBETH

Know you not he has?

MACBETH

We will proceed no further in this business:
He hath honour'd me of late; and I have bought
Golden opinions from all sorts of people,
Which would be worn now in their newest gloss,
Not cast aside so soon.

LADY MACBETH

Was the hope drunk
Wherein you dress'd yourself? hath it slept since?
And wakes it now, to look so green and pale
At what it did so freely? From this time
Such I account thy love. Art thou afeard
To be the same in thine own act and valour
As thou art in desire? Wouldst thou have that
Which thou esteem'st the ornament of life,
And live a coward in thine own esteem,
Letting 'I dare not' wait upon 'I would,'
Like the poor cat i' the adage?

MACBETH

Prithee, peace:
I dare do all that may become a man;
Who dares do more is none.

LADY MACBETH

What beast was 't then

That made you break this enterprise to me?
When you durst do it, then you were a man;
And, to be more than what you were, you would
Be so much more the man. Nor time nor place
Did then adhere, and yet you would make both:
They have made themselves, and that their fitness
    now
Does unmake you. I have given suck, and know
How tender 'tis to love the babe that milks me:
I would, while it was smiling in my face,
Have pluck'd my nipple from his boneless gums,
And dash'd the brains out, had I so sworn as you
Have done to this.

             MACBETH
       If we should fail?

             LADY MACBETH
                    We fail!
But screw your courage to the sticking-place,
And we'll not fail. When Duncan is asleep—
Whereto the rather shall his day's hard journey
Soundly invite him—his two chamberlains
Will I with wine and wassail so convince,
That memory, the warder of the brain,
Shall be a fume, and the receipt of reason
A limbec only: when in swinish sleep
Their drenched natures lie as in a death,
What cannot you and I perform upon
The unguarded Duncan? what not put upon
His spongy officers, who shall bear the guilt
Of our great quell?

             MACBETH
         Bring forth men-children only;
For thy undaunted mettle should compose
Nothing but males. Will it not be received,
When we have mark'd with blood those sleepy two
Of his own chamber, and used their very daggers,
That they have done 't?

             LADY MACBETH
          Who dares receive it other,
As we shall make our griefs and clamour roar
Upon his death?

             MACBETH
         I am settled, and bend up
Each corporal agent to this terrible feat.
Away, and mock the time with fairest show:
False face must hide what the false heart doth know.
                    [*Exeunt*

ACT II

SCENE I. *Inverness. Court of* MACBETH's *castle*

Enter BANQUO, *and* FLEANCE *bearing a torch before him*
             BANQUO
How goes the night, boy?

             FLEANCE
The moon is down; I have not heard the clock.

             BANQUO
And she goes down at twelve.

              FLEANCE
             I take 't, 'tis later, sir.

             BANQUO
Hold, take my sword. There's husbandry in heaven,
Their candles are all out. Take thee that too.
A heavy summons lies like lead upon me,
And yet I would not sleep. Merciful powers,
Restrain in me the cursed thoughts that nature
Gives way to in repose!

   Enter MACBETH, *and a* SERVANT *with a torch*
                Give me my sword.
Who's there?

             MACBETH
A friend.

             BANQUO
What, sir, not yet at rest? The king's a-bed:
He hath been in unusual pleasure, and
Sent forth great largess to your offices:
This diamond he greets your wife withal,
By the name of most kind hostess; and shut up
In measureless content.

             MACBETH
              Being unprepared,
Our will became the servant to defect,
Which else should free have wrought.

             BANQUO
                 All's well.
I dreamt last night of the three weird sisters:
To you they have show'd some truth.

             MACBETH
            I think not of them:
Yet, when we can entreat an hour to serve,
We would spend it in some words upon that busi-
    ness,
If you would grant the time.

             BANQUO
            At your kind'st leisure.

             MACBETH
If you shall cleave to my consent, when 'tis,
It shall make honour for you.

             BANQUO
              So I lose none
In seeking to augment it, but still keep
My bosom franchised and allegiance clear,
I shall be counsell'd.

             MACBETH
         Good repose the while!

             BANQUO
Thanks, sir: the like to you!
        [*Exeunt* BANQUO *and* FLEANCE

             MACBETH
Go bid thy mistress, when my drink is ready,
She strike upon the bell. Get thee to bed.
                   [*Exit* SERVANT
Is this a dagger which I see before me,
The handle toward my hand? Come, let me clutch
    thee.
I have thee not, and yet I see thee still.
Art thou not, fatal vision, sensible
To feeling as to sight? or art thou but

A dagger of the mind, a false creation,
Proceeding from the heat-oppressed brain?
I see thee yet, in form as palpable
As this which now I draw.
Thou marshall'st me the way that I was going;
And such an instrument I was to use.
Mine eyes are made the fools o' the other senses,
Or else worth all the rest: I see thee still;
And on thy blade and dudgeon gouts of blood,
Which was not so before. There's no such thing:
It is the bloody business which informs
Thus to mine eyes. Now o'er the one half-world
Nature seems dead, and wicked dreams abuse
The curtain'd sleep; witchcraft celebrates
Pale Hecate's offerings; and wither'd murder,
Alarum'd by his sentinel, the wolf,
Whose howl's his watch, thus with his stealthy pace,
With Tarquin's ravishing strides, towards his design
Moves like a ghost. Thou sure and firm-set earth,
Hear not my steps, which way they walk, for fear
Thy very stones prate of my whereabout,
And take the present horror from the time,
Which now suits with it. Whiles I threat, he lives:
Words to the heat of deeds too cold breath gives.
                                        [A bell rings
I go, and it is done: the bell invites me.
Hear it not, Duncan, for it is a knell
That summons thee to heaven, or to hell.   [Exit

SCENE II. *The same*

Enter LADY MACBETH

LADY MACBETH
That which hath made them drunk hath made me
  bold;
What hath quench'd them hath given me fire.
  Hark! Peace!
It was the owl that shriek'd, the fatal bellman,
Which gives the stern'st good-night. He is about it:
The doors are open, and the surfeited grooms
Do mock their charge with snores: I have drugg'd
  their possets,
That death and nature do contend about them,
Whether they live or die.

MACBETH
            [*Within*] Who's there? what, ho!

LADY MACBETH
Alack, I am afraid they have awaked
And 'tis not done: the attempt and not the deed
Confounds us. Hark! I laid their daggers ready;
He could not miss 'em. Had he not resembled
My father as he slept, I had done 't.
            Enter MACBETH
                        My husband!

MACBETH
I have done the deed. Didst thou not hear a noise?

LADY MACBETH
I heard the owl scream and the crickets cry.
Did not you speak?

MACBETH
            When?

LADY MACBETH
            Now.

MACBETH
                        As I descended?

LADY MACBETH
Ay.

MACBETH
Hark!
Who lies i' the second chamber?

LADY MACBETH
                        Donalbain.

MACBETH
This is a sorry sight.   [*Looking on his hands*

LADY MACBETH
A foolish thought, to say a sorry sight.

MACBETH
There's one did laugh in 's sleep, and one cried
  'Murder!'
That they did wake each other: I stood and heard
  them:
But they did say their prayers, and address'd them
Again to sleep.

LADY MACBETH
            There are two lodged together.

MACBETH
One cried 'God bless us!' and 'Amen' the other,
As they had seen me with these hangman's hands:
Listening their fear, I could not say 'Amen,'
When they did say 'God bless us!'

LADY MACBETH
Consider it not so deeply.

MACBETH
But wherefore could not I pronounce 'Amen'?
I had most need of blessing, and 'Amen'
Stuck in my throat.

LADY MACBETH
            These deeds must not be thought
After these ways; so, it will make us mad.

MACBETH
Methought I heard a voice cry 'Sleep no more!
Macbeth does murder sleep'—the innocent sleep,
Sleep that knits up the ravell'd sleave of care,
The death of each day's life, sore labour's bath,
Balm of hurt minds, great nature's second course,
Chief nourisher in life's feast,—

LADY MACBETH
                        What do you mean?

MACBETH
Still it cried 'Sleep no more!' to all the house:
'Glamis hath murder'd sleep, and therefore Cawdor
Shall sleep no more: Macbeth shall sleep no more.'

LADY MACBETH
Who was it that thus cried? Why, worthy thane,
You do unbend your noble strength, to think
So brainsickly of things. Go get some water,
And wash this filthy witness from your hand.
Why did you bring these daggers from the place?

They must lie there: go carry them, and smear
The sleepy grooms with blood.

MACBETH

                I'll go no more:
I am afraid to think what I have done;
Look on 't again I dare not.

LADY MACBETH

                Infirm of purpose!
Give me the daggers: the sleeping and the dead
Are but as pictures: 'tis the eye of childhood
That fears a painted devil. If he do bleed,
I'll gild the faces of the grooms withal,
For it must seem their guilt. [*Exit. Knocking within*

MACBETH

            Whence is that knocking?
How is 't with me, when every noise appals me?
What hands are here? ha! they pluck out mine eyes!
Will all great Neptune's ocean wash this blood
Clean from my hand? No; this my hand will rather
The multitudinous seas incarnadine,
Making the green one red.

Re-enter LADY MACBETH

LADY MACBETH

My hands are of your colour, but I shame
To wear a heart so white. [*Knocking within*] I hear a
    knocking
At the south entry: retire we to our chamber:
A little water clears us of this deed:
How easy is it then! Your constancy
Hath left you unattended. [*Knocking within*] Hark!
    more knocking:
Get on your nightgown, lest occasion call us
And show us to be watchers: be not lost
So poorly in your thoughts.

MACBETH

To know my deed, 'twere best not know myself.
                      [*Knocking within*
Wake Duncan with thy knocking! I would thou
    couldst!   [*Exeunt*

SCENE III. *The same*

Enter a PORTER. *Knocking within*

PORTER

Here's a knocking indeed! If a man were porter of
hell-gate, he should have old turning the key.
[*Knocking within*] Knock, knock, knock! Who's
there, i' the name of Beelzebub? Here's a farmer,
that hanged himself on th' expectation of plenty:
come in time; have napkins enow about you; here
you'll sweat for 't. [*Knocking within*] Knock, knock!
Who's there, in th' other devil's name? Faith, here's
an equivocator, that could swear in both the scales
against either scale; who committed treason enough
for God's sake, yet could not equivocate to heaven:
O, come in, equivocator. [*Knocking within*] Knock,
knock, knock! Who's there? Faith, here's an English
tailor come hither, for stealing out of a French hose:
come in, tailor; here you may roast your goose.
[*Knocking within*] Knock, knock; never at quiet!

What are you? But this place is too cold for hell. I'll
devil-porter it no further: I had thought to have let
in some of all professions, that go the primrose way
to the everlasting bonfire. [*Knocking within*] Anon,
anon! I pray you, remember the porter.
                          [*Opens the gate.*

Enter MACDUFF *and* LENNOX

MACDUFF

Was it so late, friend, ere you went to bed,
That you do lie so late?

PORTER

Faith, sir, we were carousing till the second cock:
and drink, sir, is a great provoker of three things.

MACDUFF

What three things does drink especially provoke?

PORTER

Marry, sir, nose-painting, sleep and urine. Lechery,
sir, it provokes and unprovokes; it provokes the
desire, but it takes away the performance: therefore
much drink may be said to be an equivocator with
lechery: it makes him and it mars him; it sets him
on and it takes him off; it persuades him and dis-
heartens him; makes him stand to and not stand to;
in conclusion, equivocates him in a sleep, and giving him the lie, leaves him.

MACDUFF

I believe drink gave thee the lie last night.

PORTER

That it did, sir, i' the very throat on me: but I requited him for his lie, and, I think, being too strong
for him, though he took up my legs sometime, yet I
made a shift to cast him.

MACDUFF

Is thy master stirring?

Enter MACBETH

Our knocking has awaked him; here he comes.

LENNOX

Good morrow, noble sir.

MACBETH

               Good morrow, both.

MACDUFF

Is the king stirring, worthy thane?

MACBETH

                         Not yet.

MACDUFF

He did command me to call timely on him:
I have almost slipp'd the hour.

MACBETH

                  I'll bring you to him.

MACDUFF

I know this is a joyful trouble to you;
But yet 'tis one.

MACBETH

The labour we delight in physics pain.
This is the door.

MACDUFF

              I'll make so bold to call,
For 'tis my limited service.   [*Exit*

LENNOX

Goes the king hence to-day?

MACBETH

He does: he did appoint so.

LENNOX

The night has been unruly: where we lay,
Our chimneys were blown down, and, as they say,
Lamentings heard i' the air, strange screams of
    death,
And prophesying with accents terrible
Of dire combustion and confused events
New hatch'd to the woful time: the obscure bird
Clamour'd the livelong night: some say, the earth
Was feverous and did shake.

MACBETH

'Twas a rough night.

LENNOX

My young remembrance cannot parallel
A fellow to it.

Re-enter MACDUFF

MACDUFF

O horror, horror, horror! Tongue nor heart
Cannot conceive nor name thee.

MACBETH *and* LENNOX

What's the matter?

MACDUFF

Confusion now hath made his masterpiece.
Most sacrilegious murder hath broke ope
The Lord's anointed temple, and stole thence
The life o' the building.

MACBETH

What is 't you say? the life?

LENNOX

Mean you his majesty?

MACDUFF

Approach the chamber, and destroy your sight
With a new Gorgon: do not bid me speak;
See, and then speak yourselves.

[*Exeunt* MACBETH *and* LENNOX
Awake, awake!

Ring the alarum-bell. Murder and treason!
Banquo and Donalbain! Malcolm! awake!
Shake off this downy sleep, death's counterfeit,
And look on death itself! up, up, and see
The great doom's image! Malcolm! Banquo!
As from your graves rise up, and walk like sprites,
To countenance this horror. Ring the bell.

[*Bell rings*

Enter LADY MACBETH

LADY MACBETH

What's the business,
That such a hideous trumpet calls to parley
The sleepers of the house? speak, speak!

MACDUFF

O gentle lady,
'Tis not for you to hear what I can speak:
The repetition, in a woman's ear,
Would murder as it fell.

Enter BANQUO

O Banquo, Banquo!
Our royal master's murder'd.

LADY MACBETH

Woe, alas!

What, in our house?

BANQUO

Too cruel any where.
Dear Duff, I prithee, contradict thyself,
And say it is not so.

Re-enter MACBETH *and* LENNOX, *with* ROSS

MACBETH

Had I but died an hour before this chance,
I had lived a blessed time; for from this instant
There's nothing serious in mortality:
All is but toys: renown and grace is dead;
The wine of life is drawn, and the mere lees
Is left this vault to brag of.

Enter MALCOLM *and* DONALBAIN

DONALBAIN

What is amiss?

MACBETH

You are, and do not know 't:
The spring, the head, the fountain of your blood
Is stopp'd; the very source of it is stopp'd.

MACDUFF

Your royal father's murder'd.

MALCOLM

O, by whom?

LENNOX

Those of his chamber, as it seem'd, had done 't:
Their hands and faces were all badged with blood;
So were their daggers, which unwiped we found
Upon their pillows:
They stared, and were distracted; no man's life
Was to be trusted with them.

MACBETH

O, yet I do repent me of my fury,
That I did kill them.

MACDUFF

Wherefore did you so?

MACBETH

Who can be wise, amazed, temperate and furious,
Loyal and neutral, in a moment? No man:
The expedition of my violent love
Outrun the pauser reason. Here lay Duncan,
His silver skin laced with his golden blood,
And his gash'd stabs look'd like a breach in nature
For ruin's wasteful entrance: there, the murderers,
Steep'd in the colours of their trade, their daggers
Unmannerly breech'd with gore: who could refrain,
That had a heart to love, and in that heart
Courage to make 's love known?

LADY MACBETH

Help me hence, ho!

MACDUFF

Look to the lady.

MALCOLM

[*Aside to* DONALBAIN] Why do we hold our tongues,
That most may claim this argument for ours?

DONALBAIN

[*Aside to* MALCOLM] What should be spoken here,
    where our fate,

Hid in an auger-hole, may rush, and seize us?
Let's away;
Our tears are not yet brew'd.

MALCOLM

[Aside to DONALBAIN] Nor our strong sorrow
Upon the foot of motion.

BANQUO

Look to the lady:

[LADY MACBETH is carried out

And when we have our naked frailties hid,
That suffer in exposure, let us meet,
And question this most bloody piece of work,
To know it further. Fears and scruples shake us:
In the great hand of God I stand, and thence
Against the undivulged pretence I fight
Of treasonous malice.

MACDUFF

And so do I.

ALL

So all.

MACBETH

Let's briefly put on manly readiness,
And meet i' the hall together.

ALL

Well contented.

[Exeunt all but MALCOLM and DONALBAIN

MALCOLM

What will you do? Let's not consort with them:
To show an unfelt sorrow is an office
Which the false man does easy. I'll to England.

DONALBAIN

To Ireland, I; our separated fortune
Shall keep us both the safer: where we are
There's daggers in men's smiles: the near in blood,
The nearer bloody.

MALCOLM

This murderous shaft that's shot
Hath not yet lighted, and our safest way
Is to avoid the aim. Therefore to horse;
And let us not be dainty of leave-taking,
But shift away: there's warrant in that theft
Which steals itself when there's no mercy left.

[Exeunt

SCENE IV. Outside MACBETH's castle

Enter ROSS with an OLD MAN

OLD MAN

Threescore and ten I can remember well:
Within the volume of which time I have seen
Hours dreadful and things strange, but this sore
    night
Hath trifled former knowings.

ROSS

Ah, good father,
Thou seest, the heavens, as troubled with man's act,
Threaten his bloody stage: by the clock 'tis day,
And yet dark night strangles the travelling lamp:
Is 't night's predominance, or the day's shame,

That darkness does the face of earth entomb,
When living light should kiss it?

OLD MAN

'Tis unnatural,
Even like the deed that's done. On Tuesday last
A falcon towering in her pride of place
Was by a mousing owl hawk'd at and kill'd.

ROSS

And Duncan's horses—a thing most strange and
    certain—
Beauteous and swift, the minions of their race,
Turn'd wild in nature, broke their stalls, flung out,
Contending 'gainst obedience, as they would make
War with mankind.

OLD MAN

'Tis said they eat each other.

ROSS

They did so, to the amazement of mine eyes,
That look'd upon 't.

Enter MACDUFF

Here comes the good Macduff.
How goes the world, sir, now?

MACDUFF

Why, see you not?

ROSS

Is 't known who did this more than bloody deed?

MACDUFF

Those that Macbeth hath slain.

ROSS

Alas, the day!
What good could they pretend?

MACDUFF

They were suborn'd:
Malcolm and Donalbain, the king's two sons,
Are stol'n away and fled, which puts upon them
Suspicion of the deed.

ROSS

'Gainst nature still:
Thriftless ambition, that wilt ravin up
Thine own life's means! Then 'tis most like
The sovereignty will fall upon Macbeth.

MACDUFF

He is already named, and gone to Scone
To be invested.

ROSS

Where is Duncan's body?

MACDUFF

Carried to Colme-kill,
The sacred storehouse of his predecessors
And guardian of their bones.

ROSS

Will you to Scone?

MACDUFF

No, cousin, I'll to Fife.

ROSS

Well, I will thither.

MACDUFF

Well, may you see things well done there: adieu!
Lest our old robes sit easier than our new!

ROSS

Farewell, father.

OLD MAN

God's benison go with you, and with those
That would make good of bad and friends of foes!
[*Exeunt*

ACT III

Scene I. *Forres. The palace*

Enter BANQUO

BANQUO

Thou hast it now: king, Cawdor, Glamis, all,
As the weird women promised, and I fear
Thou play'dst most foully for 't: yet it was said
It should not stand in thy posterity,
But that myself should be the root and father
Of many kings. If there come truth from them—
As upon thee, Macbeth, their speeches shine—
Why, by the verities on thee made good,
May they not be my oracles as well
And set me up in hope? But hush, no more.
        Sennet sounded. Enter MACBETH, *as king;* LADY
        MACBETH, *as queen;* LENNOX, ROSS, LORDS,
                LADIES, *and* ATTENDANTS

MACBETH

Here's our chief guest.

LADY MACBETH

                    If he had been forgotten,
It had been as a gap in our great feast,
And all-thing unbecoming.

MACBETH

To-night we hold a solemn supper, sir,
And I'll request your presence.

BANQUO

                    Let your highness
Command upon me, to the which my duties
Are with a most indissoluble tie
For ever knit.

MACBETH

Ride you this afternoon?

BANQUO

                Ay, my good lord.

MACBETH

We should have else desired your good advice,
Which still hath been both grave and prosperous,
In this day's council; but we'll take to-morrow.
Is 't far you ride?

BANQUO

As far, my lord, as will fill up the time
'Twixt this and supper: go not my horse the better,
I must become a borrower of the night
For a dark hour or twain.

MACBETH

                Fail not our feast.

BANQUO

My lord, I will not.

MACBETH

We hear our bloody cousins are bestow'd
In England and in Ireland, not confessing
Their cruel parricide, filling their hearers
With strange invention: but of that to-morrow,
When therewithal we shall have cause of state
Craving us jointly. Hie you to horse: adieu,
Till you return at night. Goes Fleance with you?

BANQUO

Ay, my good lord: our time does call upon 's.

MACBETH

I wish your horses swift and sure of foot,
And so I do commend you to their backs.
Farewell.   [*Exit* BANQUO
Let every man be master of his time
Till seven at night; to make society
The sweeter welcome, we will keep ourself
Till supper-time alone: while then, God be with
    you! [*Exeunt all but* MACBETH *and an* ATTENDANT
Sirrah, a word with you: attend those men
Our pleasure?

ATTENDANT

They are, my lord, without the palace-gate.

MACBETH

Bring them before us.   [*Exit* ATTENDANT
                To be thus is nothing;
But to be safely thus: our fears in Banquo
Stick deep; and in his royalty of nature
Reigns that which would be fear'd: 'tis much he
    dares,
And, to that dauntless temper of his mind,
He hath a wisdom that doth guide his valour
To act in safety. There is none but he
Whose being I do fear: and under him
My Genius is rebuked, as it is said
Mark Antony's was by Cæsar. He chid the sisters,
When first they put the name of king upon me,
And bade them speak to him; then prophet-like
They hail'd him father to a line of kings:
Upon my head they placed a fruitless crown
And put a barren sceptre in my gripe,
Thence to be wrench'd with an unlineal hand,
No son of mine succeeding. If 't be so,
For Banquo's issue have I filed my mind;
For them the gracious Duncan have I murder'd;
Put rancours in the vessel of my peace
Only for them, and mine eternal jewel
Given to the common enemy of man,
To make them kings, the seed of Banquo kings!
Rather than so, come, fate, into the list,
And champion me to the utterance! Who's there?
        Re-enter ATTENDANT, *with* TWO MURDERERS
Now go to the door, and stay there till we call.
                                [*Exit* ATTENDANT
Was it not yesterday we spoke together?

FIRST MURDERER

It was, so please your highness.

MACBETH

                        Well then, now
Have you consider'd of my speeches? Know

That it was he in the times past which held you
So under fortune, which you thought had been
Our innocent self: this I made good to you
In our last conference; pass'd in probation with you,
How you were borne in hand, how cross'd, the in-
     struments,
Who wrought with them, and all things else that
     might
To half a soul and to a notion crazed
Say 'Thus did Banquo.'

FIRST MURDERER
                    You made it known to us.
MACBETH
I did so; and went further, which is now
Our point of second meeting. Do you find
Your patience so predominant in your nature,
That you can let this go? Are you so gospell'd,
To pray for this good man and for his issue,
Whose heavy hand hath bow'd you to the grave
And beggar'd yours for ever?

FIRST MURDERER
                         We are men, my liege.
MACBETH
Ay, in the catalogue ye go for men;
As hounds and greyhounds, mongrels, spaniels, curs,
Shoughs, water-rugs and demi-wolves, are clept
All by the name of dogs: the valued file
Distinguishes the swift, the slow, the subtle,
The housekeeper, the hunter, every one
According to the gift which bounteous nature
Hath in him closed, whereby he does receive
Particular addition, from the bill
That writes them all alike: and so of men.
Now if you have a station in the file,
Not i' the worst rank of manhood, say it,
And I will put that business in your bosoms
Whose execution takes your enemy off,
Grapples you to the heart and love of us,
Who wear our health but sickly in his life,
Which in his death were perfect.

SECOND MURDERER
                         I am one, my liege,
Whom the vile blows and buffets of the world
Have so incensed that I am reckless what
I do to spite the world.

FIRST MURDERER
                    And I another
So weary with disasters, tugg'd with fortune,
That I would set my life on any chance,
To mend it or be rid on 't.

MACBETH
                    Both of you
Know Banquo was your enemy.

BOTH MURDERERS
                         True, my lord.
MACBETH
So is he mine, and in such bloody distance
That every minute of his being thrusts
Against my near'st of life: and though I could
With barefaced power sweep him from my sight

And bid my will avouch it, yet I must not,
For certain friends that are both his and mine,
Whose loves I may not drop, but wail his fall
Who I myself struck down: and thence it is
That I to your assistance do make love,
Masking the business from the common eye
For sundry weighty reasons.

SECOND MURDERER
                    We shall, my lord,
Perform what you command us.

FIRST MURDERER
                         Though our lives—
MACBETH
Your spirits shine through you. Within this hour at
     most
I will advise you where to plant yourselves,
Acquaint you with the perfect spy o' the time,
The moment on 't; for 't must be done to-night,
And something from the palace; always thought
That I require a clearness: and with him—
To leave no rubs nor botches in the work—
Fleance his son, that keeps him company,
Whose absence is no less material to me
Than is his father's, must embrace the fate
Of that dark hour. Resolve yourselves apart:
I'll come to you anon.

BOTH MURDERERS
                    We are resolved, my lord.
MACBETH
I'll call upon you straight: abide within.
                              [*Exeunt* MURDERERS
It is concluded: Banquo, thy soul's flight,
If it find heaven, must find it out to-night.   [*Exit*

SCENE II. *The palace*

Enter LADY MACBETH *and a* SERVANT
LADY MACBETH
Is Banquo gone from court?

SERVANT
Ay, madam, but returns again to-night.

LADY MACBETH
Say to the king, I would attend his leisure
For a few words.

SERVANT
                    Madam, I will.   [*Exit*
LADY MACBETH
                    Nought's had, all's spent,
Where our desire is got without content:
'Tis safer to be that which we destroy
Than by destruction dwell in doubtful joy.

Enter MACBETH
How now, my lord! why do you keep alone,
Of sorriest fancies your companions making;
Using those thoughts which should indeed have
     died
With them they think on? Things without all
     remedy
Should be without regard: what's done is done.

MACBETH

We have scotch'd the snake, not kill'd it:
She'll close and be herself, whilst our poor malice
Remains in danger of her former tooth.
But let the frame of things disjoint, both the worlds
    suffer,
Ere we will eat our meal in fear, and sleep
In the affliction of these terrible dreams
That shake us nightly: better be with the dead,
Whom we, to gain our peace, have sent to peace,
Than on the torture of the mind to lie
In restless ecstasy. Duncan is in his grave;
After life's fitful fever he sleeps well;
Treason has done his worst: nor steel, nor poison,
Malice domestic, foreign levy, nothing,
Can touch him further.

LADY MACBETH

            Come on;
Gentle my lord, sleek o'er your rugged looks;
Be bright and jovial among your guests to-night.

MACBETH

So shall I, love; and so, I pray, be you:
Let your remembrance apply to Banquo;
Present him eminence, both with eye and tongue:
Unsafe the while, that we
Must lave our honours in these flattering streams,
And make our faces visards to our hearts,
Disguising what they are.

LADY MACBETH

            You must leave this.

MACBETH

O, full of scorpions is my mind, dear wife!
Thou know'st that Banquo, and his Fleance, lives.

LADY MACBETH

But in them nature's copy's not eterne.

MACBETH

There's comfort yet; they are assailable;
Then be thou jocund: ere the bat hath flown
His cloister'd flight; ere to black Hecate's sum-
    mons
The shard-borne beetle with his drowsy hums
Hath rung night's yawning peal, there shall be done
A deed of dreadful note.

LADY MACBETH

            What's to be done?

MACBETH

Be innocent of the knowledge, dearest chuck,
Till thou applaud the deed. Come, seeling night,
Scarf up the tender eye of pitiful day,
And with thy bloody and invisible hand
Cancel and tear to pieces that great bond
Which keeps me pale! Light thickens, and the crow
Makes wing to the rooky wood:
Good things of day begin to droop and drowse,
Whiles night's black agents to their preys do rouse.
Thou marvell'st at my words: but hold thee still;
Things bad begun make strong themselves by ill:
So, prithee, go with me.   [*Exeunt*

SCENE III. *A park near the palace*

Enter THREE MURDERERS

FIRST MURDERER

But who did bid thee join with us?

THIRD MURDERER

            Macbeth.

SECOND MURDERER

He needs not our mistrust; since he delivers
Our offices, and what we have to do,
To the direction just.

FIRST MURDERER

            Then stand with us.
The west yet glimmers with some streaks of day:
Now spurs the lated traveller apace
To gain the timely inn, and near approaches
The subject of our watch.

THIRD MURDERER

            Hark! I hear horses.

BANQUO

[*Within*] Give us a light there, ho!

SECOND MURDERER

            Then 'tis he: the rest
That are within the note of expectation
Already are i' the court.

FIRST MURDERER

            His horses go about.

THIRD MURDERER

Almost a mile: but he does usually—
So all men do—from hence to the palace gate
Make it their walk.

SECOND MURDERER

            A light, a light!

Enter BANQUO, *and* FLEANCE *with a torch*

THIRD MURDERER

            'Tis he.

FIRST MURDERER

Stand to 't.

BANQUO

It will be rain to-night.

FIRST MURDERER

            Let it come down.
            [*They set upon* BANQUO

BANQUO

O, treachery! Fly, good Fleance, fly, fly, fly!
Thou mayst revenge. O slave! [*Dies.* FLEANCE *escapes*

THIRD MURDERER

Who did strike out the light?

FIRST MURDERER

            Was 't not the way?

THIRD MURDERER

There's but one down; the son is fled.

SECOND MURDERER

            We have lost
Best half of our affair.

FIRST MURDERER

Well, let's away and say how much is done. [*Exeunt*

Scene IV. *Hall in the palace*

A banquet prepared. Enter MACBETH, LADY MACBETH,
ROSS, LENNOX, LORDS, *and* ATTENDANTS

MACBETH
You know your own degrees; sit down: at first
And last the hearty welcome.

LORDS
                    Thanks to your majesty.

MACBETH
Ourself will mingle with society
And play the humble host.
Our hostess keeps her state, but in best time
We will require her welcome.

LADY MACBETH
Pronounce it for me, sir, to all our friends,
For my heart speaks they are welcome.

Enter FIRST MURDERER *to the door*

MACBETH
See, they encounter thee with their hearts' thanks.
Both sides are even: here I'll sit i' the midst:
Be large in mirth; anon we'll drink a measure
The table round. [*Approaching the door*] There's
    blood upon thy face.

MURDERER
'Tis Banquo's then.

MACBETH
'Tis better thee without than he within.
Is he dispatch'd?

MURDERER
My lord, his throat is cut; that I did for him.

MACBETH
Thou art the best o' the cut-throats: yet he's good
That did the like for Fleance: if thou didst it,
Thou art the nonpareil.

MURDERER
                    Most royal sir,
Fleance is 'scaped.

MACBETH
[*Aside*] Then comes my fit again: I had else been
    perfect,
Whole as the marble, founded as the rock,
As broad and general as the casing air:
But now I am cabin'd, cribb'd, confined, bound in
To saucy doubts and fears.—But Banquo's safe?

MURDERER
Ay, my good lord: safe in a ditch he bides,
With twenty trenched gashes on his head;
The least a death to nature.

MACBETH
                    Thanks for that.
[*Aside*] There the grown serpent lies; the worm
    that's fled
Hath nature that in time will venom breed,
No teeth for the present. Get thee gone: to-morrow
We'll hear ourselves again.   [*Exit* MURDERER

LADY MACBETH
                    My royal lord,
You do not give the cheer: the feast is sold
That is not often vouch'd, while 'tis a-making,

'Tis given with welcome: to feed were best at home;
From thence the sauce to meat is ceremony;
Meeting were bare without it.

MACBETH
                    Sweet remembrancer!
Now good digestion wait on appetite,
And health on both!

LENNOX
                    May 't please your highness sit.

The GHOST OF BANQUO *enters, and sits in* MACBETH'S
place

MACBETH
Here had we now our country's honour roof'd,
Were the graced person of our Banquo present;
Who may I rather challenge for unkindness
Than pity for mischance!

ROSS
                    His absence, sir,
Lays blame upon his promise. Please 't your high-
    ness
To grace us with your royal company.

MACBETH
The table's full.

LENNOX
                    Here is a place reserved, sir.

MACBETH
Where?

LENNOX
Here, my good lord. What is 't that moves your
    highness?

MACBETH
Which of you have done this?

LORDS
                    What, my good lord?

MACBETH
Thou canst not say I did it: never shake
Thy gory locks at me.

ROSS
Gentlemen, rise; his highness is not well.

LADY MACBETH
Sit, worthy friends: my lord is often thus,
And hath been from his youth: pray you, keep seat;
The fit is momentary; upon a thought
He will again be well: if much you note him,
You shall offend him and extend his passion:
Feed, and regard him not. Are you a man?

MACBETH
Ay, and a bold one, that dare look on that
Which might appal the devil.

LADY MACBETH
                    O proper stuff!
This is the very painting of your fear:
This is the air-drawn dagger which, you said,
Led you to Duncan. O, these flaws and starts,
Impostors to true fear, would well become
A woman's story at a winter's fire,
Authorized by her grandam. Shame itself!
Why do you make such faces? When all's done,
You look but on a stool.

MACBETH

Prithee, see there! behold! look! lo! how say you?
Why, what care I? If thou canst nod, speak too.
If charnel-houses and our graves must send
Those that we bury back, our monuments
Shall be the maws of kites.   [Exit GHOST

LADY MACBETH

What, quite unmann'd in folly?

MACBETH

If I stand here, I saw him.

LADY MACBETH

Fie, for shame!

MACBETH

Blood hath been shed ere now, i' the olden time,
Ere humane statute purged the gentle weal;
Ay, and since too, murders have been perform'd
Too terrible for the ear: the time has been,
That, when the brains were out, the man would die,
And there an end; but now they rise again,
With twenty mortal murders on their crowns,
And push us from our stools: this is more strange
Than such a murder is.

LADY MACBETH

My worthy lord,
Your noble friends do lack you.

MACBETH

I do forget.
Do not muse at me, my most worthy friends;
I have a strange infirmity, which is nothing
To those that know me. Come, love and health to
    all;
Then I'll sit down. Give me some wine, fill full.
I drink to the general joy o' the whole table,
And to our dear friend Banquo, whom we miss;
Would he were here! to all and him we thirst,
And all to all.

LORDS

Our duties, and the pledge.
Re-enter GHOST

MACBETH

Avaunt! and quit my sight! let the earth hide thee!
Thy bones are marrowless, thy blood is cold;
Thou hast no speculation in those eyes
Which thou dost glare with.

LADY MACBETH

Think of this, good peers,
But as a thing of custom: 'tis no other;
Only it spoils the pleasure of the time.

MACBETH

What man dare, I dare:
Approach thou like the rugged Russian bear,
The arm'd rhinoceros, or the Hyrcan tiger;
Take any shape but that, and my firm nerves
Shall never tremble: or be alive again,
And dare me to the desert with thy sword;
If trembling I inhabit then, protest me
The baby of a girl. Hence, horrible shadow!
Unreal mockery, hence!   [Exit GHOST

Why, so: being gone,
I am a man again. Pray you, sit still.

LADY MACBETH

You have displaced the mirth, broke the good meet-
    ing,
With most admired disorder.

MACBETH

Can such things be,
And overcome us like a summer's cloud,
Without our special wonder? You make me strange
Even to the disposition that I owe,
When now I think you can behold such sights,
And keep the natural ruby of your cheeks,
When mine is blanch'd with fear.

ROSS

What sights, my lord?

LADY MACBETH

I pray you, speak not; he grows worse and worse:
Question enrages him: at once, good night:
Stand not upon the order of your going,
But go at once.

LENNOX

Good night; and better health
Attend his majesty!

LADY MACBETH

A kind good night to all!
[Exeunt all but MACBETH and LADY MACBETH

MACBETH

It will have blood: they say blood will have blood:
Stones have been known to move and trees to speak;
Augures and understood relations have
By maggot-pies and choughs and rooks brought
    forth
The secret'st man of blood. What is the night?

LADY MACBETH

Almost at odds with morning, which is which.

MACBETH

How say'st thou, that Macduff denies his person
At our great bidding?

LADY MACBETH

Did you send to him, sir?

MACBETH

I hear it by the way, but I will send:
There's not a one of them but in his house
I keep a servant fee'd. I will to-morrow,
And betimes I will, to the weird sisters:
More shall they speak, for now I am bent to know,
By the worst means, the worst. For mine own good
All causes shall give way: I am in blood
Stepp'd in so far that, should I wade no more,
Returning were as tedious as go o'er:
Strange things I have in head that will to hand,
Which must be acted ere they may be scann'd.

LADY MACBETH

You lack the season of all natures, sleep.

MACBETH

Come, we'll to sleep. My strange and self-abuse

Is the initiate fear that wants hard use:
We are yet but young in deed.   [*Exeunt*

Scene V. *A heath*

Thunder. Enter the THREE WITCHES, *meeting* HECATE

FIRST WITCH

Why, how now, Hecate! you look angerly.

HECATE

Have I not reason, beldams as you are,
Saucy and over-bold? How did you dare
To trade and traffic with Macbeth
In riddles and affairs of death;
And I, the mistress of your charms,
The close contriver of all harms,
Was never call'd to bear my part,
Or show the glory of our art?
And, which is worse, all you have done
Hath been but for a wayward son,
Spiteful and wrathful; who, as others do,
Loves for his own ends, not for you.
But make amends now: get you gone,
And at the pit of Acheron
Meet me i' the morning: thither he
Will come to know his destiny:
Your vessels and your spells provide,
Your charms and every thing beside.
I am for the air; this night I'll spend
Unto a dismal and a fatal end:
Great business must be wrought ere noon:
Upon the corner of the moon
There hangs a vaporous drop profound;
I'll catch it ere it come to ground:
And that distill'd by magic sleights
Shall raise such artificial sprites
As by the strength of their illusion
Shall draw him on to his confusion:
He shall spurn fate, scorn death, and bear
His hopes 'bove wisdom, grace and fear:
And you all know security
Is mortals' chiefest enemy.

[*Music and a song within:*

'Come away, come away,' &c.

Hark! I am call'd; my little spirit, see,
Sits in a foggy cloud, and stays for me.   [*Exit*

FIRST WITCH

Come, let's make haste; she'll soon be back again.
          [*Exeunt*

Scene VI. *Forres. The palace*

Enter LENNOX *and another* LORD

LENNOX

My former speeches have but hit your thoughts,
Which can interpret farther: only I say
Things have been strangely borne. The gracious
    Duncan

Was pitied of Macbeth: marry, he was dead:
And the right-valiant Banquo walk'd too late;
Whom, you may say, if 't please you, Fleance kill'd,
For Fleance fled: men must not walk too late.
Who cannot want the thought, how monstrous
It was for Malcolm and for Donalbain
To kill their gracious father? damned fact!
How it did grieve Macbeth! did he not straight,
In pious rage, the two delinquents tear,
That were the slaves of drink and thralls of sleep?
Was not that nobly done? Ay, and wisely too;
For 'twould have anger'd any heart alive
To hear the men deny 't. So that, I say,
He has borne all things well: and I do think
That, had he Duncan's sons under his key—
As, an 't please heaven, he shall not—they should
    find
What 'twere to kill a father; so should Fleance.
But, peace! for from broad words, and 'cause he
    fail'd
His presence at the tyrant's feast, I hear,
Macduff lives in disgrace: sir, can you tell
Where he bestows himself?

LORD

                    The son of Duncan,
From whom this tyrant holds the due of birth,
Lives in the English court, and is received
Of the most pious Edward with such grace
That the malevolence of fortune nothing
Takes from his high respect. Thither Macduff
Is gone to pray the holy king, upon his aid
To wake Northumberland and warlike Siward:
That by the help of these, with Him above
To ratify the work, we may again
Give to our tables meat, sleep to our nights,
Free from our feasts and banquets bloody knives,
Do faithful homage and receive free honours:
All which we pine for now: and this report
Hath so exasperate the king that he
Prepares for some attempt of war.

LENNOX

                    Sent he to Macduff?

LORD

He did: and with an absolute 'Sir, not I,'
The cloudy messenger turns me his back,
And hums, as who should say 'You'll rue the time
That clogs me with this answer.'

LENNOX

                    And that well might
Advise him to a caution, to hold what distance
His wisdom can provide. Some holy angel
Fly to the court of England and unfold
His message ere he come, that a swift blessing
May soon return to this our suffering country
Under a hand accursed!

LORD

                    I'll send my prayers with him.
          [*Exeunt*

ACT IV
Scene I. *A cavern. In the middle, a boiling cauldron*

Thunder. Enter the THREE WITCHES

FIRST WITCH

Thrice the brinded cat hath mew'd.

SECOND WITCH

Thrice and once the hedge-pig whined.

THIRD WITCH

Harpier cries ''Tis time, 'tis time.'

FIRST WITCH

Round about the cauldron go:
In the poison'd entrails throw.
Toad, that under cold stone
Days and nights has thirty one
Swelter'd venom sleeping got,
Boil thou first i' the charmed pot.

ALL

Double, double toil and trouble;
Fire burn and cauldron bubble.

SECOND WITCH

Fillet of a fenny snake,
In the cauldron boil and bake;
Eye of newt and toe of frog,
Wool of bat and tongue of dog,
Adder's fork and blind-worm's sting,
Lizard's leg and howlet's wing,
For a charm of powerful trouble,
Like a hell-broth boil and bubble.

ALL

Double, double toil and trouble;
Fire burn and cauldron bubble.

THIRD WITCH

Scale of dragon, tooth of wolf,
Witches' mummy, maw and gulf
Of the ravin'd salt-sea shark,
Root of hemlock digg'd i' the dark,
Liver of blaspheming Jew,
Gall of goat and slips of yew
Sliver'd in the moon's eclipse,
Nose of Turk and Tartar's lips,
Finger of birth-strangled babe
Ditch-deliver'd by a drab,
Make the gruel thick and slab:
Add thereto a tiger's chaudron,
For the ingredients of our cauldron.

ALL

Double, double toil and trouble;
Fire burn and cauldron bubble.

SECOND WITCH

Cool it with a baboon's blood,
Then the charm is firm and good.

Enter HECATE *to the other* THREE WITCHES

HECATE

O, well done! I commend your pains;
And every one shall share i' the gains:
And now about the cauldron sing,

Like elves and fairies in a ring,
Enchanting all that you put in.

[*Music and a song:* 'Black Spirits,' &c.

[HECATE *retires*

SECOND WITCH

By the pricking of my thumbs,
Something wicked this way comes:
   Open, locks,
   Whoever knocks!

Enter MACBETH

MACBETH

How now, you secret, black, and midnight hags!
What is 't you do?

ALL

       A deed without a name.

MACBETH

I conjure you, by that which you profess,
Howe'er you come to know it, answer me:
Though you untie the winds and let them fight
Against the churches; though the yesty waves
Confound and swallow navigation up;
Though bladed corn be lodged and trees blown
   down;
Though castles topple on their warders' heads;
Though palaces and pyramids do slope
Their heads to their foundations; though the treas-
   ure
Of nature's germins tumble all together,
Even till destruction sicken; answer me
To what I ask you.

FIRST WITCH

        Speak.

SECOND WITCH

          Demand.

THIRD WITCH

               We'll answer.

FIRST WITCH

Say, if thou'dst rather hear it from our mouths,
Or from our masters?

MACBETH

        Call 'em, let me see 'em.

FIRST WITCH

Pour in sow's blood, that hath eaten
Her nine farrow; grease that's sweaten
From the murderer's gibbet throw
Into the flame.

ALL

      Come, high or low;
Thyself and office deftly show!

Thunder. FIRST APPARITION: *an armed Head*

MACBETH

Tell me, thou unknown power,—

FIRST WITCH

         He knows thy thought:
Hear his speech, but say thou nought.

FIRST APPARITION

Macbeth! Macbeth! Macbeth! beware Macduff;
Beware the thane of Fife. Dismiss me: enough.

[*Descends*

MACBETH

Whate'er thou art, for thy good caution thanks;
Thou hast harp'd my fear aright: but one word
    more,—

FIRST WITCH

He will not be commanded: here's another,
More potent than the first.

Thunder. SECOND APPARITION: *a bloody Child*

SECOND APPARITION

Macbeth! Macbeth! Macbeth!

MACBETH

Had I three ears, I'ld hear thee.

SECOND APPARITION

Be bloody, bold and resolute; laugh to scorn
The power of man, for none of woman born
Shall harm Macbeth.   [*Descends*

MACBETH

Then live, Macduff: what need I fear of thee?
But yet I'll make assurance double sure,
And take a bond of fate: thou shalt not live;
That I may tell pale-hearted fear it lies,
And sleep in spite of thunder.

Thunder. THIRD APPARITION: *a Child crowned, with a
    tree in his hand*
                    What is this,
That rises like the issue of a king,
And wears upon his baby-brow the round
And top of sovereignty?

ALL

            Listen, but speak not to 't.

THIRD APPARITION

Be lion-mettled, proud, and take no care
Who chafes, who frets, or where conspirers are:
Macbeth shall never vanquish'd be until
Great Birnam wood to high Dunsinane hill
Shall come against him.   [*Descends*

MACBETH

                That will never be:
Who can impress the forest, bid the tree
Unfix his earth-bound root? Sweet bodements!
    good!
Rebellion's head, rise never, till the wood
Of Birnam rise, and our high-placed Macbeth
Shall live the lease of nature, pay his breath
To time and mortal custom. Yet my heart
Throbs to know one thing: tell me, if your art
Can tell so much: shall Banquo's issue ever
Reign in this kingdom?

ALL

            Seek to know no more.

MACBETH

I will be satisfied: deny me this,
And an eternal curse fall on you! Let me know:
Why sinks that cauldron? and what noise is this?
                    [*Hautboys*

FIRST WITCH

Show!

SECOND WITCH

Show!

THIRD WITCH

Show!

ALL

Show his eyes, and grieve his heart;
Come like shadows, so depart!

A show of eight KINGS, *the last with a glass in his hand;*
    BANQUO'S GHOST *following*

MACBETH

Thou art too like the spirit of Banquo: down!
Thy crown does sear mine eye-balls. And thy hair,
Thou other gold-bound brow, is like the first.
A third is like the former. Filthy hags!
Why do you show me this? A fourth! Start, eyes!
What, will the line stretch out to the crack of doom?
Another yet! A seventh! I'll see no more:
And yet the eighth appears, who bears a glass
Which shows me many more; and some I see
That two-fold balls and treble sceptres carry:
Horrible sight! Now I see 'tis true;
For the blood-bolter'd Banquo smiles upon me,
And points at them for his. What, is this so?

FIRST WITCH

Ay, sir, all this is so: but why
Stands Macbeth thus amazedly?
Come, sisters, cheer we up his sprites,
And show the best of our delights:
I'll charm the air to give a sound,
While you perform your antic round,
That this great king may kindly say
Our duties did his welcome pay.

[*Music. The* WITCHES *dance, and then vanish, with*
                            HECATE

MACBETH

Where are they? Gone? Let this pernicious hour
Stand aye accursed in the calendar!
Come in, without there!

Enter LENNOX

LENNOX

            What's your grace's will?

MACBETH

Saw you the weird sisters?

LENNOX

            No, my lord.

MACBETH

Came they not by you?

LENNOX

            No indeed, my lord.

MACBETH

Infected be the air whereon they ride,
And damn'd all those that trust them! I did hear
The galloping of horse: who was 't came by?

LENNOX

'Tis two or three, my lord, that bring you word
Macduff is fled to England.

MACBETH

            Fled to England!

LENNOX

Ay, my good lord.

MACBETH

[*Aside*] Time, thou anticipatest my dread exploits:

The flighty purpose never is o'ertook
Unless the deed go with it: from this moment
The very firstlings of my heart shall be
The firstlings of my hand. And even now,
To crown my thoughts with acts, be it thought and
    done:
The castle of Macduff I will surprise;
Seize upon Fife; give to the edge o' the sword
His wife, his babes, and all unfortunate souls
That trace him in his line. No boasting like a fool;
This deed I'll do before this purpose cool:
But no more sights!—Where are these gentlemen?
Come, bring me where they are.   [*Exeunt*

SCENE II. *Fife.* MACDUFF's *castle*

Enter LADY MACDUFF, *her* SON, *and* ROSS

LADY MACDUFF
What had he done, to make him fly the land?

ROSS
You must have patience, madam.

LADY MACDUFF
                He had none:
His flight was madness: when our actions do not,
Our fears do make us traitors.

ROSS
                You know not
Whether it was his wisdom or his fear.

LADY MACDUFF
Wisdom! to leave his wife, to leave his babes,
His mansion and his titles, in a place
From whence himself does fly? He loves us not;
He wants the natural touch: for the poor wren,
The most diminutive of birds, will fight,
Her young ones in her nest, against the owl.
All is the fear and nothing is the love;
As little is the wisdom, where the flight
So runs against all reason.

ROSS
           My dearest coz,
I pray you, school yourself: but, for your husband,
He is noble, wise, judicious, and best knows
The fits o' the season. I dare not speak much further:
But cruel are the times, when we are traitors
And do not know ourselves; when we hold rumour
From what we fear, yet know not what we fear,
But float upon a wild and violent sea
Each way and move. I take my leave of you:
Shall not be long but I'll be here again:
Things at the worst will cease, or else climb upward
To what they were before. My pretty cousin,
Blessing upon you!

LADY MACDUFF
Father'd he is, and yet he's fatherless.

ROSS
I am so much a fool, should I stay longer,
It would be my disgrace and your discomfort:
I take my leave at once.   [*Exit*

LADY MACDUFF
           Sirrah, your father's dead:
And what will you do now? How will you live?

SON
As birds do, mother.

LADY MADUFF
           What, with worms and flies?

SON
With what I get, I mean; and so do they.

LADY MACDUFF
Poor bird! thou'ldst never fear the net nor lime,
The pitfall nor the gin.

SON
Why should I, mother? Poor birds they are not set
    for.
My father is not dead, for all your saying.

LADY MACDUFF
Yes, he is dead: how wilt thou do for a father?

SON
Nay, how will you do for a husband?

LADY MACDUFF
Why, I can buy me twenty at any market.

SON
Then you'll buy 'em to sell again.

LADY MACDUFF
Thou speak'st with all thy wit, and yet, i' faith,
With wit enough for thee.

SON
Was my father a traitor, mother?

LADY MACDUFF
Ay, that he was.

SON
What is a traitor?

LADY MACDUFF
Why, one that swears and lies.

SON
And be all traitors that do so?

LADY MACDUFF
Every one that does so is a traitor, and must be
hanged.

SON
And must they all be hanged that swear and lie?

LADY MACDUFF
Every one.

SON
Who must hang them?

LADY MACDUFF
Why, the honest men.

SON
Then the liars and swearers are fools; for there are
liars and swearers enow to beat the honest men and
hang up them.

LADY MACDUFF
Now, God help thee, poor monkey! But how wilt
thou do for a father?

SON
If he were dead, you'ld weep for him: if you would
not, it were a good sign that I should quickly have
a new father.

LADY MACDUFF
Poor prattler, how thou talk'st!
Enter a MESSENGER
MESSENGER
Bless you, fair dame! I am not to you known,
Though in your state of honour I am perfect.
I doubt some danger does approach you nearly:
If you will take a homely man's advice,
Be not found here; hence, with your little ones.
To fright you thus, methinks I am too savage;
To do worse to you were fell cruelty,
Which is too nigh your person. Heaven preserve
  you!
I dare abide no longer.   [*Exit*
LADY MACDUFF
      Whither should I fly?
I have done no harm. But I remember now
I am in this earthly world, where to do harm
Is often laudable, to do good sometime
Accounted dangerous folly: why then, alas,
Do I put up that womanly defence,
To say I have done no harm?—What are these
  faces?

Enter MURDERERS
FIRST MURDERER
Where is your husband?
LADY MACDUFF
I hope, in no place so unsanctified
Where such as thou mayst find him.
FIRST MURDERER
           He's a traitor.
SON
Thou liest, thou shag-ear'd villain!
FIRST MURDERER
          What, you egg!
                 [*Stabbing him*
Young fry of treachery!
SON
       He has kill'd me, mother:
Run away, I pray you!   [*Dies*
     [*Exit* LADY MACDUFF, *crying* 'Murder!'
      Exeunt MURDERERS, *following her*

SCENE III. *England. Before the* KING's *palace*

Enter MALCOLM *and* MACDUFF
MALCOLM
Let us seek out some desolate shade, and there
Weep our sad bosoms empty.
MACDUFF
         Let us rather
Hold fast the mortal sword, and like good men
Bestride our down-fall'n birthdom: each new morn
New widows howl, new orphans cry, new sorrows
Strike heaven on the face, that it resounds
As if it felt with Scotland and yell'd out
Like syllable of dolour.
MALCOLM
        What I believe, I'll wail;

What know, believe; and what I can redress,
As I shall find the time to friend, I will.
What you have spoke, it may be so perchance.
This tyrant, whose sole name blisters our tongues,
Was once thought honest: you have loved him well;
He hath not touch'd you yet. I am young; but
  something
You may deserve of him through me; and wisdom
To offer up a weak, poor, innocent lamb
To appease an angry god.
MACDUFF
I am not treacherous.
MALCOLM
        But Macbeth is.
A good and virtuous nature may recoil
In an imperial charge. But I shall crave your par-
  don;
That which you are, my thoughts cannot transpose:
Angels are bright still, though the brightest fell:
Though all things foul would wear the brows of
  grace,
Yet grace must still look so.
MACDUFF
          I have lost my hopes.
MALCOLM
Perchance even there where I did find my doubts.
Why in that rawness left you wife and child,
Those precious motives, those strong knots of love,
Without leave-taking? I pray you,
Let not my jealousies be your dishonours,
But mine own safeties. You may be rightly just,
Whatever I shall think.
MACDUFF
       Bleed, bleed, poor country:
Great tyranny, lay thou thy basis sure,
For goodness dare not check thee: wear thou thy
  wrongs;
The title is affeer'd. Fare thee well, lord:
I would not be the villain that thou think'st
For the whole space that's in the tyrant's grasp
And the rich East to boot.
MALCOLM
       Be not offended:
I speak not as in absolute fear of you.
I think our country sinks beneath the yoke;
It weeps, it bleeds, and each new day a gash
Is added to her wounds: I think withal
There would be hands uplifted in my right;
And here from gracious England have I offer
Of goodly thousands: but for all this,
When I shall tread upon the tyrant's head,
Or wear it on my sword, yet my poor country
Shall have more vices than it had before,
More suffer and more sundry ways than ever,
By him that shall succeed.
MACDUFF
       What should he be?
MALCOLM
It is myself I mean: in whom I know
All the particulars of vice so grafted

That, when they shall be open'd, black Macbeth
Will seem as pure as snow, and the poor state
Esteem him as a lamb, being compared
With my confineless harms.

MACDUFF
              Not in the legions
Of horrid hell can come a devil more damn'd
In evils to top Macbeth.

MALCOLM
              I grant him bloody,
Luxurious, avaricious, false, deceitful,
Sudden, malicious, smacking of every sin
That has a name: but there's no bottom, none,
In my vulptuousness: your wives, your daughters,
Your matrons and your maids, could not fill up
The cistern of my lust, and my desire
All continent impediments would o'erbear,
That did oppose my will: better Macbeth
Than such an one to reign.

MACDUFF
              Boundless intemperance
In nature is a tyranny; it hath been
The untimely emptying of the happy throne,
And fall of many kings. But fear not yet
To take upon you what is yours: you may
Convey your pleasures in a spacious plenty,
And yet seem cold, the time you may so hoodwink:
We have willing dames enough; there cannot be
That vulture in you, to devour so many
As will to greatness dedicate themselves,
Finding it so inclined.

MALCOLM
              With this there grows
In my most ill-composed affection such
A stanchless avarice that, were I king,
I should cut off the nobles for their lands,
Desire his jewels and this other's house:
And my more-having would be as a sauce
To make me hunger more, that I should forge
Quarrels unjust against the good and loyal,
Destroying them for wealth.

MACDUFF
              This avarice
Sticks deeper, grows with more pernicious root
Than summer-seeming lust, and it hath been
The sword of our slain kings: yet do not fear;
Scotland hath foisons to fill up your will
Of your mere own: all these are portable,
With other graces weigh'd.

MALCOLM
But I have none: the king-becoming graces,
As justice, verity, temperance, stableness,
Bounty, perseverance, mercy, lowliness,
Devotion, patience, courage, fortitude,
I have no relish of them, but abound
In the division of each several crime,
Acting it many ways. Nay, had I power, I should
Pour the sweet milk of concord into hell,
Uproar the universal peace, confound
All unity on earth.

MACDUFF
        O Scotland, Scotland!

MALCOLM
If such a one be fit to govern, speak:
I am as I have spoken.

MACDUFF
            Fit to govern!
No, not to live. O nation miserable!
With an untitled tyrant bloody-scepter'd,
When shalt thou see thy wholesome days again,
Since that the truest issue of thy throne
By his own interdiction stands accursed,
And does blaspheme his breed? Thy royal father
Was a most sainted king: the queen that bore thee,
Oftener upon her knees than on her feet,
Died every day she lived. Fare thee well!
These evils thou repeat'st upon thyself
Have banish'd me from Scotland. O my breast,
Thy hope ends here!

MALCOLM
        Macduff, this noble passion,
Child of integrity, hath from my soul
Wiped the black scruples, reconciled my thoughts
To thy good truth and honour. Devilish Macbeth
By many of these trains hath sought to win me
Into his power; and modest wisdom plucks me
From over-credulous haste: but God above
Deal between thee and me! for even now
I put myself to thy direction, and
Unspeak mine own detraction; here abjure
The taints and blames I laid upon myself,
For strangers to my nature. I am yet
Unknown to woman, never was forsworn,
Scarcely have coveted what was mine own,
At no time broke my faith, would not betray
The devil to his fellow, and delight
No less in truth than life: my first false speaking
Was this upon myself: what I am truly,
Is thine and my poor country's to command:
Whither indeed, before thy here-approach,
Old Siward, with ten thousand warlike men,
Already at a point, was setting forth.
Now we'll together, and the chance of goodness
Be like our warranted quarrel! Why are you silent?

MACDUFF
Such welcome and unwelcome things at once
'Tis hard to reconcile.

Enter a DOCTOR

MALCOLM
Well, more anon. Comes the king forth, I pray you?

DOCTOR
Ay, sir; there are a crew of wretched souls
That stay his cure: their malady convinces
The great assay of art; but at his touch,
Such sanctity hath heaven given his hand,
They presently amend.

MALCOLM
           I thank you, doctor.
                       [*Exit* DOCTOR

MACDUFF
What's the disease he means?

MALCOLM
'Tis call'd the evil:
A most miraculous work in this good king;
Which often, since my here-remain in England,
I have seen him do. How he solicits heaven,
Himself best knows: but strangely-visited people,
All swoln and ulcerous, pitiful to the eye,
The mere despair of surgery, he cures,
Hanging a golden stamp about their necks,
Put on with holy prayers: and 'tis spoken,
To the succeeding royalty he leaves
The healing benediction. With this strange virtue
He hath a heavenly gift of prophecy,
And sundry blessings hang about his throne
That speak him full of grace.

Enter ROSS

MACDUFF
See, who comes here?

MALCOLM
My countryman; but yet I know him not.

MACDUFF
My ever gentle cousin, welcome hither.

MALCOLM
I know him now: good God, betimes remove
The means that makes us strangers!

ROSS
Sir, amen.

MACDUFF
Stands Scotland where it did?

ROSS
Alas, poor country!
Almost afraid to know itself! It cannot
Be call'd our mother, but our grave: where nothing,
But who knows nothing, is once seen to smile;
Where sighs and groans and shrieks that rend the
    air,
Are made, not mark'd; where violent sorrow seems
A modern ecstasy: the dead man's knell
Is there scarce ask'd for who; and good men's lives
Expire before the flowers in their caps,
Dying or ere they sicken.

MACDUFF
O, relation
Too nice, and yet too true!

MALCOLM
What's the newest grief?

ROSS
That of an hour's age doth hiss the speaker;
Each minute teems a new one.

MACDUFF
How does my wife?

ROSS
Why, well.

MACDUFF
And all my children?

ROSS
Well too.

MACDUFF
The tyrant has not batter'd at their peace?

ROSS
No; they were well at peace when I did leave 'em.

MACDUFF
Be not a niggard of your speech: how goes 't?

ROSS
When I came hither to transport the tidings,
Which I have heavily borne, there ran a rumour
Of many worthy fellows that were out;
Which was to my belief witness'd the rather,
For that I saw the tyrant's power a-foot:
Now is the time of help; your eye in Scotland
Would create soldiers, make our women fight,
To doff their dire distresses.

MALCOLM
Be 't their comfort
We are coming thither: gracious England hath
Lent us good Siward and ten thousand men;
An older and a better soldier none
That Christendom gives out.

ROSS
Would I could answer
This comfort with the like! But I have words
That would be howl'd out in the desert air,
Where hearing should not latch them.

MACDUFF
What concern they?
The general cause? or is it a fee-grief
Due to some single breast?

ROSS
No mind that's honest
But in it shares some woe, though the main part
Pertains to you alone.

MACDUFF
If it be mine,
Keep it not from me, quickly let me have it.

ROSS
Let not your ears despise my tongue for ever,
Which shall possess them with the heaviest sound
That ever yet they heard.

MACDUFF
Hum! I guess at it.

ROSS
Your castle is surprised; your wife and babes
Savagely slaughter'd: to relate the manner,
Were, on the quarry of these murder'd deer,
To add the death of you.

MALCOLM
Merciful heaven!
What, man! ne'er pull your hat upon your brows;
Give sorrow words: the grief that does not speak
Whispers the o'er-fraught heart, and bids it break.

MACDUFF
My children too?

ROSS
Wife, children, servants, all
That could be found.

MACDUFF

And I must be from thence!
My wife kill'd too?

ROSS

I have said.

MALCOLM

Be comforted:
Let's make us medicines of our great revenge,
To cure this deadly grief.

MACDUFF

He has no children. All my pretty ones?
Did you say all? O hell-kite! All?
What, all my pretty chickens and their dam
At one fell swoop?

MALCOLM

Dispute it like a man.

MACDUFF

I shall do so;
But I must also feel it as a man:
I cannot but remember such things were,
That were most precious to me. Did heaven look on,
And would not take their part? Sinful Macduff,
They were all struck for thee! naught that I am,
Not for their own demerits, but for mine,
Fell slaughter on their souls: heaven rest them now!

MALCOLM

Be this the whetstone of your sword: let grief
Convert to anger; blunt not the heart, enrage it.

MACDUFF

O, I could play the woman with mine eyes,
And braggart with my tongue! But, gentle heavens,
Cut short all intermission; front to front
Bring thou this fiend of Scotland and myself;
Within my sword's length set him; if he 'scape,
Heaven forgive him too!

MALCOLM

This tune goes manly.
Come, go we to the king; our power is ready;
Our lack is nothing but our leave. Macbeth
Is ripe for shaking, and the powers above
Put on their instruments. Receive what cheer you
    may;
The night is long that never finds the day.   [Exeunt

ACT V

SCENE I. Dunsinane. Ante-room in the castle

Enter a DOCTOR OF PHYSIC *and a*
WAITING-GENTLEWOMAN

DOCTOR

I have two nights watched with you, but can perceive no truth in your report. When was it she last
walked?

GENTLEWOMAN

Since his majesty went into the field, I have seen her
rise from her bed, throw her nightgown upon her,
unlock her closet, take forth paper, fold it, write

upon 't, read it, afterwards seal it, and again return
to bed; yet all this while in a most fast sleep.

DOCTOR

A great perturbation in nature, to receive at once
the benefit of sleep and do the effects of watching!
In this slumbery agitation, besides her walking and
other actual performances, what, at any time, have
you heard her say?

GENTLEWOMAN

That, sir, which I will not report after her.

DOCTOR

You may to me, and 'tis most meet you should.

GENTLEWOMAN

Neither to you nor any one, having no witness to
confirm my speech.

Enter LADY MACBETH, *with a taper*
Lo you, here she comes! This is her very guise, and,
upon my life, fast asleep. Observe her; stand close.

DOCTOR

How came she by that light?

GENTLEWOMAN

Why, it stood by her: she has light by her continually; 'tis her command.

DOCTOR

You see, her eyes are open.

GENTLEWOMAN

Ay, but their sense is shut.

DOCTOR

What is it she does now? Look, how she rubs her
hands.

GENTLEWOMAN

It is an accustomed action with her, to seem thus
washing her hands: I have known her continue in
this a quarter of an hour.

LADY MACBETH

Yet here's a spot.

DOCTOR

Hark! she speaks: I will set down what comes from
her, to satisfy my remembrance the more strongly.

LADY MACBETH

Out, damned spot! out, I say! One: two: why, then
'tis time to do 't. Hell is murky. Fie, my lord, fie!
a soldier, and afeard? What need we fear who
knows it, when none can call our power to account?
Yet who would have thought the old man to have
had so much blood in him?

DOCTOR

Do you mark that?

LADY MACBETH

The thane of Fife had a wife; where is she now?
What, will these hands ne'er be clean? No more o'
that, my lord, no more o' that: you mar all with
this starting.

DOCTOR

Go to, go to; you have known what you should not.

GENTLEWOMAN

She has spoke what she should not, I am sure of
that: heaven knows what she has known.

LADY MACBETH

Here's the smell of the blood still: all the perfumes of Arabia will not sweeten this little hand. Oh, oh, oh!

DOCTOR

What a sigh is there! The heart is sorely charged.

GENTLEWOMAN

I would not have such a heart in my bosom for the dignity of the whole body.

DOCTOR

Well, well, well,—

GENTLEWOMAN

Pray God it be, sir.

DOCTOR

This disease is beyond my practice: yet I have known those which have walked in their sleep who have died holily in their beds.

LADY MACBETH

Wash your hands; put on your nightgown; look not so pale: I tell you yet again, Banquo's buried; he cannot come out on 's grave.

DOCTOR

Even so?

LADY MACBETH

To bed, to bed; there's knocking at the gate: come, come, come, come, give me your hand: what's done cannot be undone: to bed, to bed, to bed.   [*Exit*

DOCTOR

Will she go now to bed?

GENTLEWOMAN

Directly.

DOCTOR

Foul whisperings are abroad: unnatural deeds
Do breed unnatural troubles: infected minds
To their deaf pillows will discharge their secrets:
More needs she the divine than the physician.
God, God forgive us all! Look after her;
Remove from her the means of all annoyance,
And still keep eyes upon her. So good night:
My mind she has mated and amazed my sight:
I think, but dare not speak.

GENTLEWOMAN

             Good night, good doctor.

                           [*Exeunt*

SCENE II. *The country near Dunsinane*

Drum and colours. Enter MENTEITH, CAITHNESS, ANGUS,
LENNOX, *and* SOLDIERS

MENTEITH

The English power is near, led on by Malcolm,
His uncle Siward and the good Macduff:
Revenges burn in them; for their dear causes
Would to the bleeding and the grim alarm
Excite the mortified man.

ANGUS

            Near Birnam wood
Shall we well meet them; that way are they coming.

CAITHNESS

Who knows if Donalbain be with his brother?

LENNOX

For certain, sir, he is not: I have a file
Of all the gentry: there is Siward's son,
And many unrough youths, that even now
Protest their first of manhood.

MENTEITH

                 What does the tyrant?

CAITHNESS

Great Dunsinane he strongly fortifies:
Some say he's mad; others, that lesser hate him,
Do call it valiant fury: but, for certain,
He cannot buckle his distemper'd cause
Within the belt of rule.

ANGUS

               Now does he feel
His secret murders sticking on his hands;
Now minutely revolts upbraid his faith-breach;
Those he commands move only in command,
Nothing in love: now does he feel his title
Hang loose about him, like a giant's robe
Upon a dwarfish thief.

MENTEITH

               Who then shall blame
His pester'd senses to recoil and start,
When all that is within him does condemn
Itself for being there?

CAITHNESS

              Well, march we on,
To give obedience where 'tis truly owed:
Meet we the medicine of the sickly weal,
And with him pour we, in our country's purge,
Each drop of us.

LENNOX

             Or so much as it needs
To dew the sovereign flower and drown the weeds.
Make we our march towards Birnam.

                       [*Exeunt, marching*

SCENE III. *Dunsinane. A room in the castle*

Enter MACBETH, DOCTOR, *and* ATTENDANTS

MACBETH

Bring me no more reports; let them fly all:
Till Birnam wood remove to Dunsinane
I cannot taint with fear. What's the boy Malcolm?
Was he not born of woman? The spirits that know
All mortal consequences have pronounced me thus:
'Fear not, Macbeth; no man that's born of woman
Shall e'er have power upon thee.' Then fly, false thanes,
And mingle with the English epicures:
The mind I sway by and the heart I bear
Shall never sag with doubt nor shake with fear.

Enter a SERVANT

The devil damn thee black, thou cream-faced loon!
Where got'st thou that goose look?

SERVANT

There is ten thousand—

MACBETH

Geese, villain?

SERVANT

Soldiers, sir.

MACBETH

Go prick thy face and over-red thy fear,
Thou lily-liver'd boy. What soldiers, patch?
Death of thy soul! those linen cheeks of thine
Are counsellors to fear. What soldiers, whey-face?

SERVANT

The English force, so please you.

MACBETH

Take thy face hence.   [Exit SERVANT
                    Seyton!—I am sick at heart,
When I behold—Seyton, I say!—This push
Will cheer me ever, or disseat me now.
I have lived long enough: my way of life
Is fall'n into the sear, the yellow leaf,
And that which should accompany old age,
As honour, love, obedience, troops of friends,
I must not look to have; but, in their stead,
Curses, not loud but deep, mouth-honour, breath,
Which the poor heart would fain deny, and dare not.
Seyton!

Enter SEYTON

SEYTON

What's your gracious pleasure?

MACBETH

                    What news more?

SEYTON

All is confirm'd, my lord, which was reported.

MACBETH

I'll fight, till from my bones my flesh be hack'd.
Give me my armour.

SEYTON

                    'Tis not needed yet.

MACBETH

I'll put it on.
Send out moe horses, skirr the country round;
Hang those that talk of fear. Give me mine armour.
How does your patient, doctor?

DOCTOR

                    Not so sick, my lord,
As she is troubled with thick-coming fancies,
That keep her from her rest.

MACBETH

                    Cure her of that.
Canst thou not minister to a mind diseased,
Pluck from the memory a rooted sorrow,
Raze out the written troubles of the brain,
And with some sweet oblivious antidote
Cleanse the stuff'd bosom of that perilous stuff
Which weighs upon the heart?

DOCTOR

                    Therein the patient
Must minister to himself.

MACBETH

Throw physic to the dogs, I'll none of it.
Come, put mine armour on; give me my staff.
Seyton, send out. Doctor, the thanes fly from me.

Come, sir, dispatch. If thou couldst, doctor, cast
The water of my land, find her disease
And purge it to a sound and pristine health,
I would applaud thee to the very echo,
That should applaud again. Pull 't off, I say.
What rhubarb, senna, or what purgative drug,
Would scour these English hence? Hear'st thou of
  them?

DOCTOR

Ay, my good lord; your royal preparation
Makes us hear something.

MACBETH

                    Bring it after me.
I will not be afraid of death and bane
Till Birnam forest come to Dunsinane.

DOCTOR

[Aside] Were I from Dunsinane away and clear,
Profit again should hardly draw me here.   [Exeunt

SCENE IV. *Country near Birnam wood*

Drum and colours. Enter MALCOLM, *old* SIWARD *and his*
SON, MACDUFF, MENTEITH, CAITHNESS, ANGUS, LENNOX,
ROSS, *and* SOLDIERS, *marching*

MALCOLM

Cousins, I hope the days are near at hand
That chambers will be safe.

MENTEITH

                    We doubt it nothing.

SIWARD

What wood is this before us?

MENTEITH

                    The wood of Birnam.

MALCOLM

Let every soldier hew him down a bough,
And bear 't before him: thereby shall we shadow
The numbers of our host, and make discovery
Err in report of us.

SOLDIERS

It shall be done.

SIWARD

We learn no other but the confident tyrant
Keeps still in Dunsinane, and will endure
Our setting down before 't.

MALCOLM

                    'Tis his main hope:
For where there is advantage to be given,
Both more and less have given him the revolt,
And none serve with him but constrained things
Whose hearts are absent too.

MACDUFF

                    Let our just censures
Attend the true event, and put we on
Industrious soldiership.

SIWARD

                    The time approaches,
That will with due decision make us know
What we shall say we have and what we owe.

Thoughts speculative their unsure hopes relate,
But certain issue strokes must arbitrate:
Towards which advance the war. [*Exeunt, marching*

Scene V. *Dunsinane. Within the castle*

Enter MACBETH, SEYTON, *and* SOLDIERS, *with drum and colours*

MACBETH

Hang out our banners on the outward walls;
The cry is still 'They come:' our castle's strength
Will laugh a siege to scorn: here let them lie
Till famine and the ague eat them up:
Were they not forced with those that should be ours,
We might have met them dareful, beard to beard,
And beat them backward home.
                    [*A cry of women within*
                         What is that noise?

SEYTON

It is the cry of women, my good lord.   [*Exit*

MACBETH

I have almost forgot the taste of fears:
The time has been, my senses would have cool'd
To hear a night-shriek, and my fell of hair
Would at a dismal treatise rouse and stir
As life were in 't: I have supp'd full with horrors;
Direness, familiar to my slaughterous thoughts,
Cannot once start me.
                    Re-enter SEYTON
                         Wherefore was that cry?

SEYTON

The queen, my lord, is dead.

MACBETH

She should have died hereafter;
There would have been a time for such a word.
To-morrow, and to-morrow, and to-morrow,
Creeps in this petty pace from day to day,
To the last syllable of recorded time;
And all our yesterdays have lighted fools
The way to dusty death. Out, out, brief candle!
Life's but a walking shadow, a poor player
That struts and frets his hour upon the stage
And then is heard no more: it is a tale
Told by an idiot, full of sound and fury,
Signifying nothing.
                    Enter a MESSENGER
Thou comest to use thy tongue; thy story quickly.

MESSENGER

Gracious my lord,
I should report that which I say I saw,
But know not how to do it.

MACBETH

                    Well, say, sir.

MESSENGER

As I did stand my watch upon the hill,
I look'd toward Birnam, and anon, methought,
The wood began to move.

MACBETH

                    Liar and slave!

MESSENGER

Let me endure your wrath, if 't be not so:
Within this three mile may you see it coming;
I say, a moving grove.

MACBETH

                    If thou speak'st false,
Upon the next tree shalt thou hang alive,
Till famine cling thee: if thy speech be sooth,
I care not if thou dost for me as much.
I pull in resolution, and begin
To doubt the equivocation of the fiend
That lies like truth: 'Fear not, till Birnam wood
Do come to Dunsinane;' and now a wood
Comes toward Dunsinane. Arm, arm, and out!
If this which he avouches does appear,
There is nor flying hence nor tarrying here.
I 'gin to be a-weary of the sun,
And wish the estate o' the world were now undone.
Ring the alarum-bell! Blow, wind! come, wrack!
At least we'll die with harness on our back. [*Exeunt*

Scene VI. *Dunsinane. Before the castle*

Drum and colours. Enter MALCOLM, *old* SIWARD, MAC-
DUFF, *and their* ARMY, *with boughs*

MALCOLM

Now near enough; your leavy screens throw down,
And show like those you are. You, worthy uncle,
Shall, with my cousin, your right noble son,
Lead our first battle: worthy Macduff and we
Shall take upon 's what else remains to do,
According to our order.

SIWARD

                    Fare you well.
Do we but find the tyrant's power to-night,
Let us be beaten, if we cannot fight.

MACDUFF

Make all our trumpets speak; give them all breath,
Those clamorous harbingers of blood and death.
                                        [*Exeunt*

Scene VII. *Another part of the field*

Alarums. Enter MACBETH

MACBETH

They have tied me to a stake; I cannot fly,
But bear-like I must fight the course. What's he
That was not born of woman? Such a one
Am I to fear, or none.
                    Enter YOUNG SIWARD

YOUNG SIWARD

What is thy name?

MACBETH

                    Thou'lt be afraid to hear it.

YOUNG SIWARD

No; though thou call'st thyself a hotter name
Than any is in hell.

MACBETH

                    My name's Macbeth.

YOUNG SIWARD

The devil himself could not pronounce a title
More hateful to mine ear.

MACBETH

No, nor more fearful.

YOUNG SIWARD

Thou liest, abhorred tyrant; with my sword
I'll prove the lie thou speak'st.

[*They fight, and* YOUNG SIWARD *is slain*

MACBETH

Thou wast born of woman.
But swords I smile at, weapons laugh to scorn,
Brandish'd by man that's of a woman born.   [*Exit*
Alarums. Enter MACDUFF

MACDUFF

That way the noise is. Tyrant, show thy face!
If thou be'st slain and with no stroke of mine,
My wife and children's ghosts will haunt me still.
I cannot strike at wretched kerns, whose arms
Are hired to bear their staves: either thou, Macbeth,
Or else my sword, with an unbatter'd edge,
I sheathe again undeeded. There thou shouldst be;
By this great clatter, one of greatest note
Seems bruited: let me find him, fortune!
And more I beg not.   [*Exit. Alarums*
Enter MALCOLM *and old* SIWARD

SIWARD

This way, my lord; the castle's gently render'd:
The tyrant's people on both sides do fight;
The noble thanes do bravely in the war;
The day almost itself professes yours,
And little is to do.

MALCOLM

We have met with foes
That strike beside us.

SIWARD

Enter, sir, the castle.
[*Exeunt. Alarum*

SCENE VIII. *Another part of the field*
Enter MACBETH

MACBETH

Why should I play the Roman fool, and die
On mine own sword? whiles I see lives, the gashes
Do better upon them.

Enter MACDUFF

MACDUFF

Turn, hell-hound, turn!

MACBETH

Of all men else I have avoided thee:
But get thee back; my soul is too much charged
With blood of thine already.

MACDUFF

I have no words:
My voice is in my sword, thou bloodier villain
Than terms can give thee out!   [*They fight*

MACBETH

Thou losest labour:

As easy mayst thou the intrenchant air
With thy keen sword impress as make me bleed:
Let fall thy blade on vulnerable crests;
I bear a charmed life, which must not yield
To one of woman born.

MACDUFF

Despair thy charm,
And let the angel whom thou still hast served
Tell thee, Macduff was from his mother's womb
Untimely ripp'd.

MACBETH

Accursed be that tongue that tells me so,
For it hath cow'd my better part of man!
And be these juggling fiends no more believed,
That palter with us in a double sense;
That keep the word of promise to our ear,
And break it to our hope. I'll not fight with thee.

MACDUFF

Then yield thee, coward,
And live to be the show and gaze o' the time:
We'll have thee, as our rarer monsters are,
Painted upon a pole, and underwrit,
'Here may you see the tyrant.'

MACBETH

I will not yield,
To kiss the ground before young Malcolm's feet,
And to be baited with the rabble's curse.
Though Birnam wood be come to Dunsinane,
And thou opposed, being of no woman born,
Yet I will try the last: before my body
I throw my warlike shield: lay on, Macduff;
And damn'd be him that first cries 'Hold, enough!'
[*Exeunt, fighting. Alarums*
Retreat. Flourish. Enter, with drum and colours,
MALCOLM, *old* SIWARD, ROSS, *the other* THANES,
and SOLDIERS

MALCOLM

I would the friends we miss were safe arrived.

SIWARD

Some must go off: and yet, by these I see,
So great a day as this is cheaply bought.

MALCOLM

Macduff is missing, and your noble son.

ROSS

Your son, my lord, has paid a soldier's debt:
He only lived but till he was a man;
The which no sooner had his prowess confirm'd
In the unshrinking station where he fought,
But like a man he died.

SIWARD

Then he is dead?

ROSS

Ay, and brought off the field: your cause of sorrow
Must not be measured by his worth, for then
It hath no end.

SIWARD

Had he his hurts before?

ROSS

Ay, on the front.

SIWARD

Why then, God's soldier be he!
Had I as many sons as I have hairs,
I would not wish them to a fairer death:
And so his knell is knoll'd.

MALCOLM

He's worth more sorrow,
And that I'll spend for him.

SIWARD

He's worth no more:
They say he parted well and paid his score:
And so God be with him! Here comes newer comfort.

Re-enter MACDUFF, *with* MACBETH'S *head*

MACDUFF

Hail, king! for so thou art: behold, where stands
The usurper's cursed head: the time is free:
I see thee compass'd with thy kingdom's pearl,
That speak my salutation in their minds;
Whose voices I desire aloud with mine:
Hail, King of Scotland!

ALL

Hail, King of Scotland!

                     [*Flourish*

MALCOLM

We shall not spend a large expense of time
Before we reckon with your several loves,
And make us even with you. My thanes and kinsmen,
Henceforth be earls, the first that ever Scotland
In such an honour named. What's more to do,
Which would be planted newly with the time,
As calling home our exiled friends abroad
That fled the snares of watchful tyranny,
Producing forth the cruel ministers
Of this dead butcher and his fiend-like queen,
Who, as 'tis thought, by self and violent hands
Took off her life; this, and what needful else
That calls upon us, by the grace of Grace
We will perform in measure, time and place:
So thanks to all at once and to each one,
Whom we invite to see us crown'd at Scone.

                [*Flourish. Exeunt*

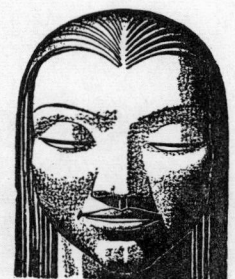

ANTONY AND CLEOPATRA

SYNOPSIS

Since the day when Cleopatra, Queen of Egypt, first met Mark Antony at Cydnus in her luxurious barge with its golden poop, silver oars and perfumed purple sails, she has held the pleasure-loving soldier-prince a willing captive at her frivolous, extravagant court, oblivious to his duty as friend, husband and triumvir of the Roman Empire. Threats of political unrest at Rome, which is being defied by the young, revengeful Pompey with his strong navy, have filtered through to Antony at Alexandria, but now comes the shock of the death of Fulvia, his high-spirited wife, who has been involved in petty wars against the other members of the triumvirate. Antony realizes that he must return to Rome and face the task of conciliating his associates and giving them military help.

At his sudden decision, Cleopatra rages impotently in her jealous disappointment, but resolves to continue her hold on her lover by daily letters sent by messenger. The conference at Rome gives little hope of permanent accord between Octavius Caesar and Antony, but, through the good offices of Lepidus, the third triumvir, and Antony's self-restraint, the atmosphere clears and the shrewd suggestion of a union between Antony and the noble Octavia, Caesar's widowed sister, is made and carried out.

Now that its great soldier has returned to the Roman triumvirate, Pompey agrees to a diplomatic settlement of all their difficulties, and gives a royal banquet in its celebration aboard one of his galleys. A soothsayer convinces Antony that he will never prosper in close association with Caesar, and he turns to the Eastern empire, sending troops to Parthia which operate so successfully, that with Octavia, he takes up residence in Athens—already halfway to Egypt where his rough-tongued soldier and companion, Enobarbus, has ever prophesied he would return.

Very soon Antony hears that Caesar, without consulting him, has renewed war on Pompey, thrown Lepidus into prison, and in other ways overlooked and slighted him. Octavia generously offers to go to Rome as mediator, but when she arrives she is told that Antony is in Alexandria, again enslaved by Cleopatra's charm, wit and constant companionship, and again heaping honors upon her. Furious over this insulting treatment of his beloved sister, Caesar speeds up preparations for war against his brother-in-law in Egypt. Antony's main advantage lies in his land forces but against his officers' advice, he takes up Caesar's challenge to a supreme sea-fight at Actium where Cleopatra accompanies him, even leading her own fleet into action. A crisis comes in the battle when the odds are even and victory may veer to either side, but, to the utter consternation of

Antony's men, Cleopatra suddenly turns her ship and flees, with her doting triumvir reluctantly following.

A ruined Antony must now negotiate with Caesar who refuses his request to live either in Egypt or Athens, but grants Cleopatra's plea for her Egyptian throne for her son, provided she will drive Antony out or put him to death. Antony replies by a foolish challenge to personal combat which Caesar disregards and sends a practised courtier to win Cleopatra to his terms by flattery and promises. Warned by Enobarbus, Antony arrives in time to see the insinuating ambassador kissing the Queen's hand in apparent triumph. He orders the man to be whipped, and rages against Cleopatra who, gradually winning him back, encourages him in his determination to fight another battle. His extravagant resolutions, his angry words, together with his infatuation, convince his followers that Antony's cause is lost, and in large numbers they desert to Caesar. Enobarbus goes, too, but only to die of a broken heart when his emperor sends after him a kindly message and the treasure he had left. The palace sentries whisper among each other that the god Hercules, whom Antony loved, is leaving him.

On the first day of battle, however, Antony is victorious on land, and returns home triumphant to feast all night at Cleopatra's court, but on the following day disaster comes with a second cowardly flight of the Egyptian fleet. Bitterly suspecting that Cleopatra is in league with Caesar, Antony resolves to kill her, but she flees from his fury to her monument and sends him word that she has ended her life. Antony orders his devoted freedman, Eros, to strike him dead, but the man, refusing, kills himself instead. His master falls on his sword and lies mortally wounded, begging his guards to dispatch him, when a second messenger comes from Cleopatra to tell him she is alive. The dying Antony is hoisted up to Cleopatra in her monument which she dares not leave for fear of capture, and dies content in her arms, the world well lost for her love.

Caesar, wanting to take the famous Egyptian queen in triumph to Rome and fearing that she may take her life, sets a close watch over her, and visits her personally to make fair promises. But Cleopatra distrusts the cold, level-headed man, against whom one of his own officers warns her, and now fully appreciating Antony's nobility her last desire is to follow him to death. She plans for a garrulous old countryman, whom the guards willingly pass, to bring her a basket of figs in which deadly asps are concealed, and, dressed again in the royal robes she wore when she first met Antony at Cydnus, she applies an asp to her breast and expires. Her loyal women, Iras and Charmian, die beside her, and Caesar orders her body placed in the same grave with Antony.

HISTORICAL DATA

The sole source of Shakespeare's version of the story of Cleopatra appears to have been Sir Thomas North's translation of Amyot's version of Plutarch's *Life of Marcus Antonius*. This account has been followed with unusual fidelity and, although the story had been frequently the basis of dramatic compositions prior to Shakespeare's play, there seems no reason to believe that he is indebted to any of his predecessors in this field. It is possible that some of the descriptions of the Nile may have been derived from Holland's translation of *Pliny* or John Pory's translation of Leo's *History of Africa*. The chief change instituted by Shakespeare is to be found in his conception of Antony whom he recreates from the vulgar libertine of Plutarch into a man of prac-

tical capacity that almost amounts to genius and a passion which is redeemed from meanness by its magnificent intensity.

Among the minor characters, that of Enobarbus is virtually an invention of Shakespeare's for although he is, of course, an historical personage, there is little premise for the rich characterization which he is given in the play.

A Book Called Antony and Cleopatra was entered in the Stationers' Register on May 20, 1608, and it is generally conceded that this records the completion of this play. Although it does not actually appear to have been printed prior to the First Folio in 1623, the date of its composition is generally assigned to the year 1607.

"*Why is my lord enrag'd against his love?*"
ANTONY AND CLEOPATRA

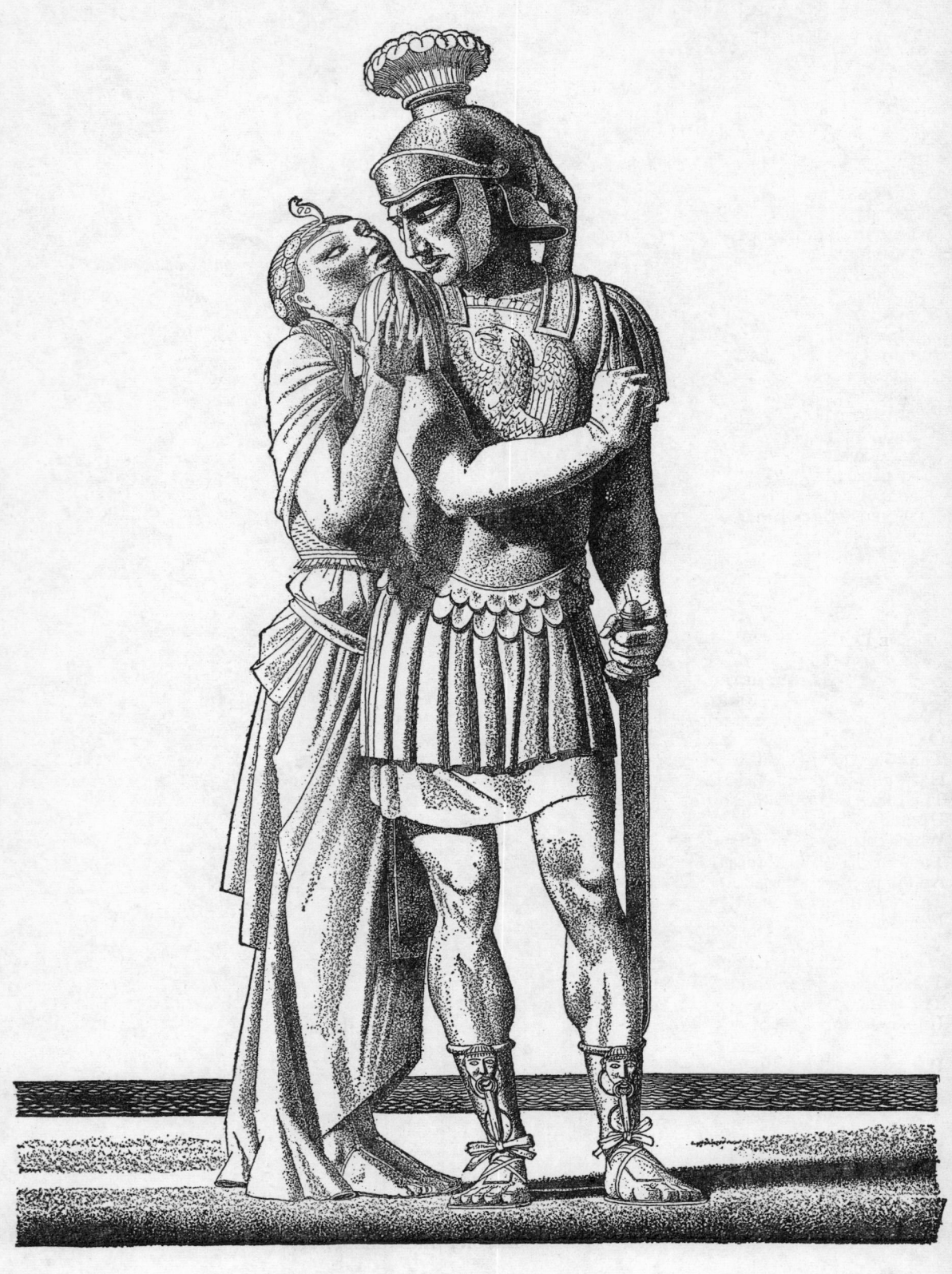

ANTONY AND CLEOPATRA

DRAMATIS PERSONÆ

ANTONY,
OCTAVIUS CÆSAR, } *triumvirs.*
LEPIDUS,
SEXTUS POMPEIUS.
DOMITIUS ENOBARBUS,
VENTIDIUS,
EROS,
SCARUS,
DERCETAS, } *friends to Antony.*
DEMETRIUS,
PHILO,
MÆCENAS,
AGRIPPA,
DOLABELLA,
PROCULEIUS, } *friends to Cæsar.*
THYREUS,
GALLUS,
MENAS,
MENECRATES, } *friends to Sextus Pompeius.*
VARRIUS,

TAURUS, *lieutenant-general to Cæsar.*
CANIDIUS, *lieutenant-general to Antony.*
SILIUS, *an officer in Ventidius's army.*
EUPHRONIUS, *an ambassador from Antony to Cæsar.*
ALEXAS,
MARDIAN, *a eunuch,* } *attendants on Cleopatra.*
SELEUCUS,
DIOMEDES,
A SOOTHSAYER.
A CLOWN.

CLEOPATRA, *queen of Egypt.*
OCTAVIA, *sister to Cæsar, and wife to Antony.*
CHARMIAN, } *attendants on Cleopatra.*
IRAS,

OFFICERS, SOLDIERS, MESSENGERS, *and other* ATTENDANTS.

SCENE—*In several parts of the Roman empire*

ACT I

SCENE I. *Alexandria. A room in* CLEOPATRA's *palace*

Enter DEMETRIUS *and* PHILO

PHILO

NAY, but this dotage of our general's
O'erflows the measure: those his goodly eyes,
That o'er the files and musters of the war
Have glow'd like plated Mars, now bend, now turn,
The office and devotion of their view
Upon a tawny front: his captain's heart,
Which in the scuffles of great fights hath burst
The buckles on his breast, reneges all temper,
And is become the bellows and the fan
To cool a gipsy's lust.
Flourish. Enter ANTONY, CLEOPATRA, *her* LADIES, *the train, with* EUNUCHS *fanning her*
                    Look, where they come:
Take but good note, and you shall see in him
The triple pillar of the world transform'd
Into a strumpet's fool: behold and see.

CLEOPATRA

If it be love indeed, tell me how much.

ANTONY

There's beggary in the love that can be reckon'd.

CLEOPATRA

I'll set a bourn how far to be beloved.

ANTONY

Then must thou needs find out new heaven, new earth.

Enter an ATTENDANT

ATTENDANT

News, my good lord, from Rome.

ANTONY

                    Grates me: the sum.

CLEOPATRA

Nay, hear them, Antony:
Fulvia perchance is angry; or, who knows
If the scarce-bearded Cæsar have not sent
His powerful mandate to you, 'Do this, or this;
Take in that kingdom, and enfranchise that;
Perform 't, or else we damn thee.'

ANTONY

                    How, my love!

CLEOPATRA

Perchance! nay, and most like:
You must not stay here longer, your dismission
Is come from Cæsar; therefore hear it, Antony.
Where's Fulvia's process? Cæsar's I would say? both?
Call in the messengers. As I am Egypt's queen,
Thou blushest, Antony, and that blood of thine
Is Cæsar's homager: else so thy cheek pays shame
When shrill-tongued Fulvia scolds. The messengers!

ANTONY

Let Rome in Tiber melt, and the wide arch
Of the ranged empire fall! Here is my space.
Kingdoms are clay: our dungy earth alike
Feeds beast as man: the nobleness of life
Is to do thus; when such a mutual pair   [*Embracing*
And such a twain can do 't, in which I bind,
On pain of punishment, the world to weet
We stand up peerless.

CLEOPATRA
Excellent falsehood!
Why did he marry Fulvia, and not love her?
I'll seem the fool I am not; Antony
Will be himself.

ANTONY
But stirr'd by Cleopatra.
Now, for the love of Love and her soft hours,
Let's not confound the time with conference harsh:
There's not a minute of our lives should stretch
Without some pleasure now. What sport to-night?

CLEOPATRA
Hear the ambassadors.

ANTONY
Fie, wrangling queen!
Whom every thing becomes, to chide, to laugh,
To weep; whose every passion fully strives
To make itself, in thee, fair and admired!
No messenger but thine; and all alone
To-night we'll wander through the streets and note
The qualities of people. Come, my queen;
Last night you did desire it. Speak not to us.
[Exeunt ANTONY and CLEOPATRA with their train

DEMETRIUS
Is Cæsar with Antonius prized so slight?

PHILO
Sir, sometimes, when he is not Antony,
He comes too short of that great property
Which still should go with Antony.

DEMETRIUS
I am full sorry
That he approves the common liar, who
Thus speaks of him at Rome: but I will hope
Of better deeds to-morrow. Rest you happy!
[Exeunt

SCENE II. *The same. Another room*

Enter CHARMIAN, IRAS, ALEXAS, *and a* SOOTHSAYER
CHARMIAN
Lord Alexas, sweet Alexas, most any thing Alexas,
almost most absolute Alexas, where's the soothsayer
that you praised so to the queen? O, that I knew this
husband, which, you say, must charge his horns
with garlands!

ALEXAS
Soothsayer!

SOOTHSAYER
Your will?

CHARMIAN
Is this the man? Is 't you, sir, that know things?

SOOTHSAYER
In nature's infinite book of secrecy
A little I can read.

ALEXAS
Show him your hand.
Enter ENOBARBUS
ENOBARBUS
Bring in the banquet quickly; wine enough
Cleopatra's health to drink.

CHARMIAN
Good sir, give me good fortune.

SOOTHSAYER
I make not, but foresee.

CHARMIAN
Pray then, foresee me one.

SOOTHSAYER
You shall be yet far fairer than you are.

CHARMIAN
He means in flesh.

IRAS
No, you shall paint when you are old.

CHARMIAN
Wrinkles forbid!

ALEXAS
Vex not his prescience; be attentive.

CHARMIAN
Hush!

SOOTHSAYER
You shall be more beloving than beloved.

CHARMIAN
I had rather heat my liver with drinking.

ALEXAS
Nay, hear him.

CHARMIAN
Good now, some excellent fortune! Let me be married to three kings in a forenoon, and widow them
all: let me have a child at fifty, to whom Herod of
Jewry may do homage: find me to marry me with
Octavius Cæsar, and companion me with my mistress.

SOOTHSAYER
You shall outlive the lady whom you serve.

CHARMIAN
O excellent! I love long life better than figs.

SOOTHSAYER
You have seen and proved a fairer former fortune
Than that which is to approach.

CHARMIAN
Then belike my children shall have no names:
prithee, how many boys and wenches must I have?

SOOTHSAYER
If every of your wishes had a womb,
And fertile every wish, a million.

CHARMIAN
Out, fool! I forgive thee for a witch.

ALEXAS
You think none but your sheets are privy to your
wishes.

CHARMIAN
Nay, come, tell Iras hers.

ALEXAS
We'll know all our fortunes.

ENOBARBUS
Mine and most of our fortunes to-night shall be—
drunk to bed.

IRAS
There's a palm presages chastity, if nothing else.

CHARMIAN
E'en as the o'erflowing Nilus presageth famine.

IRAS

Go, you wild bedfellow, you cannot soothsay.

CHARMIAN

Nay, if an oily palm be not a fruitful prognostication, I cannot scratch mine ear. Prithee, tell her but
a worky-day fortune.

SOOTHSAYER

Your fortunes are alike.

IRAS

But how, but how? give me particulars.

SOOTHSAYER

I have said.

IRAS

Am I not an inch of fortune better than she?

CHARMIAN

Well, if you were but an inch of fortune better than
I, where would you choose it?

IRAS

Not in my husband's nose.

CHARMIAN

Our worser thoughts heavens mend! Alexas,—
come, his fortune, his fortune! O, let him marry a
woman that cannot go, sweet Isis, I beseech thee!
and let her die too, and give him a worse! and let
worse follow worse, till the worst of all follow him
laughing to his grave, fifty-fold a cuckold! Good
Isis, hear me this prayer, though thou deny me a
matter of more weight; good Isis, I beseech thee!

IRAS

Amen. Dear goddess, hear that prayer of the
people! for, as it is a heart-breaking to see a handsome man loose-wived, so it is a deadly sorrow to
behold a foul knave uncuckolded: therefore, dear
Isis, keep decorum, and fortune him accordingly!

CHARMIAN

Amen.

ALEXAS

Lo, now, if it lay in their hands to make me a cuckold, they would make themselves whores, but they'ld
do 't!

ENOBARBUS

Hush! here comes Antony.

CHARMIAN

           Not he; the queen.

Enter CLEOPATRA

CLEOPATRA

Saw you my lord?

ENOBARBUS

No, lady.

CLEOPATRA

Was he not here?

CHARMIAN

No, madam.

CLEOPATRA

He was disposed to mirth; but on the sudden
A Roman thought hath struck him. Enobarbus!

ENOBARBUS

Madam?

CLEOPATRA

Seek him, and bring him hither. Where's Alexas?

ALEXAS

Here, at your service. My lord approaches.

CLEOPATRA

We will not look upon him: go with us.   [*Exeunt*

Enter ANTONY *with a* MESSENGER *and* ATTENDANTS

MESSENGER

Fulvia thy wife first came into the field.

ANTONY

Against my brother Lucius?

MESSENGER

Ay:
But soon that war had end, and the time's state
Made friends of them, jointing their force 'gainst
   Cæsar,
Whose better issue in the war from Italy
Upon the first encounter drave them.

ANTONY

           Well, what worst?

MESSENGER

The nature of bad news infects the teller.

ANTONY

When it concerns the fool or coward. On:
Things that are past are done with me. 'Tis thus;
Who tells me true, though in his tale lie death,
I hear him as he flatter'd.

MESSENGER

          Labienus—
This is stiff news—hath with his Parthian force
Extended Asia from Euphrates,
His conquering banner shook from Syria
To Lydia and to Ionia,
Whilst—

ANTONY

Antony, thou wouldst say,—

MESSENGER

          O, my lord!

ANTONY

Speak to me home, mince not the general tongue:
Name Cleopatra as she is call'd in Rome;
Rail thou in Fulvia's phrase, and taunt my faults
With such full license as both truth and malice
Have power to utter. O, then we bring forth weeds
When our quick minds lie still, and our ills told us
Is as our earing. Fare thee well awhile.

MESSENGER

At your noble pleasure.   [*Exit*

ANTONY

From Sicyon, ho, the news! Speak there!

FIRST ATTENDANT

The man from Sicyon, is there such an one?

SECOND ATTENDANT

He stays upon your will.

ANTONY

          Let him appear.
These strong Egyptian fetters I must break,
Or lose myself in dotage.

Enter another MESSENGER

          What are you?

SECOND MESSENGER

Fulvia thy wife is dead.

ANTONY
Where died she?

SECOND MESSENGER
In Sicyon:
Her length of sickness, with what else more serious
Importeth thee to know, this bears.　　　[*Gives a letter*

ANTONY
Forbear me.
[*Exit* SECOND MESSENGER
There's a great spirit gone! Thus did I desire it:
What our contempts do often hurl from us,
We wish it ours again; the present pleasure,
By revolution lowering, does become
The opposite of itself: she's good, being gone;
The hand could pluck her back that shoved her on.
I must from this enchanting queen break off:
Ten thousand harms, more than the ills I know,
My idleness doth hatch. How now! Enobarbus!

Re-enter ENOBARBUS

ENOBARBUS
What's your pleasure, sir?

ANTONY
I must with haste from hence.

ENOBARBUS
Why then we kill all our women. We see how mortal an unkindness is to them; if they suffer our departure, death's the word.

ANTONY
I must be gone.

ENOBARBUS
Under a compelling occasion let women die: it were pity to cast them away for nothing; though, between them and a great cause, they should be esteemed nothing. Cleopatra, catching but the least noise of this, dies instantly; I have seen her die twenty times upon far poorer moment: I do think there is mettle in death, which commits some loving act upon her, she hath such a celerity in dying.

ANTONY
She is cunning past man's thought.

ENOBARBUS
Alack, sir, no; her passions are made of nothing but the finest part of pure love: we cannot call her winds and waters sighs and tears; they are greater storms and tempests than almanacs can report: this cannot be cunning in her; if it be, she makes a shower of rain as well as Jove.

ANTONY
Would I had never seen her!

ENOBARBUS
O, sir, you had then left unseen a wonderful piece of work; which not to have been blest withal would have discredited your travel.

ANTONY
Fulvia is dead.

ENOBARBUS
Sir?

ANTONY
Fulvia is dead.

ENOBARBUS
Fulvia!

ANTONY
Dead.

ENOBARBUS
Why, sir, give the gods a thankful sacrifice. When it pleaseth their deities to take the wife of a man from him, it shows to man the tailors of the earth, comforting therein, that when old robes are worn out there are members to make new. If there were no more women but Fulvia, then had you indeed a cut, and the case to be lamented: this grief is crowned with consolation; your old smock brings forth a new petticoat: and indeed the tears live in an onion that should water this sorrow.

ANTONY
The business she hath broached in the state
Cannot endure my absence.

ENOBARBUS
And the business you have broached here cannot be without you; especially that of Cleopatra's, which wholly depends on your abode.

ANTONY
No more light answers. Let our officers
Have notice what we purpose. I shall break
The cause of our expedience to the queen
And get her leave to part. For not alone
The death of Fulvia, with more urgent touches,
Do strongly speak to us, but the letters too
Of many our contriving friends in Rome
Petition us at home: Sextus Pompeius
Hath given the dare to Cæsar and commands
The empire of the sea: our slippery people,
Whose love is never link'd to the deserver
Till his deserts are past, begin to throw
Pompey the Great and all his dignities
Upon his son; who, high in name and power,
Higher than both in blood and life, stands up
For the main soldier: whose quality, going on,
The sides o' the world may danger. Much is breeding,
Which, like the courser's hair, hath yet but life
And not a serpent's poison. Say, our pleasure,
To such whose place is under us, requires
Our quick remove from hence.

ENOBARBUS
I shall do 't.　　　　　　　　　　　　　　[*Exeunt*

SCENE III. *The same. Another room*

Enter CLEOPATRA, CHARMIAN, IRAS, *and* ALEXAS

CLEOPATRA
Where is he?

CHARMIAN
I did not see him since.

CLEOPATRA
See where he is, who's with him, what he does:
I did not send you: if you find him sad,

Say I am dancing; if in mirth, report
That I am sudden sick: quick, and return.

[*Exit* ALEXAS

CHARMIAN

Madam, methinks, if you did love him dearly,
You do not hold the method to enforce
The like from him.

CLEOPATRA

What should I do, I do not?

CHARMIAN

In each thing give him way, cross him in nothing.

CLEOPATRA

Thou teachest like a fool: the way to lose him.

CHARMIAN

Tempt him not so too far; I wish, forbear:
In time we hate that which we often fear.
But here comes Antony.

Enter ANTONY

CLEOPATRA

I am sick and sullen.

ANTONY

I am sorry to give breathing to my purpose,—

CLEOPATRA

Help me away, dear Charmian; I shall fall:
It cannot be thus long, the sides of nature
Will not sustain it.

ANTONY

Now, my dearest queen,—

CLEOPATRA

Pray you, stand farther from me.

ANTONY

What's the matter?

CLEOPATRA

I know, by that same eye, there's some good news.
What says the married woman? You may go:
Would she had never given you leave to come!
Let her not say 'tis I that keep you here,
I have no power upon you; hers you are.

ANTONY

The gods best know—

CLEOPATRA

O, never was there queen
So mightily betray'd! yet at the first
I saw the treasons planted.

ANTONY

Cleopatra,—

CLEOPATRA

Why should I think you can be mine and true,
Though you in swearing shake the throned gods,
Who have been false to Fulvia? Riotous madness,
To be entangled with those mouth-made vows,
Which break themselves in swearing!

ANTONY

Most sweet queen,—

CLEOPATRA

Nay, pray you, seek no colour for your going,
But bid farewell, and go: when you sued staying,
Then was the time for words: no going then;
Eternity was in our lips and eyes,

Bliss in our brows' bent, none our parts so poor
But was a race of heaven: they are so still,
Or thou, the greatest soldier of the world,
Art turn'd the greatest liar.

ANTONY

How now, lady!

CLEOPATRA

I would I had thy inches; thou shouldst know
There were a heart in Egypt.

ANTONY

Hear me, queen:
The strong necessity of time commands
Our services awhile; but my full heart
Remains in use with you. Our Italy
Shines o'er with civil swords: Sextus Pompeius
Makes his approaches to the port of Rome:
Equality of two domestic powers
Breed scrupulous faction: the hated, grown to
    strength,
Are newly grown to love: the condemn'd Pompey,
Rich in his father's honour, creeps apace
Into the hearts of such as have not thrived
Upon the present state, whose numbers threaten;
And quietness grown sick of rest would purge
By any desperate change. My more particular,
And that which most with you should safe my go-
    ing,
Is Fulvia's death.

CLEOPATRA

Though age from folly could not give me freedom,
It does from childishness: can Fulvia die?

ANTONY

She's dead, my queen:
Look here, and at thy sovereign leisure read
The garboils she awaked: at the last, best;
See when and where she died.

CLEOPATRA

O most false love!
Where be the sacred vials thou shouldst fill
With sorrowful water? Now I see, I see,
In Fulvia's death, how mine received shall be.

ANTONY

Quarrel no more, but be prepared to know
The purposes I bear, which are, or cease,
As you shall give the advice. By the fire
That quickens Nilus' slime, I go from hence
Thy soldier, servant, making peace or war
As thou affect'st.

CLEOPATRA

Cut my lace, Charmian, come;
But let it be: I am quickly ill and well,
So Antony loves.

ANTONY

My precious queen, forbear;
And give true evidence to his love, which stands
An honourable trial.

CLEOPATRA

So Fulvia told me.
I prithee, turn aside and weep for her;

Then bid adieu to me, and say the tears
Belong to Egypt: good now, play one scene
Of excellent dissembling, and let it look
Like perfect honour.

ANTONY
You'll heat my blood: no more.

CLEOPATRA
You can do better yet; but this is meetly.

ANTONY
Now, by my sword,—

CLEOPATRA
And target. Still he mends;
But this is not the best. Look, prithee, Charmian,
How this Herculean Roman does become
The carriage of his chafe.

ANTONY
I'll leave you, lady.

CLEOPATRA
Courteous lord, one word.
Sir, you and I must part, but that's not it:
Sir, you and I have loved, but there's not it:
That you know well: something it is I would,—
O, my oblivion is a very Antony,
And I am all forgotten.

ANTONY
But that your royalty
Holds idleness your subject, I should take you
For idleness itself.

CLEOPATRA
'Tis sweating labour
To bear such idleness so near the heart
As Cleopatra this. But, sir, forgive me,
Since my becomings kill me when they do not
Eye well to you. Your honour calls you hence;
Therefore be deaf to my unpitied folly,
And all the gods go with you! Upon your sword
Sit laurel victory! and smooth success
Be strew'd before your feet!

ANTONY
Let us go. Come;
Our separation so abides and flies,
That thou residing here go'st yet with me,
And I hence fleeting here remain with thee.
Away!   [Exeunt

SCENE IV. Rome. Cæsar's house

Enter OCTAVIUS CÆSAR, reading a letter, LEPIDUS, and
their train

CÆSAR
You may see, Lepidus, and henceforth know,
It is not Cæsar's natural vice to hate
Our great competitor: from Alexandria
This is the news: he fishes, drinks and wastes
The lamps of night in revel: is not more manlike
Than Cleopatra, nor the queen of Ptolemy
More womanly than he: hardly gave audience, or
Vouchsafed to think he had partners: you shall find
there

A man who is the abstract of all faults
That all men follow.

LEPIDUS
I must not think there are
Evils enow to darken all his goodness:
His faults in him seem as the spots of heaven,
More fiery by night's blackness, hereditary
Rather than purchased, what he cannot change
Than what he chooses.

CÆSAR
You are too indulgent. Let us grant it is not
Amiss to tumble on the bed of Ptolemy,
To give a kingdom for a mirth, to sit
And keep the turn of tippling with a slave,
To reel the streets at noon and stand the buffet
With knaves that smell of sweat: say this becomes
him,—
As his composure must be rare indeed
Whom these things cannot blemish,—yet must
Antony
No way excuse his soils, when we do bear
So great weight in his lightness. If he fill'd
His vacancy with his voluptuousness,
Full surfeits and the dryness of his bones
Call on him for 't: but to confound such time
That drums him from his sport and speaks as loud
As his own state and ours, 'tis to be chid
As we rate boys, who, being mature in knowledge,
Pawn their experience to their present pleasure,
And so rebel to judgement.

Enter a MESSENGER

LEPIDUS
Here's more news.

MESSENGER
Thy biddings have been done; and every hour,
Most noble Cæsar, shalt thou have report
How 'tis abroad. Pompey is strong at sea;
And it appears he is beloved of those
That only have fear'd Cæsar: to the ports
The discontents repair, and men's reports
Give him much wrong'd.

CÆSAR
I should have known no less:
It hath been taught us from the primal state,
That he which is was wish'd until he were;
And the ebb'd man, ne'er loved till ne'er worth
love,
Comes dear'd by being lack'd. This common body,
Like to a vagabond flag upon the stream,
Goes to and back, lackeying the varying tide,
To rot itself with motion.

MESSENGER
Cæsar, I bring thee word,
Menecrates and Menas, famous pirates,
Make the sea serve them, which they ear and wound
With keels of every kind: many hot inroads
They make in Italy; the borders maritime
Lack blood to think on 't, and flush youth revolt:
No vessel can peep forth, but 'tis as soon

Taken as seen; for Pompey's name strikes more
Than could his war resisted.

CÆSAR

Antony,
Leave thy lascivious wassails. When thou once
Wast beaten from Modena, where thou slew'st
Hirtius and Pansa, consuls, at thy heel
Did famine follow; whom thou fought'st against,
Though daintily brought up, with patience more
Than savages could suffer: thou didst drink
The stale of horses and the gilded puddle
Which beasts would cough at: thy palate then did
　　deign
The roughest berry on the rudest hedge;
Yea, like the stag, when snow the pasture sheets,
The barks of trees thou browsedst. On the Alps
It is reported thou didst eat strange flesh,
Which some did die to look on: and all this—
It wounds thine honour that I speak it now—
Was borne so like a soldier that thy cheek
So much as lank'd not.

LEPIDUS

'Tis pity of him.

CÆSAR

Let his shames quickly
Drive him to Rome: 'tis time we twain
Did show ourselves i' the field; and to that end
Assemble we immediate council: Pompey
Thrives in our idleness.

LEPIDUS

To-morrow, Cæsar,
I shall be furnish'd to inform you rightly
Both what by sea and land I can be able
To front this present time.

CÆSAR

Till which encounter,
It is my business too. Farewell.

LEPIDUS

Farewell, my lord: what you shall know meantime
Of stirs abroad, I shall beseech you, sir,
To let me be partaker.

CÆSAR

Doubt not, sir;
I knew it for my bond.　　　　　　　　　[Exeunt

SCENE V. *Alexandria.* CLEOPATRA's *palace*

Enter CLEOPATRA, CHARMIAN, IRAS, *and* MARDIAN

CLEOPATRA

Charmian!

CHARMIAN

Madam?

CLEOPATRA

Ha, ha!
Give me to drink mandragora.

CHARMIAN

Why, madam?

CLEOPATRA

That I might sleep out this great gap of time
My Antony is away.

CHARMIAN

You think of him too much.

CLEOPATRA

O, 'tis treason!

CHARMIAN

Madam, I trust, not so.

CLEOPATRA

Thou, eunuch Mardian!

MARDIAN

What's your highness' pleasure?

CLEOPATRA

Not now to hear thee sing; I take no pleasure
In aught an eunuch has: 'tis well for thee,
That, being unseminar'd, thy freer thoughts
May not fly forth of Egypt. Hast thou affections?

MARDIAN

Yes, gracious madam.

CLEOPATRA

Indeed!

MARDIAN

Not in deed, madam; for I can do nothing
But what indeed is honest to be done:
Yet have I fierce affections, and think
What Venus did with Mars.

CLEOPATRA

O Charmian,
Where think'st thou he is now? Stands he, or sits he?
Or does he walk? or is he on his horse?
O happy horse, to bear the weight of Antony!
Do bravely, horse! for wot'st thou whom thou
　　movest?
The demi-Atlas of this earth, the arm
And burgonet of men. He's speaking now,
Or murmuring 'Where's my serpent of old Nile?'
For so he calls me: now I feed myself
With most delicious poison. Think on me,
That am with Phœbus' amorous pinches black
And wrinkled deep in time? Broad-fronted Cæsar,
When thou wast here above the ground, I was
A morsel for a monarch: and great Pompey
Would stand and make his eyes grow in my brow;
There would he anchor his aspect and die
With looking on his life.

Enter ALEXAS

ALEXAS

Sovereign of Egypt, hail!

CLEOPATRA

How much unlike art thou Mark Antony!
Yet, coming from him, that great medicine hath
With his tinct gilded thee.
How goes it with my brave Mark Antony?

ALEXAS

Last thing he did, dear queen,
He kiss'd—the last of many doubled kisses—
This orient pearl. His speech sticks in my heart.

CLEOPATRA

Mine ear must pluck it thence.

ALEXAS

　　　　　'Good friend,' quoth he,

'Say, the firm Roman to great Egypt sends

This treasure of an oyster; at whose foot,

To mend the petty present, I will piece

Her opulent throne with kingdoms; all the east,

Say thou, shall call her mistress.' So he nodded,

And soberly did mount an arm-gaunt steed,

Who neigh'd so high, that what I would have spoke

Was beastly dumb'd by him.

CLEOPATRA

　　　　　What, was he sad or merry?

ALEXAS

Like to the time o' the year between the extremes

Of hot and cold, he was nor sad nor merry.

CLEOPATRA

O well divided disposition! Note him,

Note him, good Charmian, 'tis the man; but note

　　him:

He was not sad, for he would shine on those

That make their looks by his; he was not merry,

Which seem'd to tell them his remembrance lay

In Egypt with his joy; but between both.

O heavenly mingle! Be'st thou sad or merry,

The violence of either thee becomes,

So does it no man else. Met'st thou my posts?

ALEXAS

Ay, madam, twenty several messengers:

Why do you send so thick?

CLEOPATRA

　　　　　Who's born that day

When I forget to send to Antony,

Shall die a beggar. Ink and paper, Charmian.

Welcome, my good Alexas. Did I, Charmian,

Ever love Cæsar so?

CHARMIAN

　　　　　O that brave Cæsar!

CLEOPATRA

Be choked with such another emphasis!

Say, the brave Antony.

CHARMIAN

　　　　　The valiant Cæsar!

CLEOPATRA

By Isis, I will give thee bloody teeth,

If thou with Cæsar paragon again

My man of men.

CHARMIAN

　　　　　By your most gracious pardon,

I sing but after you.

CLEOPATRA

　　　　　My salad days,

When I was green in judgement: cold in blood,

To say as I said then! But come, away;

Get me ink and paper:

He shall have every day a several greeting,

Or I'll unpeople Egypt.　　　　　[Exeunt

ACT II

SCENE I. Messina. Pompey's house

Enter POMPEY, MENECRATES, *and* MENAS, *in warlike manner*

POMPEY

If the great gods be just, they shall assist

The deeds of justest men.

MENECRATES

　　　　　Know, worthy Pompey.

That what they do delay, they not deny.

POMPEY

Whiles we are suitors to their throne, decays

The thing we sue for.

MENECRATES

　　　　　We, ignorant of ourselves,

Beg often our own harms, which the wise powers

Deny us for our good; so find we profit

By losing of our prayers.

POMPEY

　　　　　I shall do well:

The people love me, and the sea is mine;

My powers are crescent, and my auguring hope

Says it will come to the full. Mark Antony

In Egypt sits at dinner, and will make

No wars without doors: Cæsar gets money where

He loses hearts: Lepidus flatters both,

Of both is flatter'd, but he neither loves,

Nor either cares for him.

MENAS

　　　　　Cæsar and Lepidus

Are in the field: a mighty strength they carry.

POMPEY

Where have you this? 'tis false.

MENAS

　　　　　From Silvius, sir.

POMPEY

He dreams: I know they are in Rome together,

Looking for Antony. But all the charms of love,

Salt Cleopatra, soften thy waned lip!

Let witchcraft join with beauty, lust with both!

Tie up the libertine in a field of feasts,

Keep his brain fuming; Epicurean cooks

Sharpen with cloyless sauce his appetite;

That sleep and feeding may prorogue his honour

Even till a Lethe'd dulness!

Enter VARRIUS

　　　　　How now, Varrius!

VARRIUS

This is most certain that I shall deliver:

Mark Antony is every hour in Rome

Expected: since he went from Egypt 'tis

A space for farther travel.

POMPEY

　　　　　I could have given less matter

A better ear. Menas, I did not think

This amorous surfeiter would have donn'd his helm

For such a petty war: his soldiership

Is twice the other twain: but let us rear

The higher our opinion, but our stirring
Can from the lap of Egypt's widow pluck
The ne'er-lust-wearied Antony.

MENAS

         I cannot hope
Cæsar and Antony shall well greet together:
His wife that's dead did trespasses to Cæsar;
His brother warr'd upon him; although, I think,
Not moved by Antony.

POMPEY

         I know not, Menas,
How lesser enmities may give way to greater.
Were 't not that we stand up against them all,
'Twere pregnant they should square between them-
    selves;
For they have entertained cause enough
To draw their swords: but how the fear of us
May cement their divisions and bind up
The petty difference, we yet not know.
Be 't as our gods will have 't! It only stands
Our lives upon to use our strongest hands.
Come, Menas.   [Exeunt

SCENE II. Rome. The house of LEPIDUS

Enter ENOBARBUS and LEPIDUS

LEPIDUS

Good Enobarbus, 'tis a worthy deed,
And shall become you well, to entreat your captain
To soft and gentle speech.

ENOBARBUS

         I shall entreat him
To answer like himself: if Cæsar move him,
Let Antony look over Cæsar's head
And speak as loud as Mars. By Jupiter,
Were I the wearer of Antonius' beard,
I would not shave 't to-day.

LEPIDUS

         'Tis not a time
For private stomaching.

ENOBARBUS

         Every time
Serves for the matter that is then born in 't.

LEPIDUS

But small to greater matters must give way.

ENOBARBUS

Not if the small come first.

LEPIDUS

         Your speech is passion:
But, pray you, stir no embers up. Here comes
The noble Antony.

Enter ANTONY and VENTIDIUS

ENOBARBUS

         And yonder, Cæsar.

Enter CÆSAR, MÆCENAS, and AGRIPPA

ANTONY

If we compose well here, to Parthia:
Hark, Ventidius.

CÆSAR

         I do not know,
Mæcenas; ask Agrippa.

LEPIDUS

         Noble friends,
That which combined us was most great, and let
    not
A leaner action rend us. What's amiss,
May it be gently heard: when we debate
Our trivial difference loud, we do commit
Murder in healing wounds: then, noble partners,
The rather for I earnestly beseech,
Touch you the sourest points with sweetest terms,
Nor curstness grow to the matter.

ANTONY

         'Tis spoken well.
Were we before our armies and to fight,
I should do thus.   [Flourish

CÆSAR

Welcome to Rome.

ANTONY

Thank you.

CÆSAR

Sit.

ANTONY

Sit, sir.

CÆSAR

Nay, then.

ANTONY

I learn, you take things ill which are not so,
Or being, concern you not.

CÆSAR

         I must be laugh'd at,
If, or for nothing or a little, I
Should say myself offended, and with you
Chiefly i' the world; more laugh'd at, that I should
Once name you derogately, when to sound your
    name
It not concern'd me.

ANTONY

         My being in Egypt, Cæsar,
What was 't to you?

CÆSAR

No more than my residing here at Rome
Might be to you in Egypt: yet, if you there
Did practise on my state, your being in Egypt
Might be my question.

ANTONY

         How intend you, practised?

CÆSAR

You may be pleased to catch at mine intent
By what did here befal me. Your wife and brother
Made wars upon me, and their contestation
Was theme for you, you were the word of war.

ANTONY

You do mistake your business; my brother never
Did urge me in his act: I did inquire it,
And have my learning from some true reports
That drew their swords with you. Did he not rather
Discredit my authority with yours,

And make the wars alike against my stomach,
Having alike your cause? Of this my letters
Before did satisfy you. If you'll patch a quarrel,
As matter whole you have not to make it with,
It must not be with this.

CÆSAR
            You praise yourself
By laying defects of judgement to me, but
You patch'd up your excuses.

ANTONY
            Not so, not so;
I know you could not lack, I am certain on 't,
Very necessity of this thought, that I,
Your partner in the cause 'gainst which he fought,
Could not with graceful eyes attend those wars
Which fronted mine own peace. As for my wife,
I would you had her spirit in such another:
The third o' the world is yours, which with a snaffle
You may pace easy, but not such a wife.

ENOBARBUS
Would we had all such wives, that the men might
go to wars with the women!

ANTONY
So much uncurbable, her garboils, Cæsar,
Made out of her impatience, which not wanted
Shrewdness of policy too, I grieving grant
Did you too much disquiet: for that you must
But say, I could not help it.

CÆSAR
            I wrote to you
When rioting in Alexandria; you
Did pocket up my letters, and with taunts
Did gibe my missive out of audience.

ANTONY
            Sir,
He fell upon me ere admitted: then
Three kings I had newly feasted and did want
Of what I was i' the morning: but next day
I told him of myself, which was as much
As to have ask'd him pardon. Let this fellow
Be nothing of our strife; if we contend,
Out of our question wipe him.

CÆSAR
            You have broken
The article of your oath, which you shall never
Have tongue to charge me with.

LEPIDUS
            Soft, Cæsar!

ANTONY
No, Lepidus, let him speak:
The honour is sacred which he talks on now,
Supposing that I lack'd it. But on, Cæsar;
The article of my oath.

CÆSAR
To lend me arms and aid when I required them;
The which you both denied.

ANTONY
            Neglected rather,
And then when poison'd hours had bound me up
From mine own knowledge. As nearly as I may,

I'll play the penitent to you: but mine honesty
Shall not make poor my greatness, nor my power
Work without it. Truth is that Fulvia,
To have me out of Egypt, made wars here;
For which myself, the ignorant motive, do
So far ask pardon as befits mine honour
To stoop in such a case.

LEPIDUS
            'Tis noble spoken.

MÆCENAS
If it might please you, to enforce no further
The griefs between ye: to forget them quite
Were to remember that the present need
Speaks to atone you.

LEPIDUS
            Worthily spoken, Mæcenas.

ENOBARBUS
Or, if you borrow one another's love for the instant,
you may, when you hear no more words of Pompey,
return it again: you shall have time to wrangle in
when you have nothing else to do.

ANTONY
Thou art a soldier only: speak no more.

ENOBARBUS
That truth should be silent I had almost forgot.

ANTONY
You wrong this presence; therefore speak no more.

ENOBARBUS
Go to, then; your considerate stone.

CÆSAR
I do not much dislike the matter, but
The manner of his speech; for 't cannot be
We shall remain in friendship, our conditions
So differing in their acts. Yet, if I knew
What hoop should hold us stanch, from edge to edge
O' the world I would pursue it.

AGRIPPA
            Give me leave, Cæsar.

CÆSAR
Speak, Agrippa.

AGRIPPA
Thou hast a sister by the mother's side,
Admired Octavia: great Mark Antony
Is now a widower.

CÆSAR
            Say not so, Agrippa:
If Cleopatra heard you, your reproof
Were well deserved of rashness.

ANTONY
I am not married, Cæsar: let me hear
Agrippa further speak.

AGRIPPA
To hold you in perpetual amity,
To make you brothers and to knit your hearts
With an unslipping knot, take Antony
Octavia to his wife; whose beauty claims
No worse a husband than the best of men,
Whose virtue and whose general graces speak
That which none else can utter. By this marriage
All little jealousies which now seem great,

And all great fears which now import their dangers,
Would then be nothing: truths would be tales,
Where now half tales be truths: her love to both
Would each to other and all loves to both
Draw after her. Pardon what I have spoke,
For 'tis a studied, not a present thought,
By duty ruminated.

ANTONY
               Will Cæsar speak?

CÆSAR
Not till he hears how Antony is touch'd
With what is spoke already.

ANTONY
               What power is in Agrippa,
If I would say, 'Agrippa, be it so,'
To make this good?

CÆSAR
               The power of Cæsar, and
His power unto Octavia.

ANTONY
               May I never
To this good purpose, that so fairly shows,
Dream of impediment! Let me have thy hand:
Further this act of grace; and from this hour
The heart of brothers govern in our loves
And sway our great designs!

CÆSAR
               There is my hand.
A sister I bequeath you, whom no brother
Did ever love so dearly: let her live
To join our kingdoms and our hearts; and never
Fly off our loves again!

LEPIDUS
               Happily, amen!

ANTONY
I did not think to draw my sword 'gainst Pompey;
For he hath laid strange courtesies and great
Of late upon me: I must thank him only,
Lest my remembrance suffer ill report;
At heel of that, defy him.

LEPIDUS
               Time calls upon 's:
Of us must Pompey presently be sought,
Or else he seeks out us.

ANTONY
               Where lies he?

CÆSAR
About the Mount Misenum.

ANTONY
               What's his strength
By land?

CÆSAR
Great and increasing: but by sea
He is an absolute master.

ANTONY
               So is the fame.
Would we had spoke together! Haste we for it:
Yet, ere we put ourselves in arms, dispatch we
The business we have talk'd of.

CÆSAR
               With most gladness;
And do invite you to my sister's view,
Whither straight I'll lead you.

ANTONY
               Let us, Lepidus,
Not lack your company.

LEPIDUS
               Noble Antony,
Not sickness should detain me.

[Flourish. Exeunt CÆSAR, ANTONY, and LEPIDUS

MÆCENAS
Welcome from Egypt, sir.

ENOBARBUS
Half the heart of Cæsar, worthy Mæcenas! My honourable friend, Agrippa!

AGRIPPA
Good Enobarbus!

MÆCENAS
We have cause to be glad that matters are so well digested. You stayed well by 't in Egypt.

ENOBARBUS
Ay, sir; we did sleep day out of countenance, and made the night light with drinking.

MÆCENAS
Eight wild-boars roasted whole at a breakfast, and but twelve persons there; is this true?

ENOBARBUS
This was but as a fly by an eagle: we had much more monstrous matter of feast, which worthily deserved noting.

MÆCENAS
She's a most triumphant lady, if report be square to her.

ENOBARBUS
When she first met Mark Antony, she pursed up his heart, upon the river of Cydnus.

AGRIPPA
There she appeared indeed, or my reporter devised well for her.

ENOBARBUS
I will tell you.
The barge she sat in, like a burnish'd throne,
Burn'd on the water: the poop was beaten gold;
Purple the sails, and so perfumed that
The winds were love-sick with them; the oars were silver,
Which to the tune of flutes kept stroke and made
The water which they beat to follow faster,
As amorous of their strokes. For her own person,
It beggar'd all description: she did lie
In her pavilion, cloth-of-gold of tissue,
O'er-picturing that Venus where we see
The fancy outwork nature: on each side her
Stood pretty dimpled boys, like smiling Cupids,
With divers-colour'd fans, whose wind did seem
To glow the delicate cheeks which they did cool,
And what they undid did.

AGRIPPA

O, rare for Antony!

ENOBARBUS

Her gentlewomen, like the Nereides,
So many mermaids, tended her i' the eyes,
And made their bends adornings: at the helm
A seeming mermaid steers: the silken tackle
Swell with the touches of those flower-soft hands,
That yarely frame the office. From the barge
A strange invisible perfume hits the sense
Of the adjacent wharfs. The city cast
Her people out upon her; and Antony,
Enthroned i' the market-place, did sit alone,
Whistling to the air; which, but for vacancy,
Had gone to gaze on Cleopatra too,
And made a gap in nature.

AGRIPPA

Rare Egyptian!

ENOBARBUS

Upon her landing, Antony sent to her,
Invited her to supper: she replied,
It should be better he became her guest,
Which she entreated: our courteous Antony,
Whom ne'er the word of 'No' woman heard speak,
Being barber'd ten times o'er, goes to the feast,
And, for his ordinary, pays his heart
For what his eyes eat only.

AGRIPPA

Royal wench!

She made great Cæsar lay his sword to bed:
He plough'd her, and she cropp'd.

ENOBARBUS

I saw her once

Hop forty paces through the public street;
And having lost her breath, she spoke, and panted,
That she did make defect perfection,
And breathless, power breathe forth.

MÆCENAS

Now Antony must leave her utterly.

ENOBARBUS

Never; he will not:
Age cannot wither her, nor custom stale
Her infinite variety: other women cloy
The appetites they feed, but she makes hungry
Where most she satisfies: for vilest things
Become themselves in her, that the holy priests
Bless her when she is riggish.

MÆCENAS

If beauty, wisdom, modesty, can settle
The heart of Antony, Octavia is
A blessed lottery to him.

AGRIPPA

Let us go.

Good Enobarbus, make yourself my guest
Whilst you abide here.

ENOBARBUS

Humbly, sir, I thank you.

[Exeunt

SCENE III. *The same.* CÆSAR'S *house*

Enter ANTONY, CÆSAR, OCTAVIA *between them, and*
ATTENDANTS

ANTONY

The world and my great office will sometimes
Divide me from your bosom.

OCTAVIA

All which time

Before the gods my knee shall bow my prayers
To them for you.

ANTONY

Good night, sir. My Octavia,

Read not my blemishes in the world's report:
I have not kept my square; but that to come
Shall all be done by the rule. Good night, dear lady.
Good night, sir.

CÆSAR

Good night.   [*Exeunt all but* ANTONY

Enter SOOTHSAYER

ANTONY

Now, sirrah, you do wish yourself in Egypt?

SOOTHSAYER

Would I had never come from thence, nor you
thither!

ANTONY

If you can, your reason?

SOOTHSAYER

I see it in my motion, have it not in my tongue: but
yet hie you to Egypt again.

ANTONY

Say to me, whose fortunes shall rise higher,
Cæsar's or mine?

SOOTHSAYER

Cæsar's.

Therefore, O Antony, stay not by his side:
Thy demon, that thy spirit which keeps thee, is
Noble, courageous, high, unmatchable,
Where Cæsar's is not; but near him thy angel
Becomes a fear, as being o'erpower'd: therefore
Make space enough between you.

ANTONY

Speak this no more.

SOOTHSAYER

To none but thee; no more but when to thee.
If thou dost play with him at any game,
Thou art sure to lose; and, of that natural luck,
He beats thee 'gainst the odds: thy lustre thickens,
When he shines by: I say again, thy spirit
Is all afraid to govern thee near him,
But he away, 'tis noble.

ANTONY

Get thee gone:

Say to Ventidius I would speak with him.

[*Exit* SOOTHSAYER

He shall to Parthia. Be it art or hap,
He hath spoken true: the very dice obey him,
And in our sports my better cunning faints
Under his chance: if we draw lots, he speeds;
His cocks do win the battle still of mine

When it is all to nought, and his quails ever
Beat mine, inhoop'd, at odds. I will to Egypt:
And though I make this marriage for my peace,
I' the east my pleasure lies.

Enter VENTIDIUS

O, come, Ventidius,
You must to Parthia: your commission 's ready;
Follow me, and receive 't.   [*Exeunt*

SCENE IV. *The same. A street*

Enter LEPIDUS, MÆCENAS, *and* AGRIPPA

LEPIDUS
Trouble yourselves no further: pray you, hasten
Your generals after.

AGRIPPA
Sir, Mark Antony
Will e'en but kiss Octavia, and we'll follow.

LEPIDUS
Till I shall see you in your soldier's dress,
Which will become you both, farewell.

MÆCENAS
We shall,
As I conceive the journey, be at the Mount
Before you, Lepidus.

LEPIDUS
Your way is shorter;
My purposes do draw me much about:
You'll win two days upon me.

MÆCENAS *and* AGRIPPA
Sir, good success!

LEPIDUS
Farewell.   [*Exeunt*

SCENE V. *Alexandria.* CLEOPATRA'S *palace*

Enter CLEOPATRA, CHARMIAN, IRAS, *and* ALEXAS

CLEOPATRA
Give me some music; music, moody food
Of us that trade in love.

ALL
The music, ho!

Enter MARDIAN *the Eunuch*

CLEOPATRA
Let it alone; let's to billiards: come, Charmian.

CHARMIAN
My arm is sore: best play with Mardian.

CLEOPATRA
As well a woman with an eunuch play'd
As with a woman. Come, you'll play with me, sir?

MARDIAN
As well as I can, madam.

CLEOPATRA
And when good will is show'd, though 't come too short,
The actor may plead pardon. I'll none now:
Give me mine angle; we'll to the river: there,
My music playing far off, I will betray

Tawny-finn'd fishes; my bended hook shall pierce
Their slimy jaws, and as I draw them up,
I'll think them every one an Antony,
And say 'Ah, ha! you're caught.'

CHARMIAN
'Twas merry when
You wager'd on your angling; when your diver
Did hang a salt-fish on his hook, which he
With fervency drew up.

CLEOPATRA
That time—O times!—
I laugh'd him out of patience, and that night
I laugh'd him into patience: and next morn,
Ere the ninth hour, I drunk him to his bed;
Then put my tires and mantles on him, whilst
I wore his sword Philippan.

Enter a MESSENGER

O, from Italy!
Ram thou thy fruitful tidings in mine ears,
That long time have been barren.

MESSENGER
Madam, madam,—

CLEOPATRA
Antonius dead! If thou say so, villain,
Thou kill'st thy mistress: but well and free,
If thou so yield him, there is gold, and here
My bluest veins to kiss: a hand that kings
Have lipp'd, and trembled kissing.

MESSENGER
First, madam, he is well.

CLEOPATRA
Why, there's more gold.
But, sirrah, mark, we use
To say the dead are well: bring it to that,
The gold I give thee will I melt and pour
Down thy ill-uttering throat.

MESSENGER
Good madam, hear me.

CLEOPATRA
Well, go to, I will;
But there's no goodness in thy face: if Antony
Be free and healthful,—so tart a favour
To trumpet such good tidings! If not well,
Thou shouldst come like a Fury crown'd with snakes,
Not like a formal man.

MESSENGER
Will 't please you hear me?

CLEOPATRA
I have a mind to strike thee ere thou speak'st:
Yet, if thou say Antony lives, is well,
Or friends with Cæsar, or not captive to him,
I'll set thee in a shower of gold, and hail
Rich pearls upon thee.

MESSENGER
Madam, he's well.

CLEOPATRA
Well said.

MESSENGER
And friends with Cæsar.

CLEOPATRA

        Thou'rt an honest man.

MESSENGER

Cæsar and he are greater friends than ever.

CLEOPATRA

Make thee a fortune from me.

MESSENGER

              But yet, madam,—

CLEOPATRA

I do not like 'But yet,' it does allay
The good precedence; fie upon 'But yet'!
'But yet' is as a gaoler to bring forth
Some monstrous malefactor. Prithee, friend,
Pour out the pack of matter to mine ear,
The good and bad together: he's friends with
    Cæsar,
In state of health, thou say'st, and thou say'st, free.

MESSENGER

Free, madam! no; I made no such report:
He's bound unto Octavia.

CLEOPATRA

          For what good turn?

MESSENGER

For the best turn i' the bed.

CLEOPATRA

            I am pale, Charmian.

MESSENGER

Madam, he's married to Octavia.

CLEOPATRA

The most infectious pestilence upon thee!
                [Strikes him down

MESSENGER

Good madam, patience.

CLEOPATRA

         What say you? Hence,
                [Strikes him again
Horrible villain! or I'll spurn thine eyes
Like balls before me; I'll unhair thy head:
           [She hales him up and down
Thou shalt be whipp'd with wire, and stew'd in
    brine,
Smarting in lingering pickle.

MESSENGER

             Gracious madam,
I that do bring the news made not the match.

CLEOPATRA

Say 'tis not so, a province I will give thee
And make thy fortunes proud: the blow thou hadst
Shall make thy peace for moving me to rage,
And I will boot thee with what gift beside
Thy modesty can beg.

MESSENGER

          He's married, madam.

CLEOPATRA

Rogue, thou hast lived too long.   [Draws a knife

MESSENGER

            Nay, then I'll run.
What mean you, madam? I have made no fault.
                        [Exit

CHARMIAN

Good madam, keep yourself within yourself:
The man is innocent.

CLEOPATRA

Some innocents 'scape not the thunderbolt.
Melt Egypt into Nile! and kindly creatures
Turn all to serpents! Call the slave again:
Though I am mad, I will not bite him: call.

CHARMIAN

He is afeard to come.

CLEOPATRA

         I will not hurt him.
                [Exit CHARMIAN
These hands do lack nobility, that they strike
A meaner than myself; since I myself
Have given myself the cause.
    Re-enter CHARMIAN and MESSENGER
              Come hither, sir.
Though it be honest, it is never good
To bring bad news: give to a gracious message
An host of tongues, but let ill tidings tell
Themselves when they be felt.

MESSENGER

            I have done my duty.

CLEOPATRA

Is he married?
I cannot hate thee worser than I do,
If thou again say 'Yes.'

MESSENGER

           He's married, madam.

CLEOPATRA

The gods confound thee! dost thou hold there still?

MESSENGER

Should I lie, madam?

CLEOPATRA

          O, I would thou didst,
So half my Egypt were submerged and made
A cistern for scaled snakes! Go get thee hence:
Hadst thou Narcissus in thy face, to me
Thou wouldst appear most ugly. He is married?

MESSENGER

I crave your highness' pardon.

CLEOPATRA

           He is married?

MESSENGER

Take no offence that I would not offend you:
To punish me for what you make me do
Seems much unequal: he's married to Octavia.

CLEOPATRA

O, that his fault should make a knave of thee,
That art not what thou'rt sure of! Get thee hence:
The merchandise which thou hast brought from
    Rome
Are all too dear for me: lie they upon thy hand,
And be undone by 'em!   [Exit MESSENGER

CHARMIAN

        Good your highness, patience.

CLEOPATRA

In praising Antony, I have dispraised Cæsar.

CHARMIAN

Many times, madam.

CLEOPATRA

I am paid for 't now.
Lead me from hence;
I faint: O Iras, Charmian! 'tis no matter.
Go to the fellow, good Alexas; bid him
Report the feature of Octavia, her years,
Her inclination; let him not leave out
The colour of her hair: bring me word quickly.

[*Exit* ALEXAS

Let him for ever go; let him not—Charmian,
Though he be painted one way like a Gorgon,
The other way's a Mars. [*To* MARDIAN] Bid you
  Alexas
Bring me word how tall she is. Pity me, Charmian,
But do not speak to me. Lead me to my chamber.

[*Exeunt*

SCENE VI. *Near Misenum*

Flourish. Enter POMPEY *and* MENAS *from one side, with
drum and trumpet: at another,* CÆSAR, ANTONY, LEPIDUS,
  ENOBARBUS, MÆCENAS, *with* SOLDIERS *marching*

POMPEY

Your hostages I have, so have you mine;
And we shall talk before we fight.

CÆSAR

Most meet
That first we come to words; and therefore have we
Our written purposes before us sent;
Which, if thou hast consider'd, let us know
If 'twill tie up thy discontented sword
And carry back to Sicily much tall youth
That else must perish here.

POMPEY

To you all three,
The senators alone of this great world,
Chief factors for the gods, I do not know
Wherefore my father should revengers want,
Having a son and friends; since Julius Cæsar,
Who at Philippi the good Brutus ghosted,
There saw you labouring for him. What was 't
That moved pale Cassius to conspire, and what
Made the all-honour'd honest Roman, Brutus,
With the arm'd rest, courtiers of beauteous freedom,
To drench the Capitol, but that they would
Have one man but a man? And that is it
Hath made me rig my navy, at whose burthen
The anger'd ocean foams; with which I meant
To scourge the ingratitude that despiteful Rome
Cast on my noble father.

CÆSAR

Take your time.

ANTONY

Thou canst not fear us, Pompey, with thy sails;
We'll speak with thee at sea: at land, thou know'st
How much we do o'ercount thee.

POMPEY

At land indeed

Thou dost o'ercount me of my father's house:
But since the cuckoo builds not for himself,
Remain in 't as thou mayst.

LEPIDUS

Be pleased to tell us—
For this is from the present—how you take
The offers we have sent you.

CÆSAR

There's the point.

ANTONY

Which do not be entreated to, but weigh
What it is worth embraced.

CÆSAR

And what may follow,
To try a larger fortune.

POMPEY

You have made me offer
Of Sicily, Sardinia; and I must
Rid all the sea of pirates; then, to send
Measures of wheat to Rome; this 'greed upon,
To part with unhack'd edges and bear back
Our targes undinted.

CÆSAR, ANTONY *and* LEPIDUS

That's our offer.

POMPEY

Know then,
I came before you here a man prepared
To take this offer: but Mark Antony
Put me to some impatience: though I lose
The praise of it by telling, you must know,
When Cæsar and your brother were at blows,
Your mother came to Sicily and did find
Her welcome friendly.

ANTONY

I have heard it, Pompey,
And am well studied for a liberal thanks
Which I do owe you.

POMPEY

Let me have your hand:
I did not think, sir, to have met you here.

ANTONY

The beds i' the east are soft; and thanks to you,
That call'd me timelier than my purpose hither;
For I have gain'd by 't.

CÆSAR

Since I saw you last,
There is a change upon you.

POMPEY

Well, I know not
What counts harsh fortune casts upon my face;
But in my bosom shall she never come,
To make my heart her vassal.

LEPIDUS

Well met here.

POMPEY

I hope so, Lepidus. Thus we are agreed:
I crave our composition may be written
And seal'd between us.

CÆSAR

That's the next to do.

POMPEY
We'll feast each other ere we part, and let's
Draw lots who shall begin.

ANTONY
That will I, Pompey.

POMPEY
No, Antony, take the lot:
But, first or last, your fine Egyptian cookery
Shall have the fame. I have heard that Julius Cæsar
Grew fat with feasting there.

ANTONY
You have heard much.

POMPEY
I have fair meanings, sir.

ANTONY
And fair words to them.

POMPEY
Then so much have I heard:
And I have heard, Apollodorus carried—

ENOBARBUS
No more of that: he did so.

POMPEY
What, I pray you?

ENOBARBUS
A certain queen to Cæsar in a mattress.

POMPEY
I know thee now: how farest thou, soldier?

ENOBARBUS
Well;
And well am like to do, for I perceive
Four feasts are toward.

POMPEY
Let me shake thy hand;
I never hated thee: I have seen thee fight,
When I have envied thy behaviour.

ENOBARBUS
Sir,
I never loved you much, but I ha' praised ye
When you have well deserved ten times as much
As I have said you did.

POMPEY
Enjoy thy plainness,
It nothing ill becomes thee.
Aboard my galley I invite you all:
Will you lead, lords?

CÆSAR, ANTONY and LEPIDUS
Show us the way, sir.

POMPEY
Come.
[Exeunt all but MENAS and ENOBARBUS

MENAS
[Aside] Thy father, Pompey, would ne'er have made
this treaty.—You and I have known, sir.

ENOBARBUS
At sea, I think.

MENAS
We have, sir.

ENOBARBUS
You have done well by water.

MENAS
And you by land.

ENOBARBUS
I will praise any man that will praise me; though it
cannot be denied what I have done by land.

MENAS
Nor what I have done by water.

ENOBARBUS
Yes, something you can deny for your own safety:
you have been a great thief by sea.

MENAS
And you by land.

ENOBARBUS
There I deny my land service. But give me your
hand, Menas: if our eyes had authority, here they
might take two thieves kissing.

MENAS
All men's faces are true, whatsoe'er their hands are.

ENOBARBUS
But there is never a fair woman has a true face.

MENAS
No slander; they steal hearts.

ENOBARBUS
We came hither to fight with you.

MENAS
For my part, I am sorry it is turned to a drinking.
Pompey doth this day laugh away his fortune.

ENOBARBUS
If he do, sure he cannot weep 't back again.

MENAS
You've said, sir. We looked not for Mark Antony
here: pray you, is he married to Cleopatra?

ENOBARBUS
Cæsar's sister is called Octavia.

MENAS
True, sir; she was the wife of Caius Marcellus.

ENOBARBUS
But she is now the wife of Marcus Antonius.

MENAS
Pray ye, sir?

ENOBARBUS
'Tis true.

MENAS
Then is Cæsar and he for ever knit together.

ENOBARBUS
If I were bound to divine of this unity, I would not
prophesy so.

MENAS
I think the policy of that purpose made more in the
marriage than the love of the parties.

ENOBARBUS
I think so too. But you shall find, the band that
seems to tie their friendship together will be the
very strangler of their amity: Octavia is of a holy,
cold and still conversation.

MENAS
Who would not have his wife so?

ENOBARBUS
Not he that himself is not so; which is Mark Antony.

He will to his Egyptian dish again: then shall the
sighs of Octavia blow the fire up in Cæsar; and, as
I said before, that which is the strength of their
amity shall prove the immediate author of their
variance. Antony will use his affection where it is:
he married but his occasion here.

MENAS

And thus it may be. Come, sir, will you aboard? I
have a health for you.

ENOBARBUS

I shall take it, sir: we have used our throats in
Egypt.

MENAS

Come, let's away.   [*Exeunt*

SCENE VII. *On board* POMPEY's *galley, off Misenum*

Music plays. Enter two or three SERVANTS, *with a
banquet*

FIRST SERVANT

Here they'll be, man. Some o' their plants are ill-
rooted already; the least wind i' the world will blow
them down.

SECOND SERVANT

Lepidus is high-coloured.

FIRST SERVANT

They have made him drink alms-drink.

SECOND SERVANT

As they pinch one another by the disposition, he
cries out 'No more;' reconciles them to his entreaty
and himself to the drink.

FIRST SERVANT

But it raises the greater war between him and his
discretion.

SECOND SERVANT

Why, this it is to have a name in great men's fellowship: I had as lief have a reed that will do me no
service as a partisan I could not heave.

FIRST SERVANT

To be called into a huge sphere, and not to be seen
to move in 't, are the holes where eyes should be,
which pitifully disaster the cheeks.

A sennet sounded. Enter CÆSAR, ANTONY, LEPIDUS,
POMPEY, AGRIPPA, MÆCENAS, ENOBARBUS,
MENAS, *with other* CAPTAINS

ANTONY

[*To* CÆSAR] Thus do they, sir: they take the flow o'
the Nile
By certain scales i' the pyramid; they know,
By the height, the lowness, or the mean, if dearth
Or foison follow: the higher Nilus swells,
The more it promises: as it ebbs, the seedsman
Upon the slime and ooze scatters his grain,
And shortly comes to harvest.

LEPIDUS

You've strange serpents there.

ANTONY

Ay, Lepidus.

LEPIDUS

Your serpent of Egypt is bred now of your mud by
the operation of your sun: so is your crocodile.

ANTONY

They are so.

POMPEY

Sit,—and some wine! A health to Lepidus!

LEPIDUS

I am not so well as I should be, but I'll ne'er out.

ENOBARBUS

Not till you have slept; I fear me you'll be in till
then.

LEPIDUS

Nay, certainly, I have heard the Ptolemies' pyra-
mises are very goodly things; without contradiction,
I have heard that.

MENAS

[*Aside to* POMPEY] Pompey, a word.

POMPEY

[*Aside to* MENAS] Say in mine ear: what is 't?

MENAS

[*Aside to* POMPEY] Forsake thy seat, I do beseech
thee, captain,
And hear me speak a word.

POMPEY

[*Aside to* MENAS] Forbear me till anon.—
This wine for Lepidus!

LEPIDUS

What manner o' thing is your crocodile?

ANTONY

It is shaped, sir, like itself; and it is as broad as it
hath breadth: it is just so high as it is, and moves
with it own organs: it lives by that which nourisheth
it; and the elements once out of it, it transmigrates.

LEPIDUS

What colour is it of?

ANTONY

Of it own colour too.

LEPIDUS

'Tis a strange serpent.

ANTONY

'Tis so. And the tears of it are wet.

CÆSAR

Will this description satisfy him?

ANTONY

With the health that Pompey gives him, else he is a
very epicure.

POMPEY

[*Aside to* MENAS] Go hang, sir, hang! Tell me of that?
away!
Do as I bid you.—Where's this cup I call'd for?

MENAS

[*Aside to* POMPEY] If for the sake of merit thou wilt
hear me,
Rise from thy stool.

POMPEY

[*Aside to* MENAS] I think thou'rt mad. The matter?
[*Rises, and walks aside*

MENAS

I have ever held my cap off to thy fortunes.

POMPEY

Thou hast served me with much faith. What's else
  to say?
Be jolly, lords.

ANTONY

These quick-sands, Lepidus,
Keep off them, for you sink.

MENAS

Wilt thou be lord of all the world?

POMPEY

What say'st thou?

MENAS

Wilt thou be lord of the whole world? That's twice.

POMPEY

How should that be?

MENAS

But entertain it,
And, though thou think me poor, I am the man
Will give thee all the world.

POMPEY

Hast thou drunk well?

MENAS

No, Pompey, I have kept me from the cup.
Thou art, if thou darest be, the earthly Jove:
Whate'er the ocean pales, or sky inclips,
Is thine, if thou wilt ha 't.

POMPEY

Show me which way.

MENAS

These three world-sharers, these competitors,
Are in thy vessel: let me cut the cable;
And, when we are put off, fall to their throats:
All there is thine.

POMPEY

Ah, this thou shouldst have done,
And not have spoke on 't! In me 'tis villany;
In thee 't had been good service. Thou must know,
'Tis not my profit that does lead mine honour;
Mine honour, it. Repent that e'er thy tongue
Hath so betray'd thine act: being done unknown,
I should have found it afterwards well done,
But must condemn it now. Desist, and drink.

MENAS

[Aside] For this
I'll never follow thy pall'd fortunes more.
Who seeks, and will not take when once 'tis offer'd,
Shall never find it more.

POMPEY

This health to Lepidus!

ANTONY

Bear him ashore. I'll pledge it for him, Pompey.

ENOBARBUS

Here's to thee, Menas!

MENAS

Enobarbus, welcome!

POMPEY

Fill till the cup be hid.

ENOBARBUS

There's a strong fellow, Menas.

[Pointing to the ATTENDANT who carries off LEPIDUS

MENAS

Why?

ENOBARBUS

A' bears the third part of the world, man; see'st not?

MENAS

The third part then is drunk: would it were all,
That it might go on wheels!

ENOBARBUS

Drink thou; increase the reels.

MENAS

Come.

POMPEY

This is not yet an Alexandrian feast.

ANTONY

It ripens towards it. Strike the vessels, ho!
Here's to Cæsar!

CÆSAR

I could well forbear 't.
It's monstrous labour, when I wash my brain
And it grows fouler.

ANTONY

Be a child o' the time.

CÆSAR

Possess it, I'll make answer:
But I had rather fast from all four days
Than drink so much in one.

ENOBARBUS

[To Antony] Ha, my brave emperor!
Shall we dance now the Egyptian Bacchanals,
And celebrate our drink?

POMPEY

Let's ha 't, good soldier.

ANTONY

Come, let's all take hands,
Till that the conquering wine hath steep'd our sense
In soft and delicate Lethe.

ENOBARBUS

All take hands.
Make battery to our ears with the loud music:
The while I'll place you: then the boy shall sing;
The holding every man shall bear as loud
As his strong sides can volley.

[Music plays. ENOBARBUS places them hand in hand

THE SONG

Come, thou monarch of the vine,
Plumpy Bacchus with pink eyne!
In thy fats our cares be drown'd,
With thy grapes our hairs be crown'd:
Cup us, till the world go round,
Cup us, till the world go round!

CÆSAR

What would you more? Pompey, good night. Good
  brother,
Let me request you off: our graver business
Frowns at this levity. Gentle lords, let's part;
You see we have burnt our cheeks: strong Enobarb
Is weaker than the wine; and mine own tongue
Splits what it speaks: the wild disguise hath almost

Antick'd us all. What needs more words? Good
   night.
Good Antony, your hand.
                    POMPEY
                    I'll try you on the shore.
                    ANTONY
And shall, sir: give 's your hand.
                    POMPEY
                              O Antony,
You have my father's house,—But, what? we are
   friends.
Come, down into the boat.
                    ENOBARBUS
                    Take heed you fall not.
           [Exeunt all but ENOBARBUS and MENAS
Menas, I'll not on shore.
                    MENAS
                    No, to my cabin.
These drums! these trumpets, flutes! what!
Let Neptune hear we bid a loud farewell
To these great fellows: sound and be hang'd, sound
   out!
                    [Sound a flourish, with drums
                    ENOBARBUS
Hoo! says a'. There's my cap.
                    MENAS
Hoo! Noble captain, come.   [Exeunt

ACT III

Scene I. A plain in Syria

Enter VENTIDIUS *as it were in triumph, with* SILIUS, *and
other* ROMANS, OFFICERS, *and* SOLDIERS; *the dead body
of* PACORUS *borne before him*
                    VENTIDIUS
Now, darting Parthia, art thou struck; and now
Pleased fortune does of Marcus Crassus' death
Make me revenger. Bear the king's son's body
Before our army. Thy Pacorus, Orodes,
Pays this for Marcus Crassus.
                    SILIUS
                    Noble Ventidius,
Whilst yet with Parthian blood thy sword is warm,
The fugitive Parthians follow; spur through Media,
Mesopotamia, and the shelters whither
The routed fly: so thy grand captain Antony
Shall set thee on triumphant chariots and
Put garlands on thy head.
                    VENTIDIUS
                    O Silius, Silius,
I have done enough: a lower place, note well,
May make too great an act; for learn this, Silius,
Better to leave undone than by our deed
Acquire too high a fame when him we serve's away.
Cæsar and Antony have ever won
More in their officer than person: Sossius,
One of my place in Syria, his lieutenant,

For quick accumulation of renown,
Which he achieved by the minute, lost his favour.
Who does i' the wars more than his captain can
Becomes his captain's captain: and ambition,
The soldier's virtue, rather makes choice of loss
Than gain which darkens him.
I could do more to do Antonius good,
But 'twould offend him, and in his offence
Should my performance perish.
                    SILIUS
                    Thou hast, Ventidius, that
Without the which a soldier and his sword
Grants scarce distinction. Thou wilt write to
   Antony?
                    VENTIDIUS
I'll humbly signify what in his name,
That magical word of war, we have effected;
How, with his banners and his well-paid ranks,
The ne'er-yet-beaten horse of Parthia
We have jaded out o' the field.
                    SILIUS
                    Where is he now?
                    VENTIDIUS
He purposeth to Athens: whither, with what haste
The weight we must convey with 's will permit,
We shall appear before him. On, there; pass along!
                                        [Exeunt

Scene II. Rome. An ante-chamber in CÆSAR'S house

Enter AGRIPPA *at one door, and* ENOBARBUS *at another*
                    AGRIPPA
What, are the brothers parted?
                    ENOBARBUS
They have dispatch'd with Pompey; he is gone;
The other three are sealing. Octavia weeps
To part from Rome; Cæsar is sad, and Lepidus
Since Pompey's feast, as Menas says, is troubled
With the green sickness.
                    AGRIPPA
                    'Tis a noble Lepidus.
                    ENOBARBUS
A very fine one: O, how he loves Cæsar!
                    AGRIPPA
Nay, but how dearly he adores Mark Antony!
                    ENOBARBUS
Cæsar? Why, he's the Jupiter of men.
                    AGRIPPA
What's Antony? The god of Jupiter.
                    ENOBARBUS
Spake you of Cæsar? How! the nonpareil!
                    AGRIPPA
O Antony! O thou Arabian bird!
                    ENOBARBUS
Would you praise Cæsar, say 'Cæsar': go no further.
                    AGRIPPA
Indeed, he plied them both with excellent praises.
                    ENOBARBUS
But he loves Cæsar best; yet he loves Antony:

Ho! hearts, tongues, figures, scribes, bards, poets, cannot
Think, speak, cast, write, sing, number—ho!—
His love to Antony. But as for Cæsar,
Kneel down, kneel down, and wonder.

AGRIPPA
　　　　　　　Both he loves.

ENOBARBUS
They are his shards, and he their beetle. [*Trumpet within*] So;
This is to horse. Adieu, noble Agrippa.

AGRIPPA
Good fortune, worthy soldier, and farewell.

Enter CÆSAR, ANTONY, LEPIDUS, *and* OCTAVIA

ANTONY
No further, sir.

CÆSAR
You take from me a great part of myself;
Use me well in 't. Sister, prove such a wife
As my thoughts make thee, and as my farthest band
Shall pass on thy approof. Most noble Antony,
Let not the piece of virtue which is set
Betwixt us as the cement of our love,
To keep it builded, be the ram to batter
The fortress of it; for better might we
Have loved without this mean, if on both parts
This be not cherish'd.

ANTONY
　　　　　Make me not offended
In your distrust.

CÆSAR
　　　I have said.

ANTONY
　　　　　　You shall not find,
Though you be therein curious, the least cause
For what you seem to fear: so, the gods keep you,
And make the hearts of Romans serve your ends!
We will here part.

CÆSAR
Farewell, my dearest sister, fare thee well:
The elements be kind to thee, and make
Thy spirits all of comfort! fare thee well.

OCTAVIA
My noble brother!

ANTONY
The April's in her eyes: it is love's spring,
And these the showers to bring it on. Be cheerful.

OCTAVIA
Sir, look well to my husband's house, and—

CÆSAR
　　　　　　　What,
Octavia?

OCTAVIA
I'll tell you in your ear.

ANTONY
Her tongue will not obey her heart, nor can
Her heart inform her tongue, the swan's down-feather,
That stands upon the swell at full of tide
And neither way inclines.

ENOBARBUS
[*Aside to* AGRIPPA] Will Cæsar weep?

AGRIPPA
[*Aside to* ENOBARBUS] He has a cloud in 's face.

ENOBARBUS
[*Aside to* AGRIPPA] He were the worse for that, were he a horse;
So is he, being a man.

AGRIPPA
[*Aside to* ENOBARBUS] Why, Enobarbus,
When Antony found Julius Cæsar dead,
He cried almost to roaring; and he wept
When at Philippi he found Brutus slain.

ENOBARBUS
[*Aside to* AGRIPPA] That year indeed he was troubled with a rheum;
What willingly he did confound he wail'd,
Believe 't, till I wept too.

CÆSAR
　　　　　No, sweet Octavia,
You shall hear from me still; the time shall not
Out-go my thinking on you.

ANTONY
　　　　　Come, sir, come;
I'll wrestle with you in my strength of love:
Look, here I have you; thus I let you go,
And give you to the gods.

CÆSAR
　　　　Adieu; be happy!

LEPIDUS
Let all the number of the stars give light
To thy fair way!

CÆSAR
　　　Farewell, farewell! [*Kisses* OCTAVIA

ANTONY
　　　　　　Farewell!
　　　　　　[*Trumpets sound. Exeunt*

SCENE III. *Alexandria.* CLEOPATRA's *palace*

Enter CLEOPATRA, CHARMIAN, IRAS, *and* ALEXAS

CLEOPATRA
Where is the fellow?

ALEXAS
　　　Half afeard to come.

CLEOPATRA
Go to, go to.

Enter MESSENGER
Come hither, sir.

ALEXAS
　　　　　Good majesty,
Herod of Jewry dare not look upon you
But when you are well pleased.

CLEOPATRA
　　　　　That Herod's head
I'll have: but how, when Antony is gone
Through whom I might command it? Come thou near.

MESSENGER

Most gracious majesty,—

CLEOPATRA

Didst thou behold

Octavia?

MESSENGER

Ay, dread queen.

CLEOPATRA

Where?

MESSENGER

Madam, in Rome

I look'd her in the face, and saw her led

Between her brother and Mark Antony.

CLEOPATRA

Is she as tall as me?

MESSENGER

She is not, madam.

CLEOPATRA

Didst hear her speak? is she shrill-tongued or low?

MESSENGER

Madam, I heard her speak; she is low-voiced.

CLEOPATRA

That's not so good. He cannot like her long.

CHARMIAN

Like her! O Isis! 'tis impossible.

CLEOPATRA

I think so, Charmian: dull of tongue and dwarfish.

What majesty is in her gait? Remember,

If e'er thou look'dst on majesty.

MESSENGER

She creeps:

Her motion and her station are as one;

She shows a body rather than a life,

A statue than a breather.

CLEOPATRA

Is this certain?

MESSENGER

Or I have no observance.

CHARMIAN

Three in Egypt

Cannot make better note.

CLEOPATRA

He's very knowing;

I do perceive 't: there's nothing in her yet:

The fellow has good judgement.

CHARMIAN

Excellent.

CLEOPATRA

Guess at her years, I prithee.

MESSENGER

Madam,

She was a widow—

CLEOPATRA

Widow! Charmian, hark.

MESSENGER

And I do think she's thirty.

CLEOPATRA

Bear'st thou her face in mind? is 't long or round?

MESSENGER

Round even to faultiness.

CLEOPATRA

For the most part, too, they are foolish that are so.

Her hair, what colour?

MESSENGER

Brown, madam: and her forehead

As low as she would wish it.

CLEOPATRA

There's gold for thee.

Thou must not take my former sharpness ill:

I will employ thee back again; I find thee

Most fit for business: go make thee ready;

Our letters are prepared.   [Exit MESSENGER

CHARMIAN

A proper man.

CLEOPATRA

Indeed, he is so: I repent me much

That so I harried him. Why, methinks, by him,

This creature's no such thing.

CHARMIAN

Nothing, madam.

CLEOPATRA

The man hath seen some majesty, and should know.

CHARMIAN

Hath he seen majesty? Isis else defend,

And serving you so long!

CLEOPATRA

I have one thing more to ask him yet, good Char-

mian:

But 'tis no matter; thou shalt bring him to me

Where I will write. All may be well enough.

CHARMIAN

I warrant you, madam.   [Exeunt

SCENE IV. *Athens. A room in* ANTONY'S *house*

Enter ANTONY *and* OCTAVIA

ANTONY

Nay, nay, Octavia, not only that,

That were excusable, that and thousands more

Of semblable import, but he hath waged

New wars 'gainst Pompey; made his will, and

read it

To public ear:

Spoke scantly of me: when perforce he could not

But pay me terms of honour, cold and sickly

He vented them; most narrow measure lent me;

When the best hint was given him, he not took 't,

Or did it from his teeth.

OCTAVIA

O my good lord,

Believe not all; or, if you must believe,

Stomach not all. A more unhappy lady,

If this division chance, ne'er stood between,

Praying for both parts:

The good gods will mock me presently,

When I shall pray, 'O, bless my lord and husband!'

Undo that prayer, by crying out as loud,

'O, bless my brother!' Husband win, win brother,

Prays, and destroys the prayer; no midway
'Twixt these extremes at all.

ANTONY

Gentle Octavia,
Let your best love draw to that point, which seeks
Best to preserve it; if I lose mine honour,
I lose myself: better I were not yours
Than yours so branchless. But, as you requested,
Yourself shall go between 's: the mean time, lady,
I'll raise the preparation of a war
Shall stain your brother: make your soonest haste;
So your desires are yours.

OCTAVIA

Thanks to my lord.
The Jove of power make me most weak, most weak,
Your reconciler! Wars 'twixt you twain would be
As if the world should cleave, and that slain men
Should solder up the rift.

ANTONY

When it appears to you where this begins,
Turn your displeasure that way; for our faults
Can never be so equal, that your love
Can equally move with them. Provide your going;
Choose your own company, and command what
   cost
Your heart has mind to.   [Exeunt

SCENE V. *The same. Another room*

Enter ENOBARBUS *and* EROS, *meeting*

ENOBARBUS

How now, friend Eros!

EROS

There's strange news come, sir.

ENOBARBUS

What, man?

EROS

Cæsar and Lepidus have made wars upon Pompey.

ENOBARBUS

This is old: what is the success?

EROS

Cæsar, having made use of him in the wars 'gainst
Pompey, presently denied him rivality; would not
let him partake in the glory of the action: and not
resting here, accuses him of letters he had formerly
wrote to Pompey; upon his own appeal, seizes him:
so the poor third is up, till death enlarge his confine.

ENOBARBUS

Then, world, thou hast a pair of chaps, no more;
And throw between them all the food thou hast,
They'll grind the one the other. Where's Antony?

EROS

He's walking in the garden—thus; and spurns
The rush that lies before him; cries 'Fool Lepidus!'
And threats the throat of that his officer
That murder'd Pompey.

ENOBARBUS

Our great navy's rigg'd.

EROS

For Italy and Cæsar. More, Domitius;
My lord desires you presently: my news
I might have told hereafter.

ENOBARBUS

'Twill be naught:
But let it be. Bring me to Antony.

EROS

Come, sir.   [Exeunt

SCENE VI. *Rome.* CÆSAR'S *house*

Enter CÆSAR, AGRIPPA, *and* MÆCENAS

CÆSAR

Contemning Rome, he has done all this, and more,
In Alexandria: here's the manner of 't:
I' the market-place, on a tribunal silver'd
Cleopatra and himself in chairs of gold
Were publicly enthroned: at the feet sat
Cæsarion, whom they call my father's son,
And all the unlawful issue that their lust
Since then hath made between them. Unto her
He gave the stablishment of Egypt; made her
Of lower Syria, Cyprus, Lydia,
Absolute queen.

MÆCENAS

This in the public eye?

CÆSAR

I' the common show-place, where they exercise.
His sons he there proclaim'd the kings of kings:
Great Media, Parthia and Armenia,
He gave to Alexander; to Ptolemy he assign'd
Syria, Cilicia and Phœnicia: she
In the habiliments of the goddess Isis
That day appear'd, and oft before gave audience,
As 'tis reported, so.

MÆCENAS

Let Rome be thus
Inform'd.

AGRIPPA

Who, queasy with his insolence
Already, will their good thoughts call from him.

CÆSAR

The people know it, and have now received
His accusations.

AGRIPPA

Who does he accuse?

CÆSAR

Cæsar: and that, having in Sicily
Sextus Pompeius spoil'd, we had not rated him
His part o' the isle: then does he say, he lent me
Some shipping unrestored: lastly, he frets
That Lepidus of the triumvirate
Should be deposed; and, being, that we detain
All his revenue.

AGRIPPA

Sir, this should be answer'd.

CÆSAR

'Tis done already, and the messenger gone.

I have told him, Lepidus was grown too cruel;
That he his high authority abused
And did deserve his change: for what I have con-
    quer'd,
I grant him part; but then, in his Armenia
And other of his conquer'd kingdoms, I
Demand the like.

MÆCENAS
            He'll never yield to that.

CÆSAR
Nor must not then be yielded to in this.

Enter OCTAVIA, *with her train*

OCTAVIA
Hail, Cæsar, and my lord! hail, most dear Cæsar!

CÆSAR
That ever I should call thee castaway!

OCTAVIA
You have not call'd me so, nor have you cause.

CÆSAR
Why have you stol'n upon us thus? You come not
Like Cæsar's sister: the wife of Antony
Should have an army for an usher, and
The neighs of horse to tell of her approach
Long ere she did appear; the trees by the way
Should have borne men; and expectation fainted,
Longing for what it had not; nay, the dust
Should have ascended to the roof of heaven,
Raised by your populous troops: but you are come
A market-maid to Rome; and have prevented
The ostentation of our love, which, left unshown,
Is often left unloved: we should have met you
By sea and land, supplying every stage
With an augmented greeting.

OCTAVIA
            Good my lord,
To come thus was I not constrain'd, but did it
On my free will. My lord, Mark Antony,
Hearing that you prepared for war, acquainted
My grieved ear withal; whereon, I begg'd
His pardon for return.

CÆSAR
            Which soon he granted,
Being an obstruct 'tween his lust and him.

OCTAVIA
Do not say so, my lord.

CÆSAR
            I have eyes upon him,
And his affairs come to me on the wind.
Where is he now?

OCTAVIA
            My lord, in Athens.

CÆSAR
No, my most wronged sister; Cleopatra
Hath nodded him to her. He hath given his empire
Up to a whore; who now are levying
The kings o' the earth for war: he hath assembled
Bocchus, the king of Libya; Archelaus,
Of Cappadocia; Philadelphos, king
Of Paphlagonia; the Thracian king, Adallas;
King Malchus of Arabia; King of Pont;

Herod of Jewry; Mithridates, king
Of Comagene; Polemon and Amyntas,
The kings of Mede and Lycaonia,
With a more larger list of sceptres.

OCTAVIA
            Ay me, most wretched,
That have my heart parted betwixt two friends
That do afflict each other!

CÆSAR
            Welcome hither:
Your letters did withhold our breaking forth,
Till we perceived both how you were wrong led
And we in negligent danger. Cheer your heart:
Be you not troubled with the time, which drives
O'er your content these strong necessities;
But let determined things to destiny
Hold unbewail'd their way. Welcome to Rome;
Nothing more dear to me. You are abused
Beyond the mark of thought: and the high gods,
To do you justice, make them ministers
Of us and those that love you. Best of comfort;
And ever welcome to us.

AGRIPPA
            Welcome, lady.

MÆCENAS
Welcome, dear madam.
Each heart in Rome does love and pity you:
Only the adulterous Antony, most large
In his abominations, turns you off;
And gives his potent regiment to a trull,
That noises it against us.

OCTAVIA
            Is it so, sir?

CÆSAR
Most certain. Sister, welcome: pray you,
Be ever known to patience: my dear'st sister!

            [*Exeunt*

SCENE VII. *Near Actium.* ANTONY'S *camp*

Enter CLEOPATRA *and* ENOBARBUS

CLEOPATRA
I will be even with thee, doubt it not.

ENOBARBUS
But why, why, why?

CLEOPATRA
Thou hast forspoke my being in these wars,
And say'st it is not fit.

ENOBARBUS
            Well, is it, is it?

CLEOPATRA
If not denounced against us, why should not we
Be there in person?

ENOBARBUS
            [*Aside*] Well, I could reply:
If we should serve with horse and mares together,
The horse were merely lost; the mares would bear
A soldier and his horse.

CLEOPATRA
            What is 't you say?

ENOBARBUS

Your presence needs must puzzle Antony;
Take from his heart, take from his brain, from 's
   time,
What should not then be spared. He is already
Traduced for levity; and 'tis said in Rome
That Photinus, an eunuch and your maids
Manage this war.

CLEOPATRA

            Sink Rome, and their tongues rot
That speak against us! A charge we bear i' the war,
And, as the president of my kingdom, will
Appear there for a man. Speak not against it:
I will not stay behind.

ENOBARBUS

            Nay, I have done.
Here comes the emperor.

Enter ANTONY *and* CANIDIUS

ANTONY

            Is it not strange, Canidius,
That from Tarentum and Brundusium
He could so quickly cut the Ionian sea,
And take in Toryne? You have heard on 't, sweet?

CLEOPATRA

Celerity is never more admired
Than by the negligent.

ANTONY

            A good rebuke,
Which might have well becomed the best of men,
To taunt at slackness. Canidius, we
Will fight with him by sea.

CLEOPATRA

            By sea: what else?

CANIDIUS

Why will my lord do so?

ANTONY

            For that he dares us to 't.

ENOBARBUS

So hath my lord dared him to single fight.

CANIDIUS

Ay, and to wage this battle at Pharsalia,
Where Cæsar fought with Pompey: but these offers,
Which serve not for his vantage, he shakes off,
And so should you.

ENOBARBUS

            Your ships are not well mann'd,
Your mariners are muleters, reapers, people
Ingross'd by swift impress; in Cæsar's fleet
Are those that often have 'gainst Pompey fought:
Their ships are yare, yours heavy: no disgrace
Shall fall you for refusing him at sea,
Being prepared for land.

ANTONY

            By sea, by sea.

ENOBARBUS

Most worthy sir, you therein throw away
The absolute soldiership you have by land,
Distract your army, which doth most consist
Of war-mark'd footmen, leave unexecuted
Your own renowned knowledge, quite forgo

The way which promises assurance, and
Give up yourself merely to chance and hazard
From firm security.

ANTONY

            I'll fight at sea.

CLEOPATRA

I have sixty sails, Cæsar none better.

ANTONY

Our overplus of shipping will we burn;
And, with the rest full-mann'd, from the head of
   Actium
Beat the approaching Cæsar. But if we fail,
We then can do 't at land.

Enter a MESSENGER

            Thy business?

MESSENGER

The news is true, my lord; he is descried;
Cæsar has taken Toryne.

ANTONY

Can he be there in person? 'tis impossible;
Strange that his power should be. Canidius,
Our nineteen legions thou shalt hold by land,
And our twelve thousand horse. We'll to our ship:
Away, my Thetis!

Enter a SOLDIER

           How now, worthy soldier?

SOLDIER

O noble emperor, do not fight by sea;
Trust not to rotten planks. Do you misdoubt
This sword and these my wounds? Let the Egyptians
And the Phœnicians go a-ducking: we
Have used to conquer, standing on the earth
And fighting foot to foot.

ANTONY

           Well, well: away!

[*Exeunt* ANTONY, CLEOPATRA, *and* ENOBARBUS

SOLDIER

By Hercules, I think I am i' the right.

CANIDIUS

Soldier, thou art: but his whole action grows
Not in the power on 't: so our leader's led,
And we are women's men.

SOLDIER

           You keep by land
The legions and the horse whole, do you not?

CANIDIUS

Marcus Octavius, Marcus Justeius,
Publicola and Cælius, are for sea:
But we keep whole by land. This speed of Cæsar's
Carries beyond belief.

SOLDIER

           While he was yet in Rome,
His power went out in such distractions as
Beguiled all spies.

CANIDIUS

           Who's his lieutenant, hear you?

SOLDIER

They say, one Taurus.

CANIDIUS

           Well I know the man.

Enter a MESSENGER

MESSENGER

The emperor calls Canidius.

CANIDIUS

With news the time's with labour, and throes forth
Each minute some.   [*Exeunt*

SCENE VIII. *A plain near Actium*

Enter CÆSAR, *and* TAURUS, *with his* ARMY, *marching*

CÆSAR

Taurus!

TAURUS

My lord?

CÆSAR

Strike not by land; keep whole: provoke not battle,
Till we have done at sea. Do not exceed
The prescript of this scroll: our fortune lies
Upon this jump.   [*Exeunt*

SCENE IX. *Another part of the plain*

Enter ANTONY *and* ENOBARBUS

ANTONY

Set we our squadrons on yond side o' the hill,
In eye of Cæsar's battle; from which place
We may the number of the ships behold,
And so proceed accordingly.   [*Exeunt*

SCENE X. *Another part of the plain*

Enter CANIDIUS, *marching with his land* ARMY *one way;
and* TAURUS, *the lieutenant of* CÆSAR, *with his* ARMY, *the
other way. After their going in, is heard the noise of a sea-
fight*

Alarum. Enter ENOBARBUS

ENOBARBUS

Naught, naught, all naught! I can behold no longer!
The Antoniad, the Egyptian admiral,
With all their sixty, fly and turn the rudder:
To see 't mine eyes are blasted.

Enter SCARUS

SCARUS

Gods and goddesses,
All the whole synod of them!

ENOBARBUS

What's thy passion?

SCARUS

The greater cantle of the world is lost
With very ignorance; we have kiss'd away
Kingdoms and provinces.

ENOBARBUS

How appears the fight?

SCARUS

On our side like the token'd pestilence,
Where death is sure. Yon ribaudred nag of Egypt—
Whom leprosy o'ertake!—i' the midst o' the fight,

When vantage like a pair of twins appear'd,
Both as the same, or rather ours the elder,—
The breese upon her, like a cow in June!—
Hoists sails and flies.

ENOBARBUS

That I beheld:
Mine eyes did sicken at the sight, and could not
Endure a further view.

SCARUS

She once being loof'd,
The noble ruin of her magic, Antony,
Claps on his sea-wing, and like a doting mallard,
Leaving the fight in height, flies after her:
I never saw an action of such shame;
Experience, manhood, honour, ne'er before
Did violate so itself.

ENOBARBUS

Alack, alack!

Enter CANIDIUS

CANIDIUS

Our fortune on the sea is out of breath,
And sinks most lamentably. Had our general
Been what he knew himself, it had gone well:
O, he has given example for our flight
Most grossly by his own!

ENOBARBUS

Ay, are you thereabouts? Why then good night
Indeed.

CANIDIUS

Toward Peloponnesus are they fled.

SCARUS

'Tis easy to 't; and there I will attend
What further comes.

CANIDIUS

To Cæsar will I render
My legions and my horse: six kings already
Show me the way of yielding.

ENOBARBUS

I'll yet follow
The wounded chance of Antony, though my reason
Sits in the wind against me.   [*Exeunt*

SCENE XI. *Alexandria.* CLEOPATRA'S *palace*

Enter ANTONY *with* ATTENDANTS

ANTONY

Hark! the land bids me tread no more upon 't;
It is ashamed to bear me. Friends, come hither:
I am so lated in the world that I
Have lost my way for ever. I have a ship
Laden with gold; take that, divide it; fly,
And make your peace with Cæsar.

ALL

Fly! not we.

ANTONY

I have fled myself, and have instructed cowards
To run and show their shoulders. Friends, be gone;
I have myself resolved upon a course
Which has no need of you; be gone:

My treasure's in the harbour, take it. O,
I follow'd that I blush to look upon:
My very hairs do mutiny, for the white
Reprove the brown for rashness, and they them
For fear and doting. Friends, be gone: you shall
Have letters from me to some friends that will
Sweep your way for you. Pray you, look not sad,
Nor make replies of loathness: take the hint
Which my despair proclaims; let that be left
Which leaves itself: to the sea-side straightway:
I will possess you of that ship and treasure.
Leave me, I pray, a little: pray you now:
Nay, do so; for indeed I have lost command,
Therefore I pray you: I'll see you by and by.

                            [Sits down

Enter CLEOPATRA *led by* CHARMIAN *and* IRAS; EROS
following

EROS

Nay, gentle madam, to him, comfort him.

IRAS

Do, most dear queen.

CHARMIAN

Do! why, what else?

CLEOPATRA

Let me sit down. O Juno!

ANTONY

No, no, no, no, no.

EROS

See you here, sir?

ANTONY

O fie, fie, fie!

CHARMIAN

Madam!

IRAS

Madam, O good empress!

EROS

Sir, sir!

ANTONY

Yes, my lord, yes; he at Philippi kept
His sword e'en like a dancer; while I struck
The lean and wrinkled Cassius; and 'twas I
That the mad Brutus ended: he alone
Dealt on lieutenantry and no practice had
In the brave squares of war: yet now—No matter.

CLEOPATRA

Ah! stand by.

EROS

The queen, my lord, the queen.

IRAS

Go to him, madam, speak to him:
He is unqualitied with very shame.

CLEOPATRA

Well then, sustain me: O!

EROS

Most noble sir, arise; the queen approaches:
Her head's declined, and death will seize her, but
Your comfort makes the rescue.

ANTONY

I have offended reputation,
A most unnoble swerving.

EROS

Sir, the queen.

ANTONY

O, whither hast thou led me, Egypt? See,
How I convey my shame out of thine eyes
By looking back what I have left behind
Stroy'd in dishonour.

CLEOPATRA

O my lord, my lord,
Forgive my fearful sails! I little thought
You would have follow'd.

ANTONY

Egypt, thou knew'st too well
My heart was to thy rudder tied by the strings,
And thou shouldst tow me after: o'er my spirit
Thy full supremacy thou knew'st, and that
Thy beck might from the bidding of the gods
Command me.

CLEOPATRA

O, my pardon!

ANTONY

Now I must
To the young man send humble treaties, dodge
And palter in the shifts of lowness; who
With half the bulk o' the world play'd as I pleased,
Making and marring fortunes. You did know
How much you were my conqueror, and that
My sword, made weak by my affection, would
Obey it on all cause.

CLEOPATRA

Pardon, pardon!

ANTONY

Fall not a tear, I say; one of them rates
All that is won and lost: give me a kiss;
Even this repays me. We sent our schoolmaster;
Is he come back? Love, I am full of lead.
Some wine, within there, and our viands! Fortune
    knows
We scorn her most when most she offers blows.

                             [Exeunt

SCENE XII. *Egypt.* CÆSAR'S *camp*

Enter CÆSAR, DOLABELLA, THYREUS, *with others*

CÆSAR

Let him appear that's come from Antony.
Know you him?

DOLABELLA

Cæsar, 'tis his schoolmaster:
An argument that he is pluck'd, when hither
He sends so poor a pinion of his wing,
Which had superfluous kings for messengers
Not many moons gone by.

Enter EUPHRONIUS, *ambassador from* ANTONY

CÆSAR

Approach, and speak.

EUPHRONIUS

Such as I am, I come from Antony:
I was of late as petty to his ends

As is the morn-dew on the myrtle-leaf
To his grand sea.

CÆSAR

        Be 't so: declare thine office.

EUPHRONIUS

Lord of his fortunes he salutes thee, and
Requires to live in Egypt: which not granted,
He lessens his requests, and to thee sues
To let him breathe between the heavens and earth,
A private man in Athens: this for him.
Next, Cleopatra does confess thy greatness;
Submits her to thy might, and of thee craves
The circle of the Ptolemies for her heirs,
Now hazarded to thy grace.

CÆSAR

            For Antony,
I have no ears to his request. The queen
Of audience nor desire shall fail, so she
From Egypt drive her all-disgraced friend,
Or take his life there: this if she perform,
She shall not sue unheard. So to them both.

EUPHRONIUS

Fortune pursue thee!

CÆSAR

        Bring him through the bands.

[Exit EUPHRONIUS

[To THYREUS] To try thy eloquence, now 'tis time: dispatch;
From Antony win Cleopatra: promise,
And in our name, what she requires; add more,
From thine invention, offers: women are not
In their best fortunes strong, but want will perjure
The ne'er-touch'd vestal: try thy cunning, Thyreus;
Make thine own edict for thy pains, which we
Will answer as a law.

THYREUS

        Cæsar, I go.

CÆSAR

Observe how Antony becomes his flaw,
And what thou think'st his very action speaks
In every power that moves.

THYREUS

        Cæsar, I shall.   [Exeunt

SCENE XIII. Alexandria. CLEOPATRA'S palace

Enter CLEOPATRA, ENOBARBUS, CHARMIAN, and IRAS

CLEOPATRA

What shall we do, Enobarbus?

ENOBARBUS

        Think, and die.

CLEOPATRA

Is Antony or we in fault for this?

ENOBARBUS

Antony only, that would make his will
Lord of his reason. What though you fled
From that great face of war, whose several ranges
Frighted each other, why should he follow?
The itch of his affection should not then

Have nick'd his captainship; at such a point,
When half to half the world opposed, he being
The mered question: 'twas a shame no less
Than was his loss, to course your flying flags
And leave his navy gazing.

CLEOPATRA

        Prithee, peace.

Enter ANTONY, with EUPHRONIUS the Ambassador

ANTONY

Is that his answer?

EUPHRONIUS

Ay, my lord.

ANTONY

The queen shall then have courtesy, so she
Will yield us up.

EUPHRONIUS

        He says so.

ANTONY

           Let her know 't.
To the boy Cæsar send this grizzled head,
And he will fill thy wishes to the brim
With principalities.

CLEOPATRA

        That head, my lord?

ANTONY

To him again: tell him he wears the rose
Of youth upon him, from which the world should note
Something particular: his coin, ships, legions,
May be a coward's, whose ministers would prevail
Under the service of a child as soon
As i' the command of Cæsar: I dare him therefore
To lay his gay comparisons apart
And answer me declined, sword against sword,
Ourselves alone. I'll write it: follow me.

[Exeunt ANTONY and EUPHRONIUS

ENOBARBUS

[Aside] Yes, like enough, high-battled Cæsar will
Unstate his happiness and be staged to the show
Against a sworder! I see men's judgements are
A parcel of their fortunes, and things outward
Do draw the inward quality after them,
To suffer all alike. That he should dream,
Knowing all measures, the full Cæsar will
Answer his emptiness! Cæsar, thou hast subdued
His judgement too.

Enter an ATTENDANT

ATTENDANT

        A messenger from Cæsar.

CLEOPATRA

What, no more ceremony? See, my women,
Against the blown rose may they stop their nose
That kneel'd unto the buds. Admit him, sir.

[Exit ATTENDANT

ENOBARBUS

[Aside] Mine honesty and I begin to square.
The loyalty well held to fools does make
Our faith mere folly: yet he that can endure
To follow with allegiance a fall'n lord

[1085]

Does conquer him that did his master conquer,
And earns a place i' the story.

Enter THYREUS

CLEOPATRA
                         Cæsar's will?

THYREUS
Hear it apart.

CLEOPATRA
                    None but friends: say boldly.

THYREUS
So, haply, are they friends to Antony.

ENOBARBUS
He needs as many, sir, as Cæsar has,
Or needs not us. If Cæsar please, our master
Will leap to be his friend: for us, you know,
Whose he is we are, and that is Cæsar's.

THYREUS
                                                  So.
Thus then, thou most renown'd: Cæsar entreats
Not to consider in what case thou stand'st
Further than he is Cæsar.

CLEOPATRA
                    Go on: right royal.

THYREUS
He knows that you embrace not Antony
As you did love, but as you fear'd him.

CLEOPATRA
                                                  O!

THYREUS
The scars upon your honour therefore he
Does pity as constrained blemishes,
Not as deserved.

CLEOPATRA
              He is a god and knows
What is most right: mine honour was not yielded,
But conquer'd merely.

ENOBARBUS
              [*Aside*] To be sure of that,
I will ask Antony. Sir, sir, thou art so leaky
That we must leave thee to thy sinking, for
Thy dearest quit thee.   [*Exit*

THYREUS
                    Shall I say to Cæsar
What you require of him? for he partly begs
To be desired to give. It much would please him,
That of his fortunes you should make a staff
To lean upon: but it would warm his spirits,
To hear from me you had left Antony,
And put yourself under his shroud,
The universal landlord.

CLEOPATRA
                    What's your name?

THYREUS
My name is Thyreus.

CLEOPATRA
                    Most kind messenger,
Say to great Cæsar this: in deputation
I kiss his conquering hand: tell him, I am prompt
To lay my crown at 's feet, and there to kneel:

Tell him, from his all-obeying breath I hear
The doom of Egypt.

THYREUS
              'Tis your noblest course.
Wisdom and fortune combating together,
If that the former dare but what it can,
No chance may shake it. Give me grace to lay
My duty on your hand.

CLEOPATRA
                    Your Cæsar's father oft,
When he hath mused of taking kingdoms in,
Bestow'd his lips on that unworthy place,
As it rain'd kisses.

Re-enter ANTONY *and* ENOBARBUS

ANTONY
              Favours, by Jove that thunders!
What art thou, fellow?

THYREUS
              One that but performs
The bidding of the fullest man and worthiest
To have command obey'd.

ENOBARBUS
              [*Aside*] You will be whipp'd.

ANTONY
Approach, there! Ah, you kite! Now, gods and
    devils!
Authority melts from me: of late, when I cried 'Ho!'
Like boys unto a muss, kings would start forth
And cry 'Your will?' Have you no ears?
I am Antony yet.

ENTER ATTENDANTS
              Take hence this Jack, and whip him.

ENOBARBUS
[*Aside*] 'Tis better playing with a lion's whelp
Than with an old one dying.

ANTONY
                    Moon and stars!
Whip him. Were 't twenty of the greatest tributaries
That do acknowledge Cæsar, should I find them
So saucy with the hand of she here,—what's her
    name,
Since she was Cleopatra? Whip him, fellows,
Till, like a boy, you see him cringe his face,
And whine aloud for mercy: take him hence.

THYREUS
Mark Antony,—

ANTONY
              Tug him away: being whipp'd,
Bring him again: this Jack of Cæsar's shall
Bear us an errand to him.
                    [*Exeunt* ATTENDANTS, *with* THYREUS
You were half blasted ere I knew you: ha!
Have I my pillow left unpress'd in Rome,
Forborne the getting of a lawful race,
And by a gem of women, to be abused
By one that looks on feeders?

CLEOPATRA
                    Good my lord,—

ANTONY
You have been a boggler ever:

But when we in our viciousness grow hard—
O misery on 't!—the wise gods seel our eyes;
In our own filth drop our clear judgements; make us
Adore our errors; laugh at 's while we strut
To our confusion.

CLEOPATRA
　　　　　　　O, is 't come to this?

ANTONY
I found you as a morsel cold upon
Dead Cæsar's trencher; nay, you were a fragment
Of Cneius Pompey's; besides what hotter hours,
Unregister'd in vulgar fame, you have
Luxuriously pick'd out: for I am sure,
Though you can guess what temperance should be,
You know not what it is.

CLEOPATRA
　　　　　　　Wherefore is this?

ANTONY
To let a fellow that will take rewards
And say 'God quit you!' be familiar with
My playfellow, your hand, this kingly seal
And plighter of high hearts! O, that I were
Upon the hill of Basan, to outroar
The horned herd! for I have savage cause;
And to proclaim it civilly, were like
A halter'd neck which does the hangman thank
For being yare about him.

Re-enter ATTENDANTS, *with* THYREUS

　　　　　　　Is he whipp'd?

FIRST ATTENDANT
Soundly, my lord.

ANTONY
　　　　　　Cried he? and begg'd he pardon?

FIRST ATTENDANT
He did ask favour.

ANTONY
If that thy father live, let him repent
Thou wast not made his daughter; and be thou
　　sorry
To follow Cæsar in his triumph, since
Thou hast been whipp'd for following him: hence-
　　forth
The white hand of a lady fever thee,
Shake thou to look on 't. Get thee back to Cæsar,
Tell him thy entertainment: look thou say
He makes me angry with him; for he seems
Proud and disdainful, harping on what I am,
Not what he knew I was: he makes me angry;
And at this time most easy 'tis to do 't,
When my good stars that were my former guides
Have empty left their orbs and shot their fires
Into the abysm of hell. If he mislike
My speech and what is done, tell him he has
Hipparchus, my enfranched bondman, whom
He may at pleasure whip, or hang, or torture,
As he shall like, to quit me: urge it thou:
Hence with thy stripes, begone!　　[*Exit* THYREUS

CLEOPATRA
Have you done yet?

ANTONY
　　　　　　Alack, our terrene moon
Is now eclipsed, and it portends alone
The fall of Antony.

CLEOPATRA
　　　　　　I must stay his time.

ANTONY
To flatter Cæsar, would you mingle eyes
With one that ties his points?

CLEOPATRA
　　　　　　　Not know me yet?

ANTONY
Cold-hearted toward me?

CLEOPATRA
　　　　　　Ah, dear, if I be so,
From my cold heart let heaven engender hail,
And poison it in the source, and the first stone
Drop in my neck: as it determines, so
Dissolve my life! The next Cæsarion smite!
Till by degrees the memory of my womb,
Together with my brave Egyptians all,
By the discandying of this pelleted storm
Lie graveless, till the flies and gnats of Nile
Have buried them for prey!

ANTONY
　　　　　　　I am satisfied.
Cæsar sits down in Alexandria, where
I will oppose his fate. Our force by land
Hath nobly held; our sever'd navy too
Have knit again, and fleet, threatening most sealike.
Where hast thou been, my heart? Dost thou hear,
　　lady?
If from the field I shall return once more
To kiss these lips, I will appear in blood;
I and my sword will earn our chronicle:
There's hope in 't yet.

CLEOPATRA
That's my brave lord!

ANTONY
I will be treble-sinew'd, hearted, breath'd,
And fight maliciously: for when mine hours
Were nice and lucky, men did ransom lives
Of me for jests; but now I'll set my teeth,
And send to darkness all that stop me. Come,
Let's have one other gaudy night: call to me
All my sad captains; fill our bowls once more:
Let's mock the midnight bell.

CLEOPATRA
　　　　　　　It is my birth-day:
I had thought to have held it poor, but since my
　　lord
Is Antony again, I will be Cleopatra.

ANTONY
We will yet do well.

CLEOPATRA
Call all his noble captains to my lord.

ANTONY
Do so, we'll speak to them; and to-night I'll force
The wine peep through their scars. Come on, my
　　queen;

There's sap in 't yet. The next time I do fight
I'll make death love me, for I will contend
Even with his pestilent scythe.

                [Exeunt all but ENOBARBUS

ENOBARBUS

Now he'll outstare the lightning. To be furious
Is to be frighted out of fear; and in that mood
The dove will peck the estridge; and I see still,
A diminution in our captain's brain
Restores his heart: when valour preys on reason,
It eats the sword it fights with. I will seek
Some way to leave him.   *[Exit*

ACT IV

SCENE I. *Before Alexandria.* CÆSAR's *camp*

Enter CÆSAR, AGRIPPA, *and* MÆCENAS, *with his* ARMY:
CÆSAR *reading a letter*

CÆSAR

He calls me boy, and chides as he had power
To beat me out of Egypt; my messenger
He hath whipp'd with rods; dares me to personal
    combat,
Cæsar to Antony. Let the old ruffian know
I have many other ways to die, meantime
Laugh at his challenge.

MACÆNAS

          Cæsar must think,
When one so great begins to rage, he's hunted
Even to falling. Give him no breath, but now
Make boot of his distraction. Never anger
Made good guard for itself.

CÆSAR

          Let our best heads
Know that to-morrow the last of many battles
We mean to fight. Within our files there are,
Of those that served Mark Antony but late,
Enough to fetch him in. See it done:
And feast the army; we have store to do 't,
And they have earn'd the waste. Poor Antony!

                       [Exeunt

SCENE II. *Alexandria.* CLEOPATRA's *palace*

Enter ANTONY, CLEOPATRA, ENOBARBUS, CHARMIAN,
IRAS, ALEXAS, *with others*

ANTONY

He will not fight with me, Domitius?

ENOBARBUS

               No.

ANTONY

Why should he not?

ENOBARBUS

He thinks, being twenty times of better fortune,
He is twenty men to one.

ANTONY

          To-morrow, soldier,

By sea and land I'll fight: or I will live,
Or bathe my dying honour in the blood
Shall make it live again. Woo 't thou fight well?

ENOBARBUS

I'll strike, and cry 'Take all.'

ANTONY

               Well said; come on.
Call forth my household servants: let's to-night
Be bounteous at our meal.

Enter three or four SERVITORS

               Give me thy hand,
Thou hast been rightly honest;—so hast thou;—
Thou,—and thou,—and thou: you have served me
    well,
And kings have been your fellows.

CLEOPATRA

    [Aside to ENOBARBUS] What means this?

ENOBARBUS

[Aside to CLEOPATRA] 'Tis one of those odd tricks
    which sorrow shoots
Out of the mind.

ANTONY

          And thou art honest too.
I wish I could be made so many men,
And all of you clapp'd up together in
An Antony, that I might do you service
So good as you have done.

SERVANT

          The gods forbid!

ANTONY

Well, my good fellows, wait on me to-night:
Scant not my cups, and make as much of me
As when mine empire was your fellow too
And suffer'd my command.

CLEOPATRA

    [Aside to ENOBARBUS] What does he mean?

ENOBARBUS

[Aside to CLEOPATRA] To make his followers weep.

ANTONY

             Tend me to-night;
May be it is the period of your duty:
Haply you shall not see me more; or if,
A mangled shadow: perchance to-morrow
You'll serve another master. I look on you
As one that takes his leave. Mine honest friends,
I turn you not away; but, like a master
Married to your good service, stay till death:
Tend me to-night two hours, I ask no more,
And the gods yield you for 't!

ENOBARBUS

          What mean you, sir,
To give them this discomfort? Look, they weep,
And I, an ass, am onion-eyed: for shame,
Transform us not to women.

ANTONY

          Ho, ho, ho!
Now the witch take me, if I meant it thus!
Grace grow where those drops fall! My hearty
    friends,
You take me in too dolorous a sense;

For I spake to you for your comfort, did desire you
To burn this night with torches: know, my hearts,
I hope well of to-morrow, and will lead you
Where rather I'll expect victorious life
Than death and honour. Let's to supper, come,
And drown consideration.   [*Exeunt*

SCENE III. *The same. Before the palace*

Enter two SOLDIERS *to their guard*

FIRST SOLDIER

Brother, good night: to-morrow is the day.

SECOND SOLDIER

It will determine one way: fare you well.
Heard you of nothing strange about the streets?

FIRST SOLDIER

Nothing. What news?

SECOND SOLDIER

Belike 'tis but a rumour. Good night to you.

FIRST SOLDIER

Well, sir, good night.

Enter two other SOLDIERS

SECOND SOLDIER

Soldiers, have careful watch.

THIRD SOLDIER

And you. Good night, good night.
            [*They place themselves in every corner of the stage*

FOURTH SOLDIER

Here we: and if to-morrow
Our navy thrive, I have an absolute hope
Our landmen will stand up.

THIRD SOLDIER

                    'Tis a brave army,
And full of purpose.
            [*Music of hautboys as under the stage*

FOURTH SOLDIER

            Peace! what noise?

FIRST SOLDIER

                    List, list!

SECOND SOLDIER

Hark!

FIRST SOLDIER

    Music i' the air.

THIRD SOLDIER

            Under the earth.

FOURTH SOLDIER

It signs well, does it not?

THIRD SOLDIER

                    No.

FIRST SOLDIER

                    Peace, I say!
What should this mean?

SECOND SOLDIER

'Tis the god Hercules, whom Antony loved,
Now leaves him.

FIRST SOLDIER

Walk; let's see if other watchmen
Do hear what we do.

SECOND SOLDIER

How now, masters!

ALL

[*Speaking together*] How now! How now! Do you
hear this?

FIRST SOLDIER

Ay; is 't not strange?

THIRD SOLDIER

Do you hear, masters? do you hear?

FIRST SOLDIER

Follow the noise so far as we have quarter;
Let's see how it will give off.

ALL

Content. 'Tis strange.   [*Exeunt*

SCENE IV. *The same. A room in the palace*

Enter ANTONY *and* CLEOPATRA, CHARMIAN *and others
attending*

ANTONY

Eros! mine armour, Eros!

CLEOPATRA

                    Sleep a little.

ANTONY

No, my chuck. Eros, come; mine armour, Eros!
            Enter EROS *with armour*
Come, good fellow, put mine iron on:
If fortune be not ours to-day, it is
Because we brave her: come.

CLEOPATRA

                    Nay, I'll help too.
What's this for?

ANTONY

                    Ah, let be, let be! thou art
The armourer of my heart: false, false; this, this.

CLEOPATRA

Sooth, la, I'll help: thus it must be.

ANTONY

                    Well, well;
We shall thrive now. Seest thou, my good fellow?
Go put on thy defences.

EROS

                    Briefly, sir.

CLEOPATRA

Is not this buckled well?

ANTONY

                    Rarely, rarely:
He that unbuckles this, till we do please
To daff 't for our repose, shall hear a storm.
Thou fumblest, Eros; and my queen's a squire
More tight at this than thou: dispatch. O love,
That thou couldst see my wars to-day, and knew'st
The royal occupation! thou shouldst see
A workman in 't.
            Enter an armed SOLDIER
                    Good morrow to thee; welcome:
Thou look'st like him that knows a warlike charge:
To business that we love we rise betime,
And go to 't with delight.

SOLDIER
A thousand, sir,
Early though 't be, have on their riveted trim,
And at the port expect you. [*Shout. Trumpets flourish*
Enter CAPTAINS *and* SOLDIERS
CAPTAIN
The morn is fair. Good morrow, general.
ALL
Good morrow, general.
ANTONY
'Tis well blown, lads:
This morning, like the spirit of a youth
That means to be of note, begins betimes.
So, so; come, give me that: this way; well said.
Fare thee well, dame, whate'er becomes of me:
This is a soldier's kiss: rebukeable
And worthy shameful check it were, to stand
On more mechanic compliment; I'll leave thee
Now like a man of steel. You that will fight,
Follow me close; I'll bring you to 't. Adieu.
[*Exeunt* ANTONY, EROS, CAPTAINS, *and* SOLDIERS
CHARMIAN
Please you, retire to your chamber.
CLEOPATRA
Lead me.
He goes forth gallantly. That he and Cæsar might
Determine this great war in single fight!
Then Antony—but now—Well, on.   [*Exeunt*

SCENE V. *Alexandria.* ANTONY's *camp*

Trumpets sound. Enter ANTONY *and* EROS; *a* SOLDIER
meeting them
SOLDIER
The gods make this a happy day to Antony!
ANTONY
Would thou and those thy scars had once prevail'd
To make me fight at land!
SOLDIER
Hadst thou done so,
The kings that have revolted and the soldier
That has this morning left thee would have still
Follow'd thy heels.
ANTONY
Who's gone this morning?
SOLDIER
Who!
One ever near thee: call for Enobarbus,
He shall not hear thee, or from Cæsar's camp
Say 'I am none of thine.'
ANTONY
What say'st thou?
SOLDIER
Sir,
He is with Cæsar.
EROS
Sir, his chests and treasure
He has not with him.

ANTONY
Is he gone?
SOLDIER
Most certain.
ANTONY
Go, Eros, send his treasure after; do it;
Detain no jot, I charge thee: write to him—
I will subscribe—gentle adieus and greetings;
Say that I wish he never find more cause
To change a master. O, my fortunes have
Corrupted honest men! Dispatch. Enobarbus!
[*Exeunt*

SCENE VI. *Alexandria.* CÆSAR's *camp*

Flourish. Enter CÆSAR *with* AGRIPPA, ENOBARBUS, *and*
others
CÆSAR
Go forth, Agrippa, and begin the fight:
Our will is Antony be took alive;
Make it so known.
AGRIPPA
Cæsar, I shall.   [*Exit*
CÆSAR
The time of universal peace is near:
Prove this a prosperous day, the three-nook'd world
Shall bear the olive freely.
Enter a MESSENGER
MESSENGER
Antony
Is come into the field.
CÆSAR
Go charge Agrippa
Plant those that have revolted in the van,
That Antony may seem to spend his fury
Upon himself.   [*Exeunt all but* ENOBARBUS
ENOBARBUS
Alexas did revolt, and went to Jewry
On affairs of Antony; there did persuade
Great Herod to incline himself to Cæsar
And leave his master Antony: for this pains
Cæsar hath hang'd him. Canidius and the rest
That fell away have entertainment, but
No honourable trust. I have done ill;
Of which I do accuse myself so sorely
That I will joy no more.
Enter a SOLDIER *of* CÆSAR's
SOLDIER
Enobarbus, Antony
Hath after thee sent all thy treasure, with
His bounty overplus: the messenger
Came on my guard, and at thy tent is now
Unloading of his mules.
ENOBARBUS
I give it you.
SOLDIER
Mock not, Enobarbus:
I tell you true: best you safed the bringer
Out of the host; I must attend mine office,

Or would have done 't myself. Your emperor
Continues still a Jove.   [*Exit*

ENOBARBUS
I am alone the villain of the earth,
And feel I am so most. O Antony,
Thou mine of bounty, how wouldst thou have paid
My better service, when my turpitude
Thou dost so crown with gold! This blows my heart:
If swift thought break it not, a swifter mean
Shall outstrike thought: but thought will do 't, I feel.
I fight against thee! No: I will go seek
Some ditch wherein to die; the foul'st best fits
My latter part of life.   [*Exit*

SCENE VII. *Field of battle between the camps*

Alarum. Drums and trumpets. Enter AGRIPPA *and others*
AGRIPPA
Retire, we have engaged ourselves too far:
Cæsar himself has work, and our oppression
Exceeds what we expected.   [*Exeunt*
Alarums. Enter ANTONY, *and* SCARUS *wounded*
SCARUS
O my brave emperor, this is fought indeed!
Had we done so at first, we had droven them home
With clouts about their heads.
ANTONY
                              Thou bleed'st apace.
SCARUS
I had a wound here that was like a T,
But now 'tis made an H.   [*Retreat afar off*
ANTONY
            They do retire.
SCARUS
We'll beat 'em into bench-holes: I have yet
Room for six scotches more.
Enter EROS
EROS
They are beaten, sir, and our advantage serves
For a fair victory.
SCARUS
            Let us score their backs
And snatch 'em up, as we take hares, behind:
'Tis sport to maul a runner.
ANTONY
                  I will reward thee
Once for thy spritely comfort, and ten-fold
For thy good valour. Come thee on.
SCARUS
                  I'll halt after.
                                    [*Exeunt*

SCENE VIII. *Under the walls of Alexandria*

Alarum. Enter ANTONY, *in a march;* SCARUS, *with others*
ANTONY
We have beat him to his camp: run one before,
And let the queen know of our gests. To-morrow,

Before the sun shall see 's, we'll spill the blood
That has to-day escaped. I thank you all;
For doughty-handed are you, and have fought
Not as you served the cause, but as 't had been
Each man's like mine; you have shown all Hectors.
Enter the city, clip your wives, your friends,
Tell them your feats; whilst they with joyful tears
Wash the congealment from your wounds and kiss
The honour'd gashes whole. [*To* SCARUS] Give me
      thy hand;
Enter CLEOPATRA, *attended*
To this great fairy I'll commend thy acts,
Make her thanks bless thee. O thou day o' the world,
Chain mine arm'd neck; leap thou, attire and all,
Through proof of harness to my heart, and there
Ride on the pants triumphing!

CLEOPATRA
                        Lord of lords!
O infinite virtue, comest thou smiling from
The world's great snare uncaught?
ANTONY
                        My nightingale,
We have beat them to their beds. What, girl!
      though grey
Do something mingle with our younger brown, yet
      ha' we
A brain that nourishes our nerves and can
Get goal for goal of youth. Behold this man;
Commend unto his lips thy favouring hand:
Kiss it, my warrior: he hath fought to-day
As if a god in hate of mankind had
Destroy'd in such a shape.
CLEOPATRA
                  I'll give thee, friend,
An armour all of gold; it was a king's.
ANTONY
He has deserved it, were it carbuncled
Like holy Phœbus' car. Give me thy hand:
Through Alexandria make a jolly march;
Bear our hack'd targets like the men that owe them:
Had our great palace the capacity
To camp this host, we all would sup together
And drink carouses to the next day's fate,
Which promises royal peril. Trumpeters,
With brazen din blast you the city's ear;
Make mingle with our rattling tabourines;
That heaven and earth may strike their sounds to-
      gether,
Applauding our approach.   [*Exeunt*

SCENE IX. CÆSAR'S *camp*

SENTINELS *at their post*
FIRST SOLDIER
If we be not relieved within this hour,
We must return to the court of guard: the night
Is shiny, and they say we shall embattle
By the second hour i' the morn.

SECOND SOLDIER
This last day was
A shrewd one to 's.

Enter ENOBARBUS

ENOBARBUS
O, bear me witness, night,—

THIRD SOLDIER
What man is this?

SECOND SOLDIER
Stand close, and list him.

ENOBARBUS
Be witness to me, O thou blessed moon,
When men revolted shall upon record
Bear hateful memory, poor Enobarbus did
Before thy face repent!

FIRST SOLDIER
Enobarbus!

THIRD SOLDIER
Peace!
Hark further.

ENOBARBUS
O sovereign mistress of true melancholy,
The poisonous damp of night disponge upon me,
That life, a very rebel to my will,
May hang no longer on me: throw my heart
Against the flint and hardness of my fault;
Which, being dried with grief, will break to powder,
And finish all foul thoughts. O Antony,
Nobler than my revolt is infamous,
Forgive me in thine own particular,
But let the world rank me in register
A master-leaver and a fugitive:
O Antony! O Antony!   [*Dies*

SECOND SOLDIER
Let's speak to him.

FIRST SOLDIER
Let's hear him, for the things he speaks
May concern Cæsar.

THIRD SOLDIER
Let's do so. But he sleeps.

FIRST SOLDIER
Swoons rather; for so bad a prayer as his
Was never yet for sleep.

SECOND SOLDIER
Go we to him.

THIRD SOLDIER
Awake, sir, awake; speak to us.

SECOND SOLDIER
Hear you, sir?

FIRST SOLDIER
The hand of death hath raught him. [*Drums afar off*] Hark! the drums
Demurely wake the sleepers. Let us bear him
To the court of guard; he is of note: our hour
Is fully out.

THIRD SOLDIER
Come on, then; he may recover yet.
[*Exeunt with the body*

SCENE X. *Between the two camps*

Enter ANTONY *and* SCARUS, *with their* ARMY

ANTONY
Their preparation is to-day by sea;
We please them not by land.

SCARUS
For both, my lord.

ANTONY
I would they'ld fight i' the fire or i' the air;
We'ld fight there too. But this it is; our foot
Upon the hills adjoining to the city
Shall stay with us: order for sea is given;
They have put forth the haven . . .
Where their appointment we may best discover
And look on their endeavour.   [*Exeunt*

SCENE XI. *Another part of the same*

Enter CÆSAR, *and his* ARMY

CÆSAR
But being charged, we will be still by land,
Which, as I take 't, we shall; for his best force
Is forth to man his galleys. To the vales,
And hold our best advantage.   [*Exeunt*

SCENE XII. *Hills adjoining to Alexandria*

Enter ANTONY *and* SCARUS

ANTONY
Yet they are not join'd: where yond pine does
      stand,
I shall discover all: I'll bring thee word
Straight, how 'tis like to go.   [*Exit*

SCARUS
Swallows have built
In Cleopatra's sails their nests: the augurers
Say they know not, they cannot tell; look grimly
And dare not speak their knowledge. Antony
Is valiant, and dejected, and by starts
His fretted fortunes give him hope, and fear,
Of what he has, and has not.
      [*Alarum afar off, as at a sea-fight*
Re-enter ANTONY

ANTONY
All is lost;
This foul Egyptian hath betrayed me:
My fleet hath yielded to the foe; and yonder
They cast their caps up and carouse together
Like friends long lost. Triple-turn'd whore! 'tis thou
Hast sold me to this novice, and my heart
Makes only wars on thee. Bid them all fly;
For when I am revenged upon my charm,
I have done all. Bid them all fly; begone.
      [*Exit* SCARUS
O sun, thy uprise shall I see no more:
Fortune and Antony part here, even here

Do we shake hands. All come to this? The hearts
That spaniel'd me at heels, to whom I gave
Their wishes, do discandy, melt their sweets
On blossoming Cæsar; and this pine is bark'd,
That overtopp'd them all. Betray'd I am.
O this false soul of Egypt! this grave charm,
Whose eye beck'd forth my wars and call'd them
    home,
Whose bosom was my crownet, my chief end,
Like a right gipsy hath at fast and loose
Beguiled me to the very heart of loss.
What, Eros, Eros!

Enter CLEOPATRA
              Ah, thou spell! Avaunt!

CLEOPATRA
Why is my lord enraged against his love?

ANTONY
Vanish, or I shall give thee thy deserving,
And blemish Cæsar's triumph. Let him take thee,
And hoist thee up to the shouting plebeians:
Follow his chariot, like the greatest spot
Of all thy sex: most monster-like, be shown
For poor'st diminutives, for doits; and let
Patient Octavia plough thy visage up
With her prepared nails.   [*Exit* CLEOPATRA
              'Tis well thou'rt gone,
If it be well to live; but better 'twere
Thou fell'st into my fury, for one death
Might have prevented many. Eros, ho!
The shirt of Nessus is upon me: teach me,
Alcides, thou mine ancestor, thy rage:
Let me lodge Lichas on the horns o' the moon,
And with those hands that grasp'd the heaviest club
Subdue my worthiest self. The witch shall die:
To the young Roman boy she hath sold me, and I
    fall
Under this plot: she dies for 't. Eros, ho!   [*Exit*

SCENE XIII. *Alexandria.* CLEOPATRA'S *palace*

Enter CLEOPATRA, CHARMIAN, IRAS, *and* MARDIAN
CLEOPATRA
Help me, my women! O, he is more mad
Than Telamon for his shield; the boar of Thessaly
Was never so emboss'd.

CHARMIAN
            To the monument!
There lock yourself, and send him word you are
    dead.
The soul and body rive not more in parting
Than greatness going off.

CLEOPATRA
            To the monument!
Mardian, go tell him I have slain myself;
Say that the last I spoke was 'Antony,'
And word it, prithee, piteously: hence, Mardian,
And bring me how he takes my death. To the
    monument!   [*Exeunt*

SCENE XIV. *The same. Another room*

Enter ANTONY *and* EROS
ANTONY
Eros, thou yet behold'st me?

EROS
              Ay, noble lord.

ANTONY
Sometime we see a cloud that's dragonish,
A vapour sometime like a bear or lion,
A tower'd citadel, a pendent rock,
A forked mountain, or blue promontory
With trees upon 't, that nod unto the world
And mock our eyes with air: thou hast seen these
    signs;
They are black vesper's pageants.

EROS
              Ay, my lord.

ANTONY
That which is now a horse, even with a thought
The rack dislimns and makes it indistinct
As water is in water.

EROS
           It does, my lord.

ANTONY
My good knave Eros, now thy captain is
Even such a body: here I am Antony,
Yet cannot hold this visible shape, my knave.
I made these wars for Egypt; and the queen—
Whose heart I thought I had, for she had mine,
Which, whilst it was mine, had annex'd unto 't
A million moe, now lost,—she, Eros, has
Pack'd cards with Cæsar, and false-play'd my glory
Unto an enemy's triumph.
Nay, weep not, gentle Eros; there is left us
Ourselves to end ourselves.

Enter MARDIAN
            O, thy vile lady!
She has robb'd me of my sword.

MARDIAN
             No, Antony;
My mistress loved thee, and her fortunes mingled
With thine entirely.

ANTONY
           Hence, saucy eunuch; peace!
She hath betray'd me, and shall die the death.

MARDIAN
Death of one person can be paid but once,
And that she has discharged: what thou wouldst do
Is done unto thy hand: the last she spake
Was 'Antony! most noble Antony!'
Then in the midst a tearing groan did break
The name of Antony; it was divided
Between her heart and lips: she render'd life,
Thy name so buried in her.

ANTONY
            Dead then?

MARDIAN
              Dead.

ANTONY
Unarm, Eros; the long day's task is done,
And we must sleep. [*To* MARDIAN] That thou depart'st hence safe,
Does pay thy labour richly; go. [*Exit* MARDIAN
Off, pluck off:
The seven-fold shield of Ajax cannot keep
The battery from my heart. O, cleave, my sides!
Heart, once be stronger than thy continent,
Crack thy frail case! Apace, Eros, apace!
No more a soldier. Bruised pieces, go;
You have been nobly borne. From me awhile. [*Exit* EROS
I will o'ertake thee, Cleopatra, and
Weep for my pardon. So it must be, for now
All length is torture: since the torch is out,
Lie down and stray no farther: now all labour
Mars what it does; yea, very force entangles
Itself with strength: seal then, and all is done.
Eros!—I come, my queen. Eros!—Stay for me:
Where souls do couch on flowers, we'll hand in hand,
And with our sprightly port make the ghosts gaze:
Dido and her Æneas shall want troops,
And all the haunt be ours. Come, Eros, Eros!
Re-enter EROS
EROS
What would my lord?
ANTONY
Since Cleopatra died
I have lived in such dishonour that the gods
Detest my baseness. I, that with my sword
Quarter'd the world, and o'er green Neptune's back
With ships made cities, condemn myself to lack
The courage of a woman; less noble mind
Than she which by her death our Cæsar tells
'I am conqueror of myself.' Thou art sworn, Eros,
That, when the exigent should come—which now
Is come indeed—when I should see behind me
The inevitable prosecution of
Disgrace and horror, that, on my command,
Thou then wouldst kill me: do 't; the time is come:
Thou strikest not me, 'tis Cæsar thou defeat'st.
Put colour in thy cheek.
EROS
The gods withhold me!
Shall I do that which all the Parthian darts,
Though enemy, lost aim and could not?
ANTONY
Eros,
Wouldst thou be window'd in great Rome, and see
Thy master thus with pleach'd arms, bending down
His corrigible neck, his face subdued
To penetrative shame, whilst the wheel'd seat
Of fortunate Cæsar, drawn before him, branded
His baseness that ensued?
EROS
I would not see 't.
ANTONY
Come, then; for with a wound I must be cured.

Draw that thy honest sword, which thou hast worn
Most useful for thy country.
EROS
O, sir, pardon me!
ANTONY
When I did make thee free, sworest thou not then
To do this when I bade thee? Do it at once;
Or thy precedent services are all
But accidents unpurposed. Draw, and come.
EROS
Turn from me then that noble countenance,
Wherein the worship of the whole world lies.
ANTONY
Lo thee! [*Turning from him*
EROS
My sword is drawn.
ANTONY
Then let it do at once
The thing why thou hast drawn it.
EROS
My dear master,
My captain, and my emperor, let me say,
Before I strike this bloody stroke, farewell.
ANTONY
'Tis said, man; and farewell.
EROS
Farewell, great chief. Shall I strike now?
ANTONY
Now, Eros.
EROS
Why, there then: thus I do escape the sorrow
Of Antony's death. [*Kills himself*
ANTONY
Thrice-nobler than myself!
Thou teachest me, O valiant Eros, what
I should and thou couldst not. My queen and Eros
Have by their brave instruction got upon me
A nobleness in record: but I will be
A bridegroom in my death, and run into 't
As to a lover's bed. Come then; and, Eros,
Thy master dies thy scholar: to do thus
[*Falling on his sword*
I learn'd of thee. How! not dead? not dead?
The guard, ho! O, dispatch me!
Enter DERCETAS *and* GUARD
FIRST GUARD
What's the noise?
ANTONY
I have done my work ill, friends: O, make an end
Of what I have begun.
SECOND GUARD
The star is fall'n.
FIRST GUARD
And time is at his period.
ALL
Alas, and woe!
ANTONY
Let him that loves me strike me dead.
FIRST GUARD
Not I.

SECOND GUARD

Nor I.

THIRD GUARD

Nor any one.   [*Exeunt* GUARD

DERCETAS

Thy death and fortunes bid thy followers fly.
This sword but shown to Cæsar, with this tidings,
Shall enter me with him.

Enter DIOMEDES

DIOMEDES

Where's Antony?

DERCETAS

           There, Diomed, there.

DIOMEDES

                  Lives he?
Wilt thou not answer, man?   [*Exit* DERCETAS

ANTONY

Art thou there, Diomed? Draw thy sword, and give
me
Sufficing strokes for death.

DIOMEDES

           Most absolute lord,
My mistress Cleopatra sent me to thee.

ANTONY

When did she send thee?

DIOMEDES

             Now, my lord.

ANTONY

                Where is she?

DIOMEDES

Lock'd in her monument. She had a prophesying
fear
Of what hath come to pass: for when she saw—
Which never shall be found—you did suspect
She had disposed with Cæsar, and that your rage
Would not be purged, she sent you word she was
dead;
But, fearing since how it might work, hath sent
Me to proclaim the truth; and I am come,
I dread, too late.

ANTONY

Too late, good Diomed: call my guard, I prithee.

DIOMEDES

What, ho, the emperor's guard! The guard, what,
ho!
Come, your lord calls.

Enter four or five of the GUARD *of* ANTONY

ANTONY

Bear me, good friends, where Cleopatra bides;
'Tis the last service that I shall command you.

FIRST GUARD

Woe, woe are we, sir, you may not live to wear
All your true followers out.

ALL

           Most heavy day!

ANTONY

Nay, good my fellows, do not please sharp fate
To grace it with your sorrows: bid that welcome
Which comes to punish us, and we punish it
Seeming to bear it lightly. Take me up:

I have led you oft: carry me now, good friends,
And have my thanks for all.   [*Exeunt, bearing* ANTONY

SCENE XV. *The same. A monument*

Enter CLEOPATRA, *and her maids aloft, with* CHARMIAN,
and IRAS

CLEOPATRA

O Charmian, I will never go from hence.

CHARMIAN

Be comforted, dear madam.

CLEOPATRA

                No, I will not:
All strange and terrible events are welcome,
But comforts we despise; our size of sorrow,
Proportion'd to our cause, must be as great
As that which makes it.

Enter, below, DIOMEDES

                How now! is he dead?

DIOMEDES

His death's upon him, but not dead.
Look out o' the other side your monument;
His guard have brought him thither.

Enter, below, ANTONY, *borne by the* GUARD

CLEOPATRA

                O sun,
Burn the great sphere thou movest in! darkling
stand
The varying shore o' the world. O Antony,
Antony, Antony! Help, Charmian, help, Iras, help;
Help, friends below; let's draw him hither.

ANTONY

                  Peace!
Not Cæsar's valour hath o'erthrown Antony,
But Antony's hath triumph'd on itself.

CLEOPATRA

So it should be, that none but Antony
Should conquer Antony; but woe 'tis so!

ANTONY

I am dying, Egypt, dying; only
I here importune death awhile, until
Of many thousand kisses the poor last
I lay upon thy lips.

CLEOPATRA

             I dare not, dear,
Dear my lord, pardon, I dare not,
Lest I be taken: not the imperious show
Of the full-fortuned Cæsar ever shall
Be brooch'd with me; if knife, drugs, serpents, have
Edge, sting, or operation, I am safe:
Your wife Octavia, with her modest eyes
And still conclusion, shall acquire no honour
Demuring upon me. But come, come, Antony,—
Help me, my women,—we must draw thee up;
Assist, good friends.

ANTONY

           O, quick, or I am gone.

CLEOPATRA

Here's sport indeed! How heavy weighs my lord!

Our strength is all gone into heaviness;
That makes the weight. Had I great Juno's power,
The strong-wing'd Mercury should fetch thee up
And set thee by Jove's side. Yet come a little—
Wishers were ever fools—O, come, come, come;
          [*They heave* ANTONY *aloft to* CLEOPATRA
And welcome, welcome! die where thou hast lived:
Quicken with kissing: had my lips that power,
Thus would I wear them out.

ALL

A heavy sight!

ANTONY

I am dying, Egypt, dying:
Give me some wine, and let me speak a little.

CLEOPATRA

No, let me speak, and let me rail so high,
That the false housewife Fortune break her wheel,
Provoked by my offence.

ANTONY

One word, sweet queen:
Of Cæsar seek your honour, with your safety. O!

CLEOPATRA

They do not go together.

ANTONY

Gentle, hear me:
None about Cæsar trust but Proculeius.

CLEOPATRA

My resolution and my hands I'll trust;
None about Cæsar.

ANTONY

The miserable change now at my end
Lament nor sorrow at, but please your thoughts
In feeding them with those my former fortunes
Wherein I lived, the greatest prince o' the world,
The noblest, and do now not basely die,
Not cowardly put off my helmet to
My countryman, a Roman by a Roman
Valiantly vanquish'd. Now my spirit is going;
I can no more.

CLEOPATRA

Noblest of men, woo't die?
Hast thou no care of me? shall I abide
In this dull world, which in thy absence is
No better than a sty? O, see, my women,
          [ANTONY *dies*
The crown o' the earth doth melt. My lord!
O, wither'd is the garland of the war,
The soldier's pole is fall'n: young boys and girls
Are level now with men; the odds is gone,
And there is nothing left remarkable
Beneath the visiting moon.   [*Faints*

CHARMIAN

O, quietness, lady!

IRAS

She's dead too, our sovereign.

CHARMIAN

Lady!

IRAS

Madam!

CHARMIAN

O madam, madam, madam!

IRAS

Royal Egypt, Empress!

CHARMIAN

Peace, peace, Iras!

CLEOPATRA

No more, but e'en a woman, and commanded
By such poor passion as the maid that milks
And does the meanest chares. It were for me
To throw my sceptre at the injurious gods,
To tell them that this world did equal theirs
Till they had stol'n our jewel. All's but naught;
Patience is sottish, and impatience does
Become a dog that's mad: then is it sin
To rush into the secret house of death,
Ere death dare come to us? How do you, women?
What, what! good cheer! Why, how now, Charmian!
My noble girls! Ah, women, women, look,
Our lamp is spent, it's out! Good sirs, take heart:
We'll bury him; and then, what's brave, what's
    noble,
Let's do it after the high Roman fashion,
And make death proud to take us. Come, away:
This case of that huge spirit now is cold:
Ah, women, women! Come; we have no friend
But resolution and the briefest end.
      [*Exeunt: those above bearing off* ANTONY's *body*

ACT V

Scene I. *Alexandria.* CÆSAR's *camp*

Enter CÆSAR, AGRIPPA, DOLABELLA, MÆCENAS,
GALLUS, PROCULEIUS, *and others, his council of war*

CÆSAR

Go to him, Dolabella, bid him yield;
Being so frustrate, tell him he mocks
The pauses that he makes.

DOLABELLA

Cæsar, I shall.   [*Exit*
Enter DERCETAS, *with the sword of* ANTONY

CÆSAR

Wherefore is that? and what art thou that darest
Appear thus to us?

DERCETAS

I am call'd Dercetas;
Mark Antony I served, who best was worthy
Best to be served: whilst he stood up and spoke,
He was my master, and I wore my life
To spend upon his haters. If thou please
To take me to thee, as I was to him
I'll be to Cæsar; if thou pleasest not,
I yield thee up my life.

CÆSAR

What is 't thou say'st?

DERCETAS

I say, O Cæsar, Antony is dead.

CÆSAR

The breaking of so great a thing should make
A greater crack: the round world
Should have shook lions into civil streets,
And citizens to their dens. The death of Antony
Is not a single doom; in the name lay
A moiety of the world.

DERCETAS

                    He is dead, Cæsar;
Not by a public minister of justice,
Nor by a hired knife; but that self hand,
Which writ his honour in the acts it did,
Hath, with the courage which the heart did lend it,
Splitted the heart. This is his sword;
I robb'd his wound of it; behold it stain'd
With his most noble blood.

CÆSAR

                    Look you sad, friends?
The gods rebuke me, but it is tidings
To wash the eyes of kings.

AGRIPPA

                    And strange it is
That nature must compel us to lament
Our most persisted deeds.

MÆCENAS

                    His taints and honours
Waged equal with him.

AGRIPPA

                    A rarer spirit never
Did steer humanity: but you, gods, will give us
Some faults to make us men. Cæsar is touch'd.

MÆCENAS

When such a spacious mirror's set before him,
He needs must see himself.

CÆSAR

                    O Antony!
I have follow'd thee to this. But we do lance
Diseases in our bodies: I must perforce
Have shown to thee such a declining day,
Or look on thine; we could not stall together
In the whole world: but yet let me lament,
With tears as sovereign as the blood of hearts,
That thou, my brother, my competitor
In top of all design, my mate in empire,
Friend and companion in the front of war,
The arm of mine own body and the heart
Where mine his thoughts did kindle, that our stars
Unreconciliable should divide
Our equalness to this. Hear me, good friends,—

Enter an EGYPTIAN

But I will tell you at some meeter season:
The business of this man looks out of him;
We'll hear him what he says. Whence are you?

EGYPTIAN

A poor Egyptian yet. The queen my mistress,
Confined in all she has, her monument,
Of thy intents desires instruction,
That she preparedly may frame herself
To the way she's forced to.

CÆSAR

                    Bid her have good heart:
She soon shall know of us, by some of ours,
How honourable and how kindly we
Determine for her; for Cæsar cannot live
To be ungentle.

EGYPTIAN

                    So the gods preserve thee!   [*Exit*

CÆSAR

Come hither, Proculeius. Go and say,
We purpose her no shame: give her what comforts
The quality of her passion shall require,
Lest in her greatness by some mortal stroke
She do defeat us; for her life in Rome
Would be eternal in our triumph: go,
And with your speediest bring us what she says
And how you find of her.

PROCULEIUS

                    Cæsar, I shall.   [*Exit*

CÆSAR

Gallus, go you along. [*Exit* GALLUS] Where's Dolabella,
To second Proculeius?

ALL

                    Dolabella!

CÆSAR

Let him alone, for I remember now
How he's employ'd: he shall in time be ready.
Go with me to my tent; where you shall see
How hardly I was drawn into this war;
How calm and gentle I proceeded still
In all my writings: go with me, and see
What I can show in this.   [*Exeunt*

SCENE II. *Alexandria. The monument*

Enter CLEOPATRA, CHARMIAN, *and* IRAS

CLEOPATRA

My desolation does begin to make
A better life. 'Tis paltry to be Cæsar;
Not being Fortune, he's but Fortune's knave,
A minister of her will: and it is great
To do that thing that ends all other deeds;
Which shackles accidents and bolts up change;
Which sleeps, and never palates more the dug,
The beggar's nurse and Cæsar's.

Enter, to the gates of the monument, PROCULEIUS,
GALLUS, *and* SOLDIERS

PROCULEIUS

Cæsar sends greeting to the Queen of Egypt,
And bids thee study on what fair demands
Thou mean'st to have him grant thee.

CLEOPATRA

                    What's thy name?

PROCULEIUS

My name is Proculeius.

CLEOPATRA

                    Antony
Did tell me of you, bade me trust you, but

I do not greatly care to be deceived,
That have no use for trusting. If your master
Would have a queen his beggar, you must tell him,
That majesty, to keep decorum, must
No less beg than a kingdom: if he please
To give me conquer'd Egypt for my son,
He gives me so much of mine own as I
Will kneel to him with thanks.

PROCULEIUS
                                   Be of good cheer;
You're fall'n into a princely hand; fear nothing:
Make your full reference freely to my lord,
Who is so full of grace that it flows over
On all that need. Let me report to him
Your sweet dependency, and you shall find
A conqueror that will pray in aid for kindness,
Where he for grace is kneel'd to.

CLEOPATRA
                                   Pray you, tell him
I am his fortune's vassal and I send him
The greatness he has got. I hourly learn
A doctrine of obedience, and would gladly
Look him i' the face.

PROCULEIUS
             This I'll report, dear lady.
Have comfort, for I know your plight is pitied
Of him that caused it.

GALLUS
You see how easily she may be surprised.
[*Here* PROCULEIUS *and two of the* GUARD *ascend the
monument by a ladder placed against a window, and,
having descended, come behind* CLEOPATRA. *Some of the*
                              GUARD *unbar and open the gates*
Guard her till Cæsar come.   [*Exit*

IRAS
Royal queen!

CHARMIAN
O Cleopatra! thou art taken, queen!

CLEOPATRA
Quick, quick, good hands.   [*Drawing a dagger*

PROCULEIUS
                         Hold, worthy lady, hold:
                            [*Seizes and disarms her*
Do not yourself such wrong, who are in this
Relieved, but not betray'd.

CLEOPATRA
                         What, of death too,
That rids our dogs of languish?

PROCULEIUS
                         Cleopatra,
Do not abuse my master's bounty by
The undoing of yourself: let the world see
His nobleness well acted, which your death
Will never let come forth.

CLEOPATRA
                         Where art thou, death?
Come hither, come! come, come, and take a queen
Worth many babes and beggars!

PROCULEIUS
                         O, temperance, lady!

CLEOPATRA
Sir, I will eat no meat, I'll not drink, sir;
If idle talk will once be necessary,
I'll not sleep neither: this mortal house I'll ruin,
Do Cæsar what he can. Know, sir, that I
Will not wait pinion'd at your master's court,
Nor once be chastised with the sober eye
Of dull Octavia. Shall they hoist me up
And show me to the shouting varletry
Of censuring Rome? Rather a ditch in Egypt
Be gentle grave unto me! rather on Nilus' mud
Lay me stark naked, and let the water-flies
Blow me into abhorring! rather make
My country's high pyramides my gibbet,
And hang me up in chains!

PROCULEIUS
                         You do extend
These thoughts of horror further than you shall
Find cause in Cæsar.

                    Enter DOLABELLA

DOLABELLA
                         Proculeius,
What thou hast done thy master Cæsar knows,
And he hath sent for thee: for the queen,
I'll take her to my guard.

PROCULEIUS
                         So, Dolabella,
It shall content me best: be gentle to her.
[*To* CLEOPATRA] To Cæsar I will speak what you
    shall please,
If you'll employ me to him.

CLEOPATRA
                         Say, I would die.
                    [*Exeunt* PROCULEIUS *and* SOLDIERS

DOLABELLA
Most noble empress, you have heard of me?

CLEOPATRA
I cannot tell.

DOLABELLA
             Assuredly you know me.

CLEOPATRA
No matter, sir, what I have heard or known.
You laugh when boys or women tell their dreams;
Is 't not your trick?

DOLABELLA
             I understand not, madam.

CLEOPATRA
I dream'd there was an emperor Antony:
O, such another sleep, that I might see
But such another man!

DOLABELLA
                         If it might please ye,—

CLEOPATRA
His face was as the heavens: and therein stuck
A sun and moon, which kept their course and lighted
The little O, the earth.

DOLABELLA
                         Most sovereign creature,—

CLEOPATRA
His legs bestrid the ocean: his rear'd arm

Crested the world: his voice was propertied
As all the tuned spheres, and that to friends;
But when he meant to quail and shake the orb,
He was as rattling thunder. For his bounty,
There was no winter in 't; an autumn 'twas
That grew the more by reaping: his delights
Were dolphin-like; they show'd his back above
The element they lived in: in his livery
Walk'd crowns and crownets; realms and islands
    were
As plates dropp'd from his pocket.

DOLABELLA
              Cleopatra,—

CLEOPATRA
Think you there was, or might be, such a man
As this I dream'd of?

DOLABELLA
      Gentle madam, no.

CLEOPATRA
You lie, up to the hearing of the gods.
But if there be, or ever were, one such,
It's past the size of dreaming: nature wants stuff
To vie strange forms with fancy; yet to imagine
An Antony, were nature's piece 'gainst fancy,
Condemning shadows quite.

DOLABELLA
           Hear me, good madam.
Your loss is as yourself, great; and you bear it
As answering to the weight: would I might never
O'ertake pursued success, but I do feel,
By the rebound of yours, a grief that smites
My very heart at root.

CLEOPATRA
        I thank you, sir.
Know you what Cæsar means to do with me?

DOLABELLA
I am loath to tell you what I would you knew.

CLEOPATRA
Nay, pray you, sir,—

DOLABELLA
       Though he be honourable,—

CLEOPATRA
He'll lead me then in triumph?

DOLABELLA
Madam, he will; I know 't.
[*Flourish and shout within:* 'Make way there: Cæsar!'
Enter CÆSAR, GALLUS, PROCULEIUS, MÆCENAS,
    SELEUCUS, *and others of his train*

CÆSAR
Which is the Queen of Egypt?

DOLABELLA
It is the emperor, madam.   [CLEOPATRA *kneels*

CÆSAR
Arise, you shall not kneel:
I pray you, rise; rise, Egypt.

CLEOPATRA
          Sir, the gods
Will have it thus; my master and my lord
I must obey.

CÆSAR
       Take to you no hard thoughts:
The record of what injuries you did us,
Though written in our flesh, we shall remember
As things but done by chance.

CLEOPATRA
           Sole sir o' the world,
I cannot project mine own cause so well
To make it clear; but do confess I have
Been laden with like frailties which before
Have often shamed our sex.

CÆSAR
         Cleopatra, know,
We will extenuate rather than enforce:
If you apply yourself to our intents,
Which towards you are most gentle, you shall find
A benefit in this change; but if you seek
To lay on me a cruelty by taking
Antony's course, you shall bereave yourself
Of my good purposes and put your children
To that destruction which I'll guard them from
If thereon you rely. I'll take my leave.

CLEOPATRA
And may, through all the world: 'tis yours; and we,
Your scutcheons and your signs of conquest, shall
Hang in what place you please. Here, my good lord.

CÆSAR
You shall advise me in all for Cleopatra.

CLEOPATRA
This is the brief of money, plate and jewels,
I am possess'd of: 'tis exactly valued,
Not petty things admitted. Where's Seleucus?

SELEUCUS
Here, madam.

CLEOPATRA
This is my treasurer: let him speak, my lord,
Upon his peril, that I have reserved
To myself nothing. Speak the truth, Seleucus.

SELEUCUS
Madam,
I had rather seal my lips than to my peril
Speak that which is not.

CLEOPATRA
       What have I kept back?

SELEUCUS
Enough to purchase what you have made known.

CÆSAR
Nay, blush not, Cleopatra; I approve
Your wisdom in the deed.

CLEOPATRA
        See, Cæsar! O, behold,
How pomp is follow'd! mine will now be yours,
And, should we shift estates, yours would be mine.
The ingratitude of this Seleucus does
Even make me wild. O slave, of no more trust
Than love that's hired! What, goest thou back? thou
    shalt
Go back, I warrant thee; but I'll catch thine eyes,
Though they had wings: slave, soulless villain, dog!
O rarely base!

CÆSAR

Good queen, let us entreat you.

CLEOPATRA

O Cæsar, what a wounding shame is this,
That thou vouchsafing here to visit me,
Doing the honour of thy lordliness
To one so meek, that mine own servant should
Parcel the sum of my disgraces by
Addition of his envy! Say, good Cæsar,
That I some lady trifles have reserved,
Immoment toys, things of such dignity
As we greet modern friends withal; and say,
Some nobler token I have kept apart
For Livia and Octavia, to induce
Their mediation; must I be unfolded
With one that I have bred? The gods! it smites me
Beneath the fall I have. [To SELEUCUS] Prithee, go
    hence;
Or I shall show the cinders of my spirits
Through the ashes of my chance: wert thou a man,
Thou wouldst have mercy on me.

CÆSAR

                    Forbear, Seleucus.
                    [Exit SELEUCUS

CLEOPATRA

Be it known, that we, the greatest, are misthought
For things that others do, and when we fall,
We answer others' merits in our name,
Are therefore to be pitied.

CÆSAR

                    Cleopatra,
Not what you have reserved, nor what acknowl-
    edged,
Put we i' the roll of conquest: still be 't yours,
Bestow it at your pleasure, and believe
Cæsar's no merchant, to make prize with you
Of things that merchants sold. Therefore be cheer'd;
Make not your thoughts your prisons: no, dear
    queen;
For we intend so to dispose you as
Yourself shall give us counsel. Feed, and sleep:
Our care and pity is so much upon you
That we remain your friend; and so, adieu.

CLEOPATRA

My master, and my lord!

CÆSAR

                    Not so. Adieu.
[Flourish. Exeunt CÆSAR and his train

CLEOPATRA

He words me, girls, he words me, that I should not
Be noble to myself: but, hark thee, Charmian.
                    [Whispers CHARMIAN

IRAS

Finish, good lady; the bright day is done,
And we are for the dark.

CLEOPATRA

                    Hie thee again:
I have spoke already, and it is provided;
Go put it to the haste.

CHARMIAN

Madam, I will.
Re-enter DOLABELLA

DOLABELLA

Where is the queen?

CHARMIAN

Behold, sir.   [Exit

CLEOPATRA

                    Dolabella!

DOLABELLA

Madam, as thereto sworn by your command,
Which my love makes religion to obey,
I tell you this: Cæsar through Syria
Intends his journey, and within three days
You with your children will he send before:
Make your best use of this: I have perform'd
Your pleasure and my promise.

CLEOPATRA

                    Dolabella,
I shall remain your debtor.

DOLABELLA

                    I your servant.
Adieu, good queen; I must attend on Cæsar.

CLEOPATRA

Farewell, and thanks.   [Exit DOLABELLA
                    Now, Iras, what think'st thou?
Thou, an Egyptian puppet, shalt be shown
In Rome, as well as I: mechanic slaves
With greasy aprons, rules and hammers, shall
Uplift us to the view: in their thick breaths,
Rank of gross diet, shall we be enclouded
And forced to drink their vapour.

IRAS

                    The gods forbid!

CLEOPATRA

Nay, 'tis most certain, Iras: saucy lictors
Will catch at us like strumpets, and scald rhymers
Ballad us out o' tune: the quick comedians
Extemporally will stage us and present
Our Alexandrian revels; Antony
Shall be brought drunken forth, and I shall see
Some squeaking Cleopatra boy my greatness
I' the posture of a whore.

IRAS

                    O the good gods!

CLEOPATRA

Nay, that's certain.

IRAS

I'll never see 't; for I am sure my nails
Are stronger than mine eyes.

CLEOPATRA

                    Why, that's the way
To fool their preparation, and to conquer
Their most absurd intents.
                    Re-enter CHARMIAN
                    Now, Charmian!
Show me, my women, like a queen: go fetch
My best attires: I am again for Cydnus,
To meet Mark Antony: sirrah Iras, go.
Now, noble Charmian, we'll dispatch indeed,

And when thou hast done this chare I'll give thee
    leave
To play till doomsday. Bring our crown and all.
                      [Exit IRAS. *A noise within*
Wherefore's this noise?
             Enter a GUARDSMAN

GUARDSMAN
           Here is a rural fellow
That will not be denied your highness' presence:
He brings you figs.

CLEOPATRA

Let him come in.   *[Exit* GUARDSMAN
        What poor an instrument
May do a noble deed! he brings me liberty.
My resolution's placed, and I have nothing
Of woman in me: now from head to foot
I am marble-constant; now the fleeting moon
No planet is of mine.
Re-enter GUARDSMAN, *with* CLOWN *bringing in a basket*

GUARDSMAN
        This is the man.

CLEOPATRA

Avoid, and leave him.   *[Exit* GUARDSMAN
Hast thou the pretty worm of Nilus there,
That kills and pains not?

CLOWN

Truly, I have him: but I would not be the party
that should desire you to touch him, for his biting
is immortal; those that do die of it do seldom or
never recover.

CLEOPATRA

Rememberest thou any that have died on 't?

CLOWN

Very many, men and women too. I heard of one of
them no longer than yesterday: a very honest
woman, but something given to lie; as a woman
should not do, but in the way of honesty: how she
died of the biting of it, what pain she felt: truly, she
makes a very good report o' the worm; but he that
will believe all that they say, shall never be saved
by half that they do: but this is most fallible, the
worm's an odd worm.

CLEOPATRA

Get thee hence; farewell.

CLOWN

I wish you all joy of the worm.
                   [Setting down his basket

CLEOPATRA

Farewell.

CLOWN

You must think this, look you, that the worm will
do his kind.

CLEOPATRA

Ay, ay; farewell.

CLOWN

Look you, the worm is not to be trusted but in the
keeping of wise people, for indeed there is no goodness in the worm.

CLEOPATRA

Take thou no care; it shall be heeded.

CLOWN

Very good. Give it nothing, I pray you, for it is not
worth the feeding.

CLEOPATRA

Will it eat me?

CLOWN

You must not think I am so simple but I know the
devil himself will not eat a woman: I know that a
woman is a dish for the gods, if the devil dress her
not. But, truly, these same whoreson devils do the
gods great harm in their women; for in every ten
that they make, the devils mar five.

CLEOPATRA

Well, get thee gone; farewell.

CLOWN

Yes, forsooth: I wish you joy o' the worm.   *[Exit*
    Re-enter IRAS *with a robe, crown, &c.*

CLEOPATRA

Give me my robe, put on my crown; I have
Immortal longings in me: now no more
The juice of Egypt's grape shall moist this lip:
Yare, yare, good Iras; quick. Methinks I hear
Antony call; I see him rouse himself
To praise my noble act; I hear him mock
The luck of Cæsar, which the gods give men
To excuse their after wrath. Husband, I come:
Now to that name my courage prove my title!
I am fire and air; my other elements
I give to baser life. So; have you done?
Come then and take the last warmth of my lips.
Farewell, kind Charmian; Iras, long farewell.
          [Kisses them. IRAS *falls and dies*
Have I the aspic in my lips? Dost fall?
If thou and nature can so gently part,
The stroke of death is as a lover's pinch,
Which hurts, and is desired. Dost thou lie still?
If thus thou vanishest, thou tell'st the world
It is not worth leave-taking.

CHARMIAN

Dissolve, thick cloud, and rain, that I may say
The gods themselves do weep!

CLEOPATRA
              This proves me base:
If she first meet the curled Antony,
He'll make demand of her, and spend that kiss
Which is my heaven to have. Come, thou mortal
    wretch,
     [To an asp, which she applies to her breast
With thy sharp teeth this knot intrinsicate
Of life at once untie: poor venomous fool,
Be angry, and dispatch. O, couldst thou speak,
That I might hear thee call great Cæsar ass
Unpolicied!

CHARMIAN
        O eastern star!

CLEOPATRA
              Peace, peace!
Dost thou not see my baby at my breast,
That sucks the nurse asleep?

CHARMIAN
                O, break! O, break!

CLEOPATRA
As sweet as balm, as soft as air, as gentle,—
O Antony!—Nay, I will take thee too:
            [Applying another asp to her arm
What should I stay—   [Dies

CHARMIAN
In this vile world? So, fare thee well.
Now boast thee, death, in thy possession lies
A lass unparallel'd. Downy windows, close;
And golden Phœbus never be beheld
Of eyes again so royal! Your crown's awry;
I'll mend it, and then play.
            Enter the GUARD, rushing in

FIRST GUARD
Where is the queen?

CHARMIAN
                Speak softly, wake her not.

FIRST GUARD
Cæsar hath sent—

CHARMIAN
                Too slow a messenger.
                        [Applies an asp
O, come apace, dispatch: I partly feel thee.

FIRST GUARD
Approach, ho! All's not well: Cæsar's beguiled.

SECOND GUARD
There's Dolabella sent from Cæsar; call him.

FIRST GUARD
What work is here! Charmian, is this well done?

CHARMIAN
It is well done, and fitting for a princess
Descended of so many royal kings.
Ah, soldier!   [Dies
            Re-enter DOLABELLA

DOLABELLA
How goes it here?

SECOND GUARD
All dead.

DOLABELLA
                Cæsar, thy thoughts
Touch their effects in this: thyself art coming
To see perform'd the dreaded act which thou
So sought'st to hinder.
        [Within. 'A way there, a way for Cæsar!'
        Re-enter CÆSAR and his train

DOLABELLA
O sir, you are too sure an augurer;
That you did fear is done.

CÆSAR
                Bravest at the last,
She levell'd at our purposes, and being royal
Took her own way. The manner of their deaths?
I do not see them bleed.

DOLABELLA
                Who was last with them?

FIRST GUARD
A simple countryman, that brought her figs:
This was his basket.

CÆSAR
                Poison'd then.

FIRST GUARD
                        O Cæsar,
This Charmian lived but now; she stood and spake:
I found her trimming up the diadem
On her dead mistress; tremblingly she stood,
And on the sudden dropp'd.

CÆSAR
                O noble weakness!
If they had swallow'd poison, 'twould appear
By external swelling: but she looks like sleep,
As she would catch another Antony
In her strong toil of grace.

DOLABELLA
                Here, on her breast,
There is a vent of blood, and something blown:
The like is on her arm.

FIRST GUARD
This is an aspic's trail: and these fig-leaves
Have slime upon them, such as the aspic leaves
Upon the caves of Nile.

CÆSAR
                Most probable
That so she died; for her physician tells me
She hath pursued conclusions infinite
Of easy ways to die. Take up her bed,
And bear her women from the monument:
She shall be buried by her Antony:
No grave upon the earth shall clip in it
A pair so famous. High events as these
Strike those that make them; and their story is
No less in pity than his glory which
Brought them to be lamented. Our army shall
In solemn show attend this funeral,
And then to Rome. Come, Dolabella, see
High order in this great solemnity.   [Exeunt

THE TRAGEDY OF CORIOLANUS

SYNOPSIS

Haughty, aristocratic, passionately self-willed, the Roman general, Caius Marcius, beloved of the patricians, hated by the plebeians, is a dauntless soldier whom his heroic mother, Volumnia, had sent to the wars as a stripling of sixteen years to drive back the proud Tarquin and win his first oaken garland for daring and bravery.

Just now military services are forgotten in Rome, for it is a time of famine, and the common people are clamoring for corn at their own prices and rebelling against the patrician senate, in which they are finally granted several tribunes, two of whom, Brutus and Sicinius, hate Marcius for his contemptuous attitude toward the masses. The old Menenius Agrippa reasons in his kindly, humorous way with the hostile mobs that throng the streets, but when Marcius appears he lectures them for their presumption and with brutal insolence orders them home. As he had predicted, Rome's enemies, the Volsces, are arming under his great military rival, Tullus Aufidius, and when the news is brought to the city he willingly accepts a subordinate command under the older generals, Cominius and Titus Lartius, who rely upon him for initiative and daring.

During the siege of Corioli, the Romans at first are beaten back to their trenches, but Marcius, cursing and rallying his troops in the same breath, turns the tide of battle, and as he pursues the flying Volsces he follows them alone through their gates which close behind him. When his amazed men see him emerge, bleeding but battling with incredible heroism, they rush forward with Lartius and capture the city, while Marcius moves swiftly to the aid of Cominius who is hard pressed, and a complete Roman victory is the result.

Although he cannot endure praise, and scorns any share in the spoils, Marcius is forced by his enthusiastic army to accept the oaken garland and the title of "Coriolanus," and upon his triumphant return to Rome the Senate nominates him as Consul. His friend Menenius persuades the haughty, reserved man to yield to the old Roman custom requiring the candidate to wear a gown signifying humility, stand bareheaded in the Forum, expose his wounds, and sue for the people's votes, and, in spite of his repellent manner, he gains the desired support.

Brutus and Sicinius, however, remind the citizens of his unconcealed contempt, easily convince them that they would lose their liberties under Coriolanus' rule as Consul, and while he is changing his robe they fan the mob's dislike to open hatred which is lashed into a fury when their candidate, in disdain of their fickleness, openly and obstinately derides the civic rights of the plebeian class. Denounced as a traitor, Coriolanus is saved from death by his powerful friends, who promise the incensed citizens to bring him to the market-place for public trial. Coriolanus remains obdurate until his proud patrician mother prevails upon him to stoop to tact and flattery at his hearing. But the tribunes trump up false and malicious accusations before which Coriolanus throws prudence to the winds, giving full vent to his passionate rage, and is banished from the city.

Stung by the ingratitude of the people for his military services and the desertion of the nobles, Coriolanus renounces in angry egoism his principles, his party, and his native city, and in his deadly need for revenge seeks out his old enemy, the Volscian general, Tullus Aufidius, at Antium. Astounded at Rome's lack of appreciation of its great soldier, Aufidius accepts his terms of peace and makes him his equal in command, but when he realizes how his own prestige is being undermined by Coriolanus' popularity with the Volscian troops he treacherously plots the overthrow of his former rival. When the army reaches the gates of Rome, Cominius and Menenius go out to plead for their helpless city, but Coriolanus, inflexible and relentless, turns away from all entreaties.

As the frenzied citizens threaten with death the tribunes who banished Coriolanus, his indomitable mother Volumnia, his lovely gentle wife Virgilia, and his little son Marcius, intercede on their knees before the beloved exile, and, vowing to block his way into Rome with their dead bodies, turn him from his ruthless purpose, save his soul from disgrace and his city from destruction. Relying upon Aufidius, who has witnessed the meeting, to exonerate him before the Volscian authorities, Coriolanus withdraws the troops and returns to Antium, but his fellow general denounces him to the lords of the city as a traitor who has defrauded the Volsces of victory.

Notwithstanding the angry confusion that results, his conduct before Rome is about to be judicially inquired into at Antium, but there is one last flare of an ungovernable temper, one last threat, and Coriolanus' tall, arrogant figure crumples up at the point of a conspirator's dagger. Aufidius, suddenly stricken with sorrow, orders him buried with full military honors.

HISTORICAL DATA

The source of this play is again Plutarch's *Lives* in the translation by Sir Thomas North. Shakespeare followed many of the episodes closely as they appeared in the *Life of Caius Marcius Coriolanus*. In many places the actual wording of North's translation is followed for many lines at a time with only the barest revision for metrical effect. As usual, Shakespeare made some additions—in this case, the comedy episodes and the development of the characters of Virgilia and Menenius.

There is very little evidence to establish the date of composition of the play. Internal evidences of meter and style point very definitely to its being a product of the playwright's mature years and it is generally accredited to a date about 1609–10. It appeared for the first time in the First Folio in 1623.

"*The sorrow that delivers us thus chang'd—*"
CORIOLANUS

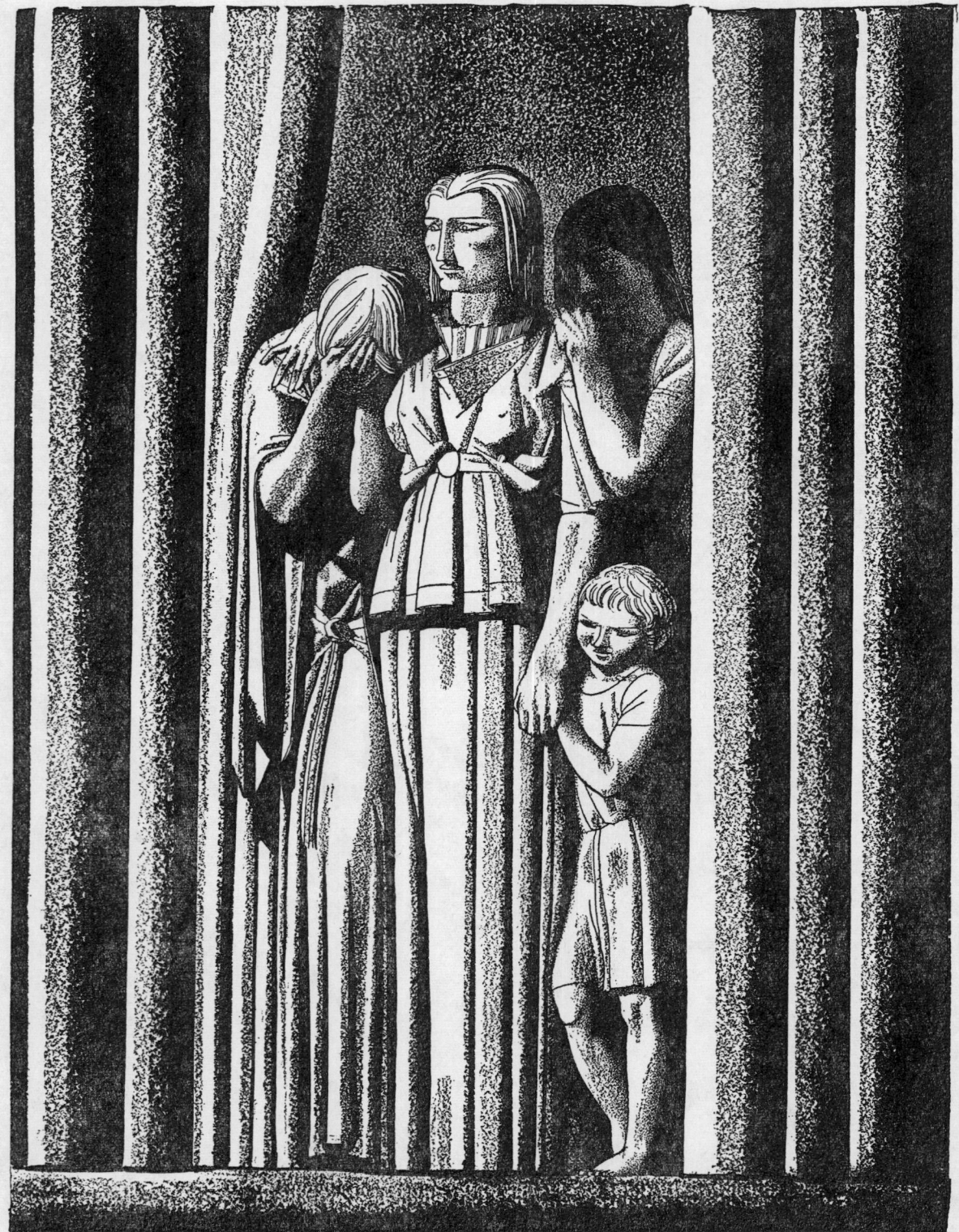

THE TRAGEDY OF CORIOLANUS

DRAMATIS PERSONÆ

CAIUS MARCIUS, *afterwards* CAIUS MARCIUS CORI-
  OLANUS.
TITUS LARTIUS,⎫ *generals against the Volscians.*
COMINIUS,⎭
MENENIUS AGRIPPA, *friend to Coriolanus.*
SICINIUS VELUTUS,⎫ *tribunes of the people.*
JUNIUS BRUTUS,⎭
YOUNG MARCIUS, *son of Coriolanus.*
A ROMAN HERALD.
TULLUS AUFIDIUS, *general of the Volscians.*
LIEUTENANT *to Aufidius.*
CONSPIRATORS *with Aufidius.*
A CITIZEN *of Antium.*
TWO VOLSCIAN GUARDS.

VOLUMNIA, *mother to Coriolanus.*
VIRGILIA, *wife to Coriolanus.*
VALERIA, *friend to Virgilia.*
GENTLEWOMAN *attending on Virgilia.*

ROMAN *and* VOLSCIAN SENATORS, PATRICIANS,
  ÆDILES, LICTORS, SOLDIERS, CITIZENS, MES-
  SENGERS, SERVANTS *to Aufidius, and other*
  ATTENDANTS.

SCENE—*Rome and the neighbourhood; Corioli and
  the neighbourhood; Antium.*

ACT I
SCENE I. *Rome. A street*

Enter a company of mutinous CITIZENS, *with staves, clubs,
  and other weapons*

FIRST CITIZEN

Before we proceed any further, hear me speak.

ALL

Speak, speak.

FIRST CITIZEN

You are all resolved rather to die than to famish?

ALL

Resolved, resolved.

FIRST CITIZEN

First, you know Caius Marcius is chief enemy to the
people.

ALL

We know 't, we know 't.

FIRST CITIZEN

Let us kill him, and we'll have corn at our own
price. Is 't a verdict?

ALL

No more talking on 't; let it be done: away, away!

SECOND CITIZEN

One word, good citizens.

FIRST CITIZEN

We are accounted poor citizens; the patricians,
good. What authority surfeits on would relieve us:
if they would yield us but the superfluity while it
were wholesome, we might guess they relieved us
humanely; but they think we are too dear: the leanness that afflicts us, the object of our misery, is as an
inventory to particularize their abundance; our
sufferance is a gain to them. Let us revenge this with
our pikes, ere we become rakes: for the gods know I
speak this in hunger for bread, not in thirst for revenge.

SECOND CITIZEN

Would you proceed especially against Caius Marcius?

ALL

Against him first: he's a very dog to the commonly-
alty.

SECOND CITIZEN

Consider you what services he has done for his
country?

FIRST CITIZEN

Very well; and could be content to give him good
report for 't, but that he pays himself with being
proud.

SECOND CITIZEN

Nay, but speak not maliciously.

FIRST CITIZEN

I say unto you, what he hath done famously, he did
it to that end: though soft-conscienced men can be
content to say it was for his country, he did it to
please his mother and to be partly proud; which he
is, even to the altitude of his virtue.

SECOND CITIZEN

What he cannot help in his nature, you account a
vice in him. You must in no way say he is covetous.

FIRST CITIZEN

If I must not, I need not be barren of accusations;
he hath faults, with surplus, to tire in repetition
[*Shouts within*] What shouts are these? The other
side o' the city is risen: why stay we prating here? to
the Capitol!

ALL

Come, come.

FIRST CITIZEN

Soft! who comes here?

Enter MENENIUS AGRIPPA

SECOND CITIZEN

Worthy Menenius Agrippa; one that hath always
loved the people.

[1105]

FIRST CITIZEN
He's one honest enough: would all the rest were so!

MENENIUS
What work's, my countrymen, in hand? where go you
With bats and clubs? the matter? speak, I pray you.

FIRST CITIZEN
Our business is not unknown to the senate; they
have had inkling, this fortnight, what we intend to
do, which now we'll show 'em in deeds. They say
poor suitors have strong breaths: they shall know we
have strong arms too.

MENENIUS
Why, masters, my good friends, mine honest neigh-
bours,
Will you undo yourselves?

FIRST CITIZEN
We cannot, sir, we are undone already.

MENENIUS
I tell you, friends, most charitable care
Have the patricians of you. For your wants,
Your suffering in this dearth, you may as well
Strike at the heaven with your staves as lift them
Against the Roman state; whose course will on
The way it takes, cracking ten thousand curbs
Of more strong link asunder than can ever
Appear in your impediment. For the dearth,
The gods, not the patricians, make it, and
Your knees to them, not arms, must help. Alack,
You are transported by calamity
Thither where more attends you, and you slander
The helms o' the state, who care for you like fathers,
When you curse them as enemies.

FIRST CITIZEN
Care for us! True, indeed! They ne'er cared for us
yet: suffer us to famish, and their store-houses
crammed with grain; make edicts for usury, to support usurers; repeal daily any wholesome act established against the rich, and provide more piercing
statutes daily, to chain up and restrain the poor. If
the wars eat us not up, they will; and there's all the
love they bear us.

MENENIUS
Either you must
Confess yourselves wondrous malicious,
Or be accused of folly. I shall tell you
A pretty tale: it may be you have heard it;
But, since it serves my purpose, I will venture
To stale 't a little more.

FIRST CITIZEN
Well, I'll hear it, sir: yet you must not think to fob
off our disgrace with a tale: but, an 't please you,
deliver.

MENENIUS
There was a time when all the body's members
Rebell'd against the belly; thus accused it:
That only like a gulf it did remain
I' the midst o' the body, idle and unactive,
Still cupboarding the viand. never bearing

Like labour with the rest; where the other instru-
ments
Did see and hear, devise, instruct, walk, feel,
And, mutually participate, did minister
Unto the appetite and affection common
Of the whole body. The belly answer'd—

FIRST CITIZEN
Well, sir, what answer made the belly?

MENENIUS
Sir, I shall tell you. With a kind of smile,
Which ne'er came from the lungs, but even thus—
For, look you, I may make the belly smile
As well as speak—it tauntingly replied
To the discontented members, the mutinous parts
That envied his receipt; even so most fitly
As you malign our senators for that
They are not such as you.

FIRST CITIZEN
                    Your belly's answer? What!
The kingly-crowned head, the vigilant eye,
The counsellor heart, the arm our soldier,
Our steed the leg, the tongue our trumpeter,
With other muniments and petty helps
In this our fabric, if that they—

MENENIUS
                    What then?
'Fore me, this fellow speaks! what then? what then?

FIRST CITIZEN
Should by the cormorant belly be restrain'd,
Who is the sink o' the body,—

MENENIUS
                    Well, what then?

FIRST CITIZEN
The former agents, if they did complain,
What could the belly answer?

MENENIUS
                    I will tell you;
If you'll bestow a small—of what you have little—
Patience awhile, you'st hear the belly's answer.

FIRST CITIZEN
You're long about it.

MENENIUS
                    Note me this, good friend;
Your most grave belly was deliberate,
Not rash like his accusers, and thus answer'd:
'True is it, my incorporate friends,' quoth he,
'That I receive the general food at first,
Which you do live upon; and fit it is,
Because I am the store-house and the shop
Of the whole body: but, if you do remember,
I send it through the rivers of your blood,
Even to the court, the heart, to the seat o' the brain;
And, through the cranks and offices of man,
The strongest nerves and small inferior veins
From me receive that natural competency
Whereby they live: and though that all at once,
You, my good friends,'—this says the belly, mark
me,—

FIRST CITIZEN
Ay, sir; well, well.

MENENIUS

'Though all at once cannot
See what I do deliver out to each,
Yet I can make my audit up, that all
From me do back receive the flour of all,
And leave me but the bran.' What say you to 't?

FIRST CITIZEN

It was an answer: how apply you this?

MENENIUS

The senators of Rome are this good belly,
And you the mutinous members: for examine
Their counsels and their cares, digest things rightly
Touching the weal o' the common, you shall find
No public benefit which you receive
But it proceeds or comes from them to you
And no way from yourselves. What do you think,
You, the great toe of this assembly?

FIRST CITIZEN

I the great toe! why the great toe?

MENENIUS

For that, being one o' the lowest, basest, poorest,
Of this most wise rebellion, thou go'st foremost:
Thou rascal, that art worst in blood to run,
Lead'st first to win some vantage.
But make you ready your stiff bats and clubs:
Rome and her rats are at the point of battle;
The one side must have bale.

Enter CAIUS MARCIUS

　　　　　　　　　Hail, noble Marcius!

MARCIUS

Thanks. What's the matter, you dissentious rogues,
That, rubbing the poor itch of your opinion,
Make yourselves scabs?

FIRST CITIZEN

　　　　　　　We have ever your good word.

MARCIUS

He that will give good words to thee will flatter
Beneath abhorring. What would you have, you curs,
That like nor peace nor war? the one affrights you,
The other makes you proud. He that trusts to you,
Where he should find you lions, finds you hares,
Where foxes, geese: you are no surer, no,
Than is the coal of fire upon the ice,
Or hailstone in the sun. Your virtue is
To make him worthy whose offence subdues him
And curse that justice did it. Who deserves greatness
Deserves your hate; and your affections are
A sick man's appetite, who desires most that
Which would increase his evil. He that depends
Upon your favours swims with fins of lead
And hews down oaks with rushes. Hang ye! Trust ye?
With every minute you do change a mind,
And call him noble that was now your hate,
Him vile that was your garland. What's the matter,
That in these several places of the city
You cry against the noble senate, who,
Under the gods, keep you in awe, which else
Would feed on one another? What's their seeking?

MENENIUS

For corn at their own rates; whereof, they say,
The city is well stored.

MARCIUS

　　　　　　　Hang 'em! They say!
They'll sit by the fire, and presume to know
What's done i' the Capitol; who's like to rise,
Who thrives and who declines; side factions and give out
Conjectural marriages; making parties strong,
And feebling such as stand not in their liking
Below their cobbled shoes. They say there's grain enough!
Would the nobility lay aside their ruth,
And let me use my sword, I'ld make a quarry
With thousands of these quarter'd slaves, as high
As I could pick my lance.

MENENIUS

Nay, these are almost thoroughly persuaded;
For though abundantly they lack discretion,
Yet are they passing cowardly. But, I beseech you,
What says the other troop?

MARCIUS

　　　　　　　They are dissolved: hang 'em!
They said they were an-hungry; sigh'd forth proverbs,
That hunger broke stone walls, that dogs must eat,
That meat was made for mouths, that the gods sent not
Corn for the rich men only: with these shreds
They vented their complainings; which being answer'd,
And a petition granted them, a strange one—
To break the heart of generosity
And make bold power look pale—they threw their caps
As they would hang them on the horns o' the moon,
Shouting their emulation.

MENENIUS

　　　　　　　What is granted them?

MARCIUS

Five tribunes to defend their vulgar wisdoms,
Of their own choice: one's Junius Brutus,
Sicinius Velutus, and I know not—'Sdeath!
The rabble should have first unroof'd the city,
Ere so prevail'd with me: it will in time
Win upon power and throw forth greater themes
For insurrection's arguing.

MENENIUS

　　　　　　　This is strange.

MARCIUS

Go get you home, you fragments!

Enter a MESSENGER, *hastily*

MESSENGER

Where's Caius Marcius?

MARCIUS

　　　　　　　Here: what's the matter?

MESSENGER

The news is, sir, the Volsces are in arms.

MARCIUS

I am glad on 't: then we shall ha' means to vent
Our musty superfluity. See, our best elders.

Enter COMINIUS, TITUS LARTIUS, *and other* SENATORS;
JUNIUS BRUTUS *and* SICINIUS VELUTUS

FIRST SENATOR

Marcius, 'tis true that you have lately told us;
The Volsces are in arms.

MARCIUS

They have a leader,
Tullus Aufidius, that will put you to 't.
I sin in envying his nobility;
And were I any thing but what I am,
I would wish me only he.

COMINIUS

You have fought together?

MARCIUS

Were half to half the world by the ears, and he
Upon my party, I'ld revolt, to make
Only my wars with him: he is a lion
That I am proud to hunt.

FIRST SENATOR

Then, worthy Marcius,
Attend upon Cominius to these wars.

COMINIUS

It is your former promise.

MARCIUS

Sir, it is;
And I am constant. Titus Lartius, thou
Shalt see me once more strike at Tullus' face.
What, art thou stiff? stand'st out?

TITUS

No, Caius Marcius;
I'll lean upon one crutch, and fight with t'other,
Ere stay behind this business.

MENENIUS

O, true-bred!

FIRST SENATOR

Your company to the Capitol; where, I know,
Our greatest friends attend us.

TITUS

[*To* COMINIUS] Lead you on.
[*To* MARCIUS] Follow Cominius; we must follow you;
Right worthy you priority.

COMINIUS

Noble Marcius!

FIRST SENATOR

[*To the* CITIZENS] Hence to your homes; be gone!

MARCIUS

Nay, let them follow:
The Volsces have much corn; take these rats thither
To gnaw their garners. Worshipful mutiners,
Your valour puts well forth: pray, follow.

[CITIZENS *steal away. Exeunt all
but* SICINIUS *and* BRUTUS

SICINIUS

Was ever man so proud as is this Marcius?

BRUTUS

He has no equal.

SICINIUS

When we were chosen tribunes for the people,—

BRUTUS

Mark'd you his lip and eyes?

SICINIUS

Nay, but his taunts.

BRUTUS

Being moved, he will not spare to gird the gods.

SICINIUS

Bemock the modest moon.

BRUTUS

The present wars devour him! he is grown
Too proud to be so valiant.

SICINIUS

Such a nature,
Tickled with good success, disdains the shadow
Which he treads on at noon: but I do wonder
His insolence can brook to be commanded
Under Cominius.

BRUTUS

Fame, at the which he aims,
In whom already he's well graced, cannot
Better be held, nor more attain'd, than by
A place below the first: for what miscarries
Shall be the general's fault, though he perform
To the utmost of a man; and giddy censure
Will then cry out of Marcius 'O, if he
Had borne the business!'

SICINIUS

Besides, if things go well,
Opinion, that so sticks on Marcius, shall
Of his demerits rob Cominius.

BRUTUS

Come:
Half all Cominius' honours are to Marcius,
Though Marcius earn'd them not; and all his faults
To Marcius shall be honours, though indeed
In aught he merit not.

SICINIUS

Let's hence, and hear
How the dispatch is made; and in what fashion,
More than his singularity, he goes
Upon this present action.

BRUTUS

Let's along. [*Exeunt*

SCENE II. *Corioli. The Senate-house*

Enter TULLUS AUFIDIUS, *with* SENATORS *of Corioli*

FIRST SENATOR

So, your opinion is, Aufidius,
That they of Rome are enter'd in our counsels,
And know how we proceed.

AUFIDIUS

Is it not yours?
What ever have been thought on in this state,
That could be brought to bodily act ere Rome
Had circumvention? 'Tis not four days gone
Since I heard thence: these are the words: I think

I have the letter here: yes, here it is:
[*Reads*] 'They have press'd a power, but it is not known
Whether for east or west: the dearth is great;
The people mutinous: and it is rumour'd,
Cominius, Marcius your old enemy,
Who is of Rome worse hated than of you,
And Titus Lartius, a most valiant Roman,
These three lead on this preparation
Whither 'tis bent: most likely 'tis for you:
Consider of it.'

FIRST SENATOR
          Our army's in the field:
We never yet made doubt but Rome was ready
To answer us.

AUFIDIUS
          Nor did you think it folly
To keep your great pretences veil'd till when
They needs must show themselves; which in the hatching,
It seem'd, appear'd to Rome. By the discovery
We shall be shorten'd in our aim, which was
To take in many towns ere almost Rome
Should know we were afoot.

SECOND SENATOR
          Noble Aufidius,
Take your commission; hie you to your bands:
Let us alone to guard Corioli:
If they set down before 's, for the remove
Bring up your army; but, I think, you'll find
They've not prepared for us.

AUFIDIUS
          O, doubt not that;
I speak from certainties. Nay, more,
Some parcels of their power are forth already,
And only hitherward. I leave your honours.
If we and Caius Marcius chance to meet,
'Tis sworn between us, we shall ever strike
Till one can do no more.

ALL
          The gods assist you!

AUFIDIUS
And keep your honours safe!

FIRST SENATOR
          Farewell.

SECOND SENATOR
          Farewell.

ALL
Farewell.   [*Exeunt*

SCENE III. *Rome. A room in* MARCIUS' *house*

Enter VOLUMNIA *and* VIRGILIA: *they set them down on two low stools, and sew*

VOLUMNIA
I pray you, daughter, sing, or express yourself in a more comfortable sort: if my son were my husband, I should freelier rejoice in that absence wherein he won honour than in the embracements of his bed where he would show most love. When yet he was but tender-bodied, and the only son of my womb; when youth with comeliness plucked all gaze his way; when, for a day of kings' entreaties, a mother should not sell him an hour from her beholding; I, considering how honour would become such a person; that it was no better than picture like to hang by the wall, if renown made it not stir, was pleased to let him seek danger where he was like to find fame. To a cruel war I sent him; from whence he returned, his brows bound with oak. I tell thee, daughter, I sprang not more in joy at first hearing he was a man-child than now in first seeing he had proved himself a man.

VIRGILIA
But had he died in the business, madam: how then?

VOLUMNIA
Then his good report should have been my son; I therein would have found issue. Hear me profess sincerely: had I a dozen sons, each in my love alike, and none less dear than thine and my good Marcius, I had rather had eleven die nobly for their country than one voluptuously surfeit out of action.

Enter a GENTLEWOMAN

GENTLEWOMAN
Madam, the Lady Valeria is come to visit you.

VIRGILIA
Beseech you, give me leave to retire myself.

VOLUMNIA
Indeed, you shall not.
Methinks I hear hither your husband's drum;
See him pluck Aufidius down by the hair;
As children from a bear, the Volsces shunning him:
Methinks I see him stamp thus, and call thus:
'Come on, you cowards! you were got in fear,
Though you were born in Rome:' his bloody brow
With his mail'd hand then wiping, forth he goes,
Like to a harvest-man that's task'd to mow
Or all, or lose his hire.

VIRGILIA
His bloody brow! O Jupiter, no blood!

VOLUMNIA
Away, you fool! it more becomes a man
Than gilt his trophy: the breasts of Hecuba,
When she did suckle Hector, look'd not lovelier
Than Hector's forehead when it spit forth blood
At Grecian sword, contemning. Tell Valeria
We are fit to bid her welcome. [*Exit* GENTLEWOMAN

VIRGILIA
Heavens bless my lord from fell Aufidius!

VOLUMNIA
He'll beat Aufidius' head below his knee,
And tread upon his neck.

Enter VALERIA, *with an* USHER *and* GENTLEWOMAN

VALERIA
My ladies both, good day to you.

VOLUMNIA
Sweet madam.

VIRGILIA
I am glad to see your ladyship.

VALERIA

How do you both? you are manifest housekeepers. What are you sewing here? A fine spot, in good faith. How does your little son?

VIRGILIA

I thank your ladyship; well, good madam.

VOLUMNIA

He had rather see the swords and hear a drum than look upon his schoolmaster.

VALERIA

O' my word, the father's son: I'll swear, 'tis a very pretty boy. O' my troth, I looked upon him o' Wednesday half an hour together; has such a confirmed countenance. I saw him run after a gilded butterfly; and when he caught it, he let it go again; and after it again; and over and over he comes, and up again; catched it again: or whether his fall enraged him, or how 'twas, he did so set his teeth, and tear it; O, I warrant, how he mammocked it!

VOLUMNIA

One on 's father's moods.

VALERIA

Indeed, la, 'tis a noble child.

VIRGILIA

A crack, madam.

VALERIA

Come, lay aside your stitchery; I must have you play the idle huswife with me this afternoon.

VIRGILIA

No, good madam; I will not out of doors.

VALERIA

Not out of doors!

VOLUMNIA

She shall, she shall.

VIRGILIA

Indeed, no, by your patience; I'll not over the threshold till my lord return from the wars.

VALERIA

Fie, you confine yourself most unreasonably: come, you must go visit the good lady that lies in.

VIRGILIA

I will wish her speedy strength, and visit her with my prayers; but I cannot go thither.

VOLUMNIA

Why, I pray you?

VIRGILIA

'Tis not to save labour, nor that I want love.

VALERIA

You would be another Penelope: yet, they say, all the yarn she spun in Ulysses' absence did but fill Ithaca full of moths. Come; I would your cambric were sensible as your finger, that you might leave pricking it for pity. Come, you shall go with us.

VIRGILIA

No, good madam, pardon me; indeed, I will not forth.

VALERIA

In truth, la, go with me, and I'll tell you excellent news of your husband.

VIRGILIA

O, good madam, there can be none yet.

VALERIA

Verily, I do not jest with you; there came news from him last night.

VIRGILIA

Indeed, madam?

VALERIA

In earnest, it's true; I heard a senator speak it. Thus it is: the Volsces have an army forth; against whom Cominius the general is gone, with one part of our Roman power: your lord and Titus Lartius are set down before their city Corioli; they nothing doubt prevailing, and to make it brief wars. This is true, on mine honour; and so, I pray, go with us.

VIRGILIA

Give me excuse, good madam; I will obey you in every thing hereafter.

VOLUMNIA

Let her alone, lady; as she is now, she will but disease our better mirth.

VALERIA

In troth, I think she would. Fare you well, then. Come, good sweet lady. Prithee, Virgilia, turn thy solemness out o' door, and go along with us.

VIRGILIA

No, at a word, madam; indeed, I must not. I wish you much mirth.

VALERIA

Well then, farewell.   [Exeunt

SCENE IV. *Before Corioli*

Enter, with drum and colours, MARCIUS, TITUS LARTIUS, CAPTAINS *and* SOLDIERS. *To them a* MESSENGER

MARCIUS

Yonder comes news: a wager they have met.

LARTIUS

My horse to yours, no.

MARCIUS

           'Tis done.

LARTIUS

                Agreed.

MARCIUS

Say, has our general met the enemy?

MESSENGER

They lie in view; but have not spoke as yet.

LARTIUS

So, the good horse is mine.

MARCIUS

           I'll buy him of you.

LARTIUS

No, I'll nor sell nor give him: lend you him I will
For half a hundred years. Summon the town.

MARCIUS

How far off lie these armies?

MESSENGER

          Within this mile and half.

MARCIUS

Then shall we hear their 'larum, and they ours.
Now, Mars, I prithee, make us quick in work,
That we with smoking swords may march from
　hence,
To help our fielded friends! Come, blow thy blast.
They sound a parley. Enter two SENATORS *with others, on
the walls*
Tullus Aufidius, is he within your walls?

FIRST SENATOR

No, nor a man that fears you less than he,
That's lesser than a little. Hark, our drums
　　　　　　　　　　　　　　[Drum afar off
Are bringing forth our youth! we'll break our walls,
Rather than they shall pound us up: our gates,
Which yet seem shut, we have but pinn'd with
　rushes;
They'll open of themselves. Hark you, far off!
　　　　　　　　　　　　　[Alarum far off
There is Aufidius; list, what work he makes
Amongst your cloven army.

MARCIUS

　　　　　　　O, they are at it!

LARTIUS

Their noise be our instruction. Ladders, ho!
Enter the army of the Volsces

MARCIUS

They fear us not, but issue forth their city.
Now put your shields before your hearts, and fight
With hearts more proof than shields. Advance,
　brave Titus:
They do disdain us much beyond our thoughts,
Which makes me sweat with wrath. Come on, my
　fellows:
He that retires, I'll take him for a Volsce,
And he shall feel mine edge.
Alarum. The ROMANS *are beat back to their trenches. Re-
enter* MARCIUS, *cursing*

MARCIUS

All the contagion of the south light on you,
You shames of Rome! you herd of— Boils **and**
　plagues
Plaster you o'er; that you may be abhorr'd
Farther than seen, and one infect another
Against the wind a mile! You souls of geese,
That bear the shapes of men, how have you run
From slaves that apes would beat! Pluto and hell!
All hurt behind; backs red, and faces pale
With flight and agued fear! Mend, and charge
　home,
Or, by the fires of heaven, I'll leave the foe,
And make my wars on you: look to 't: come on;
If you'll stand fast, we'll beat them to their wives,
As they us to our trenches followed.
Another alarum. The Volsces fly, and MARCIUS *follows
them to the gates*
So, now the gates are ope: now prove good seconds:
'Tis for the followers fortune widens them,
Not for the fliers: mark me, and do the like.
　　　　　　　　　　　　　[Enters the gates

FIRST SOLDIER

Fool-hardiness; not I.

SECOND SOLDIER

Nor I.　　　　　　　　　　*[MARCIUS is shut in*

FIRST SOLDIER

See, they have shut him in.

ALL

　　　　　　To the pot, I warrant him.
　　　　　　　　　　　　[Alarum continues
Re-enter TITUS LARTIUS

LARTIUS

What is become of Marcius?

ALL

　　　　　　　Slain, sir, doubtless.

FIRST SOLDIER

Following the fliers at the very heels,
With them he enters; who, upon the sudden,
Clapp'd to their gates: he is himself alone,
To answer all the city.

LARTIUS

　　　　　　O noble fellow!
Who sensibly outdares his senseless sword,
And, when it bows, stands up! Thou art left,
　Marcius:
A carbuncle entire, as big as thou art,
Were not so rich a jewel. Thou wast a soldier
Even to Cato's wish, not fierce and terrible
Only in strokes; but, with thy grim looks and
The thunder-like percussion of thy sounds,
Thou madest thine enemies shake, as if the world
Were feverous and did tremble.
Re-enter MARCIUS, *bleeding, assaulted by the enemy*

FIRST SOLDIER

　　　　　　　Look, sir.

LARTIUS

　　　　　　　O, 'tis Marcius!
Let's fetch him off, or make remain alike.
　　　　　　　[They fight, and all enter the city

SCENE V. *Within Corioli. A street*

Enter certain ROMANS, *with spoils*

FIRST ROMAN

This will I carry to Rome.

SECOND ROMAN

And I this.

THIRD ROMAN

A murrain on 't! I took this for silver.
　　　　　　[Alarum continues still afar off
Enter MARCIUS *and* TITUS LARTIUS *with a trumpet*

MARCIUS

See here these movers that do prize their hours
At a crack'd drachma! Cushions, leaden spoons,
Irons of a doit, doublets that hangmen would
Bury with those that wore them, these base slaves,
Ere yet the fight be done, pack up: down with them!
And hark, what noise the general makes! To him!
There is the man of my soul's hate, Aufidius,
Piercing our Romans: then, valiant Titus, take

Convenient numbers to make good the city;
Whilst I, with those that have the spirit, will haste
To help Cominius.

LARTIUS
Worthy sir, thou bleed'st;
Thy exercise hath been too violent
For a second course of fight.

MARCIUS
Sir, praise me not;
My worth hath yet not warm'd me: fare you well:
The blood I drop is rather physical
Than dangerous to me: to Aufidius thus
I will appear, and fight.

LARTIUS
Now the fair goddess, Fortune,
Fall deep in love with thee; and her great charms
Misguide thy opposers' swords! Bold gentleman,
Prosperity be thy page!

MARCIUS
Thy friend no less
Than those she placeth highest! So farewell.

LARTIUS
Thou worthiest Marcius!   [*Exit* MARCIUS
Go sound thy trumpet in the market-place;
Call thither all the officers o' the town,
Where they shall know our mind. Away!   [*Exeunt*

SCENE VI. *Near the camp of* COMINIUS

Enter COMINIUS, *as it were in retire, with* SOLDIERS
COMINIUS
Breathe you, my friends: well fought; we are come
   off
Like Romans, neither foolish in our stands,
Nor cowardly in retire: believe me, sirs,
We shall be charged again. Whiles we have struck,
By interims and conveying gusts we have heard
The charges of our friends. Ye Roman gods,
Lead their successes as we wish our own,
That both our powers, with smiling fronts en-
   countering,
May give you thankful sacrifice!
Enter a MESSENGER
Thy news?

MESSENGER
The citizens of Corioli have issued,
And given to Lartius and to Marcius battle:
I saw our party to their trenches driven,
And then I came away.

COMINIUS
Though thou speak'st truth,
Methinks thou speak'st not well. How long is 't
   since?

MESSENGER
Above an hour, my lord.

COMINIUS
'Tis not a mile; briefly we heard their drums:
How couldst thou in a mile confound an hour,
And bring thy news so late?

MESSENGER
Spies of the Volsces
Held me in chase, that I was forced to wheel
Three or four miles about; else had I, sir,
Half an hour since brought my report.
Enter MARCIUS
COMINIUS
Who's yonder,
That does appear as he were flay'd? O gods!
He has the stamp of Marcius; and I have
Before-time seen him thus.

MARCIUS
Come I too late?

COMINIUS
The shepherd knows not thunder from a tabor
More than I know the sound of Marcius' tongue
From every meaner man.

MARCIUS
Come I too late?

COMINIUS
Ay, if you come not in the blood of others,
But mantled in your own.

MARCIUS
O, let me clip ye
In arms as sound as when I woo'd; in heart
As merry as when our nuptial day was done,
And tapers burn'd to bedward!

COMINIUS
Flower of warriors,
How is 't with Titus Lartius?

MARCIUS
As with a man busied about decrees:
Condemning some to death, and some to exile;
Ransoming him or pitying, threatening the other;
Holding Corioli in the name of Rome,
Even like a fawning greyhound in the leash,
To let him slip at will.

COMINIUS
Where is that slave
Which told me they had beat you to your trenches?
Where is he? call him hither.

MARCIUS
Let him alone;
He did inform the truth: but for our gentlemen,
The common file—a plague! tribunes for them!—
The mouse ne'er shunn'd the cat as they did budge
From rascals worse than they.

COMINIUS
But how prevail'd you?

MARCIUS
Will the time serve to tell? I do not think.
Where is the enemy? are you lords o' the field?
If not, why cease you till you are so?

COMINIUS
Marcius,
We have at disadvantage fought, and did
Retire to win our purpose.

MARCIUS
How lies their battle? know you on which side
They have placed their men of trust?

COMINIUS

As I guess, Marcius,
Their bands i' the vaward are the Antiates,
Of their best trust; o'er them Aufidius,
Their very heart of hope.

MARCIUS

I do beseech you,
By all the battles wherein we have fought,
By the blood we have shed together, by the vows
We have made to endure friends, that you directly
Set me against Aufidius and his Antiates;
And that you not delay the present, but,
Filling the air with swords advanced and darts,
We prove this very hour.

COMINIUS

Though I could wish
You were conducted to a gentle bath,
And balms applied to you, yet dare I never
Deny your asking: take your choice of those
That best can aid your action.

MARCIUS

Those are they
That most are willing. If any such be here—
As it were sin to doubt—that love this painting
Wherein you see me smear'd; if any fear
Lesser his person than an ill report;
If any think brave death outweighs bad life,
And that his country's dearer than himself;
Let him alone, or so many so minded,
Wave thus, to express his disposition,
And follow Marcius.

[*They all shout, and wave their swords; take him
up in their arms, and cast up their caps*

O, me alone! make you a sword of me?
If these shows be not outward, which of you
But is four Volsces? none of you but is
Able to bear against the great Aufidius
A shield as hard as his. A certain number,
Though thanks to all, must I select from all: the rest
Shall bear the business in some other fight,
As cause will be obey'd. Please you to march;
And four shall quickly draw out my command,
Which men are best inclined.

COMINIUS

March on, my fellows:
Make good this ostentation, and you shall
Divide in all with us.   [*Exeunt*

SCENE VII. *The gates of Corioli*

TITUS LARTIUS, *having set a guard upon Corioli, going
with drum and trumpet toward* COMINIUS *and
CAIUS MARCIUS, enters with a LIEUTENANT,
other* SOLDIERS, *and a* SCOUT

LARTIUS

So, let the ports be guarded: keep your duties,
As I have set them down. If I do send, dispatch
Those centuries to our aid; the rest will serve
For a short holding: if we lose the field,
We cannot keep the town.

LIEUTENANT

Fear not our care, sir.

LARTIUS

Hence, and shut your gates upon 's.
Our guider, come; to the Roman camp conduct us.
[*Exeunt*

SCENE VIII. *A field of battle between the Roman and the
Volscian camps*

Alarum as in battle. Enter, from opposite sides, MARCIUS
and AUFIDIUS

MARCIUS

I'll fight with none but thee; for I do hate thee
Worse than a promise-breaker.

AUFIDIUS

We hate alike:
Not Afric owns a serpent I abhor
More than thy fame and envy. Fix thy foot.

MARCIUS

Let the first budger die the other's slave,
And the gods doom him after!

AUFIDIUS

If I fly, Marcius,
Holloa me like a hare.

MARCIUS

Within these three hours, Tullus,
Alone I fought in your Corioli walls,
And made what work I pleased: 'tis not my blood
Wherein thou seest me mask'd; for thy revenge
Wrench up thy power to the highest.

AUFIDIUS

Wert thou the Hector
That was the whip of your bragg'd progeny,
Thou shouldst not 'scape me here.
They fight, and certain Volsces come in the aid of
AUFIDIUS. MARCIUS *fights till they be driven in breathless*
Officious, and not valiant, you have shamed me
In your condemned seconds.   [*Exeunt*

SCENE IX. *The Roman camp*

*Flourish. Alarum. A retreat is sounded. Enter, from one
side,* COMINIUS *with the* ROMANS; *from the other side,*
MARCIUS, *with his arm in a scarf*

COMINIUS

If I should tell thee o'er this thy day's work,
Thou'lt not believe thy deeds: but I'll report it,
Where senators shall mingle tears with smiles;
Where great patricians shall attend, and shrug,
I' the end admire; where ladies shall be frighted,
And, gladly quaked, hear more; where the dull trib-
unes,
That, with the fusty plebeians, hate thine honours,
Shall say against their hearts 'We thank the gods
Our Rome hath such a soldier.'
Yet camest thou to a morsel of this feast,
Having fully dined before.

Enter TITUS LARTIUS, *with his power, from the pursuit*

LARTIUS

O general,
Here is the steed, we the caparison:
Hadst thou beheld—

MARCIUS

Pray now, no more: my mother,
Who has a charter to extol her blood,
When she does praise me grieves me. I have done
As you have done; that's what I can: induced
As you have been; that's for my country:
He that has but effected his good will
Hath overta'en mine act.

COMINIUS

You shall not be
The grave of your deserving; Rome must know
The value of her own: 'twere a concealment
Worse than a theft, no less than a traducement,
To hide your doings; and to silence that,
Which, to the spire and top of praises vouch'd,
Would seem but modest: therefore, I beseech you—
In sign of what you are, not to reward
What you have done—before our army hear me.

MARCIUS

I have some wounds upon me, and they smart
To hear themselves remember'd.

COMINIUS

Should they not,
Well might they fester 'gainst ingratitude,
And tent themselves with death. Of all the horses,
Whereof we have ta'en good, and good store, of all
The treasure in this field achieved and city,
We render you the tenth; to be ta'en forth,
Before the common distribution, at
Your only choice.

MARCIUS

I thank you, general;
But cannot make my heart consent to take
A bribe to pay my sword: I do refuse it,
And stand upon my common part with those
That have beheld the doing.

[*A long flourish. They all cry* 'Marcius! Marcius!' *cast up their caps and lances:* COMINIUS *and* LARTIUS *stand bare*

MARCIUS

May these same instruments, which you profane,
Never sound more! when drums and trumpets shall
I' the field prove flatterers, let courts and cities be
Made all of false-faced soothing!
When steel grows soft as the parasite's silk,
Let him be made a coverture for the wars!
No more, I say! For that I have not wash'd
My nose that bled, or foil'd some debile wretch,
Which without note here's many else have done,
You shout me forth
In acclamations hyperbolical;
As if I loved my little should be dieted
In praises sauced with lies.

COMINIUS

Too modest are you;

More cruel to your good report than grateful
To us that give you truly: by your patience,
If 'gainst yourself you be incensed, we'll put you,
Like one that means his proper harm, in manacles,
Then reason safely with you. Therefore, be it known,
As to us, to all the world, that Caius Marcius
Wears this war's garland: in token of the which,
My noble steed, known to the camp, I give him,
With all his trim belonging; and from this time,
For what he did before Corioli, call him,
With all the applause and clamour of the host,
CAIUS MARCIUS CORIOLANUS. Bear
The addition nobly ever!

[*Flourish. Trumpets sound, and drums*

ALL

Caius Marcius Coriolanus!

CORIOLANUS

I will go wash;
And when my face is fair, you shall perceive
Whether I blush, or no: howbeit, I thank you:
I mean to stride your steed; and at all times
To undercrest your good addition
To the fairness of my power.

COMINIUS

So, to our tent;
Where, ere we do repose us, we will write
To Rome of our success. You, Titus Lartius,
Must to Corioli back: send us to Rome
The best, with whom we may articulate
For their own good and ours.

LARTIUS

I shall, my lord.

CORIOLANUS

The gods begin to mock me. I, that now
Refused most princely gifts, am bound to beg
Of my lord general.

COMINIUS

Take 't; 'tis yours. What is 't?

CORIOLANUS

I sometime lay here in Corioli
At a poor man's house; he used me kindly:
He cried to me; I saw him prisoner;
But then Aufidius was within my view,
And wrath o'erwhelm'd my pity: I request you
To give my poor host freedom.

COMINIUS

O, well begg'd!
Were he the butcher of my son, he should
Be free as is the wind. Deliver him, Titus.

LARTIUS

Marcius, his name?

CORIOLANUS

By Jupiter, forgot:
I am weary; yea, my memory is tired.
Have we no wine here?

COMINIUS

Go we to our tent:
The blood upon your visage dries; 'tis time
It should be look'd to: come.   [*Exeunt*

SCENE X. *The camp of the Volsces*

A flourish. Cornets. Enter TULLUS AUFIDIUS, *bloody, with two or three* SOLDIERS

AUFIDIUS

The town is ta'en!

FIRST SOLDIER

'Twill be deliver'd back on good condition.

AUFIDIUS

Condition!
I would I were a Roman; for I cannot,
Being a Volsce, be that I am. Condition!
What good condition can a treaty find
I' the part that is at mercy? Five times, Marcius,
I have fought with thee; so often hast thou beat me;
And wouldst do so, I think, should we encounter
As often as we eat. By the elements,
If e'er again I meet him beard to beard,
He's mine, or I am his: mine emulation
Hath not that honour in 't it had; for where
I thought to crush him in an equal force,
True sword to sword, I'll potch at him some way,
Or wrath or craft may get him.

FIRST SOLDIER

              He's the devil.

AUFIDIUS

Bolder, though not so subtle. My valour's poison'd
With only suffering stain by him; for him
Shall fly out of itself: nor sleep nor sanctuary,
Being naked, sick, nor fane nor Capitol,
The prayers of priests nor times of sacrifice,
Embarquements all of fury, shall lift up
Their rotten privilege and custom 'gainst
My hate to Marcius: where I find him, were it
At home, upon my brother's guard, even there,
Against the hospitable canon, would I
Wash my fierce hand in 's heart. Go you to the city;
Learn how 'tis held, and what they are that must
Be hostages for Rome.

FIRST SOLDIER

              Will not you go?

AUFIDIUS

I am attended at the cypress grove: I pray you—
'Tis south the city mills—bring me word thither
How the world goes, that to the pace of it
I may spur on my journey.

FIRST SOLDIER

              I shall, sir.   [*Exeunt*

ACT II

SCENE I. *Rome. A public place*

Enter MENENIUS, *with the two* TRIBUNES *of the people,* SICINIUS *and* BRUTUS

MENENIUS

The augurer tells me we shall have news to-night.

BRUTUS

Good or bad?

MENENIUS

Not according to the prayer of the people, for they love not Marcius.

SICINIUS

Nature teaches beasts to know their friends.

MENENIUS

Pray you, who does the wolf love?

SICINIUS

The lamb.

MENENIUS

Ay, to devour him; as the hungry plebeians would the noble Marcius.

BRUTUS

He's a lamb indeed, that baes like a bear.

MENENIUS

He's a bear indeed, that lives like a lamb. You two are old men: tell me one thing that I shall ask you.

BOTH

Well, sir.

MENENIUS

In what enormity is Marcius poor in, that you two have not in abundance?

BRUTUS

He's poor in no one fault, but stored with all.

SICINIUS

Especially in pride.

BRUTUS

And topping all others in boasting.

MENENIUS

This is strange now: do you two know how you are censured here in the city, I mean of us o' the right-hand file? do you?

BOTH

Why, how are we censured?

MENENIUS

Because you talk of pride now,—will you not be angry?

BOTH

Well, well, sir, well.

MENENIUS

Why, 'tis no great matter; for a very little thief of occasion will rob you of a great deal of patience: give your dispositions the reins, and be angry at your pleasures; at the least, if you take it as a pleasure to you in being so. You blame Marcius for being proud?

BRUTUS

We do it not alone, sir.

MENENIUS

I know you can do very little alone; for your helps are many, or else your actions would grow wondrous single: your abilities are too infant-like for doing much alone. You talk of pride: O that you could turn your eyes toward the napes of your necks, and make but an interior survey of your good selves! O that you could!

BOTH

What then, sir?

MENENIUS

Why, then you should discover a brace of unmeriting, proud, violent, testy magistrates, alias fools, as any in Rome.

SICINIUS

Menenius, you are known well enough too.

MENENIUS

I am known to be a humorous patrician, and one that loves a cup of hot wine with not a drop of allaying Tiber in 't; said to be something imperfect in favouring the first complaint, hasty and tinderlike upon too trivial motion; one that converses more with the buttock of the night than with the forehead of the morning: what I think I utter, and spend my malice in my breath. Meeting two such wealsmen as you are,—I cannot call you Lycurguses—if the drink you give me touch my palate adversely, I make a crooked face at it. I can't say your worships have delivered the matter well, when I find the ass in compound with the major part of your syllables: and though I must be content to bear with those that say you are reverend grave men, yet they lie deadly that tell you you have good faces. If you see this in the map of my microcosm, follows it that I am known well enough too? what harm can your bisson conspectuities glean out of this character, if I be known well enough too?

BRUTUS

Come, sir, come, we know you well enough.

MENENIUS

You know neither me, yourselves, nor any thing. You are ambitious for poor knaves' caps and legs: you wear out a good wholesome forenoon in hearing a cause between an orange-wife and a fosset-seller, and then rejourn the controversy of three-pence to a second day of audience. When you are hearing a matter between party and party, if you chance to be pinched with the colic, you make faces like mummers; set up the bloody flag against all patience; and, in roaring for a chamber-pot, dismiss the controversy bleeding, the more entangled by your hearing: all the peace you make in their cause is, calling both the parties knaves. You are a pair of strange ones.

BRUTUS

Come, come, you are well understood to be a perfecter giber for the table than a necessary bencher in the Capitol.

MENENIUS

Our very priests must become mockers, if they shall encounter such ridiculous subjects as you are. When you speak best unto the purpose, it is not worth the wagging of your beards; and your beards deserve not so honourable a grave as to stuff a botcher's cushion, or to be entombed in an ass's pack-saddle. Yet you must be saying, Marcius is proud; who, in a cheap estimation, is worth all your predecessors since Deucalion; though peradventure some of the best of 'em were hereditary hang-men. God-den to your worships: more of your conversation would infect my brain, being the herdsmen of the beastly plebeians: I will be bold to take my leave of you.

[BRUTUS *and* SICINIUS *go aside*
Enter VOLUMNIA, VIRGILIA, *and* VALERIA

How now, my as fair as noble ladies,—and the moon, were she earthly, no nobler—whither do you follow your eyes so fast?

VOLUMNIA

Honourable Menenius, my boy Marcius approaches; for the love of Juno, let's go.

MENENIUS

Ha! Marcius coming home?

VOLUMNIA

Ay, worthy Menenius; and with most prosperous approbation.

MENENIUS

Take my cap, Jupiter, and I thank thee. Hoo! Marcius coming home?

VIRGILIA *and* VALERIA

Nay, 'tis true.

VOLUMNIA

Look, here's a letter from him: the state hath another, his wife another; and, I think, there's one at home for you.

MENENIUS

I will make my very house reel to-night: a letter for me?

VIRGILIA

Yes, certain, there's a letter for you; I saw 't.

MENENIUS

A letter for me! it gives me an estate of seven years' health; in which time I will make a lip at the physician: the most sovereign prescription in Galen is but empiricutic, and, to this preservative, of no better report than a horse-drench. Is he not wounded? he was wont to come home wounded.

VIRGILIA

O, no, no, no.

VOLUMNIA

O, he is wounded; I thank the gods for 't.

MENENIUS

So do I too, if it be not too much: brings a' victory in his pocket? the wounds become him.

VOLUMNIA

On 's brows: Menenius, he comes the third time home with the oaken garland.

MENENIUS

Has he disciplined Aufidius soundly?

VOLUMNIA

Titus Lartius writes, they fought together, but Aufidius got off.

MENENIUS

And 'twas time for him too, I'll warrant him that: an he had stayed by him, I would not have been so fidiused for all the chests in Corioli, and the gold that's in them. Is the senate possessed of this?

VOLUMNIA

Good ladies, let's go. Yes, yes, yes; the senate has letters from the general, wherein he gives my son the whole name of the war: he hath in this action outdone his former deeds doubly.

VALERIA

In troth, there's wondrous things spoke of him.

MENENIUS

Wondrous! ay, I warrant you, and not without his true purchasing.

VIRGILIA

The gods grant them true!

VOLUMNIA

True! pow, wow.

MENENIUS

True! I'll be sworn they are true. Where is he wounded? [To the TRIBUNES] God save your good worships! Marcius is coming home: he has more cause to be proud. Where is he wounded?

VOLUMNIA

I' the shoulder and i' the left arm: there will be large cicatrices to show the people, when he shall stand for his place. He received in the repulse of Tarquin seven hurts i' the body.

MENENIUS

One i' the neck, and two i' the thigh; there's nine that I know.

VOLUMNIA

He had, before this last expedition, twenty five wounds upon him.

MENENIUS

Now it's twenty seven: every gash was an enemy's grave. [A shout and flourish] Hark! the trumpets.

VOLUMNIA

These are the ushers of Marcius: before him he carries noise, and behind him he leaves tears:
Death, that dark spirit, in 's nervy arm doth lie;
Which, being advanced, declines, and then men die.
A sennet. Trumpets sound. Enter COMINIUS *and* TITUS LARTIUS; *between them,* CORIOLANUS, *crowned with an oaken garland; with* CAPTAINS *and* SOLDIERS, *and a* HERALD

HERALD

Know, Rome, that all alone Marcius did fight
Within Corioli gates: where he hath won,
With fame, a name to Caius Marcius; these
In honour follows Coriolanus.
Welcome to Rome, renowned Coriolanus! [*Flourish*

ALL

Welcome to Rome, renowned Coriolanus!

CORIOLANUS

No more of this, it does offend my heart;
Pray now, no more.

COMINIUS

Look, sir, your mother!

CORIOLANUS

O,
You have, I know, petition'd all the gods
For my prosperity!   [*Kneels*

VOLUMNIA

Nay, my good soldier, up;
My gentle Marcius, worthy Caius, and
By deed-achieving honour newly named,—

What is it?—Coriolanus must I call thee?—
But, O, thy wife!

CORIOLANUS

My gracious silence, hail!
Wouldst thou have laugh'd had I come coffin'd home,
That weep'st to see me triumph? Ah, my dear,
Such eyes the widows in Corioli wear,
And mothers that lack sons.

MENENIUS

Now, the gods crown thee!

CORIOLANUS

And live you yet? [*To* VALERIA] O my sweet lady, pardon.

VOLUMNIA

I know not where to turn: O, welcome home:
And welcome, general: and ye're welcome all.

MENENIUS

A hundred thousand welcomes. I could weep,
And I could laugh; I am light and heavy. Welcome:
A curse begin at very root on 's heart,
That is not glad to see thee! You are three
That Rome should dote on: yet, by the faith of men,
We have some old crab-trees here at home that will not
Be grafted to your relish. Yet welcome, warriors:
We call a nettle but a nettle, and
The faults of fools but folly.

COMINIUS

Ever right.

CORIOLANUS

Menenius, ever, ever.

HERALD

Give way there, and go on.

CORIOLANUS

[*To* VOLUMNIA *and* VIRGILIA] Your hand, and yours:
Ere in our own house I do shade my head,
The good patricians must be visited;
From whom I have received not only greetings,
But with them change of honours.

VOLUMNIA

I have lived
To see inherited my very wishes
And the buildings of my fancy: only
There's one thing wanting, which I doubt not but
Our Rome will cast upon thee.

CORIOLANUS

Know, good mother,
I had rather be their servant in my way
Than sway with them in theirs.

COMINIUS

On, to the Capitol!
[*Flourish. Cornets. Exeunt in state, as before.*
BRUTUS *and* SICINIUS *come forward*

BRUTUS

All tongues speak of him, and the bleared sights
Are spectacled to see him: your prattling nurse
Into a rapture lets her baby cry
While she chats him: the kitchen malkin pins
Her richest lockram 'bout her reechy neck,

Clambering the walls to eye him: stalls, bulks, win-
    dows,
Are smother'd up, leads fill'd and ridges horsed
With variable complexions, all agreeing
In earnestness to see him: seld-shown flamens
Do press among the popular throngs, and puff
To win a vulgar station: our veil'd dames
Commit the war of white and damask in
Their nicely-gawded cheeks to the wanton spoil
Of Phœbus' burning kisses: such a pother,
As if that whatsoever god who leads him
Were slily crept into his human powers,
And gave him graceful posture.

SICINIUS
               On the sudden
I warrant him consul.

BRUTUS
           Then our office may,
During his power, go sleep.

SICINIUS
He cannot temperately transport his honours
From where he should begin and end, but will
Lose those he hath won.

BRUTUS
           In that there's comfort.

SICINIUS
                Doubt not
The commoners, for whom we stand, but they
Upon their ancient malice will forget
With the least cause these his new honours; which
That he will give them make I as little question
As he is proud to do 't.

BRUTUS
           I heard him swear,
Were he to stand for consul, never would he
Appear i' the market-place, nor on him put
The napless vesture of humility,
Nor showing, as the manner is, his wounds
To the people, beg their stinking breaths.

SICINIUS
               'Tis right.

BRUTUS
It was his word: O, he would miss it rather
Than carry it but by the suit of the gentry to him,
And the desire of the nobles.

SICINIUS
            I wish no better
Than have him hold that purpose and to put it
In execution.

BRUTUS
        'Tis most like he will.

SICINIUS
It shall be to him then, as our good wills,
A sure destruction.

BRUTUS
        So it must fall out
To him or our authorities. For an end,
We must suggest the people in what hatred
He still hath held them; that to 's power he would
Have made them mules, silenced their pleaders and

Dispropertied their freedoms; holding them,
In human action and capacity,
Of no more soul nor fitness for the world
Than camels in the war, who have their provand
Only for bearing burthens, and sore blows
For sinking under them.

SICINIUS
          This, as you say, suggested
At some time when his soaring insolence
Shall touch the people—which time shall not want,
If he be put upon 't; and that's as easy
As to set dogs on sheep—will be his fire
To kindle their dry stubble; and their blaze
Shall darken him for ever.

Enter a MESSENGER

BRUTUS
           What's the matter?

MESSENGER
You are sent for to the Capitol. 'Tis thought
That Marcius shall be consul:
I have seen the dumb men throng to see him and
The blind to hear him speak: matrons flung gloves,
Ladies and maids their scarfs and handkerchers,
Upon him as he pass'd: the nobles bended,
As to Jove's statue, and the commons made
A shower and thunder with their caps and shouts:
I never saw the like.

BRUTUS
          Let's to the Capitol,
And carry with us ears and eyes for the time,
But hearts for the event.

SICINIUS
           Have with you.   [*Exeunt*

SCENE II. *The same. The Capitol*

Enter two OFFICERS, *to lay cushions*

FIRST OFFICER
Come, come, they are almost here. How many
stand for consulships?

SECOND OFFICER
Three, they say: but 'tis thought of every one
Coriolanus will carry it.

FIRST OFFICER
That's a brave fellow; but he's vengeance proud,
and loves not the common people.

SECOND OFFICER
Faith, there have been many great men that have
flattered the people, who ne'er loved them; and
there be many that they have loved, they know not
wherefore: so that, if they love they know not why,
they hate upon no better a ground: therefore, for
Coriolanus neither to care whether they love or hate
him manifests the true knowledge he has in their
disposition; and out of his noble carelessness lets
them plainly see 't.

FIRST OFFICER
If he did not care whether he had their love or no,
he waved indifferently 'twixt doing them neither

good nor harm: but he seeks their hate with greater devotion than they can render it him, and leaves nothing undone that may fully discover him their opposite. Now, to seem to affect the malice and displeasure of the people is as bad as that which he dislikes, to flatter them for their love.

SECOND OFFICER

He hath deserved worthily of his country: and his ascent is not by such easy degrees as those who, having been supple and courteous to the people, bonneted, without any further deed to have them at all into their estimation and report: but he hath so planted his honours in their eyes and his actions in their hearts, that for their tongues to be silent and not confess so much, were a kind of ingrateful injury; to report otherwise were a malice that, giving itself the lie, would pluck reproof and rebuke from every ear that heard it.

FIRST OFFICER

No more of him; he's a worthy man: make way, they are coming.

A sennet. Enter, with LICTORS *before them,* COMINIUS *the Consul,* MENENIUS, CORIOLANUS, SENATORS, SICINIUS *and* BRUTUS. *The* SENATORS *take their places; the* TRIBUNES *take their places by themselves.* CORIOLANUS *stands*

MENENIUS

Having determined of the Volsces and
To send for Titus Lartius, it remains,
As the main point of this our after-meeting,
To gratify his noble service that
Hath thus stood for his country: therefore, please you,
Most reverend and grave elders, to desire
The present consul, and last general
In our well-found successes, to report
A little of that worthy work perform'd
By Caius Marcius Coriolanus; whom
We met here, both to thank and to remember
With honours like himself.

FIRST SENATOR

Speak, good Cominius:
Leave nothing out for length, and make us think
Rather our state's defective for requital
Than we to stretch it out. [*To the* TRIBUNES] Masters o' the people,
We do request your kindest ears, and after,
Your loving motion toward the common body,
To yield what passes here.

SICINIUS

We are convented
Upon a pleasing treaty, and have hearts
Inclinable to honour and advance
The theme of our assembly.

BRUTUS

Which the rather
We shall be bless'd to do, if he remember
A kinder value of the people than
He hath hereto prized them at.

MENENIUS

That's off, that's off;

I would you rather had been silent. Please you
To hear Cominius speak?

BRUTUS

Most willingly:
But yet my caution was more pertinent
Than the rebuke you give it.

MENENIUS

He loves your people;
But tie him not to be their bedfellow.
Worthy Cominius, speak. [CORIOLANUS *offers to go away*] Nay, keep your place.

FIRST SENATOR

Sit, Coriolanus; never shame to hear
What you have nobly done.

CORIOLANUS

Your honours' pardon:
I had rather have my wounds to heal again,
Than hear say how I got them.

BRUTUS

Sir, I hope
My words disbench'd you not.

CORIOLANUS

No, sir: yet oft,
When blows have made me stay, I fled from words.
You sooth'd not, therefore hurt not: but your people,
I love them as they weigh.

MENENIUS

Pray now, sit down.

CORIOLANUS

I had rather have one scratch my head i' the sun
When the alarum were struck than idly sit
To hear my nothings monster'd. [*Exit*

MENENIUS

Masters of the people,
Your multiplying spawn how can he flatter—
That's thousand to one good one—when you now see
He had rather venture all his limbs for honour
Than one on 's ears to hear it? Proceed, Cominius.

COMINIUS

I shall lack voice: the deeds of Coriolanus
Should not be utter'd feebly. It is held
That valour is the chiefest virtue and
Most dignifies the haver: if it be,
The man I speak of cannot in the world
Be singly counterpoised. At sixteen years,
When Tarquin made a head for Rome, he fought
Beyond the mark of others: our then dictator,
Whom with all praise I point at, saw him fight,
When with his Amazonian chin he drove
The bristled lips before him: he bestrid
An o'er-press'd Roman and i' the consul's view
Slew three opposers: Tarquin's self he met,
And struck him on his knee: in that day's feats,
When he might act the woman in the scene,
He proved best man i' the field, and for his meed
Was brow-bound with the oak. His pupil age
Man-enter'd thus, he waxed like a sea;
And, in the brunt of seventeen battles since,
He lurch'd all swords of the garland. For this last,

Before and in Corioli, let me say,
I cannot speak him home: he stopp'd the fliers;
And by his rare example made the coward
Turn terror into sport: as weeds before
A vessel under sail, so men obey'd,
And fell below his stem: his sword, death's stamp,
Where it did mark, it took; from face to foot
He was a thing of blood, whose every motion
Was timed with dying cries: alone he enter'd
The mortal gate of the city, which he painted
With shunless destiny; aidless came off,
And with a sudden re-enforcement struck
Corioli like a planet: now all's his:
When, by and by, the din of war gan pierce
His ready sense; then straight his doubled spirit
Re-quicken'd what in flesh was fatigate,
And to the battle came he; where he did
Run reeking o'er the lives of men, as if
'Twere a perpetual spoil: and till we call'd
Both field and city ours, he never stood
To ease his breast with panting.

MENENIUS
　　　　　　　Worthy man!

FIRST SENATOR
He cannot but with measure fit the honours
Which we devise him.

COMINIUS
　　　　　　Our spoils he kick'd at,
And look'd upon things precious, as they were
The common muck of the world: he covets less
Than misery itself would give; rewards
His deeds with doing them, and is content
To spend the time to end it.

MENENIUS
　　　　　　　He's right noble:
Let him be call'd for.

FIRST SENATOR
　　　　Call Coriolanus

OFFICER
He doth appear.

Re-enter CORIOLANUS

MENENIUS
The senate, Coriolanus, are well pleased
To make thee consul.

CORIOLANUS
　　　　I do owe them still
My life and services.

MENENIUS
　　　　It then remains
That you do speak to the people.

CORIOLANUS
　　　　　　I do beseech you,
Let me o'erleap that custom, for I cannot
Put on the gown, stand naked, and entreat them,
For my wounds' sake, to give their suffrage: please
　you
That I may pass this doing.

SICINIUS
　　　　Sir, the people

Must have their voices; neither will they bate
One jot of ceremony.

MENENIUS
　　　　Put them not to 't:
Pray you, go fit you to the custom, and
Take to you, as your predecessors have,
Your honour with your form.

CORIOLANUS
　　　　　　It is a part
That I shall blush in acting, and might well
Be taken from the people.

BRUTUS
　　　　Mark you that?

CORIOLANUS
To brag unto them, thus I did, and thus;
Show them the unaching scars which I should hide,
As if I had received them for the hire
Of their breath only!

MENENIUS
　　　　Do not stand upon 't.
We recommend to you, tribunes of the people,
Our purpose to them: and to our noble consul
Wish we all joy and honour.

SENATORS
To Coriolanus come all joy and honour!
[*Flourish of cornets. Exeunt all but* SICINIUS *and* BRUTUS

BRUTUS
You see how he intends to use the people.

SICINIUS
May they perceive 's intent! He will require them,
As if he did contemn what he requested
Should be in them to give.

BRUTUS
　　　　　　Come, we'll inform them
Of our proceedings here: on the market-place,
I know, they do attend us.　　　　　[*Exeunt*

SCENE III. *The same. The Forum*

Enter seven or eight CITIZENS

FIRST CITIZEN
Once, if he do require our voices, we ought not to
deny him.

SECOND CITIZEN
We may, sir, if we will.

THIRD CITIZEN
We have power in ourselves to do it, but it is a
power that we have no power to do: for if he show
us his wounds and tell us his deeds, we are to put
our tongues into those wounds and speak for them;
so, if he tell us his noble deeds, we must also tell him
our noble acceptance of them. Ingratitude is monstrous: and for the multitude to be ingrateful, were
to make a monster of the multitude; of the which
we being members, should bring ourselves to be
monstrous members.

FIRST CITIZEN
And to make us no better thought of, a little help
will serve; for once we stood up about the corn, he

himself stuck not to call us the many-headed multitude.

THIRD CITIZEN

We have been called so of many; not that our heads are some brown, some black, some auburn, some bald, but that our wits are so diversely coloured: and truly I think, if all our wits were to issue out of one skull, they would fly east, west, north, south, and their consent of one direct way should be at once to all the points o' the compass.

SECOND CITIZEN

Think you so? Which way do you judge my wit would fly?

THIRD CITIZEN

Nay, your wit will not so soon out as another man's will; 'tis strongly wedged up in a blockhead; but if it were at liberty, 'twould, sure, southward.

SECOND CITIZEN

Why that way?

THIRD CITIZEN

To lose itself in a fog; where being three parts melted away with rotten dews, the fourth would return for conscience sake, to help to get thee a wife.

SECOND CITIZEN

You are never without your tricks: you may, you may.

THIRD CITIZEN

Are you all resolved to give your voices? But that's no matter, the greater part carries it. I say, if he would incline to the people, there was never a worthier man.

Enter CORIOLANUS *in a gown of humility, with*

MENENIUS

Here he comes, and in the gown of humility: mark his behaviour. We are not to stay all together, but to come by him where he stands, by ones, by twos, and by threes. He's to make his requests by particulars; wherein every one of us has a single honour, in giving him our own voices with our own tongues: therefore follow me, and I'll direct you how you shall go by him.

ALL

Content, content.   [*Exeunt* CITIZENS

MENENIUS

O sir, you are not right: have you not known
The worthiest men have done 't?

CORIOLANUS

         What must I say?—
'I pray, sir,'—Plague upon 't! I cannot bring
My tongue to such a pace. 'Look, sir, my wounds!
I got them in my country's service, when
Some certain of your brethren roar'd, and ran
From the noise of our own drums.'

MENENIUS

         O me, the gods!
You must not speak of that: you must desire them
To think upon you.

CORIOLANUS

Think upon me! hang 'em!

I would they would forget me, like the virtues
Which our divines lose by 'em.

MENENIUS

         You'll mar all:
I'll leave you: pray you, speak to 'em, I pray you,
In wholesome manner.   [*Exit*

CORIOLANUS

         Bid them wash their faces,
And keep their teeth clean. [*Re-enter two of the* CITIZENS] So, here comes a brace.

Re-enter a third CITIZEN

You know the cause, sir, of my standing here.

THIRD CITIZEN

We do, sir; tell us what hath brought you to 't.

CORIOLANUS

Mine own desert.

SECOND CITIZEN

Your own desert!

CORIOLANUS

Ay, but not mine own desire.

THIRD CITIZEN

How! not your own desire!

CORIOLANUS

No, sir, 'twas never my desire yet to trouble the poor with begging.

THIRD CITIZEN

You must think, if we give you any thing, we hope to gain by you.

CORIOLANUS

Well then, I pray, your price o' the consulship?

FIRST CITIZEN

The price is, to ask it kindly.

CORIOLANUS

Kindly! Sir, I pray, let me ha 't: I have wounds to show you, which shall be yours in private. Your good voice, sir; what say you?

SECOND CITIZEN

You shall ha 't, worthy sir.

CORIOLANUS

A match, sir. There's in all two worthy voices begged. I have your alms: adieu.

THIRD CITIZEN

But this is something odd.

SECOND CITIZEN

An 'twere to give again,—but 'tis no matter.
     [*Exeunt the three* CITIZENS

Re-enter two other CITIZENS

CORIOLANUS

Pray you now, if it may stand with the tune of your voices that I may be consul, I have here the customary gown.

FOURTH CITIZEN

You have deserved nobly of your country, and you have not deserved nobly.

CORIOLANUS

Your enigma?

FOURTH CITIZEN

You have been a scourge to her enemies, you have been a rod to her friends; you have not indeed loved the common people.

CORIOLANUS

You should account me the more virtuous, that I have not been common in my love. I will, sir, flatter my sworn brother, the people, to earn a dearer estimation of them; 'tis a condition they account gentle: and since the wisdom of their choice is rather to have my hat than my heart, I will practise the insinuating nod, and be off to them most counterfeitly; that is, sir, I will counterfeit the bewitchment of some popular man, and give it bountiful to the desirers. Therefore, beseech you, I may be consul.

FIFTH CITIZEN

We hope to find you our friend; and therefore give you our voices heartily.

FOURTH CITIZEN

You have received many wounds for your country.

CORIOLANUS

I will not seal your knowledge with showing them. I will make much of your voices, and so trouble you no farther.

BOTH CITIZENS

The gods give you joy, sir, heartily!   [*Exeunt*

CORIOLANUS

Most sweet voices!
Better it is to die, better to starve,
Than crave the hire which first we do deserve.
Why in this woolvish toge should I stand here,
To beg of Hob and Dick that do appear,
Their needless vouches? Custom calls me to 't:
What custom wills, in all things should we do 't,
The dust on antique time would lie unswept,
And mountainous error be too highly heap'd
For truth to o'er-peer. Rather than fool it so,
Let the high office and the honour go
To one that would do thus. I am half through:
The one part suffer'd, the other will I do.
     Re-enter three CITIZENS *more*
Here come moe voices.
Your voices: for your voices I have fought;
Watch'd for your voices; for your voices bear
Of wounds two dozen odd; battles thrice six
I have seen, and heard of; for your voices have
Done many things, some less, some more: your voices:
Indeed, I would be consul.

SIXTH CITIZEN

He has done nobly, and cannot go without any honest man's voice.

SEVENTH CITIZEN

Therefore let him be consul: the gods give him joy, and make him good friend to the people!

ALL

Amen, amen. God save thee, noble consul!
     [*Exeunt*

CORIOLANUS

Worthy voices!
     Re-enter MENENIUS, *with* BRUTUS *and* SICINIUS

MENENIUS

You have stood your limitation; and the tribunes

Endue you with the people's voice: remains
That in the official marks invested you
Anon do meet the senate.

CORIOLANUS

Is this done?

SICINIUS

The custom of request you have discharged:
The people do admit you, and are summon'd
To meet anon upon your approbation.

CORIOLANUS

Where? at the senate-house?

SICINIUS

     There, Coriolanus.

CORIOLANUS

May I change these garments?

SICINIUS

     You may, sir.

CORIOLANUS

That I'll straight do, and, knowing myself again,
Repair to the senate-house.

MENENIUS

I'll keep you company. Will you along?

BRUTUS

We stay here for the people.

SICINIUS

     Fare you well.
     [*Exeunt* CORIOLANUS *and* MENENIUS
He has it now; and, by his looks, methinks
'Tis warm at 's heart.

BRUTUS

     With a proud heart he wore
His humble weeds. Will you dismiss the people?
     Re-enter CITIZENS

SICINIUS

How now, my masters! have you chose this man?

FIRST CITIZEN

He has our voices, sir.

BRUTUS

We pray the gods he may deserve your loves.

SECOND CITIZEN

Amen, sir: to my poor unworthy notice,
He mock'd us when he begg'd our voices.

THIRD CITIZEN

     Certainly
He flouted us downright.

FIRST CITIZEN

No, 'tis his kind of speech; he did not mock us.

SECOND CITIZEN

Not one amongst us, save yourself, but says
He used us scornfully: he should have show'd us
His marks of merit, wounds received for 's country.

SICINIUS

Why, so he did, I am sure.

CITIZENS

No, no; no man saw 'em.

THIRD CITIZEN

He said he had wounds which he could show in private;
And with his hat, thus waving it in scorn,
'I would be consul,' says he: 'aged custom,

But by your voices, will not so permit me;
Your voices therefore.' When we granted that,
Here was 'I thank you for your voices: thank you:
Your most sweet voices: now you have left your
    voices,
I have no further with you.' Was not this mockery?

SICINIUS

Why, either were you ignorant to see 't,
Or, seeing it, of such childish friendliness
To yield your voices?

BRUTUS
                    Could you not have told him,
As you were lesson'd, when he had no power,
But was a petty servant to the state,
He was your enemy; ever spake against
Your liberties and the charters that you bear
I' the body of the weal: and now, arriving
A place of potency and sway o' the state,
If he should still malignantly remain
Fast foe to the plebeii, your voices might
Be curses to yourselves? You should have said,
That as his worthy deeds did claim no less
Than what he stood for, so his gracious nature
Would think upon you for your voices, and
Translate his malice towards you into love,
Standing your friendly lord.

SICINIUS
                    Thus to have said,
As you were fore-advised, had touch'd his spirit
And tried his inclination; from him pluck'd
Either his gracious promise, which you might,
As cause had call'd you up, have held him to;
Or else it would have gall'd his surly nature,
Which easily endures not article
Tying him to aught: so, putting him to rage,
You should have ta'en the advantage of his choler,
And pass'd him unelected.

BRUTUS
                    Did you perceive
He did solicit you in free contempt
When he did need your loves; and do you think
That his contempt shall not be bruising to you
When he hath power to crush? Why, had your
    bodies
No heart among you? or had you tongues to cry
Against the rectorship of judgement?

SICINIUS
                    Have you,
Ere now, denied the asker? and now again,
Of him that did not ask but mock, bestow
Your sued-for tongues?

THIRD CITIZEN

He's not confirm'd; we may deny him yet.

SECOND CITIZEN

And will deny him:
I'll have five hundred voices of that sound.

FIRST CITIZEN

I twice five hundred, and their friends to piece 'em.

BRUTUS

Get you hence instantly, and tell those friends,

They have chose a consul that will from them take
Their liberties, make them of no more voice
Than dogs that are as often beat for barking,
As therefore kept to do so.

SICINIUS
                    Let them assemble;
And, on a safer judgement, all revoke
Your ignorant election: enforce his pride
And his old hate unto you: besides, forget not
With what contempt he wore the humble weed,
How in his suit he scorn'd you: but your loves,
Thinking upon his services, took from you
The apprehension of his present portance,
Which most gibingly, ungravely, he did fashion
After the inveterate hate he bears you.

BRUTUS
                    Lay
A fault on us, your tribunes; that we labour'd,
No impediment between, but that you must
Cast your election on him.

SICINIUS
                    Say, you chose him
More after our commandment than as guided
By your own true affections; and that your minds,
Pre-occupied with what you rather must do
Than what you should, made you against the grain
To voice him consul: lay the fault on us.

BRUTUS

Ay, spare us not. Say we read lectures to you,
How youngly he began to serve his country,
How long continued; and what stock he springs of,
The noble house o' the Marcians, from whence came
That Ancus Marcius, Numa's daughter's son,
Who, after great Hostilius, here was king;
Of the same house Publius and Quintus were,
That our best water brought by conduits hither;
And [Censorinus] nobly named so,
Twice being [by the people chosen] censor,
Was his great ancestor.

SICINIUS
                    One thus descended,
That hath beside well in his person wrought
To be set high in place, we did commend
To your remembrances: but you have found,
Scaling his present bearing with his past,
That he's your fixed enemy, and revoke
Your sudden approbation.

BRUTUS
                    Say, you ne'er had done 't—
Harp on that still—but by our putting on:
And presently, when you have drawn your number,
Repair to the Capitol.

CITIZENS
                    We will so: almost all
Repent in their election.   [Exeunt CITIZENS

BRUTUS
                    Let them go on;
This mutiny were better put in hazard
Than stay, past doubt, for greater:
If, as his nature is, he fall in rage

With their refusal, both observe and answer
The vantage of his anger.

SICINIUS
                    To the Capitol, come:
We will be there before the stream o' the people;
And this shall seem, as partly 'tis, their own,
Which we have goaded onward.   [*Exeunt*

ACT III
SCENE I. *Rome. A street*

Cornets. Enter CORIOLANUS, MENENIUS, *all the* GENTRY,
COMINIUS, TITUS LARTIUS, *and other* SENATORS

CORIOLANUS
Tullus Aufidius then had made new head?

LARTIUS
He had, my lord; and that it was which caused
Our swifter composition.

CORIOLANUS
So then the Volsces stand but as at first;
Ready, when time shall prompt them, to make road
Upon 's again.

COMINIUS
                    They are worn, lord consul, so,
That we shall hardly in our ages see
Their banners wave again.

CORIOLANUS
                    Saw you Aufidius?

LARTIUS
On safe-guard he came to me; and did curse
Against the Volsces, for they had so vilely
Yielded the town: he is retired to Antium.

CORIOLANUS
Spoke he of me?

LARTIUS
                    He did, my lord.

CORIOLANUS
                              How? what?

LARTIUS
How often he had met you, sword to sword;
That of all things upon the earth he hated
Your person most; that he would pawn his fortunes
To hopeless restitution, so he might
Be call'd your vanquisher.

CORIOLANUS
                    At Antium lives he?

LARTIUS
At Antium.

CORIOLANUS
I wish I had a cause to seek him there,
To oppose his hatred fully. Welcome home.

Enter SICINIUS *and* BRUTUS

Behold, these are the tribunes of the people,
The tongues o' the common mouth: I do despise
    them;
For they do prank them in authority,
Against all noble sufferance.

SICINIUS
                    Pass no further.

CORIOLANUS
Ha! what is that?

BRUTUS
It will be dangerous to go on: no further.

CORIOLANUS
What makes this change?

MENENIUS
                    The matter?

COMINIUS
Hath he not pass'd the noble and the common?

BRUTUS
Cominius, no.

CORIOLANUS
                    Have I had children's voices?

FIRST SENATOR
Tribunes, give way; he shall to the market-place.

BRUTUS
The people are incensed against him.

SICINIUS
                                        Stop,
Or all will fall in broil.

CORIOLANUS
                    Are these your herd?
Must these have voices, that can yield them now,
And straight disclaim their tongues? What are your
    offices?
You being their mouths, why rule you not their
    teeth?
Have you not set them on?

MENENIUS
                    Be calm, be calm.

CORIOLANUS
It is a purposed thing, and grows by plot,
To curb the will of the nobility:
Suffer 't, and live with such as cannot rule,
Nor ever will be ruled.

BRUTUS
                    Call 't not a plot:
The people cry you mock'd them; and of late,
When corn was given them gratis, you repined,
Scandal'd the suppliants for the people, call'd them
Time-pleasers, flatterers, foes to nobleness.

CORIOLANUS
Why, this was known before.

BRUTUS
                    Not to them all.

CORIOLANUS
Have you inform'd them sithence?

BRUTUS
                              How! I inform them!

COMINIUS
You are like to do such business.

BRUTUS
                    Not unlike,
Each way, to better yours.

CORIOLANUS
Why then should I be consul? By yond clouds,

Let me deserve so ill as you, and make me
Your fellow tribune.

SICINIUS

      You show too much of that
For which the people stir: if you will pass
To where you are bound, you must inquire your
      way,
Which you are out of, with a gentler spirit;
Or never be so noble as a consul,
Nor yoke with him for tribune.

MENENIUS

      Let's be calm.

COMINIUS

The people are abused; set on. This paltering
Becomes not Rome; nor has Coriolanus
Deserved this so dishonour'd rub, laid falsely
I' the plain way of his merit.

CORIOLANUS

      Tell me of corn!
This was my speech, and I will speak 't again—

MENENIUS

Not now, not now.

FIRST SENATOR

      Not in this heat, sir, now.

CORIOLANUS

Now, as I live, I will. My nobler friends,
I crave their pardons:
For the mutable, rank-scented many, let them
Regard me as I do not flatter, and
Therein behold themselves: I say again,
In soothing them, we nourish 'gainst our senate
The cockle of rebellion, insolence, sedition,
Which we ourselves have plough'd for, sow'd and
      scatter'd,
By mingling them with us, the honour'd number;
Who lack not virtue, no, nor power, but that
Which they have given to beggars.

MENENIUS

      Well, no more.

FIRST SENATOR

No more words, we beseech you.

CORIOLANUS

      How! no more!
As for my country I have shed my blood,
Not fearing outward force, so shall my lungs
Coin words till their decay against those measles,
Which we disdain should tetter us, yet sought
The very way to catch them.

BRUTUS

      You speak o' the people,
As if you were a god to punish, not
A man of their infirmity.

SICINIUS

      'Twere well
We let the people know 't.

MENENIUS

      What, what? his choler?

CORIOLANUS

Choler!

Were I as patient as the midnight sleep,
By Jove, 'twould be my mind!

SICINIUS

      It is a mind
That shall remain a poison where it is,
Not poison any further.

CORIOLANUS

      Shall remain!
Hear you this Triton of the minnows? mark you
His absolute 'shall'?

COMINIUS

      'Twas from the canon.

CORIOLANUS

      'Shall'!
O good, but most unwise patricians! why,
You grave but reckless senators, have you thus
Given Hydra here to choose an officer,
That with his peremptory 'shall,' being but
The horn and noise o' the monster's, wants not
      spirit
To say he'll turn your current in a ditch,
And make your channel his? If he have power,
Then vail your ignorance; if none, awake
Your dangerous lenity. If you are learn'd,
Be not as common fools; if you are not,
Let them have cushions by you. You are plebeians,
If they be senators: and they are no less,
When, both your voices blended, the great'st taste
Most palates theirs. They choose their magistrate;
And such a one as he, who puts his 'shall,'
His popular 'shall,' against a graver bench
Than ever frown'd in Greece. By Jove himself,
It makes the consuls base! and my soul aches
To know, when two authorities are up,
Neither supreme, how soon confusion
May enter 'twixt the gap of both and take
The one by the other.

COMINIUS

      Well, on to the market-place.

CORIOLANUS

Whoever gave that counsel, to give forth
The corn o' the storehouse gratis, as 'twas used
Sometime in Greece,—

MENENIUS

      Well, well, no more of that.

CORIOLANUS

Though there the people had more absolute power,
I say, they nourish'd disobedience, fed
The ruin of the state.

BRUTUS

      Why, shall the people give
One that speaks thus their voice?

CORIOLANUS

      I'll give my reasons,
More worthier than their voices. They know the
      corn
Was not our recompense, resting well assured
They ne'er did service for 't: being press'd to the
      war,
Even when the navel of the state was touch'd,

They would not thread the gates. This kind of serv-
ice
Did not deserve corn gratis: being i' the war,
Their mutinies and revolts, wherein they show'd
Most valour, spoke not for them: the accusation
Which they have often made against the senate,
All cause unborn, could never be the native
Of our so frank donation. Well, what then?
How shall this bosom multiplied digest
The senate's courtesy? Let deeds express
What's like to be their words: 'We did request it;
We are the greater poll, and in true fear
They gave us our demands.' Thus we debase
The nature of our seats, and make the rabble
Call our cares fears; which will in time
Break ope the locks o' the senate, and bring in
The crows to peck the eagles.

MENENIUS
         Come, enough.

BRUTUS
Enough, with over measure.

CORIOLANUS
         No, take more:
What may be sworn by, both divine and human,
Seal what I end withal! This double worship,
Where one part does disdain with cause, the other
Insult without all reason; where gentry, title, wis-
dom,
Cannot conclude but by the yea and no
Of general ignorance,—it must omit
Real necessities, and give way the while
To unstable slightness: purpose so barr'd, it follows,
Nothing is done to purpose. Therefore, beseech
you,—
You that will be less fearful than discreet;
That love the fundamental part of state
More than you doubt the change on 't; that prefer
A noble life before a long, and wish
To jump a body with a dangerous physic
That's sure of death without it,—at once pluck out
The multitudinous tongue; let them not lick
The sweet which is their poison. Your dishonour
Mangles true judgement and bereaves the state
Of that integrity which should become 't;
Not having the power to do the good it would,
For the ill which doth control 't.

BRUTUS
         Has said enough.

SICINIUS
Has spoken like a traitor, and shall answer
As traitors do.

CORIOLANUS
         Thou wretch, despite o'erwhelm thee!
What should the people do with these bald tribunes?
On whom depending, their obedience fails
To the greater bench: in a rebellion,
When what's not meet, but what must be, was law,
Then were they chosen: in a better hour,
Let what is meet be said it must be meet,
And throw their power i' the dust.

BRUTUS
Manifest treason!

SICINIUS
         This a consul? no.

BRUTUS
The ædiles, ho!

Enter an ÆDILE
         Let him be apprehended.

SICINIUS
Go, call the people: [*Exit* ÆDILE] in whose name
myself
Attach thee as a traitorous innovator,
A foe to the public weal: obey, I charge thee,
And follow to thine answer.

CORIOLANUS
         Hence, old goat!

SENATORS, &c.
We'll surety him.

COMINIUS
         Aged sir, hands off.

CORIOLANUS
Hence, rotten thing! or I shall shake thy bones
Out of thy garments.

SICINIUS
         Help, ye citizens!

Enter a rabble of CITIZENS, *with the* ÆDILES

MENENIUS
On both sides more respect.

SICINIUS
Here's he that would take from you all your power.

BRUTUS
Seize him, ædiles!

CITIZENS
Down with him! down with him!

SENATORS, &c.
Weapons, weapons, weapons!
         [*They all bustle about* CORIOLANUS, *crying,*
'Tribunes!' 'Patricians!' 'Citizens!' 'What, ho!'
'Sicinius!' 'Brutus!' 'Coriolanus!' 'Citizens!'
'Peace, peace, peace!' 'Stay! hold! peace!'

MENENIUS
What is about to be? I am out of breath.
Confusion's near. I cannot speak. You, tribunes
To the people! Coriolanus, patience!
Speak, good Sicinius.

SICINIUS
         Hear me, people; peace!

CITIZENS
Let's hear our tribune: peace!—Speak, speak,
speak.

SICINIUS
You are at point to lose your liberties:
Marcius would have all from you; Marcius,
Whom late you have named for consul.

MENENIUS
         Fie, fie, fie!
This is the way to kindle, not to quench.

FIRST SENATOR
To unbuild the city, and to lay all flat.

SICINIUS

What is the city but the people?

CITIZENS

           True,

The people are the city.

BRUTUS

By the consent of all, we were establish'd
The people's magistrates.

CITIZENS

           You so remain.

MENENIUS

And so are like to do.

COMINIUS

That is the way to lay the city flat,
To bring the roof to the foundation,
And bury all which yet distinctly ranges,
In heaps and piles of ruin.

SICINIUS

           This deserves death.

BRUTUS

Or let us stand to our authority,
Or let us lose it. We do here pronounce,
Upon the part o' the people, in whose power
We were elected theirs, Marcius is worthy
Of present death.

SICINIUS

           Therefore lay hold of him;
Bear him to the rock Tarpeian, and from thence
Into destruction cast him.

BRUTUS

           Ædiles, seize him!

CITIZENS

Yield, Marcius, yield!

MENENIUS

           Hear me one word;
Beseech you, tribunes, hear me but a word.

ÆDILES

Peace, peace!

MENENIUS

[*To* BRUTUS] Be that you seem, truly your country's
    friend,
And temperately proceed to what you would
Thus violently redress.

BRUTUS

           Sir, those cold ways,
That seem like prudent helps, are very poisonous
Where the disease is violent. Lay hands upon him,
And bear him to the rock.

CORIOLANUS

           No, I'll die here.   [*Drawing his sword*
There's some among you have beheld me fighting:
Come, try upon yourselves what you have seen me.

MENENIUS

Down with that sword! Tribunes, withdraw awhile.

BRUTUS

Lay hands upon him.

MENENIUS

           Help Marcius, help,
You that be noble; help him, young and old!

CITIZENS

Down with him, down with him!

[*In this mutiny, the* TRIBUNES, *the* ÆDILES,
                 and the PEOPLE, *are beat in*

MENENIUS

Go, get you to your house; be gone, away!
All will be naught else.

SECOND SENATOR

           Get you gone.

COMINIUS

           Stand fast;
We have as many friends as enemies.

MENENIUS

Shall it be put to that?

FIRST SENATOR

           The gods forbid!
I prithee, noble friend, home to thy house;
Leave us to cure this cause.

MENENIUS

           For 'tis a sore upon us
You cannot tent yourself: be gone, beseech you.

COMINIUS

Come, sir, along with us.

CORIOLANUS

I would they were barbarians—as they are,
Though in Rome litter'd—not Romans—as they are
    not,
Though calved i' the porch o' the Capitol,—

MENENIUS

           Be gone:
Put not your worthy rage into your tongue:
One time will owe another.

CORIOLANUS

           On fair ground
I could beat forty of them.

MENENIUS

           I could myself
Take up a brace o' the best of them; yea, the two
    tribunes.

COMINIUS

But now 'tis odds beyond arithmetic;
And manhood is call'd foolery, when it stands
Against a falling fabric. Will you hence
Before the tag return? whose rage doth rend
Like interrupted waters, and o'erbear
What they are used to bear.

MENENIUS

           Pray you, be gone:
I'll try whether my old wit be in request
With those that have but little: this must be
    patch'd
With cloth of any colour.

COMINIUS

           Nay, come away.

[*Exeunt* CORIOLANUS, COMINIUS, *and others*

FIRST PATRICIAN

This man has marr'd his fortune.

MENENIUS

His nature is too noble for the world:
He would not flatter Neptune for his trident,

Or Jove for 's power to thunder. His heart's his
　　mouth:
What his breast forges, that his tongue must vent;
And, being angry, does forget that ever
He heard the name of death.　　　　[*A noise within*
Here's goodly work!
　　　　　　SECOND PATRICIAN
　　　　　　　I would they were a-bed!
　　　　　　MENENIUS
I would they were in Tiber! What, the vengeance,
Could he not speak 'em fair?
　　　　Re-enter BRUTUS *and* SICINIUS, *with the rabble*
　　　　　　SICINIUS
　　　　　　　Where is this viper,
That would depopulate the city, and
Be every man himself?
　　　　　　MENENIUS
　　　　　　　You worthy tribunes—
　　　　　　SICINIUS
He shall be thrown down the Tarpeian rock
With rigorous hands: he hath resisted law,
And therefore law shall scorn him further trial
Than the severity of the public power,
Which he so sets at nought.
　　　　　　FIRST CITIZEN
　　　　　　　He shall well know
The noble tribunes are the people's mouths,
And we their hands.
　　　　　　CITIZENS
He shall, sure on 't.
　　　　　　MENENIUS
　　　　　　　Sir, sir,—
　　　　　　SICINIUS
Peace!
　　　　　　MENENIUS
Do not cry havoc, where you should but hunt
With modest warrant.
　　　　　　SICINIUS
　　　　　　　Sir, how comes 't that you
Have holp to make this rescue?
　　　　　　MENENIUS
　　　　　　　Hear me speak:
As I do know the consul's worthiness,
So can I name his faults,—
　　　　　　SICINIUS
　　　　　　　Consul! what consul?
　　　　　　MENENIUS
The consul Coriolanus.
　　　　　　BRUTUS
　　　　　　　He consul!
　　　　　　CITIZENS
No, no, no, no, no.
　　　　　　MENENIUS
If, by the tribunes' leave, and yours, good people,
I may be heard, I would crave a word or two;
The which shall turn you to no further harm
Than so much loss of time.
　　　　　　SICINIUS
　　　　　　　Speak briefly then;
For we are peremptory to dispatch

This viperous traitor: to eject him hence
Were but one danger, and to keep him here
Our certain death: therefore it is decreed
He dies to-night.
　　　　　　MENENIUS
　　　　　　　Now the good gods forbid
That our renowned Rome, whose gratitude
Towards her deserved children is enroll'd
In Jove's own book, like an unnatural dam
Should now eat up her own!
　　　　　　SICINIUS
He's a disease that must be cut away.
　　　　　　MENENIUS
O, he's a limb that has but a disease;
Mortal, to cut it off; to cure it, easy.
What has he done to Rome that's worthy death?
Killing our enemies, the blood he hath lost—
Which, I dare vouch, is more than that he hath
By many an ounce—he dropp'd it for his country;
And what is left, to lose it by his country
Were to us all that do 't and suffer it
A brand to the end o' the world.
　　　　　　SICINIUS
　　　　　　　This is clean kam.
　　　　　　BRUTUS
Merely awry: when he did love his country,
It honour'd him.
　　　　　　MENENIUS
　　　　　　　The service of the foot
Being once gangrened, is not then respected
For what before it was.
　　　　　　BRUTUS
　　　　　　　We'll hear no more.
Pursue him to his house, and pluck him thence;
Lest his infection, being of catching nature,
Spread further.
　　　　　　MENENIUS
　　　　　　　One word more, one word.
This tiger-footed rage, when it shall find
The harm of unscann'd swiftness, will, too late,
Tie leaden pounds to 's heels. Proceed by process;
Lest parties, as he is beloved, break out,
And sack great Rome with Romans.
　　　　　　BRUTUS
　　　　　　　If it were so—
　　　　　　SICINIUS
What do ye talk?
Have we not had a taste of his obedience?
Our ædiles smote? ourselves resisted? Come.
　　　　　　MENENIUS
Consider this: he has been bred i' the wars
Since he could draw a sword, and is ill school'd
In bolted language; meal and bran together
He throws without distinction. Give me leave,
I'll go to him, and undertake to bring him
Where he shall answer, by a lawful form,
In peace, to his utmost peril.
　　　　　　FIRST SENATOR
　　　　　　　Noble tribunes,
It is the humane way: the other course

Will prove too bloody; and the end of it
Unknown to the beginning.

SICINIUS
Noble Menenius,
Be you then as the people's officer.
Masters, lay down your weapons.

BRUTUS
Go not home.

SICINIUS
Meet on the market-place. We'll attend you there:
Where, if you bring not Marcius, we'll proceed
In our first way.

MENENIUS
I'll bring him to you.
[To the SENATORS] Let me desire your company: he
must come,
Or what is worst will follow.

FIRST SENATOR
Pray you, let's to him.
[Exeunt

SCENE II. A room in CORIOLANUS's house

Enter CORIOLANUS with PATRICIANS

CORIOLANUS
Let them pull all about mine ears; present me
Death on the wheel, or at wild horses' heels;
Or pile ten hills on the Tarpeian rock,
That the precipitation might down stretch
Below the beam of sight; yet will I still
Be thus to them.

A PATRICIAN
You do the nobler.

CORIOLANUS
I muse my mother
Does not approve me further, who was wont
To call them woollen vassals, things created
To buy and sell with groats, to show bare heads
In congregations, to yawn, be still and wonder,
When one but of my ordinance stood up
To speak of peace or war.

Enter VOLUMNIA
I talk of you:
Why did you wish me milder? would you have me
False to my nature? Rather say, I play
The man I am.

VOLUMNIA
O, sir, sir, sir,
I would have had you put your power well on,
Before you had worn it out.

CORIOLANUS
Let go.

VOLUMNIA
You might have been enough the man you are,
With striving less to be so: lesser had been
The thwartings of your dispositions, if
You had not show'd them how ye were disposed,
Ere they lack'd power to cross you.

CORIOLANUS
Let them hang.

VOLUMNIA
Ay, and burn too.

Enter MENENIUS with the SENATORS

MENENIUS
Come, come, you have been too rough, something
too rough;
You must return and mend it.

FIRST SENATOR
There's no remedy;
Unless, by not so doing, our good city
Cleave in the midst, and perish.

VOLUMNIA
Pray, be counsell'd:
I have a heart as little apt as yours,
But yet a brain that leads my use of anger
To better vantage.

MENENIUS
Well said, noble woman!
Before he should thus stoop to the herd, but that
The violent fit o' the time craves it as physic
For the whole state, I would put mine armour on,
Which I can scarcely bear.

CORIOLANUS
What must I do?

MENENIUS
Return to the tribunes.

CORIOLANUS
Well, what then? what then?

MENENIUS
Repent what you have spoke.

CORIOLANUS
For them! I cannot do it to the gods;
Must I then do 't to them?

VOLUMNIA
You are too absolute;
Though therein you can never be too noble,
But when extremities speak. I have heard you say,
Honour and policy, like unsever'd friends,
I' the war do grow together: grant that, and tell me,
In peace what each of them by the other lose,
That they combine not there.

CORIOLANUS
Tush, tush!

MENENIUS
A good demand

VOLUMNIA
If it be honour in your wars to seem
The same you are not, which, for your best ends,
You adopt your policy, how is it less or worse,
That it shall hold companionship in peace
With honour, as in war, since that to both
It stands in like request?

CORIOLANUS
Why force you this?

VOLUMNIA
Because that now it lies you on to speak
To the people; not by your own instruction,
Nor by the matter which your heart prompts you,
But with such words that are but roted in
Your tongue, though but bastards and syllables

Of no allowance to your bosom's truth.
Now, this no more dishonours you at all
Than to take in a town with gentle words,
Which else would put you to your fortune and
The hazard of much blood.
I would dissemble with my nature, where
My fortunes and my friends at stake required
I should do so in honour. I am in this,
Your wife, your son, these senators, the nobles;
And you will rather show our general louts
How you can frown than spend a fawn upon 'em,
For the inheritance of their loves and safeguard
Of what that want might ruin.

MENENIUS
Noble lady!
Come, go with us; speak fair: you may salve so,
Not what is dangerous present, but the loss
Of what is past.

VOLUMNIA
I prithee now, my son,
Go to them, with this bonnet in thy hand;
And thus far having stretch'd it—here be with
them—
Thy knee bussing the stones—for in such business
Action is eloquence, and the eyes of the ignorant
More learned than the ears—waving thy head,
Which often, thus, correcting thy stout heart,
Now humble as the ripest mulberry
That will not hold the handling: or say to them,
Thou art their soldier, and being bred in broils
Hast not the soft way which, thou dost confess,
Were fit for thee to use, as they to claim,
In asking their good loves; but thou wilt frame
Thyself, forsooth, hereafter theirs, so far
As thou hast power and person.

MENENIUS
This but done,
Even as she speaks, why, their hearts were yours;
For they have pardons, being ask'd, as free
As words to little purpose.

VOLUMNIA
Prithee now,
Go, and be ruled: although I know thou hadst
rather
Follow thine enemy in a fiery gulf
Than flatter him in a bower.

Enter COMINIUS
Here is Cominius.

COMINIUS
I have been i' the market-place; and, sir, 'tis fit
You make strong party, or defend yourself
By calmness or by absence: all's in anger.

MENENIUS
Only fair speech.

COMINIUS
I think 'twill serve, if he
Can thereto frame his spirit.

VOLUMNIA
He must, and will.
Prithee now, say you will, and go about it.

CORIOLANUS
Must I go show them my unbarb'd sconce? must I,
With my base tongue, give to my noble heart
A lie, that it must bear? Well, I will do 't:
Yet, were there but this single plot to lose,
This mould of Marcius, they to dust should grind it,
And throw 't against the wind. To the market-
place!
You have put me now to such a part, which never
I shall discharge to the life.

COMINIUS
Come, come, we'll prompt you.

VOLUMNIA
I prithee now, sweet son, as thou hast said
My praises made thee first a soldier, so,
To have my praise for this, perform a part
Thou hast not done before.

CORIOLANUS
Well, I must do 't:
Away, my disposition, and possess me
Some harlot's spirit! my throat of war be turn'd,
Which quired with my drum, into a pipe
Small as an eunuch, or the virgin voice
That babies lulls asleep! the smiles of knaves
Tent in my cheeks, and schoolboys' tears take up
The glasses of my sight! a beggar's tongue
Make motion through my lips, and my arm'd knees,
Who bow'd but in my stirrup, bend like his
That hath received an alms! I will not do 't;
Lest I surcease to honour mine own truth,
And by my body's action teach my mind
A most inherent baseness.

VOLUMNIA
At thy choice then:
To beg of thee, it is my more dishonour
Than thou of them. Come all to ruin: let
Thy mother rather feel thy pride than fear
Thy dangerous stoutness, for I mock at death
With as big heart as thou. Do as thou list.
Thy valiantness was mine, thou suck'dst it from me,
But owe thy pride thyself.

CORIOLANUS
Pray, be content:
Mother, I am going to the market-place;
Chide me no more. I'll mountebank their loves,
Cog their hearts from them, and come home be-
loved
Of all the trades in Rome. Look, I am going:
Commend me to my wife. I'll return consul;
Or never trust to what my tongue can do
I' the way of flattery further.

VOLUMNIA
Do your will.   [*Exit*

COMINIUS
Away! the tribunes do attend you: arm yourself
To answer mildly; for they are prepared
With accusations, as I hear, more strong
Than are upon you yet.

CORIOLANUS
The word is 'mildly.' Pray you, let us go:

Let them accuse me by invention, I
Will answer in mine honour.

MENENIUS

                Ay, but mildly.

CORIOLANUS

Well, mildly be it then. Mildly!   [*Exeunt*

SCENE III. *The same. The Forum*

Enter SICINIUS *and* BRUTUS

BRUTUS

In this point charge him home, that he affects
Tyrannical power: if he evade us there,
Enforce him with his envy to the people;
And that the spoil got on the Antiates
Was ne'er distributed.

Enter an ÆDILE

What, will he come?

ÆDILE

              He's coming.

BRUTUS

                  How accompanied?

ÆDILE

With old Menenius and those senators
That always favour'd him.

SICINIUS

              Have you a catalogue
Of all the voices that we have procured,
Set down by the poll?

ÆDILE

              I have; 'tis ready.

SICINIUS

Have you collected them by tribes?

ÆDILE

                  I have.

SICINIUS

Assemble presently the people hither:
And when they hear me say 'It shall be so
I' the right and strength o' the commons,' be it
    either
For death, for fine, or banishment, then let them,
If I say fine, cry 'Fine,' if death, cry 'Death,'
Insisting on the old prerogative
And power i' the truth o' the cause.

ÆDILE

              I shall inform them.

BRUTUS

And when such time they have begun to cry,
Let them not cease, but with a din confused
Enforce the present execution
Of what we chance to sentence.

ÆDILE

              Very well.

SICINIUS

Make them be strong, and ready for this hint,
When we shall hap to give 't them.

BRUTUS

           Go about it.   [*Exit* ÆDILE
Put him to choler straight: he hath been used

Ever to conquer and to have his worth
Of contradiction: being once chafed, he cannot
Be rein'd again to temperance; then he speaks
What's in his heart; and that is there which looks
With us to break his neck.

SICINIUS

              Well, here he comes.

Enter CORIOLANUS, MENENIUS, *and* COMINIUS, *with*
SENATORS *and* PATRICIANS

MENENIUS

Calmly, I do beseech you.

CORIOLANUS

Ay, as an ostler, that for the poorest piece
Will bear the knave by the volume. The honour'd
    gods
Keep Rome in safety, and the chairs of justice
Supplied with worthy men! plant love among's!
Throng our large temples with the shows of peace,
And not our streets with war!

FIRST SENATOR

              Amen, amen.

MENENIUS

A noble wish.

Re-enter ÆDILE, *with* CITIZENS

SICINIUS

Draw near, ye people.

ÆDILE

List to your tribunes; audience: peace, I say!

CORIOLANUS

First, hear me speak.

BOTH TRIBUNES

           Well, say. Peace, ho!

CORIOLANUS

Shall I be charged no further than this present?
Must all determine here?

SICINIUS

           I do demand,
If you submit you to the people's voices,
Allow their officers, and are content
To suffer lawful censure for such faults
As shall be proved upon you.

CORIOLANUS

              I am content.

MENENIUS

Lo, citizens, he says he is content:
The warlike service he has done, consider; think
Upon the wounds his body bears, which show
Like graves i' the holy churchyard.

CORIOLANUS

              Scratches with briers,
Scars to move laughter only.

MENENIUS

              Consider further,
That when he speaks not like a citizen,
You find him like a soldier: do not take
His rougher accents for malicious sounds,
But, as I say, such as become a soldier
Rather than envy you.

COMINIUS

           Well, well, no more.

CORIOLANUS
What is the matter
That being pass'd for consul with full voice,
I am so dishonour'd that the very hour
You take it off again?

SICINIUS
Answer to us.

CORIOLANUS
Say, then: 'tis true, I ought so.

SICINIUS
We charge you, that you have contrived to take
From Rome all season'd office, and to wind
Yourself into a power tyrannical;
For which you are a traitor to the people.

CORIOLANUS
How! traitor!

MENENIUS
Nay, temperately; your promise.

CORIOLANUS
The fires i' the lowest hell fold-in the people!
Call me their traitor! Thou injurious tribune!
Within thine eyes sat twenty thousand deaths,
In thy hands clutch'd as many millions, in
Thy lying tongue both numbers, I would say
'Thou liest' unto thee with a voice as free
As I do pray the gods.

SICINIUS
Mark you this, people?

CITIZENS
To the rock, to the rock with him!

SICINIUS
Peace!
We need not put new matter to his charge:
What you have seen him do and heard him speak,
Beating your officers, cursing yourselves,
Opposing laws with strokes, and here defying
Those whose great power must try him; even this,
So criminal and in such capital kind,
Deserves the extremest death.

BRUTUS
But since he hath
Served well for Rome—

CORIOLANUS
What do you prate of service?

BRUTUS
I talk of that, that know it.

CORIOLANUS
You?

MENENIUS
Is this the promise that you made your mother?

COMINIUS
Know, I pray you,—

CORIOLANUS
I'll know no further:
Let them pronounce the steep Tarpeian death,
Vagabond exile, flaying, pent to linger
But with a grain a day, I would not buy
Their mercy at the price of one fair word,
Nor check my courage for what they can give,
To have 't with saying 'Good morrow.'

SICINIUS
For that he has,
As much as in him lies, from time to time
Envied against the people, seeking means
To pluck away their power, as now at last
Given hostile strokes, and that not in the presence
Of dreaded justice, but on the ministers
That do distribute it; in the name o' the people,
And in the power of us the tribunes, we,
Even from this instant, banish him our city,
In peril of precipitation
From off the rock Tarpeian, never more
To enter our Rome gates: i' the people's name,
I say it shall be so.

CITIZENS
It shall be so, it shall be so; let him away:
He's banish'd, and it shall be so.

COMINIUS
Hear me, my masters, and my common friends,—

SICINIUS
He's sentenced; no more hearing.

COMINIUS
Let me speak:
I have been consul, and can show for Rome
Her enemies' marks upon me. I do love
My country's good with a respect more tender,
More holy and profound, than mine own life,
My dear wife's estimate, her womb's increase
And treasure of my loins; then if I would
Speak that—

SICINIUS
We know your drift:—speak what?

BRUTUS
There's no more to be said, but he is banish'd,
As enemy to the people and his country:
It shall be so.

CITIZENS
It shall be so, it shall be so.

CORIOLANUS
You common cry of curs! whose breath I hate
As reek o' the rotten fens, whose loves I prize
As the dead carcasses of unburied men
That do corrupt my air, I banish you;
And here remain with your uncertainty!
Let every feeble rumour shake your hearts!
Your enemies, with nodding of their plumes,
Fan you into despair! Have the power still
To banish your defenders; till at length
Your ignorance, which finds not till it feels,
Making not reservation of yourselves,
Still your own foes, deliver you as most
Abated captives to some nation
That won you without blows! Despising,
For you, the city, thus I turn my back:
There is a world elsewhere.

[Exeunt CORIOLANUS, COMINIUS,
MENENIUS, SENATORS and PATRICIANS

ÆDILE
The people's enemy is gone, is gone!

CITIZENS

Our enemy is banish'd! he is gone! Hoo! hoo!
[*They all shout, and throw up their caps*

SICINIUS

Go, see him out at gates, and follow him,
As he hath follow'd you, with all despite;
Give him deserved vexation. Let a guard
Attend us through the city.

CITIZENS

Come, come, let's see him out at gates; come.
The gods preserve our noble tribunes! Come.
[*Exeunt*

ACT IV

SCENE I. *Rome. Before a gate of the city*

Enter CORIOLANUS, VOLUMNIA, VIRGILIA, MENENIUS,
      COMINIUS, *with the young Nobility of Rome*

CORIOLANUS

Come, leave your tears; a brief farewell: the beast
With many heads butts me away. Nay, mother,
Where is your ancient courage? you were used
To say extremity was the trier of spirits;
That common chances common men could bear;
That when the sea was calm all boats alike
Show'd mastership in floating; fortune's blows,
When most struck home, being gentle wounded, craves
A noble cunning: you were used to load me
With precepts that would make invincible
The heart that conn'd them.

VIRGILIA

O heavens! O heavens!

CORIOLANUS

                    Nay, I prithee, woman,—

VOLUMNIA

Now the red pestilence strike all trades in Rome,
And occupations perish!

CORIOLANUS

                    What, what, what!
I shall be loved when I am lack'd. Nay, mother,
Resume that spirit, when you were wont to say,
If you had been the wife of Hercules,
Six of his labours you'ld have done, and saved
Your husband so much sweat. Cominius,
Droop not; adieu. Farewell, my wife, my mother:
I'll do well yet. Thou old and true Menenius,
Thy tears are salter than a younger man's,
And venomous to thine eyes. My sometime general,
I have seen thee stern, and thou hast oft beheld
Heart-hardening spectacles; tell these sad women,
'Tis fond to wail inevitable strokes,
As 'tis to laugh at 'em. My mother, you wot well
My hazards still have been your solace: and
Believe 't not lightly—though I go alone,
Like to a lonely dragon, that his fen
Makes fear'd and talk'd of more than seen—your son

Will or exceed the common, or be caught
With cautelous baits and practice.

VOLUMNIA

                    My first son,
Whither wilt thou go? Take good Cominius
With thee awhile: determine on some course,
More than a wild exposture to each chance
That starts i' the way before thee.

CORIOLANUS

                    O the gods!

COMINIUS

I'll follow thee a month, devise with thee
Where thou shalt rest, that thou mayst hear of us
And we of thee: so, if the time thrust forth
A cause for thy repeal, we shall not send
O'er the vast world to seek a single man,
And lose advantage, which doth ever cool
I' the absence of the needer.

CORIOLANUS

                    Fare ye well:
Thou hast years upon thee; and thou art too full
Of the wars' surfeits, to go rove with one
That's yet unbruised: bring me but out at gate.
Come, my sweet wife, my dearest mother, and
My friends of noble touch, when I am forth,
Bid me farewell, and smile. I pray you, come.
While I remain above the ground, you shall
Hear from me still, and never of me aught
But what is like me formerly.

MENENIUS

                    That's worthily
As any ear can hear. Come, let's not weep.
If I could shake off but one seven years
From these old arms and legs, by the good gods,
I'ld with thee every foot.

CORIOLANUS

                    Give me thy hand:
Come.   [*Exeunt*

SCENE II. *The same. A street near the gate*

Enter the two TRIBUNES, SICINIUS *and* BRUTUS, *with the*
      ÆDILE

SICINIUS

Bid them all home; he's gone, and we'll no further.
The nobility are vex'd, whom we see have sided
In his behalf.

BRUTUS

                    Now we have shown our power,
Let us seem humbler after it is done
Than when it was a-doing.

SICINIUS

                    Bid them home:
Say their great enemy is gone, and they
Stand in their ancient strength.

BRUTUS

                    Dismiss them home. [*Exit* ÆDILE
Here comes his mother.

[1133]

Enter VOLUMNIA, VIRGILIA, *and* MENENIUS

SICINIUS

　　　　Let's not meet her.

BRUTUS

　　　　　　　　　　Why?

SICINIUS

They say she's mad.

BRUTUS

They have ta'en note of us: keep on your way.

VOLUMNIA

O, ye're well met: the hoarded plague o' the gods
Requite your love!

MENENIUS

　　　　Peace, peace; be not so loud.

VOLUMNIA

If that I could for weeping, you should hear,—
Nay, and you shall hear some. [*To* BRUTUS] Will you
　be gone?

VIRGILIA

[*To* SICINIUS] You shall stay too: I would I had the
　power
To say so to my husband.

SICINIUS

　　　　　　Are you mankind?

VOLUMNIA

Ay, fool; is that a shame? Note but this fool.
Was not a man my father? Hadst thou foxship
To banish him that struck more blows for Rome
Than thou hast spoken words?

SICINIUS

　　　　　　O blessed heavens!

VOLUMNIA

Moe noble blows than ever thou wise words;
And for Rome's good. I'll tell thee what; yet go:
Nay, but thou shalt stay too: I would my son
Were in Arabia, and thy tribe before him,
His good sword in his hand.

SICINIUS

　　　　　What then?

VIRGILIA

　　　　　　　　What then!

He'ld make an end of thy posterity.

VOLUMNIA

Bastards and all.
Good man, the wounds that he does bear for Rome!

MENENIUS

Come, come, peace.

SICINIUS

I would he had continued to his country
As he began, and not unknit himself
The noble knot he made.

BRUTUS

　　　　　I would he had.

VOLUMNIA

'I would he had!' 'Twas you incensed the rabble;
Cats, that can judge as fitly of his worth
As I can of those mysteries which heaven
Will not have earth to know.

BRUTUS

　　　　　Pray, let us go.

VOLUMNIA

Now, pray, sir, get you gone:
You have done a brave deed. Ere you go, hear this:
As far as doth the Capitol exceed
The meanest house in Rome, so far my son—
This lady's husband here, this, do you see?—
Whom you have banish'd, does exceed you all.

BRUTUS

Well, well, we'll leave you.

SICINIUS

　　　　　Why stay we to be baited
With one that wants her wits?

VOLUMNIA

　　　　　Take my prayers with you.
　　　　　　　　　[*Exeunt* TRIBUNES

I would the gods had nothing else to do
But to confirm my curses! Could I meet 'em
But once a-day, it would unclog my heart
Of what lies heavy to 't.

MENENIUS

　　　　　You have told them home;
And, by my troth, you have cause. You'll sup with
　me?

VOLUMNIA

Anger's my meat; I sup upon myself,
And so shall starve with feeding. Come, let's go:
Leave this faint puling, and lament as I do,
In anger, Juno-like. Come, come, come.
　　　　　[*Exeunt* VOLUMNIA *and* VIRGILIA

MENENIUS

Fie, fie, fie!　　　　　　　　[*Exit

SCENE III. *A highway between Rome and Antium*

Enter a ROMAN *and a* VOLSCE, *meeting*

A ROMAN

I know you well, sir, and you know me: your name,
I think, is Adrian.

A VOLSCIAN

It is so, sir: truly, I have forgot you.

A ROMAN

I am a Roman; and my services are, as you are,
against 'em: know you me yet?

A VOLSCIAN

Nicanor? no.

A ROMAN

The same, sir.

A VOLSCIAN

You had more beard when I last saw you; but your
favour is well appeared by your tongue. What's the
news in Rome? I have a note from the Volscian
state, to find you out there: you have well saved me
a day's journey.

A ROMAN

There hath been in Rome strange insurrections; the
people against the senators, patricians and nobles.

A VOLSCIAN

Hath been! is it ended then? Our state thinks not so:

they are in a most warlike preparation, and hope to come upon them in the heat of their division.

A ROMAN

The main blaze of it is past, but a small thing would make it flame again: for the nobles receive so to heart the banishment of that worthy Coriolanus, that they are in a ripe aptness to take all power from the people, and to pluck from them their tribunes for ever. This lies glowing, I can tell you, and is almost mature for the violent breaking out.

A VOLSCIAN

Coriolanus banished!

A ROMAN

Banished, sir.

A VOLSCIAN

You will be welcome with this intelligence, Nicanor.

A ROMAN

The day serves well for them now. I have heard it said, the fittest time to corrupt a man's wife is when she's fallen out with her husband. Your noble Tullus Aufidius will appear well in these wars, his great opposer, Coriolanus, being now in no request of his country.

A VOLSCIAN

He cannot choose. I am most fortunate, thus accidentally to encounter you: you have ended my business, and I will merrily accompany you home.

A ROMAN

I shall, between this and supper, tell you most strange things from Rome; all tending to the good of their adversaries. Have you an army ready, say you?

A VOLSCIAN

A most royal one; the centurions and their charges, distinctly billeted, already in the entertainment, and to be on foot at an hour's warning.

A ROMAN

I am joyful to hear of their readiness, and am the man, I think, that shall set them in present action. So, sir, heartily well met, and most glad of your company.

A VOLSCIAN

You take my part from me, sir; I have the most cause to be glad of yours.

A ROMAN

Well, let us go together.   [Exeunt

SCENE IV. *Antium. Before* AUFIDIUS's *house*

Enter CORIOLANUS *in mean apparel, disguised and muffled*

CORIOLANUS

A goodly city is this Antium. City,
'Tis I that made thy widows: many an heir
Of these fair edifices 'fore my wars
Have I heard groan and drop: then know me not;
Lest that thy wives with spits, and boys with stones,
In puny battle slay me.

Enter a CITIZEN

Save you, sir.

A CITIZEN

And you.

CORIOLANUS

Direct me, if it be your will,
Where great Aufidius lies: is he in Antium?

A CITIZEN

He is, and feasts the nobles of the state
At his house this night.

CORIOLANUS

Which is his house, beseech you?

A CITIZEN

This, here, before you.

CORIOLANUS

Thank you, sir: farewell.
     [Exit CITIZEN
O world, thy slippery turns! Friends now fast sworn,
Whose double bosoms seem to wear one heart,
Whose hours, whose bed, whose meal and exercise
Are still together, who twin, as 'twere, in love
Unseparable, shall within this hour,
On a dissension of a doit, break out
To bitterest enmity: so, fellest foes,
Whose passions and whose plots have broke their
     sleep
To take the one the other, by some chance,
Some trick not worth an egg, shall grow dear
     friends
And interjoin their issues. So with me:
My birth-place hate I, and my love's upon
This enemy town. I'll enter: if he slay me,
He does fair justice; if he give me way,
I'll do his country service.   [Exit

SCENE V. *The same. A hall in* AUFIDIUS's *house*

Music within. Enter a SERVINGMAN

FIRST SERVINGMAN

Wine, wine, wine!—What service is here!
I think our fellows are asleep.   [Exit

Enter another SERVINGMAN

SECOND SERVINGMAN

Where's Cotus? my master calls for him.
Cotus!   [Exit

Enter CORIOLANUS

CORIOLANUS

A goodly house: the feast smells well; but I
Appear not like a guest.

Re-enter the FIRST SERVINGMAN

FIRST SERVINGMAN

What would you have, friend? whence are you?
Here's no place for you: pray, go to the door. [Exit

CORIOLANUS

I have deserved no better entertainment,
In being Coriolanus.

Re-enter SECOND SERVINGMAN

SECOND SERVINGMAN

Whence are you, sir? Has the porter his eyes in his

head, that he gives entrance to such companions?
Pray, get you out.

CORIOLANUS

Away!

SECOND SERVINGMAN

'Away!' get you away.

CORIOLANUS

Now thou'rt troublesome.

SECOND SERVINGMAN

Are you so brave? I'll have you talked with anon.
Enter a THIRD SERVINGMAN. *The first meets him*

THIRD SERVINGMAN

What fellow's this?

FIRST SERVINGMAN

A strange one as ever I looked on: I cannot get him
out o' the house: prithee, call my master to him.
[Retires

THIRD SERVINGMAN

What have you to do here, fellow? Pray you, avoid
the house.

CORIOLANUS

Let me but stand; I will not hurt your hearth.

THIRD SERVINGMAN

What are you?

CORIOLANUS

A gentleman.

THIRD SERVINGMAN

A marvellous poor one.

CORIOLANUS

True, so I am.

THIRD SERVINGMAN

Pray you, poor gentleman, take up some other
station; here's no place for you; pray you, avoid:
come.

CORIOLANUS

Follow your function, go, and batten on cold bits.
[Pushes him away from him

THIRD SERVINGMAN

What, you will not? Prithee, tell my master what a
strange guest he has here.

SECOND SERVINGMAN

And I shall. *[Exit*

THIRD SERVINGMAN

Where dwell'st thou?

CORIOLANUS

Under the canopy.

THIRD SERVINGMAN

Under the canopy!

CORIOLANUS

Ay.

THIRD SERVINGMAN

Where's that?

CORIOLANUS

I' the city of kites and crows.

THIRD SERVINGMAN

I' the city of kites and crows! What an ass it is!
Then thou dwell'st with daws too?

CORIOLANUS

No, I serve not thy master.

THIRD SERVINGMAN

How, sir! do you meddle with my master?

CORIOLANUS

Ay; 'tis an honester service than to meddle with
thy mistress:
Thou pratest, and pratest; serve with thy trencher,
hence!
[Beats him away. Exit THIRD SERVINGMAN
Enter AUFIDIUS *with the* SECOND SERVINGMAN

AUFIDIUS

Where is this fellow?

SECOND SERVINGMAN

Here, sir: I'ld have beaten him like a dog, but for
disturbing the lords within. *[Retires*

AUFIDIUS

Whence comest thou? what wouldst thou? thy
name?
Why speak'st not? speak, man: what's thy name?

CORIOLANUS

[Unmuffling]   If, Tullus,
Not yet thou knowest me, and, seeing me, dost not
Think me for the man I am, necessity
Commands me name myself.

AUFIDIUS

               What is thy name?

CORIOLANUS

A name unmusical to the Volscians' ears,
And harsh in sound to thine.

AUFIDIUS

             Say, what's thy name?
Thou hast a grim appearance, and thy face
Bears a command in 't; though thy tackle's torn,
Thou show'st a noble vessel: what's thy name?

CORIOLANUS

Prepare thy brow to frown:—know'st thou me yet?

AUFIDIUS

I know thee not:—thy name?

CORIOLANUS

My name is Caius Marcius, who hath done
To thee particularly, and to all the Volsces,
Great hurt and mischief; thereto witness may
My surname, Coriolanus: the painful service,
The extreme dangers, and the drops of blood
Shed for my thankless country, are requited
But with that surname; a good memory,
And witness of the malice and displeasure
Which thou shouldst bear me: only that name re-
mains:
The cruelty and envy of the people,
Permitted by our dastard nobles, who
Have all forsook me, hath devour'd the rest;
And suffer'd me by the voice of slaves to be
Hoop'd out of Rome. Now, this extremity
Hath brought me to thy hearth: not out of hope—
Mistake me not—to save my life, for if
I had fear'd death, of all the men i' the world
I would have 'voided thee; but in mere spite,
To be full quit of those my banishers,
Stand I before thee here. Then if thou hast
A heart of wreak in thee, that wilt revenge

Thine own particular wrongs, and stop those maims
Of shame seen through thy country, speed thee
   straight,
And make my misery serve thy turn: so use it
That my revengeful services may prove
As benefits to thee; for I will fight
Against my canker'd country with the spleen
Of all the under fiends. But if so be
Thou darest not this and that to prove more for-
   tunes
Thou'rt tired, then, in a word, I also am
Longer to live most weary, and present
My throat to thee and to thy ancient malice;
Which not to cut would show thee but a fool,
Since I have ever follow'd thee with hate,
Drawn tuns of blood out of thy country's breast,
And cannot live but to thy shame, unless
It be to do thee service.

AUFIDIUS
              O Marcius, Marcius!
Each word thou hast spoke hath weeded from my
   heart
A root of ancient envy. If Jupiter
Should from yond cloud speak divine things,
And say ''Tis true,' I'ld not believe them more
Than thee, all noble Marcius. Let me twine
Mine arms about that body, where against
My grained ash an hundred times hath broke,
And scarr'd the moon with splinters: here I clip
The anvil of my sword, and do contest
As hotly and as nobly with thy love
As ever in ambitious strength I did
Contend against thy valour. Know thou first,
I loved the maid I married; never man
Sigh'd truer breath; but that I see thee here,
Thou noble thing! more dances my rapt heart
Than when I first my wedded mistress saw
Bestride my threshold. Why, thou Mars! I tell thee,
We have a power on foot; and I had purpose
Once more to hew thy target from thy brawn,
Or lose mine arm for 't: thou hast beat me out
Twelve several times, and I have nightly since
Dreamt of encounters 'twixt thyself and me;
We have been down together in my sleep,
Unbuckling helms, fisting each other's throat;
And waked half dead with nothing. Worthy Mar-
   cius,
Had we no quarrel else to Rome but that
Thou art thence banish'd, we would muster all
From twelve to seventy, and pouring war
Into the bowels of ungrateful Rome,
Like a bold flood o'er-beat. O, come, go in,
And take our friendly senators by the hands,
Who now are here, taking their leaves of me,
Who am prepared against your territories,
Though not for Rome itself.

CORIOLANUS
             You bless me, gods!

AUFIDIUS
Therefore, most absolute sir, if thou wilt have

The leading of thine own revenges, take
The one half of my commission, and set down—
As best thou art experienced, since thou know'st
Thy country's strength and weakness—thine own
   ways;
Whether to knock against the gates of Rome,
Or rudely visit them in parts remote,
To fright them, ere destroy. But come in:
Let me commend thee first to those that shall
Say yea to thy desires. A thousand welcomes!
And more a friend than e'er an enemy;
Yet, Marcius, that was much. Your hand: most
   welcome! [*Exeunt* CORIOLANUS *and* AUFIDIUS. *The*
            two SERVINGMEN *come forward*

FIRST SERVINGMAN
Here's a strange alteration!

SECOND SERVINGMAN
By my hand, I had thought to have strucken him
with a cudgel; and yet my mind gave me his
clothes made a false report of him.

FIRST SERVINGMAN
What an arm he has! he turned me about with his
finger and his thumb, as one would set up a top.

SECOND SERVINGMAN
Nay, I knew by his face that there was something in
him: he had, sir, a kind of face, methought,—I cannot tell how to term it.

FIRST SERVINGMAN
He had so; looking as it were—Would I were
hanged, but I thought there was more in him than
I could think.

SECOND SERVINGMAN
So did I, I'll be sworn: he is simply the rarest man
i' the world.

FIRST SERVINGMAN
I think he is: but a greater soldier than he, you wot
one.

SECOND SERVINGMAN
Who? my master?

FIRST SERVINGMAN
Nay, it's no matter for that.

SECOND SERVINGMAN
Worth six on him.

FIRST SERVINGMAN
Nay, not so neither: but I take him to be the
greater soldier.

SECOND SERVINGMAN
Faith, look you, one cannot tell how to say that: for
the defence of a town, our general is excellent.

FIRST SERVINGMAN
Ay, and for an assault too.
          Re-enter THIRD SERVINGMAN

THIRD SERVINGMAN
O slaves, I can tell you news; news, you rascals!

FIRST *and* SECOND SERVINGMAN
What, what, what? let's partake.

THIRD SERVINGMAN
I would not be a Roman, of all nations; I had as
lieve be a condemned man.

FIRST *and* SECOND SERVINGMAN
Wherefore? wherefore?

THIRD SERVINGMAN
Why, here's he that was wont to thwack our general, Caius Marcius.

FIRST SERVINGMAN
Why do you say, thwack our general?

THIRD SERVINGMAN
I do not say, thwack our general; but he was always good enough for him.

SECOND SERVINGMAN
Come, we are fellows and friends: he was ever too hard for him; I have heard him say so himself.

FIRST SERVINGMAN
He was too hard for him directly, to say the troth on 't: before Corioli he scotched him and notched him like a carbonado.

SECOND SERVINGMAN
An he had been cannibally given, he might have broiled and eaten him too.

FIRST SERVINGMAN
But, more of thy news?

THIRD SERVINGMAN
Why, he is so made on here within as if he were son and heir to Mars; set at upper end o' the table; no question asked him by any of the senators, but they stand bald before him. Our general himself makes a mistress of him; sanctifies himself with 's hand, and turns up the white o' the eye to his discourse. But the bottom of the news is, our general is cut i' the middle, and but one half of what he was yesterday; for the other has half, by the entreaty and grant of the whole table. He'll go, he says, and sowl the porter of Rome gates by the ears: he will mow all down before him, and leave his passage poll'd.

SECOND SERVINGMAN
And he's as like to do 't as any man I can imagine.

THIRD SERVINGMAN
Do 't! he will do 't; for, look you, sir, he has as many friends as enemies; which friends, sir, as it were, durst not, look you, sir, show themselves, as we term it, his friends whilst he's in directitude.

FIRST SERVINGMAN
Directitude! what's that?

THIRD SERVINGMAN
But when they shall see, sir, his crest up again and the man in blood, they will out of their burrows, like conies after rain, and revel all with him.

FIRST SERVINGMAN
But when goes this forward?

THIRD SERVINGMAN
To-morrow; to-day; presently: you shall have the drum struck up this afternoon: 'tis, as it were, a parcel of their feast, and to be executed ere they wipe their lips.

SECOND SERVINGMAN
Why, then we shall have a stirring world again. This peace is nothing, but to rust iron, increase tailors, and breed ballad-makers.

FIRST SERVINGMAN
Let me have war, say I; it exceeds peace as far as day does night; it's spritely, waking, audible, and full of vent. Peace is a very apoplexy, lethargy, mull'd, deaf, sleepy, insensible; a getter of more bastard children than war's a destroyer of men.

SECOND SERVINGMAN
'Tis so: and as war, in some sort, may be said to be a ravisher, so it cannot be denied but peace is a great maker of cuckolds.

FIRST SERVINGMAN
Ay, and it makes men hate one another.

THIRD SERVINGMAN
Reason; because they then less need one another. The wars for my money. I hope to see Romans as cheap as Volscians. They are rising, they are rising.

FIRST *and* SECOND SERVINGMAN
In, in, in, in!　　　　　　　　　　　　　[*Exeunt*]

SCENE VI. *Rome. A public place*

Enter the two TRIBUNES, SICINIUS *and* BRUTUS

SICINIUS
We hear not of him, neither need we fear him;
His remedies are tame i' the present peace
And quietness of the people, which before
Were in wild hurry. Here do we make his friends
Blush that the world goes well; who rather had,
Though they themselves did suffer by 't, behold
Dissentious numbers pestering streets than see
Our tradesmen singing in their shops and going
About their functions friendly.

BRUTUS
We stood to 't in good time.

Enter MENENIUS

　　　　　　　　　　　　　　Is this Menenius?

SICINIUS
'Tis he, 'tis he: O, he is grown most kind
Of late. Hail, sir!

MENENIUS
　　　　　　　　Hail to you both!

SICINIUS
Your Coriolanus is not much miss'd,
But with his friends: the commonwealth doth stand;
And so would do, were he more angry at it.

MENENIUS
All's well; and might have been much better, if
He could have temporized.

SICINIUS
　　　　　　　　Where is he, hear you?

MENENIUS
Nay, I hear nothing: his mother and his wife
Hear nothing from him.

Enter three or four CITIZENS

CITIZENS
The gods preserve you both!

SICINIUS
　　　　　　　God-den, our neighbours.

BRUTUS
God-den to you all, god-den to you all.
FIRST CITIZEN
Ourselves, our wives, and children, on our knees,
Are bound to pray for you both.
SICINIUS
            Live, and thrive!
BRUTUS
Farewell, kind neighbours: we wish'd Coriolanus
Had loved you as we did.
CITIZENS
            Now the gods keep you!
BOTH TRIBUNES
Farewell, farewell.   [*Exeunt* CITIZENS
SICINIUS
This is a happier and more comely time
Than when these fellows ran about the streets,
Crying confusion.
BRUTUS
            Caius Marcius was
A worthy officer i' the war, but insolent,
O'ercome with pride, ambitious past all thinking,
Self-loving,—
SICINIUS
            And affecting one sole throne,
Without assistance.
MENENIUS
            I think not so.
SICINIUS
We should by this, to all our lamentation,
If he had gone forth consul, found it so.
BRUTUS
The gods have well prevented it, and Rome
Sits safe and still without him.
Enter an ÆDILE
ÆDILE
            Worthy tribunes,
There is a slave, whom we have put in prison,
Reports, the Volsces with two several powers
Are enter'd in the Roman territories,
And with the deepest malice of the war
Destroy what lies before 'em.
MENENIUS
            'Tis Aufidius,
Who, hearing of our Marcius' banishment,
Thrusts forth his horns again into the world;
Which were inshell'd when Marcius stood for Rome,
And durst not once peep out.
SICINIUS
            Come, what talk you
Of Marcius?
BRUTUS
Go see this rumourer whipp'd. It cannot be
The Volsces dare break with us.
MENENIUS
            Cannot be!
We have record that very well it can,
And three examples of the like have been
Within my age. But reason with the fellow,
Before you punish him, where he heard this,

Lest you shall chance to whip your information,
And beat the messenger who bids beware
Of what is to be dreaded.
SICINIUS
            Tell not me:
I know this cannot be.
BRUTUS
            Not possible.
Enter a MESSENGER
MESSENGER
The nobles in great earnestness are going
All to the senate-house: some news is come
That turns their countenances.
SICINIUS
            'Tis this slave;
Go whip him 'fore the people's eyes: his raising;
Nothing but his report.
MESSENGER
            Yes, worthy sir,
The slave's report is seconded; and more,
More fearful, is deliver'd.
SICINIUS
            What more fearful?
MESSENGER
It is spoke freely out of many mouths—
How probable I do not know—that Marcius,
Join'd with Aufidius, leads a power 'gainst Rome,
And vows revenge as spacious as between
The young'st and oldest thing.
SICINIUS
            This is most likely!
BRUTUS
Raised only, that the weaker sort may wish
Good Marcius home again.
SICINIUS
            The very trick on 't.
MENENIUS
This is unlikely:
He and Aufidius can no more atone
Than violentest contrariety.
Enter a SECOND MESSENGER
SECOND MESSENGER
You are sent for to the senate:
A fearful army, led by Caius Marcius
Associated with Aufidius, rages
Upon our territories; and have already
O'erborne their way, consumed with fire, and took
What lay before them.
Enter COMINIUS
COMINIUS
O, you have made good work!
MENENIUS
            What news? what news?
COMINIUS
You have holp to ravish your own daughters, and
To melt the city leads upon your pates;
To see your wives dishonour'd to your noses,—
MENENIUS
What's the news? what's the news?

COMINIUS

Your temples burned in their cement, and
Your franchises, whereon you stood, confined
Into an auger's bore.

MENENIUS

Pray now, your news?—
You have made fair work, I fear me.—Pray, your
news?—
If Marcius should be join'd with Volscians,—

COMINIUS

If!

He is their god: he leads them like a thing
Made by some other deity than nature,
That shapes man better; and they follow him,
Against us brats, with no less confidence
Than boys pursuing summer butterflies,
Or butchers killing flies.

MENENIUS

You have made good work,
You and your apron-men; you that stood so much
Upon the voice of occupation and
The breath of garlic-eaters!

COMINIUS

He'll shake your Rome about your ears.

MENENIUS

As Hercules
Did shake down mellow fruit. You have made fair
work!

BRUTUS

But is this true, sir?

COMINIUS

Ay; and you'll look pale
Before you find it other. All the regions
Do smilingly revolt; and who resist
Are mock'd for valiant ignorance,
And perish constant fools. Who is 't can blame him?
Your enemies and his find something in him.

MENENIUS

We are all undone, unless
The noble man have mercy.

COMINIUS

Who shall ask it?
The tribunes cannot do 't for shame; the people
Deserve such pity of him as the wolf
Does of the shepherds: for his best friends, if they
Should say 'Be good to Rome,' they charged him
even
As those should do that had deserved his hate,
And therein show'd like enemies.

MENENIUS

'Tis true:
If he were putting to my house the brand
That should consume it, I have not the face
To say 'Beseech you, cease.' You have made fair
hands,
You and your crafts! you have crafted fair!

COMINIUS

You have brought
A trembling upon Rome, such as was never
So incapable of help.

BOTH TRIBUNES

Say not, we brought it.

MENENIUS

How! was it we? we loved him; but, like beasts
And cowardly nobles, gave way unto your clusters
Who did hoot him out o' the city.

COMINIUS

But I fear
They'll roar him in again. Tullus Aufidius,
The second name of men, obeys his points
As if he were his officer: desperation
Is all the policy, strength and defence,
That Rome can make against them.

Enter a troop of CITIZENS

MENENIUS

Here come the clusters
And is Aufidius with him? You are they
That made the air unwholesome, when you cast
Your stinking greasy caps in hooting at
Coriolanus' exile. Now he's coming;
And not a hair upon a soldier's head
Which will not prove a whip: as many coxcombs
As you threw caps up will he tumble down,
And pay you for your voices. 'Tis no matter;
If he could burn us all into one coal,
We have deserved it.

CITIZENS

Faith, we hear fearful news.

FIRST CITIZEN

For mine own part,
When I said, banish him, I said, 'twas pity.

SECOND CITIZEN

And so did I.

THIRD CITIZEN

And so did I; and, to say the truth, so did very
many of us: that we did, we did for the best; and
though we willingly consented to his banishment,
yet it was against our will.

COMINIUS

Ye're goodly things, you voices!

MENENIUS

You have made
Good work, you and your cry! Shall 's to the Capitol?

COMINIUS

O, ay, what else?   [*Exeunt* COMINIUS *and* MENENIUS

SICINIUS

Go, masters, get you home; be not dismay'd:
These are a side that would be glad to have
This true which they so seem to fear. Go home,
And show no sign of fear.

FIRST CITIZEN

The gods be good to us! Come, masters, let's home.
I ever said we were i' the wrong when we banished
him.

SECOND CITIZEN

So did we all. But, come, let's home.

[*Exeunt* CITIZENS

BRUTUS

I do not like this news.

SICINIUS

Nor I.

BRUTUS

Let's to the Capitol: would half my wealth
Would buy this for a lie!

SICINIUS

        Pray, let us go.   [*Exeunt*

SCENE VII. *A camp, at a small distance from Rome*

Enter AUFIDIUS *with his* LIEUTENANT

AUFIDIUS

Do they still fly to the Roman?

LIEUTENANT

I do not know what witchcraft's in him, but
Your soldiers use him as the grace 'fore meat,
Their talk at table and their thanks at end;
And you are darken'd in this action, sir,
Even by your own.

AUFIDIUS

        I cannot help it now,
Unless, by using means, I lame the foot
Of our design. He bears himself more proudlier,
Even to my person, than I thought he would
When first I did embrace him: yet his nature
In that's no changeling; and I must excuse
What cannot be amended.

LIEUTENANT

        Yet I wish, sir—
I mean for your particular—you had not
Join'd in commission with him; but either
Had borne the action of yourself, or else
To him had left it solely.

AUFIDIUS

I understand thee well; and be thou sure,
When he shall come to his account, he knows not
What I can urge against him. Although it seems,
And so he thinks, and is no less apparent
To the vulgar eye, that he bears all things fairly,
And shows good husbandry for the Volscian state,
Fights dragon-like, and does achieve as soon
As draw his sword, yet he hath left undone
That which shall break his neck or hazard mine,
Whene'er we come to our account.

LIEUTENANT

Sir, I beseech you, think you he'll carry Rome?

AUFIDIUS

All places yield to him ere he sits down;
And the nobility of Rome are his:
The senators and patricians love him too:
The tribunes are no soldiers; and their people
Will be as rash in the repeal, as hasty
To expel him thence. I think he'll be to Rome
As is the osprey to the fish, who takes it
By sovereignty of nature. First he was
A noble servant to them; but he could not
Carry his honours even: whether 'twas pride,
Which out of daily fortune ever taints
The happy man; whether defect of judgement,

To fail in the disposing of those chances
Which he was lord of; or whether nature,
Not to be other than one thing, not moving
From the casque to the cushion, but commanding
  peace
Even with the same austerity and garb
As he controll'd the war; but one of these—
As he hath spices of them all, not all,
For I dare so far free him—made him fear'd,
So hated, and so banish'd: but he has a merit,
To choke it in the utterance. So our virtues
Lie in the interpretation of the time;
And power, unto itself most commendable,
Hath not a tomb so evident as a chair
To extol what it hath done.
One fire drives out one fire; one nail, one nail;
Rights by rights fouler, strengths by strengths do
  fail.
Come, let's away. When, Caius, Rome is thine,
Thou art poor'st of all; then shortly art thou mine.

                     [*Exeunt*

ACT V

SCENE I. *Rome. A public place*

Enter MENENIUS, COMINIUS, SICINIUS *and* BRUTUS, *the two* TRIBUNES, *with others*

MENENIUS

No, I'll not go: you hear what he hath said
Which was sometime his general, who loved him
In a most dear particular. He call'd me father:
But what o' that? Go, you that banish'd him;
A mile before his tent fall down, and knee
The way into his mercy: nay, if he coy'd
To hear Cominius speak, I'll keep at home.

COMINIUS

He would not seem to know me.

MENENIUS

              Do you hear?

COMINIUS

Yet one time he did call me by my name:
I urged our old acquaintance, and the drops
That we have bled together. Coriolanus
He would not answer to: forbad all names;
He was a kind of nothing, titleless,
Till he had forged himself a name o' the fire
Of burning Rome.

MENENIUS

      Why, so: you have made good work!
A pair of tribunes that have rack'd for Rome,
To make coals cheap: a noble memory!

COMINIUS

I minded him how royal 'twas to pardon
When it was less expected: he replied,
It was a bare petition of a state
To one whom they had punish'd.

MENENIUS

              Very well:

Could he say less?

COMINIUS

I offer'd to awaken his regard
For 's private friends: his answer to me was,
He could not stay to pick them in a pile
Of noisome musty chaff: he said, 'twas folly,
For one poor grain or two, to leave unburnt,
And still to nose the offence.

MENENIUS

For one poor grain or two!
I am one of those; his mother, wife, his child,
And this brave fellow too, we are the grains:
You are the musty chaff, and you are smelt
Above the moon: we must be burnt for you.

SICINIUS

Nay, pray, be patient: if you refuse your aid
In this so never-needed help, yet do not
Upbraid 's with our distress. But sure, if you
Would be your country's pleader, your good tongue,
More than the instant army we can make,
Might stop our countryman.

MENENIUS

No, I'll not meddle.

SICINIUS

Pray you, go to him.

MENENIUS

What should I do?

BRUTUS

Only make trial what your love can do
For Rome, towards Marcius.

MENENIUS

Well, and say that Marcius
Return me, as Cominius is return'd,
Unheard; what then?
But as a discontented friend, grief-shot
With his unkindness? say 't be so?

SICINIUS

Yet your good will
Must have that thanks from Rome, after the measure
As you intended well.

MENENIUS

I'll undertake 't:
I think he'll hear me. Yet, to bite his lip
And hum at good Cominius, much unhearts me.
He was not taken well; he had not dined:
The veins unfill'd, our blood is cold, and then
We pout upon the morning, are unapt
To give or to forgive; but when we have stuff'd
These pipes and these conveyances of our blood
With wine and feeding, we have suppler souls
Than in our priest-like fasts: therefore I'll watch him
Till he be dieted to my request,
And then I'll set upon him.

BRUTUS

You know the very road into his kindness,
And cannot lose your way.

MENENIUS

Good faith, I'll prove him,

Speed how it will. I shall ere long have knowledge
Of my success.   [Exit

COMINIUS

He'll never hear him.

SICINIUS

Not?

COMINIUS

I tell you, he does sit in gold, his eye
Red as 'twould burn Rome; and his injury
The gaoler to his pity. I kneel'd before him;
'Twas very faintly he said 'Rise;' dismiss'd me
Thus, with his speechless hand: what he would do,
He sent in writing after me; what he would not,
Bound with an oath to yield to his conditions:
So that all hope is vain,
Unless his noble mother, and his wife;
Who, as I hear, mean to solicit him
For mercy to his country. Therefore, let's hence,
And with our fair entreaties haste them on. [Exeunt

SCENE II. *Entrance to the Volscian camp before Rome.*
Two SENTINELS *on guard*

Enter to them, MENENIUS

FIRST SENTINEL

Stay: whence are you?

SECOND SENTINEL

Stand, and go back.

MENENIUS

You guard like men; 'tis well: but, by your leave,
I am an officer of state, and come
To speak with Coriolanus.

FIRST SENTINEL

From whence?

MENENIUS

From Rome.

FIRST SENTINEL

You may not pass, you must return: our general
Will no more hear from thence.

SECOND SENTINEL

You'll see your Rome embraced with fire, before
You'll speak with Coriolanus.

MENENIUS

Good my friends,
If you have heard your general talk of Rome,
And of his friends there, it is lots to blanks
My name hath touch'd your ears: it is Menenius.

FIRST SENTINEL

Be it so; go back: the virtue of your name
Is not here passable.

MENENIUS

I tell thee, fellow,
Thy general is my lover: I have been
The book of his good acts, whence men have read
His fame unparallel'd haply amplified;
For I have ever verified my friends,
Of whom he's chief, with all the size that verity
Would without lapsing suffer: nay, sometimes,
Like to a bowl upon a subtle ground,

I have tumbled past the throw, and in his praise
Have almost stamp'd the leasing: therefore, fellow,
I must have leave to pass.

FIRST SENTINEL

Faith, sir, if you had told as many lies in his behalf
as you have uttered words in your own, you should
not pass here; no, though it were as virtuous to lie
as to live chastely. Therefore go back.

MENENIUS

Prithee, fellow, remember my name is Menenius,
always factionary on the party of your general.

SECOND SENTINEL

Howsoever you have been his liar, as you say you
have, I am one that, telling true under him, must
say, you cannot pass. Therefore go back.

MENENIUS

Has he dined, canst thou tell? for I would not speak
with him till after dinner.

FIRST SENTINEL

You are a Roman, are you?

MENENIUS

I am, as thy general is.

FIRST SENTINEL

Then you should hate Rome, as he does. Can you,
when you have pushed out your gates the very defender of them, and, in a violent popular ignorance,
given your enemy your shield, think to front his revenges with the easy groans of old women, the
virginal palms of your daughters, or with the palsied
intercession of such a decayed dotant as you seem to
be? Can you think to blow out the intended fire
your city is ready to flame in, with such weak breath
as this? No, you are deceived; therefore, back to
Rome, and prepare for your execution: you are
condemned; our general has sworn you out of reprieve and pardon.

MENENIUS

Sirrah, if thy captain knew I were here, he would
use me with estimation.

FIRST SENTINEL

Come, my captain knows you not.

MENENIUS

I mean, thy general.

FIRST SENTINEL

My general cares not for you. Back, I say, go; lest
I let forth your half-pint of blood;—back,—that's
the utmost of your having:—back.

MENENIUS

Nay, but, fellow, fellow,—

Enter CORIOLANUS *and* AUFIDIUS

CORIOLANUS

What's the matter?

MENENIUS

Now, you companion, I'll say an errand for you:
you shall know now that I am in estimation; you
shall perceive that a Jack guardant cannot office me
from my son Coriolanus: guess, but by my entertainment with him, if thou standest not i' the state

of hanging, or of some death more long in spectator-
ship and crueller in suffering; behold now presently, and swoon for what's to come upon thee. The
glorious gods sit in hourly synod about thy particular prosperity, and love thee no worse than thy old
father Menenius does! O my son, my son! thou art
preparing fire for us; look thee, here's water to
quench it. I was hardly moved to come to thee; but
being assured none but myself could move thee, I
have been blown out of your gates with sighs; and
conjure thee to pardon Rome and thy petitionary
countrymen. The good gods assuage thy wrath, and
turn the dregs of it upon this varlet here,—this, who,
like a block, hath denied my access to thee.

CORIOLANUS

Away!

MENENIUS

How! away!

CORIOLANUS

Wife, mother, child, I know not. My affairs
Are servanted to others: though I owe
My revenge properly, my remission lies
In Volscian breasts. That we have been familiar,
Ingrate forgetfulness shall poison rather
Than pity note how much. Therefore be gone.
Mine ears against your suits are stronger than
Your gates against my force. Yet, for I loved thee,
Take this along; I writ it for thy sake,
And would have sent it. [*Gives him a letter*] Another
    word, Menenius,
I will not hear thee speak. This man, Aufidius,
Was my beloved in Rome: yet thou behold'st.

AUFIDIUS

You keep a constant temper.

[*Exeunt* CORIOLANUS *and* AUFIDIUS

FIRST SENTINEL

Now, sir, is your name Menenius?

SECOND SENTINEL

'Tis a spell, you see, of much power: you know the
way home again.

FIRST SENTINEL

Do you hear how we are shent for keeping your
greatness back?

SECOND SENTINEL

What cause, do you think, I have to swoon?

MENENIUS

I neither care for the world nor your general: for
such things as you, I can scarce think there's any,
ye're so slight. He that hath a will to die by himself
fears it not from another: let your general do his
worst. For you, be that you are, long; and your
misery increase with your age! I say to you, as I was
said to, Away!   [*Exit*

FIRST SENTINEL

A noble fellow, I warrant him.

SECOND SENTINEL

The worthy fellow is our general: he's the rock, the
oak not to be wind-shaken.   [*Exeunt*

SCENE III. *The tent of* CORIOLANUS

Enter CORIOLANUS, AUFIDIUS, *and others*

CORIOLANUS
We will before the walls of Rome to-morrow
Set down our host. My partner in this action,
You must report to the Volscian lords how plainly
I have borne this business.

AUFIDIUS
                Only their ends
You have respected; stopp'd your ears against
The general suit of Rome; never admitted
A private whisper, no, not with such friends
That thought them sure of you.

CORIOLANUS
                This last old man,
Whom with a crack'd heart I have sent to Rome,
Loved me above the measure of a father,
Nay, godded me indeed. Their latest refuge
Was to send him; for whose old love I have,
Though I show'd sourly to him, once more offer'd
The first conditions, which they did refuse
And cannot now accept; to grace him only
That thought he could do more, a very little
I have yielded to: fresh embassies and suits,
Nor from the state nor private friends, hereafter
Will I lend ear to. [*Shout within*] Ha! what shout is
  this?
Shall I be tempted to infringe my vow
In the same time 'tis made? I will not.
Enter, in mourning habits, VIRGILIA, VOLUMNIA, *leading
  young* MARCIUS, VALERIA, *and* ATTENDANTS
My wife comes foremost; then the honour'd mould
Wherein this trunk was framed, and in her hand
The grandchild to her blood. But out, affection!
All bond and privilege of nature, break!
Let it be virtuous to be obstinate.
What is that curtsy worth? or those doves' eyes,
Which can make gods forsworn? I melt, and am not
Of stronger earth than others. My mother bows;
As if Olympus to a molehill should
In supplication nod: and my young boy
Hath an aspect of intercession, which
Great nature cries 'Deny not.' Let the Volsces
Plough Rome, and harrow Italy: I'll never
Be such a gosling to obey instinct; but stand,
As if a man were author of himself
And knew no other kin.

VIRGILIA
                My lord and husband!

CORIOLANUS
These eyes are not the same I wore in Rome.

VIRGILIA
The sorrow that delivers us thus changed
Makes you think so.

CORIOLANUS
                Like a dull actor now
I have forgot my part and I am out,
Even to a full disgrace. Best of my flesh,
Forgive my tyranny; but do not say,

For that 'Forgive our Romans.' O, a kiss
Long as my exile, sweet as my revenge!
Now, by the jealous queen of heaven, that kiss
I carried from thee, dear, and my true lip
Hath virgin'd it e'er since. You gods! I prate,
And the most noble mother of the world
Leave unsaluted: sink, my knee, i' the earth; [*Kneels*
Of thy deep duty more impression show
Than that of common sons.

VOLUMNIA
                O, stand up blest!
Whilst, with no softer cushion than the flint,
I kneel before thee, and unproperly
Show duty, as mistaken all this while
Between the child and parent.   [*Kneels*

CORIOLANUS
                What is this?
Your knees to me? to your corrected son?
Then let the pebbles on the hungry beach
Fillip the stars; then let the mutinous winds
Strike the proud cedars 'gainst the fiery sun,
Murdering impossibility, to make
What cannot be, slight work.

VOLUMNIA
                Thou art my warrior;
I holp to frame thee. Do you know this lady?

CORIOLANUS
The noble sister of Publicola,
The moon of Rome; chaste as the icicle
That's curdied by the frost from purest snow
And hangs on Dian's temple: dear Valeria!

VOLUMNIA
This is a poor epitome of yours,
Which by the interpretation of full time
May show like all yourself.

CORIOLANUS
                The god of soldiers,
With the consent of supreme Jove, inform
Thy thoughts with nobleness, that thou mayst prove
To shame unvulnerable, and stick i' the wars
Like a great sea-mark, standing every flaw
And saving those that eye thee!

VOLUMNIA
                Your knee, sirrah.

CORIOLANUS
That's my brave boy!

VOLUMNIA
Even he, your wife, this lady and myself
Are suitors to you.

CORIOLANUS
                I beseech you, peace:
Or, if you'ld ask, remember this before:
The thing I have forsworn to grant may never
Be held by you denials. Do not bid me
Dismiss my soldiers, or capitulate
Again with Rome's mechanics: tell me not
Wherein I seem unnatural: desire not
To allay my rages and revenges with
Your colder reasons.

VOLUMNIA

O, no more, no more!
You have said you will not grant us any thing;
For we have nothing else to ask, but that
Which you deny already: yet we will ask;
That, if you fail in our request, the blame
May hang upon your hardness: therefore hear us.

CORIOLANUS

Aufidius, and you Volsces, mark; for we'll
Hear nought from Rome in private. Your request?

VOLUMNIA

Should we be silent and not speak, our raiment
And state of bodies would bewray what life
We have led since thy exile. Think with thyself
How more unfortunate than all living women
Are we come hither: since that thy sight, which
　should
Make our eyes flow with joy, hearts dance with
　comforts,
Constrains them weep and shake with fear and sor-
　row;
Making the mother, wife and child, to see
The son, the husband and the father, tearing
His country's bowels out. And to poor we
Thine enmity's most capital: thou barr'st us
Our prayers to the gods, which is a comfort
That all but we enjoy; for how can we,
Alas, how can we for our country pray,
Whereto we are bound, together with thy victory,
Whereto we are bound? alack, or we must lose
The country, our dear nurse, or else thy person,
Our comfort in the country. We must find
An evident calamity, though we had
Our wish, which side should win; for either thou
Must, as a foreign recreant, be led
With manacles thorough our streets, or else
Triumphantly tread on thy country's ruin,
And bear the palm for having bravely shed
Thy wife and children's blood. For myself, son,
I purpose not to wait on fortune till
These wars determine: if I cannot persuade thee
Rather to show a noble grace to both parts
Than seek the end of one, thou shalt no sooner
March to assault thy country than to tread—
Trust to 't, thou shalt not—on thy mother's womb,
That brought thee to this world.

VIRGILIA

　　　　　　Ay, and mine,
That brought you forth this boy, to keep your name
Living to time.

BOY

　　　A' shall not tread on me;
I'll run away till I am bigger, but then I'll fight.

CORIOLANUS

Not of a woman's tenderness to be,
Requires nor child nor woman's face to see.
I have sat too long.　　　　　　　　　[Rising

VOLUMNIA

　　　Nay, go not from us thus.
If it were so that our request did tend

To save the Romans, thereby to destroy
The Volsces whom you serve, you might condemn
　us,
As poisonous of your honour: no; our suit
Is, that you reconcile them: while the Volsces
May say 'This mercy we have show'd,' the Romans,
'This we received;' and each in either side
Give the all-hail to thee, and cry 'Be blest
For making up this peace!' Thou know'st, great son,
The end of war's uncertain, but this certain,
That if thou conquer Rome, the benefit
Which thou shalt thereby reap is such a name
Whose repetition will be dogg'd with curses;
Whose chronicle thus writ: 'The man was noble,
But with his last attempt he wiped it out,
Destroy'd his country, and his name remains
To the ensuing age abhorr'd.' Speak to me, son:
Thou hast affected the fine strains of honour,
To imitate the graces of the gods;
To tear with thunder the wide cheeks o' the air,
And yet to charge thy sulphur with a bolt
That should but rive an oak. Why dost not speak?
Think'st thou it honourable for a noble man
Still to remember wrongs? Daughter, speak you:
He cares not for your weeping. Speak thou, boy:
Perhaps thy childishness will move him more
Than can our reasons. There's no man in the world
More bound to 's mother, yet here he lets me prate
Like one i' the stocks. Thou hast never in thy life
Show'd thy dear mother any courtesy;
When she, poor hen, fond of no second brood,
Has cluck'd thee to the wars, and safely home,
Loaden with honour. Say my request's unjust,
And spurn me back: but if it be not so,
Thou art not honest, and the gods will plague thee,
That thou restrain'st from me the duty which
To a mother's part belongs. He turns away:
Down, ladies; let us shame him with our knees.
To his surname Coriolanus 'longs more pride
Than pity to our prayers. Down: an end;
This is the last: so we will home to Rome,
And die among our neighbours. Nay, behold 's:
This boy, that cannot tell what he would have,
But kneels and holds up hands for fellowship,
Does reason our petition with more strength
Than thou hast to deny 't. Come, let us go:
This fellow had a Volscian to his mother;
His wife is in Corioli, and his child
Like him by chance. Yet give us our dispatch:
I am hush'd until our city be a-fire,
And then I'll speak a little.

CORIOLANUS

[After holding her by the hand, silent] O mother, mother!
What have you done? Behold, the heavens do ope,
The gods look down, and this unnatural scene
They laugh at. O my mother, mother! O!
You have won a happy victory to Rome;
But, for your son, believe it, O, believe it,
Most dangerously you have with him prevail'd,
If not most mortal to him. But let it come.

Aufidius, though I cannot make true wars,
I'll frame convenient peace. Now, good Aufidius,
Were you in my stead, would you have heard
A mother less? or granted less, Aufidius?

AUFIDIUS

I was moved withal.

CORIOLANUS

         I dare be sworn you were:
And, sir, it is no little thing to make
Mine eyes to sweat compassion. But, good sir,
What peace you'll make, advise me: for my part,
I'll not to Rome, I'll back with you; and pray you,
Stand to me in this cause. O mother! wife!

AUFIDIUS

[Aside] I am glad thou hast set thy mercy and thy
    honour
At difference in thee: out of that I'll work
Myself a former fortune.
         [The LADIES make signs to CORIOLANUS

CORIOLANUS

[To VOLUMNIA, VIRGILIA, &c.] Ay, by and by:—
But we will drink together; and you shall bear
A better witness back than words, which we
On like conditions will have counter-seal'd.
Come, enter with us. Ladies, you deserve
To have a temple built you: all the swords
In Italy, and her confederate arms,
Could not have made this peace.   [Exeunt

SCENE IV. Rome. A public place

Enter MENENIUS and SICINIUS

MENENIUS

See you yond coign o' the Capitol, yond corner-
stone?

SICINIUS

Why, what of that?

MENENIUS

If it be possible for you to displace it with your little
finger, there is some hope the ladies of Rome, especially his mother, may prevail with him. But I
say there is no hope in 't: our throats are sentenced,
and stay upon execution.

SICINIUS

Is 't possible that so short a time can alter the condition of a man?

MENENIUS

There is difference between a grub and a butterfly;
yet your butterfly was a grub. This Marcius is
grown from man to dragon: he has wings; he's more
than a creeping thing.

SICINIUS

He loved his mother dearly.

MENENIUS

So did he me: and he no more remembers his
mother now than an eight-year-old horse. The tartness of his face sours ripe grapes: when he walks, he
moves like an engine, and the ground shrinks before
his treading: he is able to pierce a corslet with his
eye; talks like a knell, and his hum is a battery. He
sits in his state, as a thing made for Alexander.
What he bids be done, is finished with his bidding.
He wants nothing of a god but eternity and a
heaven to throne in.

SICINIUS

Yes, mercy, if you report him truly.

MENENIUS

I paint him in the character. Mark what mercy his
mother shall bring from him: there is no more
mercy in him than there is milk in a male tiger; that
shall our poor city find: and all this is long of you.

SICINIUS

The gods be good unto us!

MENENIUS

No, in such a case the gods will not be good unto us.
When we banished him, we respected not them;
and, he returning to break our necks, they respect
not us.

Enter a MESSENGER

MESSENGER

Sir, if you'ld save your life, fly to your house:
The plebeians have got your fellow-tribune,
And hale him up and down, all swearing, if
The Roman ladies bring not comfort home,
They'll give him death by inches.

Enter another MESSENGER

SICINIUS

         What's the news?

SECOND MESSENGER

Good news, good news; the ladies have prevail'd,
The Volscians are dislodged, and Marcius gone:
A merrier day did never yet greet Rome,
No, not the expulsion of the Tarquins.

SICINIUS

         Friend,
Art thou certain this is true? is it most certain?

SECOND MESSENGER

As certain as I know the sun is fire:
Where have you lurk'd, that you make doubt of it?
Ne'er through an arch so hurried the blown tide,
As the recomforted through the gates. Why, hark
    you!
         [Trumpets; hautboys; drums beat; all together
The trumpets, sackbuts, psalteries and fifes,
Tabors and cymbals and the shouting Romans,
Make the sun dance. Hark you!   [A shout within

MENENIUS

         This is good news:
I will go meet the ladies. This Volumnia
Is worth of consuls, senators, patricians,
A city full; of tribunes, such as you,
A sea and land full. You have pray'd well to-day:
This morning for ten thousand of your throats
I'ld not have given a doit. Hark, how they joy!
         [Music still, with shouts

SICINIUS

First, the gods bless you for your tidings; next,
Accept my thankfulness.

SECOND MESSENGER
          Sir, we have all
Great cause to give great thanks.
                    SICINIUS
                    They are near the city?
                    SECOND MESSENGER
Almost at point to enter.
                    SICINIUS
                    We will meet them,
And help the joy.   [Exeunt

SCENE V. *The same. A street near the gate*

Enter two SENATORS *with* VOLUMNIA, VIRGILIA,
VALERIA, *&c. passing over the stage, followed by*
PATRICIANS *and others*
                    FIRST SENATOR
Behold our patroness, the life of Rome!
Call all your tribes together, praise the gods,
And make triumphant fires; strew flowers before
     them:
Unshout the noise that banish'd Marcius,
Repeal him with the welcome of his mother;
Cry 'Welcome, ladies, welcome!'
                    ALL
                              Welcome, ladies,
Welcome!   [A flourish with drums and trumpets. Exeunt

SCENE VI. *Corioli. A public place*

Enter TULLUS AUFIDIUS, *with* ATTENDANTS
                    AUFIDIUS
Go tell the lords o' the city I am here:
Deliver them this paper: having read it,
Bid them repair to the market-place, where I,
Even in theirs and in the commons' ears,
Will vouch the truth of it. Him I accuse
The city ports by this hath enter'd, and
Intends to appear before the people, hoping
To purge himself with words: dispatch.
                              [Exeunt ATTENDANTS
Enter three or four CONSPIRATORS *of* AUFIDIUS' *faction*
Most welcome!
                    FIRST CONSPIRATOR
                    How is it with our general?
                    AUFIDIUS
                              Even so
As with a man by his own alms empoison'd,
And with his charity slain.
                    SECOND CONSPIRATOR
                              Most noble sir,
If you do hold the same intent wherein
You wish'd us parties, we'll deliver you
Of your great danger.
                    AUFIDIUS
                    Sir, I cannot tell:
We must proceed as we do find the people.

THIRD CONSPIRATOR
The people will remain uncertain whilst
'Twixt you there's difference; but the fall of either
Makes the survivor heir of all.
                    AUFIDIUS
                              I know it,
And my pretext to strike at him admits
A good construction. I raised him, and I pawn'd
Mine honour for his truth: who being so heighten'd,
He water'd his new plants with dews of flattery,
Seducing so my friends; and, to this end,
He bow'd his nature, never known before
But to be rough, unswayable and free.
                    THIRD CONSPIRATOR
Sir, his stoutness
When he did stand for consul, which he lost
By lack of stooping,—
                    AUFIDIUS
                    That I would have spoke of:
Being banish'd for 't, he came unto my hearth;
Presented to my knife his throat: I took him,
Made him joint-servant with me, gave him way
In all his own desires, nay, let him choose
Out of my files, his projects to accomplish,
My best and freshest men, served his designments
In mine own person, holp to reap the fame
Which he did end all his; and took some pride
To do myself this wrong: till at the last
I seem'd his follower, not partner, and
He waged me with his countenance, as if
I had been mercenary.
                    FIRST CONSPIRATOR
                    So he did, my lord:
The army marvell'd at it, and in the last,
When he had carried Rome and that we look'd
For no less spoil than glory—
                    AUFIDIUS
                              There was it:
For which my sinews shall be stretch'd upon him.
At a few drops of women's rheum, which are
As cheap as lies, he sold the blood and labour
Of our great action: therefore shall he die,
And I'll renew me in his fall. But hark!
[Drums and trumpets sound, with great shouts of the people
                    FIRST CONSPIRATOR
Your native town you enter'd like a post,
And had no welcomes home; but he returns,
Splitting the air with noise.
                    SECOND CONSPIRATOR
                              And patient fools,
Whose children he hath slain, their base throats tear
With giving him glory.
                    THIRD CONSPIRATOR
                    Therefore, at your vantage,
Ere he express himself, or move the people
With what he would say, let him feel your sword,
Which we will second. When he lies along,
After your way his tale pronounced shall bury
His reasons with his body.

AUFIDIUS

          Say no more:

Here come the lords.

Enter the LORDS *of the city*

ALL THE LORDS

You are most welcome home.

AUFIDIUS

          I have not deserved it.

But, worthy lords, have you with heed perused

What I have written to you?

LORDS

          We have.

FIRST LORD

          And grieve to hear 't.

What faults he made before the last, I think

Might have found easy fines: but there to end

Where he was to begin, and give away

The benefit of our levies, answering us

With our own charge, making a treaty where

There was a yielding,—this admits no excuse.

AUFIDIUS

He approaches: you shall hear him.

Enter CORIOLANUS, *marching with drum and colours; the*
commoners being with him

CORIOLANUS

Hail, lords! I am return'd your soldier;

No more infected with my country's love

Than when I parted hence, but still subsisting

Under your great command. You are to know,

That prosperously I have attempted, and

With bloody passage led your wars even to

The gates of Rome. Our spoils we have brought
   home

Do more than counterpoise a full third part

The charges of the action. We have made peace,

With no less honour to the Antiates

Than shame to the Romans: and we here deliver,

Subscribed by the consuls and patricians,

Together with the seal o' the senate, what

What we have compounded on.

AUFIDIUS

          Read it not, noble lords;

But tell the traitor, in the highest degree

He hath abused your powers.

CORIOLANUS

Traitor! how now!

AUFIDIUS

          Ay, traitor, Marcius!

CORIOLANUS

          Marcius!

AUFIDIUS

Ay, Marcius, Caius Marcius: dost thou think

I'll grace thee with that robbery, thy stol'n name

Coriolanus, in Corioli?

You lords and heads o' the state, perfidiously

He has betray'd your business, and given up,

For certain drops of salt, your city Rome,

I say 'your city,' to his wife and mother;

Breaking his oath and resolution, like

A twist of rotten silk; never admitting

Counsel o' the war; but at his nurse's tears

He whined and roar'd away your victory;

That pages blush'd at him, and men of heart

Look'd wondering each at other.

CORIOLANUS

          Hear'st thou, Mars?

AUFIDIUS

Name not the god, thou boy of tears!

CORIOLANUS

          Ha!

AUFIDIUS

No more.

CORIOLANUS

Measureless liar, thou hast made my heart

Too great for what contains it. 'Boy!' O slave!

Pardon me, lords, 'tis the first time that ever

I was forced to scold. Your judgements, my grave
   lords,

Must give this cur the lie: and his own notion—

Who wears my stripes impress'd upon him; that

Must bear my beating to his grave—shall join

To thrust the lie unto him.

FIRST LORD

Peace, both, and hear me speak.

CORIOLANUS

Cut me to pieces, Volsces; men and lads,

Stain all your edges on me. 'Boy!' false hound!

If you have writ your annals true, 'tis there,

That, like an eagle in a dove-cote, I

Flutter'd your Volscians in Corioli;

Alone I did it. 'Boy!'

AUFIDIUS

          Why, noble lords,

Will you be put in mind of his blind fortune,

Which was your shame, by this unholy braggart,

'Fore your own eyes and ears?

ALL CONSPIRATORS

Let him die for 't.

ALL THE PEOPLE

'Tear him to pieces.' 'Do it presently.' 'He killed

my son.' 'My daughter.' 'He killed my cousin

Marcus.' 'He killed my father.'

SECOND LORD

Peace, ho! no outrage: peace!

The man is noble, and his fame folds-in

This orb o' the earth. His last offences to us

Shall have judicious hearing. Stand, Aufidius,

And trouble not the peace.

CORIOLANUS

          O that I had him,

With six Aufidiuses, or more, his tribe,

To use my lawful sword!

AUFIDIUS

          Insolent villain!

ALL CONSPIRATORS

Kill, kill, kill, kill, kill him!

[*The* CONSPIRATORS *draw, and kill* CORIOLANUS:
          AUFIDIUS *stands on his body*

LORDS

          Hold, hold, hold, hold!

AUFIDIUS
My noble masters, hear me speak.
FIRST LORD
O Tullus,—
SECOND LORD
Thou hast done a deed whereat valour will weep.
THIRD LORD
Tread not upon him. Masters all, be quiet;
Put up your swords.
AUFIDIUS
My lords, when you shall know—as in this rage
Provoked by him, you cannot—the great danger
Which this man's life did owe you, you'll rejoice
That he is thus cut off. Please it your honours
To call me to your senate, I'll deliver
Myself your loyal servant, or endure
Your heaviest censure.
FIRST LORD
Bear from hence his body;
And mourn you for him: let him be regarded
As the most noble corse that ever herald
Did follow to his urn.
SECOND LORD
His own impatience
Takes from Aufidius a great part of blame.
Let's make the best of it.
AUFIDIUS
My rage is gone,
And I am struck with sorrow. Take him up:
Help, three o' the chiefest soldiers; I'll be one.
Beat thou the drum, that it speak mournfully:
Trail your steel pikes. Though in this city he
Hath widow'd and unchilded many a one,
Which to this hour bewail the injury,
Yet he shall have a noble memory.
Assist. [*Exeunt, bearing the body of* CORIOLANUS.
A dead march sounded

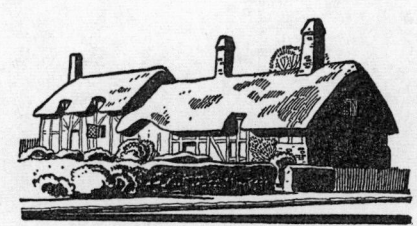

THE LIFE OF TIMON OF ATHENS

SYNOPSIS

Timon, a wealthy lord of Athens, revels in the joy of ostentatious giving as a generous friend, a kindly master, a liberal patron of the arts, and a lavish entertainer. Being naturally of a frank, cordial nature, he dispenses his favors with entire lack of discrimination and esteems as friends all the throng of flatterers and dependents his bountiful spending draws around him.

Although the cynical philosopher, Apemantus, ridicules the motives of these hangers-on and warns his credulous friend against them, and Flavius, his true honest steward, tries to curb his reckless extravagance, Timon foolishly refuses to be crossed in his generosity, paying· to ransom a follower, Ventidius, from prison, bestowing a fortune on a servant so that he may marry, and giving precious stones as favors at a gorgeous banquet to his friends.

Presently Timon's creditors begin to suspect his actual financial state, and send their agents to press him with bills. The importunities of these men at length force Timon to listen to his faithful steward who proves to him that he is not only a bankrupt but his credit is gone, Flavius having already applied to the Senate for a loan for his master which has been refused. Thunderstruck, Timon consoles himself with the thought that he can draw upon all the friends he has helped in the past, but one by one his fair-weather followers deny his request for a small loan, as they try to bribe the servant to say they were out, regret their lack of funds, and affect anger at not being the first to be approached. Timon's eyes are at last opened to the parasitic nature of his worthless friends, and he invites them to a final banquet to which they all come with lame excuses for denying his appeal. Covered dishes are brought in filled with warm water which Timon throws in his guests' faces as he curses them, and in lieu of money he pelts them with stones.

Timon's philanthropy passes into the extreme of universal hatred of mankind whom he bitterly denounces as he leaves Athens forever for a hermit's life in a cave near the sea, where one day, while digging for the roots that constitute his food, he discovers a vast hidden treasure of gold.

Meanwhile, Athenian ingratitude has shown itself again when Alcibiades, a famous general and true friend of Timon, is banished by angry senators because of his persistent pleading for the life of a condemned soldier who has fought valiantly for the state. In leaving, he rails against the city's injustice and lack of appreciation of his services, but, unlike Timon, he plans at once to avenge his wrongs by collecting his discontented soldiers for a march on Athens. With his army and his two mistresses, Timandra and Phrynia, he happens to pass by the cave of his old friend, whose changed fortunes and appearance shock him so deeply that he offers Timon gold, in spite of the fact that his soldiers are deserting him for lack of pay. When Timon hears that Alcibiades is advancing against Athens to humiliate the city for his unjust banishment, he shares his treasure with the general and his mistresses, cursing them all roundly as he gives out the gold and assuring Alcibiades that, notwithstanding their friendship, he wishes never to see him again.

The old misanthrope, Apemantus, visits Timon who jeers at his companion together with the rest of the world. Two thieves, hearing of his treasure, seek out his cave and are given money by Timon who sardonically praises their thievery and encourages them to continue it. His devoted steward, Flavius, who has shared his remaining wealth with Timon's dismissed servants, now comes to aid his master and comfort him, and succeeds, after enduring his curses, in convincing him of his honesty, but Timon will not allow him to remain and gives him a huge sum of money on the condition that he will never return, nor show charity to any living person.

Word has spread in Athens that Timon's withdrawal from society is merely a subterfuge to test his friends and hoping to share his treasure, two former followers, a dissembling poet and a painter, arrive with protestations of continued devotion which are received with wrath and malediction.

The Athenian senate, worried by the approach of Alcibiades' army, sends delegates to ask Timon's financial aid, promising him greater honors and dignities than he previously held, but they receive only messages of utter scorn and indifference to his fellow Athenians. Alcibiades, on the other hand, shows a willingness to arbitrate, and, after a parley before the walls of Athens, is permitted to enter the city, provided he will spare the innocent and confine his vengeance to his enemies and those of Timon. As this agreement is reached, word is brought by a soldier who has been seeking for Timon that he is dead and buried in a rude sea-washed tomb.

HISTORICAL DATA

The story of the misanthrope Timon appears to have been well-known to Elizabethan writers. Allusions to the theme are to be found in *Skialetheia* (1598), *Jack Drum's Entertainment* (1601), and in Richard Barckley's *Felicity of Man*. A play on Timon, dated in manuscript form about 1600, seems to have been the only predecessor of Shakespeare's work that contained a banquet scene and a faithful steward, but there is no evidence that it was ever produced or was known to Shakespeare. More direct source material was probably the parenthetical account of Timon in Plutarch's *Life of Marcus Antonius*, familiar to the playwright either in North's translation, or as retold in Paynter's *Palace of*

Pleasure (1567). There is also reason to believe that Shakespeare was familiar in some form with Lucian's dialogue of *Timon, or the Misanthrope*.

The play is generally thought to be only in part Shakespeare's, although authorities differ as to whether it is an old play in part rewritten, or an original work, unfinished, and completed by another hand. There is no record of its presentation and it first appears in printed form in the First Folio. There is little real evidence to help fix the time of its composition, but various internal indications have helped scholars to agree in general on a date about 1607.

"*Let me look back upon thee, O thou wall,*"
TIMON OF ATHENS

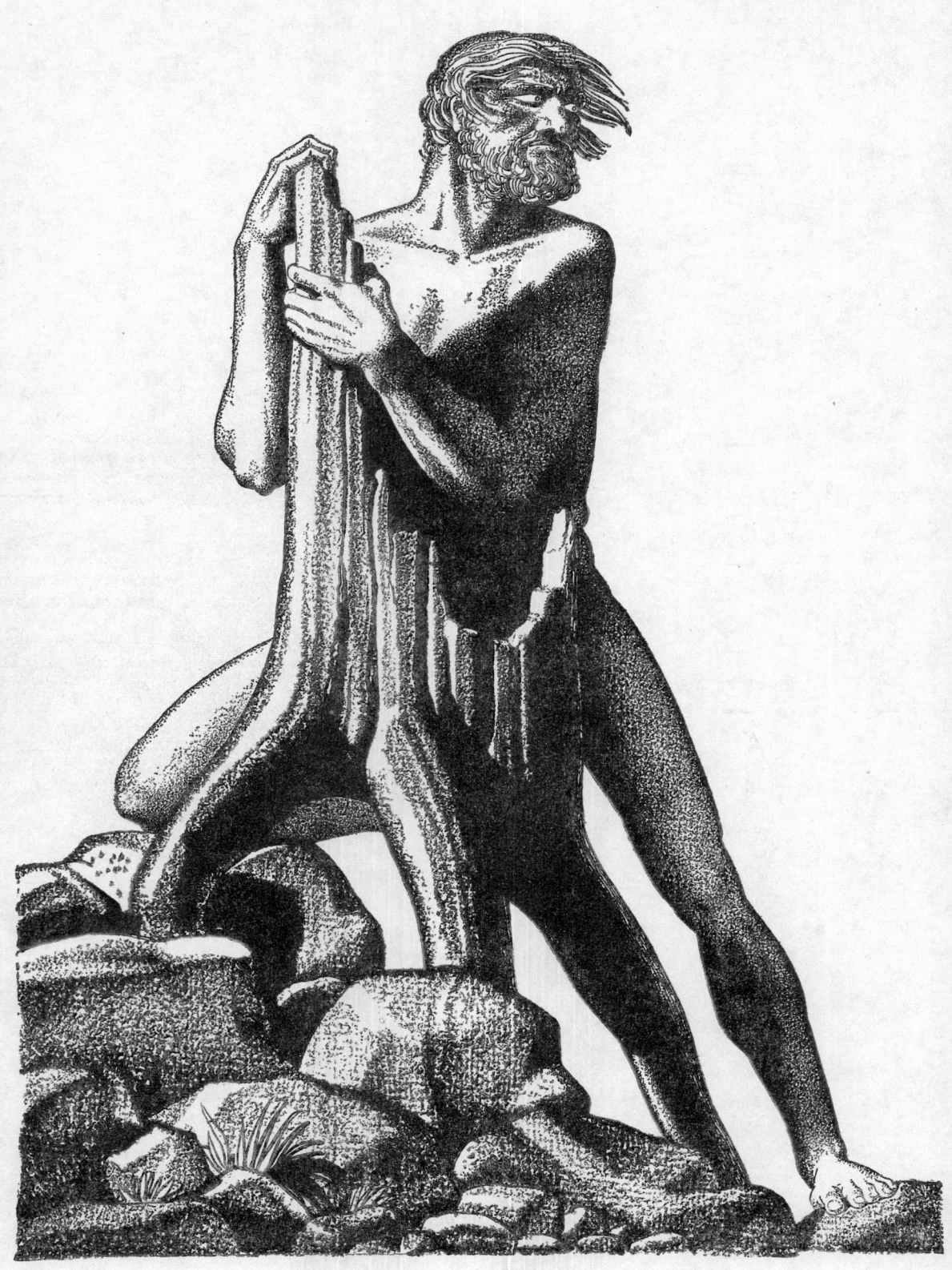

THE LIFE OF TIMON OF ATHENS

DRAMATIS PERSONÆ

TIMON, *a noble Athenian.*
LUCIUS,
LUCULLUS, } *flattering lords.*
SEMPRONIUS,
VENTIDIUS, *one of Timon's false friends.*
ALCIBIADES, *an Athenian captain.*
APEMANTUS, *a churlish philosopher.*
FLAVIUS, *steward to Timon.*
POET.
PAINTER.
JEWELLER.
MERCHANT.
AN OLD ATHENIAN.
FLAMINIUS,
LUCILIUS, } *servants to Timon.*
SERVILIUS,

CAPHIS,
PHILOTUS,
TITUS, } *servants to Timon's creditors and to*
HORTENSIUS, *the Lords.*
And others,
A PAGE.
A FOOL.
THREE STRANGERS.

PHRYNIA,
TIMANDRA, } *mistresses to Alcibiades.*

CUPID *and* AMAZONS *in the mask.*

Other LORDS, SENATORS, OFFICERS, BANDITTI,
and ATTENDANTS.

SCENE—*Athens, and the neighbouring woods.*

ACT I

SCENE I. *Athens. A hall in* TIMON's *house*

Enter POET, PAINTER, JEWELLER, MERCHANT, *and
others, at several doors*

POET

Good day, sir.

PAINTER

        I am glad you're well.

POET

I have not seen you long: how goes the world?

PAINTER

It wears, sir, as it grows.

POET

            Ay, that's well known:
But what particular rarity? what strange,
Which manifold record not matches? See,
Magic of bounty! all these spirits thy power
Hath conjured to attend. I know the merchant.

PAINTER

I know them both; th' other's a jeweller.

MERCHANT

O, 'tis a worthy lord!

JEWELLER

        Nay, that's most fix'd.

MERCHANT

A most incomparable man, breathed, as it were,
To an untirable and continuate goodness:
He passes.

JEWELLER

I have a jewel here—

MERCHANT

O, pray, let's see 't: for the Lord Timon, sir?

JEWELLER

If he will touch the estimate: but, for that—

POET

[Reciting to himself] 'When we for recompense have
    praised the vile,
It stains the glory in that happy verse
Which aptly sings the good.'

MERCHANT

[Looking on the jewel] 'Tis a good form.

JEWELLER

And rich: here is a water, look ye.

PAINTER

You are rapt, sir, in some work, some dedication
To the great lord.

POET

        A thing slipp'd idly from me.
Our poesy is as a gum, which oozes
From whence 'tis nourish'd: the fire i' the flint
Shows not till it be struck; our gentle flame
Provokes itself, and, like the current, flies
Each bound it chafes. What have you there?

PAINTER

A picture, sir. When comes your book forth?

POET

Upon the heels of my presentment, sir
Let's see your piece.

PAINTER

        'Tis a good piece.

POET

So 'tis: this comes off well and excellent.

PAINTER

Indifferent.

POET

        Admirable: how this grace
Speaks his own standing! what a mental power
This eye shoots forth! how big imagination
Moves in this lip! to the dumbness of the gesture
One might interpret.

PAINTER

It is a pretty mocking of the life.
Here is a touch; is 't good?

POET

I will say of it,
It tutors nature: artificial strife
Lives in these touches, livelier than life.

Enter certain SENATORS, *and pass over*

PAINTER

How this lord is follow'd!

POET

The senators of Athens: happy man!

PAINTER

Look, moe!

POET

You see this confluence, this great flood of visitors.
I have, in this rough work, shaped out a man,
Whom this beneath world doth embrace and hug
With amplest entertainment: my free drift
Halts not particularly, but moves itself
In a wide sea of wax: no levell'd malice
Infects one comma in the course I hold;
But flies an eagle flight, bold and forth on,
Leaving no tract behind.

PAINTER

How shall I understand you?

POET

I will unbolt to you.
You see how all conditions, how all minds,
As well of glib and slippery creatures as
Of grave and austere quality, tender down
Their services to Lord Timon: his large fortune,
Upon his good and gracious nature hanging,
Subdues and properties to his love and tendance
All sorts of hearts; yea, from the glass-faced flatterer
To Apemantus, that few things loves better
Than to abhor himself: even he drops down
The knee before him, and returns in peace
Most rich in Timon's nod.

PAINTER

I saw them speak together.

POET

Sir, I have upon a high and pleasant hill
Feign'd Fortune to be throned: the base o' the mount
Is rank'd with all deserts, all kind of natures,
That labour on the bosom of this sphere
To propagate their states: amongst them all,
Whose eyes are on this sovereign lady fix'd,
One do I personate of Lord Timon's frame,
Whom Fortune with her ivory hand wafts to her;
Whose present grace to present slaves and servants
Translates his rivals.

PAINTER

'Tis conceived to scope.
This throne, this Fortune, and this hill, methinks,
With one man beckon'd from the rest below,
Bowing his head against the steepy mount
To climb his happiness, would be well express'd
In our condition.

POET

Nay, sir, but hear me on.
All those which were his fellows but of late,
Some better than his value, on the moment
Follow his strides, his lobbies fill with tendance,
Rain sacrificial whisperings in his ear,
Make sacred even his stirrup, and through him
Drink the free air.

PAINTER

Ay, marry, what of these?

POET

When Fortune in her shift and change of mood
Spurns down her late beloved, all his dependants
Which labour'd after him to the mountain's top
Even on their knees and hands, let him slip down,
Not one accompanying his declining foot.

PAINTER

'Tis common:
A thousand moral paintings I can show,
That shall demonstrate these quick blows of Fortune's
More pregnantly than words. Yet you do well
To show Lord Timon that mean eyes have seen
The foot above the head.

Trumpets sound. Enter LORD TIMON, *addressing himself
courteously to every suitor; a* MESSENGER *from* VENTIDIUS
talking with him; LUCILIUS *and other servants following*

TIMON

Imprison'd is he, say you?

MESSENGER

Ay, my good lord: five talents is his debt;
His means most short, his creditors most strait:
Your honourable letter he desires
To those have shut him up; which failing,
Periods his comfort.

TIMON

Noble Ventidius! Well,
I am not of that feather to shake off
My friend when he must need me. I do know him
A gentleman that well deserves a help:
Which he shall have: I'll pay the debt and free him.

MESSENGER

Your lordship ever binds him.

TIMON

Commend me to him: I will send his ransom;
And, being enfranchised, bid him come to me:
'Tis not enough to help the feeble up,
But to support him after. Fare you well.

MESSENGER

All happiness to your honour!   [*Exit*

Enter an OLD ATHENIAN

OLD ATHENIAN

Lord Timon, hear me speak.

TIMON

Freely, good father.

OLD ATHENIAN

Thou hast a servant named Lucilius.

TIMON

I have so: what of him?

OLD ATHENIAN
Most noble Timon, call the man before thee.
TIMON
Attends he here, or no? Lucilius!
LUCILIUS
Here, at your lordship's service.
OLD ATHENIAN
This fellow here, Lord Timon, this thy creature,
By night frequents my house. I am a man
That from my first have been inclined to thrift,
And my estate deserves an heir more raised
Than one which holds a trencher.
TIMON
                    Well, what further?
OLD ATHENIAN
One only daughter have I, no kin else,
On whom I may confer what I have got:
The maid is fair, o' the youngest for a bride,
And I have bred her at my dearest cost
In qualities of the best. This man of thine
Attempts her love: I prithee, noble lord,
Join with me to forbid him her resort;
Myself have spoke in vain.
TIMON
                    The man is honest.
OLD ATHENIAN
Therefore he will be, Timon:
His honesty rewards him in itself;
It must not bear my daughter.
TIMON
                    Does she love him?
OLD ATHENIAN
She is young and apt:
Our own precedent passions do instruct us
What levity's in youth.
TIMON
[To LUCILIUS] Love you the maid?
LUCILIUS
Ay, my good lord; and she accepts of it.
OLD ATHENIAN
If in her marriage my consent be missing,
I call the gods to witness, I will choose
Mine heir from forth the beggars of the world,
And dispossess her all.
TIMON
                    How shall she be endow'd,
If she be mated with an equal husband?
OLD ATHENIAN
Three talents on the present; in future, all.
TIMON
This gentleman of mine hath served me long:
To build his fortune I will strain a little,
For 'tis a bond in men. Give him thy daughter:
What you bestow, in him I'll counterpoise,
And make him weigh with her.
OLD ATHENIAN
                    Most noble lord,
Pawn me to this your honour, she is his.
TIMON
My hand to thee; mine honour on my promise.

LUCILIUS
Humbly I thank your lordship: never may
That state or fortune fall into my keeping,
Which is not owed to you!
[Exeunt LUCILIUS and OLD ATHENIAN
POET
Vouchsafe my labour, and long live your lordship!
TIMON
I thank you; you shall hear from me anon:
Go not away. What have you there, my friend?
PAINTER
A piece of painting, which I do beseech
Your lordship to accept.
TIMON
                    Painting is welcome.
The painting is almost the natural man;
For since dishonour traffics with man's nature,
He is but outside: these pencill'd figures are
Even such as they give out. I like your work,
And you shall find I like it: wait attendance
Till you hear further from me.
PAINTER
                    The gods preserve ye!
TIMON
Well fare you, gentleman: give me your hand;
We must needs dine together. Sir, your jewel
Hath suffer'd under praise.
JEWELLER
                    What, my lord! dispraise?
TIMON
A mere satiety of commendations.
If I should pay you for 't as 'tis extoll'd,
It would unclew me quite.
JEWELLER
                    My lord, 'tis rated
As those which sell would give: but you well know
Things of like value, differing in the owners,
Are prized by their masters: believe 't, dear lord,
You mend the jewel by the wearing it.
TIMON
Well mock'd.
MERCHANT
No, my good lord; he speaks the common tongue,
Which all men speak with him.
TIMON
Look, who comes here: will you be chid?
Enter APEMANTUS
JEWELLER
We'll bear, with your lordship.
MERCHANT
                    He'll spare none.
TIMON
Good morrow to thee, gentle Apemantus!
APEMANTUS
Till I be gentle, stay thou for thy good morrow;
When thou art Timon's dog, and these knaves hon-
est.
TIMON
Why dost thou call them knaves? thou know'st them
not.

APEMANTUS
Are they not Athenians?

TIMON
Yes.

APEMANTUS
Then I repent not.

JEWELLER
You know me, Apemantus?

APEMANTUS
Thou know'st I do; I call'd thee by thy name.

TIMON
Thou art proud, Apemantus.

APEMANTUS
Of nothing so much as that I am not like Timon.

TIMON
Whither art going?

APEMANTUS
To knock out an honest Athenian's brains.

TIMON
That's a deed thou'lt die for.

APEMANTUS
Right, if doing nothing be death by the law.

TIMON
How likest thou this picture, Apemantus?

APEMANTUS
The best, for the innocence.

TIMON
Wrought he not well that painted it?

APEMANTUS
He wrought better that made the painter; and yet
he's but a filthy piece of work.

PAINTER
You're a dog.

APEMANTUS
Thy mother's of my generation: what's she, if I be a
dog?

TIMON
Wilt dine with me, Apemantus?

APEMANTUS
No; I eat not lords.

TIMON
An thou shouldst, thou'ldst anger ladies.

APEMANTUS
O, they eat lords; so they come by great bellies.

TIMON
That's a lascivious apprehension.

APEMANTUS
So thou apprehend'st it: take it for thy labour.

TIMON
How dost thou like this jewel, Apemantus?

APEMANTUS
Not so well as plain-dealing, which will not cost a
man a doit.

TIMON
What dost thou think 'tis worth?

APEMANTUS
Not worth my thinking. How now, poet!

POET
How now, philosopher!

APEMANTUS
Thou liest.

POET
Art not one?

APEMANTUS
Yes.

POET
Then I lie not.

APEMANTUS
Art not a poet?

POET
Yes.

APEMANTUS
Then thou liest: look in thy last work, where thou
hast feigned him a worthy fellow.

POET
That's not feigned; he is so.

APEMANTUS
Yes, he is worthy of thee, and to pay thee for thy
labour: he that loves to be flattered is worthy o' the
flatterer. Heavens, that I were a lord!

TIMON
What wouldst do then, Apemantus?

APEMANTUS
E'en as Apemantus does now; hate a lord with my
heart.

TIMON
What, thyself?

APEMANTUS
Ay.

TIMON
Wherefore?

APEMANTUS
That I had no angry wit to be a lord. Art not thou a
merchant?

MERCHANT
Ay, Apemantus.

APEMANTUS
Traffic confound thee, if the gods will not!

MERCHANT
If traffic do it, the gods do it.

APEMANTUS
Traffic's thy god; and thy god confound thee!
            Trumpet sounds. Enter a MESSENGER

TIMON
What trumpet's that?

MESSENGER
'Tis Alcibiades, and some twenty horse,
All of companionship.

TIMON
Pray, entertain them; give them guide to us.
            [*Exeunt some* ATTENDANTS
You must needs dine with me: go not you hence
Till I have thank'd you: when dinner's done,
Show me this piece. I am joyful of your sights.
            Enter ALCIBIADES, *with the rest*
Most welcome, sir!

APEMANTUS
            So, so, there!
Aches contract and starve your supple joints!

That there should be small love 'mongst these sweet
　　knaves,
And all this courtesy! The strain of man's bred out
Into baboon and monkey.
ALCIBIADES
Sir, you have saved my longing, and I feed
Most hungerly on your sight.
TIMON
　　　　　　　　　Right welcome, sir!
Ere we depart, we'll share a bounteous time
In different pleasures. Pray you, let us in.
　　　　　　　　　　　　　　[Exeunt all but APEMANTUS
Enter two LORDS
FIRST LORD
What time o' day is 't, Apemantus?
APEMANTUS
Time to be honest.
FIRST LORD
That time serves still.
APEMANTUS
The most accursed thou, that still omitt'st it.
SECOND LORD
Thou art going to Lord Timon's feast?
APEMANTUS
Ay, to see meat fill knaves and wine heat fools.
SECOND LORD
Fare thee well, fare thee well.
APEMANTUS
Thou art a fool to bid me farewell twice.
SECOND LORD
Why, Apemantus?
APEMANTUS
Shouldst have kept one to thyself, for I mean to give
thee none.
FIRST LORD
Hang thyself!
APEMANTUS
No, I will do nothing at thy bidding: make thy re-
quests to thy friend.
SECOND LORD
Away, unpeaceable dog, or I'll spurn thee hence!
APEMANTUS
I will fly, like a dog, the heels o' the ass. 　　[Exit
FIRST LORD
He's opposite to humanity. Come, shall we in,
And taste Lord Timon's bounty? he outgoes
The very heart of kindness.
SECOND LORD
He pours it out; Plutus, the god of gold,
Is but his steward: no meed, but he repays
Sevenfold above itself; no gift to him,
But breeds the giver a return exceeding
All use of quittance.
FIRST LORD
　　　　　　　　The noblest mind he carries
That ever govern'd man.
SECOND LORD
Long may he live in fortunes! Shall we in?
FIRST LORD
I'll keep you company. 　　　　　　　　[Exeunt

SCENE II. *A banqueting-room in* TIMON'*s house*

Hautboys playing loud music. A great banquet served in;
FLAVIUS *and others attending; and then enter* LORD TIMON,
ALCIBIADES, LORDS, SENATORS, *and* VENTIDIUS. *Then
comes, dropping after all,* APEMANTUS, *discontentedly, like
himself*
VENTIDIUS
Most honour'd Timon,
It hath pleased the gods to remember my father's
　　age,
And call him to long peace.
He is gone happy, and has left me rich:
Then, as in grateful virtue I am bound
To your free heart, I do return those talents,
Doubled with thanks and service, from whose help
I derived liberty.
TIMON
　　　　　　　O, by no means,
Honest Ventidius; you mistake my love:
I gave it freely ever; and there's none
Can truly say he gives, if he receives:
If our betters play at that game, we must not dare
To imitate them; faults that are rich are fair.
VENTIDIUS
A noble spirit!
TIMON
Nay, my lords, ceremony was but devised at first
To set a gloss on faint deeds, hollow welcomes,
Recanting goodness, sorry ere 'tis shown;
But where there is true friendship, there needs none.
Pray, sit; more welcome are ye to my fortunes
Than my fortunes to me. 　　　　　　　[*They sit*
FIRST LORD
My lord, we always have confess'd it.
APEMANTUS
Ho, ho, confess'd it! hang'd it, have you not?
TIMON
O, Apemantus, you are welcome.
APEMANTUS
　　　　　　　　　　　　No;
You shall not make me welcome:
I come to have thee thrust me out of doors.
TIMON
Fie, thou'rt a churl; ye've got a humour there
Does not become a man; 'tis much to blame.
They say, my lords, 'ira furor brevis est;' but yond
man is ever angry. Go, let him have a table by him-
self; for he does neither affect company, nor is he fit
for 't indeed.
APEMANTUS
Let me stay at thine apperil, Timon:
I come to observe; I give thee warning on 't.
TIMON
I take no heed of thee; thou'rt an Athenian, there-
fore welcome: I myself would have no power;
prithee, let my meat make thee silent.
APEMANTUS
I scorn thy meat; 'twould choke me, for I should
ne'er flatter thee. O you gods, what a number of

men eat Timon, and he sees 'em not! It grieves me
to see so many dip their meat in one man's blood;
and all the madness is, he cheers them up too.
I wonder men dare trust themselves with men:
Methinks they should invite them without knives;
Good for their meat, and safer for their lives.
There's much example for 't; the fellow that sits
next him now, parts bread with him, pledges the
breath of him in a divided draught, is the readiest
man to kill him: 't has been proved. If I were a
huge man, I should fear to drink at meals;
Lest they should spy my windpipe's dangerous
  notes:
Great men should drink with harness on their
  throats.

TIMON

My lord, in heart; and let the health go round.

SECOND LORD

Let it flow this way, my good lord.

APEMANTUS

Flow this way! A brave fellow! he keeps his tides
well. Those healths will make thee and thy state
look ill, Timon. Here's that which is too weak to be
a sinner, honest water, which ne'er left man i' the
mire:
This and my food are equals; there's no odds:
Feasts are too proud to give thanks to the gods.

APEMANTUS's *Grace*

> Immortal gods, I crave no pelf;
> I pray for no man but myself:
> Grant I may never prove so fond,
> To trust man on his oath or bond,
> Or a harlot for her weeping,
> Or a dog that seems a-sleeping,
> Or a keeper with my freedom,
> Or my friends, if I should need 'em.
> Amen. So fall to 't:
> Rich men sin, and I eat root.   [*Eats and drinks*

Much good dich thy good heart, Apemantus!

TIMON

Captain Alcibiades, your heart's in the field now.

ALCIBIADES

My heart is ever at your service, my lord.

TIMON

You had rather be at a breakfast of enemies than a
dinner of friends.

ALCIBIADES

So they were bleeding-new, my lord, there's no
meat like 'em: I could wish my best friend at such a
feast.

APEMANTUS

Would all those flatterers were thine enemies, then,
that then thou mightst kill 'em and bid me to 'em!

FIRST LORD

Might we but have that happiness, my lord, that
you would once use our hearts, whereby we might
express some part of our zeals, we should think ourselves for ever perfect.

TIMON

O, no doubt, my good friends, but the gods themselves have provided that I shall have much help

from you: how had you been my friends else? why
have you that charitable title from thousands, did
not you chiefly belong to my heart? I have told
more of you to myself than you can with modesty
speak in your own behalf; and thus far I confirm
you. O you gods, think I, what need we have any
friends, if we should ne'er have need of 'em? they
were the most needless creatures living, should we
ne'er have use for 'em, and would most resemble
sweet instruments hung up in cases, that keep their
sounds to themselves. Why, I have often wished myself poorer, that I might come nearer to you. We are
born to do benefits: and what better or properer can
we call our own than the riches of our friends? O,
what a precious comfort 'tis, to have so many, like
brothers, commanding one another's fortunes! O
joy, e'en made away ere 't can be born! Mine eyes
cannot hold out water, methinks: to forget their
faults, I drink to you.

APEMANTUS

Thou weep'st to make them drink, Timon.

SECOND LORD

Joy had the like conception in our eyes,
And at that instant like a babe sprung up.

APEMANTUS

Ho, ho! I laugh to think that babe a bastard.

THIRD LORD

I promise you, my lord, you moved me much.

APEMANTUS

Much!   [*Tucket, within*

TIMON

What means that trump?

Enter a SERVANT

                    How now!

SERVANT

Please you, my lord, there are certain ladies most
desirous of admittance.

TIMON

Ladies! what are their wills?

SERVANT

There comes with them a forerunner, my lord,
which bears that office, to signify their pleasures.

TIMON

I pray, let them be admitted.

Enter CUPID

CUPID

Hail to thee, worthy Timon! and to all
That of his bounties taste! The five best senses
Acknowledge thee their patron, and come freely
To gratulate thy plenteous bosom: th' ear,
Taste, touch, and smell, pleased from thy table rise;
They only now come but to feast thine eyes.

TIMON

They're welcome all; let 'em have kind admittance:
Music, make their welcome!   [*Exit* CUPID

FIRST LORD

You see, my lord, how ample you're beloved.
Music. Re-enter CUPID, *with a mask of* LADIES *as Amazons, with lutes in their hands, dancing and playing*

[1158]

APEMANTUS

Hoy-day, what a sweep of vanity comes this way!
They dance! they are mad women.
Like madness is the glory of this life,
As this pomp shows to a little oil and root.
We make ourselves fools, to disport ourselves,
And spend our flatteries, to drink those men
Upon whose age we void it up again
With poisonous spite and envy.
Who lives, that's not depraved or depraves?
Who dies, that bears not one spurn to their graves
Of their friends' gift?
I should fear those that dance before me now
Would one day stamp upon me: 't has been done;
Men shut their doors against a setting sun.

The LORDS *rise from table, with much adoring of* TIMON;
and to show their loves, each singles out an AMAZON, *and
all dance, men with women, a lofty strain or two to the
hautboys, and cease*

TIMON

You have done our pleasures much grace, fair
   ladies,
Set a fair fashion on our entertainment,
Which was not half so beautiful and kind;
You have added worth unto 't and lustre,
And entertain'd me with mine own device:
I am to thank you for 't.

FIRST LADY

My lord, you take us even at the best.

APEMANTUS

Faith, for the worst is filthy, and would not hold
taking, I doubt me.

TIMON

Ladies, there is an idle banquet attends you:
Please you to dispose yourselves.

ALL LADIES

Most thankfully, my lord.

                [*Exeunt* CUPID *and* LADIES

TIMON

Flavius!

FLAVIUS

My lord?

TIMON

The little casket bring me hither.

FLAVIUS

Yes, my lord. [*Aside*] More jewels yet!
There is no crossing him in 's humour;
Else I should tell him—well, i' faith, I should—
When all's spent, he'ld be cross'd then, an he could.
'Tis pity bounty had not eyes behind,
That man might ne'er be wretched for his mind.
                            [*Exit*

FIRST LORD

Where be our men?

SERVANT

Here, my lord, in readiness.

SECOND LORD

Our horses!

Re-enter FLAVIUS, *with the casket*

TIMON

O my friends,
I have one word to say to you: look you, my good
   lord,
I must entreat you, honour me so much
As to advance this jewel; accept it and wear it,
Kind my lord.

FIRST LORD

I am so far already in your gifts,—

ALL

So are we all.

Enter a SERVANT

SERVANT

My lord, there are certain nobles of the senate
newly alighted and come to visit you.

TIMON

They are fairly welcome.

FLAVIUS

I beseech your honour, vouchsafe me a word; it
does concern you near.

TIMON

Near! why, then, another time I'll hear thee:
I prithee, let's be provided to show them entertainment.

FLAVIUS

[*Aside*] I scarce know how.

Enter another SERVANT

SECOND SERVANT

May it please your honour, Lord Lucius
Out of his free love hath presented to you
Four milk-white horses, trapp'd in silver.

TIMON

I shall accept them fairly: let the presents
Be worthily entertain'd.

Enter a THIRD SERVANT

How now! what news?

THIRD SERVANT

Please you, my lord, that honourable gentleman,
Lord Lucullus, entreats your company to-morrow
to hunt with him, and has sent your honour two
brace of greyhounds.

TIMON

I'll hunt with him; and let them be received,
Not without fair reward.

FLAVIUS

[*Aside*] What will this come to?
He commands us to provide and give great gifts,
   and all out of an empty coffer:
Nor will he know his purse, or yield me this,
To show him what a beggar his heart is,
Being of no power to make his wishes good:
His promises fly so beyond his state
That what he speaks is all in debt, he owes
For every word: he is so kind that he now
Pays interest for 't; his land's put to their books.
Well, would I were gently put out of office,
Before I were forced out!
Happier is he that has no friend to feed
Than such that do e'en enemies exceed.
I bleed inwardly for my lord.   [*Exit*

TIMON
You do yourselves
Much wrong, you bate too much of your own
merits.
Here, my lord, a trifle of our love.

SECOND LORD
With more than common thanks I will receive it.

THIRD LORD
O, he's the very soul of bounty!

TIMON
And now I remember, my lord, you gave good
words the other day of a bay courser I rode on.
'Tis yours, because you liked it.

THIRD LORD
O, I beseech you, pardon me, my lord, in that.

TIMON
You may take my word, my lord; I know, no man
can justly praise, but what he does affect: I weigh
my friend's affection with mine own: I'll tell you
true. I'll call to you.

ALL LORDS
O, none so welcome.

TIMON
I take all and your several visitations
So kind to heart, 'tis not enough to give:
Methinks, I could deal kingdoms to my friends,
And ne'er be weary. Alcibiades,
Thou art a soldier, therefore seldom rich;
It comes in charity to thee: for all thy living
Is 'mongst the dead, and all the lands thou hast
Lie in a pitch'd field.

ALCIBIADES
Ay, defiled land, my lord.

FIRST LORD
We are so virtuously bound—

TIMON
And so am I to you.

SECOND LORD
So infinitely endear'd—

TIMON
All to you. Lights, more lights!

FIRST LORD
The best of happiness, honour and fortunes, keep
with you, Lord Timon!

TIMON
Ready for his friends.
[Exeunt all but APEMANTUS and TIMON

APEMANTUS
What a coil's here!
Serving of becks and jutting-out of bums!
I doubt whether their legs be worth the sums
That are given for 'em. Friendship's full of dregs:
Methinks, false hearts should never have sound legs.
Thus honest fools lay out their wealth on court'sies.

TIMON
Now, Apemantus, if thou wert not sullen,
I would be good to thee.

APEMANTUS
No, I'll nothing: for if I should be bribed too, there
would be none left to rail upon thee; and then thou

wouldst sin the faster. Thou givest so long, Timon,
I fear me thou wilt give away thyself in paper
shortly: what needs these feasts, pomps and vain-
glories?

TIMON
Nay, an you begin to rail on society once, I am
sworn not to give regard to you. Farewell; and come
with better music. [Exit

APEMANTUS
So: thou wilt not hear me now; thou shalt not them:
I'll lock thy heaven from thee.
O, that men's ears should be
To counsel deaf, but not to flattery! [Exit

ACT II

SCENE I. A SENATOR's house

Enter a SENATOR, *with papers in his hands*

SENATOR
And late five thousand: to Varro and to Isidore
He owes nine thousand; besides my former sum,
Which makes it five and twenty. Still in motion
Of raging waste? It cannot hold; it will not.
If I want gold, steal but a beggar's dog
And give it Timon, why, the dog coins gold:
If I would sell my horse and buy twenty moe
Better than he, why, give my horse to Timon;
Ask nothing, give it him, it foals me straight
And able horses: no porter at his gate,
But rather one that smiles and still invites
All that pass by. It cannot hold; no reason
Can found his state in safety. Caphis, ho!
Caphis, I say!

Enter CAPHIS

CAPHIS
Here, sir; what is your pleasure?

SENATOR
Get on your cloak, and haste you to Lord Timon;
Importune him for my moneys; be not ceased
With slight denial; nor then silenced, when—
'Commend me to your master'—and the cap
Plays in the right hand, thus: but tell him,
My uses cry to me, I must serve my turn
Out of mine own; his days and times are past,
And my reliances on his fracted dates
Have smit my credit: I love and honour him,
But must not break my back to heal his finger:
Immediate are my needs; and my relief
Must not be toss'd and turn'd to me in words,
But find supply immediate. Get you gone:
Put on a most importunate aspect,
A visage of demand; for, I do fear,
When every feather sticks in his own wing,
Lord Timon will be left a naked gull,
Which flashes now a phœnix. Get you gone.

CAPHIS
I go, sir.

SENATOR
'I go, sir!' Take the bonds along with you,
And have the dates in compt.
CAPHIS
I will, sir.
SENATOR
Go. [Exeunt

SCENE II. *A hall in* TIMON'S *house*

Enter FLAVIUS, *with many bills in his hand*
FLAVIUS
No care, no stop! so senseless of expense,
That he will neither know how to maintain it,
Nor cease his flow of riot: takes no account
How things go from him; nor resumes no care
Of what is to continue: never mind
Was to be so unwise, to be so kind.
What shall be done? he will not hear till feel:
I must be round with him, now he comes from
    hunting.
Fie, fie, fie, fie!
Enter CAPHIS, *with the* SERVANTS *of* ISIDORE *and* VARRO
CAPHIS
Good even, Varro: what, you come for money?
VARRO'S SERVANT
Is 't not your business too?
CAPHIS
It is: and yours too, Isidore?
ISIDORE'S SERVANT
It is so.
CAPHIS
Would we were all discharged!
VARRO'S SERVANT
I fear it.
CAPHIS
Here comes the lord.
Enter TIMON, ALCIBIADES, LORDS, *and others*
TIMON
So soon as dinner's done, we'll forth again,
My Alcibiades. With me? what is your will?
CAPHIS
My lord, here is a note of certain dues.
TIMON
Dues! Whence are you?
CAPHIS
Of Athens here, my lord.
TIMON
Go to my steward.
CAPHIS
Please it your lordship, he hath put me off
To the succession of new days this month:
My master is awaked by great occasion
To call upon his own, and humbly prays you
That with your other noble parts you'll suit
In giving him his right.
TIMON
Mine honest friend,
ɤ prithee but repair to me next morning.

CAPHIS
Nay, good my lord,—
TIMON
Contain thyself, good friend.
VARRO'S SERVANT
One Varro's servant, my good lord,—
ISIDORE'S SERVANT
From Isidore; he humbly prays your speedy payment.
CAPHIS
If you did know, my lord, my master's wants,—
VARRO'S SERVANT
'Twas due on forfeiture, my lord, six weeks and
past.
ISIDORE'S SERVANT
Your steward puts me off, my lord, and I
Am sent expressly to your lordship.
TIMON
Give me breath.
I do beseech you, good my lords, keep on;
I'll wait upon you instantly.
[*Exeunt* ALCIBIADES, LORDS, &c.
[*To* FLAVIUS] Come hither: pray you,
How goes the world, that I am thus encounter'd
With clamorous demands of date-broke bonds,
And the detention of long-since-due debts,
Against my honour?
FLAVIUS
Please you, gentlemen,
The time is unagreeable to this business:
Your importunacy cease till after dinner,
That I may make his lordship understand
Wherefore you are not paid.
TIMON
Do so, my friends. See them well entertain'd. [*Exit*
FLAVIUS
Pray, draw near. [*Exit*
Enter APEMANTUS *and* FOOL
CAPHIS
Stay, stay, here comes the fool with Apemantus:
let's ha' some sport with 'em.
VARRO'S SERVANT
Hang him, he'll abuse us.
ISIDORE'S SERVANT
A plague upon him, dog!
VARRO'S SERVANT
How dost, fool?
APEMANTUS
Dost dialogue with thy shadow?
VARRO'S SERVANT
I speak not to thee.
APEMANTUS
No, 'tis to thyself. [*To the* FOOL] Come away.
ISIDORE'S SERVANT
There's the fool hangs on your back already.
APEMANTUS
No, thou stand'st single, thou'rt not on him yet.
CAPHIS
Where's the fool now?

APEMANTUS

He last asked the question. Poor rogues, and usurers' men! bawds between gold and want!

ALL SERVANTS

What are we, Apemantus?

APEMANTUS

Asses.

ALL SERVANTS

Why?

APEMANTUS

That you ask me what you are, and do not know yourselves. Speak to 'em, fool.

FOOL

How do you, gentlemen?

ALL SERVANTS

Gramercies, good fool: how does your mistress?

FOOL

She's e'en setting on water to scald such chickens as you are. Would we could see you at Corinth!

APEMANTUS

Good! gramercy.

Enter PAGE

FOOL

Look you, here comes my mistress' page.

PAGE

[To the FOOL] Why, how now, captain! what do you in this wise company? How dost thou, Apemantus?

APEMANTUS

Would I had a rod in my mouth, that I might answer thee profitably.

PAGE

Prithee, Apemantus, read me the superscription of these letters: I know not which is which.

APEMANTUS

Canst not read?

PAGE

No.

APEMANTUS

There will little learning die then, that day thou art hang'd. This is to Lord Timon; this to Alcibiades. Go; thou wast born a bastard, and thou'lt die a bawd.

PAGE

Thou wast whelped a dog, and thou shalt famish a dog's death. Answer not, I am gone.   [Exit

APEMANTUS

E'en so thou outrun'st grace. Fool, I will go with you to Lord Timon's.

FOOL

Will you leave me there?

APEMANTUS

If Timon stay at home. You three serve three usurers?

ALL SERVANTS

Ay; would they served us!

APEMANTUS

So would I,—as good a trick as ever hangman served thief.

FOOL

Are you three usurers' men?

ALL SERVANTS

Ay, fool.

FOOL

I think no usurer but has a fool to his servant: my mistress is one, and I am her fool. When men come to borrow of your masters, they approach sadly and go away merry; but they enter my mistress' house merrily and go away sadly: the reason of this?

VARRO'S SERVANT

I could render one.

APEMANTUS

Do it then, that we may account thee a whoremaster and a knave; which notwithstanding, thou shalt be no less esteemed.

VARRO'S SERVANT

What is a whoremaster, fool?

FOOL

A fool in good clothes, and something like thee. 'Tis a spirit: sometime 't appears like a lord; sometime like a lawyer; sometime like a philosopher, with two stones moe than 's artificial one: he is very often like a knight; and, generally, in all shapes that man goes up and down in from fourscore to thirteen, this spirit walks in.

VARRO'S SERVANT

Thou art not altogether a fool.

FOOL

Nor thou altogether a wise man: as much foolery as I have, so much wit thou lack'st.

APEMANTUS

That answer might have become Apemantus.

ALL SERVANTS

Aside, aside; here comes Lord Timon.

Re-enter TIMON and FLAVIUS

APEMANTUS

Come with me, fool, come.

FOOL

I do not always follow lover, elder brother, and woman; sometime the philosopher.

[Exeunt APEMANTUS and FOOL

FLAVIUS

Pray you, walk near: I'll speak with you anon.

[Exeunt SERVANTS

TIMON

You make me marvel; wherefore, ere this time, Had you not fully laid my state before me, That I might so have rated my expense As I had leave of means?

FLAVIUS

You would not hear me, At many leisures I proposed.

TIMON

Go to: Perchance some single vantages you took. When my indisposition put you back; And that unaptness made your minister, Thus to excuse yourself.

FLAVIUS

O my good lord, At many times I brought in my accounts,

Laid them before you; you would throw them off,
And say, you found them in mine honesty.
When for some trifling present you have bid me
Return so much, I have shook my head and wept;
Yea, 'gainst the authority of manners pray'd you
To hold your hand more close: I did endure
Not seldom nor no slight checks, when I have
Prompted you in the ebb of your estate
And your great flow of debts. My loved lord,
Though you hear now, too late!—yet now's a time—
The greatest of your having lacks a half
To pay your present debts.

TIMON

               Let all my land be sold.

FLAVIUS

'Tis all engaged, some forfeited and gone,
And what remains will hardly stop the mouth
Of present dues: the future comes apace:
What shall defend the interim? and at length
How goes our reckoning?

TIMON

To Lacedæmon did my land extend.

FLAVIUS

O my good lord, the world is but a word:
Were it all yours to give it in a breath,
How quickly were it gone!

TIMON

               You tell me true.

FLAVIUS

If you suspect my husbandry or falsehood,
Call me before the exactest auditors,
And set me on the proof. So the gods bless me,
When all our offices have been oppress'd
With riotous feeders, when our vaults have wept
With drunken spilth of wine, when every room
Hath blazed with lights and bray'd with minstrelsy,
I have retired me to a wasteful cock,
And set mine eyes at flow.

TIMON

               Prithee, no more.

FLAVIUS

Heavens, have I said, the bounty of this lord!
How many prodigal bits have slaves and peasants
This night englutted! Who is not Timon's?
What heart, head, sword, force, means, but is Lord
    Timon's?
Great Timon, noble, worthy, royal Timon!
Ah, when the means are gone that buy this praise,
The breath is gone whereof this praise is made:
Feast-won, fast-lost; one cloud of winter showers,
These flies are couch'd.

TIMON

               Come, sermon me no further:
No villanous bounty yet hath pass'd my heart,
Unwisely, not ignobly, have I given.
Why dost thou weep? Canst thou the conscience
    lack,
To think I shall lack friends? Secure thy heart;
If I would broach the vessels of my love,
And try the argument of hearts by borrowing,

Men and men's fortunes could I frankly use
As I can bid thee speak.

FLAVIUS

            Assurance bless your thoughts!

TIMON

And in some sort these wants of mine are crown'd,
That I account them blessings; for by these
Shall I try friends: you shall perceive how you
Mistake my fortunes; I am wealthy in my friends.
Within there! Flaminius! Servilius!

Enter FLAMINIUS, SERVILIUS, *and other* SERVANTS

SERVANTS

My lord? my lord?

TIMON

I will dispatch you severally: you to Lord Lucius: to
Lord Lucullus you: I hunted with his honour to-
day: you to Sempronius: commend me to their
loves; and, I am proud, say, that my occasions have
found time to use 'em toward a supply of money: let
the request be fifty talents.

FLAMINIUS

As you have said, my Lord.

FLAVIUS

[*Aside*] Lord Lucius and Lucullus? hum!

TIMON

Go you, sir, to the senators—
Of whom, even to the state's best health, I have
Deserved this hearing—bid 'em send o' the instant
A thousand talents to me.

FLAVIUS

            I have been bold,
For that I knew it the most general way,
To them to use your signet and your name,
But they do shake their heads, and I am here
No richer in return.

TIMON

            Is 't true? can 't be?

FLAVIUS

They answer, in a joint and corporate voice,
That now they are at fall, want treasure, cannot
Do what they would; are sorry—you are honour-
    able,—
But yet they could have wish'd—they know not—
Something hath been amiss—a noble nature
May catch a wrench—would all were well—'tis
    pity:—
And so, intending other serious matters,
After distasteful looks and these hard fractions,
With certain half-caps and cold-moving nods
They froze me into silence.

TIMON

            You gods, reward them!
Prithee, man, look cheerly. These old fellows
Have their ingratitude in them hereditary:
Their blood is caked, 'tis cold, it seldom flows;
'Tis lack of kindly warmth they are not kind;
And nature, as it grows again toward earth,
Is fashion'd for the journey, dull and heavy.
[*To a* SERVANT] Go to Ventidius. [*To* FLAVIUS]
    Prithee, be not sad;

Thou art true and honest; ingeniously I speak,
No blame belongs to thee. [*To* SERVANT] Ventidius lately
Buried his father, by whose death he's stepp'd
Into a great estate: when he was poor,
Imprison'd, and in scarcity of friends,
I clear'd him with five talents: greet him from me;
Bid him suppose some good necessity
Touches his friend, which craves to be remember'd
With those five talents. [*Exit* SERVANT] [*To* FLAVIUS]
　　That had, give 't these fellows
To whom 'tis instant due. Ne'er speak or think
That Timon's fortunes 'mong his friends can sink.

FLAVIUS

I would I could not think it: that thought is bounty's foe;
Being free itself, it thinks all others so.　　[*Exeunt*

ACT III

SCENE I. *A room in* LUCULLUS's *house*

FLAMINIUS *waiting. Enter a* SERVANT *to him*

SERVANT

I have told my lord of you; he is coming down to you.

FLAMINIUS

I thank you, sir.

Enter LUCULLUS

SERVANT

Here's my lord.

LUCULLUS

[*Aside*] One of Lord Timon's men? a gift, I warrant. Why, this hits right; I dreamt of a silver basin and ewer to-night. Flaminius, honest Flaminius; you are very respectively welcome, sir. Fill me some wine. [*Exit* SERVANT] And how does that honourable, complete, free-hearted gentleman of Athens, thy very bountiful good lord and master?

FLAMINIUS

His health is well, sir.

LUCULLUS

I am right glad that his health is well, sir: and what hast thou there under thy cloak, pretty Flaminius?

FLAMINIUS

Faith, nothing but an empty box, sir; which, in my lord's behalf, I come to entreat your honour to supply; who, having great and instant occasion to use fifty talents, hath sent to your lordship to furnish him, nothing doubting your present assistance therein.

LUCULLUS

La, la, la, la! 'nothing doubting,' says he? Alas, good lord! a noble gentleman 'tis, if he would not keep so good a house. Many a time and often I ha' dined with him, and told him on 't; and come again to supper to him, of purpose to have him spend less; and yet he would embrace no counsel, take no

warning by my coming. Every man has his fault, and honesty is his: I ha' told him on 't, but I could ne'er get him from 't.

Re-enter SERVANT, *with wine*

SERVANT

Please your lordship, here is the wine.

LUCULLUS

Flaminius, I have noted thee always wise. Here's to thee.

FLAMINIUS

Your lordship speaks your pleasure.

LUCULLUS

I have observed thee always for a towardly prompt spirit—give thee thy due—and one that knows what belongs to reason; and canst use the time well, if the time use thee well: good parts in thee. [*To* SERVANT] Get you gone, sirrah. [*Exit* SERVANT] Draw nearer, honest Flaminius. Thy lord's a bountiful gentleman: but thou art wise; and thou knowest well enough, although thou comest to me, that this is no time to lend money, especially upon bare friendship, without security. Here's three solidares for thee: good boy, wink at me, and say thou saw'st me not. Fare thee well.

FLAMINIUS

Is 't possible the world should so much differ,
And we alive that lived? Fly, damned baseness,
To him that worships thee! [*Throwing back the money*

LUCULLUS

Ha! now I see thou art a fool, and fit for thy master.
　　　　　　　　　　　　　　　　　　　　[*Exit*

FLAMINIUS

May these add to the number that may scald thee!
Let molten coin be thy damnation,
Thou disease of a friend, and not himself!
Has friendship such a faint and milky heart,
It turns in less than two nights? O you gods,
I feel my master's passion! this slave,
Unto his honour, has my lord's meat in him:
Why should it thrive and turn to nutriment,
When he is turn'd to poison?
O, may diseases only work upon 't!
And, when he's sick to death, let not that part of nature
Which my lord paid for, be of any power
To expel sickness, but prolong his hour!　　[*Exit*

SCENE II. *A public place*

Enter LUCIUS, *with three* STRANGERS

LUCIUS

Who, the Lord Timon? he is my very good friend, and an honourable gentleman.

FIRST STRANGER

We know him for no less, though we are but strangers to him. But I can tell you one thing, my lord, and which I hear from common rumours: now Lord Timon's happy hours are done and past, and his estate shrinks from him.

LUCIUS

Fie, no, do not believe it; he cannot want for money.

SECOND STRANGER

But believe you this, my lord, that not long ago one of his men was with the Lord Lucullus to borrow so many talents; nay, urged extremely for 't, and showed what necessity belonged to 't, and yet was denied.

LUCIUS

How!

SECOND STRANGER

I tell you, denied, my lord.

LUCIUS

What a strange case was that! now, before the gods, I am ashamed on 't. Denied that honourable man! there was very little honour showed in 't. For my own part, I must needs confess, I have received some small kindnesses from him, as money, plate, jewels, and such-like trifles, nothing comparing to his; yet, had he mistook him and sent to me, I should ne'er have denied his occasion so many talents.

Enter SERVILIUS

SERVILIUS

See, by good hap, yonder's my lord; I have sweat to see his honour. My honoured lord!

LUCIUS

Servilius! you are kindly met, sir. Fare thee well: commend me to thy honourable virtuous lord, my very exquisite friend.

SERVILIUS

May it please your honour, my lord hath sent—

LUCIUS

Ha! what has he sent? I am so much endeared to that lord; he's ever sending: how shall I thank him, think'st thou? And what has he sent now?

SERVILIUS

Has only sent his present occasion now, my lord; requesting your lordship to supply his instant use with so many talents.

LUCIUS

I know his lordship is but merry with me; He cannot want fifty five hundred talents.

SERVILIUS

But in the mean time he wants less, my lord. If his occasion were not virtuous, I should not urge it half so faithfully.

LUCIUS

Dost thou speak seriously, Servilius?

SERVILIUS

Upon my soul, 'tis true, sir.

LUCIUS

What a wicked beast was I to disfurnish myself against such a good time, when I might ha' shown myself honourable! how unluckily it happened, that I should purchase the day before for a little part, and undo a great deal of honour! Servilius, now, before the gods, I am not able to do—the more

beast, I say:—I was sending to use Lord Timon myself, these gentlemen can witness; but I would not, for the wealth of Athens, I had done 't now. Commend me bountifully to his good lordship; and I hope his honour will conceive the fairest of me, because I have no power to be kind: and tell him this from me, I count it one of my greatest afflictions, say, that I cannot pleasure such an honourable gentleman. Good Servilius, will you befriend me so far as to use mine own words to him?

SERVILIUS

Yes, sir, I shall.

LUCIUS

I'll look you out a good turn, Servilius.

[*Exit* SERVILIUS

True, as you said, Timon is shrunk indeed;
And he that's once denied will hardly speed.　[*Exit*

FIRST STRANGER

Do you observe this, Hostilius?

SECOND STRANGER

Ay, too well.

FIRST STRANGER

Why, this is the world's soul; and just of the same piece
Is every flatter's spirit. Who can call him
His friend that dips in the same dish? for, in
My knowing, Timon has been this lord's father,
And kept his credit with his purse;
Supported his estate; nay, Timon's money
Has paid his men their wages: he ne'er drinks,
But Timon's silver treads upon his lip;
And yet—O, see the monstrousness of man
When he looks out in an ungrateful shape!—
He does deny him, in respect of his,
What charitable men afford to beggars.

THIRD STRANGER

Religion groans at it.

FIRST STRANGER

　　　　　　For mine own part,
I never tasted Timon in my life,
Nor came any of his bounties over me,
To mark me for his friend; yet, I protest,
For his right noble mind, illustrious virtue,
And honourable carriage,
Had his necessity made use of me,
I would have put my wealth into donation,
And the best half should have return'd to him,
So much I love his heart: but, I perceive,
Men must learn now with pity to dispense;
For policy sits above conscience.　　　[*Exeunt*

SCENE III. *A room in* SEMPRONIUS' *house*

Enter SEMPRONIUS, *and a* SERVANT OF TIMON'S

SEMPRONIUS

Must he needs trouble me in 't,—hum!—'bove all others?
He might have tried Lord Lucius or Lucullus:
And now Ventidius is wealthy too,

Whom he redeem'd from prison: all these
Owe their estates unto him.

SERVANT

My lord,
They have all been touch'd and found base metal,
for
They have all denied him.

SEMPRONIUS

How! have they denied him?
Has Ventidius and Lucullus denied him?
And does he send to me? Three? hum!
It shows but little love or judgement in him:
Must I be his last refuge? His friends, like physicians,
Thrive, give him over: must I take the cure upon
me?
Has much disgraced me in 't; I'm angry at him,
That might have known my place: I see no sense
for 't,
But his occasions might have woo'd me first;
For, in my conscience, I was the first man
That e'er received gift from him:
And does he think so backwardly of me now,
That I'll requite it last? No:
So it may prove an argument of laughter
To the rest, and 'mongst lords I be thought a fool.
I'd rather than the worth of thrice the sum,
Had sent to me first, but for my mind's sake;
I'd such a courage to do him good. But now return,
And with their faint reply this answer join;
Who bates mine honour shall not know my coin.

[*Exit*

SERVANT

Excellent! Your lordship's a goodly villain.
The devil knew not what he did when he made man
politic; he crossed himself by 't: and I cannot think
but in the end the villanies of man will set him clear.
How fairly this lord strives to appear foul! takes vir-
tuous copies to be wicked; like those that under hot
ardent zeal would set whole realms on fire:
Of such a nature is his politic love.
This was my lord's best hope; now all are fled,
Save only the gods: now his friends are dead,
Doors, that were ne'er acquainted with their wards
Many a bounteous year, must be employ'd
Now to guard sure their master.
And this is all a liberal course allows;
Who cannot keep his wealth must keep his house.

[*Exit*

SCENE IV. *A hall in* TIMON'S *house*

Enter two SERVANTS OF VARRO, *and the* SERVANT OF
LUCIUS, *meeting* TITUS, HORTENSIUS, *and other* SERVANTS
of Timon's creditors, waiting his coming out

FIRST VARRO SERVANT

Well met; good morrow, Titus and Hortensius.

TITUS

The like to you, kind Varro.

HORTENSIUS

Lucius!

What, do we meet together?

LUCIUS' SERVANT

Ay, and I think
One business does command us all; for mine
Is money.

TITUS

So is theirs and ours.

Enter PHILOTUS

LUCIUS' SERVANT

And Sir Philotus too!

PHILOTUS

Good day at once.

LUCIUS' SERVANT

Welcome, good brother.
What do you think the hour?

PHILOTUS

Labouring for nine.

LUCIUS' SERVANT

So much?

PHILOTUS

Is not my lord seen yet?

LUCIUS' SERVANT

Not yet.

PHILOTUS

I wonder on 't; he was wont to shine at seven.

LUCIUS' SERVANT

Ay, but the days are wax'd shorter with him:
You must consider that a prodigal course
Is like the sun's; but not, like his, recoverable.
I fear
'Tis deepest winter in Lord Timon's purse;
That is, one may reach deep enough and yet
Find little.

PHILOTUS

I am of your fear for that.

TITUS

I'll show you how to observe a strange event.
Your lord sends now for money.

HORTENSIUS

Most true, he does.

TITUS

And he wears jewels now of Timon's gift,
For which I wait for money.

HORTENSIUS

It is against my heart.

LUCIUS' SERVANT

Mark, how strange it shows,
Timon in this should pay more than he owes:
And e'en as if your lord should wear rich jewels,
And send for money for 'em.

HORTENSIUS

I'm weary of this charge, the gods can witness:
I know my lord hath spent of Timon's wealth,
And now ingratitude makes it worse than stealth.

FIRST VARRO SERVANT

Yes, mine's three thousand crowns: what's yours?

LUCIUS' SERVANT

Five thousand mine.

FIRST VARRO SERVANT

'Tis much deep: and it should seem by the sum
Your master's confidence was above mine;
Else, surely, his had equall'd.

Enter FLAMINIUS

TITUS

One of Lord Timon's men.

LUCIUS' SERVANT

Flaminius! Sir, a word: pray, is my lord ready to
come forth?

FLAMINIUS

No, indeed he is not.

TITUS

We attend his lordship: pray, signify so much.

FLAMINIUS

I need not tell him that; he knows you are too
diligent.   [*Exit*

Enter FLAVIUS *in a cloak, muffled*

LUCIUS' SERVANT

Ha! is not that his steward muffled so?
He goes away in a cloud: call him, call him.

TITUS

Do you hear, sir?

SECOND VARRO SERVANT

By your leave, sir,—

FLAVIUS

What do ye ask of me, my friend?

TITUS

We wait for certain money here, sir.

FLAVIUS

Ay,
If money were as certain as your waiting,
'Twere sure enough.
Why then preferr'd you not your sums and bills,
When your false masters eat of my lord's meat?
Then they could smile and fawn upon his debts,
And take down the interest into their gluttonous
     maws.
You do yourselves but wrong to stir me up;
Let me pass quietly:
Believe 't, my lord and I have made an end;
I have no more to reckon, he to spend.

LUCIUS' SERVANT

Ay, but this answer will not serve.

FLAVIUS

If 'twill not serve, 'tis not so base as you;
For you serve knaves.   [*Exit*

FIRST VARRO SERVANT

How! what does his cashiered worship mutter?

SECOND VARRO SERVANT

No matter what; he's poor, and that's revenge
enough. Who can speak broader than he that has
no house to put his head in? such may rail against
great buildings.

Enter SERVILIUS

TITUS

O, here's Servilius; now we shall know some answer.

SERVILIUS

If I might beseech you, gentlemen, to repair some

other hour, I should derive much from 't; for, take 't
of my soul, my lord leans wondrously to discontent:
his comfortable temper has forsook him; he's much
out of health and keeps his chamber.

LUCIUS' SERVANT

Many do keep their chambers are not sick:
And if it be so far beyond his health,
Methinks he should the sooner pay his debts,
And make a clear way to the gods.

SERVANT

Good gods!

TITUS

We cannot take this for answer, sir.

FLAMINIUS

[*Within*] Servilius, help! My lord! my lord!

Enter TIMON, *in a rage;* FLAMINIUS *following*

TIMON

What, are my doors opposed against my passage?
Have I been ever free, and must my house
Be my retentive enemy, my gaol?
The place which I have feasted, does it now,
Like all mankind, show me an iron heart?

LUCIUS' SERVANT

Put in now, Titus.

TITUS

My lord, here is my bill.

LUCIUS' SERVANT

Here's mine.

HORTENSIUS

And mine, my lord.

BOTH VARRO SERVANTS

And ours, my lord.

PHILOTUS

All our bills.

TIMON

Knock me down with 'em: cleave me to the girdle.

LUCIUS' SERVANT

Alas, my lord,—

TIMON

Cut my heart in sums.

TITUS

Mine, fifty talents.

TIMON

Tell out my blood.

LUCIUS' SERVANT

Five thousand crowns, my lord.

TIMON

Five thousand drops pays that. What yours?—and
yours?

FIRST VARRO SERVANT

My lord,—

SECOND VARRO SERVANT

My lord,—

TIMON

Tear me, take me, and the gods fall upon you! [*Exit*

HORTENSIUS

Faith, I perceive our masters may throw their caps
at their money: these debts may well be called desperate ones, for a madman owes 'em.   [*Exeunt*

Re-enter TIMON *and* FLAVIUS

TIMON

They have e'en put my breath from me, the slaves.
Creditors? devils!

FLAVIUS

My dear lord,—

TIMON

What if it should be so?

FLAVIUS

My lord,—

TIMON

I'll have it so. My steward!

FLAVIUS

Here, my lord.

TIMON

So fitly? Go, bid all my friends again,
Lucius, Lucullus, and Sempronius: all:
I'll once more feast the rascals.

FLAVIUS

          O my lord,
You only speak from your distracted soul;
There is not so much left, to furnish out
A moderate table.

TIMON

         Be it not in thy care;
Go,
I charge thee, invite them all: let in the tide
Of knaves once more; my cook and I'll provide.

[*Exeunt*

SCENE V. *The Senate-house*

The Senate sitting

FIRST SENATOR

My lord, you have my voice to it; the fault's
Bloody; 'tis necessary he should die:
Nothing emboldens sin so much as mercy.

SECOND SENATOR

Most true; the law shall bruise him.

Enter ALCIBIADES, *attended*

ALCIBIADES

Honour, health, and compassion to the senate!

FIRST SENATOR

Now, captain?

ALCIBIADES

I am an humble suitor to your virtues;
For pity is the virtue of the law,
And none but tyrants use it cruelly.
It pleases time and fortune to lie heavy
Upon a friend of mine, who in hot blood
Hath stepp'd into the law, which is past depth
To those that without heed do plunge into 't.
He is a man, setting his fate aside,
Of comely virtues:
Nor did he soil the fact with cowardice—
An honour in him which buys out his fault—
But with a noble fury and fair spirit,
Seeing his reputation touch'd to death,
He did oppose his foe:
And with such sober and unnoted passion

He did behave his anger, ere 'twas spent,
As if he had but proved an argument.

FIRST SENATOR

You undergo too strict a paradox,
Striving to make an ugly deed look fair:
Your words have took such pains, as if they labour'd
To bring manslaughter into form, and set quarrelling
Upon the head of valour; which indeed
Is valour misbegot and came into the world
When sects and factions were newly born:
He's truly valiant that can wisely suffer
The worst that man can breathe, and make his wrongs
His outsides, to wear them like his raiment, carelessly,
And ne'er prefer his injuries to his heart,
To bring it into danger.
If wrongs be evils and enforce us kill,
What folly 'tis to hazard life for ill!

ALCIBIADES

My lord,—

FIRST SENATOR

        You cannot make gross sins look clear:
To revenge is no valour, but to bear.

ALCIBIADES

My lords, then, under favour, pardon me,
If I speak like a captain.
Why do fond men expose themselves to battle,
And not endure all threats? sleep upon 't,
And let the foes quietly cut their throats,
Without repugnancy? If there be
Such valour in the bearing, what make we
Abroad? why then women are more valiant
That stay at home, if bearing carry it;
And the ass more captain than the lion, the felon
Loaden with irons wiser than the judge,
If wisdom be in suffering. O my lords,
As you are great, be pitifully good:
Who cannot condemn rashness in cold blood?
To kill, I grant, is sin's extremest gust;
But in defence, by mercy, 'tis most just.
To be in anger is impiety;
But who is man that is not angry?
Weigh but the crime with this.

SECOND SENATOR

You breathe in vain.

ALCIBIADES

        In vain! His service done
At Lacedæmon and Byzantium
Were a sufficient briber for his life.

FIRST SENATOR

What's that?

ALCIBIADES

        I say, my lords, has done fair service,
And slain in fight many of your enemies:
How full of valour did he bear himself
In the last conflict, and made plenteous wounds!

SECOND SENATOR

He has made too much plenty with 'em;

He's a sworn rioter: he has a sin
That often drowns him and takes his valour prisoner:
If there were no foes, that were enough
To overcome him: in that beastly fury
He has been known to commit outrages
And cherish factions: 'tis inferr'd to us,
His days are foul and his drink dangerous.
      FIRST SENATOR
He dies.
     ALCIBIADES
    Hard fate! he might have died in war.
My lords, if not for any parts in him—
Though his right arm might purchase his own time
And be in debt to none—yet, more to move you,
Take my deserts to his and join 'em both:
And, for I know your reverend ages love
Security, I'll pawn my victories, all
My honours to you, upon his good returns.
If by this crime he owes the law his life,
Why, let the war receive 't in valiant gore;
For law is strict, and war is nothing more.
      FIRST SENATOR
We are for law: he dies; urge it no more,
On height of our displeasure: friend or brother,
He forfeits his own blood that spills another.
     ALCIBIADES
Must it be so? it must not be. My lords,
I do beseech you, know me.
     SECOND SENATOR
How!
     ALCIBIADES
Call me to your remembrances.
     THIRD SENATOR
What!
     ALCIBIADES
I cannot think but your age has forgot me;
It could not else be I should prove so base
To sue and be denied such common grace:
My wounds ache at you.
     FIRST SENATOR
      Do you dare our anger?
'Tis in few words, but spacious in effect;
We banish thee for ever.
     ALCIBIADES
      Banish me!
Banish your dotage; banish usury,
That makes the senate ugly.
     FIRST SENATOR
If, after two days' shine, Athens contain thee,
Attend our weightier judgement. And, not to swell
 our spirit,
He shall be executed presently. [Exeunt SENATORS
     ALCIBIADES
Now the gods keep you old enough, that you may
 live
Only in bone, that none may look on you!
I'm worse than mad: I have kept back their foes,
While they have told their money and let out
Their coin upon large interest, I myself
Rich only in large hurts. All those for this?

Is this the balsam that the usuring senate
Pours into captains' wounds? Banishment!
It comes not ill; I hate not to be banish'd;
It is a cause worthy my spleen and fury,
That I may strike at Athens. I'll cheer up
My discontented troops, and lay for hearts.
'Tis honour with most lands to be at odds;
Soldiers should brook as little wrongs as gods. [Exit

SCENE VI. *A banqueting-room in* TIMON'S *house*

Music. Tables set out: SERVANTS *attending. Enter divers*
 LORDS, SENATORS *and others, at several doors*
     FIRST LORD
The good time of day to you, sir.
     SECOND LORD
I also wish it to you. I think this honourable lord
did but try us this other day.
     FIRST LORD
Upon that were my thoughts tiring when we encountered: I hope it is not so low with him as he
made it seem in the trial of his several friends.
     SECOND LORD
It should not be, by the persuasion of his new feasting.
     FIRST LORD
I should think so: he hath sent me an earnest inviting, which many my near occasions did urge me to
put off; but he hath conjured me beyond them, and
I must needs appear.
     SECOND LORD
In like manner was I in debt to my importunate
business, but he would not hear my excuse. I am
sorry, when he sent to borrow of me, that my pro-
vision was out.
     FIRST LORD
I am sick of that grief too, as I understand how all
things go.
     SECOND LORD
Every man here's so. What would he have borrowed
of you?
     FIRST LORD
A thousand pieces.
     SECOND LORD
A thousand pieces!
     FIRST LORD
What of you?
     SECOND LORD
He sent to me, sir,—Here he comes.
   Enter TIMON *and* ATTENDANTS
     TIMON
With all my heart, gentlemen both: and how fare
you?
     FIRST LORD
Ever at the best, hearing well of your lordship.
     SECOND LORD
The swallow follows not summer more willing than
we your lordship.

TIMON

[*Aside*] No more willingly leaves winter; such summer-birds are men.—Gentlemen, our dinner will not recompense this long stay: feast your ears with the music awhile, if they will fare so harshly o' the trumpet's sound; we shall to 't presently.

FIRST LORD

I hope it remains not unkindly with your lordship, that I returned you an empty messenger.

TIMON

O, sir, let it not trouble you.

SECOND LORD

My noble lord,—

TIMON

Ah, my good friend, what cheer?

SECOND LORD

My most honourable lord, I am e'en sick of shame, that, when your lordship this other day sent to me, I was so unfortunate a beggar.

TIMON

Think not on 't, sir.

SECOND LORD

If you had sent but two hours before—

TIMON

Let it not cumber your better remembrance. [*The banquet brought in*] Come, bring in all together.

SECOND LORD

All covered dishes!

FIRST LORD

Royal cheer, I warrant you.

THIRD LORD

Doubt not that, if money and the season can yield it.

FIRST LORD

How do you? What's the news?

THIRD LORD

Alcibiades is banished: hear you of it?

FIRST *and* SECOND LORDS

Alcibiades banished!

THIRD LORD

'Tis so, be sure of it.

FIRST LORD

How? how?

SECOND LORD

I pray you, upon what?

TIMON

My worthy friends, will you draw near?

THIRD LORD

I'll tell you more anon. Here's a noble feast toward.

SECOND LORD

This is the old man still.

THIRD LORD

Will 't hold? will 't hold?

SECOND LORD

It does: but time will—and so—

THIRD LORD

I do conceive.

TIMON

Each man to his stool, with that spur as he would to the lip of his mistress: your diet shall be in all places alike. Make not a city feast of it, to let the meat cool ere we can agree upon the first place: sit, sit. The gods require our thanks.

You great benefactors, sprinkle our society with thankfulness. For your own gifts, make yourselves praised: but reserve still to give, lest your deities be despised. Lend to each man enough, that one need not lend to another; for, were your godheads to borrow of men, men would forsake the gods. Make the meat be beloved more than the man that gives it. Let no assembly of twenty be without a score of villains: if there sit twelve women at the table, let a dozen of them be—as they are. The rest of your fees, O gods,—the senators of Athens, together with the common lag of people,—what is amiss in them, you gods, make suitable for destruction. For these my present friends, as they are to me nothing, so in nothing bless them, and to nothing are they welcome.

Uncover, dogs, and lap.

[*The dishes are uncovered and seen to be full of warm water*]

SOME SPEAK

What does his lordship mean?

SOME OTHER

I know not.

TIMON

May you a better feast never behold,
You knot of mouth-friends! smoke and luke-warm water
Is your perfection. This is Timon's last;
Who stuck and spangled you with flatteries,
Washes it off, and sprinkles in your faces
Your reeking villany.

[*Throwing the water in their faces*]

Live loathed, and long,
Most smiling, smooth, detested parasites,
Courteous destroyers, affable wolves, meek bears,
You fools of fortune, trencher-friends, time's flies,
Cap-and-knee slaves, vapours, and minute-jacks!
Of man and beast the infinite malady
Crust you quite o'er! What, dost thou go?
Soft! take thy physic first—thou too—and thou:—
Stay, I will lend thee money, borrow none.

[*Throws the dishes at them, and drives them out*]

What, all in motion? Henceforth be no feast,
Whereat a villain's not a welcome guest.
Burn, house! sink, Athens! henceforth hated be
Of Timon man and all humanity!   [*Exit*

Re-enter the LORDS, SENATORS, &c.

FIRST LORD

How now, my lords!

SECOND LORD

Know you the quality of Lord Timon's fury?

THIRD LORD

Push! did you see my cap?

FOURTH LORD

I have lost my gown.

FIRST LORD

He's but a mad lord, and nought but humour sways him. He gave me a jewel th' other day, and now he has beat it out of my hat. Did you see my jewel?

THIRD LORD

Did you see my cap?

SECOND LORD

Here 'tis.

FOURTH LORD

Here lies my gown.

FIRST LORD

Let's make no stay.

SECOND LORD

Lord Timon's mad.

THIRD LORD

    I feel 't upon my bones.

FOURTH LORD

One day he gives us diamonds, next day stones.

                            [Exeunt

ACT IV

SCENE I. *Without the walls of Athens*

Enter TIMON

TIMON

Let me look back upon thee. O thou wall,
That girdlest in those wolves, dive in the earth,
And fence not Athens! Matrons, turn incontinent!
Obedience fail in children! Slaves and fools,
Pluck the grave wrinkled senate from the bench,
And minister in their steads! To general filths
Convert o' the instant, green virginity!
Do 't in your parents' eyes! Bankrupts, hold fast;
Rather than render back, out with your knives,
And cut your trusters' throats! Bound servants, steal!
Large-handed robbers your grave masters are
And pill by law. Maid, to thy master's bed!
Thy mistress is o' the brothel. Son of sixteen,
Pluck the lined crutch from thy old limping sire,
With it beat out his brains! Piety and fear,
Religion to the gods, peace, justice, truth,
Domestic awe, night-rest and neighbourhood,
Instruction, manners, mysteries and trades,
Degrees, observances, customs and laws,
Decline to your confounding contraries,
And let confusion live! Plagues incident to men,
Your potent and infectious fevers heap
On Athens, ripe for stroke! Thou cold sciatica,
Cripple our senators, that their limbs may halt
As lamely as their manners! Lust and liberty
Creep in the minds and marrows of our youth,
That 'gainst the stream of virtue they may strive,
And drown themselves in riot! Itches, blains,
Sow all the Athenian bosoms, and their crop
Be general leprosy! Breath infect breath,
That their society, as their friendship, may
Be merely poison! Nothing I'll bear from thee
But nakedness, thou detestable town!
Take thou that too, with multiplying bans!
Timon will to the woods, where he shall find
The unkindest beast more kinder than mankind.

The gods confound—hear me, you good gods all!—
The Athenians both within and out that wall!
And grant, as Timon grows, his hate may grow
To the whole race of mankind, high and low!
Amen.
                            [Exit

SCENE II. *Athens.* TIMON's *house*

Enter FLAVIUS, *with two or three* SERVANTS

FIRST SERVANT

Hear you, master steward, where's our master?
Are we undone? cast off? nothing remaining?

FLAVIUS

Alack, my fellows, what should I say to you?
Let me be recorded by the righteous gods,
I am as poor as you.

FIRST SERVANT

           Such a house broke!
So noble a master fall'n! All gone! and not
One friend to take his fortune by the arm,
And go along with him!

SECOND SERVANT

           As we do turn our backs
From our companion thrown into his grave,
So his familiars to his buried fortunes
Slink all away; leave their false vows with him,
Like empty purses pick'd; and his poor self,
A dedicated beggar to the air,
With his disease of all-shunn'd poverty,
Walks, like contempt, alone. More of our fellows.

Enter other SERVANTS

FLAVIUS

All broken implements of a ruin'd house.

THIRD SERVANT

Yet do our hearts wear Timon's livery;
That see I by our faces; we are fellows still,
Serving alike in sorrow: leak'd is our bark,
And we, poor mates, stand on the dying deck,
Hearing the surges threat: we must all part
Into this sea of air.

FLAVIUS

           Good fellows all,
The latest of my wealth I'll share amongst you.
Wherever we shall meet, for Timon's sake
Let's yet be fellows; let's shake our heads, and say,
As 'twere a knell unto our master's fortunes,
'We have seen better days.' Let each take some.
Nay, put out all your hands. Not one word more:
Thus part we rich in sorrow, parting poor.

    [SERVANTS embrace, and part several ways

O, the fierce wretchedness that glory brings us!
Who would not wish to be from wealth exempt,
Since riches point to misery and contempt?
Who would be so mock'd with glory? or to live
But in a dream of friendship?
To have his pomp and all what state compounds
But only painted, like his varnish'd friends?
Poor honest lord, brought low by his own heart,
Undone by goodness! Strange, unusual blood,
When man's worst sin is, he does too much good!

Who then dares to be half so kind again?
For bounty, that makes gods, does still mar men.
My dearest lord, blest to be most accursed,
Rich only to be wretched, thy great fortunes
Are made thy chief afflictions. Alas, kind lord!
He's flung in rage from this ingrateful seat
Of monstrous friends; nor has he with him to
Supply his life, or that which can command it.
I'll follow, and inquire him out:
I'll ever serve his mind with my best will;
Whilst I have gold, I'll be his steward still.   [*Exit*

SCENE III. *Woods and cave, near the sea-shore*

Enter TIMON, *from the cave*

TIMON

O blessed breeding sun, draw from the earth
Rotten humidity; below thy sister's orb
Infect the air! Twinn'd brothers of one womb,
Whose procreation, residence and birth
Scarce is dividant, touch them with several fortunes,
The greater scorns the lesser: not nature,
To whom all sores lay siege, can bear great fortune
But by contempt of nature.
Raise me this beggar and deny 't that lord,
The senator shall bear contempt hereditary,
The beggar native honour.
It is the pasture lards the rother's sides,
The want that makes him lean. Who dares, who
    dares,
In purity of manhood stand upright,
And say 'This man's a flatterer'? if one be,
So are they all; for every grise of fortune
Is smooth'd by that below: the learned pate
Ducks to the golden fool: all is oblique;
There's nothing level in our cursed natures
But direct villany. Therefore be abhorr'd
All feasts, societies and throngs of men!
His semblable, yea, himself, Timon disdains:
Destruction fang mankind! Earth, yield me roots!
                                        [*Digging*
Who seeks for better of thee, sauce his palate
With thy most operant poison! What is here?
Gold? yellow, glittering, precious gold? No, gods,
I am no idle votarist: roots, you clear heavens!
Thus much of this will make black white, foul fair,
Wrong right, base noble, old young, coward valiant.
Ha, you gods! why this? what this, you gods? Why,
    this
Will lug your priests and servants from your sides,
Pluck stout men's pillows from below their heads:
This yellow slave
Will knit and break religions; bless the accursed;
Make the hoar leprosy adored; place thieves,
And give them title, knee and approbation
With senators on the bench: this is it
That makes the wappen'd widow wed again;
She, whom the spital-house and ulcerous sores
Would cast the gorge at, this embalms and spices

To the April day again. Come, damned earth,
Thou common whore of mankind, that put'st odds
Among the rout of nations, I will make thee
Do thy right nature. [*March afar off*] Ha! a drum?
    Thou'rt quick,
But yet I'll bury thee: thou'lt go, strong thief,
When gouty keepers of thee cannot stand:
Nay, stay thou out for earnest.   [*Keeping some gold*
Enter ALCIBIADES, *with drum and fife, in warlike manner;*
        PHRYNIA *and* TIMANDRA

ALCIBIADES
                    What art thou there? speak.
TIMON
A beast, as thou art. The canker gnaw thy heart,
For showing me again the eyes of man!
ALCIBIADES
What is thy name? Is man so hateful to thee,
That art thyself a man?
TIMON
I am misanthropos, and hate mankind.
For thy part, I do wish thou wert a dog,
That I might love thee something.
ALCIBIADES
                    I know thee well;
But in thy fortunes am unlearn'd and strange.
TIMON
I know thee too; and more than that I know thee
I not desire to know. Follow thy drum;
With man's blood paint the ground, gules, gules:
Religious canons, civil laws are cruel;
Then what should war be? This fell whore of thine
Hath in her more destruction than thy sword,
For all her cherubin look.
PHRYNIA
        Thy lips rot off!
TIMON
I will not kiss thee; then the rot returns
To thine own lips again.
ALCIBIADES
How came the noble Timon to this change?
TIMON
As the moon does, by wanting light to give:
But then renew I could not, like the moon;
There were no suns to borrow of.
ALCIBIADES
Noble Timon, what friendship may I do thee?
TIMON
None, but to maintain my opinion.
ALCIBIADES
What is it, Timon?
TIMON
Promise me friendship, but perform none: if thou
wilt not promise, the gods plague thee, for thou art
a man: if thou dost perform, confound thee, for thou
art a man!
ALCIBIADES
I have heard in some sort of thy miseries.
TIMON
Thou saw'st them when I had prosperity.

ALCIBIADES

I see them now; then was a blessed time.

TIMON

As thine is now, held with a brace of harlots.

TIMANDRA

Is this the Athenian minion whom the world
Voiced so regardfully?

TIMON

        Art thou Timandra?

TIMANDRA

Yes.

TIMON

Be a whore still: they love thee not that use thee;
Give them diseases, leaving with thee their lust.
Make use of thy salt hours: season the slaves
For tubs and baths; bring down rose-cheeked youth
To the tub-fast and the diet.

TIMANDRA

        Hang thee, monster!

ALCIBIADES

Pardon him, sweet Timandra, for his wits
Are drown'd and lost in his calamities.
I have but little gold of late, brave Timon,
The want whereof doth daily make revolt
In my penurious band: I have heard, and grieved,
How cursed Athens, mindless of thy worth,
Forgetting thy great deeds, when neighbour states,
But for thy sword and fortune, trod upon them—

TIMON

I prithee, beat thy drum, and get thee gone.

ALCIBIADES

I am thy friend and pity thee, dear Timon.

TIMON

How dost thou pity him whom thou dost trouble?
I had rather be alone.

ALCIBIADES

        Why, fare thee well:
Here is some gold for thee.

TIMON

        Keep it, I cannot eat it.

ALCIBIADES

When I have laid proud Athens on a heap—

TIMON

Warr'st thou 'gainst Athens?

ALCIBIADES

        Ay, Timon, and have cause.

TIMON

The gods confound them all in thy conquest,
And thee after, when thou hast conquer'd!

ALCIBIADES

Why me, Timon?

TIMON

        That by killing of villains
Thou wast born to conquer my country.
Put up thy gold: go on,—here's gold,—go on;
Be as a planetary plague, when Jove
Will o'er some high-viced city hang his poison
In the sick air: let not thy sword skip one:
Pity not honour'd age for his white beard;
He is an usurer: strike me the counterfeit matron;

It is her habit only that is honest,
Herself's a bawd: let not the virgin's cheek
Make soft thy trenchant sword; for those milk-paps,
That through the window-bars bore at men's eyes,
Are not within the leaf of pity writ,
But set them down horrible traitors: spare not the
   babe
Whose dimpled smiles from fools exhaust their
   mercy;
Think it a bastard whom the oracle
Hath doubtfully pronounced thy throat shall cut,
And mince it sans remorse: swear against objects;
Put armour on thine ears and on thine eyes,
Whose proof nor yells of mothers, maids, nor babes,
Nor sight of priests in holy vestments bleeding,
Shall pierce a jot. There's gold to pay thy soldiers:
Make large confusion; and, thy fury spent,
Confounded be thyself! Speak not, be gone.

ALCIBIADES

Hast thou gold yet? I'll take the gold thou givest me,
Not all thy counsel.

TIMON

Dost thou or dost thou not, heaven's curse upon
   thee!

PHRYNIA and TIMANDRA

Give us some gold, good Timon: hast thou more?

TIMON

Enough to make a whore forswear her trade,
And to make whores, a bawd. Hold up, you sluts,
Your aprons mountant: you are not oathable;
Although, I know, you'll swear, terribly swear,
Into strong shudders and to heavenly agues,
The immortal gods that hear you; spare your oaths,
I'll trust to your conditions: be whores still;
And he whose pious breath seeks to convert you,
Be strong in whore, allure him, burn him up;
Let your close fire predominate his smoke,
And be no turncoats: yet may your pains, six
   months,
Be quite contrary: and thatch your poor thin roofs
With burdens of the dead;—some that were hang'd,
No matter:—wear them, betray with them: whore
   still;
Paint till a horse may mire upon your face:
A pox of wrinkles!

PHRYNIA and TIMANDRA

Well, more gold: what then?
Believe 't that we'll do any thing for gold.

TIMON

Consumptions sow
In hollow bones of man; strike their sharp shins,
And mar men's spurring. Crack the lawyer's voice,
That he may never more false title plead,
Nor sound his quillets shrilly: hoar the flamen,
That scolds against the quality of flesh
And not believes himself: down with the nose,
Down with it flat; take the bridge quite away
Of him that, his particular to foresee,
Smells from the general weal: make curl'd-pate
   ruffians bald;

And let the unscarr'd braggarts of the war
Derive some pain from you: plague all;
That your activity may defeat and quell
The source of all erection. There's more gold:
Do you damn others, and let this damn you,
And ditches grave you all!

PHRYNIA *and* TIMANDRA

More counsel with more money, bounteous Timon.

TIMON

More whore, more mischief first; I have given you earnest.

ALCIBIADES

Strike up the drum towards Athens! Farewell, Timon:
If I thrive well, I'll visit thee again.

TIMON

If I hope well, I'll never see thee more.

ALCIBIADES

I never did thee harm.

TIMON

Yes, thou spokest well of me.

ALCIBIADES

Call'st thou that harm?

TIMON

Men daily find it. Get thee away, and take
Thy beagles with thee.

ALCIBIADES

We but offend him. Strike!
[*Drum beats. Exeunt* ALCIBIADES, PHRYNIA,
and TIMANDRA

TIMON

That nature, being sick of man's unkindness,
Should yet be hungry! Common mother, thou,
[*Digging*
Whose womb unmeasurable and infinite breast
Teems, and feeds all; whose self-same mettle,
Whereof thy proud child, arrogant man, is puff'd,
Engenders the black toad and adder blue,
The gilded newt and eyeless venom'd worm,
With all the abhorred births below crisp heaven
Whereon Hyperion's quickening fire doth shine;
Yield him, who all thy human sons doth hate,
From forth thy plenteous bosom one poor root!
Ensear thy fertile and conceptious womb,
Let it no more bring out ingrateful man!
Go great with tigers, dragons, wolves and bears;
Teem with new monsters, whom thy upward face
Hath to the marbled mansion all above
Never presented!—O, a root! dear thanks!—
Dry up thy marrows, vines, and plough-torn leas;
Whereof ingrateful man, with liquorish draughts
And morsels unctuous, greases his pure mind,
That from it all consideration slips!
Enter APEMANTUS
More man? plague, plague!

APEMANTUS

I was directed hither: men report
Thou dost affect my manners, and dost use them.

TIMON

'Tis then because thou dost not keep a dog,
Whom I would imitate: consumption catch thee!

APEMANTUS

This is in thee a nature but infected;
A poor unmanly melancholy sprung
From change of fortune. Why this spade? this place?
This slave-like habit? and these looks of care?
Thy flatterers yet wear silk, drink wine, lie soft,
Hug their diseased perfumes and have forgot
That ever Timon was. Shame not these woods
By putting on the cunning of a carper.
Be thou a flatterer now, and seek to thrive
By that which has undone thee: hinge thy knee,
And let his very breath whom thou'lt observe
Blow off thy cap; praise his most vicious strain,
And call it excellent: thou wast told thus;
Thou gavest thine ears like tapsters that bade welcome
To knaves and all approachers: 'tis most just
That thou turn rascal; hadst thou wealth again,
Rascals should have 't. Do not assume my likeness.

TIMON

Were I like thee, I'ld throw away myself.

APEMANTUS

Thou hast cast away thyself, being like thyself,
A madman so long, now a fool. What, think'st
That the bleak air, thy boisterous chamberlain,
Will put thy shirt on warm? will these moss'd trees,
That have outlived the eagle, page thy heels,
And skip when thou point'st out? will the cold brook,
Candied with ice, caudle thy morning taste,
To cure thy o'er-night's surfeit? Call the creatures
Whose naked natures live in all the spite
Of wreakful heaven, whose bare unhoused trunks,
To the conflicting elements exposed,
Answer mere nature; bid them flatter thee;
O, thou shalt find—

TIMON

A fool of thee: depart.

APEMANTUS

I love thee better now than e'er I did.

TIMON

I hate thee worse.

APEMANTUS

Why?

TIMON

Thou flatter'st misery.

APEMANTUS

I flatter not, but say thou art a caitiff.

TIMON

Why dost thou seek me out?

APEMANTUS

To vex thee.

TIMON

Always a villain's office or a fool's.
Dost please thyself in 't?

APEMANTUS
Ay.
TIMON
What! a knave too?
APEMANTUS
If thou didst put this sour-cold habit on
To castigate thy pride, 'twere well: but thou
Dost it enforcedly; thou'ldst courtier be again,
Wert thou not beggar. Willing misery
Outlives incertain pomp, is crown'd before:
The one is filling still, never complete,
The other at high wish: best state, contentless,
Hath a distracted and most wretched being,
Worse than the worst, content.
Thou shouldst desire to die, being miserable.
TIMON
Not by his breath that is more miserable.
Thou art a slave, whom Fortune's tender arm
With favour never clasp'd, but bred a dog.
Hadst thou, like us from our first swath, proceeded
The sweet degrees that this brief world affords
To such as may the passive drugs of it
Freely command, thou wouldst have plunged thy-
self
In general riot, melted down thy youth
In different beds of lust, and never learn'd
The icy precepts of respect, but follow'd
The sugar'd game before thee. But myself,
Who had the world as my confectionary,
The mouths, the tongues, the eyes and hearts of
men
At duty, more than I could frame employment;
That numberless upon me struck, as leaves
Do on the oak, have with one winter's brush
Fell from their boughs, and left me open, bare
For every storm that blows: I, to bear this,
That never knew but better, is some burden:
Thy nature did commence in sufferance, time
Hath made thee hard in 't. Why shouldst thou hate
men?
They never flatter'd thee: what hast thou given?
If thou wilt curse, thy father, that poor rag,
Must be thy subject, who in spite put stuff
To some she beggar and compounded thee
Poor rogue hereditary. Hence, be gone!
If thou hadst not been born the worst of men,
Thou hadst been a knave and flatterer.
APEMANTUS
Art thou proud yet?
TIMON
Ay, that I am not thee.
APEMANTUS
I, that I was
No prodigal.
TIMON
I, that I am one now:
Were all the wealth I have shut up in thee,
I'ld give thee leave to hang it. Get thee gone.
That the whole life of Athens were in this!
Thus would I eat it. [Eating a root

APEMANTUS
Here; I will mend thy feast.
[Offering him a root
TIMON
First mend my company; take away thyself.
APEMANTUS
So I shall mend mine own, by the lack of thine.
TIMON
'Tis not well mended so, it is but botch'd;
If not, I would it were.
APEMANTUS
What wouldst thou have to Athens?
TIMON
Thee thither in a whirlwind. If thou wilt,
Tell them there I have gold; look, so I have.
APEMANTUS
Here is no use for gold.
TIMON
The best and truest;
For here it sleeps, and does no hired harm.
APEMANTUS
Where liest o' nights, Timon?
TIMON
Under that's above me. Where feed'st thou o' days,
Apemantus?
APEMANTUS
Where my stomach finds meat; or, rather, where
I eat it.
TIMON
Would poison were obedient and knew my mind!
APEMANTUS
Where wouldst thou send it?
TIMON
To sauce thy dishes.
APEMANTUS
The middle of humanity thou never knewest, but
the extremity of both ends: when thou wast in thy
gilt and thy perfume, they mocked thee for too
much curiosity; in thy rags thou know'st none, but
art despised for the contrary. There's a medlar for
thee; eat it.
TIMON
On what I hate I feed not.
APEMANTUS
Dost hate a medlar?
TIMON
Ay, though it look like thee.
APEMANTUS
An thou hadst hated meddlers sooner, thou shouldst
have loved thyself better now. What man didst
thou ever know unthrift that was beloved after his
means?
TIMON
Who, without those means thou talk'st of, didst
thou ever know beloved?
APEMANTUS
Myself.
TIMON
I understand thee; thou hadst some means to keep
a dog.

APEMANTUS

What things in the world canst thou nearest compare to thy flatterers?

TIMON

Women nearest; but men, men are the things themselves. What wouldst thou do with the world, Apemantus, if it lay in thy power?

APEMANTUS

Give it the beasts, to be rid of the men.

TIMON

Wouldst thou have thyself fall in the confusion of men, and remain a beast with the beasts?

APEMANTUS

Ay, Timon.

TIMON

A beastly ambition, which the gods grant thee t' attain to! If thou wert the lion, the fox would beguile thee: if thou wert the lamb, the fox would eat thee: if thou wert the fox, the lion would suspect thee, when peradventure thou wert accused by the ass: if thou wert the ass, thy dulness would torment thee, and still thou livedst but as a breakfast to the wolf: if thou wert the wolf, thy greediness would afflict thee, and oft thou shouldst hazard thy life for thy dinner: wert thou the unicorn, pride and wrath would confound thee, and make thine own self the conquest of thy fury: wert thou a bear, thou wouldst be killed by the horse: wert thou a horse, thou wouldst be seized by the leopard: wert thou a leopard, thou wert german to the lion, and the spots of thy kindred were jurors on thy life: all thy safety were remotion, and thy defence absence. What beast couldst thou be that were not subject to a beast? and what a beast art thou already, that seest not thy loss in transformation!

APEMANTUS

If thou couldst please me with speaking to me, thou mightst have hit upon it here: the commonwealth of Athens is become a forest of beasts.

TIMON

How has the ass broke the wall, that thou art out of the city?

APEMANTUS

Yonder comes a poet and a painter: the plague of company light upon thee! I will fear to catch it, and give way: when I know not what else to do, I'll see thee again.

TIMON

When there is nothing living but thee, thou shalt be welcome. I had rather be a beggar's dog than Apemantus.

APEMANTUS

Thou art the cap of all the fools alive.

TIMON

Would thou wert clean enough to spit upon!

APEMANTUS

A plague on thee! thou art too bad to curse.

TIMON

All villains that do stand by thee are pure.

APEMANTUS

There is no leprosy but what thou speak'st.

TIMON

If I name thee.
I'll beat thee; but I should infect my hands.

APEMANTUS

I would my tongue could rot them off!

TIMON

Away, thou issue of a mangy dog!
Choler does kill me that thou art alive;
I swoon to see thee.

APEMANTUS

Would thou wouldst burst!

TIMON

Away, thou tedious rogue! I am sorry I shall lose a stone by thee.   [*Throws a stone at him*

APEMANTUS

Beast!

TIMON

Slave!

APEMANTUS

Toad!

TIMON

Rogue, rogue, rogue!
I am sick of this false world, and will love nought
But even the mere necessities upon 't.
Then, Timon, presently prepare thy grave;
Lie where the light foam of the sea may beat
Thy grave-stone daily: make thine epitaph,
That death in me at others' lives may laugh.
[*To the gold*] O thou sweet king-killer, and dear divorce
'Twixt natural son and sire! thou bright defiler
Of Hymen's purest bed! thou valiant Mars!
Thou ever young, fresh, loved, and delicate wooer,
Whose blush doth thaw the consecrated snow
That lies on Dian's lap! thou visible god,
That solder'st close impossibilities,
And makest them kiss! that speak'st with every tongue,
To every purpose! O thou touch of hearts!
Think thy slave man rebels; and by thy virtue
Set them into confounding odds, that beasts
May have the world in empire!

APEMANTUS

Would 'twere so!
But not till I am dead. I'll say thou hast gold:
Thou wilt be throng'd to shortly.

TIMON

Throng'd to!

APEMANTUS

Ay,

TIMON

Thy back, I prithee.

APEMANTUS

Live, and love thy misery!

TIMON

Long live so, and so die! [*Exit* APEMANTUS] I am quit.
Moe things like men? Eat, Timon, and abhor them.

[1176]

Enter BANDITTI

FIRST BANDITTI

Where should he have this gold? It is some poor
fragment, some slender ort of his remainder: the
mere want of gold, and the falling-from of his
friends, drove him into this melancholy.

SECOND BANDITTI

It is noised he hath a mass of treasure.

THIRD BANDITTI

Let us make the assay upon him: if he care not for
't, he will supply us easily; if he covetously reserve
it, how shall 's get it?

SECOND BANDITTI

True; for he bears it not about him; 'tis hid.

FIRST BANDITTI

Is not this he?

BANDITTI

Where?

SECOND BANDITTI

'Tis his description.

THIRD BANDITTI

He; I know him.

BANDITTI

Save thee, Timon.

TIMON

Now, thieves?

BANDITTI

Soldiers, not thieves.

TIMON

Both too; and women's sons.

BANDITTI

We are not thieves, but men that much do want.

TIMON

Your greatest want is, you want much of meat.
Why should you want? Behold, the earth hath roots;
Within this mile break forth a hundred springs;
The oaks bear mast, the briers scarlet hips;
The bounteous housewife, nature, on each bush
Lays her full mess before you. Want! why want?

FIRST BANDITTI

We cannot live on grass, on berries, water,
As beasts and birds and fishes.

TIMON

Nor on the beasts themselves, the birds and fishes;
You must eat men. Yet thanks I must you con
That you are thieves profess'd, that you work not
In holier shapes: for there is boundless theft
In limited professions. Rascal thieves,
Here's gold. Go, suck the subtle blood o' the grape,
Till the high fever seethe your blood to froth,
And so 'scape hanging: trust not the physician;
His antidotes are poison, and he slays
Moe than you rob: take wealth and lives together;
Do villany, do, since you protest to do 't,
Like workmen. I'll example you with thievery:
The sun's a thief, and with his great attraction
Robs the vast sea: the moon's an arrant thief,
And her pale fire she snatches from the sun:
The sea's a thief, whose liquid surge resolves

The moon into salt tears: the earth's a thief,
That feeds and breeds by a composture stol'n
From general excrement: each thing's a thief:
The laws, your curb and whip, in their rough power
Have uncheck'd theft. Love not yourselves; away,
Rob one another. There's more gold. Cut throats:
All that you meet are thieves: to Athens go,
Break open shops; nothing can you steal,
But thieves do lose it: steal not less for this
I give you; and gold confound you howsoe'er!
Amen.

THIRD BANDITTI

Has almost charmed me from my profession by
persuading me to it.

FIRST BANDITTI

'Tis in the malice of mankind that he thus advises
us; not to have us thrive in our mystery.

SECOND BANDITTI

I'll believe him as an enemy, and give over my
trade.

FIRST BANDITTI

Let us first see peace in Athens: there is no time so
miserable but a man may be true.

[*Exeunt* BANDITTI

Enter FLAVIUS

FLAVIUS

O you gods!
Is yond despised and ruinous man my lord?
Full of decay and failing? O monument
And wonder of good deeds evilly bestow'd!
What an alteration of honour
Has desperate want made!
What viler thing upon the earth than friends
Who can bring noblest minds to basest ends!
How rarely does it meet with this time's guise,
When man was wish'd to love his enemies!
Grant I may ever love, and rather woo
Those that would mischief me than those that do!
Has caught me in his eye: I will present
My honest grief unto him, and, as my lord,
Still serve him with my life. My dearest master!

TIMON

Away! what art thou?

FLAVIUS

Have you forgot me, sir?

TIMON

Why dost ask that? I have forgot all men;
Then, if thou grant'st thou'rt a man, I have forgot
thee.

FLAVIUS

An honest poor servant of yours.

TIMON

Then I know thee not:
I never had honest man about me, I; all
I kept were knaves, to serve in meat to villains.

FLAVIUS

The gods are witness,
Ne'er did poor steward wear a truer grief
For his undone lord than mine eyes for you.

TIMON

What, dost thou weep? come nearer; then I love
  thee,
Because thou art a woman, and disclaim'st
Flinty mankind, whose eyes do never give
But thorough lust and laughter. Pity's sleeping:
Strange times, that weep with laughing, not with
  weeping!

FLAVIUS

I beg of you to know me, good my lord,
To accept my grief, and whilst this poor wealth
  lasts
To entertain me as your steward still.

TIMON

Had I a steward
So true, so just, and now so comfortable?
It almost turns my dangerous nature mild.
Let me behold thy face. Surely this man
Was born of woman.
Forgive my general and exceptless rashness,
You perpetual-sober gods! I do proclaim
One honest man—mistake me not—but one;
No more, I pray,—and he's a steward.
How fain would I have hated all mankind!
And thou redeem'st thyself: but all, save thee,
I fell with curses.
Methinks thou art more honest now than wise;
For, by oppressing and betraying me,
Thou mightst have sooner got another service:
For many so arrive at second masters,
Upon their first lord's neck. But tell me true—
For I must ever doubt, though ne'er so sure—
Is not thy kindness subtle, covetous,
If not a usuring kindness and as rich men deal gifts,
Expecting in return twenty for one?

FLAVIUS

No, my most worthy master; in whose breast
Doubt and suspect, alas, are placed too late:
You should have fear'd false times when you did
  feast:
Suspect still comes where an estate is least.
That which I show, heaven knows, is merely love,
Duty and zeal to your unmatched mind,
Care of your food and living; and, believe it,
My most honour'd lord,
For any benefit that points to me,
Either in hope or present, I'ld exchange
For this one wish, that you had power and wealth
To requite me by making rich yourself.

TIMON

Look thee, 'tis so! Thou singly honest man,
Here, take: the gods, out of my misery,
Have sent thee treasure. Go, live rich and happy;
But thus condition'd: thou shalt build from men,
Hate all, curse all, show charity to none,
But let the famish'd flesh slide from the bone
Ere thou relieve the beggar: give to dogs
What thou deniest to men; let prisons swallow 'em,
Debts wither 'em to nothing: be men like blasted
  woods,

And may diseases lick up their false bloods!
And so farewell, and thrive.

FLAVIUS

          O, let me stay
And comfort you, my master.

TIMON

            If thou hatest curses
Stay not: fly, whilst thou art blest and free:
Ne'er see thou man, and let me ne'er see thee.

                    [Exeunt severally

ACT V

SCENE I. *The woods. Before* TIMON's *cave*

Enter POET *and* PAINTER; TIMON *watching them from his
cave*

PAINTER

As I took note of the place, it cannot be far where he
abides.

POET

What's to be thought of him? does the rumour hold
for true, that he's so full of gold?

PAINTER

Certain: Alcibiades reports it; Phrynia and Timandra had gold of him: he likewise enriched poor
straggling soldiers with great quantity: 'tis said he
gave unto his steward a mighty sum.

POET

Then this breaking of his has been but a try for his
friends.

PAINTER

Nothing else: you shall see him a palm in Athens
again, and flourish with the highest. Therefore 'tis
not amiss we tender our loves to him in this supposed distress of his: it will show honestly in us, and
is very likely to load our purposes with what they
travail for, if it be a just and true report that goes
of his having.

POET

What have you now to present unto him?

PAINTER

Nothing at this time but my visitation: only I will
promise him an excellent piece.

POET

I must serve him so too, tell him of an intent that's
coming toward him.

PAINTER

Good as the best. Promising is the very air o' the
time: it opens the eyes of expectation: performance
is ever the duller for his act; and, but in the plainer
and simpler kind of people, the deed of saying is
quite out of use. To promise is most courtly and
fashionable: performance is a kind of will or testament which argues a great sickness in his judgement
that makes it.   *[TIMON comes from his cave, behind*

TIMON

[Aside] Excellent workman! thou canst not paint a
man so bad as is thyself.

POET

I am thinking what I shall say I have provided for
him: it must be a personating of himself; a satire
against the softness of prosperity, with a discovery
of the infinite flatteries that follow youth and
opulency.

TIMON

[Aside] Must thou needs stand for a villain in thine
own work? wilt thou whip thine own faults in other
men? Do so, I have gold for thee.

POET

Nay, let's seek him:
Then do we sin against our own estate,
When we may profit meet, and come too late.

PAINTER

True;
When the day serves, before black-corner'd night,
Find what thou want'st by free and offer'd light.
Come.

TIMON

[Aside] I'll meet you at the turn. What a god's gold,
That he is worshipp'd in a baser temple
Than where swine feed!
'Tis thou that rigg'st the bark and plough'st the
    foam,
Settlest admired reverence in a slave:
To thee be worship! and thy saints for aye
Be crown'd with plagues, that thee alone obey!
Fit I meet them.   [Coming forward

POET

Hail, worthy Timon!

PAINTER

Our late noble master!

TIMON

Have I once lived to see two honest men?

POET

Sir,
Having often of your open bounty tasted,
Hearing you were retired, your friends fall'n off,
Whose thankless natures—O abhorred spirits!—
Not all the whips of heaven are large enough—
What! to you,
Whose star-like nobleness gave life and influence
To their whole being! I am rapt, and cannot cover
The monstrous bulk of this ingratitude
With any size of words.

TIMON

Let it go naked, men may see 't the better:
You that are honest, by being what you are,
Make them best seen and known.

PAINTER

He and myself
Have travail'd in the great shower of your gifts,
And sweetly felt it.

TIMON

Ay, you are honest men.

PAINTER

We are hither come to offer you our service.

TIMON

Most honest men! Why, how shall I requite you?
Can you eat roots, and drink cold water? no.

BOTH

What we can do, we'll do, to do you service.

TIMON

Ye're honest men: ye've heard that I have gold;
I am sure you have: speak truth; ye're honest men.

PAINTER

So it is said, my noble lord: but therefore
Came not my friend nor I.

TIMON

Good honest men! Thou draw'st a counterfeit
Best in all Athens: thou'rt indeed the best;
Thou counterfeit'st most lively.

PAINTER

So, so, my lord.

TIMON

E'en so, sir, as I say. And, for thy fiction,
Why, thy verse swells with stuff so fine and smooth
That thou art even natural in thine art.
But, for all this, my honest-natured friends,
I must needs say you have a little fault:
Marry, 'tis not monstrous in you; neither wish I
You take much pains to mend.

BOTH

Beseech your honour
To make it known to us.

TIMON

You'll take it ill.

BOTH

Most thankfully, my lord.

TIMON

Will you, indeed?

BOTH

Doubt it not, worthy lord.

TIMON

There's never a one of you but trusts a knave
That mightily deceives you.

BOTH

Do we, my lord?

TIMON

Ay, and you hear him cog, see him dissemble,
Know his gross patchery, love him, feed him,
Keep in your bosom: yet remain assured
That he's a made-up villain.

PAINTER

I know none such, my lord.

POET

Nor I.

TIMON

Look you, I love you well; I'll give you gold,
Rid me these villains from your companies:
Hang them or stab them, drown them in a draught,
Confound them by some course, and come to me,
I'll give you gold enough.

BOTH

Name them, my lord, let's know them.

TIMON

You that way, and you this, but two in company:

Each man apart, all single and alone,
Yet an arch-villain keeps him company.
If, where thou art, two villains shall not be,
Come not near him. If thou wouldst not reside
But where one villain is, then him abandon.
Hence, pack! there's gold; you came for gold, ye
    slaves:
[*To* PAINTER] You have work for me, there's pay-
    ment: hence!
[*To* POET] You are an alchemist, make gold of that:
Out, rascal dogs!
           [*Beats them out, and then retires into his cave*
      Enter FLAVIUS *and two* SENATORS

FLAVIUS
It is in vain that you would speak with Timon;
For he is set so only to himself
That nothing but himself which looks like man
Is friendly with him.

FIRST SENATOR
          Bring us to his cave:
It is our part and promise to the Athenians
To speak with Timon.

SECOND SENATOR
          At all times alike
Men are not still the same: 'twas time and griefs
That framed him thus: time, with his fairer hand,
Offering the fortunes of his former days,
The former man may make him. Bring us to him,
And chance it as it may.

FLAVIUS
          Here is his cave.
Peace and content be here! Lord Timon! Timon!
Look out, and speak to friends: the Athenians
By two of their most reverend senate greet thee:
Speak to them, noble Timon.
       TIMON *comes from his cave*

TIMON
Thou sun, that comfort'st, burn! Speak, and be
    hang'd:
For each true word, a blister! and each false
Be as a cauterizing to the root o' the tongue,
Consuming it with speaking!

FIRST SENATOR
          Worthy Timon,—

TIMON
Of none but such as you, and you of Timon.

FIRST SENATOR
The senators of Athens greet thee, Timon.

TIMON
I thank them, and would send them back the
    plague,
Could I but catch it for them.

FIRST SENATOR
          O, forget
What we are sorry for ourselves in thee.
The senators with one consent of love
Entreat thee back to Athens; who have thought
On special dignities, which vacant lie
For thy best use and wearing.

SECOND SENATOR
          They confess
Toward thee forgetfulness too general, gross:
Which now the public body, which doth seldom
Play the recanter, feeling in itself
A lack of Timon's aid, hath sense withal
Of it own fail, restraining aid to Timon;
And send forth us, to make their sorrowed render,
Together with a recompense more fruitful
Than their offence can weigh down by the dram;
Ay, even such heaps and sums of love and wealth,
As shall to thee blot out what wrongs were theirs,
And write in thee the figures of their love,
Ever to read them thine.

TIMON
          You witch me in it,
Surprise me to the very brink of tears:
Lend me a fool's heart and a woman's eyes,
And I'll beweep these comforts, worthy senators.

FIRST SENATOR
Therefore, so please thee to return with us,
And of our Athens, thine and ours, to take
The captainship, thou shalt be met with thanks,
Allow'd with absolute power, and thy good name
Live with authority: so soon we shall drive back
Of Alcibiades the approaches wild;
Who, like a boar too savage, doth root up
His country's peace.

SECOND SENATOR
          And shakes his threatening sword
Against the walls of Athens.

FIRST SENATOR
          Therefore, Timon,—

TIMON
Well, sir, I will; therefore, I will, sir; thus:
If Alcibiades kill my countrymen,
Let Alcibiades know this of Timon,
That Timon cares not. But if he sack fair Athens,
And take our goodly aged men by the beards,
Giving our holy virgins to the stain
Of contumelious, beastly, mad-brain'd war;
Then let him know, and tell him Timon speaks it,
In pity of our aged and our youth,
I cannot choose but tell him, that I care not,
And let him take 't at worst; for their knives care
    not,
While you have throats to answer: for myself,
There's not a whittle in the unruly camp,
But I do prize it at my love before
The reverend'st throat in Athens. So I leave you
To the protection of the prosperous gods,
As thieves to keepers.

FLAVIUS
          Stay not; all's in vain.

TIMON
Why, I was writing of my epitaph;
It will be seen to-morrow: my long sickness
Of health and living now begins to mend,
And nothing brings me all things. Go, live still;

Be Alcibiades your plague, you his,
And last so long enough!

FIRST SENATOR
          We speak in vain.

TIMON
But yet I love my country, and am not
One that rejoices in the common wreck,
As common bruit doth put it.

FIRST SENATOR
          That's well spoke.

TIMON
Commend me to my loving countrymen,—

FIRST SENATOR
These words become your lips as they pass through
     them.

SECOND SENATOR
And enter in our ears like great triumphers
In their applauding gates.

TIMON
          Commend me to them;
And tell them that, to ease them of their griefs,
Their fears of hostile strokes, their aches, losses,
Their pangs of love, with other incident throes
That nature's fragile vessel doth sustain
In life's uncertain voyage, I will some kindness do
     them:
I'll teach them to prevent wild Alcibiades' wrath.

FIRST SENATOR
I like this well; he will return again.

TIMON
I have a tree, which grows here in my close,
That mine own use invites me to cut down,
And shortly must I fell it: tell my friends,
Tell Athens, in the sequence of degree
From high to low throughout, that whoso please
To stop affliction, let him take his haste,
Come hither ere my tree hath felt the axe,
And hang himself: I pray you, do my greeting.

FLAVIUS
Trouble him no further; thus you still shall find him.

TIMON
Come not to me again: but say to Athens,
Timon hath made his everlasting mansion
Upon the beached verge of the salt flood;
Who once a day with his embossed froth
The turbulent surge shall cover: thither come,
And let my grave-stone be your oracle.
Lips, let sour words go by and language end:
What is amiss, plague and infection mend!
Graves only be men's works, and death their gain!
Sun, hide thy beams! Timon hath done his reign.
          [Retires to his cave

FIRST SENATOR
His discontents are unremoveably
Coupled to nature.

SECOND SENATOR
Our hope in him is dead: let us return,
And strain what other means is left unto us
In our dear peril.

FIRST SENATOR
          It requires swift foot.   [Exeunt

SCENE II. Before the walls of Athens

Enter two SENATORS and a MESSENGER

FIRST SENATOR
Thou hast painfully discover'd: are his files
As full as thy report?

MESSENGER
          I have spoke the least:
Besides, his expedition promises
Present approach.

SECOND SENATOR
We stand much hazard, if they bring not Timon.

MESSENGER
I met a courier, one mine ancient friend;
Whom, though in general part we were opposed,
Yet our old love made a particular force,
And made us speak like friends: this man was riding
From Alcibiades to Timon's cave,
With letters of entreaty, which imported
His fellowship i' the cause against your city,
In part for his sake moved.

FIRST SENATOR
          Here come our brothers.

Enter SENATORS from TIMON

THIRD SENATOR
No talk of Timon, nothing of him expect.
The enemies' drum is heard, and fearful scouring
Doth choke the air with dust: in, and prepare:
Ours is the fall, I fear, our foes the snare.   [Exeunt

SCENE III. The woods. TIMON'S cave, and a rude tomb
     seen

Enter a SOLDIER, seeking TIMON

SOLDIER
By all description this should be the place.
Who's here? speak, ho! No answer! What is this?
Timon is dead, who hath outstretch'd his span:
Some beast read this; there does not live a man.
Dead, sure; and this his grave. What's on this tomb
I cannot read; the character I'll take with wax:
Our captain hath in every figure skill,
An aged interpreter, though young in days:
Before proud Athens he's set down by this,
Whose fall the mark of his ambition is.   [Exit

SCENE IV. Before the walls of Athens

Trumpets sound. Enter ALCIBIADES with his powers

ALCIBIADES
Sound to this coward and lascivious town
Our terrible approach.   [A parley sounded
     Enter SENATORS upon the walls
Till now you have gone on and fill'd the time
With all licentious measure, making your wills

The scope of justice; till now myself and such
As slept within the shadow of your power
Have wander'd with our traversed arms and breathed
Our sufferance vainly: now the time is flush,
When crouching marrow in the bearer strong
Cries of itself 'No more:' now breathless wrong
Shall sit and pant in your great chairs of ease;
And pursy insolence shall break his wind
With fear and horrid flight.

FIRST SENATOR
                    Noble and young,
When thy first griefs were but a mere conceit,
Ere thou hadst power or we had cause of fear,
We sent to thee, to give thy rages balm,
To wipe out our ingratitude with loves
Above their quantity.

SECOND SENATOR
                    So did we woo
Transformed Timon to our city's love
By humble message and by promised means:
We were not all unkind, nor all deserve
The common stroke of war.

FIRST SENATOR
                    These walls of ours
Were not erected by their hands from whom
You have received your griefs: nor are they such
That these great towers, trophies and schools should fall
For private faults in them.

SECOND SENATOR
                    Nor are they living
Who were the motives that you first went out;
Shame, that they wanted cunning, in excess
Hath broke their hearts. March, noble lord,
Into our city with thy banners spread:
By decimation and a tithed death—
If thy revenges hunger for that food
Which nature loathes—take thou the destined tenth,
And by the hazard of the spotted die
Let die the spotted.

FIRST SENATOR
                    All have not offended;
For those that were, it is not square to take,
On those that are, revenges: crimes, like lands,
Are not inherited. Then, dear countryman,
Bring in thy ranks, but leave without thy rage:
Spare thy Athenian cradle and those kin
Which, in the bluster of thy wrath, must fall
With those that have offended: like a shepherd
Approach the fold and cull the infected forth,
But kill not all together.

SECOND SENATOR
                    What thou wilt,
Thou rather shalt enforce it with thy smile
Than hew to 't with thy sword.

FIRST SENATOR
                    Set but thy foot
Against our rampired gates, and they shall ope;
So thou wilt send thy gentle heart before,
To say thou'lt enter friendly.

SECOND SENATOR
                    Throw thy glove,
Or any token of thine honour else,
That thou wilt use the wars as thy redress
And not as our confusion, all thy powers
Shall make their harbour in our town, till we
Have seal'd thy full desire.

ALCIBIADES
                    Then there's my glove;
Descend, and open your uncharged ports:
Those enemies of Timon's, and mine own,
Whom you yourselves shall set out for reproof,
Fall, and no more: and, to atone your fears
With my more noble meaning, not a man
Shall pass his quarter, or offend the stream
Of regular justice in your city's bounds,
But shall be render'd to your public laws
At heaviest answer.

BOTH
                    'Tis most nobly spoken.

ALCIBIADES
Descend, and keep your words.
                    [The SENATORS descend, and open the gates
                    Enter SOLDIER

SOLDIER
My noble general, Timon is dead;
Entomb'd upon the very hem o' the sea;
And on his grave-stone this insculpture, which
With wax I brought away, whose soft impression
Interprets for my poor ignorance.

ALCIBIADES
[Reads]
'Here lies a wretched corse, of wretched soul bereft:
Seek not my name: a plague consume you wicked caitiffs left!
Here lie I, Timon; who, alive, all living men did hate:
Pass by and curse thy fill; but pass and stay not here thy gait.'

These well express in thee thy latter spirits:
Though thou abhorr'dst in us our human griefs,
Scorn'dst our brain's flow and those our droplets which
From niggard nature fall, yet rich conceit
Taught thee to make vast Neptune weep for aye
On thy low grave, on faults forgiven. Dead
Is noble Timon: of whose memory
Hereafter more. Bring me into your city,
And I will use the olive with my sword,
Make war breed peace, make peace stint war, make each
Prescribe to other as each other's leech.
Let our drums strike.   [Exeunt

PERICLES, PRINCE OF TYRE

SYNOPSIS

GOWER, who presents each act of the drama, discloses the adventurous Pericles, Prince of Tyre, at the court of Antioch, suing for the hand of the beautiful daughter of King Antiochus who, in order to keep her unmarried on account of their incestuous relations, subjects all her suitors to the penalty of death when they fail to solve a certain riddle.

Many have already perished in the endeavor, but Pericles guesses the meaning of the riddle which contains the story of Antiochus' sin. Fearing for his life, he first flees to his own country, but, realizing that he will be pursued by assassins, he leaves his kingdom in the hands of the faithful Helicanus and sails for Tarsus, carrying a shipload of provisions to its famine-stricken people. Here Pericles is gratefully welcomed by the governor, Cleon, and may remain as long as he wishes, but word comes from Tyre that he still is in danger. In his next voyage he is wrecked in a storm and cast alone, destitute and despairing, on the coast of Pentapolis where he is befriended by some fishermen whom he soon sees struggling with a net in which his suit of armor has been caught. Again in knightly array, Pericles decides to enter the lists of a tournament which the fishermen have told him King Simonides is holding to celebrate the birthday of his daughter Thaisa. His accomplishments are so distinguished and chivalrous that Thaisa falls in love with him and although he insists that he is poor and unknown, the King consents to their marriage.

Several months later, having received word from Tyre that Antiochus and his daughter had been killed in their chariot by a thunder-bolt of the gods, and that his nobles in Tyre, thinking him dead, wish to make Helicanus king, Pericles reveals his identity to his wife and her father, and sets sail with Thaisa for Tyre. During a furious storm Thaisa gives birth to a daughter, and apparently dies. The superstitious sailors demand that the dead woman be thrown overboard to calm the seas, and the grieving husband places his wife's body, clad in royal robes, in a heavy chest which the great waves wash to the shores of Ephesus.

Thaisa is found and revived by a kind, skillful physician, Lord Cerimon, who, taking her to be the sole survivor of her husband's wrecked ship, helps the forlorn woman to become a priestess in Diana's temple. Pericles' vessel proceeds to Tyre by way of Tarsus where he leaves his infant daughter Marina to be brought up in the care of his good friends, Cleon and his wife Dionyza.

In the next fourteen years Marina develops into rare beauty and becomes highly accomplished, but unfortunately she overshadows Cleon's only daughter Philoten, and Dionyza is gradually aroused to such jealous fury that she bribes a villain to murder the girl as she is walking by the seashore. Just as the assassin makes his attempt, some pirates appear, seize Marina and carry her to Mytilene where they sell her to the keeper of a brothel. The girl's courage does not fail her, however, and she preserves her innocence by persuading those who frequent the resort to reform their habits. Among them is Lysimachus, Governor of Mytilene, who supplies her with enough gold to buy her freedom and pledges his future help.

Just at this time, Pericles goes with Helicanus to fetch his daughter home from Tarsus where he is told a false story of her death, is shown the monument erected to her memory, and departs bowed down with grief. His ship is driven before the winds to Mytilene and anchors in the harbor, with Pericles lying on a couch in the pavilion on his deck, refusing to speak to anyone or to eat. Lysimachus, as governor of Mytilene, coming to pay a call of courtesy upon the King, is told of his melancholy and suggests to Helicanus that if the gifted Marina who has become noted for her dancing and singing be brought to perform before Pericles, he might be aroused from his stupor. Helicanus assents doubtfully, and Marina asks for the King to be left alone with her and a companion-maid. After singing, she tells him that she also has had great misfortunes and that she once stood equal with mighty kings. Having interested him to the point of questioning her, she relates her history, even telling the names of her parents, and Pericles, galvanized into new life, accepts her with delight as his daughter and heiress. Exhausted, he drops into a deep slumber in which Diana appears and commands him to make a sacrifice at her temple at Ephesus where he must recite the story of his life. Obediently changing his plans, he proceeds to Ephesus and with Marina, Lysimachus, Helicanus and his train he does the goddess' bidding.

As he concludes his tale at the altar, the High Priestess, who is Thaisa, collapses in a faint, and Lord Cerimon, assuring Pericles that she is his wife, explains the manner of her rescue. There is a joyful reunion of the family, and Pericles announces the betrothal of Marina and Lysimachus who are made rulers of Tyre, Pericles and Thaisa returning to Pentapolis to take the place of King Simonides who has just died. When the people of Tarsus learn of the evil plot against the daughter of the honored Pericles, they burn Cleon and Dionyza in their palace.

HISTORICAL DATA

The story of Apollonius of Tyre, of which this play is a dramatic version, appears frequently in the early literature of several nations. Shakespeare probably derived his plot from Laurence Twine's *Patterne of Painful Adventures* (1576) and from the poetical account by John Gower in his *Confessio Amantis*, Book VIII. A resemblance also has been pointed out between the play and Sir Philip Sidney's romance *Arcadia* (1590) in which the character, "Pyrocles" may have been the prototype of the *Pericles* of Shakespeare.

Gower appears as Chorus in the play and it is generally believed that the speeches spoken by him are not the work of Shakespeare. As a matter of fact, there is considerable doubt as to the authorship of *Pericles*. Although much of it is beyond doubt the work of Shakespeare, there is, nevertheless, a substantial portion which is equally certainly the product of other writers. This doubtful material has been variously assigned, perhaps with the most reason to George Wilkins who, in 1608, published a novel, *The Painful Adventures of Pericles, Prince of Tyre. Being the True History of the Play of Pericles as it Was Lately Presented by the Worthy and Ancient Poet, John Gower.*

The play was not included in either the First or Second Folio which may be in part due to the doubts cast upon its authorship. It was, however, entered in the Stationers' Register in 1608 and published in a Quarto Edition with Shakespeare's name on the title page as author in 1609. There is no internal evidence that helps fix the date of its composition and it is accordingly generally attributed to 1607–8.

"*These roving thieves serve the great pirate Valdes*";
PERICLES

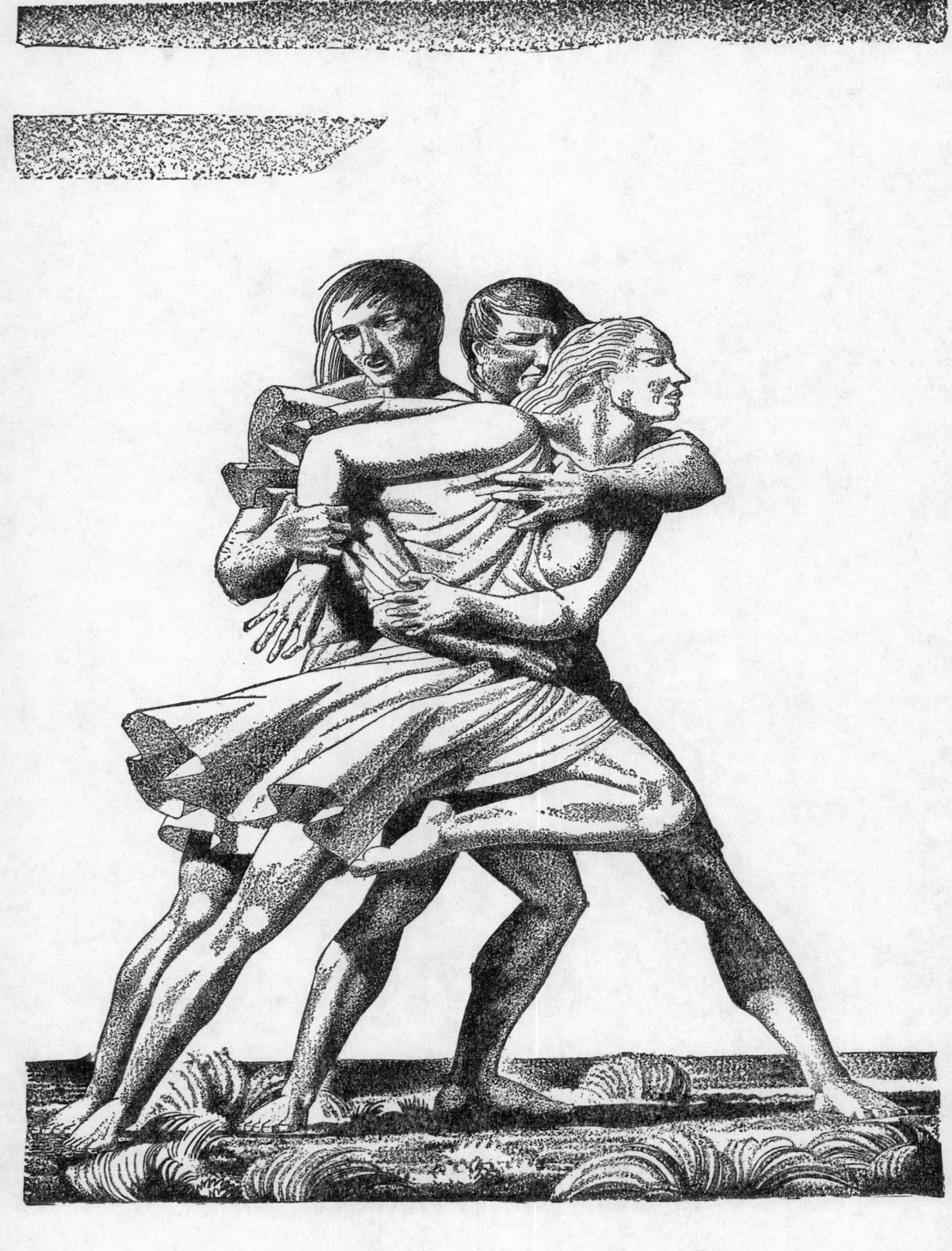

PERICLES, PRINCE OF TYRE

DRAMATIS PERSONÆ

ANTIOCHUS, *king of Antioch.*
PERICLES, *prince of Tyre.*
HELICANUS, } *two lords of Tyre.*
ESCANES,
SIMONIDES, *king of Pentapolis.*
CLEON, *governor of Tarsus.*
LYSIMACHUS, *governor of Mytilene.*
CERIMON, *a lord of Ephesus.*
THALIARD, *a lord of Antioch.*
PHILEMON, *servant to Cerimon.*
LEONINE, *servant to Dionyza.*
MARSHAL.
A PANDAR.
BOULT, *his servant.*

THE DAUGHTER *of Antiochus.*
DIONYZA, *wife to Cleon.*
THAISA, *daughter to Simonides.*
MARINA, *daughter to Pericles and Thaisa.*
LYCHORIDA, *nurse to Marina.*
A BAWD.

LORDS, KNIGHTS, GENTLEMEN, SAILORS, PIRATES,
FISHERMEN, *and* MESSENGERS.

DIANA.
GOWER, *as Chorus.*

SCENE—*Dispersedly in various countries.*

ACT I

Enter GOWER

Before the palace of Antioch

To SING a song that old was sung,
From ashes ancient Gower is come,
Assuming man's infirmities,
To glad your ear and please your eyes.
It hath been sung at festivals,
On ember-eves and holy-ales;
And lords and ladies in their lives
Have read it for restoratives:
The purchase is to make men glorious;
Et bonum quo antiquius, eo melius.
If you, born in these latter times
When wit's more ripe, accept my rhymes,
And that to hear an old man sing
May to your wishes pleasure bring,
I life would wish, and that I might
Waste it for you like taper-light.
This Antioch then Antiochus the Great
Built up, this city, for his chiefest seat,
The fairest in all Syria:
I tell you what mine authors say:
This king unto him took a fere,
Who died and left a female heir,
So buxom, blithe and full of face
As heaven had lent her all his grace;
With whom the father liking took,
And her to incest did provoke:
Bad child, worse father! to entice his own
To evil should be done by none:
But custom what they did begin
Was with long use account no sin.
The beauty of this sinful dame
Made many princes thither frame,
To seek her as a bed-fellow,
In marriage-pleasures play-fellow:

Which to prevent he made a law,
To keep her still and men in awe,
That whoso ask'd her for his wife,
His riddle told not, lost his life:
So for her many a wight did die,
As yon grim looks do testify.
What now ensues, to the judgement of your eye
I give, my cause who best can justify. *[Exit*

SCENE I. *Antioch. A room in the palace*

Enter ANTIOCHUS, PRINCE PERICLES *and* FOLLOWERS

ANTIOCHUS
Young prince of Tyre, you have at large received
The danger of the task you undertake.

PERICLES
I have, Antiochus, and, with a soul
Embolden'd with the glory of her praise,
Think death no hazard in this enterprise.

ANTIOCHUS
Bring in our daughter, clothed like a bride,
For the embracements even of Jove himself;
At whose conception, till Lucina reign'd,
Nature this dowry gave, to glad her presence,
The senate-house of planets all did sit,
To knit in her their best perfections.
Music. Enter ANTIOCHUS' DAUGHTER

PERICLES
See where she comes, apparell'd like the spring,
Graces her subjects, and her thoughts the king
Of every virtue gives renown to men!
Her face the book of praises, where is read
Nothing but curious pleasures, as from thence
Sorrow were ever razed, and testy wrath
Could never be her mild companion.
You gods that made me man and sway in love,
That have inflamed desire in my breast

[1185]

To taste the fruit of yon celestial tree
Or die in the adventure, be my helps,
As I am son and servant to your will,
To compass such a boundless happiness!

ANTIOCHUS

Prince Pericles,—

PERICLES

That would be son to great Antiochus.

ANTIOCHUS

Before thee stands this fair Hesperides,
With golden fruit, but dangerous to be touch'd;
For death-like dragons here affright thee hard:
Her face, like heaven, enticeth thee to view
Her countless glory, which desert must gain;
And which, without desert, because thine eye
Presumes to reach, all thy whole heap must die.
Yon sometimes famous princes, like thyself,
Drawn by report, adventurous by desire,
Tell thee, with speechless tongues and semblance
   pale,
That without covering, save yon field of stars,
Here they stand martyrs, slain in Cupid's wars;
And with dead cheeks advise thee to desist
For going on death's net, whom none resist.

PERICLES

Antiochus, I thank thee, who hath taught
My frail mortality to know itself,
And by those fearful objects to prepare
This body, like to them, to what I must;
For death remember'd should be like a mirror,
Who tells us life's but breath, to trust it error.
I'll make my will then, and, as sick men do,
Who know the world, see heaven, but feeling woe
Gripe not at earthly joys as erst they did,
So I bequeath a happy peace to you
And all good men, as every prince should do;
My riches to the earth from whence they came;
But my unspotted fire of love to you.
                   [*To the* PRINCESS
Thus ready for the way of life or death,
I wait the sharpest blow.

ANTIOCHUS

Scorning advice: read the conclusion then:
Which read and not expounded, 'tis decreed,
As these before thee thou thyself shalt bleed.

DAUGHTER

Of all 'say'd yet, mayst thou prove prosperous!
Of all 'say'd yet, I wish thee happiness!

PERICLES

Like a bold champion I assume the lists,
Nor ask advice of any other thought
But faithfulness and courage.

He reads the riddle

  'I am no viper, yet I feed
    On mother's flesh which did me breed.
  I sought a husband, in which labour
  I found that kindness in a father:
  He's father, son, and husband mild;
  I mother, wife, and yet his child.
  How they may be, and yet in two,
  As you will live, resolve it you.'

[*Aside*] Sharp physic is the last: but, O you powers
That give heaven countless eyes to view men's acts,
Why cloud they not their sights perpetually,
If this be true, which makes me pale to read it?
Fair glass of light, I loved you, and could still,
Were not this glorious casket stored with ill:
But I must tell you, now my thoughts revolt;
For he's no man on whom perfections wait
That, knowing sin within, will touch the gate.
You are a fair viol and your sense the strings,
Who, finger'd to make man his lawful music,
Would draw heaven down and all the gods, to
   hearken,
But being play'd upon before your time,
Hell only danceth at so harsh a chime.
Good sooth, I care not for you.

ANTIOCHUS

Prince Pericles, touch not, upon thy life,
For that's an article within our law,
As dangerous as the rest. Your time's expired:
Either expound now or receive your sentence.

PERICLES

Great king,
Few love to hear the sins they love to act;
'Twould braid yourself too near for me to tell it.
Who has a book of all that monarchs do,
He's more secure to keep it shut than shown:
For vice repeated is like the wandering wind,
Blows dust in others' eyes, to spread itself;
And yet the end of all is bought thus dear,
The breath is gone, and the sore eyes see clear
To stop the air would hurt them. The blind mole
   casts
Copp'd hills towards heaven, to tell the earth is
   throng'd
By man's oppression; and the poor worm doth die
   for 't.
Kings are earth's gods; in vice their law's their will;
And if Jove stray, who dares say Jove doth ill?
It is enough you know; and it is fit,
What being more known grows worse, to smother it.
All love the womb that their first being bred,
Then give my tongue like leave to love my head.

ANTIOCHUS

[*Aside*] Heaven, that I had thy head! He has found
   the meaning:
But I will gloze with him.—Young prince of Tyre,
Though by the tenour of our strict edict,
Your exposition misinterpreting,
We might proceed to cancel of your days;
Yet hope, succeeding from so fair a tree
As your fair self, doth tune us otherwise:
Forty days longer we do respite you;
If by which time our secret be undone,
This mercy shows we'll joy in such a son:
And until then your entertain shall be
As doth befit our honour and your worth.
              [*Exeunt all but* PERICLES

PERICLES

How courtesy would seem to cover sin,

When what is done is like an hypocrite,
The which is good in nothing but in sight!
If it be true that I interpret false,
Then were it certain you were not so bad
As with foul incest to abuse your soul;
Where now you're both a father and a son,
By your untimely claspings with your child,
Which pleasure fits a husband, not a father;
And she an eater of her mother's flesh,
By the defiling of her parent's bed;
And both like serpents are, who though they feed
On sweetest flowers, yet they poison breed.
Antioch, farewell! for wisdom sees, those men
Blush not in actions blacker than the night,
Will shun no course to keep them from the light.
One sin, I know, another doth provoke;
Murder's as near to lust as flame to smoke:
Poison and treason are the hands of sin,
Ay, and the targets, to put off the shame:
Then, lest my life be cropp'd to keep you clear,
By flight I'll shun the danger which I fear.   [*Exit*

Re-enter ANTIOCHUS

ANTIOCHUS

He hath found the meaning, for the which we mean
To have his head.
He must not live to trumpet forth my infamy,
Nor tell the world Antiochus doth sin
In such a loathed manner;
And therefore instantly this prince must die;
For by his fall my honour must keep high.
Who attends us there?

Enter THALIARD

THALIARD

Doth your highness call?

ANTIOCHUS

Thaliard,
You are of our chamber, and our mind partakes
Her private actions to your secrecy:
And for your faithfulness we will advance you.
Thaliard, behold, here's poison, and here's gold;
We hate the prince of Tyre, and thou must kill him:
It fits thee not to ask the reason why,
Because we bid it. Say, is it done?

THALIARD

                    My lord,
'Tis done.

ANTIOCHUS

    Enough.

Enter a MESSENGER

Let your breath cool yourself, telling your haste.

MESSENGER

My lord, prince Pericles is fled.   [*Exit*

ANTIOCHUS

               As thou
Wilt live, fly after: and like an arrow shot
From a well experienced archer hits the mark
His eye doth level at, so thou ne'er return
Unless thou say 'Prince Pericles is dead.'

THALIARD

My lord,

If I can get him within my pistol's length,
I'll make him sure enough: so, farewell to your
highness.

ANTIOCHUS

Thaliard, adieu! [*Exit* THALIARD] Till Pericles be
dead,
My heart can lend no succour to my head.   [*Exit*

SCENE II. *Tyre. A room in the palace*

Enter PERICLES

PERICLES

[*To* LORDS *without*] Let none disturb us. Why should
this change of thoughts,
The sad companion, dull-eyed melancholy,
Be my so used a guest as not an hour,
In the day's glorious walk, or peaceful night,
The tomb where grief should sleep, can breed me
quiet?
Here pleasures court mine eyes, and mine eyes shun
them,
And danger, which I fear'd, is at Antioch,
Whose arm seems far too short to hit me here:
Yet neither pleasure's art can joy my spirits,
Nor yet the other's distance comfort me.
Then it is thus: the passions of the mind,
That have their first conception by mis-dread,
Have after-nourishment and life by care;
And what was first but fear what might be done,
Grows elder now and cares it be not done.
And so with me: the great Antiochus,
'Gainst whom I am too little to contend,
Since he's so great can make his will his act,
Will think me speaking, though I swear to silence;
Nor boots it me to say I honour him,
If he suspect I may dishonour him:
And what may make him blush in being known,
He'll stop the course by which it might be known:
With hostile forces he'll o'erspread the land,
And with the ostent of war will look so huge,
Amazement shall drive courage from the state,
Our men be vanquish'd ere they do resist,
And subjects punish'd that ne'er thought offence:
Which care of them, not pity of myself,
Who am no more but as the tops of trees
Which fence the roots they grow by and defend
them,
Makes both my body pine and soul to languish,
And punish that before that he would punish.

Enter HELICANUS, *with other* LORDS

FIRST LORD

Joy and all comfort in your sacred breast!

SECOND LORD

And keep your mind, till you return to us,
Peaceful and comfortable!

HELICANUS

Peace, peace, and give experience tongue.
They do abuse the king that flatter him:
For flattery is the bellows blows up sin;

The thing the which is flatter'd, but a spark,
To which that blast gives heat and stronger glow-
  ing;
Whereas reproof, obedient and in order,
Fits kings, as they are men, for they may err.
When Signior Sooth here does proclaim a peace,
He flatters you, makes war upon your life.
Prince, pardon me, or strike me, if you please;
I cannot be much lower than my knees.
                PERICLES
All leave us else; but let your cares o'erlook
What shipping and what lading's in our haven,
And then return to us. [*Exeunt* LORDS] Helicanus,
  thou
Hast moved us: what seest thou in our looks?
                HELICANUS
An angry brow, dread lord.
                PERICLES
If there be such a dart in princes' frowns,
How durst thy tongue move anger to our face?
                HELICANUS
How dare the plants look up to heaven, from
  whence
They have their nourishment?
                PERICLES
            Thou know'st I have power
To take thy life from thee.
                HELICANUS
[*Kneeling*] I have ground the axe myself;
Do you but strike the blow.
                PERICLES
Rise, prithee, rise: sit down: thou art no flatterer:
I thank thee for it; and heaven forbid
That kings should let their ears hear their faults hid!
Fit counsellor and servant for a prince,
Who by thy wisdom makest a prince thy servant,
What wouldst thou have me do?
                HELICANUS
            To bear with patience
Such griefs as you yourself do lay upon yourself.
                PERICLES
Thou speak'st like a physician, Helicanus,
That minister'st a potion unto me
That thou wouldst tremble to receive thyself.
Attend me then: I went to Antioch,
Where, as thou know'st, against the face of death,
I sought the purchase of a glorious beauty,
From whence an issue I might propagate,
Are arms to princes and bring joys to subjects.
Her face was to mine eye beyond all wonder;
The rest—hark in thine ear—as black as incest:
Which by my knowledge found, the sinful father
Seem'd not to strike, but smooth: but thou know'st
  this,
'Tis time to fear when tyrants seem to kiss.
Which fear so grew in me, I hither fled,
Under the covering of a careful night,
Who seem'd my good protector; and, being here,
Bethought me what was past, what might succeed.
I knew him tyrannous; and tyrants' fears

Decrease not, but grow faster than the years:
And should he doubt it, as no doubt he doth,
That I should open to the listening air
How many worthy princes' bloods were shed,
To keep his bed of blackness unlaid ope,
To lop that doubt, he'll fill this land with arms,
And make pretence of wrong that I have done him;
When all, for mine, if I may call offence,
Must feel war's blow, who spares not innocence:
Which love to all, of which thyself art one,
Who now reprovest me for it,—
                HELICANUS
              Alas, sir!
                PERICLES
Drew sleep out of mine eyes, blood from my cheeks,
Musings into my mind, with thousand doubts
How I might stop this tempest ere it came;
And finding little comfort to relieve them,
I thought it princely charity to grieve them.
                HELICANUS
Well, my lord, since you have given me leave to
  speak,
Freely will I speak. Antiochus you fear,
And justly too, I think, you fear the tyrant,
Who either by public war or private treason
Will take away your life.
Therefore, my lord, go travel for a while,
Till that his rage and anger be forgot,
Or till the Destinies do cut his thread of life.
Your rule direct to any; if to me,
Day serves not light more faithful than I'll be.
                PERICLES
I do not doubt thy faith;
But should he wrong my liberties in my absence?
                HELICANUS
We'll mingle our bloods together in the earth,
From whence we had our being and our birth.
                PERICLES
Tyre, I now look from thee then, and to Tarsus
Intend my travel, where I'll hear from thee;
And by whose letters I'll dispose myself.
The care I had and have of subjects' good
On thee I lay, whose wisdom's strength can bear it.
I'll take thy word for faith, not ask thine oath:
Who shuns not to break one will sure crack both:
But in our orbs we'll live so round and safe,
That time of both this truth shall ne'er convince,
Thou show'dst a subject's shine, I a true prince.
                        [*Exeunt*

SCENE III. *Tyre. An ante-chamber in the palace*

Enter THALIARD
                THALIARD
So, this is Tyre, and this the court. Here must I kill
King Pericles; and if I do it not, I am sure to be
hanged at home: 'tis dangerous. Well, I perceive he
was a wise fellow and had good discretion, that,
being bid to ask what he would of the king, desired

he might know none of his secrets: now do I see he
had some reason for 't; for if a king bid a man be a
villain, he's bound by the indenture of his oath to be
one. Hush! here come the lords of Tyre.

Enter HELICANUS *and* ESCANES, *with other* LORDS

HELICANUS
You shall not need, my fellow peers of Tyre,
Further to question me of your king's departure:
His seal'd commission left in trust with me
Doth speak sufficiently he's gone to travel.

THALIARD
[*Aside*] How! the king gone!

HELICANUS
If further yet you will be satisfied,
Why, as it were unlicensed of your loves,
He would depart, I'll give some light unto you.
Being at Antioch—

THALIARD
[*Aside*] What from Antioch?

HELICANUS
Royal Antiochus—on what cause I know not—
Took some displeasure at him; at least he judged so:
And doubting lest that he had err'd or sinn'd,
To show his sorrow, he'ld correct himself;
So puts himself unto the shipman's toil,
With whom each minute threatens life or death.

THALIARD
[*Aside*] Well, I perceive I shall not be hanged now,
although I would; but since he's gone, the king's
seas must please: he 'scaped the land, to perish at
the sea. I'll present myself. Peace to the lords of
Tyre!

HELICANUS
Lord Thaliard from Antiochus is welcome.

THALIARD
From him I come
With message unto princely Pericles;
But since my landing I have understood
Your lord has betook himself to unknown travels,
My message must return from whence it came.

HELICANUS
We have no reason to desire it,
Commended to our master, not to us:
Yet, ere you shall depart, this we desire,
As friends to Antioch, we may feast in Tyre. [*Exeunt*

SCENE IV. *Tarsus. A room in the Governor's house*

Enter CLEON *the Governor of Tarsus, with* DIONYZA
and others

CLEON
My Dionyza, shall we rest us here,
And by relating tales of others' griefs,
See if 'twill teach us to forget our own?

DIONYZA
That were to blow at fire in hope to quench it;
For who digs hills because they do aspire
Throws down one mountain to cast up a higher.
O my distressed lord, even such our griefs are;

Here they're but felt, and seen with mischief's eyes,
But like to groves, being topp'd, they higher rise.

CLEON
O Dionyza,
Who wanteth food, and will not say he wants it,
Or can conceal his hunger till he famish?
Our tongues and sorrows do sound deep
Our woes into the air; our eyes do weep,
Till tongues fetch breath that may proclaim them
　　louder;
That, if heaven slumber while their creatures want,
They may awake their helps to comfort them.
I'll then discourse our woes, felt several years,
And wanting breath to speak help me with tears.

DIONYZA
I'll do my best, sir.

CLEON
This Tarsus, o'er which I have the government,
A city on whom plenty held full hand,
For riches strew'd herself even in the streets;
Whose towers bore heads so high they kiss'd the
　　clouds,
And strangers ne'er beheld but wonder'd at;
Whose men and dames so jetted and adorn'd,
Like one another's glass to trim them by:
Their tables were stored full, to glad the sight,
And not so much to feed on as delight;
All poverty was scorn'd, and pride so great,
The name of help grew odious to repeat.

DIONYZA
O, 'tis too true.

CLEON
But see what heaven can do! By this our change,
These mouths, who but of late earth, sea and air,
Were all too little to content and please,
Although they gave their creatures in abundance,
As houses are defiled for want of use,
They are now starved for want of exercise:
Those palates who, not yet two summers younger,
Must have inventions to delight the taste,
Would now be glad of bread, and beg for it:
Those mothers who, to nousle up their babes,
Thought nought too curious, are ready now
To eat those little darlings whom they loved.
So sharp are hunger's teeth, that man and wife
Draw lots who first shall die to lengthen life:
Here stands a lord, and there a lady weeping;
Here many sink, yet those which see them fall
Have scarce strength left to give them burial.
Is not this true?

DIONYZA
Our cheeks and hollow eyes do witness it.

CLEON
O, let those cities that of plenty's cup
And her prosperities so largely taste,
With their superfluous riots, hear these tears!
The misery of Tarsus may be theirs.

Enter a LORD

LORD
Where's the lord governor?

CLEON

Here.
Speak out thy sorrows which thou bring'st in haste,
For comfort is too far for us to expect.

LORD

We have descried, upon our neighbouring shore,
A portly sail of ships make hitherward.

CLEON

I thought as much.
One sorrow never comes but brings an heir,
That may succeed as his inheritor;
And so in ours: some neighbouring nation,
Taking advantage of our misery,
Hath stuff'd these hollow vessels with their power,
To beat us down, the which are down already,
And make a conquest of unhappy me,
Whereas no glory's got to overcome.

LORD

That's the least fear; for, by the semblance
Of their white flags display'd, they bring us peace,
And come to us as favourers, not as foes.

CLEON

Thou speak'st like him 's untutor'd to repeat:
Who makes the fairest show means most deceit.
But bring they what they will and what they can,
What need we fear?
The ground's the lowest, and we are half way there.
Go tell their general we attend him here,
To know for what he comes and whence he comes
And what he craves.

LORD

I go, my lord.   [Exit

CLEON

Welcome is peace, if he on peace consist;
If wars, we are unable to resist.

Enter PERICLES *with* ATTENDANTS

PERICLES

Lord governor, for so we hear you are,
Let not our ships and number of our men
Be like a beacon fired to amaze your eyes,
We have heard your miseries as far as Tyre,
And seen the desolation of your streets:
Nor come we to add sorrow to your tears,
But to relieve them of their heavy load;
And these our ships, you happily may think
Are like the Trojan horse was stuff'd within
With bloody veins expecting overthrow,
Are stored with corn to make your needy bread,
And give them life whom hunger starved half dead.

ALL

The gods of Greece protect you!
And we'll pray for you.

PERICLES

Arise, I pray you, rise:
We do not look for reverence, but for love
And harbourage for ourself, our ships and men.

CLEON

The which when any shall not gratify,
Or pay you with unthankfulness in thought,
Be it our wives, our children, or ourselves,

The curse of heaven and men succeed their evils!
Till when,—the which I hope shall ne'er be seen—
Your grace is welcome to our town and us.

PERICLES

Which welcome we'll accept; feast here awhile,
Until our stars that frown lend us a smile.   [*Exeunt*

ACT II

Enter GOWER

GOWER

Here have you seen a mighty king
His child, I wis, to incest bring;
A better prince and benign lord,
That will prove awful both in deed and word.
Be quiet then as men should be,
Till he hath pass'd necessity.
I'll show you those in troubles reign,
Losing a mite, a mountain gain.
The good in conversation,
To whom I give my benison,
Is still at Tarsus, where each man
Thinks all is writ he speken can;
And, to remember what he does,
Build his statue to make him glorious:
But tidings to the contrary
Are brought your eyes; what need speak I?

DUMB SHOW

Enter, at one door, PERICLES, *talking with* CLEON; *all the
train with them. Enter, at another door, a* GENTLEMAN,
with a letter to PERICLES; PERICLES *shows the letter to*
CLEON; *gives the* MESSENGER *a reward, and knights him.*
     Exit PERICLES *at one door, and* CLEON *at another*

Good Helicane, that stay'd at home,
Not to eat honey like a drone
From others' labours; for though he strive
To killen bad, keep good alive;
And to fulfil his prince' desire,
Sends word of all that haps in Tyre:
How Thaliard came full bent with sin
And had intent to murder him;
And that in Tarsus was not best
Longer for him to make his rest.
He, doing so, put forth to seas,
Where when men been, there's seldom ease;
For now the wind begins to blow;
Thunder above and deeps below
Make such unquiet that the ship
Should house him safe is wreck'd and split;
And he, good prince, having all lost,
By waves from coast to coast is tost:
All perishen of man, of pelf,
Ne aught escapen but himself;
Till fortune, tired with doing bad,
Threw him ashore, to give him glad:
And here he comes. What shall be next,
Pardon old Gower,—this longs the text.   [*Exit*

SCENE I. *Pentapolis. An open place by the sea-side*

Enter PERICLES, *wet*

PERICLES

Yet cease your ire, you angry stars of heaven!
Wind, rain, and thunder, remember, earthly man
Is but a substance that must yield to you;
And I, as fits my nature, do obey you:
Alas, the sea hath cast me on the rocks,
Wash'd me from shore to shore, and left me breath
Nothing to think on but ensuing death:
Let it suffice the greatness of your powers
To have bereft a prince of all his fortunes;
And having thrown him from your watery grave,
Here to have death in peace is all he'll crave.

Enter THREE FISHERMEN

FIRST FISHERMAN

What, ho, Pilch!

SECOND FISHERMAN

Ha, come and bring away the nets!

FIRST FISHERMAN

What, Patchbreech, I say!

THIRD FISHERMAN

What say you, master?

FIRST FISHERMAN

Look how thou stirrest now! come away, or I'll
fetch thee with a wanion.

THIRD FISHERMAN

Faith, master, I am thinking of the poor men that
were cast away before us even now.

FIRST FISHERMAN

Alas, poor souls, it grieved my heart to hear what
pitiful cries they made to us to help them, when,
well-a-day, we could scarce help ourselves.

Nay, master, said not I as much when I saw the
porpus, how he bounced and tumbled? they say
they're half fish, half flesh: a plague on them, they
ne'er come but I look to be washed. Master, I marvel how the fishes live in the sea.

FIRST FISHERMAN

Why, as men do a-land; the great ones eat up the
little ones: I can compare our rich misers to nothing
so fitly as to a whale; a' plays and tumbles, driving
the poor fry before him, and at last devours them
all at a mouthful: such whales have I heard on o'
the land, who never leave gaping till they've swallowed the whole parish, church, steeple, bells, and
all.

PERICLES

[Aside] A pretty moral.

THIRD FISHERMAN

But, master, if I had been the sexton, I would have
been that day in the belfry.

SECOND FISHERMAN

Why, man?

THIRD FISHERMAN

Because he should have swallowed me too: and
when I had been in his belly, I would have kept
such a jangling of the bells, that he should never

have left till he cast bells, steeple, church, and
parish, up again. But if the good King Simonides
were of my mind,—

PERICLES

[Aside] Simonides!

THIRD FISHERMAN

We would purge the land of these drones, that rob
the bee of her honey.

PERICLES

[Aside] How from the finny subject of the sea
These fishers tell the infirmities of men;
And from their watery empire recollect
All that may men approve or men detect!—
Peace be at your labour, honest fishermen.

SECOND FISHERMAN

Honest! good fellow, what's that? If it be a day fits
you, search out of the calendar, and nobody look
after it.

PERICLES

May see the sea hath cast upon your coast.

SECOND FISHERMAN

What a drunken knave was the sea to cast thee in
our way!

PERICLES

A man whom both the waters and the wind,
In that vast tennis-court, have made the ball
For them to play upon, entreats you pity him;
He asks of you, that never used to beg.

FIRST FISHERMAN

No, friend, cannot you beg? Here's them in our
country of Greece gets more with begging than we
can do with working.

SECOND FISHERMAN

Canst thou catch any fishes then?

PERICLES

I never practised it.

SECOND FISHERMAN

Nay, then thou wilt starve, sure; for here's nothing
to be got now-a-days, unless thou canst fish for 't.

PERICLES

What I have been I have forgot to know;
But what I am, want teaches me to think on:
A man throng'd up with cold: my veins are chill,
And have no more of life than may suffice
To give my tongue that heat to ask your help;
Which if you shall refuse, when I am dead,
For that I am a man, pray see me buried.

FIRST FISHERMAN

Die quoth-a? Now gods forbid 't! And I have a
gown here; come, put it on; keep thee warm. Now,
afore me, a handsome fellow! Come, thou shalt go
home, and we'll have flesh for holidays, fish for
fasting-days, and moreo'er puddings and flap-jacks,
and thou shalt be welcome.

PERICLES

I thank you, sir.

SECOND FISHERMAN

Hark you, my friend; you said you could not beg.

PERICLES

I did but crave.

SECOND FISHERMAN

But crave! Then I'll turn craver too, and so I shall 'scape whipping.

PERICLES

Why, are all your beggars whipped then?

SECOND FISHERMAN

O, not all, my friend, not all; for if all your beggars were whipped, I would wish no better office than to be beadle. But, master, I'll go draw up the net.

[Exit with THIRD FISHERMAN

PERICLES

[Aside] How well this honest mirth becomes their labour!

FIRST FISHERMAN

Hark you, sir, do you know where ye are?

PERICLES

Not well.

FIRST FISHERMAN

Why, I'll tell you: this is called Pentapolis, and our king the good Simonides.

PERICLES

The good Simonides, do you call him?

FIRST FISHERMAN

Ay, sir; and he deserves so to be called for his peaceable reign and good government.

PERICLES

He is a happy king, since he gains from his subjects the name of good by his government. How far is his court distant from this shore?

FIRST FISHERMAN

Marry, sir, half a day's journey: and I'll tell you, he hath a fair daughter, and to-morrow is her birthday; and there are princes and knights come from all parts of the world to just and tourney for her love.

PERICLES

Were my fortunes equal to my desires, I could wish to make one there.

FIRST FISHERMAN

O, sir, things must be as they may; and what a man cannot get, he may lawfully deal for—his wife's soul.

Re-enter SECOND and THIRD FISHERMAN, drawing up a net

SECOND FISHERMAN

Help, master, help! here's a fish hangs in the net, like a poor man's right in the law; 'twill hardly come out. Ha! bots on 't, 'tis come at last, and 'tis turned to a rusty armour.

PERICLES

An armour, friends! I pray you, let me see it.
Thanks, fortune, yet, that after all thy crosses
Thou givest me somewhat to repair myself;
And though it was mine own, part of my heritage,
Which my dead father did bequeath to me,
With this strict charge, even as he left his life,
'Keep it, my Pericles; it hath been a shield
'Twixt me and death:'—and pointed to this brace—
'For that it saved me, keep it; in like necessity—

The which the gods protect thee from!—may defend thee.'
It kept where I kept, I so dearly loved it;
Till the rough seas, that spare not any man,
Took it in rage, though calm'd have given 't again:
I thank thee for 't: my shipwreck now's no ill,
Since I have here my father's gift in 's will.

FIRST FISHERMAN

What mean you, sir?

PERICLES

To beg of you, kind friends, this coat of worth,
For it was sometime target to a king;
I know it by this mark. He loved me dearly,
And for his sake I wish the having of it;
And that you'ld guide me to your sovereign's court,
Where with it I may appear a gentleman;
And if that ever my low fortune's better,
I'll pay your bounties; till then rest your debtor.

FIRST FISHERMAN

Why, wilt thou tourney for the lady?

PERICLES

I'll show the virtue I have borne in arms.

FIRST FISHERMAN

Why, do 'e take it, and the gods give thee good on 't!

SECOND FISHERMAN

Ay, but hark you, my friend; 'twas we that made up this garment through the rough seams of the waters: there are certain condolements, certain vails. I hope, sir, if you thrive, you'll remember from whence you had them.

PERICLES

Believe 't, I will.
By your furtherance I am clothed in steel;
And spite of all the rapture of the sea
This jewel holds his building on my arm:
Unto thy value I will mount myself
Upon a courser, whose delightful steps
Shall make the gazer joy to see him tread.
Only, my friend, I yet am unprovided
Of a pair of bases.

SECOND FISHERMAN

We'll sure provide: thou shalt have my best gown to make thee a pair; and I'll bring thee to the court myself.

PERICLES

Then honour be but a goal to my will,
This day I'll rise, or else add ill to ill.   [Exeunt

SCENE II. The same. A public way or platform leading to the lists. A pavilion by the side of it for the reception of the KING, PRINCESS, LORDS, &c.

Enter SIMONIDES, THAISA, LORDS, and ATTENDANTS

SIMONIDES

Are the knights ready to begin the triumph?

FIRST LORD

They are, my liege,
And stay your coming to present themselves.

SIMONIDES

Return them, we are ready; and our daughter,
In honour of whose birth these triumphs are,
Sits here, like beauty's child, whom nature gat
For men to see and seeing wonder at. [*Exit a* LORD

THAISA

It pleaseth you, my royal father, to express
My commendations great, whose merit's less.

SIMONIDES

It's fit it should be so; for princes are
A model which heaven makes like to itself:
As jewels lose their glory if neglected,
So princes their renowns if not respected.
'Tis now your honour, daughter, to entertain
The labour of each knight in his device.

THAISA

Which, to preserve mine honour, I'll perform.
Enter a KNIGHT; *he passes over, and his* SQUIRE *presents
his shield to the* PRINCESS

SIMONIDES

Who is the first that doth prefer himself?

THAISA

A knight of Sparta, my renowned father;
And the device he bears upon his shield
Is a black Ethiope reaching at the sun;
The word, 'Lux tua vita mihi.'

SIMONIDES

He loves you well that holds his life of you.
[*The* SECOND KNIGHT *passes*
Who is the second that presents himself?

THAISA

A prince of Macedon, my royal father;
And the device he bears upon his shield
Is an arm'd knight that's conquer'd by a lady;
The motto thus, in Spanish, 'Piu por dulzura que
por fuerza.' [*The* THIRD KNIGHT *passes*

SIMONIDES

And what's the third?

THAISA

The third of Antioch;
And his device, a wreath of chivalry;
The word, 'Me pompæ provexit apex.'
[*The* FOURTH KNIGHT *passes*

SIMONIDES

What is the fourth?

THAISA

A burning torch that's turned upside down;
The word, 'Quod me alit, me extinguit.'

SIMONIDES

Which shows that beauty hath his power and will,
Which can as well inflame as it can kill.
[*The* FIFTH KNIGHT *passes*

THAISA

The fifth, an hand environed with clouds,
Holding out gold that's by the touchstone tried;
The motto thus, 'Sic spectanda fides.'
[*The* SIXTH KNIGHT, PERICLES, *passes*

SIMONIDES

And what's

The sixth and last, the which the knight himself
With such a graceful courtesy deliver'd?

THAISA

He seems to be a stranger; but his present is
A wither'd branch, that's only green at top;
The motto, 'In hac spe vivo.'

SIMONIDES

A pretty moral;
From the dejected state wherein he is,
He hopes by you his fortunes yet may flourish.

FIRST LORD

He had need mean better than his outward show
Can any way speak in his just commend;
For by his rusty outside he appears
To have practised more the whipstock than the
lance.

SECOND LORD

He well may be a stranger, for he comes
To an honour'd triumph strangely furnished.

THIRD LORD

And on set purpose let his armour rust
Until this day, to scour it in the dust.

SIMONIDES

Opinion's but a fool, that makes us scan
The outward habit by the inward man.
But stay, the knights are coming: we will withdraw
Into the gallery. [*Exeunt*
[*Great shouts within, and all cry* 'The mean knight!'

SCENE III. *The same. A hall of state: a banquet
prepared*

Enter SIMONIDES, THAISA, LORDS, KNIGHTS, *and*
ATTENDANTS

SIMONIDES

Knights,
To say you're welcome were superfluous.
To place upon the volume of your deeds,
As in a title-page, your worth in arms,
Were more than you expect, or more than's fit,
Since every worth in show commends itself.
Prepare for mirth, for mirth becomes a feast:
You are princes and my guests.

THAISA

But you, my knight and guest,
To whom this wreath of victory I give,
And crown you king of this day's happiness.

PERICLES

'Tis more by fortune, lady, than my merit.

SIMONIDES

Call it by what you will, the day is yours;
And here, I hope, is none that envies it.
In framing an artist, art hath thus decreed,
To make some good, but others to exceed;
And you are her labour'd scholar. Come, queen o'
the feast,—
For, daughter, so you are,—here take your place:
Marshal the rest as they deserve their grace.

KNIGHTS

We are honour'd much by good Simonides.

SIMONIDES

Your presence glads our days: honour we love;
For who hates honour hates the gods above.

MARSHAL

Sir, yonder is your place.

PERICLES

           Some other is more fit.

FIRST KNIGHT

Contend not, sir; for we are gentlemen
That neither in our hearts nor outward eyes
Envy the great nor do the low despise.

PERICLES

You are right courteous knights.

SIMONIDES

           Sit, sir, sit.
[Aside] By Jove, I wonder, that is king of thoughts,
These cates resist me, he not thought upon.

THAISA

[Aside] By Juno, that is queen of marriage,
All viands that I eat do seem unsavoury,
Wishing him my meat.—Sure he's a gallant gentle-
man.

SIMONIDES

He's but a country gentleman;
Has done no more than other knights have done;
Has broken a staff or so; so let it pass.

THAISA

[Aside] To me he seems like diamond to glass.

PERICLES

[Aside] Yon king's to me like to my father's picture,
Which tells me in that glory once he was;
Had princes sit, like stars, about his throne,
And he the sun, for them to reverence;
None that beheld him but, like lesser lights,
Did vail their crowns to his supremacy:
Where now his son's like a glow-worm in the night,
The which hath fire in darkness, none in light:
Whereby I see that Time's the king of men;
He's both their parent, and he is their grave,
And gives them what he will, not what they crave.

SIMONIDES

What, are you merry, knights?

KNIGHTS

Who can be other in this royal presence?

SIMONIDES

Here, with a cup that's stored unto the brim,—
As you do love, fill to your mistress' lips,—
We drink this health to you.

KNIGHTS

           We thank your grace.

SIMONIDES

Yet pause awhile:
Yon knight doth sit too melancholy,
As if the entertainment in our court
Had not a show might countervail his worth.
Note it not you, Thaisa?

THAISA

What is 't to me, my father?

SIMONIDES

O, attend, my daughter:
Princes, in this, should live like gods above,
Who freely give to every one that comes
To honour them:
And princes not doing so are like to gnats,
Which make a sound, but kill'd are wonder'd at.
Therefore to make his entrance more sweet,
Here, say we drink this standing-bowl of wine to
him.

THAISA

Alas, my father, it befits not me
Unto a stranger knight to be so bold:
He may my proffer take for an offence,
Since men take women's gifts for impudence.

SIMONIDES

How!
Do as I bid you, or you'll move me else.

THAISA

[Aside] Now, by the gods, he could not please me
better.

SIMONIDES

And furthermore tell him, we desire to know of him,
Of whence he is, his name and parentage.

THAISA

The king my father, sir, has drunk to you.

PERICLES

I thank him.

THAISA

Wishing it so much blood unto your life.

PERICLES

I thank both him and you, and pledge him freely.

THAISA

And further he desires to know of you
Of whence you are, your name and parentage.

PERICLES

A gentleman of Tyre; my name, Pericles;
My education been in arts and arms;
Who, looking for adventures in the world,
Was by the rough seas reft of ships and men,
And after shipwreck driven upon this shore.

THAISA

He thanks your grace; names himself Pericles,
A gentleman of Tyre,
Who only by misfortune of the seas
Bereft of ships and men, cast on this shore.

SIMONIDES

Now, by the gods, I pity his misfortune,
And will awake him from his melancholy.
Come, gentlemen, we sit too long on trifles,
And waste the time, which looks for other revels.
Even in your armours, as you are address'd,
Will very well become a soldier's dance.
I will not have excuse, with saying this
Loud music is too harsh for ladies' heads,
Since they love men in arms as well as beds.
           [The KNIGHTS dance
So, this was well ask'd, 'twas so well perform'd.
Come, sir, here's a lady that wants breathing too:
And I have heard, you knights of Tyre

Are excellent in making ladies trip,
And that their measures are as excellent.

PERICLES

In those that practise them they are, my lord.

SIMONIDES

O, that's as much as you would be denied
Of your fair courtesy.

[The KNIGHTS and LADIES dance
Unclasp, unclasp:
Thanks, gentlemen, to all; all have done well,
[To PERICLES] But you the best. Pages and lights, to
  conduct
These knights unto their several lodgings! Yours,
  sir,
We have given order to be next our own.

PERICLES

I am at your grace's pleasure.

SIMONIDES

Princes, it is too late to talk of love,
And that's the mark I know you level at:
Therefore each one betake him to his rest;
To-morrow all for speeding do their best. [Exeunt

SCENE IV. *Tyre. A room in the Governor's house*

Enter HELICANUS *and* ESCANES

HELICANUS

No, Escanes, know this of me,
Antiochus from incest lived not free:
For which, the most high gods not minding longer
To withhold the vengeance that they had in store,
Due to this heinous capital offence,
Even in the height and pride of all his glory,
When he was seated in a chariot
Of an inestimable value, and his daughter with him,
A fire from heaven came, and shrivell'd up
Their bodies, even to loathing; for they so stunk,
That all those eyes adored them ere their fall
Scorn now their hand should give them burial.

ESCANES

'Twas very strange.

HELICANUS

        And yet but justice; for though
This king were great, his greatness was no guard
To bar heaven's shaft, but sin had his reward.

ESCANES

'Tis very true.

Enter two or three LORDS

FIRST LORD

See, not a man in private conference
Or council has respect with him but he.

SECOND LORD

It shall no longer grieve without reproof.

THIRD LORD

And cursed be he that will not second it.

FIRST LORD

Follow me then. Lord Helicane, a word.

HELICANUS

With me? and welcome: happy day, my lords.

FIRST LORD

Know that our griefs are risen to the top,
And now at length they overflow their banks.

HELICANUS

Your griefs! for what? wrong not your prince you
  love.

FIRST LORD

Wrong not yourself, then, noble Helicane;
But if the prince do live, let us salute him,
Or know what ground's made happy by his breath.
If in the world he live, we'll seek him out;
If in his grave he rest, we'll find him there;
And be resolved he lives to govern us,
Or dead, give 's cause to mourn his funeral,
And leave us to our free election.

SECOND LORD

Whose death's indeed the strongest in our censure:
And knowing this kingdom is without a head,—
Like goodly buildings left without a roof
Soon fall to ruin—your noble self,
That best know how to rule and how to reign,
We thus submit unto, our sovereign.

ALL

Live, noble Helicane!

HELICANUS

For honour's cause, forbear your suffrages:
If that you love Prince Pericles, forbear.
Take I your wish, I leap into the seas,
Where's hourly trouble for a minute's ease.
A twelvemonth longer, let me entreat you
To forbear the absence of your king;
If in which time expired he not return,
I shall with aged patience bear your yoke.
But if I cannot win you to this love,
Go search like nobles, like noble subjects,
And in your search spend your adventurous worth;
Whom if you find and win unto return,
You shall like diamonds sit about his crown.

FIRST LORD

To wisdom he's a fool that will not yield;
And since Lord Helicane enjoineth us,
We with our travels will endeavour it.

HELICANUS

Then you love us, we you, and we'll clasp hands:
When peers thus knit, a kingdom ever stands.

[Exeunt

SCENE V. *Pentapolis. A room in the palace*

Enter SIMONIDES, *reading a letter, at one door: the*
KNIGHTS *meet him*

FIRST KNIGHT

Good morrow to the good Simonides.

SIMONIDES

Knights, from my daughter this I let you know,
That for this twelvemonth she'll not undertake
A married life.
Her reason to herself is only known,
Which from her by no means can I get.

SECOND KNIGHT
May we not get access to her, my lord?
SIMONIDES
Faith, by no means; she hath so strictly
Tied her to her chamber, that 'tis impossible.
One twelve moons more she'll wear Diana's livery;
This by the eye of Cynthia hath she vow'd,
And on her virgin honour will not break it.
THIRD KNIGHT
Loath to bid farewell, we take our leaves.
[Exeunt KNIGHTS
SIMONIDES
So,
They are well dispatch'd; now to my daughter's
     letter:
She tells me here, she'll wed the stranger knight,
Or never more to view nor day nor light.
'Tis well, mistress; your choice agrees with mine;
I like that well: nay, how absolute she's in 't,
Not minding whether I dislike or no!
Well, I do commend her choice;
And will no longer have it be delay'd.
Soft! here he comes: I must dissemble it.

Enter PERICLES
PERICLES
All fortune to the good Simonides!
SIMONIDES
To you as much, sir! I am beholding to you
For your sweet music this last night: I do
Protest my ears were never better fed
With such delightful pleasing harmony.
PERICLES
It is your grace's pleasure to commend;
Not my desert.
SIMONIDES
          Sir, you are music's master.
PERICLES
The worst of all her scholars, my good lord.
SIMONIDES
Let me ask you one thing: what do you think of my
daughter, sir?
PERICLES
A most virtuous princess.
SIMONIDES
And she is fair too, is she not?
PERICLES
As a fair day in summer, wondrous fair.
SIMONIDES
Sir, my daughter thinks very well of you;
Ay, so well, that you must be her master,
And she will be your scholar: therefore look to it.
PERICLES
I am unworthy for her schoolmaster.
SIMONIDES
She thinks not so; peruse this writing else.
PERICLES
[Aside] What's here?
A letter, that she loves the knight of Tyre!
'Tis the king's subtilty to have my life.—
O, seek not to entrap me, gracious lord,

A stranger and distressed gentleman,
That never aim'd so high to love your daughter,
But bent all offices to honour her.
SIMONIDES
Thou hast bewitch'd my daughter, and thou art
A villain.
PERICLES
By the gods, I have not:
Never did thought of mine levy offence;
Nor never did my actions yet commence
A deed might gain her love or your displeasure.
SIMONIDES
Traitor, thou liest.
PERICLES
          Traitor!
SIMONIDES
                    Ay, traitor.
PERICLES
Even in his throat—unless it be the king—
That calls me traitor, I return the lie.
SIMONIDES
[Aside] Now, by the gods, I do applaud his courage
PERICLES
My actions are as noble as my thoughts,
That never relish'd of a base descent.
I came unto your court for honour's cause,
And not to be a rebel to her state;
And he that otherwise accounts of me,
This sword shall prove he's honour's enemy.
SIMONIDES
No?
Here comes my daughter, she can witness it.

Enter THAISA
PERICLES
Then, as you are as virtuous as fair,
Resolve your angry father, if my tongue
Did e'er solicit, or my hand subscribe
To any syllable that made love to you.
THAISA
Why, sir, say if you had,
Who takes offence at that would make me glad?
SIMONIDES
Yea, mistress, are you so peremptory?
[Aside] I am glad on 't with all my heart.—
I'll tame you; I'll bring you in subjection.
Will you, not having my consent,
Bestow your love and your affections
Upon a stranger? [Aside] who, for aught I know,
May be, nor can I think the contrary,
As great in blood as I myself.—
Therefore hear you, mistress; either frame
Your will to mine,—and you, sir, hear you,
Either be ruled by me, or I'll make you—
Man and wife:
Nay, come, your hands and lips must seal it too:
And being join'd, I'll thus your hopes destroy;
And for a further grief,—God give you joy!
What, are you both pleased?
THAISA
          Yes, if you love me, sir.

PERICLES
Even as my life my blood that fosters it.
SIMONIDES
What, are you both agreed?
BOTH
Yes, if 't please your majesty.
SIMONIDES
It pleaseth me so well, that I will see you wed;
And then, with what haste you can, get you to bed.
[*Exeunt*

ACT III

Enter GOWER
GOWER
Now sleep y-slaked hath the rout;
No din but snores the house about,
Made louder by the o'er-fed breast
Of this most pompous marriage-feast.
The cat, with eyne of burning coal,
Now couches 'fore the mouse's hole;
And crickets sing at the oven's mouth,
E'er the blither for their drouth.
Hymen hath brought the bride to bed,
Where, by the loss of maidenhead,
A babe is moulded. Be attent,
And time that is so briefly spent
With your fine fancies quaintly eche:
What's dumb in show I'll plain with speech.

DUMB SHOW
Enter PERICLES *and* SIMONIDES *at one door, with* AT-
TENDANTS; *a* MESSENGER *meets them, kneels, and gives*
PERICLES *a letter:* PERICLES *shows it* SIMONIDES; *the*
LORDS *kneel to the former. Then enter* THAISA *with child,*
with LYCHORIDA, *a nurse: the* KING *shows her the letter;*
she rejoices: she and PERICLES *take leave of her father, and*
depart with LYCHORIDA *and their* ATTENDANTS. *Then*
exeunt SIMONIDES *and the rest*

By many a dern and painful perch
Of Pericles the careful search,
By the four opposing coigns
Which the world together joins,
Is made with all due diligence
That horse and sail and high expense
Can stead the quest. At last from Tyre,
Fame answering the most strange inquire,
To the court of King Simonides
Are letters brought, the tenour these:
Antiochus and his daughter dead;
The men of Tyrus on the head
Of Helicanus would set on
The crown of Tyre, but he will none:
The mutiny he there hastes t' oppress;
Says to 'em, if King Pericles
Come not home in twice six moons,
He, obedient to their dooms,
Will take the crown. The sum of this,
Brought hither to Pentapolis,

Y-ravished the regions round,
And every one with claps can sound,
'Our heir-apparent is a king!
Who dream'd, who thought of such a thing?'
Brief, he must hence depart to Tyre:
His queen with child makes her desire—
Which who shall cross?—along to go.
Omit we all their dole and woe:
Lychorida, her nurse, she takes,
And so to sea: their vessel shakes
On Neptune's billow; half the flood
Hath their keel cut: but fortune's mood
Varies again; the grisled north
Disgorges such a tempest forth,
That, as a duck for life that dives,
So up and down the poor ship drives:
The lady shrieks and well-a-near
Does fall in travail with her fear:
And what ensues in this fell storm
Shall for itself itself perform.
I nill relate, action may
Conveniently the rest convey;
Which might not what by me is told.
In your imagination hold
This stage the ship, upon whose deck
The sea-tost Pericles appears to speak.   [*Exit*

SCENE I

Enter PERICLES, *on shipboard*
PERICLES
Thou god of this great vast, rebuke these surges,
Which wash both heaven and hell; and thou, that
   hast
Upon the winds command, bind them in brass,
Having call'd them from the deep! O, still
Thy deafening dreadful thunders; gently quench
Thy nimble sulphurous flashes! O, how, Lychorida,
How does my queen? Thou stormest venomously;
Wilt thou spit all thyself? The seaman's whistle
Is as a whisper in the ears of death,
Unheard. Lychorida!—Lucina, O
Divinest patroness and midwife gentle
To those that cry by night, convey thy deity
Aboard our dancing boat; make swift the pangs
Of my queen's travails! Now, Lychorida!
Enter LYCHORIDA, *with an Infant*
LYCHORIDA
Here is a thing too young for such a place,
Who, if it had conceit, would die, as I
Am like to do: take in your arms this piece
Of your dead queen.
PERICLES
      How, how, Lychorida!
LYCHORIDA
Patience, good sir; do not assist the storm.
Here's all that is left living of your queen,
A little daughter: for the sake of it,
Be manly, and take comfort.

PERICLES

O you gods!

Why do you make us love your goodly gifts,
And snatch them straight away? We here below
Recall not what we give, and therein may
Use honour with you.

LYCHORIDA

Patience, good sir,
Even for this charge.

PERICLES

Now, mild may be thy life!
For a more blustrous birth had never babe:
Quiet and gentle thy conditions! for
Thou art the rudeliest welcome to this world
That ever was prince's child. Happy what follows!
Thou hast as chiding a nativity
As fire, air, water, earth and heaven can make,
To herald thee from the womb: even at the first
Thy loss is more than can thy portage quit,
With all thou canst find here. Now, the good gods
Throw their best eyes upon 't!

Enter two SAILORS

FIRST SAILOR

What courage, sir? God save you!

PERICLES

Courage enough: I do not fear the flaw;
It hath done to me the worst. Yet, for the love
Of this poor infant, this fresh-new sea-farer,
I would it would be quiet.

FIRST SAILOR

Slack the bolins there! Thou wilt not, wilt thou?
Blow, and split thyself.

SECOND SAILOR

But sea-room, an the brine and cloudy billow kiss
the moon, I care not.

FIRST SAILOR

Sir, your queen must overboard: the sea works
high, the wind is loud, and will not lie till the ship
be cleared of the dead.

PERICLES

That's your superstition.

FIRST SAILOR

Pardon us, sir; with us at sea it hath been still observed; and we are strong in custom. Therefore
briefly yield her; for she must overboard straight.

PERICLES

As you think meet. Most wretched queen!

LYCHORIDA

Here she lies, sir.

PERICLES

A terrible childbed hast thou had, my dear;
No light, no fire: the unfriendly elements
Forgot thee utterly; nor have I time
To give thee hallow'd to thy grave, but straight
Must cast thee, scarcely coffin'd, in the ooze;
Where, for a monument upon thy bones,
And aye-remaining lamps, the belching whale
And humming water must o'erwhelm thy corpse,

Lying with simple shells. O Lychorida,
Bid Nestor bring me spices, ink and paper,
My casket and my jewels; and bid Nicander
Bring me the satin coffer: lay the babe
Upon the pillow: hie thee, whiles I say
A priestly farewell to her: suddenly, woman.

[*Exit* LYCHORIDA

SECOND SAILOR

Sir, we have a chest beneath the hatches, caulked
and bitumed ready.

PERICLES

I thank thee. Mariner, say what coast is this?

SECOND SAILOR

We are near Tarsus.

PERICLES

Thither, gentle mariner,
Alter thy course for Tyre. When canst thou reach it?

SECOND SAILOR

By break of day, if the wind cease.

PERICLES

O, make for Tarsus!
There will I visit Cleon, for the babe
Cannot hold out to Tyrus: there I'll leave it
At careful nursing. Go thy ways, good mariner:
I'll bring the body presently. [*Exeunt*

SCENE II. *Ephesus. A room in* CERIMON'*s house*

Enter CERIMON, *a* SERVANT, *and some Persons who have
been shipwrecked*

CERIMON

Philemon, ho!

Enter PHILEMON

PHILEMON

Doth my lord call?

CERIMON

Get fire and meat for these poor men:
'T has been a turbulent and stormy night.

SERVANT

I have been in many; but such a night as this,
Till now, I ne'er endured.

CERIMON

Your master will be dead ere you return;
There's nothing can be minister'd to nature
That can recover him. [*To* PHILEMON] Give this to
 the 'pothecary,
And tell me how it works. [*Exeunt all but* CERIMON

Enter two GENTLEMEN

FIRST GENTLEMAN

Good morrow.

SECOND GENTLEMAN

Good morrow to your lordship.

CERIMON

Gentlemen,
Why do you stir so early?

FIRST GENTLEMAN

Sir,
Our lodgings, standing bleak upon the sea

Shook as the earth did quake;
The very principals did seem to rend
And all-to topple: pure surprise and fear
Made me to quit the house.

SECOND GENTLEMAN

That is the cause we trouble you so early;
'Tis not our husbandry.

CERIMON

O, you say well.

FIRST GENTLEMAN

But I much marvel that your lordship, having
Rich tire about you, should at these early hours
Shake off the golden slumber of repose.
'Tis most strange,
Nature should be so conversant with pain,
Being thereto not compell'd.

CERIMON

I hold it ever,
Virtue and cunning were endowments greater
Than nobleness and riches: careless heirs
May the two latter darken and expend,
But immortality attends the former,
Making a man a god. 'Tis known, I ever
Have studied physic, through which secret art,
By turning o'er authorities, I have,
Together with my practice, made familiar
To me and to my aid the blest infusions
That dwell in vegetives, in metals, stones;
And I can speak of the disturbances
That nature works, and of her cures; which doth
    give me
A more content in course of true delight
Than to be thirsty after tottering honour,
Or tie my treasure up in silken bags,
To please the fool and death.

SECOND GENTLEMAN

Your honour has through Ephesus pour'd forth
Your charity, and hundreds call themselves
Your creatures, who by you have been restored:
And not your knowledge, your personal pain, but
    even
Your purse, still open, hath built Lord Cerimon
Such strong renown as time shall never . . .

Enter two or three SERVANTS *with a chest*

FIRST SERVANT

So; lift there.

CERIMON

What's that?

FIRST SERVANT

Sir,
Even now did the sea toss up upon our shore
This chest: 'tis of some wreck.

CERIMON

Set 't down, let's look upon 't.

SECOND GENTLEMAN

'Tis like a coffin, sir.

CERIMON

Whate'er it be,
'Tis wondrous heavy. Wrench it open straight:

If the sea's stomach be o'ercharged with gold,
'Tis a good constraint of fortune it belches upon us.

SECOND GENTLEMAN

'Tis so, my lord.

CERIMON

How close 'tis caulk'd and bitumed! Did the sea
cast it up?

FIRST SERVANT

I never saw so huge a billow, sir, as toss'd it upon
shore.

CERIMON

Wrench it open: soft! it smells most sweetly in my
sense.

SECOND GENTLEMAN

A delicate odour.

CERIMON

As ever hit my nostril. So, up with it.
O you most potent gods! what's here? a corse!

FIRST GENTLEMAN

Most strange!

CERIMON

Shrouded in cloth of state; balmed and entreasured
with full bags of spices! A passport too! Apollo, perfect me in the characters!   [*Reads from a scroll*

'Here I give to understand,
    If e'er this coffin drive a-land,
    I, King Pericles, have lost
    This queen, worth all our mundane cost.
    Who finds her, give her burying;
    She was the daughter of a king:
    Besides this treasure for a fee,
    The gods requite his charity!'

If thou livest, Pericles, thou hast a heart
That even cracks for woe! This chanced to-night.

SECOND GENTLEMAN

Most likely, sir.

CERIMON

Nay, certainly to-night;
For look how fresh she looks! They were too rough
That threw her in the sea. Make a fire within:
Fetch hither all my boxes in my closet.

[*Exit a* SERVANT

Death may usurp on nature many hours,
And yet the fire of life kindle again
The o'erpress'd spirits. I heard of an Egyptian
That had nine hours lien dead,
Who was by good appliance recovered.

Re-enter a SERVANT, *with boxes, napkins, and fire*

Well said, well said; the fire and cloths.
The rough and woful music that we have,
Cause it to sound, beseech you.
The viol once more: how thou stirr'st, thou block!
The music there! I pray you, give her air.
Gentlemen,
This queen will live: nature awakes; a warmth
Breathes out of her: she hath not been entranced
Above five hours: see how she 'gins to blow
Into life's flower again!

FIRST GENTLEMAN

The heavens,

Through you, increase our wonder, and set up
Your fame for ever.

CERIMON
She is alive; behold,
Her eyelids, cases to those heavenly jewels
Which Pericles hath lost, begin to part
Their fringes of bright gold: the diamonds
Of a most praised water do appear
To make the world twice rich. Live,
And make us weep to hear your fate, fair creature,
Rare as you seem to be.   [*She moves*

THAISA
O dear Diana,
Where am I? Where's my lord? What world is this?

SECOND GENTLEMAN
Is not this strange?

FIRST GENTLEMAN
Most rare.

CERIMON
Hush, my gentle neighbours!
Lend me your hands; to the next chamber bear her.
Get linen: now this matter must be look'd to,
For her relapse is mortal. Come, come;
And Æsculapius guide us! [*Exeunt, carrying her away*

SCENE III. *Tarsus. A room in the Governor's house*

Enter PERICLES, CLEON, DIONYZA, *and* LYCHORIDA *with*
MARINA *in her arms*

PERICLES
Most honour'd Cleon, I must needs be gone;
My twelve months are expired, and Tyrus stands
In a litigious peace. You, and your lady,
Take from my heart all thankfulness! The gods
Make up the rest upon you!

CLEON
Your shafts of fortune, though they hurt you mor-
tally,
Yet glance full wanderingly on us.

DIONYZA
O your sweet queen!
That the strict fates had pleased you had brought
her hither,
To have bless'd mine eyes with her!

PERICLES
We cannot but obey
The powers above us. Could I rage and roar
As doth the sea she lies in, yet the end
Must be as 'tis. My gentle babe Marina, whom,
For she was born at sea, I have named so, here
I charge your charity withal, leaving her
The infant of your care; beseeching you
To give her princely training, that she may be
Manner'd as she is born.

CLEON
Fear not, my lord, but think

Your grace, that fed my country with your corn,
For which the people's prayers still fall upon you,
Must in your child be thought on. If neglection
Should therein make me vile, the common body,
By you relieved, would force me to my duty:
But if to that my nature need a spur,
The gods revenge it upon me and mine,
To the end of generation!

PERICLES
I believe you;
Your honour and your goodness teach me to 't,
Without your vows. Till she be married, madam,
By bright Diana, whom we honour, all
Unscissar'd shall this hair of mine remain,
Though I show ill in 't. So I take my leave.
Good madam, make me blessed in your care
In bringing up my child.

DIONYZA
I have one myself,
Who shall not be more dear to my respect
Than yours, my lord.

PERICLES
Madam, my thanks and prayers

CLEON
We'll bring your grace e'en to the edge o' the shore,
Then give you up to the mask'd Neptune and
The gentlest winds of heaven.

PERICLES
I will embrace
Your offer. Come, dearest madam. O, no tears,
Lychorida, no tears:
Look to your little mistress, on whose grace
You may depend hereafter. Come, my lord. [*Exeunt*

SCENE IV. *Ephesus. A room in* CERIMON's *house*

Enter CERIMON *and* THAISA

CERIMON
Madam, this letter, and some certain jewels,
Lay with you in your coffer: which are
At your command. Know you the character?

THAISA
It is my lord's.
That I was shipp'd at sea, I well remember,
Even on my eaning time; but whether there
Delivered, by the holy gods,
I cannot rightly say. But since King Pericles,
My wedded lord, I ne'er shall see again,
A vestal livery will I take me to,
And never more have joy.

CERIMON
Madam, if this you purpose as ye speak,
Diana's temple is not distant far,
Where you may abide till your date expire.
Moreover, if you please, a niece of mine
Shall there attend you.

THAISA

My recompense is thanks, that's all;
Yet my good will is great, though the gift small.

[*Exeunt*

ACT IV

Enter GOWER

GOWER

Imagine Pericles arrived at Tyre,
Welcomed and settled to his own desire.
His woeful queen we leave at Ephesus,
Unto Diana there as a votaress.
Now to Marina bend your mind,
Whom our fast-growing scene must find
At Tarsus, and by Cleon train'd
In music, letters; who hath gain'd
Of education all the grace,
Which makes her both the heart and place
Of general wonder. But, alack,
That monster envy, oft the wrack
Of earned praise, Marina's life
Seeks to take off by treason's knife.
And in this kind hath our Cleon
One daughter, and a wench full grown,
Even ripe for marriage rite; this maid
Hight Philoten: and it is said
For certain in our story, she
Would ever with Marina be:
Be 't when she weaved the sleided silk
With fingers long, small, white as milk;
Or when she would with sharp needle wound
The cambric, which she made more sound
By hurting it; or when to the lute
She sung, and made the night-bird mute,
That still records with moan; or when
She would with rich and constant pen
Vail to her mistress Dian; still
This Philoten contends in skill
With absolute Marina: so
With the dove of Paphos might the crow
Vie feathers white. Marina gets
All praises, which are paid as debts,
And not as given. This so darks
In Philoten all graceful marks,
That Cleon's wife, with envy rare,
A present murderer does prepare
For good Marina, that her daughter
Might stand peerless by this slaughter.
The sooner her vile thoughts to stead,
Lychorida, our nurse, is dead:
And cursed Dionyza hath
The pregnant instrument of wrath
Prest for this blow. The unborn event
I do commend to your content:
Only I carry winged time
Post on the lame feet of my rhyme;
Which never could I so convey,
Unless your thoughts went on my way.
Dionyza does appear,
With Leonine, a murderer.

[*Exit*

SCENE I. *Tarsus. An open place near the sea-shore*

Enter DIONYZA *with* LEONINE

DIONYZA

Thy oath remember; thou hast sworn to do 't:
'Tis but a blow, which never shall be known.
Thou canst not do a thing in the world so soon,
To yield thee so much profit. Let not conscience,
Which is but cold, inflaming love i' thy bosom,
Inflame too nicely; nor let pity, which
Even women have cast off, melt thee, but be
A soldier to thy purpose.

LEONINE

I will do 't; but yet she is a goodly creature.

DIONYZA

The fitter then the gods should have her. Here she
comes weeping for her only mistress' death. Thou
art resolved?

LEONINE

I am resolved.

Enter MARINA, *with a basket of flowers*

MARINA

No, I will rob Tellus of her weed,
To strew thy green with flowers: the yellows, blues,
The purple violets, and marigolds,
Shall, as a carpet, hang upon thy grave,
While summer-days do last. Ay me! poor maid,
Born in a tempest, when my mother died,
This world to me is like a lasting storm,
Whirring me from my friends.

DIONYZA

How now, Marina! why do you keep alone?
How chance my daughter is not with you?
Do not consume your blood with sorrowing:
You have a nurse of me. Lord, how your favour's
Changed with this unprofitable woe!
Come, give me **your** flowers, ere the sea mar it.
Walk with Leonine; the air is quick there,
And it pierces and sharpens the stomach.
Come, Leonine, take her by the arm, walk with her.

MARINA

No, I pray you; I'll not bereave you of your servant.

DIONYZA

Come, come;
I love the king your father and yourself
With more than foreign heart. We every day
Expect him here: when he shall come, and find
Our paragon to all reports thus blasted,
He will repent the breadth of his great voyage;
Blame both my lord and me, that we have taken
No care to your best courses. Go, I pray you,
Walk, and be cheerful once again; reserve
That excellent complexion, which did steal
The eyes of young and old. Care not for me;
I can go home alone.

MARINA
Well, I will go;
But yet I have no desire to it.

DIONYZA
Come, come, I know 'tis good for you.
Walk half an hour, Leonine, at the least:
Remember what I have said.

LEONINE
I warrant you, madam.

DIONYZA
I'll leave you, my sweet lady, for a while:
Pray, walk softly, do not heat your blood:
What! I must have care of you.

MARINA
My thanks, sweet madam.
[Exit DIONYZA
Is this wind westerly that blows?

LEONINE
South-west.

MARINA
When I was born, the wind was north.

LEONINE
Was 't so?

MARINA
My father, as nurse said, did never fear,
But cried 'Good seamen!' to the sailors, galling
His kingly hands, haling ropes;
And, clasping to the mast, endured a sea
That almost burst the deck.

LEONINE
When was this?

MARINA
When I was born:
Never was waves nor wind more violent;
And from the ladder-tackle washes off
A canvas-climber. 'Ha!' says one, 'wilt out?'
And with a dropping industry they skip
From stem to stern: the boatswain whistles, and
The master calls and trebles their confusion.

LEONINE
Come, say your prayers.

MARINA
What mean you?

LEONINE
If you require a little space for prayer,
I grant it: pray; but be not tedious,
For the gods are quick of ear, and I am sworn
To do my work with haste.

MARINA
Why will you kill me?

LEONINE
To satisfy my lady.

MARINA
Why would she have me kill'd?
Now, as I can remember, by my troth,
I never did her hurt in all my life:
I never spake bad word, nor did ill turn
To any living creature: believe me, la,
I never kill'd a mouse, nor hurt a fly:
I trod upon a worm against my will,

But I wept for it. How have I offended,
Wherein my death might yield her any profit,
Or my life imply her any danger?

LEONINE
My commission
Is not to reason of the deed, but do 't.

MARINA
You will not do 't for all the world, I hope.
You are well favour'd, and your looks foreshow
You have a gentle heart. I saw you lately,
When you caught hurt in parting two that fought:
Good sooth, it show'd well in you: do so now:
Your lady seeks my life; come you between,
And save poor me, the weaker.

LEONINE
I am sworn,
And will dispatch.   [He seizes her
Enter PIRATES

FIRST PIRATE
Hold, villain!   [LEONINE runs away

SECOND PIRATE
A prize! a prize!

THIRD PIRATE
Half-part, mates, half-part. Come let's have her
aboard suddenly.   [Exeunt PIRATES with MARINA
Re-enter LEONINE

LEONINE
These roguing thieves serve the great pirate Valdes;
And they have seized Marina. Let her go:
There's no hope she will return. I'll swear she's
    dead,
And thrown into the sea. But I'll see further:
Perhaps they will but please themselves upon her,
Not carry her aboard. If she remain,
Whom they have ravish'd must by me be slain. [Exit

SCENE II. Mytilene. A room in a brothel

Enter PANDAR, BAWD, and BOULT

PANDAR
Boult!

BOULT
Sir?

PANDAR
Search the market narrowly; Mytilene is full of
gallants. We lost too much money this mart by being
too wenchless.

BAWD
We were never so much out of creatures. We have
but poor three, and they can do no more than they
can do; and they with continual action are even as
good as rotten.

PANDAR
Therefore let's have fresh ones, whate'er we pay for
them. If there be not a conscience to be used in
every trade, we shall never prosper.

BAWD
Thou sayest true: 'tis not our bringing up of poor

bastards,—as, I think, I have brought up some eleven—

BOULT

Ay, to eleven; and brought them down again. But shall I search the market?

BAWD

What else, man? The stuff we have, a strong wind will blow it to pieces, they are so pitifully sodden.

PANDAR

Thou sayest true; they're too unwholesome, o' conscience. The poor Transylvanian is dead, that lay with the little baggage.

BOULT

Ay, she quickly pooped him; she made him roast-meat for worms. But I'll go search the market. [Exit

PANDAR

Three or four thousand chequins were as pretty a proportion to live quietly, and so give over.

BAWD

Why to give over, I pray you? is it a shame to get when we are old?

PANDAR

O, our credit comes not in like the commodity, nor the commodity wages not with the danger: therefore, if in our youths we could pick up some pretty estate, 'twere not amiss to keep our door hatched. Besides, the sore terms we stand upon with the gods will be strong with us for giving o'er.

BAWD

Come, other sorts offend as well as we.

PANDAR

As well as we! ay, and better too; we offend worse. Neither is our profession any trade; it's no calling. But here comes Boult.

Re-enter BOULT, *with the* PIRATES *and* MARINA

BOULT

[*To* MARINA] Come your ways. My masters, you say she's a virgin?

FIRST PIRATE

O, sir, we doubt it not.

BOULT

Master, I have gone through for this piece, you see: if you like her, so; if not, I have lost my earnest.

BAWD

Boult, has she any qualities?

BOULT

She has a good face, speaks well, and has excellent good clothes: there's no farther necessity of qualities can make her be refused.

BAWD

What's her price, Boult?

BOULT

I cannot be bated one doit of a thousand pieces.

PANDAR

Well, follow me, my masters, you shall have your money presently. Wife, take her in; instruct her what she has to do, that she may not be raw in her entertainment. [*Exeunt* PANDAR *and* PIRATES

BAWD

Boult, take you the marks of her, the colour of her

hair, complexion, height, her age, with warrant of her virginity; and cry 'He that will give most shall have her first.' Such a maidenhead were no cheap thing, if men were as they have been. Get this done as I command you.

BOULT

Performance shall follow. [*Exit*

MARINA

Alack that Leonine was so slack, so slow!
He should have struck, not spoke; or that these pirates,
Not enough barbarous, had not o'erboard thrown me
For to seek my mother!

BAWD

Why lament you, pretty one?

MARINA

That I am pretty.

BAWD

Come, the gods have done their part in you.

MARINA

I accuse them not.

BAWD

You are light into my hands, where you are like to live.

MARINA

The more my fault,
To 'scape his hands where I was like to die.

BAWD

Ay, and you shall live in pleasure

MARINA

No.

BAWD

Yes, indeed shall you, and taste gentlemen of all fashions: you shall fare well; you shall have the difference of all complexions. What! do you stop your ears?

MARINA

Are you a woman?

BAWD

What would you have me be, an I be not a woman?

MARINA

An honest woman, or not a woman.

BAWD

Marry, whip thee, gosling: I think I shall have something to do with you. Come, you're a young foolish sapling, and must be bowed as I would have you.

MARINA

The gods defend me!

BAWD

If it please the gods to defend you by men, then men must comfort you, men must feed you, men must stir you up. Boult's returned.

Re-enter BOULT

Now, sir, hast thou cried her through the market?

BOULT

I have cried her almost to the number of her hairs; I have drawn her picture with my voice.

BAWD

And I prithee tell me, how dost thou find the inclination of the people, especially of the younger sort?

BOULT

Faith, they listened to me as they would have hearkened to their father's testament. There was a Spaniard's mouth so watered, that he went to bed to her very description.

BAWD

We shall have him here to-morrow with his best ruff on.

BOULT

To-night, to-night. But, mistress, do you know the French knight that cowers i' the hams?

BAWD

Who, Monsieur Veroles?

BOULT

Ay, he: he offered to cut a caper at the proclamation; but he made a groan at it, and swore he would see her to-morrow.

BAWD

Well, well; as for him, he brought his disease hither: here he does but repair it. I know he will come in our shadow, to scatter his crowns in the sun.

BOULT

Well, if we had of every nation a traveller, we should lodge them with this sign.

BAWD

Pray you, come hither awhile. You have fortunes coming upon you. Mark me: you must seem to do that fearfully which you commit willingly, despise profit where you have most gain. To weep that you live as ye do makes pity in your lovers: seldom but that pity begets you a good opinion, and that opinion a mere profit.

MARINA

I understand you not.

BOULT

O, take her home, mistress, take her home: these blushes of hers must be quenched with some present practice.

BAWD

Thou sayest true, i' faith, so they must; for your bride goes to that with shame which is her way to go with warrant.

BOULT

Faith, some do, and some do not. But, mistress, if I have bargained for the joint,—

BAWD

Thou mayst cut a morsel off the spit.

BOULT

I may so.

BAWD

Who should deny it? Come, young one, I like the manner of your garments well.

BOULT

Ay, by my faith, they shall not be changed yet.

BAWD

Boult, spend thou that in the town: report what a

sojourner we have; you'll lose nothing by custom. When nature framed this piece, she meant thee a good turn; therefore say what a paragon she is, and thou hast the harvest out of thine own report.

BOULT

I warrant you, mistress, thunder shall not so awake the beds of eels as my giving out her beauty stir up the lewdly-inclined. I'll bring home some to-night.

BAWD

Come your ways; follow me.

MARINA

If fires be hot, knives are sharp, or waters deep,
Untied I still my virgin knot will keep.
Diana, aid my purpose!

BAWD

What have we to do with Diana? Pray you, will you go with us?　　　　　　　　　　　　[Exeunt

SCENE III. Tarsus. A room in the Governor's house

Enter CLEON and DIONYZA

DIONYZA

Why, are you foolish? Can it be undone?

CLEON

O Dionyza, such a piece of slaughter
The sun and moon ne'er look'd upon!

DIONYZA

　　　　　　　　　　　　　　　I think

You'll turn a child again.

CLEON

Were I chief lord of all this spacious world,
I'ld give it to undo the deed. O lady,
Much less in blood than virtue, yet a princess
To equal any single crown o' the earth
I' the justice of compare! O villain Leonine!
Whom thou hast poison'd too:
If thou hadst drunk to him, 't had been a kindness
Becoming well thy fact: what canst thou say
When noble Pericles shall demand his child?

DIONYZA

That she is dead. Nurses are not the fates,
To foster it, nor ever to preserve.
She died at night; I'll say so. Who can cross it?
Unless you play the pious innocent,
And for an honest attribute cry out
'She died by foul play.'

CLEON

　　　　　　　O, go to. Well, well,
Of all the faults beneath the heavens, the gods
Do like this worst.

DIONYZA

　　　　　　　　Be one of those that think
The petty wrens of Tarsus will fly hence
And open this to Pericles. I do shame
To think of what a noble strain you are
And of how coward a spirit.

CLEON

　　　　　　　　　To such proceeding
Who ever but his approbation added,

[1204]

Though not his prime consent, he did not flow
From honourable sources.

DIONYZA

Be it so, then:
Yet none does know, but you, how she came dead,
Nor none can know, Leonine being gone.
She did distain my child, and stood between
Her and her fortunes: none would look on her,
But cast their gazes on Marina's face;
Whilst ours was blurted at, and held a malkin,
Not worth the time of day. It pierced me thorough;
And though you call my course unnatural,
You not your child well loving, yet I find
It greets me as an enterprise of kindness
Perform'd to your sole daughter.

CLEON

Heavens forgive it!

DIONYZA

And as for Pericles,
What should he say? We wept after her hearse,
And yet we mourn: her monument
Is almost finish'd, and her epitaphs
In glittering golden characters express
A general praise to her, and care in us
At whose expense 'tis done.

CLEON

Thou art like the harpy,
Which, to betray, dost, with thine angel's face,
Seize with thine eagle's talons.

DIONYZA

You are like one that superstitiously
Doth swear to the gods that winter kills the flies:
But yet I know you'll do as I advise.　　　[Exeunt

SCENE IV

Enter GOWER, *before the monument of* MARINA *at Tarsus*

GOWER

Thus time we waste, and longest leagues make
　　short;
Sail seas in cockles, have and wish but for 't;
Making, to take our imagination,
From bourn to bourn, region to region.
By you being pardon'd, we commit no crime
To use one language in each several clime
Where our scenes seem to live. I do beseech you
To learn of me, who stand i' the gaps to teach you
The stages of our story. Pericles
Is now again thwarting the wayward seas,
Attended on by many a lord and knight,
To see his daughter, all his life's delight.
Old Helicanus goes along: behind
Is left to govern it, you bear in mind
Old Escanes, whom Helicanus late
Advanced in time to great and high estate.
Well-sailing ships and bounteous winds have
　　brought
This king to Tarsus,—think his pilot thought;

So with his steerage shall your thoughts grow on,—
To fetch his daughter home, who first is gone.
Like motes and shadows see them move awhile;
Your ears unto your eyes I'll reconcile.

DUMB SHOW

Enter PERICLES *at one door, with all his train;* CLEON
and DIONYZA *at the other.* CLEON *shows* PERICLES *the
tomb; whereat* PERICLES *makes lamentation, puts on sackcloth, and in a mighty passion departs. Then exeunt* CLEON,
DIONYZA, *and the rest*

See how belief may suffer by foul show!
This borrow'd passion stands for true old woe;
And Pericles, in sorrow all devour'd,
With sighs shot through and biggest tears o'er-
　　shower'd,
Leaves Tarsus and again embarks. He swears
Never to wash his face, nor cut his hairs:
He puts on sackcloth, and to sea. He bears
A tempest, which his mortal vessel tears,
And yet he rides it out. Now please you wit
The epitaph is for Marina writ
By wicked Dionyza.

[Reads the inscription on MARINA'S *monument*

'The fairest, sweet'st and best, lies here,
　Who wither'd in her spring of year,
　She was of Tyrus the king's daughter,
　On whom foul death hath made this slaughter;
　Marina was she call'd; and at her birth,
　Thetis, being proud, swallow'd some part o' the earth:
　Therefore the earth, fearing to be o'erflow'd,
　Hath Thetis' birth-child on the heavens bestow'd:
　Wherefore she does, and swears she'll never stint,
　Make raging battery upon shores of flint.'

No visor does become black villany
So well as soft and tender flattery.
Let Pericles believe his daughter's dead,
And bear his courses to be ordered
By Lady Fortune; while our scene must play
His daughter's woe and heavy well-a-day
In her unholy service. Patience, then,
And think you now are all in Mytilene.　　　[Exit

SCENE V. *Mytilene. A street before the brothel*

Enter, from the brothel, two GENTLEMEN

FIRST GENTLEMAN

Did you ever hear the like?

SECOND GENTLEMAN

No, nor never shall do in such a place as this, she
being once gone.

FIRST GENTLEMAN

But to have divinity preached there! did you ever
dream of such a thing?

SECOND GENTLEMAN

No, no. Come, I am for no more bawdy-houses:
shall 's go hear the vestals sing?

FIRST GENTLEMAN

I'll do any thing now that is virtuous; but I am out
of the road of rutting for ever.　　　[Exeunt

SCENE VI. *The same. A room in the brothel*

Enter PANDAR, BAWD, *and* BOULT

PANDAR

Well, I had rather than twice the worth of her she had ne'er come here.

BAWD

Fie, fie upon her! she's able to freeze the god Priapus, and undo a whole generation. We must either get her ravished or be rid of her. When she should do for clients her fitment and do me the kindness of our profession, she has me her quirks, her reasons, her master reasons, her prayers, her knees; that she would make a puritan of the devil, if he should cheapen a kiss of her.

BOULT

Faith, I must ravish her, or she'll disfurnish us of all our cavaliers and make all our swearers priests.

PANDAR

Now, the pox upon her green-sickness for me!

BAWD

Faith, there's no way to be rid on 't but by the way to the pox. Here comes the Lord Lysimachus disguised.

BOULT

We should have both lord and lown, if the peevish baggage would but give way to customers.

Enter LYSIMACHUS

LYSIMACHUS

How now! How a dozen of virginities?

BAWD

Now, the gods to-bless your honour!

BOULT

I am glad to see your honour in good health.

LYSIMACHUS

You may so; 'tis the better for you that your resorters stand upon sound legs. How now, wholesome iniquity have you that a man may deal withal, and defy the surgeon?

BAWD

We have here one, sir, if she would—but there never came her like in Mytilene.

LYSIMACHUS

If she'ld do the deed of darkness, thou wouldst say.

BAWD

Your honour knows what 'tis to say well enough.

LYSIMACHUS

Well, call forth, call forth.

BOULT

For flesh and blood, sir, white and red, you shall see a rose; and she were a rose indeed, if she had but—

LYSIMACHUS

What, prithee?

BOULT

O, sir, I can be modest.

LYSIMACHUS

That dignifies the renown of a bawd, no less than it gives a good report to a number to be chaste.

[*Exit* BOULT

BAWD

Here comes that which grows to the stalk; never plucked yet, I can assure you.

Re-enter BOULT *with* MARINA

Is she not a fair creature?

LYSIMACHUS

Faith, she would serve after a long voyage at sea. Well, there's for you: leave us.

BAWD

I beseech your honour, give me leave: a word, and I'll have done presently.

LYSIMACHUS

I beseech you, do.

BAWD

[*To* MARINA] First, I would have you note, this is an honourable man.

MARINA

I desire to find him so, that I may worthily note him.

BAWD

Next, he's the governor of this country, and a man whom I am bound to.

MARINA

If he govern the country, you are bound to him indeed; but how honourable he is in that, I know not.

BAWD

Pray you, without any more virginal fencing, will you use him kindly? He will line your apron with gold.

MARINA

What he will do graciously, I will thankfully receive.

LYSIMACHUS

Ha' you done?

BAWD

My lord, she's not paced yet: you must take some pains to work her to your manage. Come, we will leave his honour and her together. Go thy ways.

[*Exeunt* BAWD, PANDAR, *and* BOULT

LYSIMACHUS

Now, pretty one, how long have you been at this trade?

MARINA

What trade, sir?

LYSIMACHUS

Why, I cannot name 't but I shall offend.

MARINA

I cannot be offended with my trade. Please you to name it.

LYSIMACHUS

How long have you been of this profession?

MARINA

E'er since I can remember.

LYSIMACHUS

Did you go to 't so young? Were you a gamester at five or at seven?

MARINA

Earlier too, sir, if now I be one.

LYSIMACHUS

Why, the house you dwell in proclaims you to be a creature of sale.

MARINA

Do you know this house to be a place of such resort, and will come into 't? I hear say you are of honourable parts and are the governor of this place.

LYSIMACHUS

Why, hath your principal made known unto you who I am?

MARINA

Who is my principal?

LYSIMACHUS

Why, your herb-woman; she that sets seeds and roots of shame and iniquity. O, you have heard something of my power, and so stand aloof for more serious wooing. But I protest to thee, pretty one, my authority shall not see thee, or else look friendly upon thee. Come, bring me to some private place: come, come.

MARINA

If you were born to honour, show it now;
If put upon you, make the judgement good
That thought you worthy of it.

LYSIMACHUS

How's this? how's this? Some more; be sage.

MARINA

                   For me
That am a maid, though most ungentle fortune
Have placed me in this sty, where, since I came,
Diseases have been sold dearer than physic,
O, that the gods
Would set me free from this unhallow'd place,
Though they did change me to the meanest bird
That flies i' the purer air!

LYSIMACHUS

          I did not think
Thou couldst have spoke so well; ne'er dream'd thou couldst.
Had I brought hither a corrupted mind,
Thy speech had alter'd it. Hold, here's gold for thee.
Persever in that clear way thou goest,
And the gods strengthen thee!

MARINA

           The good gods preserve you!

LYSIMACHUS

For me, be you thoughten
That I came with no ill intent; for to me
The very doors and windows savour vilely.
Fare thee well. Thou art a piece of virtue, and
I doubt not but thy training hath been noble.
Hold, here's more gold for thee.
A curse upon him, die he like a thief,
That robs thee of thy goodness! If thou dost
Hear from me, it shall be for thy good.

Re-enter BOULT

BOULT

I beseech your honour, one piece for me.

LYSIMACHUS

Avaunt, thou damned door-keeper!
Your house, but for this virgin that doth prop it,
Would sink, and overwhelm you. Away!   [*Exit*

BOULT

How's this? We must take another course with you. If your peevish chastity, which is not worth a breakfast in the cheapest country under the cope, shall undo a whole household, let me be gelded like a spaniel. Come your ways.

MARINA

Whither would you have me?

BOULT

I must have your maidenhead taken off, or the common hangman shall execute it. Come your ways. We'll have no more gentlemen driven away. Come your ways, I say.

Re-enter BAWD

BAWD

How now! what's the matter?

BOULT

Worse and worse, mistress; she has here spoken holy words to the Lord Lysimachus.

BAWD

O abominable!

BOULT

She makes our profession as it were to stink afore the face of the gods.

BAWD

Marry, hang her up for ever!

BOULT

The nobleman would have dealt with her like a nobleman, and she sent him away as cold as a snowball, saying his prayers too.

BAWD

Boult, take her away; use her at thy pleasure: crack the glass of her virginity, and make the rest malleable.

BOULT

An if she were a thornier piece of ground than she is, she shall be ploughed.

MARINA

Hark, hark, you gods!

BAWD

She conjures: away with her! Would she had never come within my doors! Marry, hang you! She's born to undo us. Will you not go the way of womenkind? Marry, come up, my dish of chastity with rosemary and bays!   [*Exit*

BOULT

Come, mistress; come your ways with me.

MARINA

Whither wilt thou have me?

BOULT

To take from you the jewel you hold so dear.

MARINA
Prithee, tell me one thing first.

BOULT
Come now, your one thing.

MARINA
What canst thou wish thine enemy to be?

BOULT
Why, I could wish him to be my master, or rather,
my mistress.

MARINA
Neither of these are so bad as thou art,
Since they do better thee in their command.
Thou hold'st a place, for which the pained'st fiend
Of hell would not in reputation change:
Thou art the damned door-keeper to every
Coistrel that comes inquiring for his Tib;
To the choleric fisting of every rogue
Thy ear is liable; thy food is such
As hath been belch'd on by infected lungs.

BOULT
What would you have me do? go to the wars, would
you? where a man may serve seven years for the
loss of a leg, and have not money enough in the end
to buy him a wooden one?

MARINA
Do any thing but this thou doest. Empty
Old receptacles, or common shores, of filth;
Serve by indenture to the common hangman:
Any of these ways are yet better than this;
For what thou professest, a baboon, could he speak,
Would own a name too dear. O, that the gods
Would safely deliver me from this place!
Here, here's gold for thee.
If that thy master would gain by me,
Proclaim that I can sing, weave, sew, and dance,
With other virtues, which I'll keep from boast;
And I will undertake all these to teach.
I doubt not but this populous city will
Yield many scholars.

BOULT
But can you teach all this you speak of?

MARINA
Prove that I cannot, take me home again,
And prostitute me to the basest groom
That doth frequent your house.

BOULT
Well, I will see what I can do for thee: if I can place
thee, I will.

MARINA
But amongst honest women.

BOULT
Faith, my acquaintance lies little amongst them.
But since my master and mistress have bought you,
there's no going but by their consent: therefore I
will make them acquainted with your purpose, and
I doubt not but I shall find them tractable enough.
Come, I'll do for thee what I can; come your ways.
[Exeunt

ACT V

Enter GOWER

GOWER
Marina thus the brothel 'scapes, and chances
Into an honest house, our story says.
She sings like one immortal, and she dances
As goddess-like to her admired lays;
Deep clerks she dumbs, and with her needle com-
    poses
Nature's own shape, of bud, bird, branch, or berry,
That even her art sisters the natural roses;
Her inkle, silk, twin with the rubied cherry:
That pupils lacks she none of noble race,
Who pour their bounty on her, and her gain
She gives the cursed bawd. Here we her place;
And to her father turn our thoughts again,
Where we left him, on the sea. We there him lost:
Whence, driven before the winds, he is arrived
Here where his daughter dwells; and on this coast
Suppose him now at anchor. The city strived
God Neptune's annual feast to keep: from whence
Lysimachus our Tyrian ship espies,
His banners sable, trimm'd with rich expense;
And to him in his barge with fervour hies.
In your supposing once more put your sight
Of heavy Pericles; think this his bark:
Where what is done in action, more, if might,
Shall be discover'd; please you, sit, and hark. [*Exit*

SCENE I. *On board* PERICLES' *ship, off Mytilene. A close
pavilion on deck, with a curtain before it;* PERICLES *within
it, reclined on a couch. A barge lying beside the Tyrian
vessel*

Enter two SAILORS, *one belonging to the Tyrian vessel,
the other to the barge; to them* HELICANUS

TYRIAN SAILOR
[*To the* SAILOR *of Mytilene*] Where is Lord Helicanus?
    he can resolve you.
O, here he is.
Sir, there is a barge put off from Mytilene,
And in it is Lysimachus the governor,
Who craves to come aboard. What is your will?

HELICANUS
That he have his. Call up some gentlemen.

TYRIAN SAILOR
Ho, gentlemen! my lord calls.

Enter two or three GENTLEMEN

FIRST GENTLEMAN
Doth your lordship call?

HELICANUS
Gentlemen, there is some of worth would come
aboard; I pray, greet him fairly.
[*The* GENTLEMEN *and the two* SAILORS *descend, and go
    on board the barge*
Enter from thence, LYSIMACHUS, *and* LORDS; *with the*
GENTLEMEN *and the two* SAILORS

TYRIAN SAILOR

Sir,
This is the man that can, in aught you would,
Resolve you.

LYSIMACHUS

Hail, reverend sir! the gods preserve you!

HELICANUS

And you, sir, to outlive the age I am,
And die as I would do.

LYSIMACHUS

        You wish me well.
Being on shore, honouring of Neptune's triumphs,
Seeing this goodly vessel ride before us,
I made to it, to know of whence you are.

HELICANUS

First, what is your place?

LYSIMACHUS

        I am the governor
Of this place you lie before.

HELICANUS

Sir,
Our vessel is of Tyre, in it the king;
A man who for this three months hath not spoken
To any one, nor taken sustenance
But to prorogue his grief.

LYSIMACHUS

Upon what ground is his distemperature?

HELICANUS

'Twould be too tedious to repeat;
But the main grief springs from the loss
Of a beloved daughter and a wife.

LYSIMACHUS

May we not see him?

HELICANUS

You may;
But bootless is your sight; he will not speak
To any.

LYSIMACHUS

Yet let me obtain my wish.

HELICANUS

Behold him. [PERICLES discovered] This was a goodly
    person,
Till the disaster that, one mortal night,
Drove him to this.

LYSIMACHUS

Sir king, all hail! the gods preserve you!
Hail, royal sir!

HELICANUS

It is in vain; he will not speak to you.

FIRST LORD

Sir,
We have a maid in Mytilene, I durst wager,
Would win some words of him.

LYSIMACHUS

        'Tis well bethought.
She, questionless, with her sweet harmony
And other chosen attractions, would allure,
And make a battery through his deafen'd parts,
Which now are midway stopp'd:

She is all happy as the fairest of all,
And with her fellow maids is now upon
The leafy shelter that abuts against
The island's side.   [Whispers
a LORD, who goes off in the barge of LYSIMACHUS

HELICANUS

Sure, all's effectless; yet nothing we'll omit
That bears recovery's name. But, since your kind-
    ness
We have stretch'd thus far, let us beseech you
That for our gold we may provision have,
Wherein we are not destitute for want,
But weary for the staleness.

LYSIMACHUS

        O, sir, a courtesy
Which if we should deny, the most just gods
For every graff would send a caterpillar,
And so inflict our province. Yet once more
Let me entreat to know at large the cause
Of your king's sorrow.

HELICANUS

      Sit, sir, I will recount it to you.
But, see, I am prevented.
Re-enter, from the barge, LORD, with MARINA, and a
      young LADY

LYSIMACHUS

        O, here is
The lady that I sent for. Welcome, fair one!—
Is 't not a goodly presence?

HELICANUS

        She's a gallant lady.

LYSIMACHUS

She's such a one, that, were I well assured
Came of a gentle kind and noble stock,
I'ld wish no better choice, and think me rarely wed.
Fair one, all goodness that consists in bounty
Expect even here, where is a kingly patient:
If that thy prosperous and artificial feat
Can draw him but to answer thee in aught,
Thy sacred physic shall receive such pay
As thy desires can wish.

MARINA

        Sir, I will use
My utmost skill in his recovery, provided
That none but I and my companion maid
Be suffer'd to come near him.

LYSIMACHUS

       Come, let us leave her;
And the gods make her prosperous!   [MARINA sings

LYSIMACHUS

Mark'd he your music?

MARINA

No, nor look'd on us.

LYSIMACHUS

See, she will speak to him.

MARINA

Hail, sir! my lord, lend ear.

PERICLES

Hum, ha!

MARINA

I am a maid,
My lord, that ne'er before invited eyes,
But have been gazed on like a comet: she speaks,
My lord, that, may be, hath endured a grief
Might equal yours, if both were justly weigh'd.
Though wayward fortune did malign my state,
My derivation was from ancestors
Who stood equivalent with mighty kings:
But time hath rooted out my parentage,
And to the world and awkward casualties
Bound me in servitude. [Aside] I will desist;
But there is something glows upon my cheek,
And whispers in mine ear 'Go not till he speak.'

PERICLES

My fortunes—parentage—good parentage—
To equal mine!—was it not thus? what say you?

MARINA

I said, my lord, if you did know my parentage,
You would not do me violence.

PERICLES

I do think so. Pray you, turn your eyes upon me.
You are like something that—What countrywoman?
Here of these shores?

MARINA

No, nor of any shores:
Yet I was mortally brought forth, and am
No other than I appear.

PERICLES

I am great with woe, and shall deliver weeping.
My dearest wife was like this maid, and such a one
My daughter might have been: my queen's square
brows;
Her stature to an inch; as wand-like straight,
As silver-voiced; her eyes as jewel-like
And cased as richly; in pace another Juno;
Who starves the ears she feeds, and makes them
hungry,
The more she gives them speech. Where do you
live?

MARINA

Where I am but a stranger: from the deck
You may discern the place.

PERICLES

Where were you bred?
And how achieved you these endowments, which
You make more rich to owe?

MARINA

If I should tell my history, it would seem
Like lies disdain'd in the reporting.

PERICLES

Prithee, speak:
Falseness cannot come from thee; for thou look'st
Modest as Justice, and thou seem'st a palace
For the crown'd Truth to dwell in: I will believe
thee,
And make my senses credit thy relation
To points that seem impossible; for thou look'st
Like one I loved indeed. What were thy friends?
Didst thou not say, when I did push thee back—

Which was when I perceived thee—that thou
camest
From good descending?

MARINA

So indeed I did.

PERICLES

Report thy parentage. I think thou said'st
Thou hadst been toss'd from wrong to injury,
And that thou thought'st thy griefs might equal
mine,
If both were open'd.

MARINA

Some such thing
I said, and said no more but what my thoughts
Did warrant me was likely.

PERICLES

Tell thy story;
If thine consider'd prove the thousandth part
Of my endurance, thou art a man, and I
Have suffer'd like a girl: yet thou dost look
Like Patience gazing on kings' graves and smiling
Extremity out of act. What were thy friends?
How lost thou them? Thy name, my most kind vir-
gin?
Recount, I do beseech thee: come, sit by me.

MARINA

My name is Marina.

PERICLES

O, I am mock'd,
And thou by some incensed god sent hither
To make the world to laugh at me.

MARINA

Patience, good sir,
Or here I'll cease.

PERICLES

Nay, I'll be patient.
Thou little know'st how thou dost startle me,
To call thyself Marina.

MARINA

The name
Was given me by one that had some power,
My father, and a king.

PERICLES

How! a king's daughter?
And call'd Marina?

MARINA

You said you would believe me;
But, not to be a troubler of your peace,
I will end here.

PERICLES

But are you flesh and blood?
Have you a working pulse? and are no fairy?
Motion! Well; speak on. Where were you born?
And wherefore call'd Marina?

MARINA

Call'd Marina
For I was born at sea.

PERICLES

At sea! what mother?

MARINA

My mother was the daughter of a king;
Who died the minute I was born,
As my good nurse Lychorida hath oft
Deliver'd weeping.

PERICLES

O, stop there a little!
[*Aside*] This is the rarest dream that e'er dull sleep
Did mock sad fools withal: this cannot be:
My daughter's buried.—Well: where were you
  bred?
I'll hear you more, to the bottom of your story,
And never interrupt you.

MARINA

You scorn: believe me, 'twere best I did give o'er.

PERICLES

I will believe you by the syllable
Of what you shall deliver. Yet, give me leave:
How came you in these parts? where were you bred?

MARINA

The king my father did in Tarsus leave me;
Till cruel Cleon, with his wicked wife,
Did seek to murder me: and having woo'd
A villain to attempt it, who having drawn to do 't,
A crew of pirates came and rescued me;
Brought me to Mytilene. But, good sir,
Whither will you have me? Why do you weep? It
  may be,
You think me an impostor: no, good faith;
I am the daughter to King Pericles,
If good King Pericles be.

PERICLES

Ho, Helicanus!

HELICANUS

Calls my lord?

PERICLES

Thou art a grave and noble counsellor,
Most wise in general: tell me, if thou canst,
What this maid is, or what is like to be,
That thus hath made me weep.

HELICANUS

I know not; but
Here is the regent, sir, of Mytilene
Speaks nobly of her.

LYSIMACHUS

She never would tell
Her parentage; being demanded that,
She would sit still and weep.

PERICLES

O Helicanus, strike me, honour'd sir;
Give me a gash, put me to present pain;
Lest this great sea of joys rushing upon me
O'erbear the shores of my mortality,
And drown me with their sweetness. O, come hither,
Thou that beget'st him that did thee beget;
Thou that wast born at sea, buried at Tarsus,
And found at sea again! O Helicanus,
Down on thy knees; thank the holy gods as loud
As thunder threatens us: this is Marina.
What was thy mother's name? tell me but that,

For truth can never be confirm'd enough,
Though doubts did ever sleep.

MARINA

First, sir, I pray, what is your title?

PERICLES

I
Am Pericles of Tyre: but tell me now
My drown'd queen's name, as in the rest you said
Thou hast been godlike perfect, the heir of king
  doms,
And another like to Pericles thy father.

MARINA

Is it no more to be your daughter than
To say my mother's name was Thaisa?
Thaisa was my mother, who did end
The minute I began.

PERICLES

Now, blessing on thee! rise; thou art my child.
Give me fresh garments. Mine own, Helicanus:
She is not dead at Tarsus, as she should have been,
By savage Cleon: she shall tell thee all;
When thou shalt kneel, and justify in knowledge
She is thy very princess. Who is this?

HELICANUS

Sir, 'tis the governor of Mytilene,
Who, hearing of your melancholy state,
Did come to see you.

PERICLES

I embrace you.
Give me my robes. I am wild in my beholding.
O heavens bless my girl! But, hark, what music?
Tell Helicanus, my Marina, tell him
O'er, point by point, for yet he seems to doubt,
How sure you are my daughter. But, what music?

HELICANUS

My lord, I hear none.

PERICLES

None!
The music of the spheres! List, my Marina.

LYSIMACHUS

It is not good to cross him; give him way.

PERICLES

Rarest sounds! Do ye not hear?

LYSIMACHUS

My lord, I hear.
[*Music*

PERICLES

Most heavenly music!
It nips me unto listening, and thick slumber
Hangs upon mine eyes: let me rest.   [*Sleeps*

LYSIMACHUS

A pillow for his head:
So, leave him all. Well, my companion friends,
If this but answer to my just belief,
I'll well remember you.   [*Exeunt all but* PERICLES
DIANA *appears to* PERICLES *in a vision*

DIANA

My temple stands in Ephesus: hie thee thither,
And do upon mine altar sacrifice.
There, when my maiden priests are met together,

Before the people all,
Reveal how thou at sea didst lose thy wife:
To mourn thy crosses, with thy daughter's, call,
And give them repetition to the life.
Or perform my bidding, or thou livest in woe;
Do it, and happy; by my silver bow!
Awake, and tell thy dream.   [*Disappears*

PERICLES

Celestial Dian, goddess argentine,
I will obey thee. Helicanus!

     Re-enter HELICANUS, LYSIMACHUS, *and* MARINA

HELICANUS

         Sir?

PERICLES

My purpose was for Tarsus, there to strike
The inhospitable Cleon; but I am
For other service first: toward Ephesus
Turn our blown sails; eftsoons I'll tell thee why.
[*To* LYSIMACHUS] Shall we refresh us, sir, upon your
     shore,
And give you gold for such provision
As our intents will need?

LYSIMACHUS

Sir,
With all my heart; and, when you come ashore,
I have another suit.

PERICLES

       You shall prevail,
Were it to woo my daughter; for it seems
You have been noble towards her.

LYSIMACHUS

       Sir, lend me your arm.

PERICLES

Come, my Marina.   [*Exeunt*

SCENE II

Enter GOWER, *before the temple of* DIANA *at Ephesus*

GOWER

Now our sands are almost run;
More a little, and then dumb.
This, my last boon, give me,
For such kindness must relieve me,
That you aptly will suppose
What pageantry, what feats, what shows,
What minstrelsy and pretty din,
The regent made in Mytilene,
To greet the king. So he thrived,
That he is promised to be wived
To fair Marina; but in no wise
Till he had done his sacrifice,
As Dian bade: whereto being bound,
The interim, pray you, all confound.
In feather'd briefness sails are fill'd,
And wishes fall out as they're will'd.
At Ephesus, the temple see,
Our king and all his company.
That he can hither come so soon,
Is by your fancies' thankful doom.   [*Exit*

SCENE III. *The temple of* DIANA *at Ephesus;* THAISA
standing near the altar, as high priestess; a number of
VIRGINS *on each side;* CERIMON *and other Inhabitants of*
Ephesus attending

Enter PERICLES, *with his train;* LYSIMACHUS,
HELICANUS, MARINA, *and a* LADY

PERICLES

Hail, Dian! to perform thy just command,
I here confess myself the king of Tyre;
Who, frighted from my country, did wed
At Pentapolis the fair Thaisa.
At sea in childbed died she, but brought forth
A maid-child call'd Marina; who, O goddess,
Wears yet thy silver livery. She at Tarsus
Was nursed with Cleon; who at fourteen years
He sought to murder: but her better stars
Brought her to Mytilene; 'gainst whose shore
Riding, her fortunes brought the maid aboard us,
Where, by her own most clear remembrance, she
Made known herself my daughter.

THAISA

       Voice and favour!
You are, you are—O royal Pericles!—   [*Faints*

PERICLES

What means the nun? she dies! help, gentlemen!

CERIMON

Noble sir,
If you have told Diana's altar true,
This is your wife.

PERICLES

       Reverend appearer, no;
I threw her overboard with these very arms.

CERIMON

Upon this coast, I warrant you.

PERICLES

       'Tis most certain.

CERIMON

Look to the lady. O, she's but overjoy'd.
Early in blustering morn this lady was
Thrown upon this shore. I oped the coffin,
Found there rich jewels; recover'd her, and placed
     her
Here in Diana's temple.

PERICLES

       May we see them?

CERIMON

Great sir, they shall be brought you to my house,
Whither I invite you. Look, Thaisa is
Recovered.

THAISA

       O, let me look!
If he be none of mine, my sanctity
Will to my sense bend no licentious ear,
But curb it, spite of seeing. O, my lord,
Are you not Pericles? Like him you spake,
Like him you are: did you not name a tempest,
A birth, and death?

PERICLES

       The voice of dead Thaisa!

THAISA
That Thaisa am I, supposed dead
And drown'd.

PERICLES
Immortal Dian!

THAISA
          Now I know you better.
When we with tears parted Pentapolis,
The king my father gave you such a ring.
                 [Shows a ring

PERICLES
This, this: no more, you gods! your present kindness
Makes my past miseries sports: you shall do well,
That on the touching of her lips I may
Melt, and no more be seen. O, come, be buried
A second time within these arms.

MARINA
              My heart
Leaps to be gone into my mother's bosom.
               [Kneels to THAISA

PERICLES
Look, who kneels here! Flesh of thy flesh, Thaisa;
Thy burden at the sea, and call'd Marina
For she was yielded there.

THAISA
            Blest, and mine own!

HELICANUS
Hail, madam, and my queen!

THAISA
              I know you not.

PERICLES
You have heard me say, when I did fly from Tyre,
I left behind an ancient substitute:
Can you remember what I call'd the man?
I have named him oft.

THAISA
            'Twas Helicanus then.

PERICLES
Still confirmation:
Embrace him, dear Thaisa; this is he.
Now do I long to hear how you were found;
How possibly preserved; and who to thank,
Besides the gods, for this great miracle.

THAISA
Lord Cerimon, my lord; this man,
Through whom the gods have shown their power;
   that can
From first to last resolve you.

PERICLES
            Reverend sir,

The gods can have no mortal officer
More like a god than you. Will you deliver
How this dead queen re-lives?

CERIMON
            I will, my lord.
Beseech you, first go with me to my house,
Where shall be shown you all was found with her;
How she came placed here in the temple;
No needful thing omitted.

PERICLES
Pure Dian, bless thee for thy vision! I
Will offer night-oblations to thee. Thaisa,
This prince, the fair-betrothed of your daughter,
Shall marry her at Pentapolis. And now,
This ornament
Makes me look dismal will I clip to form;
And what this fourteen years no razor touch'd,
To grace thy marriage-day, I'll beautify.

THAISA
Lord Cerimon hath letters of good credit, sir,
My father's dead.

PERICLES
Heavens make a star of him! Yet there, my queen,
We'll celebrate their nuptials, and ourselves
Will in that kingdom spend our following days:
Our son and daughter shall in Tyrus reign.
Lord Cerimon, we do our longing stay
To hear the rest untold: sir, lead 's the way. *[Exeunt*
                Enter GOWER

GOWER
In Antiochus and his daughter you have heard
Of monstrous lust the due and just reward:
In Pericles, his queen and daughter, seen,
Although assail'd with fortune fierce and keen,
Virtue preserved from fell destruction's blast,
Led on by heaven and crown'd with joy at last:
In Helicanus may you well descry
A figure of truth, of faith, of loyalty:
In reverend Cerimon there well appears
The worth that learned charity aye wears:
For wicked Cleon and his wife, when fame
Had spread their cursed deed and honour'd name
Of Pericles, to rage the city turn,
That him and his they in his palace burn;
The gods for murder seemed so content
To punish, although not done, but meant.
So, on your patience evermore attending,
New joy wait on you! Here our play has ending.
                        [Exit

CYMBELINE

SYNOPSIS

THE palace of the British king, Cymbeline, is filled with frowning courtiers who dutifully reflect his intense anger and displeasure over the private marriage of his daughter Imogen, heir to the throne, to a poor but distinguished gentleman of the court, named Posthumus, whom she has loved since childhood. Cymbeline, whose two infant sons were stolen from their nursery and never recovered, wishes Imogen to marry Cloten, the loutish son of his second wife, and he cruelly banishes Posthumus forever from his native land.

In parting, the anguished couple give each other keepsakes with which they vow never to part. Imogen presents her husband with a fine diamond ring, an heirloom, while Posthumus clasps a rare bracelet on his wife's arm. Wishing to place her son on the British throne, the scheming, treacherous Queen urges Cloten to press his attentions upon Imogen, who tells him that she hates him.

Meanwhile Posthumus arrives in Rome, his destination, and meets at a friend's house an evil-minded Italian, Iachimo, who is scoffing at the chastity of women in general, and, after a lengthy argument with Posthumus, expresses his doubt of the constancy of even the Briton's highly praised wife. In a fury of exasperation, Posthumus accepts the man's wager of a large sum of money against Imogen's gift, the diamond ring, that he will accomplish her dishonor and get possession of the bracelet given her by her husband.

Iachimo is graciously received in Britain by Imogen as a friend of Posthumus, but his love-making is repulsed with utter disdain. Craftily, he recovers her goodwill in order to gain admittance to her bedchamber that night in a large trunk, which she agrees to protect for him since it contains, according to his pretence, a rich present for the Roman emperor. While she sleeps, he makes accurate mental notes of her room and person, especially of an unusual mole on her neck, and slips the bracelet from her arm. With his testimony artfully presented, and enhanced with downright lies, Iachimo succeeds in breaking down Posthumus' faith in his wife's loyalty, and the diamond ring is delivered to him.

Nothing now can exceed Posthumus' jealous rage. He plans his wife's death by directing her to go to Milford Haven, ostensibly to meet him but actually to be killed by his order which he sends to his man, Pisanio, whom he informs of his wife's infidelity. Imogen joyfully starts out, accompanied by Pisanio, who, on the way to Milford Haven, shows her Posthumus' inhuman letter of instructions. He begs the heartbroken woman to consider her husband deceived; to punish him by thinking her dead; then to seek him out in Rome. He persuades her to disguise herself in the boy's clothing he has brought, and enlist in the service of the Roman Ambassador now going to Italy. Pisanio speeds back to court to avoid suspicion. Before he goes, however, he urges Imogen to use, when fatigued, what he thinks is a soothing cordial which the malicious Queen has given him, wishing to kill him and believing that the court physician had concocted a poison at her request, whereas it is only a sleeping draught that stupefies for a time.

Imogen loses her way in the Welsh mountains and comes, faint and hungry, to a cave where Belarius, a banished nobleman, lives disguised as a peasant. With him are the King's two sons, now grown to manhood, whom he abducted in their infancy in revenge for his unjust banishment. They are strongly attracted to Imogen and entertain her so delightfully that she lingers in their cave.

Pisanio is beset with the revengeful Cloten's threats of death and, thinking Imogen has escaped, gives him information of her flight and a suit of Posthumus' clothes in which he starts on a venomous errand to Milford Haven, where he encounters and insults one of Imogen's mountaineer brothers, who cuts off his head, throws it into the sea, and covers the body lightly with leaves in a grove. Sorrowing and distracted over her husband's acts, Imogen drinks the cordial and falls into a death-like sleep. Her grieving brothers, with beautiful ceremony, place her body near Cloten's. Awakening, she discovers what she mistakes for Posthumus' headless body, and in her despair she enlists as a page in the service of the Roman general, Lucius, who is invading Britain to exact the lawful tribute which the Queen has persuaded Cymbeline to disregard.

With the Roman forces come Iachimo and Posthumus. The latter, disguised as a peasant, fights with great bravery for Britain, while, at a critical juncture, Belarius and the two princes splendidly turn the tide of battle into complete victory for their country. When the prisoners are assembled in Cymbeline's tent, Imogen, still as a Roman page, espies her diamond ring on Iachimo's hand, and wins the King's help to force the man's confession. The frustrated Queen has just died, and her full intrigue is revealed. Posthumus, who has been praying for death, is united with the forgiving Imogen, and pardons Iachimo. The King joyfully receives his newly-found sons, and pardons Belarius. He releases the Roman general, Lucius, and, notwithstanding the British victory, promises payment to Rome of her tribute, in order to guarantee peace.

HISTORICAL DATA

The pseudo-historical elements of *Cymbeline* are derived from Holinshed, in whose *Chronicles* is the legendary story of the British king "Cunobelinus." The names of his two sons are used by Shakespeare and the original tale loosely followed. The story of Imogen and Posthumus is taken from the ninth novel of the second day of Boccaccio's *Decameron*. Shakespeare may have taken this from a French translation or possibly from the English version as it appears in "The Tale Told by the Fishwife of the Stand on the Green" in *Westward for Smelts*. A number of subsidiary sources have been suggested, and the stepmother motive and, more particularly, the

episode in the cave are notably similar to the fairy story of "Little Snow White."

There is no definite assurance of the date of composition of the play but Simon Forman in his *Booke of Plaies and Notes Thereof* records a performance witnessed by him. He died in 1611 and this fixes a later limit on the play. Inasmuch as his entry comes between notes of performances of *Macbeth* and *The Winter's Tale*, which belong respectively to 1610 and 1611, it is safe to assume that 1610 is the probable date of *Cymbeline*.

It first appeared in printed form in the First Folio in 1623.

"By Jupiter, an angel!"
CYMBELINE

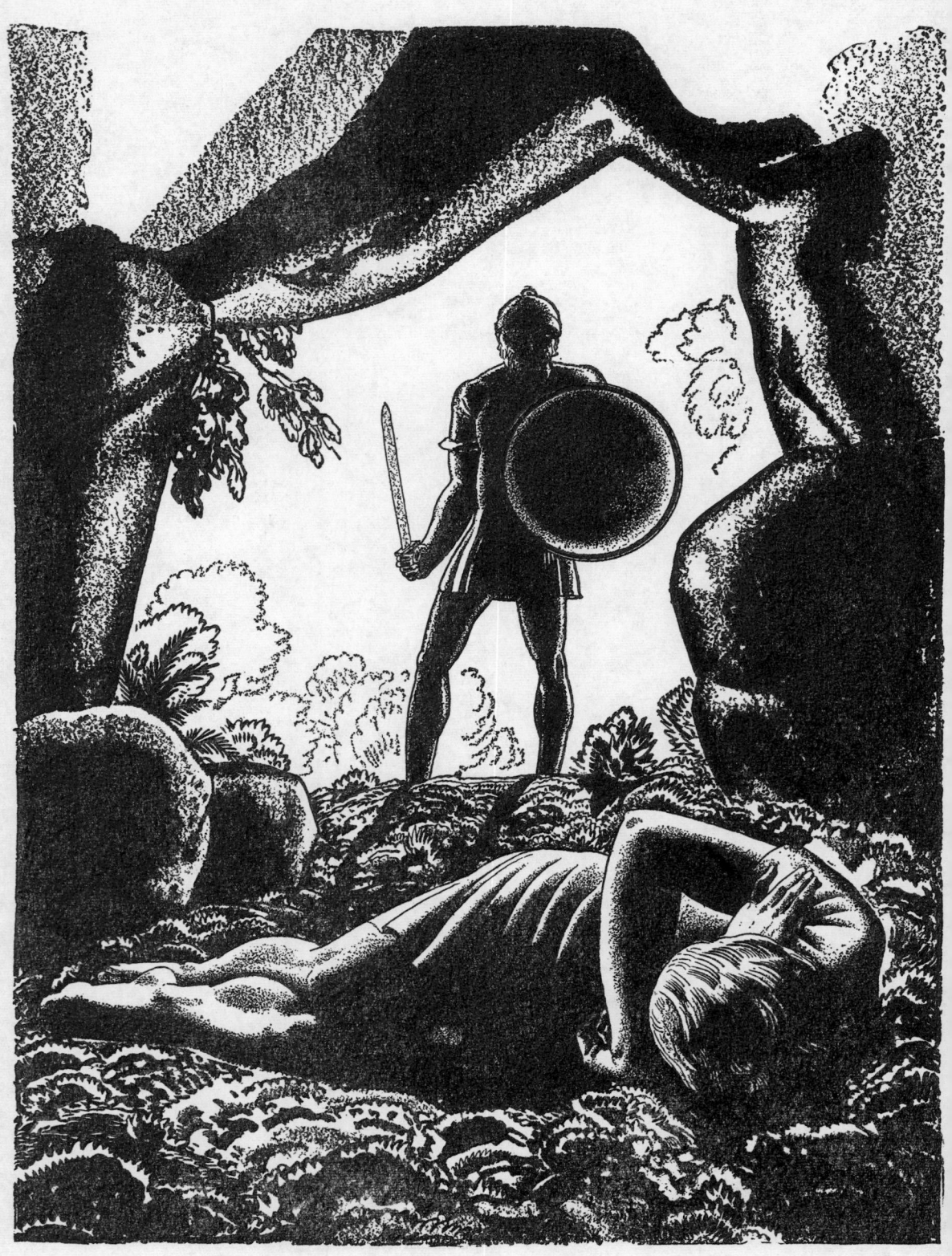

CYMBELINE

DRAMATIS PERSONÆ

CYMBELINE, *king of Britain.*
CLOTEN, *son to the Queen by a former husband.*
POSTHUMUS LEONATUS, *a gentleman, husband to Imogen.*
BELARIUS, *a banished lord, disguised under the name of Morgan.*
GUIDERIUS,
ARVIRAGUS, } *sons to Cymbeline, disguised under the names of Polydore and Cadwal, supposed sons to Morgan.*
PHILARIO, *friend to Posthumus,* }
IACHIMO, *friend to Philario,* } *Italians.*
CAIUS LUCIUS, *general of the Roman forces.*
PISANIO, *servant to Posthumus.*
CORNELIUS, *a physician.*
A ROMAN CAPTAIN.
TWO BRITISH CAPTAINS.

A FRENCHMAN, *friend to Philario.*
TWO LORDS *of Cymbeline's court.*
TWO GENTLEMEN *of the same.*
TWO GAOLERS.

QUEEN, *wife to Cymbeline.*
IMOGEN, *daughter to Cymbeline by a former queen.*
HELEN, *a lady attending on Imogen.*

LORDS, LADIES, ROMAN SENATORS, TRIBUNES, *a* SOOTHSAYER, *a* DUTCHMAN, *a* SPANIARD, MUSICIANS, OFFICERS, CAPTAINS, SOLDIERS, MESSENGERS, *and other* ATTENDANTS APPARITIONS.

SCENE—*Britain: Rome.*

ACT I

SCENE I. *Britain. The garden of* CYMBELINE's *palace*

Enter two GENTLEMEN

FIRST GENTLEMAN

You do not meet a man but frowns: our bloods
No more obey the heavens than our courtiers
Still seem as does the king.

SECOND GENTLEMAN
But what's the matter?

FIRST GENTLEMAN

His daughter, and the heir of 's kingdom, whom
He purposed to his wife's sole son—a widow
That late he married—hath referr'd herself
Unto a poor but worthy gentleman: she's wedded;
Her husband banish'd; she imprison'd: all
Is outward sorrow; though I think the king
Be touch'd at very heart.

SECOND GENTLEMAN
None but the king?

FIRST GENTLEMAN

He that hath lost her too: so is the queen,
That most desired the match: but not a courtier,
Although they wear their faces to the bent
Of the king's looks, hath a heart that is not
Glad at the thing they scowl at.

SECOND GENTLEMAN
And why so?

FIRST GENTLEMAN

He that hath miss'd the princess is a thing
Too bad for bad report: and he that hath her,
I mean, that married her,—alack, good man!—
And therefore banish'd, is a creature such
As, to seek through the regions of the earth
For one his like, there would be something failing
In him that should compare. I do not think

So fair an outward and such stuff within
Endows a man but he.

SECOND GENTLEMAN
You speak him far.

FIRST GENTLEMAN

I do extend him, sir, within himself,
Crush him together rather than unfold
His measure duly.

SECOND GENTLEMAN
What's his name and birth?

FIRST GENTLEMAN

I cannot delve him to the root: his father
Was call'd Sicilius, who did join his honour
Against the Romans with Cassibelan,
But had his titles by Tenantius, whom
He served with glory and admired success,
So gain'd the sur-addition Leonatus:
And had, besides this gentleman in question,
Two other sons, who in the wars o' the time
Died with their swords in hand; for which their father,
Then old and fond of issue, took such sorrow
That he quit being, and his gentle lady,
Big of this gentleman, our theme, deceased
As he was born. The king he takes the babe
To his protection, calls him Posthumus Leonatus,
Breeds him and makes him of his bed-chamber:
Puts to him all the learnings that his time
Could make him the receiver of; which he took,
As we do air, fast as 'twas minister'd,
And in 's spring became a harvest: lived in court—
Which rare it is to do—most praised, most loved:
A sample to the youngest, to the more mature
A glass that feated them, and to the graver
A child that guided dotards; to his mistress,
For whom he now is banish'd, her own price

Proclaims how she esteem'd him and his virtue;
By her election may be truly read
What kind of man he is.
SECOND GENTLEMAN
　　　　　I honour him
Even out of your report. But, pray you, tell me,
Is she sole child to the king?
FIRST GENTLEMAN
　　　　　His only child.
He had two sons,—if this be worth your hearing,
Mark it,—the eldest of them at three years old,
I' the swathing clothes the other, from their nursery
Were stolen, and to this hour no guess in knowledge
Which way they went.
SECOND GENTLEMAN
　　　　How long is this ago?
FIRST GENTLEMAN
Some twenty years.
SECOND GENTLEMAN
That a king's children should be so convey'd!
So slackly guarded! and the search so slow,
That could not trace them!
FIRST GENTLEMAN
　　　　Howsoe'er 'tis strange,
Or that the negligence may well be laugh'd at,
Yet is it true, sir.
SECOND GENTLEMAN
　　　I do well believe you.
FIRST GENTLEMAN
We must forbear: here comes the gentleman,
The queen and princess.　　　　　[Exeunt
　Enter the QUEEN, POSTHUMUS and IMOGEN
QUEEN
No, be assured you shall not find me, daughter,
After the slander of most stepmothers,
Evil-eyed unto you: you're my prisoner, but
Your gaoler shall deliver you the keys
That lock up your restraint. For you, Posthumus,
So soon as I can win the offended king,
I will be known your advocate: marry, yet
The fire of rage is in him, and 'twere good
You lean'd unto his sentence with what patience
Your wisdom may inform you.
POSTHUMUS
　　　　　Please your highness,
I will from hence to-day.
QUEEN
　　　　You know the peril.
I'll fetch a turn about the garden, pitying
The pangs of barr'd affections, though the king
Hath charged you should not speak together. [Exit
IMOGEN
　　　　　　　　O
Dissembling courtesy! How fine this tyrant
Can tickle where she wounds! My dearest husband,
I something fear my father's wrath; but nothing—
Always reserved my holy duty—what
His rage can do on me: you must be gone,
And I shall here abide the hourly shot
Of angry eyes, not comforted to live,

But that there is this jewel in the world
That I may see again.
POSTHUMUS
　　　　My queen! my mistress!
O lady, weep no more, lest I give cause
To be suspected of more tenderness
Than doth become a man! I will remain
The loyal'st husband that did e'er plight troth:
My residence in Rome at one Philario's,
Who to my father was a friend, to me
Known but by letter: thither write, my queen,
And with mine eyes I'll drink the words you send,
Though ink be made of gall.
　　　　Re-enter QUEEN
QUEEN
　　　　Be brief, I pray you:
If the king come, I shall incur I know not
How much of his displeasure. [Aside] Yet I'll move
　him
To walk this way: I never do him wrong
But he does buy my injuries, to be friends;
Pays dear for my offences.　　　　　[Exit
POSTHUMUS
　　　　Should we be taking leave
As long a term as yet we have to live,
The loathness to depart would grow. Adieu!
IMOGEN
Nay, stay a little:
Were you but riding forth to air yourself,
Such parting were too petty. Look here, love;
This diamond was my mother's: take it, heart;
But keep it till you woo another wife,
When Imogen is dead.
POSTHUMUS
　　　　How, how! another?
You gentle gods, give me but this I have,
And sear up my embracements from a next
With bonds of death! [Putting on the ring] Remain,
　remain thou here
While sense can keep it on! And, sweetest, fairest,
As I my poor self did exchange for you
To your so infinite loss, so in our trifles
I still win of you: for my sake wear this;
It is a manacle of love; I'll place it
Upon this fairest prisoner.
　　　　[Putting a bracelet on her arm
IMOGEN
　　　　O the gods!
When shall we see again?
　Enter CYMBELINE and LORDS
POSTHUMUS
　　　　Alack, the king!
CYMBELINE
Thou basest thing, avoid! hence, from my sight!
If after this command thou fraught the court
With thy unworthiness, thou diest: away!
Thou'rt poison to my blood.
POSTHUMUS
　　　　The gods protect you,

And bless the good remainders of the court!
I am gone.   [*Exit*

IMOGEN
There cannot be a pinch in death
More sharp than this is.

CYMBELINE
          O disloyal thing,
That shouldst repair my youth, thou heap'st
A year's age on me!

IMOGEN
          I beseech you, sir,
Harm not yourself with your vexation:
I am senseless of your wrath; a touch more rare
Subdues all pangs, all fears.

CYMBELINE
          Past grace? obedience?

IMOGEN
Past hope, and in despair; that way, past grace.

CYMBELINE
That mightst have had the sole son of my queen!

IMOGEN
O blessed, that I might not! I chose an eagle,
And did avoid a puttock.

CYMBELINE
Thou took'st a beggar; wouldst have made my throne
A seat for baseness.

IMOGEN
          No; I rather added
A lustre to it.

CYMBELINE
          O thou vile one!

IMOGEN
          Sir,
It is your fault that I have loved Posthumus:
You bred him as my playfellow, and he is
A man worth any woman, overbuys me
Almost the sum he pays.

CYMBELINE
          What, art thou mad!

IMOGEN
Almost, sir: heaven restore me! Would I were
A neat-herd's daughter, and my Leonatus
Our neighbour-shepherd's son!

CYMBELINE
          Thou foolish thing!
Re-enter QUEEN
They were again together: you have done
Not after our command. Away with her,
And pen her up.

QUEEN
          Beseech your patience. Peace,
Dear lady daughter, peace! Sweet sovereign,
Leave us to ourselves, and make yourself some comfort
Out of your best advice.

CYMBELINE
          Nay, let her languish
A drop of blood a day; and, being aged,
Die of this folly!   [*Exeunt* CYMBELINE *and* LORDS

QUEEN
Fie! you must give way.
Enter PISANIO
Here is your servant. How now, sir! What news?

PISANIO
My lord your son drew on my master.

QUEEN
          Ha!
No harm, I trust, is done?

PISANIO
          There might have been,
But that my master rather play'd than fought,
And had no help of anger: they were parted
By gentlemen at hand.

QUEEN
          I am very glad on 't.

IMOGEN
Your son's my father's friend; he takes his part.
To draw upon an exile! O brave sir!
I would they were in Afric both together;
Myself by with a needle, that I might prick
The goer-back. Why came you from your master?

PISANIO
On his command: he would not suffer me
To bring him to the haven: left these notes
Of what commands I should be subject to
When 't pleased you to employ me.

QUEEN
          This hath been
Your faithful servant: I dare lay mine honour
He will remain so.

PISANIO
          I humbly thank your highness.

QUEEN
Pray, walk awhile.

IMOGEN
          About some half-hour hence,
I pray you, speak with me: you shall at least
Go see my lord aboard: for this time leave me.
                 [*Exeunt*

SCENE II. *The same. A public place*

Enter CLOTEN *and two* LORDS
FIRST LORD
Sir, I would advise you to shift a shirt; the violence
of action hath made you reek as a sacrifice: where
air comes out, air comes in: there's none abroad so
wholesome as that you vent.

CLOTEN
If my shirt were bloody, then to shift it. Have I hurt
him?

SECOND LORD
[*Aside*] No, faith; not so much as his patience.

FIRST LORD
Hurt him! his body's a passable carcass, if he be not
hurt: it is a throughfare for steel, if it be not hurt.

SECOND LORD
[*Aside*] His steel was in debt; it went o' the backside
the town.

[1219]

CLOTEN

The villain would not stand me.

SECOND LORD

[Aside] No; but he fled forward still, toward your
face.

FIRST LORD

Stand you! You have land enough of your own: but
he added to your having; gave you some ground.

SECOND LORD

[Aside] As many inches as you have oceans. Puppies!

CLOTEN

I would they had not come between us.

SECOND LORD

[Aside] So would I, till you had measured how long
a fool you were upon the ground.

CLOTEN

And that she should love this fellow, and refuse me!

SECOND LORD

[Aside] If it be a sin to make a true election, she is
damned.

FIRST LORD

Sir, as I told you always, her beauty and her brain
go not together: she's a good sign, but I have seen
small reflection of her wit.

SECOND LORD

[Aside] She shines not upon fools, lest the reflection
should hurt her.

CLOTEN

Come, I'll to my chamber. Would there had been
some hurt done!

SECOND LORD

[Aside] I wish not so; unless it had been the fall of an
ass, which is no great hurt.

CLOTEN

You'll go with us?

FIRST LORD

I'll attend your lordship.

CLOTEN

Nay, come, let's go together.

SECOND LORD

Well, my lord.   [Exeunt

SCENE III. *A room in* CYMBELINE'S *palace*

Enter IMOGEN *and* PISANIO

IMOGEN

I would thou grew'st unto the shores o' the haven,
And question'dst every sail: if he should write
And I not have it, 'twere a paper lost,
As offer'd mercy is. What was the last
That he spake to thee?

PISANIO

       It was, his queen, his queen!

IMOGEN

Then waved his handkerchief?

PISANIO

       And kiss'd it, madam.

IMOGEN

Senseless linen! happier therein than I!
And that was all?

PISANIO

       No, madam; for so long
As he could make me with this eye or ear
Distinguish him from others, he did keep
The deck, with glove, or hat, or handkerchief,
Still waving, as the fits and stirs of 's mind
Could best express how slow his soul sail'd on,
How swift his ship.

IMOGEN

       Thou shouldst have made him
As little as a crow, or less, ere left
To after-eye him.

PISANIO

       Madam, so I did.

IMOGEN

I would have broke mine eye-strings, crack'd them,
but
To look upon him, till the diminution
Of space had pointed him sharp as my needle;
Nay, follow'd him, till he had melted from
The smallness of a gnat to air; and then
Have turn'd mine eye, and wept. But, good Pisanio,
When shall we hear from him?

PISANIO

       Be assured, madam,
With his next vantage.

IMOGEN

I did not take my leave of him, but had
Most pretty things to say: ere I could tell him
How I would think on him at certain hours,
Such thoughts and such; or I could make him swear
The shes of Italy should not betray
Mine interest and his honour; or have charged him,
At the sixth hour of morn, at noon, at midnight,
To encounter me with orisons, for then
I am in heaven for him; or ere I could
Give him that parting kiss which I had set
Betwixt two charming words, comes in my father,
And, like the tyrannous breathing of the north,
Shakes all our buds from growing.

Enter a LADY

LADY

       The queen, madam,
Desires your highness' company.

IMOGEN

Those things I bid you do, get them dispatch'd.
I will attend the queen.

PISANIO

       Madam, I shall.   [Exeunt

SCENE IV. *Rome.* PHILARIO'S *house*

Enter PHILARIO, IACHIMO, *a* FRENCHMAN, *a* DUTCH-
MAN, *and a* SPANIARD

IACHIMO

Believe it, sir, I have seen him in Britain: he was

then of a crescent note; expected to prove so worthy as since he hath been allowed the name of: but I could then have looked on him without the help of admiration, though the catalogue of his endowments had been tabled by his side and I to peruse him by items.

PHILARIO

You speak of him when he was less furnished than now he is with that which makes him both without and within.

FRENCHMAN

I have seen him in France: we had very many there could behold the sun with as firm eyes as he.

IACHIMO

This matter of marrying his king's daughter, wherein he must be weighed rather by her value than his own, words him, I doubt not, a great deal from the matter.

FRENCHMAN

And then his banishment.

IACHIMO

Ay, and the approbation of those that weep this lamentable divorce under her colours are wonderfully to extend him; be it but to fortify her judgement, which else an easy battery might lay flat, for taking a beggar without less quality. But how comes it he is to sojourn with you? how creeps acquaintance?

PHILARIO

His father and I were soldiers together; to whom I have been often bound for no less than my life. Here comes the Briton: let him be so entertained amongst you as suits, with gentlemen of your knowing, to a stranger of his quality.

Enter POSTHUMUS

I beseech you all, be better known to this gentleman; whom I commend to you as a noble friend of mine: how worthy he is I will leave to appear hereafter, rather than story him in his own hearing.

FRENCHMAN

Sir, we have known together in Orleans.

POSTHUMUS

Since when I have been debtor to you for courtesies, which I will be ever to pay and yet pay still.

FRENCHMAN

Sir, you o'er-rate my poor kindness: I was glad I did atone my countryman and you; it had been pity you should have been put together with so mortal a purpose as then each bore, upon importance of so slight and trivial a nature.

POSTHUMUS

By your pardon, sir, I was then a young traveller; rather shunned to go even with what I heard than in my every action to be guided by others' experiences: but upon my mended judgement—if I offend not to say it is mended—my quarrel was not altogether slight.

FRENCHMAN

Faith, yes, to be put to the arbitrement of swords,

and by such two that would, by all likelihood, have confounded one the other, or have fallen both.

IACHIMO

Can we with manners ask what was the difference?

FRENCHMAN

Safely, I think: 'twas a contention in public, which may without contradiction suffer the report. It was much like an argument that fell out last night, where each of us fell in praise of our country mistresses; this gentleman at that time vouching—and upon warrant of bloody affirmation—his to be more fair, virtuous, wise, chaste, constant-qualified and less attemptable than any the rarest of our ladies in France.

IACHIMO

That lady is not now living, or this gentleman's opinion, by this, worn out.

POSTHUMUS

She holds her virtue still and I my mind.

IACHIMO

You must not so far prefer her 'fore ours of Italy.

POSTHUMUS

Being so far provoked as I was in France, I would abate her nothing, though I profess myself her adorer, not her friend.

IACHIMO

As fair and as good—a kind of hand-in-hand comparison—had been something too fair and too good for any lady in Britany. If she went before others I have seen, as that diamond of yours outlustres many I have beheld, I could not but believe she excelled many: but I have not seen the most precious diamond that is, nor you the lady.

POSTHUMUS

I praised her as I rated her: so do I my stone.

IACHIMO

What do you esteem it at?

POSTHUMUS

More than the world enjoys.

IACHIMO

Either your unparagoned mistress is dead, or she's outprized by a trifle.

POSTHUMUS

You are mistaken: the one may be sold or given, if there were wealth enough for the purchase or merit for the gift: the other is not a thing for sale, and only the gift of the gods.

IACHIMO

Which the gods have given you?

POSTHUMUS

Which, by their graces, I will keep.

IACHIMO

You may wear her in title yours: but, you know, strange fowl light upon neighbouring ponds. Your ring may be stolen too: so your brace of unprizeable estimations, the one is but frail and the other casual; a cunning thief, or a that way accomplished courtier, would hazard the winning both of first and last.

POSTHUMUS

Your Italy contains none so accomplished a courtier

to convince the honour of my mistress; if, in the holding or loss of that, you term her frail. I do nothing doubt you have store of thieves; notwithstanding, I fear not my ring.

PHILARIO
Let us leave here, gentlemen.

POSTHUMUS
Sir, with all my heart. This worthy signior, I thank him, makes no stranger of me; we are familiar at first.

IACHIMO
With five times so much conversation, I should get ground of your fair mistress, make her go back even to the yielding, had I admittance and opportunity to friend.

POSTHUMUS
No, no.

IACHIMO
I dare thereupon pawn the moiety of my estate to your ring, which in my opinion o'ervalues it something: but I make my wager rather against your confidence than her reputation: and, to bar your offence herein too, I durst attempt it against any lady in the world.

POSTHUMUS
You are a great deal abused in too bold a persuasion, and I doubt not you sustain what you're worthy of by your attempt.

IACHIMO
What's that?

POSTHUMUS
A repulse: though your attempt, as you call it, deserve more; a punishment too.

PHILARIO
Gentlemen, enough of this: it came in too suddenly; let it die as it was born, and, I pray you, be better acquainted.

IACHIMO
Would I had put my estate and my neighbour's on the approbation of what I have spoke!

POSTHUMUS
What lady would you choose to assail?

IACHIMO
Yours; whom in constancy you think stands so safe. I will lay you ten thousand ducats to your ring, that, commend me to the court where your lady is, with no more advantage than the opportunity of a second conference, and I will bring from thence that honour of hers which you imagine so reserved.

POSTHUMUS
I will wage against your gold, gold to it: my ring I hold dear as my finger; 'tis part of it.

IACHIMO
You are afraid, and therein the wiser. If you buy ladies' flesh at a million a dram, you cannot preserve it from tainting: but I see you have some religion in you, that you fear.

POSTHUMUS
This is but a custom in your tongue; you bear a graver purpose, I hope.

IACHIMO
I am the master of my speeches, and would undergo what's spoken, I swear.

POSTHUMUS
Will you? I shall but lend my diamond till your return: let there be covenants drawn between 's: my mistress exceeds in goodness the hugeness of your unworthy thinking: I dare you to this match: here's my ring.

PHILARIO
I will have it no lay.

IACHIMO
By the gods, it is one. If I bring you no sufficient testimony that I have enjoyed the dearest bodily part of your mistress, my ten thousand ducats are yours; so is your diamond too: if I come off, and leave her in such honour as you have trust in, she your jewel, this your jewel, and my gold are yours; provided I have your commendation for my more free entertainment.

POSTHUMUS
I embrace these conditions; let us have articles betwixt us. Only, thus far you shall answer: if you make your voyage upon her, and give me directly to understand you have prevailed, I am no further your enemy; she is not worth our debate: if she remain unseduced, you not making it appear otherwise, for your ill opinion and the assault you have made to her chastity, you shall answer me with your sword.

IACHIMO
Your hand; a covenant: we will have these things set down by lawful counsel, and straight away for Britain, lest the bargain should catch cold and starve: I will fetch my gold, and have our two wagers recorded.

POSTHUMUS
Agreed.   [Exeunt POSTHUMUS and IACHIMO

FRENCHMAN
Will this hold, think you?

PHILARIO
Signior Iachimo will not from it. Pray, let us follow 'em.   [Exeunt

SCENE V. Britain. A room in CYMBELINE's palace

Enter QUEEN, LADIES, and CORNELIUS

QUEEN
Whiles yet the dew's on ground, gather those flowers;
Make haste: who has the note of them?

FIRST LADY
                                                    I, madam.

QUEEN
Dispatch.   [Exeunt LADIES
Now, master doctor, have you brought those drugs?

CORNELIUS
Pleaseth your highness, ay: here they are, madam:
                                        [Presenting a small box

But I beseech your grace, without offence,—
My conscience bids me ask—wherefore you have
Commanded of me these most poisonous com-
    pounds,
Which are the movers of a languishing death,
But, though slow, deadly.

QUEEN
            I wonder, doctor,
Thou ask'st me such a question. Have I not been
Thy pupil long? Hast thou not learn'd me how
To make perfumes? distil? preserve? yea, so
That our great king himself doth woo me oft
For my confections? Having thus far proceeded,—
Unless thou think'st me devilish—is 't not meet
That I did amplify my judgement in
Other conclusions? I will try the forces
Of these thy compounds on such creatures as
We count not worth the hanging, but none human,
To try the vigour of them and apply
Allayments to their act, and by them gather
Their several virtues and effects.

CORNELIUS
                Your highness
Shall from this practice but make hard your heart:
Besides, the seeing these effects will be
Both noisome and infectious.

QUEEN
            O, content thee.

Enter PISANIO

[*Aside*] Here comes a flattering rascal; upon him
Will I first work: he's for his master,
And enemy to my son. How now, Pisanio!
Doctor, your service for this time is ended;
Take your own way.

CORNELIUS
        [*Aside*] I do suspect you, madam;
But you shall do no harm.

QUEEN
        [*To* PISANIO] Hark thee, a word.

CORNELIUS
[*Aside*] I do not like her. She doth think she has
Strange lingering poisons: I do know her spirit,
And will not trust one of her malice with
A drug of such damn'd nature. Those she has
Will stupefy and dull the sense awhile;
Which first, perchance, she'll prove on cats and
    dogs,
Then afterward up higher: but there is
No danger in what show of death it makes,
More than the locking up the spirits a time,
To be more fresh, reviving. She is fool'd
With a most false effect; and I the truer,
So to be false with her.

QUEEN
            No further service, doctor,
Until I send for thee.

CORNELIUS
        I humbly take my leave. [*Exit*

QUEEN
Weeps she still, say'st thou? Dost thou think in time

She will not quench and let instructions enter
Where folly now possesses? Do thou work:
When thou shalt bring me word she loves my son,
I'll tell thee on the instant thou art then
As great as is thy master; greater, for
His fortunes all lie speechless, and his name
Is at last gasp: return he cannot, nor
Continue where he is: to shift his being
Is to exchange one misery with another,
And every day that comes comes to decay
A day's work in him. What shalt thou expect,
To be depender on a thing that leans,
Who cannot be new built, nor has no friends,
So much as but to prop him? [*The* QUEEN *drops the
    box:* PISANIO *takes it up*] Thou takest up
Thou know'st not what; but take it for thy labour:
It is a thing I made, which hath the king
Five times redeem'd from death: I do not know
What is more cordial: nay, I prithee, take it;
It is an earnest of a further good
That I mean to thee. Tell thy mistress how
The case stands with her; do 't as from thyself.
Think what a chance thou changest on; but think
Thou hast thy mistress still, to boot, my son,
Who shall take notice of thee: I'll move the king
To any shape of thy preferment, such
As thou'lt desire; and then myself, I chiefly,
That set thee on to this desert, am bound
To load thy merit richly. Call my women:
Think on my words.   [*Exit* PISANIO
                A sly and constant knave;
Not to be shaked: the agent for his master;
And the remembrancer of her to hold
The hand-fast to her lord. I have given him that
Which, if he take, shall quite unpeople her
Of liegers for her sweet; and which she after,
Except she bend her humour, shall be assured
To taste of too.

Re-enter PISANIO *with* LADIES
            So, so; well done, well done:
The violets, cowslips, and the primroses,
Bear to my closet. Fare thee well, Pisanio;
Think on my words.   [*Exeunt* QUEEN *and* LADIES

PISANIO
            And shall do:
But when to my good lord I prove untrue,
I'll choke myself: there's all I'll do for you.   [*Exit*

SCENE VI. *The same. Another room in the palace*

Enter IMOGEN *alone*

IMOGEN
A father cruel, and a step-dame false;
A foolish suitor to a wedded lady,
That hath her husband banish'd;—O, that husband!
My supreme crown of grief! and those repeated
Vexations of it! Had I been thief-stol'n,
As my two brothers, happy! but most miserable
Is the desire that's glorious: blest be those,

How mean soe'er, that have their honest wills,
Which seasons comfort. Who may this be? Fie!

Enter PISANIO *and* IACHIMO

PISANIO
Madam, a noble gentleman of Rome,
Comes from my lord with letters.

IACHIMO
               Change you, madam?
The worthy Leonatus is in safety,
And greets your highness dearly.   [*Presents a letter*

IMOGEN
              Thanks, good sir:
You're kindly welcome.

IACHIMO
[*Aside*] All of her that is out of door most rich!
If she be furnish'd with a mind so rare,
She is alone the Arabian bird, and I
Have lost the wager. Boldness be my friend!
Arm me, audacity, from head to foot!
Or, like the Parthian, I shall flying fight;
Rather, directly fly.

IMOGEN
[*Reads*] 'He is one of the noblest note, to whose kindnesses I am
most infinitely tied. Reflect upon him accordingly, as you
value your trust—   LEONATUS.'

So far I read aloud:
But even the very middle of my heart
Is warm'd by the rest, and takes it thankfully.
You are as welcome, worthy sir, as I
Have words to bid you, and shall find it so
In all that I can do.

IACHIMO
           Thanks, fairest lady.
What, are men mad? Hath nature given them eyes
To see this vaulted arch and the rich crop
Of sea and land, which can distinguish 'twixt
The fiery orbs above and the twinn'd stones
Upon the number'd beach, and can we not
Partition make with spectacles so precious
'Twixt fair and foul?

IMOGEN
         What makes your admiration?

IACHIMO
It cannot be i' the eye; for apes and monkeys,
'Twixt two such shes, would chatter this way and
Contemn with mows the other: nor i' the judgement;
For idiots, in this case of favour, would
Be wisely definite: nor i' the appetite;
Sluttery, to such neat excellence opposed,
Should make desire vomit emptiness,
Not so allured to feed.

IMOGEN
What is the matter, trow?

IACHIMO
         The cloyed will,
That satiate yet unsatisfied desire, that tub
Both fill'd and running, ravening first the lamb,
Longs after for the garbage.

IMOGEN
        What, dear sir,
Thus raps you? Are you well?

IACHIMO
             Thanks, madam; well.
[*To* PISANIO] Beseech you, sir,
Desire my man's abode where I did leave him:
He's strange and peevish.

PISANIO
          I was going, sir,
To give him welcome.   [*Exit*

IMOGEN
Continues well my lord? His health, beseech you?

IACHIMO
Well, madam.

IMOGEN
Is he disposed to mirth? I hope he is.

IACHIMO
Exceeding pleasant; none a stranger there
So merry and so gamesome: he is call'd
The Briton reveller.

IMOGEN
        When he was here
He did incline to sadness, and oft-times
Not knowing why.

IACHIMO
        I never saw him sad.
There is a Frenchman his companion, one
An eminent monsieur, that, it seems, much loves
A Gallian girl at home: he furnaces
The thick sighs from him; whiles the jolly Briton,
Your lord, I mean, laughs from 's free lungs, cries,
'O,
Can my sides hold, to think that man, who knows
By history, report, or his own proof,
What woman is, yea, what she cannot choose
But must be, with his free hours languish for
Assured bondage?'

IMOGEN
       Will my lord say so?

IACHIMO
Ay, madam; with his eyes in flood with laughter:
It is a recreation to be by
And hear him mock the Frenchman. But, heavens
    know,
Some men are much to blame.

IMOGEN
         Not he, I hope.

IACHIMO
Not he: but yet heaven's bounty towards him might
Be used more thankfully. In himself 'tis much;
In you, which I account his beyond all talents,
Whilst I am bound to wonder, I am bound
To pity too.

IMOGEN
       What do you pity, sir?

IACHIMO
Two creatures heartily.

IMOGEN
         Am I one, sir?

You look on me: what wreck discern you in me
Deserves your pity?

IACHIMO

Lamentable! What,
To hide me from the radiant sun, and solace
I' the dungeon by a snuff?

IMOGEN

I pray you, sir,
Deliver with more openness your answers
To my demands. Why do you pity me?

IACHIMO

That others do,
I was about to say, enjoy your——But
It is an office of the gods to venge it,
Not mine to speak on 't.

IMOGEN

You do seem to know
Something of me, or what concerns me: pray you,—
Since doubting things go ill often hurts more
Than to be sure they do; for certainties
Either are past remedies, or, timely knowing,
The remedy then born,—discover to me
What both you spur and stop.

IACHIMO

Had I this cheek
To bathe my lips upon; this hand, whose touch,
Whose every touch, would force the feeler's soul
To the oath of loyalty; this object, which
Takes prisoner the wild motion of mine eye,
Fixing it only here; should I, damn'd then,
Slaver with lips as common as the stairs
That mount the Capitol; join gripes with hands
Made hard with hourly falsehood—falsehood, as
With labour; then by-peeping in an eye
Base and unlustrous as the smoky light
That's fed with stinking tallow; it were fit
That all the plagues of hell should at one time
Encounter such revolt.

IMOGEN

My lord, I fear,
Has forgot Britain.

IACHIMO

And himself. Not I
Inclined to this intelligence pronounce
The beggary of his change, but 'tis your graces
That from my mutest conscience to my tongue
Charms this report out.

IMOGEN

Let me hear no more.

IACHIMO

O dearest soul, your cause doth strike my heart
With pity, that doth make me sick! A lady
So fair, and fasten'd to an empery,
Would make the great'st king double, to be part-
ner'd
With tomboys hired with that self exhibition
Which your own coffers yield! with diseased ven-
tures
That play with all infirmities for gold

Which rottenness can lend nature! such boil'd stuff
As well might poison poison! Be revenged,
Or she that bore you was no queen and you
Recoil from your great stock.

IMOGEN

Revenged!
How should I be revenged? If this be true,—
As I have such a heart that both mine ears
Must not in haste abuse,—if it be true,
How should I be revenged?

IACHIMO

Should he make me
Live like Diana's priest, betwixt cold sheets,
Whiles he is vaulting variable ramps,
In your despite, upon your purse? Revenge it.
I dedicate myself to your sweet pleasure,
More noble than that runagate to your bed,
And will continue fast to your affection,
Still close as sure.

IMOGEN

What ho, Pisanio!

IACHIMO

Let me my service tender on your lips.

IMOGEN

Away! I do condemn mine ears that have
So long attended thee. If thou wert honourable,
Thou wouldst have told this tale for virtue, not
For such an end thou seek'st, as base as strange.
Thou wrong'st a gentleman who is as far
From thy report as thou from honour, and
Solicit'st here a lady that disdains
Thee and the devil alike. What ho, Pisanio!
The king my father shall be made acquainted
Of thy assault: if he shall think it fit
A saucy stranger in his court to mart
As in a Romish stew, and to expound
His beastly mind to us, he hath a court
He little cares for, and a daughter who
He not respects at all. What ho, Pisanio!

IACHIMO

O happy Leonatus! I may say:
The credit that thy lady hath of thee
Deserves thy trust, and thy most perfect goodness
Her assured credit. Blessed live you long!
A lady to the worthiest sir that ever
Country call'd his! and you his mistress, only
For the most worthiest fit! Give me your pardon.
I have spoke this to know if your affiance
Were deeply rooted, and shall make your lord
That which he is new o'er: and he is one
The truest manner'd, such a holy witch
That he enchants societies into him;
Half all men's hearts are his.

IMOGEN

You make amends.

IACHIMO

He sits 'mongst men like a descended god:
He hath a kind of honour sets him off,
More than a mortal seeming. Be not angry,

Most mighty princess, that I have adventured
To try your taking of a false report, which hath
Honour'd with confirmation your great judgement
In the election of a sir so rare,
Which you know cannot err. The love I bear him
Made me to fan you thus, but the gods made you,
Unlike all others, chaffless. Pray, your pardon.

IMOGEN

All's well, sir: take my power i' the court for yours.

IACHIMO

My humble thanks. I had almost forgot
To entreat your grace but in a small request,
And yet of moment too, for it concerns
Your lord; myself and other noble friends
Are partners in the business.

IMOGEN

         Pray, what is 't?

IACHIMO

Some dozen Romans of us, and your lord—
The best feather of our wing—have mingled sums
To buy a present for the emperor;
Which I, the factor for the rest, have done
In France: 'tis plate of rare device and jewels
Of rich and exquisite form, their values great;
And I am something curious, being strange,
To have them in safe stowage: may it please you
To take them in protection?

IMOGEN

         Willingly;
And pawn mine honour for their safety: since
My lord hath interest in them, I will keep them
In my bedchamber.

IACHIMO

         They are in a trunk,
Attended by my men: I will make bold
To send them to you, only for this night;
I must aboard to-morrow.

IMOGEN

         O, no, no.

IACHIMO

Yes, I beseech; or I shall short my word
By lengthening my return. From Gallia
I cross'd the seas on purpose and on promise
To see your grace.

IMOGEN

         I thank you for your pains:
But not away to-morrow!

IACHIMO

         O, I must, madam:
Therefore I shall beseech you, if you please
To greet your lord with writing, do 't to-night:
I have outstood my time, which is material
To the tender of our present.

IMOGEN

         I will write.
Send your trunk to me; it shall safe be kept
And truly yielded you. You're very welcome.

                     [*Exeunt*

ACT II

SCENE I. *Britain. Before* CYMBELINE's *palace*

Enter CLOTEN *and two* LORDS

CLOTEN

Was there ever man had such luck! when I kissed
the jack, upon an up-cast to be hit away! I had a
hundred pound on 't: and then a whoreson jacka-
napes must take me up for swearing; as if I borrowed
mine oaths of him, and might not spend them at my
pleasure.

FIRST LORD

What got he by that? You have broke his pate with
your bowl.

SECOND LORD

[*Aside*] If his wit had been like him that broke it, it
would have run all out.

CLOTEN

When a gentleman is disposed to swear, it is not for
any standers-by to curtail his oaths, ha?

SECOND LORD

No, my lord; [*Aside*] nor crop the ears of them.

CLOTEN

Whoreson dog! I give him satisfaction? Would he
had been one of my rank!

SECOND LORD

[*Aside*] To have smelt like a fool.

CLOTEN

I am not vexed more at any thing in the earth: a
pox on 't! I had rather not be so noble as I am; they
dare not fight with me, because of the queen my
mother: every Jack-slave hath his bellyful of fighting, and I must go up and down like a cock that nobody can match.

SECOND LORD

[*Aside*] You are cock and capon too; and you crow,
cock, with your comb on.

CLOTEN

Sayest thou?

SECOND LORD

It is not fit your lordship should undertake every
companion that you give offence to.

CLOTEN

No, I know that: but it is fit I should commit offence
to my inferiors.

SECOND LORD

Ay, it is fit for your lordship only.

CLOTEN

Why, so I say.

FIRST LORD

Did you hear of a stranger that's come to court to-
night?

CLOTEN

A stranger, and I not know on 't!

SECOND LORD

[*Aside*] He's a strange fellow himself, and knows it
not.

FIRST LORD

There's an Italian come, and 'tis thought one of
Leonatus' friends.

CLOTEN

Leonatus! a banished rascal; and he's another,
whatsoever he be. Who told you of this stranger?

FIRST LORD

One of your lordship's pages.

CLOTEN

Is it fit I went to look upon him? is there no deroga-
tion in 't?

SECOND LORD

You cannot derogate, my lord.

CLOTEN

Not easily, I think.

SECOND LORD

[Aside] You are a fool granted; therefore your issues,
being foolish, do not derogate.

CLOTEN

Come, I'll go see this Italian: what I have lost to-
day at bowls I'll win to-night of him. Come, go.

SECOND LORD

I'll attend your lordship.

[Exeunt CLOTEN and FIRST LORD

That such a crafty devil as is his mother
Should yield the world this ass! a woman that
Bears all down with her brain; and this her son
Cannot take two from twenty, for his heart,
And leave eighteen. Alas, poor princess,
Thou divine Imogen, what thou endurest,
Betwixt a father by thy step-dame govern'd,
A mother hourly coining plots, a wooer
More hateful than the foul expulsion is
Of thy dear husband, than that horrid act
Of the divorce he'ld make! The heavens hold firm
The walls of thy dear honour; keep unshaked
That temple, thy fair mind; that thou mayst stand,
To enjoy thy banish'd lord and this great land! [Exit

SCENE II. IMOGEN'S bedchamber in CYMBELINE'S palace:
a trunk in one corner of it

IMOGEN in bed, reading; a LADY attending

IMOGEN

Who's there? my woman Helen?

LADY

Please you, madam.

IMOGEN

What hour is it?

LADY

Almost midnight, madam.

IMOGEN

I have read three hours then: mine eyes are weak:
Fold down the leaf where I have left: to bed:
Take not away the taper, leave it burning;
And if thou canst awake by four o' the clock,
I prithee, call me. Sleep hath seized me wholly.

[Exit LADY

To your protection I commend me, gods!
From fairies and the tempters of the night
Guard me. beseech ye!

[Sleeps. IACHIMO comes from the trunk

IACHIMO

The crickets sing, and man's o'er-labour'd sense
Repairs itself by rest. Our Tarquin thus
Did softly press the rushes, ere he waken'd
The chastity he wounded. Cytherea,
How bravely thou becomest thy bed! fresh lily!
And whiter than the sheets! That I might touch!
But kiss; one kiss! Rubies unparagon'd,
How dearly they do 't! 'Tis her breathing that
Perfumes the chamber thus: the flame o' the taper
Bows toward her, and would under-peep her lids
To see the enclosed lights, now canopied
Under these windows, white and azure, laced
With blue of heaven's own tinct. But my design,
To note the chamber: I will write all down:
Such and such pictures; there the window; such
The adornment of her bed; the arras, figures,
Why, such and such; and the contents o' the story.
Ah, but some natural notes about her body
Above ten thousand meaner moveables
Would testify, to enrich mine inventory.
O sleep, thou ape of death, lie dull upon her!
And be her sense but as a monument,
Thus in a chapel lying! Come off, come off:

[Taking off her bracelet

As slippery as the Gordian knot was hard!
'Tis mine; and this will witness outwardly,
As strongly as the conscience does within,
To the madding of her lord. On her left breast
A mole cinque-spotted, like the crimson drops
I' the bottom of a cowslip: here's a voucher,
Stronger than ever law could make: this secret
Will force him think I have pick'd the lock and ta'en
The treasure of her honour. No more. To what end?
Why should I write this down, that's riveted,
Screw'd to my memory? She hath been reading late
The tale of Tereus; here the leaf's turn'd down
Where Philomel gave up. I have enough:
To the trunk again, and shut the spring of it.
Swift, swift, you dragons of the night, that dawning
May bare the raven's eye! I lodge in fear;
Though this a heavenly angel, hell is here.

[Clock strikes

One, two, three: time, time!

[Goes into the trunk. The scene closes

SCENE III. An ante-chamber adjoining IMOGEN'S
apartments

Enter CLOTEN and LORDS

FIRST LORD

Your lordship is the most patient man in loss, the
most coldest that ever turned up ace.

CLOTEN

It would make any man cold to lose.

FIRST LORD

But not every man patient after the noble temper of
your lordship. You are most hot and furious when
you win.

CLOTEN

Winning will put any man into courage. If I could
get this foolish Imogen, I should have gold enough.
It's almost morning, is 't not?

FIRST LORD

Day, my lord.

CLOTEN

I would this music would come: I am advised to
give her music o' mornings; they say it will penetrate.

Enter MUSICIANS

Come on; tune: if you can penetrate her with your
fingering, so; we'll try with tongue too: if none will
do, let her remain; but I'll never give o'er. First, a
very excellent good-conceited thing; after, a wonderful sweet air, with admirable rich words to it:
and then let her consider.

SONG

Hark, hark! the lark at heaven's gate sings,
    And Phœbus 'gins arise,
His steeds to water at those springs
    On chaliced flowers that lies;
And winking Mary-buds begin
    To ope their golden eyes;
With every thing that pretty is,
    My lady sweet, arise:
        Arise, arise!

CLOTEN

So, get you gone. If this penetrate, I will consider
your music the better: if it do not, it is a vice in her
ears, which horse-hairs and calves'-guts, nor the
voice of unpaved eunuch to boot, can never amend.

[Exeunt MUSICIANS

SECOND LORD

Here comes the king.

CLOTEN

I am glad I was up so late; for that's the reason I
was up so early: he cannot choose but take this service I have done fatherly.

Enter CYMBELINE *and* QUEEN

Good morrow to your majesty and to my gracious
mother.

CYMBELINE

Attend you here the door of our stern daughter?
Will she not forth?

CLOTEN

I have assailed her with music, but she vouchsafes
no notice.

CYMBELINE

The exile of her minion is too new;
She hath not yet forgot him: some more time
Must wear the print of his remembrance out,
And then she's yours.

QUEEN

You are most bound to the king,
Who lets go by no vantages that may
Prefer you to his daughter. Frame yourself
To orderly soliciting, and be friended
With aptness of the season; make denials
Increase your services; so seem as if
You were inspired to do those duties which

You tender to her; that you in all obey her,
Save when command to your dismission tends,
And therein you are senseless.

CLOTEN

Senseless! not so.

Enter a MESSENGER

MESSENGER

So like you, sir, ambassadors from Rome;
The one is Caius Lucius.

CYMBELINE

A worthy fellow,
Albeit he comes on angry purpose now;
But that's no fault of his: we must receive him
According to the honour of his sender;
And towards himself, his goodness forespent on us,
We must extend our notice. Our dear son,
When you have given good morning to your mis-
    tress,
Attend the queen and us; we shall have need
To employ you towards this Roman. Come, our
    queen.   *[Exeunt all but* CLOTEN

CLOTEN

If she be up, I'll speak with her; if not,
Let her lie still and dream. By your leave, ho!
                                    [Knocks

I know her women are about her: what
If I do line one of their hands? 'Tis gold
Which buys admittance; oft it doth; yea, and makes
Diana's rangers false themselves, yield up
Their deer to the stand o' the stealer; and 'tis gold
Which makes the true man kill'd and saves the thief;
Nay, sometime hangs both thief and true man: what
Can it not do and undo? I will make
One of her women lawyer to me, for
I yet not understand the case myself.
By your leave.   *[Knocks*

Enter a LADY

LADY

Who's there that knocks?

CLOTEN

A gentleman.

LADY

No more?

CLOTEN

Yes, and a gentlewoman's son.

LADY

That's more
Than some whose tailors are as dear as yours
Can justly boast of. What's your lordship's pleasure?

CLOTEN

Your lady's person: is she ready?

LADY

Ay,
To keep her chamber.

CLOTEN

There is gold for you;
Sell me your good report.

LADY

How! my good name? or to report of you
What I shall think is good? The princess! *[Exit* LADY

Enter IMOGEN

CLOTEN

Good morrow, fairest: sister, your sweet hand.

IMOGEN

Good morrow, sir. You lay out too much pains
For purchasing but trouble: the thanks I give
Is telling you that I am poor of thanks
And scarce can spare them.

CLOTEN

　　　　　　　Still I swear I love you.

IMOGEN

If you but said so, 'twere as deep with me:
If you swear still, your recompense is still
That I regard it not.

CLOTEN

　　　　　This is no answer.

IMOGEN

But that you shall not say I yield being silent,
I would not speak. I pray you, spare me: faith,
I shall unfold equal discourtesy
To your best kindness: one of your great knowing
Should learn, being taught, forbearance.

CLOTEN

'To leave you in your madness, 'twere my sin:
I will not.

IMOGENE

Fools are not mad folks.

CLOTEN

　　　　　Do you call me fool?

IMOGEN

As I am mad, I do:
If you'll be patient, I'll no more be mad;
That cures us both. I am much sorry, sir,
You put me to forget a lady's manners,
By being so verbal: and learn now for all
That I, which know my heart, do here pronounce,
By the very truth of it, I care not for you,
And am so near the lack of charity—
To accuse myself—I hate you; which I had rather
You felt than make 't my boast.

CLOTEN

　　　　　You sin against
Obedience, which you owe your father. For
The contract you pretend with that base wretch,
One bred of alms and foster'd with cold dishes,
With scraps o' the court, it is no contract, none:
And though it be allow'd in meaner parties—
Yet who than he more mean?—to knit their souls,
On whom there is no more dependency
But brats and beggary, in self-figured knot;
Yet you are curb'd from that enlargement by
The consequence o' the crown, and must not soil
The precious note of it with a base slave,
A hilding for a livery, a squire's cloth,
A pantler, not so eminent.

IMOGEN

　　　　　Profane fellow!
Wert thou the son of Jupiter, and no more
But what thou art besides, thou wert too base
To be his groom: thou wert dignified enough,

Even to the point of envy, if 'twere made
Comparative for your virtues to be styled
The under-hangman of his kingdom, and hated
For being preferr'd so well.

CLOTEN

　　　　　The south-fog rot him!

IMOGEN

He never can meet more mischance than come
To be but named of thee. His meanest garment,
That ever hath but clipp'd his body, is dearer
In my respect than all the hairs above thee,
Were they all made such men. How now, Pisanio!

Enter PISANIO

CLOTEN

'His garment!' Now, the devil—

IMOGEN

To Dorothy my woman hie thee presently,—

CLOTEN

'His garment!'

IMOGEN

　　　　　I am sprited with a fool,
Frighted and anger'd worse: go bid my woman
Search for a jewel that too casually
Hath left mine arm: it was thy master's: 'shrew me,
If I would lose it for a revenue
Of any king's in Europe! I do think
I saw 't this morning: confident I am
Last night 'twas on mine arm; I kiss'd it:
I hope it be not gone to tell my lord
That I kiss aught but he.

PISANIO

　　　　　'Twill not be lost.

IMOGEN

I hope so: go and search.　　　　[*Exit* PISANIO

CLOTEN

　　　　　You have abused me:
'His meanest garment!'

IMOGEN

　　　　　Ay, I said so, sir:
If you will make 't an action, call witness to 't.

CLOTEN

I will inform your father.

IMOGEN

　　　　　Your mother too:
She's my good lady, and will conceive, I hope,
But the worst of me. So, I leave you, sir,
To the worst of discontent.　　　　[*Exit*

CLOTEN

　　　　　I'll be revenged:
'His meanest garment!' Well.　　　　[*Exit*

SCENE IV. *Rome.* PHILARIO'S *house*

Enter POSTHUMUS *and* PHILARIO

POSTHUMUS

Fear it not, sir: I would I were so sure
To win the king as I am bold her honour
Will remain hers.

PHILARIO
What means do you make to him?

POSTHUMUS
Not any; but abide the change of time;
Quake in the present winter's state, and wish
That warmer days would come: in these fear'd
   hopes,
I barely gratify your love; they failing,
I must die much your debtor.

PHILARIO
Your very goodness and your company
O'erpays all I can do. By this, your king
Hath heard of great Augustus: Caius Lucius
Will do 's commission throughly: and I think
He'll grant the tribute, send the arrearages,
Or look upon our Romans, whose remembrance
Is yet fresh in their grief.

POSTHUMUS
              I do believe,
Statist though I am none, nor like to be,
That this will prove a war; and you shall hear
The legions now in Gallia sooner landed
In our not-fearing Britain than have tidings
Of any penny tribute paid. Our countrymen
Are men more order'd than when Julius Cæsar
Smiled at their lack of skill, but found their courage
Worthy his frowning at: their discipline,
Now mingled with their courages, will make known
To their approvers they are people such
That mend upon the world.

Enter IACHIMO

PHILARIO
           See! Iachimo!

POSTHUMUS
The swiftest harts have posted you by land,
And winds of all the corners kiss'd your sails,
To make your vessel nimble.

PHILARIO
           Welcome, sir.

POSTHUMUS
I hope the briefness of your answer made
The speediness of your return.

IACHIMO
           Your lady
Is one of the fairest that I have look'd upon.

POSTHUMUS
And therewithal the best, or let her beauty
Look through a casement to allure false hearts,
And be false with them.

IACHIMO
         Here are letters for you.

POSTHUMUS
Their tenour good, I trust.

IACHIMO
         'Tis very like.

PHILARIO
Was Caius Lucius in the Britain court
When you were there?

IACHIMO
        He was expected then,
But not approach'd.

POSTHUMUS
        All is well yet.
Sparkles this stone as it was wont? or is 't not
Too dull for your good wearing?

IACHIMO
           If I had lost it,
I should have lost the worth of it in gold.
I'll make a journey twice as far, to enjoy
A second night of such sweet shortness which
Was mine in Britain; for the ring is won.

POSTHUMUS
The stone's too hard to come by.

IACHIMO
           Not a whit,
Your lady being so easy.

POSTHUMUS
         Make not, sir,
Your loss your sport: I hope you know that we
Must not continue friends.

IACHIMO
         Good sir, we must,
If you keep covenant. Had I not brought
The knowledge of your mistress home, I grant
We were to question farther: but I now
Profess myself the winner of her honour,
Together with your ring, and not the wronger
Of her or you, having proceeded but
By both your wills.

POSTHUMUS
        If you can make 't apparent
That you have tasted her in bed, my hand
And ring is yours: if not, the foul opinion
You had of her pure honour gains or loses
Your sword or mine, or masterless leaves both
To who shall find them.

IACHIMO
        Sir, my circumstances,
Being so near the truth as I will make them,
Must first induce you to believe: whose strength
I will confirm with oath; which, I doubt not,
You'll give me leave to spare, when you shall find
You need it not.

POSTHUMUS
        Proceed.

IACHIMO
        First, her bedchamber,—
Where, I confess, I slept not, but profess
Had that was well worth watching,—it was hang'd
With tapestry of silk and silver; the story
Proud Cleopatra, when she met her Roman,
And Cydnus swell'd above the banks, or for
The press of boats or pride: a piece of work
So bravely done, so rich, that it did strive
In workmanship and value; which I wonder'd
Could be so rarely and exactly wrought,
Since the true life on 't was—

POSTHUMUS
             This is true;
And this you might have heard of here, by me,
Or by some other.

IACHIMO
             More particulars
Must justify my knowledge.

POSTHUMUS
             So they must,
Or do your honour injury.

IACHIMO
             The chimney
Is south the chamber; and the chimney-piece,
Chaste Dian bathing: never saw I figures
So likely to report themselves: the cutter
Was as another nature, dumb; outwent her,
Motion and breath left out.

POSTHUMUS
             This is a thing
Which you might from relation likewise reap,
Being, as it is, much spoke of.

IACHIMO
             The roof o' the chamber
With golden cherubins is fretted: her andirons—
I had forgot them—were two winking Cupids
Of silver, each on one foot standing, nicely
Depending on their brands.

POSTHUMUS
             This is her honour!
Let it be granted you have seen all this,—and praise
Be given to your remembrance—the description
Of what is in her chamber nothing saves
The wager you have laid.

IACHIMO
             Then, if you can,
             [Showing the bracelet
Be pale: I beg but leave to air this jewel; see!
And now 'tis up again: it must be married
To that your diamond; I'll keep them.

POSTHUMUS
             Jove!
Once more let me behold it: is it that
Which I left with her?

IACHIMO
             Sir,—I thank her—that:
She stripp'd it from her arm; I see her yet;
Her pretty action did outsell her gift,
And yet enrich'd it too: she gave it me
And said she prized it once.

POSTHUMUS
             May be she pluck'd it off
To send it me.

IACHIMO
She writes so to you, doth she?

POSTHUMUS
O, no, no, no! 'tis true. Here, take this too;
             [Gives the ring
It is a basilisk unto mine eye,

Kills me to look on 't. Let there be no honour
Where there is beauty: truth, where semblance; love,
Where there's another man: the vows of women
Of no more bondage be to where they are made
Than they are to their virtues; which is nothing.
O, above measure false!

PHILARIO
             Have patience, sir,
And take your ring again; 'tis not yet won:
It may be probable she lost it, or
Who knows if one of her women, being corrupted,
Hath stol'n it from her?

POSTHUMUS
             Very true;
And so, I hope, he came by 't. Back my ring:
Render to me some corporal sign about her
More evident than this; for this was stol'n.

IACHIMO
By Jupiter, I had it from her arm.

POSTHUMUS
Hark you, he swears; by Jupiter he swears.
'Tis true:—nay, keep the ring—'tis true: I am sure
She would not lose it: her attendants are
All sworn and honourable:—they induced to steal it!
And by a stranger!—No, he hath enjoy'd her:
The cognizance of her incontinency
Is this: she hath bought the name of whore thus dearly.
There, take thy hire; and all the fiends of hell
Divide themselves between you!

PHILARIO
             Sir, be patient:
This is not strong enough to be believed
Of one persuaded well of—

POSTHUMUS
             Never talk on 't;
She hath been colted by him.

IACHIMO
             If you seek
For further satisfying, under her breast—
Worthy the pressing—lies a mole, right proud
Of that most delicate lodging: by my life,
I kiss'd it, and it gave me present hunger
To feed again, though full. You do remember
This stain upon her?

POSTHUMUS
             Ay, and it doth confirm
Another stain, as big as hell can hold,
Were there no more but it.

IACHIMO
             Will you hear more?

POSTHUMUS
Spare your arithmetic; never count the turns;
Once, and a million!

IACHIMO
             I'll be sworn—

POSTHUMUS

No swearing.
If you will swear you have not done 't you lie,
And I will kill thee if thou dost deny
Thou'st made me cuckold.

IACHIMO

I'll deny nothing.

POSTHUMUS

O, that I had her here, to tear her limb-meal!
I will go there and do 't; i' the court; before
Her father. I'll do something—   [Exit

PHILARIO

Quite besides
The government of patience! You have won:
Let's follow him and pervert the present wrath
He hath against himself.

IACHIMO

With all my heart. [Exeunt

SCENE V. *Another room in* PHILARIO's *house*

Enter POSTHUMUS

POSTHUMUS

Is there no way for men to be, but women
Must be half-workers? We are all bastards;
And that most venerable man which I
Did call my father, was I know not where
When I was stamp'd; some coiner with his tools
Made me a counterfeit: yet my mother seem'd
The Dian of that time: so doth my wife
The nonpareil of this. O, vengeance, vengeance!
Me of my lawful pleasure she restrain'd,
And pray'd me oft forbearance; did it with
A pudency so rosy, the sweet view on 't
Might well have warm'd old Saturn; that I thought
    her
As chaste as unsunn'd snow. O, all the devils!
This yellow Iachimo, in an hour,—was 't not?—
Or less,—at first?—perchance he spoke not, but
Like a full-acorn'd boar, a German one,
Cried 'O!' and mounted; found no opposition
But what he look'd for should oppose and she
Should from encounter guard. Could I find out
The woman's part in me! For there's no motion
That tends to vice in man but I affirm
It is the woman's part: be it lying, note it,
The woman's; flattering, hers; deceiving, hers;
Lust and rank thoughts, hers, hers; revenges, hers;
Ambitions, covetings, change of prides, disdain,
Nice longing, slanders, mutability,
All faults that may be named, nay, that hell knows,
Why, hers, in part or all, but rather all;
For even to vice
They are not constant, but are changing still
One vice, but of a minute old, for one
Not half so old as that. I'll write against them,
Detest them, curse them: yet 'tis greater skill
In a true hate, to pray they have their will:
The very devils cannot plague them better.   [Exit

ACT III

SCENE I. *Britain. A hall in* CYMBELINE's *palace*

Enter in state, CYMBELINE, QUEEN, CLOTEN, *and* LORDS
at one door, and at another, CAIUS LUCIUS *and*
ATTENDANTS

CYMBELINE

Now say, what would Augustus Cæsar with us?

LUCIUS

When Julius Cæsar, whose remembrance yet
Lives in men's eyes and will to ears and tongues
Be theme and hearing ever, was in this Britain
And conquer'd it, Cassibelan, thine uncle,—
Famous in Cæsar's praises, no whit less
Than in his feats deserving it—for him
And his succession granted Rome a tribute,
Yearly three thousand pounds; which by thee lately
Is left untender'd.

QUEEN

And, to kill the marvel,
Shall be so ever.

CLOTEN

There be many Cæsars
Ere such another Julius. Britain is
A world by itself, and we will nothing pay
For wearing our own noses.

QUEEN

That opportunity,
Which then they had to take from 's, to resume
We have again. Remember, sir, my liege,
The kings your ancestors, together with
The natural bravery of your isle, which stands
As Neptune's park, ribbed and paled in
With rocks unscaleable and roaring waters,
With sands that will not bear your enemies' boats,
But suck them up to the topmast. A kind of con-
    quest
Cæsar made here; but made not here his brag
Of 'Came, and saw, and overcame:' with shame—
The first that ever touch'd him—he was carried
From off our coast, twice beaten; and his shipping—
Poor ignorant baubles!—on our terrible seas,
Like egg-shells moved upon their surges, crack'd
As easily 'gainst our rocks: for joy whereof
The famed Cassibelan, who was once at point—
O giglot fortune!—to master Cæsar's sword,
Made Lud's town with rejoicing fires bright
And Britons strut with courage.

CLOTEN

Come, there's no more tribute to be paid: our kingdom is stronger than it was at that time; and, as I
said, there is no moe such Cæsars: other of them
may have crooked noses, but to owe such straight
arms, none.

CYMBELINE

Son, let your mother end.

CLOTEN

We have yet many among us can gripe as hard as
Cassibelan: I do not say I am one; but I have a
hand. Why tribute? why should we pay tribute? If

Cæsar can hide the sun from us with a blanket, or
put the moon in his pocket, we will pay him tribute
for light; else, sir, no more tribute, pray you now.
CYMBELINE
You must know,
Till the injurious Romans did extort
This tribute from us, we were free: Cæsar's ambi-
tion,
Which swell'd so much that it did almost stretch
The sides o' the world, against all colour here
Did put the yoke upon 's; which to shake off
Becomes a warlike people, whom we reckon
Ourselves to be.
CLOTEN and LORDS
We do.
CYMBELINE
　　　　　Say then to Cæsar,
Our ancestor was that Mulmutius which
Ordain'd our laws, whose use the sword of Cæsar
Hath too much mangled; whose repair and fran-
chise
Shall, by the power we hold, be our good deed,
Though Rome be therefore angry. Mulmutius made
　　our laws,
Who was the first of Britain which did put
His brows within a golden crown, and call'd
Himself a king.
LUCIUS
I am sorry, Cymbeline,
That I am to pronounce Augustus Cæsar—
Cæsar, that hath moe kings his servants than
Thyself domestic officers—thine enemy:
Receive it from me, then: war and confusion
In Cæsar's name pronounce I 'gainst thee: look
For fury not to be resisted. Thus defied,
I thank thee for myself.
CYMBELINE
　　　　　Thou art welcome, Caius.
Thy Cæsar knighted me; my youth I spent
Much under him; of him I gather'd honour;
Which he to seek of me again, perforce,
Behoves me keep at utterance. I am perfect
That the Pannonians and Dalmatians for
Their liberties are now in arms; a precedent
Which not to read would show the Britons cold:
So Cæsar shall not find them.
LUCIUS
　　　　　Let proof speak.
CLOTEN
His majesty bids you welcome. Make pastime with
us a day or two, or longer: if you seek us afterwards
in other terms, you shall find us in our salt-water
girdle: if you beat us out of it, it is yours; if you fall
in the adventure, our crows shall fare the better for
you; and there's an end.
LUCIUS
So, sir.
CYMBELINE
I know your master's pleasure, and he mine:
All the remain is 'Welcome.'　　　　　[Exeunt

SCENE II. _Another room in the palace_

Enter PISANIO, _with a letter_
PISANIO
How! of adultery? Wherefore write you not
What monster's her accuser? Leonatus!
O master! what a strange infection
Is fall'n into thy ear! What false Italian,
As poisonous-tongued as handed, hath prevail'd
On thy too ready hearing? Disloyal! No:
She's punish'd for her truth, and undergoes,
More goddess-like than wife-like, such assaults
As would take in some virtue. O my master!
Thy mind to her is now as low as were
Thy fortunes. How! that I should murder her?
Upon the love and truth and vows which I
Have made to thy command? I, her? her blood?
If it be so to do good service, never
Let me be counted serviceable. How look I,
That I should seem to lack humanity
So much as this fact comes to? [_Reading_]
　　　　　　　　　　'Do't: the letter
　　That I have sent her, by her own command
　　Shall give thee opportunity.'
　　　　　　　　　　O damn'd paper!
Black as the ink that's on thee! Senseless bauble,
Art thou a feodary for this act, and look'st
So virgin-like without? Lo, here she comes.
I am ignorant in what I am commanded.
Enter IMOGEN
IMOGEN
How now, Pisanio!
PISANIO
Madam, here is a letter from my lord.
IMOGEN
Who? thy lord? that is my lord Leonatus!
O, learn'd indeed were that astronomer
That knew the stars as I his characters;
He'ld lay the future open. You good gods,
Let what is here contain'd relish of love,
Of my lord's health, of his content, yet not
That we two are asunder; let that grieve him:
Some griefs are medicinable; that is one of them,
For it doth physic love: of his content,
All but in that! Good wax, thy leave. Blest be
You bees that make these locks of counsel! Lovers
And men in dangerous bonds pray not alike:
Though forfeiters you cast in prison, yet
You clasp young Cupid's tables. Good news, gods!
[_Reads_] 'Justice, and your father's wrath, should he take me
in his dominion, could not be so cruel to me, as you, O the
dearest of creatures, would even renew me with your eyes.
Take notice that I am in Cambria, at Milford-Haven: what
your own love will out of this advise you, follow. So he wishes
you all happiness, that remains loyal to his vow, and your,
increasing in love,
　　　　　　　　　　LEONATUS POSTHUMUS.'
O, for a horse with wings! Hear'st thou, Pisanio?
He is at Milford-Haven: read, and tell me
How far 'tis thither. If one of mean affairs
May plod it in a week, why may not I

Glide thither in a day? Then, true Pisanio,—
Who long'st, like me, to see thy lord; who long'st—
O, let me bate,—but not like me—yet long'st,
But in a fainter kind:—O, not like me;
For mine's beyond beyond: say, and speak thick,—
Love's counsellor should fill the bores of hearing,
To the smothering of the sense—how far it is
To this same blessed Milford: and by the way
Tell me how Wales was made so happy as
To inherit such a haven: but, first of all,
How we may steal from hence: and for the gap
That we shall make in time, from our hence-going
And our return, to excuse: but first, how get hence.
Why should excuse be born or ere begot?
We'll talk of that hereafter. Prithee, speak,
How many score of miles may we well ride
'Twixt hour and hour?

PISANIO

                    One score 'twixt sun and sun,
Madam, 's enough for you, and too much too.

IMOGEN

Why, one that rode to 's execution, man,
Could never go so slow: I have heard of riding
    wagers,
Where horses have been nimbler than the sands
That run i' the clock's behalf. But this is foolery:
Go bid my woman feign a sickness, say
She'll home to her father: and provide me presently
A riding-suit, no costlier than would fit
A franklin's housewife.

PISANIO

                    Madam, you're best consider.

IMOGEN

I see before me, man: nor here, nor here,
Nor what ensues, but have a fog in them,
That I cannot look through. Away, I prithee;
Do as I bid thee: there's no more to say;
Accessible is none but Milford way.   [Exeunt

SCENE III. *Wales: a mountainous country with a cave*

Enter BELARIUS, GUIDERIUS, *and* ARVIRAGUS

BELARIUS

A goodly day not to keep house with such
Whose roof's as low as ours! Stoop, boys: this gate
Instructs you how to adore the heavens, and bows
    you
To a morning's holy office: the gates of monarchs
Are arch'd so high that giants may jet through
And keep their impious turbans on, without
Good morrow to the sun. Hail, thou fair heaven!
We house i' the rock, yet use thee not so hardly
As prouder livers do.

GUIDERIUS

Hail, heaven!

ARVIRAGUS

                    Hail, heaven!

BELARIUS

Now for our mountain sport: up to yond hill!

Your legs are young: I'll tread these flats. Consider,
When you above perceive me like a crow,
That it is place which lessens and sets off:
And you may then revolve what tales I have told
    you
Of courts, of princes, of the tricks in war:
This service is not service, so being done,
But being so allow'd: to apprehend thus,
Draws us a profit from all things we see;
And often, to our comfort, shall we find
The sharded beetle in a safer hold
Than is the full-wing'd eagle. O, this life
Is nobler than attending for a check,
Richer than doing nothing for a bauble,
Prouder than rustling in unpaid-for silk:
Such gain the cap of him that makes 'em fine,
Yet keeps his book uncross'd: no life to ours.

GUIDERIUS

Out of your proof you speak: we, poor unfledged,
Have never wing'd from view o' the nest, nor know
    not
What air's from home. Haply this life is best
If quiet life be best, sweeter to you
That have a sharper known, well corresponding
With your stiff age: but unto us it is
A cell of ignorance, travelling a-bed,
A prison for a debtor that not dares
To stride a limit.

ARVIRAGUS

                    What should we speak of
When we are old as you? when we shall hear
The rain and wind beat dark December, how
In this our pinching cave shall we discourse
The freezing hours away? We have seen nothing:
We are beastly; subtle as the fox for prey,
Like warlike as the wolf for what we eat:
Our valour is to chase what flies; our cage
We make a quire, as doth the prison'd bird,
And sing our bondage freely.

BELARIUS

                    How you speak!
Did you but know the city's usuries,
And felt them knowingly: the art o' the court,
As hard to leave as keep: whose top to climb
Is certain falling, or so slippery that
The fear's as bad as falling: the toil o' the war,
A pain that only seems to seek out danger
I' the name of fame and honour, which dies i' the
    search,
And hath as oft a slanderous epitaph
As record of fair act; nay, many times,
Doth ill deserve by doing well; what's worse,
Must court'sy at the censure:—O boys, this story
The world may read in me: my body's mark'd
With Roman swords, and my report was once
First with the best of note: Cymbeline loved me;
And when a soldier was the theme, my name
Was not far off: then was I as a tree
Whose boughs did bend with fruit: but in one night,
A storm, or robbery, call it what you will,

Shook down my mellow hangings, nay, my leaves,
And left me bare to weather.

GUIDERIUS
Uncertain favour!

BELARIUS
My fault being nothing, as I have told you oft,
But that two villains, whose false oaths prevail'd
Before my perfect honour, swore to Cymbeline
I was confederate with the Romans; so
Follow'd my banishment; and this twenty years
This rock and these demesnes have been my world:
Where I have lived at honest freedom, paid
More pious debts to heaven than in all
The fore-end of my time. But up to the mountains!
This is not hunters' language: he that strikes
The venison first shall be the lord o' the feast;
To him the other two shall minister;
And we will fear no poison, which attends
In place of greater state. I'll meet you in the valleys.
[Exeunt GUIDERIUS and ARVIRAGUS
How hard it is to hide the sparks of nature!
These boys know little they are sons to the king;
Nor Cymbeline dreams that they are alive.
They think they are mine: and though train'd up
    thus meanly
I' the cave wherein they bow, their thoughts do hit
The roofs of palaces, and nature prompts them
In simple and low things to prince it much
Beyond the trick of others. This Polydore,
The heir of Cymbeline and Britain, who
The king his father call'd Guiderius,—Jove!
When on my three-foot stool I sit and tell
The warlike feats I have done, his spirits fly out
Into my story: say 'Thus mine enemy fell,
And thus I set my foot on 's neck,' even then
The princely blood flows in his cheek, he sweats,
Strains his young nerves, and puts himself in pos-
    ture
That acts my words. The younger brother, Cadwal,
Once Arviragus, in as like a figure
Strikes life into my speech and shows much more
His own conceiving. Hark, the game is roused!
O Cymbeline! heaven and my conscience knows
Thou didst unjustly banish me: whereon,
At three and two years old, I stole these babes,
Thinking to bar thee of succession as
Thou reft'st me of my lands. Euriphile,
Thou wast their nurse; they took thee for their
    mother,
And every day do honour to her grave:
Myself, Belarius, that am Morgan call'd,
They take for natural father. The game is up. [Exit

SCENE IV. Country near Milford-Haven

Enter PISANIO and IMOGEN

IMOGEN
Thou told'st me, when we came from horse, the
    place

Was near at hand: ne'er long'd my mother so
To see me first, as I have now. Pisanio! man!
Where is Posthumus? What is in thy mind,
That makes thee stare thus? Wherefore breaks that
    sigh
From the inward of thee? One but painted thus
Would be interpreted a thing perplex'd
Beyond self-explication: put thyself
Into a haviour of less fear, ere wildness
Vanquish my staider senses. What's the matter?
Why tender'st thou that paper to me, with
A look untender? If 't be summer news,
Smile to 't before; if winterly, thou need'st
But keep that countenance still. My husband's hand!
That drug-damn'd Italy hath out-craftied him,
And he's at some hard point. Speak, man: thy
    tongue
May take off some extremity, which to read
Would be even mortal to me.

PISANIO
Please you, read;
And you shall find me, wretched man, a thing
The most disdain'd of fortune.

IMOGEN
[Reads] 'Thy mistress, Pisanio, hath played the strumpet in
my bed; the testimonies whereof lie bleeding in me. I speak not
out of weak surmises; but from proof as strong as my grief, and
as certain as I expect my revenge. That part thou, Pisanio,
must act for me, if thy faith be not tainted with the breach of
hers. Let thine own hands take away her life: I shall give thee
opportunity at Milford-Haven: she hath my letter for the purpose: where, if thou fear to strike, and to make me certain it is
done, thou art the pandar to her dishonour, and equally to me
disloyal.'

PISANIO
What shall I need to draw my sword? the paper
Hath cut her throat already. No, 'tis slander;
Whose edge is sharper than the sword; whose tongue
Outvenoms all the worms of Nile; whose breath
Rides on the posting winds, and doth belie
All corners of the world: kings, queens, and states,
Maids, matrons, nay, the secrets of the grave
This viperous slander enters. What cheer, madam?

IMOGEN
False to his bed! What is it to be false?
To lie in watch there, and to think on him?
To weep 'twixt clock and clock? if sleep charge
    nature,
To break it with a fearful dream of him,
And cry myself awake? that's false to 's bed, is it?

PISANIO
Alas, good lady!

IMOGEN
I false! Thy conscience witness: Iachimo,
Thou didst accuse him of incontinency;
Thou then look'dst like a villain; now, methinks,
Thy favour's good enough. Some jay of Italy,
Whose mother was her painting, hath betray'd him:
Poor I am stale, a garment out of fashion;
And, for I am richer than to hang by the walls,
I must be ripp'd:—to pieces with me!—O.

Men's vows are women's traitors! All good seeming,
By the revolt, O husband, shall be thought
Put on for villany; not born where 't grows,
But worn a bait for ladies.

PISANIO
                Good madam, hear me.

IMOGEN
True honest men being heard, like false Æneas,
Were in his time thought false; and Sinon's weeping
Did scandal many a holy tear, took pity
From most true wretchedness: so thou Posthumus,
Wilt lay the leaven on all proper men;
Goodly and gallant shall be false and perjured
From thy great fail. Come, fellow, be thou honest:
Do thou thy master's bidding. When thou see'st him,
A little witness my obedience. Look!
I draw the sword myself: take it, and hit
The innocent mansion of my love, my heart:
Fear not; 'tis empty of all things but grief:
Thy master is not there, who was indeed
The riches of it. Do his bidding; strike.
Thou mayst be valiant in a better cause,
But now thou seem'st a coward.

PISANIO
                Hence, vile instrument!
Thou shalt not damn my hand.

IMOGEN
                Why, I must die;
And if I do not by thy hand, thou art
No servant of thy master's. Against self-slaughter
There is a prohibition so divine
That cravens my weak hand. Come, here's my heart;—
Something's afore 't. Soft, soft! we'll no defence;—
Obedient as the scabbard. What is here?
The scriptures of the loyal Leonatus,
All turn'd to heresy? Away, away,
Corrupters of my faith! you shall no more
Be stomachers to my heart. Thus may poor fools
Believe false teachers: though those that are betray'd
Do feel the treason sharply, yet the traitor
Stands in worse case of woe.
And thou, Posthumus, thou that didst set up
My disobedience 'gainst the king my father,
And make me put into contempt the suits
Of princely fellows, shalt hereafter find
It is no act of common passage, but
A strain of rareness: and I grieve myself
To think, when thou shalt be disedged by her
That now thou tirest on, how thy memory
Will then be pang'd by me. Prithee, dispatch:
The lamb entreats the butcher: where's thy knife?
Thou art too slow to do thy master's bidding,
When I desire it too.

PISANIO
             O gracious lady,
Since I received command to do this business
I have not slept one wink.

IMOGEN
             Do 't and to bed then.

PISANIO
I'll wake mine eye-balls blind first.

IMOGEN
                Wherefore then
Didst undertake it? Why hast thou abused
So many miles with a pretence? this place?
Mine action, and thine own? our horses' labour?
The time inviting thee? the perturb'd court,
For my being absent? whereunto I never
Purpose return. Why hast thou gone so far,
To be unbent when thou hast ta'en thy stand,
The elected deer before thee?

PISANIO
                But to win time
To lose so bad employment; in the which
I have consider'd of a course. Good lady,
Hear me with patience.

IMOGEN
             Talk thy tongue weary; speak:
I have heard I am a strumpet; and mine ear,
Therein false struck, can take no greater wound,
Nor tent to bottom that. But speak.

PISANIO
                Then, madam,
I thought you would not back again.

IMOGEN
                Most like,
Bringing me here to kill me.

PISANIO
                Not so, neither:
But if I were as wise as honest, then
My purpose would prove well. It cannot be
But that my master is abused: some villain,
Ay, and singular in his art, hath done you both
This cursed injury.

IMOGEN
Some Roman courtezan.

PISANIO
              No, on my life.
I'll give but notice you are dead, and send him
Some bloody sign of it; for 'tis commanded
I should do so: you shall be miss'd at court,
And that will well confirm it.

IMOGEN
            Why, good fellow,
What shall I do the while? where bide? how live?
Or in my life what comfort, when I am
Dead to my husband?

PISANIO
            If you'll back to the court—

IMOGEN
No court, no father; nor no more ado
With that harsh, noble, simple nothing,
That Cloten, whose love-suit hath been to me
As fearful as a siege.

PISANIO
            If not at court,
Then not in Britain must you bide.

IMOGEN
                Where then?

Hath Britain all the sun that shines? Day, night,
Are they not but in Britain? I' the world's volume
Our Britain seems as of it, but not in 't;
In a great pool a swan's nest: prithee, think
There's livers out of Britain.

PISANIO
　　　　　　　　I am most glad
You think of other place. The ambassador,
Lucius the Roman, comes to Milford-Haven
To-morrow: now, if you could wear a mind
Dark as your fortune is, and but disguise
That which, to appear itself, must not yet be
But by self-danger, you should tread a course
Pretty and full of view; yea, haply, near
The residence of Posthumus; so nigh at least
That though his actions were not visible, yet
Report should render him hourly to your ear
As truly as he moves.

IMOGEN
　　　　　　　　O, for such means,
Though peril to my modesty, not death on 't,
I would adventure!

PISANIO
　　　　　　　　Well then, here's the point:
You must forget to be a woman; change
Command into obedience; fear and niceness—
The handmaids of all women, or, more truly,
Woman it pretty self—into a waggish courage;
Ready in gibes, quick-answer'd, saucy and
As quarrelous as the weasel; nay, you must
Forget that rarest treasure of your cheek,
Exposing it—but, O, the harder heart!
Alack, no remedy!—to the greedy touch
Of common-kissing Titan, and forget
Your laboursome and dainty trims, wherein
You made great Juno angry.

IMOGEN
　　　　　　　　Nay, be brief:
I see into thy end, and am almost
A man already.

PISANIO
　　　　　　　　First, make yourself but like one.
Fore-thinking this, I have already fit—
'Tis in my cloak-bag—doublet, hat, hose, all
That answer to them: would you, in their serving
And with what imitation you can borrow
From youth of such a season, 'fore noble Lucius
Present yourself, desire his service, tell him
Wherein you're happy,—which you'll make him
　　know,
If that his head have ear in music,—doubtless
With joy he will embrace you; for he's honourable,
And, doubling that, most holy. Your means abroad,
You have me, rich; and I will never fail
Beginning nor supplyment.

IMOGEN
　　　　　　　　Thou art all the comfort
The gods will diet me with. Prithee, away:
There's more to be consider'd; but we'll even
All that good time will give us: this attempt

I am soldier to, and will abide it with
A prince's courage. Away, I prithee.

PISANIO
Well, madam, we must take a short farewell,
Lest, being miss'd, I be suspected of
Your carriage from the court. My noble mistress,
Here is a box; I had it from the queen:
What's in 't is precious; if you are sick at sea,
Or stomach-qualm'd at land, a dram of this
Will drive away distemper. To some shade,
And fit you to your manhood: may the gods
Direct you to the best!

IMOGEN
　　　　　　　　Amen: I thank thee.
　　　　　　　　　　　　　[Exeunt severally

SCENE V. A room in CYMBELINE's palace

Enter CYMBELINE, QUEEN, CLOTEN, LUCIUS, and LORDS
CYMBELINE
Thus far; and so farewell.

LUCIUS
　　　　　　　　Thanks, royal sir.
My emperor hath wrote, I must from hence;
And am right sorry that I must report ye
My master's enemy.

CYMBELINE
　　　　　　　　Our subjects, sir,
Will not endure his yoke; and for ourself
To show less sovereignty than they, must needs
Appear unkinglike.

LUCIUS
　　　　　　　　So, sir: I desire of you
A conduct over-land to Milford-Haven.
Madam, all joy befal your grace, and you!

CYMBELINE
My lords, you are appointed for that office;
The due of honour in no point omit.
So farewell, noble Lucius.

LUCIUS
　　　　　　　　Your hand, my lord.

CLOTEN
Receive it friendly; but from this time forth
I wear it as your enemy.

LUCIUS
　　　　　　　　Sir, the event
Is yet to name the winner: fare you well.

CYMBELINE
Leave not the worthy Lucius, good my lords,
Till he have cross'd the Severn. Happiness!
　　　　　　　　　　[Exeunt LUCIUS and LORDS

QUEEN
He goes hence frowning: but it honours us
That we have given him cause.

CLOTEN
　　　　　　　　'Tis all the better;
Your valiant Britons have they wishes in it.

CYMBELINE
Lucius hath wrote already to the emperor

How it goes here. It fits us therefore ripely
Our chariots and our horsemen be in readiness:
The powers that he already hath in Gallia
Will soon be drawn to head, from whence he moves
His war for Britain.

QUEEN
                        'Tis not sleepy business,
But must be look'd to speedily and strongly.

CYMBELINE
Our expectation that it would be thus
Hath made us forward. But, my gentle queen,
Where is our daughter? She hath not appear'd
Before the Roman, nor to us hath tender'd
The duty of the day: she looks us like
A thing more made of malice than of duty:
We have noted it. Call her before us, for
We have been too slight in sufferance.
                        [Exit an ATTENDANT

QUEEN
                        Royal sir,
Since the exile of Posthumus, most retired
Hath her life been; the cure whereof, my lord,
'Tis time must do. Beseech your majesty,
Forbear sharp speeches to her: she's a lady
So tender of rebukes that words are strokes,
And strokes death to her.

Re-enter ATTENDANT

CYMBELINE
                        Where is she, sir? How
Can her contempt be answer'd?

ATTENDANT
                        Please you, sir,
Her chambers are all lock'd, and there's no answer
That will be given to the loud'st of noise we make.

QUEEN
My lord, when last I went to visit her,
She pray'd me to excuse her keeping close;
Whereto constrain'd by her infirmity,
She should that duty leave unpaid to you,
Which daily she was bound to proffer: this
She wish'd me to make known; but our great court
Made me to blame in memory.

CYMBELINE
                        Her doors lock'd?
Not seen of late? Grant, heavens, that which I fear
Prove false!   [Exit

QUEEN
Son, I say, follow the king.

CLOTEN
That man of hers, Pisanio, her old servant,
I have not seen these two days.

QUEEN
                        Go, look after.
                        [Exit CLOTEN
Pisanio, thou that stand'st so for Posthumus!
He hath a drug of mine; I pray his absence
Proceed by swallowing that; for he believes
It is a thing most precious. But for her,
Where is she gone? Haply, despair hath seized her;
Or, wing'd with fervour of her love, she's flown

To her desired Posthumus: gone she is
To death or to dishonour; and my end
Can make good use of either: she being down,
I have the placing of the British crown.

Re-enter CLOTEN

How now, my son!

CLOTEN
                        'Tis certain she is fled.
Go in and cheer the king: he rages; none
Dare come about him.

QUEEN
                        [Aside] All the better: may
This night forestall him of the coming day!   [Exit

CLOTEN
I love and hate her: for she's fair and royal,
And that she hath all courtly parts more exquisite
Than lady, ladies, woman; from every one
The best she hath, and she, of all compounded,
Outsells them all; I love her therefore: but
Disdaining me and throwing favours on
The low Posthumus slanders so her judgement
That what's else rare is choked; and in that point
I will conclude to hate her, nay, indeed,
To be revenged upon her. For when fools
Shall—

Enter PISANIO

                Who is here? What, are you packing, sirrah?
Come hither: ah, you precious pandar! Villain,
Where is thy lady? In a word; or else
Thou art straightway with the fiends.

PISANIO
                        O, good my lord!

CLOTEN
Where is thy lady? or, by Jupiter,—
I will not ask again. Close villain,
I'll have this secret from thy heart, or rip
Thy heart to find it. Is she with Posthumus?
From whose so many weights of baseness cannot
A dram of worth be drawn.

PISANIO
                        Alas, my lord,
How can she be with him? When was she miss'd?
He is in Rome.

CLOTEN
                        Where is she, sir? Come nearer;
No farther halting: satisfy me home
What is become of her.

PISANIO
O, my all-worthy lord!

CLOTEN
                        All-worthy villain!
Discover where thy mistress is at once,
At the next word: no more of 'worthy lord!'
Speak, or thy silence on the instant is
Thy condemnation and thy death.

PISANIO
                        Then, sir,
This paper is the history of my knowledge
Touching her flight.   [Presenting a letter

CLOTEN

          Let's see 't. I will pursue her
Even to Augustus' throne.

PISANIO

         [Aside] Or this, or perish.
She's far enough; and what he learns by this
May prove his travel, not her danger.

CLOTEN

             Hum!

PISANIO

[Aside] I'll write to my lord she's dead. O Imogen,
Safe mayst thou wander, safe return again!

CLOTEN

Sirrah, is this letter true?

PISANIO

Sir, as I think.

CLOTEN

It is Posthumus' hand; I know 't. Sirrah, if thou
wouldst not be a villain, but do me true service,
undergo those employments wherein I should have
cause to use thee with a serious industry, that is,
what villany soe'er I bid thee do, to perform it
directly and truly, I would think thee an honest
man: thou shouldst neither want my means for thy
relief, nor my voice for thy preferment.

PISANIO

Well, my good lord.

CLOTEN

Wilt thou serve me? for since patiently and constantly thou hast stuck to the bare fortune of that
beggar Posthumus, thou canst not, in the course of
gratitude, but be a diligent follower of mine. Wilt
thou serve me?

PISANIO

Sir, I will.

CLOTEN

Give me thy hand; here's my purse. Hast any of thy
late master's garments in thy possession?

PISANIO

I have, my lord, at my lodging the same suit he
wore when he took leave of my lady and mistress.

CLOTEN

The first service thou dost me, fetch that suit hither:
let it be thy first service; go.

PISANIO

I shall, my lord.   [Exit

CLOTEN

Meet thee at Milford-Haven!—I forgot to ask him
one thing; I'll remember 't anon:—even there, thou
villain Posthumus, will I kill thee. I would these
garments were come. She said upon a time—the
bitterness of it I now belch from my heart—that she
held the very garment of Posthumus in more respect
than my noble and natural person, together with
the adornment of my qualities. With that suit upon
my back, will I ravish her: first kill him, and in her
eyes; there shall she see my valour, which will then
be a torment to her contempt. He on the ground,
my speech of insultment ended on his dead body,
and when my lust hath dined—which, as I say, to

vex her I will execute in the clothes that she so
praised—to the court I'll knock her back, foot her
home again. She hath despised me rejoicingly, and
I'll be merry in my revenge.

        Re-enter PISANIO, with the clothes
Be those the garments?

PISANIO

Ay, my noble lord.

CLOTEN

How long is 't since she went to Milford-Haven?

PISANIO

She can scarce be there yet.

CLOTEN

Bring this apparel to my chamber; that is the second
thing that I have commanded thee: the third is,
that thou wilt be a voluntary mute to my design. Be
but duteous, and true preferment shall tender itself
to thee. My revenge is now at Milford: would I had
wings to follow it! Come, and be true.   [Exit

PISANIO

Thou bid'st me to my loss: for, true to thee
Were to prove false, which I will never be,
To him that is most true. To Milford go,
And find not her whom thou pursuest. Flow, flow,
You heavenly blessings, on her! This fool's speed
Be cross'd with slowness; labour be his meed! [Exit

SCENE VI. Wales: before the cave of BELARIUS

       Enter IMOGEN, in boy's clothes

IMOGEN

I see a man's life is a tedious one:
I have tired myself; and for two nights together
Have made the ground my bed. I should be sick,
But that my resolution helps me. Milford,
When from the mountain-top Pisanio show'd thee,
Thou wast within a ken: O Jove! I think
Foundations fly the wretched; such, I mean,
Where they should be relieved. Two beggars told
   me
I could not miss my way: will poor folks lie,
That have afflictions on them, knowing 'tis
A punishment or trial? Yes; no wonder,
When rich ones scarce tell true: to lapse in fulness
Is sorer than to lie for need; and falsehood
Is worse in kings than beggars. My dear lord!
Thou art one o' the false ones: now I think on thee,
My hunger's gone; but even before, I was
At point to sink for food. But what is this?
Here is a path to 't: 'tis some savage hold:
I were best not call; I dare not call: yet famine,
Ere clean it o'erthrow nature, makes it valiant.
Plenty and peace breeds cowards; hardness ever
Of hardiness is mother. Ho! who's here?
If any thing that's civil, speak; if savage,
Take or lend. Ho! No answer? then I'll enter.
Best draw my sword; and if mine enemy
But fear the sword like me, he'll scarcely look on 't.
Such a foe, good heavens!   [Exit, to the cave

Enter BELARIUS, GUIDERIUS, *and* ARVIRAGUS

BELARIUS

You, Polydore, have proved best woodman and
Are master of the feast: Cadwal and I
Will play the cook and servant; 'tis our match:
The sweat of industry would dry and die,
But for the end it works to. Come; our stomachs
Will make what's homely savoury: weariness
Can snore upon the flint, when resty sloth
Finds the down pillow hard. Now, peace be here,
Poor house, that keep'st thyself!

GUIDERIUS

                    I am throughly weary.

ARVIRAGUS

I am weak with toil, yet strong in appetite.

GUIDERIUS

There is cold meat i' the cave; we'll browse on that,
Whilst what we have kill'd be cook'd.

BELARIUS

[*Looking into the cave*] Stay; come not in.
But that it eats our victuals, I should think
Here were a fairy.

GUIDERIUS

                    What's the matter, sir?

BELARIUS

By Jupiter, an angel! or, if not,
An earthly paragon! Behold divineness
No elder than a boy!

Re-enter IMOGEN

IMOGEN

Good masters, harm me not:
Before I enter'd here, I call'd; and thought
To have begg'd or bought what I have took: good
    troth,
I have stol'n nought; nor would not, though I had
    found
Gold strew'd i' the floor. Here's money for my meat:
I would have left it on the board so soon
As I had made my meal, and parted
With prayers for the provider.

GUIDERIUS

                    Money, youth?

ARVIRAGUS

All gold and silver rather turn to dirt!
As 'tis no better reckon'd, but of those
Who worship dirty gods.

IMOGEN

                    I see you're angry:
Know, if you kill me for my fault, I should
Have died had I not made it.

BELARIUS

                    Whither bound?

IMOGEN

To Milford-Haven.

BELARIUS

What's your name?

IMOGEN

Fidele, sir. I have a kinsman who
Is bound for Italy; he embark'd at Milford;

To whom being going, almost spent with hunger,
I am fall'n in this offence.

BELARIUS

                    Prithee, fair youth,
Think us no churls, nor measure our good minds
By this rude place we live in. Well encounter'd!
'Tis almost night: you shall have better cheer
Ere you depart; and thanks to stay and eat it.
Boys, bid him welcome.

GUIDERIUS

                    Were you a woman, youth,
I should woo hard but be your groom. In honesty,
I bid for you as I'ld buy.

ARVIRAGUS

                    I'll make 't my comfort
He is a man; I'll love him as my brother:
And such a welcome as I'ld give to him
After long absence, such is yours: most welcome!
Be sprightly, for you fall 'mongst friends.

IMOGEN

                    'Mongst friends,
If brothers. [*Aside*] Would it had been so, that they
Had been my father's sons! then had my prize
Been less, and so more equal ballasting
To thee, Posthumus.

BELARIUS

He wrings at some distress.

GUIDERIUS

Would I could free 't!

ARVIRAGUS

                    Or I; whate'er it be,
What pain it cost, what danger! Gods!

BELARIUS

                    Hark, boys.
                                        [*Whispering*

IMOGEN

Great men,
That had a court no bigger than this cave,
That did attend themselves and had the virtue
Which their own conscience seal'd them—laying by
That nothing-gift of differing multitudes—
Could not out-peer these twain. Pardon me, gods!
I'ld change my sex to be companion with them,
Since Leonatus' false.

BELARIUS

                    It shall be so.
Boys, we'll go dress our hunt. Fair youth, come in:
Discourse is heavy, fasting; when we have supp'd,
We'll mannerly demand thee of thy story,
So far as thou wilt speak it.

GUIDERIUS

                    Pray, draw near.

ARVIRAGUS

The night to the owl and morn to the lark less
    welcome.

IMOGEN

Thanks, sir.

ARVIRAGUS

I pray, draw near.   [*Exeunt*

[1240]

SCENE VII. *Rome. A public place*

Enter two SENATORS *and* TRIBUNES
FIRST SENATOR

This is the tenour of the emperor's writ:
That since the common men are now in action
'Gainst the Pannonians and Dalmatians,
And that the legions now in Gallia are
Full weak to undertake our wars against
The fall'n-off Britons, that we do incite
The gentry to this business. He creates
Lucius proconsul: and to you the tribunes,
For this immediate levy, he commends
His absolute commission. Long live Cæsar!

FIRST TRIBUNE

Is Lucius general of the forces?

SECOND SENATOR

　　　　　　Ay.

FIRST TRIBUNE

Remaining now in Gallia?

FIRST SENATOR

　　　　　　With those legions
Which I have spoke of, whereunto your levy
Must be supplyant: the words of your commission
Will tie you to the numbers and the time
Of their dispatch.

FIRST TRIBUNE

　　　We will discharge our duty.
　　　　　　　　　　　　[*Exeunt*

ACT IV

SCENE I. *Wales: near the cave of* BELARIUS

Enter CLOTEN *alone*
CLOTEN

I am near to the place where they should meet, if
Pisanio have mapped it truly. How fit his garments
serve me! Why should his mistress, who was made
by him that made the tailor, not be fit too? the
rather—saving reverence of the word—for 'tis said
a woman's fitness comes by fits. Therein I must play
the workman. I dare speak it to myself—for it is not
vain-glory for a man and his glass to confer in his
own chamber—I mean, the lines of my body are as
well drawn as his; no less young, more strong, not
beneath him in fortunes, beyond him in the advantage of the time, above him in birth, alike conversant in general services, and more remarkable in
single oppositions: yet this imperceiverant thing
loves him in my despite. What mortality is! Posthumus, thy head, which now is growing upon thy
shoulders, shall within this hour be off; thy mistress
enforced; thy garments cut to pieces before thy face:
and all this done, spurn her home to her father; who
may haply be a little angry for my so rough usage;
but my mother, having power of his testiness, shall
turn all into my commendations. My horse is tied
up safe: out, sword, and to a sore purpose! Fortune,

put them into my hand! This is the very description
of their meeting-place; and the fellow dares not deceive me.
　　　　　　　　　　　　[*Exit*

SCENE II. *Before the cave of* BELARIUS

Enter, from the cave, BELARIUS, GUIDERIUS, ARVIRAGUS,
and IMOGEN
BELARIUS

[*To* IMOGEN] You are not well: remain here in the
　cave;
We'll come to you after hunting.

ARVIRAGUS

　　　　　[*To* IMOGEN] Brother, stay here:
Are we not brothers?

IMOGEN

　　　　　　So man and man should be;
But clay and clay differs in dignity,
Whose dust is both alike. I am very sick.

GUIDERIUS

Go you to hunting; I'll abide with him.

IMOGEN

So sick I am not, yet I am not well;
But not so citizen a wanton as
To seem to die ere sick: so please you, leave me;
Stick to your journal course: the breach of custom
Is breach of all. I am ill, but your being by me
Cannot amend me: society is no comfort
To one not sociable: I am not very sick,
Since I can reason of it. Pray you, trust me here:
I'll rob none but myself; and let me die,
Stealing so poorly.

GUIDERIUS

　　　　　I love thee; I have spoke it:
How much the quantity, the weight as much,
As I do love my father.

BELARIUS

　　　　　What! how! how!

ARVIRAGUS

If it be sin to say so, sir, I yoke me
In my good brother's fault: I know not why
I love this youth; and I have heard you say,
Love's reason's without reason: the bier at door
And a demand who is 't shall die, I'ld say
'My father, not this youth.'

BELARIUS

　　　　　[*Aside*] O noble strain!
O worthiness of nature! breed of greatness!
Cowards father cowards and base things sire base:
Nature hath meal and bran, contempt and grace.
I'm not their father; yet who this should be,
Doth miracle itself, loved before me.—
'Tis the ninth hour o' the morn.

ARVIRAGUS

　　　　　　Brother, farewell.

IMOGEN

I wish ye sport.

ARVIRAGUS

　　　You health. So please you, sir.

IMOGEN

[*Aside*] These are kind creatures. Gods, what lies I
 have heard!
Our courtiers say all's savage but at court:
Experience, O, thou disprovest report!
The imperious seas breed monsters; for the dish
Poor tributary rivers as sweet fish.
I am sick still, heart-sick. Pisanio,
I'll now taste of thy drug.   [*Swallows some*

GUIDERIUS

     I could not stir him:
He said he was gentle, but unfortunate;
Dishonestly afflicted, but yet honest.

ARVIRAGUS

Thus did he answer me: yet said, hereafter
I might know more.

BELARIUS

    To the field, to the field!
We'll leave you for this time: go in and rest.

ARVIRAGUS

We'll not be long away.

BELARIUS

     Pray, be not sick,
For you must be our housewife.

IMOGEN

      Well or ill,
I am bound to you.

BELARIUS

    And shalt be ever.
      [*Exit* IMOGEN, *to the cave*
This youth, howe'er distress'd, appears he hath had
Good ancestors.

ARVIRAGUS

    How angel-like he sings!

GUIDERIUS

But his neat cookery! he cut our roots
In characters;
And sauced our broths, as Juno had been sick,
And he her dieter.

ARVIRAGUS

     Nobly he yokes
A smiling with a sigh, as if the sigh
Was that it was, for not being such a smile;
The smile mocking the sigh, that it would fly
From so divine a temple, to commix
With winds that sailors rail at.

GUIDERIUS

      I do note
That grief and patience, rooted in him both,
Mingle their spurs together.

ARVIRAGUS

      Grow, patience!
And let the stinking elder, grief, untwine
His perishing root with the increasing vine!

BELARIUS

It is great morning. Come, away!—Who's there?
    Enter CLOTEN
I cannot find those runagates; that villain
Hath mock'd me: I am faint.

BELARIUS

     'Those runagates!'
Means he not us? I partly know him; 'tis
Cloten, the son o' the queen. I fear some ambush.
I saw him not these many years, and yet
I know 'tis he. We are held as outlaws: hence!

GUIDERIUS

He is but one: you and my brother search
What companies are near: pray you, away;
Let me alone with him.
    [*Exeunt* BELARIUS *and* ARVIRAGUS

CLOTEN

     Soft! What are you
That fly me thus? some villain mountaineers?
I have heard of such. What slave art thou?

GUIDERIUS

       A thing
More slavish did I ne'er than answering
A slave without a knock.

CLOTEN

     Thou art a robber,
A law-breaker, a villain: yield thee, thief.

GUIDERIUS

To who? to thee? What art thou? Have not I
An arm as big as thine? a heart as big?
Thy words, I grant, are bigger; for I wear not
My dagger in my mouth. Say what thou art,
Why I should yield to thee.

CLOTEN

     Thou villain base,
Know'st me not by my clothes?

GUIDERIUS

     No, nor thy tailor, rascal,
Who is thy grandfather: he made those clothes,
Which, as it seems, make thee.

CLOTEN

     Thou precious varlet,
My tailor made them not.

GUIDERIUS

     Hence then, and thank
The man that gave them thee. Thou art some fool;
I am loath to beat thee.

CLOTEN

     Thou injurious thief,
Hear but my name, and tremble.

GUIDERIUS

      What's thy name?

CLOTEN

Cloten, thou villain.

GUIDERIUS

Cloten, thou double villain, be thy name,
I cannot tremble at it: were it Toad, or Adder,
 Spider,
'Twould move me sooner.

CLOTEN

     To thy further fear,
Nay, to thy mere confusion, thou shalt know
I am son to the queen.

GUIDERIUS
                    I am sorry for 't; not seeming
So worthy as thy birth.
CLOTEN
                    Art not afeard?
GUIDERIUS
Those that I reverence, those I fear, the wise:
At fools I laugh, not fear them.
CLOTEN
                              Die the death:
When I have slain thee with my proper hand,
I'll follow those that even now fled hence,
And on the gates of Lud's town set your heads:
Yield, rustic mountaineer.   [*Exeunt, fighting*

Re-enter BELARIUS *and* ARVIRAGUS

BELARIUS
No companies abroad?
ARVIRAGUS
None in the world: you did mistake him, sure.
BELARIUS
I cannot tell: long is it since I saw him,
But time hath nothing blurr'd those lines of favour
Which then he wore; the snatches in his voice,
And burst of speaking, were as his: I am absolute
'Twas very Cloten.
ARVIRAGUS
                    In this place we left them:
I wish my brother make good time with him,
You say he is so fell.
BELARIUS
                    Being scarce made up,
I mean, to man, he had not apprehension
Of roaring terrors: for defect of judgement
Is oft the cause of fear. But see, thy brother.

Re-enter GUIDERIUS *with* CLOTEN'S *head*

GUIDERIUS
This Cloten was a fool, an empty purse;
There was no money in 't: not Hercules
Could have knock'd out his brains, for he had none:
Yet I not doing this, the fool had borne
My head as I do his.
BELARIUS
                    What hast thou done?
GUIDERIUS
I am perfect what: cut off one Cloten's head,
Son to the queen, after his own report;
Who call'd me traitor, mountaineer; and swore,
With his own single hand he'ld take us in,
Displace our heads where—thank the gods!—they
   grow,
And set them on Lud's town.
BELARIUS
                    We are all undone.
GUIDERIUS
Why, worthy father, what have we to lose,
But that he swore to take, our lives? The law
Protects not us: then why should we be tender
To let an arrogant piece of flesh threat us,
Play judge and executioner, all himself,

For we do fear the law? What company
Discover you abroad?
BELARIUS
                    No single soul
Can we set eye on; but in all safe reason
He must have some attendants. Though his humour
Was nothing but mutation, ay, and that
From one bad thing to worse, not frenzy, not
Absolute madness could so far have raved,
To bring him here alone: although perhaps
It may be heard at court that such as we
Cave here, hunt here, are outlaws, and in time
May make some stronger head; the which he hear-
   ing—
As it is like him—might break out, and swear
He'ld fetch us in; yet is 't not probable
To come alone, either he so undertaking,
Or they so suffering: then on good ground we fear,
If we do fear this body hath a tail
More perilous than the head.
ARVIRAGUS
                    Let ordinance
Come as the gods foresay it: howsoe'er,
My brother hath done well.
BELARIUS
                    I had no mind
To hunt this day: the boy Fidele's sickness
Did make my way long forth.
GUIDERIUS
                    With his own sword,
Which he did wave against my throat, I have ta'en
His head from him: I'll throw 't into the creek
Behind our rock, and let it to the sea,
And tell the fishes he's the queen's son, Cloten:
That's all I reck.   [*Exit*
BELARIUS
                    I fear 'twill be revenged:
Would, Polydore, thou hadst not done 't! though
   valour
Becomes thee well enough.
ARVIRAGUS
                    Would I had done 't,
So the revenge alone pursued me! Polydore,
I love thee brotherly, but envy much
Thou hast robb'd me of this deed: I would revenges,
That possible strength might meet, would seek us
   through
And put us to our answer.
BELARIUS
                    Well, 'tis done:
We'll hunt no more to-day, nor seek for danger
Where there's no profit. I prithee, to our rock;
You and Fidele play the cooks: I'll stay
Till hasty Polydore return, and bring him
To dinner presently.
ARVIRAGUS
                    Poor sick Fidele!
I'll willingly to him: to gain his colour
I'ld let a parish of such Clotens blood,
And praise myself for charity.   [*Exit*

BELARIUS

O thou goddess,
Thou divine Nature, how thyself thou blazon'st
In these two princely boys! They are as gentle
As zephyrs blowing below the violet,
Not wagging his sweet head; and yet as rough,
Their royal blood enchafed, as the rudest wind
That by the top doth take the mountain pine
And make him stoop to the vale. 'Tis wonder
That an invisible instinct should frame them
To royalty unlearn'd, honour untaught,
Civility not seen from other, valour
That wildly grows in them, but yields a crop
As if it had been sow'd. Yet still it's strange
What Cloten's being here to us portends,
Or what his death will bring us.

Re-enter GUIDERIUS

GUIDERIUS

Where's my brother?
I have sent Cloten's clotpoll down the stream,
In embassy to his mother: his body's hostage
For his return.   [*Solemn music*

BELARIUS

My ingenious instrument!
Hark, Polydore, it sounds! But what occasion
Hath Cadwal now to give it motion? Hark!

GUIDERIUS

Is he at home?

BELARIUS

He went hence even now.

GUIDERIUS

What does he mean? Since death of my dear'st
    mother
It did not speak before. All solemn things
Should answer solemn accidents. The matter?
Triumphs for nothing and lamenting toys
Is jollity for apes and grief for boys.
Is Cadwal mad?

Re-enter ARVIRAGUS *with* IMOGEN, *as dead, bearing her
in his arms*

BELARIUS

Look, here he comes,
And brings the dire occasion in his arms
Of what we blame him for!

ARVIRAGUS

The bird is dead
That we have made so much on. I had rather
Have skipp'd from sixteen years of age to sixty,
To have turn'd my leaping-time into a crutch,
Than have seen this.

GUIDERIUS

O sweetest, fairest lily!
My brother wears thee not the one half so well
As when thou grew'st thyself.

BELARIUS

O melancholy!
Who ever yet could sound thy bottom? find
The ooze, to show what coast thy sluggish crare
Might easiliest harbour in? Thou blessed thing!

Jove knows what man thou mightst have made; but
    I,
Thou diedst, a most rare boy, of melancholy.
How found you him?

ARVIRAGUS

Stark, as you see:
Thus smiling, as some fly had tickled slumber,
Not as death's dart, being laugh'd at; his right
    cheek
Reposing on a cushion.

GUIDERIUS

Where?

ARVIRAGUS

O' the floor;
His arms thus leagued: I thought he slept, and put
My clouted brogues from off my feet, whose rude-
    ness
Answer'd my steps too loud.

GUIDERIUS

Why, he but sleeps:
If he be gone, he'll make his grave a bed;
With female fairies will his tomb be haunted,
And worms will not come to thee.

ARVIRAGUS

With fairest flowers,
Whilst summer lasts, and I live here, Fidele,
I'll sweeten thy sad grave: thou shalt not lack
The flower that's like thy face, pale primrose, nor
The azured harebell, like thy veins; no, nor
The leaf of eglantine, whom not to slander,
Out-sweeten'd not thy breath: the ruddock would
With charitable bill—O bill, sore shaming
Those rich-left heirs that let their fathers lie
Without a monument!—bring thee all this;
Yea, and furr'd moss besides, when flowers are none,
To winter-ground thy corse.

GUIDERIUS

Prithee, have done;
And do not play in wench-like words with that
Which is so serious. Let us bury him,
And not protract with admiration what
Is now due debt. To the grave!

ARVIRAGUS

Say, where shall 's lay him?

GUIDERIUS

By good Euriphile, our mother.

ARVIRAGUS

Be 't so:
And let us, Polydore, though now our voices
Have got the mannish crack, sing him to the ground,
As once our mother; use like note and words,
Save that 'Euriphile' must be 'Fidele.'

GUIDERIUS

Cadwal,
I cannot sing: I'll weep, and word it with thee;
For notes of sorrow out of tune are worse
Than priests and fanes that lie.

ARVIRAGUS

We'll speak it then.

BELARIUS

Great griefs, I see, medicine the less; for Cloten
Is quite forgot. He was a queen's son, boys:
And though he came our enemy, remember
He was paid for that: though mean and mighty, rotting
Together, have one dust, yet reverence,
That angel of the world, doth make distinction
Of place 'tween high and low. Our foe was princely;
And though you took his life as being our foe,
Yet bury him as a prince.

GUIDERIUS

             Pray you, fetch him hither.
Thersites' body is as good as Ajax',
When neither are alive.

ARVIRAGUS

             If you'll go fetch him,
We'll say our song the whilst. Brother, begin.

[Exit BELARIUS

GUIDERIUS

Nay, Cadwal, we must lay his head to the east;
My father hath a reason for 't.

ARVIRAGUS

             'Tis true.

GUIDERIUS

Come on then and remove him.

ARVIRAGUS

             So. Begin.

GUIDERIUS

SONG

Fear no more the heat o' the sun,
   Nor the furious winter's rages;
Thou thy worldly task hast done,
     Home art gone and ta'en thy wages:
Golden lads and girls all must,
As chimney-sweepers, come to dust.

ARVIRAGUS

Fear no more the frown o' the great;
   Thou art past the tyrant's stroke;
Care no more to clothe and eat;
     To thee the reed is as the oak:
The sceptre, learning, physic, must
All follow this and come to dust.

GUIDERIUS

Fear no more the lightning-flash,

ARVIRAGUS

   Nor the all-dreaded thunder-stone;

GUIDERIUS

Fear not slander, censure rash;

ARVIRAGUS

   Thou hast finish'd joy and moan:

BOTH

All lovers young, all lovers must
Consign to thee and come to dust.

GUIDERIUS

No exorciser harm thee!

ARVIRAGUS

Nor no witchcraft charm thee!

GUIDERIUS

Ghost unlaid forbear thee!

ARVIRAGUS

Nothing ill come near thee!

BOTH

Quiet consummation have;
And renowned be thy grave!

Re-enter BELARIUS *with the body of* CLOTEN

GUIDERIUS

We have done our obsequies: come, lay him down.

BELARIUS

Here's a few flowers, but 'bout midnight more:
The herbs that have on them cold dew o' the night
Are strewings fitt'st for graves. Upon their faces.
You were as flowers, now wither'd: even so
These herblets shall, which we upon you strow.
Come on, away: apart upon our knees.
The ground that gave them first has them again:
Their pleasures here are past, so is their pain.

[*Exeunt* BELARIUS, GUIDERIUS, *and* ARVIRAGUS

IMOGEN

[*Awaking*] Yes, sir, to Milford-Haven; which is the way?—
I thank you.—By yond bush?—Pray, how far thither?
'Ods pittikins! can it be six mile yet?—
I have gone all night:—faith, I'll lie down and sleep.
But, soft! no bedfellow! O gods and goddesses!

[*Seeing the body of* CLOTEN

These flowers are like the pleasures of the world;
This bloody man, the care on 't. I hope I dream;
For so I thought I was a cave-keeper,
And cook to honest creatures: but 'tis not so;
'Twas but a bolt of nothing, shot at nothing,
Which the brain makes of fumes: our very eyes
Are sometimes like our judgements, blind. Good faith,
I tremble still with fear: but if there be
Yet left in heaven as small a drop of pity
As a wren's eye, fear'd gods, a part of it!
The dream's here still: even when I wake, it is
Without me, as within me; not imagined, felt.
A headless man! The garments of Posthumus!
I know the shape of 's leg: this is his hand;
His foot Mercurial; his Martial thigh;
The brawns of Hercules: but his Jovial face—
Murder in heaven?—How!—'Tis gone. Pisanio,
All curses madded Hecuba gave the Greeks,
And mine to boot, be darted on thee! Thou,
Conspired with that irregulous devil, Cloten,
Hast here cut off my lord. To write and read
Be henceforth treacherous! Damn'd Pisanio
Hath with his forged letters—damn'd Pisanio—
From this most bravest vessel of the world
Struck the main-top! O Posthumus! alas,
Where is thy head? where's that? Ay me! where's that?
Pisanio might have kill'd thee at the heart,
And left this head on. How should this be? Pisanio?
'Tis he and Cloten: malice and lucre in them
Have laid this woe here. O, 'tis pregnant, pregnant!
The drug he gave me, which he said was precious
And cordial to me, have I not found it
Murderous to the senses? That confirms it home:

This is Pisanio's deed, and Cloten's: O!
Give colour to my pale cheek with thy blood,
That we the horrider may seem to those
Which chance to find us: O, my lord, my lord!

[Falls on the body

Enter LUCIUS, *a* CAPTAIN *and other* OFFICERS, *and a*
SOOTHSAYER

CAPTAIN

To them the legions garrison'd in Gallia
After your will have cross'd the sea, attending
You here at Milford-Haven with your ships:
They are in readiness.

LUCIUS

       But what from Rome?

CAPTAIN

The senate hath stirr'd up the confiners
And gentlemen of Italy, most willing spirits
That promise noble service: and they come
Under the conduct of bold Iachimo,
Syenna's brother.

LUCIUS

       When expect you them?

CAPTAIN

With the next benefit o' the wind.

LUCIUS

       This forwardness
Makes our hopes fair. Command our present num-
     bers
Be muster'd; bid the captains look to 't. Now, sir,
What have you dream'd of late of this war's purpose?

SOOTHSAYER

Last night the very gods show'd me a vision—
I fast and pray'd for their intelligence—thus:
I saw Jove's bird, the Roman eagle, wing'd
From the spongy south to this part of the west,
There vanish'd in the sunbeams: which portends—
Unless my sins abuse my divination—
Success to the Roman host.

LUCIUS

       Dream often so,
And never false. Soft, ho! what trunk is here
Without his top? The ruin speaks that sometime
It was a worthy building. How! a page!
Or dead, or sleeping on him? But dead rather;
For nature doth abhor to make his bed
With the defunct, or sleep upon the dead.
Let's see the boy's face.

CAPTAIN

       He's alive, my lord.

LUCIUS

He'll then instruct us of this body. Young one,
Inform us of thy fortunes, for it seems
They crave to be demanded. Who is this
Thou makest thy bloody pillow? Or who was he
That, otherwise than noble nature did,
Hath alter'd that good picture? What's thy interest
In this sad wreck? How came it? Who is it?
What art thou?

IMOGEN

       I am nothing: or if not,

Nothing to be were better. This was my master,
A very valiant Briton and a good,
That here by mountaineers lies slain. Alas!
There is no more such masters: I may wander
From east to occident, cry out for service,
Try many, all good, serve truly, never
Find such another master.

LUCIUS

       'Lack, good youth!
Thou movest no less with thy complaining than
Thy master in bleeding: say his name, good friend.

IMOGEN

Richard du Champ. *[Aside]* If I do lie, and do
No harm by it, though the gods hear, I hope
They'll pardon it. Say you, sir?

LUCIUS

Thy name?

IMOGEN

Fidele, sir.

LUCIUS

Thou dost approve thyself the very same:
Thy name well fits thy faith, thy faith thy name.
Wilt take thy chance with me? I will not say
Thou shalt be so well master'd, but be sure,
No less beloved. The Roman emperor's letter
Sent by a consul to me should not sooner
Than thine own worth prefer thee: go with me.

IMOGEN

I'll follow, sir. But first, an 't please the gods,
I'll hide my master from the flies, as deep
As these poor pickaxes can dig: and when
With wild wood-leaves and weeds I ha' strew'd his
     grave
And on it said a century of prayers,
Such as I can, twice o'er, I'll weep and sigh,
And leaving so his service, follow you,
So please you entertain me.

LUCIUS

       Ay, good youth;
And rather father thee than master thee.
My friends,
The boy hath taught us manly duties: let us
Find out the prettiest daisied plot we can,
And make him with our pikes and partisans
A grave: come, arm him. Boy, he is preferr'd
By thee to us, and he shall be interr'd
As soldiers can. Be cheerful; wipe thine eyes:
Some falls are means the happier to arise.   *[Exeunt*

SCENE III. *A room in* CYMBELINE'S *palace*

Enter CYMBELINE, LORDS, PISANIO, *and* ATTENDANTS

CYMBELINE

Again; and bring me word how 'tis with her.

[Exit an ATTENDANT

A fever with the absence of her son;
A madness, of which her life's in danger. Heavens,
How deeply you at once do touch me! Imogen,
The great part of my comfort, gone; my queen

Upon a desperate bed, and in a time
When fearful wars point at me; her son gone,
So needful for this present: it strikes me, past
The hope of comfort. But for thee, fellow,
Who needs must know of her departure and
Dost seem so ignorant, we'll enforce it from thee
By a sharp torture.

PISANIO
           Sir, my life is yours,
I humbly set it at your will: but, for my mistress,
I nothing know where she remains, why gone,
Nor when she purposes return. Beseech your high-
    ness,
Hold me your loyal servant.

FIRST LORD
           Good my liege,
The day that she was missing he was here:
I dare be bound he's true and shall perform
All parts of his subjection loyally. For Cloten,
There wants no diligence in seeking him,
And will, no doubt, be found.

CYMBELINE
           The time is troublesome.
[To PISANIO] We'll slip you for a season; but our
    jealousy
Does yet depend.

FIRST LORD
           So please your majesty,
The Roman legions, all from Gallia drawn,
Are landed on your coast, with a supply
Of Roman gentlemen by the senate sent.

CYMBELINE
Now for the counsel of my son and queen!
I am amazed with matter.

FIRST LORD
           Good my liege,
Your preparation can affront no less
Than what you hear of: come more, for more you're
    ready:
The want is but to put those powers in motion
That long to move.

CYMBELINE
           I thank you. Let's withdraw;
And meet the time as it seeks us. We fear not
What can from Italy annoy us, but
We grieve at chances here. Away!
                  [Exeunt all but PISANIO

PISANIO
I heard no letter from my master since
I wrote him Imogen was slain: 'tis strange:
Nor hear I from my mistress, who did promise
To yield me often tidings; neither know I
What is betid to Cloten, but remain
Perplex'd in all. The heavens still must work.
Wherein I am false I am honest; not true, to be true.
These present wars shall find I love my country,
Even to the note o' the king, or I'll fall in them.
All other doubts, by time let them be clear'd:
Fortune brings in some boats that are not steer'd.
                           [Exit

SCENE IV. *Wales. Before the cave of* BELARIUS

Enter BELARIUS, GUIDERIUS, *and* ARVIRAGUS

GUIDERIUS
The noise is round about us.

BELARIUS
           Let us from it.

ARVIRAGUS
What pleasure, sir, find we in life, to lock it
From action and adventure?

GUIDERIUS
           Nay, what hope
Have we in hiding us? This way, the Romans
Must or for Britons slay us or receive us
For barbarous and unnatural revolts
During their use, and slay us after.

BELARIUS
           Sons,
We'll higher to the mountains; there secure us.
To the king's party there's no going: newness
Of Cloten's death—we being not known, not mus-
    ter'd
Among the bands—may drive us to a render
Where we have lived, and so extort from 's that
Which we have done, whose answer would be death
Drawn on with torture.

GUIDERIUS
           This is, sir, a doubt
In such a time nothing becoming you,
Nor satisfying us.

ARVIRAGUS
           It is not likely
That when they hear the Roman horses neigh,
Behold their quarter'd fires, have both their eyes
And ears so cloy'd importantly as now,
That they will waste their time upon our note,
To know from whence we are.

BELARIUS
           O, I am known
Of many in the army: many years,
Though Cloten then but young, you see, not wore
    him
From my remembrance. And besides, the king
Hath not deserved my service nor your loves;
Who find in my exile the want of breeding,
The certainty of this hard life; aye hopeless
To have the courtesy your cradle promised,
But to be still hot summer's tanlings and
The shrinking slaves of winter.

GUIDERIUS
           Than be so
Better to cease to be. Pray, sir, to the army:
I and my brother are not known; yourself
So out of thought, and thereto so o'ergrown,
Cannot be question'd.

ARVIRAGUS
           By this sun that shines,
I'll thither: what thing is it that I never
Did see man die! scarce ever look'd on blood,
But that of coward hares, hot goats, and venison!

Never bestrid a horse, save one that had
A rider like myself, who ne'er wore rowel
Nor iron on his heel! I am ashamed
To look upon the holy sun, to have
The benefit of his blest beams, remaining
So long a poor unknown.

GUIDERIUS
        By heavens, I'll go:
If you will bless me, sir, and give me leave,
I'll take the better care, but if you will not,
The hazard therefore due fall on me by
The hands of Romans!

ARVIRAGUS
        So say I: amen.

BELARIUS
No reason I, since of your lives you set
So slight a valuation, should reserve
My crack'd one to more care. Have with you, boys!
If in your country wars you chance to die,
That is my bed too, lads, and there I'll lie:
Lead, lead. [*Aside*] The time seems long; their blood
   thinks scorn,
Till it fly out and show them princes born. [*Exeunt*

ACT V

Scene I. *Britain. The Roman camp*

Enter POSTHUMUS, *with a bloody handkerchief*
POSTHUMUS
Yea, bloody cloth, I'll keep thee; for I wish'd
Thou shouldst be colour'd thus. You married ones,
If each of you should take this course, how many
Must murder wives much better than themselves
For wrying but a little! O Pisanio!
Every good servant does not all commands:
No bond but to do just ones. Gods! if you
Should have ta'en vengeance on my faults, I never
Had lived to put on this: so had you saved
The noble Imogen to repent, and struck
Me, wretch more worth your vengeance. But, alack,
You snatch some hence for little faults; that's love,
To have them fall no more: you some permit
To second ills with ills, each elder worse,
And make them dread it, to the doers' thrift.
But Imogen is your own: do your best wills,
And make me blest to obey! I am brought hither
Among the Italian gentry, and to fight
Against my lady's kingdom: 'tis enough
That, Britain, I have kill'd thy mistress; peace!
I'll give no wound to thee. Therefore, good heavens,
Hear patiently my purpose: I'll disrobe me
Of these Italian weeds, and suit myself
As does a Briton peasant: so I'll fight
Against the part I come with; so I'll die
For thee, O Imogen, even for whom my life
Is, every breath, a death: and thus, unknown,
Pitied nor hated, to the face of peril
Myself I'll dedicate. Let me make men know

More valour in me than my habits show.
Gods, put the strength o' the Leonati in me!
To shame the guise o' the world, I will begin
The fashion, less without and more within.   [*Exit*

Scene II. *Field of battle between the British and Roman camps*

Enter, from one side, LUCIUS, IACHIMO, IMOGEN, *and the* ROMAN ARMY; *from the other side, the* BRITISH ARMY; LEONATUS POSTHUMUS *following, like a poor soldier. They march over and go out. Then enter again, in skirmish,* IACHIMO *and* POSTHUMUS: *he vanquisheth and disarmeth* IACHIMO, *and then leaves him*

IACHIMO
The heaviness and guilt within my bosom
Takes off my manhood: I have belied a lady,
The princess of this country, and the air on 't
Revengingly enfeebles me; or could this carl,
A very drudge of nature's, have subdued me
In my profession? Knighthoods and honours, borne
As I wear mine, are titles but of scorn.
If that thy gentry, Britain, go before
This lout as he exceeds our lords, the odds
Is that we scarce are men and you are gods.   [*Exit*
The battle continues; the BRITONS *fly;* CYMBELINE *is taken: then enter, to his rescue,* BELARIUS, GUIDERIUS, *and* ARVIRAGUS

BELARIUS
Stand, stand! We have the advantage of the ground;
The lane is guarded: nothing routs us but
The villany of our fears.

GUIDERIUS *and* ARVIRAGUS
        Stand, stand, and fight!
Re-enter POSTHUMUS, *and seconds the* BRITONS: *they rescue* CYMBELINE *and exeunt. Then re-enter* LUCIUS, IACHIMO, *and* IMOGEN

LUCIUS
Away, boy, from the troops, and save thyself;
For friends kill friends, and the disorder's such
As war were hoodwink'd.

IACHIMO
        'Tis their fresh supplies.

LUCIUS
It is a day turn'd strangely: or betimes
Let's re-inforce, or fly.   [*Exeunt*

Scene III. *Another part of the field*

Enter POSTHUMUS *and a* BRITISH LORD

LORD
Camest thou from where they made the stand?

POSTHUMUS
              I did.
Though you, it seems, come from the fliers.

LORD
              I did.

POSTHUMUS
No blame be to you, sir; for all was lost,
But that the heavens fought: the king himself

Of his wings destitute, the army broken,
And but the backs of Britons seen, all flying
Through a strait lane; the enemy full-hearted,
Lolling the tongue with slaughtering, having work
More plentiful than tools to do 't, struck down
Some mortally, some slightly touch'd, some falling
Merely through fear; that the strait pass was
    damm'd
With dead men hurt behind, and cowards living
To die with lengthen'd shame.

LORD
                Where was this lane?

POSTHUMUS
Close by the battle, ditch'd, and wall'd with turf;
Which gave advantage to an ancient soldier,
An honest one, I warrant; who deserved
So long a breeding as his white beard came to,
In doing this for 's country. Athwart the lane,
He, with two striplings—lads more like to run
The country base than to commit such slaughter;
With faces fit for masks, or rather fairer
Than those for preservation cased, or shame—
Made good the passage; cried to those that fled,
'Our Britain's harts die flying, not our men:
To darkness fleet souls that fly backwards. Stand;
Or we are Romans, and will give you that
Like beasts which you shun beastly, and may save
But to look back in frown: stand, stand!' These
    three,
Three thousand confident, in act as many,—
For three performers are the file when all
The rest do nothing,—with this word 'Stand, stand,'
Accommodated by the place, more charming
With their own nobleness, which could have turn'd
A distaff to a lance, gilded pale looks,
Part shame, part spirit renew'd; that some, turn'd
    coward
But by example,—O, a sin in war,
Damn'd in the first beginners!—'gan to look
The way that they did, and to grin like lions
Upon the pikes o' the hunters. Then began
A stop i' the chaser, a retire; anon
A rout, confusion thick: forthwith they fly
Chickens, the way which they stoop'd eagles; slaves,
The strides they victors made: and now our cowards,
Like fragments in hard voyages, became
The life o' the need; having found the back-door
    open
Of the unguarded hearts, heavens, how they wound!
Some slain before, some dying, some their friends
O'er-borne i' the former wave: ten chased by one
Are now each one the slaughter-man of twenty:
Those that would die or ere resist are grown
The mortal bugs o' the field.

LORD
             This was strange chance:
A narrow lane, an old man, and two boys.

POSTHUMUS
Nay, do not wonder at it: you are made
Rather to wonder at the things you hear

Than to work any. Will you rhyme upon 't,
And vent it for a mockery? Here is one:
'Two boys, an old man twice a boy, a lane,
Preserved the Britons, was the Romans' bane.'

LORD
Nay, be not angry, sir.

POSTHUMUS
            'Lack, to what end?
Who dares not stand his foe, I'll be his friend;
For if he'll do as he is made to do,
I know he'll quickly fly my friendship too.
You have put me into rhyme.

LORD
           Farewell; you're angry. [Exit

POSTHUMUS
Still going? This is a lord! O noble misery!
To be i' the field, and ask 'what news?' of me!
To-day how many would have given their honours
To have saved their carcasses! took heel to do 't,
And yet died too! I, in mine own woe charm'd,
Could not find death where I did hear him groan,
Nor feel him where he struck. Being an ugly monster,
'Tis strange he hides him in fresh cups, soft beds,
Sweet words; or hath moe ministers than we
That draw his knives i' the war. Well, I will find
    him:
For being now a favourer to the Briton,
No more a Briton, I have resumed again
The part I came in: fight I will no more,
But yield me to the veriest hind that shall
Once touch my shoulder. Great the slaughter is
Here made by the Roman; great the answer be
Britons must take. For me, my ransom's death:
On either side I come to spend my breath,
Which neither here I'll keep nor bear again,
But end it by some means for Imogen.

Enter two BRITISH CAPTAINS *and* SOLDIERS

FIRST CAPTAIN
Great Jupiter be praised! Lucius is taken:
'Tis thought the old man and his sons were angels.

SECOND CAPTAIN
There was a fourth man, in a silly habit,
That gave the affront with them.

FIRST CAPTAIN
                  So 'tis reported:
But none of 'em can be found. Stand! who's there?

POSTHUMUS
A Roman;
Who had not now been drooping here if seconds
Had answer'd him.

SECOND CAPTAIN
           Lay hands on him; a dog!
A leg of Rome shall not return to tell
What crows have peck'd them here. He brags his
    service
As if he were of note: bring him to the king.

Enter CYMBELINE, BELARIUS, GUIDERIUS, ARVIRAGUS,
PISANIO, *and* ROMAN CAPTIVES. *The* CAPTAINS *present*
POSTHUMUS *to* CYMBELINE, *who delivers him over to a*
GAOLER: *then exeunt omnes*

SCENE IV. *A British prison*

Enter POSTHUMUS *and two* GAOLERS

FIRST GAOLER

You shall not now be stol'n, you have locks upon you:
So graze as you find pasture.

SECOND GAOLER

　　　　　　　Ay, or a stomach.

[*Exeunt* GAOLERS

POSTHUMUS

Most welcome, bondage! for thou art a way,
I think, to liberty: yet am I better
Than one that's sick o' the gout; since he had rather
Groan so in perpetuity than be cured
By the sure physician, death, who is the key
To unbar these locks. My conscience, thou art fetter'd
More than my shanks and wrists: you good gods, give me
The penitent instrument to pick that bolt,
Then, free for ever! Is 't enough I am sorry?
So children temporal fathers do appease;
Gods are more full of mercy. Must I repent?
I cannot do it better than in gyves,
Desired more than constrain'd: to satisfy,
If of my freedom 'tis the main part, take
No stricter render of me than my all.
I know you are more clement than vile men,
Who of their broken debtors take a third,
A sixth, a tenth, letting them thrive again
On their abatement: that's not my desire:
For Imogen's dear life take mine; and though
'Tis not so dear, yet 'tis a life; you coin'd it:
'Tween man and man they weigh not every stamp;
Though light, take pieces for the figure's sake:
You rather mine, being yours: and so, great powers,
If you will take this audit, take this life,
And cancel these cold bonds. O Imogen!
I'll speak to thee in silence.　　　　　[*Sleeps*

Solemn music. Enter, as in an apparition, SICILIUS
LEONATUS, *father to* POSTHUMUS, *an old man, attired like
a warrior; leading in his hand an ancient matron, his wife
and mother to* POSTHUMUS, *with music before them: then,
after other music, follow the two young* LEONATI, *brothers
to* POSTHUMUS, *with wounds as they died in the wars. They
circle* POSTHUMUS *round as he lies sleeping.*

SICILIUS

No more, thou thunder-master, show
　　Thy spite on mortal flies:
With Mars fall out, with Juno chide,
　　That thy adulteries
　　　Rates and revenges.
Hath my poor boy done aught but well,
　　Whose face I never saw?
I died whilst in the womb he stay'd
　　Attending nature's law:
Whose father then—as men report
　　Thou orphans' father art—
Thou shouldst have been, and shielded him
　　From this earth-vexing smart.

MOTHER

Lucina lent not me her aid,
　　But took me in my throes;
That from me was Posthumus ript,
　　Came crying 'mongst his foes,
　　　A thing of pity!

SICILIUS

Great nature, like his ancestry,
　　Moulded the stuff so fair,
That he deserved the praise o' the world,
　　As great Sicilius' heir.

FIRST BROTHER

When once he was mature for man,
　　In Britain where was he
That could stand up his parallel,
　　Or fruitful object be
In eye of Imogen, that best
　　Could deem his dignity?

MOTHER

With marriage wherefore was he mock'd,
　　To be exiled, and thrown
From Leonati seat, and cast
　　From her his dearest one,
　　　Sweet Imogen?

SICILIUS

Why did you suffer Iachimo,
　　Slight thing of Italy,
To taint his nobler heart and brain
　　With needless jealousy;
And to become the geck and scorn
　　O' the other's villany?

SECOND BROTHER

For this, from stiller seats we came,
　　Our parents and us twain,
That striking in our country's cause
　　Fell bravely and were slain,
Our fealty and Tenantius' right
　　With honour to maintain.

FIRST BROTHER

Like hardiment Posthumus hath
　　To Cymbeline perform'd:
Then, Jupiter, thou king of gods,
　　Why hast thou thus adjourn'd
The graces for his merits due;
　　Being all to dolours turn'd?

SICILIUS

Thy crystal window ope; look out;
　　No longer exercise
Upon a valiant race thy harsh
　　And potent injuries.

MOTHER

Since, Jupiter, our son is good,
　　Take off his miseries.

SICILIUS

Peep through thy marble mansion; help;
　　Or we poor ghosts will cry
To the shining synod of the rest
　　Against thy deity.

BOTH BROTHERS

Help, Jupiter; or we appeal,
　　And from thy justice fly.

JUPITER *descends in thunder and lightning, sitting upon an
eagle: he throws a thunderbolt. The* GHOSTS *fall on their
knees*

JUPITER

No more, you petty spirits of region low,
  Offend our hearing; hush! How dare you ghosts
Accuse the thunderer, whose bolt, you know,
  Sky-planted, batters all rebelling coasts?
Poor shadows of Elysium, hence, and rest
  Upon your never-withering banks of flowers:
Be not with mortal accidents opprest;
  No care of yours it is; you know 'tis ours.

Whom best I love I cross; to make my gift,
  The more delay'd, delighted. Be content;
Your low-laid son our godhead will uplift:
  His comforts thrive, his trials well are spent.
Our Jovial star reign'd at his birth, and in
  Our temple was he married. Rise, and fade.
He shall be lord of lady Imogen,
  And happier much by his affliction made.
This tablet lay upon his breast, wherein
  Our pleasure his full fortune doth confine:
And so away: no farther with your din
  Express impatience, lest you stir up mine.
  Mount, eagle, to my palace crystalline.

                                  [*Ascends*

SICILIUS

He came in thunder; his celestial breath
Was sulphurous to smell: the holy eagle
Stoop'd, as to foot us: his ascension is
More sweet than our blest fields: his royal bird
Prunes the immortal wing and cloys his beak,
As when his god is pleased.

ALL
          Thanks, Jupiter!

SICILIUS

The marble pavement closes, he is enter'd
His radiant roof. Away! and, to be blest,
Let us with care perform his great behest.

                  [*The* GHOSTS *vanish*

POSTHUMUS

[*Waking*] Sleep, thou hast been a grandsire, and begot
A father to me; and thou hast created
A mother and two brothers: but, O scorn!
Gone! they went hence so soon as they were born:
And so I am awake. Poor wretches that depend
On greatness' favour dream as I have done;
Wake, and find nothing. But, alas, I swerve:
Many dream not to find, neither deserve,
And yet are steep'd in favours; so am I,
That have this golden chance, and know not why.
What fairies haunt this ground? A book? O rare one!
Be not, as is our fangled world, a garment
Nobler than that it covers: let thy effects
So follow, to be most unlike our courtiers,
As good as promise.

[*Reads*] 'When as a lion's whelp shall, to himself unknown, without seeking find, and be embraced by a piece of tender air, and when from a stately cedar shall be lopped branches, which, being dead many years, shall after revive, be jointed to the old stock and freshly grow, then shall Posthumus end his miseries, Britain be fortunate and flourish in peace and plenty.'

'Tis still a dream; or else such stuff as madmen
Tongue, and brain not: either both, or nothing:
Or senseless speaking, or a speaking such
As sense cannot untie. Be what it is,

The action of my life is like it, which
I'll keep, if but for sympathy.

          Re-enter GAOLERS

FIRST GAOLER

Come, sir, are you ready for death?

POSTHUMUS

Over-roasted rather; ready long ago.

FIRST GAOLER

Hanging is the word, sir: if you be ready for that, you are well cooked.

POSTHUMUS

So, if I prove a good repast to the spectators, the dish pays the shot.

FIRST GAOLER

A heavy reckoning for you, sir. But the comfort is, you shall be called to no more payments, fear no more tavern-bills; which are often the sadness of parting, as the procuring of mirth: you come in faint for want of meat, depart reeling with too much drink; sorry that you have paid too much, and sorry that you are paid too much; purse and brain both empty, the brain the heavier for being too light, the purse too light, being drawn of heaviness: of this contradiction you shall now be quit. O, the charity of a penny cord! it sums up thousands in a trice: you have no true debitor and creditor but it; of what's past, is, and to come, the discharge: your neck, sir, is pen, book, and counters; so the acquittance follows.

POSTHUMUS

I am merrier to die than thou art to live.

FIRST GAOLER

Indeed, sir, he that sleeps feels not the toothache: but a man that were to sleep your sleep, and a hangman to help him to bed, I think he would change places with his officer; for, look you, sir, you know not which way you shall go.

POSTHUMUS

Yes, indeed do I, fellow.

FIRST GAOLER

Your death has eyes in 's head then; I have not seen him so pictured: you must either be directed by some that take upon them to know, or to take upon yourself that which I am sure you do not know, or jump the after-inquiry on your own peril: and how you shall speed in your journey's end, I think you'll never return to tell one.

POSTHUMUS

I tell thee, fellow, there are none want eyes to direct them the way I am going, but such as wink and will not use them.

FIRST GAOLER

What an infinite mock is this, that a man should have the best use of eyes to see the way of blindness! I am sure hanging's the way of winking.

          Enter a MESSENGER

MESSENGER

Knock off his manacles; bring your prisoner to the king.

POSTHUMUS

Thou bringest good news, I am called to be made free.

FIRST GAOLER

I'll be hanged then.

POSTHUMUS

Thou shalt be then freer than a gaoler; no bolts for the dead.   [*Exeunt all but* FIRST GAOLER

FIRST GAOLER

Unless a man would marry a gallows and beget young gibbets, I never saw one so prone. Yet, on my conscience, there are verier knaves desire to live, for all he be a Roman: and there be some of them too, that die against their wills; so should I, if I were one. I would we were all of one mind, and one mind good; O, there were desolation of gaolers and gallowses! I speak against my present profit, but my wish hath a preferment in 't.   [*Exit*

SCENE V. CYMBELINE'S *tent*

Enter CYMBELINE, BELARIUS, GUIDERIUS, ARVIRAGUS, PISANIO, LORDS, OFFICERS, *and* ATTENDANTS

CYMBELINE

Stand by my side, you whom the gods have made
Preservers of my throne. Woe is my heart,
That the poor soldier, that so richly fought,
Whose rags shamed gilded arms, whose naked breast
Stepp'd before targes of proof, cannot be found:
He shall be happy that can find him, if
Our grace can make him so.

BELARIUS

     I never saw
Such noble fury in so poor a thing;
Such precious deeds in one that promised nought
But beggary and poor looks.

CYMBELINE

     No tidings of him?

PISANIO

He hath been search'd among the dead and living,
But no trace of him.

CYMBELINE

     To my grief, I am
The heir of his reward; [*To* BELARIUS, GUIDERIUS,
and ARVIRAGUS] which I will add
To you, the liver, heart, and brain of Britain,
By whom I grant she lives. 'Tis now the time
To ask of whence you are: report it.

BELARIUS

     Sir,
In Cambria are we born, and gentlemen:
Further to boast were neither true nor modest,
Unless I add we are honest.

CYMBELINE

     Bow your knees.
Arise my knights o' the battle: I create you
Companions to our person, and will fit you
With dignities becoming your estates.

Enter CORNELIUS *and* LADIES

There's business in these faces. Why so sadly
Greet you our victory? you look like Romans,
And not o' the court of Britain.

CORNELIUS

     Hail, great king!
To sour your happiness, I must report
The queen is dead.

CYMBELINE

     Who worse than a physician
Would this report become? But I consider,
By medicine life may be prolong'd, yet death
Will seize the doctor too. How ended she?

CORNELIUS

With horror, madly dying, like her life;
Which, being cruel to the world, concluded
Most cruel to herself. What she confess'd
I will report, so please you: these her women
Can trip me if I err; who with wet cheeks
Were present when she finish'd.

CYMBELINE

     Prithee, say.

CORNELIUS

First, she confess'd she never loved you, only
Affected greatness got by you, not you:
Married your royalty, was wife to your place,
Abhorr'd your person.

CYMBELINE

     She alone knew this;
And, but she spoke in dying, I would not
Believe her lips in opening it. Proceed.

CORNELIUS

Your daughter, whom she bore in hand to love
With such integrity, she did confess
Was as a scorpion to her sight; whose life,
But that her flight prevented it, she had
Ta'en off by poison.

CYMBELINE

     O most delicate fiend!
Who is 't can read a woman? Is there more?

CORNELIUS

More, sir, and worse. She did confess she had
For you a mortal mineral; which, being took,
Should by the minute feed on life and lingering
By inches waste you: in which time she purposed,
By watching, weeping, tendance, kissing, to
O'ercome you with her show, and in time,
When she had fitted you with her craft, to work
Her son into the adoption of the crown:
But, failing of her end by his strange absence,
Grew shameless-desperate; open'd, in despite
Of heaven and men, her purposes; repented
The evils she hatch'd were not effected; so
Despairing died.

CYMBELINE

     Heard you all this, her women?

LADIES

We did, so please your highness.

CYMBELINE

     Mine eyes
Were not in fault, for she was beautiful,

Mine ears that heard her flattery, nor my heart
That thought her like her seeming; it had been
   vicious
To have mistrusted her: yet, O my daughter!
That it was folly in me, thou mayst say,
And prove it in thy feeling. Heaven mend all!
Enter LUCIUS, IACHIMO, *the* SOOTHSAYER, *and other*
ROMAN PRISONERS, *guarded;* POSTHUMUS *behind, and*
IMOGEN

Thou comest not, Caius, now for tribute; that
The Britons have razed out, though with the loss
Of many a bold one; whose kinsmen have made suit
That their good souls may be appeased with slaugh-
   ter
Of you their captives, which ourself have granted:
So think of your estate.

               LUCIUS
Consider, sir, the chance of war: the day
Was yours by accident; had it gone with us,
We should not, when the blood was cool, have
   threaten'd
Our prisoners with the sword. But since the gods
Will have it thus, that nothing but our lives
May be call'd ransom, let it come: sufficeth
A Roman with a Roman's heart can suffer:
Augustus lives to think on 't: and so much
For my peculiar care. This one thing only
I will entreat; my boy, a Briton born,
Let him be ransom'd: never master had
A page so kind, so duteous, diligent,
So tender over his occasions, true,
So feat, so nurse-like: let his virtue join
With my request, which I'll make bold your high-
   ness
Cannot deny; he hath done no Briton harm,
Though he have served a Roman: save him, sir,
And spare no blood beside.

             CYMBELINE
                 I have surely seen him:
His favour is familiar to me. Boy,
Thou hast look'd thyself into my grace,
And art mine own. I know not why, nor wherefore,
To say, live, boy: ne'er thank thy master; live:
And ask of Cymbeline what boon thou wilt,
Fitting my bounty and thy state, I'll give it;
Yea, though thou do demand a prisoner,
The noblest ta'en.

             IMOGEN
              I humbly thank your highness.

             LUCIUS
I do not bid thee beg my life, good lad,
And yet I know thou wilt.

             IMOGEN
               No, no: alack,
There's other work in hand: I see a thing
Bitter to me as death: your life, good master,
Must shuffle for itself.

             LUCIUS
              The boy disdains me,
He leaves me, scorns me: briefly die their joys

That place them on the truth of girls and boys.
Why stands he so perplex'd?

             CYMBELINE
              What wouldst thou, boy?
I love thee more and more: think more and more
What's best to ask. Know'st him thou look'st on?
   speak,
Wilt have him live? Is he thy kin? thy friend?

             IMOGEN
He is a Roman; no more kin to me
Than I to your highness; who, being born your
   vassal,
Am something nearer.

             CYMBELINE
             Wherefore eyest him so?

             IMOGEN
I'll tell you, sir, in private, if you please
To give me hearing.

             CYMBELINE
              Ay, with all my heart,
And lend my best attention. What's thy name?

             IMOGEN
Fidele, sir.

             CYMBELINE
             Thou'rt my good youth, my page;
I'll be thy master: walk with me; speak freely.
             [CYMBELINE *and* IMOGEN *converse apart*

             BELARIUS
Is not this boy revived from death?

             ARVIRAGUS
                One sand another
Not more resembles that sweet rosy lad
Who died, and was Fidele. What think you?

             GUIDERIUS
The same dead thing alive.

             BELARIUS
Peace, peace! see further; he eyes us not; forbear;
Creatures may be alike: were 't he, I am sure
He would have spoke to us.

             GUIDERIUS
              But we saw him dead.

             BELARIUS
Be silent; let's see further.

             PISANIO
             [*Aside*] It is my mistress:
Since she is living, let the time run on
To good or bad.
             [CYMBELINE *and* IMOGEN *come forward*

             CYMBELINE
             Come, stand thou by our side;
Make thy demand aloud. [*To* IACHIMO] Sir, step
   you forth;
Give answer to this boy, and do it freely;
Or, by our greatness and the grace of it,
Which is our honour, bitter torture shall
Winnow the truth from falsehood. On, speak to him.

             IMOGEN
My boon is that this gentleman may render
Of whom he had this ring.

POSTHUMUS

[Aside] What's that to him?

CYMBELINE

That diamond upon your finger, say
How came it yours?

IACHIMO

Thou'lt torture me to leave unspoken that
Which, to be spoke, would torture thee.

CYMBELINE

How! me?

IACHIMO

I am glad to be constrain'd to utter that
Which torments me to conceal. By villany
I got this ring: 'twas Leonatus' jewel;
Whom thou didst banish; and—which more may
    grieve thee,
As it doth me,—a nobler sir ne'er lived
'Twixt sky and ground. Wilt thou hear more, my
    lord?

CYMBELINE

All that belongs to this.

IACHIMO

That paragon, thy daughter,
For whom my heart drops blood and my false spirits
Quail to remember—Give me leave; I faint.

CYMBELINE

My daughter! what of her? Renew thy strength:
I had rather thou shouldst live while nature will
Than die ere I hear more: strive, man, and speak.

IACHIMO

Upon a time—unhappy was the clock
That struck the hour!—it was in Rome,—accurst
The mansion where!—'twas at a feast,—O, would
Our viands had been poison'd, or at least
Those which I heaved to head!—the good Post-
    humus,—
What should I say? he was too good to be
Where ill men were; and was the best of all
Amongst the rarest of good ones—sitting sadly,
Hearing us praise our loves of Italy
For beauty that made barren the swell'd boast
Of him that best could speak; for feature, laming
The shrine of Venus, or straight-pight Minerva,
Postures beyond brief nature; for condition,
A shop of all the qualities that man
Loves woman for; besides that hook of wiving,
Fairness which strikes the eye—

CYMBELINE

I stand on fire:
Come to the matter.

IACHIMO

All too soon I shall,
Unless thou wouldst grieve quickly. This Posthumus,
Most like a noble lord in love and one
That had a royal lover, took his hint,
And not dispraising whom we praised,—therein
He was as calm as virtue—he began
His mistress' picture; which by his tongue being
    made,

And then a mind put in 't, either our brags
Were crack'd of kitchen-trulls, or his description
Proved us unspeaking sots.

CYMBELINE

Nay, nay, to the purpose.

IACHIMO

Your daughter's chastity—there it begins.
He spake of her, as Dian had hot dreams,
And she alone were cold: whereat I, wretch,
Made scruple of his praise, and wager'd with him
Pieces of gold 'gainst this which then he wore
Upon his honour'd finger, to attain
In suit the place of 's bed and win this ring
By hers and mine adultery: he, true knight,
No lesser of her honour confident
Than I did truly find her, stakes this ring;
And would so, had it been a carbuncle
Of Phœbus' wheel; and might so safely, had it
Been all the worth of 's car. Away to Britain
Post I in this design: well may you, sir,
Remember me at court; where I was taught
Of your chaste daughter the wide difference
'Twixt amorous and villanous. Being thus quench'd
Of hope, not longing, mine Italian brain
'Gan in your duller Britain operate
Most vilely; for my vantage, excellent;
And, to be brief, my practice so prevail'd,
That I return'd with simular proof enough
To make the noble Leonatus mad,
By wounding his belief in her renown
With tokens thus, and thus; averring notes
Of chamber-hanging, pictures, this her bracelet,—
O cunning, how I got it!—nay, some marks
Of secret on her person, that he could not
But think her bond of chastity quite crack'd,
I having ta'en the forfeit. Whereupon—
Methinks I see him now—

POSTHUMUS

[Advancing] Ay, so thou dost,
Italian fiend! Ay me, most credulous fool,
Egregious murderer, thief, any thing
That's due to all the villains past, in being,
To come! O, give me cord, or knife, or poison,
Some upright justicer! Thou, king, send out
For torturers ingenious: it is I
That all the abhorred things o' the earth amend
By being worse than they. I am Posthumus,
That kill'd thy daughter: villain-like, I lie;
That caused a lesser villain than myself,
A sacrilegious thief, to do 't. The temple
Of virtue was she; yea, and she herself.
Spit, and throw stones, cast mire upon me, set
The dogs o' the street to bay me: every villain
Be call'd Posthumus Leonatus, and
Be villany less than 'twas! O Imogen!
My queen, my life, my wife! O Imogen,
Imogen, Imogen!

IMOGEN

Peace, my lord; hear, hear—

POSTHUMUS
Shall 's have a play of this? Thou scornful page,
There lie thy part.   [*Striking her: she falls*

PISANIO
O, gentlemen, help!
Mine and your mistress! O, my lord Posthumus!
You ne'er kill'd Imogen till now. Help, help!
Mine honour'd lady!

CYMBELINE
Does the world go round?

POSTHUMUS
How come these staggers on me?

PISANIO
          Wake, my mistress!

CYMBELINE
If this be so, the gods do mean to strike me
To death with mortal joy.

PISANIO
          How fares my mistress?

IMOGEN
O, get thee from my sight;
Thou gavest me poison: dangerous fellow, hence!
Breathe not where princes are.

CYMBELINE
          The tune of Imogen!

PISANIO
Lady,
The gods throw stones of sulphur on me, if
That box I gave you was not thought by me
A precious thing: I had it from the queen.

CYMBELINE
New matter still?

IMOGEN
        It poison'd me.

CORNELIUS
          O gods!
I left out one thing which the queen confess'd,
Which must approve thee honest: 'If Pisanio
Have' said she 'given his mistress that confection
Which I gave him for cordial, she is served
As I would serve a rat.'

CYMBELINE
          What's this, Cornelius?

CORNELIUS
The queen, sir, very oft importuned me
To temper poisons for her, still pretending
The satisfaction of her knowledge only
In killing creatures vile, as cats and dogs,
Of no esteem: I, dreading that her purpose
Was of more danger, did compound for her
A certain stuff, which being ta'en would cease
The present power of life, but in short time
All offices of nature should again
Do their due functions. Have you ta'en of it?

IMOGEN
Most like I did, for I was dead.

BELARIUS
          My boys,
There was our error.

GUIDERIUS
This is, sure, Fidele.

IMOGEN
Why did you throw your wedded lady from you?
Think that you are upon a rock, and now
Throw me again.   [*Embracing him*

POSTHUMUS
      Hang there like fruit, my soul,
Till the tree die!

CYMBELINE
      How now, my flesh, my child!
What, makest thou me a dullard in this act?
Wilt thou not speak to me?

IMOGEN
      [*Kneeling*] Your blessing, sir.

BELARIUS
[*To* GUIDERIUS *and* ARVIRAGUS] Though you did love
this youth, I blame ye not;
You had a motive for 't.

CYMBELINE
      My tears that fall
Prove holy water on thee! Imogen,
Thy mother's dead.

IMOGEN
      I am sorry for 't, my lord.

CYMBELINE
O, she was naught; and long of her it was
That we meet here so strangely: but her son
Is gone, we know not how nor where.

PISANIO
          My lord,
Now fear is from me, I'll speak troth. Lord Cloten,
Upon my lady's missing, came to me
With his sword drawn; foam'd at the mouth, and
  swore,
If I discover'd not which way she was gone,
It was my instant death. By accident,
I had a feigned letter of my master's
Then in my pocket; which directed him
To seek her on the mountains near to Milford;
Where, in a frenzy, in my master's garments,
Which he enforced from me, away he posts
With unchaste purpose, and with oath to violate
My lady's honour: what became of him
I further know not.

GUIDERIUS
      Let me end the story:
I slew him there.

CYMBELINE
      Marry, the gods forfend!
I would not thy good deeds should from my lips
Pluck a hard sentence: prithee, valiant youth,
Deny 't again.

GUIDERIUS
      I have spoke it, and I did it.

CYMBELINE
He was a prince.

GUIDERIUS
A most incivil one: the wrongs he did me
Were nothing prince-like; for he did provoke me

With language that would make me spurn the sea,
If it could so roar to me: I cut off 's head;
And am right glad he is not standing here
To tell this tale of mine.

CYMBELINE

            I am sorry for thee:
By thine own tongue thou art condemn'd, and must
Endure our law: thou'rt dead.

IMOGEN

            That headless man
I thought had been my lord.

CYMBELINE

            Bind the offender,
And take him from our presence.

BELARIUS

            Stay, sir king:
This man is better than the man he slew,
As well descended as thyself, and hath
More of thee merited than a band of Clotens
Had ever scar for. [*To the* GUARD] Let his arms alone;
They were not born for bondage.

CYMBELINE

            Why, old soldier,
Wilt thou undo the worth thou art unpaid for,
By tasting of our wrath? How of descent
As good as we?

ARVIRAGUS

     In that he spake too far.

CYMBELINE

And thou shalt die for 't.

BELARIUS

          We will die all three:
But I will prove that two on 's are as good
As I have given out him. My sons, I must
For mine own part unfold a dangerous speech,
Though haply well for you.

ARVIRAGUS

         Your danger's ours.

GUIDERIUS

And our good his.

BELARIUS

        Have at it then, by leave.
Thou hadst, great king, a subject who
Was call'd Belarius.

CYMBELINE

       What of him? he is
A banish'd traitor.

BELARIUS

      He it is that hath
Assumed this age, indeed a banish'd man;
I know not how a traitor.

CYMBELINE

        Take him hence:
The whole world shall not save him.

BELARIUS

         Not too hot:
First pay me for the nursing of thy sons;
And let it be confiscate all, so soon
As I have received it.

CYMBELINE

     Nursing of my sons!

BELARIUS

I am too blunt and saucy: here's my knee:
Ere I arise I will prefer my sons;
Then spare not the old father. Mighty sir,
These two young gentlemen, that call me father
And think they are my sons, are none of mine;
They are the issue of your loins, my liege,
And blood of your begetting.

CYMBELINE

          How! my issue!

BELARIUS

So sure as you your father's. I, old Morgan,
Am that Belarius whom you sometime banish'd:
Your pleasure was my mere offence, my punishment
Itself, and all my treason: that I suffer'd
Was all the harm I did. These gentle princes—
For such and so they are—these twenty years
Have I train'd up: those arts they have as I
Could put into them; my breeding was, sir, as
Your highness knows. Their nurse, Euriphile,
Whom for the theft I wedded, stole these children
Upon my banishment: I moved her to 't,
Having received the punishment before
For that which I did then: beaten for loyalty
Excited me to treason: their dear loss,
The more of you 'twas felt, the more it shaped
Unto my end of stealing them. But, gracious sir,
Here are your sons again; and I must lose
Two of the sweet'st companions in the world.
The benediction of these covering heavens
Fall on their heads like dew! for they are worthy
To inlay heaven with stars.

CYMBELINE

        Thou weep'st, and speak'st.
The service that you three have done is more
Unlike than this thou tell'st. I lost my children:
If these be they, I know not how to wish
A pair of worthier sons.

BELARIUS

         Be pleased awhile.
This gentleman, whom I call Polydore,
Most worthy prince, as yours, is true Guiderius:
This gentleman, my Cadwal, Arviragus,
Your younger princely son; he, sir, was lapp'd
In a most curious mantle, wrought by the hand
Of his queen mother, which for more probation
I can with ease produce.

CYMBELINE

        Guiderius had
Upon his neck a mole, a sanguine star;
It was a mark of wonder.

BELARIUS

         This is he;
Who hath upon him still that natural stamp:
It was wise nature's end in the donation,
To be his evidence now.

CYMBELINE

            O, what am I?

A mother to the birth of three? Ne'er mother
Rejoiced deliverance more. Blest pray you be,
That, after this strange starting from your orbs,
You may reign in them now! O Imogen,
Thou hast lost by this a kingdom.

IMOGEN

               No, my lord;
I have got two worlds by 't. O my gentle brothers,
Have we thus met? O, never say hereafter
But I am truest speaker: you call'd me brother,
When I was but your sister; I you brothers,
When ye were so indeed.

CYMBELINE

           Did you e'er meet?

ARVIRAGUS

Ay, my good lord.

GUIDERIUS

           And at first meeting loved,
Continued so, until we thought he died.

CORNELIUS

By the queen's dram she swallow'd.

CYMBELINE

             O rare instinct!
When shall I hear all through? This fierce abridgement
Hath to it circumstantial branches, which
Distinction should be rich in. Where? how lived you?
And when came you to serve our Roman captive?
How parted with your brothers? how first met them?
Why fled you from the court? and whither? These,
And your three motives to the battle, with
I know not how much more, should be demanded;
And all the other by-dependances,
From chance to chance: but nor the time nor place
Will serve our long inter'gatories. See,
Posthumus anchors upon Imogen;
And she, like harmless lightning, throws her eye
On him, her brothers, me, her master, hitting
Each object with a joy: the counterchange
Is severally in all. Let's quit this ground,
And smoke the temple with our sacrifices.
[To BELARIUS] Thou art my brother; so we'll hold
    thee ever.

IMOGEN

You are my father too; and did relieve me,
To see this gracious season.

CYMBELINE

            All o'erjoy'd,
Save these in bonds: let them be joyful too,
For they shall taste our comfort.

IMOGEN

             My good master,
I will yet do you service.

LUCIUS

          Happy be you!

CYMBELINE

The forlorn soldier that so nobly fought,
He would have well becomed this place and graced
The thankings of a king.

POSTHUMUS

          I am, sir,
The soldier that did company these three
In poor beseeming; 'twas a fitment for
The purpose I then follow'd. That I was he,
Speak, Iachimo: I had you down, and might
Have made you finish.

IACHIMO

[Kneeling] I am down again:
But now my heavy conscience sinks my knee,
As then your force did. Take that life, beseech you,
Which I so often owe: but your ring first;
And here the bracelet of the truest princess
That ever swore her faith.

POSTHUMUS

          Kneel not to me:
The power that I have on you is to spare you;
The malice towards you to forgive you: live,
And deal with others better.

CYMBELINE

          Nobly doom'd!
We'll learn our freeness of a son-in-law;
Pardon's the word to all.

ARVIRAGUS

          You holp us, sir,
As you did mean indeed to be our brother;
Joy'd are we that you are.

POSTHUMUS

Your servant, princes. Good my lord of Rome,
Call forth your soothsayer: as I slept, methought
Great Jupiter, upon his eagle back'd,
Appear'd to me, with other spritely shows
Of mine own kindred: when I waked, I found
This label on my bosom; whose containing
Is so from sense in hardness that I can
Make no collection of it: let him show
His skill in the construction.

LUCIUS

          Philarmonus!

SOOTHSAYER

Here, my good lord.

LUCIUS

          Read, and declare the meaning.

SOOTHSAYER

[Reads] 'When as a lion's whelp shall, to himself unknown,
without seeking find, and be embraced by a piece of tender air,
and when from a stately cedar shall be lopped branches,
which, being dead many years, shall after revive, be jointed to
the old stock and freshly grow, then shall Posthumus end his
miseries, Britain be fortunate and flourish in peace and plenty.'

Thou, Leonatus, art the lion's whelp;
The fit and apt construction of thy name,
Being Leo-natus, doth import so much.
[To CYMBELINE] The piece of tender air, thy virtu-
    ous daughter,
Which we call 'mollis aer;' and 'mollis aer'
We term it 'mulier:' which 'mulier' I divine
Is this most constant wife; who even now,
Answering the letter of the oracle,

Unknown to you, unsought, were clipp'd about
With this most tender air.

CYMBELINE

             This hath some seeming.

SOOTHSAYER

The lofty cedar, royal Cymbeline,
Personates thee: and thy lopp'd branches point
Thy two sons forth; who, by Belarius stol'n,
For many years thought dead, are now revived,
To the majestic cedar join'd, whose issue
Promises Britain peace and plenty.

CYMBELINE

             Well;
My peace we will begin. And, Caius Lucius,
Although the victor, we submit to Cæsar
And to the Roman empire, promising
To pay our wonted tribute, from the which
We were dissuaded by our wicked queen;
Whom heavens in justice both on her and hers
Have laid most heavy hand.

SOOTHSAYER

The fingers of the powers above do tune

The harmony of this peace. The vision,
Which I made known to Lucius ere the stroke
Of this yet scarce-cold battle, at this instant
Is full accomplish'd; for the Roman eagle,
From south to west on wing soaring aloft,
Lessen'd herself and in the beams o' the sun
So vanish'd: which foreshow'd our princely eagle,
The imperial Cæsar, should again unite
His favour with the radiant Cymbeline,
Which shines here in the west.

CYMBELINE

             Laud we the gods;
And let our crooked smokes climb to their nostrils
From our blest altars. Publish we this peace
To all our subjects. Set we forward: let
A Roman and a British ensign wave
Friendly together: so through Lud's town march:
And in the temple of great Jupiter
Our peace we'll ratify; seal it with feasts.
Set on there! Never was a war did cease,
Ere bloody hands were wash'd, with such a peace.
                   [Exeunt

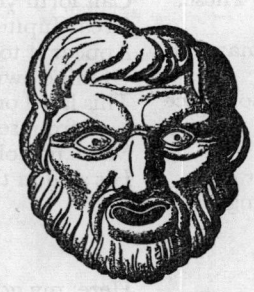

THE WINTER'S TALE

SYNOPSIS

Polixenes, King of Bohemia, has made an extended visit of many months at the court of Leontes, King of Sicilia, the dear friend of his boyhood, with whom he finds it very hard to part, but now that his fleet is waiting to convey him home he feels that he must leave. Leontes begs him to remain another week but Polixenes firmly refuses until Queen Hermione, when bidden by her husband, seconds the invitation in her gay, friendly way, and the visitor yields. No sooner has he complied, however, than a dark shadow of suspicion crosses Leontes' mind as he broods over the fact that his old friend would not stay for his urging but consented at Hermione's asking. Continuing in sheer unreasonableness to misconstrue every act of courtesy between the pair, he becomes so obsessed by his jealous conviction of their guilty intimacy that he summons Camillo, his faithful counsellor, who at first contends against the King's black thoughts but finally appears to agree, as Polixenes' cup-bearer, to poison their guest.

Polixenes notices Leontes' changed demeanor and learning its reason in a chance meeting with Camillo, who has no intention of obeying his King's order, they both escape on the Bohemian ships. Their flight together serves to confirm Leontes' wildest suspicions and he vents his fury on Hermione, branding her publicly as an adulteress, depriving her of her little son, and throwing her into prison, in spite of her declarations of innocence and the fact that she will soon bear a child. Hermione holds the sympathies of the court by her patient dignity and when her little daughter is born, her gentlewoman Paulina, hoping to touch the King's heart by the sight of the innocent baby, forces her way into his presence with the child. A violent scene follows in which Leontes disowns the infant princess as Polixenes' bastard, and Paulina retaliates by plainly telling him what the world thinks of him.

The King wishes the child killed, but instead orders Antigonus, the husband of Paulina, to take it to some desert place outside of his dominions and abandon it. The distressed courtier obeys by leaving the baby princess unprotected on the seacoast of Bohemia, but he places beside her a bag of gold and jewels with the instructions he has just received in a vision that her name shall be Perdita. A bear kills Antigonus, his ship is wrecked in a storm, and no news ever reaches Sicilia of the expedition, but a kindly, honest shepherd finds the baby, and his son witnesses the death of Antigonus and his mariners.

Convinced himself of Hermione's guilt, the King plans to silence the protests of his courtiers forever by appealing for judgment to the oracle at Delphi, and, as the Queen at her public trial again affirms her fidelity to her husband, the ambassadors arrive with the sealed oracle of Apollo which reveals the truth, stating that Hermione is chaste, Polixenes blameless, Camillo true, Leontes a jealous tyrant, his babe truly begotten, and adding that the King shall live without an heir until the lost child is found. As the raging King declares the oracle false and orders the sessions to proceed, the death of his beloved little son, a child of great promise, is announced. Hermione falls down in a deathlike swoon, Paulina swears she is dead, and the King is left in bitter loneliness to repent his blind, insane jealousy.

Sixteen years pass by. Leontes is a broken, grieving man; the little Princess Perdita, grown to womanhood in the shepherd's home, is both good and beautiful; Florizel, the Bohemian prince and heir to the throne, is deeply in love with her; and his father, after consulting Camillo, now high in the King's service, about the rumors of his son's entanglement with the supposed daughter of a shepherd, goes in disguise with his old counsellor to visit a festive midsummer sheep-shearing, where he sees his son dressed as a shepherd dancing with a charming girl of noble bearing. As Florizel is about to ask for a betrothal, and the old shepherd offers a substantial dowry, the angry Polixenes reveals himself and threatens to punish the Prince, whereupon Florizel decides to elope with Perdita to some foreign country. The good Camillo advises him to go to Sicilia on the pretext that he comes with greetings from Bohemia, and gives him letters of introduction and ample instructions on the best method of winning Leontes' heart.

Meanwhile, the shepherd, to save himself from the King's wrath and explain the mystery of his wealth, resolves to tell Polixenes about finding Perdita and the bag of gold, but when on his way to the palace with the jewels and her baby garments he is intercepted and with his son is taken aboard the Prince's ship sailing for Sicilia. A cordial reception is given the lovers at Leontes' court, where they are quickly joined by Polixenes and Camillo.

The evidence of the shepherd and his son proves beyond doubt that Perdita is the lost princess. Polixenes and his friend are reconciled, Camillo is warmly welcomed home, Florizel and Perdita are formally betrothed, and nothing now mars the reunion but the memory of the sacrificed Hermione. One day, Paulina, who has continually cautioned the King against a second marriage, invites the company to see a finely-executed statue of the Queen which stands in her chapel. As the King and Perdita, with their guests and courtiers, marvel at the wonderful work of art, music is heard and Hermione herself, who has spent all these years in seclusion waiting for the return of her daughter, steps down to embrace her repentant husband and the long-lost princess.

HISTORICAL DATA

The story of the play is taken from the popular Elizabethan romance, *Pandosto: The Triumph of Time* (1588). This romance, later known as *The History of Dorastus and Fawnia*, by Robert Greene, was sufficiently popular to run through fourteen editions. Its own origin is unidentifiable. Shakespeare made certain minor changes in the plot, most important of which was the ultimate saving of the life of Hermione who, as Bellaria in Greene's tale, had died of grief over the death of her son. More important, however, is the elevating and ennobling of the character of Hermione, and the invention of several additional characters including Paulina, Antigonus and the rogue Autolycus. Several of the theatrical devices, such as bringing the apparent statue to life, may have been derived from a number of sources for they occur not infrequently in English and continental fiction.

The earliest notice of *The Winter's Tale* is found in Simon Forman's *Booke of Plaies and Notes Thereof*, in which is recorded a performance at the Globe Theatre on May 15, 1611. It is subsequently referred to by Sir George Buck, Master of the Revels, who noted a performance of "The King's Players" at Whitehall in November 1611. The dance of the twelve satyrs (Act IV, Scene iv), three of whom had "danced before the King," has been thought to have been borrowed from the antimasque in Jonson's *Masque of Oberon* performed at court, January 1, 1611. This, combined with the mature metrical and stylistic features which are in themselves evidence of a late date for the composition of this play, helps support the generally accepted theory that it was written in the early part of 1611.

No quarto was published, nor is the title found in the *Stationers' Register* before the edition in the First Folio, 1623.

"*He tells her something*
That makes her blood look out."
THE WINTER'S TALE

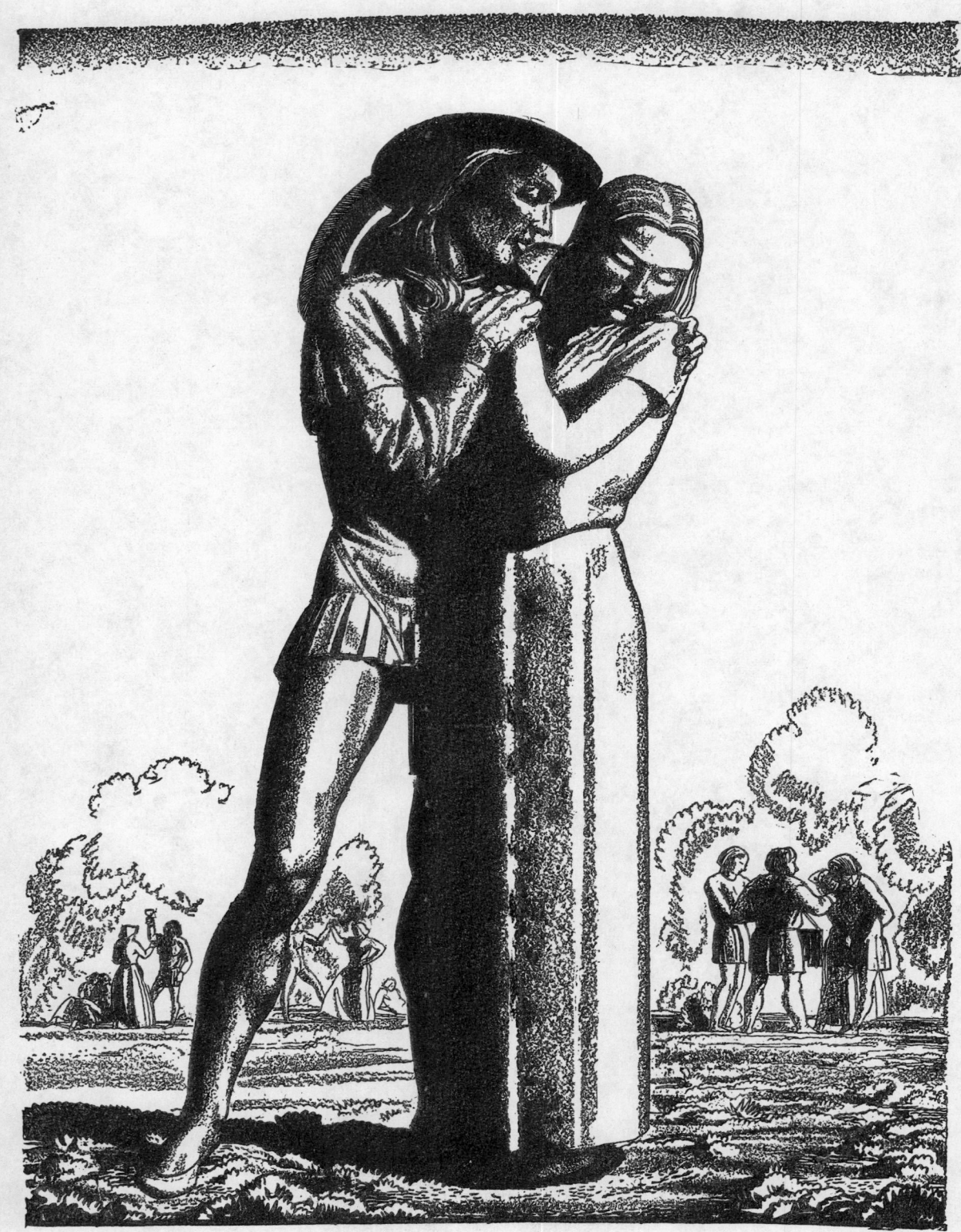

THE WINTER'S TALE

DRAMATIS PERSONÆ

LEONTES, *king of Sicilia.*
MAMILLIUS, *young prince of Sicilia.*
CAMILLO,
ANTIGONUS,
CLEOMENES, } *Four lords of Sicilia.*
DION,
POLIXENES, *king of Bohemia.*
FLORIZEL, *prince of Bohemia.*
ARCHIDAMUS, *a lord of Bohemia.*
OLD SHEPHERD, *reputed father of Perdita.*
CLOWN, *his son.*
AUTOLYCUS, *a rogue.*
A MARINER.

A GAOLER.

HERMIONE, *queen to Leontes.*
PERDITA, *daughter to Leontes and Hermione.*
PAULINA, *wife to Antigonus.*
EMILIA, *a lady attending on Hermione.*
MOPSA,
DORCAS, } *Shepherdesses.*

Other LORDS *and* GENTLEMEN, LADIES, OFFICERS
and SERVANTS, SHEPHERDS, *and* SHEPHERDESSES.

Time, as Chorus

SCENE—*Partly in Sicilia, and partly in Bohemia.*

ACT I

SCENE I. *Antechamber in* LEONTES' *palace*

Enter CAMILLO *and* ARCHIDAMUS

ARCHIDAMUS

IF you shall chance, Camillo, to visit Bohemia, on
the like occasion whereon my services are now on
foot, you shall see, as I have said, great difference
betwixt our Bohemia and your Sicilia.

CAMILLO

I think, this coming summer, the King of Sicilia
means to pay Bohemia the visitation which he justly
owes him.

ARCHIDAMUS

Wherein our entertainment shall shame us we will
be justified in our loves; for indeed—

CAMILLO

Beseech you,—

ARCHIDAMUS

Verily, I speak it in the freedom of my knowledge:
we cannot with such magnificence—in so rare—I
know not what to say. We will give you sleepy drinks,
that your senses, unintelligent of our insufficience,
may, though they cannot praise us, as little accuse
us.

CAMILLO

You pay a great deal too dear for what's given
freely.

ARCHIDAMUS

Believe me, I speak as my understanding instructs
me, and as mine honesty puts it to utterance.

CAMILLO

Sicilia cannot show himself over-kind to Bohemia.
They were trained together in their childhoods; and
there rooted betwixt them then such an affection,
which cannot choose but branch now. Since their
more mature dignities and royal necessities made
separation of their society, their encounters, though

not personal, have been royally attorneyed with interchange of gifts, letters, loving embassies; that
they have seemed to be together, though absent;
shook hands, as over a vast; and embraced, as it
were, from the ends of opposed winds. The heavens
continue their loves!

ARCHIDAMUS

I think there is not in the world either malice or
matter to alter it. You have an unspeakable comfort
of your young prince Mamillius: it is a gentleman
of the greatest promise that ever came into my note.

CAMILLO

I very well agree with you in the hopes of him: it is a
gallant child; one that indeed physics the subject,
makes old hearts fresh: they that went on crutches
ere he was born desire yet their life to see him a
man.

ARCHIDAMUS

Would they else be content to die?

CAMILLO

Yes; if there were no other excuse why they should
desire to live.

ARCHIDAMUS

If the king had no son, they would desire to live on
crutches till he had one. [*Exeunt*

SCENE II. *A room of state in the same*

Enter LEONTES, HERMIONE, MAMILLIUS, POLIXENES,
CAMILLO, *and* ATTENDANTS

POLIXENES

Nine changes of the watery star hath been
The shepherd's note since we have left our throne
Without a burthen: time as long again
Would be fill'd up, my brother, with our thanks;
And yet we should, for perpetuity,
Go hence in debt: and therefore, like a cipher,
Yet standing in rich place, I multiply

With one 'We thank you,' many thousands moe
That go before it.

LEONTES
            Stay your thanks a while;
And pay them when you part.

POLIXENES
                        Sir, that's to-morrow.
I am question'd by my fears, of what may chance
Or breed upon our absence; that may blow
No sneaping winds at home, to make us say
'This is put forth too truly:' besides, I have stay'd
To tire your royalty.

LEONTES
            We are tougher, brother,
Than you can put us to't.

POLIXENES
            No longer stay.

LEONTES
One seven-night longer.

POLIXENES
            Very sooth, to-morrow.

LEONTES
We'll part the time between's, then: and in that
I'll no gainsaying.

POLIXENES
            Press me not, beseech you, so.
There is no tongue that moves, none, none i' the
    world,
So soon as yours could win me: so it should now,
Were there necessity in your request, although
'Twere needful I denied it. My affairs
Do even drag me homeward: which to hinder
Were in your love a whip to me; my stay
To you a charge and trouble: to save both,
Farewell, our brother.

LEONTES
            Tongue-tied our queen? speak you.

HERMIONE
I had thought, sir, to have held my peace until
You had drawn oaths from him not to stay. You, sir,
Charge him too coldly. Tell him, you are sure
All in Bohemia's well; this satisfaction
The by-gone day proclaim'd: say this to him,
He's beat from his best ward.

LEONTES
            Well said, Hermione.

HERMIONE
To tell, he longs to see his son, were strong:
But let him say so then, and let him go;
But let him swear so, and he shall not stay,
We'll thwack him hence with distaffs.
Yet of your royal presence I'll adventure
The borrow of a week. When at Bohemia
You take my lord, I'll give him my commission
To let him there a month behind the gest
Prefix'd for's parting: yet, good deed, Leontes,
I love thee not a jar o' the clock behind
What lady she her lord. You'll stay?

POLIXENES
            No, madam.

HERMIONE
Nay, but you will?

POLIXENES
            I may not, verily.

HERMIONE
Verily!
You put me off with limber vows; but I,
Though you would seek to unsphere the stars with
    oaths,
Should yet say 'Sir, no going.' Verily,
You shall not go: a lady's 'Verily' 's
As potent as a lord's. Will you go yet?
Force me to keep you as a prisoner,
Not like a guest; so you shall pay your fees
When you depart, and save your thanks. How say
    you?
My prisoner? or my guest? by your dread 'Verily,'
One of them you shall be.

POLIXENES
            Your guest, then, madam:
To be your prisoner should import offending;
Which is for me less easy to commit
Than you to punish.

HERMIONE
            Not your gaoler, then,
But your kind hostess. Come, I'll question you
Of my lord's tricks and yours when you were boys:
You were pretty lordings then?

POLIXENES
            We were, fair queen,
Two lads that thought there was no more behind,
But such a day to-morrow as to-day,
And to be boy eternal.

HERMIONE
            Was not my lord
The verier wag o' the two?

POLIXENES
We were as twinn'd lambs that did frisk i' the sun,
And bleat the one at the other: what we changed
Was innocence for innocence; we knew not
The doctrine of ill-doing, nor dream'd
That any did. Had we pursued that life,
And our weak spirits ne'er been higher rear'd
With stronger blood, we should have answer'd
    heaven
Boldly 'not guilty;' the imposition clear'd
Hereditary ours.

HERMIONE
            By this we gather
You have tripp'd since.

POLIXENES
            O my most sacred lady!
Temptations have since then been born to's: for
In those unfledged days was my wife a girl;
Your precious self had then not cross'd the eyes
Of my young play-fellow.

HERMIONE
            Grace to boot!
Of this make no conclusion, lest you say
Your queen and I are devils: yet go on;

The offences we have made you do we'll answer,
If you first sinn'd with us, and that with us
You did continue fault, and that you slipp'd not
With any but with us.

LEONTES

                Is he won yet?

HERMIONE

He'll stay, my lord.

LEONTES

          At my request he would not.
Hermione, my dearest, thou never spokest
To better purpose.

HERMIONE

         Never?

LEONTES

              Never, but once.

HERMIONE

What! have I twice said well? when was't before?
I prithee tell me; cram's with praise, and make's
As fat as tame things: one good deed dying tongue-
    less
Slaughters a thousand waiting upon that.
Our praises are our wages: you may ride's
With one soft kiss a thousand furlongs ere
With spur we heat an acre. But to the goal:
My last good deed was to entreat his stay:
What was my first? it has an elder sister,
Or I mistake you: O, would her name were Grace!
But once before I spoke to the purpose: when?
Nay, let me have't; I long.

LEONTES

              Why, that was when
Three crabbed months had sour'd themselves to
    death,
Ere I could make thee open thy white hand,
And clap thyself my love: then didst thou utter
'I am yours for ever.'

HERMIONE

          'Tis Grace indeed.
Why, lo you now, I have spoke to the purpose twice:
The one for ever earn'd a royal husband;
The other for some while a friend.

LEONTES

              [Aside] Too hot, too hot!
To mingle friendship far is mingling bloods.
I have tremor cordis on me: my heart dances;
But not for joy; not joy. This entertainment
May a free face put on, derive a liberty
From heartiness, from bounty, fertile bosom,
And well become the agent; 't may, I grant;
But to be paddling palms and pinching fingers,
As now they are, and making practised smiles,
As in a looking-glass, and then to sigh, as 'twere
The mort o' the deer; O, that is entertainment
My bosom likes not, nor my brows! Mamillius,
Art thou my boy?

MAMILLIUS

        Ay, my good lord.

LEONTES

                I' fecks!

Why, that's my bawcock. What, hast smutch'd thy
    nose?
They say it is a copy out of mine. Come, captain,
We must be neat; not neat, but cleanly, captain:
And yet the steer, the heifer and the calf
Are all call'd neat.—Still virginalling
Upon his palm!—How now, you wanton calf!
Art thou my calf?

MAMILLIUS

        Yes, if you will, my lord.

LEONTES

Thou want'st a rough pash and the shoots that I
    have,
To be full like me: yet they say we are
Almost as like as eggs; women say so,
That will say any thing: but were they false
As o'er-dyed blacks, as wind, as waters, false
As dice are to be wish'd by one that fixes
No bourn 'twixt his and mine, yet were it true
To say this boy were like me. Come, sir page,
Look on me with your welkin eye: sweet villain!
Most dear'st! my collop! Can thy dam?—may't be?—
Affection! thy intention stabs the centre:
Thou dost make possible things not so held,
Communicatest with dreams;—how can this be?—
With what's unreal thou coactive art,
And fellow'st nothing: then 'tis very credent
Thou mayst co-join with something; and thou dost,
And that beyond commission, and I find it,
And that to the infection of my brains
And hardening of my brows.

POLIXENES

           What means Sicilia?

HERMIONE

He something seems unsettled.

POLIXENES

              How, my lord!
What cheer? how is't with you, best brother?

HERMIONE

                You look
As if you held a brow of much distraction:
Are you moved, my lord?

LEONTES

           No, in good earnest.
How sometimes nature will betray its folly,
Its tenderness, and make itself a pastime
To harder bosoms! Looking on the lines
Of my boy's face, methoughts I did recoil
Twenty-three years, and saw myself unbreech'd,
In my green velvet coat, my dagger muzzled,
Lest it should bite its master, and so prove,
As ornaments oft do, too dangerous:
How like, methought, I then was to this kernel,
This squash, this gentleman. Mine honest friend,
Will you take eggs for money?

MAMILLIUS

No, my lord, I'll fight.

LEONTES

You will! why, happy man be's dole! My brother,

Are you so fond of your young prince, as we
Do seem to be of ours?

POLIXENES

              If at home, sir,
He's all my exercise, my mirth, my matter:
Now my sworn friend, and then mine enemy;
My parasite, my soldier, statesman, all:
He makes a July's day short as December;
And with his varying childness cures in me
Thoughts that would thick my blood.

LEONTES

                So stands this squire
Officed with me: we two will walk, my lord,
And leave you to your graver steps. Hermione,
How thou lovest us, show in our brother's welcome;
Let what is dear in Sicily be cheap:
Next to thyself and my young rover, he's
Apparent to my heart.

HERMIONE

             If you would seek us,
We are yours i' the garden: shall's attend you there?

LEONTES

To your own bents dispose you: you'll be found,
Be you beneath the sky. [Aside] I am angling now,
Though you perceive me not how I give line.
Go to, go to!
How she holds up the neb, the bill to him!
And arms her with the boldness of a wife
To her allowing husband!

     [Exeunt POLIXENES, HERMIONE, and ATTENDANTS
            Gone already!
Inch-thick, knee-deep, o'er head and ears a fork'd
     one!
Go, play, boy, play: thy mother plays, and I
Play too; but so disgraced a part, whose issue
Will hiss me to my grave: contempt and clamour
Will be my knell. Go, play, boy, play. There have
     been,
Or I am much deceived, cuckolds ere now;
And many a man there is, even at this present,
Now, while I speak this, holds his wife by the arm,
That little thinks she has been sluiced in's absence
And his pond fish'd by his next neighbour, by
Sir Smile, his neighbour: nay, there's comfort in't,
Whiles other men have gates and those gates open'd,
As mine, against their will. Should all despair
That have revolted wives, the tenth of mankind
Would hang themselves. Physic for't there is none;
It is a bawdy planet, that will strike
Where 'tis predominant; and 'tis powerful, think it,
From east, west, north and south: be it concluded,
No barricado for a belly; know't;
It will let in and out the enemy
With bag and baggage: many thousand on's
Have the disease, and feel't not. How now, boy!

MAMILLIUS

I am like you, they say.

LEONTES

            Why, that's some comfort.
What, Camillo there?

CAMILLO

Ay, my good lord.

LEONTES

Go play, Mamillius; thou'rt an honest man.
                    [Exit MAMILLIUS
Camillo, this great sir will yet stay longer.

CAMILLO

You had much ado to make his anchor hold:
When you cast out, it still came home.

LEONTES

                     Didst note it?

CAMILLO

He would not stay at your petitions; made
His business more material.

LEONTES

                 Didst perceive it?
[Aside] They're here with me already; whispering,
     rounding
'Sicilia is a so-forth:' 'tis far gone,
When I shall gust it last.—How came't, Camillo,
That he did stay?

CAMILLO

            At the good queen's entreaty.

LEONTES

At the queen's be't: 'good' should be pertinent;
But, so it is, it is not. Was this taken
By any understanding pate but thine?
For thy conceit is soaking, will draw in
More than the common blocks: not noted, is't,
But of the finer natures? by some severals
Of head-piece extraordinary? lower messes
Perchance are to this business purblind? say.

CAMILLO

Business, my lord! I think most understand
Bohemia stays here longer.

LEONTES

            Ha!

CAMILLO

                Stays here longer.

LEONTES

Ay, but why?

CAMILLO

To satisfy your highness, and the entreaties
Of our most gracious mistress.

LEONTES

               Satisfy!
The entreaties of your mistress! satisfy!
Let that suffice. I have trusted thee, Camillo,
With all the nearest things to my heart, as well
My chamber-councils; wherein, priest-like, thou
Hast cleansed my bosom, I from thee departed
Thy penitent reform'd: but we have been
Deceived in thy integrity, deceived
In that which seems so.

CAMILLO

            Be it forbid, my lord!

LEONTES

To bide upon't, thou art not honest; or,
If thou inclinest that way, thou art a coward,

Which hoxes honesty behind, restraining
From course required; or else thou must be counted
A servant grafted in my serious trust
And therein negligent; or else a fool
That seest a game play'd home, the rich stake drawn,
And takest it all for jest.

CAMILLO

My gracious lord,
I may be negligent, foolish and fearful;
In every one of these no man is free,
But that his negligence, his folly, fear,
Among the infinite doings of the world,
Sometime puts forth. In your affairs, my lord,
If ever I were wilful-negligent,
It was my folly; if industriously
I play'd the fool, it was my negligence,
Not weighing well the end; if ever fearful
To do a thing, where I the issue doubted,
Whereof the execution did cry out
Against the non-performance, 'twas a fear
Which oft infects the wisest: these, my lord,
Are such allow'd infirmities that honesty
Is never free of. But, beseech your Grace,
Be plainer with me; let me know my trespass
By its own visage: if I then deny it,
'Tis none of mine.

LEONTES

Ha' not you seen, Camillo,—
But that's past doubt, you have, or your eye-glass
Is thicker than a cuckold's horn,—or heard,—
For to a vision so apparent rumour
Cannot be mute,—or thought,—for cogitation
Resides not in that man that does not think,—
My wife is slippery? If thou wilt confess,
Or else be impudently negative,
To have nor eyes nor ears nor thought, then say
My wife's a hobby-horse; deserves a name
As rank as any flax-wench that puts to
Before her troth-plight: say't and justify't.

CAMILLO

I would not be a stander-by to hear
My sovereign mistress clouded so, without
My present vengeance taken: 'shrew my heart,
You never spoke what did become you less
Than this; which to reiterate were sin
As deep as that, though true.

LEONTES

Is whispering nothing?
Is leaning cheek to cheek? is meeting noses?
Kissing with inside lip? stopping the career
Of laughter with a sigh?—a note infallible
Of breaking honesty;—horsing foot on foot?
Skulking in corners? wishing clocks more swift?
Hours, minutes? noon, midnight? and all eyes
Blind with the pin and web but theirs, theirs only,
That would unseen be wicked? is this nothing?
Why, then the world and all that's in't is nothing;
The covering sky is nothing; Bohemia nothing;
My wife is nothing; nor nothing have these nothings,
If this be nothing.

CAMILLO

Good my lord, be cured
Of this diseased opinion, and betimes;
For 'tis most dangerous.

LEONTES

Say it be, 'tis true.

CAMILLO

No, no, my lord.

LEONTES

It is; you lie, you lie:
I say thou liest, Camillo, and I hate thee,
Pronounce thee a gross lout, a mindless slave,
Or else a hovering temporizer, that
Canst with thine eyes at once see good and evil,
Inclining to them both: were my wife's liver
Infected as her life, she would not live
The running of one glass.

CAMILLO

Who does infect her?

LEONTES

Why, he that wears her like her medal, hanging
About his neck, Bohemia: who, if I
Had servants true about me, that bare eyes
To see alike mine honour as their profits,
Their own particular thrifts, they would do that
Which should undo more doing: ay, and thou,
His cupbearer,—whom I from meaner form
Have bench'd and rear'd to worship, who mayst see
Plainly as heaven sees earth and earth sees heaven,
How I am gall'd,—mightst bespice a cup,
To give mine enemy a lasting wink;
Which draught to me were cordial.

CAMILLO

Sir, my lord,
I could do this, and that with no rash potion,
But with a lingering dram, that should not work
Maliciously like poison: but I cannot
Believe this crack to be in my dread mistress,
So sovereignly being honourable.
I have loved thee,—

LEONTES

Make that thy question, and go rot!
Dost think I am so muddy, so unsettled,
To appoint myself in this vexation; sully
The purity and whiteness of my sheets,
Which to preserve is sleep, which being spotted
Is goads, thorns, nettles, tails of wasps;
Give scandal to the blood o' the prince my son,
Who I do think is mine and love as mine,
Without ripe moving to 't? Would I do this?
Could man so blench?

CAMILLO

I must believe you, sir:
I do; and will fetch off Bohemia for 't;
Provided that, when he's removed, your highness
Will take again your queen as yours at first,
Even for your son's sake; and thereby for sealing
The injury of tongues in courts and kingdoms
Known and allied to yours.

LEONTES
                    Thou dost advise me
Even so as I mine own course have set down:
I'll give no blemish to her honour, none.

CAMILLO
My lord,
Go then; and with a countenance as clear
As friendship wears at feasts, keep with Bohemia
And with your queen. I am his cupbearer:
If from me he have wholesome beverage,
Account me not your servant.

LEONTES
                    This is all:
Do 't, and thou hast the one half of my heart;
Do 't not, thou splitt'st thine own.

CAMILLO
                    I'll do 't, my lord.

LEONTES
I will seem friendly, as thou hast advised me. [Exit

CAMILLO
O miserable lady! But, for me,
What case stand I in? I must be the poisoner
Of good Polixenes: and my ground to do 't
Is the obedience to a master, one
Who, in rebellion with himself, will have
All that are his so too. To do this deed,
Promotion follows. If I could find example
Of thousands that had struck anointed kings
And flourish'd after, I 'ld not do 't; but since
Nor brass nor stone nor parchment bears not one,
Let villany itself forswear 't. I must
Forsake the court: to do 't, or no, is certain
To me a break-neck. Happy star reign now!
Here comes Bohemia.

Re-enter POLIXENES

POLIXENES
                    This is strange: methinks
My favour here begins to warp. Not speak?
Good day, Camillo.

CAMILLO
                    Hail, most royal sir!

POLIXENES
What is the news i' the court?

CAMILLO
                    None rare, my lord.

POLIXENES
The king hath on him such a countenance
As he had lost some province, and a region
Loved as he loves himself: even now I met him
With customary compliment; when he,
Wafting his eyes to the contrary, and falling
A lip of much contempt, speeds from me and
So leaves me, to consider what is breeding
That changes thus his manners.

CAMILLO
I dare not know, my lord.

POLIXENES
How! dare not! do not. Do you know, and dare not?
Be intelligent to me: 'tis thereabouts;

For, to yourself, what you do know, you must,
And cannot say, you dare not. Good Camillo,
Your changed complexions are to me a mirror
Which shows me mine changed too; for I must be
A party in this alteration, finding
Myself thus alter'd with 't.

CAMILLO
                    There is a sickness
Which puts some of us in distemper; but
I cannot name the disease; and it is caught
Of you that yet are well.

POLIXENES
                    How! caught of me!
Make me not sighted like the basilisk:
I have look'd on thousands, who have sped the better
By my regard, but kill'd none so. Camillo,—
As you are certainly a gentleman; thereto
Clerk-like experienced, which no less adorns
Our gentry than our parents' noble names,
In whose success we are gentle,—I beseech you,
If you know aught which does behove my knowledge
Thereof to be inform'd, imprison 't not
In ignorant concealment.

CAMILLO
                    I may not answer.

POLIXENES
A sickness caught of me, and yet I well!
I must be answer'd. Dost thou hear, Camillo?
I conjure thee, by all the parts of man
Which honour does acknowledge, whereof the least
Is not this suit of mine, that thou declare
What incidency thou dost guess of harm
Is creeping toward me; how far off, how near;
Which way to be prevented, if to be;
If not, how best to bear it.

CAMILLO
                    Sir, I will tell you;
Since I am charged in honour and by him
That I think honourable: therefore mark my coun-
    sel,
Which must be ev'n as swiftly follow'd as
I mean to utter it, or both yourself and me
Cry lost, and so good night!

POLIXENES
                    On, good Camillo.

CAMILLO
I am appointed him to murder you.

POLIXENES
By whom, Camillo?

CAMILLO
                    By the king.

POLIXENES
                    For what?

CAMILLO
He thinks, nay, with all confidence he swears,
As he had seen 't, or been an instrument
To vice you to 't, that you have touch'd his queen
Forbiddenly.

POLIXENES

O then, my best blood turn
To an infected jelly, and my name
Be yoked with his that did betray the Best!
Turn then my freshest reputation to
A savour that may strike the dullest nostril
Where I arrive, and my approach be shunn'd,
Nay, hated too, worse than the great'st infection
That e'er was heard or read!

CAMILLO

Swear his thought over
By each particular star in heaven and
By all their influences, you may as well
Forbid the sea for to obey the moon,
As or by oath remove or counsel shake
The fabric of his folly, whose foundation
Is piled upon his faith, and will continue
The standing of his body.

POLIXENES

How should this grow?

CAMILLO

I know not: but I am sure 'tis safer to
Avoid what's grown than question how 'tis born.
If therefore you dare trust my honesty,
That lies enclosed in this trunk which you
Shall bear along impawn'd, away to-night!
Your followers I will whisper to the business;
And will by twos and threes at several posterns,
Clear them o' the city. For myself, I'll put
My fortunes to your service, which are here
By this discovery lost. Be not uncertain;
For, by the honour of my parents, I
Have utter'd truth: which if you seek to prove,
I dare not stand by; nor shall you be safer
Than one condemn'd by the king's own mouth,
        thereon
His execution sworn.

POLIXENES

I do believe thee:
I saw his heart in's face. Give me thy hand:
Be pilot to me and thy places shall
Still neighbour mine. My ships are ready, and
My people did expect my hence departure
Two days ago. This jealousy
Is for a precious creature: as she's rare,
Must it be great; and, as his person's mighty,
Must it be violent; and as he does conceive
He is dishonour'd by a man which ever
Profess'd to him, why, his revenges must
In that be made more bitter. Fear o'ershades me:
Good expedition be my friend, and comfort
The gracious queen, part of his theme, but nothing
Of his ill-ta'en suspicion! Come, Camillo;
I will respect thee as a father if
Thou bear'st my life off hence: let us avoid.

CAMILLO

It is in mine authority to command
The keys of all the posterns: please your highness
To take the urgent hour. Come, sir, away. [Exeunt

ACT II

Scene I. *A room in* LEONTES' *palace*

Enter HERMIONE, MAMILLIUS, *and* LADIES

HERMIONE

Take the boy to you: he so troubles me,
'Tis past enduring.

FIRST LADY

Come, my gracious lord,
Shall I be your playfellow?

MAMILLIUS

No, I'll none of you.

FIRST LADY

Why, my sweet lord?

MAMILLIUS

You'll kiss me hard, and speak to me as if
I were a baby still. I love you better.

SECOND LADY

And why so, my lord?

MAMILLIUS

Not for because
Your brows are blacker; yet black brows, they say,
Become some women best, so that there be not
Too much hair there, but in a semicircle,
Or a half-moon made with a pen.

SECOND LADY

Who taught you this?

MAMILLIUS

I learn'd it out of women's faces. Pray now
What colour are your eyebrows?

FIRST LADY

Blue, my lord.

MAMILLIUS

Nay, that's a mock: I have seen a lady's nose
That has been blue, but not her eyebrows.

FIRST LADY

Hark ye;
The queen your mother rounds apace: we shall
Present our services to a fine new prince
One of these days; and then you'ld wanton with us,
If we would have you.

SECOND LADY

She is spread of late
Into a goodly bulk: good time encounter her!

HERMIONE

What wisdom stirs amongst you? Come, sir, now
I am for you again: pray you, sit by us,
And tell 's a tale.

MAMILLIUS

Merry or sad shall 't be?

HERMIONE

As merry as you will.

MAMILLIUS

A sad tale's best for winter: I have one
Of sprites and goblins.

HERMIONE

Let's have that, good sir.
Come on, sit down: come on, and do your best
To fright me with your sprites; you're powerful at it.

MAMILLIUS

There was a man—

HERMIONE

Nay, come, sit down; then on.

MAMILLIUS

Dwelt by a churchyard: I will tell it softly;
Yon crickets shall not hear it.

HERMIONE

Come on, then,
And give 't me in mine ear.

Enter LEONTES, *with* ANTIGONUS, LORDS, *and* OTHERS

LEONTES

Was he met there? his train? Camillo with him?

FIRST LORD

Behind the tuft of pines I met them; never
Saw I men scour so on their way: I eyed them
Even to their ships.

LEONTES

How blest am I
In my just censure, in my true opinion!
Alack, for lesser knowledge! how accursed
In being so blest! There may be in the cup
A spider steep'd, and one may drink, depart,
And yet partake no venom; for his knowledge
Is not infected: but if one present
The abhorr'd ingredient to his eye, make known
How he hath drunk, he cracks his gorge, his sides,
With violent hefts. I have drunk, and seen the spider.
Camillo was his help in this, his pandar:
There is a plot against my life, my crown;
All's true that is mistrusted: that false villain
Whom I employ'd was pre-employ'd by him:
He has discover'd my design, and I
Remain a pinch'd thing; yea, a very trick
For them to play at will. How came the posterns
So easily open?

FIRST LORD

By his great authority;
Which often hath no less prevail'd than so
On your command.

LEONTES

I know 't too well.
Give me the boy: I am glad you did not nurse him:
Though he does bear some signs of me, yet you
Have too much blood in him.

HERMIONE

What is this? sport?

LEONTES

Bear the boy hence; he shall not come about her;
Away with him! and let her sport herself
With that she's big with; for 'tis Polixenes
Has made thee swell thus.

HERMIONE

But I'ld say he had not,
And I'll be sworn you would believe my saying,
Howe'er you lean to the nayward.

LEONTES

You, my lords,
Look on her, mark her well; be but about

To say 'she is a goodly lady,' and
The justice of your hearts will thereto add
''Tis pity she's not honest, honourable:'
Praise her but for this her without-door form,
Which on my faith deserves high speech, and straight
The shrug, the hum or ha, these petty brands
That calumny doth use; O, I am out,
That mercy does, for calumny will sear
Virtue itself: these shrugs, these hums and ha's,
When you have said 'she's goodly,' come between
Ere you can say 'she's honest:' but be 't known,
From him that has most cause to grieve it should be,
She's an adulteress.

HERMIONE

Should a villain say so,
The most replenish'd villain in the world,
He were as much more villain: you, my lord,
Do but mistake.

LEONTES

You have mistook, my lady,
Polixenes for Leontes: O thou thing!
Which I'll not call a creature of thy place,
Lest barbarism, making me the precedent,
Should a like language use to all degrees,
And mannerly distinguishment leave out
Betwixt the prince and beggar: I have said
She's an adulteress; I have said with whom:
More, she's a traitor and Camillo is
A federary with her; and one that knows,
What she should shame to know herself
But with her most vile principal, that she's
A bed-swerver, even as bad as those
That vulgars give bold'st titles; ay, and privy
To this their late escape.

HERMIONE

No, by my life,
Privy to none of this. How will this grieve you,
When you shall come to clearer knowledge, that
You thus have publish'd me! Gentle my lord,
You scarce can right me throughly then to say
You did mistake.

LEONTES

No; if I mistake
In those foundations which I build upon,
The centre is not big enough to bear
A school-boy's top. Away with her, to prison!
He who shall speak for her is afar off guilty
But that he speaks.

HERMIONE

There's some ill planet reigns:
I must be patient till the heavens look
With an aspect more favourable. Good my lords,
I am not prone to weeping, as our sex
Commonly are; the want of which vain dew
Perchance shall dry your pities: but I have
That honourable grief lodged here which burns
Worse than tears drown: beseech you all, my lords,
With thoughts so qualified as your charities
Shall best instruct you, measure me; and so
The king's will be perform'd!

LEONTES

Shall I be heard?

HERMIONE

Who is 't that goes with me? Beseech your highness,
My women may be with me; for you see
My plight requires it. Do not weep, good fools;
There is no cause: when you shall know your mistress
Has deserved prison, then abound in tears
As I come out: this action I now go on
Is for my better grace. Adieu, my lord:
I never wish'd to see you sorry; now
I trust I shall. My women, come; you have leave.

LEONTES

Go, do our bidding; hence!

[Exit QUEEN, guarded; with LADIES

FIRST LORD

Beseech your highness, call the queen again.

ANTIGONUS

Be certain what you do, sir, lest your justice
Prove violence; in the which three great ones suffer,
Yourself, your queen, your son.

FIRST LORD

For her, my lord,
I dare my life lay down and will do't, sir,
Please you to accept it, that the queen is spotless
I' the eyes of heaven and to you; I mean,
In this which you accuse her.

ANTIGONUS

If it prove
She's otherwise, I'll keep my stables where
I lodge my wife; I'll go in couples with her;
Than when I feel and see her no farther trust her;
For every inch of woman in the world,
Ay, every dram of woman's flesh is false,
If she be.

LEONTES

Hold your peaces.

FIRST LORD

Good my lord,—

ANTIGONUS

It is for you we speak, not for ourselves:
You are abused, and by some putter-on
That will be damn'd for 't; would I knew the villain,
I would land-damn him. Be she honour-flaw'd,
I have three daughters; the eldest is eleven;
The second and the third, nine, and some five;
If this prove true, they'll pay for 't: by mine honour,
I'll geld 'em all; fourteen they shall not see,
To bring false generations: they are co-heirs;
And I had rather glib myself than they
Should not produce fair issue.

LEONTES

Cease; no more.
You smell this business with a sense as cold
As is a dead man's nose: but I do see 't and feel 't,
As you feel doing thus; and see withal
The instruments that feel.

ANTIGONUS

If it be so,

We need no grave to bury honesty:
There's not a grain of it the face to sweeten
Of the whole dungy earth.

LEONTES

What! lack I credit?

FIRST LORD

I had rather you did lack than I, my lord,
Upon this ground; and more it would content me
To have her honour true than your suspicion,
Be blamed for 't how you might.

LEONTES

Why, what need we
Commune with you of this, but rather follow
Our forceful instigation? Our prerogative
Calls not your counsels, but our natural goodness
Imparts this; which if you, or stupified
Or seeming so in skill, cannot or will not
Relish a truth like us, inform yourselves
We need no more of your advice: the matter,
The loss, the gain, the ordering on 't, is all
Properly ours.

ANTIGONUS

And I wish, my liege,
You had only in your silent judgement tried it,
Without more overture.

LEONTES

How could that be?
Either thou art most ignorant by age,
Or thou wert born a fool. Camillo's flight,
Added to their familiarity,
Which was as gross as ever touch'd conjecture,
That lack'd sight only, nought for approbation
But only seeing, all other circumstances
Made up to the deed,—doth push on this proceeding:
Yet, for a greater confirmation,
For in an act of this importance 'twere
Most piteous to be wild, I have dispatch'd in post
To sacred Delphos, to Apollo's temple,
Cleomenes and Dion, whom you know
Of stuff'd sufficiency: now from the oracle
They will bring all; whose spiritual counsel had,
Shall stop or spur me. Have I done well?

FIRST LORD

Well done, my lord.

LEONTES

Though I am satisfied and need no more
Than what I know, yet shall the oracle
Give rest to the minds of others, such as he
Whose ignorant credulity will not
Come up to the truth. So have we thought it good
From our free person she should be confined,
Lest that the treachery of the two fled hence
Be left her to perform. Come, follow us;
We are to speak in public; for this business
Will raise us all.

ANTIGONUS

[Aside] To laughter, as I take it,
If the good truth were known.   [Exeunt

SCENE II. *A prison*

Enter PAULINA, *a* GENTLEMAN, *and* ATTENDANTS

PAULINA

The keeper of the prison, call to him;
Let him have knowledge who I am.

[*Exit* GENTLEMAN

Good lady,
No court in Europe is too good for thee;
What dost thou then in prison?

Re-enter GENTLEMAN, *with the* GAOLER

Now, good sir,
You know me, do you not?

GAOLER

For a worthy lady
And one who much I honour.

PAULINA

Pray you, then,
Conduct me to the queen.

GAOLER

I may not, madam:
To the contrary I have express commandment.

PAULINA

Here's ado,
To lock up honesty and honour from
The access of gentle visitors! Is 't lawful, pray you,
To see her women? any of them? Emilia?

GAOLER

So please you, madam,
To put apart these your attendants, I
Shall bring Emilia forth.

PAULINA

I pray now, call her.
Withdraw yourselves.

[*Exeunt* GENTLEMAN *and* ATTENDANTS

GAOLER

And, madam,
I must be present at your conference.

PAULINA

Well, be 't so, prithee.

[*Exit* GAOLER

Here's such ado to make no stain a stain
As passes colouring.

Re-enter GAOLER, *with* EMILIA

Dear gentlewoman,
How fares our gracious lady?

EMILIA

As well as one so great and so forlorn
May hold together: on her frights and griefs,
Which never tender lady hath borne greater,
She is something before her time deliver'd.

PAULINA

A boy?

EMILIA

A daughter; and a goodly babe,
Lusty and like to live: the queen receives
Much comfort in't; says 'My poor prisoner,
I am innocent as you.'

PAULINA

I dare be sworn:

These dangerous unsafe lunes i' the king, beshrew
them!
He must be told on't, and he shall: the office
Becomes a woman best; I'll take 't upon me:
If I prove honey-mouth'd, let my tongue blister,
And never to my red-look'd anger be
The trumpet any more. Pray you, Emilia,
Commend my best obedience to the queen:
If she dares trust me with her little babe,
I'll show't the king and undertake to be
Her advocate to the loud'st. We do not know
How he may soften at the sight o' the child:
The silence often of pure innocence
Persuades when speaking fails.

EMILIA

Most worthy madam,
Your honour and your goodness is so evident,
That your free undertaking cannot miss
A thriving issue: there is no lady living
So meet for this great errand. Please your ladyship
To visit the next room, I'll presently
Acquaint the queen of your most noble offer;
Who but to-day hammer'd of this design,
But durst not tempt a minister of honour,
Lest she should be denied.

PAULINA

Tell her, Emilia,
I'll use that tongue I have: if wit flow from 't
As boldness from my bosom, let 't not be doubted
I shall do good.

EMILIA

Now be you blest for it!
I'll to the queen: please you, come something nearer.

GAOLER

Madam, if 't please the queen to send the babe,
I know not what I shall incur to pass it,
Having no warrant.

PAULINA

You need not fear it, sir:
This child was prisoner to the womb, and is
By law and process of great nature thence
Freed and enfranchised; not a party to
The anger of the king, nor guilty of,
If any be, the trespass of the queen.

GAOLER

I do believe it.

PAULINA

Do not you fear: upon mine honour, I
Will stand betwixt you and danger.

[*Exeunt*

SCENE III. *A room in* LEONTES' *palace*

Enter LEONTES, ANTIGONUS, LORDS, *and* SERVANTS

LEONTES

Nor night nor day no rest: it is but weakness
To bear the matter thus; mere weakness. If
The cause were not in being,—part o' the cause,
She the adulteress; for the harlot king
Is quite beyond mine arm, out of the blank

And level of my brain, plot-proof; but she
I can hook to me: say that she were gone,
Given to the fire, a moiety of my rest
Might come to me again. Who's there?

FIRST SERVANT

My lord?

LEONTES

How does the boy?

FIRST SERVANT

He took good rest to-night;
'Tis hoped his sickness is discharged.

LEONTES

To see his nobleness!
Conceiving the dishonour of his mother,
He straight declined, droop'd, took it deeply,
Fasten'd and fix'd the shame on 't in himself,
Threw off his spirit, his appetite, his sleep,
And downright languish'd. Leave me solely: go,
See how he fares. [*Exit* SERVANT] Fie, fie! no thought
    of him:
The very thought of my revenges that way
Recoil upon me: in himself too mighty,
And in his parties, his alliance; let him be
Until a time may serve: for present vengeance,
Take it on her. Camillo and Polixenes
Laugh at me, make their pastime at my sorrow:
They should not laugh if I could reach them, nor
Shall she within my power.

Enter PAULINA, *with a* CHILD

FIRST LORD

You must not enter.

PAULINA

Nay, rather, good my lords, be second to me:
Fear you his tyrannous passion more, alas,
Than the queen's life? a gracious innocent soul,
More free than he is jealous.

ANTIGONUS

That's enough.

SECOND SERVANT

Madam, he hath not slept to-night; commanded
None should come at him.

PAULINA

Not so hot, good sir:
I come to bring him sleep. 'Tis such as you,
That creep like shadows by him, and do sigh
At each his needless heavings, such as you
Nourish the cause of his awaking: I
Do come with words as medicinal as true,
Honest as either, to purge him of that humour
That presses him from sleep.

LEONTES

What noise there, ho?

PAULINA

No noise, my lord; but needful conference
About some gossips for your highness.

LEONTES

How!
Away with that audacious lady! Antigonus,
I charged thee that she should not come about me:
I knew she would.

ANTIGONUS

I told her so, my lord,
On your displeasure's peril and on mine,
She should not visit you.

LEONTES

What, canst not rule her?

PAULINA

From all dishonesty he can: in this,
Unless he take the course that you have done,
Commit me for committing honour, trust it,
He shall not rule me.

ANTIGONUS

La you now, you hear:
When she will take the rein I let her run;
But she'll not stumble.

PAULINA

Good my liege, I come;
And, I beseech you, hear me, who professes
Myself your loyal servant, your physician,
Your most obedient counsellor, yet that dares
Less appear so in comforting your evils,
Than such as most seem yours: I say, I come
From your good queen.

LEONTES

Good queen!

PAULINA

Good queen, my lord,
Good queen; I say good queen;
And would by combat make her good, so were I
A man, the worst about you.

LEONTES

Force her hence.

PAULINA

Let him that makes but trifles of his eyes
First hand me: on mine own accord I'll off;
But first I'll do my errand. The good queen,
For she is good, hath brought you forth a daughter;
Here 'tis; commends it to your blessing.

[*Laying down the* CHILD

LEONTES

Out!
A mankind witch! Hence with her, out o' door:
A most intelligencing bawd!

PAULINA

Not so:
I am as ignorant in that as you
In so entitling me, and no less honest
Than you are mad; which is enough, I'll warrant,
As this world goes, to pass for honest.

LEONTES

Traitors!
Will you not push her out? Give her the bastard.
Thou dotard! thou art woman-tired, unroosted
By thy dame Partlet here. Take up the bastard;
Take 't up, I say; give 't to thy crone.

PAULINA

For ever
Unvenerable be thy hands, if thou
Takest up the princess by that forced baseness
Which he has put upon 't!

LEONTES
He dreads his wife.

PAULINA
So I would you did; then 'twere past all doubt
You'ld call your children yours.

LEONTES
A nest of traitors!

ANTIGONUS
I am none, by this good light.

PAULINA
Nor I; nor any
But one that's here, and that's himself; for he
The sacred honour of himself, his queen's,
His hopeful son's, his babe's, betrays to slander,
Whose sting is sharper than the sword's; and will
not,—
For, as the case now stands, it is a curse
He cannot be compell'd to 't,—once remove
The root of his opinion, which is rotten
As ever oak or stone was sound.

LEONTES
A callat
Of boundless tongue, who late hath beat her hus-
band
And now baits me! This brat is none of mine;
It is the issue of Polixenes:
Hence with it, and together with the dam
Commit them to the fire!

PAULINA
It is yours;
And, might we lay the old proverb to your charge,
So like you, 'tis the worse. Behold, my lords,
Although the print be little, the whole matter
And copy of the father, eye, nose, lip;
The trick of 's frown; his forehead; nay, the valley,
The pretty dimples of his chin and cheek; his smiles;
The very mould and frame of hand, nail, finger:
And thou, good goddess Nature, which hast made it
So like to him that got it, if thou hast
The ordering of the mind too, 'mongst all colours
No yellow in 't, lest she suspect, as he does,
Her children not her husband's!

LEONTES
A gross hag!
And, lozel, thou art worthy to be hang'd,
That wilt not stay her tongue.

ANTIGONUS
Hang all the husbands
That cannot do that feat, you'll leave yourself
Hardly one subject.

LEONTES
Once more, take her hence.

PAULINA
A most unworthy and unnatural lord
Can do no more.

LEONTES
I'll ha' thee burnt.

PAULINA
I care not:
It is an heretic that makes the fire,

Not she which burns in 't. I'll not call you tyrant;
But this most cruel usage of your queen—
Not able to produce more accusation
Than your own weak-hinged fancy—something
savours
Of tyranny, and will ignoble make you,
Yea, scandalous to the world.

LEONTES
On your allegiance,
Out of the chamber with her! Were I a tyrant,
Where were her life? she durst not call me so,
If she did know me one. Away with her!

PAULINA
I pray you, do not push me; I'll be gone.
Look to your babe, my lord; 'tis yours: Jove send her
A better guiding spirit! What needs these hands?
You, that are thus so tender o'er his follies,
Will never do him good, not one of you.
So, so: farewell; we are gone.   [Exit

LEONTES
Thou, traitor, hast set on thy wife to this.
My child? away with 't! Even thou, that hast
A heart so tender o'er it, take it hence
And see it instantly consumed with fire;
Even thou and none but thou. Take it up straight:
Within this hour bring me word 'tis done,
And by good testimony, or I'll seize thy life,
With what thou else call'st thine. If thou refuse
And wilt encounter with my wrath, say so;
The bastard brains with these my proper hands
Shall I dash out. Go, take it to the fire;
For thou set'st on thy wife.

ANTIGONUS
I did not, sir:
These lords, my noble fellows, if they please,
Can clear me in 't.

LORDS
We can: my royal liege,
He is not guilty of her coming hither.

LEONTES
You're liars all.

FIRST LORD
Beseech your highness, give us better credit;
We have always truly served you; and beseech you
So to esteem of us: and on our knees we beg,
As recompense of our dear services
Past and to come, that you do change this purpose,
Which being so horrible, so bloody, must
Lead on to some foul issue: we all kneel.

LEONTES
I am a feather for each wind that blows:
Shall I live on to see this bastard kneel
And call me father? better burn it now
Than curse it then. But be it; let it live.
It shall not neither. You, sir, come you hither;
You that have been so tenderly officious
With Lady Margery, your midwife there,
To save this bastard's life,—for 'tis a bastard,

So sure as this beard's grey,—what will you adven-
ture
To save this brat's life?
                    ANTIGONUS
                              Any thing, my lord,
That my ability may undergo,
And nobleness impose: at least thus much:
I'll pawn the little blood which I have left
To save the innocent: any thing possible.
                    LEONTES
It shall be possible. Swear by this sword
Thou wilt perform my bidding.
                    ANTIGONUS
                              I will, my lord.
                    LEONTES
Mark and perform it: seest thou? for the fail
Of any point in 't shall not only be
Death to thyself but to thy lewd-tongued wife,
Whom for this time we pardon. We enjoin thee,
As thou art liege-man to us, that thou carry
This female bastard hence, and that thou bear it
To some remote and desert place, quite out
Of our dominions; and that there thou leave it,
Without more mercy, to it own protection
And favour of the climate. As by strange fortune
It came to us, I do in justice charge thee,
On thy soul's peril and thy body's torture,
That thou commend it strangely to some place
Where chance may nurse or end it. Take it up.
                    ANTIGONUS
I swear to do this, though a present death
Had been more merciful. Come on, poor babe:
Some powerful spirit instruct the kites and ravens
To be thy nurses! Wolves and bears, they say,
Casting their savageness aside have done
Like offices of pity. Sir, be prosperous
In more than this deed does require! And blessing
Against this cruelty fight on thy side,
Poor thing, condemn'd to loss! [*Exit with the* CHILD
                    LEONTES
                              No, I'll not rear
Another's issue.
                    Enter a SERVANT
                    SERVANT
            Please your highness, posts
From those you sent to the oracle are come
An hour since: Cleomenes and Dion,
Being well arrived from Delphos, are both landed,
Hasting to the court.
                    FIRST LORD
                    So please you, sir, their speed
Hath been beyond account.
                    LEONTES
                              Twenty three days
They have been absent: 'tis good speed; foretells
The great Apollo suddenly will have
The truth of this appear. Prepare you, lords;
Summon a session, that we may arraign
Our most disloyal lady; for, as she hath
Been publicly accused, so shall she have

A just and open trial. While she lives
My heart will be a burthen to me. Leave me,
And think upon my bidding.   [*Exeunt*

ACT III
Scene I. *A sea-port in Sicilia*

Enter CLEOMENES *and* DION
                    CLEOMENES
The climate's delicate, the air most sweet,
Fertile the isle, the temple much surpassing
The common praise it bears.
                    DION
                              I shall report,
For most it caught me, the celestial habits,
Methinks I so should term them, and the reverence
Of the grave wearers. O, the sacrifice!
How ceremonious, solemn and unearthly
It was i' the offering!
                    CLEOMENES
                              But of all, the burst
And the ear-deafening voice o' the oracle,
Kin to Jove's thunder, so surprised my sense,
That I was nothing.
                    DION
                    If the event o' the journey
Prove as successful to the queen,—O be 't so!—
As it hath been to us rare, pleasant, speedy,
The time is worth the use on 't.
                    CLEOMENES
                              Great Apollo
Turn all to the best! These proclamations,
So forcing faults upon Hermione,
I little like.
                    DION
                    The violent carriage of it
Will clear or end the business: when the oracle,
Thus by Apollo's great divine seal'd up,
Shall the contents discover, something rare
Even then will rush to knowledge. Go: fresh horses!
And gracious be the issue!   [*Exeunt*

Scene II. *A court of Justice*

Enter LEONTES, LORDS, *and* OFFICERS
                    LEONTES
This sessions, to our great grief we pronounce,
Even pushes 'gainst our heart: the party tried
The daughter of a king, our wife, and one
Of us too much beloved. Let us be clear'd
Of being tyrannous, since we so openly
Proceed in justice, which shall have due course,
Even to the guilt or the purgation.
Produce the prisoner.
                    OFFICER
It is his highness' pleasure that the queen
Appear in person here in court. Silence!

Enter HERMIONE *guarded;* PAULINA *and* LADIES
attending

LEONTES

Read the indictment.

OFFICER

[*Reads*] Hermione, queen to the worthy Leontes, king of Sicilia, thou art here accused and arraigned of high treason, in committing adultery with Polixenes, king of Bohemia, and conspiring with Camillo to take away the life of our sovereign lord the king, thy royal husband: the pretence whereof being by circumstances partly laid open, thou, Hermione, contrary to the faith and allegiance of a true subject, didst counsel and aid them, for their better safety, to fly away by night.

HERMIONE

Since what I am to say must be but that
Which contradicts my accusation, and
The testimony on my part no other
But what comes from myself, it shall scarce boot me
To say 'not guilty:' mine integrity,
Being counted falsehood, shall, as I express it,
Be so received. But thus, if powers divine
Behold our human actions, as they do,
I doubt not then but innocence shall make
False accusation blush, and tyranny
Tremble at patience. You, my lord, best know,
Who least will seem to do so, my past life
Hath been as continent, as chaste, as true,
As I am now unhappy; which is more
Than history can pattern, though devised
And play'd to take spectators. For behold me
A fellow of the royal bed, which owe
A moiety of the throne, a great king's daughter,
The mother to a hopeful prince, here standing
To prate and talk for life and honour 'fore
Who please to come and hear. For life, I prize it
As I weigh grief, which I would spare: for honour,
'Tis a derivative from me to mine,
And only that I stand for. I appeal
To your own conscience, sir, before Polixenes
Came to your court, how I was in your grace,
How merited to be so; since he came,
With what encounter so uncurrent I
Have strain'd, to appear thus: if one jot beyond
The bound of honour, or in act or will
That way inclining, harden'd be the hearts
Of all that hear me, and my near'st of kin
Cry fie upon my grave!

LEONTES

        I ne'er heard yet
That any of these bolder vices wanted
Less impudence to gainsay what they did
Than to perform it first.

HERMIONE

        That's true enough;
Though 'tis a saying, sir, not due to me.

LEONTES

You will not own it.

HERMIONE

        More than mistress of
Which comes to me in name of fault, I must not
At all acknowledge. For Polixenes,

With whom I am accused, I do confess
I loved him as in honour he required,
With such a kind of love as might become
A lady like me, with a love even such,
So and no other, as yourself commanded:
Which not to have done I think had been in me
Both disobedience and ingratitude
To you and toward your friend; whose love had
   spoke,
Even since it could speak, from an infant, freely
That it was yours. Now, for conspiracy,
I know not how it tastes; though it be dish'd
For me to try how: all I know of it
Is that Camillo was an honest man;
And why he left your court, the gods themselves,
Wotting no more than I, are ignorant.

LEONTES

You knew of his departure, as you know
What you have underta'en to do in 's absence.

HERMIONE

Sir,
You speak a language that I understand not:
My life stands in the level of your dreams,
Which I'll lay down.

LEONTES

        Your actions are my dreams;
You had a bastard by Polixenes,
And I but dream'd it. As you were past all shame,—
Those of your fact are so,—so past all truth:
Which to deny concerns more than avails; for as
Thy brat hath been cast out, like to itself,
No father owning it,—which is, indeed,
More criminal in thee than it,—so thou
Shalt feel our justice, in whose easiest passage
Look for no less than death.

HERMIONE

        Sir, spare your threats:
The bug which you would fright me with I seek.
To me can life be no commodity:
The crown and comfort of my life, your favour,
I do give lost; for I do feel it gone,
But know not how it went. My second joy
And first-fruits of my body, from his presence
I am barr'd, like one infectious. My third comfort,
Starr'd most unluckily, is from my breast,
The innocent milk in it most innocent mouth,
Haled out to murder: myself on every post
Proclaim'd a strumpet: with immodest hatred
The child-bed privilege denied, which 'longs
To women of all fashion; lastly, hurried
Here to this place, i' the open air, before
I have got strength of limit. Now, my liege,
Tell me what blessings I have here alive,
That I should fear to die? Therefore proceed.
But yet hear this; mistake me not; no life,
I prize it not a straw, but for mine honour,
Which I would free, if I shall be condemn'd
Upon surmises, all proofs sleeping else
But what your jealousies awake, I tell you
'Tis rigour and not law. Your honours all,

I do refer me to the oracle:
Apollo be my judge!

FIRST LORD
This your request
Is altogether just: therefore bring forth,
And in Apollo's name, his oracle.

[*Exeunt certain* OFFICERS

HERMIONE
The Emperor of Russia was my father:
O that he were alive, and here beholding
His daughter's trial! that he did but see
The flatness of my misery, yet with eyes
Of pity, not revenge!

Re-enter OFFICERS, *with* CLEOMENES *and* DION

OFFICER
You here shall swear upon this sword of justice,
That you, Cleomenes and Dion, have
Been both at Delphos, and from thence have brought
This seal'd-up oracle, by the hand deliver'd
Of great Apollo's priest, and that since then
You have not dared to break the holy seal
Nor read the secrets in't.

CLEOMENES *and* DION
All this we swear.

LEONTES
Break up the seals and read.

OFFICER
[*Reads*] Hermione is chaste; Polixenes blameless; Camillo a
true subject; Leontes a jealous tyrant; his innocent babe truly
begotten; and the king shall live without an heir, if that which
is lost be not found.

LORDS
Now blessed be the great Apollo!

HERMIONE
Praised!

LEONTES
Hast thou read truth?

OFFICER
Ay, my lord; even so
As it is here set down.

LEONTES
There is no truth at all i' the oracle:
The sessions shall proceed: this is mere falsehood.

Enter SERVANT

SERVANT
My lord the king, the king!

LEONTES
What is the business?

SERVANT
O sir, I shall be hated to report it!
The prince your son, with mere conceit and fear
Of the queen's speed, is gone.

LEONTES
How! gone!

SERVANT
Is dead.

LEONTES
Apollo's angry; and the heavens themselves
Do strike at my injustice. [HERMIONE *faints*] How
now there!

PAULINA
This news is mortal to the queen: look down
And see what death is doing.

LEONTES
Take her hence:
Her heart is but o'ercharged; she will recover:
I have too much believed mine own suspicion:
Beseech you, tenderly apply to her
Some remedies for life.

[*Exeunt* PAULINA *and* LADIES, *with* HERMIONE
Apollo, pardon
My great profaneness 'gainst thine oracle!
I'll reconcile me to Polixenes;
New woo my queen; recall the good Camillo,
Whom I proclaim a man of truth, of mercy;
For, being transported by my jealousies
To bloody thoughts and to revenge, I chose
Camillo for the minister to poison
My friend Polixenes: which had been done,
But that the good mind of Camillo tardied
My swift command, though I with death and with
Reward did threaten and encourage him,
Not doing it and being done: he, most humane
And fill'd with honour, to my kingly guest
Unclasp'd my practice, quit his fortunes here,
Which you knew great, and to the hazard
Of all incertainties himself commended,
No richer than his honour: how he glisters
Thorough my rust! and how his piety
Does my deeds make the blacker!

Re-enter PAULINA

PAULINA
Woe the while!
O, cut my lace, lest my heart, cracking it,
Break too!

FIRST LORD
What fit is this, good lady?

PAULINA
What studied torments, tyrant, hast for me?
What wheels? racks? fires? what flaying? boiling?
In leads or oils? what old or newer torture
Must I receive, whose every word deserves
To taste of thy most worst? Thy tyranny
Together working with thy jealousies,
Fancies too weak for boys, too green and idle
For girls of nine, O, think what they have done
And then run mad indeed, stark mad! for all
Thy by-gone fooleries were but spices of it.
That thou betray'dst Polixenes, 'twas nothing;
That did but show thee, of a fool, inconstant
And damnable ingrateful: nor was 't much,
Thou wouldst have poison'd good Camillo's honour
To have him kill a king; poor trespasses,
More monstrous standing by: whereof I reckon
The casting forth to crows thy baby-daughter
To be or none or little; though a devil
Would have shed water out of fire ere done 't:
Nor is 't directly laid to thee, the death
Of the young prince, whose honourable thoughts,
Thoughts high for one so tender, cleft the heart

That could conceive a gross and foolish sire
Blemish'd his gracious dam: this is not, no,
Laid to thy answer: but the last,—O lords,
When I have said, cry 'woe!'—the queen, the queen,
The sweet'st, dear'st creature's dead, and venge-
   ance for 't
Not dropp'd down yet.

FIRST LORD
               The higher powers forbid!

PAULINA
I say she's dead, I'll swear 't. If word nor oath
Prevail not, go and see: if you can bring
Tincture or lustre in her lip, her eye,
Heat outwardly or breath within, I'll serve you
As I would do the gods. But, O thou tyrant!
Do not repent these things, for they are heavier
Than all thy woes can stir: therefore betake thee
To nothing but despair. A thousand knees
Ten thousand years together, naked, fasting,
Upon a barren mountain, and still winter
In storm perpetual, could not move the gods
To look that way thou wert.

LEONTES
               Go on, go on:
Thou canst not speak too much; I have deserved
All tongues to talk their bitterest.

FIRST LORD
               Say no more:
Howe'er the business goes, you have made fault
I' the boldness of your speech.

PAULINA
               I am sorry for 't:
All faults I make, when I shall come to know them,
I do repent. Alas! I have show'd too much
The rashness of a woman: he is touch'd
To the noble heart. What's gone and what's past
   help
Should be past grief: do not receive affliction
At my petition; I beseech you, rather
Let me be punish'd, that have minded you
Of what you should forget. Now, good my liege,
Sir, royal sir, forgive a foolish woman:
The love I bore your queen, lo, fool again!
I'll speak of her no more, nor of your children;
I'll not remember you of my own lord,
Who is lost too: take your patience to you,
And I'll say nothing.

LEONTES
               Thou didst speak but well
When most the truth; which I receive much better
Than to be pitied of thee. Prithee, bring me
To the dead bodies of my queen and son:
One grave shall be for both; upon them shall
The causes of their death appear, unto
Our shame perpetual. Once a day I'll visit
The chapel where they lie, and tears shed there
Shall be my recreation: so long as nature
Will bear up with this exercise, so long
I daily vow to use it. Come and lead me
To these sorrows.   [Exeunt

SCENE III. *Bohemia. A desert country near the sea*

Enter ANTIGONUS *with a* CHILD, *and a* MARINER

ANTIGONUS
Thou art perfect, then, our ship hath touch'd upon
The deserts of Bohemia?

MARINER
               Ay, my lord; and fear
We have landed in ill time: the skies look grimly
And threaten present blusters. In my conscience,
The heavens with that we have in hand are angry
And frown upon 's.

ANTIGONUS
Their sacred wills be done! Go, get aboard;
Look to thy bark: I'll not be long before
I call upon thee.

MARINER
Make your best haste, and go not
Too far i' the land: 'tis like to be loud weather;
Besides, this place is famous for the creatures
Of prey that keep upon 't.

ANTIGONUS
               Go thou away:
I'll follow instantly.

MARINER
               I am glad at heart
To be so rid o' the business.

ANTIGONUS
               Come, poor babe:
I have heard, but not believed, the spirits o' the dead
May walk again: if such thing be, thy mother
Appear'd to me last night, for ne'er was dream
So like a waking. To me comes a creature,
Sometimes her head on one side, some another;
I never saw a vessel of like sorrow,
So fill'd and so becoming: in pure white robes,
Like very sanctity, she did approach
My cabin where I lay; thrice bow'd before me,
And, gasping to begin some speech, her eyes
Became two spouts: the fury spent, anon
Did this break from her: 'Good Antigonus,
Since fate, against thy better disposition,
Hath made thy person for the thrower-out
Of my poor babe, according to thine oath,
Places remote enough are in Bohemia,
There weep and leave it crying; and, for the babe
Is counted lost for ever, Perdita,
I prithee, call 't. For this ungentle business,
Put on thee by my lord, thou ne'er shalt see
Thy wife Paulina more.' And so, with shrieks,
She melted into air. Affrighted much,
I did in time collect myself, and thought
This was so, and no slumber. Dreams are toys:
Yet for this once, yea, superstitiously,
I will be squared by this. I do believe
Hermione hath suffer'd death; and that
Apollo would, this being indeed the issue
Of King Polixenes, it should here be laid,
Either for life or death, upon the earth
Of its right father. Blossom, speed thee well!

There lie, and there thy character: there these;
Which may, if fortune please, both breed thee,
  pretty,
And still rest thine. The storm begins: poor wretch,
That for thy mother's fault art thus exposed
To loss and what may follow! Weep I cannot,
But my heart bleeds; and most accursed am I
To be by oath enjoin'd to this. Farewell!
The day frowns more and more: thou'rt like to have
A lullaby too rough: I never saw
The heavens so dim by day. A savage clamour!
Well may I get aboard! This is the chase:
I am gone for ever.   [*Exit, pursued by a bear*

                Enter a SHEPHERD
                    SHEPHERD

I would there were no age between ten and three-
and-twenty, or that youth would sleep out the rest;
for there is nothing in the between but getting
wenches with child, wronging the ancientry, stealing, fighting—Hark you now! Would any but these
boiled brains of nineteen and two-and-twenty hunt
this weather? They have scared away two of my
best sheep, which I fear the wolf will sooner find
than the master: if any where I have them, 'tis by
the sea-side, browzing of ivy. Good luck, an't be thy
will! what have we here? Mercy on's, a barne; a
very pretty barne! A boy or a child, I wonder? A
pretty one; a very pretty one: sure, some scape:
though I am not bookish, yet I can read waiting-
gentlewoman in the scape. This has been some stair-
work, some trunk-work, some behind-door-work:
they were warmer that got this than the poor thing
is here. I'll take it up for pity: yet I'll tarry till my
son come; he hallooed but even now. Whoa, ho,
hoa!

                Enter CLOWN
                    CLOWN
Hilloa, loa!

                    SHEPHERD
What, art so near? If thou'lt see a thing to talk on
when thou art dead and rotten, come hither.
What ailest thou, man?

                    CLOWN
I have seen two such sights, by sea and by land! but
I am not to say it is a sea, for it is now the sky: betwixt the firmament and it you cannot thrust a
bodkin's point.

                    SHEPHERD
Why, boy, how is it?

                    CLOWN
I would you did but see how it chafes, how it rages,
how it takes up the shore! but that's not to the point.
O, the most piteous cry of the poor souls! sometimes to see 'em, and not to see 'em; now the ship
boring the moon with her main-mast, and anon
swallowed with yest and froth, as you'ld thrust a
cork into a hogshead. And then for the land-service,
to see how the bear tore out his shoulder-bone; how
he cried to me for help and said his name was Antigonus, a nobleman. But to make an end of the ship,

to see how the sea flap-dragoned it: but, first, how
the poor souls roared, and the sea mocked them; and
how the poor gentleman roared and the bear
mocked him, both roaring louder than the sea or
weather.

                    SHEPHERD
Name of mercy, when was this, boy?

                    CLOWN
Now, now: I have not winked since I saw these
sights: the men are not yet cold under water, nor
the bear half dined on the gentleman: he's at it now.

                    SHEPHERD
Would I had been by, to have helped the old man!

                    CLOWN
I would you had been by the ship side, to have
helped her: there your charity would have lacked
footing.

                    SHEPHERD
Heavy matters! heavy matters! but look thee here,
boy. Now bless thyself: thou mettest with things
dying, I with things new-born. Here's a sight for
thee; look thee, a bearing-cloth for a squire's child!
look thee here; take up, take up, boy; open't. So,
let's see: it was told me I should be rich by the fairies. This is some changeling: open't. What's within,
boy?

                    CLOWN
You're a made old man: if the sins of your youth are
forgiven you, you're well to live. Gold! all gold!

                    SHEPHERD
This is fairy gold, boy, and 'twill prove so: up with't,
keep it close: home, home, the next way. We are
lucky, boy; and to be so still requires nothing but
secrecy. Let my sheep go: come, good boy, the next
way home.

                    CLOWN
Go you the next way with your findings. I'll go see
if the bear be gone from the gentleman and how
much he hath eaten: they are never curst but when
they are hungry: if there be any of him left, I'll bury
it.

                    SHEPHERD
That's a good deed. If thou mayest discern by that
which is left of him what he is, fetch me to the sight
of him.

                    CLOWN
Marry, will I; and you shall help to put him i' the
ground.

                    SHEPHERD
'Tis a lucky day, boy, and we'll do good deeds on't.
                                        [*Exeunt*

                    ACT IV
                    SCENE I

                Enter TIME, *the Chorus*
                    TIME
I, that please some, try all, both joy and terror

Of good and bad, that makes and unfolds error,
Now take upon me, in the name of Time,
To use my wings. Impute it not a crime
To me or my swift passage, that I slide
O'er sixteen years and leave the growth untried
Of that wide gap, since it is in my power
To o'erthrow law and in one self-born hour
To plant and o'erwhelm custom. Let me pass
The same I am, ere ancient'st order was
Or what is now received: I witness to
The times that brought them in; so shall I do
To the freshest things now reigning, and make stale
The glistering of this present, as my tale
Now seems to it. Your patience this allowing,
I turn my glass and give my scene such growing
As you had slept between: Leontes leaving,
The effects of his fond jealousies so grieving
That he shuts up himself, imagine me,
Gentle spectators, that I now may be
In fair Bohemia; and remember well,
I mentioned a son o' the king's, which Florizel
I now name to you; and with speed so pace
To speak of Perdita, now grown in grace
Equal with wondering: what of her ensues
I list not prophesy; but let Time's news
Be known when 'tis brought forth. A shepherd's
     daughter,
And what to her adheres, which follows after,
Is the argument of Time. Of this allow,
If ever you have spent time worse ere now;
If never, yet that Time himself doth say
He wishes earnestly you never may.   [Exit

Scene II. *Bohemia. The palace of* POLIXENES

Enter POLIXENES *and* CAMILLO
POLIXENES
I pray thee, good Camillo, be no more importunate:
'tis a sickness denying thee any thing; a death to
grant this.

CAMILLO
It is fifteen years since I saw my country: though I
have for the most part been aired abroad, I desire
to lay my bones there. Besides, the penitent king,
my master, hath sent for me; to whose feeling sorrows I might be some allay, or I o'erween to think
so, which is another spur to my departure.

POLIXENES
As thou lovest me, Camillo, wipe not out the rest of
thy services by leaving me now: the need I have of
thee, thine own goodness hath made; better not to
have had thee than thus to want thee: thou, having
made me businesses, which none without thee can
sufficiently manage, must either stay to execute
them thyself, or take away with thee the very services thou hast done; which if I have not enough
considered, as too much I cannot, to be more thankful to thee shall be my study; and my profit therein,
the heaping friendships. Of that fatal country, Sici-

lia, prithee speak no more; whose very naming pun-
ishes me with the remembrance of that penitent, as
thou callest him, and reconciled king, my brother;
whose loss of his most precious queen and children
are even now to be afresh lamented. Say to me,
when sawest thou the Prince Florizel, my son?
Kings are no less unhappy, their issue not being
gracious, than they are in losing them when they
have approved their virtues.

CAMILLO
Sir, it is three days since I saw the prince. What his
happier affairs may be, are to me unknown: but I
have missingly noted, he is of late much retired from
court and is less frequent to his princely exercises
than formerly he hath appeared.

POLIXENES
I have considered so much, Camillo, and with some
care; so far, that I have eyes under my service which
look upon his removedness; from whom I have this
intelligence, that he is seldom from the house of a
most homely shepherd; a man, they say, that from
very nothing, and beyond the imagination of his
neighbours, is grown into an unspeakable estate.

CAMILLO
I have heard, sir, of such a man, who hath a daughter of most rare note: the report of her is extended
more than can be thought to begin from such a
cottage.

POLIXENES
That's likewise part of my intelligence; but, I fear,
the angle that plucks our son thither. Thou shalt accompany us to the place; where we will, not appearing what we are, have some question with the
shepherd; from whose simplicity I think it not uneasy to get the cause of my son's resort thither.
Prithee, be my present partner in this business, and
lay aside the thoughts of Sicilia.

CAMILLO
I willingly obey your command.

POLIXENES
My best Camillo! We must disguise ourselves.
          [Exeunt

Scene III. *A road near the* SHEPHERD's *cottage*

Enter AUTOLYCUS, *singing*
When daffodils begin to peer,
     With heigh! the doxy over the dale,
Why, then comes in the sweet o' the year;
     For the red blood reigns in the winter's pale.

The white sheet bleaching on the hedge,
     With heigh! the sweet birds, O, how they sing!
Doth set my pugging tooth on edge;
     For a quart of ale is a dish for a king.

The lark, that tirra-lyra chants,
     With heigh! with heigh! the thrush and the jay,
Are summer songs for me and my aunts,
     While we lie tumbling in the hay.

I have served Prince Florizel and in my time wore three-pile; but now I am out of service:

But shall I go mourn for that, my dear?
The pale moon shines by night:
And when I wander here and there,
I then do most go right.

If tinkers may have leave to live,
And bear the sow-skin budget,
Then my account I well may give,
And in the stocks avouch it.

My traffic is sheets; when the kite builds, look to lesser linen. My father named me Autolycus; who being, as I am, littered under Mercury, was likewise a snapper-up of unconsidered trifles. With die and drab I purchased this caparison, and my revenue is the silly cheat. Gallows and knock are too powerful on the highway: beating and hanging are terrors to me: for the life to come, I sleep out the thought of it. A prize! a prize!

Enter CLOWN

CLOWN

Let me see: every 'leven wether tods; every tod yields pound and odd shilling; fifteen hundred shorn, what comes the wool to?

AUTOLYCUS

[*Aside*] If the springe hold, the cock's mine.

CLOWN

I cannot do't without counters. Let me see; what am I to buy for our sheep-shearing feast? Three pound of sugar; five pound of currants; rice—what will this sister of mine do with rice? But my father hath made her mistress of the feast, and she lays it on. She hath made me four and twenty nosegays for the shearers, three-man song-men all, and very good ones; but they are most of them means and bases; but one puritan amongst them, and he sings psalms to hornpipes. I must have saffron to colour the warden pies; mace; dates, none, that's out of my note; nutmegs, seven; a race or two of ginger, but that I may beg; four pound of prunes, and as many of raisins o' the sun.

AUTOLYCUS

O that ever I was born!   [*Grovelling on the ground*

CLOWN

I' the name of me—

AUTOLYCUS

O, help me, help me! pluck but off these rags; and then, death, death!

CLOWN

Alack, poor soul! thou hast need of more rags to lay on thee, rather than have these off.

AUTOLYCUS

O sir, the loathsomeness of them offends me more than the stripes I have received, which are mighty ones and millions.

CLOWN

Alas, poor man! a million of beating may come to a great matter.

AUTOLYCUS

I am robbed, sir, and beaten; my money and ap-

parel ta'en from me, and these detestable things put upon me.

CLOWN

What, by a horseman, or a footman?

AUTOLYCUS

A footman, sweet sir, a footman.

CLOWN

Indeed, he should be a footman by the garments he has left with thee: if this be a horseman's coat, it hath seen very hot service. Lend me thy hand, I'll help thee: come, lend me thy hand. [*Helping him up*

AUTOLYCUS

O, good sir, tenderly, O!

CLOWN

Alas, poor soul!

AUTOLYCUS

O, good sir, softly, good sir! I fear, sir, my shoulder-blade is out.

CLOWN

How now! canst stand?

AUTOLYCUS

Softly, dear sir [*picks his pocket*]; good sir, softly. You ha' done me a charitable office.

CLOWN

Dost lack any money? I have a little money for thee.

AUTOLYCUS

No, good sweet sir; no, I beseech you, sir: I have a kinsman not past three quarters of a mile hence, unto whom I was going; I shall there have money, or any thing I want: offer me no money, I pray you; that kills my heart.

CLOWN

What manner of fellow was he that robbed you?

AUTOLYCUS

A fellow, sir, that I have known to go about with troll-my-dames: I knew him once a servant of the prince: I cannot tell, good sir, for which of his virtues it was, but he was certainly whipped out of the court.

CLOWN

His vices, you would say; there's no virtue whipped out of the court: they cherish it to make it stay there; and yet it will no more but abide.

AUTOLYCUS

Vices I would say, sir. I know this man well: he hath been since an ape-bearer; then a process-server, a bailiff; then he compassed a motion of the Prodigal Son, and married a tinker's wife within a mile where my land and living lies; and, having flown over many knavish professions, he settled only in rogue: some call him Autolycus.

CLOWN

Out upon him! prig, for my life, prig: he haunts wakes, fairs and bear-baitings.

AUTOLYCUS

Very true, sir; he, sir, he; that's the rogue that put me into this apparel.

CLOWN

Not a more cowardly rogue in all Bohemia: if you had but looked big and spit at him, he'ld have run.

AUTOLYCUS

I must confess to you, sir, I am no fighter: I am false
of heart that way; and that he knew, I warrant him.

CLOWN

How do you now?

AUTOLYCUS

Sweet sir, much better than I was; I can stand and
walk: I will even take my leave of you, and pace
softly towards my kinsman's.

CLOWN

Shall I bring thee on the way?

AUTOLYCUS

No, good-faced sir; no, sweet sir.

CLOWN

Then fare thee well: I must go buy spices for our
sheep-shearing.

AUTOLYCUS

Prosper you, sweet sir! [*Exit* CLOWN] Your purse is
not hot enough to purchase your spice. I'll be with
you at your sheep-shearing too: if I make not this
cheat bring out another and the shearers prove
sheep, let me be unrolled and my name put in the
book of virtue!

SONG

Jog on, jog on, the foot-path way,
    And merrily hent the stile-a:
A merry heart goes all the day,
    Your sad tires in a mile-a.   [*Exit*

SCENE IV. *The* SHEPHERD'S *cottage*

Enter FLORIZEL *and* PERDITA

FLORIZEL

These your unusual weeds to each part of you
Do give a life: no shepherdess, but Flora
Peering in April's front. This your sheep-shearing
Is as a meeting of the petty gods,
And you the queen on't.

PERDITA

                    Sir, my gracious lord,
To chide at your extremes it not becomes me:
O, pardon, that I name them! Your high self,
The gracious mark o' the land, you have obscured
With a swain's wearing, and me, poor lowly maid,
Most goddess-like prank'd up: but that our feasts
In every mess have folly and the feeders
Digest it with a custom, I should blush
To see you so attired, sworn, I think,
To show myself a glass.

FLORIZEL

                    I bless the time
When my good falcon made her flight across
Thy father's ground.

PERDITA

                    Now Jove afford you cause!
To me the difference forges dread; your greatness
Hath not been used to fear. Even now I tremble
To think your father, by some accident,
Should pass this way as you did: O, the Fates!

How would he look, to see his work, so noble,
Vilely bound up? What would he say? Or how
Should I, in these my borrow'd flaunts, behold
The sternness of his presence?

FLORIZEL

                    Apprehend
Nothing but jollity. The gods themselves,
Humbling their deities to love, have taken
The shapes of beasts upon them: Jupiter
Became a bull, and bellow'd; the green Neptune
A ram, and bleated; and the fire-robed god,
Golden Apollo, a poor humble swain,
As I seem now. Their transformations
Were never for a piece of beauty rarer,
Nor in a way so chaste, since my desires
Run not before mine honour, nor my lusts
Burn hotter than my faith.

PERDITA

                    O, but, sir,
Your resolution cannot hold, when 'tis
Opposed, as it must be, by the power of the king:
One of these two must be necessities,
Which then will speak, that you must change this
    purpose,
Or I my life.

FLORIZEL

                    Thou dearest Perdita,
With these forced thoughts, I prithee, darken not
The mirth o' the feast. Or I'll be thine, my fair,
Or not my father's. For I cannot be
Mine own, nor any thing to any, if
I be not thine. To this I am most constant,
Though destiny say no. Be merry, gentle;
Strangle such thoughts as these with any thing
That you behold the while. Your guests are coming:
Lift up your countenance, as it were the day
Of celebration of that nuptial which
We two have sworn shall come.

PERDITA

                    O lady Fortune,
Stand you auspicious!

FLORIZEL

                    See, your guests approach:
Address yourself to entertain them sprightly,
And let's be red with mirth.

Enter SHEPHERD, CLOWN, MOPSA, DORCAS, *and others,
with* POLIXENES *and* CAMILLO *disguised*

SHEPHERD

Fie, daughter! when my old wife lived, upon
This day she was both pantler, butler, cook,
Both dame and servant; welcomed all, served all;
Would sing her song and dance her turn; now here,
At upper end o' the table, now i' the middle;
On his shoulder, and his; her face o' fire
With labour and the thing she took to quench it,
She would to each one sip. You are retired,
As if you were a feasted one and not
The hostess of the meeting: pray you, bid
These unknown friends to's welcome; for it is
A way to make us better friends, more known.

Come, quench your blushes and present yourself
That which you are, mistress o' the feast: come on,
And bid us welcome to your sheep-shearing,
As your good flock shall prosper.

PERDITA
                    [To POLIXENES] Sir, welcome:
It is my father's will I should take on me
The hostess-ship o' the day. [To CAMILLO] You're
    welcome, sir.
Give me those flowers there, Dorcas. Reverend sirs,
For you there's rosemary and rue; these keep
Seeming and savour all the winter long:
Grace and remembrance be to you both,
And welcome to our shearing!

POLIXENES
                              Shepherdess,
A fair one are you, well you fit our ages
With flowers of winter.

PERDITA
                    Sir, the year growing ancient,
Not yet on summer's death, nor on the birth
Of trembling winter, the fairest flowers o' the season
Are our carnations and streak'd gillyvors,
Which some call nature's bastards: of that kind
Our rustic garden's barren; and I care not
To get slips of them.

POLIXENES
              Wherefore, gentle maiden,
Do you neglect them?

PERDITA
                For I have heard it said
There is an art which in their piedness shares
With great creating nature.

POLIXENES
                    Say there be;
Yet nature is made better by no mean,
But nature makes that mean: so, over that art
Which you say adds to nature, is an art
That nature makes. You see, sweet maid, we marry
A gentler scion to the wildest stock,
And make conceive a bark of baser kind
By bud of nobler race: this is an art
Which does mend nature, change it rather, but
The art itself is nature.

PERDITA
            So it is.

POLIXENES
Then make your garden rich in gillyvors,
And do not call them bastards.

PERDITA
                    I'll not put
The dibble in earth to set one slip of them;
No more than were I painted I would wish
This youth should say 'twere well, and only there-
    fore
Desire to breed by me. Here's flowers for you;
Hot lavender, mints, savory, marjoram;
The marigold, that goes to bed wi' the sun
And with him rises weeping: these are flowers

Of middle summer, and I think they are given
To men of middle age. You're very welcome.

CAMILLO
I should leave grazing, were I of your flock,
And only live by gazing.

PERDITA
                Out, alas!
You'ld be so lean, that blasts of January
Would blow you through and through. Now, my
    fair'st friend,
I would I had some flowers o' the spring that might
Become your time of day; and yours, and yours,
That wear upon your virgin branches yet
Your maidenheads growing: O Proserpina,
For the flowers now, that frighted thou let'st fall
From Dis's waggon! daffodils,
That come before the swallow dares, and take
The winds of March with beauty; violets dim,
But sweeter than the lids of Juno's eyes
Or Cytherea's breath; pale primroses,
That die unmarried, ere they can behold
Bright Phœbus in his strength, a malady
Most incident to maids; bold oxlips and
The crown imperial; lilies of all kinds,
The flower-de-luce being one! O, these I lack,
To make you garlands of; and my sweet friend,
To strew him o'er and o'er!

FLORIZEL
                    What, like a corse?

PERDITA
No, like a bank for love to lie and play on;
Not like a corse; or if, not to be buried,
But quick and in mine arms. Come, take your
    flowers:
Methinks I play as I have seen them do
In Whitsun pastorals: sure this robe of mine
Does change my disposition.

FLORIZEL
                    What you do
Still betters what is done. When you speak, sweet,
I'ld have you do it ever: when you sing,
I'ld have you buy and sell so, so give alms,
Pray so; and, for the ordering your affairs,
To sing them too: when you do dance, I wish you
A wave o' the sea, that you might ever do
Nothing but that; move still, still so,
And own no other function: each your doing,
So singular in each particular,
Crowns what you are doing in the present deeds,
That all your acts are queens.

PERDITA
                    O Doricles,
Your praises are too large: but that your youth,
And the true blood which peeps fairly through't,
Do plainly give you out an unstain'd shepherd,
With wisdom I might fear, my Doricles,
You woo'd me the false way.

FLORIZEL
                    I think you have
As little skill to fear as I have purpose

To put you to't. But come; our dance, I pray:
Your hand, my Perdita: so turtles pair,
That never mean to part.

PERDITA
              I'll swear for 'em.

POLIXENES
This is the prettiest low-born lass that ever
Ran on the green-sward: nothing she does or seems
But smacks of something greater than herself,
Too noble for this place.

CAMILLO
              He tells her something
That makes her blood look out: good sooth, she is
The queen of curds and cream.

CLOWN
              Come on, strike up!

DORCAS
Mopsa must be your mistress: marry, garlic,
To mend her kissing with!

MOPSA
              Now, in good time!

CLOWN
Not a word, a word; we stand upon our manners.
Come, strike up!

[*Music. Here a dance of* SHEPHERDS *and* SHEPHERDESSES

POLIXENES
Pray, good shepherd, what fair swain is this
Which dances with your daughter?

SHEPHERD
They call him Doricles; and boasts himself
To have a worthy feeding: but I have it
Upon his own report and I believe it;
He looks like sooth. He says he loves my daughter:
I think so too; for never gazed the moon
Upon the water, as he'll stand and read
As 'twere my daughter's eyes: and, to be plain,
I think there is not half a kiss to choose
Who loves another best.

POLIXENES
              She dances featly.

SHEPHERD
So she does any thing; though I report it,
That should be silent: if young Doricles
Do light upon her, she shall bring him that
Which he not dreams of.

Enter SERVANT

SERVANT
O master, if you did but hear the pedlar at the door,
you would never dance again after a tabor and
pipe; no, the bagpipe could not move you: he sings
several tunes faster than you'll tell money; he utters
them as he had eaten ballads and all men's ears
grew to his tunes.

CLOWN
He could never come better; he shall come in. I love
a ballad but even too well, if it be doleful matter
merrily set down, or a very pleasant thing indeed
and sung lamentably.

SERVANT
He hath songs for man or woman, of all sizes; no

milliner can so fit his customers with gloves: he has
the prettiest love-songs for maids; so without bawdry,
which is strange; with such delicate burthens of dil-
dos and fadings, 'jump her and thump her;' and
where some stretch-mouthed rascal would, as it
were, mean mischief and break a foul gap into the
matter, he makes the maid to answer 'Whoop, do
me no harm, good man;' puts him off, slights him,
with 'Whoop, do me no harm, good man.'

POLIXENES
This is a brave fellow.

CLOWN
Believe me, thou talkest of an admirable conceited
fellow. Has he any unbraided wares?

SERVANT
He hath ribbons of all the colours i' the rainbow;
points more than all the lawyers in Bohemia can
learnedly handle, though they come to him by the
gross: inkles, caddisses, cambrics, lawns: why, he
sings 'em over as they were gods or goddesses; you
would think a smock were a she-angel, he so chants
to the sleeve-hand and the work about the square
on't.

CLOWN
Prithee bring him in; and let him approach singing.

PERDITA
Forewarn him that he use no scurrilous words in's
tunes.   [*Exit* SERVANT

CLOWN
You have of these pedlars, that have more in them
than you'ld think, sister.

PERDITA
Ay, good brother, or go about to think.

Enter AUTOLYCUS, *singing*

Lawn as white as driven snow;
Cypress black as e'er was crow;
Gloves as sweet as damask roses;
Masks for faces and for noses;
Bugle bracelet, necklace amber,
Perfume for a lady's chamber;
Golden quoifs and stomachers,
For my lads to give their dears;
Pins and poking-sticks of steel,
What maids lack from head to heel:
Come buy of me, come; come buy, come buy;
Buy, lads, or else your lasses cry:
Come buy.

CLOWN
If I were not in love with Mopsa, thou shouldst take
no money of me; but being enthralled as I am, it
will also be the bondage of certain ribbons and
gloves.

MOPSA
I was promised them against the feast; but they
come not too late now.

DORCAS
He hath promised you more than that, or there be
liars.

MOPSA
He hath paid you all he promised you: may be, he
has paid you more, which will shame you to give
him again.

CLOWN

Is there no manners left among maids? will they wear their plackets where they should bear their faces? Is there not milking-time, when you are going to bed, or kiln-hole, to whistle off these secrets, but you must be tittle-tattling before all our guests? 'tis well they are whispering: clamour your tongues, and not a word more.

MOPSA

I have done. Come, you promised me a tawdry-lace and a pair of sweet gloves.

CLOWN

Have I not told thee how I was cozened by the way and lost all my money?

AUTOLYCUS

And indeed, sir, there are cozeners abroad; therefore it behoves men to be wary.

CLOWN

Fear not thou, man, thou shalt lose nothing here.

AUTOLYCUS

I hope so, sir; for I have about me many parcels of charge.

CLOWN

What hast here? ballads?

MOPSA

Pray now, buy some: I love a ballad in print o' life, for then we are sure they are true.

AUTOLYCUS

Here's one to a very doleful tune, how a usurer's wife was brought to bed of twenty money-bags at a burthen, and how she longed to eat adders' heads and toads carbonadoed.

MOPSA

Is it true, think you?

AUTOLYCUS

Very true, and but a month old.

DORCAS

Bless me from marrying a usurer!

AUTOLYCUS

Here's the midwife's name to't, one Mistress Taleporter, and five or six honest wives that were present. Why should I carry lies abroad?

MOPSA

Pray you now, buy it.

CLOWN

Come on, lay it by: and let's first see moe ballads; we'll buy the other things anon.

AUTOLYCUS

Here's another ballad of a fish, that appeared upon the coast, on Wednesday the fourscore of April, forty thousand fathom above water, and sung this ballad against the hard hearts of maids: it was thought she was a woman, and was turned into a cold fish for she would not exchange flesh with one that loved her: the ballad is very pitiful and as true.

DORCAS

Is it true too, think you?

AUTOLYCUS

Five justices' hands at it, and witnesses more than my pack will hold

CLOWN

Lay it by too: another.

AUTOLYCUS

This is a merry ballad, but a very pretty one.

MOPSA

Let's have some merry ones.

AUTOLYCUS

Why, this is a passing merry one and goes to the tune of 'Two maids wooing a man:' there's scarce a maid westward but she sings it; 'tis in request, I can tell you.

MOPSA

We can both sing it: if thou'lt bear a part, thou shalt hear; 'tis in three parts.

DORCAS

We had the tune on't a month ago.

AUTOLYCUS

I can bear my part; you must know 'tis my occupation: have at it with you.

SONG

A. Get you hence, for I must go
    Where it fits not you to know.
        D. Whither? M. O, whither? D. Whither?
M. It becomes thy oath full well,
    Thou to me thy secrets tell:
        D. Me too, let me go thither.

M. Or thou goest to the grange or mill:
D. If to either, thou dost ill.
        A. Neither. D. What, neither? A. Neither.
D. Thou hast sworn my love to be;
M. Thou hast sworn it more to me:
    Then whither goest? say, whither?

CLOWN

We'll have this song out anon by ourselves: my father and the gentlemen are in sad talk, and we'll not trouble them. Come, bring away thy pack after me. Wenches, I'll buy for you both. Pedlar, let's have the first choice. Follow me, girls.

[Exit with DORCAS and MOPSA

AUTOLYCUS

And you shall pay well for 'em.   [Follows singing

Will you buy any tape,
    Or lace for your cape,
My dainty duck, my dear-a?
    Any silk, any thread,
    Any toys for your head,
Of the new'st, and finest, finest wear-a?
    Come to the pedlar;
    Money's a medler,
That doth utter all men's ware-a.   [Exit

Re-enter SERVANT

SERVANT

Master, there is three carters, three shepherds, three neat-herds, three swine-herds, that have made themselves all men of hair, they call themselves Saltiers, and they have a dance which the wenches say is a gallimaufry of gambols, because they are not in't; but they themselves are o' the mind, if it be not too rough for some that know little but bowling, it will please plentifully.

SHEPHERD

Away! we'll none on't: here has been too much
homely foolery already. I know, sir, we weary you.

POLIXENES

You weary those that refresh us: pray, let's see these
four threes of herdsmen.

SERVANT

One three of them, by their own report, sir, hath
danced before the king; and not the worst of the
three but jumps twelve foot and a half by the squier.

SHEPHERD

Leave your prating: since these good men are
pleased, let them come in; but quickly now.

SERVANT

Why, they stay at door, sir.   [*Exit*
Here a dance of twelve SATYRS

POLIXENES

O, father, you'll know more of that hereafter.
[*To* CAMILLO] Is it not too far gone? 'Tis time to
    part them.
He's simple and tells much. How now, fair shepherd!
Your heart is full of something that does take
Your mind from feasting. Sooth, when I was young
And handed love as you do, I was wont
To load my she with knacks: I would have ran-
    sack'd
The pedlar's silken treasury and have pour'd it
To her acceptance; you have let him go
And nothing marted with him. If your lass
Interpretation should abuse and call this
Your lack of love or bounty, you were straited
For a reply, at least if you make a care
Of happy holding her.

FLORIZEL

                    Old sir, I know
She prizes not such trifles as these are:
The gifts she looks from me are pack'd and lock'd
Up in my heart; which I have given already,
But not deliver'd. O, hear me breathe my life
Before this ancient sir, who, it should seem,
Hath sometime loved! I take thy hand, this hand,
As soft as dove's down and as white as it,
Or Ethiopian's tooth, or the fann'd snow that's
    bolted
By the northern blasts twice o'er.

POLIXENES

                    What follows this?
How prettily the young swain seems to wash
The hand was fair before! I have put you out:
But to your protestation; let me hear
What you profess.

FLORIZEL

                    Do, and be witness to't.

POLIXENES

And this my neighbour too?

FLORIZEL

                    And he, and more
Than he, and men, the earth, the heavens, and all:
That, were I crown'd the most imperial monarch,
Thereof most worthy, were I the fairest youth

That ever made eye swerve, had force and knowl-
    edge
More than was ever man's, I would not prize them
Without her love; for her employ them all;
Commend them and condemn them to her service
Or to their own perdition.

POLIXENES

                    Fairly offer'd.

CAMILLO

This shows a sound affection.

SHEPHERD

                    But, my daughter,
Say you the like to him?

PERDITA

                    I cannot speak
So well, nothing so well; no, nor mean better:
By the pattern of mine own thoughts I cut out
The purity of his.

SHEPHERD

                    Take hands, a bargain!
And, friends unknown, you shall bear witness to't:
I give my daughter to him, and will make
Her portion equal his.

FLORIZEL

                    O, that must be
I' the virtue of your daughter: one being dead,
I shall have more than you can dream of yet;
Enough then for your wonder. But, come on,
Contract us 'fore these witnesses.

SHEPHERD

                    Come, your hand;
And, daughter, yours.

POLIXENES

                    Soft, swain, awhile, beseech you;
Have you a father?

FLORIZEL

                    I have: but what of him?

POLIXENES

Knows he of this?

FLORIZEL

                    He neither does nor shall.

POLIXENES

Methinks a father
Is at the nupital of his son a guest
That best becomes the table. Pray you once more,
Is not your father grown incapable
Of reasonable affairs? is he not stupid
With age and altering rheums? can he speak? hear?
Know man from man? dispute his own estate?
Lies he not bed-rid? and again does nothing
But what he did being childish?

FLORIZEL

                    No, good sir;
He has his health and ampler strength indeed
Than most have of his age.

POLIXENES

                    By my white beard,
You offer him, if this be so, a wrong
Something unfilial: reason my son
Should choose himself a wife, but as good reason

The father all whose joy is nothing else
But fair posterity, should hold some counsel
In such a business.

FLORIZEL
I yield all this;
But for some other reasons, my grave sir,
Which 'tis not fit you know, I not acquaint
My father of this business.

POLIXENES
Let him know't.

FLORIZEL
He shall not.

POLIXENES
Prithee, let him.

FLORIZEL
No, he must not.

SHEPHERD
Let him, my son: he shall not need to grieve
At knowing of thy choice.

FLORIZEL
Come, come, he must not.
Mark our contract.

POLIXENES
Mark your divorce, young sir,
[Discovering himself
Whom son I dare not call; thou art too base
To be acknowledged: thou a sceptre's heir,
That thus affects a sheep-hook! Thou old traitor,
I am sorry that by hanging thee I can
But shorten thy life one week. And thou, fresh piece
Of excellent witchcraft, who of force must know
The royal fool thou copest with,—

SHEPHERD
O, my heart!

POLIXENES
I'll have thy beauty scratch'd with briers, and made
More homely than thy state. For thee, fond boy,
If I may ever know thou dost but sigh
That thou no more shalt see this knack, as never
I mean thou shalt, we'll bar thee from succession;
Not hold thee of our blood, no, not our kin,
Far than Deucalion off: mark thou my words:
Follow us to the court. Thou churl, for this time,
Though full of our displeasure, yet we free thee
From the dead blow of it. And you, enchantment,—
Worthy enough a herdsman; yea, him too,
That makes himself, but for our honour therein,
Unworthy thee,—if ever henceforth thou
These rural latches to his entrance open,
Or hoop his body more with thy embraces,
I will devise a death as cruel for thee
As thou art tender to't.   [Exit

PERDITA
Even here undone!
I was not much afeard; for once or twice
I was about to speak and tell him plainly,
The selfsame sun that shines upon his court
Hides not his visage from our cottage, but
Looks on alike. Will't please you, sir, be gone?
I told you what would come of this: beseech you,

Of your own state take care: this dream of mine,—
Being now awake, I'll queen it no inch farther,
But milk my ewes and weep.

CAMILLO
Why, how now, father!
Speak ere thou diest.

SHEPHERD
I cannot speak, nor think,
Nor dare to know that which I know. O sir!
You have undone a man of fourscore three,
That thought to fill his grave in quiet; yea,
To die upon the bed my father died,
To lie close by his honest bones: but now
Some hangman must put on my shroud and lay me
Where no priest shovels in dust. O cursed wretch,
That knew'st this was the prince, and wouldst adventure
To mingle faith with him! Undone! undone!
If I might die within this hour, I have lived
To die when I desire.   [Exit

FLORIZEL
Why look you so upon me?
I am but sorry, not afeard; delay'd,
But nothing alter'd: what I was, I am;
More straining on for plucking back, not following
My leash unwillingly.

CAMILLO
Gracious my lord,
You know your father's temper: at this time
He will allow no speech, which I do guess
You do not purpose to him; and as hardly
Will he endure your sight as yet, I fear:
Then, till the fury of his highness settle,
Come not before him.

FLORIZEL
I not purpose it.
I think, Camillo?

CAMILLO
Even he, my lord.

PERDITA
How often have I told you 'twould be thus!
How often said, my dignity would last
But till 'twere known!

FLORIZEL
It cannot fail but by
The violation of my faith; and then
Let nature crush the sides o' the earth together
And mar the seeds within! Lift up thy looks:
From my succession wipe me, father, I
Am heir to my affection.

CAMILLO
Be advised.

FLORIZEL
I am, and by my fancy: if my reason
Will thereto be obedient, I have reason;
If not, my senses, better pleased with madness,
Do bid it welcome.

CAMILLO
This is desperate, sir.

FLORIZEL

So call it: but it does fulfil my vow;
I needs must think it honesty. Camillo,
Not for Bohemia, nor the pomp that may
Be thereat glean'd; for all the sun sees, or
The close earth wombs, or the profound seas hide
In unknown fathoms, will I break my oath
To this my fair beloved: therefore, I pray you,
As you have ever been my father's honour'd friend,
When he shall miss me,—as, in faith, I mean not
To see him any more,—cast your good counsels
Upon his passion: let myself and fortune
Tug for the time to come. This you may know
And so deliver, I am put to sea
With her whom here I cannot hold on shore;
And most opportune to our need I have
A vessel rides fast by, but not prepared
For this design. What course I mean to hold
Shall nothing benefit your knowledge, nor
Concern me the reporting.

CAMILLO

O my lord!
I would your spirit were easier for advice,
Or stronger for your need.

FLORIZEL

Hark, Perdita. [*Drawing her aside*
I'll hear you by and by.

CAMILLO

He's irremovable,
Resolved for flight. Now were I happy, if
His going I could frame to serve my turn,
Save him from danger, do him love and honour,
Purchase the sight again of dear Sicilia
And that unhappy king, my master, whom
I so much thirst to see.

FLORIZEL

Now, good Camillo;
I am so fraught with curious business that
I leave out ceremony.

CAMILLO

Sir, I think
You have heard of my poor services, i' the love
That I have borne your father?

FLORIZEL

Very nobly
Have you deserved: it is my father's music
To speak your deeds, not little of his care
To have them recompensed as thought on.

CAMILLO

Well, my lord,
If you may please to think I love the king,
And through him what is nearest to him, which is
Your gracious self, embrace but my direction,
If your more ponderous and settled project
May suffer alteration, on mine honour
I'll point you where you shall have such receiving
As shall become your highness; where you may
Enjoy your mistress, from the whom, I see,
There's no disjunction to be made, but by
As heavens forefend! your ruin; marry her,

And, with my best endeavours in your absence,
Your discontenting father strive to qualify
And bring him up to liking.

FLORIZEL

How, Camillo,
May this, almost a miracle, be done?
That I may call thee something more than man
And after that trust to thee.

CAMILLO

Have you thought on
A place whereto you'll go?

FLORIZEL

Not any yet:
But as the unthought-on accident is guilty
To what we wildly do, so we profess
Ourselves to be the slaves of chance, and flies
Of every wind that blows.

CAMILLO

Then list to me:
This follows, if you will not change your purpose
But undergo this flight, make for Sicilia,
And there present yourself and your fair princess,
For so I see she must be, 'fore Leontes:
She shall be habited as it becomes
The partner of your bed. Methinks I see
Leontes opening his free arms and weeping
His welcomes forth; asks thee the son forgiveness,
As 'twere i' the father's person; kisses the hands
Of your fresh princess; o'er and o'er divides him
'Twixt his unkindness and his kindness; the one
He chides to hell and bids the other grow
Faster than thought or time.

FLORIZEL

Worthy Camillo,
What colour for my visitation shall I
Hold up before him?

CAMILLO

Sent by the king your father
To greet him and to give him comforts. Sir,
The manner of your bearing towards him, with
What you as from your father shall deliver,
Things known betwixt us three, I'll write you down:
The which shall point you forth at every sitting
What you must say; that he shall not perceive
But that you have your father's bosom there
And speak his very heart.

FLORIZEL

I am bound to you:
There is some sap in this.

CAMILLO

A course more promising
Than a wild dedication of yourselves
To unpath'd waters, undream'd shores, most certain
To miseries enough: no hope to help you,
But as you shake off one to take another:
Nothing so certain as your anchors, who
Do their best office, if they can but stay you
Where you'll be loath to be: besides you know
Prosperity's the very bond of love,

Whose fresh complexion and whose heart together
Affliction alters.

PERDITA
                    One of these is true:
I think affliction may subdue the cheek,
But not take in the mind.

CAMILLO
                    Yea, say you so?
There shall not at your father's house these seven
  years
Be born another such.

FLORIZEL
                    My good Camillo,
She is as forward of her breeding as
She is i' the rear o' her birth.

CAMILLO
                    I cannot say 'tis pity
She lacks instructions, for she seems a mistress
To most that teach.

PERDITA
                    Your pardon, sir; for this
I'll blush you thanks.

FLORIZEL
                    My prettiest Perdita!
But O, the thorns we stand upon! Camillo,
Preserver of my father, now of me,
The medicine of our house, how shall we do?
We are not furnish'd like Bohemia's son,
Nor shall appear in Sicilia.

CAMILLO
                    My lord,
Fear none of this: I think you know my fortunes
Do all lie there: it shall be so my care
To have you royally appointed as if
The scene you play were mine. For instance, sir,
That you may know you shall not want, one word.
                    [They talk aside

Re-enter AUTOLYCUS

AUTOLYCUS
Ha, ha! what a fool Honesty is! and Trust, his sworn
brother, a very simple gentleman! I have sold all
my trumpery; not a counterfeit stone, not a ribbon,
glass, pomander, brooch, table-book, ballad, knife,
tape, glove, shoe-tie, bracelet, horn-ring, to keep
my pack from fasting: they throng who should buy
first, as if my trinkets had been hallowed and
brought a benediction to the buyer: by which means
I saw whose purse was best in picture; and what I
saw, to my good use I remembered. My clown, who
wants but something to be a reasonable man, grew
so in love with the wenches' song, that he would not
stir his pettitoes till he had both tune and words;
which so drew the rest of the herd to me, that all
their other senses stuck in ears: you might have
pinched a placket, it was senseless; 'twas nothing to
geld a codpiece of a purse; I would have filed keys
off that hung in chains: no hearing, no feeling, but
my sir's song, and admiring the nothing of it. So
that in this time of lethargy I picked and cut most
of their festival purses; and had not the old man

come in with a whoo-bub against his daughter and
the king's son and scared my choughs from the
chaff, I had not left a purse alive in the whole army.
                    [CAMILLO, FLORIZEL, and PERDITA come forward

CAMILLO
Nay, but my letters, by this means being there
So soon as you arrive, shall clear that doubt.

FLORIZEL
And those that you'll procure from King Leontes—

CAMILLO
Shall satisfy your father.

PERDITA
                    Happy be you!
All that you speak shows fair.

CAMILLO
                    Who have we here? [Seeing AUTOLYCUS
We'll make an instrument of this; omit
Nothing may give us aid.

AUTOLYCUS
If they have overheard me now, why, hanging.

CAMILLO
How now, good fellow! why shakest thou so?
Fear not, man; here's no harm intended to thee.

AUTOLYCUS
I am a poor fellow, sir.

CAMILLO
Why, be so still; here's nobody will steal that from
thee: yet for the outside of thy poverty we must
make an exchange; therefore discase thee instantly,
—thou must think there's a necessity in't,—and
change garments with this gentleman: though the
pennyworth on his side be the worst, yet hold thee,
there's some boot.

AUTOLYCUS
I am a poor fellow, sir. [Aside] I know ye well
enough.

CAMILLO
Nay, prithee, dispatch: the gentleman is half flayed
already.

AUTOLYCUS
Are you in earnest, sir? [Aside] I smell the trick on't.

FLORIZEL
Dispatch, I prithee.

AUTOLYCUS
Indeed, I have had earnest; but I cannot with conscience take it.

CAMILLO
Unbuckle, unbuckle.
                    [FLORIZEL and AUTOLYCUS exchange garments
Fortunate mistress,—let my prophecy
Come home to ye!—you must retire yourself
Into some covert: take your sweetheart's hat
And pluck it o'er your brows, muffle your face,
Dismantle you, and, as you can, disliken
The truth of your own seeming; that you may—
For I do fear eyes over—to shipboard
Get undescried.

PERDITA
                    I see the play so lies
That I must bear a part.

CAMILLO
No remedy.
Have you done there?

FLORIZEL
Should I now meet my father,
He would not call me son.

CAMILLO
Nay, you shall have no hat.   [*Giving it to* PERDITA
Come, lady, come. Farewell, my friend.

AUTOLYCUS
Adieu, sir.

FLORIZEL
O Perdita, what have we twain forgot!
Pray you, a word.

CAMILLO
[*Aside*] What I do next, shall be to tell the king
Of this escape and whither they are bound;
Wherein my hope is I shall so prevail
To force him after: in whose company
I shall review Sicilia, for whose sight
I have a woman's longing.

FLORIZEL
Fortune speed us!
Thus we set on, Camillo, to the sea-side.

CAMILLO
The swifter speed the better.
[*Exeunt* FLORIZEL, PERDITA, *and* CAMILLO

AUTOLYCUS
I understand the business, I hear it: to have an open
ear, a quick eye, and a nimble hand, is necessary for
a cut-purse; a good nose is requisite also, to smell
out work for the other senses. I see this is the time
that the unjust man doth thrive. What an exchange
had this been without boot! What a boot is here
with this exchange! Sure the gods do this year con-
nive at us, and we may do any thing extempore.
The prince himself is about a piece of iniquity,
stealing away from his father with his clog at his
heels: if I thought it were a piece of honesty to acquaint the king withal, I would not do't: I hold it
the more knavery to conceal it; and therein am I
constant to my profession.

Re-enter CLOWN *and* SHEPHERD
Aside, aside; here is more matter for a hot brain:
every lane's end, every shop, church, session, hanging, yields a careful man work.

CLOWN
See, see; what a man you are now! There is no
other way but to tell the king she's a changeling and
none of your flesh and blood.

SHEPHERD
Nay, but hear me.

CLOWN
Nay, but hear me.

SHEPHERD
Go to, then.

CLOWN
She being none of your flesh and blood, your flesh
and blood has not offended the king; and so your
flesh and blood is not to be punished by him. Show

those things you found about her, those secret things,
all but what she has with her: this being done, let
the law go whistle: I warrant you.

SHEPHERD
I will tell the king all, every word, yea, and his
son's pranks too; who, I may say, is no honest man,
neither to his father nor to me, to go about to make
me the king's brother-in-law.

CLOWN
Indeed, brother-in-law was the farthest off you
could have been to him and then your blood had
been the dearer by I know how much an ounce.

AUTOLYCUS
[*Aside*] Very wisely, puppies!

SHEPHERD
Well, let us to the king: there is that in this fardel
will make him scratch his beard.

AUTOLYCUS
[*Aside*] I know not what impediment this complaint
may be to the flight of my master.

CLOWN
Pray heartily he be at palace.

AUTOLYCUS
[*Aside*] Though I am not naturally honest, I am so
sometimes by chance: let me pocket up my pedlar's
excrement. [*Takes off his false beard*] How now,
rustic! whither are you bound?

SHEPHERD
To the palace, as it like your worship.

AUTOLYCUS
Your affairs there, what, with whom, the condition
of that fardel, the place of your dwelling, your
names, your ages, of what having, breeding, and
any thing that is fitting to be known, discover.

CLOWN
We are but plain fellows, sir.

AUTOLYCUS
A lie; you are rough and hairy. Let me have no
lying: it becomes none but tradesmen, and they often give us soldiers the lie: but we pay them for it
with stamped coin, not stabbing steel; therefore
they do not give us the lie.

CLOWN
Your worship had like to have given us one, if you
had not taken yourself with the manner.

SHEPHERD
Are you a courtier, an't like you, sir?

AUTOLYCUS
Whether it like me or no, I am a courtier. Seest thou
not the air of the court in these enfoldings? hath not
my gait in it the measure of the court? receives not
thy nose court-odour from me? reflect I not on thy
baseness court-contempt? Thinkest thou, for that
I insinuate, or toaze from thee thy business, I am
therefore no courtier? I am courtier cap-a-pe; and
one that will either push on or pluck back thy business there: whereupon I command thee to open thy
affair.

SHEPHERD
My business, sir, is to the king.

AUTOLYCUS
What advocate hast thou to him?

SHEPHERD
I know not, an't like you.

CLOWN
Advocate's the court-word for a pheasant: say you have none.

SHEPHERD
None, sir; I have no pheasant, cock nor hen.

AUTOLYCUS
How blessed are we that are not simple men!
Yet nature might have made me as these are,
Therefore I will not disdain.

CLOWN
This cannot be but a great courtier.

SHEPHERD
His garments are rich, but he wears them not handsomely.

CLOWN
He seems to be the more noble in being fantastical: a great man, I'll warrant; I know by the picking on's teeth.

AUTOLYCUS
The fardel there? what's i' the fardel? Wherefore that box?

SHEPHERD
Sir, there lies such secrets in this fardel and box, which none must know but the king; and which he shall know within this hour, if I may come to the speech of him.

AUTOLYCUS
Age, thou hast lost thy labour.

SHEPHERD
Why, sir?

AUTOLYCUS
The king is not at the palace; he is gone aboard a new ship to purge melancholy and air himself: for, if thou beest capable of things serious, thou must know the king is full of grief.

SHEPHERD
So 'tis said, sir; about his son, that should have married a shepherd's daughter.

AUTOLYCUS
If that shepherd be not in hand-fast, let him fly: the curses he shall have, the tortures he shall feel, will break the back of man, the heart of monster.

CLOWN
Think you so, sir?

AUTOLYCUS
Not he alone shall suffer what wit can make heavy and vengeance bitter; but those that are germane to him, though removed fifty times, shall all come under the hangman: which though it be great pity, yet it is necessary. An old sheep-whistling rogue, a ram-tender, to offer to have his daughter come into grace! Some say he shall be stoned; but that death is too soft for him, say I: draw our throne into a sheep-cote! all deaths are too few, the sharpest too easy.

CLOWN
Has the old man e'er a son, sir, do you hear, an't like you, sir?

AUTOLYCUS
He has a son, who shall be flayed alive; then, 'nointed over with honey, set on the head of a wasp's nest; then stand till he be three quarters and a dram dead; then recovered again with aqua-vitæ or some other hot infusion; then, raw as he is, and in the hottest day prognostication proclaims, shall he be set against a brick-wall, the sun looking with a southward eye upon him, where he is to behold him with flies blown to death. But what talk we of these traitorly rascals, whose miseries are to be smiled at, their offences being so capital? Tell me, for you seem to be honest plain men, what you have to the king: being something gently considered, I'll bring you where he is aboard, tender your persons to his presence, whisper him in your behalfs; and if it be in man besides the king to effect your suits, here is man shall do it.

CLOWN
He seems to be of great authority: close with him, give him gold; and though authority be a stubborn bear, yet he is oft led by the nose with gold: show the inside of your purse to the outside of his hand, and no more ado. Remember 'stoned,' and 'flayed alive.'

SHEPHERD
An't please you, sir, to undertake the business for us, here is that gold I have: I'll make it as much more and leave this young man in pawn till I bring it you.

AUTOLYCUS
After I have done what I promised?

SHEPHERD
Ay, sir.

AUTOLYCUS
Well, give me the moiety. Are you a party in this business?

CLOWN
In some sort, sir: but though my case be a pitiful one, I hope I shall not be flayed out of it.

AUTOLYCUS
O, that's the case of the shepherd's son: hang him, he'll be made an example.

CLOWN
Comfort, good comfort! We must to the king and show our strange sights: he must know 'tis none of your daughter nor my sister; we are gone else. Sir, I will give you as much as this old man does when the business is performed, and remain, as he says, your pawn till it be brought you.

AUTOLYCUS
I will trust you. Walk before toward the seaside; go on the right hand: I will but look upon the hedge and follow you.

CLOWN
We are blest in this man, as I may say, even blest.

SHEPHERD

Let's before as he bids us: he was provided to do us
good.   [*Exeunt* SHEPHERD *and* CLOWN

AUTOLYCUS

If I had a mind to be honest, I see Fortune would
not suffer me: she drops booties in my mouth. I am
courted now with a double occasion, gold and a
means to do the prince my master good; which who
knows how that may turn back to my advancement? I will bring these two moles, these blind ones,
aboard him: if he think it fit to shore them again
and that the complaint they have to the king concerns him nothing, let him call me rogue for being
so far officious; for I am proof against that title and
what shame else belongs to't. To him will I present
them: there may be matter in it.   [*Exit*

ACT V

SCENE I. *A room in* LEONTES' *palace*

Enter LEONTES, CLEOMENES, DION, PAULINA, *and*
SERVANTS

CLEOMENES

Sir, you have done enough, and have perform'd
A saint-like sorrow: no fault could you make,
Which you have not redeem'd; indeed, paid down
More penitence than done trespass: at the last,
Do as the heavens have done, forget your evil;
With them forgive yourself.

LEONTES

      Whilst I remember
Her and her virtues, I cannot forget
My blemishes in them, and so still think of
The wrong I did myself: which was so much,
That heirless it hath made my kingdom; and
Destroy'd the sweet'st companion that e'er man
Bred his hopes out of.

PAULINA

      True, too true, my lord:
If, one by one, you wedded all the world,
Or from the all that are took something good,
To make a perfect woman, she you kill'd
Would be unparallel'd.

LEONTES

      I think so. Kill'd!
She I kill'd! I did so: but thou strikest me
Sorely, to say I did; it is as bitter
Upon thy tongue as in my thought: now, good now,
Say so but seldom.

CLEOMENES

      Not at all, good lady:
You might have spoken a thousand things that
would
Have done the time more benefit and graced
Your kindness better.

PAULINA

      You are one of those
Would have him wed again.

DION

      If you would not so,
You pity not the state, nor the remembrance
Of his most sovereign name; consider little
What dangers, by his highness' fail of issue,
May drop upon his kingdom and devour
Incertain lookers on. What were more holy
Than to rejoice the former queen is well?
What holier than, for royalty's repair,
For present comfort and for future good,
To bless the bed of majesty again
With a sweet fellow to't?

PAULINA

      There is none worthy,
Respecting her that's gone. Besides, the gods
Will have fulfill'd their secret purposes;
For has not the divine Apollo said,
Is't not the tenor of his oracle,
That King Leontes shall not have an heir
Till his lost child be found? which that it shall,
Is all as monstrous to our human reason
As my Antigonus to break his grave
And come again to me; who, on my life,
Did perish with the infant. 'Tis your counsel
My lord should to the heavens be contrary,
Oppose against their wills. [*To* LEONTES] Care not
 for issue;
The crown will find an heir: great Alexander
Left his to the worthiest; so his successor
Was like to be the best.

LEONTES

      Good Paulina,
Who hast the memory of Hermione,
I know, in honour, O, that ever I
Had squared me to thy counsel! —then, even now,
I might have look'd upon my queen's full eyes;
Have taken treasure from her lips,—

PAULINA

      And left them
More rich for what they yielded.

LEONTES

      Thou speak'st truth.
No more such wives; therefore, no wife: one worse,
And better used, would make her sainted spirit
Again possess her corpse, and on this stage,
Where we offenders now, appear soul-vex'd,
And begin, 'Why to me?'

PAULINA

      Had she such power,
She had just cause.

LEONTES

      She had; and would incense me
To murder her I married.

PAULINA

      I should so.
Were I the ghost that walk'd, I'ld bid you mark
Her eye, and tell me for what dull part in't

You chose her; then I'ld shriek, that even your ears
Should rift to hear me; and the words that follow'd
Should be 'Remember mine.'

LEONTES
                              Stars, stars,
And all eyes else dead coals! Fear thou no wife;
I'll have no wife, Paulina.

PAULINA
                              Will you swear
Never to marry but by my free leave?

LEONTES
Never, Paulina; so be blest my spirit!

PAULINA
Then, good my lords, bear witness to his oath.

CLEOMENES
You tempt him over-much.

PAULINA
                              Unless another,
As like Hermione as is her picture,
Affront his eye.

CLEOMENES
              Good madam,—

PAULINA
                              I have done.
Yet, if my lord will marry,—if you will, sir,
No remedy, but you will,—give me the office
To choose you a queen: she shall not be so young
As was your former; but she shall be such
As, walk'd your first queen's ghost, it should take
      joy
To see her in your arms.

LEONTES
                              My true Paulina,
We shall not marry till thou bid'st us.

PAULINA
                              That
Shall be when your first queen's again in breath;
Never till then.

Enter a GENTLEMAN

GENTLEMAN
One that gives out himself Prince Florizel,
Son of Polixenes, with his princess, she
The fairest I have yet beheld, desires access
To your high presence.

LEONTES
                    What with him? he comes not
Like to his father's greatness: his approach,
So out of circumstance and sudden, tells us
'Tis not a visitation framed, but forced
By need and accident. What train?

GENTLEMAN
                              But few,
And those but mean.

LEONTES
                    His princess, say you, with him?

GENTLEMAN
Ay, the most peerless piece of earth, I think,
That e'er the sun shone bright on.

PAULINA
                              O Hermione,

As every present time doth boast itself
Above a better gone, so must thy grave
Give way to what's seen now! Sir, you yourself
Have said and writ so, but your writing now
Is colder than that theme, 'She had not been,
Nor was not to be equall'd;'—thus your verse
Flow'd with her beauty once: 'tis shrewdly ebb'd
To say you have seen a better.

GENTLEMAN
                              Pardon, madam:
The one I have almost forgot,—your pardon,—
The other, when she has obtain'd your eye,
Will have your tongue too. This is a creature,
Would she begin a sect, might quench the zeal
Of all professors else; make proselytes
Of who she but bid follow.

PAULINA
                              How! not women?

GENTLEMAN
Women will love her, that she is a woman
More worth than any man; men, that she is
The rarest of all women.

LEONTES
                              Go, Cleomenes;
Yourself, assisted with your honour'd friends,
Bring them to our embracement.

                    [*Exeunt* CLEOMENES *and others*
                              Still, 'tis strange
He thus should steal upon us.

PAULINA
                              Had our prince,
Jewel of children, seen this hour, he had pair'd
Well with this lord: there was not full a month
Between their births.

LEONTES
Prithee, no more; cease; thou know'st
He dies to me again when talk'd of: sure,
When I shall see this gentleman, thy speeches
Will bring me to consider that which may
Unfurnish me of reason. They are come.

Re-enter CLEOMENES *and others, with* FLORIZEL
                    and PERDITA

Your mother was most true to wedlock, prince;
For she did print your royal father off,
Conceiving you: were I but twenty one,
Your father's image is so hit in you,
His very air, that I should call you brother,
As I did him, and speak of something wildly
By us perform'd before. Most dearly welcome!
And your fair princess,—goddess!—O, alas!
I lost a couple, that 'twixt heaven and earth
Might thus have stood begetting wonder, as
You, gracious couple, do: and then I lost,
All mine own folly, the society,
Amity too, of your brave father, whom,
Though bearing misery, I desire my life
Once more to look on him.

FLORIZEL
                              By his command
Have I here touch'd Sicilia, and from him

Give you all greetings, that a king, at friend,
Can send his brother: and, but infirmity,
Which waits upon worn times, hath something
    seized
His wish'd ability, he had himself
The lands and waters 'twixt your throne and his
Measured to look upon you; whom he loves,
He bade me say so, more than all the sceptres
And those that bear them living.

LEONTES
                  O my brother,
Good gentleman! the wrongs I have done thee stir
Afresh within me; and these thy offices,
So rarely kind, are as interpreters
Of my behind-hand slackness! Welcome hither,
As is the spring to the earth. And hath he too
Exposed this paragon to the fearful usage,
At least ungentle, of the dreadful Neptune,
To greet a man not worth her pains, much less
The adventure of her person?

FLORIZEL
              Good my lord,
She came from Libya.

LEONTES
              Where the warlike Smalus,
That noble honour'd lord, is fear'd and loved?

FLORIZEL
Most royal sir, from thence; from him, whose
    daughter
His tears proclaim'd his, parting with her: thence,
A prosperous south-wind friendly, we have cross'd,
To execute the charge my father gave me,
For visiting your highness: my best train
I have from your Sicilian shores dismiss'd;
Who for Bohemia bend, to signify
Not only my success in Libya, sir,
But my arrival, and my wife's, in safety
Here where we are.

LEONTES
           The blessed gods
Purge all infection from our air whilst you
Do climate here! You have a holy father,
A graceful gentleman; against whose person,
So sacred as it is, I have done sin:
For which the heavens, taking angry note,
Have left me issueless; and your father's blest,
As he from heaven merits it, with you
Worthy his goodness. What might I have been,
Might I a son and daughter now have look'd on,
Such goodly things as you!

Enter a LORD

LORD
             Most noble sir,
That which I shall report will bear no credit,
Were not the proof so nigh. Please you, great sir,
Bohemia greets you from himself by me;
Desires you to attach his son, who has—
His dignity and duty both cast off—
Fled from his father, from his hopes, and with
A shepherd's daughter.

LEONTES
           Where's Bohemia? speak.

LORD
Here in your city; I now came from him:
I speak amazedly; and it becomes
My marvel and my message. To your court
Whiles he was hastening, in the chase, it seems,
Of this fair couple, meets he on the way
The father of this seeming lady and
Her brother, having both their country quitted
With this young prince.

FLORIZEL
           Camillo has betray'd me;
Whose honour and whose honesty till now
Endured all weathers.

LORD
           Lay't so to his charge:
He's with the king your father.

LEONTES
             Who? Camillo?

LORD
Camillo, sir; I spake with him; who now
Has these poor men in question. Never saw I
Wretches so quake: they kneel, they kiss the earth;
Forswear themselves as often as they speak:
Bohemia stops his ears, and threatens them
With divers deaths in death.

PERDITA
           O my poor father!
The heaven sets spies upon us, will not have
Our contract celebrated.

LEONTES
           You are married?

FLORIZEL
We are not, sir, nor are we like to be;
The stars, I see, will kiss the valleys first:
The odds for high and low's alike.

LEONTES
           My lord,
Is this the daughter of a king?

FLORIZEL
           She is,
When once she is my wife.

LEONTES
That 'once,' I see by your good father's speed,
Will come on very slowly. I am sorry,
Most sorry, you have broken from his liking
Where you were tied in duty, and as sorry
Your choice is not so rich in worth as beauty,
That you might well enjoy her.

FLORIZEL
           Dear, look up:
Though Fortune, visible an enemy,
Should chase us with my father, power no jot
Hath she to change our loves. Beseech you, sir,
Remember since you owed no more to time
Than I do now: with thought of such affections,
Step forth mine advocate; at your request
My father will grant precious things as trifles.

LEONTES

Would he do so, I'ld beg your precious mistress,
Which he counts but a trifle.

PAULINA

              Sir, my liege,
Your eye hath too much youth in't: not a month
'Fore your queen died, she was more worth such
    gazes
Than what you look on now.

LEONTES

              I thought of her,
Even in these looks I made. [*To* FLORIZEL] But your
    petition
Is yet unanswer'd. I will to your father:
Your honour not o'erthrown by your desires,
I am friend to them and you: upon which errand
I now go toward him; therefore follow me
And mark what way I make: come, good my lord.
                                 [*Exeunt*

SCENE II. *Before* LEONTES' *palace*

Enter AUTOLYCUS *and a* GENTLEMAN

AUTOLYCUS

Beseech you, sir, were you present at this relation?

FIRST GENTLEMAN

I was by at the opening of the fardel, heard the old
shepherd deliver the manner how he found it:
whereupon, after a little amazedness, we were all
commanded out of the chamber; only this methought I heard the shepherd say, he found the
child.

AUTOLYCUS

I would most gladly know the issue of it.

FIRST GENTLEMAN

I make a broken delivery of the business; but the
changes I perceived in the king and Camillo were
very notes of admiration: they seemed almost, with
staring on one another, to tear the cases of their
eyes; there was speech in their dumbness, language
in their very gesture; they looked as they had heard
of a world ransomed, or one destroyed: a notable
passion of wonder appeared in them; but the wisest
beholder, that knew no more but seeing, could not
say if the importance were joy or sorrow; but in the
extremity of the one, it must needs be.

Enter another GENTLEMAN

Here comes a gentleman that haply knows more.
The news, Rogero?

SECOND GENTLEMAN

Nothing but bonfires: the oracle is fulfilled; the
king's daughter is found: such a deal of wonder is
broken out within this hour, that ballad-makers
cannot be able to express it.

Enter a third GENTLEMAN

Here comes the Lady Paulina's steward: he can deliver you more. How goes it now, sir? this news
which is called true is so like an old tale, that the
verity of it is in strong suspicion: has the king found
his heir?

THIRD GENTLEMAN

Most true, if ever truth were pregnant by circumstance: that which you hear you'll swear you see,
there is such unity in the proofs. The mantle of
Queen Hermione's, her jewel about the neck of it,
the letters of Antigonus found with it, which they
know to be his character, the majesty of the creature
in resemblance of the mother, the affection of nobleness which nature shows above her breeding, and
many other evidences proclaim her with all certainty to be the king's daughter. Did you see the
meeting of the two kings?

SECOND GENTLEMAN

No.

THIRD GENTLEMAN

Then have you lost a sight, which was to be seen,
cannot be spoken of. There might you have beheld
one joy crown another, so and in such manner, that
it seemed sorrow wept to take leave of them, for
their joy waded in tears. There was casting up of
eyes, holding up of hands, with countenance of such
distraction, that they were to be known by garment, not by favour. Our king, being ready to leap
out of himself for joy of his found daughter, as if
that joy were now become a loss, cries 'O, thy
mother, thy mother!' then asks Bohemia forgiveness; then embraces his son-in-law; then again
worries he his daughter with clipping her; now he
thanks the old shepherd, which stands by like a
weather-bitten conduit of many kings' reigns. I
never heard of such another encounter, which lames
report to follow it and undoes description to do it.

SECOND GENTLEMAN

What, pray you, became of Antigonus, that carried
hence the child?

THIRD GENTLEMAN

Like an old tale still, which will have matter to rehearse, though credit be asleep and not an ear open.
He was torn to pieces with a bear: this avouches the
shepherd's son; who has not only his innocence,
which seems much, to justify him, but a handkerchief and rings of his that Paulina knows.

FIRST GENTLEMAN

What became of his bark and his followers?

THIRD GENTLEMAN

Wrecked the same instant of their master's death
and in the view of the shepherd: so that all the instruments which aided to expose the child were even
then lost when it was found. But O, the noble combat that 'twixt joy and sorrow was fought in Paulina!
She had one eye declined for the loss of her husband, another elevated that the oracle was fulfilled:
she lifted the princess from the earth, and so locks
her in embracing, as if she would pin her to her
heart that she might no more be in danger of losing.

FIRST GENTLEMAN

The dignity of this act was worth the audience of
kings and princes; for by such was it acted.

THIRD GENTLEMAN

One of the prettiest touches of all and that which angled for mine eyes, caught the water though not the fish, was when, at the relation of the queen's death, with the manner how she came to't bravely confessed and lamented by the king, how attentiveness wounded his daughter; till, from one sign of dolour to another, she did, with an 'Alas,' I would fain say, bleed tears, for I am sure my heart wept blood. Who was most marble there changed colour; some swooned, all sorrowed: if all the world could have seen't, the woe had been universal.

FIRST GENTLEMAN

Are they returned to the court?

THIRD GENTLEMAN

No: the princess hearing of her mother's statue, which is in the keeping of Paulina,—a piece many years in doing and now newly performed by that rare Italian master, Julio Romano, who, had he himself eternity and could put breath into his work, would beguile Nature of her custom, so perfectly he is her ape: he so near to Hermione hath done Hermione, that they say one would speak to her and stand in hope of answer:—thither with all greediness of affection are they gone, and there they intend to sup.

SECOND GENTLEMAN

I thought she had some great matter there in hand; for she hath privately twice or thrice a day, ever since the death of Hermione, visited that removed house. Shall we thither and with our company piece the rejoicing?

FIRST GENTLEMAN

Who would be thence that has the benefit of access? every wink of an eye, some new grace will be born: our absence makes us unthrifty to our knowledge. Let's along.   [*Exeunt* GENTLEMEN

AUTOLYCUS

Now, had I not the dash of my former life in me, would preferment drop on my head. I brought the old man and his son aboard the prince; told him I heard them talk of a fardel and I know not what: but he at that time, overfond of the shepherd's daughter, so he then took her to be, who began to be much sea-sick, and himself little better, extremity of weather continuing, this mystery remained undiscovered. But 'tis all one to me; for had I been the finder out of this secret, it would not have relished among my other discredits.

Enter SHEPHERD *and* CLOWN

Here come those I have done good to against my will, and already appearing in the blossoms of their fortune.

SHEPHERD

Come, boy; I am past moe children, but thy sons and daughters will be all gentlemen born.

CLOWN

You are well met, sir. You denied to fight with me this other day, because I was no gentleman born. See you these clothes? say you see them not and

think me still no gentleman born: you were best say these robes are not gentlemen born: give me the lie, do, and try whether I am not now a gentleman born.

AUTOLYCUS

I know you are now, sir, a gentleman born.

CLOWN

Ay, and have been so any time these four hours.

SHEPHERD

And so have I, boy.

CLOWN

So you have: but I was a gentleman born before my father; for the king's son took me by the hand, and called me brother; and then the two kings called my father brother; and then the prince my brother and the princess my sister called my father father; and so we wept, and there was the first gentleman-like tears that ever we shed.

SHEPHERD

We may live, son, to shed many more.

CLOWN

Ay; or else 'twere hard luck, being in so preposterous estate as we are.

AUTOLYCUS

I humbly beseech you, sir, to pardon me all the faults I have committed to your worship, and to give me your good report to the prince my master.

SHEPHERD

Prithee, son, do; for we must be gentle, now we are gentlemen.

CLOWN

Thou wilt amend thy life?

AUTOLYCUS

Ay, an it like your good worship.

CLOWN

Give me thy hand: I will swear to the prince thou art as honest a true fellow as any is in Bohemia.

SHEPHERD

You may say it, but not swear it.

CLOWN

Not swear it, now I am a gentleman? Let boors and franklins say it, I'll swear it.

SHEPHERD

How if it be false, son?

CLOWN

If it be ne'er so false, a true gentleman may swear it in the behalf of his friend: and I'll swear to the prince thou art a tall fellow of thy hands and that thou wilt not be drunk; but I know thou art no tall fellow of thy hands and that thou wilt be drunk: but I'll swear it, and I would thou wouldst be a tall fellow of thy hands.

AUTOLYCUS

I will prove so, sir, to my power.

CLOWN

Ay, by any means prove a tall fellow: if I do not wonder how thou darest venture to be drunk, not being a tall fellow, trust me not. Hark! the kings and the princes, our kindred, are going to see the

queen's picture. Come, follow us: we'll be thy good
masters.   [*Exeunt*

SCENE III. *A chapel in* PAULINA's *house*

Enter LEONTES, POLIXENES, FLORIZEL, PERDITA,
CAMILLO, PAULINA, LORDS, *and* ATTENDANTS

LEONTES
O grave and good Paulina, the great comfort
That I have had of thee!

PAULINA
                    What, sovereign sir,
I did not well, I meant well. All my services
You have paid home: but that you have vouchsafed
With your crown'd brother and these your con-
    tracted
Heirs of your kingdoms, my poor house to visit,
It is a surplus of your grace, which never
My life may last to answer.

LEONTES
            O Paulina,
We honour you with trouble: but we came
To see the statue of our queen: your gallery
Have we pass'd through, not without much content
In many singularities; but we saw not
That which my daughter came to look upon,
The statue of her mother.

PAULINA
            As she lived peerless,
So her dead likeness, I do well believe,
Excels whatever yet you look'd upon
Or hand of man hath done; therefore I keep it
Lonely, apart. But here it is: prepare
To see the life as lively mock'd as ever
Still sleep mock'd death: behold, and say 'tis well.
[PAULINA *draws a curtain, and discovers* HERMIONE
                              standing like a statue
I like your silence, it the more shows off
Your wonder: but yet speak; first, you, my liege.
Comes it not something near?

LEONTES
            Her natural posture!
Chide me, dear stone, that I may say indeed
Thou art Hermione; or rather, thou art she
In thy not chiding, for she was as tender
As infancy and grace. But yet, Paulina,
Hermione was not so much wrinkled, nothing
So aged as this seems.

POLIXENES
            O, not by much.

PAULINA
So much the more our carver's excellence;
Which lets go by some sixteen years and makes her
As she lived now.

LEONTES
            As now she might have done,
So much to my good comfort, as it is
Now piercing to my soul. O, thus she stood,
Even with such life of majesty, warm life,

As now it coldly stands, when first I woo'd her!
I am ashamed: does not the stone rebuke me
For being more stone than it? O royal piece,
There's magic in thy majesty, which has
My evils conjured to remembrance, and
From thy admiring daughter took the spirits,
Standing like stone with thee.

PERDITA
            And give me leave,
And do not say 'tis superstition, that
I kneel and then implore her blessing. Lady,
Dear queen, that ended when I but began,
Give me that hand of yours to kiss.

PAULINA
            O, patience!
The statue is but newly fix'd, the colour's
Not dry.

CAMILLO
My lord, your sorrow was too sore laid on,
Which sixteen winters cannot blow away,
So many summers dry: scarce any joy
Did ever so long live; no sorrow
But kill'd itself much sooner.

POLIXENES
            Dear my brother,
Let him that was the cause of this have power
To take off so much grief from you as he
Will piece up in himself.

PAULINA
            Indeed, my lord,
If I had thought the sight of my poor image
Would thus have wrought you, for the stone is mine,
I'ld not have show'd it.

LEONTES
            Do not draw the curtain.

PAULINA
No longer shall you gaze on't, lest your fancy
May think anon it moves.

LEONTES
            Let be, let be.
Would I were dead, but that, methinks, already—
What was he that did make it? See, my lord,
Would you not deem it breathed? and that those
    veins
Did verily bear blood?

POLIXENES
            Masterly done:
The very life seems warm upon her lip.

LEONTES
The fixure of her eye has motion in't,
As we are mock'd with art.

PAULINA
            I'll draw the curtain:
My lord's almost so far transported that
He'll think anon it lives.

LEONTES
            O sweet Paulina,
Make me to think so twenty years together!
No settled senses of the world can match
The pleasure of that madness. Let't alone.

PAULINA

I am sorry, sir, I have thus far stirr'd you: but
I could afflict you farther.

LEONTES

Do, Paulina;
For this affliction has a taste as sweet
As any cordial comfort. Still, methinks,
There is an air comes from her: what fine chisel
Could ever yet cut breath? Let no man mock me,
For I will kiss her.

PAULINA

Good my lord, forbear:
The ruddiness upon her lip is wet;
You'll mar it if you kiss it, stain your own
With oily painting. Shall I draw the curtain?

LEONTES

No, not these twenty years.

PERDITA

So long could I
Stand by, a looker on.

PAULINA

Either forbear,
Quit presently the chapel, or resolve you
For more amazement. If you can behold it,
I'll make the statue move indeed, descend
And take you by the hand: but then you'll think,
Which I protest against, I am assisted
By wicked powers.

LEONTES

What you can make her do,
I am content to look on: what to speak,
I am content to hear; for 'tis as easy
To make her speak as move.

PAULINA

It is required
You do awake your faith. Then all stand still;
On: those that think it is unlawful business
I am about, let them depart.

LEONTES

Proceed:
No foot shall stir.

PAULINA

Music, awake her; strike! [Music
'Tis time; descend; be stone no more; approach;
Strike all that look upon with marvel. Come,
I'll fill your grave up: stir, nay, come away,
Bequeath to death your numbness, for from him
Dear life redeems you. You perceive she stirs:
[HERMIONE comes down
Start not; her actions shall be holy as
You hear my spell is lawful: do not shun her
Until you see her die again; for then
You kill her double. Nay, present your hand:
When she was young you woo'd her; now in age
Is she become the suitor?

LEONTES

O, she's warm!
If this be magic, let it be an art
Lawful as eating.

POLIXENES

She embraces him.

CAMILLO

She hangs about his neck:
If she pertain to life let her speak too.

POLIXENES

Ay, and make't manifest where she has lived,
Or how stolen from the dead.

PAULINA

That she is living,
Were it but told you, should be hooted at
Like an old tale: but it appears she lives,
Though yet she speak not. Mark a little while.
Please you to interpose, fair madam: kneel
And pray your mother's blessing. Turn, good lady,
Our Perdita is found.

HERMIONE

You gods, look down,
And from your sacred vials pour your graces
Upon my daughter's head! Tell me, mine own,
Where hast thou been preserved? where lived? how
found
Thy father's court? for thou shalt hear that I,
Knowing by Paulina that the oracle
Gave hope thou wast in being, have preserved
Myself to see the issue.

PAULINA

There's time enough for that;
Lest they desire upon this push to trouble
Your joys with like relation. Go together,
You precious winners all; your exultation
Partake to every one. I, an old turtle,
Will wing me to some wither'd bough and there
My mate, that's never to be found again,
Lament till I am lost.

LEONTES

O, peace, Paulina!
Thou shouldst a husband take by my consent,
As I by thine a wife: this is a match,
And made between's by vows. Thou hast found
mine;
But how, is to be question'd; for I saw her,
As I thought, dead; and have in vain said many
A prayer upon her grave. I'll not seek far,—
For him, I partly know his mind,—to find thee
An honourable husband. Come, Camillo,
And take her by the hand, whose worth and honesty
Is richly noted and here justified
By us, a pair of kings. Let's from this place.
What! look upon my brother: both your pardons,
That e'er I put between your holy looks
My ill suspicion. This your son-in-law,
And son unto the king, whom heavens directing,
Is troth-plight to your daughter. Good Paulina,
Lead us from hence, where we may leisurely
Each one demand, and answer to his part
Perform'd in this wide gap of time, since first
We were dissever'd: hastily lead away. [Exeunt

THE TEMPEST

SYNOPSIS

Prospero, Duke of Milan, had been a ruler who preferred a life of studious penetration into Nature's secrets to one of state business and diplomacy. He had placed the entire management of ducal affairs in the hands of his brother Antonio, but this false, ambitious man, with the aid of the powerful Alonso, King of Naples, who wished to annex Milan, ousted Prospero from his dukedom. The conspirators did not dare to kill the Prince outright, so he and his three-year-old daughter were spirited away and set adrift in the open sea in a small boat. Death would have been inevitable, had it not been for the humane firmness of Gonzalo, the Counsellor, who stocked the boat with the necessities of life, including also some rich garments and Prospero's books of magic.

They at last reached a desert island with one lone inhabitant, the misshapen monster, Caliban, son of the wicked witch Sycorax. Prospero released the good spirits imprisoned by Sycorax, trained both them and Caliban to obey his will, and devoted himself to the intensive study of magic and the education of his little daughter Miranda.

Twelve years pass, and Miranda is now an utterly unsophisticated girl of peerless beauty. As the play opens, she is watching with compassionate concern a fine large ship off the coast blazing with flames in a sudden tempest. Prospero tells her it is full of human beings like themselves, and assures her of their safety. Putting aside his magic mantle, he relates to her the whole story of his life, and at the end comes the surprising information that all his enemies are in the vessel which his art has apparently wrecked.

Ariel, chief of the spirits, comes to report gleefully that the ship is safe in harbor; the mariners are asleep under the hatches; and the passengers dispersed over the island, with King Alonso and his party vainly seeking for his lost son Ferdinand. Ariel, by singing, guides the young prince to Prospero's cave where he is startled by the appearance of Miranda whom he thinks the island goddess, while she, in turn, thinks this new creature of noble bearing must be divine. Their mutual attraction delights Prospero, but he resolves to test Ferdinand's strength of character and his avowed love for Miranda, first by challenging him sternly as a spy and traitor, then setting him to work as a prisoner piling heavy logs of wood. Miranda begs Ferdinand to rest, but, despite the lovemaking, the young man works steadily, to Prospero's entire satisfaction.

In one part of the island, ever pursued by Ariel, wanders the disconsolate King. Gonzalo advises him to rest, and, under Ariel's influence, they both fall asleep. The King's brother, Sebastian, and Prospero's false brother, Antonio, plot the death of the two sleeping men, but Ariel frustrates their plans by whispering in Gonzalo's ear. Later, with Prospero present, though invisible, Ariel tantalizes the hungry tired group with the sight of a delicious banquet spread before them, then causes the food to vanish and upbraids them for their cruel treatment in former years of Prospero and his infant daughter.

He tells them they are being punished for their past sins, and leaves them almost senseless with fear. Ariel has also been following the movements of the monster Caliban, who hates Prospero for his mastery of the island. He has been discovered by two sailors who escaped from the wreck and found a cask of wine that had been washed ashore. After they are all drunk, they plot to kill Prospero, with Caliban as their guide, and take possession of the island for themselves. Ariel gives his master full information of Caliban's treachery, but Prospero proceeds with the celebration he has planned in honor of the betrothal of Ferdinand and Miranda.

The beautiful pageant is suddenly cut short by Prospero when he recalls Ariel's warnings of the plot against his life. The conspirators are easily routed by spirits in the shapes of dogs and hounds. The penitent King appears, fetched by Ariel, with Prospero's brother and the others. Prospero recalls to them their guilty deeds, then forgives them, first addressing himself to the kindly Gonzalo, and the King promises to restore him to his dukedom. He leads Alonso to a cell where the astonished King sees his son Ferdinand, given up as lost, playing chess with Miranda. Both father and son are overwhelmed with joy, and the King takes great delight in Miranda who is marvelling at these people from the brave new world in which she is going to live. Ariel escorts their ship safely to Naples, where he is given his freedom by Prospero who forsakes forever his magic art.

HISTORICAL DATA

For the main thread of the plot of this play no source has been discovered. There is a notable resemblance in some particulars to a German comedy *Die Schöne Sidea* by Jacob Ayrer, but it is more probable that both derived from the same source than that Shakespeare is indebted to the continental author. The story of the storm and "the still vex'd Bermoothes" were undoubtedly taken from the various accounts of the shipwreck of Sir George Somers' "Sea Venture" off the Bermudas, and the subsequent escape to Virginia in 1609–10. The god Setebos is taken from Eden's *History of Travaile* (1577), a translation of Magellan's *Voyage to the South Pole*. Gonzalo's ideal commonwealth (Act II, Scene i) comes from Florio's translation (1603) of Montaigne's *Essays*, and Prospero's speech renouncing magic was probably suggested by a passage in Goldring's translation of Ovid's *Metamorphoses*. The supernatural episodes and most of the names are almost certainly Shakespeare's invention. It has been ingeniously suggested that Caliban is merely an anagram for "cannibal."

The play could not very well have been written prior to 1609, the year of Somers' wreck, and it was performed during the marriage festivities of King James' daughter, Elizabeth, in 1613. Malone stated that the play was in existence in 1611, and, although an entry in the Revels accounts stating that it had been performed at Whitehall on Hallowmass night during that year is known to be a forgery, faith in Malone's accuracy has generally caused scholars to agree to this year as its date of composition. It did not appear in published form until the First Folio.

"*I have done nothing but in care of thee,—*"
THE TEMPEST

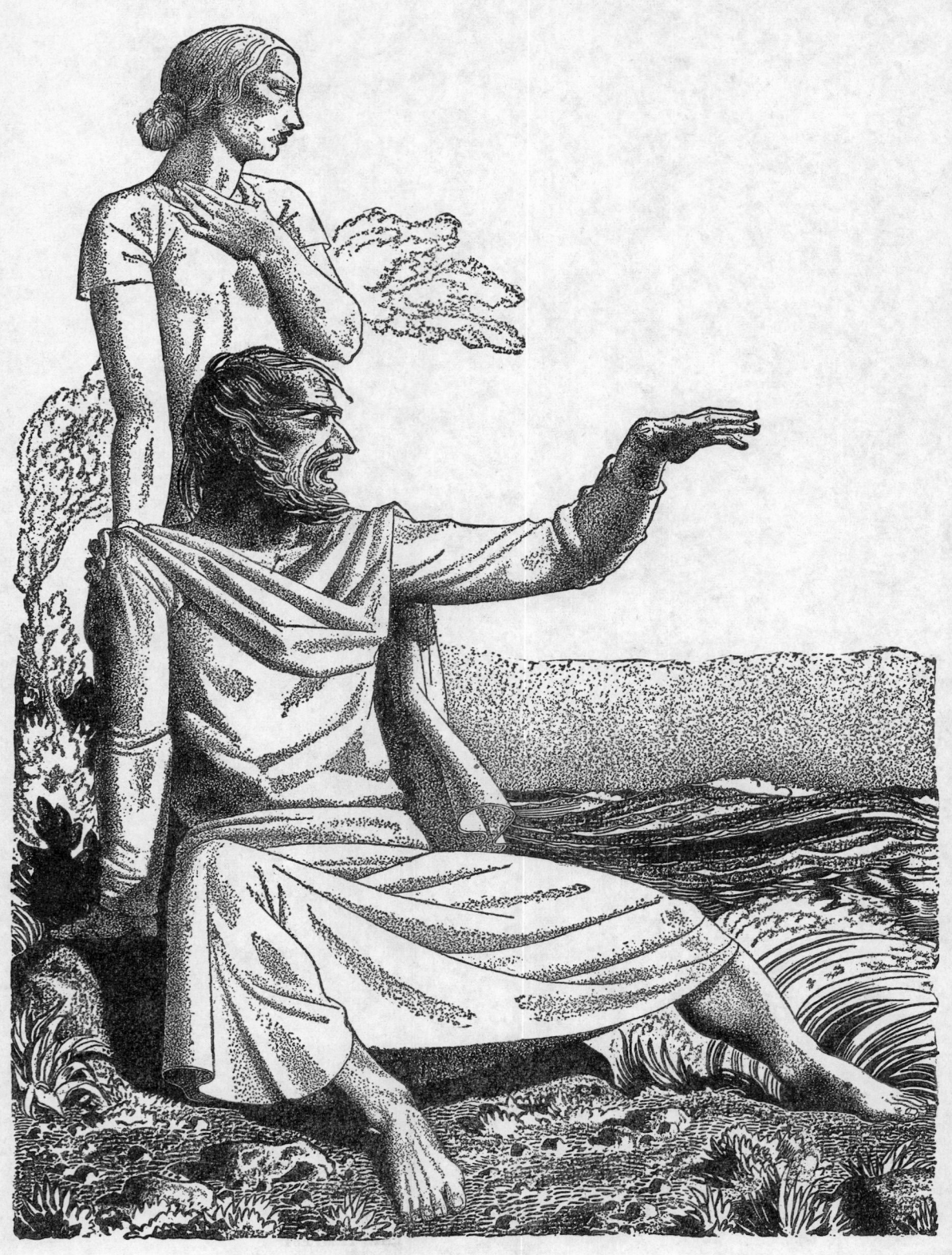

THE TEMPEST

DRAMATIS PERSONÆ

ALONSO, *King of Naples.*
SEBASTIAN, *his brother.*
PROSPERO, *the right Duke of Milan.*
ANTONIO, *his brother, the usurping Duke of Milan.*
FERDINAND, *son to the King of Naples.*
GONZALO, *an honest old Counsellor.*
ADRIAN,
FRANCISCO, } *Lords.*
CALIBAN, *a savage and deformed Slave.*
TRINCULO, *a Jester.*
STEPHANO, *a drunken Butler.*
MASTER *of a Ship.*
BOATSWAIN.

MARINERS.

MIRANDA, *daughter to Prospero.*

ARIEL, *an airy Spirit.*
IRIS,
CERES,
JUNO, } *presented by Spirits.*
NYMPHS,
REAPERS,

OTHER SPIRITS, *attending on Prospero.*

SCENE—*A ship at sea: an uninhabited island.*

ACT I

SCENE I. *On a ship at sea: a tempestuous noise of thunder and lightning heard*

Enter a SHIPMASTER *and a* BOATSWAIN

MASTER

Boatswain!

BOATSWAIN

Here, master: what cheer?

MASTER

Good, speak to the mariners: fall to't, yarely, or we run ourselves aground: bestir, bestir. [*Exit*

Enter MARINERS

BOATSWAIN

Heigh, my hearts! cheerly, cheerly, my hearts! yare, yare! Take in the topsail. Tend to the master's whistle. Blow, till thou burst thy wind, if room enough!

Enter ALONSO, SEBASTIAN, ANTONIO, FERDINAND, GONZALO, *and others*

ALONSO

Good boatswain, have care. Where's the master? Play the men.

BOATSWAIN

I pray now, keep below.

ANTONIO

Where is the master, boatswain?

BOATSWAIN

Do you not hear him? You mar our labour: keep your cabins: you do assist the storm.

GONZALO

Nay, good, be patient.

BOATSWAIN

When the sea is. Hence! What cares these roarers for the name of king? To cabin: silence! trouble us not.

GONZALO

Good, yet remember whom thou hast aboard.

BOATSWAIN

None that I more love than myself. You are a counsellor; if you can command these elements to silence, and work the peace of the present, we will not hand

a rope more; use your authority: if you cannot, give thanks you have lived so long, and make yourself ready in your cabin for the mischance of the hour, if it so hap. Cheerly, good hearts! Out of our way, I say. [*Exit*

GONZALO

I have great comfort from this fellow: methinks he hath no drowning mark upon him; his complexion is perfect gallows. Stand fast, good Fate, to his hanging: make the rope of his destiny our cable, for our own doth little advantage. If he be not born to be hanged, our case is miserable. [*Exeunt*

Re-enter BOATSWAIN

BOATSWAIN

Down with the topmast! yare! lower, lower! Bring her to try with main-course. [*A cry within*] A plague upon this howling! they are louder than the weather or our office.

Re-enter SEBASTIAN, ANTONIO, *and* GONZALO

Yet again! what do you here? Shall we give o'er, and drown? Have you a mind to sink?

SEBASTIAN

A pox o' your throat, you bawling, blasphemous, incharitable dog!

BOATSWAIN

Work you, then.

ANTONIO

Hang, cur! hang, you whoreson, insolent noisemaker. We are less afraid to be drowned than thou art.

GONZALO

I'll warrant him for drowning; though the ship were no stronger than a nutshell, and as leaky as an unstanched wench.

BOATSWAIN

Lay her a-hold, a-hold! set her two courses; off to sea again; lay her off.

Enter MARINERS *wet*

MARINERS

All lost! to prayers, to prayers! all lost!

BOATSWAIN

What, must our mouths be cold?

GONZALO

The king and prince at prayers! let's assist them,
For our case is as theirs.

SEBASTIAN

I'm out of patience.

ANTONIO

We are merely cheated of our lives by drunkards:
This wide-chapp'd rascal,—would thou mightst lie
drowning the washing of ten tides!

GONZALO

He'll be hang'd yet,
Though every drop of water swear against it,
And gape at widest to glut him.
[A confused noise within: 'Mercy on us!'—
'We split, we split!'—'Farewell my wife and chil-
dren!'—'Farewell, brother!'—'We split, we split, we
split!']

ANTONIO

Let's all sink with the king.

SEBASTIAN

Let's take leave of him.
[Exeunt ANTONIO and SEBASTIAN

GONZALO

Now would I give a thousand furlongs of sea for an
acre of barren ground, long heath, brown furze, any
thing. The wills above be done! but I would fain die
a dry death. [Exeunt

SCENE II. *The island. Before* PROSPERO'S *cell*

Enter PROSPERO *and* MIRANDA

MIRANDA

If by your art, my dearest father, you have
Put the wild waters in this roar, allay them.
The sky, it seems, would pour down stinking pitch,
But that the sea, mounting to the welkin's cheek,
Dashes the fire out. O, I have suffer'd
With those that I saw suffer! a brave vessel,
Who had, no doubt, some noble creature in her,
Dash'd all to pieces. O, the cry did knock
Against my very heart! Poor souls, they perish'd!
Had I been any god of power, I would
Have sunk the sea within the earth, or ere
It should the good ship so have swallow'd and
The fraughting souls within her.

PROSPERO

Be collected:
No more amazement: tell your piteous heart
There's no harm done.

MIRANDA

O, woe the day!

PROSPERO

No harm.
I have done nothing but in care of thee,
Of thee, my dear one, thee, my daughter, who
Art ignorant of what thou art, nought knowing
Of whence I am, nor that I am more better

Than Prospero, master of a full poor cell,
And thy no greater father.

MIRANDA

More to know
Did never meddle with my thoughts.

PROSPERO

'Tis time
I should inform thee farther. Lend thy hand,
And pluck my magic garment from me.—So:
[Lays down his mantle
Lie there, my art. Wipe thou thine eyes; have com-
fort.
The direful spectacle of the wreck, which touch'd
The very virtue of compassion in thee,
I have with such provision in mine art
So safely order'd, that there is no soul,
No, not so much perdition as an hair
Betid to any creature in the vessel
Which thou heard'st cry, which thou saw'st sink. Sit
down;
For thou must now know farther.

MIRANDA

You have often
Begun to tell me what I am; but stopp'd,
And left me to a bootless inquisition,
Concluding 'Stay: not yet.'

PROSPERO

The hour's now come;
The very minute bids thee ope thine ear;
Obey, and be attentive. Canst thou remember
A time before we came unto this cell?
I do not think thou canst, for then thou wast not
Out three years old.

MIRANDA

Certainly, sir, I can.

PROSPERO

By what? by any other house or person?
Of any thing the image tell me, that
Hath kept with thy remembrance.

MIRANDA

'Tis far off,
And rather like a dream than an assurance
That my remembrance warrants. Had I not
Four or five women once that tended me?

PROSPERO

Thou hadst, and more, Miranda. But how is it
That this lives in thy mind? What seest thou else
In the dark backward and abysm of time?
If thou remember'st aught ere thou camest here,
How thou camest here thou mayst.

MIRANDA

But that I do not.

PROSPERO

Twelve year since, Miranda, twelve year since,
Thy father was the Duke of Milan, and
A prince of power.

MIRANDA

Sir, are not you my father?

PROSPERO

Thy mother was a piece of virtue, and

She said thou wast my daughter; and thy father
Was Duke of Milan; and his only heir
A princess, no worse issued.

MIRANDA

O the heavens!
What foul play had we, that we came from thence?
Or blessed was't we did?

PROSPERO

Both, both, my girl:
By foul play, as thou say'st, were we heaved thence;
But blessedly holp hither.

MIRANDA

O, my heart bleeds
To think o' the teen that I have turn'd you to,
Which is from my remembrance! Please you, farther.

PROSPERO

My brother, and thy uncle, call'd Antonio,—
I pray thee, mark me,—that a brother should
Be so perfidious!—he whom, next thyself,
Of all the world I loved, and to him put
The manage of my state; as at that time
Through all the signories it was the first,
And Prospero the prime duke, being so reputed
In dignity, and for the liberal arts
Without a parallel; those being all my study,
The government I cast upon my brother,
And to my state grew stranger, being transported
And rapt in secret studies. Thy false uncle—
Dost thou attend me?

MIRANDA

Sir, most heedfully.

PROSPERO

Being once perfected how to grant suits,
How to deny them, who to advance, and who
To trash for over-topping, new created
The creatures that were mine, I say, or changed 'em,
Or else new form'd 'em; having both the key
Of officer and office, set all hearts i' the state
To what tune pleased his ear; that now he was
The ivy which had hid my princely trunk,
And suck'd my verdure out on't. Thou attend'st not.

MIRANDA

O, good sir, I do.

PROSPERO

I pray thee, mark me.
I, thus neglecting worldly ends, all dedicated
To closeness and the bettering of my mind
With that which, but by being so retired,
O'er-prized all popular rate, in my false brother
Awaked an evil nature; and my trust,
Like a good parent, did beget of him
A falsehood in its contrary, as great
As my trust was; which had indeed no limit,
A confidence sans bound. He being thus lorded,
Not only with what my revenue yielded,
But what my power might else exact, like one
Who having into truth, by telling of it,
Made such a sinner of his memory,
To credit his own lie, he did believe
He was indeed the duke; out o' the substitution,

And executing the outward face of royalty,
With all prerogative:—hence his ambition growing,—
Dost thou hear?

MIRANDA

Your tale, sir, would cure deafness.

PROSPERO

To have no screen between this part he play'd
And him he play'd it for, he needs will be
Absolute Milan. Me, poor man, my library
Was dukedom large enough: of temporal royalties
He thinks me now incapable; confederates,
So dry he was for sway, wi' the King of Naples
To give him annual tribute, do him homage,
Subject his coronet to his crown, and bend
The dukedom, yet unbow'd,—alas, poor Milan!—
To most ignoble stooping.

MIRANDA

O the heavens!

PROSPERO

Mark his condition, and the event; then tell me
If this might be a brother.

MIRANDA

I should sin
To think but nobly of my grandmother:
Good wombs have borne bad sons.

PROSPERO

Now the condition.
This King of Naples, being an enemy
To me inveterate, hearkens my brother's suit;
Which was, that he, in lieu o' the premises,
Of homage and I know not how much tribute,
Should presently extirpate me and mine
Out of the dukedom, and confer fair Milan,
With all the honours, on my brother: whereon,
A treacherous army levied, one midnight
Fated to the purpose, did Antonio open
The gates of Milan; and, i' the dead of darkness,
The ministers for the purpose hurried thence
Me and thy crying self.

MIRANDA

Alack, for pity!
I, not remembering how I cried out then,
Will cry it o'er again: it is a hint
That wrings mine eyes to't.

PROSPERO

Hear a little further,
And then I'll bring thee to the present business
Which now's upon 's; without the which, this story
Were most impertinent.

MIRANDA

Wherefore did they not
That hour destroy us?

PROSPERO

Well demanded, wench:
My tale provokes that question. Dear, they durst not,
So dear the love my people bore me; nor set
A mark so bloody on the business; but
With colours fairer painted their foul ends.
In few, they hurried us aboard a bark,

Bore us some leagues to sea; where they prepared
A rotten carcass of a butt, not rigg'd,
Nor tackle, sail, nor mast; the very rats
Instinctively have quit it: there they hoist us,
To cry to the sea that roar'd to us; to sigh
To the winds, whose pity, sighing back again,
Did us but loving wrong.

MIRANDA
　　　　　　　Alack, what trouble
Was I then to you!

PROSPERO
　　　　　　　O, a cherubin
Thou wast that did preserve me. Thou didst smile,
Infused with a fortitude from heaven,
When I have deck'd the sea with drops full salt,
Under my burthen groan'd; which raised in me
An undergoing stomach, to bear up
Against what should ensue.

MIRANDA
　　　　　　　How came we ashore?

PROSPERO
By Providence divine.
Some food we had, and some fresh water, that
A noble Neapolitan, Gonzalo,
Out of his charity, who being then appointed
Master of this design, did give us, with
Rich garments, linens, stuffs and necessaries,
Which since have steaded much; so, of his gentleness,
Knowing I loved my books, he furnish'd me
From mine own library with volumes that
I prize above my dukedom.

MIRANDA
　　　　　　　Would I might
But ever see that man!

PROSPERO
　　　　　　　Now I arise:
[Resumes his mantle
Sit still, and hear the last of our sea-sorrow.
Here in this island we arrived; and here
Have I, thy schoolmaster, made thee more profit
Than other princess' can, that have more time
For vainer hours, and tutors not so careful.

MIRANDA
Heavens thank you for't! And now, I pray you, sir,
For still 'tis beating in my mind, your reason
For raising this sea-storm?

PROSPERO
　　　　　　　Know thus far forth.
By accident most strange, bountiful Fortune,
Now my dear lady, hath mine enemies
Brought to this shore; and by my prescience
I find my zenith doth depend upon
A most auspicious star, whose influence
If now I court not, but omit, my fortunes
Will ever after droop. Here cease more questions:
Thou art inclined to sleep; 'tis a good dulness,
And give it way: I know thou canst not choose.
[MIRANDA sleeps

Come away, servant, come. I am ready now.
Approach, my Ariel, come.

Enter ARIEL

ARIEL
All hail, great master! grave sir, hail! I come
To answer thy best pleasure; be't to fly,
To swim, to dive into the fire, to ride
On the curl'd clouds, to thy strong bidding task
Ariel and all his quality.

PROSPERO
　　　　　　　Hast thou, spirit,
Perform'd to point the tempest that I bade thee?

ARIEL
To every article.
I boarded the king's ship; now on the beak,
Now in the waist, the deck, in every cabin,
I flamed amazement: sometime I'ld divide,
And burn in many places; on the topmast,
The yards and bowsprit, would I flame distinctly,
Then meet and join. Jove's lightnings, the precursors
O' the dreadful thunder-claps, more momentary
And sight-outrunning were not: the fire and cracks
Of sulphurous roaring the most mighty Neptune
Seem to besiege, and make his bold waves tremble,
Yea, his dread trident shake.

PROSPERO
　　　　　　　My brave spirit!
Who was so firm, so constant, that this coil
Would not infect his reason?

ARIEL
　　　　　　　Not a soul
But felt a fever of the mad, and play'd
Some tricks of desperation. All but mariners
Plunged in the foaming brine, and quit the vessel,
Then all afire with me: the king's son, Ferdinand,
With hair up-staring,—then like reeds, not hair,—
Was the first man that leap'd; cried, 'Hell is empty,
And all the devils are here.'

PROSPERO
　　　　　　　Why, that's my spirit!
But was not this nigh shore?

ARIEL
　　　　　　　Close by, my master.

PROSPERO
But are they, Ariel, safe?

ARIEL
　　　　　　　Not a hair perish'd;
On their sustaining garments not a blemish,
But fresher than before: and, as thou badest me,
In troops I have dispersed them 'bout the isle.
The king's son have I landed by himself;
Whom I left cooling of the air with sighs
In an odd angle of the isle, and sitting,
His arms in this sad knot.

PROSPERO
　　　　　　　Of the king's ship,
The mariners, say how thou hast disposed,
And all the rest o' the fleet.

ARIEL
　　　　　　　Safely in harbour

[1302]

Is the king's ship; in the deep nook, where once
Thou call'dst me up at midnight to fetch dew
From the still-vex'd Bermoothes, there she's hid:
The mariners all under hatches stow'd;
Who, with a charm join'd to their suffer'd labour,
I have left asleep: and for the rest o' the fleet,
Which I dispersed, they all have met again,
And are upon the Mediterranean flote,
Bound sadly home for Naples;
Supposing that they saw the king's ship wreck'd,
And his great person perish.

PROSPERO

           Ariel, thy charge
Exactly is perform'd: but there's more work.
What is the time o' the day?

ARIEL

           Past the mid season.

PROSPERO

At least two glasses. The time 'twixt six and now
Must by us both be spent most preciously.

ARIEL

Is there more toil? Since thou dost give me pains,
Let me remember thee what thou hast promised,
Which is not yet perform'd me.

PROSPERO

           How now? moody?
What is't thou canst demand?

ARIEL

           My liberty.

PROSPERO

Before the time be out? no more!

ARIEL

           I prithee,
Remember I have done thee worthy service;
Told thee no lies, made thee no mistakings, served
Without or grudge or grumblings: thou didst promise
To bate me a full year.

PROSPERO

           Dost thou forget
From what a torment I did free thee?

ARIEL

           No.

PROSPERO

Thou dost; and think'st it much to tread the ooze
Of the salt deep,
To run upon the sharp wind of the north,
To do me business in the veins o' the earth
When it is baked with frost.

ARIEL

           I do not, sir.

PROSPERO

Thou liest, malignant thing! Hast thou forgot
The foul witch Sycorax, who with age and envy
Was grown into a hoop? hast thou forgot her?

ARIEL

No, sir.

PROSPERO

Thou hast. Where was she born? speak; tell
     me.

ARIEL

Sir, in Argier.

PROSPERO

           O, was she so? I must
Once in a month recount what thou hast been,
Which thou forget'st. This damn'd witch Sycorax,
For mischiefs manifold, and sorceries terrible
To enter human hearing, from **Argier,**
Thou know'st, was banish'd: for one thing she did
They would not take her life. Is not this true?

ARIEL

Ay, sir.

PROSPERO

This blue-eyed hag was hither brought with child,
And here was left by the sailors. Thou, my slave,
As thou report'st thyself, wast then her servant;
And, for thou wast a spirit too delicate
To act her earthy and abhorr'd commands,
Refusing her grand hests, she did confine thee,
By help of her more potent ministers,
And in her most unmitigable rage,
Into a cloven pine; within which rift
Imprison'd thou didst painfully remain
A dozen years; within which space she died,
And left thee there; where thou didst vent thy groans
As fast as mill-wheels strike. Then was this island—
Save for the son that she did litter here,
A freckled whelp hag-born—not honour'd with
A human shape.

ARIEL

           Yes, Caliban her son.

PROSPERO

Dull thing, I say so; he, that Caliban,
Whom now I keep in service. Thou best know'st
What torment I did find thee in; thy groans
Did make wolves howl, and penetrate the breasts
Of ever-angry bears: it was a torment
To lay upon the damn'd, which Sycorax
Could not again undo: it was mine art,
When I arrived and heard thee, that made gape
The pine, and let thee out.

ARIEL

           I thank thee, master.

PROSPERO

If thou more murmur'st, I will rend an oak,
And peg thee in his knotty entrails, till
Thou hast howl'd away twelve winters.

ARIEL

           Pardon, master:
I will be correspondent to command,
And do my spiriting gently.

PROSPERO

           Do so; and after two days
I will discharge thee.

ARIEL

           That's my noble master!
What shall I do? say what; what shall I do?

PROSPERO

Go make thyself like a nymph o' the sea:
Be subject to no sight but thine and mine; invisible

To every eyeball else. Go take this shape,
And hither come in't: go, hence with diligence!
                              [*Exit* ARIEL
Awake, dear heart, awake! thou hast slept well;
Awake!

MIRANDA
          The strangeness of your story put
Heaviness in me.

PROSPERO
          Shake it off. Come on;
We'll visit Caliban my slave, who never
Yields us kind answer.

MIRANDA
                    'Tis a villain, sir,
I do not love to look on.

PROSPERO
                    But, as 'tis,
We cannot miss him: he does make our fire,
Fetch in our wood, and serves in offices
That profit us. What, ho! slave! Caliban!
Thou earth, thou! speak.

CALIBAN [*within*]
                    There's wood enough within.

PROSPERO
Come forth, I say! there's other business for thee:
Come, thou tortoise! when?

Re-enter ARIEL *like a water-nymph*

Fine apparition! My quaint Ariel,
Hark in thine ear.

ARIEL
          My lord, it shall be done.   [*Exit*

PROSPERO
Thou poisonous slave, got by the devil himself
Upon thy wicked dam, come forth!

Enter CALIBAN

CALIBAN
As wicked dew as e'er my mother brush'd
With raven's feather from unwholesome fen
Drop on you both! a south-west blow on ye
And blister you all o'er!

PROSPERO
For this, be sure, to-night thou shalt have cramps,
Side-stitches that shall pen thy breath up; urchins
Shall, for that vast of night that they may work,
All exercise on thee; thou shalt be pinch'd
As thick as honeycomb, each pinch more stinging
Than bees that made 'em.

CALIBAN
                    I must eat my dinner.
This island's mine, by Sycorax my mother,
Which thou takest from me. When thou camest first,
Thou strokedst me, and madest much of me;
     wouldst give me
Water with berries in't; and teach me how
To name the bigger light, and how the less,
That burn by day and night: and then I loved thee,
And show'd thee all the qualities o' th' isle,
The fresh springs, brine-pits, barren place and fer-
     tile:
Cursed be I that did so! All the charms

Of Sycorax, toads, beetles, bats, light on you!
For I am all the subjects that you have,
Which first was mine own king: and here you sty me
In this hard rock, whiles you do keep from me
The rest o' th' island.

PROSPERO
          Thou most lying slave,
Whom stripes may move, not kindness! I have used
     thee,
Filth as thou art, with human care; and lodged thee
In mine own cell, till thou didst seek to violate
The honour of my child.

CALIBAN
O ho, O ho! would 't had been done!
Thou didst prevent me; I had peopled else
This isle with Calibans.

PROSPERO
          Abhorred slave,
Which any print of goodness wilt not take,
Being capable of all ill! I pitied thee,
Took pains to make thee speak, taught thee each
     hour
One thing or other: when thou didst not, savage,
Know thine own meaning, but wouldst gabble like
A thing most brutish, I endow'd thy purposes
With words that made them known. But thy vile
     race,
Though thou didst learn, had that in't which good
     natures
Could not abide to be with; therefore wast thou
Deservedly confined into this rock,
Who hadst deserved more than a prison.

CALIBAN
You taught me language; and my profit on't
Is, I know how to curse. The red plague rid you
For learning me your language!

PROSPERO
          Hag-seed, hence!
Fetch us in fuel; and be quick, thou'rt best,
To answer other business. Shrug'st thou, malice?
If thou neglect'st, or dost unwillingly
What I command, I'll rack thee with old cramps,
Fill all thy bones with aches, make thee roar,
That beasts shall tremble at thy din.

CALIBAN
                    No, pray thee.
[*Aside*] I must obey: his art is of such power,
It would control my dam's god, Setebos,
And make a vassal of him.

PROSPERO
          So, slave; hence!
                              [*Exit* CALIBAN
Re-enter ARIEL, *invisible, playing and singing;*
          FERDINAND *following*

ARIEL's *song.*
Come unto these yellow sands,
     And then take hands:
Courtsied when you have and kiss'd
     The wild waves whist:

Foot it featly here and there;
And, sweet sprites, the burthen bear.
           Hark, hark!

BURTHEN [*dispersedly*]
Bow-wow.

ARIEL
The watch-dogs bark:

BURTHEN [*dispersedly*]
Bow-wow.

ARIEL
Hark, hark! I hear
The strain of strutting chanticleer
Cry, Cock-a-diddle-dow.

FERDINAND
Where should this music be? i' th' air or th' earth?
It sounds no more: and, sure, it waits upon
Some god o' th' island. Sitting on a bank,
Weeping again the king my father's wreck,
This music crept by me upon the waters,
Allaying both their fury and my passion
With its sweet air: thence I have follow'd it,
Or it hath drawn me rather. But 'tis gone.
No, it begins again.

ARIEL
[*Sings*] Full fathom five thy father lies;
      Of his bones are coral made;
      Those are pearls that were his eyes:
          Nothing of him that doth fade,
      But doth suffer a sea-change
      Into something rich and strange.
      Sea-nymphs hourly ring his knell:

BURTHEN:
                  Ding-dong.

ARIEL
Hark! now I hear them,—Ding-dong, bell.

FERDINAND
The ditty does remember my drown'd father.
This is no mortal business, nor no sound
That the earth owes:—I hear it now above me.

PROSPERO
The fringed curtains of thine eye advance,
And say what thou seest yond.

MIRANDA
               What is't? a spirit?
Lord, how it looks about! Believe me, sir,
It carries a brave form. But 'tis a spirit.

PROSPERO
No, wench; it eats and sleeps and hath such senses
As we have, such. This gallant which thou seest
Was in the wreck; and, but he's something stain'd
With grief, that's beauty's canker, thou mightst call
   him
A goodly person: he hath lost his fellows,
And strays about to find 'em.

MIRANDA
              I might call him
A thing divine; for nothing natural
I ever saw so noble.

PROSPERO
       [*Aside*] It goes on, I see,
As my soul prompts it. Spirit, fine spirit! I'll free thee
Within two days for this.

FERDINAND
              Most sure, the goddess
On whom these airs attend! Vouchsafe my prayer
May know if you remain upon this island;
And that you will some good instruction give
How I may bear me here: my prime request,
Which I do last pronounce, is, O you wonder!
If you be maid or no?

MIRANDA
             No wonder, sir;
But certainly a maid.

FERDINAND
           My language! heavens!
I am the best of them that speak this speech,
Were I but where 'tis spoken.

PROSPERO
             How? the best?
What wert thou, if the King of Naples heard thee?

FERDINAND
A single thing, as I am now, that wonders
To hear thee speak of Naples. He does hear me;
And that he does I weep: myself am Naples,
Who with mine eyes, never since at ebb, beheld
The king my father wreck'd.

MIRANDA
            Alack, for mercy!

FERDINAND
Yes, faith, and all his lords; the Duke of Milan
And his brave son being twain.

PROSPERO
       [*Aside*] The Duke of Milan
And his more braver daughter could control thee,
If now 'twere fit to do't. At the first sight
They have changed eyes. Delicate Ariel,
I'll set thee free for this. [*To* FERDINAND] A word,
   good sir;
I fear you have done yourself some wrong: a word.

MIRANDA
Why speaks my father so ungently? This
Is the third man that e'er I saw; the first
That e'er I sigh'd for: pity move my father
To be inclined my way!

FERDINAND
           O, if a virgin,
And your affection not gone forth, I'll make you
The queen of Naples.

PROSPERO
          Soft, sir! one word more.
[*Aside*] They are both in either's powers: but this
   swift business
I must uneasy make, lest too light winning
Make the prize light. [*To* FERDINAND] One word
   more; I charge thee
That thou attend me: thou dost here usurp
The name thou owest not; and hast put thyself
Upon this island as a spy, to win it
From me, the lord on't.

FERDINAND
          No, as I am a man.

MIRANDA

There's nothing ill can dwell in such a temple:
If the ill spirit have so fair a house,
Good things will strive to dwell with't.

PROSPERO

              Follow me.
Speak not you for him; he's a traitor. Come;
I'll manacle thy neck and feet together:
Sea-water shalt thou drink; thy food shall be
The fresh-brook muscles, wither'd roots, and husks
Wherein the acorn cradled. Follow.

FERDINAND

            No;
I will resist such entertainment till
Mine enemy has more power.

[Draws, and is charmed from moving

MIRANDA

          O dear father,
Make not too rash a trial of him, for
He's gentle, and not fearful.

PROSPERO

          What! I say,
My foot my tutor? Put thy sword up, traitor;
Who makest a show, but darest not strike, thy con-
science
Is so possess'd with guilt: come from thy ward;
For I can here disarm thee with this stick
And make thy weapon drop.

MIRANDA

        Beseech you, father.

PROSPERO

Hence! hang not on my garments.

MIRANDA

          Sir, have pity;
I'll be his surety.

PROSPERO

        Silence! one word more
Shall make me chide thee, if not hate thee. What!
An advocate for an impostor! hush!
Thou think'st there is no more such shapes as he,
Having seen but him and Caliban: foolish wench!
To the most of men this is a Caliban,
And they to him are angels.

MIRANDA

        My affections
Are, then, most humble; I have no ambition
To see a goodlier man.

PROSPERO

        Come on; obey:
Thy nerves are in their infancy again,
And have no vigour in them.

FERDINAND

        So they are:
My spirits, as in a dream, are all bound up.
My father's loss, the weakness which I feel,
The wreck of all my friends, nor this man's threats,
To whom I am subdued, are but light to me,
Might I but through my prison once a day
Behold this maid: all corners else o' th' earth

Let liberty make use of; space enough
Have I in such a prison.

PROSPERO

       [Aside] It works.
          [To FERDINAND] Come on.
Thou hast done well, fine Ariel!
          [To FERDINAND] Follow me.
[To ARIEL] Hark what thou else shalt do me.

MIRANDA

        Be of comfort;
My father's of a better nature, sir,
Than he appears by speech: this is unwonted
Which now came from him.

PROSPERO

        Thou shalt be as free
As mountain winds: but then exactly do
All points of my command.

ARIEL

        To the syllable.

PROSPERO

Come, follow. Speak not for him. *[Exeunt*

ACT II

SCENE I. *Another part of the island*

Enter ALONSO, SEBASTIAN, ANTONIO, GONZALO,
ADRIAN, FRANCISCO, *and others*

GONZALO

Beseech you, sir, be merry; you have cause,
So have we all, of joy; for our escape
Is much beyond our loss. Our hint of woe
Is common; every day, some sailor's wife,
The masters of some merchant, and the merchant,
Have just our theme of woe; but for the miracle,
I mean our preservation, few in millions
Can speak like us: then wisely, good sir, weigh
Our sorrow with our comfort.

ALONSO

        Prithee, peace.

SEBASTIAN

He receives comfort like cold porridge.

ANTONIO

The visitor will not give him o'er so.

SEBASTIAN

Look, he's winding up the watch of his wit; by and
by it will strike.

GONZALO

Sir,—

SEBASTIAN

One: tell.

GONZALO

When every grief is entertain'd that's offer'd,
Comes to the entertainer—

SEBASTIAN

A dollar.

GONZALO

Dolour comes to him, indeed: you have spoken truer
than you purposed.

SEBASTIAN

You have taken it wiselier than I meant you should.

GONZALO

Therefore, my lord,—

ANTONIO

Fie, what a spendthrift is he of his tongue!

ALONSO

I prithee, spare.

GONZALO

Well, I have done: but yet,—

SEBASTIAN

He will be talking.

ANTONIO

Which, of he or Adrian, for a good wager, first begins to crow?

SEBASTIAN

The old cock.

ANTONIO

The cockerel.

SEBASTIAN

Done. The wager?

ANTONIO

A laughter.

SEBASTIAN

A match!

ADRIAN

Though this island seem to be desert,—

SEBASTIAN

Ha, ha, ha!—So, you're paid.

ADRIAN

Uninhabitable, and almost inaccessible,—

SEBASTIAN

Yet,—

ADRIAN

Yet,—

ANTONIO

He could not miss't.

ADRIAN

It must needs be of subtle, tender and delicate temperance.

ANTONIO

Temperance was a delicate wench.

SEBASTIAN

Ay, and a subtle; as he most learnedly delivered.

ADRIAN

The air breathes upon us here most sweetly.

SEBASTIAN

As if it had lungs, and rotten ones.

ANTONIO

Or as 'twere perfumed by a fen.

GONZALO

Here is every thing advantageous to life.

ANTONIO

True; save means to live.

SEBASTIAN

Of that there's none, or little.

GONZALO

How lush and lusty the grass looks! how green!

ANTONIO

The ground, indeed, is tawny.

SEBASTIAN

With an eye of green in't.

ANTONIO

He misses not much.

SEBASTIAN

No; he doth but mistake the truth totally.

GONZALO

But the rarity of it is,—which is indeed almost beyond credit,—

SEBASTIAN

As many vouched rarities are.

GONZALO

That our garments, being, as they were, drenched in the sea, hold, notwithstanding, their freshness and glosses, being rather new-dyed than stained with salt water.

ANTONIO

If but one of his pockets could speak, would it not say he lies?

SEBASTIAN

Ay, or very falsely pocket up his report.

GONZALO

Methinks our garments are now as fresh as when we put them on first in Afric, at the marriage of the king's fair daughter Claribel to the King of Tunis.

SEBASTIAN

'Twas a sweet marriage, and we prosper well in our return.

ADRIAN

Tunis was never graced before with such a paragon to their queen.

GONZALO

Not since widow Dido's time.

ANTONIO

Widow! a pox o' that! How came that widow in? widow Dido!

SEBASTIAN

What if he had said 'widower Æneas' too? Good Lord, how you take it!

ADRIAN

'Widow Dido' said you? you make me study of that: she was of Carthage, not of Tunis.

GONZALO

This Tunis, sir, was Carthage.

ADRIAN

Carthage?

GONZALO

I assure you, Carthage.

ANTONIO

His word is more than the miraculous harp.

SEBASTIAN

He hath raised the wall, and houses too.

ANTONIO

What impossible matter will he make easy next?

SEBASTIAN

I think he will carry this island home in his pocket, and give it his son for an apple.

ANTONIO

And, sowing the kernels of it in the sea, bring forth more islands.

GONZALO

Ay.

ANTONIO

Why, in good time.

GONZALO

Sir, we were talking that our garments seem now as
fresh as when we were at Tunis at the marriage of
your daughter, who is now queen.

ANTONIO

And the rarest that e'er came there.

SEBASTIAN

Bate, I beseech you, widow Dido.

ANTONIO

O, widow Dido! ay, widow Dido.

GONZALO

Is not, sir, my doublet as fresh as the first day I wore
it? I mean, in a sort.

ANTONIO

That sort was well fished for.

GONZALO

When I wore it at your daughter's marriage?

ALONSO

You cram these words into mine ears against
The stomach of my sense. Would I had never
Married my daughter there! for, coming thence,
My son is lost, and, in my rate, she too,
Who is so far from Italy removed
I ne'er again shall see her. O thou mine heir
Of Naples and of Milan, what strange fish
Hath made his meal on thee?

FRANCISCO

           Sir, he may live:
I saw him beat the surges under him,
And ride upon their backs; he trod the water,
Whose enmity he flung aside, and breasted
The surge most swoln that met him; his bold head
'Bove the contentious waves he kept, and oar'd
Himself with his good arms in lusty stroke
To the shore, that o'er his wave-worn basis bow'd,
As stooping to relieve him: I not doubt
He came alive to land.

ALONSO

           No, no, he's gone.

SEBASTIAN

Sir, you may thank yourself for this great loss,
That would not bless our Europe with your daughter,
But rather lose her to an African;
Where she, at least, is banish'd from your eye,
Who hath cause to wet the grief on't.

ALONSO

           Prithee, peace.

SEBASTIAN

You were kneel'd to, and importuned otherwise,
By all of us; and the fair soul herself
Weigh'd between loathness and obedience, at
Which end o' the beam should bow. We have lost
     your son,
I fear, for ever: Milan and Naples have
Mo widows in them of this business' making

Than we bring men to comfort them:
The fault's your own.

ALONSO

           So is the dear'st o' the loss.

GONZALO

My lord Sebastian,
The truth you speak doth lack some gentleness,
And time to speak it in: you rub the sore,
When you should bring the plaster.

SEBASTIAN

           Very well.

ANTONIO

And most chirurgeonly.

GONZALO

It is foul weather in us all, good sir,
When you are cloudy.

SEBASTIAN

           Foul weather?

ANTONIO

           Very foul.

GONZALO

Had I plantation of this isle, my lord,—

ANTONIO

He'ld sow't with nettle-seed.

SEBASTIAN

           Or docks, or mallows.

GONZALO

And were the king on't, what would I do?

SEBASTIAN

'Scape being drunk for want of wine.

GONZALO

I' the commonwealth I would by contraries
Execute all things; for no kind of traffic
Would I admit; no name of magistrate;
Letters should not be known; riches, poverty,
And use of service, none; contract, succession,
Bourn, bound of land, tilth, vineyard, none;
No use of metal, corn, or wine, or oil;
No occupation; all men idle, all;
And women too, but innocent and pure;
No sovereignty;—

SEBASTIAN

           Yet he would be king on't.

ANTONIO

The latter end of his commonwealth forgets the beginning.

GONZALO

All things in common nature should produce
Without sweat or endeavour: treason, felony,
Sword, pike, knife, gun, or need of any engine,
Would I not have; but nature should bring forth,
Of it own kind, all foison, all abundance,
To feed my innocent people.

SEBASTIAN

No marrying 'mong his subjects?

ANTONIO

None, man; all idle; whores and knaves.

GONZALO

I would with such perfection govern, sir,
To excel the golden age.

SEBASTIAN
'Save his majesty!

ANTONIO
Long live Gonzalo!

GONZALO
And,—do you mark me, sir?

ALONSO
Prithee, no more: thou dost talk nothing to me.

GONZALO
I do well believe your highness; and did it to minister occasion to these gentlemen, who are of such
sensible and nimble lungs that they always use to
laugh at nothing.

ANTONIO
'Twas you we laughed at.

GONZALO
Who in this kind of merry fooling am nothing to
you: so you may continue, and laugh at nothing
still.

ANTONIO
What a blow was there given!

SEBASTIAN
An it had not fallen flat-long.

GONZALO
You are gentlemen of brave mettle; you would lift
the moon out of her sphere, if she would continue in
it five weeks without changing.

Enter ARIEL *(invisible) playing solemn music*

SEBASTIAN
We would so, and then go a bat-fowling.

ANTONIO
Nay, good my lord, be not angry.

GONZALO
No, I warrant you; I will not adventure my discretion so weakly. Will you laugh me asleep, for I am
very heavy?

ANTONIO
Go sleep, and hear us.

[*All sleep except* ALONSO, SEBASTIAN, *and* ANTONIO

ALONSO
What, all so soon asleep! I wish mine eyes
Would, with themselves, shut up my thoughts: I find
They are inclined to do so.

SEBASTIAN
Please you, sir,
Do not omit the heavy offer of it:
It seldom visits sorrow; when it doth,
It is a comforter.

ANTONIO
We two, my lord,
Will guard your person while you take your rest,
And watch your safety.

ALONSO
Thank you.—Wondrous heavy.

[ALONSO *sleeps. Exit* ARIEL

SEBASTIAN
What a strange drowsiness possesses them!

ANTONIO
It is the quality o' the climate.

SEBASTIAN
Why
Doth it not then our eyelids sink? I find not
Myself disposed to sleep.

ANTONIO
Nor I; my spirits are nimble.
They fell together all, as by consent;
They dropp'd, as by a thunder-stroke. What might,
Worthy Sebastian?—O, what might?—No more:—
And yet methinks I see it in thy face,
What thou shouldst be: the occasion speaks thee; and
My strong imagination sees a crown
Dropping upon thy head.

SEBASTIAN
What, art thou waking?

ANTONIO
Do you not hear me speak?

SEBASTIAN
I do; and surely
It is a sleepy language, and thou speak'st
Out of thy sleep. What is it thou didst say?
This is a strange repose, to be asleep
With eyes wide open; standing, speaking, moving,
And yet so fast asleep.

ANTONIO
Noble Sebastian,
Thou let'st thy fortune sleep—die, rather; wink'st
Whiles thou art waking.

SEBASTIAN
Thou dost snore distinctly;
There's meaning in thy snores.

ANTONIO
I am more serious than my custom: you
Must be so too, if heed me; which to do
Trebles thee o'er.

SEBASTIAN
Well, I am standing water.

ANTONIO
I'll teach you how to flow.

SEBASTIAN
Do so: to ebb
Hereditary sloth instructs me.

ANTONIO
O,
If you but knew how you the purpose cherish
Whiles thus you mock it! how, in stripping it,
You more invest it! Ebbing men, indeed,
Most often do so near the bottom run
By their own fear or sloth.

SEBASTIAN
Prithee, say on:
The setting of thine eye and cheek proclaim
A matter from thee; and a birth, indeed,
Which throes thee much to yield,

ANTONIO
Thus, sir:
Although this lord of weak remembrance, this,
Who shall be of as little memory
When he is earth'd, hath here almost persuaded,—
For he's a spirit of persuasion, only

[1309]

Professes to persuade,—the king his son's alive,
'Tis as impossible that he's undrown'd
As he that sleeps here swims.

SEBASTIAN
                              I have no hope
That he's undrown'd.

ANTONIO
                              O, out of that 'no hope'
What great hope have you! no hope that way is
Another way so high a hope that even
Ambition cannot pierce a wink beyond,
But doubt discovery there. Will you grant with me
That Ferdinand is drown'd?

SEBASTIAN
                              He's gone.

ANTONIO
                              Then, tell me,
Who's the next heir of Naples?

SEBASTIAN
                              Claribel.

ANTONIO
She that is queen of Tunis; she that dwells
Ten leagues beyond man's life; she that from Naples
Can have no note, unless the sun were post,—
The man i' the moon's too slow,—till new-born chins
Be rough and razorable; she that from whom
We all were sea-swallow'd, though some cast again,
And by that destiny, to perform an act
Whereof what's past is prologue; what to come,
In yours and my discharge.

SEBASTIAN
                              What stuff is this! How say you?
'Tis true, my brother's daughter's queen of Tunis;
So is she heir of Naples; 'twixt which regions
There is some space.

ANTONIO
                              A space whose every cubit
Seems to cry out, 'How shall that Claribel
Measure us back to Naples? Keep in Tunis,
And let Sebastian wake.' Say, this were death
That now hath seized them; why, they were no worse
Than now they are. There be that can rule Naples
As well as he that sleeps; lords that can prate
As amply and unnecessarily
As this Gonzalo; I myself could make
A chough of as deep chat. O, that you bore
The mind that I do! what a sleep were this
For your advancement! Do you understand me?

SEBASTIAN
Methinks I do.

ANTONIO
                              And how does your content
Tender your own good fortune?

SEBASTIAN
                              I remember
You did supplant your brother Prospero.

ANTONIO
                              True:
And look how well my garments sit upon me;

Much feater than before: my brother's servants
Were then my fellows; now they are my men.

SEBASTIAN
But, for your conscience.

ANTONIO
Ay, sir; where lies that? if 'twere a kibe,
'Twould put me to my slipper: but I feel not
This deity in my bosom: twenty consciences,
That stand 'twixt me and Milan, candied be they,
And melt, ere they molest! Here lies your brother,
No better than the earth he lies upon,
If he were that which now he's like, that's dead;
Whom I, with this obedient steel, three inches of it,
Can lay to bed for ever; whiles you, doing thus,
To the perpetual wink for aye might put
This ancient morsel, this Sir Prudence, who
Should not upbraid our course. For all the rest,
They'll take suggestion as a cat laps milk;
They'll tell the clock to any business that
We say befits the hour.

SEBASTIAN
                              Thy case, dear friend,
Shall be my precedent; as thou got'st Milan,
I'll come by Naples. Draw thy sword: one stroke
Shall free thee from the tribute which thou payest;
And I the king shall love thee.

ANTONIO
                              Draw together;
And when I rear my hand, do you the like,
To fall it on Gonzalo.

SEBASTIAN
                              O, but one word.
                              [They talk apart

Re-enter ARIEL invisible

ARIEL
My master through his art foresees the danger
That you, his friend, are in; and sends me forth,—
For else his project dies,—to keep them living.
                              [Sings in GONZALO'S ear

        While you here do snoring lie,
        Open-eyed conspiracy
                His time doth take.
        If of life you keep a care,
        Shake off slumber, and beware:
        Awake, awake!

ANTONIO
Then let us both be sudden.

GONZALO
                              Now, good angels
Preserve the king!   [They wake

ALONSO
Why, how now? ho, awake!—why are you drawn?
Wherefore this ghastly looking?

GONZALO
                              What's the matter?

SEBASTIAN
Whiles we stood here securing your repose,
Even now, we heard a hollow burst of bellowing
Like bulls, or rather lions: did't not wake you?
It struck mine ear most terribly.

ALONSO

             I heard nothing.

ANTONIO

O, 'twas a din to fright a monster's ear,
To make an earthquake! sure, it was the roar
Of a whole herd of lions.

ALONSO

             Heard you this, Gonzalo?

GONZALO

Upon mine honour, sir, I heard a humming,
And that a strange one too, which did awake me:
I shaked you, sir, and cried: as mine eyes open'd,
I saw their weapons drawn:—there was a noise,
That's verily. 'Tis best we stand upon our guard,
Or that we quit this place: let's draw our weapons.

ALONSO

Lead off this ground; and let's make further search
For my poor son.

GONZALO

             Heavens keep him from these beasts!
For he is, sure, i' th' island.

ALONSO

             Lead away.

ARIEL

Prospero my lord shall know what I have done:
So, king, go safely on to seek thy son.   [Exeunt

SCENE II. *Another part of the island*

Enter CALIBAN *with a burden of wood. A noise of thunder
heard*

CALIBAN

All the infections that the sun sucks up
From bogs, fens, flats, on Prosper fall, and make him
By inch-meal a disease! His spirits hear me,
And yet I needs must curse. But they'll nor pinch,
Fright me with urchin-shows, pitch me i' the mire,
Nor lead me, like a firebrand, in the dark
Out of my way, unless he bid 'em: but
For every trifle are they set upon me;
Sometime like apes, that mow and chatter at me,
And after bite me; then like hedgehogs, which
Lie tumbling in my barefoot way, and mount
Their pricks at my footfall; sometime am I
All wound with adders, who with cloven tongues
Do hiss me into madness.

Enter TRINCULO

             Lo, now, lo!
Here comes a spirit of his, and to torment me
for bringing wood in slowly. I'll fall flat;
Perchance he will not mind me.

TRINCULO

Here's neither bush nor shrub, to bear off any
weather at all, and another storm brewing; I hear it
sing i' the wind: yond same black cloud, yond huge
one, looks like a foul bombard that would shed his
liquor. If it should thunder as it did before, I know
not where to hide my head: yond same cloud cannot choose but fall by pailfuls. What have we here?

a man or a fish? dead or alive? A fish: he smells like
a fish; a very ancient and fish-like smell; a kind of
not of the newest Poor-John. A strange fish! Were I
in England now, as once I was, and had but this fish
painted, not a holiday fool there but would give a
piece of silver: there would this monster make a man;
any strange beast there makes a man: when they will
not give a doit to relieve a lame beggar, they will
lay out ten to see a dead Indian. Legged like a man!
and his fins like arms! Warm o' my troth! I do now
let loose my opinion; hold it no longer: this is no fish,
but an islander, that hath lately suffered by a thunderbolt. [*Thunder*] Alas, the storm is come again!
best way is to creep under his gaberdine; there is no
other shelter hereabout: misery acquaints a man
with strange bedfellows. I will here shroud till the
dregs of the storm be past.

Enter STEPHANO, *singing: a bottle in his hand*

STEPHANO

     I shall no more to sea, to sea,
     Here shall I die a-shore,—

This is a very scurvy tune to sing at a man's funer l:
well, here's my comfort.   [*Drinks*

[*Sings*] The master, the swabber, the boatswain, and I,
     The gunner, and his mate,
   Loved Mall, Meg, and Marian, and Margery,
     But none of us cared for Kate;
     For she had a tongue with a tang,
     Would cry to a sailor, Go hang!
  She loved not the savour of tar nor of pitch;
  Yet a tailor might scratch her where'er she did itch.
   Then, to sea, boys, and let her go hang!

This is a scurvy tune too: but here's my comfort.
                                [*Drinks*

CALIBAN

Do not torment me:—O!

STEPHANO

What's the matter? Have we devils here? Do you put
tricks upon 's with salvages and men of Ind, ha? I
have not scaped drowning, to be afeard now of your
four legs; for it hath been said, As proper a man as
ever went on four legs cannot make him give ground;
and it shall be said so again, while Stephano breathes
at nostrils.

CALIBAN

The spirit torments me:—O!

STEPHANO

This is some monster of the isle with four legs, who
hath got, as I take it, an ague. Where the devil should
he learn our language? I will give him some relief, if
it be but for that. If I can recover him, and keep him
tame, and get to Naples with him, he's a present for
any emperor that ever trod on neat's-leather.

CALIBAN

Do not torment me, prithee; I'll bring my wood
home faster.

STEPHANO

He's in his fit now, and does not talk after the wisest.
He shall taste of my bottle: if he have never drunk
wine afore, it will go near to remove his fit. If I can

recover him, and keep him tame, I will not take too much for him; he shall pay for him that hath him, and that soundly.

CALIBAN

Thou dost me yet but little hurt; thou wilt anon, I know it by thy trembling: now Prosper works upon thee.

STEPHANO

Come on your ways; open your mouth; here is that which will give language to you, cat: open your mouth; this will shake your shaking, I can tell you, and that soundly: you cannot tell who's your friend: open your chaps again.

TRINCULO

I should know that voice: it should be—but he is drowned; and these are devils:—O defend me!

STEPHANO

Four legs and two voices,—a most delicate monster! His forward voice, now, is to speak well of his friend; his backward voice is to utter foul speeches and to detract. If all the wine in my bottle will recover him, I will help his ague. Come:—Amen! I will pour some in thy other mouth.

TRINCULO

Stephano!

STEPHANO

Doth thy other mouth call me? Mercy, mercy! This is a devil, and no monster: I will leave him; I have no long spoon.

TRINCULO

Stephano! If thou beest Stephano, touch me, and speak to me; for I am Trinculo,—be not afeard,— thy good friend Trinculo.

STEPHANO

If thou beest Trinculo, come forth: I'll pull thee by the lesser legs: if any be Trinculo's legs, these are they. Thou art very Trinculo indeed! How camest thou to be the siege of this moon-calf? can he vent Trinculos?

TRINCULO

I took him to be killed with a thunder-stroke. But art thou not drowned, Stephano? I hope, now, thou art not drowned. Is the storm overblown? I hid me under the dead moon-calf's gaberdine for fear of the storm. And art thou living, Stephano? O Stephano, two Neapolitans scaped!

STEPHANO

Prithee, do not turn me about; my stomach is not constant.

CALIBAN

[Aside] These be fine things, an if they be not sprites. That's a brave god, and bears celestial liquor: I will kneel to him.

STEPHANO

How didst thou 'scape? How camest thou hither? swear, by this bottle, how thou camest hither. I escaped upon a butt of sack, which the sailors heaved o'erboard, by this bottle! which I made of the bark of a tree with mine own hands, since I was cast ashore.

CALIBAN

I'll swear, upon that bottle, to be thy true subject; for the liquor is not earthly.

STEPHANO

Here; swear, then, how thou escapedst.

TRINCULO

Swum ashore, man, like a duck: I can swim like a duck, I'll be sworn.

STEPHANO

Here, kiss the book. Though thou canst swim like a duck, thou art made like a goose.

TRINCULO

O Stephano, hast any more of this?

STEPHANO

The whole butt, man: my cellar is in a rock by the sea-side, where my wine is hid. How now, moon-calf! how does thine ague?

CALIBAN

Hast thou not dropp'd from heaven?

STEPHANO

Out o' the moon, I do assure thee: I was the man i' the moon when time was.

CALIBAN

I have seen thee in her, and I do adore thee: my mistress show'd me thee, and thy dog, and thy bush.

STEPHANO

Come, swear to that; kiss the book: I will furnish it anon with new contents: swear.

TRINCULO

By this good light, this is a very shallow monster! I afeard of him! A very weak monster! The man i' the moon! A most poor credulous monster! Well drawn, monster, in good sooth!

CALIBAN

I'll show thee every fertile inch o' th' island; and I will kiss thy foot: I prithee, be my god.

TRINCULO

By this light, a most perfidious and drunken monster! when's god's asleep, he'll rob his bottle.

CALIBAN

I'll kiss thy foot; I'll swear myself thy subject.

STEPHANO

Come on, then; down, and swear.

TRINCULO

I shall laugh myself to death at this puppy-headed monster. A most scurvy monster! I could find in my heart to beat him,—

STEPHANO

Come, kiss.

TRINCULO

But that the poor monster's in drink. An abominable monster!

CALIBAN

I'll show thee the best springs; I'll pluck thee berries; I'll fish for thee, and get thee wood enough.
A plague upon the tyrant that I serve!
I'll bear him no more sticks, but follow thee,
Thou wondrous man.

TRINCULO

A most ridiculous monster, to make a wonder of a
poor drunkard!

CALIBAN

I prithee, let me bring thee where crabs grow;
And I with my long nails will dig thee pig-nuts;
Show thee a jay's nest, and instruct thee how
To snare the nimble marmoset; I'll bring thee
To clustering filberts, and sometimes I'll get thee
Young scamels from the rock. Wilt thou go with me?

STEPHANO

I prithee now, lead the way, without any more talking. Trinculo, the king and all our company else being drowned, we will inherit here: here; bear my
bottle: fellow Trinculo, we'll fill him by and by
again.

CALIBAN *sings drunkenly*

Farewell, master; farewell, farewell!

TRINCULO

A howling monster; a drunken monster!

CALIBAN

No more dams I'll make for fish;
   Nor fetch in firing
   At requiring;
Nor scrape trencher, nor wash dish:
   'Ban, 'Ban, Cacaliban
Has a new master:—get a new man.

Freedom, hey-day! hey-day, freedom! freedom, hey-
day, freedom!

STEPHANO

O brave monster! Lead the way.   [*Exeunt*

ACT III

SCENE I. *Before* PROSPERO's *cell*

Enter FERDINAND, *bearing a log*

FERDINAND

There be some sports are painful, and their labour
Delight in them sets off: some kinds of baseness
Are nobly undergone, and most poor matters
Point to rich ends. This my mean task
Would be as heavy to me as odious, but
The mistress which I serve quickens what's dead,
And makes my labours pleasures: O, she is
Ten times more gentle than her father's crabbed,
And he's composed of harshness. I must remove
Some thousands of these logs, and pile them up,
Upon a sore injunction: my sweet mistress
Weeps when she sees me work, and says, such base-
   ness
Had never like executor. I forget:
But these sweet thoughts do even refresh my labours,
Most busy lest, when I do it.

Enter MIRANDA; *and* PROSPERO *at a distance, unseen*

MIRANDA

          Alas, now, pray you,
Work not so hard: I would the lightning had

Burnt up those logs that you are enjoin'd to pile!
Pray, set it down, and rest you: when this burns,
'Twill weep for having wearied you. My father
Is hard at study; pray, now, rest yourself;
He's safe for these three hours.

FERDINAND

          O most dear mistress,
The sun will set before I shall discharge
What I must strive to do.

MIRANDA

          If you'll sit down,
I'll bear your logs the while: pray, give me that;
I'll carry it to the pile.

FERDINAND

          No, precious creature;
I had rather crack my sinews, break my back,
Than you should such dishonour undergo,
While I sit lazy by.

MIRANDA

          It would become me
As well as it does you: and I should do it
With much more ease; for my good will is to it,
And yours it is against.

PROSPERO

          Poor worm, thou art infected!
This visitation shows it.

MIRANDA

          You look wearily.

FERDINAND

No, noble mistress; 'tis fresh morning with me
When you are by at night. I do beseech you,—
Chiefly that I might set it in my prayers,—
What is your name?

MIRANDA

          Miranda.—O my father,
I have broke your hest to say so!

FERDINAND

          Admired Miranda!
Indeed the top of admiration! worth
What's dearest to the world! Full many a lady
I have eyed with best regard, and many a time
The harmony of their tongues hath into bondage
Brought my too diligent ear: for several virtues
Have I liked several women; never any
With so full soul, but some defect in her
Did quarrel with the noblest grace she owed,
And put it to the foil: but you, O you,
So perfect and so peerless, are created
Of every creature's best!

MIRANDA

          I do not know
One of my sex; no woman's face remember,
Save, from my glass, mine own; nor have I seen
More that I may call men than you, good friend,
And my dear father: how features are abroad,
I am skilless of; but, by my modesty,
The jewel in my dower, I would not wish
Any companion in the world but you;
Nor can imagination form a shape,
Besides yourself, to like of. But I prattle

Something too wildly, and my father's precepts
I therein do forget.

FERDINAND

　　　　　　I am, in my condition,
A prince, Miranda; I do think, a king;
I would, not so!—and would no more endure
This wooden slavery than to suffer
The flesh-fly blow my mouth. Hear my soul speak:
The very instant that I saw you, did
My heart fly to your service; there resides,
To make me slave to it; and for your sake
Am I this patient log-man.

MIRANDA

　　　　　　　　Do you love me?

FERDINAND

O heaven, O earth, bear witness to this sound,
And crown what I profess with kind event,
If I speak true! if hollowly, invert
What best is boded me to mischief! I,
Beyond all limit of what else i' the world,
Do love, prize, honour you.

MIRANDA

　　　　　　　　I am a fool
To weep at what I am glad of.

PROSPERO

　　　　　　　Fair encounter
Of two most rare affections! Heavens rain grace
On that which breeds between 'em!

FERDINAND

　　　　　　　　Wherefore weep you?

MIRANDA

At mine unworthiness, that dare not offer
What I desire to give; and much less take
What I shall die to want. But this is trifling;
And all the more it seeks to hide itself,
The bigger bulk it shows. Hence, bashful cunning!
And prompt me, plain and holy innocence!
I am your wife, if you will marry me;
If not, I'll die your maid: to be your fellow
You may deny me; but I'll be your servant,
Whether you will or no.

FERDINAND

　　　　　　　My mistress, dearest;
And I thus humble ever.

MIRANDA

　　　　　　　My husband, then?

FERDINAND

Ay, with a heart as willing
As bondage e'er of freedom: here's my hand.

MIRANDA

And mine, with my heart in't: and now farewell
Till half an hour hence.

FERDINAND

　　　　　　A thousand thousand!

[Exeunt FERDINAND and MIRANDA severally

PROSPERO

So glad of this as they I cannot be,
Who are surprised withal; but my rejoicing
At nothing can be more. I'll to my book;

For yet, ere supper-time, must I perform
Much business appertaining.　　　　　[Exit

SCENE II. *Another part of the island*

Enter CALIBAN, STEPHANO, *and* TRINCULO

STEPHANO

Tell not me;—when the butt is out, we will drink
water; not a drop before: therefore bear up, and
board 'em. Servant-monster, drink to me.

TRINCULO

Servant-monster! the folly of this island! They say
there's but five upon this isle: we are three of them;
if th' other two be brained like us, the state totters.

STEPHANO

Drink, servant-monster, when I bid thee: thy eyes
are almost set in thy head.

TRINCULO

Where should they be set else? he were a brave monster indeed, if they were set in his tail.

STEPHANO

My man-monster hath drowned his tongue in sack:
for my part, the sea cannot drown me; I swam, ere
I could recover the shore, five-and-thirty leagues off
and on. By this light, thou shalt be my lieutenant,
monster, or my standard.

TRINCULO

Your lieutenant, if you list; he's no standard.

STEPHANO

We'll not run, Monsieur Monster.

TRINCULO

Nor go neither; but you'll lie, like dogs, and yet say
nothing neither.

STEPHANO

Moon-calf, speak once in thy life, if thou beest a good
moon-calf.

CALIBAN

How does thy honour? Let me lick thy shoe.
I'll not serve him, he is not valiant.

TRINCULO

Thou liest, most ignorant monster: I am in case to
justle a constable. Why, thou deboshed fish, thou,
was there ever man a coward that hath drunk so
much sack as I to-day? Wilt thou tell a monstrous
lie, being but half a fish and half a monster?

CALIBAN

Lo, how he mocks me! wilt thou let him, my lord?

TRINCULO

'Lord,' quoth he! That a monster should be such a
natural!

CALIBAN

Lo, lo, again! bite him to death, I prithee.

STEPHANO

Trinculo, keep a good tongue in your head: if you
prove a mutineer,—the next tree! The poor monster's my subject, and he shall not suffer indignity.

CALIBAN

I thank my noble lord. Wilt thou be pleased to
hearken once again to the suit I made to thee?

STEPHANO

Marry, will I: kneel and repeat it; I will stand, and so shall Trinculo.

Enter ARIEL, *invisible*

CALIBAN

As I told thee before, I am subject to a tyrant, a sorcerer, that by his cunning hath cheated me of the island.

ARIEL

Thou liest.

CALIBAN

       Thou liest, thou jesting monkey, thou:
I would my valiant master would destroy thee!
I do not lie.

STEPHANO

Trinculo, if you trouble him any more in's tale, by this hand, I will supplant some of your teeth.

TRINCULO

Why, I said nothing.

STEPHANO

Mum, then, and no more. Proceed.

CALIBAN

I say, by sorcery he got this isle;
From me he got it. If thy greatness will
Revenge it on him,—for I know thou darest,
But this thing dare not,—

STEPHANO

That's most certain.

CALIBAN

Thou shalt be lord of it, and I'll serve thee.

STEPHANO

How now shall this be compassed? Canst thou bring me to the party?

CALIBAN

Yea, yea, my lord: I'll yield him thee asleep,
Where thou mayst knock a nail into his head.

ARIEL

Thou liest; thou canst not.

CALIBAN

What a pied ninny's this! Thou scurvy patch!
I do beseech thy greatness, give him blows,
And take his bottle from him: when that's gone,
He shall drink nought but brine; for I'll not show him
Where the quick freshes are.

STEPHANO

Trinculo, run into no further danger: interrupt the monster one word further, and, by this hand, I'll turn my mercy out o' doors, and make a stock-fish of thee.

TRINCULO

Why, what did I? I did nothing. I'll go farther off.

STEPHANO

Didst thou not say he lied?

ARIEL

Thou liest.

STEPHANO

Do I so? take thou that. [*Beats him*] As you like this, give me the lie another time.

TRINCULO

I did not give the lie. Out o' your wits, and hearing too? A pox o' your bottle! this can sack and drinking do. A murrain on your monster, and the devil take your fingers!

CALIBAN

Ha, ha, ha!

STEPHANO

Now, forward with your tale.—Prithee, stand farther off.

CALIBAN

Beat him enough: after a little time,
I'll beat him too.

STEPHANO

       Stand farther.—Come, proceed.

CALIBAN

Why, as I told thee, 'tis a custom with him
I' th' afternoon to sleep: there thou mayst brain him,
Having first seized his books; or with a log
Batter his skull, or paunch him with a stake,
Or cut his wezand with thy knife. Remember
First to possess his books; for without them
He's but a sot, as I am, nor hath not
One spirit to command: they all do hate him
As rootedly as I. Burn but his books.
He has brave utensils,—for so he calls them,—
Which, when he has a house, he'll deck withal.
And that most deeply to consider is
The beauty of his daughter; he himself
Calls her a nonpareil: I never saw a woman,
But only Sycorax my dam and she;
But she as far surpasseth Sycorax
As great'st does least.

STEPHANO

       Is it so brave a lass?

CALIBAN

Ay, lord; she will become thy bed, I warrant,
And bring thee forth brave brood.

STEPHANO

Monster, I will kill this man: his daughter and I will be king and queen,—save our Graces!—and Trinculo and thyself shall be viceroys. Dost thou like the plot, Trinculo?

TRINCULO

Excellent.

STEPHANO

Give me thy hand: I am sorry I beat thee; but, while thou livest, keep a good tongue in thy head.

CALIBAN

Within this half hour will he be asleep:
Wilt thou destroy him then?

STEPHANO

       Ay, on mine honour,

ARIEL

This will I tell my master.

CALIBAN

Thou makest me merry; I am full of pleasure:
Let us be jocund: will you troll the catch
You taught me but while-ere?

STEPHANO

At thy request, monster, I will do reason, any reason.
—Come on, Trinculo, let us sing.   [Sings

Flout 'em and scout 'em, and scout 'em and flout 'em;
      Thought is free.

CALIBAN

That's not the tune.
                    [ARIEL plays the tune on a tabor and pipe

STEPHANO

What is this same?

TRINCULO

This is the tune of our catch, played by the picture
of Nobody.

STEPHANO

If thou beest a man, show thyself in thy likeness: if
thou beest a devil, take't as thou list.

TRINCULO

O, forgive me my sins!

STEPHANO

He that dies pays all debts: I defy thee. Mercy upon
us!

CALIBAN

Art thou afeard?

STEPHANO

No, monster, not I.

CALIBAN

Be not afeard; the isle is full of noises,
Sounds and sweet airs, that give delight, and hurt
      not.
Sometimes a thousand twangling instruments
Will hum about mine ears; and sometime voices,
That, if I then had waked after long sleep,
Will make me sleep again: and then, in dreaming,
The clouds methought would open, and show riches
Ready to drop upon me; that, when I waked,
I cried to dream again.

STEPHANO

This will prove a brave kingdom to me, where I shall
have my music for nothing.

CALIBAN

When Prospero is destroyed.

STEPHANO

That shall be by and by: I remember the story.

TRINCULO

The sound is going away; let's follow it, and after do
our work.

STEPHANO

Lead, monster; we'll follow. I would I could see this
taborer; he lays it on.

TRINCULO

Wilt come? I'll follow, Stephano.   [Exeunt

SCENE III. *Another part of the island*

Enter ALONSO, SEBASTIAN, ANTONIO, GONZALO,
      ADRIAN, FRANCISCO, *and others*

GONZALO

By'r lakin, I can go no further, sir;
My old bones ache: here's a maze trod, indeed,
Through forth-rights and meanders! By your pa-
      tience,
I needs must rest me.

ALONSO

                    Old lord, I cannot blame thee,
Who am myself attach'd with weariness,
To the dulling of my spirits: sit down, and rest.
Even here I will put off my hope, and keep it
No longer for my flatterer: he is drown'd
Whom thus we stray to find; and the sea mocks
Our frustrate search on land. Well, let him go.

ANTONIO

[*Aside to* SEBASTIAN] I am right glad that he's so out
      of hope.
Do not, for one repulse, forgo the purpose
That you resolved to effect.

SEBASTIAN

                    [*Aside to* ANTONIO] The next advantage
Will we take throughly.

ANTONIO

[*Aside to* SEBASTIAN] Let it be to-night;
For, now they are oppress'd with travel, they
Will not, nor cannot, use such vigilance
As when they are fresh.

SEBASTIAN

[*Aside to* ANTONIO] I say, to-night: no more.
                    [Solemn and strange music

ALONSO

What harmony is this?—My good friends, hark!

GONZALO

Marvellous sweet music!
Enter PROSPERO *above, invisible. Enter several strange
Shapes, bringing in a banquet: they dance about it with
gentle actions of salutation; and, inviting the King, &c.
      to eat, they depart*

ALONSO

Give us kind keepers, heavens!—What were these?

SEBASTIAN

A living drollery. Now I will believe
That there are unicorns; that in Arabia
There is one tree, the phœnix' throne; one phœnix
At this hour reigning there.

ANTONIO

                    I'll believe both;
And what does else want credit, come to me,
And I'll be sworn 'tis true: travellers ne'er did lie,
Though fools at home condemn 'em.

GONZALO

                    If in Naples
I should report this now, would they believe me?
If I should say, I saw such islanders,—
For, certes, these are people of the island,—
Who, though they are of monstrous shape, yet, note
Their manners are more gentle-kind than of
Our human generation you shall find
Many, nay, almost any.

PROSPERO

[Aside] Honest lord,
Thou hast said well; for some of you there present
Are worse than devils.

ALONSO

I cannot too much muse
Such shapes, such gesture, and such sound, express-
ing—
Although they want the use of tongue—a kind
Of excellent dumb discourse.

PROSPERO

[Aside] Praise in departing.

FRANCISCO

They vanish'd strangely.

SEBASTIAN

No matter, since
They have left their viands behind; for we have
stomachs.—
Will't please you taste of what is here?

ALONSO

Not I.

GONZALO

Faith, sir, you need not fear. When we were boys,
Who would believe that there were mountaineers
Dew-lapp'd like bulls, whose throats had hanging at
'em
Wallets of flesh? or that there were such men
Whose heads stood in their breasts? which now we
find
Each putter-out of five for one will bring us
Good warrant of.

ALONSO

I will stand to, and feed,
Although my last: no matter, since I feel
The best is past. Brother, my lord the duke,
Stand to, and do as we.
Thunder and lightning. Enter ARIEL, *like a harpy; claps
his wings upon the table; and, with a quaint device, the
banquet vanishes*

ARIEL

You are three men of sin, whom Destiny,—
That hath to instrument this lower world
And what is in't,—the never-surfeited sea
Hath caused to belch up you; and on this island,
Where man doth not inhabit,—you 'mongst men
Being most unfit to live. I have made you mad;
And even with such-like valour men hang and drown
Their proper selves.

*[*ALONSO, SEBASTIAN *&c. draw their swords*
You fools! I and my fellows
Are ministers of Fate: the elements,
Of whom your swords are temper'd, may as well
Wound the loud winds, or with bemock'd-at stabs
Kill the still-closing waters, as diminish
One dowle that's in my plume: my fellow-ministers
Are like invulnerable. If you could hurt,
Your swords are now too massy for your strengths,
And will not be uplifted. But remember,—
For that's my business to you,—that you three

From Milan did supplant good Prospero;
Exposed unto the sea, which hath requit it,
Him and his innocent child: for which foul deed
The powers, delaying, not forgetting, have
Incensed the seas and shores, yea, all the creatures,
Against your peace. Thee of thy son, Alonso,
They have bereft; and do pronounce by me:
Lingering perdition—worse than any death
Can be at once—shall step by step attend
You and your ways; whose wraths to guard you
from,—
Which here, in this most desolate isle, else falls
Upon your heads,—is nothing but heart-sorrow
And a clear life ensuing.
*He vanishes in thunder; then, to soft music, enter the Shapes
again, and dance, with mocks and mows, and carrying out
the table*

PROSPERO

Bravely the figure of this harpy hast thou
Perform'd, my Ariel; a grace it had, devouring:
Of my instruction hast thou nothing bated
In what thou hadst to say: so, with good life
And observation strange, my meaner ministers
Their several kinds have done. My high charms
work,
And these mine enemies are all knit up
In their distractions: they now are in my power;
And in these fits I leave them, while I visit
Young Ferdinand, — whom they suppose is
drown'd,—
And his and mine loved darling. *[Exit above*

GONZALO

I' the name of something holy, sir, why stand you
In this strange stare?

ALONSO

O, it is monstrous, monstrous!
Methought the billows spoke, and told me of it;
The winds did sing it to me; and the thunder,
That deep and dreadful organ-pipe, pronounced
The name of Prosper: it did bass my trespass.
Therefore my son i' th' ooze is bedded; and
I'll seek him deeper than e'er plummet sounded,
And with him there lie mudded. *[Exit*

SEBASTIAN

But one fiend at a time,
I'll fight their legions o'er.

ANTONIO

I'll be thy second.
[Exeunt SEBASTIAN *and* ANTONIO

GONZALO

All three of them are desperate: their great guilt,
Like poison given to work a great time after,
Now 'gins to bite the spirits. I do beseech you,
That are of suppler joints, follow them swiftly,
And hinder them from what this ecstasy
May now provoke them to.

ADRIAN

Follow, I pray you.
[Exeunt

ACT IV

SCENE I. *Before* PROSPERO'S *cell*

Enter PROSPERO, FERDINAND, *and* MIRANDA

PROSPERO

If I have too austerely punish'd you,
Your compensation makes amends; for I
Have given you here a third of mine own life,
Or that for which I live; who once again
I tender to thy hand: all thy vexations
Were but my trials of thy love, and thou
Hast strangely stood the test: here, afore Heaven,
I ratify this my rich gift. O Ferdinand,
Do not smile at me that I boast her off,
For thou shalt find she will outstrip all praise,
And make it halt behind her.

FERDINAND

           I do believe it
Against an oracle.

PROSPERO

Then, as my gift, and thine own acquisition
Worthily purchased, take my daughter: but
If thou dost break her virgin-knot before
All sanctimonious ceremonies may
With full and holy rite be minister'd,
No sweet aspersion shall the heavens let fall
To make this contract grow; but barren hate,
Sour-eyed disdain and discord shall bestrew
The union of your bed with weeds so loathly
That you shall hate it both: therefore take heed,
As Hymen's lamps shall light you.

FERDINAND

           As I hope
For quiet days, fair issue and long life,
With such love as 'tis now, the murkiest den,
The most opportune place, the strong'st suggestion
Our worser Genius can, shall never melt
Mine honour into lust, to take away
The edge of that day's celebration
When I shall think, or Phœbus' steeds are founder'd,
Or Night kept chain'd below.

PROSPERO

           Fairly spoke.
Sit, then, and talk with her; she is thine own.
What, Ariel! my industrious servant, Ariel!

Enter ARIEL

ARIEL

What would my potent master? here I am.

PROSPERO

Thou and thy meaner fellows your last service
Did worthily perform; and I must use you
In such another trick. Go bring the rabble,
O'er whom I give thee power, here to this place:
Incite them to quick motion; for I must
Bestow upon the eyes of this young couple
Some vanity of mine art: it is my promise,
And they expect it from me.

ARIEL

           Presently?

PROSPERO

Ay, with a twink.

ARIEL

Before you can say, 'come,' and 'go,'
And breathe twice, and cry, 'so, so,'
Each one, tripping on his toe,
Will be here with mop and mow.
Do you love me, master? no?

PROSPERO

Dearly, my delicate Ariel. Do not approach
Till thou dost hear me call.

ARIEL

           Well, I conceive.   [*Exit*

PROSPERO

Look thou be true; do not give dalliance
Too much the rein: the strongest oaths are straw
To the fire i' the blood: be more abstemious,
Or else, good night your vow!

FERDINAND

           I warrant you, sir;
The white cold virgin snow upon my heart
Abates the ardour of my liver.

PROSPERO

           Well.
Now come, my Ariel! bring a corollary,
Rather than want a spirit: appear, and pertly!
No tongue! all eyes! be silent.   [*Soft music*

Enter IRIS

IRIS

Ceres, most bounteous lady, thy rich leas
Of wheat, rye, barley, vetches, oats, and pease;
Thy turfy mountains, where live nibbling sheep,
And flat meads thatch'd with stover, them to keep;
Thy banks with pioned and twilled brims,
Which spongy April at thy hest betrims,
To make cold nymphs chaste crowns; and thy broom-groves,
Whose shadow the dismissed bachelor loves,
Being lass-lorn; thy pole-clipt vineyard;
And thy sea-marge, sterile and rocky-hard,
Where thou thyself dost air;—the queen o' the sky,
Whose watery arch and messenger am I,
Bids thee leave these; and with her sovereign grace,
Here on this grass-plot, in this very place,
To come and sport:—her peacocks fly amain:
Approach, rich Ceres, her to entertain.

Enter CERES

CERES

Hail, many-colour'd messenger, that ne'er
Dost disobey the wife of Jupiter;
Who, with they saffron wings, upon my flowers
Diffusest honey-drops, refreshing showers;
And with each end of thy blue bow dost crown
My bosky acres and my unshrubb'd down,
Rich scarf to my proud earth;—why hath thy queen
Summon'd me hither, to this short-grass'd green?

IRIS

A contract of true love to celebrate;
And some donation freely to estate
On the blest lovers.

CERES

           Tell me, heavenly bow,
If Venus or her son, as thou dost know,
Do now attend the queen? Since they did plot
The means that dusky Dis my daughter got,
Her and her blind boy's scandal'd company
I have forsworn.

IRIS

Of her society
Be not afraid: I met her Deity
Cutting the clouds towards Paphos, and her son
Dove-drawn with her. Here thought they to have done
Some wanton charm upon this man and maid,
Whose vows are, that no bed-right shall be paid
Till Hymen's torch be lighted: but in vain;
Mars's hot minion is returned again;
Her waspish-headed son has broke his arrows,
Swears he will shoot no more, but play with sparrows,
And be a boy right out.

CERES

High'st queen of state,
Great Juno, comes; I know her by her gait.

Enter JUNO

JUNO

How does my bounteous sister? Go with me
To bless this twain, that they may prosperous be,
And honour'd in their issue.   [*They sing:*

JUNO

Honour, riches, marriage-blessing,
Long continuance, and increasing,
Hourly joys be still upon you!
Juno sings her blessings on you.

CERES

Earth's increase, foison plenty,
Barns and garners never empty;
Vines with clustering bunches growing;
Plants with goodly burthen bowing;
Spring come to you at the farthest
In the very end of harvest!
Scarcity and want shall shun you;
Ceres' blessing so is on you.

FERDINAND

This is a most majestic vision, and
Harmonious charmingly. May I be bold
To think these spirits?

PROSPERO

Spirits, which by mine art
I have from their confines call'd to enact
My present fancies.

FERDINAND

Let me live here ever;
So rare a wonder'd father and a wise
Makes this place Paradise.

[JUNO *and* CERES *whisper, and send* IRIS *on employment*

PROSPERO

Sweet, now, silence!
Juno and Ceres whisper seriously;
There's something else to do: hush, and be mute,
Or else our spell is marr'd.

IRIS

You nymphs, call'd Naiads, of the windring brooks,
With your sedged crowns and ever-harmless looks,
Leave your crisp channels, and on this green land
Answer your summons; Juno does command:
Come, temperate nymphs, and help to celebrate
A contract of true love; be not too late.

Enter certain NYMPHS

You sunburn'd sicklemen, of August weary,
Come hither from the furrow, and be merry:
Make holiday; your rye-straw hats put on,
And these fresh nymphs encounter every one
In country footing.

Enter certain REAPERS, *properly habited: they join with
the* NYMPHS *in a graceful dance; towards the end whereof*
PROSPERO *starts suddenly, and speaks; after which, to a
strange, hollow, and confused noise, they heavily vanish*

PROSPERO

[*Aside*] I had forgot that foul conspiracy
Of the beast Caliban and his confederates
Against my life: the minute of their plot
Is almost come. [*To the* SPIRITS] Well done! avoid;
no more!

FERDINAND

This is strange: your father's in some passion
That works him strongly.

MIRANDA

Never till this day
Saw I him touch'd with anger so distemper'd.

PROSPERO

You do look, my son, in a moved sort,
As if you were dismay'd: be cheerful, sir.
Our revels now are ended. These our actors,
As I foretold you, were all spirits, and
Are melted into air, into thin air:
And, like the baseless fabric of this vision,
The cloud-capp'd towers, the gorgeous palaces,
The solemn temples, the great globe itself,
Yea, all which it inherit, shall dissolve,
And, like this insubstantial pageant faded,
Leave not a rack behind. We are such stuff
As dreams are made on; and our little life
Is rounded with a sleep. Sir, I am vex'd;
Bear with my weakness; my old brain is troubled:
Be not disturb'd with my infirmity:
If you be pleased, retire into my cell,
And there repose: a turn or two I'll walk,
To still my beating mind.

FERDINAND *and* MIRANDA

We wish your peace.
[*Exeunt*

PROSPERO

Come with a thought. I thank thee, Ariel: come.

Enter ARIEL

ARIEL

Thy thoughts I cleave to. What's thy pleasure?

PROSPERO

Spirit,
We must prepare to meet with Caliban.

ARIEL

Ay, my commander: when I presented Ceres,
I thought to have told thee of it; but I fear'd
Lest I might anger thee.

PROSPERO

Say again, where didst thou leave these varlets?

ARIEL

I told you, sir, they were red-hot with drinking;
So full of valour that they smote the air
For breathing in their faces; beat the ground
For kissing of their feet; yet always bending
Towards their project. Then I beat my tabor;
At which, like unback'd colts, they prick'd their ears,
Advanced their eyelids, lifted up their noses

As they smelt music: so I charm'd their ears,
That, calf-like, they my lowing follow'd through
Tooth'd briers, sharp furzes, pricking goss, and
   thorns,
Which enter'd their frail shins: at last I left them
I' the filthy-mantled pool beyond your cell,
There dancing up to the chins, that the foul lake
O'erstunk their feet.

PROSPERO
          This was well done, my bird.
Thy shape invisible retain thou still:
The trumpery in my house, go bring it hither,
For stale to catch these thieves.

ARIEL
             I go, I go.   [Exit

PROSPERO
A devil, a born devil, on whose nature
Nurture can never stick; on whom my pains,
Humanely taken, all, all lost, quite lost;
And as with age his body uglier grows,
So his mind cankers. I will plague them all,
Even to roaring.
   Re-enter ARIEL, loaden with glistering apparel, &c.
        Come, hang them on this line.

PROSPERO and ARIEL remain, invisible. Enter CALIBAN,
    STEPHANO, and TRINCULO, all wet

CALIBAN
Pray you, tread softly, that the blind mole may not
Hear a foot fall: we now are near his cell.

STEPHANO
Monster, your fairy, which you say is a harmless
fairy, has done little better than played the Jack
with us.

TRINCULO
Monster, I do smell all horse-piss; at which my nose
is in great indignation.

STEPHANO
So is mine. Do you hear, monster? If I should take a
displeasure against you, look you,—

TRINCULO
Thou wert but a lost monster.

CALIBAN
Good my lord, give me thy favour still.
Be patient, for the prize I'll bring thee to
Shall hoodwink this mischance: therefore speak
   softly.
All's hush'd as midnight yet.

TRINCULO
Ay, but to lose our bottles in the pool,—

STEPHANO
There is not only disgrace and dishonour in that,
monster, but an infinite loss.

TRINCULO
That's more to me than my wetting: yet this is your
harmless fairy, monster.

STEPHANO
I will fetch off my bottle, though I be o'er ears for
my labour.

CALIBAN
Prithee, my king, be quiet. See'st thou here,

This is the mouth o' the cell: no noise, and enter.
Do that good mischief which may make this island
Thine own for ever, and I, thy Caliban,
For aye thy foot-licker.

STEPHANO
Give me thy hand. I do begin to have bloody
thoughts.

TRINCULO
O King Stephano! O peer! O worthy Stephano!
look what a wardrobe here is for thee!

CALIBAN
Let it alone, thou fool; it is but trash.

TRINCULO
O, ho, monster! we know what belongs to a frippery.
O King Stephano!

STEPHANO
Put off that gown, Trinculo; by this hand, I'll have
that gown.

TRINCULO
Thy Grace shall have it.

CALIBAN
The dropsy drown this fool! what do you mean
To dote thus on such luggage? Let's alone,
And do the murder first: if he awake,
From toe to crown he'll fill our skins with pinches,
Make us strange stuff.

STEPHANO
Be you quiet, monster. Mistress line, is not this my
jerkin? Now is the jerkin under the line: now, jerkin,
you are like to lose your hair, and prove a bald
jerkin.

TRINCULO
Do, do: we steal by line and level, an't like your
Grace.

STEPHANO
I thank thee for that jest; here's a garment for't: wit
shall not go unrewarded while I am king of this
country. 'Steal by line and level' is an excellent pass
of pate; there's another garment for't.

TRINCULO
Monster, come, put some lime upon your fingers,
and away with the rest.

CALIBAN
I will have none on't: we shall lose our time,
And all be turn'd to barnacles, or to apes
With foreheads villanous low.

STEPHANO
Monster, lay-to your fingers: help to bear this away
where my hogshead of wine is, or I'll turn you out of
my kingdom: go to, carry this.

TRINCULO
And this.

STEPHANO
Ay, and this.
A noise of hunters heard. Enter divers SPIRITS, in shape of
dogs and hounds, hunting them about; PROSPERO and
       ARIEL setting them on

PROSPERO
Hey, Mountain, hey!

ARIEL

Silver! there it goes, Silver!

PROSPERO

Fury, Fury! there, Tyrant, there! hark, hark!

[CALIBAN, STEPHANO, *and* TRINCULO *are driven out*

Go charge my goblins that they grind their joints

With dry convulsions; shorten up their sinews

With aged cramps; and more pinch-spotted make them

Than pard or cat o' mountain.

ARIEL

Hark, they roar!

PROSPERO

Let them be hunted soundly. At this hour

Lie at my mercy all mine enemies:

Shortly shall all my labours end, and thou

Shalt have the air at freedom: for a little

Follow, and do me service.   [*Exeunt*

ACT V

SCENE I. *Before the cell of* PROSPERO

Enter PROSPERO *in his magic robes, and* ARIEL

PROSPERO

Now does my project gather to a head:

My charms crack not; my spirits obey; and time

Goes upright with his carriage. How's the day?

ARIEL

On the sixth hour; at which time, my lord,

You said our work should cease.

PROSPERO

I did say so,

When first I raised the tempest. Say, my spirit,

How fares the king and's followers?

ARIEL

Confined together

In the same fashion as you gave in charge,

Just as you left them; all prisoners, sir,

In the line-grove which weather-fends your cell;

They cannot budge till your release. The king,

His brother, and yours, abide all three distracted,

And the remainder mourning over them,

Brimful of sorrow and dismay; but chiefly

Him that you term'd, sir, 'The good old lord, Gonzalo;'

His tears run down his beard, like winter's drops

From eaves of reeds. Your charm so strongly works 'em,

That if you now beheld them, your affections

Would become tender.

PROSPERO

Dost thou think so, spirit?

ARIEL

Mine would, sir, were I human.

PROSPERO

And mine shall.

Hast thou, which art but air, a touch, a feeling

Of their afflictions, and shall not myself,

One of their kind, that relish all as sharply,

Passion as they, be kindlier moved than thou art?

Though with their high wrongs I am struck to the quick,

Yet with my nobler reason 'gainst my fury

Do I take part: the rarer action is

In virtue than in vengeance: they being penitent,

The sole drift of my purpose doth extend

Not a frown further. Go release them, Ariel:

My charms I'll break, their senses I'll restore,

And they shall be themselves.

ARIEL

I'll fetch them, sir.

[*Exit*

PROSPERO

Ye elves of hills, brooks, standing lakes, and groves;

And ye that on the sands with printless foot

Do chase the ebbing Neptune, and do fly him

When he comes back; you demi-puppets that

By moonshine do the green sour ringlets make,

Whereof the ewe not bites; and you whose pastime

Is to make midnight mushrooms, that rejoice

To hear the solemn curfew; by whose aid—

Weak masters though ye be—I have bedimm'd

The noontide sun, call'd forth the mutinous winds,

And 'twixt the green sea and the azured vault

Set roaring war: to the dread rattling thunder

Have I given fire, and rifted Jove's stout oak

With his own bolt; the strong-based promontory

Have I made shake, and by the spurs pluck'd up

The pine and cedar: graves at my command

Have waked their sleepers, oped, and let 'em forth

By my so potent art. But this rough magic

I here abjure; and, when I have required

Some heavenly music,—which even now I do,—

To work mine end upon their senses, that

This airy charm is for, I'll break my staff,

Bury it certain fathoms in the earth,

And deeper than did ever plummet sound

I'll drown my book.   [*Solemn music*

Re-enter ARIEL *before: then* ALONSO, *with a frantic gesture, attended by* GONZALO; SEBASTIAN *and* ANTONIO *in like manner, attended by* ADRIAN *and* FRANCISCO: *they all enter the circle which* PROSPERO *had made, and there stand charmed; which* PROSPERO *observing, speaks:*

A solemn air, and the best comforter

To an unsettled fancy, cure thy brains,

Now useless, boil'd within thy skull! There stand,

For you are spell-stopp'd.

Holy Gonzalo, honourable man,

Mine eyes, even sociable to the show of thine,

Fall fellowly drops. The charm dissolves apace;

And as the morning steals upon the night,

Melting the darkness, so their rising senses

Begin to chase the ignorant fumes that mantle

Their clearer reason. O good Gonzalo,

My true preserver, and a loyal sir

To him thou follow'st! I will pay thy graces

Home both in word and deed. Most cruelly

Didst thou, Alonso, use me and my daughter:
Thy brother was a furtherer in the act.
Thou art pinch'd for't now, Sebastian. Flesh and
  blood,
You, brother mine, that entertain'd ambition,
Expell'd remorse and nature; who, with Sebastian,—
Whose inward pinches therefore are most strong,—
Would here have kill'd your king; I do forgive thee,
Unnatural though thou art. Their understanding
Begins to swell; and the approaching tide
Will shortly fill the reasonable shore,
That now lies foul and muddy. Not one of them
That yet looks on me, or would know me: Ariel,
Fetch me the hat and rapier in my cell:
I will discase me, and myself present
As I was sometime Milan: quickly, spirit;
Thou shalt ere long be free.

      ARIEL *sings and helps to attire him*
      Where the bee sucks, there suck I:
      In a cowslip's bell I lie;
      There I couch when owls do cry.
      On the bat's back I do fly
      After summer merrily.
      Merrily, merrily shall I live now
      Under the blossom that hangs on the bough.

      PROSPERO
Why, that's my dainty Ariel! I shall miss thee;
But yet thou shalt have freedom: so, so, so.
To the king's ship, invisible as thou art:
There shalt thou find the mariners asleep
Under the hatches; the master and the boatswain
Being awake, enforce them to this place,
And presently, I prithee.

      ARIEL
I drink the air before me, and return
Or ere your pulse twice beat.   [*Exit*

      GONZALO
All torment, trouble, wonder and amazement
Inhabits here: some heavenly power guide us
Out of this fearful country!

      PROSPERO
      Behold, sir king,
The wronged Duke of Milan, Prospero:
For more assurance that a living prince
Does now speak to thee, I embrace thy body;
And to thee and thy company I bid
A hearty welcome.

      ALONSO
      Whether thou be'st he or no,
Or some enchanted trifle to abuse me,
As late I have been, I not know: thy pulse
Beats, as of flesh and blood; and, since I saw thee,
The affliction of my mind amends, with which,
I fear, a madness held me: this must crave—
An if this be at all—a most strange story.
Thy dukedom I resign, and do entreat
Thou pardon me my wrongs.—But how should
  Prospero
Be living and be here?

      PROSPERO
      First, noble friend,
Let me embrace thine age, whose honour cannot
Be measured or confined.

      GONZALO
      Whether this be
Or be not, I'll not swear.

      PROSPERO
      You do yet taste
Some subtilties o' the isle, that will not let you
Believe things certain. Welcome, my friends all!
[*Aside to* SEBASTIAN *and* ANTONIO] But you, my brace
  of lords, were I so minded,
I here could pluck his Highness' frown upon you,
And justify you traitors: at this time
I will tell no tales.

      SEBASTIAN
[*Aside*] The devil speaks in him.

      PROSPERO
      No.
For you, most wicked sir, whom to call brother
Would even infect my mouth, I do forgive
Thy rankest fault,—all of them; and require
My dukedom of thee, which perforce, I know,
Thou must restore.

      ALONSO
      If thou be'st Prospero,
Give us particulars of thy preservation;
How thou hast met us here, who three hours since
Were wreck'd upon this shore; where I have lost—
How sharp the point of this remembrance is!—
My dear son Ferdinand.

      PROSPERO
      I am woe for't, sir.

      ALONSO
Irreparable is the loss; and patience
Says it is past her cure.

      PROSPERO
      I rather think
You have not sought her help, of whose soft grace
For the like loss I have her sovereign aid,
And rest myself content.

      ALONSO
      You the like loss!

      PROSPERO
As great to me as late; and, supportable
To make the dear loss, have I means much weaker
Than you may call to comfort you, for I
Have lost my daughter.

      ALONSO
      A daughter?
O heavens, that they were living both in Naples,
The king and queen there! that they were, I wish
Myself were mudded in that oozy bed
Where my son lies. When did you lose your daughter?

      PROSPERO
In this last tempest. I perceive, these lords
At this encounter do so much admire,
That they devour their reason, and scarce think
Their eyes do offices of truth, their words

Are natural breath: but, howsoe'er you have
Been justled from your senses, know for certain
That I am Prospero, and that very duke
Which was thrust forth of Milan; who most strangely
Upon this shore, where you were wreck'd, was
 landed,
To be the lord on't. No more yet of this;
For 'tis a chronicle of day by day,
Not a relation for a breakfast, nor
Befitting this first meeting. Welcome, sir;
This cell's my court: here have I few attendants,
And subjects none abroad: pray you, look in.
My dukedom since you have given me again,
I will requite you with as good a thing;
At least bring forth a wonder, to content ye
As much as me my dukedom.

Here PROSPERO *discovers* FERDINAND *and* MIRANDA
playing at chess

MIRANDA
Sweet lord, you play me false.

FERDINAND
     No, my dear'st love,
I would not for the world.

MIRANDA
Yes, for a score of kingdoms you should wrangle,
And I would call it fair play.

ALONSO
     If this prove
A vision of the island, one dear son
Shall I twice lose.

SEBASTIAN
    A most high miracle!

FERDINAND
'Though the seas threaten, they are merciful;
I have cursed them without cause.   [*Kneels*

ALONSO
     Now all the blessings
Of a glad father compass thee about!
Arise, and say how thou camest here.

MIRANDA
     O, wonder!
How many goodly creatures are there here!
How beauteous mankind is! O brave new world,
That has such people in't!

PROSPERO
    'Tis new to thee.

ALONSO
What is this maid with whom thou wast at play?
Your eld'st acquaintance cannot be three hours:
Is she the goddess that hath sever'd us,
And brought us thus together?

FERDINAND
     Sir, she is mortal;
But by immortal Providence she's mine:
I chose her when I could not ask my father
For his advice, nor thought I had one. She
Is daughter to this famous Duke of Milan,
Of whom so often I have heard renown,
But never saw before; of whom I have

Received a second life; and second father
This lady makes him to me.

ALONSO
     I am hers:
But, O, how oddly will it sound that I
Must ask my child forgiveness!

PROSPERO
     There, sir, stop:
Let us not burthen our remembrances with
A heaviness that's gone.

GONZALO
     I have inly wept,
Or should have spoke ere this. Look down, you gods,
And on this couple drop a blessed crown!
For it is you that have chalk'd forth the way
Which brought us hither.

ALONSO
     I say, Amen, Gonzalo!

GONZALO
Was Milan thrust from Milan, that his issue
Should become kings of Naples? O, rejoice
Beyond a common joy! and set it down
With gold on lasting pillars: In one voyage
Did Claribel her husband find at Tunis,
And Ferdinand, her brother, found a wife
Where he himself was lost, Prospero his dukedom
In a poor isle, and all of us ourselves
When no man was his own.

ALONSO
[*To* FERDINAND *and* MIRANDA] Give me your hands:
Let grief and sorrow still embrace his heart
That doth not wish you joy!

GONZALO
     Be it so! Amen!

Re-enter ARIEL, *with the* MASTER *and* BOATSWAIN
amazedly following

O, look, sir, look, sir! here is more of us:
I prophesied, if a gallows were on land,
This fellow could not drown. Now, blasphemy,
That swear'st grace o'erboard, not an oath on shore?
Hast thou no mouth by land? What is the news?

BOATSWAIN
The best news is, that we have safely found
Our king and company; the next, our ship—
Which, but three glasses since, we gave out split—
Is tight and yare and bravely rigg'd, as when
We first put out to sea.

ARIEL
[*Aside to* PROSPERO] Sir, all this service
Have I done since I went.

PROSPERO
[*Aside to* ARIEL] My tricksy spirit!

ALONSO
These are not natural events; they strengthen
From strange to stranger. Say, how came you hither?

BOATSWAIN
If I did think, sir, I were well awake,
I'ld strive to tell you. We were dead of sleep,
And—how we know not—all clapp'd under hatches;
Where, but even now, with strange and several noises

Of roaring, shrieking, howling, jingling chains,
And mo diversity of sounds, all horrible,
We were awaked; straightway, at liberty;
Where we, in all her trim, freshly beheld
Our royal, good, and gallant ship; our master
Capering to eye her:—on a trice, so please you,
Even in a dream, were we divided from them,
And were brought moping hither.

ARIEL

[Aside to PROSPERO] Was't well done?

PROSPERO

[Aside to ARIEL] Bravely, my diligence. Thou shalt
be free.

ALONSO

This is as strange a maze as e'er men trod;
And there is in this business more than nature
Was ever conduct of: some oracle
Must rectify our knowledge.

PROSPERO

Sir, my liege,
Do not infest your mind with beating on
The strangeness of this business; at pick'd leisure
Which shall be shortly, single I'll resolve you,
Which to you shall seem probable, of every
These happen'd accidents; till when, be cheerful,
And think of each thing well. [Aside to ARIEL] Come
hither, spirit:
Set Caliban and his companions free;
Untie the spell. [Exit ARIEL] How fares my gracious
sir?
There are yet missing of your company
Some few odd lads that you remember not.

Re-enter ARIEL, driving in CALIBAN, STEPHANO, and
TRINCULO, in their stolen apparel

STEPHANO

Every man shift for all the rest, and let no man take
care for himself; for all is but fortune.—Coragio,
bully-monster, coragio!

TRINCULO

If these be true spies which I wear in my head,
here's a goodly sight.

CALIBAN

O Setebos, these be brave spirits indeed!
How fine my master is! I am afraid
He will chastise me.

SEBASTIAN

Ha, ha!
What things are these, my lord Antonio?
Will money buy 'em?

ANTONIO

Very like; one of them
Is a plain fish, and, no doubt, marketable.

PROSPERO

Mark but the badges of these men, my lords,
Then say if they be true. This mis-shapen knave,
His mother was a witch; and one so strong
That could control the moon, make flows and ebbs,
And deal in her command, without her power.
These three have robb'd me; and this demi-devil—
For he's a bastard one—had plotted with them

To take my life. Two of these fellows you
Must know and own; this thing of darkness I
Acknowledge mine.

CALIBAN

I shall be pinch'd to death.

ALONSO

Is not this Stephano, my drunken butler?

SEBASTIAN

He is drunk now: where had he wine?

ALONSO

And Trinculo is reeling ripe: where should they
Find this grand liquor that hath gilded 'em?—
How camest thou in this pickle?

TRINCULO

I have been in such a pickle, since I saw you last,
that, I fear me, will never out of my bones: I shall
not fear fly-blowing.

SEBASTIAN

Why, how now, Stephano!

STEPHANO

O, touch me not;—I am not Stephano, but a cramp.

PROSPERO

You'ld be king o' the isle, sirrah?

STEPHANO

I should have been a sore one, then.

ALONSO

This is a strange thing as e'er I look'd on.
[Pointing to CALIBAN

PROSPERO

He is as disproportion'd in his manners
As in his shape. Go, sirrah, to my cell;
Take with you your companions; as you look
To have my pardon, trim it handsomely.

CALIBAN

Ay, that I will; and I'll be wise hereafter,
And seek for grace. What a thrice-double ass
Was I, to take this drunkard for a god,
And worship this dull fool!

PROSPERO

Go to; away!

ALONSO

Hence, and bestow your luggage where you found it.

SEBASTIAN

Or stole it, rather.
[Exeunt CALIBAN, STEPHANO, and TRINCULO

PROSPERO

Sir, I invite your Highness and your train
To my poor cell, where you shall take your rest
For this one night; which, part of it, I'll waste
With such discourse as, I not doubt, shall make it
Go quick away: the story of my life,
And the particular accidents gone by
Since I came to this isle: and in the morn
I'll bring you to your ship, and so to Naples,
Where I have hope to see the nuptial
Of these our dear-beloved solemnized;
And thence retire me to my Milan, where
Every third thought shall be my grave.

ALONSO

I long

[1324]

To hear the story of your life, which must
Take the ear strangely.

PROSPERO

               I'll deliver all;
And promise you calm seas, auspicious gales,
And sail so expeditious, that shall catch
Your royal fleet far off. [*Aside to* ARIEL] My Ariel,
   chick,
That is thy charge: then to the elements
Be free, and fare thou well! Please you, draw near.
                        [*Exeunt*

EPILOGUE

SPOKEN BY PROSPERO

Now my charms are all o'erthrown,
And what strength I have's mine own,

Which is most faint: now, 'tis true,
I must be here confined by you,
Or sent to Naples. Let me not,
Since I have my dukedom got,
And pardon'd the deceiver, dwell
In this bare island by your spell;
But release me from my bands
With the help of your good hands:
Gentle breath of yours my sails
Must fill, or else my project fails,
Which was to please. Now I want
Spirits to enforce, art to enchant;
And my ending is despair,
Unless I be relieved by prayer,
Which pierces so, that it assaults
Mercy itself, and frees all faults.
As you from crimes would pardon'd be,
Let your indulgence set me free.

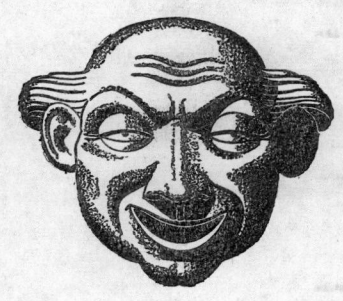

THE FAMOUS HISTORY OF THE LIFE OF KING HENRY VIII

SYNOPSIS

THE gorgeous splendor and pageantry of the peace meeting between King Henry and the French King at the Field of the Cloth of Gold in France soon becomes only a glowing memory, and in a short time astute English statesmen are discussing in London the futility and inordinate cost of the impressive spectacle, and pointing out the growing power of its sponsor, the arrogant ambitious Wolsey, Cardinal of York and Lord Chancellor of England.

Already rumors come of the seizure of English merchantmen by the French, and the powerful Duke of Buckingham, Wolsey's avowed enemy, hears of the Cardinal's treacherous connivance with the Emperor Charles V to alter the feared French-English treaty without Henry's knowledge, provided the way is well paved with gold for Wolsey's own pocket. Against the advice of friends, the honest Buckingham is on the point of exposing the Cardinal to the King when he is arrested with his son-in-law, Lord Abergavenny, for high treason. The good Queen Katharine happens to come to Henry at this moment to protest against some of Wolsey's unjust taxes which are causing bitter suffering and discord among the King's subjects, and, with a sharp rebuke to the Cardinal, Henry orders the repeal of the laws and pardons all resisters, the wily churchman contriving, however, to get full credit to himself for the King's clemency. Graciously invited by the King, Katharine remains for the hearing of the charges against Buckingham, for whom she has also interceded, and points out that the principal witness against the Duke is his late surveyor who was dismissed upon the complaints of tenants. Henry's mind, however, is completely obsessed by the details of the evidence produced by Wolsey's bribed followers, particularly the elaborated story of Buckingham's intention to gain the crown even at the cost of the King's life.

The Earl of Surrey, the Duke's son-in-law, is transferred by Wolsey to Ireland to prevent him from helping his father, and the weight of the trumped-up evidence proves sufficient to secure Buckingham's conviction, in spite of the love and esteem in which he is held by the Commons, and he is ordered to execution. The Cardinal's dislike of Queen Katharine having increased with the refusal of her nephew, the Emperor, to appoint him to the archbishopric of Toledo, generally regarded as the stepping-stone to the papacy, he insinuates to Henry that his marriage twenty years ago to Katharine, the widow of his brother Arthur, is illegal, and secretly plans the King's divorce and re-marriage to the Duchess of Alençon, the French King's sister.

Meanwhile, however, at a great banquet and masked ball given by Cardinal Wolsey at his palace, York Place, the King meets and falls in love with the fair young Anne Bullen, one of the

Queen's gentlewomen and daughter of Sir Thomas Bullen, creates her Marchioness of Pembroke, and immediately takes up the Cardinal's suggestion of nice scruples over the validity of his marriage to his brother's widow. Summoned to public trial for divorce, with Wolsey and a papal legate as judges, the Queen affirms her fidelity as a wife and asks for proceedings to be delayed until ratification of her marriage may be received from her native Spain. The King does not help her, and, naming Wolsey as the instigator of the divorce, she appeals over his head to Rome and sweeps from the court.

Wolsey, publicly exonerated by Henry of Katharine's accusation, is dismayed to learn that the King intends marrying the protestant Anne Bullen, sends a message to Rome to delay the divorce, and secretly offers his aid to the Queen. But the letter to Rome is miscarried and reaches Henry's hands together with an inventory of the Cardinal's vast wealth which he has prepared to show the authorities of the Church his desirability as the next pope. Forced to yield all his possessions to the Crown, Wolsey is dismissed from the court, and later, a sick repentant man, is arrested for high treason, but dies on his way to London at an abbey in Leicester.

Cranmer, the Archbishop of Canterbury, is persuaded by the King to annul his marriage to Katharine, and Anne Bullen, already secretly married to Henry, is crowned Queen of England. Katharine dies, forgiving her enemies and commending to the King's mercy her daughter Mary and her faithful attendants.

A certain group of noblemen who are suspicious of Cranmer's influence with the King accuse him of introducing heresies into the teachings of the Church, but Henry, although consenting to his trial, is satisfied of the Archbishop's integrity and presents him with a ring of authority with which to protect himself. Watching from a place of vantage, the King sees the patient churchman being kept waiting in an anteroom with lackeys and footmen and treated with other indignities, and interrupting the council, formally censures the noblemen, commands them to treat the Archbishop with friendliness, and confers upon him the special favor of standing as godfather at the baptism of the newly-born Princess Elizabeth.

HISTORICAL DATA

The chief historical basis for the play is Holinshed's *Chronicles*, although some details seem to have come direct from Halle's *Union of the Families of Lancaster and Yorke* (1548). Some details may have been suggested by Samuel Rowley's *When you see me you know me* (1605), and perhaps Shakespeare borrowed somewhat from *The Life of Wolsey* by George Cavendish. The fifth act seems to have been based largely on Foxe's *Actes and Monuments*, better known as *The Book of Martyrs* (1563). An almost literal transcription of much of the actual diction from prose to verse form is evident in the first three scenes of this act.

There has been some controversy as to the authenticity of this play as a work of Shakespeare. Not only is there a striking lack of unity in the play itself, but there are obvious variations of style and workmanship that give rise to the belief that it was in any case the product of more than one author. It is generally conceded that John Fletcher is probably responsible for a considerable portion of the play. Some extremists have tried to divorce it altogether from the list of Shakespeare's works, but its unchallenged appearance in the First Folio denies support of so radical a view.

The Globe Theatre on June 29, 1613, caught fire and was burned down. The then current production was a play called *Henry VIII or All is True*. There seems little doubt that this was the present play. It was referred to at that time in contemporary comment as "a new play." It is difficult to conjecture exactly how long prior to this date Shakespeare may have written the play, but it is obviously in his later manner. Certain allusions to King James and the settlements in Virginia (Act V, Scene v) lend color to the theory that it may have been written as late as 1612. In any event, it is in all probability the last of Shakespeare's extant work.

It was first printed in the First Folio in 1623.

"*Sweet partner,*
I must not yet forsake you."
HENRY VIII

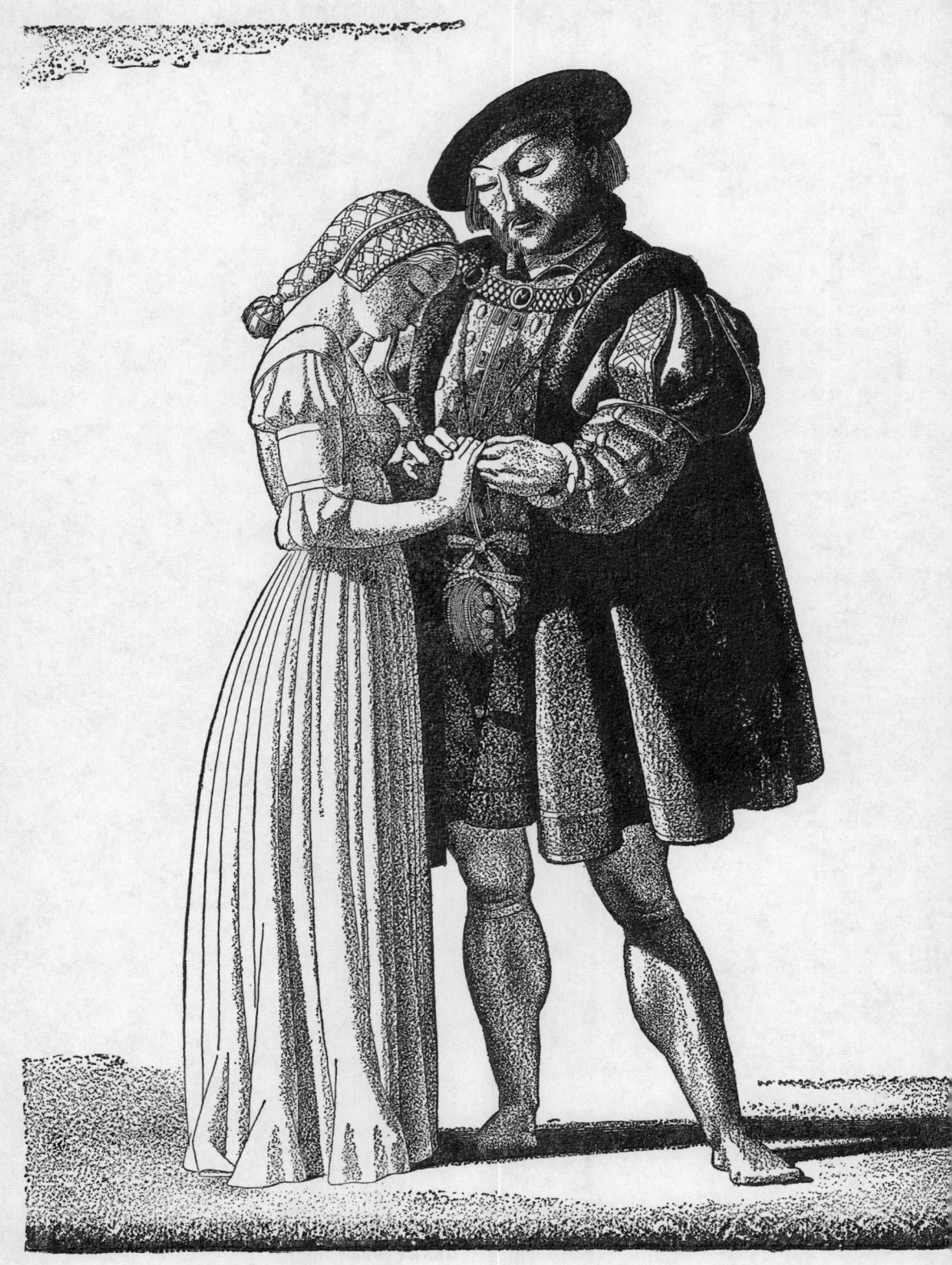

THE FAMOUS HISTORY OF
THE LIFE OF KING HENRY VIII

DRAMATIS PERSONÆ

KING HENRY *the Eighth*.
CARDINAL WOLSEY.
CARDINAL CAMPEIUS.
CAPUCIUS, *Ambassador from the Emperor Charles V.*
CRANMER, *Archbishop of Canterbury*.
DUKE OF NORFOLK.
DUKE OF BUCKINGHAM.
DUKE OF SUFFOLK.
EARL OF SURREY.
LORD CHAMBERLAIN.
LORD CHANCELLOR.
GARDINER, *Bishop of Winchester*.
BISHOP *of Lincoln*.
LORD ABERGAVENNY.
LORD SANDS.
SIR HENRY GUILDFORD.
SIR THOMAS LOVELL.
SIR ANTHONY DENNY.
SIR NICHOLAS VAUX.
SECRETARIES *to Wolsey*.
CROMWELL, *Servant to Wolsey*.
GRIFFITH, *Gentleman-usher to Queen Katharine*.
THREE GENTLEMEN.

DOCTOR BUTTS, *Physician to the King*.
GARTER *King-at-Arms*.
SURVEYOR *to the Duke of Buckingham*.
BRANDON.
SERGEANT-AT-ARMS.

DOOR-KEEPER *of the Council-chamber*.
PORTER, *and his* MAN.
PAGE *to Gardiner*.
A CRIER.

QUEEN KATHARINE, *wife to King Henry, after-wards divorced*.
ANNE BULLEN, *her Maid of Honour, afterwards Queen*.
AN OLD LADY, *friend to Anne Bullen*.
PATIENCE, *woman to Queen Katharine*.

Several LORDS *and* LADIES *in the Dumb Shows;* WOMEN *attending upon the* QUEEN; SCRIBES, OFFICERS, GUARDS, *and other* ATTENDANTS

SPIRITS.

SCENE—*London; Westminster; Kimbolton*.

THE PROLOGUE

I COME no more to make you laugh: things now,
That bear a weighty and a serious brow,
Sad, high and working, full of state and woe,
Such noble scenes as draw the eye to flow,
We now present. Those that can pity, here
May, if they think it well, let fall a tear;
The subject will deserve it. Such as give
Their money out of hope they may believe,
May here find truth too. Those that come to see
Only a show or two, and so agree
The play may pass, if they be still and willing,
I'll undertake may see away their shilling
Richly in two short hours. Only they
That come to hear a merry bawdy play,
A noise of targets, or to see a fellow
In a long motley coat guarded with yellow,
Will be deceived; for, gentle hearers, know,
To rank our chosen truth with such a show
As fool and fight is, beside forfeiting
Our own brains and the opinion that we bring
To make that only true we now intend,
Will leave us never an understanding friend.
Therefore, for goodness' sake, and as you are known
The first and happiest hearers of the town,
Be sad, as we would make ye: think ye see
The very persons of our noble story

As they were living; think you see them great,
And follow'd with the general throng and sweat
Of thousand friends; then, in a moment, see
How soon this mightiness meets misery:
And if you can be merry then, I'll say
A man may weep upon his wedding-day.

ACT I

SCENE I. *London. An ante-chamber in the palace*

Enter the DUKE OF NORFOLK *at one door; at the other, the* DUKE OF BUCKINGHAM *and the* LORD ABERGAVENNY

BUCKINGHAM
Good morrow, and well met. How have ye done
Since last we saw in France?

NORFOLK
              I thank your grace,
Healthful, and ever since a fresh admirer
Of what I saw there.

BUCKINGHAM
             An untimely ague
Stay'd me a prisoner in my chamber, when
Those suns of glory, those two lights of men,
Met in the vale of Andren.

NORFOLK
             'Twixt Guynes and Arde:

I was then present, saw them salute on horseback;
Beheld them, when they 'lighted, how they clung
In their embracement, as they grew together;
Which had they, what four throned ones could have
　weigh'd
Such a compounded one?

BUCKINGHAM
　　　　　All the whole time
I was my chamber's prisoner.

NORFOLK
　　　　　Then you lost
The view of earthly glory: men might say,
Till this time pomp was single, but now married
To one above itself. Each following day
Became the next day's master, till the last
Made former wonders its. To-day the French,
All clinquant, all in gold, like heathen gods,
Shone down the English; and to-morrow they
Made Britain India: every man that stood
Show'd like a mine. Their dwarfish pages were
As cherubins, all gilt: the madams too,
Not used to toil, did almost sweat to bear
The pride upon them, that their very labour
Was to them as a painting: now this masque
Was cried incomparable; and the ensuing night
Made it a fool and beggar. The two kings,
Equal in lustre, were now best, now worst,
As presence did present them; him in eye
Still him in praise; and being present both,
'Twas said they saw but one, and no discerner
Durst wag his tongue in censure. When these suns—
For so they phrase 'em—by their heralds challenged
The noble spirits to arms, they did perform
Beyond thought's compass; that former fabulous
　story,
Being now seen possible enough, got credit,
That Bevis was believed.

BUCKINGHAM
　　　　　O, you go far.

NORFOLK
As I belong to worship, and affect
In honour honesty, the tract of every thing
Would by a good discourser lose some life,
Which action's self was tongue to. All was royal;
To the disposing of it nought rebell'd;
Order gave each thing view; the office did
Distinctly his full function.

BUCKINGHAM
　　　　　Who did guide,
I mean, who set the body and the limbs
Of this great sport together, as you guess?

NORFOLK
One, certes, that promises no element
In such a business.

BUCKINGHAM
　　　　　I pray you, who, my lord?

NORFOLK
All this was order'd by the good discretion
Of the right reverend Cardinal of York.

BUCKINGHAM
The devil speed him! no man's pie is freed
From his ambitious finger. What had he
To do in these fierce vanities? I wonder
That such a keech can with his very bulk
Take up the rays o' the beneficial sun,
And keep it from the earth.

NORFOLK
　　　　　Surely, sir,
There's in him stuff that puts him to these ends;
For, being not propp'd by ancestry, whose grace
Chalks successors their way, nor call'd upon
For high feats done to the crown; neither allied
To eminent assistants; but, spider-like,
Out of his self-drawing web, he gives us note,
The force of his own merit makes his way;
A gift that heaven gives for him, which buys
A place next to the king.

ABERGAVENNY
　　　　　I cannot tell
What heaven hath given him; let some graver eye
Pierce into that; but I can see his pride
Peep through each part of him: whence has he that?
If not from hell, the devil is a niggard,
Or has given all before, and he begins
A new hell in himself.

BUCKINGHAM
　　　　　Why, the devil,
Upon this French going out, took he upon him,
Without the privity o' the king, to appoint
Who should attend on him? He makes up the file
Of all the gentry; for the most part such
To whom as great a charge as little honour
He meant to lay upon: and his own letter,
The honourable board of council out,
Must fetch him in he papers.

ABERGAVENNY
　　　　　I do know
Kinsmen of mine, three at the least, that have
By this so sicken'd their estates that never
They shall abound as formerly.

BUCKINGHAM
　　　　　O, many
Have broke their backs with laying manors on 'em
For this great journey. What did this vanity
But minister communication of
A most poor issue?

NORFOLK
　　　　　Grievingly I think,
The peace between the French and us not values
The cost that did conclude it.

BUCKINGHAM
　　　　　Every man,
After the hideous storm that follow'd, was
A thing inspired, and not consulting broke
Into a general prophecy: That this tempest,
Dashing the garment of this peace, aboded
The sudden breach on 't.

NORFOLK
　　　　　Which is budded out;

For France hath flaw'd the league, and hath attach'd
Our merchants' goods at Bourdeaux.

ABERGAVENNY

                   Is it therefore
The ambassador is silenced?

NORFOLK

               Marry, is 't.

ABERGAVENNY

A proper title of a peace, and purchased
At a superfluous rate!

BUCKINGHAM

            Why, all this business
Our reverend cardinal carried.

NORFOLK

               Like it your grace,
The state takes notice of the private difference
Betwixt you and the cardinal. I advise you—
And take it from a heart that wishes towards you
Honour and plenteous safety—that you read
The cardinal's malice and his potency
Together; to consider further that
What his high hatred would effect wants not
A minister in his power. You know his nature,
That he's revengeful, and I know his sword
Hath a sharp edge; it's long and 't may be said
It reaches far, and where 'twill not extend,
Thither he darts it. Bosom up my counsel;
You'll find it wholesome. Lo, where comes that rock
That I advise your shunning.

Enter CARDINAL WOLSEY, *the purse borne before him, certain of the* GUARD, *and two* SECRETARIES *with papers.*
The CARDINAL *in his passage fixeth his eye on* BUCKINGHAM, *and* BUCKINGHAM *on him, both full of disdain*

WOLSEY

The Duke of Buckingham's surveyor, ha?
Where's his examination?

FIRST SECRETARY

            Here, so please you.

WOLSEY

Is he in person ready?

FIRST SECRETARY

          Ay, please your grace.

WOLSEY

Well, we shall then know more; and Buckingham
Shall lessen this big look.

            [*Exeunt* WOLSEY *and his train*

BUCKINGHAM

This butcher's cur is venom-mouth'd, and I
Have not the power to muzzle him; therefore best
Not wake him in his slumber. A beggar's book
Outworths a noble's blood.

NORFOLK

           What, are you chafed?
Ask God for temperance; that's the appliance only
Which your disease requires.

BUCKINGHAM

            I read in 's looks
Matter against me, and his eye reviled
Me as his abject object: at this instant

He bores me with some trick: he's gone to the king;
I'll follow and outstare him.

NORFOLK

              Stay, my lord,
And let your reason with your choler question
What 'tis you go about: to climb steep hills
Requires slow pace at first: anger is like
A full-hot horse, who being allow'd his way,
Self-mettle tires him. Not a man in England
Can advise me like you: be to yourself
As you would to your friend.

BUCKINGHAM

            I'll to the king;
And from a mouth of honour quite cry down
This Ipswich fellow's insolence, or proclaim
There's difference in no persons.

NORFOLK

              Be advised;
Heat not a furnace for your foe so hot
That it do singe yourself: we may outrun,
By violent swiftness, that which we run at,
And lose by over-running. Know you not,
The fire that mounts the liquor till 't run o'er
In seeming to augment it wastes it? Be advised:
I say again, there is no English soul
More stronger to direct you than yourself,
If with the sap of reason you would quench,
Or but allay, the fire of passion.

BUCKINGHAM

              Sir,
I am thankful to you; and I'll go along
By your prescription: but this top-proud fellow—
Whom from the flow of gall I name not, but
From sincere motions—by intelligence
And proofs as clear as founts in July when
We see each grain of gravel, I do know
To be corrupt and treasonous.

NORFOLK

           Say not 'treasonous.'

BUCKINGHAM

To the king I'll say 't; and make my vouch as strong
As shore of rock. Attend. This holy fox,
Or wolf, or both—for he is equal ravenous
As he is subtle, and as prone to mischief
As able to perform 't; his mind and place
Infecting one another, yea, reciprocally—
Only to show his pomp as well in France
As here at home, suggests the king our master
To this last costly treaty, the interview,
That swallow'd so much treasure, and like a glass
Did break i' the rinsing.

NORFOLK

           Faith, and so it did.

BUCKINGHAM

Pray, give me favour, sir. This cunning cardinal
The articles o' the combination drew
As himself pleased; and they were ratified
As he cried 'Thus let be,' to as much end
As give a crutch to the dead: but our count-cardinal
Has done this, and 'tis well; for worthy Wolsey,

Who cannot err, he did it. Now this follows—
Which, as I take it, is a kind of puppy
To the old dam, treason—Charles the emperor,
Under pretence to see the queen his aunt—
For 'twas indeed his colour, but he came
To whisper Wolsey—here makes visitation:
His fears were that the interview betwixt
England and France might through their amity
Breed him some prejudice; for from this league
Peep'd harms that menaced him: he privily
Deals with our cardinal; and, as I trow—
Which I do well, for I am sure the emperor
Paid ere he promised; whereby his suit was granted
Ere it was ask'd—but when the way was made
And paved with gold, the emperor thus desired,
That he would please to alter the king's course,
And break the foresaid peace. Let the king know,
As soon he shall by me, that thus the cardinal
Does buy and sell his honour as he pleases,
And for his own advantage.

NORFOLK
           I am sorry
To hear this of him, and could wish he were
Something mistaken in 't.

BUCKINGHAM
           No, not a syllable:
I do pronounce him in that very shape
He shall appear in proof.

Enter BRANDON, *a* SERGEANT-AT-ARMS *before him, and
two or three of the* GUARD

BRANDON
Your office, sergeant; execute it.

SERGEANT
           Sir,
My lord the Duke of Buckingham, and Earl
Of Hereford, Stafford, and Northampton, I
Arrest thee of high treason, in the name
Of our most sovereign king.

BUCKINGHAM
           Lo you, my lord,
The net has fall'n upon me! I shall perish
Under device and practice.

BRANDON
           I am sorry
To see you ta'en from liberty, to look on
The business present: 'tis his highness' pleasure
You shall to the Tower.

BUCKINGHAM
           It will help me nothing
To plead mine innocence; for that dye is on me
Which makes my whitest part black. The will of
  heaven
Be done in this and all things! I obey.
O my Lord Abergavenny, fare you well!

BRANDON
Nay, he must bear you company. [*To* ABER-
GAVENNY] The king
Is pleased you shall to the Tower, till you know
How he determines further.

ABERGAVENNY
           As the duke said,
The will of heaven be done, and the king's pleasure
By me obey'd!

BRANDON
           Here is a warrant from
The king to attach Lord Montacute; and the bodies
Of the duke's confessor, John de la Car,
One Gilbert Peck, his chancellor,—

BUCKINGHAM
           So, so;
These are the limbs o' the plot: no more, I hope.

BRANDON
A monk o' the Chartreux.

BUCKINGHAM
           O, Nicholas Hopkins?

BRANDON
           He.

BUCKINGHAM
My surveyor is false; the o'er-great cardinal
Hath show'd him gold; my life is spann'd already:
I am the shadow of poor Buckingham,
Whose figure even this instant cloud puts on,
By darkening my clear sun. My lord, farewell.
                    [*Exeunt*

SCENE II. *The same. The council-chamber*

Cornets. Enter KING HENRY, *leaning on the* CARDINAL'S
shoulder; the Nobles, and SIR THOMAS LOVELL: *the* CAR-
DINAL *places himself under the* KING'S *feet on his right side*

KING
My life itself, and the best heart of it,
Thanks you for this great care: I stood i' the level
Of a full-charged confederacy, and give thanks
To you that choked it. Let be call'd before us
That gentleman of Buckingham's; in person
I'll hear him his confessions justify;
And point by point the treasons of his master
He shall again relate.

A noise within, crying 'Room for the Queen!' *Enter*
QUEEN KATHARINE, *ushered by the* DUKE OF NORFOLK,
and the DUKE OF SUFFOLK: *she kneels. The* KING *riseth
from his state, takes her up, kisses and placeth her by him*

QUEEN KATHARINE
Nay, we must longer kneel: I am a suitor.

KING
Arise, and take place by us: half your suit
Never name to us; you have half our power:
The other moiety ere you ask is given;
Repeat your will and take it.

QUEEN KATHARINE
           Thank your majesty.
That you would love yourself, and in that love
Not unconsider'd leave your honour nor
The dignity of your office, is the point
Of my petition.

KING
           Lady mine, proceed.

QUEEN KATHARINE
I am solicited, not by a few,
And those of true condition, that your subjects
Are in great grievance: there have been commission
Sent down among 'em, which hath flaw'd the heart
Of all their loyalties: wherein although,
My good lord cardinal, they vent reproaches
Most bitterly on you as putter on
Of these exactions, yet the king our master—
Whose honour heaven shield from soil!—even he
    escapes not
Language unmannerly, yea, such which breaks
The sides of loyalty, and almost appears
In loud rebellion.

NORFOLK
           Not almost appears;
It doth appear; for, upon these taxations,
The clothiers all, not able to maintain
The many to them 'longing, have put off
The spinsters, carders, fullers, weavers, who,
Unfit for other life, compell'd by hunger
And lack of other means, in desperate manner
Daring the event to the teeth, are all in uproar,
And danger serves among them.

KING
           Taxation!
Wherein? and what taxation? My lord cardinal,
You that are blamed for it alike with us,
Know you of this taxation?

WOLSEY
           Please you, sir,
I know but of a single part in aught
Pertains to the state, and front but in that file
Where others tell steps with me.

QUEEN KATHARINE
           No, my lord,
You know no more than others: but you frame
Things that are known alike, which are not whole-
    some
To those which would not know them, and yet must
Perforce be their acquaintance. These exactions,
Whereof my sovereign would have note, they are
Most pestilent to the hearing; and, to bear 'em,
The back is sacrifice to the load. They say
They are devised by you; or else you suffer
Too hard an exclamation.

KING
           Still exaction!
The nature of it? in what kind, let's know,
Is this exaction?

QUEEN KATHARINE
    I am much too venturous
In tempting of your patience, but am bolden'd
Under your promised pardon. The subjects' grief
Comes through commissions, which compel from
    each
The sixth part of his substance, to be levied
Without delay; and the pretence for this

Is named your wars in France: this makes bold
    mouths:
Tongues spit their duties out, and cold hearts freeze
Allegiance in them; their curses now
Live where their prayers did; and it's come to pass,
This tractable obedience is a slave
To each incensed will. I would your highness
Would give it quick consideration, for
There is no primer business.

KING
           By my life,
This is against our pleasure.

WOLSEY
           And for me,
I have no further gone in this than by
A single voice, and that not pass'd me but
By learned approbation of the judges. If I am
Traduced by ignorant tongues, which neither know
My faculties nor person, yet will be
The chronicles of my doing, let me say
'Tis but the fate of place, and the rough brake
That virtue must go through. We must not stint
Our necessary actions, in the fear
To cope malicious censurers; which ever,
As ravenous fishes, do a vessel follow
That is new-trimm'd, but benefit no further
Than vainly longing. What we oft do best,
By sick interpreters, once weak ones, is
Not ours or not allow'd; what worst, as oft,
Hitting a grosser quality, is cried up
For our best act. If we shall stand still,
In fear our notion will be mock'd or carp'd at,
We should take root here where we sit, or sit
State-statues only.

KING
           Things done well,
And with a care, exempt themselves from fear;
Things done without example, in their issue
Are to be fear'd. Have you a precedent
Of this commission? I believe, not any.
We must not rend our subjects from our laws,
And stick them in our will. Sixth part of each?
A trembling contribution! Why, we take
From every tree lop, bark, and part o' the timber,
And though we leave it with a root, thus hack'd,
The air will drink the sap. To every county
Where this is question'd send our letters, with
Free pardon to each man that has denied
The force of this commission: pray, look to 't;
I put it to your care.

WOLSEY
[To the SECRETARY] A word with you.
Let there be letters writ to every shire,
Of the king's grace and pardon. The grieved com-
    mons
Hardly conceive of me: let it be noised
That through our intercession this revokement
And pardon comes: I shall anon advise you
Further in the proceeding.   [Exit SECRETARY
           Enter SURVEYOR

QUEEN KATHARINE

I am sorry that the Duke of Buckingham
Is run in your displeasure.

KING

         It grieves many:
The gentleman is learn'd and a most rare speaker;
To nature none more bound; his training such
That he may furnish and instruct great teachers,
And never seek for aid out of himself. Yet see,
When these so noble benefits shall prove
Not well disposed, the mind growing once corrupt,
They turn to vicious forms, ten times more ugly
Than ever they were fair. This man so complete,
Who was enroll'd 'mongst wonders, and when we,
Almost with ravish'd listening, could not find
His hour of speech a minute; he, my lady,
Hath into monstrous habits put the graces
That once were his, and is become as black
As if besmear'd in hell. Sit by us; you shall hear—
This was his gentleman in trust—of him
Things to strike honour sad. Bid him recount
The fore-recited practices; whereof
We cannot feel too little, hear too much.

WOLSEY

Stand forth, and with bold spirit relate what you,
Most like a careful subject, have collected
Out of the Duke of Buckingham.

KING

         Speak freely.

SURVEYOR

First, it was usual with him, every day
It would infect his speech, that if the king
Should without issue die, he'll carry it so
To make the sceptre his: these very words
I've heard him utter to his son-in-law,
Lord Abergavenny, to whom by oath he menaced
Revenge upon the cardinal.

WOLSEY

         Please your highness, note
This dangerous conception in this point.
Not friended by his wish, to your high person
His will is most malignant, and it stretches
Beyond you to your friends.

QUEEN KATHARINE

         My learn'd lord cardinal,
Deliver all with charity.

KING

         Speak on:
How grounded he his title to the crown
Upon our fail? to this point hast thou heard him
At any time speak aught?

SURVEYOR

         He was brought to this
By a vain prophecy of Nicholas Henton.

KING

What was that Henton?

SURVEYOR

         Sir, a Chartreux friar,
His confessor, who fed him every minute
With words of sovereignty.

KING

         How know'st thou this?

SURVEYOR

Not long before your highness sped to France,
The duke being at the Rose, within the parish
Saint Lawrence Poultney, did of me demand
What was the speech among the Londoners
Concerning the French journey: I replied,
Men fear'd the French would prove perfidious,
To the king's danger. Presently the duke
Said, 'twas the fear indeed, and that he doubted
'Twould prove the verity of certain words
Spoke by a holy monk; 'that oft,' says he,
'Hath sent to me, wishing me to permit
John de la Car, my chaplain, a choice hour
To hear from him a matter of some moment:
Whom after under the confession's seal
He solemnly had sworn, that what he spoke
My chaplain to no creature living but
To me should utter, with demure confidence
This pausingly ensued: Neither the king nor 's heirs,
Tell you the duke, shall prosper: bid him strive
To gain the love o' the commonalty: the duke
Shall govern England.'

QUEEN KATHARINE

         If I know you well,
You were the duke's surveyor and lost your office
On the complaint o' the tenants: take good heed
You charge not in your spleen a noble person
And spoil your nobler soul: I say, take heed;
Yes, heartily beseech you.

KING

         Let him on.
Go forward.

SURVEYOR

         On my soul, I'll speak but truth.
I told my lord the duke, by the devil's illusions
The monk might be deceived; and that 'twas dan-
    gerous for him
To ruminate on this so far, until
It forged him some design, which, being believed,
It was much like to do: he answer'd 'Tush,
It can do me no damage;' adding further,
That, had the king in his last sickness fail'd,
The cardinal's and Sir Thomas Lovell's heads
Should have gone off.

KING

         Ha! what, so rank? Ah, ha!
There's mischief in this man: canst thou say further?

SURVEYOR

I can, my liege.

KING

         Proceed.

SURVEYOR

         Being at Greenwich,
After your highness had reproved the duke
About Sir William Bulmer,—

KING

         I remember

Of such a time: being my sworn servant,
The duke retain'd him his. But on; what hence?

SURVEYOR

'If' quoth he 'I for this had been committed,
As to the Tower I thought, I would have play'd
The part my father meant to act upon
The usurper Richard; who, being at Salisbury,
Made suit to come in 's presence; which if granted,
As he made semblance of his duty, would
Have put his knife into him.'

KING

A giant traitor!

WOLSEY

Now, madam, may his highness live in freedom,
And this man out of prison?

QUEEN KATHARINE

God mend all!

KING

There's something more would out of thee; what
say'st?

SURVEYOR

After 'the duke his father,' with the 'knife,'
He stretch'd him, and with one hand on his dagger,
Another spread on 's breast, mounting his eyes,
He did discharge a horrible oath, whose tenour
Was, were he evil used, he would outgo
His father by as much as a performance
Does an irresolute purpose.

KING

There's his period,
To sheathe his knife in us. He is attach'd;
Call him to present trial: if he may
Find mercy in the law, 'tis his; if none,
Let him not seek 't of us: by day and night!
He's traitor to the height.

[Exeunt

SCENE III. An antechamber in the palace

Enter the LORD CHAMBERLAIN and LORD SANDS

CHAMBERLAIN

Is 't possible the spells of France should juggle
Men into such strange mysteries?

SANDS

New customs,
Though they be never so ridiculous,
Nay, let 'em be unmanly, yet are follow'd.

CHAMBERLAIN

As far as I see, all the good our English
Have got by the late voyage is but merely
A fit or two o' the face; but they are shrewd ones;
For when they hold 'em, you would swear directly
Their very noses had been counsellors
To Pepin or Clotharius, they keep state so.

SANDS

They have all new legs, and lame ones: one would
take it,
That never saw 'em pace before, the spavin
Or springhalt reign'd among 'em.

CHAMBERLAIN

Death! my lord,
Their clothes are after such a pagan cut too,
That, sure, they've worn out Christendom.

Enter SIR THOMAS LOVELL

How now!
What news, Sir Thomas Lovell?

LOVELL

Faith, my lord,
I hear of none but the new proclamation
That's clapp'd upon the court-gate.

CHAMBERLAIN

What is 't for?

LOVELL

The reformation of our travell'd gallants,
That fill the court with quarrels, talk, and tailors.

CHAMBERLAIN

I'm glad 'tis there: now I would pray our monsieurs
To think an English courtier may be wise,
And never see the Louvre.

LOVELL

They must either,
For so run the conditions, leave those remnants
Of fool and feather that they got in France,
With all their honourable points of ignorance
Pertaining thereunto, as fights and fireworks,
Abusing better men than they can be
Out of a foreign wisdom, renouncing clean
The faith they have in tennis and tall stockings,
Short blister'd breeches and those types of travel,
And understand again like honest men,
Or pack to their old playfellows: there, I take it,
They may, 'cum privilegio,' wear away
The lag end of their lewdness, and be laugh'd at.

SANDS

'Tis time to give 'em physic, their diseases
Are grown so catching.

CHAMBERLAIN

What a loss our ladies
Will have of these trim vanities!

LOVELL

Ay, marry,
There will be woe indeed, lords: the sly whoresons
Have got a speeding trick to lay down ladies;
A French song and a fiddle has no fellow.

SANDS

The devil fiddle 'em! I am glad they are going,
For, sure, there's no converting of 'em: now
An honest country lord, as I am, beaten
A long time out of play, may bring his plain-song,
And have an hour of hearing; and, by 'r lady,
Held current music too.

CHAMBERLAIN

Well said, Lord Sands;
Your colt's tooth is not cast yet.

SANDS

No, my lord;
Nor shall not, while I have a stump.

CHAMBERLAIN

Sir Thomas,

Whither were you a-going?

LOVELL

To the cardinal's:

Your lordship is a guest too.

CHAMBERLAIN

O, 'tis true:

This night he makes a supper, and a great one,
To many lords and ladies; there will be
The beauty of this kingdom, I'll assure you.

LOVELL

That churchman bears a bounteous mind indeed,
A hand as fruitful as the land that feeds us;
His dews fall every where.

CHAMBERLAIN

No doubt he's noble;

He had a black mouth that said other of him.

SANDS

He may, my lord; has wherewithal: in him
Sparing would show a worse sin than ill doctrine:
Men of his way should be most liberal;
They are set here for examples.

CHAMBERLAIN

True, they are so;

But few now give so great ones. My barge stays;
Your lordship shall along. Come, good Sir Thomas,
We shall be late else; which I would not be,
For I was spoke to, with Sir Henry Guildford
This night to be comptrollers.

SANDS

I am your lordship's. [Exeunt

SCENE IV. *A hall in York place*

Hautboys. A small table under a state for the CARDINAL, *a longer table for the guests. Then enter* ANNE BULLEN *and divers other* LADIES *and* GENTLEMEN *as guests, at one door; at another door, enter* SIR HENRY GUILDFORD

GUILDFORD

Ladies, a general welcome from his grace
Salutes ye all; this night he dedicates
To fair content and you: none here, he hopes,
In all this noble bevy, has brought with her
One care abroad; he would have all as merry
As, first, good company, good wine, good welcome,
Can make good people.

Enter LORD CHAMBERLAIN, LORD SANDS, *and*
SIR THOMAS LOVELL

O, my lord, you're tardy:

The very thought of this fair company
Clapp'd wings to me.

CHAMBERLAIN

You are young, Sir Harry Guildford.

SANDS

Sir Thomas Lovell, had the cardinal
But half my lay thoughts in him, some of these
Should find a running banquet ere they rested,

I think would better please 'em: by my life,
They are a sweet society of fair ones.

LOVELL

O, that your lordship were but now confessor
To one or two of these!

SANDS

I would I were;

They should find easy penance.

LOVELL

Faith, how easy?

SANDS

As easy as a down-bed would afford it.

CHAMBERLAIN

Sweet ladies, will it please you sit? Sir Harry,
Place you that side; I'll take the charge of this:
His grace is entering. Nay, you must not freeze;
Two women placed together makes cold weather:
My Lord Sands, you are one will keep 'em waking;
Pray, sit between these ladies.

SANDS

By my faith,

And thank your lordship. By your leave, sweet
ladies:
If I chance to talk a little wild, forgive me;
I had it from my father.

ANNE

Was he mad, sir?

SANDS

O, very mad, exceeding mad, in love too:
But he would bite none; just as I do now,
He would kiss you twenty with a breath. [*Kisses her*

CHAMBERLAIN

Well said, my lord.

So, now you're fairly seated. Gentlemen,
The penance lies on you, if these fair ladies
Pass away frowning.

SANDS

For my little cure,

Let me alone.

Hautboys. Enter CARDINAL WOLSEY, *and takes his state*

WOLSEY

You're welcome, my fair guests: that noble lady
Or gentleman that is not freely merry,
Is not my friend: this, to confirm my welcome;
And to you all, good health.   [*Drinks*

SANDS

Your grace is noble:

Let me have such a bowl may hold my thanks,
And save me so much talking.

WOLSEY

My Lord Sands,

I am beholding to you: cheer your neighbours.
Ladies, you are not merry: gentlemen,
Whose fault is this?

SANDS

The red wine first must rise

In their fair cheeks, my lord; then we shall have 'em
Talk us to silence.

ANNE

You are a merry gamester,
My Lord Sands.

SANDS

Yes, if I make my play.
Here's to your ladyship: and pledge it, madam,
For 'tis to such a thing—

ANNE

You cannot show me.

SANDS

I told your grace they would talk anon.
    [Drum and trumpet: chambers discharged

WOLSEY

What's that?

CHAMBERLAIN

Look out there, some of ye.   [Exit SERVANT

WOLSEY

What warlike voice,
And to what end, is this? Nay, ladies, fear not;
By all the laws of war you're privileged.
    Re-enter SERVANT

CHAMBERLAIN

How now! what is 't?

SERVANT

A noble troop of strangers;
For so they seem: they've left their barge, and
    landed;
And hither make, as great ambassadors
From foreign princes.

WOLSEY

Good lord chamberlain,
Go, give 'em welcome; you can speak the French
    tongue;
And, pray, receive 'em nobly and conduct 'em
Into our presence, where this heaven of beauty
Shall shine at full upon them. Some attend him.
    [Exit CHAMBERLAIN, attended.
    All rise, and tables removed
You have now a broken banquet; but we'll mend it.
A good digestion to you all: and once more
I shower a welcome on ye; welcome all.
Hautboys. Enter the KING and others, as masquers, habited
like shepherds, ushered by the LORD CHAMBERLAIN. They
pass directly before the CARDINAL, and gracefully salute
    him
A noble company! what are their pleasures?

CHAMBERLAIN

Because they speak no English, thus they pray'd
To tell your grace, that, having heard by fame
Of this so noble and so fair assembly
This night to meet here, they could do no less,
Out of the great respect they bear to beauty,
But leave their flocks, and under your fair conduct
Crave leave to view these ladies and entreat
An hour of revels with 'em.

WOLSEY

Say, lord chamberlain,
They have done my poor house grace; for which I
    pay 'em

A thousand thanks and pray 'em take their pleasures. [They choose. The KING chooses ANNE BULLEN

KING

The fairest hand I ever touch'd! O beauty,
Till now I never knew thee!   [Music. Dance

WOLSEY

My lord!

CHAMBERLAIN

Your grace?

WOLSEY

Pray, tell 'em thus much from me:
There should be one amongst 'em, by his person,
More worthy this place than myself; to whom,
If I but knew him, with my love and duty
I would surrender it.

CHAMBERLAIN

I will, my lord. [Whispers the Masquers

WOLSEY

What say they?

CHAMBERLAIN

Such a one, they all confess,
There is indeed; which they would have your grace
Find out, and he will take it.

WOLSEY

Let me see then.
By all your good leaves, gentlemen; here I'll make
My royal choice.

KING

[Unmasking] Ye have found him, cardinal:
You hold a fair assembly; you do well, lord:
You are a churchman, or, I'll tell you, cardinal,
I should judge now unhappily.

WOLSEY

I am glad
Your grace is grown so pleasant.

KING

My lord chamberlain,
Prithee, come hither: what fair lady's that?

CHAMBERLAIN

An 't please your grace, Sir Thomas Bullen's
    daughter,
The Viscount Rochford, one of her highness'
    women.

KING

By heaven, she is a dainty one. Sweetheart,
I were unmannerly, to take you out,
And not to kiss you. A health, gentlemen!
Let it go round.

WOLSEY

Sir Thomas Lovell, is the banquet ready
I' the privy chamber?

LOVELL

Yes, my lord.

WOLSEY

Your grace,
I fear, with dancing is a little heated.

KING

I fear, too much.

WOLSEY
There's fresher air, my lord,
In the next chamber.

KING
Lead in your ladies, every one. Sweet partner,
I must not yet forsake you. Let's be merry,
Good my lord cardinal: I have half a dozen healths
To drink to these fair ladies, and a measure
To lead 'em once again; and then let's dream
Who's best in favour. Let the music knock it.

[Exeunt with trumpets

ACT II

SCENE I. *Westminster. A street*

Enter two GENTLEMEN, *meeting*

FIRST GENTLEMAN
Whither away so fast?

SECOND GENTLEMAN
O, God save ye!
Even to the hall, to hear what shall become
Of the great Duke of Buckingham.

FIRST GENTLEMAN
I'll save you
That labour, sir. All's now done, but the ceremony
Of bringing back the prisoner.

SECOND GENTLEMAN
Were you there?

FIRST GENTLEMAN
Yes, indeed was I.

SECOND GENTLEMAN
Pray, speak what has happen'd.

FIRST GENTLEMAN
You may guess quickly what.

SECOND GENTLEMAN
Is he found guilty?

FIRST GENTLEMAN
Yes, truly is he, and condemn'd upon 't.

SECOND GENTLEMAN
I am sorry for 't.

FIRST GENTLEMAN
So are a number more.

SECOND GENTLEMAN
But, pray, how pass'd it?

FIRST GENTLEMAN
I'll tell you in a little. The great duke
Came to the bar; where to his accusations
He pleaded still not guilty, and alleged
Many sharp reasons to defeat the law.
The king's attorney on the contrary
Urged on the examinations, proofs, confessions
Of divers witnesses; which the duke desired
To have brought viva voce to his face:
At which appear'd against him his surveyor;
Sir Gilbert Peck his chancellor; and John Car,
Confessor to him; with that devil monk,
Hopkins, that made this mischief.

SECOND GENTLEMAN
That was he
That fed him with his prophecies?

FIRST GENTLEMAN
The same.
All these accused him strongly; which he fain
Would have flung from him, but indeed he could
not:
And so his peers upon his evidence
Have found him guilty of high treason. Much
He spoke, and learnedly, for life, but all
Was either pitied in him or forgotten.

SECOND GENTLEMAN
After all this, how did he bear himself?

FIRST GENTLEMAN
When he was brought again to the bar, to hear
His knell rung out, his judgement, he was stirr'd
With such an agony, he sweat extremely,
And something spoke in choler, ill and hasty:
But he fell to himself again and sweetly
In all the rest show'd a most noble patience.

SECOND GENTLEMAN
I do not think he fears death.

FIRST GENTLEMAN
Sure, he does not;
He never was so womanish; the cause
He may a little grieve at.

SECOND GENTLEMAN
Certainly
The cardinal is the end of this.

FIRST GENTLEMAN
'Tis likely,
By all conjectures: first, Kildare's attainder,
Then deputy of Ireland; who removed,
Earl Surrey was sent thither, and in haste too,
Lest he should help his father.

SECOND GENTLEMAN
That trick of state
Was a deep envious one.

FIRST GENTLEMAN
At his return
No doubt he will requite it. This is noted,
And generally, whoever the king favours,
The cardinal instantly will find employment,
And far enough from court too.

SECOND GENTLEMAN
All the commons
Hate him perniciously, and, o' my conscience,
Wish him ten fathom deep: this duke as much
They love and dote on; call him bounteous Buck-
ingham,
The mirror of all courtesy—

FIRST GENTLEMAN
Stay there, sir,
And see the noble ruin'd man you speak of.
Enter BUCKINGHAM *from his arraignment, tipstaves before
him, the axe with the edge towards him, halberds on each
side, accompanied with* SIR THOMAS LOVELL, SIR NICHO-
LAS VAUX, SIR WILLIAM SANDS, *and common people, &c.*

SECOND GENTLEMAN

Let's stand close, and behold him.

BUCKINGHAM

All good people,

You that thus far have come to pity me,
Hear what I say, and then go home and lose me.
I have this day received a traitor's judgement,
And by that name must die: yet, heaven bear wit-
ness,
And if I have a conscience, let it sink me,
Even as the axe falls, if I be not faithful!
The law I bear no malice for my death;
'T has done upon the premisses but justice:
But those that sought it I could wish more Chris-
tians:
Be what they will, I heartily forgive 'em:
Yet let 'em look they glory not in mischief,
Nor build their evils on the graves of great men;
For then my guiltless blood must cry against 'em.
For further life in this world I ne'er hope,
Nor will I sue, although the king have mercies
More than I dare make faults. You few that loved
me
And dare be bold to weep for Buckingham,
His noble friends and fellows, whom to leave
Is only bitter to him, only dying,
Go with me, like good angels, to my end,
And, as the long divorce of steel falls on me,
Make of your prayers one sweet sacrifice
And lift my soul to heaven. Lead on, o' God's name.

LOVELL

I do beseech your grace, for charity,
If ever any malice in your heart
Were hid against me, now to forgive me frankly.

BUCKINGHAM

Sir Thomas Lovell, I as free forgive you
As I would be forgiven: I forgive all;
There cannot be those numberless offences
'Gainst me, that I cannot take peace with: no black
envy
Shall mark my grave. Commend me to his grace,
And if he speak of Buckingham, pray tell him
You met him half in heaven: my vows and prayers
Yet are the king's, and, till my soul forsake,
Shall cry for blessings on him: may he live
Longer than I have time to tell his years!
Ever beloved and loving may his rule be!
And when old time shall lead him to his end,
Goodness and he fill up one monument!

LOVELL

To the water side I must conduct your grace;
Then give my charge up to Sir Nicholas Vaux,
Who undertakes you to your end.

VAUX

Prepare there;

The duke is coming: see the barge be ready,
And fit it with such furniture as suits
The greatness of his person.

BUCKINGHAM

Nay, Sir Nicholas,

Let it alone; my state now will but mock me.
When I came hither, I was lord high constable
And Duke of Buckingham; now, poor Edward
Bohun:
Yet I am richer than my base accusers,
That never knew what truth meant: I now seal it;
And with that blood will make 'em one day groan
for 't.
My noble father, Henry of Buckingham,
Who first raised head against usurping Richard,
Flying for succour to his servant Banister,
Being distress'd, was by that wretch betray'd,
And without trial fell; God's peace be with him!
Henry the Seventh succeeding, truly pitying
My father's loss, like a most royal prince,
Restored me to my honours, and out of ruins
Made my name once more noble. Now his son,
Henry the Eighth, life, honour, name and all
That made me happy, at one stroke has taken
For ever from the world. I had my trial,
And must needs say, a noble one; which makes me
A little happier than my wretched father:
Yet thus far we are one in fortunes: both
Fell by our servants, by those men we loved most;
A most unnatural and faithless service!
Heaven has an end in all: yet; you that hear me,
This from a dying man receive as certain:
Where you are liberal of your loves and counsels
Be sure you be not loose; for those you make friends
And give your hearts to, when they once perceive
The least rub in your fortunes, fall away
Like water from ye, never found again
But where they mean to sink ye. All good people,
Pray for me! I must now forsake ye: the last hour
Of my long weary life is come upon me.
Farewell:
And when you would say something that is sad,
Speak how I fell. I have done; and God forgive me!

[*Exeunt* DUKE *and train*

FIRST GENTLEMAN

O, this is full of pity! Sir, it calls,
I fear, too many curses on their heads
That were the authors.

SECOND GENTLEMAN

If the duke be guiltless,

'Tis full of woe: yet I can give you inkling
Of an ensuing evil, if it fall,
Greater than this.

FIRST GENTLEMAN

Good angels keep it from us!

What may it be? You do not doubt my faith, sir?

SECOND GENTLEMAN

This secret is so weighty, 'twill require
A strong faith to conceal it.

FIRST GENTLEMAN

Let me have it;

I do not talk much.

SECOND GENTLEMAN

I am confident;

You shall, sir: did you not of late days hear

A buzzing of a separation
Between the king and Katharine?

FIRST GENTLEMAN

              Yes, but it held not:
For when the king once heard it, out of anger
He sent command to the lord mayor straight
To stop the rumour and allay those tongues
That durst disperse it.

SECOND GENTLEMAN

              But that slander, sir,
Is found a truth now: for it grows again
Fresher than e'er it was, and held for certain
The king will venture at it. Either the cardinal,
Or some about him near, have, out of malice
To the good queen, possess'd him with a scruple
That will undo her: to confirm this too,
Cardinal Campeius is arrived, and lately;
As all think, for this business.

FIRST GENTLEMAN

              'Tis the cardinal;
And merely to revenge him on the emperor,
For not bestowing on him at his asking
The archbishopric of Toledo, this is purposed.

SECOND GENTLEMAN

I think you have hit the mark: but is 't not cruel
That she should feel the smart of this? The cardinal
Will have his will, and she must fall.

FIRST GENTLEMAN

              'Tis woeful.
We are too open here to argue this;
Let's think in private more.   [Exeunt

SCENE II. *An ante-chamber in the palace*

Enter the LORD CHAMBERLAIN, *reading a letter*

CHAMBERLAIN

'My lord, the horses your lordship sent for, with all the care I
had, I saw well chosen, ridden, and furnished. They were
young and handsome, and of the best breed in the north.
When they were ready to set out for London, a man of my lord
cardinal's, by commission and main power, took 'em from me;
with this reason: His master would be served before a subject,
if not before the king; which stopped our mouths, sir.'

I fear he will indeed: well, let him have them:
He will have all, I think.

Enter to the LORD CHAMBERLAIN, *the* DUKES OF
NORFOLK *and* SUFFOLK

NORFOLK

Well met, my lord chamberlain.

CHAMBERLAIN

Good day to both your graces.

SUFFOLK

How is the king employ'd?

CHAMBERLAIN

              I left him private,
Full of sad thoughts and troubles.

NORFOLK

                 What's the cause?

CHAMBERLAIN

It seems the marriage with his brother's wife
Has crept too near his conscience.

SUFFOLK

              No, his conscience
Has crept too near another lady.

NORFOLK

              'Tis so:
This is the cardinal's doing, the king-cardinal:
That blind priest, like the eldest son of fortune,
Turns what he list. The king will know him one day.

SUFFOLK

Pray God he do! he'll never know himself else.

NORFOLK

How holily he works in all his business!
And with what zeal! for, now he has crack'd the
league
Between us and the emperor, the queen's great
nephew,
He dives into the king's soul, and there scatters
Dangers, doubts, wringing of the conscience,
Fears and despairs; and all these for his marriage:
And out of all these to restore the king,
He counsels a divorce; a loss of her
That, like a jewel, has hung twenty years
About his neck, yet never lost her lustre,
Of her that loves him with that excellence
That angels love good men with, even of her
That, when the greatest stroke of fortune falls,
Will bless the king: and is not this course pious?

CHAMBERLAIN

Heaven keep me from such counsel! 'Tis most true
These news are every where; every tongue speaks
'em,
And every true heart weeps for 't: all that dare
Look into these affairs see this main end,
The French king's sister. Heaven will one day open
The king's eyes, that so long have slept upon
This bold bad man.

SUFFOLK

              And free us from his slavery.

NORFOLK

We had need pray,
And heartily, for our deliverance;
Or this imperious man will work us all
From princes into pages: all men's honours
Lie like one lump before him, to be fashion'd
Into what pitch he please.

SUFFOLK

              For me, my lords,
I love him not, nor fear him; there's my creed:
As I am made without him, so I'll stand,
If the king please; his curses and his blessings
Touch me alike; they're breath I not believe in.
I knew him, and I know him; so I leave him
To him that made him proud, the pope.

NORFOLK

              Let's in;
And with some other business put the king

From these sad thoughts that work too much upon
 him:
My lord, you'll bear us company?
      CHAMBERLAIN
          Excuse me;
The king has sent me otherwhere: besides,
You'll find a most unfit time to disturb him:
Health to your lordships.
      NORFOLK
     Thanks, my good lord chamberlain.
[*Exit* LORD CHAMBERLAIN; *and the* KING *draws the
curtain and sits reading pensively*
      SUFFOLK
How sad he looks! sure, he is much afflicted.
      KING
Who's there, ha?
      NORFOLK
     Pray God he be not angry.
      KING
Who's there, I say? How dare you thrust yourselves
Into my private meditations?
Who am I? ha?
      NORFOLK
A gracious king that pardons all offences
Malice ne'er meant: our breach of duty this way
Is business of estate, in which we come
To know your royal pleasure.
      KING
         Ye are too bold:
Go to; I'll make ye know your times of business:
Is this an hour for temporal affairs, ha?
  Enter WOLSEY *and* CAMPEIUS, *with a commission*
Who's there? my good lord cardinal? O my Wolsey,
The quiet of my wounded conscience,
Thou art a cure fit for a king. [*To* CAMPEIUS] You're
 welcome,
Most learned reverend sir, into our kingdom:
Use us and it. [*To* WOLSEY] My good lord, have
 great care
I be not found a talker.
      WOLSEY
     Sir, you cannot.
I would your grace would give us but an hour
Of private conference.
      KING
  [*To* NORFOLK *and* SUFFOLK] We are busy; go.
      NORFOLK
[*Aside to* SUFFOLK] This priest has no pride in him?
      SUFFOLK
    [*Aside to* NORFOLK] Not to speak of:
I would not be so sick though for his place:
But this cannot continue.
      NORFOLK
    [*Aside to* SUFFOLK] If it do,
I'll venture one have-at-him.
      SUFFOLK
    [*Aside to* NORFOLK] I another.
    [*Exeunt* NORFOLK *and* SUFFOLK
      WOLSEY
Your grace has given a precedent of wisdom

Above all princes, in committing freely
Your scruple to the voice of Christendom:
Who can be angry now? what envy reach you?
The Spaniard, tied by blood and favour to her,
Must now confess, if they have any goodness,
The trial just and noble. All the clerks,
I mean the learned ones, in Christian kingdoms
Have their free voices: Rome, the nurse of judge-
 ment,
Invited by your noble self, hath sent
One general tongue unto us, this good man,
This just and learned priest, Cardinal Campeius;
Whom once more I present unto your highness.
      KING
And once more in mine arms I bid him welcome,
And thank the holy conclave for their loves:
They have sent me such a man I would have wish'd
 for.
      CAMPEIUS
Your grace must needs deserve all strangers' loves,
You are so noble. To your highness' hand
I tender my commission; by whose virtue,
The court of Rome commanding, you, my lord
Cardinal of York, are join'd with me their servant
In the unpartial judging of this business.
      KING
Two equal men. The queen shall be acquainted
Forthwith for what you come. Where's Gardiner?
      WOLSEY
I know your majesty has always loved her
So dear in heart, not to deny her that
A woman of less place might ask by law,
Scholars allow'd freely to argue for her.
      KING
Ay, and the best she shall have; and my favour
To him that does best: God forbid else. Cardinal,
Prithee, call Gardiner to me, my new secretary:
I find him a fit fellow.   [*Exit* WOLSEY
   Re-enter WOLSEY, *with* GARDINER
      WOLSEY
[*Aside to* GARDINER] Give me your hand: much joy
 and favour to you:
You are the king's now.
      GARDINER
    [*Aside to* WOLSEY] But to be commanded
For ever by your grace, whose hand has raised me.
      KING
Come hither, Gardiner.   [*Walks and whispers*
      CAMPEIUS
My Lord of York, was not one Doctor Pace
In this man's place before him?
      WOLSEY
         Yes, he was.
      CAMPEIUS
Was he not held a learned man?
      WOLSEY
         Yes, surely.
      CAMPEIUS
Believe me, there's an ill opinion spread then,
Even of yourself, lord cardinal.

WOLSEY
How! of me?

CAMPEIUS
They will not stick to say you envied him,
And fearing he would rise, he was so virtuous,
Kept him a foreign man still; which so grieved him
That he ran mad and died.

WOLSEY
Heaven's peace be with him!
That's Christian care enough: for living murmurers
There's places of rebuke. He was a fool;
For he would needs be virtuous: that good fellow,
If I command him, follows my appointment:
I will have none so near else. Learn this, brother,
We live not to be griped by meaner persons.

KING
Deliver this with modesty to the queen.
                                        [Exit GARDINER
The most convenient place that I can think of
For such receipt of learning is Black-Friars;
There ye shall meet about this weighty business.
My Wolsey, see it furnish'd. O, my lord,
Would it not grieve an able man to leave
So sweet a bedfellow? But, conscience, conscience!
O, 'tis a tender place; and I must leave her. [Exeunt

SCENE III. An ante-chamber of the QUEEN's apartments

Enter ANNE BULLEN and an OLD LADY

ANNE
Not for that neither: here's the pang that pinches:
His highness having lived so long with her, and she
So good a lady that no tongue could ever
Pronounce dishonour of her—by my life,
She never knew harm-doing—O, now, after
So many courses of the sun enthroned,
Still growing in a majesty and pomp, the which
To leave a thousand-fold more bitter than
'Tis sweet at first to acquire—after this process,
To give her the avaunt! it is a pity
Would move a monster.

OLD LADY
Hearts of most hard temper
Melt and lament for her.

ANNE
O, God's will! much better
She ne'er had known pomp: though 't be temporal,
Yet, if that quarrel, fortune, do divorce
It from the bearer, 'tis a sufferance panging
As soul and body's severing.

OLD LADY
Alas, poor lady!
She's a stranger now again.

ANNE
So much the more
Must pity drop upon her. Verily,
I swear, 'tis better to be lowly born,
And range with humble livers in content,

Than to be perk'd up in a glistering grief
And wear a golden sorrow.

OLD LADY
Our content
Is our best having.

ANNE
By my troth and maidenhead,
I would not be a queen.

OLD LADY
Beshrew me, I would,
And venture maidenhead for 't; and so would you,
For all this spice of your hypocrisy:
You, that have so fair parts of woman on you,
Have too a woman's heart; which ever yet
Affected eminence, wealth, sovereignty;
Which, to say sooth, are blessings; and which gifts—
Saving your mincing—the capacity
Of your soft cheveril conscience would receive,
If you might please to stretch it.

ANNE
Nay, good troth.

OLD LADY
Yes, troth, and troth; you would not be a queen?

ANNE
No, not for all the riches under heaven.

OLD LADY
'Tis strange: a three-pence bow'd would hire me,
Old as I am, to queen it: but, I pray you,
What think you of a duchess? have you limbs
To bear that load of title?

ANNE
No, in truth.

OLD LADY
Then you are weakly made: pluck off a little;
I would not be a young count in your way,
For more than blushing comes to: if your back
Cannot vouchsafe this burthen, 'tis too weak
Ever to get a boy.

ANNE
How you do talk!
I swear again, I would not be a queen
For all the world.

OLD LADY
In faith, for little England
You'ld venture an emballing: I myself
Would for Carnarvonshire, although there 'long'd
No more to the crown but that. Lo, who comes here?

Enter the LORD CHAMBERLAIN

CHAMBERLAIN
Good morrow, ladies. What were 't worth to know
The secret of your conference?

ANNE
My good lord,
Not your demand; it values not your asking:
Our mistress' sorrows we were pitying.

CHAMBERLAIN
It was a gentle business, and becoming
The action of good women: there is hope
All will be well.

ANNE
Now, I pray God, amen!
CHAMBERLAIN
You bear a gentle mind, and heavenly blessings
Follow such creatures. That you may, fair lady,
Perceive I speak sincerely, and high note's
Ta'en of your many virtues, the king's majesty
Commends his good opinion of you, and
Does purpose honour to you no less flowing
Than Marchioness of Pembroke; to which title
A thousand pound a year, annual support,
Out of his grace he adds.
ANNE
　　　　　　I do not know
What kind of my obedience I should tender;
More than my all is nothing: nor my prayers
Are not words duly hallowed, nor my wishes
More worth than empty vanities; yet prayers and
　　wishes
Are all I can return. Beseech your lordship,
Vouchsafe to speak my thanks and my obedience,
As from a blushing handmaid, to his highness,
Whose health and royalty I pray for.
CHAMBERLAIN
　　　　　　　Lady,
I shall not fail to approve the fair conceit
The king hath of you. [Aside] I have perused her
　　well;
Beauty and honour in her are so mingled
That they have caught the king: and who knows
　　yet
But from this lady may proceed a gem
To lighten all this isle?—I'll to the king,
And say I spoke with you.
ANNE
　　　　　　My honour'd lord.
　　　　　　[Exit LORD CHAMBERLAIN
OLD LADY
Why, this it is; see, see!
I have been begging sixteen years in court,
Am yet a courtier beggarly, nor could
Come pat betwixt too early and too late
For any suit of pounds; and you, O fate!
A very fresh fish here—fie, fie, fie upon
This compell'd fortune!—have your mouth fill'd up
Before you open it.
ANNE
　　　　　　This is strange to me.
OLD LADY
How tastes it? is it bitter? forty pence, no.
There was a lady once, 'tis an old story,
That would not be a queen, that would she not,
For all the mud in Egypt: have you heard it?
ANNE
Come, you are pleasant.
OLD LADY
　　　　　　With your theme, I could
O'ermount the lark. The Marchioness of Pembroke!
A thousand pounds a year for pure respect!
No other obligation! By my life,

That promises mo thousands: honour's train
Is longer than his foreskirt. By this time
I know your back will bear a duchess: say,
Are you not stronger than you were?
ANNE
　　　　　　　Good lady,
Make yourself mirth with your particular fancy,
And leave me out on 't. Would I had no being,
If this salute my blood a jot: it faints me,
To think what follows.
The queen is comfortless, and we forgetful
In our long absence: pray, do not deliver
What here you've heard to her.
OLD LADY
　　　　　　What do you think me? [Exeunt

SCENE IV. A hall in Black-Friars

Trumpets, sennet and cornets. Enter two VERGERS, *with short silver wands; next them, two* SCRIBES, *in the habit of doctors; after them, the* ARCHBISHOP OF CANTERBURY *alone; after him, the* BISHOPS OF LINCOLN, ELY, ROCH- ESTER, *and* SAINT ASAPH; *next them, with some small distance, follows a* GENTLEMAN *bearing the purse, with the great seal, and a cardinal's hat; then two* PRIESTS, *bearing each a silver cross; then a* GENTLEMAN USHER *bare- headed, accompanied with a* SERGEANT-AT-ARMS *bearing a silver mace; then two* GENTLEMAN *bearing two great silver pillars; after them, side by side, the two* CARDINALS; *two* NOBLEMEN *with the sword and mace. The* KING *takes place under the cloth of state; the two* CARDINALS *sit under him as judges. The* QUEEN *takes place some dis- tance from the* KING. *The* BISHOPS *place themselves on each side the court, in manner of a consistory; below them, the* SCRIBES. *The* LORDS *sit next the* BISHOPS. *The rest of the* ATTENDANTS *stand in convenient order about the stage*
WOLSEY
Whilst our commission from Rome is read,
Let silence be commanded.
KING
　　　　　　What's the need?
It hath already publicly been read,
And on all sides the authority allow'd;
You may then spare that time.
WOLSEY
　　　　　　　Be 't so. Proceed.
SCRIBE
Say, Henry King of England, come into the court.
CRIER
Henry King of England, &c.
KING
Here.
SCRIBE
Say, Katharine Queen of England, come into the
court.
CRIER
Katharine Queen of England, &c.
[*The* QUEEN *makes no answer, rises out of her chair, goes about the court, comes to the* KING, *and kneels at his feet;*
　　　　　　　　then speaks

QUEEN KATHARINE

Sir, I desire you do me right and justice,
And to bestow your pity on me; for
I am a most poor woman, and a stranger,
Born out of your dominions; having here
No judge indifferent, nor no more assurance
Of equal friendship and proceeding. Alas, sir,
In what have I offended you? what cause
Hath my behaviour given to your displeasure,
That thus you should proceed to put me off,
And take your good grace from me? Heaven wit-
  ness,
I have been to you a true and humble wife,
At all times to your will conformable,
Ever in fear to kindle your dislike,
Yea, subject to your countenance, glad or sorry
As I saw it inclined: when was the hour
I ever contradicted your desire,
Or made it not mine too? Or which of your friends
Have I not strove to love, although I knew
He were mine enemy? what friend of mine
That had to him derived your anger, did I
Continue in my liking? nay, gave notice
He was from thence discharged? Sir, call to mind
That I have been your wife, in this obedience,
Upward of twenty years, and have been blest
With many children by you: if in the course
And process of this time you can report,
And prove it too, against mine honour aught,
My bond to wedlock or my love and duty,
Against **your** sacred person, in God's name,
Turn me away, and let the foul'st contempt
Shut door upon me, and so give me up
To the sharp'st kind of justice. Please you, sir,
The king, your father, was reputed for
A prince most prudent, of an excellent
And unmatch'd wit and judgement: Ferdinand,
My father, king of Spain, was reckon'd one
The wisest prince that there had reign'd by many
A year before: it is not to be question'd
That they had gather'd a wise council to them
Of every realm, that did debate this business,
Who deem'd our marriage lawful: wherefore I
  humbly
Beseech you, sir, to spare me, till I may
Be by my friends in Spain advised, whose counsel
I will implore: if not, i' the name of God,
Your pleasure be fulfill'd!

WOLSEY

                    You have here, lady,
And of your choice, these reverend fathers; men
Of singular integrity and learning,
Yea, the elect o' the land, who are assembled
To plead your cause: it shall be therefore bootless
That longer you desire the court, as well
For your own quiet, as to rectify
What is unsettled in the king.

CAMPEIUS

                              His grace
Hath spoken well and justly: therefore, madam,

It's fit this royal session do proceed,
And that without delay their arguments
Be now produced and heard.

QUEEN KATHARINE

                          Lord cardinal,
To you I speak.

WOLSEY

              Your pleasure, madam?

QUEEN KATHARINE

                                  Sir,
I am about to weep; but, thinking that
We are a queen, or long have dream'd so, certain
The daughter of a king, my drops of tears
I'll turn to sparks of fire.

WOLSEY

                    Be patient yet.

QUEEN KATHARINE

I will, when you are humble; nay, before,
Or God will punish me. I do believe,
Induced by potent circumstances, that
You are mine enemy, and make my challenge
You shall not be my judge: for it is you
Have blown this coal betwixt my lord and me;
Which God's dew quench! Therefore I say again,
I utterly abhor, yea, from my soul
Refuse you for my judge; whom, yet once more,
I hold my most malicious foe, and think not
At all a friend to truth.

WOLSEY

                  I do profess
You speak not like yourself; who ever yet
Have stood to charity and display'd the effects
Of disposition gentle, and of wisdom
O'ertopping woman's power. Madam, you do me
  wrong:
I have no spleen against you, nor injustice
For you or any: how far I have proceeded,
Or how far further shall, is warranted
By a commission from the consistory,
Yea, the whole consistory of Rome. You charge me
That I have blown this coal: I do deny it:
The king is present: if it be known to him
That I gainsay my deed, how may he wound,
And worthily, my falsehood! yea, as much
As you have done my truth. If he know
That I am free of your report, he knows
I am not of your wrong. Therefore in him
It lies to cure me; and the cure is to
Remove these thoughts from you: the which before
His highness shall speak in, I do beseech
You, gracious madam, to unthink your speaking,
And to say so no more.

QUEEN KATHARINE

                  My lord, my lord,
I am a simple woman, much too weak
To oppose your cunning. You're meek and humble-
  mouth'd;
You sign your place and calling, in full seeming,
With meekness and humility; but your heart
Is cramm'd with arrogancy, spleen, and pride

You have, by fortune and his highness' favours,
Gone slightly o'er low steps, and now are mounted
Where powers are your retainers, and your words,
Domestics to you, serve your will as 't please
Yourself pronounce their office. I must tell you,
You tender more your person's honour than
Your high profession spiritual; that again
I do refuse you for my judge, and here,
Before you all, appeal unto the pope,
To bring my whole cause 'fore his holiness,
And to be judged by him.

[She curtsies to the KING, *and offers to depart*

CAMPEIUS
　　　　　　　　The queen is obstinate,
Stubborn to justice, apt to accuse it, and
Disdainful to be tried by 't: 'tis not well.
She's going away.

KING
Call her again.

CRIER
Katharine Queen of England, come into the court.

GENTLEMAN USHER
Madam, you are call'd back.

QUEEN KATHARINE
What need you note it? pray you, keep your way:
When you are call'd, return. Now the Lord help!
They vex me past my patience. Pray you, pass on:
I will not tarry, no, nor ever more
Upon this business my appearance make
In any of their courts.

[Exeunt QUEEN, *and her* ATTENDANTS

KING
　　　　　　　Go thy ways, Kate:
That man i' the world who shall report he has
A better wife, let him in nought be trusted,
For speaking false in that: thou art, alone,
If thy rare qualities, sweet gentleness,
Thy meekness saint-like, wife-like government,
Obeying in commanding, and thy parts
Sovereign and pious else, could speak thee out,
The queen of earthly queens. She's noble born,
And like her true nobility she has
Carried herself towards me.

WOLSEY
　　　　　　　Most gracious sir,
In humblest manner I require your highness,
That it shall please you to declare in hearing
Of all these ears—for where I am robb'd and bound,
There must I be unloosed, although not there
At once and fully satisfied—whether ever I
Did broach this business to your highness, or
Laid any scruple in your way which might
Induce you to the question on 't? or ever
Have to you, but with thanks to God for such
A royal lady, spake one the least word that might
Be to the prejudice of her present state
Or touch of her good person?

KING
　　　　　　　My lord cardinal,
I do excuse you; yea, upon mine honour,

I free you from 't. You are not to be taught
That you have many enemies that know not
Why they are so, but, like to village curs,
Bark when their fellows do: by some of these
The queen is put in anger. You're excused:
But will you be more justified? you ever
Have wish'd the sleeping of this business, never de-
　sired
It to be stirr'd, but oft have hinder'd, oft,
The passages made toward it: on my honour,
I speak my good lord cardinal to this point,
And thus far clear him. Now, what moved me to 't,
I will be bold with time and your attention:
Then mark the inducement. Thus it came; give
　heed to 't:
My conscience first received a tenderness,
Scruple, and prick, on certain speeches utter'd
By the Bishop of Bayonne, then French ambassador;
Who had been hither sent on the debating
A marriage 'twixt the Duke of Orleans and
Our daughter Mary: i' the progress of this business,
Ere a determinate resolution, he,
I mean the bishop, did require a respite,
Wherein he might the king his lord advertise
Whether our daughter were legitimate,
Respecting this our marriage with the dowager,
Sometimes our brother's wife. This respite shook
The bosom of my conscience, enter'd me,
Yea, with a splitting power, and made to tremble
The region of my breast; which forced such way
That many mazed considerings did throng
And press'd in with this caution. First, methought
I stood not in the smile of heaven, who had
Commanded nature that my lady's womb,
If it conceived a male-child by me, should
Do no more offices of life to 't than
The grave does to the dead; for her male issue
Or died where they were made, or shortly after
This world had air'd them: hence I took a thought,
This was a judgement on me, that my kingdom,
Well worthy the best heir o' the world, should not
Be gladded in 't by me: then follows that
I weigh'd the danger which my realms stood in
By this my issue's fail; and that gave to me
Many a groaning throe. Thus hulling in
The wild sea of my conscience, I did steer
Toward this remedy whereupon we are
Now present here together; that's to say,
I meant to rectify my conscience, which
I then did feel full sick and yet not well,
By all the reverend fathers of the land
And doctors learn'd. First I began in private
With you, my Lord of Lincoln; you remember
How under my oppression I did reek,
When I first moved you.

LINCOLN
　　　　　　　Very well, my liege.

KING
I have spoke long: be pleased yourself to say
How far you satisfied me.

LINCOLN
                    So please your highness,
The question did at first so stagger me,
Bearing a state of mighty moment in 't
And consequence of dread, that I committed
The daring'st counsel which I had to doubt,
And did entreat your highness to this course
Which you are running here.

KING
                              I then moved you,
My Lord of Canterbury, and got your leave
To make this present summons: unsolicited
I left no reverend person in this court;
But by particular consent proceeded
Under your hands and seals: therefore, go on;
For no dislike i' the world against the person
Of the good queen, but the sharp thorny points
Of my alleged reasons, drive this forward:
Prove but our marriage lawful, by my life
And kingly dignity, we are contented
To wear our mortal state to come with her,
Katharine our queen, before the primest creature
That's paragon'd o' the world.

CAMPEIUS
                    So please your highness,
The queen being absent, 'tis a needful fitness
That we adjourn this court till further day:
Meanwhile must be an earnest motion
Made to the queen, to call back her appeal
She intends unto his holiness.

KING
        [Aside] I may perceive
These cardinals trifle with me: I abhor
This dilatory sloth and tricks of Rome.
My learn'd and well-beloved servant, Cranmer,
Prithee, return; with thy approach, I know,
My comfort comes along.—Break up the court:
I say, set on.

                    [Exeunt in manner as they entered

ACT III

SCENE I. London. The QUEEN's apartments

The QUEEN and her WOMEN, as at work

QUEEN KATHARINE
Take thy lute, wench: my soul grows sad with
    troubles;
Sing, and disperse 'em, if thou canst: leave working.

SONG

Orpheus with his lute made trees,
And the mountain tops that freeze,
    Bow themselves when he did sing:
To his music plants and flowers
Ever sprung, as sun and showers
    There had made a lasting spring.

Every thing that heard him play,
Even the billows of the sea,
    Hung their heads, and then lay by.
In sweet music is such art,
Killing care and grief of heart
Fall asleep, or hearing die.

Enter a GENTLEMAN

QUEEN KATHARINE
How now!

GENTLEMAN
An 't please your grace, the two great cardinals
Wait in the presence.

QUEEN KATHARINE
                Would they speak with me?

GENTLEMAN
They will'd me say so, madam.

QUEEN KATHARINE
                            Pray their graces
To come near. [Exit GENTLEMAN] What can be their
    business
With me, a poor weak woman, fall'n from favour?
I do not like their coming. Now I think on 't,
They should be good men, their affairs as righteous:
But all hoods make not monks.

Enter the two CARDINALS, WOLSEY and CAMPEIUS

WOLSEY
                        Peace to your highness!

QUEEN KATHARINE
Your graces find me here part of a housewife;
I would be all, against the worst may happen.
What are your pleasures with me, reverend lords?

WOLSEY
May it please you, noble madam, to withdraw
Into your private chamber, we shall give you
The full cause of our coming.

QUEEN KATHARINE
                        Speak it here;
There's nothing I have done yet, o' my conscience,
Deserves a corner: would all other women
Could speak this with as free a soul as I do!
My lords, I care not, so much I am happy
Above a number, if my actions
Were tried by every tongue, every eye saw 'em,
Envy and base opinion set against 'em,
I know my life so even. If your business
Seek me out, and that way I am wife in,
Out with it boldly: truth loves open dealing.

WOLSEY
Tanta est erga te mentis integritas, regina serenissima,—

QUEEN KATHARINE
O, good my lord, no Latin;
I am not such a truant since my coming,
As not to know the language I have lived in:
A strange tongue makes my cause more strange,
    suspicious;
Pray speak in English: here are some will thank you,
If you speak truth, for their poor mistress' sake;
Believe me, she has had much wrong: lord cardinal,
The willing'st sin I ever yet committed
May be absolved in English.

WOLSEY

Noble lady,
I am sorry my integrity should breed,
And service to his majesty and you,
So deep suspicion, where all faith was meant.
We come not by the way of accusation,
To taint that honour every good tongue blesses,
Nor to betray you any way to sorrow—
You have too much, good lady—but to know
How you stand minded in the weighty difference
Between the king and you, and to deliver,
Like free and honest men, our just opinions
And comforts to your cause.

CAMPEIUS

Most honour'd madam,
My Lord of York, out of his noble nature,
Zeal and obedience he still bore your grace,
Forgetting, like a good man, your late censure
Both of his truth and him, which was too far,
Offers, as I do, in a sign of peace,
His service and his counsel.

QUEEN KATHARINE

[*Aside*] To betray me.—
My lords, I thank you both for your good wills;
Ye speak like honest men; pray God, ye prove so!
But how to make ye suddenly an answer,
In such a point of weight, so near mine honour,
More near my life, I fear, with my weak wit,
And to such men of gravity and learning,
In truth, I know not. I was set at work
Among my maids, full little, God knows, looking
Either for such men or such business.
For her sake that I have been—for I feel
The last fit of my greatness—good your graces,
Let me have time and counsel for my cause:
Alas, I am a woman, friendless, hopeless!

WOLSEY

Madam, you wrong the king's love with these fears:
Your hopes and friends are infinite.

QUEEN KATHARINE

In England
But little for my profit: can you think, lords,
That any Englishman dare give me counsel?
Or be a known friend, 'gainst his highness' pleasure—
Though he be grown so desperate to be honest—
And live a subject? Nay, forsooth, my friends,
They that must weigh out my afflictions,
They that my trust must grow to, live not here:
They are, as all my other comforts, far hence
In mine own country, lords.

CAMPEIUS

I would your grace
Would leave your griefs, and take my counsel.

QUEEN KATHARINE

How, sir?

CAMPEIUS

Put your main cause into the king's protection;
He's loving and most gracious: 'twill be much
Both for your honour better and your cause;

For if the trial of the law o'ertake ye,
You'll part away disgraced.

WOLSEY

He tells you rightly.

QUEEN KATHARINE

Ye tell me what ye wish for both, my ruin:
Is this your Christian counsel? out upon ye!
Heaven is above all yet; there sits a judge
That no king can corrupt.

CAMPEIUS

Your rage mistakes us.

QUEEN KATHARINE

The more shame for ye: holy men I thought ye,
Upon my soul, two reverend cardinal virtues;
But cardinal sins and hollow hearts I fear ye:
Mend 'em, for shame, my lords. Is this your com-
fort?
The cordial that ye bring a wretched lady,
A woman lost among ye, laugh'd at, scorn'd?
I will not wish ye half my miseries;
I have more charity: but say, I warn'd ye;
Take heed, for heaven's sake, take heed, lest at once
The burthen of my sorrows fall upon ye.

WOLSEY

Madam, this is a mere distraction;
You turn the good we offer into envy.

QUEEN KATHARINE

Ye turn me into nothing: woe upon ye,
And all such false professors! would you have me—
If you have any justice, any pity,
If ye be any thing but churchmen's habits—
Put my sick cause into his hands that hates me?
Alas, has banish'd me his bed already,
His love, too long ago! I am old, my lords,
And all the fellowship I hold now with him
Is only my obedience. What can happen
To me above this wretchedness? all your studies
Make me a curse like this.

CAMPEIUS

Your fears are worse.

QUEEN KATHARINE

Have I lived thus long—let me speak myself,
Since virtue finds no friends—a wife, a true one?
A woman, I dare say without vain-glory,
Never yet branded with suspicion?
Have I with all my full affections
Still met the king? loved him next heaven? obey'd
him?
Been, out of fondness, superstitious to him?
Almost forgot my prayers to content him?
And am I thus rewarded? 'tis not well, lords.
Bring me a constant woman to her husband,
One that ne'er dream'd a joy beyond his pleasure,
And to that woman, when she has done most,
Yet will I add an honour, a great patience.

WOLSEY

Madam, you wander from the good we aim at.

QUEEN KATHARINE

My lord, I dare not make myself so guilty,
To give up willingly that noble title

Your master wed me to: nothing but death
Shall e'er divorce my dignities.

WOLSEY

             Pray, hear me.

QUEEN KATHARINE

Would I had never trod this English earth,
Or felt the flatteries that grow upon it!
Ye have angels' faces, but heaven knows your hearts.
What will become of me now, wretched lady!
I am the most unhappy woman living.
Alas, poor wenches, where are now your fortunes?
Shipwreck'd upon a kingdom, where no pity,
No friends, no hope; no kindred weep for me;
Almost no grave allow'd me: like the lily,
That once was mistress of the field and flourish'd,
I'll hang my head and perish.

WOLSEY

             If your grace
Could but be brought to know our ends are honest,
You'ld feel more comfort: why should we, good
     lady,
Upon what cause, wrong you? alas, our places,
The way of our profession is against it:
We are to cure such sorrows, not to sow 'em.
For goodness' sake, consider what you do;
How you may hurt yourself, ay, utterly
Grow from the king's acquaintance, by this carriage.
The hearts of princes kiss obedience,
So much they love it; but to stubborn spirits
They swell, and grow as terrible as storms.
I know you have a gentle, noble temper,
A soul as even as a calm: pray think us
Those we profess, peace-makers, friends and serv-
     ants.

CAMPEIUS

Madam, you'll find it so. You wrong your virtues
With these weak women's fears: a noble spirit,
As yours was put into you, ever casts
Such doubts, as false coin, from it. The king loves
     you;
Beware you lose it not: for us, if you please
To trust us in your business, we are ready
To use our utmost studies in your service.

QUEEN KATHARINE

Do what ye will, my lords: and pray forgive me,
If I have used myself unmannerly;
You know I am a woman, lacking wit
To make a seemly answer to such persons.
Pray do my service to his majesty:
He has my heart yet, and shall have my prayers
While I shall have my life. Come, reverend fathers,
Bestow your counsels on me: she now begs,
That little thought, when she set footing here,
She should have bought her dignities so dear.

                     [Exeunt

SCENE II. Ante-chamber to the KING'S apartment

Enter the DUKE OF NORFOLK, the DUKE OF SUFFOLK, the
EARL OF SURREY, and the LORD CHAMBERLAIN

NORFOLK

If you will now unite in your complaints
And force them with a constancy, the cardinal
Cannot stand under them: if you omit
The offer of this time, I cannot promise
But that you shall sustain moe new disgraces,
With these you bear already.

SURREY

                  I am joyful
To meet the least occasion that may give me
Remembrance of my father-in-law, the duke,
To be revenged on him.

SUFFOLK

            Which of the peers
Have uncontemn'd gone by him, or at least
Strangely neglected? when did he regard
The stamp of nobleness in any person
Out of himself?

CHAMBERLAIN

       My lords, you speak your pleasures:
What he deserves of you and me I know;
What we can do to him, though now the time
Gives way to us, I much fear. If you cannot
Bar his access to the king, never attempt
Any thing on him; for he hath a witchcraft
Over the king in 's tongue.

NORFOLK

               O, fear him not;
His spell in that is out: the king hath found
Matter against him that for ever mars
The honey of his language. No, he's settled,
Not to come off, in his displeasure.

SURREY

                  Sir,
I should be glad to hear such news as this
Once every hour.

NORFOLK

          Believe it, this is true:
In the divorce his contrary proceedings
Are all unfolded; wherein he appears
As I would wish mine enemy.

SURREY

               How came
His practices to light?

SUFFOLK

Most strangely.

SURREY

                  O, how, how?

SUFFOLK

The cardinal's letters to the pope miscarried,
And came to the eye o' the king: wherein was read
How that the cardinal did entreat his holiness
To stay the judgement o' the divorce; for if
It did take place, 'I do' quoth he 'perceive
My king is tangled in affection to
A creature of the queen's, Lady Anne Bullen.'

SURREY

Has the king this?

SUFFOLK

        Believe it.

SURREY
Will this work?

CHAMBERLAIN
The king in this perceives him, how he coasts
And hedges his own way. But in this point
All his tricks founder, and he brings his physic
After his patient's death: the king already
Hath married the fair lady.

SURREY
Would he had!

SUFFOLK
May you be happy in your wish, my lord!
For, I profess, you have it.

SURREY
Now, all my joy
Trace the conjunction!

SUFFOLK
My amen to 't!

NORFOLK
All men's!

SUFFOLK
There's order given for her coronation:
Marry, this is yet but young, and may be left
To some ears unrecounted. But, my lords,
She is a gallant creature and complete
In mind and feature: I persuade me, from her
Will fall some blessing to this land, which shall
In it be memorized.

SURREY
But will the king
Digest this letter of the cardinal's?
The Lord forbid!

NORFOLK
Marry, amen!

SUFFOLK
No, no;
There be moe wasps that buzz about his nose
Will make this sting the sooner. Cardinal Campeius
Is stol'n away to Rome; hath ta'en no leave;
Has left the cause o' the king unhandled, and
Is posted as the agent of our cardinal,
To second all his plot. I do assure you
The king cried 'Ha!' at this.

CHAMBERLAIN
Now God incense him,
And let him cry 'Ha!' louder!

NORFOLK
But, my lord,
When returns Cranmer?

SUFFOLK
He is return'd in his opinions, which
Have satisfied the king for his divorce,
Together with all famous colleges
Almost in Christendom: shortly, I believe,
His second marriage shall be publish'd, and
Her coronation: Katharine no more
Shall be call'd queen, but princess dowager
And widow to Prince Arthur.

NORFOLK
This same Cranmer's

A worthy fellow, and hath ta'en much pain
In the king's business.

SUFFOLK
He has; and we shall see him
For it an archbishop.

NORFOLK
So I hear.

SUFFOLK
'Tis so.
The cardinal!

Enter WOLSEY *and* CROMWELL

NORFOLK
Observe, observe, he's moody.

WOLSEY
The packet, Cromwell,
Gave 't you the king?

CROMWELL
To his own hand, in 's bedchamber.

WOLSEY
Look'd he o' the inside of the paper?

CROMWELL
Presently
He did unseal them, and the first he view'd,
He did it with a serious mind; a heed
Was in his countenance. You he bade
Attend him here this morning.

WOLSEY
Is he ready
To come abroad?

CROMWELL
I think, by this he is.

WOLSEY
Leave me awhile.   [*Exit* CROMWELL
[*Aside*] It shall be to the Duchess of Alençon,
The French king's sister: he shall marry her.
Anne Bullen! No; I'll no Anne Bullens for him:
There's more in 't than fair visage. Bullen!
No, we'll no Bullens. Speedily I wish
To hear from Rome. The Marchioness of Pembroke!

NORFOLK
He's discontented.

SUFFOLK
May be, he hears the king
Does whet his anger to him.

SURREY
Sharp enough,
Lord, for thy justice!

WOLSEY
[*Aside*] The late queen's gentlewoman, a knight's
daughter,
To be her mistress' mistress! the queen's queen!
This candle burns not clear: 'tis I must snuff it;
Then out it goes. What though I know her virtuous
And well deserving? yet I know her for
A spleeny Lutheran, and not wholesome to
Our cause, that she should lie i' the bosom of
Our hard-ruled king. Again, there is sprung up
An heretic, an arch one, Cranmer, one
Hath crawl'd into the favour of the king,
And is his oracle.

NORFOLK
He is vex'd at something.

SURREY
I would 'twere something that would fret the string,
The master-cord on 's heart!

Enter KING, *reading of a schedule, and* LOVELL

SUFFOLK
The king, the king!

KING
What piles of wealth hath he accumulated
To his own portion! and what expense by the hour
Seems to flow from him! How, i' the name of thrift,
Does he rake this together? Now, my lords,
Saw you the cardinal?

NORFOLK
My lord, we have
Stood here observing him: some strange commotion
Is in his brain: he bites his lip, and starts;
Stops on a sudden, looks upon the ground,
Then lays his finger on his temple; straight
Springs out into fast gait; then stops again,
Strikes his breast hard, and anon he casts
His eye against the moon: in most strange postures
We have seen him set himself.

KING
It may well be;
There is a mutiny in 's mind. This morning
Papers of state he sent me to peruse,
As I required: and wot you what I found
There, on my conscience, put unwittingly?
Forsooth, an inventory, thus importing,
The several parcels of his plate, his treasure,
Rich stuffs, and ornaments of household, which
I find at such proud rate that it out-speaks
Possession of a subject.

NORFOLK
It's heaven's will:
Some spirit put this paper in the packet,
To bless your eye withal.

KING
If we did think
His contemplation were above the earth,
And fix'd on spiritual object, he should still
Dwell in his musings: but I am afraid
His thinkings are below the moon, not worth
His serious considering.

[KING *takes his seat; whispers* LOVELL, *who goes to the*
CARDINAL

WOLSEY
Heaven forgive me!
Ever God bless your highness!

KING
Good my lord,
You are full of heavenly stuff, and bear the inventory
Of your best graces in your mind; the which
You were now running o'er: you have scarce time
To steal from spiritual leisure a brief span
To keep your earthly audit: sure, in that

I deem you an ill husband, and am glad
To have you therein my companion.

WOLSEY
Sir,
For holy offices I have a time; a time
To think upon the part of business which
I bear i' the state; and nature does require
Her times of preservation, which perforce
I, her frail son, amongst my brethren mortal,
Must give my tendance to.

KING
You have said well.

WOLSEY
And ever may your highness yoke together,
As I will lend you cause, my doing well
With my well saying!

KING
'Tis well said again;
And 'tis a kind of good deed to say well:
And yet words are no deeds. My father loved you:
He said he did, and with his deed did crown
His word upon you. Since I had my office,
I have kept you next my heart; have not alone
Employ'd you where high profits might come home,
But pared my present havings, to bestow
My bounties upon you.

WOLSEY
[*Aside*] What should this mean?

SURREY
[*Aside*] The Lord increase this business!

KING
Have I not made you
The prime man of the state? I pray you, tell me,
If what I now pronounce you have found true:
And, if you may confess it, say withal,
If you are bound to us or no. What say you?

WOLSEY
My sovereign, I confess your royal graces,
Shower'd on me daily, have been more than could
My studied purposes requite; which went
Beyond all man's endeavours: my endeavours
Have ever come too short of my desires,
Yet filed with my abilities: mine own ends
Have been mine so that evermore they pointed
To the good of your most sacred person and
The profit of the state. For your great graces
Heap'd upon me, poor undeserver, I
Can nothing render but allegiant thanks,
My prayers to heaven for you, my loyalty,
Which ever has and ever shall be growing,
Till death, that winter, kill it.

KING
Fairly answer'd;
A loyal and obedient subject is
Therein illustrated: the honour of it
Does pay the act of it; as, i' the contrary,
The foulness is the punishment. I presume
That, as my hand has open'd bounty to you,
My heart dropp'd love, my power rain'd honour, more

[1350]

On you than any; so your hand and heart,
Your brain and every function of your power,
Should, notwithstanding that your bond of duty,
As 'twere in love's particular, be more
To me, your friend, than any.

WOLSEY
                                        I do profess
That for your highness' good I ever labour'd
More than mine own; that am, have, and will be—
Though all the world should crack their duty to
    you,
And throw it from their soul; though perils did
Abound, as thick as thought could make 'em, and
Appear in forms more horrid—yet my duty,
As doth a rock against the chiding flood,
Should the approach of this wild river break,
And stand unshaken yours.

KING
                              'Tis nobly spoken.
Take notice, lords, he has a loyal breast,
For you have seen him open 't. [Giving him papers]
    Read o'er this;
And after, this: and then to breakfast with
What appetite you have.
[Exit KING, frowning upon the CARDINAL: the nobles
    throng after him, smiling and whispering

WOLSEY
                      What should this mean?
What sudden anger's this? how have I reap'd it?
He parted frowning from me, as if ruin
Leap'd from his eyes. So looks the chafed lion
Upon the daring huntsman that has gall'd him;
Then makes him nothing. I must read this paper;
I fear, the story of his anger. 'Tis so;
This paper has undone me: 'tis the account
Of all that world of wealth I have drawn together
For mine own ends; indeed, to gain the popedom,
And fee my friends in Rome. O negligence!
Fit for a fool to fall by: what cross devil
Made me put this main secret in the packet
I sent the king? Is there no way to cure this?
No new device to beat this from his brains?
I know 'twill stir him strongly; yet I know
A way, if it take right, in spite of fortune
Will bring me off again. What's this? 'To the Pope!'
The letter, as I live, with all the business
I writ to 's holiness. Nay then, farewell!
I have touch'd the highest point of all my greatness;
And, from that full meridian of my glory,
I haste now to my setting: I shall fall
Like a bright exhalation in the evening,
And no man see me more.

    Re-enter to WOLSEY the DUKES OF NORFOLK and
    SUFFOLK, the EARL OF SURREY, and the LORD
                    CHAMBERLAIN

NORFOLK
Hear the king's pleasure, cardinal: who commands
    you
To render up the great seal presently
Into our hands; and to confine yourself

To Asher-house, my Lord of Winchester's,
Till you hear further from his highness.

WOLSEY
                                        Stay:
Where's your commission, lords? words cannot carry
Authority so weighty.

SUFFOLK
              Who dare cross 'em,
Bearing the king's will from his mouth expressly?

WOLSEY
Till I find more than will or words to do it—
I mean your malice—know, officious lords,
I dare, and must deny it. Now I feel
Of what coarse metal ye are moulded—envy:
How eagerly ye follow my disgraces,
As if it fed ye! and how sleek and wanton
Ye appear in every thing may bring my ruin!
Follow your envious courses, men of malice;
You have Christian warrant for 'em, and, no doubt,
In time will find their fit rewards. That seal
You ask with such a violence, the king,
Mine and your master, with his own hand gave me;
Bade me enjoy it, with the place and honours,
During my life; and, to confirm his goodness,
Tied it by letters-patents: now, who'll take it?

SURREY
The king, that gave it.

WOLSEY
                  It must be himself, then.

SURREY
Thou art a proud traitor, priest.

WOLSEY
                      Proud lord, thou liest:
Within these forty hours Surrey durst better
Have burnt that tongue than said so.

SURREY
                              Thy ambition,
Thou scarlet sin, robb'd this bewailing land
Of noble Buckingham, my father-in-law:
The heads of all thy brother cardinals,
With thee and all thy best parts bound together,
Weigh'd not a hair of his. Plague of your policy!
You sent me deputy for Ireland;
Far from his succour, from the king, from all
That might have mercy on the fault thou gavest
    him;
Whilst your great goodness, out of holy pity,
Absolved him with an axe.

WOLSEY
                      This, and all else
This talking lord can lay upon my credit,
I answer, is most false. The duke by law
Found his deserts. How innocent I was
From any private malice in his end,
His noble jury and foul cause can witness.
If I loved many words, lord, I should tell you
You have as little honesty as honour,
That in the way of loyalty and truth
Toward the king, my ever royal master,

Dare mate a sounder man than Surrey can be,
And all that love his follies.

SURREY

By my soul,
Your long coat, priest, protects you; thou shouldst feel
My sword i' the life-blood of thee else. My lords,
Can ye endure to hear this arrogance?
And from this fellow? If we live thus tamely,
To be thus jaded by a piece of scarlet,
Farewell nobility; let his grace go forward,
And dare us with his cap like larks.

WOLSEY

All goodness
Is poison to thy stomach.

SURREY

Yes, that goodness
Of gleaning all the land's wealth into one,
Into your own hands, cardinal, by extortion;
The goodness of your intercepted packets
You writ to the pope against the king: your goodness,
Since you provoke me, shall be most notorious.
My Lord of Norfolk, as you are truly noble,
As you respect the common good, the state
Of our despised nobility, our issues,
Who, if he live, will scarce be gentlemen,
Produce the grand sum of his sins, the articles
Collected from his life. I'll startle you
Worse than the sacring bell, when the brown wench
Lay kissing in your arms, lord cardinal.

WOLSEY

How much, methinks, I could despise this man,
But that I am bound in charity against it!

NORFOLK

Those articles, my lord, are in the king's hand:
But, thus much, they are foul ones.

WOLSEY

So much fairer
And spotless shall mine innocence arise,
When the king knows my truth.

SURREY

This cannot save you:
I thank my memory, I yet remember
Some of these articles, and out they shall.
Now, if you can blush and cry 'guilty,' cardinal,
You'll show a little honesty.

WOLSEY

Speak on, sir;
I dare your worst objections: if I blush,
It is to see a nobleman want manners.

SURREY

I had rather want those than my head. Have at you!
First that, without the king's assent or knowledge,
You wrought to be a legate; by which power
You maim'd the jurisdiction of all bishops.

NORFOLK

Then that in all you writ to Rome, or else
To foreign princes, 'Ego et Rex meus'

Was still inscribed; in which you brought the king
To be your servant.

SUFFOLK

Then that, without the knowledge
Either of king or council, when you went
Ambassador to the emperor, you made bold
To carry into Flanders the great seal.

SURREY

Item, you sent a large commission
To Gregory de Cassado, to conclude,
Without the king's will or the state's allowance,
A league between his highness and Ferrara.

SUFFOLK

That, out of mere ambition, you have caused
Your holy hat to be stamp'd on the king's coin.

SURREY

Then, that you have sent innumerable substance—
By what means got, I leave to your own conscience—
To furnish Rome, and to prepare the ways
You have for dignities, to the mere undoing
Of all the kingdom. Many more there are;
Which, since they are of you and odious,
I will not taint my mouth with.

CHAMBERLAIN

O my lord!
Press not a falling man too far; 'tis virtue:
His faults lie open to the laws; let them,
Not you, correct him. My heart weeps to see him
So little of his great self.

SURREY

I forgive him.

SUFFOLK

Lord cardinal, the king's further pleasure is—
Because all those things you have done of late,
By your power legatine, within this kingdom,
Fall into the compass of a præmunire—
That therefore such a writ be sued against you;
To forfeit all your goods, lands, tenements,
Chattels, and whatsoever, and to be
Out of the king's protection. This is my charge.

NORFOLK

And so we'll leave you to your meditations
How to live better. For your stubborn answer
About the giving back the great seal to us,
The king shall know it, and, no doubt, shall thank you.
So fare you well, my little good lord cardinal.

[Exeunt all but WOLSEY

WOLSEY

So farewell to the little good you bear me.
Farewell! a long farewell, to all my greatness!
This is the state of man: to-day he puts forth
The tender leaves of hopes; to-morrow blossoms,
And bears his blushing honours thick upon him;
The third day comes a frost, a killing frost,
And, when he thinks, good easy man, full surely
His greatness is a-ripening, nips his root,
And then he falls, as I do. I have ventured,
Like little wanton boys that swim on bladders,
This many summers in a sea of glory,

But far beyond my depth: my high-blown pride
At length broke under me, and now has left me,
Weary and old with service, to the mercy
Of a rude stream that must for ever hide me.
Vain pomp and glory of this world, I hate ye:
I feel my heart new open'd. O, how wretched
Is that poor man that hangs on princes' favours!
There is, betwixt that smile we would aspire to,
That sweet aspect of princes, and their ruin,
More pangs and fears than wars or women have:
And when he falls, he falls like Lucifer,
Never to hope again.
            Enter CROMWELL, *and stands amazed*
            Why, how now, Cromwell!
                    CROMWELL
I have no power to speak, sir.
                    WOLSEY
                    What, amazed
At my misfortunes? can thy spirit wonder
A great man should decline? Nay, an you weep,
I am fall'n indeed.
                    CROMWELL
            How does your grace?
                    WOLSEY
                    Why, well;
Never so truly happy, my good Cromwell.
I know myself now; and I feel within me
A peace above all earthly dignities,
A still and quiet conscience. The king has cured me,
I humbly thank his grace; and from these shoulders,
These ruin'd pillars, out of pity, taken
A load would sink a navy, too much honour.
O, 'tis a burden, Cromwell, 'tis a burden
Too heavy for a man that hopes for heaven!
                    CROMWELL
I am glad your grace has made that right use of it.
                    WOLSEY
I hope I have: I am able now, methinks,
Out of a fortitude of soul I feel,
To endure more miseries and greater far
Than my weak-hearted enemies dare offer.
What news abroad?
                    CROMWELL
            The heaviest and the worst
Is your displeasure with the king.
                    WOLSEY
                    God bless him!
                    CROMWELL
The next is, that Sir Thomas More is chosen
Lord chancellor in your place.
                    WOLSEY
                    That's somewhat sudden:
But he's a learned man. May he continue
Long in his highness' favour, and do justice
For truth's sake and his conscience; that his bones,
When he has run his course and sleeps in blessings,
May have a tomb of orphans' tears wept on 'em!
What more?

                    CROMWELL
That Cranmer is return'd with welcome,
Install'd lord archbishop of Canterbury.
                    WOLSEY
That's news indeed.
                    CROMWELL
            Last, that the Lady Anne,
Whom the king hath in secrecy long married,
This day was view'd in open as his queen,
Going to chapel; and the voice is now
Only about her coronation.
                    WOLSEY
There was the weight that pull'd me down. O
    Cromwell,
The king has gone beyond me: all my glories
In that one woman I have lost for ever:
No sun shall ever usher forth mine honours,
Or gild again the noble troops that waited
Upon my smiles. Go, get thee from me, Cromwell;
I am a poor fall'n man, unworthy now
To be thy lord and master: seek the king;
That sun, I pray, may never set! I have told him
What and how true thou art: he will advance thee;
Some little memory of me will stir him—
I know his noble nature—not to let
Thy hopeful service perish too: good Cromwell,
Neglect him not; make use now, and provide
For thine own future safety.
                    CROMWELL
            O my lord,
Must I then leave you? must I needs forgo
So good, so noble and so true a master?
Bear witness, all that have not hearts of iron,
With what a sorrow Cromwell leaves his lord.
The king shall have my service, but my prayers
For ever and for ever shall be yours.
                    WOLSEY
Cromwell, I did not think to shed a tear
In all my miseries; but thou hast forced me,
Out of thy honest truth, to play the woman.
Let's dry our eyes: and thus far hear me, Cromwell;
And, when I am forgotten, as I shall be,
And sleep in dull cold marble, where no mention
Of me more must be heard of, say, I taught thee;
Say, Wolsey, that once trod the ways of glory,
And sounded all the depths and shoals of honour,
Found thee a way, out of his wreck, to rise in;
A sure and safe one, though thy master miss'd it.
Mark but my fall and that that ruin'd me.
Cromwell, I charge thee, fling away ambition:
By that sin fell the angels; how can man then,
The image of his Maker, hope to win by it?
Love thyself last: cherish those hearts that hate thee;
Corruption wins not more than honesty.
Still in thy right hand carry gentle peace,
To silence envious tongues. Be just, and fear not
Let all the ends thou aim'st at be thy country's,
Thy God's, and truth's; then if thou fall'st, O
    Cromwell,
Thou fall'st a blessed martyr! Serve the king;

And prithee, lead me in:
There take an inventory of all I have,
To the last penny; 'tis the king's: my robe,
And my integrity to heaven, is all
I dare now call mine own. O Cromwell, Cromwell!
Had I but served my God with half the zeal
I served my king, he would not in mine age
Have left me naked to mine enemies.

CROMWELL
Good sir, have patience.

WOLSEY
              So I have. Farewell
The hopes of court! my hopes in heaven do dwell.
                                        [*Exeunt*

ACT IV

SCENE I. *A street in Westminster*

Enter two GENTLEMEN, *meeting one another*

FIRST GENTLEMAN
You're well met once again.

SECOND GENTLEMAN
              So are you.

FIRST GENTLEMAN
You come to take your stand here and behold
The Lady Anne pass from her coronation?

SECOND GENTLEMAN
'Tis all my business. At our last encounter,
The Duke of Buckingham came from his trial.

FIRST GENTLEMAN
'Tis very true: but that time offer'd sorrow;
This, general joy.

SECOND GENTLEMAN
              'Tis well: the citizens,
I am sure, have shown at full their royal minds—
As, let 'em have their rights, they are ever forward—
In celebration of this day with shows,
Pageants and sights of honour.

FIRST GENTLEMAN
              Never greater,
Nor, I'll assure you, better taken, sir.

SECOND GENTLEMAN
May I be bold to ask what that contains,
That paper in your hand?

FIRST GENTLEMAN
              Yes; 'tis the list
Of those that claim their offices this day
By custom of the coronation.
The Duke of Suffolk is the first, and claims
To be high-steward; next, the Duke of Norfolk,
He to be earl marshal: you may read the rest.

SECOND GENTLEMAN
I thank you, sir: had I not known those customs,
I should have been beholding to your paper.
But, I beseech you, what's become of Katharine,
The princess dowager? how goes her business?

FIRST GENTLEMAN
That I can tell you too. The Archbishop
Of Canterbury, accompanied with other

Learned and reverend fathers of his order,
Held a late court at Dunstable, six miles off
From Ampthill, where the princess lay; to which
She was often cited by them, but appear'd not:
And, to be short, for not appearance and
The king's late scruple, by the main assent
Of all these learned men she was divorced,
And the late marriage made of none effect:
Since which she was removed to Kimbolton,
Where she remains now sick.

SECOND GENTLEMAN
              Alas, good lady! [*Trumpets*
The trumpets sound: stand close, the queen is
coming.   [*Hautboys*

THE ORDER OF THE CORONATION

1. *A lively Flourish of Trumpets.*
2. *Then two* JUDGES.
3. LORD CHANCELLOR, *with purse and mace before him.*
4. CHORISTERS, *singing.*   MUSICIANS.
5. MAYOR OF LONDON, *bearing the mace. Then* GARTER, *in his coat of arms, and on his head he wears a gilt copper crown.*
6. MARQUESS DORSET, *bearing a sceptre of gold, on his head a demi-coronal of gold. With him, the* EARL OF SURREY, *bearing the rod of silver with the dove, crowned with an earl's coronet. Collars of SS.*
7. DUKE OF SUFFOLK, *in his robe of estate, his coronet on his head, bearing a long white wand, as high-steward. With him, the* DUKE OF NORFOLK, *with the rod of marshalship, a coronet on his head. Collars of SS.*
8. *A canopy borne by four of the* CINQUE-PORTS; *under it, the* QUEEN *in her robe; in her hair richly adorned with pearl, crowned. On each side her, the* BISHOPS OF LONDON *and* WINCHESTER.
9. *The old* DUCHESS OF NORFOLK, *in a coronal of gold, wrought with flowers, bearing the* QUEEN'S *train.*
10. *Certain* LADIES *or* COUNTESSES, *with plain circlets of gold without flowers.*

They pass over the stage in order and state.

SECOND GENTLEMAN
A royal train, believe me. These I know:
Who's that that bears the sceptre?

FIRST GENTLEMAN
              Marquess Dorset:
And that the Earl of Surrey, with the rod.

SECOND GENTLEMAN
A bold brave gentleman. That should be
The Duke of Suffolk?

FIRST GENTLEMAN
              'Tis the same: high-steward.

SECOND GENTLEMAN
And that my Lord of Norfolk?

FIRST GENTLEMAN
              Yes.

SECOND GENTLEMAN
[*Looking on the* QUEEN] Heaven bless thee!
Thou hast the sweetest face I ever look'd on.
Sir, as I have a soul, she is an angel;

Our king has all the Indies in his arms,
And more and richer, when he strains that lady:
I cannot blame his conscience.

FIRST GENTLEMAN
                                    They that bear
The cloth of honour over her, are four barons
Of the Cinque-ports.

SECOND GENTLEMAN
Those men are happy; and so are all are near her.
I take it, she that carries up the train
Is that old noble lady, Duchess of Norfolk.

FIRST GENTLEMAN
It is; and all the rest are countesses.

SECOND GENTLEMAN
Their coronets say so. These are stars indeed,
And sometimes falling ones.

FIRST GENTLEMAN
                                    No more of that.

[*Exit procession; and then a great flourish of trumpets
Enter a* THIRD GENTLEMAN

God save you, sir! where have you been broiling?

THIRD GENTLEMAN
Among the crowd i' the abbey; where a finger
Could not be wedged in more: I am stifled
With the mere rankness of their joy.

SECOND GENTLEMAN
                                    You saw
The ceremony?

THIRD GENTLEMAN
That I did.

FIRST GENTLEMAN
                    How was it?

THIRD GENTLEMAN
Well worth the seeing.

SECOND GENTLEMAN
                    Good sir, speak it to us.

THIRD GENTLEMAN
As well as I am able. The rich stream
Of lords and ladies, having brought the queen
To a prepared place in the choir, fell off
A distance from her; while her grace sat down
To rest awhile, some half an hour or so,
In a rich chair of state, opposing freely
The beauty of her person to the people.
Believe me, sir, she is the goodliest woman
That ever lay by man: which when the people
Had the full view of, such a noise arose
As the shrouds make as sea in a stiff tempest,
As loud and to as many tunes: hats, cloaks,—
Doublets, I think,—flew up; and had their faces
Been loose, this day they had been lost. Such joy
I never saw before. Great-bellied women,
That had not half a week to go, like rams
In the old time of war, would shake the press,
And make 'em reel before 'em. No man living
Could say 'This is my wife' there, all were woven
So strangely in one piece.

SECOND GENTLEMAN
                                    But what follow'd?

THIRD GENTLEMAN
At length her grace rose, and with modest paces
Came to the altar, where she kneel'd and saintlike
Cast her fair eyes to heaven and pray'd devoutly;
Then rose again and bow'd her to the people;
When by the Archbishop of Canterbury
She had all the royal makings of a queen,
As holy oil, Edward Confessor's crown,
The rod, and bird of peace, and all such emblems
Laid nobly on her: which perform'd, the choir,
With all the choicest music of the kingdom,
Together sung 'Te Deum.' So she parted,
And with the same full state paced back again
To York-place, where the feast is held.

FIRST GENTLEMAN
                                    Sir,
You must no more call it York-place; that's past;
For, since the cardinal fell, that title's lost:
'Tis now the king's, and call'd Whitehall.

THIRD GENTLEMAN
                                    I know it;
But 'tis so lately alter'd, that the old name
Is fresh about me.

SECOND GENTLEMAN
                    What two reverend bishops
Were those that went on each side of the queen?

THIRD GENTLEMAN
Stokesly and Gardiner; the one of Winchester,
Newly preferr'd from the king's secretary,
The other, London.

SECOND GENTLEMAN
                    He of Winchester
Is held no great good lover of the archbishop's,
The virtuous Cranmer.

THIRD GENTLEMAN
                    All the land knows that:
However, yet there is no great breach; when it comes,
Cranmer will find a friend will not shrink from him.

SECOND GENTLEMAN
Who may that be, I pray you?

THIRD GENTLEMAN
                    Thomas Cromwell;
A man in much esteem with the king, and truly
A worthy friend. The king has made him master
O' the jewel house,
And one, already, of the privy council.

SECOND GENTLEMAN
He will deserve more.

THIRD GENTLEMAN
                    Yes, without all doubt.
Come, gentlemen, ye shall go my way,
Which is to the court, and there ye shall be my guests:
Something I can command. As I walk thither,
I'll tell ye more.

BOTH
                    You may command us, sir. [*Exeunt*

SCENE II. *Kimbolton*

Enter KATHARINE, *Dowager, sick; led between* GRIFFITH, *her* GENTLEMAN USHER, *and* PATIENCE, *her woman*

GRIFFITH
How does your grace?

KATHARINE
O Griffith, sick to death!
My legs, like loaden branches, bow to the earth,
Willing to leave their burthen. Reach a chair.
So; now, methinks, I feel a little ease.
Didst thou not tell me, Griffith, as thou led'st me,
That the great child of honour, Cardinal Wolsey,
Was dead?

GRIFFITH
Yes, madam; but I think your grace,
Out of the pain you suffer'd, gave no ear to 't.

KATHARINE
Prithee, good Griffith, tell me how he died:
If well, he stepp'd before me, happily,
For my example.

GRIFFITH
Well, the voice goes, madam:
For after the stout Earl Northumberland
Arrested him at York, and brought him forward,
As a man sorely tainted, to his answer,
He fell sick suddenly, and grew so ill
He could not sit his mule.

KATHARINE
Alas, poor man!

GRIFFITH
At last, with easy roads, he came to Leicester,
Lodged in the abbey; where the reverend abbot,
With all his covent, honourably received him;
To whom he gave these words, 'O father abbot,
An old man, broken with the storms of state,
Is come to lay his weary bones among ye;
Give him a little earth for charity!'
So went to bed; where eagerly his sickness
Pursued him still; and three nights after this,
About the hour of eight, which he himself
Foretold should be his last, full of repentance,
Continual meditations, tears and sorrows,
He gave his honours to the world again,
His blessed part to heaven, and slept in peace.

KATHARINE
So may he rest; his faults lie gently on him!
Yet thus far, Griffith, give me leave to speak him,
And yet with charity. He was a man
Of an unbounded stomach, ever ranking
Himself with princes; one that by suggestion
Tied all the kingdom: simony was fair-play:
His own opinion was his law: i' the presence
He would say untruths, and be ever double
Both in his words and meaning: he was never,
But where he meant to ruin, pitiful:
His promises were, as he then was, mighty;
But his performance, as he is now, nothing:
Of his own body he was ill, and gave
The clergy ill example.

GRIFFITH
Noble madam,
Men's evil manners live in brass; their virtues
We write in water. May it please your highness
To hear me speak his good now?

KATHARINE
Yes, good Griffith;
I were malicious else.

GRIFFITH
This cardinal,
Though from an humble stock, undoubtedly
Was fashion'd to much honour from his cradle.
He was a scholar, and a ripe and good one;
Exceeding wise, fair-spoken and persuading:
Lofty and sour to them that loved him not,
But to those men that sought him, sweet as summer.
And though he were unsatisfied in getting,
Which was a sin, yet in bestowing, madam,
He was most princely: ever witness for him
Those twins of learning that he raised in you,
Ipswich and Oxford! one of which fell with him,
Unwilling to outlive the good that did it;
The other, though unfinish'd, yet so famous,
So excellent in art and still so rising,
That Christendom shall ever speak his virtue.
His overthrow heap'd happiness upon him;
For then, and not till then, he felt himself,
And found the blessedness of being little:
And, to add greater honours to his age
Than man could give him, he died fearing God.

KATHARINE
After my death I wish no other herald,
No other speaker of my living actions,
To keep mine honour from corruption,
But such an honest chronicler as Griffith.
Whom I most hated living, thou hast made me,
With thy religious truth and modesty,
Now in his ashes honour: peace be with him!
Patience, be near me still; and set me lower:
I have not long to trouble thee. Good Griffith,
Cause the musicians play me that sad note
I named my knell, whilst I sit meditating
On that celestial harmony I go to.
[*Sad and solemn music*

GRIFFITH
She is asleep: good wench, let's sit down quiet,
For fear we wake her: softly, gentle Patience.
The vision. Enter, solemnly tripping one after another, six personages, clad in white robes, wearing on their heads garlands of bays, and golden vizards on their faces; branches of bays or palm in their hands. They first congee unto her, then dance; and, at certain changes, the first two hold a spare garland over her head; at which the other four make reverent curtsies; then the two that held the garland deliver the same to the other next two, who observe the same order in their changes, and holding the garland over her head: which done, they deliver the same garland to the last two, who likewise observe the same order: at which, as it were by inspiration, she makes in her sleep signs of rejoicing, and holdeth up her hands to heaven: and so in their dancing

vanish, carrying the garland with them. The music
continues
KATHARINE
Spirits of peace, where are ye? are ye all gone,
And leave me here in wretchedness behind ye?
GRIFFITH
Madam, we are here.
KATHARINE
It is not you I call for:
Saw ye none enter since I slept?
GRIFFITH
None, madam.
KATHARINE
No? Saw you not even now a blessed troop
Invite me to a banquet, whose bright faces
Cast thousand beams upon me, like the sun?
They promised me eternal happiness,
And brought me garlands, Griffith, which I feel
I am not worthy yet to wear: I shall, assuredly.
GRIFFITH
I am most joyful, madam, such good dreams
Possess your fancy.
KATHARINE
Bid the music leave;
They are harsh and heavy to me.   [*Music ceases*
PATIENCE
Do you note
How much her grace is alter'd on the sudden?
How long her face is drawn! how pale she looks,
And of an earthy cold! Mark her eyes!
GRIFFITH
She is going, wench: pray, pray.
PATIENCE
Heaven comfort her!
Enter a MESSENGER
MESSENGER
An 't like your grace,—
KATHARINE
You are a saucy fellow:
Deserve we no more reverence?
GRIFFITH
You are to blame,
Knowing she will not lose her wonted greatness,
To use so rude behaviour: go to, kneel.
MESSENGER
I humbly do entreat your highness' pardon;
My haste made me unmannerly. There is staying
A gentleman, sent from the king, to see you.
KATHARINE
Admit him entrance, Griffith: but this fellow
Let me ne'er see again.
[*Exeunt* GRIFFITH *and* MESSENGER
Re-enter GRIFFITH, *with* CAPUCIUS
If my sight fail not,
You should be lord ambassador from the emperor,
My royal nephew, and your name Capucius.
CAPUCIUS
Madam, the same; your servant.
KATHARINE
O, my lord,

The times and titles now are alter'd strangely
With me since first you knew me. But, I pray you,
What is your pleasure with me?
CAPUCIUS
Noble lady,
First, mine own service to your grace; the next,
The king's request that I would visit you;
Who grieves much for your weakness, and by me
Sends you his princely commendations,
And heartily entreats you take good comfort.
KATHARINE
O my good lord, that comfort comes too late;
'Tis like a pardon after execution:
That gentle physic, given in time, had cured me;
But now I am past all comforts here but prayers.
How does his highness?
CAPUCIUS
Madam, in good health.
KATHARINE
So may he ever do! and ever flourish,
When I shall dwell with worms, and my poor name
Banish'd the kingdom! Patience, is that letter,
I caused you write, yet sent away?
PATIENCE
No, madam.
[*Giving it to* KATHARINE
KATHARINE
Sir, I most humbly pray you to deliver
This to my lord the king.
CAPUCIUS
Most willing, madam.
KATHARINE
In which I have commended to his goodness
The model of our chaste loves, his young daughter,—
The dews of heaven fall thick in blessings on her!—
Beseeching him to give her virtuous breeding—
She is young and of a noble modest nature:
I hope she will deserve well—and a little
To love her for her mother's sake, that loved him,
Heaven knows how dearly. My next poor petition
Is that his noble grace would have some pity
Upon my wretched women, that so long
Have follow'd both my fortunes faithfully:
Of which there is not one, I dare avow,—
And now I should not lie—but will deserve,
For virtue and true beauty of the soul,
For honesty and decent carriage,
A right good husband, let him be a noble:
And, sure, those men are happy that shall have 'em.
The last is, for my men; they are the poorest,
But poverty could never draw 'em from me;
That they may have their wages duly paid 'em,
And something over to remember me by:
If heaven had pleased to have given me longer life
And able means, we had not parted thus.
These are the whole contents: and, good my lord,
By that you love the dearest in this world,
As you wish Christian peace to souls departed,
Stand these poor people's friend, and urge the king
To do me this last right.

CAPUCIUS
By heaven, I will,
Or let me lose the fashion of a man!

KATHARINE
I thank you, honest lord. Remember me
In all humility unto his highness:
Say his long trouble now is passing
Out of this world; tell him, in death I bless'd him,
For so I will. Mine eyes grow dim. Farewell,
My lord. Griffith, farewell. Nay, Patience,
You must not leave me yet: I must to bed;
Call in more women. When I am dead, good wench,
Let me be used with honour: strew me over
With maiden flowers, that all the world may know
I was a chaste wife to my grave: embalm me,
Then lay me forth; although unqueen'd, yet like
A queen, and daughter to a king, inter me.
I can no more.   [Exeunt, leading KATHARINE

ACT V

SCENE I. London. A gallery in the palace

Enter GARDINER, BISHOP OF WINCHESTER, *a* PAGE *with a torch before him, met by* SIR THOMAS LOVELL

GARDINER
It's one o'clock, boy, is 't not?

BOY
It hath struck.

GARDINER
These should be hours for necessities,
Not for delights; times to repair our nature
With comforting repose, and not for us
To waste these times. Good hour of night, Sir
    Thomas!
Whither so late?

LOVELL
Came you from the king, my lord?

GARDINER
I did, Sir Thomas, and left him at primero
With the Duke of Suffolk.

LOVELL
I must to him too,
Before he go to bed. I'll take my leave.

GARDINER
Not yet, Sir Thomas Lovell. What's the matter?
It seems you are in haste: an if there be
No great offence belongs to 't, give your friend
Some touch of your late business: affairs that walk,
As they say spirits do, at midnight, have
In them a wilder nature than the business
That seeks dispatch by day.

LOVELL
My lord, I love you;
And durst commend a secret to your ear
Much weightier than this work. The queen's in
    labour,

They say, in great extremity; and fear'd
She'll with the labour end.

GARDINER
The fruit she goes with
I pray for heartily, that it may find
Good time, and live: but for the stock, Sir Thomas,
I wish it grubb'd up now.

LOVELL
Methinks I could
Cry the amen; and yet my conscience says
She's a good creature, and, sweet lady, does
Deserve our better wishes.

GARDINER
But, sir, sir,
Hear me, Sir Thomas: you're a gentleman
Of mine own way; I know you wise, religious;
And, let me tell you, it will ne'er be well,
'Twill not, Sir Thomas Lovell, take 't of me,
Till Cranmer, Cromwell, her two hands, and she,
Sleep in their graves.

LOVELL
Now, sir, you speak of two
The most remark'd i' the kingdom. As for Cromwell,
Beside that of the jewel house, is made master
O' the rolls, and the king's secretary; further, sir,
Stands in the gap and trade of moe preferments,
With which the time will load him. The archbishop
Is the king's hand and tongue; and who dare speak
One syllable against him?

GARDINER
Yes, yes, Sir Thomas,
There are that dare; and I myself have ventured
To speak my mind of him: and indeed this day,
Sir, I may tell it you, I think I have
Incensed the lords o' the council that he is—
For so I know he is, they know he is—
A most arch-heretic, a pestilence
That does infect the land: with which they moved
Have broken with the king; who hath so far
Given ear to our complaint, of his great grace
And princely care foreseeing those fell mischiefs
Our reasons laid before him, hath commanded
To-morrow morning to the council-board
He be convented. He's a rank weed, Sir Thomas,
And we must root him out. From your affairs
I hinder you too long: good night, Sir Thomas.

LOVELL
Many good nights, my lord: I rest your servant.
        [Exeunt GARDINER and PAGE
        Enter KING and SUFFOLK

KING
Charles, I will play no more to-night;
My mind's not on 't; you are too hard for me.

SUFFOLK
Sir, I did never win of you before.

KING
But little, Charles,
Nor shall not, when my fancy's on my play.
Now, Lovell, from the queen what is the news?

LOVELL

I could not personally deliver to her
What you commanded me, but by her woman
I sent your message; who return'd her thanks
In the great'st humbleness, and desired your high-
ness
Most heartily to pray for her.

KING

What say'st thou, ha?
To pray for her? what, is she crying out?

LOVELL

So said her woman, and that her sufferance made
Almost each pang a death.

KING

Alas, good lady!

SUFFOLK

God safely quit her of her burthen, and
With gentle travail, to the gladding of
Your highness with an heir!

KING

'Tis midnight, Charles;
Prithee, to bed; and in thy prayers remember
The estate of my poor queen. Leave me alone;
For I must think of that which company
Would not be friendly to.

SUFFOLK

I wish your highness
A quiet night, and my good mistress will
Remember in my prayers.

KING

Charles, good night.
[Exit SUFFOLK
Enter SIR ANTHONY DENNY
Well, sir, what follows?

DENNY

Sir, I have brought my lord the archbishop,
As you commanded me.

KING

Ha! Canterbury?

DENNY

Ay, my good lord.

KING

'Tis true: where is he, Denny?

DENNY

He attends your highness' pleasure.

KING

Bring him to us.
[Exit DENNY

LOVELL

[Aside] This is about that which the bishop spake:
I am happily come hither.
Re-enter DENNY, with CRANMER

KING

Avoid the gallery. [LOVELL seems to stay] Ha! I have
said. Be gone.
What! [Exeunt LOVELL and DENNY

CRANMER

[Aside] I am fearful: wherefore frowns he thus?
'Tis his aspect of terror. All's not well.

KING

How now, my lord! you do desire to know
Wherefore I sent for you.

CRANMER

[Kneeling] It is my duty
To attend your highness' pleasure.

KING

Pray you, arise,
My good and gracious Lord of Canterbury.
Come, you and I must walk a turn together;
I have news to tell you: come, come, give me your
hand.
Ah, my good lord, I grieve at what I speak,
And am right sorry to repeat what follows:
I have, and most unwillingly, of late
Heard many grievous, I do say, my lord,
Grievous complaints of you; which, being con-
sider'd,
Have moved us and our council, that you shall
This morning come before us; where, I know,
You cannot with such freedom purge yourself,
But that, till further trial in those charges
Which will require your answer, you must take
Your patience to you and be well contented
To make your house our Tower: you a brother of
us,
It fits we thus proceed, or else no witness
Would come against you.

CRANMER

[Kneeling] I humbly thank your highness;
And am right glad to catch this good occasion
Most throughly to be winnow'd, where my chaff
And corn shall fly asunder: for, I know,
There's none stands under more calumnious tongues
Than I myself, poor man.

KING

Stand up, good Canterbury:
Thy truth and thy integrity is rooted
In us, thy friend: give me thy hand, stand up:
Prithee, let's walk. Now, by my holidame,
What manner of man are you? My lord, I look'd
You would have given me your petition, that
I should have ta'en some pains to bring together
Yourself and your accusers, and to have heard you,
Without indurance further.

CRANMER

Most dread liege,
The good I stand on is my truth and honesty:
If they shall fail, I, with mine enemies,
Will triumph o'er my person; which I weigh not,
Being of those virtues vacant. I fear nothing
What can be said against me.

KING

Know you not
How your state stands i' the world, with the whole
world?
Your enemies are many, and not small; their prac-
tices
Must bear the same proportion; and not ever
The justice and the truth o' the question carries

The due o' the verdict with it: at what ease
Might corrupt minds procure knaves as corrupt
To swear against you? Such things have been done.
You are potently opposed, and with a malice
Of as great size. Ween you of better luck,
I mean, in perjured witness, than your master,
Whose minister you are, whiles here he lived
Upon this naughty earth? Go to, go to;
You take a precipice for no leap of danger,
And woo your own destruction.

CRANMER
               God and your majesty
Protect mine innocence, or I fall into
The trap is laid for me!

KING
               Be of good cheer;
They shall no more prevail than we give way to.
Keep comfort to you; and this morning see
You do appear before them. If they shall chance,
In charging you with matters, to commit you,
The best persuasions to the contrary
Fail not to use, and with what vehemency
The occasion shall instruct you: if entreaties
Will render you no remedy, this ring
Deliver them, and your appeal to us
There make before them. Look, the good man
   weeps!
He's honest, on mine honour. God's blest mother!
I swear he is true-hearted, and a soul
None better in my kingdom. Get you gone,
And do as I have bid you. [*Exit* CRANMER] He has
   strangled
His language in his tears.

      Enter OLD LADY; LOVELL *following*
GENTLEMAN
     [*Within*] Come back: what mean you?
OLD LADY
I'll not come back; the tidings that I bring
Will make my boldness manners. Now, good angels
Fly o'er thy royal head, and shade thy person
Under their blessed wings!

KING
            Now, by thy looks
I guess thy message. Is the queen deliver'd?
Say, ay, and of a boy.

OLD LADY
          Ay, ay, my liege;
And of a lovely boy: the God of heaven
Both now and ever bless her! 'tis a girl,
Promises boys hereafter. Sir, your queen
Desires your visitation, and to be
Acquainted with this stranger: 'tis as like you
As cherry is to cherry.

KING
           Lovell!
LOVELL
           Sir?
KING
Give her an hundred marks. I'll to the queen.
                            [*Exit*

OLD LADY
An hundred marks! By this light, I'll ha' more.
An ordinary groom is for such payment.
I will have more, or scold it out of him.
Said I for this, the girl was like to him?
I will have more, or else unsay 't; and now,
While it is hot, I'll put it to the issue.   [*Exeunt*

SCENE II. *Before the council-chamber*

PURSUIVANTS, PAGES, &*c. attending*
Enter CRANMER, *Archbishop of Canterbury*
CRANMER
I hope I am not too late; and yet the gentleman
That was sent to me from the council pray'd me
To make great haste. All fast? what means this? Ho!
Who waits there? Sure, you know me?

          Enter KEEPER
KEEPER
                    Yes, my lord;
But yet I cannot help you.

CRANMER
Why?

        Enter DOCTOR BUTTS
KEEPER
Your grace must wait till you be call'd for.

CRANMER
                   So.

BUTTS
[*Aside*] This is a piece of malice. I am glad
I came this way so happily: the king
Shall understand it presently.   [*Exit*

CRANMER
          [*Aside*] 'Tis Butts,
The king's physician: as he pass'd along,
How earnestly he cast his eyes upon me!
Pray heaven, he sound not my disgrace! For certain,
This is of purpose laid by some that hate me—
God turn their hearts! I never sought their malice—
To quench mine honour: they would shame to
   make me
Wait else at door, a fellow-councillor,
'Mong boys, grooms and lackeys. But their pleasures
Must be fulfill'd, and I attend with patience.
     Enter the KING *and* BUTTS *at a window above*
BUTTS
I'll show your grace the strangest sight—
KING
                What's that, Butts?
BUTTS
I think your highness saw this many a day.
KING
Body o' me, where is it?
BUTTS
             There, my lord:
The high promotion of his grace of Canterbury;
Who holds his state at door, 'mongst pursuivants,
Pages and footboys.

KING

Ha! 'tis he, indeed:
Is this the honour they do one another?
'Tis well there's one above 'em yet. I had thought
They had parted so much honesty among 'em,
At least good manners, as not thus to suffer
A man of his place and so near our favour
To dance attendance on their lordships' pleasures,
And at the door too, like a post with packets.
By holy Mary, Butts, there's knavery:
Let 'em alone, and draw the curtain close;
We shall hear more anon.   [Exeunt

SCENE III. *The council-chamber*

Enter LORD CHANCELLOR, *places himself at the upper
end of the table on the left hand; a seat being left void above
him, as for* CANTERBURY'S *seat;* DUKE OF SUFFOLK,
DUKE OF NORFOLK, SURREY, LORD CHAMBERLAIN,
GARDINER, *seat themselves in order on each side.* CROM-
WELL *at lower end, as secretary.* KEEPER *at the door*

CHANCELLOR

Speak to the business, master secretary:
Why are we met in council?

CROMWELL

Please your honours,
The chief cause concerns his grace of Canterbury.

GARDINER

Has he had knowledge of it?

CROMWELL

Yes.

NORFOLK

Who waits there?

KEEPER

Without, my noble lords?

GARDINER

Yes.

KEEPER

My lord archbishop;
And has done half an hour, to know your pleasures.

CHANCELLOR

Let him come in.

KEEPER

Your grace may enter now.

CRANMER *enters and approaches the council-table*

CHANCELLOR

My good lord archbishop, I'm very sorry
To sit here at this present and behold
That chair stand empty: but we all are men,
In our own natures frail and capable
Of our flesh; few are angels: out of which frailty
And want of wisdom, you, that best should teach us,
Have misdemean'd yourself, and not a little,
Toward the king first, then his laws, in filling
The whole realm, by your teaching and your chap-
    lains,—
For so we are inform'd,—with new opinions,
Divers and dangerous; which are heresies,
And, not reform'd, may prove pernicious.

GARDINER

Which reformation must be sudden too,
My noble lords; for those that tame wild horses
Pace 'em not in their hands to make 'em gentle,
But stop their mouths with stubborn bits and spur
    'em,
Till they obey the manage. If we suffer,
Out of our easiness and childish pity
To one man's honour, this contagious sickness,
Farewell all physic: and what follows then?
Commotions, uproars, with a general taint
Of the whole state: as of late days our neighbours,
The upper Germany, can dearly witness,
Yet freshly pitied in our memories.

CRANMER

My good lords, hitherto, in all the progress
Both of my life and office, I have labour'd,
And with no little study, that my teaching
And the strong course of my authority
Might go one way, and safely; and the end
Was ever to do well: nor is there living,
I speak it with a single heart, my lords,
A man that more detests, more stirs against,
Both in his private conscience and his place,
Defacers of a public peace, than I do.
Pray heaven, the king may never find a heart
With less allegiance in it! Men that make
Envy and crooked malice nourishment
Dare bite the best. I do beseech your lordships,
That, in this case of justice, my accusers,
Be what they will, may stand forth face to face,
And freely urge against me.

SUFFOLK

Nay, my lord,
That cannot be: you are a councillor,
And, by that virtue, no man dare accuse you.

GARDINER

My lord, because we have business of more moment,
We will be short with you. 'Tis his highness' pleasure,
And our consent, for better trial of you,
From hence you be committed to the Tower;
Where, being but a private man again,
You shall know many dare accuse you boldly,
More than, I fear, you are provided for.

CRANMER

Ah, my good Lord of Winchester, I thank you;
You are always my good friend; if your will pass,
I shall both find your lordship judge and juror,
You are so merciful. I see your end;
'Tis my undoing. Love and meekness, lord,
Become a churchman better than ambition:
Win straying souls with modesty again,
Cast none away. That I shall clear myself,
Lay all the weight ye can upon my patience,
I make as little doubt as you do conscience
In doing daily wrongs. I could say more,
But reverence to your calling makes me modest.

GARDINER

My lord, my lord, you are a sectary;

That's the plain truth: your painted gloss discovers,
To men that understand you, words and weakness.

CROMWELL

My Lord of Winchester, you are a little,
By your good favour, too sharp; men so noble,
However faulty, yet should find respect
For what they have been: 'tis a cruelty
To load a falling man.

GARDINER

          Good master secretary,
I cry your honour mercy; you may, worst
Of all this table, say so.

CROMWELL

          Why, my lord?

GARDINER

Do not I know you for a favourer
Of this new sect? ye are not sound.

CROMWELL

          Not sound?

GARDINER

Not sound, I say.

CROMWELL

          Would you were half so honest!
Men's prayers then would seek you, not their fears.

GARDINER

I shall remember this bold language.

CROMWELL

          Do.
Remember your bold life too.

CHANCELLOR

          This is too much;
Forbear, for shame, my lords.

GARDINER

          I have done.

CROMWELL

          And I.

CHANCELLOR

Then thus for you, my lord: it stands agreed,
I take it, by all voices, that forthwith
You be convey'd to the Tower a prisoner;
There to remain till the king's further pleasure
Be known unto us: are you all agreed, lords?

ALL

We are.

CRANMER

          Is there no other way of mercy,
But I must needs to the Tower, my lords?

GARDINER

          What other
Would you expect? you are strangely troublesome.
Let some o' the guard be ready there.

Enter GUARD

CRANMER

          For me?
Must I go like a traitor thither?

GARDINER

          Receive him,
And see him safe i' the Tower.

CRANMER

          Stay, good my lords,

I have a little yet to say. Look there, my lords;
By virtue of that ring, I take my cause
Out of the gripes of cruel men, and give it
To a most noble judge, the king my master.

CHAMBERLAIN

This is the king's ring.

SURREY

          'Tis no counterfeit.

SUFFOLK

'Tis the right ring, by heaven: I told ye all,
When we first put this dangerous stone a-rolling,
'Twould fall upon ourselves.

NORFOLK

          Do you think, my lords,
The king will suffer but the little finger
Of this man to be vex'd?

CHAMBERLAIN

          'Tis now too certain:
How much more is his life in value with him?
Would I were fairly out on 't!

CROMWELL

          My mind gave me,
In seeking tales and informations
Against this man, whose honesty the devil
And his disciples only envy at,
Ye blew the fire that burns ye: now have at ye!

Enter KING, frowning on them; takes his seat

GARDINER

Dread sovereign, how much are we bound to
     heaven
In daily thanks, that gave us such a prince,
Not only good and wise, but most religious:
One that, in all obedience, makes the church
The chief aim of his honour; and, to strengthen
That holy duty, out of dear respect,
His royal self in judgement comes to hear
The cause betwixt her and this great offender.

KING

You were ever good at sudden commendations,
Bishop of Winchester. But know, I come not
To hear such flattery now, and in my presence
They are too thin and bare to hide offences.
To me you cannot reach you play the spaniel,
And think with wagging of your tongue to win me;
But, whatsoe'er thou takest me for, I'm sure
Thou hast a cruel nature and a bloody.
[To CRANMER] Good man, sit down. Now let me see
     the proudest
He, that dares most, but wag his finger at thee:
By all that's holy, he had better starve
Than but once think this place becomes thee not.

SURREY

May it please your grace,—

KING

          No, sir, it does not please me.
I had thought I had had men of some understand-
     ing
And wisdom of my council; but I find none.

Was it discretion, lords, to let this man,
This good man,—few of you deserve that title,—
This honest man, wait like a lousy footboy
At chamber-door? and one as great as you are?
Why, what a shame was this! Did my commission
Bid ye so far forget yourselves? I gave ye
Power as he was a councillor to try him,
Not as a groom: there's some of ye, I see,
More out of malice than integrity,
Would try him to the utmost, had ye mean;
Which ye shall never have while I live.

CHANCELLOR
　　　　　　　　　　Thus far,
My most dread sovereign, may it like your grace
To let my tongue excuse all. What was purposed
Concerning his imprisonment, was rather,
If there be faith in men, meant for his trial
And fair purgation to the world, than malice,
I'm sure, in me.

KING
　　　　　　Well, well, my lords, respect him;
Take him and use him well; he's worthy of it.
I will say thus much for him, if a prince
May be beholding to a subject, I
Am, for his love and service, so to him.
Make me no more ado, but all embrace him:
Be friends, for shame, my lords! My Lord of Canterbury,
I have a suit which you must not deny me;
That is, a fair young maid that yet wants baptism;
You must be godfather, and answer for her.

CRANMER
The greatest monarch now alive may glory
In such an honour: how may I deserve it,
That am a poor and humble subject to you?

KING
Come, come, my lord, you'ld spare your spoons:
you shall have two noble partners with you; the old
Duchess of Norfolk, and Lady Marquess Dorset:
will these please you?
Once more, my Lord of Winchester, I charge you,
Embrace and love this man.

GARDINER
　　　　　　　　With a true heart
And brother-love I do it.

CRANMER
　　　　　　　　And let heaven
Witness how dear I hold this confirmation.

KING
Good man, those joyful tears show thy true heart:
The common voice, I see, is verified
Of thee, which says thus: 'Do my Lord of Canterbury
A shrewd turn, and he is your friend for ever.'
Come, lords, we trifle time away; I long
To have this young one made a Christian.
As I have made ye one, lords, one remain;
So I grow stronger, you more honour gain. [Exeunt

SCENE IV. *The palace yard*

Noise and tumult within. Enter PORTER *and his* MAN

PORTER
You'll leave your noise anon, ye rascals: do you take
the court for Paris-garden? ye rude slaves, leave
your gaping.
[*Within*] 'Good master porter, I belong to the
larder.'

PORTER
Belong to the gallows, and be hanged, ye rogue!
Is this a place to roar in? Fetch me a dozen crab-
tree staves, and strong ones: these are but switches
to 'em. I'll scratch your heads: you must be seeing
christenings? do you look for ale and cakes here,
you rude rascals?

MAN
Pray, sir, be patient: 'tis as much impossible—
Unless we sweep 'em from the door with cannons—
To scatter 'em, as 'tis to make 'em sleep
On May-day morning; which will never be:
We may as well push against Powle's as stir 'em.

PORTER
How got they in, and be hang'd?

MAN
Alas, I know not; how gets the tide in?
As much as one sound cudgel of four foot—
You see the poor remainder—could distribute,
I made no spare, sir.

PORTER
　　　　　　You did nothing, sir.

MAN
I am not Samson, nor Sir Guy, nor Colbrand,
To mow 'em down before me: but if I spared any
That had a head to hit, either young or old,
He or she, cuckold or cuckold-maker,
Let me ne'er hope to see a chine again;
And that I would not for a cow, God save her!
[*Within*] 'Do you hear, master porter?'

PORTER
I shall be with you presently, good master puppy.
Keep the door close, sirrah.

MAN
What would you have me do?

PORTER
What should you do, but knock 'em down by the
dozens? Is this Moorfields to muster in? or have we
some strange Indian with the great tool come to
court, the women so besiege us? Bless me, what a fry
of fornication is at door! On my Christian conscience, this one christening will beget a thousand;
here will be father, godfather, and all together.

MAN
The spoons will be the bigger, sir. There is a fellow
somewhat near the door, he should be a brazier by
his face, for, o' my conscience, twenty of the dog-
days now reign in 's nose; all that stand about him
are under the line, they need no other penance:
that fire-drake did I hit three times on the head,

and three times was his nose discharged against me; he stands there, like a mortar-piece, to blow us. There was a haberdasher's wife of small wit near him, that railed upon me till her pinked porringer fell off her head, for kindling such a combustion in the state. I missed the meteor once, and hit that woman, who cried out 'Clubs!' when I might see from far some forty truncheoners draw to her succour, which were the hope o' the Strand, where she was quartered. They fell on; I made good my place: at length they came to the broomstaff to me; I defied 'em still: when suddenly a file of boys behind 'em, loose shot, delivered such a shower of pebbles, that I was fain to draw mine honour in and let 'em win the work: the devil was amongst 'em, I think, surely.

PORTER

These are the youths that thunder at a playhouse and fight for bitten apples; that no audience, but the tribulation of Tower-hill, or the limbs of Limehouse, their dear brothers, are able to endure. I have some of 'em in Limbo Patrum, and there they are like to dance these three days; besides the running banquet of two beadles that is to come.

Enter LORD CHAMBERLAIN

CHAMBERLAIN

Mercy o' me, what a multitude are here!
They grow still too; from all parts they are coming,
As if we kept a fair here. Where are these porters,
These lazy knaves? Ye have made a fine hand,
    fellows!
There's a trim rabble let in: are all these
Your faithful friends o' the suburbs? We shall have
Great store of room, no doubt, left for the ladies,
When they pass back from the christening.

PORTER

                    An 't please your honour,
We are but men; and what so many may do,
Not being torn a-pieces, we have done:
An army cannot rule 'em.

CHAMBERLAIN

                    As I live,
If the king blame me for 't, I'll lay ye all
By the heels, and suddenly; and on your heads
Clap round fines for neglect: ye're lazy knaves;
And here ye lie baiting of bombards when
Ye should do service. Hark! the trumpets sound;
They're come already from the christening:
Go, break among the press, and find a way out
To let the troop pass fairly, or I'll find
A Marshalsea shall hold ye play these two months.

PORTER

Make way there for the princess.

MAN

                    You great fellow,
Stand close up, or I'll make your head ache.

PORTER

You i' the camlet, get up o' the rail;
I'll peck you o'er the pales else.   [*Exeunt*

SCENE V. *The palace*

Enter Trumpets, sounding; then two ALDERMEN, LORD MAYOR, GARTER, CRANMER, DUKE OF NORFOLK *with his marshal's staff,* DUKE OF SUFFOLK, *two* NOBLEMEN *bearing great standing-bowls for the christening gifts; then four* NOBLEMEN *bearing a canopy, under which the* DUCHESS OF NORFOLK, *godmother, bearing the child richly habited in a mantle, &c., train borne by a* LADY; *then follows the* MARCHIONESS DORSET, *the other godmother, and* LADIES. *The troop pass once about the stage, and* GARTER *speaks*

GARTER

Heaven, from thy endless goodness, send prosperous life, long, and ever happy, to the high and mighty princess of England, Elizabeth!

Flourish. Enter KING *and* GUARD

CRANMER

[*Kneeling*] And to your royal grace, and the good
    queen,
My noble partners and myself thus pray:
All comfort, joy, in this most gracious lady,
Heaven ever laid up to make parents happy,
May hourly fall upon ye!

KING

                    Thank you, good lord archbishop;
What is her name?

CRANMER

                    Elizabeth.

KING

                    Stand up, lord.
                    [*The* KING *kisses the child*
With this kiss take my blessing: God protect thee!
Into whose hand I give thy life.

CRANMER

                    Amen.

KING

My noble gossips, ye have been too prodigal:
I thank ye heartily; so shall this lady,
When she has so much English.

CRANMER

                    Let me speak, sir,
For heaven now bids me; and the words I utter
Let none think flattery, for they'll find 'em truth.
This royal infant—heaven still move about her!—
Though in her cradle, yet now promises
Upon this land a thousand thousand blessings,
Which time shall bring to ripeness: she shall be—
But few now living can behold that goodness—
A pattern to all princes living with her,
And all that shall succeed: Saba was never
More covetous of wisdom and fair virtue
Than this pure soul shall be: all princely graces,
That mould up such a mighty piece as this is,
With all the virtues that attend the good,
Shall still be doubled on her: truth shall nurse her,
Holy and heavenly thoughts still counsel her:
She shall be loved and fear'd: her own shall bless
    her;
Her foes shake like a field of beaten corn.

And hang their heads with sorrow. Good grows
   with her:
In her days every man shall eat in safety,
Under his own vine, what he plants, and sing
The merry songs of peace to all his neighbours:
God shall be truly known; and those about her
From her shall read the perfect ways of honour,
And by those claim their greatness, not by blood.
Nor shall this peace sleep with her; but, as when
The bird of wonder dies, the maiden phœnix,
Her ashes new create another heir
As great in admiration as herself,
So shall she leave her blessedness to one—
When heaven shall call her from this cloud of dark-
   ness—
Who from the sacred ashes of her honour
Shall star-like rise, as great in fame as she was,
And so stand fix'd. Peace, plenty, love, truth, terror,
That were the servants to this chosen infant,
Shall then be his, and like a vine grow to him
Wherever the bright sun of heaven shall shine,
His honour and the greatness of his name
Shall be, and make new nations: he shall flourish,
And, like a mountain cedar, reach his branches
To all the plains about him. Our children's children
Shall see this, and bless heaven.

            KING
                Thou speakest wonders.
          CRANMER
She shall be, to the happiness of England,
An aged princess; many days shall see her,
And yet no day without a deed to crown it.
Would I had known no more! but she must die;
She must; the saints must have her; yet a virgin,
A most unspotted lily shall she pass
To the ground. and all the world shall mourn her.

            KING
O lord archbishop,
Thou hast made me now a man! never, before
This happy child, did I get any thing.
This oracle of comfort has so pleased me,
That when I am in heaven I shall desire
To see what this child does, and praise my Maker.
I thank ye all. To you, my good lord mayor,
And your good brethren, I am much beholding;
I have received much honour by your presence,
And ye shall find me thankful. Lead the way, lords:
Ye must all see the queen, and she must thank ye;
She will be sick else. This day, no man think
Has business at his house; for all shall stay:
This little one shall make it holiday.   *[Exeunt*

THE EPILOGUE

 'Tis ten to one this play can never please
All that are here: some come to take their ease,
And sleep an act or two; but those, we fear,
We have frighted with our trumpets; so, 'tis clear,
They'll say 'tis naught: others, to hear the city
Abused extremely, and to cry 'That's witty!'
Which we have not done neither; that, I fear,
All the expected good we're like to hear
For this play at this time, is only in
The merciful construction of good women;
For such a one we show'd 'em: if they smile,
And say 'twill do, I know, within a while
All the best men are ours; for 'tis ill hap,
If they hold when their ladies bid 'em clap.

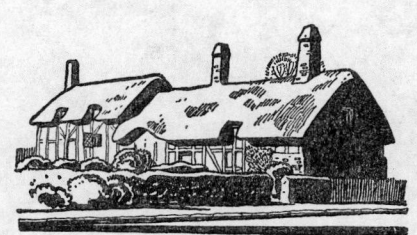

And hang their heads with sorrow. Good grows
with her.

In her days every man shall eat in safety
Under his own vine, what he plants, and sing
The merry songs of peace to all his neighbours.
God shall be truly known, and those about her
From her shall read the perfect ways of honour,
And by those claim their greatness, not by blood.
Nor shall this peace sleep with her; but as when
The bird of wonder dies, the maiden phoenix,
Her ashes new create another heir
As great in admiration as herself;
So shall she leave her blessedness to one—
When heaven shall call her from this cloud of dark-
ness—
Who from the sacred ashes of her honour
Shall star-like rise, as great in fame as she was,
And so stand fix'd. Peace, plenty, love, truth, terror,
That were the servants to this chosen infant,
Shall then be his, and like a vine grow to him;
Wherever the bright sun of heaven shall shine,
His honour and the greatness of his name
Shall be, and make new nations. He shall flourish,
And, like a mountain cedar, reach his branches
To all the plains about him. Our children's children
Shall see this, and bless heaven.

KING.   Thou speakest wonders.

CRANMER.
She shall be, to the happiness of England,
An aged princess; many days shall see her,
And yet no day without a deed to crown it.
Would I had known no more! but she must die,
She must, the saints must have her; yet a virgin,
A most unspotted lily shall she pass
To the ground, and all the world shall mourn her.

KING. O lord archbishop,
Thou hast made me now a man! never, before
This happy child, did I get any thing.
This oracle of comfort has so pleas'd me,
That when I am in heaven I shall desire
To see what this child does, and praise my Maker.
I thank ye all. To you, my good lord mayor,
And your good brethren, I am much beholding;
I have received much honour by your presence,
And ye shall find me thankful. Lead the way, lords:
Ye must all see the queen, and she must thank ye;
She will be sick else. This day, no man think
Has business at his house; for all shall stay:
This little one shall make it holiday.   [Exeunt.

THE EPILOGUE

'Tis ten to one this play can never please
All that are here: some come to take their ease,
And sleep an act or two; but those, we fear,
We have frighted with our trumpets; so, 'tis clear,
They'll say 'tis naught: others, to hear the city
Abus'd extremely, and to cry 'That's witty!'
Which we have not done neither: that, I fear,
All the expected good we are like to hear
For this play at this time, is only in
The merciful construction of good women;
For such a one we show'd 'em: if they smile,
And say 'twill do, I know, within a while
All the best men are ours; for 'tis ill hap,
If they hold when their ladies bid 'em clap.

VENUS AND ADONIS

TO THE

RIGHT HONORABLE HENRIE WRIOTHESLEY,

EARLE OF SOUTHAMPTON, AND BARON OF TITCHFIELD

RIGHT HONOURABLE,

I KNOW not how I shall offend in dedicating my vn-
polisht lines to your Lordship, nor how the worlde will
censure me for choosing so strong a proppe to support so
weake a burthen, onelye if your Honour seeme but
pleased, I account myselfe highly praised, and vowe to
take aduantage of all idle houres, till I haue honoured
you with some grauer labour. But if the first heire of my
inuention proue deformed, I shall be sorie it had so noble
a god-father: and neuer after eare so barren a land, for
fear it yeeld me still so bad a haruest, I leaue it to your
Honourable suruey, and your Honor to your hearts
content which I wish may alwaies answere your owne
wish, and the worlds hopefull expectation.

Your Honors in all dutie,

WILLIAM SHAKESPEARE.

HISTORICAL DATA

In 1593 this poem was printed on the press of Richard Field. It was the first work of Shakespeare to achieve formal publication.

Not only was it the first product of Shakespeare's pen to appear in print, but it seems also to have been the first of his creative work, if his own phrase in the dedication, "the first heir of my invention", may be so interpreted. In any case it attained rapid success and during the next fifty years at least twelve editions of the poem appeared.

The source of the classical legend which is the basis of the poem was probably the *Metamorphoses* of Ovid, which was the reference work in this field most generally used by Elizabethan poets. Thomas Lodge in his *Glaucus and Scilla* (1589) described a situation very similar to that used by Shakespeare and was almost certainly the most important immediate contributor to the composition of this poem, even the verse-form corresponding.

"She hearkens for his hounds and for his horn."
VENUS AND ADONIS

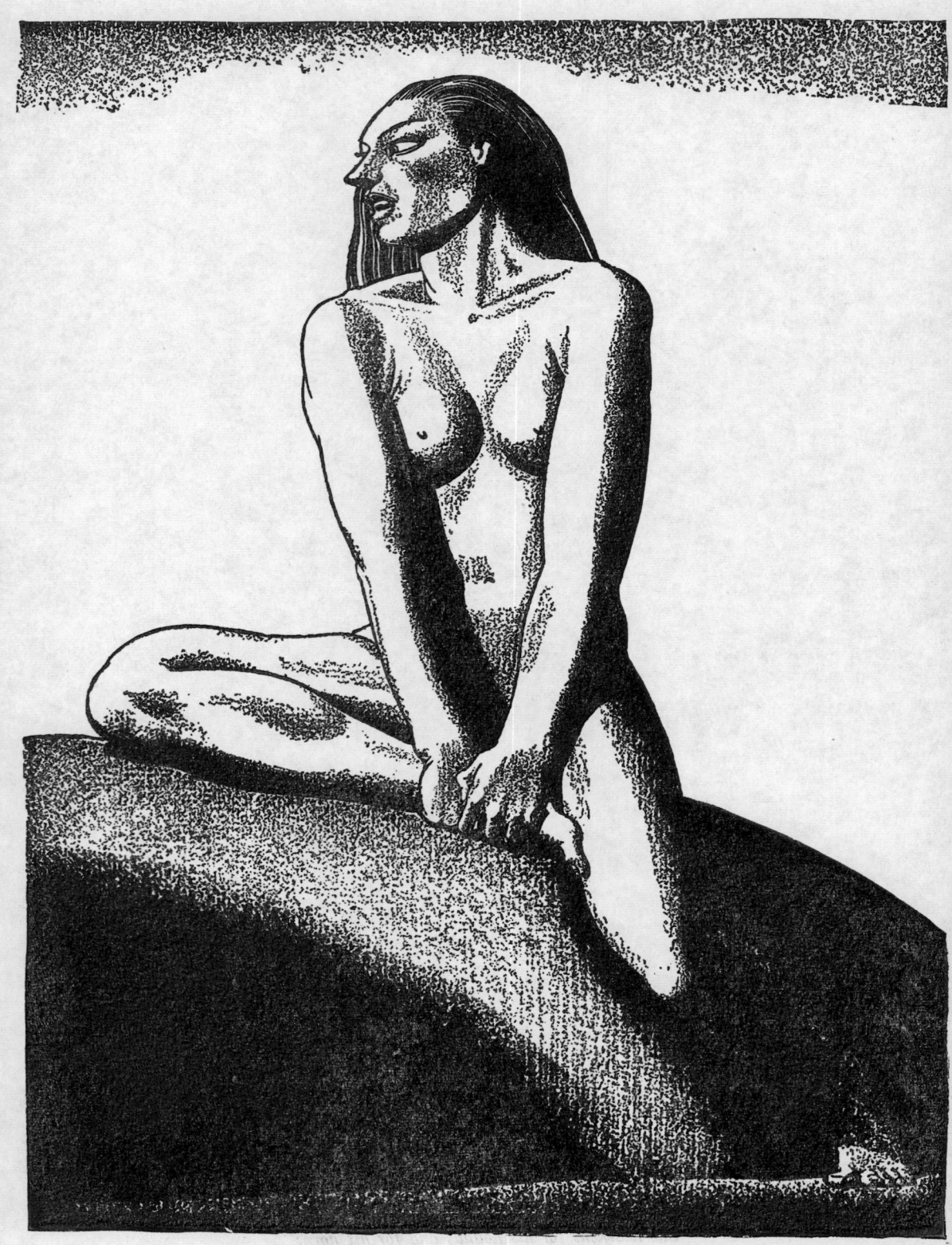

VENUS AND ADONIS

Even as the sun with purple-colour'd face
Had ta'en his last leave of the weeping morn,
Rose-cheek'd Adonis hied him to the chase;
Hunting he loved, but love he laugh'd to scorn:
 Sick-thoughted Venus makes amain unto him,
 And like a bold-faced suitor 'gins to woo him.

'Thrice fairer than myself,' thus she began,
'The field's chief flower, sweet above compare,
Stain to all nymphs, more lovely than a man,
More white and red than doves or roses are;
 Nature that made thee, with herself at strife,
 Saith that the world hath ending with thy life.

'Vouchsafe, thou wonder, to alight thy steed,
And rein his proud head to the saddle-bow;
If thou wilt deign this favour, for thy meed
A thousand honey secrets shalt thou know:
 Here come and sit, where never serpent hisses,
 And being set, I'll smother thee with kisses;

'And yet not cloy thy lips with loathed satiety,
But rather famish them amid their plenty,
Making them red and pale with fresh variety;
Ten kisses short as one, one long as twenty:
 A summer's day will seem an hour but short,
 Being wasted in such time-beguiling sport.'

With this she seizeth on his sweating palm,
The precedent of pith and livelihood,
And, trembling in her passion, calls it balm,
Earth's sovereign salve to do a goddess good:
 Being so enraged, desire doth lend her force
 Courageously to pluck him from his horse.

Over one arm the lusty courser's rein,
Under her other was the tender boy,
Who blush'd and pouted in a dull disdain,
With leaden appetite, unapt to toy;
 She red and hot as coals of glowing fire,
 He red for shame, but frosty in desire.

The studded bridle on a ragged bough
Nimbly she fastens—O, how quick is love!—
The steed is stalled up, and even now
To tie the rider she begins to prove:
 Backward she push'd him, as she would be thrust,
 And govern'd him in strength, though not in lust.

So soon was she along as he was down,
Each leaning on their elbows and their hips:
Now doth she stroke his cheek, now doth he frown,
And 'gins to chide, but soon she stops his lips;
 And kissing speaks, with lustful language broken,
 'If thou wilt chide, thy lips shall never open.'

He burns with bashful shame; she with her tears
Doth quench the maiden burning of his cheeks;
Then with her windy sighs and golden hairs
To fan and blow them dry again she seeks:
 He saith she is immodest, blames her miss;
 What follows more she murders with a kiss.

Even as an empty eagle, sharp by fast,
Tires with her beak on feathers, flesh and bone,
Shaking her wings, devouring all in haste,
Till either gorge be stuff'd or prey be gone;
 Even so she kiss'd his brow, his cheek, his chin,
 And where she ends she doth anew begin.

Forced to content, but never to obey,
Panting he lies and breatheth in her face;
She feedeth on the steam as on a prey,
And calls it heavenly moisture, air of grace;
 Wishing her cheeks were gardens full of flowers,
 So they were dew'd with such distilling showers.

Look, how a bird lies tangled in a net,
So fasten'd in her arms Adonis lies;
Pure shame and awed resistance made him fret,
Which bred more beauty in his angry eyes:
 Rain added to a river that is rank
 Perforce will force it overflow the bank.

Still she entreats, and prettily entreats,
For to a pretty ear she tunes her tale;
Still is he sullen, still he lours and frets,
'Twixt crimson shame, and anger ashy-pale;
 Being red, she loves him best; and being white,
 Her best is better'd with a more delight.

Look how he can, she cannot choose but love;
And by her fair immortal hand she swears,
From his soft bosom never to remove,
Till he take truce with her contending tears,
 Which long have rain'd, making her cheeks all
  wet;
 And one sweet kiss shall pay this countless debt.

Upon this promise did he raise his chin,
Like a dive-dapper peering through a wave,
Who, being look'd on, ducks as quickly in;
So offers he to give what she did crave;
    But when her lips were ready for his pay,
    He winks, and turns his lips another way.

Never did passenger in summer's heat
More thirst for drink than she for this good turn.
Her help she sees, but help she cannot get;
She bathes in water, yet her fire must burn:
    'O, pity,' 'gan she cry, 'flint-hearted boy!
    'Tis but a kiss I beg; why art thou coy?

'I have been woo'd, as I entreat thee now,
Even by the stern and direful god of war,
Whose sinewy neck in battle ne'er did bow,
Who conquers where he comes in every jar;
    Yet hath he been my captive and my slave,
    And begg'd for that which thou unask'd shalt
    have.

'Over my altars hath he hung his lance,
His batter'd shield, his uncontrolled crest,
And for my sake hath learn'd to sport and dance,
To toy, to wanton, dally, smile and jest;
    Scorning his churlish drum and ensign red,
    Making my arms his field, his tent my bed.

'Thus he that overruled I overswayed,
Leading him prisoner in a red-rose chain:
Strong-temper'd steel his stronger strength obeyed,
Yet was he servile to my coy disdain.
    O, be not proud, nor brag not of thy might,
    For mastering her that foil'd the god of fight!

'Touch but my lips with those fair lips of thine—
Though mine be not so fair, yet are they red—
The kiss shall be thine own as well as mine:
What see'st thou in the ground? hold up thy head:
    Look in mine eyeballs, there thy beauty lies;
    Then why not lips on lips, since eyes in eyes?

'Art thou ashamed to kiss? then wink again,
And I will wink; so shall the day seem night;
Love keeps his revels where there are but twain;
Be bold to play, our sport is not in sight:
    These blue-vein'd violets whereon we lean
    Never can blab, nor know not what we mean.

'The tender spring upon thy tempting lip
Shews thee unripe; yet mayst thou well be tasted:
Make use of time, let not advantage slip;
Beauty within itself should not be wasted:
    Fair flowers that are not gather'd in their prime
    Rot and consume themselves in little time.

'Were I hard-favour'd, foul, or wrinkled-old,
Ill-nurtured, crooked, churlish, harsh in voice,
O'erworn, despised, rheumatic and cold,
Thick-sighted, barren, lean, and lacking juice,

Then mightst thou pause, for then I were not for
    thee;
    But having no defects, why dost abhor me?

'Thou canst not see one wrinkle in my brow;
Mine eyes are grey and bright and quick in turning;
My beauty as the spring doth yearly grow,
My flesh is soft and plump, my marrow burning;
    My smooth moist hand, were it with thy hand felt,
    Would in thy palm dissolve, or seem to melt.

'Bid me discourse, I will enchant thine ear,
Or, like a fairy, trip upon the green,
Or, like a nymph, with long dishevell'd hair,
Dance on the sands, and yet no footing seen:
    Love is a spirit all compact of fire,
    Not gross to sink, but light, and will aspire.

'Witness this primrose bank whereon I lie;
These forceless flowers like sturdy trees support me;
Two strengthless doves will draw me through the
    sky,
From morn till night, even where I list to sport me:
    Is love so light, sweet boy, and may it be
    That thou shouldst think it heavy unto thee?

'Is thine own heart to thine own face affected?
Can thy right hand seize love upon thy left?
Then woo thyself, be of thyself rejected,
Steal thine own freedom, and complain on theft.
    Narcissus so himself himself forsook,
    And died to kiss his shadow in the brook.

'Torches are made to light, jewels to wear,
Dainties to taste, fresh beauty for the use,
Herbs for their smell, and sappy plants to bear;
Things growing to themselves are growth's abuse:
    Seeds spring from seeds and beauty breedeth
    beauty;
    Thou wast begot; to get it is thy duty.

'Upon the earth's increase why shouldst thou feed,
Unless the earth with thy increase be fed?
By law of nature thou art bound to breed,
That thine may live when thou thyself art dead;
    And so, in spite of death, thou dost survive,
    In that thy likeness still is left alive.'

By this, the love-sick queen began to sweat,
For, where they lay, the shadow had forsook them,
And Titan, tired in the mid-day heat,
With burning eye did hotly overlook them,
    Wishing Adonis had his team to guide,
    So he were like him and by Venus' side.

And now Adonis, with a lazy spright,
And with a heavy, dark, disliking eye,
His louring brows o'erwhelming his fair sight,
Like misty vapours when they blot the sky,
    Souring his cheeks, cries 'Fie, no more of love!
    The sun doth burn my face; I must remove.'

'Ay me,' quoth Venus, 'young, and so unkind!
What bare excuses makest thou to be gone!
I'll sigh celestial breath, whose gentle wind
Shall cool the heat of this descending sun:
    I'll make a shadow for thee of my hairs;
    If they burn too, I'll quench them with my tears.

'The sun that shines from heaven shines but warm,
And, lo, I lie between that sun and thee:
The heat I have from thence doth little harm,
Thine eye darts forth the fire that burneth me;
    And were I not immortal, life were done
    Between this heavenly and earthly sun.

'Art thou obdurate, flinty, hard as steel?
Nay, more than flint, for stone at rain relenteth:
Art thou a woman's son, and canst not feel
What 'tis to love? how want of love tormenteth?
    O, had thy mother borne so hard a mind,
    She had not brought forth thee, but died unkind.

'What am I, that thou shouldst contemn me this?
Or what great danger dwells upon my suit?
What were thy lips the worse for one poor kiss?
Speak, fair; but speak fair words, or else be mute:
    Give me one kiss, I'll give it thee again,
    And one for interest, if thou wilt have twain.

'Fie, lifeless picture, cold and senseless stone,
Well painted idol, image dull and dead,
Statue contenting but the eye alone,
Thing like a man, but of no woman bred!
    Thou art no man, though of a man's complexion,
    For men will kiss even by their own direction.'

This said, impatience chokes her pleading tongue,
And swelling passion doth provoke a pause;
Red cheeks and fiery eyes blaze forth her wrong;
Being judge in love, she cannot right her cause:
    And now she weeps, and now she fain would
      speak,
    And now her sobs do her intendments break.

Sometimes she shakes her head, and then his hand,
Now gazeth she on him, now on the ground;
Sometimes her arms infold him like a band:
She would, he will not in her arms be bound;
    And when from thence he struggles to be gone,
    She locks her lily fingers one in one.

'Fondling,' she saith, 'since I have hemm'd thee
    here
Within the circuit of this ivory pale,
I'll be a park, and thou shalt be my deer;
Feed where thou wilt, on mountain or in dale:
    Graze on my lips, and if those hills be dry,
    Stray lower, where the pleasant fountains lie.

'Within this limit is relief enough,
Sweet bottom-grass and high delightful plain,
Round rising hillocks, brakes obscure and rough,
To shelter thee from tempest and from rain:
    Then be my deer, since I am such a park;
    No dog shall rouse thee, though a thousand bark.'

At this Adonis smiles as in disdain,
That in each cheek appears a pretty dimple:
Love made those hollows, if himself were slain,
He might be buried in a tomb so simple;
    Foreknowing well, if there he came to lie,
    Why, there Love lived, and there he could not die.

These lovely caves, these round enchanting pits,
Open'd their mouths to swallow Venus' liking.
Being mad before, how doth she now for wits?
Struck dead at first, what needs a second striking?
    Poor queen of love, in thine own law forlorn,
    To love a cheek that smiles at thee in scorn!

Now which way shall she turn? what shall she say?
Her words are done, her woes the more increasing;
The time is spent, her object will away
And from her twining arms doth urge releasing.
    'Pity,' she cries, 'some favour, some remorse!'
    Away he springs, and hasteth to his horse.

But, lo, from forth a copse that neighbours by,
A breeding jennet, lusty, young and proud,
Adonis' trampling courser doth espy,
And forth she rushes, snorts and neighs aloud:
    The strong-neck'd steed, being tied unto a tree,
    Breaketh his rein and to her straight goes he.

Imperiously he leaps, he neighs, he bounds,
And now his woven girths he breaks asunder;
The bearing earth with his hard hoof he wounds,
Whose hollow womb resounds like heaven's thun-
      der;
    The iron bit he crusheth 'tween his teeth,
    Controlling what he was controlled with.

His ears up-prick'd; his braided hanging mane
Upon his compass'd crest now stand on end;
His nostrils drink the air, and forth again,
As from a furnace, vapours doth he send:
    His eye, which scornfully glisters like fire,
    Shows his hot courage and his high desire.

Sometime he trots, as if he told the steps,
With gentle majesty and modest pride;
Anon he rears upright, curvets and leaps,
As who should say 'Lo, thus my strength is tried;
    And this I do to captivate the eye
    Of the fair breeder that is standing by.'

What recketh he his rider's angry stir,
His flattering 'Holla' or his 'Stand, I say'?
What cares he now for curb or pricking spur?
For rich caparisons or trappings gay?
    He sees his love, and nothing else he sees,
    For nothing else with his proud sight agrees.

Look, when a painter would surpass the life,
In limning out a well proportion'd steed,
His art with nature's workmanship at strife,
As if the dead the living should exceed;
    So did this horse excel a common one
    In shape, in courage, colour, pace and bone.

Round-hoof'd, short-jointed, fetlocks shag and long,
Broad breast, full eye, small head and nostril wide,
High crest, short ears, straight legs and passing
    strong,
Thin mane, thick tail, broad buttock, tender hide:
    Look, what a horse should have he did not lack,
    Save a proud rider on so proud a back.

Sometime he scuds far off, and there he stares;
Anon he starts at stirring of a feather;
To bid the wind a base he now prepares,
And whether he run or fly they know not whether;
    For through his mane and tail the high wind sings,
    Fanning the hairs, who wave like feather'd wings.

He looks upon his love and neighs unto her;
She answers him, as if she knew his mind:
Being proud, as females are, to see him woo her,
She puts on outward strangeness, seems unkind,
    Spurns at his love and scorns the heat he feels,
    Beating his kind embracements with her heels.

Then, like a melancholy malcontent,
He vails his tail, that, like a falling plume,
Cool shadow to his melting buttock lent:
He stamps, and bites the poor flies in his fume.
    His love, perceiving how he was enraged,
    Grew kinder, and his fury was assuaged.

His testy master goeth about to take him;
When, lo, the unback'd breeder, full of fear,
Jealous of catching, swiftly doth forsake him,
With her the horse, and left Adonis there:
    As they were mad, unto the wood they hie them,
    Out-stripping crows that strive to over-fly them.

All swoln with chafing, down Adonis sits,
Banning his boisterous and unruly beast:
And now the happy season once more fits,
That love-sick Love by pleading may be blest;
    For lovers say, the heart hath treble wrong
    When it is barr'd the aidance of the tongue.

An oven that is stopp'd, or river stay'd,
Burneth more hotly, swelleth with more rage:
So of concealed sorrow may be said;
Free vent of words love's fire doth assuage;
    But when the heart's attorney once is mute,
    The client breaks, as desperate in his suit.

He sees her coming, and begins to glow,
Even as a dying coal revives with wind,
And with his bonnet hides his angry brow,
Looks on the dull earth with disturbed mind,

Taking no notice that she is so nigh,
For all askance he holds her in his eye.

O, what a sight it was, wistly to view
How she came stealing to the wayward boy!
To note the fighting conflict of her hue,
How white and red each other did destroy!
    But now her cheek was pale, and by and by
    It flash'd forth fire, as lightning from the sky.

Now was she just before him as he sat,
And like a lowly lover down she kneels;
With one fair hand she heaveth up his hat,
Her other tender hand his fair cheek feels:
    His tenderer cheek receives her soft hand's print,
    As apt as new-fall'n snow takes any dint.

O, what a war of looks was then between them!
Her eyes petitioners to his eyes suing;
His eyes saw her eyes as they had not seen them;
Her eyes woo'd still, his eyes disdain'd the wooing:
    And all this dumb play had his acts made plain
    With tears, which chorus-like her eyes did rain.

Full gently now she takes him by the hand,
A lily prison'd in a gaol of snow,
Or ivory in an alabaster band;
So white a friend engirts so white a foe:
    This beauteous combat, wilful and unwilling,
    Show'd like two silver doves that sit a-billing.

Once more the engine of her thoughts began:
'O fairest mover on this mortal round,
Would thou wert as I am, and I a man,
My heart all whole as thine, thy heart my wound;
    For one sweet look thy help I would assure thee,
    Though nothing but my body's bane would cure
      thee.'

'Give me my hand,' saith he; 'why dost thou feel it?'
'Give me my heart,' saith she, 'and thou shalt have
    it;
O, give it me, lest thy hard heart do steel it,
And being steel'd, soft sighs can never grave it:
    Then love's deep groans I never shall regard,
    Because Adonis' heart hath made mine hard.

'For shame,' he cries, 'let go, and let me go;
My day's delight is past, my horse is gone,
And 'tis your fault I am bereft him so:
I pray you hence, and leave me here alone;
    For all my mind, my thought, my busy care,
    Is how to get my palfrey from the mare.'

Thus she replies: 'Thy palfrey, as he should,
Welcomes the warm approach of sweet desire:
Affection is a coal that must be cool'd;
Else, suffer'd, it will set the heart on fire:
    The sea hath bounds, but deep desire hath none;
    Therefore no marvel though thy horse be gone.

'How like a jade he stood, tied to the tree,
Servilely master'd with a leathern rein!
But when he saw his love, his youth's fair fee,
He held such petty bondage in disdain;
    Throwing the base thong from his bending crest,
    Enfranchising his mouth, his back, his breast.

'Who sees his true-love in her naked bed,
Teaching the sheets a whiter hue than white,
But, when his glutton eye so full hath fed,
His other agents aim at like delight?
    Who is so faint, that dares not be so bold
    To touch the fire, the weather being cold?

'Let me excuse thy courser, gentle boy;
And learn of him, I heartily beseech thee,
To take advantage on presented joy;
Though I were dumb, yet his proceedings teach
        thee:
    O, learn to love; the lesson is but plain,
    And once made perfect, never lost again.'

'I know not love,' quoth he, 'nor will not know it,
Unless it be a boar, and then I chase it;
'Tis much to borrow, and I will not owe it;
My love to love is love but to disgrace it;
    For I have heard it is a life in death,
    That laughs, and weeps, and all but with a
        breath.

'Who wears a garment shapeless and unfinish'd?
Who plucks the bud before one leaf put forth?
If springing things be any jot diminish'd,
They wither in their prime, prove nothing worth:
    The colt that's back'd and burthen'd being
        young
    Loseth his pride, and never waxeth strong.

'You hurt my hand with wringing; let us part,
And leave this idle theme, this bootless chat:
Remove your siege from my unyielding heart;
To love's alarms it will not ope the gate:
    Dismiss your vows, your feigned tears, your flat-
        tery;
    For where a heart is hard they make no battery.'

'What! canst thou talk?' quoth she, 'hast thou a
        tongue?
O, would thou hadst not, or I had no hearing!
Thy mermaid's voice hath done me double wrong;
I had my load before, now press'd with bearing:
    Melodious discord, heavenly tune harsh-sounding,
    Ear's deep-sweet music, and heart's deep-sore
        wounding.

'Had I no eyes but ears, my ears would love
That inward beauty and invisible;
Or were I deaf, thy outward parts would move
Each part in me that were but sensible:

Though neither eyes nor ears, to hear nor see,
Yet should I be in love by touching thee.

'Say, that the sense of feeling were bereft me,
And that I could not see, nor hear, nor touch,
And nothing but the very smell were left me,
Yet would my love to thee be still as much;
    For from the stillitory of thy face excelling
    Comes breath perfumed, that breedeth love by
        smelling.

'But, O, what banquet wert thou to the taste,
Being nurse and feeder of the other four!
Would they not wish the feast might ever last,
And bid Suspicion double-lock the door,
    Lest Jealousy, that sour unwelcome guest,
    Should by his stealing in disturb the feast?'

Once more the ruby-colour'd portal open'd,
Which to his speech did honey passage yield;
Like a red morn, that ever yet betoken'd
Wreck to the seaman, tempest to the field,
    Sorrow to shepherds, woe unto the birds,
    Gusts and foul flaws to herdmen and to herds.

This ill presage advisedly she marketh:
Even as the wind is hush'd before it raineth,
Or as the wolf doth grin before he barketh,
Or as the berry breaks before it staineth,
    Or like the deadly bullet of a gun,
    His meaning struck her ere his words begun.

And at his look she flatly falleth down,
For looks kill love, and love by looks reviveth:
A smile recures the wounding of a frown;
But blessed bankrupt, that by love so thriveth!
    The silly boy, believing she is dead,
    Claps her pale cheek, till clapping makes it red;

And all amazed brake off his late intent,
For sharply he did think to reprehend her,
Which cunning love did wittily prevent:
Fair fall the wit that can so well defend her!
    For on the grass she lies as she were slain,
    Till his breath breatheth life in her again.

He wrings her nose, he strikes her on the cheeks,
He bends her fingers, holds her pulses hard,
He chafes her lips; a thousand ways he seeks
To mend the hurt that his unkindness marr'd:
    He kisses her; and she, by her good will,
    Will never rise, so he will kiss her still.

The night of sorrow now is turn'd to day:
Her two blue windows faintly she up-heaveth,
Like the fair sun, when in his fresh array
He cheers the morn, and all the earth relieveth:
    And as the bright sun glorifies the sky,
    So is her face illumined with her eye;

Whose beams upon his hairless face are fix'd,
As if from thence they borrowed all their shine.
Were never four such lamps together mix'd,
Had not his clouded with his brow's repine;
    But hers, which through the crystal tears gave
      light,
    Shone like the moon in water seen by night.

'O, where am I?' quoth she; 'in earth or heaven,
Or in the ocean drench'd, or in the fire?
What hour is this? or morn or weary even?
Do I delight to die, or life desire?
    But now I lived, and life was death's annoy;
    But now I died, and death was lively joy.

'O, thou didst kill me: kill me once again:
Thy eyes' shrewd tutor, that hard heart of thine,
Hath taught them scornful tricks, and such disdain,
That they have murder'd this poor heart of mine;
    And these mine eyes, true leaders to their queen,
    But for thy piteous lips no more had seen.

'Long may they kiss each other, for this cure!
O, never let their crimson liveries wear!
And as they last, their verdure still endure,
To drive infection from the dangerous year!
    That the star-gazers, having writ on death,
    May say, the plague is banish'd by thy breath.

'Pure lips, sweet seals in my soft lips imprinted,
What bargains may I make, still to be sealing?
To sell myself I can be well contented,
So thou wilt buy, and pay, and use good dealing;
    Which purchase if thou make, for fear of slips
    Set thy seal-manual on my wax-red lips.

'A thousand kisses buys my heart from me;
And pay them at thy leisure, one by one.
What is ten hundred touches unto thee?
Are they not quickly told and quickly gone?
    Say, for non-payment that the debt should
      double,
    Is twenty hundred kisses such a trouble?'

'Fair queen,' quoth he, 'if any love you owe me,
Measure my strangeness with my unripe years:
Before I know myself, seek not to know me;
No fisher but the ungrown fry forbears:
    The mellow plum doth fall, the green sticks fast,
    Or being early pluck'd is sour to taste.

'Look, the world's comforter, with weary gait,
His day's hot task hath ended in the west;
The owl, night's herald, shrieks, 'tis very late;
The sheep are gone to fold, birds to their nest;
    And coal-black clouds that shadow heaven's light
    Do summon us to part, and bid good night.

'Now let me say "Good night," and so say you;
If you will say so, you shall have a kiss.'

'Good night,' quoth she; and, ere he says 'Adieu,'
The honey fee of parting tender'd is:
    Her arms do lend his neck a sweet embrace;
    Incorporate then they seem; face grows to face.

Till breathless he disjoin'd, and backward drew
The heavenly moisture, that sweet coral mouth,
Whose precious taste her thirsty lips well knew,
Whereon they surfeit, yet complain on drouth:
    He with her plenty press'd, she faint with dearth,
    Their lips together glued, fall to the earth.

Now quick desire hath caught the yielding prey,
And glutton-like she feeds, yet never filleth;
Her lips are conquerors, his lips obey,
Paying what ransom the insulter willeth;
    Whose vulture thought doth pitch the price so
      high,
    That she will draw his lips' rich treasure dry.

And having felt the sweetness of the spoil,
With blindfold fury she begins to forage;
Her face doth reek and smoke, her blood doth boil,
And careless lust stirs up a desperate courage,
    Planting oblivion, beating reason back,
    Forgetting shame's pure blush and honour's
      wrack.

Hot, faint and weary, with her hard embracing,
Like a wild bird being tamed with too much han-
      dling,
Or as the fleet-foot roe that's tired with chasing,
Or like the froward infant still'd with dandling,
    He now obeys, and now no more resisteth,
    While she takes all she can, not all she listeth.

What wax so frozen but dissolves with tempering,
And yields at last to every light impression?
Things out of hope are compass'd oft with ventur-
     ing,
Chiefly in love, whose leave exceeds commission:
    Affection faints not like a pale-faced coward,
    But then woos best when most his choice is fro-
     ward.

When he did frown, O, had she then gave over,
Such nectar from his lips she had not suck'd.
Foul words and frowns must not repel a lover;
What though the rose have prickles, yet 'tis pluck'd:
    Were beauty under twenty locks kept fast,
    Yet love breaks through, and picks them all at
     last.

For pity now she can no more detain him;
The poor fool prays her that he may depart:
She is resolved no longer to restrain him;
Bids him farewell, and look well to her heart,
    The which, by Cupid's bow she doth protest,
    He carries thence incaged in his breast.

'Sweet boy,' she says, 'this night I'll waste in sorrow,
For my sick heart commands mine eyes to watch.
Tell me, love's master, shall we meet to-morrow?
Say, shall we? shall we? wilt thou make the match?'
    He tells her, no; to-morrow he intends
    To hunt the boar with certain of his friends.

'The boar!' quoth she; whereat a sudden pale,
Like lawn being spread upon the blushing rose,
Usurps her cheeks; she trembles at his tale,
And on his neck her yoking arms she throws:
    She sinketh down, still hanging by his neck,
    He on her belly falls, she on her back.

Now is she in the very lists of love,
Her champion mounted for the hot encounter:
All is imaginary she doth prove,
He will not manage her, although he mount her;
    That worse than Tantalus' is her annoy,
    To clip Elysium, and to lack her joy.

Even so poor birds, deceived with painted grapes,
Do surfeit by the eye and pine the maw,
Even so she languisheth in her mishaps
As those poor birds that helpless berries saw.
    The warm effects which she in him finds missing
    She seeks to kindle with continual kissing.

But all in vain; good queen, it will not be:
She hath assay'd as much as may be proved;
Her pleading hath deserved a greater fee;
She's Love, she loves, and yet she is not loved.
    'Fie, fie,' he says, 'you crush me; let me go;
    You have no reason to withhold me so.'

'Thou hadst been gone,' quoth she, 'sweet boy, ere
    this,
But that thou told'st me thou wouldst hunt the boar.
O, be advised: thou know'st not what it is
With javelin's point a churlish swine to gore,
    Whose tushes never sheathed he whetteth still,
    Like to a mortal butcher, bent to kill.

'On his bow-back he hath a battle set
Of bristly pikes, that ever threat his foes;
His eyes, like glow-worms, shine when he doth fret;
His snout digs sepulchres where'er he goes;
    Being moved, he strikes whate'er is in his way,
    And whom he strikes his crooked tushes slay.

'His brawny sides, with hairy bristles armed,
Are better proof than thy spear's point can enter;
His short thick neck cannot be easily harmed;
Being ireful, on the lion he will venture:
    The thorny brambles and embracing bushes,
    As fearful of him, part; through whom he rushes.

'Alas, he nought esteems that face of thine,
To which Love's eyes pay tributary gazes;
Nor thy soft hands, sweet lips and crystal eyne,
Whose full perfection all the world amazes;

But having thee at vantage—wondrous dread!—
Would root these beauties as he roots the mead.

'O, let him keep his loathsome cabin still;
Beauty hath nought to do with such foul fiends:
Come not within his danger by thy will;
They that thrive well take counsel of their friends.
    When thou didst name the boar, not to dissemble,
    I fear'd thy fortune, and my joints did tremble.

'Didst thou not mark my face? was it not white?
Saw'st thou not signs of fear lurk in mine eye?
Grew I not faint? and fell I not downright?
Within my bosom, whereon thou dost lie,
    My boding heart pants, beats, and takes no rest,
    But, like an earthquake, shakes thee on my breast.

'For where Love reigns, disturbing Jealousy
Doth call himself Affection's sentinel;
Gives false alarms, suggesteth mutiny,
And in a peaceful hour doth cry "Kill, kill!"
    Distempering gentle Love in his desire,
    As air and water do abate the fire.

'This sour informer, this bate-breeding spy,
This canker that eats up Love's tender spring,
This carry-tale, dissentious Jealousy,
That sometime true news, sometime false doth
    bring,
    Knocks at my heart, and whispers in mine ear,
    That if I love thee, I thy death should fear:

'And more than so, presenteth to mine eye
The picture of an angry-chafing boar,
Under whose sharp fangs on his back doth lie
An image like thyself, all stain'd with gore;
    Whose blood upon the fresh flowers being shed
    Doth make them droop with grief and hang the
    head.

'What should I do, seeing thee so indeed,
That tremble at the imagination?
The thought of it doth make my faint heart bleed,
And fear doth teach it divination:
    I prophesy thy death, my living sorrow,
    If thou encounter with the boar to-morrow.

'But if thou needs wilt hunt, be ruled by me;
Uncouple at the timorous flying hare,
Or at the fox which lives by subtlety,
Or at the roe which no encounter dare:
    Pursue these fearful creatures o'er the downs,
    And on thy well-breath'd horse keep with thy
    hounds.

'And when thou hast on foot the purblind hare,
Mark the poor wretch, to overshoot his troubles,
How he outruns the wind, and with what care
He cranks and crosses with a thousand doubles:
    The many musits through the which he goes
    Are like a labyrinth to amaze his foes.

'Sometime he runs among a flock of sheep,
To make the cunning hounds mistake their smell,
And sometime where earth-delving conies keep,
To stop the loud pursuers in their yell;
　　And sometime sorteth with a herd of deer:
　　Danger deviseth shifts; wit waits on fear:

'For there his smell with others being mingled,
The hot scent-snuffing hounds are driven to doubt,
Ceasing their clamorous cry till they have singled
With much ado the cold fault cleanly out;
　　Then do they spend their mouths: Echo replies,
　　As if another chase were in the skies.

'By this, poor Wat, far off upon a hill,
Stands on his hinder legs with listening ear,
To hearken if his foes pursue him still:
Anon their loud alarums he doth hear;
　　And now his grief may be compared well
　　To one sore sick that hears the passing-bell.

'Then shalt thou see the dew-bedabbled wretch
Turn, and return, indenting with the way;
Each envious brier his weary legs doth scratch,
Each shadow makes him stop, each murmur stay:
　　For misery is trodden on by many,
　　And being low never relieved by any.

'Lie quietly, and hear a little more;
Nay, do not struggle, for thou shalt not rise:
To make thee hate the hunting of the boar,
Unlike myself thou hear'st me moralize,
　　Applying this to that, and so to so;
　　For love can comment upon every woe.

'Where did I leave?' 'No matter where,' quoth he;
'Leave me, and then the story aptly ends:
The night is spent.' 'Why, what of that?' quoth she.
'I am,' quoth he, 'expected of my friends;
　　And now 'tis dark, and going I shall fall.'
　　'In night,' quoth she, 'desire sees best of all.

'But if thou fall, O, then imagine this,
The earth, in love with thee, thy footing trips,
And all is but to rob thee of a kiss.
Rich preys make true men thieves; so do thy lips
　　Make modest Dian cloudy and forlorn,
　　Lest she should steal a kiss, and die forsworn.

'Now of this dark night I perceive the reason:
Cynthia for shame obscures her silver shine,
Till forging Nature be condemn'd of treason,
For stealing moulds from heaven that were divine;
　　Wherein she framed thee, in high heaven's
　　　despite,
　　To shame the sun by day and her by night.

'And therefore hath she bribed the Destinies
To cross the curious workmanship of nature,

To mingle beauty with infirmities
And pure perfection with impure defeature;
　　Making it subject to the tyranny
　　Of mad mischances and much misery;

'As burning fevers, agues pale and faint,
Life-poisoning pestilence and frenzies wood,
The marrow-eating sickness, whose attaint
Disorder breeds by heating of the blood:
　　Surfeits, imposthumes, grief and damn'd despair,
　　Swear Nature's death for framing thee so fair.

'And not the least of all these maladies
But in one minute's fight brings beauty under:
Both favour, savour, hue and qualities,
Whereat the impartial gazer late did wonder,
　　Are on the sudden wasted, thaw'd and done,
　　As mountain snow melts with the midday sun.

'Therefore, despite of fruitless chastity,
Love-lacking vestals and self-loving nuns,
That on the earth would breed a scarcity
And barren dearth of daughters and of sons,
　　Be prodigal: the lamp that burns by night
　　Dries up his oil to lend the world his light.

'What is thy body but a swallowing grave,
Seeming to bury that posterity
Which by the rights of time thou needs must have,
If thou destroy them not in dark obscurity?
　　If so, the world will hold thee in disdain,
　　Sith in thy pride so fair a hope is slain.

'So in thyself thyself art made away;
A mischief worse than civil home-bred strife,
Or theirs whose desperate hands themselves do slay,
Or butcher-sire that reaves his son of life.
　　Foul cankering rust the hidden treasure frets,
　　But gold that's put to use more gold begets.'

'Nav. then,' quoth Adon, 'you will fall again
Into your idle over-handled theme:
The kiss I gave you is bestow'd in vain,
And all in vain you strive against the stream;
　　For, by this black-faced night, desire's foul nurse,
　　Your treatise makes me like you worse and worse.

'If love have lent you twenty thousand tongues,
And every tongue more moving than your own,
Bewitching like the wanton mermaid's songs,
Yet from mine ear the tempting tune is blown;
　　For know, my heart stands armed in mine ear,
　　And will not let a false sound enter there;

'Lest the deceiving harmony should run
Into the quiet closure of my breast;
And then my little heart were quite undone,
In his bedchamber to be barr'd of rest.
　　No, lady, no; my heart longs not to groan,
　　But soundly sleeps, while now it sleeps alone

'What have you urged that I cannot reprove?
The path is smooth that leadeth on to danger:
I hate not love, but your device in love
That lends embracements unto every stranger.
    You do it for increase: O strange excuse,
    When reason is the bawd to lust's abuse!

'Call it not love, for Love to heaven is fled
Since sweating Lust on earth usurp'd his name;
Under whose simple semblance he hath fed
Upon fresh beauty, blotting it with blame;
    Which the hot tyrant stains and soon bereaves,
    As caterpillars do the tender leaves.

'Love comforteth like sunshine after rain,
But Lust's effect is tempest after sun;
Love's gentle spring doth always fresh remain,
Lust's winter comes ere summer half be done;
    Love surfeits not, Lust like a glutton dies;
    Love is all truth, Lust full of forged lies.

'More I could tell, but more I dare not say;
The text is old, the orator too green.
Therefore, in sadness, now I will away;
My face is full of shame, my heart of teen:
    Mine ears, that to your wanton talk attended,
    Do burn themselves for having so offended.'

With this, he breaketh from the sweet embrace
Of those fair arms which bound him to her breast,
And homeward through the dark lawnd runs apace;
Leaves Love upon her back deeply distress'd.
    Look, how a bright star shooteth from the sky,
    So glides he in the night from Venus' eye:

Which after him she darts, as one on shore
Gazing upon a late-embarked friend,
Till the wild waves will have him seen no more,
Whose ridges with the meeting clouds contend:
    So did the merciless and pitchy night
    Fold in the object that did feed her sight.

Whereat amazed, as one that unaware
Hath dropp'd a precious jewel in the flood,
Or 'stonish'd as night-wanderers often are,
Their light blown out in some mistrustful wood;
    Even so confounded in the dark she lay,
    Having lost the fair discovery of her way.

And now she beats her heart, whereat it groans,
That all the neighbour caves, as seeming troubled,
Make verbal repetition of her moans;
Passion on passion deeply is redoubled:
    'Ay me!' she cries, and twenty times, 'Woe, woe!'
    And twenty echoes twenty times cry so.

She, marking them, begins a wailing note,
And sings extemporally a woeful ditty;
How love makes young men thrall, and old men
    dote;
How love is wise in folly, foolish-witty:

Her heavy anthem still concludes in woe,
And still the choir of echoes answer so.

Her song was tedious, and outwore the night,
For lovers' hours are long, though seeming short:
If pleased themselves, others, they think, delight
In such-like circumstance, with such-like sport:
    Their copious stories, oftentimes begun,
    End without audience, and are never done.

For who hath she to spend the night withal,
But idle sounds resembling parasites;
Like shrill-tongued tapsters answering every call,
Soothing the humour of fantastic wits?
    She says ''Tis so:' they answer all ''Tis so;'
    And would say after her, if she said 'No.'

Lo, here the gentle lark, weary of rest,
From his moist cabinet mounts up on high,
And wakes the morning, from whose silver breast
The sun ariseth in his majesty;
    Who doth the world so gloriously behold,
    That cedar-tops and hills seem burnish'd gold.

Venus salutes him with this fair good-morrow:
'O thou clear god, and patron of all light,
From whom each lamp and shining star doth bor-
    row
The beauteous influence that makes him bright,
    There lives a son, that suck'd an earthly mother,
    May lend thee light, as thou dost lend to other.'

This said, she hasteth to a myrtle grove,
Musing the morning is so much o'erworn,
And yet she hears no tidings of her love:
She hearkens for his hounds and for his horn:
    Anon she hears them chant it lustily,
    And all in haste she coasteth to the cry.

And as she runs, the bushes in the way
Some catch her by the neck, some kiss her face,
Some twine about her thigh to make her stay:
She wildly breaketh from their strict embrace,
    Like a milch doe, whose swelling dugs do ache,
    Hasting to feed her fawn hid in some brake.

By this she hears the hounds are at a bay;
Whereat she starts, like one that spies an adder
Wreathed up in fatal folds just in his way,
The fear whereof doth make him shake and shud-
    der;
    Even so the timorous yelping of the hounds
    Appals her senses and her spirit confounds.

For now she knows it is no gentle chase,
But the blunt boar, rough bear, or lion proud,
Because the cry remaineth in one place,
Where fearfully the dogs exclaim aloud:
    Finding their enemy to be so curst,
    They all strain courtesy who shall cope him first.

This dismal cry rings sadly in her ear,
Through which it enters to surprise her heart;
Who, overcome by doubt and bloodless fear,
With cold-pale weakness numbs each feeling part:
    Like soldiers, when their captain once doth yield,
    They basely fly, and dare not stay the field.

Thus stands she in a trembling ecstasy;
Till, cheering up her senses all dismay'd,
She tells them 'tis a causeless fantasy,
And childish error, that they are afraid;
    Bids them leave quaking, bids them fear no more:
    And with that word she spied the hunted boar;

Whose frothy mouth, bepainted all with red,
Like milk and blood being mingled both together,
A second fear through all her sinews spread,
Which madly hurries her she knows not whither:
    This way she runs, and now she will no further,
    But back retires to rate the boar for murther.

A thousand spleens bear her a thousand ways;
She treads the path that she untreads again;
Her more than haste is mated with delays,
Like the proceedings of a drunken brain,
    Full of respects, yet nought at all respecting:
    In hand with all things, nought at all effecting.

Here kennell'd in a brake she finds a hound,
And asks the weary caitiff for his master;
And there another licking of his wound,
'Gainst venom'd sores the only sovereign plaster;
    And here she meets another sadly scowling,
    To whom she speaks, and he replies with howling.

When he hath ceased his ill-resounding noise,
Another flap-mouth'd mourner, black and grim,
Against the welkin volleys out his voice;
Another and another answer him,
    Clapping their proud tails to the ground below,
    Shaking their scratch'd ears, bleeding as they go.

Look, how the world's poor people are amazed
At apparitions, signs and prodigies,
Whereon with fearful eyes they long have gazed,
Infusing them with dreadful prophecies;
    So she at these sad signs draws up her breath,
    And, sighing it again, exclaims on Death.

'Hard-favour'd tyrant, ugly, meagre, lean,
Hateful divorce of love,'—thus chides she Death,—
'Grim-grinning ghost, earth's worm, what dost thou
    mean
To stifle beauty and to steal his breath,
    Who when he lived, his breath and beauty set
    Gloss on the rose, smell to the violet?

'If he be dead,—O no, it cannot be,
Seeing his beauty, thou shouldst strike at it;—
O yes, it may; thou hast no eyes to see,
But hatefully at random dost thou hit.

Thy mark is feeble age; but thy false dart
Mistakes that aim, and cleaves an infant's heart.

'Hadst thou but bid beware, then he had spoke,
And, hearing him, thy power had lost his power.
The Destinies will curse thee for this stroke;
They bid thee crop a weed, thou pluck'st a flower:
    Love's golden arrow at him should have fled,
    And not Death's ebon dart, to strike him dead.

'Dost thou drink tears, that thou provokest such
    weeping?
What may a heavy groan advantage thee?
Why hast thou cast into eternal sleeping
Those eyes that taught all other eyes to see?
    Now Nature cares not for thy mortal vigour,
    Since her best work is ruin'd with thy rigour.'

Here overcome, as one full of despair,
She vail'd her eyelids, who, like sluices, stopp'd
The crystal tide that from her two cheeks fair
In the sweet channel of her bosom dropp'd;
    But through the flood-gates breaks the silver rain,
    And with his strong course opens them again.

O, how her eyes and tears did lend and borrow!
Her eye seen in the tears, tears in her eye;
Both crystals, where they view'd each other's sor-
    row,
Sorrow that friendly sighs sought still to dry;
    But like a stormy day, now wind, now rain,
    Sighs dry her cheeks, tears make them wet again.

Variable passions throng her constant woe,
As striving who should best become her grief;
All entertain'd, each passion labours so
That every present sorrow seemeth chief,
    But none is best: then join they all together,
    Like many clouds consulting for foul weather.

By this, far off she hears some huntsman holloa;
A nurse's song ne'er pleased her babe so well:
The dire imagination she did follow
This sound of hope doth labour to expel;
    For now reviving joy bids her rejoice,
    And flatters her it is Adonis' voice.

Whereat her tears began to turn their tide,
Being prison'd in her eye like pearls in glass:
Yet sometimes falls an orient drop beside,
Which her cheek melts, as scorning it should pass
    To wash the foul face of the sluttish ground,
    Who is but drunken when she seemeth drown'd.

O hard-believing love, how strange it seems
Not to believe, and yet too credulous!
Thy weal and woe are both of them extremes;
Despair, and hope, makes thee ridiculous:
    The one doth flatter thee in thoughts unlikely,
    In likely thoughts the other kills thee quickly.

Now she unweaves the web that she hath wrought;
Adonis lives, and Death is not to blame;
It was not she that call'd him all to nought:
Now she adds honours to his hateful name;
    She clepes him king of graves, and grave for kings,
    Imperious supreme of all mortal things.

'No, no,' quoth she, 'sweet Death, I did but jest;
Yet pardon me, I felt a kind of fear
When as I met the boar, that bloody beast,
Which knows no pity, but is still severe;
    Then, gentle shadow,—truth I must confess,—
    I rail'd on thee, fearing my love's decease.

''Tis not my fault: the boar provoked my tongue;
Be wreak'd on him, invisible commander;
'Tis he, foul creature, that hath done thee wrong;
I did but act, he's author of thy slander:
    Grief hath two tongues; and never woman yet
    Could rule them both without ten women's wit.'

Thus hoping that Adonis is alive,
Her rash suspect she doth extenuate;
And that his beauty may the better thrive,
With Death she humbly doth insinuate;
    Tells him of trophies, statues, tombs, and stories
    His victories, his triumphs and his glories.

'O Jove,' quoth she, 'how much a fool was I
To be of such a weak and silly mind
To wail his death who lives and must not die
Till mutual overthrow of mortal kind!
    For he being dead, with him is beauty slain,
    And, beauty dead, black chaos comes again.

'Fie, fie, fond love, thou art so full of fear
As one with treasure laden, hemm'd with thieves;
Trifles unwitnessed with eye or ear
Thy coward heart with false bethinking grieves.'
    Even at this word she hears a merry horn,
    Whereat she leaps that was but late forlorn.

As falcons to the lure, away she flies;
The grass stoops not, she treads on it so light;
And in her haste unfortunately spies
The foul boar's conquest on her fair delight;
    Which seen, her eyes, as murder'd with the view,
    Like stars ashamed of day, themselves withdrew;

Or, as the snail, whose tender horns being hit,
Shrinks backward in his shelly cave with pain,
And there all smother'd up in shade doth sit,
Long after fearing to creep forth again;
    So, at his bloody view, her eyes are fled
    Into the deep-dark cabins of her head:

Where they resign their office and their light
To the disposing of her troubled brain;
Who bids them still consort with ugly night,
And never wound the heart with looks again;
    Who, like a king perplexed in his throne,
    By their suggestion gives a deadly groan,

Whereat each tributary subject quakes;
As when the wind, imprison'd in the ground,
Struggling for passage, earth's foundation shakes,
Which with cold terror doth men's minds confound.
    This mutiny each part doth so surprise,
    That from their dark beds once more leap her eyes;

And being open'd threw unwilling light
Upon the wide wound that the boar had trench'd
In his soft flank; whose wonted lily white
With purple tears, that his wound wept, was drench'd:
    No flower was nigh, no grass, herb, leaf or weed,
    But stole his blood and seem'd with him to bleed.

This solemn sympathy poor Venus noteth;
Over one shoulder doth she hang her head;
Dumbly she passions, frantically she doteth;
She thinks he could not die, he is not dead:
    Her voice is stopp'd, her joints forget to bow;
    Her eyes are mad that they have wept till now.

Upon his hurt she looks so steadfastly
That her sight dazzling makes the wound seem three;
And then she reprehends her mangling eye,
That makes more gashes where no breach should be:
    His face seems twain, each several limb is doubled;
    For oft the eye mistakes, the brain being troubled.

'My tongue cannot express my grief for one,
And yet,' quoth she, 'behold two Adons dead!
My sighs are blown away, my salt tears gone,
Mine eyes are turn'd to fire, my heart to lead:
    Heavy heart's lead, melt at mine eyes' red fire!
    So shall I die by drops of hot desire.

'Alas, poor world, what treasure hast thou lost!
What face remains alive that's worth the viewing?
Whose tongue is music now? what canst thou boast
Of things long since, or any thing ensuing?
    The flowers are sweet, their colours fresh and trim;
    But true-sweet beauty lived and died with him.

'Bonnet nor veil henceforth no creature wear!
Nor sun nor wind will ever strive to kiss you:
Having no fair to lose, you need not fear;
The sun doth scorn you, and the wind doth hiss you:
    But when Adonis lived, sun and sharp air
    Lurk'd like two thieves, to rob him of his fair.

'And therefore would he put his bonnet on,
Under whose brim the gaudy sun would peep;
The wind would blow it off, and, being gone,
Play with his locks: then would Adonis weep;
    And straight, in pity of his tender years,
    They both would strive who first should dry his tears.

'To see his face the lion walk'd along
Behind some hedge, because he would not fear him;
To recreate himself when he hath sung,
The tiger would be tame and gently hear him;
　　If he had spoke, the wolf would leave his prey,
　　And never fright the silly lamb that day.

'When he beheld his shadow in the brook,
The fishes spread on it their golden gills;
When he was by, the birds such pleasure took,
That some would sing, some other in their bills
　　Would bring him mulberries and ripe-red cherries;
　　He fed them with his sight, they him with berries.

'But this foul, grim, and urchin-snouted boar,
Whose downward eye still looketh for a grave,
Ne'er saw the beauteous livery that he wore;
Witness the entertainment that he gave:
　　If he did see his face, why then I know
　　He thought to kiss him, and hath kill'd him so.

''Tis true, 'tis true; thus was Adonis slain:
He ran upon the boar with his sharp spear,
Who did not whet his teeth at him again,
But by a kiss thought to persuade him there;
　　And nuzzling in his flank, the loving swine
　　Sheathed unaware the tusk in his soft groin.

'Had I been tooth'd like him, I must confess,
With kissing him I should have kill'd him first;
But he is dead, and never did he bless
My youth with his; the more am I accurst.'
　　With this, she falleth in the place she stood,
　　And stains her face with his congealed blood.

She looks upon his lips, and they are pale;
She takes him by the hand, and that is cold;
She whispers in his ears a heavy tale,
As if they heard the woeful words she told;
　　She lifts the coffer-lids that close his eyes,
　　Where, lo, two lamps, burnt out, in darkness lies:

Two glasses, where herself herself beheld
A thousand times, and now no more reflect;
Their virtue lost, wherein they late excell'd,
And every beauty robb'd of his effect:
　　'Wonder of time,' quoth she, 'this is my spite,
　　That, thou being dead, the day should yet be
　　　light.

'Since thou art dead, lo, here I prophesy,
Sorrow on love hereafter shall attend:
It shall be waited on with jealousy,
Find sweet beginning but unsavoury end;
　　Ne'er settled equally, but high or low,
　　That all love's pleasure shall not match his woe.

'It shall be fickle, false and full of fraud;
Bud, and be blasted, in a breathing-while;
The bottom poison, and the top o'erstraw'd
With sweets that shall the truest sight beguile:

The strongest body shall it make most weak,
Strike the wise dumb, and teach the fool to speak.

'It shall be sparing and too full of riot,
Teaching decrepit age to tread the measures;
The staring ruffian shall it keep in quiet,
Pluck down the rich, enrich the poor with treasures;
　　It shall be raging-mad, and silly-mild,
　　Make the young old, the old become a child.

'It shall suspect where is no cause of fear;
It shall not fear where it should most mistrust;
It shall be merciful and too severe,
And most deceiving when it seems most just;
　　Perverse it shall be where it shows most toward,
　　Put fear to valour, courage to the coward.

'It shall be cause of war and dire events,
And set dissension 'twixt the son and sire;
Subject and servile to all discontents,
As dry combustious matter is to fire:
　　Sith in his prime death doth my love destroy,
　　They that love best their loves shall not enjoy.'

By this the boy that by her side lay kill'd
Was melted like a vapour from her sight,
And in his blood, that on the ground lay spill'd,
A purple flower sprung up, chequer'd with white,
　　Resembling well his pale cheeks and the blood
　　Which in round drops upon their whiteness stood.

She bows her head, the new-sprung flower to smell,
Comparing it to her Adonis' breath;
And says, within her bosom it shall dwell,
Since he himself is reft from her by death:
　　She crops the stalk, and in the breach appears
　　Green-dropping sap, which she compares to tears.

'Poor flower,' quoth she, 'this was thy father's guise—
Sweet issue of a more sweet-smelling sire—
For every little grief to wet his eyes:
To grow unto himself was his desire,
　　And so 'tis thine; but know, it is as good
　　To wither in my breast as in his blood.

'Here was thy father's bed, here in my breast;
Thou art the next of blood, and 'tis thy right:
Lo, in this hollow cradle take thy rest;
My throbbing heart shall rock thee day and night:
　　There shall not be one minute in an hour
　　Wherein I will not kiss my sweet love's flower.'

Thus weary of the world, away she hies,
And yokes her silver doves; by whose swift aid
Their mistress, mounted, through the empty skies
In her light chariot quickly is convey'd;
　　Holding their course to Paphos, where their
　　　queen
　　Means to immure herself and not be seen.

THE RAPE OF LUCRECE

THE RAPE OF LUCRECE

TO THE

RIGHT HONOURABLE HENRIE WRIOTHESLEY,

EARLE OF SOUTHAMPTON, AND BARON OF TITCHFIELD

THE loue I dedicate to your Lordship is without end:
wherof this Pamphlet without beginning is but a superfluous Moity. The warrant I haue of your Honourable
disposition, not the worth of my vntutord Lines makes it
assured of acceptance. What I haue done is yours, what
I haue to doe is yours, being part in all I haue, deuoted
yours. Were my worth greater, my duety would shew
greater, meane time, as it is, it is bound to your Lordship; To whom I wish long life still lengthned with all
happinesse.

Your Lordships in all duety.

WILLIAM SHAKESPEARE.

HISTORICAL DATA

Richard Field, the publisher of *Venus and Adonis*, also gave to the world the first printed version of *The Rape of Lucrece*, which appeared in 1594. It was presumably written immediately after the former poem, and was probably the "graver labour" referred to in the dedication of its predecessor.

The story of Lucrece, or Lucretia, is one of the oldest and most famous of the Roman legends. In Elizabethan times it had appeared in dozens of forms, so many of which may have been familiar to Shakespeare that it is impossible to cite any as the immediate source material for his poem. In structure, however, it most nearly resembles Daniel's *Complaint of Rosamond* (1592), which treats a closely parallel theme and is also written in the seven-lined stanza form. In addition to this Shakespeare in all likelihood drew upon the omissions of Ovid and Livy, and probably that of Chaucer in the *Legend of Good Women*.

"Short time seems long in sorrow's sharp sustaining:"
THE RAPE OF LUCRECE

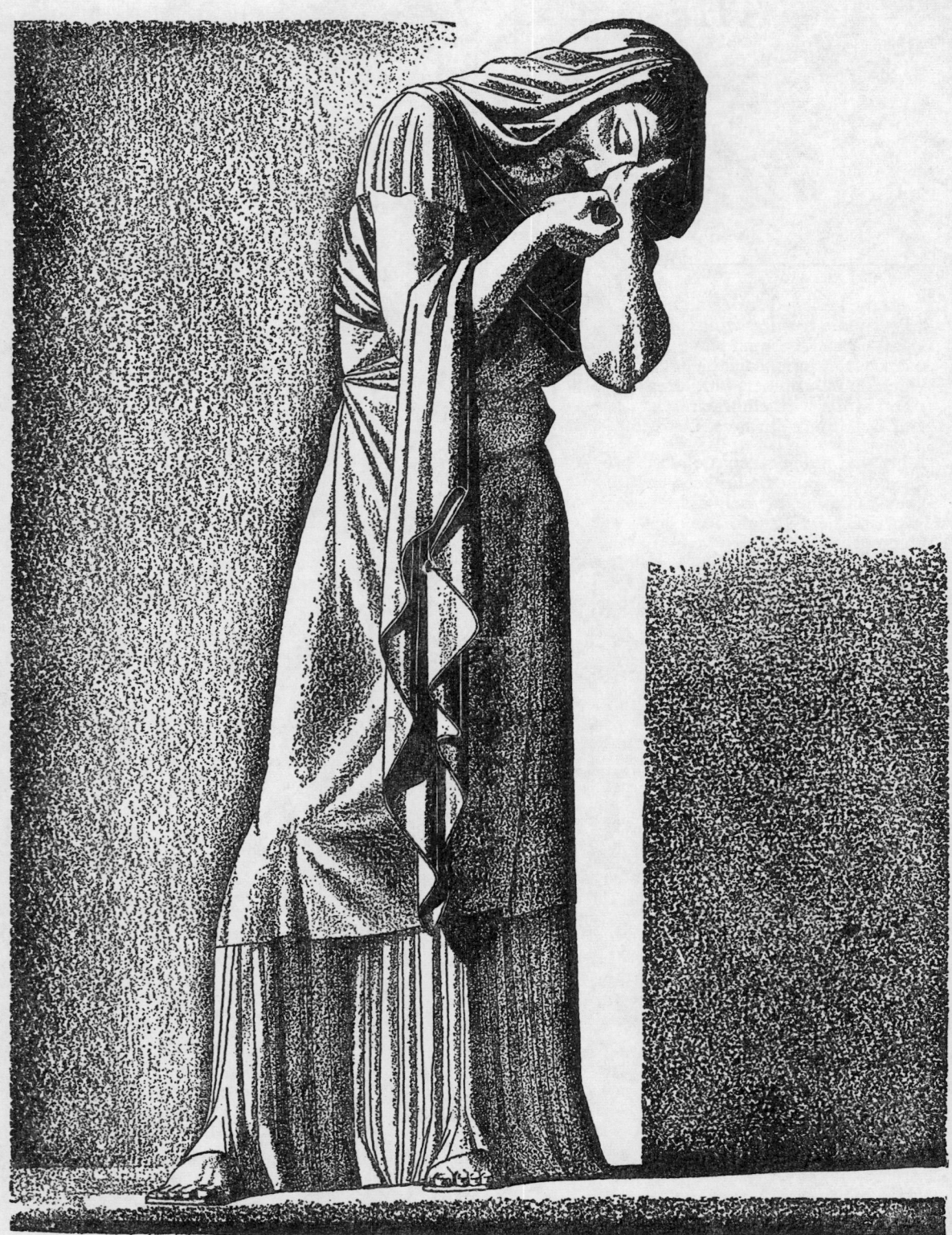

THE RAPE OF LUCRECE

From the besieged Ardea all in post,
Borne by the trustless wings of false desire,
Lust-breathed Tarquin leaves the Roman host,
And to Collatium bears the lightless fire,
Which, in pale embers hid, lurks to aspire,
  And girdle with embracing flames the waist
  Of Collatine's fair love, Lucrece the chaste.

Haply that name of 'chaste' unhappily set
This bateless edge on his keen appetite;
When Collatine unwisely did not let
To praise the clear unmatched red and white
Which triumph'd in that sky of his delight,
  Where mortal stars, as bright as heaven's beauties,
  With pure aspects did him peculiar duties.

For he the night before, in Tarquin's tent,
Unlock'd the treasure of his happy state;
What priceless wealth the heavens had him lent
In the possession of his beauteous mate;
Reckoning his fortune at such high-proud rate,
  That kings might be espoused to more fame,
  But king nor peer to such a peerless dame.

O happiness enjoy'd but of a few!
And, if possess'd, as soon decay'd and done
As is the morning's silver-melting dew
Against the golden splendour of the sun!
An expired date, cancell'd ere well begun:
  Honour and beauty, in the owner's arms,
  Are weakly fortress'd from a world of harms.

Beauty itself doth of itself persuade
The eyes of men without an orator;
What needeth then apologies be made,
To set forth that which is so singular?
Or why is Collatine the publisher
  Of that rich jewel he should keep unknown
  From thievish ears, because it is his own?

Perchance his boast of Lucrece' sovereignty
Suggested this proud issue of a king;
For by our ears our hearts oft tainted be:
Perchance that envy of so rich a thing,
Braving compare, disdainfully did sting
  His high-pitch'd thoughts, that meaner men
    should vaunt
  That golden hap which their superiors want.

But some untimely thought did instigate
His all-too-timeless speed, if none of those:
His honour, his affairs, his friends, his state,
Neglected all, with swift intent he goes
To quench the coal which in his liver glows.
  O rash-false heat, wrapp'd in repentant cold,
  Thy hasty spring still blasts, and ne'er grows old!

When at Collatium this false lord arrived,
Well was he welcomed by the Roman dame,
Within whose face beauty and virtue strived
Which of them both should underprop her fame:
When virtue bragg'd, beauty would blush for shame;
  When beauty boasted blushes, in despite
  Virtue would stain that o'er with silver white.

But beauty, in that white intituled,
From Venus' doves doth challenge that fair field:
Then virtue claims from beauty beauty's red,
Which virtue gave the golden age to gild
Their silver cheeks, and call'd it then their shield;
  Teaching them thus to use it in the fight,
  When shame assail'd, the red should fence the
    white.

This heraldry in Lucrece' face was seen,
Argued by beauty's red and virtue's white:
Of either's colour was the other queen,
Proving from world's minority their right:
Yet their ambition makes them still to fight;
  The sovereignty of either being so great,
  That oft they interchange each other's seat.

This silent war of lilies and of roses,
Which Tarquin view'd in her fair face's field,
In their pure ranks his traitor eye encloses;
Where, lest between them both it should be kill'd,
The coward captive vanquished doth yield
  To those two armies, that would let him go
  Rather than triumph in so false a foe.

Now thinks he that her husband's shallow tongue,
The niggard prodigal that praised her so,
In that high task hath done her beauty wrong,
Which far exceeds his barren skill to show:
Therefore that praise which Collatine doth owe
  Enchanted Tarquin answers with surmise,
  In silent wonder of still-gazing eyes.

This earthly saint, adored by this devil,
Little suspecteth the false worshipper;
For unstain'd thoughts do seldom dream on evil;
Birds never limed no secret bushes fear:
So guiltless she securely gives good cheer
    And reverend welcome to her princely guest,
    Whose inward ill no outward harm express'd:

For that he colour'd with his high estate,
Hiding base sin in plaits of majesty;
That nothing in him seem'd inordinate,
Save sometime too much wonder of his eye,
Which, having all, all could not satisfy;
    But, poorly rich, so wanteth in his store,
    That, cloy'd with much, he pineth still for more.

But she, that never coped with stranger eyes,
Could pick no meaning from their parling looks,
Nor read the subtle-shining secrecies
Writ in the glassy margents of such books:
She touch'd no unknown baits, nor fear'd no hooks;
    Nor could she moralize his wanton sight,
    More than his eyes were open'd to the light.

He stories to her ears her husband's fame,
Won in the fields of fruitful Italy;
And decks with praises Collatine's high name,
Made glorious by his manly chivalry
With bruised arms and wreaths of victory:
    Her joy with heaved-up hand she doth express,
    And wordless so greets heaven for his success.

Far from the purpose of his coming hither,
He makes excuses for his being there:
No cloudy show of stormy blustering weather
Doth yet in his fair welkin once appear;
Till sable Night, mother of dread and fear,
    Upon the world dim darkness doth display,
    And in her vaulty prison stows the day.

For then is Tarquin brought unto his bed,
Intending weariness with heavy spright;
For after supper long he questioned
With modest Lucrece, and wore out the night:
Now leaden slumber with life's strength doth fight;
    And every one to rest themselves betake,
    Save thieves and cares and troubled minds that
    wake.

As one of which doth Tarquin lie revolving
The sundry dangers of his will's obtaining;
Yet ever to obtain his will resolving,
Though weak-built hopes persuade him to abstaining:
Despair to gain doth traffic oft for gaining,
    And when great treasure is the meed proposed,
    Though death be adjunct, there's no death supposed.

Those that much covet are with gain so fond
That what they have not, that which they possess,
They scatter and unloose it from their bond,
And so, by hoping more, they have but less;
Or, gaining more, the profit of excess
    Is but to surfeit, and such griefs sustain,
    That they prove bankrupt in this poor-rich gain.

The aim of all is but to nurse the life
With honour, wealth and ease, in waning age;
And in this aim there is such thwarting strife
That one for all or all for one we gage;
As life for honour in fell battle's rage;
    Honour for wealth; and oft that wealth doth cost
    The death of all, and all together lost.

So that in venturing ill we leave to be
The things we are for that which we expect;
And this ambitious foul infirmity,
In having much, torments us with defect
Of that we have: so then we do neglect
    The thing we have, and, all for want of wit,
    Make something nothing by augmenting it.

Such hazard now must doting Tarquin make,
Pawning his honour to obtain his lust;
And for himself himself he must forsake:
Then where is truth, if there be no self-trust?
When shall he think to find a stranger just,
    When he himself himself confounds, betrays
    To slanderous tongues and wretched hateful days?

Now stole upon the time the dead of night,
When heavy sleep had closed up mortal eyes:
No comfortable star did lend his light,
No noise but owls' and wolves' death-boding cries;
Now serves the season that they may surprise
    The silly lambs: pure thoughts are dead and still,
    While lust and murder wakes to stain and kill.

And now this lustful lord leap'd from his bed,
Throwing his mantle rudely o'er his arm;
Is madly toss'd between desire and dread;
Th' one sweetly flatters, th' other feareth harm;
But honest fear, bewitch'd with lust's foul charm,
    Doth too too oft betake him to retire,
    Beaten away by brain-sick rude desire.

His falchion on a flint he softly smiteth,
That from the cold stone sparks of fire do fly;
Whereat a waxen torch forthwith he lighteth,
Which must be lode-star to his lustful eye;
And to the flame thus speaks advisedly:
    'As from this cold flint I enforced this fire,
    So Lucrece must I force to my desire.'

Here pale with fear he doth premeditate
The dangers of his loathsome enterprise,
And in his inward mind he doth debate
What following sorrow may on this arise:
Then looking scornfully he doth despise
    His naked armour of still-slaughter'd lust,
    And justly thus controls his thoughts unjust:

'Fair torch, burn out thy light, and lend it not
To darken her whose light excelleth thine:
And die, unhallow'd thoughts, before you blot
With your uncleanness that which is divine:
Offer pure incense to so pure a shrine:
    Let fair humanity abhor the deed
    That spots and stains love's modest snow-white
       weed.

'O shame to knighthood and to shining arms!
O foul dishonour to my household's grave!
O impious act, including all foul harms!
A martial man to be soft fancy's slave!
True valour still a true respect should have;
    Then my digression is so vile, so base,
    That it will live engraven in my face.

'Yea, though I die, the scandal will survive,
And be an eye-sore in my golden coat;
Some loathsome dash the herald will contrive,
To cipher me how fondly I did dote;
That my posterity, shamed with the note,
    Shall curse my bones, and hold it for no sin
    To wish that I their father had not bin.

'What win I, if I gain the thing I seek?
A dream, a breath, a froth of fleeting joy.
Who buys a minute's mirth to wail a week?
Or sells eternity to get a toy?
For one sweet grape who will the vine destroy?
    Or what fond beggar, but to touch the crown,
    Would with the sceptre straight be strucken down?

'If Collatinus dream of my intent,
Will he not wake, and in a desperate rage
Post hither, this vile purpose to prevent?
This siege that hath engirt his marriage,
This blur to youth, this sorrow to the sage,
    This dying virtue, this surviving shame,
    Whose crime will bear an ever-during blame.

'O what excuse can my invention make,
When thou shalt charge me with so black a deed?
Will not my tongue be mute, my frail joints shake,
Mine eyes forgo their light, my false heart bleed?
The guilt being great, the fear doth still exceed;
    And extreme fear can neither fight nor fly,
    But coward-like with trembling terror die.

'Had Collatinus kill'd my son or sire,
Or lain in ambush to betray my life,
Or were he not my dear friend, this desire
Might have excuse to work upon his wife,
As in revenge or quittal of such strife:
    But as he is my kinsman, my dear friend,
    The shame and fault finds no excuse nor end.

'Shameful it is; ay, if the fact be known:
Hateful it is; there is no hate in loving:

I'll beg her love; but she is not her own:
The worst is but denial and reproving:
My will is strong, past reason's weak removing.
    Who fears a sentence or an old man's saw
    Shall by a painted cloth be kept in awe.'

Thus graceless holds he disputation
'Tween frozen conscience and hot-burning will,
And with good thoughts makes dispensation,
Urging the worser sense for vantage still;
Which in a moment doth confound and kill
    All pure effects, and doth so far proceed
    That what is vile shows like a virtuous deed.

Quoth he, 'She took me kindly by the hand,
And gazed for tidings in my eager eyes,
Fearing some hard news from the warlike band,
Where her beloved Collatinus lies.
O, how her fear did make her colour rise!
    First red as roses that on lawn we lay,
    Then white as lawn, the roses took away.

'And how her hand, in my hand being lock'd,
Forced it to tremble with her loyal fear!
Which struck her sad, and then it faster rock'd,
Until her husband's welfare she did hear;
Whereat she smiled with so sweet a cheer
    That had Narcissus seen her as she stood
    Self-love had never drown'd him in the flood.

'Why hunt I then for colour or excuses?
All orators are dumb when beauty pleadeth;
Poor wretches have remorse in poor abuses;
Love thrives not in the heart that shadows dreadeth:
Affection is my captain, and he leadeth;
    And when his gaudy banner is display'd,
    The coward fights, and will not be dismay'd.

'Then, childish fear avaunt! debating die!
Respect and reason wait on wrinkled age!
My heart shall never countermand mine eye:
Sad pause and deep regard beseems the sage;
My part is youth, and beats these from the stage:
    Desire my pilot is, beauty my prize;
    Then who fears sinking where such treasure lies?'

As corn o'ergrown by weeds, so heedful fear
Is almost choked by unresisted lust.
Away he steals with open listening ear,
Full of foul hope and full of fond mistrust;
Both which, as servitors to the unjust,
    So cross him with their opposite persuasion,
    That now he vows a league, and now invasion.

Within his thought her heavenly image sits,
And in the self-same seat sits Collatine:
That eye which looks on her confounds his wits;
That eye which him beholds, as more divine,
Unto a view so false will not incline;
    But with a pure appeal seeks to the heart,
    Which once corrupted takes the worser part;

And therein heartens up his servile powers,
Who, flatter'd by their leader's jocund show,
Stuff up his lust, as minutes fill up hours;
And as their captain, so their pride doth grow,
Paying more slavish tribute than they owe.
    By reprobate desire thus madly led,
    The Roman lord marcheth to Lucrece' bed.

The locks between her chamber and his will,
Each one by him enforced, retires his ward;
But, as they open, they all rate his ill,
Which drives the creeping thief to some regard:
The threshold grates the door to have him heard;
    Night-wandering weasels shriek to see him there;
    They fright him, yet he still pursues his fear.

As each unwilling portal yields him way,
Through little vents and crannies of the place
The wind wars with his torch to make him stay,
And blows the smoke of it into his face,
Extinguishing his conduct in this case;
    But his hot heart, which fond desire doth scorch,
    Puffs forth another wind that fires the torch:

And being lighted, by the light he spies
Lucretia's glove, wherein her needle sticks:
He takes it from the rushes where it lies,
And griping it, the needle his finger pricks;
As who should say 'This glove to wanton tricks
    Is not inured; return again in haste;
    Thou see'st our mistress' ornaments are chaste.'

But all these poor forbiddings could not stay him;
He in the worst sense construes their denial:
The doors, the wind, the glove, that did delay him,
He takes for accidental things of trial;
Or as those bars which stop the hourly dial,
    Who with a lingering stay his course doth let,
    Till every minute pays the hour his debt.

'So, so,' quoth he, 'these lets attend the time,
Like little frosts that sometime threat the spring,
To add a more rejoicing to the prime,
And give the sneaped birds more cause to sing.
Pain pays the income of each precious thing;
    Huge rocks, high winds, strong pirates, shelves
      and sands,
    The merchant fears, ere rich at home he lands.'

Now is he come unto the chamber door,
That shuts him from the heaven of his thought,
Which with a yielding latch, and with no more,
Hath barr'd him from the blessed thing he sought.
So from himself impiety hath wrought,
    That for his prey to pray he doth begin,
    As if the heavens should countenance his sin.

But in the midst of his unfruitful prayer,
Having solicited the eternal power

That his foul thoughts might compass his fair fair,
And they would stand auspicious to the hour,
Even there he starts: quoth he, 'I must deflower:
    The powers to whom I pray abhor this fact;
    How can they then assist me in the act?

'Then Love and Fortune be my gods, my guide!
My will is back'd with resolution:
Thoughts are but dreams till their effects be tried;
The blackest sin is clear'd with absolution;
Against love's fire fear's frost hath dissolution.
    The eye of heaven is out, and misty night
    Covers the shame that follows sweet delight.'

This said, his guilty hand pluck'd up the latch,
And with his knee the door he opens wide.
The dove sleeps fast that this night-owl will catch:
Thus treason works ere traitors be espied.
Who sees the lurking serpent steps aside;
    But she, sound sleeping, fearing no such thing,
    Lies at the mercy of his mortal sting.

Into the chamber wickedly he stalks
And gazeth on her yet unstained bed.
The curtains being close, about he walks,
Rolling his greedy eyeballs in his head:
By their high treason is his heart misled;
    Which gives the watch-word to his hand full soon
    To draw the cloud that hides the silver moon.

Look, as the fair and fiery-pointed sun,
Rushing from forth a cloud, bereaves our sight;
Even so, the curtain drawn, his eyes begun
To wink, being blinded with a greater light:
Whether it is that she reflects so bright,
    That dazzleth them, or else some shame supposed;
    But blind they are, and keep themselves enclosed.

O, had they in that darksome prison died!
Then had they seen the period of their ill;
Then Collatine again, by Lucrece' side,
In his clear bed might have reposed still:
But they must ope, this blessed league to kill;
    And holy-thoughted Lucrece to their sight
    Must sell her joy, her life, her world's delight.

Her lily hand her rosy cheek lies under,
Cozening the pillow of a lawful kiss;
Who, therefore angry, seems to part in sunder,
Swelling on either side to want his bliss;
Between whose hills her head entombed is:
    Where, like a virtuous monument, she lies,
    To be admired of lewd unhallow'd eyes.

Without the bed her other fair hand was,
On the green coverlet; whose perfect white
Show'd like an April daisy on the grass,
With pearly sweat, resembling dew of night.
Her eyes, like marigolds, had sheathed their light,
    And canopied in darkness sweetly lay,
    Till they might open to adorn the day.

Her hair, like golden threads, play'd with her
       breath;
O modest wantons! wanton modesty!
Showing life's triumph in the map of death,
And death's dim look in life's mortality:
Each in her sleep themselves so beautify
   As if between them twain there were no strife,
   But that life lived in death and death in life.

Her breasts, like ivory globes circled with blue,
A pair of maiden worlds unconquered,
Save of their lord no bearing yoke they knew,
And him by oath they truly honoured.
These worlds in Tarquin new ambition bred;
   Who, like a foul usurper, went about
   From this fair throne to heave the owner out.

What could he see but mightily he noted?
What did he note but strongly he desired?
What he beheld, on that he firmly doted,
And in his will his wilful eye he tired.
With more than admiration he admired
   Her azure veins, her alabaster skin,
   Her coral lips, her snow-white dimpled chin.

As the grim lion fawneth o'er his prey,
Sharp hunger by the conquest satisfied,
So o'er this sleeping soul doth Tarquin stay,
His rage of lust by gazing qualified;
Slack'd, not suppress'd; for standing by her side,
   His eye, which late this mutiny restrains,
   Unto a greater uproar tempts his veins:

And they, like straggling slaves for pillage fighting,
Obdurate vassals fell exploits effecting,
In bloody death and ravishment delighting,
Nor children's tears nor mothers' groans respecting,
Swell in their pride, the onset still expecting:
   Anon his beating heart, alarum striking,
   Gives the hot charge, and bids them do their
       liking.

His drumming heart cheers up his burning eye,
His eye commends the leading to his hand;
His hand, as proud of such a dignity,
Smoking with pride, march'd on to make his stand
On her bare breast, the heart of all her land;
   Whose ranks of blue veins, as his hand did scale,
   Left their round turrets destitute and pale.

They, mustering to the quiet cabinet
Where their dear governess and lady lies,
Do tell her she is dreadfully beset,
And fright her with confusion of their cries:
She, much amazed, breaks ope her lock'd-up eyes,
   Who, peeping forth this tumult to behold,
   Are by his flaming torch dimm'd and controll'd.

Imagine her as one in dead of night
From forth dull sleep by dreadful fancy waking,

That thinks she hath beheld some ghastly sprite,
Whose grim aspect sets every joint a-shaking;
What terror 'tis! but she, in worser taking,
   From sleep disturbed, heedfully doth view
   The sight which makes supposed terror true.

Wrapp'd and confounded in a thousand fears,
Like to a new-kill'd bird she trembling lies;
She dares not look; yet, winking, there appears
Quick-shifting antics, ugly in her eyes:
Such shadows are the weak brain's forgeries;
   Who, angry that the eyes fly from their lights,
   In darkness daunts them with more dreadful
       sights.

His hand, that yet remains upon her breast,—
Rude ram, to batter such an ivory wall!—
May feel her heart, poor citizen! distress'd,
Wounding itself to death, rise up and fall,
Beating her bulk, that his hand shakes withal.
   This moves in him more rage and lesser pity,
   To make the breach and enter this sweet city.

First, like a trumpet, doth his tongue begin
To sound a parley to his heartless foe;
Who o'er the white sheet peers her whiter chin,
The reason of this rash alarm to know,
Which he by dumb demeanour seeks to show;
   But she with vehement prayers urgeth still
   Under what colour he commits this ill.

Thus he replies: 'The colour in thy face,
That even for anger makes the lily pale
And the red rose blush at her own disgrace,
Shall plead for me and tell my loving tale:
Under that colour am I come to scale
   Thy never-conquer'd fort: the fault is thine,
   For those thine eyes betray thee unto mine.

'Thus I forestall thee, if thou mean to chide:
Thy beauty hath ensnared thee to this night,
Where thou with patience must my will abide;
My will that marks thee for my earth's delight,
Which I to conquer sought with all my might;
   But as reproof and reason beat it dead,
   By thy bright beauty was it newly bred.

'I see what crosses my attempt will bring;
I know what thorns the growing rose defends;
I think the honey guarded with a sting;
All this beforehand counsel comprehends:
But will is deaf and hears no heedful friends;
   Only he hath an eye to gaze on beauty,
   And dotes on what he looks, 'gainst law or duty.

'I have debated, even in my soul,
What wrong, what shame, what sorrow I shall
       breed;
But nothing can affection's course control,
Or stop the headlong fury of his speed.
I know repentant tears ensue the deed,

Reproach, disdain and deadly enmity;
Yet strive I to embrace mine infamy.'

This said, he shakes aloft his Roman blade,
Which, like a falcon towering in the skies,
Coucheth the fowl below with his wings' shade,
Whose crooked beak threats if he mount he dies:
So under his insulting falchion lies
    Harmless Lucretia, marking what he tells
    With trembling fear, as fowl hear falcon's bells.

'Lucrece,' quoth he, 'this night I must enjoy thee:
If thou deny, then force must work my way,
For in thy bed I purpose to destroy thee:
That done, some worthless slave of thine I'll slay,
To kill thine honour with thy life's decay;
    And in thy dead arms do I mean to place him,
    Swearing I slew him, seeing thee embrace him.

'So thy surviving husband shall remain
The scornful mark of every open eye;
Thy kinsmen hang their heads at this disdain,
Thy issue blurr'd with nameless bastardy:
And thou, the author of their obloquy,
    Shalt have thy trespass cited up in rhymes
    And sung by children in succeeding times.

'But if thou yield, I rest thy secret friend:
The fault unknown is as a thought unacted;
A little harm done to a great good end
For lawful policy remains enacted.
The poisonous simple sometime is compacted
    In a pure compound; being so applied,
    His venom in effect is purified.

'Then, for thy husband and thy children's sake,
Tender my suit: bequeath not to their lot
The shame that from them no device can take,
The blemish that will never be forgot;
Worse than a slavish wipe or birth-hour's blot:
    For marks descried in men's nativity
    Are nature's faults, not their own infamy.'

Here with a cockatrice' dead-killing eye
He rouseth up himself, and makes a pause;
While she, the picture of true piety,
Like a white hind under the gripe's sharp claws,
Pleads, in a wilderness where are no laws,
    To the rough beast that knows no gentle right,
    Nor aught obeys but his foul appetite.

But when a black-faced cloud the world doth threat,
In his dim mist the aspiring mountains hiding,
From earth's dark womb some gentle gust doth get,
Which blows these pitchy vapours from their biding,
Hindering their present fall by this dividing;
    So his unhallow'd haste her words delays,
    And moody Pluto winks while Orpheus plays.

Yet, foul night-waking cat, he doth but dally,
While in his hold-fast foot the weak mouse panteth:
Her sad behaviour feeds his vulture folly,
A swallowing gulf that even in plenty wanteth:
His ear her prayers admits, but his heart granteth
    No penetrable entrance to her plaining:
    Tears harden lust, though marble wear with rain-
      ing.

Her pity-pleading eyes are sadly fixed
In the remorseless wrinkles of his face;
Her modest eloquence with sighs is mixed,
Which to her oratory adds more grace.
She puts the period often from his place,
    And midst the sentence so her accent breaks
    That twice she doth begin ere once she speaks.

She conjures him by high almighty Jove,
By knighthood, gentry, and sweet friendship's oath,
By her untimely tears, her husband's love,
By holy human law and common troth,
By heaven and earth, and all the power of both,
    That to his borrow'd bed he make retire,
    And stoop to honour, not to foul desire.

Quoth she: 'Reward not hospitality
With such black payment as thou hast pretended;
Mud not the fountain that gave drink to thee;
Mar not the thing that cannot be amended;
End thy ill aim before thy shoot be ended;
    He is no woodman that doth bend his bow
    To strike a poor unseasonable doe.

'My husband is thy friend; for his sake spare me:
Thyself art mighty; for thine own sake leave me:
Myself a weakling; do not then ensnare me:
Thou look'st not like deceit; do not deceive me.
My sighs, like whirlwinds, labour hence to heave
    thee:
    If ever man were moved with woman's moans,
    Be moved with my tears, my sighs, my groans:

'All which together, like a troubled ocean,
Beat at thy rocky and wreck-threatening heart,
To soften it with their continual motion;
For stones dissolved to water do convert.
O, if no harder than a stone thou art,
    Melt at my tears, and be compassionate!
    Soft pity enters at an iron gate.

'In Tarquin's likeness I did entertain thee:
Hast thou put on his shape to do him shame?
To all the host of heaven I complain me,
Thou wrong'st his honour, wound'st his princely
    name.
Thou art not what thou seem'st; and if the same,
    Thou seem'st not what thou art, a god, a king;
    For kings, like gods, should govern every thing.

'How will thy shame be seeded in thine age,
When thus thy vices bud before thy spring!
If in thy hope thou darest do such outrage,
What darest thou not when once thou art a king?
O, be remember'd, no outrageous thing
    From vassal actors can be wiped away;
    Then kings' misdeeds cannot be hid in clay.

'This deed will make thee only loved for fear;
But happy monarchs still are fear'd for love:
With foul offenders thou perforce must bear,
When they in thee the like offences prove:
If but for fear of this, thy will remove;
    For princes are the glass, the school, the book,
    Where subjects' eyes do learn, do read, do look.

'And wilt thou be the school where Lust shall learn?
Must he in thee read lectures of such shame?
Wilt thou be glass wherein it shall discern
Authority for sin, warrant for blame,
To privilege dishonour in thy name?
    Thou back'st reproach against long-living laud,
    And makest fair reputation but a bawd.

'Hast thou command? by him that gave it thee,
From a pure heart command thy rebel will:
Draw not thy sword to guard iniquity,
For it was lent thee all that brood to kill.
Thy princely office how canst thou fulfil,
    When, pattern'd by thy fault, foul sin may say
    He learn'd to sin and thou didst teach the way?

'Think but how vile a spectacle it were,
To view thy present trespass in another.
Men's faults do seldom to themselves appear;
Their own transgressions partially they smother:
This guilt would seem death-worthy in thy brother.
    O, how are they wrapp'd in with infamies
    That from their own misdeeds askance their eyes!

'To thee, to thee, my heaved-up hands appeal,
Not to seducing lust, thy rash relier:
I sue for exiled majesty's repeal;
Let him return, and flattering thoughts retire:
His true respect will prison false desire,
    And wipe the dim mist from thy doting eyne,
    That thou shalt see thy state and pity mine.'

'Have done,' quoth he: 'my uncontrolled tide
Turns not, but swells the higher by this let.
Small lights are soon blown out, huge fires abide,
And with the wind in greater fury fret:
The petty streams that pay a daily debt
    To their salt sovereign, with their fresh falls' haste
    Add to his flow, but alter not his taste.'

'Thou art,' quoth she, 'a sea, a sovereign king;
And, lo, there falls into thy boundless flood
Black lust, dishonour, shame, misgoverning,
Who seek to stain the ocean of thy blood.

If all these petty ills shall change thy good,
    Thy sea within a puddle's womb is hearsed,
    And not the puddle in thy sea dispersed.

'So shall these slaves be king, and thou their slave;
Thou nobly base, they basely dignified;
Thou their fair life, and they thy fouler grave:
Thou loathed in their shame, they in thy pride:
The lesser thing should not the greater hide;
    The cedar stoops not to the base shrub's foot,
    But low shrubs wither at the cedar's root.

'So let thy thoughts, low vassals to thy state'—
'No more,' quoth he; 'by heaven, I will not hear
    thee:
Yield to my love; if not, enforced hate,
Instead of love's coy touch, shall rudely tear thee:
That done, despitefully I mean to bear thee
    Unto the base bed of some rascal groom,
    To be thy partner in this shameful doom.'

This said, he sets his foot upon the light,
For light and lust are deadly enemies:
Shame folded up in blind concealing night,
When most unseen, then most doth tyrannize.
The wolf hath seized his prey, the poor lamb cries;
    Till with her own white fleece her voice controll'd
    Entombs her outcry in her lips' sweet fold:

For with the nightly linen that she wears
He pens her piteous clamours in her head,
Cooling his hot face in the chastest tears
That ever modest eyes with sorrow shed.
O, that prone lust should stain so pure a bed!
    The spots whereof could weeping purify,
    Her tears should drop on them perpetually.

But she hath lost a dearer thing than life,
And he hath won what he would lose again:
This forced league doth force a further strife;
This momentary joy breeds months of pain;
This hot desire converts to cold disdain:
    Pure Chastity is rifled of her store,
    And Lust, the thief, far poorer than before.

Look, as the full-fed hound or gorged hawk,
Unapt for tender smell or speedy flight,
Make slow pursuit, or altogether balk
The prey wherein by nature they delight,
So surfeit-taking Tarquin fares this night:
    His taste delicious, in digestion souring,
    Devours his will, that lived by foul devouring.

O, deeper sin than bottomless conceit
Can comprehend in still imagination!
Drunken Desire must vomit his receipt,
Ere he can see his own abomination.
While Lust is in his pride, no exclamation
    Can curb his heat or rein his rash desire,
    Till, like a jade, Self-will himself doth tire.

And then with lank and lean discolour'd cheek,
With heavy eye, knit brow, and strengthless pace,
Feeble Desire, all recreant, poor and meek,
Like to a bankrupt beggar wails his case:
　The flesh being proud, Desire doth fight with Grace,
　　For there it revels, and when that decays
　　The guilty rebel for remission prays.

So fares it with this faultful lord of Rome,
Who this accomplishment so hotly chased;
For now against himself he sounds this doom,
That through the length of times he stands disgraced:
　Besides, his soul's fair temple is defaced,
　　To whose weak ruins muster troops of cares,
　　To ask the spotted princess how she fares.

She says, her subjects with foul insurrection
Have batter'd down her consecrated wall,
And by their mortal fault brought in subjection
Her immortality, and made her thrall
To living death and pain perpetual:
　Which in her prescience she controlled still,
　　But her foresight could not forestall their will.

Even in this thought through the dark night he
　　stealeth,
A captive victor that hath lost in gain;
Bearing away the wound that nothing healeth,
The scar that will, despite of cure, remain;
Leaving his spoil perplex'd in greater pain.
　She bears the load of lust he left behind,
　　And he the burthen of a guilty mind.

He like a thievish dog creeps sadly thence;
She like a wearied lamb lies panting there;
He scowls, and hates himself for his offence;
She, desperate, with her nails her flesh doth tear;
He faintly flies, sweating with guilty fear;
　She stays, exclaiming on the direful night;
　　He runs, and chides his vanish'd, loathed delight.

He thence departs a heavy convertite;
She there remains a hopeless cast-away;
He in his speed looks for the morning light;
She prays she never may behold the day,
'For day,' quoth she, 'night's 'scapes doth open lay,
　And my true eyes have never practised how
　　To cloak offences with a cunning brow.

'They think not but that every eye can see
The same disgrace which they themselves behold;
And therefore would they still in darkness be,
To have their unseen sin remain untold;
For they their guilt with weeping will unfold,
　And grave, like water that doth eat in steel,
　　Upon my cheeks what helpless shame I feel.'

Here she exclaims against repose and rest,
And bids her eyes hereafter still be blind.
She wakes her heart by beating on her breast,

And bids it leap from thence, where it may find
Some purer chest to close so pure a mind.
　Frantic with grief thus breathes she forth her spite
　　Against the unseen secrecy of night:

'O comfort-killing Night, image of hell!
Dim register and notary of shame!
Black stage for tragedies and murders fell!
Vast sin-concealing chaos! nurse of blame!
Blind muffled bawd! dark harbour for defame!
　Grim cave of death! whispering conspirator
　　With close-tongued treason and the ravisher!

'O hateful, vaporous and foggy Night!
Since thou art guilty of my cureless crime,
Muster thy mists to meet the eastern light,
Make war against proportion'd course of time;
Or if thou wilt permit the sun to climb
　His wonted height, yet ere he go to bed,
　　Knit poisonous clouds about his golden head.

'With rotten damps ravish the morning air;
Let their exhaled unwholesome breaths make sick
The life of purity, the supreme fair,
Ere he arrive his weary noon-tide prick;
And let thy misty vapours march so thick
　That in their smoky ranks his smother'd light
　　May set at noon and make perpetual night.

'Were Tarquin Night, as he is but Night's child,
The silver-shining queen he would distain;
Her twinkling handmaids too, by him defiled,
Through Night's black bosom should not peep
　　again:
So should I have co-partners in my pain;
　And fellowship in woe doth woe assuage,
　　As palmers' chat makes short their pilgrimage.

'Where now I have no one to blush with me,
To cross their arms and hang their heads with mine,
To mask their brows and hide their infamy;
But I alone alone must sit and pine,
Seasoning the earth with showers of silver brine,
　Mingling my talk with tears, my grief with groans,
　　Poor wasting monuments of lasting moans.

'O Night, thou furnace of foul-reeking smoke,
Let not the jealous Day behold that face
Which underneath thy black all-hiding cloak
Immodestly lies martyr'd with disgrace!
Keep still possession of thy gloomy place,
　That all the faults which in thy reign are made
　　May likewise be sepulchred in thy shade!

'Make me not object to the tell-tale Day!
The light will show, character'd in my brow,
The story of sweet chastity's decay,
The impious breach of holy wedlock vow:
Yea, the illiterate, that know not how
　To cipher what is writ in learned books,
　　Will quote my loathsome trespass in my looks.

'The nurse, to still her child, will tell my story,
And fright her crying babe with Tarquin's name;
The orator, to deck his oratory,
Will couple my reproach to Tarquin's shame;
Feast-finding minstrels, tuning my defame,
  Will tie the hearers to attend each line,
  How Tarquin wronged me, I Collatine.

'Let my good name, that senseless reputation,
For Collatine's dear love be kept unspotted:
If that be made a theme for disputation,
The branches of another root are rotted,
And undeserved reproach to him allotted
  That is as clear from this attaint of mine
  As I, ere this, was pure to Collatine.

'O unseen shame! invisible disgrace!
O unfelt sore! crest-wounding, private scar!
Reproach is stamp'd in Collatinus' face,
And Tarquin's eye may read the mot afar,
How he in peace is wounded, not in war.
  Alas, how many bear such shameful blows,
  Which not themselves, but he that gives them
    knows!

'If, Collatine, thine honour lay in me,
From me by strong assault it is bereft.
My honey lost, and I, a drone-like bee,
Have no perfection of my summer left,
But robb'd and ransack'd by injurious theft:
  In thy weak hive a wandering wasp hath crept,
  And suck'd the honey which thy chaste bee kept.

'Yet am I guilty of thy honour's wrack;
Yet for thy honour did I entertain him;
Coming from thee, I could not put him back,
For it had been dishonour to disdain him:
Besides, of weariness he did complain him,
  And talk'd of virtue: O unlook'd-for evil,
  When virtue is profaned in such a devil!

'Why should the worm intrude the maiden bud?
Or hateful cuckoos hatch in sparrows' nests?
Or toads infect fair founts with venom mud?
Or tyrant folly lurk in gentle breasts?
Or kings be breakers of their own behests?
  But no perfection is so absolute
  That some impurity doth not pollute.

'The aged man that coffers up his gold
Is plagued with cramps and gouts and painful fits,
And scarce hath eyes his treasure to behold,
But like still-pining Tantalus he sits
And useless barns the harvest of his wits,
  Having no other pleasure of his gain
  But torment that it cannot cure his pain.

'So then he hath it when he cannot use it,
And leaves it to be master'd by his young;
Who in their pride do presently abuse it:

Their father was too weak, and they too strong,
To hold their cursed-blessed fortune long.
  The sweets we wish for turn to loathed sours
  Even in the moment that we call them ours.

'Unruly blasts wait on the tender spring;
Unwholesome weeds take root with precious flowers;
The adder hisses where the sweet birds sing;
What virtue breeds iniquity devours:
We have no good that we can say is ours
  But ill-annexed Opportunity
  Or kills his life or else his quality.

'O Opportunity, thy guilt is great!
'Tis thou that executest the traitor's treason;
Thou set'st the wolf where he the lamb may get;
Whoever plots the sin, thou point'st the season;
'Tis thou that spurn'st at right, at law, at reason;
  And in thy shady cell, where none may spy him,
  Sits Sin, to seize the souls that wander by him.

'Thou makest the vestal violate her oath;
Thou blow'st the fire when temperance is thaw'd;
Thou smother'st honesty, thou murder'st troth;
Thou foul abettor! thou notorious bawd!
Thou plantest scandal and displacest laud:
  Thou ravisher, thou traitor, thou false thief,
  Thy honey turns to gall, thy joy to grief!

'Thy secret pleasure turns to open shame,
Thy private feasting to a public fast,
Thy smoothing titles to a ragged name,
Thy sugar'd tongue to bitter wormwood taste:
Thy violent vanities can never last.
  How comes it then, vile Opportunity,
  Being so bad, such numbers seek for thee?

'When wilt thou be the humble suppliant's friend,
And bring him where his suit may be obtained?
When wilt thou sort an hour great strifes to end?
Or free that soul which wretchedness hath chained?
Give physic to the sick, ease to the pained?
  The poor, lame, blind, halt, creep, cry out for
    thee;
  But they ne'er meet with Opportunity.

'The patient dies while the physician sleeps;
The orphan pines while the oppressor feeds;
Justice is feasting while the widow weeps;
Advice is sporting while infection breeds:
Thou grant'st no time for charitable deeds:
  Wrath, envy, treason, rape, and murder's rages,
  Thy heinous hours wait on them as their pages.

'When Truth and Virtue have to do with thee,
A thousand crosses keep them from thy aid:
They buy thy help, but Sin ne'er gives a fee;
He gratis comes, and thou art well appaid
As well to hear as grant what he hath said.
  My Collatine would else have come to me
  When Tarquin did, but he was stay'd by thee.

'Guilty thou art of murder and of theft,
Guilty of perjury and subornation,
Guilty of treason, forgery and shift,
Guilty of incest, that abomination;
An accessary by thine inclination
    To all sins past and all that are to come,
    From the creation to the general doom.

'Mis-shapen Time, copesmate of ugly Night,
Swift subtle post, carrier of grisly care,
Eater of youth, false slave to false delight,
Base watch of woes, sin's pack-horse, virtue's snare;
Thou nursest all and murder'st all that are:
    O, hear me then, injurious, shifting Time!
    Be guilty of my death, since of my crime.

'Why hath thy servant Opportunity
Betray'd the hours thou gavest me to repose,
Cancell'd my fortunes and enchained me
To endless date of never-ending woes?
Time's office is to fine the hate of foes,
    To eat up errors by opinion bred,
    Not spend the dowry of a lawful bed.

'Time's glory is to calm contending kings,
To unmask falsehood and bring truth to light,
To stamp the seal of time in aged things,
To wake the morn and sentinel the night,
To wrong the wronger till he render right,
    To ruinate proud buildings with thy hours
    And smear with dust their glittering golden
        towers;

'To fill with worm-holes stately monuments,
To feed oblivion with decay of things,
To blot old books and alter their contents,
To pluck the quills from ancient ravens' wings,
To dry the old oak's sap and cherish springs,
    To spoil antiquities of hammer'd steel
    And turn the giddy round of Fortune's wheel;

'To show the beldam daughters of her daughter,
To make the child a man, the man a child,
To slay the tiger that doth live by slaughter,
To tame the unicorn and lion wild,
To mock the subtle in themselves beguiled,
    To cheer the ploughman with increaseful crops,
    And waste huge stones with little water-drops.

'Why work'st thou mischief in thy pilgrimage,
Unless thou couldst return to make amends?
One poor retiring minute in an age
Would purchase thee a thousand thousand friends,
Lending him wit that to bad debtors lends:
    O, this dread night, wouldst thou one hour come
        back,
    I could prevent this storm and shun thy wrack!

'Thou ceaseless lackey to eternity,
With some mischance cross Tarquin in his flight:
Devise extremes beyond extremity,

To make him curse this cursed crimeful night:
Let ghastly shadows his lewd eyes affright,
    And the dire thought of his committed evil
    Shape every bush a hideous shapeless devil.

'Disturb his hours of rest with restless trances,
Afflict him in his bed with bedrid groans;
Let there bechance him pitiful mischances,
To make him moan; but pity not his moans:
Stone him with harden'd hearts, harder than stones;
    And let mild women to him lose their mildness,
    Wilder to him than tigers in their wildness.

'Let him have time to tear his curled hair,
Let him have time against himself to rave,
Let him have time of time's help to despair,
Let him have time to live a loathed slave,
Let him have time a beggar's orts to crave,
    And time to see one that by alms doth live
    Disdain to him disdained scraps to give.

'Let him have time to see his friends his foes,
And merry fools to mock at him resort;
Let him have time to mark how slow time goes
In time of sorrow, and how swift and short
His time of folly and his time of sport;
    And ever let his unrecalling crime
    Have time to wail the abusing of his time.

'O Time, thou tutor both to good and bad,
Teach me to curse him that thou taught'st this ill!
At his own shadow let the thief run mad,
Himself himself seek every hour to kill!
Such wretched hands such wretched blood should
        spill;
    For who so base would such an office have
    As slanderous deathsman to so base a slave?

'The baser is he, coming from a king,
To shame his hope with deeds degenerate:
The mightier man, the mightier is the thing
That makes him honour'd or begets him hate;
For greatest scandal waits on greatest state.
    The moon being clouded presently is miss'd,
    But little stars may hide them when they list.

'The crow may bathe his coal-black wings in mire,
And unperceived fly with the filth away;
But if the like the snow-white swan desire,
The stain upon his silver down will stay.
Poor grooms are sightless night, kings glorious day:
    Gnats are unnoted wheresoe'er they fly,
    But eagles gazed upon with every eye.

'Out, idle words, servants to shallow fools!
Unprofitable sounds, weak arbitrators!
Busy yourselves in skill-contending schools;
Debate where leisure serves with dull debaters;
To trembling clients be you mediators:
    For me, I force not argument a straw,
    Since that my case is past the help of law.

'In vain I rail at Opportunity,
At Time, at Tarquin, and uncheerful Night;
In vain I cavil with mine infamy,
In vain I spurn at my confirm'd despite:
This helpless smoke of words doth me no right.
　　The remedy indeed to do me good
　　Is to let forth my foul-defiled blood.

'Poor hand, why quiver'st thou at this decree?
Honour thyself to rid me of this shame;
For if I die, my honour lives in thee,
But if I live, thou livest in my defame:
Since thou couldst not defend thy loyal dame
　　And wast afeard to scratch her wicked foe,
　　Kill both thyself and her for yielding so.'

This said, from her be-tumbled couch she starteth,
To find some desperate instrument of death:
But this no slaughterhouse no tool imparteth
To make more vent for passage of her breath;
Which, thronging through her lips, so vanisheth
　　As smoke from Ætna that in air consumes,
　　Or that which from discharged cannon fumes.

'In vain,' quoth she, 'I live, and seek in vain
Some happy mean to end a hapless life.
I fear'd by Tarquin's falchion to be slain,
Yet for the self-same purpose seek a knife:
But when I fear'd I was a loyal wife:
　　So am I now: O no, that cannot be;
　　Of that true type hath Tarquin rifled me.

'O, that is gone for which I sought to live,
And therefore now I need not fear to die.
To clear this spot by death, at least I give
A badge of fame to slander's livery,
A dying life to living infamy:
　　Poor helpless help, the treasure stol'n away,
　　To burn the guiltless casket where it lay!

'Well, well, dear Collatine, thou shalt not know
The stained taste of violated troth;
I will not wrong thy true affection so,
To flatter thee with an infringed oath;
This bastard graff shall never come to growth:
　　He shall not boast who did thy stock pollute
　　That thou art doting father of his fruit.

'Nor shall he smile at thee in secret thought,
Nor laugh with his companions at thy state;
But thou shalt know thy interest was not bought
Basely with gold, but stol'n from forth thy gate.
For me, I am the mistress of my fate,
　　And with my trespass never will dispense,
　　Till life to death acquit my forced offence.

'I will not poison thee with my attaint,
Nor fold my fault in cleanly-coin'd excuses;
My sable ground of sin I will not paint,
To hide the truth of this false night's abuses:
My tongue shall utter all; mine eyes, like sluices,

As from a mountain-spring that feeds a dale,
Shall gush pure streams to purge my impure tale.'

By this, lamenting Philomel had ended
The well tuned warble of her nightly sorrow,
And solemn night with slow sad gait descended
To ugly hell; when, lo, the blushing morrow
Lends light to all fair eyes that light will borrow:
　　But cloudy Lucrece shames herself to see,
　　And therefore still in night would cloister'd be.

Revealing day through every cranny spies,
And seems to point her out where she sits weeping;
To whom she sobbing speaks: 'O eye of eyes,
Why pry'st thou through my window? leave thy peeping:
Mock with thy tickling beams eyes that are sleeping:
　　Brand not my forehead with thy piercing light,
　　For day hath nought to do what's done by night.'

Thus cavils she with every thing she sees:
True grief is fond and testy as a child,
Who wayward once, his mood with nought agrees:
Old woes, not infant sorrows, bear them mild;
Continuance tames the one; the other wild,
　　Like an unpractised swimmer plunging still
　　With too much labour drowns for want of skill.

So she, deep-drenched in a sea of care,
Holds disputation with each thing she views,
And to herself all sorrow doth compare;
No object but her passion's strength renews,
And as one shifts, another straight ensues:
　　Sometime her grief is dumb and hath no words;
　　Sometime 'tis mad and too much talk affords.

The little birds that tune their morning's joy
Make her moans mad with their sweet melody:
For mirth doth search the bottom of annoy;
Sad souls are slain in merry company;
Grief best is pleased with grief's society:
　　True sorrow then is feelingly sufficed
　　When with like semblance it is sympathized.

'Tis double death to drown in ken of shore;
He ten times pines that pines beholding food;
To see the salve doth make the wound ache more;
Great grief grieves most at that would do it good;
Deep woes roll forward like a gentle flood,
　　Who, being stopp'd, the bounding banks o'er-flows;
　　Grief dallied with nor law nor limit knows.

'You mocking birds,' quoth she, 'your tunes entomb
Within your hollow-swelling feather'd breasts,
And in my hearing be you mute and dumb:
My restless discord loves no stops nor rests;
A woeful hostess brooks not merry guests:
　　Relish your nimble notes to pleasing ears;
　　Distress like dumps when time is kept with tears.

'Come, Philomel, that sing'st of ravishment,
Make thy sad grove in my dishevell'd hair:
As the dank earth weeps at thy languishment,
So I at each sad strain will strain a tear,
And with deep groans the diapason bear;
    For burden-wise I'll hum on Tarquin still,
    While thou on Tereus descant'st better skill.

'And whiles against a thorn thou bear'st thy part,
To keep thy sharp woes waking, wretched I,
To imitate thee well, against my heart
Will fix a sharp knife, to affright mine eye;
Who, if it wink, shall thereon fall and die.
    These means, as frets upon an instrument,
    Shall tune our heart-strings to true languishment.

'And for, poor bird, thou sing'st not in the day,
As shaming any eye should thee behold,
Some dark deep desert, seated from the way,
That knows not parching heat nor freezing cold,
Will we find out; and there we will unfold
    To creatures stern sad tunes, to change their
      kinds:
    Since men prove beasts, let beasts bear gentle
      minds.'

As the poor frighted deer, that stands at gaze,
Wildly determining which way to fly,
Or one encompass'd with a winding maze,
That cannot tread the way out readily;
So with herself is she in mutiny,
    To live or die, which of the twain were better,
    When life is shamed and death reproach's debtor.

'To kill myself,' quoth she, 'alack, what were it,
But with my body my poor soul's pollution?
They that lose half with greater patience bear it
Than they whose whole is swallow'd in confusion.
That mother tries a merciless conclusion
    Who, having two sweet babes, when death takes
      one,
    Will slay the other and be nurse to none.

'My body or my soul, which was the dearer,
When the one pure, the other made divine?
Whose love of either to myself was nearer,
When both were kept for heaven and Collatine?
Ay me! the bark peel'd from the lofty pine,
    His leaves will wither and his sap decay;
    So must my soul, her bark being peel'd away.

'Her house is sack'd, her quiet interrupted,
Her mansion batter'd by the enemy;
Her sacred temple spotted, spoil'd, corrupted,
Grossly engirt with daring infamy:
Then let it not be call'd impiety,
    If in this blemish'd fort I make some hole
    Through which I may convey this troubled soul.

'Yet die I will not till my Collatine
Have heard the cause of my untimely death;

That he may vow, in that sad hour of mine,
Revenge on him that made me stop my breath.
My stained blood to Tarquin I'll bequeath,
    Which by him tainted shall for him be spent,
    And as his due writ in my testament.

'My honour I'll bequeath unto the knife
That wounds my body so dishonoured.
'Tis honour to deprive dishonour'd life;
The one will live, the other being dead:
So of shame's ashes shall my fame be bred;
    For in my death I murder shameful scorn:
    My shame so dead, mine honour is new-born.

'Dear lord of that dear jewel I have lost,
What legacy shall I bequeath to thee?
My resolution, love, shall be thy boast,
By whose example thou revenged mayst be.
How Tarquin must be used, read it in me:
    Myself, thy friend, will kill myself, thy foe,
    And, for my sake, serve thou false Tarquin so.

'This brief abridgement of my will I make:
My soul and body to the skies and ground;
My resolution, husband, do thou take;
Mine honour be the knife's that makes my wound;
My shame be his that did my fame confound;
    And all my fame that lives disbursed be
    To those that live and think no shame of me.

'Thou, Collatine, shalt oversee this will;
How was I overseen that thou shalt see it!
My blood shall wash the slander of mine ill;
My life's foul deed, my life's fair end shall free it
Faint not, faint heart, but stoutly say "So be it:"
    Yield to my hand; my hand shall conquer thee:
    Thou dead, both die and both shall victors be.'

This plot of death when sadly she had laid,
And wiped the brinish pearl from her bright eyes,
With untuned tongue she hoarsely calls her maid,
Whose swift obedience to her mistress hies;
For fleet-wing'd duty with thought's feathers flies.
    Poor Lucrece' cheeks unto her maid seem so
    As winter meads when sun doth melt their snow.

Her mistress she doth give demure good-morrow,
With soft slow tongue, true mark of modesty,
And sorts a sad look to her lady's sorrow,
For why her face wore sorrow's livery,
But durst not ask of her audaciously
    Why her two suns were cloud-eclipsed so,
    Nor why her fair cheeks over-wash'd with woe.

But as the earth doth weep, the sun being set,
Each flower moisten'd like a melting eye,
Even so the maid with swelling drops 'gan wet
Her circled eyne, enforced by sympathy
Of those fair suns set in her mistress' sky,
    Who in a salt-waved ocean quench their light,
    Which makes the maid weep like the dewy night

A pretty while these pretty creatures stand,
Like ivory conduits coral cisterns filling:
One justly weeps; the other takes in hand
No cause, but company, of her drops spilling:
Their gentle sex to weep are often willing,
    Grieving themselves to guess at others' smarts,
    And then they drown their eyes or break their
        hearts.

For men have marble, women waxen, minds,
And therefore are they form'd as marble will;
The weak oppress'd, the impression of strange kinds
Is form'd in them by force, by fraud, or skill:
Then call them not the authors of their ill,
    No more than wax shall be accounted evil
    Wherein is stamp'd the semblance of a devil.

Their smoothness, like a goodly champaign plain,
Lays open all the little worms that creep;
In men, as in a rough-grown grove, remain
Cave-keeping evils that obscurely sleep:
Through crystal walls each little mote will peep:
    Though men can cover crimes with bold stern
        looks,
    Poor women's faces are their own faults' books.

No man inveigh against the withered flower,
But chide rough winter that the flower hath kill'd:
Not that devour'd, but that which doth devour,
Is worthy blame. O, let it not be hild
Poor women's faults, that they are so fulfill'd
    With men's abuses: those proud lords to blame
    Make weak-made women tenants to their shame.

The precedent whereof in Lucrece view,
Assail'd by night with circumstances strong
Of present death, and shame that might ensue
By that her death, to do her husband wrong:
Such danger to resistance did belong,
    That dying fear through all her body spread;
    And who cannot abuse a body dead?

By this, mild patience bid fair Lucrece speak
To the poor counterfeit of her complaining:
'My girl,' quoth she, 'on what occasion break
Those tears from thee, that down thy cheeks are
    raining?
If thou dost weep for grief of my sustaining,
    Know, gentle wench, it small avails my mood:
    If tears could help, mine own would do me good.

'But tell me, girl, when went'—and there she stay'd
Till after a deep groan—'Tarquin from hence?'
'Madam, ere I was up,' replied the maid,
'The more to blame my sluggard negligence:
Yet with the fault I thus far can dispense;
    Myself was stirring ere the break of day,
    And ere I rose was Tarquin gone away.

'But, lady, if your maid may be so bold,
She would request to know your heaviness.'
'O, peace!' quoth Lucrece: 'if it should be told,

The repetition cannot make it less,
For more it is than I can well express:
    And that deep torture may be call'd a hell
    When more is felt than one hath power to tell.

'Go, get me hither paper, ink and pen:
Yet save that labour, for I have them here.
What should I say? One of my husband's men
Bid thou be ready by and by to bear
A letter to my lord, my love, my dear:
    Bid him with speed prepare to carry it;
    The cause craves haste and it will soon be writ.'

Her maid is gone, and she prepares to write,
First hovering o'er the paper with her quill:
Conceit and grief an eager combat fight;
What wit sets down is blotted straight with will;
This is too curious-good, this blunt and ill:
    Much like a press of people at a door,
    Throng her inventions, which shall go before.

At last she thus begins: 'Thou worthy lord
Of that unworthy wife that greeteth thee,
Health to thy person! next vouchsafe t' afford—
If ever, love, thy Lucrece thou wilt see—
Some present speed to come and visit me.
    So, I commend me from our house in grief:
    My woes are tedious, though my words are brief.'

Here folds she up the tenour of her woe,
Her certain sorrow writ uncertainly.
By this short schedule Collatine may know
Her grief, but not her grief's true quality:
She dares not thereof make discovery,
    Lest he should hold it her own gross abuse,
    Ere she with blood had stain'd her stain'd excuse.

Besides, the life and feeling of her passion
She hoards, to spend when he is by to hear her,
When sighs and groans and tears may grace the
    fashion
Of her disgrace, the better so to clear her
From that suspicion which the world might bear her.
    To shun this blot, she would not blot the letter
    With words, till action might become them better.

To see sad sights moves more than hear them told;
For then the eye interprets to the ear
The heavy motion that it doth behold,
When every part a part of woe doth bear.
'Tis but a part of sorrow that we hear:
    Deep sounds make lesser noise than shallow fords,
    And sorrow ebbs, being blown with wind of words.

Her letter now is seal'd and on it writ
'At Ardea to my lord with more than haste.'
The post attends, and she delivers it,
Charging the sour-faced groom to hie as fast
As lagging fowls before the northern blast:
    Speed more than speed but dull and slow she
        deems:
    Extremity still urgeth such extremes.

The homely villain court'sies to her low,
And blushing on her, with a steadfast eye
Receives the scroll without or yea or no,
And forth with bashful innocence doth hie.
But they whose guilt within their bosoms lie
    Imagine every eye beholds their blame;
    For Lucrece thought he blush'd to see her shame:

When, silly groom! God wot, it was defect
Of spirit, life and bold audacity.
Such harmless creatures have a true respect
To talk in deeds, while others saucily
Promise more speed but do it leisurely:
    Even so this pattern of the worn-out age
    Pawn'd honest looks, but laid no words to gage.

His kindled duty kindled her mistrust,
That two red fires in both their faces blazed;
She thought he blush'd, as knowing Tarquin's lust,
And blushing with him, wistly on him gazed;
Her earnest eye did make him more amazed:
    The more she saw the blood his cheeks replenish,
    The more she thought he spied in her some blemish.

But long she thinks till he return again,
And yet the duteous vassal scarce is gone.
The weary time she cannot entertain,
For now 'tis stale to sigh, to weep and groan:
So woe hath wearied woe, moan tired moan,
    That she her plaints a little while doth stay,
    Pausing for means to mourn some newer way.

At last she calls to mind where hangs a piece
Of skilful painting, made for Priam's Troy;
Before the which is drawn the power of Greece,
For Helen's rape the city to destroy,
Threatening cloud-kissing Ilion with annoy;
    Which the conceited painter drew so proud,
    As heaven, it seem'd, to kiss the turrets bow'd.

A thousand lamentable objects there,
In scorn of nature, art gave lifeless life:
Many a dry drop seem'd a weeping tear,
Shed for the slaughter'd husband by the wife:
The red blood reek'd, to show the painter's strife;
    And dying eyes gleam'd forth their ashy lights,
    Like dying coals burnt out in tedious nights.

There might you see the labouring pioner
Begrimed with sweat and smeared all with dust;
And from the towers of Troy there would appear
The very eyes of men through loop-holes thrust,
Gazing upon the Greeks with little lust:
    Such sweet observance in this work was had
    That one might see those far-off eyes look sad.

In great commanders grace and majesty
You might behold, triumphing in their faces,
In youth, quick bearing and dexterity;
And here and there the painter interlaces
Pale cowards, marching on with trembling paces;

Which heartless peasants did so well resemble
That one would swear he saw them quake and
    tremble.

In Ajax and Ulysses, O, what art
Of physiognomy might one behold!
The face of either cipher'd either's heart;
Their face their manners most expressly told:
In Ajax' eyes blunt rage and rigour roll'd;
    But the mild glance that sly Ulysses lent
    Show'd deep regard and smiling government.

There pleading might you see grave Nestor stand,
As 'twere encouraging the Greeks to fight,
Making such sober action with his hand
That it beguiled attention, charm'd the sight:
In speech, it seem'd, his beard all silver white
    Wagg'd up and down, and from his lips did fly
    Thin winding breath which purl'd up to the sky.

About him were a press of gaping faces,
Which seem'd to swallow up his sound advice;
All jointly listening, but with several graces,
As if some mermaid did their ears entice,
Some high, some low, the painter was so nice;
    The scalps of many, almost hid behind,
    To jump up higher seem'd, to mock the mind.

Here one man's hand lean'd on another's head,
His nose being shadow'd by his neighbour's ear;
Here one being throng'd bears back, all boll'n and
    red;
Another smother'd seems to pelt and swear;
And in their rage such signs of rage they bear
    As, but for loss of Nestor's golden words,
    It seem'd they would debate with angry swords.

For much imaginary work was there;
Conceit deceitful, so compact, so kind,
That for Achilles' image stood his spear
Griped in an armed hand; himself behind
Was left unseen, save to the eye of mind:
    A hand, a foot, a face, a leg, a head,
    Stood for the whole to be imagined.

And from the walls of strong-besieged Troy
When their brave hope, bold Hector, march'd to
    field,
Stood many Trojan mothers sharing joy
To see their youthful sons bright weapons wield;
And to their hope they such odd action yield
    That through their light joy seemed to appear,
    Like bright things stain'd, a kind of heavy fear.

And from the strand of Dardan, where they fought,
To Simois' reedy banks the red blood ran,
Whose waves to imitate the battle sought
With swelling ridges; and their ranks began
To break upon the galled shore, and than
    Retire again, till meeting greater ranks
    They join and shoot their foam at Simois' banks.

To this well-painted piece is Lucrece come,
To find a face where all distress is stell'd.
Many she sees where cares have carved some,
But none where all distress and dolour dwell'd,
Till she despairing Hecuba beheld,
  Staring on Priam's wounds with her old eyes,
  Which bleeding under Pyrrhus' proud foot lies.

In her the painter had anatomized
Time's ruin, beauty's wreck, and grim care's reign:
Her cheeks with chaps and wrinkles were disguised;
Of what she was no semblance did remain:
Her blue blood changed to black in every vein,
  Wanting the spring that those shrunk pipes had fed,
  Show'd life imprison'd in a body dead.

On this sad shadow Lucrece spends her eyes,
And shapes her sorrow to the beldam's woes,
Who nothing wants to answer her but cries,
And bitter words to ban her cruel foes:
The painter was no god to lend her those;
  And therefore Lucrece swears he did her wrong,
  To give her so much grief and not a tongue.

'Poor instrument,' quoth she, 'without a sound,
I'll tune thy woes with my lamenting tongue,
And drop sweet balm in Priam's painted wound,
And rail on Pyrrhus that hath done him wrong,
And with my tears quench Troy that burns so long,
  And with my knife scratch out the angry eyes
  Of all the Greeks that are thine enemies.

'Show me the strumpet that began this stir,
That with my nails her beauty I may tear.
Thy heat of lust, fond Paris, did incur
This load of wrath that burning Troy doth bear:
Thy eye kindled the fire that burneth here;
  And here in Troy, for trespass of thine eye,
  The sire, the son, the dame and daughter die.

'Why should the private pleasure of some one
Become the public plague of many moe?
Let sin, alone committed, light alone
Upon his head that hath transgressed so;
Let guiltless souls be freed from guilty woe:
  For one's offence why should so many fall,
  To plague a private sin in general?

'Lo, here weeps Hecuba, here Priam dies,
Here manly Hector faints, here Troilus swounds,
Here friend by friend in bloody channel lies,
And friend to friend gives unadvised wounds,
And one man's lust these many lives confounds:
  Had doting Priam check'd his son's desire,
  Troy had been bright with fame and not with fire.'

Here feelingly she weeps Troy's painted woes:
For sorrow, like a heavy-hanging bell
Once set on ringing, with his own weight goes;
Then little strength rings out the doleful knell:

So Lucrece, set a-work, sad tales doth tell
  To pencill'd pensiveness and colour'd sorrow;
  She lends them words, and she their looks doth borrow.

She throws her eyes about the painting round,
And who she finds forlorn she doth lament.
At last she sees a wretched image bound,
That piteous looks to Phrygian shepherds lent:
His face, though full of cares, yet show'd content;
  Onward to Troy with the blunt swains he goes,
  So mild that Patience seem'd to scorn his woes.

In him the painter labour'd with his skill
To hide deceit and give the harmless show
An humble gait, calm looks, eyes wailing still,
A brow unbent, that seem'd to welcome woe;
Cheeks neither red nor pale, but mingled so
  That blushing red no guilty instance gave,
  Nor ashy pale the fear that false hearts have.

But, like a constant and confirmed devil,
He entertain'd a show so seeming just,
And therein so ensconced his secret evil,
That jealousy itself could not mistrust
False-creeping craft and perjury should thrust
  Into so bright a day such black-faced storms,
  Or blot with hell-born sin such saint-like forms.

The well-skill'd workman this mild image drew
For perjured Sinon, whose enchanting story
The credulous old Priam after slew;
Whose words, like wildfire, burnt the shining glory
Of rich-built Ilion, that the skies were sorry,
  And little stars shot from their fixed places,
  When their glass fell wherein they view'd their faces.

This picture she advisedly perused,
And chid the painter for his wondrous skill,
Saying, some shape in Sinon's was abused;
So fair a form lodged not a mind so ill:
And still on him she gazed, and gazing still
  Such signs of truth in his plain face she spied
  That she concludes the picture was belied.

'It cannot be,' quoth she, 'that so much guile'—
She would have said 'can lurk in such a look;'
But Tarquin's shape came in her mind the while,
And from her tongue 'can lurk' from 'cannot' took:
'It cannot be' she in that sense forsook,
  And turn'd it thus, 'It cannot be, I find,
  But such a face should bear a wicked mind:

'For even as subtle Sinon here is painted,
So sober-sad, so weary and so mild,
As if with grief or travail he had fainted,
To me came Tarquin armed; so beguiled
With outward honesty, but yet defiled
  With inward vice: as Priam him did cherish,
  So did I Tarquin; so my Troy did perish.

'Look, look, how listening Priam wets his eyes,
To see those borrow'd tears that Sinon sheds!
Priam, why art thou old and yet not wise?
For every tear he falls a Trojan bleeds:
His eye drops fire, no water thence proceeds;
   Those round clear pearls of his that move thy pity
   Are balls of quenchless fire to burn thy city.

'Such devils steal effects from lightless hell;
For Sinon in his fire doth quake with cold,
And in that cold hot-burning fire doth dwell;
These contraries such unity do hold,
Only to flatter fools and make them bold:
   So Priam's trust false Sinon's tears doth flatter,
   That he finds means to burn his Troy with water.'

Here, all enraged, such passion her assails,
That patience is quite beaten from her breast.
She tears the senseless Sinon with her nails,
Comparing him to that unhappy guest
Whose deed hath made herself herself detest:
   At last she smilingly with this gives o'er;
   'Fool, fool!' quoth she, 'his wounds will not be
   sore.'

Thus ebbs and flows the current of her sorrow,
And time doth weary time with her complaining.
She looks for night, and then she longs for morrow,
And both she thinks too long with her remaining:
Short time seems long in sorrow's sharp sustaining:
   Though woe be heavy, yet it seldom sleeps,
   And they that watch see time how slow it creeps.

Which all this time hath overslipp'd her thought,
That she with painted images hath spent;
Being from the feeling of her own grief brought
By deep surmise of others' detriment,
Losing her woes in shows of discontent.
   It easeth some, though none it ever cured,
   To think their dolour others have endured.

But now the mindful messenger come back
Brings home his lord and other company;
Who finds his Lucrece clad in mourning black:
And round about her tear-distained eye
Blue circles stream'd, like rainbows in the sky:
   These water-galls in her dim element
   Foretell new storms to those already spent.

Which when her sad-beholding husband saw,
Amazedly in her sad face he stares:
Her eyes, though sod in tears, look'd red and raw,
Her lively colour kill'd with deadly cares.
He hath no power to ask her how she fares:
   Both stood, like old acquaintance in a trance,
   Met far from home, wondering each other's
   chance.

At last he takes her by the bloodless hand,
And thus begins: 'What uncouth ill event

Hath thee befall'n, that thou dost trembling stand?
Sweet love, what spite hath thy fair colour spent?
Why art thou thus attired in discontent?
   Unmask, dear dear, this moody heaviness,
   And tell thy grief, that we may give redress.'

Three times with sighs she gives her sorrow fire,
Ere once she can discharge one word of woe:
At length address'd to answer his desire,
She modestly prepares to let 'hem know
Her honour is ta'en prisoner by the foe;
   While Collatine and his consorted lords
   With sad attention long to hear her words.

And now this pale swan in her watery nest
Begins the sad dirge of her certain ending:
'Few words,' quoth she, 'shall fit the trespass best,
Where no excuse can give the fault amending:
In me moe woes than words are now depending;
   And my laments would be drawn out too long,
   To tell them all with one poor tired tongue.

'Then be this all the task it hath to say:
Dear husband, in the interest of thy bed
A stranger came, and on that pillow lay
Where thou wast wont to rest thy weary head;
And what wrong else may be imagined
   By foul enforcement might be done to me,
   From that, alas, thy Lucrece is not free.

'For in the dreadful dead of dark midnight,
With shining falchion in my chamber came
A creeping creature, with a flaming light,
And softly cried "Awake, thou Roman dame,
And entertain my love; else lasting shame
   On thee and thine this night I will inflict,
   If thou my love's desire do contradict.

'"For some hard-favour'd groom of thine," quoth he,
"Unless thou yoke thy liking to my will,
I'll murder straight, and then I'll slaughter thee,
And swear I found you where you did fulfil
The loathsome act of lust, and so did kill
   The lechers in their deed: this act will be
   My fame, and thy perpetual infamy."

'With this, I did begin to start and cry;
And then against my heart he set his sword,
Swearing, unless I took all patiently,
I should not live to speak another word;
So should my shame still rest upon record,
   And never be forgot in mighty Rome
   The adulterate death of Lucrece and her groom.

'Mine enemy was strong, my poor self weak,
And far the weaker with so strong a fear:
My bloody judge forbade my tongue to speak;
No rightful plea might plead for justice there:
His scarlet lust came evidence to swear
   That my poor beauty had purloin'd his eyes;
   And when the judge is robb'd, the prisoner dies.

'O, teach me how to make mine own excuse!
Or, at the least, this refuge let me find;
Though my gross blood be stain'd with this abuse,
Immaculate and spotless is my mind;
That was not forced; that never was inclined
    To accessary yieldings, but still pure
    Doth in her poison'd closet yet endure.'

Lo, here, the hopeless merchant of this loss,
With head declined, and voice damm'd up with woe,
With sad-set eyes and wretched arms across,
From lips new-waxen pale begins to blow
The grief away that stops his answer so:
    But, wretched as he is, he strives in vain;
    What he breathes out his breath drinks up again.

As through an arch the violent roaring tide
Outruns the eye that doth behold his haste,
Yet in the eddy boundeth in his pride
Back to the strait that forced him on so fast,
In rage sent out, recall'd in rage, being past:
    Even so his sighs, his sorrows, make a saw,
    To push grief on and back the same grief draw.

Which speechless woe of his poor she attendeth
And his untimely frenzy thus awaketh:
'Dear lord, thy sorrow to my sorrow lendeth
Another power; no flood by raining slaketh.
My woe too sensible thy passion maketh
    More feeling-painful: let it then suffice
    To drown one woe, one pair of weeping eyes.

'And for my sake, when I might charm thee so,
For she that was thy Lucrece, now attend me:
Be suddenly revenged on my foe,
Thine, mine, his own: suppose thou dost defend me
From what is past: the help that thou shalt lend me
    Comes all too late, yet let the traitor die;
    For sparing justice feeds iniquity.

'But ere I name him, you fair lords,' quoth she,
Speaking to those that came with Collatine
'Shall plight your honourable faiths to me,
With swift pursuit to venge this wrong of mine;
For 'tis a meritorious fair design
    To chase injustice with revengeful arms:
    Knights, by their oaths, should right poor ladies'
        harms.'

At this request, with noble disposition
Each present lord began to promise aid,
As bound in knighthood to her imposition,
Longing to hear the hateful foe bewray'd.
But she, that yet her sad task hath not said,
    The protestation stops. 'O, speak,' quoth she,
    'How may this forced stain be wiped from me?

'What is the quality of my offence,
Being constrain'd with dreadful circumstance?
May my pure mind with the foul act dispense,
My low-declinéd honour to advance?

May any terms acquit me from this chance?
    The poison'd fountain clears itself again;
    And why not I from this compelled stain?'

With this, they all at once began to say,
Her body's stain her mind untainted clears;
While with a joyless smile she turns away
The face, that map which deep impression bears
Of hard misfortune, carved in it with tears.
    'No, no,' quoth she, 'no dame hereafter living
    By my excuse shall claim excuse's giving.'

Here with a sigh, as if her heart would break,
She throws forth Tarquin's name: 'He, he,' she says,
But more than 'he' her poor tongue could not speak;
Till after many accents and delays,
Untimely breathings, sick and short assays,
    She utters this: 'He, he, fair lords, 'tis he,
    That guides this hand to give this wound to me.'

Even here she sheathed in her harmless breast
A harmful knife, that thence her soul unsheathed:
That blow did bail it from the deep unrest
Of that polluted prison where it breathed:
Her contrite sighs unto the clouds bequeathed
    Her winged sprite, and through her wounds doth
        fly
    Life's lasting date from cancell'd destiny.

Stone-still, astonish'd with this deadly deed,
Stood Collatine and all his lordly crew;
Till Lucrece' father, that beholds her bleed,
Himself on her self-slaughter'd body threw;
And from the purple fountain Brutus drew
    The murderous knife, and, as it left the place,
    Her blood, in poor revenge, held it in chase;

And bubbling from her breast, it doth divide
In two slow rivers, that the crimson blood
Circles her body in on every side,
Who, like a late-sack'd island, vastly stood
Bare and unpeopled in this fearful flood.
    Some of her blood still pure and red remain'd,
    And some look'd black, and that false Tarquin
        stain'd.

About the mourning and congealed face
Of that black blood a watery rigol goes,
Which seems to weep upon the tainted place:
And ever since, as pitying Lucrece' woes,
Corrupted blood some watery token shows;
    And blood untainted still doth red abide,
    Blushing at that which is so putrified.

'Daughter, dear daughter,' old Lucretius cries,
'That life was mine which thou hast here deprived.
If in the child the father's image lies,
Where shall I live now Lucrece is unlived?
Thou wast not to this end from me derived.
    If children pre-decease progenitors,
    We are their offspring, and they none of ours.

'Poor broken glass, I often did behold
In thy sweet semblance my old age new born;
But now that fair fresh mirror, dim and old,
Shows me a bare-boned death by time outworn:
O, from thy cheeks my image thou hast torn,
    And shiver'd all the beauty of my glass,
    That I no more can see what once I was.

'O time, cease thou thy course and last no longer,
If they surcease to be that should survive.
Shall rotten death make conquest of the stronger,
And leave the faltering feeble souls alive?
The old bees die, the young possess their hive:
    Then live, sweet Lucrece, live again, and see
    Thy father die, and not thy father thee!'

By this, starts Collatine as from a dream,
And bids Lucretius give his sorrow place;
And then in key-cold Lucrece' bleeding stream
He falls, and bathes the pale fear in his face,
And counterfeits to die with her a space;
    Till manly shame bids him possess his breath,
    And live to be revenged on her death.

The deep vexation of his inward soul
Hath served a dumb arrest upon his tongue;
Who, mad that sorrow should his use control
Or keep him from heart-easing words so long,
Begins to talk; but through his lips do throng
    Weak words, so thick come in his poor heart's aid
    That no man could distinguish what he said.

Yet sometime 'Tarquin' was pronounced plain,
But through his teeth, as if the name he tore.
This windy tempest, till it blow up rain,
Held back his sorrow's tide, to make it more;
At last it rains, and busy winds give o'er:
    Then son and father weep with equal strife
    Who should weep most, for daughter or for wife.

The one doth call her his, the other his,
Yet neither may possess the claim they lay.
The father says 'She's mine.' 'O, mine she is,'
Replies her husband: 'do not take away
My sorrow's interest; let no mourner say
    He weeps for her, for she was only mine,
    And only must be wail'd by Collatine.'

'O,' quoth Lucretius, 'I did give that life
Which she too early and too late hath spill'd.'
'Woe, woe,' quoth Collatine, 'she was my wife;
I owed her, and 'tis mine that she hath kill'd.'
'My daughter' and 'my wife' with clamours fill'd
    The dispersed air, who, holding Lucrece' life,
    Answer'd their cries, 'my daughter' and 'my wife.'

Brutus, who pluck'd the knife from Lucrece' side,
Seeing such emulation in their woe,
Began to clothe his wit in state and pride,
Burying in Lucrece' wound his folly's show.
He with the Romans was esteemed so
    As silly-jeering idiots are with kings,
    For sportive words and uttering foolish things:

But now he throws that shallow habit by
Wherein deep policy did him disguise,
And arm'd his long-hid wits advisedly
To check the tears in Collatinus' eyes.
'Thou wronged lord of Rome,' quoth he, 'arise:
    Let my unsounded self, supposed a fool,
    Now set thy long-experienced wit to school.

'Why, Collatine, is woe the cure for woe?
Do wounds help wounds, or grief help grievous
    deeds?
Is it revenge to give thyself a blow
For his foul act by whom thy fair wife bleeds?
Such childish humour from weak minds proceeds:
    Thy wretched wife mistook the matter so,
    To slay herself, that should have slain her foe.

'Courageous Roman, do not steep thy heart
In such relenting dew of lamentations,
But kneel with me and help to bear thy part
To rouse our Roman gods with invocations
That they will suffer these abominations,
    Since Rome herself in them doth stand disgraced,
    By our strong arms from forth her fair streets
    chased.

'Now, by the Capitol that we adore,
And by this chaste blood so unjustly stained,
By heaven's fair sun that breeds the fat earth's store,
By all our country rights in Rome maintained,
And by chaste Lucrece' soul that late complained
    Her wrongs to us, and by this bloody knife,
    We will revenge the death of this true wife!'

This said, he struck his hand upon his breast,
And kiss'd the fatal knife, to end his vow,
And to his protestation urged the rest,
Who, wondering at him, did his words allow:
Then jointly to the ground their knees they bow;
    And that deep vow, which Brutus made before,
    He doth again repeat, and that they swore.

When they had sworn to this advised doom,
They did conclude to bear dead Lucrece thence,
To show her bleeding body thorough Rome,
And so to publish Tarquin's foul offence:
Which being done with speedy diligence,
    The Romans plausibly did give consent
    To Tarquin's everlasting banishment.

SONNETS

TO . THE . ONLIE . BEGETTER . OF .
THESE . INSVING . SONNETS .
M⁼ W. H. ALL . HAPPINESSE .
AND . THAT . ETERNITIE .
PROMISED .
BY .
OVR . EVER-LIVING . POET .
WISHETH .
THE . WELL-WISHING .
ADVENTVRER . IN .
SETTING .
FORTH .

T. T.

HISTORICAL DATA

The first edition of Shakespeare's Sonnets was entered on the Stationers' Register May 20, 1609, published by Thomas Thorpe under the title *Shakespeare's Sonnets never before Imprinted*. In addition to the 154 Sonnets, it contained the elegiac poem *A Lover's Complaint*, a poem which is sometimes doubted to have been composed by Shakespeare. It appears that this edition was not authorized, and there was no second publication until the Sonnets subsequently appeared with much miscellaneous additional material by other authors in an edition published in 1640 by John Benson. The order of the Sonnets in the second edition was altogether different from that in the earlier one.

Probably none of the writings of Shakespeare has ever caused the controversy that arose over the date, character and literary history of the Sonnets. In general they are thought to be, in a very considerable measure, autobiographical. Attempts to decide their "sincerity" are largely futile, partially because many of the poems belong, in form, to well-recognized literary conventions, and more particularly because the essentially poetic mind of the author and his imaginative fervor make exaggeration and a distorted picture of the poet inevitable.

A large number of the Sonnets, generally defined as Nos. 1–126, are addressed to a man; subsequent ones are, many of them, apparently directed to a woman. The two groups are not mutually exclusive, however, and a great many of the Sonnets are mere generalities of an apostrophic character.

The identity of the persons addressed has always caused a storm of conjecture and controversy. The matter of "Mr. W. H.", to whom the publisher dedicated his volume, has been the subject of years of research and study, but no satisfactory result has ever been obtained. Two names most generally discussed in this connection are William Herbert, Earl of Pembroke, and the Earl of Southampton, Henry Wriothesley, both of whom were well-known to Shakespeare, and the latter the recipient of the dedication of both *Venus and Adonis* and *The Rape of Lucrece*. The Pembroke theory has the advantage of having the initials in the indicated order rather than by the process of metathesis which would be necessary to have it apply to the Earl of Southampton, and perhaps this has lent credence to the theory that "the dark lady" referred to in the Sonnets was his mistress, Mary Fitton, regardless of the fact that she appears to have been blonde. The rival poets referred to in Sonnets 78–86 are generally considered to have been Spenser, Marlowe, Chapman, Jonson, and possibly Peel and Drayton.

The question of the date of the Sonnets is also in dispute. Meres in *Palladis Tamia* in 1598 referred to "sugred sonnets among his private friends", but there is no indication as to how many of those contained in the first edition might have been referred to. It is probable that the composition of the book as it first appeared occupied a matter of several years, and presumably many of them were written prior to the turn of the century. Thorpe published the book with the above dedication.

SONNETS

I

FROM fairest creatures we desire increase,
That thereby beauty's rose might never die,
But as the riper should by time decease,
His tender heir might bear his memory:
But thou, contracted to thine own bright eyes,
Feed'st thy light's flame with self-substantial fuel,
Making a famine where abundance lies,
Thyself thy foe, to thy sweet self too cruel.
Thou that art now the world's fresh ornament
And only herald to the gaudy spring,
Within thine own bud buriest thy content
And, tender churl, makest waste in niggarding.
  Pity the world, or else this glutton be,
  To eat the world's due, by the grave and thee.

II

When forty winters shall besiege thy brow
And dig deep trenches in thy beauty's field,
Thy youth's proud livery, so gazed on now,
Will be a tatter'd weed, of small worth held:
Then being ask'd where all thy beauty lies,
Where all the treasure of thy lusty days,
To say, within thine own deep-sunken eyes,
Were an all-eating shame and thriftless praise.
How much more praise deserved thy beauty's use,
If thou couldst answer 'This fair child of mine
Shall sum my count and make my old excuse,'
Proving his beauty by succession thine!
  This were to be new made when thou art old,
  And see thy blood warm when thou feel'st it cold.

III

Look in thy glass, and tell the face thou viewest
Now is the time that face should form another;
Whose fresh repair if now thou not renewest,
Thou dost beguile the world, unbless some mother.
For where is she so fair whose unear'd womb
Disdains the tillage of thy husbandry?
Or who is he so fond will be the tomb
Of his self-love, to stop posterity?
Thou art thy mother's glass, and she in thee
Calls back the lovely April of her prime:
So thou through windows of thine age shalt see,
Despite of wrinkles, this thy golden time.
  But if thou live, remember'd not to be,
  Die single, and thine image dies with thee.

IV

Unthrifty loveliness, why dost thou spend
Upon thyself thy beauty's legacy?
Nature's bequest gives nothing, but doth lend,
And being frank, she lends to those are free.
Then, beauteous niggard, why dost thou abuse
The bounteous largess given thee to give?
Profitless usurer, why dost thou use
So great a sum of sums, yet canst not live?
For having traffic with thyself alone,
Thou of thyself thy sweet self dost deceive.
Then how, when nature calls thee to be gone,
What acceptable audit canst thou leave?
  Thy unused beauty must be tomb'd with thee,
  Which, used, lives th' executor to be.

V

Those hours that with gentle work did frame
The lovely gaze where every eye doth dwell,
Will play the tyrants to the very same
And that unfair which fairly doth excel:
For never-resting time leads summer on
To hideous winter and confounds him there;
Sap check'd with frost and lusty leaves quite gone,
Beauty o'ersnow'd and bareness every where:
Then, were not summer's distillation left,
A liquid prisoner pent in walls of glass,
Beauty's effect with beauty were bereft,
Nor it, nor no remembrance what it was:
  But flowers distill'd, though they with winter meet,
  Leese but their show; their substance still lives sweet.

VI

Then let not winter's ragged hand deface
In thee thy summer, ere thou be distill'd:
Make sweet some vial; treasure thou some place
With beauty's treasure, ere it be self-kill'd.
That use is not forbidden usury,
Which happies those that pay the willing loan;
That's for thyself to breed another thee,
Or ten times happier, be it ten for one;
Ten times thyself were happier than thou art,
If ten of thine ten times refigured thee:
Then what could death do, if thou shouldst depart,
Leaving thee living in posterity?

Be not self-will'd, for thou art much too fair
To be death's conquest and make worms thine
    heir.

VII

Lo, in the orient when the gracious light
Lifts up his burning head, each under eye
Doth homage to his new-appearing sight,
Serving with looks his sacred majesty;
And having climb'd the steep-up heavenly hill,
Resembling strong youth in his middle age,
Yet mortal looks adore his beauty still,
Attending on his golden pilgrimage;
But when from highmost pitch, with weary car,
Like feeble age, he reeleth from the day,
The eyes, 'fore duteous, now converted are
From his low tract, and look another way:
    So thou, thyself out-going in thy noon,
    Unlook'd on diest, unless thou get a son.

VIII

Music to hear, why hear'st thou music sadly?
Sweets with sweets war not, joy delights in joy.
Why lovest thou that which thou receivest not
    gladly,
Or else receivest with pleasure thine annoy?
If the true concord of well tuned sounds,
By unions married, do offend thine ear,
They do but sweetly chide thee, who confounds
In singleness the parts that thou shouldst bear.
Mark how one string, sweet husband to another,
Strikes each in each by mutual ordering;
Resembling sire and child and happy mother,
Who, all in one, one pleasing note do sing:
    Whose speechless song, being many, seeming one,
    Sings this to thee: 'Thou single wilt prove none.'

IX

Is it for fear to wet a widow's eye
That thou consumest thyself in single life?
Ah! if thou issueless shalt hap to die,
The world will wail thee, like a makeless wife;
The world will be thy widow, and still weep
That thou no form of thee hast left behind,
When every private widow well may keep
By children's eyes her husband's shape in mind.
Look, what an unthrift in the world doth spend
Shifts but his place, for still the world enjoys it;
But beauty's waste hath in the world an end,
And kept unused, the user so destroys it.
    No love toward others in that bosom sits
    That on himself such murderous shame commits.

X

For shame! deny that thou bear'st love to any,
Who for thyself art so unprovident.
Grant, if thou wilt, thou art beloved of many,
But that thou none lovest is most evident;
For thou art so possess'd with murderous hate
That 'gainst thyself thou stick'st not to conspire,

Seeking that beauteous roof to ruinate
Which to repair should be thy chief desire.
O, change thy thought, that I may change my mind!
Shall hate be fairer lodged than gentle love?
Be, as thy presence is, gracious and kind,
Or to thyself at least kind-hearted prove:
    Make thee another self, for love of me,
    That beauty still may live in thine or thee.

XI

As fast as thou shalt wane, so fast thou grow'st
In one of thine, from that which thou departest;
And that fresh blood which youngly thou bestow'st
Thou mayst call thine when thou from youth con-
    vertest.
Herein lives wisdom, beauty and increase;
Without this, folly, age and cold decay:
If all were minded so, the times should cease
And threescore year would make the world away.
Let those whom Nature hath not made for store,
Harsh, featureless and rude, barrenly perish:
Look, whom she best endow'd she gave the more;
Which bounteous gift thou shouldst in bounty
    cherish:
    She carved thee for her seal, and meant thereby
    Thou shouldst print more, not let that copy die.

XII

When I do count the clock that tells the time,
And see the brave day sunk in hideous night;
When I behold the violet past prime,
And sable curls all silver'd o'er with white;
When lofty trees I see barren of leaves,
Which erst from heat did canopy the herd,
And summer's green all girded up in sheaves,
Borne on the bier with white and bristly beard,
Then of thy beauty do I question make,
That thou among the wastes of time must go,
Since sweets and beauties do themselves forsake
And die as fast as they see others grow;
    And nothing 'gainst Time's scythe can make de-
      fence
    Save breed, to brave him when he takes thee
      hence.

XIII

O, that you were yourself! but, love, you are
No longer yours than you yourself here live:
Against this coming end you should prepare,
And your sweet semblance to some other give.
So should that beauty which you hold in lease
Find no determination; then you were
Yourself again, after yourself's decease,
When your sweet issue your sweet form should bear.
Who lets so fair a house fall to decay,
Which husbandry in honour might uphold
Against the stormy gusts of winter's day
And barren rage of death's eternal cold?
    O, none but unthrifts: dear my love, you know
    You had a father; let your son say so.

XIV

Not from the stars do I my judgement pluck;
And yet methinks I have astronomy,
But not to tell of good or evil luck,
Of plagues, of dearths, or seasons' quality;
Nor can I fortune to brief minutes tell,
Pointing to each his thunder, rain and wind,
Or say with princes if it shall go well,
By oft predict that I in heaven find:
But from thine eyes my knowledge I derive,
And, constant stars, in them I read such art,
As truth and beauty shall together thrive,
If from thyself to store thou wouldst convert;
   Or else of thee this I prognosticate:
   Thy end is truth's and beauty's doom and date.

XV

When I consider every thing that grows
Holds in perfection but a little moment,
That this huge stage presenteth nought but shows
Whereon the stars in secret influence comment;
When I perceive that men as plants increase,
Cheered and check'd even by the self-same sky,
Vaunt in their youthful sap, at height decrease,
And wear their brave state out of memory;
Then the conceit of this inconstant stay
Sets you most rich in youth before my sight,
Where wasteful Time debateth with Decay,
To change your day of youth to sullied night;
   And all in war with Time for love of you,
   As he takes from you, I engraft you new.

XVI

But wherefore do not you a mightier way
Make war upon this bloody tyrant, Time?
And fortify yourself in your decay
With means more blessed than my barren rhyme?
Now stand you on the top of happy hours,
And many maiden gardens, yet unset,
With virtuous wish would bear your living flowers
Much liker than your painted counterfeit:
So should the lines of life that life repair,
Which this, Time's pencil, or my pupil pen,
Neither in inward worth nor outward fair,
Can make you live yourself in eyes of men.
   To give away yourself keeps yourself still;
   And you must live, drawn by your own sweet skill.

XVII

Who will believe my verse in time to come,
If it were fill'd with your most high deserts?
Though yet, heaven knows, it is but as a tomb
Which hides your life and shows not half your parts.
If I could write the beauty of your eyes
And in fresh numbers number all your graces,
The age to come would say 'This poet lies;
Such heavenly touches ne'er touch'd earthly faces.'
So should my papers, yellowed with their age,
Be scorn'd, like old men of less truth than tongue,

And your true rights be term'd a poet's rage
And stretched metre of an antique song:
   But were some child of yours alive that time,
   You should live twice, in it and in my rhyme.

XVIII

Shall I compare thee to a summer's day?
Thou art more lovely and more temperate:
Rough winds do shake the darling buds of May,
And summer's lease hath all too short a date:
Sometime too hot the eye of heaven shines,
And often is his gold complexion dimm'd;
And every fair from fair sometime declines,
By chance or nature's changing course untrimm'd;
But thy eternal summer shall not fade,
Nor lose possession of that fair thou owest;
Nor shall Death brag thou wander'st in his shade,
When in eternal lines to time thou grow'st:
   So long as men can breathe, or eyes can see,
   So long lives this, and this gives life to thee.

XIX

Devouring Time, blunt thou the lion's paws,
And make the earth devour her own sweet brood;
Pluck the keen teeth from the fierce tiger's jaws,
And burn the long-lived phœnix in her blood;
Make glad and sorry seasons as thou fleet'st,
And do whate'er thou wilt, swift-footed Time,
To the wide world and all her fading sweets;
But I forbid thee one most heinous crime:
O, carve not with thy hours my love's fair brow,
Nor draw no lines there with thine antique pen;
Him in thy course untainted do allow
For beauty's pattern to succeeding men.
   Yet do thy worst, old Time: despite thy wrong,
   My love shall in my verse ever live young.

XX

A woman's face with Nature's own hand painted
Hast thou, the master-mistress of my passion;
A woman's gentle heart, but not acquainted
With shifting change, as is false women's fashion;
An eye more bright than theirs, less false in rolling,
Gilding the object whereupon it gazeth;
A man in hue, all 'hues' in his controlling,
Which steals men's eyes and women's souls amazeth.
And for a woman wert thou first created;
Till Nature, as she wrought thee, fell a-doting,
And by addition me of thee defeated,
By adding one thing to my purpose nothing.
   But since she prick'd thee out for women's
     pleasure,
   Mine be thy love, and thy love's use their treasure.

XXI

So is it not with me as with that Muse
Stirr'd by a painted beauty to his verse,
Who heaven itself for ornament doth use
And every fair with his fair doth rehearse,

Making a couplement of proud compare,
With sun and moon, with earth and sea's rich gems,
With April's first-born flowers, and all things rare
That heaven's air in this huge rondure hems.
O, let me, true in love, but truly write,
And then believe me, my love is as fair
As any mother's child, though not so bright
As those gold candles fix'd in heaven's air:
  Let them say more that like of hearsay well;
  I will not praise that purpose not to sell.

XXII

My glass shall not persuade me I am old,
So long as youth and thou are of one date;
But when in thee time's furrows I behold,
Then look I death my days should expiate.
For all that beauty that doth cover thee
Is but the seemly raiment of my heart,
Which in thy breast doth live, as thine in me:
How can I then be elder than thou art?
O, therefore, love, be of thyself so wary
As I, not for myself, but for thee will;
Bearing thy heart, which I will keep so chary
As tender nurse her babe from faring ill.
  Presume not on thy heart when mine is slain;
  Thou gavest me thine, not to give back again.

XXIII

As an unperfect actor on the stage,
Who with his fear is put besides his part,
Or some fierce thing replete with too much rage,
Whose strength's abundance weakens his own heart;
So I, for fear of trust, forget to say
The perfect ceremony of love's rite,
And in mine own love's strength seem to decay,
O'ercharged with burthen of mine own love's might.
O, let my books be then the eloquence
And dumb presagers of my speaking breast;
Who plead for love, and look for recompense,
More than that tongue that more hath more
    express'd.
  O, learn to read what silent love hath writ:
  To hear with eyes belongs to love's fine wit.

XXIV

Mine eye hath play'd the painter and hath stell'd
Thy beauty's form in table of my heart;
My body is the frame wherein 'tis held,
And perspective it is best painter's art.
For through the painter must you see his skill,
To find where your true image pictured lies;
Which in my bosom's shop is hanging still,
That hath his windows glazed with thine eyes.
Now see what good turns eyes for eyes have done:
Mine eyes have drawn thy shape, and thine for me
Are windows to my breast, where-through the sun
Delights to peep, to gaze therein on thee;
  Yet eyes this cunning want to grace their art,
  They draw but what they see, know not the
    heart.

XXV

Let those who are in favour with their stars
Of public honour and proud titles boast,
Whilst I, whom fortune of such triumph bars,
Unlook'd for joy in that I honour most.
Great princes' favourites their fair leaves spread
But as the marigold at the sun's eye,
And in themselves their pride lies buried,
For at a frown they in their glory die.
The painful warrior famoused for fight,
After a thousand victories once foil'd,
Is from the book of honour razed quite,
And all the rest forgot for which he toil'd:
  Then happy I, that love and am beloved
  Where I may not remove nor be removed.

XXVI

Lord of my love, to whom in vassalage
Thy merit hath my duty strongly knit,
To thee I send this written ambassage,
To witness duty, not to show my wit:
Duty so great, which wit so poor as mine
May make seem bare, in wanting words to show it,
But that I hope some good conceit of thine
In thy soul's thought, all naked, will bestow it:
Till whatsoever star that guides my moving,
Points on me graciously with fair aspect,
And puts apparel on my tatter'd loving,
To show me worthy of thy sweet respect:
  Then may I dare to boast how I do love thee;
  Till then not show my head where thou mayst
    prove me.

XXVII

Weary with toil, I haste me to my bed,
The dear repose for limbs with travel tired;
But then begins a journey in my head,
To work my mind, when body's work's expired:
For then my thoughts, from far where I abide,
Intend a zealous pilgrimage to thee,
And keep my drooping eyelids open wide,
Looking on darkness which the blind do see:
Save that my soul's imaginary sight
Presents thy shadow to my sightless view,
Which, like a jewel hung in ghastly night,
Makes black night beauteous and her old face new.
  Lo, thus, by day my limbs, by night my mind,
  For thee and for myself no quiet find.

XXVIII

How can I then return in happy plight,
That am debarr'd the benefit of rest?
When day's oppression is not eased by night,
But day by night, and night by day, oppress'd?
And each, though enemies to either's reign,
Do in consent shake hands to torture me;
The one by toil, the other to complain
How far I toil, still farther off from thee.
I tell the day, to please him thou art bright,
And dost him grace when clouds do blot the heaven:

So flatter I the swart-complexion'd night;
When sparkling stars twire not thou gild'st the even.
But day doth daily draw my sorrows longer,
And night doth nightly make grief's strength seem stronger.

XXIX

When, in disgrace with fortune and men's eyes,
I all alone beweep my outcast state,
And trouble deaf heaven with my bootless cries,
And look upon myself, and curse my fate,
Wishing me like to one more rich in hope,
Featured like him, like him with friends possess'd,
Desiring this man's art and that man's scope,
With what I most enjoy contented least;
Yet in these thoughts myself almost despising,
Haply I think on thee, and then my state,
Like to the lark at break of day arising
From sullen earth, sings hymns at heaven's gate;
    For thy sweet love remember'd such wealth brings
    That then I scorn to change my state with kings.

XXX

When to the sessions of sweet silent thought
I summon up remembrance of things past,
I sigh the lack of many a thing I sought,
And with old woes new wail my dear time's waste:
Then can I drown an eye, unused to flow,
For precious friends hid in death's dateless night,
And weep afresh love's long since cancell'd woe,
And moan the expense of many a vanish'd sight:
Then can I grieve at grievances foregone,
And heavily from woe to woe tell o'er
The sad account of fore-bemoaned moan,
Which I new pay as if not paid before.
    But if the while I think on thee, dear friend,
    All losses are restored and sorrows end.

XXXI

Thy bosom is endeared with all hearts,
Which I by lacking have supposed dead;
And there reigns love, and all love's loving parts,
And all those friends which I thought buried.
How many a holy and obsequious tear
Hath dear religious love stol'n from mine eye,
As interest of the dead, which now appear
But things removed that hidden in thee lie!
Thou art the grave where buried love doth live,
Hung with the trophies of my lovers gone,
Who all their parts of me to thee did give;
That due of many now is thine alone:
    Their images I loved I view in thee,
    And thou, all they, hast all the all of me.

XXXII

If thou survive my well-contented day,
When that churl Death my bones with dust shall cover,
And shalt by fortune once more re-survey

These poor rude lines of thy deceased lover,
Compare them with the bettering of the time,
And though they be outstripp'd by every pen,
Reserve them for my love, not for their rhyme,
Exceeded by the height of happier men.
O, then vouchsafe me but this loving thought:
'Had my friend's Muse grown with this growing age,
A dearer birth than this his love had brought,
To march in ranks of better equipage:
    But since he died, and poets better prove,
    Theirs for their style I'll read, his for his love.'

XXXIII

Full many a glorious morning have I seen
Flatter the mountain-tops with sovereign eye,
Kissing with golden face the meadows green,
Gilding pale streams with heavenly alchemy;
Anon permit the basest clouds to ride
With ugly rack on his celestial face,
And from the forlorn world his visage hide,
Stealing unseen to west with this disgrace:
Even so my sun one early morn did shine
With all-triumphant splendour on my brow;
But, out, alack! he was but one hour mine,
The region cloud hath mask'd him from me now.
    Yet him for this my love no whit disdaineth;
    Suns of the world may stain when heaven's sun staineth.

XXXIV

Why didst thou promise such a beauteous day,
And make me travel forth without my cloak,
To let base clouds o'ertake me in my way,
Hiding thy bravery in their rotten smoke?
'Tis not enough that through the cloud thou break,
To dry the rain on my storm-beaten face,
For no man well of such a salve can speak
That heals the wound and cures not the disgrace:
Nor can thy shame give physic to my grief;
Though thou repent, yet I have still the loss:
The offender's sorrow lends but weak relief
To him that bears the strong offence's cross.
    Ah, but those tears are pearl which thy love sheds,
    And they are rich and ransom all ill deeds.

XXXV

No more be grieved at that which thou hast done:
Roses have thorns, and silver fountains mud;
Clouds and eclipses stain both moon and sun,
And loathsome canker lives in sweetest bud.
All men make faults, and even I in this,
Authorizing thy trespass with compare,
Myself corrupting, salving thy amiss,
Excusing thy sins more than thy sins are;
For to thy sensual fault I bring in sense—
Thy adverse party is thy advocate—
And 'gainst myself a lawful plea commence:
Such civil war is in my love and hate,
    That I an accessary needs must be
    To that sweet thief which sourly robs from me.

XXXVI

Let me confess that we two must be twain,
Although our undivided loves are one:
So shall those blots that do with me remain,
Without thy help, by me be borne alone.
In our two loves there is but one respect,
Though in our lives a separable spite,
Which though it alter not love's sole effect,
Yet doth it steal sweet hours from love's delight.
I may not evermore acknowledge thee,
Lest my bewailed guilt should do thee shame,
Nor thou with public kindness honour me,
Unless thou take that honour from thy name:
   But do not so; I love thee in such sort,
   As thou being mine, mine is thy good report.

XXXVII

As a decrepit father takes delight
To see his active child do deeds of youth,
So I, made lame by fortune's dearest spite,
Take all my comfort of thy worth and truth;
For whether beauty, birth, or wealth, or wit,
Or any of these all, or all, or more,
Entitled in thy parts do crowned sit,
I make my love engrafted to this store:
So then I am not lame, poor, nor despised,
Whilst that this shadow doth such substance give
That I in thy abundance am sufficed
And by a part of all thy glory live.
   Look, what is best, that best I wish in thee:
   This wish I have; then ten times happy me!

XXXVIII

How can my Muse want subject to invent,
While thou dost breathe, that pour'st into my verse
Thine own sweet argument, too excellent
For every vulgar paper to rehearse?
O, give thyself the thanks, if aught in me
Worthy perusal stand against thy sight;
For who's so dumb that cannot write to thee,
When thou thyself dost give invention light?
Be thou the tenth Muse, ten times more in worth
Than those old nine which rhymers invocate;
And he that calls on thee, let him bring forth
Eternal numbers to outlive long date.
   If my slight Muse do please these curious days,
   The pain be mine, but thine shall be the praise.

XXXIX

O, how thy worth with manners may I sing,
When thou art all the better part of me?
What can mine own praise to mine own self bring?
And what is 't but mine own when I praise thee?
Even for this let us divided live,
And our dear love lose name of single one,
That by this separation I may give
That due to thee which thou deservest alone.
O absence, what a torment wouldst thou prove,
Were it not thy sour leisure gave sweet leave
To entertain the time with thoughts of love,

Which time and thoughts so sweetly doth deceive,
   And that thou teachest how to make one twain,
   By praising him here who doth hence remain!

XL

Take all my loves, my love, yea, take them all;
What hast thou then more than thou hadst before?
No love, my love, that thou mayst true love call;
All mine was thine before thou hadst this more.
Then, if for my love thou my love receivest,
I cannot blame thee for my love thou usest;
But yet be blamed, if thou thyself deceivest
By wilful taste of what thyself refusest.
I do forgive thy robbery, gentle thief,
Although thou steal thee all my poverty;
And yet, love knows, it is a greater grief
To bear love's wrong than hate's known injury.
   Lascivious grace, in whom all ill well shows,
   Kill me with spites; yet we must not be foes.

XLI

Those pretty wrongs that liberty commits,
When I am sometime absent from thy heart,
Thy beauty and thy years full well befits,
For still temptation follows where thou art.
Gentle thou art, and therefore to be won,
Beauteous thou art, therefore to be assailed;
And when a woman woos, what woman's son
Will sourly leave her till she have prevailed?
Ay me! but yet thou mightst my seat forbear,
And chide thy beauty and thy straying youth,
Who lead thee in their riot even there
Where thou art forced to break a twofold truth,
   Hers, by thy beauty tempting her to thee,
   Thine, by thy beauty being false to me.

XLII

That thou hast her, it is not all my grief,
And yet it may be said I loved her dearly;
That she hath thee, is of my wailing chief,
A loss in love that touches me more nearly.
Loving offenders, thus I will excuse ye:
Thou dost love her, because thou know'st I love her;
And for my sake even so doth she abuse me,
Suffering my friend for my sake to approve her.
If I lose thee, my loss is my love's gain,
And losing her, my friend hath found that loss;
Both find each other, and I lose both twain,
And both for my sake lay on me this cross:
   But here's the joy; my friend and I are one;
   Sweet flattery! then she loves but me alone.

XLIII

When most I wink, then do mine eyes best see,
For all the day they view things unrespected;
But when I sleep, in dreams they look on thee,
And, darkly bright, are bright in dark directed.
Then thou, whose shadow shadows doth make bright,
How would thy shadow's form form happy show

To the clear day with thy much clearer light,
When to unseeing eyes thy shade shines so!
How would, I say, mine eyes be blessed made
By looking on thee in the living day,
When in dead night thy fair imperfect shade
Through heavy sleep on sightless eyes doth stay!
    All days are nights to see till I see thee,
    And nights bright days when dreams do show
      thee me.

XLIV

If the dull substance of my flesh were thought,
Injurious distance should not stop my way;
For then, despite of space, I would be brought,
From limits far remote, where thou dost stay.
No matter then although my foot did stand
Upon the farthest earth removed from thee;
For nimble thought can jump both sea and land,
As soon as think the place where he would be.
But, ah, thought kills me, that I am not thought,
To leap large lengths of miles when thou art gone,
But that, so much of earth and water wrought,
I must attend time's leisure with my moan;
    Receiving nought by elements so slow
    But heavy tears, badges of either's woe.

XLV

The other two, slight air and purging fire,
Are both with thee, wherever I abide;
The first my thought, the other my desire,
These present-absent with swift motion slide.
For when these quicker elements are gone
In tender embassy of love to thee,
My life, being made of four, with two alone
Sinks down to death, oppress'd with melancholy;
Until life's composition be recured
By those swift messengers return'd from thee,
Who even but now come back again, assured
Of thy fair health, recounting it to me:
    This told, I joy; but then no longer glad,
    I send them back again, and straight grow sad.

XLVI

Mine eye and heart are at a mortal war,
How to divide the conquest of thy sight;
Mine eye my heart thy picture's sight would bar,
My heart mine eye the freedom of that right.
My heart doth plead that thou in him dost lie,
A closet never pierced with crystal eyes,
But the defendant doth that plea deny,
And says in him thy fair appearance lies.
To 'cide this title is impanneled
A quest of thoughts, all tenants to the heart;
And by their verdict is determined
The clear eye's moiety and the dear heart's part:
    As thus; mine eye's due is thine outward part,
    And my heart's right thine inward love of heart.

XLVII

Betwixt mine eye and heart a league is took,
And each doth good turns now unto the other:
When that mine eye is famish'd for a look,
Or heart in love with sighs himself doth smother,
With my love's picture then my eye doth feast
And to the painted banquet bids my heart;
Another time mine eye is my heart's guest
And in his thoughts of love doth share a part:
So, either by thy picture or my love,
Thyself away art present still with me;
For thou not farther than my thoughts canst move,
And I am still with them and they with thee;
    Or, if they sleep, thy picture in my sight
    Awakes my heart to heart's and eye's delight.

XLVIII

How careful was I, when I took my way,
Each trifle under truest bars to thrust,
That to my use it might unused stay
From hands of falsehood, in sure wards of trust!
But thou, to whom my jewels trifles are,
Most worthy comfort, now my greatest grief,
Thou, best of dearest and mine only care,
Art left the prey of every vulgar thief.
Thee have I not lock'd up in any chest,
Save where thou art not, though I feel thou art,
Within the gentle closure of my breast,
From whence at pleasure thou mayst come and part;
    And even thence thou wilt be stol'n, I fear,
    For truth proves thievish for a prize so dear.

XLIX

Against that time, if ever that time come,
When I shall see thee frown on my defects,
When as thy love hath cast his utmost sum,
Call'd to that audit by advised respects;
Against that time when thou shalt strangely pass,
And scarcely greet me with that sun, thine eye,
When love, converted from the thing it was,
Shall reasons find of settled gravity;
Against that time do I ensconce me here
Within the knowledge of mine own desert,
And this my hand against myself uprear,
To guard the lawful reasons on thy part:
    To leave poor me thou hast the strength of laws,
    Since why to love I can allege no cause.

L

How heavy do I journey on the way,
When what I seek, my weary travel's end,
Doth teach that ease and that repose to say,
'Thus far the miles are measured from thy friend!'
The beast that bears me, tired with my woe,
Plods dully on, to bear that weight in me,
As if by some instinct the wretch did know
His rider loved not speed, being made from thee:
The bloody spur cannot provoke him on
That sometimes anger thrusts into his hide;
Which heavily he answers with a groan,
More sharp to me than spurring to his side;
    For that same groan doth put this in my mind;
    My grief lies onward, and my joy behind.

LI

Thus can my love excuse the slow offence
Of my dull bearer when from thee I speed:
From where thou art why should I haste me thence?
Till I return, of posting is no need.
O, what excuse will my poor beast then find,
When swift extremity can seem but slow?
Then should I spur, though mounted on the wind,
In winged speed no motion shall I know:
Then can no horse with my desire keep pace;
Therefore desire, of perfect'st love being made,
Shall neigh—no dull flesh—in his fiery race;
But love, for love, thus shall excuse my jade;
  Since from thee going he went wilful-slow,
  Towards thee I'll run and give him leave to go.

LII

So am I as the rich, whose blessed key
Can bring him to his sweet up-locked treasure,
The which he will not every hour survey,
For blunting the fine point of seldom pleasure.
Therefore are feasts so solemn and so rare,
Since, seldom coming, in the long year set,
Like stones of worth they thinly placed are,
Or captain jewels in the carcanet.
So is the time that keeps you as my chest,
Or as the wardrobe which the robe doth hide,
To make some special instant special blest,
By new unfolding his imprison'd pride.
  Blessed are you, whose worthiness gives scope,
  Being had, to triumph, being lack'd, to hope.

LIII

What is your substance, whereof are you made,
That millions of strange shadows on you tend?
Since every one hath, every one, one shade,
And you, but one, can every shadow lend.
Describe Adonis, and the counterfeit
Is poorly imitated after you;
On Helen's cheek all art of beauty set,
And you in Grecian tires are painted new:
Speak of the spring and foison of the year,
The one doth shadow of your beauty show,
The other as your bounty doth appear;
And you in every blessed shape we know.
  In all external grace you have some part,
  But you like none, none you, for constant heart.

LIV

O, how much more doth beauty beauteous seem
By that sweet ornament which truth doth give!
The rose looks fair, but fairer we it deem
For that sweet odour which doth in it live.
The canker-blooms have full as deep a dye
As the perfumed tincture of the roses,
Hang on such thorns, and play as wantonly
When summer's breath their masked buds discloses:
But, for their virtue only is their show,
They live unwoo'd and unrespected fade;

Die to themselves. Sweet roses do not so;
Of their sweet deaths are sweetest odours made:
  And so of you, beauteous and lovely youth,
  When that shall vade, by verse distills your truth.

LV

Not marble, nor the gilded monuments
Of princes, shall outlive this powerful rhyme;
But you shall shine more bright in these contents
Than unswept stone, besmear'd with sluttish time.
When wasteful war shall statues overturn,
And broils root out the work of masonry,
Nor Mars his sword nor war's quick fire shall burn
The living record of your memory.
'Gainst death and all-oblivious enmity
Shall you pace forth; your praise shall still find room
Even in the eyes of all posterity
That wear this world out to the ending doom.
  So, till the judgement that yourself arise,
  You live in this, and dwell in lovers' eyes.

LVI

Sweet love, renew thy force; be it not said
Thy edge should blunter be than appetite,
Which but to-day by feeding is allay'd,
To-morrow sharpen'd in his former might:
So, love, be thou; although to-day thou fill
Thy hungry eyes even till they wink with fulness,
To-morrow see again, and do not kill
The spirit of love with a perpetual dulness.
Let this sad interim like the ocean be
Which parts the shore, where two contracted new
Come daily to the banks, that, when they see
Return of love, more blest may be the view;
  Or call it winter, which, being full of care,
  Makes summer's welcome thrice more wish'd,
    more rare.

LVII

Being your slave, what should I do but tend
Upon the hours and times of your desire?
I have no precious time at all to spend,
Nor services to do, till you require.
Nor dare I chide the world-without-end hour
Whilst I, my sovereign, watch the clock for you,
Nor think the bitterness of absence sour
When you have bid your servant once adieu;
Nor dare I question with my jealous thought
Where you may be, or your affairs suppose,
But, like a sad slave, stay and think of nought
Save, where you are how happy you make those.
  So true a fool is love that in your will,
  Though you do any thing, he thinks no ill.

LVIII

That god forbid that made me first your slave,
I should in thought control your times of pleasure,
Or at your hand the account of hours to crave,
Being your vassal, bound to stay your leisure!

O, let me suffer, being at your beck,
The imprison'd absence of your liberty;
And patience, tame to sufferance, bide each check,
Without accusing you of injury.
Be where you list, your charter is so strong
That you yourself may privilege your time
To what you will; to you it doth belong
Yourself to pardon of self-doing crime.
  I am to wait, though waiting so be hell,
  Not blame your pleasure, be it ill or well.

LIX

If there be nothing new, but that which is
Hath been before, how are our brains beguiled,
Which, labouring for invention, bear amiss
The second burthen of a former child!
O, that record could with a backward look,
Even of five hundred courses of the sun,
Show me your image in some antique book,
Since mind at first in character was done.
That I might see what the old world could say
To this composed wonder of your frame;
Whether we are mended, or whether better they,
Or whether revolution be the same.
  O, sure I am, the wits of former days
  To subjects worse have given admiring praise.

LX

Like as the waves make towards the pebbled shore,
So do our minutes hasten to their end;
Each changing place with that which goes before,
In sequent toil all forwards do contend.
Nativity, once in the main of light,
Crawls to maturity, wherewith being crown'd,
Crooked eclipses 'gainst his glory fight,
And Time that gave doth now his gift confound.
Time doth transfix the flourish set on youth
And delves the parallels in beauty's brow,
Feeds on the rarities of nature's truth,
And nothing stands but for his scythe to mow:
  And yet to times in hope my verse shall stand,
  Praising thy worth, despite his cruel hand.

LXI

Is it thy will thy image should keep open
My heavy eyelids to the weary night?
Dost thou desire my slumbers should be broken,
While shadows like to thee do mock my sight?
Is it thy spirit that thou send'st from thee
So far from home into my deeds to pry,
To find out shames and idle hours in me,
The scope and tenour of thy jealousy?
O, no! thy love, though much, is not so great:
It is my love that keeps mine eye awake;
Mine own true love that doth my rest defeat,
To play the watchman ever for thy sake:
  For thee watch I whilst thou dost wake elsewhere,
  From me far off, with others all too near.

LXII

Sin of self-love possesseth all mine eye
And all my soul and all my every part;
And for this sin there is no remedy,
It is so grounded inward in my heart.
Methinks no face so gracious is as mine,
No shape so true, no truth of such account,
And for myself mine own worth do define,
As I all other in all worths surmount.
But when my glass shows me myself indeed,
Beated and chopp'd with tann'd antiquity,
Mine own self-love quite contrary I read;
Self so self-loving were iniquity.
  'Tis thee, myself, that for myself I praise,
  Painting my age with beauty of thy days.

LXIII

Against my love shall be, as I am now,
With Time's injurious hand crush'd and o'erworn;
When hours have drain'd his blood and fill'd his
    brow
With lines and wrinkles; when his youthful morn
Hath travell'd on to age's steepy night,
And all those beauties whereof now he's king
Are vanishing or vanish'd out of sight,
Stealing away the treasure of his spring;
For such a time do I now fortify
Against confounding age's cruel knife,
That he shall never cut from memory
My sweet love's beauty, though my lover's life:
  His beauty shall in these black lines be seen,
  And they shall live, and he in them still green.

LXIV

When I have seen by Time's fell hand defaced
The rich-proud cost of outworn buried age;
When sometime lofty towers I see down-razed,
And brass eternal slave to mortal rage;
When I have seen the hungry ocean gain
Advantage on the kingdom of the shore,
And the firm soil win of the watery main,
Increasing store with loss and loss with store:
When I have seen such interchange of state,
Or state itself confounded to decay;
Ruin hath taught me thus to ruminate,
That Time will come and take my love away.
  This thought is as a death, which cannot choose
  But weep to have that which it fears to lose.

LXV

Since brass, nor stone, nor earth, nor boundless sea
But sad mortality o'er-sways their power,
How with this rage shall beauty hold a plea,
Whose action is no stronger than a flower?
O, how shall summer's honey breath hold out
Against the wreckful siege of battering days,
When rocks impregnable are not so stout,
Nor gates of steel so strong, but Time decays?

O fearful meditation! where, alack,
Shall Time's best jewel from Time's chest lie hid?
Or what strong hand can hold his swift foot back?
Or who his spoil of beauty can forbid?
　　O, none, unless this miracle have might,
　　That in black ink my love may still shine bright.

LXVI

Tired with all these, for restful death I cry,
As, to behold desert a beggar born,
And needy nothing trimm'd in jollity,
And purest faith unhappily forsworn,
And gilded honour shamefully misplaced,
And maiden virtue rudely strumpeted,
And right perfection wrongfully disgraced,
And strength by limping sway disabled,
And art made tongue-tied by authority,
And folly, doctor-like, controlling skill,
And simple truth miscall'd simplicity,
And captive good attending captain ill:
　　Tired with all these, from these would I be gone,
　　Save that, to die, I leave my love alone.

LXVII

Ah, wherefore with infection should he live
And with his presence grace impiety,
That sin by him advantage should achieve
And lace itself with his society?
Why should false painting imitate his cheek,
And steal dead seeing of his living hue?
Why should poor beauty indirectly seek
Roses of shadow, since his rose is true?
Why should he live, now Nature bankrupt is,
Beggar'd of blood to blush through lively veins?
For she hath no exchequer now but his,
And, proud of many, lives upon his gains.
　　O, him she stores, to show what wealth she had
　　In days long since, before these last so bad.

LXVIII

Thus is his cheek the map of days outworn,
When beauty lived and died as flowers do now,
Before these bastard signs of fair were born,
Or durst inhabit on a living brow;
Before the golden tresses of the dead,
The right of sepulchres, were shorn away,
To live a second life on second head;
Ere beauty's dead fleece made another gay:
In him those holy antique hours are seen,
Without all ornament, itself and true,
Making no summer of another's green,
Robbing no old to dress his beauty new;
　　And him as for a map doth Nature store,
　　To show false Art what beauty was of yore.

LXIX

Those parts of thee that the world's eye doth view
Want nothing that the thought of hearts can mend;
All tongues, the voice of souls, give thee that due,
Uttering bare truth, even so as foes commend.
Thy outward thus with outward praise is crown'd;
But those same tongues, that give thee so thine own,
In other accents do this praise confound
By seeing farther than the eye hath shown.
They look into the beauty of thy mind,
And that, in guess, they measure by thy deeds;
Then, churls, their thoughts, although their eyes
　　　　were kind,
To thy fair flower add the rank smell of weeds:
　　But why thy odour matcheth not thy show,
　　The soil is this, that thou dost common grow.

LXX

That thou art blamed shall not be thy defect,
For slander's mark was ever yet the fair;
The ornament of beauty is suspect,
A crow that flies in heaven's sweetest air.
So thou be good, slander doth but approve
Thy worth the greater, being woo'd of time;
For canker vice the sweetest buds doth love,
And thou present'st a pure unstained prime.
Thou hast pass'd by the ambush of young days,
Either not assail'd, or victor being charged;
Yet this thy praise cannot be so thy praise,
To tie up envy evermore enlarged:
　　If some suspect of ill mask'd not thy show,
　　Then thou alone kingdoms of hearts shouldst owe.

LXXI

No longer mourn for me when I am dead
Than you shall hear the surly sullen bell
Give warning to the world that I am fled
From this vile world, with vilest worms to dwell:
Nay, if you read this line, remember not
The hand that writ it; for I love you so,
That I in your sweet thoughts would be forgot,
If thinking on me then should make you woe.
O, if, I say, you look upon this verse
When I perhaps compounded am with clay,
Do not so much as my poor name rehearse,
But let your love even with my life decay;
　　Lest the wise world should look into your moan,
　　And mock you with me after I am gone.

LXXII

O, lest the world should task you to recite
What merit lived in me, that you should love
After my death, dear love, forget me quite,
For you in me can nothing worthy prove;
Unless you would devise some virtuous lie,
To do more for me than mine own desert,
And hang more praise upon deceased I
Than niggard truth would willingly impart:
O, lest your true love may seem false in this,
That you for love speak well of me untrue,
My name be buried where my body is,
And live no more to shame nor me nor you.
　　For I am shamed by that which I bring forth,
　　And so should you, to love things nothing worth.

LXXIII

Tha time of year thou mayst in me behold
When yellow leaves, or none, or few, do hang
Up n those boughs which shake against the cold,
Bar ruin'd choirs, where late the sweet birds sang.
In ne thou see'st the twilight of such day
As after sunset fadeth in the west;
Which by and by black night doth take away,
Death's second self, that seals up all in rest.
In me thou see'st the glowing of such fire,
That on the ashes of his youth doth lie,
As the death-bed whereon it must expire,
Consumed with that which it was nourish'd by.
    This thou perceivest, which makes thy love more
       strong,
    To love that well which thou must leave ere long.

LXXIV

But be contented: when that fell arrest
Without all bail shall carry me away,
My life hath in this line some interest,
Which for memorial still with thee shall stay.
When thou reviewest this, thou dost review
The very part was consecrate to thee:
The earth can have but earth, which is his due;
My spirit is thine, the better part of me:
So then thou hast but lost the dregs of life,
The prey of worms, my body being dead;
The coward conquest of a wretch's knife,
Too base of thee to be remembered.
    The worth of that is that which it contains,
    And that is this, and this with thee remains.

LXXV

So are you to my thoughts as food to life,
Or as sweet-season'd showers are to the ground;
And for the peace of you I hold such strife
As 'twixt a miser and his wealth is found;
Now proud as an enjoyer, and anon
Doubting the filching age will steal his treasure,
Now counting best to be with you alone,
Then better'd that the world may see my pleasure:
Sometime all full with feasting on your sight,
And by and by clean starved for a look;
Possessing or pursuing no delight,
Save what is had or must from you be took.
    Thus do I pine and surfeit day by day,
    Or gluttoning on all, or all away.

LXXVI

Why is my verse so barren of new pride,
So far from variation or quick change?
Why with the time do I not glance aside
To new-found methods and to compounds strange?
Why write I still all one, ever the same,
And keep invention in a noted weed,
That every word doth almost tell my name,
Showing their birth and where they did proceed?
O, know, sweet love, I always write of you,
And you and love are still my argument;
So all my best is dressing old words new,
Spending again what is already spent:
    For as the sun is daily new and old,
    So is my love still telling what is told.

LXXVII

Thy glass will show thee how thy beauties wear,
Thy dial how thy precious minutes waste;
The vacant leaves thy mind's imprint will bear,
And of this book this learning mayst thou taste.
The wrinkles which thy glass will truly show
Of mouthed graves will give thee memory;
Thou by thy dial's shady stealth mayst know
Time's thievish progress to eternity.
Look, what thy memory cannot contain
Commit to these waste blanks, and thou shalt find
Those children nursed, deliver'd from thy brain,
To take a new acquaintance of thy mind.
    These offices, so oft as thou wilt look,
    Shall profit thee and much enrich thy book.

LXXVIII

So oft have I invoked thee for my Muse
And found such fair assistance in my verse
As every alien pen hath got my use
And under thee their poesy disperse.
Thine eyes, that taught the dumb on high to sing
And heavy ignorance aloft to fly,
Have added feathers to the learned's wing
And given grace a double majesty.
Yet be most proud of that which I compile,
Whose influence is thine and born of thee:
In others' works thou dost but mend the style,
And arts with thy sweet graces graced be;
    But thou art all my art, and dost advance
    As high as learning my rude ignorance.

LXXIX

Whilst I alone did call upon thy aid,
My verse alone had all thy gentle grace;
But now my gracious numbers are decay'd,
And my sick Muse doth give another place.
I grant, sweet love, thy lovely argument
Deserves the travail of a worthier pen;
Yet what of thee thy poet doth invent
He robs thee of, and pays it thee again.
He lends thee virtue, and he stole that word
From thy behaviour; beauty doth he give,
And found it in thy cheek: he can afford
No praise to thee but what in thee doth live.
    Then thank him not for that which he doth say,
    Since what he owes thee thou thyself dost pay.

LXXX

O, how I faint when I of you do write,
Knowing a better spirit doth use your name,
And in the praise thereof spends all his might,
To make me tongue-tied, speaking of your fame!

But since your worth, wide as the ocean is,
The humble as the proudest sail doth bear,
My saucy bark, inferior far to his,
On your broad main doth wilfully appear.
Your shallowest help will hold me up afloat,
Whilst he upon your soundless deep doth ride;
Or, being wreck'd, I am a worthless boat,
He of tall building and of goodly pride:
    Then if he thrive and I be cast away,
    The worst was this; my love was my decay.

LXXXI

Or I shall live your epitaph to make,
Or you survive when I in earth am rotten;
From hence your memory death cannot take,
Although in me each part will be forgotten.
Your name from hence immortal life shall have,
Though I, once gone, to all the world must die:
The earth can yield me but a common grave,
When you entombed in men's eyes shall lie.
Your monument shall be my gentle verse,
Which eyes not yet created shall o'er-read;
And tongues to be your being shall rehearse,
When all the breathers of this world are dead;
    You still shall live—such virtue hath my pen—
    Where breath most breathes, even in the mouths
      of men.

LXXXII

I grant thou wert not married to my Muse,
And therefore mayst without attaint o'erlook
The dedicated words which writers use
Of their fair subject, blessing every book.
Thou art as fair in knowledge as in hue,
Finding thy worth a limit past my praise;
And therefore art enforced to seek anew
Some fresher stamp of the time-bettering days.
And do so, love; yet when they have devised
What strained touches rhetoric can lend,
Thou truly fair wert truly sympathized
In true plain words by thy true-telling friend;
    And their gross painting might be better used
    Where cheeks need blood; in thee it is abused.

LXXXIII

I never saw that you did painting need,
And therefore to your fair no painting set;
I found, or thought I found, you did exceed
The barren tender of a poet's debt:
And therefore have I slept in your report,
That you yourself, being extant, well might show
How far a modern quill doth come too short,
Speaking of worth, what worth in you doth grow.
This silence for my sin you did impute,
Which shall be most my glory, being dumb;
For I impair not beauty being mute,
When others would give life and bring a tomb.
    There lives more life in one of your fair eyes
    Than both your poets can in praise devise.

LXXXIV

Who is it that says most? which can say more
Than this rich praise, that you alone are you?
In whose confine immured is the store
Which should example where your equal grew.
Lean penury within that pen doth dwell
That to his subject lends not some small glory;
But he that writes of you, if he can tell
That you are you, so dignifies his story.
Let him but copy what in you is writ,
Not making worse what nature made so clear,
And such a counterpart shall fame his wit,
Making his style admired every where.
    You to your beauteous blessings add a curse,
    Being fond on praise, which makes your praises
      worse.

LXXXV

My tongue-tied Muse in manners holds her still,
While comments of your praise, richly compiled,
Reserve their character with golden quill,
And precious phrase by all the Muses filed.
I think good thoughts, whilst other write good
    words,
And, like unletter'd clerk, still cry 'Amen'
To every hymn that able spirit affords,
In polish'd form of well refined pen.
Hearing you praised, I say, ' 'Tis so, 'tis true,'
And to the most of praise add something more;
But that is in my thought, whose love to you,
Though words come hindmost, holds his rank be-
    fore.
    Then others for the breath of words respect,
    Me for my dumb thoughts, speaking in effect.

LXXXVI

Was it the proud full sail of his great verse,
Bound for the prize of all too precious you,
That did my ripe thoughts in my brain inhearse,
Making their tomb the womb wherein they grew?
Was it his spirit, by spirits taught to write
Above a mortal pitch, that struck me dead?
No, neither he, nor his compeers by night
Giving him aid, my verse astonished.
He, nor that affable familiar ghost
Which nightly gulls him with intelligence,
As victors, of my silence cannot boast;
I was not sick of any fear from thence:
    But when your countenance fill'd up his line,
    Then lack'd I matter; that enfeebled mine.

LXXXVII

Farewell! thou art too dear for my possessing,
And like enough thou know'st thy estimate:
The charter of thy worth gives thee releasing;
My bonds in thee are all determinate.
For how do I hold thee but by thy granting?
And for that riches where is my deserving?
The cause of this fair gift in me is wanting,
And so my patent back again is swerving.

Thyself thou gavest, thy own worth then not know-
    ing,
Or me, to whom thou gavest it, else mistaking;
So thy great gift, upon misprision growing,
Comes home again, on better judgement making.
    Thus have I had thee, as a dream doth flatter,
    In sleep a king, but waking no such matter.

LXXXVIII

When thou shalt be disposed to set me light,
And place my merit in the eye of scorn,
Upon thy side against myself I'll fight,
And prove thee virtuous, though thou art forsworn.
With mine own weakness being best acquainted,
Upon thy part I can set down a story
Of faults conceal'd, wherein I am attainted;
That thou in losing me shalt win much glory:
And I by this will be a gainer too;
For bending all my loving thoughts on thee,
The injuries that to myself I do,
Doing thee vantage, double-vantage me.
    Such is my love, to thee I so belong,
    That for thy right myself will bear all wrong.

LXXXIX

Say that thou didst forsake me for some fault,
And I will comment upon that offence:
Speak of my lameness, and I straight will halt,
Against thy reasons making no defence.
Thou canst not, love, disgrace me half so ill,
To set a form upon desired change,
As I'll myself disgrace; knowing thy will,
I will acquaintance strangle and look strange;
Be absent from thy walks; and in my tongue
Thy sweet beloved name no more shall dwell,
Lest I, too much profane, should do it wrong,
And haply of our old acquaintance tell.
    For thee, against myself I'll vow debate,
    For I must ne'er love him whom thou dost hate.

XC

Then hate me when thou wilt; if ever, now;
Now, while the world is bent my deeds to cross,
Join with the spite of fortune, make me bow,
And do not drop in for an after-loss:
Ah, do not, when my heart hath 'scaped this sorrow,
Come in the rearward of a conquer'd woe;
Give not a windy night a rainy morrow,
To linger out a purposed overthrow.
If thou wilt leave me, do not leave me last,
When other petty griefs have done their spite,
But in the onset come: so shall I taste
At first the very worst of fortune's might;
    And other strains of woe, which now seem woe,
    Compared with loss of thee will not seem so.

XCI

Some glory in their birth, some in their skill,
Some in their wealth, some in their body's force;
Some in their garments, though new-fangled ill;

Some in their hawks and hounds, some in their
    horse;
And every humour hath his adjunct pleasure,
Wherein it finds a joy above the rest:
But these particulars are not my measure;
All these I better in one general best.
Thy love is better than high birth to me,
Richer than wealth, prouder than garments' cost,
Of more delight than hawks or horses be;
And having thee, of all men's pride I boast:
    Wretched in this alone, that thou mayst take
    All this away and me most wretched make.

XCII

But do thy worst to steal thyself away,
For term of life thou art assured mine;
And life no longer than thy love will stay,
For it depends upon that love of thine.
Then need I not to fear the worst of wrongs,
When in the least of them my life hath end.
I see a better state to me belongs
Than that which on thy humour doth depend:
Thou canst not vex me with inconstant mind,
Since that my life on thy revolt doth lie.
O, what a happy title do I find,
Happy to have thy love, happy to die!
    But what's so blessed-fair that fears no blot?
    Thou mayst be false, and yet I know it not.

XCIII

So shall I live, supposing thou art true,
Like a deceived husband; so love's face
May still seem love to me, though alter'd new;
Thy looks with me, thy heart in other place:
For there can live no hatred in thine eye,
Therefore in that I cannot know thy change.
In many's looks the false heart's history
Is writ in moods and frowns and wrinkles strange,
But heaven in thy creation did decree
That in thy face sweet love should ever dwell;
Whate'er thy thoughts or thy heart's workings be,
Thy looks should nothing thence but sweetness tell.
    How like Eve's apple doth thy beauty grow,
    If thy sweet virtue answer not thy show!

XCIV

They that have power to hurt and will do none,
That do not do the thing they most do show,
Who, moving others, are themselves as stone,
Unmoved, cold and to temptation slow;
They rightly do inherit heaven's graces
And husband nature's riches from expense;
They are the lords and owners of their faces,
Others but stewards of their excellence.
The summer's flower is to the summer sweet,
Though to itself it only live and die,
But if that flower with base infection meet,
The basest weed outbraves his dignity:
    For sweetest things turn sourest by their deeds;
    Lilies that fester smell far worse than weeds.

XCV

How sweet and lovely dost thou make the shame
Which, like a canker in the fragrant rose,
Doth spot the beauty of thy budding name!
O, in what sweets dost thou thy sins inclose!
That tongue that tells the story of thy days,
Making lascivious comments on thy sport,
Cannot dispraise but in a kind of praise;
Naming thy name blesses an ill report.
O, what a mansion have those vices got
Which for their habitation chose out thee,
Where beauty's veil doth cover every blot
And all things turn to fair that eyes can see!
　　Take heed, dear heart, of this large privilege;
　　The hardest knife ill used doth lose his edge.

XCVI

Some say, thy fault is youth, some wantonness;
Some say, thy grace is youth and gentle sport;
Both grace and faults are loved of more and less:
Thou makest faults graces that to thee resort.
As on the finger of a throned queen
The basest jewel will be well esteem'd,
So are those errors that in thee are seen
To truths translated and for true things deem'd.
How many lambs might the stern wolf betray,
If like a lamb he could his looks translate!
How many gazers mightst thou lead away,
If thou wouldst use the strength of all thy state!
　　But do not so; I love thee in such sort,
　　As thou being mine, mine is thy good report.

XCVII

How like a winter hath my absence been
From thee, the pleasure of the fleeting year!
What freezings have I felt, what dark days seen!
What old December's bareness every where!
And yet this time removed was summer's time;
The teeming autumn, big with rich increase,
Bearing the wanton burthen of the prime,
Like widowed wombs after their lords' decease:
Yet this abundant issue seem'd to me
But hope of orphans and unfather'd fruit;
For summer and his pleasures wait on thee,
And, thou away, the very birds are mute;
　　Or, if they sing, 'tis with so dull a cheer
　　That leaves look pale, dreading the winter's near.

XCVIII

From you have I been absent in the spring,
When proud-pied April, dress'd in all his trim,
Hath put a spirit of youth in every thing,
That heavy Saturn laugh'd and leap'd with him.
Yet nor the lays of birds, nor the sweet smell
Of different flowers in odour and in hue,
Could make me any summer's story tell,
Or from their proud lap pluck them where they
　　grew:
Nor did I wonder at the lily's white,
Nor praise the deep vermilion in the rose;

They were but sweet, but figures of delight,
Drawn after you, you pattern of all those.
　　Yet seem'd it winter still, and, you away,
　　As with your shadow I with these did play.

XCIX

The forward violet thus did I chide:
Sweet thief, whence didst thou steal thy sweet that
　　smells,
If not from my love's breath? The purple pride
Which on thy soft cheek for complexion dwells
In my love's veins thou hast too grossly dyed.
The lily I condemned for thy hand,
And buds of marjoram had stol'n thy hair;
The roses fearfully on thorns did stand,
One blushing shame, another white despair;
A third, nor red nor white, had stol'n of both,
And to his robbery had annex'd thy breath;
But, for his theft, in pride of all his growth
A vengeful canker eat him up to death.
　　More flowers I noted, yet I none could see
　　But sweet or colour it had stol'n from thee.

C

Where art thou, Muse, that thou forget'st so long
To speak of that which gives thee all thy might?
Spend'st thou thy fury on some worthless song,
Darkening thy power to lend base subjects light?
Return, forgetful Muse, and straight redeem
In gentle numbers time so idly spent;
Sing to the ear that doth thy lays esteem
And gives thy pen both skill and argument.
Rise, resty Muse, my love's sweet face survey,
If Time have any wrinkle graven there;
If any, be a satire to decay,
And make Time's spoils despised every where.
　　Give my love fame faster than Time wastes life;
　　So thou prevent'st his scythe and crooked knife.

CI

O truant Muse, what shall be thy amends
For thy neglect of truth in beauty dyed?
Both truth and beauty on my love depends;
So dost thou too, and therein dignified.
Make answer, Muse: wilt thou not haply say,
'Truth needs no colour, with his colour fix'd;
Beauty no pencil, beauty's truth to lay;
But best is best, if never intermix'd'?
Because he needs no praise, wilt thou be dumb?
Excuse not silence so, for 't lies in thee
To make him much outlive a gilded tomb
And to be praised of ages yet to be.
　　Then do thy office, Muse; I teach thee how
　　To make him seem long hence as he shows now.

CII

My love is strengthen'd, though more weak in seem-
　　ing;
I love not less, though less the show appear:

That love is merchandized whose rich esteeming
The owner's tongue doth publish every where.
Our love was new, and then but in the spring,
When I was wont to greet it with my lays;
As Philomel in summer's front doth sing,
And stops her pipe in growth of riper days:
Not that the summer is less pleasant now
Than when her mournful hymns did hush the night,
But that wild music burthens every bough,
And sweets grown common lose their dear delight.
 Therefore, like her, I sometime hold my tongue,
 Because I would not dull you with my song.

CIII

Alack, what poverty my Muse brings forth,
That having such a scope to show her pride,
The argument, all bare, is of more worth
Than when it hath my added praise beside!
O, blame me not, if I no more can write!
Look in your glass, and there appears a face
That over-goes my blunt invention quite,
Dulling my lines and doing me disgrace.
Were it not sinful then, striving to mend,
To mar the subject that before was well?
For to no other pass my verses tend
Than of your graces and your gifts to tell;
 And more, much more, than in my verse can sit,
 Your own glass shows you when you look in it.

CIV

To me, fair friend, you never can be old,
For as you were when first your eye I eyed,
Such seems your beauty still. Three winters cold
Have from the forests shook three summers' pride,
Three beauteous springs to yellow autumn turn'd
In process of the seasons have I seen,
Three April perfumes in three hot Junes burn'd,
Since first I saw you fresh, which yet are green.
Ah, yet doth beauty, like a dial-hand,
Steal from his figure, and no pace perceived;
So your sweet hue, which methinks still doth stand,
Hath motion, and mine eye may be deceived:
 For fear of which, hear this, thou age unbred;
 Ere you were born was beauty's summer dead.

CV

Let not my love be call'd idolatry,
Nor my beloved as an idol show,
Since all alike my songs and praises be
To one, of one, still such, and ever so.
Kind is my love to-day, to-morrow kind,
Still constant in a wondrous excellence;
Therefore my verse to constancy confined,
One thing expressing, leaves out difference.
'Fair, kind, and true,' is all my argument,
'Fair, kind, and true,' varying to other words;
And in this change is my invention spent,
Three themes in one, which wondrous scope affords.
 'Fair, kind, and true,' have often lived alone,
 Which three till now never kept seat in one.

CVI

When in the chronicle of wasted time
I see descriptions of the fairest wights,
And beauty making beautiful old rhyme
In praise of ladies dead and lovely knights,
Then, in the blazon of sweet beauty's best,
Of hand, of foot, of lip, of eye, of brow,
I see their antique pen would have express'd
Even such a beauty as you master now.
So all their praises are but prophecies
Of this our time, all you prefiguring;
And, for they look'd but with divining eyes,
They had not skill enough your worth to sing:
 For we, which now behold these present days,
 Have eyes to wonder, but lack tongues to praise.

CVII

Not mine own fears, nor the prophetic soul
Of the wide world dreaming on things to come,
Can yet the lease of my true love control,
Supposed as forfeit to a confined doom.
The mortal moon hath her eclipse endured,
And the sad augurs mock their own presage;
Incertainties now crown themselves assured,
And peace proclaims olives of endless age.
Now with the drops of this most balmy time
My love looks fresh, and Death to me subscribes,
Since, spite of him, I'll live in this poor rhyme,
While he insults o'er dull and speechless tribes:
 And thou in this shalt find thy monument,
 When tyrants' crests and tombs of brass are spent.

CVIII

What's in the brain, that ink may character,
Which hath not figured to thee my true spirit?
What's new to speak, what new to register,
That may express my love, or thy dear merit?
Nothing, sweet boy; but yet, like prayers divine,
I must each day say o'er the very same;
Counting no old thing old, thou mine, I thine,
Even as when first I hallowed thy fair name.
So that eternal love in love's fresh case
Weighs not the dust and injury of age,
Nor gives to necessary wrinkles place,
But makes antiquity for aye his page;
 Finding the first conceit of love there bred,
 Where time and outward form would show it
 dead.

CIX

O, never say that I was false of heart,
Though absence seem'd my flame to qualify.
As easy might I from myself depart
As from my soul, which in thy breast doth lie:
That is my home of love: if I have ranged,
Like him that travels, I return again;
Just to the time, not with the time exchanged,
So that myself bring water for my stain.
Never believe, though in my nature reign'd
All frailties that besiege all kinds of blood,

That it could so preposterously be stain'd,
To leave for nothing all thy sum of good;
   For nothing this wide universe I call,
   Save thou, my rose; in it thou art my all.

CX

Alas, 'tis true I have gone here and there,
And made myself a motley to the view,
Gored mine own thoughts, sold cheap what is most
    dear,
Made old offences of affections new;
Most true it is that I have look'd on truth
Askance and strangely: but, by all above,
These blenches gave my heart another youth,
And worse essays proved thee my best of love.
Now all is done, have what shall have no end:
Mine appetite I never more will grind
On newer proof, to try an older friend,
A god in love, to whom I am confined.
   Then give me welcome, next my heaven the best,
   Even to thy pure and most most loving breast.

CXI

O, for my sake do you with Fortune chide,
The guilty goddess of my harmful deeds,
That did not better for my life provide
Than public means which public manners breeds.
Thence comes it that my name receives a brand,
And almost thence my nature is subdued
To what it works in, like the dyer's hand:
Pity me then and wish I were renew'd;
Whilst, like a willing patient, I will drink
Potions of eisel 'gainst my strong infection;
No bitterness that I will bitter think,
Nor double penance, to correct correction.
   Pity me then, dear friend, and I assure ye
   Even that your pity is enough to cure me.

CXII

Your love and pity doth the impression fill
Which vulgar scandal stamp'd upon my brow;
For what care I who calls me well or ill,
So you o'er-green my bad, my good allow?
You are my all the world, and I must strive
To know my shames and praises from your tongue;
None else to me, nor I to none alive,
That my steel'd sense or changes right or wrong.
In so profound abysm I throw all care
Of others' voices, that my adder's sense
To critic and to flatterer stopped are.
Mark how with my neglect I do dispense:
   You are so strongly in my purpose bred
   That all the world besides methinks are dead.

CXIII

Since I left you mine eye is in my mind,
And that which governs me to go about
Doth part his function and is partly blind,
Seems seeing, but effectually is out;

For it no form delivers to the heart
Of bird, of flower, or shape, which it doth latch:
Of his quick objects hath the mind no part,
Nor his own vision holds what it doth catch;
For if it see the rudest or gentlest sight,
The most sweet favour or deformed'st creature,
The mountain or the sea, the day or night,
The crow or dove, it shapes them to your feature:
   Incapable of more, replete with you,
   My most true mind thus maketh mine untrue.

CXIV

Or whether doth my mind, being crown'd with you,
Drink up the monarch's plague, this flattery?
Or whether shall I say, mine eye saith true,
And that your love taught it this alchemy,
To make of monsters and things indigest
Such cherubins as your sweet self resemble,
Creating every bad a perfect best,
As fast as objects to his beams assemble?
O, 'tis the first; 'tis flattery in my seeing,
And my great mind most kingly drinks it up:
Mine eye well knows what with his gust is 'greeing,
And to his palate doth prepare the cup:
   If it be poison'd, 'tis the lesser sin
   That mine eye loves it and doth first begin.

CXV

Those lines that I before have writ do lie,
Even those that said I could not love you dearer:
Yet then my judgement knew no reason why
My most full flame should afterwards burn clearer.
But reckoning Time, whose million'd accidents
Creep in 'twixt vows, and change decrees of kings,
Tan sacred beauty, blunt the sharp'st intents,
Divert strong minds to the course of altering things;
Alas, why, fearing of Time's tyranny,
Might I not then say 'Now I love you best,'
When I was certain o'er incertainty,
Crowning the present, doubting of the rest?
   Love is a babe; then might I not say so,
   To give full growth to that which still doth grow?

CXVI

Let me not to the marriage of true minds
Admit impediments. Love is not love
Which alters when it alteration finds,
Or bends with the remover to remove:
O, no! it is an ever-fixed mark,
That looks on tempests and is never shaken;
It is the star to every wandering bark,
Whose worth 's unknown, although his height be
    taken.
Love's not Time's fool, though rosy lips and cheeks
Within his bending sickle's compass come;
Love alters not with his brief hours and weeks,
But bears it out even to the edge of doom.
   If this be error and upon me proved,
   I never writ, nor no man ever loved.

CXVII

Accuse me thus: that I have scanted all
Wherein I should your great deserts repay,
Forgot upon your dearest love to call,
Whereto all bonds do tie me day by day;
That I have frequent been with unknown minds,
And given to time your own dear-purchased right;
That I have hoisted sail to all the winds
Which should transport me farthest from your sight.
Book both my wilfulness and errors down,
And on just proof surmise accumulate;
Bring me within the level of your frown,
But shoot not at me in your waken'd hate;
   Since my appeal says I did strive to prove
   The constancy and virtue of your love.

CXVIII

Like as, to make our appetites more keen,
With eager compounds we our palate urge;
As, to prevent our maladies unseen,
We sicken to shun sickness when we purge;
Even so, being full of your ne'er-cloying sweetness,
To bitter sauces did I frame my feeding;
And sick of welfare found a kind of meetness
To be diseased, ere that there was true needing.
Thus policy in love, to anticipate
The ills that were not, grew to faults assured,
And brought to medicine a healthful state,
Which, rank of goodness, would by ill be cured:
   But thence I learn, and find the lesson true,
   Drugs poison him that so fell sick of you.

CXIX

What potions have I drunk of Siren tears,
Distill'd from limbecks foul as hell within,
Applying fears to hopes and hopes to fears,
Still losing when I saw myself to win!
What wretched errors hath my heart committed,
Whilst it hath thought itself so blessed never!
How have mine eyes out of their spheres been fitted,
In the distraction of this madding fever!
O benefit of ill! now I find true
That better is by evil still made better;
And ruin'd love, when it is built anew,
Grows fairer than at first, more strong, far greater.
   So I return rebuked to my content,
   And gain by ill thrice more than I have spent.

CXX

That you were once unkind befriends me now,
And for that sorrow which I then did feel
Needs must I under my transgression bow,
Unless my nerves were brass or hammer'd steel.
For if you were by my unkindness shaken,
As I by yours, you've pass'd a hell of time;
And I, a tyrant, have no leisure taken
To weigh how once I suffer'd in your crime.
O, that our night of woe might have remember'd
My deepest sense, how hard true sorrow hits,

And soon to you, as you to me, then tender'd
The humble salve which wounded bosoms fits!
   But that your trespass now becomes a fee;
   Mine ransoms yours, and yours must ransom me.

CXXI

'Tis better to be vile than vile esteemed,
When not to be receives reproach of being;
And the just pleasure lost, which is so deemed
Not by our feeling, but by others' seeing:
For why should others' false adulterate eyes
Give salutation to my sportive blood?
Or on my frailties why are frailer spies,
Which in their wills count bad what I think good?
No, I am that I am, and they that level
At my abuses reckon up their own:
I may be straight, though they themselves be bevel;
By their rank thoughts my deeds must not be shown;
   Unless this general evil they maintain,
   All men are bad and in their badness reign.

CXXII

Thy gift, thy tables, are within my brain
Full character'd with lasting memory,
Which shall above that idle rank remain,
Beyond all date, even to eternity:
Or, at the least, so long as brain and heart
Have faculty by nature to subsist;
Till each to razed oblivion yield his part
Of thee, thy record never can be miss'd.
That poor retention could not so much hold,
Nor need I tallies thy dear love to score;
Therefore to give them from me was I bold,
To trust those tables that receive thee more:
   To keep an adjunct to remember thee
   Were to import forgetfulness in me.

CXXIII

No, Time, thou shalt not boast that I do change:
Thy pyramids built up with newer might
To me are nothing novel, nothing strange;
They are but dressings of a former sight.
Our dates are brief, and therefore we admire
What thou dost foist upon us that is old;
And rather make them born to our desire
Than think that we before have heard them told.
Thy registers and thee I both defy,
Not wondering at the present nor the past,
For thy records and what we see doth lie,
Made more or less by thy continual haste.
   This I do vow, and this shall ever be,
   I will be true, despite thy scythe and thee.

CXXIV

If my dear love were but the child of state,
It might for Fortune's bastard be unfather'd,
As subject to Time's love or to Time's hate,
Weeds among weeds, or flowers with flowers
    gather'd.

No, it was builded far from accident;
It suffers not in smiling pomp, nor falls
Under the blow of thralled discontent,
Whereto the inviting time our fashion calls:
It fears not policy, that heretic,
Which works on leases of short-number'd hours,
But all alone stands hugely politic,
That it nor grows with heat nor drowns with show-
    ers.
    To this I witness call the fools of time,
    Which die for goodness, who have lived for crime.

CXXXV

Were 't aught to me I bore the canopy,
With my extern the outward honouring,
Or laid great bases for eternity,
Which prove more short than waste or ruining?
Have I not seen dwellers on form and favour
Lose all, and more, by paying too much rent,
For compound sweet forgoing simple savour,
Pitiful thrivers, in their gazing spent?
No, let me be obsequious in thy heart,
And take thou my oblation, poor but free,
Which is not mix'd with seconds, knows no art
But mutual render, only me for thee.
    Hence, thou suborn'd informer! a true soul
    When most impeach'd stands least in thy control.

CXXXVI

O thou, my lovely boy, who in thy power
Dost hold Time's fickle glass, his sickle, hour;
Who hast by waning grown, and therein show'st
Thy lovers withering as thy sweet self grow'st;
If Nature, sovereign mistress over wrack,
As thou goest onwards, still will pluck thee back,
She keeps thee to this purpose, that her skill
May time disgrace and wretched minutes kill.
Yet fear her, O thou minion of her pleasure!
She may detain, but not still keep, her treasure:
    Her audit, though delay'd, answer'd must be,
    And her quietus is to render thee.

CXXXVII

In the old age black was not counted fair,
Or if it were, it bore not beauty's name;
But now is black beauty's successive heir,
And beauty slander'd with a bastard shame:
For since each hand hath put on nature's power,
Fairing the foul with art's false borrow'd face,
Sweet beauty hath no name, no holy bower,
But is profaned, if not lives in disgrace.
Therefore my mistress' eyes are raven black,
Her eyes so suited, and they mourners seem
At such who, not born fair, no beauty lack,
Slandering creation with a false esteem:
    Yet so they mourn, becoming of their woe,
    That every tongue says beauty should look so.

CXXXVIII

How oft, when thou, my music, music play'st,
Upon that blessed wood whose motion sounds

With thy sweet fingers, when thou gently sway'st
The wiry concord that mine ear confounds,
Do I envy those jacks that nimble leap
To kiss the tender inward of thy hand,
Whilst my poor lips, which should that harvest reap,
At the wood's boldness by thee blushing stand!
To be so tickled, they would change their state
And situation with those dancing chips,
O'er whom thy fingers walk with gentle gait,
Making dead wood more blest than living lips.
    Since saucy jacks so happy are in this,
    Give them thy fingers, me thy lips to kiss.

CXXXIX

The expense of spirit in a waste of shame
Is lust in action; and till action, lust
Is perjured, murderous, bloody, full of blame,
Savage, extreme, rude, cruel, not to trust;
Enjoy'd no sooner but despised straight;
Past reason hunted; and no sooner had,
Past reason hated, as a swallowed bait,
On purpose laid to make the taker mad:
Mad in pursuit, and in possession so;
Had, having, and in quest to have, extreme;
A bliss in proof, and proved, a very woe;
Before, a joy proposed; behind, a dream.
    All this the world well knows; yet none knows well
    To shun the heaven that leads men to this hell.

CXXX

My mistress' eyes are nothing like the sun;
Coral is far more red than her lips' red:
If snow be white, why then her breasts are dun;
If hairs be wires, black wires grow on her head.
I have seen roses damask'd, red and white,
But no such roses see I in her cheeks;
And in some perfumes is there more delight
Than in the breath that from my mistress reeks.
I love to hear her speak, yet well I know
That music hath a far more pleasing sound:
I grant I never saw a goddess go,
My mistress, when she walks, treads on the ground:
    And yet, by heaven, I think my love as rare
    As any she belied with false compare.

CXXXI

Thou art as tyrannous, so as thou art,
As those whose beauties proudly make them cruel;
For well thou know'st to my dear doting heart
Thou art the fairest and most precious jewel.
Yet, in good faith, some say that thee behold,
Thy face hath not the power to make love groan:
To say they err I dare not be so bold,
Although I swear it to myself alone.
And to be sure that is not false I swear,
A thousand groans, but thinking on thy face,
One on another's neck, do witness bear
Thy black is fairest in my judgement's place.
    In nothing art thou black save in thy deeds,
    And thence this slander, as I think, proceeds.

CXXXII

Thine eyes I love, and they, as pitying me,
Knowing thy heart torments me with disdain,
Have put on black and loving mourners be,
Looking with pretty ruth upon my pain.
And truly not the morning sun of heaven
Better becomes the grey cheeks of the east,
Nor that full star that ushers in the even
Doth half that glory to the sober west,
As those two mourning eyes become thy face:
O, let it then as well beseem thy heart
To mourn for me, since mourning doth thee grace,
And suit thy pity like in every part.
   Then will I swear beauty herself is black,
   And all they foul that thy complexion lack.

CXXXIII

Beshrew that heart that makes my heart to groan
For that deep wound it gives my friend and me!
Is 't not enough to torture me alone,
But slave to slavery my sweet'st friend must be?
Me from myself thy cruel eye hath taken,
And my next self thou harder hast engrossed:
Of him, myself, and thee, I am forsaken;
A torment thrice threefold thus to be crossed.
Prison my heart in thy steel bosom's ward,
But then my friend's heart let my poor heart bail;
Whoe'er keeps me, let my heart be his guard;
Thou canst not then use rigour in my gaol:
   And yet thou wilt; for I, being pent in thee,
   Perforce am thine, and all that is in me.

CXXXIV

So, now I have confess'd that he is thine
And I myself am mortgaged to thy will,
Myself I'll forfeit, so that other mine
Thou wilt restore, to be my comfort still:
But thou wilt not, nor he will not be free,
For thou art covetous and he is kind;
He learn'd but surety-like to write for me,
Under that bond that him as fast doth bind.
The statute of thy beauty thou wilt take,
Thou usurer, that put'st forth all to use,
And sue a friend came debtor for my sake;
So him I lose through my unkind abuse.
   Him have I lost; thou hast both him and me:
   He pays the whole, and yet am I not free.

CXXXV

Whoever hath her wish, thou hast thy 'Will,'
And 'Will' to boot, and 'Will' in overplus;
More than enough am I that vex thee still,
To thy sweet will making addition thus.
Wilt thou, whose will is large and spacious,
Not once vouchsafe to hide my will in thine?
Shall will in others seem right gracious,
And in my will no fair acceptance shine?
The sea, all water, yet receives rain still,
And in abundance addeth to his store;

So thou, being rich in 'Will,' add to thy 'Will'
One will of mine, to make thy large 'Will' more.
   Let no unkind, no fair beseechers kill;
   Think all but one, and me in that one 'Will.'

CXXXVI

If thy soul check thee that I come so near,
Swear to thy blind soul that I was thy 'Will,'
And will, thy soul knows, is admitted there;
Thus far for love, my love-suit, sweet, fulfil.
'Will' will fulfil the treasure of thy love,
Ay, fill it full with wills, and my will one.
In things of great receipt with ease we prove
Among a number one is reckon'd none:
Then in the number let me pass untold,
Though in thy store's account I one must be;
For nothing hold me, so it please thee hold
That nothing me, a something sweet to thee:
   Make but my name thy love, and love that still,
   And then thou lovest me, for my name is 'Will.'

CXXXVII

Thou blind fool, Love, what dost thou to mine eyes,
That they behold, and see not what they see?
They know what beauty is, see where it lies,
Yet what the best is take the worst to be.
If eyes, corrupt by over-partial looks,
Be anchor'd in the bay where all men ride,
Why of eyes' falsehood hast thou forged hooks,
Whereto the judgement of my heart is tied?
Why should my heart think that a several plot
Which my heart knows the wide world's common
    place?
Or mine eyes seeing this, say this is not,
To put fair truth upon so foul a face?
   In things right true my heart and eyes have erred,
   And to this false plague are they now transferred.

CXXXVIII

When my love swears that she is made of truth,
I do believe her, though I know she lies,
That she might think me some untutor'd youth,
Unlearned in the world's false subtleties.
Thus vainly thinking that she thinks me young,
Although she knows my days are past the best,
Simply I credit her false-speaking tongue:
On both sides thus is simple truth suppress'd.
But wherefore says she not she is unjust?
And wherefore say not I that I am old?
O, love's best habit is in seeming trust,
And age in love loves not to have years told:
   Therefore I lie with her and she with me,
   And in our faults by lies we flatter'd be.

CXXXIX

O, call not me to justify the wrong
That thy unkindness lays upon my heart;
Wound me not with thine eye, but with thy tongue;
Use power with power, and slay me not by art.

Tell me thou lovest elsewhere; but in my sight,
Dear heart, forbear to glance thine eye aside:
What need'st thou wound with cunning, when thy
  might
Is more than my o'er-press'd defence can bide?
Let me excuse thee: ah, my love well knows
Her pretty looks have been mine enemies;
And therefore from my face she turns my foes,
That they elsewhere might dart their injuries:
 Yet do not so; but since I am near slain,
 Kill me outright with looks, and rid my pain.

CXL

Be wise as thou art cruel; do not press
My tongue-tied patience with too much disdain;
Lest sorrow lend me words, and words express
The manner of my pity-wanting pain.
If I might teach thee wit, better it were,
Though not to love, yet, love, to tell me so;
As testy sick men, when their deaths be near,
No news but health from their physicians know;
For, if I should despair, I should grow mad,
And in my madness might speak ill of thee:
Now this ill-wresting world is grown so bad,
Mad slanderers by mad ears believed be.
 That I may not be so, nor thou belied,
 Bear thine eyes straight, though thy proud heart
  go wide.

CXLI

In faith, I do not love thee with mine eyes,
For they in thee a thousand errors note;
But 'tis my heart that loves what they despise,
Who, in despite of view, is pleased to dote;
Nor are mine ears with thy tongue's tune delighted;
Nor tender feeling, to base touches prone,
Nor taste, nor smell, desire to be invited
To any sensual feast with thee alone:
But my five wits nor my five senses can
Dissuade one foolish heart from serving thee,
Who leaves unsway'd the likeness of a man,
Thy proud heart's slave and vassal wretch to be:
 Only my plague thus far I count my gain,
 That she that makes me sin awards me pain.

CXLII

Love is my sin, and thy dear virtue hate,
Hate of my sin, grounded on sinful loving:
O, but with mine compare thou thine own state,
And thou shalt find it merits not reproving;
Or, if it do, not from those lips of thine,
That have profaned their scarlet ornaments
And seal'd false bonds of love as oft as mine,
Robb'd others' beds' revenues of their rents.
Be it lawful I love thee, as thou lovest those
Whom thine eyes woo as mine importune thee:
Root pity in thy heart, that, when it grows,
Thy pity may deserve to pitied be.
 If thou dost seek to have what thou dost hide,
 By self-example mayst thou be denied!

CXLIII

Lo, as a careful housewife runs to catch
One of her feather'd creatures broke away,
Sets down her babe, and makes all swift dispatch
In pursuit of the thing she would have stay;
Whilst her neglected child holds her in chase,
Cries to catch her whose busy care is bent
To follow that which flies before her face,
Not prizing her poor infant's discontent:
So runn'st thou after that which flies from thee,
Whilst I thy babe chase thee afar behind;
But if thou catch thy hope, turn back to me,
And play the mother's part, kiss me, be kind:
 So will I pray that thou mayst have thy 'Will,'
 If thou turn back and my loud crying still.

CXLIV

Two loves I have of comfort and despair,
Which like two spirits do suggest me still:
The better angel is a man right fair,
The worser spirit a woman colour'd ill.
To win me soon to hell, my female evil
Tempteth my better angel from my side,
And would corrupt my saint to be a devil,
Wooing his purity with her foul pride.
And whether that my angel be turn'd fiend
Suspect I may, yet not directly tell;
But being both from me, both to each friend,
I guess one angel in another's hell:
 Yet this shall I ne'er know, but live in doubt,
 Till my bad angel fire my good one out.

CXLV

Those lips that Love's own hand did make
Breathed forth the sound that said 'I hate,'
To me that languish'd for her sake:
But when she saw my woeful state,
Straight in her heart did mercy come,
Chiding that tongue that ever sweet
Was used in giving gentle doom;
And taught it thus anew to greet;
'I hate' she alter'd with an end,
That follow'd it as gentle day
Doth follow night, who, like a fiend,
From heaven to hell is flown away;
 'I hate' from hate away she threw,
 And saved my life, saying 'not you.'

CXLVI

Poor soul, the centre of my sinful earth,
............these rebel powers that thee array,
Why dost thou pine within and suffer dearth,
Painting thy outward walls so costly gay?
Why so large cost, having so short a lease,
Dost thou upon thy fading mansion spend?
Shall worms, inheritors of this excess,
Eat up thy charge? is this thy body's end?
Then, soul, live thou upon thy servant's loss,
And let that pine to aggravate thy store;

Buy terms divine in selling hours of dross;
Within be fed, without be rich no more:
  So shalt thou feed on Death, that feeds on men,
  And Death once dead, there's no more dying then.

CXLVII

My love is as a fever, longing still
For that which longer nurseth the disease;
Feeding on that which doth preserve the ill,
The uncertain sickly appetite to please.
My reason, the physician to my love,
Angry that his prescriptions are not kept,
Hath left me, and I desperate now approve
Desire is death, which physic did except.
Past cure I am, now reason is past care,
And frantic-mad with evermore unrest;
My thoughts and my discourse as madmen's are,
At random from the truth vainly express'd;
  For I have sworn thee fair, and thought thee
    bright,
  Who art as black as hell, as dark as night.

CXLVIII

O me, what eyes hath Love put in my head,
Which have no correspondence with true sight!
Or, if they have, where is my judgement fled,
That censures falsely what they see aright?
If that be fair whereon my false eyes dote,
What means the world to say it is not so?
If it be not, then love doth well denote
Love's eye is not so true as all men's: no,
How can it? O, how can Love's eye be true,
That is so vex'd with watching and with tears?
No marvel then, though I mistake my view;
The sun itself sees not till heaven clears.
  O cunning Love! with tears thou keep'st me blind,
  Lest eyes well-seeing thy foul faults should find.

CXLIX

Canst thou, O cruel! say I love thee not,
When I against myself with thee partake?
Do I not think on thee, when I forgot
Am of myself, all tyrant, for thy sake?
Who hateth thee that I do call my friend?
On whom frown'st thou that I do fawn upon?
Nay, if thou lour'st on me, do I not spend
Revenge upon myself with present moan?
What merit do I in myself respect,
That is so proud thy service to despise,
When all my best doth worship thy defect,
Commanded by the motion of thine eyes?
  But, love, hate on, for now I know thy mind;
  Those that can see thou lovest, and I am blind.

CL

O, from what power hast thou this powerful might
With insufficiency my heart to sway?

To make me give the lie to my true sight,
And swear that brightness doth not grace the day?
Whence hast thou this becoming of things ill,
That in the very refuse of thy deeds
There is such strength and warrantise of skill,
That, in my mind, thy worst all best exceeds?
Who taught thee how to make me love thee more,
The more I hear and see just cause of hate?
O, though I love what others do abhor,
With others thou shouldst not abhor my state:
  If thy unworthiness raised love in me,
  More worthy I to be beloved of thee.

CLI

Love is too young to know what conscience is;
Yet who knows not conscience is born of love?
Then, gentle cheater, urge not my amiss,
Lest guilty of my faults thy sweet self prove:
For, thou betraying me, I do betray
My nobler part to my gross body's treason;
My soul doth tell my body that he may
Triumph in love; flesh stays no farther reason,
But rising at thy name doth point out thee
As his triumphant prize. Proud of this pride,
He is contented thy poor drudge to be,
To stand in thy affairs, fall by thy side.
  No want of conscience hold it that I call
  Her 'love' for whose dear love I rise and fall.

CLII

In loving thee thou know'st I am forsworn,
But thou art twice forsworn, to me love swearing;
In act thy bed-vow broke, and new faith torn,
In vowing new hate after new love bearing.
But why of two oaths' breach do I accuse thee,
When I break twenty? I am perjured most;
For all my vows are oaths but to misuse thee,
And all my honest faith in thee is lost:
For I have sworn deep oaths of thy deep kindness,
Oaths of thy love, thy truth, thy constancy;
And, to enlighten thee, gave eyes to blindness,
Or made them swear against the thing they see;
  For I have sworn thee fair; more perjured I,
  To swear against the truth so foul a lie!

CLIII

Cupid laid by his brand and fell asleep:
A maid of Dian's this advantage found,
And his love-kindling fire did quickly steep
In a cold valley-fountain of that ground;
Which borrow'd from this holy fire of Love
A dateless lively heat, still to endure,
And grew a seething bath, which yet men prove
Against strange maladies a sovereign cure.
But at my mistress' eye Love's brand new-fired,
The boy for trial needs would touch my breast;
I, sick withal, the help of bath desired,
And thither hied, a sad distemper'd guest,

But found no cure: the bath for my help lies
Where Cupid got new fire, my mistress' eyes.

CLIV

The little Love-god lying once asleep
Laid by his side his heart-inflaming brand,
Whilst many nymphs that vow'd chaste life to keep
Came tripping by; but in her maiden hand
The fairest votary took up that fire

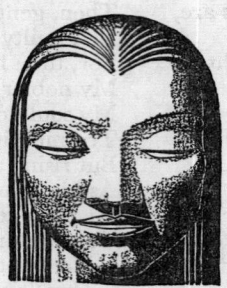

Which many legions of true hearts had warm'd;
And so the general of hot desire
Was sleeping by a virgin hand disarm'd.
This brand she quenched in a cool well by,
Which from Love's fire took heat perpetual,
Growing a bath and healthful remedy
For men diseased; but I, my mistress' thrall,
Came there for cure, and this by that I prove,
Love's fire heats water, water cools not love.

A LOVER'S COMPLAINT

From off a hill whose concave womb re-worded
A plaintful story from a sistering vale,
My spirits to attend this double voice accorded,
And down I laid to list the sad-tuned tale;
Ere long espied a fickle maid full pale,
Tearing of papers, breaking rings a-twain,
Storming her world with sorrow's wind and rain.

Upon her head a platted hive of straw,
Which fortified her visage from the sun,
Whereon the thought might think sometime it saw
The carcass of a beauty spent and done:
Time had not scythed all that youth begun,
Nor youth all quit; but, spite of heaven's fell rage,
Some beauty peep'd through lattice of sear'd age.

Oft did she heave her napkin to her eyne,
Which on it had conceited characters,
Laundering the silken figures in the brine
That season'd woe had pelleted in tears,
And often reading what contents it bears;
As often shrieking undistinguish'd woe,
In clamours of all size, both high and low.

Sometimes her levell'd eyes their carriage ride,
As they did battery to the spheres intend;
Sometime diverted their poor balls are tied
To the orbed earth; sometimes they do extend
Their view right on; anon their gazes lend
To every place at once, and nowhere fix'd
The mind and sight distractedly commix'd.

Her hair, nor loose nor tied in formal plat,
Proclaim'd in her a careless hand of pride;
For some, untuck'd, descended her sheaved hat,
Hanging her pale and pined cheek beside;
Some in her threaden fillet still did bide,
And, true to bondage, would not break from thence,
Though slackly braided in loose negligence.

A thousand favours from a maund she drew
Of amber, crystal, and of beaded jet,
Which one by one she in a river threw,
Upon whose weeping margent she was set;
Like usury, applying wet to wet,
Or monarch's hands that lets not bounty fall
Where want cries some, but where excess begs all.

Of folded schedules had she many a one,
Which she perused, sigh'd, tore, and gave the flood;
Crack'd many a ring of posied gold and bone,
Bidding them find their sepulchres in mud;
Found yet moe letters sadly penn'd in blood,
With sleided silk feat and affectedly
Enswathed, and seal'd to curious secrecy.

These often bathed she in her fluxive eyes,
And often kiss'd, and often 'gan to tear;
Cried 'O false blood, thou register of lies,
What unapproved witness dost thou bear!
Ink would have seem'd more black and damned
    here!'
This said, in top of rage the lines she rents,
Big discontent so breaking their contents.

A reverend man that grazed his cattle nigh—
Sometime a blusterer, that the ruffle knew
Of court, of city, and had let go by
The swiftest hours, observed as they flew—
Towards this afflicted fancy fastly drew;
And, privileged by age, desires to know
In brief the grounds and motives of her woe.

So slides he down upon his grained bat,
And comely-distant sits he by her side;
When he again desires her, being sat,
Her grievance with his hearing to divide:
If that from him there may be aught applied
Which may her suffering ecstasy assuage,
'Tis promised in the charity of age.

'Father,' she says, 'though in me you behold
The injury of many a blasting hour,
Let it not tell your judgement I am old;
Not age, but sorrow, over me hath power:
I might as yet have been a spreading flower,
Fresh to myself, if I had self-applied
Love to myself, and to no love beside.

'But, woe is me! too early I attended
A youthful suit—it was to gain my grace—
Of one by nature's outwards so commended,
That maidens' eyes stuck over all his face:
Love lack'd a dwelling and made him her place:
And when in his fair parts she did abide,
She was new lodged and newly deified.

'His browny locks did hang in crooked curls;
And every light occasion of the wind
Upon his lips their silken parcels hurls.
What's sweet to do, to do will aptly find:
Each eye that saw him did enchant the mind;
For on his visage was in little drawn
What largeness thinks in Paradise was sawn.

'Small show of man was yet upon his chin;
His phœnix down began but to appear,
Like unshorn velvet, on that termless skin,
Whose bare out-bragg'd the web it seem'd to wear:
Yet show'd his visage by that cost more dear;
And nice affections wavering stood in doubt
If best were as it was, or best without.

'His qualities were beauteous as his form,
For maiden-tongued he was, and thereof free;
Yet, if men moved him, was he such a storm
As oft 'twixt May and April is to see,
When winds breathe sweet, unruly though they be.
His rudeness so with his authorized youth
Did livery falseness in a pride of truth.

'Well could he ride, and often men would say,
"That horse his mettle from his rider takes:
Proud of subjection, noble by the sway,
What rounds, what bounds, what course, what stop
　　he makes!"
And controversy hence a question takes,
Whether the horse by him became his deed,
Or he his manage by the well-doing steed.

'But quickly on this side the verdict went:
His real habitude gave life and grace
To appertainings and to ornament,
Accomplish'd in himself, not in his case:
All aids, themselves made fairer by their place,
Came for additions; yet their purposed trim
Pieced not his grace, but were all graced by him.

'So on the tip of his subduing tongue
All kind of arguments and question deep,
All replication prompt and reason strong,
For his advantage still did wake and sleep:
To make the weeper laugh, the laugher weep,
He had the dialect and different skill,
Catching all passions in his craft of will;

'That he did in the general bosom reign
Of young, of old, and sexes both enchanted,
To dwell with him in thoughts, or to remain
In personal duty, following where he haunted:
Consents bewitch'd, ere he desire, have granted,
And dialogued for him what he would say,
Ask'd their own wills and made their wills obey.

'Many there were that did his picture get,
To serve their eyes, and in it put their mind;
Like fools that in the imagination set

The goodly objects which abroad they find
Of lands and mansions, theirs in thought assign'd;
And labouring in moe pleasures to bestow them
Than the true gouty landlord which doth owe them:

'So many have, that never touch'd his hand,
Sweetly supposed them mistress of his heart.
My woeful self, that did in freedom stand,
And was my own fee-simple, not in part,
What with his art in youth and youth in art,
Threw my affections in his charmed power,
Reserved the stalk and gave him all my flower.

'Yet did I not, as some my equals did,
Demand of him, nor being desired yielded;
Finding myself in honour so forbid,
With safest distance I mine honour shielded:
Experience for me many bulwarks builded
Of proofs new-bleeding, which remain'd the foil
Of this false jewel, and his amorous spoil.

'But, ah, who ever shunn'd by precedent
The destined ill she must herself assay?
Or forced examples, 'gainst her own content,
To put the by-past perils in her way?
Counsel may stop awhile what will not stay;
For when we rage, advice is often seen
By blunting us to make our wits more keen.

'Nor gives it satisfaction to our blood,
That we must curb it upon others' proof;
To be forbod the sweets that seem so good,
For fear of harms that preach in our behoof.
O appetite, from judgement stand aloof!
The one a palate hath that needs will taste,
Though Reason weep, and cry "It is thy last."

'For further I could say "This man's untrue,"
And knew the patterns of his foul beguiling;
Heard where his plants in others' orchards grew,
Saw how deceits were gilded in his smiling;
Knew vows were ever brokers to defiling;
Thought characters and words merely but art,
And bastards of his foul adulterate heart.

'And long upon these terms I held my city,
Till thus he 'gan besiege me: 'Gentle maid,
Have of my suffering youth some feeling pity,
And be not of my holy vows afraid:
That's to ye sworn to none was ever said;
For feasts of love I have been call'd unto,
Till now did ne'er invite, nor never woo.

'"All my offences that abroad you see
Are errors of the blood, none of the mind;
Love made them not: with acture they may be,
Where neither party is nor true nor kind:
They sought their shame that so their shame did find;
And so much less of shame in me remains
By how much of me their reproach contains.

' "Among the many that mine eyes have seen,
Not one whose flame my heart so much as warmed,
Or my affection put to the smallest teen,
Or any of my leisures ever charmed:
Harm have I done to them, but ne'er was harmed;
Kept hearts in liveries, but mine own was free,
And reign'd, commanding in his monarchy.

' "Look here, what tributes wounded fancies sent me,
Of paled pearls and rubies red as blood;
Figuring that they their passions likewise lent me
Of grief and blushes, aptly understood
In bloodless white and the encrimson'd mood;
Effects of terror and dear modesty,
Encamp'd in hearts, but fighting outwardly.

' "And, lo, behold these talents of their hair,
With twisted metal amorously impleach'd,
I have received from many a several fair,
Their kind acceptance weepingly beseech'd,
With the annexions of fair gems enrich'd,
And deep-brain'd sonnets that did amplify
Each stone's dear nature, worth and quality.

' "The diamond, why, 'twas beautiful and hard,
Whereto his invised properties did tend;
The deep-green emerald, in whose fresh regard
Weak sights their sickly radiance do amend;
The heaven-hued sapphire and the opal blend
With objects manifold: each several stone,
With wit well blazon'd, smiled or made some moan.

' "Lo, all these trophies of affections hot,
Of pensived and subdued desires the tender,
Nature hath charged me that I hoard them not,
But yield them up where I myself must render,
That is, to you, my origin and ender;
For these, of force, must your oblations be,
Since I their altar, you enpatron me.

' "O, then, advance of yours that phraseless hand,
Whose white weighs down the airy scale of praise;
Take all these similes to your own command,
Hallow'd with sighs that burning lungs did raise;
What me your minister, for you obeys,
Works under you; and to your audit comes
Their distract parcels in combined sums.

' "Lo, this device was sent me from a nun,
Or sister sanctified, of holiest note;
Which late her noble suit in court did shun,
Whose rarest havings made the blossoms dote;
For she was sought by spirits of richest coat,
But kept cold distance, and did thence remove,
To spend her living in eternal love.

' "But, O my sweet, what labour is 't to leave
The thing we have not, mastering what not strives,
Playing the place which did no form receive,
Playing patient sports in unconstrained gyves?

She that her fame so to herself contrives,
The scars of battle 'scapeth by the flight.
And makes her absence valiant, not her might.

' "O, pardon me, in that my boast is true:
The accident which brought me to her eye
Upon the moment did her force subdue,
And now she would the caged cloister fly:
Religious love put out Religion's eye:
Not to be tempted, would she be immured,
And now, to tempt all, liberty procured.

' "How mighty then you are, O, hear me tell!
The broken bosoms that to me belong
Have emptied all their fountains in my well,
And mine I pour your ocean all among:
I strong o'er them, and you o'er me being strong,
Must for your victory us all congest,
As compound love to physic your cold breast.

' "My parts had power to charm a sacred nun,
Who disciplined, ay, dieted in grace,
Believed her eyes when they to assail begun,
All vows and consecrations giving place:
O most potential love! vow, bond, nor space,
In thee hath neither sting, knot, nor confine,
For thou art all, and all things else are thine.

' "When thou impressest, what are precepts worth
Of stale example? When thou wilt inflame,
How coldly those impediments stand forth
Of wealth, of filial fear, law, kindred, fame!
Love's arms are peace, 'gainst rule, 'gainst sense,
        'gainst shame;
And sweetens, in the suffering pangs it bears,
The aloes of all forces, shocks and fears.

' "Now all these hearts that do on mine depend,
Feeling it break, with bleeding groans they pine;
And supplicant their sighs to you extend,
To leave the battery that you make 'gainst mine,
Lending soft audience to my sweet design,
And credent soul to that strong-bonded oath
That shall prefer and undertake my troth."

'This said, his watery eyes he did dismount,
Whose sights till then were levell'd on my face;
Each cheek a river running from a fount
With brinish current downward flow'd apace:
O, how the channel to the stream gave grace!
Who glazed with crystal gate the glowing roses
That flame through water which their hue encloses.

'O father, what a hell of witchcraft lies
In the small orb of one particular tear!
But with the inundation of the eyes
What rocky heart to water will not wear?
What breast so cold that is not warmed here?
O cleft effect! cold modesty, hot wrath,
Both fire from hence and chill extincture hath.

'For, lo, his passion, but an art of craft,
Even there resolved my reason into tears;
There my white stole of chastity I daff'd,
Shook off my sober guards and civil fears;
Appear to him, as he to me appears,
All melting; though our drops this difference bore,
His poison'd me, and mine did him restore.

'In him a plenitude of subtle matter,
Applied to cautels, all strange forms receives,
Of burning blushes, or of weeping water,
Or swounding paleness; and he takes and leaves,
In either's aptness, as it best deceives,
To blush at speeches rank, to weep at woes,
Or to turn white and swound at tragic shows:

'That not a heart which in his level came
Could 'scape the hail of his all-hurting aim
Showing fair nature is both kind and tame

And, veil'd in them, did win whom he would maim:
Against the thing he sought he would exclaim;
When he most burn'd in heart-wish'd luxury,
He preach'd pure maid and praised cold chastity.

'Thus merely with the garment of a Grace
The naked and concealed fiend he cover'd;
That the unexperient gave the tempter place,
Which, like a cherubin, above them hover'd.
Who, young and simple, would not be so lover'd?
Ay me! I fell, and yet do question make
What I should do again for such a sake.

'O, that infected moisture of his eye,
O, that false fire which in his cheek so glow'd,
O, that forced thunder from his heart did fly,
O, that sad breath his spongy lungs bestow'd,
O, all that borrow'd motion seeming owed,
Would yet again betray the fore-betray'd,
And new pervert a reconciled maid!'

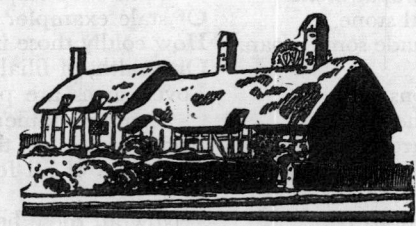

THE PASSIONATE PILGRIM

I

When my love swears that she is made of truth,
I do believe her, though I know she lies,
That she might think me some untutor'd youth,
Unskilful in the world's false forgeries.
Thus vainly thinking that she thinks me young,
Although I know my years be past the best,
I smiling credit her false-speaking tongue,
Outfacing faults in love with love's ill rest.
But wherefore says my love that she is young?
And wherefore say not I that I am old?
O, love's best habit is a soothing tongue,
And age, in love, loves not to have years told.
   Therefore I'll lie with love, and love with me,
   Since that our faults in love thus smother'd be.

II

Two loves I have, of comfort and despair,
That like two spirits do suggest me still;
My better angel is a man right fair,
My worser spirit a woman colour'd ill.
To win me soon to hell, my female evil
Tempteth my better angel from my side,
And would corrupt my saint to be a devil,
Wooing his purity with her fair pride.
And whether that my angel be turn'd fiend,
Suspect I may, yet not directly tell:
For being both to me, both to each friend,
I guess one angel in another's hell:
   The truth I shall not know, but live in doubt,
   Till my bad angel fire my good one out.

III

Did not the heavenly rhetoric of thine eye,
'Gainst whom the world could not hold argument,
Persuade my heart to this false perjury?
Vows for thee broke deserve not punishment.
A woman I forswore; but I will prove,
Thou being a goddess, I forswore not thee:
My vow was earthly, thou a heavenly love;
Thy grace being gain'd cures all disgrace in me.
My vow was breath, and breath a vapour is;
Then, thou fair sun, that on this earth doth shine,
Exhale this vapour vow; in thee it is:
If broken, then it is no fault of mine.
   If by me broke, what fool is not so wise
   To break an oath, to win a paradise?

IV

Sweet Cytherea, sitting by a brook
With young Adonis, lovely, fresh and green,
Did court the lad with many a lovely look,
Such looks as none could look but beauty's queen.
She told him stories to delight his ear,
She show'd him favours to allure his eye;
To win his heart, she touch'd him here and there;
Touches so soft still conquer chastity.
But whether unripe years did want conceit,
Or he refused to take her figured proffer,
The tender nibbler would not touch the bait,
But smile and jest at every gentle offer:
   Then fell she on her back, fair queen, and toward:
   He rose and ran away; ah, fool too froward.

V

If love make me forsworn, how shall I swear to love?
O never faith could hold, if not to beauty vowed:
Though to myself forsworn, to thee I'll constant prove;
Those thoughts, to me like oaks, to thee like osiers bowed.
Study his bias leaves, and make his book thine eyes,
Where all those pleasures live that art can comprehend.
If knowledge be the mark, to know thee shall suffice;
Well learned is that tongue that well can thee commend:
All ignorant that soul that sees thee without wonder;
Which is to me some praise, that I thy parts admire:
Thine eye Jove's lightning seems, thy voice his dreadful thunder,
Which, not to anger bent, is music and sweet fire.
   Celestial as thou art, O do not love that wrong,
   To sing heaven's praise with such an earthly tongue.

VI

Scarce had the sun dried up the dewy morn,
And scarce the herd gone to the hedge for shade,
When Cytherea, all in love forlorn,
A longing tarriance for Adonis made
Under an osier growing by a brook,
A brook where Adon used to cool his spleen:
Hot was the day; she hotter that did look
For his approach, that often there had been.

[1429]

Anon he comes, and throws his mantle by,
And stood stark naked on the brook's green brim:
The sun look'd on the world with glorious eye,
Yet not so wistly as this queen on him.
　He, spying her, bounced in, whereas he stood:
　'O Jove,' quoth she, 'why was not I a flood!'

VII

Fair is my love, but not so fair as fickle,
Mild as a dove, but neither true nor trusty,
Brighter than glass and yet, as glass is, brittle,
Softer than wax and yet as iron rusty,
　A lily pale, with damask dye to grace her,
　None fairer, nor none falser to deface her.

Her lips to mine how often hath she joined,
Between each kiss her oaths of true love swearing!
How many tales to please me hath she coined,
Dreading my love, the loss thereof still fearing!
　Yet in the midst of all her pure protestings,
　Her faith, her oaths, her tears, and all were jest-
　　ings.

She burn'd with love, as straw with fire flameth;
She burn'd out love, as soon as straw out-burneth;
She framed the love, and yet she foil'd the framing;
She bade love last, and yet she fell a-turning.
　Was this a lover, or a lecher whether?
　Bad in the best, though excellent in neither.

VIII

If music and sweet poetry agree,
As they must needs, the sister and the brother,
Then must the love be great 'twixt thee and me,
Because thou lovest the one and I the other.
Dowland to thee is dear, whose heavenly touch
Upon the lute doth ravish human sense;
Spenser to me, whose deep conceit is such
As passing all conceit needs no defence.
Thou lovest to hear the sweet melodious sound
That Phœbus' lute, the queen of music, makes;
And I in deep delight am chiefly drown'd
When as himself to singing he betakes.
　One god is god of both, as poets feign;
　One knight loves both, and both in thee remain.

IX

Fair was the morn when the fair queen of love,
. . . .
Paler for sorrow than her milk-white dove,
For Adon's sake, a youngster proud and wild;
Her stand she takes upon a steep-up hill:
Anon Adonis comes with horn and hounds;
She, silly queen, with more than love's good will,
Forbade the boy he should not pass those grounds:
'Once,' quoth she, 'did I see a fair sweet youth
Here in these brakes deep-wounded with a boar,
Deep in the thigh, a spectacle of ruth!
See, in my thigh,' quoth she, 'here was the sore.'
　She showed hers: he saw more wounds than one,
　And blushing fled, and left her all alone.

X

Sweet rose, fair flower, untimely pluck'd, soon
　vaded,
Pluck'd in the bud and vaded in the spring!
Bright orient pearl, alack, too timely shaded!
Fair creature, kill'd too soon by death's sharp sting!
　Like a green plum that hangs upon a tree,
　And falls through wind before the fall should be.

I weep for thee and yet no cause I have;
For why thou left'st me nothing in thy will:
And yet thou left'st me more than I did crave;
For why I craved nothing of thee still:
　O yes, dear friend, I pardon crave of thee,
　Thy discontent thou didst bequeath to me.

XI

Venus, with young Adonis sitting by her
Under a myrtle shade, began to woo him:
She told the youngling how god Mars did try her,
And as he fell to her, so fell she to him.
'Even thus,' quoth she, 'the warlike god embraced
　me,'
And then she clipp'd Adonis in her arms;
'Even thus,' quoth she, 'the warlike god unlaced
　me,'
As if the boy should use like loving charms;
'Even thus,' quoth she, 'he seized on my lips,'
And with her lips on his did act the seizure:
And as she fetched breath, away he skips,
And would not take her meaning nor her pleasure.
　Ah, that I had my lady at this bay,
　To kiss and clip me till I run away!

XII

Crabbed age and youth cannot live together:
Youth is full of pleasance, age is full of care;
Youth like summer morn, age like winter weather;
Youth like summer brave, age like winter bare.
Youth is full of sport, age's breath is short;
　Youth is nimble, age is lame;
Youth is hot and bold, age is weak and cold;
　Youth is wild, and age is tame.
Age, I do abhor thee; youth, I do adore thee;
　O, my love, my love is young!
Age, I do defy thee: O, sweet shepherd, hie thee,
　For methinks thou stay'st too long.

XIII

Beauty is but a vain and doubtful good;
A shining gloss that vadeth suddenly;
A flower that dies when first it 'gins to bud;
A brittle glass that's broken presently:
　A doubtful good, a gloss, a glass, a flower,
　Lost, vaded, broken, dead within an hour.

And as goods lost are seld or never found,
As vaded gloss no rubbing will refresh,
As flowers dead lie wither'd on the ground,
As broken glass no cement can redress,

So beauty blemish'd once's for ever lost,
In spite of physic, painting, pain and cost.

XIV

Good night, good rest. Ah, neither be my share:
She bade good night that kept my rest away;
And daff'd me to a cabin hang'd with care,
To descant on the doubts of my decay.
  'Farewell,' quoth she, 'and come again to-
    morrow:'
  Fare well I could not, for I supp'd with sorrow.

Yet at my parting sweetly did she smile,
In scorn or friendship, nill I construe whether:
'T may be, she joy'd to jest at my exile,
'T may be, again to make me wander thither:
  'Wander,' a word for shadows like myself,
  As take the pain, but cannot pluck the pelf.

XV

Lord, how mine eyes throw gazes to the east!
My heart doth charge the watch; the morning rise
Doth cite each moving sense from idle rest.
Not daring trust the office of mine eyes,
  While Philomela sits and sings, I sit and mark,
  And wish her lays were tuned like the lark;

For she doth welcome daylight with her ditty,
And drives away dark dreaming night:
The night so pack'd, I post unto my pretty;
Heart hath his hope and eyes their wished sight;
  Sorrow changed to solace and solace mixed with
    sorrow;
  For why, she sigh'd, and bade me come to-
    morrow.

Were I with her, the night would post too soon;
But now are minutes added to the hours;
To spite me now, each minute seems a moon;
Yet not for me, shine sun to succour flowers!
  Pack night, peep day; good day, of night now
    borrow:
  Short, night, to-night, and length thyself to-
    morrow.

[XVI.]

It was a lording's daughter, the fairest one of three,
That liked of her master as well as well might be,
Till looking on an Englishman, the fair'st that eye
  could see,
  Her fancy fell a-turning.
Long was the combat doubtful that love with love
  did fight,
To leave the master loveless, or kill the gallant
  knight:
To put in practice either, alas, it was a spite
  Unto the silly damsel!
But one must be refused; more mickle was the pain
That nothing could be used to turn them both to
  gain,

For of the two the trusty knight was wounded with
  disdain:
  Alas, she could not help it!
Thus art with arms contending was victor of the
  day,
Which by a gift of learning did bear the maid away:
Then, lullaby, the learned man hath got the lady
  gay;
  For now my song is ended.

XVII

On a day, alack the day!
Love, whose month was ever May,
Spied a blossom passing fair,
Playing in the wanton air:
Through the velvet leaves the wind
All unseen 'gan passage find;
That the lover, sick to death,
Wish'd himself the heaven's breath,
'Air,' quoth he, 'thy cheeks may blow;
Air, would I might triumph so!
But, alas! my hand hath sworn
Ne'er to pluck thee from thy thorn:
Vow, alack! for youth unmeet,
Youth, so apt to pluck a sweet.
Thou for whom Jove would swear
Juno but an Ethiope were;
And deny himself for Jove,
Turning mortal for thy love.'

[XVIII.]

My flocks feed not,
My ewes breed not,
My rams speed not;
  All is amiss:
Love's denying,
Faith's defying,
Heart's renying,
  Causer of this.
All my merry jigs are quite forgot,
All my lady's love is lost, God wot:
Where her faith was firmly fix'd in love,
There a nay is placed without remove.
One silly cross
Wrought all my loss;
  O frowning Fortune, cursed, fickle dame!
For now I see
Inconstancy
  More in women than in men remain.

In black mourn I,
All fears scorn I,
Love hath forlorn me,
  Living in thrall:
Heart is bleeding,
All help needing,
O cruel speeding,
  Fraughted with gall.
My shepherd's pipe can sound no deal:
My wether's bell rings doleful knell;

My curtal dog, that wont to have play'd,
Plays not at all, but seems afraid;
My sighs so deep
Procure to weep,
    In howling wise, to see my doleful plight.
How sighs resound
Through heartless ground,
    Like a thousand vanquish'd men in bloody fight!

Clear wells spring not,
Sweet birds sing not,
Green plants bring not
    Forth their dye;
Herds stand weeping,
Flocks all sleeping,
Nymphs back peeping
    Fearfully:
All our pleasure known to us poor swains,
All our merry meetings on the plains,
All our evening sport from us is fled,
All our love is lost, for Love is dead.
Farewell, sweet lass,
They like ne'er was
    For a sweet content, the cause of all my moan:
Poor Corydon
Must live alone;
    Other help for him I see that there is none.

XIX

When as thine eye hath chose the dame,
And stall'd the deer that thou shouldst strike,
Let reason rule things worthy blame,
As well as fancy, partial wight:
    Take counsel of some wiser head,
    Neither too young nor yet unwed.

And when thou comest thy tale to tell,
Smooth not thy tongue with filed talk,
Lest she some subtle practice smell,—
A cripple soon can find a halt;—
    But plainly say thou lovest her well,
    And set thy person forth to sell.

What though her frowning brows be bent,
Her cloudy looks will calm ere night:
And then too late she will repent
That thus dissembled her delight;
    And twice desire, ere it be day,
    That which with scorn she put away.

What though she strive to try her strength,
And ban and brawl, and say thee nay,
Her feeble force will yield at length,
When craft hath taught her thus to say;
    'Had women been so strong as men,
    In faith, you had not had it then.'

And to her will frame all thy ways;
Spare not to spend, and chiefly there
Where thy desert may merit praise,
By ringing in thy lady's ear:

The strongest castle, tower and town,
The golden bullet beats it down.

Serve always with assured trust,
And in thy suit be humble true;
Unless thy lady prove unjust,
Press never thou to choose anew:
    When time shall serve, be thou not slack
    To proffer, though she put thee back.

The wiles and guiles that women work,
Dissembled with an outward show,
The tricks and toys that in them lurk,
The cock that treads them shall not know.
    Have you not heard it said full oft,
    A woman's nay doth stand for nought?

Think women still to strive with men,
To sin and never for to saint:
There is no heaven, by holy then,
When time with age shall them attaint.
    Were kisses all the joys in bed,
    One woman would another wed.

But, soft! enough—too much, I fear—
Lest that my mistress hear my song:
She will not stick to round me on th' ear,
To teach my tongue to be so long:
    Yet will she blush, here be it said,
    To hear her secrets so bewray'd.

[XX.]

Live with me, and be my love,
And we will all the pleasures prove
That hills and valleys, dales and fields,
And all the craggy mountains yields.
There will we sit upon the rocks,
And see the shepherds feed their flocks,
By shallow rivers, by whose falls
Melodious birds sing madrigals.

There will I make thee a bed of roses,
With a thousand fragrant posies,
A cap of flowers, and a kirtle
Embroider'd all with leaves of myrtle.

A belt of straw and ivy buds,
With coral clasps and amber studs;
And if these pleasures may thee move,
Then live with me and be my love.

LOVE'S ANSWER

If that the world and love were young,
And truth in every shepherd's tongue,
These pretty pleasures might me move
To live with thee and be thy love.

[XXI.]

As it fell upon a day
In the merry month of May,

Sitting in a pleasant shade
Which a grove of myrtles made,
Beasts did leap and birds did sing,
Trees did grow and plants did spring;
Every thing did banish moan,
Save the nightingale alone:
She, poor bird, as all forlorn,
Lean'd her breast up-till a thorn,
And there sung the dolefull'st ditty,
That to hear it was great pity:
'Fie, fie, fie,' now would she cry;
'Tereu, Tereu!' by and by;
That to hear her so complain,
Scarce I could from tears refrain;
For her griefs so lively shown
Made me think upon mine own.
Ah, thought I, thou mourn'st in vain!
None takes pity on thy pain:
Senseless trees they cannot hear thee;
Ruthless beasts they will not cheer thee:
King Pandion he is dead;
All thy friends are lapp'd in lead;
All thy fellow birds do sing,
Careless of thy sorrowing.
Even so, poor bird, like thee,
None alive will pity me.
Whilst as fickle Fortune smiled,
Thou and I were both beguiled.

Every one that flatters thee
Is no friend in misery.
Words are easy, like the wind;
Faithful friends are hard to find:
Every man will be thy friend
Whilst thou hast wherewith to spend;
But if store of crowns be scant,
No man will supply thy want.
If that one be prodigal,
Bountiful they will him call,
And with such-like flattering,
'Pity but he were a king;'
If he be addict to vice,
Quickly him they will entice;
If to women he be bent,
They have at commandment:
But if Fortune once do frown,
Then farewell his great renown;
They that fawn'd on him before
Use his company no more.
He that is thy friend indeed,
He will help thee in thy need:
If thou sorrow, he will weep;
If thou wake, he cannot sleep;
Thus of every grief in heart
He with thee doth bear a part.
These are certain signs to know
Faithful friend from flattering foe.

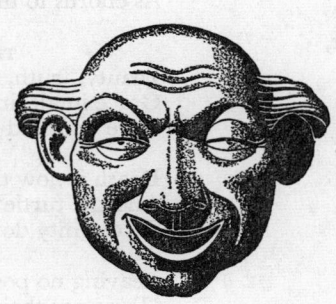

THE PHŒNIX AND TURTLE

LET the bird of loudest lay,
On the sole Arabian tree,
Herald sad and trumpet be,
To whose sound chaste wings obey.

But thou shrieking harbinger,
Foul precurrer of the fiend,
Augur of the fever's end,
To this troop come thou not near!

From this session interdict
Every fowl of tyrant wing,
Save the eagle, feather'd king:
Keep the obsequy so strict.

Let the priest in surplice white,
That defunctive music can,
Be the death-diving swan,
Lest the requiem lack his right.

And thou treble-dated crow,
That thy sable gender makest
With the breath thou givest and takest,
'Mongst our mourners shalt thou go.

Here the anthem doth commence:
Love and constancy is dead;
Phœnix and the turtle fled
In a mutual flame from hence.

So they loved, as love in twain
Had the essence but in one;
Two distincts, division none:
Number there in love was slain.

Hearts remote, yet not asunder;
Distance, and no space was seen
'Twixt the turtle and his queen:
But in them it were a wonder.

So between them love did shine,
That the turtle saw his right

Flaming in the phœnix' sight;
Either was the other's mine.

Property was thus appalled,
That the self was not the same;
Single nature's double name
Neither two nor one was called.

Reason, in itself confounded,
Saw division grow together,
To themselves yet either neither,
Simple were so well compounded;

That it cried, How true a twain
Seemeth this concordant one!
Love hath reason, reason none,
If what parts can so remain.

Whereupon it made this threne
To the phœnix and the dove,
Co-supremes and stars of love,
As chorus to their tragic scene.

THRENOS

Beauty, truth, and rarity,
Grace in all simplicity,
Here enclosed in cinders lie.

Death is now the phœnix' nest;
And the turtle's loyal breast
To eternity doth rest,

Leaving no posterity:
'Twas not their infirmity,
It was married chastity.

Truth may seem, but cannot be;
Beauty brag, but 'tis not she;
Truth and beauty buried be.

To this urn let those repair
That are either true or fair;
For these dead birds sigh a prayer.

NOTES

NOTES

THE FIRST PART OF KING HENRY VI

I. i. 3. '*crystal*,' unnecessarily changed by Hanmer to '*crisped*'; Warburton, '*cristed*' or '*crested*'; Roderick, '*tristful tresses in the sky*,' or 'tresses in the crystal sky.'

I. i. 6. '*King Henry the Fifth*'; Pope, '*Henry the Fifth*'; Walker, '*King Henry Fifth*'; Pope's reading has been generally followed by modern editors.

I. i. 12. '*wrathful*'; Rowe, '*awful.*'

I. i. 24. '*glory's*'; Folios, '*Glories.*'

I. i. 27. '*By magic verses have contrived his end*'; alluding to the old notion "that life might be taken away by metrical charms" (Johnson). Folios 2, 3, 4, '*Verse*'; Pope, '*verse have thus.*'

I. i. 33. '*had not*'; Vaughan proposed '*had but*' (but *cp.* ll. 41-43).

I. i. 49. '*moist*'; so Folios 2, 3, 4; Folio 1, '*moistned.*'

I. i. 56. '*or bright——*'; various attempts have been made to fill up the blank, which some editors explain as due to the inability of the compositor to read the name in the MS.; Francis Drake, Berenice, Cassiopeia, Alexander, &c., have been suggested. Probably the speech is interrupted by the entrance of the messenger.

I. i. 60. '*Rheims*'; Folios, '*Rheimes*'; evidently intended as a dissyllable; but Capell's '*Rheims. Roan,*' derives some support from the fact that '*Roan*,' *i.e.* '*Rouen*,' is mentioned by Gloucester in line 65 (Cambridge ed.).

I. i. 65. '*Rouen*'; Folio 1, '*Roan.*'

I. i. 76. '*A third*'; Folios 2, 3, 4, '*A third man*'; Walker, '*A third one*'; Delius, '*A third thinketh*'; Keightley, '*A third thinks that*'; Dyce, '*And a third thinks*,' &c. Surely a simpler solution of the difficulty is to read '*third*' as a dissyllable with a trilled r.

I. i. 78. '*Awake, awake*'; Folio 2, '*Awake, away.*'

I. i. 83. '*their*'; Theobald's emendation; Folios, '*her*'; Anon. conjectured '*our.*'

I. i. 94. '*Reignier*'; Rowe's emendation of '*Reynold*' of the Folios.

I. i. 95. '*The Duke of Alençon*'; Walker omits '*of*,' to improve the rhythm of the line.

I. i. 96. '*crowned*'; Rowe's emendation; '*crown'd*,' the reading of the Folios.

I. i. 124. '*flew*,' Rowe's correction; Folios, '*slew.*'

I. i. 128. '*A Talbot! a Talbot! cried out amain.*' The line has been variously emended as being defective, metrically. Pope, '*A Talbot! Talbot! cried*'; Seymour, '*A Talbot! cried, a Talbot!*'; Vaughan, '*Talbot! a Talbot! cried.*' If, however, '*cried*' is read as a dissyllable, the movement of the line is parallel to that of '*prevent it, resist it, let it not be so*,' in Richard II. iv., and no correction seems necessary—

A Tálbot! | A Tálbot! crí|ed óut | amáin | .

I. i. 131. '*Sir John Fastolfe*'; Theobald's emendation here and elsewhere of Folios, '*Sir John Falstaffe*'; but in all probability Falstaff was the popular form of the name and it is questionable whether the text should be altered here. "He was a lieutenant-general, deputy regent to the Duke of Bedford in Normandy, and a Knight of the Garter."

I. i. 176. '*steal*,' Mason's conjecture; Folios, '*send*'; Keightley '*fetch.*'

I. ii. 1. '*Mars his true moving*'; *cp.* "You are as ignorant in the true *movings* of my muse as the astronomers are in the *true movings of Mars*, which to this day they could not attain to," quoted by Steevens from one of Nash's prefaces to '*Gabriel Harvey's Hunt's Up*,' 1596. Kepler's work on Mars (*Comment. de Motibus Stellæ Martis*) was published in 1609.

I. ii. 13. '*live*'; Capell, '*sit*'; Walker, '*lie.*'

I. ii. 30. '*bred*'; Folios, '*bread.*'

I. ii. 56. '*nine sibyls of old Rome.*' The number of the Sibyls is variously given as three, four, seven, ten; possibly the '*nine*' is here due to confusion with the nine Sibylline books.

I. ii. 86. '*which you see*,' reading of Folios 2, 3, 4; Folio 1, '*which you may see.*'

I. ii. 99. '*five*'; Folios, '*fine.*'

I. ii. 101. '*Out of a great deal of old iron*'; Dyce's conjecture, '*out of a deal old iron*,' seems the best of the emendations proposed.

I. ii. 103. '*ne'er fly from a man*'; so Folio 1; Folios 2, 3, 4, '*ne're flye no man*'; Collier MS., '*ne'er fly from no man*'; there was probably some jingle intended:—

CHAR. *Then come, o' God's name; I fear no woman.*
PUC. *And while I live, I'll ne'er fly from no man.*

I. ii. 108. '*thy desire*,' = desire for thee.

I. ii. 131. '*Except Saint Martin's summer*'; "except prosperity after misfortune, like fair weather at Martlemas, after winter has begun" (Johnson). St. Martin's Day is November 11th.

I. ii. 138. '*That proud insulting ship, Which Cæsar and his fortune bare at once*,' evidently suggested by the following passage in North's translation of Plutarch's "Life of Cæsar":— "Cæsar hearing that, straight discovered himself unto the faster of the pynnace, who at first was amazed when he saw him; but Cæsar, then taking him by the hand, said unto him, good fellow, be of good cheer, . . . and fear not, for *thou hast Cæsar and his fortune with thee.*"

I. ii. 140. '*Mohamet inspired with a dove*'; *cp.* "he (Mahomet) used to feed (a dove) with wheat out of his ear; which dove, when it was hungry, lighted on Mahomet's shoulder, and thrust its bill in to find its breakfast; Mahomet persuading the rude and simple Arabians that it was the Holy Ghost that gave him advice" (Raleigh's "History of the World"), I. i. vi.

I. ii. 143. '*Saint Philip's daughters*'; "the four daughters of Philip mentioned in the Acts" (Hanmer).

I. ii. 145. '*reverently worship*'; Capell, '*ever worship*'; Steevens, '*reverence, worship*'; Dyce (Collier MS.), '*reverent worship*'; the last seems the only plausible reading.

I. ii. 148. '*Orleans*,' Folios, '*Orleance*'; Capell, '*hence.*'

I. iii. 4. '*'tis Gloucester*'; Pope's emendation; Folios, "*'tis Gloster*'; Steevens, '*it is Gloster*,' &c.; *cp.* l. 62 below, where Folios similarly read '*Gloster.*'

I. iii. 29. '*ambitious Humphry*'; Folio 4, '*ambition*'; '*Humphrey*,' Theobald's emendation; Folio 1, '*Vmpheir*'; Folios 2, 3, 4, '*Umpire.*'

I. iii. 35. '*indulgences to sin*'; "the public stews were formerly under the jurisdiction of the bishop of Winchester" (Pope).

[1437]

I. iii. 72. '*as e'er thou canst; Cry*'; Folios, '*as e're thou canst, cry*'; Collier MS., '*as thou canst cry*.'

I. iii. 81. '*cost*,' Folios 2, 3, 4, '*deare cost*.'

I. iii. 87. '*it ere long*'; so Folios 1, 2; Folios 3, 4, '*it e're be long*'; Capell, '*it ere 't be long*'; Collier MS., '*it off, ere long*'; Orson, '*at it*.'

I. iv. 22. '*on the turrets*,' Folios, '*in an upper chamber of a tower*' (Malone).

I. iv. 27. '*Duke*'; Theobald's emendation of '*Earle*' of the Folios.

I. iv. 33. '*so vile-esteem'd*'; Pope, '*so vilde esteem'd*'; Folios, '*so pil'd esteem'd*'; Capell, '*so pill'd esteem'd*'; Mason, '*so ill-esteemed*,' &c.

I. iv. 95. '*like thee, Nero*,' Malone; Folio 1, '*like thee*'; Folio 2, '*Nero like will*'; Folios 3, 4, '*Nero like, will*'; Pope, '*Nero-like*,' &c.

I. iv. 101. '*Joan la Pucelle*'; Folios, '*Joan de Puzel*' (and elsewhere).

I. v. 6. '*Blood will I draw on thee, thou art a witch*'; "the superstition of those times taught that he that could draw the witch's blood was free from her power" (Johnson).

I. v. 21. '*like Hannibal*,' who, in order to escape, devised the stratagem of fixing lighted twigs to the horns of oxen. (*Cp.* Livy, xxii. 16.)

I. v. 30. '*treacherous from*'; so Folios 3, 4; Folios 1, 2, '*trecherous from*'; Pope, '*tim'rous from*.'

I. vi. 2. '*English*' (trisyllabic), so Folio 1; Folios 2, 3, 4, '*English wolves*'; Staunton, '*English dogs*.'

I. vi. 6. '*Adonis' gardens*.' "The proverb alluded to seems always to have been used in a bad sense, for things which make a fair show for a few days, and then wither away; but the author of this play, desirous of making a show of his learning, without considering its propriety, has made the Dauphin apply it as an encomium" (Blakeway). *Cp.* Faerie Queene, III. vi. 29; Folio 1, '*Garden*.'

I. vi. 22. '*Than Rhodope's or Memphis*' ' Hanmer's emendation; Folios '*or Memphis*'; Capell's '*of Memphis*' has been generally adopted. Pliny, writing of the pyramids near Memphis, records that "the fairest and most commended for workmanship was built at the cost and charges of *one Rhodope*, a verie strumpet."

I. vi. 25. '*the rich-jewel'd coffer of Darius*'; referred to by Plutarch in his "Life of Alexander," as the "preciousest thing, and the richest that was gotten of all spoyls and riches, taken at the overthrow of Darius . . . he said he would put the Iliads of Homer into it, as the worthiest thing."

II. i. 8. '*redoubted Burgundy*'; Duke of Burgundy, surnamed Philip the Good.

II. i. 20. '*all together*'; Rowe's emendation of '*altogether*' of Folios.

II. i. 40. '*ay, and glad*'; Folios, '*I and glad*'; Pope, '*I am glad*.'

II. i. 63. '*your quarters*'; '*your*,' so Folio 1; Folios 2, 3, 4, '*our*'; '*quarters*'; so Folios 1, 2, 3; Folio 4, '*Quarter*.'

II. ii. 20. '*Arc*,' Rowe's emendation of '*acre*' of Folios.

II. ii. 38. '*Awergne*'; Rowe's emendation of Folio 1, '*Ouergne*'; Folios 2, 3, '*Auergne*'; Folio 4, '*Avergne*.'

II. iii. 49. '*I substance*'; Vaughan proposed to read, '*I shadow, aye and substance*.'

II. iv. 6. '*in the error*'; Johnson (adopted by Capell), '*i' the right*'; Hudson, '*in error*.'

II. iv. 83. '*His grandfather was Lionel Duke of Clarence*'; this is erroneous; Duke Lionel was his maternal great-great-grandfather.

II. iv. 91. '*executed*'; Pope, '*headed*'; Steevens, '*execute*' (probably to be read as a dissyllable).

II. iv. 117. '*wiped*'; Folios 2, 3, 4, '*wip't*'; Folio 1, '*whipt*.'

II. iv. 127. '*a thousand*'; Collier MS., '*Ten thousand*.'

II. iv. 132. '*gentle sir*'; so Folios 2, 3, 4; Folio 1, '*gentle*.' Anon. conjectured '*gentlemen*.'

II. v. '*enter Mortimer*'; Edmund Mortimer served under Henry V. in 1422, and died in his castle in Ireland in 1424.

II. v. 6. '*an age of care*'; Collier MS., '*a cage of care*.'

II. v. 74. '*For by my mother I derived am*'; '*mother*' should strictly be '*grandmother*,' *i.e.* his father's mother.

II. v. 113. '*fair be all*'; Theobald, '*fair befal*.'

II. v. 123. '*choked with ambition of the meaner sort*,' *i.e.* "shifted

by the ambition of those whose right to the crown was inferior to his own" (Clarke).

II. v. 129. '*ill the advantage*'; '*ill*,' Theobald's emendation of '*will*' of the Folios. Collier MS., '*will the advancer*.'

III. i. 53. '*Ay, see*'; Rowe's emendation of '*I, see*' of the Folios; Hanmer, '*I'll see*.'

III. i. 141. '*kind*'; Pope, '*gentle*'; Capell, '*kind, kind*'; Collier MS., '*and kind*'; probably the line should be read:

"*O loving úncle.* || *Kind Dúke* | *of Glóucéster.*"

III. i. 197. '*lose*,' should lose; Folio 1, '*loose*'; Folios 2, 3, 4, '*should lose*.'

III. ii. 14. '*Paysans, pauvres gens de France*'; Rowe's emendation of Folios, '*Peasauns la pouure*,' &c.

III. ii. 40. '*the pride*'; Theobald, '*the prize*'; Hanmer, '*being prize*'; Jackson, '*the bride*'; Vaughan, '*the gripe*.'

III. ii. 52. '*all despite*'; Collier MS., '*hell's despite*.'

III. ii. 73. '*God be wi' you*'; Rowe's emendation of Folios, '*God b' uy*.'

III. ii. 118. '*and martial*'; Collier MS., '*and matchless*'; Vaughan, '*unmatchable*.'

III. iii. 85. '*Done like a Frenchman: turn, and turn again*'; "the inconstancy of the French was always a subject of satire. I have read a dissertation to prove that the index of the wind upon our steeples was made in form of a cock to ridicule the French for their frequent changes" (Johnson).

III. iv. 18. '*I do remember*'; "Henry was but nine months old when his father died, and never even saw him" (Malone).

III. iv. 38. '*the law of arms is such*'; "By the ancient law before the Conquest, fighting in the king's palace, or before the king's judges, was punished with death. And by Statute 33, Henry VIII., malicious striking in the king's palace, whereby blood is drawn, is punishable by perpetual imprisonment and fine at the king's pleasure and also with loss of the offender's right hand" (Blackstone).

IV. i. 19. '*at the battle of Patay*'; Capell's emendation (adopted by Malone) of '*Poictiers*' of the Folios. The battle of Poictiers was fought 1357; the date of the present scene is 1428.

IV. i. 181. '*An if I wist he did*,' Capell; Folios, '*And if I wish he did*'; Rowe, '*And if I wish he did.—*'; Theobald (in text), '*An if I wis he did.—*'; (in note), '*And if I wis, he did.—*'; Johnson, '*And if—I wish—he did—*' or '*And if he did,—I wish—*'; Steevens, '*And, if I wist, he did,—*.'

IV. ii. 14. '*their love*'; Hanmer, '*our love*.'

IV. ii. 22. '*war*'; Capell, '*death*.'

IV. ii. 26. '*spoil*'; Vaughan, '*steel*.'

IV. iii. 51. '*That ever living man of memory*,' *i.e.* that ever man of living memory. Lettsom, '*man of ever-living*.'

IV. iv. 16. '*legions*,' Rowe's emendation of Folios. '*Regions*.'

IV. iv. 19. '*in advantage lingering*'; Staunton, '*in disadvantage ling'ring*'; Lettsom, '*in disvantage lingering*'; Vaughan, '*disadvantage ling'ring*.' Johnson explains the phrase, "Protracting his resistance by the advantage of a strong post"; Malone, "Endeavouring by every means, with advantage to himself, to linger out the action."

IV. iv. 31. '*host*'; so Folios 3, 4; Folios 1, 2, '*hoast*'; Theobald's conjecture (adopted by Hanmer), '*horse*.'

IV. iv. 42. '*rescue: he is*'; Folios 1, 2, '*rescue, he is*'; Folios 3, 4, '*rescue, if he is*'; Rowe (ed. 1), '*rescue, if he's*'; (ed. 2) '*rescue, he's*'; Pope, '*rescue now, he's*.'

IV. v. 39. '*shame*'; Walker, '*sham'd*.'

IV. vi. 44. '*On that advantage*,' so the Folios; Theobald conjectured '*On that bad vantage*,' but subsequently read, '*Out on that vantage*'; Hanmer, '*Oh! what advantage*'; Vaughan, '*Oh, hated vantage!*' &c.

IV. vii. 4.

"*Triumphant Death, smear'd with captivity,*
Young Talbot's valour makes me smile at thee";

the phrase '*smear'd with captivity*,' has not been clearly explained; at first sight it is difficult to determine its exact force, and whether the words refer to Death or to the speaker (Talbot). Leo explains that '*Death is supposed to go triumphantly over the battlefield, *smeared* with the *terrible* aspect of captivity'; but possibly the reference is to the Christian belief that Christ took Death captive. Death the Victor is, from this point of view, Death the Victim; it is, as it were, unconsciously smeared (*i.e.* smirched) with the wretched (not the *terrible*) aspect of captivity.

IV. vii. 60. '*But where's*'; so Folios; Rowe, '*Where is*'; Lettsom proposed, '*First, where's*.'

IV. vii. 70. '*Henry*'; so Folio 1; Folios 2, 3, 4, '*our King Henry*.' The line is probably to be read:—

'*Great mareshal to Henry the Sixth.*'

V. i. 17. '*Knit*,' the reading of the Folios; Pope first suggested '*kin*,' which was also adopted by Theobald, Hanmer, Warburton, and Johnson; Capell restored '*knit*,' which was adopted by Steevens and Malone. The Cambridge editions see in '*knit*,' "a conceit suggested by the 'Knot of amity' in the preceding line."

V. i. 21. '*Marriage, uncle! alas, my years are young!*' Pope reads, '*Marriage, alas! my years are yet too young*'; Capell, '*Marriage, good uncle! alas, my years are young*'; Walker, '*Marriage, uncle, 'las my years are young.*'

V. i. 21. '*My years are young*'; "His majesty was, however, twenty-four years old" (Malone).

V. iii. 49. '*where inshipp'd*'; the reading of Folio 4; Folios 1, 2, '*wherein ship'd*'; Folio 3, '*wherein shipp'd.*'

V. iii. 8. '*speedy and quick*'; Pope, '*speedy quick*'; Walker, '*speed and quick.*' '*argues*'; Vaughan, '*urges.*'

V. iii. 10. '*cull'd*'; Collier MS., '*call'd.*'

V. iii. 11. '*regions*'; Folios, '*Regions*'; Warburton, '*legions.*'

V. iii. 48, 49. '*I kiss . . . side*'; Capell and other editors transpose these lines:—'*And lay . . . side. I kiss . . .* [kissing her hand] *. . . peace.*'

V. iii. 57. '*Keeping them prisoner underneath her wings*'; Folios 1, 2, '*prisoner*'; Folios 3, 4, '*prisoners*'; Vaughan, '*prisoned*'; '*her wings*,' Folios 3, 4; Folio 1, '*his wings*'; Folio 2, '*hir wings*'; Vaughan, '*its wings.*'

V. iii. 63. '*Twinkling another counterfeited beam*'; Vaughan, '*Kindling another counterfeited beam*'; or '*Twinkling in other counterfeited beams.*'

V. iii. 68. '*Hast not a tongue? is she not here?*' Anon. conjectured

'*tongue to speak?*' '*here?*'; Folio 1, '*heere?*'; Folios 2, 3, 4, '*heere thy prisoner*'; Keightley, '*here alone*'; Lettsom, '*here in place,*' or '*here beside thee*'; Vaughan, '*present here.*'

V. iii. 71. '*makes the senses rough*'; so the Folios; Hanmer, '*makes the senses crouch*'; Capell, '*make . . . crouch*'; Jackson, '*makes the senses touch*'; Collier MS., '*mocks the sense of touch.*'

V. iii. 78, 79. '*She's beautiful, and therefore to be woo'd,*' &c. These lines were evidently proverbial; *cp. Richard III.*, I. ii, 227, 228, and *Titus Andronicus*, II. i. 82, 83.

V. iii. 108. '*Lady*'; Capell, '*Nay, hear me, Lady*'; Collier MS., '*Lady, pray tell me*'; Lettsom, '*Lady, sweet lady*'; Dyce, '*I prithee, lady.*'

V. iii. 145. '*And here I will expect thy coming*'; Dyce, '*here, my lord*'; Folio 4, '*coming*'; Folios 1, 2, 3, '*comming*'; Capell, '*coming, Reignier*'; Collier MS., '*coming down*'; Anon. conjectured '*coming, king*'; Anon. conjectured '*communing.*'

V. iii. 154. '*country*'; so the Folios; Theobald, '*counties*'; Capell, '*countries*'; Malone, '*county.*'

V. iii. 179. '*modestly*'; Folio 1, '*modestie.*'

V. iii. 192. '*And natural*'; Perring, '*Maid-natural*'; Capell, '*And*'; Folio 1, '*Mad*'; Folios 2, 3, 4, '*Made*'; Pope, '*Her*'; Collier, '*Mid*'; Jackson conjectured '*Man*'; Barry, '*Made*'; Vaughan, '*Mild.*'

V. iv. 37. '*Not me begotten*'; Anon. conjectured '*Me, not begotten*'; Malone, '*Not one begotten*'; Anon. conjectured '*Not mean-begotten.*'

V. iv. 49. '*No, misconceived!*'; so Steevens; Folios 1, 2, 3, '*No misconceived,*' Folio 4, '*no, misconceived Joan*'; Capell, '*No, misconceivers*'; Vaughan, '*No, misconceited!*'

V. iv. 121. '*Poison'd*'; Theobald, '*prison'd.*'

V. iv. 150. '*Stand'st thou aloof upon comparison?*' "Do you stand to compare your present state, a state which you have neither right nor power to maintain, with the terms which we offer?" (Johnson).

V. v. 39. '*Yes, my lord*'; so Folio 1; Folios 2, 3, 4, '*Yes, my good lord*'; Anon. conjectured, '*Yes, yes, my lord,*' or '*Why, yes, my lord*'; Dyce, '*O, yes, my lord*'; Vaughan, '*Yes, my lord—more.*'

V. v. 55. '*Marriage*'; so Folio 1; Folios 2, 3, 4, read '*But marriage*'; perhaps we should read '*marriage.*'

V. v. 64. '*bringeth*,' the reading of Folio 1; Folios 2, 3, 4, '*bringeth forth*'; perhaps the difficulty of the line is due to the quadrisyllabic nature of the word '*contrary*' '*cónteráry.*'

V. v. 90. '*To cross*'; Walker, '*Across.*'

THE SECOND PART OF KING HENRY VI

I. i. 1. '*As by your high,*' &c.; '*The Contention*' reads:—'*As by your high imperial majesty's command.*'

I. i. 7. '*and*'; the reading of Folio 1; Folios 2, 3, 4, omit it.

I. i. 19. '*lends*'; Rowe, '*lend'st.*'

I. i. 48, 49. '*duchy of Anjou and the county of Maine*'; changed by Capell from Quartos to '*dutchies of Anjou and Maine.*'

I. i. 60. '*kneel down*'; Pope reads '*kneel you down*'; Keightley, Collier MS., '*kneel thee down.*' Perhaps '*kneel*' is to be read as a dissyllable.

I. i. 85. '*Beaufort*'; Folios read '*Beauford*'; Rowe, '*Bedford.*'

I. i. 90. '*And had his highness in his infancy Crowned*'; Grant White's emendation of Folios, '*And hath . . . Crowned*'; Rowe reads '*And was . . . Crowned*'; Capell, '*O hath . . . Been crown'd*'; Malone, '*And hath . . . Been crown'd.*'

I. i. 99. '*Defacing*'; Capell reads, '*Reversing,*' following, '*The Contention.*'

I. i. 244. '*humours fits*'; so Folios, Quartos; Rowe reads '*humour fits*'; Malone, '*humours fit.*'

I. ii. 22. '*My troublous dream this night doth make me sad*'; Capell's emendation of Folios, '*My troublous dreames . . . doth,*' &c.

I. ii. 38. '*And in that chair where kings and queens are crown'd*'; '*are*,' Hanmer's correction from Quartos; Folios 1, 2, read '*wer*'; Folios 3, 4, '*were.*'

I. ii. 59. '*thou wilt ride with us*'; Dyce, from Quartos, '*thou 'lt ride with us, I'm sure*'; Hanmer, '*thou too wilt ride with us*'; Vaughan, '*thou; thou wilt ride with us.*'

I. ii. 71. '*What say'st thou? majesty!*'; Capell reads from Quartos, '*My majesty! why, man*'; Vaughan, '*What say'st thou, "Majesty"?*' &c.

I. ii. 100. '*A crafty knave does need no broker*'; an old proverb given in Ray's collection.

I. iii. 3. '*In the quill*'; Hanmer, '*in quill*'; Jackson, '*in quiet*'; Singer, '*in the coil*'; Collier MS., '*in sequel,*' &c. In Ainsworth's Latin Dictionary, 1761, the phrase is rendered, '*ex compacto agunt.*' Halliwell and others explain it also as 'all together in a body.' This interpretation is borne out by a passage in '*The Devonshire Damsel's Frolic,*' one of the 'Songs and Sonnets' in the collection called 'Choyce Drollery,' &c. (1656):—

"*Thus those females were all in a quill
And following on their pastimes still.*"

No satisfactory explanation has yet been given of the origin of the phrase. The following solution is suggested:—"*the quill*" I take to be a popular elaboration of the more correct phrase "*a quill*," which occurs in the ballad quoted; the latter seems to be a corruption of French *accueil*, O. F. *acueil, acoil, akel, achoil,* &c., 'a gathering together.' It is noteworthy that a verb '*aquyle*' occurs in one passage in Middle English, where in all probability it is the English form of the verb "*accueillir.*" (*Cp. Pearl,* ed. Gollancz, p. 122.)

I. iii. 29. '*master was*'; Warburton's emendation of Folios, '*mistress was*.'

I. iii. 66. '*haughty*'; probably an error for '*haught*,' the reading of Folios 2, 3, 4; Pope, '*proud*.'

I. iii. 88. '*to the lays*'; Rowe, '*their lays*.'

I. iii. 143. '*most master wear*'; '*master*,' Halliwell, '*master*'; '*wear*,' so Folio 1; Folios 2, 3, 4, '*wears*,' '*most master*' = 'the one who is most master,' *i.e.* 'the queen.'

I. iii. 147. '*fume needs*'; Grant White (Dyce and Walker conjectured) '*fury*,' which seems a most plausible emendation; '*needs*,' the reading of Folio 1; Folios 2, 3, 4, '*can need*'; Keightley, '*needs now*.'

I. iii. 148. '*far*'; Pope reads '*fast*,' adopted by many editors.

I. iii. 201. '*This doom, my lord, if I may judge*'; Capell reads, '*This do, my lord, if I may be the judge*'; Dyce from Quartos, '*This is my doom, my lord, if I may judge*'; Vaughan conjectured, '*This doom, my lord, if I may judge, is law*'; Collier MS., '*This doom, my gracious lord, if I may judge*.'

I. iii. 211. '*the spite of man*'; Capell reads '*the sight of my master*'; Folios 2, 3, read '*the spite of my man*'; Folio 4, '*the spite of my master*'; Collier MS., '*the spite of this man*'; Steevens, '*the spite of a man*'; Vaughan conjectured '*the spite of many*.'

I. iv. 32. '*What fates await*'; so Folios; Pope reads '*Tell me what fates await*'; Capell, '*What fate awaits*'; Vaughan, '*What fate awaiteth then*'; Wordsworth, '*Tell me what fate awaits*.'

I. iv. 42. '*we watch'd you at an inch*'; Daniel, '*we've catch'd you in the nick*,' or '*at the nick*.'

I. iv. 62. '*Aio te Æacida, Romanos vincere posse*'; the ambiguous answer which Pyrrhus received from the oracle at Delphi before his war against the Romans; meaning either 'I say that thou the descendant of Æacus, mayest conquer the Romans,' or 'I say that the Romans may conquer thee, descendant of Æacus'; '*te*' inserted by Warburton; Folios 1, 2, read, '*Æacida*'; Folios 3, 4 '*Æacide*'; Rowe, '*te Æacidem*.'

II. i. 24. '*Tantæne animis cælestibus iræ?*' 'Is such resentment found in heavenly minds?' (*Æneid*, i. 15). Omitted by Pope.

II. i. 26. '*With such holiness can you do it*'; omitted by Pope. Warburton, '*With such holiness can you not do it?*'; Johnson, '*A churchman, with such*,' &c.; Collier MS., '*And with such holiness you well can do it*'; the old play '*dote*' for '*do it*.' Many emendations have been proposed. If the original reading is retained, it must be considered ironical.

II. i. 29. '*you*'; Pope, '*yourself*.'

II. i. 34. '*furious*'; Folio 2, '*too-too furious*.'

II. i. 47. given in Folios to Gloucester; corrected by Theobald.

II. i. 53. '*Medice, teipsum—*'; "Physician, heal thyself"; from the Vulgate (Luke iv. 23). Folios read '*Medice teipsum*'; Rowe, '*Medice cura teipsum*'; &c. omitted by Pope.

II. i. 69. '*To present your highness with the man*'; Pope reads, '*Before your highness to present the man*'; Capell, '*Come to present your highness with the man*,' &c.

II. i. 91. '*Simpcox*'; Pope's emendation (Theobald conjecture) of Folios '*Symon*'; Capell, '*Saunder*.'

II. i. 135. '*things called whips*'; Halliwell and others quote from Armin's *Nest of Ninnies* (1608); "There are, as Hamlet saies, *things cold whips in store*"; this cannot refer, as has been supposed, to Hamlet's '*whips and scorns of time*,' but may well have occurred in the pre-Shakespearian *Hamlet*. The actual words are to be found in Kyd's *Spanish Tragedy*:—

> "Well heaven is heaven still!
> And there is Nemesis, and furies,
> And things call'd whips."

Perhaps Armin wrote 'Hamlet' when he meant 'Jeronimy.'

II. i. 178. '*vanquished*'; Walker, '*languish'd*'; Vaughan, '*banish'd*.'

II. ii. 6. '*at full*'; Folios 3, 4, '*thus at full*'; Capell, '*at the full*'; Keightley, '*at full length*'; Marshall, '*told at full*.'

II. ii. 15. '*Edmund*'; Folio 1 reads '*Edmond*'; Folios 2, 3, 4, '*Edward*.'

II. ii. 27. '*Richard was murder'd traitorously*'; Folio 1 reads '*Richard . . . traiterously*'; Folios 2, 3, 4, '*King Richard . . . traiter-

ously*'; Pope, '*King Richard trait'rously was murther'd*'; Dyce, '*was harmless Richard murder'd traitorously*.'

II. ii. 28. '*told the truth*'; Hanmer reads '*told the very truth*'; Capell, '*surely told the truth*'; Keightley, '*told the truth in this*'; Marshall, '*the Duke of York hath told the truth*.'

II. ii. 35. '*Philippe*,' Hanmer's correction; Folio 1, '*Phillip*'; Folios 2, 3, 4, '*Philip*'; Collier MS., '*Philippa*.'

II. ii. 42. '*Who kept him in captivity till he died*'; "it was really his son-in-law, Lord Grey of Ruthvyn, and not Edmund Mortimer, whom, according to Hall, Owen Glendower kept in captivity till he died" (Malone).

II. ii. 55. '*York claims*'; Pope, '*York here claims*'; Capell, '*but York claims*'; Dyce, '*while York claims*'; Hudson, '*York doth claim*.'

II. iii. 3. '*sins*'; Theobald's emendation of '*sinne*'; Folios 1, 2; '*sin*' Folio 3.

II. iii. 14. '*Welcome is banishment; welcome were my death*'; Pope reads '*Welcome is exile*,' &c.; Anon. conjecture '*Welcome is banishment; welcomer my death*'; Wordsworth, '*Welcome is banishment; welcome were death*'; '*banishment*' is probably to be considered a dissyllable.

II. iii. 20. '*I beseech*'; Hanmer, '*Beseech*.'

II. iii. 21. '*ease*,' the reading of Folios 1, 4; Folios 2, 3, '*cease*.'

II. iii. 29. '*Should be to be protected like a child*'; Collier MS. reads '*Should be protected like a child by peers*.' '*Should be to be*' = 'should need to be.'

II. iii. 30. '*God and King Henry govern England's realm*'; omitted by Capell; '*Realm*,' the reading of Folios; Steevens (Johnson conjectured), '*helm*'; Dyce and Staunton, '*helm!*' In the next line Keightley proposed '*helm*' for '*realm*.'

II. iii. 32. Collier MS. inserts after l. 32, '*To think I fain would keep it makes me laugh*.'

II. iii. 35. '*willingly*'; Pope, '*willing*' (from Quartos).

II. iii. 46. '*youngest*'; so Folios 1, 2; Folios 3, 4, '*younger*'; Singer (Anon. conjectured MS.), '*strongest*'; Collier MS., '*proudest*'; Staunton, '*haughtiest*'; Kinnear, '*highest*.' Perhaps '*her*' may be taken to refer to '*pride*.'

II. iii. 55. '*defend*'; Pope, '*guard*'; Vaughan, '*feed*.'

II. iii. 89. '*blow*'; Warburton adds, from Quartos, '*as Bevis of Southampton fell upon Ascapart*.'

II. iii. 97. '*Go, take hence that traitor from our sight*'; Hanmer, '*Go, and take hence*,' &c.; perhaps '*traitor*' should be read as a trisyllable.

II. iv. 3. '*Barren winter, with his wrathful nipping cold*'; Pope, '*The barren winter, with his nipping cold*'; Capell, '*Bare winter with his wrathful nipping cold*'; Mitford, '*The barren winter with his wrathful cold*.'

II. iv. 5. '*ten*'; Steevens, "*Tis ten o'clock*'; Lettsom, from Quartos, "*Tis almost ten*.'

II. iv. 12. '*laughing*'; so Folio 1; Folios 2, 3, 4, '*still laughing*'; Hudson (Lettsom conj.), '*and laughing*.'

II. iv. 25. '*thine enemies*'; Folios 4, '*their enemies*'; Rowe, '*our enemies*.'

II. iv. 31. '*with papers on my back*'; "criminals undergoing punishment usually wore papers on their backs containing their offence."

II. iv. 87. '*gone too?*'; so Folios 2, 3, 4; Folio 1, '*gone to?*'; Collier MS., '*gone so?*'

III. i. 78. '*as is the ravenous wolf*'; Rowe's correction of Folios, '*as is . . . Wolues*'; Malone, '*as are . . . wolves*'; Vaughan, '*as the ravenous wolves*.'

III. i. 98. '*Well, Suffolk, thou shalt not see me blush*'; the reading of Folio 1; Folios 2, 3, 4, '*Well, Suffolk, yet thou*,' &c.; Malone, from Quartos, '*Well, Suffolk's duke, thou*,' &c.; Dyce (Walker conj.), '*Well, Suffolk, well, thou*,' &c.

III. i. 133. '*easy*'; Collier MS., '*easily*'; Walker, '*very*'; omitted by Wordsworth.

III. i. 151. '*But mine is*,' &c.; Hudson (Lettsom conj.), from Quartos, reads, '*But I am*,' &c.; '*mine*' = 'my death.'

III. i. 211. '*strays*'; Theobald (adopting the conj. Thirlby), '*strives*'; Vaughan, '*strains*.'

III. i. 223. '*Free lords*'; Hanmer, '*See, lords*'; Dyce (Collier MS.), '*Fair lords*'; Cambridge editors suggest '*My lords*.'

III. i. 280. '*spoke*'; so Folios; Hanmer, '*spoken*.'

III. i. 348. 'nourish' (monosyllabic), = 'nurse' (verb); (Collier MS. reads 'march').

III. i. 357. 'John Cade of Ashford'; Seymour adds, 'with a headlong crew.'

III. ii. 26. 'Nell'; Theobald, 'Well'; Capell, 'Meg'; Malone, 'Margaret'; Clark MS., 'well.' The playwright here, as in other places (cp. below, ll. 79, 100, 120), seems, by some strange error, to have thought of Eleanor instead of Margaret.

III. ii. 70. 'ay me'; Pope reads 'ah me.'

III. ii. 78. ll. 78 to 121 struck out in Collier MS.

III. ii. 79. 'Eleanor'; cp. supra, Note, III. ii. 26.

III. ii. 80. 'Statuë and worship it'; Keightley correction of Folios, 'Statue, and worship it'; Rowe reads 'statue, and do worship to it'; Capell, 'statue then, and worship it'; Dyce, 'statua and worship it.'

III. ii. 88. 'gentle'; Singer (Anon. MS. conj. and Collier MS.) reads 'ungentle'; destroying the whole point of the passage.

III. ii. 89. 'he,' i.e. Æolus, the God of the winds.

III. ii. 100, 120. 'Eleanor', cp. supra, Note, III. ii. 26.

III. ii. 152. 'For seeing him I see my life in death'; Folio 4 reads 'For . . . life is Death'; Johnson 'For . . . death in life'; Capell, 'And . . . death in life'; Rann, 'And . . . life in death'; Vaughan, 'So . . . my self in death.'

III. ii. 163. 'being all descended,' i.e. "the blood being."

III. ii. 182. 'And both of you were vow'd Duke Humphrey's foes,' the reading of Folio 1; Folio 2, 'were . . . death'; Folios 3, 4, 'have . . . death'; Capell first suggested true reading.

III. ii. 192. 'was dead'; Vaughan, 'is dead,' or 'was deaded,' or 'was ended.'

III. ii. 244. 'Lord Suffolk'; the reading of Folios; Malone reads from Quartos, 'false Suffolk.'

III. ii. 262. 'harmful'; Folios 2, 3, 4 read 'harmless.'

III. ii. 308. 'enemy'; Capell (from Quartos), 'enemies.'

III. ii. 322. 'daintiest that'; Theobald, 'daintiest meat'; Hanmer (from Quarto), 'daintiest thing'; Vaughan, 'daintiest cate.'

III. ii. 344-5. 'That thou mightst think,' &c. "That by the impression of my kiss forever remaining on thy hand, thou mightest think on those lips through which a thousand sighs will be breathed for thee" (Johnson).

III. ii. 359. 'thence,' away from the land; Folios 2, 3, 4, 'hence.'

III. ii. 366. 'no joy'; Singer (Collier MS.), 'to joy'; 'nought,' Folios 3, 4, 'ought.'

III. iii. 4. 'and feel no pain'; Theobald reads, from Quartos, 'but one whole year.'

IV. i. 21, 22. 'The lives of those,' &c., so Folios, with the exception of the note of exclamation, added by Grant White; Knight prints a note of interrogation; Nicholson, 'Shall the lives . . . sum?'; Marshall, 'The lives . . . shall they Be counterpoised,' &c.

IV. i. 48. Omitted in Folios; restored by Pope (from Quartos).

IV. i. 50. In Folios this line is made part of preceding speech, with 'lowsie' for 'lowly,' restored by Pope (from Quartos).

IV. i. 70. 'Cap. Yes, Pole. Suf. Pole!' added by Capell from Quartos.

IV. i. 85. 'mother's bleeding,' Rowe's correction of Folios, 'Mother-bleeding.'

IV. i. 117. 'Gelidus timor occupat artus,' i.e. "chill fear seizes my limbs"; the reading of Folios 2, 3, 4; Folio 1 reads, 'Pine gelidus'; Theobald, 'Pæne gelidus,' &c. (cp. Æneid, vii. 446).

IV. i. 129. Lloyd, 'Exempt from fear is true nobility.'

IV. i. 136. 'Brutus' bastard hand'; Theobald proposed 'dastard,' but afterwards withdrew his suggestion; Servilia, the mother of Brutus, became, it is true, the mistress of Julius Cæsar, but not until after the birth of Brutus.

IV. i. 137, 138. 'savage islanders Pompey the Great'; the story of Pompey's death is given in Plutarch; the murderers were Achillas, an Egyptian, and Septimius, who had served under him; perhaps they are described as 'islanders,' because the murder was committed at Pelusium, an island-like spot in the midst of morasses, easternmost mouth of the Nile.

IV. ii. 80. 'Chatham'; Rowe's emendation. Folio 1, 'Chartam'; Folios 2, 3, 4, 'Chattam,' &c.

IV. iii. 7. 'a hundred lacking one'; Malone, 'a hundred lacking one, a week,' from Quartos. In the reign of Elizabeth butchers were not allowed to sell flesh-meat in Lent; by special licenses, however, a limited number of beasts might be killed each week.

IV. iv. 22. Pope, 'Lamenting still and mourning Suffolk's death?'

IV. iv. 43. 'Lord Say, the traitors hate thee'; Folio 1, 'hateth'; Capell, 'traitor rebel hateth'; Marshall, 'the traitor Jack Cade hateth thee.'

IV. vii. 33, 34. 'thou hast caused printing to be used'; printing was not really introduced into England until twenty years later.

IV. vii. 57, 58. Cæsar says in Book V. of the "Commentaries," 'Ex his omnibus sunt humanissimi qui Cantium incolunt,' which Golding rendered (1590), 'Of all the inhabitants of this isle, the civilest are the Kentish folke.'

IV. vii. 59. 'because full'; Hanmer reads 'beauteous, full'; Vaughan, 'bounteous, full,' &c.

IV. vii. 67. 'But to maintain' (Johnson; Rann); 'Kent to m.,' the reading of Folios; Steevens, 'Bent to m.'; Malone, 'Kent to m.,' &c.

IV. vii. 85, 86. 'The help of hatchet'; so Folio 1; Folios 2, 3, 4, 'the help of a hatchet'; Farmer, 'pap with a hatchet,' a singularly happy emendation, &c.

IV. vii. 106. 'Sir James Cromer'; it was Sir William Cromer whom Cade beheaded.

IV. viii. 13. 'rebel'; Singer's emendation (Collier MS. and Anon. MS.) of Folios, 'rabble'; Vaughan, 'ribald.'

IV. ix. 26. 'Of gallowglasses and stout kernes'; Hanmer reads, 'Of desp'rate gallowglasses,' &c.; Capell, 'Of nimble g.,' &c.; Dyce, 'Of savage g.,' &c.; 'stout'; Mitford, 'stout Irish'; 'kernes'; Keightley, 'kernes, he'; Vaughan, 'kernes supplied.'

IV. ix. 29. 'arms'; Folio 1, 'Armes'; Folios 2, 3, 4, 'Armies.'

IV. ix. 33. 'calm'd'; the reading of Folio 4; Folio 1, 'calme'; Folio 2, 'claimd'; Folio 3, 'claim'd'; Beckett, 'cramp'd'; Walker, 'chased.'

IV. ix. 36. 'I pray thee, Buckingham, go and meet him'; Staunton, 'Go, I pray thee, B.,' &c.; Rowe reads, 'go and meet with him'; Malone, 'to go and meet him'; Steevens (1793), 'go forth and meet him'; Collier (Collier MS.), 'then go and meet him'; Dyce, 'go thou and meet him.'

IV. x. 1. 'Fie on ambition'; so the later Folios; Folio 1, 'Ambitions.'

IV. x. 42. 'That Alexander Iden, an esquire of Kent'; Capell, 'squir'; Marshall omits 'an,' following Hall.

IV. x. 52. 'As for words, whose greatness answers words'; Rowe reads, 'As for more words,' &c.; Mason, 'As for mere words,' &c.; Dyce (Anon. conj.), 'But as for words,' &c., &c.

IV. x. 57. 'God'; Malone's correction (from Quartos) of 'Ioue' of the Folios.

IV. x. 78. 'And as I thrust thy body in with my sword'; Dyce (Lloyd conj.) omits 'in.'

V. i. 74. 'Alexander Iden, that's my name'; Capell, 'My name is Alexander Iden, sir'; Hanmer, 'Ev'n Alexander,' &c.; Edd, 'Iden, Alexander Iden,' &c.; Keightley, 'Alexander Iden, that's my name, my liege,' &c.

V. i. 78. 'Iden, kneel down. Rise up a knight'; Hanmer reads, 'Iden kneel down; and rise thou up a knight'; Dyce (Lettsom conj.), 'Iden, kneel down. Iden, rise up a knight'; Vaughan, 'Iden, kneel down; and now rise up Sir Alexander.'

V. i. 95. 'darest'; monosyllabic; Folio 1, 'dar'st'; Folios 2, 3, 4, 'durst.'

V. i. 109. 'these'; Theobald's correction of 'thee' of the Folios.

V. i. 130. 'mistakest'; so Folios 2, 3, 4; Folio 1, 'mistakes.'

V. i. 146. 'fell-lurking'; Roderick, 'fell-barking'; Hudson (Heath conj.), 'fell-lurching'; Collier (Collier MS.), 'fell-looking'; Capell, 'fell lurking.'

V. i. 170. 'shame'; Dyce (Walker conj.), 'stain.'

V. i. 211. 'victorious'; so Folio 1; Folios 2, 3, 4, read 'victorious noble.'

V. ii. 28. 'La fin couronne les œuvres'; i.e. 'the end crowns the work'; Folio 1 reads, 'Corrone les eumenes'; Folios 2, 3, 4, 'Corronne les oevres.'

V. ii. 42. 'Knit earth and heaven together'; Vaughan adds 'in one blase.'

V. ii. 66. 'So, lie thou there'; Malone supposes that a line has been omitted here, equivalent to '*Behold the prophecy is come to pass*'; Vaughan's conjecture adds '*fulfilling prophecy.*'

V. ii. 87. '*parts*'; Hanmer reads '*powers*'; Warburton, '*party*'; Collier MS., '*frends*'; Dyce (Walker conj.), '*part.*'

V. iii. 1. '*of*'; Collier MS. (from Quartos), '*Old*,' adopted by Dyce.

V. iii. 29. '*faith*'; Malone's correction (from Quartos); Folios, '*hand.*'

THE THIRD PART OF KING HENRY VI

I. i. 11. '*dangerously*,' Theobald's correction (from Quartos); Folios, '*dangerous.*'

I. i. 18. '*But is your grace*'; Pope, '*Is his grace*'; Capell, '*Is your grace*'; Malone from (Quartos), '*What, is your grace*'; Steevens, '*What, 's your grace*'; Lettsom, '*What, Is your grace.*'

I. i. 19. '*hope*'; Capell, '*end*'; Dyce (Anon. conj.), '*hap.*'

I. i. 34. '*thrust you out perforce*'; Rowe, '*thrust you out by force*'; Capell (from Quartos), '*put us out by force.*'

I. i. 36. '*council*'; Pope's emendation of Folios 1, 2, '*counsaile*'; Folio 3, '*counsell*'; Folio 4, '*counsel.*'

I. i. 41. '*And bashful Henry deposed, whose cowardice*'; Quartos, '*be deposde*'; as the line stands in the Folios 'Henry' must be either dissyllabic or monosyllabic.

I. i. 55. '*You both have vow'd*'; Folio 4, '*you have both vow'd*'; Pope, '*you vow'd*'; Collier MS., '*you have both vow'd*'; Collier conjectured '*both have vow'd*'; Vaughan conjectured '*you both vow'd.*'

I. i. 56. '*favourites*'; Capell, '*favourers.*'

I. i. 62. '*poltroons, such as he*'; Folio 1, '*Poultroones, such as he*'; Folios 2, 3, '*Poultroones, and such is he*'; Folio 4, '*Poltroons, and such is he*'; Capell, '*poltroons, and such as he.*'

I. i. 70. '*Far be the thought of this from Henry's heart*'; Capell (from Quartos), '*Far be it from the thoughts of Henry's heart.*'

I. i. 76. '*I am thine*'; Rowe, '*Henry, I am thine*'; Theobald (from Quartos), '*Thou 'rt deceiv'd, I'm thine.*'

I. i. 78. '*The earldom was,*' *i.e.* the earldom of March, by which he claimed the throne; Theobald (from Quartos), '*The kingdom is.*'

I. i. 83. '*and that's,*' the reading of Folios 2, 3, 4; Folio 1, '*that's*'; Quartos, '*and that is*'; Collier, '*that is.*'

I. i. 105. '*Thy father*'; '*Thy,*' Rowe's correction (from Quartos) of Folios, '*My*'; '*father*'; Capell conjectured '*uncle.*'

I. i. 144. '*his crown*'; Johnson, '*his son*'; Dr. Percy pointed out that Richard II. had no son; Capell (from Quartos), '*the crown*'; Vaughan, '*his line*'; Wordsworth, '*the throne.*'

I. i. 171. '*for this my life-time reign as king,*' the reading of Folio 1; Folios 2, 3, 4, '*for this time,*' &c.; Theobald (from Quartos), '*but reign in quiet, while I live.*'

I. i. 261. '*from,*' the reading of Folios 2, 3, 4, and Quartos; Folio 1, '*to.*'

I. i. 268. '*cost,*' so Folios; Hanmer, '*truss*'; Warburton, '*coast,*' *i.e.* 'watch and follow, or hover round'; Steevens, '*cote*'; Jackson, '*court*'; Dyce, '*souse.*' Warburton's emendation is generally adopted by modern editors.

I. ii. 16. '*any*'; Dyce, '*an.*' (?) '*But for a kingdom may an oath be broken.*'

I. ii. 38. '*shalt to the Duke of Norfolk*'; the reading of Folios 1, 2, 3; Folio 4, '*shalt be D. of N.*'; Rowe, '*shall go to the D. of N.*'; Pope, '*shalt to th' D. of N. go*'; Steevens, '*shalt unto the D. of N.*'; Vaughan, '*shalt straight to the D. of N.*'

I. ii. 40. '*Lord Cobham*'; Hanmer, '*Lord of Cobham.*'

I. iii. 48. '*Di faciant laudis summa sit ista tuæ*'; *i.e.* 'The gods grant that this be the sum of thy glory'; (Ovid, *Epistle from Phillis to Demophoon*).

I. iv. 109. '*sake*'; Capell (from Quartos), '*death.*'

I. iv. 150. '*passion moves*'; Folios 2, 3, 4, '*passions move*'; Folio 1, '*passions moues.*'

I. iv. 152, 153. '*That face of his the hungry cannibals Would not have touch'd, would not have stain'd with blood*'; Warburton's arrangement (from Quartos); printed as three lines in Folios, ending '*his . . . touch't . . . blood.*' For '*with blood*' Folios 2, 3, 4 read '*the roses just with blood*'; Theobald, '*the roses juic'd with blood*'; Hanmer, '*the roses just i' th' bud*'; Collier MS., '*the rose's 'ues with blood.*'

I. iv. 169. '*to all*'; Capell (from Quartos), '*of all.*'

II. i. 20. '*Methinks, 'tis prize enough to be his son*'; so Folios; Warburton (from Quartos), '*pride.*'

II. i. 113. Omitted in Folios, added by Steevens (from Quartos).

II. i. 131. '*idle,*' Capell's emendation (from Quartos) of Folios, '*lazy.*'

II. i. 146. '*Your kind aunt, Duchess of Burgundy,*' *i.e.* Isabel, daughter of John I., King of Portugal, by Philippa of Lancaster, eldest daughter of John of Gaunt; she was, therefore, really third cousin to Edward, and not aunt.

II. i. 182. '*to London will we march amain*'; Theobald's emendation (from Quartos); Folios read '*to London will we march*'; Hanmer, '*straight to London will we march.*'

II. i. 190. '*fail'st*'; Steevens, '*fall'st*'; Quartos, '*faints.*'

II. ii. 47-48. *cp.* Greene's *Royal Exchange:*—"It hath been an old proverb, that happy is that son whose father goes to the devil," &c.

II. ii. 147. '*Although thy husband may be Menelaus,*' *cp.* *Troilus and Cressida*, V. i. 53, where Thersites calls Menelaus "the primitive statue and oblique memorial of cuckolds."

II. ii. 172. '*deniest,*' Warburton's correction (from Quartos); Folios 1, 2, '*denied'st*'; Folios 3, 4, '*deni'dst.*'

II. ii. 177. '*these*'; Capell (from Quartos), '*thy.*'

II. iii. 37. '*Thou setter up and plucker down of kings*'; *cp.* Daniel ii. 21, "He removeth kings and setteth up kings."

II. iii. 43. '*in earth*'; the reading of Folios 1, 2; Folios 3, 4, '*in the earth*'; Pope, '*on earth.*'

II. iii. 49. '*all together,*' Rowe's emendation of Folios, '*altogether.*'

II. iii. 53. '*wear*'; Collier MS., '*wore*'; Collier (ed. 2), '*ware.*'

II. v. 26. '*make*'; Folios, '*makes.*'

II. v. 38. '*months*'; Rowe, '*weeks, months.*'

II. v. 60. '*as this dead man doth me*'; Hanmer, '*as this dead man to me*'; Wordsworth, '*as this dead doth me.*'

II. v. 80. '*hast,*' the reading of Folios 3, 4; Folios 1, 2, '*hath.*'

II. v. 87. '*kill,*' Rowe's correction of Folios, '*kills.*'

II. v. 92, 93. '*O boy, thy father gave thee life too soon, And hath bereft thee of thy life too late*'; much has been written on these lines, the difficulty being in the words '*too late*'; the simplest meaning of the phrase seems to be '*when too late*'; others explain '*too late*' ≅ '*too recently.*' The Quartos read '*too late*' in the first line, and '*too soon*' in the second.

The force of the crude couplet seems to be:—O boy, too soon thy father gave thee life (better thou had'st never been born!); too late he discovers that the fatal blow was aimed at thee.

II. v. 119. '*Even,*' Capell's emendation; Folios 1, 2, 3, '*Men*'; Folio 4, '*Man*'; Rowe, '*Sad*'; Mitford, '*Mere*'; Delius (Mitford conj.), '*Son*'; Collier MS., '*E'en*'; Keightley conjectured, "*Fore men*' or '*To men*'; Anonymous conjecture, '*Main,*' &c.

II. v. 6. '*And, now I fall, thy tough commixture melts,*' Rowe's reading; Folios, '*fall. Thy*'; Rann, '*fall, that*'; Johnson conjectured '*fall, the*'; '*commixture melts,*' Steevens' correction (from Quartos); Folio 1, '*Commixtures melt*'; Folios 2, 3, 4, '*Commixtures melt.*'

II. vi. 8. Omitted in Folios. Restored by Theobald (from Quartos).

II. vi. 17. Omitted by Capell, following Quartos.

II. vi. 42, 45. The assignment to the speakers is due to Capell, following Quartos, which here are more correct than Folios.

II. vi. 80. '*If this right hand would buy two hours' life*'; Capell (from Quartos), '*would this right hand buy but an hour's life*'; Folio 1, '*two hours*' '; Folios 2, 3, 4, '*but two hours*'.'

II. vi. 82. '*This hand should*'; Capell (from Quartos), '*I'd.*'

II. vi. 100. *'in thy shoulder'*; so Folio 1; Folios 2, 3, 4, *'on thy s.'*

III. i. *'Enter two keepers'*; Folios, *'Enter Sinklo and Humfrey'*; "as Sinklo is certainly the name of an Actor who is mentioned in the stage directions in the *Taming of the Shrew* (Ind. i. 81), and in *Henry IV.*, Part II. (Act v. Sc. 4), there is a great probability that Humphrey is the name of another Actor; perhaps, as Malone suggests, Humfrey Jeaffes. Neither of these is mentioned in the list of 'Principall Actors' prefixed to the first Folio" (Camb. Editors).

III. i. 13. *'Enter King Henry, disguised, with a Prayer-book'*, Malone's emendation; Folios, *'Enter the King with a Prayer booke'*; Collier MS. adds, *'disguised as a Churchman'*; Capell (from Quartos), *'Enter King Henrie disguisde.'*

III. i. 14. *'To greet mine own land with my wishful sight'*; Rann (from Quartos), *'and thus disguis'd to greet my native land.'*

III. i. 17. *'wast,'* the reading of Folios 3, 4; Folios, 1, 2, *'was.'*

III. i. 24. *'thee, sour adversity'*; Dyce's emendation; *'the sower Adversaries'*; Pope, *'these sour adversities'*; Clarke's Concordance, *'these sour adversaries'*; Delius, *'the sour adversities.'*

III. i. 55. *'thou that talk'st,'* &c.; Rowe's emendation; Quartos, *'thou that talkes,'* &c.; Folios, *'thou talk'st,'* &c.; Collier, *'thou talkest,'* &c.

III. i. 60. *'and that's enough'*; Rann (from Quartos), *'though not in shew.'*

III. i. 97. *'We charge you, in God's name, and the king's'*; *'You'*; Anonymous conjecture, *'you now'* or *'you then'*; *'and the king's'*; Rowe, *'and in the king's.'*

III. ii. 2. *'Richard'*; the reading of Folios and Quartos; Pope (from Hall), *'John.'*

III. ii. 3. *'lands'*; Capell's correction (from Quartos); Folios, *'land.'*

III. ii. 6-7. *'In quarrel of the house of York,'* &c.; but in reality Sir John Grey fell in the second battle of St. Albans, fighting on the side of King Henry.

III. ii. 32. *'then'*; Quartos, *'them.'*

III. ii. 108. *''twas for shift'*; so Folios 1, 2; Folio 3 reads, *''twas for a shift'*; Folio 4, *'it was for a shift.'*

III. ii. 110. *'very sad'*; so Folio 1; Folios 2, 3, 4, *'sad.'*

III. ii. 119. *'your prisoner'*; the reading of Folios, Capell (from Quartos), *'as prisoner'*; Id. conj. *'a prisoner.'*

III. ii. 143. *'Flattering me with impossibilities'*; Pope, *'Flatt'ring my mind with things impossible'* (*'me'* = *'myself'*).

III. ii. 156. *'shrub'*; Quartos, *'shrimpe.'*

III. ii. 170. *'Until my mis-shaped trunk that bears this head'*; the reading of Folios 1, 2; Folios 3, 4, *'Until this . . . head'*; Pope, *'Until! the . . . head'*; Thirlby, *'Until the head of this mis-shapen trunk'*; Hanmer, *'Until the head this mis-shap'd trunk doth bear,'* &c.

III. ii. 193. *'the murderous Machiavel'*; Warburton (from Quartos), *'th' aspiring Catiline'*; Folios 1, 2, *'Macheuill'*; Folio 4, *'Matchevil.'*

III. iii. 3. *'while Lewis doth sit'*; Rowe, *'whiles Lewis sits'*; Pope, *'while Lewis sits.'*

III. iii. 11. *'seat'*; Walker conjectured *'state.'*

III. iii. 42. *'waiteth on true sorrow'*; Warburton, *'waiting rues to-morrow.'*

III. iii. 45. *'Our'*; Collier MS., *'The'*; Vaughan conjectured *'Proud.'*

III. iii. 75. *'thy'*; Johnson, *'thee.'*

III. iii. 96. *'thirty and six years'*; Quartos, *'thirtie and eight'*; the correct number according to Malone.

III. iii. 124. *'an eternal plant'*; Warburton's emendation (from Quartos); Folios read *'an externall p.'*; Hanmer, *'a perennial p.'*

III. iii. 127. *'Exempt from envy, but not from disdain'*; *i.e.* not liable to malice or hatred, altho' not secured from female disdain.

III. iii. 133. *'tempted'*; Vaughan, *'temper'd.'*

III. iii. 156. *'Warwick, peace'*; the reading of Folios 2, 3, 4; Folio 1, *'Warwick.'*

III. iii. 228. *'I'll,'* Capell (from Quartos); Folios read *'I.'*

III. iii. 233, 234. *'But, Warwick, Thou and Oxford, with five thousand men'*; Theobald, *'But, Warwick, Thyself and . . . men'*; Hanmer, *'But Warwick, thou Thyself and . . . men'*; Steevens, *'But, Warwick, thou And . . . men'*; Collier MS., *'But, Warwick, thou And . . . warlike men'*; Keightley, *'But, Warwick, Thou and

Lord . . . men'*; Anon. conjectured *'But, Warwick, thou And . . . men of mine.'* Perhaps, as an anonymous scholar has suggested, the line should be read as an Alexandrine.

III. iii. 242. *'Mine eldest daughter'*; the reading of Folios (following Quartos); Theobald (from Holinshed), *'my younger d.'* It was, however, Anne, Warwick's second daughter, whom Edward married.

III. iii. 253. *'Shalt,'* the reading of Folios 2, 3, 4; Folio 1, *'Shall.'*

IV. i. 13. *'our'*; Capell, *'your.'*

IV. i. 17. *'And shall'*; Rowe, *'And you shall'*; Walker, *'Ay, and shall,'* or *'Marry, and shall.'*

IV. i. 41. *'But the safer'*; Folios 2, 3, 4, *'Yes, but the safer'*; S. Walker conjectured *'But then the safer'*; Keightley, *'Ay, but the safer'*; Anon. conjectured *'But yet the safer'*; Vaughan, *'But all the safer'*; Folio 2, *'safter.'*

IV. i. 42. *'using'*; Vaughan, *'losing.'*

IV. i. 66. *'brother's'*; Rowe's emendation of Folios, *'Brothers'*; Anon. conjectured *'brothers'.'*

IV. i. 73, 74. *'dislike . . . Doth'*; Folios, *'dislikes . . . Doth'*; Rowe, *'dislikes . . . Do.'*

IV. i. 89, 90. *'therefore, in brief, Tell me'*; Folio 1, *'Therefore, in briefe, tell me'*; Folios 2, 3, 4, *'Therefore, in briefe, tell'*; Pope, *'So tell.'*

IV. i. 93. *'thy'*; Rowe (from Quartos); Folios, *'the.'*

IV. i. 118. *'elder . . . younger'*; Folios (from Quartos); Theobald, *'younger . . . elder.'*

IV. i. 126. *'the love'*; Pope, *'love.'*

IV. i. 128. *'Yet am I arm'd'*; Vaughan, *'Yet am I warn'd.'*

IV. ii. 12. *'Sweet Clarence'*; Pope, *'friend'*; Capell, *'Clarence.'* Many modern editions omit *'but.'*

IV. ii. 15. *'towns'*; Theobald (Thirlby conj.); Folios, *'town.'*

IV. ii. 21. It had been prophesied that if the horses of the Thracian Rhesus drank of the Xanthus and grazed on the Trojan plains, the Greeks would never take Troy. Wherefore Diomede and Ulysses killed him at night, and carried off his horses. Vide Iliad, x.; Ovid, *Metamorphoses*, xiii. 98-108, 249-252; Virgil, *Æneid*, i. 469-473.

IV. iii. 14. *'keeps'*; so Folios 3, 4; Folios 1, 2, *'keepes'*; Theobald, *'keepeth'*; Hanmer, *'keeps here'*; Vaughan, *'keeps out'*; Keightley, *'field here.'*

IV. iii. 15. *'more dangerous'*; so Folios 1, 2; Folios 3, 4, *'the more d.'*; Hanmer, *'dangerous.'*

IV. iii. 42. *'Yea, brother of Clarence, art thou here too?'*; Pope, *'Brother of C., and art thou here too?'*; Capell, *'Yea, brother of C., and art thou here too?'*

IV. iii. 55. *'tell what answer'*; Pope, *'tell you what reply'*; Capell, *'tell his grace what answer'*; Keightley, *'tell him what answer'*; Anon. conjectured *'tell the duke what answer'*; Dyce, *'tell him there what answer.'*

IV. iv. 11. *'new committed'*; Rowe, *'now committed.'*

IV. iv. 19. *'is it that makes me bridle passion'*; the reading of Folio 1; Folios 2, 3, *'is it . . . my passion'*; Folio 4, *'is . . . my passion'*; Rowe, *'is it . . . in my passion'*; Pope, *'is 't . . . in my passion'*; Vaughan, *'is it, makes . . . passion.'*

IV. v. 16. *'brother of Gloucester, Lord Hastings'*; Pope, *'brother Glo'ster, Hastings'*; Collier MS., *'brother of Gloster, Hastings.'*

IV. v. 21. *'Flanders'*; Vaughan suggests the addition of the words, *'as I guess.'*

IV. vi. 55. *'be confiscate'*; Malone's emendation, Folio 1, *'confiscate'*; Folios 2, 3, 4, *'confiscated.'*

IV. vii. 8. *Ravenspurgh*, the name of a seaport in Yorkshire; the reading of Folios 2, 3, 4; Folio 1, *'Rauenspurre'*; Quarto 1, 3, *'Raunspur'*; Quarto 2, *'Ravenspurgh haven before'*; Pope omits *'haven'*; Steevens conjectured *'fore.'*

IV. vii. 30. *'A wise stout captain, and soon persuaded'*; *'captain'* probably trisyllabic; Keightley, *'I' faith, a wise'*; Collier MS., *'captain he'*; Delius (Lettsom conj.), *'captain'*; Cartwright, *'captain, faith'*; Pope, *'persuaded soon.'*

IV. vii. 57. *'shall'*; Capell (from Quartos), *'should.'*

IV. viii. In the Folios, Somerset is named in the stage direction, though he had gone with young Richmond into Brittany. The mistake arose, as the Cambridge Eds. point out, from the Quartos, in which Scenes vi. and viii. form but one.

IV. viii. 2. '*hasty Germans*'; S. Walker, '*lusty*'; Cartwright, '*hardy.*'

IV. viii. 43. '*water-flowing tears*': Capell, '*water-flowing eyes*'; Collier MS., '*bitter-flowing tears*'; Vaughan, '*wet o'erflowing tears.*'

IV. viii. 61. '*hoped-for hay*'; Quartos, '*hope for haie*'; Malone proposed, altogether unnecessarily, to change the words to '*hope for aye.*'

V. i. 6. '*Daintry,*' popular pronunciation of Daventry.

V. i. 50. '*I had*'; Pope, '*I'd.*'

V. i. 73. '*Two of thy name, both Dukes of Somerset*'; "Edmund slain at battle of St. Alban's, 1455; and Henry, his son, beheaded after the battle of Hexham, 1463" (Ritson).

V. i. 78. '*whom an*'; Rowe's emendation; Folios 2, 3, 4, '*whom, an*'; Folio 1, '*whom, in.*'

V. i. 86. '*That Clarence is*'; Steevens conjectured '*Clarence, so harsh, so blunt*'; Quartos, '*so harsh*' (*so blunt* omitted); Collier conjectured '*so harsh, so blind*'; Mitford, '*so harsh*' or '*so blunt*'; S. Walker, '*blunt-unnatural*'; Anon. conjectured '*brute-unnatural.*'

V. i. 91. '*Jephthah's*'; Rowe, '*Jepthah's*'; Folios 1, 2, '*Iephah*'; Folios 3, 4, '*Jepthah.*'

V. ii. 44. '*clamour,*' Warburton's reading from Quartos; Folios, '*cannon.*'

V. ii. 47-49. The arrangement of the lines in the Quartos; they form three lines in Folios, and have been variously arranged by editors.

V. iii. 5. '*our glorious sun,*' alluding to the cognizance of Edward.

V. iv. 18. '*The friends of France our shrouds and tacklings*'; S. Walker, '*Our . . . our,*' or '*These . . . our,*' &c.; Cartwright, '*Our . . . the,*' &c.; Pope, '*tacklings still*'; Johnson, '*tackling still*'; '*tacklings*' is evidently trisyllabic in this passage.

V. iv. 75. '*mine eyes*'; Capell (from Quartos); Folios, '*my eye.*'

V. v. 1. '*Now here*'; the reading of Folio 1; Folios 2, 3, 4, '*Now here's*'; Capell (from Quartos), '*Lo, here.*'

V. v. 2. '*Hames*'; the reading of Quartos and Folios; 'Ham" in Picardy; Rowe reads '*Hammes*'; Hanmer, '*Holmes*'; Capell, '*Hammes*'; Delius, '*Ham's.*'

V. v. 38. '*thou*'; Rowe (from Quarto 3); Folios (Quartos 1, 2), '*the.*'

V. v. 50. '*The Tower, the Tower*'; Capell's reading; Folios, '*Tower, the Tower*'; Theobald (from Quartos), '*The Tower, man, the Tower!—I'll root 'em out*'; Steevens, '*The Tower, man, Tower!*'

V. v. 77, 78. Steevens' reading, which is nearest to Quartos; Folio 1, '*Where is that devil's butcher, Richard? Hard favor'd Richard,*' &c.

V. vi. 20. '*fool*'; Seymour conjectured (from Quartos), '*fowl.*'

V. vi. 41. '*Men for their sons, wives for their husbands*'; Anon. conjectured (from Quartos), '*Wives for their husbands, fathers for their sons*'; Folio 1, '*sonnes, . . . husbands*'; Folio 2, '*sonnes, . . . husbands fate*'; Folios 3, 4, '*sons . . . husbands fate*'; Warburton, '*sons . . . husbands fate*'; Knight, '*sons*' . . . husbands,' &c.

V. vi. 45. '*boding luckless time*'; Quartos, '*aboding . . . tune*'; Theobald, '*a boding . . . tune.*'

V. vi. 48. '*discords*'; Grant White (from Quartos), '*discord.*'

V. vi. 51. '*To wit, an indigested and deformed lump*'; Capell (from Quartos), '*to wit an indigest deformed lump*'; Dyce (Capell conj.) omits '*to wit.*'

V. vi. 79. After this line, Theobald inserts from Quartos, '*I had no father, I am like no father.*'

V. vii. 30. The Camb. editor quotes from Steevens:—"In my copy of the second Folio, which had belonged to King Charles the First, his Majesty has erased *Cla.* and written *King* in its stead. Shakespeare, therefore, in the catalogue of his restorers, may boast a Royal name."

THE TRAGEDY OF KING RICHARD III

I. i. 2. '*Sun of York*'; probably an allusion to the device of a sun, the cognizance of Edward IV. Quartos, '*sonne*'; Folios, '*Son*'; Rowe, '*sun.*'

I. i. 15. '*to court an amorous looking-glass*'; Vaughan thought the line might be improved by a slight emendation:—'*an amorous looking lass.*' (!).

I. i. 26. '*spy*'; so Quartos; Folios, '*see.*'

I. i. 61. '*have*'; so Quartos and Folio 4; Folios 1, 2, 3, '*hath.*'

I. i. 65. '*That tempers him to this extremity*'; so Quarto 1; Quartos 2-8 read, '*That tempts him,*' &c. (Quarto 3, '*tempts*'); Folios read, '*That tempts him to this harsh extremity*'; Anon. conjectured, '*That tempts him now to this extremity.*'

I. i. 75. '*was to her for his*'; so Quartos; Folio 1, '*was, for her*'; Folios 2, 3, '*was, for his.*'

I. i. 132. '*eagle*'; so Quartos; Folios, '*Eagles.*'

I. i. 133. '*prey*'; so Quartos; Folios, '*play.*'

I. i. 138. '*by Saint Paul*'; the reading of Quartos; Folios, '*by S. Iohn,*' a favourite oath of Richard's.

I. ii. 8. '*be it,*' monosyllabic.

I. ii. 14. '*Cursed be the hand that made these fatal holes*'; Quartos, '*Curst*'; Folios, '*O cursed*'; Quartos 1, 2, '*these fatal*'; Quartos 3-8, '*the fatall*'; Folios, '*these.*'

I. ii. ll. 16, 25. Omitted in Quartos.

I. ii. 19. '*to adders, spiders*'; the reading of Quartos; Folios read, '*to wolves, to spiders.*'

I. ii. 60, 61. '*Thy deed . . . Provokes*'; so Quartos; Folios 1, 2, 3, '*Deeds . . . Prouokes*'; Folio 4, '*deeds . . . Provoke.*'

I. ii. 76. '*evils*'; so Quartos; Folios, '*crimes.*'

I. ii. 89. '*Why, then they are not dead*'; the reading of Quartos; Folios read, '*Then say they were not slaine.*'

I. ii. 127. '*These eyes could never endure sweet beauty's wreck*'; Quartos, '*never*'; Folios read, '*not*'; Quartos, '*sweet*'; Folios 1, 2, '*yt*'; Folios 3, 4, '*that*'; '*wreck,*' Theobald's emendation of '*wrack*' of Quartos and Folios.

I. ii. 135. '*you*'; Folios, '*thee.*'

I. ii. 147. '*Never hung poison on a fouler toad*'; alluding to the old belief that toads were venomous.

I. ii. 156, 167. Omitted in Quartos.

I. ii. 179. '*for I did kill King Henry*'; Quartos read, '*twas I that kild your husband.*'

I. ii. 181. '*twas I that stabb'd young Edward*'; Quartos read, '*twas I that kild King Henry.*'

I. ii. 185. '*the*'; Folios, '*thy.*'

I. ii. 202. Omitted in Folios.

I. ii. 206. '*devoted suppliant*'; so Quarto 1; Folios read, '*devoted servant*'; the rest, '*suppliant.*'

I. ii. 210. '*would,*' the reading of Quartos; Folios, '*may*'; '*thee,*' so Quartos; Folios, '*you.*'

I. ii. 211. '*more*'; so Quartos; Folios, '*most.*'

I. ii. 225. '*Sirs, take up the corse*'; omitted in Folios.

I. ii. 227, 228:—

"*Was ever woman in this humour woo'd?*
Was ever woman in this humour won?"

cp. "*She is a woman, therefore may be woo'd;*
She is a woman, therefore may be won."
Titus And., II. i. 82, 83.

"*She's beautiful, and therefore to be woo'd;*
She is a woman, therefore to be won."
1 *Henry VI.,* V. iii. 78, 79.

I. ii. 235. '*nothing*'; so Quartos; Folios, '*no Friends.*'

I. iii. 5. '*words*'; so Quartos; Folios read '*eyes.*'

I. iii. 7. '*harm*'; Folios 1, 2, 3, '*harmes.*'

I. iii. 17. '*Here come the lords*'; so Quartos 1, 2; Quartos 3-8, '*Here comes the Lords*'; Folios, '*Here comes the Lord*'; Theobald altered '*Derby*' to '*Stanley,*' as Thomas, Lord Stanley, was not created Earl of Derby till after the accession of Henry VII.

I. iii. 36. '*Madam, we did*'; Folios 1, 2, 3, '*I (i.e. Aye) Madam*'; Quartos, '*Madame we did.*'

I. iii. 43. '*who are they that complain*'; the reading of Quartos; Folios read, '*who is it that complaines.*'

I. iii. 58. '*person*'; so Quartos; Folios, '*Grace.*'

I. iii. 67. '*kindred*'; so Quartos 1, 6, 7, 8; Quartos 2, 3, 4, 5, read '*kinred*'; Folios, '*children.*'

I. iii. 68, 69. '*Makes him to send; that thereby he may gather The ground of your ill-will, and to remove it,*' the reading of Quartos 1-6. (Quarto 6, '*grounds*'); Folios read, '*Makes him to send, that he may learn the ground*'; Pope, "*Makes him to send that he may learn the ground Of your ill-will, and thereby to remove it*"; Capell, "*Hath sent for you; that thereby he may gather The ground of your ill-will, and so remove it,*" &c.

I. iii. 77. '*we*'; so Quartos; Folios, '*I.*'

I. iii. 80. '*whilst many fair promotions*'; the reading of Quartos; Folios, '*while great promotions*'; (evidently to be read as a quadrisyllable).

I. iii. 90. '*cause*'; so Quartos; Folios, '*meane.*'

I. iii. 106. '*With those gross taunts I often have endured*'; so Quartos; Folios read, '*Of those . . . that oft I have e.*'.

I. iii. 109. '*thus taunted, scorn'd, and baited at*'; the reading of Quartos; Folios read, '*so baited, scorn'd, and stormed at.*'

I. iii. 114. Omitted in Folios.

I. iii. 116. Omitted in Quartos.

I. iii. 130. '*Margaret's battle at St. Alban's,*' *i.e.* the second battle of St. Albans, Feb. 17, 1461.

I. iii. 161. '*I being queen*'; so the Quartos; Folios read, '*I am queen.*'

I. iii. 167-169. Omitted in Quartos.

I. iii. 219. '*them,*' *i.e.* heaven, used in plural sense.

I. iii. 287. '*I'll not believe*'; so Quartos; Folios, '*I will not thinke.*'

I. iii. 321. '*And for your grace; and you, my noble lords*'; Folios, '*And for your Grace, and yours my gracious Lord.*'

I. iii. 337. '*old odd ends stolen out*'; so Quartos; Folios, '*odde old ends stolen forth.*'

I. iii. 354. '*Your eyes drop millstones, when fools' eyes drop tears,*' a proverbial expression; '*drop tears*'; the reading of Quartos; Folios, '*fall Teares.*'

I. iv. 3. '*So full of ugly sights, of ghastly dreams*'; so Quartos; Folios, '*So full of fearefull Dreames, of ugly sights.*'

I. iv. 9, 10. '*Methoughts that I had broken from the Tower, And was embark'd to cross to Burgundy*'; so Folios; Quartos read, '*Me thoughts I was imbarkt for Burgundy.*'

I. iv. 25. '*ten thousand*'; so Quartos; Folios, '*a thousand.*'

I. iv. 28. Omitted in Quartos.

I. iv. 36, 37. '*and often . . . ghost*'; omitted in Quartos.

I. iv. 38. '*kept in*'; so Quartos; Folios, '*Stop'd.*'

I. iv. 45. '*who*'; so Quartos; Folios, '*I*'; '*flood,*' river ('*melancholy flood,*'*i.e.,* the river Styx).

I. iv. 46. '*grim ferryman*'; *i.e.* Charon; so Quartos; Folios, '*sowre f.*'

I. iv. 57. '*to your torments*'; so Quartos; Folios, '*unto Torment.*'

I. iv. 59. '*environ'd me about*'; so Quartos; Folios omit '*about.*'

I. iv. 65. '*I promise you, I am afraid to hear you tell it*'; so the Quartos; Folios read, '*I am affraid (me thinks) to hear you tell it.*'

I. iv. 66. '*O Brakenbury*'; Quartos read, '*O Brokenbury*'; Folios, '*Ah Keeper, Keeper!*' '*those,*' so Quartos; Folios, '*these.*'

I. iv. 69-72. Omitted in Quartos.

I. iv. 72. '*My guiltless wife*'; Clarence's wife died before this date.

I. iv. 73. '*I pray thee, gentle Keeper, stay by me*'; the reading of Quartos; Folios read, '*Keeper, I prythee sit by me a-while.*'

I. iv. 85. '*In God's name what are you, and how came you hither?*'; the reading of Quartos; Folios, '*What would'st thou, Fellow? And how camm'st thou hither?*'

I. iv. 94. '*Here are the keys, there sits the duke asleep*'; so Quartos; Folios read, '*There lies the Duke asleepe, and there the Keyes.*'

I. iv. 100. '*till the judgement-day*'; so Quartos; Folios, '*til the great judgement-day.*'

I. iv. 107-108. Omitted in Folios.

I. iv. 110. '*my holy humour*'; so Quartos; Folios read, '*this passionate humor of mine.*'

I. iv. 124. '*it . . . thing*'; omitted in Folios.

I. iv. 142. '*shalt we to this gear?*' so Quartos; Folios read, '*shall we fall to worke.*'

I. iv. 144. '*we will chop him in*'; so Quartos; Folios read, '*throw him into.*'

I. iv. 157. Omitted in Quartos.

I. iv. 169. '*call'd forth from out*'; so Quartos; Folios, '*drawne forth among.*'

I. iv. 177. '*to have redemption*'; so Quartos read; Folios, '*for any goodness.*'

I. iv. 178, 227. Omitted in Folios.

I. iv. 206. Omitted in Quartos.

I. iv. 239. '*this world's*'; so Quartos; Folios, '*this earth's.*'

I. iv. 248, 259. '*Relent! 'tis,*' &c.; Folios, '*Relent? no: 'Tis,*' &c.; the text is due to a blending of the readings of Quartos and Folios, first suggested by Tyrwhitt (*vide* Note vii., Camb. ed.).

I. iv. 263. '*like Pilate*'; *cp.* Matthew xxvii. 24.

I. iv. 264. '*grievous guilty murder done*'; so Quartos; Folios, '*grievous murther.*'

I. iv. 272. '*Until the duke take*'; so Quartos; Folios, '*Till that the Duke give.*'

II. i. 5. '*now in peace*'; so Quartos; Folios read, '*more to peace.*'

II. i. 7. '*Rivers and Hastings*'; so Quartos; Folios read, '*Dorset and Rivers.*'

II. i. 33. '*On you or yours*'; the reading of Quartos; Folios read, '*Vpon your Grace.*'

II. i. 40. '*zeal*'; so Quartos; Folios, '*loue.*'

II. i. 44. '*perfect*'; so Quartos; Folios, '*blessed.*'

II. i. 45. '*And in good time, here comes the noble duke*'; so Quartos; Folios read, '*And in good time, Heere comes Sir Richard Ratcliffe, and the Duke.*'

II. i. 56. '*unwittingly*'; so Quartos; Folios read, '*unwillingly.*'

II. i. 66. '*Of you, Lord Rivers, and, Lord Grey, of you*'; so Quartos 1-4; Folios read, '*Of you and you, Lord Riuers and of Dorset.*'

II. i. 67. '*have frown'd on me*'; the reading of Quartos; Folios read, '*have frown'd on me, Of you Lord Wooduill, and Lord Scales of you.*'

II. i. 69-72. Quoted by Milton in *Iconoclastes* by way of illustrating his statement that "the poets, and some English, have been in this point so mindful of decorum, as to put never nine pious words in the mouth of any person, than of a tyrant."

II. i. 98. '*Then speak at once what is it thou demand'st*'; '*speak,*' the reading of Quartos; Folios, '*say*'; *demand'st*,' the reading of Quartos; Folios, '*requests.*'

II. i. 103. '*that tongue*'; so Folios; Quartos read, '*the same.*'

II. i. 104. '*slew*'; so Quartos; Folios, '*kill'd.*'

II. i. 105. '*cruel*'; Quartos; Folios, '*bitter.*'

II. i. 116. '*his own garments*'; Quartos 6, 7, 8, '*his owne armes*'; Folios, '*his Garments*'; '*gave,*' so Quartos; Folios, '*did give.*'

II. ii. 11. '*sorrow to wail*'; so Folios; Quartos read, '*labour to weepe for.*'

II. ii. 15. '*daily*'; so Quartos; Folios, '*earnest*'; Pope, '*daily earnest,*' omitting '*all to that effect.*'

II. ii. 16. Omitted in Quartos.

II. ii. 46. '*perpetual rest*'; so Quartos; Folios read, '*nere-changing night*'; Collier MS., '*nere-changing light.*'

II. ii. 84-85. '*So do I; I for an Edward weep*'; omitted in Folios.

II. ii. ll. 89-100, 123-140. Omitted in Quartos.

II. ii. 101. '*Madam*'; so Quartos; Folios, '*Sister.*'

II. ii. 144. '*weighty*'; reading of Quartos; Folios omit it.

II. iii. 4. '*Seldom comes the better*'; a proverbial expression; found in Ray's *Proverbs.*

II. iii. 11. '*Woe to that land that's govern'd by a child*'; *cp.* Ecclesiastes, x. 16.

II. iii. 28. '*sons and brothers haught*'; so Folios; Quartos, '*kindred hauty*'; Capell conjectured, '*kindred hauty are.*'

II. iv. 20. '*if this rule were true*'; so the Cambridge Editors; Quartos 1, 2, '*if this were a true rule*'; Quartos 3-8, '*if this were a rule*'; Folios, '*if his rule were true.*'

II. iv. 62, 63. '*blood against blood, Self,*' &c.; so Quartos; Folios, '*Brother to Brother; Blood to blood, selfe,*' &c.

II. iv. 67. '*Madam, farewell*'; omitted in Quartos.

III. i. 82. '*formal vice, Iniquity*'; Hanmer reads, '*formal wiss antiquary*'; Warburton, '*formal-wise antiquity*'; '*Iniquity*' was not uncommon as name of the formal (*i.e.* conventional) comic character, the *Vice*, of the Morality plays (*cp. e.g.* '*The Nice Wanton*').

III. i. 110, 111; observe this instance of dramatic irony.

III. i. 171, 172. Omitted in Quartos.

III. i. 175. '*icy-cold*'; Ingleby's conjecture; Quartos and Folios read, '*icie, cola.*'

III. i. 192. '*Chop off his head, man; somewhat we will do*'; so Quartos; Folios read, '*Chop off his Head: something wee will determine.*'

III. ii. 11. '*razed*'; Quartos 1-4, '*raste*'; Quarto 5, '*caste*'; Folios 1, 2, '*rased off*'; Folios 3, 4, '*raised off.*' Quoted in Nares '*rashed.*' *To rase or rash* seems to have been an old hunting term used specially for the violence of the boar.

III. ii. 55. '*I will not do it, to the death*'; *i.e.* though death be the consequence.

III. ii. 108. '*fellow*'; Quartos read, '*Hastings.*'

III. iii. 7, 8. Omitted in Quartos.

III. iii. 15. After this line Folios insert:— '*When she exclaim'd on Hastings, you, and I*'; omitted in Quartos.

III. iii. 23. '*Make haste; the hour of death is expiate*'; so Folio 1; Folios 2-4, '*is now expired*' (*cp. supra* l. 8): *expiate* = ended, terminated; Quartos read, '*Come, come, dispatch; the limit of your liues is out*'; Steevens, '*expirate.*'

III. iv. 1. '*My lords, at once*'; so Quartos; Folios, '*Now, Noble Peers.*'

III. iv. 10. '*Who, I, my lord,*' &c., so Quartos; the Folios:—

> '*We know each other's Faces; for our Hearts*
> *He knowes no more of mine, then I of yours,*
> *Or I of his, my Lord, then you of mine.*'

III. iv. 76. '*Tellest thou me of "if"*'; so Quartos; Folios, '*Talk'st thou to me of "ifs."*'

III. iv. 83. '*raze his helm*'; Quartos read, '*race his helme*'; Folios 1, 2, '*rowse our Helmes*'; Folios 3, 4, '*rowze our Helmes*'; Rowe, '*rase our helms*'; *cp. supra* III. ii. 11.

III. iv. 84. '*But I disdain'd it, and did scorn to fly*'; so Quartos; Folios, '*And I did scorne it, and disdaine to flye.*'

III. iv. 97. '*grace of mortal*'; so Folios; Quartos, '*state of worldly.*'

III. iv. 103-106. Omitted in Quartos.

III. v. 5. '*Tut, I can*'; so Folios; Quartos, '*Tut feare not me, I can.*'

III. v. 7. Omitted in Quartos.

III. v. 10-21. The first Quarto differs in many points from this, the reading of the Folios, especially in making Catesby enter with Hastings' head, though previously Gloster has ordered him 'to overlook the walls.' A similar discrepancy occurs in Scene IV., ll. 80, 81.

III. v. 51-60. Gloucester's speech given to 'Buckingham' in Folios.

III. v. 69, 70. '*Yet witness . . . farewell*'; so Folios; Quartos read, '*Yet witnesse what we did intend, and so my Lord adue.*'

III. v. 96. '*and . . . adieu*'; 103-105. Omitted in Quartos.

III. v. 100-101. '*I go . . . affords*'; so Folios; Quartos read, '*About three or four a clocke looke to heare What news Guildhall affordeth, and so my Lord farewell.*'

III. vi. 12. '*blind*'; so Quartos; Folios, '*bold.*'

III. vii. 24. '*they spake not a word,*' omitted in Quartos.

III. vii. 25. '*breathing stones,*' *i.e.* they were able to breathe, but without the power of speech; later Quartos, '*breathlesse s.*'

III. vii. ll. 98, 99, 120, 127, 144-153, 202, omitted in Quartos.

III. vii. 220. Omitted in Folios, where the previous line reads, '*Come, citizens, we will entreat no more.*'

III. vii. 240. '*Richard, England's royal king*'; so Quartos; Folios, '*King Richard, England's worthie king.*'

IV. i. 7. '*As much to you, good sister! Whither away?*' the reading of Folios; Quartos, which omit ll. 2-6, read, '*Sister, well met, whether awaie so fast?*'

IV. i. 14. '*How doth the prince, and my young son of York?*' so Folios; Quartos read, '*How fares the Prince?*'

IV. i. 15. '*Right well, dear Madam. By your patience*'; the reading of Folios; Quartos read, '*Well Madam, and in health, but by your leave.*'

IV. i. 18. '*why, who's that?*'; the reading of Quartos; Folios, '*who's that?*'

IV. i. 25. '*Then bring me to their sights*'; so Folios; Quartos read, '*Then feare not thou.*'

IV. i. 51. '*To meet you on the way, and welcome you*'; so Quartos; Folios read, '*In your behalfe, to meet you on the way.*'

IV. i. 61. '*red-hot steel*'; Steevens says, "She seems to allude to the ancient mode of punishing a regicide, or any other egregious criminal, viz. by placing a crown of iron, heated red-hot, upon his head."

IV. i. 66. '*Why?*'; so Folios; omitted in Quartos.

IV. i. 76-77. '*As miserable by the death of thee As thou hast made me by my dear lord's death*'; so Quartos; Folios read, '*More miserable by the life of thee, Then,*' &c.; *cp.* I. ii. 27.

IV. i. 96. '*Eighty odd years*'; the Duchess was actually only sixty-eight at this time.

IV. i. 98-104. Omitted in Quartos.

IV. ii. 16. '*That Edward still should live true noble prince*'; so Quartos and Folios; Theobald, '*That Edward still should live, True noble Prince.*'

IV. ii. 46-53. In the lines the Cambridge text follows substantially the reading of the Quartos in preference to the Folios, where the passage is carelessly printed.

IV. ii. 57. '*The boy is foolish*'; *i.e.* Edward Plantagenet, who had been kept imprisoned in the Tower almost from his tenderest years.

IV. ii. 103-120. Omitted in Folios.

IV. iii. 5. '*this ruthless piece of butchery*'; so Quartos 1, 2; Quarto 3, '*thir ruthfull . . . ,*' &c.; Quartos 4-8, '*this ruthfull*,' &c.; Folios, '*This peece of ruthfull Butchery.*'

IV. iii. 11. '*innocent alabaster*'; so Quarto 8; Quartos 1-7, '*innocent alabaster*'; Folios 1, 2, 3 read, '*Alabaster innocent*'; Folio 4, '*Alabaster innocent.*'

IV. iii. 40. '*the Breton Richmond*'; "after the battle of Tewkesbury he had taken refuge in the court of Francis II., Duke of Bretagne" (Malone).

IV. iv. 17-19, placed after line 34 in Folios.

IV. iv. ll. 20, 21, 28. Omitted in Quartos.

IV. iv. 41. '*Harry*'; Quartos, '*Richard*'; Folios, '*Husband.*'

IV. iv. 52-53. Omitted in Quartos; transposed in Folios.

IV. iv. 72. '*their,*' *i.e.* hell's; *cp.* the use of 'heaven,' I. iii. 219.

IV. iv. 88-90. The reading of the Quartos is followed in these lines in preference to that of the Folios:—

> "*A dreame of what thou wast, a garish Flagg,*
> *To be the aymne of every dangerous shot;*
> *A sign of dignity, a Breath, a Bubble.*"

IV. iv. ll. 102-104 transposed; l. 103 omitted in Quartos; Folios, '*she*' for '*one.*'

IV. iv. 175. '*Humphrey Hour*'; perhaps a mere personification, as it were, of some particular Hour, formed on the analogy of such phrases as '*Tom Trott,*' &c. According to some, there is an allusion to the phrase 'to dine with Duke Humphrey.'

IV. iv. 179-182. '*I prithee . . . So.*'; so Folios; Quartos read, '*DU. O hear me speake, for I shall never see thee more.* KING. *Come, come, you are too bitter.*'

IV. iv. 221-234. Omitted in Quartos.

IV. iv. 235-236. '*my enterprise, And dangerous success of bloody wars*'; so Folios; Quartos read, '*my dangerous attempt of hostile armes.*'

IV. iv. 275, 276. '*steep'd in Rutland's blood,—A handkerchief*'; so Folios; Quartos read '*a handkercher steept in Rutlands bloud.*'

IV. iv. 276-277, 288-342. Omitted in Quartos.

IV. iv. 324. '*Of ten times*'; Theobald's correction of Folios, '*Oftentimes.*'

IV. iv. 387. '*What canst thou swear by now?*'; omitted in Quartos.

IV. iv. 511-516. So the Folios; the Quartos differ materially in the phraseology of the lines.

V. ii. 17. '*Every man's conscience is a thousand swords*'; Folios, '*men*' for '*swords*'; the words paraphrase '*Conscientia nulle testes.*'

V. iii. 2. '*My Lord of Surrey, why look you so sad?*'; so the Folios;

Quarto I reads, '*Whie, how now Catesbie, whie lookst thou so bad?*'; the other Quartos, '*Whie . . . so sad?*'

V. iii. 22. '*Sir William Brandon, you shall bear my standard*'; so Folios; Quartos read, '*Where is Sir William Brandon, he shall beare my standerd.*'

V. iii. 23-26. In Quartos these lines are inserted between ll. 43 and 44, and ll. 27, 28, 43 are omitted.

V. iii. 40. '*Good Captain Blunt, bear my good-night to him*'; so Quartos; Folios, '*Sweet Blunt, make some good meanes to speak with him.*'

V. iii. 95. '*tender George*'; George Stanley was at this time already married, tho' Shakespeare, following Hall and Holinshed, makes him a child.

V. iii. 125. '*By thee was punched full of deadly holes*'; this has been described as one of the worst lines in all Shakespeare, but this is due to the fact that critics have confused (i.) 'punch,' the technical word for making use of the *puncheon*, a shoemaker's tool for making holes with (Fr. *poinson*, a bodkin, L. *punctionem*), with (ii.) *punch*, to beat, *which* is a distinct word, and is merely an abbreviation of *punish*.

V. iii. 143. '*Let fall thy lance: despair, and die!*'; Capell reads, '*hurtless lance*'; Collier MS., '*pointless lance*'; but no change is necessary; the line is probably intentionally abrupt, *cp.* 148.

V. iii. 152. '*lead*'; so Quarto I; all other eds., '*laid.*'

V. iii. 162-163. These lines are Lettsom's conjecture, the true lines being lost.

V. iii. 173. '*I died for hope*'; i.e. 'for want of hope,' *cp.* '*dead for hope*' (Greene's *James IV., V., VI.*) = 'dead to hope.' Various unnecessary emendations have been proposed (v. Glossary).

V. iii. 180. '*the lights burn blue,*' alluding to the old superstitious belief that when a spirit was present the lights burnt blue.

V. iii. 204-206. '*Methought . . . Richard*'; Johnson proposed to place these lines after line 192.

V. iii. 212-214. '*KING RICH. O Ratcliff . . . my lord,*' omitted in Folios.

V. iii. 221. '*eaves-dropper*'; so Folio 4; Quarto I, '*ease dropper*'; Quarto 2, '*ewse dropper*'; Folios I, 2, 3, '*Ease-dropper.*'

V. iii. 317. '*Bretons*'; Capell's emendation; Quartos I, 2, 3, 5, '*Brittains*'; Folios 3, 4, '*Britains*'; Pope, '*Britons.*'

V. iii. 322. '*restrain*'; so Quartos and Folios. Warburton proposed '*distrain,*' and this reading has been adopted by several modern editors.

V. iii. 324. '*mother's cost,*' should be '*brother's cost*'; the error —a mere printer's error—was due to the 2nd edition of Holinshed; *cp.* Hall, '*brought up by my brother's* (i.e. Richard's brother-in-law, the Duke of Burgundy) *meanes and mine.*'

V. iii. 345. '*the enemy is past the marsh*'; "There was a large marsh in Bosworth plaine between the two armies, which Richard passed, and arranged his forces so that it protected his right wing. He thus also compelled the enemy to fight with the sun in their faces, a great disadvantage when bows and arrows were in use" (Malone).

V. v. 9. '*But tell me, is young George Stanley living?*'; so Folios and Quartos; Pope, '*tell me first*'; Keightley, '*tell me, pray,*' &c. There is no need to emend; '*George*' is evidently dissyllabic.

THE COMEDY OF ERRORS

I. i. 79. '*The latter-born;*' line 125 below seems to imply that this should be 'elder-born,' a change adopted by Rowe; but probably 'the children became exchanged in the confusion during the breaking-up of the ship.'

I. ii. 41. '*The almanac of my true date,*' because both were born in the same hour.

I. ii. 64. '*I shall be post indeed;*' a post stood in the middle of the shop, on which the scores of the customers were *scored*, or marked with chalk or notches.

I. ii. 66. '*Clock;*' Pope's emendation for '*cook,*' the reading of the Folios.

II. i. 109-113. These lines read as follows in the Folio:—

> '*I see the Iewell best enameled*
> *Will loose his lustre; yet the gold bides still*
> *That others touch, and often touching will,*
> *Where gold and no man that hath a name,*' &c.

The change of *where* to *wear* in the last line has been generally accepted, as also *and though* for *yet* in the second line; *yet* for *and* in the third; *and so a man* for *and no man* in the fourth; Warburton paraphrases this passage thus emended:—"Gold, indeed, will long bear the handling; however, often *touching* (i.e. assaying) will wear even gold: just so the greatest character, though as pure as gold itself, may in time be injured by the repeated attacks of falsehood and corruption." The Cambridge editors wisely abstain from these wholesale emendations, though so far no satisfactory explanation has been given of the lines. May not the meaning of the passage depend on some such interpretation as this:—The wife (the jewel) soon loses her beauty and ceases to attract, but man (the gold) still stands the test, assayed by other women, and although gold wears out if assayed too often, yet a man of good reputation is not shamed by his falsehood and corruption. 'Wherefore,' says Adriana, 'since I (the jewel) cannot please his eye, I'll weep what's left away,' &c.

II. ii. 87. '*Jollity;*' Staunton suggested that the reading is an error for '*policy,*' and the reading has been adopted by some modern editors.

II. ii. 116. As the line stands, it reads as an Alexandrine. Walker suggested *carv'd thee* for *carved to thee;* others propose the omission of *to thee;* neither change seems desirable.

II. ii. 144. '*I live distain'd, thou undishonoured;*' so read the Folios; *distain'd* has been changed to *unstain'd* in most modern editions; Heath proposed '*I live unstained, thou dishonoured.*' The line as it stands in the text seems to mean, 'I live distained (i.e. stained), if untrue to my marriage vows; you, however, live undishonoured, however false you may be.'

II. ii. 183. '*this sure uncertainty,*' i.e. 'This to her surely a thing uncertain.'

II. ii. 188. The second Folio reads '*and Elves Sprites,*' which Rowe altered to '*Elvish sprites,*' a reading adopted by most editors. Theobald proposed to change *owls* to *ouphes.*

II. ii. 197. "'*tis to an ass;*' the words remind one of Bottom's transformation in the *Midsummer-Night's Dream.*

III. i. 54. '*If thy name be called Luce:*' '*Luce*' = 'pike;' there is perhaps a play upon 'pike' in the sense of 'spear,' *cp.* '*Shall I set in my staff?*' line 52.

III. i. 55. Probably a line has been lost rhyming with this; the rhyming word was perhaps *rope.*

III. ii. 66. '*I am thee;*' this reading of the Folio may surely, without risk, be emended:—'*I aim thee,*' i.e. 'I aim at thee;' the transitive use of *aim* is found in Elizabethan writers.

III. ii. 120, 121. '*armed and reverted, making war against her heir;*' Folio 2 substituted *hair* for *heir*, but the play upon words is the whole point of the passage, an allusion being intended to the War of the League against Henry of Navarre, the heir of Henry III. of France, whose cause was supported by Elizabeth; in 1591 she sent a body of 4000 men under Essex to help him. "Mistress Nell's brazen forehead seemed to push back her rough and rebellious hair, as France resisted the claim of the Protestant heir to the throne" (Clarke).

English enthusiasm for Henry of Navarre found expression, too, in Shakespeare's *Love's Labour's Lost.*

As regards the peculiar use of *reverted,* i.e. 'turned back,' Schmidt suggests that there may be a play upon the sense of 'fallen to another proprietor.'

IV. i. 21. '*I buy a thousand pound a year;*' some point in these words, familiar to Shakespeare's audience, is lost to us, and no satisfactory explanation has as yet been given, though Halliwell's comparison of the line with 3 *Henry VI*. II. ii. 144, is noteworthy:—

> "*A wisp of straw were worth a thousand crowns,*
> *To make this shameless callet know herself.*"

IV. ii. 35. '*A fiend, a fury;*' the Folios read '*fairy,*' corrected by Theobald, who had been followed by most editors, including the Cambridge editors; a strong case can, however, be made for the original reading (*e.g. cp.* Hamlet I. i. 161-163).

IV. ii. 61. '*If Time be in debt;*' the Folios read '*If I,*' where *I* is probably an error for '*a* (*i.e. he*) or *he;* the reading in the text is Rowe's emendation.

IV. iii. 12, 13. '*What, have you got the picture of old Adam new-apparelled?*' '*The picture of old Adam*' = the sergeant, who was clad '*in buff;*' in Elizabethan slang this latter phrase was used in the sense of 'bare skin,' *i.e.* 'naked;' hence the quibble. *New-apparelled* offers some difficulty, and depends on the general construction of the whole line. It has been ingeniously suggested that the idea is 'got him a new *suit,*' *i.e.* 'got rid of him.' On the other hand, there is a possibility that the phrase '*What have you got?*' is a vulgarism for '*What have you done with?*' Theobald proposed to read '*What, have you got rid of the picture,*' &c. In the latter cases *new-apparelled* must be regarded as merely a descriptive epithet, the whole phrase '*the picture of old Adam new-apparelled*' being an elaborate circumlocution for 'sergeant.'

IV. iii. 57. '*We'll mend our dinner,*' *i.e.* 'we'll buy something more for our dinner.'

IV. iv. 39, 40. '*The prophecy like the parrot, beware the rope's-end;*' the Cambridge editors most ingeniously conjecture that we should read:—

> "*or, rather, 'prospice funem,' beware the rope's end.*
> *Antipholus of E.   Wilt thou still talk like the parrot?*"

Dyce proposed, '*or, rather, to prophecy, like,*' &c.
Parrots were taught uncomplimentary remarks in Elizabethan times, as they are at present; there are many allusions to the very phrase in the text: Ralpho, in Butler's Hudibras,

> "*Could tell what subtlest parrots mean,*
> *That speak, but think contrary clean;*
> *What member 't is of whom they talk,*
> *When they cry* rope, *and* walk, knave, walk."

V. i. 46. '*And much different,*' &c., the second Folio, for the sake of the metre, reads *much much;* a reading which does not commend itself; *too much* has been conjectured. The line as it stands is certainly doubtful: *différent* does not occur in Shakespeare.

V. i. 66. '*Glanced it;*' Pope's conjectural *at it* is unnecessary, though *glance* in the sense *to hint,* used transitively, does not otherwise occur; Folio I does not elide the *ed* of *glanced.*

V. i. 79. '*But moody and dull melancholy;*' something is obviously amiss with the line; *moody moping* has been suggested. *Kinsman* in the next line is used in its general sense of *akin,* which some editors have unnecessarily substituted; it has even been changed to *kinswoman.*

V. i. 170. '*Beaten the maids,*' &c. *i.e. have beaten;* but the previous verb has *are,*—a confusion of constructions which causes little difficulty, and fairly common in Elizabethan English.

V. i. 309. '*My feeble key of untuned cares;*' *i.e.* 'the feeble tone of my voice, which gives utterance to nothing but unharmonious grief.'

V. i. 387. '*These* ERRORS *are arose,*' so the Folios; *are* has been variously changed by scholars into *all, rare,* but no change is necessary; as far as rhythm is concerned the Folio reading is certainly preferable.

V. i. 399. '*Thirty-three years;*' this reading of the Folios has been changed to *twenty-five* by most editors, following Theobald, who calculates the age of the twins by putting together what Ægeon says in Act I. i. 126 and in line 319 of Act V. Capell suggested *twenty-three,* from Act I. i. line 126 and line 133. On the other hand, the Duke states in line 325 of the present Act that he has been patron to Antipholus for 'twenty years;' it looks as though Shakespeare changed his idea as to the age of the twins towards the end of the play, without troubling to make all his references fit in with one another.

V. i. 403. '*And you the calendars of their nativity;*' *i.e.*, the two Dromios; *cp.* 'Here comes the almanac of my true date,' I. ii. 41.

V. i. 405. '*After so long grief, such nativity;*' the labouring line harmonises well with the emotion of the speaker; the line is evidently intended to be read as follows:—

> '*After | so long | grief, súch | nativ | ity.*'

There seems no reason for changing *nativity,* though Hanmer's conjecture *felicity* has been accepted by most editors; Johnson proposed *festivity.*

THE TRAGEDY OF TITUS ANDRONICUS

I. i. 5-6. '*I am his first-born son, that was the last That ware*'; so Quartos; Folios 1, 2, 3 read '*I was the first-born son, that was the last That wore*'; Folio 4, '*I was the first-born Son of him that last Wore*'; Pope, '*I am the firstborn son of him that last Wore*'; Collier, '*I am his son That wore*'; Collier MS., '*I am the first borne Sonne, of him the last That wore.*'

I. i. 62. '*gates*'; Capell reads '*gates, tribunes*'; Collier MS., '*brazen gates.*'

I. i. 138. '*his tent*'; Theobald reads '*her tent*' (alluding to Hecuba beguiling Polymnestor into the tent where she and the other Trojan captives were).

I. i. 154. '*drugs*'; Quarto 1, '*drugges*'; Quarto 2, '*grudgges*'; Folios, '*grudges.*'

I. i. 484. '*stand up*'; perhaps these words were, as Pope suggested, merely a stage-direction.

II. i. 83, 84. *cf.* Henry VI, Part I, V. iii. 78, 79; Richard III, I. ii. 227, 228.

II. iii. 20. '*yellowing*'; so Quartos; Folios read '*yelping*'; Pope, '*yelling.*'

II. iii. 93. '*barren detested*'; Rowe reads '*barren and detested*'; Capell, '*bare, detested.*'

II. iii. 126. '*painted hope braves your mightiness*'; so Quartos; Folio I; Folios 2, 3, 4, '*painted hope, she . . .*'; Warburton,

'*painted cope she . . .*'; Capell, '*paint now braves your mightness*'; Steevens conjectured '*painted, braves your . . .*'; &c. &c.

II. iii. 132. '*outlive us*'; Theobald's pointing; Quartos, Folios, '*outliue us*'; Dyce (ed. 2), '*outlive ye.*'

II. iii. 152. '*paws*'; Collier MS., '*claws.*'

II. iv. 5. '*scrowl*'; Quartos, '*scrowle*'; Folios 1, 2, '*scowle*'; Folios 3, 4, '*scowl*'; Delius, '*scrawl.*'

II. iv. 9. '*case*'; Pope's emendation of Quartos, Folios, '*cause.*'

II. iv. 49. '*Which that sweet tongue hath made*'; so Quartos, Folios; Hanmer, '*Which that sweet tongue of thine hath often made*'; Collier MS., '*Which that sweet tongue hath made in minstrelsy*'; &c.

III. i. 12. '*For these, tribunes*'; so Quartos, Folio I; Folio 4, '*For these, these Tribunes*'; Malone, '*For these, good tribunes*'; Jackson conjectured '*For these two tribunes*'; Collier conjectured '*For these, O tribunes.*'

III. i. 17. '*urns*'; Hanmer's emendation of Quartos, Folios 1, 2, 3, '*ruines*'; Folio 4, '*ruins.*'

III. i. 34-36. Quarto 2 reads '*or if they did marke, All bootlesse unto them*'; Folios, '*oh if they did heare They would not pity me*'; Capell, '*or, if they did mark, All bootless unto them, they would not pity me,*' &c.

III. i. 67. '*sight*'; Theobald, '*spight.*'

III. i. 86. '*Sweet varied notes, enchanting every ear*'; Collier MS.

reads 'Rich varied notes, enchanting old and young'; Folio 4, 'Sweet various . . .'; &c.

III. i. 125. 'as'; the reading of Collier, from Collier MS. and Long MS.; Quartos, Folios, 'in'; Rowe, 'like.'

III. i. 210. 'would'; so Quartos; Folios read 'wilt'; Capell conjectured 'wou't.'

III. i. 226. 'blow'; the reading of Folios 2, 3, 4; Folio 1, Quartos, 'flow.'

III. i. 282-3. 'employ'd in these things', &c.; so Folios; Quartos, 'imployds in these Armes'; perhaps, as the Cambridge editors suggest, the original MS. had as follows:—

> "And thou, Lavinia, shalt be imployd,
> Bear thou my hand, sweet wench, between thy teeth,"

the Quarto reading being due to a correction of 'teeth' to 'armes'; the latter being taken by the printer as belonging to the previous line.

III. i. 292. 'leaves'; Rowe's emendation of Quartos, Folios, 'loues.'

III. ii. The whole of this scene is omitted in Quartos.

III. ii. 13. 'with outrageous beating'; Folio 1 reads 'without ragious beating.'

IV. i. 9. 'Fear her not'; so Quartos; Folios read 'Feare not'; Rowe, 'Fear thou not.'

IV. i. 45. 'Soft! so busily'; Quartos, Folios, read 'Soft, so busily'; Rowe, 'Soft! see how busily'; Capell, 'Soft, soft; how busily'; Knight, 'Soft! how busily'; Keightley, 'Soft, soft! so busily'; Collier MS., 'Soft! see how busily.'

IV. i. 82, 83. 'Magni Dominator poli, Tam lentus audis scelera? tam lentus vides?'; i.e. Great ruler of the skies, dost thou so tardily hear and see crimes committed? (Seneca's Hippolytus, ii. 671); Theobald, 'Magne Dominator'; Hanmer, 'Magne Regnator.'

IV. i. 130. 'Revenge, ye heavens'; Johnson conjectured, 'Reuenge the heauens,' so Quarto, Folios.

IV. ii. 8, 76; omitted in Folios.

IV. ii. 20-21. "He who is pure in life, and free from sin, needs not the darts of the Moor, nor the bow" (Horace, Odes, I. 22).

IV. ii. 26. 'sound'; Theobald conjectured 'Fond,' i.e. foolish; but 'sound' is probably to be taken ironically.

IV. ii. 166. 'take no longer days'; Collier MS., 'make no longer delays.'

IV. iii. 2. 'let'; so Quartos, Folio 1; Folios 2, 3, 4, 'now let.'

IV. iii. 4. 'Terras Astræa reliquit'; i.e. Astræa (the goddess of Justice) left the earth (Ovid. Metam. i. 150).

IV. iii. 56. 'To Saturn, Caius'; Capell's emendation; Quartos, Folios read 'To Saturnine, to Caius'; Rowe (ed. 1), 'To Cœlus and to Saturn'; (ed. 2), 'To Saturn and to Cœlus.'

IV. iv. 37. 'Thy life-blood out'; Folio 2, 'ont'; Folio 3, 'on't'; Walker suggested that a previous line had been lost, but the text seems correct, = "and drawn thy life-blood out."

IV. iv. 103. Omitted in Quarto 2 and Folios; the reading of Quarto 1.

V. i. 17. 'All the Goths,' should be 'The other Goths,' as 'the first Goth' is kept distinct.

V. i. 42. An allusion to the old proverb, "A black man is a pearl in a fair woman's eye" (Malone).

V. i. 93. 'And cut her hands'; so Quartos; Folios, 'And cut her hands off'; Collier MS., 'Cut her hands off.'

V. i. 122. A proverb found in Ray's collection.

V. i. 132. 'break their necks'; Malone conjectured 'break their necks and die'; Jackson conjectured 'stray and break their necks'; Collier MS., 'ofttimes break their necks,' &c.

V. ii. 80. 'ply'; so Quartos; Folios, 'play.'

V. ii. 162; iii. 52. Omitted in Folios.

V. iii. 73. 'Lest Rome'; Capell's reading; Quartos, Folios, 'Let Rome'; Malone, 'Lest Rome.'

V. iii. 124. 'And as he is'; so Quartos, Folios; Theobald reads 'Damn'd as he is.'

THE TAMING OF THE SHREW

INDUCT. i. 9. 'go by, Jeronimy'; a popular phrase from Kyd's Spanish Tragedy—"the common butt of raillery to all the poets in Shakespeare's time."

Induct. i. 17. 'Brach Merriman'; 'brach' usually means a female hound, as in the next line; the sequence of thought requires 'brach' to be a verb: perhaps it is used in the sense of 'couple,' 'mate.' Hanmer proposed 'leech'; Keightley, 'bathe'; Singer (ed. 2), 'trash,' &c.

Induct. i. 63. 'And when he says he is,' &c., so the old eds. The reading is probably correct; the line means 'when he says he is mad, say that he dreams.' Rowe proposed 'And when he says he's poor'; Keightley 'And when he says what he is,' &c.

Induct. i. 87. The Folios and Quarto prefix 'Sincklo,' the name of an actor in Shakespeare's company, who is mentioned also in stage-directions of Quarto edition (1600) of 2 Henry IV., V. iv., and in the Folio, 3 Henry VI., III. i.

Induct. i. 88. 'Soto' is a character in Beaumont and Fletcher's Women Pleased.

I. i. 32. Cp. The Taming of a Shrew:—

> 'Welcome to Athens, my beloved friend,
> To Plato's school and Aristotle's walks.'

I. i. 42. 'If Biondello, thou wert'; the Collier MS. reads 'now were'; Dyce adopts this emendation.

I. i. 63. 'To comb your noddle with a three-legg'd stool'; an old expression occurring in Skelton's Merrie Tales. "Hys wife would divers times in the weeke kimbe his head with a iii. footed stoole."

I. i. 234. 'I, sir! ne'er a whit.' Rowe proposed 'Ay, sir, ne'er,' &c.; Dyce, 'Ay, sir.—Ne'er.' It is difficult to determine whether 'I' is the personal pronoun, or stands, as is often the case, for 'Ay.'

I. i. 247. 'The presenters,' i.e. Sly and his attendants in the balcony above.

I. ii. 28. 'what he 'leges in Latin'; the Folios and Quarto, 'leges,' an authorised form for 'alleges'; Grumio, strange to say, though an Italian, mistakes Italian for Latin.

I. ii. 149-150. 'paper' . . . 'them'; changed by Pope to 'papers': Mr. Daniel considers 'paper' to be the note of the 'books,' and 'them' the books.

II. i. 75-83, arranged as verse in the Folios and Quarto, first printed as prose by Pope.

II. i. 201. 'no such jade as you'; probably an error for 'no jade for such as you,' as conjectured by Hudson: many other less obvious emendations have been proposed, e.g. "no such load as you, sir" (Singer), &c.

II. i. 206-208. 'buzzard' in this passage is a crux: its three senses are, I think, punned on by the speakers:—(i.) a simpleton (l. 206); (ii.) a mean hawk (ll. 207, 208); in the latter case Petruchio interprets it as (iii.) 'a buzzing insect,' hence 'you wasp' (l. 209). Katharine's reply seems to mean:—'that, in calling her a turtle, he has mistaken a hawk for a dove'; underlying this retort there may be a suggestion of the proverbial 'blind buzzard.'

II. i. 288. 'morn'; cp. Troilus, I. iii. 229:—

> 'Modest as morning when she coldly eyes
> The youthful Phœbus.'

The Collier MS. has 'moone.'

II. i. 317. 'We will have rings and things,' probably a fragment of an old ballad. Collier quotes some lines bearing a very strong resemblance to these "from the recitation of an old lady"—a vague authority.

II. i. 369. 'Marseilles' road,' Folio 1 and Quarto, 'Marcellus'; the other Folios 'Marsellis'; the word is obviously trisyllabic; the apostrophe is not needed, cp. 'Venice gold,' 'Pisa walls' in the previous speech.

III. i. 4. Theobald proposed 'she is a shrew, but, wrangling *pedant, this is*'; evidently some words are lost, but it is useless to attempt the restoration of the line, as there is no evidence.

III. ii. 16. '*make friends, invite, and proclaim the banns*'; so Folio 1 and Quarto; Folios 2 and 3 insert '*yes*' before '*and.*' The more noteworthy suggestions are:— " *Make friends invite, Yes*" (Singer); "*make friends invite guests*" (Dyce); "*make feasts, invite friends*" (Dyce, ed. 2).

IV. i. 128. '*Where is the life that late I led*'; a line of an old song, quoted also by Pistol; *cp.* 2 *Henry IV.,* V. iii. 137. Similarly '*It was the friar of orders grey,*' &c., is a bit of an old ballad, now lost.

IV. i. 196. '*to kill a wife with kindness,*' a proverbial expression. Heywood's play, *A Woman Killed with Kindness,* was first produced in 1602.

IV. ii. 45. '*longeth*'; the Folios and Quartos correct '*longeth,*' without apostrophe; '*to long*' in the sense of '*to belong*' is common in older English writings. Similarly '*pointed*' in old eds., III. ii. 1.

IV. ii. 61. '*An ancient angel*'; so the Folios and Quartos; Theobald suggested '*engle*' (a gull); other proposals have been *ayeul, gentle, morsel, antick,* &c., but no change is necessary.

Cotgrave renders *Angelot à la grosse escaille* by "an old angeil; and by metaphor, a fellow of the old, sound, honest and worthie stamp."

IV. iii. 60. '*ruffling treasure*'; Pope changed '*ruffling*' to '*rustling*'; perhaps we should read '*russling*' (for '*rustling*'). *Cp. Lear,* II. iv. 299, where the Quarto reading is '*russel,*' while the Folios have '*ruffle.*' Mrs. Quickly's '*rushling in silk and gold*' (*Merry Wives,* II. ii. 63) seems to be an important piece of evidence in favour of '*rustling.*'

IV. iv. 62. '*Cambio,*' probably an error for '*Biondello,*' as suggested by the Cambridge editors, and more satisfactory from a metrical point of view. Again, "the supposed Cambio was not acting as Baptista's servant, and moreover, had he been sent on such an errand, he would have 'flown on the wings of love' to perform it. We must suppose that Biondello apparently makes his exit, but really waits till the stage is clear for an interview with his disguised master."

V. i. 27. '*his father has come from Padua,*' so the Folios and Quartos; various changes have been proposed, *e.g.* '*to Padua,*' '*from Pisa,*' &c., but the Pedant means that he has been staying at Padua.

THE TWO GENTLEMEN OF VERONA

DRAMATIS PERSONÆ. 'The names of all the actors' are given at the end of the play in the Folios; the form 'Protheus' is invariably used for 'Proteus,' 'Athonio' for 'Antonio,' and 'Panthion' for 'Panthino.'

I. i. 19. '*On a love-book pray for my success;*' an allusion to the Roman Catholic custom of placing the beads on the prayer-book, and of counting the beads with the prayers. 'The love-book' is in this case to take the place of the prayer-book; some have supposed that Shakespeare is here referring to Marlowe's 'Hero and Leander,' which, however, though entered on the Stationers' Registers in 1593, was not printed till 1598, after which date many references occur to it in contemporary literature; Shakespeare directly quotes from it in *As You Like It,* IV. i. 100.

I. ii. 53. '*What fool is she;*' the first three Folios read 'what 'fool is she,' indicating the omission of the indefinite article, a not uncommon Elizabethan idiom.

I. ii. 137. '*I see you have a month's mind to them;*' Schmidt in his 'Shakespeare Lexicon' explains the phrase 'month's mind' as 'a woman's longing,' as though the expression had its origin in the longing for particular articles of food shown by women, but this interpretation seems to have no authority. Johnson rightly remarks on this passage:—'A *month's mind,* in the ritual sense, signifies not desire or inclination, but remembrance; yet I suppose this is the true original of expression.'

I. iii. 27. "Shakespeare has been guilty of no mistake in placing the emperor's court at Milan. Several of the first German Emperors held their courts there occasionally, it being at that time their immediate property, and the chief town of their Italian dominions."—STEEVENS.

II. i. 35. '*none else would;*' *i.e.* 'no one else would perceive them.'

II. i. 73, 74. '*to put on your hose;*' various suggestions have been made for the emendation of these words:—'to beyond your nose,' 'to put spectacles on your nose,' 'to put on your shoes,' 'to button your hose.' It is not certain that a rhyming couplet was intended. Probably 'unable to see to put on one's hose' was a proverbial expression meaning 'unable to tell which leg to put into one's hose first,' *i.e.* 'not to have one's wits about one.'

II. i. 157. '*for in print I found it.*' Probably these lines are quoted from some old ballad or play, though their source has not yet been found. One cannot help thinking that Shakespeare is quoting from some play of the 'Two Italian Gentlemen' type; the reprinted extracts contain passages strongly reminding one of these lines.

II. iii. 28. '*a wood woman;*' the Folios read 'a would woman;'

Theobald first changed 'would' into 'wood' (*i.e.* mad); others 'an ould (*i.e.* old) woman.'

II. iv. 112. The Folios give this line to 'Thurio;' if the reading be right, he must have quitted the stage during the scene, probably immediately before the entrance of Proteus, after line 99.

II. iv. 126. '*Whose high imperious thoughts have punished me;*' Johnson proposed to read 'those' for 'whose,' as if the 'imperious thoughts' are Valentine's and not 'Love's;' the word 'thoughts' certainly presents a difficulty, being used here probably in the sense of 'dispositions of the mind.'

II. iv. 192. '*Is it mine, or Valentine's praise;*' the first Folio reads, 'It is mine or Valentine's praise;' the later Folios, 'Is it mine then, or Valentineans praise?' Theobald's suggestion, 'mine eye,' has been generally adopted; 'if this were unsatisfactory,' the Camb. editors remark, 'another guess might be hazarded:—

Is it mine unstaid mind or Valentine's praise.'

In the latter case 'Valentine's' must be read as a dissyllable; in the former as a quadrisyllable; it is not necessary to read, as has been proposed, 'Valentino's' or 'Valentinus.' Two other ingenious emendations are noteworthy:—'her mien,' 'mine eyne,' ('thine eyne' occurs as a rhyme in *Midsummer-Night's Dream,* III. ii. 138).

II. v. 1; III. i. 81; V. iv. 129. The Cambridge editors have retained the reading of the Folios in these lines, 'Padua' in the first passage, and 'Verona' in the second and third, 'because it is impossible that the words can be a mere printer's, or transcriber's error. These inaccuracies are interesting as showing that Shakespeare had written the whole of the play before he had finally determined where the scene was to be laid;' the scene is in each case undoubtedly Milan (perhaps 'Milano,' *metri causa*).

III. i. 272. '*Condition;*' so the first three Folios; the fourth Folio reads 'conditions,' adopted in many editions; 'condition' is generally used by Shakespeare in the sense of 'temper,' 'quality.'

III. ii. 77. Malone suggests that some such line as the following has been lost after 'integrity:'—'as her obdurate heart may penetrate,' but the meaning is perhaps rightly explained by Steevens:—"such ardour and sincerity as would be manifested by practising the directions given in the four preceding lines."

IV. i. 36. '*Robin Hood's fat friar,*' *i.e.* Friar Tuck. This allusion to 'Robin Hood's friar' by the Italian outlaw is somewhat unexpected; in the later play of *As You Like It* there is also an allusion to 'Robin Hood,' but Shakespeare is careful to add 'of England' ('they live like the old Robin Hood of England,' I. i. 115).

IV. i. 49. *'An heir, and near allied;'* the Folios read 'niece,' for which Theobald suggested 'near,' a reading generally accepted; possibly, but doubtfully, 'niece' may after all be correct, being used occasionally by Elizabethan writers to signify almost any relationship.

IV. iv. 55. *'Hangman boys;'* the Folios read 'hangman's boys;' the reading in the text was given by Singer from a MS. note in a copy of the second Folio in his possession.

IV. iv. 73. The first Folio misprints, 'not leave her token.'

V. iv. 2. Probably a better reading than the folio is that generally adopted, due to Collier's MS.:—

'these shadowy, desert, unfrequented woods.'

V. iv. 47-50. *'Rend thy faith . . . perjury, to love me. Thou . . .'* The lines seem clear as they stand; a suggestion by Mr. Daniel is perhaps worthy of mention:—'rain . . . perjury. To love me Thou,' *or* 'hail . . . Discandied into perjury. To love me Thou . . .'

V. iv. 71. A difficult line to scan; Johnson proposed 'O time most curst;' others omit 'most' or 'O;' perhaps we have here an Alexandrine, 'O' counting as a monosyllabic foot; the second syllable of 'deepest' being an extra syllable before the pause:—

The pri'/vate wou'nd/ is de'epest;|| O'-/ time mo'st/ accur'st,/

LOVE'S LABOUR'S LOST

There is no list of 'Dramatis Personæ' in the Quartos and Folios: it should be remembered that 'Biron' is spelt 'Berowne,' rhyming with 'moon' in Act IV. iii. 227; 'Moth' was probably pronounced 'Mote' (*cp.* the quibble on 'nothing' in *Much Ado*, II. iii. 57, and on 'Goths' in *As You Like It*, III. iii. 6); 'Mercade' is generally 'Marcade'; 'Armado' is sometimes given as 'Armatho'; 'Boyet' rhymes with 'debt' in V. ii. 334; 'Longaville' with 'ill' in IV. iii. 120, and with 'mile' in V. ii. 53.

I. i. 62. *'feast'*; Quartos and Folios *'fast,'* corrected by Theobald.

I. i. 82. *'Who dazzling so'*; "that when he *dazzles*, that is, has his eye made weak, by fixing his eye upon a *fairer* eye, that *fairer* eye shall be his *heed*, his direction or *lodestar*, and give him light that was blinded by it" (Johnson).

I. i. 104. *'Any abortive,'* the reading of the Quartos and Folios; probably an error for 'an' as corrected by Pope.

I. i. 106. *'shows'*; Theobald substituted *'earth'* for the sake of the rhyme; Walker proposed *'mirth.'* Malone supposes a line to be lost after line 104.

I. i. 108-109. *'So you to study . . . little gate'*; this is one of the instances where the reading of the first Quarto is better than that of the Folio:—

'So you to studie now it is too late,
That were to clymbe ore the house to unlocke the gate.'

Various emendations have been proposed; the only real difficulty is in the loose use of the word 'so.' Biron says that he likes of each thing that in season grows; 'so' presupposes, however, some statement to this effect; 'to wish for, or to do, a thing out of season is huge folly'; (*so* you, now that it is too late to study, climb o'er the house, &c.).

I. i. 184. *'Tharborough'*; the reading of the Quarto *'farborough'* probably gives us Dull's actual pronunciation of his office.

I. i. 193. *'heaven,'* so Quartos and Folios. Theobald proposed *'having'*; whatever may be the exact force of the phrase, it seems most probable that *'heaven'* is the right word, and no emendation is necessary.

I. ii. 85. *'A green wit'*; a probable allusion, according to the Cambridge editors, to the 'green withes' with which Samson was bound (*cp.* note *supra* on pronunciation of 'Moth').

I. ii. 103, 104. The ballad of *King Cophetua and the Beggar-Maid* may be found in Percy's *Reliques.*

II. i. 45. *'Well fitted in arts'*; the second Folio inserts 'the,' omitted in the earlier editions.

II. i. 113-127. The speakers in Quarto 1 are 'Berowne' and 'Katharine.'

II. i. 128. Shakespeare may have got a hint for this passage from Monstrelet's *Chronicles*, according to which Charles, King of Navarre, surrendered to the King of France the castle of Cherbourg, the country of Evreux, and other lordships for the Duchy of Nemours and a promise of 200,000 gold crowns (*vide Shakespeare's Library*, ed. Hazlitt, Part I. Vol. i.).

II. i. 237. *'Impatient to speak and not see,'* i.e., 'not able to endure merely the faculty of speech without that of sight.'

III. i. 16, 17. "It was a common trick among some of the most indolent of the ancient masters, to place the hands in the bosom or the pockets, or conceal them in some part of the drapery, to avoid the labour of representing them, or to disguise their own want of skill to employ them with grace and propriety" (Steevens).

IV. i. 1-4. These lines, as Spedding pointed out, were most probably introduced in the corrected copy. "It was thus that Shakespeare learnt to shade off his scenes, to carry the action beyond the stage."

IV. i. 138. *'Armado o' th' one side'*; the reading is due to Rowe; the first Quarto has *'Armatho ath toothen side,'* and the Folio *'Armathor ath to the side.'* Possibly the whole passage from 'O my troth . . . nit' should have been printed in the previous scene, after line 136, and some editors make the transposition.

IV. ii. 42. *'The allusion holds in the exchange,'* i.e., 'the riddle is as good when I use the name of Adam as when I use the name of Cain.'

IV. ii. 60. *'one sorel'*; the first Quarto has *'o sorell,'* and the Folios *'O sorell'*; Capell proposed *'O sore L,'* which is generally adopted.

IV. ii. 95, 96. The first Quarto and Folio give the following reading:—

'Vermiche, vencha, que non te vnde, que non te perreche';

the reading adopted by the Cambridge editors is from Florio's *Second Frutes* (1591), whence Shakespeare probably took it.

IV. ii. 117. *'apostrophas'*; this is taken by some editors to refer to the apostrophes in *vow'd* and *bow'd* (ll. 104, 106), and the words are accordingly printed *'vowed'* and *'bowed'*; this interpretation seems unsatisfactory, but so far nothing better has been advanced. Does not Holofernes' criticism bear directly on the last line of the canzonet? Nathaniel should have read:—

'That singës heaven's praise with such an earthly tongue.'

It was usual to mark *es* with two dots when sounded: Holofernes may mean by *'apostrophas,' 'diæreses.'* The poem is printed with a few variant readings (*e.g.* 'to sing') in the *Passionate Pilgrim*, where also are found ll. 57-70 and ll. 98-117 of the next scene, also with some interesting points of difference.

IV. iii. 105. *'Wish,'* so the Quartos and first Folio; in the *Passionate Pilgrim* 'wish'd'; similarly in the line 109 'thorn' is due to the version printed in *England's Helicon;* the other editions read *'throne.'* Rowe first proposed the change.

IV. iii. 139. The second Folio omits *one.* Walker's suggestion *'One's'* makes the line rhythmic.

IV. iii. 143. *'Faith infringed,'* the reading of the Quartos and the Folio; *'faith so infringed'* seems the most satisfactory emendation proposed.

IV. iii. 163. '*a gnat*,' perhaps alluding to the fact that it sings, as it flies. Biron refers probably to the King's sonnets.

IV. iii. 245. '*wood*'; Quartos and Folios read '*word*.'

IV. iii. 252. '*School of night*'; so the early editions; '*scowl*,' '*stole*,' '*soul*,' '*scroll*,' '*seal*,' '*shade*,' have been proposed by various scholars; possibly, as the Cambridge editors suggest, '*school*' is an error for '*shoote, i.e. suit*.'

V. i. 28, 29. In Quarto and Folio the line reads:—

'*Bome boon for boon priscian*, a little scratcht 'twill serve.'

V. i. 128. Capell proposed '*or*' for '*and*'; the passage is evidently corrupt.

V. ii. 67. '*perttaunt-like*'; this word is the *crux* of the play, the early editions read '*perttaunt-like*' and '*pertaunt-like*.' Theobald reads '*pedant-like*,' and other editors suggest '*portent-like*,' '*pageant-like*,' '*potently*,' '*persuant-like*.' It is perhaps worth while suggesting that the phrase (*tant*) *pour tant* (*quasi* 'tit for tat') perhaps underlies the word: it may well have been used in some game: Mr. Marshall quotes *pur Tant* from a poetical description of an old game, but no explanation has as yet been advanced.

V. ii. 333. '*To show his teeth as white as whale's bone*'; this should certainly be printed *whalës bone*, the regular name for walrus tusk in old English.

V. ii. 339. '*Madman*,' obviously an error for '*man*'; '*mad*' probably due to '*madam*' in the next line.

V. ii. 564, 565. According to Plutarch, Alexander's head had a twist towards the left; he states also that Alexander's skin had "a marvellous good savour."

V. ii. 587. '*Canis*'; '*canus*' in the old editions, required for the sake of the rhyme.

V. ii. 734, 735. The meaning of these somewhat obscure lines seems to be that 'the latest minute of the hour often fashions or moulds all causes or questions to the purposes of his speed, that is, to his own intents'; "the extreme parts are the end parts, '*extremities*'—as, of our body, fingers; of chains, the final links; of given portions of time, the last of those units into which we choose to divide them." Observe '*forms*' for '*form*' by attraction of '*time*.' In the next lines the metaphor is derived from archery.

V. ii. 746. '*Double*'; so Quartos and Folios; many modern editors adopt '*dull*' from the Collier MS.

V. ii. 757. '*Strange*'; the Quartos and Folios read '*straying*,' probably merely a variant spelling of '*strange*.'

V. ii. 769. '*Jack hath not Jill*,' *cp.* *Midsummer-Night's Dream*, III. ii. 462:—

"*Jack shall have Jill:*
Nought shall go ill:
The man shall have his mare again, and all shall be well."

THE TRAGEDY OF ROMEO AND JULIET

PROLOGUE, omitted in Folios.

I. i. 21. '*cruel*'; so Quartos 4, 5; Quartos 2, 3, Folios read '*ciuil*,' and '*civil*.'

I. i. 97. '*father*'; so Quartos 2, 4; Quarto 5, '*further*'; Quarto 3, Folios 1, 2, 3, '*Fathers*'; Folio 4, '*Father's*.'

I. i. 116. '*drave me to walk abroad*'; Pope (from Quarto 1), '*drew me from company*'; Theobald, '*drew me to walk abroad*.'

I. i. 123. '*Which then most sought where most might not be found*'; Pope (from Quarto 1), '*That most are busied, when they 're most alone*'; Keightley, '*Which there . . .* ,' &c. Herr conjectured '*Which then most sought where many . . .*'; Allen conjectured '*which then most sought where more . . .*'

I. i. 149. '*sun*'; Theobald's emendation of Quartos and Folios, '*same*.'

I. i. 168. '*see pathways to his will*'; Staunton conjectured '*set pathways to our will*'; Hanmer, '*. . . ill*.'

I. i. 181. '*Why such is*'; Seymour conjectured '*Why such is, merely*'; Collier MS., '*Why such, Benvolio, is*'; Mommsen conjectured '*Why, such, Benvolio, such is*'; Keightley, '*Why, gentle cousin, such is*'; Orger conjectured '*Why, such a love is*.'

I. i. 186. '*raised*'; Pope's correction (from Quarto 1); Quartos, Folios, '*made*.'

I. i. 198. '*Bid a sick man in sadness make*'; so (Quarto 1) Quartos 4, 5; Quartos 2, 3, Folio 1, read '*A sicke man in sadnesse makes*'; Folios 2, 3, 4, '*A sicke man in good sadnesse makes*.'

I. i. 207. '*From love's weak childish bow she lives unharm'd*'; Grant White conjectured '*Gainst . . . encharm'd*'; Quartos, Folios, '*vncharmd*'; Collier MS., '*encharm'd*.'

I. i. 212. '*with beauty dies her store*'; Theobald reads '*with her dies Beauty's Store*'; Keightley, '*with her dies beauty store*.'

I. ii. 15. '*She is the hopeful lady of my earth*'; Johnson conjectured '*She is the hope and stay of my full years*.'

I. ii. 25. '*made dark heaven light*'; Theobald reads '*make dark heaven's light*'; Warburton, '*make dark even light*'; Jackson conjectured '*mask dark heaven's light*'; Daniel conjectured '*mock dark heaven's light*.'

I. ii. 26. '*young men*'; Johnson conjectured '*yeomen*.'

I. ii. 32. '*Which on more view*,' &c.; so Quartos 4, 5; Quartos 2, 3, Folios, '*one*' for '*on*'; (Quarto 1) '*Such, amongst view of many myne being one*'; perhaps we should read with Mason, '*Whilst on more view of many, mine being one*'; many readings have been proposed.

I. iii. 34. '*Shake, quoth the dove-house*,' referring to the effects of the earthquake; Daniel conjectured '*goeth*' for '*quoth*.'

I. iii. 67, 68. '*honour*'; Pope's emendation (from Quarto 1); Quartos, Folios, '*houre*' and '*hour*.'

I. iv. 39. '*The game was ne'er so fair, and I am done*'; "an allusion to an old proverbial saying which advises to give over when the game is at the fairest" (Ritson).

I. iv. 41. *Cp.* Chaucer's *Manciple's Prologue*:—

"*Ther gan our hoste for to jape and pleye,*
And seyde, sirs, what!
Dun is in the myre!"

A proverbial expression originally used in an old rural sport, and meaning, "we are all at a standstill!" or, "let us make an effort to move on" (*vide* Prof. Skeat's *Notes to Canterbury Tales*, Vol v. p. 435-6).

I. iv. 42. '*Of this sir-reverence love*'; Singer's emendation (from Quarto 1); Quartos read '*Or saue you reuerence loue*'; Folios 1, 2, 3, '*Or saue your reuerence loue*.'

I. iv. 45. Capell's emendation; (Quarto 1) reads '*We burne our lights by night, like Lampes by day*'; Quartos, '*We waste our lights in vaine, lights lights by day*'; Folios, '*We wast our lights in vaine, lights, lights, by day*.'

I. iv. 66. '*Maid*'; Pope's reading (from Quarto 1); Quartos, Folio 1, '*man*'; Folios 2, 3, 4, '*woman*'; Ulrici (from Collier MS.), '*milk-maid*.'

I. iv. 77. '*Courtier's*'; Pope (from Quarto 1) reads '*lawyer's*'; Theobald conjectured '*taylor's*.'

I. iv. 85. '*Of healths*'; Thrilby conjectured '*Of delves*'; Keightley conjectured '*Trenches*'; Clark MS., '*Of hilts*.'

I. iv. 91. '*Untangled*'; '*which once u.*', the untangling of which.

I. iv. 103. '*Face*'; Pope's reading (from Quarto 1); Quartos, Folios, '*side*'; Collier MS., '*tide*.'

I. v. 16. '*Will have a bout*'; (Quarto 1); '*will haue about*'; Quartos, Folios, '*will walke about*'; Pope, '*we'll have a bout*; Daniel, '*will walke a bout*.'

I. v. 44. '*It seems she*'; so (Quarto 1); Quartos, Folio 1; Folios 2, 3, 4, read '*Her beauty*'; Bulloch conjectured '*In streams she*'; &c.

II. i. 10. '*pronounce*'; Quartos 2, 3, '*prouaunt*'; Folio 1, '*Prouant*'; Folios 2, 3, 4, '*Couply*'; Rowe, '*couple*.'

II. i. 13. 'trim,' Steevens (from Quarto 1); Quartos, Folios, 'true.'

II. i. 13. 'Young Adam Cupid, he that shot so trim'; all the early editions read 'Abraham Cupid'; Theobald conjectured 'auborn'; Upton, 'Adam,' referring to Adam Bell, the famous archer. It must be borne in mind, however, that 'Abram,' 'Abraham,' was a regular corrupt form of auburn, formerly often written abern, abron.

II. ii. 41-42. 'nor any other part Belonging to a man. O, be some other name!' Malone's emendation; Pope (from Quarto 1) reads 'nor any other part'; Quartos, Folios, 'O be some other name Belonging to a man.'

II. ii. 44. 'name,' so Pope (from Quarto 1); Quartos, Folios, 'word.'

II. ii. 61. 'fair maid, if either thee dislike'; so Quartos, Folios; Pope (from Quarto 1) reads 'fair saint . . . displease'; Theobald, 'fair saint . . . dislike'; Grant White, 'fair maid . . . displease'; Anon. conjectured 'fair maid . . . mislike.'

II. ii. 107. 'blessed moon I swear'; so (Quarto 1) Quartos; Folios read 'moon I vow.'

II. ii. 153. 'suit'; so Quarto 5; Quarto 4, 'sute'; Quartos 2, 3, Folios, 'strife.'

II. ii. 190. 'father's cell'; Capell's reading (from Quarto 1); Quartos, Folios 3, 4, 'Friers close cell'; Folios 1, 2, 'Fries close cell.'

II. iii. 1-4. Omitted in Folios 2, 3, 4.

II. iii. 4. 'day's path and Titan's fiery wheels'; Malone's reading (from Quarto 1); Quartos, Folio 1, 'day's path, and Titans burning wheels'; Pope, 'day's pathway, made by Titan's wheels.'

II. iii. 23. 'small,' so Pope (from Quarto 1); Quartos, Folios, 'weake.'

II. iv. 149, 150. 'I am none of his skains-mates'; 'skains-mates' occurs nowhere else, its origin is uncertain; it is perhaps connected with skein, skein, 'as if associated in winding yarns' (or skain's = gen. of skain, skean = dagger; 'as if a brother in arms').

II. vi. 34. 'sum up sum of half my'; so Quartos 2, 3; Quartos 4, 5, 'summe up some of halfe my'; Folios, 'sum up some of halfe my,' &c.

III. i. 114. 'kinsman,' Capell's reading (from Quarto 1); Quarto 5, other texts, 'cousin.'

III. i. 167. 'agile'; (Quarto 1) Quartos 4, 5, 'agill'; Quartos 2, 3, Folio 1, 'aged'; Folios 2, 3, 4, 'able.'

III. i. 190. 'hate's'; Knight's emendation; Quartos, Folios, read 'hearts'; Hanmer, 'heats' '; Johnson, 'hearts'.'

III. ii. 6. 'That runaways' eyes may wink'; an epitome of the various interpretations of these words filling no less than twenty-eight pages of Furness' variorum edition; the Quartos and Folios do not mark the possessive, and scholars are divided on the subject of the singular or plural possessive. The Cambridge editors evidently make 'runaways' = runagates, night-prowlers. The present editor cannot bring himself to believe that Shakespeare intended this reading, and would fain substitute 'Runaway's' in the sense of 'Day's'; 'Runaway' may have belonged to the playful phraseology of Elizabethan girls, and savours of the expressive language of children's rhymes.

III. ii. 66. 'dear-loved'; Pope's reading (from Quarto 1); Quartos, Folios, read 'dearest.'

III. ii. 76. 'Dove-feather'd raven'; Theobald's emendation of Quartos 2, 3, Folio 1, 'Rauenous douefeathered Rauen'; Quartos 4, 5, Folios 2, 3, 4, 'Rauenous doue, feathred Rauen.'

III. ii. 79. 'damned saint'; so Quartos 4, 5, Folios 2, 3, 4; Quartos 2, 3, 'dimme saint'; Folio 1, 'dimne saint.'

III. iii. 52. 'Thou fond mad man, hear me but speak a word'; Malone's emendation (from Quarto 1); Quartos 2, 3, 'Then fond mad man, heare me a little speake'; Quartos 4, 5, 'Thou fond mad man, heare me a little speake'; Folio 1, 'Then fond mad man, heare me speake'; Folios 2, 3, 4, 'Fond mad man, heare me speake.'

III. v. 31. According to Warburton there is a popular saying to this effect, due to the fact that the toad has very fine eyes and the lark very ugly ones.

III. v. 55. 'below'; Pope's reading (from Quarto 1); Quartos, Folios, 'so lowe.'

III. v. 152. Omitted in Folios.

III. v. 166. 'lent'; Pope (from Quarto 1) reads 'sent'; Cowden Clarke conjectured 'left.'

III. v. 177-179. So Quarto 2 and the other Quartos; Quarto 1 reads:—

> "Gods blessed mother wife it mads me,
> Day, night, early, late, at home, abroad.
> Alone, in company, waking or sleeping,
> Still my care hath been to see her matcht."

Many attempts have been made to smooth the lines, but perhaps they express Capulet's excitement.

III. v. 182. 'train'd'; Capell's reading (from Quarto 1); Quartos 3, 4, 5, Folios 'allied'; Quarto 2, 'liand'; &c.

IV. i. 3. 'nothing slow to slack his haste'; Collier conjectured 'something slow,' &c.; Quarto 1, 'nothing slack to slow his haste'; Johnson conjectured 'nothing slow to back his haste.'

IV. i. 16. Omitted in Quartos, Folios.

IV. i. 45. 'cure,' so (Quarto 1) Quarto 5; Quartos 2, 3, 4, Folios, 'care.'

IV. i. 115-116. 'and he and I Will watch thy waking'; the reading of Quartos 3, 4, 5; omitted in Folios.

IV. v. 104-105. 'O play me some merry dump, to comfort me'; the reading of Quartos; omitted in Folios.

IV. v. 122-124. These lines are from Richard Edwards' Paradise of Dainty Devises, 1576.

V. i. 1. 'flattering truth'; so Quartos, Folios; Malone following (Quarto 1) reads 'flattering eye'; Collier MS., 'flattering death'; Grant White, 'flattering sooth'; &c.

V. i. 24. 'I defy you'; Pope's reading; (Quarto 1), 'I defie my'; Quartos 2, 3, 4, Folio 1, 'I denie you'; Folios 2, 3, 4, Quarto 5, 'I deny you.'

V. i. 27. 'I do beseech you, sir, have patience'; Pope (from Quarto 1) reads 'Pardon me sir, I dare not leave you thus'; Steevens (1793) reads 'Pardon me, sir, I will not leave you thus.'

V. iii. 122. 'Stumbled at graves,' &c:—

> 'For many men that stumble at the threshold
> Are well foretold that danger lurks within';
> 3 Henry VI., IV. vii. 11, 12

V. iii. 170. 'rust'; so Quartos, Folios; Hazlitt (from Quarto 1) reads 'rest.'

V. iii. 206. 'it,' i.e. the dagger; so Quarto 2; the rest read 'is.'

—— 'mis-sheathed'; the reading of Folio 4; Folios 1, 2, 3, Quarto 5, 'misheathed'; Quarto 3, 4, 'missheath'd'; Jackson conjectured 'mi-sheath'd.'

V. iii. 212. After this line (Quarto 1) reads 'and young Benvolio is deceased too.'

THE TRAGEDY OF KING RICHARD II

I. i. 1. 'Old John of Gaunt'; Gaunt was only fifty-eight years old at the time when the play opens, but Shakespeare refers to him throughout as an old man.

I. i. 20. 'Many years of happy days befal'; Pope suggested 'May many'; Tate, 'Now many'; Collier, 'Full many'; others suggest that 'years' is to be read as a dissyllable. No change is necessary; the emphatic monosyllabic foot at the beginning of the speech is not very remarkable, and may easily be paralleled.

I. i. 65. 'inhabitable'; Theobald suggested 'unhabitable.'

I. i. 77. 'What I have spoke, or thou canst worse deuise; this is the reading of Quarto 1; Quarto 2, 'spoke, or thou canst deuise'; Quartos 3, 4, 'spoke, or what thou canst deuise'; Folios and Quarto 5, 'spoken, or thou canst deuise'; Hanmer conjectured, 'spoke, as what thou hast devised.'

I. i. 95. 'for these eighteen years'; since the insurrection of Wat Tyler, in 1381.

I. i. 189. 'beggar-fear'; so Quartos 1, 5, and Folios 1, 2; Quartos 2, 3, 4, 'beggar-face'; Folios 3, 4, 'beggar'd fear'; Hanmer proposed 'haggard fear'; others have suggested, 'bugbear fear'; 'bug-bear-face'; 'stagger'd fear.'

I. i. 199. 'Saint Lambert's day'; thus Quartos 1, 5, and Folios; Quartos 2, 3, 4, 'St Lambards Day.' This was September 17th.

I. i. 204. 'Lord marshal'; Norfolk was himself Earl Marshal of England; this was therefore a deputy appointed for the occasion: Holinshed tells us that he was Thomas Holland, Duke of Surrey. Capell suggested 'Marshal' for 'Lord Marshal' in order to normalise the scansion of the line: otherwise 'marshal' must be taken as equivalent to a monosyllable, or a monosyllable with an unessential extra syllable before a pause.

I. ii. 1. 'Woodstock's blood'; thus Quartos 1, 2, 3, 4; Folios 1, 2, 3, read 'Gloursters'; Folio 4 and Quarto 5, 'Glosters.' The Duke of Gloucester was also called Thomas of Woodstock.

I. ii. 47. 'sit'; so the Folios and Quarto 5; Quartos 1, 2, 3, 4, 'set.'

I. ii. 66. 'Plashy'; the seat of Thomas of Woodstock, as Lord High Constable, near Dunmow, in Essex.

I. ii. 70. 'hear there'; so Quarto 2; Quarto 1 reads 'cheere there.'

I. iii. 20. 'and my succeeding issue'; so Quartos 1, 2, 3, 4; the Folios and Quarto 5, 'and his succeeding issue.'

I. iii. 43. 'daring-hardy'; Theobald's emendation of the Quartos and Folios; Quarto 1, 'daring, hardy'; Quartos 2, 3, 4, 'daring hardie'; Folios 1, 2, 'daring hardie'; Quarto 5 and Folios 3, 4, 'daring hardy.'

I. iii. 58. 'thee dead'; Quartos 1, 2, 'the dead.'

I. iii. 67, 68. 'at English feasts, . . . The daintiest last'; referring to the English custom of having sweets as the last course at a dinner.

I. iii. 84. 'innocency'; the Quartos and Folios, 'innocence,' changed by Capell to 'innocency.'

I. iii. 128. 'Of civil wounds plough'd up with neighbours' sword'; Quarto 1, 'cruell' for 'civil'; Quartos 1, 2, 3, 4, 'sword'; the Folios and Quarto 5, 'swords'; Theobald conjectured 'neighbour' for 'neighbours'.'

I. iii. 136. 'wrathful iron arms'; Quarto 1 reads 'harsh resounding arms.'

I. iii. 138. 'kindred's'; Quartos 1, 2, read 'kinreds.'

I. iii. 140. 'upon pain of life'; the reading of Quartos 1, 2, 3, 4; the Folios and Quarto 5, 'upon pain of death.'

I. iii. 193. 'so far'; the Quartos and Folio 1, 'so fare'; Folios 2, 3, and Quarto 5, 'so farre'; Folio 4, 'so far.'

I. iii. 276. 'wise man'; written as one word in the first two Quartos, and evidently pronounced with the accent on the first syllable.

I. iv. 23. 'Bagot here and Green'; omitted in Quartos 1, 2, 3, 4; inserted in the Folios and Quarto 5.

I. iv. 58. 'Ely House'; the Bishop of Ely's palace in Holborn. 'Ely-Place' marks its site.

II. i. 18. 'of whose taste the wise are fond'; Quarto 1 reads 'of whose taste the wise are fond'; Quarto 2, 'of whose state the wise are found'; Quartos 3, 4, 5 and Folios read 'of his state: then there are found'; Folio 1, 'sound'; the reading in the text was first suggested by Collier.

II. i. 40-55. 'This royal throne . . . Jewry'; with the exception of line 50, this passage is quoted more or less correctly in England's Parnassus (1600), but is attributed by mistake to Michael Drayton.

II. i. 73-83. These famous lines suggest comparison with the word play of Ajax upon his name in Sophocles' drama.

II. i. 102. 'incaged'; the reading of Folios 1, 2; Quartos 1, 2, 3, 4 read 'inraged'; Quarto 5 reads 'encaged'; Folios 3, 4 read 'ingaged.'

II. i. 113. 'thou now, not king'; Theobald's emendation of the Quartos and Folios; Quartos 1, 2, 3 read 'thou now not, not king'; Quarto 4 reads 'thou now not, nor king'; the Folios and Quarto 5 read 'thou and not king.'

II. i. 115. 'And thou'— King Richard. 'A lunatic,' &c. Quarto 1, 'And thou.' King. 'A lunatike'; Quarto 2, 'And thou.' King. 'A lunatick'; Quartos 3, 4 read 'And thou.' King 'Ah lunaticke'; the Folios and Quarto 5, 'And—' Rich. 'And thou, a lunaticke'; Warburton, 'And thou—' K. Rich. 'And thou, a lunatick.'

II. i. 246. ''Gainst us, our lives'; Vaughan conjectured 'Against ourselves'; Collier MS., ''Gainst us, our wives.'

II. i. 248. Pope proposed the omission of 'quite' in order to improve the scansion of the line. It has been suggested that Shakespeare may have written 'The gentlemen and nobles hath he fined.' Sidney Walker rearranged the passage thus:—

'The commons hath he pill'd
With grievous taxes, and quite lost their hearts;
The nobles hath he fined for ancient quarrels.'

The text as it stands is better than the readings which result from these emendations.

II. i. 253. 'Wars have,' &c.; Rowe's emendation; Quartos 1, 2, and the Folios read 'Wars hath,' &c.; Capell conjectured 'War hath,' &c.

II. i. 254. "The allusion here is to the treaty which Richard made with Charles VI. of France in the year 1393."

II. i. 255. The Folios omit 'noble' but there are many similar quasi-Alexandrines in the play.

II. i. 277. 'Then thus: I have from le Port Blanc.' The first Quarto reads:—

'Then thus, I have from le Port Blan
A Bay in Brittaine,' &c.

Dr. Wright notes that as the Quartos have 'le Port Blan,' and Holinshed 'le Porte Blanc,' he adopts the reading 'le Port Blanc,' which is the name of a small port in the department of Côtes du Nord, near Tréguier.

II. i. 279. Malone, having Holinshed before him, assumed that a line has been lost, and introduced the following words after 'Cobham':—

'The son of Richard Earl of Arundel.'

II. i. 282. 'Sir John Ramston'; according to Holinshed 'Sir Thomas,' not 'Sir John.'

II. i. 283. 'Quoint'; Quartos 1, 2, 3, 4 read 'Coines.'

II. ii. 18. 'perspectives'; "at the right Honourable the Lord Gerards at Gerards Bromley, there are the pictures of Henry the Great of France and his Queen, both upon the same indented board, which if beheld directly, you only perceive a confused piece of work; but, if obliquely, of one side you see the King's, and on the other the Queen's picture"; Plot's Natural History of Staffordshire (quoted by Staunton).

II. ii. 31. 'though'; Quarto 1 reads 'thought'; 'on thinking on'; Folios 3, 4 read 'one thinking, on'; Collier MS., 'unthinking on'; 'no thought'; Lettsom conjectured 'no thing.'

II. ii. 57. 'all the rest'; the reading of Quarto 1; Quartos 2, 3, 4, 5 and Folios 1, 2 read 'the rest of the'; Folios 3, 4, 'the rest of that'; Pope, 'all of that,' 'revolt'; Quartos 3, 4 read 'revolting'; 'faction'; Daniel conjectured 'factious.'

II. ii. 58. 'The Earl of Worcester'; Thomas Percy, Steward of the King's household: he was brother to the Earl of Northumberland.

II. iii. 9. 'Cotswold'; Quartos 1, 2, 3, 4 read 'Cotshall'; the Folios and Quarto 5 read 'Coltshold.'

II. iii. 100. The Clarendon Press editors suggest that this passage bears considerable resemblance to the speech of Nestor (Iliad, vii. 157). (Hall's translation of Homer was published in 1581.)

II. iii. 164. 'Bristol'; the reading of Quarto 5; all the rest Quartos and Folios 'Bristow.'

III. ii. 1. 'Barkloughly'; the name was derived from Holinshed, where it was undoubtedly a copyist's or printer's error for 'Hertlowli,' i.e. Harlech.

III. ii. 14. Alluding to the old idea that spiders were venomous.

III. ii. 40. 'boldly'; Collier's conjecture; Quarto 1, 'bouldly'; Quarto 2, 'bloudy'; Quartos 3, 4, 5, and Folios, 'bloody.'

III. ii. 156. 'sad stories of the death of kings'; Shakespeare was probably thinking of the Mirror for Magistrates with its 'tragedies' of English princes, Richard among the earliest of them.

III. ii. 160-163. Douce plausibly suggested that this image was suggested to Shakespeare by the seventh print in the *Imagines Mortis*, where "*a King is represented sitting on his throne, sword in hand, with courtiers round him, while from his crown rises a grinning skeleton.*"

III. iii. 105. '*the honourable tomb*'; the tomb of Edward III. in Westminster Abbey.

III. iv. 11. '*joy*'; Rowe's emendation; Quarto and Folios, '*griefe.*'

III. iv. 22. '*And I could sing*'; Pope's emendation; '*weep*,' has been generally adopted, but the Cambridge editors adhere to the reading of the Quartos and Folios. They explain that "the Queen speaks with an emphasis on '*sing*.' 'And I could even sing for joy if thy troubles were only such as weeping could alleviate, and then I could not ask you weep for me.' "

IV. i. 55. '*sun to sun*'; Capell's emendation of '*sinne to sinne*' of the Quartos.

IV. i. 148. '*Prevent it, resist it*'; Pope proposed '*prevent, resist it*'; others scan '*resist*' by apocope ('*sist*'); the natural movement of the line suggests:—

'*prevént it, | resist it, | —lét | it nót | be so.*'

IV. i. 154-318. This part of the 'deposition scene' appeared for the first time in the Quarto of 1608. In the earlier editions line 319 reads: '*Let it be so, and lo on Wednesday next We solemnly proclaim.*'

IV. i. 215. '*that swear*'; *i.e.* 'of those that swear'; Folios and Quarto 5, '*are made.*'

IV. i. 270. '*torment'st*'; Rowe's emendation of Quartos 3, 4, 5 and Folios, '*torments.*'

IV. i. 281-288. A reminiscence of Marlowe's famous lines in Faustus: '*Was this the face that launch'd a thousand ships,*' &c.

V. i. 88. '*Better far off than near, be ne'er the near,*' *i.e.* 'better to be far apart than to be near, and yet never the nearer.'

V. iii. 43. '*secure, foolhardy king*'; Quartos, '*secure foole hardy king*'; Folio 4, '*secure foul-hardy king.*'

V. iii. 88. '*Love loving not itself,*' &c.; *i.e.* 'love which is indifferent to the claims of kindred can be loving to none.'

V. iii. 144. The reading of Quarto 5; the other editions omit '*too.*'

V. v. 9. '*this little world*'; alluding to the conception of man as a 'microcosm,' *i.e.* 'an abstract or model of the world.'

V. v. 31. '*person*'; so Quarto 1; the rest '*prison.*'

A MIDSUMMER-NIGHT'S DREAM

I. i. 10. '*new-bent*'; Rowe's correction of '*now bent,*' the reading of the Quartos and Folios.

I. i. 11. '*Philostrate*' is the name assumed by Arcite in Chaucer's *Knight's Tale;* it occurs too in Plutarch's *Lives*, where are to be found also the names, Lysander, and Demetrius.

I. i. 27. The second Folio reads, '*this hath bewitched*'; the earlier edition '*this man*'; perhaps we should read '*this man hath 'witched.*'

I. i. 44. '*our law*'; Solon's laws gave a father the power of life and death over his child.

I. i. 159, 160. These lines should perhaps be transposed.

I. i. 167. '*to do observance to a morn of May,*' *cp. Knight's Tale*, 1500; '*And for to doon his observance to May.*'

I. i. 219. '*stranger companies*'; Theobald's emendation of '*strange companions,*' which is the reading of the Quartos and Folios.

I. ii. 11. '*The most lamentable comedy,*' &c. *Cp.* the title of Preston's *Cambyses*, '*a lamentable tragedy mixed full of pleasant mirth*'; &c.

I. ii. 48. '*Thisne, Thisne,*' so the Quartos and Folios: perhaps this spelling was intentional to represent Bottom's attempt to speak the name 'in a monstrous little voice.' The words may, however, be an error for '*thisne, thisne,*' *i.e.* 'in this manner, in this manner,' '*thissen*' being used in this sense in various dialects.

II. i. 54, 55. The Quartos and Folios read '*coffe . . . loffe,*' for the sake of the rhyme.

II. i. 58. '*room*'; probably pronounced as a dissyllable.

II. i. 78. '*Perigenia,*' called '*Perigouna*' in North's *Plutarch;* she was the daughter of the famous robber Sinnis, by whom Theseus had a son, Menaloppus.

II. i. 79. '*Ægle*'; Rowe's correction for '*Eagles*' of the Quartos and Folios; probably '*Eagles*' was for '*Ægles,*' a form due to North's *Plutarch*, where it is stated that some think Theseus left Ariadne "because he was in love with another, as by these verses should appear,

'*Ægles the nymph was lov'd of Theseus,
Who was the daughter of Panopeus.*' "

II. i. 80. '*Antiopa,*' said to be the name of the Amazon queen, and the mother of Hippolytus.

II. i. 231. '*Daphne holds the chase*'; the story tells how Apollo pursued Daphne, who was changed into a laurel-tree as he reached her.

III. i. 35-45. This was probably suggested by an actual incident which occurred during the Kenilworth festivities, when one Harry Goldingham, who was to represent Arion upon the Dolphin's back, tore off his disguise and swore he was none of Arion (*cp.* Scott's use of this story in *Kenilworth*).

III. i. 179. '*Squash,*' *i.e.* an unripe peascod.

III. ii. 36. '*latch'd*'; the word '*latch*' in this passage, as Prof. Skeat has pointed out, is not connected with the ordinary '*latch,*' 'to catch,' but is etymologically the casual form of '*leak,*' and means 'to cause to drop, to drip.'

III. ii. 119. '*sport alone,*' *i.e.* 'by itself, without anything else'; others render 'alone' by 'above all things, without a parallel.'

III. ii. 188. '*oes*'; *o* was used for anything round, among other things for circular discs of metal used for ornaments, *cp.* Bacon, Essay xxxvii.: "And Oes, and Spangs, as they are of no great cost, so they are of most glory."

III. ii. 204. '*needles,*' a monosyllable; '*needle*' was often spelt '*neeld*' in Old English.

III. ii. 212-214. "Helena says, 'we had two seeming bodies but one heart.' She then exemplifies her position by a simile—'we had two of the first, *i.e.* bodies, like the double coats in heraldry that belong to man and wife as one person, but which, like our single heart, have but one crest.' "

III. ii. 257. '*No no; he'll . . . seem*'; the first Quarto '*heele seem*'; the second '*hee'l seem*'; the first Folio '*No, no, Sir, seem.*' The passage is clearly corrupt in the old editions. I am inclined to accept Mr. Orson's ingenious suggestion:—

"*No no, sir; still
Seeme to breake loose,*"

'*heele*' being an easy misreading of '*stille.*'

IV. i. 28. '*a reasonable good ear in music*'; weavers were supposed to be fond of music, more especially of psalm-singing; *cp.* 1 *Henry IV.*, II. iv. 130, 131. '*I would I were a weaver, I could sing psalms.*'

IV. i. 41. '*So doth the woodbine the sweet honeysuckle*'; commonly '*woodbine*' is identical with '*honeysuckle,*' but it is also used by Elizabethans for 'convolvulus' and 'ivy.' Shakespeare, however, uses the word in two other passages (II. i. 251 and *Much Ado*, III. i. 30) in the sense of 'honeysuckle'; hence Warburton suggested:—

"*So doth the woodbine, the sweet honeysuckle,
Gently entwist the maple, ivy so,*" &c.

Johnson thought that '*woodbine*' was the plant, and '*honeysuckle*' the flower. These suggestions are not satisfactory: the simplest way out of the difficulty is to take '*woodbine*' as

[1455]

equivalent to 'convolvulus' or 'bindweed'; *cp.* Ben Jonson's *Vision of Delight*:—

> "*behold!*
> *How the blue bindweed doth itself unfold*
> *With honeysuckle.*"

IV. i. 72. '*Dian's bud*'; it has been thought that perhaps '*Dian's bud*' = 'Diana's rose,' 'the rose of England's Virgin Queen'; '*Diana's Rose*' is actually used in this complimentary sense in Greene's *Friar Bacon*.

IV. i. 82. '*Than common sleep*,' &c.; the Quartos and first two Folios read '*sleepe: of all these, fine the sense*'; the correction is Theobald's.

IV. i. 90. '*prosperity*'; so the first Quarto; the second and Folios '*posterity.*'

IV. i. 116. '*fountains*'; perhaps an error for '*mountains.*'

V. i. 47. '*my kinsman Hercules*'; *cp.* North's *Plutarch, Life of Theseus*: "they (Theseus and Hercules) were near kinsmen, being cousins removed by the mother's side."

V. i. 54. '*critical,*' *i.e.* 'censorious' as in the well-known utterance of Iago, '*I am nothing, if not critical*' (*Othello*, II. i. 119).

V. i. 59. '*wondrous strange snow*'; '*strange*' is hardly the epithet one would expect, and various emendations have been suggested:—'*strange black,*' '*strong snow,*' '*swarthy snow,*' '*sable-snow,*' 'and, *wondrous strange! yet snow.*' Perhaps the most plausible conjecture is Mr. S. W. Orson's '*wondrous flaming snow,*' *cp.* "What strange fits be these, Philautus, that burne thee with such a heat, that thou shakest for cold, and all thy body in a shivering sweat, in a *flaming ice*, melteth like wax and hardeneth like the adamant" (Lyly's *Euphues*, ed. Arber, p. 311).

V. i. 91. '*And what poor duty,*' &c.; Coleridge proposed:—

> "*And what poor duty cannot do, yet would,*
> *Noble respect takes it,*" &c.

The metre is defective as the lines stand. Theobald read '*poor willing duty . . . Noble respect.*' The meaning is sufficiently clear, and recalls *Love's Labour's Lost*, V. ii. 517, '*That sport best pleases that doth least know how,*' &c. *Takes it in might* = regards the ability or effort of the performance.

V. i. 118. '*stand upon points*'; Quince's punctuation reminds one of the reading of Roister Doister's letter to Mistress Constance in the old comedy (*cp. Roister Doister*, iii. 3).

V. i. 138. '*name*'; as there is no rhyme to *name*, the loss of a line is to be inferred, or perhaps we should read '*which by name Lion hight.*'

V. i. 205. '*mural down*'; the Quartos read '*Moon used*'; the Folios '*morall downe*'; the emendation '*mural*' was due to Pope.

V. i. 221. '*a lion-fell*'; the Quartos and Folios read '*a lion fell,*' *i.e.* a fierce lion, but Snug wishes to say 'he is not a lion,' wherefore the words have been hyphened by most modern editors, 'lion-fell,' *i.e.* 'a lion's skin.' Johnson understood '*neither*' before '*a lion fell*'; Rowe read '*No lion fell.*' There is, I think, a more obvious emendation, and I propose:—

> "*Then know that I, one Snug the joiner, n'am*
> *A lion fell, nor else no lions dam,*"

'*n'am*' being an archaic form, like *nill* (*i.e.* ne will). In Gascoigne's *Steele Glas* the following couplet occurs, remarkably suggestive of our text:—

> "*I n'am a man, as some do think I am;*
> (*Laugh not good lord*), *I am indede a dame.*"

V. i. 261, 262. Spedding proposed to invert these lines.

V. i. 265. '*gleams*'; the Quartos and Folio 1 read '*beams*'; Folio 2 '*streams.*'

V. i. 309, 310. '*he for a man—God bless us,*' omitted in the Folios, probably in consequence of the statute of James I. forbidding profane speaking, or use of 'the holy name of God.'

V. i. 312. '*means,*' changed by Theobald to '*moans.*' '*Mean*' n the sense of 'to lament,' an archaic form, is really more correct than 'moan,' and probably intentionally used by Shakespeare to harmonise with the archaisms of the interlude.

V. i. 360. '*behowls*'; Theobald's emendation of '*beholds,*' the reading of the Quartos and Folios.

V. i. 383. '*this ditty*'; Johnson supposes that two songs are lost, one led by Titania, and one by Oberon.

THE LIFE AND DEATH OF KING JOHN

I. i. 20. According to the Cambridge editors the line must probably be scanned as an Alexandrine, reading the first '*controlment*' in the time of a trisyllable and the second as a quadrisyllable. This seems very doubtful; the irregularity of the line is not remarkable; there is merely an extra syllable before the pause:—

> *Contról|ment fór| contrólment || so áns|wer Fránce.|*

I. i. 28. '*sullen presage of your own decay*'; there is perhaps an allusion here to the dismal passing-bell, as Steevens suggested; according to Delius, the trumpet of doom is alluded to. There is, however, no difficulty in the thought as it stands, without these references to a secondary idea.

I. i. 49. '*expedition's*'; first Folio *expeditious*; an obvious misprint.

I. i. 54. '*Cœur-de-lion*'; '*Cordelion*' in the Folios and old play; perhaps the spelling should be kept as the popular form of the name.

'*knighted in the field*'; in '*The Troublesome Reign*' he is knighted at the siege of Acon or Acre, by the title of Sir Robert Fauconbridge of Montbery.

I. i. 85. '*trick*'; it has been suggested that '*trick*' is used here in the heraldic sense of 'copy'; it would seem, however, to be used in a less definite sense.

I. i. 139. '*sir Robert's his,*' so the Folios; Theobald proposed '*sir Robert his,*' regarding '*his*' as the old genitive form; Vaughan '*just sir Robert's shape*'; Schmidt takes the "'*s his*' as a reduplica-

tive possessive. Surely '*his*' is used substantively with that rollicking effect which is so characteristic of Faulconbridge. There is no need to explain the phrase as equivalent to 'his shape, which is also his father Sir Robert's'; 'sir Robert's his' = '*sir Robert's shape,*' '*his*' emphasizing substantively the previous pronominal use of the word.

I. i. 143. '*Look, where three-farthings goes*'; three-farthing pieces of silver were coined in 1561 (discontinued in 1582); they were very thin, and were distinguished from the silver pence by an impression of the queen's profile, with a rose behind her ear

I. i. 147. '*I would not*'; Folio 1 reads '*It would not,*' probably a misprint, though Delius makes '*it*' refer to '*His face.*'

I. i. 234-5. '*eat his part in me upon Good-Friday*'; evidently a popular proverb, *cp.* Heywood's *Dialogue upon Proverbs*:

> "*He may his part on Good Friday eat,*
> *And fast never the wurs for ought he shall geat*" (*i.e.* get).

I. i. 244. '*Knight, knight, good mother, Basilisco-like*'; an allusion to the old play called '*Soliman and Perseda*' (printed 1599, written probably some ten years before); Piston the buffoon, representing the old Vice of the Morality Plays, jumps on the back of Basilisco, the bragging coward, and makes him take oath on his dagger:—

BAS. '*I, the aforesaid Basilisco,—knight, good fellow, knight, knight,—*

PIST. *Knave, good fellow, knave, knave.'*

(*cp.* Dodsley's *Old Plays*, ed. Hazlitt, *Vol. v.* 271-2.)

II. i. 2. *'that great forerunner of thy blood'*; Shakespeare, by some oversight, here makes Arthur directly descended from Richard.

II. i. 5. *'by this brave duke,'* so the old play. Richard was, however, slain by an arrow at the siege of Chaluz, some years after the Duke's death.

II. i. 64. *'her niece, the Lady Blanch of Spain,'* *i.e.* her grand-daughter; Blanch was the daughter of John's sister Eleanor and Alphonso VIII. King of Castile.

II. i. 65. *'of the king's deceased,'* *i.e.* *'of the deceased king'*; Folios 2, 3, 4, *'king'*; but Folio 1, *'kings'* = *'king's'* is idiomatically correct.

II. i. 103. *'huge'*; Rowe read *'large,'* doubtless a misprint for *'huge'* restored by Capell.

II. i. 113. *'breast';* Folio 1, *'beast.'*

II. i. 119. *'Excuse; it is,'* &c.; Malone's correction of the Folios, *'Excuse it is'*; Rowe (ed. 2) *'Excuse it, 'tis.'*

II. i. 137. *'of whom the proverb goes',* *i.e.* *'Mortuo leoni et lepores insultant'*; *cp.* Kyd's *Spanish Tragedy*, *'Hares may pull dead lions by the beard.'*

II. i. 144. *'Great Alcides' shows upon an ass'*; alluding to the skin of the Nemean lion won by Hercules. The Folios read *'shooes'*; the reading of the text was first proposed by Theobald.

II. i. 149. *'King Philip,'* &c.; the line is printed in the Folios as part of Austria's speech, with *'King Lewis'* instead of *'King Philip'*; the error was first corrected by Theobald.

II. i. 152. *'Anjou,'* Theobald's correction of *'Angiers'* of the Folios.

II. i. 156. *'Bretagne'*; Folios 1, 2, *'Britaine'*; Folio 3, *'Britain'*; Folio 4, *'Brittain'*.

II. i. 159. ll. 159 to 197 considered as spurious by Pope.

II. i. 160, 161. *'it,'* old form of possessive, so Folios 2, 3, 4; Folio 1, *'yt . . . it'*; Johnson, *'it' . . . it' '*; Capell, *'it's . . . it's.'* In the Lancashire dialect *'hit'* is still the common form of the possessive, an archaism used here in imitation of the language of the nursery.

II. i. 167. *'whether,'* monosyllabic; Folios 1, 2, 3, *'where'*; Folio 4, *'whe're.'*

II. i. 177. *'this is thy eld'st'*; Capell's emendation of the Folios, *'this is thy eldest'*; Fleay proposed *'this' thy eld'st'*; Ritson, *'thy eld'st,'* omitting *'this is.'*

II. i. 180. *'the canon of the law,'* *cp.* Exodus xx. 5.

II. i. 187. *'And with her plague; her sin his injury,'* &c.; the Folios, *'And with her plague her sin: his injury,'* &c. The punctuation adopted was first proposed by Mr. Roby, who explains the passage thus:—"God hath made her sin and herself to be a plague to this distant child, who is punished for her and with the punishment belonging to her: God has made her sin to be an injury to Arthur, and her injurious deeds to be the executioner to punish her sin: all which (viz., her first sin and her now injurious deeds) are punished in the person of this child."

II. i. 196. *'aim'*; Folio 1, *'ayme'*; Folios 2, 3, 4, *'ay me'*; Rowe conjectured *'amen'*; Moberly, *'hem'*; Jackson, *'shame'*; Johnson, *'j'aime.'*

II. i. 215. *'Confronts your,'* Capell's emendation; Folios 1, 2, *'Comfort yours'*; Folios 3, 4, *'Comfort your'*; Rowe suggested, *'Confront your'*; Collier, *'Come 'fore your.'*

II. i. 217. *'waist'*; Folios 1, 2, 3, *'waste'*; Folio 4, *'waiste'*; *'doth'*; the singular by attraction to the preceding word; Rowe, *'do.'*

II. i. 234. *'Crave,'* so Pope; Folios read *'Craues.'*

II. i. 259. *'roundure,'* so Capell; Folios read *'rounder'*; Singer, *'rondure.'*

II. i. 262. *'rude'*; Williams conjectured *'wide.'*

II. i. 323. *'Dyed'*; Folios 1, 2, 3, *'Dide'*; Folio 4, *'dy'd.'* Pope suggested *'Stain'd'*; Vaughan, *'Dipp'd.'*

II. i. 325. In the Folios *'the first citizen'* is throughout named *'Hubert,'* in all probability owing to the fact that the actor of the part of Hubert also took this minor character of the play.

II. i. 335. *'run,'* so Folios 2, 3, 4; Folio 1, *'rome'*; Malone reads, *'roam'*; Nicholson conjectured, *'foam.'*

II. i. 353. *'fangs,'* Steevens' spelling for *'phangs'* of the Folios.

II. i. 358. *'equal potents'*; Collier reads *'equal potent'*; Delius, *'equal-potents'*; Dyce, *'equal-potent.'*

'fiery kindled,' so Folios 2, 3, 4; Folio 1, *'fierie kindled'*; Pope, *'fiery-kindled'*; Collier (ed. 2), *'fire-ykindled'*; Lettsom conjectures *'fire-enkindled.'*

II. i. 371. *'King'd of our fears'*; the Folios, *'Kings of our fear'*; the excellent emendation adopted in the text was first proposed by Tyrwhitt.

II. i. 378. *'the mutines of Jerusalem,'* *i.e.* the mutineers of Jerusalem, evidently alluding to John of Giscala and Simon bar Gioras, the leaders of the opposing factions, who combined in order to resist the Roman attack. Shakespeare probably derived his knowledge from Peter Morwyng's translation (1558) of the spurious Josephus, the 'joseppon,' as it is called: Josephus was first Englished in 1602.

II. i. 425. *'Dauphin,'* so Rowe; Folios, *'Dolphin'* (*passim*).

II. i. 584. *'aid'*; Collier (ed. 2, Mason's conjecture) *'aim.'*

III. i, 16-17. *'thou didst but jest, With my vex'd spirits,'* &c.; Rowe's emendation of the punctuation of the Folios, *'jest . . . spirits.'*

III. i. 148. *'task,'* Theobald's correction of the Folios; Folios 1, 2, *'tast'*; Folios 3, 4, *'taste'*; Rowe conjectured *'tax.'*

III. i. 210. *'new untrimmed bride'*; so the Folios; Theobald, *'new and trimmed,'* or *'new untamed,'* *'new betrimmed'*; Dyce *'new-uptrimmed.'* Staunton was probably right when he suggested that *'untrimmed'* is descriptive of the bride with her hair hanging loose.

III. i. 260. *'chafed lion'*; Theobald's correction of the Folios, *'cased.'*

III. i. 281-285. In the first Folio the reading is:—

'But thou hast sworn against religion;
By what thou swear'st against the thing thou swear'st,
And mak'st an oath the surety for thy truth,
Against an oath the truth, thou art unsure
To swear, sweares only not to be foresworn.'

In line 281 a plausible emendation is *'swar'st'* (= *'swor'st'*) for the second *'swear'st.'* *'By what'* = *'in so far as'*; lines 281, 282 are evidently parallel in sense; a slight obscurity may perhaps be cleared away by taking the first *'truth'* as used with a suggestion of the secondary meaning *'troth'*: lines 283, 284 are considered the crux of the passage, but possibly all difficulty is removed by placing a semicolon after *'unsure,'* and rendering *'to swear'* with the force of *'if a man swear.'*

III. ii. 4. *'Philip'*; Theobald, *'Richard'*; the error was probably Shakespeare's; *'Philip'* was *'Sir Richard.'*

III. iii. 26. *'time,'* Pope's emendation for *'tune'* of the Folios.

III. iii. 40. *'Sound on into the drowsy ear of night'*; the Folios, *'race'*; Dyce and Staunton, *'ear'*; Bulloch, *'face,'* &c. Theobald suggested *'sound one unto,'* as plausible an emendation as so many of his excellent readings.

III. iii. 53. *'brooded watchful day'*; Pope's *'broad-ey'd,'* Mitford's *'broad and,'* and various emendations have been proposed, but *'brooded'* = *'having a brood to watch over,'* hence *'brooding'* = *'sitting on brood.'*

III. iii. 73. *'attend on you,'* so Folios 1, 2; Folios 3, 4, *'to attend'*; Pope reads *'t' attend.'*

III. iv. 2. *'convicted,'* *i.e.* *'overcome'*; there is perhaps a reference here to the Spanish Armada. Pope proposed *'collected'*; other suggestions have been *'convented,'* *'connected,'* *'combined,'* *'convexed,'* &c.

III. iv. 6. *'Is not Angiers lost?'* &c. Arthur was made prisoner at the capture of Mirabeau in 1202. Angiers was captured by John four years later.

III. iv. 44. *'not holy,'* so Folio 4; Folios 1, 2, 3, *'holy'*; Delius and Staunton (Steevens' conjecture) *'unholy.'*

III. iv. 64. *'friends,'* Rowe's emendation of *'fiends'* of the Folios.

III. iv. 98. *'Then have I reason to be fond of grief,'* Rowe's reading; Folios 1, 2, 3 read *'Then, have I reason to be fond of grief?'*; Folio 4, *'Then . . . grief?'*

III. iv. 110. *'world's taste,'* Pope's emendation of the Folios, *'words taste'*; Jackson's conjecture, *'word, state.'*

III. iv. 182. '*strong actions*,' so Folios 2, 3, 4. Folio 1 misprints '*strange actions*.'

IV. i. 92. '*mote*,' Steevens' emendation for '*moth*' of the Folios, a frequent spelling of the word.

IV. ii. 42. '*then lesser is my fear*,' so Folio 1; '*then*' a common spelling of '*than*' in Elizabethan English; Folios 2, 3, 4, '*then less is my fear*'; Pope, '*the lesser is my fear*.'

IV. ii. 50. '*myself and them*' = (perhaps) '*myself and themselves*'; hence the ungrammatical '*them*.'

IV. ii. 65. '*than whereupon our weal*,' &c. The meaning of the passage seems to be, 'we ask for his liberty only in so far as the commonwealth (*i.e.* '*our weal, on you depending*') counts it your welfare,' &c.

IV. ii. 117. '*care*'; it is impossible to determine whether the first Folio reads '*eare*' or '*care*'; the other Folios '*care*.' There is considerable doubt as to whether the first letter is Roman or Italic, and taking all the evidence into account it seems possible that '*care*' was corrected to '*eare*' in some copies of the first Folio.

IV. ii. 120. '*first of April*'; according to history, Eleanor died in 1204 in the month of July.

IV. ii. 123. '*Three days before*'; Constance died in reality three years, and not three days before, in August, 1201.

IV. ii. 147. '*a prophet*,' *i.e.* Peter of Pomfret (Pontefract).

IV. iii. 11. '*him*' = the Dauphin.

V. i. 8. '*counties*'; it is difficult to determine whether '*counties*' = (i.) 'counts,' *i.e.* 'the nobility,' or (ii.) 'the divisions of the country': probably the former.

V. ii. 1. '*this*,' *i.e.* 'this compact with the English lords.'

V. ii. 27. '*step after a stranger, march*,' so the Folios; Theobald '*stranger march*,' but the original reading seems preferable.

V. ii. 36. '*grapple*,' Pope's emendation of '*cripple*' of the Folios; Steevens conjectured '*gripple*,' Gould '*souple*.'

V. ii. 59. '*Full of warm blood*,' Heath's conjecture for '*Full warm of blood*' of the Folios.

V. ii. 64. '*an angel spake*'; '*angel*' used probably equivocally with a play upon '*angel*' the gold coin, the quibble being suggested by the previous '*purse*,' '*nobles*.'

V. ii. 133. '*unhair'd*,' Theobald's correction of Folios; Folio 1, '*vnheard*'; Folios 2, 3, 4, '*unheard*'; Keightley proposed '*unbeard*.'

V. iii. 8. '*Swinstead*,' so in '*The Troublesome Reign*'; '*Swinstead*' = Swineshead, near Spalding, in Lincolnshire.

V. iv. 15. '*He*,' *i.e.* the Dauphin; perhaps '*lords*' in the previous line is an error for '*lord*.'

V. iv. 24-5. '*even as a form of wax Resolveth from his figure 'gainst the fire*,' alluding to the images of wax used in witchcraft; as the figure melted before the fire, so the person it represented dwindled away.

V. iv. 60. '*Right in thine eye*'; it has been suggested that '*right*' is a misprint for '*riot*'; '*pight*,' '*fight*,' '*fright*.' &c., have been proposed: there is no reason at all for emending the word.

V. vi. 12. '*eyeless night*,' Theobald's emendation of the Folios, '*endles*.'

V. vii. 16. '*Leaves them invisible, and his siege*'; so Folio 1; the other Folios, '*and her siege*'; Pope, '*leaves them; invisible his siege*'; Hanmer, '*leaves them insensible; his siege*'; Steevens, '*invisible*'; &c.

V. vii. 21. '*cygnet*'; Rowe's correction of '*Symet*' of the Folios.

THE MERCHANT OF VENICE

THE name '*Shylock*' may have been derived by Shakespeare from a pamphlet called '*Caleb Shillocke his prophecies, or the Jewes Prediction*'; the Pepysian ballad on this subject belongs to the year 1607; to the same year belongs a prose piece printed at the end of a rare tract called '*A Jewes prophecie, or Newes from Rome of two mighty armies,*' &c. Its ultimate origin is unknown; it may have been an Italian name *Sciolocca*. According to Hunter, *Scialac* was the name of a Maronite of Mount Libanus, who was living in 1614.

I. i. 27. '*dock'd*'; Rowe's emendation for '*docks*,' the reading of the Quartos and Folios.

I. i. 113. '*Is that any thing new?*' The old editions read '*Is that any thing now*,' changed to '*new*' by Johnson. Rowe first suggested the interrogation.

I. ii. 76. '*the Scottish lord*'; in the first Folio '*Scottish*' is changed to '*other*.'

I. ii. 79-81. "Alluding to the constant assistance, or rather, constant promises of assistance, that the French gave the Scots in their quarrels with the English" (Warburton).

I. ii. 120. '*The four strangers*'; allusion has been made to six strangers. An interesting oversight on the poet's part.

I. iii. 60, 61. '*Is he yet possess'd How much ye would*,' so read the second and third Quartos; the Folios read '*he would*'; the first Quarto '*are you resolv'd how much he would have*': this is one of the important points in which the second Quarto is superior to the first.

I. iii. 67. *Cp.* Genesis xxx.

I. iii. 70. '*the third*,' *i.e.* 'reckoning Abraham himself as the first.'

I. iii. 130. '*A breed for barren metal*'; the reading of the Folio '*a breed of*'; '*for*' must be equivalent to 'in exchange for'; '*breed*' = 'interest money bred from the principal' (*cp.* Gr. τόκος).

II. i. The old stage direction ran as follows:—'*Enter Morochus a tawnie Moore all in white, and three or four followers accordingly, with Portia, Nerissa and their traine.*'

II. i. 25. '*the Sophy*,' *cp.* "*Sofi*, and *Sofito*, an ancient word signifying a wise man, learned and skillful in Magike Naturale. It has grown to be the common name of the Emperour of Persia" (Abraham Hartwell's translation of Minadoi's *History of the Wars between the Turks and the Persians*).

The '*Sefii of Persia*' is mentioned in the German play *Der Jude von Venedig*.

II. i. 35. '*page*'; Theobald's emendation for 'rage,' the reading of all the old editions.

II. ii. 88. Gobbo's 'you,' as a mark of respect, changes to 'thou,' after the recognition.

II. ii. 154. "Long and deep lines from the Mount of Venus (the ball of the thumb) towards the line of life, signifieth so many wives. . . . These lines visible and deep, so many wives the party shall have" (Saunder's *Chiromancie*, quoted by Halliwell).

II. iii. 11. '*did*'; the Quartos and first Folio read 'doe'; the reading 'did' was first given in the second Folio; if this is adopted, '*get*' = 'beget.'

II. v. 25. '*Black-Monday*,' *i.e.* Easter Monday, so called, because of a storm which occurred on April 14, 1360, being Easter Monday, when Edward III was lying with his army before Paris, and when many of his men-at-arms died of cold (Stowe).

II. v. 36. '*Jacob's staff*'; *cp.* Gen. xxxii. and Heb. xi. 21. 'A Jacob's staff' was generally used in the sense of 'a pilgrim's staff,' because St. James (or Jacob) was the patron saint of pilgrims.

II. v. 43. '*A Jewess' eye*'; the Quartos and Folios read '*a Jewes eye*,' probably pronounced '*Jewës*;' 'worth a Jew's eye' was a proverbial phrase: 'that worth was the price which the Jews paid for immunity from mutilation and death.' The reading "*Jewess*' " seems very doubtful.

II. vi. 51. '*by my hood*'; this phrase is found nowhere else in Shakespeare; according to Malone, Gratiano is in a masqued habit, to which it is probable that formerly, as at present, a large cape or hood was affixed.

II. vii. 41. '*the Hyrcanian deserts*'; Shakespeare three times mentions the tigers of Hyrcania, 'the name given to a district of indefinite extent south of the Caspian,' where, according to Pliny, tigers were bred.

II. vii. 53. '*undervalued*'; "in the beginning of Elizabeth's reign, gold was to silver in the proportion of 11 to 1; in the forty-third year of her reign it was in the proportion of 10 to 1'' (Clarendon).

II. vii. 69. '*tombs do*'; Johnson's emendation for the old reading '*timber do.*'

II. vii. 75. Halliwell notes that this line is a paraphrastical inversion of the common old proverb: 'Farewell, frost,' which was used in the absence or departure of anything that was unwelcome or displeasing.

III. i. 9. '*Knapped ginger*'; perhaps '*to knap ginger*' is to 'nibble ginger'; old women were fond of this condiment: Cotgrave invariably gives '*knap*' as a synonym of '*gnaw*' or '*nibble.*'

III. i. 64, 65. '*humility*,' rightly explained by Schmidt as 'kindness, benevolence, humanity.'

III. i. 115. The special value of the 'turquoise' was its supposed virtue in indicating the health of the wearer: it was said to brighten or fade as its wearer was well or ill, and to give warning of approaching danger.

III. ii. 54. '*more love*'; because Hercules rescued Hesione not for love of the lady, but for the sake of the horses promised him by Laomedon.

III. ii. 99. '*veiling an Indian beauty*'; it has been pointed out that Montaigne in his Essay on 'Beauty' says: "The Indians describe it black and swarthy, with blabbered thick lips, with a broad and flat nose." If Shakespeare gives us a reminiscence of this, he must have read Montaigne in French, as Florio's translation was not published until 1603.

III. ii. 102. '*Hard food for Midas,*' who prayed that everything he touched might turn to gold, and soon regretted his prayer.

III. ii. 106. '*paleness*'; as Bassanio uses 'pale' of silver a few lines before, Theobald, on Warburton's suggestion, proposed to read '*plainness*'; but '*pale*' is a regular epithet of lead, and there seems no reason for changing the reading here.

III. ii. 112. '*rain*'; the reading of the second Quarto, '*rein*,' is generally preferred.

III. v. 72, 73. '*And if on earth he do not mean it, then In reason*'; the second Quarto '*it, it*'; the Folios '*it, it is.*'

Various emendations have been suggested for '*mean,*' but no change is necessary: '*mean*' = 'aim at.' A kind correspondent, Mr. S. W. Orson, calls attention to Herbert's use of the word in '*The Church Porch*' (E. Stock's reprint of the first edition) "Shoots higher much than he that *means* a tree" (p. 12), and "Scorns his first bed of dirt, and *means* the sky" (p. 163).

IV. i. 36. '*Our holy Sabbath*'; so the first Quarto; the second reads '*Sabaoth*'; it is just possible that Shakespeare might have been misled by the expression, 'Lord God of Sabaoth,' which occurs in the New Testament. 'Sabbath' and 'Sabaoth' (*i.e.* 'hosts,' in the phrase 'Lord of hosts') were confused even by Sir Walter Scott, when in *Ivanhoe*, ch. x. he refers to "the gains of a week, aye the space between two Sabaoths." Similarly Spenser (F. Q. viii. 2):—

'*But henceforth all shall rest eternally*
With him that is the God of Sabaoth hight'

Dr. Johnson treated the two words as identical in the first edition of his Dictionary.

IV. i. 50, 51. '*affection, Mistress of passion*'; the Quartos and Folios read '*affection. Master of passion.*' The reading now generally adopted was first suggested by Thrilby; '*Maistres*' or '*mastres*,' the old spelling of '*mistress*' evidently produced the error. 'Affection,' when contrasted with 'passion,' seems to denote 'emotions produced through the senses by external objects.'

IV. i. 56. '*a wollen bag-pipe*'; the reading of all the old editions; 'wawling,' 'swollen,' 'bollen,' have been variously suggested; '*woollen*' probably refers to the covering of the windbag.

IV. i. 179, 180. *Cp.* "Mercy is seasonable in the time of affliction, as clouds of rain in the time of drought," Ecclesiasticus, xxxv. 20.

IV. i. 251. '*Are there balance*'; '*balance*' was frequently treated as a plural by Elizabethan writers, though this is the only instance in Shakespeare.

V. i. 4. '*Troilus*'; the image is from Chaucer's *Troilus and Cresseide*: "Upon the wallis fast eke would he walke" (Bk. v. 666).

V. i. 7-14. '*Thisbe*,' &c. Hunter (*New Illustrations*, i. 309) ingeniously suggests that the old Folio of Chaucer was lying open before Shakespeare when he wrote this dialogue, and that there he found Thisbe, Dido, and Medea, as well as Troilus. It is certainly striking that Thisbe, Dido, and Medea follow each other in the '*Legend of Good Women.*' Shakespeare has seemingly transferred to Dido what he found in Chaucer's *Legend* concerning Ariadne ('*And to the stronde bare-fote faste she went*'—'*And turne agayne, and on the stronde hire fyinde.*'). Chaucer's *Medea* directed Shakespeare's mind to Ovid, *Metam.* VII.

V. i. 15. '*Jessica*'; Medea, who stole away from her father Æetes, with the golden fleece, suggests Jessica's own story to Lorenzo.

V. i. 60, &c. "The corresponding passage in Plato is in his tenth book *De Republica*, where he speaks of the harmony of the Spheres, and represents a syren sitting on each of the eight orbs, and singing to each in its proper tone, while they are thus guided through the heavens, and consent in a diapason of perfect harmony, the Fates themselves chanting to this celestial music" (Du Bois, *The Wreath*, p. 60, quoted by Furness). The Platonic doctrine is, however, blended with reminiscences of Job xxxviii. 7, "The morning stars sang together."

V. i. 65. '*close it in*'; Quarto 1 and Folios read '*in it*,' which some editors have taken as equivalent to '*close-in-it.*'

V. i. 194. A similar repetition of the word '*love*' at the end of ten consecutive lines is found in '*The Fayre Mayde of the Exchange*' (1607); *cp.* *Edward III.* Act II. sc. i., where '*the sun*' ends eight consecutive lines.

THE FIRST PART OF KING HENRY IV

I. i. 5. '*No more the thirsty entrance of this soil*,' &c.; Folio 4, '*entrails*' for '*entrance*'; Steevens, '*entrants*'; Mason '*Erinnys*'; Malone compares Genesis iv. 11: "And now art thou cursed from the earth, which hath opened *her mouth* to receive thy brother's blood from thy hand"; '*entrance*' probably = '*the mouth* of the earth or *soil.*'

I. i. 28. '*now is twelve month old*,' so Quartos 1, 2; Folios, '*is a twelvemonth old*'; Quartos 7, 8, '*is but twelve months old.*'

I. i. 69. '*Mordake the Earl of Fife*'; this was "Murdach Stewart, *not* the son of Douglas, but the eldest son of Robert, Duke of Albany, Regent of Scotland, third son of King Robert II." ('the' first supplied by Pope).

I. ii. 15. '*that wandering knight so fair*,' an allusion to 'El Donzel del Febo,' the 'Knight of the Sun,' whose adventures were translated from the Spanish:—"*The First Part of the Mirrour of Princely deeds and Knighthood: Wherein is shewed the Worthiness of the Knight of the Sunne and his brother Rosicleer.*"

Now newly translated out of Spanish into our vulgar English tongue, by M(argaret) T(iler)"; eight parts of the book were published between 1579 and 1601. Shirley alludes to the Knight in the *Gamester* (iii. 1):—

"*He has knocked the flower of chivalry, the very Donzel del Phebo of the time.*"

I. ii. 42. '*Of Hybla*,' reading of Quartos; omitted in Folios; '*my old lad of the castle*'; probably a pun on the original name of Falstaff (*cp.* Preface).

I. ii. 86, 87. '*For wisdom cries out in the streets, and no man regards it*'; an adaptation of Proverbs i. 20, omitted in Folios.

I. iii. 128. '*Albeit I make a hazard of my head*'; the reading of Quartos; Folios, '*Although it be with hazard of my head.*'

I. iii. 201, &c. This rant of Hotspur has been compared with the similar sentiment put into the mouth of Eteocles by Euripides—"I will not disguise my thoughts; I would scale heaven; I would descend to the very entrails of the earth, if so be that by that price I could obtain a kingdom."

In *The Knight of the Burning Pestle* (Induction), Beaumont and Fletcher put these lines into the mouth of Ralph, the apprentice, "apparently with the design of raising a good-natured laugh at Shakespeare's expense" (Johnson).

I. iii. 253. *'when his . . . age,' cp. Richard II.* Act II. iii. 48, 49, 'as my fortune ripens with thy love, It shall be still thy true love's recompense.'

II. i. 76, 77. *'great oneyers,'* probably a jocose term for 'great ones,' with perhaps a pun on *'owners'*; various emendations have been proposed, *e.g.* *'oneraires,' 'moneyers,' 'seignors,' 'owners,' 'mynheers,' 'overseers,'* &c.

II. iii. 86. *'I'll break thy little finger,'* an ancient token of amorous dalliance, as Steevens has shown by quotations.

II. iv. *'Boar's-Head Tavern,'* the original tavern in Eastcheap was burnt down in the great fire, but was subsequently rebuilt, and stood until 1757, when it was demolished. Goldsmith visited the tavern, and wrote of it enthusiastically in his *Essays.*

II. iv. 119. *'pitiful-hearted Titan,'* so the early eds.: Theobald suggested *'butter'* for *'Titan,'* and the emendation has been generally adopted.

II. iv. 122. *'here's lime in this sack,' cp.* Sir Richard Hawkins' statement in his *Voyages,* that the Spanish sacks "for conservation are mingled with the lime in the making," and hence give rise to "the stone, the dropsy, and infinite other distempers, not heard of before this wine came into frequent use."

II. iv. 130, 131. *'I would I were a weaver'*; weavers were good singers, especially of psalms, most of them being Calvinists who had fled from Flanders to escape persecution.

II. iv. 135. *'dagger of lath,'* like that carried by the Vice in the old Morality plays.

II. iv. 239. *'you elf-skin'*; so the Quartos and Folios; Hanmer, *'eel-skin' (cp. 2 Henry IV.* III. ii. 322); Johnson, *'elfkin.'*

II. iv. 334. *'O, Glendower,'* (?) perhaps we should read, *'Owen Glendower.'*

II. iv. 380. *'King Cambyses' vein'*; an allusion to a ranting play called *'A Lamentable Tragedie, mixed full of pleasant mirth, containing the Life of Cambises, King of Persia'* (1570).

II. iv. **393.** *'The camomile,'* &c., *cp.* Lyly's *Euphues* (quoted by Farmer): "Though the camomile the more it is trodden and pressed down, the more it spreadeth; yet the violet the oftener it is handled and touched, the sooner it withereth and decayeth."

II. iv. 445. *'that reverend vice,'* &c., alluding to the *Vice* of the Morality plays; 'Iniquity' and 'Vanity' were among the names given to the character, according to the particular *'Vice'* held up to ridicule.

II. iv. 484. *'mad,'* Folios 3, 4; the rest *'made.'*

II. iv. 496. *'Peto'*; probably 'Poins,' according to Johnson; perhaps, the prefix in the MS. was simply 'P.' The Cambridge editors, however, remark that the formal address is appropriate to Peto rather than to Poins.

III. i. 147, &c. *'telling me of the mold-warp.' cp. Legend of Glendour* (stanza 23) in *The Mirror for Magistrates,* 1559:—

"And for it to sit us hereon more agog,
A prophet came (a vengeance take them all!)
Affirming Henry to be Gogmagog,
Whom Merlin doth a mouldwarp ever call,
Accurst of God, that must be brought in thrall
By a wolf, a dragon, and a lion strong,
Which should divide his kingdom them among."

III. i. 158, 159. Compare Chaucer, *Canterbury Tales,* 5860:—

"Thou saist, that dropping houses, and eek smoke,
And chiding wives maken men to flee
Out of her owen hous";

Vaughan adds the following:—"It is singular that Shakespeare should have combined two annoyances commemorated together by an old Welsh proverb, which I would translate:

*'Three things will drive a man from home:
A roof that leaks,
A house that reeks,
A wife who scolds whene'er she speaks.'"*

III. ii. 32. *'Thy place in council thou hast rudely lost,' i.e.* 'by thy rude or violent conduct'; there is an anachronism here, as the Prince was removed from the council for striking the Chief-Justice in 1403, some years after the battle of Shrewsbury.

III. ii. 38. *'doth'*; Quartos and Folios, *'do,'* which may be explained as due to the plural implied in *'every man'*; Rowe, *'does'*; Collier MS., *'doth.'*

III. ii. 62. *'carded his state'*; *'to card'* is often used in Elizabethan English in the sense of 'to mix, or debase by mixing' *(e.g.* "You card your beer if you see your guests begin to get drunk, half small, half strong." Green's *Quip for an Upstart Courtier*); Warburton suggested *'carded,'* *"scarded,' i.e. 'discarded'*; but the former explanation is undoubtedly correct. 'To stir and mix with cards, to stir together, to mix,' the meaning is brought out by 1607 quotation from Topsell, Four-foot Beasts, "As for his diet, let it be warm mashes, sodden wheat and hay, thoroughly carded with wool-cards."

III. ii. 154. *'If He be pleased I shall perform'*; the reading of Quartos; Folio 1, *'if I performe, and doe survive'*; Folios 2, 3, 4, *'if I promise, and doe survive,'* &c.

III. ii. 164. *'Lord Mortimer of Scotland,'* a mistake for Lord March of Scotland, George Dunbar, who took sides with the English.

III. iii. 34. *'By this fire, that's God's angel'*; the latter words omitted in Folios and Quartos after Quarto 2; evidently a familiar expression. Vaughan thinks the allusion is to Hebrews i. 7; but it is more probably to Exodus iii. 2.

III. iii. 126. *'neither fish nor flesh,'* alluding to the old proverb, "Neither fish nor flesh, nor good red herring."

III. iii. 150. *'I pray God my girdle break'*; an allusion to the old adage, "ungirt, unblessed"; the breaking of the girdle was formerly a serious matter, as the purse generally hung on to the girdle, and would, in the event of the girdle breaking, probably be lost.

IV. i. 31. *'that inward sickness—'*; Rowe first suggested the dash in place of the comma of the early editions; the sentence is suddenly broken off.

IV. i. 85. *'term of fear'*; the Folios and later Quartos (7 and 8), *'dream'* for *'term.'*

IV. i. 98.

*'All plumed like estridges that with the wind
Baited like eagles having lately bathed'*:

This, the reading of the early editions, has been variously emended; Steevens and Malone suggested that a line has dropped out after *wind,* and the former (too boldly) proposed as the missing line:—

"Run on, in gallant trim they now advance":

on the other hand, Rowe's proposal to read *'wing the wind'* for *'with'* has had many supporters, though it is said that *'wing the wind'* applies to ostriches less than to any other birds; Dyce, however, quotes a passage from Claudian (*In Eutropium II.,* 310-313) to justify it:—

*"Vasta velut Libyæ venantum vocibus ales
Cum premitur, calidas cursu transmittet arenas,
Inque modum veli sinuatis flamina pennis
Pulverulenta volat"*;

the Cambridge editors maintain that this means that the bird spreads its wings like a sail bellying with the wind—a different thing from *'winging the wind.'* "But the Cambridge editors," Dyce replies, "take no notice of the important word *volat,* by which Claudian means, of course, that the ostrich, *when once her wings are filled with the wind, flies* along the ground (though she does not mount into the air)"; he adds the following apt quotation from Rogers:—

"*Such to their grateful ear the gush of springs*
Who course the ostrich, as away she wings."
COLUMBUS, Canto VIII.

baited = *baiting; to bait* or *bate* = "to flap the wings, as the hawk did when unhooded and ready to fly."
'*having lately bathed*'; "writers on falconry," says Steevens, "often mention the bathing of hawks and eagles as highly necessary for their health and spirits. All birds, after bathing, spread out their wings to catch the wind, and flutter violently with them in order to dry themselves. This, in the falconer's language, is called *bating*."
IV. ii. 28, 29. '*younger sons to younger brothers*,' i.e. 'men of desperate fortune and wild adventure'; the phrase, as Johnson pointed out, occurs in Raleigh's *Discourse on War*.
V. i. *Stage direction*. The Quartos and Folios make the Earl of Westmoreland one of the characters; but, as Malone pointed out, he was in the rebel camp as a pledge for Worcester's safe conduct.
V. i. 13. '*old limbs*'; Henry was, in reality, only thirty years old at this time.
V. ii. 8. '*suspicion*'; Rowe's emendation for '*supposition*' of the early editions. Johnson points out that the same image of '*suspicion*' is exhibited in a Latin tragedy, called *Roxana*, written about the same time by Dr. William Alabaster.
V. ii. 18. '*adopted name of privilege,*' i.e. the name of *Hotspur* will suggest that his temperament must be his excuse.

V. ii. 33. '*Douglas*' must here be read as a trisyllable.
V. ii. 60. '*By still dispraising praise valued with you*'; omitted by Pope and others as 'foolish,' but defended by Johnson:—"to vilify praise, compared or valued with merit, superior to praise, is no harsh expression."
V. ii. 72. '*so wild a libertine*'; Capell's emendation for the reading of the Folios, '*at libertie,*' and Quartos 1-4, '*a libertie*'; Theobald punctuated the line thus: '*of any prince, so wild, at liberty*'; others proposed '*wild o' liberty,*' which Collier erroneously declared to be the reading of the three oldest Quartos.
V. iii. 45. '*Turk Gregory never did such deeds in arms*'; Warburton observes:—"Fox, in his *History*, hath made Gregory (*i.e.* Pope Gregory VII., called Hildebrand) so odious that I don't doubt but the good Protestants of that time were well pleased to hear him thus characterized, as uniting the attributes of their two great enemies, the Turk and Pope, in one."
V. iv. 81. '*But thought's the slave of life,*' &c.; Dyce and others prefer the reading of Quarto 1:—

'*But thoughts the slaves of life, and life time's fool,*
And time that takes survey of all the world,
Must have a stop.'

i.e. "Thoughts, which are the slaves of life, aye, and life itself, which is but the fool of Time, aye, and Time itself, which measures the existence of the whole world, must come to an end" (Vaughan).
V. iv. 163. '*Grow great,*' so Quartos; Folios, '*grow great again.*'
V. v. 41. '*sway*'; Folios and later Quartos, '*way.*'

THE SECOND PART OF KING HENRY IV

INDUCTION. '*Enter Rumour, painted full of tongues,*' so Quarto; Folios, '*Enter Rumour.*' In ancient pageants Rumour was often represented as apparelled in a robe 'full of toongs'; Stephen Hawes, in his *Pastimes of Pleasure*, describes Rumour as

"*A goodly lady, environed about*
With tongues of fire."

Similarly Chaucer, *House of Fame*, 298-300. Probably the idea was ultimately derived from Virgil, *Æneid*, IV. 173-188.
Induct. 6. '*tongues,*' so Quarto; Folios, '*tongue.*'
Induct. 8. '*men,*' so Quarto; Folios, '*them.*'
I. i. 62. '*whereon,*' so Quarto; Folios, '*when.*'
I. i. 164. '*Lean*'; Quarto, '*leaue*'; '*your*'; Quarto, '*you.*'
I. i. 166-179; 189-190; omitted in Quarto.
I. ii. 8. '*foolish-compounded clay, man*'; Quarto and Folios, '*foolish compounded clay-man.*'
I. ii. 34, 35. '*his tongue be hotter,*' alluding to the rich man in the Parable, Luke xvi. 24.
I. ii. 35, 36. '*a rascally yea-forsooth knave*'; Quarto, '*rascall.*'
I. ii. 55, 56. '*here comes the nobleman who committed the Prince,*' &c.; this was Sir William Gascoigne, Chief-Justice of the King's Bench.
I. ii. 163, 164. '*I cannot go; I cannot tell*'; Johnson was probably right in seeing here a play on *go* and *tell* in the sense of '*pass current*' and '*count as good money.*'
I. ii. 209. '*Spit white*'; *cp. Batman uppon Bartholome*, ed. 1582 (quoted by Dr. Furnivall):—"*If the spittle be white viscus, the sickness cometh of fleam; if black, of melancholy; the white spittle not knottie signifieth health.*" Other passages indicate that it was also regarded as a sign of thirst.
I. ii. 211-218. Omitted in Folios.
I. iii. 36-55. Omitted in Quarto.
I. iii. 36, &c.

'*If this present quality of war*
Indeed the instant action: a cause on foot,' &c.

Various attempts have been made to restore the meaning of the lines. Malone's reading has been generally accepted:—

"*Yes, in this present quality of war:*
Indeed the instant action—a cause on foot—
Lives so in hope as in an early spring."

which Grant White paraphrases, "Yes, in this present quality, function, or business of war, it is harmful to lay down likelihoods, etc. Indeed this very action or affair—a cause on foot —is no more hopeful for fruition than the buds of an unseasonably early spring." Pope proposed '*Impede the instant act*'; Johnson, "*in this present. . . . Indeed of instant action*"; Mason, "*if this prescient quality of war Induc'd the instant action,*" &c.
I. iii. 71. '*against the French.*' A French army of 12,000 men landed at Mitford Haven in Wales, for the aid of Glendower, during this rebellion.
I. iii. 85-108. Omitted in Quarto.
II. i. 151, 152. '*so God save me, la!*'; Quarto, '*so God save me law*'; Folios, '*in good earnest la.*'
II. ii. 25-27. Omitted in Folios.
II. ii. 71. '*virtuous*'; Folios, '*pernicious*'; Capell conjectured '*precious.*'
II. ii. 84. '*Althæa*'; the boy here confounds Althæa's firebrand with Hecuba's; perhaps the blunder was the poet's.
II. ii. 109. '*borrower's cap*'; Theobald's emendation; Folios and Quartos, '*borrowed cap.*'
II. ii. 161. '*leathern jerkins,*' commonly worn by vintners and tapsters.
III. ii. 12. '*heart's dear Harry*'; Folios, '*heart-deere-Harry.*'
II. iii. 19. '*the grey vault of heaven*'; *cp.* the use of '*grey*' applied to the eyes, where we generally use '*blue*'; '*grey-eyed morn*' (*Romeo and Juliet*, II. iii. 1) may perhaps illustrate the same fact.
II. iv. 33. '*When Arthur's first in court*'; from the ballad of *Sir Lancelot du Lake*, printed in Percy's *Reliques*.
II. iv. 49. '*your brooches, pearls, and ouches*'; a scrap of an old ballad, first marked as a quotation by Capell.
II. iv. 54. Omitted in Folios.
II. iv. 110. PISTOL has been likened to the character of 'the swaggering ruffian,' CENTURIO, in the famous Spanish play by Rojas, called *Celestina*, which was translated into English by James Mabbe; and though entered on the Stationers' Regis-

ters in 1598, the translation was not issued till 1630. It is more than probable that Mabbe was one of Shakespeare's friends; at all events, the dramatist may easily have read the English *Tragicke-Comedye of Celestina* in MS. (Mabbe's fascinating book has recently been reprinted as a volume of Mr. Nutt's *Tudor Translations*.)

II. iv. 130. *'Since when, I pray you, sir?'* a scoffing form of enquiry.

II. iv. 132, 133. Omitted in Folios.

II. iv. 157. *'Have we not Hiren here?'* probably a quotation from a lost play by George Peele called *The Turkish Mahomet and Hyren the Fair Greek;* 'Hiren,' a corruption of 'Irene.'

II. iv. 161. *'And hollow pamper'd jades of Asia';* cp. 2 *Tamburlaine*, IV. iv:—

> "Holla, ye pamper'd jades of Asia!
> What! can ye draw but twenty miles a day?"

II. iv. 165. *'Let the welkin roar';* a commonplace tag in old ballads of the time.

II. iv. 175. *'Then feed, and be fat, my fair Calipolis';* a burlesque of passages in Peele's *Battle of Alcazar* (1594); Muley Mahomet enters to his wife with lion's flesh on his sword, and says, 'Feed then, and faint not, my fair Calipolis.'

II. iv. 177. *'Si fortune me tormente, sperato me contento';* the line probably purposely corrupted, was restored by Hanmer:—'Si fortuna me tormenta, il sperare me contenta' (*i.e.* 'If fortune torments me, hope contents me'). "Pistol is only a copy of Hannibal Gonsaga," remarked Farmer, "who vaunted on yielding himself a prisoner, as you may read in an old collection of tales, called *Wits, Fits, Fancies:*—

> 'Si Fortuna me tormenta,
> Il speranza me contenta.'"

II. iv. 194. *'Then death rock me asleep,'* &c.; said to be a fragment of an old song written by Anne Boleyn.

II. iv. 196. *'Untwine the Sisters Three';* cp. *Midsummer-Night's Dream*, V. i. 325-330, where there is a reference to the 'shears' of Atropos, the Fate that cut the thread of human destiny.

II. iv. 261. *'Fiery Trigon';* alluding to the astrological division of the zodiacal signs into four *trigons* or *triplicities;* one consisting of the three *fiery* signs (Aries, Leo, and Sagittarius); the others, respectively, of three airy, three watery, and three earthly signs. When the three superior planets were in the three fiery signs they formed a *fiery trigon;* when in Cancer, Scorpio, and Pisces, a *watery* one, &c.

III. i. The whole scene omitted in Quarto 1 (*i.e.* the earlier copies of the edition).

III. i. 30. *'Then happy low, lie down!';* Quarto reads 'Then (happy) low lie downe'; Coleridge suggested 'Then, happy low-lie-down'; Warburton, 'happy lowly clown.' The Folio seems to make the meaning quite clear:—'Then happy Lowe, lye downe'; 'low' is used substantively, 'You who are happy in your humble situations, lay down your heads to rest,' &c.

III. i. 43. *'little,' i.e.* 'a little.'

III. i. 53-56. Omitted in Folios.

III. i. 66. *'cousin Nevil';* the earldom of Warwick did not come into the family of the Nevilles till the latter part of the reign of Henry IV.; at this time it was in the family of Beauchamp.

III. ii. *'Justice Shallow';* the character has, with much reason, been identified with Sir Thomas Lucy of Charlecote (*cp. The Merry Wives of Windsor*); perhaps there is a reference to his arms in the words, *'If the young dace be a bait for the old pike, I see no reason in the law of nature but I may snap at him'* (*cp. infra*, ll. 356, 357; 'luce' = 'pike,' *cp.* Note, line 1, *Merry Wives of Windsor*).

III. ii. 24-26. *'Then was Jack Falstaff, now Sir John, a boy, and page to Thomas Mowbray, Duke of Norfolk.'* This is generally given as one of the points of evidence that Falstaff was originally called Oldcastle, Sir John Oldcastle having actually been in his youth page to the Duke of Norfolk: but it would seem that the same is true of Sir John Fastolf.

III. ii. 29. *'I see* (Folios 'saw') *him break Skogan's heal'* =

(Quarto *Skoggins;* Folio 1, 'Scoggans'); two Scogans must be carefully differentiated, though probably both are confused by Shakespeare in this passage:—(i.) Henry Scogan, the poet, Chaucer's Scogan, described by Ben Jonson in *The Fortunate Isles*, as

> "a fine gentleman, and master of arts
> Of Henry the Fourth's times, that made disguises
> For the King's sons, and writ in ballad royal
> Daintily well";

(ii.) John Scogan, "an excellent mimick, and of great pleasantry in conversation, the favourite buffoon of the court of Edward IV." A book of *'Scogins Jests'* was published in 1565 by Andrew Borde, and probably suggested the name to Shakespeare.

III. ii. 32, 33. *'but much of the father's substance';* so Quarto; Folios, 'not'; the Variorum of 1821 proposed 'not much'; the Quarto reading must be understood as ironical.

III. ii. 276. *'Dagonet in Arthur's show';* Sir Dagonet is Arthur's fool in the story of Tristram de Lyonesse; *'Arthur's show'* was an exhibition of archery by a society of 58 members which styled itself "*The Ancient Order, Society, and Unitie laudable of Prince Arthur and his Knightly Armory of the Round Table*," and took the names of the knights of the old romance. Mulcaster referred to it in his *Positions, concerning the training up of children* (1581). The meeting-place of the society was Mile-end Green.

III. ii. 308. *'invisible';* Rowe's emendation; Quarto and Folios, 'invincible,' *i.e.* (?) "not to be evinced, not to be made out, indeterminable" (Schmidt).

III. ii. 309, 310. *'yet . . . mandrake';* 310-314, 'a' came . . . good-nights'; omitted in Folios.

III. ii. 325, 326. *'philosopher's two stones';* "one of which was an universal medicine, the other a transmuter of base metals into gold"; so Warburton; Malone explains:—"I will make him of *twice* the value of the philosopher's stone."

IV. i. 55-79. Omitted in Quarto.

IV. i. 71. *'there';* the reading of the Folios; Hanmer conjectured 'sphere'; Collier 'chair.'

IV. i. 93. Neither this line nor 95 is to be found in the Folios, and they are omitted in some copies of the Quarto. To some corruption of the text is due the obscurity of ll. 94-96, which Clarke paraphrases:—"The grievances of my brother general, the commonwealth, and the home cruelty to my born brother, cause me to make this quarrel my own." The archbishop's brother had been beheaded by the King's order.

IV. i. 103-139. Omitted in Quarto.

IV. i. 173. *'true substantial form,' i.e.* 'in due form and legal validity.'

IV. iii. 41. *'hook-nosed fellow of Rome';* Quarto adds 'there cosin' before 'I came,' which Johnson took to be a corruption of 'there, Cæsar.'

IV. iii. 116, 117. *'commences it and sets it in act and use';* Tyrwhitt saw in these words an allusion "to the Cambridge *Commencement* and the Oxford *Act;* for by those different names the two Universities have long distinguished the season at which each gives to her respective students a complete authority to use *those hoards of learning* which have entitled them to their several degrees."

IV. iv. 35. *'as flaws congealed in the spring of day';* according to Warburton the allusion is "to the opinion of some philosophers that the vapours being congealed in the air by the cold (which is most intense in the morning), and being afterwards rarefied and let loose by the warmth of the sun, occasion those sudden and impetuous gusts of wind which are called flaws"; Malone explained *'flaws'* to mean "small blades of ice which are stuck on the edges of the water in winter mornings."

IV. iv. 122. *'loathly births of nature,' i.e.* unnatural births.

IV. v. 204. *'And all my friends';* Tyrwhitt's conjecture for 'thy friends' of the Folios and Quarto. Dyce, 'my foes.' Clarke explains the original reading thus:—"By the first *thy friends* the King means those who are friendly inclined to the prince, and who, he goes on to say, must be made securely friends."

IV. v. 234. "'Tis called Jerusalem'; probably from the tapestries of the history of Jerusalem with which it was hung; now used for the meetings of Convocation.

V. i. 28, 29. 'A friend i' court is better than a penny in purse'; cp. The Romaunt of the Rose, 5540:—

"For frende in court aie better is
Than peny is in purse, certis";

Camden gives the same proverbial expression.

V. ii. 38. 'A ragged and forestall'd remission'; 'forestall'd' has been variously interpreted; the simplest interpretation seems to be 'anticipated, asked for before being granted,' not necessarily by the Chief-Justice himself, but by his friends; the explanation fits in well with the dignified utterance of the speaker. Others explain, 'a pardon that is sure not to be granted, the case having been prejudged'; 'a pardon which is precluded from being absolute, by the refusal of the offender to accuse or alter his conduct,' &c.

V. iii. 71. 'Do me right'; 'to do a man right' was formerly, according to Steevens, the usual expression in pledging healths.

'And dub me knight'; it was a custom in Shakespeare's day to drink a bumper kneeling to the health of one's mistress. He who performed this exploit was dubbed a knight for the evening, cp. A Yorkshire Tragedy. "They call it knighting in London when they drink upon their knees" (Malone).

V. iii. 117, 118. 'Dead? As nail in door'; an ancient proverbial expression; the door-nail was probably the nail on which the knocker struck. "It is therefore used as a comparison to any one irrevocably dead, one who has fallen (as Virgil says) multa morte, that is, with abundant death, such as iteration of strokes on the head would naturally produce."

V. iii. 137. 'Where is the life that late I led'; a scrap of an old song; cp. Taming of the Shrew, IV. i.

V. v. 28. 'obsque hoc nihil est,' "'tis all in every part'; the second and later Folios correct 'obsque' to 'absque,' but the error may have been intentional on the author's part. Pistol uses a Latin expression 'ever the same, for without this there is nothing,' and then goes on to allude to an English proverbial expression,

"All in all, and all in every part," which he seems to give as its free rendering.

V. v. 108. 'I heard a bird so sing'; a proverbial expression still extant.

EPILOGUE. Shakespeare's authorship of this epilogue has been doubted, and it has been described as 'a manifest and poor imitation of the epilogue to As You Like It.' It is noteworthy that it occurs already in the Quarto (1600), though with one important difference; the words 'and so kneel down . . . queen' (ll. 33, 34) are printed there at the end of the first paragraph, after 'infinitely.' It seems probable, therefore, that the epilogue originally ended there, and that the remaining lines were added somewhat later. One is strongly tempted to infer that the additions to the epilogue were called forth by the success of the first and second parts of the play of Sir John Oldcastle, written evidently to vindicate the character of Falstaff's original, and put on the stage as a counter-attraction to Henry IV., hence the words, added in a spirit of playful defiance, 'for Oldcastle died a martyr, and this is not the man' (l. 31). The first part of Sir John Oldcastle was performed for the first time about the 1st of November, 1599, the second part, dealing with the Lollard's death, was evidently written by the end of the year. The First Part of the true and honourable history of the Life of Sir John Oldcastle, the good Lord Cobham, appeared in two editions in 1600; Shakespeare's name had been impudently printed on the title-page of the former and less correct edition; the authors were Munday, Drayton, Wilson, and Chettle. The 'Second Part' is not known to exist.

l. 26-28. 'our humble author will continue the story, with Sir John in it, and make you merry with fair Katherine in France'; Shakespeare changed his mind. "The public was not to be indulged in laughter for laughter's sake at the expense of his play. The tone of the entire play of Henry V. would have been altered if Falstaff had been allowed to appear in it. . . . Agincourt is not the field for splendid mendacity. . . . There is no place for Falstaff any longer on earth; he must find refuge 'in Arthur's bosom.'" But the public would not absolve "our humble author of his promise, and they were to make merry again with their favourite

'round about the oak
Of Herne the hunter.'"

THE LIFE OF KING HENRY V

PROLOGUE. 9. 'spirits that have dared'; so Staunton; Folios 1, 2, 3, 'hath'; Folio 4, 'spirit, that hath.'

I. ii. 45, 52. 'Elbe,' restored by Capell; Folios, 'Elue'; (Holinshed, 'Elbe'; Hall, 'Elve').

I. ii. 61-64. Theobald (Warburton); cp. Montaigne's Essays, III. 9 (vide Florio's translation).

I. ii. 77. 'Lewis the tenth'; the reading of Folios, following Holinshed; Pope, from Hall, reads 'ninth.'

I. ii. 94. 'amply to imbar'; so Folios (Folios 1, 2, 'imbarre'); Quartos 1, 2, 'imbace,' Quarto 3, 'imbrace'; Rowe, 'make bare'; Theobald (Warburton), 'imbare'; Pope, 'openly imbrace,' &c. Schmidt explains the lines:—"They strive to exclude you, instead of excluding amply, i.e. without restriction or subterfuge, their own false titles." Perhaps Mr. W. A. Wright's explanation is the truer, taking 'imbar' in the sense of 'to bar in,' 'secure':—"The Kings of France, says the Archbishop, whose own right is derived only through the female line, prefer to shelter themselves under the flimsy protection of an appeal to the Salic law, which would exclude Henry's claim, instead of fully securing and defending their own titles by maintaining that though, like Henry's, derived through the female line, their claim was stronger than his."

I. ii. 98. 'in the Book of Numbers'; cp. Numbers xxvii. 1-11.

I. ii. 99. 'man'; the reading of Folios; Quartos, 'sonne.'

I. ii. 110. 'Forage in,' Folios, 'Forrage in'; Quarto 1, 'Foraging'; Quarto 3, 'Forraging the.'

I. ii. 125. 'Your grace hath cause and means.' Hanmer reads 'Your race hath had cause, means.' Various readings have been suggested, but there seems to be no difficulty whatever in understanding the text as it stands.

I. ii. 131. 'blood'; so Folios 3, 4; Folio 1, 'Bloods'; Folio 2, 'Blouds.'

I. ii. 150. 'with ample and brim fulness'; probably 'brim' is here adjectival; Pope reads 'brimfulness'; but the accent favours the present reading.

I. ii. 154. 'the ill neighbourhood'; Boswell, from Quartos, reads 'the bruit thereof.'

I. ii. 163. 'her chronicle'; Capell, Johnson conjectured; Folios read, 'their C.'; Quartos, 'your Chronicles'; Rowe, 'his Chronicle.'

I. ii. 173. 'tear'; so Rowe, ed. 2; Folios, 'tame'; Quartos, 'spoil'; Theobald, 'taint.'

I. ii. 180-183. Theobald first compared these lines with Cicero, De Republica, ii. 42, and thought that Shakespeare had perhaps borrowed from Cicero.

I. ii. 187-203. Lyly, in his Euphues (Arber's Reprint, pp. 262-4), has a similar description of the common-wealth of the bees: its ultimate source is probably Pliny's Natural History, Book xi. (n.b., Holland's translation did not appear till 1601).

I. ii. 197. 'majesty'; so Rowe from Quartos; Folios, 'Maiesties.'

I. ii. 208. 'Come,' so Folios; Capell, from Quartos, 'fly'; 'as many ways meet in one town'; Capell, from Quartos, reads 'As many seuerall wayes meete in one towne'; Dyce, Lettsom conjectured 'As many several streets,' &c.

I. ii. 209. 'meet in one salt sea'; Capell, from Quartos, reads 'run in one self sea'; Vaughan conjectured 'run in one salt sea.'

I. ii. 212. '*End*'; Pope's emendation from Quartos; Folios, '*And.*'

I. ii. 255. '*This tun of treasure*'; probably suggested by the corresponding words in *The Famous Victories*.

I. ii. 263. '*shall strike his father's crown into the hazard*'; '*hazard*' used technically, "the hazard in a tennis-court"; glosses, '*grille de tripot*' in old French dictionaries.

Prol. II. Pope transferred the Prologue to the end of the first scene.

Prol. II. 32. '*The abuse of distance; force a play*': so Folios; Pope, '*while we force a play*'; Warburton conjectured '*while we farce a play,*' &c.; 'to force a play' is interpreted by Steevens to mean 'to produce a play by compressing many circumstances into a narrow compass.' Various emendations have been proposed, but in spite of the imperfection of the line as it stands, no suggestions seem to improve upon it. Perhaps, after all, the line is correct as it stands, with a pause for a syllable at the cæsura, and with a vocalic *r* in '*force*,' making the word dissyllabic; *cp.* '*fierce*,' II. iv. 100.

Prol. II. 41. '*But, till the king come forth,*' &c., *i.e.* 'until the King come forth we shall not shift our scene unto Southampton.'

II. i. 5. '*there shall be smiles*'; Hanmer conjectures, Warburton, '*there shall be—*(smiles)'; Farmer, Collier, 2 ed., '*smites*' (*i.e.* blows).

II. i. 22. '*mare*'; restored by Theobald from Quartos; Folios read '*name*'; Hanmer, '*dame*'; Collier MS., '*jade.*'

II. i. 26. '*How now, mine host Pistol!*' Quartos, '*How do you my Hoste?*' giving the words to Nym.

II. i. 34, 35. '*O well a day, Lady, if he be not drawn now*'; '*drawn,*' Theobald's emendation; Folios, '*hewne*'; Malone from Quarto I, '*O Lord! here's corporal Nym's——.*'

II. i. 39. '*Iceland dog!*' Steevens, Johnson conjectured; Folios read '*Island dog*'; Quartos, '*Iseland.*' There are several allusions to "these shaggy, sharp-eared, white dogs, much imported formerly as favourites for ladies."

II. i. 73. '*lazar kite of Cressid's kind*'; probably a scrap from some old play. In certain parallel passages the readings vary between '*Kite*,' '*Kit*,' '*Catte*'; '*Kit*,' too, is the spelling of Folio 4.

II. i. 78, 79. '*and you, hostess*'; Folios, '*and your Hostesse*'; Folio 4, '*Hostes you must come straight to my master, and you Hoste Pistole.*'

II. i. 92. '*Base is the slave that pays,*' a quotation from an old play. Steevens quotes "My motto shall be, Base is the man that pays" (Heywood's *Fair Maid of the West*).

II. i. 101, 102. Omitted in Folios.

II. ii. 9. '*Whom he hath dull'd and cloy'd with gracious favours*'; Folios 3, 4, '*lull'd.*' Quartos, followed by Steevens, '*whom he hath cloy'd and grac'd with princely favours.*'

II. ii. 61. '*Who are the late commissioners?*'; Vaughan conjectured '*Who ask the late commissions?*' Collier MS. '*the state c.*'; but no change is necessary; '*late commissioners*' = 'lately appointed commissioners.'

II. ii. 63. '*for it,*' *i.e.* for my commission.

II. ii. 114. '*by treasons*'; Mason conjectured '*to treasons*'; Moberly conjectured '*by reasons.*'

II. ii. 118. '*But he that bade thee bade thee stand up*'; Moberly conjectured '*But he that tempter-fiend that stirr'd thee up*'; Dyce, Johnson conjectured '*tempted*'; Folios, '*bad*'; Vaughan conjectured '*sin thus.*' No emendation is necessary, tho' it is uncertain what the exact force of '*bade thee stand up*' may be, whether (1) 'like an honest-man,' or (2) 'rise in rebellion.'

II. ii. 139-140. '*To mark the full-fraught man and best indued With some suspicion*'; Malone's emendation; Theobald, '*The best,*' &c.; Folios, '*To make thee full fraught man, and best indued,*' &c.; Pope, '*To make the full-fraught man, the best, endu'd With,*' &c.

II. ii. 46. '*Henry*'; Theobald's correction from Quartos; Folios, '*Thomas.*'

II. ii. 173. '*you have*'; so Knight, from Quartos; Folios 2, 3, 4, '*you three*'; Folio 1, '*you.*'

II. ii. 10. '*A*' made a finer end'; Folios 1, 2, '*a finer*'; Folios 3, 4, '*finer*'; Capell, '*a fine*'; Johnson conjectured '*a final*'; Vaughan conjectured '*a fair.*' Probably Mistress Quickly's words are correctly reported, and should not be edited.

II. iii. 14. '*fumble with the sheets*'; popularly supposed to be a sign of approaching death.

II. iii. 16, 17. '*and a' babbled of green fields*'; Theobald's famous correction of Folios, '*and a Table of greene fields*'; Theobald's reading was suggested to him by a MS. note written in a copy of Shakespeare by 'a gentleman sometime deceased,' who proposed '*And a' talked of green fields.*' The Quartos omit the line, giving the passage thus:—

> "*His nose was as sharp as a pen,*
> *For when I saw him fumble with the sheetes,*
> *And talk of floures, and smile vpo his fingers ends,*
> *I knew there was no way but one*"

(*n.b.* '*talk of floures*'). Many suggestions have been put forward since Pope explained that the words were part of a stage direction, and that 'Greenfield was the name of the property-man in that time who furnished implements, &c., for the actors.' The marginal stage-direction was, according to him, '*A table of green-fields.*' Malone, '*in a table of green fields*,' Collin MSS., '*on a table of green freese.*' Recently M. Henry Bradley has pointed out that 'green field' was occasionally used for the exchequer table, a table of green baize. A combination of this suggestion with the reading of the Collier MS. would require merely the change of '*and*' to '*on*,' but one cannot easily give up one's perfect faith in Theobald's most brilliant conjecture.

II. iii. 51. '*Let senses rule*'; *i.e.* 'let prudence govern you' (Steevens).

II. iii. 53. '*And hold-fast is the only dog*'; *cp.* 'Brag is a good dog, but holdfast is a better.'

II. iii. 54. '*Caveto,*' Quartos, '*cophetua.*'

II. iv. 58. '*mountain sire*'; Theobald, '*mounting sire*'; Collier, Mitford conjectured '*mighty sire*'; '*mountain*' evidently means 'huge as a mountain.'

Prol. III. 4. '*Hampton,*' Theobald's correction of Folios, '*Dover.*'

Prol. III. 6. '*fanning*'; Rowe's emendation of Folios 1, 2, '*fayning,*' Folios 3, 4, '*faining*'; Gould conjectured '*playing.*'

Prol. III. 35. '*Eke*'; the first Folio, '*eech*'; the others, '*ech*'; probably representing the pronunciation of the word.

III. i. 7. '*summon up,*' Rowe's emendation of Folios, '*commune up.*'

III. i. 15. '*nostril*'; Rowe's emendation of Folios, '*nosthrill.*'

III. i. 32. '*straining*'; Rowe's emendation of Folios, '*Straying.*'

III. ii. 19. '*Up to the breach, you dogs! avaunt, you cullions!*'; so Folios; Capell reads, from Quartos, '*God's plud!—Up to the preaches you rascals! will you not up to the preaches?*'

III. v. 46. '*Knights*'; Theobald's emendation of Folios, '*Kings.*'

III. v. 54. '*Rouen*'; Malone's emendation of '*Rone,*' Quartos; '*Roan,*' Folios.

III. vi. 27. '*And giddy Fortune's furious fickle wheel,*' &c.; *cp.* '*Fortune is blind . . . whose foot is standing on a rolling stone,*' Kyd's *Spanish Tragedy*.

III. vi. 30, 31. '*Fortune is painted blind*'; Warburton proposed the omission of '*blind,*' which may have been caught up from the next line.

III. vi. 40. '*Fortune is Bardolph's foe*'; a reference to the old ballad, '*Fortune, my foe!*'

III. vi. 77. '*new-tuned*'; Pope reads '*new-turned*'; Collier MS., '*new-coined*'; Grant White, '*new-found.*'

III. vi. 101-106. Fluellen's description of Bardolph forcibly recalls Chaucer's Sompnour in the *Prologue to the Canterbury Tales* (Quartos, '*whelkes, and knubs, and pumples*' for '*bubukles, and whelks, and knobs*').

III. vi. 112. '*lenity,*' Rowe's emendation from Quartos; Folios, '*Levity.*'

III. vi. 14. '*habit*'; *i.e.* sleeveless coat, the herald's tabard.

III. vii. 14. '*chez les narines*'; Capell, '*qui a*'; Folios, '*ches*'; Heath conjectured '*voyez,*' &c.

III. vii. 41, 42. '*Wonder of Nature,*' probably the first words of a sonnet or lyric of the time.

III. vii. 65, 66. '*Le chien . . . au bourbier*'; 'the dog is returned to his own vomit, and the washed out sow to the mire,' *cp.* 2 Peter ii. 22.

Prol. IV. 16. '*name*'; Tyrwhitt's conjecture; Folios, '*nam'd.*'

Prol. IV. 20. '*cripple tardy-gaited*'; Folios, '*creeple-tardy-gated.*'

Prol. IV. 26. '*Investing lank-lean cheeks and war-worn coats*'; Capell, '*And war-worn coats, investing lank-lean cheeks*'; Hanmer, '*In wasted*'; Warburton, '*Invest in*'; Beckett conjectured '*Infesting,*' &c.

IV. i. 35. '*Qui va là*'; Rowe's emendation of Folios, '*Che vous la?*'

IV. i. 65. '*speak lower*'; so Quarto 3, adopted by Malone; Quartos 1, 2, '*lewer*'; Folios, '*fewer*'; *cp*. 'to speak few,' a provincialism for 'to speak low,' (according to Steevens, who prefers the Folio reading).

IV. i. 92. '*Sir Thomas*'; Theobald's correction of Folios, '*John.*'

IV. i. 47. '*sinfully miscarry upon the sea*'; Pope reads from Quartos, '*fall into some lewd action and miscarry.*'

IV. i. 180. '*mote*'; Malone's emendation of Folios, '*Moth*'; Quartos, '*moath.*'

IV. i. 244. '*What is thy soul of adoration?*'; Knight's reading; Folio 1 reads, '*What? is thy Soule of Odoration?*'; Folios 2, 3, 4, '*Adoration*'; Warburton, '*What is thy toll*, O adoration?'; Hanmer, '*What is thy shew of adoration?*'; Johnson, '*What is thy soul, O adoration?*'; &c., &c. (*v.* Glossary).

IV. i. 289, 290. '*take from them now the sense of reckoning, if the opposed numbers*'; Tyrwhitt's reading; Folios, '*take . . . reck'ning of the opposed numbers:*'; Theobald, '*take . . . reck'ning; lest th' opposed numbers,*' &c. &c.

IV. iii. 40. '*the feast of Crispian*' falls upon the 25th October.

IV. iii. 44. '*He that shall live this day, and see*'; Pope's reading; Folios, '*He that shall see this day and live*'; Quartos, '*He that outlives this day and sees.*'

IV. iii. 48. Omitted in Folios.

IV. iii. 52. '*his mouth*'; so Folios; Quartos, '*their mouths*'; Pope, '*their mouth.*'

IV. iv. 4. '*Qualtitie calmie custure me*'; probably Pistol catches the last word of the French soldier's speech, repeats it, and adds the refrain of a popular Irish song, '*Galen, O custure me*' = 'colleen oge astore,' *i.e.* 'young girl, my treasure.' The popularity of the song is evidenced by the following heading of one of the songs in Robinson's *Handful of Pleasant Delights* (*cp.* Arber's Reprint, p. 33): '*A Sonet of a Lover in the praise of his lady.| To Galen o custure me; sung at eurie lines end*'; first pointed out by Malone.

IV. iv. 69. '*this roaring devil? the old play*'; alluding to the standing character of the Devil in the Morality plays.

IV. v. 11. '*Let us die in honour; once*'; Knight's emendation; Folio 1, '*Let us dye in once*'; Folios 2, 3, 4, '*Let us flye in once*'; &c. Omitted by Pope.

IV. v. 18. '*our lives*'; Steevens adds from Quartos, '*Unto these English, or else die with fame*'; Vaughan conjectured '*Unto these English, or else die with shame.*'

IV. vii. 26. '*alike*'; so Folios; Rowe reads '*as like.*'

IV. vii. 43. '*made*'; Capell, following Quartos, reads '*made an end.*'

IV. vii. 62. '*Assyrian slings*'; Theobald compared Judith ix. 7, and defended the reading against Warburton's proposed '*Balearian*' (afterwards withdrawn).

IV. vii. 68. '*what means this, herald?*' Steevens' reading; Folio 1, '*what meanes this herald?*'; Folios 2, 3, 4, '*what means their herald*'; Hanmer conjectured '*what mean'st thou, herald?*'

IV. vii. 78. '*their wounded steeds*'; Folios, '*with,*' corrected by Malone. The Quartos omit the line.

Prol. V. 30–35. The allusion is to Robert Devereux, Earl of Essex, who was sent to Ireland in 1599 to suppress Tyrone's rebellion; he left London on March 27, and returned on September 28 (*v.* Preface).

Prol. V. 38. '*The emperor's coming*'; *i.e.* 'the emperor is coming,' or (better) 'the emperor's coming,' parallel to 'the King of England's stay at home.' The line refers to the visit of Sigismund, Emperor of Germany, 1st May 1416. Malone supposed that a line had dropped out before '*The Emperor,*' &c.; Capell re-wrote the passage. It seems, however, that if instead of a semi-colon, a comma is placed after '*at home,*' the lines are perfectly intelligible as they stand.

V. i. 80. '*Doll*'; Capell, '*Nell*'; which is probably the correct reading, though Shakespeare may himself have made the mistake.

V. ii. 7. '*Burgundy*'; Rowe's emendation, from Quartos, of Folio 1, '*Burgogne*'; Folios 2, 4, '*Burgoigne*'; Folio 3, '*Bargoigne.*'

V. ii. 11. '*So are you, princes English, every one*'; Folios 1, 2, 3, '*So are you princes (English) every one*'; Folio 4, '*So are you princes (English every one).*'

V. ii. 12. '*England*'; so Folios 2, 3, 4; Folio 1 reads '*Ireland.*'

V. ii. 50. '*all*'; Rowe's reading; Folios, '*withall.*'

V. ii. 82. '*Pass our accept*'; Warburton reads, '*Pass, or accept*'; Malone conjectured '*Pass, or except,*' &c.

V. ii. 45, 46. '*queen of all, Katharine*'; Capell conjectured, adopted by Dyce, '*queen of all Katharines.*'

V. ii. 39. '*Héritier*'; Folios read '*Heretere*'; '*Præclarissimus*'; so Folios; Rann reads '*Percarissimus*'; the error is, however, copied from Holinshed.

V. ii. 373. '*Sennet*'; Folio 1, '*Senet*'; Folio 2, '*Sonet*,' as though referring to the fourteen lines of the Epilogue.

Epil. 13. '*Which oft our stage hath shown*'; *vide* Preface to 1, 2, 3 *Henry VI.*

MUCH ADO ABOUT NOTHING

I. i. 199, 200. The English story of "Mr. Fox" alluded to here was first written down by Blakeway, who contributed to Malone's Variorum Edition a version of the tale he had heard from an old aunt (*cp.* Jacobs' *English Fairy Tales*).

II. i. 196, 197. '*As melancholy as a lodge in a warren*': the phrase suggests "The daughter of Zion is left as a cottage in a vineyard, as a lodge in a garden of cucumbers." Isaiah i. 8.

II. ii. 41. Some editors substitute 'Borachio' for 'Claudio' in order to relieve the difficulty here, but, as the Cambridge editors point out, "Hero's supposed offence would not be enhanced by calling one lover by the name of the other. . . . Perhaps the author meant that Borachio should persuade her to play, as children say, at being Hero and Claudio."

II. iii. 37. The Folio reads:—'*Enter Prince, Leonato, Claudio and Jack Wilson*'; the latter was probably the singer who took the part of Balthasar.

III. ii. 25. '*Where is but a humour or a worm*': toothache was popularly supposed to be caused by a worm at the root of the tooth.

III. iii. It is an interesting fact that 'Dogberry,' the vulgar name of the *dogwood*, was used as a surname as far back as the time of Richard II., and that 'Verges,' a provincial corruption

of *verjuice*, occurs in an ancient MS. (MS. Ashmol. 38) as the name of a usurer whose epitaph is given:—

> "Here lies father Varges
> Who died to save charges."

III. iii. 81, 82. '*Keep your fellows' counsels and your own.*' It has been pointed out by students of Shakespeare's legal acquirements that these words still form part of the oath administered by judges' marshal to the grand jurymen at the present day.

III. v. 15. '*Comparisons are odorous.*' An elaborate extension of this joke occurs in the old play of *Sir Gyles Goosecappe* (c. 1603).

III. v. 33. '*When the age is in, the wit is out*'; a blunder for the old proverbial expression, "when the ale is in, wit is out"—

> "When ale is in, wit is out,
> When ale is out, wit is in,
> The first thou showest out of doubt,
> The last in thee hath not been."
> HEYWOOD'S *Epigrams and Proverbs.*

IV. ii. Nearly all the speeches of Dogberry throughout the scene are given to the famous comedian 'Kemp,' those of Verges to 'Cowley.' William Kempe and Richard Cowley are among the 'principall actors' enumerated in the first Folio. The retention of the names of the actors "supplies a measure of the editorial care to which the several Folios were submitted." Dogberry's speech is assigned to 'Andrew,' probably a familiar appellation of Kempe, who, according to the Cambridge Edition, often played the part of 'Merry Andrew.'

IV. ii. 5, 6. 'We have the exhibition to examine.' Verges' blunder is not quite clear: possibly 'exhibition' is used in the sense of 'allowance' or permission; otherwise he perhaps means 'examination to exhibit.'

V. i. 16. 'Bid sorrow wag, cry "hem!"' The Quarto and the first and second Folios read, 'And sorrow wagge, crie hem': Folio 3, 'And hallow, wag, cry hem': Folio 4, 'And hollow wag, cry hem.' Many emendations have been suggested. Capell's 'bid sorrow

wag,' is now generally adopted. Johnson proposed 'Cry, sorrow wag! and hem.' ('Sorrow wag,' like 'care away,' was probably a proverbial phrase.) One other suggestion is perhaps noteworthy:—'And, sorry wag, cry "hem."'

V. iii. 18, 21. 'Heavily, heavily'; so reads the Quarto; the Folios 'Heavenly, heavenly,' adopted by many editors. The same error, however, of 'heavenly' for 'heavily' occurs in the Folio reading of Hamlet II. ii. 296.

"The slayers of the virgin knight are performing a solemn requiem on the body of Hero, and they invoke Midnight and the shades of the dead to assist, until her death be uttered, that is, proclaimed, published, sorrowfully, sorrowfully" (Halliwell).

V. iv. 121, 122. 'There is no staff more reverend than one tipped with horn'; i.e. having a ferrule of horn; there is, of course, a quibbling allusion in the words of the favourite Elizabethan joke.

THE TRAGEDY OF JULIUS CÆSAR

I. i. 24. 'with awl. I'; Folios, 'withal I'; the correction was made by Farmer.

I. ii. 19. The line is evidently to be read thus:—

"A soothsay'r bids you 'ware the ides of March."

I. ii. 155. 'walls'; Rowe's emendation of Folios, 'walkes.'

I. ii. 254. "Tis very like: he hath'; Theobald's emendation; Folios, "Tis very like he hath.'

I. ii. 315. 'He should not humour me'; i.e. 'he (Brutus) should not influence me, as I have been influencing him'; others take 'he' to refer to Cæsar, and Johnson explains the passage as follows:—"Cæsar loves Brutus, but if Brutus and I were to change places, his (Cæsar's love) should not humour me, so as to make me forget my principles."

I. iii. 30. 'These are their reasons'; Jervis conjectured 'These have their seasons'; Collier MS., 'These are the seasons.'

I. iii. 65. 'Why old men fool and'; Mitford conjectured; Folios, 'Why old men. Fools, and'; Blackstone conjectured 'Why old men fools, and.'

I. iii. 129. 'In favour's like'; Johnson reads 'In favour's, like'; Folios 1, 2, 'Is Fauors, like'; Folios 3, 4, 'Is Favours, like'; Rowe, 'Is feaw'rous, like'; Capell, 'Is favour'd like'; &c. &c.

II. i. 40. 'the ides of March'; Theobald's correction of Folios, 'the first of March.'

II. i. 83. 'For if thou path, thy native semblance on'; so Folio 2; Folios 1, 3, 4, 'For if thou path thy . . .'; Pope, 'For if thou march, thy . . .'; Singer conjectured 'For if thou put'st thy . . .' &c.; but there is no need to improve on the reading of Folio 2.

II. ii. 19. 'fight'; so Folios; Dyce, 'fought'; Keightley, 'did fight.'

II. ii. 46. 'are'; Upton conjectured; Folios 1, 2, 'heare'; Folios 3, 4, 'hear'; Rowe, 'heard'; Theobald, 'were.'

III. i. 39. 'law of children'; Johnson's emendation of Folios, 'lane of children'; Steevens conjectured 'line of c.'; Mason conjectured 'play of c.' Mr. Fleay approves of the Folio reading, and explains 'lane' in the sense of 'narrow conceits'; he compares the following lines from Jonson's Staple of News:—

"A narrow-minded man! my thoughts do dwell
All in a lane."

III. i. 47, 48. 'Know, Cæsar, doth not wrong, nor without cause Will he be satisfied'; there is an interesting piece of literary history connected with these lines. In Ben Jonson's Sylva or Discoveries occurs the famous criticism on Shakespeare, where Jonson, after speaking of his love for Shakespeare, "on this side of idolatry, expresses a wish 'that he had blotted more.'" "His wit was in his own power; would the rule of it had been so too! Many times he fell into those things which could not escape laughter: as when he said in the person of Cæsar, one speaking to him, 'Cæsar, thou dost me wrong,' he replied, 'Cæsar did

never wrong but with just cause,' and such like; which were ridiculous. But he redeemed his vices with his virtues. There was ever more in him to be praised than to be pardoned." Again in his Staple of News (acted 1625), a character says, "Cry you mercy, you never did wrong, but with just cause." From these references it is inferred that in its original form the passage stood thus:—

"METELLUS. Cæsar, thou dost me wrong.
CÆSAR. Know, Cæsar doth not wrong, but with just cause,
Nor without cause will he be satisfied."

It is impossible to determine whether Jonson misquoted, or whether (as seems more likely) his criticism effected its purpose, and the lines were changed by Shakespeare or by his editors.

III. i. 77. 'Et tu, Brute'; according to Plutarch, Cæsar called out in Latin to Casca, 'O vile traitor, Casca, what doest thou?' Suetonius, however, states that Cæsar addressed Brutus in Greek:—'"καὶ οὐ, τεκνον," i.e. 'and thou, too, my son.' The words 'Et tu, Brute,' proverbial in Elizabethan times, must have been derived from the Greek; they are found in at least three works published earlier than Julius Cæsar:—(i.) Eedes' Latin play, Cæsaris interfecti, 1582; (ii.) The True Tragedie of Richard, Duke of York, 1595; (iii.) Acolastus, his Afterwitte, 1600. In Cæsar's Legend, Mirror for Magistrates, 1587, these lines occur:—

"O this, quoth I, is violence: then Cassius pierced my breast;
And Brutus thou, my son, quoth I, whom erst I loved best."

III. i. 105-110. These lines are given to Casca by Pope.

III. i. 175. 'in strength of malice'; so Folios; Pope, 'exempt from malice'; Capell, 'no strength of malice'; Seymour, 'reproof of malice'; Collier MS., adopted by Craik, 'in strength of welcome'; Badham conjectured 'unstring their malice,' &c. If any emendation is necessary, Capell's suggestion commends itself most; but 'in strength of malice' may mean 'in the intensity of their hatred to Cæsar's tyranny,' and this, as Grant White points out, suits the context.

III. i. 263. 'limbs of men', so Folios; Hanmer, 'kind of men'; Johnson conjectured 'lives of' or 'lymmes of men'; Jackson, 'imps of men'; Collier MS., adopted by Craik, 'loins of men'; Bulloch, 'limbs of Rome,' &c.

III. ii. 251. 'On this side Tiber'; Theobald proposed 'that' for 'this'; Cæsar's gardens were on the left bank of the river. Shakespeare followed North's Plutarch, and North merely translated the words in Amyot.

IV. i. 37. 'abjects, orts'; Staunton's reading; Theobald, 'abject orts'; Folios, 'Obiects, Arts'; Beckett conjectured 'abject arts'; Gould conjectured 'objects, orts.'

IV. i. 44. 'our means stretch'd'; Folio 1, 'our meanes stretcht'; Folios 2, 3, 4, 'and our best meanes stretcht out'; Johnson, 'our best means stretcht'; Malone, 'our means stretch'd to the utmost.'

IV. ii. 50, 52. Craik's suggestion that 'Lucilius' and 'Lucius' have been transposed in these lines has been accepted by many Editors. The Cambridge editors are of opinion that the error is due to the author and not to a transcriber, and have, therefore, not tampered with the text.

IV. iii. 129. Cp. "This Phaonius . . . came into the chamber, and with a certain scoffing and mocking gesture, which he counterfeited of purpose, he rehearsed the verses which old Nestor said in Homer":—

"My lords I pray you hearken both to me,
For I have seen more years than suchie three."

(North's Plutarch).

IV. iii. 132. 'vilely'; so Folio 4; Folios 1, 2, 'vildely'; Folio 3, 'vildly.'

V. i. 20. 'I will do so,' i.e. 'I will do as you wish, and keep on the left'; according to some Editors, the words may mean 'I will not wrangle, but will have my way.'

V. i. 53. 'three and thirty'; Theobald, 'three and twenty' (the number given in Plutarch).

V. iii. 98. 'The last'; Rowe unnecessarily suggested, 'Thou last'; but cp. North's Plutarch, "he (Brutus) lamented the death of Cassius, calling him the last of all the Romans."

V. v. 33. 'Farewell to thee too, Strato. Countrymen'; Theobald's emendation of Folios, 'Farewell to thee, to Strato, Countrymen.'

V. v. 71. 'in a general honest thought And'; Collier MS., adopted by Craik, reads 'in a generous honest thought Of.'

AS YOU LIKE IT

DRAMATIS PERSONAE. The pronunciation of 'Jaques' is still somewhat doubtful, though the metrical test makes it certain that it is always a dissyllable in Shakespeare: there is evidence that the name was well known in England, and ordinarily pronounced as a monosyllable; hence Harrington's Metamorphosis of A-jax (1596). The name of the character was probably rendered 'Jakës'; the modern stage practice is in favour of 'Jaqowes.'

I. i. 1. 'it was upon this fashion: bequeathed,' &c. The Folio does not place a stop at 'fashion,' but makes 'bequeathed' a past participle; the words 'charged' . . . 'on his blessing' presuppose 'he' or 'my father'; the nominative may, however, be easily supplied from the context, or possibly, but doubtfully, 'a' (= 'he') has been omitted before 'charged.' There is very much to be said in favour of the Folio reading; a slight confusion of two constructions seems to have produced the difficulty. Warburton, Hanmer, and Capell proposed to insert 'my father' before 'bequeathed.' Others punctuate in the same way as in the present text, but read 'he bequeathed' or 'my father bequeathed'; the Cambridge editors hold that the subject of the sentence is intentionally omitted.

I. ii. 76. The Folio prefixes 'Rosalind' to the speech: Theobald first proposed the change to 'Celia,' and he has been followed by most editors. Capell suggested 'Fernandine' for 'Frederick' in the previous speech. Shakespeare does not give us the name of Rosalind's father: he is generally referred to as 'Duke Senior'; Celia's father is mentioned as 'Frederick' in two other places (l. 219 of this scene, and V. iv. 151). One has, however, a shrewd suspicion that Touchstone is referring to the exiled king as 'old Frederick,' and that Rosalind speaks the words 'my father's love is enough to honour him;' the expression is so much in harmony with her subsequent utterance, ll. 220:—

'My father loved Sir Rowland as his soul.'

And again, in the next scene, l. 28:—

'The Duke my father loved his father dearly.'

I. ii. 193. 'You mean'; Theobald proposed 'An' you mean,' and the Cambridge editors suggest that 'and' for 'an' (= if) may be the right reading, omitted by the printer, who mistook it for part of the stage-direction 'Orl. and' for 'Orland.'

I. ii. 257. 'the taller'; but Rosalind is later on described as 'more than common tall,' and Celia as 'the woman low, and browner than her brother'; probably 'taller' is a slip of Shakespeare's pen: 'shorter,' 'smaller,' 'lesser,' 'lower,' have been variously proposed; of these 'lesser' strikes one perhaps as most Shakespearian.

I. iii. 99. 'change,' &c., Folio 1; the other Folios read 'charge,' i.e. 'burden,' probably the true reading.

I. iii. 125. There has been much discussion of the scansion of this line; several critics, in their anxiety to save Shakespeare

from the serious charge of using a false quantity, propose to accent 'Aliena' on the penultimate, but for all that it seems most likely that the line is to be read:—

'No lóng|er Cél|ya bút|Ali|ena.'

II. i. 5. 'here feel we but'; Theobald first conjectured 'but' for 'not' of the Folios, and his emendation has been accepted by many scholars, though violently opposed by others. Most of the discussions turn on 'the penalty of Adam,' which ordinarily suggests toil—'in the sweat of thy brow shalt thou eat bread'—but in this passage Shakespeare makes the penalty to be "the seasons' difference," cp. Paradise Lost, x. 678, 9:—

'Else had the spring Perpetual smiled on earth with vernant flowers.'

II. i. 13-14. 'like the toad, ugly and venomous,' &c. A favourite Euphuistic conceit, e.g. 'The foul toade hath a faire stone in his head,' Euphues, p. 53 (ed. Arber), based on an actual belief in toadstones. The origin of the belief is traced back to Pliny's description of a stone as 'of the colour of a frog.'

II. ii. 12. 'no more do yours,' a somewhat loose construction, but one easily understood, the force of the previous sentence being 'to some kind of men their graces serve them not as friends.'

II. iii. 71. 'seventeen'; Rowe's emendation for 'seaventie' of the Folios.

II. iv. 1. 'weary'; Theobald's emendation for 'merry' of the Folios, and generally adopted; some scholars are in favour of the Folio reading, and put it down to Rosalind's assumed merriment; her subsequent confession as to her weariness must then be taken as an aside.

II. iv. 48. 'from whom,' i.e. from the peascod; similarly 'her' in the next line: he was wooing the peascod instead of his mistress.

II. v. 3. 'turn,' so the Folios: Pope substituted 'tune'; but the change is unnecessary; according to Steevens 'to turn a tune or note' is still a current phrase among vulgar musicians.

II. v. 57, 58. 'I'll rail against all the first-born of Egypt.' According to Johnson 'the first-born of Egypt' was a proverbial expression for high-born persons, but it has not been found elsewhere. Nares suggests that perhaps Jaques is only intended to say that, if he cannot sleep, he will, like other discontented persons, rail against his betters. There is no doubt some subtler meaning in the words, and the following is possibly worthy of consideration:—Jaques says if he cannot sleep he'll rail again all first-borns, for it is the question of birthright which has caused him 'leave his wealth and ease,' merely as he had previously put it 'to please a stubborn will'; this idea has perhaps suggested Pharaoh's stubbornness, and by some such association 'all first-borns' became 'all the first-born of Egypt;' or, by mere association, the meaningless tag 'of Egypt' is added by Jaques to round off the phrase, and to give it some sort of colour.

II. vii. 19. Touchstone of course alludes to the common saying 'Fortune favours fools,' cp. 'Every man out of his humour,' I. i.

Sogliardo. Why, who am I, sir?
Macilente. One of those that fortune favours.
Carlo. [Aside] The periphrasis of a fool.

II. vii. 34, 36. 'A worthy fool' . . . 'O, worthy fool': the 'A' and 'O' should probably change places, according to an anonymous conjecture noted in the Cambridge Edition.

II. vii. 55. 'Not to seem'; the words 'not to' were first added by Theobald: the Folios read 'seem'; Collier, following his MS. corrections, proposed 'but to seem'; the meaning is the same in both cases. Mr. Furness follows Ingleby in maintaining the correctness of the text, and paraphrases thus:—"He who is hit the hardest by me must laugh the hardest, and that he must do so is plain; because if he is a wise man he must seem foolishly senseless of the bob by laughing it off. Unless he does this, viz., shows his insensibility by laughing it off, any chance hit of the fool will expose every nerve and fibre of his folly."

II. vii. 73. 'the weary very means,' the reading of the Folios (Folios 1 and 2 'wearie'; Folios 3, 4, 'weary'). Pope proposed 'very very'; Collier (MS.) 'the very means of wear'; Staunton 'weary-very,' or 'very-weary.' Others maintain the correctness of the original reading, and explain, 'until that its very means, being weary or exhausted, do ebb.' A very plausible emendation was suggested by Singer, viz., 'wearer's' for 'weary,' and it has rightly been adopted by several editors: cp. Henry VIII. I. i. 83-85:—

'O, many
Have broke their backs with laying manors on 'em
For this great journey.'

II. vii. 178. 'because thou art not seen,' i.e. "as thou art an enemy that dost not brave us with thy presence" (Johnson): several unnecessary emendations have been proposed, e.g. 'Thou causest not that teen' (Hanmer); 'Because thou art foreseen' (Staunton), &c.

II. vii. 189. 'As friend remember'd not,' i.e. 'as forgotten friendship,' or 'as want an unremembered friend feels': cp. 'benefits forgot,' supra.

III. ii. 112. 'the very false gallop,' cp. Nashe's Four Letters Confuted, "I would trot a false gallop through the rest of his ragged verses but that if I should retort his rime dogrell aright, I must make my verses (as he doth his) run hobling like a Brewer's Cart upon the stones, and observe no length in their feet."

III. ii. 154. 'pulpiter': Spedding's suggestion for 'Jupiter' of the Folios.

III. ii. 405. 'living,' i.e. lasting, permanent; the antithesis seems to require 'loving,' which has been substituted by some editors: it is noteworthy that in some half-dozen instances in Shakespeare 'live' has been printed for 'love,' but it is questionable whether any change is justifiable here.

III. iii. 4. 'your features! . . . what features?' Farmer's conjecture 'feature! . . . what's feature' seems singularly plausible; cp. l. 17, 'I do not know what "poetical" is.'

III. iii. 72. 'her,' so Folios 1, 2: 'his,' Folios 3, 4: the female bird was the falcon; the male was called 'tercel' or 'tassel.'

III. iv. 40. 'noble goose'; Hanmer substituted 'nose-quilled' for 'noble,' which is, of course, used ironically.

III. v. 7. 'dies and lives,' i.e. 'lives and dies,' i.e. 'subsists from the cradle to the grave'; the inversion of the words seems to have been an old idiom; cp. 'Romaunt of the Rose,' v. 5790:—

"With sorwe they both die and live,
That unto Richesse her hertis yive."

Other passages in later literature might be adduced where the exigencies of metre do not exist.

IV. i. 142, 143. 'like Diana in the fountain.' Stow mentions in his Survey of London (1603) that there was set up in 1596 on the east side of the cross in Cheapside "a curiously wrought tabernacle of grey marble, and in the same an alabaster image of Diana, and water conveyed from the Thames prilling from her naked breast." It is very doubtful whether Shakespeare is referring to this particular 'Diana,' as some have supposed.

IV. ii. 12. The words 'Then sing him home, the rest shall bear this burden,' are printed as one line in the Folios. Theobald was the first to re-arrange, as in the text. Knight, Collier, Dyce, and others take the whole to be a stage-direction. Knight first called attention to the fact that possibly the original music for this song is to be found in John Hilton's 'Catch that Catch Can; or, a Choice Collection of Catches, Rounds,' &c., 1652 (printed Furness, p. 230, 231).

IV. iii. 75. 'fair ones'; Mr. Wright suggests that perhaps we should read 'fair one,' and Mr. Furness assents to the view that 'Shakespeare seems to have forgotten that Celia was apparently the only woman present.' But surely it is noteworthy that Oliver a few lines lower down gives the description:— 'The boy is fair,' &c.

IV. iii. 87. 'like a ripe sister: the woman low'; the pause at the woman low cæsura takes the place of a syllable.

IV. iii. 101. 'chewing the food,' usually quoted as 'chewing the cud,' a correction of the line first suggested by Scott (cp. Introduction to Quentin Durward).

V. ii. 18. 'fair sister'; Oliver addresses 'Ganymede' thus for he is Orlando's counterfeit Rosalind (cp. IV. iii. 92). Some interpreters of Shakespeare are of opinion that Oliver knows the whole secret of the situation.

V. ii. 70. 'which I tender dearly'; probably an allusion to the Act "against Conjuracons, Inchantments, and Witchcraftes," passed under Elizabeth, which enacted that all persons using witchcraft, &c., whereby death ensued, should be put to death without benefit of clergy, &c.

V. iii. 15. Chappell printed the music of the song from a MS., now in the Advocates' Library, Edinburgh, belonging to the early part of the seventeenth century (cp. Furness, pp. 262, 263). In the Folios the last stanza is made the second. Mr. Roffe is of opinion that Shakespeare contemplated a trio between the Pages and Touchstone.

V. iv. 4. 'As those that fear they hope, and know they fear.' A large number of unnecessary emendations have been proposed for this plausible reading of the Folios; e.g. 'fear, they hope, and know they fear'; 'fear their hope and hope their fear'; 'fear their hope and know their fear,' &c. The last of these gives the meaning of the line as it stands in the text.

V. iv. 87. 'we quarrel in print, by the book'; Shakespeare probably refers to "Vincentio Saviolo his Practise. In two Bookes. The first intreating the use of the Rapier and Dagger. The second of Honor and honorable Quarrels"; printed in 1594.

V. iv. 88. 'books for good manners,' e.g. "A lytle Booke of Good Manners for Chyldren with interpritation into the vulgare Englysshe tongue by R. Whittinton, Poet Laureat"; printed at London in 1554; (cp. Dr. Furnivall's Book of Norture of John Russell, &c., published by the Early English Text Society, 1868). Cp. Hamlet, V. ii. 149, 'he (i.e. Laertes) is the card of calendar of gentry,' a probable allusion to the title of some such 'book of manners.'

V. iv. 111. 'her hand with his'; the first and second Folios 'his hand'; corrected to 'her' in the second and third Folios.

V. iv. 145. 'even daughter, welcome'; Theobald proposed 'daughter-welcome,' i.e. 'welcome as a daughter.' Folios 1, 2, 3, read 'daughter welcome'; Folio 4, 'daughter, welcome.' The sense is clear whichever reading is adopted, though the rhythm seems in favour of the reading in the text: 'O my dear niece,' says the Duke, 'nay, daughter, welcome to me in no less degree than daughter.'

Epilogue. 17. 'If I were a woman'; the part of Rosalind was of course originally taken by a boy-actor: women's parts were not taken by women till after the Restoration.

TWELFTH NIGHT; OR, WHAT YOU WILL

I. i. 5. '*sound*'; so the Folios; Pope changed it to '*south*,' and editors have generally accepted this emendation, but it seems unnecessary: Grant White appropriately asks, "Did Pope, or the editors who have followed him, ever lie musing on the sward at the edge of a wood, and hear the low sweet hum of the summer air, as it kissed the coyly-shrinking wild flowers upon the banks, and passed on loaded with fragrance from the sweet salute?"

I. i. 22. '*like fell and cruel hounds*'; referring to the story of Actæon.

I. i. 38. '*all supplied, and filled*'; the comma after '*supplied*' is not in the Folio: its insertion simplifies the lines. Others leave the Folio reading, but bracket '*her sweet perfections*' in the next line; making them appositional to '*thrones*.'

I. ii. 15. '*Arion on the dolphin's back*'; the Folios misprint '*Orion*' for '*Arion*.'

I. iii. 64, 65. '*bring your hand to the buttery-bar and let it drink*'; "a proverbial phrase among Abigails, to ask at once for a kiss and a present" (Kenrick).

I. iii. 89. '*Then hadst thou had an excellent head of hair*'; Sir Toby evidently plays upon '*tongues*' and '*tongs*' (*i.e.* curling-tongs).

I. iii. 110. '*an old man*'; Theobald proposed to read '*a noble man*,' taking the allusion to be to Orsino. Clarke explains '*an old man*' as '*a man of experience*'; "the word *old*," he adds, "gives precisely that absurd effect of refraining from competing in dancing, fencing, &c., with exactly the antagonist incapacitated by age over whom Sir Andrew might hope to prove his superiority."

I. iii. 130. '*That's sides and heart*'; Sir Andrew and Sir Toby are wrong in the parts assigned to Taurus in the old astrological figures of the human body. Taurus was supposed to govern the neck and throat.

I. iv. 3. '*three days*'; Mr. Daniel points out in his 'Time-Analysis' that this statement is inconsistent with the Duke's words in V. i. 102, '*Three months this youth hath tended upon me*.'

II. i. 17. '*Messaline*'; possibly an error for Mitylene, as Capell conjectured.

II. iii. 17. '*the picture of "we three"*'; "a common sign, in which two wooden heads are exhibited with this inscription under it, '*We three loggerheads be*,' the spectator being supposed to make the third" (Malone).

II. iii. 23, 24. '*Pigrogromitus . . . of Queubus*,' &c. Mr. Swinburne sees in these 'freaks of nomenclature' the direct influence of Rabelais (*cp. A Study of Shakespeare*, pp. 155, 156).

II. iii. 37. '*O mistress mine*,' &c. "this tune is contained in both the editions of Morley's *Consort Lessons*, 1599 and 1611. It is also found in Queen Elizabeth's Virginal Book, arranged by Boyd. As it is to be found in print in 1599, it proves either that Shakespeare's *Twelfth Night* was written in or before that year, or that, in accordance with the then prevailing custom, '*O mistress mine*,' was an old song, introduced into the play" (Chappell's *Popular Music of the Olden Time*).

II. iii. 107. '*Out o' tune, sir: ye lie*'; Theobald proposed '*time, sir?*' which has been very generally adopted. The reading of the Folios may well stand without change. Sir Toby says to the Clown that he is out of tune and lies in declaring '*no, no, no, you dare not*' (*i.e.* dare not bid Malvolio go). Hence next words '*Art any more than a steward*,' addressed to Malvolio.

II. v. 36. '*the lady of the Strachy*'; this is one of the unsettled problems in Shakespeare. Hunter ingeniously suggested that Shakespeare ridicules, in the scene between the Clown, as Sir Topas, and Malvolio (IV. ii.), the exorcisms by Puritan ministers, in the case of a family named *Starchy* (1596-99), and that the difficult *Strachy* was a hint to the audience to expect subsequent allusion to the Starchy affair. Others suggest '*Strozzi*,' '*Stracci*,' '*Stratarch*.' Halliwell refers to a Russian word meaning lawyer or judge. The incident of a lady of high rank marrying her steward is the subject of Webster's *Duchess of Malfy*.

II. v. 60. '*with cars*'; so Folio 1; the later Folios, '*with cares*'; Johnson, '*with carts*'; many emendations have been proposed.

Clarke defends the original reading, and compares '*A team of horse shall not pluck that from me*' (*Two Gentlemen*, III. i. 264, 265). Hanmer's suggestion '*by th' ears*' has been generally adopted.

II. v. 157. '*yellow stockings*'; these were much worn in Shakespeare's time, and have still survived to our own day in the yellow stockings worn by the 'Blue Coat boys.'

III. i. 49. '*these*,' *i.e.* these coins which Viola has given him.

III. i. 55. '*Cressida was a beggar*'; 'according to the story Cressida finally became a leper and begged by the roadside.'

III. i. 63. '*And, like the haggard, check at every feather*'; so the Folios; Johnson proposed '*not*' for '*and*,' and this reading has reasonably been adopted by most editors; '*to check*' is "a term in falconry, applied to a hawk when she forsakes her proper game, and follows some other of inferior kind that crosses her in her flight"; the meaning therefore of the Folio reading would be 'that he must catch at every opportunity,' but this does not suit the context: the wise Clown must be discriminative; hence Johnson's '*not*.'

III. i. 67. '*wise men, folly-fall'n, quite taint their wit*'; Folio 1, '*wisemens folly falne*'; Hanmer and Warburton, '*wise men's folly shown*'; the text is Theobald's, and is generally adopted.

III. i. 119. '*a cypress, not a bosom, Hides my heart*'; the force of these words has, it would seem, been missed; the point of the '*cypress*' is not its blackness but its transparency. *Cp.* '*The Ballad of Robin Hood, Scarlet and John*':

> "*Cypress over her face,*
> *Through which her rose-like cheeks did blush*
> *All in a comely grace.*"

'*Bosom*' must, I think, be used in this passage in the sense of 'the bosom of the dress' which conceals the body. Olivia says, 'you can see my heart; a thin gauze as it were hides it, not a stomacher.'

III. ii. 24. '*sailed into the north*,' &c.; perhaps this is a reference to the discovery of Northern Nova Zembla by the Dutchman Barenz in 1596. (*Cp.* C. H. Coote's paper on '*the new map*,' l. 85. *New Shakespeare Society Publications*, 1878.)

III. ii. 62. '*youngest wren of nine*'; Folio, '*mine*,' emended by Theobald. The wren is said to lay nine or ten eggs at a time, and the last hatched nestling is usually the smallest of the whole brood.

III. ii. 74, 75. '*the new map with the augmentation of the Indies*'; no doubt a reference to the map which Hallam, in his *Literature of Europe*, calls 'the best map of the 16th century': it is found in the first edition of Hakluyt's *Voyages* (1589), but as it records discoveries made at least seven years later, it was in all probability a separate map, well known at the time, and made so as to be inserted in Hakluyt: the author was probably Mr. Emmerie Mollineux, who was also the first Englishman to make a terrestrial globe. It is noteworthy that the map shows a marked development of the geography of India proper, &c. (*Cp. Transactions of New Shakespeare Society*, 1877-79.)

III. iii. 15. '*And thanks; and ever . . . oft good turns*.' The Cambridge editors hold that some word has dropped out between '*ever*' and '*oft*.' Many emendations have been proposed; perhaps the simplest reading is that of the Old spelling Shakespeare:—

'*And thanks, and, ever oft, good turns . . .*'

'*ever oft*' in the sense of 'with perpetual frequency.' Theobald proposed:—

'*And thanks, and ever thanks; and oft good turns.*'

IV. i. 13-15. '*I am afraid this great lubber, the world, will prove a cockney*'; so the Folios; the lines evidently mean "I am afraid affectation and foppery will overspread the world" (Johnson); it has been proposed to change '*world*' into '*word*' (*i.e.* with reference to 'vent'): others read '*this great lubberly world*'; Knight explains that the words are spoken aside, and mean, 'I am afraid the world will prove this great lubber (Sebastian) a cockney.' This seems very strained, and probably the simplest reading of the passage is the best.

IV. ii. 12-13. '*the old hermit of Prague*'; Douce points out that the allusion is "not to the celebrated heresiarch, Jerome of Prague, but another of that name, born likewise at Prague, and called the *hermit* of Camaldoli in Tuscany."

IV. ii. 37. '*clearstories*'; Folio 1, '*cleere stores*'; Folio 2, '*cleare stones*'; the reading adopted is Blakeway's conjecture in Boswell: '*clerestory*' is the name given to the windows above the arches of the nave of a Gothic church.

IV. ii. 132. '*goodman devil*'; Folio 1, '*good man diuell*'; Rowe's '*goodman Drivel*,' seems the most plausible emendation, if any is necessary; Folio 2 reads '*good man Direll.*'

V. i. 110. '*My soul the faithfull'st offerings hath breathed out*';

the Folios '*have*,' corrected by Capell, but probably Shakespeare's own reading; the plural for the singular, owing to the plural object ('*faithfull'st offerings*') preceding the verb.

V. i. 194. '*a passy measures pavin*'; Folio 1, '*panym*'; Folio 2, '*Pavin*'; various emendations have been suggested, but there is little doubt that the reading in the text is the correct one. '*Passy measures*' is a corruption of the Italian '*passamezzo*,' which word Florio explains as 'a *passa-measure* in dancing, a cinque pace'; it was a slow dance, differing little from the action of walking. '*Pavin*' was a grave Spanish dance. According to Halliwell, the *passy measures pavin* is described as follows in an early MS. list of dances:—"*The passinge measure Pavyon*—2 singles and a double forward, and 2 singles syde.—Reprince back." Sir Toby means, therefore, that 'the surgeon is a rogue and a grave solemn coxcomb.'

V. i. 353. '*against.*' Tyrwhitt's conjecture '*in*' has a good deal in its favour; '*against*' may have been caught from line 368.

THE TRAGEDY OF HAMLET, PRINCE OF DENMARK

I. i. 63. '*He smote the sledded Polacks on the ice*'; Quarto 1, Quarto 2, Folio 1, '*pollax*,' variously interpreted as '*Polaeks*,' '*poleauxe*,' &c.; there is very little to be said against the former interpretation, unless it be that 'the ambitious Norway' in the previous sentence would lead one to expect 'the sledded Polack,' a commendable reading originally proposed by Pope.

I. i. 108-125. These lines occur in the Quartos, but are omitted in Folios.

I. i. 167. '*eastward*,' so Quartos; Folios, '*easterne*'; the latter reading was perhaps in Milton's mind, when he wrote:—

"*Now morn her rosy steps in th' eastern clime*
Advancing, sowed the earth with orient pearls."
Par. Lost, v. 1.

I. ii. 9. '*to*'; the reading of Quartos; Folios, '*of.*'
I. ii. 58-60. Omitted in Folios.
I. iii. 13. '*this temple*'; so Quartos; Folios, '*his temple.*'
I. iii. 17. '*will*,' so Quartos; Folios, '*fear.*'
I. iii. 19. Omitted in Quartos.
I. iii. 26. '*particular act and place*,' so Quartos; Folios, '*peculiar sect and force.*'
I. iii. 58. Polonius' precepts have been traced back to Euphues' advice to Philautus; the similarity is certainly striking (*vide* Rushton's *Shakespeare's Euphuism*); others see in the passage a reference to Lord Burleigh's 'ten precepts,' enjoined upon Robert Cecil when about to set out on his travels (French's *Shakespeareana Genealogica*, v. Furness, Vol. II., p. 239).
I. iii. 65. '*comrade*' (accented on the second syllable), so Folio 1; Quartos (also Quarto 1), '*cowrage.*'
I. iii. 74. '*Are of a most select and generous chief in that*'; so Folio 1; Quarto 1, '*are of a most select and general chiefe in that*'; Quarto 2, '*Or of a most select and generous chiefe in that*'; the line is obviously incorrect; the simplest emendation of the many proposed is the omission of the words '*of a*' and '*chief*,' which were probably due to marginal corrections of '*in*' and '*best*' in the previous line:—

"*Are most select and generous in that.*"

(Collier '*choice*' for '*chief*'; Staunton '*sheaf*,' *i.e.* set, clique, suggested by the Euphuistic phrase "gentlemen of the best sheaf").
I. iii. 109. '*Running*,' Collier's conjecture; Quartos, '*Wrong*'; Folio 1, '*Roaming*'; Pope, '*Wronging*'; Warburton, '*Wronging*'; Theobald, '*Ranging*,' &c.
I. iii. 130. '*bawds*'; Theobald's emendation of '*bonds*,' the reading of Quartos and Folio 1.
I. iv. 17-38. Omitted in Folio 1 (also Quarto 1).
I. iv. 36-38.

'*the dram of eale*
Doth all the noble substance of a doubt
To his own scandal';

this famous crux has taxed the ingenuity of generations of scholars, and some fifty various readings and interpretations have been proposed. The general meaning of the words is clear, emphasizing as they do the previous statement that as a man's virtues, be they as pure as grace, shall in the general censure take corruption from one particular fault, even so 'the dram of eale' reduces all the noble substance to its own low level.

The difficulty of the passage lies in (i.) '*eale*' and (ii.) '*doth . . . of a doubt*'; a simple explanation of (i.) is that '*eale*' = '*e'il*,' *i.e.* '*evil*' (similarly in Quarto 2, II. ii. 627, '*deale*' = '*de'ile*' = '*devil*'). The chief objection to this plausible conjecture is that one would expect something rather more definite than 'dram of evil'; it is said, however, that '*eale*' is still used in the sense of 'reproach' in the western counties. Theobald proposed 'base,' probably having in mind the lines in *Cymbeline* (III. v. 88):—

"*From whose so many weights of baseness cannot*
A dram of worth be drawn."

As regards (ii.), no very plausible emendation has been proposed; '*of a doubt*' has been taken to be a printer's error for '*often dout*,' '*oft endoubt*,' '*offer doubt*,' '*oft work out*,' &c. To the many questions which these words have called forth, the present writer is rash enough to add one more:—Could, perhaps, 'doth of a doubt' = deprives of the benefit of a doubt? Is there any instance of 'do' in XVIth century English = 'deprive'; the usage is common in modern English slang.
I. iv. 75-78. Omitted in Folio 1.
I. v. 22. '*List, list, O list!*' so Quartos; Folio 1, '*list, Hamlet, oh list.*'
II. i. The stage direction in Quartos:—*Enter old Polonius, with his man or two;* Folios, *Polonius and Reynaldo;* in Quarto 1, *Reynaldo* is called *Montano,* hence perhaps the reading of the later Quarto.
II. i. 4. '*to make inquire*'; so Quartos; Folios read, '*you make inquiry.*'
II. ii. 17. Omitted in Folios.
II. ii. 73. '*three*'; so Quarto 1 and Folios; Quartos read '*threescore.*'
II. ii. 209-211. The reading of Folios; omitted in Quartos.
II. ii. 322-323. '*the clown . . . sere*,' omitted in Quartos; *vide* Glossary, "TICKLE O' THE SERE."
II. ii. 330, 331. '*I think their inhibition comes by the means of the late innovation*'; *vide* PREFACE.
II. ii. 335-358. Omitted in Quartos.
II. ii. 336-340.

"I saw the children of Powles last night:
And troth they pleas'd me pretty, pretty well,
The apes, in time, will do it handsomely.
—I like the audience that frequenteth there
With much applause."
           Jack Drum's Entertainment (1601).

II. ii. 444. '*Æneas' tale to Dido*'; one cannot but believe that Hamlet's criticism of the play is throughout ironical, and that the speeches quoted are burlesque. "The fancy that a burlesque was intended," wrote Coleridge, "sinks below criticism; the lines, as epic narrative, are superb"; perhaps he would have changed his mind, and would have recognised them as mere parody, if he had read *Dido, Queen of Carthage*, a play left incomplete by Marlowe and finished by Nash (*cp.* e.g. Act II, Sc. i, which seems to be the very passage Shakespeare had in view).

II. ii. 463. Omitted in Folios.

II. ii. 472. '*Then senseless Ilium*'; 527, '*mobled . . . good*'; omitted in Quartos.

II. ii. 517. '*whether,*' Malone emendation; Quartos, Folios, '*where*' (*i.e. 'wh'ere* = *whether*).

II. ii. 537. '*a speech of some dozen or sixteen lines*'; there was much throwing about of brains in the attempt to find these lines in the play-scene in Act III. Sc. ii. "The discussion," as Furness aptly puts it, "is a tribute to Shakespeare's consummate art," and the view of this scholar commends itself—viz., that "in order to give an air of probability to what everyone would feel [otherwise] highly improbable, Shakespeare represents Hamlet as adapting an old play to his present needs by inserting in it some pointed lines."

II. ii. 586, 587:—

"Hum, I have heard
That guilty creatures, sitting at a play," &c.,

vide Heywood's *Apology for Actors*, where a number of these stories are collected; perhaps, however, Shakespeare had in mind the plot of *A Warning for Faire Women*, a play on this theme published in 1599, referring to a *cause célèbre* which befell at Lynn in Norfolk.

III. i. 13-14. '*Niggard of question, but of our own demands most free*'; Hanmer, '*Most free of our question, but to our demands most niggard*'; Warburton, '*Most free of question, but of our demands most niggard*'; Collier MS., '*niggard of our question, but to our demands most free.*'

III. i. 59. '*to take arms against a sea of troubles,*' &c.; the alleged confusion of metaphors in this passage was due to the commentator's ignorance, not to Shakespeare's; *vide* Glossary, '*take arms.*'

III. i. 79, 80:—

"The undiscovered country from whose bourn
No traveller returns."

In Catullus' *Elegy on a Sparrow*, occur the words:—

"Qui nunc it per iter tenebricosum
Illuc unde negant redire quenquam."

III. i. 144. '*paintings*'; so (Quarto 1) Quartos; Folio 1, '*pratlings*'; Folios 2, 3, 4, '*pratling*'; Pope, '*painting*'; Macdonald conjectured '*prancings.*'

III. ii. 33. '*nor man*'; so Quartos; Folios, '*or Norman.*'

III. ii. 45, 46. There is a striking passage in Quarto 1, omitted in Quarto 2 and Folio, concerning those 'that keep one suit of jests, as a man is known by one suit of apparell'; the lines have a Shakespearian note, and are probably of great interest.

III. ii. 134. Much has been said to explain the introduction of the dumb-show; from the historical point of view its place in a court-play is not surprising, *vide* Glossary, '*Dumb Show.*'

III. ii. 164. The reading of the Folios; Quarto is:—

"For women feare too much, even as they love,
And women's fear and love holds quantity."

Johnson believed that a line was lost rhyming with '*love.*'

III. ii. 165. '*In neither ought, or in extremity*'; Malone's emendation; Folios, '*In neither ought,*' &c.; Quartos, '*Eyther none, in neither ought,*' &c.

III. ii. 201. '*favourite*'; Folio 1, '*favourites,*' a reading for which much is to be said.

III. ii. 245. '*Vienna*'; Quarto 1, '*Guyana*'; for '*Gonzago,*' Quarto 1 reads *Albertus*, who is throughout called Duke; in Quarto 2 it is always *King;* except here where Hamlet says '*Gonzago is the Duke's name.*'

III. ii. 250. '*The croaking raven doth bellow for revenge*';

cp. "*The screeking raven sits croaking for revenge,*
Whole herds of beasts comes bellowing for revenge."
        The True Tragedie of Rich. III.

III. ii. 384. '*bitter business as the day*'; so Folios; Quartos read '*business as the bitter day.*'

III. iii. 7. '*lunacies*'; so Folios; Quartos—'*browes.*'

III. iii. 79. '*hire and salary*'; so Folios; Quartos misprint, '*base and silly.*'

III. iv. 71-76, 78-81, 161-165, 167-170, 202-210, omitted in Folios.

III. iv. 169. '*And either . . . the devil*'; some such word as '*master*', '*quell*', '*shame,*' has been omitted in Quartos, which read '*and either the devil.*'

IV. i. 4. Omitted in Folios.

IV. i. 40-44. Folio 1 omits these lines, and ends scene with the words:—

"And what's untimely done. Oh, come away,
My soul is full of discord and dismay."

Theobald proposed to restore the line by adding '*for, haply, slander.*'

IV. ii. 17. '*like an ape*'; so Folios; Quartos, '*like an apple*'; Farmer conjectured '*like an ape, an apple*'; Singer, from Quarto 1, '*like an ape doth nuts*'; Hudson (1879), '*as an ape doth nuts.*'

IV. ii. 23, 24. '*A knavish speech sleeps in a foolish ear*'; a sentence proverbial since Shakespeare's time, but not known earlier.

IV. ii. 30. *cp.* Psalm cxliv., '*Man is like a thing of naught*'; 30, 31. '*Hide fox, and all after,*' the reading of Folios; omitted in Quarto.

IV. iii. 26-28. Omitted in Folios.

IV. iii. 40. '*this deed, for thine*'; so Quartos; Folios, '*deed of thine, for thine.*'

IV. iii. 43. '*with fiery quickness*'; so Folios; omitted in Quartos.

IV. iii. 68. '*my haps, my joys were ne'er begun*'; so Folios; Quartos, '*my haps, my joys will nere begin*'; Johnson conjectured '*my hopes, my joys are not begun*'; Heath conjectured "*t may hap, my joys will ne'er begin*'; Collier MS., '*my hopes, my joyes were ne're begun*'; Tschischwitz, '*my joys will ne'er begun.*'

IV. iv. 3. '*Craves*'; so Quartos; Folios 1, 2, '*Claimes.*'

IV. iv. 9-66. The reading of the Quartos; omitted in Folios.

IV. v. 38. '*grave*'; so Quarto 1, Folios; Quartos, '*ground*'; '*did go*'; Pope's emendation of Quartos; Folios, '*did not go.*'

IV. v. 47-54. Song in Quartos; omitted in Folios.

IV. v. 74. '*death. O*'; Quartos, '*death, and now behold.*'

IV. v. 86. '*Feeds on his wonder*'; Johnson's emendation; Quartos, '*Feeds on this wonder*'; Folios, '*Keepes on his wonder*'; Hanmer, '*Feeds on his anger.*'

IV. v. 93. '*Alack, what noise is this*', omitted in Quartos.

IV. v. 116. '*unsmirched brows*'; Grant White's emendation; Folio 1, '*unsmirched brow.*'

IV. v. 157-160, 162, omitted in Quartos.

IV. v. 163. '*rain'd*'; so Quartos; Folios 1, 2, '*raines.*'

IV. v. 169, 170. '*It is the false steward,*' &c.; the story has not yet been identified.

IV. v. 190. *cp.* '*Eastward Hoe*' (1604), by Jonson, Marston, and Chapman, for a travesty of the scene and this song (Act III. Sc. i.).

IV. vi. 2. '*Sea-faring men*'; so Quartos; Folios read '*Sailors.*'

IV. vii. 14. '*She's so conjunctive*'; so Folios; Quartos read '*She is so concline*'; Quarto, 1676, '*She is so precious.*'

IV. vii. 22. '*loud a wind*,' so Folios; Quartos 2, 3, '*loued Arm'd*'; Quartos 4, 5, '*loued armes*.'

IV. vii. 67-80. '*my lord . . . graveness*'; omitted in Folios; so, too, ll. 115-124.

IV. vii. 161. '*But stay, what noise?*'; the reading of Quartos; omitted in Folios.

IV. vii. 177. '*tunes*'; so Folio 1 and Quarto 1; Quarto 2, '*lauds*' (*i.e.* chants).

IV. vii. 191. '*douts*'; Knight's emendation; Folio 1, '*doubts*'; Quartos, '*drownes*.'

V. i. 34-36, 104-105. '*is this . . . recoveries*'; 119, 179, omitted in Quartos.

V. i. 241. '*treble woe*'; the reading of Quartos 2, 3, 6; Folio 1, '*terrible woer*'; Folios 2, 3, 4, '*terrible wooer*.'

V. i. 272. '*woo't drink up eisel*'; vide Glossary, '*eisel*'; the various emendations '*Weissel*,' '*Yssel*' (a northern branch of the Rhine), '*Nile*,' '*Nilus*,' are all equally unnecessary.

V. ii. 9. '*pall*'; so Quarto 2; Folio 1, '*parle*'; Pope, '*fall*.'

V. ii. 31. '*they*,' *i.e.* my brains.

V. ii. 57, 68-80. Omitted in Quartos.

V. ii. 78. '*court*'; Rowe's emendation of Folios, '*count*'.

V. ii. 96. '*or*'; Folios read '*for*.'

V. ii. 104-138. These lines are omitted in Folios, which read, '*Sir, you are not ignorant of what excellence Laertes is at his weapon*.'

V. ii. 123. '*another tongue*'; Johnson conjectured '*a mother tongue*'; Heath conjectured '*a mother tongue?*' No change is necessary; it's a bit of sarcasm.

V. ii. 150-151. Omitted in Folios.

V. ii. 183. '*many more of the same breed*'; so Quartos; Folio 1 reads, '*mine more of the same Beauy*'; Folios 2, 3, 4, '*nine more of the same Beavy*.'

V. ii. 190-202. Omitted in Folios.

V. ii. 217. '*Since no man has aught of what he leaves, what is't to leave betimes? Let be*.' The reading is taken partly from the Folios and partly from the Quartos; a long list of proposed emendations is given by the Cambridge editors.

V. ii. 234. Omitted in Quartos.

V. ii. 238. '*brother*'; so Quartos; Folios read '*mother*.'

V. ii. 281. '*He's fat and scant of breath*'; vide Glossary, '*FAT*.'

V. ii. 339. '*live*'; so Folios; Quartos, '*I leave*.'

V. ii. 377. '*forced cause*'; so Folios; Quartos read '*for no cause*.'

THE MERRY WIVES OF WINDSOR

I. i. 20. '*The luce is the fresh fish; the salt fish is an old coat*.' No satisfactory explanation of this passage has as yet been offered; various suggestions have been made, *e.g.* 'salt-fish' = the hake borne by the stockfishmongers; 'same' for 'salt'; ''tis ott fish' (assigned to Evans), &c. May not, however, the whole point of the matter lie in Shallow's use of 'salt' in the sense of 'saltant,' the heraldic term, used especially for vermin? If so, 'salt fish' = 'the leaping louse,' with a quibble on 'salt' as opposed to 'fresh fish.' There is further allusion to the proverbial predilection of vermin for 'old coats,' used quibblingly in the sense of 'coat-of-arms.'

I. i. 79. '*Outrun on Cotsall*,' *i.e.* on the Cotswold hills (in Gloucestershire); probably an allusion to the famous Cotswold Games, which were revived at the beginning of the seventeenth century, though evidently instituted earlier; the allusion does not occur in the first and second Quartos.

I. i. 153. '*Scarlet and John*'; Robin Hood's boon companion; an allusion to Bardolph's red face.

I. iii. 24. '*A minute's rest*'; "a minim's rest" is the ingenious suggestion of Bennet Langton; *cp. Romeo and Juliet*, II. iv. 22, "rests me his minim rest."

I. iii. 39. '*Carves*'; probably used here in the sense of 'to show favour by expressive gestures'; *cp.* "A carver: chironomus . . . one that useth apish motions with his hands."—Littleton's *Latin-English Dictionary* (1675).

I. iii. 61. '*Region of Guiana*.' Sir Walter Raleigh returned from his expedition to South America in 1596, and published his book on "The Discovery of the large, rich, and beautiful Empire of Guiana" in the same year.

I. iii. 83. '*By welkin and her star*.' This is no doubt the correct reading of the line, and there is no need to read *stars*, as has been suggested; 'star' is obviously used here for 'the sun'; the Quartos read 'fairies.'

II. i. 4, 5. '*Though Love use Reason for his physician*.' The Folios read '*precisian*'; the emendation adopted in the text was first suggested by Johnson, and has been generally accepted; *cp.* Sonnet CXLVII.: "My reason the physician to my love."

II. i. 195, 197. In the Folios the name 'Broome' is given instead of 'Brooke'; but Falstaff's pun, "Such Brooks are welcome to me, that overflow with liquor," removes all doubt as to the correct reading, which is actually found in the Quartos.

II. i. 198. '*Will you go, An-hires?*' so the Folios and Quartos; Theobald's correction 'mynheers' has been adopted by many modern editors. Other suggestions are "on, here;" "on, hearts;" "on, heroes;" "cavaleires;" &c.

II. iii. 81. '*Cried I aim?*' The Folios and Quartos read 'cried

game;' the ingenious emendation, due to Douce, was first adopted by Dyce.

III. i. 16, &c. Sir Hugh oddly confuses Marlowe's famous ditty, "Come live with me and be my love," and the old version of the 137th Psalm, "When we did sit in Babylon."

III. i. 90. '*Gallia and Gaul*'; so the Folios; the first and second Quartos read 'Gawle and Gawlia;' Farmer's conjecture "Gaullia and Gaul" was adopted by Malone and other editors. Gallia = Wales.

III. ii. 68. '*He shall not knit a knot in his fortunes*' (which are now as it were unravelled).

III. iii. 36. '*Have I caught thee*'; probably the reading of the Quarto which omits 'thee' is the more correct; Falstaff quotes from the second song in Sydney's *Astrophel and Stella*:—

"Have I caught my heav'nly jewell,
Teaching sleep most faire to be?
Now will I teach her that she
When she wakes is too-too cruell."

III. v. 4. The reading of the Quartos is seemingly preferable: —'Have I lived to be carried in a basket, and thrown into the Thames like a barrow of butcher's offal.'

III. v. 8, 9. '*The rogues slighted me into the river*,' *i.e.* 'Threw me' in contemptuously; the Quartos read 'slided me in.'

IV. i. 40. '*Hang-hog is Latin for bacon*'; probably suggested by the famous story told of Sir Nicholas Bacon. A prisoner named Hog, who had been condemned to death, prayed for mercy on the score of kindred. "Aye but," replied the judge, "you and I cannot be of kindred unless you are hanged; for Hog is not Bacon till it be well hanged" (Bacon's *Apophthegms*).

IV. ii. 17. '*Old lunes*'; the Folios and third Quarto read 'lines;' the first and second Quartos 'vaine;' the correction is Theobald's; the same error occurs in *Troilus and Cressida*, II. iii. 128.

IV. ii. 86. '*The witch of Brentford*'; an actual personage of the sixteenth century. A tract is extant entitled "Jyl of Breyntford's Testament," whence it appears that the witch kept a tavern at Brentford; in Dekker & Webster's *Westward Ho* the following allusion is found:—"I doubt that old hag Gillian of Brainford has bewitched me."

IV. iv. 41. '*That Falstaff at that oak shall meet with us*.' After this line the following words from the Quartos have been added in many editions:—

"We'll send him word to meet us in the field,
Disguised like Horne with huge horns on his head."

IV. iv. 56. '*To pinch*'; probably the correct reading should be 'to-pinch,' where 'to' is the intensitive prefix so common in old English, though it is possible to explain it as the ordinary infinitive prefix, omitted in the case of the former verb in the sentence.

IV. iv. 81. '*Send quickly to Sir John.*' Theobald ingeniously suggested 'Quickly' for 'quickly.'

IV. v. 69, 70. '*Cozen-germans*'; the first Quarto reads:—

"For there is three sorts of cosen garmombles,
Is cosen all the Host of Maidenhead and Readings,"

where 'garmombles' is very possibly a perversion of Mömpelgard; Count Frederick of Mömpelgard visited Windsor in 1592; free post-horses were granted him by a passport of Lord Howard.

The Count became a "Duke of Jamany" (Wirtemberg) in 1593; considerable interest must have been taken in the Duke about 1598. A letter to the Queen, dated August 14, 1598, is extant, in which the following passage occurs:—"I have heard with extreme regret that some of my enemies endeavour to calumniate me and prejudice your majesty against me. I have given them no occasion for this. I hope that when your majesty has discovered this report to be false, you will have greater reason to continue your affection towards me, and give neither faith nor credit to such vipers." In the year 1602 appeared "An Account of the Duke's Bathing Excursion to the far-famed Kingdom of England" (*vide* Rye's *England as seen by Foreigners*).

V. v. 22. '*Bribe buck*'; the Folios read 'brib'd buck,' which is probably the right reading: 'a bribed buck' was a buck cut up into portions, (Old French *bribes* = 'portions of meat to be given away').

V. v. 37. '*Orphan heirs.*' Theobald suggested 'ouphen' (elvish) for 'orphan,' and he has been followed by many editors, but the change is unnecessary. *Cp.* 'unfather'd heirs' 2 *Henry IV.* iv. 122.

V. v. 40, 42. '*Toys*,' evidently to be read 'toyës,' rhyming with 'O-yes' in the previous line; similarly 'unswept' should probably be 'unswep' rhyming with 'leap.'

V. v. 105. '*These fair yokes*'; the first Folio reads 'yoakes,' the second 'okes.' 'Yokes' must refer to the resemblance of the buck's horns to a yoke; a sort of sense can be got out of 'oaks,' the antlers resembling the branches of oaks, but the first Folio reading seems preferable.

TROILUS AND CRESSIDA

Prol. 15. '*six-gated city*'; Theobald, '*six gates i' th' city.*'

Prol. 16. '*Timbria, Helias, Chetas, Troien,*' so Folios; Theobald reads '*Thymbria, Ilia, Scæa, Troian;*' Capell, '*Thymbria, Ilias, Chetas, Troyan.*'

Prol. 17. '*Antenorides*'; Theobald's emendation of Folios, '*Antenonidus*'; Pope reads '*Anteroridas.*'

Prol. 23. '*A prologue arm'd*'; *i.e.* clad in armour instead of in a black cloak, which was the usual garb of the speaker of the Prologue.

Prol. 28. '*Beginning in the middle*'; Theobald reads "*Ginning i' th' middle.*'

I. i. 31. '*So, traitor!—"When she comes!"—When is she thence?*'; Quarto, '*So traitor then she comes when she is thence*'; Folios, '*So (Traitor) then she comes, when she is thence.*'

I. i. 37. '*a storm*'; Rowe's correction of Quarto, '*a scorne*'; Folios 1, 2, '*a-scorne*'; Folios 3, 4, '*a-scorn.*'

I. i. 44. '*praise her*'; so Quarto; Folios read '*praise it.*'

I. i. 55. '*Handlest in thy discourse, O, that her hand,*' &c.; Theobald, '*discourse—how white her hand*'; similar emendations have been proposed, but probably '*that her hand*' = 'that hand of hers.'

I. i. 75, 76. '*as fair on Friday as Helen is on Sunday*'; *i.e.* as beautiful in her worst dress as Helen in her 'Sunday best.'

I. ii. 153. '*two and fifty*'; so Quarto, Folios; Theobald reads '*one and fifty*': 'hairs'; Quarto reads '*heires.*'

I. ii. 234. '*an eye*'; so Quarto; Folios read '*money*'; Collier conjectured '*one eye.*'

I. ii. 282. '*joy's soul lies in the doing,*' so Quarto, Folio 1; Folios 2, 3, 4 read '*the soules joy lyes in dooing.*' Mason conjectured '*dies*'; Seymour conjectured '*lives,*' &c.

I. iii. 31. '*thy godlike*'; Theobald's emendation; Quarto, '*the godlike*'; Folios, '*thy godly*'; Pope, '*thy goodly.*'

I. iii. 54. '*Retorts*'; Dyce's emendation; Quarto, Folios read '*Retires.*'

I. iii. 70-75. Omitted in Quarto.

I. iii. 73. '*Mastic,*' perhaps a corrupt form of *L. mastigia,* a rascal that ought to be whipped; later, a scourge; the more usual form of the word was 'mastix,' *cp.* '*Histriomastix.*'

I. iii. 92. '*ill aspects of planets evil*'; so Folios; Quarto, '*influence of euill Planets.*'

I. iii. 220. '*Achilles*'; Johnson conjectured '*Alcides.*'

I. iii. 238. '*And, Jove's accord,*' *i.e.* 'And, Jove granting or favouring'; various emendations have been proposed on the supposition that the passage is corrupt.

I. iii. 315, 354-356. Omitted in Quarto.

II. i. 29, 30. Omitted in Folios.

II. i. 114. '*brooch*'; Rowe, '*brach*'; Malone conjectured '*brock.*'

II. ii. 77. '*an old aunt whom the Greeks held captive,*' *i.e.* "Priam's sister, Hesione, whom Hercules, being enraged at Priam's breach of faith, gave to Telamon, who by her had Ajax" (Malone).

II. ii. 110. '*Our firebrand brother, Paris,*' alluding to Hecuba's dream that she should be delivered of a burning torch.

II. ii. 166. '*Aristotle thought*'; Rowe and Pope proposed '*graver sages think,*' to save Shakespeare from the terrible anachronism. It has been pointed out that Aristotle speaks of political and not of moral philosophy; and, further, that Bacon makes the same mistake in his *Advancement of Learning,* Book II. (published 1605).

II. iii. 65. '*of the prover,*' the reading of Quarto; Folios read '*to the Creator*'; Rowe (ed. 2), '*to thy creator*'; Capell, '*of thy creator.*'

II. iii. 77. '*He shent our,*' Theobald's emendation; Quarto reads '*He sate our*'; Folios, '*He sent our.*'

II. iii. 140. '*Enter you*'; so Folios; Quarto reads '*entertaine.*'

III. i. 106. The reading of Folios omitted in Quarto.

III. ii. 65. '*fears*'; so Folio 3; Quarto, Folios 1, 2, '*teares*'; Folio 4, '*tears.*'

III. ii. 146. '*show*'; Folios 1, 2, 3, '*shew*' = 'showed.'

III. iii. 4. '*through the sight I bear in things to love*'; (?) 'through my peculiar knowledge as to where it is well to place affection'; Johnson proposed '*Jove*' for '*love,*' reading, 'through the sight I bear in things, to Jove I have abandoned,' &c., but Jove favoured the Trojans. No very satisfactory explanation has been advanced.

III. iii. 30. '*In most accepted pain,*' = trouble willingly undergone. Hanmer suggested '*pay*' for '*pain.*'

III. iii. 110. '*mirror'd,*' the reading of Singer MS. and Collier MS.; Quarto, Folios, '*married*'; Keightley, '*arrived*'; &c.

III. iii. 175. '*One touch of nature makes the whole world kin,*' *i.e.* one touch of human nature, one natural trait, shows the kinship of all mankind, viz. that they praise new-born gawds, and are always hankering after novelty.

III. iii. 194. '*one of Priam's daughters*'; *i.e.* 'Polyxena, in the act of marrying whom she was afterwards killed by Paris.'

IV. ii. 72. '*secrets of nature*'; so Folios; Quarto, '*secrets of neighbor Pandar*'; Theobald, '*secret'st things of nature*'; Hanmer '*secretest of natures,*' &c., &c.

IV. iv. 4. '*violenteth in a sense as strong, As that which*'; so Quarto; Folios read '*no lesse in . . . As that which,*' &c.; Pope, '*in its sense is no less strong, than that Which.*'

IV. iv. 77-80. The reading in the text is Staunton's; many

emendations have been proposed, but this is generally accepted by modern editors.

IV. iv. 146-150; v. 165-170. Omitted in Quarto.

IV. v. 29. Omitted in Folios; the reading of Quarto; Collier MS. reads *And parted you and your same argument.*

IV. v. 59. '*accosting,*' Theobald's conjecture; Quarto, Folios, '*a coasting*'; Collier MS., '*occasion*'; &c.

IV. v. 142. '*Neoptolemus so mirable*'; Hanmer reads '*Neoptolemus' sire so mirable*'; Warburton, '*Neoptolemus's sire irascible*'; Collier conjectured '*Neoptolemus so admirable,*' &c.

V. i. 19-22. '*raw . . . tetter,*' the reading of Quarto; omitted in Folios, substituting '*and the like.*'

V. i. 55. '*hanging at his brother's leg*'; so Folios; Quarto reads '*at his bare leg.*'

V. iii. 20-21. '*as lawful, For we would give much, to use violent thefts*'; Tyrwhitt's conjecture; Folios read, '*as lawfull: For we would count give much to as violent thefts.*'

V. iii. 112. The Folio here inserts:—

"PAND. Why, but heare you?
TROY. Hence brother lackie; ignomie and shame
Pursue thy life, and live aye with thy name."

Cf. Sc. x.

V. vii. 6. '*aims*'; so Capell; Quarto, Folio 2, '*armes*'; Folio 1, '*arme*'; Folios 3, 4, '*arms.*'

ALL'S WELL THAT ENDS WELL

I. i. 77, 78.

'*These great tears grace his remembrance more
Than those I shed for him;*'

i.e. "the big and copious tears she then shed herself, which were caused in reality by Bertram's departure, though attributed by Lafeu and the Countess to the loss of her father; and from this misapprehension of theirs graced his remembrance more than those she actually shed for him."

I. i. 107-160. These lines are struck out by some editors; the Cambridge editors rightly call them 'a blot on the play;' they were probably "an interpolation, 'to tickle the ears of the groundlings.'" The opening words of the speech which follows are obscure, and the enumeration of 'the loves' looks like 'the nonsense of some foolish conceited player.' Hanmer proposed:—

'*Not my virginity yet.—You're for the Court:
There shall your master,*' &c.

I. ii. 54. '*He scatter'd not in ears, but grafted them,*'; *cp.* the Collect in the Liturgy: "Grant we beseech thee, Almighty God, that the words which we have heard this day with our outward ears may through thy grace be so grafted inwardly in our hearts, that they may bring forth the fruit of good living," &c.

I. ii. 56. '*this,*' so the Folio; Pope read '*Thus,*' possibly the right word here.

I. ii. 22. '*service is no heritage*'; the idea seems to be that, 'if service is no blessing, children are'; Psalm cxxvii. 3 has been appropriately cited in connection with this expression:—"Lo, children are an heritage of the Lord."

I. iii. 51, 52. '*Young Charbon the puritan and old Poysam the papist*'; '*Charbon*' possibly for '*Chair-bonne,*' and '*Poysam*' for '*Poisson,*' alluding to the respective lenten fares of the Puritan and Papist (*cp.* the old French proverb, '*Jeune chair et viel poisson*' = *young* flesh and *old* fish are the best).

I. iii. 109. '. . . *queen of virgins*'; Theobald inserted '*Dian no*' before '*queen.*'

II. i. 1, 2. '*lords*' . . . '*lords*'; probably the young noblemen are divided into two sections according as they intend to take service with the 'Florentines' or the 'Senoys' (*cp.* Note vi. Cambridge edition).

II. i. 12, 13. '*let higher Italy,—Those bated,*' &c.; the passage is probably corrupt. '*Higher Italy*' has been variously interpreted to mean (1) Upper Italy; (2) the side of Italy next to the Adriatic (but both Florence and Siena are on the other side); (3) Italy higher in rank and dignity than France; (4) the noblest of Italy, the worthiest among Italians. Johnson paraphrased as follows:—'Let upper Italy, *where you are to exercise your valour,* see that you come to gain honour, to the *abatement,* that is, to the disgrace and depression of those *that have now lost their ancient military fame,* and inherit but the fall of the last monarchy.' Schmidt proposed '*high*' for '*higher*': Coleridge '*hired*': Hanmer '*bastards*' for '*bated.*' Knight took '*bated*' to mean '*excepted,*' Schmidt '*beaten down.*'

II. i. 32-3. '*No sword worn but one to dance with*'; alluding to the light swords worn for dancing.

II. i. 62. '*I'll fee*'; Theobald's emendation. Folios, '*Ile see.*'

II. i. 73. '*To give great Charlemain a pen in 's hand*'; Charlemagne late in life attempted to learn to write.

II. i. 74, 75.

'*ne worse of worst extended,
With vilest torture let my life be ended*';

So Folio 1; the other Folios read '*no*' for '*ne.*' Malone's '*nay*' for '*ne*' commends itself, though his explanation of '*extended*' as 'my body being extended on the rack' seems weak: it is probably used here simply in the sense of 'meted out to me,' or merely used for the purpose of emphasising '*worse of worst.*' A mass of conjectural emendations are recorded in the Cambridge edition of the play.

II. ii. 22, 23. '*Tib's rush for Tom's forefinger*'; 'Tib and Tom' were used like 'Jack and Jill'; Tib was a cant term for any low or vulgar woman. 'Rush rings' were sometimes used at marriage ceremonies, especially where the marriages were somewhat doubtful (*cp.* Douce's *Illustrations,* p. 196).

II. iii. 1-39. Johnson changed the distribution of the speakers, so as to bring out 'the whole merriment of the scene,' which, according to him, "consists in the pretensions of Parolles to knowledge and sentiments which he has not." Johnson has been generally followed by modern editors. The Folio arrangement has been kept in the Cambridge text.

II. iii. 23. '*a showing of a heavenly effect in an earthly actor*'; the title of some pamphlet is evidently ridiculed in these words.

II. iii. 74. '*Imperial Love*'; Folio 1, '*imperiall loue*'; Folio 2, '*imperiall Ioue*'; Folio 3, '*impartiall Jove.*'

II. iii. 77. '*ames-ace,*' *i.e.* two aces; the lowest throw at dice; one would expect it, from the context, to mean just the contrary, but Lafeu is probably making 'a comparison by contraries,'—'an ironical comparison,' used with humorous effect. "One lauding a sweet-songed prima donna," aptly observed Brinsley Nicholson, "says, I'd rather hear her than walk a hundred miles with peas in my boots."

II. v. 26. '*end*'; the Folios have '*And*'; the correction, from the Ellesmere copy of the first Folio, has been generally adopted.

II. v. 47, 48. '*Have or will to deserve*'; Malone proposed '*have qualities or will,*' &c.; Singer, '*wit or will*'; the later Folios omit '*to,*' and read '*have, or will deserve*'; the reading in the text is that of Folio 1.

III. i. 12-13.

'*That the great figure of a council frames
By self-unable motion*';

probably Clarke's explanation of these difficult lines is the best:—"The reasons of our state I cannot give you, excepting as an ordinary and uninitiated man, whom the august body of a government-council creates with power unable of itself to act, or with power incapable of acting of its own accord or independently." Others make '*that*' the subject of '*frames*,' explaining '*motion*' as 'mental sight,' or 'intuition.'

III. ii. 9. '*sold*'; so Folios 3, 4; Folios 1, 2, '*hold*'; Harness proposed '*holds a goodly manner for*.'

III. ii. 62. '*If thou engrossest all the griefs are thine*'; the omission of the relative is common in Shakespeare. Rowe unnecessarily altered the line to '*all the griefs as thine*.'

III. ii. 87. '*holds him much to have*'; so the Folios; Theobald conjectured '*soils him much to have*'; others suggested '*hoves him not much to have*'; '*fouls him much to have*,' &c. Rolfe's view of the passage seems by far the most satisfactory:—"He has a deal of that too-much, *i.e.* excess of vanity, which makes him fancy he has many good qualities."

III. ii. 107. '*still-peering air*'; so Folio 1; Folio 2, '*still-piercing*'; probably an error for '*still-piecing*,' *i.e.* '*still-closing*.' A passage in *The Wisdom of Solomon* has been appropriately compared, and may be the source of the thought:—"*As when an arrow is shot at a mark, it pareth the air, which immediately cometh together again, so that a man cannot know where it went through*."

III. v. 66. '*I write, good creature*,' so Folio 1; Folios 2, 3, 4, '*I right*'; Rowe, '*Ah! right good creature!*' The Globe edition, '*I warrant, good creature*'; Kinnear, '*I war'nt* (= warrant), *good creature*' (*cp.* *Hamlet*, I. ii. 242, Quarto 2, '*I war'nt*').

III. vi. 35. '*John Drum's Entertainment*'; 'to give a person John Drum's Entertainment' probably meant to give him such an entertainment as the drum gets; hence 'to give a person a drumming,' to turn him forcibly out of your company. Theobald quotes the following from Holinshed's *Description of Ireland*:— "His porter, or none other officer, durst not, for both his ears, give the simplest man that resorted to his house, *Tom Drum his entertainment*, which is to hale a man in by the head, and thrust him out by both the shoulders." In Marston's interlude, *Jack Drum's Entertainment* (1601), Jack Drum is a servant who is constantly baffled in his knavish tricks.

IV. i. 42. '*Bajazet's mule*'; the allusion has not yet been explained; perhaps '*Bajazet's*' is a blunder on the part of Parolles for '*Balaam's*.'

IV. ii. 25. '*Jove's*,' probably substituted for the original '*God's*,' in obedience to the statute against profanity. Johnson conjectured '*Love's*.'

IV. ii. 36. '*Who then recover*'; the Folios read, '*who then recovers*,' changed unnecessarily by Pope to '*which then recover*,' but '*who*' is often used for 'an irrational antecedent personified,' though in this passage the antecedent may be '*of me*' implied in '*my*'; '*my sick desires*' = 'the sick desires of me'; in this latter case 'recovers' is the more common third person singular, instead of the first person after '*who*.'

IV. ii. 38. '*I see that men make rope's in such a scarre*,' the reading of Folios 1, 2; Folio 3, '*make ropes*'; Folio 4, '*make ropes . . . scar*.' This is one of the standing cruxes in the text of Shakespeare; some thirty emendations have been proposed for '*ropes*' and '*scarre*,' *e.g.* '*hopes . . . affairs*'; '*hopes . . . scenes*'; '*hopes . . . scare*'; '*slopes scarre*': other suggestions are, '*may cope's . . . sorte*'; '*may rope's . . . snarle*'; '*may rope's . . . snare*,' &c. The apostrophe in the first and second Folios makes it almost certain that "*s*" stands for '*us*.' Possibly '*make*' is used as an auxiliary; '*make rope's*,' would then mean 'do constrain, or ensnare us.' Or is '*make rope*' a compound verb? '*Scarre*' may be '*scare*' (*i.e.* 'fright'). The general sense seems to be, 'I see that men may reduce us to such a fright, that we'll forsake ourselves.'

IV. iii. 238. '*He will steal, sir, an egg out of a cloister*,' *i.e.* 'anything, however trifling, from any place, however holy.'

IV. iii. 268, 269. '*and a perpetual succession for it*'; some such verb as '*grant*' is to be supplied. Hanmer altered '*for it*' to '*in it*'; Kinnear conjectured '*free in perpetuity*.'

IV. iv. 34. '*revives*'; so the Folios; '*eviles*,' '*invites*,' '*requires*' have been variously proposed; it is doubtful whether any change is necessary: 'Time,' says Helena, 'gives us fresh courage.'

IV. v. 35. '*an English name*'; Folios 1, 2, '*maine*'; Folio 3, '*main*'; Folio 4, '*mean*'; Rowe first suggested '*name*'; the allusion is obviously to the Black Prince.

IV. v. 36. '*his fisnomy is more hotter*'; Hanmer's proposal '*honour'd*' for '*hotter*' seems to be a most plausible emendation.

V. i. 6. '*Enter a Gentleman*'; Folio 1 reads '*A gentle Astringer*'; Folio 2, '*A gentle Astranger*'; Folios 3, 4, '*A Gentleman a stranger*.' '*Astringer*' = a keeper of goshawks; the word occurs nowhere else in Shakespeare. There seems, however, no very particular reason for its omission in modern editions, though it is true that in the Folio the speeches given to 'the Astringer' all have the prefix '*Gent*.'

V. ii. 1. '*Good Monsieur Lavache*'; Folio 1, '*Lauatch*'; Folio 2, '*Lavatch*'; Folios 3, 4, '*Levatch*'; Tollet's conjecture '*Lavache*' has been generally adopted. Clarke suggests that it may have been intended for *Lavage*, which, in familiar French, is used to express 'slop,' 'puddle,' 'washiness.' Something is to be said in favour of Jervis' proposed reading, '*Lapatch*,' *i.e.* '*patch*' = clown, with the prefix '*la*' in imitation of '*Lafeu*.'

V. ii. 26. '*Similes of comfort*'; Theobald's certain emendation for the reading of the Folios, '*smiles of comfort*.'

V. iii. 65, 66.

'*Our own love waking cries to see what 's done,*
While shameful hate sleeps out the afternoon.'

Johnson conjectured '*slept*' for '*sleeps*,' *i.e.* 'love cries to see what was done while hatred slept, and suffered mischief to be done.' Mason proposed '*old*' for '*own*.' W. G. Clarke ingeniously emended '*shameful hate*' into '*shame full late*,' but the emendation destroys the antithesis between '*love*' and '*hate*.' It is best to leave the lines as they stand, though the words '*our own love*' are somewhat doubtful: the general meaning is simple enough.

V. iii. 121. '*my fore-past proofs*,' &c.; *i.e.* "the proofs which I have already had are sufficient to show that my *fears* were not *vain* and irrational. I have rather been hitherto more easy than sought, and have *unreasonably* had *too little fear*" (Johnson).

V. iii. 193. '*He blushes, and 'tis it*'; Folios "*'tis hit*,' which has been variously explained as an Archaic form of 'it': as an error for "*'tis his*,' or '*is hit*.' It seems unnecessary to alter the Folio; "*'tis hit*' can very well mean 'the blow has been well aimed, it has struck home,' 'it' being used impersonally.

V. iii. 214. '*Her infinite cunning, with her modern grace*'; Walker's certain emendation of the Folio reading '*her insuite comming*'; other suggestions have been made:—'*Her instant comity*' (Bubier); '*Her Jesuit cunning*' (Bulloch); '*Her own suit, coming*' (Perring).

Epil. 1. '*The King's a beggar*'; an allusion to the old story of 'The King and the Beggar' (*cp.* Percy's *Reliques*), often referred to by Shakespeare; *cp.* '*Is there not a ballad, boy, of the King and the Beggar*'? (*Love's Labour's Lost*, I. ii. 114); similarly *Richard II.*, V. iii. 79, 80:—

'*Our scene is alter'd from a serious thing,*
And now chang'd to "The Beggar and the King." '

MEASURE FOR MEASURE

I. i. 8. There is no gap in the Folios, which is due to Theobald's plausible theory that the obscurity of the passage is due to some careless omission on the part of the printers. Various attempts have been made to explain the lines, *e.g.* "But that to your sufficiencies your worth is abled" (Johnson); "But your sufficiency as worth is able" (Farmer); Theobald supplied the missing words thus—

"*But that to your sufficiency you add*
Due diligency as your worth is able."

I. i. 42. '*Hold therefore, Angelo;*' the Duke probably says these words on tendering commission to Angelo.

I. ii. 27. '*There went but a pair of shears between us;*' *i.e.* 'we are of one piece.'

I. ii. 111. *Cp. St. Paul to the Romans* ix. 15, 18: "For He saith to Moses, I will have mercy *on whom I will* have mercy," and again, "Therefore hath He mercy *on whom He will* have mercy, and *whom He will* He hardeneth."

I. ii. 123. '*Morality;*' the Folios misprint '*mortality.*'

I. ii. 139. '*Propagation;*' Folio 1 reads *propogation*, corrected in Folio 2; *prorogation, procuration, preservation*, have been suggested by various editors, but the text as it stands is probably correct, though not altogether clear; '*propagation*' = 'increase;' perhaps the word implies 'increase of interest,' and '*for propagation*' = 'that she might continue to receive the interest, which was to be hers while she remained unmarried.'

I. iii. 43. '*To do in slander;*' so the Folios; '*me*' and '*it*' have been suggested for '*in*,' but no change is necessary; '*do in*' = 'bring in, bring upon me.'

II. i. 39. '*Some run from brakes of ice, and answer none;*' the line as it stands in the Folios is obviously corrupt, and has occasioned much discussion. Shakespeare probably wrote '*brakes of vice;*' brakes = thickets, hence 'entanglements;' '*brakes of vice*' is antithetical to '*a fault alone,*' *cp. Henry VIII.* I. ii. 75—

> "the rough brake
> That virtue must go through."

The line therefore means 'some escape from whole thickets of sin, and pay no penalty.' Judging by the passage in *Henry VIII*, *through* for *from* would perhaps be an improvement.

II. i. 127. '*An open room;*' Schmidt, "public room;" perhaps it means 'open to sun, light, cheerful.'

II. ii. 78. '*Like man new made;*' commentators are strongly tempted to refer the words to '*new made man,*' *i.e.* Adam; Holt White paraphrased thus:—"And you, Angelo, will breathe new life into Claudio, as the Creator animated Adam, by breathing into his nostrils the breath of life." Malone explains:—"You will then appear as tender-hearted and merciful as the first man was in his days of innocence, immediately after his creation." Schmidt and others, "like man redeemed and regenerated by divine grace." The lines are perhaps capable of this interpretation:—And mercy will breathe within your lips, even as Mercy (*i.e.* God) breathed within the lips of new made man.

II. ii. 89. "*Dormiunt aliquando leges, moriuntur nunquam,*" is a well-known maxim in law (Holt White).

II. ii. 156. '*Where prayers cross,*' *i.e.* where his prayer to possess Isabella crosses with hers, "Heaven keep your *honour* safe!"

II. iii. 11. '*The flaws of her own youth;*' possibly Warburton's correction "*flames*" should be adopted; *cp.*

> '*To flaming youth let virtue be as wax,*
> *And melt in her own fire.*'
> —HAMLET, III. iv. 84, 85.

II. iii. 40. '*O injurious love*' (Folios '*loue*'); Hanmer's suggestion, "*law*" for "*loue*," has been generally accepted; the law respited her 'a life whose very comfort' was 'a dying horror.'

II. iv. 9. '*Feared;*' probably an error of '*feared*,' *i.e.* '*seared*,' which, according to Collier, is the reading of Lord Ellesmere's copy of the first Folio.

II. iv. 103. '*That longing have been sick for;*' Rowe suggested, "I've been sick for."

II. iv. 172. '*O perilous mouths;*' the line is defective as it stands (?) "*O pernicious mouths*" (Walker), or "*these perilous*" (Seymour).

III. i. 94, 97. '*Prenzie;*' the source of this strange word has baffled students; it seems identical with the Scottish *primsie*, 'demure, precise,' which in its turn is connected with *prim* (in Old French *prin, pren*): under any circumstances there is no reason why the word should be changed, as has been proposed, to 'princely,' the reading of the second Folio, or 'priestly,' 'pensive,' &c.

III. ii. 9. "The passage seems to us to imply, furred (that is,

lined with lamb-skin fur inside, and trimmed with fox-skin fur outside) with both kinds of fur, to show that craft (fox-skin), being richer than innocency (lamb-skin), is used for decoration" (Clarke).

III. ii. 12, 13. '*Good father friar*' . . . '*good brother father;*' the joke, as Tyrwhitt pointed out, would be clearer in French, '*mon père frère*' . . . '*mon frère père.*'

III. ii. 39. '*From our faults, as faults from seeming, free!*' So Folio 1, Folio 2 and Folio 3, '*Free from our faults,*' &c.; Hanmer corrects the latter part of the line, '*As from faults seeming free.*' As it stands in the text, it would seem to mean "Would that we were so free from faults, as our faults are from seeming (hypocrisy)." One feels inclined to hazard—

> '*Free from our faults, as from false seeming, free!*'

(*Cp.* II. iv. 15. '*thy false seeming.*')

III. ii. 219, 220. '*Security enough to make fellowships accurst;*' *cp. Prov.* xi. 15.

III. ii. 252-273. These lines are in all probability not Shakespeare's, but by another hand.

III. ii. 255. '*Grace to stand, and virtue go;*' *i.e.* 'To have grace to stand firm, and virtue to go forward.'

III. ii. 264-267. '*How may likeness made in crimes,*' &c.; these lines do not readily admit of interpretation, and some corruption has probably crept into the text; Malone suggested *wade* for *made*, *i.e.* "How may hypocrisy wade in crimes;" Hanmer, "that likeness shading crimes," &c. None of the suggestions seems very satisfactory. Perhaps '*to draw*' = '*to-draw*,' *i.e.* 'pull to pieces' (?).

IV. i. This song appears in Beaumont and Fletcher's *Bloody Brother*, with the addition of the following stanza, assuredly not Shakespeare's, though found in the spurious edition of his poems, (1640)—

> "*Hide, O hide those hills of snow*
> *Which thy frozen bosom bears,*
> *On whose tops the pinks that grow*
> *Are of those that April wears;*
> *But first set my poor heart free,*
> *Bound by those icy chains by thee.*"

IV. i. 13. "Though the music soothed my sorrows, it had no tendency to produce light merriment" (Johnson).

IV. ii. 41, 42. '*If it be too little—thief;*' the Folios give this to *Clo.* (Pompey); Capell first transferred it to Abhorson, and he has been followed by most editors. Cowden Clarke defends the Folio arrangement; among other arguments he maintains that "the speech is much more in character with the clown's snip-snap style of chop-logic than with Abhorson's manner, which is remarkably curt and bluff."

IV. iv. 5. '*redeliver;*' Folio 1, '*re-liuer;*' Folio 2, '*deliuer;*' Capell first suggested '*redeliver.*'

IV. iv. 24. '*bears of a credent bulk;*' so Folios 1, 2, 3; many emendations have been proposed; Dyce's seems the most plausible—'bears so credent bulk;' '*credent bulk*' = 'weight of credit.'

V. i. 64. '*Do not banish reason, For inequality;*' *i.e.* because of 'improbability,' 'incongruity,' or, according to some, 'partiality.'

V. i. 320. "These shops," according to Nares, "were places of great resort, for passing away time in an idle manner. By way of enforcing some kind of regularity, and perhaps at least as much to promote drinking, certain laws were usually hung up, the transgression of which was to be punished by specific *forfeitures*. It is not to be wondered, that laws of that nature were as often laughed at as obeyed."

V. i. 352, 353. '*be hanged an hour*' seems to have been a cant phrase, meaning little more than 'be hanged!'

V. i. 491. '*Give me your hand;*' *i.e.* 'if you give me your hand.'

THE TRAGEDY OF OTHELLO, THE MOOR OF VENICE

I. i. 15. Omitted in Folios and Quartos 2, 3.

I. i. 21. 'A fellow almost damn'd in a fair wife'; if this alludes to Bianca, the phrase may possibly mean 'very near being married to a most fair wife.' Some explain, "A fellow whose ignorance of war would be condemned in a fair woman." The emendations proposed are unsatisfactory, and probably unnecessary.

I. i. 73. 'changes'; Folios read 'chances.'

I. ii. 72-78; iii. 18; 38; 65; 120; 125; 196; omitted Quarto 1.

I. ii. 75. 'weaken motion'; Rowe's emendation; Folios and Quartos 2, 3, 'weakens motion'; Pope (Ed. 2, Theobald) 'weaken notion'; Hanmer, 'waken motion'; Keightley, 'wakens motion'; Anon. conjecture in Furness, 'wake emotion,' &c.

I. iii. 69. 'bloody book of law'; "By the Venetian law the giving of love-potions was highly criminal" (Clarke).

I. iii. 89. 'feats of broil'; Capell's emendation; Quarto 1, 'feate of broile'; Folio 1, 'Feats of Broiles,' &c.

I. iii. 109. 'Certain'; so Quartos; Folios 'wider.'

I. iii. 141. 'portance in my'; so Folios and Quarto 2; Quarto 3, 'portence in my'; Quarto 1, 'with it all my'; Johnson conjectured 'portance in't; my' &c.; 'travels' ; the reading of Modern Ed. (Globe Ed.); Quartos, 'trauells'; Pope, 'travel's'; Folio 1, 'Trauellours'; Folios 2, 3, 'Travellers'; Folio 4, 'Traveller's'; Richardson conjectured 'travellous' or 'travailous.'

I. iii. 161. 'sighs'; Folios, 'kisses'; Southern MS., 'thanks.'

I. iii. 251. 'and storm of fortunes'; Quarto 1, 'and scorne of Fortunes,' &c.

I. iii. 262. 'Let her have your voices,' Dyce's correction; Folios, 'Let her have your voice'; Quartos read:—

> "Your voyces Lords; beseech you let her will
> Haue a free way."

I. iii. 265, 266. 'the young affects in me defunct'; Quartos, 'the young affects In my defunct'; so Folio 1; Folios 2, 3, 4 ('effects'). The reading of the text is the simplest and most plausible emendation of the many proposed, the words meaning 'the passions of youth which I have now outlived': 'proper satisfaction' = 'my own gratification.'

I. iii. 328. 'balance'; Folios, 'brain' and 'braine'; Theobald, 'beam.'

I. iii. 350. 'luscious as locusts'; "perhaps so mentioned from being placed together with wild honey in St. Matthew iii. 4" (Schmidt).

I. iii. 353, 354. Omitted in Folios.

I. iii. 381. The reading in the text is that of the second and third Quartos; Quarto 1 adds after the words 'I am chang'd':—

> "Goe to, farewell, put money enough in your purse";

omitting 'I'll go sell all my land.'

II. i. 39-40; 158; 255, 256 ('didst not mark that?'); omitted in Quarto 1.

II. i. 65. 'tire the ingener'; Knight, Steevens conjectured; Folio 1, 'tyre the Ingeniuer'; Folios 2, 3, 4, 'tire the Ingeniver'; Quarto 1, 'beare all Excellency—'; Quartos 2, 3, 'beare an excelency':—Johnson conjectured 'tire the ingenious verse'; Pope, 'beare all excellency—'.

II. i. 82. 'And . . . Cyprus'; omitted in Folios.

II. i. 245. 'a devilish knave'; omitted in Quartos.

II. i. 254. 'blest pudding'; Folios, 'Bless'd pudding'; omitted in Quartos.

II. i. 263. 'comes the master and main'; so Folios; Quarto 1 reads 'comes the maine'; Quartos 2, 3, 'comes Roderigo, the master and the maine.'

II. i. 274. 'haply may'; Quartos read 'haply with his Trunchen may.'

II. i. 303. 'poor trash of Venice, whom I trash'; Steevens' emendation; Quarto 1, 'poor trash . . . I crush'; Folios, Quartos 2, 3, 'poor Trash . . . I trace'; Theobald, Warburton conjectured 'poor

brach . . . I trace'; Warburton (later conjectured) 'poor brach . . . I cherish.'

II. iii. 38. 'here,' i.e. in my head.

II. iii. 84-91. These lines are from an old song called 'Take thy old cloak about thee,' to be found in Percy's Reliques.

II. iii. 161. 'sense of place'; Hanmer's emendation of Quartos, Folios, 'place of sense.'

II. iii. 306. 'some time'; so Quartos; Folios, 'a time'; Grant White, 'one time.'

III. i. 12, 13. 'for love's sake'; Quarto 1, 'of all loues.'

III. i. 41. 'Florentine,' i.e. 'even a Florentine'; Iago was a Venetian.

III. i. 50. Omitted in Folios.

III. iii. 23. 'watch him tame,' i.e. tame him by keeping him from sleep (as was done with hawks).

III. iii. 110. 'By heaven, he echoes me'; Quarto 1, 'By heauen he ecchoes me'; Folios, 'Alas, thou echo'st me'; Quartos 2, 3, 'why dost thou ecchoe me.'

III. iii. 136. 'thy worst of thoughts'; so Folios, Quarto 2; Quarto 1 reads 'the worst of thoughts'; Quarto 3, 'thy thoughts'; perhaps we should read:—

> "As thou dost rum'nate, give thy worst of thoughts."

III. iii. 174. 'strongly'; so Quartos; Folios, 'soundly'; Knight, 'fondly.'

III. iii. 281. 'Desdemona comes'; so Quartos; Folios read 'Looke where she comes.'

III. iii. 330; 388-395; 458-465; iv. 7-9; 197, 198. Omitted in Quarto 1.

III. iii. 445. 'any that was hers'; Malone's emendation; Quartos, 'any, it was hers'; Folio 1, 'any, it was hers'; Folios 2, 3, 4, 'any if 't was hers'; Anon. conjecture 'any "it" was hers.'

III. iii. 452. 'thy hollow cell'; so Quartos; Folios read 'the hollow hell'; Warburton, 'th' unhallow'd cell.'

III. iii. 461. Steevens compares the following passage in Holland's Pliny:—"And the sea Pontus ever more floweth and runneth out from Propontes, but the sea never retireth back again within Pontus."

III. iii. 474. 'business ever'; Quartos, 'worke so euer'; Collier, 'work soe'er'; &c.

III. iv. 45. 'our new heraldry' (vide Preface).

III. iv. 66. 'her,' i.e. to my wife (implied in 'wive').

III. iv. 123. 'shut myself up in,' &c., i.e. 'Confine myself to some other course of life, awaiting fortune's charity'; Quarto 1, 'shoote my selfe up in'; Capell, 'shoot myself upon'; Rann, 'shape myself upon'; Collier MS., 'shift myself upon.'

III. iv. 153. 'warrior'; Hanmer, 'wrangler'; cp. 'O my fair warrior' (II. i. 184).

IV. i. 76. 'here o'erwhelmed'; Quarto 1, 'here ere while, mad.'

IV. i. 119. ('What, a customer!'); ii. 74-77, 85-102; omitted in Quarto 1.

IV. i. 134. 'and, by this hand, she falls me'; so Collier; Quarto 1 reads 'by this hand she fals'; Folios, 'and falls me'; Quartos 2, 3, 'fals me.'

IV. i. 263. 'This the nature'; Pope's reading; Quartos, 'This the noble nature'; Folios, 'Is this the nature.'

IV. ii. 110. 'least misuse'; Quarto 1, 'greatest abuse'; Collier MS., 'least misdeede.'

IV. ii. 171. 'The messengers of Venice stay the meat'; Knight's reading; Folio 1, 'The Messengers of Venice staies the meate'; Folios 2, 3, 4, 'The Messenger of Venice staies the meate'; Quarto 1, 'And the great Messengers of Venice stay'; Quartos 2, 3, 'The meate, great Messengers of Venice stay.'

IV. iii. 23. 'All's one. Good faith'; Quarto 1, 'All's one good faith'; Quartos 2, 3, 'All's one; gooc father'; Folios, 'All's one: good Father.'

IV. iii. 26. 'Barbara'; Quartos read, 'Barbary'; Folio 1, 'Barbarie.'

IV. iii. 40. &c.; the original of Desdemona's song is to be

found in Percy's *Reliques* under the title of '*A Lover's Complaint, being forsaken of his Love*,' where the plaintive lover is a man.

IV. iii. 40. '*sighing*'; Folios, '*singing*'; Quarto 3, '*singhing*'; Folio 1 (Dev.), '*sining*.'

V. i. 82-83; ii. 86, 188-197, 270-276; omitted in Quarto 1.

V. i. 104. '*gentlemen*'; the reading of Folios; Quartos, '*Gentlewoman*.'

V. i. 106. '*if you stare*'; so Folios; Quartos 1, 2, '*an you stirre*'; Quarto 3, '*an you stirr*'; Anon. conjecture '*if you stay*.'

V. ii. 7. '*Put out the light, and then put out the light*'; *i.e.* 'put out the light, and then put out the light of life.' The Cambridge Editors give some dozen variant methods of punctuating and reading the line, but it is perfectly clear as it stands.

V. ii. 155. '*made mocks with love*'; "taken advantage to play upon the weakness of passion" (Johnson).

V. ii. 176. '*Disprove this villain*'; Capell, '*Disprove it, villain*.'

V. ii. 341. '*bring away*'; Quartos, '*bring him away*'; Collier MS., '*bring them away*.'

V. ii. 351. '*Indian*'; Folio 1, '*Iudean*'; Theobald proposed '*Judian*,' adding, "I am satisfied in his *Judian* he is alluding to Herod, who, in a fit of blind jealosie, threw away such a jewel of a wife as *Mariamne* was to him." This interpretation was Warburton's. "This it is," as Coleridge put it, "for no-poets to comment on the greatest of poets! To make Othello say that he, who had killed his wife, was like Herod who had killed Mariamne!" Boswell aptly quotes from Habington's *Castara*—

> "*So the unskilful Indian those bright gems*
> *Which might add majesty to diadems,*
> *'Mong the waves scatters.*"

THE TRAGEDY OF KING LEAR

I. i. 38. '*from our age*'; so Folios; Quartos '*of our state*.'

I. i. 39-44. ('*while we . . . now*'); 50-51, 164; I. ii. 18 ('*fine word, legitimate*'); 48 ('*and reverence*'); 119-124; I. iv. 6 ('*so may it come*'); 296; 345-356; omitted in Quartos.

I. i. 52. '*Where nature doth with merit challenge. Goneril*'; so Folios; Quartos read '*Where merit doth most challenge it.*'

I. i. 61. '*do*'; so Quartos; Folios read '*speak*.'

I. i. 77. '*Ponderous*'; so Folios; Quartos, '*richer*.'

I. i. 82. '*the last, not least*'; so Quartos; Folios read '*our last and least*.'

I. i. 103; ii. 94-96; ii. 143-150 ('*as of unnaturalness . . . come*'); 170 ('*go armed*'); I. iii. 17-21; 25, 26; I. iv. 138-153; 218; 231-235; omitted in Folios.

I. i. 109. '*mysteries*,' the reading of Folios 2, 3, 4; Quartos, '*mistresse*'; Folio 1, '*miseries*.'

I. i. 145. '*What wouldst thou do, old man?*'; "This is spoken on seeing his master put his hand to his sword" (Capell); Folios 1, 2, 3, '*wouldest*'; Quartos, '*wilt*.'

I. i. 148. '*stoops to folly*'; so Quartos; Folios, '*falls to folly*' (Folio 3, '*fall to folly*'); '*Reverse thy doom*'; so Quarto; Folios read, '*reserue thy state*.'

I. i. 166. '*recreant*'; omitted in Quartos.

I. i. 173. '*five*'; so Folios; Quartos, '*Foure*.'

I. i. 175. '*sixth*,' so Folios; Quartos, '*fift*.'

I. i. 191. This line is given to Cordelia in Folios.

I. i. 232. '*Better*'; so Folios; Quartos, '*go to, go to, better*.'

I. i. 247. '*respects of fortune*'; so Quartos; Folios, '*respect and fortunes*.'

I. i. 278. '*want*'; Quartos, '*worth*.' Theobald explains the Folio reading, "You well deserve to meet with that *want* of love from your husband, which you have professed to want for our Father."

I. i. 280. '*shame them derides*'; so Quartos; Folios, '*with shame derides*'; Warburton, '*with shame abides*,' &c.

I. i. 288. '*hath not been*'; so Quartos; Folios, '*hath been*.'

I. ii. 10. So Folios; Quartos read, '*with base, base bastardie*.'

I. ii. 21. '*top the*'; Edward's conjecture of Quartos 1, 2, '*tooth*'; Quarto 3, '*too h*'; Folios 1, 2, '*to'th*'; Folios 3, 4, '*to th*,' &c.

I. ii. 63. '*that*,' *i.e.* the matter, contents.

I. ii. 102. '*These late eclipses in the sun and moon portend no good*'; *v.* Preface.

I. ii. 118. '*surfeit*'; so Quarto 1; Quartos 2, 3, '*surfet*'; Folios 1, 2, 3, '*surfets*'; Folio 4, '*surfeits*'; Collier conjectured '*forefeit*.'

I. ii. 181-188. '*That's my fear . . . Brother*,' so Folios; Quartos read '*That's my feare brother*,' omitting rest of speech.

I. iii. 21. '*With checks as flatteries, when they are seen abused*'; Tyrwhitt's explanation seems the most plausible, "with checks, as well as flatterers, when they (*i.e.* flatterers) are seen to be abused." The emendators have been busy with the line without much success.

I. iv. 96. '*Kent Why, fool?*'; the reading of Quartos; Folios read '*Lear. Why m*y *Boy?*'

I. iv. 152. '*Ladies* ; Capell's emendation; Quartos, '*lodes*'; Collier, '*loads*.'

I. iv. 228. '*Ha! waking?*' Quartos read '*sleeping or waking; ha! sure.*'

II. i. 10-11. Omitted in Quartos 2, 3.

II. i. 47. '*their thunders*'; so the Quartos; Folios, '*the thunder*'; Johnson, '*their thunder*.'

II. i. 59. '*dispatch*'; *i.e.* 'dispatch him'; or perhaps, 'dispatch is the word.'

II. i. 71. '*what I should deny*'; so Quartos; Folios, '*What should I deny*'; Rowe, '*by what I should deny*'; Hanmer, '*what I'd deny*'; Warburton, '*when I should deny*'; Schmidt, '*what, should I deny*.'

II. i. 79. '*I never got him*'; so Quartos; Folios, '*said he?*'

II. i. 98. '*of that consort*'; so Folios; omitted in Quartos.

II. i. 101. '*the waste and spoil of his*'; Quarto 1, '*the wast and spoyle of his*'; Quartos 2, 3, '*these—and waste of this his*'; Quarto 1 (Dev. and Cap.) '*these—and waste of this his*'; Folio 1, '*th' expence and wast of his*'; Folios 2, 3, 4, '*th' expence and wast of*.'

II. ii. 57. '*hours*'; Folios, '*years*.'

II. ii. 72. '*Which are too intrinse to unloose*'; Folio 1, '*are t' intrince*'; Folios 2, 3, 4, '*art t'intrince*'; Quartos, '*are to intrench*'; Pope, '*Too intricate*'; Theobald, '*Too 'intrinsecate*'; Hanmer, '*too intrinsick*'; '*to unloose*'; Folios, '*t'unloose*'; Quartos, '*toinloose*'; Seymour conjectured '*to enloose*.'

II. ii. 138-142. '*His fault . . . punish'd with*'; omitted in Folios.

II. ii. 142. '*the king must take it ill*'; Folios read '*the King his Master, needs must take it ill*.'

II. ii. 147. Omitted in Folios.

II. ii. 158, 159. '*out of heaven's benediction comest To the warm sun*'; *cp.* Heywood's '*Dialogues on Proverbs*'; '*In your rennyng from hym to me, ye runne out of God's blessing into the warm sunne*'; *i.e.* from good to worse. Professor Skeat suggests to me that the proverb refers to the haste of the congregation to leave the shelter of the church, immediately after the priest's benediction, running from God's blessing into the warm sun. This explanation seems by far the best that has been suggested.

II. ii. 162. '*miracles*'; so Folios; Quartos 1, 2, 3, '*my wracke*'; Quarto 1 (Bodl.), '*my rackles*.'

II. ii. 165-167. '*and shall . . . remedies*'; many emendations have been proposed to remove the obscurity of the lines, but none can be considered satisfactory. Kent, it must be remembered, is 'all weary and o'er-watched.' Jennens suggested that Kent is reading disjointed fragments of Cordelia's letter. '*From this enormous state*' seems to mean 'in this abnormal state of affairs.'

II. iv. 18, 19. Omitted in Folios.

II. iv. 95, 96; 137-142. Omitted in Quartos.

II. iv. 99. '*commands her service*'; so Quartos; Folios, '*commands, tends, service*.'

II. iv. 165. '*and blast her pride*'; so Quartos; Folios, '*and blister*'; Collier MS. and S. Walker conjectured '*and blast her*'; Schmidt conjectured '*and blister pride*.'

II. iv. 169. '*tender-hefted*'; so Folios; Quarto 2, '*tender hested*'; Quarto 1, '*teder hested*'; Quarto 3, '*tender hasted*'; Rowe (Ed. 2) and Pope, '*tender hearted*'; &c.

II. iv. 298. '*bleak*'; so Quartos; Folios, '*high*.'

III. i. 7-15; vi. 17-55; 97-101 ('*oppressed . . . behind*'); 102-115; vii. 99-107; omitted in the Folios.

III. i. 22-29; ii. 79-96; iv. 17-18; 26-27; 37-38; vi. 12-16; 84; omitted in the Quartos.

III. ii. 7. '*smite*'; so Quartos; Folios, '*strike.*'

III. ii. 9. '*make*'; Folios, '*makes.*'

III. ii. 22. '*have . . . join'd*'; the reading of Quartos; Folios read '*will . . . join.*'

III. ii. 37. '*No I will be the pattern of all patience*'; cp. the description of Leir by Perillus in the old play:—'*But he, the myrrour of mild patience, Puts up all wrongs, and never gives reply.*'

III. ii. 64. '*More harder than the stones*'; so Folios; Quartos '*More hard then is the stone.*'

III. ii. 73. '*That's sorry*'; so Folios; Quartos, '*That sorrowes.*'

III. ii. 74-77. Cp. Clown's song in *Twelfth Night*, V. vi. 379.

III. ii. 95-96. '*I live before his time*'; according to the legend, Lear was contemporary with Joash, King of Judah. The whole prophecy, which does not occur in the Quartos, was probably an interpolation, tacked on by the actor who played the fool. The passage is an imitation of some lines formerly attributed to Chaucer, called '*Chaucer's Prophecy.*'

III. iv. 6. '*contentious*'; so Folios; Quarto 1 (some copies) '*tempestious*'; Quartos 2, 3, and Quarto 1 (some copies) '*crulentious.*'

III. iv. 29. '*storm*'; so Quartos; Folios, '*night.*'

III. iv. 46. '*Through the sharp hawthorn blows the cold wind*'; probably the burden of an old song.

III. iv. 53-54. '*knives under his pillow and halters in his pew*' (to tempt him to suicide). Theobald pointed out that the allusion is to an incident mentioned in Harsnet's *Declaration.*

III. iv. 81. '*thy word justly*'; Pope's emendation; Quartos read, '*thy words justly*'; Folio 1, '*thy words Justice.*'

III. iv. 101. '*sessa*'; Malone's emendation; Folio 1, '*Sesey,*' Quarto 1, '*cease*'; Quarto 2, '*cease*'; Capell, '*sesse*'; &c.

III. iv. 138, 139. Cp. '*The Romance of Sir Bevis of Hamptoun*';—

> "Rattes and myce and suche small dere,
> Was his meate that seuen yere."

III. iv. 182-184. '*Child Rowland to the dark tower came,*' &c. Jamieson, in his *Illustrations of Northern Antiquities* (1814) has preserved the story as told him by a tailor in his youth; this Scottish Version has since been reprinted and studied (Cp. Childs' *English and Scottish Ballads*, and Jacob's *English Fairy Tales*).

III. iv. 183. '*His word was still*' refers, of course, to the giant, and not to Childe Rowland. The same story (with the refrain *Fee fo fum, Here is the Englishman*) is alluded to in Peele's *Old Wives Tale*, and it is just possible that it may be the ultimate original of the plot of Milton's *Comus* (v. Preface, on *British* for *English*).

III. vi. 25. '*Come o'er the bourn, Bessy, to me.*' Mr. Chappell (*Popular Music of the Olden Time*, p. 305, note) says, "The allusion is to an English ballad by William Birch, entitled, 'A Songe betwene the Quene's Majestie and England,' a copy of which is in the library of the Society of Antiquaries. England commences the dialogue, inviting Queen Elizabeth in the following words:—

> "Come over the born, Bessy, come over the born, Bessy,
> Swete Bessy, come over to me."

The date of Birch's song is 1558, and it is printed in full in the *Harleian Miscellany*, X. 260.

III. vi. 41-44. Put into verse by Theobald. Steevens quotes a line from an old song,

> "Sleepeyst thou, makyst thou, Jeffery Coke."

found in *The Interlude of the Four Elements* (1519).

III. vi. 73. '*Thy horn is dry*,' "A horn was usually carried about by every Tom of Bedlam, to receive such drink as the charitable might afford him, with whatever scraps of food they might give him" (Malone), &c.

III. vi. 89-102. "Every editor from Theobald downwards," as the Cambridge Editors observe, "except Hanmer, has

reprinted this speech from the Quartos. In deference to this consensus of authority we have retained it, though, as it seems to us, internal evidence is conclusive against the supposition that the lines were written by Shakespeare."

III. vii. 58. '*stick*'; the reading of Folios; Quartos, '*rash.*'

III. vii. 63. '*howl'd that stern*'; Quartos, '*heard that dearne*': Capell, '*howl'd that dearn*'; ('dearn' = obscure, dark, gloomy).

III. vii. 65. '*All cruels else subscribed*'; so Quartos; Folios '*subscribe.*' The passage has been variously interpreted; the weight of authority favouring the Folio reading, Schmidt's explanation being perhaps the most plausible:—"Everything which is at other times cruel, shows feeling or regard; you alone have not done so." Furness makes the words part of the speech addressed to the porter, "acknowledge the claims of all creatures, however cruel they may be at other times," or "give up all cruel things else; *i.e.*, forget that they are cruel." This approximates to the interpretation given by Mr. Wright to the reading in the text, "all their other cruelties being yielded or forgiven."

IV. i. 6-9. '*Welcome . . . blasts*'; vi. 166-171 ('*Plate . . . lips*'); vii. 61; omitted in the Quartos.

IV. i. 12. '*Life would not yield to age,*' *i.e.* life would not gladly lapse into old age and death.

IV. i. 38. '*Kill*'; Quarto 1, '*bitt*'; Quartos 2, 3, '*bit*'; (probably an error for '*hit*').

IV. i. 60-64. ii. 31-50, 53-59, 62-68, 69; iii. (the whole scene); vii. 24-25, 33-36, 79-80, 85-98, omitted in the Folios.

IV. ii. 28. '*My fool usurps my body*'; so Folios; Quarto 1, '*A foole usurps my bed*'; Quarto 2, '*My foote usurps my head*'; Malone, '*My fool usurps my bed.*'

IV. ii. 47. '*tame these vile offences*'; Schmidt conjectured '*take the vild offenders*'; Heath conjectured '*these vile*'; Quarto 1, '*this vild*'; Pope, '*the vile.*'

IV. ii. 57. '*thy state begins to threat*'; Jennens conjectured; Quarto 1, '*thy state begins thereat*'; Quartos 2, 3, '*thy slaier begins threats*'; Theobald, '*thy slayer begins his threats,*' &c.

IV. ii. 68. '*your manhood! mew!*'; some copies of Quarto 1 read '*manhood mew*'; others '*manhood now*'; so the later Quartos; according to the present reading '*mew*' is evidently a cat-like interjection of contempt.

IV. iii. 19. '*like a better way*'; so Quartos; the passage seems to mean that her smiles and tears resembled sunshine and rain, but in a more beautiful manner; many emendations have been proposed—'*like a wetter May*' (Warburton); '*like a better May*' (Malone); '*like;—a better way*' (Boaden), &c.

IV. iii. 29. '*Let pity not be believed*'; Pope, '*Let pity ne'er believe it*'; Capell, '*Let it not be believed*' (but '*believed*' = "believed to exist').

IV. iii. 31. '*clamour moisten'd*'; Capell's reading; Quartos '*And clamour moistened her*'; Theobald, '*And, clamour-motion'd*'; Grant White, '*And, clamour-moisten'd,*' &c.

IV. v. 4. '*lord*'; so Folios; Quartos read '*lady.*'

IV. vi. 97-98. '*I had white hairs in my beard ere the black ones were there*'; *i.e.*, "I had the wisdom of age before I had attained to that of youth" (Capell).

IV. vi. 225. '*tame to*'; so Folios; Quartos, '*lame by.*'

IV. vii. 32. '*opposed against the warring winds*'; Quartos, '*Exposed*'; Folios, '*jarring.*'

IV. vii. 36. '*Mine enemy's*'; Folios '*Mine Enemies*'; Quartos 1, 2, '*Mine injurious*'; Quarto 2, '*Mine injurious*'; Theobald, '*My very enemy's,*' &c.

IV. vii. 79. '*kill'd*'; so Folios; Quartos '*cured*'; Collier conjectured '*quell'd.*'

V. i. 11-13, 18-19, 23-28, 33; iii. 39-40, 48, 55-60, 103, 110, 205-222, omitted in the Folios.

V. i. 26. Mason's conjecture '*Not the old king*' for '*not bolds the king*' is worthy of mention. Albany's point is that the invading enemy is France and not the wronged king, together with others whom heavy causes compel to fight against them; otherwise '*not bolds the king*' = 'not as it emboldens the king'; an awkward and harsh construction.

V. i. 46. '*and . . . ceases*'; iii. 77, 91, 145, 282, omitted in the Quartos.

V. ii. 5. Mr. Spedding (*News Sh. Soc. Trans.*, Part I.) plausibly suggested that the Fifth Act really begins here, and that the battle takes place between Edgar's exit and re-entrance, the imagination having leisure to fill with anxiety for the issue.

V. iii. 77. '*the walls are thine*'; Theobald conjectured '*they all are thine*'; (but perhaps the castle-walls are referred to).

V. iii. 94. '*prove it*'; so Quartos; Folios, '*make it*'; Anon. conjecture '*mark it*'; Collier MS., '*make good*.'

V. iii. 97. '*medicine*,' Folios; Quartos, '*poyson*.'

V. iii. 129. '*the priuilege of mine honours*'; Pope's reading; Quartos read '*the priuiledge of my tongue*'; Folios, '*my priuiledge, The pruiledge of mine Honours*.' Edgar refers to '*the right of bringing the charge*' as the privilege of his profession as knight.

V. iii. 147. Omitted in Quarto 2; Quarto 1 reads '*Heere do I tosse those treasons to thy head.*'

V. iii. 157. '*name*'; Quartos read '*thing*.'

V. iii. 160. '*Most monstrous! know'st*'; Steevens' emendation; Quarto 1 reads '*Most monstrous knowst*'; Quartos 2, 3, '*Monster, knowst*'; Folios, '*Most monstrous! O know'st*'; Capell, '*Most monsterous! know'st*'; Edd. Globe Ed., '*Most monstrous! Oh! know'st*.'

V. iii. 161. '*Ask me not what I know*'; the Folios give this line to Edmund; the Quartos to Goneril.

V. iii. 171, 172. '*vices . . . plague us*'; so Folios; Quartos read *vertues . . . scourge us*; Hanmer, '*vices . . . plague and punish us*'; Keightley, '*vices . . . plague us in their time*'; Anon. conjecture '*vices . . . scourge us and to plague us*'; *cp*. 'Wherewith a man sinneth, by the same also shall he be punished,' *Wisdom* xi. 16.

V. iii. 206. '*but another*,' &c., *i.e.* "one more such circumstance only, by amplifying what is already too much, would add to it, and so exceed what seemed to be the limit of sorrow" (Wright).

V. iii. 282. '*One of them we behold*,' *i.e.* each beholding the other sees one of fortune's two notable objects of love and hate; (? for '*we*' read '*ye*,' as has been suggested).

V. iii. 311. '*Look on her, look, her lips*'; Johnson's emendation; Folio 1 reads '*Looke her lips*'; Folios, '*looke (or look) on her lips.*'

V. iii. 324. This speech is given in the Folios to Edgar, and probably it was so intended by the poet. It has been suggested that the first two lines should be given to Edgar, the last two to Albany.

THE TRAGEDY OF MACBETH

I. i. 1. Perhaps we should follow the punctuation of the Folio, and place a note of interrogation after '*again*.'

I. ii. 14. '*damned quarrel*'; Johnson's, perhaps unnecessary, emendation of Folios, '*damned quarry*' (*cp*. IV. iii. 206); but Holinshed uses '*quarrel*' in the corresponding passage.

I. ii. 20-21. Many emendations and interpretations have been advanced for this passage; Koppel's explanation (*Shakespeare Studien*, 1896) is as follows:—"he faced the slave, who never found time for the preliminary formalities of a duel, *i.e.* shaking hands with and bidding farewell to the opponent"; seemingly, however, '*which*' should have '*he*' (*i.e.* Macbeth) and not '*slave*' as its antecedent.

I. iii. 15. '*And the very ports they blow*'; Johnson conjectured '*various*' for '*very*'; Pope reads '*points*' for '*ports*'; Clar. Press ed. '*orts*'; '*blow*' = 'blow upon.'

I. iii. 32. '*weird*'; Folios, '*weyward*' (prob. = '*weird*'); Keightley, '*weyard*.'

I. iii. 98, 99. '*As thick as hail Came post*'; Rowe's emendation; Folios read '*As thick as tale Can post*.'

I. v. 21-23. The difficulty of these lines arises from the repeated words '*that which*' in line 22, and some editors have consequently placed the inverted commas after '*undone*'; but '*that which*' is probably due to the same expression in the previous line, and we should perhaps read '*and that's which*' or '*and that's what*.'

I. vi. 4. '*martlet*'; Rowe's emendation of Folios, '*Barlet*.'

I. vi. 5. '*loved mansionry*'; Theobald's emendation of Folios, '*loved mansonry*'; Pope (ed. 2), '*loved masonry*.'

I. vi. 6. '*jutty, frieze*'; Pope, '*jutting frieze*'; Staunton conjectured '*jutty, nor frieze*,' &c.

I. vi. 9. '*most*'; Rowe's emendation of Folios, '*must*'; Collier MS. '*much*.'

I. vii. 6. '*shoal*'; Theobald's emendation of Folios 1, 2, '*schoole*.'

I. vii. 45. '*Like the poor cat i' the adage*'; 'The cat would eat fyshe, and would not wet her feete,' Heywood's *Proverbs*; the low Latin form of the same proverb is:—

"*Catus amat pisces, sed non vult tingere plantas.*"

I. vii. 47. '*do more*'; Rowe's emendation of Folios, '*no more.*'

II. i. 51. '*sleep*'; Steevens conjectured '*sleeper*,' but no emendation is necessary; the pause after '*sleep*' is evidently equivalent to a syllable.

II. i. 55. '*Tarquin's ravishing strides*'; Pope's emendation; Folios, '*Tarquins ravishing sides*.'

II. i. 56. '*sure*'; Pope's conjecture, adopted by Capell; Folios 1, 2, '*sowre*.'

II. i. 57. '*which way they walk*'; Rowe's emendation; Folios, '*which way they may walk.*'

II. ii. 35-36. There are no inverted commas in the Folios. The arrangement in the text is generally followed (similarly, ll. 41-43).

III. i. 129. '*you with the perfect spy o' the time*'; Johnson conjectured '*you with a*'; Tyrwhitt conjectured '*you with the perfect spot, the time*'; Beckett conjectured '*you with the perfectry o' the time*'; Grant White, from Collier MS., '*you, with a perfect spy, o' the time*'; Schmidt interprets '*spy*' to mean "an advanced guard; that time which will precede the time of the deed, and indicate that it is at hand"; according to others '*spy*' = the person who gives the information; the simplest explanation is, perhaps, 'the exact spying out of the time,' *i.e.* 'the moment on't,' which in the text follows in apposition.

III. ii. 20. '*our peace*'; so Folio 1; Folios 2, 3, 4, '*our place*.'

III. iv. 14. '*'Tis better thee without than he within*'; probably '*he*' instead of '*him*' for the sake of effective antithesis with '*thee*'; unless, as is possible, '*he within*' = 'he in this room.'

III. iv. 78. '*time has*'; Folio 1, '*times has*'; Folios 2, 3, 4, '*times have*'; the reading of the First Folio is probably what Shakespeare intended.

III. iv. 105-106. '*If trembling I inhabit then*'; various emendations have been proposed, *e.g.* '*I inhibit*,' = '*me inhibit*,' '*I inhibit thee*,' '*I inherit*,' &c.; probably the text is correct, and the words mean 'If I then put on the habit of trembling,' *i.e.* 'If I invest myself in trembling' (*cp*. Koppel, p. 76).

III. iv. 122. The Folios read:—

"*It will have blood they say;
Blood will have blood.*"

III. iv. 144. '*in deed*'; Theobald's emendation of Folios, '*indeed*'; Hanmer, '*in deeds*.'

III. v. 13. '*Loves*'; Halliwell conjectured '*Lives*'; Staunton conjectured '*Loves evil*.'

III. vi. 27. '*the most pious Edward*,' *i.e.* Edward the Confessor.

IV. i. 97. '*Rebellion's head*'; Theobald's conjecture, adopted by Hanmer; Folios read '*Rebellious dead*'; Warburton's conjecture, adopted by Theobald, '*Rebellious head*.'

IV. ii. 18, 19. '*when we are traitors And do not know ourselves*,' *i.e.* 'when we are accounted traitors, and do not know that we are, having no consciousness of guilt'. Hanmer, '*know't o.*'; Keightley, '*know it ourselves*'; but no change seems necessary.

IV. ii. 19-20. '*when we hold rumour*,' &c.; *i.e.* 'when we interpret rumour in accordance with our fear, yet know not exactly what it is we fear.'

IV. ii. 22. '*Each way and move*'; Theobald conjectured '*Each way and wave*'; Capell, '*And move each way*'; Steevens conjectured 'And each way move'; Johnson conjectured 'Each way, and move—'; Jackson conjectured 'Each wail and moan'; Ingleby conjectured 'Which way we move'; Anonymous conjecture, 'And move each wave'; Staunton conjectured 'Each sway and move'; Daniel conjectured 'Each way it moves'; Camb. eds. conjectured 'Each way and none'; perhaps 'Each way we move' is the simplest reading of the words.

IV. ii. 70. 'do worse,' i.e. "let her and her children be destroyed without warning" (Johnson); (Hanmer, 'do less'; Capell, 'do less').

IV. iii. 15. 'deserve'; Warburton's emendation, adopted by Theobald; Folios 1, 2, 'discerne'; Folios 3, 4, 'discern'; ——, 'and wisdom'; there is some corruption of text here, probably a line has dropped out. Hanmer reads ''tis wisdom'; Steevens conjectured 'and wisdom is it'; Collier conjectured 'and 'tis wisdom'; Staunton conjectured 'and wisdom 'tis' or 'and wisdom bids'; Keightley, 'and wisdom 'twere.'

IV. iii. 111. 'Died every day she lived,' "lived a life of daily mortification" (Delius).

IV. iii. 235. 'tune'; Rowe's emendation of Folios, 'time.'

V. i. 24. 'sense is shut'; Rowe's emendation of Folios, 'sense are shut'; S. Walker's conjecture, adopted by Dyce, 'sense are shut.' The reading of the Folio probably gives the right reading, 'sense' being taken as a plural.

V. iii. 1. 'them,' i.e. the thanes.

V. iii. 21. 'cheer'; Percy's conjecture, adopted by Dyce, 'chair'; ——, 'disseat,' Jennens's and Capell's conjecture, adopted by Steevens; Folio 1, 'dis-eate'; Folios 2, 3, 4, 'disease'; Bailey conjectured 'disseize'; Daniel conjectured 'defeat'; Furness, 'dis-ease'; Perring conjectured 'disheart.'

V. iii. 22. 'way of life'; Johnson proposed the unnecessary emendation 'May of life,' and several editors have accepted the conjecture.

V. iii. 43. 'stuff'd'; Folios 2, 3, 4, 'stuft'; Pope, 'full'; Steevens' conjecture, adopted by Hunter, 'foul'; Anonymous conjecture, 'fraught,' 'press'd'; Bailey conjectured 'stain'd'; Mull conjectured 'steep'd'; ——; 'stuff'; so Folios 3, 4; Jackson conjectured 'tuft'; Collier (ed. 2), from Collier MS., 'grief'; Keightley, 'matter'; Anonymous conjecture, 'slough,' 'freight'; Kinnear conjectured 'fraught.'

V. iii. 54. 'senna'; so Folio 4; Folio 1, 'Cyme'; Folios 2, 3, 'Caeny'; Bulloch conjectured 'sirrah.'

V. iii. 57. 'it,' i.e. the armour.

ANTONY AND CLEOPATRA

I. i. 18. 'Grates me: the sum'; Folio 1, 'Grates me, the summe'; Folios 2, 3, 'Rate me, the summe'; Rowe, 'Rate me the sum'; Pope, 'It grates me. Tell the sum'; Capell, ''T grates me:—The sum'; Steevens (1793), "Grates me:—The Sum.'

I. i. 60-61. 'liar, who Thus speaks of him'; Pope reads 'liar Fame, Who speaks him thus.'

I. ii. 4. 'charge'; Warburton and Southern MS. conjectures, adopted by Theobald; Folios, 'change'; Jackson conjectured 'chain'; Williams conjectured ''hang.'

I. ii. 38. 'fertile'; Warburton conjecture, adopted by Theobald; Folios 'foretell' and 'foretel'; Pope, 'foretold'; Collier MS. 'fruitful.'

I. ii. 59-60. 'Alexas,—come'; Theobald's reading of the Folio text, where Alexas is erroneously printed as though the name of the speaker.

I. ii. 77. 'Saw you my lord?'; so Folios 2, 3, 4; Folio 1 reads 'Saue you, my lord.'

I. ii. 98-103. The arrangement of the text was first given by Steevens.

I. ii. 110. 'minds'; Warburton conjecture, adopted by Hanmer; Folios 1, 2, 'windes'; Collier conjectured 'wints.'

I. ii. 128. 'enchanting'; so Folio 1: omitted in Folios 2, 3, 4; Rowe reads 'Ægyptian.'

I. ii. 137. 'a compelling occasion'; Rowe's emendation of Folios, 'a compelling an occasion'; Nicholson conjectured 'so compelling as occasion,' &c.

I. ii. 193. 'like the courser's hair,' &c., alluding to the popular notion that horsehair put into water will turn into a snake or worm.

I. iv. 3. 'Our'; Heath and Johnson conjecture, adopted by Singer; Folios, 'One'; Hanmer, 'A.'

I. iv. 22. 'as'; Johnson conjectured 'and.'

I. iv. 46. 'lackeying'; 'lacquying,' Theobald's correction, from Anon. MS.: Folios, 'lacking'; Pope, 'lashing'; Southern MS., 'backing.'

I. v. 48. 'an arm-gaunt'; Folios, 'an Arme-gaunt'; Hanmer, 'an arm-girt'; Mason conjecture, adopted by Steevens, 1793, 'a termagant'; Jackson conjectured 'a war-gaunt'; Borden conjectured, adopted by Singer, 'an arrogant'; Lettsom conjectured 'a rampaunt'; the latter ingenious emendation certainly commends itself; unless 'arm-gaunt' = 'having lean fore-limbs.'

I. v. 50. 'beastly'; Hanmer, 'beast-like'; Collier MS., 'boastfully'; Becket conjectured 'basely.'

II. i. 10. 'powers are crescent'; Theobald reads 'pow'r's a crescent'; Becket conjectured 'power is crescent'; Anon. conjectured 'power's a-crescent.'

II. ii. 48. 'Was theme for you,' i.e. 'had you for its theme'; Johnson conjectured 'Had theme from you'; Collier (ed. 2), 'For theme was you'; Staunton conjectured 'Had you for theme'; Orson conjectured 'Was known for yours,' &c.

II. ii. 114. 'your considerate stone,' i.e. 'I am silent as a stone'; Heath conjectured 'your confederates love'; Johnson, 'your considerate ones'; Blackstone conjectured 'your consideratest one,' &c., &c.

II. ii. 213. 'And made their bends adornings'; i.e. "and made their very act of obeisance an improvement on their beauty" (Steevens); the passage has been variously interpreted, but this seems the simplest solution.

II. iii. 3. 'my prayers'; Rowe reads 'in prayers'; Collier MS., 'with prayers.'

II. iii. 23. 'a fear'; Collier (ed. 2). Thirlby conjectured 'afeard'; S. Walker conjectured 'afear.'

II. iii. 31. 'he away, 'tis'; Pope's emendation of Folio 1, 'he alway 'tis'; Folios 2, 3, 4, 'he always is.'

II. iii. 39. 'inhoop'd,' i.e. enclosed in a hoop; Hanmer, 'in-coop'd'; Seward conjecture, adopted by Capell, 'in whoop'd-at.'

II. v. 12. 'Tawny-finn'd'; Theobald's emendation of Folios, 'Tawny-fine'; Rowe reads 'Tawny-fin.'

II. v. 103. 'That art not what thou'rt sure of!'; Hanmer, 'That say'st but what thou'rt sure of'; Johnson conjectured 'That art—not what?—Thou'rt sure on't,' &c.; perhaps the words of the text mean 'that art not the evil thing of which thou art so certain'; other interpretations have been advanced.

II. v. 116. 'Though he be painted one way like a Gorgon,' alluding to the old 'perspective' pictures showing one picture from one point of view, another from another standpoint.

II. vii. 74. 'there'; Pope, 'then'; Steevens conjectured 'theirs.'

II. vii. 94. 'increase the reels'; Steevens conjectured 'and grease the wheels'; Douce conjectured 'increase the revels.'

II. vii. 111. 'bear'; Theobald's emendation; Folios, 'beat.'

III. v. 12. 'Then, world, thou hast'; Hanmer's emendation; Folios, 'Then would thou hadst'; Warburton MS., 'Then would thou hast': 'chaps, no,' Theobald's reading of Folios, 'chaps no.'

III. vi. 54. 'left unloved'; Collier MS., 'held unloved'; Singer conjectured, adopted by Hudson, 'felt unloved'; Seymour conjectured 'left unvalued'; Staunton conjectured 'left unpriz'd.'

III. vii. 5. 'If not denounced against us'; Hanmer reads, 'Is't not denounc'd 'gainst us?'; Jackson conjectured 'Is't not? Denounce against us!'; &c.

III. vii. 68, 69. 'his whole action grows Not in the power on't,' i.e. "his whole conduct in the war is not founded upon that which is his greatest strength, namely, his land force, but on the caprice of a woman," &c. (Malone).

III. xii. 28-29. '*And in our name, what she requires; add more, From thine invention, offers*'; Grant White conjectured '*What she requires; and in our name add more Offers from thine invention*'; Walker, '*and more . . . From thine invention offer.*'

III. xiii. 162. '*Cæsarion smite*'; Hanmer's emendation; Folios, '*Cæsarian smile.*'

IV. iv. 3. '*mine*'; Folios, '*thine.*'

IV. iv. 5-8. The text follows Malone's arrangement and reading (*vide* Cambridge Edition, Note VI.).

IV. v. 17. '*Dispatch. Enobarbus!*'; Steevens' (1773) reading; Folio 1, '*Dispatch Enobarbus*'; Folio 2, '*Dispatch Eros*'; Folios 3, 4, '*Dispatch, Eros*'; Pope '*dispatch my Eros*'; Johnson conjectured '*Dispatch! To Enobarbus!*'; Capell, '*Dispatch.—O Enobarbus!*'; Rann, '*Eros! Dispatch*'; Ritson conjectured, adopted by Steevens 1793, '*Eros, despatch*'; Anon. conjecture, '*Domitius Enobarbus!*'

IV. vi. 13. '*persuade*'; Rowe's correction of Folios, '*disswade.*'

IV. viii. 23. '*favouring*'; Theobald's emendation of Folios '*savouring.*'

IV. xii. 25. '*soul*'; Capell, '*soil*'; Singer (ed. 2) from Collier MS., '*spell*'; S. Walker conjectured '*snake: grave*'; Pope reads '*gay*'; Collier (ed. 2) from Collier MS., '*great*'; Singer (ed. 2), '*grand.*'

IV. xiv. 87. '*Lo thee*'; Grant White conjectured '*Lo there.*'

IV. xv. 10. '*Burn the great sphere*'; Hanmer, '*Turn from the sphere*'; Warburton, '*Turn from th' great sphere.*'

IV. xv. 11. '*shore*'; Staunton conjecture, adopted by Hudson, '*star.*'

IV. xv. 21. '*I dare not*'; Malone conjectured '*I dare not descend*'; Ritson conjecture, adopted by Wordsworth, '*I dare not come down*'; Anon. conjecture, from Plutarch, '*I dare not ope the gates*'; &c.

IV. xv. 73. '*No more, but e'en a woman*'; Capell's version; Folios read '*No more but in a Woman*'; Rowe, '*No more but a meer woman*'; Johnson conjecture, adopted by Steevens, 1773, 1778, '*No more—but e'en a woman.*'

V. i. 15. '*crack: the round world.*'; Steevens conjectured '*crack than this: the ruin'd world*'; Singer conjectured '*crack: the round world convulsive*'; Nicholson conjectured '*crack: the round world in rending*'; Daniel conjectured '*crack in the round world*'; &c., &c.

V. i. 24. '*Splitted the heart*'; Collier MS., '*Split that self noble heart*'; Elze conjectured '*Splitted that very heart.*'

V. i. 59-60. '*live To be ungentle,*' Rowe (ed. 2) and Southern MS.; Folios read '*leaue to be ungentle*'; Capell, '*Leave to be gentle*'; Tyrwhitt conjectured '*learn To be ungentle*'; Gould conjectured '*bear to be ungentle.*'

V. ii. 7. '*dug*'; Warburton conjecture, adopted by Theobald, '*dugg*'; Folios, '*dung*'; Nicholson conjectured '*tongue*'; Cartwright conjectured '*wrong*'; Bailey conjectured '*doom.*'

V. ii. 50. '*necessary*'; Hanmer, '*accessory*'; Malone conjectured '*necessary, I'll not so much as syllable a word*'; Ritson conjectured '*necessary, I will not speak; if sleep be necessary.*'

V. ii. 87. '*an autumn 'twas*'; Theobald and Thirlby conjectured; Folios read '*an Anthony it was*'; &c.

V. ii. 104. '*smites*'; Capell's emendation; Folios 1, 2, '*suites*'; Folios 3, 4, '*suits*'; Pope, '*shoots.*'

V. ii. 173. '*my chance,*' i.e. my changed fortune, lot; Hanmer reads '*mischance*'; S. Walker conjectured '*my change*'; Ingleby conjecture, adopted by Hudson, '*my glance.*'

V. ii. 177-178. '*We answer others' merits in our name, Are*'; Malone's reading; Folios, '*We answer others merits, in our name Are*'; &c.

V. ii. 351. '*caves*'; so Folios 2, 3, 4; Folio 1, '*caues*'; Barry conjectured '*canes*'; Anon. conjecture '*caves*'; Perring conjectured '*course.*'

THE TRAGEDY OF CORIOLANUS

I. i. 169-171. '*your virtue,*' &c.; "your virtue is to speak well of him whom his own offences have subjected to justice; and to rail at those laws by which he whom you praise was punished" (Johnson).

I. iii. 15. '*bound with oak,*' as a mark of honour for saving the life of a citizen.

I. iii. 43. '*At Grecian sword, contemning,*' &c.; Folio 1 reads '*At Grecian sword. Contemning, tell Valeria,*' &c.; the reading in the text is substantially Collier's; many emendations have been proposed; perhaps a slightly better version of the line would be gained by the omission of the comma.

I. iv. 14. '*that fears you less*'; Johnson conjectured '*but fears you less*'; Johnson and Capell conjectured '*that fears you more*'; Schmidt, '*that fears you,—less.*' The meaning is obvious, though there is a confusion, due to the case of the double negative in '*nor*' and '*less.*'

I. iv. 31. '*you herd of—Boils,*' Johnson's emendation. Folios 1, 2, '*you Heard of Byles*'; Folios 3, 4, '*you Herd of Biles*'; Rowe, '*you herds of biles*'; Pope (ed. 1), '*you herds; of boils*'; Pope (ed. 2), Theobald, '*you! herds of boils*'; Collier MS., '*unheard of boils*'; &c., &c.

I. iv. 42. '*trenches followed*'; so Folios 2, 3, 4; Folio 1, '*trenches followes*'; Collier (ed. 1), '*trenches follow*'; (ed. 2), '*trenches. Follow!*'; Dyce, Lettsom conjectured '*trenches: follow me*'; &c.

I. iv. 58. '*Cato's*'; Theobald's emendation of Folios, '*Calues*' and '*Calves*'; Rowe, '*Calvus.*'

I. vi. 6. '*ye*'; Folios, '*the.*'

I. vi. 76. Folios, '*O, me alone! make you a sword of me?*'; the punctuation in the text is Capell's. Clarke's explanation, making the line imperative, seems the most plausible:—"O take me alone for weapon among you all! make yourselves a sword of me."

I. ix. 41-53. The chief departure from the folios in this doubtful passage is the substitution of '*coverture*' for '*overture,*' as conjectured by Tyrwhitt; '*him*' is seemingly used here instead of the neuter '*it.*'

II. i. 223. '*end,*' i.e. to where he should end.

II. i. 253. '*touch,*' Hanmer's emendation; Folios, '*teach*'; Theobald, '*reach.*'

II. iii. 58-59. '*virtues Which our divines lose by 'em,*' i.e. 'which our divines preach to men in vain'; but the line is possibly corrupt.

II. iii. 113. '*woolvish toge*'; Steevens' conjecture, adopted by Malone; Folio 1 reads '*Wooluish tongue*'; Folios 2, 3, 4, '*Woolvish gowne*'; Capell, '*wolfish gown*'; Mason conjectured '*woollen gown,*' or '*foolish gown*'; Beckett conjectured '*woolish gown*'; Steevens conjectured '*woolvish tongue*'; Grant White conjectured '*foolish togue*'; Clarke, (?) '*wool'nish,*' i.e. '*woolenish.*'

II. iii. 241-243. vide Preface.

III. i. 93. '*Hydra here*'; i.e. 'the many-headed multitude'; so Folio 2.

III. i. 98-101. i.e. "let your admitted ignorance take a lower tone and defer to their admitted superiority" (Clarke).

III. i. 230. '*your*'; Rowe's emendation of Folios, '*our.*'

III. ii. 21. '*thwartings of*'; Theobald's reading; Folios, '*things of*'; Rowe, '*things that thwart*'; Wright conjectured '*things that cross.*'

III. ii. 32. '*to the herd*'; Warburton's suggestion, adopted by Theobald; Folios, '*to the heart*'; Collier MS., '*o' th' heart*'; &c.

III. ii. 56. '*though but bastards and syllables*'; Capell, '*but bastards*'; Seymour conjectured '*although but bastards, syllables*'; Badham conjectured '*thought's bastards, and but syllables.*'

III. ii. 64. '*I am in this*'; Warburton, '*In this advice I speak as your wife, your son,*' &c.

III. ii. 69. '*that want,*' i.e. the want of that inheritance.

III. ii. 78. '*Which often, thus, correcting thy stout heart*'; Johnson, '*With often,*' &c.; Capell, '*And often*'; Staunton conjectured '*While often*'; Nicholson conjectured '*Whiles-often*'; Warburton, '*Which soften.*'

III. iii. 35. '*among's,*' i.e. among us; Folio 1, '*amongs*'; Folios 2, 3, 4, '*amongst you*'; Pope, '*amongst you*'; Capell, '*among us.*'

III. iii. 36. '*throng*,' Theobald's and Warburton's emendation of Folios, '*Through.*'

III. iii. 55. '*accents*,' Theobald's correction of Folios, '*actions.*'

III. iii. 131. '*not*'; Capell's correction of Folios, '*but.*'

IV. i. 7-9. '*fortune's blows, When most struck home, being gentle wounded, craves A noble cunning*'; *i.e.* "When Fortune's blows are most struck home, to be gentle, although wounded, demands a noble philosophy" (Clarke). Pope, '*gently warded*'; Hanmer, '*greatly warded*'; Collier MS., '*gentle-minded.*'

IV. iv. 23. '*My birth-place hate I, and my love's upon*'; Capell's emendation. Folio 1 reads, '*My Birth-place have I, and my loues upon*'; Folios 2, 3, '*My Birth-lace have I, and my lover upon*'; Folio 4, '*My Birth-place have I, and my Lover left; upon*'; Pope, '*My birth-place have I and my lovers left*'; Beckett conjectured '*My country have I and my lovers lost,*' &c.

IV. vii. 51-53. The sense of the lines should be to this effect:—"Power is in itself most commendable, but the orator's chair, from which a man's past actions are extolled, is the inevitable tomb of his power." The passage is crude, and many suggestions have been advanced.

IV. vii. 55. '*fouler*'; Dyce's ingenious reading, '*falter*,' is the best conjectural emendation of the line.

V. i. 68, 69. Many emendations have been proposed to clear up the obscurity of the line. It appears to mean either (i.) that Coriolanus bound Cominius by an oath to yield to his conditions; or (ii.) that Coriolanus was bound by an oath as *to what he would not*, unless the Romans should yield to his conditions. Johnson proposed to read—

"*What he would not,*
Bound by an oath. To yield to his conditions,"—

the rest being omitted. Many attempts have been made to improve the passage, but no proposal carries conviction with it.

V. ii. 73. '*your*'; so Folio 1, 2, 3; Folio 4, '*our.*'

V. ii. 81, 82. '*though I owe My revenge properly,*' *i.e.* 'though revenge is my own, remission belongs to the Volscians.'

THE LIFE OF TIMON OF ATHENS

I. i. 23. '*gum, which oozes*'; Johnson's reading; Folios read '*grown, which uses*'; Pope, '*gum which issues.*'

I. i. 26, 27. '*flies Each bound it chafes*'; Folios, '*chases*'; Becket conjectured '*flies. Eche (bound) it chafes*'; Schmidt '*chafes with.*'

I. i. 33, 34. '*grace Speaks his own standing*'; Johnson conjectured '*standing . . . graces*' or '*grace Speaks understanding*'; Mason conjectured '*Grace Speaks its own standing*'; Jackson conjectured '*grace Speaks! 'tis one standing*'; Orger conjectured '*grace . . . seeming.*'

I. i. 43. '*happy man*'; Theobald's emendation of Folios, '*happy men.*'

I. i. 50. '*sea of wax*'; Bailey conjectured '*sweep of taxing*'; Collier MS., '*sea of verse*'; &c.; but there is evidently a reference to writing-tablets covered with wax.

I. i. 90. '*slip*'; Folios, '*sit*'; Delius conjectured '*sink.*'

I. i. 132. The line is supposed by some to be corrupt, and many emendations have been proposed, but Coleridge's interpretation commends itself:—"The meaning of the first line the poet himself explains, or rather unfolds, in the second. 'The man is honest!'—True; and for that very cause, and with no additional or extrinsic motive, he will be so. No man can be justly called honest, who is not so for honesty's sake, itself including its reward.''

I. i. 234. '*That I had no angry wit to be a lord*'; Blackstone conjectured '*Angry that I had no wit,—to be a lord*'; Malone conjectured '*That I had no angry wit.—To be a lord!*'; Anon. conjectured '*That I had no ampler wit than be a lord*'; Warburton, '*That I had so hungry a wit to be a lord*'; Heath conjectured '*That . . . so wrong'd my wit to be a lord*'; &c., &c.

I. ii. 43. Alluding to the then custom of each guest bringing his own knife to a feast.

I. ii. 70. '*sin*'; Farmer conjectured '*sing*'; Singer conjectured '*dine*'; Kinnear conjectured '*surfeit.*'

I. ii. 119-124. The arrangement of these lines was first suggested by Rann, and followed by Steevens in his edition of 1793.

I. ii. 126. '*Music, make their welcome*'; Pope reads '*Let musick make their welcome*'; Capell, '*Musick, make known their welcome.*'

II. i. 10. '*And able horses*'; so Folios 1, 2; Folios 3, 4, '*An able horse*'; Theobald, '*ten able horse*'; Jackson conjectured '*Ay, able horses*'; Collier MS., '*a stable o' horses*'; Singer conjectured '*Two able horses.*'

II. i. 13. '*found his state in safety*'; Hanmer's reading; Folios, '*sound . . .*'; Capell, '*found . . . on safety*'; Capell conjectured '*find . . . in safety.*'

II. ii. 6. '*Was to be*'; Heath conjectured '*Was made to be*'; Long MS., '*Was*'; Mason conjectured '*Was formed*'; Singer MS., '*Was truly*'; Collier MS., '*Was surely.*'

II. ii. 74. '*mistress*'; (so l. 102).

II. ii. 143. '*loved lord*'; Folios 2, 3, 4, '*dear lov'd lord*'; S. Walker conjectured '*belov'd.*'

II. ii. 144. Folios read '*Though you heare now (too late) yet nowes a time, The*'; Hanmer, '*Though . . . yet now's too late a time*'; Collier MS., '*Though . . . yet now's a time too late.*'

II. ii. 163. '*wasteful cock*'; Pope reads '*lonely room*'; Collier MS., '*wasteful nook*'; Jackson conjectured '*wakeful cock*'; Jervis conjectured '*wakeful couch*'; Keightley, '*wasteful cock-loft*'; Daniel conjectured '*wakeful cot*'; Jackson's conjecture seems best, '*wakeful cock,*' *i.e.* 'cock-loft,' unless '*cock*' = wine-tap.

III. i. 47. '*And we alive that lived*'; *i.e.* in so short a time.

III. i. 51. '*Let molten coin be thy damnation*'; *cp.* the old ballad "The Dead Man's Song":

"*And ladles full of melted gold*
Were poured down their throats."

III. i. 55-56. '*slave, Unto his honour*'; Steevens' reading; Folios, '*Slave unto his honour*'; Pope, '*slave Unto this hour*'; Collier MS., '*slave unto his humour*'; Staunton, '*slave Unto dishonour*'; but the words are probably spoken ironically.

III. ii. 11, 12. '*so many*'; changed by Theobald to '*fifty*'; so, too, in l. 37; but the figures are very doubtful, and '*fifty-five hundred talents,*' in l. 39, is obviously a mere exaggeration.

III. ii. 23. '*mistook him,*' &c., *i.e.* 'made the mistake and applied to me'; Hanmer, '*o'erlook'd*'; Warburton, '*mislook'd*'; Johnson conjectured '*not mistook.*'

III. ii. 48, 49. '*for a little part*'; Theobald, '*for a little dirt*'; Hanmer, '*a little dirt*'; Heath conjectured '*for a little profit*'; Johnson conjectured '*for a little park*'; Mason conjectured '*for a little port*'; Jackson conjectured '*for a little part*'; Bailey conjectured '*for a little sport*'; Kinnear conjectured '*for a little pomp.*' Steevens explains the passage thus:—"By purchasing what brought me little honour, I have lost the more honourable opportunity of supplying the wants of my friends."

III. ii. 67. '*spirit,*' Theobald's correction of Folios, '*sport*'; Collier MS., '*port.*'

III. ii. 76. '*in respect of his*'; Staunton conjectured '*this.*'

III. iii. 12. '*Thrive, give him over*'; so Folio 1; Folios 2, 3, 4, '*That thriv'd, give him over*'; Pope, '*Three give him over?*'; Hanmer, '*Tried give him over*'; Theobald, '*Thriv'd, give him over?*'; Tyrwhitt conjectured '*Shriv'd give him over:*'; Johnson conjectured '*Thrice give him over,*' &c.

III. iii. 14. '*sense*'; Collier conjectured '*'scuse.*'

III. iv. 110. '*Sempronius: all:*'; so Folios 3, 4; Folio 1, '*Sempronius Vllorxa: All*'; Folio 2, '*Semprovius: All*'; Malone, '*Sempronius: Ullorxa, all*'; Grant White suggested that '*Vllorxa*' was a misprint for '*Ventidius.*'

III. v. 22. '*behave his anger, ere 'twas spent*'; Folios, '*behooue*

[1483]

his . . .'; Johnson conjectured '*behold his adversary shent*'; Steevens conjectured '*behave, ere was his anger spent*'; Becket conjectured '*behave; his anger was, 'ere spent*'; Hanmer, '*behave in's . . .*'; Malone conjectured '*behave his . . .*'; Collier MS., '*reprove his, . . .*', &c.

III. v. 62. '*I say, my lords, has*'; Pope reads '*I say my lords ha's*'; Folio 1, '*Why say my Lords ha's*'; Folios 2, 3, '*Why I say my Lords ha's*'; Folio 4, '*Why, I say my Lords ha's*'; Capell, '*Why I say, my lords, he has*'; Dyce, '*Why, I say, my lords, has*'; Globe ed., '*I say my lords, he has.*'

III. v. 102. '*And, not to swell our spirit,*' *i.e.* 'not to swell our spirit with anger, not to become exasperated'; Theobald, '*And note, to swell your spirit*'; Capell, '*And, not to swell your spirit*'; Singer, '*quell*'; Kinnear, '*quail.*'

III. v. 105. '*Only in bone,*' *i.e.* 'as a mere skeleton'; Staunton conjectured '*Only at home,*' or '*Only in doors*'; Ingleby conjectured '*only in bed*'; Hudson conjectured '*only alone.*'

III. v. 116. '*most lands*'; Warburton, '*most hands*'; Malone conjectured '*most lords*'; Mason conjectured '*my stains*'; Becket conjectured '*most brands*'; Jackson conjectured, '*most bands.*'

III. vi. 33, 34. '*harshly o' the trumpet's*'; Rowe, '*harshly as o' the Trumpets*'; Steevens (1793), '*harshly on the trumpet's*'; Grant White conjectured '*harshly. O, the trumpets,*' &c.

III. vi. 89. '*you with flatteries*'; so Folios; Warburton, '*with your flatteries*'; Keightley, '*by you with flatteries*'; Folio 2 reads '*flatteries*'; S. Walker conjectured '*flattery.*'

IV. i. 21. '*let*'; Hanmer's emendations of Folios, '*yet.*'

IV. ii. 35. '*what state compounds*'; S. Walker conjectured '*state comprehends*'; Grant White conjectured '*that state compounds*'; Watkiss Lloyd conjectured '*whate'er state comprehends.*'

IV. iii. 9. '*deny't*'; Warburton, '*denude*'; Hanmer, '*degrade*'; Heath conjectured '*deprive*'; Steevens conjectured '*devest*'; Collier MS., '*decline*'; &c.; the indefinite '*it*' refers to the implied noun in '*raise,*' *i.e.* 'give elevation to.'

IV. iii. 12. '*pasture lards the rother's sides*'; '*rother,*' Singer's emendation for Folios, '*brothers.*' Folio 1, '*Pastour*'; Folios 2, 3, 4, '*pastor*'; Farmer and Steevens conjectured '*pasterer*': '*lards*'; Rowe's reading, Folio 1, '*Lards*'; Folios 2, 3, 4, '*Lords.*'

IV. iii. 18. '*all is oblique*'; Pope's emendation, Folio 1, '*All's obliquie*'; Folios 2, 3, '*Alls obliquy*'; Folio 4, '*All's obliquy*'; Rowe, '*all's obloquy*'; Lettsom conjectured '*all, all's oblique.*'

IV. iii. 38. '*wappen'd*'; so Folios 1, 2; Folios 3, 4, '*wapen'd*'; Warburton, '*waped*'; Johnson conjectured '*wained*'; Malone conjectured '*wapper'd*'; Anon. conjectured, '*Wapping*'; Steevens conjectured '*weeping*'; Seymour conjectured '*vapid*'; Staunton conjectured '*woe-pin'd*'; Fleay, '*wop-eyed*'; *i.e.* having waterish eyes (*vide* Glossary).

IV. iii. 106. '*conquer my country*'; Kinnear conjectured '*confound my countrymen*'; Hanmer, '*make conquest of my country*'; Capell, '*conquer thy own country*'; S. Walker conjectured '*scourge thy country*'; Hudson, '*scourge my country.*'

IV. iii. 116. '*window-bars*'; Johnson conjectured; Folios, '*window Barn*'; Pope, '*window-barn*'; Warburton, '*window-lawn*'; Tyrwhitt conjectured '*widow's barb.*'

IV. iii. 153. '*spurring*'; Hanmer, '*sparring*'; Long MS., '*spurning*'; Seymour conjectured '*springing*'; there is no need to emend the text.

IV. iii. 215. '*bade*'; Folio 1, '*bad*'; Folios 2, 3, 4, '*bid.*'

IV. iii. 225. '*when*'; S. Walker conjectured '*where.*'

IV. iii. 243. '*Outlives incertain*'; Rowe's emendation; Folio 1 reads '*Out-lives: incertaine*'; Folios 2, 3, 4, '*Out-lives: in certaine*'; Hanmer, '*Out-strips incertain*'; Capell, '*Out-vies uncertain.*'

IV. iii. 254. '*drugs*'; Folios 1, 2, '*drugges*'; Mason conjectured

'*drudges*'; Collier MS., '*dugs*'; Capell conjectured MS. '*dregs*'; '*drugs*' = '*drudges.*'

IV. iii. 283. '*my*'; Rowe's correction of Folios, '*thy.*'

IV. iii. 311, 312. '*after his means,*' *i.e.* '*after his means were gone.*'

IV. iii. 418. '*meat*'; Theobald, '*meet*' (*i.e.* 'what you ought to be'); Hanmer, '*men*'; Steevens conjectured '*me*'; &c.

IV. iii. 419-423. '*Behold, the earth hath roots,*' &c.; *cp.* Hall's *Satires,* III. 1 (pub. 1598):—

> "*Time was that, whiles the autumn full did last*
> *Our hungry sires gap'd for the falling mast,*" &c.

IV. iii. 436. '*villany*'; Rowe's correction of Folios 1, 2, '*villaine.*'

IV. iii. 442. '*moon*'; Theobald, '*mounds*'; Capell, '*earth*'; Tollet conjectured '*main.*'

IV. iii. 496. '*dangerous nature mild*'; Thirlby conjectured; Folios, '*wild*'; Becket conjectured '*nature dangerous-wild*'; Jackson conjectured '*dolorous nature wild.*'

V. i. 45. '*black-corned'd,*' *i.e.* 'hiding things in dark corners'; Hanmer, '*black-corneted*'; Warburton conjectured '*black-cornette*'; Farmer conjectured MS. '*black-coroned*'; Mason conjectured '*black-crowned*'; Jackson conjectured '*dark-horned*'; Singer conjectured, '*black-curtain'd,*' &c.

V. i. 114. '*You have work*'; so Folios; Hanmer, '*You have work'd*'; Malone, '*You have done work*'; Steevens conjectured '*You've work'd.*'

V. i. 134. '*as a cauterizing*'; Rowe's emendation; Folio 1, '*as a Cantherizing*'; Folios 2, 3, 4, '*as a Catherizing*'; Pope, '*cauterizing*'; Capell, '*cancerizing.*'

V. i. 145. '*general, gross:*' Pope's emendation of Folios, '*generall grosse:*' S. Walker's conjecture, adopted by Dyce, '*general-gross.*'

V. i. 211. '*haste*'; Pope, '*taste*'; Warburton conjectured MS., '*tatch*'; Collier MS., '*halter.*'

V. ii. 7. '*whom,*' instead of '*who,*' owing to confusion of construction; Pope, '*Who*'; Hanmer, '*And*'; Singer, '*When*'; &c.

V. ii. 8. '*made a particular force*'; Hanmer reads '*had . . . force*'; Staunton conjectured '*took . . . truce*'; Bailey conjectured '*had . . . force with*'; &c.

V. iii. 3-4. These words are in all probability the reflection of the soldier; this view is certainly more acceptable than to believe them to be an inscription placed by Timon somewhere near the tomb. Nor is it necessary, with Warburton, to change '*read*' into '*rear'd.*' The soldier, seeing the tomb, infers that Timon is dead, but he cannot read the inscription; 'some beast read this! there does not live a man able to do so' (*v.* Preface).

V. iv. 28. '*Shame, that they wanted cunning, in excess*'; Theobald's emendation ('extreme shame for their folly in banishing you hath broken their hearts'); Folio 1 reads '(*Shame that they wanted, cunning in excesse*)'; Folios 2, 3, 4, '*Shame (that they wanted cunning in excesse)*'; Johnson conjectured '*Shame that they wanted, coming in excess.*'

V. iv. 62. '*render'd to your*'; the conjecture of '*Chedworth,*' adopted by Dyce; Folio 1 reads '*remedied to your*'; Folios 2, 3, 4, '*remedied by your*'; Pope, '*remedied by*'; Johnson, '*remedied to*'; Malone, '*remedy'd, to your*'; Singer (ed. 2), '*remitted to your.*'

V. iv. 79. '*On thy low grave, on faults forgiven. Dead*'; the reading of Folios; Theobald reads '*On thy low grave.—On: faults forgiven.—Dead*'; Hanmer, '*On thy low grave our faults—forgiv'n, since dead.*'

PERICLES, PRINCE OF TYRE

I. i. 24. '*boundless*'; Rowe's emendation of Quartos; Folios 3, 4, '*bondlesse.*'

I. i. 29. '*death-like dragons here affright*'; Daniel conjectured '*death, like dragons, here affrights*'; S. Walker conjectured '*affront*'; Hudson conjectured '*affronts.*'

I. i. 55-57. The arrangement of the text, confused in Quartos and Folios, was first made by Malone.

I. i. 59, 60. '*Of all 'say'd yet*'; Mason conjectured '*In all, save that*'; Mitford conjectured '*O false! and yet.*'

I. i. 113. '*cancel of*'; Malone's emendation; Folios 3, 4, '*cancel off*'; Quartos 1, 2, 3, 4, 6, '*counsell of*'; Quarto 5, '*counsel of.*'

I. i. 128. '*untimely*'; Wilkins, in the Novel, writes '*uncomely,*' which may, perhaps, give the correct reading of the line.

I. i. 135. '*blush,*' *i.e.* '*who blush*'; the omission of the pronoun, personal or relative, is characteristic of the non-Shakespearian portions of the play.

I. ii. 1. '*change of thoughts,*' *i.e.* perturbation of thought; Steevens conjectured '*charge of thoughts?*'; Mason conjectured '*change of thoughts?*'; Singer (ed. 2), '*charge our thoughts?*'; Staunton conjectured '*change our thoughts?*'; Bailey conjectured '*child of thought*'; Daniel conjectured '*cast of thought.*'

I. ii. 3. '*Be my so used a guest as*'; Dyce's emendation; Quarto 1, '*By me so vsde a guest, as*'; Malone (1780), '*By me's so us'd a guest, as*'; Jackson conjectured '*Be by me so us'd a guest?*'

I. ii. 8. '*arm*'; so Folio 4; Dyce reads '*aim.*'

I. ii. 30. '*Who am*'; Farmer conjectured; Quartos, Folios 3, 4, '*Who once*'; Malone (1780), '*Who owe*'; (1790), '*Who wants.*'

I. ii. 41. '*blast*'; Mason conjectured; Quartos, Folios 3, 4, '*spark*'; Malone (1790), '*breath*'; Steevens conjectured '*wind.*'

I. ii. 55. '*plants*'; so Quarto 1; Malone's emendation of Quartos and Folios, '*planets.*'

I. ii. 86. '*doubt it*'; Steevens conjectured; Quartos 1, 2, 3, '*doo't*'; Quartos 4, 5, 6, and Folios, '*thinke.*'

I. ii. 93. '*spares*'; so Quarto 1; Quartos 2-6, and Folios 3, 4, '*feares*' and '*fears.*'

I. ii. 95. '*reprovest*'; Malone, '*reprov'st*'; Quartos 1, 2, 3, '*reprou'dst*'; Quartos 4, 5, 6, '*reprovedst*'; Folios 3, 4, '*reproved'st.*'

I. iii. 3-6. *Cp.* "I will therefore commend the poet Philipides, who, being demanded by King Lisimachus what favour he might do unto him, for that he loved him, made him answer to the king, that your Majesty would never impart unto me any of your secrets."—Barnabie Riche's *Soldiers' Wish to Briton's Welfare.*

I. iii. 27-28. '*but since he's gone, the king's seas must please*'; Mason conjectured '*But since he is gone, the king, seas must please*'; Percy conjectured '*But since he's gone, the king it sure must please*'; Collier (ed. 2), '*But since he is gone the king's ease must please*'; Perring conjectured '*But since he's gone, the king this news must please*'; Dyce conjectured '*But since he's gone the king's ears it must please.*'

I. iv. 8. '*mischief's eyes*'; Steevens, '*mistful eyes*'; Anonymous conjecture (1814), '*mischief-size*'; Singer (ed. 2), '*mistie eyes*'; S. Walker conjectured '*misery's eyes*'; Kinnear conjectured '*weakness' eyes*'; Mr. T. Tyler's suggestion, '*not seen with mischief's eyes,*' *i.e.* 'not seen with the eyes of despair,' seems to be the most ingenious correction of the line, if any change is necessary.

I. iv. 13-14. '*Our tongues and sorrows do sound deep Our woes*'; Hudson reads '*Our tongues do sound our sorrows and deep woes*': ——; '*sorrows do*'; Cartwright conjectured '*sobbings do*'; Bailey conjectured '*bosoms too*'; Anonymous conjecture, '*sorrowing bosoms do.*'

I. iv. 15. '*tongues*'; Quartos 1, 2, 3, '*toungs*'; Steevens conjectured '*lungs.*'

I. iv. 39. '*yet two summers younger*'; Mason conjectured; Quarto 1, '*yet too sauers younger*'; Folios 3, 4, '*yet to savers younger.*'

I. iv. 69. '*of unhappy me*'; Malone (1780), '*of unhappy men*'; Steevens conjectured '*of unhappy we*'; Jackson conjectured '*O unhappy me.*'

I. iv. 74. '*him's,*' *i.e.* '*him who is*'; Malone's reading; Quarto 1, '*himnes*'; Quarto 2, 3, Folio 3, '*hymnes*'; Quartos 4, 5, '*hymnes*'; Quarto 6, '*hywmes*'; Folio 4, '*hymns*'; Steevens conjectured '*him who is.*'

Prol. II. 19. '*for though*'; Steevens, '*forth*'; Singer (ed. 2), '*for thy*'; Nicholson conjectured '*for-though*'; Kinnear conjectured '*for through.*'

Prol. II. 22. '*Sends word*'; Steevens conjectured; Quartos 1-5 read '*Sau'd one*'; Quarto 6, Folios 3, 4, '*Sav'd one.*'

II. i. 49. '*finny*'; Steevens conjectured (from Wilkins' novel); Quartos, Folios 3, 4, '*fenny.*'

II. i. 55. '*search*'; Steevens conjectured '*scratch it*'; Singer (ed. 2), '*scratch't*'; Staunton, '*scratch*'; Anonymous conjecture, '*steal it*'; Hudson, '*steal't.*'

II. i. 57. '*May see the sea hath cast upon your coast*'; so Quartos; Folios 3, 4, '*I' may see the sea hath cast me upon your coast*'; Malone (1780), '*You may see the sea hath cast me on your coast*'; Steevens, adopted by Malone (1790), '*Nay, see, the sea hath cast upon your coast——.*'

II. ii. 14. '*entertain*'; Steevens conjectured '*explain*'; Anony-

mous conjecture, '*entreat*'; Anonymous conjecture, '*emblazon*'; Schmidt conjectured '*interpret.*'

II. iii. 19. '*Marshal*'; Malone's emendation; Quartos, Folio 3, '*Martiall*'; Folio 4, '*Martial.*'

II. iii. 29. '*resist*'; Collier conjectured '*distaste.*'

——, '*he not*'; so Quartos 2-6, Folios 3, 4; Malone, '*she not*'; Malone conjectured '*he now*'; Steevens conjectured '*be not*'; Mason conjectured '*she but*'; Dyce conjectured '*he but.*'

II. iii. 50. '*stored*'; Steevens conjectured; Quartos 1, 2, 3, 6, '*stur'd*'; Folios 3, 4, '*stirr'd*'; Mason conjectured '*stow'd.*'

II. iii. 64. '*kill'd are wonder'd at*'; Daniel, '*still ne'er wondered at*'; Anonymous conjecture, '*kill'd are scorned at*'; Kinnear, '*little are wonder'd at.*'

II. iv. 41. '*For honour's cause*'; Dyce's reading; Quartos, Folios 3, 4, '*Try honours cause*'; Steevens conjectured '*Try honour's course*'; Jackson conjectured '*Cry, honour's cause!*'; Anonymous conjecture '*By honour's cause.*'

Prol. III. 35. '*Y-ravished*'; Steevens conjectured; Quarto 1, '*Iranyshed*'; Quarto 2, '*Irany shed*'; the rest, '*Irony shed.*'

III. i. 7-8. '*Thou stormest venomously; Wilt*'; Dyce's reading; Quartos, Folios 3, 4, '*then storme venomously, Wilt*'; Malone, '*Thou storm, venomously, Wilt*'; Steevens, '*Thou, storm, thou! venomously Wilt*'; Collier, '*Thou storm, venomously Wilt.*'

III. i. 14. '*travails*'; Folio 3, '*travels*'; Dyce, '*travail.*'

III. i. 26. '*Use honour with you*'; Steevens reads '*Vie honour with yourselves*'; Mason conjectured '*Vie honour with you.*'

III. i. 62. '*aye-remaining lampes*'; Malone's conjecture; Quarto 1, 2, 3, '*ayre remayning lampes*'; Quartos 4, 5, 6, '*ayre remaining lampes*'; Folio 3, '*ayre remaining lamps*'; Folio 4, '*air remaining lamps*'; Jackson conjectured '*area-manesing,*' &c.

III. ii. 17. '*all-to topple*'; Singer (ed. 2), '*al-to topple*'; Quartos, Folios 3, 4, '*all to topple*'; Dyce, '*all to-topple.*'

III. ii. 22. '*Rich tire*'; Steevens conjectured '*Such towers*'; Quartos 1, 2, 3, '*Rich tire*'; the rest, '*Rich attire*'; Jackson conjectured '*Rich Tyre*'; Collier (ed. 2), '*Rich 'tire.*'

III. ii. 41. '*treasure*'; Steevens' emendation for '*pleasures*' and '*pleasure*' of Quartos, Folios 3, 4.

III. ii. 42. Steevens explained the words as an allusion to an old print exhibiting *Death* in the act of plundering a miser of his bags, and the *Fool* standing behind, and grinning at the process.

III. ii. 48. '*time shall never. . . .*'; so Quartos 1, 2, 3; Quartos 4, 5, 6, Folios 3, 4, '*neuer shall decay*'; Malone, '*time shall never—*'; Dyce, '*time shall never raze*'; Staunton, '*time shall ne'er decay*'; Anonymous conjecture, '*time shall never end.*'

III. iii. 7. '*wanderingly*'; Quartos, Folios 3, 4, '*wondringly*'; Schmidt conjectured '*woundingly.*'

III. iii. 29. '*Unscissar'd shall this hair*'; Steevens' emendation; Quartos 1-4, '*vnsisterd . . . heyre*'; Quarto 5, '*unsisterd shall his heyres*'; Quarto 6, '*unsisterd . . . heire*'; Folios 3, 4, '*unsister'd . . . heir.*'

III. iii. 30. '*show ill*'; Quartos and Folios read '*show will*'; the correction was made independently by Malone and Dyce; this and the previous emendations are confirmed by the corresponding passage in the Novel.

Prol. IV. 17. '*marriage rite*'; Collier's reading; Percy conjectured '*marriage rites*'; Quartos, Folios 3, 4, '*marriage sight*'; Steevens conjecture, adopted by Malone, '*marriage fight*'; Steevens conjectured '*marriage night.*'

Prol. IV. 26. '*night-bird*'; Malone's emendation of Quartos, Folios 3, 4, '*night-bed.*'

IV. i. 5. '*inflaming love i' thy bosom*'; Knight's emendation of Quarto 1, '*in flaming, thy loue bosome,*' &c.

IV. i. 11. '*only mistress' death*'; Malone (1790), '*old mistress' death*'; Percy conjectured '*old nurse's death*'; &c., &c.

IV. i. 64. '*stem to stern*'; Malone's emendation; Quartos, '*sterne to sterne*'; Folios 3, 4, '*stern to stern.*'

IV. i. 97. '*the great pirate Valdes*'; "perhaps there is here a scornful allusion to Don Pedro de Valdes, a Spanish admiral taken by Drake in 1588" (Malone).

IV. iii. 17. '*pious*'; Mason conjecture and Wilkins' novel, adopted by Collier; Quartos 1, 2, 3, '*impious*'; the rest omit the word.

IV. iii. 47-48. '*dost, with thine angel's face, Seize*'; Malone conjectured '*dost wear thine angel's face; Seize*'; Steevens, '*doth wear an angel's face, Seize*'; Hudson (1881), '*doth use an angel's face, Then seize.*'

IV. iii. 48. '*talons*'; Rowe's emendation of Quartos, Folios 3, 4, '*talents.*'

IV. iv. 13-16. The arrangement of the lines is according to Hudson's edition (1881).

IV. iv. 18. '*his pilot thought*'; Steevens conjectured '*his pilot wrought*'; Mason conjectured '*this pilot-thought*'; Quartos 1, 2, 3, '*this Pilot thought*'; the rest, '*this Pilate thought.*'

IV. iv. 48. '*scene must play*'; Malone's emendation (1790); Quartos, Folios 3, 4 read '*Steare must play*'; Steevens conjecture, adopted by Malone (1780), '*tears must play*'; Malone conjectured '*stage must play*'; Steevens, '*scenes display.*'

V. i. 47. '*deafen'd*'; Malone's emendation; Quarto 1, '*defend*'; the rest, '*defended.*'

V. i. 72. '*prosperous and artificial feat*'; i.e. '*gracefully and skilfully performed*'; Mason conjectured '*prosperous artifice and fate*'; Steevens, '*prosperous-artificial feat*':

———; '*feat*'; Percy conjecture, adopted by Steevens, Quartos, Folios 3, 4, '*fate.*'

V. i. 206, 207. The passage is so corrupt that the Cambridge editors found themselves obliged to leave it as it stands in the Quartos and Folios.

V. i. 233. '*nips*'; Collier conjectured '*raps.*'

V. i. 245. '*life*'; Charlemont conjectured, adopted by Malone; Quartos, Folios 3, 4, '*like.*'

CYMBELINE

I. i. 3. '*does the king*'; Tyrwhitt's conjecture; Folios, '*do's the Kings*'; Hanmer, '*do the kings.*'

I. i. 134. '*A year's age*'; this reading seems weak; one expects some stronger expression. Warburton, adopted by Theobald, '*a yare [i.e. speedy] age*'; Hanmer, '*many A year's age*'; Nicholson, '*more than Thy years' age*'; &c., &c.

I. iii. 9. '*make me with this eye or ear*'; Folios, '*his*' for '*this.*'

I. iv. 19, 20. '*are wonderfully to*'; Warburton conjectured '*aids wonderfully to*'; Capell conjectured '*are wonderful to*'; Eccles, '*and wonderfully do.*'

I. iv. 72. '*could not but*'; Malone's emendation of Folios, '*could not.*'

I. iv. 110. '*herein too*'; so Folios 3, 4; Folios 1, 2, '*heerein to*'; Grant White, '*hereinto*'; Anon. conjecture, '*hereunto*'; Vaughan conjectured '*herein, so.*'

I. iv. 132. '*afraid*'; Warburton's emendation, adopted by Theobald; Folios, '*a Friend*'; Becket conjectured '*affied*'; Jackson conjectured '*affianc'd*'; Collier MS., '*afeard*'; Ingleby conjectured '*her friend.*'

I. v. 68. '*chance thou changest on*'; so Folios; Rowe reads '*chance thou chancest on*'; Theobald, '*change thou chancest on.*'

I. vi. 24. '*trust—*'; Boswell's reading, Folios, '*trust*'; Hanmer, '*truest*'; Rann, '*truest*'; Thirlby conjectured '*trusty.*'

I. vi. 35. '*number'd*'; (?) '*rich in numbers*'; Theobald, '*unnumber'd*'; Warburton, '*humbl'd*'; Farmer conjectured '*umber'd*'; Jackson conjectured '*member'd*'; Theobald's excellent emendation has much to commend it.

I. vi. 44. '*desire vomit emptiness*'; Johnson explained these difficult words as follows:—"*Desire*, when it approached *sluttery*, and considered it in comparison with *such neat* excellence, would not only be *not so allured to feed*, but seized with a fit of loathing, would *vomit emptiness*, would feel the convulsions of disgust, though being unfed, it had no object." Pope, '*desire vomit ev'n emptiness*'; Capell, '*desire vomit to emptiness*'; Hudson, '*desire vomit from emptiness.*'

I. vi. 108. '*unlustrous*'; Rowe's emendation of Folios, '*illustrious*'; Ingleby, '*ill-lustrous.*'

II. ii. 49. '*bare the raven's eye*'; Theobald's conjecture, adopted by Steevens; Folios, '*beare the Rauens eye.*'

II. iii. 26. '*With every thing that pretty is*'; Hanmer (unnecessarily, for the sake of the rhyme), '*With all the things that pretty bin*'; Warburton, '*With everything that pretty bin.*'

II. iii. 30. '*vice*'; Rowe's emendation of Folios, '*voyce.*'

II. iii. 49. '*soliciting*'; the reading of Collier (ed. 2); Folio 1 reads '*solicity*'; Folios 2, 3, 4, '*solicits*'; Pope, '*solicits.*'

II. iii. 103. '*Are not*'; Warburton's conjecture, adopted by Theobald, '*cure not*'; but no change is necessary.

III. i. 20. '*rocks*'; Seward conjecture, adopted by Hanmer; Folios, '*Oakes.*'

III. i. 53. '*We do*'; these words are part of Cymbeline's speech in Folios; Collier MS. assigns them to Cloten, and the arrangement has been generally adopted.

III. iii. 2. '*Stoop*'; Hanmer's emendation of Folios, '*Sleepe.*'

III. iii. 6. '*turbans*'; Folio 1, '*Turbonds*'; Folios 2, 3, 4, '*Turbands.*'

III. iii. 23. '*bauble*'; Rowe's emendation of Folios, '*Babe*';

Hanmer, '*bribe*'; the latter suggestion has been accepted by many modern editors; Brae, '*badge*,' i.e. decoration, ribbon.

III. iii. 34. '*prison for*'; Pope's emendation of Folio 1, '*Prison, or*'; Folios 2, 3, 4, '*Prison or*'; Anon. conjecture, and Vaughan conjecture, '*prison of.*'

III. iii. 83. '*I' the cave wherein they bow*'; Warburton's emendation; Folios, '*I' th' Cave, whereon the Bowe*'; Rowe, '*I' th' cave, where on the bow*'; Pope, '*Here in the cave, wherein*'; Theobald, '*I' th' cave, there, on the brow*,' &c.

III. iv. 49. '*Whose mother was her painting*,' i.e. 'who owed her beauty to her painted face'; or, perhaps, 'whose painted face was the sum of her woman-like qualities'; according to others, 'whose mother aided and abetted her daughter in her trade.'

III. iv. 78. '*afore't*'; Rowe's emendation of Folios, '*a-foot.*'

III. iv. 101. '*I'll wake mine eye-balls blind first*'; Hanmer's emendation; Folios read '*I'll wake mine eye-balles first*'; Rowe, '*I'll break mine eye-balles first*'; Johnson conjecture, adopted by Ingleby, '*I'll wake mine eye-balls out first*'; Collier MS., '*I'll crack mine eye-balls first.*'

III. iv. 132. Vaughan proposed '*With that harsh noble—noble simply in nothing*'; Spence, '*trash noble*' (i.e. base coin); Elze, '*that ignoble*,' &c.

III. iv. 135. '*Where then?*' perhaps these words should be assigned to Pisanio.

III. iv. 174. '*Which you'll make him know*'; Hanmer's reading; Folios read '*Which will make him know*'; Theobald, '*Which will make him so.*'

III. v. 44. '*loud'st of noise*'; Capell's emendation; Folios 1, 2, '*lowd of noise*'; Rowe, '*loudest noise.*'

III. v. 73. Possibly, as explained by Johnson, these words are to be explained as meaning, 'than any lady, than all ladies, than all womankind'; Hanmer, '*than any lady, winning from each one.*'

III. vi. 71. Perhaps should read, with Hanmer, '*I bid*'; i.e. 'I'd bid for you and make up my mind to have you.'

III. vii. 9. '*commends*'; Warburton's emendation, adopted by Theobald; Folios, '*commands*' (perhaps = 'commands to be given').

IV. ii. 133. '*humour*'; Theobald's emendation of Folios, '*honor.*'

IV. ii. 169. '*parish*'; Hanmer, '*marish*'; Garrick's version, '*river*'; Becket conjectured '*parage.*'

IV. ii. 225. '*The ruddock*,' &c.; the kindly service of the Robin Redbreast is often referred to in Elizabethan literature, e.g.

"*Covering with moss the dead's unclosed eye,*
The little redbreast teacheth charitie."
Drayton, *The Owl.*

It is worth while noting that the story of *The Babes in the Wood* was dramatised as early as 1600 in Yarrington's *Two Lamentable Tragedies.*

IV. iii. 36. '*I heard no letter*,' i.e. (?) 'I've not had a line'; Hanmer reads '*I've had*'; Capell, '*I have had*'; Mason conjecture, and Warburton conjecture, adopted by Collier (ed. 2), '*I had.*'

V. i. 15. '*dread it, to the doers' thrift*'; perhaps this means that the guilty benefit by their dread, for their dread makes them repent, and repentance brings them salvation. Theobald suggested '*dreaded . . . thrift*'; but the text, though somewhat difficult, may be correct.

V. iii. 26. '*that*,' *i.e.* 'that death.'

V. iii. 43. '*they*'; Theobald's correction of Folios, '*the*'; *i.e.* 'retracing as slaves the strides they made as victors.'

V. iii. 53. '*Nay, do not wonder*'; Theobald reads '*Nay, do but wonder*'; Staunton conjectured '*Ay, do but wonder*'; "Posthumus first bids him not wonder, then tells him in another mode of reproach that wonder was all he was made for" (Johnson).

V. v. 54. '*and in time*'; so Folio 1; Folios 2, 3, 4, '*yes and in time*,' S. Walker conjectured '*and in due time*,' &c.

V. v. 263. The stage-direction was first inserted by Hanmer,

and explains the meaning of the lines, and gets rid of a long series of unnecessary emendations.

V. v. 305. '*scar*'; '*had ever s. for*,' *i.e.* had ever received a scar for; Folios 1, 2, '*scarre*'; Collier conjectured '*sense*'; Singer (ed. 2), '*score*'; Bailey conjectured '*soar*.'

V. v. 378. '*When ye*'; Rowe's emendation of Folios, '*When we*'; Capell, '*When you*.'

V. v. 382. '*fierce*,' disordered; (?) vehement, rapid; Collier conjectured '*forc'd*'; Bailey conjectured '*brief*.'

V. v. 384. '*distinction should be rich in*,' *i.e.* "Ought to be rendered distinct by a liberal amplitude of narrative" (Steevens).

V. v. 392. '*our long inter'gatories*'; Tyrwhitt conjecture, adopted by Malone; Folios, '*our long Interrogatories*.'

THE WINTER'S TALE

I. ii. 44. '*What lady she her lord*'; 'she' has been variously interpreted; Collier and Dyce proposed 'should,' destroying the beauty of the line; Schmidt makes the phrase 'lady she' = 'a woman that is a lady,' taking 'she' ≅ 'woman'; others print 'lady-she'; perhaps the word may be best explained as the pleonastic pronoun so common in popular poetry; the rhythm seems to favour this latter view.

I. ii. 70. '*The doctrine of ill-doing, nor dream'd*'; so Folio 1; the later Folios, '*no nor dream'd*'; Spedding, '*neither dream'd*'; perhaps '*doctrine*' should be read as a trisyllable; a harsh line would, however, result; and the reading of the later Folios has much to commend it.

I. ii. 131-2. '*false As o'er-dyed blacks*'; Folios 1, 2, 3, '*o're dy'd*'; the words have been variously interpreted to mean 'fabrics dyed over with some other colour,' or, 'dyed too much'; Steevens saw in the phrase an allusion to the fact that black will receive no other hue without discovering itself through it; the passage may simply contain the idea, 'the blacker the garb, the less sincere the mourning.'

I. ii. 154. '*methoughts*'; so the Folios in this and other places; this erroneous form was probably due to '*methinks*'; it is noteworthy that the correct '*methought*' occurs a few lines below.

I. ii. 284. '*that*,' *i.e.* 'that of which you accuse her.'

II. i. 11. '*Who taught you this?*' Rowe's emendation of the reading of Folio 1, '*taught 'this*' (with an apostrophe before '*this*,' indicating an elision); the later Folios, '*taught this*.'

II. i. 25. '*A sad tale's best for winter*,' hence the title of the play.

II. i. 39-41. '*There may be in the cup A spider*,' &c.; it was formerly believed that spiders were venomous.

II. i. 134, 135. '*I'll keep my stables where I lodge my wife*'; *i.e.* 'I'll degrade my wife's chamber into a stable or dog kennel.'

II. i. 143. '*I would land-damn him*'; so the Folios; '*land-damm*,' '*laudanum*,' '*lamback*,' (*i.e.* 'ebat'), '*half-damn*,' '*live-damn*,' '*landan (lantan, rantan)*,' '*lant-dam*,' are among the various emendations proposed; Schmidt suggests '*I would—Lord, damn him!*' In all probability the reading of the Folios should not be departed from, and it seems likely that Antigonus, having in the previous phrase used the word '*damn'd*,' here uses 'land-damn,' as a sort of grim quibble for '*landan*,'—a Gloucestershire word still in use "to express the punishment meted out to slanderers and adulterers by rustics traversing from house to house along the country side, blowing trumpets and beating drums or pans and kettles; when an audience was assembled the delinquents' names were proclaimed, and they were said to be landanned" (*cp.* Halliwell's *Dictionary of Archaic Words*, and *Notes and Queries* iii. 464).': landan, lantan, rantan, were variants of the same word, which was probably imitative in its origin.

II. i. 153. '*As you feel doing thus*,' probably = my doing thus to you (*i.e.* touching him, or perhaps pulling his beard); '*the instruments that feel*' = my fingers.

II. iii. 177. '*to it own protection*,' so Folios 1, 2; Folios 3, 4,

'*its*'; the old possessive form '*it*,' still in use in Lancashire, occurs again in this play (III. ii. 101); there are some dozen instances elsewhere: '*it own*,' may be regarded as a sort of idiomatic compound, the combination helping to maintain the archaism; '*its*' (Folio, *it 's*) *own*,' to be found in Act I. ii. 266 is said to be the only instance of its use in Shakespeare.

III. iii. 119. '*You 're a made old man*'; Theobald's emendation of the Folio reading '*mad*,' confirmed by a passage in Shakespeare's original:—"The goodman desired her to be quiet . . . if she could hold her peace they were made for ever."

IV. i. 15. '*to it*,' *i.e.* 'the present.'

IV. ii. 4. '*It is fifteen years since*,' &c.; changed by Hanmer to '*sixteen*,' the number intended by Shakespeare.

IV. iii. 23, 24. '*when the kite builds, look to lesser linen*'; alluding to this bird's habit of carrying off small linen garments hung out to dry; Autolycus preferred more substantial prey.

IV. iii. 51. '*I' the name of me——*'; probably, as has been suggested, the Clown's exclamation of '*Mercy*' is interrupted by Autolycus.

IV. iv. 247. '*clamour your tongues*'; Hanmer's emendation '*charm*' has been generally adopted, but '*clamour*' is almost certainly correct (Taylor, the Water-Poet, wrote '*Clamour the promulgation of your tongues*'); '*clamour*' or rather '*clammer*,' is probably radically identical with '*clamber*,' the Scandinavian original of which '*klambra*' = 'to pinch closely together, to clamp.'

IV. iv. 274. '*another ballad of a fish*'; *cp. e.g.* "A strange report of a monstrous fish that appeared in the form of a woman from her waist upward, seen in the sea"; entered in the Stationers' Registers in 1604.

IV. iv. 429. '*Far than Deucalion off*'; '*far*' = 'farther'; the Folios all correctly read '*farre*,' *i.e.* the old form of the comparative of '*far*.'

IV. iv. 579. '*i' the rear o' her birth*'; Folios 1, 2, 3, '*our birth*'; Rowe first emended the line as in the text, though in his second edition he read 'o' our' for 'o' her.'

IV. iv. 587. '*appear*,' *i.e.* appear so (like Bohemia's son).

IV. iv. 707. '*at palace*'; Folio 1, '*at 'Pallace*'; probably the apostrophe indicates "the omission of the article or its absorption in rapid pronunciation."

V. ii. 57. '*weather-bitten conduit*'; changed to '*weather-beaten*' in Folio 3; but '*weather-bitten*' is undoubtedly the correct form (*cp.* Skeat's *Etymological Dictionary*): conduits were frequently in the form of human figures.

V. ii. 95, 96. '*that rare Italian master*'; Giulio Pippi, known as 'Giulio Romano,' was born in 1492, and died in 1546; his fame as a painter was widespread; Shakespeare, taking him as 'a type of artistic excellence,' makes him a sculptor; it must, however, be remembered that the statue was a 'painted picture.' Much has been made of this reference by the advocates of Shakespeare's alleged Italian journeys (*cp.* Elze's *Essays on Shakespeare*).

THE TEMPEST

I. i. 65. '*long heath, brown furze*'; so the folios; Hanmer's emendation has been generally accepted:—'ling, heath, broom, furze.'

I. ii. 100. '*Who having into truth*'; 'into,' used in the sense of 'unto,' and so emended in most editions; the sentence though very involved is intelligible without any alteration; 'into truth' depends upon 'a sinner'; and 'it' refers vaguely to 'his own lie'; 'to credit' = 'as to credit.'

I. ii. 169. '*Now I arise*'; probably derived from astrology; 'now my star is in the ascendent;' it should be noted that the stage direction 'Resumes his mantle' is not in the Folios.

I. ii. 266. '*for one thing she did*'; Shakespeare does not tell us what he refers to here; perhaps he merely added the point in order to account for her preservation, or the incident may have been mentioned in his original.

I. ii. 377, 378. '*Kiss'd the wild waves*'; so the Folios, *i.e.*, 'Kissed the wild waves into silence;' often printed with a comma after 'kissed.'

II. i. 5. '*The masters of some merchant*'; *i.e.*, 'the owners of some merchantman'; Steevens suggested 'mistress' (old spelling 'maistres'); the Cambridge editors 'master's' (*i.e.*, 'master's wife').

II. i. 27. '*which, of he or Adrian*'; 'he' for 'him,' used somewhat substantively, probably owing to the use of the word in the previous sentence, 'he will be talking.'

II. i. 35. The Folios read: 'Seb. *Ha, ha, ha!* Ant. *So you're paid.*' Theobald gives the whole line to Sebastian; and his reading is adopted by the Camb. ed. Possibly a better emendation is the transposition of the prefixes to the speeches; the point of the quibble is no doubt the old proverb 'let them laugh that win.' Capell ingeniously suggested that the Folio reading should stand with the slight change of 'you've paid' for 'you're paid.'

II. i. 122. '*who hath cause*'; the antecedent of 'who' is most probably 'she'; some make the relative refer to 'eye,' *i.e.* 'which hath cause to weep.'

II. i. 126. '*should bow*'; so Folios; seemingly unnecessary corrections have been made, *e.g.* 'she'd bow'; 'which end the beam should bow'; the omission of the pronoun 'it' or 'she' before 'should' can easily be paralleled in Shakespeare.

II. i. 237. '*But doubt discovery there*'; *i.e.* 'Cannot but doubt that anything can be discovered there.'

II. i. 244. '*She that from whom*'; the unnecessary 'that' is perhaps intentionally repeated, owing to the previous repetition of 'she that.'

II. i. 273. '*candied*'; generally explained as 'sugared over, and so insensible'; perhaps a better interpretation is 'made sweet as sugar,' as in the phrase 'the candied tongue.' Is Antonio possibly playing on 'candied' and 'candid' (a word not yet fully naturalised in the language, but probably familiar)?

II. ii. 76, 77. '*I will not take too much for him*'; *i.e.* 'I will take as much as I can possibly get.'

II. ii. 170. '*Scamels*'; not found elsewhere in Shakespeare. Many emendations have been made; staniel (a species of hawk) has been adopted by some editors; the word occurs probably in *Twelfth Night* (II. v. 106), though the editions read 'stallion.' 'Scamel' is evidently the name of a rock-breeding bird; Mr. Wright has pointed out that, according to Stevenson's "Birds of Norfolk," "the female Bar-tailed Godwit is called a 'Scamell' by the gunners of Blakeney."

III. i. 15. '*Most busy lest, when I do it*'; so the first Folio. Various readings have been suggested; Pope, 'least busy when I do it'; Theobald, 'most busie-less when I do it'; Holt, 'most busiest, when I do it'; Spedding 'most busiest when idlest,' &c., &c. It seems likely that the reading of the second, third, and fourth Folios throws light on the real meaning of the line —'most busy least, when I do it'; *i.e.*, 'most busy when I indulge my thoughts, least busy when I am actually at work.' A comma after 'busy' instead of after 'least' would simplify this reading, but it is possible to understand it as punctuated in the Folios; Shakespeare probably wished to make the superlatives as antithetical as possible; perhaps we should read 'labour' for 'labours.'

III. iii. 39. '*Praise in departing*'; a proverbial expression; "stay your praises till you see how your entertainment will end."

IV. i. 64. '*pioned and twilled*'; various emendations have been suggested for these difficult words of the Folio:—'peonied and lilied,' 'tulip'd,' 'tilled,' &c. It is noted that 'piony' is an old spelling of 'peony,' and that the flower was formerly spoken of as 'the mayden piony' and 'virgin peonie.' In all probability the meaning of the words has not yet been discovered; they are evidently technical terms of horticulture. (*Cp.* Glossary.)

IV. i. 110. Mr. Wright suggests that 'earths' should be read as a dissyllable, 'earthes'; the second, third, and fourth Folios read '*and*' before 'foison.'

IV. i. 147. &c. In *The Tragedy of Darius*, by William Alexander, afterwards Earl of Sterling, published in the year 1603, occurs the following passage, which, according to Steevens, may have been the original of Shakespeare's Speech:

"Let greatnesse of her glascie sceptre vaunt:
Not scepters, no, but reeds, soone brus'd, soone broken
And let this worldlie pomp our wits inchant.
All fades, and scarcelie leaues behind a token.
  Those golden pallaces, those gorgeous halles
With fourniture superfluouslie faire:
  Those statelie courts, those sky-encountering walles
Evanish all like vapours in the aire."

IV. i. 193. The Folios read 'hang on them.'

IV. i. 221. '*O King Stephano! O Peer!*' an allusion to the old song, often referred to in Elizabethan literature, "Take thy old cloak about thee":—

"King Stephen was a worthy peere,
  His breeches cost him but a crowne,
He held them sixpence all too deere;
  Therefore he called the taylor Lowne."

The ballad is printed in Percy's Reliques; Shakespeare quotes it also in Othello, II. iii. 84.

IV. i. 230. '*Let's alone*'; some verb of motion must be understood, *i.e.*, 'let us go alone' (leaving Trinculo behind); 'alone' is possibly an error of the Folios for 'along,' as suggested by Theobald.

IV. i. 236. "An allusion to what often happens to people who pass the line. The violent fevers which they contract in that hot climate make them lose their hair."—STEEVENS.

V. i. 23-24. The first and second Folios place a comma after 'sharply,' making 'passion' a verb; the comma is omitted in the third and fourth Folios.

V. i. 310. The line is to be read, according to the Folios, "to see our dear belov'd solémnizéd."

THE FAMOUS HISTORY OF THE LIFE OF KING HENRY VIII

Prol. 3. 'high and working'; Staunton reads 'and high-working.'

Prol. 12. 'shilling'; the usual price for a seat on or next the stage.

Prol. 16. 'a long motley coat'; the professional garb of the fool or jester.

Prol. 21. The line is either to be taken as a parenthesis, 'that' referring to 'opinion' (= reputation); or as following directly on 'opinion,' i.e. 'the reputation we bring of making what we represent strictly in accordance with truth.'

I. i. 6. 'Those suns of glory'; i.e. Francis I., King of France, and Henry VIII., King of England; Folios 3, 4 read 'sons.'

I. i. 7. 'the vale of Andren.' 'Twizt Guynes and Arde.' Guynes, a town in Picardy belonging to the English; Arde, a town in Picardy belonging to the French; the vale of Andren between the two towns was the scene of the famous 'Field of the Cloth of Gold.'

I. i. 62, 63. Capell's reading of Folio 1, 'but spider-like, Out of his selfe-drawing web, O gives us note.' Further, Capell and Rowe substituted 'self-drawn' for 'self-drawing.'

I. i. 79, 80. 'The honourable . . . out, . . . him in he papers'; Folios 1, 2, read 'The Council, out . . . him in, he papers,' &c. Pope's explanation of these awkward lines is probably correct:—"His own letter, by his own single authority, and without the concurrence of the council, must fetch him in whom he papers" (i.e. registers on the paper). Various emendations have been proposed; e.g. 'the papers'; 'he paupers.' (Collier MS., 'wrensing').

I. i. 86. 'minister communication'; Collier MS., 'the consummation'; but the phrase is Holinshed's.

I. i. 90. 'the hideous storm'; "On Mondaie, the eighteenth of June, was such an hideous storme of wind and weather, that manie conjectured it did prognosticate trouble and hatred shortlie after to follow betweene princes" (Holinshed).

I. i. 115. The Duke of Buckingham's surveyor was his cousin, Charles Knevet, or Knyvet, grandson of Humphrey Stafford, First Duke of Buckingham.

I. i. 120. 'venom-mouth'd'; Pope's reading; Folios read 'venom'd-mouth'd.'

I. i. 152. 'Whom from the flow of gall I name not,' &c.; i.e. 'whom I mention, not because I am still angry'; &c.

I. i. 167. 'rinsing,' Pope's unnecessary emendation of the Folio reading 'wrenching,' which is evidently an error for 'renching,' a provincial English cognate of 'rinse,' both words being ultimately derived from the same Scandinavian original, rinse, through the medium of French, rench, a direct borrowing; (Collier MS., 'wrensing').

I. i. 172. 'count-cardinal'; Pope proposed 'court-cardinal.'

I. i. 176. 'Charles the emperor,' viz., Charles V., Emperor of Germany; Katherine was his mother's sister.

I. i. 200. 'Hereford'; Capell's reading; Folios, 'Hertford.'

I. i. 204-206. The meaning of these unsatisfactory lines seems to be, as Johnson explained, "I am sorry to be present and an eye-witness of your loss of liberty."

I. i. 211. 'Abergavenny'; Folios, 'Aburgany,' the usual pronunciation of the name.

I. i. 217. 'Montacute'; Folios read 'Mountacute'; Rowe reads 'Montague.'

I. i. 219. 'chancellor'; Theobald's correction; Folios 1, 2 read 'Councellour.'

I. i. 221. 'Nicholas Hopkins'; Theobald's correction (from Holinshed) of Folios, 'Michaell' (probably due to printer's confusion of 'Nich' with 'Mich').

I. ii. 67. 'business'; Warburton's emendation of Folios, 'baseness.'

I. ii. 147. 'Henton'; i.e. Nicholas Hopkins, "a monk of an house of the Chartreux Order beside Bristow, called Henton" (Holinshed); there is no need to amend the text.

I. ii. 164. 'confession's seal'; Theobald's emendation (following Holinshed) of Folios, 'commissions.'

I. ii. 170. 'To gain'; the reading of Folio 4; Folios 1, 2, 3, read 'To'; Collier MS. reads 'To get'; Grant White, 'To win.'

I. ii. 179. 'for him'; Capell's emendation of 'For this' of the Folios; Collier MS. reads 'From this'; &c.

I. ii. 190. 'Bulmer'; Folios read 'Blumer'; Pope, 'Blomer.'

I. iii. 13. 'Or springhalt'; Verplank's (Collier conj.) emendation of Folios, 'A springhalt'; Pope, 'And springhalt.'

I. iii. 34. 'wear'; the reading of Folios 2, 3, 4; Folio 1 reads 'wee'; Anon. conjecture 'oui.'

I. iii. 59. 'has wherewithal'; Folios, 'ha's,' probably an error for ''has,' i.e. '(he) has.'

I. iv. 6. 'As, first, good company'; so Folios 1, 2, 3; Folio 4 reads 'As, first good company'; Theobald, 'as, first-good company'; Halliwell, 'as far as good company,' &c.

II. i. 29. 'was either pitied in him or forgotten'; i.e. "either produced no effect, or only ineffectual pity" (Malone).

II. i. 54. 'Sir William Sands'; Theobald's emendation (from Holinshed) of Folio 1, 'Sir Walter Sands'; Folios 2, 3, 4, 'Walter Sands.'

II. i. 85. 'mark'; Warburton's emendation of Folios, 'make.'

II. i. 104. 'I now seal it,' i.e. my truth,—with blood.

II. ii. 82. 'one have-at-him'; Folio 1, 'one; haue at him'; Folios 2, 3, 4, 'one heave at him'; Knight, 'one;—have at him.'

II. ii. 91. 'Have their free voices,' i.e. 'have liberty to express their opinions freely'; (Grant White, 'Gave' for 'Have').

II. iii. 14. 'that quarrel, fortune, do'; Folio 1 reads 'that quarrell. Fortune, do'; Collier MS., 'that cruel fortune do'; Keightley, 'that quarrel, by fortune, do'; Lettsom conjectured 'that fortunes quarrel do'; Hanmer, 'that quarr'ler, fortune do'; &c.

II. iii. 46. 'little England'; Steevens pointed out that Pembrokeshire was known as 'little England'; and as Anne Bullen was about to be made Marchioness of Pembroke, there may be a special point in the phrase.

II. iii. 92. 'the mud in Egypt,' i.e. 'the land fertilized by the Nile's overflow.'

II. iv. 61. 'That longer you desire the court,' i.e. desire the court to delay its proceedings; Folio 4, 'defer'; Keightley conjectured 'court delay'd.'

II. iv. 171. 'The Bishop of Bayonne'; strictly it should be 'the Bishop of Tarbes,' but the mistake was Holinshed's.

II. iv. 173. 'The Duke of Orleans,' was the second son of Francis I., King of France.

II. iv. 181. 'the bosom of my conscience'; Holinshed's use of 'secret bottom of my conscience' justified Theobald's emendation of 'bosom' to 'bottom.'

II. iv. 198. 'throe'; Pope's emendation of Folios, 'throw.'

II. iv. 203. 'yet not,' i.e. not yet.

II. iv. 224. 'drive'; Pope's emendation of Folios, 'drives.'

III. i. 38. 'and that way I am wife in'; i.e. 'concerning my conduct as a wife.' (Rowe proposed 'wise' for 'wife.')

III. i. 40, 41. 'Tanta est erga te mentis integritas, regina serenissima'; 'So great is our integrity of purpose towards thee, most serene princess.'

III. ii. 64. 'He is returned in his opinions,' i.e. having sent in advance the opinions he has gathered.

III. ii. 66. 'Together with all famous colleges'; Rowe reads, 'Gather'd from all the famous colleges.'

III. ii. 172. 'been mine so'; so Folio 1; Folios 2, 3, 4 read 'been so.'

III. ii. 192. 'that am, have, and will be,' &c.; the reading of the Folios of these lines, which have taxed the ingenuity of scholars; some two dozen various emendations are recorded in the Cambridge Shakespeare, but probably the text as we have it represents the author's words; the meaning of the passage is clear, and the difficulty is due to the change in construction. Instead of 'that am, have, and will be,' it has been proposed to read, 'that am your slave, and will be'; this would get rid of the awkward 'have' = 'have been,' but probably the line is correct as it stands.

III. ii. 282. 'And dare us with his cap like larks'; "One of the methods of daring larks was by small mirrors fastened on scarlet cloth, which engaged the attention of these birds while the fowler drew his net over them" (Steevens).

III. ii. 321. '*Cassado*'; so Folios, following Hall and Holinshed; Rowe reads the correct form, '*Cassalis.*'

III. ii. 343. '*Chattels*'; Theobald's emendation of Folios, '*Castles.*'

IV. ii. 58-59. '*Those twins of learning . . . Ipswich and Oxford*'; Wolsey's College, Ipswich, of which the gateway still remains, was founded by Wolsey. Christ Church College, Oxford, was founded by Wolsey: it was first called Cardinal College.

IV. ii. 60. '*the good that did it*'; Pope reads, '*the good he did it*'; Collier MS., '*the good man did it*'; Staunton, '*the good that rear'd it,*' &c. The words, if not corrupt, must mean the 'good man (for the goodness) that caused it, *i.e.* founded it.'

V. i. 34. '*is*'; Theobald, '*he's.*'

V. i. 107. '*you a brother to us,*' *i.e.* being a Privy Councillor.

V. iii. 11-12. '*frail and capable of our flesh*'; Keightley, '*culpable and frail,*' &c.; Pope, '*and capable Of frailty*'; Malone, '*incapable; Of our flesh*'; Mason conj. '*and culpable: Of our flesh,*' &c.

V. iii. 22. '*pace 'em not in their hands*'; *i.e.* 'leading them by the bridle.'

V. iii. 30. '*The upper Germany*'; alluding to Thomas Munzer's insurrection in Saxony (1521-1522), or to the Anabaptist rising in Munster (1535); the passage is from Foxe.

V. iii. 66. '*Lay,*' *i.e.* 'though ye lay.'

V. iii. 85. '*This is too much*'; the Folios give the speech to the Chamberlain, evidently due to confusion of '*Cham.*' and '*Chan.*'

V. iii. 125. '*bare*'; Malone's emendation of Folios, '*base.*'

V. iii. 166. '*You 'ld spare your spoons,*' *i.e.* 'you wish to save your spoons'; alluding to the old custom of giving spoons as christening presents.

V. iv. 26. '*And that I would not for a cow, God save her!*' a proverbial expression still used in the South of England.

V. iv. 62, 63. '*The tribulation of Towerhill, or the limbs of Limehouse.*' There is no evidence for finding in these words the names of Puritan congregations, as commentators have supposed; the alternative phrases are sufficiently expressive without any such supposition, and were perhaps coined for the occasion; they are not found elsewhere.

V. v. 70. '*And your good brethren*'; Thirlby's conjecture, adopted by Theobald; Folios read '*and you good brethren.*'

V. v. 75. '*has*'; *i.e.* he has; Folios, "*Has.*'

VENUS AND ADONIS

156. '*shouldst*'; Quarto 1, '*should.*'

171. *cp.* Sonnet I.

211. '*lifeless*'; Quartos 1, 2, 3, '*liuelesse.*'

213. '*Statue*'; Quartos 1, 2, 3, '*Statüe*'; *cp.* l. 1013; Quartos 3, 4, '*statües.*'

231; 239; 689. '*deer*'; Quartos 1, 2, 3, '*deare.*'

272. '*stand,*' so Quartos 1-4; the rest '*stands.*'

283. '*stir*'; Quartos 1, 2, 3, '*sturre.*'

304. '*And whether*'; Quartos, '*And where*' (*i.e.* 'wher'er').

334; 402. '*fire*'; Quartos 1, 2, 3, '*fier*'; but '*fire,*' l. 494 (rhyming with '*desire*').

353. '*tenderer*'; Quarto 1, '*tendrer*'; the rest, '*tender.*'

362. '*goal*'; Quartos, '*gaile*'; '*Iaile.*'

392. '*master'd*'; Quartos 1, 2, 3, '*maister'd*'; *cp.* l. 114; '*mastering*'; Quartos 1, 2, 3, '*maistring.*'

——, '*rein*'; Quartos 1-10, '*raine.*'

429. '*mermaid's*'; early Quartos, '*marmaides*'; '*marmaids*'; *cp.* l. 777; Quartos 1, 2, 3, '*marmaids*'; Quarto 4, '*mirmaides.*'

434. '*invisible*'; Steevens conjectured '*invincible.*'

454. '*wreck*'; Quartos. '*wracke,*' '*wrack*' (*cp.* l. 558).

466. '*bankrupt*'; Quartos, '*bankrout,*' '*banckrout,*' '*banquerout.*'

466. '*love*'; S. Walker conjectured '*loss.*'

507. '*verdure*'; Quartos 1, 2, 3, '*verdour.*'

529. '*gait*'; Quartos, '*gate.*'

547. '*prey*'; Quartos, '*pray*' (though rhyming with 'obey'); so '*prayes,*' l. 724, and '*pray*'; (rhyming with '*day*'), l. 1097.

567. '*venturing*'; Quartos, '*ventring.*'

599. '*Tantalus*' '; Quartos, '*Tantalus.*'

628. '*venture*'; Quartos, '*venter*' (rhyming with '*enter*').

632. '*eyes pay*'; Quartos 1, 2, '*eye paies.*'

680. '*overshoot,*' Steevens conjecture; Quartos 1, 2, 3, '*overshut.*'

705. '*doth*'; Quartos 1, 2, 3, '*do.*'

743. '*imposthumes*'; Quartos, '*impostumes.*'

781. '*run*'; Quartos 1, 2, 3, '*ronne*' (rhyming with '*undone*').

832. '*deeply*'; S. Walker conjectured '*doubly.*'

902. '*together*'; Quartos, '*togither*' (rhyming with '*whither*'); *cp.* l. 971; Quartos 1, 2, 3, '*all together*' (rhyming with '*weather*'); Quarto 4, '*altogither.*'

940. '*random*'; Quartos 1-4, '*randon.*'

993. '*all to nought*' (rhyming with '*wrought*'); Dyce, '*all-to nought*'; Delius, '*all-to naught.*'

1002. '*decease*'; early Quartos, '*decesse*' (rhyming with '*confess*').

1013-1014. '*stories His*'; Theobald's conjecture; Quartos, '*stories, His.*'

1041. '*ugly*'; Quarto 1, '*oughly.*'

1067. '*limb*'; Quarto 1, '*lim.*'

1117. '*been*'; Quarto 1, '*bin.*'

1155. '*severe*'; early Quartos, '*seveare*' (rhyming with '*fear*').

1161. '*servile*'; Quartos 1, 2, '*seruill*'; *cp.* line 392, '*servilely*'; Quartos 1, 2, 3, '*seruilly.*'

THE RAPE OF LUCRECE

8. '*unhappily*'; Quartos 1, 2, 3, '*vnhap'ly.*'

24. '*morning's*'; Quarto 1 (Bodl. 1), '*morning.*'

31. '*apologies*'; Quarto 1 (Bodl. 1), '*appologie.*'

56. '*o'er*'; Quartos 1, 2, 3, 'ore'; Quarto 4, '*or'e*'; Malone (1780), '*or*' (*i.e.* gold).

134-136. Many emendations have been proposed to render clear the meaning of these lines, but no change is necessary: "the covetous have not, *i.e.* do not possess, that which they possess, longing for the possessions of others"; the second clause of line 135 is in apposition to the first.

195. '*let*'; Schmidt conjectured '*lest.*'

239. '*ay, if*'; early Quartos, '*I, if.*'

637. *i.e.* "who, in consequence of their own misdeeds, look with indifference on the offences of others" (Schmidt).

649. '*debt*'; early Quartos, '*det*' (rhyming with '*fret*'); similarly l. 696, '*balk*'; Quartos, '*bauk*' (rhyming with '*hawk*').

782. '*misty*'; Quartos 1, 2, '*mustie.*'

841. '*guilty*'; Malone, '*guiltless,*' but no change is necessary; Lucrece's self-reproach at first assigns the guilt to herself.

930. Perhaps we should read, '*injurious-shifting Time.*'

1134. '*descant'st*'; Quartos, '*descants.*'

1338. '*court'sies*'; Quartos, '*cursies.*'

1662. '*wretched*'; S. Walker conjectured '*wreathed.*'

SONNETS

XII. 4. '*And . . . all*'; so Malone. Quarto, '*And . . . or.*'

XVI. 10. '*this, . . . pen*'; Quarto, '*this (Time's pensel or my pupill pen).*' Massey conjectured '*this time's pencil, or my pupil pen*'; this reading is accepted by several editors, who interpret the first clause to refer either to some particular artist, or to any painter of the time.

XIX. 5. '*fleet'st*'; so Quarto; Dyce, '*fleets*' (rhyming with '*sweets*'); cp. VIII. 7.

XX. 7. '*hue, all "hues"*'; Quarto, '*hew all Hews*' (*Hews* in italics).

XXI. 5. '*couplement*'; Quarto, '*coopelment.*'

XXV. 9-11. '*fight . . . quite*'; Malone (Theobald conjectured); Quarto, '*worth . . . quite.*' Theobald conjectured '*worth . . . forth*'; Capell MS., '*might . . . quite.*'

XXVII. 10. '*thy*'; Quarto, '*their*'; a common mistake in the Sonnets, evidently due to the '*y*' being taken for '*e*' with the mark of contraction for '*ir.*'

XXVIII. 13, 14. '*longer . . . strength seem stronger*'; Capell MS. and Collier conjecture; Quarto, '*longer . . . length seeme stronger.*'

XXXI. 8. '*thee*'; Quarto, '*there.*'

XXXIV. 10-12. '*loss . . . cross*'; Quarto, '*losse . . . losse.*'

XXXIV. 13. '*sheds*'; Quarto, '*sheeds*' (rhyming with '*deeds*').

XXXIX. 12. '*doth*'; Quarto, '*dost.*'

XL. 7. '*thyself*'; Quarto, '*this selfe.*'

XLI. 8. '*she have*'; Tyrwhitt conjectured; Quarto, '*he haue*'; Ewing, '*he has.*'

XLVII. 11. '*not*', so ed. 1640; Quarto, '*nor.*'

XLIX. 10. '*desert*'; Quarto, '*desart*' (rhyming with '*part*').

LI. 11. '*neigh—no dull flesh—*' (Malone); Quarto, '*naigh noe dull flesh*'; probably the reading of the Quarto is correct. '*neigh*' = 'neigh after,' 'neigh to,' cp. "They were fed horses in the morning; everyone neighed after his neighbour's wife," Jeremiah v. 8.

LV. 1. '*monuments*'; Quarto, '*monument.*'

LVI. 13. '*Or*'; Tyrwhitt conjecture and Capell MS.; Quarto, '*As*'; Anonymous conjecture, '*Ah!*'; '*Else.*'

LVII. 13. '*will*'; Quarto, '*Will*'; Massey conjectured "'*Will.*'"

LXII. 7. '*And for myself,*' i.e. 'and for my own satisfaction,' or perhaps the words merely emphasize the statement.

LXV. 12. '*of*'; Malone; Quarto, '*or*'; Capell MS., '*o'er*'; Gildon, '*on.*'

LXIX. 3. '*that due*'; Capell MS. and Tyrwhitt conjecture; Quarto '*that end*'; Sewell (ed. 2), '*thy due.*'

LXX. 1. '*art*,' ed. 1640; Quarto, '*are.*'

6. '*Thy*'; Capell MS.; Quarto, '*their.*'

LXXIII. 4. '*Bare ruin'd choirs*'; Quarto, '*Bare rn'wd quiers.*'

LXXIV. 14. '*that is this,*' i.e. my spirit is my poetry.

LXXVI. 7. '*tell,*' Capell MS., Quarto, '*fel*'; Lintott, '*fell*'; Nicholson conjectured '*spell.*'

LXXVII. "Probably this sonnet was designed to accompany a present of a book consisting of blank paper" (Steevens).

LXXXV. 3. '*Reserve their*'; Tyler (Anon. conj. MS.), '*Rehearse thy,*' a more plausible reading than '*preserve their,*' '*deserve their,*' &c., and other suggestions which have been advanced: there is probably some error in the text as printed.

LXXXVI. 13. '*fill'd*'; Quarto, '*fild*'; Malone, '*fil'd.*'

XCIV. 14. cp. Edward III. ii. 1 (printed in 1596):—

> "*Poison shows worst in a golden cup;*
> *Dark night seems darker by the lightning flash;*
> *Lilies that fester seem far worse than weeds;*
> *And every glory, that inclines to sin,*
> *The same is treble by the opposite.*"

XCV. 12. '*turn*'; Quarto, '*turnes.*'

XCIX. A fifteen-lined sonnet; the first line serves as a sort of introduction, standing outside the sonnet.

XCIX. 15. '*sweet*'; S. Walker conjectured, '*scent.*'

CII. 8. '*her,*' Houseman; Quarto, '*his.*'

CVI. 12. '*skill*'; Tyrwhitt conjecture and Capell MS.; Quarto, '*still.*'

CVII. 8. It has been suggested that this is a possible allusion to the peace completed in 1609, which ended the war between Spain and the United Provinces; but this is merely a random suggestion.

CVIII. 3. '*new . . . new,*' Malone; Quarto, '*new . . . now*'; S. Walker conjectured '*now . . . now.*'

CXII. 8. '*or changes*'; Malone conjectured '*e'er changes*'; Knight conjectured '*so changes.*'

14. '*besides methinks are,*' Capell MS. and Steevens conjecture; Quarto, '*besides me thinkes y' are*'; Dyce, '*besides methinks they're.*'

CXIII. 6. '*latch*'; Quarto, '*lack.*'

14. '*maketh mine untrue*'; so Quarto; Capell MS., and Malone conjecture '*makes mine eye untrue*'; Collier conjectured '*maketh my eyne untrue*'; Malone conjectured '*thy most true mind maketh mine untrue.*'

CXIX. 14. '*ill,*' Malone; Quarto, '*ills.*'

CXX. 6. '*you've*'; Quarto, '*y'haue.*'

CXXIII. 7. '*them,*' i.e. '*what thou dost foist upon us.*'

CXXIV. 13-14. '*The fools of time,*' &c. Tyler sees in these lines a reference to the popular repute of Essex as the "good earl," notwithstanding the "crimes" for which he and certainly his companions were executed; the allusion is probably more general, and perhaps, as Palgrave observes, to "the plotters and political martyrs of the time."

CXXVI. This short poem is of six rhymed couplets; it was evidently not intended to pass as an ordinary sonnet, though after the last line an omission of two lines is marked in the Quarto by two pairs of parentheses. It is the *envoy*, the conclusion of one series of sonnets.

2. '*sickle, hour*'; Quarto, '*sickle, hower*'; perhaps we should read '*sickle hour*'; other suggestions, unsatisfactory for the most part, are, '*fickle mower*'; '*fickle hoar*'; '*sickle hoar*'; &c.

CXXVII. 9-10. '*eyes . . . eyes,*' Quarto; Capell MS., '*eyes . . . hairs*'; S. Walker and Delius conjecture '*hairs . . . eyes*'; Staunton and Brae conjecture '*brows . . . eyes,*' &c.

CXXIX. 11. '*proved, a very,*' Capell MS.; Quarto, '*proud and very.*'

CXXXV. 13. '*no unkind, no*'; Dowden conjectured '*no unkind "No"*'; Rossetti proposed '*skill,*' i.e. '*avail*' instead of '*kill.*'

CXXXVII. cp. PASSIONATE PILGRIM, i.

CXLII. 6-7. cp. EDWARD III. ii. 1:—'*His cheeks put on their scarlet ornaments.*'

CXLIII. 1. '*housewife*'; Quarto, '*huswife.*'

13. '*have thy "Will"*': i.e. Shakespeare's friend Will, not himself.

CXLIV. cp. PASSIONATE PILGRIM, ii.

6. '*side,*' so Passionate Pilgrim, and Capell MS.; Quarto, '*sight.*'

9. '*fiend*'; Quarto, '*finde*'; Passionate Pilgrim, '*feend.*'

CXLV. The only sonnet in Shakespeare in eight-syllable verse.

CXLVI. 1-2. '*earth . . . these rebel*'; Quarto, '*earth, My sinfull earth these rebbell*'; Malone, '*earth, Fool'd by those rebel*'; Steevens, '*earth, Starv'd by the rebel*'; Dowden, '*earth [Press'd by] these rebel,*' &c. Probably any one of these readings comes near the original; in this case *array* = clothe. Ingleby renders the word "abuse, afflict, ill-treat"; he reads, '*leagu'd with,*' and takes the participle in close conjunction with '*earth.*' This rendering is ingenious, but very doubtful.

CLII. 13. '*I*'; Quarto, '*eye.*'

A LOVER'S COMPLAINT

12. 'scythed'; Quarto, 'sithed.'

37. 'beaded'; Quarto, 'bedded' (? = "imbedded, set").

39. 'weeping margent'; Malone conjectured 'margent weeping.'

51. 'gan to tear'; Quarto, 'gaue to teare'; Gildon, 'gave a tear.'

60. 'observed as they flew'; the clause is probably connected with 'hours'; "the reverend man had not let the swift hours pass by without gaining some knowledge of the world"; it is possible, however, that 'they' refers to the torn-up letters.

112. 'manage'; Quarto, 'mannad'g.'

118. 'came'; Sewell's correction; Quarto, 'can'; Sewell's 2nd ed., 'can for additions get their purpose trim.'

164. 'woo'; Quarto, 'vow.'

182. 'sweets that seem'; Quarto, 'sweets that seemes'; Capell MS., 'sweet that seems.'

228. 'Hallow'd'; Quarto, 'hollowed'; Sewell's correction.

241. 'playing the place'; some error due to the printer has spoilt the line; the first word of the line has been caught up by the compositor's eye from the first of the next line, or vice versa: the most ingenious and plausible emendation is 'paling' for 'playing.'

260. 'nun'; Quarto, 'Sunne.'

261. 'ay'; Quarto, 'I.'

271. 'Love's arms are peace'; so Quarto; Capell MS. and Malone conjecture, 'proof' for 'peace,' a plausible change, if any is necessary; other readings are:—'Love aims at peace'; 'Love charms our peace'; 'Love aims a piece'; &c.

286. 'who glazed with crystal gate'; Malone, 'who, glaz'd with crystal, gate' (i.e. gate = "the ancient perfect tense of the verb to get," flame being its object).

308. 'swound'; Quarto, 'sound,' cp. 305, 'swounding'; Quarto, 'sounding.'

THE PASSIONATE PILGRIM

I., II.; cp. SONNETS, cxxxviii., cxliv.

III. V. XVII.; cp. LOVE'S LABOUR'S LOST, IV. iii. 57-70; IV. ii. 103-116; IV. iii. 98-117.

VIII. 5. John Dowland was one of the most famous of Elizabethan musicians; his song-books appeared in 1597, 1600, and 1603; his "Pilgrim's Solace," 1612. There are many references to him in Elizabethan and later literature, more especially to his 'Lachrymæ, or, Seven Tears figured in seven heavenlie Pavans' (1605); (cp. Bullen's Lyrics from Elizabethan Song-Books.)

XII. 12. 'stay'st'; old eds. 'staies.'

XIII. Two copies of this poem "from a corrected MS." were printed in Gent. Mag. xx. 521; xxx. 39; the variants do not improve the poem.

XV. 8. 'And drives'; perhaps we should read, 'And daylight drives' (Anon. conj.).

XVIII. 5. 'Love's denying'; Malone's conjecture; old eds., 'Love is dying'; England's Helicon, 'Love is denying.'

7. 'renying'; ed. 1599, 'nenying.'

21. 'Love hath forlorn me'; Steevens conjectured 'Love forlorn I.'

31-32. My sighs . . . Procure to'; edd. 1599, 1612, 'With sighes . . . procures to'; the reading of the text is Malone's.

43. 'back peeping'; edd. 1599, 1612, 'blacke peeping.'

XIX. 4. 'fancy, partial wight'; Capell MS. and Malone conjecture withdrawn; edd. 1599, 1612, 'fancy (party all might)'; ed. 1640, 'fancy (partly all might)'; Malone (from MS. copy), 'fancy, partial like,' Collier (from MS. copy), 'partial fancy like'; Steevens conjectured 'fancy, partial tike'; Furnivall conjectured 'fancy's partial might.'

45. 'There is no heaven, by holy then'; the line has been variously emended; Malone reads from an old MS.:—

"Here is no heaven; they holy then
Begin, when," &c.

No satisfactory emendation has been proposed, and perhaps the original reading may be allowed to stand without the comma after 'heaven':—'there is no heaven by holy then,' i.e. "by that holy time"; others suggest, 'be holy then,' or 'by the holy then,' &c.

XX. 1. 'Live with me, and be my love'; in England's Helicon and other early versions the line runs, 'Come live with me,' &c., and in this way it is usually quoted. Two verses found in England's Helicon are omitted in the present version, but included in the 1640 ed., where "Love's Answer" is also in six quatrains; the additional matter was evidently also derived from England's Helicon. After l. 12 the following lines are inserted:—

"A gown made of the finest wool,
Which from our pretty Lambs we pull.
Fair lined slippers for the cold,
With buckles of the purest gold."

The last stanza runs thus:—

"The shepherd's swains shall dance and sing,
For thy delight each May morning;
If these delights thy mind may move,
Then live with me and be my love."

GLOSSARY

Abate, to depress, sink, subdue
Abc-book, a catechism
Able, to qualify or uphold
Absolute, highly accomplished, perfect
Aby, to pay retribution for
Abysm, abyss
Action, direction by mute signs, charge or accusation
Action-taking, litigious
Additions, titles or descriptions
Address, to make ready
Addressed or *addrest*, ready
Adversity, contrariety
Advertisement, admonition
Advertising, attentive
Advise, to consider, recollect
Advised, not precipitant, cautious
Affect, love
Affection, affectation, imagination, disposition, quality
Affections, passions, desires
Affeered, confirmed
Affied, betrothed
Affined, joined by affinity
Affront, to meet or face
Affy, to betroth in marriage
Aglet-baby, a diminutive being
Agnize, acknowledge, confess
A-good, in good earnest
Aim, guess, encouragement, suspicion
Alder-liefest, most dear of all things
Ale, a merry meeting
Allow, to approve
Allowance, approbation
Ames-ace, lowest chance of the dice
Amort, sunk and dispirited
Anchor, anchoret
Ancient, an ensign
Anight, in the night
Answer, retaliation
Antick, the fool of the old farces
Antiquity, old age
Antres, caves and dens
Appeal, to accuse
Appointment, preparation
Apprehensive, quick to understand
Approbation, entry on probation

Approof, proof, approbation
Approve, to justify, to make good, to establish, to recommend to approbation
Approved, felt, convicted by proof
Approvers, persons who try
Aqua-vitæ, brandy, *eau-de-vie*
Arch, chief
Argentine, silvery
Argier, Algiers
Argosies, great ships, galleons
Argument, subject for conversation, evidence, proof
Arm, to take up in the arms
Aroint, avaunt, begone
A-row, successively, one after another
Articulate, to enter into articles
Articulated, exhibited in articles
Artificial, ingenious, artful
Aspersion, sprinkling
Assinego, a he-ass
Assurance, conveyance or deed
Assured, affianced
Astringer, a falconer
Ates, instigation from Ate, the mischievous goddess that incites bloodshed
Atomies, minute particles discernible in a stream of sunshine that breaks into a darkened room, atoms
Attasked, reprehended, corrected
Attended, waited for
Attent, attentive
Attorney, deputation
Attorneyship, the discretional agency of another
Attornied, supplied by substitution of embassies
Avaunt, contemptuous dismission
Audacious, spirited, animated
Audrey, a corruption of Etheldreda
Authentic, an epithet applied to the learned

Baccare, stand back, give place
Bale, misery, calamity
Baleful, baneful
Balked, bathed or piled up
Balm, the oil of consecration
Band, bond
Bank, to sail along the banks
Bar, barrier
Barbed, caparisoned in a warlike manner

Barful, full of impediments
Barn or *bairn*, a child
Base, a rustic game, called prison-base
Bases, a kind of dress used by knights on horseback
Basilisks, a species of cannon
Basta, Spanish, 'tis enough
Bastard, raisin wine
Bat, a club or staff
Bate, strife, contention
Bate, to flutter as a hawk
Batlet, an instrument used by washers of clothes
Battle, army
Bavin, brushwood
Bawcock, a jolly cock
Bay, the space between the main beams of a roof
Beak, the forecastle, or the boltsprit
Beard, to oppose in a hostile manner, to set at defiance
Bearing-cloth, a mantle used at christenings
Beat, in falconry, to flutter
Beetle, to hang over the base
Being, abode
Belongings, endowments
Be-mete, be-measure
Be-moiled, be-draggled, be-mired
Bending, unequal to the weight
Benefit, beneficiary
Bent, the utmost degree of any passion
Best, bravest
Bestowed, left, stowed, or lodged
Bestraught, distraught or distracted
Beteem, to give, to pour out, to permit or suffer
Bewray, betray, discover
Bezonian, a term of reproach
Biding, place, abiding
Bigging, a kind of cap
Bilbo, a Spanish blade of peculiar excellence
Bilboes, a species of fetters
Bill, a weapon carried by watchmen
Bird-bolt, a species of arrow
Bisson, blind
Blank, the white mark at which an arrow is shot
Blast, burst
Blear, to deceive
Blench, to start off
Blent, blended, mixed
Blood-boltered, daubed with blood
Blows, swells
Blunt, stupid, insensible
Board, to accost, to address
Bobb, to trick, to make a fool of
Bodged, boggled, made bungling work
Bolting-hatch, the receptacle in which the meal is bolted
Bombard, or *bumbard*, a barrel
Bombast, the stuffing of clothes
Bona-robas, strumpets
Bond, bounden duty
Book, paper of conditions
Bore, demeaned

Bore, the calibre of a gun
Bores, stabs or wounds
Bosom, wish, heart's desire
Bots, worms in the stomach of a horse
Bourn, boundary, rivulet
Bow, yoke
Brace, armour for the arm, state of defence
Brach, a species of hound
Braid, crafty or deceitful
Bravery, showy dress
Brawl, a kind of dance
Breach, of the sea, breaking of the sea
Breast, voice, surface
Breathed, inured by constant practice
Breathing, complimentary
Breeched, sheathed
Breeching, liable to school-boy punishment
Brize, the gad or horse-fly
Broached, spitted, transfixed
Broke, to deal with a pander
Broken, toothless
Broker, a matchmaker, a procuress or pimp
Brow, height
Bruited, reported with clamour
Brush, detrition, decay
Buckle, to bend, to yield to pressure
Bugs, bugbears, terrors
Bulk, the body
Bunting, a bird like a skylark
Burgonet, a kind of helmet
Bush, the sign of a public-house
Butt-shaft, an arrow to shoot at butts
Buxom, obedient, under command
By'rlakin, by our ladykin, or little lady

Caddis, a narrow worsted galloon
Cade, a barrel
Cadent, falling
Cage, a prison
Cain-coloured, yellow
Caliver, a species of musket
Callet, a lewd woman
Calling, appellation
Calm, qualm
Canary, a sprightly nimble dance
Candle-wasters, those who sit up all night to drink
Canker, the dog-rose
Canstick, candlestick
Cantle, a piece of anything
Cantons, cantos
Cap, the top, the principal
Cap, to salute by taking off the cap
Capitulate, to make head
Capon, metaphor for a letter
Capricious, lascivious
Captious, capacious or recipient
Carack, a ship of great bulk
Carbonadoed, scotched like meat for the gridiron
Care, inclination
Careires, the motion of a horse

Carkanet, necklace or chain
Carl, clown or husbandman
Carlot, peasant
Carpet-consideration, on a carpet, a festivity
Carren, a critic
Carriage, import
Carry, to prevail over
Case, skin, outside garb
Case, to strip naked
Cast, to empty, to dismiss or reject
Castilian, an opprobrious term
Castiliano vulgo, a term of contempt
Cataian, some kind of sharper
Catling, a lute-string made of catgut
Cautelous, insidious, cautious
Cavaleroes, airy, gay fellows
Caviare, a delicacy made of the roe of sturgeon
Cease, decease, die, to stop
Censure, to judge
Centuries, companies of an hundred
Ceremonies, honorary ornaments, tokens of respect
Ceremonious, superstitious
Cess, measure
Chace, a term at tennis
Chair, throne
Chamber, ancient name for London
Chamber, a species of great gun
Chamberers, men of intrigue
Character, to write, to infix strongly
Charactery, the matter with which letters are made
Chares, taskwork
Charge-house, the free-school
Charitable, dear, endearing
Charneco, a sort of sweet wine
Chaudron, entrails
Cheater, escheator, an officer in the exchequer, a gamester
Check, command, control
Cheer, countenance
Cherry-pit, a play with cherry-stones
Cheveril, soft or kid leather
Chew, to ruminate, consider
Chewet, a noisy chattering bird
Chide, to resound, to echo
Chiding, sound
Childing, unseasonably pregnant
Chopin, a high shoe or clog
Christom, the white cloth put on a new-baptized child
Chrystals, eyes
Chuck, chicken, a term of endearment
Chuff, rich, avaricious
Cite, to incite, to show, to prove
Civil, grave or solemn
Civil, human creature, anything human
Clack-dish, a beggar's dish
Claw, to flatter
Clinquant, glittering, shining
Clip, to embrace, to infold
Clout, the mark archers aim at

Coach-fellow, one who draws with a confederate
Coasting, conciliatory, inviting
Cobloaf, a crusty, uneven loaf
Cock, cock-boat
Cockle, a weed
Cockled, inshelled like a cockle
Cockshut-time, twilight
Codling, anciently an immature apple
Coffin, the cavity of a raised pie
Cog, to falsify, to lie, to defraud
Coigne, corner
Coil, bustle, stir
Collect, to assemble by observation
Collection, corollary, consequence
Collied, black, smutted with coal
Collier, a term of the highest reproach
Colt, to fool, to trick
Co-mart, a joint bargain
Combinate, betrothed
Comforting, aiding
Commended, committed
Commonty, a comedy
Compact, made up of
Company, companion
Comparative, a dealer in comparisons
Compassed, round
Complexion, humour
Compliments, accomplishments
Comply, to compliment
Compose, to come to a composition
Composition, contract or bargain, consistency, concordancy
Composture, composition, compost
Comptible, submissive
Con, to know
Conclusions, experiments
Concupy, concupiscence
Condolement, sorrow
Coney-catched, cheated
Coney-catcher, a cheat, or sharper
Confession, profession
Confound, to destroy, to expend, to consume
Confounded, worn or wasted
Conject, conjecture
Consigned, sealed
Consist, to stand upon
Continent, the thing which contains
Continents, banks of rivers
Contraction, marriage contract
Contrive, to spend and wear out
Control, to confute
Convent, to serve or agree
Convented, cited, summoned
Converse, interchange
Convey, to perform sleight-of-hand
Conveyance, theft, fraud
Convince, to overpower, subdue, convict
Convive, to feast
Cope, covering
Copped, rising to a cope, or head

Copy, theme
Coragio, a word of encouragement
Corinthian, a wencher
Corky, dry, withered, husky
Corollary, surplus
Corrigible, corrected
Costard, the head
Coster-monger, meanly, mercenary
Cote, to overtake
Coted, quoted, observed, or regarded
Cotsale, Cotswold in Gloucestershire
Count Confect, a specious nobleman
Countenance, false appearance, hypocrisy
Counterpoints, counterpanes
County, count, earl
Covered, hollow
Cower, to sink by bending the hams
Cowl-staff, a staff for carrying a tub
Coy, to soothe or stroke
Coyed, condescended unwillingly
Coystril, a coward cock, a mean or drunken fellow
Cozier, a tailor or botcher
Crack, dissolution
Crack, a boy, or child, a boy-child
Cranks, windings
Crants, chants
Crare, a small trading vessel
Create, compounded, or made up
Credit, a light set upon a beacon
Cressive, increasing
Crestless, having no right to arms
Crisp, curling, winding, curled, bent
Critic, cynic
Crosses, money stamped with a cross
Crow-keeper, a scarecrow
Crown, to conclude
Crowned, dignified, adorned
Crownet, last purpose
Cry, a troop or pack
Cue, in stage cant, the last words of the preceding speech
Cuisses, armour for the thighs
Cullion, a despicable fellow
Cunning, sagacity, knowledge
Curb, to bend or truckle
Curiosity, finical delicacy, scrupulousness or captiousness
Curious, scrupulous
Curled, ostentatiously dressed
Currents, occurrences
Curst, crabbed, shrewish, angry
Curtail, a cur of little value
Curtal, a docked horse
Curtle-axe, or *cutlass*, a short sword
Custard-coffin, the crust of a pie
Customer, a common woman
Cut, a horse
Cyprus, a transparent stuff

Daff, or *doff*, to do off, to put aside

Danger, reach or control
Danskers, natives of Denmark
Dark-house, a house made gloomy by discontent
Darraign, to arrange, put in order
Daub, to disguise
Daubery, falsehood and imposition
Day-bed, a couch
Day-woman, dairy-maid
Dear, best, important, dire
Dearn, lonely, solitary
Death-tokens, spots appearing on those infected by the plague
Decay, misfortunes
Deck, to cover, a pack
Decline, to run through from first to last
Deem, opinion, surmise
Defeat, destruction
Defence, art of fencing
Defend, to forbid
Defiance, refusal
Delay, to let slip
Demise, to grant
Denay, denial
Denier, the twelfth part of a French sou
Denotements, indications or discoveries
Depend, to be in service
Deracinate, to force up by the roots
Derogate, degraded, blasted
Descant, a term in music
Dich, dit or do it
Dickon, familiarly for Richard
Die, gaming
Diffused, extravagant, irregular
Digression, transgression
Dint, impression
Direction, judgment, skill
Disable, to undervalue
Disappointed, unprepared
Disclose, to hatch
Discontenting, discontented
Discourse, reason
Disease, uneasiness, discontent
Diseases, sayings
Disgrace, hardship, injury
Dislimns, unpaints, obliterates
Dispose, to make terms, to settle matters
Distaste, to corrupt, to change to a worse state
Distemper, intoxication
Distemperature, perturbation
Distractions, detachments, separate bodies
Division, the pauses or parts of musical composition
Doctrine, skill
Dole, lot, allowance
Dolphin, the Dauphin of France
Don, to do on, to put on
Dotant, dotard
Dout, to do out, extinguish
Dowle, a feather
Down-gyved, hanging down like what confines the fetters round the ankles

Drab, whoring
Drawn, embowelled, exenterated
Dread, epithet applied to kings
Drew, assembled
Dribbling, a term of contempt
Drive, to fly with impetuosity
Drollery, a show performed by puppets
Drugs, drudges
Drumble, to act lazily and stupidly
Ducdame, duc ad me, bring him to me
Dudgeon, the handle of a dagger
Due, to endue, to deck, to grace
Dump, a mournful elegy
Dup, to do up, to lift up

Eager, sour, sharp, harsh
Eanlings, lambs just dropped
Ear, to plough
Easy, slight, inconsiderable
Eche, to eke out
Ecstasy, alienation of mind, madness
Effects, affects, actions, deeds effected
Eftest, deftest, readiest
Egypt, a gipsy
Eld, old time or persons
Element, initiation, previous practice
Embossed, enclosed, swollen, puffy
Embowelled, exhausted
Embraced, indulged in
Empery, dominion, sovereign command
Emulous, jealous of higher authority
Encave, to hide
Engross, to fatten, to pamper
Engrossments, accumulations
Enmew, to coop up
Ensconce, to protect as with a fort
Enseamed, greasy
Entertain, to retain in service
Entertainment, the pay of an army, admission to office
Ephesian, a cant term for a toper
Equipage, stolen goods
Erring, wandering
Escoted, paid
Esil, a river so called, or vinegar
Esperance, the motto of the Percy family
Essential, existent, real
Estimate, price
Estimation, conjecture
Excrement, the beard
Excrements, the hair, nails, feathers of birds, etc.
Execute, to employ, to put to use
Execution, employment of exercise
Executors, executioners
Exercise, exhortation, lecture, or confession
Exhale, hale or lug out
Exhibition, allowance
Exigent, end
Expedient, expeditious
Expiate, fully completed
Exposture, exposure

Express, to reveal
Expulsed, expelled
Exsufflicate, contemptible, abominable
Extend, to seize
Extent, in law, violence in general
Extravagant, wandering
Eyases, young nestlings
Eyas musket, infant lilliputian
Eye, a small shade of colour
Eyliads, glances, looks. See *Oeiliads*
Eyne, eyes

Face, to carry a foolish appearance
Facinorous, wicked
Fact, guilt
Factious, active
Faculties, medicinal virtues, office, exercise of power
Fadge, to suit or fit
Fading, the burthen of a song
Faithful, not an infidel
Faitors, traitors, rascals
Fall, an ebb
Falsing, falsifying
Fancy, love
Fans, ancient
Fap, drunk
Far, extensively
Farced, stuffed
Fashions, farcens or farcy
Fast, determined, fixed
Fat, dull
Favour, countenance, features, indulgence, pardon, appearance
Feat, ready, dexterous
Feated, formed, made neat
Federary, a confederate
Fee-grief, a peculiar sorrow
Feeder, an eater, a servant
Feere, or *Pheere,* a companion, a husband
Feet, footing
Fell, skin
Fell-feats, savage practices
Feodary, an accomplice, a confederate
Festinately, hastily
Festival term, splendid phraseology
Fet, fetched
Fico, a fig
Fielded, in the field of battle
Fig, to insult
Fights, clothes hung round a ship to conceal the men from the enemy
Filed, gone an equal pace with
Fills, the shafts
Filths, common sewers
Fine, full of fineness, artful
Fine, to make showy or specious
Fire-new, bran-new, new from the forge
Firk, to chastise
Fit, a division of a song
Fitchew, a pole-cat

Fives, a distemper in horses
Flap-dragon, a small inflammable substance which topers swallow in a glass of wine
Flap-jacks, pancakes
Fleet, to float
Fleshment, first act of military service
Flewed, having the flews or chaps of a hound
Flight, a sort of shooting
Flourish, ornament
Flote, wave
Flush, mature, ripe
Foin, to thrust in fencing
Foison, plenty
Folly, depravity of mind
Fond, foolish, or prized by folly
Fonder, more weak or foolish
Fondly, foolishly
Fools' zanies, baubles with the head of a fool
Foot-cloth, a housing covering the body of the horse, and almost reaching to the ground
Forced, false
Fordid, destroyed
Fordo, to undo, to destroy
Foredone, overcome
Foreslow, to be dilatory, to loiter
Forgetive, inventive, imaginative
Forked, horned
Former, foremost
Forspoke, contradicted, spoken against
Forthcoming, in custody
Foul, homely, not fair
Fox, a cant word for a sword
Foxship, mean, cunning
Frampold, peevish, fretful, or cross
Frank, a sty
Franklin, a little gentleman or freeholder
Fret, the stop of a musical instrument, which regulates the vibration of the string
Frippery, a shop where old clothes were sold
Frize, a cloth made in Wales
Frontier, forehead
Frush, to break or bruise
Fulfilling, filling till there be no room for more
Fullams, loaded dice
Fumiter, fumitory

Gabardine, a loose felt cloak
Gain-giving, misgiving
Galliard, an ancient dance
Galliasses, a species of galleys
Gallow, to scare or frighten
Gallowglasses, heavy armed foot
Gallymawfry, a medley
Gamester, a frolicsome person, a wanton
Garboils, commotion, stir
Gasted, frightened
Gaudy, a festival day
Gawds, baubles, toys
Geck, a fool
Generosity, high birth

Generous, most noble
Gentility, urbanity
Gentle, noble, high-minded
Gentry, complaisance
German, akin
Gest, a stage or journey
Gib, a cat
Giglot, a wanton wench
Gild, gilding, golden money
Gilder, a coin valued at 1s. 6d. or 2s.
Gimmal, a ring or engine
Ging, a gang
Gird, a sarcasm or gibe, emotion
Gleek, to joke or scoff, to beguile
Gloze, to expound, to comment upon
Good-deed, indeed, in very deed
Good-den, good-evening
Good-life, of a moral or jovial turn
Good-jer, gougere, morbus gallicus
Gorbellied, fat and corpulent
Gourds, a species of dice
Gouts, drops
Government, evenness of temper, decency of manners
Grammercy, grand mercy, great thanks
Grange, the farm-house of a monastery
Gratillity, gratuity
Grave, to entomb
Graves, or *greaves*, armour for the legs
Greasily, grossly
Greek, a bawd or pander
Greenly, awkwardly, unskilfully
Greets, pleases
Grise, a step
Grossly, palpably
Groundlings, the frequenters of the pit in the playhouse
Growing, accruing
Guard, to fringe or lace
Guarded, ornamented
Guards, badges of dignity
Guinea-hen, a prostitute
Gules, red, a term in heraldry
Gulf, the swallow, the throat
Gun-stones, cannon-balls
Gust, taste, rashness
Gyve, to catch, to shackle

Haggard, a species of hawk
Hair, complexion or character
Hardiment, bravery, stoutness
Harlocks, wild mustard
Harlot, a cheat
Harrow, to conquer, to subdue
Harry, to use roughly, to harass
Having, estate or fortune
Haunt, company
Hay, a term in the fencing-school
Head, body of forces
Heart, the most valuable part
Heat, violence of resentment

Heavy, slow
Hebenon, henbane
Hefted, heaved
Hefts, heavings
Hell, an obscure dungeon in a prison
Helmed, steered through
Hent, seized or taken possession of
Hereby, as it may happen
Hermits, beadsmen
Hest, behest, command
Hight, called
Hilding, a paltry cowardly fellow
Hiren, a harlot
His, often used for *its*
Hit, to agree
Hold, to esteem
Holla, a term of the manege
Holy, faithful
Home, completely, in full extent
Honey-stalks, clover flowers
Hoop, a measure
Hox, to hamstring
Hull, to drive to and fro upon the water without sails or rudder
Humorous, changeable, humid, moist
Hungry, sterile, unprolific
Hunt-counter, base tyke, worthless dog
Hunt-sup, the name of a tune
Hurley, noise
Hurtling, merry with impetuosity
Husbandry, thrift, frugality
Huswife, a jilt

Images, children, representatives
Imbare, to lay open or display to view
Immanity, barbarity, savageness
Immediacy, close connection
Imp, to supply
Imp, progeny
Impair, unsuitable
Impartial, sometimes used for partial
Imperious, imperial
Impeticos, to impetticoat or impocket
Importance, importunacy
Importance, the thing imported
Impress, a device or motto
Incapable, unintelligent
Incarnardine, to stain of a red colour
Incensed, incited, suggested
Inclip, to embrace
Include, to shut up, to conclude
Incony, or *kony*, fine, delicate
Incorrect, ill-regulated
Indent, to bargain and article
Index, something preparatory to
Indifferent, sometimes for different, impartial
Indite, to convict
Induction, entrance, preparations
Indurance, delay, procrastination
Ingaged, sometimes for unengaged

Inkhorn-mate, a book-mate
Inkle, tape, crewel, or worsted
Inland, civilized, not rustic
Insconce, to fortify
Insuit, solicitation
Intend, to pretend
Intending, regarding
Intendment, intention or disposition
Intenible, incapable of retaining
Intention, eagerness of desire
Interessed, interested
Intrenchant, that which cannot be cut
Intrinse, intrinsicate
Inwardness, intimacy, confidence
Iron, clad in armour
Irregulous, lawless, licentious

Jack, a term of contempt
Jack-a-lent, a puppet thrown at in Lent
Jack guardant, a jack in office
Jaded, treated with contempt, worthless
Jar, the noise made by the pendulum of a clock
Jauncing, jaunting
Jesses, straps of leather by which the hawk is held on the fist
Jest, to play a part in a mask
Jet, to strut
Jovial, belonging to Jove
Journal, daily
Jump, to agree with, to agitate
Jump, hazard, to venture at
Jump, just

Kam, awry, crooked
Keech, a solid lump or mass
Keel, to cool
Keisar, Cæsar
Kerns, light-armed Irish foot
Key, the key for tuning
Kicksy-wicksy, a wife
Kiln-hole, a place into which coals are put under a stove
Kind, nature, species, child
Kindless, unnatural
Kindly, naturally
Kindly, kindred
Kinged, ruled by
Kirtle, part of a woman's dress
Knave, servant
Knots, figures planted in box
Know of, to consider

Labras, lips
Laced mutton, a woman of the town
Lackeying, moving like a lackey or page
Lag, the meanest persons
Land-damn, to destroy in some way
Lands, landing-places
Large, licentious
Latch, to lay hold of

Latched, or *letched,* licked over
Latten, thin as a lath
Laund, lawn
Lavoltas, a kind of dance
Lay, a wager
Leather-coats, a species of apple
Leave, to part with, to give away
Leech, a physician
Leer, feature, complexion
Leet, court-leet, or court of the manor
Legerity, lightness, nimbleness
Leges, alleges
Leiger, resident
Lenten, short and spare
L'envoy, moral, or conclusion of a poem
Let, to hinder
Lethe, death
Libbard, or *lubbar,* a leopard
Liberal, licentious or gross in language
Liberty, libertinism
License, an appearance of licentiousness
Liefest, dearest
Lifter, a thief
Light o' love, a dance tune
Livelihood, appearance of life
Lodged, laid by the wind
Loffe, to laugh
Loggats, a game played with pins of wood
Longly, longingly
Loof, to bring a vessel close to the wind
Lop, the branches
Lot, a prize
Lottery, allotment
Lowted, treated with contempt
Lowts, clowns
Lozel, worthless, dishonest
Lullaby, sleeping-house, *i.e.,* cradle
Lunes, lunacy, frenzy
Lurch, to win
Lustick, lusty, cheerful, pleasant
Lym, a species of dog

Made, enriched
Magnificent, glorying, boasting
Make, to bar, to shut
Makest, dost
Mall, Mrs. *alias* Mary Frith, or Moll Cutpurse
Mallecho, mischief
Mammock, to cut in pieces
Man, to tame a hawk
Marchpane, a species of sweetmeat
Martial-hand, a careless scrawl
Martlemas, the latter spring
Match, an appointment, a compact
Mate, to confound
Mated, amated, dismayed
Meacock, a dastardly creature
Mean, the tenor in music
Means, interest, pains
Measure, the reach

Measure, means
Meazels, lepers
Medicine, a she-physician
Meet, a match
Meiny, people, domestics
Mephistophilus, the name of a spirit or familiar
Mercatanté, a merchant
Mered, mere
Mermaid, syren
Messes, degrees about court
Micher, a truant, a lurking thief
Misery, avarice
Mistress, the jack in bowling
Mobled, or *mabled,* vailed, grossly covered
Modern, trite, common, meanly pretty
Modesty, moderation
Moe, to make mouths
Mome, a blockhead, a dolt
Month's mind, a popish anniversary
Mortal-staring, that which stares fatally
Motion, a kind of puppet-show
Motion, divinatory agitation
Motions, indignation
Mouse-hunt, a weasel
Mousing, gorging, devouring
Moy, a piece of money or a measure of corn
Much, an expression of disdain
Much, strange, wonderful
Muleters, muleteers
Mummy, balsamic liquor
Mure, a wall
Musit or *muset,* a gap in a hedge
Muss, a scramble

Nay-word, a watchword or by-word
Neat, finical
Neeld, needle
Neglection, neglect
Neif, fist
Nephew, a grandson, or any lineal descendant
Nether-stocks, stockings
Nicely, scrupulously
Nick, reckoning or count
Nick, to set a mark of folly on
Nicked, emasculated
Night-rule, frolic of the night
Nill, will not
Nine men's morris, a game
Noble, a coin
Noddy, a game at cards; also, a noodle
Noise, music
Nonce, on purpose, for the turn
Nook-shotten, that which shoots into capes
Northern man, vir borealis, a clown
Novum, some game at dice
Nowl, a head
Nuthook, a thief

Ob, obolum, a halfpenny
Obdicut, a fiend

Obsequious, serious, as at funeral obsequies, careful of
Observing, religiously attentive
Obstacle, obstinate
Oddly, unequally
Odds, quarrel
Od's pittikins, God me pity
Oe, a circle
Oeiliad, a cast or glance of the eye
O'er-raught, over-reached
Of, through
Offering, the assailant
Old, frequent, more than enough
Oneyers, accountants, bankers
Opinion, obstinacy, conceit, character
Opposition, combat
Or, before
Orbs, circles made by the fairies on the ground
Order, to take, to adapt measures
Ordinance, rank
Orgulous, proud, disdainful
Orient, pellucid, lustrous
Orts, scraps
Ostent, show, ostentation
Ousel-cock, the blackbird
Overblow, to drive away, to keep off
Overlook, to bewitch
Oversee, to execute, to superintend
Ouph, fairy, goblin
Out, full, complete
Outlook, to face down
Outvied, a term at the game of gleek
Outward, not in the secret of affairs
Owches, bosses of gold set in diamonds

Packed, confederate
Paddock, a toad
Pagan, a loose vicious person
Paid, punished
Pajock, peacock
Palabras, words
Pale, to empale, encircle with a crown
Palliament, a robe
Palter, to juggle or shuffle
Pantaloon, the Italian
Paper, to write down, or appoint by writing
Paper, written securities
Parcel, reckon up
Parcel-gilt, gilt only on certain parts
Parish-top, a large top formerly kept in every village to be whipped for exercise
Paritor, an apparitor, an officer of the bishop's court
Parle, speech
Parlous, keen, shrewd
Partake, to impart, to participate
Parted, endowed with parts
Partisan, a pike
Parts, party
Pash, a head
Pash, to strike with violence
Pashed, bruised, crushed

Pass, to decide, to assure or convey
Passed, excelling, past all expression or bounds
Passes, what has passed
Passing, eminent, egregious
Passionate, a prey to mournful sensations
Passioning, being in a passion
Passy-measure, a dance
Pastry, the room where pastry was made
Patch, a term of reproach
Patchery, roguery, villany
Patine, a dish used in the Eucharist
Paucas, few
Pavin, a dance
Pay, to beat, to hit
Peat, a pet
Pedant, a schoolmaster
Pedascule, a pedant
Peize, to balance, to keep in suspense
Pelting, paltry, petty, inconsiderable
Penthesilea, Amazon
Perfections, liver, brain, and heart
Periapts, charms worn about the neck
Perjure, a perjurer
Pestered, impeded
Pheeze, to teaze, comb, or curry
Philip, a name for the sparrow
Physical, medicinal
Pick, to pitch
Pickers, the hands
Picking, piddling, insignificant
Pickt-hatch, a place noted for brothels
Pied ninny, a jester, a fool
Piel'd, shaven
Pight, pitched, fixed
Pilcher, an outer garment of leather
Pin and web, disorders of the eye
Placket, a petticoat
Plain song, the chant, *in plano cantu*
Planched, made of brands
Plant, the foot
Plantage, the moon's influence over plants
Plates, silver coin
Platforms, plans, schemes
Pleached, folded together
Plurisy, repletion
Point, hook for the hose or breeches
Point-device, with the utmost exactness
Poize, weight or moment
Polacks, Polanders
Pomander, a ball of perfume
Pomewater, a species of apple
Porpentine, porcupine
Port, show, state, appearance
Portage, portholes
Portance, carriage, behaviour
Potch, to push violently
Poulter, a poulterer
Pouncet-box, a small box for perfumes
Powder, to salt
'Praise, to appraise

Prank, to dress ostentatiously, to plume
Precedent, original draft
Precepts, warrants
Pregnancy, readiness
Pregnant, ready, evident, apposite
Pregnant enemy, the enemy of mankind
Premised, sent before the time
Prenominate, forenamed
Presence, the presence-chamber
Prest, ready
Pretence, design, device
Pretty, petty, little
Prevent, to anticipate
Pricks, prickles, skewers
Prime, prompt
Primero, a game at cards
Principality, first or principal of women
Principals, rafters of a building
Princox, a coxcomb, or spoiled child
Prize, privilege
Proface, much good may it do you
Profession, end and purpose of coming
Project, to shape
Prompture, suggestion, temptation
Prone, sometimes humble
Proof, confirmed state of manhood
Proper-false, fair, false, deceitful
Propertied, taken possession of
Property, due performance
Prorogue, to deaden or benumb
Prune, to plume
Pugging, thievish
Pun, to pound
Purchase, stolen goods
Purchased, acquired by unjust methods

Quaint-mazes, a game running the figure of eight
Quaintly, clever, adroit
Quality, confederates
Quarry, a pile of slaughtered game
Quart d'ecu, fourth of a French crown
Quat, a pimple
Quell, to murder, to destroy
Question, to converse
Questrist, one who seeks for another
Quests, reports
Quick, alive, quickening, quick-witted
Quiddits, subtilties
Quillets, law chicane
Quilt, a flock bed
Quintain, post for various exercises
Quit, to requite
Quittance, requital, to make requital
Quiver, nimble, active

Rabato, an ornament for the neck
Rack, to exaggerate
Rack, the fleeting away of the clouds
Racking, in rapid motion
Rag, a term of contempt

Rank, rate or pace
Rapture, a fit
Rascal, applied to lean deer
Raught, reached
Ravined, glutted with prey
Rayed, bewrayed
Razed, slashed, opened
Razes, roots
Rear-mouse, a bat
Reason, to discourse
Rebeck, an old musical instrument
Receiving, ready apprehension
Recheate, a sound to call back dogs
Reck, to care for, to mind, to attend to
Record, to sing
Recorder, a kind of flute or flageolet
Recure, to recover
Rede, counsel, advice
Red-lattice, the sign of an alehouse
Reduce, to bring back
Reechy, discoloured by smoke, greasy
Refell, to refute
Regard, reflection
Regret, exchange of salutation
Reguerdon, recompense, return
Remembered, reminded
Remotion, removal or remoteness
Removed, remote, private
Render, a confession, an account
Renege, to renounce
Repeal, to recall from exile
Reports, reporters
Reproof, confutation
Repugn, to resist
Reputing, boasting of
Resolve, to dissolve
Respective, cool, considerate
'Rest, arrest
Retire, to withdraw
Reword, to echo
Rib, to enclose
Rigol, a circle
Rim, a part of the intestines
Rivage, the bank or shore
Rivality, equal rank
Rivals, partners
Romage, rummage
Rondure, circle
Ronyon, a scurvy woman
Rook, to squat down
Ropery, roguery
Rope-tricks, abusive language
Rounded, whispered
Roundel, a country dance
Rouse, a draught of jollity
Roynish, mangy or scabby
Ruddock, the redbreast
Rudesby, blusterer, swaggerer
Ruff, the folding of the tops of boots
Ruffle, to riot, to create disturbance

Ruth, pity, compassion

Sacred, accursed
Sag, or *swagg*, to sink down
Sallet, a helmet
Saltiers, corruption of satyrs
Saucy, lascivious
Saw, the whole tenor of any discourse
Say, silk, a sample, a taste, or relish
Scaffoldage, gallery of the theatre
Scald, a word of contempt, poor, filthy
Scaling, weighing
Scall, an old word of reproach
Scamels, or *sea-mells*, sea-birds
Scotched, cut slightly
Scrimers, fencers
Scroyles, scabby fellows
Sculls, numbers of fish together
Scutched, whipped, carted
Seam, lard
Sear, to stigmatize, to close
Sect, a cutting in gardening
Secure, to assure
Seeling, blinding
Septentrion, the north
Sequester, a separation
Serpigo, a kind of tetter
Serve, to accompany
Set, a term in music
Setebos, a species of devil
Shale, a case, a shell
Shard-borne, borne by scaly wings
Shards, broken pots, a beetle's wings
Sheer, pellucid, transparent
Shent, ruined, rebuked, ashamed
Shot, shooter
Shoughs, shocks, a species of dog
Siege, stool, seat, rank
Sightless, unsightly
Single, weak, small, void of guile
Sink-a-pace, cinque-pace, a dance
Sir-reverence, save-your-reverence
Sithence, thence
Sizes, allowances of victuals
Skains-mates, loose companions
Skill, cunning, design, reason
Skills not, is of no importance
Skirr, to scour, to ride hastily
Sledded, riding in a sled or sledge
Sliver, to cut a piece or slice
Slower, more serious
Smoke, to discover
Smoothed, fawned on
Sneap, to check or rebuke, a rebuke
Sneaping, nipping
Sneck-up, cant phrase, "go hang yourself"
Snipe, a fool, a blockhead
Snuffs, tiffs
Solicit, to excite
Solidares, ancient coin

Sooth, sweetness
Sort, the lot
Sort and suit, figure and rank
Sot, a fool
Sowl, to pull by the ears
Speak to, to aspire or lay claim to
Sped, done, settled
Speed, event
Sperr, to shut up, defend by bars, etc.
Spotted, wicked
Sprag or *spackt*, apt to learn
Sprighted, haunted
Sprightly, ghostly
Square, to quarrel
Squash, an immature peascod
Squire, a square or rule
Stale, a bait or decoy to catch birds
Standing bowls, bowls elevated on feet
Stannyel, a kind of hawk
Star, a scar of that appearance
Starve, to perish
Station, the act of standing
Sternage, steerage, course
Sticking-place, the stop in a machine
Sticklers, arbitrators, judges, sidesmen
Stigmatic, one on whom nature has set a mark of deformity
Still, constant or continual
Stoup, somewhat more than half a gallon
Stover, a kind of thatch
Strachy, a kind of domestic office
Strain, lineage, difficulty, doubt
Stratagem, great or dreadful event
Stuck, a thrust in fencing
Subscribe, to yield, to surrender
Sur-reined, over-worked, or ridden
Swashing, noisy, bullying
Swath, the dress of a new-born child
Sway, the whole weight, momentum
Sweeting, a species of apple
Swinge-bucklers, rakes, rioters

Table, the palm of the hand extended
Table, a picture
Tables, table-books, memoranda
Tabourines, drums
Take, to strike with a disease, to blast
Take-up, to contradict, call to account
Take-up, to levy
Talents, riches
Tallow keech, the fat of an ox or cow
Tarre, to stimulate, to excite, provoke
Tartar, Tartarus, the fabled place of future punishment
Task, to keep busied with scruples
Taurus, heart in medical astrology
Taxation, censure or satire
Teen, sorrow, grief
Tent, to take up residence
Tercel, the male hawk

Testern, to gratify with a sixpence
Tharborough, a peace-officer
Thick-pleached, thickly interwoven
Thought, melancholy
Thrasonical, boastful, bragging
Three-man-beetle, for driving piles
Thrummed, made of coarse woollen cloth
Tib, a strumpet
Tickle-brain, some strong liquor
Tightly, briskly, promptly
Tilly-valley, an interjection of contempt
Tire, to fasten, to fix the talons on
Tod, to yield a tod, or 28 pounds
Tokened, spotted as in the plague
Touch, exploit, particle, touchstone
Touches, features
Touched, tried
Toys, rumours, idle reports, fancies
Toze, to pull or pluck
Tranect, a ferry
Tray-trap, some kind of game
Treachers, treacherous persons
Trick, peculiarity of voice, face, etc.
Trick, smeared, painted, in heraldry
Tricking, dress
Trojan, cant word for a thief
Troll-my-dames, a game
Turleygood, or *turlupin*, a gipsy
Turn, to become sour
Twangling, an expression of contempt
Twigging, wickered

Umbered, discovered by gleam of fire
Unaccustomed, unseemly, indecent
Unaneled, without extreme unction
Unbarbed, untrimmed, unshaven
Unbated, not blunted
Unbolt, to explain
Unbolted, coarse
Uncoined, real, unrefined, unadorned
Under-generation, the antipodes
Under-skinker, a tapster
Undertaker, one who takes upon himself the quarrel of another
Uneath, scarcely, not easily
Unhappy, waggish, unlucky
Unhoused, free from domestic cares
Unhouseled, not having received the sacrament
Union, a species of pearl
Unmastered, licentious
Unproper, common
Unqualitied, disarmed of his faculties
Unrough, smooth-faced, unbearded
Unsisted, untried
Unsisting, always opening, never at rest
Unsquared, unadapted to their subject
Unstanched, incontinent
Untented, unsearchable
Untraced, singular, not in common use
Utis, a merry festival

Utterance, a phrase in combat

Valanced, fringed with a beard
Vantbrace, armour for the arm
Vaunt, the avaunt, what went before
Velure, velvet
Venew, a bout, a term in fencing
Venies, hits in fencing
Via, a cant phrase of exultation
Virtue, the most efficacious part, valour
Virtuous, salutiferous
Vixen, or *fixen*, a female fox
Vozaments, advisements

Wannion, vengeance
Warden, a species of pears
Watch, a watch-light
Water-work, water colours
Way of life, periphrasis for life
Weet, to know
Wheel, refrain, burden of a ballad
Whelked, having protuberances
Whiffler, the first in processions
Whiles, until
Whip, the crack, the best
Whipping-cheer, flogging
Whist, silent, at peace, hushed
White death, the chlorosis
Whiting-time, bleaching time, spring
Whitsters, the bleachers of linen
Whoobub, hubbub
Whooping, measure or reckoning
Wilderness, wildness
Windows, eye-lids
Winter-ground, to protect from winter
Wish, to recommend
Wistly, wistfully
Wit-snapper, one who affects repartee
Wittol, knowing, conscious of
Woman-tired, henpecked
Wondered, able to perform wonders
Wood, crazy, frantic
Woodcock, a simpleton
Woolward, a phrase appropriated to pilgrims and penitentiaries
Workings, labours of thought
World, to go to the, to be married
Worm, a serpent
Wrest, an instrument for tuning the harp
Writhled, wrinkled
Wroth, misfortune

Yarely, readily, nimbly
Yeild, inform, condescend, reward
Yellowness, jealousy
Yeoman, a sheriff's officer
Yerk, to jerk, to thrust with a quick motion
Yexen, or *waxen*, to hiccough
Yield, to report

Zany, a fool or gull
Zealous, pious

INDEX TO THE CHARACTERS

AARON,	A Moor, beloved by Tamora,	*Titus Andronicus.*
ABBOT OF WESTMINSTER,		*Richard II.*
ABERGAVENNY, LORD,		*King Henry VIII.*
ABHORSON,	An Executioner,	*Measure for Measure.*
ABRAM,	Servant of Montague,	*Romeo and Juliet.*
ACHILLES,	A Grecian Commander,	*Troilus and Cressida.*
ADAM,	Servant to Oliver,	*As You Like It.*
ADRIAN,	A Lord of Naples,	*Tempest.*
ADRIANA,	Wife of Antipholus of Ephesus,	*Comedy of Errors.*
ÆGEON,	A Merchant of Syracuse,	*Comedy of Errors.*
ÆMILIA,	An Abbess at Ephesus,	*Comedy of Errors.*
ÆMILIUS,	A Noble Roman,	*Titus Andronicus.*
ÆMILIUS LEPIDUS,	A Roman Triumvir,	*Julius Cæsar.*
ÆNEAS,	A Trojan Commander,	*Troilus and Cressida.*
AGAMEMNON,	A Grecian General,	*Troilus and Cressida.*
AGRIPPA,	A Friend of Cæsar,	*Antony and Cleopatra.*
AGRIPPA, MENENIUS,	Friend of Coriolanus,	*Coriolanus.*
AGUE-CHEEK, SIR ANDREW,		*Twelfth Night.*
AJAX,	A Grecian Commander,	*Troilus and Cressida.*
ALARBUS,	Son of Tamora,	*Titus Andronicus.*
ALBANY, DUKE OF,		*King Lear.*
ALCIBIADES,	An Athenian General,	*Timon of Athens.*
ALENÇON, DUKE OF,		*King Henry VI., Part 1.*
ALEXANDER,	Servant to Cressida,	*Troilus and Cressida.*
ALEXANDER IDEN,	A Kentish Gentleman,	*King Henry VI., Part II.*
ALEXAS,	Attendant on Cleopatra,	*Antony and Cleopatra.*
ALICE,	Attendant on Princess Katharine,	*King Henry V.*
ALONSO,	King of Naples,	*Tempest.*
AMIENS,	A Lord Attendant on the Exiled Duke,	*As You Like It.*
ANDROMACHE,	Wife of Hector,	*Troilus and Cressida.*
ANDRONICUS, MARCUS,	Tribune, Brother of Titus,	*Titus Andronicus.*
ANDRONICUS, TITUS,	General against the Goths,	*Titus Andronicus.*
ANGELO,	A Goldsmith,	*Comedy of Errors.*
ANGELO,	Deputy of Duke of Vienna,	*Measure for Measure.*
ANGUS,	A Scottish Nobleman,	*Macbeth.*
ANNE, LADY,	Widow of Edward Prince of Wales,	*King Richard III.*
ANNE BULLEN,	Afterwards Queen,	*King Henry VIII.*
ANTENOR,	A Trojan Commander,	*Troilus and Cressida.*
ANTIGONUS,	A Sicilian Lord,	*Winter's Tale.*
ANTIOCHUS,	King of Antioch,	*Pericles.*
ANTIOCHUS, DAUGHTER OF,		*Pericles.*
ANTIPHOLUS OF EPHESUS,	Twin Brothers; Sons of Ægeon, but un-	Comedy of Errors.
ANTIPHOLUS OF SYRACUSE,	known to each other,	
ANTONIO,	The Merchant of Venice,	*Merchant of Venice.*
ANTONIO,	Usurping Duke of Milan,	*Tempest.*
ANTONIO.	A Sea Captain,	*Twelfth Night.*

BIGOT, ROBERT,	Earl of Norfolk,	*King John.*
BIONDELLO,	Servant of Lucentio,	*Taming of the Shrew.*
BIRON,	A Lord Attendant on the King of Navarre,	*Love's Labour's Lost.*
BISHOP OF CARLISLE,		*King Richard II.*
BISHOP OF ELY,		*King Henry V.*
BISHOP OF ELY,	John Morton,	*King Richard III.*
BISHOP OF LINCOLN,		*King Henry VIII.*
BISHOP OF WINCHESTER,	Gardiner,	*King Henry VIII.*
BLANCH,	Niece of King John,	*King John.*
BLOUNT, SIR JAMES,		*King Richard III.*
BLUNT, SIR WALTER,	Friend of Henry IV.,	*King Henry IV., Pts. I., II.*
BOLINGBROKE,	A Conjuror,	*King Henry VI., Part II.*
BOLINGBROKE,	Afterwards Henry IV.,	*King Richard II.*
BONA,	Sister of the French Queen,	*King Henry VI., Part III.*
BORACHIO,	Follower of Don John,	*Much Ado About Nothing.*
BOTTOM,	The Weaver,	*Midsummer-Night's Dream.*
BOULT,	A Servant,	*Pericles.*
BOURBON, DUKE OF,		*King Henry V.*
BOUCHIER, CARDINAL,	Archbishop of Canterbury,	*King Richard III.*
BOYET,	A Lord attending on the Princess of France,	*Love's Labour's Lost.*
BRABANTIO,	A Senator,	*Othello.*
BRAKENBURY, SIR ROBERT,	Lieutenant of the Tower,	*King Richard III.*
BRANDON,		*King Henry VIII.*
BRUTUS, JUNIUS,	Tribune of the People,	*Coriolanus.*
BRUTUS, MARCUS,	A Roman Conspirator,	*Julius Cæsar.*
BUCKINGHAM, DUKE OF,		*King Richard III.*
BUCKINGHAM, DUKE OF,	Of the King's Party,	*King Henry VI., Part II.*
BUCKINGHAM, DUKE OF,		*King Henry VIII.*
BULLCALF,	A Recruit,	*King Henry IV., Part II.*
BULLEN, ANNE,	Afterwards Queen,	*King Henry VIII.*
BURGUNDY, DUKE OF,		*King Henry V.*
BURGUNDY, DUKE OF,		*King Henry VI., Part I.*
BURGUNDY, DUKE OF,		*King Lear.*
BUSHY,	"Creature" of Richard II.,	*King Richard II.*
BUTTS, DR.,	Physician to Henry VIII.,	*King Henry VIII.*
CADE, JACK,	A Rebel,	*King Henry VI., Part II.*
CADWAL,	Arviragus in Disguise,	*Cymbeline.*
CÆSAR, OCTAVIUS,	A Triumvir,	*Antony and Cleopatra.*
CAITHNESS,	A Scottish Nobleman,	*Macbeth.*
CAIUS, DR.,	A French Physician,	*Merry Wives of Windsor.*
CAIUS, LUCIUS,	General of Roman Forces,	*Cymbeline.*
CAIUS MARCIUS CORIOLANUS,	A Noble Roman,	*Coriolanus.*
CALCHAS,	A Trojan Priest,	*Troilus and Cressida.*
CALIBAN,	A Savage and Deformed Slave,	*The Tempest.*
CALPURNIA,	Wife of Cæsar,	*Julius Cæsar.*
CAMBRIDGE, EARL OF,	A Conspirator,	*King Henry V.*
CAMILLO,	A Sicilian Lord,	*Winter's Tale.*
CAMPEIUS, CARDINAL,		*King Henry VIII.*
CANIDIUS,	Lieutenant-General of Antony,	*Antony and Cleopatra.*
CANTERBURY, ARCHBISHOP OF,	Cardinal Bouchier,	*King Richard III.*
CANTERBURY, ARCHBISHOP OF		*King Henry V.*
CANTERBURY, ARCHBISHOP OF,	Cranmer,	*King Henry VIII.*
CAPHIS,	A Servant,	*Timon of Athens.*
CAPUCIUS,	Ambassador from Charles V.,	*King Henry VIII.*
CAPULET,	At variance with Montague,	*Romeo and Juliet.*
CAPULET, LADY,	Wife of Capulet,	*Romeo and Juliet.*
CARDINAL BEAUFORT,	Bishop of Winchester,	*King Henry VI., Part II.*
CARDINAL BOUCHIER,	Archbishop of Canterbury,	*King Richard III.*
CARDINAL CAMPEIUS.		*King Henry VIII.*

CARDINAL PANDULPH,	The Pope's Legate,	*King John.*
CARDINAL WOLSEY,		*King Henry VIII.*
CARLISLE, BISHOP OF,		*King Richard II.*
CASCA,	A Roman Conspirator,	*Julius Cæsar.*
CASSANDRA,	Daughter of Priam,	*Troilus and Cressida.*
CASSIO,	Lieutenant to Othello,	*Othello.*
CASSIUS,	A Roman Conspirator,	*Julius Cæsar.*
CATESBY, SIR WILLIAM,		*King Richard III.*
CATO, YOUNG,	Friend of Brutus and Cassius,	*Julius Cæsar.*
CELIA,	Daughter of Frederick,	*As You Like It.*
CERES,	A Spirit,	*The Tempest.*
CERIMON,	A Lord of Ephesus,	*Pericles.*
CHARLES,	A Wrestler,	*As You Like It.*
CHARLES,	The Dauphin,	*King Henry VI., Part I.*
CHARLES VI.,	King of France,	*King Henry V.*
CHARMIAN,	Attendant on Cleopatra,	*Antony and Cleopatra.*
CHATILLON,	Ambassador from France,	*King John.*
CHIRON,	Son of Tamora,	*Titus Andronicus.*
CHORUS,	As a Prologue,	*King Henry V.*
CHRISTOPHER SLY,	A Drunken Tinker,	*Taming of the Shrew.*
CHRISTOPHER URSWICK,	A Priest,	*King Richard III.*
CICERO,	A Roman Senator,	*Julius Cæsar.*
CINNA,	A Poet,	*Julius Cæsar.*
CINNA,	A Roman Conspirator,	*Julius Cæsar.*
CLARENCE, DUKE OF,	Brother of Edward IV.,	*King Richard III.*
CLARENCE, THOMAS, DUKE OF,	Son of Henry IV.,	*King Henry IV., Part II.*
CLAUDIO,	A Young Gentleman,	*Measure for Measure.*
CLAUDIO,	A Young Florentine Lord,	*Much Ado About Nothing.*
CLAUDIUS,	King of Denmark,	*Hamlet.*
CLAUDIUS,	Servant of Brutus,	*Julius Cæsar.*
CLEOMENES,	A Sicilian Lord,	*Winter's Tale.*
CLEON,	Governor of Tharsus	*Pericles.*
CLEOPATRA,	Queen of Egypt,	*Antony and Cleopatra.*
CLIFFORD, LORD,	Of the King's Party,	*King Henry VI., Pts. II., III.*
CLIFFORD, YOUNG,	Son of Lord Clifford,	*King Henry VI., Part II.*
CLITUS,	Servant of Brutus,	*Julius Cæsar.*
CLOTEN,	Son of the Queen,	*Cymbeline.*
CLOWN,	Servant to Mrs. Overdone,	*Measure for Measure.*
CLOWN,	Servant to Olivia,	*Twelfth Night.*
COBWEB,	A Fairy,	*Midsummer-Night's Dream.*
COLVILLE, SIR JOHN,	Enemy to the King,	*King Henry IV., Part II.*
COMINIUS,	General against the Volscians,	*Coriolanus.*
CONRADE,	Follower of Don John,	*Much Ado About Nothing.*
CONSTABLE OF FRANCE,		*King Henry V.*
CONSTANCE,	Mother of Arthur,	*King John.*
CORDELIA,	Daughter of Lear,	*King Lear.*
CORIN,	A Shepherd,	*As You Like It.*
CORIOLANUS,	A Noble Roman,	*Coriolanus.*
CORNELIUS,	A Courtier,	*Hamlet.*
CORNELIUS,	A Physician,	*Cymbeline.*
CORNWALL, DUKE OF,		*King Lear.*
COSTARD,	A Clown,	*Love's Labour's Lost.*
COUNT OF ROUSILLON,		*All's Well that Ends Well.*
COUNTESS OF AUVERGNE,		*King Henry VI., Part I.*
COUNTESS OF ROUSILLON,	Mother to Bertram,	*All's Well that Ends Well.*
COURT,	Soldier in the King's Army,	*King Henry V.*
CRANMER,	Archbishop of Canterbury,	*King Henry VIII.*
CRESSIDA,	Daughter to Calchas,	*Troilus and Cressida.*
CROMWELL,	Servant to Wolsey,	*King Henry VIII.*
CUPID,	Presenter in the Masque,	*Timon of Athens.*

FRANCISCA,	A Nun,	*Measure for Measure.*
FRANCISCO,	A Soldier,	*Hamlet.*
FRANCISCO,	A Lord of Naples,	*The Tempest.*
FREDERICK,	Brother to the Exiled Duke,	*As You Like It.*
FRIAR FRANCIS,	A Franciscan,	*Much Ado About Nothing.*
FRIAR JOHN,	A Franciscan,	*Romeo and Juliet.*
FRIAR LAWRENCE,	A Franciscan,	*Romeo and Juliet.*
FROTH,	A Foolish Gentleman,	*Measure for Measure.*
GADSHILL,	Follower of Sir John Falstaff,	*King Henry IV., Part I.*
GALLUS,	Friend to Cæsar,	*Antony and Cleopatra.*
GARDINER,	Bishop of Winchester,	*King Henry VIII.*
GARGRAVE, SIR THOMAS,		*King Henry VI., Part I.*
GEOFFREY FITZ-PETER,	Earl of Essex,	*King John.*
GEORGE,	A Follower of Cade,	*King Henry VI., Part II.*
GEORGE,	Duke of Clarence,	*King Henry VI., Part III.*
GEORGE,	Duke of Clarence,	*King Richard III.*
GERTRUDE,	Queen of Denmark,	*Hamlet.*
GHOST OF HAMLET'S FATHER,		*Hamlet.*
GLANSDALE, SIR WILLIAM,		*King Henry VI., Part I.*
GLENDOWER, OWEN,		*King Henry IV., Part I.*
GLOUCESTER, DUCHESS OF,		*King Richard II.*
GLOUCESTER, DUKE OF,	Brother to King Henry V.,	*King Henry V.*
GLOUCESTER, DUKE OF,	Uncle and Protector to King Henry VI.,	*King Henry VI., Part III.*
GLOUCESTER, DUKE OF,	Afterwards King Richard III.,	*King Richard III.*
GLOUCESTER, EARL OF,		*King Lear.*
GLOUCESTER, PRINCE HUMPHREY OF,	Son to King Henry IV.,	*King Henry IV., Part III.*
GOBBO, LAUNCELOT,	Servant to Shylock,	*Merchant of Venice.*
GOBBO, OLD,	Father to Launcelot Gobbo,	*Merchant of Venice.*
GONERIL,	Daughter to King Lear,	*King Lear.*
GONZALO,	Councillor of Naples,	*The Tempest.*
GOWER,	As Chorus,	*Pericles.*
GOWER,	Of the King's Party,	*King Henry IV., Part II.*
GOWER,	Officer in the King's Army,	*King Henry V.*
GRANDPRÉ,	A French Lord,	*King Henry V.*
GRATIANO,	Brother to Brabantio,	*Othello.*
GRATIANO,	Friend to Antonio and Bassanio,	*Merchant of Venice.*
GREEN,	"Creature" to King Richard II.,	*King Richard II.*
GREGORY,	Servant to Capulet,	*Romeo and Juliet.*
GREMIO,	Suitor to Bianca,	*Taming of the Shrew.*
GREY, LADY,	Queen to King Edward IV.,	*King Henry VI., Part III.*
GREY, LORD,		*King Richard III.*
GREY, SIR THOMAS,	A Conspirator,	*King Henry V.*
GRIFFITH,	Gentleman-Usher to Queen Katharine,	*King Henry VIII.*
GRUMIO,	Servant to Petruchio,	*Taming of the Shrew.*
GUIDERIUS,	Son to Cymbeline,	*Cymbeline.*
GUILDENSTERN,	A Courtier,	*Hamlet.*
GUILDFORD, SIR HENRY,		*King Henry VIII.*
GURNEY, JAMES,	Servant to Lady Falconbridge,	*King John.*
HAMLET,	Prince of Denmark,	*Hamlet.*
HARCOURT,	Of the King's Party,	*King Henry IV., Part II.*
HASTINGS, LORD,	Enemy to the King,	*King Henry IV., Part II.*
HASTINGS, LORD,	Of the Duke's Party,	*King Henry VI., Part III.*
HASTINGS, LORD,		*King Richard III.*
HECATE,	A Witch,	*Macbeth.*
HECTOR,	Son to Priam,	*Troilus and Cressida.*
HELEN,	Woman to Imogen,	*Cymbeline.*
HELEN,	Wife to Menelaus,	*Troilus and Cressida.*
HELENA,	A Gentlewoman,	*All's Well that Ends Well.*

JULIET,		*Measure for Measure.*
JULIET,	Daughter to Capulet,	*Romeo and Juliet.*
JULIUS CÆSAR,		*Julius Cæsar.*
JUNIUS BRUTUS,	Tribune of the People,	*Coriolanus.*
JUNO,	A Spirit,	*The Tempest.*
JUSTICE SHALLOW,	A Country Justice,	*King Henry IV., Part II.*
KATHARINA,	The Shrew,	*Taming of the Shrew.*
KATHARINE,	A Lady attending on the Princess of France,	*Love's Labour's Lost.*
KATHARINE, PRINCESS,	Daughter to Chas. VI., King of France,	*King Henry V.*
KATHARINE, QUEEN,	Wife to King Henry VIII.,	*King Henry VIII.*
KENT, EARL OF,		*King Lear.*
KING EDWARD IV.,		*King Richard III.*
KING HENRY IV.,		*King Henry IV., Pts. I., II*
KING HENRY V.,		*King Henry V.*
KING HENRY VI.,		*Henry VI., Pts. I., II., III.*
KING HENRY VIII.,		*King Henry VIII.*
KING JOHN,		*King John.*
KING OF FRANCE,		*All's Well that Ends Well.*
KING OF FRANCE,		*King Lear.*
KING RICHARD II.,		*King Richard II.*
KING RICHARD III.,		*King Richard III.*
LADY ANNE,	Widow to Edward Prince of Wales,	*King Richard III.*
LADY CAPULET,	Wife to Capulet,	*Romeo and Juliet.*
LADY FALCONBRIDGE,	Mother to Robert and Philip Falconbridge,	*King John.*
LADY GREY,	Afterwards Queen to King Edward IV.,	*King Henry VI., Part III.*
LADY MACBETH,	Wife to Macbeth,	*Macbeth.*
LADY MACDUFF,	Wife to Macduff,	*Macbeth.*
LADY MONTAGUE,	Wife to Montague,	*Romeo and Juliet.*
LADY MORTIMER,	Daughter to Glendower,	*King Henry IV., Part I.*
LADY NORTHUMBERLAND,		*King Henry IV., Part II.*
LADY PERCY,	Wife to Hotspur,	*King Henry IV., Part I.*
LAERTES,	Son to Polonius,	*Hamlet.*
LAFEU,	An Old Lord,	*All's Well that Ends Well.*
LANCASTER, DUKE OF,	Uncle to King Richard II.,	*King Richard II.*
LANCASTER, PRINCE JOHN OF,	Son to King Henry IV.,	*King Henry IV., Pts. I., II.*
LAUNCE,	Servant to Proteus,	*Two Gentlemen of Verona.*
LAUNCELOT GOBBO,	Servant to Shylock,	*Merchant of Venice.*
LAVACHE,	A Clown,	*All's Well that Ends Well.*
LAVINIA,	Daughter to Titus,	*Titus Andronicus.*
LAWRENCE, FRIAR,	A Franciscan,	*Romeo and Juliet.*
LEAR,	King of Britain,	*King Lear.*
LE BEAU,	A Courtier,	*As You Like It.*
LENNOX,	A Scottish Nobleman,	*Macbeth.*
LEONARDO,	Servant to Bassanio,	*Merchant of Venice.*
LEONATO,	Governor of Messina,	*Much Ado About Nothing.*
LEONATUS, POSTHUMUS,	Husband to Imogen,	*Cymbeline.*
LEONINE,	Servant to Dionyza,	*Pericles.*
LEONTES,	King of Sicilia,	*Winter's Tale.*
LEPIDUS, M. ÆMILIUS,	A Triumvir,	*Antony and Cleopatra.*
LEWIS, THE DAUPHIN,		*King John.*
LEWIS, THE DAUPHIN,		*King Henry V.*
LEWIS XI.,	King of France,	*King Henry VI., Part III.*
LIGARIUS,	A Roman Conspirator,	*Julius Cæsar.*
LINCOLN, BISHOP OF,		*King Henry VIII.*
LION,	A Character in the Interlude,	*Midsummer-Night's Dream.*
LODOVICO,	Kinsman to Brabantio,	*Othello.*
LONGAVILLE,	A Lord Attendant on the King of Navarre,	*Love's Labour's Lost.*
LONGSWORD, WILLIAM,	Earl of Salisbury,	*King John.*

LORD, A,	Character in the Induction,	*Taming of the Shrew.*
LORD ABERGAVENNY,		*King Henry VIII.*
LORD BARDOLPH,	Enemy to the King,	*King Henry IV., Part II.*
LORD CHIEF-JUSTICE,	Of the King's Bench,	*King Henry IV., Part II.*
LORD CLIFFORD,	Of the King's Party,	*King Henry VI., Pts. II., III.*
LORD FITZWATER,		*King Richard II.*
LORD GREY,	Son to Lady Grey,	*King Richard III.*
LORD HASTINGS		*King Richard III.*
LORD HASTINGS,	Enemy to the King,	*King Henry IV., Part II.*
LORD HASTINGS,	Of the Duke's Party,	*King Henry VI., Part III.*
LORD LOVEL,		*King Richard III.*
LORD MOWBRAY,	Enemy to the King,	*King Henry IV., Part II.*
LORD RIVERS,	Brother to Lady Grey,	*King Henry VI., Part III.*
LORD ROSS,		*King Richard II.*
LORD SANDS,		*King Henry VIII.*
LORD SAY,		*King Henry VI., Part II.*
LORD SCALES,	Governor of the Tower,	*King Henry VI., Part II.*
LORD SCROOP,	A Conspirator,	*King Henry V.*
LORD STAFFORD,	Of the Duke's Party,	*King Henry VI., Part III.*
LORD STANLEY,		*King Richard III.*
LORD TALBOT,	Afterwards Earl of Shrewsbury,	*King Henry VI., Part I.*
LORD WILLOUGHBY,		*King Richard II.*
LORENZO,	The Lover of Jessica,	*Merchant of Venice.*
LOVEL, LORD,		*King Richard III.*
LOVELL, SIR THOMAS,		*King Henry VIII.*
LUCE,	Servant to Luciana,	*Comedy of Errors.*
LUCENTIO,	Son to Vincentio,	*Taming of the Shrew.*
LUCETTA,	Waiting-woman to Julia,	*Two Gentlemen of Verona.*
LUCIANA,	Sister to Adriana,	*Comedy of Errors.*
LUCILIUS,	Friend to Brutus and Cassius,	*Julius Cæsar.*
LUCILIUS,	Servant to Timon,	*Timon of Athens.*
LUCIO,	A Fantastic,	*Measure for Measure.*
LUCIUS,	A Lord: Flatterer of Timon,	*Timon of Athens.*
LUCIUS,	A Servant,	*Timon of Athens.*
LUCIUS,	Servant to Brutus,	*Julius Cæsar.*
LUCIUS,	Son to Titus,	*Titus Andronicus.*
LUCULLUS,	A Lord: Flatterer of Timon,	*Timon of Athens.*
LUCY, SIR WILLIAM,		*King Henry VI., Part I.*
LYCHORIDA,	Nurse to Marina,	*Pericles.*
LYMOGES,	Duke of Austria,	*King John.*
LYSANDER,	In Love with Hermione,	*Midsummer-Night's Dream.*
LYSIMACHUS,	Governor of Mitylene,	*Pericles.*
MACBETH,	General of the King's Army,	*Macbeth.*
MACBETH, LADY,	Wife to Macbeth,	*Macbeth.*
MACDUFF,	A Scottish Nobleman,	*Macbeth.*
MACDUFF, LADY,	Wife to Macduff,	*Macbeth.*
MACMORRIS,	Officer in the King's Army,	*King Henry V.*
MALCOLM,	Son to King Duncan,	*Macbeth.*
MALVOLIO,	Steward to Olivia,	*Twelfth Night.*
MAMILLIUS,	Son to Leontes,	*Winter's Tale.*
MARC ANTONY,	A Triumvir,	*Antony and Cleopatra.*
MARCELLUS,	An Officer,	*Hamlet.*
MARCH, EARL OF,	Edward Mortimer,	*King Henry IV., Part I.*
MARCIUS, YOUNG,	Son of Coriolanus,	*Coriolanus.*
MARCUS ANDRONICUS,	Tribune: Brother to Titus,	*Titus Andronicus.*
MARCUS ANTONIUS,	A Roman Triumvir,	*Julius Cæsar.*
MARCUS BRUTUS,	A Roman Conspirator,	*Julius Cæsar.*
MARDIAN,	Attendant on Cleopatra,	*Antony and Cleopatra.*
MARESHALL, WILLIAM,	Earl of Pembroke,	*King John.*

SNARE,	A Sheriff's Officer,	*King Henry IV., Part II.*
SNOUT,	The Tinker,	*Midsummer-Night's Dream.*
SNUG,	The Joiner,	*Midsummer-Night's Dream.*
SOLINUS,	Duke of Ephesus,	*Comedy of Errors.*
SOMERSET, DUKE OF,	Of the King's Party,	*King Henry VI., Pts. II., III.*
SOMERVILLE, SIR JOHN,		*King Henry VI., Part III.*
SOUTHWELL,	A Priest,	*King Henry VI., Part II.*
SPEED,	A Clownish Servant,	*Two Gentlemen of Verona.*
STAFFORD, LORD,	Of the Duke's Party,	*King Henry VI., Part III.*
STAFFORD, SIR HUMPHREY,		*King Henry VI., Part II.*
STANLEY, LORD,		*King Richard III.*
STANLEY, SIR JOHN,		*King Henry VI., Part II.*
STANLEY, SIR WILLIAM,		*King Henry VI., Part II.*
STARVELING,	The Tailor,	*Midsummer-Night's Dream.*
STEPHANO,	A Drunken Butler,	*The Tempest.*
STEPHANO,	Servant to Portia,	*Merchant of Venice.*
STRATO,	Servant to Brutus,	*Julius Cæsar.*
SUFFOLK, DUKE OF,	Of the King's Party,	*King Henry VI., Part II.*
SUFFOLK, DUKE OF,		*King Henry VIII.*
SUFFOLK, EARL OF,		*King Henry VI., Part I.*
SURREY, DUKE OF,		*King Richard II.*
SURREY, EARL OF,	Son to Duke of Norfolk,	*King Richard III.*
SURREY, EARL OF,		*King Henry VIII.*
TALBOT, JOHN,	Son to Lord Talbot,	*King Henry VI., Part I.*
TALBOT, LORD,	Afterwards Earl of Shrewsbury,	*King Henry VI., Part I.*
TAMORA,	Queen of the Goths,	*Titus Andronicus.*
TAURUS,	Lieutenant-General to Cæsar,	*Antony and Cleopatra.*
TEARSHEET, DOLL,	A Bawd,	*King Henry IV., Part II.*
THAISA,	Daughter to Simonides,	*Pericles.*
THALIARD,	A Lord of Antioch,	*Pericles.*
THERSITES,	A Deformed Grecian,	*Troilus and Cressida.*
THESEUS,	Duke of Athens,	*Midsummer-Night's Dream.*
THISBE,	A Character in the Interlude,	*Midsummer-Night's Dream.*
THOMAS,	A Friar,	*Measure for Measure.*
THOMAS, DUKE OF CLARENCE,	Son to King Henry IV.,	*King Henry IV., Part II.*
THOMAS HORNER,	An Armourer,	*King Henry VI., Part II.*
THREE WITCHES,		*Macbeth.*
THURIO,	Rival to Valentine,	*Two Gentlemen of Verona.*
THYREUS,	Friend to Cæsar,	*Antony and Cleopatra.*
TIMANDRA,	Mistress to Alcibiades,	*Timon of Athens.*
TIME,	As Chorus,	*Winter's Tale.*
TIMON,	A Noble Athenian,	*Timon of Athens.*
TITANIA,	Queen of the Fairies,	*Midsummer-Night's Dream.*
TITINIUS,	Friend to Brutus and Cassius,	*Julius Cæsar.*
TITUS ANDRONICUS,	General against the Goths,	*Titus Andronicus.*
TITUS LARTIUS,	General against the Volscians,	*Coriolanus.*
TOUCHSTONE,	A Clown,	*As You Like It.*
TRANIO,	Servant to Lucentio,	*Taming of the Shrew.*
TRAVERS,	Servant to Northumberland,	*King Henry IV., Part II.*
TREBONIUS,	A Roman Conspirator,	*Julius Cæsar.*
TRESSEL,	Attendant on Lady Anne,	*Richard III.*
TRINCULO,	A Jester,	*The Tempest.*
TROILUS,	Son to Priam,	*Troilus and Cressida.*
TUBAL,	A Jew, Friend to Shylock,	*Merchant of Venice.*
TULLUS AUFIDIUS,	Volscian General,	*Coriolanus.*
TYBALT,	Nephew to Capulet,	*Romeo and Juliet.*
TYRREL, SIR JAMES,		*King Richard III.*
ULYSSES,	A Grecian Commander,	*Troilus and Cressida.*
URSULA,	Attendant on Hero,	*Much Ado About Nothing.*

INDEX OF FIRST LINES

SONGS

SONNETS

F42

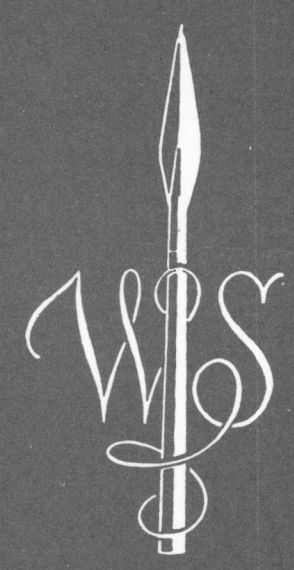